WHAT DO CHILDREN AND YOUNG ADULTS READ NEXT?

A Reader's Guide to Fiction for Children and Young Adults

ISSN 1540-5060

WHAT DO CHILDREN AND YOUNG ADULTS

READ NEXT?

A Reader's Guide to Fiction for Children and Young Adults

VOLUME 6

JANIS ANSELL
PAM SPENCER HOLLEY

THOMSON

GALE

Detroit • New York • San Francisco • San Diego • New Haven, Conn. • Waterville, Maine • London • Munich

(3)

R
I
016.813008
W555
v.6

THOMSON

———★———
™
GALE

What Do Children and Young Adults Read Next? Volume 6

Project Editor
Dana Ferguson

Editorial
Prindle LaBarge
Kathleen Meek

Editorial Support Services
Tom Potts

Manufacturing
Drew Kalasky
Lori Kessler

ISBN 0-7876-6580-0
ISSN 1540-5060

Printed in the United States of America
10 9 8 7 6 5 4 3

Contents

Preface

Thousands of books aimed at children and young adults are published each year, and with that number growing every year, parents and their children often wonder, "What do I read next?" *What Do Children and Young Adults Read Next?* is a reader's advisory tool designed to match readers from preschool through high school with books that reflect their interests and concerns. It guides both reluctant and avid readers to new authors and new titles for further reading. *What Do Children and Young Adults Read Next?* allows readers quick and easy access to specific information on recent titles. In addition, each entry provides alternate reading selections, giving children, parents and librarians the answer to the frequently-asked question: "What do I read next?"

Highlights

- Compiled by Janis Ansell and Pam Spencer Holley, both experts in the field of juvenile and young adult literature.
- Overview essay describes recent trends in young peoples' literature.
- "Other books you might like" included in each entry, leads to the exploration of additional authors or titles.
- Twelve indexes help locate specific titles or offer suggestions for reading in favorite time periods or geographic locales, about special subjects or characters, or for a particular age level.
- All authors and titles listed in entries under "Other books by the author" and "Other books you might like" are indexed, allowing easy access to thousands of books recommended for further reading.

Details on over 1,500 Titles

What Do Children and Young Adults Read Next? contains entries for over 1,500 books published between 2002-2003 aimed at young readers. Titles have been selected on the basis of their currency, appeal to readers, and literary merit. The entries are listed alphabetically by author. Books by authors with more than one entry are then subarranged by title. The following information is provided where applicable:

- **Author or editor's name** and real name if a pseudonym is used. Co-authors, co-editors, translators and illustrators are also listed where applicable.
- **Book title.**
- **Date and place of publication; name of publisher.**

- **Series name.**
- **Age Range:** Indicates the grade levels for which the title is best suited.
- **Subject(s):** Gives the subject matter covered by the title.
- **Major character(s):** Names and brief descriptions of the characters featured in the title.
- **Time period(s):** Tells when the story takes place.
- **Locale(s):** Tells where the story takes place.
- **What the book is about:** A brief plot summary.
- **Where it's reviewed:** Citations to reviews of the book, including the source of the review, date of the source, and the page on which the review appears. Included are reviews from sources such as *Booklist* and *Publishers Weekly*.
- **Other books by the author:** Titles and publication dates of other books the author has written, useful for those wanting to read more by a particular author.
- **Other books you might like:** Titles by other authors written on a similar theme or in a similar style. These titles further the reader's exploration of the genre.

Indexes Answer Readers' Questions

The twelve indexes in *What Do Children and Young Adults Read Next?* used separately or in conjunction with each other, create many pathways to the featured titles, answering general questions or locating specific titles. For example:

"Are there any new in the Amber series?"

The SERIES INDEX lists entries by the name of the series of which they are a part.

"I would like to read a book that has won an award recently."

The AWARDS INDEX lists awards and citations given by experts in the field of children and young adult literature.

"Do you know of any young adult stories set during the 18th century?"

The TIME PERIOD INDEX is a chronological listing of the time settings in which the main entry titles take place.

"I'm looking for a story set in the Arctic."

The GEOGRAPHIC INDEX lists titles by their locale. This can help readers pinpoint an area in which they may have a particular interest, such as their hometown, another country, or even space.

"My daughter needs a book about life in the military"

The SUBJECT INDEX is an alphabetical listing of all the subjects covered by the main entry titles. Topics include such things as fiction genres (e.g. Fantasy, Ghost Stories, Amateur Detective Stories), life and relationships (e.g. Self-Perception, Friendship, School Life), and subjects of interest to today's children and young adults (e.g. Sports, Clothes, Movies).

"Do you have any books with a character whose name is the same as mine?"

The CHARACTER NAME INDEX lists the major characters named in the entries. This can help readers who remember some information about a book, but not an author or title.

"What books are available that feature ducks?"

The CHARACTER DESCRIPTION INDEX identifies the major characters by occupation (e.g. Beekeeper, Police Officer) or persona (e.g. Toy, Dog).

"Which books are appropiate for my fifth-grade son?"

The AGE LEVEL INDEX lists titles by grade levels for which they are best suited. The ability of individual readers may not necessarily reflect their actual age; the wide variety of age ranges allows the user to select titles for slower or more advanced readers.>

"I need to write a book report on a 150 page book. What do you suggest?"

The PAGE COUNT INDEX groups titles according to their page count ranges, allowing readers to select individual titles with specific page counts.>

"Which picture books are illustrated by Cat Bowman Smith?"

The ILLUSTRATOR INDEX is an alphabetical listing of the illustrators of the main entry titles.>

"What has Caroline B. Cooney written recently?"

The AUTHOR INDEX contains the names of all authors featured in the entries and those listed under "Other books you might like.">

"I want to read a book that's similar to the Harry Potter books."

The TITLE INDEX includes all main entry titles and all titles recommended under "Other books by the author" and "Other books you might like" in one alphabetical listing. Thus a reader can find a specific title, new or old, then go to that entry to find out what new titles are similar.

The indexes can also be used to narrow down or broaden choices. A reader interested in 50 page stories set in England during World War II would consult the PAGE COUNT, SUBJECT, and GEOGRAPHIC indexes to see which titles appear in all three. Someone interested in detective stories set during the 1930s could compare titles in the TIME PERIOD and CHARACTER DESCRIPTION indexes. And with the AUTHOR and TITLE indexes, which include all books listed under "Other books by the author" and "Other books you might like," it is easy to compile an extensive list of titles for further reading, not only with the titles recommended in a main entry, but also by seeing other titles to which the main entry or its recommended titles are similar.

About the Authors

Janis Ansell's writing of the children's entries for *What Do Children and Young Adults Read Next?* reflects her life-long interest in reading and her ability to adapt knowledge gained in one subject area to another. Beyond a personal interest in reading she seeks to develop children's literacy and share her love of reading with them. Janis, a public library volunteer in Virginia Beach and a former school psychologist and early childhood teacher, and her husband Charles, a self-employed architect, have brought up three enthusiastic readers—their children Jonathan, Carrie, and Laurie.

Professional expertise and affiliations and volunteer participation in libraries and classrooms augment her natural interest in books, especially those for children. Ansell is a former children's book reviewer for *ForeWord Magazine.* Professionally affiliated with the Randolph-Macon Woman's College Alumnae Association Board, Ansell has been named an Honorary Life Member of the Virginia Congress of Parents and Teachers and a Volunteer of the Year at Alanton Elementary School. She has served on the Lynnhaven Middle School Planning Council and is a past board member of the Tidewater Association of Hearing Impaired Children and of the Alanton PTA. Ansell is a member of the American Library Association (ALA) and the Association of Library Service to Children (ALSC). She is a library and classroom volunteer at Virginia Beach Friends School.

Janis Ansell's psychological insight into young children, her love of books, and her practical experience as a professional, a parent, and a volunteer make her entries in *What Do Children and Young Adults Read Next?* exceptionally informative and useful.

Pam Spencer Holley, coordinator and author of the young adult entries for *What Do Children and Young Read Next?,* and retired coordinator of library services for the Fairfax County Public schools in Virginia, is a recognized expert in young adult literature. A past member of the Margaret A. Edwards Award Committee and the Alex Award Committee of the Young Adult Library Services Association of the American Library Association, she recently chaired the 2004 Michael L. Printz Award Committee which selects the finest books for young adults, based solely on literary quality. She is the current Vice President/President Elect of the Young Adult Library Services Association of ALA. Pam is a member of the Advisory Committee for H.W. Wilson's Senior High School Library Catalog. She is also an occasional contributing reviewer to *School Library Journal* and served as a past chair of the column "Adult Books for Young Adults" for that publication. Serving as a member of the Advisory Board for the professional publication *Voice of Youth Advocates,* more commonly known as VOYA, she also writes their "Audiobooks, It Is! column."

Acknowledgments

Janis Ansell would like to thank the following: Carrie Ansell, my daughter, future librarian, and contributor of 250 entries to this volume I extend my gratitude. I wouldn't have made it without you, Carrie! Collaborating with my sister and co-author Pam Spencer Holley on Volumes 5 and 6 has been a terrific experience. Thanks to my husband Charles, son Jonathan and daughter Laurie for being understanding, patient and supportive. To my parents, my thanks for all those phone calls gently reminding me to get back to work. Many American and Canadian publishers provided review copies of their 2002 and 2003 titles. Great Neck Branch Library processed hundreds of reserve requests for titles available only at other branches in the Virginia Beach Public Library system. Thanks Dana and Deb for putting up with me and not complaining when I failed, yet again, to meet a deadline.

      Pam Spencer Holley would like to thank the following: Once again, special thanks to my dad, Boyd "Gus" Gustafson, for his delivery service of young adult titles from the Williamsburg Regional Library to my home on Virginia's Eastern Shore, and to my mom, Jane Gustafson, for the treats that often arrived with the books. Thanks to my husband for Rick Holley, not only for his patience with me when deadline nears, but also for maintaining the database of entries for *What Do Children and Young Adults Read Next?* In addition to the Williamsburg Regional Library, copies of books were also obtained from Arcadia High School, purchased from bookstores, or received through the generosity of our wonderful American and Canadian publishers of children's and young adult books. I am grateful to Cathy Chauvette, public librarian with Fairfax County (VA) and long-time friend, for continuing to write the majority of the science fiction and fantasy entries. It was again a special treat to work more closely with co-author Janis Ansell, who also happens to be my sister, in this continued combining of the children's and young adult books into the single edition of *What Do Children and Young Adults Read Next?* As we began Volume 6, we didn't realize it would be our last volume but increasing family commitments have forced us to relinquish this wonderful project. And to editor Dana Ferguson, (Vols. 3-6), my continued thanks for being so knowledgeable and caring; it has been a pleasure to work with you; and the previous editors, Neil E. Walker (Vol. 1) and Shelly Dickey (Vol. 2).

Also Available Online

The entries in this book can also be found in the online version of *What Do I Read Next?* Online on GaleNet. This electronic product encompasses over 112,000 books, including genre fiction, mainstream fiction, and nonfiction. All the books included in the online version are recommended by librarians or other experts, award winners, or appear on bestseller lists. The user-friendly functionality allows users to refine their searching by using several criteria, while making it easy to identify similar titles for further research and reading. The online version is updated with new information two times a year. For more information about *What Do I Read Next?* Online or GaleNet, please contact Gale.

Suggestions Are Welcome

The editors welcome any comments and suggestions for enhancing and improving *What Do Children and Young Adults Read Next?* Please address correspondence to the Editors, *What Do Children and Young Adults Read Next?*, at the following address:

    Gale Group
    27500 Drake Rd.
    Farmington Hills, MI 48331-3535
    Phone: 248-699-GALE
    Toll-free: 800-347-GALE
    Fax: 248-699-8054

Introduction

As the year 2002 finally arrived and the United States tried to move past, though never forget, the terrorist attack of 9/11, publishers put into play "The 4/11 Call to Action on 9/11." An ad hoc committee of publishers met right after 9/11 to see what they could do to provide some measure of comfort to children and in response to the need of their authors and illustrators who wanted to do something to help, from writing a book to painting a poster. In 2001 this committee, including Brenda Bowen at Simon & Schuster, Marc Aronson then at Cricket, Andrea Pinkney then at Hyperion, Paula Wiseman at Harcourt and many others, held a silent auction at the National Book Awards and then at Christmas gave books to the children who'd lost family members in the attacks. In 2002 they arranged author and illustrator visits in the three communities directly affected by the 9/11 attacks, featuring such book people as Newbery Award winning Linda Sue Park and Caldecott Honor Book illustrator Brian Selznick. Not wishing to lose the momentum, they all agreed they want to continue the campaign of "Find Comfort in Books, Read Together" which serves as a watchword for all of us who love to read and share books.

Articles Not to Be Missed

Armstrong, Jennifer. "Narrative and Violence." *Horn Book*, March/April, 2003, pp. 191-194.

> *For young readers, books and reading are important means of coping with unexpected world violence.*

Aronson, Marc. "Coming of Age." *Publishers Weekly*, February 11, 2002, pp. 82-86.

> *An overview of the development of young adult literature in the U.S.*

Atkinson, Nathalie. "A Timely Trilogy." *Publishers Weekly*, November 17, 2003, pp. 22-23.

> *A trip to Afghanistan to collect information for a non-fiction adult title led to a children's trilogy.*

Bader, Barbara. "How the Little House Gave Ground: The Beginnings of Multiculturalism in a New, Black Children's Literature." *Horn Book*, November/December 2002, pp. 657-673.

> *This is the first of three articles by the author on the subject of multiculturalism in children's literature. The other two appear in Horn Book, March/April 223, pp. 143-162 and Horn Book, May/June 2002, pp. 265-291.*

Bauer, Joan. "On the Job." *Riverbank Review*, Winter 2002-2003, pp. 29-31.

> *Author commentary on the world of work in her novels.*

Carter, Betty. "Alex: The Why and the How." *Booklist*, April 1, 2003, p. 1389.

> *An explanation of the Alex Award, which annually lists ten top adult books for young adults.*

Cooper, Susan. "There and Back Again: Tolkien Reconsidered." *Horn Book*, March/April 2002, pp. 143-150.

> *A former student of Professor Tolkien comments on her rereading of* The Lord of the Rings.

Devereaux, Elizabeth. "An Appetite for Alice." *Publishers Weekly*, September 30, 2002, pp. 26-27.

> *Commentary on the Phyllis Reynolds Naylor series.*

Goldsmith, Francisca. "Earphone English." *School Library Journal*, May 2002, pp. 50-53.

> *ESL teens turn to audiobooks for book discussions and reading improvement.*

Hade, Daniel. "Storyselling: Are Publishers Changing the Way Children Read?" *Horn Book*, September/October 2002, pp. 509-517.

> *Publishing house mergers and the profit-motive driven merchandising spin-offs of book characters impact the way books are selected and marketed.*

Heppermann, Christine. "William Steig." *Riverbank Review*, Summer 2002, pp. 10-13.

> *Author/illustrator Steig's characters share their creators joy for life.*

Horning, Kathleen T. "A Lifetime of Stories." *Riverbank Review*, Summer 2002, pp. 7-8.

> *A tribute to the great teller of stories, Virginia Hamilton.*

Isaacs, Kathleen I. "Reality Check." *School Library Journal*, October 2003, pp. 50-51.

> *New books for teens show increased violence.*

"Left on the Cutting Room Floor." *Publishers Weekly*, February 10, 2003, pp. 78-79.

> *Some titles for children's books never leave the office.*

Lowry, Lois. "The Remembered Gate and the Unopened Door." *Horn Book*, March/April 2002, pp. 159-177.

The author discusses her works and some of her early memories as part of the annual Zena Sutherland lecture.

Muse, Daphne. "The World She Dreamed, Generations She Shared, Visions She Wrote: A Tribute to Virginia Hamilton 1936-2002." *The New Advocate*, Summer 2002, pp. 171-173

The article's title says it all, a tribute to a deserving author who opened the world to many readers.

Park, Linda Sue. "Staying on Past Canal Street: Reflections on Asian Identity." *Booklist*, January 1 & 15, 2002, pp. 832-833.

A Korean American reflects on the varied Asian American cultures.

Pavao, Kate. "Out of the Closet." *Publishers Weekly*, December 1, 2003, pp. 23-25.

The increased presence in YA literature of gay and lesbian characters.

Sawyer, Jenny. "Feed Me." *Riverbank Review*, Spring 2003, pp. 13-14.

An analysis of the consumer-driven world created by author M.T. Anderson.

Scieszka, Jon. "Guys and Reading." *Riverbank Review*, Summer 2002, pp. 4-6.

The author asks, "What does it take to get boys and books together?" and proposes some answers.

Shader, Robin. "The Butler Did It." *School Library Journal*, June 2002, p. 37.

Attracting students to the library through discussions of mystery books.

Smith, Robin. "Teaching New Readers to Love Books." *Horn Book*, September/October 2003, pp. 537-543.

Reading to children develops capable readers who also love to read.

Sullivan, Ed. "Fiction or Poetry?" *School Library Journal*, August 2003, pp. 44-45.

A look at the increased number of novels written in verse.

Sullivan, Ed. "Race Matters." *School Library Journal*, June 2002, pp. 40-41.

Essay on books about racial identity and relationships.

Sullivan, Ed. "Wrestling with Faith in Young Adult Fiction." *Booklist*, October 1, 2003, p. 331.

Overview of books about teens grappling with their faith.

Varley, Pamela. "As Good as Reading? Kids and the Audiobook Revolution." *Horn Book*, May/June 2002, pp. 251-262.

Discusses the differences in the ways in which readers and listeners experience a book.

Weisman, Kay. "Reflection on Fiction Spin-offs: Should Harriet Spy Again?" *Booklist*, December 1, 2002, page 667.

The pros and cons of spin-offs from classics and other beloved tales.

Wynne-Jones, Tim. "Where Ideas Really Come From." *Horn Book*, September/October 2002, pp. 625-629.

The author describes how serendipity, circuitous routes and getting lost all lead to ideas for writing.

Articles by authors of the books that win, or are named honor books, of the Boston Globe-Horn Book awards can be found in the January/February issues of *Horn Book* magazine. Likewise, the speeches of Newbery and Caldecott winners in the July/August issues. "Carte Blanche," a monthly column in *Booklist*, is written by author and critic Michael Cart and offers wide-ranging essays on books and publishing.

Author/Editor/Illustrator Interviews

Allende, Isabel

Rochman, Hazel. "The Booklist Interview: Isabel Allende." *Booklist*, November 15, 2002, p. 591.

Almond, David

Comerford, Lynda Brill. "The British Invasion: David Almond." *Publishers Weekly*, July 1, 2002, p. 26.

Avi

Cooper, Ilene. "The Booklist Interview: Avi." *Booklist*, May 15, 2002, p. 1609.

Roback, Diane. "Going Gold." *Publishers Weekly*, February 10, 2003, p. 81.

Bear, Greg

Moltz, Sandy. "Forging Futures with Teens and Science Fiction: A Conversation with Greg Bear and David Brin." *Voice of Youth Advocates*, April 2003, pp. 15-18.

Boughton, Simon

Cooper, Ilene. "The Booklist Interview: Simon Boughton." *Booklist*, March 15, 2003, p. 1325.

Bray, Libba

Brown, Jennifer M. "Flying Starts: Libba Bray." *Publishers Weekly*, December 22, 2003, p.31.

Brin, David

Moltz, Sandy. "Forging Futures with Teens and Science Fiction: A Conversation with Greg Bear and David Brin." *Voice of Youth Advocates*, April 2003, pp. 15-18.

Burgess, Melvin

Jenkins, Emily. "The British Invasion: Melvin Burgess." *Publishers Weekly*, July 1, 2002, pp. 28-29

Chambers, Aidan

Alderdice, Kit. "The British Invasion: Aidan Chambers." *Publishers Weekly*, July 1, 2002, pp. 27-28

Rochman, Hazel. "The Booklist Interview: Aidan Chambers." *Booklist*, March 15, 2003, p. 1321.

Clements, Andrew

Lodge, Sally. "Spring Attractions: Andrew Clements." *Publishers Weekly*, April 1, 2002, pp. 25-26.

Collier, Bryan

Willis, Arlette Ingram and Violet J. Harris. "Threads of Connection: A Conversation with Bryan Collier, Illustrator." *The New Advocate*, Spring 2003, pp. 97-103.

Cross, Gillian

Alderdice, Kit. "The British Invasion: Gillian Cross." *Publishers Weekly*, July 1, 2002, p. 28

Crossley-Holland, Kevin

Zvirin, Stephanie. "The Booklist Interview: Kevin Crossley-Holland." *Booklist*, April 15, 2002, p. 1414.

Crutcher, Chris

Shoemaker, Joel. "Crutch, Davis, & Will: That Was Them, This Is Now." *Voice of Youth Advocates*, June 2002, pp. 94-99.

Davis, Will

Shoemaker, Joel. "Crutch, Davis, & Will: That Was Them, This Is Now." *Voice of Youth Advocates*, June 2002, pp. 94-99.

Dessen, Sarah

O'Dell, Katie. "Ringing True: The Authentic Voice of Sarah Dessen." *Voice of Youth Advocates*, June 2002, pp. 100-102.

Donnelly, Jennifer

Maughan, Shannon. "PW Talks with Jennifer Donnelly: Donnelly's Light Shines." *Publishers Weekly*, May 12, 2003, p. 31.

Doyle, Brian

Beck, Martha Davis. "Brian Doyle." *Riverbank Review*, Spring 2003, pp. 4-8.

Dunkle, Clare B.

Devereaux, Elizabeth. "Flying Starts: Clare B. Dunkle." *Publishers Weekly* , December 22, 2003, p. 30.

Farmer, Nancy

Brown, Jennifer M. "Nancy Farmer: Voices of Experience." *Publishers Weekly*, July 22, 2002, pp. 154-155.

Horning, Kathleen T. "The House of Farmer." *School Library Journal*, February 2003, pp. 48-50.

Fleischman, Paul

Kruse-Field, Deb. "Paul Fleischman." *Riverbank Review*, Spring 2002, pp. 10-12.

Foster, Frances

Marcus, Leonard S. "An Interview with Frances Foster." *Horn Book*, September/October, 2003, pp. 545-560.

Gaiman, Neil

Olson, Ray. "The Booklist Interview: Neil Gaiman." *Booklist*, August 2002, p. 1949.

Zaleski, Jeff. "Comics! Books! Films!" *Publishers Weekly*, July 28, 2003, pp. 46-57.

Gantos, Jack

Comerford, Lynda Brill. "Spring Attractions: Jack Gantos." *Publishers Weekly*, April 1, 2002, pp. 24-25.

Shoemaker, Joel. "Filling Holes with Words: An Interview with Jack Gantos." *Voice of Youth Advocates*, June 2003, pp. 100-103.

Garden, Nancy

Jenkins, Christine A. "Annie on Her Mind." *School Library Journal*, June, 2003, pp. 48-50.

Haddix, Margaret Peterson

Pavao, Kate. "Spring Attractions: Margaret Peterson Haddix." *Publishers Weekly*, April 1, 2002, p. 26.

Hidier, Tanuja Desai

Comerford, Lynda Brill. "Flying Starts: Tanuja Desai Hidier." *Publishers Weekly*, December 23, 2002, pp. 32-33.

Horvath, Polly

Kruse-Field, Deb. "Polly Horvath." *Riverbank Review*, Summer 2002, pp. 17-20.

Jimemez, Francisco

Barrera, Rosalinda B. "Secrets Shared: A Conversation with Francisco Jimemez." *The New Advocate*, Winter 2003, pp. 1-8.

Johnson, Kathleen Jeffrie

Pavao, Kate. "Flying Starts: Kathleen Jeffrie Johnson." *Publishers Weekly*, December 23, 2003, p. 36.

Johnston, Tim

Maughan, Shannon. "Flying Starts: Tim Johnston." *Publishers Weekly*, December 23, 2003, p. 34.

Kalman, Maira

Cooper, Ilene. "The Booklist Interview: Maira Kalman." *Booklist*, January 2003, p. 896.

King-Smith, Dick

Frederick, Heather Vogel. "A Life Filled with Tails." *Publishers Weekly*, September 30, 2002, p. 73.

Lowry, Lois

Roper, Ingrid. "PW Talks with Lois Lowry: Picturing the Turn of the 20th Century." *Publishers Weekly*, p. 77.

Marsden, John

Devereaux, Elizabeth. "PW Talks with John Marsden: Bestseller Down Under." *Publishers Weekly*, August 26, 2003, p. 70.

Marzollo, Jean

Spodek, Bernard, Rosalinda B. Barrera and Violet J. Harris. "In Touch with Kids: A Conversation with Jean Marzollo." *The New Advocate*, Spring 2002, pp. 91-99.

McDonald, Janet

Engberg, Gillian. "The Booklist Interview: Janet McDonald." *Booklist*, February 15, 2002, p. 1026.

Na, An

Rochman, Hazel. "The Booklist Interview: An Na." *Booklist*, March 15, 2002, p. 1253.

Naidoo, Beverley

Rochman, Hazel. "The Booklist Interview: Beverley Naidoo." *Booklist*, January 1 & 15, 2002, p. 630.

Paolini, Christopher

Bickers, James. "Flying Starts: Christopher Paolini." *Publishers Weekly*, December 22, 2003, p. 28.

Park, Linda Sue

Horning, Kathleen T. "Discovering Linda Sue Park." *School Library Journal*, July 2002, pp. 48-50.

Swanson, Susan Marie. "Interview: Linda Sue Park." *Riverbank Review*, Fall 2002, pp. 23-26.

Peck, Richard

Brown, Jennifer M. "A Long Way from Decatur." *Publishers Weekly*, July 21, 2003, pp. 169-170.

Prose, Francine

Comerford, Lynda Brill. "PW Talks with Francine Prose: What Price Protection?" *Publishers Weekly*, February 24, 2003, p. 72.

Rennison, Louise

Roback, Diane. "Spring Attractions: Louise Rennison." *Publishers Weekly*, April 1, 2002, p. 24.

Rohmann, Eric

Roback, Diane. "Going Gold." *Publishers Weekly*, February 10, 2003, p. 81.

Sachar, Louis

Alfano, Christine. "Louis Sachar." *Riverbank Review*, Summer 2003, pp. 17-19.

Say, Allen

Brown, Jennifer M. "PW Talks with Allen Say." *Publishers Weekly*, February 25, 2002, p. 65.

Sendak, Maurice

Sutton, Roger. "An Interview with Maurice Sendak." *Horn Book*, November/December 2003, pp. 687-699.

Sis, Peter

Devereaux, Elizabeth. "PW Talks with Peter Sis: Discovering the World." *Publishers Weekly*, October 13, 2003, p. 78.

op de Beeck, Nathalie. "Interview: Peter Sis." *Riverbank Review*, Spring 2002, pp. 17-21.

Steig, William

Cotler, Joanna. "William Steig at 95." *Publishers Weekly*, April 21, 2003, p. 24.

Teague, Mark

Britton, Jason. "In the Studio with Mark Teague." *Publishers Weekly*, September 16, 2002, pp. 23-24.

Van Draanen, Wendelin

Lodge, Sally. "Spring Attractions: Wendelin Van Draanen." *Publishers Weekly*, April 1, 2002, p. 25.

Weaver, Will

Shoemaker, Joel. "Crutch, Davis, & Will: That Was Them, This Is Now." *Voice of Youth Advocates*, June 2002, pp. 94-99.

Wilson, Jacqueline

Britton, Jason. "The British Invasion: Jacqueline Wilson." *Publishers Weekly*, July 1, 2002, pp. 26-27.

Wittlinger, Ellen

Moltz, Sandy. "How Art Can Save You: An Interview with Ellen Wittlinger." *Voice of Youth Advocates*, December 2003, pp. 372-373.

Wolff, Virginia Euwer

Colburn, Nell. "The Incomparable Wolff." *School Library Journal*, February 2002, pp. 54-56.

Woodson, Jacqueline

Brown, Jennifer M. "From Outsider to Insider." *Publishers Weekly*, February 11, 2002, pp. 156-157.

Zindel, Paul

Scales, Pat. "The Pigman and Me." *School Library Journal*, June, 2002, pp. 52-54.

Awards: 2002

Canada

The Canadian Library Association's Best Book of the Year for Young Adults was *Before Wings* written by Beth Goobie.

International

The Americas Award, sponsored by the Consortium of Latin American Studies Programs, is to honor titles that "authentically and engagingly" portray Latin America, the Caribbean or Latinos in the U.S. *Before We Were Free* by Julia Alvarez was presented the award while *Behind the Mountains* by Edwidge Danticat received an honorable mention.

The International Board on Books for Young People, commonly referred to as IBBY, presented the Hans Christian Andersen Award to Aidan Chambers in recognition of the "important and lasting contribution" to children's literature made by his body of work. Illustrator Quentin Blake was also recognized with this biennial award.

United Kingdom

The Amazing Maurice and His Educated Rodents by Terry Pratchett received the Carnegie Medal, which is presented annually to the author of the best book for children.

The Kate Greenaway Medal for distinguished illustration in a book for children was awarded to Bob Graham, author and illustrator of *Jethro Byrd, Fairy Child*.

The British Book Award, the Nibbies, was awarded to *Saffy's Angel* by Hilary McKay. The shortlist included *Sorceress* by Celia Rees and *Mortal Engines* by Philip Reeve.

Sponsored by the independent charity Booktrust, which supports books and reading, the Smarties Book Prize for the best children's book published in the United Kingdom was awarded to Philip Reeve for *Mortal Engines* in the 9-11 age category. In the 5-8 age group, the award went to *That Pesky Rat*, written and illustrated by Lauren Child and, in the 5 and under age group, author/illustrator Lucy Cousin's *Jazzy in the Jungle* claimed the prize.

The Whitbread Book of the Year was Philip Pullman's *The Amber Spyglass*.

United States

Beverley Naidoo's *The Other Side of Truth* received the Jane Addams Children's Book Award while Rachna Gilmore's *A Group of One* and Virginia Euwer Wolff's *True Believer* were named Honor Books.

The Assembly on Literature for Adolescents, of the National Council of Teachers of English, presented its ALAN Award to Paul Zindel for his contribution to the field of adolescent literature. Zindel also received the Margaret A. Edwards Award.

The winner of the Henry Bergh Book Award for Fiction/Companion Animals, given by the American Society for the Prevention of Cruelty to Animals (ASPCA), is *Stray Dog* by Kathe Koja. Three picture books were also recognized with the Henry Bergh Book Award: *Goose's Story* by Cari Best in the Fiction Environment and Ecology category; Gloria Rand's *Little Flower* and Sanna Stanley's *Monkey for Sale* in the Fiction Humane Heroes category.

Lord of the Deep by Graham Salisbury received the Boston Globe-Horn Book Award for Fiction and Poetry while *Saffy's Angel* by Hilary McKay was named an Honor Book, as was *Amber was Brave, Essie Was Smart* by author/illustrator Vera B. Williams. In the Picture Book category *"Let's Get a Pup!" Said Kate*, written and illustrated by Bob Graham, claimed the award while honor recognition went to *I Stink!* by Kate McMullan with illustrations by Jim McMullan and *Little Rat Sets Sail* by Monika Bang-Campbell, illustrated by Molly Bang.

The Christopher Awards honor distinguished media, including books, films and television programs, that remind readers and viewers "of their worth, individuality and power to positively impact and shape our world." They were presented to Sharon Creech for *Love That Dog* for ages 8-10; *Uncle Daddy* by Ralph Fletcher for ages 10-12; and in the young adult category to *Soldier X* by Don Wulffson and *Witness* by Karen Hesse. In the preschool category, *Kiss Good Night* by Amy Hest, with illustrations by Anita Jeram, claimed the prize; *Beatrice's Goat*, written by Page McBrier and illustrated by Lori Lohstoeter, won for ages 6-8.

The Mystery Writers of America awarded its Edgar Award in the Young Adult category to Tim Wynne-Jones for *The Boy in the Burning House*, while Lillian Eige's *Dangling* won in the Juvenile category.

The New York Library Association honored Jerry Pinkney with the Empire State Award for Excellence in Literature for Young People in recognition of the body of his work.

The Southern California Children's Booksellers' Association presented its annual Golden Dolphin Award for excellence in children's literature to Sid Fleischman.

The Society of Children's Book Writers and Illustrators awarded its Golden Kite fiction prize to Jaira Placide for her work entitled *Fresh Girl*. The Golden Kite picture book text award went to *George Hogglesberry: Grade School Alien* by Sarah Wilson with the honor award in the category claimed by Barbara Joosee's *Stars in the Darkness*. *Mrs. Biddlebox* by Linda Smith, illustrated by Marla Frazee, received the picture book illustration award and Lisa Wheeler's *Sailor Moo: Cow at Sea* with illustrations by Ponder Goembel was named an honor book.

The Dolly Gray Awards, given biannually, recognize fictional books that provide a positive portrayal of youngsters with developmental disabilities. Barbara O'Connor's book *Me and Rupert Goody* received this an award.

The International Reading Association Award for Young Adult Fiction was presented to *A Step from Heaven* by An Na. *Coolies*, written by Yin and illustrated by Chris Soentpiet, received the award for Intermediate Fiction and the Primary Fiction award went to *Silver Seeds* by Paolilli and Dan Brewer. The award is given for an author's first or second published book and is given the year following its publication.

The Los Angeles Times Book Prize for Young Adult Fiction was given to *Feed*, written by M.T. Anderson.

Following in the footsteps of Virginia Hamilton, who was a 1995 recipient, Karen Hesse recently received the MacArthur Fellowship which grants the chosen individual $500,000 over five years with "no strings attached." Hesse was cited for "expanding the possibilities of literature for children and young adults."

Allen Say received the David McCord Citation in honor of work that "has made a significant contribution in the field of children's literature."

The National Book Award went to Nancy Farmer for her work *The House of the Scorpion*. Finalists included *Feed* by M.T. Anderson and *Hush* by Jacqueline Woodson.

Patricia MacLachlan, author of the Newbery winner *Sarah, Plain and Tall*, received a National Humanities Medal for her "numerous critically acclaimed books for children of all ages." The National Humanities Medal is awarded to individuals or organizations that have "deepened the nation's understanding of the humanities."

The New England Booksellers Association presented its New England Book Award to Leonard Everett Fisher in honor of the contribution his body of work has made to the region's literature.

The Scott O'Dell Award, which recognizes a work written by a U.S. author and set in the Americas, was given to *The Land* by Mildred Taylor. The PEN Center USA Literary Award, given for an outstanding book written by an author living in the Western United States, was also won by Mildred D. Taylor for her work *The Land*.@p:

The PEN/Phyllis Naylor Working Writer Fellowship, given to "recognize new writing talents of special promise," was given to Lori Aurelia Williams, author of *When Kambia Elaine Flew in from Neptune* and *Shayla's Double Brown Baby Blues*.

The Phoenix Award, given to books of high literary merit that didn't receive major awards when they were first published, was presented to *A Formal Feeling* by Zibby O'Neal.

The Regina Medal, presented by the Catholic Library Association, was given to editor and author Charlotte Zolotow for her lifetime achievement in children's literature.

The *Riverbank Review* of fiction for young readers awarded its Books of Distinction title to *Seek* by Paul Fleischman, *A Step from Heaven* by An Na and *True Believer* by Virginia Euwer Wolff. Picture books receiving the award included *The Journey* by Sarah Stewart, with illustrations by David Small; *The Other Side* written by Jacqueline Woodson and illustrated by E.B. Lewis; and *The Stray Dog*, written and illustrated by Marc Simont.

The Association of Jewish Libraries honored *Chicken Soup by Heart*, written by Esther Hershenhorn with illustrations by

Rosanne Litzinger, with the Sidney Taylor Book Award for Young Readers.

Time of Wonder award, bestowed by Maine's Discovery Museum to a work that captures the "sense of wonder and imagination" in children's literature, was given to *Ruby Holler* by Sharon Creech.

The WILLA Literary Award, named after Willa Cather, was given to Marisa Montes for *Circle of Time*, an outstanding women's story set in the West in the Children's/Young Adult category.

The Wordcraft Circle of Native Writers and Storytellers presented its Children's Prose Award to Cynthia Leitich Smith, author of *Rain Is Not My Indian Name*. Further information is available at www.wordcraftcircle.org.

The Charlotte Zolotow Award for "outstanding writing in a children's picture book" went to *Clever Beatrice* written by Margaret Willey with illustrations by Heather Solomon. One honor award title, *Five Creatures* by Emily Jenkins and illustrated by Tomek Bogacki, was chosen.

Awards: 2003-2004

Canada

The Canadian Library Association's Best Book of the Year for Young Adults was awarded to *True Confessions of a Heartless Girl* written by Martha Brooks.

International

Judith Ortiz Cofer received the Americas Award for *The Meaning of Consuelo*, while *Cuba 15* by Nancy Osa received an Honorable Mention and Gary Soto's *The Afterlife* was Commended.

United Kingdom

The British Book Award, called the Nibbies, was given to *The Curious Incident of the Dog in the Night-Time* by Mark Haddon, which was published as an adult title in the United States. Jonathan Stroud's *The Amulet of Samarkand* was shortlisted.

The Carnegie Medal was awarded to Sharon Creech for her book *Ruby Holler*. Creech is the first American to win the United Kingdom's distinguished honor and is also the first author to win both a Carnegie and a Newbery Medal for *Walk Two Moons*. A 2003 title that won the 2004 Carnegie Medal is Jennifer Donnelly's *A Gathering Light*, released in the United States as *A Northern Light*.

The royal title of Commander of the British Empire, or CBE, was presented to Philip Pullman on December 12 for his contribution to literature.

The Nestle Smarties Book Prize for ages 9-11 was awarded to David Almond for *The Fire-Eaters* while S.F. Said received it for ages 6-8 for his work entitled *Varjak Paw*. In the 5 and under age group, the prize went to *The Witch's Children and the Queen* by Ursula Jones with illustrations by Russell Ayto.

United States

Parvana's Journey by Deborah Ellis received a Jane Addams Children's Book Award in the older children's category while *The Same Stuff as Stars* by Katherine Paterson and *When My Name Was Keoko* by Linda Sue Park were named Honor Books. *The Village That Vanished* by Ann Grifalconi, with illustrations by Kadir Nelson, was named a Picture Book Honor Book.

The recipients of the ALAN Award were Norma Fox Mazer and Harry Mazer for their contribution to adolescent literature.

Honor Book recognitions in the Fiction category of the Boston Globe-Horn Book Awards were cited for *Feed* by M.T. Anderson and Jacqueline Woodson's *Locomotion*. The Fiction and Poetry Award winner was *The Jamie and Angus Stories* by Anne Fine with illustrations by Penny Dale. In the Picture Book category, *Big Momma Makes the World*, written by Phyllis Root and illustrated by Helen Oxenbury, received the award while honor recognition went to *Dahlia*, written and illustrated by Barbara McClintock, and *Blues Journey* by Walter Dean Myers with illustrations by Christopher Myers.

This year's Christopher Awards in the Books category were presented to *Pictures of Hollis Wood*, written by Patricia Reilly Giff and *Left for Dead* by Pete Nelson. Picture books named to receive the 54th annual Christopher Medal were *Mole and the Baby Bird* by Marjorie Newman, with illustrations by Patrick Benson; *Dear Mrs. LaRue: Letters from Obedience School* by author/illustrator Mark Teague; and Margaret Gray's *The Ugly Princess and the Wise Fool*, with illustrations by Randy Cecil.

Volumes 1-3 of *The Wessex Paper*, written by Daniel Parker, received the 2003 Edgar in the Young Adult Category while *Acceleration* by Graham McNamee received the same award in 2004. The 2004 Edgar Award for Best Juvenile Mystery went to *Bernie Magruder and the Bats in the Belfry* by Phyllis Reynolds Naylor. The 2003 Edgar Award for Best Juvenile Mystery was *Harriet Spies Again* by Helen Ericson.

Milkweed by Jerry Spinelli received a Golden Kite Award while *Breath* by Donna Jo Napoli was cited as an Honor Book. The Golden Kite Picture Book Illustrator Award went to Angela Johnson's *I Dream of Trains* with illustrations by Loren Long. In the same category, *Just a Minute: A Trickster Tale and Counting Book* by Yuyi Morales received an honor. *On Sand Island* written by Jacqueline Griggs Martin was designated a Golden Kite Picture Book Text Honor Book.

The International Reading Association presented its Young Adult Fiction Award to Chris Crowe for *Mississippi Trial, 1955* and its Intermediate Fiction Award to Marlene Carvel for *Who Will Tell My Brother?*. The Primary Fiction Award went to *One Leaf Rides the Wind* by Celeste Davidson Mannis.

The Bank Street College of Education presented its Claudia Lewis Award for poetry to *Yesterday I Had the Blues* by new author Jeron Ashford Frame and a Lifetime Achievement Award to Karla Kuskin.

The Book Prize from the Los Angeles Times was awarded to first time young adult novelist Jennifer Donnelly for *A Northern Light*. Finalists included *True Confessions of a Heartless Girl* by Martha Brooks; *Olive's Ocean* by Kevin Henkes; Richard Peck's *The River Between Us* and *After* by Francise Prose.

Angela Johnson and Peter Sis both received MacArthur Fellowships, also known as "Genius Awards." Sis was the first illustrator to receive the honor.

This year's David McCord Literature Citation was awarded to Patricia and Fredrick McKissack.

The national Medal of Arts was awarded to Newbery medallist Beverly Cleary, only the second children's book author to win this award for artistic excellence.

The National Book Award for Young People's Literature was presented to Polly Horvath for *The Canning Season* while finalists included Paul Fleischman's *Breakout*, Richard Peck's *The River Between Us* and *Locomotion* by Jacqueline Woodson.

Jean Fritz was the recipient of this year's National Humanities Medal presented to her in a White House ceremony.

The first recipient of the NSK Neustadt Prize for Children's Literature, presented by the University of Oklahoma and its international journal *World Literature Today*, was presented to Mildred Taylor. The award, which carries a $25,000 purse, is given every other year to a "living writer with significant achievement, either over a lifetime or in a particular publication," that has a "positive impact on the quality of children's literature."

Shelley Pearsall received the Scott O'Dell Award for Historical Fiction for *Trouble Don't' Last*.

The PEN/Phyllis Naylor Working Writer Fellowship was awarded this year to Franny Billingsley.

Zipped by Laura and Tom McNeal received the PEN Center USA Literary Award in the category of Children's Literature.

Author and illustrator Eric Carle received the Laura Ingalls Wilder Award which is presented to "a children's book creator whose books have made a substantial and lasting contribution to literature for children."

Receiving a Phoenix Award is *The Long Night Watch* by Ivan Southall.

Jean Craighead George received the Regina Medal, awarded by the Catholic Library Association.

Rodzina by Karen Cushman received the WILLA Award in the Children's/Young Adult Category.

The 2003 Charlotte Zolotow Award for outstanding writing in a picture book published in the United States during the preceding year went to Holly Keller, author and illustrator of *Farfallina & Marcel*. *The First Thing My Mama Told Me*, written by Susan Marie Swanson and illustrated by Christine Davenier, was recognized as a Charlotte Zolotow Honor Book. The same title was named a New York Times Best Illustrated Book in 2002.

For complete lists of Newbery, Caldecott, Coretta Scott King, Pura Belpre, Notables, Best Books for Young Adults, Quick Picks, Michael L. Printz and Alex Award recipients, search the ALA website at www.ala.org.

Censorship, or, You Win Some, You Lose Some

2002 – 2003

As one reviews these censorship cases, it should be noted that some complaints are valid and point out the need for librarians to review and evaluate materials they add to their libraries so that books meant for older audiences don't end up on the elementary shelves. At the same time, parents often seize on one issue in a book and then try to restrict that book for all students, instead of working with their child and his/her reading habits and interests. The best preparation that a librarian can make is to broaden his or her reading horizons .

ALABAMA: A grandparent's complaint led to the removal of *Breaking Boxes* by A.M. Jenkins from all its elementary school libraries. *Breaking Boxes* was selected as a Quick Pick for Young Adults and won the 1996 Delacorte Prize for literature written for 12 to 18-year-olds.

ARKANSAS: The Cedarville School Board, against the recommendation of its elementary school library committee,

decided to make J.K. Rowling's Harry Potter series available only to those students who had parental permission. A parent filed a lawsuit claiming the School Board was in violation of a student's "fundamental right to receive information and ideas." The Harry Potter series was ordered returned to library shelves by a federal judge after the school board ban was ruled unconstitutional.

CALIFORNIA: *Sophie's Choice* by William Styron was returned to the library shelves in La Mirada, California after the ACLU threatened to sue if the missing book was not returned.

FLORIDA: Though *The Adventures of Huckleberry Finn* by Mark Twain will be restricted to teachers of grades 11 or higher, the book will remain on the library shelves of both middle and high schools. Judy Blume's *Deenie* is being challenged in Hernando County by a parent who considers it unsuitable for elementary school students.

ILLINOIS: After five years *Forever* by Judy Blume is back in the middle school libraries in Elgin and available for checkout. However, its shelf life may be short-lived as opponents plan to wait out the two-year grace period and then re-challenge the book.

LOUISIANA: In Shreveport the Caddo Parish School Board committee has recommended the return of two books to the high school reading list. In each case it's added a requirement for parental permission before eleventh grade students can read either *The Chocolate War* by Robert Cormier, which is listed as optional reading, or *The Great Santini* by Pat Conroy.

MAINE: In Lewiston Rev. Douglas Taylor, minister of the Jesus Party, held a second shredding ceremony of a Harry Potter book, this time *Harry Potter and the Chamber of Secrets*, prior to the nationwide opening day of the movie. In 2001 the group shredded copies of *Harry Potter and the Sorcerer's Stone*. Approximately 30 followers joined him at the event.

MASSACHUSETTS: A public librarian who visited Duxbury High School to give booktalks also distributed a summer reading list. When several parents complained about certain titles on the list, the librarian was asked to booktalk only titles from the school's required summer reading list and not provide other suggestions. Parents had concerns about such titles as Steve Chobosky's *The Perks of Being a Wallflower* and the anonymously authored *Go Ask Alice*. In Cromwell a group tried to ban witchcraft titles from local schools, including two Newbery titles, *The Witch of Blackbird Pond* by Elizabeth George Speare and *Bridge to Terabithia* by Katherine Paterson. The group failed to request the required curriculum review and no action was taken.

MISSISSIPPI: The school board in George County, responding to a grandparent's complaint of profanity in books, has banned *Of Mice and Men* by John Steinbeck, along with *Fallen Angels* by Walter Dean Myers and *The Things They Carried* by Tim O'Brien, from classrooms and libraries. When another parent asked to have the ban lifted, the George County School Board stood firm stating that *Of Mice and Men* is the second most banned book in American high schools.

MISSOURI: The popular Harry Potter series always seems to be in the news and in 54 school libraries in Springfield, Missouri, the titles have been returned to the shelves following a grandmother's complaint about witchcraft. In Webb City a complaint about the Alice series by Phyllis Reynolds Naylor led to the removal of *Achingly Alice* and *The Grooming of Alice,* while three other titles were made available only to sixth graders and above.

NOVA SCOTIA: Three books that had the term "nigger," were removed after a complaint that the term was demeaning and encouraged racism. *To Kill a Mockingbird* by Harper Lee, *In the Heat of the Night* by John Dudley Ball and *Underground to Canada* by Barbara Smucker were reinstated after the school board was chastised by Nova Scotia's Education Minister.

OHIO: School officials removed three of an order of Accelerated Reader titles, which set into motion a review of the entire shipment of AR titles received by L.T. Ball Junior High Library in Tipp City. The School Board intends to review its materials selection policy.

SOUTH CAROLINA: In Horry County, South Carolina, a complaint has been filed against Bette Green's *The Drowning of Stephan Jones*, stating that the book promotes homosexuality.

TENNESSEE: Like Missouri, complaints about *Alice on the Outside* were made in Murfreesboro about the book being too sexually explicit and the book committee was considering whether to remove it.

TEXAS: The independent Gregory-Portland School District voted to retain *Athletic Shorts* by Chris Crutcher after a parent complained about foul and racist language as well as sexual content. In Crawford County, the school board will consider whether to remove *Extreme Elvin* by Chris Crutcher and R.L. Stine's *Double Date* from middle school libraries following a parental complaint. Statewide the most frequently banned books were *Alice on the Outside*, one of the titles in the popular Alice series written by Phyllis Reynolds Naylor, and *Forever* by Judy Blume.

VIRGINIA: PABBIS, the Fairfax County group Parents Against Bad Books in Schools, continues to mount book challenges. This time there are 18 challenges, the most ever received at one time by Fairfax County Public Schools, and questioned titles include *Girl Goddess* and *Witch Baby* by Francesca Lia Block, *The Chocolate War* by Robert Cormier, *Shogun* by James Clavell, *Fallen Angels* by Walter Dean Myers and Alice Walker's *The Color Purple*. At an approximate cost to the system of $2600 for staff time for reviewing each incident, the total review cost nears $50,000. Thus far the Fairfax County school has voted to retain *Witch Baby* with a young adult sticker.

WISCONSIN: In Oregon, following a parent complaint about Louise Rennison's book *Knocked Out by My Nunga-Nungas,* a school committee has decided to retain the book in the middle school library.

WYOMING: The Jackson School Board found Julius Lester's *When Dad Killed Mom* to be inappropriate and pulled it from library shelves.

Between 1999 and 2002 Harry Potter books were the most frequently challenged works according to ALA's Office of Intellectual Freedom. In response to censorship charges against Harry, some booksellers urged their peers to donate a percentage of the sales from *Harry Potter and the Order of the Phoenix* to the American Bookseller's Foundation for Free Expression which has helped stave off attempts to remove Harry from library shelves. Harry has been bumped to second

place as the Alice series by Phyllis Reynolds Naylor received the greatest number of challenges during 2003 for its sexual content. Alice has aged in the series and is now in high school, a time when thinking, talking and wondering about sexual matters is a natural occurrence, but one that raises concerns in parents.

Further information about intellectual freedom, censorship and Banned Books Week can be found at the American Library Association web site: www.ala.org.

Books to Film

J.R.R. Tolkien's The Lord of the Rings series, first published in the mid-1950s, has been a bonanza for both its film producers and Houghton Mifflin, which owned the copyright to the titles. Special events in stores, display units featuring the characters and many related items have captured the interest of fans, along with their money. *The Whale Rider*, a 1987 book from a New Zealand author, was made available in the U.S. in 2003 to coincide with the film's release. Based on mythology, it tells of a young girl who grows up to become the legendary whale rider of her people.

According to people involved in the film industry, children's books, from the classics to the new series, are currently popular as everyone's interested in family-oriented films. The classic by Natalie Babbitt about immortality, *Tuck Everlasting*, came out in the fall of 2002 and featured William Hurt, Sissy Spacek and Ben Kingsley. April 2003 saw the release of the film based on Louis Sacher's Newbery award-winning novel *Holes*. In addition to stars Sigourney Weaver, Jon Voight and Shia LaBoeuf, who plays the protagonist Stanley Yelnats, Sachar himself has a cameo role in this film for which he wrote the screenplay. Daniel Handler, who writes as Lemony Snicket, is the author of A Series of Unfortunate Events series, books about the tragic happenings in the lives of the Baudelaire orphans. Scheduled to be released in late 2004, Meryl Streep, Jude Law, and Jim Carrey are listed as the current stars of this feature.

The popularity of fantasy books is evident also in some of the movies being made, spurred no doubt by the success of the Harry Potter series in both book and film format. Miramax has quite a few fantasy-based projects including *Artemis Fowl* by Eoin Colfer, Jonathan Stroud's *The Amulet of Samarkand* and *Ella Enchanted* by Gail Carson Levine, which was released in 2004. At Walden Media, future productions include such classics as C.W. Lewis's The Chronicles of Narnia and Lois Lowry's *The Giver*. Universal Pictures released *Dr. Seuss' The Cat in the Hat* starring Mike Myers as the cat, with child stars Spencer Breslin and Dakota Fanning. A complete listing of what's been optioned and what's in production is available in *Publishers Weekly*, October 6, 2003, pages 24-25.

American Girl produces high-quality dolls, which are very popular with young girls who often have sizable collections. Samantha, one of the first released dolls, will have a made-for-TV movie released in 2004 based on her character and is the first TV attempt for the Pleasant Company. The stage is a site for book activity as Tomie dePaola's *Oliver Button Is a Sissy*, a work featuring a boy who loves to dance and dislikes football, is sung by choruses nationwide with performances scheduled for Kennedy Center and Carnegie Hall. The Houston Grand Opera performed *The Little Prince* by Antoine de Saint-

Exupery in Texas after which the production embarked on an out-of-state road tour. Arnold Lobel's award-winning characters, who already have Newbery and Caldecott Medals to their credit, are now starring on Broadway in a musical stage adaptation entitled *A Year with Frog and Toad*.

Debuts

First time authors and illustrators garnered their share of awards in 2002 and 2003. A Caldecott Honor was one of several awards claimed by first timer Mo Willems for his humorous, audience-participation picture book *Don't Let the Pigeon Drive the Bus!*, a title which he also illustrated. Brenda Woods received a Coretta Scott King Author Honor Book designation for her first novel *The Red Rose Box*, a story of family tragedy that begins in 1950s segregated Louisiana. Three siblings in a kitchen make for a lively breakfast in Tamson Weston's award-winning debut title, *Hey, Pancakes!* with illustrations by Stephen Gammell. Colors describe the many moods of a little boy and his family members in *Yesterday I Had the Blues* by first-time author Jeron Ashford Frame, winner of the Claudia Lewis Award and a Blue Ribbon from the *Bulletin of the Center for Children's Books*. Also receiving *Bulletin of the Center for Children's Books* Blue Ribbon Awards were *The Witch's Children* by Ursula Jones with illustrations by Russell Ayto and *Slow Loris*, written and illustrated by Alexis Deacon. Both titles were originally published in the United Kingdom.

Several titles by new authors offer a glimpse of other cultures. Inspired by her grandmother's stories, Shirin Yim Bridges created *Ruby's Wish* about a young girl in China who longs for an education. The title, illustrated by Sophie Blackall was named a *Publishers Weekly* Best Children's Book for 2002. *Dream Carver*, a Smithsonian Notable Book for Children written by Diana Cohn with illustrations by Amy Cordova, is set in Oaxaca. A grouchy Moroccan bachelor contends with an imp, a magic pot and a thief in *The Bachelor and the Bean*, adapted and illustrated by Shelley Fowles and selected as a Best Book by the Center for Children's Books. *The Gold-Threaded Dress*, a *Booklist* Editors' Choice by Carolyn Marsden deals with the challenges faced by a young Thai-American and her search for acceptance in a new school. In a Smithsonian Notable Book for Children, Japanese immigrants in 19th-century California solve a ghostly mystery in *Ghosts for Breakfast* by Stanley Todd Terasaki with illustrations by Shelly Shinjo. In *Suki's Kimono*, a first grader's older sisters go to the first day of school in modern fashions but Suki wears her Japanese kimono, a gift from her grandmother. Selected as an International Reading Association Teacher's Choice, the debut title by Cheri Uegaki, with illustrations by Stephane Jorisch, captures Suki's unselfconscious delight in and appreciation for this cultural attire. The life of migrant workers is portrayed in a Notable Social Studies Trade Book for Young People *The Hard-Times Jar* illustrated by first-timer John Holyfield. The book's author, Ethel Footman Smothers, based her story about Emma on family history. The art of another new children's book illustrator, Stacey Dressen-McQueen is seen in the award-winning picture book set in Holland in 1945, *Boxes for Katje*, written by Candace Fleming.

Animals have important roles in many of the award-winning picture books written by first time authors. In *Puss in Cowboy Boots*, a retelling of a classic fairy tale, Jan Huling moves the story of a upwardly mobile cat from France to Texas and claims a Parent's Choice Award for the story illustrated by Phil Huling. Animals cower in a barn, fearing the arrival of "Storm" in the IRA Children's Choice selection *Storm Is Coming!* written by Heather Tekavec and illustrated by Margaret Spengler. Selected as a Best Book by the Center for Children's Books, *Hungry Hen* by Richard Waring with illustrations by Caroline Jayne Church features a hen with a voracious appetite and a hungry, but greedy fox that waits just a bit too long to dine. Animals and food also take center stage in the ALA Notable Children's Book *Bear Snores On* written by Karma Wilson and illustrated by Jane Chapman. Parent animals and their offspring follow bedtime rituals guaranteed to lull any child to sleep in a Center for Children's Books Best Book by Katherine Riley Nakamura, *Song of Night: It's Time to Go to Bed* with illustrations by Linnea Riley.

In the field of young adult books, several first time novelists emerged as stars over the last several years including two Printz Honor Book winners, Jennifer Donnelly and K.L. Going. Donnelly garnered an incredible number of awards for her first YA novel *A Northern Light*, including recognition as an ALA Best Books for Young Adults; Borders Original Voices; Best Book status from *Publishers Weekly*, *School Library Journal*, and the *Los Angeles Times*; an Editor's Choice from *Booklist*; and was a recipient of the 2004 Carnegie Medal. Donnelly's heroine Mattie Gokey is a young woman who, at the beginning of the 20th century, is faced with decisions. Should she follow in her mother's footsteps and settle down to life as a farmer's wife or follow her dream and attend college to prepare for a writing career? Her decision comes easily after witnessing the murder of a young girl at an Adirondack hotel. Going also garnered numerous awards fo rher book *Fat Kid Rules the World*, which in addition to the Printz, was also recognized as an ALA Best Books for Young Adults; earned Best Book status from *School Library Journal*; received an Editor's Choice from *Booklist*; and was a Blue Ribbon winner from *Bulletin of the Center for Children's Books*. K.L.'s hero Troy is a 300-pound blob of insecurity who's prevented from jumping in front of the subway by scrawny, hyper Curt MacRae, guitarist extraordinaire. The unique friendship that develops between these two boys leads to positive changes for both of them.

More and more YA books feature or include gay or lesbian characters, but David Levithan takes a different approach in his award-winning *Boy Meets Boy* which received an ALA Best Books for Young Adults and an ALA Quick Picks for Reluctant Young Adult Readers recognition in addition to being named a *Booklist* Editor's Choice, a *Bulletin of the Center for Children's Books* Blue Ribbon and a Notable Social Studies Trade Book. In Levithan's work, Paul meets Noah in the book store and falls in love instantly, but best of all, no one's concerned that the teens are gay. Paul lives in a town where the Boy Scouts organization became the Joy Scouts, the football quarterback is also the homecoming queen and being gay is no big deal. Nancy Osa describes another culture in *Cuba 15* where Violeta turns 15 and, somewhat against her wishes, prepares for her quinceanera, a traditional Latin American party that turns out to be more special than she thought it could be. Named a Pura Belpre Honor Book, a Notable Social Studies Trade Book, an ALA Children's Notable Book, an ALA Best Books for Young Adults, a *Booklist* Editor's Choice and winner of the Delacorte Press Prize, Osa is a writer to watch in the years ahead. First author Rachel Cohn looked at the ever more prevalent problem of stepfamilies in *Gingerbread* which walked away with such honors as an ALA Best Books for Young Adults and an ALA Quick Picks for Reluctant Young Adult Readers, as well as a Best Book from *School Library Journal*, an Editor's Choice from *Booklist* and a Blue Ribbon winner from *Bulletin of the Center for Children's Books* . Cyd Charisse, described as a hellion by her parents, leaves San Francisco to stay with her biological father in New York City, an experience that allows her to think about what being a family really means to her.

Proving that family abuse knows no boundaries, there were books exploring that subject written by Nigerian, British and American authors. Nigerian Chimama Adichie's first novel, *Purple Hibiscus*, named an ALA Best Books for Young Adults, tells of teenage Kambili and her older brother who see how their father is revered by their townspeople, yet only they and their mother know how abusive he is at home. A visit to their Aunty's home lets them see that reading books, enjoying good meals and laughing together are the way a family should act. In *Martyn Pig* by British author Kevin Brooks, Martyn's mother has left and he's alone with his alcoholic father until the day the two struggle, his father falls, hits his head and dies. In this ALA Best Books for Young Adults, Martyn fears he'll be accused of murder so he doesn't call for help and, the more he puts it off, the harder it is to tell anyone until he finally dumps the body in a quarry. *Bottled Up* by Jaye Murray, which was also recognized as an ALA Best Books for Young Adults, illustrates how easy it is for Pip to fall into the habit of smoking dope, drinking too much and emulating his abusive father, until he sees how damaging his behavior is to his adored younger brother Mikey.

Though there were many works of historical fiction published during this time, most of them were written by seasoned authors. Shelley Pearsall won the Scott O'Dell award and was named a *Booklist* Editor's Choice for *Trouble Don't Last*, a work featuring 11-year-old Samuel, a slave who's aided in escaping on the Underground Railroad by the older, father-figure slave Harrison. In *Bloody Jack* by L.A. Meyer, young Mary Faber finds herself homeless and without a gang leader to protect her, so she dresses as a boy and takes to the seas where she helps hunt pirates in this ALA Best Books for Young Adults. Kristi Collier's *Jericho Walls* takes a look at the racism so common in the south in the 1950s and received recognition as a Smithsonian Notable Book.

The quandary of a relationship in which one feels obligated to stay is explored in the adult title *Dive from Clausen's Pier*, where Carrie is bored and ready to leave her fiancé Mike, but then on Memorial Day he breaks his neck diving from Clausen's Pier. Written by Ann Packer and recipient of the ALA Alex Award, in addition to being named a *Publishers Weekly* Best Book, Carrie flees to New York City where she struggles to decide whether she needs to stay in NYC or return to her Wisconsin home and Mike. Kate, Mary Lawson's central character in *Crow Lake*, also worries about relationships, though her's are in her family as she feels that her brother Matt threw away his career when he dropped out of school to marry a neighbor. This ALA Alex winner, which was also named a *Publishers Weekly* Best Book, finds Kate eventually accepting her brother's decision, which frees her to enjoy her relationship with her boyfriend Daniel.

The problems of high school life took center stage in several works. Manhattan teenagers with too much money fill the pages of an ALA Best Books for Young Adults winner in Jake Coburn's *Prep* while the travails of ninth grade, friendship, and crushes are explored in *True Meaning of Cleavage* by Mariah Fredericks, recipient of a place on the *Booklist* Editor's Choice listing. Manipulating a geek to become Mr. Popularity backfires, with tragic results, in Gail Giles's *Shattering Glass*, recognized as both an ALA Best Books for Young Adults and an ALA Quick Picks for Reluctant Young Adult Readers. The suicide of a young girl, despite the round-the-clock efforts of her friends to prevent it, leads to a murder trial for the unnamed narrator in the ALA Best Books for Young Adults *Aimee* by Mary Beth Miller.

Publishing News 2002-2003

The past few years have seen new publishers spring up and others forced to file for Chapter 11 Bankruptcy. Located in Dublin, Ohio, Darby Creek Publishing started up in 2003 and plans to produce both fiction and nonfiction titles, with one of its first titles being *The Warriors* by the acclaimed author Joseph Bruchac. In some cases, publishers add imprints, which was the case with Millbrook, a noted nonfiction publisher, which started the children's book imprint Roaring Brook Press. Unfortunately Millbrook entered into bankruptcy proceedings and the fate of Roaring Brook was up in the air until the imprint became part of Holt in 2004. As the publisher for the 2003 Caldecott winner, *My Friend Rabbit* by Eric Rohmann, plus the recipient of some ALA Best Books for Young Adults titles, Roaring Brook Press appears to have found a permanent home.

Following the success of its adult division, British publisher Bloomsbury sent its children division to the United States. In the U.K. Bloomsbury was the original publisher of the Harry Potter series, though in the United States Scholastic assumes that role.

Hoping to reach children and teens, Winslow Press integrated its children's and young adult titles with its web site. Unfortunately Winslow, which produced the popular series Dear Mr. President and a time travel series for middle school students, the Hourglass Adventures, filed for Chapter 11 bankruptcy protection. The Troll Book Club also filed for Chapter 11 though its administration indicated it would like to remain in business if financing could help turn the losses around.

Paperback imprints have become increasingly popular and Tor's Starscape was designed to make their already popular adult fantasy and science fiction books more easily available to younger readers. In addition to the Tor titles, works from other publishers and original pieces will become part of Starscape. In 2003 the company began Tor Teen, an imprint designed for science fiction and fantasy readers aged 13 and up, which will begin with Tor's backlist titles that have proven appeal to teens. "Where Fantasy Takes Flight" is the tag line for Firebird, a paperback imprint from Penguin Putnam, that also consists of backlist science fiction and fantasy with appeal for both teens and adults. Editor Sharyn November noted that the teens she hears from the most are those who find their science fiction and fantasy books in the adult section. Two advisory boards have been set up to assist November, one from teen readers and the other from librarians, authors, and editors who read widely in and are knowledgeable about this genre.

At Scholastic, senior editor David Levithan noticed a lack of books written for older teens and launched the PUSH line which concentrates on works by first-time authors that "speak straight to teens." Pocket Books and MTV collaborate on original books for older teens that might be considered a little "edgy," while Simon & Schuster's Pulse imprint includes TV tie-ins, award-winning fiction titles and nonfiction. In 2003 all the media tie-ins were consolidated into the single imprint Simon Spotlight, which before had been structured for younger readers. The Dell Laurel-Leaf imprint from Random House has a program called Readers Circle that publishes rack-sized copies of award-winning and established YA books, each of which contains a section on discussion questions, interviews with the author and biographical information. To launch the program, Random House sent out seven Readers Circle authors on tour including Louis Sachar, Jennifer Armstrong, Lois Lowry and Adam Bagdasarian, to name a few.

Adult authors are venturing into the children's and young adult fields in ever increasing numbers and four who were recent entries enjoyed great success. Carl Hiaasen produced the award winning *Hoot*, Michael Chabon wrote the equally respected *Summerland* while Neil Gaiman entered the field with *Coraline*. The first young adult novel for Joyce Carol Oates was *Big Mouth and Ugly Girl*, Clive Barker is writing a four-book series beginning with *Abarat* and Isabel Allende has penned *City of the Beast*.

Publishers are aware that other people besides librarians buy books and they're customizing their wares for teachers. Books useful for classroom reading are often accompanied by such additional items as posters, activity sheets, online information and guides in addition to the teacher's guides tipped into the book. Book Clubs and book fairs, book-based television programs, and special mailings all entice and hold the interest of teachers.

An entirely new product has emerged in the arena of young adult literature: *Rush Hour*, a semi-annual journal with Michael Cart as the founding editor. Published by Random House and based on the British magazine *Granta*, this literary journal plans to feature established authors but offers them the chance to stretch and try experimental pieces if they wish. Ten years in conception, the first volume was titled "Sin," and included works by Ron Koertge, Marc Aronson, Joan Bauer and Nikki Grimes. Published in hardback for schools and public libraries, it will also be available in trade paperback for the retail market. Designed for older young adults, the journal is "unique" and the material will be "sophisticated" according to editor Cart.

Characters, from the Unusual to the Unforgettable

There's seems to be no limit to the innovation that authors bring to the creation of characters. Who would have expected a doughnut to star in a picture book? That's just what happens in *Arnie the Doughnut* by author/illustrator Laurie Keller. Arnie achieves his fondest dream when he's purchased from the bakery. His dream soon becomes a nightmare when he discovers that his new owner plans to eat him. It takes some sweet-talking for Arnie to save himself in this humorous story. Jerdine Nolen's *Plantzilla* with illustrations by David Catrow features another object that influences a household. The class plant, spending the summer in a student's home, doesn't have much to say, but the growth pattern of Plantzilla and some mysterious disappearances in the home prompt frantic communication

from the student's mother to his vacationing teacher. A loud, proud garbage truck struts his stuff in *I Stink!* by Kate and James McMullan. This title, featuring an anthropomorphized truck that collects all the garbage from "A" to "Z," has won ten children's book awards. A doll is a more familiar character in a children's book but it's unlikely readers have met one like the Princess Mimi Doll, a.k.a. Mean Mimi, introduced in *The Meanest Doll in the World*, the sequel to Ann M. Martin and Laura Godwin's *The Doll People* with illustrations by Brian Selznick.

Unusual animals star in humorous and award winning books also. Mo Willems, in his first picture book *Don't Let the Pigeon Drive the Bus!*, introduces a mischievous blue pigeon that is determined to drive a bus. Neither whining, wheedling, cajoling nor throwing a major temper tantrum achieves the pigeon's goal, but as the unsuccessful, dejected bird walks away it spots an even larger vehicle that inspires a bigger dream and possibly another story. A worm sporting a red baseball cap keeps a record of life from a worm's point of view in Doreen Cronin's *Diary of a Worm* with illustrations by Harry Bliss. Life can be dangerous for such a character, especially during fishing season, and school presents additional challenges. The Australian import *Diary of a Wombat* written by Jackie French and illustrated by Bruce Whatley presents life down under from the perspective of one of the hungry little creatures that actually believes it is providing a service to the human inhabitants of the home it seems to be claiming as its own. Readers will find humor in the award-winning title but one wonders if life with a wombat in the yard is quite as enjoyable. A lost alien tries to find its mother after crash-landing on Earth in *Beegu*, written and illustrated by Alexis Deacon. The New York Times Best Illustrated Book presents a sympathetic character that can't seem to find acceptance, but does find a way home again. Rodents star in other titles. In an easy-reader chapter book, *Little Rat Sets Sail* by Monika Bang-Campbell with illustrations by Molly Bang, frightened Little Rat tries to get out of sailing lessons but by summer's end she's conquered her fear of the water and looks forward to mastering a more challenging vessel next year. The title character of *The Tale of Despereaux*, Kate DiCamillo's Newbery Medal winning novel, is unlike other mice in the castle and hence he is banished to the dungeon. The very uniqueness of Despereaux's sensitive nature, his literacy, and his appreciation of music enable him to conquer his fears, save a princess, and bring light and soup back into castle life.

Folktale characters appear in adaptations that stretch the originals in new directions. Mary Pope Osborne's *The Brave Little Seamstress* with illustrations by Giselle Potter remains true to the Grimm Brother's original story of a tailor with the exception of casting the protagonist as a woman and twisting the ending a bit. Two authors take the same Aesop's fable and "fracture" it in different directions. Gail Carson Levine, in her book *Betsy Who Cried Wolf* with illustrations by Scott Nash, cast eight-year-old Betsy in the role of the traditionally male character who cried wolf once too often. In this story Betsy solves the dilemma of the wolf on her own by offering the starving creature her dinner. *The Wolf Who Cried Boy* by Bob Hartman with illustrations by Tim Raglin turns the situation around. Little Wolf is tired of the family's steady fare of lamb and other game; he wants some Boy for dinner. After ruining the unappetizing dinner prepared by his mom twice with his cries of "Boy!" Little Wolf gets no response from his annoyed parents when a Scout Troop marches through the nearby woods. A wolf also appears in a parody of the *Three Little Pigs* titled *Where's the Big Bad Wolf* that is written and illustrated by Eileen Christelow. In this take on the tale Detective Doggedly, investigating the destruction of three little pigs' homes, gets help from residents at the Home for Elderly Cows in finding the masquerading culprit. Author/Illustrator Diane Stanley concludes her award-winning adaptation entitled *Goldie and the Three Bears* with Goldie (who stumbles into the bears' home seeking help after getting off the bus at the wrong stop) and the littlest bear becoming playmates. In Lane Smith's title *Pinocchio the Boy: or Incognito in Collodi* the author/illustrator extends the story of puppet Pinocchio by surmising what happens after the Blue Fairy changes the puppet into a real boy.

Series

Series abound in fantasyland and several come from non-American authors. Australian Garth Nix's *Sabriel* from HarperCollins was published in 1996 and readers entered a fascinating world of necromancers and the undead. *Sabriel* was followed by *Lirael* in 2001 and concludes with *Abhorsen* in 2003. Both adults and teens enjoy this series and booksellers feel that word of mouth and handselling have contributed to its large sales. Bats have intrigued readers since Canadian Kenneth Oppel's first work *Silverwing* appeared in 1997. The book wasn't signed as a series but editorial director David Gale of Simon & Schuster said when books two and three arrived, he was thrilled and wouldn't minding seeing more. Though Oppel's books sell well in the U.S., they haven't reached the level they attained in Canada where Cheerios boxes recently carried photos of the author along with covers of his books.

British author Jonathan Stroud is writing The Bartimaeus Trilogy and the first in the series, *The Amulet of Samarkand*, was published by Hyperion and was recently named a 2004 Boston Globe-Horn Book Honor Book. Starring a centuries-old djinn named Bartimaeus, it also features a young magician and a girl who's not affected by some of the magic of the time. Also from Britain, though not scheduled to be published in the U.S. until 2004, is *LionBoy* by the mother-daughter writing team of Louisa Young and her 10-year-old daughter Isabel, who write under the name of Zizou Corder, a pen name derived from the moniker of Isabel's pet lizard. From the United States is Christopher Paolini's work *Eragon*, the first in the Inheritance trilogy, which attracted a lot of attention after it was revealed that he wrote it when he was 15 and initially self-published it, until the title was picked up by Knopf.

Two new series may appeal to Harry Potter fans as they await the release of Rowling's next title. The Spiderwick Chronicles written by Holly Black and Tony DiTerlizzi with illustrations by DiTerlizzi describes unusual adventures involving strange creatures (think boggarts, goblins and trolls) that are experienced by nine-year-old twins and their teen-aged sister when they move into a great-aunt's old mansion. The first title, *The Field Guide* was awarded a Center for Children's Books Best Book designation in 2003. The five books comprising the series, each about 100 pages, give a reader who may not be up to the length of Rowling's works an alternative in the fantasy genre. In 2002, Jenny Nimmo's new series Children of the Red King began with *Midnight for Charlie Bone* about a ten-year-old boy's discovery that he's inherited some magical abilities.

After Charlie enters Bloor's Academy, an elite boarding school, more surprising discoveries await him.

Humor can be found in series works, and Meg Cabot's Princess Diaries is a good example, with its young teenager who discovers she's really a princess and readjusts to life as a royal. From Britain comes the Mates, Dates series featuring Lucy, Izzie and Nesta who escapades were probably inspired by Louise Rennison's Georgia Nicolson series.

Milestones, Anniversaries, Events and Birthdays

2002

E.P. Dutton and Company, Inc.: This company first began publishing 150 years ago in 1852.

Peter Rabbit: 100 years ago Beatrix Potter introduced this character in her classic book *The Tale of Peter Rabbit*.

Margaret K. McElderry: Renowned children's book editor celebrated her 90th birthday in July.

The Velveteen Rabbit: Margery Williams' title character has been well loved for 80 years.

The Boxcar Children: The Alden children have solved mysteries for 60 years.

The Little House: Virginia Lee Burton's Caldecott Medal winner has been enjoyed for 60 years.

Charlotte's Web: The friendship between a remarkable pig and a creative spider has continued for 50 years.

New York Times Best Illustrated Children's Book Award: For 50 years the award has been presented.

From the Mixed-Up Files of Mrs. Basil E. Frankweiler: Jamie and Claudia first ran through the halls of the Metropolitan Museum of Art 35 years ago.

Fudge: First introduced 30 years ago by Judy Blume in *Tales of a Fourth Grade Nothing*, Fudge returned this year in *Double Fudge*.

Nate the Great: The beginning reader series about this detective and his dog began 30 years ago.

Jumanji: 20 years after the mysterious board game was first played, author Chris Van Allsburg produced the sequel *Zathura*.

Bruce Coville: His first novel *The Monster's Ring: A Magic Shop Book* was published 20 years ago.

Froggy: It's been 10 years since *Froggy Gets Dressed*, the first of 13 titles about Jonathan London's appealing character Froggy.

Dr. Seuss: The Dr. Seuss National Memorial Sculpture Garden opened in Springfield, MA with 22 sculptures of the author/illustrator's famous characters.

The Hatchet: The Twin Cities of Minneapolis and St. Paul celebrated the selection of Gary Paulsen's title for their One Book Project, a two month program where residents of all ages in these two cities read this tale of survival in the Canadian wilderness.

Dora the Explorer: Dora and her ever-present backpack have moved from television to the printed page in a new series published by Simon & Schuster Children's Publishing.

Virginia Lee Burton: A display of the author and illustrator's art was held at the Haggerty Museum of Art in Wisconsin. Burton is known for the Caldecott Medal winner title *The Little House* and other classics such as *Mike Mulligan and His Steam Shovel*.

2003

Clifford the Big Red Dog: 40 years ago Emily Elizabeth introduced her adorable, fast-growing puppy to readers.

Cricket Magazine: The children's literature magazine celebrated its 30th year with a retrospective title *Celebrate Cricket*.

Little Bear: 10 years ago Little Bear first struggled to fall asleep in *Can't You Sleep Little Bear?* by Martin Waddell.

Eric Carle: Artwork from five of the renowned author/illustrator's picture books was recreated in flowers at the 29th annual Macy's Flower Show in New York.

Goosebumps: Twenty-five of R.L. Stine's most popular titles have been re-released by Scholastic Children's Books.

Gryphon Award: The Center for Children's Books at the University of Illinois in Urbana-Champaign announced the establishment of a new children's literature award to recognize transitional books, those intended for readers between kindergarten and fourth grade. The first award will be announced in March 2004.

J.K. Rowling: Rowling meets a famous cartoon family when *The Simpsons* visit London in an episode of this popular television series.

Books on Buses: In Rochester, New York, this program has installed racks filled with children's books on the city's public buses. Over 50,000 books have been collected and the success of this project has led Anchorage, Alaska to try a similar program.

Obituaries

January 28, 2002: Astrid Lindgren, 1958 recipient of the Hans Christian Andersen medal for her contribution to children's literature and best known for her books about Pippi Longstocking died in Stockholm at the age of 94.

January 2002: In St. Paul Minnesota, 70-old Judy Delton, author of more than two hundred children's books passed away.

February 9, 2002: Isabelle Holland author of *Man Without a Face* died in New York City.

February 16, 2002: Carol Fenner died in Battle Creek, MI at the age of 72. Her book *Yolanda's Genius* was named a Newbery Honor Book in 1996.

February 19, 2002: Virginia Hamilton, the first African-American winner of the Newbery Medal whose works also garnered two Newbery Honors, the National Book Award, the Laura Ingalls Wilder Award, the Hans Christian Anderson Award and three Coretta Scott King Awards succumbed to breast cancer at the age of 65 in Dayton, Ohio.

May 5, 2002: Eighty-six-year-old Franklyn M. Branley co-founder of the *Let's-Read-and-Find-Out* series and author of many children's books on astronomy died in Brunswick, ME.

May 11, 2002: Bill Peet, 87-year-old picture book author and illustrator, passed away at his home in California. His 1989 title *Bill Peet: An Autobiography* was chosen as a Caldecott Honor Book.

May 28, 2002: The ghostwriter for many of the original Nancy Drew stories, Mildred Wirt Benson, died in Toledo, Ohio at the age of 96. Paid $125 for each of the 23 Nancy Drew stories, she never collected royalties. She was still a columnist for the local newspaper "The Blade" and became ill at work.

June 12, 2002: A reviewer and professor of children's literature, Zena Bailey Sutherland died in Chicago at the age of 86. She was the editor at *The Bulletin of the Center for Children's Books*, taught at the University of Chicago Library School and wrote five editions of the well-used textbook *Children and Books*.

June 13, 2002 - Maia Wojciechowska winner of the 1965 Newbery Medal for *Shadow of a Bull* died at the age of 74.

July 4, 2002: Joan Bodger, a children's book author, editor, storyteller, and an educator, died at the age of 79 in British Columbia.

July 21, 2002: Esphyr Slobodkina, author and illustrator of the well-known *Caps for Sale*, originally published in 1938 died at the age of 93.

July 23, 2002: Chaim Potok died at his home in Pennsylvania; though best known as an adult author, many of his titles had direct appeal to teens including *The Chosen* and *My Name Is Asher Lev*.

August 8, 2002: Doris Buchanan Smith, remembered for her award-winning novel *A Taste of Blackberries* died at the age of 68. In addition to her four children, she took in more than 200 foster children.

September 11, 2002: David Wisniewski, winner of the 1997 Caldecott Medal for *The Golem* died in Maryland after a brief illness. He was 49 years old.

September 27, 2002: Glen Rounds, renowned author and illustrator and recipient of the Kerlan Award for "singular achievement in creation of children's literature" died at the age of 96 in Pinehurst, NC.

November 2, 2002: Science fiction author Charles Sheffield died in Maryland. A scientist who worked for NASA, Sheffield turned to science fiction writing in the late 1970s, producing over 30 novels and more than 100 short stories.

December 2, 2002: Aileen Fisher 96-year-old author of award-winning children's poetry, picture books, plays and biographies died in Boulder, CO.

March 7, 2003: Born in England but an immigrant to Canada, Monica Hughes died at the age of 77. She was the author of many young adult science fiction novels.

March 27, 2003: Paul Zindel, 2002 recipient of the Margaret A. Edwards Award for lifetime contributions to young people's literature, died at the age of 66 in Manhattan. Zindel's first novel *The Pigman* received the Boston Globe-Horn Book Award for fiction.

June 28, 2003: Joan Lowery Nixon, four-time winner of the Edgar Allan Poe Award for Best Juvenile Mystery and author of many historical novels for children, died at the age of 76 in Houston, TX.

June 30, 2003: Author and illustrator Robert McCloskey, recipient of the Regina Medal and winner of two Caldecott Medals, in 1942 for *Make Way for Ducklings* and in 1958 for *Time of Wonder* as well as two Caldecott Honors for *Blueberries for Sale* and *One Morning in Maine* died in Deer Isle, ME at the age of 88.

August 2003: Tom Feelings author of *The Middle Passage* and one who "brought the African experience to American Children," passed away at the age of 70.

September 29, 2003: Beloved Vice President and Library Promotion Director at HarperCollins, Bill Morris died at the age of 74. A friend to everyone, his loss was widely mourned by the library and publishing community.

October 3, 2003: William Steig died in Boston at the age of 95. Winner of the Caldecott Medal for *Sylvester and the Magic Pebble*, and a Caldecott Honor for *The Amazing Bone* author and illustrator Steig also had two books recognized as Newbery Honor Books, *Dr. DeSoto* and *Abel's Island*. Steig's character Shrek, created in a picture book of the same name, has gained new fame as the star of a movie.

October 11, 2003: Vivien Alcock writer of fantasies and mysteries died in London at the age of 79.

October 29, 2003: Harry C. Stubbs died at the age of 81. Under the pen name of Hal Clement, he wrote a dozen science fiction novels.

December 3, 2003: The author of *Flat Stanley* and its sequels, Jeff Brown, died at the age of 77.

In conclusion

As the Children's Book Council noted with the theme for the 84th observance of Children's Book Week in 2003, we are "Free to Read." The more than 1,500 titles in this sixth volume of *What Do Children and Young Adults Read Next?* include those that may interest, challenge, soothe, inform, frighten, delight, inspire, provoke, or console readers who are, fortunately, free to read.

A

1

ALMA FLOR ADA
G. BRIAN KARAS, Illustrator

Daniel's Pet

(San Diego: Harcourt, Inc., 2002)

Series: Green Light Reader. Level 1
Subject(s): Pets; Animals/Chickens; Farm Life
Age range(s): Grades K-1
Major character(s): Daniel, Child, Son; Jen, Chicken; Mama, Mother
Time period(s): 2000s
Locale(s): United States

Summary: Daniel asks Mama if the soft baby chick in his hands can be his pet. He names her Jen and gives her special attention as he cares for all the hens on the family farm. It's exciting for Daniel to see Jen grow and a bit alarming the day he can't find her. Mama shows Daniel that Jen is sitting on a nest full of eggs. Lucky Daniel! Now he'll have lots of pets. (20 pages)

Where it's reviewed:
Bulletin of the Center for Children's Books, December 2002, page 140
Horn Book Guide, Fall 2003, page 348

Other books by the same author:
I Love Saturdays Y Domingos, 2002
With Love, Little Red Hen, 2001
Daniel's Mystery Egg, 2000 (Green Light Reader Level 2)

Other books you might like:
Antonia Barber, *Gemma and the Baby Chick*, 1993
   Gemma warms a rejected egg until it hatches and then returns the baby chick to its sleeping mother.
Jenny Nimmo, *Something Wonderful*, 2001
   Little Hen does something wonderful when she gathers the eggs abandoned by the other chickens and sits on them until they hatch.

Mary Wormell, *Hilda Hen's Search*, 1994
   Hilda Hen confidently searches until she finds a perfectly original spot for her nest.

2

ALMA FLOR ADA
ELIVIA SAVADIER, Illustrator

I Love Saturdays Y Domingos

(New York: Atheneum Books for Young Readers, 2002)

Subject(s): Grandparents; Bilingualism; Heritage
Age range(s): Grades K-3
Major character(s): Unnamed Character, 6-Year-Old, Daughter (granddaughter); Grandpa, Grandfather; Abuelita, Grandmother
Time period(s): 2000s
Locale(s): United States

Summary: A little girl visits her father's parents on Saturday and her mother's parents on Sunday. With one set of grandparents she speaks English and with the other she speaks Spanish. Grandpa tells stories of his parents and older brother coming to America from Europe. Abuelita proudly relates experiences of her Native American heritage. Cultures and family come together to celebrate the little girl's sixth birthday with a party and a lot of love. (32 pages)

Where it's reviewed:
Booklist, February 1, 2002, page 944
Horn Book Guide, Fall 2002, page 318
Kirkus Reviews, December 1, 2001, page 1680
Publishers Weekly, December 10, 2001, page 69
School Library Journal, January 2002, page 89

Other books by the same author:
With Love, Little Red Hen, 2001
The Three Golden Oranges, 1999
Jordi's Star, 1996

Other books you might like:

Helen Buckley, *Grandfather and I*, 1994
  Grandfather makes a perfect companion because he always has time to spare.
Carmen Santiago Nodar, *Abuelita's Paradise*, 1992
  Marita sits in her deceased grandmother's rocker recalling her stories about Puerto Rican life.
Effin Older, *My Two Grandmothers*, 2000
  During visits with each of her grandmothers Lilly learns about different family traditions.

3

GEORGIE ADAMS
EMILY BOLAN, Illustrator

The Three Little Witches Storybook
(New York: Hyperion Books for Children, 2002)

Subject(s): Witches and Witchcraft; Magic; Halloween
Age range(s): Grades 1-3
Major character(s): Zara, Student, Witch; Ziggy, Student, Witch; Zoe, Student, Witch
Time period(s): Indeterminate
Locale(s): Magic Wood, Fictional Country (Cauldron Cottage)

Summary: Zara, Ziggy and Zoe excitedly plan a Halloween party and use a spell to send the invitations to each guest. Then they clean the house, or try to. Some of the spells don't do exactly what the novice witches expect the first time they try. One day a talking signpost gives them a clue as to the location of the school, a magical building that moves about the community. Finally the night of the party arrives along with the invited guests. After games, and food and lots of fun, the guests depart and Zara, Ziggy and Zoe bid each other good night. Originally published in England in 2001. (92 pages)

Where it's reviewed:

Booklist, September 1, 2002, page 138
Horn Book Guide, Spring 2003, page 64
Publishers Weekly, September 23, 2002, page 22
School Librarian, Summer 2002, page 73
School Library Journal, December 2002, page 84

Awards the book has won:
Smithsonian's Notable Books for Children, 2002

Other books by the same author:
Highway Builders, 1996
Nanny Fox and the Christmas Surprise, 1996
Fish, Fish, Fish, 1993

Other books you might like:

Marion Dane Bauer, *Alison's Fierce and Ugly Halloween*, 1997
  Alison's attempt to be scary on Halloween creates friction with her friend Cindy who has different ideas about the holiday.
Arthur Howard, *Hoodwinked*, 2001
  Little witch Mitzi wants a creepy pet but after her first two choices are unsatisfactory, she adopts a stray kitten that seems just right.
Dav Pilkey, *Dragon's Halloween*, 1993
  In the fifth easy reader about Dragon, the kindly creature

scares himself with his pumpkin monster and then with sounds from his hungry stomach.
James Stevenson, *Emma*, 1985
  Not a typical witch, Emma even needs flying lessons.

C.S. ADLER

The No Place Cat
(New York: Clarion Books, 2002)

Subject(s): Animals/Cats; Runaways; Stepfamilies
Age range(s): Grades 4-8
Major character(s): Tess, 12-Year-Old; Annie, Stepsister, Child
Time period(s): 2000s
Locale(s): Tucson, Arizona

Summary: Her father remarries and suddenly only child Tess is surrounded by three stepsiblings, a stepmother with rules and a father who is extremely rigid and efficient. Messy Tess doesn't stand a chance in their house, but the final blow comes when her little stepsister Annie destroys her extra-credit project for social studies. Sick of living by rules, she packs some clothes and walks across Tucson, even spending one night at a state camp ground, to stay with her mother. Befriended by a little cat at the campground, Tess is surprised at the feeling she develops for the cat and is very upset when her mother's hatred of cats becomes obvious. At first, life seems great staying with her mother but Tess eventually becomes lonely as her mother's either busy socializing or away on a business trip, reasons that kept her from seeking custody of Tess in the first place. Eventually her father convinces her to return home and suddenly a few rules sound good to Tess, especially when her stepmother helps her try to find the cat that initially befriended Tess. (153 pages)

Where it's reviewed:

Bulletin of the Center for Children's Books, April 2002, page 270
Children's Bookwatch, July 2002, page 3
Horn Book Guide, Fall 2002, page 367
Kirkus Reviews, March 15, 2002, page 404
School Library Journal, March 2002, page 225

Other books by the same author:
The Unhappy Horse, 2002
Winning, 1999
Not Just a Summer Crush, 1998
Her Blue Straw Hat, 1997
More than a Horse, 1997

Other books you might like:

Berlie Doherty, *Holly Starcross*, 2002
  Ever since her mother remarried and had three children, Holly has felt left out, so she's delighted to have a chance to meet and stay with her father.
Deborah Moulton, *Summer Girl*, 1992
  Ten years after her parents divorce, Tommy is sent to live with her father. It's awkward at first, but gradually they work out their relationship.
Debra Seely, *Grasslands*, 2002
  After his father remarries, Thomas lives with his new

stepfamily but is miserable because he's slower than his stepsiblings at chores.

5

DAVID A. ADLER
CHRIS O'LEARY, Illustrator

Mama Played Baseball

(San Diego: Gulliver Books/Harcourt, Inc., 2003)

Subject(s): Sports/Baseball; World War II; Working Mothers
Age range(s): Grades K-3
Major character(s): Amy, Child, Daughter; Unnamed Character, Mother, Baseball Player; Unnamed Character, Father, Military Personnel
Time period(s): 1940s
Locale(s): United States

Summary: While Amy's father is overseas fighting in World War II, her mother has to get a job to help support the family. Amy's mother is hired to play baseball in the All-American Girl's Professional Baseball League. Amy is proud of her mother, helps her practice and attends all of her mother's home games. One day, Amy's mother puts on her uniform and tells Amy to come with her to the bus station. Amy thinks they are going to an away game together but, instead, they go to greet Amy's father who has made it home safely from the war. (32 pages)

Where it's reviewed:
Bulletin of the Center for Children's Books, April 2003, page 302
School Library Journal, April 2003, page 114

Other books by the same author:
A Picture Book of Lewis and Clark, 2003
The Babe & I, 1999 (Smithsonian's Notable Books for Children)
Lou Gehrig: The Luckiest Man, 1997
Cam Jansen and the Mystery of the Stolen Diamonds, 1980

Other books you might like:
Shana Corey, *Players in Pigtails*, 2003
    Katie Casey is chosen to play in the All-American Girls Professional Baseball League.
Deborah Hopkinson, *Girl Wonder: A Baseball Story in Nine Innings*, 2003
    A fictionalized account of Alta Weiss, the first woman to pitch baseball for a semi-professional men's team, is set in 1907.
Doreen Rappaport, *Dirt on Their Skirts*, 2000
    Margaret cheers on her favorite players during the 1946 All-American Girls Professional Baseball League championship. Lyndall Callan, co-author.

6

JON AGEE, Author/Illustrator

Z Goes Home

(New York: Michael Di Capua Books/Hyperion, 2003)

Subject(s): Letters; Zoos; Work
Age range(s): Grades 1-3

Major character(s): Z, Object
Time period(s): Indeterminate
Locale(s): Fictional Country

Summary: At the end of the workday Z climbs down from his position as part of the sign "City Zoo" and begins his commute to his home. His trip takes him past, over, into and around the other 25 letters of the alphabet. When Z reaches his home he announces his arrival to O, W, I and E! As a group, Z's family is clearly Zowie! (32 pages)

Where it's reviewed:
Booklist, September 1, 2003, page 127
Bulletin of the Center for Children's Books, October 2003, page 48
Horn Book, November 2003, page 727
Publishers Weekly, June 16, 2003, page 68
School Library Journal, September 2003, page 166

Other books by the same author:
Milo's Hat Trick, 2001 (Publishers Weekly Best Children's Books)
Dmitri the Astronaut, 1996
Ludlow Laughs, 1985

Other books you might like:
Shirley Glaser, *The Alphazeds*, 2003
    As individual letters fill a room it becomes increasingly chaotic until some of the letters discover that by working together they can make a word.
Andy Rash, *Agent A to Agent Z*, 2004
    Agent A is on a mission through the alphabet to locate a mole (the spy kind).
June Sobel, *B Is for Bulldozer: A Construction ABC*, 2003
    A year-long work project to construct an amusement park uses equipment representing each letter of the alphabet.

7

CHARLOTTE AGELL, Author/Illustrator

Welcome Home or Someplace Like It

(New York: Holt, 2003)

Subject(s): Country Life; Grandfathers; Diaries
Age range(s): Grades 5-8
Major character(s): Aggie Wing, 13-Year-Old; Thorne Wing, 15-Year-Old; Eugene Belicose, Grandfather
Time period(s): 2000s
Locale(s): Ludwig, Maine

Summary: Moving around so much, supposedly so her mother can research the romances she writes, Aggie keeps a journal about each location; she's now on Notebook 27. This time she and her brother Thorne have been dropped off at their grandfather's in Maine and they feel a little uncomfortable as they'd never before met him. Aggie and Thorne gradually settle into life in this tiny town, populated with a good share of eccentrics, and pretty soon Aggie learns to raise chickens and teacher her 91-year-old grandfather to swim. Discovering why her mother fled Ludwig when she was only seventeen explains many oddities in Aggie's life and helps her understand her mother's restlessness. As August nears, she realizes how much she likes Ludwig and hopes they can stay longer in this author's first novel. (231 pages)

Where it's reviewed:
Booklist, November 15, 2003, page 607
Bulletin of the Center for Children's Books, January 2004, page 178
Publishers Weekly, November 24, 2003, page 65
School Library Journal, November 2003, page 134
Voice of Youth Advocates, October 2003, page 300

Other books you might like:
Polly Horvath, *The Canning Season*, 2003
  Ratchet spends the summer in Maine with her two great aunts, Tilly and PenPen, whose eccentricities match their age.
Katherine Paterson, *The Same Stuff as Stars*, 2002
  Dumped by her mother on her great-grandmother's doorstep, Angel once again assumes responsibility for running a household.
Richard Peck, *A Long Way from Chicago*, 1998
  Warm and funny stories are shared during the summer Joey and his sister Mary Alice spend with their grandmother.

8

ALLAN AHLBERG
RAYMOND BRIGGS, Illustrator

A Bit More Bert

(New York: Farrar Straus Giroux, 2002)

Subject(s): Humor; Short Stories; Pets
Age range(s): Preschool-Grade 1
Major character(s): Bert, Father, Spouse; Bert, Dog
Time period(s): 2000s
Locale(s): England

Summary: In six brief chapters affable Bert introduces his dog, also named Bert, allows the readers to cut his hair when the barbershop is closed, shares his snack chips with everyone in the family and visits his mother. When Bert the dog runs off, Bert searches futilely and then reports the loss to the police before going home to find Bert on the doorstep awaiting his return. Finally, after a busy day, Bert and family settle down to sleep in their cozy home, bidding good night to the many other ''Berts'' they've come across that day. (32 pages)

Where it's reviewed:
Booklist, November 1, 2002, page 502
Bulletin of the Center for Children's Books, November 2002, page 96
Horn Book, September 2002, page 548
Publishers Weekly, August 19, 2002, page 92
School Library Journal, November 2002, page 110

Awards the book has won:
Bulletin of the Center for Children's Books Blue Ribbons, 2002
Horn Book Fanfare, 2002

Other books by the same author:
The Adventures of Bert, 2001 (Bulletin of the Center for Children's Books Blue Ribbons)
The Snail House, 2001 (Smithsonian's Notable Books for Children)
The Bravest Ever Bear, 2000

Other books you might like:
Joy Cowley, *Agapanthus Hum and Major Bark*, 2001
  Agapanthus Hum intends to select a kitten from the animal shelter but a small dog steals her heart instead.
Mary Ann Hoberman, *The Two Sillies*, 2000
  Two silly people use complicated methods to solve simple problems.
Margaret Wild, *The Pocket Dogs*, 2001
  Despite Biff and Buff's attempts to alert Mr. Pockets, he fails to notice the hole in one of his coat pockets and poor little Biff falls out.

9

ALLAN AHLBERG
KATHARINE MCEWEN, Illustrator

The Cat Who Got Carried Away

(Cambridge, MA: Candlewick Press, 2003)

Subject(s): Family Life; Pets; Babies
Age range(s): Grades 2-4
Major character(s): Gus Gaskitt, Brother, Student—Elementary School; Gloria Gaskitt, Sister, Student—Elementary School; Horace, Cat, Kidnap Victim; Randolph, Rat, Kidnap Victim
Time period(s): 2000s
Locale(s): England

Summary: The Gaskitts notice many strange things happening. The class pet Randolph vanishes, the teacher is injured while searching for the pet and the substitute teacher is a fitness buff. A strange baby carriage roams the streets making odd sounds, such as bark, squeak, and even a meow. That last sound might have something to do with the fact that Gus and Gloria cannot find Horace. Also, they notice that their mother is often in bed and eats strange things such as fried egg and pineapple sandwiches. Meanwhile, abducted Horace and Randolph plot their escape with help from a captured guinea pig. Gus, Gloria, their classmates and substitute teacher, while on their morning run, notice the theft of penguins from the zoo and follow the getaway car to the fake pet shop, ending the animal theft ring. While all this is going on, Gus and Gloria's parents are at the hospital where their mother is delivering their little brother. Soon enough the Gaskitt family is complete again as Horace returns home and the baby leaves the hospital, ready for adventure. (80 pages)

Where it's reviewed:
Booklist, June 2003, page 1782
Bulletin of the Center for Children's Books, June 2003, page 389
Publishers Weekly, March 17, 2003, page 78
School Library Journal, September 2003, page 166

Other books by the same author:
The Woman Who Won Things, 2002 (IRA Children's Choices)
The Man Who Wore All His Clothes, 2001
The Better Brown Stories, 1996 (Smithsonian's Notable Books for Children)

Other books you might like:
Denys Cazet, *Minnie and Moo and the Seven Wonders of the World*, 2003
  With a thinker like Moo and a friend like Minnie this farm is a place of nonstop action and adventure.
Barbara Park, *Junie B., First Grader: One Man Band*, 2003
  A sore toe might keep Junie B. from playing in a big kickball game but it won't keep her out of the action.
Lane Smith, *The Happy Hocky Family Moves to the Country!*, 2003
  New experiences await the members of the Hocky family as they adjust to life in the country.

10

ALLAN AHLBERG
GILLIAN TYLER, Illustrator

Treasure Hunt

(Cambridge, MA: Candlewick Press, 2002)

Subject(s): Games; Playing; Parent and Child
Age range(s): Preschool-Kindergarten
Major character(s): Tilly, Child, Daughter
Time period(s): 2000s
Locale(s): England

Summary: Tilly's family makes a game of everyday things by hiding "treasures" in the house, the yard or the garage with Tilly searching until she finds the item. On snowy days Tilly's cat hides in the garden, but Tilly hunts until she finds her treasure. At bedtime Tilly hides herself and her parents search and search for their treasure so they can have a cuddle before she sleeps. (24 pages)

Where it's reviewed:
Booklist, March 15, 2002, page 1261
Bulletin of the Center for Children's Books, April 2002, page 271
Horn Book, May 2002, page 311
Publishers Weekly, March 25, 2002, page 63
School Library Journal, April 2002, page 100

Other books by the same author:
The Snail House, 2001 (Smithsonian's Notable Books for Children)
The Bravest Ever Bear, 2000
Monkey Do!, 1998

Other books you might like:
Marisabina Russo, *Where Is Ben?*, 1990
  While Ben's mother is busy in the kitchen he tries to get some attention by engaging her in a game of hide-and-seek.
William Steig, *Toby, Where Are You?*, 1997
  Toby's parents play along with his game of hiding from his family.
Caroline Uff, *Lulu's Busy Day*, 2000
  After a busy day of play Lulu cleans up her toys, has a bubble bath and settles into bed for a story and a good night's sleep.

11

ALLAN AHLBERG
KATHARINE MCEWEN, Illustrator

The Woman Who Won Things

(Cambridge, MA: Candlewick Press, 2002)

Subject(s): Humor; Contests; Stealing
Age range(s): Grades 2-4
Major character(s): Mrs. Gaskitt, Mother, Spouse; Gus Gaskitt, 9-Year-Old, Twin; Gloria Gaskitt, 9-Year-Old, Twin; Mrs. Plum, Teacher (substitute), Thief
Time period(s): 2000s
Locale(s): England

Summary: While Mrs. Gaskitt seems to be having one lucky day after another—winning prizes from the many contests that she enters—Gus and Gloria, other students and even the teachers are having nothing but bad luck. Since elderly Mrs. Plum begins substituting in the classroom shoes, bracelets, umbrellas and cell phones are simply vanishing. When the suitcase that Mrs. Plum carries with her at all times begins ringing, Gus and Gloria suspect that she may have something to do with the missing items. As luck would have it, an accidental meeting between Mrs. Gaskitt and Mrs. Plum provides confirmation to their suspicions. (80 pages)

Where it's reviewed:
Booklist, August 2002, page 1955
Bulletin of the Center for Children's Books, June 2002, page 354
Horn Book Guide, Fall 2002, page 355
Publishers Weekly, April 15, 2002, page 66
School Library Journal, June 2002, page 80

Awards the book has won:
IRA Children's Choices, 2003

Other books by the same author:
The Man Who Wore All His Clothes, 2001
The Better Brown Stories, 1996 (Smithsonian's Notable Books for Children)
The Giant Baby, 1994

Other books you might like:
David A. Adler, *The Cam Jansen Series*, 1980-
  Cam Jansen relies on her photographic memory to solve mysteries at school and in her daily life.
Howard Goldsmith, *The Twiddle Twins Music Box Mystery*, 1997
  Timothy and Tabitha discover the identity of the thief who takes a family's music box.
Elizabeth Levy, *The Snack Attack Mystery*, 1996
  The third entry in the Invisible, Inc. series discovers the reason snacks are vanishing from a classroom.

12

INGMARIE AHVANDER
MATI LEPP, Illustrator
ELISABETH KALLICK DYSSEGAARD, Translator

Pancake Dreams

(New York: R & S Books/Farrar Straus Giroux, 2002)

Subject(s): Food; Grandparents; Travel
Age range(s): Grades K-2
Major character(s): Stefan, Child; Unnamed Character, Grandmother, Cook
Time period(s): 2000s (2002)
Locale(s): Jordan; Sweden

Summary: Since moving with his family to Jordan, Stefan misses his grandmother—and the special Swedish pancakes she used to make for him. When Stefan finds a box that's perfect for transporting pancakes, he begins to work on a plan to get them delivered to him. His visiting aunt brings the box back to his grandmother along with a note requesting the pancakes. His grandmother then advertises for a ''responsible person for pancake transportation.'' A Swedish businessman delivers the pancakes to Stefan, who enjoys the treats—and the anticipation of a visit from his grandmother. (28 pages)

Where it's reviewed:
Booklist, November 15, 2002, page 607
Horn Book Guide, Spring 2003, page 23
Horn Book, January 2003, page 51
Kirkus Reviews, August 1, 2002, page 1120
School Library Journal, December 2002, page 84

Other books you might like:
Eric Carle, *Pancakes, Pancakes!*, 1970
    Jack goes to great lengths to have homemade pancakes for breakfast.
Tomie De Paola, *Pancakes for Breakfast*, 1978
    A little, old lady makes pancakes for breakfast.
Tamson Weston, *Hey, Pancakes!*, 2003
    Three siblings take over the kitchen to make pancakes for breakfast.

13

JOAN AIKEN

Midwinter Nightingale

(New York: Delacorte, 2003)

Series: Wolves Chronicles
Subject(s): Adventure and Adventurers; Kings, Queens, Rulers, etc.
Age range(s): Grades 5-8
Major character(s): Dido Twite, Adventurer; Simon, Nobleman (Duke of Battersea); The Baron, Werewolf; Richard IV, Royalty (king)
Time period(s): Indeterminate Past
Locale(s): London, England

Summary: Having enjoyed a vacation in the Americas, Dido returns to London where she discovers that her good friend Simon is missing, along with King Richard, but before she can find them, Dido's kidnapped. Simon not only hides King

Richard, who's dying and will likely be replaced by Simon, but also tries to find a missing coronet, which is needed to crown the next king. Aggravating Simon and King Richard is the Baron, a werewolf who would like to place his own son on the English throne. Adding to the adventure are Dido's escape, horrendous floods, Russian bears and a strange army in this fast-paced read. (248 pages)

Where it's reviewed:
Booklist, June 2003, page 1774
Horn Book Guide, Fall 2003, page 361
Kirkus Reviews, June 1, 2003, page 799
Publishers Weekly, June 9, 2003, page 52
School Library Journal, June 2003, page 136

Other books by the same author:
The Witch of Clatteringshaws, 2005 (Wolves Chronicles)
Dido and Pa, 2003 (Wolves Chronicles)
Midnight Is a Place, 2002
The Cuckoo Tree, 2000
Dangerous Games, 1999 (Wolves Chronicles)

Other books you might like:
Richard W. Jennings, *Mystery in Mt. Mole*, 2003
    Though Andy knows Mr. Farley is one of the least popular teachers at his school, he can't believe that no one seems to care about Mr. Farley's disappearance.
Lemony Snicket, *Unfortunate Events Series*, 1999-
    The Baudelaire children live up to the name of the series as their lives go from bad to worse after their parents are killed in a fire.
Jean Thesman, *Love Among the Walnuts*, 1998
    Evil uncles try to get their hands on Sandy's parents' money, but their plan to poison everyone fails when Sandy and his valet bypass dessert.

14

JEZ ALBOROUGH, Author/Illustrator

Captain Duck

(New York: HarperCollins Publishers, 2002)

Subject(s): Animals; Boats and Boating; Stories in Rhyme
Age range(s): Preschool-Grade 1
Major character(s): Duck, Duck; Goat, Goat; Frog, Frog; Sheep, Sheep
Time period(s): Indeterminate
Locale(s): Fictional Country

Summary: When Duck's truck runs out of gas he walks to Goat's house to borrow some. Goat doesn't answer his door so Duck takes a gas can from his shed. While walking back to the truck he sees Frog, sets down the can and follows Frog to Goat's boat. Without waiting for Goat, Duck jumps in the boat with Frog and Sheep, ignores their warnings and does everything that Goat has just said not to do. Soon, the boat is roaring over the water with Duck at the controls, Frog and Sheep hanging on for dear life and Goat on shore. Duck's madcap adventure ends when the boat runs out of gas, far from shore and the friends must wait to drift back to Goat's dock. (34 pages)

Where it's reviewed:
Books, Christmas 2002, page 26

Publishers Weekly, May 5, 2003, page 224
School Library Journal, July 2003, page 86
Times Educational Supplement, October 25, 2002, page 14*

Other books by the same author:
Fix-It Duck, 2002
Duck in the Truck, 2000
My Friend Bear, 1998

Other books you might like:
Doreen Cronin, *Duck for President*, 2004
   Ambitious Duck, known for making trouble on the farm, grows tired of the routine of farm chores and enters politics.
Amy Hest, *Baby Duck and the Bad Eyeglasses*, 1996
   Although Baby Duck doesn't like her new glasses, she is happy to be able to read her name on the hull of her very own rowboat.
Eric Rohmann, *My Friend Rabbit*, 2002
   Mouse tolerates well-meaning Rabbit's tendency to create problems because friends accept each other as they are. Caldecott Medal
David Shannon, *Duck on a Bike*, 2002
   Duck has a mind to ride a bike and soon has the opportunity to do so; all the other animals join him for a ride around the barnyard.

15

JEZ ALBOROUGH, Author/Illustrator

Fix-It Duck
(New York: HarperCollins Publishers, 2002)

Subject(s): Animals/Ducks; Problem Solving; Stories in Rhyme
Age range(s): Preschool-Grade 1
Major character(s): Duck, Duck, Friend; Sheep, Sheep, Friend; Frog, Frog, Friend
Time period(s): Indeterminate
Locale(s): Fictional Country

Summary: Duck fancies himself a repairman so when water drips into his cup as he relaxes in the living room he decides his roof needs fixing. With toolbox in wing, he becomes "Fix-It Duck." Duck can't reach the roof so he drives to Sheep's home to borrow a ladder. As he sips tea with Sheep explaining the problem at his home, he discovers Sheep's window is in need of repair and Fix-It Duck hops into action again. Duck's solutions to every problem create new and more serious ones. By the conclusion of the book, Sheep's trailer home is rolling out of control down the hill and almost runs over Frog before landing in the lake and Duck's house is flooded with the bathwater that he forgot to turn off. The good news is, Duck's roof isn't leaking after all. Originally published in Great Britain in 2001. (36 pages)

Where it's reviewed:
Booklist, April 1, 2002, page 1331
Horn Book Guide, Fall 2002, page 293
Kirkus Reviews, March 1, 2002, page 328
Publishers Weekly, March 18, 2002, page 105
School Library Journal, May 2002, page 104

Other books by the same author:
Duck in the Truck, 2000
Hug, 2000
My Friend Bear, 1998

Other books you might like:
Doreen Cronin, *Giggle, Giggle, Quack*, 2002
   While the farmer vacations, Duck substitutes his own written instructions for those left by the farmer and creates hilarious chaos.
Sally Grindley, *Mucky Duck*, 2003
   As a pristine white duck plays with its human companion Oliver she soon takes on an appearance worthy of the title Mucky Duck.
David Shannon, *Duck on a Bike*, 2002
   Duck's able to realize his idea of riding a bike when the kids leave some in the farm yard and he inspires other animals to join him.

16

ARLENE ALDA
MARYANN KOVALSKI, Illustrator

Morning Glory Monday
(Plattsburgh, NY: Tundra Books, 2003)

Subject(s): Gardens and Gardening; Emigration and Immigration; Italian Americans
Age range(s): Grades K-3
Major character(s): Unnamed Character, Child, Narrator; Mama, Mother
Time period(s): 1930s
Locale(s): New York, New York

Summary: When the young narrator's mother becomes homesick for Italy one summer the girl and her father try to cheer Mama up. On a trip to Coney Island, the girl wins some seeds that she plants in window boxes certain that the flowers will make Mama smile. Sure enough, as the morning glories grow and spread up the fire escape and through the entire Lower East Side, Mama gets happier and happier. The flowers eventually bring joy to the entire neighborhood. (32 pages)

Where it's reviewed:
Booklist, January 2004, page 872
Bulletin of the Center for Children's Books, November 2003, page 92
School Library Journal, November 2003, page 88

Other books by the same author:
Hurry Granny Annie, 1999
Pig, Horse, or Cow, Don't Wake Me Now, 1994
Sheep, Sheep, Sheep, Help Me Fall Asleep, 1992

Other books you might like:
Lisa Bruce, *Fran's Flower*, 2000
   When Fran finds a flowerpot with a little bud she is determined to help it grow.
Eve Bunting, *Flower Garden*, 1994
   A young girl and her father plant a window box for her mother's birthday.
Sarah Stewart, *The Gardener*, 1997
   In this Caldecott Honor Book, Lydia moves to the city

---

during the Great Depression to help her uncle, but she keeps the farm alive through window boxes.

17

ELIZABETH ALDER

Crossing the Panther's Path

(New York: Farrar Straus Giroux, 2002)

Subject(s): War of 1812; Indians of North America
Age range(s): Grades 7-10
Major character(s): Billy Calder, 15-Year-Old, Linguist (interpreter); Tecumseh, Indian (Shawnee), Chieftain; William Henry Harrison, Government Official (governor)
Time period(s): 1800s; 1810s (1809-1814)
Locale(s): Midwest (Mississippi River Valley)

Summary: After the Revolutionary War, Americans have time to explore their country and soon settlers move into the Mississippi Valley and encroach on Indian lands. Tecumseh, a Shawnee Chief, wants to mobilize the Indian tribes in the Mississippi River Valley in defense of their land. Billy is the son of a British Army officer and a Mohawk Indian mother and, after meeting Tecumseh when he requests British help, is eager to use his translating skills to help this fiery chief. The Indians successfully defeat the Americans in the early stages of the War of 1812, but that's largely due to the help of the British. As the campaign continues, many of the British and the Indians defect until Tecumseh eventually sends a letter to Governor Harrison suggesting the two of them meet on a field of combat in this work based on historical fact. (230 pages)

Where it's reviewed:
Booklist, May 15, 2002, page 1604
Bulletin of the Center for Children's Books, September 2002, page 4
Horn Book Guide, Fall 2002, page 367
School Library Journal, July 2002, page 113
Voice of Youth Advocates, June 2002, page 112

Awards the book has won:
IRA Teachers' Choices/Advanced, 2003

Other books by the same author:
The King's Shadow, 1995

Other books you might like:
Ann Rinaldi, *The Second Bend in the River*, 1997
   Rebecca and her family become friends with Tecumseh when he returns to his boyhood home in Ohio, a spot now occupied by settlers.
Gloria Whelan, *Once on This Island*, 1995
   When their father leaves to fight in the War of 1812, a young girl and her brothers assume responsibility for their family's Michigan farm.
Patricia Willis, *Danger Along the Ohio*, 1997
   Landing on the Shawnee side of the Ohio River, three children care for a wounded Indian boy as they journey down the river in search of their father.

18

LLOYD ALEXANDER

The Rope Trick

(New York: Dutton, 2002)

Subject(s): Supernatural; Adventure and Adventurers; Magicians
Age range(s): Grades 4-7
Major character(s): Lidi, Magician; Daniella, Orphan, Psychic; Ferramondo, Magician; Jericho, Worker (roustabout); Julian, Farmer
Time period(s): Indeterminate Past
Locale(s): Campania, Fictional Country

Summary: Following the death of her verbally abusive, magician father, Lidi continues the family tradition and travels from town to town entertaining crowds with her magic tricks. Accompanying her are Jericho, her canvasmaster, and later Daniella who predicts the future and Julian, a tenant farmer who's been badly beaten. Lidi travels in search of Ferramondo, the famous magician who performs the rope trick, where the magician climbs a stiff rope and disappears when he reaches the top. This little troupe meets both good and bad people on the road but, when Scabbia and his cronies descend upon them and burn their wagons, they replicate the rope trick and are whisked away to another land where Ferramondo awaits them. (195 pages)

Where it's reviewed:
Bulletin of the Center for Children's Books, January 2003, page 186
Horn Book, November 2002, page 743
Publishers Weekly, November 4, 2002, page 84
School Library Journal, September 2002, page 219
Voice of Youth Advocates, December 2002, page 393

Other books by the same author:
The Gawgon and the Boy, 2001 (ALA Notable Children's Books)
Gypsy Rizka, 1999
The Iron Ring, 1997
The Arkadians, 1994
The Remarkable Journey of Prince Jen, 1991

Other books you might like:
Avi, *Midnight Magic*, 1999
   Summoned to the palace of the King of Pergamentioto to exorcise the ghost of Princess Teresina's murdered brother, magician Mangus finds more than a ghost.
Diana Wynne Jones, *The Lives of Christopher Chant*, 1988
   As he dreams, Christopher travels to strange and fascinating worlds.
D. Anne Love, *The Puppeteer's Apprentice*, 2003
   Running away from her abusive home situation, Mouse meets and apprentices with a traveling puppeteer.
Paul Theroux, *Millroy the Magician*, 1994
   Performing his magic at fairs and on television programs, Millroy really wants to promote good eating so he opens a restaurant chain of vegetarian foods.

19

MARTHA ALEXANDER, Author/Illustrator

I'll Never Share You, Blackboard Bear

(Cambridge, MA: Candlewick Press, 2003)

Subject(s): Animals/Bears; Sharing; Imagination
Age range(s): Preschool-Grade 1
Major character(s): Anthony, Child, Friend; Gloria, Child, Friend; Stewart, Child (older), Bully; Blackboard Bear, Bear (imaginary)
Time period(s): Indeterminate
Locale(s): United States

Summary: When Anthony and Blackboard Bear go out for a walk Gloria approaches Anthony and offers to trade all her toys for Blackboard Bear. Anthony refuses. Stewart approaches when he hears the commotion and tries to bully Anthony into sharing his bear. Anthony and Blackboard Bear go home and Blackboard Bear shares an idea with Anthony that will enable Anthony to share his friend without completely letting go. (26 pages)

Where it's reviewed:
Booklist, January 2004, page 872
Publishers Weekly, November 17, 2003, page 67
School Library Journal, February 2004, page 102

Other books by the same author:
I Sure Am Glad to See You, Blackboard Bear, 2001 (reissue of a 1976 title)
And My Mean Old Mother Will Be Sorry, Blackboard Bear, 2000 (reissue of a 1969 title)
We're in Big Trouble, Blackboard Bear, 1980

Other books you might like:
Richard Hamilton, *Polly's Picnic*, 2003
    After hungry animals devour sleeping Polly's picnic lunch they feel some remorse in this rhyming tale and cook food to replace what they've taken.
Kevin Henkes, *Sheila Rae's Peppermint Stick*, 2001
    Sheila Rae challenges sister Louise's request that she share her peppermint stick, but her efforts backfire and Louise gets a share.
Kevin Luthardt, *Mine!*, 2001
    When a new toy breaks as two brothers fight over it, they realize sharing their toys is a better idea.

20

DAVID ALMOND

Counting Stars

(New York: Delacorte, 2002)

Subject(s): Short Stories; Small Town Life; Family Life
Age range(s): Grades 9-12
Time period(s): 1950s
Locale(s): Felling, England

Summary: This collection of eighteen stories is made up of the bits and pieces, remembered and imagined, of Almond's life as a child in a small town in England. Raised in a Catholic home with his many siblings, his tales reveal the small events that are so important in day-to-day life: the death of his sister,

his father's illness, the teachings of their priest; their interchangeable aunts; and the various eccentric townspeople. (205 pages)

Where it's reviewed:
Booklist, February 1, 2002, page 934
Bulletin of the Center for Children's Books, March 2002, page 232
Horn Book, March 2002, page 207
School Library Journal, March 2002, page 225
Voice of Youth Advocates, August 2002, page 188

Other books by the same author:
Secret Heart, 2002
Heaven Eyes, 2001
Kit's Wilderness, 2000
Skellig, 1999

Other books you might like:
Robert Cormier, *Frenchtown Summer*, 1999
    Eugene's twelfth summer in his small town of Monument marks his coming of age as he begins a relationship with his father.
Gerald Hausman, *Doctor Moledinky's Castle: A Hometown Tale*, 1995
    One summer Andy and his friend Pauly explore their town of Berkeley Bend and discover the strange yet heart-warming characters that live there.
Jim Heynen, *Fishing for Chickens: Short Stories about Rural Youth*, 2001
    Assorted authors contributed to this anthology of stories about the reality of farm life for young people.
Tim Wynne-Jones, *The Book of Changes: Stories*, 1995
    Seven stories narrated by teens tell of ordinary dilemmas in their lives, from school assignments to divorce.

21

DAVID ALMOND

Secret Heart

(New York: Delacorte, 2002)

Subject(s): Circus; Self-Perception; Animals
Age range(s): Grades 6-9
Major character(s): Joe Maloney, Handicapped (stutterer); Corinna, Entertainer (trapeze artist); Nanty Solo, Blind Person, Entertainer (fortuneteller); Hackenschmidt "Lion of Russia", Wrestler (professional)
Time period(s): 2000s
Locale(s): Helmouth, England

Summary: The outcast of his motley little village, stuttering Joe hears voices of animals in his head and often skips school to explore the woods and the fields in search of those animals. One night he dreams of a tiger and the next day a ragtag circus comes to town, a circus that pulls Joe to its blue tent scattered with stars. Joe meets the performers Corinna and Nanty Solo, outcasts like himself, and is befriended by them. Blind Nanty tells Joe his fortune and urges him to follow what's in his mind and his "secret heart." And it's to Joe that the performers all turn when the circus disbands and they want the soul of their tiger returned to the woods in this work that merges dreams and reality. (199 pages)

Where it's reviewed:
Booklist, October 1, 2002, page 322
Bulletin of the Center for Children's Books, December 2002, page 140
Kliatt, November 2002, page 5
School Library Journal, October 2002, page 154
Voice of Youth Advocates, December 2002, page 393

Other books by the same author:
Fire-Eaters, 2004
Counting Stars, 2002
Heaven Eyes, 2001 (ALA Notable Children's Books)
Kit's Wilderness, 2000 (Printz Award)
Skellig, 1999 (Printz Honor Book)

Other books you might like:
Kate DiCamillo, *The Tiger Rising*, 2001
   Taking pity on a caged tiger he's been hired to feed, Rob releases him, but that leads to unexpected tragedy.
Bill Littlefield, *The Circus in the Woods*, 2001
   One summer Molly finds a circus in the middle of the woods where she meets the fortuneteller Nell.
Marilyn Singer, *The Circus Lunicus*, 2000
   A toy lizard transforms to a fairy lizard and Solly becomes a star of Circus Lunicus, finds his mother, and sees his life become wild and wacky.

22

ELAINE MARIE ALPHIN

Picture Perfect

(Minneapolis, MN: Carolrhoda Books, Inc., 2003)

Subject(s): Multiple Personalities; Abuse; Missing Persons
Age range(s): Grades 7-10
Major character(s): Ian Slater, 9th Grader, Photographer; Teddy Camden, 9th Grader; Chris Slater, Principal
Time period(s): 2000s
Locale(s): Sawville, California

Summary: Ian's best friend Teddy disappears and he's the last one to see him, making Ian the Sawville sheriff's best suspect. Living under the rule of an abusive, domineering father, Ian survives either by zoning out or escaping with Teddy to a hideout they've created in a nearby redwood forest. When Ian's memory of those last few hours before Teddy vanished gradually returns, he's not sure he's strong enough to reveal his father's role in the disappearance. (244 pages)

Where it's reviewed:
Booklist, August 2003, page 1970
Bulletin of the Center for Children's Books, October 2003, page 49
Publishers Weekly, August 4, 2003, page 81
School Library Journal, October 2003, page 158

Other books by the same author:
Simon Says, 2002
Ghost Soldier, 2001
Counterfeit Son, 2000

Other books you might like:
Robert Cormier, *The Rag and Bone Shop*, 2001
   As the last to have seen murdered Alicia, Jason begins to wonder if he did indeed kill her.

E.L. Konigsburg, *Silent to the Bone*, 2000
   Falsely accused of hurting his sister, mute Branwell is not able to defend himself until his best friend devises a way to break through his silence.
Kristen D. Randle, *The Only Alien on the Planet*, 1995
   New student Ginny finally breaks through Smitty's shell, but doing so leads to his hospitalization in a story of sibling abuse.

23

ELAINE MARIE ALPHIN

Simon Says

(San Diego: Harcourt, 2002)

Subject(s): Identity; Schools/Boarding Schools; Artists and Art
Age range(s): Grades 9-12
Major character(s): Charles Weston, 11th Grader, Artist; Graeme Brandt, 12th Grader, Writer; Adrian Lawson, Songwriter, 11th Grader; Rachel Holland, Editor (student journal)
Time period(s): 2000s
Locale(s): Houston, Texas

Summary: Tired of the ''Simon Says'' games of conformity that people play, Charlies expects to avoid them by transferring to the Whitman High School for the Arts. In this boarding school he wants to meet Graeme, a senior who wrote and sold a young adult novel when he was only in the 9th grade. Unfortunately, Graeme doesn't have the answers Charles seeks and proves only that he, too, plays the ''Simon Says'' game. Ironically when Charles shares some of his oil paintings with Graeme, it serves as inspiration for Graeme, to finally complete his second novel. Unfortunately Graeme is unable to erase his self-doubts about his writing and eventually commits suicide. Only then does Charles realize that some of the most individualistic people at the school are his roommate Adrian and Rachel, the editor of the student journal. (258 pages)

Where it's reviewed:
Booklist, April 15, 2002, page 1394
Bulletin of the Center for Children's Books, June 2002, page 355
Kirkus Reviews, April 1, 2002, page 486
Publishers Weekly, May 20, 2002, page 68
School Library Journal, June 2002, page 130

Other books by the same author:
Ghost Soldier, 2001
Counterfeit Son, 2000
The Ghost Cadet, 1991

Other books you might like:
Alice Hoffman, *The River King*, 2000
   Gus is befriended by beautiful Carlin at post Haddan school, but is disliked by his fellow students which leads to tragedy.
Scott Johnson, *Overnight Sensation*, 1994
   When Kerry's new group of friends leads her away from her old, individualistic friend Madeline, she realizes she's made a mistake.

Nancy Werlin, *Black Mirror*, 2001
  Scholarship students at a boarding school, loner Frances doesn't believe the story that her brother committed suicide from a drug overdose.

24

JULIA ALVAREZ

Before We Were Free

(New York: Knopf/Random House, 2002)

Subject(s): Family Life; Revolutions; Dictators
Age range(s): Grades 6-10
Major character(s): Anita de la Torre, 12-Year-Old; Mundin de la Torre, Brother; Rafael ''El Jefe'' Trujillo, Historical Figure (dictator)
Time period(s): 1960s
Locale(s): Dominican Republic

Summary: After 30 years of living under the dictatorship of Rafael Trujillo, many people in the Dominican Republic want to overthrow him and build new lives. Anita doesn't understand how deeply involved her family is in the conspiracy and when her favorite cousins leave the family compound for New York, she doesn't realize they're escaping while they can. Gradually it becomes apparent that the secret police watch them and their maid spies on the family. When Trujillo is assassinated, his son takes over and is crueler than his father. Anita's father and uncle are arrested for being part of the assassination plot, her older brother Mundin hides in the Italian Embassy, and she and her mother spend two months hiding in a friend's bedroom closet until they can escape to America. Alvarez explains her reasons for writing this book, her first young adult novel, as it's the life she might have led if her family hadn't escaped, as described in *How the Garcia Girls Lost Their Accents*. (167 pages)

Where it's reviewed:
Booklist, August 2002, page 1945
Bulletin of the Center for Children's Books, November 2002, page 97
Horn Book, September 2002, page 563
Publishers Weekly, July 22, 2002, page 180
School Library Journal, August 2002, page 182

Awards the book has won:
ALA Best Books for Young Adults, 2003
ALA Notable Children's Books, 2003

Other books by the same author:
Finding Miracles, 2004
Woman I Kept to Myself: Poems, 2004
Something to Declare, 1998 (adult nonfiction)
In the Time of the Butterflies, 1994 (adult fiction)
How the Garcia Girls Lost Their Accents, 1991 (ALA Notable Children's Books)

Other books you might like:
Anne Frank, *The Diary of Anne Frank*, 1952
  Anne's diary covers the years during World War II when she hides from the Nazis in an Amsterdam warehouse. Biography.
Lyll Becerra de Jenkins, *The Honorable Prison*, 1988
  Because of her father's stand as a newspaper editor, Marta and her family are imprisoned by their South American government.
Beverley Naidoo, *The Other Side of Truth*, 2001
  Her father's job as a journalist marks him for assassination by the Nigerian government; his wife is shot instead and his children are sent to England.
James Watson, *Talking in Whispers*, 1984
  Chilean teen Andres Larreta escapes the death squad that captures his father and brother, but then is left on his own to search for them.

25

STEPHEN E. AMBROSE

This Vast Land: A Young Man's Journal of the Lewis and Clark Expedition

(New York: Simon & Schuster, 2003)

Subject(s): American West; Voyages and Travels; Diaries
Age range(s): Grades 7-10
Major character(s): George Shannon, Teenager, Historical Figure; Peme, Indian (Shoshone); William Clark, Historical Figure, Explorer; Meriwether Lewis, Historical Figure, Explorer
Time period(s): 1800s (1803-1806)
Locale(s): West (expedition traveled from Pittsburgh, PA to Fort Clatsop, WA)

Summary: When Lewis and Clark begin their famous journey, George Shannon at 17 years old is the youngest member of the Corps of Discovery. His thoughts and events of the expedition fill a diary as the reader learns about the Shoshone squaw with whom George falls in love and fathers a son; the racism against the Indians shown by some of the Corps, and how the expedition members are forced to sell the buttons off their uniforms for food. Similar to Ambrose's nonfiction *Undaunted Courage*, this fictionalized condensation will appeal to teens. (293 pages)

Where it's reviewed:
Booklist, September 1, 2003, page 77
Bulletin of the Center for Children's Books, January 2004, page 179
Horn Book, January 2004, page 78
School Library Journal, September 2003, page 209
Voice of Youth Advocates, December 2003, page 388

Other books by the same author:
Mississippi and the Making of a Nation: From the Louisiana Purchase to Today, 2002
To America: Personal Reflections of an Historian, 2002
Lewis & Clark: Voyage of Discovery, 1998
Undaunted Courage: Meriwether Lewis, Thomas Jefferson and the Opening of the American West, 1996

Other books you might like:
Joseph Bruchac, *Sacajawea: The Story of Bird Woman and the Lewis and Clark Expedition*, 2000
  In alternating chapters, Sacajawea and William Clark ''narrate'' the legendary story of the celebrated Lewis and Clark Expedition.
Gail Langer Karwoski, *Seaman: The Dog Who Explored the West with Lewis & Clark*, 1999

Thinking Seaman's guard dog abilities will help on the expedition, Lewis buys him for $20, but the men regard Seaman as a mascot.

Roland Smith, *The Captain's Dog*, 1999
Big, black Newfoundland dog Seaman adds his own interpretation of the Lewis and Clark expedition to notes found in Lewis's journal.

26

JANET S. ANDERSON

The Last Treasure
(New York: Dutton, 2003)

Subject(s): Treasure, Buried; Mystery and Detective Stories; Family Life
Age range(s): Grades 5-9
Major character(s): Ellsworth Duncan Smith, 13-Year-Old; Jessica Emily ''Jess'' Smith, Cousin (of Ellsworth), 13-Year-Old; John Matthew Smith, Spirit
Time period(s): 2000s
Locale(s): Smiths Mills, New York

Summary: Growing up the only son of a widower, Ellsworth has been told of the ten family homes surrounding a square that were built in the late 1800s by the family patriarch John Matthew Smith. Seven of these homes were occupied, while the other three were the treasure houses, built to hide unusual wealth for the families but only to be used in time of great need. Because the eyes of a child are needed to find these treasures, a distant aunt sends a birthday card to Ellsworth containing $300 and the plea to come visit. When Ellsworth arrives, he's introduced to his cousin Jess, who's also been summoned through the ministrations of John Matthew's ghost, and the two teens find they must help patch up the family quarrels before they can begin to understand the clues to locate the treasure. (257 pages)

Where it's reviewed:
Booklist, March 15, 2003, page 1326
Bulletin of the Center for Children's Books, May 2003, page 348
Publishers Weekly, May 5, 2003, page 222
School Library Journal, June 2003, page 136
Voice of Youth Advocates, April 2003, page 40

Other books by the same author:
The Monkey Tree, 1998
Going through the Gate, 1997

Other books you might like:
David A. Crossman, *The Secret of the Missing Grave*, 1999
On his summer visit to Penobscot Island, Ab and his friend Bean find the missing treasure in a tunnel connecting the Webster and the Winthrop house.
Jean Ferris, *All That Glitters*, 1996
Brian's summer takes an upward turn when he and his dad are part of a scuba diving team searching for a sunken Spanish galleon.
Will Hobbs, *Ghost Canoe*, 1997
The discovery of a hidden canoe sets off an adventure for young Nathan that involves murder and buried treasure.

27

LAURIE HALSE ANDERSON
DAVID GORDON, Illustrator

The Big Cheese of Third Street
(New York: Simon & Schuster Books for Young Readers, 2002)

Subject(s): Neighbors and Neighborhoods; Teasing; Self-Esteem
Age range(s): Grades K-3
Major character(s): Little Benny Antonelli, Child, Bullied Child
Time period(s): 2000s
Locale(s): Third Street

Summary: Little Benny is surrounded by enormous family members who use him as the ball when they play keep away with the equally large Sorensons from Second Street. In order to keep himself away from all their games Little Benny learns to climb. Whenever the big kids chase him he climbs up the nearest pole, street sign, or drain pipe. Little Benny's skill comes in handy during the annual block party. None of the big Antonellis or Sorensons can climb the greased pole to get the cheese on top. Little Benny ignores their laughter and starts up the pole. He climbs until he reaches the big cheese high atop the pole and then slides down to everyone's cheers. (32 pages)

Where it's reviewed:
Booklist, December 1, 2001, page 644
Bulletin of the Center for Children's Books, March 2002, page 233
Horn Book Guide, Fall 2002, page 318
Publishers Weekly, November 19, 2001, page 67
School Library Journal, February 2002, page 96

Other books by the same author:
Thank You Sarah: The Woman Who Saved Thanksgiving, 2002
No Time for Mother's Day, 1999
Ndito Runs, 1996
Turkey Pox, 1996

Other books you might like:
Judith Caseley, *Bully*, 2001
To stop his former friend Jack's bullying behavior Mickey tries all his family's suggestions and adds one of his own.
Patty Lovell, *Stand Tall, Molly Lou Melon*, 2001
Molly Lou's acceptance of what the class bully considers her shortcomings enables her to impress the other students and teach Ronald a lesson.
John Nickle, *The Ant Bully*, 1999
After being squirted by a bully, frustrated Lucas turns his squirt gun on some ants and suffers the consequences when he shrinks to ant size.

28

LAURIE HALSE ANDERSON

Catalyst

(New York: Viking, 2002)

Subject(s): Fathers and Daughters; Neighbors and Neighborhoods; Schools/High Schools

Age range(s): Grades 9-12

Major character(s): Kate Malone, 12th Grader, 18-Year-Old; Teri Litch, Bully, 12th Grader; Jack Malone, Religious, Father (of Kate); Michael ''Mikey'' Litch, Child

Time period(s): 2000s

Locale(s): United States

Summary: A senior in high school, Kate's dream is to attend MIT, the alma mater of her deceased mother. So sure is she that she'll be accepted, she has no back-up schools. When her rejection letter arrives, she is stranded, unsure of what to do next. Her plight diminishes when her kind father offers a temporary home to school outcast Teri Litch and her little brother Mikey as they wait for their burned home to be rebuilt. When Mikey is accidentally electrocuted and dies, the truth about his illegitimate birth and the incestuous rape of Teri by her convict father emerges. Some catalytic spark emerges between the two girls and Kate postpones college to help Teri recover. (240 pages)

Where it's reviewed:

Booklist, September 15, 2002, page 222

Bulletin of the Center for Children's Books, December 2002, page 141

Horn Book, November 2002, page 746

School Library Journal, October 2002, page 154

Voice of Youth Advocates, December 2002, page 372

Awards the book has won:

ALA Best Books for Young Adults, 2003

Other books by the same author:

Storm Rescue, 2001 (Wild at Heart Book 6)

Fever 1793, 2000

Speak, 1999 (Printz Honor Book)

Other books you might like:

Sue Ellen Bridgers, *Keeping Christina*, 1993

   Annie befriends bedraggled, waif-like Christina but then doesn't know how to get rid of her when Christina becomes too controlling.

Caroline B. Cooney, *The Party's Over*, 1991

   Hallie's at loose ends in her small Maine town when all her friends go to college and she's left at home realizing ''the party's over.''

Sarah Dessen, *Someone Like You*, 1998

   During Halley's junior year, she and her best friend Scarlett become very close, especially after Scarlett realizes she's pregnant.

29

M.T. ANDERSON

Feed

(Cambridge, MA: Candlewick Press, 2002)

Subject(s): Friendship; Biotechnology; Internet

Age range(s): Grades 8-12

Major character(s): Titus, Teenager; Violet, Teenager

Time period(s): Indeterminate Future

Locale(s): Earth

Summary: Now that everyone who can afford it has a computer feed directly into their cerebral cortex, Titus and his friends discover it's difficult to find truly different entertainment. That's why Titus finds home-schooled Violet so intriguing when he meets her. Violet didn't receive the feed when she was a child, so she really does see the world differently and, for a short while, Violet is spectacularly amusing to Titus. Then a random act of violence damages her less effective feed and suddenly, she's too different. Titus has fallen in love and is determined to remain true to Violet, but he's part of the feed and Violet is all by herself. (237 pages)

Where it's reviewed:

Booklist, October 15, 2002, page 400

Library Media Connection, January 2003, page 89

New York Times Book Review, November 17, 2002, page 47

School Library Journal, September 2002, page 21

Voice of Youth Advocates, December 2002, page 394

Awards the book has won:

ALA Best Books for Young Adults, 2003

Boston Globe-Horn Book Honor Book, 2003

Other books by the same author:

The Game of Sunken Places, 2004

Burger Wuss, 1999

Thirsty, 1997

Other books you might like:

Pat Cadigan, *Synners*, 2001

   Virtual reality, hackers and implants make for a dangerous world in the near future.

George Alec Effinger, *When Gravity Fails*, 1987

   Despite his best efforts, Marid finds himself enhanced with implants that allow him to control both his knowledge and his personality.

Nancy Farmer, *The House of the Scorpion*, 2002

   Cloning leads an old drug lord to believe that he can avoid death, but what about the life of his young clone?

30

PEGGY PERRY ANDERSON, Author/Illustrator

Let's Clean Up!

(Boston: Houghton Mifflin Company, 2002)

Subject(s): Cleanliness; Animals/Frogs and Toads; Stories in Rhyme

Age range(s): Preschool-Grade 1

Major character(s): Joe, Frog, Son; Mother, Frog, Mother

Time period(s): Indeterminate

Locale(s): Fictional Country

Summary: Thanks to Mother, Joe has a clean room in which to play. He finds and plays with all his toys and games, leaving the room a cluttered mess once again. Mother's not happy to see Joe's messy room and she gives him the task of cleaning it this time. Although Joe soon proudly shows Mother his neat room, she quickly sees that Joe's pick-up strategy leaves the two of them with an even bigger job—cleaning the yard. (32 pages)

Where it's reviewed:
Booklist, March 1, 2002, page 1138
Horn Book Guide, Fall 2002, page 318
Publishers Weekly, March 25, 2002, page 66
School Library Journal, April 2002, page 100

Other books by the same author:
Out to Lunch, 1998
To the Tub, 1996
Time for Bed, the Babysitter Said, 1995

Other books you might like:
Jonathan London, *Froggy Bakes a Cake*, 2000
    Assisting his father with a birthday celebration for his mother, Froggy unintentionally creates a large mess.
Elise Petersen, *Tracy's Mess*, 1995
    Tracy appears to be fastidious— but wait until you see what's behind her bedroom door!
Rosemary Wells, *Max Cleans Up*, 2000
    Each time Ruby hands Max some trash from his room to throw away he stuffs it in his overall pocket.

31

LAURENCE ANHOLT
CATHERINE ANHOLT, Illustrator

Chimp and Zee and the Big Storm

(New York: Phyllis Fogelman Books, 2002)

Subject(s): Animals/Chimpanzees; Weather; Sibling Rivalry
Age range(s): Grades K-2
Major character(s): Chimp, Chimpanzee, Twin; Zee, Chimpanzee, Twin; Papakey, Father, Chimpanzee; Mumkey, Mother, Chimpanzee
Time period(s): Indeterminate
Locale(s): Jungletown, Fictional Country

Summary: As storm winds rattle the windows Chimp and Zee are stuck inside squabbling rather than playing. Eagerly they go outside to help Papakey get the forgotten wash off the line. While folding a sheet, the wind carries Chimp and Zee away and they sail over Jungletown screaming for help. Just when it looks as if they'll be carried out to sea, Mumkey stands on Papakey's shoulders and uses her umbrella to hook one twin's long tail and the family returns to the safety of their home. (32 pages)

Where it's reviewed:
Booklist, October 1, 2002, page 330
Horn Book Guide, Spring 2003, page 6
Publishers Weekly, July 15, 2002, page 75
School Library Journal, September 2002, page 180
Smithsonian, December 2002, page 123

Awards the book has won:
Smithsonian's Notable Books for Children, 2002

Other books by the same author:
Chimp and Zee, 2001
Harry's Home, 2000
Sophie and the New Baby, 2000 (Smithsonian's Notable Books for Children)

Other books you might like:
Debi Gliori, *Mr. Bear to the Rescue*, 2000
    On a stormy night Mr. Bear responds to Mr. Rabbit-Bunn's plea for help after the destruction of a tree that housed his family.
Olof Landstrom, *Boo and Baa Get Wet*, 2000
    As a storm approaches Boo and Baa hurry outside to gather in their forgotten croquet set.
Teddy Slater, *Winnie the Pooh and the Blustery Day*, 1993
    Winnie the Pooh tries to save Piglet by grasping a thread from his scarf as the wind carries him away on a blustery day.

32

KATHI APPELT
JON GOODELL, Illustrator

The Alley Cat's Meow

(San Diego: Harcourt, Inc., 2002)

Subject(s): Animals/Cats; Music and Musicians; Dancing
Age range(s): Grades K-2
Major character(s): Red, Cat; Ginger, Cat
Time period(s): 1940s
Locale(s): Alleytown

Summary: One night at the Alley Cat's Meow, Red meets a beautiful cat named Ginger and asks her to dance. It's love at first sight and soon, Red and Ginger are dancing their way around the globe, on Broadway, the Silver Screen, and all over the world. (32 pages)

Where it's reviewed:
Booklist, January 2003, page 904
Kirkus Reviews, September 1, 2002, page 1301
School Library Journal, October 2002, page 98

Other books by the same author:
Piggies in a Polka, 2003
Bubbles, Bubbles, 2001
Watermelon Day, 1996

Other books you might like:
Petra Mathers, *Sophie and Lou*, 1991
    A dance studio opens across the street and Sophie wants to learn, but is too shy to take lessons.
Dyan Sheldon, *Clara and Buster Go Moondancing*, 2001
    Cat Clara and dog Buster try their hand at ballroom dancing but create a mess in the house with their moves; they have much better success outside.
Joan Sweeney, *Bijou, Bonbon & Beau: The Kittens Who Danced for Degas*, 1998
    Three kittens make a home for themselves in a Parisian theatre, where Degas sketches them dancing with the ballerinas.

33

KATHI APPELT
ARTHUR HOWARD, Illustrator

Bubba and Beau Go Night-Night
(San Diego: Harcourt, Inc., 2003)

Subject(s): Babies; Animals/Dogs; Bedtime
Age range(s): Grades K-2
Major character(s): Beau, Dog; Bubba, Baby, Son; Big Bubba, Father; Mama Pearl, Mother
Time period(s): 2000s (2003)
Locale(s): United States

Summary: There's nothing Bubba and Beau love more than a ride to town with Big Bubba. On any given day they might visit the seed store, thump watermelons at the produce stand or stop by the post office for stamps. The final errand is always the purchase of ice cream cones. After a busy day in town Big Bubba's tired and so is Mama Pearl and she didn't even go to town. Bubba and Beau aren't at all tired and say so in loud wails and howls. Big Bubba's got the solution—another ride. (32 pages)

Where it's reviewed:
Booklist, May 1, 2003, page 1604
Bulletin of the Center for Children's Books, May 2003, page 349
Horn Book Guide, Fall 2003, page 294
Publishers Weekly, March 17, 2003, page 78
School Library Journal, April 2003, page 114

Awards the book has won:
Center for Children's Books Best Books, 2003

Other books by the same author:
Bubba and Beau Meet the Relatives, 2004
Piggies in a Polka, 2003
Bubba and Beau, Best Friends, 2002

Other books you might like:
Russell Hoban, *Bedtime for Frances*, 1960
    Frances is a master at avoiding sleep, but her patient parents have a response for every problem.
Kate Lum, *What! Cried Granny: An Almost Bedtime Story*, 1999
    Before Patrick can go to bed at Granny's she has to make a bed for him; then he needs a blanket, a pillow and a teddy bear.
Peggy Rathmann, *10 Minutes till Bedtime*, 1998
    When a child's father announces "10 minutes till bedtime," the hamster tour guide springs into action with the "Bedtime Tour."
Caroline Uff, *Lulu's Busy Day*, 2000
    After a busy day of play Lulu cleans up her toys, has a bubble bath and settles into bed for a story and a good night's sleep.

34

KATHI APPELT
ARTHUR HOWARD, Illustrator

Bubba and Beau, Best Friends
(San Diego: Harcourt, Inc., 2002)

Subject(s): Cleanliness; Babies; Animals/Dogs
Age range(s): Preschool-Grade 1
Major character(s): Bubba, Baby, Son; Beau, Dog, Friend; Mama Pearl, Mother, Housewife
Time period(s): 2000s (2002)
Locale(s): Texas

Summary: Bubba and Beau have a lot in common. They're about the same age; they both have proud parents; they move around on all fours; they share the same pink blankie. Bubba likes the soft blankie because it smells just like Beau. Beau likes the blankie that smells just like Bubba and also for the sound it makes when he snaps it. At least those are the reasons Bubba and Beau like the blankie before Mama Pearl washes it. When the friends confront their wet, cold, soapy-smelling blankie they both howl with sadness. While the blankie hangs on the clothesline, Mama Pearl bathes Bubba and Beau until they both smell of soap. Then Mama Pearl gives Bubba and Beau the dry blankie that is, once again, soft, warm and smelling just right. (32 pages)

Where it's reviewed:
Booklist, April 2002, page 1331
Bulletin of the Center for Children's Books, April 2002, page 271
Horn Book Guide, Fall 2002, page 293
Publishers Weekly, April 8, 2002, page 225
School Library Journal, July 2002, page 76

Awards the book has won:
School Library Journal Best Books, 2002
Center for Children's Books Best Books, 2002

Other books by the same author:
Where, Where Is Swamp Bear?, 2002
Bubbles, Bubbles, 2001
Oh My Baby, Little One, 2000 (Parents' Choice Recommended Book)

Other books you might like:
Lindsey Gardiner, *Here Come Poppy and Max*, 2000
    Poppy enjoys imaginative play with her pet dog, Max.
Madeleine L'Engle, *The Other Dog*, 2001
    A poodle named Touche looks upon the new baby in the house as another dog of an inferior breed and pities his family for the poor selection.
Rosemary Wells, *McDuff and the Baby*, 1997
    McDuff's idyllic life with Fred and Lucy changes dramatically when they bring home a tiny, crying, time-consuming stranger.

35

KATHI APPELT
LEUYEN PHAM, Illustrator

Piggies in a Polka

(San Diego: Harcourt, Inc., 2003)

Subject(s): Animals/Pigs; Music and Musicians; Farm Life
Age range(s): Grades K-2
Major character(s): Porcina, Pig, Singer
Time period(s): 2000s (2002)
Locale(s): United States

Summary: All the pigs in the ''holler'' arrive for the yearly hootenanny. Serenaded by the beautiful Porcina, the pigs polka, square dance, do the hokey ''porkey'' and finally end up in a piggy mosh pit. After an evening of music and dancing, the pigs head home, already looking forward to next year's hootenanny. (40 pages)

Where it's reviewed:
Publishers Weekly, August 25, 2003, page 63
School Library Journal, September 2003, page 166

Other books by the same author:
Incredible Me!, 2003
Bubbles, Bubbles, 2001
Bats around the Clock, 2000

Other books you might like:
James Marshall, *Swine Lake*, 1999
    A porcine dance troupe performs Swine Lake.
Bill Martin Jr., *Barn Dance*, 1995
    A young farm boy discovers the barnyard animals having a dance in the middle of the night.
Carole Lexa Schaefer, *Full Moon Barnyard Dance*, 2003
    One night when the farm animals can't sleep, they decide to have a dance by the pond.
Elizabeth Winthrop, *Dumpy La Rue*, 2001
    Dumpy La Rue wants to be a ballerina, but he's told, ''Pigs don't dance.''

36

KATHI APPELT
MEGAN HALSEY, Illustrator

Where, Where Is Swamp Bear?

(New York: HarperCollins, 2002)

Subject(s): Animals/Bears; Swamps; Stories in Rhyme
Age range(s): Preschool-Grade 1
Major character(s): Pierre, Child, Relative (grandson of Granpere); Granpere, Grandfather, Fisherman
Time period(s): Indeterminate Past
Locale(s): Louisiana

Summary: When Pierre and his grandfather go fishing in the Louisiana swamp, the Cajun boy is curious about the elusive swamp bear. As Granpere explains about the bear, the swamp, and all its other inhabitants throughout the day, attentive readers will be able to spot the swamp bear hidden in the landscape. Pierre never does see the swamp bear, even though he's always nearby. The book concludes with a note about the real swamp bear, the Louisiana black bear now recognized as an endangered species. (32 pages)

Where it's reviewed:
Booklist, February 15, 2002, page 1018
Horn Book Guide, Fall 2002, page 293
Kirkus Reviews, November 15, 2001, page 60
Publishers Weekly, November 26, 2001, page 60
School Library Journal, January 2002, page 89

Other books by the same author:
Incredible Me!, 2003
Bubbles, Bubbles, 2001
Oh My Baby, Little One, 2000

Other books you might like:
Kevin Henkes, *Grandpa and Bo*, 2002
    Bo enjoys exploring nature with his grandfather during his summer on Grandpa's farm.
Amy Hest, *Rosie's Fishing Trip*, 1994
    After a fishing trip with Grampa, Rosie learns that actually catching fish is not the most important reason for such excursions.
Sheryl McFarlane, *Waiting for Whales*, 1991
    A man teaches his granddaughter to watch for the whales that pass by every summer. After he dies, the granddaughter and her mother continue the tradition.
Jan Bourdeau Waboose, *Morning on the Lake*, 1998
    A Native American boy spends a whole day exploring the wilderness with his grandfather.

37

DAWN APPERLEY, Author/Illustrator

Good Night, Sleep Tight, Little Bunnies

(New York: Cartwheel/Scholastic Press, 2002)

Subject(s): Bedtime; Animals; Family
Age range(s): Preschool-Kindergarten
Major character(s): Unnamed Character, Child
Time period(s): 2000s (2002)
Locale(s): United States

Summary: All over the world, young animals are put to bed. The animals, ranging from bunnies to camels to ducks to tigers and more are shown in the wild. On the final page, they are revealed to be the stuffed animals surrounding a little girl as she is tucked in by her mom. (32 pages)

Where it's reviewed:
Horn Book Guide, Fall 2002, page 294
Publishers Weekly, April 22, 2002, page 72
School Library Journal, May 2002, page 104

Other books by the same author:
Don't Wake the Baby, 2001
Flip and Flop, 2001
Hello Little Lamb, 2000

Other books you might like:
Margaret Wise Brown, *Goodnight Moon*, 1947
    A little bunny gets ready for bed by saying good night to all the beloved objects in his room.

Barbara Shook Hazen, *Where Do Bears Sleep?*, 1970
   Different animals do different things as they prepare to go
   to sleep.
Ann Purmell, *Where Wild Babies Sleep*, 2003
   This book looks at where a wide variety of "wild" babies
   sleep, ending with the wildest baby of them all—a human
   child.

38

JENNIFER ARMSTRONG, Co-Author
NANCY BUTCHER, Co-Author

The Kindling
(New York: HarperCollins, 2003)

Series: Fire-Us. Book 1
Subject(s): Survival
Age range(s): Grades 7-12
Major character(s): Teacher, Teenager; Mommy, Teenager;
   Hunter, Teenager; Anchorman "Angerman", Teenager
Time period(s): 2000s
Locale(s): Lazarus, Florida

Summary: In this first book of the Fire-Us Series, three teenagers create a life for several small children in a post-apoca-
lyptic Florida. Mommy provides the meals and maintains
standards of cleanliness and discipline, while Hunter scavenges among the abandoned buildings of the town for whatever goods are needed. Teacher assembles "The Book," part
scrapbook, part history and part tool of prophecy, to school
the little ones in knowledge of the time before the "Fire-Us"
took all the grown-ups. Their lives have taken on a frightening
semblance of normalcy, but the three teens are aware that
supplies are running out. Then a stranger arrives who calls
himself Anchorman and frequently launches angry diatribes
that he frames as though he were a television anchorman. The
small children quickly rename him Angerman, and the name
is so apt, it sticks. Angerman may seem out of touch with
reality, but he does know that the group needs to leave, and he
persuades them to join him on a journey to find a Grown Up,
the President. The subsequent books, *The Keepers of the
Flame* and *The Kiln*, deal with the quest and its dangers, and
solve the mystery of the virus that has eliminated virtually the
entire adult population. (224 pages)

Where it's reviewed:
Booklist, April 15, 2002, page 1412
Bulletin of the Center for Children's Books, June 2002, page
   355
Kliatt, March 2002, page 6
School Library Journal, October 2002, page 154
Voice of Youth Advocates, June 2002, page 125

Awards the book has won:
Booklist Editors' Choice/Books for Youth, 2002

Other books by the same author:
The Kiln, 2003 (Fire-Us Book 3)
The Keepers of the Flame, 2002 (Fire-Us Book 2)

Other books you might like:
Octavia Butler, *The Parable of the Sower*, 1993
   Lauren can see what no one else will admit; that the city is
   on the verge of collapse.

Alice Hoffman, *Green Angel*, 2003
   Green slowly recovers a sense of life after her entire family
   is lost when the city goes up in flame.
Jean Ure, *Plague*, 1991
   Fran returns from a wilderness trip to find that her entire
   city has died of a plague.

39

JENNIFER ARMSTRONG, Editor

Shattered: Stories of Children and War
(New York: Knopf, 2002)

Subject(s): War; Short Stories
Age range(s): Grades 6-9

Summary: Teenagers and war is the theme of this collection of
a dozen stories written by noted authors about many different
wars. Joseph Bruchac tells of his Abenaki great-grandfather
who fought for the Union side during America's Civil War in
"Sounds of Thunder" while Lisa Rowe Fraustino, in
"Things Happen," tells of a young girl who helped hide a
draft dodger during the Vietnam War. Palestinian Ibtisam
Barakat's tale, "The Second Day," is more personal as it tells
of her family's flight to Jordan at the beginning of the Six-Day
War. From Graham Salisbury comes "A Bad Day for Base-
ball," an account of the young ROTC students who were
pressed into battle following the bombing of Pearl Harbor.
Other authors include Jennifer Armstrong, Marilyn Singer,
M.E. Kerr, Dian Curtis Regan, Lois Metzger, Suzanne Fisher
Staples, David Lubar and Gloria D. Miklowitz. (166 pages)

Where it's reviewed:
Bulletin of the Center for Children's Books, May 2002, page
   309
Horn Book, May 2002, page 323
Kirkus Reviews, December 1, 2001, page 1681
Publishers Weekly, January 21, 2002, page 90
School Library Journal, January 2002, page 131

Awards the book has won:
ALA Best Books for Young Adults, 2003
Center for Children's Books Best Books, 2002

Other books by the same author:
The Kindling, 2002 (Fire-Us Trilogy, Book 1)
Thomas Jefferson: Letters from a Philadelphia Schoolgirl,
   2000
Mary Mehan Awake, 1997
Steal Away, 1992

Other books you might like:
Bernard Ashley, *Little Soldier*, 2002
   Rescued from the strife of his homeland, Kaninda finds
   that London is just as dangerous as gang warfare erupts in
   his neighborhood.
James Howe, *The Color of Absence: Twelve Stories about
   Loss and Hope*, 2001
   These stories illustrate the rainbow that always follows sad
   events.
Anne Mazer, *A Walk in My World: International Short Stories
   about Youth*, 1998
   Young people worldwide share similar experiences as
   shown in these sixteen stories by international authors.

40

JIM ARNOSKY, Author/Illustrator

Armadillo's Orange

(New York: G.P. Putnam's Sons, 2003)

Subject(s): Animals/Armadillos; Animals; Food
Age range(s): Grades K-2
Major character(s): Armadillo, Armadillo
Time period(s): Indeterminate
Locale(s): Earth

Summary: Armadillo crafts a burrow in an orange grove, depending on a fallen orange to mark the entrance. Each day as he wanders down the path in search of food he pays little attention to the other animals he sees along the way. Armadillo doesn't worry about finding his way home again because he knows he can spot the brightly colored orange. On a very windy day, while Armadillo searches for insects to eat, the orange blows away, down the hill and into a ditch. Poor Armadillo! He's lost because he can't find the orange. Gradually he uses his senses to hear, smell and see what is familiar in the vicinity of his burrow. Now he doesn't need the orange because he has his neighbors to help him locate his home. (32 pages)

Where it's reviewed:
Booklist, August 2003, page 1986
Publishers Weekly, June 16, 2003, page 73
School Library Journal, July 2003, page 86

Other books by the same author:
Beachcombing, 2004
Following the Coast, 2004
Raccoon on His Own, 2001
Little Lions, 1998
Rabbits and Raindrops, 1997

Other books you might like:
Jan Brett, *Armadillo Rodeo*, 1995
 Bo, a nearsighted armadillo, mistakenly thinks a cowgirl's red boots are a cute armadillo and follows them to a rodeo.
Lynne Cherry, *The Armadillo from Amarillo*, 1994
 Trying to get a sense of his place in space an armadillo hitches rides on an eagle and the space shuttle.
Pam Munoz Ryan, *Armadillos Sleep in Dugouts: And Other Places Animals Live*, 1997
 Rhyming text in a picture book describes different "homes" built or selected by a variety of animals.

41

KERRY ARQUETTE
NANCY HAYASHI, Illustrator

What Did You Do Today?

(San Diego: Harcourt, Inc., 2002)

Subject(s): Stories in Rhyme; Farm Life; Animals
Age range(s): Preschool-Kindergarten
Major character(s): Unnamed Character, Child
Time period(s): 2000s (2002)
Locale(s): United States

Summary: A little boy explores his farm, asking the animals what they are doing today. In turn, the family pets, farm animals, wild animals and insects all describe their day's activities. Finally, the little boy describes his own day that ends with him in bed and ready to go to sleep. (32 pages)

Where it's reviewed:
Booklist, May 15, 2002, page 1599
Horn Book Guide, Fall 2002, page 294
Kirkus Reviews, April 1, 2002, page 486
Publishers Weekly, March 18, 2002, page 102
School Library Journal, June 2002, page 80

Other books by the same author:
Daddy Promises, 1999

Other books you might like:
Suzanne Tanner Chitwood, *Wake Up, Big Barn!*, 2002
 A picture book gives a look at farm life from sun-up to sun-down.
Kes Gray, *Cluck O'Clock*, 2004
 Chickens give an hour-by-hour account of their life on the farm.
Merrily Kutner, *Down on the Farm*, 2004
 Kid, a young goat, explores his farm.

42

AILEEN ARRINGTON

Camp of the Angel

(New York: Philomel/Penguin Putnam, 2003)

Subject(s): Single Parent Families; Child Abuse; Islands
Age range(s): Grades 4-7
Major character(s): Elizabeth "Jordan", 11-Year-Old; Carson "Brother", Child; White Cat, Cat
Time period(s): 2000s
Locale(s): South Carolina (barrier island)

Summary: Jordan and Brother's mother left four years ago and ever since Papa's been drinking and beating them, often just because their tone was wrong when they tried to explain something to him. They're usually able to hide the bruises from their teachers, but one day Jordan disobeys her shiftless father and goes to school because it's her turn to be the All Day Helper. This time her bruise can't be hidden and she's sent to the nurse's office, which results in the social worker visiting their home. The only happiness the two children have is a white cat they find by their home and, even though they know their father wouldn't let them keep it, they feed and pet it. The day Jordan's father kicks their cat is the day Jordan yells back at him and then tells the police about her father's little nighttime burglaries. When their father lands in jail, their aunt and uncle come to stay with them, fixing up the little summer cottage, cleaning up the yard, repairing the dock and providing the love and safety Jordan and Brother have needed on their island home. (154 pages)

Where it's reviewed:
Booklist, March 1, 2003, page 1197
Bulletin of the Center for Children's Books, June 2003, page 390
Kirkus Reviews, March 1, 2003, page 379
Library Media Connection, November 2003, page 52

School Library Journal, March 2003, page 228

Other books you might like:

Robbie Branscum, *The Girl*, 1986

Raised by uncaring grandparents on a dirt-poor farm, ''the girl'' and her siblings gather strength from one another.

Jane Buchanan, *Hank's Story*, 2001

Sent on the Orphan Train and placed with the Olson family, Hank flees from abusive Mr. Olson to the shelter of animal lover Holly McIntire.

Patricia Hermes, *Cheat the Moon*, 1998

With her mother dead, her father an alcoholic and the responsibility of her brother Will on her shoulders, young Gabby has to grow up quickly.

Phyllis Reynolds Naylor, *Shiloh*, 1991

A boy's need to protect an abused dog is the catalyst for a painful maturation.

43

FRANCES ARRINGTON

Prairie Whispers

(New York: Philomel, 2003)

Subject(s): Frontier and Pioneer Life; Babies; Family Life
Age range(s): Grades 5-8
Major character(s): Colleen McCall, 12-Year-Old; Bonnie McCall, Baby; Mary Kathleen O'Brien, Mother (of Bonnie); Clay O'Brien, Father (of Bonnie)
Time period(s): 1860s
Locale(s): South Dakota (prairie along the Missouri River)

Summary: With her father away for a few days, responsibility falls on Colleen's shoulders when her mother goes into premature labor. Her baby sister is stillborn and her mother comatose after labor, so Colleen hurries to a neighbor's house for help. Hearing a cry from a covered wagon, she checks and finds a dying Mary Kathleen who has just given birth to a healthy daughter. Wanting to help, Colleen agrees to hide the baby from the woman's abusive husband, as well as take a gold watch and strongbox as legacy for the child. Returning home, Colleen swaps the babies and fully intends to tell her mother the truth when she is better. But the lies pile up and suddenly the baby's father returns, demanding his strongbox and his daughter, and Colleen doesn't know what to do. (184 pages)

Where it's reviewed:

Booklist, May 15, 2003, page 1663
Bulletin of the Center for Children's Books, May 2003, page 349
Horn Book, July 2003, page 450
School Library Journal, May 2003, page 144
Voice of Youth Advocates, June 2003, page 126

Awards the book has won:

Booklist Editors' Choice/Books for Youth, 2003

Other books by the same author:

Bluestem, 2000

Other books you might like:

Patricia Hermes, *Calling Me Home*, 1998

Abbie likes some parts of prairie life, but when her baby

brother dies of cholera, she feels guilty that she didn't find the doctor in time.

Sonia Levitin, *Clem's Chances*, 2001

Clem finally finds his father, who headed West in search of gold, but realizes Pierre doesn't have room in his life for a son.

Kathryn Reiss, *Riddle of the Prairie Bride*, 2001

Ida Kate can hardly wait for the arrival of her father's mail-order bride, but after the bride arrives, worries that the woman's an imposter.

Laura Ingalls Wilder, *The Long Winter*, 1953

Winter is a hard time for the Ingalls family as they have only seed grain for food.

44

LENA ARRO
CATARINA KRUUSVAL, Illustrator
JOAN SANDIN, Translator

Good Night, Animals

(New York: R&S Books/Farrar Straus Giroux, 2002)

Subject(s): Camps and Camping; Animals; Sleep
Age range(s): Preschool-Grade 1
Major character(s): Bubble, Child; Pearl, Child
Time period(s): 2000s (2002)
Locale(s): Sweden

Summary: In this cumulative tale, Bubble and Pearl take pillows and sleeping bags for a sleepover in their tent. Once they get settled in for the night though, they hear a strange noise that makes them nervous. Fortunately, it's just a few mice that Bubble and Pearl agree to let in for the night. This starts a string of visitors as a cat, rabbits, a dog, a sheep, a hen and finally a horse all join Bubble and Pearl in the tent. Finally with a crowded and cozy tent, Bubble and Pearl go to sleep. (28 pages)

Where it's reviewed:

Booklist, December 15, 2002, page 766
Bulletin of the Center for Children's Books, December 2002, page 142
Horn Book Guide, Spring 2003, page 6
Kirkus Reviews, August 1, 2002, page 1121
School Library Journal, February 2003, page 102

Awards the book has won:

Center for Children's Books Best Books, 2002

Other books by the same author:

By Geezers and Galoshes!, 2001

Other books you might like:

Mem Fox, *Where Is the Green Sheep?*, 2004

The sheep are ready to go to bed, but they can't find the green sheep.

Libba Moore Gray, *Is There Room on the Feather Bed?*, 1997

During a storm, the farm animals seek shelter in the teeny, tiny house of the wee fat woman and her wee fat husband.

Peggy Rathmann, *Good Night, Gorilla*, 1994

Unbeknownst to a zookeeper making his final rounds a little gorilla steals his keys and releases all the animals to follow the unsuspecting man home.

Karma Wilson, *Bear Snores On*, 2002
    One cold winter night, a mouse sneaks into a bear's lair and is soon joined by other woodland creatures.
Audrey Wood, *The Napping House*, 1984
    In this cumulative story, a sleepy household congregates in Granny's bed.

45

FRANK ASCH
JOHN KANZLER, Illustrator

The Ghost of P.S. 42

(New York: Simon & Schuster Books for Young Readers, 2002)

Series: Class Pets. #1
Subject(s): Animals/Mice; Ghosts; School Life
Age range(s): Grades 2-4
Major character(s): Molly, Mouse, Sister; Jake, Mouse, Brother; Gino, Hamster, Spirit
Time period(s): 2000s
Locale(s): United States

Summary: For three days Molly and Jake search for an acceptable home. It's too crowded to go back to their family at the deli in which they were born. When they come to P.S. 42 Molly is able to squeeze through a foundation crack to get inside, but pudgy Jake has to find a larger opening. As he searches he runs into a cat intent on eating him and an owl that hopes to beat the cat to a meal. When he leaps down the chimney he lands in a furnace and is almost incinerated before he gets out and finds Molly. Her adventures have been less life threatening than Jake's, but no less interesting. Gino has introduced Molly to the pets in his classroom and is giving her a tour and computer instructions when Jake appears. The evening becomes really interesting when the cat Jake got away from earlier leaps through an open window in the classroom. With Gino's help and the early arrival of the classroom teacher, they avoid being eaten and settle into a space in the wall to sleep for the day. (89 pages)

Where it's reviewed:
Booklist, December 15, 2002, page 759
Publishers Weekly, September 2, 2002, page 76
School Library Journal, October 2002, page 98

Other books by the same author:
Survival School, 2004 (Class Pets #3)
Battle in a Bottle, 2003 (Class Pets #2)
Hands around Lincoln School, 1994

Other books you might like:
Avi, *Poppy*, 1995
    With help from other animals a young mouse courageously journeys into the unknown and defeats an evil owl.
Errol Broome, *Magnus Maybe*, 1998
    Young Magnus, newly purchased from a pet shop, gets out of his cage seeking freedom and a home of his own.
Dick King-Smith, *The School Mouse*, 1995
    In the school building that is her family's home Flora takes advantage of the daily lessons and uses her literacy to save her family.

Elizabeth Spires, *The Mouse of Amherst*, 1999
    When Emmaline moves into the Dickinson household unexpected adventures become part of her life.

46

FRANK ASCH, Author/Illustrator
DEVIN ASCH, Illustrator

Like a Windy Day

(San Diego: Gulliver Books/Harcourt, Inc., 2003)

Subject(s): Weather; Playing; Fall
Age range(s): Grades K-2
Major character(s): Unnamed Character, Young Woman
Time period(s): 2000s (2002)
Locale(s): United States

Summary: A young girl wants to "play like a windy day." She imagines scattering seeds, turning windmills, flying kites and stealing hats. She pictures all the fun activities she could do if she were the wind, ending her day by turning into a gentle breeze. (32 pages)

Where it's reviewed:
Booklist, October 1, 2002, page 330
Publishers Weekly, October 14, 2002, page 82
School Library Journal, October 2002, page 98

Other books by the same author:
Mr. Maxwell's Mouse, 2004
Baby Duck's New Friend, 2001

Other books you might like:
Arthur Dorros, *Feel the Wind*, 1989
    This non-fiction book describes what causes wind and its effects on the world around us.
Robert McCloskey, *Time of Wonder*, 1957
    This winner of the Caldecott Medal describes the habitat and weather of a Maine island where a family is spending the summer.
Robin Mitchell, *Windy*, 2002
    Windy is happy to wake up on a windy morning, because it means she can fly her kite. Judith Steedman, co-author.
Phoebe Stone, *When the Wind Bears Go Dancing*, 1997
    A little girl, hearing a storm outside her window at bedtime, decides that it's the wind bears dancing.

47

JOHN ASHBY

Sea Gift

(New York: Clarion Books, 2003)

Subject(s): Treasure, Buried; Coming-of-Age; Fishing
Age range(s): Grades 6-9
Major character(s): Lauchie, 14-Year-Old, Fisherman; Ian, Fisherman, Aged Person; Angus, 14-Year-Old, Fisherman
Time period(s): 2000s
Locale(s): Cape Breton, Nova Scotia, Canada

Summary: Lauchie's father died at sea so it's taken some convincing for his mother to let him assist their neighbor Ian with his lobstering. When she finally agrees, Lauchie is thrilled, especially when Ian presents him with his father's old bait knife, Ian's wife knits him a pair of fisherman's rough gray wool gloves and his mother buys him a new set of yellow oilers. Just like his father, Lauchie loves the smell of the salt air, the feel of the sea, and the setting and baiting of the lobster traps. When pulling traps one day, Lauchie finds a trap that has a sealed crock inside with a letter written 400 years earlier by a shipwrecked doctor. The letter contains directions to a cave containing hidden gold coins. This information sends Lauchie and his good friend Angus on a search for the cave, though Lauchie finds more than gold that summer as he begins to grow up in this author's first novel. (202 pages)

Where it's reviewed:
Booklist, September 15, 2003, page 229
Bulletin of the Center for Children's Books, February 2004, page 222
Kirkus Reviews, October 15, 2003, page 1268
School Library Journal, December 2003, page 144

Other books you might like:
Joachim Friedrich, *4 1/2 Friends and the Secret Cave*, 2001
    Collin and Steffi set up a detective agency but have to admit her twin brother Radish when he finds a cave with a 1950s treasure map.
Pete Fromm, *Blood Knot*, 1998
    This unusual collection of short stories focuses on fishing and the relationships that develop, or come close to ending, because of the sport.
Ethan Howland, *The Lobster War*, 2001
    Following in the footsteps of his deceased father, Dain learns some hard lessons on his way to becoming a lobsterman.

48

BERNARD ASHLEY

Little Soldier
(New York: Scholastic, 2002)

Subject(s): Gangs; Foster Homes; Blacks
Age range(s): Grades 7-10
Major character(s): Kaninda Bulumba, Orphan; Laura Rose, 13-Year-Old; Captain Betty Rose, Foster Parent
Time period(s): 2000s
Locale(s): Lasai, Fictional Country (in Africa); London, England

Summary: Left for dead after witnessing the massacre of his parents and younger sister, Kaninda joins the Kibu rebels to avenge his anger against the murderous Yusulu clan. He's soon picked up by the Red Cross and finds himself in the custody of Captain Betty, part of the God's Force Christian group, who offers him a new home in London. Violence finds Kaninda there, too, when his foster sister Laura rebels against her parents and joyrides in a car, which leads to an accident and the death of a young girl. That incident sparks a gang riot and soon Kaninda is caught up in another type of war, even as he longs to return home to Lasai to finish his task there. (230 pages)

Where it's reviewed:
Booklist, May 1, 2002, page 1518

Bulletin of the Center for Children's Books, July 2002, page 394
Publishers Weekly, January 21, 2002, page 91
School Library Journal, June 2002, page 130
Voice of Youth Advocates, August 2002, page 188

Awards the book has won:
School Library Journal Best Books, 2002

Other books by the same author:
Dodgem, 1981
Break in the Sun, 1980
Terry on the Fence, 1977

Other books you might like:
Chinua Achebe, *Girls at War, and Other Stories*, 1973
    Stories that recount the problems that occur when Nigerian customs clash with the emerging culture of modern Africa.
Peter Dickinson, *AK*, 1990
    Paul's tired of the fighting in his African country, but the reader gets to choose how the story will end: either peace or more bloodshed.
Louise Moeri, *The Forty-Third War*, 1989
    Teen Uno and two of his friends become battle initiates in the eight days they help the revolutionaries of their Central American country.
Beverley Naidoo, *The Other Side of Truth*, 2001
    Whisked to London after an assassination attempt on their Nigerian father, Sade and Femi accidentally become part of the foster system.

49

LINDA ASHMAN
JANE DYER, Illustrator

Babies on the Go
(San Diego: Harcourt, Inc., 2003)

Subject(s): Animals; Babies; Stories in Rhyme
Age range(s): Preschool
Time period(s): 2000s (2003)
Locale(s): Earth

Summary: Although some babies can move on their own very shortly after birth, most need a little help to get around. From human babies pushed in strollers to kangaroo babies in their mother's pouch to crocodile babies riding in their mother's mouth, babies have many modes of transportation. (32 pages)

Where it's reviewed:
Bulletin of the Center for Children's Book, June 2003, page 390
Horn Book Guide, Fall 2003, page 294

Other books by the same author:
Rub-a-Dub Sub, 2003
Can You Make a Piggy Giggle?, 2002
Castles, Caves, and Honeycombs, 2001 (Booklist Editors' Choice)

Other books you might like:
Eric Carle, *Does a Kangaroo Have a Mother, Too?*, 2000
    Just like human babies, animals have mothers too.
Susan Meyers, *Everywhere Babies*, 2001
    Babies all over the world experience the same things,

eating, sleeping, playing, and, most importantly, having the love of their family.

Tara Jaye Morrow, *Mommy Loves Her Baby/Daddy Loves His Baby*, 2003
Mommy and Daddy love their baby as much as various animals love their favorite activities.

50

LINDA ASHMAN
HENRY COLE, Illustrator

Can You Make a Piggy Giggle?
(New York: Dutton Children's Books, 2002)

Subject(s): Animals/Pigs; Animals; Stories in Rhyme
Age range(s): Preschool-Kindergarten
Major character(s): Unnamed Character, Child, Narrator; Unnamed Character, Pig
Time period(s): 2000s
Locale(s): United States

Summary: It's obvious to one active young boy that, while it's possible to make a chick snicker or a calf laugh, nothing will make a pig giggle. Neither riddles nor fiddles nor waddling in puddles causes a pig to chuckle in the way a duck might. The inventive boy soon has the farm animals rolling with laughter, but the pig barely cracks a smile. (32 pages)

Where it's reviewed:
Booklist, July 2002, page 1853
Bulletin of the Center for Children's Books, April 2002, page 271
Horn Book Guide, Fall 2002, page 294
Kirkus Reviews, April 15, 2002, page 560
School Library Journal, June 2002, page 80

Awards the book has won:
IRA Children's Choices, 2003

Other books by the same author:
Castles, Caves, and Honeycombs, 2001 (Booklist Editors' Choice)
Sailing Off to Sleep, 2001
Maxwell's Magic Mix-Up, 2001

Other books you might like:
Stella Blackstone, *There's a Cow in the Cabbage Patch*, 2001
In a rhyming tale, a farmer convinces all his wandering animals to return to their usual spaces.
David Martin, *Five Little Piggies*, 1998
The author interprets the familiar nursery rhyme to show what really happens with each of those pigs.
David McPhail, *Pigs Aplenty, Pigs Galore!*, 1993
Laughter is not on one man's mind when pigs seeking pizza invade his home. He'd simply like them to clean up their mess.
Phyllis Root, *Meow Monday*, 2000
Bonnie tries to quiet her blooming pussy willows because their noise bothers the farm animals.

51

LINDA ASHMAN
JEFF MACK, Illustrator

Rub-a-Dub Sub
(San Diego: Harcourt, Inc., 2003)

Subject(s): Underwater Exploration; Submarines; Stories in Rhyme
Age range(s): Grades K-2
Major character(s): Unnamed Character, Child
Time period(s): 2000s (2003)
Locale(s): United States

Summary: A boy in a submarine explores the ocean depths starting with playful seals near the surface and heading down past an octopus, lobster and other sea creatures. Near the ocean floor, the boy runs into a big blue shark and begins a hasty ascent to the surface saying goodbye to all the creatures he meets along the way. Finally he surfaces safely and the illustrations show that he's really in his bathtub. (40 pages)

Where it's reviewed:
Booklist, June 2003, page 1782
Publishers Weekly, April 7, 2003, page 64
School Library Journal, July 2003, page 86

Other books by the same author:
Babies on the Go, 2003
Can You Make a Piggy Giggle?, 2002
Sailing Off to Sleep, 2001

Other books you might like:
Joan Anderson, *Sally's Submarine*, 1995
Sally enters her cardboard submarine for a day of imaginative adventure.
Kathleen W. Kranking, *The Ocean Is . . .*, 2003
Underwater photographs show the varied plant and animal life of the ocean.
Milly Jane Limmer, *Where Will You Swim Tonight?*, 1991
At bathtime a young girl imagines growing a tail and swimming with various sea creatures.
Christine Loomis, *Scuba Bunnies*, 2004
After their bath time, the scuba bunnies go on an undersea adventure.
Bethany Roberts, *Follow Me!*, 1998
Octopus Mom and her eight children journey through the ocean to visit their grandmother.

52

CATHERINE ATKINS

Alt Ed
(New York: Putnam, 2003)

Subject(s): Schools/Junior High School; Interpersonal Relations; Behavior
Age range(s): Grades 8-10
Major character(s): Susan Callaway, 10th Grader, Narrator; Brendan Slater, 11th Grader, Homosexual; Randy Callahan, Football Player; Amber Hawkins, Student—High School; Tracee Ellison, 11th Grader, Cheerleader; Kale Krasner, Bully; Roy Duffy, Counselor

Time period(s): 2000s
Locale(s): United States

Summary: Susan and Brendan agree to take part in an after-school counseling group, rather than to being expelled for their role in trashing bully Kale's beloved truck. Susan rationalizes her actions for the destruction as Kale's teased her about her weight ever since she started school. Though Brendan hasn't been in school as long, he's heckled for being gay. Brendan and Susan are joined in the group by the none-too-smart Kale, perfect student Tracee, party girl Amber and jock Randy. Initially resisting the efforts of their guidance counselor, the group slowly opens up to one another, reveals their past problems and even discusses the school rules they disobeyed that almost expelled each one of them. Though gaining in confidence, they don't magically become perfect teens through this session, but do begin to make strides toward learning to like themselves and one another. Narrator Susan works on gaining control of her weight but, more importantly, reaches out to her distant father who subconsciously still grieves over the death of his wife. (198 pages)

Where it's reviewed:
Booklist, January 2003, page 870
Horn Book, March 2003, page 209
Publishers Weekly, April 21, 2003, page 63
School Library Journal, March 2003, page 228
Voice of Youth Advocates, April 2003, page 40

Other books by the same author:
When Jeff Comes Home, 1999

Other books you might like:
Sarah Dessen, *Keeping the Moon*, 1999
　Though Colie's lost 45 pounds, she hasn't shed her insecurity, especially when a classmate tries to say she has an "easy" reputation.
James Howe, *The Misfits*, 2001
　Tired of being called names, four friends decide to run for office at their school; though they don't win, they focus attention on the problem.
Robert Lipsyte, *One Fat Summer*, 1977
　Bobby Marks spends his summer dreaming of food while mowing lawns; amazingly, his extra pounds disappear.

53

MARTHA ATTEMA

When the War Is Over
(Custer, WA: Orca Book Publishers, 2003)

Subject(s): World War II; Resistance Movements; Romance
Age range(s): Grades 7-10
Major character(s): Janke Visser, 16-Year-Old, Resistance Fighter; Helmut, Military Personnel (German); Jan Visser, Brother (of Janke), Resistance Fighter
Time period(s): 1940s (1943-1945)
Locale(s): Bishopville, Netherlands

Summary: The Nazis come to Janke's little town in the Netherlands and her brother Jan and their father immediately become part of the resistance movement, though her mother's nervousness about the occupation wears her down so that she often spends days in bed. Janke does her part too by being a courier, riding her bicycle all over the surrounding countryside to deliver messages, helping people escape, picking up dynamite and doing anything else that can help destroy the Nazis. She hates the Germans and what they're doing to her country, until the day she meets Helmut. Hating him, yet strangely attracted to him, Janke meets him occasionally and finds that he's as dissatisfied with the Nazis as she is, and wants only to move to Canada to be with his uncle. Janke is captured while on a mission and it falls to Helmut to either save or betray her in a detailed look at the courage many young people showed during World War II. (246 pages)

Where it's reviewed:
Resource Links, February 2003, page 36
Voice of Youth Advocates, August 2003, page 216

Other books by the same author:
Hero, 2003
Daughter of Light, 2001
A Light in the Dunes, 1997
A Time to Choose, 1995

Other books you might like:
Laura Malone Elliott, *Under a War-Torn Sky*, 2001
　Shot down behind enemy lines during World War II, members of the French Resistance help return Henry to safety.
Michael O. Tunnell, *Brothers in Valor: A Story of Resistance*, 2001
　Three brave teenagers listen to BBC broadcasts and then prepare handbills detailing the truth about Hitler, but are arrested for their efforts.
Elizabeth Van Steenwyk, *A Traitor Among Us*, 1998
　Not to be left out, young Pieter helps the Resistance fighters in his village and exposes a traitor.

54

AMELIA ATWATER-RHODES

Hawksong
(New York: Delacorte, 2003)

Subject(s): Fantasy
Age range(s): Grades 7-10
Major character(s): Danica Shardae, Shape-Shifter, 19-Year-Old; Zane Cobriana, Shape-Shifter
Time period(s): Indeterminate
Locale(s): Fictional Country

Summary: For generations two different clans of shape shifters have fought one another until almost everyone in Danica's family has been killed. A member of the avian shape shifters, Danica changes between human and golden hawk form. Her counterpart in the serpiente clan is Zane, a person she's always feared, whose animal form is that of a cobra. But Danica is so tired of this war between the two groups that she's ready to try the impossible: marry Zane and bring a halt to the strife between their groups. Though each teen is willing to try to bring about peace, rebels could undermine their good efforts. (243 pages)

Where it's reviewed:
Kirkus Reviews, June 15, 2003, page 855
Publishers Weekly, June 30, 2003, page 80

School Library Journal, August 2003, page 154
Voice of Youth Advocates, June 2003, page 145

Other books by the same author:
Snakecharm, 2004
Midnight Predator, 2002
Shattered Mirror, 2001

Other books you might like:
Barbara Hambly, *Dragonshadow*, 1999
  John and Jenny try to return to the lives they led before
  slaying a dragon, but nothing is the same since Jenny
  discovered her ability to become a dragon.
Gillian Rubenstein, *Foxspell*, 1996
  Unhappy after his father deserts his family, Tod meets a
  fox-man who can shift between fox and human form, a
  talent Tod quickly learns.
Jean Thesman, *The Other Ones*, 1999
  Bridget finally acknowledges her powers when she helps a
  friend shape shift to falcon form so she can escape from
  her human body.

55

MARY JANE AUCH, Author/Illustrator
HERM AUCH, Illustrator

Poultrygeist
(New York: Holiday House, 2003)

Subject(s): Animals/Roosters; Animals; Halloween
Age range(s): Grades K-2
Major character(s): Rudy, Rooster, Friend; Ralph, Rooster,
  Friend; Sophie, Pig; Clarissa, Cow
Time period(s): Indeterminate
Locale(s): Fictional Country

Summary: Rudy and Ralph are so competitive that simply
vying to be first to crow in the morning is not enough. All day
they argue and contend to see who is bigger, stronger or
louder. The noise bothers Sophie and Clarissa, but Ralph is
not particularly sensitive to their concerns. Rudy tries to be
quiet for an entire day, but when the animals gather to make
their Halloween costumes, his squawk is added to the caco-
phony of sounds in the barn. Suddenly all is quiet as a huge
scary figure rises from a dark corner of the barn. Everyone
races out of the barn to the safety of a nearby hill. Clarissa
blames Ralph and Rudy's noise for waking the poultrygeist.
The next morning Ralph and Rudy hold each other's beaks to
prevent any sound from emerging as the sun rises without
their help. After the Halloween party, the animals return to the
barn to sleep. Rudy and Ralph argue so loudly about their
roosting spots that the poultrygeist again emerges from the
shadows. (32 pages)

Where it's reviewed:
Booklist, September 1, 2003, page 133
Publishers Weekly, August 4, 2003, page 78
School Library Journal, September 2003, page 168

Other books by the same author:
Souperchicken, 2003
The Princess and the Pizza, 2002 (Children's Choices, Begin-
  ning and Young Readers)
The Nutquacker, 1999

Other books you might like:
Denys Cazet, *Minnie and Moo Meet Frankenswine*, 2001
  Lightning strikes the barn revealing a monster devouring
  one of the pigs—or at least that's what the frightened
  animals tell Minnie and Moo.
Ragnhild Scamell, *Rooster Crows*, 1994
  Pompous Rooster is so confident that his crowing causes
  the sun to rise that he challenges Bluebird to a contest.
Mary Wormell, *Hilda Hen's Scary Night*, 1996
  Fearfully, Hilda Hen crosses the dark farmyard, safely
  passing the snakes (garden hose) and monsters (toys) to
  reach the refuge of the hen house.

56

MARY JANE AUCH, Author/Illustrator
HERM AUCH, Illustrator

The Princess and the Pizza
(New York: Holiday House, 2002)

Subject(s): Princes and Princesses; Fairy Tales; Humor
Age range(s): Grades K-3
Major character(s): Paulina, Royalty (princess); Drupert,
  Royalty (prince); Zelda, Royalty
Time period(s): Indeterminate Past
Locale(s): Blom Castle, Fictional Country

Summary: Princess Paulina is bored. Her father's renounced
his throne for a quiet life as a wood-carver and Paulina misses
her life as a princess. The announcement that Queen Zelda
seeks a princess for her son Prince Drupert to marry, gives
Princess Paulina an idea. She finds her ex-princess attire and
hurries to Blom Castle where she finds eleven other want-to-
be princesses. Paulina and four others pass Queen Zelda's first
challenge by being unable to sleep atop sixteen mattresses.
The glass slipper test eliminates two others and the remaining
three are told to create a feast. As the last to reach the supplies
Paulina uses the limited ingredients remaining to create a
messy concoction of dough, tomatoes, cheese and spices that
she bakes over an open fire. Although Paulina's pizza wins
the prize of marriage to Prince Drupert she rejects the offer
and hurries away to open her own business. (32 pages)

Where it's reviewed:
Bulletin of the Center for Children's Books, March 2002,
  page 234
Horn Book Guide, Fall 2002, page 318
The New Advocate, Spring 2003, page 219
Publishers Weekly, January 28, 2002, page 289
School Library Journal, May 2002, page 104

Other books by the same author:
The Nutquacker, 1999
Bantam of the Opera, 1997
Eggs Mark the Spot, 1996

Other books you might like:
Ellen Jackson, *Cinder Edna*, 1994
  Cinderella and Cinder Edna have different philosophies of
  life yet each meets the prince of her dreams at the ball in
  this twist on a classic tale.
Marjorie Priceman, *Princess Picky*, 2002
  Known to be a picky eater, Princess Nicki accepts a wiz-

ard's plan to eat vegetables in order to achieve her goals to be tall, smart and long-haired.

Alain Vaes, *The Princess and the Pea*, 2001

Not your typical princess, this one is a mechanic but Opal wins the heart of Prince Ralph and manages to charm his demanding mother too.

57

MARY JANE AUCH, Author/Illustrator
HERM AUCH, Illustrator

Souperchicken

(New York: Holiday House, 2003)

Subject(s): Animals/Chickens; Animals; Books and Reading
Age range(s): Grades K-3
Major character(s): Henrietta, Chicken
Time period(s): Indeterminate
Locale(s): New York

Summary: As the only literate chicken on her farm Henrietta is the only one able to read the sign on the truck carrying her aunties off on vacation. Henrietta realizes that the "Souper Soup Company" has plans other than recreation and she's determined to save her relatives. By consulting soup cans at the store and a map she hitches rides on trucks going in the right direction. On the way she advises truckloads of pigs and cows that the vacation promises they were given are fake and recommends they escape. Finally she reaches the Souper Soup Company, locates the crates of relatives and releases them. After escaping she searches each mailbox they pass for clues to the farm on which they want to seek refuge. Finally finding someone that subscribes to a vegetarian magazine, Henrietta leads the flock to a life of bug eating in the farmer's garden. (32 pages)

Where it's reviewed:
Booklist, March 15, 2003, page 1329
Bulletin of the Center for Children's Books, June 2003, page 391
Publishers Weekly, February 24, 2003, page 71
School Library Journal, May 2003, page 108

Other books by the same author:
The Nutquacker, 1999
Bantam of the Opera, 1997
Eggs Mark the Spot, 1996

Other books you might like:
Deborah Bruss, *Book! Book! Book!*, 2001
Bored farm animals enjoy reading a story now and then but only the librarians understand the chickens' request for a book.
Doreen Cronin, *Click, Clack, Moo: Cows That Type*, 2000
By using an old typewriter, cows have no difficulty communicating their needs to Farmer Brown; soon the hens make demands too.
Niki Daly, *What's Cooking, Jamela?*, 2001
Jamela grows so fond of the chicken she's feeding in order to fatten it for a special meal that she can't bear to allow it to be slaughtered.

58

AVI (Pseudonym of Avi Wortis)

Crispin: The Cross of Lead

(New York: Hyperion, 2002)

Subject(s): Orphans; Middle Ages; Identity
Age range(s): Grades 6-9
Major character(s): Crispin "Asta's son", 13-Year-Old; Bear, Entertainer (juggler); John Aycliff, Steward; Lord Furnival, Nobleman, Father (of Crispin)
Time period(s): 14th century (1377)
Locale(s): Great Wexley, England

Summary: After his village outcast mother dies and is buried, "Asta's son" finally learns from the priest that his baptized name is Crispin. The priest is murdered before he's able to discuss Crispin's birth origins and Crispin learns that Aycliff has put a bounty on his head with instructions that anyone may kill him. Running away, with only a loaf of bread and his mother's cross of lead, he meets up with the itinerant juggler Bear and becomes his servant. Working together, the two exchange ideas and Bear puts the thought of freedom into Crispin's head; knowing only the life of a serf, such a concept had never occurred to him. The two travel to Great Wexley for both the Midsummer's Day festivities and some clandestine meetings of Bear's, where Crispin realizes Aycliff still pursues him. Bear is kidnapped and Crispin learns that his father is actually Lord Furnival; since his death Aycliff is worried that Crispin will make a claim on the estate. Faced with demanding the estate or freeing Bear, Crispin makes the right decision for his new life in this Newbery Award winner. (262 pages)

Where it's reviewed:
Bulletin of the Center for Children's Books, October 2002, page 46
Horn Book, September 2002, page 566
Riverbank Review, Spring 2003, page 41
School Library Journal, June 2002, page 130
Voice of Youth Advocates, June 2002, page 112

Awards the book has won:
IRA Children's Choices/Advanced Readers, 2003
Newbery Medal, 2003

Other books by the same author:
The Mayor of Central Park, 2003
Don't You Know There's a War On?, 2001
The Secret School, 2001
Second Sight: Stories for a New Millennium, 1999
The Barn, 1994

Other books you might like:
Malcolm Bosse, *Captives of Time*, 1987
During the Middle Ages, Anne supports herself and her mute brother by learning to make clocks.
Michael Cadnum, *The Book of the Lion*, 2000
Fearing he will face the same punishment as his counterfeiting master who loses his hand, Edmund eagerly agrees to become a squire.
Karen Cushman, *The Midwife's Apprentice*, 1995
A nameless orphan calls herself Alyce and apprentices to

the local midwife, though not without lots of teasing from the village children.

Elizabeth Gray, *Adam of the Road*, 1942
This Newbery winner portrays a 13th century minstrel lad who searches for both his father and his dog.

59

AVI
BRIAN FLOCA, Illustrator

The Mayor of Central Park

(New York: HarperCollins Publishers, 2003)

Subject(s): Animals/Squirrels; Animals/Rats; Animals
Age range(s): Grades 3-6
Major character(s): Oscar Westerwit, Squirrel; Dudley ''Big Daddy Duds'' Throckmorton, Rat, Organized Crime Figure; Maud Throckmorton, Rat, Daughter
Time period(s): 1900s (1900)
Locale(s): New York, New York (Central Park)

Summary: Known as the unofficial mayor of Central Park, Oscar also manages the Central Park Green Sox for which he plays shortstop. Not long after Oscar's pitcher goes missing more trouble starts when Big Daddy Duds and his followers invade Central Park, seeing it as prime territory for jewel thefts. Maud doesn't agree with her father's way of doing business and, seeking independence, moves uptown to take a position as a private duty nurse. The gun-toting rats evict the park families and take over their homes and Oscar feels powerless to right this injustice. Maud, however, has no qualms about taking on her father and his henchmen and proposes that the issue of rights to Central Park be settled by a baseball game. (193 pages)

Where it's reviewed:
Booklist, August 2003, page 1976
Bulletin of the Center for Children's Books, December 2003, page 140
Publishers Weekly, August 11, 2003, page 280
School Library Journal, December 2003, page 144

Other books by the same author:
Abigail Takes the Wheel, 1999
Perloo the Bold, 1998
Poppy, 1995

Other books you might like:
Johanna Hurwitz, *Lexi's Tale*, 2001
Lexi, a squirrel, tries to teach a guinea pig who's recently arrived the way of life in Central Park.
Brian Jacques, *Redwall Series*, 1987-
This series features the mice of Redwall that defend their abbey against scurrilous animals and offer refuge to friends.
Cynthia Rylant, *Gooseberry Park*, 1995
A dog, a cat and a hermit crab are stuck babysitting for young squirrels whose mother is lost after an ice storm destroys their tree home.

60

AVI (Pseudonym of Avi Wortis)
C.B. MORDAN, Illustrator

Silent Movie

(New York: Anne Schwartz/Atheneum Books for Young Readers, 2003)

Subject(s): Emigration and Immigration; Movies; Family
Age range(s): Grades 2-5
Major character(s): Papa, Father, Immigrant; Gustave, Immigrant, Son; Mama, Mother, Immigrant; Bartholomew Bunting, Producer, Businessman
Time period(s): 1900s (1909)
Locale(s): New York, New York

Summary: Like scenes from a silent movie the story of an emigrant family unfolds. Six months after Papa sails to America, Mama and Gustave sail to join him but they do not find each other on the crowded arrival docks. Gustave and Mama venture into the strange city alone, afraid, and reduced to begging a few coins in order to survive until a friend from the old country finds them and offers shelter. Bartholomew Bunting spots Gustave identifying a thief to a policeman and hires the boy to act in a silent movie. Papa, taking a break from his daily search for his family, sees the movie, recognizes his son, and hurries to the movie studio. Dramatically, Gustave, Mama, and Papa are reunited and enjoy prosperity in this new country because Gustave is such a successful and well-paid actor. (48 pages)

Where it's reviewed:
Booklist, March 1, 2003, page 1196
Bulletin of the Center for Children's Books, April 2003, page 303
Horn Book, March 2003, page 197
Publishers Weekly, December 16, 2002, page 66
School Library Journal, March 2003, page 176

Awards the book has won:
ALA Notable Children's Books, 2004

Other books by the same author:
Prairie School, 2001
Abigail Takes the Wheel, 1999 (I Can Read Book)
Finding Providence: The Story of Roger Williams, 1997 (I Can Read Book)

Other books you might like:
Don Brown, *Mack Made Movies*, 2003
A picture book biography of Mack Sennett describes the producer's role in the early years of the film industry.
Eve Bunting, *Dreaming of America: An Ellis Island Story*, 2000
A fictionalized account of the first immigrant processed at Ellis Island tells of Annie and her brothers trying to join their parents in America.
Amy Hest, *When Jessie Came Across the Sea*, 1997
Thirteen-year-old Jessie travels alone to America and works for three years to save enough money for her grandmother to join her.
Riki Levinson, *Soon, Annala*, 1993
Anna and her parents eagerly await the arrival of the ship bringing Anna's two younger brothers to join the family in America.

61

JIM AYLESWORTH
BARBARA MCCLINTOCK, Illustrator

Goldilocks and the Three Bears

(New York: Scholastic Press, 2003)

Subject(s): Folklore; Animals/Bears; Behavior
Age range(s): Grades K-3
Major character(s): Goldilocks, Child, Daughter
Time period(s): Indeterminate Past
Locale(s): Fictional Country

Summary: Goldilocks is a good girl, though sometimes forgetful of her mother's instructions, and that is how she came to follow a path into the woods, a place that she is not allowed to go. Curiosity overpowers her memory again when Goldilocks happens upon a little house and goes inside to investigate. Once inside, Goldilocks really forgets her manners by sampling porridge (and completely eating one bowl) and trying out three chairs. Breaking the little chair does not restore her memory and Goldilocks wanders upstairs and samples the three beds. The little one is so comfy that she falls asleep—and that's where a bear family finds her after their morning walk. When Goldilocks opens her eyes and discovers she is face-to-face with bears she suddenly remembers not to talk to strangers and runs all the way home and she never ever forgets her mother's directions again. (32 pages)

Where it's reviewed:
Booklist, November 1, 2003, page 498
Bulletin of the Center for Children's Books, December 2003, page 141
Horn Book, November 2003, page 757
Publishers Weekly, August 18, 2003, page 77
School Library Journal, October 2003, page 143

Awards the book has won:
Publishers Weekly Best Children's Books, 2003
School Library Journal Best Books, 2003

Other books by the same author:
The Tale of Tricky Fox: A New England Trickster Tale, 2001
The Full Belly Bowl, 1999 (Booklist Editors' Choice)
The Gingerbread Man, 1998 (School Library Journal Best Books)

Other books you might like:
Jan Brett, *Goldilocks and the Three Bears*, 1987
    This illustrated retelling is true to the original tale of a young girl who seeks shelter in a home, falls asleep and is found by three bears.
James Marshall, *Goldilocks and the Three Bears*, 1988
    In a humorous version of the tale, three bears returning from a walk discover someone sleeping in Baby Bear's bed.
Melodye Benson Rosales, *Leola and the Honeybears: An African-American Retelling of Goldilocks and the Three Bears*, 1999
    Lost in the woods, Leola wanders into the Honeybear's Inn for some food and a nap.

Diane Stanley, *Goldie and the Three Bears*, 2003
    After getting off the school bus at the wrong stop Goldie enters an empty cottage and finds a friend when the occupants return.

62

KATHERINE AYRES

Macaroni Boy

(New York: Delacorte, 2003)

Subject(s): Depression (Economic); Family Life; Bullies
Age range(s): Grades 4-8
Major character(s): Mike Costa, 6th Grader; Joseph ''Joe'' Ryan, 6th Grader; Andy Simms, Bully; Mr. Costa ''Grandpap'', Grandfather
Time period(s): 1930s (1933)
Locale(s): Pittsburgh, Pennsylvania

Summary: Living near the Warehouse district of Pittsburgh is Mike Costa, whose father and three uncles own and run Costa Brothers Fine Foods; though it's the Depression era, the warehouse means that Mike's family always has food. However, Mike has other problems right now, beginning with the decreasing number of rats he finds in his traps, and the increasing number he sees dead on the streets. Then there's Andy the bully who calls him ''Macaroni Boy,'' or, even worse, ''Rat Boy.'' But these problems pale in his concern for his grandfather who is becoming increasingly senile; when he begins to vomit blood, Mike and his good friend Joe try to find out why. They make the connection between the dead rats, two dead hoboes and his grandfather's bloody vomit and eventually track it back to poisoned fish in the Allegheny River in this historical piece. (182 pages)

Where it's reviewed:
Booklist, January 2003, page 887
Bulletin of the Center for Children's Books, March 2003, page 265
Publishers Weekly, January 20, 2003, page 82
School Library Journal, February 2003, page 140
Voice of Youth Advocates, April 2003, page 40

Other books by the same author:
Stealing South: A Story of the Underground Railroad, 2001
Silver Dollar Girl, 2000
Under Copp's Hill, 2000
Voices at Whisper Bend, 1999
North by Night: A Story of the Underground Railroad, 1998

Other books you might like:
Carol Flynn Harris, *A Place for Joey*, 2001
    When Joey saves a policeman from the syrup of the exploding molasses tank, he realizes he will always stay in Boston, and maybe become a policeman.
Gayle Pearson, *The Coming Home Cafe*, 1988
    During the Depression, Elizabeth looks for coal at the train yard where she meets Eddie and rides the rails with him to find work.
Lee Wardlaw, *Seventh Grade Weirdo*, 1992
    The school bully, aka ''The Shark,'' pegs seventh grader Rob as the perfect weirdo victim.

B

ADAM BAGDASARIAN

First French Kiss and Other Traumas
(New York: Melanie Kroupa Books/Farrar Straus Giroux, 2002)

Subject(s): Short Stories; Coming-of-Age
Age range(s): Grades 7-10
Major character(s): Will, Narrator
Time period(s): 20th century
Locale(s): Beverly Hills, California

Summary: Ranging from humorous to poignant, these moments from Will's life trace the years of every boy who safely navigates elementary, middle and high school. Arranged in random order, Will recounts the time his bravado embroiled him in a fight against classmate Mike, who'd unfortunately grown several inches and many pounds over the summer. There's also his dismay at receiving a gumball machine and realizing that the only thing he'd ever receive from it is gum. The title story occurs in sixth grade when he kisses Maggie in a Spin the Bottle game, but then continues to kiss Maggie until he discovers the difficulty of breathing and kissing at the same time. Opening his mouth to gasp some air, Maggie's tongue slides in his mouth, which wasn't the air he needed; still unable to breathe, the matter is resolved by returning to the party. The dilemma of never being able to win against an older brother, the problems involved with going steady, his sadness at seeing his older brother depart for college and his grief over the unexpected death of his father are snippets of everyday life that have meaning for all. (134 pages)

Where it's reviewed:
Booklist, August 2002, page 1945
Horn Book, November 2002, page 747
Publishers Weekly, September 9, 2002, page 69
School Library Journal, October 2002, page 154
Voice of Youth Advocates, December 2002, page 372

Other books by the same author:
Forgotten Fire, 2000

Other books you might like:
Rick Book, *Necking with Louise*, 1999
  From his first date with Louise to his love for his grandfather and his final ice hockey game of the season, all are contained in seven chapters.
Jim Heynen, *The Boys' House: New and Selected Stories*, 2001
  Eccentric characters and new discoveries await two boys who live on a farm, as this collection of over 60 stories reveals.
M. Jerry Weiss, *Lost and Found: Award-Winning Authors Sharing Real-Life Experiences through Fiction*, 2000
  Thirteen young adult authors write about ''lost and found'' experiences encountered while growing up in this collection of stories.
Tim Wynne-Jones, *The Book of Changes: Stories*, 1995
  Seven stories narrated by teens tell of ordinary dilemmas in their lives, from school assignments to divorce.

64

ALI BAHRAMPOUR, Author/Illustrator

Otto: The Story of a Mirror
(New York: Farrar Straus Giroux, 2003)

Subject(s): Travel; Employment; Runaways
Age range(s): Grades K-3
Major character(s): Otto, Object (mirror); Miranda, Object (mirror)
Time period(s): Indeterminate
Locale(s): Fictional Country

Summary: Otto has a good job reflecting the customers in Topper's Hat Store, but he'd rather be traveling to the exotic locales he reads about once the shop is closed. Bored with his job, Otto begins showing distorted reflections and when a particularly irate customer threatens to smash him, he runs away, eventually ending up on the open sea. Otto finds the island of his dreams and meets Miranda who shares his dream of seeing the world. This is the author's first book. (32 pages)

Where it's reviewed:
Horn Book, March/April 2003, page 198
Publishers Weekly, March 17, 2003, page 75
School Library Journal, July 2003, page 86

Other books by the same author:
Luna Likes Bugs, 2005

Other books you might like:
Marjorie Flack, *The Story about Ping*, 1933
    One night when duck Ping doesn't make it back to his houseboat in time, he has an adventure on the Yangtze River.
Deb Lund, *Dinosailors*, 2003
    Dinosaurs decide they are bored with village life and set off for the sea.
Dian Curtis Regan, *Chance*, 2003
    Bored with baby stuff, an infant named Chance takes to the road.

65

LINDA BAILEY
BILL SLAVIN, Illustrator

Stanley's Party

(Tonawanda, NY: Kids Can Press, 2003)

Subject(s): Animals/Dogs; Pets; Humor
Age range(s): Grades 1-3
Major character(s): Stanley, Dog
Time period(s): 2000s
Locale(s): Canada

Summary: Stanley's people go out almost every night leaving him alone. When Stanley discovers that he can get on the couch in their absence and no one yells at him to get off, a new world of secret privilege opens to him. Stanley learns to open the refrigerator and to push buttons with his nose to get music playing on the stereo. Of course, he always cleans up before his people arrive home at midnight. In time Stanley realizes that he still feels lonely so he invites friends from the dog park to join him. Each invited guest invites other dogs, all of which Stanley welcomes to his people's house. What a great party! The only problem is that his people arrive home early and discover what Stanley does in secret. After that, Stanley is invited along on their evenings out and Stanley's party becomes legendary in the world of dogs. (32 pages)

Where it's reviewed:
Booklist, July 2003, page 1895
Bulletin of the Center for Children's Books, May 2003, page 350
School Library Journal, July 2003, page 87

Other books by the same author:
Adventures with the Vikings, 2001
Best Figure Skater in the Whole World, 2001
When Addie Was Scared, 1999

Other books you might like:
Michael Garland, *Last Night at the Zoo*, 2001
    Bored zoo animals plan a getaway, don costumes and spend the evening dancing at a club and dining out before taking a bus back to the zoo.

Nina Laden, *The Night I Followed the Dog*, 1994
    While a family sleeps, their pet dog secretly leads an exciting nightlife.
Maggie Smith, *Argo, You Lucky Dog*, 1994
    While Argo's owners are out of town he wins the lottery and uses the proceeds to redecorate the house.

66

MARY BRYANT BAILEY
ELIZABETH SAYLES, Illustrator

Jeoffry's Halloween

(New York: Farrar Straus Giroux, 2003)

Subject(s): Animals/Cats; Halloween; Stories in Rhyme
Age range(s): Grades K-3
Major character(s): Jeoffry, Cat, Friend
Time period(s): 2000s (2003)
Locale(s): United States

Summary: On Halloween night, Jeoffry and his hound friend explore the bogs, fields and forests surrounding their farm. The outdoor world is suddenly scary on Halloween night as normal sights such as fog and geese take on a spookier hue. Jeoffry catches up with some trick-or-treaters and, when they get lost in the woods, Jeoffry is able to guide them home. (32 pages)

Where it's reviewed:
Horn Book Guide, Spring 2004, page 29
School Library Journal, September 1, 2003, page 168

Other books by the same author:
Jeoffry's Christmas, 2002

Other books you might like:
Margaret Wise Brown, *The Fierce Yellow Pumpkin*, 2003
    A small green pumpkin gets its wish to be able to scare away the field mice when it grows into a large orange pumpkin that is made into a Jack-o-Lantern.
Eve Bunting, *Scary, Scary Halloween*, 1986
    A cat watches the trick-or-treaters passing by him.
Cynthia Rylant, *Moonlight: The Halloween Cat*, 2003
    Moonlight explores his neighborhood on Halloween.

67

E.D. BAKER

The Frog Princess

(New York: Bloomsbury, 2002)

Subject(s): Fairy Tales; Animals/Frogs and Toads; Princes and Princesses
Age range(s): Grades 5-8
Major character(s): Emeralda, 14-Year-Old, Royalty (princess); Jorge, Royalty (prince); Eadric, Royalty (prince); Grassina, Aunt (of Emeralda's), Witch
Time period(s): Indeterminate
Locale(s): Fictional Country

Summary: Escaping from the odious Prince Jorge, whom everyone thinks she should marry, Princess Emeralda heads to the swamp whereupon seeing a snake, she promptly loses her balance and falls in the water. When a voice complains that she's chased away the grasshoppers he was planning to eat for lunch, she looks around and sees-a frog! Claiming to be Prince Eadric, turned into a frog by a malicious witch, Frog asks for the requisite kiss to return him to his human form. Finally persuaded, Emeralda kisses him but whoa! After feeling dizzy and bubbly inside, she realizes the ground is closer than usual and she has short, stubby, green legs. Oh no! She's turned into a frog. Somehow the kiss malfunctioned and the two frogs need to find a witch to turn them back to their human forms. Hopping back to the castle, on what is now a treacherous journey, Emeralda knows her aunt Grassina will be able to help. In a twist on the ''happily ever after'' ending, Emeralda discovers that Eadric is not the handsome prince she expected, though that really doesn't matter in this first novel. (214 pages)

Where it's reviewed:
Booklist, November 15, 2002, page 597
Bulletin of the Center for Children's Books, February 2003, page 226
Publishers Weekly, November 18, 2002, page 61
School Library Journal, January 2003, page 133
Voice of Youth Advocates, December 2002, page 394

Other books by the same author:
Dragon's Breath, 2003

Other books you might like:
Ellen Conford, *The Frog Princess of Pelham*, 1997
    School heartthrob Danny Malone, trying to collect on a bet, kisses Chandler and, to their horror, turns Chandler into a frog!
Gail Carson Levine, *Ella Enchanted*, 1997
    In this retelling of *Cinderella*, Ella's been blessed with obedience by a fairy; when she meets Prince Charmant, she needs the curse removed.
Patricia C. Wrede, *Dealing with Dragons*, 1990
    Princess Cimorene refuses to be proper, even going so far as to volunteer to be a dragon's captive princess.

68

JULIE BAKER

Up Molasses Mountain

(New York: Wendy Lamb/Random House, 2002)

Subject(s): Miners and Mining; Prejudice; Physically Handicapped
Age range(s): Grades 6-9
Major character(s): Elizabeth Braxton, 15-Year-Old; Clarence Henderson, 14-Year-Old; John ''Johnny'' Beasley, Football Player
Time period(s): 1950s (1953)
Locale(s): Clay, West Virginia

Summary: Like many of the small towns in West Virginia, Clay is a mining town and has been relatively peaceful, except for mine accidents, until the United Mine Workers arrive and try to unionize. The town is immediately split as Elizabeth sees her father and brother take opposing stances and notices that Clarence's father is on the side of the UMW. Elizabeth is one of the few people in her town who's nice to Clarence, for he's shunned and teased by everyone else who think he's

retarded because his harelip impairs his speech. The two become friends and enjoy the beauty of the woods surrounding their homes, but also find their lives affected by the dissension in Clay. Some miners try to strike, a runaway train strikes and kills Elizabeth's boyfriend Johnny, explosions are set off in the mine and families reel from the trauma. Elizabeth's grandmother wisely compares overcoming this heartache to climbing ''up molasses mountain.'' This impressive first novel explores the feelings of two young teens, each of whom wants more than working in the mines, against the backdrop of miners, unions and a beautiful countryside. (209 pages)

Where it's reviewed:
Booklist, May 15, 2002, page 1604
Kirkus Reviews, May 1, 2002, page 648
Publishers Weekly, May 27, 2002, page 61
School Library Journal, July 2002, page 113
Voice of Youth Advocates, August 2002, page 189

Other books you might like:
Carla Joinson, *Diamond in the Dust*, 2001
    Katy's father has selected the mine foreman for her to marry, but when her brother is killed in the mines she leaves Buckeye City.
Phyllis Reynolds Naylor, *Send No Blessings*, 1990
    Beth doesn't want to spend her whole life in a doublewide trailer in West Virginia and is afraid she'll never achieve her dream of college.
N.A. Perez, *Breaker*, 1988
    After Pat's father is killed in a mining accident, he begins working in the mines while his brother fights for improved labor conditions.
Gloria Skurzynski, *Rockbuster*, 2001
    Orphaned young, Tommy toils in the mines but resists involvement in the labor movement, choosing instead to become a lawyer and help all people.

69

KAGE BAKER

Black Projects, White Knights: The Company Dossiers

(Urbana, IL: Golden Gryphon Press, 2002.)

Subject(s): Short Stories; Science Fiction; Time Travel
Age range(s): Grades 9-Adult
Time period(s): Indeterminate
Locale(s): Earth

Summary: A treat not only for fans of the Company, that quasi-omniscient future corporation, but also for those who would like to sample the Company's reality, this short story collection offers new outrages while filling in some background. For those who came in late, the Company is the sole owner of both time travel and eternal life technologies. Despite some painful limitations, which have resulted in lower profitability, the Company has found a way to make it pay as they alter the past to their advantage in the future. In one story, Facilitator Joseph bullies a feverish Robert Louis Stevenson into coming up with ideas for a screenplay. Some of the secret of what has happened to the oldest Company operatives is revealed in another. Several of the most entertaining stories involve Alec, a lonely little boy who subverts the virtual friend who has been sent to socialize him. As Alec grows up, his remarkable computer gifts allow him to stay one step ahead of his oppressors. (288 pages)

Where it's reviewed:
Analog Science Fiction and Fact, March 2003, page 137
Booklist, September 1, 2002, page 69
Publishers Weekly, September 2, 2002, page 59

Other books by the same author:
The Graveyard Game, 2001
Mendoza in Hollywood: A Novel of the Company, 2000
Sky Coyote: A Novel of the Company, 1999
In the Garden of Iden, 1997

Other books you might like:
Max Barry, *Jennifer Government*, 2003
　　Corporate affiliations now identify people and unscrupulous John Nike tries to outwit government agent Jennifer with horrifying and hilarious results.
Terry Bisson, *Bears Discover Fire: And Other Stories*, 1993
　　What the bears decide to do with their new discovery is just one of the surprising twists in this short story collection.
Ursula K. Le Guin, *Changing Planes*, 2003
　　Emotions are powerful, and in this collection of connected short stories, they send a number of travelers on visits to other realities.

70

KEITH BAKER, Author/Illustrator

Meet Mr. and Mrs. Green

(San Diego: Harcourt, Inc., 2002)

Subject(s): Animals/Alligators; Camps and Camping; Fairs
Age range(s): Grades K-2
Major character(s): Mr. Green, Alligator; Mrs. Green, Alligator
Time period(s): 2000s (2002)
Locale(s): United States

Summary: Mr. and Mrs. Green know how to have a good time and they do so in the three separate stories in this book. In the first, ''Camping,'' Mrs. Green thinks it would be fun to go camping. The Greens get all their camping supplies together, but then Mr. Green gets nervous. Luckily, Mrs. Green leads him on a convoluted trek back to their back yard. In ''100 Pancakes,'' Mr. Green declares that he's so hungry he could eat 100 pancakes, but requires a little encouragement from Mrs. Green to finish the 100th. Finally, in ''County Fair,'' Mr. and Mrs. Green plan to enter their creations (a floral arrangement for Mr. Green and a painting for Mrs. Green) in the county fair. Even though Mr. Green's flowers blow right out of the vase on the trip, they both still manage to win blue ribbons, thanks to flowers Mr. Green arranges in Mrs. Green's hat. (48 pages)

Where it's reviewed:
Kirkus Reviews, September 1, 2002, page 1302
Publishers Weekly, September 23, 2002, page 71
School Library Journal, November 2002, page 111

Other books by the same author:
More Mr. and Mrs. Green, 2004
Quack and Count, 1999
Hide and Snake, 1991

Other books you might like:
Arnold Lobel, *Frog and Toad Are Friends*, 1979
　　Frog and Toad share a series of adventures in this early chapter book.
James Marshall, *George and Martha*, 1974
　　Best friends, George and Martha, have a series of adventures, told in five separate vignettes.
Bernard Waber, *Lyle, Lyle Crocodile*, 1965
　　A cranky neighbor forces Lyle to live in the Central Park Zoo.

71

ROBIN BALLARD, Author/Illustrator

I Used to Be the Baby

(New York: Greenwillow Books/HarperCollins Publishers, 2002)

Subject(s): Babies; Brothers; Mothers and Sons
Age range(s): Preschool-Kindergarten
Major character(s): Mommy, Mother; Unnamed Character, Baby, Brother; Unnamed Character, Brother, Narrator
Time period(s): 2000s (2002)
Locale(s): United States

Summary: A little boy, obviously proud of his size and maturity, relates how he helps Mommy take care of his baby brother. When the baby tries to take his toys, the brother substitutes something age-appropriate for a baby and plays with him. At naptime both are very quiet but in the car baby cries because he doesn't like riding so his brother sings to him. Each situation the big brother confronts is a learning experience with Mommy patiently guiding him into the appropriate way to respond to a younger sibling. After the baby is fast asleep it's time for the big brother to climb into Mommy's lap for a bedtime story and a little ''baby'' time of his own. (24 pages)

Where it's reviewed:
Booklist, May 1, 2002, page 1530
Horn Book Guide, Fall 2002, page 294
Kirkus Reviews, March 15, 2002, page 405
Publishers Weekly, March 18, 2002, page 102
School Library Journal, May 2002, page 104

Other books by the same author:
My Day, Your Day, 2001
Tonight and Tomorrow, 2000
When We Get Home, 1999
When I Am a Sister, 1998

Other books you might like:
Judith Caseley, *Mama, Coming and Going*, 1994
　　Jenna is a big help to Mama after baby Mickey is born.
Russell Hoban, *A Baby Sister for Frances*, 1976
　　Frances is not sure how she will fit into the family now that baby Gloria is here.
Holly Keller, *Geraldine's Baby Brother*, 1994
　　Gradually, Geraldine becomes more accepting of her noisy baby brother and all the attention he receives.

Marisabina Russo, *Hannah's Baby Sister*, 1998
  Hannah looks forward to a new baby in the family.
Susan Winter, *A Baby Just Like Me*, 1994
  Martha feels disappointed that her baby sister is not able to be her playmate immediately.

72

MONIKA BANG-CAMPBELL
MOLLY BANG, Illustrator

Little Rat Sets Sail
(San Diego: Harcourt, Inc., 2002)

Subject(s): Animals/Rats; Fear; Sailing
Age range(s): Grades 1-3
Major character(s): Little Rat, Rat, Daughter; Buzzy Bear, Bear, Teacher
Time period(s): Indeterminate
Locale(s): Fictional Country

Summary: Little Rat's parents give her no choice; despite her fears they enroll her in a sailing class. Reluctantly, Little Rat attends the first class where her expectations are confirmed. Buzzy Bear, recognizing her discomfort, assigns others to the single occupant prams while Little Rat and another student join Buzzy Bear in a larger boat. Gradually, Little Rat becomes comfortable and capable on the water. Her greatest accomplishment, in her view, is simply surviving the lessons. Maybe next year she'll try sailing a solo pram. (48 pages)

Where it's reviewed:
Booklist, April 1, 2002, page 1326
Bulletin of the Center for Children's Books, May 2002, page 309
Horn Book, July 2002, page 452
Publishers Weekly, January 7, 2002, page 65
School Library Journal, June 2002, page 80

Awards the book has won:
Boston Globe-Horn Book Picture Book Honor Book, 2002
Bulletin of the Center for Children's Books Blue Ribbons, 2002

Other books you might like:
Susan Hill, *Stuart Sets Sail*, 2001
  Tiny Stuart Little sails away in this "I Can Read" book based on the movie adaptation of E.B. White's classic story.
Leonard Kessler, *Last One in Is a Rotten Egg*, 1999
  Freddy's fear of swimming keeps him from enjoying the deep end with friends in an "I Can Read" newly illustrated reissue of a 1969 title.
Rosemary Wells, *Mama, Don't Go!*, 2001
  With support from a sensitive teacher Yoko gradually overcomes her fear of separating from her mother.

73

MICHAEL BANIA, Author/Illustrator

Kumak's House: A Tale of the Far North
(Portland, OR: Alaska Northwest Books, 2002)

Subject(s): Folklore; Family; Problem Solving

Age range(s): Grades K-2
Major character(s): Kumak, Spouse, Eskimo; Aana Lulu, Eskimo, Aged Person
Time period(s): Indeterminate Past
Locale(s): Arctic

Summary: Because Kumak's house is too small no one in his family is happy. Kumak takes his problem to Aana Lulu, the old wise woman of the village. She advises him to invite a rabbit to live with him. Kumak complies and the problem grows worse so he visits Aana Lulu again. Each time she instructs him to add another animal to his home and each time after he does so he returns to Aana Lulu with the same complaint. After adding a rabbit, fox, caribou, porcupine, otter, bear and whale and not noticing any change in his family circumstances Kumak goes once more to Aana Lulu. Wisely she proclaims that the animal guests have stayed too long. After Kumak evicts the animals his house seems just right and his happy family members agree. A concluding author's note gives background information for the story and describes the culture and customs of the Arctic region. (32 pages)

Where it's reviewed:
Booklist, September 1, 2002, page 136
Horn Book Guide, Fall 2002, page 408
Publishers Weekly, June 10, 2002, page 63
School Library Journal, January 2003, page 93

Awards the book has won:
Notable Social Studies Trade Books for Young People, 2003

Other books by the same author:
Kumak's Fish, 2004

Other books you might like:
Jan Brett, *The Mitten*, 1989
  In an award-winning adaptation of a folktale, animals find temporary shelter by crowding into a lost mitten.
Lydia Dabcovich, *The Polar Bear Son: An Inuit Tale*, 1997
  An elderly Inuit woman adopts an orphaned polar bear cub that hunts and fishes for her.
Ann McGovern, *Too Much Noise*, 1967
  An old man complains that his noisy house interferes with his sleep; the advice of the village wise man helps him find the quiet he seeks.

74

KATE BANKS
GEORG HALLENSLEBEN, Illustrator

Close Your Eyes
(New York: Frances Foster Books/Farrar Straus Giroux, 2002)

Subject(s): Animals/Tigers; Bedtime; Dreams and Nightmares
Age range(s): Preschool
Major character(s): Unnamed Character, Tiger (cub); Unnamed Character, Tiger, Mother
Time period(s): Indeterminate
Locale(s): Fictional Country

Summary: A little tiger has many reasons why he cannot close his eyes. The tiger cub's mother has a response for every excuse that gently reassures her cub and reminds him to close his eyes. Each time the little tiger expresses fear that he may fall or become lost while dreaming, his mother confidently states how she will protect him. Finally, the little tiger surrenders to the darkness, closes his eyes, and allows sleep to overtake him, sure of the presence of his mother when he awakens. (36 pages)

Where it's reviewed:
Booklist, October 15, 2002, page 409
Horn Book, September 2002, page 549
Publishers Weekly, September 2, 2002, page 74
School Library Journal, July 2002, page 767
Smithsonian, December 2002, page 123

Awards the book has won:
School Library Journal Best Books, 2002
Smithsonian's Notable Books for Children, 2002

Other books by the same author:
A Gift from the Sea, 2001 (Smithsonian's Notable Books for Children)
The Night Worker, 2000 (ALA Notable Children's Book)
And If the Moon Could Talk, 1998 (Boston Globe-Horn Book Award)

Other books you might like:
Margaret Wise Brown, *Goodnight Moon*, 1947
In a classic of bedtime stories, a little rabbit's evening ritual is to say goodnight to everything in sight, including the moon, shining outside.
Russell Hoban, *Bedtime for Frances*, 1960
Frances is a master at avoiding sleep, but her patient parents have a response for every problem.
Martin Waddell, *Can't You Sleep, Little Bear?*, 1988
Big Bear comforts Little Bear when a fear of the dark keeps him from dozing off.

KATE BANKS

Dillon Dillon
(New York: Frances Foster/Farrar Straus Giroux, 2002)

Subject(s): Identity; Family; Adoption
Age range(s): Grades 4-6
Major character(s): Dillon Dillon, 10-Year-Old, Adoptee; Didier Dillon, 13-Year-Old, Brother; Daisy Dillon, 5-Year-Old, Sister
Time period(s): 2000s
Locale(s): Lake Waban; Rock Falls, New Hampshire

Summary: When Dillon views his tenth birthday present, a red rowboat with his repetitive name painted on the stern, he finally voices the question that he's pondered for years and receives an unexpected answer. At birth, Dillon was given his mother's maiden name and he began life as Dillon McDermott. Tragically, his birth parents died in a plane crash when he was very young and, following his adoption by his mother's brother and sister-in-law, Dillon's name became Dillon Dillon. The news stuns Dillon who spends the summer vacation rowing his new boat across the lake to a small island where he befriends a pair of loons and slowly explores his identity, his place in the family, his relationship with Didier and Daisy and the power of love to overcome unforeseen

obstacles. This is the first novel for the author of many award-winning picture books. (150 pages)

Where it's reviewed:
Booklist, September 15, 2002, page 230
Bulletin of the Center for Children's Books, October 2002, page 47
Horn Book, November 2002, page 747
Publishers Weekly, September 30, 2002, page 72
School Library Journal, October 2002, page 154

Awards the book has won:
Parenting's Books of the Year, 2002

Other books by the same author:
A Gift from the Sea, 2001 (Smithsonian's Notable Books for Children)
The Night Worker, 2000 (ALA Notable Children's Book)
And If the Moon Could Talk, 1998 (Boston Globe-Horn Book Award)

Other books you might like:
Alane Ferguson, *Secrets*, 1997
In rapid succession, 12-year-old T.J. learns he is adopted, meets his birthmother and learns he has a biological sister.
Charlene C. Gianetti, *Who Am I?: And Other Questions of Adopted Kids*, 1999
A nonfiction title addresses common questions of adopted preteens and teens.
Jean Davies Okimoto, *Molly by Any Other Name*, 2000
Adopted Molly's search for identity includes locating her Asian birth mother.

76

KATE BANKS
TOMEK BOGACKI, Illustrator

Mama's Coming Home
(New York: Frances Foster Books/Farrar Straus Giroux, 2003)

Subject(s): Working Mothers; Gender Roles; Family Life
Age range(s): Grades K-2
Major character(s): Mama, Mother, Businesswoman; Papa, Father, Spouse
Time period(s): 2000s (2003)
Locale(s): United States

Summary: It's that time of day when Papa heads to the kitchen to begin cooking dinner and Mama hurries to the subway. Children are playing, pets are roaming, everyone's thinking about Mama coming home. Papa makes pizza and the kids set the table as Mama walks in the rain from the subway to their apartment. Finally, Mama's home and everyone can enjoy pizza! (32 pages)

Where it's reviewed:
Booklist, April 15, 2003, page 1474
Bulletin of the Center for Children's Books, April 2003, page 304
Horn Book, March 2003, page 199
Publishers Weekly, December 9, 2002, page 82
School Library Journal, March 2003, page 176

Other books by the same author:

A Gift from the Sea, 2001 (Smithsonian's Notable Books for Children)

The Night Worker, 2000 (ALA Notable Children's Books)

And If the Moon Could Talk, 1998 (Boston Globe-Horn Book Award)

Other books you might like:

Karen Ackerman, *By the Dawn's Early Light*, 1994
   Mom works the graveyard shift at a box factory, arriving home to her children "by the dawn's early light."

Doris Dorrie, *Lottie's Princess Dress*, 1999
   Mom's trying to leave for work but first she has to convince Lottie to get dressed for school.

Marisabina Russo, *When Mama Gets Home*, 1998
   Three children eagerly await their mother's return from work so they can tell her about their day.

Eileen Spinelli, *When Mama Comes Home Tonight*, 1998
   In the evening, after arriving home from work, Mama and her child complete the household chores together.

77

KATE BANKS
TOMEK BOGACKI, Illustrator

The Turtle and the Hippopotamus
(New York: Frances Foster/Farrar Straus Giroux, 2002)

Subject(s): Animals; Fear; Problem Solving
Age range(s): Preschool-Grade 1
Major character(s): Turtle, Turtle; Hippopotamus, Hippopotamus
Time period(s): Indeterminate
Locale(s): Fictional Country

Summary: Using the same rebus format introduced in *The Bird, the Monkey and the Snake in the Jungle,* the author and illustrator tell the tale of fearful Turtle's attempts to cross a river. Other animals suggest she swim across, but Turtle is afraid to swim past Hippopotamus so she uses other strategies. She tries to fly like a bird, hop like a grasshopper, blow across like a dandelion seed and build a bridge. Nothing works. When Turtle uses a rope as a tail in hopes of swinging across, she falls into the river where Hippopotamus catches her, gives her a ride to shore and suggests she swim over the next time. (28 pages)

Where it's reviewed:

Booklist, August 2002, page 1969
Horn Book Guide, Fall 2002, page 294
Horn Book, May 2002, page 312
Publishers Weekly, April 29, 2002, page 72
School Library Journal, August 2002, page 146

Other books by the same author:

A Gift from the Sea, 2001 (Smithsonian's Notable Books for Children)

The Night Worker, 2000 (ALA Notable Children's Book)

The Bird, the Monkey, and the Snake in the Jungle, 1999

Other books you might like:

Alyssa Satin Capucilli, *Inside a Zoo in the City: A Rebus Read-Along Story*, 2000

In a rhyming story, the alarm wakes the parrot first as zoo animals begin their day.

Elizabeth Falconer, *The House that Jack Built: A Rebus Book*, 1990
   The traditional tale is retold with rebuses to show what happens when Jack builds a house.

Shirley Neitzel, *I'm Taking a Trip on My Train*, 1999
   A young boy pretends to be the engineer of a train. As the cumulative tale develops each pictured item becomes a rebus in the ever-lengthening text.

78

KATE BANKS

Walk Softly, Rachel
(New York: Frances Foster Books/Farrar Straus and Giroux, 2003)

Subject(s): Emotional Problems; Family Problems; Secrets
Age range(s): Grades 6-9
Major character(s): Rachel One, Grandmother (of Rachel Three); Rachel Two, Mother (of Rachel Three); Rachel Three, 14-Year-Old; Jake, Brother (deceased)
Time period(s): 2000s
Locale(s): United States

Summary: When Rachel Two mentions she's looking for a new house because Rachel One may need to live with them, Rachel Three unknowingly disrupts tightly held feelings when she asks why her grandmother can't have Jake's bedroom. Seven years earlier her older brother Jake, then 17, died in a car accident and his bedroom has been preserved as a shrine ever since. Wishing she'd known her brother, Rachel explores his room and finds the journal where Jake reveals the pressure he feels from his parents' expectations and his own deep depression. Rachel finally understands that her brother committed suicide and her family has never learned to grieve and move on. (149 pages)

Where it's reviewed:

Booklist, October 15, 2003, page 402
Bulletin of the Center for Children's Books, October 2003, page 50
Publishers Weekly, September 1, 2003, page 90
School Library Journal, September 2003, page 209

Awards the book has won:

School Library Journal Best Books, 2003

Other books by the same author:

Dillon Dillon, 2002

Other books you might like:

Stella Pevsner, *How Could You Do It, Diane?*, 1989
   A family is torn apart after their daughter dies because they don't know if her overdose is an accident or suicide.

Susan Beth Pfeffer, *The Year Without Michael*, 1987
   Michael leaves home to play softball and never returns. Was he kidnapped or did he run away?

Adrienne Ross, *In the Quiet*, 2000
   Searching for her mother's spirit, Sammy realizes that digging holes isn't needed as her mother's memory has been there "in the quiet."

Carol Lynch Williams, *Carolina Autumn*, 2000
   A year after losing her father and sister in a plane crash,

Carolina's just beginning to show enthusiasm for the outside world.

79

LYNNE REID BANKS

The Dungeon

(New York: HarperCollins, 2002)

Subject(s): Revenge; Voyages and Travels
Age range(s): Grades 6-9
Major character(s): Bruce MacLennan, Laird; Archibald MacInnes, Laird; Peony, Child, Servant; Finlay ''Fin'' MacLean, Servant (stable boy)
Time period(s): 14th century
Locale(s): Scotland; China

Summary: Archibald MacInnes raids the home of Bruce MacLennan, kills his children and abducts his wife. Mourning their loss, Bruce MacLennan orders a new castle to be built around a dark dungeon where he plans to one day imprison Archibald. During the castle's construction, MacLennan travels to China, partly for the adventure and partly to forget the horror of his losses. He buys a young Chinese girl to serve him tea, names her Peony, removes the bindings from her feet and brings her with him when he returns home. Though he feels some tenderness toward her, he squashes those feelings when his planned revenge against Archibald fails and he blames his defeat on Peony. Tossing her in the just-built dungeon, he leaves her there for several days during which time Peony kills herself. Checking on her, MacLennan finds her dead and doesn't understand why she couldn't wait for him to free her. For the next several weeks he's haunted by Peony's death, but when he returns to the dungeon, Peony's body is gone. And before Laird MacLennan returns aboveground, the stable boy Fin, Peony's one friend, locks him in his own dungeon in this tale of retribution. (279 pages)

Where it's reviewed:
Booklist, October 1, 2002, page 311
Horn Book, September 2002, page 566
Publishers Weekly, October 28, 2002, page 73
School Library Journal, December 2002, page 132
Voice of Youth Advocates, October 2002, page 268

Other books by the same author:
Fair Exchange, 1998
Angela and Diabola, 1997
Broken Bridge, 1994
One More River, 1992
Melusine: A Mystery, 1989

Other books you might like:
Mollie Hunter, *The King's Swift Rider*, 1998
    Though Martin never uses a weapon, his aid to Robert the Bruce as he fights for independence from England is incalculable.
Katherine Paterson, *Rebels of the Heavenly Kingdom*, 1988
    Wang Lee is kidnapped by bandits and then rescued by Mei Lin, a girl warrior, in this tale of China's Taiping Rebellion.
James VanOosting, *The Last Payback*, 1997
    When her twin is killed, Dimple knows she must follow

their motto of ''never delay a payback'' and goes after Ronnie, their friend who had a gun.

80

CLIVE BARKER

Abarat

(New York: Joanna Cotler Books/HarperCollins, 2002)

Series: Abarat. Book 1
Subject(s): Quest; Fables
Age range(s): Grades 8-12
Major character(s): Candy Quackenbush, Teenager; John Mischief, Mythical Creature; Christopher ''Lord of Midnight'' Carrion, Mythical Creature
Time period(s): Indeterminate
Locale(s): Abarat, Fictional Country (The Sea of Izabella and its islands)

Summary: Candy Quackenbush, like a lot of people, isn't sure what she does like, but she is certain that she doesn't like her life as it is. So when the mysterious Sea of Izabella comes rolling across the prairie outside her boring hometown, Candy is ready to take a chance. She's acquired an ally, the weird John Mischief, who's a friendly sort of monster with seven brothers growing out of his head. They have already saved her from an even scarier creature who was clearly trying to kill her, so when Candy is swept away in the retreating sea, she is inclined to treat John Mischief as a friend. Candy will need all the friends she can find as she travels the islands of the Sea of Izabella, each of which exists forever at a particular hour of the day. The Lord of Midnight, Christopher Carrion, is out for Candy's blood, although she doesn't yet know it. (388 pages)

Where it's reviewed:
Book World, November 24, 2002, page 9
Booklist, September 1, 2002, page 120
Library Media Connection, February 2003, page 78
Publishers Weekly, June 24, 2002, page 58
School Library Journal, October 2002, page 154

Awards the book has won:
ALA Best Books for Young Adults 2003

Other books by the same author:
Everville: The Second Book of the Art, 1994
The Thief of Always: A Fable, 1992
The Great and Secret Show: The First Book of the Art, 1989
The Books of Blood, 1984 (three volumes)

Other books you might like:
Peter Dickinson, *The Ropemaker*, 2001
    An oddly assorted group sets out to an unknown destination to find a wizard so old he may not even exist.
David Lindsay, *Voyage to Arcturus*, 2002
    The bizarre tale of a journey across a distant world echoes the story of a man's journey within himself.
William Nicholson, *The Wind Singer: An Adventure*, 2000
    Kestrel chaffs at her oppressive society and suddenly finds herself a criminal outcast on a quest for freedom.

81

STEVEN BARNES

Lion's Blood: A Novel of Slavery and Freedom in an Alternate America

(New York: Warner Books, 2002)

Subject(s): Alternate History; Slavery; Friendship
Age range(s): Grades 9-Adult
Major character(s): Aidan O'Dere, Slave; Kai ibn Jallaled-dinibn Rashid, Nobleman
Time period(s): 1860s; 1870s (1863-1876)
Locale(s): Bilalistan, Fictional Country

Summary: In this alternate history, the Islamic and African cultures rule a world in which Europe never emerged from the Dark Ages and the vast plantations of the new world are run by wealthy Moslems. Of course, the same problem of a sufficient work force exists in this new reality, and it has been solved in a familiar way with slaves imported from the European countries. Aidan O'Dere is a young Irish boy who grows to manhood as a favored slave and best friend to his owner's son, Kai. The two boys find little difference between them, but as Aidan grows older, his awareness of the oppression of his race comes between the friends. Kai, meantime, experiences discomfort at his growing realization of the enormous gulf between them. As they age, every milestone pushes them further apart. But Kai and Aidan are determined to find common ground and a war with the Aztecs seems the perfect opportunity. (528 pages)

Where it's reviewed:
Black Issues Book Review, May-June 2002, page 42
Booklist, January 1, 2002, page 824
Bookpage, February 2002, page 23
Publishers Weekly, January 21, 2002, page 69
Science Fiction Chronicle, May 2002, page 36

Other books by the same author:
Zulu Heart, 2003
Charisma, 2002
Far Beyond the Stars, 1998
Iron Shadows, 1998

Other books you might like:
Orson Scott Card, *Seventh Son*, 1987
  The first of a series set in an alternate America where magic is real, and evil stalks the land and Alvin Maker.
Len Deighton, *SS-GB*, 1978
  Germany wins World War II, and the SS now handles the murder investigations in London.
Mary Gentle, *The Book of Ash*, 1999-2000
  Ash, a sort of profane Joan of Arc, is a famous historical heroine, or perhaps she never existed; time and reality keep shifting in this challenging series.

82

STEVEN BARNES

Zulu Heart

(New York: Warner Books, 2003)

Subject(s): Alternate History; Friendship; Slavery

Age range(s): Grades 9-Adult
Major character(s): Aidan O'Dere, Slave; Kai ibn Jallaled-dinibn Rashid, Nobleman
Time period(s): 1870s
Locale(s): Bilalistan, Fictional Country

Summary: Aidan's invaluable service during the recent war wins him his freedom. Although he was a slave, he helped his nobleman master, Kai ibn Rashid, win a decisive battle, which would otherwise have been lost. Now Aidan has taken his family and led a group of former slaves to a settlement where they hope to pioneer a free way of life for whites, but fate doesn't intend for Aidan to live quietly. First there are rumors that the sister he lost when they were enslaved still lives in the distant east. Then Kai comes to him with a proposal for Aidan to go east to search for his sister with his help. The price for Kai's help is high, however. Aidan must allow himself to be sold back into slavery to act as a spy for Kai's group of revolution-leaning slave owners in this sequel to *Lion's Blood*. (463 pages)

Where it's reviewed:
Chronicle, May 2003, page 41
Publishers Weekly, February 24, 2003, page 57

Other books by the same author:
Charisma, 2002
Lion's Blood: A Novel of Slavery and Freedom in an Alternate America, 2002
Far Beyond the Stars, 1998
Iron Shadows, 1998

Other books you might like:
Octavia Butler, *Kindred*, 1979
  Time travel allows a slave's descendant to experience slavery first hand.
William Gibson, *The Difference Engine*, 1991
  Charles Babbage gets his primitive computer to work and the Victorians find appalling uses for the machine.
Harry Turtledove, *Guns of the South*, 1992
  With better guns, the South might have won the Civil War; in this novel, they do.

83

TRACY BARRETT

Cold in Summer

(New York: Holt, 2003)

Subject(s): Ghosts; Moving, Household
Age range(s): Grades 4-7
Major character(s): Ariadne "Addy" Fellowes, 7th Grader; May Butler, Spirit
Time period(s): 2000s
Locale(s): Dobbin, Tennessee

Summary: When her mother accepts a position at a college in Tennessee, Ariadne is miserable about leaving the ocean, her best friend and their Florida home. She's hesitant to make friends with the girls in her school but one day after swimming in Cedar Point Lake, she meets and talks to May, a girl dressed in old-fashioned clothes. It's only when Ariadne researches the local history of Dobbin that she finds a book called *The Strange Case of Little May Butler* and realizes that

May is a ghost who needs to find her body before she can return home. Ariadne is determined to help May, just as May initially helped her. (203 pages)

Where it's reviewed:
Booklist, April 1, 2003, page 1395
Bulletin of the Center for Children's Books, September 2003, page 6
Horn Book, May 2003, page 338
Publishers Weekly, May 5, 2003, page 221
School Library Journal, July 2003, page 123

Other books by the same author:
Anna of Byzantium, 1999

Other books you might like:
Elaine Marie Alphin, *Ghost Soldier*, 2001
    Alexander researches the Chamblee family history for the ghost of Civil War soldier Richeson Francis.
Dick King-Smith, *The Roundhill*, 2000
    A girl named Alice, who appears and disappears without making a sound, visits Evan in his special beech grove.
Phyllis Reynolds Naylor, *Jade Green: A Ghost Story*, 2000
    Judith's green-framed photo of her mother awakens the ghost of a former serving girl; luckily the ghost protects her from a murderous relative.
Ken Radford, *A Haunting of Mill Lane*, 1988
    Scared by noises in her new home, Sarah befriends Sally-Anne, the ghost of a murder victim from 100 years ago.
Brenda Seabrooke, *The Haunting at Stratton Falls*, 2000
    Living with relatives after her father's was declared missing, Abby is miserable; a ghost appears just when Abby needs her help.

84

WILLIAM BARRINGER
KIM LAFAVE , Illustrator

Gregory and Alexander
(Custer, WA: Orca Books, 2003)

Subject(s): Animals/Insects; Seasons; Friendship
Age range(s): Grades K-2
Major character(s): Gregory, Mouse, Friend; Al, Insect, Friend
Time period(s): 2000s (2003)
Locale(s): Perambulator Park, Canada

Summary: Best friends Gregory and Al love playing together in the park where they live. More than anything however, Gregory would like to be able to fly a kite. When Al encloses himself in a cocoon one night, Gregory waits patiently for his friend to reappear. Finally, after Gregory has almost given up, a beautiful butterfly arrives and introduces himself as his old friend Al, now known as Alexander. Alexander acts as Gregory's kite, until he is forced to fly south for the winter. The next year, Gregory makes a new caterpillar friend. (32 pages)

Where it's reviewed:
Horn Book Guide, Fall 2003, page 315
School Library Journal, September 2003, page 168

Other books you might like:
Eric Carle, *The Very Hungry Caterpillar*, 1979
    Preparing for its change into a butterfly, a hungry caterpillar eats everything in sight.
Lois Ehlert, *Waiting for Wings*, 2001
    Rhyming text follows the life cycle of four butterflies.
Anne Rockwell, *Becoming Butterflies*, 2002
    A school class watches as three caterpillars turn into monarch butterflies.
Sam Swope, *Gotta Go! Gotta Go!*, 2000
    A small caterpillar knows that she must make her way to Mexico. When she turns into a butterfly, the trip becomes much easier.

85

MAX BARRY

Jennifer Government
(New York: Doubleday, 2003)

Subject(s): Satire; Business; Government
Age range(s): Grades 10-Adult
Major character(s): Jennifer Government, Government Official, Mother; John Nike, Businessman; Hack Nike, Office Worker
Time period(s): Indeterminate Future
Locale(s): United States; London, England; Australia

Summary: In a near future world where your last name represents your corporate affiliation, Hack Nike, an unhappy cog in the corporate machine, is overjoyed to be approached by two executives from Nike's marketing department. John Nike quickly bullies Hack into signing a contract, which Hack then discovers requires him to commit murder. It's all part of John's clever plan to make the latest Nikes really desirable—as he puts it, to give them *street cred*. What Hack doesn't know is that the ambitious and amoral John Nike has a serious problem and her name is Jennifer Government. Jennifer has a mysterious past, but she takes her job as a government agent seriously, and when John's murderous plans get rolling, Jennifer won't give up until she gets her man. (321 pages)

Where it's reviewed:
Booklist, December 1, 2002, page 644
Kirkus Reviews, November 1, 2002, page 1546
Publishers Weekly, January 6, 2003, page 38
School Library Journal, August 2003, page 187
Time, February 10, 2003, page 80

Awards the book has won:
School Library Journal Best Books, 2003
Booklist Books for Youth Editors' Choice/Adult Books for Young Adults,

Other books by the same author:
Syrup: A Novel, 1999

Other books you might like:
M.T. Anderson, *Feed*, 2002
    Violet's less-than-perfect implant seems like an amusing flaw that makes her quirky until it malfunctions and begins to kill her.
Terry Bisson, *Pirates of the Universe*, 1996
    Good workers are rewarded with a permanent residence at

the retirement community/theme park Pirates of the Universe.

William Gibson, *Pattern Recognition*, 2003

Cayce's response to corporate logos provides her with both a source of income as well as acute mental discomfort.

86

SUSAN CAMPBELL BARTOLETTI
BEPPE GIACOBBE, Illustrator

Nobody's Nosier Than a Cat

(New York: Hyperion Books for Children, 2003)

Subject(s): Animals/Cats; Pets; Stories in Rhyme
Age range(s): Grades K-3
Major character(s): Unnamed Character, Child, Narrator
Time period(s): 2000s (2003)
Locale(s): United States

Summary: In this celebration of cats, a boy describes the many attributes of a cat from sleeping to exploring and from making a mess to curling up on your lap. The main cat in the narrator's life highlights all these activities and then comes home to curl up with its devoted owner. (40 pages)

Where it's reviewed:
Booklist, November 1, 2003, page 499
Horn Book Guide, Spring 2004, page 29

Other books by the same author:
The Christmas Promise, 2001
A Coal Miner's Bride: The Diary of Anetka Kaminska, 2000 (Dear America Series)
Dancing with Dziadzu, 1997

Other books you might like:
Patricia Hubbell, *I Like Cats*, 2004
Rhyming text celebrates all the things cats do.
Nancy Jewell, *Five Little Kittens*, 1999
Cat parents care for five little kittens throughout the day.
Leslea Newman, *Cats, Cats, Cats*, 2001
Every night when Mrs. Brown goes to sleep, her many cats have a party.

87

NORA RALEIGH BASKIN

Almost Home

(New York: Little, Brown, 2003)

Subject(s): Family Problems; Stepmothers; Self-Acceptance
Age range(s): Grades 4-7
Major character(s): Leah Baer, 6th Grader; Will Hiller, 6th Grader; Gail Baer, Stepmother; Annie Baer, Stepsister; Karen Baer, Stepmother
Time period(s): 2000s
Locale(s): New Paltz, New York

Summary: Leah's mother Karen has gone to California taking Leah's little sister Annie with her, while Leah lives with her father and waits for Karen to send for her. However, as the months add up, it becomes obvious that Karen, who's been revealed as her stepmother, isn't going to be sending for her. Leah feels alone, both with her father and his new wife Gail,

as well as in her new school, until Will befriends her. Wary at first, Leah and Will spend lunchtime together and as they talk, Leah begins to develop trust in him. His interest in drama intrigues her and she eventually tries out for a part in a play, accepts that she's not moving to California, begins to like her stepmother Gail and waits for a visit from her little sister Annie whom she adores. (173 pages)

Where it's reviewed:
Booklist, May 1, 2003, page 1591
Bulletin of the Center for Children's Books, May 2003, page 351
Publishers Weekly, April 21, 2003, page 63
School Library Journal, July 2003, page 123
Voice of Youth Advocates, August 2003, page 216

Other books by the same author:
Basketball (or Something Like It), 2005
What Every Girl (Except Me) Knows, 2001

Other books you might like:
C.S. Adler, *The No Place Cat*, 2002
Feeling out of place when her father remarries and she gains three stepsiblings, Tess moves in with her mom, but that doesn't work either.
Berlie Doherty, *Holly Starcross*, 2002
Ever since her mother remarried and had three children, Holly has felt left out, so she's delighted to have a chance to meet and stay with her father.
Susan Glick, *One Shot*, 2003
When her erratic mother moves to California, Lorrie opts to live with her father and his new wife Elaine and enjoys a wonderful summer.

88

TANYA ROBYN BATT
NICOLETTA CECCOLI, Illustrator

The Faerie's Gift

(Cambridge, MA: Barefoot Books, 2003)

Subject(s): Fairies; Folklore; Wishes
Age range(s): Grades 1-4
Major character(s): Unnamed Character, Woodsman; Unnamed Character, Mythical Creature (fairy)
Time period(s): Indeterminate Past
Locale(s): Fictional Country

Summary: A poor, childless woodcutter saves the life of a fairy while working in the forest and receives one glowing wish in appreciation. Hurrying home to tell his family of his good fortune, the woodcutter soon realizes that the one wish is more of a burden than a blessing as each family member has a different suggestion for what he should wish. Each request seems valid to the woodcutter, but also impossible to honor. After walking alone through the forest and contemplating his dilemma the woodcutter realizes that, with careful wording, he can satisfy everyone's desires and so he does. (32 pages)

Where it's reviewed:
Booklist, February 15, 2003, page 1070
Bulletin of the Center for Children's Books, April 2003, page 304
Publishers Weekly, December 23, 2002, page 69

School Library Journal, June 2003, page 124

Other books by the same author:
The Princess and the White Bear King, 2004
A Child's Book of Faeries, 2002
The Fabrics of Fairy Tale, 2000

Other books you might like:
Teresa Bateman, *Harp O' Gold*, 2001
  After becoming a prisoner of his own foolish wish for fame and fortune Tom tries to locate his original battered harp and trade the gold one for it.
J. Patrick Lewis, *At the Wish of the Fish: A Russian Folktale*, 1999
  A simple peasant accepts a fish's bargain, chooses his wishes thoughtfully and ends up with a bride, a home and more wits than at the beginning of the tale.
Uri Shulevitz, *The Treasure*, 1979
  A man searches far and wide for a treasure and learns that true riches are close to home.

89

JOAN BAUER

Stand Tall

(New York: Penguin Putnam, 2002)

Subject(s): Divorce; Grandfathers; Individuality
Age range(s): Grades 5-8
Major character(s): Sam ''Tree'' Benton, 7th Grader; Sophia ''Sophie'' Santack, 8th Grader; Leo Benton, Grandfather
Time period(s): 2000s
Locale(s): Ripley

Summary: Sam, nicknamed Tree because he's six foot three inches tall and still growing, finds that being tall leads to a whole new set of expectations. His coach expects him to lead the basketball team and Tree's not even very athletic. Now his parents divorce, and he's expected to adjust to alternating weeks between his mother's new apartment and his house where his father and grandfather live. Luckily Tree and his grandfather are good friends and when old Vietnam War injuries force his grandfather to have a leg amputated, it's Tree who helps him with his prosthesis. Tree also worries about his lack of abilities, yet when classmates dump smelly garbage in new student Sophie's locker, he's the one who stands up for this outspoken girl. When a flood forces evacuation in his neighborhood, it's Tree who makes sure all the pets have a safe, dry spot in the shelter. Slowly but surely his self-confidence builds and when he and his brothers help tear down their home's water-soaked walls, Tree realizes he's good at physical labor, solving problems and making damaged items whole again. (182 pages)

Where it's reviewed:
Booklist, September 15, 2002, page 230
Publishers Weekly, July 29, 2002, page 73
Riverbank Review, Fall 2002, page 45
School Library Journal, August 2002, page 182
Voice of Youth Advocates, October 2002, page 268

Awards the book has won:
Smithsonian's Notable Books for Children/Older Readers, 2002

ALA Notable Children's Books, 2003

Other books by the same author:
Thwonk, 2001
Hope Was Here, 2000
Backwater, 1999
Rules of the Road, 1998
Sticks, 1996

Other books you might like:
Caroline Janover, *How Many Days Until Tomorrow?*, 2000
  Certain Gramps likes his brother Simon better, it's Josh who helps Gramps when he falls, dislocates his hip and must be rescued from a rising tide.
Richard Mosher, *Zazoo: A Novel*, 2001
  Learning about her Grand-Pierre's heroics during World War II is all news to Zazoo, though she's lived with him for 11 years.
Barbara Garland Polikoff, *Life's a Funny Proposition, Horatio*, 1992
  Grieving over the loss of his father, Horatio is upset that his grandfather moves in with them, until he sees O.P.'s grief when his dog dies.

90

MARION DANE BAUER

Runt

(New York: Clarion Books, 2002)

Subject(s): Animals/Wolves
Age range(s): Grades 4-6
Major character(s): Runt, Wolf; King, Wolf, Father (of Runt); Bider, Wolf
Time period(s): 2000s
Locale(s): Minnesota

Summary: Born last, and the smallest in the litter, Runt strives to emulate his brothers and sisters in hopes of earning a real name based on a skill, but never seems able to please his father King. When he tries to follow the pack and hunt for food, he becomes lost; during a storm, he doesn't seek shelter in the cave with his siblings; and when he tries to grab hold of a porcupine, he winds up with quills in his muzzle and one of his siblings dies. It seems that Runt can do nothing right, until the day Bider, a disgruntled male kicked out of his own pack, attempts to usurp leadership from King and then Runt's name becomes Singer. (138 pages)

Where it's reviewed:
Booklist, October 15, 2002, page 406
Kirkus Reviews, October 1, 2002, page 1463
Publishers Weekly, October 14, 2002, page 84
School Library Journal, September 2002, page 219

Other books by the same author:
An Early Winter, 1999
Beyond the Playhouse Wall, 1997
A Question of Trust, 1994
Am I Blue?: Coming Out from the Silence, 1994
A Taste of Smoke, 1993

Other books you might like:
Melvin Burgess, *The Cry of the Wolf*, 1992
  When the Hunter kills the pack leader and its mate, Ben

wishes he'd never told him about the wolves that live near his family's farm.

Jean Craighead George, *Julie of the Wolves*, 1972
  Julie becomes lost on the ice, but luckily she's found by wolves and learns survival skills from them.

Elizabeth Hall, *Child of the Wolves*, 1996
  Disliking the man who's bought him, puppy Granite runs into the woods where Snowflake, a wolf who's lost one of her pups, "adopts" him into her pack.

Jack London, *The Call of the Wild*, 1903
  This classic tale describes how the dog Buck becomes the leader of a pack of wolves.

91

FLEUR BEALE

I Am Not Esther

(New York: Hyperion, 2002)

Subject(s): Mothers and Daughters; Cults; Christian Life
Age range(s): Grades 7-10
Major character(s): Ellen Greenland, Widow(er), Nurse; Kirby "Esther Pilgrim" Greenland, 14-Year-Old; Caleb Pilgrim, Uncle, Religious; Naomi Pilgrim, Aunt; Daniel Pilgrim, Cousin
Time period(s): 2000s
Locale(s): Wellington, New Zealand

Summary: When Kirby's mother Ellen suddenly announces that she's leaving in a few days to work with the refugees in Africa, Kirby's shocked for she wouldn't expect her flaky mother to work there. Kirby's further shocked when she meets Uncle Caleb, Aunt Naomi, and their family, with whom she's supposed to stay until her mother returns, and discovers they belong to a sect called the Fellowship of the Children of the Faith. From being an independent, organized child who does the grocery shopping, plans the budget and keeps an eye on her mother, Kirby is now renamed Esther, for everyone in the family has a Biblical name, wears dowdy long skirts and an apron, and takes part in extended prayer sessions. Resistant at first, and quick to swear, Esther quickly learns to drop the cussing, speak without contractions and follow the family rules, for when she doesn't everyone suffers in the prayer vigils for her soul. Attending a public school, Kirby's guidance counselor, Mrs. Fletcher, is familiar with the Children of the Faith religious sect and offers help when Kirby and her cousin Daniel are forced to leave the Fellowship. Though Kirby misses the feeling of being part of a large family, she knows their way of life is not the way she wants to live. Finally locating her mother leads to more problems, but also hope for resolution and the beginning of a new and better life together. (250 pages)

Where it's reviewed:
Booklist, October 15, 2002, page 401
Bulletin of the Center for Children's Books, December 2002, page 143
Publishers Weekly, September 30, 2002, page 72
School Library Journal, November 2002, page 154
Voice of Youth Advocates, February 2003, page 464

Awards the book has won:
ALA Quick Picks for Reluctant Young Adult Readers, 2003

Other books by the same author:
Against the Tide, 1993

Other books you might like:
Linda Crew, *Brides of Eden*, 2001
  Joshua mesmerizes the women of Corvallis, Oregon and they join his church, eager to become the "Second Mary" with Joshua ready to father the child.

Margaret Peterson Haddix, *Leaving Fishers*, 1997
  Dorry joins the religious group Fishers of Men, but knows it's time to leave the organization when she tries to convert the children she's babysitting.

Marilyn Levy, *No Way Home*, 1990
  Billy's mother is part of a fanatical religious cult, which won't let him leave when his three-week visit ends.

Jane Yolen, *Armageddon Summer*, 1998
  Two teens meet as each tries to be a buffer between a parent and cult leader Beelson who predicts the end of the world on July 27, 2000.

92

MARGARET BEAMES
SUE HITCHCOCK, Illustrator

Night Cat

(New York: Orchard Books/Scholastic, Inc., 2003)

Subject(s): Animals/Cats; Pets; Gardens and Gardening
Age range(s): Grades K-3
Major character(s): Oliver, Cat
Time period(s): 2000s (2003)
Locale(s): New Zealand

Summary: One night when his owner calls him in for the evening Oliver decides that he wants to stay out and prowl the garden. At first Oliver has fun chasing moths, but then he accidentally pounces on a porcupine. Ouch! Oliver also learns that other nighttime creatures, including an owl and opossum, are large and scary. Finally, Oliver begs to be let in the house. First book published in the US for this New Zealand author. (40 pages)

Where it's reviewed:
Horn Book, December 2003, page 141
Publishers Weekly, May 19, 2003, page 73
School Library Journal, September 2003, page 163

Other books you might like:
Tomek Bogacki, *Cat and Mouse in the Night*, 1998
  Cat and Mouse like to play in the fields, but at night the world seems scary.

Lois Duncan, *I Walk at Night*, 2000
  A mild-mannered house cat enjoys great adventures at night.

Hazel Hutchins, *One Dark Night*, 2001
  On a dark, stormy night, a stray cat seeks shelter for her kittens.

93

DARLEEN BAILEY BEARD

The Babbs Switch Story

(New York: Farrar Straus Giroux, 2002)

Subject(s): Sisters; Mentally Handicapped; Fires
Age range(s): Grades 5-8
Major character(s): Ruth Ann ''Ruthie'' Tillman, 12-Year-Old; Daphne Sue Tillman, 16-Year-Old, Mentally Ill Person
Time period(s): 1920s (1924)
Locale(s): Babbs Switch, Oklahoma

Summary: It's sometimes hard for Ruthie to accept her older sister Daphne as she acts younger than she is, carries around a one-armed doll and likes to hug soft things, a habit that's killed the family kittens. When the Larrs family find their youngest daughter Elizabeth in Daphne's arms, they fear she might accidentally suffocate her. For that reason, her parents forbid Ruthie to sing the solo in their town's Christmas pageant; with Elizabeth portraying the baby Jesus, her parents don't want the town stirred up about Daphne. That night a terrible fire breaks out in the schoolhouse where the pageant's being held and Ruthie can't find her sister. When she thinks of Daphne dead, Ruthie understands how much she really means to her, mental afflictions and all. Luckily tragedy turns to happiness when it's discovered that Daphne is alive and has saved little Elizabeth in this sweet period piece. (166 pages)

Where it's reviewed:
Booklist, March 15, 2002, page 1255
Kirkus Reviews, March 15, 2002, page 406
Publishers Weekly, March 18, 2002, page 105
School Library Journal, March 2002, page 225
Voice of Youth Advocates, April 2002, page 36

Other books by the same author:
Operation Clean Sweep, 2004
Twister, 1999
The Flimflam Man, 1998

Other books you might like:
Betsy Byars, *Summer of the Swans*, 1970
   Sara has always cared for her handicapped brother Charlie and gathers her friends to help her look for him when he runs away to see the swans.
Jeanette Ingold, *The Big Burn*, 2002
   Three teens find their lives intertwined when the ''big burn'' forest fire blazes through the Northwest.
Ruth White, *Memories of Summer*, 2000
   After they move to Michigan, Lyric realizes that her sister Summer's tics and phobias are worsening as her mental condition deteriorates.

94

MARGARET BECHARD

Hanging on to Max

(Brookfield, CT: Roaring Brook/Millbrook, 2002)

Subject(s): Fathers and Sons; Parenthood; Teen Parents
Age range(s): Grades 8-12

Major character(s): Sam Pettigrew, 17-Year-Old, Single Father; Max Pettigrew, Baby; Claire Bailey, Single Mother, 12th Grader
Time period(s): 1980s
Locale(s): United States

Summary: Sam's senior year isn't quite what he and his best friend used to dream about. Instead of playing varsity football and preparing for college, he's filling baby bottles, changing diapers and playing with Max, his son. Earlier when his girlfriend decided to give the baby up for adoption, Sam knew he couldn't let go of his son. Afraid the courts won't let him adopt Max, since it is just Sam and his taciturn father, his aunt moves in for several months until Max is a little older. Now Sam attends an alternative high school, picks up Max from the school's childcare and lives with his dad until he graduates, at which time he will start a construction job. But is he doing what's best for him? For Max? Eventually Sam must make the hardest decision of his life in this poignant tale of fatherhood. (142 pages)

Where it's reviewed:
Booklist, May 1, 2002, page 1518
Horn Book, May 2002, page 324
Publishers Weekly, June 3, 2002, page 89
School Library Journal, May 2002, page 146
Voice of Youth Advocates, April 2002, page 36

Awards the book has won:
School Library Journal Best Books, 2002
ALA Best Books for Young Adults, 2003

Other books by the same author:
If It Doesn't Kill You, 1999
My Mom Married the Principal, 1997
Really No Big Deal, 1994

Other books you might like:
Norma Klein, *No More Saturday Nights*, 1988
   Though college becomes more difficult, Tim Weber fights to keep his son rather than let his girlfriend give him up for adoption.
Marilyn Reynolds, *Too Soon for Jeff*, 1994
   Jeff finally leaves college to return home and split the parenting responsibilities for his newborn son Ethan.
Hope Wurmfeld, *Baby Blues*, 1992
   After Annie's father dies, her only friend is her boyfriend Jimmy; when she becomes pregnant, they both know their baby should be adopted.

95

IAN BECK, Author/Illustrator

Teddy's Snowy Day

(New York: Scholastic Press, 2002)

Subject(s): Winter; Toys; Christmas
Age range(s): Preschool-Grade 1
Major character(s): Teddy, Toy, Bear
Time period(s): 2000s (2002)
Locale(s): United Kingdom

Summary: When Teddy's owner goes out to play, she puts him on the windowsill so that he can watch without getting lost. When the little girl's mother shuts the window Teddy goes flying. Out in the winter wonderland, Teddy enjoys snow-boarding, building a ''snowbear,'' and ice sliding, before realizing that it has gotten dark and he is cold and lost. A never-fully-identified Santa takes him home in his sleigh, where he is reunited with his owner. This book was originally published in Great Britain in 1998. (32 pages)

Where it's reviewed:
Booklist, October 1, 2002, page 332
Horn Book Guide, Spring 2003, page 7
Kirkus Reviews, November 1, 2002, page 1610
Publishers Weekly, September 23, 2002, page 38
School Library Journal, October 2002, page 98

Other books by the same author:
The Happy Bee, 2002
Home Before Dark, 2001
Tom and the Island of Dinosaurs, 1995

Other books you might like:
Kevin Henkes, *Oh!*, 1999
  Both children and animals are delighted by the first snow-fall and enjoy playing outside.
Mick Inkpen, *Kipper's Snowy Day*, 1996
  With his friend Tiger, Kipper plays all day in the snow.
Ezra Jack Keats, *The Snowy Day*, 1963
  In this Caldecott winner, Peter explores his snow-draped city.
Dayal Kaur Khalsa, *The Snow Cat*, 1992
  When Elsie, a little girl who lives alone in the woods, wishes for a cat, God sends her a snow cat.

96

SUSAN WILLIAMS BECKHORN

The Kingfisher's Gift
(New York: Philomel/Penguin Putnam, 2002)

Subject(s): Mothers and Daughters; Grandmothers; Fairies
Age range(s): Grades 4-6
Major character(s): Fanny Morrow, 12-Year-Old; Grandmother Morrow, Grandmother; Henry, Chauffeur; Ida, Servant (maid); Tamarack, Mythical Creature (fairy); Iris, Mythical Creature (fairy); Meadowsweet, Mythical Creature (fairy)
Time period(s): 1900s
Locale(s): Boston, Massachusetts

Summary: Franny's father tells the most wonderful stories about fairies, little spirits that he and Franny can see, but then he dies and Franny is heartbroken. Her mother tries to burn the fairy stories, but Franny pulls them from the fire, burning her hands in the process. Now Franny's hands are healing, her mother's parents take her on a rest trip to Europe, and Franny stays with her father's mother, Grandmother Morrow. Traveling in a wee basket are three fairies, King Tamarack, Queen Iris and their daughter Princess Meadowsweet, who accompany Franny to her grandmother's home. For some reason Princess Meadowsweet can't fly and Franny knows if she finds the magic feather, Meadowsweet will finally be able to fly. Though the search keeps her occupied, she becomes aware of the attraction between Ida and Henry and her stern grandmother's attempt to bring them together. By summer's

end Franny learns that the fairies enrich her life, but also enable her to live in the real world as she learns to grieve over her father's death and await her mother's return in this old-fashioned, charming story. (182 pages)

Where it's reviewed:
Booklist, April 15, 2002, page 1418
Horn Book Guide, Fall 2002, page 367
Kirkus Reviews, April 15, 2002, page 562
School Library Journal, July 2002, page 113

Other books by the same author:
In the Morning of the World: Six Woodland Why Stories, 2000

Other books you might like:
Frances Hodgson Burnet, *The Secret Garden*, 1912
  Mary and her invalid cousin explore a locked garden in Yorkshire and find themselves changed by their experience.
Janet Taylor Lisle, *Afternoon of the Elves*, 1989
  Sara-Kate invites Hillary to her decrepit home and among the weeds in her yard, shows her the wonderful village the elves have built.
Josepha Sherman, *Windleaf*, 1993
  Thierry falls in love with a girl who's half human and half faerie; to win her hand, he must accomplish three dangerous quests.

97

HILARI BELL

Flame
(New York: Simon & Schuster, 2003)

Series: Book of Sorahb. Book 1
Subject(s): Fantasy
Age range(s): Grades 6-10
Major character(s): Soraya, Daughter (of Merahb), 15-Year-Old; Jiaan, Bastard Son (of Merahb), 17-Year-Old; Kavi, Spy, 19-Year-Old; Merahb, Military Personnel, Father; Sorahb, Mythical Creature, Warrior
Time period(s): Indeterminate Past
Locale(s): Farsala, Fictional Country

Summary: For years the Persian-like country of Farsala enjoys peace but it also becomes complacent about its borders, unwilling to listen to the warnings of its High Commander Merahb who alerts them to the probable invasion by their neighbors the Hrum. Three teens find themselves involved in the upcoming conflict, beginning with Merahb's daughter Soraya who faces sacrifice to appease the djinn of war. Her half-brother Jiaan is dispatched to ensure Soraya's safety while Kavi is to report to Merahb on Jiaan's success in hiding Soraya. Unfortunately Kavi is also conscripted by the Hrum to report on the Farsala military strength. The three teens wonder if the old legacy about the mighty warrior Sorahb returning to help Farsala in time of need might be coming true as they fear Farsala's destruction. In the midst of the confusion over who reports to whom, Commander Merahb dies and the Farsalan cavalry is defeated in this first of a trilogy. (344 pages)

Where it's reviewed:
Booklist, September 1, 2003, page 122

Horn Book, September 2003, page 607
Publishers Weekly, October 27, 2003, page 70
School Library Journal, November 2003, page 134
Voice of Youth Advocates, October 2003, page 321

Other books by the same author:
Wheel, 2004 (Book of Sorahb Book Two)
Wizard Test, 2004
The Goblin Wood, 2003
A Matter of Profit, 2001

Other books you might like:
Catherine Jinks, *Pagan's Crusade*, 2003
    Pagan, squire to Lord Roland, makes good use of his streetwise fast-talk to spring his knight from Saladin's capture.
Tanith Lee, *Gold Unicorn*, 1994
    When Tanaquil breathes life into a gold unicorn, she accidentally opens the gate to an alternate world where war is fought nonstop.
Tamora Pierce, *The Realms of the Gods*, 1996
    As battle rolls around them and Daine and her mentor face immediate death, Daine's parents spirit them away to the land of the gods.

98

HILARI BELL

The Goblin Wood

(New York: EOS/HarperCollins, 2003)

Subject(s): Fantasy; Witches and Witchcraft; Knights and Knighthood
Age range(s): Grades 6-9
Major character(s): Makenna, Witch, 16-Year-Old; Sir Tobin, Knight; Master Lazur, Religious (priest); Cogswallop, Mythical Creature (goblin)
Time period(s): Indeterminate Past
Locale(s): Realm of the Bright Gods, Fictional Country

Summary: From the south, barbarians invade the Realm of the Bright Gods, pushing Realm inhabitants into the Northern ice fields. Unfortunately these fields are populated by goblins that moved there as a result of the Decree of Bright Magic, which ordered the death of hedgewitches, seers and others of their kind. Five years earlier, this decree led to the death of Makenna's mother, a skilled hedgewitch, who successfully healed many of the occupants of her village. Declaring revenge for her mother's death, Makenna flooded the fields of her village and headed north where she met Cogswallop, a mischievous goblin. Now Makenna finds herself the leader of the goblins as they fight to retain their Northern lands against the army of the Hierarch of their realm. Meanwhile, Sir Tobin is accused of treachery and, to regain his good name, accepts Master Lazur's offer to hunt down and capture Makenna. Captured by the goblins, Sir Tobin alters his opinion of the fearless leader and her loyal army; unfortunately Tobin is unable to halt the plan to capture Makenna in this stirring adventure. (294 pages)

Where it's reviewed:
Booklist, June 2003, page 1758

Bulletin of the Center for Children's Books, June 2003, page 392
Horn Book, May 2003, page 339
Publishers Weekly, March 24, 2003, page 76
School Library Journal, July 2003, page 123

Awards the book has won:
ALA Best Books for Young Adults, 2004

Other books by the same author:
Wheel, 2004 (Book of Sorahb Book 2)
Flame, 2003 (Book of Sorahb Book 1)
A Matter of Profit, 2001
Navohar, 2000
Songs of Power, 2000

Other books you might like:
Robin McKinley, *The Blue Sword*, 1982
    Bored with her proper life, Harry discovers magic she never knew existed when a king kidnaps her.
Tamora Pierce, *Alanna: The First Adventure*, 1983
    Disguised as a boy, Alanna trains to be a knight, becomes squire to a young heir and uses her magical powers to save his life.
Sherwood Smith, *Court Duel*, 1998
    Mel prefers being on the battlefield, but encounters war in another medium when her future sister-in-law entices her to join life at court.

99

WILLIAM BELL

Death Wind

(Custer, WA: Orca Book Publishers, 2002)

Series: Orca Soundings
Subject(s): Weather; Runaways
Age range(s): Grades 7-10
Major character(s): Allie, Runaway; Razz, 17-Year-Old, Sports Figure (skaterboarder)
Time period(s): 1980s
Locale(s): Barrie, Ontario, Canada; Ottawa, Ontario, Canada

Summary: Upset about her failing grades, tired of her parents' continual arguing, and scared that she might be pregnant, Allie decides the best thing is to get away. Leaving a note for her parents, she and Razz take off for the few days of his skateboarding meet. Though Razz wins, he needs to return to their hometown for a television commercial, which petrifies Allie, but bigger problems arise as they become caught in the famous ''Barrie tornado.'' Seeing her home destroyed, Allie and Razz rush to the shelter to find her parents where Allie ends up manning the phone for missing and lost persons while Razz ferries the injured to the hospital and there finds Allie's parents. A tearful reunion sets the stage for the three of them to discuss Allie's problems and work together to find a solution. (92 pages)

Where it's reviewed:
Book Report, November 2002, page 45
Kliatt, July 2002, page 15
Resource Links, October 2002, page 26
School Library Journal, October 2002, page 158
Voice of Youth Advocates, December 2002, page 372

Other books by the same author:
Alma, 2003
Stones, 2001
Zack, 1999
Absolutely Invincible, 1997
Crabbe, 1997

Other books you might like:
Tom Bodett, *Williwaw!*, 1999
  Two young people are caught on Bag Bay when a huge storm, called a ''williwaw,'' rears up and threatens to swamp their boat.
Matthew Olshan, *Finn: A Novel*, 2001
  To escape her crazy mother, Finn runs away with her grandparents' pregnant maid as the two head for California in search of the baby's father.
Marilyn Reynolds, *Detour for Emmy*, 1993
  Deserted by the father of her child, Emmy decides to have her baby and make the best life she can for both of them.

100

SANDRA BELTON
BENNY ANDREWS, Illustrator

Pictures for Miss Josie
(New York: Greenwillow Books/HarperCollins Publishers, 2003)

Subject(s): African Americans; Self-Esteem; Intergenerational Saga
Age range(s): Grades 1-4
Major character(s): Josephine Carroll ''Miss Josie'' Smith, Friend, Teacher; Unnamed Character, Son, Artist; Unnamed Character, Father, Friend
Time period(s): Indeterminate Past
Locale(s): Washington, District of Columbia

Summary: A young boy's father introduces him to Miss Josie when he is so young that Miss Josie seems to tower above him. Miss Josie is known for befriending young African American men pursuing an education and now she welcomes the opportunity to mentor the man's son. Over the years the relationship ebbs and flows with Miss Josie steadfastly introducing the growing boy to the city in which she lives and to the potential that resides within him. As the boy grows, Miss Josie's career as an educator also advances but she still makes time for him. While the father sees no future in his son's art, Miss Josie insists that he put his gift to good use. Despite advancing age, Miss Josie is present at important moments in his life such as his college graduation and his marriage. One day he returns to introduce his son and to bring Miss Josie pictures of all the proud moments they shared over the years. The book concludes with a brief biographical sketch of Josephine Carroll Smith on whom the story is based. (40 pages)

Where it's reviewed:
Booklist, May 1, 2003, page 1604
Bulletin of the Center for Children's Books, June 2003, page 392
Horn Book, May 2003, page 325
Publishers Weekly, March 17, 2003, page 76
School Library Journal, May 2003, page 108

Other books by the same author:
Beauty, Her Basket, 2004
May'naise Sandwiches & Sunshine Tea, 1994
From Miss Ida's Front Porch, 1993

Other books you might like:
Nikki Grimes, *Talkin' about Bessie: The Story of Aviator Elizabeth Coleman*, 2002
  A picture book biography poetically relates the life story of the first female African American pilot.
Elizabeth Fitzgerald Howard, *Virgie Goes to School with Us Boys*, 2000
  Virgie's desire for an education gives her the resolve to walk seven miles to the Quaker school and stay away from home for a week.
Andrea Davis Pinkney, *Ella Fitzgerald: The Tale of a Vocal Virtuosa*, 2002
  The story of the life and music of a renowned African American vocalist is illustrated with lively scratchboard art.
Pam Munoz Ryan, *When Marian Sang: The True Recital of Marian Anderson*,
  Despite the segregation of 1939, Marian Anderson, singer and civil rights activist, is the first African American to perform at the Metropolitan Opera.

101

TEA BENDUHN

Gravel Queen
(New York: Simon & Schuster, 2003)

Subject(s): Friendship; Homosexuality/Lesbianism
Age range(s): Grades 9-12
Major character(s): Aurin Jondiss, 12th Grader, Lesbian; Kenney, 12th Grader; Fred Wallace, 12th Grader, Homosexual; Nelia, Lesbian; Grant Grayson, Cousin (of Nelia)
Time period(s): 2000s
Locale(s): Greensboro, North Carolina

Summary: Ever since they were in sixth grade together, Aurin, Kenney and Fred have been good friends. Now, the summer before their senior year, they hang out in the park and watch some teens play Ultimate Frisbee. Aurin is inexplicably attracted to one of the players and eventually, through taking dance lessons, meets Nelia, cousin of Grant. The dynamics of the trio of friends change when both glamorous, straight Kenney and gay Fred fall for Nelia's cousin Grant in this author's first novel. (152 pages)

Where it's reviewed:
Booklist, June 3, 2003, page 1759
Bulletin of the Center for Children's Books, April 2003, page 305
Publishers Weekly, January 20, 2003, page 83
School Library Journal, March 2003, page 228
Voice of Youth Advocates, April 2003, page 41

Other books you might like:
Nancy Garden, *Lark in the Morning*, 1991
  Gillian's concerned when the family's tool shed is burglarized for it contains her diary with private thoughts about her lesbianism.

M.E. Kerr, *Deliver Us from Evie*, 1994
When Evie's brother Parr discloses her lesbianism, Evie joins her lover Patsy and moves to New York.

Sara Ryan, *Empress of the World*, 2001
Nic is amazed that she and Battle fall for one another in a relationship that moves easily from friendship to kissing to romance.

Shelley Stoehr, *Tomorrow Wendy: A Love Story*, 1998
After Cary has dated Danny for a year she thinks she'd rather date his twin sister Wendy, but realizes she's confused about her sexual identity.

102

JAMES BENNETT

Faith Wish

(New York: Holiday House, 2003)

Subject(s): Pregnancy; Cults; Christian Life
Age range(s): Grades 9-12
Major character(s): Anne-Marie Morgan, 12th Grader, Cheerleader; Brother Jackson, Religious (evangelist)
Time period(s): 2000s
Locale(s): Chicago, Illinois (suburbs); Camp Shaddai, Illinois

Summary: Accompanying her best friend to a revival meeting, Anne-Marie is mesmerized by the words and sound of the evangelist Brother Jackson, so much so that she turns to reading the Bible instead of her textbooks. When she's finally able to meet him alone, she gives in to his seduction, an act that leads to her pregnancy. Anne-Marie's life veers off course as she fails her senior year, is sent to summer school and realizes she's pregnant with Brother Jackson's baby. Borrowing her parent's car, Anne-Marie takes off in search of Brother Jackson, finds him and, at his suggestion, attends Camp Shaddai which is populated by other girls who need counseling. Submitting to the Camp Shaddai counseling, and now unsure about even having sex with Brother Jackson, Anne-Marie becomes Sister Ruth Anne before tragedy strikes. (247 pages)

Where it's reviewed:
Publishers Weekly, June 2, 2003, page 53
School Library Journal, July 2003, page 123
Voice of Youth Advocates, August 2003, page 216

Other books by the same author:
The Squared Circle, 2002

Other books you might like:
Linda Crew, *Brides of Eden*, 2001
Joshua mesmerizes the women of Corvallis, Oregon into joining his church, all eager to become the "Second Mary" ready to father Joshua's child.

Margaret Peterson Haddix, *Leaving Fishers*, 1997
Dorry joins the religious group Fishers of Men, but knows it's time to leave the organization when she tries to convert the children she's babysitting.

Sheri Reynolds, *The Rapture of Canaan*, 1996
Belonging to a fundamentalist church founded by her grandfather, Ninah endures his wrath when she becomes pregnant by her prayer partner James.

Patricia H. Rushford, *Stranded*, 2001
Jennie and her grandmother are kept in the religious settlement Desert Colony after their Piper Cherokee crashes.

Jane Yolen, *Armageddon Summer*, 1998
Two teens meet as each tries to be a buffer between a parent and cult leader Beelson, who predicts the end of the world on July 27, 2000.

103

JIM BENTON, Author/Illustrator

Lunch Walks Among Us

(New York: Simon & Schuster Books for Young Readers, 2003)

Series: Franny K. Stein, Mad Scientist. Book 1
Subject(s): Scientific Experiments; Humor; School Life
Age range(s): Grades 2-5
Major character(s): Franny K. Stein, Student, Scientist; Miss Shelly, Teacher
Time period(s): Indeterminate
Locale(s): Fictional Country

Summary: Miss Shelly notices that Franny's having a hard time making friends at school. She also notes Franny enjoys science experiments and she suggests Franny approach the process of making friends as an experiment. Franny studies what the other students wear, eat and play with and then she goes home and creates a concoction that transforms her into a sweet little girl. She has her mother pack a peanut butter and jelly sandwich on white bread for lunch and she carries a doll that she has modified so it no longer bites off the heads of other dolls. Franny discovers that students seem more comfortable around her in this transformed state than when she was herself, a mad scientist. However, when Miss Shelly is captured by a monster that rises out of an unintentional brew in the classroom trash can, Franny drinks the antidote to the potion and gets the students to help her create a monster out of luncheon meat to rescue their teacher. Though Franny, the mad scientist, is unconventional and a bit scary, the students learn that they can like her just the way she is. (102 pages)

Where it's reviewed:
Bulletin of the Center for Children's Books, December 2003, page 142
Publishers Weekly, September 29, 2003, page 65

Awards the book has won:
IRA Children's Choices, 2004

Other books by the same author:
Attack of the 50-Foot Cupid, 2004 (Franny K. Stein, Mad Scientist Book 2)
Invisible Fran, 2004 (Franny K. Stein, Mad Scientist Book 3)

Other books you might like:
Andrew Clements, *Jake Drake, Know-It-All*, 2001
Jake tries to prove himself by winning the school's first science fair.

Jeanne Marie Grunwell, *Mind Games*, 2003
Members of Mr. Ennis's Mad Science Club prepare a science fair project on ESP.

Dav Pilkey, *Ricky Ricotta's Giant Robot*, 2000
Dr. Stinky creates a destructive Robot but forgets to pro-

gram his invention to be nasty and mean so the giant Robot becomes the friend Ricky seeks.

104

BARBARA HELEN BERGER, Author/Illustrator

All the Way Lhasa: A Tale from Tibet
(New York: Philomel Books, 2002)

Subject(s): Folklore; Determination; Travel
Age range(s): Grades K-3
Major character(s): Unnamed Character, Child, Traveler; Unnamed Character, Aged Person
Time period(s): Indeterminate Past
Locale(s): Tibet

Summary: Two travelers pass an old woman sitting beside the road and ask how far the journey to the holy city of Lhasa is. To the first, galloping on horseback, the woman replies that the distance is so far that the rider will not reach it by nightfall. To the second, a boy walking with a yak carrying a load, the old woman replies that, though Lhasa is very far away, the boy and his yak will arrive before night. By putting one foot in front of another and having the determination to reach his goal despite the challenges of the journey, the boy and his yak do get to Lhasa where the old woman greets them as they enter the holy city. A concluding author's note gives supporting information about the Tibetan culture. (32 pages)

Where it's reviewed:
Booklist, October 1, 2002, page 346
Bulletin of the Center for Children's Books, October 2002, page 49
Publishers Weekly, August 19, 2002, page 88
Riverbank Review, Winter 2002-2003, page 32
School Library Journal, September 2002, page 209

Awards the book has won:
Notable Social Studies Trade Books for Young People, 2003

Other books by the same author:
Angels on a Pin, 1999
A Lot of Otters, 1997 (School Library Journal Best Books)
The Jewel Heart, 1994

Other books you might like:
Don Brown, *Far Beyond the Garden Gate: Alexandra David-Neel's Journey to Lhasa*, 2002
   A picture book biography describes the 1924 adventure of the first Western woman to enter Lhasa.
Lotta Carswell Hume, *Favorite Children's Stories from China and Tibet*, 1989
   A newly formatted reissue of a 1962 title includes many stories from Chinese folklore.
Gioia Timpanelli, *Tales from the Roof of the World: Folktales of Tibet*, 1984
   A collection illustrated with Tibetan symbols retells four folktales.

105

MARA BERGMAN
MARJOLEIN POTTIE, Illustrator

Musical Beds
(New York: Margaret K. McElderry Books, 2002)

Subject(s): Family; Parent and Child; Bedtime
Age range(s): Preschool-Grade 1
Major character(s): Dad, Father, Spouse; Josie, Child, Daughter; Ruby, Child, Daughter; Little Rick, Child, Son
Time period(s): 2000s (2002)
Locale(s): England

Summary: Dad's in charge of bedtime but no one seems able to sleep. Josie thinks there's a witch in her room, but Dad assures her it's only the shadow of a tree on the wall. Josie sneaks into her parents' bed and soon falls asleep. Ruby hears a ghost in her room but Dad assures her that it's only the wind. Still Ruby is happier in her parents' bed and soon she too is asleep. Little Rick is thirsty so Dad gives him water and tucks him into bed. Then Dad tries to sleep in Ruby's bed, but Little Rick is lonely and climbs in too. After trying the top bunk, Dad decides he really wants his own bed so he carries all the sleeping children back to their own beds and settles into his to sleep before his wife gets home. (32 pages)

Where it's reviewed:
Booklist, October 15, 2002, page 409
Bulletin of the Center for Children's Books, January 2003, page 187
Publishers Weekly, October 7, 2002, page 71
School Library Journal, December 2002, page 85

Other books by the same author:
Bears, Bears, Everywhere, 1999

Other books you might like:
Marie-Louise Gay, *Good Night Sam*, 2003
   Sam gets help from big sister Stella to locate his missing dog so he can sleep.
Russell Hoban, *Bedtime for Frances*, 1960
   Frances is a master at avoiding bedtime but her patient parents have a response for every problem.
Mary Beth Lundgren, *Seven Scary Monsters*, 2003
   Cleverly, a young boy figures out how to rid his room of seven monsters so he can sleep comfortably.

106

CARI BEST
HOLLY MEADE, Illustrator

Goose's Story
(New York: Melanie Kroupa/Farrar Straus Giroux, 2002)

Subject(s): Animals/Geese; Physically Handicapped; Animals, Treatment of
Age range(s): Grades K-3
Major character(s): Unnamed Child, Daughter, Narrator; Unnamed Character, Goose, Amputee; Henry, Dog
Time period(s): 2000s
Locale(s): Connecticut

Summary: In the spring, Henry is the first to be aware of the imminent return of the geese. His barking alerts his young owner and together they watch the geese settle into the pond near their home. One goose seems isolated from the others and then the girl sees that it is injured. Shaken and concerned for the goose the girl watches it closely all summer while trying not to offer too much help. She treats the goose as her parents treat her when she is ill by telling it stories and speaking soft assurances. Finally the goose ventures into the pond where she is more accepted by the others in the flock. Sometime in the fall while the girl is at school, all the geese fly south. All winter the girl wonders if the one-footed goose is alive and in the spring, Henry's barking precedes the answer she's been awaiting. (32 pages)

Where it's reviewed:
Booklist, May 1, 2002, page 1520
Bulletin of the Center for Children's Books, September 2002, page 6
Horn Book Guide, Fall 2002, page 319
Horn Book, May 2002, page 312
School Library Journal, July 2002, page 77

Awards the book has won:
Center for Children's Books Best Books, 2002

Other books by the same author:
Shrinking Violet, 2001 (School Library Journal Best Books)
Last Licks: A Spaldeen Story, 1999
Three Cheers for Catherine the Great!, 1999 (Booklist Editors' Choice)
Getting Used to Harry, 1996

Other books you might like:
Nan Parson Rossiter, *The Way Home*, 1999
    After Dad rescues an injured goose, Samuel cares for Chicory so she is able to fly south with her mate for the winter and return the next spring.
Pirkko Vainio, *The Snow Goose*, 1993
    A little girl raises a gosling hatched from the egg of a dying goose only to watch it join a flock and fly away as the summer ends.
Jane Yolen, *Honkers*, 1993
    A lonely young girl and three abandoned geese share a summer of activity before being separated by the approach of winter.

107

CARI BEST
GISELLE POTTER, Illustrator

When Catherine the Great and I Were Eight!

(New York: Melanie Kroupa Books/Farrar Straus Giroux, 2003)

Subject(s): Grandmothers; Automobiles; Neighbors and Neighborhoods
Age range(s): Grades K-3
Major character(s): Catherine "Grandma", Grandmother, Immigrant; Sara, Daughter (granddaughter), 8-Year-Old; Mr. Minsky, Neighbor, Driver
Time period(s): Indeterminate Past
Locale(s): New York, New York

Summary: To escape the summer heat in the city Sara, Grandma and lots of neighbors pile into Mr. Minsky's big car to drive to the beach. After an eventful trip, delayed by a forgotten bathing suit, a problem with the car and lots of traffic, the group finally arrives at the seashore long after the crowds have departed. The picnic lunch is eaten along the way, but there is still enough daylight for everyone to enjoy the beach and the water. As promised, Grandma teaches Sara to float just as she did as eight-year-old Catherine, in a big black sea far away from America. (32 pages)

Where it's reviewed:
Booklist, August 2003, page 1986
Bulletin of the Center for Children's Books, October 2003, page 51
Horn Book, September 2003, page 590
School Library Journal, September 2003, page 169

Other books by the same author:
Goose's Story, 2002
Shrinking Violet, 2001
Three Cheers for Catherine the Great!, 1999 (Booklist Editors' Choice)

Other books you might like:
Stephanie Calmenson, *Hotter than a Hot Dog!*, 1994
    To escape the summer heat, Granny takes her granddaughter to the beach for the day.
Phyllis Root, *Rattletrap Car*, 2001
    It takes persistence, ingenuity and a few children's toys for a family's old car to transport them from the heat of their farm to the cool relief of a lake.
Cynthia Rylant, *Mr. Putter and Tabby Row the Boat*, 1997
    Mr. Putter anticipates cooling relief from the heat by boating on the pond with Tabby, but his idea fails to help either feel better.

108

PHIL BILDNER
C.F. PAYNE, Illustrator

Shoeless Joe & Black Betsy

(New York: Simon & Schuster Books for Young Readers, 2002)

Subject(s): Sports/Baseball; Historical; Superstition
Age range(s): Grades 2-4
Major character(s): Joseph "Shoeless Joe" Jackson, Baseball Player; Charlie Ferguson, Artisan, Aged Person
Time period(s): 1900s; 1910s
Locale(s): South Carolina; Pennsylvania; Ohio

Summary: To achieve his dream of a major league baseball career, Shoeless Joe must break out of his hitting slump so he visits his friend and renowned maker of bats, Charlie Ferguson to order a new bat. The handcrafted oak bat looks good, but still Shoeless Joe is not hitting. He returns to Charlie and insists that the bat be made of hickory and stained with tobacco juice so it will intimidate pitchers. The bat, named Black Betsy by its owner, works well for Shoeless Joe until he moves up to the majors. Each time he hits another slump Shoeless Joe returns to Charlie. Now, Charlie knows he's made a fine bat and he also knows ball players are superstitious so he gives Shoeless Joe instructions in proper bat care.

Sure enough when Joe sleeps with Black Betsy, massages the bat with oil, wraps it in cotton if he's sent to a northern ballpark and brings her home each winter to the warmth of the South, he continues his hitting success. An ''Afterword'' gives factual background to the story including the statistics of Shoeless Joe's career. (40 pages)

Where it's reviewed:
Booklist, February 15, 2002, page 1014
Bulletin of the Center for Children's Books, February 2002, page 200
Kirkus Reviews, December 15, 2001, page 1754
Publishers Weekly, January 7, 2002, page 64
School Library Journal, April 2002, page 100

Other books you might like:
David A. Adler, *Lou Gehrig: The Luckiest Man*, 1997
    A picture book biography details the life and baseball career of the star player for the Yankees.
Donald Hall, *When Willard Met Babe Ruth*, 1996
    In 1917 a young baseball fan and his farmer father unexpectedly meet Babe Ruth when his car goes into the ditch while avoiding their flock of geese.
Ernest Lawrence Thayer, *Casey at the Bat: A Ballad of the Republic Sung in the Year 1888*, 2000
    Illustrator Christopher Bing augments the legendary poem about Casey's ninth inning strike out with fictional news articles. Caldecott Honor Book.

109

TOM BIRDSEYE

Attack of the Mutant Underwear

(New York: Holiday House, 2003)

Subject(s): School Life; Interpersonal Relations; Diaries
Age range(s): Grades 4-6
Major character(s): Cody Lee Carson, 5th Grader; Amy, 5th Grader; Ms. B, Teacher
Time period(s): 2000s (2003)
Locale(s): Benton, Oregon

Summary: Moving to Benton gives Cody the opportunity to begin the school year as the ''New Me.'' No one knows the ''Old Me'' Cody, prone to embarrassing moments and frequent trips to the principal's office. In Cody's new class Ms. B sees potential in him—his grades are good and cute Amy might have some interest in getting to know him better. Each time Cody suffers one of childhood's inevitable embarrassing moments (that often seem to involve underwear) he senses the ''Old Me'' returning and his grades and deportment begin slipping. A disastrous mix-up between the Valentine's Day gift planned for Amy and the gag gift for his sister seems to ruin his chances of ''New Me'' love and he abandons hope of reform. Pairing up with a classmate known for unruly behavior on the end-of-the-year camping trip almost spoils the adventure for everyone but the ''New Me'' hero Cody comes through in the end. (198 pages)

Where it's reviewed:
Booklist, January 2004, page 852
Bulletin of the Center for Children's Books, January 2004, page 181

Publishers Weekly, December 8, 2003, page 62
School Library Journal, January 2004, page 124

Other books by the same author:
The Eye of the Stone, 2000
Tarantula Shoes, 1995
Just Call Me Stupid, 1993

Other books you might like:
Judy Blume, *Double Fudge*, 2002
    In the fourth story about the Hatcher family, seventh grader Peter discovers he has a cousin with the same name and behavior as his younger brother Fudge.
Andrew Clements, *Frindle*, 1996
    Frustrated by his teacher's extensive use of the dictionary Nick invents a new word for pen.
Phyllis Reynolds Naylor, *Alice in Blunderland*, 2003
    Fourth grader Alice has the best of intentions but still seems to end up in one embarrassing predicament after another.

110

ANNE BISHOP

Shadows and Light

(New York: ROC, 2002)

Series: Tir Alainn Trilogy. Book 2
Subject(s): Fantasy; Fairies; Prejudice
Age range(s): Grades 9-Adult
Major character(s): Liam, Nobleman, Witch; Brenna, Witch, Sister; Aiden, Mythical Creature (fairy); Lyrra, Mythical Creature (muse); Ashk, Mythical Creature (fairy)
Time period(s): Indeterminate
Locale(s): Sylvalan, Fictional Country

Summary: Parts of the land of Faerie are disappearing. At the same time in the human world, a sinister Inquisitor is killing the witches, which are vital to maintain the magic needed for Faerie to remain as it is and keep open the roads between Faerie and the human world. Neglect by their human kin has led to indifference and even active dislike by many in Faerie, and three of the most powerful figures in the land are hard-pressed to get fairy-kind to take action. Aiden, the fairy Bard, and his wife Lyrra, the Muse, spend much of their time in the human world trying to salvage the situation. Currently their travels bring them into contact with a brother and sister who personify the human side of the dilemma. Brenna has always known and accepted her difference as a witch. Her brother Liam, protected by his status both as a man and as a nobleman, is blind to the persecution. At first he denies that Brenna needs protection, then he denies that he shares her gifts, but finally Liam is forced to recognize the danger that exists in his world. Meanwhile, the powerful fairy Ashk tires of watching harm befall those for whom she feels responsible. Ashk's title is the Hunter and she's ready to go hunting for Inquisitors. (420 pages)

Where it's reviewed:
Booklist, October 1, 2002, page 307
Kliatt, March 2003, page 30
Voice of Youth Advocates, June 2003, page 146

Other books by the same author:
The House of Gaian, 2003 (Tir Alainn Trilogy Book 3)
The Pillars of the World, 2001 (Tir Alainn Trilogy Book 1)
The Invisible Ring, 2000

Other books you might like:
Lynn Abbey, *Jerlayne*, 1999
   Willful Jerlayne demands to know the whole truth of the fairy people, even if it involves goblins and humans.
Emma Bull, *Finder: A Novel of the Borderlands*, 2003
   Living on the edge of Faerie is a dangerous business, even when Faerie is right next door to the known world.
Katherine Kurtz, *Chronicles of the Deryni*, 1987-
   In this on-going series, the religious persecution of the magically gifted causes war, murder and political upheaval.

111

HOLLY BLACK

Tithe: A Modern Faerie Tale

(New York: Simon & Schuster, 2002)

Subject(s): Fantasy; Fairies
Age range(s): Grades 8-12
Major character(s): Kaye Fierch, Teenager, Mythical Creature; Rath Roiben Rye, Knight, Mythical Creature
Time period(s): 2000s
Locale(s): New Jersey

Summary: Kaye doesn't quite fit together, with her blond hair, Asian eyes, foul mouth, punk attitude and belief in fairies. She doesn't quite fit in, either, and her unconventional mother, who still chases her dream of rock-and-roll stardom, doesn't help Kaye feel any more normal. When her mother's latest gig falls through, Kaye finds herself back in the small New Jersey shore town where she spent her early childhood. It is the place, in fact, where Kaye learned to believe in fairies, because they often visited her. Walking home late one night, Kaye hears a noise in the trees and upon investigation, knows immediately that the gorgeous man lying wounded is no man, but a fairy. In return for her help pulling out the arrow in his side, he agrees to answer three questions. It's only spite and luck that make Kaye demand his name as the last of the three questions. Rath Roiben Rye is a powerful knight of the Unseelie Court, hostage from one fairy queen to another. Soon, it will be his task to seek a human being to offer in sacrifice as the seven-year tithe. Only the fact that neither Kaye nor Roiben are at all what they seem offers them the least chance for survival. (320 pages)

Where it's reviewed:
Booklist, February 15, 2003, page 1064
Bulletin of the Center for Children's Books, January 2003, page 188
Horn Book Guide, Spring 2003, page 91
School Library Journal, October 2002, page 158
Voice of Youth Advocates, October 2002, page 292

Awards the book has won:
ALA Best Books for Young Adults, 2003
Center for Children's Books Best Books, 2002

Other books by the same author:
The Spiderwick Chronicles, 2003- (Tony DiTerlizzi, co-author)

Other books you might like:
Emma Bull, *War for the Oaks*, 1987
   A rock musician is chosen by the Faerie Courts to bring blood to their battleground.
Charles de Lint, *Someplace to be Flying*, 1998
   The mythical Crow Girls, who are both human and bird, bring gossip and chaos to the streets of Newford.
Annette Curtis Klause, *Blood and Chocolate*, 1997
   Vivian finds life as a teen is complicated by the fact that she is a werewolf.

112

SUSAN BLACKABY
MARY NEWELL DEPALMA, Illustrator

Rembrandt's Hat

(Boston: Houghton Mifflin Company, 2002)

Subject(s): Clothes; Lost and Found; Animals/Bears
Age range(s): Grades K-3
Major character(s): Rembrandt, Bear; Boo, Cat; Tip, Rabbit
Time period(s): Indeterminate
Locale(s): Fictional Country

Summary: The wind takes Rembrandt's blue hat and the substitutes he tries simply aren't suitable replacements. The bird that agrees to perch on his head is too fidgety and flies away in fright when Boo approaches, admiring the tasty looking hat. Boo volunteers for hat duty but the cat is too big and heavy for kindly Rembrandt. When Tip spots Rembrandt he suggests a trip to the hat store. Rembrandt tries on lots of hats and purchases the one recommended by Tip but it doesn't seem to suit him either so he gives it away to the clown in the park. Then he sees a souvenir vendor who has just the right cap to become Rembrandt's new hat as the author's first picture book concludes. (32 pages)

Where it's reviewed:
Booklist, April 15, 2002, page 1405
Bulletin of the Center for Children's Books, May 2002, page 310
Horn Book Guide, Fall 2002, page 319
Publishers Weekly, January 14, 2002, page 59
School Library Journal, July 2002, page 83

Other books you might like:
Catherine Bancroft, *Felix's Hat*, 1993
   Sensitive parents and supportive siblings help Felix overcome the loss of his favorite orange hat. Hannah Coale Gruenberg, co-author.
Joan L. Nodeset, *Who Took the Farmer's Hat?*, 1963
   A farmer searches for his lost hat, carried away by the wind and put to good use.
Tracey Campbell Pearson, *The Purple Hat*, 1997
   A bird finds Annie's beloved purple hat and uses it for a nest.

113

TERENCE BLACKER

The Angel Factor

(New York: Simon & Schuster, 2002)

Subject(s): Adoption; Aliens; Angels
Age range(s): Grades 6-9
Major character(s): Thomas Wisdom, 12-Year-Old; Gip Sanchez, Alien
Time period(s): 2000s
Locale(s): London, England

Summary: Living the perfect life of a good-looking, bright kid, Thomas is happy except for the fear that his parents are CIA agents. Using the talents of his best friend Gip, the two boys break open an encrypted file on his parents' computer where Thomas finds that his parents are not CIA agents, but angels. They're not the angels discussed in the Bible, but aliens from another world who have come to Earth to prevent humans from destroying themselves. The Seraph organization plans for angels to adopt humans and teach them how to live so that the violence will cease, but in doing so they're removing the very essence of humanity. The future of the project rests on Thomas's shoulders and when he rejects becoming an angel, the aliens retreat in this thriller. (216 pages)

Where it's reviewed:
Booklist, August 2002, page 1945
Bulletin of the Center for Children's Books, January 2003, page 189
Publishers Weekly, July 22, 2002, page 180
School Library Journal, August 2002, page 182
Voice of Youth Advocates, October 2002, page 292

Awards the book has won:
IRA Children's Choices/Advanced Readers, 2003

Other books by the same author:
Kill Your Darlings, 2000 (adult fiction)
Reverence, 1996 (adult fiction)
Homebird, 1993

Other books you might like:
Catherine Dexter, *Alien Game*, 1995
    Zoe is convinced that new student Christina is an alien and enlists the help of her friend Norton to prove it.
William Sleator, *Interstellar Pig*, 1984
    Barney joins three neighbors for a game of Interstellar Pig, not realizing his neighbors are aliens playing for control of Earth.
Sylvia Waugh, *Space Race*, 2000
    Thomas is upset to learn that he and his father must return to their planet Ormingat after living on Earth for five years.

114

GARY BLACKWOOD

Shakespeare's Spy

(New York: Dutton, 2003)

Series: Shakespeare Stealer. Book 3
Subject(s): Theater; Actors and Actresses; Apprentices
Age range(s): Grades 5-8
Major character(s): Widge, Actor, Orphan; William Shakespeare, Historical Figure, Writer (playwright); Judith Shakespeare, Historical Figure, Daughter (of Shakespeare)
Time period(s): 17th century (1602)
Locale(s): London, England

Summary: A former street urchin who's now part of the actors comprising Lord Chamberlain's Men, Widge is one of the first suspects when costumes and scripts disappear from the Globe Theater. Tension is already high among the cast members for they're worried about Queen Elizabeth's failing health; if she dies, more than likely the Puritans will take charge and close down the Globe, along with all the other theaters. Knowing he's innocent, and hoping to settle at least one mystery, Widge lets it be known that he's been dismissed by Shakespeare and heads to their rival company, Admiral's Men, to find the robber. His uncanny ability with words and codes helps him decipher a note that leads to the thief, which restores some balance to Lord Chamberlain's Men. In addition to spying, Widge falls for Shakespeare's daughter Judith, and to impress her he tries to complete the writing of a discarded play of Shakespeare's in this authentic look at life in the 1600s. (281 pages)

Where it's reviewed:
Booklist, September 1, 2003, page 119
Horn Book, November 2003, page 739
Kirkus Reviews, October 15, 2003, page 1269
School Library Journal, October 2003, page 158

Other books by the same author:
Shakespeare's Scribe, 2000 (Shakespeare Stealer Book 2)
The Shakespeare Stealer, 1998 (Shakespeare Stealer Book 1)

Other books you might like:
J.B. Cheaney, *The Playmaker*, 2000
    After his mother's death, Richard travels to London where he's lucky enough to find a job as an actor with Lord Chamberlain's Men.
Susan Cooper, *King of Shadows*, 1999
    Selected to act in the newly-renovated Globe Theater, Nat falls through time to play Puck against Will Shakespeare as Oberon.
Lynne Kositsky, *A Question of Will*, 2000
    Part of a field trip to London, Perin rushes to catch up with her group only to land in 16th century London as apprentice to William Shakespeare.

115

GARY BLACKWOOD

The Year of the Hangman

(New York: Dutton, 2002)

Subject(s): Alternate History; Spies; Revolutionary War
Age range(s): Grades 7-10
Major character(s): Benedict Arnold, Historical Figure; Benjamin Franklin, Historical Figure; Creighton Brown, 17-Year-Old, Spy; Hugh Gower, Uncle (of Creighton), Government Official, governor of South Carolina Col
Time period(s): 1770s (1777)
Locale(s): New Orleans, Louisiana; HMS *Amity*, Atlantic Ocean

Summary: The year is 1777, called the "year of the hangman" because of the resemblance of the 7's to a tiny gallows, and in this alternative history the Continental Army has been defeated by the British. George Washington is held captive and slated for execution; Benedict Arnold leads a band of patriots who have escaped to New Orleans, which is under French control; and Benjamin Franklin has set up his printing press to print broadsides for the revolutionaries. Into this stewpot comes Creighton Brown, a spoiled English teen who has so little purpose in life that his mother arranges for him to be abducted and taken to his uncle, a colonial governor. Arnold and his privateers attack them off Florida, Creighton's uncle is taken into custody and Creighton is sent to work for Franklin, who doesn't know that Creighton's been asked to spy for the British. For the first time in his life Creighton has a purpose and feels pride in producing the broadsides and the newspaper, but he's unsure of loyalties as he finds himself rooting for the Americans. (261 pages)

Where it's reviewed:
Booklist, August 2002, page 1945
Bulletin of the Center for Children's Books, December 2002, page 144
Publishers Weekly, September 16, 2002, page 70
School Library Journal, September 2002, page 219
Voice of Youth Advocates, October 2002, page 269

Awards the book has won:
School Library Journal Best Books, 2002
ALA Best Books for Young Adults, 2003

Other books by the same author:
Shakespeare's Spy, 2003
Shakespeare's Scribe, 2000
Moonshine, 1999
The Shakespeare Stealer, 1998
Dying Sun, 1989

Other books you might like:
Orson Scott Card, *Seventh Son*, 1987
  The lucky seventh son of a seventh son, Alvin is born with special powers on the frontier of a United States where magic works.
Philip K. Dick, *The Man in the High Castle*, 1962
  World War II ends with the other side winning and the Japanese in control of the western half of the United States.
William Gibson, *The Difference Engine*, 1991
  Charles Babbage's success enables the Victorians to use computer technology, which they put to frightening uses.

116
QUENTIN BLAKE, Author/Illustrator

Mrs. Armitage: Queen of the Road
(Atlanta: Peachtree, 2003)

Subject(s): Automobiles; Motorcycles; Transportation
Age range(s): Grades K-2
Major character(s): Mrs. Anastasia Armitage, Niece, Driver; Breakspear, Dog; Cosmo, Uncle, Motorcyclist
Time period(s): 2000s
Locale(s): England

Summary: Uncle Cosmo decides to buy a motorcycle and gives his old car to Mrs. Armitage. In her opinion the car doesn't look very exciting, but with Breakspear as a companion, Mrs. Armitage gives it a try. On a bumpy road the hubcaps fall off so Mrs. Armitage takes them to the junkyard. On the way she crunches a fender, then loses a bumper. Each time she accidentally crumples a piece of car she discards it. By the time Mrs. Armitage and Breakspear meet Uncle Cosmo and other motorcyclists on the road the car resembles a four-wheeled motorcycle. The motorcyclists admire it and invite her to come along with them on their ride to the Crazy Duck Cafe. (32 pages)

Where it's reviewed:
Booklist, November 15, 2003, page 598
School Library Journal, October 2003, page 114

Other books by the same author:
Tell Me a Picture, 2003
Loveykins, 2002
Ten Frogs, 2000
Mrs. Armitage and the Big Wave, 1998
Mrs. Armitage on Wheels, 1988

Other books you might like:
Don Brown, *Alice Ramsey's Grand Adventure*, 1997
  A picture book biography describes the 1909 journey of the first woman to travel by automobile from New York to San Francisco.
Faye Gibbons, *Mama and Me and the Model T*, 1999
  When Mr. Long arrives home with the family's first car Mama takes everyone for an exciting ride about the farm.
Margaret Mahy, *The Rattlebang Picnic*, 1994
  When a wheel falls off the McTavishes' old car they use Granny's too-hard-to-eat pizza as a spare.

117
ROBERT J. BLAKE, Author/Illustrator

Togo
(New York: Philomel Books, 2002)

Subject(s): Animals/Dogs; Rescue Work; Historical
Age range(s): Grades 2-4
Major character(s): Leonhard Seppala, Animal Trainer (dog sledder); Togo, Dog
Time period(s): 1910s; 1920s (1925)
Locale(s): Alaska

Summary: As a pup, Togo is clearly too independent, too small and too unruly to become a sled dog so Leonhard Seppala gives him away to be a pet. Togo, true to Seppala's estimation of his independent character, has other plans and he's given a chance to prove his value as a sled dog. Soon Seppala is known as the owner of the fastest sled dog team in North America. When a crisis arises in Nome and diphtheria serum must be rushed to the city, Seppala and his team are asked to carry it. Under Togo's leadership the team fights through blinding snow and across treacherous ice for over 350 miles to reach the next team in the relay of the serum run. A concluding epilogue and author's note give additional information about the historic event, now commemorated annually as the Iditarod Race. (44 pages)

Where it's reviewed:
Booklist, September 15, 2002, page 230
Horn Book Guide, Spring 2003, page 25
Kirkus Reviews, August 15, 2002, page 1216
School Library Journal, September 2002, page 181
Smithsonian, December 2002, page 126

Awards the book has won:
ALA Notable Children's Books, 2003
Smithsonian's Notable Books for Children, 2002

Other books by the same author:
Fledgling, 2000
Akiak: A Tale from the Iditarod, 1997 (School Library Journal Best Books)
Spray, 1996

Other books you might like:
Margo Lundell, *Lad to the Rescue*, 1997
    While saving an invalid child from a poisonous snake Lad is bitten and almost dies.
Gary Paulsen, *Dogteam*, 1993
    On a moonlit night, a team of dogs enjoys a dogsled run through the snowy woods.
Patricia Seibert, *Mush! Across Alaska in the World's Longest Sled-Dog Race*, 1992
    The dogs that pull the sleds are the focal point in a story about the Iditarod Race.
Rosemary Wells, *Lassie Come Home*, 1995
    The picture book adaptation of Eric Knight's classic story tells of the power of love binding pet to owner and Lassie's determination to return to Joe.

118

LUCY JANE BLEDSOE

Hoop Girlz
(New York: Holiday House, 2002)

Subject(s): Sports/Basketball; Self-Confidence; Brothers and Sisters
Age range(s): Grades 4-7
Major character(s): River Borowitz-Jacobs, 11-Year-Old, Basketball Player; Zacj Borowitz-Jacobs, Coach, Brother (of River); Emily Hargraves, Basketball Player (professional)
Time period(s): 2000s
Locale(s): Azalea, Oregon

Summary: Hearing that the local high school coach is setting up a sixth grade team to compete in a tournament where the most valuable player will meet professional basketball player Emily Hargraves, River is immediately interested. When she doesn't make the "A Team," she's disappointed about blowing her chance to meet her idol, but also realizes that she doesn't have that "win at any cost" mentality. Instead she stays with the B Team, renames them "Hoop Girlz," and silk-screens some wild purple t-shirts. They make up for their lack of height, wheelchair-bound player and fourth grade teammate by working together while still having a lot of fun. In strange ways, River achieves her dream. (162 pages)

Where it's reviewed:
Booklist, September 1, 2002, page 129

Horn Book Guide, Fall 2003, page 362
Kirkus Reviews, September 1, 2002, page 1304
Reading Teacher, April 2003, page 706
School Library Journal, December 2002, page 132

Other books by the same author:
Antarctic Scoop, 2003
This Wild Silence: A Novel, 2003
Cougar Canyon, 2001
Tracks in the Snow, 1997

Other books you might like:
Paul Baczewski, *Just for Kicks*, 1990
    Brandon makes the school football team a family affair when he talks his sister into going out for the position of kicker.
Jan Cheripko, *Rat*, 2002
    Rat's withered arm reduces him to being team manager for his basketball team; he's a good player if someone would only give him a chance.
David Klass, *A Different Season*, 1988
    Jim's in love with Jennifer, but he's not happy when she earns a place on his baseball team.

119

SUZANNE BLOOM, Author/Illustrator

No Place for a Pig
(Honesdale, PA: Boyds Mills Press, 2003)

Subject(s): Animals/Pigs; Neighbors and Neighborhoods; Pets
Age range(s): Grades K-3
Major character(s): Mrs. Taffy, Neighbor; Serena, Pig
Time period(s): 2000s (2003)
Locale(s): United States

Summary: Mrs. Taffy loves pigs. When she wins one in a radio contest, she thinks that she has the perfect place for it on her shelf. However, when Mrs. Taffy gets out to Hog Heaven, she finds that she's won a real piglet. She brings piglet Serena back (on the subway) to her city apartment and her neighbors help take care of Serena. Soon, however, Serena has outgrown Mrs. Taffy's third-floor walk-up apartment and Mrs. Taffy is worried that she'll have to move to the country. Her neighbors come up with a solution and turn an empty lot into a vegetable garden, complete with a pigsty for Serena. (32 pages)

Where it's reviewed:
Booklist, January, 2004, page 872
Publishers Weekly, November 10, 2003, page 61
School Library Journal, November 2003, page 88

Other books by the same author:
Piggy Monday: A Tale about Manners, 2001
The Bus for Us, 2001
We Keep a Pig in the Parlor, 1988

Other books you might like:
Judi Barrett, *Old MacDonald Had an Apartment House*, 1998
    The super of a city apartment building turns the vacant apartments into a farm.
Arthur Dorros, *City Chicken*, 2003
    Henry has lived in a city chicken coop all her life. Lured by descriptions of the country, Henry visits, but decides that city life is for her.

Diane Goode, *Tiger Trouble!*, 2001
Jack and his pet tiger Lily face eviction when his apartment building is sold and a new landlord begins managing it.
Mary Stolz, *Emmett's Pig*, 1959
Emmett lives in an urban apartment, but he still wants a pig for a pet.
Karen Wallace, *City Pig*, 2000
Dolores has a fancy life in the big city, but after a vacation in the country, she decides to join the pigs in the country pond.

120

JUDY BLUME

Double Fudge

(New York: Dutton, 2002)

Subject(s): Humor; Money; Family Life
Age range(s): Grades 4-7
Major character(s): Peter "Pete" Hatcher, 7th Grader; Farley Drexel "Fudge" Hatcher, Child; Flora Hatcher, Cousin (of Pete), 7th Grader; Fauna Hatcher, Cousin (of Pete and Fudge), 7th Grader; Farley Drexel Hatcher, Cousin (of Pete and Fudge)
Time period(s): 2000s
Locale(s): New York, New York; Washington, District of Columbia

Summary: Pete and his annoying little brother Fudge are back! For some reason, Fudge has become obsessed with money. He makes "fudge bucks," dresses up as a miser for Halloween and asks everyone the rudest questions about their money. But if Pete thinks Fudge is bad, he changes his mind after meeting another Farley Drexel. The Hatchers travel to Washington, DC, to allow Fudge to see where America's money is made at the Bureau of Engraving and Printing, and there they run into their cousins, the Honolulu Hatchers. A more annoying set of relatives couldn't be found beginning with a set of twins Pete's age, named Flora and Fauna, who burst out with corny songs and call themselves the Heavenly Hatchers. There's also their four-year-old brother, who shares Fudge's real name Farley Drexel and growls at people and then licks them, mimicking a dog. Worst of all, the Honolulu Hatchers visit Pete and his family in Manhattan where the twins show up at his school to sing at a special assembly. (213 pages)

Where it's reviewed:
Booklist, September 15, 2002, page 235
Bulletin of the Center for Children's Books, November 2002, page 99
Horn Book, November 2002, page 748
Publishers Weekly, June 24, 2002, page 57
School Library Journal, September 2002, page 181

Other books by the same author:
Fudge-a-Mania, 1990
Superfudge, 1980

Other books you might like:
Julia Alvarez, *How Tia Lola Came to Visit/Stay*, 2001
Miguel is mortified that his Tia Lola cares for him while his mother works and tries to hide her, but Tia Lola charms everyone in his town.

Sharon G. Flake, *Money Hungry*, 2001
Forced to live on the streets for a few weeks, Raspberry has become obsessed about money, never again wanting to be without a home.
Dyan Sheldon, *My Brother Is a Visitor from Another Planet*, 1993
Adam's older brother Keith takes advantage of his trusting nature and convinces Adam that he's an alien needing assistance to reach his spaceship.

121

DIANE CAIN BLUTHENTHAL, Author/Illustrator

I'm Not Invited?

(New York: Richard Jackson Book/Atheneum Books for Young Readers, 2003)

Subject(s): Friendship; Family; School Life
Age range(s): Grades 1-3
Major character(s): Minnie, Student—Elementary School, Friend; Charles, Student—Elementary School, Friend
Time period(s): 2000s (2003)
Locale(s): United States

Summary: Overhearing a brief conversation between Charles and another student makes Minnie think she's being excluded from a party being held on Saturday. All week Minnie searches the mailbox for an invitation, feeling more and more miserable when nothing appears. She tries to ask Charles but he seems oblivious to her anxieties. On Saturday morning she rides by Charles's house and sees the balloon decorations, confirming her worst fears. Then another friend invites her to play ball and when she arrives at the field she notices Charles is there. When Minnie questions why he's not at the party, he replies that he'd rather play with his friends than go to his sister's party. Minnie agrees. (32 pages)

Where it's reviewed:
Booklist, April 15, 2003, page 1475
Bulletin of the Center for Children's Books, April 2003, page 306
Publishers Weekly, December 16, 2002, page 66

Other books by the same author:
Matilda the Moocher, 1997

Other books you might like:
Holly Hobbie, *Toot & Puddle: You Are My Sunshine*, 1999
The sun shines but Toot mopes so Puddle and Tulip try to cheer their friend.
Matt Novak, *No Zombies Allowed*, 2002
While viewing photos of the previous year's party two witches decide to exclude some misbehaving groups; finally they decide it's easier to ban cameras.
Nancy Elizabeth Wallace, *Tell-a-Bunny*, 2000
Sunny's whispered phone communications with friends lead to a surprise birthday party for her brother that is not what she'd planned.

122

DON BOLOGNESE, Author/Illustrator

The Warhorse
(New York: Simon & Schuster, 2003)

Subject(s): Animals/Horses; Artists and Art; Kings, Queens, Rulers, etc.
Age range(s): Grades 5-8
Major character(s): Lorenzo Arrighi, Apprentice, Artist; Renato Arrighi, Artisan (armorer), Father; Beatrice, Teenager
Time period(s): 16th century
Locale(s): Italy

Summary: Apprenticed to his father, the master armorer for the Duke, Lorenzo wants to do more than make the armor, he wants to don it and then take part in the battle. His father forbids him to do so but when the Duke is threatened, Lorenzo mounts his horse Scoppio and rides out to assist. Entering the middle of a battle fray, Lorenzo's romanticized view is quickly dashed when he witnesses the injuries of the wounded men and sees the severed body parts lying on the ground, though he battles admirably. When mercenaries attack a family of lepers, he leaps to their assistance and is immediately taken with their daughter Beatrice, the only unmarked one of the four. Though she is considered an untouchable, Lorenzo never forgets her as he leaves the fields of battle and pursues his career as an artist, painting all the faces of the Virgin Mary with Beatrice's image. (165 pages)

Where it's reviewed:
Kirkus Reviews, May 15, 2003, page 746
Publishers Weekly, June 30, 2003, page 80
School Library Journal, August 2003, page 154

Other books by the same author:
Printmaking, 1987 (nonfiction)
Charcoal and Pastel, 1986 (nonfiction)
Drawing Spaceships and Other Spacecraft, 1982 (nonfiction)

Other books you might like:
Patricia Beatty, *Charley Skedaddle*, 1987
    Charley earns his nickname when he skedaddles from the horror of his first Civil War battle.
Michael Cadnum, *The Book of the Lion*, 2000
    Fearing he will face the same punishment as his counterfeiting master who loses his hand, Edmund eagerly agrees to be a squire.
Mirjam Pressler, *Shylock's Daughter*, 2001
    The desire to escape her Jewish ghetto is so strong that Jessica leaves behind her religion and her father, though she takes his savings.

123

REBECCA BOND, Author/Illustrator

When Marcus Moore Moved In
(New York: Megan Tingley Books/Little, Brown and Company, 2003)

Subject(s): Moving, Household; Friendship; Neighbors and Neighborhoods
Age range(s): Grades K-3
Major character(s): Marcus Moore, Child; Katherine "Kate" Brown, Child
Time period(s): 2000s
Locale(s): Brooklyn, New York

Summary: When Marcus moves to a new neighborhood he's surrounded by boxes and furniture but still lonely. As the hours pass, a girl comes into view. She's also playing alone and doesn't seem to notice Marcus as he makes a house on the sidewalk out of empty boxes. But Kate has spotted Marcus and introduces herself. Thus begins an afternoon of imaginary, noisy, joyful play on MacDougal Street. (32 pages)

Where it's reviewed:
Booklist, May 15, 2003, page 1669
Bulletin of the Center for Children's Books, July 2003, page 437
Publishers Weekly, June 16, 2003, page 68
School Library Journal, August 2003, page 122

Other books by the same author:
Bravo, Maurice!, 2000
Just Like a Baby, 1999

Other books you might like:
Nancy Carlson, *My Best Friend Moved Away*, 2001
    A little girl is left with only memories of good times she and her best friend shared . . . until the new neighbors arrive.
Joyce Champion, *Emily and Alice*, 1993
    When Alice moves into the house next door to Emily, the two girls quickly become friends.
Chris Raschka, *Yo! Yes?*, 1993
    An award-winning celebration of friendship shows the tentative first steps as two boys of different races become acquainted.

124

SUSAN BONNERS

Making Music
(New York: Farrar Straus Giroux, 2002)

Subject(s): Music and Musicians; Moving, Household; Single Parent Families
Age range(s): Grades 3-5
Major character(s): Annie Howard, Child of Divorced Parents, 4th Grader; Mrs. Bergstrom, Neighbor, Musician (pianist)
Time period(s): 2000s (2002)
Locale(s): United States

Summary: Adjusting to a move to an urban neighborhood in a new city is challenging for Annie. Every evening as she roller skates on the sidewalk Annie finds comfort in the piano music emanating from one house. Annie would like to learn to play but she knows her recently divorced mother has no extra money for lessons. During the summer, when she's not busy helping her mother get the house and yard in order, Annie visits with Mrs. Bergstrom and listens to her play the piano. Annie teaches Mrs. Bergstrom how to operate her new VCR and Mrs. Bergstrom agrees to give her piano lessons in exchange for help with her yard work. (88 pages)

Where it's reviewed:
Booklist, November 1, 2002, page 489
Horn Book Guide, Spring 2003, page 64
Kirkus Reviews, September 1, 2002, page 1304
Publishers Weekly, November 4, 2002, page 84
School Library Journal, October 2002, page 99

Other books by the same author:
Edwina Victorious, 2000
Why Does a Cat Do That?, 1998
The Silver Balloon, 1997 (Christopher Award)

Other books you might like:
Amy Hest, *The Private Notebook of Katie Roberts, Age 11*, 1995
    Katie keeps a record of her thoughts and feelings when her widowed mother remarries, moving them from New York to Texas.
Susan Patron, *Maybe Yes, Maybe No, Maybe Maybe*, 1993
    In an award-winning title, middle child PK begrudgingly adjusts to a move to a new apartment with her mother and two sisters.
Vera B. Williams, *Scooter*, 1993
    When Lanny, her scooter and her mother move to a new apartment in the city, Lanny's outgoing personality helps her make new friends.

125

TONY BONNING
SALLY HOBSON, Illustrator

Fox Tale Soup

(New York: Simon & Schuster Books for Young Readers, 2002)

Subject(s): Folklore; Animals/Foxes; Food
Age range(s): Grades K-2
Major character(s): Fox, Fox, Trickster
Time period(s): Indeterminate Past
Locale(s): Fictional Country

Summary: First published in Great Britain in 2001 as *Stone Soup,* this retelling uses animals in the familiar tale. Fox is a tired, hungry traveler whose initial request for food is refused by animals that are, at least, willing to give him water for his pot. Into the pot of boiling water Fox places a carefully selected stone. Each time Fox tastes the soup in front of the audience of curious animals he places a request for a single item to make the soup more palatable. Before the soup is ready the animals add seasonings, carrots, cabbage, corn, and a turnip to the Fox's pot. Finally, after everyone eats they express their surprise that such a delicious soup could be made from only a stone. (32 pages)

Where it's reviewed:
Booklist, February 1, 2002, page 942
Bulletin of the Center for Children's Books, March 2002, page 235
Kirkus Reviews, December 15, 2001, page 1754
Publishers Weekly, December 17, 2001, page 90
School Library Journal, March 2002, page 172

Other books by the same author:
Another Fine Mess, 1998

Other books you might like:
Marcia Brown, *Stone Soup*, 1986
    In one of many retellings of the tale, three hungry soldiers claiming to make soup from water and a stone outwit villagers hoarding food.
Susan Stevens Crummel, *Tumbleweed Stew*, 2000
    Jack Rabbit tricks a rancher into providing the vegetables needed for a pot of tumbleweed stew in an easy reader set in Texas.
Paul Brett Johnson, *A Perfect Pork Stew*, 1998
    Baba Yaga's poor eyesight allows Ivan to get away with her pig while making pork stew from a load of dirt and all Baba Yaga's vegetables.

126

TEENA BOOTH

Falling from Fire

(New York: Wendy Lamb/Random House, 2002)

Subject(s): Fires; Identity; Family Life
Age range(s): Grades 6-9
Major character(s): Teresa "Teri" Dinsmore, 15-Year-Old, 9th Grader; Samantha Dinsmore, 18-Year-Old; Andrew Rickman, Child, Brother (of Teri and Samantha); Doug Stewart, 9th Grader; Wesley Wilton, 9th Grader; Gramma, Grandmother
Time period(s): 2000s
Locale(s): Timberville, California

Summary: Teri's a nobody at school, unlike her sister Samantha who fits right in with the "rowdy" crowd. The only other clique are the "holy rollers" and Teri doesn't fit in there either, though her heartthrob Doug does. At home, her mother's a natural platinum beauty who's pursuing husband number four and consequently isn't around much. It falls to Teri to watch her little brother Andrew and visit her Gramma who lives nearby. On Teri's fifteenth birthday, Andrew plays with the matches from the birthday candles and sets the house on fire. With no house, the family is split up with Teri and Samantha sleeping at their Gramma's house, Andrew at his father's house and her mother with her latest conquest. Almost guiltily, Teri enjoys the new attention that's paid to her at school as she dresses better than ever before, thanks to the donation of clothes from the community. Doug even asks her out, which thrills her before she discovers how shallow he is. Finally she looks twice at Wesley, the classic nerd who's only interested in politics and has been her friend forever, and realizes what a wonderful person he is, in this author's first novel. (201 pages)

Where it's reviewed:
Booklist, June 2002, page 1704
Kliatt, July 2002, page 7
Publishers Weekly, June 3, 2002, page 89
School Library Journal, August 2002, page 182
Voice of Youth Advocates, October 2002, page 269

Other books you might like:
Laurie Halse Anderson, *Catalyst*, 2002
    Opening up their home to Teri Litch and her young brother after fire destroys their house prompts Kate to postpone college for one year.

Deborah Froese, *Out of the Fire*, 2002
  Badly burned when a bonfire ignites suddenly, Dayle recuperates and rethinks her life until she's able to forgive the boy who tossed the gasoline.
Marcus Sedgwick, *Witch Hill*, 2001
  A fire destroys Jamie's home and he's left traumatized by the thought that he didn't rescue his baby sister.

127

RUTH LERCHER BORNSTEIN

Butterflies and Lizards, Beryl and Me

(Tarrytown, NY: Marshall Cavendish, 2002)

Subject(s): Depression (Economic); Moving, Household; Old Age
Age range(s): Grades 4-7
Major character(s): Charlotte ''Charley'' Gordon, 11-Year-Old, Artist; Beryl Stubbs, Aged Person; Walt, Streetperson (hobo)
Time period(s): 1930s (1936)
Locale(s): Valley Junction, Missouri

Summary: It's the middle of the Depression and Charley's dad has lost another job. This time he abandons the family, leaving Charley and her mother to move to a rural part of Missouri where her mother works long hours at the cannery. Left alone, Charley tries to make friends with some neighborhood children, but they want nothing to do with a poor kid who wears raggedy clothes and sports a hacked-off hair cut. Though everyone tells her to stay away from ''crazy Beryl,'' who rocks and holds a teddy bear that belonged to her dead son, Charley and elderly Beryl become friends and enjoy tea and graham crackers together in the afternoon. Charley finds that Beryl is a wonderful person who not only teaches her about the lizards and butterflies in her garden, but also loves life and her hobo boyfriend, Walt. When Beryl dies, she leaves a special legacy to encourage Charley to develop her artistic talent in this author's first novel. (144 pages)

Where it's reviewed:
Book Report, September 2002, page 51
Booklist, May 15, 2002, page 1606
Kirkus Reviews, April 15, 2002, page 562
School Library Journal, May 2002, page 146

Other books you might like:
Martha Brooks, *Being with Henry*, 2000
  Kicked out of his house, Laker meets and does yard work for elderly Henry, beginning a friendship that helps keep Henry out of a nursing home.
Pat Derby, *Visiting Miss Pierce*, 1986
  As part of a school project, Barry visits nursing home resident Miss Pierce and finds his life changed by her stories.
Kenneth E. Ethridge, *Viola, Furgy, Bobbi, and Me*, 1989
  Old Mrs. Viola Spencer hires Stephen to do her yard work, but their mutual interest in baseball quickly leads to friendship.
E. Cody Kimmel, *Visiting Miss Caples*, 2000
  Jenna discovers her elderly friend Miss Caples had the same problem she has, a manipulative friend who is unkind to others.

128

BARBARA BOTTNER
VICTORIA CHESS, Illustrator

The Scaredy Cats

(New York: Simon & Schuster Books for Young Readers, 2003)

Subject(s): Animals/Cats; Fear; Behavior
Age range(s): Grades K-2
Major character(s): Baby Scaredy Cat, Cat, Child; Mrs. Scaredy Cat, Mother, Cat; Mr. Scaredy Cat, Father, Cat
Time period(s): 2000s (2003)
Locale(s): United States

Summary: The Scaredy Cats worry so much about all the potential negative consequences of their actions that they don't do anything at all. Mr. Scaredy Cat doesn't want to awaken Baby for fear Baby will jump out of bed, knocking him over. When Baby Scaredy Cat suggests reading a book, her parents worry that they won't like the story, so the family ends up sitting around bored. When Mrs. Scaredy Cat thinks about frying eggs, she worries about getting burned, so the family ends up spending their day hungry. Finally, at the end of the day Baby makes her parents realize that good things could happen too and the family dreams about being braver tomorrow. (32 pages)

Where it's reviewed:
Bulletin of the Center for Children's Books, June 2003, page 393
Horn Book, March/April 2003, page 199
Publishers Weekly, March 17, 2003, page 76
School Library Journal, April 2003, page 116

Other books by the same author:
Rosa's Room, 2004
Be Brown!, 2002
Bootsie Barker Bites, 1992

Other books you might like:
Harry Allard, *The Stupids Step Out*, 1974
  The Stupids plan a day out, but everyday tasks prove a challenge to achieving their goal.
Ed Boxall, *Francis the Scaredy Cat*, 2002
  Francis is scared of everything. When he thinks a monster has captured his best friend, he is able to face his fears for his friend's sake.
Joan Rankin, *Scaredy Cat*, 1996
  A scared kitten is reassured by its mother.

129

TIM BOWLER

Storm Catchers

(New York: Simon & Schuster/Atheneum, 2003)

Subject(s): Kidnapping; Family Problems; Suspense
Age range(s): Grades 6-10
Major character(s): Ella Parnell, 13-Year-Old, Kidnap Victim; Fin Parnell, Teenager, Brother; Sam Parnell, Child; Ricky Prescott, Kidnapper, Teenager
Time period(s): 2000s
Locale(s): Cornwall, England

Summary: With his parents visiting at the local pub, Fin sneaks off to his friend's house, leaving siblings Ella and Sam home alone. While he's gone Ella is kidnapped and a ransom note is left behind. Their father scrambles to collect the ransom money but when Fin delivers it and Ricky tells him to rip up the bills, he realizes the kidnapping is for revenge, not money. Between Sam's conversations with an invisible friend and Fin's use of a dowsing pendulum, the family succeeds in locating Ella, but not without discovering the truth about a past misdeed of Mr. Parnell's which leaves the family structure in disarray. (200 pages)

Where it's reviewed:
Booklist, September 1, 2003, page 112
Bulletin of the Center for Children's Books, July 2003, page 437
Publishers Weekly, June 2, 2003, page 53
School Library Journal, May 2003, page 144
Voice of Youth Advocates, August 2003, page 216

Other books by the same author:
Apocalypse, 2004
Firmament, 2004
Starseeker, 2002
River Boy, 2000

Other books you might like:
Robert Cormier, *In the Middle of the Night*, 1995
   Because of an incident several years earlier, Denny's family moves often, changing houses, phone numbers and schools.
Lois Duncan, *The Twisted Window*, 1987
   Tracy agrees to help a young man kidnap his half-sister but has no idea how much she'll regret her decision.
Norma Fox Mazer, *The Solid Gold Kid*, 1977
   A rich boy is kidnapped, along with four other teens, and all of them are held for ransom.
David Patneaude, *Someone Was Watching*, 1993
   Though everyone thinks Chris's sister Molly drowned, Chris is convinced she was kidnapped and travels to Florida to rescue her.

130

C.J. BOX

Savage Run

(New York: Putnam, 2002)

Subject(s): Environmental Problems; Conspiracies; Mystery and Detective Stories
Age range(s): Grades 10-Adult
Major character(s): Joe Pickett, Game Warden; Marybeth Pickett, Spouse (of Joe Pickett); Stewie Woods, Activist; Jim Finotta, Rancher
Time period(s): 2000s
Locale(s): Saddlestring, Wyoming

Summary: Stewie Woods and his new bride are in the Bighorn National Forest of Wyoming, spiking trees to hamper the logging industry, when a cow explodes, taking Stewie and his new bride too. What seems at first just a weird occurrence bothers Joe Pickett, who tends to track down answers to questions and ignore all the folks he angers along the way. He begins his search with hobbyist rancher Jim Finotta, who owned the exploding cow, and steps up his investigation after hearing of the deaths of a congressman, writer, lawyer and animal rights activist, all of whom were involved with environmental issues. Then his wife Marybeth receives phone calls from Stewie, who is miraculously alive, and Joe arranges a meeting with him. The meeting goes awry when Joe and Stewie are ambushed and the two are forced to escape across Savage Run, a secret escape route last used by Cheyenne fleeing from Pawnee warriors in another exciting mystery starring a down-to-earth hero. (272 pages)

Where it's reviewed:
Booklist, May 1, 2002, page 1470
Kirkus Reviews, May 1, 2002, page 614
Library Journal, August 15, 2002, page 149
New York Times Book Review, August 25, 2002, page 18
Publishers Weekly, May 20, 2002, page 50

Other books by the same author:
Trophy Hunt, 2004
Winterkill, 2003
Open Season, 2001

Other books you might like:
Nevada Barr, *Endangered Species*, 1997
   Sabotage, a plane crash, and loggerhead turtles combine as Anna Pigeon searches for the murderer of two men.
Steve Hamilton, *Winter of the Wolf Moon*, 2000
   Thinking too much about his failures as a cop, Alex wants to hibernate but trying to help an Ojibway leads to confrontation with a drug dealer.
Clinton McKinzie, *The Edge of Justice*, 2002
   Investigating the death of a young climber, Antonio realizes her death wasn't an accident and suspects problems in the climbing community.

131

ED BOXALL, Author/Illustrator

Francis the Scaredy Cat

(Cambridge, MA: Candlewick Press, 2002)

Subject(s): Animals/Cats; Fear; Courage
Age range(s): Preschool-Kindergarten
Major character(s): Francis, Cat; Ben, Child, Friend
Time period(s): 2000s
Locale(s): England

Summary: Francis enjoys many of life's simple pleasures such as reading, bubble baths and Ben. Yet, Francis harbors a secret fear. Not even Ben knows that Francis is afraid of the dark, especially dark, stormy nights when Francis hears a monster in a tree in the garden. One such stormy evening Ben is late arriving home and Francis fears the tree's monster has captured Ben. To save his beloved friend Francis courageously goes out into the storm and climbs the tree where he comes face to face with the terrifying monster that turns out to be a cat, just like him only bigger, darker, and wilder. The cat kindly leads Francis down the tree and into the arms of Ben who's quite content to hug Francis. (32 pages)

Where it's reviewed:
Booklist, December 15, 2002, page 759

Magpies, July 2002, page 29
Publishers Weekly, July 8, 2002, page 48
School Library Journal, September 2002, page 181
Tribune Books, October 13, 2002, page 4

Other books by the same author:
Scoot on Top of the World, 2004

Other books you might like:
Barbara Bottner, *The Scaredy Cats*, 2003
    Mr. and Mrs. Scaredy Cat are so frightened of the imagined negative consequences of their actions that they are unable to do anything.
Katie Davis, *Scared Stiff*, 2001
    After discovering the non-threatening reality behind her many imagined fears a little girl looks forward to living a fright-free life.
Ellen Stoll Walsh, *Pip's Magic*, 1994
    Unexpectedly, while searching for answers to his fear of the dark, Pip overcomes his problem.

132

MARIE BRADBY
TED RAND, Illustrator

Once Upon a Farm
(New York: Orchard Books/Scholastic, Inc., 2002)

Subject(s): Family; Farm Life; Stories in Rhyme
Age range(s): Grades K-2
Major character(s): Sue, Sister (younger), Daughter; Unnamed Character, Brother (older), Narrator; Daddy, Father, Farmer
Time period(s): Indeterminate
Locale(s): United States

Summary: Memories of life on a farm include plowing behind a mule, hauling produce to market in a pick-up, dipping water from a well and watching Daddy drive the combine. Sue grooms a pony while her brother mucks stalls and both dream of winning a blue ribbon at the State Fair. The opportunity to pick apples, milk cows, and run from an ornery goat happen only in the memories of the farm children after the farm is sold to make way for roads, buildings and a shopping mall. Progress for some is the end of a way of life for others. (32 pages)

Where it's reviewed:
Horn Book Guide, Fall 2002, page 320
Publishers Weekly, February 11, 2002, page 186
School Library Journal, March 2002, page 172

Other books by the same author:
Momma, Where Are You From?, 2000 (Notable Social Studies Trade Books for Young People)
The Longest Wait, 1998
More Than Anything Else, 1995 (ALA Notable Children's Book)

Other books you might like:
Thomas Locker, *Family Farm*, 1988
    A family must work together and change with the times to maintain a successful farm.

Patricia MacLachlan, *All the Places to Love*, 1994
    Three generations live on a farm that holds "all the places to love" that anyone could every want.
David McPhail, *Farm Morning*, 1991
    Father and daughter spend a special morning on the farm feeding their animals.

133

KARLEEN BRADFORD
LESLIE ELIZABETH WATTS, Illustrator

You Can't Rush a Cat
(Custer, WA: Orca Book Publishers, 2003)

Subject(s): Animals/Cats; Grandparents; Pets
Age range(s): Grades 1-3
Major character(s): Jessica, Child; Granddaddy, Grandfather
Time period(s): 2000s (2003)
Locale(s): Ontario, Canada

Summary: When Jessica visits Granddaddy she discovers that he is trying to lure a stray cat out of hiding and into his house. With dishes of milk and fish, Jessica and Granddaddy manage to lure the cat inside, but not out into the open. Disappointed that she has still not seen the cat and wanting her grandfather, who lives alone, to have a companion when she leaves, Jessica decides to coax the cat out of hiding by singing every cat song she knows. By the afternoon, Granddaddy and the cat are fast friends. (32 pages)

Where it's reviewed:
Booklist, February 1, 2004, page 979
School Library Journal, February 2004, page 103

Other books by the same author:
Dragonfire, 1997
There Will Be Wolves, 1996
Thirteenth Child, 1995

Other books you might like:
Ragnhild Scamell, *Wish Come True Cat*, 2001
    When Holly wishes on a star for a kitten, she's not expecting the scraggly-looking stray that winds up on her windowsill.
Charlotte Voake, *Ginger Finds a Home*, 2003
    A little girl encourages a stray cat to come home and live with her.
Martin Waddell, *A Kitten Called Moonlight*, 2001
    Charlotte and her mother remember how they discovered their stray kitten.

134

KIMBERLY BRUBAKER BRADLEY

For Freedom: The Story of a French Spy
(New York: Delacorte, 2004)

Subject(s): Spies; World War II; Underground Resistance Movements
Age range(s): Grades 6-9
Major character(s): Suzanne David, Spy, Singer (opera)
Time period(s): 1940s
Locale(s): Cherbourg, France

Summary: As a young teen, Suzanne's main desire is to become an opera singer. It's not until a neighbor is killed in a bombing raid and Germans gain control of her French town and evict her family from their home, that she understands the impact of World War II on her world. Realizing that Suzanne's opera singing allows her to travel, her doctor recruits her as a spy for the French Resistance, warning her to tell no one, even her parents. When she's ultimately betrayed, her luck holds and the problems of D-Day convince the Germans to release her. (181 pages)

Where it's reviewed:
Bulletin of the Center for Children's Books, July 2003, page 438
Horn Book, July 2003, page 450
Publishers Weekly, June 2, 2003, page 51
School Library Journal, June 2003, page 136
Voice of Youth Advocates, June 2003, page 126

Other books by the same author:
Halfway to the Sky, 2002

Other books you might like:
Laura Malone Elliott, *Under a War-Torn Sky*, 2001
    Shot down behind enemy lines, pilot Henry Forester is aided by members of the French Resistance who return him to America.
Lois Lowry, *Number the Stars*, 1989
    Annemarie fears for her Jewish friend's life when the Germans occupy her Copenhagen neighborhood.
Bjarne B. Reuter, *The Boys of St. Petri*, 1994
    Sons of a local minister, Lars and Gunnar lead their Danish classmates in acts of resistance against the Nazis.
Elizabeth Van Steenwyk, *A Traitor Among Us*, 1998
    Not wanting to be left out, young Pieter helps the Resistance fighters in his village by exposing a traitor.

135

KIMBERLY BRUBAKER BRADLEY

Halfway to the Sky
(New York: Delacorte, 2002)

Subject(s): Hiking; Mothers and Daughters; Grief
Age range(s): Grades 5-8
Major character(s): Katahdin "Dani" Brown, 12-Year-Old; Springer Brown, 13-Year-Old (deceased), Handicapped (muscular dystrophy); Susan Brown, Mother
Time period(s): 2000s
Locale(s): Bristol, Tennessee; Appalachian Trail, Appalachians

Summary: Upset that her parents stayed together for her brother Springer, but can't remain married for her, Dani decides to hike the entire Appalachian Trail on her own. The Trail has special significance for her family as she was named for a mountain in Maine and her brother for one in Georgia. Now Springer's dead, her parents are divorced and her dad's remarried and expecting a new child. Having trained secretly for six months, Dani tells her mother she's staying at her dad's house, rides a bus out of town and arrives at the trailhead at Amicalola Falls State Park. Within a few days, her mother catches up with her and, though they're both mad, agrees to hike for a few days, then two weeks and finally for two months, allowing them to walk and talk. They talk about their family, their happy and sad memories, and the way Springer kept them all together in this tale of grief and renewal. (167 pages)

Where it's reviewed:
Book Report, November 2002, page 45
Booklist, April 1, 2002, page 1326
Bulletin of the Center for Children's Books, May 2002, page 310
Kirkus Reviews, January 15, 2002, page 100
School Library Journal, April 2002, page 142

Other books by the same author:
The President's Daughter, 2004
For Freedom: The Story of a French Spy, 2003
Weaver's Daughter, 2000

Other books you might like:
C.S. Adler, *The No Place Cat*, 2002
    Unhappy living with her father and his new family, Tess walks across Tucson to live with her mother.
Richard E. Allen, *Ozzy on the Outside*, 1989
    When Ozzy's mother is killed in a freak accident, he is so shattered with grief that he runs away.
Julie Reece Deaver, *Say Goodnight, Gracie*, 1988
    Morgan's life comes to an abrupt halt when her best friend Jimmy is killed in an automobile accident.
Ivy Ruckman, *No Way Out*, 1988
    Hiking through Utah's Zion Narrows, a group of campers are trapped in a canyon when a heavy downpour produces a flash flood.

136

HENRIETTA BRANFORD
CLAUDIO MUNOZ, Illustrator

Little Pig Figwort Can't Get to Sleep
(New York: Clarion Books, 2002)

Subject(s): Animals/Pigs; Bedtime; Sleep
Age range(s): Grades K-2
Major character(s): Pig Figwort, Pig
Time period(s): Indeterminate
Locale(s): Fictional Country

Summary: Little Pig Figwort's siblings are fast asleep, but Pig Figwort is simply not sleepy. He needs adventure so he goes on a deep-sea dive to find someone ready to play. Unfortunately, the mermaids and other undersea residents are trying to sleep so Pig Figwort goes home and tries to do the same. Still not successful he leaves for the North Pole in hopes of adventure, but the seals and polar bears are sleeping so little Pig Figwort returns home. Alas, he's still not sleepy so he tries a trip to the moon. Finally, he finds moon pigs at play and little Pig Figwort joins them in many games until he simply can't play anymore. Then he gets back in his rocket and goes home to join his siblings in slumber. Originally published in Great Britain in 2000. (32 pages)

Where it's reviewed:
Booklist, June 2002, page 1733

Bulletin of the Center for Children's Books, May 2002, page 311

Publishers Weekly, January 14, 2002, page 59

School Library Journal, July 2002, page 84

Awards the book has won:

Center for Children's Books Best Books, 2002

Other books by the same author:

The Theft of Thor's Hammer, 1996

Other books you might like:

Caroline Castle, *Naughty!*, 2001

Little Zeb is not sleepy. When he runs off to play he meets Little Hippo. Together they frolic until they settle down to sleep under the banana tree.

Debi Gliori, *Polar Bolero: A Bedtime Dance*, 2001

Too warm to sleep a young polar bear slips out of bed and goes to the place where the ''wide-awake'' gather to dance the Polar Bolero.

Sharon Pierce McCullough, *Bunbun at Bedtime*, 2001

When Bunbun hears bedtime announced he races to play some more before finally getting ready for bed just in time for a good night kiss.

Veronica Uribe, *Buzz Buzz Buzz*, 2001

Juliana and Andres are unable to sleep because of the annoying buzzing of a mosquito in their room.

137

ANN BRASHARES

The Second Summer of the Sisterhood

(New York: Delacorte, 2003)

Subject(s): Summer; Mothers and Daughters; Friendship

Age range(s): Grades 7-10

Major character(s): Lena Kaligaris, 16-Year-Old, Clerk (clothing store); Bridget ''Bee'' Vreeland, 16-Year-Old; Carmen Lucille Lowell, 16-Year-Old, Babysitter; Tabitha ''Tibby'' Tomko-Rollins, Student (filmmaking); Kostos Dounas, Boyfriend (of Lena)

Time period(s): 2000s

Locale(s): Burgess, Alabama; Bethesda, Maryland; Williamston College, North Carolina

Summary: Four friends, Tibby, Bee, Lena and Carmen, confront another summer of separation with only their traveling pants to unite them. Carmen's mother borrows the pants for a date and Carmen realizes she doesn't want some man disrupting their lives. Bee visits her estranged grandmother in Alabama and is relieved to realize she's not like her suicidal mother. Tibby's at film school where she has her eye on a fellow while also working on a documentary about her mother. Still smitten over Kostos, Lena's a clerk in a clothing store and wrangling with her mother. In this sequel to *The Sisterhood of the Traveling Pants*, the four girls learn the difficulties of growing up. (373 pages)

Where it's reviewed:

Booklist, April 15, 2003, page 1461

Bulletin of the Center for Children's Books, May 2003, page 351

Horn Book, May 2003, page 339

Publishers Weekly, March 3, 2003, page 77

School Library Journal, May 2003, page 144

Other books by the same author:

The Sisterhood of the Traveling Pants, 2001

Other books you might like:

Catherine Clark, *Truth or Dairy*, 2000

When her boyfriend dumps her, Courtney throws herself into student government activities and working, but no more boys!

Alice Hoffman, *Local Girls*, 1999

Interconnected stories trace Gretel's life from preteen years to career woman status and reflect the ups and downs of suburban life.

Jaclyn Moriarty, *Feeling Sorry for Celia*, 2001

Elizabeth worries about Celia who always runs away, but after rescuing her from the circus, Celia steals Elizabeth's boyfriend

Rosie Rushton, *Just Don't Make a Scene, Mum*, 1999

In this first of a series, five British teens find their lives connected through a radio show that lets them describe embarrassing moments.

138

LIBBA BRAY

A Great and Terrible Beauty

(New York: Delacorte/Random House, 2003)

Subject(s): Supernatural; Schools/Boarding Schools; Victorian Period

Age range(s): Grades 9-12

Major character(s): Gemma Doyle, 16-Year-Old; Pippa, Student—Boarding School; Felicity Worthington, Student—Boarding School; Ann Bradshaw, Student—Boarding School

Time period(s): 1890s

Locale(s): Bombay, India; London, England

Summary: Gemma really wants to attend school in London but not under the circumstances in which she arrives at Spence School. Walking with her mother in Bombay, she's told to go back home but when she leaves her mother, Gemma can ''see'' her mother's death. Returning to England with her opium-addicted father, Gemma's visions increase when she's at boarding school. One night she and Pippa, Ann and Felicity sneak out to a cave where they find the journal of a former student that explains the Order, an ancient group of women who control the power of the realms. They also learn about the murder of a Gypsy girl and the resulting evil that was unleashed. For these students, more horror awaits with the upcoming debutante season where they'll be paraded before ''suitable'' gentlemen in that never ending Victorian quest to find a proper husband. (403 pages)

Where it's reviewed:

Booklist, November 15, 2003, page 606

Kirkus Reviews, November 15, 2003, page 1358

Library Media Connection, March 2004, page 66

Publishers Weekly, December 8, 2003, page 62

School Library Journal, February 2004, page 141

Awards the book has won:

ALA Best Books for Young Adults, 2004

Other books by the same author:
Kari, 2000
Other books you might like:
Maeve Binchey, *Echoes*, 1986
 Class differences spell the end of a marriage in this novel set in Ireland.
Leon Garfield, *Footsteps*, 1980
 In Victorian London, William tries to correct an error made by his father, but finds his life almost ruined instead.
Victoria Holt, *The India Fan*, 1988
 Traveling to India as companion to the wealthy Lavinia Framling, Drusilla is intrigued by a mysterious bejeweled fan.
Philip Pullman, *The Ruby in the Smoke*, 1987
 Sally finds her father's Indian past comes to haunt her in Victorian London.

139

PATRICIA BRAY

Devlin's Luck

(New York: Bantam, 2002)

Subject(s): Fantasy; Adventure and Adventurers
Age range(s): Grades 9-Adult
Major character(s): Devlin Stonehand, Blacksmith, Farmer
Time period(s): Indeterminate
Locale(s): Jorsk, Fictional Country

Summary: Devlin appears unannounced in the middle of a festival and demands to take the oath of the Chosen One. The once-mighty kingdom of Jorsk has historically had a defender, the Chosen One of the Gods, sworn to justice and driven to seek it by means of a deadly gas. When Devlin makes his oath, to the astonishment of everyone, including himself, he is not immolated on the spot, which disappoints him. For reasons that are only gradually revealed, Devlin is a bitter man who mourns his past; he finds his new life as Chosen One difficult and yearns to die on a quest. However, as he survives challenge after challenge, it becomes obvious that there is more to Devlin than he has admitted and he may be just what the kingdom needs if it is going to survive. For those hoping to gain from Jorsk's collapse, however, Devlin is a disaster who needs to die. (480 pages)

Where it's reviewed:
Booklist, May 1, 2002, page 1513
Library Journal, May 15, 2002, page 130
Voice of Youth Advocates, August 2002, page 199

Other books by the same author:
Devlin's Honor, 2003
The Wrong Mr. Wright, 2002
An Unlikely Alliance, 1998

Other books you might like:
Lois McMaster Bujold, *The Curse of Chalion*, 2001
 A disillusioned warrior, hoping only to rest, finds himself saddled with the welfare of a princess.
Chris Bunch, *Corsair*, 2001
 Robbed of his family by slavers, a young man grows up to take his revenge on the high seas.

Lawrence Watt-Evans, *Touched by the Gods*, 1997
 A young man from a remote backwater is the chosen vehicle of the gods to intervene in human affairs; his personal reluctance means nothing.

140

MIRIAM BRENAMAN

Evvy's Civil War

(New York: Putnam, 2002)

Subject(s): Underground Railroad; Gender Roles; Civil War
Age range(s): Grades 7-10
Major character(s): Evelyn "Evvy" Chamberlyn, 14-Year-Old; Sapphire Jewell, Slave, Aunt (of Evvy's); Atha Shipson, Teacher, Quaker; Sophie Shipson, Teacher, Quaker
Time period(s): 1860s
Locale(s): Virginia

Summary: The oldest of six, Evvy turns 14 and suddenly crinolines, corsets and curls are supposed to be part of her daily life, though she doesn't understand why, especially since boys don't have to worry about these social obligations. Evvy's been taught by her mother, whose Quaker background emphasizes the importance of education for women, and runs her own illegal school for slaves. When her father leaves to fight in the Civil War, and her mother edges into depression following the accidental death of her youngest daughter, responsibility for the household falls on Evvy's shoulders, along with the secrets she's recently learned. Her mother's slave Sapphire is also Evvy's aunt, with the two women joined by a common grandfather. Sapphire is a conductor on the Underground Railroad and both Evvy's parents know and support this role. With all this knowledge and work to do, Evvy's happy to have her Philadelphia cousins Atha and Sophie nearby. (209 pages)

Where it's reviewed:
Book Report, September 2002, page 52
Booklist, April 15, 2002, page 1398
Kliatt, March 2002, page 6
School Library Journal, February 2002, page 129
Voice of Youth Advocates, February 2002, page 432

Other books you might like:
Jennifer L. Holm, *Boston Jane: An Adventure*, 2001
 Miss Heppelwhite's proper training doesn't matter now to Jane as she embarks on her new life in the Washington territory.
Trudy Krisher, *Uncommon Faith*, 2003
 Able to speak her mind when most women are sedate and soft-spoken, Faith won't spend her life darning socks or spinning and weaving.
Philip Pullman, *The Ruby in the Smoke*, 1987
 Sally, an orphaned 16-year-old, outmaneuvers a host of villainous 19th-century figures to claim her inheritance and her independence.
Ann Rinaldi, *Or Give Me Death*, 2003
 Patsy assumes responsibility while her father Patrick Henry travels and her mother is confined to the basement for the safety of everyone.

141

HERBIE BRENNAN

Faerie Wars

(New York: Bloomsbury, 2003)

Subject(s): Fantasy; Fairies
Age range(s): Grades 8-10
Major character(s): Henry Atherton, Teenager; Alan Fogarty, Criminal, Scientist; Pyrgus Malvae, Mythical Creature (fairy), Royalty
Time period(s): 2000s
Locale(s): England

Summary: Bet you thought fairyland was just a fairy tale. It turns out it's a parallel world and when one passes from one dimension to the other weird things happen, like growing small and acquiring wings, as Pyrgus is about to find out. Sent to the Analogue World to escape from the machinations of the Dark Court in his world, something goes amiss. Pyrgus is well and truly caught, by a boy bored enough, that's Henry, and a man crazy enough, that's Mr. Fogarty, to believe he's a fairy. At home Pyrgus is a prince and he suspects foul play in fairyland, for someone has tampered with the portals between the dimensions. After some brief difficulties in convincing the two humans to take him seriously, Pyrgus enlists Henry and Mr. Fogarty on a mission to Faerie to find out what's going on. (367 pages)

Where it's reviewed:
Booklist, April 15, 2003, page 1464
New York Times Book Review, June 22, 2003, page 22
Publishers Weekly, May 26, 2003, page 72
School Library Journal, July 2003, page 123
Voice of Youth Advocates, June 2003, page 146

Awards the book has won:
ALA Best Books for Young Adults, 2004

Other books by the same author:
Fairy Nuff: A Tale of Bluebell Wood, 2002
Nuff Said: Another Tale of Bluebell Wood, 2002
Letters From a Mouse, 1997

Other books you might like:
Emma Bull, *War for the Oaks*, 1996
    A hapless rock musician finds herself caught in the middle of a battle between the Seelie and Unseelie courts.
Barbara Hambly, *The Silent Tower*, 1986
    Alone late at night in her office, a computer programmer hears a noise and follows a barely seen figure into another world of wizards and danger.
Margaret Mahy, *Alchemy*, 2003
    Roland wonders what's going on when a teacher blackmails him to spy on another student's experiments in alchemy.

142

NOEL-ANNE BRENNAN

The Sword of the Land

(New York: Ace Books, 2003)

Subject(s): Fantasy; Coming-of-Age

Age range(s): Grades 9-Adult
Major character(s): Rislin sae Becha, Noblewoman; Sithli sae Sudit, Royalty (queen), Cousin
Time period(s): Indeterminate
Locale(s): Saeditin, Fictional Country

Summary: Rislin is happy to swear allegiance to her cousin Sithli. After all, they have long been friends and when Rislin's mother was deposed in a brutal coup, it was Sithli who intervened and prevented Rislin from joining her mother in death. The girls grow up together, with Rislin shouldering the dangerous or difficult tasks shirked by her cousin, now destined for the throne. When Sithli becomes queen, it's increasingly difficult for Rislin to ignore the fact that Sithli has her own pleasure rather than the welfare of her people at heart. Rislin feels more and more that she ought to lead the disillusioned populace, which is ready to rebel, but the oath she swore to Sithli leaves Rislin debating her next step. (368 pages)

Where it's reviewed:
Booklist, February 15, 2003, page 1059
Chronicle, February 2003, page 62

Other books by the same author:
Blood of the Land, 2004
Winter Reckoning, 1986

Other books you might like:
Teresa Edgerton, *The Queen's Necklace*, 2001
    The Captain of the Guard and his intrepid wife discover that it may take more than mere loyalty to save the Queen.
Sharon Shinn, *Summers at Castle Auburn*, 2001
    When they were children, Corie was content for her half-sister Elisandra to inherit the throne, but her view changes as she grows up.
Elizabeth Wiley, *A Sorcerer and a Gentleman*, 1995
    A clandestine romance leads to a sorcerer's war.

143

THERESA BRESLIN

Remembrance

(New York: Delacorte, 2002)

Subject(s): World War I; Interpersonal Relations; Nursing
Age range(s): Grades 7-10
Major character(s): John Malcolm Dundas, Twin, Military Personnel; Maggie Dundas, Twin, Nurse; Alex Dundas, Military Personnel; Charlotte Armstrong-Barnes, 15-Year-Old, Nurse; Francis Armstrong-Barnes, Military Personnel, Pacifist
Time period(s): 1910s (1915-1918)
Locale(s): Scotland; France

Summary: Five teenagers in a small town in Scotland find their lives impacted forever by World War I and the resulting changes in the social classes of their country. Charlotte and Francis are teens who live in the village's manor house and are considered upper class. As war breaks out, Charlotte trains as a nurse while Francis thinks war is a waste of bodies and says so, which his mother considers disloyal to England. In the house of shopkeeper Dundas, his oldest son John is able to enlist while his youngest son Alex wants to lie about his age as he fears the war will end before he's old enough to join. Maggie initially works in a munitions factory, but later trains as a nurse where she becomes friends with Charlotte as the two are sent to the battlefields in France. Charlotte meets and falls in love with John, killed at the battle of the Somme, though she knows he would have never been considered a ''proper'' husband for her. Pacifist Francis, an officer in the trenches, writes Maggie, which allows him to air all his anti-war views. Young Alex, who sees only the glamour of war, enlists to avenge his brother's death in this Scottish author's tale of patriotism, class differences and family apprehensions. (296 pages)

Where it's reviewed:
Booklist, December 15, 2002, page 752
Library Media Connection, April 2003, page 74
Publishers Weekly, October 28, 2002, page 73
School Library Journal, October 2002, page 158
Voice of Youth Advocates, December 2002, page 374

Awards the book has won:
ALA Best Books for Young Adults, 2003

Other books by the same author:
Kezzie, 2002
Dream Master, 1999
Whispers in the Graveyard, 1994 (Carnegie Medal)
Time to Reap, 1991
Simon's Challenge, 1988

Other books you might like:
Iain Lawrence, *Lord of the Nutcracker Men*, 2001
    His father fights in the trenches during World War I and sends home soldier carvings for his son Johnny that grow more horrific as the war continues.
Linda Newbery, *The Shell House*, 2002
    Linked by Graveney Hall are Edmund, who fights in World War I, and Greg who later photographs the burned-out shell of Edmund's family home.
Erich Marie Remarque, *All Quiet on the Western Front*, 1929
    Of four German friends, only Paul survives the battles of World War I.

144

JAN BRETT, Author/Illustrator

Daisy Comes Home

(New York: G.P. Putnam's Sons, 2002)

Subject(s): Animals/Chickens; Bullies; Adventure and Adventurers
Age range(s): Grades K-3
Major character(s): Daisy, Chicken, Runaway; Mei Mei, Child
Time period(s): 2000s
Locale(s): Li River, China

Summary: Daisy, the smallest of Mei Mei's six hens, is bullied off the hen house's roosting shelf every night and forced to sleep on the cold, damp floor. When Daisy tires of the floor she sneaks out of the hen house to sleep in one of Mei Mei's market baskets. In her sleep Daisy is unaware that the river is rising and soon she's floating down the Li River in the basket. A dog on a houseboat barks at her, a water buffalo splashes

her and curious monkeys try to grab the basket but each time the basket carries Daisy to safety. When the current pushes the basket against a raft poled by a cormorant fisherman, he throws a net over Daisy and carries her to market to sell. Sad Mei Mei is also at the market selling her hen's eggs and, when she's alerted to Daisy's predicament, she rescues the hen from the protesting fisherman. Daisy's experiences on the river help her claim her space in the hen house and she never sleeps on a cold floor again. (32 pages)

Where it's reviewed:
Booklist, March 15, 2002, page 1256
Bulletin of the Center for Children's Books, March 2002, page 235
Kirkus Reviews, December 15, 2001, page 1754
Publishers Weekly, December 3, 2001, page 60
School Library Journal, March 2002, page 172

Other books by the same author:
Hedgie's Surprise, 2000
Gingerbread Baby, 1999
Comet's Nine Lives, 1996

Other books you might like:
Marjorie Flack, *The Story about Ping*, 1933
    The classic tale of a young duck's adventures on the Yangtze River inspired Brett's creation of *Daisy Come Home*.
David Martin, *Little Chicken Chicken*, 1996
    Imaginative Little Chicken Chicken entertains the other birds in the henhouse with her juggling and tightrope walking.
Janet Morgan Stoeke, *Minerva Louise at the Fair*, 2000
    Curious Minerva Louise leaves the comfort of the henhouse to explore the source of the sounds emanating from the county fair.

145

JAN BRETT, Author/Illustrator

Who's That Knocking on Christmas Eve?

(New York: G.P. Putnam's Sons, 2002)

Subject(s): Christmas; Animals/Bears; Folklore
Age range(s): Grades K-2
Major character(s): Kyri, Child, Daughter; Unnamed Character, Traveler; Unnamed Character, Bear
Time period(s): Indeterminate Past
Locale(s): Norway

Summary: On a journey from Finnmark to Oslo a boy and his ice bear note smoke curling from a chimney in the distance. They walk to the house and the boy requests shelter. Kyri welcomes him with the warning that in past years trolls have invaded the home to devour the Christmas cooking. This year is no different. The boy refuses to open the door so the trolls tunnel under the house and burst through the cellar door. Kyri and the boy flee, but the ice bear is asleep under the warm stove. A small troll pokes the bear's nose with a bit of hot sausage, waking the bear and causing the rapid exodus of all the trolls. Next year's Christmas Eve should be much quieter. (32 pages)

Where it's reviewed:
Booklist, September 1, 2002, page 138
Bulletin of the Center for Children's Books, October 2002, page 49
Publishers Weekly, September 23, 2002, page 36
School Library Journal, October 2002, page 56

Other books by the same author:
Jan Brett's Christmas Treasury, 2001
Hedgie's Surprise, 2000
Christmas Trolls, 1993
Trouble with Trolls, 1992
Goldilocks and the Three Bears, 1987

Other books you might like:
Ingri D'Aulaire, *D'Aulaire's Trolls*, 1972
    A collection of folklore describes trolls of Norway's mountains and stories about them.
Rebecca Hickox, *Per and the Dala Horse*, 1995
    The youngest of three brothers, with help from his toy horse, is the one able to outwit trolls in this story based on Swedish folklore.
Edward Marshall, *Troll Country*, 1996
    After wandering into the darkest part of the woods, Elsie Fay encounters a troll and tries to outsmart it.

146

JANEEN BRIAN
STEPHEN MICHAEL KING, Illustrator

Where Does Thursday Go?
(New York: Clarion Books, 2002)

Subject(s): Animals/Bears; Animals/Birds; Friendship
Age range(s): Grades K-1
Major character(s): Bruno, Bear, Friend; Bert, Bird, Friend
Time period(s): Indeterminate
Locale(s): Fictional Country

Summary: Bruno's Thursday birthday is so much fun he's reluctant to see it end. Determined to say goodbye to the special day before it vanishes Bruno and Bert sneak out into the night to search for Thursday. He calls to a gurgling river, a hooting owl, a whistling train and swishing ocean waves but hears no response to his question, ''Is that you, Thursday?'' Finally, sitting with Bert on his front steps Bruno lists the characteristics of Thursday that are reminiscent of his birthday and there high above in the night sky Bert spots just what Bruno is seeking: something big and round like a cake, as bright as candles and floating like a balloon. Happily Bruno waves goodbye as a cloud slowly covers the full moon and then Bruno and Bert climb into bed, satisfied. (32 pages)

Where it's reviewed:
Booklist, March 1, 2002, page 1139
Horn Book Guide, Fall 2002, page 296
Magpies, November 2001, page 26
Publishers Weekly, January 28, 2002, page 289
School Library Journal, April 2002, page 100

Awards the book has won:
Children's Book Council of Australia Notable Book, 2002

Other books by the same author:
Silly Galah!, 2001

Andrea's Cubby, 1998
Leaves for Mr. Walter, 1998 (Children's Book Council of Australia Notable Book)

Other books you might like:
Frank Asch, *Mooncake*, 1978
    Believing the moon is made of cake Bear builds a rocket to fly himself there in order to taste it.
Nancy White Carlstrom, *Happy Birthday, Jesse Bear!*, 1994
    From the first preparations to the party fun Jesse Bear excitedly describes his fourth birthday.
Mem Fox, *Sleepy Bears*, 1999
    As winter nears Mother Bear calls her children inside for a bedtime rhyme before they sleep.

147

KATE BRIAN

The Princess and the Pauper
(New York: Simon & Schuster, 2003)

Subject(s): Princes and Princesses
Age range(s): Grades 6-8
Major character(s): Carina, Royalty (princess), 16-Year-Old; Julia Johnson, 16-Year-Old; Ingrid, 16-Year-Old, Friend (of Carina); Markus Ingvoldsson, 16-Year-Old
Time period(s): 2000s
Locale(s): Los Angeles, California

Summary: Princess Carina is in Los Angeles on a goodwill visit to America, where she hopes to meet up with Ribbit, the punk rocker she's met via e-mail, whose band Toadmuffin is slated for a concert while she's in town. Unfortunately, she can't think of any way to escape her chaperone until she bumps into Julia while sharing the bathroom at Julia's school. As Carina's good friend Ingrid points out, the two are almost mirror images of each other and when Carina offers Julia $10,000 to swap places with her for one night, scholarship student Julia leaps at the offer. Pretty soon Julia's swathed in jewels and a long gown, attending an embassy ball with Markus Ingvaldsson, son of one of Vineland's ministers, while Carina's riding to the Toadmuffin concert with one of Ribbit's roadies. The evening starts out well, but the big question remains: will Julia and Carina make it through the night without revealing their true identities? (266 pages)

Where it's reviewed:
Booklist, October 15, 2003, page 404
Publishers Weekly, June 16, 2003, page 72
School Library Journal, August 2003, page 154

Awards the book has won:
ALA Quick Picks for Reluctant Young Adult Readers, 2004

Other books you might like:
Meg Cabot, *The Princess Diaries*, 2000
    Raised by her artist mother in Greenwich Village, Mia is dismayed to learn she's a princess and heir to her father's throne in Genovia.
Ellen Conford, *A Royal Pain*, 1986
    Abby discovers the wrong parents have brought her up for she's really a princess from Saxony Coburn.
Francess Lantz, *A Royal Kiss*, 2000
    While shopping in a vintage clothing store, Samantha hap-

pens to meet Prince Sebastian which leads to a fairy-tale romance.

ANITA BRIGGS
MARY RAYNER, Illustrator

Hobart
(New York: Simon & Schuster Books for Young Readers, 2002)

Subject(s): Animals/Pigs; Farm Life; Talent
Age range(s): Grades 2-4
Major character(s): Hobart, Pig, Dancer (aspiring); Wilfred, Pig, Singer; Byron, Pig, Writer (poet); Violet, Pig, Acrobat
Time period(s): 2000s
Locale(s): United States

Summary: In the author's first book barnyard gossipers warn four talented pigs that their idyllic life will change with their imminent sale to a meat processing plant. Rather than see his dreams of becoming a tap dancer end on a dinner plate, optimistic Hobart leads his siblings in an escape from the farm. In their hideout in the hills each practices until they become skilled with their chosen art. Recognizing that their former farmer owner still has bills to pay, the pigs devise a plan to return to the farm and market their talents to his benefit. With Violet providing an acrobatic introduction, Wilfred singing lyrics created by poetic Byron and Hobart tap-dancing along, the ''Performing Pigs'' offer a timely tribute of appreciation that assures them a long, happy life on the farm. (57 pages)

Where it's reviewed:
Booklist, May 1, 2002, page 1525
Bulletin of the Center for Children's Books, June 2002, page 356
Horn Book Guide, Fall 2002, page 355
Publishers Weekly, April 29, 2002, page 71
School Library Journal, June 2002, page 88

Other books you might like:
Dick King-Smith, *Lady Lollipop*, 2001
The responsibility of caring for her pet pig Lollipop transforms a spoiled princess into a gentler, more obedient person.
Mary Stolz, *Emmett's Pig*, 1987
Although Emmett lives in an apartment he really would like to have a pig for a pet.
E.B. White, *Charlotte's Web*, 1952
Ingenious Charlotte uses her talents to save the life of her friend Wilbur, who is ''Some Pig.''

PATRICIA BRIGGS

Dragon Blood
(New York: Ace, 2003)

Subject(s): Fantasy; Magic; Romance
Age range(s): Grades 9-Adult
Major character(s): Wardwick ''Ward'', Nobleman; Tisala, Noblewoman, Spy; Jakoven, Royalty; Oreg, Wizard, Dragon
Time period(s): Indeterminate
Locale(s): Five Kingdoms, Fictional Country

148

SHIRIN YIM BRIDGES
SOPHIE BLACKALL, Illustrator

Ruby's Wish
(San Francisco: Chronicle Books, 2002)

Subject(s): Gender Roles; Education; China
Age range(s): Grades K-3
Major character(s): Ruby, Child, Relative (granddaughter); Grandfather, Grandfather, Aged Person
Time period(s): 19th century
Locale(s): China

Summary: The limited expectations of a young girl in Ruby's society are not satisfying to her. She chooses to wear red every day rather than reserving it for the traditional celebratory occasion. While fortunate that Grandfather provides a teacher for all his many grandchildren, Ruby feels resentful that, unlike the boys, she has to learn cooking, embroidery and housekeeping in addition to her studies. Ruby expresses her frustration in a poem that the teacher shares with Grandfather prompting a discussion in which Ruby remarks that, one day, she'd like to go to university as the boys do and not simply be forced into a marriage. Grandfather remembers her request and, when one day arrives, Ruby learns that she will be one of the first female students at the university. The author's first children's book is based on her grandmother's family history. (30 pages)

Where it's reviewed:
Booklist, November 15, 2002, page 608
Bulletin of the Center for Children's Books, October 2002, page 49
Publishers Weekly, August 19, 2002, page 88
Riverbank Review, Winter 2002-2003, page 35
School Library Journal, February 2003, page 102

Awards the book has won:
Publishers Weekly Best Children's Books, 2002

Other books you might like:
Elizabeth Fitzgerald Howard, *Virgie Goes to School with Us Boys*, 2000
Virgie lives in another country and time, but she shares with Ruby a determination to receive an education just as her brothers do.
Page McBrier, *Beatrice's Goat*, 2001
Money, not tradition, prevents Beatrice from attending school until an international aid organization donates an income-producing goat to her family.
Robert D. San Souci, *Fa Mulan: The Story of a Woman Warrior*, 1998
In a retelling of a Chinese poem a courageous young girl disguises her gender by wearing male clothing and goes to battle in her father's place.

Summary: Ward works to rebuild Hurog, but elsewhere in the kingdom deterioration sets in as his obsession for magical artifacts corrupt King Jakoven. He has lost much support from his nobility and an active rebellion is underway. Tisala, who appeared briefly in *Dragon Bones*, is captured and tortured while spying in the capital. Able to escape, she needs to hide without betraying any one else, and uses Hurog as a refuge. As Tisala recovers from the effects of her torture, Ward realizes how strongly he feels about her. Jakoven arrests Ward believing that he can awaken his new toy, an ancient, evil artifact, although he has no idea Tisala is hiding in Hurog. While Jakoven tries to break Ward in his prison, Tisala and Oreg hurry to the rescue. By the time they arrive, Ward discovers why he must fight Jakoven, whether or not he is ready. (275 pages)

Where it's reviewed:
Booklist, January 1, 2003, page 860
Chronicle, January 2003, page 29
Kliatt, March 2003, page 30
Voice of Youth Advocates, June 2003, page 146

Other books by the same author:
Dragon Bones, 2002
The Hob's Bargain, 2001
When Demons Walk, 1998

Other books you might like:
Joanne Bertin, *The Last Dragonlord*, 1998
    The last man able to become a dragon has been alone since his transformation, and longs for another to be called.
Barbara Hambly, *Dragonshadow*, 1999
    The wizard and knight who once saved the kingdom from a dragon now find themselves allied with it against a greater enemy.
Robin Hobb, *Fool's Errand*, 2002
    The prince has disappeared and the Fool is dispatched to beg Fitz, former royal assassin, to use his unique talents to recover the heir to the throne.

`151`

PATRICIA BRIGGS

Dragon Bones
(New York: Ace, 2002)

Subject(s): Fantasy; Magic; Coming-of-Age
Age range(s): Grades 9-Adult
Major character(s): Wardwick "Ward", Nobleman; Hurogmeten, Ruler, Father (of Ward); Oreg, Wizard, Dragon
Time period(s): Indeterminate
Locale(s): Five Kingdoms, Fictional Country

Summary: Wardwick of Hurog has convinced everyone, especially his father, that he is as dumb and slow as he looks. Ward's father is Hurogmeten, the ruler of his mountainous part of the Five Kingdoms. Unfortunately, he is also cruel and insane, and much of his madness is directed at his family. Ward is practically an adult and has stayed alive by pretending to have been seriously injured by his father so that he has little wit; everyone knows this so Ward is no threat. Now Ward's father dies and Ward inherits the kingdom. Almost immediately, Ward discovers secrets of Hurog only the Hurogmeten knows and must decide who can be trusted with the knowledge that Ward of Hurog is not an idiot. First and foremost is the bizarre ghost Oreg, who appears to Ward as his father is dying. Oreg is clearly deciding whether or not to trust Ward, too. Oreg has immense power, enormous secrets, and is a slave to the Hurogmeten. But Ward doesn't want a slave; he'd rather have a friend. (292 pages)

Where it's reviewed:
Kliatt, May 2002, page 23
Voice of Youth Advocates, October 2002, page 292

Other books by the same author:
Dragon Blood, 2003
The Hob's Bargain, 2001
When Demons Walk, 1998

Other books you might like:
Mary Brown, *The Unlikely Ones*, 1986
    A bizarre group of slaves escapes from an evil witch and decides to fight for their freedom.
C.J. Cherryh, *The Curse of Chalion*, 2001
    Magical means and personal sacrifice will be required if the princess is to be protected.
Robin Hobb, *The Farseer Saga*, 1995-1997
    This trilogy follows the career of the royal bastard FitzChivalry Farseer as he trains to be a royal assassin and discovers the magic he has inherited.

`152`

RAYMOND BRIGGS, Author/Illustrator

Ug: Boy Genius of the Stone Age
(New York: Alfred A. Knopf, 2002)

Subject(s): Cartoons and Comics; Family; Problem Solving
Age range(s): Grades 3-6
Major character(s): Ug, Son, Genius; Dug, Father, Prehistoric Human; Dugs, Mother, Prehistoric Human
Time period(s): Indeterminate Past
Locale(s): Earth

Summary: Ug's parents have no patience for his persistent questions, especially his request for softer trousers. As Dug explains, because they live in the Stone Age everything is made of stone, including Ug's hand-carved britches. Ug imagines a life of soft pants, cooked food and balls that bounce. To Dugs, Ug's ideas are disgusting and she often wishes that he would simply stop thinking. Gradually Dug develops some sympathy for Ug's desire for soft and warm trousers and he cuts some mammoth skin with a sharp stone but since sewing has not yet been invented, Ug can only look longingly at the pieces of skin and imagine their potential. (32 pages)

Where it's reviewed:
Booklist, November 15, 2002, page 600
Bulletin of the Center for Children's Books, January 2003, page 190
Horn Book, November 2002, page 734
Publishers Weekly, August 19, 2002, page 89
School Library Journal, October 2002, page 158

Awards the book has won:
School Library Journal Best Books, 2002

Other books by the same author:
Ethel and Ernest, 1999
The Bear, 1994
Jim and the Beanstalk, 1989

Other books you might like:
Paul Fleischman, *Weslandia*, 1999
　Contented nonconformist Wesley uses his genius and his summer vacation to transform his backyard into a new civilization.
Charles Higham, *Life in the Old Stone Age*, 1989
　Based on archeological evidence this nonfiction title for youth describes the early life of man.
Fiona MacDonald, *The Stone Age News*, 1998
　Using a newspaper format, a youth nonfiction title reports on inventions, climate, lifestyles and progress during the Stone Age.

153

PAUL BRIGHT
GUY PARKER-REES, Illustrator

Quiet!

(New York: Orchard/Scholastic, 2003)

Subject(s): Bedtime; Animals/Lions; Family
Age range(s): Preschool-Grade 1
Major character(s): Papa Lion, Lion, Father; Mama Lion, Lion, Mother; Baby Leo, Lion, Baby
Time period(s): 2000s (2003)
Locale(s): Africa

Summary: Mama and Papa Lion are putting Baby Leo down for a nap, but the jungle is too noisy for him to sleep. As king of the animals, Papa Lion orders all of the animals to be quiet or risk being eaten! Although a few animals have little outbursts, none wakes Baby Leo so Papa Lion has nothing to eat to satisfy his growing hunger. Finally, a loud noise does wake Baby Leo but Papa Lion can do nothing about it because the noise is his stomach growling! (32 pages)

Where it's reviewed:
Horn Book Guide, Spring 2004, page 11
School Library Journal, December 2003, page 104

Awards the book has won:
IRA Children's Choices, 2004

Other books by the same author:
Under the Bed, 2004

Other books you might like:
Claire Freedman, *Hushabye Lily*, 2003
　Lily can't fall asleep because of all of the noise in the farmyard, so the animals offer various sleep solutions.
Mingfong Ho, *Hush!: A Thai Lullaby*, 2000
　As a mother puts her baby to sleep, she implores the nearby animals to be quiet.
Bernard Waber, *The Mouse That Snored*, 2000
　The sound of a mouse's snoring wakens the residents of a quiet house.

154

LARRY DANE BRIMNER
JOSE ARUEGO, Illustrator
ARIANE DEWEY, Illustrator

The Littlest Wolf

(New York: HarperCollins Publishers, 2002)

Subject(s): Animals/Wolves; Growing Up; Self-Esteem
Age range(s): Preschool-Grade 1
Major character(s): Little One, Wolf, Son; Big Gray, Wolf, Father
Time period(s): Indeterminate
Locale(s): Fictional Country

Summary: Big Gray notices the smallest of his offspring does not join the others in play. Little One says his siblings do not want to play with him because he cannot roll in a straight line or run fast or pounce high. Big Gray observes Little One perform each action and notes that what Little One is doing is just right for now because straight rolls and fast running and high pounces come later. Little One's confidence grows as Big Gray affirms his development and reminds him that the acorn is just right when it is a tiny acorn waiting to become a big oak. (34 pages)

Where it's reviewed:
Bulletin of the Center for Children's Books, July 2002, page 395
Horn Book Guide, Fall 2002, page 321
Kirkus Reviews, March 15, 2002, page 406
Publishers Weekly, March 11, 2002, page 71
School Library Journal, May 2002, page 105

Awards the book has won:
IRA Children's Choices, 2003

Other books by the same author:
The Big Tee Ball Game, 2001
The Big, Beautiful Brown Box, 2001
The Sparkle Thing, 2001

Other books you might like:
Syd Hoff, *Bernard on His Own*, 1993
　Bernard's parents reassure him that one day he'll be able to climb a tree, catch a fish and gather honey on his own.
Holly Keller, *Jacob's Tree*, 1999
　Little bear Jacob hates being too small to do what other bears can do; the marks Papa makes on the elm tree show how much he's growing.
Robert Kraus, *Leo the Late Bloomer*, 1971
　Father is impatient for Leo to learn to do things, but Mother knows that Leo will bloom in his own time.
Ellen Stoll Walsh, *Hop Jump*, 1993
　Bored with hopping and jumping like all the other frogs, Betsy dances instead, starting a trend in frog movement.

155

PAT BRISSON
MAXIE CHAMBLISS, Illustrator

Hobbledy-Clop
(Honesdale, PA: Boyds Mills Press, 2003)

Subject(s): Grandparents; Animals; Animals/Reptiles
Age range(s): Preschool-Kindergarten
Major character(s): Brendan O'Doyle, Child; Grandma, Grandmother
Time period(s): 2000s (2003)
Locale(s): United States

Summary: In this cumulative tale, Brendan O'Doyle pulls his little, red wagon full of tea party supplies to Grandma's house. On his way to surprise Grandma with a tea party, Brendan picks up his pet snake, dog, cat and horse. Once at Grandma's house, the snake causes chaos by tickling her and causing a fit of giggles. With tea and giggles finished, Brendan packs up his wagon and heads back home to the sound of the wagon going hoppledy-clop down the hill. (32 pages)

Where it's reviewed:
Horn Book Guide, Fall 2003, page 296
School Library Journal, February 2003, page 102

Other books by the same author:
Star Blanket, 2003
Wanda's Roses, 1994
Your Best Friend, Kate, 1992

Other books you might like:
Kathy Henderson, *And the Good Brown Earth*, 2004
  Joe and his grandmother work together tending their garden.
David Kirk, *Miss Spider's Tea Party*, 1994
  Miss Spider invites the other insects over for tea.
Reeve Lindbergh, *My Hippie Grandmother*, 2003
  A young boy enjoys spending time with his hippie grandmother.

156

PAT BRISSON
ERICA MAGNUS, Illustrator

Star Blanket
(Honesdale, PA: Boyds Mills Press, 2003)

Subject(s): Storytelling; Bedtime; Family
Age range(s): Preschool-Grade 1
Major character(s): Laura, Child, Daughter; Unnamed Character, Father
Time period(s): 2000s (2003)
Locale(s): United States

Summary: When Laura's dad puts her to bed at night, he always tells her the story of the star blanket that she holds as she sleeps. The blanket was originally a present to Laura's father when his little sister was born and there are 41 stars, one each for every member of the family at that time. Each star represents a relative. Being able to name them all guarantees a good night sleep. (32 pages)

Where it's reviewed:
Publishers Weekly, December 15, 2003, page 72
School Library Journal, December 2003, page 104

Other books by the same author:
Hobbledy-Clop, 2003
Bertie's Picture Day, 2000
The Summer My Father Was Ten, 1999

Other books you might like:
Debi Gliori, *Flora's Blanket*, 2001
  Flora can't sleep without her security blanket and it's gone missing!
Patricia Polacco, *The Keeping Quilt*, 1991
  A quilt made by a Jewish immigrant family from their old clothes is passed down from generation to generation.
Phyllis Root, *The Name Quilt*, 2003
  Sadie's grandmother tells her bedtime stories from a quilt embroidered with the names of her relatives.

157

KEVIN BROCKMEIER, Author/Illustrator

City of Names
(New York: Viking, 2002)

Subject(s): Space and Time; Names, Personal; Fantasy
Age range(s): Grades 4-7
Major character(s): Howie Quackenbush, 10-Year-Old, 5th Grader; Kevin Bugg, 5th Grader, Friend (Howie's); Casey Robinson, 5th Grader, Friend (Howie's)
Time period(s): 1990s
Locale(s): North Mellwood

Summary: With the last name Quackenbush, Howie experiences a lot of teasing so he's keenly interested in how names affect people. Perhaps that's the reason his school book order includes not the joke book he orders, but a book entitled *Secret Guide to North Mellwood*, with a map showing the "true" name of every building in town. By using one of the designated "portals" on the map, Howie discovers that he can be magically transported around town and back to his portal of origin simply by reciting the building's "true" name. Howie shares the secret of the strange map with Kevin and Casey so the friends can join the adventures with Howie in the author's first book. (137 pages)

Where it's reviewed:
Booklist, June 2002, page 1720
Bulletin of the Center for Children's Books, May 2002, page 312
Horn Book Guide, Fall 2002, page 368
Publishers Weekly, May 27, 2002, page 60
School Library Journal, July 2002, page 113

Other books you might like:
Edward Eager, *Seven-Day Magic*, 1962
  Susan checks out a library book that unexpectedly brings magic into her life.
Adam Osterweil, *The Comic Book Kid*, 2001
  A comic book with blank pages and a magic ring carry Brian and Paul through time and space as the blank pages fill with their adventures.

Jon Scieszka, *Summer Reading Is Killing Me!*, 1998
  The Time Warp Trio becomes stuck in a battle waged by good and evil characters from their summer reading list.

158

BRUCE BROOKS

Dolores: Seven Stories about Her
(New York: HarperCollins, 2002)

Subject(s): Identity; Brothers and Sisters; Coming-of-Age
Age range(s): Grades 7-10
Major character(s): Dolores "Do", 16-Year-Old; Jimmy, Brother (of Dolores)
Time period(s): 2000s
Locale(s): New York, New York

Summary: Meet Dolores, a quirky, self-confident loner who is her own best company, in seven stories that cover her actions from ages seven through 16. Beginning and ending with an abduction, Dolores's older brother Jimmy saves her when she's only seven and two women try to kidnap her from Wal-Mart; when Do is 16, she's able to extricate herself from the clutches of a would-be rapist when he tries to abduct her in New York City. In between one has the chance to become friends with Do and admire her ability to withstand peer pressure, especially when she becomes a cheerleader and doesn't conform to "cookie cutter" expectations, or her calmness when facing gossip and turning the other cheek to rumors. Meeting Dolores is a coming-of-age experience for every reader. (135 pages)

Where it's reviewed:
Bulletin of the Center for Children's Books, May 2002, page 312
Publishers Weekly, February 18, 2002, page 97
School Library Journal, April 2002, page 142
School Library Journal, May 15, 2002, page 1591
Voice of Youth Advocates, June 2002, page 114

Other books by the same author:
All That Remains, 2001
Asylum for Nightface, 1996
What Hearts, 1992
Everywhere, 1990
The Moves Make the Man, 1984

Other books you might like:
Scott Johnson, *Overnight Sensation*, 1994
  Kerry realizes she's made a mistake when she lets her friends lead her away from her old buddy Madeline, an individual who refuses to follow the crowd.
Kathe Koja, *Buddha Boy*, 2003
  Jinsen tries to live by Buddhist principles, which makes him different from his classmates and sets him up for their bullying.
Jerry Spinelli, *Stargirl*, 2000
  Stargirl rocks Mica High School, but her naivete doesn't prepare her for the fickle roller coaster of popularity that lurks for nonconformists.

159

KEVIN BROOKS

Lucas
(New York: Scholastic/The Chicken House, 2003)

Subject(s): Islands; Prejudice; Good and Evil
Age range(s): Grades 9-12
Major character(s): Caitlin "Cait" McCann, 15-Year-Old; Dominic "Dom" McCann, Brother (of Cait), Student—College; Lucas, Teenager, Drifter; Jamie Tait, Wealthy, Bully
Time period(s): 2000s
Locale(s): Hale Island, England

Summary: Summertime finds Cait in a quandary as her friends suddenly become too worldly and explore make-up, provocative clothing and illegal substances. Living on an island off the coast of England, friendships and teen activities are limited and there's a small-mindedness to the population. When a teenage drifter named Lucas appears, only Cait befriends this gentle soul while a group of bullies, led by wealthy, spoiled Jamie, harass and bedevil him. Cait is further frustrated by her brother Dominic's friendship with Jamie. A vicious attack on a young girl sets up Lucas as the scapegoat and Cait is powerless to halt the mob mentality she witnesses in this British import. (423 pages)

Where it's reviewed:
Booklist, May 1, 2003, page 1595
Bulletin of the Center for Children's Books, June 2003, page 393
Horn Book, March 2003, page 210
Publishers Weekly, February 10, 2003, page 188
Voice of Youth Advocates, April 2003, page 42

Awards the book has won:
ALA Best Books for Young Adults, 2004
Booklist Editors' Choice/Books for Youth, 2003

Other books by the same author:
Kissing the Rain, 2004
Martyn Pig, 2002

Other books you might like:
Joe Cardillo, *Pulse*, 1996
  Kris and Jason's student environmental group attracts hecklers who turn a camping trip into tragedy.
Harper Lee, *To Kill a Mockingbird*, 1960
  Scout witnesses injustice first hand when her father defends a black man accused of raping a white woman.
Norma Fox Mazer, *Out of Control*, 1993
  Mean-spirited physical revenge for an imagined insult haunts the victim and her attackers, even when they try to pretend nothing happened.
Carol Plum-Ucci, *The Body of Christopher Creed*, 2000
  Christopher's disappearance is just one of many secrets in his hometown.
Robert Westall, *Yaxley's Cat*, 1992
  Rose and her children rent an isolated beach house and discover a murder, but are saved by the previous owner's cat who enjoys more than nine lives.

160

KEVIN BROOKS

Martyn Pig

(New York: Chicken House/Scholastic, 2002)

Subject(s): Death; Alcoholism; Family Problems
Age range(s): Grades 7-10
Major character(s): Martyn Pig, 15-Year-Old; Alexandra "Alex" Freeman, 17-Year-Old; Dean, Boyfriend (of Alex); William Pig, Alcoholic; Jean Pig, Aunt (of Martyn)
Time period(s): 2000s
Locale(s): England

Summary: To Martyn, life doesn't seem quite fair. First there's his dreadful name Martyn Pig, often shortened to "Porky," but then he also has to live with his drunken, abusive father. His father did stay sober for two months, right after his mother left, when Aunty Jean filed for custody of Martyn. Afraid that his drinking would cause him to lose custody of Martyn, and his accompanying welfare check, William stayed sober until the custody hearing ended at which point he disappeared for three drunken days. One night, right before Christmas, William moves toward Martyn to strike him and, in self-defense, Martyn pushes him away. William falls, strikes his head on the fireplace and dies, but Martyn doesn't call the police. Afraid he'll be suspected of murder, or worse yet have to live with Aunty Jean, Martyn pretends nothing has happened. With the help of his neighbor Alex and her scummy boyfriend Dean, they stuff his dad in a sleeping bag, weigh it with stones and toss it in the quarry. An unexpected inheritance provides Martyn with money to live on and he thinks everything's wonderful. Little does he realize that his troubles are just beginning as he tries to maintain the facade that his father's still alive and Alex and Dean try to blackmail him in this author's first novel. (230 pages)

Where it's reviewed:
Booklist, May 1, 2002, page 1459
Bulletin of the Center for Children's Books, September 2002, page 7
Publishers Weekly, May 27, 2002, page 61
School Library Journal, May 2002, page 147
Voice of Youth Advocates, April 2002, page 37

Awards the book has won:
School Library Journal Best Books, 2002

Other books by the same author:
Kissing the Rain, 2004
Lucas, 2003

Other books you might like:
Robert Cormier, *Tenderness*, 1997
When a girl he cares for accidentally drowns, a serial killer knows the police will claim he murdered her.
Lois Duncan, *I Know What You Did Last Summer*, 1973
Four teens take a vow of silence after a hit-and-run accident, but are later tracked down for their involvement.
Maurice Gee, *The Fat Man*, 1997
Colin is caught when he steals a chocolate bar from the "fat man," which is really a set-up to enable Herbert Muskie to retaliate against Colin's parents.

Judy Waite, *Shopaholic*, 2003
Concerned that she's lost her best friends, Taylor is thrilled to hang out with Kat and almost too late realizes how she's being used.

161

MARTHA BROOKS

True Confessions of a Heartless Girl

(New York: Farrar Straus Giroux/Melanie Kroupa Books, 2003)

Subject(s): City and Town Life; Interpersonal Relations; Pregnancy
Age range(s): Grades 9-12
Major character(s): Noreen Stall, 17-Year-Old, Pregnant Teenager; Wesley Cuthand, Indian, Boyfriend (of Noreen); Lynda Bradley, Restaurateur; Delbert "Del" Armstrong, Farmer; Dolores Harper, Waiter/Waitress, Aged Person; Seth Bradley, Child (son of Lynda)
Time period(s): 2000s
Locale(s): Pembina Lake, Manitoba, Canada

Summary: Stealing her boyfriend Wesley's truck along with his cash, Noreen winds up in a small cafi where kindly owner Lynda offers her a place to sleep. In the morning, wild, foul-mouthed Noreen meets some of the other residents of Pembina Lake, each of whom has his or her own secret problem. Noreen doesn't mean to be heartless, she just doesn't know any other way to behave after enduring a childhood of abuse by her stepfather and neglect from her mother. Neither act excuses Noreen from willfully wounding her boyfriend, verbally hurting Lynda's young son Seth or generally being a pain to everyone else as she rejects people before they have a chance to hurt her. Noreen affects everyone in the town and in good ways, from Del resigning himself to his brother's earlier death, to Dolores accepting the inevitability of her daughter's cancer and Lynda saying yes to Del's love for her. Even poor Wesley, who puts up with all of Noreen's edginess, finally hears an "I love you" from Noreen as she struggles to overcome her heartlessness. (181 pages)

Where it's reviewed:
Booklist, April 1, 2003, page 1396
Horn Book, May 2003, page 340
Publishers Weekly, February 17, 2003, page 76
School Library Journal, February 2003, page 140
Voice of Youth Advocates, June 2003, page 126

Awards the book has won:
ALA Best Books for Young Adults, 2004
School Library Journal Best Books, 2003

Other books by the same author:
Being with Henry, 2000
Bone Dance, 1997
Two Moons in August, 1992
Paradise Cafe and Other Stories, 1990

Other books you might like:
James Bennett, *Plunking Reggie Jackson*, 2001
Worry about his girlfriend's possible pregnancy distracts Coley from his grades and his baseball pitching.

Alex Flinn, *Breathing Underwater*, 2001
    Only a court order and an anger management class help
    Nick understand why he hits his girlfriend Caitlin.
Laura Hendrie, *Remember Me*, 1999
    Orphaned and living in a small town where she's an
    outsider, Rose's friendship with the motel owner Bird
    gives her a sense of belonging.

162

DON BROWN

Our Time on the River

(Boston: Houghton Mifflin, 2003)

Subject(s): Brothers; Canoeing; Rivers
Age range(s): Grades 7-10
Major character(s): David, 19-Year-Old, Military Personnel;
    Steve, 14-Year-Old
Time period(s): 1960s (1968)
Locale(s): Susquehanna River, New York; Susquehanna
    River, Pennsylvania

Summary: With David Vietnam-bound, which dredges up
memories of a relative who didn't return from World War II,
his father has wisely asked David to take a canal trip down the
Susquehanna River with his younger brother Steve. The trip
begins easily enough as they paddle and choose their nighttime campsites, where they have only to contend with insects
and hungry raccoons. A drinking spree for David, an injury to
Steve and then too fast a current for David force the brothers
to look out for, and help, one another. As these two brothers
gradually become friends, the changing current of the river
reflects the uneasy feeling of the times. (135 pages)

Where it's reviewed:
Booklist, April 1, 2003, page 1386
Kliatt, March 2003, page 8
Publishers Weekly, February 3, 2003, page 76
School Library Journal, April 2003, page 157
Voice of Youth Advocates, August 2003, page 218

Other books by the same author:
Kid Blink Beats the World, 2004 (nonfiction)

Other books you might like:
Alden R. Carter, *Between a Rock and a Hard Place*, 1995
    A rite-of-passage canoe trip for two cousins almost turns to
    disaster when Randy loses his insulin and Mark must find
    help fast.
Will Hobbs, *Down the Yukon*, 2001
    Jason and his friend Jamie enter a race down the Yukon
    River from Dawson City to Nome, Alaska to win $20,000
    and buy back a sawmill.
Ethan Howland, *The Lobster War*, 2001
    Working to be a lobsterman like his father, Dain is disap-
    pointed when he realizes his older brother Eddie cut his
    lobster traps.
Gary Paulsen, *The Beet Fields: Memories of a Sixteenth
    Summer*, 2000
    Running away from home and his alcoholic mother, a
    young boy spends the summer working, hoeing beets, join-
    ing a carnival and enlisting in the Army.

163

JEFF BROWN
SCOTT NASH, Illustrator

Stanley, Flat Again!

(New York: HarperCollins Publishers, 2003)

Subject(s): Boats and Boating; Humor; Sailing
Age range(s): Grades 2-4
Major character(s): Stanley Lambchop, Son, Brother (older);
    Arthur Lambchop, Son, Brother (younger); Emma Weeks,
    Classmate, Accident Victim
Time period(s): Indeterminate
Locale(s): Fictional Country

Summary: While playing with Arthur, Stanley suddenly becomes flat again. The doctor thinks Stanley suffers from a rare
disorder called OBP that causes unexpected flatness when two
points on the body are struck simultaneously. Neither Stanley
nor Arthur likes the attention Stanley's condition generates.
Arthur feels left out and Stanley feels embarrassed. Stanley's
flatness does prove helpful when the spinnaker rips during a
sailing race and Stanley fills in, assuring victory. Next, a
building collapses trapping Emma Weeks and only Stanley is
able to get to the pocket of debris in which she's trapped and
lead her out to safety. A congratulatory slap on the back and
Emma's poke in the ribs trigger the OBP and Stanley unexpectedly returns to his normal shape. (87 pages)

Where it's reviewed:
Booklist, May 15, 2003, page 1660
Bulletin of the Center for Children's Books, April 2003, page
    307
Publishers Weekly, February 17, 2003, page 78
School Library Journal, March 2003, page 178

Other books by the same author:
Invisible Stanley, 1996
Stanley and the Magic Lamp, 1996
Flat Stanley, 1964

Other books you might like:
David Elliott, *The Transmogrification of Roscoe Wizzle*, 2001
    Roscoe is changing into a bug and he wonders if it's
    because he's eating too many Jungle Burgers at the town's
    newest restaurant.
Mary James, *Shoebag*, 1990
    Life changes dramatically but temporarily for Shoebag, a
    young cockroach that becomes a boy.
Simon Mason, *The Quigleys at Large*, 2003
    In the sequel to *The Quigleys*, four stories describe the
    continuing adventures of a wacky British family.
James Proimos, *Johnny Mutton, He's So Him!*, 2003
    Johnny, a sheep dressed as a boy, is a unique, enthusiastic
    individual, unconcerned about his appearance.

164

MARGARET WISE BROWN
DAN YACCARINO, Illustrator

The Good Little Bad Little Pig

(New York: Hyperion Books for Children, 2002)

Subject(s): Animals/Pigs; Pets; Behavior
Age range(s): Preschool-Grade 1
Major character(s): Peter, Child
Time period(s): 1950s
Locale(s): United States

Summary: Peter wants a pet pig, specifically one that's not too good and not too bad. His parents help him write a letter to a farmer asking for a good little bad little pig and the farmer fulfills Peter's request. Once the pig arrives, Peter takes responsibility for bathing and feeding him and his parents see that even though the pig sometimes misbehaves, he can also be a joy. Originally published in the 1939 collection *The Fish with the Deep Sea Smile*, the story is posthumously issued as a stand-alone picture book. (24 pages)

Where it's reviewed:
BookPage, October 2002, page 29
Publishers Weekly, September 30, 2002, page 70
School Library Journal, November 2002, page 112

Other books by the same author:
Big Red Barn, 1948
Goodnight Moon, 1947
The Runaway Bunny, 1942

Other books you might like:
David McPhail, *Pigs Aplenty, Pigs Galore!*, 1993
    Pigs throw a party in the narrator's house and then unexpectedly help with the clean up.
Elizabeth Spurr, *A Pig Named Perrier*, 2002
    Perrier, pet pig of a movie starlet, discovers his love for mud on a trip to the starlet's country home.
Mark Teague, *Pigsty*, 1994
    When Wendell's mother declares his room a ''pigsty,'' he heads upstairs to clean it only to discover that two pigs have moved in.

165

MARGARET WISE BROWN
LORETTA KRUPINSKI, Illustrator

My World of Color

(New York: Hyperion Books for Children, 2002)

Subject(s): Artists and Art; Nature; Animals/Mice
Age range(s): Preschool-Grade 1
Major character(s): Unnamed Character, Mouse, Artist
Time period(s): 2000s (2002)
Locale(s): United States

Summary: An artist and his apprentice explore the world of colors. Each page describes one of the following colors: red, orange, yellow, green, blue, purple, white, black, brown, pink and gray. At the story's conclusion, the artist displays his paintings that reflect the colors he finds in nature. (32 pages)

Where it's reviewed:
Book World, September 22, 2002, page 11
Booklist, May 1, 2002, page 1531
Horn Book Guide, Fall 2002, page 296
Publishers Weekly, March 25, 2002, page 62
School Library Journal, June 2002, page 88

Other books by the same author:
The Diggers, 1960
The Color Kittens, 1949
Two Little Trains, 1949

Other books you might like:
Ann Jonas, *Color Dance*, 1989
    Three children make all the colors of the rainbow while performing a dance with colored scarves.
Laura Leuck, *Teeny, Tiny Mouse: A Book About Colors*, 1998
    A mouse mother asks her child to name all the colors in their teeny, tiny house.
Leo Lionni, *Little Blue and Little Yellow*, 1959
    This book explains the concept of color mixing through the friendship of Little Blue and Little Yellow, who become green when they hug.
Bill Martin Jr., *Brown Bear, Brown Bear, What Do You See?*, 1983
    Animals introduce the world of colors.
Ellen Stoll Walsh, *Mouse Paint*, 1989
    Three white mice fall in and out of jars of primary colored paint, confusing a cat as they change colors.

166

MARGARET WISE BROWN
STEVE JOHNSON, Illustrator
LOU FANCHER, Illustrator

Robin's Room

(New York: Hyperion Books for Children, 2002)

Subject(s): Independence; Imagination; Individuality
Age range(s): Preschool-Kindergarten
Major character(s): Robin, Child
Time period(s): 2000s (2002)
Locale(s): United States

Summary: Robin is a little boy who gets into everything from painting pictures on the walls, to planting flowers in the bathtub, to all manner of fun projects. His parents decide that the solution to this is to give Robin his own room. Robin renovates the room, with the help of three carpenters, to his fantastic specifications—and the creatively destructive projects around the house finally stop. (32 pages)

Where it's reviewed:
Booklist, April 15, 2002, page 1406
Horn Book Guide, Fall 2002, page 321
Horn Book, September 2002, page 8
Kirkus Reviews, April 1, 2002, page 487
Publishers Weekly, May 20, 2002, page 65

Other books by the same author:
Two Little Trains, 2001
Goodnight Moon, 1947
The Runaway Bunny, 1942

Other books you might like:

Elizabeth Starr Hill, *Evan's Corner*, 1967
  In his family's crowded apartment Evan tries to find a space that's all his own.
Amada Irma Perez, *My Very Own Room*, 2000
  Crowded into a room with her five brothers, a little girl longs for a room of her own.
Uri Shulevitz, *The Moon in My Room*, 1963
  A little boy loves the private world of his very own room.
Audrey Wood, *The Flying Dragon Room*, 1996
  Patrick borrows tools from Mrs. Jenkins to create a fantastic subterranean realm that he willingly shares with his parents.

167

MARGARET WISE BROWN
DAN ANDREASEN, Illustrator

Sailor Boy Jig

(New York: Margaret K. McElderry Books/Simon & Schuster, 2002)

Subject(s): Animals/Dogs; Dancing; Stories in Rhyme
Age range(s): Preschool-Kindergarten
Major character(s): Unnamed Character, Dog, Sailor
Time period(s): Indeterminate
Locale(s): Fictional Country

Summary: The legacy of an esteemed author continues in a previously unpublished tale. A lively sailor's feet barely touch the deck as he dances his jig. Whether stomping, jumping, stepping or dancing the sailor's actions vary from big movements to little ones and loud ones to soft as the font size and illustrations vary to support the text. After an active day the cheerful sailor falls into his bunk for a good night's sleep. (32 pages)

Where it's reviewed:
Booklist, March 15, 2002, page 1261
Horn Book Guide, Fall 2002, page 296
Publishers Weekly, April 1, 2002, page 81
School Library Journal, June 2002, page 90

Other books by the same author:
Two Little Trains, 2001 (Publishers Weekly Best Children's Books)
Another Important Book, 1999 (School Library Journal Best Books)
Goodnight Moon, 1947

Other books you might like:
Debi Gliori, *Polar Bolero: A Bedtime Dance*, 2001
  Unable to sleep a young polar bear slips outside and joins with others to dance the Polar Bolero until they are all ready to drift back to bed.
Rhonda Gowler Greene, *Jamboree Day*, 2001
  The jungle is rocking for Jamboree Day, a lively event that's held every May.
Elizabeth Winthrop, *Dumpy La Rue*, 2001
  Dumpy's got rhythm and he wants to dance despite the objections of his family that pigs simply don't do that sort of thing.

168

N.M. BROWNE

Warriors of Alavna

(New York: Bloomsbury, 2002)

Subject(s): Space and Time; Fantasy; War
Age range(s): Grades 7-10
Major character(s): Dan "Bear Sark", Warrior; Ursula, 15-Year-Old, Sorceress; Rhonwen, Sorceress; Macsen, Warrior
Time period(s): 2000s; 1st century (75)
Locale(s): England

Summary: On a school field trip to the site of the Battle of Hastings, Dan is paired with Ursula and the two set off to explore the grounds, until Ursula disappears into a thick yellow mist. Following her, Dan finds himself in a strange world with murdered bodies, heavy, ornate swords and people speaking Latin. Eventually he's captured, reunited with Ursula and told they've been summoned by Rhonwen to help her brother Macsen defeat an invading tribe, the Ravens. Dan's athletic ability and his agility and strength earn him the name "Bear Sark" for his prowess in battle. Ursula discovers unknown powers, similar to those of Rhonwen, as she calls up a Roman legion to help Macsen and is known as "Boar Skull." Eventually defeating the Ravens, Dan and Ursula prepare to return to their own world, but wonder if they'll ever see the Cambrogi people again. (308 pages)

Where it's reviewed:
Bulletin of the Center for Children's Books, October 2002, page 50
Kirkus Reviews, September 1, 2002, page 1305
Reading Time, November 2000, page 11
School Library Journal, January 2003, page 133

Other books by the same author:
Basilisk, 2004
Warriors of Camlann, 2003
Hunted, 2002

Other books you might like:
Michael Crichton, *Timelines*, 1999
  Excavating a 14th-century French fortress town, Professor Johnston meets disaster when he asks to be sent back to the time the town flourished.
Pamela Smith Hill, *The Last Grail Keeper*, 2001
  Accompanying her mother to Glastonbury where she's working on a dig, Felicity time travels and discovers she's one of the Grail Keepers.
Terry Kretzer-Malvehy, *Passage to Little Bighorn*, 1999
  At a reenactment of the Little Bighorn battle, Dakota finds he's traveled back in time and is captured by Sitting Bull's warriors.
Jane Yolen, *Sister Light, Sister Dark*, 1988
  A sisterhood of warrior women finds it useful to have a shadow sister to watch their backs; unfortunately, bright sunlight undoes the magic.

169

N.M. BROWNE

Warriors of Camlann
(New York: Bloomsbury, 2003)

Subject(s): Arthurian Legends; Time Travel; Coming-of-Age
Age range(s): Grades 7-12
Major character(s): Dan, Teenager, Warrior; Ursula, Teenager, Warrior; Taliesin, Wizard; Arturus, Royalty (king)
Time period(s): 5th century
Locale(s): England

Summary: This retelling of the Matter of Britain will appeal to everyone who always thought that King Arthur was a little too good. Dan and Ursula, having proven themselves as heroes in *Warriors of Alavna*, attempt to return to their own time in 21st century Britain. Unknown to them, they are pulled off course to the fifth century by the druid Taliesin, who has also been time traveling. Taliesin intends to preserve what he can of the 1st century tribes, for which he, Dan and Ursula have previously fought, and has chosen a leader to pull together the tribes and accept two heroes from outside of time. But Ursula has lost her magic, although not her warrior-strength, during their journey through the time-bending mist, and Dan no longer has the berserker rage that allowed him to conquer any enemy. Worst of all, both find a multitude of things to dislike in Arturus, Taliesin's chosen leader. They long to abandon Taliesin and just go home, but do they dare, when it seems they have arrived just in time to save the man who will be remembered as King Arthur? (396 pages)

Where it's reviewed:
Horn Book Guide, Fall 2003, page 379
Kirkus Reviews, May 15, 2003, page 746
Publishers Weekly, April 14, 2003, page 72
School Library Journal, July 2003, page 124
Voice of Youth Advocates, June 2003, page 146

Other books by the same author:
Basilisk, 2004
Hunted, 2002
Warriors of Alavna, 2002

Other books you might like:
Catherine Christian, *The Pendragon*, 1978
　Bedwyr is the narrator for this version of Arthur's story, which focuses on the relationships of the Knights of the Round Table.
Jo Walton, *The King's Name*, 2001
　Sulien, a woman warrior, joins the king who's fighting to preserve civilization in this story, which parallels the Arthurian legend.
Jack Whyte, *The Singing Sword*, 1999
　The Matter of Britain is retold as a story of the survival of Roman military tactics.

170

JOSEPH BRUCHAC

The Warriors
(Plain City, OH: Darby Creek, 2003)

Subject(s): Sports; Schools/Boarding Schools; Indians of North America
Age range(s): Grades 5-8
Major character(s): Jake Forrest, Indian (Iroquois), Sports Figure (lacrosse player); Coach Scott, Coach (of lacrosse)
Time period(s): 2000s
Locale(s): Maryland

Summary: Raised on an Iroquois Reservation, Jake isn't happy when his mother accepts a position as a lawyer in Washington, DC, and he's sent to boarding school because of all her traveling. He discovers that one reason he's had no trouble being admitted to Weltimore Academy is his prowess as a lacrosse player, yet he finds that his teammates play for different reasons than he does. On the rez, lacrosse is considered almost a sacred game that goes beyond competition and ritual, yet on his new school team, Jake is unhappy that his coach doesn't understand that lacrosse is more than a game. He also doesn't like being called "Chief" by boys who don't understand how demeaning that makes him feel. His coach is also his history teacher and much of what he teaches about the Indians in America isn't accurate, which just leaves Jake feeling more lonely than ever. Jake revises his feelings about the man when Coach Scott is wounded protecting a mother and her child during a robbery, and even organizes a special lacrosse game as a prayer of healing for him, a lacrosse game in which everyone at the school, from student to staff, takes part. (117 pages)

Where it's reviewed:
Booklist, December 15, 2003, page 664
Bulletin of the Center for Children's Books, October 2003, page 52
Publishers Weekly, July 21, 2003, page 195
School Library Journal, October 2003, page 158

Other books by the same author:
A Code Talker's Story, 2004
Hidden Roots, 2004
Pocahontas, 2003
The Winter People, 2002
Journal of Jesse Smoke: A Cherokee Boy, 2001

Other books you might like:
Jennifer Owings Dewey, *Navajo Summer*, 1998
　Not wishing to spend the summer with either parent while they're divorcing, Jamie stays with a Navajo family she's met and enjoys the pace of their lives.
Will Hobbs, *Bearstone*, 1990
　Cloyd discovers his Indian heritage as he battles for survival in the Colorado Mountains.
Hazel Krantz, *Walks in Beauty*, 1997
　Anita is worn down from the stress of remaining a true Navajo in the face of the white man's world.

171

JOSEPH BRUCHAC

The Winter People
(New York: Dial Books/Penguin Putnam, 2002)

Subject(s): Indians of North America; Coming-of-Age; French and Indian War
Age range(s): Grades 5-9
Major character(s): Saxso, Indian (Abenaki); Robert Rogers, Military Personnel
Time period(s): 1750s (1759)
Locale(s): St. Francis, Quebec, Canada

Summary: During the French and Indian War, a raid on a small village inhabited by ancestors of the author is recreated here in a blending of fact and fiction. The village is St. Francis and a mixture of Catholic Indians and Frenchmen live there. The young Indian Saxso is warned of the raid and rushes back to the village to save his mother and sisters, but loses them when he helps someone else save a child. Led by Major Rogers, the Rogers Rangers capture many women and children and flee south with their hostages. Saxso refuses to give up his family and follows them south, tracking the group even though he's wounded, in a story finally told from the Indians' viewpoint. (168 pages)

Where it's reviewed:
Booklist, October 1, 2002, page 322
Kliatt, September 2002, page 6
Library Media Connection, April 2003, page 72
School Library Journal, November 2002, page 154
Voice of Youth Advocates, October 2002, page 269

Awards the book has won:
Smithsonian's Notable Books for Children/Older Readers, 2002
School Library Journal Best Books, 2002

Other books by the same author:
A Code Talker's Story, 2004
Hidden Roots, 2004
Pocahontas, 2003
The Warriors, 2003
The Heart of a Chief, 1998

Other books you might like:
Michael Dorris, *Morning Girl*, 1992
    Morning Girl, an Arawak Indian, finds everything in her life changes after the arrival of Columbus and the ''round'' strangers.
Sally M. Keehn, *I Am Regina*, 1991
    Captured by the Delaware Indians during the French and Indian War, after nine years of captivity Regina can barely recognize her mother.
Elizabeth George Speare, *The Sign of the Beaver*, 1983
    After the French and Indian wars, Matt is left alone for a while, but Indians help him survive while his family is away.

172

JEFF BRUMBEAU
GAIL DE MARCKEN, Illustrator

Miss Hunnicutt's Hat
(New York: Orchard Books/Scholastic, Inc., 2003)

Subject(s): Self-Confidence; Fashion Design; Animals/Chickens
Age range(s): Grades K-3
Major character(s): Miss Hunnicutt, Neighbor
Time period(s): Indeterminate
Locale(s): Littleton, Fictional Country

Summary: Miss Hunnicutt is quite pleased with her stylish new hat, topped with a live chicken and coming to her all the way from Paris. However, when she wears it on the day the queen is expected to come through town, her neighbors work themselves into a tizzy over her unorthodox fashion choice. Miss Hunnicutt stands up for her right to wear what she likes and her assertiveness is rewarded when the queen emerges from her car attired in a hat topped by a live turkey. (48 pages)

Where it's reviewed:
Booklist, January 2003, page 904
School Library Journal, March 2003, page 178

Other books by the same author:
The Quiltmaker's Journey, 2004
The Quiltmaker's Gift, 1999 (Notable Social Studies Trade Books for Young People)
The Man-in-the-Moon in Love, 1992

Other books you might like:
Elaine Greenstein, *Mattie's Hats Won't Wear That!*, 1997
    Hatmaker Mattie's hats are sick of her wild decorations so Mattie decides to let the hats decorate themselves.
Ezra Jack Keats, *Jennie's Hat*, 1966
    A rather plain new hat is beautifully adorned by Jennie's bird friends who add themselves to the decorations.
Helen Lester, *Tacky the Penguin*, 1988
    Non-conformist Tacky doesn't fit in with his oh-so-proper neighbors, but his uniqueness saves the day in the end.
Melissa Milich, *Miz Fannie Mae's Fine New Easter Hat*, 1997
    Mama's fine new Easter hat becomes the site of a ''miracle'' when the decorative eggs begin hatching during church.
Sam Swope, *The Araboolies of Liberty Street*, 2001
    When the unorthodox Araboolies move on to Liberty Street, General Pinch tries to force the family to conform or move.

173

JENNIFER BRUTSCHY
CAT BOWMAN SMITH, Illustrator

Just One More Story
(New York: Orchard Books/Scholastic, Inc., 2002)

Subject(s): Storytelling; Bedtime; Music and Musicians
Age range(s): Grades K-2

Major character(s): Austin, Child, Son; Dad, Musician, Story-teller; Mom, Mother, Singer
Time period(s): Indeterminate
Locale(s): San Antonio, Texas; Tuscaloosa, Alabama; Lafayette, Louisiana

Summary: Austin's family is known as "The Swamp Snakes," a traveling country-western musical group. Despite constant travel to different towns Austin can depend on the sameness of the trailer in which they live, Dad's nightly bedtime story and his own nightly plea for just one more story. When they stop to visit an uncle in Tuscaloosa their overnight stay in his two-story house gives Austin the rationale to win his argument for an additional story. In Lafayette, Dad wins a fiddling contest and Mom suggests an overnight stay in a hotel when they reach the next big city. Austin sees great potential in being assigned a hotel room on the eleventh floor. (32 pages)

Where it's reviewed:
Bulletin of the Center for Children's Books, July 2002, page 395
Horn Book Guide, Fall 2002, page 321
Horn Book, July 2002, page 441
Publishers Weekly, May 13, 2002, page 70
School Library Journal, July 2002, page 84

Other books by the same author:
Celeste and Crabapple Sam, 1994
Winter Fox, 1993

Other books you might like:
Allan Ahlberg, *It Was a Dark and Stormy Night*, 1994
    With tongue-in-cheek humor, a young boy uses storytelling to orchestrate his escape from a band of brigands.
Kate Duke, *Aunt Isabel Makes Trouble*, 1996
    Penelope assures that Aunt Isabel's storytelling lasts a long time by throwing in a timely "BUT" whenever Aunt Isabel seems to be nearing a conclusion.
Dugald Steer, *Just One More Story*, 1999
    Mother Pig's four piglets beg for just one more of her piggy versions of familiar fairy tales before they go to bed.

174

SHARON BRYANT

The Earth Kitchen
(New York: HarperCollins, 2002)

Subject(s): Mental Illness
Age range(s): Grades 5-8
Major character(s): Gwendolyn Mary "Gwen" Brace, 12-Year-Old, Mentally Ill Person; Dr. Stone, Doctor (psychiatrist)
Time period(s): 1960s
Locale(s): United States

Summary: The continual air-raid drills and sirens, so prevalent in America during the Cold War, have taken a toll on Gwen. Several years earlier she was the only survivor of an automobile accident that killed her parents, yet her mind has now convinced her they died in an atomic bomb blast. Currently hospitalized at Unity State Hospital, she recedes into a fantasy world where, with the help of a gold key dropped by a bird, she unlocks a mental forest and hides in a room in a tree, a space she calls "the earth kitchen." It's only there that Gwen, with the help of her psychiatrist, begins to heal until she's able to return to reality and the kitchen of her favorite aunt, in a haunting first novel. (148 pages)

Where it's reviewed:
Horn Book, March 2002, page 208
Kirkus Reviews, March 15, 2002, page 407
Publishers Weekly, January 28, 2002, page 292
School Library Journal, March 2002, page 225
Voice of Youth Advocates, April 2002, page 38

Other books you might like:
Margaret Buffie, *Angels Turn Their Backs*, 1998
    A combination of counseling, a parrot and an incomplete needlepoint angel help Addy overcome her panic attacks.
Patricia McCormick, *Cut*, 2000
    Callie finally understands that she's not to blame for her brother's asthma attack and takes the first step to heal and no longer cut herself.
Louise Plummer, *A Dance for Three*, 2000
    When her boyfriend won't accept his role in her pregnancy, Hannah ends up in an adolescent psychiatric ward.

175

JANE BUCHANAN
LESLIE BOWMAN, Illustrator

The Berry-Picking Man
(New York: Farrar Straus Giroux, 2003)

Subject(s): Old Age; Conduct of Life; Family Life
Age range(s): Grades 3-5
Major character(s): Old Sam, Aged Person, Mentally Ill Person; Meggie, 9-Year-Old, Daughter; Mama, Mother, Photographer
Time period(s): 2000s (2003)
Locale(s): United States

Summary: Meggie wishes Old Sam, released from a mental hospital after 25 years, had not come to her town to live. The lonely man with no family calls her mother when he needs a ride, help or someone to eat the berries that he picks. As the youngest, Meggie is stuck riding along with Mama when she responds to Sam's calls while her sisters stay out of sight to avoid being included. Meggie is torn between fear, disgust, compassion, and guilt each time she sees Sam. When Sam is struck by a car and hospitalized just before Christmas, it is Meggie who agrees with Sam's notion that he should spend Christmas day with her family. Though her sisters protest, her father transports Sam from the hospital to their home for the day. As Meggie's understanding of Mama's message of charity to all deepens she also brings her sisters to a greater appreciation of the value of empathy. (88 pages)

Where it's reviewed:
Booklist, August 2003, page 1980
Bulletin of the Center for Children's Books, May 2003, page 353
School Library Journal, June 2003, page 97

Awards the book has won:
Booklist Editors' Choice, 2003

Other books by the same author:
Goodbye, Charley, 2004
Hank's Story, 2001
Gratefully Yours, 1997

Other books you might like:
Sara Harrell Banks, *Under the Shadow of Wings*, 1997
Tatnall defends her slow cousin Obie from bullies but she cannot protect him from his own inner turmoil and ultimately, he determines his fate.
Kimberly Willis Holt, *My Louisiana Sky*, 1998
Bright Tiger loves her parents but doesn't realize they're mentally handicapped until she's older and her grandmother dies.
Donna Jo Napoli, *April Flowers*, 2000
Following a stroke, Maggie's grandmother must move into Maggie's home, challenging Maggie to understand the changes in grandmother and her family.
Barbara O'Connor, *Me and Rupert Goody*, 1999
Uncle Beau's General Store provides Jennalee a refuge from an unstable family life, until Rupert Goody arrives and Jennalee must adjust to change.

176

LOIS MCMASTER BUJOLD

Diplomatic Immunity: A Comedy of Terrors

(Riverdale, NY: Baen Books, 2002)

Subject(s): Science Fiction; Detection; Cultural Conflict
Age range(s): Grades 9-Adult
Major character(s): Miles Vorkosigan, Spouse, Government Official (lord auditor); Ekaterin Vorkosigan, Spouse
Time period(s): Indeterminate Future
Locale(s): Graf Station, Space Station

Summary: Irrepressible adventurer Miles Vorkosigan is now Lord Miles, an important government figure who, as an auditor, represents the Emperor and reports to him directly. He also marries, having persuaded Ekaterin of his noble intentions. But he hasn't completely abandoned his old ways as he investigates a crime while on his honeymoon. Luckily Ekaterin understands Miles and loves him in spite of his overactive brain. Assured this will just be a minor detour in their private bliss, Miles and Ekaterin find themselves in the midst of a full-fledged diplomatic incident involving firefights on a quaddie space station. It's a good thing Ekaterin will be there to tell everyone to shut up when Miles needs to think or no one will survive. (311 pages)

Where it's reviewed:
Booklist, April 15, 2002, page 1386
Library Journal, May 15, 2002, page 130
Publishers Weekly, April 1, 2002, page 58
School Library Journal, January 2003, page 174
Voice of Youth Advocates, October 2002, page 292

Other books by the same author:
Paladin of Souls, 2003
The Curse of Chalion, 2001
A Civil Campaign: A Comedy of Biology, 1999

Other books you might like:
C.J. Cherryh, *Explorer*, 2003
Linguist Bren Cameron has his hands full when he serves as ambassador to a new group of suspicious aliens, in addition to the humans and alien atevi.
Elizabeth Moon, *Trading in Danger*, 2003
Expelled from space academy, a cadet finds she needs every skill she's learned to pilot one of her family's merchant vessels.
Dorothy L. Sayers, *Busman's Honeymoon*, 1937
Like Miles Vorkosigan, Lord Peter Wimsey investigates a murder in his honeymoon house, while his new bride Harriet helps the investigation move along.

177

EVE BUNTING
KURT CYRUS, Illustrator

The Bones of Fred McFee

(San Diego: Harcourt, Inc., 2002)

Subject(s): Halloween; Stories in Rhyme; Brothers and Sisters
Age range(s): Grades K-3
Major character(s): Jessie, Child, Sister; Unnamed Character, Child, Brother (older)
Time period(s): 2000s
Locale(s): United States

Summary: A plastic skeleton named Fred McFee by Jessie and her brother hangs in a sycamore tree in their yard. The wind rattles the bones of the skeleton making it seem so authentic that the dog won't go near the tree and the family's rooster vanishes. With plans to take the skeleton down after Halloween and store it to use again next year, the siblings carve their jack o' lanterns and place them below the tree on Halloween night. The next morning the plastic skeleton is gone, a rectangular mound covers the ground below the tree and no one knows what's become of Fred McFee. (32 pages)

Where it's reviewed:
Booklist, September 1, 2002, page 139
Bulletin of the Center for Children's Books, October 2002, page 50
Horn Book Guide, Spring 2003, page 27
Publishers Weekly, September 23, 2002, page 23
School Library Journal, September 2002, page 181

Awards the book has won:
Center for Children's Books Best Books, 2002

Other books by the same author:
The Days of Summer, 2001
Butterfly House, 1999 (Notable Social Studies Trade Books for Young People)
Smoky Night, 1994 (Caldecott Medal)
Scary, Scary Halloween, 1986

Other books you might like:
Cynthia De Felice, *The Dancing Skeleton*, 1989
Because he does not yet ''feel dead,'' Aaron will not stay in his coffin.
Tony Johnston, *The Ghost of Nicholas Greebe*, 1996
For 100 years the ghost of Nicholas Grebe haunts the

house in which he once lived awaiting the return of his leg bone.

Robert D. San Souci, *Cinderella Skeleton*, 2000
  In a ghoulish retelling of the fairy tale, the prince gets Cinderella's shoe with the foot still inside so he finds her by matching bone to bone.

Judy Sierra, *The House That Drac Built*, 1995
  A rhyming cumulative tale introduces such unusual creatures as a manticore and the fiend of Bloodygore living in the house that Drac built.

Erica Silverman, *The Halloween House*, 1997
  On Halloween two prison escapees seek refuge in what they think is an unoccupied house but which is actually a haunted one.

178

EVE BUNTING
TIMOTHY BUSH, Illustrator

Christmas Cricket

(New York: Clarion Books, 2002)

Subject(s): Animals/Insects; Christmas; Self-Esteem
Age range(s): Grades K-2
Major character(s): Cricket, Cricket; Dad, Father; Unnamed Character, Child
Time period(s): 2000s
Locale(s): California

Summary: Unhappy Cricket seeks shelter from the dark, wet, cold night by hopping into a house. He finds shelter in a tree covered with stars and begins a sad song. A child notices the singing and Dad peers into the branches of the family's Christmas tree for its source. Telling the child that the songs of animals and insects carry the voices of angels, Dad suggests that they sing along too and they join joyful Cricket in a Christmas carol. (32 pages)

Where it's reviewed:
Booklist, September 15, 2002, page 245
Horn Book Guide, Spring 2003, page 27
Kirkus Reviews, November 1, 2002, page 1616
Publishers Weekly, September 23, 2002, page 32
School Library Journal, October 2002, page 57

Awards the book has won:
IRA Children's Choices, 2003

Other books by the same author:
The Days of Summer, 2001
We Were There: A Nativity Story, 2001
Ducky, 1997

Other books you might like:
Odds Bodkin, *The Christmas Cobwebs*, 2001
  While a poor cobbler and his family sleep, spiders decorate their Christmas tree with carefully spun ornaments.
Larry Dane Brimner, *Merry Christmas, Old Armadillo*, 1995
  While lonely Old Armadillo naps on Christmas Eve his friends prepare a surprise just for him.
Michael Cutting, *The Little Crooked Christmas Tree*, 1990
  Because a tree shelters a dove it grows crookedly and cannot be chosen as a Christmas tree although it has the true spirit of the season.

179

EVE BUNTING
LEUYEN PHAM, Illustrator

Little Badger's Just-About Birthday

(San Diego: Harcourt, Inc., 2002)

Subject(s): Animals/Badgers; Birthdays; Animals
Age range(s): Grades K-2
Major character(s): Old Badger, Badger, Grandfather; Little Badger, Badger, Friend
Time period(s): Indeterminate
Locale(s): Fictional Country

Summary: Old Badger awakens Little Badger with the news that it is his ''just-about'' birthday, so named because it was just about this time of year that he was born. Together Old Badger and Little Badger prepare invitations, set refreshments on the log table, and welcome Little Badger's friends to the party. Each animal arrives with a special gift such as an acorn, a shiny moonstone or a grub. During the course of the party Little Badger learns that all his friends were born at just about this time of year too so he declares it is a party for everyone and generously allows each one to take home one of his gifts. Finally, when it's just-about bedtime, Little Badger realizes that it's also Old Badger's just-about birthday and he concludes a satisfying day by giving Old Badger a token of his love. (32 pages)

Where it's reviewed:
Booklist, March 15, 2002, page 1261
Horn Book Guide, Fall 2002, page 296
Publishers Weekly, March 18, 2002, page 106
School Library Journal, April 2002, page 101

Other books by the same author:
Little Badger, Terror of the Seven Seas, 2001
Can You Do This, Old Badger?, 2000
Butterfly House, 1999 (Notable Social Studies Trade Books for Young People)

Other books you might like:
Holly Hobbie, *Toot & Puddle: A Present for Toot*, 1998
  Toot's birthday is coming and Puddle is trying to find the best gift for his friend.
Pat Hutchins, *It's MY Birthday!*, 1999
  Unlike generous Little Badger, little monster Billy has difficulty sharing the gifts he receives at his birthday party.
Vivian Sathre, *Three Kind Mice*, 1997
  Three mice bake a cake as a birthday surprise for a cat.

180

EVE BUNTING
K. WENDY POPP, Illustrator

One Candle

(New York: Joanna Cotler/HarperCollins Publishers, 2002)

Subject(s): Holidays, Jewish; Holocaust; Jews
Age range(s): Grades 1-4
Major character(s): Grandma, Grandmother
Time period(s): 2000s (2002); 1940s
Locale(s): United States; Buchenwald, Germany

Summary: Every year during the family Hanukkah celebration, Grandma tells the story of her experience celebrating Hanukkah at Buchenwald concentration camp. As a twelve-year-old girl working in the soldiers' kitchen, Grandma and her sister managed to smuggle out a small potato, a pat of margarine and two matches. By carving out the potato and lighting the margarine, the girls were able to create a Hanukkah candle. Every year, Grandma makes a candle from a carved-out potato to remember that time. (32 pages)

Where it's reviewed:
Booklist, September 1, 2002, page 139
Horn Book Guide, Spring 2003, page 27
Kirkus Reviews, November 1, 2002, page 1616
Publishers Weekly, September 23, 2002, page 28
School Library Journal, October 2002, page 57

Other books by the same author:
Anna's Table, 2003
I Have an Olive Tree, 1999
Someday a Tree, 1993

Other books you might like:
David A. Adler, *One Yellow Daffodil: A Hanukkah Story*, 1995
  A Holocaust survivor is invited to share Hanukkah with customers of his flower shop.
Paula Kurzband Feder, *The Feather-Bed Journey*, 1995
  A brother and sister accidentally tear open a feather pillow and learn about its significance to their grandmother's experiences during the Holocaust.
Marci Stillerman, *Nine Spoons: A Chanukah Story*, 1998
  In a Nazi concentration camp, a woman manages to make a menorah from nine spoons.

181

EVE BUNTING

The Presence: A Ghost Story
(New York: Clarion Books, 2003)

Subject(s): Ghosts; Guilt; Grandmothers
Age range(s): Grades 6-10
Major character(s): Catherine Miller, 17-Year-Old; Eunice Larrimer, Grandmother; Collin Miller, Teenager; Noah Vanderhorst, Spirit
Time period(s): 2000s
Locale(s): Pasadena, California

Summary: Several months ago Catherine and her best friend Kirsty were in a terrible car accident; Catherine survived and Kirsty didn't. When her parents have a chance for a European trip over Christmas, it's decided that Catherine will stay with her grandmother. Now in Pasadena, Catherine hopes for some quiet time at her grandmother's church, St. Matthew's, but it isn't to be. She hears someone call her name, feels an area of cold as she moves around the church and sees notes written to her that no one else can see. She's warned away from the church by an elderly parishioner and hears of girls who resemble her who have disappeared, but doesn't connect anything menacing with that information. Meeting a good-looking young man inside the church, she's led to believe he can contact her friend Kirsty. Catherine eventually puts all the pieces together and realizes the young man trapped in the church for over 100 years is the ghost Noah who searches for his girlfriend Lydia, but will anyone else believe her? (195 pages)

Where it's reviewed:
Booklist, October 15, 2003, page 404
Bulletin of the Center for Children's Books, November 2003, page 95
Library Media Connection, February 2004, page 71
School Library Journal, October 2003, page 162
Voice of Youth Advocates, February 2004, page 500

Other books by the same author:
Snowboarding on Monster Mountain, 2003
Spying on Miss Muller, 1995
For Always, 1993
The Ghost Children, 1989
The Haunting of Safekeep, 1985

Other books you might like:
Meg Cabot, *Haunted: A Tale of the Mediator*, 2003
  Suze finds her plate full with mediating between the living and the dead.
Judd Holt, *A Promise to Catie*, 1992
  Billy falls in love with a young girl he sees around his Texas farmhouse, not realizing she's a ghost.
Phyllis Reynolds Naylor, *Jade Green: A Ghost Story*, 2000
  Judith's green-framed photo of her mother awakens the ghost of a former serving girl; luckily the ghost protects her from a murderous relative.
Vivian Vande Velde, *There's a Dead Person Following My Sister Around*, 1999
  A ghost who wants to return to life takes over Vicki's body and Ted must oust the ghost so his sister can return.
Robert Westall, *The Promise*, 1990
  Valerie dies during World War II, a bomb obliterates her grave and Bob recalls a promise to find her if she's ever lost; her ghost remembers, too.

182

MELVIN BURGESS

The Ghost Behind the Wall
(New York: Holt, 2003)

Subject(s): Ghosts; Memory; Old Age
Age range(s): Grades 5-7
Major character(s): David Withington, 12-Year-Old; Robert Alveston, Aged Person
Time period(s): 2000s
Locale(s): London, England

Summary: Small for his age and very mischievous, David learns he can create chaos when he crawls through the air ducts of his apartment building. Spying on neighbors, he plays most of his tricks on elderly Mr. Alveston, who's already having memory problems. One day he's caught and part of his punishment is to visit the elderly gentleman. An unusual friendship develops between David and Mr. Alveston and it's David who helps when the ghost of Mr. Alveston's youth unleashes a malevolent plan. (161 pages)

Where it's reviewed:
Booklist, April 15, 2003, page 1470
Bulletin of the Center for Children's Books, February 2003, page 227
Publishers Weekly, April 14, 2003, page 70
School Library Journal, July 2003, page 124
Voice of Youth Advocates, April 2003, page 61

Awards the book has won:
Center for Children's Books Best Books, 2003

Other books by the same author:
Kite, 2000
An Angel for May, 1995
Earth Giant, 1995
Burning Issy, 1994
The Cry of the Wolf, 1992

Other books you might like:
Eileen Dunlop, *The Ghost by the Sea*, 1996
  Two cousins try to solve the mysterious drowning of an ancestor so Milly's spirit will stop haunting their grandparent's home.
Neil Gaiman, *Coraline*, 2002
  Opening a door leading into the other half of her old house, Coraline meets mirror images of her parents who want to keep her on their side.
Eva Ibbotson, *Dial-a-Ghost*, 2001
  The Dial-a-Ghost Agency mixes up an order and sends screaming ghosts to a convent and a loving ghost family to an orphan who needs tenderness.
Vivian Vande Velde, *There's a Dead Person Following My Sister Around*, 1999
  A ghost who wants to return to life takes over Vicki's body and Ted must oust the ghost so his sister can come back.

183

MELVIN BURGESS

Lady: My Life as a Bitch

(New York: Holt, 2002)

Subject(s): Animals/Dogs; Alcoholism; Magic
Age range(s): Grades 9-12
Major character(s): Sandra ''Lady'' Francy, 17-Year-Old, Dog
Time period(s): 2000s
Locale(s): Manchester, England

Summary: Fun and parties! Why would Sandra want her life to be saddled with work, responsibility and more studying? She unknowingly changes her life when she curses the wrong homeless drunk and is transformed into Lady, a fun-loving dog. Wow-she's now free and can run wherever she wants. A half-hearted attempt to return to her family is squashed when they want nothing to do with this wild dog, so Sandra/Lady now decides to make the most of her new life. There's no one to tell her what she can or can't do with a boyfriend, no alarm clock signals the beginning of another school day and there are no rules to follow. Sandra/Lady decides she's now living the perfect life,'a dog's life.' (235 pages)

Where it's reviewed:
Booklist, June 2002, page 1716

Kirkus Reviews, May 15, 2002, page 728
Publishers Weekly, March 4, 2002, page 81
School Library Journal, July 2002, page 114
Voice of Youth Advocates, August 2002, page 199

Other books by the same author:
Bloodtide, 2001
Smack, 1998
The Baby and Fly Pie, 1996
An Angel for May, 1994

Other books you might like:
T.E. Bethancourt, *The Dog Days of Arthur Cane*, 1976
  Changed into a stray dog, Arthur learns more than he wishes when he's caught by the dog catcher and awaits his dismal fate.
Scott Bradfield, *Animal Planet*, 1995
  A satirical novel of talking animals who decide to take action after tiring of lives as pets or caged animals in a zoo.
Meredith Ann Pierce, *The Woman Who Loved Reindeer*, 1985
  Caribou raises and then falls in love with Reindeer, a trangl who shape shifts between reindeer and human form.

184

JOHN BURNINGHAM, Author/Illustrator

The Magic Bed

(New York: Alfred A. Knopf, 2003)

Subject(s): Magic; Shopping; Fantasy
Age range(s): Grades K-2
Major character(s): Georgie, Child, Son; Unnamed Character, Grandmother
Time period(s): 2000s
Locale(s): England

Summary: When Georgie's granny insists that he get a new bed, he shops in a used furniture store where he finds a magic bed. After cleaning the bed he can read all but one word of the inscription and he repeats variations of the missing word until his bed magically begins to float over the city. Nightly Georgie travels to distant lands but he doesn't tell his family about the bed's magical properties. Unfortunately, while Georgie's on holiday with his family, Georgie's granny replaces the old bed with a new one. Upon arriving home and discovering the magic bed is missing, Georgie races to the dump, finds the bed, repeats the magic word and flies away. (40 pages)

Where it's reviewed:
Booklist, November 15, 2003, page 598
Publishers Weekly, September 29, 2003, page 64
School Library Journal, October 2003, page 114

Other books by the same author:
Colors, 2003
Hushabye, 2001 (Parenting's Reading Magic Award)
Shopping Basket, 1999

Other books you might like:
Catherine Ann Cullen, *The Magical, Mystical, Marvelous Coat*, 2001
  Each of six buttons on a little girl's coat reveals unexpected problem-solving capabilities as she gives them one by one to others in need.

Tim Egan, *Burnt Toast on Davenport Street*, 1997
   Belatedly, Arthur realizes that the fly offering to grant him three wishes must be magic; the performance of the toaster would suggest as much.
Richard Egielski, *Three Magic Balls*, 2000
   Rudy discovers that three ordinary-looking balls in his uncle's toyshop have magical properties.

185
KRISTIN BUTCHER

Cairo Kelly and the Mann
(Custer, WA: Orca Books, 2002)

Subject(s): Sports/Baseball; Loyalty; Literacy
Age range(s): Grades 4-8
Major character(s): Michael "Midge" Ridge, 13-Year-Old, Baseball Player; Cairo Kelly Romani, Baseball Player (pitcher); Harold "the Mann" Mann, Maintenance Worker, Sports Figure (umpire)
Time period(s): 2000s
Locale(s): Canada

Summary: Midge and his buddy Cairo Kelly spend alot of time in the principal's office, so it's a good thing they excel at baseball. Their school custodian Hal Mann is the best umpire their league has, so they're pretty upset when Hal refuses to take the newly-mandated written test for all officials. Cairo Kelly is such a good pitcher that scouts are starting to come around and the boys want to have the best umpire behind the plate. Midge and Cairo Kelly immediately start a protest and lead the other teams in a player strike. After some checking around, Midge and Cairo Kelly discover that Hal can't read or write, which is why he's refused to take the test. They wisely decide it's time to change their battle strategy and make sure Hal returns to call strikes and balls for them. (172 pages)

Where it's reviewed:
Booklist, September 1, 2002, page 129
Kliatt, November 2002, page 17
Quill & Quire, April 2002, page 38
Resource Links, June 2002, page 10
Voice of Youth Advocates, April 2003, page 46

Other books by the same author:
The Trouble with Liberty, 2003
The Hemingway Tradition, 2002
The Gramma War, 2001
The Runaways, 1997

Other books you might like:
Matt Christopher, *Hit-Away Kid*, 1988
   Though Barry sometimes bends the rules, he receives a lesson in sports ethics from an opposing pitcher who wants to win at any cost.
Mame Farrell, *Bradley and the Billboard*, 1998
   Bradley feels great after hitting a home run over 300 feet; he's brought back to reality when his girlfriend repeats the feat.
Chris Lynch, *Gold Dust*, 2000
   Richard's dream of he and Napoleon being star baseball players shatters during the racist 1970s.

186
KRISTIN BUTCHER

The Hemingway Tradition
(Custer, WA: Orca Books, 2002)

Subject(s): Suicide; Fathers and Sons; School Newspapers
Age range(s): Grades 9-12
Major character(s): Shaw Sebring, 16-Year-Old, Volleyball Player; Jai Dhillon, Volleyball Player, 11th Grader; Tess Petersen, 11th Grader
Time period(s): 2000s
Locale(s): Winnipeg, Manitoba, Canada

Summary: Shaw doesn't want to remember his father as a suicide victim, especially since he was the one who found him after he'd eaten a bullet; instead he wants to concentrate on the fun times they had fishing, skiing and sharing favorite books and authors. To start anew, he and his mother leave Vancouver for Winnipeg where Shaw makes friends with Jai and Tess the first day at his new school and, with Jai's insistence, joins the volleyball team. Jai's enthusiasm and East Indian heritage sometimes set him up for racist remarks, and when Shaw sees Jai under attack, he steps into the fray. With Tess's encouragement, Shaw follows in his father's writing footsteps as he composes an article about racism for the school paper and then follows it up with other articles. Slowly but surely he comes to terms with his father's death as he and his mother both make new lives for themselves. (92 pages)

Where it's reviewed:
Kliatt, January 2003, page 18
Quill & Quire, September 2002, page 59
School Library Journal, April 2003, page 157

Other books by the same author:
Zee's Way, 2004
The Trouble with Liberty, 2003
Cairo Kelly and the Mann, 2002

Other books you might like:
Eleanor Cameron, *The Private Worlds of Julia Redfern*, 1988
   Introspective Julia writes a short story that helps ease her grief over her father's accidental death.
Katherine Holubitsky, *Alone at Ninety Foot*, 1999
   Pam's drawn to the pool called Ninety Foot for it's there her mother committed suicide after the SIDS death of Pam's little sister.
Kathe Koja, *Buddha Boy*, 2003
   Jinsen tries to live by Buddhist principles, which makes him different from his classmates and sets him up for their bullying.
Don Trembath, *The Tuesday Cafe*, 1996
   Enrolled in a writing class, Harper doesn't realize he's in with the newly literate and learning disabled, for it's the best class he's ever taken.

187

KRISTIN BUTCHER

The Trouble with Liberty

(Custer, WA: Orca Book Publishers, 2003)

Series: Orca Soundings
Subject(s): Moving, Household; Teacher-Student Relationships
Age range(s): Grades 7-10
Major character(s): Valerie Gail ''Val'' MacQueen, 15-Year-Old; Cody MacQueen, Brother (of Val); Liberty Hayes, 10th Grader
Time period(s): 2000s
Locale(s): Sutter's Crossing, British Columbia, Canada

Summary: Liberty Hayes blows into Sutter's Crossing and nothing is ever quite the same. Val meets gorgeous Liberty at the rodeo and is happy to discover they're in the same grade. That first day of school, Val, her brother Cody and their mom pick up Liberty for school and it's obvious that Cody's smitten. Though Liberty enjoys having Cody as a boyfriend, she's after bigger and better things, like their band teacher or, when that doesn't work out, the chance to spread a rumor about the school principal raping her. Val, Cody and the rest of the townspeople believe Liberty, at least at the beginning. By the time her lies are revealed, a lot of people are hurt, the principal resigns and Liberty's family moves out of town, just as fast as they moved in. (88 pages)

Where it's reviewed:
Resource Links, June 2003, page 24
School Library Journal, July 2003, page 124
Voice of Youth Advocates, August 2003, page 212

Other books by the same author:
Zee's Way, 2004 (Orca Soundings)
Cairo Kelly and the Mann, 2002
The Hemingway Tradition, 2002
The Gramma War, 2001

Other books you might like:
Sarah Dessen, *Dreamland*, 2000
    Her parents are so concerned about their older daughter that they don't see the bruises on Caitlin, bruises inflicted by her boyfriend Rogerson.
E.R. Frank, *Friction*, 2003
    New student Stacy upsets Alex's Forest Alternative School when she accused their teacher Simon of molesting her.
Rob Thomas, *Rats Saw God*, 1996
    Steve York falls in love with Dub and then sees that love die when Dub betrays him with their creative writing teacher.

188

AMY BUTLER

Virginia Bound

(New York: Clarion, 2003)

Subject(s): Orphans; Indians of North America; Servants
Age range(s): Grades 4-8

Major character(s): Rob Brackett, 13-Year-Old, Orphan; Nell Cranston, Child, Orphan; Captain Holt, Farmer (tobacco); Mattoume, 12-Year-Old, Indian (Pamunkey)
Time period(s): 17th century (1620s)
Locale(s): London, England; Jamestown, Virginia

Summary: Orphaned and living on the streets of London, Rob also looks out for orphaned Nell, but her inexperience leads to their kidnapping and transport to Jamestown to work as indentured servants. Rob is spoken for by Captain Holt, a cruel tobacco farmer, and separated from Nell. Miserable, Rob's angry at his owner and wary of Mattoume, a young Indian girl who also helps Holt, as he considers her to be a savage. When Mattoume saves him from a snake while they work in the fields, he begins to reconsider his feelings and sees that she misses her tribe as much as he misses England. Together they plot to escape and luckily, as they flee, Holt is mauled and killed by a bear before he can stop them. Escaping to Mattoume's home, Rob is reunited with Nell and learns to adjust to a new way of life in this author's first novel. (188 pages)

Where it's reviewed:
Booklist, March 1, 2003, page 1197
Horn Book Guide, Fall 2003, page 363
Kirkus Reviews, February 15, 2003, page 301
Library Media Connection, March 2004, page 63
School Library Journal, June 2003, page 136

Other books you might like:
Sandra Forrester, *Wheel of the Moon*, 2000
    Living with a group of fellow orphans, Pen's group is caught, tossed aboard ship and sent to Jamestown to be indentured servants.
Gail Langer Karwoski, *Surviving Jamestown: The Adventures of Young Sam Collier*, 2001
    Sam Collier, 12-year-old page to John Smith, witnesses the hardship of life in the New World settlement in North America.
Elizabeth Massie, *1609: Winter of the Dead: A Novel about the Founding of Jamestown*, 2000
    Two orphans sail to the New World in exchange for labor aboard ship, confident their previous survival by living on their wits can be repeated.
Megan McDonald, *Shadows in the Glasshouse*, 2000
    Tempted by a hot meat pie, Merry is kidnapped and put aboard ship, headed for life as an indentured servant in Jamestown.

189

DORI HILLSTAD BUTLER

Sliding into Home

(Atlanta: Peachtree, 2003)

Subject(s): Sports/Baseball; Gender Roles; Moving, Household
Age range(s): Grades 5-8
Major character(s): Joelle Cunningham, Baseball Player, 13-Year-Old
Time period(s): 2000s
Locale(s): Iowa

Summary: Moving from Minneapolis, where she was a star on the boys' baseball team, to Iowa, Joelle is appalled to learn she's not allowed to play on the boys' team. Though she's encouraged to play on the girls' softball team, she really prefers baseball, as she faithfully explains the differences between the two sports. After speaking to all levels of school system bureaucracy, from coach to principal to superintendent, Joelle is finally convinced that she's never going to be allowed to play baseball for her school team, so she tries a different approach. Instead she sets up a girls baseball league and pulls in potential players from surrounding towns; when the school board reconsiders their stance, and Joelle is invited to join the boys' team, she declines and returns to concentrate on the girls' baseball league she formed. (218 pages)

Where it's reviewed:
Booklist, May 1, 2003, page 1591
Horn Book Guide, Fall 2003, page 363
Kirkus Reviews, May 15, 2003, page 747
School Library Journal, January 2004, page 124

Other books by the same author:
Trading Places with Tank Talbott, 2003

Other books you might like:
Lucy Jane Bledsoe, *Hoop Girlz*, 2002
    Disappointed at not making the A-team, River sets up her own basketball team that compensates for its lack of height and talent by working as a team.
David Klass, *A Different Season*, 1987
    A female second baseman on the boys' baseball team affects star pitcher Jim Roark's usually perfect throw.
Sue Macy, *Girls Got Game: Sports Stories & Poems*, 2001
    Nine poems and an equal number of short stories describe some of the vast array of sports in which women are now able to participate.
Virginia Euwer Wolff, *Bat 6*, 1998
    Two Oregon farm communities play softball against each other every summer, but this year racist feelings from World War II create trouble for both teams.

190

TONI BUZZEO
MARY GRANDPRE, Illustrator

The Sea Chest
(New York: Dial Books for Young Readers, 2002)

Subject(s): Lighthouses; Islands; Sisters
Age range(s): Grades 1-4
Major character(s): Maita, 10-Year-Old, Relative (great-granddaughter); Maita, Aged Person, Aunt; Seaborne, Adoptee, Sister
Time period(s): Indeterminate Past
Locale(s): Halley's Head Light, Maine

Summary: Elderly Auntie Maita remembers her childhood in a story told to a young girl. The only child of lighthouse keepers, young Maita recalls a happy but lonely life on her island home. After one particularly frightening storm Maita and her father walk the shoreline and find a large bundle wrapped in down mattresses. The sounds coming from the bundle lead Maita to hope for a kitten, but once they untie the ropes and remove the down covering they find a leather sea chest with a baby inside. Maita names her new sister Seaborne. Auntie Maita shares the story with Seaborne's great granddaughter, as she awaits the arrival of a sister being adopted from a country across the sea. A concluding author's note in the author's first picture book gives historical background for the legend on which the story is based. (32 pages)

Where it's reviewed:
Booklist, September 15, 2002, page 238
Kirkus Reviews, July 1, 2002, page 949
Publishers Weekly, August 5, 2002, page 72
School Library Journal, August 2002, page 147

Other books you might like:
George Ella Lyon, *One Lucky Girl*, 2000
    A tornado picks up Becky's crib and carries it away, depositing it in a field where her family finds her, still sleeping.
Gloria Rand, *Baby in a Basket*, 1997
    Trappers find a baby, securely bundled in a basket, hours after a sleigh tips over during an Alaskan snowstorm and the basket falls out.
Gretchen Woelfle, *Katje, the Windmill Cat*, 2001
    Flood waters sweep a cradle out of a home. Katje saves the baby by leaping from side to side of the cradle to balance it in the swirling water.

191

MARCIA BYALICK

Quit It
(New York: Delacorte, 2002)

Subject(s): Friendship; Family Life; Mental Health
Age range(s): Grades 4-8
Major character(s): Carrie Kravitz, 7th Grader, Handicapped (Tourette Syndrome); Clyde Paskoff, 6th Grader; Rebecca Peters, 6th Grader
Time period(s): 2000s
Locale(s): Long Island, New York

Summary: Recently diagnosed with Tourette Syndrome, Carrie's spent the summer trying different medications to control her neurological disorder that displays itself through uncontrollable tics, throat clearings, coughs and jerks. She feels like a zombie from the medications and worries about being conspicuous as she starts seventh grade. But she goes ahead and signs up for "Lunch Bunch," a peer counseling group, and the school play; sits with her good friend Clyde, who is obsessive compulsive about mosquitoes and West Nile Virus; and makes friends with new student Rebecca, who doesn't care for Clyde. Carrie wishes her parents would feel more comfortable about her Tourette syndrome, for she certainly works hard at trying to control her tics and throat clearing, and finally becomes bold enough to speak to them about her concern. The problem with Clyde and Rebecca becomes easy to solve once Carrie realizes what makes a real friend; she's lucky Clyde never stopped being one. (171 pages)

Where it's reviewed:
Booklist, October 1, 2002, page 324

Bulletin of the Center for Children's Books, December 2002, page 146

Kirkus Reviews, August 1, 2002, page 123

Library Media Connection, March 2003, page 75

School Library Journal, November 2002, page 158

Other books by the same author:

It's a Matter of Trust, 1995

Other books you might like:

E.R. Frank, *Friction*, 2003

New student Stacy ruins Alex's 8th grade year with her lies and gossip about Alex and their teacher Simon.

Adele Griffin, *Hannah, Divided*, 2002

Away from the family farm, math genius Hannah is miserable at boarding school and becomes obsessively annoying with her counting and tapping.

George Harrar, *Not as Crazy as I Seem*, 2003

Wrongfully accused of tagging lockers upsets Devon, but also forces him to learn techniques to manage his obsessive mannerisms.

Terry Spencer Hesser, *Kissing Doorknobs*, 1998

Tara's behavior becomes so controlling that it takes 30 minutes to complete the doorknob ritual when leaving her house.

Amy Goldman Koss, *The Girls*, 2000

Ringleader Candace manages to whittle her clique from five to four when she decides Maya is out; now the others wonder who's next?

192

BETSY BYARS

Keeper of the Doves

(New York: Viking, 2002)

Subject(s): Sisters; Family Life; Fathers

Age range(s): Grades 3-6

Major character(s): Amen ''Amie'' McBee, Sister (youngest), Daughter; Albert ''Papa'' McBee, Father, Businessman; Mr. Tominski, Recluse, Immigrant

Time period(s): 1890s (1891-1899)

Locale(s): The Willows, Kentucky

Summary: Amie's older twin sisters make fun of Mr. Tominski and try to frighten her with tales about the old man who lives on the family property and keeps doves. Papa does not tolerate their stories because he owes Mr. Tominski a great debt. As Papa tells Amie, Mr. Tominski saved his life after finding him in the woods, injured from a hunting accident, and carrying him home. Since then, Mr. Tominski has been allowed to live at The Willows and Papa provides all his care. Sensitive Amie comes to appreciate the keeper of the doves as a gentle, harmless soul although not everyone in the family shares her opinion. (121 pages)

Where it's reviewed:

Booklist, October 1, 2002, page 322

Bulletin of the Center for Children's Books, January 2003, page 190

Publishers Weekly, August 19, 2002, page 90

Riverbank Review, Winter 2002-2003, page 39

School Library Journal, October 2002, page 158

Other books by the same author:

Little Horse on His Own, 2004

Little Horse, 2002

Me Tarzan, 2000

Disappearing Acts, 1998

Other books you might like:

Jane Buchanan, *The Berry-Picking Man*, 2003

Her mother's insistence on reaching out to eccentric Old Sam angers Meggie but from her example, Meggie learns compassion.

Katherine Paterson, *Preacher's Boy*, 1999

Robbie wrestles with his conscience when he realizes that his foolish actions could lead to the death of an innocent man.

Helen Recorvits, *Goodbye, Walter Malinski*, 1999

A horrible accident unites an immigrant family and the Polish-American community to which they belong.

193

BETSY BYARS
DAVID MCPHAIL, Illustrator

Little Horse

(New York: Henry Holt and Company, 2002)

Series: Early Chapter Book

Subject(s): Animals/Horses; Adventure and Adventurers; Fantasy

Age range(s): Grades 2-3

Major character(s): Little Horse, Horse; Unnamed Character, Child; Unnamed Character, Farmer

Time period(s): Indeterminate

Locale(s): Fictional Country

Summary: Little Horse's sheltered life in his valley ends when he tumbles into the stream while viewing his reflection. Despite his desperate attempts to swim to shore the swift current carries him downstream. Little Horse survives a plunge over a waterfall and a raptor's claws. His refuge in a forest of flowers becomes a place of danger when a very large animal pins him to the ground with his paw. Soon an animal so large his movement shakes the ground retrieves Little Horse and carries him to a large ''cave'' with many very big horses. Little Horse is surprised to discover how small he is in relation to other horses. The farmer passes him to a smaller ''animal'' and Little Horse receives a wooden ''cave'' with hay and oats. Little Horse settles in comfortably while planning his return to the Valley of the Little Horses as soon as he is strong and wise enough for the journey. (45 pages)

Where it's reviewed:

Booklist, March 15, 2002, page 1255

Bulletin of the Center for Children's Books, June 2002, page 357

Horn Book Guide, Fall 2002, page 355

Horn Book, May 2002, page 325

School Library Journal, April 2002, page 101

Other books by the same author:

Me Tarzan, 2000

Ant Plays Bear, 1997

The Joy Boys, 1996 (Yearling First Choice Chapter Book)

Tornado, 1996

Other books you might like:

Hans Christian Andersen, *Thumbelina*, 1997
  A translation by Haugard tells of tiny Thumbelina's near disasters before she's flown to safety by a kind sparrow.
Syd Hoff, *Chester*, 1989
  An "I Can Read Book" describes a wild horse's quest to find a loving home.
Ursula K. Le Guin, *Jane on Her Own: A Catwings Tale*, 1999
  Farm life bores Jane who puts her wings to good use and flies off to find a home more suited to her.
John Petersen, *The Littles*, 1967
  The Tiny family lives a relatively safe life in the walls of the Bigg family's home, but must take special precautions to avoid the house cat.

194

JANIE BYNUM, Author/Illustrator

Pig Enough

(San Diego: Harcourt, Inc., 2003)

Subject(s): Animals/Guinea Pigs; Animals/Pigs; Scouting
Age range(s): Grades K-2
Major character(s): Willy, Guinea Pig, Scout (aspiring); Peyton, Pig, Bully
Time period(s): Indeterminate
Locale(s): Fictional Country

Summary: Sociable Willy tries many activities unsuccessfully. He's not a capable trumpet player, he forgets his lines in the play and he's not able to pitch for the baseball team. When Willy spots a sign announcing sign-ups for a Pig Scout troop he joins the line. Peyton mocks his interest saying Willy doesn't even look like a pig. Willy proclaims that he is "pig enough" and the scout leader adds him to the troop. On the troop's first hike, Willy and Peyton become partners by default, but Peyton doesn't stay with Willy as required. Fortunately, Willy remembers the rules, searches for Peyton and uses his unique guinea pig traits to attract rescuers. Apparently Willy is right; he is "pig enough" and now the entire troop agrees. (32 pages)

Where it's reviewed:
Booklist, October 15, 2003, page 416
Publishers Weekly, August 11, 2003, page 278
School Library Journal, September 2003, page 175

Other books by the same author:
Altoona Up North, 2001
Otis, 2000
Altoona Baboona, 1999

Other books you might like:

Ian Falconer, *Olivia Saves the Circus*, 2001
  Confident Olivia is pig enough to fill the roles of every circus performer when ear infections keep them from performing—or so she says.
Brian Lies, *Hamlet and the Magnificent Sandcastle*, 2001
  Idealist Hamlet is fortunate to have a friend like Quince when a rising tide threatens his safety as the little pig builds a large sandcastle.
Elizabeth Winthrop, *Dumpy La Rue*, 2001
  Dumpy ignores his family's objections and follows his desire to become a dancer.

C

195

MEG CABOT

All-American Girl

(New York: HarperCollins, 2002)

Subject(s): Presidents; Heroes and Heroines; Humor
Age range(s): Grades 6-10
Major character(s): Samantha "Sam" Madison, 10th Grader, Artist; Lucy Madison, Sister (of Sam), Cheerleader; Rebecca Madison, Sister (of Sam); David, Artist, Teenager
Time period(s): 2000s
Locale(s): Washington, District of Columbia

Summary: Individualistic Samantha, with her hair and clothes dyed black, is ensconced between two sisters, a popular cheerleader and a gifted younger one. With art as Sam's main talent, her parents sign her up for a drawing class which she skips on the second day. Waiting outside for her ride, she inadvertently saves the President's life by jumping on an assassin's back, breaking her wrist in her struggle. Suddenly Sam's the coolest kid in school and even has a date with the President's son David, in another hilarious adventure from a popular author. (247 pages)

Where it's reviewed:

Booklist, October 1, 2002, page 311
Bulletin of the Center for Children's Books, December 2002, page 147
Publishers Weekly, June 24, 2002, page 58
School Library Journal, October 2002, page 158
Voice of Youth Advocates, October 2002, page 270

Awards the book has won:
ALA Quick Picks for Reluctant Young Adult Readers, 2003

Other books by the same author:
Mia Tells It Like It Is, 2004
Princess in Pink, 2004
Teen Idol, 2004
Princess in Waiting, 2003
Princess in the Spotlight, 2001
The Princess Diaries, 2000

Other books you might like:
Catherine Clark, *Truth or Dairy*, 2000
    When her boyfriend dumps her, Courtney throws herself into student government, work, and boy-hating.
Julian F. Thompson, *Simon Pure*, 1987
    Simon is the youngest student at Riddle University and his involvement with the daughter of a professor leads to hilarious moments.
Ellen Wittlinger, *Razzle*, 2001
    Kenyon almost gives up tall and independent Razzle for a self-centered sexpot who throws him aside when he can't help her with a modeling career.

196

MEG CABOT

Haunted: A Tale of the Mediator

(New York: HarperCollins, 2003)

Subject(s): Supernatural; Ghosts; Romance
Age range(s): Grades 7-10
Major character(s): Susannah "Suze" Simon, 16-Year-Old, 11th Grader; Paul Slater, 17-Year-Old; Hector "Jesse" De Silva, Spirit
Time period(s): 2000s
Locale(s): Carmel, California

Summary: Being a mediator between the living and the dead poses enough difficulties without Suze having to attend school with a mediator who tried to kill her last summer. Unfortunately, Paul's a real looker and Suze finds herself unwillingly drawn to him, even though she's already fallen for Jesse, the ghost of a cowboy who died in her room over a century ago. And to make matters worse, her brother returns home from college bringing a friend whose revenge-seeking ghost brother accompanies him. This fifth of the series is the first to be published under Meg Cabot's real name. (246 pages)

Where it's reviewed:
Booklist, March 1, 2003, page 1192

Bulletin of the Center for Children's Books, February 2003, page 228

Kliatt, January 2003, page 6

School Library Journal, January 2003, page 133

Voice of Youth Advocates, April 2003, page 61

Other books by the same author:

Darkest Hour, 2001 (written as Jenny Carroll)

Ninth Key, 2001 (written as Jenny Carroll)

Reunion, 2001 (written as Jenny Carroll)

Shadowland, 2000 (written as Jenny Carroll)

Other books you might like:

Lawrence Gordon, *Haunted High*, 2000

Eddie's asked to solve a 1978 car crash because of his ability to communicate with ghosts using his laptop.

Phyllis Reynolds Naylor, *Jade Green: A Ghost Story*, 2000

Judith's green-framed photo of her mother awakens the ghost of a former serving girl; luckily the ghost protects her from a murderous relative.

Stephanie S. Tolan, *The Face in the Mirror*, 1998

Acting in *Richard III*, Jared realizes he must stop the ghost of a 19th-century actor from smothering his half-brother.

Vivian Vande Velde, *There's a Dead Person Following My Sister Around*, 1999

A ghost who wants to return to life takes over Vicki's body and Ted has to figure out how to oust the ghost so his sister can come back.

197

MEG CABOT

Princess in Love

(New York: HarperCollins, 2002)

Series: Princess Diaries. Volume 3

Subject(s): Princes and Princesses; Humor; Identity

Age range(s): Grades 7-10

Major character(s): Amelia "Mia" Renaldo, Royalty (princess), 9th Grader; Lilly Moscovitz, 9th Grader, Entertainer (host of cable program); Frank Gianini, Stepfather, Teacher (algebra); Michael Moscovitz, 12th Grader; Kenny, Boyfriend; Grandmere, Grandmother (of Mia)

Time period(s): 2000s

Locale(s): New York, New York (Manhattan)

Summary: Beginning with the required school assignment on how Thanksgiving was spent in her house, which Mia describes in full detail including her diatribe on the mass genocide of the Indians by the early Pilgrims, the heir to Genovia is back in her third book. Since Mia's father finally admitted to having an heir, albeit an illegitimate one, Mia's life has been forever changed. Her Grandmere supervises her rigorous training to become a princess while Mia continues as a freshman at Albert Einstein High School. Even her school life is different for her algebra teacher, Mr. Gianini, is now her stepfather, Frank. Kenny thinks he's Mia's boyfriend and he likes her as much as she likes the brother of her best friend Lilly, who, to Mia's dismay, seems to be in love with his brilliant lab partner. Through her diary entries, Mia records her life: normal life for any teen who's also a princess, especially one who'll be leaving soon to be introduced to her Genovia subjects. (229 pages)

Where it's reviewed:

Booklist, July 2002, page 1837

Bulletin of the Center for Children's Books, May 2002, page 314

Kliatt, March 2002, page 6

School Library Journal, October 2002, page 160

Voice of Youth Advocates, June 2002, page 114

Other books by the same author:

Mia Tells It Like It Is, 2004 (Princess Diaries Volumes 1-2)

Princess in Pink, 2004 (Princess Diaries Volume 5)

Princess in Waiting, 2003 (Princess Diaries Volume 4)

Princess in the Spotlight, 2001 (Princess Diaries Volume 2)

The Princess Diaries, 2000

Other books you might like:

Kate Brian, *The Princess and the Pauper*, 2003

Princess Carina swaps identities with Julia so she can attend a Toadmuffin concert and Julia can take her place at an embassy ball.

Ellen Conford, *A Royal Pain*, 1986

Abby discovers the wrong parents have brought her up for she's really a princess from Saxony Coburn.

Louise Rennison, *Angus, Thongs and Full-Frontal Snogging: Confessions of Georgia Nicolson*, 2000

In her diary Georgia records her interest in kissing, her appearance and her opposition to most of what the adult world thinks is important.

198

MEG CABOT

Princess in Waiting

(New York: HarperCollins, 2003)

Series: Princess Diaries. Volume 4

Subject(s): Princes and Princesses; Dating (Social Customs)

Age range(s): Grades 5-9

Major character(s): Amelia "Mia" Renaldo, Royalty (princess), 14-Year-Old; Michael Moskowitz, Boyfriend; Grandmere, Grandmother

Time period(s): 2000s

Locale(s): Genovia, Fictional Country; New York, New York

Summary: Over Christmas break Princess Mia travels to Genovia where she's introduced to the Genovian people and stumbles more than a few times as she tries to act like a princess. Somehow the Genovians don't like being lectured to about pollution from the yachts in their harbor, or hearing punny jokes or seeing their admiral accidentally bumped into the ocean. Perhaps because her mind's on her boyfriend Michael, she embroils herself in a parking meter snafu and argues on a regular basis with her Grandmere about a suitor. Her biggest problem arises when Grandmere wants to attend a fancy ball and Mia plans to spend the evening with Michael. (240 pages)

Where it's reviewed:

Booklist, May 15, 2003, page 1660

Bulletin of the Center for Children's Books, May 2003, page 353

School Library Journal, May 2003, page 148

Voice of Youth Advocates, June 2003, page 127

Other books by the same author:
Princess in Pink, 2005 (Princess Diaries Volume 5)
Princess in Training, 2005 (Princess Diaries Volume 6)
Boy Meets Girl, 2004

Other books you might like:
Francess Lantz, *A Royal Kiss*, 2000
   A chance meeting with Prince Sebastian while shopping in a vintage clothing store leads to a fairy-tale romance for Samantha.
Louise Rennison, *Angus, Thongs and Full-Frontal Snogging: Confessions of Georgia Nicolson*, 2000
   In her diary Georgia records her interest in kissing, her appearance and her opposition to most of what the adult world thinks is important.
Patricia C. Wrede, *Dealing with Dragons*, 1990
   Princess Cimorene would rather be a dragon's captive princess than be forced to meet more boring suitors.
Rona S. Zable, *Love at the Laundromat*, 1986
   Joanne finds love at her mother's laundromat but only after hilarious communications about the contents of a laundry basket.

199

MICHAEL CADNUM

Daughter of the Wind

(New York: Orchard Books/Scholastic, 2003)

Subject(s): Vikings; Adventure and Adventurers; Coming-of-Age
Age range(s): Grades 7-10
Major character(s): Hallgerd, Kidnap Victim; Gauk, 17-Year-Old; Hego, Artisan (knife sharpener)
Time period(s): Indeterminate Past
Locale(s): Spjothhof, Norway; Denmark

Summary: In this companion to *Raven of the Waves* the Danes look for a bride for their leader's son and, while raiding Spjothhof, kidnap Hallgerd as their prize. Daughter of a wealthy leader, Hallgerd knows her villagers will rescue her so she stalls for time with her captors. Meanwhile Hego witnesses the kidnapping and, though slow in mind, follows the attackers as far as their boats. Finally returning to the village, he encounters Gauk who believes he's now a berserker, or warrior, since killing a bear and feeling its spirit enter him. The two young men set out in pursuit of Hallgerd and are there just as she manages to escape in a time when violence is part of everyday life. (266 pages)

Where it's reviewed:
Booklist, November 15, 2003, page 591
Bulletin of the Center for Children's Books, December 2003, page 144
Publishers Weekly, July 14, 2003, page 78
School Library Journal, December 2003, page 144
Voice of Youth Advocates, December 2003, page 389

Other books by the same author:
Blood Gold, 2004
Ship of Fire, 2003
The Leopard Sword, 2002
Raven of the Waves, 2001

Redhanded, 2000

Other books you might like:
Henrietta Branford, *The Fated Sky*, 1999
   Though Ran is scheduled to be sacrificed to Odin, she is rescued by the blind harper Toki and taken to Iceland where the two fall in love.
Eloise McGraw, *The Striped Ships*, 1991
   Young Jilly tells the story of the Norman invasion of Saxon England through her work on the famed Bayeux Tapestry.
Gary Paulsen, *Brian's Hunt*, 2003
   Realizing his Cree friends have been killed by a bear, Brian arms himself with bow and arrow and hunts down the marauder.
Rebecca Tingle, *The Edge on the Sword*, 2001
   Traveling to her wedding, Flaed uses all the defensive techniques she's learned when Danish raiders attack her train.

200

MICHAEL CADNUM

Forbidden Forest: The Story of Little John and Robin Hood

(New York: Orchard/Scholastic, 2002)

Subject(s): Middle Ages; Historical; Robbers and Outlaws
Age range(s): Grades 7-10
Major character(s): Robin Hood, Outlaw; John "Little John" Little, Outlaw; Margaret Lea, Widow(er), 16-Year-Old; Red Roger, Outlaw
Time period(s): 12th century
Locale(s): Nottingham, England; Sherwood Forest, England

Summary: After accidentally killing a knight, who was about to do the same to his employer the ferry master, John Little takes off for the forest with a band of angry ferry passengers at his heels. A small-time thief since his father died three years earlier, John first meets the outlaw Red Roger, but quickly abandons him once he realizes the man is dishonorable. Trying to survive, but knowing he will do better with a group of people, John encounters the legendary Robin Hood and, after their battle with quarterstaffs, becomes part of Robin's group of "merry men." At the same time, Margaret Lea is newly wed to a wealthy knight who is murdered on their wedding night; accused of the crime, Margaret and her maid also flee to the forest where they join up with Robin Hood. Margaret and John, now called Little John, find they are drawn to one another in this author's second book about Robin Hood. (218 pages)

Where it's reviewed:
Booklist, April 15, 2002, page 1394
Bulletin of the Center for Children's Books, June 2002, page 357
Horn Book, July 2002, page 453
School Library Journal, June 2002, page 130
Voice of Youth Advocates, April 2002, page 38

Awards the book has won:
Smithsonian's Notable Books for Children, 2002

Other books by the same author:
Raven of the Waves, 2001
The Book of the Lion, 2000
In a Dark Wood, 1998

Other books you might like:
Robin McKinley, *The Outlaws of Sherwood*, 1988
    A realistic reworking of the story of Robin Hood with Robin portrayed as an ordinary man.
Nancy Springer, *Rowan Hood: Outlaw Girl of Sherwood Forest*, 2001
    Daughter of the famed Robin Hood, Rowan seeks him out after her mother is killed, though she prefers to establish her own band of outlaws.
Theresa Tomlinson, *The Forestwife*, 1995
    Running away from an arranged marriage, Mary finds shelter with the Forestwife from whom she learns to be an herbalist in this Robin Hood retelling.
Jane Yolen, *Sherwood: Original Stories from the World of Robin Hood*, 2000
    Eight stories explore the life around Sherwood Forest, though not necessarily from the original Robin Hood's perspective.

201

MICHAEL CADNUM

The Leopard Sword

(New York: Viking, 2002)

Subject(s): Knights and Knighthood; Middle Ages; Crusades
Age range(s): Grades 7-10
Major character(s): Hubert, 18-Year-Old, Servant (squire); Edmund, Servant (squire); Nigel, Knight; Rannulf, Knight; John, Royalty (prince)
Time period(s): 12th century
Locale(s): *San Raffaello*, At Sea; Rome, Italy; London, England

Summary: Following the Battle of Acre in the 12th century, squires Hubert and Edmund accompany their knights Sir Nigel and Sir Rannulf back to England. Their sea voyage is treacherous as they continually dodge harassing Saracens and then must reach the safety of shore after their ship sinks. Seeking shelter in Rome, they manage to avoid the outlaws and drunks who plague the streets of Rome, and continue on to England. Arriving there, they discover more problems, for Prince John has assumed power and Edmund's crime, though to have been erased by his servitude in the Crusades, holds the threat of imprisonment. To save his friend, Hubert must enter into a trial by combat in this sequel to *The Book of the Lion*. (195 pages)

Where it's reviewed:
Booklist, August 2002, page 1945
Bulletin of the Center for Children's Books, January 2003, page 191
Kliatt, September 2002, page 8
School Library Journal, October 2002, page 160
Voice of Youth Advocates, December 2002, page 374

Other books by the same author:
Blood Gold, 2004

Daughter of the Wind, 2003
Ship of Fire, 2003
Raven of the Waves, 2001 (Smithsonian's Notable Books for Children)
The Book of the Lion, 2000

Other books you might like:
Joan Elizabeth Goodman, *The Winter Hare*, 1996
    Will has always wanted to be a knight; his dream comes true when he helps Empress Matilda escape and is allowed to use the winter hare on his shield.
Gerald Morris, *The Squire, His Knight & His Lady*, 1999
    The squire to one of the knights of the Round Table hopes that someday he can be a bit more important.
Katherine Paterson, *Parzival: The Quest of the Grail Knight*, 1998
    An unsophisticated lad, Parzival mounts a sway-backed nag and goes in search of King Arthur; his desire to excel overcomes his bumbling moments.
Frances Temple, *The Ramsay Scallop*, 1994
    Two young people go on a pilgrimage on behalf of their village in the aftermath of the Crusades.

202

DEB CALETTI

The Queen of Everything

(New York: Simon Pulse/Simon & Schuster, 2002)

Subject(s): Family Problems; Murder
Age range(s): Grades 9-12
Major character(s): Jordan McKenzie, 17-Year-Old; Melissa Beene, 17-Year-Old; Kal Kramer, Boyfriend (of Jordan); Gayle D'Angelo, Neighbor, Wealthy; Vince McKenzie, Father (of Jordan); Claire, Mother (of Jordan)
Time period(s): 2000s
Locale(s): Parrish Island, Washington (fictional island as part of the San Juan Islands in Puget Sound)

Summary: Eventually living with her hippie mother becomes too much for Jordan and she decides to leave the boarding house, with its eccentric roomers, her mother's boyfriend and their new baby, and move in with her ordinary father. Life with her father seems normal, and if anyone had asked, Jordan would have said her mother Claire was the crazy one while her father Vince was a sane, normal parent. Jordan makes friends with Melissa down the street, dates bad boy Kal, and worries when she notices how obsessed her father is with their wealthy neighbor Mrs. D'Angelo. Jordan even speaks to her grandfather about her concerns, but when her grandfather dies, she immediately fears it's her fault. Then her father's obsession turns to murder when Mrs. D'Angelo manipulates him into killing her husband. Now Vince McKenzie awaits trial and Jordan returns home to her mother to ponder how this "nice, sweet man" could have committed murder in this author's first novel. (372 pages)

Where it's reviewed:
Bulletin of the Center for Children's Books, January 2003, page 185
Kliatt, January 2003, page 13
Publishers Weekly, November 18, 2002, page 62
School Library Journal, November 2002, page 158

Voice of Youth Advocates, February 2003, page 465

Other books by the same author:
Honey, Baby, Sweetheart, 2004

Other books you might like:
Robert Cormier, *Tenderness*, 1997
    When a girl he cares for accidentally drowns, a serial killer knows the police will claim he murdered her.
Julius Lester, *When Dad Killed Mom*, 2001
    Siblings Jeremy and Jenna struggle to understand why their father killed their mother and then lied about it in the courtroom.
C.D. Payne, *Youth in Revolt: The Journals of Nick Twisp*, 1996
    Nick's diaries reveal his struggle to deal with his parents' divorce, figure out what high school's all about and examine his widening world.
Alan Watt, *Diamond Dogs*, 2000
    When Neil's sheriff father hides the evidence of an accidental death caused by Neil, they are forever linked in a chilling, destructive bond.
Ellen Wittlinger, *The Long Night of Leo and Bree*, 2002
    Upset about his sister's murder, Leo kidnaps Bree planning to kill her, but a night of talking changes his mind.

203

DIA CALHOUN

White Midnight

(New York: Farrar Straus Giroux, 2003)

Subject(s): Social Classes; Tolerance
Age range(s): Grades 7-10
Major character(s): Rose Chandler, 15-Year-Old; Mr. Brae, Landowner; Raymont Brae, Teenager
Time period(s): Indeterminate Past
Locale(s): Greengarden, Fictional Country

Summary: Timid, asthmatic, fearful and told she's unattractive, it's no wonder Rose is happiest when she's gardening in Greengarden Orchard, owned and neglected by Mr. Brae. Daughter of a bondfamily who are indebted to Mr. Brae, the Chandlers can hardly say no when he offers them freedom, status and money if they'll allow Rose to marry his grandson and bear him an heir. Though this sounds like an appealing offer, the reality is that "The Thing" has been kept locked in the attic since his birth, which killed his mother Amberly. Rose agrees, for there isn't much else she can say, and at first works in Mr. Brae's home until she feels comfortable there. Finally the time comes for her to meet "The Thing" and she wonders if she'll be brave enough in this prequel to *Firegold*. (289 pages)

Where it's reviewed:
Booklist, September 15, 2003, page 231
Library Media Connection, March 2004, page 66
Publishers Weekly, December 1, 2003, page 59
School Library Journal, March 2004, page 203
Voice of Youth Advocates, December 2003, page 410

Awards the book has won:
ALA Best Books for Young Adults, 2004

Other books by the same author:
Aria of the Sea, 2000
Firegold, 1999

Other books you might like:
Robin McKinley, *Beauty: A Retelling of the Story of Beauty and the Beast*, 1978
    A romantic reworking of the classic story of the young girl who overlooks the beast's ugliness and sees his kind heart.
Robin McKinley, *Rose Daughter*, 1997
    Twenty years after the publication of *Beauty*, the author returns to the story of Beauty and the Beast with a more powerful, mature version.
Donna Jo Napoli, *Beast*, 2000
    Transformed into a lion, Persian Prince Orasmyn wanders until the scent of roses draws him to an abandoned castle in France where he meets Belle.

204

ANNIE CALLAN

Taf: A Novel

(Chicago: Cricket Books, 2002)

Subject(s): Runaways; Coming-of-Age
Age range(s): Grades 8-11
Major character(s): Taffy "Taf" Stetson, Teenager
Time period(s): 1910s (1915-1918)
Locale(s): Pacific Northwest

Summary: Living with her mother and abusive stepfather, Taffy accidentally drops one of her twin brothers one day and, afraid that she's killed him, runs away from home. Thinking she'll find her father who abandoned his family to travel to Oregon, Taf sets out and meets more than one intriguing character. First she falls in love with a bead artist who's part Nez Perce and Chinese, then with a policeman who has twins and is looking for a wife. Over a span of four years, she roams the Pacific Northwest, never finding her father, but finally accepting that she's enjoying her growing self-confidence, in this first novel from a poet. (248 pages)

Where it's reviewed:
Kirkus Reviews, November 1, 2001, page 1546
Kliatt, March 2002, page 7
Publishers Weekly, November 19, 2001, page 68
School Library Journal, January 2002, page 131
Voice of Youth Advocates, April 2002, page 38

Other books by the same author:
The Back Door: Poems, 1995

Other books you might like:
Kathleen Karr, *Gold-Rush Phoebe*, 1998
    Phoebe runs away to the gold fields of California, doesn't find gold, and opens a restaurant instead.
Gayle Pearson, *The Coming Home Cafe*, 1988
    During the Depression Elizabeth looks for coal at the Chicago train yard where she meets Eddie and rides the rails with him in search of work.
Rodman Philbrick, *Max the Mighty*, 1998
    Abused by her stepfather, Rachel is kidnapped by Max and together they travel to a Montana ghost town where she hopes to find her real father.

Betrayed!

(New York: Atheneum/Simon & Schuster, 2002)

Subject(s): Frontier and Pioneer Life; Indians of North America; Animals/Dogs

Age range(s): Grades 5-8

Major character(s): Tyler Bohannon, 14-Year-Old; Isaac Peerce, Slave (freed); Sooner, Dog; Captain Little, Shipowner; Iron Shell, Chieftain, Indian (Sioux); Mary ''Many Horses'' Burden, Captive

Time period(s): 1860s (1867)

Locale(s): St. Joseph, Missouri; Fort Benton, Montana

Summary: With the blessings of his mother and stepfather, Tyler, his dog Sooner and his good friend Isaac set out West to make their fortune. They find work about the keelboat *Darlin' Nell* which is heading toward the Montana Territory to trade with the Indians. The trading gathering explodes in violence and to maintain relations, Tyler and Isaac are given as a peace offering in exchange for a dead warrior of the Sioux. Tyler can't believe they're being traded and that he has to go with Iron Shell and leave behind his dog, his rifle and his money. Once in the Indian camp, Tyler finds that his white skin works against him as the Indians naturally prefer Isaac with his darker coloring, and Tyler's life is now one of slavery. Befriending Many Horses, Tyler's amazed to discover she's also white but has been raised by the Sioux following an Indian raid. Though Many Horses doesn't wish to leave her Indian family, she secures horses for Tyler and Isaac so they can escape and continue on their way to the West, now happily joined by Sooner. (212 pages)

Where it's reviewed:

Booklist, July 2002, page 1841
Horn Book Guide, Fall 2002, page 368
Kirkus Reviews, April 1, 2002, page 488
School Library Journal, June 2002, page 130
Voice of Youth Advocates, April 2002, page 38

Other books by the same author:

Michael, Wait for Me, 2000
Sooner, 1998
The American Frontier, 1997 (Nonfiction)
Glennis, Before and After, 1996
Bigger, 1994

Other books you might like:

Marty Crisp, *Private Captain: A Novel of Gettysburg*, 2001
When Ben can't find his brother Reuben at Gettysburg, he returns home but leaves behind Reuben's dog to search for him.
Kristiana Gregory, *The Legend of Jimmy Spoon*, 1990
Two Shoshone boys offer Jimmy a horse to come visit their camp; he doesn't realize his stay is meant to be permanent.
Brian Jacques, *Castaways of the Flying Dutchman*, 2001
Neb and his dog Den are tossed overboard from the *Flying Dutchman* just after an angel curses its crew to forever sail the sea.

Gary Paulsen, *Call Me Francis Tucket*, 1995
Captured by Pawnee Indians and then rescued by Mr. Grimes, Francis continues west across the prairie looking for his parents' wagon train.
Mark Twain, *The Adventures of Huckleberry Finn*, 1885
The classic adventure of the slave Jim and young Huck, two runaways who flee Huck's abusive father and float down the Mississippi River.

206

ANN CAMERON

Colibri

(New York: Frances Foster Books/Farrar Straus Giroux, 2003)

Subject(s): Kidnapping; Indians of Central America

Age range(s): Grades 5-8

Major character(s): Tzunun ''Rosa Garcia'' Chumil, 12-Year-Old, Crime Victim; Baltasar Om, Kidnapper, Con Artist; Celestina Tuc, Friend (seer)

Time period(s): 2000s

Locale(s): San Sebastian, Guatemala

Summary: Stolen from her parents when she was young, Tzunun, now called Rosa, can barely remember her early life, remembering only the time she has spent with Uncle. Told that Rosa will bring him a fortune, Uncle has kept her by his side as they travel from village to village begging; sometimes Uncle is blind and sometimes he's lame, but he's always a thief and a cheat. This bothers Rosa immensely as one memory from her childhood is her mother admonishing her to ''be honest.'' Consulting the fortune teller Dona Celestina, Uncle decides have Rosa help him steal a valuable statue, Holy Maria of the Lilies, from a church in San Sebastian. This dishonesty is beyond what Rosa can tolerate and she gathers her courage to tell the plan to the priest, though she's terrified of Uncle's possible retribution. Uncle is caught and jailed and Rosa travels to Dona Celestina's home where she's taken in; one final confrontation with Uncle reveals the secrets of her early life and offers Rosa the chance to be reunited with her family. (227 pages)

Where it's reviewed:

Booklist, October 1, 2003, page 324
Bulletin of the Center for Children's Books, October 2003, page 52
Horn Book, September 2003, page 607
Publishers Weekly, July 21, 2003, page 196
School Library Journal, October 2003, page 162

Awards the book has won:

ALA Notable Children's Books, 2004
School Library Journal Best Books, 2003

Other books by the same author:

The Secret Life of Amanda K. Woods, 1998

Other books you might like:

Caroline B. Cooney, *What Janie Found*, 2000
Kidnapped and living with the family that raised her rather than her biological one, Janie has finally come to terms with her own feelings.
Ben Mikaelsen, *Red Midnight*, 2002
Fleeing their village when soldiers kill his family, Santiago

and Angelina sail from Guatemala to Florida seeking safety.

Susan Beth Pfeffer, *Twice Taken*, 1994

> While watching a television show, Brooks recognizes her father's picture and realizes he took her from her mother's custody eleven years ago.

207

ANN CAMERON
LIS TOFT, Illustrator

Gloria Rising

(New York: Frances Foster Books/Farrar Straus Giroux, 2002)

Subject(s): Self-Awareness; Schools; African Americans
Age range(s): Grades 2-4
Major character(s): Gloria Jones, 4th Grader, Friend; Julian Bates, 4th Grader, Friend; Grace Street, Astronaut; Mrs. Yardley, Teacher
Time period(s): 2000s
Locale(s): United States

Summary: Sent to the store to buy an onion, Gloria happens to meet Dr. Grace Street when she catches the onion Gloria tosses in the air while waiting in line. That chance encounter becomes a tremendous help to Gloria, Julian and their classmates during a challenging academic year with Mrs. Yardley, a strict, judgmental teacher who does not believe that Gloria actually met Dr. Street. At Mrs. Yardley's suggestion Gloria writes to Dr. Street asking her to confirm their meeting. No letter comes in response, but one day Dr. Street appears as a guest visitor in the class. Her lesson about overcoming fear and changing behavior is a turning point for the students and Mrs. Yardley. A concluding author's note gives web links for additional information about astronauts and NASA. (98 pages)

Where it's reviewed:

Booklist, February 15, 2002, page 1032
Bulletin of the Center for Children's Books, April 2002, page 273
New York Times Book Review, June 2, 2002, page 30
Publishers Weekly, April 1, 2002, page 85
School Library Journal, March 2002, page 172

Other books by the same author:

Gloria's Way, 2000
More Stories Huey Tells, 1997
More Stories Julian Tells, 1986

Other books you might like:

David A. Adler, *School Trouble for Andy Russell*, 1999
> The substitute in Andy's classroom blames the creative underachiever for mishaps that are the work of another student.

Beverly Cleary, *Ramona Quimby, Age 8*, 1981
> Spirited Ramona continues her adventures as she enters third grade in this Newbery Honor book.

Trisha Magraw, *Cowgirl Megan*, 1995
> In a title in the Magic Attic Club series, Megan's friends doubt she'll be able to achieve her dream of becoming a diplomat.

208

ANN CAMPBELL
HOLLY MEADE, Illustrator

Queenie Farmer Had Fifteen Daughters

(San Diego: Silver Whistle/Harcourt, Inc., 2002)

Subject(s): Mothers and Daughters; Single Parent Families; Tall Tales
Age range(s): Grades K-2
Major character(s): Queenie Farmer, Single Mother
Time period(s): Indeterminate Past
Locale(s): Fictional Country

Summary: After giving birth to fifteen daughters, Queenie Farmer loses her prized herd of cows and her husband who takes off after the cows and never returns. Undaunted, Queenie Farmer tackles the job of raising fifteen girls, dressing them in black and white spotted dresses so they are somewhat reminiscent of the lost cow herd. The monotonous passage of time is marked by Queenie's "super mom" response to her daughters' few requests. On their sixth birthday she bakes each one an individual cake, after grinding the flour, milking the cow, churning the butter and gathering the eggs. By the time the girls are 12 they are no longer willing to sleep in the barn's hayloft so Queenie single-handedly builds beds, weaves bedspreads and stuffs pillows with feathers for their individually decorated rooms. Queenie's zealous efforts continue through dating, marriages and the arrival of 55 grandchildren who visit Queenie every Sunday. The other days of the week Queenie indulges herself for a change. (32 pages)

Where it's reviewed:

Booklist, March 1, 2002, page 1148
Horn Book Guide, Fall 2002, page 321
Horn Book, July 2002, page 442
Publishers Weekly, April 1, 2002, page 82
School Library Journal, August 2002, page 148

Other books by the same author:

Dora's Box, 1998

Other books you might like:

Benedicte Guettier, *The Father Who Had 10 Children*, 1999
> A single father with 10 children is one busy man who discovers, when he takes a little time for himself, how much he misses his children.

Mary Ann Hoberman, *The Seven Silly Eaters*, 1997
> Patient Mrs. Peters indulgently prepares food to satisfy each of her seven persnickety, hungry children.

Kate Lum, *What! Cried Granny: An Almost Bedtime Story*, 1999
> Granny goes to great lengths to solve the problems that threaten to keep Patrick's first sleepover at her house from being successful.

209

F. ISABEL CAMPOY
JOSE ARUEGO, Illustrator
ARIANE DEWEY, Illustrator

Rosa Raposa

(San Diego: Gulliver Books/Harcourt, Inc., 2002)

Subject(s): Trickster Tales; Animals/Foxes; Animals/Jaguars
Age range(s): Grades K-3
Major character(s): Rosa Raposa, Fox, Trickster; Chango-
monkey, Monkey, Friend; Jaguar, Jaguar
Time period(s): Indeterminate
Locale(s): Amazon Jungle, Brazil

Summary: Three times Rosa Raposa faces the feared Jaguar and each time she lives to tell the tale. Jaguar tricks Chango-monkey into freeing him from a pit trap with the intention of eating his rescuer. Rosa Raposa saves Chango-monkey by tricking the boastful Jaguar into showing how he was rescued and then trapping him again. Later, when Jaguar finds Rosa Raposa happily swinging from a liana vine the little fox must quickly outfox Jaguar again and she does. Finally, Rosa Raposa's plan to quench her thirst while avoiding Jaguar almost causes her to suffer bee stings but a quick leap in the river sends the bees to vent their anger on Jaguar. (32 pages)

Where it's reviewed:
Booklist, September 1, 2002, page 136
Bulletin of the Center for Children's Books, November 2002, page 100
Horn Book, January 2003, page 53
Publishers Weekly, September 9, 2002, page 66
School Library Journal, September 2002, page 181

Other books by the same author:
Flying Dragons, 2001 (Alma Flor Ada, co-author)
Rimas/Rhymes, 1999 (Alma Flor Ada, co-author)

Other books you might like:
Jim Aylesworth, *The Tale of Tricky Fox: A New England Trickster Tale*, 2001
   Tricky Fox attempts to win a bet with Brother Fox but meets his comeuppance before he succeeds.
Gerald McDermott, *The Fox and the Stork*, 1999
   Fox's trick on Stork backfires and when she returns his dinner invitation, Fox goes home hungry.
Tim Myers, *Basho and the Fox*, 2000
   A fox tricks Basho into a haiku contest to determine who has the right to eat the cherries from a tree near Basho's hut.

210

KATE CANN

Hard Cash

(New York: Simon Pulse, 2003)

Subject(s): Wealth; Art
Age range(s): Grades 9-12
Major character(s): Richard Steele, 17-Year-Old, Artist
Time period(s): 2000s
Locale(s): England

Summary: Ironically called Rich, he's sick of always being broke with no money for dates, art supplies or a pint at the pub and no hope of lots of cash in the future. Unexpectedly his artistic talent pays off when he's wooed by the head of an ad agency who gives him wads of money. Suddenly Rich is able to do all he's ever wanted, from attending great parties to wearing expensive threads, but he discovers that having cash and knowing how to spend it is just as difficult as having none in this first of a trilogy. (327 pages)

Where it's reviewed:
Booklist, February 1, 2004, page 968
Bulletin of the Center for Children's Books, December 2003, page 145
Kliatt, November 2003, page 12
Publishers Weekly, October 13, 2003, page 80
School Library Journal, November 2003, page 134

Other books by the same author:
Diving In, 2005
In the Deep End, 2005
Sink or Swim, 2005
Shacked Up, 2004
Speeding, 2004

Other books you might like:
Robin Brancato, *Uneasy Money*, 1986
   When 18-year-old Mike wins $2.5 million in the lottery, his friends brim with suggestions on ways to spend it.
Rosie Rushton, *Just Don't Make a Scene, Mum*, 1999
   In this first of a series, five British teens find their lives connected through a radio show that lets them describe embarrassing moments.
Neal Shusterman, *The Eyes of Kid Midas*, 1992
   The magical sunglasses Kevin finds on a sacred mountain answer his every wish, but his problems expand with each granted request.

211

A.E. CANNON
ELWOOD H. SMITH, Illustrator

On the Go with Pirate Pete and Pirate Joe

(New York: Puffin Books, 2002)

Series: Puffin Easy-to-Read. Level 3
Subject(s): Pirates; Humor; Conduct of Life
Age range(s): Grades 1-3
Major character(s): Pete, Pirate; Joe, Pirate
Time period(s): Indeterminate Past
Locale(s): Fictional Country

Summary: Despite their intention to be pirates, Pirate Pete and Pirate Joe are lacking some of the necessary pirate accoutrements such as a ship. When they spot one for sale they both realize that they are afraid of the water so maybe using a ship for transportation is not a good idea. The pirate captain of the ship sells them his pirate van instead and Pirate Joe and Pirate Pete happily drive to the pet shop to purchase a parrot. After seeing what's available they decide to buy the gray one with the patch over its eye despite the shop owner's concern that the parrot knows only one word. For Pirate Pete and Pirate Joe the parrot and its vocabulary are perfect. Yo ho! (32 pages)

Where it's reviewed:

Bulletin of the Center for Children's Books, September 2002, page 8
Horn Book Guide, Fall 2002, page 351
Kirkus Reviews, May 1, 2002, page 650
School Library Journal, August 2002, page 148
Tribune Books, June 30, 2002, page 5

Other books by the same author:

Let the Good Times Roll with Pirate Pete and Pirate Joe, 2004
I Know What You Do When I Go to School, 1996

Other books you might like:

Ariane Dewey, *Lafitte, the Pirate*, 1985
    Historical fiction in a beginning reader explores the exploits of a famous pirate.
Leonard Kessler, *The Pirates Adventure on Spooky Island*, 1979
    A bumbling pirate captain depends on his capable parrot to help him capture Bad Bart.
Danier Laurence, *Captain and Matey Set Sail*, 2001
    Four brief stories in a beginning reader capture the individuality of Captain and Matey.

212

NAN WILLARD CAPPO

Cheating Lessons

(New York: Simon & Schuster, 2002)

Subject(s): Cheating; Contests; Schools/High Schools
Age range(s): Grades 7-10
Major character(s): Bernadette Ternell, 11th Grader; Mr. Malory, Teacher (English)
Time period(s): 2000s
Locale(s): Michigan

Summary: Bernadette can't believe that she had the highest marks on the qualifying test for the statewide competition called the Classics Bowl. Though she's thrilled, and eager to beat her debating rivals from a snooty private school, she can't figure out how she, and her teammates, could possibly have answered enough questions to achieve their score. Concerned that something's amiss, Bernadette snoops around and realizes that her gorgeous English teacher Mr. Malory, on whom every girl in school has a crush, may be responsible for the shenanigans. Talking to her parents, she's further dismayed to realize her mother thinks Bernadette should keep her mouth shut and compete. What is it with adults and cheating? Luckily Bernadette is clever enough to figure out how to maintain her self-respect in this first novel that examines the pervasive problem of cheating. (234 pages)

Where it's reviewed:

Booklist, March 15, 2002, page 1250
Horn Book, March 2002, page 209
Publishers Weekly, January 7, 2002, page 65
School Library Journal, March 2002, page 226
Voice of Youth Advocates, February 2002, page 432

Other books you might like:

Linda Ellerbee, *Girl Reporter Sinks School!*, 2000
    An overheard conversation in gym class about selling

answers to the math test gives Casey an idea for her next school newspaper article.
E.L. Konigsburg, *The View from Saturday*, 1996
    Chosen by their teacher for the Academic Bowl, four sixth-graders relate their individual stories, which are intriguingly interwoven.
Zilpha Keatley Snyder, *Libby on Wednesday*, 1990
    Libby hates meeting on Wednesdays with four other writing contest winners, but eventually appreciates their help with both writing and family problems.

213

ALYSSA SATIN CAPUCILLI
PAT SCHORIES, Illustrator

Biscuit Goes to School

(New York: HarperCollins Publishers, 2002)

Series: I Can Read Book
Subject(s): Animals/Dogs; Schools; Pets
Age range(s): Grades K-1
Major character(s): Biscuit, Dog
Time period(s): 2000s (2002)
Locale(s): United States

Summary: Biscuit wants to follow his young owner to school, but of course dogs aren't allowed in school. However, after the girl leaves on the bus, Biscuit manages to find his own way to her school. Soon the whole school has made friends with Biscuit, including the girl's teacher. (32 pages)

Where it's reviewed:

Booklist, August 2002, Page 1969
Horn Book Guide, Spring 2003, page 60
Kirkus Reviews, June 15, 2002, page 877

Other books by the same author:

Bathtime for Biscuit, 1998
Biscuit Finds a Friend, 1997
Biscuit, 1996

Other books you might like:

Jonathan London, *Shawn and Keeper: Show and Tell*, 2000
    Shawn brings his dog Keeper to school for show-and-tell and unexpected chaos ensues.
Grace Maccarone, *Mr. Rover Takes Over*, 2001
    When an elementary school class's teacher gets sick the principal sends an unlikely substitute—a dog named Mr. Rover.
Cynthia Rylant, *Henry and Mudge*, 1987
    A lonely little boy adopts a dog and discovers a true friend.

214

ELISA CARBONE

The Pack

(New York: Viking, 2003)

Subject(s): Feral Children; Animals/Wolves; Violence
Age range(s): Grades 7-10
Major character(s): Akhil Vyas, Orphan, Feral Child; Becky Tuttle, 15-Year-Old, 9th Grader; Omar, 9th Grader; Kyle Metzger, Bully

Time period(s): 2000s
Locale(s): Washington, District of Columbia (suburbs of Washington, DC)

Summary: High school misfits, overweight Becky and biracial Omar, befriend new student Akhil, a scarred Hindu. It's difficult for Akhil to adapt to high school rules as he doesn't want to sit in a chair or ask permission to go to the bathroom; when Becky and Omar learn that Akhil was raised by wolves and is being studied by the National Institutes of Health, they better understand his difficulty in adjusting as well as his unique senses. The three learn of white supremacist Kyle Metzger's plan to detonate a bomb at their school and they rely on Akhil's senses to foil this massacre attempt. (153 pages)

Where it's reviewed:
Booklist, February 15, 2003, page 1064
Bulletin of the Center for Children's Books, March 2003, page 267
Publishers Weekly, March 17, 2003, page 77
School Library Journal, March 2003, page 228
Voice of Youth Advocates, April 2003, page 46

Other books by the same author:
Sarah and the Naked Truth, 2000
Starting School with an Enemy, 1998
Stealing Freedom, 1998

Other books you might like:
Mordicai Gerstein, *Victor: A Novel Based on the Life of Victor, the Savage of Aveyron*, 1998
  Captured by woodcutters during the French Revolution, feral child Victor is raised in a school for the deaf in Paris.
Karen Hesse, *The Music of Dolphins*, 1996
  A feral child raised by dolphins is studied by language experts in Boston, but is returned to her real home and family when she sickens.
Ron Koertge, *The Brimstone Journals*, 2001
  Fifteen seniors reveal their thoughts in a series of poems, but one is so angry he wants to retaliate against anyone who's ever made him mad.
Todd Strasser, *Give a Boy a Gun*, 2000
  Student interviews, coupled with facts about shootings, describe two unhappy boys who attend a school dance to shoot students and teachers.

215

ORSON SCOTT CARD

Shadow Puppets

(New York: Tor, 2002)

Subject(s): Self-Acceptance; Political Thriller; Love
Age range(s): Grades 10-Adult
Major character(s): Julian "Bean" Delphiki, Genius; Petra Arkanian, Genius; Peter Wiggin, Genius; Achilles Flandres, Genius
Time period(s): Indeterminate Future
Locale(s): Earth

Summary: The Hegemony is on increasingly shaky ground, in spite of the fact that the mad genius Achilles is being sent to prison by the Chinese. Peter Wiggin, the Hegemon, struggles

to regain political power and believes that he can use Achilles to reassert control. Peter's plan is to stay one step ahead of Achilles' machinations and, at the appropriate moment, reveal that he has saved the world from the madman. When he orders Achilles rescued, Bean promptly resigns. Bean knows that no one has ever used Achilles successfully, so he and Petra flee, hoping to remain unworthy of Achilles' attention. Petra has fallen in love with Bean and, as they travel, begins to convince him that with help, they can have children who do not share Bean's genetically fatal mutation. While Peter is planning and Petra and Bean are breeding, Achilles springs his plot. But the ties of Battle School are immensely powerful, and from within the closed Islamic empire, there is an offer of help. (352 pages)

Where it's reviewed:
Analog Science Fiction and Fact, February 2003, page 136
Booklist, July 2002, page 1796
Kirkus Reviews, June 15, 2002, page 846
Library Journal, August 2002, page 152
Publishers Weekly, July 15, 2002, page 59

Other books by the same author:
The Crystal City, 2003
Saints, 2001
The Shadow of the Hegemon, 2000

Other books you might like:
Nancy Farmer, *The House of the Scorpion*, 2002
  A drug lord dreams of living forever by taking the body of the boy he has had cloned from himself, in a near future where drug cartels run countries.
William Gibson, *All Tomorrow's Parties*, 1999
  The disturbance in the future that Laney feels in Tokyo is the artificial intelligence struggling to be born in flesh in San Francisco.
Eva Hoffman, *The Secret*, 2002
  Iris begins to doubt her humanity when she discovers her mother's secret, that Iris is a clone.

216

JANET LEE CAREY

Wenny Has Wings

(New York: Atheneum/Simon & Schuster, 2002)

Subject(s): Brothers and Sisters; Grief; Near-Death Experience
Age range(s): Grades 4-7
Major character(s): Will North, 11-Year-Old; Wenny North, Child, Sister (of Will); Mr. James, Religious (church youth leader)
Time period(s): 2000s
Locale(s): United States

Summary: Will and his sister Wenny are walking to the store when a runaway truck hits them. As Will later relates, after being struck he saw Wenny heading toward the light and was following her into the tunnel when he thought of his parents and was pulled back to life; actually, it was Dr. Westfall using electric paddles on his heart that brought him back. Now Will is left as the survivor to deal with his parents' grief as well as his own, which can be overwhelming at times. Given a notebook by Mr. James who explains that he often writes letters to God when he's troubled, Will instead writes to his sister explaining how much he misses her and how mad he is that she left him. He even tries to contact her through messages in helium balloons and seances; eventually his entire family receives counseling so Will can deal with his near-death experience and his parents with their grief. (232 pages)

Where it's reviewed:
Booklist, July 2002, page 1841
Bulletin of the Center for Children's Books, July 2002, page 396
Kirkus Reviews, June 1, 2002, page 801
Publishers Weekly, July 15, 2002, page 74
School Library Journal, July 2002, page 114

Other books by the same author:
The Double Life of Zoe Flynn, 2004
Molly's Fire, 2000

Other books you might like:
Mary E. Pearson, *David v. God*, 2000
    Killed on a biology field trip, David isn't ready to die so he challenges God to a debate; luckily the captain of the debate team is there to coach him.
Frederick Reiken, *The Odd Sea*, 1998
    Philip has a birdwatching class so he doesn't join his brother Ethan on a walk around the pond, which is the last time Ethan is ever seen.
Cynthia Rylant, *The Heavenly Village*, 1999
    For those people not quite ready for Heaven, God has provided the Heavenly Village where one is able to live partly on Earth and partly in Heaven.
William Sleator, *Rewind*, 1999
    Hit by a car, Peter is told he's not "permanently dead," instead he has twelve hours to "rewind" and change events preceding his accident.

217

ERIC CARLE, Author/Illustrator

Slowly, Slowly, Slowly, said the Sloth
(New York: Philomel Books, 2002)

Subject(s): Behavior; Animals
Age range(s): Grades K-3
Major character(s): Unnamed Character, Sloth
Time period(s): Indeterminate
Locale(s): South America (Amazon Rain Forest)

Summary: Sloth eats, crawls and ponders in a slow, slow way. Day and night, rain or shine, the sloth hangs upside down in a tree. Other animals in the forest wonder why the sloth is so quiet, slow and boring but the sloth has no answers. Finally, when asked why it is lazy, the sloth considers the question carefully (and slowly) and replies with a list of descriptive adjectives that identify its nature as anything but lazy. Then the relaxed, peaceful creature states, "That's just the way I am. I like to do things slowly, slowly, slowly." (28 pages)

Where it's reviewed:
Horn Book Guide, Spring 2003, page 9
Kirkus Reviews, August 1, 2002, page 1123
Publishers Weekly, July 1, 2002, page 77

School Library Journal, September 2002, page 181
Smithsonian, December 2002, page 123

Awards the book has won:
ALA Notable Children's Books, 2003
Smithsonian's Notable Books for Children, 2002

Other books by the same author:
The Very Clumsy Click Beetle, 1999
The Very Lonely Firefly, 1995
The Very Quiet Cricket, 1990

Other books you might like:
Helen Lester, *Score One for the Sloths*, 2001
    Student sloths content to sleep and reap the teachers' praise learn a different approach to slothful behavior when perky Sparky enrolls in the class.
Ann Turnbull, *Too Tired*, 1994
    The sloths are almost left behind because they are too tired to climb aboard Noah's Ark.
Jeanne Willis, *Sloth's Shoes*, 1998
    Sloth's friends make a pair of shoes for his fifth birthday that he receives when he finally arrives for the party a year late.

218

RON CARLSON

The Speed of Light
(New York: HarperCollins, 2003)

Subject(s): Summer; Coming-of-Age; Scientific Experiments
Age range(s): Grades 7-10
Major character(s): Witt Dimmick, 12-Year-Old; Rafferty, 12-Year-Old; Lawrence "Larry", 12-Year-Old; Ferguson, Alligator
Time period(s): 1960s
Locale(s): United States

Summary: The trio of Larry, Witt and Rafferty devour summer, with baseball games, enlivened with plugged bats; bike riding; sleep outs in weedy fields; and exploration of the world around them, usually with household chemicals and dangerous experiments. Their best experiment occurs when they try to revive Ferguson, a 5-year-old alligator who was killed by Witt's abusive father. A combination of chemicals, wires and one dead alligator inside a TV cabinet lead to a masterful explosion. Hi-jinks abound as the boys travel effortlessly through one dusty summer day after another. But changes occur, as is inevitable when one is growing up, and Larry's attention turns to girls, Rafferty's to other friends and Witt's to survival as he seeks refuge at his uncle's home in this author's first novel for young people. (280 pages)

Where it's reviewed:
Booklist, August 2003, page 1976
Kirkus Reviews, June 1, 2003, page 801
Publishers Weekly, July 7, 2003, page 73
School Library Journal, July 2003, page 124
Voice of Youth Advocates, October 2003, page 301

Other books by the same author:
A Kind of Flying: Selected Stories, 2003
At the Jim Bridger: Stories, 2002

Other books you might like:
Morse Hamilton, *The Garden of Eden Motel*, 1999
  Falling in love, working in the bean fields, and getting to
  know his stepfather add up to a top-notch summer for Del.
Sid Hite, *Cecil in Space*, 1999
  Cecil bemoans summertime in a boring town, but finds
  there's lots to do as he watches baseball, helps his friend
  Isaac, and notices girls.
Gary Paulsen, *Harris and Me: A Summer Remembered*, 1994
  A summer of pig wrestling, outmaneuvering a testy barn
  cat and peeing on an electric fence make many memories
  for ''Harris and Me.''
Clay Reynolds, *Monuments*, 2000
  Hugh's quiet summer disappears when his town decides to
  demolish an ugly old building.

219

WILLIAM CARMAN, Author/Illustrator

What's That Noise?

(New York: Random House, 2002)

Subject(s): Imagination; Bedtime
Age range(s): Grades K-3
Major character(s): Unnamed Character, Child, Son
Time period(s): 2000s (2002)
Locale(s): United States

Summary: In the author's first children's book a strange sound
awakens a little boy. He wonders if it's the neighbor's lawn
mower but a quick check out the window assures him that's
not it. Then his imagination takes off and he suspects an alien
spaceship, a monster in his closet or an octopus in the bathtub.
As he investigates each possibility and rules it out he's drawn
closer and closer to his parents' room. Apparently there is a
bear in the room so he sneaks in to warn his parents. That's
when he discovers the source of all the noise-his snoring
father. (34 pages)

Where it's reviewed:
Booklist, September 15, 2002, page 238
Children's Bookwatch, November 2002, page 5
Kirkus Reviews, June 1, 2002, page 802
Publishers Weekly, June 17, 2002, page 63
School Library Journal, August 2002, page 148

Other books you might like:
Andrea Beck, *Elliot's Noisy Night*, 2002
  Although his friend assures him that he's hearing only
  normal night sounds in his house, Elliot still finds it hard to
  fall asleep.
Michelle Edwards, *What's That Noise?*, 2002
  When strange sounds scare two brothers, the older one
  wonders if he can muster the courage to walk to his
  brother's bed in the dark.
Melinda Long, *When Papa Snores*, 2000
  There's no question about the source of the racket in this
  house. It's definitely Nana and Papa. The question is,
  which one snores louder?

220

MICHAEL CART, Editor

Necessary Noise: Stories about Our Families as They Really Are

(New York: Joanna Cotler/HarperCollins, 2003)

Subject(s): Short Stories; Family Life
Age range(s): Grades 7-10

Summary: What constitutes a family these days when families
have evolved far beyond the traditional notion of mother,
father and two children? This anthology offers a wide range of
family experiences including sibling rivalry, extended families, estranged family members and parent-child relationships. A daughter brings home her rude, minimalist boyfriend
just as the family is trapped inside by weather in Lois Lowry's
hilarious ''Snowstorm.'' ''Visit'' by Walter Dean Myers tells
of a father who abandoned his son 25 years earlier and now is
the last visitor to Death Row to see his son before execution.
Joan Bauer describes a family's attempt to save their small
store against an encroaching ''big box'' superstore in ''Hard-
ware.'' Seven other top young adult authors are included:
Nikki Grimes, Joyce Carol Oates, Sonya Sones, Norma
Howe, Emma Donoghue, Rita Williams-Garcia and editor
Michael Cart. (239 pages)

Where it's reviewed:
Booklist, May 15, 2003, page 1659
Bulletin of the Center for Children's Books, July 2003, page
  439
Horn Book, July 2003, page 452
School Library Journal, June 2003, page 137
Voice of Youth Advocates, June 2003, page 141

Other books by the same author:
911: The Book of Help, 2002
Love and Sex: Ten Stories of Truth, 2001
Tomorrowland: Ten Stories about the Future, 1999
My Father's Scar, 1996

Other books you might like:
Lisa Rowe Fraustino, *Dirty Laundry: Stories about Family
  Secrets*, 1998
  As these 11 original short stories indicate, every family has
  some ''dirty laundry'' they want to keep hidden.
David Gifaldi, *Rearranging and Other Stories*, 1998
  Teenagers mature in many ways and the author captures
  the essence of coming-of-age in these stories.
Chris Lynch, *All the Old Haunts*, 2001
  Short stories revolve around that moment when teens be-
  come aware of the realities of life and have to make
  personal decisions.
Tim Wynne-Jones, *The Book of Changes: Stories*, 1995
  Seven stories narrated by teens tell of ordinary dilemmas
  in their lives, from school assignments to divorce.

221

ANNE LAUREL CARTER
ALAN DANIEL, Illustrator
LEA DANIEL, Illustrator

Under a Prairie Sky

(Custer, WA: Orca, 2002)

Subject(s): Brothers; Animals/Horses; Responsibility
Age range(s): Grades K-3
Major character(s): Unnamed Character, Child, Brother (older); Unnamed Character, Child, Brother (younger)
Time period(s): Indeterminate Past
Locale(s): Canada

Summary: A young boy dreams of joining the Royal Canadian Mounted Police someday, but for now he just helps his parents on their farm. With a thunderstorm approaching, the boy's father tells him to find his younger brother. The boy searches for his brother on horseback and finally finds him at a stream catching frogs. The two boys race back to the barn chased by thunder and lightning, arriving safely just in time. (32 pages)

Where it's reviewed:
Booklist, May 15, 2002, page 1600
Horn Book Guide, Fall 2002, page 322
Resource Links, June 2002, page 1
School Library Journal, June 2002, page 90

Other books by the same author:
My Home Bay, 2004
In the Clear, 2001
Tall in the Saddle, 1999

Other books you might like:
Ann Blade, *A Boy of Tache*, 1977
  When a Canadian Indian boy's grandfather falls ill on a beaver hunt, the boy must go for help.
David Bouchard, *If You're Not from the Prairie*, 1995
  A boy describes all the joys of growing up on the prairie.
Marilyn Reynolds, *The Prairie Fire*, 2001
  Percy must help his father save their home and livestock from the advancing prairie fire.

222

DON CARTER, Author/Illustrator

Get to Work, Trucks!

(Brookfield, CT: Roaring Brook Press, 2002)

Subject(s): Transportation; Work; Construction
Age range(s): Preschool-Kindergarten
Time period(s): 2000s
Locale(s): United States

Summary: Simple, brightly colored illustrations and limited text follow a day in the life of a variety of trucks. As the trucks roll down the road to the construction site numbers and colors are introduced. Working cranes, dump trucks, loaders and bulldozers conceptually communicate opposites such as high/low and big/little. At the end of day the many trucks stop working and go home. This is the first book written and illustrated by this children's book illustrator. (24 pages)

Where it's reviewed:
Booklist, March 1, 2002, page 440
Bulletin of the Center for Children's Books, May 2002, page 314
The New Advocate, Winter 2002, page 80
Publishers Weekly, January 14, 2002, page 58
School Library Journal, March 2002, page 173

Awards the book has won:
Center for Children's Books Best Books, 2002

Other books you might like:
Donald Crews, *Truck*, 1980
  A wordless Caldecott Honor Book follows a truck from the loading of its cargo to delivery destination.
Kate McMullan, *I Stink!*, 2002
  A garbage truck narrates its route through the streets of New York, graphically describing the alphabet of trash it collects.
Peter Sis, *Trucks Trucks Trucks*, 1999
  After cleaning up his large collection of toy trucks, Matt goes outside to watch real trucks in action in an award-winning title.
Sam Williams, *101 Trucks*, 2003
  By lifting the flaps, readers discover what's inside the 101 different trucks rolling down the road.

223

MARLENE CARVELL

Who Will Tell My Brother?

(New York: Hyperion, 2002)

Subject(s): Schools/High Schools; Indians of North America; Identity
Age range(s): Grades 7-10
Major character(s): Evan Hill, 12th Grader, Indian (part Mohawk)
Time period(s): 2000s
Locale(s): New York

Summary: As his father reconnects with his Mohawk relatives on the reservation, Evan realizes the pride he takes in his own part-Mohawk heritage and decides to resume his older brother's attempt to remove his high school's Indian mascot. He's tired and embarrassed having to watch the school cheerleaders don war paint and place paper feather headdresses atop their heads, to look at the fans making tomahawk chopping motions and listen to what the crowds imagine are war whoops. Evan talks to faculty members, the school principal and even the school board, but all he manages to stir up is resentment and an unwillingness to forfeit the mascot. Students come after him with scissors to cut his hair and his brother's dog is found dead lying atop a paper headdress, yet Evan still doesn't let go of his belief that the mascot is wrong in this poignant free verse novel based on an incident in the lives of the author's two sons. (150 pages)

Where it's reviewed:
Book Report, February 2003, page 79
Booklist, July 2002, page 1837
Bulletin of the Center for Children's Books, October 2002, page 51

School Library Journal, July 2002, page 114
Voice of Youth Advocates, June 2002, page 114

Other books you might like:
Avi, *Nothing but the Truth*, 1991
   Philip's attempt to get out of Miss Narwin's class by humming during the playing of the National Anthem is blown out of proportion by the media.
A.E. Cannon, *The Shadow Brothers*, 1990
   When Henry's Navajo heritage is challenged, he leaves his white foster brother to live on the reservation and find his identity.
Jan Cheripko, *Rat*, 2002
   Rat earns the disdain of all his teammates when he tells the judge about their basketball coach's attempt to rape a cheerleader.
Will Hobbs, *Bearstone*, 1990
   Cloyd finds his Indian heritage as he battles for survival in the Colorado mountains.
Hazel Krantz, *Walks in Beauty*, 1997
   It's difficult for young Anita to remain a Navajo while also interacting with segments of the white man's world.
Marsha Qualey, *Revolutions of the Heart*, 1993
   When Cory shows interest in Native American Mac, she becomes the recipient of outrage, disdain and lewd notes from members of her community.

224

MARY CASANOVA
JEAN-PAUL TIBBLES, Illustrator

Cecile: Gates of Gold

(Middleton, WI: American Girl/Pleasant Company, 2002)

Series: Girls of Many Lands
Subject(s): Kings, Queens, Rulers, etc.; Servants
Age range(s): Grades 4-7
Major character(s): Louis I4, Royalty (king); Cecile Revel, 12-Year-Old; Elizabeth Charlotte ''Madame'' d'Orleans, Noblewoman
Time period(s): 18th century
Locale(s): Rileaux, France; Versailles, France

Summary: Living in a small village in France, Cecile helps a noblewoman who injured herself when she fell from her horse. Unbeknownst to Cecile, this woman is the sister-in-law of King Louis I4 and to thank Cecile, lands her a job at court tending to her dogs. The opulence of life at court at first overwhelms Cecile, especially as she has to quickly learn court etiquette, ignore the gossip she overhears and be careful to stay friends with everyone. Cecile also learns that it's important to stay in favor at court, which can be a very difficult task. (191 pages)

Where it's reviewed:
Booklist, October 15, 2002, page 404
Catholic Library World, June 2003, page 283
Horn Book Guide, Spring 2003, page 76
Ruminator Review, Winter 2002, page 41
School Library Journal, September 2002, page 220

Other books by the same author:
When Eagles Fall, 2002

Curse of a Winter Moon, 2000
Stealing Thunder, 1999

Other books you might like:
Karen Cushman, *Catherine, Called Birdy*, 1994
   Although she knows her opinion means nothing, Birdy fights to control her destiny and marriage during the Middle Ages.
Kristiana Gregory, *Eleanor: Crown Jewel of Aquitaine, France, 1136*, 2002
   Eleanor's diary covers her teen years up until she becomes the Queen of France, remembered for her independence and political activism.
Kathryn Lasky, *Marie Antoinette: Princess of Versailles*, 2000
   Two years of Marie Antoinette's life are revealed when she is engaged to the Dauphin of France and gives up childhood ways to become a young wife.

225

MARY CASANOVA
ARD HOYT, Illustrator

One-Dog Canoe

(New York: Melanie Kroupa Books/Farrar Straus Giroux, 2003)

Subject(s): Canoeing; Animals; Stories in Rhyme
Age range(s): Preschool-Grade 1
Major character(s): Unnamed Character, Child; Unnamed Character, Dog
Time period(s): 2000s (2003)
Locale(s): United States

Summary: As a girl loads a picnic basket into her little red canoe her pet climbs in too. Happily the girl paddles away on her trip for two. First one animal and then another, larger too, ask to come aboard and each time the girl agrees until the canoe is so overloaded that a leaping frog, eager to join the activity, causes it to capsize. Now all the animals and the poor picnic basket are in the water enjoying a nice swim. (32 pages)

Where it's reviewed:
Booklist, February 15, 2003, page 1072
Kirkus Reviews, December 15, 2002, page 1846
Publishers Weekly, December 9, 2002, page 81
School Library Journal, March 2003, page 178

Other books by the same author:
The Hunter: A Chinese Folktale, 2000 (ALA Notable Children's Books)

Other books you might like:
Jan Brett, *The Mitten*, 1989
   In an award-winning adaptation of a folktale animals seeking warmth crowd into a lost mitten.
Bernard Waber, *Bearsie Bear and the Surprise Sleepover Party*, 1997
   On a cold winter night, Bearsie Bear's friends come knocking at the door asking to share his warm bed.
Sarah Weeks, *Splish, Splash!*, 1999
   Chub's ''the more the merrier'' attitude soon has his tub overflowing with animals eager to join the fish in the tub.

226

MARY CASANOVA

When Eagles Fall

(New York: Hyperion, 2002)

Subject(s): Animals/Birds; Wilderness Survival; Wildlife Rescue
Age range(s): Grades 5-8
Major character(s): Alexis ''Alex'' Castille-Reed, 13-Year-Old; Russell Reed, Scientist
Time period(s): 2000s
Locale(s): International Falls, Minnesota (Rainy Lake)

Summary: Alex's younger brother died recently from cancer and each of her family members reacts differently to the loss, though each is unable to articulate the link between grief and behavior. Alex drinks too much at a pool party and her mother ''banishes'' her to Minnesota to stay with her father, a noted expert on bald eagles. Up at Rainy Lake he and his team band the eagles and describe their environment. Alex enjoys working with these birds, though she resents her father and the respect his team pays him. Trying to prove her usefulness, she canoes to an island where an eagle nest had been spotted but is difficult to reach because of the fishing lure entangled in its sticks. Alex climbs the tree and removes the lure but accidentally knocks an eaglet to the ground. Realizing its wing is broken, Alex knows she must take it to a wildlife center but a storm comes up and she loses the paddle for her canoe. Stranded on the island, she encounters a bear, hunger, and hundreds of bats before she resourcefully sets a fire to attract attention. Two days of Alex being missing brings her mother to Minnesota and the family finally talks about their loss and their grief in this tale of survival. (152 pages)

Where it's reviewed:
Booklist, June 2002, page 1704
Horn Book Guide, Fall 2002, page 388
Kirkus Reviews, June 15, 2002, page 877
School Library Journal, July 2002, page 114
Voice of Youth Advocates, February 2003, page 465

Other books by the same author:
Cecile: Gates of Gold, 2002
Curse of a Winter Moon, 2000
Stealing Thunder, 1999
Wolf Shadows, 1997
Moose Tracks, 1995

Other books you might like:
Melvin Burgess, *Kite*, 2000
    Told to destroy the eggs of an endangered kite, Tom keeps them; when one hatches, he raises the bird but needs help to train her.
Jean Craighead George, *On the Far Side of the Mountain*, 1990
    Choosing outdoor living as a way of life, Sam battles the elements every day but now must fight illegal trafficking of peregrine falcons.
Sue Mayfield, *I Carried You on Eagle's Wings*, 1991
    Tony and his friend Clare find and care for an injured seagull that they release the same day Tony's mother dies of multiple sclerosis.

227

JUDITH CASELEY, Author/Illustrator

On the Town: A Community Adventure

(New York: Greenwillow Books/HarperCollins Publishers, 2002)

Subject(s): Community Helpers; Neighbors and Neighborhoods; Mothers and Sons
Age range(s): Grades K-3
Major character(s): Charlie, Student—Elementary School, Son; Mama, Mother; Papa, Father
Time period(s): 2000s (2002)
Locale(s): United States

Summary: A school assignment to record the names of people and places in the community fits right in with an afternoon of errands for Charlie and Mama. At each stop Charlie notes the person and the place with a captioned drawing. With his teacher as the first entry, Charlie adds to his book a garbage collector, the police station, a barber, the post office, the pharmacist, a bank teller, a librarian, the waitress at the luncheonette, a fire station where his uncle works, and the train station where he meets Papa returning home from work. At bedtime Charlie remembers that he needs to add one more very important place in the community—home. (32 pages)

Where it's reviewed:
Booklist, April 15, 2002, page 1406
Bulletin of the Center for Children's Books, June 2002, page 358
Horn Book Guide, Fall 2002, page 322
Publishers Weekly, May 20, 2002, page 69
School Library Journal, May 2002, page 105

Awards the book has won:
Notable Social Studies Trade Books for Young People, 2003

Other books by the same author:
Bully, 2001
Field Day Friday, 2000
Mickey's Class Play, 1998

Other books you might like:
Robin Ballard, *My Day, Your Day*, 2001
    Illustrations show the play activities of children in a day care setting paralleling the actual work experiences of their parents.
Kate Banks, *The Night Worker*, 2000
    Many community helpers work at night while the rest of the town sleeps.
Andrea Zimmerman, *Trashy Town*, 1999
    As Mr. Gilly drives the trash truck on its rounds he collects trash from the school, the doctor's office, the park and the pizza parlor.

228

DOMINIC CATALANO, Author/Illustrator

Mr. Basset Plays

(Honesdale, PA: Boyds Mills Press, 2003)

Subject(s): Animals/Dogs; Wealth; Playing
Age range(s): Grades K-3
Major character(s): Reginald E. Basset, Dog, Wealthy

Time period(s): 2000s (2003)
Locale(s): United States

Summary: Mr. Reginald E. Basset has everything money can buy, but he still feels something is missing from his life. After seeing some neighborhood children playing, Mr. Basset decides that play is what he needs. He tries out all the activities that the children are doing, but he is still unsatisfied. With a little help from his butler, Mr. Basset realizes that what he's missing is friends and he joins the neighborhood baseball game for fun and companionship. (32 pages)

Where it's reviewed:
Booklist, March 1, 2003, page 1201
School Library Journal, March 2003, page 179

Other books by the same author:
Hush!, 2003
Santa and the Three Bears, 2003
Wolf Plays Alone, 1992

Other books you might like:
Susin Nielsen-Fernlund, *Hank and Fergus*, 2003
    Hank loves his imaginary best friend, but when a new little boy moves in next door, Hank discovers what he's been missing.
Danny Shanahan, *Buckledown the Workhound*, 1993
    After working himself to the bone, successful but dog-tired Buckledown realizes his life is incomplete and retires to become a full-time family dog.
Helen Stephens, *Blue Horse*, 2003
    Shy Tilly longs for friends and with the help (and encouragement) of her blue horse toy, she's able to reach out to a girl on the playground.
Pirkko Vainio, *The Dream House*, 1997
    Lucas builds his dream house, but then discovers he is lonely. When children arrive to play, his wishes are fulfilled.

229

PETER CATALANOTTO, Author/Illustrator

Matthew A.B.C.

(New York: A Richard Jackson Book/Atheneum Books for Young Readers, 200)

Subject(s): Names, Personal; Identity; Schools
Age range(s): Grades K-2
Major character(s): Mrs. Tuttle, Teacher; Principal Nozzet, Principal; Matthew Zee, Child, Student—Elementary School
Time period(s): 2000s (2002)
Locale(s): United States

Summary: Mrs. Tuttle's ability to distinguish the identity of each of the 25 students in her class amazes Principal Nozzet. To Mrs. Tuttle it is easy. Although each pupil is named Matthew, each has a last name beginning with a different letter of the alphabet and a distinguishing characteristic associated with that letter. When Principal Nozzet brings a new student to the room, he wonders how the child will fit in, but Mrs. Tuttle and her class recognize that Matthew Zee in his zippered outfit is just what they need. (32 pages)

Where it's reviewed:
Booklist, July 2002, page 1854
Horn Book, July 2002, page 442
Publishers Weekly, May 20, 2002, page 64
Riverbank Review, Fall 2002, page 32
School Library Journal, June 2002, page 90

Awards the book has won:
Horn Book Fanfare, 2003

Other books by the same author:
Emily's Art, 2001
Dad & Me, 1999
The Painter, 1995

Other books you might like:
Eve Bunting, *Girls A to Z*, 2002
    Each of 26 girls imagines being in an occupation that is perfectly suited to her name.
Woody Jackson, *The Cow's Alfa-bet*, 2003
    Cows give an alphabetic tour of the Vermont countryside.
Jacqueline Rogers, *Kindergarten A B C*, 2002
    Kindergarteners try to locate items associated with each letter of the alphabet in this search and find book.

230

KARIN CATES
NANCY CARPENTER, Illustrator

A Far-Fetched Story

(New York: Greenwillow Books/HarperCollins Publishers, 2002)

Subject(s): Quilts; Grandmothers; Storytelling
Age range(s): Grades K-2
Major character(s): Grandmother, Grandmother, Seamstress
Time period(s): Indeterminate Past
Locale(s): Fictional Country

Summary: One by one Grandmother sends members of the family out to fetch one last armload of wood for the long winter ahead. Each one comes home empty handed with torn clothes and a tale of barely escaping from some animal. Grandmother considers each excuse to be "a far-fetched story" and tosses the ragged clothes into the wood box for burning. By evening she's got a pile of torn clothing and no additional wood. Instead of burning the clothes, Grandmother cuts and sews the pieces until she creates a warm quilt that does as much good as firewood to keep the family warm all winter. (32 pages)

Where it's reviewed:
Booklist, February 15, 2002, page 1019
Horn Book Guide, Fall 2002, page 322
Publishers Weekly, December 10, 2001, page 70
School Library Journal, January 2002, page 95

Other books by the same author:
The Secret Remedy Book: A Story of Comfort and Love, 2003

Other books you might like:
Jeff Brumbeau, *The Quiltmaker's Gift*, 2000
    A talented quiltmaker refuses to sell her creations, but generously gives them away to anyone in need of warmth, comfort or shelter.

Ann Whitford Paul, *The Seasons Sewn: A Year in Patchwork*, 1996
An award-winning overview presents quilt patterns and their place in 19th-century American life.
Patricia Polacco, *The Keeping Quilt*, 1988
A special quilt connects four generations of one family.

231

KARIN CATES
WENDY ANDERSON HALPERIN, Illustrator

The Secret Remedy Book: A Story of Comfort and Love

(New York: Orchard/Scholastic, Inc., 2003)

Subject(s): Homesickness; Aunts and Uncles; Rural Life
Age range(s): Grades K-3
Major character(s): Lolly, Child, Niece; Zep, Aunt
Time period(s): 2000s (2003)
Locale(s): United States

Summary: Lolly loves visiting her Auntie Zep with her parents, but the first time she is allowed to go for a summer visit alone, she gets homesick. Luckily Auntie Zep knows just what to do and she heads for the Secret Remedy Book. The process of following the seven remedies (from drinking apple juice slowly to planting some seeds) in the book keeps Lolly busy and she goes to bed tired and happy. (32 pages)

Where it's reviewed:
Booklist, June 2003, page 1783
School Library Journal, August 2003, page 124

Other books by the same author:
A Far-Fetched Story, 2002

Other books you might like:
Kay Chorao, *The Good-bye Book*, 1988
A young boy doesn't want his parents to leave him home with a babysitter.
Colleen Cydor, *Smarty Pants*, 1999
Norah has a great time when she goes to visit her great-aunt for a week.
John Warren Stewig, *Making Plum Jam*, 2002
While staying alone with his aunts for a week one summer Jackie enjoys several adventures, including making plum jam.

232

DENYS CAZET, Author/Illustrator

Elvis the Rooster Almost Goes to Heaven

(New York: HarperCollins Publishers, 2003)

Series: I Can Read Book
Subject(s): Animals/Roosters; Animals/Chickens; Humor
Age range(s): Grades 1-3
Major character(s): Elvis, Rooster; Little Willie, Chicken, Detective; Rocky, Duck
Time period(s): Indeterminate
Locale(s): Fictional Country

Summary: Elvis takes his job of bringing up the sun every morning very seriously. The morning that a bug flies into his mouth and chokes him, Elvis is unable to crow. When the sun rises anyway, Elvis faints. The chickens contact Little Willie and Rocky to find Elvis. Rocky locates him atop the roof and carries him to the chicken coop. Sure that he is dying, Elvis languishes all day surrounded by the chickens while Little Willie figures out a way to restore his confidence. Finally it's almost dawn again and they lead Elvis to the rooftop. Once again as he opens his beak to crow he inhales a bug but this time a quick Heimlich maneuver expels the bug, allowing Elvis to get his cock-a-doodle-doo going again. (48 pages)

Where it's reviewed:
Bulletin of the Center for Children's Books, May 2003, page 354
Publishers Weekly, March 17, 2003, page 77
School Library Journal, May 2003, page 109

Other books by the same author:
Elvis the Rooster and the Magic Words, 2004
Minnie and Moo and the Attack of the Easter Bunnies, 2004
Minnie and Moo: The Night of the Living Bed, 2003

Other books you might like:
Sheila Crow, *The Hen That Crowed*, 1993
The town of Bean Blossom learns that there are advantages to having a rooster that crows at first light.
Bill Peet, *Cock-a-Doodle Dudley*, 1990
Cocky Dudley thinks that he controls the daily rising of the sun.
Ragnhild Scamell, *Rooster Crows*, 1994
Pompous Rooster is so confident that his crowing causes the sun to rise that he challenges Bluebird to a contest.

233

DENYS CAZET, Author/Illustrator

Minnie and Moo and the Potato from Planet X

(New York: HarperCollins Publishers, 2002)

Series: I Can Read Book
Subject(s): Aliens; Animals/Cows; Space Travel
Age range(s): Grades 1-2
Major character(s): Minnie, Cow; Moo, Cow; Spud, Alien
Time period(s): Indeterminate
Locale(s): Fictional Country

Summary: When Spud crash lands his spaceship in Minnie and Moo's pasture they do all they can to help him become airborne again in time to deliver the package of Anti-Bump Cream. Failure will mean the planets will bump into each other and life, as Minnie and Moo know it, will end. By modifying the farmer's tractor and locating ''space fuel'' that only a rescuer such as Minnie can supply, they succeed and Spud takes off to complete his important delivery. (48 pages)

Where it's reviewed:
Horn Book Guide, Fall 2002, page 351
Kirkus Reviews, March 1, 2002, page 331
School Library Journal, June 2002, page 90

Other books by the same author:
Minnie and Moo: The Attack of the Easter Bunnies, 2004
Minnie and Moo Meet Frankenswine, 2001
Minnie and Moo and the Musk of Zorro, 2000
Minnie and Moo and the Thanksgiving Tree, 2000

Other books you might like:
Tony Johnston, *Alien & Possum: Friends No Matter What*, 2001
    Possum's quiet evening of stargazing becomes interesting when a spaceship crashes nearby and a strange creature wanders out of it.
David McPhail, *Tinker and Tom and the Star Baby*, 1998
    Tinker repairs a spaceship that lands in his yard while the alien Star Baby eats the cat's food and levitates kitchen objects.
Dan Yaccarino, *First Day on a Strange New Planet*, 2000
    The first entry in the ''Blast Off Boy and Blorp'' series introduces the exchange students as each begins adjusting to life in an alien world.

234

DENYS CAZET, Author/Illustrator

Minnie and Moo and the Seven Wonders of the World

(New York: Richard Jackson Book/Atheneum Books for Young Readers, 2003)

Subject(s): Animals/Cows; Farm Life; Humor
Age range(s): Grades 2-4
Major character(s): Minnie, Cow; Moo, Cow; Irene, Rhinoceros
Time period(s): Indeterminate
Locale(s): Fictional Country

Summary: Convinced that their farm will be sold Moo enlists Minnie's help in her bright idea to raise funds by giving tours of the Seven Wonders of the World right here on their farm. While doing so the animals discover Irene, a zoo escapee that reports a conversation she's overheard while hiding in the woods, and the animals discover that it's not their farm that will be sold, but the neighboring farm so they give all the money they collect to the neighbors. To save Irene, Moo breaks her promise to stop thinking and comes up with a plan to hide the lonely rhino. (134 pages)

Where it's reviewed:
Bulletin of the Center for Children's Books, December 2003, page 145
Horn Book, January 2004, page 79
Publishers Weekly, December 22, 2003, page 61
School Library Journal, November 2003, page 90

Other books by the same author:
Minnie and Moo and the Potato from Planet X, 2002
Minnie and Moo Meet Frankenswine, 2001
Minnie and Moo Go to Paris, 1999

Other books you might like:
Allan Ahlberg, *The Cat Who Got Carried Away*, 2003
    A kidnapped cat, rat and guinea pig plot their own escape from thieves in a humorous, episodic title.

Alan Arkin, *Cassie Loves Beethoven*, 2000
    A farm family plays classical music to their new cow to encourage milk production; instead they foster Cassie's interest in producing music.
Julius Lester, *Ackamarackus: Julius Lester's Sumptuously Silly Fantastically Funny Fables*, 2001
    Six original fables offer lessons based on the problem-solving strategies of animals.

235

DENYS CAZET, Author/Illustrator

Minnie and Moo: The Night Before Christmas

(New York: HarperCollins Publishers, 2002)

Series: I Can Read Book
Subject(s): Animals/Cows; Christmas; Humor
Age range(s): Grades 1-2
Major character(s): Minnie, Cow; Moo, Cow; John, Farmer
Time period(s): Indeterminate
Locale(s): Fictional Country

Summary: It's Christmas Eve and Moo has a plan to help Farmer John. Once again the forgetful farmer has hidden a bag of gifts for his grandchildren in the barn and now can't remember where they are. Moo, with a book by ''Clement Moose'' as her guide, dresses Minnie in a Santa suit, ties plastic forks as antlers to eight chickens and a red-nosed rooster and uses a wheelless wheelbarrow as a sleigh. Out the barn door the entourage flies with guide Moo in the role of Mrs. Claus. Because the chimney is too small for Minnie, she uses the front door and soon has the presents under the tree. Before Minnie and Moo can escape the grandchildren run in to discover the very best Christmas surprise ever! (48 pages)

Where it's reviewed:
Booklist, October 1, 2002, page 332
Bulletin of the Center for Children's Books, December 2002, page 148
Horn Book, November 2002, page 750
Publishers Weekly, September 23, 2002, page 39
School Library Journal, October 2002, page 58

Other books by the same author:
Minnie and Moo and the Potato from Planet X, 2002
Minnie and Moo Meet Frankenswine, 2001
Minnie and Moo and the Musk of Zorro, 2000
Minnie and Moo Go to Paris, 1999

Other books you might like:
Nola Buck, *Santa's Short Suit Shrunk and Other Christmas Tongue Twisters*, 1997
    Silly sketches supplement short sayings seasonally celebrating Santa sights and sounds.
Claudia Mills, *Gus and Grandpa and the Christmas Cookies*, 1997
    As they bake piles of Christmas cookies, Gus and Grandpa decide that they have enough to give away to people less fortunate.
Dav Pilkey, *Dragon's Merry Christmas*, 1991
    Dragon enjoys a variety of Christmas activities including sharing his gifts with needy animals in a beginning reader.

236

MICHAEL CHABON

Summerland

(New York: Hyperion, 2002)

Subject(s): Sports/Baseball; Fantasy; Good and Evil
Age range(s): Grades 6-12
Major character(s): Ethan Feld, 11-Year-Old, Baseball Player; Jennifer T. Rideout, Baseball Player; Thor Wignutt, Baseball Player; Ringfinger Brown, Aged Person; Coyote, Mythical Creature (evil)
Time period(s): 2000s
Locale(s): Clam Island, Washington

Summary: Following the death of his mother, Ethan and his father move to Clam Island, a rainy island in Puget Sound. One tiny piece of the western end of the island enjoys sunny days and is referred to as "Summerland" by the natives. Ethan's father is a rabid baseball fan so Ethan, even knowing he's a dreadful athlete, plays for the local team. Ringfinger Brown recruits Ethan as the hero needed to beat back Coyote, an evil shape-shifter who uses Summerland as the gateway to other worlds where he holds power. Ethan agrees to help Ringfinger after Coyote kidnaps his inventor father, who he thinks has made a substance to help melt the underlying structure of the world. Going in search of his dad, Ethan is accompanied by Jennifer, Thor, a tiny giant, a Sasquatch, a talking rat, a major league ballplayer, a fairy princess and a host of others. Luckily Ethan has enough helpers to form a baseball team who find themselves playing against the Coyote All-Stars, where striking out has deadly ramifications in this author's first novel for young people. (492 pages)

Where it's reviewed:
Booklist, August 2002, page 1884
Bulletin of the Center for Children's Books, January 2003, page 193
Horn Book, November 2002, page 751
School Library Journal, November 2002, page 159
Voice of Youth Advocates, February 2003, page 485

Awards the book has won:
Smithsonian's Notable Books for Children/Older Readers, 2002
School Library Journal Best Books, 2002

Other books you might like:
W.P. Kinsella, *Shoeless Joe*, 1982
    Fantasy, time travel, and one man's dream combine to produce an incredible baseball game.
Ursula K. Le Guin, *A Wizard of Earthsea*, 1968
    An apprentice wizard accidentally releases an evil power.
Michael Molloy, *The Time Witches*, 2002
    Wolfbane returns to plot revenge against the Light Witch Abby Clover, but finds himself lost in time thanks to Abby and her Grand Master.
J.K. Rowling, *Harry Potter and the Sorcerer's Stone*, 1998
    Raised by his aunt and uncle, Harry is thrilled to be selected for the Hogwarts School of Witchcraft and Wizardry.

237

AIDAN CHAMBERS

Postcards from No Man's Land

(New York: Dutton, 2002)

Subject(s): World War II; Coming-of-Age; Unmarried Mothers
Age range(s): Grades 9-12
Major character(s): Jacob Todd, 17-Year-Old; Geertrui "Maria" Wesseling, Aged Person; Daan van Riet, Homosexual
Time period(s): 1940s (1944); 1990s
Locale(s): Amsterdam, Netherlands; Oosterbeek, Netherlands

Summary: With his grandmother too ill to attend, Jacob agrees to represent her at a commemorative ceremony in the Netherlands for participants in the Battle of Arnhem, the battle that led to his grandfather's death. He also plans to speak with Geertrui, daughter of the family that hid his grandfather from the Nazis and tended to his wounds. When Jacob arrives in Amsterdam, he's a typical teen, unsure of himself and absolutely taken with the idea of Anne Frank, her diary and her nearby house. At the end of the first day, he's had tea with a girl who he later realizes is a transsexual, been mugged, and is now in the uncomfortable position of being the unexpected houseguest of Daan, Geertrui's grandson. This is a difficult time for the van Riet family as Geertrui is dying of excruciatingly painful stomach cancer and has requested an assisted suicide; before that, she tells Jacob of her involvement with his grandfather and the love they shared for one another, a fact unknown to him. Jacob, too, meets several people that he cares for which forces him to confront his own sexuality, in this powerful, coming-of-age, award-winning novel. (312 pages)

Where it's reviewed:
Bulletin of the Center for Children's Books, September 2002, page 9
Horn Book, July 2002, page 454
Publishers Weekly, April 22, 2002, page 72
School Library Journal, July 2002, page 114
Voice of Youth Advocates, August 2002, page 189

Awards the book has won:
Michael L. Printz Award, 2003
ALA Best Books for Young Adults, 2003

Other books by the same author:
Favorite Ghost Stories, 2002
The Toll Bridge, 1995
Nik: Now I Know, 1987
Out of Time: Stories of the Future, 1984
Dance on My Grave: A Life and a Death in Four Parts, 1983

Other books you might like:
Robert Cormier, *Heroes*, 1998
    After being wounded in World War II, Francis finds there are many different kinds of heroes.
Anne Frank, *The Diary of Anne Frank*, 1952
    Anne's diary covers the years during World War II when she hides from the Nazis in an Amsterdam warehouse. Biography.
Don Wulffson, *Soldier X*, 2001
    German soldier Erik is wounded, swaps uniforms with a

dead Russian and, at a Russian hospital, falls in love with Tamara who knows his identity.

REMY CHARLIP, Author/Illustrator
TAMARA RETTENMUND, Illustrator

Little Old Big Beard and Big Young Little Beard: A Short and Tall Tale

(New York: Marshall Cavendish, 2003)

Subject(s): Cowboys/Cowgirls; Lost and Found; Humor
Age range(s): Grades K-2
Major character(s): Little Beard, Cowboy, Friend; Big Beard, Cowboy, Aged Person; Grace, Cow
Time period(s): Indeterminate Past
Locale(s): United States

Summary: Best friends Little Old Big Beard and Big Young Little Beard enjoy nightly hilltop sunsets and dinner with Grace until the day Grace vanishes. The saddened cowboys mount their horses and search up one hill, around the other and through a forest looking for Grace. When they don't find her the pals begin crying so much that they are soon standing in puddles of tears. As the water rises, they hear a loud "MOOOOOOO" and know that Grace is nearby. With their beloved cow they wind their way up their favorite hill and enjoy their usual dinner of beans in the contented company of Grace and each other. (32 pages)

Where it's reviewed:
Booklist, December 1, 2003, page 683
Bulletin of the Center for Children's Books, January 2004, page 183
Publishers Weekly, August 11, 2003, page 278
School Library Journal, October 2003, page 115

Other books by the same author:
Baby Hearts & Baby Flowers, 2002
Why I Will Never Ever Ever Ever Have Enough Time to Read This Book, 2000
I Love You, 1999

Other books you might like:
Roy Gerrard, *Rosie and the Rustlers*, 1989
    A story in rhyme describes how Rosie catches the rustlers who have stolen her cattle.
Stephen Gulbis, *Cowgirl Rosie and Her Five Baby Bison*, 2001
    Cowgirl Rosie is so sad to lose her five baby bison that her profuse tears help Sheriff Joe solve the mystery of their disappearance.
Tres Seymour, *Hunting the White Cow*, 1993
    A wayward cow becomes a legend in a mountain community as attempts to capture her fail.

CHIH-YUAN CHEN, Author/Illustrator

On My Way to Buy Eggs

(La Jolla, CA: Kane/Miller Book Publishers, 2003)

Subject(s): Imagination; Responsibility; Playing

Age range(s): Grades K-1
Major character(s): Shau-yu, Child, Daughter
Time period(s): 1990s
Locale(s): Taiwan

Summary: On her way to buy eggs Shau-yu imaginatively incorporates play into her walk. She follows the cat, woofs at the dog, and peeks at the world through a clear blue marble making her feel as if she's in a big, blue sea. Shau-yu dons a pair of glasses she finds under a tree and decides she looks just like her mother. Despite her blurry vision the now be-spectacled Shau-yu makes her way to the shop and, pretending to be her mother, requests the eggs she's been sent to buy. The shopkeeper plays along with her game and offers some gum for the shopper's "daughter" Shau-yu. Contentedly Shau-yu returns home to report a busy day and a successful shopping trip. Originally published in Taiwan in 2001. (36 pages)

Where it's reviewed:
Booklist, October 15, 2003, page 416
Horn Book, January 2004, page 68
Publishers Weekly, August 25, 2003, page 62
School Library Journal, October 2003, page 115

Awards the book has won:
Publishers Weekly Best Children's Books, 2003

Other books you might like:
Crockett Johnson, *Harold and the Purple Crayon*, 1958
    Harold has a magic purple crayon, a vivid imagination, and a talent for drawing himself into and out of trouble.
Carole Lexa Schaefer, *The Squiggle*, 1996
    A "squiggle" of red string found while walking becomes for an imaginative child a dragon, a tightrope and fire-works.
Alice Schertle, *Down the Road*, 1995
    Mama sends Hetty down the road on her first solo errand to buy eggs from the general store for Papa's breakfast.
Peter Sis, *Madlenka*, 2000
    Walking about her neighborhood sharing news of a loose tooth, Madlenka imagines traveling to the home countries of each neighbor.

DA CHEN

Wandering Warrior

(New York: Delacorte, 2003)

Subject(s): Martial Arts; Adventure and Adventurers
Age range(s): Grades 7-10
Major character(s): Luka, 11-Year-Old, Warrior; Atami Baba, Religious (monk), Martial Arts Expert; Gulan, Religious (monk), Martial Arts Expert; Ulanbaat Ghengi, Ruler (emperor)
Time period(s): Indeterminate Past
Locale(s): China

Summary: Son of a now-deceased Chinese woman and the Mogo Emperor Ulanbaat Ghengi, Luka conceals his identity in the persona of a beggar and lives with his mentor Atami. Luka is educated and trained in Kung Fu by Atami who tells him of his predestination to be the Holy Emperor of China.

Atami is captured by the enemy and Luka is held in a Mogo prison where he meets Atami's former master Gulan, who continues Luka's Kung Fu training. The two finally escape; Gulan is severely wounded and Luka confronts many dangers before facing his own father in battle in this author's first novel. (322 pages)

Where it's reviewed:
Booklist, February 15, 2003, page 1064
Bulletin of the Center for Children's Books, April 2003, page 307
Publishers Weekly, December 16, 2002, page 68
School Library Journal, February 2003, page 140
Voice of Youth Advocates, June 2003, page 127

Other books by the same author:
Sounds of the River: A Memoir, 2002 (adult fiction)
China's Son: Growing Up in the Cultural Revolution, 2001

Other books you might like:
Malcolm Bosse, *The Examination*, 1994
  Brothers Hong, the practical one, and Chen, the scholar, travel to Beijing so Chen may take the examination that will decide their futures.
Alexandre Dumas, *The Three Musketeers*, 1844
  Meet the original swashbucklers who rip through adventure after adventure.
Erik Christian Haugaard, *The Boy and the Samurai*, 1991
  Saru, a street urchin, reminisces about how his life and the life of a samurai intertwined in sixteenth-century Japan.
Eric A. Kimmel, *Sword of the Samurai: Adventure Stories from Japan*, 1999
  Eleven stories relate the culture of these Japanese warriors who lived by strict rules and traditions.
Francine Pascal, *Fearless*, 1999
  Born missing the gene for fear, Gaia excels in the art of self-defense and is honorable in the use of her skills.
James Raven, *Entering the Way*, 1993
  When a gang tries to take over a San Francisco neighborhood, four karate students form the Dojo Rats to oppose them.

241

ANDREA CHENG

Marika

(Asheville, NC: Front Street Books, 2002)

Subject(s): Jews; World War II; Identity
Age range(s): Grades 7-10
Major character(s): Maria "Marika" Schnurmacher, Teenager; Andras Schnurmacher, Brother (of Maria); Apa Schnurmacher, Father (of Marika), Stock Broker
Time period(s): 1930s; 1940s (1934-1945)
Locale(s): Budapest, Hungary

Summary: As a child, Marika's biggest concern is the wall that suddenly appears dividing her family's apartment into her father's side and her mother's side, which is where Marika and her brother Andras live. Then she turns 11 and her father hears the warnings against the Jews, so Marika forges birth certificates for everyone in the family to show they are Catholic. For the most part this is true as the Schnurmachers

celebrate Christmas and Easter, as well as attend Mass, though they are Jewish. But even their lapsed Jewishness brings them into Hitler's fold just as it does those who regularly attend temple. Marika is picked up one day by the Germans and fears she'll be sent to a concentration camp; thanks to her father's wealth, she's released to his custody in this work based on the life of the author's mother. (163 pages)

Where it's reviewed:
Booklist, November 15, 2002, page 590
Horn Book, November 2002, page 752
Publishers Weekly, September 16, 2002, page 69
School Library Journal, December 2002, page 132
Voice of Youth Advocates, February 2003, page 466

Other books by the same author:
Honeysuckle House, 2003

Other books you might like:
Kimberly Brubaker Bradley, *For Freedom: The Story of a French Spy*, 2003
  Intent upon a career singing opera, Suzanne is unaware of the war until the Germans gain control of her French town and evict her family.
Gudrun Pausewang, *The Final Journey*, 1996
  Sheltered from Nazi terrorism, young Alice rides a cattle car to Auschwitz where she's happy to go to the showers and wash away the grime of the trip.
Jerry Spinelli, *Milkweed*, 2003
  A young Gypsy boy is at first enamored of the "jack boots" who take over his city, but later realizes the horror of the Nazis.

242

JAN CHERIPKO

Rat

(Honesdale, PA: Boyds Mills Press, 2002)

Subject(s): Sports/Basketball; Adolescence; School Life
Age range(s): Grades 7-9
Major character(s): Jeremy "Rat" Chandler, 15-Year-Old; Simpson Theodore III, Bully, Basketball Player; Patrick O'Connor, Coach, Teacher (earth science); Mary O'Connor, Artist
Time period(s): 2000s
Locale(s): Sparrowburg, New York

Summary: Called "Rat," short for gym rat because he's always in the gym playing basketball, Jeremy was born with a withered arm, which reduces his team involvement to manager. Even that position is shaky after he testifies against the team's basketball coach who he found trying to rape one of their school's cheerleaders. Though Jeremy feels he acted correctly, his teammates are furious that their coach has been convicted and fired just at the beginning of basketball season. Into his place comes Mr. O'Connor, the school's earth science teacher and former basketball player, and a new, fairer regime begins. Bully Simpson, who's made Jeremy's life miserable, leaves the team and Jeremy and Mr. O'Connor's pregnant wife Mary strike up a friendship. The team learns several important lessons during this memorable season. (205 pages)

Where it's reviewed:
Childhood Education, Winter 2002, page 109
Journal of Adolescent and Adult Literacy, April 2003, page 609
Kirkus Reviews, September 1, 2002, page 1306
School Library Journal, August 2002, page 183
Voice of Youth Advocates, October 2002, page 270

Awards the book has won:
IRA Children's Choices/Advanced Readers, 2003

Other books by the same author:
Imitate the Tiger, 1996
Voices of the River: Adventures on the Delaware, 1993

Other books you might like:
Edward Bloor, *Tangerine*, 1997
 Legally blind Paul and his family move to Florida where Paul plays soccer and slowly faces the truth about his blindness and his brother's culpability.
Carl Deuker, *Painting the Black*, 1997
 Ryan must decide whether or not to turn in his friend Josh whom he saw assaulting a girl; if he does, his school will lose their baseball title.
Walter Dean Myers, *Hoops*, 1981
 Just as Cal is set to demonstrate his basketball prowess for scouts in the city's Tournament of Champions, his coach is accused of gambling.
Stephen Roos, *The Gypsies Never Came*, 2001
 Augie has learned to ignore the disparaging comments of some of his classmates who like to tease him about his deformed left hand.

243

LYNNE CHERRY, Author/Illustrator

How Groundhog's Garden Grew
(New York: Blue Sky Press/Scholastic, Inc., 2003)

Subject(s): Animals; Gardens and Gardening; Environmental Problems
Age range(s): Grades K-3
Major character(s): Little Groundhog, Groundhog; Squirrel, Squirrel
Time period(s): 2000s (2003)
Locale(s): United States

Summary: When Little Groundhog is caught eating a neighbor's garden, Squirrel offers to help him plant his own. Little Groundhog and Squirrel collect seeds and then settle down for their winter hibernation. When they wake up in the spring, they get right to work planting their gardens. With careful tending through the summer, Little Groundhog has a bumper crop and invites his neighbors to a feast to share the bounty. (40 pages)

Where it's reviewed:
Booklist, February 2003, page 1000
Publishers Weekly, December 16, 2002, page 67
School Library Journal, February 2003, page 103

Awards the book has won:
IRA Children's Choices, 2004

Other books by the same author:
A River Ran Wild: An Environmental History, 1992
The Great Kapok Tree, 1990
Where the Butterflies Grow, 1989

Other books you might like:
Henry Cole, *Jack's Garden*, 1995
 In a take-off of "This is the House that Jack Built," Jack plants a garden.
Lois Ehlert, *Growing Vegetable Soup*, 1987
 A father and his child grow the ingredients needed for vegetable soup.
Ruth Krauss, *The Carrot Seed*, 1945
 A young boy plants a carrot seed and waits patiently for it to grow.

244

C.J. CHERRYH

Explorer
(New York: DAW, 2002)

Subject(s): Aliens; Cultural Conflict
Age range(s): Grades 9-Adult
Major character(s): Bren Cameron, Linguist; Ilisidi, Alien, Noblewoman
Time period(s): Indeterminate Future
Locale(s): *Phoenix*, Spaceship; *Reunion*, Space Station

Summary: The spaceship *Phoenix* has at long last arrived at its destination, the space station *Reunion*, from which the humans once fled to the planet of the alien atevi. Now carrying both humans and atevi, the *Phoenix* is on a rescue mission of any humans left alive on the space station, for they are in danger from hostile aliens. In fact, as they arrive, they find the station besieged. Bren Cameron, who has long played a principle role in mediating between humans and atevi, now needs to act as a go-between with a third species. Matters are infinitely complicated by the presence of that redoubtable atevi, Ilisidi, grandmother to the atevi ruler, who can be counted on to behave in a completely unpredictable way. (408 pages)

Where it's reviewed:
Analog Science Fiction and Fact, May 2003, page 132
Booklist, November 11, 2002, page 583
Library Journal, November 15, 2002, page 106
Publishers Weekly, October 28, 2002, page 56
Voice of Youth Advocates, April 2003, page 62

Other books by the same author:
At the Edge of Space, 2003
Defender, 2001
Downbelow Station, 2001

Other books you might like:
Eleanor Arnason, *Ring of Swords*, 1993
 Violence seems inevitable when humankind meets an alien species that believes heterosexuality is perverse.
Mary Doria Russell, *The Sparrow*, 1996
 A Jesuit believes God has sent him to meet an alien race, but finds his faith challenged when he disastrously misinterprets the culture.

Sheri S. Tepper, *After Long Silence*, 1987

    The music that seems to affect seismic activity turns out to be communication with a crystalline race.

245

MICHAEL CHESWORTH, Author/Illustrator

Alphaboat

(New York: Farrar Straus Giroux, 2002)

Subject(s): Boats and Boating; Stories in Rhyme; Treasure
Age range(s): Grades 2-4
Major character(s): Captain T, Sea Captain, Object (letter)
Time period(s): Indeterminate Past
Locale(s): At Sea

Summary: Captain T and all the letters set sail on the Alphaboat in search of buried treasure. Despite all the problems with shipbuilding and stormy weather, the letters discover the buried treasure, which is a dictionary. Filled with visual and verbal puns, readers will discover something new with every reading. (32 pages)

Where it's reviewed:
Booklist, October 15, 2002, page 410
Kirkus Reviews, August 1, 2002, page 1124
Publishers Weekly, August 12, 2002, page 299
School Library Journal, September 2002, page 182

Other books by the same author:
Archibald Frisby, 1996
Rainy Day Dream, 1992

Other books you might like:
Mary Murphy, *The Alphabet Keeper*, 2003
    One day the letters escape from the Alphabet Keeper when she is cleaning their cage.
William Steig, *CDB!*, 1968
    Caldecott winning cartoonist Steig captions illustrations with letters that any child who knows the alphabet can read. C D B, for example, is See the Bee!
Audrey Wood, *Alphabet Adventure*, 2001
    The letters of the alphabet set off to teach a child his letters, but on the way ''i'' loses her dot, delaying the group's arrival.

246

EMMA CHICHESTER CLARK, Author/Illustrator

No More Kissing!

(New York: A Doubleday Book for Young Readers, 2002)

Subject(s): Love; Family; Babies
Age range(s): Preschool-Grade 1
Major character(s): Momo, Monkey, Brother (older); Unnamed Character, Monkey, Baby
Time period(s): Indeterminate
Locale(s): Fictional Country

Summary: Momo is appalled at all the kissing he observes, especially in his own family. He recalls just how bad it was when he was a baby so he's grateful that the amount of kissing has been reduced now that he's older. However, he cannot convince his family to stop the practice all together. As Momo fears, when his baby brother is born, the kissing begins again in earnest. Finally, listening to his little brother cry, Momo has had enough and he takes the baby away from the kissing relatives to play with him. Still, the baby cries and just once, quite by accident, Momo kisses him. First published in Great Britain in 2001. (32 pages)

Where it's reviewed:
Booklist, January 1, 2002, page 863
Horn Book, March, 2002, page 201
Kirkus Reviews, December 15, 2001, page 1755
Publishers Weekly, December 3, 2001, page 58
School Library Journal, January 2002, page 96

Other books by the same author:
Where Are You, Blue Kangaroo?, 2001
I Love You, Blue Kangaroo!, 1999
Across the Blue Mountains, 1993

Other books you might like:
Holly Keller, *Geraldine's Baby Brother*, 1994
    It takes some time for Geraldine to adjust to her noisy baby brother and all the attention he receives.
Phyllis Root, *What Baby Wants*, 1998
    While Mama naps everyone in the family tries to determine what will soothe the crying baby.
Vera B. Williams, *More More More, Said the Baby: 3 Love Stories*, 1990
    The Caldecott Honor Book beautifully portrays the playful expressions of love between parent and child.

247

EMMA CHICHESTER CLARK, Author/Illustrator

What Shall We Do, Blue Kangaroo?

(New York: A Doubleday Book for Young Readers, 2003)

Subject(s): Toys; Family; Self-Reliance
Age range(s): Grades K-1
Major character(s): Lily, Child, Daughter; Blue Kangaroo, Toy (stuffed animal); Tiny Teddy, Toy (stuffed animal), Bear
Time period(s): 2000s (2002)
Locale(s): England

Summary: Lily asks Blue Kangaroo for ideas, but he doesn't know what to do next. Lily asks family members to do various activities with her but no one has time so Lily does it herself. Each time Blue Kangaroo notices how well Lily performs the task or activity. During the course of the day, Lily draws pictures of dinosaurs, has a tea party for her animal friends, masters the reading of a book and rescues the animals left outside from a sudden rainstorm. Only Blue Kangaroo notices that Lily's forgotten one little tea party guest. After Lily falls asleep, Blue Kangaroo realizes he'll have to retrieve Tiny Teddy from the yard himself and he does. Originally published in Great Britain in 2002. (32 pages)

Where it's reviewed:
Booklist, May 15, 2003, page 1669
Horn Book, September 2003, page 592
Publishers Weekly, May 5, 2003, page 224
School Library Journal, July 2003, page 88

Other books by the same author:
It Was You, Blue Kangaroo!, 2002
Where Are You, Blue Kangaroo?, 2001
I Love You, Blue Kangaroo!, 1999 (Christopher Medal)

Other books you might like:
Jane Hissey, *Old Bear*, 1997
  Old Bear is stuck in the attic and some stuffed animal friends work to free him.
Barbro Lindgren, *Sam's Teddy Bear*, 1982
  Sam's dog helps recover his special teddy bear.
Rosemary Wells, *Bunny Party*, 2001
  Max and Ruby can't agree on which toys are invited to the party they're planning for Grandma's birthday.

248

LAUREN CHILD, Author/Illustrator

That Pesky Rat

(Cambridge, MA: Candlewick Press, 2002)

Subject(s): Pets; Animals/Rats; Names, Personal
Age range(s): Grades K-3
Major character(s): Unnamed Character, Rat; Mrs. Trill, Store Owner; Mr. Fortesque, Aged Person
Time period(s): 2000s
Locale(s): Grubby Alley, England

Summary: The lonely resident of trash can number three wants nothing more than to be someone's pet and to have a name. As it is now, his home is periodically emptied of all its contents and he must begin again. That pesky rat, as residents of the neighborhood call the misunderstood creature, knows the local pets and the pros and cons of their lives with their respective owners. Desperately, the rat writes and posts a notice in the window of Mrs. Trill's pet shop describing its personal attributes and its desire for a home. When Mr. Fortesque squints to read the notice through his thick glasses he assumes he's found the cat of his dreams. Neither Mrs. Trill nor the pesky rat correct Mr. Fortesque's misunderstanding and the rat goes home with near-sighted Mr. Fortesque to become a contented pet with a name. First published in Great Britain in 2002. (32 pages)

Where it's reviewed:
Booklist, September 1, 2002, page 120
Horn Book Guide, Spring 2003, page 28
Kirkus Reviews, July 1, 2002, page 950
Publishers Weekly, July 1, 2002, page 79
School Library Journal, August 2002, page 148

Awards the book has won:
Booklist Editors' Choice, 2002

Other books by the same author:
Beware of the Storybook Wolves, 2001 (IRA Children's Choices)
Clarice Bean, Guess Who's Babysitting?, 2001 (School Library Journal Best Books)
I Will Never Not Ever Eat a Tomato, 2000 (Kate Greenaway Medal)

Other books you might like:
Becky Bloom, *Crackers*, 2001
  Crackers is a hard-working cat that doesn't fit the expectations of his employers because he actually likes mice.
Helen Lester, *Hooway for Wodney Wat*, 1999
  Rodney Rat cleverly uses his inability to make the ''R'' sound to trick the class bully into leaving him and his classmates alone.
Tres Seymour, *I Love My Buzzard*, 1994
  A young boy who loves his buzzard as well as his squid, slugs and warthog reconsiders his priorities when his mom moves out to escape the menagerie.

249

LAUREN CHILD, Author/Illustrator

Utterly Me, Clarice Bean

(Cambridge, MA: Candlewick Press, 2003)

Subject(s): Schools; Contests; Family Life
Age range(s): Grades 3-5
Major character(s): Clarice Bean, Student—Elementary School, Friend (Betty's); Betty Moody, Student—Elementary School, Friend; Karl Wrenbury, Student—Elementary School, Classmate
Time period(s): 2000s (2002)
Locale(s): England

Summary: Best friends Clarice and Betty draw comparisons between their situation in the class of a grumpy, vengeful teacher and that of their favorite book character, Ruby Redfort, secret agent. In her daydreams Clarice compares each situation to those Ruby faces in the books. When Betty goes on an unexpected trip just as partners are being chosen for a very important class project, the teacher wrongly accuses Karl of taking the winner's cup and, as punishment, assigns him to work with Clarice. A situation that seems to Clarice to be utterly the worst actually works out well when Clarice discovers that, out of class, Karl the troublemaker has some clever ideas for their project. When Betty returns from her trip, she and Clarice use knowledge gained from their favorite reading material to solve the mystery of the missing prize in time for the reading contest award to be presented. Though Clarice, Karl and Betty do not win, they do have an utterly memorable project. Originally published in Great Britain in 2002. (190 pages)

Where it's reviewed:
Booklist, September 15, 2003, page 235
Bulletin of the Center for Children's Books, November 2003, page 96
Magpies, November 2002, page 33
Publishers Weekly, September 15, 2003, page 65
School Library Journal, November 2003, page 90

Awards the book has won:
IRA Children's Choices, 2004

Other books by the same author:
Clarice Bean, Guess Who's Babysitting?, 2001 (School Library Journal Best Books)
I Will Never Not Ever Eat a Tomato, 2000 (Kate Greenaway Medal)

Clarice Bean, That's Me, 1999

Other books you might like:

David A. Adler, *School Trouble for Andy Russell*, 1999
   The substitute in Andy's classroom blames the creative underachiever for mishaps that are the work of another student.
Beverly Cleary, *Ramona Quimby, Age 8*, 1981
   Spirited Ramona keeps her family guessing about her next adventure as she enters third grade in this Newbery Honor Book.
Marissa Moss, *Oh Boy, Amelia!*, 2001
   Her older sister's first crush causes Amelia to wonder about gender roles.

`250`
LAUREN CHILD, Author/Illustrator

What Planet Are You from, Clarice Bean?
(Cambridge, MA: Candlewick Press, 2002)

Subject(s): Schools; Family; Environment
Age range(s): Grades 2-4
Major character(s): Clarice Bean, Sister, Student; Kurt Bean, Brother, Environmentalist; Robert Granger, Student, Classmate
Time period(s): 2000s (2001)
Locale(s): Navarino Street, England

Summary: Arriving just a little late for school Clarice finds that not only is she stuck with Robert Granger as a partner for an environmental project but also she is forced to accept Robert's idea to study the relative speed of snails and worms. When Kurt decides to prevent the destruction of an ancient tree on their street by camping in the tree with a friend, Clarice and her family lend support by making posters and climbing the tree to eat dinner with Kurt. Clarice's activism makes her late to school and lacking a snail and worm project. Though her teacher is doubtful, Robert shows the newspaper picture of Clarice's family and Clarice is allowed to give a report about her week as an "ecowarrior." (32 pages)

Where it's reviewed:
Booklist, April 15, 2002, page 1406
Horn Book Guide, Fall 2002, page 322
Publishers Weekly, February 4, 2002, page 78
School Library Journal, March 2002, page 173

Other books by the same author:
Clarice Bean, Guess Who's Babysitting?, 2001 (School Library Journal Best Book)
I Am NOT Sleepy and I Will NOT Go to Bed, 2001 (IRA Children's Choice)
I Will Never Not Ever Eat a Tomato, 2000 (Kate Greenaway Medal)

Other books you might like:
Lisa Campbell Ernst, *Squirrel Park*, 1993
   Stuart Ivey and a friendly squirrel make sure that development plans spare the last big oak tree in town.
Arthur A. Levine, *Pearl Moscowitz's Last Stand*, 1993
   When elderly Pearl learns that the last tree on her street is to be cut down, she encourages her neighbors to be environmental activists and save it.

Janice May Udry, *A Tree Is Nice*, 1956
   The Caldecott Medal winner celebrates the many simple pleasures that a tree offers.

`251`
LAUREN CHILD, Author/Illustrator

Who's Afraid of the Big Bad Book?
(New York: Hyperion Books for Children, 2003)

Subject(s): Books and Reading; Imagination; Fairy Tales
Age range(s): Grades 1-3
Major character(s): Herb, Child, Friend; Ezzie, Child, Friend
Time period(s): Indeterminate
Locale(s): Fictional Country

Summary: The night Ezzie sleeps over Herb falls asleep while reading a book of fairy tales. He's awakened by a loud shriek and realizes that he's fallen into the book. He races out of the home of three bears into a series of adventures, some of his own making because of the liberties he's taken with his book. An important character has been cut out to make a card for his mother and others have mustaches drawn on their faces. Herb soon learns how unhappy the characters are with his treatment. With angry characters in hot pursuit, Herb tries to find a way out of the book when it slides off his bed and he falls out, waking Ezzie. After explaining what happened, Herb and Ezzie try to repair the book so the characters can live out their stories in the intended way. Originally published in England in 2002. (36 pages)

Where it's reviewed:
Booklist, January 2004, page 872
Bulletin of the Center for Children's Books, January 2004, page 183
Magpies, November 2002, page 4
Publishers Weekly, November 24, 2003, page 63

Other books by the same author:
That Pesky Rat, 2002 (Booklist Editors' Choice)
What Planet Are You from, Clarice Bean?, 2002 (Children's Choices, Intermediate Readers)
Beware of the Storybook Wolves, 2001
Clarice Bean, Guess Who's Babysitting?, 2001

Other books you might like:
John Stadler, *What's So Scary?*, 2001
   After the illustrator spills paint on the book, slips, and drops his brush a character picks it up and draws an ending he likes to the story.
Janet Stevens, *And the Dish Ran Away with the Spoon*, 2001
   Cat, Dog and Cow search for the missing Dish and Spoon before it's time for their nursery rhyme to be read again.
Ellen Stoll Walsh, *Jack's Tale*, 1997
   Jack agrees to walk through a tale only to please the author. In the end he marries the princess and lives happily ever after.
Bruce Whatley, *Wait! No Paint!*, 2001
   The illustrator changes the outcome of a familiar story when he spills his juice and runs out of red paint.
David Wiesner, *The Three Pigs*, 2001
   Characters set the direction in a Caldecott Medal retelling

as they wander in and out of the pages of different stories with varying illustrative styles.

252

SUZANNE TANNER CHITWOOD, Author/Illustrator

Wake Up, Big Barn!

(New York: Cartwheel/Scholastic, Inc., 2002)

Subject(s): Farm Life; Animals; Stories in Rhyme
Age range(s): Preschool-Kindergarten
Time period(s): Indeterminate
Locale(s): United States

Summary: A rooster crows to awaken the barn and its inhabitants. Donkeys bray, cows moo and young pigs enjoy a mud bath. A peacock struts, showing off colorful feathers as frogs hop nearby. Horses race for hay and a crow dines on corn. Ripe cherries fall from the tree and reappear in a tasty pie as the sun goes down. Owl begins its nightly vigil near the big barn as the author/illustrator's first book draws to a close. (40 pages)

Where it's reviewed:
Booklist, February 1, 2002, page 945
Horn Book Guide, Fall 2002, page 297
Publishers Weekly, April 1, 2002, page 82
School Library Journal, April 2002, page 101

Other books you might like:
Stella Blackstone, *There's a Cow in the Cabbage Patch*, 2001
 All the farm animals are out of place but the farmer knows just what to do to get them back where they belong.
Margaret Wise Brown, *Big Red Barn*, 1995
 A day in the life of a barn introduces the many types of animals who live there.
Nancy Tafuri, *Silly Little Goose!*, 2001
 As Goose searches for a suitable spot to build her nest readers have a tour of a farm and its animals.

253

MARGARET CHODOS-IRVINE, Author/Illustrator

Ella Sarah Gets Dressed

(San Diego: Harcourt, Inc., 2003)

Subject(s): Clothes; Individuality; Parent and Child
Age range(s): Preschool-Kindergarten
Major character(s): Ella Sarah, Child, Sister (younger)
Time period(s): 2000s (2003)
Locale(s): United States

Summary: Ella Sarah knows exactly what she wants to wear today. Her parents and older sister suggest alternate outfits, but to each proposal Ella Sarah simply repeats the list of garments she wants to wear. Finally, a frustrated Ella Sarah gets herself dressed in her pink polka-dot pants, flowered dress, striped socks, yellow shoes and red hat. She's ready just in time to answer the doorbell as three similarly attired friends arrive for a tea party. They agree that Ella Sarah's outfit is just right for the occasion. (36 pages)

Where it's reviewed:
Booklist, June 2003, page 1768

Horn Book Guide, Fall 2003, page 297
Publishers Weekly, April 28, 2003, page 68
Riverbank Review, Summer 2003, page 30
School Library Journal, July 203, page 88

Awards the book has won:
Caldecott Honor Book, 2004
ALA Notable Children's Books, 2004

Other books you might like:
Doris Dorrie, *Lottie's Princess Dress*, 1999
 Lottie convinces her mother to let her wear her sparkly, gold princess dress to school.
Jennifer A. Ericsson, *The Most Beautiful Kid in the World*, 1996
 Annie doesn't agree with Mama's choice of outfit so she changes into something that will make her "the most beautiful kid" for Grandma's birthday.
Marthe Jocelyn, *Hannah and the Seven Dresses*, 1999
 Hannah has such a hard time deciding which dress to wear for her birthday that she tries to wear all seven at once.
Andrea Spalding, *Sarah May and the New Red Dress*, 1999
 Sarah May has her heart set on a new red dress so she is disappointed when her mother buys dark blue material.
Harriet Ziefert, *Clara Ann Cookie*, 1999
 Clara wakes in a grumpy mood and refuses to get dressed, so Mother has to creatively convince her to don her outfit.

254

EILEEN CHRISTELOW, Author/Illustrator

Where's the Big Bad Wolf?

(New York: Clarion Books, 2002)

Subject(s): Animals/Dogs; Animals/Wolves; Mystery and Detective Stories
Age range(s): Grades 1-2
Major character(s): Phineas T. Doggedly, Detective—Police, Dog; BBW, Wolf
Time period(s): Indeterminate
Locale(s): Fictional Country

Summary: A cloud of straw engulfs Detective Doggedly's patrol car and he's certain the cause must be BBW, breaking his promise to stay out of trouble. When Doggedly gets to the scene he finds the three little pigs whose house has just been destroyed being assisted by a friendly sheep. Despite Detective Doggedly's insistence that this must be the work of BBW no one has seen a wolf in the vicinity. The huffing and puffing incident happens again after the pigs build a house of sticks and still there is no wolf in sight, only the same helpful sheep. By the third time, Detective Doggedly follows the sheep and finds the real culprit. This time BBW (without his sheep disguise) ends up behind bars for a few days. (32 pages)

Where it's reviewed:
Booklist, October 15, 2002, page 410
Kirkus Reviews, July 15, 2002, page 1028
Publishers Weekly, July 8, 2002, page 49
School Library Journal, September 2002, page 182
Smithsonian, December 2002, page 123

Awards the book has won:
Smithsonian's Notable Books for Children, 2002

Other books by the same author:
The Great Pig Search, 2001 (School Library Journal Best Books)
Jerome Camps Out, 1998
The Great Pig Escape, 1994 (Book Links Good Book)

Other books you might like:
Gavin Bishop, *The Three Little Pigs*, 1989
In this retelling of the three little pigs in search of their fortunes the hip wolf with sunglasses and Walkman still meets the stew pot in the end.
Steven Kellogg, *The Three Little Pigs*, 1997
The pigs in this humorous retelling face a tough-looking hungry wolf trying to order piglet from their waffle wagon.
Barry Moser, *The Three Little Pigs*, 2001
The traditional tale is retold with adherence to the familiar text while the illustrations add humor.
Jon Scieszka, *The True Story of the 3 Little Pigs!*, 1989
Misunderstood A. Wolf presents his side of the story about just what happened between him and those three pigs.
Eugene Trivizas, *The Three Little Wolves and the Big Bad Pig*, 1993
A familiar tale takes a new turn when the big, bad pig tries to outmaneuver the three little wolves and ends up surprising himself.
David Wiesner, *The Three Pigs*, 2001
Three pigs take control of events in the story by simply walking (or flying) off the page and into another tale where they seek refuge from the wolf.

255

LISA CINDRICH

In the Shadow of the Pali: A Story of the Hawaiian Leper Colony
(New York: Putnam, 2002)

Subject(s): Survival; Conduct of Life; Diseases
Age range(s): Grades 6-9
Major character(s): Liliha, 12-Year-Old; Kaalani, Bully; Hana, Friend (of Liliha); Manukekua, Friend
Time period(s): 1860s
Locale(s): Kalaupapa Leprosy Colony, Hawaii

Summary: Forced by her uncle to care for her diseased grandmother, Liliha contracts the dreaded leprosy and is sent to the Kalaupapa Leprosy Colony on Molokai. Begun by the Hawaiian Islands legislature in the 1860s, the leper colony is initially chaotic with no rules, no shelter, minimal rations and only a drunk in charge. Liliha manages to anger the island's biggest bully, Kaalani, who's in charge of doling out the rations, which means she struggles to find enough food to stay alive. Luckily she's befriended by Hana, who accompanied her leper husband to the island, and Manukekua, who together teach Liliha to stand up to Kaalani. Liliha also gains strength from her carving and weaving and, though her disease worsens, surprises herself by accepting her fate and making the most of her shortened life in this author's first novel. (245 pages)

Where it's reviewed:
Bulletin of the Center for Children's Books, October 2002, page 52
Kirkus Reviews, June 15, 2002, page 878
Kliatt, July 2002, page 7
School Library Journal, June 2002, page 134
Voice of Youth Advocates, August 2002, page 190

Other books you might like:
T. Degens, *On the Third Ward*, 1990
Only the stories told by the Empress of China relieve Wanda's day-to-day monotony of life spent in a hospital for tubercular teens.
James Michener, *Hawaii*, 1959
A fictionalized account of the birth and growth of Hawaii and its peoples.
Mette Newth, *The Dark Light*, 1998
Stuck in a leprosy hospital, Tora reads to all the patients which helps them leave the hospital by a way other than death.

256

CATHERINE CLARK

Frozen Rodeo
(New York: HarperCollins, 2003)

Subject(s): Humor; Family Life; Sports/Ice Skating
Age range(s): Grades 8-12
Major character(s): Peggy Fleming Farrell, 17-Year-Old
Time period(s): 2000s
Locale(s): Lindville

Summary: Summertime and Fleming's life is anything but easy. Saddled with baby-sitting her younger siblings, also named after figure skaters; working at a coffee bar at the local Git-n-Go gas station to repay her parents for totaling their car; taking French in summer school; and assisting her pregnant mother with Lamaze classes, Fleming's ready to return to regular school to relax. Instead she partners with her dad for a rodeo-style ice capade, foils a robber and then roller blades off to the hospital to help her mother give birth to Elvis in a tale laced with humor. (287 pages)

Where it's reviewed:
Booklist, February 15, 2003, page 1064
Kirkus Reviews, February 15, 2003, page 302
Kliatt, January 2003, page 7
School Library Journal, March 2003, page 228
Voice of Youth Advocates, April 2003, page 46

Other books by the same author:
The Alison Rules, 2004
Wurst Case Scenario, 2001
Truth or Dairy (2000)

Other books you might like:
Meg Cabot, *The Princess Diaries*, 2000-
Raised in Greenwich Village by her artist mother, Mia is dismayed to learn she's princess and heir to her father's Genovian throne.
Louise Rennison, *Angus, Thongs and Full-Frontal Snogging: Confessions of Georgia Nicolson*, 2000
In her diary, Georgia records her interest in kissing, her

appearance and her opposition to most of what the adult world thinks is important.

Ellen Wittlinger, *Zigzag*, 2003
Robin's miserable summer turns into an adventure when she accompanies her aunt and two cousins on a trip that zigzags across America.

Rona S. Zable, *Love at the Laundromat*, 1986
Joanne finds love at her mother's laundromat, but not without hilarious miscommunications about the contents of a laundry basket.

257

CLARA GILLOW CLARK

Hill Hawk Hattie

(Cambridge, Massachusetts: Candlewick Press, 2003)

Subject(s): Fathers and Daughters; Gender Roles; Lumber Industry

Age range(s): Grades 4-7

Major character(s): Hattie Basket, 11-Year-Old; Amos Basket, Father, Lumberjack

Time period(s): 19th century (late 1800s)

Locale(s): Delaware River, New York; Delaware River, Pennsylvania

Summary: When Hattie's mom dies, her father becomes mean and crotchety and so does Hattie, but who can blame her when she's had to quit school and take over all the running of the house? Her father's a "Hill Hawk" lumberman, which means he spends a lot of time on his own felling, trimming and preparing trees to sell down river after the ice melts. This year he decides that he needs Hattie's help but he doesn't want anyone to know his daughter's undertaking such a dangerous task, so he dresses her as a boy and calls her Harley. As the two ride a raft downriver, shepherding the logs that represent a year's work and wages, the taciturn Amos finally talks to Hattie and, just before he leaves her at her grandmother's for schooling, is able to express his love for her. Hattie's not happy about staying with her grandmother, but knows deep down she's still a "Hill Hawker" and will return home as soon as school's out. (163 pages)

Where it's reviewed:
Booklist, July 2003, page 1886
Horn Book Guide, Fall 2003, page 380
Library Media Connection, January 2004, page 64
School Library Journal, August 2003, page 158
Voice of Youth Advocates, August 2003, page 218

Other books by the same author:
Nellie Bishop, 1997
Willie and the Rattlesnake King, 1997
Annie's Choice, 1993

Other books you might like:
William Durbin, *Blackwater Ben*, 2003
Once his mother dies, Ben quits seventh grade to assist his father who cooks for the loggers at the Blackwater Logging Camp.

Gary Paulsen, *The Cookcamp*, 1991
For a young boy, World War II means disruption of his family when he's sent to live with his grandmother, the cook for a logging company.

Patricia Curtis Pfitsch, *Riding the Flume*, 2002
When Carrie needs to travel quickly to St. Joseph, she takes a chance and rides down the wet and dangerous 30-mile log flume.

Gloria Whelan, *The Wanigan: A Life on the River*, 2002
Annabel can't believe she has to help her mother cook for loggers and ride in this flimsy shack, built on a barge, while floating downriver with the logs.

258

JUDITH CLARKE

Starry Nights

(Asheville, NC: Front Street, 2003)

Subject(s): Ghosts; Brothers and Sisters; Haunted Houses

Age range(s): Grades 7-10

Major character(s): Jess Sinclair, Child; Vida Sinclair, 14-Year-Old; Clement David "Clem" Sinclair, 17-Year-Old; Amy Atlee, Spirit

Time period(s): 2000s

Locale(s): Australia

Summary: Jess doesn't understand what's happening to her family. They used to live in a wonderful house by the bay, but now they've moved inland because her mother's had a nervous breakdown. Her sister Vida is angry all the time and wants to attend *siances*, Jess never sees her father because he's commuting and Clem hasn't even unpacked. One day Jess glimpses a faint hint of blue and senses the presence of a ghostly figure. From conversations Clem has with this ghostly presence, one learns that her name is Amy and she was their mother's best friend. By the end of this book, an intriguing blend of the real world and the spiritual world, the reader understands the relationship between Clem and Amy. (148 pages)

Where it's reviewed:
Booklist, June 2003, page 1759
Horn Book, September 2003, page 608
Publishers Weekly, May 12, 2003, page 67
Riverbank Review, Summer 2003, page 43
Voice of Youth Advocates, February 2004, page 500

Other books by the same author:
Wolf on the Fold, 2001
Night Train, 2000
The Lost Day, 1999
Al Capsella Takes a Vacation, 1993
The Heroic Life of Al Capsella, 1990

Other books you might like:
Peni R. Griffin, *The Ghost Sitter*, 2001
Promising her sister that she won't leave, Susie waits for her family to return until two young girls help release her from her pledge.

Judd Holt, *A Promise to Catie*, 1992
Billy falls in love with a young girl he sees around his Texas farmhouse, not realizing she's a ghost.

Alice Sebold, *The Lovely Bones*, 2002
Murdered on her way home from school, Suzy watches

from heaven as her family and friends all react differently to her death.

Gary Soto, *The Afterlife*, 2003

Ready to dance the night away, Chuy is murdered in the men's room and drifts over his hometown seeing how much he's loved.

259

JUDITH CLARKE

Wolf on the Fold

(Asheville, NC: Front Street Books, 2002)

Subject(s): Family Life; Short Stories; Family Saga
Age range(s): Grades 9-12
Major character(s): Kenny Sinclair, 14-Year-Old
Time period(s): 20th century; 21st century (1935-2002)
Locale(s): Australia

Summary: These interconnected stories follow Kenny Sinclair and his succeeding generations as they battle or witness poverty, racism, emigration and war. Following the death of his father, 14-year-old Kenny is now the sole support for his family. Heading out to find work, he stops to warm his hands over a fire and almost loses his life to a serial killer. Succeeding chapters follow his daughters, their children and their grandchildren over a 70-year span. Their lives are played out against local and world events as they see war begin, witness neighbors forced to tolerate racist remarks, struggle through the Vietnam War, lose family members and endure all the day-to-day crises that occur to families in this interwoven collection of six tales. (169 pages)

Where it's reviewed:
Booklist, September 1, 2002, page 112
Bulletin of the Center for Children's Books, October 2002, page 52
Publishers Weekly, June 10, 2002, page 61
School Library Journal, September 2002, page 220
Voice of Youth Advocates, October 2002, page 270

Other books by the same author:
Starry Nights, 2003
Night Train, 2000
The Lost Day, 1999
Al Capsella Takes a Vacation, 1993
The Heroic Life of Al Capsella, 1990

Other books you might like:
Louisa May Alcott, *Little Women*, 1868
    This classic story of family life stars the four March sisters—Jo, Meg, Beth and Amy.
Berlie Doherty, *White Peak Farm*, 1984
    Several generations are bound together by their ties to the land of White Peak Farm.
Robin Klein, *Dresses of Red and Gold*, 1993
    The three sisters and cousin of the Australian Melling family fill their summer with rich activities as they endure World War II.
Joanne Rocklin, *Strudel Stories*, 1999
    In tribute to their deceased grandfather, Lori and her sister make the family's favorite dish of strudel and recount the flight of their family from Odessa.

260

ANDREW CLEMENTS
DOLORES AVENDANO, Illustrator

Jake Drake, Class Clown

(New York: Simon & Schuster Books for Young Readers, 2002)

Series: Jake Drake
Subject(s): School Life; Teacher-Student Relationships; Behavior
Age range(s): Grades 2-5
Major character(s): Jake Drake, 10-Year-Old, Student—Elementary School; Mrs. Brattle, Teacher; Miss Bruce, Teacher (student)
Time period(s): 2000s
Locale(s): United States

Summary: From the vantage point of fourth grade, Jake reminisces about his year in second grade during the time that a student teacher is assigned to teach his class. From serious, rigid Miss Bruce Jake learns that being the class clown is a way to get attention, if not from the teacher, at least from the other students. His behavior creates a challenge for Miss Bruce and she turns to Mrs. Brattle for help. The experienced teacher sends Miss Bruce back to the classroom and assures that Jake understands the behavior expected of him for the remainder of the year. Jake feels content to have made a memorable impression on Miss Bruce, but decides being the class clown is not a role he wishes to continue. (72 pages)

Where it's reviewed:
Horn Book Guide, Fall 2002, page 356
Publishers Weekly, April 1, 2002, page 86
School Library Journal, July 2002, page 86

Other books by the same author:
Jake Drake, Bully Buster, 2001 (Jake Drake)
Jake Drake, Teacher's Pet, 2001 (Jake Drake)
Jake Drake, Know-It-All, 2001 (Jake Drake)

Other books you might like:
Betsy Duffey, *How to Be Cool in the Third Grade*, 1993
    Learning to be more understanding of others helps Robbie achieve his goal of being "cool" this year.
Patricia Reilly Giff, *The Secret at the Polk Street School*, 1987
    One title in a series tells about one of many adventures experienced by students at Polk Street School.
Stephanie Greene, *Show and Tell*, 1998
    The student teacher in Woody's second grade class doesn't like his show-and-tell presentation.

261

ANDREW CLEMENTS

Things Not Seen

(New York: Philomel Books, 2002)

Subject(s): Blindness; Friendship; Physically Handicapped
Age range(s): Grades 6-8
Major character(s): Bobby Phillips, 15-Year-Old; Alicia Van Horn, Blind Person, Teenager; Emily Phillips, Mother (of Bobby); Dr. Phillips, Scientist (physicist)
Time period(s): 2000s

Locale(s): Chicago, Illinois

Summary: What would you do if you awoke one morning and discovered you were invisible? That's what happens to Bobby and neither he nor his parents can figure out how the invisibility happened or what to do to change him back. While his scientist father thinks of solutions, his mother calls the school to report her son being ill. An automobile accident puts his parents in the hospital and cabin fever forces Bobby out of his house. Because it's warm outside clothing is a problem, so he takes advantage of his invisibility and goes naked. Heading to the university library, he selects a listening room where he meets Alicia, a young girl his age who's blind. Once he convinces Alicia of his invisibility, the two are linked for Alicia can relate to feeling that no one sees her. Meanwhile the police become involved when they think Bobby's disappeared and foul play might be involved. Concerned that his parents may be charged with his murder, Bobby must find a way to shed his invisibility. (251 pages)

Where it's reviewed:
Bulletin of the Center for Children's Books, June 2002, page 358
Horn Book, March 2002, page 210
Publishers Weekly, January 28, 2002, page 291
School Library Journal, March 2002, page 226
Voice of Youth Advocates, February 2002, page 443

Awards the book has won:
ALA Best Books for Young Adults, 2003

Other books by the same author:
The Jacket, 2002
The School Story, 2001
The Janitor's Boy, 2000
Frindle, 1996

Other books you might like:
James DeVita, *Blue*, 2001
    Bored and dreaming of the blue marlin fish that leap out of the water, Morgan awakens to find he's turning into one.
Jeanette Ingold, *The Window*, 1996
    Blinded in a car accident and living with unfamiliar relatives, Mandy hears and ''sees'' enough to piece together the missing bits of her life.
H.G. Wells, *The Invisible Man*, 1897
    A crazed scientist makes himself invisible but then goes on to commit murder; only when he is killed does his body return to visibility.

262

ANDREW CLEMENTS

A Week in the Woods

(New York: Simon & Schuster Books for Young Readers, 2002)

Subject(s): Survival; Camps and Camping; Teacher-Student Relationships
Age range(s): Grades 4-6
Major character(s): Mark Robert Chelmsley, 5th Grader, Son; Mr. Maxwell, Teacher
Time period(s): 2000s (2002)
Locale(s): Scarsdale, New York; Whitson, New Hampshire

Summary: Mark's unhappy to be forced to leave his friends in Scarsdale and attend a new school in Whitson for a few months before being sent to a preppy boarding school. Being driven to school by a chauffeur doesn't help Mark's acceptance by the students. Neither do rumors about the renovations on the farm purchased by his wealthy, often absent parents. Mark's indifferent attitude for the first two weeks in his new school causes Mr. Maxwell to label him a spoiled, rich kid. Although Mark changes and grows in this new rural environment where, for the first time in his life, he has free time, Mr. Maxwell chooses not to see any difference. A weeklong school camping trip proves how wrong Mr. Maxwell's judgment has been when Mark's courage, intelligence and careful preparation for the trip prevent a possible tragedy. (190 pages)

Where it's reviewed:
Booklist, October 1, 2002, page 324
Horn Book Guide, Spring 2003, page 76
Kirkus Reviews, August 1, 2002, page 1124
Publishers Weekly, August 12, 2002, page 301
School Library Journal, November 2002, page 160

Awards the book has won:
IRA Children's Choices, 2003

Other books by the same author:
Jake Drake, Know-It-All, 2001 (Jake Drake)
The School Story, 2001
The Janitor's Boy, 2000
The Landry News, 1999 (School Library Journal Best Books)

Other books you might like:
Kristine L. Franklin, *Lone Wolf*, 1997
    In a remote wooded area Perry's solitary life with his dog and divorced father ends when a family with many children moves in nearby.
Jean Craighead George, *Julie of the Wolves*, 1974
    In a Newbery Award winning title, a pack of wolves comes to Julie's rescue during her trek across the Alaskan wilderness.
Kirkpatrick Hill, *Winter Camp*, 1993
    Recently orphaned Toughboy and his younger sister struggle to survive the winter in an Alaskan trapping camp with an elderly Athabascan caretaker.
Gary Paulsen, *Hatchet*, 1987
    In a Newbery Honor book, a 13-year-old survives a plane crash into a remote Canadian lake. Can Brian survive alone until rescued?

263

BRUCE CLEMENTS

A Chapel of Thieves

(New York: Farrar Straus Giroux, 2002)

Subject(s): Humor; Religion; Voyages and Travels
Age range(s): Grades 6-8
Major character(s): Clayton Desant, Religious, Brother (of Henry); Henry Desant, 15-Year-Old, Brother (of Clayton); Victor Hugo, Historical Figure (writer)
Time period(s): 1840s (1849)
Locale(s): Paris, France; St. Louis, Missouri

Summary: Letters from Clayton, who is preaching in France, arrive back in Missouri for his brother Henry who quickly reads between the lines and realizes Clayton's congregation is nothing but a pack of thieves who are setting up his brother as a fall guy. To save his naïve, inept brother, Henry travels down the Mississippi River to New Orleans and then across the Atlantic to Paris where he locates Clayton, who's not exactly happy to see him. Humor, riots, and scenes with Victor Hugo add to the charm of this very funny sequel to *I Tell a Lie Every So Often*. (210 pages)

Where it's reviewed:
Book Report, September 2002, page 52
Booklist, March 15, 2002, page 1255
Bulletin of the Center for Children's Books, April 2002, page 274
Publishers Weekly, April 8, 2002, page 228
School Library Journal, May 2002, page 147

Other books by the same author:
Tom Loves Anna Loves Tom, 1990
Treasure of Plunderell Manor, 1987
Coming About, 1984
Anywhere Else But Here, 1980
I Tell a Lie Every So Often, 1974

Other books you might like:
Cathryn Clinton, *The Calling*, 2001
   Setting out on a revival tour, 12-year-old Esta Lea worries that her sister is only interested in boys and her uncle steals money from the collection.
Sid Fleischman, *Bandit's Moon*, 1998
   Orphaned and left in the care of a scoundrel, Annyrose dresses like a boy and escapes, only to be captured by the outlaw Joaquin Murieta.
Kathleen Karr, *Skullduggery*, 2000
   Matthew accompanies Dr. ABC to Europe where he hopes to obtain the skull of Voltaire as part of his phrenology research.

264

JESSICA CLERK
LAURA RANKIN, Illustrator

The Wriggly, Wriggly Baby

(New York: Arthur A. Levine/Scholastic, Inc., 2002)

Subject(s): Babies; Stories in Rhyme; Parent and Child
Age range(s): Preschool-Grade 1
Major character(s): Unnamed Character, Baby
Time period(s): 2000s (2002)
Locale(s): United States

Summary: Wriggling on the rug isn't enough for this high-energy baby. Soon the baby with the family dog and cat in tow has wriggled right out the front door and on to the zoo, the circus, the fair and the ocean. Meanwhile, his worried parents trail behind looking for him without success. Finally, the tired baby finds his way home. (32 pages)

Where it's reviewed:
Booklist, October 1, 2002, page 334
Detroit Free Press, August 18, 2002, page 5E
Kirkus Reviews, July 15, 2002, page 1029

School Library Journal, September 2002, page 182

Other books you might like:
Pat Hutchins, *Where's the Baby?*, 1998
   A baby monster's family tries to find him before he can turn the house upside-down.
Peggy Rathmann, *The Day the Babies Crawled Away*, 2003
   When their parents aren't watching, babies crawl away from the fair.
James Stevenson, *Rolling Rose*, 1992
   Toddler Rose escapes her house for an adventure in her walker.

265

KATIE COBB

Happenings

(New York: HarperCollins, 2002)

Subject(s): Teachers; Brothers and Sisters; Schools/High Schools
Age range(s): Grades 7-10
Major character(s): Kelsey Gene Blackwell, 12th Grader; Russ Blackwell, Guardian, Police Officer
Time period(s): 2000s
Locale(s): United States

Summary: Kelsey can't believe the difference in her AP English class. What used to be an exciting, challenging class, with timed writing assignments and demanding books to read, has degenerated into nothing but worksheets. Tired of Mrs. Delaney's lack of teaching, and concerned about their upcoming test, the AP English seniors decide to do just what Mrs. Delaney does, nothing. When Kelsey's older brother and guardian Russ hears about the class's shenanigans, he immediately punishes Kelsey by taking away her driving privileges, reminds her of how upset their deceased father would be, and has her check in with him by e-mail at regularly scheduled times. The administration intervenes and threatens the athletic eligibility and graduation of the class members. Kelsey's caught between her brother Russ, who wants her to abandon the protest, and her allegiance to her friends who want to continue their work stoppage in this first novel. (250 pages)

Where it's reviewed:
Booklist, March 1, 2002, page 1131
Kliatt, May 2002, page 16
Publishers Weekly, January 14, 2002, page 61
School Library Journal, March 2002, page 226
Voice of Youth Advocates, February 2002, page 433

Other books you might like:
Jean Ferris, *Across the Grain*, 1990
   When his older sister Paige, who is also his guardian, decides to move to the desert, Will has no choice but to accompany her.
Rob Thomas, *Rats Saw God*, 1996
   One English credit shy of graduation, Steve's guidance counselor suggests he write a 100-page essay about anything he knows.

Don Trembath, *The Tuesday Cafe*, 1996

Harper learns a lot about himself through his writing class, never realizing it's for newly literate and learning disabled.

266

JAKE COBURN

Prep

(New York: Dutton, 2003)

Subject(s): Gangs; Interpersonal Relations; Self-Perception
Age range(s): Grades 9-12
Major character(s): Nick, Student—High School; Kris Conway, Student—High School; Daniel H. "Danny" Conway, 9th Grader; Greg Carmichael, Student—High School, Gang Member; Charles "Kodak" Kohn, Student—High School
Time period(s): 2000s
Locale(s): New York, New York (Manhattan)

Summary: Once part of a tagging team, spraying graffiti over the walls of New York City buildings, Nick pulls away from Greg and Kodak after Kodak is almost killed. Now Nick concentrates on winning his best friend Kris for his girlfriend, until her brother Danny runs afoul of a gang leader. Pressed to save Danny from serious damage by the MKII gang, Nick reconnects with Greg and his gang for a little help. These gangs aren't the ones from poor neighborhoods; instead they're populated by rich, prep school kids get a kick out of their prowess with butterfly knives, crazed partying, alcoholism, drug addiction, and name brand clothing. Though Nick reenters that world for a while, it's not one in which he wants to stay in this author's first novel. (182 pages)

Where it's reviewed:
Booklist, November 1, 2003, page 489
Bulletin of the Center for Children's Books, January 2004, page 184
New York Times Book Review, January 18, 2004, page 18
School Library Journal, October 2003, page 162
Voice of Youth Advocates, December 2003, page 389

Awards the book has won:
ALA Best Books for Young Adults, 2004

Other books you might like:
Dennis Foon, *Skud*, 2003
Three of four seniors see their life-long plans fall apart before they graduate: one dies, one is jailed and the third loses a chance at pro ice hockey.
Gordon Korman, *Jake, Reinvented*, 2003
In an attempt to win the hand of DiDi, Jacob reinvents himself as Jake, cool long snapper of the football team and fabulous party thrower.
Walter Dean Myers, *The Beast*, 2003
Returning home to Harlem from his prep school, Spoon finds that his girlfriend Gabi has become involved with heroin.

267

MARYANN COCCA-LEFFLER, Author/Illustrator

Bravery Soup

(Morton Grove, IL: Albert Whitman & Company, 2002)

Subject(s): Fear; Animals/Bears; Problem Solving
Age range(s): Grades K-2
Major character(s): Carlin, Raccoon; Big Bear, Bear, Cook
Time period(s): Indeterminate
Locale(s): Fictional Country

Summary: To conquer his many fears Carlin seeks out Big Bear who, coincidentally, is brewing a large pot of bravery soup. The soup needs one more important ingredient to make it complete and Carlin agrees to retrieve it from a distant cave if Big Bear will help him become brave. Big Bear's instructions to travel alone through the forest and up a mountain to the cave terrify Carlin but Big Bear assures him that he is braver than he suspects he is. Carlin's friends offer help and share items that they think will assist Carlin. In the end, Carlin's wits and courage get him to the cave and back to Big Bear with the soup's missing ingredient and Big Bear rewards him with a bowl of well-earned bravery soup. (32 pages)

Where it's reviewed:
Booklist, April 15, 2002, page 1406
Horn Book Guide, Fall 2002, page 323
Publishers Weekly, March 11, 2002, page 70
School Library Journal, March 2002, page 173

Other books by the same author:
Bus Route to Boston, 2000
Mr. Tanen's Ties, 1999
Missing: One Stuffed Rabbit, 1998

Other books you might like:
Kevin Henkes, *Sheila Rae, the Brave*, 1987
When brave Sheila Rae and her timid sister Louise become lost it is Louise who courageously finds the way home.
Holly Keller, *Brave Horace*, 1998
After being invited to a monster-movie party fearful Horace practices being brave enough to attend.
Ellen Stoll Walsh, *Pip's Magic*, 1994
While searching for answers to his fear of the dark, Pip unwittingly overcomes his problem.

268

MARYANN COCCA-LEFFLER, Author/Illustrator

Mr. Tanen's Tie Trouble

(Morton Grove, IL: Albert Whitman & Company, 2003)

Subject(s): Schools; Clothes; Problem Solving
Age range(s): Grades K-3
Major character(s): Mr. Tanen, Principal; Mr. Apple, Administrator
Time period(s): 2000s (2003)
Locale(s): Lynnhurst School

Summary: Renowned for his extensive tie collection, Mr. Tanen proves himself to also be a generous leader. When Mr. Tanen returns to school following winter vacation he's pleased to note the repairs of the furnace and refrigerator and the newly painted classrooms. Then he settles down to select the new playground equipment purchased with the money saved by the school. A call from Mr. Apple informs him that all the money was used making repairs and improvements and there is not enough left for playground equipment. Rather than disappoint his students, Mr. Tanen holds an auction of his 975 ties and earns enough money from their sale to purchase and install the new playground. At the official Opening Day ceremony for the playground Mr. Tanen is surprised to see his ties reappear as the official ceremonial ''ribbon'' around the playground. (32 pages)

Where it's reviewed:
Booklist, June 2003, page 1783
School Library Journal, May 2003, page 110

Other books by the same author:
Bravery Soup, 2002
Jungle Halloween, 2000
Mr. Tanen's Ties, 1999

Other books you might like:
Stephanie Calmenson, *The Frog Principal*, 2001
   A magician's error turns a school principal into a frog that kindly offers to substitute until the principal returns.
Sharon Creech, *A Fine, Fine School*, 2001
   Proud of his fine school, Mr. Keene thinks that more, more, more of the same will make the school even better so the principal holds Saturday school.
Patricia Polacco, *Mr. Lincoln's Way*, 2001
   Loved for being a ''cool'' principal by everyone but the school bully, Mr. Lincoln learns the bully's interests and uses them to help him.

269

ESME RAJI CODELL

Sahara Special
(New York: Hyperion, 2003)

Subject(s): Self-Esteem; Teacher-Student Relationships; Authorship
Age range(s): Grades 4-7
Major character(s): Sahara ''Sahara Special'' Jones, 5th Grader; Madame Poitier ''Miss Pointy'', Teacher
Time period(s): 2000s
Locale(s): United States

Summary: Missing her father who abandoned his family, Sahara spends her time at school writing him letters rather than completing any classwork. Trying to help, the school places Sahara with a special needs teacher, hence the nickname ''Sahara Special.'' When her mother objects to this placement, Sahara repeats fifth grade. Madame Poitier is her new teacher and, with her dislike of bureaucracy and unusual but creative teaching style, she energizes her students. Sahara has always said she's a writer and with Miss Pointy, she's able to prove it. (175 pages)

Where it's reviewed:
Booklist, April 1, 2003, page 1397
Bulletin of the Center for Children's Books, April 2003, page 308
Horn Book, May 2003, page 340

Publishers Weekly, March 17, 2003, page 77
School Library Journal, July 2003, page 124

Other books by the same author:
Education Esme: Diary of a Teacher's First Year, 1999 (adult fiction)

Other books you might like:
Lloyd Alexander, *The Gawgon and the Boy*, 2001
   Apprehensive about being tutored at home by his Aunt Annie, David finds she sparks his imagination better than any other teacher he's had.
Sharon Creech, *Love That Dog*, 2001
   Inspired by the gentle guidance of his teacher Miss Stretchberry, Jack evolves from a poetry hater to an admirer and writer of poems.
Amy McDonald, *No More Nasty*, 2001
   Though Simon is relieved his class's ''nasty'' teacher is retiring, he's not sure about the substitute who's his unconventional great aunt.

270

PETER COHEN
OLOF LANDSTROM, Illustrator
JOAN SANDIN, Translator

Boris's Glasses
(New York: R&S Books/Farrar Straus Giroux, 2003)

Subject(s): Animals/Hamsters; Factories; Cleanliness
Age range(s): Grades 1-3
Major character(s): Boris, Hamster
Time period(s): 2000s (2003)
Locale(s): Sweden

Summary: Boris visits the optometrist to determine why he struggles to see his TV. After he receives glasses Boris is amazed at all he can see from fingers on babies to sugar roses on cakes and the pretty girl at the bakery. Boris gets a management job at the factory overseeing the production of radios. After a day of clear vision, Boris decides that working is tedious and he doesn't want to see how dirty his house is. He decides to take the glasses off, but to keep them in case he wants to see a baby's fingers and the like in the future. (28 pages)

Where it's reviewed:
Bulletin of the Center for Children's Books, October 2003, page 54
Publishers Weekly, September 8, 2003, page 76
School Library Journal, September 2003, page 176

Other books by the same author:
Mr. Bohm and the Herring, 1992
Olson's Meat Pies, 1989

Other books you might like:
Shirley Day, *Luna and the Big Blur: A Story for Children Who Wear Glasses*, 2000
   Luna hates wearing her glasses, but when she doesn't a series of mishaps occur.
Ainslie Manson, *Ballerinas Don't Wear Glasses*, 2001
   A boy convinces his sister not to wear her glasses for her ballet recital, because if she can't see the audience, she won't have stage fright.

Lane Smith, *Glasses: Who Needs 'Em?*, 1991
An optometrist tries to convince a young boy to wear the glasses he needs to correct his vision.

271

DIANA COHN
AMY CORDOVA, Illustrator

Dream Carver

(San Francisco: Chronicle Books, 2002)

Subject(s): Imagination; Artists and Art; Fathers and Sons
Age range(s): Grades 1-3
Major character(s): Mateo, Son, Artisan; Unnamed Character, Father, Artisan
Time period(s): Indeterminate Past
Locale(s): Mexico

Summary: From his father Mateo learns to carve small wooden animal figures to sell at local fiestas and in the shops in Oaxaca just as Mateo's father learned to do from his father. In Mateo's dreams though he sees brightly colored, life-size carved animals. When Mateo shares his dreams his father cannot understand why he would want to change the carving techniques the family has used for centuries. Despite his father's admonitions Mateo secretly masters the art of carving larger animals and painting them with bright colors. When Mateo displays his work at the next fiesta, the crowds eagerly buy his carvings and his father acknowledges that it is time for Mateo to teach him a new style. Background information on Oaxacan woodcarving is appended in the author's first book. (32 pages)

Where it's reviewed:
Booklist, June 2002, page 1721
Bulletin of the Center for Children's Books, October 2002, page 53
Horn Book Guide, Fall 2002, page 323
School Library Journal, July 2002, page 86
Smithsonian, December 2002, page 124

Awards the book has won:
Smithsonian's Notable Books for Children, 2002

Other books you might like:
Patricia Grossman, *Saturday Market*, 1994
Artisans display a variety of wares at a weekly Mexican market.
Patricia Maloney Markun, *The Little Painter of Sabana Grande*, 1993
A shortage of paper does not deter a young Panamanian artist who uses his adobe home as his canvas.
Jeanette Winter, *Josefina*, 1996
In her Mexican village Josefina creates unique pieces of brightly painted clay figures.

272

RACHEL COHN

Gingerbread

(New York: Simon & Schuster, 2002)

Subject(s): Mothers and Daughters; Stepfamilies; Abortion

Age range(s): Grades 9-12
Major character(s): Cyd Charisse, 16-Year-Old; Frank, Father (of Cyd Charisse); Danny, Stepbrother (of Cyd Charisse); Rhonda, Stepsister (of Cyd Charisse); Shrimp, Boyfriend (of Cyd Charisse)
Time period(s): 2000s
Locale(s): San Francisco, California; New York, New York

Summary: Sent home from boarding school for "sexual indiscretions," Cyd Charisse quickly wears out her welcome in San Francisco with her mother and stepfather, especially when she thumbs her nose at their curfews, creates chaos in the family and dates the surfer Shrimp. So Cyd Charisse is sent to New York for the summer where she will not only live with her biological father, with whom her mother had an affair seventeen years ago, but also finally meet her older half-brother Danny and half-sister Rhonda. Cyd Charisse's fairy tale dream of her distant family and their perfect reunion doesn't hold up as her father barely has time for her, Danny has a gay partner and Rhonda, called Lisbeth by the family, wants no part of her. Making the most of being in New York, Cyd Charisse puts a move on her father's chauffeur, works for Danny as a barista in his cafi and begins to consider her California family in a different light. Throughout her stay, she clings to the rag doll her real father gave her years ago, a doll she calls Gingerbread, though on the way home she merges her thoughts of Gingerbread with Shrimp in this way-hip, first novel. (172 pages)

Where it's reviewed:
Booklist, April 15, 2002, page 1394
Kliatt, March 2002, page 7
Publishers Weekly, January 21, 2002, page 91
School Library Journal, February 2002, page 129
Voice of Youth Advocates, April 2002, page 40

Awards the book has won:
ALA Best Books for Young Adults, 2003
School Library Journal Best Books, 2002

Other books by the same author:
The Steps, 2003

Other books you might like:
Francesca Lia Block, *Weetzie Bat*, 1989
Offbeat Weetzie and Dirk each find their true love, though not with one another, in this witty, bizarre, modern-day fairy tale.
Sid Fleischman, *Bo and Mzzz Mad*, 2001
When Bo's orphaned, he's unsure whether or not to contact his Martinka relatives who've always feuded with his Gamage side of the family.
Mavis Jukes, *Cinderella 2000*, 1999
A modern-day Cinderella, who's saddled with baby-sitting her twin stepsisters on New Years Eve, needs a fairy godmother fast!
Susan Whitcher, *The Fool Reversed*, 2000
Anna's tarot cards warn, but don't save, her from falling from an older man; luckily fellow teen Dylan rescues her from this sticky situation.

273

RACHEL COHN

The Steps

(New York: Simon & Schuster, 2003)

Subject(s): Stepfamilies; Family Life
Age range(s): Grades 5-8
Major character(s): Annabel Whoopi Schubert, 12-Year-Old; Lucy Crosswell, 12-Year-Old, Stepsister; Angus Crosswell, Child, Stepbrother; Jack Schubert, Father; Beatrice Schubert, Baby
Time period(s): 2000s
Locale(s): New York, New York; Sydney, Australia

Summary: All of a sudden families, specifically step families, begin taking over Annabel's life. Born to free-wheeling parents, who she calls Angelina and Jack, Annabel doesn't even mind when they separate as it stops the arguing and she sees Jack more than when he lived at home. But now he's married Penny and moved to Australia where he lives with Penny's children Lucy and Angus and their baby Beatrice. Her mother Angelina is madly in love with the father of the biggest dweeb in Annabel's school and headed to Hawaii with him over Christmas vacation, so it's off to Australia for Annabel. She's certain that she can talk Jack into returning to New York with her, so is a little taken aback when she arrives and hears Lucy and Angus calling him Dad. Annabel's instant hostility to Lucy gradually changes to friendship as she realizes Lucy's not happy either with having to move to Sydney. By book's end, Annabel's adjusted to her Australian stepfamily, which is a good thing because her mother calls with the news that she's pregnant and plans to marry the dweeb's father. (144 pages)

Where it's reviewed:
Booklist, January 2003, page 887
Bulletin of the Center for Children's Books, February 2003, page 229
Horn Book, May 2003, page 341
Publishers Weekly, December 23, 2003, page 71
School Library Journal, February 2003, page 140

Other books by the same author:
Shrimp, 2005
Pop Princess, 2004
Gingerbread, 2002

Other books you might like:
Anne Fine, *My War with Goggle-Eyes*, 1989
    Kitty brings out all her artillery in an attempt to get rid of Gerald Faulkner, the man her mother is dating.
P.J. Petersen, *White Water*, 1997
    Stepbrothers learn to work together when a rattlesnake bites their father while they're on a canoe trip.
J.P. Reading, *The Summer of Sassy Jo*, 1989
    Sent to live with her mother, insecure Sally Jo goes out of her way to antagonize her new family.
Todd Strasser, *Pastabilities*, 2000
    Though the Rand family's nanny is a little unusual with her spiked hair, body piercings and tattoos, she's the only one who can control their blended family. ·

274

BABETTE COLE, Author/Illustrator

Truelove

(New York: Dial Books for Young Readers, 2002)

Subject(s): Animals/Dogs; Babies; Love
Age range(s): Grades K-2
Major character(s): Truelove, Dog
Time period(s): 2000s
Locale(s): England

Summary: After a new baby joins the family, the family pet Truelove tries to assure there is enough love for everyone. The new parents don't seem to agree that "love is sharing" when Truelove offers the baby a dead mouse. When Truelove expresses joy by "singing" a love song the unappreciated dog is sent out to the doghouse. Truelove runs away and satisfies his loving instincts caring for strays. About the time the new parents notice Truelove is missing, the police are apprehending the dog and his companions. When Truelove is rescued, he gets permission for all the other dogs to join the family too because he's sure there is enough love to go around in this title originally published in Great Britain in 2001. (32 pages)

Where it's reviewed:
Booklist, December 1, 2001, page 647
Kirkus Reviews, November 15, 2001, page 1611
Magpies, March 2001, page 30
Publishers Weekly, December 3, 2001, page 59
School Library Journal, January 2002, page 96

Other books by the same author:
Bad Habits!, 1999 (IRA Children's Choice)
Drop Dead, 1997
Dr. Dog, 1994

Other books you might like:
Madeleine L'Engle, *The Other Dog*, 2001
    A misunderstanding of the difference between dogs and babies has a family's pet wondering why the family would acquire a dog as inadequate as Jo.
Rosemary Wells, *McDuff and the Baby*, 1997
    McDuff's idyllic life with Fred and Lucy changes dramatically when they bring home a tiny, crying, time-consuming stranger.
Harriet Ziefert, *Pushkin Minds the Bundle*, 2000
    Pushkin is understandably jealous of the bundle named Pierre that receives so much attention and even claims Pushkin's favorite seat in the car.

275

SHEILA COLE

The Canyon

(New York: HarperCollins, 2002)

Subject(s): Endangered Species; Environmental Problems; Conduct of Life
Age range(s): Grades 4-7
Major character(s): Zachary James "Zach" Barnes, 6th Grader; Trevor, 6th Grader

Time period(s): 2000s
Locale(s): San Ramon, California

Summary: The San Ramon Canyon is a favorite spot for hiking or picnicking, so Zach's community is upset when they hear the Bowen Corporation will be leveling it to build 95 luxury homes. Zach fights against the development by taking photographs of the canyon as well as enlisting his schoolmates and neighbors to sign petitions and present their case to the local government. When that doesn't work, Zach and his friend Trevor pull up the surveyor stakes, though Trevor goes a little overboard with vandalism. Upset that this will hurt their cause, Zach sells his baseball cards on the Internet and links it to saving the San Ramon Canyon. Zach's pleas and his discovery of the endangered pocket mouse prompt the owner of the property to set aside half the canyon for a nature preserve and the other half for a scaled down housing development. (146 pages)

Where it's reviewed:
Booklist, August 2002, page 1958
Horn Book Guide, Fall 2002, page 369
Kirkus Reviews, May 15, 2002, page 729
School Library Journal, June 2002, page 134

Other books by the same author:
What Kind of Love?: The Diary of a Pregnant Teenager, 1995 (ALA Recommended Book for Reluctant Young Adult Readers)
The Dragon in the Cliff, 1991
Meaning Well, 1974

Other books you might like:
Joe Cardillo, *Pulse*, 1996
When Jason and Kris discover a plan to turn their favorite woodland area into a mall, they form a student environmental group called Pulse.
Carl Hiaasen, *Hoot*, 2002
Roy and a strange kid named Mullet Fingers try to save the nesting area of the burrowing owls from construction of an American Pancake House.
Monte Killingsworth, *Eli's Song*, 1991
Upset that an old-growth forest is to be cut, young Eli "tree sits" until a lawyer agrees to take his case to court.
David Klass, *California Blue*, 1994
Thrilled to discover a new species of butterfly, John's delight ends when he realizes the butterfly's rarity will cost his father his lumber job.

276

EOIN COLFER

Artemis Fowl: The Arctic Incident

(New York: Hyperion/Talk Miramax, 2002)

Subject(s): Fairies; Kidnapping; Magic
Age range(s): Grades 5-8
Major character(s): Artemis Fowl Jr., 13-Year-Old; Artemis Fowl Sr., Father (of Artemis), Kidnap Victim; Butler, Servant; Captain Holly Short, Fairy, Police Officer
Time period(s): Indeterminate Future
Locale(s): Ireland; Murmansk, Russia; Lower Elements, Fictional Country

Summary: Artemis returns in an attempt to rescue his long-missing father from the Russian Mafiya. To be successful, he and Butler need the help of his former-kidnap victim, Captain Holly Short of the LEPrecon (Lower Elements Police Reconnaissance), who for once is eager to work with him. Don't think that Artemis is on Captain Holly's friends list; matter of fact she planned to bring in Artemis and Butler on charges of smuggling. Instead Captain Holly is forced to seek Artemis's help when one of her LEPrecon officers, Briar Cudgeons, attempts to overthrow fairyland in this second outrageous adventure. (277 pages)

Where it's reviewed:
Book World, July 14, 2002, page 12
Booklist, May 1, 2002, page 1518
Bulletin of the Center for Children's Books, June 2002, page 358
Publishers Weekly, April 15, 2002, page 65
School Library Journal, July 2002, page 118

Other books by the same author:
Artemis Fowl: The Eternity Code, 2003
Artemis Fowl, 2001
Benny and Omar, 2001

Other books you might like:
Debi Gliori, *Pure Dead Magic*, 2001
Siblings Pandora and Titus must evade assassins as they search for and try to rescue their kidnapped father.
J.K. Rowling, *The Harry Potter Series*, 1998-
Raised by his aunt and uncle, Harry is thrilled to be invited to attend Hogwarts School and begin his studies of wizardry.
Lemony Snicket, *Unfortunate Events Series*, 1999-
The Baudelaire children live up to the name of the series as their lives go from bad to worse following their parents' death in a fire.

277

EOIN COLFER

Artemis Fowl: The Eternity Code

(New York: Hyperion/Miramax, 2003)

Subject(s): Adventure and Adventurers; Magic; Computers
Age range(s): Grades 5-8
Major character(s): Artemis Fowl, Teenager, Con Artist; Butler, Servant; Jon Spiro, Businessman; Holly Short, Police Officer; Juliet Butler, Sister (of Butler); Mulch Diggums, Dwarf
Time period(s): Indeterminate Future
Locale(s): London, England; Ireland (Fowl Manor); Chicago, Illinois

Summary: With his father rescued from the Russians and recovering in a hospital in Helsinki, and his mother proclaiming that the Fowl family will no longer engage in illegal activities, Artemis has to work quickly to move his last extortion plan into action. Using fairy technology he builds a new supercomputer, called the C Cube, which he plans to hold off the market if shyster businessman Jon Spiro will pay him a metric ton of gold. But his scheme backfires, the C Cube is stolen, Butler is mortally wounded, and Artemis stashes his friend away cryogenically until medical help can arrive. Until then, Artemis calls on Butler's sister Juliet, his reluctant ally Holly Short from the fairy police, and Mulch, to storm the Spiro Needle in Chicago and retrieve the C Cube in another action-filled adventure. (309 pages)

Where it's reviewed:
Booklist, June 2003, page 1759
Bulletin of the Center for Children's Books, July 2003, page 440
Publishers Weekly, March 31, 2003, page 68
School Library Journal, July 2003, page 128
Voice of Youth Advocates, October 2003, page 322

Other books by the same author:
Artemis Fowl Files, 2004
Artemis Fowl: The Arctic Incident, 2002
Artemis Fowl, 2001

Other books you might like:
Will Allen, *Swords for Hire: Two of the Most Unlikely Heroes*, 2003
 Rather than farming, Sam opts to be a knight; as his attempts at rescue with compatriot Rigby Skeet prove, he's not a very good one.
Anthony Dana Arkin, *Captain Hawaii*, 1994
 Exploding rafts, swarming spiders and a severed hand aren't what Arron expects to find when he and his parents vacation in Hawaii.
Anthony Horowitz, *Point Blank: An Alex Rider Adventure*, 2002
 Attending an elite finishing school, Alex finds a crazed scientist is replacing the sons of important men with docile clones.

278

EOIN COLFER

The Wish List
(New York: Miramax/Hyperion, 2003)

Subject(s): Humor; Ghosts; Good and Evil
Age range(s): Grades 7-10
Major character(s): Meg Finn, 14-Year-Old, Spirit; Lowrie McCall, Aged Person; Belch, Criminal; Raptor, Dog (pit bull); Beelzebub, Demon; Saint Peter, Religious
Time period(s): 2000s
Locale(s): Ireland

Summary: After her mother dies and her abusive stepfather kicks Meg out of the house, she turns to a life of crime with Belch and his pit bull Raptor. The three try to rob her elderly neighbor Lowrie McCall but when a gas tank explodes, the three robbers are blown out of their bodies and wind up headed to heaven and hell. Belch and Raptor end up below where they're put to work by Beelzebub to lure Meg into more trouble, for Satan wants her as part of his contingent. Meg is nicely balanced between good deeds and evil deeds, partly because she tried to protect Lowrie, so neither St. Peter nor Beelzebub can decide where she should reside. She's sent back to Earth with instructions to help Lowrie attain all the items on his wish list, a task which could help her attain heavenly status. Knowing that he doesn't have many more

days on Earth, Lowrie wants to kick a soccer goal, kiss a woman he didn't dare kiss when he was young and exact revenge on a bully from his childhood days. Meg works hard to help him, but Belch works equally hard to keep her from succeeding, in this humorous tale that mixes reality and fantasy. (252 pages)

Where it's reviewed:
Bulletin of the Center for Children's Books, December 2003, page 146
Kliatt, January 2004, page 6
Publishers Weekly, October 13, 2003, page 80
School Library Journal, December 2003, page 148
Voice of Youth Advocates, December 2003, page 410

Other books by the same author:
The Legend of Spud Murphy, 2004
The Supernaturalist, 2004
Artemis Fowl: The Eternity Code, 2003
Artemis Fowl: The Arctic Incident, 2002
Artemis Fowl, 2001 (Bulletin of the Center for Children's Books Blue Ribbons)

Other books you might like:
Cherie Bennett, *Heaven Can't Wait*, 1996
 Teens Cisco, Nicole and Melody die before learning life's lessons and must now help other teens before being admitted to Ultimate Heaven.
Lael Littke, *Haunted Sister*, 1998
 Janine "dies" in an automobile accident, but instead has a near-death experience; when she returns to earth, her dead twin Lenore comes back with her.
Barbara Timberlake Russell, *Blue Lightning*, 1997
 Struck by lightning, Calvin floats above his body but doesn't die; returning to life, he's followed by Rory's ghost who makes life miserable for him.

279

JAMES LINCOLN COLLIER

Wild Boy
(Tarrytown, NY: Marshall Cavendish, 2002)

Subject(s): Mountain Life; Anger; Fathers and Sons
Age range(s): Grades 5-8
Major character(s): Jesse, 12-Year-Old; Larry, Mountain Man, Trapper; Billings, Mountain Man
Time period(s): Indeterminate Past
Locale(s): United States

Summary: Jesse's mother leaves the family and Jesse now loses his temper all the time. When he swings an ax handle at his father and knocks him unconscious, Jesse takes off for the mountains, intending to live there. After just three days he's starving and stealing animals out of someone's traps. Trapper Larry catches Jesse and decides to teach him survival skills, beginning with chopping firewood for the winter months. Jesse learns there's more to being a mountain man than just having food and shelter as he contends with a bear and a mentally unbalanced man who thinks he's chasing all the game away. Jesse eventually sorts out his feelings about his family and realizes why his mother abandoned them; when he finally feels self-confident and able to restrain his temper, he returns home to his father in this look at life on the frontier. (159 pages)

Where it's reviewed:
Booklist, November 1, 2002, page 490
Horn Book Guide, Fall 2003, page 364
School Library Journal, November 2002, page 160

Other books by the same author:
Me and Billy, 2004
To Live Among Strangers, 2004
Chipper, 2001
The Corn Raid, 2000
The Jazz Kid, 1994

Other books you might like:
William Durbin, *Blackwater Ben*, 2003
   After his mother dies, Ben quits seventh grade to assist his father who cooks for the loggers at the Blackwater Logging Camp.
Deb Vanesse, *A Distant Enemy*, 1997
   Part Eskimo and part white, Joseph is an angry young man trying to live in the ways of his Eskimo culture, but going about everything the wrong way.
Luke Wallin, *The Redneck Poacher's Son*, 1981
   All his life Jesse's wanted to escape from the swamps, where his father makes moonshine and traps and hunts illegally.

280

KRISTI COLLIER

Jericho Walls

(New York: Holt, 2002)

Subject(s): Race Relations; Segregation; African Americans
Age range(s): Grades 6-9
Major character(s): Josephine ''Jo'' Clawson, 11-Year-Old; Lucas Jefferson, 12-Year-Old; Abilene Jefferson, Housekeeper
Time period(s): 1950s (1957)
Locale(s): Jericho, South Carolina

Summary: Moving from Indiana back to her preacher father's hometown, Jo and her mother are not familiar with, or even aware of, the unwritten rules for black and white interchanges. Jo's part Cherokee mother works with some members of the black community but her husband, to ingratiate himself with his racist congregation, asks her to withdraw her help. The combination of tomboy and preacher's kid keeps Jo from becoming friendly with kids in her neighborhood and she hangs around with Lucas, the son of their family's housekeeper, Abilene. Jo is appalled when Lucas is not granted a library card and she and her brother organize a sit-in until Lucas receives his card. This author's first novel offers an objective, realistic peek at life before the days of Civil Rights when racism and prejudice were once commonplace. (213 pages)

Where it's reviewed:
Bulletin of the Center for Children's Books, September 2002, page 10
Horn Book, July 2002, page 456
Publishers Weekly, April 15, 2002, page 65

School Library Journal, April 2002, page 142
Voice of Youth Advocates, June 2002, page 115

Awards the book has won:
Smithsonian's Notable Books for Children/Older Readers, 2002

Other books you might like:
Christopher Paul Curtis, *The Watsons Go to Birmingham—1963*, 1995
   Heading south to visit Grandmother, the Watson family's high spirits falter when a church in Birmingham blows up and four children are killed.
Trudy Krisher, *Spite Fences*, 1994
   The summer Maggie Pugh is 13 remains embedded in her memory as the summer she realizes how racist her town is.
Carolyn Meyer, *White Lilacs*, 1993
   The black community of Freedomtown opposes being moved to the sewer flats, but violence and marches by the Ku Klux Klan stop their action.
Harriette Gillem Robinet, *Walking to the Bus-Rider Blues*, 2000
   During the Montgomery bus boycott, Alfa, Zinnia and Big Mama walk everywhere and see some wrongs righted as they adjust to the ''bus-rider-blues.''
Ouida Sebestyen, *Words by Heart*, 1979
   Young black Lena upsets her local community when she beats a white boy in a spelling bee at the turn of the century.

281

PAT LOWERY COLLINS

The Fattening Hut

(Boston: Houghton Mifflin, 2003)

Subject(s): Runaways; Gender Roles; Islands
Age range(s): Grades 9-12
Major character(s): Helen, 14-Year-Old; Margaret, Aunt
Time period(s): 20th century
Locale(s): Fictional Country (primitive tropical island)

Summary: In Helen's mythical island culture in the early 1900s, after being promised as a bride to an older man in her village, she follows custom and enters the ''fattening hut.'' Here her favorite foods are prepared for her to ensure a plumb bride, but finds she's unable to eat. Her aunt Margaret, outcast of the family, learned to read English from British visitors and in turn taught Helen to do the same; now she smuggles in a piece she wrote entitled ''An Island Story,'' which gives a brief history of the fattening hut. Helen is startled to read about the ceremonial cutting—she doesn't really understand what it means, but knows she wants no part of it and runs away. There aren't many places to hide on an island, but she travels as far away from her family as possible and fortuitously meets some Englishmen who offer her asylum. (186 pages)

Where it's reviewed:
Booklist, November 1, 2003, page 490
Library Media Connection, March 2004, page 66
Publishers Weekly, October 20, 2003, page 55
School Library Journal, November 2003, page 134

Voice of Youth Advocates, February 2004, page 484

Other books by the same author:
Just Imagine, 2001
Signs and Wonders, 1999

Other books you might like:
Nancy Farmer, *A Girl Named Disaster*, 1996
Raised by a cruel aunt, 11-year-old Nhamofaces marriage to an older man with three wives; instead she runs away to locate her father in Zimbabwe.
Christina Kessler, *No Condition Is Permanent*, 2000
Accompanying her Peace Corps mother to Sierra Leone, Jolie offends the villagers when she stops her friend Khadi's initiation into a women's secret society.
Lensey Namioka, *Ties That Bind, Ties That Break*, 1999
The young Chinese girl Ailin first defies tradition by refusing to have her feet bound then, when older, cancels her arranged marriage.
Suzanne Fisher Staples, *Haveli*, 1993
Forced to marry elderly Rahim, Shabanu and her child run away after he dies.

282

PAUL COLLINS

The Earthborn
(New York: Tor, 2003)

Subject(s): Science Fiction; Feral Children; Survival
Age range(s): Grades 9-Adult
Major character(s): Welkin Quinn, 14-Year-Old, Military Personnel; Sarah, Teenager
Time period(s): Indeterminate Future
Locale(s): Melbourne, Australia

Summary: Though Welkin was born aboard the starship *Colony*, he still thinks of Earth as his home planet, though he's never been near its surface. He finally has his chance when his spacecraft returns to Earth after a failed attempt at colonizing Tau Ceti III. Part of a reconnaissance team made up of "expendables," Welkin finds himself on a devastated, wasted Earth and under attack by murderous feral Earthborn. Sarah, another Earthborn who tries to unite families, unexpectedly rescues him and he quickly realizes that much of what he's been told by his commanding officers aboard the ship has been incorrect. Sarah's barbaric way of life, which is the only way to survive on Earth, is an eye opener for Welkin who's used to the elite lifestyle enjoyed aboard the *Colony* by the Skyborns in a novel by an Australian author. (240 pages)

Where it's reviewed:
Analog, September 2003, page 134
Booklist, March 15, 2003, page 1285
Chronicle, April 2003, page 40
Publishers Weekly, March 3, 2003, page 76
Voice of Youth Advocates, June 2003, page 147

Other books by the same author:
Metaworlds: Best Australian Science Fiction, 1994
Alien Worlds, 1979

Other books you might like:
C.J. Cherryh, *Precursor*, 1999
Three cultures, two human and one alien, struggle for supremacy and control of an orbiting space station.
John Marsden, *Tomorrow, When the War Began Series*, 1995-2002
Teen friends become guerrillas and assist the army when terrorists overrun their homeland of New Zealand.
Gary Paulsen, *The White Fox Chronicles: Escape, Return, Breakout*, 2000
Cody is part of a resistance group of Americans fighting to regain control of their country from the Confederation of Consolidated Republics.

283

ROSS COLLINS, Author/Illustrator

Alvie Eats Soup
(New York: Scholastic Press, 2002.)

Subject(s): Food; Grandparents; Obstinacy
Age range(s): Grades K-2
Major character(s): Alvie, Child, Brother; Delilah, Child, Sister; Gourmet Granny Franny, Cook, Grandmother
Time period(s): 2000s (2002)
Locale(s): Chowderville, United Kingdom

Summary: Alvie only eats soup. He likes soup so much that his first word was "Mulligatawny." This dismays his parents who worry about his health and the fact that his Granny Franny is a gourmet chef. When they learn that she is coming for a visit, Alvie's parents try everything to get him to eat something other than soup—but to no avail. However, once Granny Franny arrives, they discover that she only eats peas. Alvie decides to follow suit. (32 pages)

Where it's reviewed:
Booklist, November 1, 2002, page 505
Horn Book Guide, Spring 2003, page 29
Kirkus Reviews, September 1, 2002, page 1306
Publishers Weekly, October 14, 2002, page 83
School Library Journal, October 1, 2002, page 99

Other books by the same author:
Busy Night, 2003
I Live in the Jungle, 2000
Sea Hole, 1997

Other books you might like:
Jackie French, *Too Many Pears!*, 2003
Pamela the cow loves pears and doesn't want to eat anything else.
Russell Hoban, *Bread and Jam for Frances*, 1964
Frances only likes to eat bread and jam, but when her mother starts feeding her bread and jam at every meal, she soon gets sick of it.
Mary Ann Hoberman, *The Seven Silly Eaters*, 2000
The seven Peters children each have a favorite food and will only eat that. For Mom's birthday they come up with a surprise.
Mitchell Sharmat, *Gregory, the Terrible Eater*, 1980
Gregory the goat doesn't like to eat shoes and tin cans, he

wants to eat fruits and vegetables, much to his parents' dismay.

284

SUZANNE COLLINS

Gregor the Overlander
(New York: Scholastic, 2003)

Subject(s): Fantasy; Brothers and Sisters; Missing Persons
Age range(s): Grades 5-8
Major character(s): Gregor, 11-Year-Old; Boots, Sister, Child
Time period(s): 2000s
Locale(s): New York, New York; Underland, Fictional Country (city of Regalia)

Summary: Watching his little sister one day while doing the family laundry in the basement of their apartment building, Gregor sees Boots crawl into an air shaft and disappear. He quickly follows her and finds himself falling through the shaft, landing in an underground world filled with huge, talking cockroaches, giant spiders and translucent skinned humans. Wanting to leave as quickly as he arrived, Gregor discovers he's the leader that's been promised to help the Underland inhabitants battle the giant, gnawing rats. He's not totally convinced he needs to stay until he realizes his father, who disappeared three years ago, is held captive by these rats. Together with Boots, who charms all the strange creatures, one large rat and all the cockroaches and spiders, Gregor successfully defeats the rats and frees his father in a robust fantasy by a new author. (311 pages)

Where it's reviewed:
Booklist, November 15, 2003, page 608
Bulletin of the Center for Children's Books, January 2004, page 185
Horn Book, September 2003, page 609
School Library Journal, November 2003, page 134
Voice of Youth Advocates, October 2003, page 322

Other books by the same author:
Gregor the Overlander and the Prophecy of Bane, 2004

Other books you might like:
Joan Aiken, *Is Underground*, 1993
    Searching for her cousin Arun, Is finds him held captive in the underground mines and foundries of Holderness.
Jeanne DuPrau, *The City of Ember*, 2003
    The underground city in which Lina and Doon live is wearing out, but only they seem concerned about finding the instructions to leave.
Brian Jacques, *Redwall Series*, 1987-
    A series that features the mice of Redwall who defend their abbey against scurrilous animals and offer refuge to friends.
Robin Jarvis, *The Final Reckoning*, 2002
    The despicable sewer cat Jupiter returns from the dead to seize control of the world but is sent into the astral void by Audrey and the other Deptford mice.

285

ELLEN CONFORD
RENEE W. ANDRIANI, Illustrator

Annabel the Actress, Starring in Hound of the Barkervilles
(New York: Simon & Schuster Books for Young Readers, 2002)

Subject(s): Actors and Actresses; Animals/Dogs; Humor
Age range(s): Grades 2-4
Major character(s): Annabel, Child, Actress (aspiring); Binky, Dog (Newfoundland)
Time period(s): 2000s (2002)
Locale(s): United States

Summary: The opportunity to perform in a real play is so exciting to Annabel that she overcomes her fear of Binky, a dog much larger than his name suggests. Getting accustomed to Binky is the first hurdle. Then, Annabel sees her costume, bunny pajamas, and wonders how she can take the stage in such a humiliating outfit. Despite those setbacks, Annabel performs like a professional, learning her lines and improvising when the unexpected happens during the show. Annabel doesn't break a leg but she does prove to be a trouper! (83 pages)

Where it's reviewed:
Booklist, July 2002, page 1844
Bulletin of the Center for Children's Books, October 2002, page 53
Publishers Weekly, July 8, 2002, page 51
School Library Journal, July 2002, page 86

Other books by the same author:
Annabel the Actress Starring in Camping It Up, 2004
Annabel the Actress Starring in Just a Little Extra, 2000
Annabel the Actress Starring in Gorilla My Dreams, 1999

Other books you might like:
Diane DeGroat, *Annie Pitts, Burger Kid*, 2000
    Annie, aspiring actress, feels confident that she'll win the Burger Barn poster contest and fulfill her desire for fame.
Patricia Reilly Giff, *Poopsie Pomerantz, Pick Up You Feet*, 1989
    Poopsie's self esteem drops when she is chosen to play a pig in the class play.
Phyllis Reynolds Naylor, *The Girl's Revenge*, 1998
    Caroline's plan seems perfect to the actress wannabe and it does give her attention, but not what she expects.

286

JANE LESLIE CONLY

The Rudest Alien on Earth
(New York: Holt, 2002)

Subject(s): Science Fiction; Aliens; Animals
Age range(s): Grades 4-7
Major character(s): Oluu, Alien, Shape-Shifter; Molly Harkin, 10-Year-Old; Jack Molloy, 10-Year-Old
Time period(s): 2000s
Locale(s): Vermont

Summary: Sent to Earth on a fact-finding mission to find out about its life forms, Oluu is sent out with strict rules to follow, but not to interact with, or form attachments to, the life forms. However, Oluu's always been a little careless and apt to follow her heart instead of her head, so as soon as she lands she shape shifts into the form of a border collie. Then she befriends Molly and amazes her when she can speak to her in English. Though Molly tries to keep Oluu a secret, her loner friend Jack eventually figures it out. Oluu doesn't remain as a border collie but shape shifts as the circumstances warrant, from a bird, a fly or even a pony. Oluu's also not very good about remaining in contact with her planet, so when it's time to return home no one answers the call. Eventually Oluu reaches a point where she must decide whether to remain on Earth as a human or return to her predictable, controlled planet. (264 pages)

Where it's reviewed:
Booklist, September 1, 2002, page 122
Bulletin of the Center for Children's Books, November 2002, page 101
Horn Book, January 2003, page 68
Publishers Weekly, September 30, 2002, page 72
School Library Journal, October 2002, page 160

Other books by the same author:
What Happened on Planet Kid, 2000
While No One Was Watching, 1998
Trout Summer, 1995

Other books you might like:
Kate Gilmore, *The Exchange Student*, 1999
  A young alien with an obsessive fondness for animals leaves his planet to stay with an Earth family.
Kathy Mackel, *Can of Worms*, 1999
  Mike opens a "can of worms" when he sends out a message to space requesting rescue; all of a sudden he's surrounded by aliens who want to help.
Richard Scrimger, *The Nose from Jupiter*, 1998
  Alan appreciates the help he receives from the alien living in his nose; when Norbert's no longer needed, one giant sneeze sends him to Jupiter.
William Sleator, *Interstellar Pig*, 1984
  Barney plays the board game Interstellar Pig with three neighbors who happen to be aliens playing for control of the Earth.
Sylvia Waugh, *Earthborn*, 2002
  Nesta is shocked to learn that being born on Earth doesn't mean she's human and that she has to return to her parents' planet of Ormingat.

287

NEIL CONNELLY

St. Michael's Scales
(New York: Arthur A. Levine/Scholastic, 2002)

Subject(s): Guilt; Sports/Wrestling; Schools/Catholic Schools
Age range(s): Grades 8-10
Major character(s): Keegan Flannery, 15-Year-Old, Twin; Michael Flannery, Twin (deceased)
Time period(s): 1970s
Locale(s): United States

Summary: Filled with guilt that he survived his premature birth and his twin Michael didn't, Keegan is convinced that his twin's death was all his fault; his guilt even includes his mother's institutionalization in a mental hospital. Small of stature with few friends at school, an older brother who ran away, and a too-sad, distant father, Keegan decides that his twin wants him to commit suicide before he turns sixteen. With only two weeks to that birthday, Keegan begins to plot his death. Meanwhile, the wrestling coach at Our Lady of Perpetual Health High School needs a wrestler for the 98-pound class and at 84-pounds, Keegan is a natural. After daily wrestling practice and bonding with his teammates, Keegan feels part of a group for the first time in his life. When a classmate commits suicide, Keegan rethinks his plans and approaches his dad to talk about the reasons for his guilt in this author's first novel. (309 pages)

Where it's reviewed:
Booklist, March 15, 2002, page 1250
Horn Book, May 2002, page 324
Publishers Weekly, March 25, 2002, page 66
School Library Journal, June 2002, page 134
Voice of Youth Advocates, April 2002, page 40

Other books by the same author:
Buddy Cooper Finds a Way, 2004

Other books you might like:
Leon Garfield, *The Empty Sleeve*, 1988
  Robust Peter and frail Paul, though twins, are as different mentally as they are physically.
Joyce McDonald, *Swallowing Stones*, 1997
  Michael fires his new rifle in the air, not realizing that the bullet kills Jenna Ward's father. Once he knows, he buries the rifle.
Han Nolan, *When We Were Saints*, 2003
  Told by his grandfather that he's a saint, Archie wonders if sainthood is his destiny; to find out, he accompanies Clare on a pilgrimage.
Peter Pohl, *I Miss You, I Miss You!*, 1999
  After her twin is killed in a car crash, Tina's life turns upside down.

288

GLEN COOK

Angry Lead Skies
(New York: NAL/Roc, 2002)

Series: Garrett Files
Subject(s): Fantasy; Magic; Detection
Age range(s): Grades 9-Adult
Major character(s): Garrett, Detective—Private; Kip Prose, Teenager
Time period(s): Indeterminate
Locale(s): Tunfaire, Fictional City

Summary: Garrett's got a new case, or perhaps the case has got him. Fans of the long running series will know that despite his hard-boiled attitude, Garrett is rarely in control. In part, that's because he works in Tunfaire, that magical city where humans, fairies, gods and assorted other beings all live, though certainly not in harmony. And that's where Garrett enters, for he's always ready to get to the bottom of a problem, for a reasonable fee. This time, extremely unlovable teen Kip Prose turns up and claims his life is being threatened by elves that are actually after his friends. His description of big-eyed little guys with slick skin and skinny gray bodies sure doesn't sound like any elves Garrett has met. Kip is so repulsive that Garrett is tempted to just let it go when he's grabbed again, this time right under Garrett's nose. Darn it, the kid's got this beautiful sister, and Garrett can never disappoint a gorgeous woman. (368 pages)

Where it's reviewed:
Booklist, April 1, 2002, page 1313
Library Journal, April 15, 2002, page 128
Voice of Youth Advocates, August 2002, page 200

Other books by the same author:
Soldiers Live, 2000
Faded Steel Heat, 1999 (Garrett Files)
Water Sleeps, 1999

Other books you might like:
Jasper Fforde, *The Eyre Affair: A Novel*, 2002
    Lituratec Thursday Next is no Garrett, but she's pretty tough in her own way as she chases the villain into the pages of *Jane Eyre*.
Eric Garcia, *Anonymous Rex*, 2000
    Dinosaurs walk among us, cleverly disguised in people suits; when one of these guys gets out of line, one of their own is on the case.
Tanya Huff, *Summon the Keeper*, 1998
    Accompanied by her smart-mouthed cat Austin, Keeper Claire attempts to close a gate to hell.

289

LISA BROADIE COOK
ADAM MCCAULEY, Illustrator

Martin MacGregor's Snowman

(New York: Walker & Company, 2003)

Subject(s): Weather; Problem Solving; Imagination
Age range(s): Grades K-3
Major character(s): Martin MacGregor, Child, Son
Time period(s): 2000s
Locale(s): United States

Summary: In the author's first book, single-minded Martin MacGregor wants snow. What is winter without enough snow to build a snowman? Daily, Martin is disappointed. In desperation, imaginative Martin tries making snowmen with flour, cotton balls, soap bubbles, shaving cream, mashed potatoes and even grass clippings. Not only are the attempts unsatisfying but also they frequently lead to trouble for Martin. By April 1st, Martin has given up all hope of a snowfall, but when he awakens that morning he discovers the ground is covered with snow, enough snow to cause schools to close and to allow Martin and his family to make a snowman, a snowlady, a snowbaby, a snowboy and a snowgirl. Is Martin satisfied? Only until the rain falls in May when what he'd really like to do is build sand castles at the beach. (32 pages)

Where it's reviewed:
Booklist, October 1, 2003, page 326

Bulletin of the Center for Children's Books, January 2004, page 185
Publishers Weekly, November 24, 2003, page 64
School Library Journal, October 2003, page 116

Other books you might like:
Lois Ehlert, *Snowballs*, 1995
    Simple text and clear collages tell of the creation of a snow family and the inevitable result as the weather warms.
Kevin O'Malley, *Straight to the Pole*, 2003
    This cold youngster has too much of a good thing as he struggles through a blizzard, trying to get to the bus stop.
Carole Lexa Schaefer, *Snow Pumpkin*, 2000
    An early snowfall supplies almost enough snow for a snowman. Lily and Jesse get a pumpkin from Gram's field to finish the job.

290

KAZ COOKE, Author/Illustrator

The Terrible Underpants

(New York: Hyperion Books for Children, 2003)

Subject(s): Pets; Clothes; Humor
Age range(s): Grades K-2
Major character(s): Wanda-Linda, Child, Daughter; Glenda, Animal (wombat); Mom, Mother
Time period(s): 2000s
Locale(s): Australia

Summary: Poor Wanda-Linda! All her underwear is drying on the clothesline and it's time to get dressed for school. Mom won't let her use the wet underwear from the clothesline so she offers a pair of old underpants. Wanda-Linda recognizes these terrible, baggy, stained underpants and wishes she had another choice. Her parents assure her that no one will notice, but Wanda-Linda thinks otherwise and events prove Wanda-Linda right. Gusts of wind, playing on the monkey bars and even running through the sprinkler at home reveal glimpses of the terrible underwear under her purple dress. Finally, by the end of the day, while enjoying a tea party with Glenda, Wanda-Linda solves the problem by simply removing the offensive garment. Originally published in Australia in 2000. (36 pages)

Where it's reviewed:
Bulletin of the Center for Children's Books, May 2003, page 356
Observer, February 18, 2001, page 16*
Publishers Weekly, March 10, 2003, page 72
School Library Journal, August 2003, page 124

Other books by the same author:
Get Another Grip, 1998
Crocodile Club, 1997
Get a Grip, 1996

Other books you might like:
Marc Brown, *Arthur's Underwear*, 1999
    In his dreams, Arthur pictures the humiliation he'd suffer if he should forget to don underwear before going to school.
Sam Lloyd, *What Color Is Your Underwear?*, 2004
    A lift-the-flap book shows the colorful underwear worn by various animals.

Mary Monsell, *Underwear!*, 1988

   Wearing colorful underwear improves the mood of a grumpy buffalo.

Todd Parr, *Underwear Do's and Don'ts*, 2000

   A humorous colorful book lists rules for the proper use of underwear.

291

TRISH COOKE
PAUL HOWARD, Illustrator

Full, Full, Full of Love

(Cambridge, MA: Candlewick Press, 2003)

Subject(s): Grandmothers; Food; African Americans
Age range(s): Grades K-2
Major character(s): Jay Jay, Child, Son; Grannie, Grandmother, Cook; Mama, Mother, Spouse
Time period(s): 2000s (2003)
Locale(s): United States

Summary: Mama drops Jay Jay off at Grannie's house and then hurries to pick up his dad so they can join the family for Sunday dinner. Jay Jay is hungry dinner smells good. Each time Jay Jay asks if dinner is ready, Grannie distracts him with a task because it's not quite time to eat. They set the table, look at the fish in Grannie's aquarium, and watch out the window for the arrival of the other family members. Finally, Mama returns and others drive up too. Jay Jay is sure this is the sign the dinner is finally ready. He's right! Soon everyone is full, full, full of food and love and hugs and kisses. (26 pages)

Where it's reviewed:
Booklist, February 15, 2003, page 1083
Bulletin of the Center for Children's Books, March 2003, page 268
Publishers Weekly, November 25, 2002, page 66
School Library Journal, February 2003, page 103

Other books by the same author:
The Grandad Tree, 2000
So Much, 1994 (Booklist Editors' Choice)
When I Grow Bigger, 1994

Other books you might like:
Melrose Cooper, *I Got a Family*, 1993
   A young girl describes the unique affection she receives from each individual in her caring family.
Valerie Flournoy, *Tanya's Reunion*, 1995
   Tanya helps Grandma prepare for the arrival of extended family for a reunion at the Virginia farm Grandma lived on as a child.
bell hooks, *Homemade Love*, 2002
   Sweet, sweet Girlpie rejoices in the love of her family shown by endearing nicknames, loving hugs, and forgiveness for imperfections.
Gloria Jean Pinkney, *The Sunday Outing*, 1994
   During weekly visits to the north Philadelphia Station, Ernestine and Great-Aunt Odessa share family stories and dreams for the future.

292

CAROLINE B. COONEY

Goddess of Yesterday

(New York: Delacorte, 2002)

Subject(s): Courage; Mythology
Age range(s): Grades 6-10
Major character(s): Anaxandra, 12-Year-Old; Callisto, Royalty (princess), Handicapped; Helen, Royalty (queen); King Menelaus, Royalty (king), Spouse (husband of Helen); Pleisthenes, Royalty (prince); Paris, Lover (of Helen)
Time period(s): 13th century B.C.
Locale(s): Siphnos, Mediterranean (island in the Aegean Sea); Sparta, Greece; Troy, Turkey

Summary: Young Anaxandra is taken hostage to serve as a companion to the king's crippled daughter Callisto. Later pirates attack the island in search of treasure and ruthlessly slaughter anyone they stumble on; luckily Anaxandra has hidden herself well and is the only survivor. King Menelaus finds her and, thinking she is Princess Callisto, takes her to his home in Sparta. Keeping up the facade that she is Callisto, Anaxandra witnesses Paris's visit to Sparta when he falls in love with Menelaus's wife Helen. Helen betrays her husband by fleeing with Paris to Troy, bringing Anaxandra with them to care for Helen's youngest son Pleisthenes, making Anaxandra a witness to the intrigue and peril that signal the beginning of the war between Troy and Sparta. (263 pages)

Where it's reviewed:
Booklist, June 2002, page 1704
Bulletin of the Center for Children's Books, July 2002, page 397
Publishers Weekly, July 8, 2002, page 50
School Library Journal, June 2002, page 134
Voice of Youth Advocates, August 2002, page 200

Awards the book has won:
ALA Notable Children's Books, 2003
Center for Children's Books Best Books, 2002

Other books by the same author:
For All Time, 2001
The Ransom of Mercy Carter, 2001
What Janie Found, 2000
Prisoner of Time, 1998
The Voice on the Radio, 1996

Other books you might like:
Vivien Alcock, *Singer to the Sea God*, 1993
   Perseus needs a way to kill the dreadful Gorgon, a creature with snakes for hair.
Adele Geras, *Troy*, 2001
   As the tragedy of the fall of Troy plays out, the various Greek gods and goddesses appear before the doomed inhabitants to explain their motives.
Clemence McLaren, *Inside the Walls of Troy: A Novel of the Women Who Lived the Trojan War*, 1996
   A tale of the fall of Troy from the perspective of Helen and Cassandra.

293

DOUG COONEY
TONY DITERLIZZI, Illustrator

The Beloved Dearly

(New York: Simon & Schuster, 2002)

Subject(s): Pets; Business Enterprises
Age range(s): Grades 4-7
Major character(s): Ernest "Ernie" Castellano, 12-Year-Old, Businessman; Dusty, Child, Artisan (coffin maker); Tony, Child (gravedigger); Swimming Pool, Child (professional mourner); Mister Doggie, Dog (Ernie's pet)
Time period(s): 2000s
Locale(s): United States

Summary: Ernie's been too creative with his get-rich-quick schemes and his father threatens to ground him if he hears of any more money making shenanigans. But Ernie likes money too much to quit and when he realizes his father had to pay for his mother's funeral, sees another business opportunity. With an available vacant lot, Ernie lights on the idea of pet funerals and lines up Dusty as his coffin maker, Tony as the grave-digger and Swimming Pool as the professional mourner. Business booms for ant farms, cats, iguanas and various other pets. Unfortunately greed takes over, Ernie doesn't pay his helpers their promised raises and his own dog, Mister Doggie, sickens and dies in this first novel, originally a stage play. (183 pages)

Where it's reviewed:
Booklist, January 2002, page 858
Bulletin of the Center for Children's Books, May 2002, page 315
Horn Book Guide, Fall 2002, page 369
Publishers Weekly, December 10, 2001, page 71
School Library Journal, January 2002, page 132

Other books by the same author:
I Know Who Likes You, 2004

Other books you might like:
Lucy Frank, *Just Ask Iris*, 2001
  Spunky Iris sets up her own business, called "Just Ask Iris," and runs errands or walks dogs to earn money to buy her first bra.
Gordon Korman, *Son of Interflux*, 1986
  Simon uses Student Government funds to buy a piece of land for a Cultural Center and Worm Shop, land his father's company needs to expand.
Johnniece Marshall Wilson, *Poor Girl, Rich Girl*, 1992
  Convinced she'll look better with contact lenses rather than her glasses, Miranda works at odd jobs to pay for this luxury.

294

HELEN COOPER
TED DEWAN, Illustrator

Sandmare

(New York: Farrar Straus Giroux, 2003)

Subject(s): Animals/Horses; Beaches; Wishes

Age range(s): Grades 2-4
Major character(s): Sandmare, Horse; Polly, Child
Time period(s): 2000s (2003)
Locale(s): United Kingdom

Summary: One day, Polly asks her father to draw a horse for her on the beach. Polly and the newly drawn Sandmare wish that the horse could run free. Because of the strength of the wish, the sun gives Sandmare one night to escape being washed away by the waves. With the help of a dog, a herd of beach ponies, carousel seahorses, a plastic gorilla and many others, Sandmare is able to reach Polly's house where Polly draws wings for the horse to fly away and become part of a "mare's tail cloud." (72 pages)

Where it's reviewed:
Booklist, May 1, 2003, page 1591
Horn Book Guide, April 2003, page 309
School Library Journal, July 2003, page 88
Times Educationa Supplement, November 16, 2001, page 20*

Awards the book has won:
Center for Children's Books Best Books, 2003

Other books by the same author:
The Boy Who Wouldn't Go to Bed, 2001 (Kate Greenaway Medal)
Pumpkin Soup, 1999 (Kate Greenaway Medal)
The Bear under the Stairs, 1993

Other books you might like:
Betsy Byars, *Little Horse*, 2002
  When Little Horse falls in a river and is swept away, he must find his way back home.
Helen Cresswell, *The Little Sea Pony*, 1997
  Molly must save the sea pony from captivity.
Jessie Haas, *Runaway Radish*, 2001
  Judy learns to take care of Radish, a small pony, when he comes to live with her.
Magdalen Nabb, *The Enchanted Horse*, 1993
  Irina's toy horse comes alive at night, carrying her across the moor on secret moonlit rides.

295

HELEN COOPER, Author/Illustrator

Tatty Ratty

(New York: Farrar Straus Giroux, 2002)

Subject(s): Lost and Found; Toys; Imagination
Age range(s): Preschool-Kindergarten
Major character(s): Tatty Ratty, Rabbit, Toy (stuffed animal); Molly, Child, Daughter; Mom, Mother, Spouse; Dad, Father, Spouse
Time period(s): 2000s (2001); Indeterminate
Locale(s): England; Fictional Country

Summary: Sadly Molly realizes that Tatty Ratty is once again lost, possibly forgotten on the bus. Mom helps Molly look in the house and calls the bus company to check the lost and found. At bedtime, Dad's suggestion that Tatty Ratty may have hopped off the bus to find his way back to Molly begins an imaginative discussion about Tatty Ratty's adventures. Over the course of a few days Molly proposes that Tatty Ratty is eating porridge with the Three Bears, riding in Cinderella's carriage and being saved from pirates by a dragon. Mom and Dad participate in the imaginary adventures, each one designed to bring Tatty Ratty closer to home. Finally, Molly agrees that Tatty Ratty is very near, waiting to be found on the shelves of a toy store looking just like new. Originally published in Great Britain in 2001. (32 pages)

Where it's reviewed:

Booklist, February 15, 2002, page 1019
Horn Book Guide, Fall 2002, page 323
Kirkus Reviews, February 1, 2002, page 178
School Librarian, Spring 2002, page 17
School Library Journal, April 2002, page 102

Awards the book has won:

IRA Children's Choices, 2003

Other books by the same author:

Pumpkin Soup, 1999
The Boy Who Wouldn't Go to Bed, 1997
Little Monster Did It!, 1996

Other books you might like:

Emma Chichester Clark, *Where Are You, Blue Kangaroo?*, 2001
Lily loses Blue Kangaroo so often that he decides to hide rather than risk a trip to the seashore.
Debi Gliori, *Flora's Blanket*, 2001
When Flora loses her special blanket the entire family helps search for it.
Martin Waddell, *Small Bear Lost*, 1996
After Small Bear is accidentally left on a train he manages to find his way home to the little girl who lost him.

296

SUSAN COOPER
JANE BROWNE, Illustrator

Frog

(New York: Margaret K. McElderry Books, 2002)

Subject(s): Problem Solving; Animals/Frogs and Toads; Family

Age range(s): Grades K-2

Major character(s): Little Joe, Child, Brother (younger); Frog, Frog

Time period(s): 2000s (2002)

Locale(s): United States

Summary: All the members of Little Joe's family are accomplished swimmers and enjoy the family's pool. Little Joe simply splashes and his siblings laugh at his feeble attempts to swim. The day that Frog leaps into the pool and cannot get out Little Joe studies its movements carefully. Other members of the family try a variety of methods to get Frog out of the pool but they soon tire of the activity. Then Little Joe quietly stands near Frog, scoops him out of the water and puts him on the ground, pointed in the direction of his own pond. Frog hops away happily and Little Joe puts his observations to work and swims, just like Frog, all the way across the pool. (32 pages)

Where it's reviewed:

Booklist, June 2002, page 1733
Bulletin of the Center for Children's Books, July 2002, page 398

Horn Book, July 2002, page 443
Publishers Weekly, May 13, 2002, page 70
School Library Journal, June 2002, page 92

Other books you might like:

Betsy Jay, *Swimming Lessons*, 1998
Fearful Jane is not motivated by Mom's logical reasons for learning how to swim but Jimmy's teasing prompts her to jump into the pool.
Martha Weston, *Tuck in the Pool*, 1995
Tuck's need to rescue his lucky spider from the pool bottom helps the reluctant swimmer gain confidence.
Tim Winton, *The Deep*, 2000
Though Alice can swim she's afraid to go into the deep water near the fascinating dolphins.

297

SUSAN COOPER

Green Boy

(New York: McElderry/Simon & Schuster, 2002)

Subject(s): Environmental Problems; Brothers; Mutism

Age range(s): Grades 5-8

Major character(s): Trey, 12-Year-Old; Lou, Child

Locale(s): Lucaya Island, Bahamas; Long Pond Cay, Bahamas; Pangaia, Fictional Country

Summary: Living on the beautiful island of Lucaya with their grandparents, Trey and his younger brother Lou help them fight off the developers who want to turn the nearby island of Long Pond Cay into a resort. While playing one day, Trey and Lou, who elects to be mute, are transported to Pangaia, an alternate world that has been destroyed by pollution and development. Pangaian rebels are fighting against the destruction of their world and realize that Lou is the prophesied Green Man who will help them. Trey and Lou travel between the two worlds as they help to clean up Pangaia and, on their beloved island, watch as a hurricane swallows up all the changes made by the developers and restores the beaches. (195 pages)

Where it's reviewed:

Booklist, March 1, 2002, page 1136
Bulletin of the Center for Children's Books, May 2002, page 315
New York Times Book Review, May 12, 2002, page 32
Publishers Weekly, January 14, 2002, page 61
School Library Journal, February 2002, page 130

Other books by the same author:

Magician's Boy, 2004
The Boggart and the Monster, 1997
The Boggart, 1993

Other books you might like:

Sue Pace, *The Last Oasis*, 1993
In a land blighted by environmental pollution, Madonna and Phoenix head for Idaho where they've heard the air and water are free from poisons.
Ruth Park, *My Sister Sif*, 1991
Riko and her sister Sif are related to the merpeople who live in an underwater city, but pollution threatens their home.

Joyce Sweeney, *The Spirit Window*, 1998
  Miranda is delighted that her grandmother Lila, helped by teen Adam, is able to keep the developers away from her Florida land.

298

TOM COPPINGER
DIRK ZIMMER, Illustrator

Curse in Reverse
(New York: Atheneum Books for Young Readers, 2003)

Subject(s): Fairy Tales; Witches and Witchcraft
Age range(s): Grades K-3
Major character(s): Agneeza, Witch, Aged Person; Mr. Tretter, Spouse; Mrs. Tretter, Spouse
Time period(s): Indeterminate Past
Locale(s): Humborg, Fictional Country

Summary: In the author's first picture book, the first two residents of Humborg with whom Agnezza seeks shelter from the cold refuse to admit her. Mr. and Mrs. Tretter generously welcome the old woman into their home, share their meager meal and insist she sleep in the only bed. In the morning, when Agnezza learns the couple is childless she gives them the only thing she has, a curse. Puzzled as to why their kindness would be repaid with the "Curse of the One-Armed Man," the Tretters fear the arrival of the one-armed man and the misfortune he will surely bring. Mr. and Mrs. Tretter are soon blessed with birth of a baby boy, but are afraid to tempt fate by celebrating. A year after her initial visit, Agnezza returns to visit the Tretters. Mr. Tretter asks why Agnezza cursed them and she explains that, as a witch, she cannot give blessings so she gave a curse, in reverse. Mr. Tretter, trying to cook and do household chores while holding his son, is the one-armed man. (34 pages)

Where it's reviewed:
Booklist, September 1, 2003, page 128
Horn Book, September 2003, page 593
Publishers Weekly, June 9, 2003, page 50
Riverbank Review, Summer 2003, page 29
School Library Journal, July 2003, page 89

Other books you might like:
Alma Flor Ada, *The Three Golden Oranges*, 1999
  Two selfish brothers who ignore the advice of an old woman to work with their younger brother to achieve a goal suffer the consequences.
Joanna Cole, *Bony-Legs*, 1983
  A girl's kindness to mistreated animals gives her the magical items she needs to escape from a wicked witch who wants to eat her.
Arthur Ransome, *The Fool of the World and the Flying Ship*, 1968
  In a Caldecott Medal winning folktale a peasant reveals that he is no fool as his attention to good advice enables him to marry the princess.

299

ROBERT CORBET

Fifteen Love
(New York: Walker, 2003)

Subject(s): Romance; Family Problems; Sports/Tennis
Age range(s): Grades 7-10
Major character(s): Will Holland, Tennis Player, 15-Year-Old; Mia Foley, Musician (violinist), 15-Year-Old; Dave Holland, Paraplegic; Harriet, Dog (beagle)
Time period(s): 2000s
Locale(s): Australia

Summary: Will likes Mia and Mia likes Will, but they have trouble connecting. Told in alternating chapters, Will relates the pressure he feels from his father, a very demanding tennis coach who thinks his son could be a professional. Mia plays the viola and is upset about her father's late nights at work, which she discovers are due to his affair. As Mia watches her family fall apart, she swears off all men. Meanwhile Will finds himself tongue-tied whenever he sees Mia and, when they finally have a date, miscommunications hamper everything. It takes Will's younger brother Dave and Mia's beagle Harriet to accidentally bring them both together in this humorous Australian import. (186 pages)

Where it's reviewed:
Bulletin of the Center for Children's Books, April 2003, page 309
Horn Book, July 2003, page 453
Publishers Weekly, February 17, 2003, page 76
School Library Journal, May 2003, page 148
Voice of Youth Advocates, August 2003, page 218

Other books by the same author:
The Passenger Seat, 2000

Other books you might like:
Louise Plummer, *The Unlikely Romance of Kate Bjorkman*, 1995
  When Kate falls in love for the first time, she records her memories by writing a romance novel, relying on *The Romance Writers Phrase Book*.
Carol Lynch Williams, *My Angelica*, 1999
  Entering a writing contest, Sage pens a romance and George enters some of his love poems, but the best love story of all is theirs.
Ellen Wittlinger, *Lombardo's Law*, 1993
  Justine never imagines her first real romance will be with a boy who's two years younger and two inches shorter than she.
Karen Romano Young, *The Beetle and Me: A Love Story*, 1999
  Daisy's first love is a 1957 purple Volkswagen beetle, but beetle love and real love coalesce when Daisy and Billy sign up for an auto mechanics class.

300

SUE CORBETT

12 Again

(New York: Dutton/Penguin Putnam, 2002)

Subject(s): Wishes; Mothers and Sons; Humor
Age range(s): Grades 4-7
Major character(s): Patrick McBride, 12-Year-Old; Bernadette "Detta" McBride, Mother, 12-Year-Old
Time period(s): 2000s; 1970s
Locale(s): United States

Summary: On the night before her fortieth birthday, Bernadette McBride feels stressed out with trying to complete a writing project and take care of her family, so she heads to the home of her recently deceased Irish mother for a good night's sleep in peaceful, quiet surroundings. Finding some liquor in the pantry, she toasts her birthday and makes a wish to be young again. Waking up the next morning, she's once again a 12-year-old living in her childhood home and being waited on by her mother. Outside her home, however, the world has moved on to 2002 so Bernadette enrolls in her son's school and soon shares the same class with Patrick. Back at the McBride's home, Patrick finds all the household responsibilities heaped on his shoulders and he struggles to keep up his schoolwork while also caring for his brothers and assuming the household chores. Everyone thinks Bernadette has just walked out and can't find a way to communicate with her family until she resorts to e-mailing Patrick, asking for his help in reversing her mother's spell in a book that's part Irish magic. (227 pages)

Where it's reviewed:
Booklist, September 1, 2002, page 122
Bulletin of the Center for Children's Books, October 2002, page 54
Publishers Weekly, July 22, 2002, page 180
School Library Journal, July 2002, page 118
Voice of Youth Advocates, August 2002, page 200

Other books you might like:
Jackie French Koller, *If I Had One Wish*, 1991
　Alec wishes he'd never had a younger brother and, horror of horrors, his wish comes true!
Francine Pascal, *Hangin' Out with Cici*, 1977
　When Victoria hits her head, she time travels back a generation, meets Cici, and discovers that Cici is her mother.
Cynthia Voigt, *Building Blocks*, 1984
　Brann travels back in time to witness his father's childhood, which helps them build a better relationship.

301

SHANA COREY
MARK TEAGUE, Illustrator

First Graders from Mars: Episode 2: The Problem with Pelly

(New York: Scholastic Press, 2002)

Subject(s): Self-Acceptance; Individuality; Schools

Age range(s): Grades 1-2
Major character(s): Pelly, 1st Grader; Horus, 1st Grader, Friend (Pelly's); Tera, 1st Grader, Bully; Madama DaLuna, Singer
Time period(s): Indeterminate
Locale(s): Mars

Summary: Pelly's pod excitedly prepares for the visit of an opera singer by cleaning their thinking capsules, practicing instruments and decorating the walls with their artwork. Poor Pelly stands out from the others in school because her head is adorned with a fluffernobbin and not a "normal" cluster of tentacles. Native Martian Tera teases her and calls her weird while Horus defends non-native Pelly's appearance as simply being different. On the morning of Madama Da Luna's visit, Pelly wraps her fluffernobbin in three rubber bands so she will look the same as the others. A sneeze dislodges Pelly's rubber bands, freeing her fluffernobbin just before Madama Da Luna arrives and removes her coat and scarf—revealing her beautiful fluffernobbin! (32 pages)

Where it's reviewed:
Booklist, February 15, 2002, page 1019
Horn Book Guide, Fall 2002, page 324
Kirkus Reviews, December 1, 2001, page 1683
Publishers Weekly, January 28, 2002, page 293
School Library Journal, April 2002, page 102

Other books by the same author:
First Graders from Mars: Episode 3: Nergal and the Great Space Race, 2002
Milly and the Macy's Parade, 2002
First Graders from Mars: Episode 1: Horus's Horrible Day, 2001

Other books you might like:
Amy Hest, *Baby Duck and the Bad Eyeglasses*, 1996
　Baby Duck feels ugly and different in her new glasses but Grampa helps her appreciate how nice it is to see clearly.
Helen Lester, *Hooway for Wodney Wat*, 1999
　Rodney Rat uses his speech impediment to get the best of a class bully during a game of Simon Says.
Rosemary Wells, *Yoko*, 1998
　Yoko enjoys finding her favorite food in her lunchbox but classmates tease her for being the only one to eat sushi.

302

SHANA COREY
MARK TEAGUE, Illustrator

First Graders from Mars: Episode 3: Nergal and the Great Space Race

(New York: Scholastic Press, 2002)

Subject(s): Self-Esteem; Contests; Schools
Age range(s): Grades 1-3
Major character(s): Nergal, 1st Grader, Alien; Ms. Vortex, Teacher, Alien
Time period(s): Indeterminate
Locale(s): Mars

Summary: Nergal dreads the race culminating the school's Martian Health Week because he remembers his dismal showing the previous year. Ms. Vortex's reminder to Nergal is that it's not necessary to be good, but it is important to try one's Martian best. By the day's conclusion it's clear that Nergal has learned the lesson. After Ms. Vortex offers the class some homemade goodies as a treat someone notes that they taste burnt and Ms. Vortex admits that she's not a good cook. Nergal consoles her by reminding her that she's a very good teacher and it's only important that she tried her Martian best when she baked the treats. (32 pages)

Where it's reviewed:
Horn Book Guide, Spring 2003, page 60
Publishers Weekly, July 1, 2002, page 81
School Library Journal, January 2003, page 94

Other books by the same author:
First Graders from Mars: Episode 4: Tera, Star Student, 2003
First Graders from Mars: Episode 2: The Problem with Pelly, 2002
First Graders from Mars: Episode 1: Horus's Horrible Day, 2001

Other books you might like:
Marc Brown, *Arthur and the Popularity Test*, 1998
    Results of a magazine's popularity contest cause some of Arthur's friends to change in hopes of being more likeable.
Jamie McEwan, *The Heart of Cool*, 2001
    In a new school, Bobby tries to emulate the ''cool'' behavior of Harry and ignore the taunts of a bully in order to find acceptance.
Dan Yaccarino, *The Big Science Fair*, 2002
    Blast Off Boy, exchange student on planet Meep, worries about the science fair while alien Blorp is excited to participate in one on Earth.

303

SHANA COREY
BRETT HELQUIST, Illustrator

Milly and the Macy's Parade

(New York: Scholastic Press, 2002)

Subject(s): Christmas; Department Stores; Historical
Age range(s): Grades K-3
Major character(s): Milly, Immigrant, Child; Mr. Macy, Businessman; Papa, Father, Immigrant
Time period(s): 1920s (1924)
Locale(s): New York, New York

Summary: Milly loves the Christmas splendor of Macy's where her father works the delivery docks with other immigrants. Papa and his coworkers seem depressed by the holiday preparations, which makes them remember the customs of the countries they left behind when they emigrated. To cheer them Milly asks Mr. Macy to hold a holiday parade; once convinced of the advantage to his business Mr. Macy agrees to do so. Papa, Milly and other immigrants along with Macy's employees dress in costumes to participate in the first Macy's Parade. A concluding author's note identifies the fact and fiction of the story. (40 pages)

Where it's reviewed:
Booklist, September 1, 2002, page 139
Bulletin of the Center for Children's Books, November 2002, page 101

Kirkus Reviews, October 1, 2002, page 1464
Publishers Weekly, September 23, 2002, page 36
School Library Journal, October 2002, page 99

Other books by the same author:
First Graders from Mars: Episode 1: Horus's Horrible Day, 2001
You Forgot Your Skirt, Amelia Bloomer!, 2000 (Booklist Editors' Choice)
Brave Pig, 1999 (Step into Reading)

Other books you might like:
Elisa Bartone, *American Too*, 1996
    When immigrant Rosie is chosen to be Queen of the San Gennaro Feast she dresses as the Statue of Liberty to show that she is American too.
Pamela Pease, *Macy's on Parade: A Pop-Up Celebration of Macy's Thanksgiving Day Parade*, 2002
    The text gives background information about the production of the annual parade while the pop-ups bring it to life.
Tom Shachtman, *Parade!*, 1985
    A nonfiction title uses photographs to illustrate the descriptions of the year of planning needed for each performance of the Macy's Parade.

304

SHANA COREY
REBECCA GIBBON, Illustrator

Players in Pigtails

(New York: Scholastic, Inc., 2003)

Subject(s): Sports/Baseball; Women; World War II
Age range(s): Grades 1-4
Major character(s): Katie Casey, Baseball Player
Time period(s): 1940s (1943)
Locale(s): United States

Summary: Katie Casey lives and breathes baseball, but the boys at her high school won't let her try out for the team. During World War II, as all the professional baseball players are called up to fight, Katie is scouted to try out for the All-American Girls Professional Baseball League. Chosen to play for the Kenosha Comets, Katie thrills in the chance to play baseball professionally. (40 pages)

Where it's reviewed:
Booklist, June 2003, page 1768
Bulletin of the Center for Children's Books, July/August 2003, page 44
Publishers Weekly, February 17, 2003, page 74
School Library Journal, April 2003, page 117

Awards the book has won:
Center for Children's Books Best Books, 2003

Other books by the same author:
Milly and the Macy's Parade, 2002
You Forgot Your Skirt, Amelia Bloomer!, 2000 (Booklist Editors' Choice)
Babe's Bathtime, 1999

Other books you might like:
David A. Adler, *Mama Played Baseball*, 2003
    While Amy's father is serving in the army during World

War II her mother gets a job playing baseball in the All-American Girls Professional Baseball League.

Deborah Hopkinson, *Girl Wonder: A Baseball Story in Nine Innings*, 2003

A fictionalized account of Alta Weiss, the first woman to pitch baseball for a semi-professional men's team, back in 1907.

Doreen Rappaport, *Dirt on Their Skirts*, 2000

Margaret cheers on her favorite players during the 1946 All-American Girls Professional Baseball League championship. Lyndall Callan, co-author.

305

NANCY COTE, Author/Illustrator

It Feels Like Snow

(Honesdale, PA: Boyds Mills Press, 2003)

Subject(s): Weather; Neighbors and Neighborhoods; Old Age
Age range(s): Preschool-Grade 1
Major character(s): Alice, Aged Person, Neighbor
Time period(s): 2000s (2003)
Locale(s): United States

Summary: Alice can feel in her bones the coming of the snow, but when she tries to warn her neighbors they scoff at her. Each time it happens though, Alice is proven right. Finally after a particularly big snowstorm, Alice invites her neighbors over for soup and a cozy fire and they apologize for doubting her. (32 pages)

Where it's reviewed:
Publishers Weekly, November 17, 2003, page 64
School Library Journal, November 2003, page 91

Other books by the same author:
Flip-Flops, 1998
Palm Trees, 1993

Other books you might like:
Ezra Jack Keats, *The Snowy Day*, 1963
This Caldecott Medal winner tells the story of a little boy's enjoyment of the season's first snowfall.
Nancy Poydar, *Snip, Snip . . . Snow!*, 1997
As Sophie and her classmates make paper snowflakes they look out the window and discover that real snow is falling.
Nathaniel Tripp, *Snow Comes to the Farm*, 2001
A boy and his older brother explore the natural clues to the coming snowfall.
Neil Waldman, *The Snowflake: A Water Cycle Story*, 2003
This non-fiction book follows a drop of water throughout one year.

306

AUDREY COULOUMBIS

Say Yes

(New York: Putnam, 2002)

Subject(s): Stepmothers; Missing Persons; Stealing
Age range(s): Grades 6-9

Major character(s): Casey Drummond, 12-Year-Old; Sylvia Drummond, Stepmother; Paulie, 16-Year-Old, Foster Child; Fran Capotosto, Aged Person (Sylvia's mother)
Time period(s): 2000s
Locale(s): New York, New York

Summary: Returning home from school one day, Casey finds her stepmother missing, $55 in an envelope and extra TV dinners in the freezer. Certain that Sylvia's probably off with her no-good boyfriend, a replacement for Casey's deceased dad, and not wanting to make trouble for Sylvia, she doesn't tell anyone. But the building superintendent's foster son Paulie figures it out and, having learned street smarts, talks Casey into helping him rob the apartments of old ladies for food money. Casey is saved from a life of crime when Sylvia's mother Fran shows up and manages to help both Casey and Paulie, who's been beaten one too many times by the super. The return of a very contrite Sylvia signals a new beginning for Casey as the three women sort out how to build a life together. (200 pages)

Where it's reviewed:
Booklist, May 1, 2002, page 1518
Bulletin of the Center for Children's Books, July 2002, page 398
Publishers Weekly, May 6, 2002, page 58
School Library Journal, July 2002, page 118
Voice of Youth Advocates, April 2002, page 40

Awards the book has won:
Bulletin of the Center for Children's Books Blue Ribbons, 2002
Center for Children's Books Best Books, 2002

Other books by the same author:
Getting Near to Baby, 1999
Just Before Daybreak, 1987

Other books you might like:
Margaret Peterson Haddix, *Don't You Dare Read This, Mrs. Dunphrey*, 1996
Abandoned by their abusive father and depressed mother, Tish works after school to make enough money to feed herself and her younger brother.
Dean Hughes, *Team Picture*, 1996
David doesn't know what to do when his foster father comes home drunk; if David tells anyone, he'll be back in the welfare system and he doesn't want that.
Donna Jo Napoli, *Three Days*, 2001
Jackie is kidnapped while her father's having a heart attack along a deserted road in Italy; after three days with her captors she manages to escape.

307

LUCY COUSINS, Author/Illustrator

Jazzy in the Jungle

(Cambridge, MA: Candlewick Press, 2002)

Subject(s): Animals; Rain Forest; Games
Age range(s): Preschool
Major character(s): Baby Jazzy, Animal (lemur); Mama JoJo, Mother, Animal (lemur)
Time period(s): Indeterminate

Locale(s): Fictional Country

Summary: Mama JoJo looks for Jazzy all over the jungle. In their game of Hide and Seek she is ''It'' and Jazzy is hiding. Holes in pages cut to match the outlines of leaves and flowers give clues to something but each time Mama JoJo peeks behind the bush or tree she finds another jungle animal, not her baby. Each animal, bird, insect or reptile suggests another place to look until finally the elephant sends Mama JoJo to the big boo tree and there she finds Jazzy nestled in its branches waiting to be found. (26 pages)

Where it's reviewed:
Kirkus Reviews, October 1, 2002, page 1464
Magpies, November 2002, page 26
Publishers Weekly, October 21, 2002, page 77
School Library Journal, December 2002, page 86
Smithsonian, December 2002, page 123

Awards the book has won:
Smithsonian's Notable Books for Children, 2002

Other books by the same author:
Maisy Goes Camping, 2004
Maisy Loves You, 2003
Maisy Cleans Up, 2002

Other books you might like:
Laurence Anholt, *Chimp and Zee*, 2001
    While shopping with Mumkey, Chimp and Zee rest on a rock that they learn, too late, is actually an elephant. Catherine Anholt, co-author.
Rhonda Gowler Greene, *Jamboree Day*, 2001
    The jungle is rocking for Jamboree Day as animals hop, fly, march, bounce and leap to the annual event.
Nancy Tafuri, *Where Did Bunny Go?*, 2001
    During a game of ''Hide and Seek'' Bird finds Chipmunk and Squirrel but cannot find Bunny.

308

BRUCE COVILLE

Juliet Dove, Queen of Love

(San Diego: Harcourt, 2003)

Series: Magic Book Shop
Subject(s): Magic; Mythology; Shyness
Age range(s): Grades 4-8
Major character(s): Juliet Dove, Student—Middle School; Cupid, Deity; Psyche, Deity; Iris, Deity; Roxanne, Rat; Jerome, Rat; S.H. Elives, Magician
Time period(s): 2000s
Locale(s): Venus Harbor

Summary: Very shy Juliet and her arch enemy toss insults at one another before Juliet runs away, only to discover she's on a street she's not seen before. Intrigued by the shop of magic supplies run by S.H. Elives, she wanders in and meets Iris who convinces her she wants an amulet. When Juliet touches the amulet, she is surprised to discover that she does want it, but later is horrified to find she can't remove it from around her neck. Even worse, all the boys in her class are suddenly love-struck, call her, follow her everywhere, and sit in clumps on her front lawn. When the talking rats Roxanne and Jerome appear in her bedroom, she's startled to learn that the amulet was once worn by Helen of Troy and she's now part of the love story of Cupid and Psyche. Now it's up to Juliet, with help from the rats and a few goddesses, to remove the amulet and set Cupid free. (190 pages)

Where it's reviewed:
Booklist, January 2004, page 854
Publishers Weekly, November 24, 2003, page 66
School Library Journal, December 2003, page 148

Other books by the same author:
Evil Elves, 2004
The Monster's Ring, 2002
The Monsters of Morley Manor: A Madcap Adventure, 2001

Other books you might like:
Adele Geras, *Troy*, 2001
    As the tragedy of the fall of Troy plays out, the various Greek gods and goddesses appear before the doomed inhabitants to explain their motives.
Clemence McLaren, *Aphrodite's Blessings*, 2001
    The mythical tales of the tribulations of marriage for Atalanta, Andromeda and Psyche are retold in these three love stories.
Doris Orgel, *The Princess and the God*, 1996
    In this retelling of the Cupid and Psyche myth, Psyche is unhappy that her great beauty arouses jealousy in her two sisters.
Jane Yolen, *Atalanta and the Arcadian Beast*, 2003
    Aided by the bear that found her, young Atalanta hunts the winged lion that killed her guardian in this third of the Young Herroes series.

309

JOY COWLEY
JENNIFER PLECAS, Illustrator

Agapanthus Hum and the Angel Hoot

(New York: Philomel Books, 2003)

Subject(s): Parent and Child; Growing Up
Age range(s): Grades 1-3
Major character(s): Agapanthus Hum, Child, Daughter; Major Bark, Dog; Daddy, Father, Spouse; Orville, Child, Friend
Time period(s): 2000s (2003)
Locale(s): United States

Summary: When Agapanthus Hum's woggly tooth falls out she's no longer able to make her bumblebee buzz sound. Instead she makes a sound like a train's toot. Daddy says it's an ''angel hoot.'' Each time Major Bark hears it he howls. Agapanthus Hum takes her ''hoot and howl'' show to school for Show and Tell and impresses her classmates. When her permanent tooth grows in Agapanthus Hum can no longer make an ''angel hoot'' sound, but Orville's lost a tooth and he can so he asks to borrow Major Bark. (48 pages)

Where it's reviewed:
Booklist, February 15, 2003, page 1072
Bulletin of the Center for Children's Books, March 2003, page 268
Publishers Weekly, February 17, 2003, page 78
School Library Journal, February 2003, page 103

Other books by the same author:
Wishing of Biddy Malone, 2004
Mr. Wishy-Washy, 2003
Agapanthus Hum and Major Bark, 2001
Agapanthus Hum and the Eyeglasses, 1999

Other books you might like:
Stephen Krensky, *My Loose Tooth*, 1999
    A rhyming ''Step into Reading'' series entry describes a child's experiences with a loose tooth.
Kate McMullan, *Fluffy Meets the Tooth Fairy*, 2000
    In a beginning reader guinea pig Fluffy tries to assure that Wade's tooth gets under his pillow before the Tooth Fairy arrives.
Barbara Park, *Junie B., First Grader: Toothless Wonder*, 2002
    Junie B. is not happy to be the first student in class to have a loose upper tooth. She fears looking like her toothless elderly uncle.

310

JUDY COX
BLANCHE SIMS, Illustrator

Cool Cat, School Cat

(New York: Holiday House, 2002)

Subject(s): Animals/Cats; Animals, Treatment of; Schools
Age range(s): Grades 2-4
Major character(s): Gus Zander, Student—Elementary School, Animal Lover; Pamela Kennedy, Student—Elementary School, Animal Lover; Leo, Cat
Time period(s): 2000s
Locale(s): United States

Summary: As Gus walks to his new school on the first day of class he meets Pamela and a stray cat. Thus begins a tentative friendship and a cat rescue operation. When Gus eventually is able to grab the cat he knows he can't take the forlorn stray home to his ''no pets allowed'' apartment. He hides Leo in an empty office and sneaks in to feed him at recess. Within a few days the office is a smelly mess, Pamela discovers what he's doing and, rather than admit it to the teacher, they both work together to save the cat. Gus has a poor memory and benefits from Pamela's organizational ability, as does Leo since she provides proper cat food and a makeshift litter box. Leo can't stay there forever, but they do convince their teacher that he needs a pet so Leo at least has a good home. (84 pages)

Where it's reviewed:
Bulletin of the Center for Children's Books, February 2003, page 231
Kirkus Reviews, October 1, 2002, page 183
School Library Journal, September 2002, page 182

Other books by the same author:
Butterfly Buddies, 2001
Mean, Mean Maureen Green, 2000
Third Grade Pet, 1998

Other books you might like:
Betsy Duffey, *Throw-Away Pets*, 1993
    Evie and Megan have 24 hours to find homes for aban-

doned pets at the animal shelter or the animals will be destroyed.
Julie Andrews Edwards, *Little Bo: The Story of Bonnie Boadicea*, 1999
    Sailor Billy Bates rescues kitten Little Bo from the snow and then must hide her from his ship's captain.
Bill Wallace, *A Dog Called Kitty*, 1980
    Ricky overcomes his fear of dogs and the taunts of a bully to save a starving stray pup found in his barn.

311

JOHN COY
CAROLYN FISHER, Illustrator

Two Old Potatoes and Me

(New York: Alfred A. Knopf, 2003)

Subject(s): Fathers and Daughters; Gardens and Gardening; Divorce
Age range(s): Grades K-3
Major character(s): Dad, Father, Divorced Person; Unnamed Character, Child of Divorced Parents, Daughter
Time period(s): 2000s (2003)
Locale(s): United States

Summary: A young girl staying with her Dad discovers two potatoes so old they have sprouts so she throws them away. Dad retrieves them, gets information from his father on growing potatoes and then leads his daughter to the garden where they prepare the soil. By cutting each old potato into smaller chunks, they are able to plant nine hills of potatoes. All summer they tend them carefully, pulling weeds, picking off bugs, and watering the plants. Finally, in September they dig their crop and find that the two old potatoes have become 67 fresh, edible potatoes. That's a lot of mashed potatoes! (34 pages)

Where it's reviewed:
Bulletin of the Center for Children's Books, October 2003, page 54
Publishers Weekly, May 19, 2003, page 74
Riverbank Review, Spring 2003, page 39
School Library Journal, June 2003, page 98

Awards the book has won:
Center for Children's Books Best Books, 2003

Other books by the same author:
Vroomaloom Zoom, 2000
Strong to the Hoop, 1999 (ALA Notable Children's Book)
Night Driving, 1996 (Marion Vannett Ridgway Award)

Other books you might like:
Joan Holub, *The Garden That We Grew*, 2001
    A group of children carefully plant and tend a garden. Then they harvest enough pumpkins for pies, cookies and jack-o'-lanterns.
Kate Lied, *Potato: A Tale from the Great Depression*, 1997
    After picking potatoes for two weeks, a previously unemployed father is able to glean enough potatoes to barter for other items the family needs.
Barbara Santucci, *Loon Summer*, 2001
    After her parents' divorce Rainie's summer at the family's

lake cabin seems strange but together she and her dad create new memories.

Andrea Spalding, *Me and Mr. Mah*, 1999

His parents' divorce forces a young boy to leave his farm home on the prairie and move to a city far from his father.

MAHLON F. CRAFT
K.Y. CRAFT, Illustrator

Sleeping Beauty
(New York: SeaStar Books, 2002)

Subject(s): Folklore; Fairy Tales; Princes and Princesses
Age range(s): Grades 2-4
Major character(s): Aurora, Royalty (princess), Daughter; Prince, Royalty, Rescuer
Time period(s): Indeterminate Past
Locale(s): Fictional Country

Summary: This romantically illustrated retelling of the classic Grimm tale of a beloved princess cursed as an infant by an angry fairy remains true to the original story. On her sixteenth birthday, as foretold, Princess Aurora pricks her finger on a spindle and falls asleep. Instantly, briars grow over the now enchanted castle and local legend describes the sleeping princess in the tower as Briar Rose. One hundred years later Prince, traveling from a far-away kingdom, happens upon the briar-covered castle and decides to rescue the sleeping princess. Unlike those that have gone before, Prince notes the briars parting to allow his entry. Prince finds Princess Aurora in the castle's high tower and awakens her with a kiss. (32 pages)

Where it's reviewed:
Booklist, September 15, 2002, page 236
Bulletin of the Center for Children's Books, January 2003, page 194
Kirkus Reviews, October 1, 2002, page 1465
Publishers Weekly, September 30, 2002, page 71
School Library Journal, October 2002, page 142

Awards the book has won:
Center for Children's Books Best Books, 2002

Other books by the same author:
Christmas Moon, 2003

Other books you might like:
Margaret Early, *Sleeping Beauty*, 1993
Exquisite illustrations distinguish Early's retelling of the classic fairy tale.
Vivian French, *The Thistle Princess*, 1998
The wall a king and queen build to protect their beloved child actually stifles her and deprives her of happiness.
Jacob Grimm, *Sleeping Beauty*, 1984
One of many traditional retellings of the classic story is illustrated by Mercer Mayer. Wilhelm Grimm, co-author.
Paul O. Zelinsky, *Rapunzel*, 1997
This retelling of the classic story of the pain and power of love captured the Caldecott Medal.

SHARON CREECH

Ruby Holler
(New York: HarperCollins, 2002)

Subject(s): Orphans; Twins; Voyages and Travels
Age range(s): Grades 4-7
Major character(s): Dallas Carter, 13-Year-Old, Twin; Florida Carter, 13-Year-Old, Twin; Sairy Morey, Aged Person, Artisan (woodcarver); Tiller Morey, Aged Person, Artisan (woodcarver); Mr. Trepid, Businessman (owner of the orphanage)
Time period(s): 2000s
Locale(s): Ruby Holler

Summary: "Trouble twins" Dallas and Florida have lived the longest in the Boxton Creek Home for Children, and have probably broken the most rules and received the most hours of punishment. Though they've been placed in foster homes, they're always returned to Boxton Creek Home where the Trepids are not happy to see them. An elderly couple, Sairy and Tiller Morey, want companions for separate trips they plan to take and offer a foster home to Dallas and Florida. Initially skeptical and always ready to run away, the magical effects of Ruby Holler and the Moreys work to break down the defensiveness of the twins. Dreamy Dallas is to accompany Sairy on a hiking trip in search of an exotic bird while his sister, feisty Florida, will be Tiller's canoeing companion. Mr. Trepid supports this arrangement as he plans to steal the Morey's treasure, said to be hidden under rocks around their home in Ruby Holler, while they're away. In a classic ending, Mr. Trepid receives his comeuppance and the twins find a loving couple with whom to live as Dallas loses his dreaminess and Florida her feistiness. (310 pages)

Where it's reviewed:
Booklist, April 1, 2002, page 1328
Bulletin of the Center for Children's Books, July 2002, page 399
Horn Book, May 2002, page 326
Publishers Weekly, March 4, 2002, page 80
School Library Journal, April 2002, page 142

Awards the book has won:
ALA Notable Children's Books, 2003
School Library Journal Best Books, 2002

Other books by the same author:
Heartbeat, 2004
The Wanderer, 2000 (Newbery Honor Book)
Bloomability, 1998
Chasing Redbird, 1997
Walk Two Moons, 1994 (Newbery Medal)

Other books you might like:
Patricia Reilly Giff, *Pictures of Hollis Woods*, 2002
Living with foster parent Josie, Hollis worries that Josie's increasing senility will mean she has to find another foster home.
Eva Ibbotson, *Island of the Aunts*, 2000
When Aunts Etta, Coral and Myrtle need help caring for their creatures, they return to England and kidnap several children to be assistants.

Lemony Snicket, *Unfortunate Events Series*, 1999-
   The Baudelaire children live up to the name of the series as their lives go from bad to worse after their parents are killed.

314

CAROLYN CRIMI
MARSHA GRAY CARRINGTON, Illustrator

Tessa's Tip-Tapping Toes

(New York: Orchard Books/Scholastic, Inc., 2002)

Subject(s): Dancing; Singing; Animals/Mice
Age range(s): Grades K-2
Major character(s): Tessa, Mouse, Dancer; Oscar, Cat, Singer
Time period(s): 2000s (2002)
Locale(s): United States

Summary: Tessa is a mouse that loves to dance. Her mother wishes she would scurry like all the other mice and when a new house cat moves in she forbids Tessa to dance. New cat, Oscar, loves to sing, but after the neighbors complain his owner forbids it. Both animals try to suppress their creative impulses, but during a rainstorm one night, Oscar starts singing, Tessa starts dancing and pretty soon the rest of the house is joining in. (32 pages)

Where it's reviewed:
Booklist, March 1, 2002, page 1140
Horn Book Guide, Fall 2002, page 324
Kirkus Reviews, January 15, 2002, page 102
Publishers Weekly, December 3, 2001, page 75

Other books by the same author:
Boris and Bella, 2004
Don't Need Friends, 1999
Outside, Inside, 1995

Other books you might like:
Marsha Diane Arnold, *Prancing, Dancing Lily*, 2004
   Dancing Lily doesn't fit in with the rest of the cows in her herd, so she sets off to find out where she belongs.
Helen Craig, *Angelina Ballerina*, 1988
   All Angelina wants to do is dance, so her parents send her to ballet school.
Karma Wilson, *Hilda Must Be Dancing*, 2004
   Hilda the Hippo loves to dance, but her foot-stomping rhythms are too loud for her friends and neighbors.
Elizabeth Winthrop, *Dumpy La Rue*, 2001
   When Dumpy is told that pigs don't dance he sets out to prove the entire barnyard wrong. Soon they all want to join Dumpy.

315

CRAIG CRIST-EVANS

Amaryllis

(Cambridge, MA: Candlewick Press, 2003)

Subject(s): Brothers; Vietnam War; Fathers and Sons
Age range(s): Grades 7-10
Major character(s): Frank Staples, 18-Year-Old, Military Personnel; Jimmy Staples, Surfer (15-Year-Old)
Time period(s): 1960s
Locale(s): Singer Island, Florida; Vietnam

Summary: The wreck of the *Amaryllis* off the coast of their Florida home results in perfect surfing waves for Frank and his younger brother Jimmy. Being out on the water is about the only way they can escape the abuse of their alcoholic father, until Frank turns eighteen and joins the army to fight in Vietnam. That first year Jimmy receives lots of letter from Frank that reveal his ignorance about what he's fighting for or even why he's there. After being wounded, he admits to an addiction to heroin, an addiction that Jimmy isn't about to reveal to their father. When a letter arrives from the Army telling them that Frank is missing, Jimmy's father realizes that his alcoholism probably contributed to his son's likely death in a moving tale of a dysfunctional family. (184 pages)

Where it's reviewed:
Booklist, November 1, 2003, page 490
Bulletin of the Center for Children's Books, January 2004, page 187
Publishers Weekly, December 15, 2003, page 75
School Library Journal, November 2003, page 138
Voice of Youth Advocates, December 2003, page 390

Other books by the same author:
North of Everything, 2004
Moon Over Tennessee: A Boy's Civil War Journal, 1999 (Bonnie Christensen, illustrator)

Other books you might like:
Valerie Hobbs, *Sonny's War*, 2002
   Though Cory considered protesting the Vietnam War, she rethinks her concerns when her brother Sonny returns home wounded, but alive.
Walter Dean Myers, *Fallen Angels*, 1988
   Lacking money for college, Richie Perry enlists and is sent ''in country'' where he quickly learns about the horror and tediousness of war.
S.L. Rottman, *Stetson*, 2002
   After too many years of living with his alcoholic father, Stet finally leaves home when his dad causes an accident that injures his sister.

316

DOREEN CRONIN
HARRY BLISS, Illustrator

Diary of a Worm

(New York: Joanna Cotler Books/HarperCollins Publishers, 2003)

Subject(s): Animals/Worms; Diaries; Humor
Age range(s): Grades 1-3
Major character(s): Unnamed Character, Worm, Student; Spider, Spider, Friend
Time period(s): Indeterminate
Locale(s): Fictional Country

Summary: Dated entries humorously describe information (worms can't walk upside down), parental words of wisdom (during fishing season, dig deeper) and the details of a young worm's days (playing on the sidewalk after a rain is fun). Through his entries, the worm reveals scientific facts about the benefits of worms to the earth. While the worm, in his red ball cap, sometimes wishes to have legs like his pal Spider he's basically satisfied with life as a worm—no baths, no complaints about mud in the house, and no trips to the dentist. (36 pages)

Where it's reviewed:
Booklist, October 1, 2003, page 326
Bulletin of the Center for Children's Books, October 2003, page 55
Horn Book, November 2003, page 728
Publishers Weekly, July 21, 2003, page 194
School Library Journal, October 2003, page 116

Awards the book has won:
School Library Journal Best Books, 2003
Center for Children's Books Best Books, 2003

Other books by the same author:
Giggle, Giggle, Quack, 2002 (Publishers Weekly Best Children's Books)
Click, Clack, Moo: Cows That Type, 2000 (Caldecott Honor Book)

Other books you might like:
Kathy Caple, *Wow, It's Worm!*, 2001
    Worm returns in a beginning reader to enjoy movies on TV, building with blocks, and cooling off on a sunny day.
Theresa Greenaway, *Worms*, 1999
    A nonfiction title describes the habitat and life cycle of worms and how to care for them as pets.
Jay O'Callahan, *Herman and Marguerite: An Earth Story*, 1996
    Earthworm Herman and Caterpillar Marguerite build a friendship and bring life back to an orchard.
Chris Raschka, *Wormy Worm*, 2000
    The wiggling antics of Wormy Worm make it difficult to figure out which end is which.

317

DOREEN CRONIN
BETSY LEWIN, Illustrator

Giggle, Giggle, Quack
(New York: Simon & Schuster Books for Young Readers, 2002)

Subject(s): Animals; Farm Life; Humor
Age range(s): Grades K-2
Major character(s): Duck, Duck, Rebel; Farmer Brown, Farmer, Brother; Bob, Brother
Time period(s): 2000s (2002)
Locale(s): United States

Summary: Bob diligently follows the written directions provided by the vacationing Farmer Brown without realizing that Duck, pencil in beak, has substituted other notes for the official ones. Thus, the animals are treated to pizza delivered to the barn on Tuesday night. Wednesday, as instructed, Bob bathes the pigs in the tub with Farmer Brown's favorite bubble bath. Thursday, as the animals settle down to watch a video, Farmer Brown calls. As soon as he hears the giggling animal sounds in the background he knows Duck is up to something and quickly ends his vacation. (32 pages)

Where it's reviewed:
Bulletin of the Center for Children's Books, June 2002, page 360
Horn Book, May 2002, page 313
New York Times Book Review, August 11, 2002, page 19
Publishers Weekly, April 15, 2002, page 63
School Library Journal, June 2002, page 92

Awards the book has won:
Publishers Weekly Best Children's Books, 2002
School Library Journal Best Books, 2002

Other books by the same author:
Click, Clack, Moo: Cows That Type, 2000 (Caldecott Honor Book)

Other books you might like:
Eileen Christelow, *The Great Pig Search*, 2001
    Farmer Bert plans a vacation to Florida with the intention of locating his runaway pigs but they continue to elude him.
Paul Brett Johnson, *The Goose Who Went Off in a Huff*, 2001
    In the third book about Miss Rosemary's rebellious farm animals, Magnolia satisfies her maternal instincts by mothering a lost circus elephant.
David Small, *George Washington's Cows*, 1994
    According to this tale Washington's outlandish animals are the reason he gave politics a try.

318

GILLIAN CROSS

Phoning a Dead Man
(New York: Holiday, 2002)

Subject(s): Organized Crime; Mystery and Detective Stories; Physically Handicapped
Age range(s): Grades 7-10
Major character(s): Hayley Cox, Student—High School; Annie Glasgow, Fiance(e), Handicapped; John Cox, Brother (of Hayley), Amnesiac; Frosya, Care Giver
Time period(s): 2000s
Locale(s): England; Russia (Siberia)

Summary: When Hayley's family receives the news that her brother John has been killed while demolishing a building in Russia, she can't believe he's really dead. Her parents, in turn, burn all his belongings as they try to ease their grief. His fiancee Annie can't imagine that John, a demolitions expert, would endanger himself and decides to travel to Russia to hear first-hand what happened. Wheelchair-bound, Annie asks Hayley to accompany her and the two find themselves helped by the Russian Mafia as they search Siberia for John. Unbeknownst to them, John is now an amnesiac being cared for by a simple, kindly villager called Frosya. The only clue the two women have to his location is the satellite tracking station of his cell phone, and the knowledge the Mafia may want to find John before they do. (252 pages)

Where it's reviewed:
Booklist, May 1, 2002, page 1459
Bulletin of the Center for Children's Books, May 2002, page 315
Publishers Weekly, March 4, 2002, page 81

School Library Journal, May 2002, page 147
Voice of Youth Advocates, June 2002, page 115

Other books by the same author:
Tightrope, 1999
Pictures in the Dark, 1996
Wolf, 1991
On the Edge, 1988

Other books you might like:
Margaret Buffie, *The Dark Garden*, 1997
 An accident leaves Thea an amnesiac after which her dreams blend with those of Susan, a previous occupant of Thea's house.
Robert Cormier, *I Am the Cheese*, 1977
 A children's nursery song has a sinister significance for a young amnesiac victim.
Michelle Kavanaugh, *Emerald Explosion*, 1988
 Patrick travels to the Soviet Union when he's told his mother's been killed; though she's really alive, something is amiss.
Neal Shusterman, *Dissidents*, 1989
 Derek lives in Moscow with his mother, the US Ambassador to the Soviet Union, where he smuggles Soviet Anna out of the country.

319

KEVIN CROSSLEY-HOLLAND

At the Crossing Places
(New York: Arthur A. Levine/Scholastic, 2002)

Series: Arthur Trilogy. Book 2
Subject(s): Arthurian Legends; Growing Up; Crusades
Age range(s): Grades 6-10
Major character(s): Arthur de Caldicott, Teenager, Nobleman; Stephen de Holt, Nobleman; Winnie de Verdon, Teenager, Noblewoman
Time period(s): 13th century
Locale(s): Shropshire, England

Summary: Arthur is finally old enough to be sent to train as squire with Lord Stephen, who intends to take Arthur on crusade. There's plenty to learn first, and not all of it has to do with the skill of becoming a squire. Arthur still watches the mysterious seeing stone for clues to his future, discovering that little he sees can be taken at face value. He realizes that this is true in his own life as well, as he becomes aware of cruelty and ignorance that seem senseless and willful. But there is pleasure too, as Arthur is attracted to his pretty neighbor Winnie. Arthur wants to know more about his parentage to further his cause with Winnie, but there are clearly secrets, and they may spell doom for Arthur's hopes. (394 pages)

Where it's reviewed:
Booklist, November 1, 2002, page 494
Horn Book, November 2002, page 752
Kliatt, November 2002, page 6
School Library Journal, November 2002, page 160
Voice of Youth Advocates, February 2003, page 485

Other books by the same author:
The Seeing Stone, 2000 (Arthur Trilogy Book 1)

Other books you might like:
Michael Cadnum, *The Book of the Lion*, 2000
 With little choice in the matter, Edmund finds himself enlisted in the Crusades.
Sarah Thomson, *The Dragon's Son*, 2001
 Several of the characters from the Arthurian legends, including Mordred, tell their side of the story.
Jane Yolen, *Sword of the Rightful King: A Novel of King Arthur*, 2003
 A squire becomes a central figure in this version of the story of King Arthur.

320

CHRIS CROWE

Mississippi Trial, 1955
(New York: Penguin Putnam, 2002)

Subject(s): Grandfathers; Racism; Fathers and Sons
Age range(s): Grades 7-10
Major character(s): Hiram Hillburn, 15-Year-Old; Harlan Hillburn, Father; Earl Hillburn, Grandfather, Racist; Emmett Till, 14-Year-Old, Historical Figure; R.C. Rydell, 18-Year-Old, Bully
Time period(s): 1950s (1955)
Locale(s): Greenwood, Mississippi

Summary: As a child Hiram spends a lot of time with his grandparents in the Mississippi Delta, while his father serves overseas in World War II and then later attends graduate school. Hiram doesn't understand why his dad hates the South and takes a job in Arizona after graduation. Now that Hiram's 16, and Grandfather Earl has been ill, he returns to Greenwood to spend the summer and help out. This is also the summer that Chicago teenager Emmett Till visits and is accused of talking "ugly" to a white woman, a charge for which he's tortured and murdered. Two white men are put on trial, but are found innocent. For the first time in Hiram's young life he witnesses racism at its worst, and feels terrible because he and Emmett crossed paths and Hiram found him to be very nice. Looking into the tragedy a little more deeply, Hiram discovers that his childhood friend R.C. is not the one who murdered Emmett and is forced to look more closely at the political maneuvering of his grandfather. In this author's first novel, Hiram learns why his father distances himself from his Southern hometown. (231 pages)

Where it's reviewed:
Bulletin of the Center for Children's Books, April 2002, page 276
Kliatt, May 2002, page 8
Publishers Weekly, July 17, 2002, page 66
School Library Journal, May 2002, page 147
Voice of Youth Advocates, April 2002, page 40

Awards the book has won:
ALA Best Books for Young Adults, 2003

Other books by the same author:
More than a Game: Sports Literature for Young Adults, 2004
Getting Away with Murder: The True Story of the Emmett Till Case, 2003

From the Outside Looking In: Short Stories for LDS Teenagers, 1998

Other books you might like:

Christopher Paul Curtis, *The Watsons Go to Birmingham—1963*, 1995

Heading south to visit Grandmother, the Watson family's high spirits falter when a church in Birmingham blows up and four children die.

Carolyn Meyer, *White Lilacs*, 1993

The black community of Freedomtown opposes being moved to the sewer flats, but violence and marches by the Ku Klux Klan stop their action.

Mildred D. Taylor, *The Gold Cadillac*, 1987

Visiting relatives, an African-American family from Ohio confronts the racism that is part of everyday life in the South in the 1950s.

321

SHUTTA CRUM

Spitting Image

(New York: Clarion Books, 2003)

Subject(s): Family Life; Fathers; Poverty
Age range(s): Grades 5-8
Major character(s): Jessica Kay ''Jessie'' Bovey, 12-Year-Old; Miss Woodruff, Volunteer (for VISTA); Robert E. Ketchum, 12-Year-Old
Time period(s): 1960s
Locale(s): Baylor, Kentucky

Summary: Growing up in her tiny town of Baylor, Jessie wonders about her father's identity and why her grandmother's so testy and irritable. Told to stop always using her fists when she's angry, Jessie tries to be a better person. She gets her chance when VISTA volunteer Miss Woodruff comes to their town as part of the government's War on Poverty. She learns that the government can help with schooling and other needs, so she tries to earn money to buy her friend Robert a pair of glasses. Showing a newsman around her town adds ten dollars to her glasses fund, but also draws the anger of her community when photos depicting the ugly side of their poverty appear nationally. By book's end, Jessie learns the identity of her father, finds a grandfather and works on controlling her temper in this author's first novel. (218 pages)

Where it's reviewed:

Booklist, March 1, 2003, page 1206
Bulletin of the Center for Children's Books, April 2003, page 310
Kirkus Reviews, April 15, 2003, page 605
Publishers Weekly, April 21, 2003, page 62
School Library Journal, April 2003, page 157

Other books you might like:

Vicki Grove, *Destiny*, 2000

Destiny's family is mired in poverty, each child has a different father and their house was purchased through insurance from a car accident.

Kimberly Willis Holt, *My Louisiana Sky*, 1998

Bright Tiger loves her parents but doesn't realize they're

mentally handicapped until she's older and her grandmother dies.

Delia Ray, *Ghost Girl: A Blue Ridge Mountain Story*, 2003

President Hoover builds a school in her community, but April's mother won't let her attend until her aunt intervenes.

322

MITTIE CUETARA, Author/Illustrator

Baby Business

(New York: Dutton Children's Books, 2003)

Subject(s): Babies; Behavior; Stories in Rhyme
Age range(s): Preschool-Grade 1
Time period(s): 2000s
Locale(s): United States

Summary: From the moment any baby wakes, the action is nonstop. Simple illustrations expand the vignettes as one baby after another demonstrates making a mess while eating, courageously taking first steps, swinging, crying and crawling away from searching parents. Daytime activities from play to eating to the natural consequences of that action with a bath and a story thrown in all add up to one tired baby at bedtime. (28 pages)

Where it's reviewed:

Booklist, June 2003, page 1784
Bulletin of the Center for Children's Books, September 2003, page 9
Publishers Weekly, May 12, 2003, page 65
School Library Journal, June 2003, page 98

Awards the book has won:

Center for Children's Books Best Books, 2003

Other books by the same author:

The Crazy Crawler Crane and Other Very Short Truck Stories, 1998
Terrible Teresa and Other Very Short Stories, 1997

Other books you might like:

Eve Bunting, *Girls A to Z*, 2002

The little girls in this picture book enjoy varied activities just as babies do but are a bit less messy—and potty-trained too.

Susan Meyers, *Everywhere Babies*, 2001

Despite differences in appearance babies share a myriad of common experiences.

Charles R. Smith Jr., *Brown Sugar Babies*, 2000

The babies in this photographic essay come in all shades of brown—some peanut butter creamy, some cinnamon spice and some sweet as honey.

323

CATHERINE ANN CULLEN
DAVID MCPHAIL, Illustrator

Thirsty Baby

(New York: Little, Brown and Company, 2003)

Subject(s): Babies; Stories in Rhyme; Family
Age range(s): Preschool-Kindergarten

Major character(s): Unnamed Character, Baby, Son; Grandpa, Grandfather
Time period(s): Indeterminate
Locale(s): Earth

Summary: A very thirsty baby starts with a sip and finishes with a sup as he consumes his bottle, the bath water, a pond in the park, a river and the silver sea. At that point Grandpa is wondering where he'll find something else for the thirsty baby to drink, but the baby finally seems satisfied. He burps and claims he's had enough, at least until bedtime. (24 pages)

Where it's reviewed:
Booklist, April 1, 2003, page 1400
Bulletin of the Center for Children's Books, April 2003, page 310
School Library Journal, April 2003, page 118

Other books by the same author:
The Magical, Mystical, Marvelous Coat, 2001

Other books you might like:
Kathy Henderson, *The Baby Dances*, 1999
    As the seasons change, a baby grows under the watchful eyes of a loving family.
Susan Myers, *Everywhere Babies*, 2001
    Babies of all shapes, sizes and colors are everywhere, playing, eating, sleeping and most of all, being loved.
Margaret Wild, *Midnight Babies*, 2001
    Baby Brenda meets her baby friends at the Midnight Cafe for a night of dancing and eating before crawling home to bed.

324

LYNN CULLEN
JACQUELINE ROGERS, Illustrator

Little Scraggly Hair: A Dog on Noah's Ark
(New York: Holiday House, 2003)

Subject(s): Animals/Dogs; Biblical Fiction; Floods
Age range(s): Grades K-3
Major character(s): Little Scraggly Hair, Dog; Noah, Biblical Figure
Time period(s): Indeterminate Past
Locale(s): Earth

Summary: An author's note cites the literary sources for this retelling of Noah's Ark combined with the story of how dogs become man's best friend. Set in the Appalachian Mountains Noah is ridiculed by his neighbors for building an ark, a situation understood by Little Scraggly Hair, an outcast in the dog world in the days when dogs were not friendly with people. By the time the ark is finished and the rains begin, only Little Scraggly Hair will help round up the pairs of animals. The Ark is so loaded that Little Scraggly Hair spends 40 days squished between a buffalo and a bear with his nose stuck in a knothole. Dogs have had cold, wet noses since that time. (32 pages)

Where it's reviewed:
Booklist, November 1, 2003, page 500

Bulletin of the Center for Children's Books, February 2004, page 226
Publishers Weekly, November 10, 2003, page 61
School Library Journal, December 2003, page 112

Other books by the same author:
Godiva, 2001
Mightiest Heart, 1998

Other books you might like:
Pippa Goodhart, *Noah Makes a Boat*, 1997
    Noah lacks experience with boat building but he's obedient and resourceful so he completes the task just as the rains begin.
Patricia Hooper, *A Stormy Ride on Noah's Ark*, 2001
    To soothe the fears of some animals on the storm-tossed ark a sparrow sings, a mouse tells a tale and spider weaves a web of sleep.
Peter Spier, *Noah's Ark*, 1977
    The Caldecott Medal winner pictorially reenacts the story of the flood.

325

LYNN CULLEN

Nelly in the Wilderness
(New York: HarperCollins, 2002)

Subject(s): Frontier and Pioneer Life; Stepmothers; Grief
Age range(s): Grades 5-8
Major character(s): Nelly Vandorn, 12-Year-Old; Cornelius Vandorn, 14-Year-Old; Margery Vandorn, Stepmother; Frank Vandorn, Father, Trapper; John "Johnny Appleseed" Chapman, Frontiersman
Time period(s): 1820s
Locale(s): Indiana

Summary: After Nelly's mother dies, their father takes off and Nelly and her brother Cornelius, raised on the belief that trouble comes in threes, wait for the third bit of trouble to arrive. It does, when their father returns with Margery, his new wife whose curled hair and fancy clothes reveal a knowledge of the frontier garnered from romantic books. Both siblings take an instant dislike to her and make Margery's life miserable as she tries to adjust to a life that is so unlike her city upbringing. When John Chapman stops by their cabin, Nelly even hopes that he'll take her stepmother away; alas, that doesn't happen. Gradually Nelly sees the good in Margery, especially when she helps her care for a wildcat cub or tells her about city life, but it's not soon enough for them to build a relationship before Margery dies in childbirth. (184 pages)

Where it's reviewed:
Booklist, April 1, 2002, page 1328
Bulletin of the Center for Children's Books, May 2002, page 316
Horn Book, July 2002, page 457
Publishers Weekly, February 25, 2002, page 67
School Library Journal, February 2002, page 130

Other books by the same author:
Stink Bomb, 1998
The Three Lives of Harris Harper, 1996

The Backyard Ghost, 1993

Other books you might like:

Frances Arrington, *Bluestem*, 2000
  Depressed from living on the prairie and losing babies in two successive winters, Polly and Jessie's mother walks out of their home one day and never returns.

Pam Conrad, *Prairie Songs*, 1985
  Young Louisa is upset when her friend, the doctor's wife, loses touch with reality after enduring the harsh life of the Nebraska plains.

Patricia MacLachlan, *Sarah, Plain and Tall*, 1986
  Caleb and Anna are entranced by the mail-order bride from Maine who travels West to be a new mother for them.

Kathryn Reiss, *Riddle of the Prairie Bride*, 2001
  When her father's mail-order bride arrives, Ida Kate worries she's an imposter as she's different from the description she wrote of herself in her letters.

326

PAT CUMMINGS, Author/Illustrator

Ananse and the Lizard: A West African Tale

(New York: Henry Holt and Company, 2002)

Subject(s): Folklore; Legends; Animals/Spiders
Age range(s): Grades K-3
Major character(s): Ananse, Spider; Lizard, Lizard, Trickster
Time period(s): Indeterminate Past
Locale(s): Ghana

Summary: Self-confident Ananse believes he will be the one to guess the name of the village Chief's daughter and thus win her hand in marriage. Although Ananse does learn the name, in his desire to impress the king he unwittingly allows Lizard to outsmart him. Lizard offers to announce Ananse's impending arrival, but requests the daughter's name in order to add legitimacy to the mission. Instead of announcing Ananse, Lizard uses the information to win the daughter's hand and half the chief's land. Ananse departs in anger, threatening to destroy Lizard when next they meet. To this day, lizards everywhere seem a bit nervous and stretch their necks back and forth. They're really on the lookout for Ananse. (40 pages)

Where it's reviewed:
Booklist, November 1, 2002, page 500
Bulletin of the Center for Children's Books, January 2003, page 195
Publishers Weekly, October 14, 2002, page 83
School Library Journal, October 2002, page 142
Tribune Books, November 3, 2002, page 5

Other books by the same author:
Angel Baby, 2000
Purrrrr, 1999
My Aunt Came Back, 1998

Other books you might like:

Virginia Hamilton, *A Ring of Tricksters: Animal Tales from America, the West Indies, and Africa*, 1997
  Eleven read-aloud tales include tricksters from spiders to

rabbits and the unwitting animals that bear the brunt of their cleverness.

Eric A. Kimmel, *Anasi and the Talking Melon*, 1994
  Anansi tricks the other animals into thinking that the melon in which he's hiding is actually speaking.

Tololwa M. Mollel, *Ananse's Feast: An Ashanti Tale*, 1997
  Turtle Akye finds a way to give trickster Ananse a taste of his medicine.

327

PRISCILLA CUMMINGS

Saving Grace

(New York: Dutton, 2003)

Subject(s): Family Life; Depression (Economic); Deafness
Age range(s): Grades 4-8
Major character(s): Grace McFarland, 11-Year-Old; Louise ''Miss Louise'' Showalter, Secretary
Time period(s): 1930s
Locale(s): Washington, District of Columbia

Summary: The McFarland family feels the effects of the Depression when they're evicted from their home and cast out on the street. Realizing the family can no longer be together, their parents send Grace and her two younger brothers to a children's charity shelter, while everyone else disperses to relatives, shelters or a hospital. At Christmas, Grace is invited to the home of the Hammonds where she eats good food, is finally warm and enjoys being with a happy, loving family, though she feels guilty knowing her own family is suffering. She also feels needed as she uses her sign language to communicate with the Hammond's youngest daughter who is deaf. When Miss Louise, the oldest Hammond daughter, wants to adopt her, Grace understands the hard decision she must make. (240 pages)

Where it's reviewed:
Booklist, May 15, 2003, page 1665
Bulletin of the Center for Children's Books, September 2003, page 10
Kirkus Reviews, June 1, 2003, page 801
School Library Journal, June 2003, page 137
Voice of Youth Advocates, October 2003, page 302

Other books by the same author:
Red Kayak, 2004
A Face First, 2001
Autumn Journey, 1997

Other books you might like:

Barbara Corcoran, *The Sky Is Falling*, 1988
  Annah's middle class world comes crashing down during the Depression when her father loses his banking job.

Cynthia DeFelice, *Nowhere to Call Home*, 1999
  Her father's suicide sends Frankie to the rails dressed as a hobo, but she decides she's better off living with her aunt.

Elizabeth Winthrop, *Franklin Delano Roosevelt: Letters from a Mill Town Girl*, 2001
  The Depression reduces her family's income, which spurs Emma to write the President asking why their lives are changing.

`328`

MARIANNE CURLEY

The Dark

(New York: Bloomsbury, 2003)

Series: Guardians of Time
Subject(s): Space and Time; Fantasy; Adventure and Adventurers
Age range(s): Grades 7-10
Major character(s): Akarian, Kidnap Victim, Wizard; Lathenia, Deity; Ethan Robert, 16-Year-Old, Student—High School; Isabel Becket, 16-Year-Old, Healer; Matt Becket, Brother (of Isabel)
Time period(s): 2000s; Indeterminate Past
Locale(s): Australia; Fictional Country (the Underworld)

Summary: In this sequel to *The Named*, Isabel, Ethan and Matt, a new member of the Named, search for their mentor, Arkarian, who's been kidnapped by Lathenia in retaliation for their eliminating her second in command. Lathenia oversees the Order of Chaos, which attempts to change history, while the Named fight against her destructive Order. Though expressly forbidden to follow Arkarian, the three teenagers have a few side trips to medieval France and ancient Rome before descending to the Underworld with its monsters and unanticipated dangers. Though their first priority is to find and rescue Arkarian, Isabel needs to decide if she's in love with him while Ethan and Matt need to mend their differences in this swashbuckling adventure. (334 pages)

Where it's reviewed:
Booklist, October 1, 2003, page 310
Kirkus Reviews, October 1, 2003, page 1222
Publishers Weekly, November 24, 2003, page 66
School Library Journal, January 2004, page 128
Voice of Youth Advocates, December 2003, page 410

Other books by the same author:
The Named, 2002
Old Magic, 2000

Other books you might like:
Lynn Ewing, *Into the Cold Fire*, 2000
    The members of the Daughters of the Moon need to use all their powers to rescue fellow witch Sirena from the Dark Side.
Christopher Tebbetts, *The Viking Series*, 2003
    In this quartet of books Zack lands in a world parallel to his own and filled with Vikings who encounter some of the same problems that Zack does.
Mark London Williams, *Ancient Fire*, 2001
    Eli stumbles into one of his father's time spheres and lands in the middle of a riot in ancient Alexandria.

`329`

MARIANNE CURLEY

The Named

(New York: Bloomsbury, 2002)

Series: Guardians of Time. Book 1
Subject(s): Space and Time; Fantasy

Age range(s): Grades 7-10
Major character(s): Ethan Robert, 16-Year-Old, Student—High School; Isabel Becket, 16-Year-Old, Student—High School
Time period(s): 2000s; Indeterminate Past
Locale(s): Australia

Summary: To keep history intact, the Guardians battle constantly against the Order of Chaos whose members want to change history to allow more evil to occur while the Guard constantly time travels to prevent Chaos from occurring. Ethan is a member of the Guard who's made several dangerous time travel trips and now is given the chance to train an apprentice so that he can climb to the elevated Guardian status. His apprentice is Isabel, sister of his former best friend, who shows healing powers that will make her a valuable member of the Guard. In this first of a trilogy, Ethan learns that as his assignments become more dangerous it's becoming harder to know whom to trust. (333 pages)

Where it's reviewed:
Booklist, November 15, 2002, page 590
Magpies, July 2002, page 40
Publishers Weekly, September 16, 2002, page 69
School Library Journal, January 2003, page 134
Voice of Youth Advocates, February 2003, page 486

Other books by the same author:
The Dark, 2003 (Guardians of Time Book 2)
Old Magic, 2000

Other books you might like:
Terry Brooks, *Running with the Demon*, 1997
    Nest is caught in the middle of a struggle between good and evil in Hopewell, Illinois.
Philip Pullman, *The Subtle Knife*, 1997
    A magical tool that can cut between universes draws an innocent into a battle between good and evil.
Silver RavenWolf, *Witches' Night Out*, 2000
    Bethany's Thursday night group usually gathers for innocuous charms, but tonight they call up the Hounds of the Wild Hunt to locate a killer.

`330`

JANE LOUISE CURRY

The Egyptian Box

(New York: Margaret K. McElderry/Simon & Schuster, 2002)

Subject(s): Supernatural; Magic; Family Life
Age range(s): Grades 4-7
Major character(s): Leticia Ann "Tee" Woodie, Student—Middle School; Charles Woodie, Student—Middle School; Sebastian "Uncle Bass" Fall, Uncle (great-great-great uncle)
Time period(s): 2000s
Locale(s): Oasis Wells, Southwest

Summary: Tee is unhappy living in the desert, where her family moves after her Great Uncle Sebastian leaves them his home, antique store and video shop. She'd rather be in Maine where the weather is cooler and she has friends. Uncle Bass wills her a carved wooden Egyptian statue, called a Shabti, whose purpose was to serve the dead in their Afterlife. Her younger brother Charles is intrigued by the hieroglyphics written on the statue and, using the Internet, manages to decipher the symbols, saying them aloud to Tee as he does. The words are potent for they bring the statue to life and Tee now has a servant to wash the dishes or do her math homework. The Shabti emulates Tee's movements and clothing styles so well that Tee decides to send her to school so that she can stay home and watch videos and eat junk food. Luckily Tee realizes before it's too late that Shabti has a plan to make the transformation permanent; altering the hieroglyphs and donating the statue to the Egyptian Museum solves her problem very handily. (186 pages)

Where it's reviewed:
Book Report, September 2002, page 53
Booklist, June 2002, page 1722
Bulletin of the Center for Children's Books, May 2002, page 316
Publishers Weekly, March 4, 2002, page 80
School Library Journal, March 2002, page 226

Other books by the same author:
Black Canary, 2005
Stolen Life, 1999
Dark Shade, 1998
Moon Window, 1996
Lotus Cup, 1986

Other books you might like:
Kate McMullan, *Under the Mummy's Spell*, 1992
    Kissing the 3,000-year-old mummy mask of Princess Nephia, Peter accidentally releases the spirit of the princess's evil Aunt Tachu.
Pamela F. Service, *The Reluctant God*, 1988
    Lorna discovers the unembalmed body of a young pharaoh's son, Ameni, and helps him recover a stolen urn.
William Sleator, *The Duplicate*, 1988
    David finds a gadget on the beach that duplicates himself; when there are three Davids, he knows the gadget's out of control.
Cynthia Voigt, *The Vandemark Mummy*, 1991
    Althea and Phineas assist their father in locating a stolen mummy.

331

KAREN CUSHMAN

Rodzina

(New York: Clarion Books, 2003)

Subject(s): Orphans; Survival
Age range(s): Grades 5-8
Major character(s): Rodzina Clara Jadqiga Anastozy Brodski, Orphan, 12-Year-Old; Catriona Anabel ''Miss Doctor'' Wellington, Guardian, Doctor
Time period(s): 1880s (1881)
Locale(s): West

Summary: A husky, stubborn girl, Rodzina leaves Chicago aboard an orphan train convinced no loving family will ever adopt her. For a while Rodzina's exactly correct as she watches some of her favorite younger orphans leave with their jubilant families. Her biggest fears are confirmed when two elderly sisters adopt her to be their servant, and again when Mr. Clence adopts her intending to wed her and secure a mother for his 13 motherless children; luckily she escapes from each situation. As the orphan train nears the end of its trek, Rodzina's only choice is the Boys' and Girls' Training School, though she'd really like to be adopted by Miss Doctor, the group's guardian. (215 pages)

Where it's reviewed:
Booklist, January 1, 2004, page 780
Bulletin of the Center for Children's Books, March 2003, page 269
Horn Book, May 2003, page 342
Publishers Weekly, January 13, 2003, page 60
School Library Journal, April 2003, page 157

Awards the book has won:
Booklist Editors' Choice/Books for Middle Readers, 2003

Other books by the same author:
Matilda Bone, 2000
The Ballad of Lucy Whipple, 1996
The Midwife's Apprentice, 1995
Catherine, Called Birdy, 1994

Other books you might like:
Jane Buchanan, *Hank's Story*, 2001
    Sent on the Orphan Train and placed with the Olson family, Hank flees from abusive Mr. Olson to the shelter of animal lover Holly McIntire.
David DeVries, *Home at Last*, 1994
    New York-bred Billy has a hard time fitting in with the Nebraska Andersen family, after being sent there by the Children's Aid Society.
Joan Lowery Nixon, *The Orphan Train Quartet*, 1987-1989
    A series of books featuring the Kelly children who are sent West on the Orphan Train when their mother can no longer care for them.

332

JANE CUTLER
TRACEY CAMPBELL PEARSON, Illustrator

Leap, Frog

(New York: Farrar Straus Giroux, 2002)

Series: Fraser Brothers Adventure. Book 4
Subject(s): Animals/Frogs and Toads; Contests; Brothers
Age range(s): Grades 2-5
Major character(s): Edward Fraser, 3rd Grader, Brother (younger); Charley O'Hara, 1st Grader, Neighbor; Jason Fraser, Brother, 6th Grader
Time period(s): 2000s (2002)
Locale(s): California

Summary: Anyone other than good-hearted Edward might be bothered to have active Charley move in next door, but Edward knows how to humor the younger child so his presence is positive for everyone in this episodic chapter book. Together Edward and Charley catch a frog from the lake and enter a frog-jumping contest. Edward uses his art skills to make faces on the ''egg babies'' of two middle-school friends. When Jason reacts angrily to a class schedule that assigns him to an acting class because his chosen elective is full, Edward feels puzzled. To celebrate Edward's birthday, his family attends a children's play and Edward can see that Jason is as spellbound by the performance as Charley is though Jason doesn't admit that to his little brother. (198 pages)

Where it's reviewed:
Booklist, November 1, 2002, page 490
Bulletin of the Center for Children's Books, December 2002, page 139
Horn Book, September 2002, page 569
Kirkus Reviews, October 15, 2002, page 1527
School Library Journal, October 2002, page 100

Awards the book has won:
Center for Children's Books Best Books, 2002

Other books by the same author:
'Gator Aid, 1999 (Fraser Brothers Adventure)
Rats, 1996 (Fraser Brothers Adventure)
No Dogs Allowed, 1992 (Fraser Brothers Adventure)

Other books you might like:
Judy Blume, *Superfudge*, 1980
    Peter's life is filled with the unexpected as the family tries to stay one step ahead of little brother Fudge.
Johanna Hurwitz, *Hurray for Ali Baba Bernstein*, 1989
    Expect the unexpected could be the motto for nine-year-old Ali Baba who seems able to rise above the turmoil.
Elizabeth Levy, *Night of the Living Gerbil*, 2001
    Sam's effort to soothe his younger brother's grief about the death of his gerbil leads Robert to think his pet has become a zombie.

333

LEAH CUTTER

Paper Mage
(New York: NAL/Roc, 2003)

Subject(s): Fantasy; Magic; Coming-of-Age
Age range(s): Grades 9-Adult
Major character(s): Xiao Yen, Teenager, Wizard
Time period(s): 7th century (Tang Dynasty)
Locale(s): China

Summary: As family fortunes wane, Xiao Yen is sent to train with the paper mages, wizards who use origami techniques to achieve their magic. This is an act of desperation on her family's part for although Xiao Yen is talented, only boys should be trained as mages and her family fears that she'll never find a husband. Xiao Yen loves magic, but she also wants to make her mother happy, and her divided family loyalties cause her pain until her aunt, the family matriarch, decrees that she should accept a commission to protect two travelers. It's bad enough that she will be traveling alone without a chaperone, but to make things worse, the two travelers are foreigners. Xiao Yen leaves behind her family and everything familiar to fulfill her duty. At first all goes well and her magic is adequate to the task, but soon a disguised goddess makes an appearance and Xiao Yen discovers she needs to find strength she never suspected she had. (352 pages)

Where it's reviewed:
Booklist, February 15, 2003, page 1059
Chronicle, February 2003, page 63
Kliatt, May 2003, page 24

Other books by the same author:
The Caves of Buda, 2004

Other books you might like:
Barry Hughart, *The Bridge of Birds*, 1984
    Number Ten Ox is an apprentice to a Chinese magician who is expected to carry his master on his back—literally.
Kim Stanley Robinson, *The Years of Rice and Salt*, 2002
    In this alternate history, China and the Islamic world dominate Earth after a debilitating plague.
David Wingrove, *Chung Kuo: the Middle Kingdom*, 1990
    Welcome to a future world ruled by a China still practicing ancient social conventions.

334

MARGERY CUYLER
S.D. SCHINDLER, Illustrator

Skeleton Hiccups
(New York: Margaret K. McElderry Books, 2002)

Subject(s): Ghosts; Problem Solving; Humor
Age range(s): Grades K-2
Major character(s): Skeleton, Spirit; Ghost, Spirit
Time period(s): Indeterminate
Locale(s): Fictional Country

Summary: Skeleton awakens with hiccups that greatly impact his ability to perform his usual daily grooming. The hiccups cause him to be so jittery that he makes a mess of the pumpkin he carves and misses the ball while playing catch with Ghost. To help his friend Ghost recommends all the standard hiccup cures such as holding your breath, swallowing sugar and drinking water upside down. None of those solutions work because Skeleton, lacking skin or organs, is unable to contain air, sugar or water. Even Ghost's attempts to scare Skeleton don't work until he finds a mirror. While looking at Ghost isn't scary to Skeleton, seeing his own reflection in a mirror startles him enough to get those hiccups to flee. (32 pages)

Where it's reviewed:
Booklist, September 15, 2002, page 245
Bulletin of the Center for Children's Books, September 2002, page 11
Horn Book, September 2002, page 549
Publishers Weekly, September 23, 2002, page 22
School Library Journal, October 2002, page 100

Awards the book has won:
Center for Children's Books Best Books, 2002

Other books by the same author:
Big Friends, 2004
Ah-Choo!, 2002
100th Day Worries, 2000

Other books you might like:
Melinda Long, *Hiccup Snickup*, 2001
    A girl with the hiccups tries the advice offered by each member of her family.

Mercer Mayer, *Hiccup*, 1976
  Mr. Hippopotamus irritates the friend with hiccups he's trying to help and then he starts hiccupping too.
Virginia Mueller, *Monster's Birthday Hiccups*, 1991
  Hiccups almost spoil Monster's birthday party until he has an idea to get rid of them.

335

MARGERY CUYLER
DAVID CATROW, Illustrator

That's Good! That's Bad! In The Grand Canyon

(New York: Henry Holt and Company, 2002)

Subject(s): Grandmothers; Travel; Tall Tales
Age range(s): Grades K-2
Major character(s): Unnamed Character, Child, Traveler; Unnamed Character, Grandmother, Traveler
Time period(s): 2000s
Locale(s): Grand Canyon, Arizona

Summary: One accident after another transforms a little boy's hike with his grandmother into a series of near calamities. Each change in the action that seems for the better turns out to be for the worse as the boy falls off a cliff, onto a horse, that throws him into a white water raft from which the boy tumbles into the water—and that's not all. The nonstop, improbable adventures continue until the boy reconnects with his grandmother for one very big and very good hug after another. (32 pages)

Where it's reviewed:
Booklist, May 15, 2002, page 1600
Horn Book Guide, Fall 2002, page 324
Publishers Weekly, March 18, 2002, page 106
School Library Journal, June 2002, page 92

Other books by the same author:
Stop, Drop, and Roll, 2001
100th Day Worries, 2000 (IRA Teachers' Choice)
That's Good! That's Bad!, 1993

Other books you might like:
Jules Feiffer, *Meanwhile . . .* , 1997
  Raymond discovers that, with a little imagination and the word ''meanwhile,'' he can enjoy an adventure in the Wild West and other unplanned locations.
Margaret Mahy, *A Busy Day for a Good Grandmother*, 1993
  Mrs. Oberon, grandmother extraordinaire, overcomes unusual obstacles to reach and soothe her teething grandson.
John Winch, *Keeping Up with Grandma*, 2000
  The activities Grandma plans to add a little excitement to her life with Grandpa causes a bit more than Grandpa finds appealing.

D

336
DEBBIE DADEY

Whistler's Hollow
(New York: Bloomsbury, 2002)

Subject(s): Aunts and Uncles; Secrets
Age range(s): Grades 4-6
Major character(s): Lillie Mae Worth, Orphan, 11-Year-Old; Paul Garrett, Student—Middle School, Neighbor; Esther Worth, Aunt (great aunt); Dallas Worth, Uncle (great uncle)
Time period(s): 1920s
Locale(s): Henderson, Kentucky (Whistler's Hollow)

Summary: When her mother dies, Lillie Mae's Aunt Helen wastes no time in rounding up all her mother's belongings for herself and then sending Lillie Mae off to live with her father's aunt and uncle, even though they're strangers to her. She finds her Uncle Dallas and Aunt Esther to be kind, just as they were to her father when they brought him up, but her neighbor and classmate Paul is rude and nasty, and turns the other students in their classroom against her. Many mysteries confront Lillie Mae, including her father's whereabouts; everyone tells her he died in World War I but she never saw any telegram saying he died, so she thinks he'll return any day. There's also a rotten food smell that emanates from the forbidden attic, which concerns Lillie Mae. When she discovers that Uncle Dallas helps pay Aunt Esther's medical bills by making moonshine in the attic, with the help of rude Paul, she understands Paul's fear that she'd learn about the moonshine. Receiving a box of her mother's things from her mother's sister, she finds a telegram from her father explaining his whereabouts. (112 pages)

Where it's reviewed:
Kirkus Reviews, June 1, 2002, page 803
Library Media Connection, February 2003, page 71
Publishers Weekly, June 10, 2002, page 61
School Library Journal, July 2002, page 118

Other books by the same author:
Cherokee Sister, 2000

Other books you might like:
Carole Crowe, *Groover's Heart*, 2001
    Raised by her Aunt Viola, surrounded by material goods but no real love, Charlotte covets the simple life of her recovering alcoholic uncle.
Iain Lawrence, *Lord of the Nutcracker Men*, 2001
    His father fights in the trenches during World War I and sends Johnny carvings of soldiers that grow more horrific as the war continues.
Janet Taylor Lisle, *The Art of Keeping Cool*, 2000
    Staying with his grandfather while his father fights in World War II, Robert wonders why there are no photos of his dad in his grandfather's home.
Cynthia Rylant, *I Had Seen Castles*, 1993
    An elderly man remembers how his experiences in World War I haunted him and changed his life.

337
MAURINE F. DAHLBERG

The Spirit and Gilly Bucket
(New York: Farrar Straus Giroux, 2002)

Subject(s): Slavery; Underground Railroad; Aunts and Uncles
Age range(s): Grades 5-8
Major character(s): Mary Gillian "Gilly" Bucket, 11-Year-Old; Rissy, Slave; Laura Hayden, Aunt; Henry Hayden, Uncle, Plantation Owner; Sarah Hayden, Cousin; Edward "Neddy" Hayden, Cousin, Child; Simon Craiky, Plantation Owner
Time period(s): 1850s (1859)
Locale(s): Glencaren Plantation, Virginia

Summary: Her mother dies, her father leaves to hunt for gold in California, and Gilly moves to Virginia, where she lives with her aunt and uncle. Used to speaking her mind and unbound by formality, Gilly has a hard time adjusting to the ways of a Virginia plantation, especially the use of slaves, which she's always been taught is wrong. Needlework, petticoats, and a clean face are all hard for her to manage. She enjoys her cousins Sarah and Neddy, but would be truly miserable without Rissy. Becoming friends, Gilly teaches Rissy to read and both girls talk about going in search of their fathers. When Rissy hears that she's to be sold to their neighbor Mr. Craiky, who beats his slaves, she runs away. Worried about her friend, Gilly's happy to be asked to help Rissy reach the Underground Railroad, though she's very surprised to see who the conductor is, in this authentic look at a pre-Civil War time. (234 pages)

Where it's reviewed:
Booklist, January 2003, page 888
Kirkus Reviews, October 15, 2002, page 1528
Library Media Connection, February 2003, page 73
School Library Journal, December 2002, page 132
Voice of Youth Advocates, February 2003, page 466

Other books by the same author:
Even the Spiders Fled West, 2004
Play to the Angel, 2000

Other books you might like:
Jennifer Armstrong, *Steal Away*, 1992
    Yankee Susannah and Bethlehem, the slave given to her, both escape north from their Virginia home.
Miriam Brenaman, *Evvy's Civil War*, 2002
    Saddled with much of the responsibility for her home, Evvy also runs an illegal school for slaves.
Louann Gaeddert, *Breaking Free*, 1994
    Though Richard is grateful to his uncle for raising him, he is distressed that his uncle keeps slaves as this practice is outlawed at his home in Vermont.

338

JULIET DALLAS-CONTE
ALISON BARTLETT, Illustrator

Cock-a-Moo-Moo

(Boston: Little, Brown and Company, 2002)

Subject(s): Animals; Animals/Roosters; Memory Loss
Age range(s): Preschool-Grade 1
Major character(s): Rooster, Rooster
Time period(s): Indeterminate
Locale(s): Fictional Country

Summary: In the author's first book, originally published in England in 2001, Rooster faces a predicament as the sun rises. He's forgotten how to crow correctly and his attempts produce the sounds of other barnyard animals rather than his distinctive call. Cows, sheep, ducks, pigs and even the chickens let him know that he's not sounding right. By nightfall, Rooster is feeling mighty discouraged but at the sight of a fox sneaking into the henhouse, he cries out with all the other animals' sounds, attracting them and scaring off the fox. In delight, Rooster crows out a loud cock-a-doodle-doo! (32 pages)

Where it's reviewed:
Booklist, June 2002, page 1734
Bulletin of the Center for Children's Books, April 2002, page 277
Horn Book Guide, Fall 2002, page 298
Publishers Weekly, March 4, 2002, page 78
School Library Journal, May 2002, page 111

Awards the book has won:
IRA Children's Choices, 2003

Other books you might like:
Mary Jane Auch, *Bantam of the Opera*, 1997
    Luigi's variations on the cock-a-doodle-doo theme anger the head rooster so Luigi joins the opera in order to express himself.
David McPhail, *The Day the Cow Said, ''Cock-a-Doodle-Doo!''*, 1997
    On a particularly windy day, the sounds of the farm animals get mixed up so that each is making another's sound.
Bill Peet, *Cock-a-Doodle Dudley*, 1990
    Cocky Dudley thinks that he controls the daily rising of the sun.
Janet Stevens, *Cook-a-Doodle-Doo!*, 1999
    Bored with a steady diet of chicken feed, Big Brown Rooster takes charge in the kitchen and makes strawberry shortcake.

339

ANNIE DALTON
MARK ELLIOTT, Illustrator

Isabel: Taking Wing

(Middleton, WI: American Girl/Pleasant Company, 2002)

Series: Girls of Many Lands
Subject(s): Aunts and Uncles; Theater; Adventure and Adventurers
Age range(s): Grades 5-8
Major character(s): Isabel Campion, 12-Year-Old; Elinor, Aunt; Aunt de Vere, Healer
Time period(s): 16th century
Locale(s): London, England; Northamptonshire, England

Summary: Unhappy about all the restrictions a girl faces, Isabel defies her father and her aunt when she sneaks out at night to attend a play at the Rose Theater. Caught, she's sent to live with Aunt de Vere, but while traveling to her aunt's home, Isabel is robbed and abandoned in the forest. A traveling troupe of actors finds her and offers protection as well as a chance to act. Reaching her aunt's home, she learns the power of healing as well as the inborn strength exhibited by so many other women. When she receives a letter from her older sister asking her to return home and help with her younger siblings who may have the plague, Isabel is eager to do so in this richly detailed work. (182 pages)

Where it's reviewed:
Booklist, November 1, 2002, page 491
Catholic Library World, December 2002, page 144
Horn Book Guide, Spring 2003, page 78
Ruminator Review, Winter 2002, page 41
School Library Journal, October 2002, page 160

Other books by the same author:
Flying High, 2003
Losing the Plot, 2002
Winging It, 2002

Other books you might like:
Berthe Amoss, *Lost Magic*, 1993
    Ceridwen, an orphaned child, is adopted by an old woman

who helps her use her healing powers so that she becomes the Wise Woman at Castle Bedevere.

J.B. Cheaney, *The Playmaker*, 2000
   After his mother's death, Richard travels to London where he's lucky enough to find a job as an actor with Lord Chamberlain's Men.

Karen Cushman, *Matilda Bone*, 2000
   Orphan Matilda is deposited on Blood and Bone Alley to help a bonesetter, but has difficulty adjusting and prays to every saint to save her.

Theresa Tomlinson, *The Forestwife*, 1995
   In a retelling of Robin Hood, Mary runs away from an arranged marriage, finds shelter with the Forestwife and learns to be an herbalist.

340

NIKI DALY, Author/Illustrator

Old Bob's Brown Bear

(New York: Farrar Straus Giroux, 2002)

Subject(s): Grandparents; Dolls and Dollhouses; Gifts
Age range(s): Preschool-Grade 1
Major character(s): Old Bob, Grandfather, Aged Person; Emma, Child, Daughter
Time period(s): 2000s (2002)
Locale(s): South Africa

Summary: Old Bob asks for a teddy bear for his birthday, because, as a child, he'd always wanted an old fuzzy bear. The bear Old Bob gets, of course, is new and Emma can tell that Old Bob doesn't love his bear, so she takes the teddy bear home with her to love. She takes it to the beach and on picnics, gives it a bubble bath and generally loves it, until she grows older and plays with it less and less. When Old Bob notices the bear a few years later, he asks to have the old, fuzzy bear back because now it's just like Bob always wanted it to be. (32 pages)

Where it's reviewed:
Booklist, October 1, 2002, page 334
Books for Keeps, January 2002, page 20
Kirkus Reviews, October 1, 2002, page 1466
School Library Journal, November 2002, page 121
Tribune Books, September 22, 2002, page 4

Other books by the same author:
Once Upon a Time, 2003
Jamela's Dress, 1999 (ALA Notable Children's Books)
Not So Fast, Songololo, 1986

Other books you might like:
Don Freeman, *Corduroy*, 1968
   Lonely Corduroy, a department store teddy bear, finally finds the home he's always wanted.
Tony Johnston, *My Best Friend Bear*, 2002
   When a little girl loves the stuffing right out of her bear, her mother repairs it.
David McPhail, *The Teddy Bear*, 2002
   After a young boy forgets his teddy bear at a diner a homeless man finds it and adopts it as his own.

Brigitte Weninger, *Ragged Bear*, 1996
   Poor Teddy is ignored and finally left in the park, where a new child finds him and loves him.

341

NIKI DALY, Author/Illustrator

Once Upon a Time

(New York: Farrar Straus Giroux, 2003)

Subject(s): Storytelling; Schools; Books and Reading
Age range(s): Grades K-2
Major character(s): Sarie, Child, Student—Elementary School; Anna, Aunt
Time period(s): 2000s (2003)
Locale(s): Little Karoo, South Africa

Summary: Sarie hates reading. She stumbles over the words in class and the other children make fun of her. Everyday after school Sarie escapes to her Auntie Anna's and tells her all about her problems. One day, she discovers a book in Auntie Anna's old car and they read the Cinderella story out loud together. As the story comes alive—with Sarie as the princess, her tormentors as the evil stepsisters and a kind classmate as the prince—Sarie's reading improves, until one day she is able to read beautifully in front of the entire class and the school principal. (40 pages)

Where it's reviewed:
Booklist, February 15, 2003, page 1083
Bulletin of the Center for Children's Books, April 2003, page 311
Horn Book, May/June 2003, page 327
Kirkus Reviews, January 1, 2003, page 59
School Library Journal, May 2003, page 112

Other books by the same author:
Jamela's Dress, 1999 (ALA Notable Children's Books)
Bravo Zan Angelo!, 1998
Not So Fast, Songololo, 1986

Other books you might like:
Marie Leonard, *Tibili: The Little Boy Who Didn't Want to Go to School*,
   Tibili, growing up on the African Savannah, learns from the animals about the importance of reading and writing.
Pat Mora, *Tomas and the Library Lady*, 1997
   In this true story, Tomas, son of migrant farm workers, learns to read and love books with the help of a librarian in Iowa.
John Steptoe, *Mufaro's Beautiful Daughters*, 1987
   This Caldecott Honor Book tells an African Cinderella story.

342

DAN DANKO, Co-Author
TOM MASON, Co-Author
BARRY GOTT, Illustrator

Sidekicks

(New York: Little, Brown and Co., 2003)

Series: Sidekicks. Book 1

Subject(s): Heroes and Heroines; Adventure and Adventurers; Humor
Age range(s): Grades 5-8
Major character(s): Guy "Speedy" Martin, 13-Year-Old, Hero; "Pumpkin" Pete, Hero; Spelling Beatrice, Hero
Time period(s): 2000s
Locale(s): United States

Summary: As the fastest runner in the world, Guy, better known as Speedy, is eligible to be a superhero, but first has to go through an apprentice program as a sidekick for the League of Justice. Of course, all this superhero stuff has to coexist with being a kid, going to school, and completing homework, but that's not Speedy's biggest problem. No, it's having to serve his apprenticeship as a sidekick to Pumpkin Pete, whose superpowers equate to those of a pumpkin. Part of the secret organization the League of Big Justice, Speedy and Pumpkin Pete, as well as all the other superheroes, lunge into action when the Brotherhood of Rottenness blows up the headquarters of the League of Big Justice and kidnaps some of their members. Now it's up to the sidekicks to try to save the superheroes, so one can only hope that running, spelling and a few other trivial powers will be enough to overcome the Brotherhood of Rottenness in this wacky tale. (97 pages)

Where it's reviewed:
Bulletin of the Center for Children's Books, October 2003, page 47
School Library Journal, November 2003, page 138

Other books by the same author:
The Brotherhood of Rotten Baby-sitters, 2005 (Sidekicks Book 5)
Attack of the Mole Master, 2004 (Sidekicks Book 3)
The Candy Man Cometh, 2004 (Sidekicks Book 4)
Operation Squish, 2003 (Sidekicks, Book 2)

Other books you might like:
Mel Gilden, *Harry Newberry and the Raiders of the Red Drink*, 1989
  Harry thinks his mother is the heroine of his favorite comic book until she's kidnapped by evil Bonnie Android who's looking for a lost recipe.
Kathy Mackel, *Can of Worms*, 1999
  Mike opens a "can of worms" when he sends out a message to space requesting rescue; suddenly he's surrounded by aliens who want to help him.
William Sleator, *Interstellar Pig*, 1984
  Barney plays the board game Interstellar Pig with three neighbors who happen to be aliens playing for control of the Earth.

343

EDWIDGE DANTICAT

Behind the Mountains: The Diary of Celiane Esperance

(New York: Orchard/Scholastic, 2002)

Series: First Person Fiction. Number 1
Subject(s): Emigration and Immigration; Diaries
Age range(s): Grades 5-9
Major character(s): Celiane Esperance, 13-Year-Old, Immigrant; Moy Esperance, 19-Year-Old, Immigrant
Time period(s): 2000s
Locale(s): Beau Jour, Haiti; New York, New York (Brooklyn)

Summary: Given a small notebook by her teacher, Celiane records her daily life in a small village in the mountains of Haiti. Her father moved to New York five years ago to earn a living and the family exists on what he's able to send them. A trip to Port-au-Prince causes injury for Celiane and her mother when a pipe bomb explodes as part of a political demonstration. This catalyst causes the family to seek plane tickets and visas so the Esperance family can join their father and husband in New York, but Celiane finds that leaving is saying goodbye to everything that's familiar, from family and friends to objects and the mountains. Celiane's brother Moy joins the exodus but moving to Brooklyn is difficult as the family adjusts to the cold, the school, and the problems they encounter with their father who forgets his children have grown up in the five years they've been separated. An author's note explains Danticat's own immigrant experience. (192 pages)

Where it's reviewed:
Booklist, October 1, 2002, page 312
Bulletin of the Center for Children's Books, February 2003, page 232
Publishers Weekly, October 28, 2002, page 72
School Library Journal, October 2002, page 160
Voice of Youth Advocates, February 2003, page 472

Other books by the same author:
Dew Breaker, 2004
Krik? Krak!, 1995
Breath, Eyes, Memory, 1994

Other books you might like:
Julia Alvarez, *How the Garcia Girls Lost Their Accents*, 1991
  A sensitive story of four sisters and their adjustment to life in America after fleeing the Dominican Republic. Adult fiction.
Frances Temple, *A Taste of Salt*, 1992
  While hospitalized recovering from a terrorist firebombing, Djo tells his story of Haitian oppression.
Ana Veciana-Suarez, *Flight to Freedom*, 2002
  When Yara's family is spied upon in Cuba and her father is sent out of town, the family decides to flee to Miami for a safer life.

344

DENNIS DANVERS

The Watch

(New York, HarperCollins/Eos, 2002)

Subject(s): Time Travel; Politics
Age range(s): Grades 9-Adult
Major character(s): Peter Kropotnik, Philosopher, Time Traveler; Rachel Pederson, Government Official; Jonah, Slave, Time Traveler; Anchee Mahur, Time Traveler
Time period(s): 1990s
Locale(s): Richmond, Virginia

Summary: As the elderly Russian anarchist Peter Kropotnik lies dying, a bizarre visitor interrupts him. Anchee Mahur claims to be from the far future and says he will restore Peter to his youth, but only in a time and place of Anchee's choosing. Peter hesitates briefly, but chooses life, and finds himself in Richmond, Virginia in 1999. Sure enough, he is young again, and like any good revolutionary, he has basic urban survival skills. He finds a job and uses the local libraries to research the changes in the world. His near-destitute state, and need to study English as a second language, brings him into contact with Rachel, who runs an agency for refugees and immigrants. Rachel knows almost immediately there is something very different about Peter, for he's the most self disciplined and directed man she has ever met. Together they work with the homeless of Richmond and soon, Peter meets another time traveler who is far more disoriented than he, and with good reason for Jonah is a slave from the heart of the Confederacy. Through his friendship with Jonah, Peter begins to dream of new political action; Anchee's purpose, however, remains a mystery. (353 pages)

Where it's reviewed:
Booklist, December 1, 2001, page 636
Library Journal, January 2002, page 159
New York Times Book Review, February 24, 2002, page 19
Publishers Weekly, December 24, 2001, page 47
School Library Journal, June 2002, page 172

Other books by the same author:
The Fourth World, 2000
End of Days, 1999
Circuit of Heaven, 1998

Other books you might like:
Kage Baker, *In the Garden of Iden*, 1997
   Mendoza, a time traveling cyborg, falls in love with a firebrand cleric during the persecutions of Bloody Mary.
Orson Scott Card, *Pastwatch: The Redemption of Christopher Columbus*, 1996
   The ability to time travel leads some to question whether an attempt should be made to change the past to make history more equitable.
Connie Willis, *To Say Nothing of the Dog; or How We Found the Bishop's Bird Stump at Last*, 1997
   Time traveling Oxford history students are sent scrambling though the past looking for an object that obsesses a wealthy benefactor.

345

PAULA DANZIGER
TONY ROSS, Illustrator

Amber Brown Is Green with Envy

(New York: Putnam, 2003)

Subject(s): Divorce; Moving, Household; Stepfamilies
Age range(s): Grades 2-4
Major character(s): Amber Brown, Child of Divorced Parents, 4th Grader; Unnamed Character, Single Mother; Unnamed Character, Single Father
Time period(s): 2000s (2003)
Locale(s): New York

Summary: Just when Amber thinks she's gotten used to her new life being split between her two parents, life changes again. Amber's mom plans to remarry and move the entire family into a new house. This upsets Amber because the new house might not be in the same town and Amber might have to switch schools and leave all of her friends. Then her dad goes on a date during their weekend together, leaving Amber with a babysitter. Reassurance comes where Amber least expects it, the principal's office. In the end Amber and her dad reconcile and the new house does end up being in town. (160 pages)

Where it's reviewed:
Booklist, September 1, 2003, page 119
Publishers Weekly, July 21, 2003, page 198
School Library Journal, September 2003, page 176

Awards the book has won:
IRA Children's Choices, 2004

Other books by the same author:
Amber Brown Is Feeling Blue, 1998
Amber Brown Sees Red, 1997
Amber Brown Is Not a Crayon, 1994

Other books you might like:
Robin Cruise, *The Top-Secret Journal of Fiona Claire Jardin*, 1998
   Fiona writes about her parents' divorce and the experience of shared custody in her journal.
Marissa Moss, *Max's Logbook*, 2003
   Max struggles when his parents decide to separate and his dad moves out of the house.
Vera B. Williams, *Scooter*, 1993
   When her parents divorce, Elana and her mother move into a new apartment in New York City.

346

PAULA DANZIGER
TONY ROSS, Illustrator

Get Ready for Second Grade, Amber Brown

(New York: G.P. Putnam's Sons, 2002)

Series: A Is for Amber
Subject(s): Schools; Teachers; Fear
Age range(s): Grades 1-3
Major character(s): Amber Brown, 2nd Grader; Justin Daniels, Friend, 2nd Grader; Ms. Light, Teacher
Time period(s): 1990s
Locale(s): United States

Summary: When the teacher Amber expects to have for second grade moves just before school opens Amber faces the beginning of the year with fears of the unknown. She's comforted by the familiar presence of Justin and other friends as she imagines a horrible teacher who is an alien, or someone who gives lots of homework or a teacher who does not give out bathroom passes. When Amber and the other nervous students meet Ms. Light their fears vanish and their expectations for a terrific year return. Amber concludes the day assured that she is ready for second grade! (48 pages)

Where it's reviewed:
Booklist, November 1, 2002, page 505
Horn Book Guide, Fall 2002, page 351
Publishers Weekly, July 1, 2002, page 81
School Library Journal, July 2002, page 87

Awards the book has won:
Parenting's Books of the Year, 2002

Other books by the same author:
It's a Fair Day, Amber Brown, 2002 (A Is for Amber)
It's Justin Time, Amber Brown, 2001 (A Is for Amber)
What a Trip, Amber Brown, 2001 (A Is for Amber)

Other books you might like:
Jack Gantos, *Back to School for Rotten Ralph*, 1998
    Jealous Ralph, lonely to be left behind on the first day of
    school makes Sarah's life difficult when the cat follows her
    to school.
Megan McDonald, *Judy Moody*, 2000
    The first day of third grade is a particularly grouchy day for
    Judy as she lives up to her name.
Suzanne Williams, *Emily at School*, 1996
    Emily learns that second grade has some unexpected chal-
    lenges, including new student Alex.

347

PAULA DANZIGER

United Tates of America

(New York: Scholastic, 2002)

Subject(s): Aunts and Uncles; Death; Artists and Art
Age range(s): Grades 4-6
Major character(s): Sarah Kate ''Skate'' Tate, 6th Grader,
    Artist; Susie Seinfeld, Cousin, 6th Grader; Mort ''GUM'',
    Uncle
Time period(s): 2000s
Locale(s): Chelsea, New Jersey; Plymouth, Massachusetts

Summary: Middle school looms ahead of Skate and she worries about all the change that entails, especially with her
friends. Her best friend Susie loses interest in Skate and their
scrapbook club ''The Happy Scrappers;'' industrial arts is her
least favorite subject; and her locker never opens properly.
One person remains true and that is her beloved, world-
traveling uncle, GUM, which makes his unexpected death so
sad. Even in death GUM knows how to keep the Tates happy
as his bequest encourages them to take a fun, family trip,
shown in Skate's scrapbook which is bound in this book. (144
pages)

Where it's reviewed:
Booklist, April 15, 2002, page 1400
Bulletin of the Center for Children's Books, September 2002,
    page 12
Horn Book, March 2002, page 210
Publishers Weekly, February 4, 2002, page 77
School Library Journal, June 2002, page 136

Other books by the same author:
Snail Mail No More, 2000
P.S. Longer Letter Later, 1998
Thames Doesn't Rhyme with James, 1994
This Place Has No Atmosphere, 1989

The Cat Ate My Gymsuit, 1987

Other books you might like:
Margaret Peterson Haddix, *Takeoffs and Landings*, 2001
    Their mother travels giving motivational speeches; accom-
    panying her for two weeks allows Lori and Chuck the
    chance to know her better.
Kevin Henkes, *The Birthday Room*, 1999
    Ben gives up his studio to turn it into a guest bedroom so
    that his estranged uncle will come visit Ben's family.
Amy Goldman Koss, *Stolen Words*, 2001
    On their first family vacation since the death of their
    beloved aunt Beth, Robyn details not only their sightsee-
    ing, but also their attempts to grieve.

348

SHARON DARROW

The Painters of Lexieville

(Cambridge, MA: Candlewick Press, 2003)

Subject(s): Poverty; Family Problems; Country Life
Age range(s): Grades 7-10
Major character(s): Pertrisha ''Pert'' Lexie, 17-Year-Old;
    Jobe Lexie, 18-Year-Old, Worker (painter); John Lexie,
    Father (of Pert and Jobe), Worker (painter); Orris Lexie,
    Uncle, Worker (painter); Alice Turnbull, Social Worker;
    Truly Lexie, Mother (of Pert and Jobe)
Time period(s): Indeterminate Past
Locale(s): Lexieville, Arkansas

Summary: Pert wants nothing more than to escape the shotgun
shacks, poverty and air of defeat that comprise her pitiful
community in Arkansas, and hopes for a chance to attend
beauty school in Little Rock. Their social worker Mrs. Turnbull finds painting jobs for her father, brother Jobe and Uncle
Orris which helps ease some of their misery, but nothing helps
Pert's biggest problem—Uncle Orris. As Pert becomes older,
her uncle's once playful teasing turns sexual in nature and her
mother doesn't believe Pert when she explains what he's
doing. Finally Pert tells Uncle Orris's girlfriend about his
sexual abuse and he comes after Pert, beating her savagely.
For a while her family falls apart when her mother commits
suicide and Jobe, thinking he's beaten Orris to death, feels he
must become a snake-handling preacher in order to be for-
given. But time, and help from Mrs. Turnbull, sets the Lexies
in the right direction in this author's first novel for teens. (182
pages)

Where it's reviewed:
Booklist, November 15, 2003, page 606
Bulletin of the Center for Children's Books, January 2004,
    page 188
Kirkus Reviews, September 15, 2003, page 1173
Library Media Connection, January 2004, page 67
Publishers Weekly, December 1, 2003, page 57

Other books you might like:
Vicki Grove, *Destiny*, 2000
    Destiny's family is mired in poverty, each child has a
    different father and their house was purchased through
    insurance from a car accident.

Linda Holeman, *Mercy's Birds*, 1998
Garbed in black, Mercy tries to hide her painful life with her depressed mother, alcoholic aunt, and her aunt's sexual harassing boyfriend.

Phyllis Reynolds Naylor, *Send No Blessings*, 1990
Beth doesn't want to spend her whole life in a doublewide trailer in West Virginia and is afraid she'll never achieve her dream of college.

349

ELLEN DATLOW, Co-Editor
TERRI WINDLING, Co-Editor
CHARLES VESS, Illustrator

The Green Man: Tales from the Mythic Forest

(New York: Viking, 2002)

Subject(s): Short Stories; Fantasy
Age range(s): Grades 7-12

Summary: Datlow and Windling, anthologizers extraordinaire, have assembled a collection of fantasy stories that focus on the mysteries of green places, wildernesses, forests, or even the trees in suburban yards. Delia Sherman's memorable tale is set in Central Park where her heroine draws on all the lore that is dear to fairytale lovers; no trip to New York's great green space will ever be the same after having read *Grand Central Park*. Stories from such well-known authors as Gaiman, Yolen, De Lint and McKillip, as well as many others, are also found on these pages. Vess's lovely line drawing head-pieces add to the haunting touch of these tales. (384 pages)

Where it's reviewed:
Booklist, April 15, 2002, page 1412
Kirkus Reviews, May 1, 2002, page 651
Publishers Weekly, May 27, 2002, page 62
School Library Journal, July 2002, page 118
Voice of Youth Advocates, June 2002, page 126

Awards the book has won:
ALA Best Books for Young Adults, 2003

Other books by the same author:
Black Heart, Ivory Bones, 2000
Silver Birch, Blood Moon, 1999
Snow White, Blood Red, 1993

Other books you might like:
Charles de Lint, *Waifs and Strays*, 2002
A collection that includes stories of all types, many of which use mythology as background.

Rosemary Edghill, *Paying the Piper at the Gates of Dawn*, 2003
This quirky collection includes an interesting twist on the *Tam Lin* tale.

Robin McKinley, *Water: Tales of Elemental Spirits*, 2002
This collection revolves around the theme of water spirits.
Peter Dickinson, co-author

350

KATIE DAVIS, Author/Illustrator

Mabel the Tooth Fairy and How She Got Her Job

(San Diego: Harcourt, Inc., 2003)

Subject(s): Fairies; Dentistry; Friendship
Age range(s): Grades K-2
Major character(s): Mabel Becaharuvic, Mythical Creature
Time period(s): 2000s (2003)
Locale(s): United States

Summary: Mabel begins her career as a run-of-the-mill fairy, but after she neglects her teeth, she decides that she'll begin taking the teeth that kids lose to make a new set. Although that plan doesn't work, she loves the kids. While on vacation, Mabel meets a dentist who fixes her teeth and gives her a job as his hygienist. Mabel is able to keep her night job too. (40 pages)

Where it's reviewed:
Publishers Weekly, October 13, 2003, page 79
School Library Journal, January 2004, page 96

Other books by the same author:
Party Animals, 2002
Who Hoots?, 2000
Who Hops?, 1998

Other books you might like:
Ann Fitzpatrick Alper, *Harry McNairy, Tooth Fairy*, 1998
When Harry McNairy gets to Michael's house, he is surprised that Michael refuses to trade his tooth for money.

Pamela Duncan Edwards, *Dear Tooth Fairy*, 2003
Worried that she still hasn't lost her first tooth, 6-year-old Claire writes to the tooth fairy.

Lois G. Grambling, *This Whole Tooth Fairy Thing's Nothing but a Big Rip-Off!*, 2003
Little Hippo waits eagerly for the tooth fairy to arrive.

Charlotte Middleton, *Tabitha's Terrifically Tough Tooth*, 2001
Tabitha tries everything to get her loose tooth out, but it won't budge until she sneezes. Then it flies across the room.

Katherine Tillotson, *Nice Try, Tooth Fairy*, 2000
When Emma asks for her tooth back to show her Grandpa, the tooth fairy brings a series of animals' teeth by mistake.

351

KATIE DAVIS, Author/Illustrator

Party Animals

(San Diego: Harcourt, Inc., 2002)

Subject(s): Animals/Ants; Surprises; Farm Life
Age range(s): Grades K-2
Major character(s): Unnamed Character, Insect (ant)
Time period(s): 2000s (2002)
Locale(s): United States

Summary: In this brightly colored counting book, an ant follows the barnyard animals around, offering to help and trying to wangle a party invitation. He is largely ignored however by the pigs making mud pies, the mice slicing cheese, the cows baking a cake and all the other animals in the midst of the preparations. In the end, it turns out that the party is a surprise for the ant so he goes to the party after all. (40 pages)

Where it's reviewed:
Kirkus Reviews, September 15, 2002, page 1387
Publishers Weekly, August 12, 2002, page 298
School Library Journal, December 2002, page 86

Other books by the same author:
Scared Stiff, 2001
Who Hoots?, 2000
Who Hops?, 1998

Other books you might like:
Emma Dodd, *Dog's Colorful Day: A Messy Story About Colors and Counting*, 2001
    Throughout the day, Dog adds colorful spots to his coat.
Bonnie MacKain, *One Hundred Hungry Ants*, 1993
    One hundred ants, on their way to a picnic, show off the basics of division.
Anne Miranda, *Monster Math*, 1999
    In this counting book, one little monster invites 50 friends to her birthday bash.

352

REBECCA FJELLAND DAVIS

Jake Riley: Irreparably Damaged
(New York: HarperCollins, 2003)

Subject(s): Emotional Problems; Farm Life; Schools/Junior High School
Age range(s): Grades 8-12
Major character(s): Elaine ''Lainey'', 14-Year-Old; Jake Riley, 15-Year-Old
Time period(s): 2000s
Locale(s): Iowa

Summary: Living on a farm, Lainey's used to its rhythm of chores and animal care which, though hard work, offers a continuity and sense of peace. All that changes when the son of her father's tenant farmer returns home from reform school where he's been serving time for manslaughter. Attending her high school, Jake's been labeled ''irreparably damaged'' by the guidance counselor, though Lainey has seen the good side of him. Unfortunately Jake has many serious emotional problems and he becomes obsessed with Lainey, at first harassing her with sexual suggestions, but then switching to threats of killing her. Lainey complains to her parents, but they think she's imagining the threats until her father sees Jake with a shotgun pointed directly at Lainey, in a chilling first novel. (265 pages)

Where it's reviewed:
Booklist, September 1, 2003, page 112
Bulletin of the Center for Children's Books, July 2003, page 441
Publishers Weekly, June 30, 2003, page 81
School Library Journal, July 2003, page 128
Voice of Youth Advocates, October 2003, page 302

Awards the book has won:
Bulletin of the Center for Children's Books Blue Ribbons, 2003

Other books you might like:
Amy Efaw, *Battle Dress*, 2000
    Andi thinks she's escaped her mother's craziness by attending West Point, but finds that the harassment from upperclassmen is unending.
Alex Flinn, *Breaking Point*, 2002
    As a new scholarship student at a ritzy private school, Paul longs to be part of a group and doesn't see how he's being set up.
Gail Giles, *Shattering Glass*, 2002
    As the alpha male in his new school, Rob decides to transform nerdy Simon Glass, but underestimates Simon's deviousness.

353

MARGUERITE W. DAVOL
YUMI HEO, Illustrator

The Snake's Tales
(New York: Orchard Books/Scholastic Inc., 2002)

Subject(s): Animals/Reptiles; Storytelling; Folklore
Age range(s): Grades 1-4
Major character(s): Papa, Father, Spouse; Mama, Mother, Spouse; Beno, Son, Brother; Allita, Daughter, Sister; Unnamed Character, Snake, Storyteller
Time period(s): Indeterminate Past
Locale(s): Fictional Country

Summary: An original story inspired by a Seneca tale is set in a time before stories. The routine of tending goats and weaving wool makes up each day until Mama sends Beno to pick strawberries. Returning home with his full basket, Beno rests on a flat stone and a snake offers to tell him stories in exchange for the berries. Mesmerized by the stories, Beno listens until his basket is empty. When raspberries are ripe Mama sends Allita but she also arrives home with an empty basket and the same excuse: the snake ate them. So, when the apples are ripe, Mama sends both children to do the picking. Again the snake comes and tells more stories as Beno and Allita eagerly listen. This time after eating the apples, the snake is barely able to crawl away. At dinner Papa tells the family about a lumpy snake he's just seen. And from that day on, stories have been shared and enjoyed by everyone. (32 pages)

Where it's reviewed:
Booklist, January 2003, page 904
BookPage, December 2002, page 23
Publishers Weekly, July 22, 2002, page 177
School Library Journal, September 2002, page 183

Other books by the same author:
Why Butterflies Go By on Silent Wings, 2001
The Loudest, Fastest, Best Drummer in Kansas, 2000
The Paper Dragon, 1997 (ALA Notable Children's Books)

Other books you might like:

Allan Ahlberg, *It Was a Dark and Stormy Night*, 1994
With tongue-in-cheek humor, a young boy uses storytelling to orchestrate his escape from a band of brigands.
Richard Buckley, *The Greedy Python*, 1985
A rhyming folk tale describes a python so greedy that he eats everything in reach—including himself.
Walter Dean Myers, *The Story of the Three Kingdoms*, 1995
The wisdom in the People's stories gives them the strength to share the kingdoms of earth, sky and water with the creatures living there.

354

MICHAEL DE GUZMAN

Melonhead

(New York: Farrar Straus Giroux, 2002)

Subject(s): Runaways; Voyages and Travels; Family Problems
Age range(s): Grades 5-8
Major character(s): Sidney T. Mellon, 12-Year-Old; Alice, Grandmother
Time period(s): 2000s
Locale(s): Seattle, Washington; Los Angeles, California; New York, New York

Summary: Six years of shuttling back and forth between his divorced parents is wearing thin for Sidney. When he's in Seattle, he puts up with his abusive stepfather, nasty stepbrother and ineffective mother, but when he heads to Los Angeles to see his father, he lives with a man who has absolutely no ambition. On top of his two disastrous home situations, Sidney is very unattractive. He has skinny legs, bright red hair that tends to stick out in odd places and a head that's much too large for his body, which earns him the nickname "Melonhead." The fact that his last name is Mellon just adds to the jokes and teasing he receives from other kids. Sick of his life and tired of being laughed at, he boards a bus for the East Coast, arrives in New York and remembers that his grandmother lives there. Ah, finally, a place for Sidney! (238 pages)

Where it's reviewed:
Booklist, October 15, 2002, page 404
Library Media Connection, March 2003, page 81
Publishers Weekly, October 21, 2002, page 76
School Library Journal, September 2002, page 220
Voice of Youth Advocates, February 2003, page 472

Other books by the same author:
The Bamboozlers, 2005
Beekman's Big Deal, 2004

Other books you might like:

Lesley Howarth, *Maphead*, 1994
Maphead leaves his parallel universe to come to Earth to find his human mother, but first must learn to speak English.
Janet Taylor Lisle, *How I Became a Writer and Oggie Learned to Drive*, 2002
To distract his brother from shuttling back and forth be-

tween their divorced parents' homes, Archie tells Oogie stories about the Mole People.
Ruth White, *Tadpole*, 2003
Rather than return to his abusive uncle's home, Tadpole leaves his cousins and runs away again, this time to Nashville where he finds a job.

355

CHARLES DE LINT

Spirits in the Wires

(New York: Tor, 2003)

Subject(s): Fantasy; Computers
Age range(s): Grades 9-Adult
Major character(s): Saskia Madding, Mythical Creature, Writer; Christy Riddel, Musician; Christiana Tree, Mythical Creature; Holly Rue, Store Owner
Time period(s): 2000s
Locale(s): Newford, Fictional City (Wordwood, part of cyberspace)

Summary: The Wordwood is the Web Site created by a group of word and literature loving friends who share an interest in mythology, legend and fairy tales. Originally, they planned to enter the text of as many of their favorite stories as possible to share with the world. Holly Rue used to keep the site running from her bookstore, but after a certain point, the Wordwood seemed to be able to take care of itself. In fact, the Wordwood appeared to be actively managing itself. Of course, Holly wasn't too surprised; after all, a human with a brownie for a business partner expects the unexpected. Saskia Madding, a poet with no memories of her early life, comes to believe the Wordwood created her. Christy Riddel may love mystery and fairy tales in his music, but he isn't so sure about this claim of Saskia's, even though he loves her. Christy shouldn't be so skeptical for Christiana is his shadow-self, the female part of his original personality who should exist only in fantasies, but who has made a place for herself in Christy's world. When things go wrong in the Wordwood, both Saskia and Christiana disappear, leaving the others to send a rescue party after them. But when the rescuers disappear as well, Christy and Holly face the challenge of going into the Wordwood themselves. (448 pages)

Where it's reviewed:
Booklist, August 2003, page 1967
Library Journal, August 2003, page 140
Publishers Weekly, July 7, 2003, page 57

Other books by the same author:
Seven Wild Sisters, 2002
Tapping the Dream Tree, 2002
Waifs and Strays, 2002

Other books you might like:

Pat Cadigan, *Dervish Is Digital*, 2002
A determined policewoman tracks a virtual stalker, with extraordinary powers, through cyberspace.
Neil Gaiman, *Stardust*, 1998
When his bride-to-be demands a fallen star as a wedding present a young man crosses the border into Faerie, where the rules of his world don't apply.

William Gibson, *All Tomorrow's Parties*, 1999
> The artificial intelligence who inhabits greater cyberspace wants to create a real world body for herself.

356

CHARLES DE LINT

Tapping the Dream Tree
(New York: Tor, 2002)

Subject(s): Short Stories; Fantasy
Age range(s): Grades 9-Adult
Time period(s): Indeterminate
Locale(s): Newford, Fictional City

Summary: Many of the familiar characters from de Lint's other Newford fantasies appear in these stories. Christy Riddel meets the ghost of a young woman's dreams in ''The Words that Remain.'' If you are curious about how Holly Rue met the brownie in her bookstore, ''Pixel Pixies'' introduces him as well as the vandalizing pixies who invade from cyberspace. Those who have never walked the streets of Newford, but who enjoy dark urban fantasy, will like ''Wingless Angels.'' ''Sign Here,'' is a biting and funny new take on the compact with the devil story. By turns frightening, romantic, and satiric, there's something here for everyone who wants to believe they might still meet magic on their city or suburban street. (541 pages)

Where it's reviewed:
Analog Science Fiction and Fact, March 2003, page 34
Booklist, November 15, 2002, page 584
Kirkus Reviews, September 15, 2002, page 1357
Library Journal, November 15, 2002, page 106
Publishers Weekly, October 28, 2002, page 56

Other books by the same author:
Spirits in the Wires, 2003
Seven Wild Sisters, 2002
The Onion Girl, 2001

Other books you might like:
Kage Baker, *Black Projects, White Knights: The Company Dossiers*, 2002
> Like de Lint's Newford tales, Baker's stories about the Company, that exploitive time traveling business, are linked by shared characters and ideas.
George Alec Effinger, *Budayeen Nights*, 2003
> Marid, enhanced private investigator, roams the near-future streets of a corrupt middle eastern city in these stories.
Ursula K. Le Guin, *Changing Planes*, 2003
> Although each of these stories takes place on a different world, every world is reached by becoming unbearably bored while waiting in an airport.

357

CHARLES DE LINT

Waifs and Strays
(New York: Viking, 2002)

Subject(s): Short Stories; Fantasy
Age range(s): Grades 9-Adult

Time period(s): Indeterminate

Summary: The thread connecting these stories is the gritty and recognizable real world familiar to everyone, and its separation by the thinnest veil from another, quite different reality. In some tales, this other world draws on Native American myths, and in others traditional European legends. At some past time, Lily helps an artist who has stumbled out of our time and into Faerie in ''Somewhere in My Mind There Is a Painting Box.'' Perhaps last year, Apples protected her little sister Cassie from a predatory babysitter as only a vampire can in ''There's No Such Thing.'' Sometime in the near future, Jorey, of ''A Tattoo on Her Heart,'' discovers her identity and her totem during a revel night. Past, present and future all share themes of belonging, coming-of-age, and making a moral choice. (391 pages)

Where it's reviewed:
Booklist, October 2002, page 312
Bulletin of the Center for Children's Books, December 2002, page 151
Kirkus Reviews, August 15, 2002, page 1221
School Library Journal, November 2002, page 160
Voice of Youth Advocates, December 2002, page 395

Other books by the same author:
Tapping the Dream Tree, 2002
Forests of the Heart, 2000
Someplace to be Flying, 1998

Other books you might like:
Ellen Datlow, *Black Swan, White Raven*, 1997
> One of the titles in the Fairy Tale Anthologies Series, collection of modern fairytales ranges from gentle to gritty. Teri Windling, co-editor.
Rosemary Edghill, *Paying the Piper at the Gates of Dawn*, 2003
> Writers trapped in worlds of their own imagining, a fairy detective and an retelling of ''Tam Lin'' make this an enjoyable collection of short fiction.
Robin McKinley, *Water: Tales of Elemental Spirits*, 2002
> All the stories in this anthology involve water and the mythical creatures associated with it. Peter Dickinson, co-author.

358

TOMIE DE PAOLA, Author/Illustrator

Adelita: A Mexican Cinderella Story
(New York: G.P. Putnam's Sons, 2002)

Subject(s): Fairy Tales; Folklore; Stepfamilies
Age range(s): Grades K-3
Major character(s): Adelita Mercado Martinez, Stepdaughter, Servant; Esperanza, Aged Person, Servant; Javier, Young Man, Friend; Dona Micaela, Stepmother
Time period(s): Indeterminate Past
Locale(s): Mexico

Summary: Orphaned Adelita's life becomes even sadder when Dona Micaela dismisses Esperanza from the home, leaving Adelita without her only lifelong companion. Alone Adelita serves the vengeful Dona Micaela and her two unkind daughters. Denied the opportunity to attend a fiesta to celebrate the homecoming of Javier, her childhood friend, Adelita weeps in misery. Then, Esperanza appears at the door, inspired by a dream, and helps Adelita find clothes and get to the fiesta. With her hair braided with flowers Adelita is not recognizable to others at the party. After Adelita's arrival, Javier dances with no other, but still she leaves without identifying herself. When Adelita overhears Dona Micaela say that Javier is searching for the mystery girl, Adelita initiates a plan that assures he will find her. (32 pages)

Where it's reviewed:
Booklist, August 2002, page 1967
Bulletin of the Center for Children's Books, December 2002, page 150
Kirkus Reviews, September 1, 2002, page 1307
Publishers Weekly, July 1, 2002, page 79
School Library Journal, September 2002, page 210

Awards the book has won:
Notable Social Studies Trade Books for Young People, 2003

Other books by the same author:
Jamie O'Rourke and the Pooka, 2000
Strega Nona Takes a Vacation, 2000
Days of the Blackbird: A Tale of Northern Italy, 1997

Other books you might like:
Jewell Reinhart Coburn, *Domitila: A Cinderella Tale from the Mexican Tradition*, 2000
   In a variant based on Mexican folklore the mystery girl is the former cook at the governor's home who's sought by the governor's son.
Ellen Jackson, *Cinder Edna*, 1994
   In a Cinderella tale with a feminist twist Cinder Edna doesn't wait for a fairy godmother; she takes charge of her life and gets the prince herself.
Charles Perrault, *Cinderella*, 1954
   In one of many retellings of a classic tale of love and inner beauty, Cinderella survives years of torment to win a prince's hand in marriage. Marcia Brown, illustrator.
Robert D. San Souci, *Cendrillon: A Caribbean Cinderella*, 1998
   Cendrillon seeks assistance from the washerwoman with the magic wand when she needs help getting to a fancy ball in proper attire.
Robert D. San Souci, *Little Gold Star: A Spanish American Cinderella Tale*, 2000
   A gold star is Teresa's reward for being kind; the star's magic enables Teresa to fulfill her stepmother's demands and find happiness.

359

TOMIE DE PAOLA, Author/Illustrator

A New Barker in the House
(New York: G.P. Putnam's Sons, 2002)

Subject(s): Adoption; Brothers and Sisters; Twins
Age range(s): Grades K-2
Major character(s): Moffat ''Moffie'', Dog, Sister (twin); Morgan ''Morgie'', Dog, Brother (twin); Marcos, 3-Year-Old, Adoptee
Time period(s): Indeterminate

Locale(s): Fictional Country

Summary: When Moffie and Morgie's parents announce that the family's hopes to adopt a sibling are coming true the twins excitedly make plans. Patiently their parents explain that Marcos comes from another country and speaks only Spanish. As Morgie and Moffie play with Marcos they introduce him to their favorite activities and learn the corresponding Spanish words as Marcos learns the English term. By story's end they are on their way to being one bigger, still happy, bilingual *familia*. (32 pages)

Where it's reviewed:
Booklist, July 2002, page 1856
Horn Book Guide, Fall 2002, page 325
Kirkus Reviews, March 15, 2002, page 409
Publishers Weekly, April 8, 2002, page 229
School Library Journal, June 2002, page 92

Other books by the same author:
Meet the Barkers: Morgan and Moffat Go to School, 2001
Strega Nona Takes a Vacation, 2000
Bill and Pete to the Rescue, 1998

Other books you might like:
James Howe, *Pinky and Rex and the New Baby*, 1993
   Content as the only child, Rex feels threatened by the arrival of an adopted baby brother and copes by becoming the perfect big sister.
Jean Little, *Emma's Yucky Brother*, 2001
   Everyone makes some adjustments when Emma's family adopts a four-year-old foster child.
Fred Rogers, *Let's Talk About Adoption*, 1995
   A straightforward title examines the possible feelings adopted children might have.

360

ALEXIS DEACON, Author/Illustrator

Beegu
(New York: Farrar Straus Giroux, 2003)

Subject(s): Aliens; Lost and Found; Loneliness
Age range(s): Grades K-2
Major character(s): Beegu, Alien
Time period(s): Indeterminate
Locale(s): Earth

Summary: Beegu's spaceship crashes, stranding her on a strange planet with creatures that cannot understand her. Alone and lonely, Beegu seeks friends but each time she thinks she finds a place to belong the big creatures chase her away although the little ones are happy to have her near. Beegu falls asleep thinking she hears her mother's voice calling to her and she's right. A spaceship locates her and she is reunited with her parents. As she eagerly tells them of her unexpected visit to Earth the spaceship sails away leaving Beegu with only memories of the small ones on Earth that were kind to her. (36 pages)

Where it's reviewed:
Booklist, December 1, 2003, page 684
New York Times Book Review, November 16, 2003, page 31
Publishers Weekly, September 8, 2003, page 74
School Library Journal, November 2003, page 91

Awards the book has won:
New York Times Best Illustrated Books, 2003

Other books by the same author:
Slow Loris, 2002

Other books you might like:
Neal Layton, *Smile If You're Human*, 1999
    An alien family comes to Earth to photograph a human but
    they land in a zoo and have difficulty determining which
    creature is human.
David McPhail, *Tinker and Tom and the Star Baby*, 1998
    Tinker repairs a spaceship that lands in his yard while the
    alien Star Baby eats the cat's food and levitates kitchen
    objects.
Arthur Yorinks, *Company's Coming*, 1988
    Moe and Shirley have surprise visitors—friendly aliens—
    on the very day they are expecting relatives for dinner.

361

ALEXIS DEACON, Author/Illustrator

Slow Loris

(La Jolla, CA: Kane/Miller Book Publishers, 2002)

Subject(s): Zoos; Animals; Behavior
Age range(s): Grades K-2
Major character(s): Slow Loris, Animal
Time period(s): 2000s
Locale(s): England

Summary: Slow Loris is an unusually lethargic member of his
species or so it seems to the zoo's daytime visitors. Even the
other animals think Slow Loris is boring. They don't know
that at night, when the visitors are gone and the zoo animals
are asleep, Slow Loris comes to life. One night Slow Loris is
so loud with his exuberant activity that he awakens some of
the other animals. Soon all the animals hear about the wild
behavior of nocturnal Slow Loris and join his nightly activity
in the author's first book. (32 pages)

Where it's reviewed:
Booklist, June 2002, page 1734
Bulletin of the Center for Children's Books, May 2002, page
    317
Horn Book Guide, Fall 2002, page 324
Publishers Weekly, January 21, 2002, page 89
School Library Journal, July 2002, page 88

Awards the book has won:
Bulletin of the Center for Children's Books Blue Ribbons,
    2002
Center for Children's Books Best Books, 2002

Other books you might like:
Eric Carle, *Slowly, Slowly, Slowly, said the Sloth*, 2002
    To other jungle animals the sloth may appear to be slow,
    quiet and boring but they learn not to suggest he's also
    lazy.
Michael Garland, *Last Night at the Zoo*, 2001
    Bored zoo animals plan a night on the town, returning to
    the zoo before anyone notices they are missing.
Peggy Rathmann, *Good Night, Gorilla*, 1994
    Unbeknownst to a zookeeper making his final rounds, a

little gorilla steals his keys and releases all the animals to
follow the unsuspecting man home.

362

ERIN DEALEY
HANAKO WAKIYAMA, Illustrator

Goldie Locks Has Chicken Pox

(New York: Atheneum Books for Young Readers, 2002)

Subject(s): Illness; Brothers and Sisters; Stories in Rhyme
Age range(s): Grades K-2
Major character(s): Goldie Locks, Daughter, Child; Brother
    Locks, Brother (younger), Child
Time period(s): Indeterminate
Locale(s): Fictional Country

Summary: While Goldie suffers from the chicken pox her
parents phone the bears to check on baby bear's health and
decline visits from an assortment of other storybook characters. All the while, Brother is bothering Goldie until she's sure
he's a bigger pest than the chicken pox. Brother declares that
he has super powers to protect him but, by story's end, the
telltale spots are popping out on his face too. This is the
author's first picture book. (32 pages)

Where it's reviewed:
Bulletin of the Center for Children's Books, April 2002, page
    278
Publishers Weekly, January 21, 2002, page 88
School Library Journal, February 2002, page 97

Other books you might like:
Laurie Halse Anderson, *Turkey Pox*, 1996
    Charity's family fails to notice that she has developed
    chicken pox, until they arrive at Nana's house for dinner.
Marc Brown, *Arthur's Chicken Pox*, 1994
    D.W. is jealous of the attention that chicken pox brings to
    her brother Arthur.
True Kelley, *I've Got Chicken Pox*, 1994
    Initially euphoric about missing school because of the
    chicken pox, Jess soon tires of ice cream, ginger ale and
    itching!
Maggie Smith, *Dear Daisy, Get Well Soon*, 2000
    Peter's friend can't play because she has the chicken pox
    so he writes to her or sends a gift every day until she's
    better.

363

CAROLEE DEAN

Comfort

(Boston: Houghton Mifflin, 2002)

Subject(s): Poetry; Alcoholism; Family Problems
Age range(s): Grades 7-10
Major character(s): Kenny Roy Willson, 15-Year-Old, Writer
    (poet); Maggie Willson, Mother; Roy Willson, Convict,
    Father
Time period(s): 2000s
Locale(s): Comfort, Texas

Summary: It's hard to be a sane, sensible teenager when your parents are out of control, yet this is what Kenny manages to do. His life has been pretty normal, playing on the football team and in the band, but now his mother alters his birth certificate so he's eligible for a driver's license and can drive his soon-to-be-released-from-prison father to his AA meetings. In addition, because she's struggling with a small cafe, she makes Kenny quit both football and band to help the cafe be successful, and tries to mold Kenny's father into becoming a country music star. Kenny's wise enough to know he needs to leave home and hopes his love of writing will aid him, in addition to the money he takes from the cafe for the salary his mother doesn't pay him. A winning piece of poetry in the University Interscholastic League competition provides a good starting point for his "Dallas Fund" in this author's first novel. (230 pages)

Where it's reviewed:
Book World, July 28, 2002, page 11
Kirkus Reviews, February 15, 2002, page 254
Kliatt, March 2002, page 10
School Library Journal, March 2002, page 230
Voice of Youth Advocates, April 2002, page 40

Other books you might like:
Jack Gantos, *What Would Joey Do?*, 2002
    Joey discovers that all his family members need more help than he can give, including his beloved Grandma who tells him to make a friend.
Ron Koertge, *Shakespeare Bats Cleanup*, 2003
    Recovering from mono, Kevin tries writing a little haiku, then a sonnet and even a sestina, discovering that poetry is "almost as cool as baseball."
Phyllis Reynolds Naylor, *Send No Blessings*, 1990
    Beth doesn't want to spend her whole life in a doublewide trailer in West Virginia and is afraid she'll never achieve her dream of college.

364

JULIE REECE DEAVER

The Night I Disappeared
(New York: Simon Pulse, 2002)

Subject(s): Psychological Thriller; Suspense; Emotional Problems
Age range(s): Grades 7-10
Major character(s): Jamie Tessman, 17-Year-Old; Morgan Hackett, 18-Year-Old; Webb, Friend (imaginary); Dr. Hackett, Doctor (psychiatrist)
Time period(s): 2000s
Locale(s): Chicago, Illinois

Summary: Disappointed at spending the summer apart from Webb, her almost-boyfriend who's backpacking in Europe, Jamie accompanies her attorney mother to Chicago where she argues a high-profile case. At first Jamie is able to control her thoughts about Webb, but she finds herself so engrossed in her fantasies about him that she is unaware of her surroundings and eventually ends up in the hospital following a bike accident. There she meets Morgan who looks after her, giving her the first friend she can remember since Webb. When Jamie's fantasies finally overwhelm her, her mother seeks psychiatric help from Dr. Hackett, who happens to be Morgan's aunt. Just as Dr. Hackett was able to help Morgan over her grief at the loss of her best friend in *Say Goodnight, Gracie*, so she is able to assist Jamie in reliving the trauma that forced her to create her imaginary friend Webb. (242 pages)

Where it's reviewed:
Booklist, May 1, 2002, page 1429
Bulletin of the Center for Children's Books, May 2002, page 318
Kliatt, July 2002, page 16
Publishers Weekly, April 22, 2002, page 71
School Library Journal, May 2002, page 148

Other books by the same author:
Chicago Blues, 1995
First Wedding, Once Removed, 1995
Say Goodnight, Gracie, 1988

Other books you might like:
Margaret Buffie, *Angels Turn Their Backs*, 1998
    A combination of counseling, a parrot and an incomplete needlepoint angel help Addy overcome her panic attacks.
Betty Hyland, *The Girl with the Crazy Brother*, 1987
    Attending a new school is difficult for Dana, but she's more concerned about her brother who develops signs of schizophrenia.
Ruth White, *Memories of Summer*, 2000
    After they move to Michigan, Lyric realizes her sister Summer's mental condition is deteriorating as her tics and phobias worsen.

365

NICHOLAS DEBON, Author/Illustrator

A Brave Soldier
(Toronto: Groundwood/Douglas & McIntyre, 2002)

Subject(s): Military Life; World War I; Courage
Age range(s): Grades 2-5
Major character(s): Frank, Military Personnel
Time period(s): 1910s (1914-1918)
Locale(s): Canada; England; France

Summary: Although Frank knows nothing about the war being waged in Europe he doesn't want to be considered a coward so he enlists along with other young men from his town. The new enlistees board a ship for England where they receive training through the winter and spring and then are sent to the battlefront in France. Life in the trenches is monotonous, smelly, crowded and dirty. When the order for battle comes Frank advances with the others until a large explosion stops him. Wounded, while others died from the artillery shell, Frank is treated for shrapnel wounds and sent home. Not everyone in his town is as lucky. (32 pages)

Where it's reviewed:
Booklist, November 1, 2002, page 491
Books in Canada, November 2002, page 39
Horn Book Guide, Spring 2003, page 65
Resource Links, December 2002, page 4
School Library Journal, February 2003, page 104

Awards the book has won:
Notable Social Studies Trade Books for Young People, 2003

Other books by the same author:
Four Pictures by Emily Carr, 2003

Other books you might like:
Michael Foreman, *War Game*, 1994
 A memorial to the author's four uncles who fought in World War I depicts war as alluring and terrifying, at times boring, grim and ultimately deadly.
Dr. Seuss, *The Butter Battle Book*, 1984
 The stupidity of war is obvious as Zooks and Yooks take sides against each other because of the different way in which each group butters bread.
James Stevenson, *Don't You Know There's a War On?*, 1992
 In a nonfiction picture book the author recalls his childhood during World War II when his brother joins the Navy and gas and food are rationed.

366

CYNTHIA DEFELICE
CAT BOWMAN SMITH, Illustrator

Old Granny and the Bean Thief

(New York: Farrar Straus Giroux, 2003)

Subject(s): Grandmothers; Food; Robbers and Outlaws
Age range(s): Grades K-3
Major character(s): Old Granny, Aged Person, Grandmother; Unnamed Character, Raccoon, Thief
Time period(s): Indeterminate Past
Locale(s): Fictional Country

Summary: Old Granny has no quarrel with living alone out in the country dining on beans. To assure her daily supply Old Granny has some beans soaking and some baking in the oven at all times. When a thief steals her beans three days in a row, Old Granny becomes angry enough to walk to town and report the problem to the sheriff. On the way she meets a talking snake, pecan, cow patty, prickly pear cactus, and alligator. All are sympathetic to her story and promise to help her if she puts them in her sack on her journey home. As luck would have it, the sheriff is gone fishing and Old Granny has to solve her problem without his help. So, as she walks home, she picks up the talking animals, plant and objects and places them around her house just as she's told. Wouldn't you know it, they knew just what to do and when the raccoon sneaks in the house to steal the beans he's scared away and never comes back again. (32 pages)

Where it's reviewed:
Booklist, July 2003, page 1896
Bulletin of the Center for Children's Books, November 2003, page 98
Horn Book, September 2003, page 594
Publishers Weekly, August 11, 2003, page 279
School Library Journal, September 2003, page 176

Other books by the same author:
The Real, True Dulcie Campbell, 2002
Cold Feet, 2000 (ALA Notable Children's Books)
Clever Crow, 1998

Other books you might like:
Lisa Campbell Ernst, *Hannah Mae O'Hannigan's Wild West Show*, 2003

City girl Hannah Mae dreams of life as a cowgirl. A visit to Uncle Coot's ranch provides an opportunity to realize her goal.
Marcia Vaughan, *Whistling Dixie*, 1995
 For each argument against the swamp creatures she brings home as pets, Dixie Lee can identify their protective purpose; events prove her right.
Bernadette Watts, *The Bremen Town Musicians: A Tale by Jacob and Wilhelm Grimm*, 1992
 In an illustrated adaptation about four old animals that outwit a gang of robbers and make a new home together.

367

CYNTHIA DEFELICE
R.W. ALLEY, Illustrator

The Real, True Dulcie Campbell

(New York: Farrar Straus Giroux, 2002)

Subject(s): Family; Princes and Princesses; Books and Reading
Age range(s): Grades 1-3
Major character(s): Dulcie Campbell, Child, Daughter; Unnamed Character, Brother, Son; Dad, Father, Farmer
Time period(s): 2000s (2002)
Locale(s): Hollyhock, Iowa

Summary: As Dulcie begins yet another day of chores she considers the error that surely was made at the time of her birth. It's clear to Dulcie that someone in the hospital took her from her royal crib and sent her home with farmers when she actually should be living in a palace. After informing her family that her true name is Princess Dulcinea, Dulcie sets off to find her real home. Dulcie's parents play along with her idea while her brother seems simply grateful to see her go. Dulcie begins her search by researching princesses in a book of fairy tales while sitting in a ''palace,'' that to her unimaginative family is actually the barn. After learning the fate of the princesses in the stories—mistreatment, wicked witch spells, loneliness, and frog kisses—Dulcie reconsiders her life on the farm and hurries home. Dad greets her by letting her know that, to him, she's a princess. (32 pages)

Where it's reviewed:
Booklist, August 2002, page 1969
Bulletin of the Center for Children's Books, December 2002, page 150
Kirkus Reviews, July 1, 2002, page 952
Publishers Weekly, July 15, 2002, page 73
School Library Journal, September 2002, page 183

Other books by the same author:
Old Granny and the Bean Thief, 2003
Cold Feet, 2000 (Horn Book Fanfare)
Clever Crow, 1998

Other books you might like:
Lois Duncan, *The Longest Hair in the World*, 1999
 The fulfillment of Emily's birthday wish to have long hair in order to be a princess in the school play has unexpected consequences.

Fred Hiatt, *If I Were Queen of the World*, 1997
  A young girl imagines that as queen she could eat lollipops without sharing and stay up as late as she wants.
Carol Diggory Shields, *I Am Really a Princess*, 1993
  A young girl discovers that her imagined life as a princess will have drawbacks she has not considered previously.

368

CYNTHIA DEFELICE

Under the Same Sky
(New York: Farrar Straus Giroux, 2003)

Subject(s): Farm Life; Fathers and Sons; Migrant Labor
Age range(s): Grades 7-10
Major character(s): Joe Pedersen, 14-Year-Old; Manuel, 16-Year-Old, Migrant Worker
Time period(s): 2000s
Locale(s): New York

Summary: Wanting an expensive motorbike for his birthday, Joe is astounded that his parents won't buy it for him, even though he explains that all his friends are getting one. His father suggests Joe work on the family farm this summer and earn the money to buy a Thunderbird motorbike; Joe agrees after he figures it'll take about eight weeks. Though Joe is aware migrant workers cared for the cabbage and strawberry crops, he'd never worked with them and finds he has to earn their respect. Hoeing and weeding are much harder than he thought and it takes weeks to build up his muscles, muscles that are puny compared to crew boss Manuel who is only two years older than Joe. In addition to gaining muscles, Joe sees that his own friends are petty and unkind, especially to the migrant workers whom he's come to admire in this coming-of-age tale. (215 pages)

Where it's reviewed:
Booklist, June 2003, page 1759
Bulletin of the Center for Children's Books, May 2003, page 358
Publishers Weekly, March 10, 2003, page 72
School Library Journal, March 2003, page 232
Voice of Youth Advocates, April 2003, page 47

Other books by the same author:
The Ghost of Cutler Creek, 2004
Death at Devil's Bridge, 2000
Nowhere to Call Home, 1999 (Notable Social Studies Trade Books for Young People)
The Ghost of Fossil Glen, 1998 (School Library Journal Best Books)
The Apprenticeship of Lucas Whitaker, 1996 (School Library Journal Best Books)

Other books you might like:
Jim Heynen, *Fishing for Chickens: Short Stories about Rural Youth*, 2001
  The realities of farm life are portrayed in this collection of short stories by both well-known and lesser-known authors.
Francisco Jimenez, *The Circuit: Stories from the Life of a Migrant Child*, 1997
  Accompanying his parents as they head North to follow the crops, Panchito alternates between attending school and picking crops.
Gretchen Olson, *Joyride*, 1998
  A summer spent with migrant workers teaches Jeff the value of their friendship, compared to the shallowness of his tennis-playing buddies.

369

DIANE DEGROAT, Author/Illustrator

Good Night, Sleep Tight, Don't Let the Bedbugs Bite!
(New York: SeaStarBooks, 2002)

Subject(s): Animals; Camps and Camping; Courage
Age range(s): Grades K-2
Major character(s): Gilbert, Opossum, Camper; Frank, Raccoon, Friend (Gilbert's); Lewis, Camper, Bully
Time period(s): Indeterminate
Locale(s): Fictional Country

Summary: Gilbert's excitement about the day camp's overnight adventure wanes when he boards the bus. Lewis teases Gilbert and Frank for being afraid of the stories about a camp ghost and he taunts them all day at camp. The ghost stories told around the campfire that evening make Frank and Gilbert a little nervous in their bunks. Unfortunately, Gilbert drinks too much juice at dinner and in the middle of the night he has to go to the bathroom. Using his flashlight, Gilbert follows the path to the building but he trips, drops his flashlight and knocks over some garbage cans. When he reaches the bathroom and turns on the light he finds Lewis cowering under the sinks convinced that the clanking noise is the camp ghost. Gilbert handles Lewis's fear and embarrassment diplomatically and by the time they board the bus to return home there's some hope that Lewis learned his lesson. (32 pages)

Where it's reviewed:
Booklist, July 2002, page 1856
Horn Book Guide, Fall 2002, page 325
Horn Book, July 2002, page 444
Publishers Weekly, April 8, 2002, page 227
School Library Journal, August 2002, page 149

Other books by the same author:
We Gather Together . . . Now Please Get Lost!, 2001
Jingle Bell, Homework Smells, 2000 (IRA Children's Choice)
Happy Birthday to You, You Belong in a Zoo, 1999 (IRA Children's Choice)

Other books you might like:
Stan Berenstain, *The Berenstain Bears Go to Camp*, 1982
  The cubs enjoy day camp but they are not eager to attend the final event, a sleep-out atop Skull Rock. Co-author Jan Berenstain.
Patricia Reilly Giff, *Ronald Morgan Goes to Camp*, 1995
  Although Ronald is a reluctant camper he seems to know just how to help his friends whenever a problem appears.
John Himmelman, *Lights Out!*, 1995
  Imagined fears of six campers keep them from falling asleep.

370

ALICE DELACROIX
CYNTHIA FISHER, Illustrator

The Hero of Third Grade

()

Age range(s): Grades 2-4
Major character(s): Randall, Child of Divorced Parents, 3rd Grader; Mrs. Hubbard, Teacher; Max, 3rd Grader, Friend
Time period(s): 2000s (2002)
Locale(s): Rushport

Summary: Poor Randall! It's bad enough that his parents have divorced but his mother's new job requires them to move and Randall must enter a new school in April. Missing his old friends and feeling shy and alone in Mrs. Hubbard's class, Randall adopts the secret persona of the ''Scarlet Pimpernel'' by writing notes solving small classroom problems and signing them with a rose stamp. Until Randall finds a friend in Max and develops a sense of acceptance in his new class he gains confidence and satisfaction through his secret ''Scarlet Pimpernel'' notes. By the time the year comes to an end, Randall no longer needs to be a secret hero because his classmates like him just the way he is. (72 pages)

Where it's reviewed:
Bulletin of the Center for Children's Books, November 2002, page 102
School Library Journal, December 2002, page 86

Other books by the same author:
Mattie's Whisper, 1992

Other books you might like:
Kate Banks, *Howie Bowles, Secret Agent*, 1999
    After his third move on one year Howie becomes Secret Agent Bean Burger rather than expend energy adjusting to a new group of classmates.
Paula Danziger, *Amber Brown Is Not a Crayon*, 1994
    Amber's third grade year is made more difficult when she learns that her best friend Justin is moving.
Betsy Duffey, *Hey, New Kid!*, 1996
    To impress classmates in his new school Cody makes up a new identity so he doesn't have to tell people the truthful, but boring story of his life.
Suzy Kline, *Song Lee and the I Hate You Notes*, 1999
    An anonymous sender of two ''I hate you'' notes finally admits to her wrongdoing.

371

MICHAEL DELANEY, Author/Illustrator

Birdbrain Amos

(New York: Philomel Books, 2002)

Subject(s): Animals/Hippos; Animals/Birds; Humor
Age range(s): Grades 3-5
Major character(s): Amos, Hippopotamus; Kumba, Bird, Mother; Amoeba, Bird
Time period(s): Indeterminate
Locale(s): Africa

Summary: In order to be rid of annoying bugs, Amos advertises for a bird to eat them. When Kumba responds to the ad and demonstrates her prodigious appetite Amos suggests that she ''make herself at home,'' and she does so quite literally by building a nest on Amos's head. When three eggs appear in the nest, a very unhappy Amos hasn't the heart to evict the avian squatter, but he's so embarrassed that he avoids the other hippos rather than face their ridicule. Eventually he tires of the constant presence of the noisy birds and sends them all away. When he discovers a python ready to eat Amoeba, Amos reconsiders and rescues the offspring who repays his kindness by taking up residence and eating the ticks off his back. (153 pages)

Where it's reviewed:
Booklist, April 1, 2002, page 1323
Bulletin of the Center for Children's Books, April 2002, page 278
Horn Book Guide, Fall 2002, page 356
Horn Book, March 2002, page 211
School Library Journal, April 2002, page 102

Awards the book has won:
Booklist Editors' Choice, 2002

Other books by the same author:
Deep Doo-Doo and the Mysterious E-Mail, 2001
Deep Doo-Doo, 1998
Henry's Special Delivery, 1984

Other books you might like:
Avi, *Ereth's Birthday*, 2000
    A dying fox begs cantankerous Ereth to save and care for her three kits; not an easy task for a vegetarian porcupine with no hunting skills.
Brooks Hansen, *Caesar's Antlers*, 1997
    Kindly Caesar uses his antlers to transport a sparrow with her nest of babies as she searches for her lost mate.
Cynthia Rylant, *Gooseberry Park*, 1995
    A dog, a bat and a hermit crab are stuck babysitting for young squirrels whose mother is lost after an ice storm destroys their tree home.

372

BARRY DENENBERG

Elisabeth: The Princess Bride

(New York: Scholastic, 2003)

Series: Royal Diaries
Subject(s): Diaries; Princes and Princesses
Age range(s): Grades 5-8
Major character(s): Elisabeth Amelie Eugenie ''Sisi'', Royalty (Empress of Austria); Franz Joseph I, Royalty (Emperor of Austria); Helene, Sister (of Elisabeth)
Time period(s): 19th century (1853-1854)
Locale(s): Possenhofen, Germany (formerly part of Bavaria); Bad Ischl, Austria

Summary: Though a minor character in the realm of royalty, Elisabeth was married to Franz Joseph, the Emperor of Austria, during a time of change in Europe. In her diary, Elisabeth is a teenager whose interests lie in horseback riding, her family, their pets and the family home Possenhofen. Her older sister Helene is to be introduced to Franz Joseph I with the intention of marrying him, but at the last minute it is decided that Elisabeth will accompany Helene to meet Franz Joseph's younger brother. This plan backfires when Franz Joseph I is more interested in Elisabeth than Helene, which causes great consternation for everyone as Elisabeth reveals in her writings. Elisabeth knows one doesn't turn down an emperor and six months later she marries him. Unfortunately the marriage proves unhappy for her in later years, though Elisabeth has always been regarded as one of the great beauties of Europe. (151 pages)

Where it's reviewed:
School Library Journal, April 2003, page 158

Other books by the same author:
Mirror, Mirror on the Wall: The Diary of Bess Brennan, 2002 (Dear America)
Early Sunday Morning: The Pearl Harbor Diary of Amber Billows, 2001 (Dear America)
One Eye Laughing, the Other Weeping: The Diary of Julie Weiss, 2000 (Dear America)
The Journal of Ben Uchida: Citizen 13559 Mirror Lake Internment Camp, 1999 (My Name Is America)
The Journal of William Thomas Emerson: A Revolutionary War Patriot, 1998 (My Name Is America)

Other books you might like:
Kristiana Gregory, *Cleopatra VII: Daughter of the Nile*, 1999
    Diary entries for Cleopatra, ruler of Egypt, cover her early teen years when she was preparing to be Egypt's ruler.
Kristiana Gregory, *Eleanor: Crown Jewel of Aquitaine, France, 1136*, 2002
    Eleanor records her early life of needlework, court gossip and riding before she marries Louis the Younger and becomes Queen of France.
Kathryn Lasky, *Elizabeth I: Red Rose of the House of Tudor*, 1999
    A series of fictionalized diary entries provides a look at Elizabeth's life during her early teen years as she strives for her father's attention.

373

BARRY DENENBERG

Mirror, Mirror on the Wall: The Diary of Bess Brennan

(New York: Scholastic, 2002)

Series: Dear America
Subject(s): Blindness; Diaries; Twins
Age range(s): Grades 4-8
Major character(s): Bess Brennan, Blind Person, 12-Year-Old; Elin Brennan, Twin (of Bess), 12-Year-Old
Time period(s): 1930s (1932)
Locale(s): Boston, Massachusetts

Summary: Sledding down a hill, with some hooligan schoolmates veering too close to her, Bess swings away from them and crashes into a tree. Rushed to the hospital by ambulance, with her twin sister beside her, Bess undergoes several weeks of tests, diagnosis of detached retinas and then two operations to repair them. When neither surgery is successful and Bess

can no longer detect day or night, she's sent to the Perkins School for the Blind. Returning home on weekends, she and her twin work together on Bess's diary, started when she was seven and written in faithfully ever since. Bess dictates and Elin writes of Bess's adventures at Perkins, dealing with roommates, enduring a not-so-nice housemother and learning to write with Braille. (142 pages)

Where it's reviewed:
Booklist, October 1, 2002, page 325
School Library Journal, October 2002, page 161

Other books by the same author:
Elisabeth: The Princess Bride, 2003 (Royal Diaries)
Early Sunday Morning: The Pearl Harbor Diary of Amber Billows, 2001 (Dear America)
One Eye Laughing, the Other Weeping: The Diary of Julie Weiss, 2000 (Dear America)
The Journal of Ben Uchida: Citizen 13559 Mirror Lake Internment Camp, 1999 (My Name Is America)
The Journal of William Thomas Emerson: A Revolutionary War Patriot, 1998 (My Name Is America)

Other books you might like:
Jeanette Ingold, *The Window*, 1996
    Though blind, Mandy hears and "sees" family events through her bedroom window and pieces together all the missing parts of her family life.
Patrick J. Quinn, *Matthew Pinkowski's Special Summer*, 1991
    Matthew and his friends all have a handicap of some sort, but that doesn't stop them from having an adventure-filled summer.
Susan Shreve, *The Gift of the Girl Who Couldn't Hear*, 1991
    Deaf Lucy uses an intricate ploy to make sure her good friend Eliza stars in the school musical.

374

SHARON PHILLIPS DENSLOW
LYNNE RAE PERKINS, Illustrator

Georgie Lee

(New York: Greenwillow Books/HarperCollins, 2002)

Subject(s): Farm Life; Grandmothers; Animals/Cows
Age range(s): Grades 2-4
Major character(s): J.D., 8-Year-Old; Grandmother, Grandmother, Aged Person; Georgie Lee, Cow
Time period(s): 2000s
Locale(s): United States

Summary: A summer visit to Grandmother's farm is always a time of adventure for J.D., one he looks forward too, if only he didn't have to put up with Georgie Lee. That ornery, independent cow thinks she should go everywhere J.D. and Grandmother go and J.D. just can't get used to this big animal popping up in the most unlikely places. Grandmother has endless patience with Georgie Lee even though she gets onto the porch, eats all the freshly picked corn and scares Grandmother and J.D. by clomping through the brush as they explore a haunted house. By summer's end, Georgie Lee also alerts Grandmother and J.D. to a neighbor's need for assistance after falling in her pasture and J.D. develops a new appreciation for Grandmother's cow. (91 pages)

Where it's reviewed:
Booklist, July 2002, page 1856
Bulletin of the Center for Children's Books, June 2002, page 360
Horn Book, July 2002, page 458
School Library Journal, May 2002, page 111
Smithsonian, December 2002, page 124

Awards the book has won:
Smithsonian's Notable Books for Children, 2002
ALA Notable Children's Books, 2003

Other books by the same author:
Big Wolf and Little Wolf, 2000
On the Trail with Miss Pace, 1995
Woollybear Good-bye, 1994

Other books you might like:
Alan Arkin, *Cassie Loves Beethoven*, 2000
    Hallie and David's unusual pet is a talking cow that loves Beethoven's music and learns to play it on a special keyboard.
Jessie Haas, *Runaway Radish*, 2001
    Radish is a pony with a great deal to teach his young owners.
Mary Downing Hahn, *Anna on the Farm*, 2001
    Anna's week on Uncle George and Aunt Aggie's farm allows her unexpected freedom from the rigid social conventions of city life.
Dick King-Smith, *Lady Lollipop*, 2001
    Spoiled Princess Penelope learns a great deal about manners from the pig she selects as a pet.

375

GRACE DENT

LBD: It's a Girl Thing

(New York: Putnam, 2003)

Subject(s): Rock Music; Music and Musicians; Schools/High Schools
Age range(s): Grades 7-10
Major character(s): Veronica "Ronnie" Ripperton, 14-Year-Old; Claudette "Claude" Cassiera, 14-Year-Old; Fleur Swan, 14-Year-Old
Time period(s): 2000s
Locale(s): England

Summary: The LBD, or Les Bambinos Dangereuses, can't believe their ancient parents won't let them attend the Astlebury Music Festival and are outraged when it's suggested the loud music will damage their eardrums. Ronnie's father's offer to take the LBD to Walrus World instead caps their disappointment. Not willing to give up, the LBD, consisting of Ronnie, Claude and Fleur, decide if they can't go to the music, they'll bring the music to Blackwell with an open-air music event. Organizing an event for over two thousand people, scouring out local talent, advertising at their school, and selling tickets are all tasks the LBD shoulder as they put on a smashing extravaganza in this author's first novel. (275 pages)

Where it's reviewed:
Booklist, November 15, 2003, page 606

Bulletin of the Center for Children's Books, November 2003, page 98
Kliatt, September 2003, page 7
Publishers Weekly, September 22, 2003, page 105
Voice of Youth Advocates, October 2003, page 303

Other books you might like:
Chad Henry, *Dogbreath Victorious*, 1999
    Tim and his alternate-rock band Dogbreath can't believe they're competing against his mother's band, The Angry Housewives.
Louise Rennison, *Angus, Thongs and Full-Frontal Snogging: Confessions of Georgia Nicolson*, 2000
    In her diary Georgia records her interest in kissing, her appearance and her opposition to most of what the adult world thinks is important.
Cherry Whytock, *My Cup Runneth Over: The Life of Angelica Cookson Potts*, 2003
    Though told by her friends otherwise, Angel loves food and knows she is endowed with many "wobbly bits."

376

LISA DESIMINI, Author/Illustrator

Policeman Lou and Policewoman Sue

(New York: Blue Sky Press/Scholastic, Inc., 2003)

Subject(s): Police Procedural; Small Town Life; Work
Age range(s): Grades K-2
Major character(s): Lou, Police Officer; Sue, Police Officer
Time period(s): 2000s (2003)
Locale(s): United States

Summary: Police partners Lou and Sue work hard to keep their small town safe. They help children cross the street to school, rescue stray dogs, write parking tickets, and finally catch a purse-snatcher. Lou and Sue end the day with a chicken dinner at Sue's place. A list of safety tips follows the text. (40 pages)

Where it's reviewed:
Booklist, May 15, 2003, page 1670
Publishers Weekly, May 26, 2003, page 68
School Library Journal, June 2003, page 98

Awards the book has won:
IRA Children's Choices, 2004

Other books by the same author:
My Beautiful Child, 2004
Dot the Fire Dog, 2001
Sun & Moon, 1999

Other books you might like:
Paulette Bourgeois, *Police Officers*, 1999
    As they solve a bike theft case, two neighborhood police officers explain the legal process, the different types of officers and the duties of each.
Carol Greene, *Police Officers Protect People*, 1997
    Photographs illustrate the duties of police officers.
Peggy Rathmann, *Officer Buckle and Gloria*, 1995
    Officer Buckle's school safety talks are pretty dull, until police dog Gloria gets in on the action. Caldecott winner.

377

SARAH DESSEN

This Lullaby

(New York: Viking, 2002)

Subject(s): Mothers and Daughters; Music and Musicians; Dating (Social Customs)
Age range(s): Grades 9-12
Major character(s): Remy Starr, 18-Year-Old; Dexter Jones, Singer
Time period(s): 2000s
Locale(s): Lakeview

Summary: With a mother who's a romance writer and collector of husbands, Remy's learned to keep boys at a distance. Her icy resolve is further aided by the song her disappearing father wrote on the day she was born; called ''This Lullaby,'' it contains the line ''even if I let you down.'' Remy knows not to allow any guy to let her down, especially this summer before she leaves for Stanford. All her plans leap out the window when she meets curly-haired, messy, unorganized but lovable Dexter, a musician whose goal in life is to play in a successful band. Resisting all the way, Remy's swept up into a romance with a guy who's unlike anyone she's ever dated and with whom she slowly but surely falls in love. Knowing Remy, however, she'll blow off Dexter before the end of the summer, but will he let her go? (345 pages)

Where it's reviewed:
Booklist, April 1, 2002, page 1319
Horn Book, July 2002, page 459
Publishers Weekly, May 20, 2002, page 66
School Library Journal, April 2002, page 146
Voice of Youth Advocates, June 2002, page 116

Awards the book has won:
Publishers Weekly Best Children's Books, 2002
Best Books for Young Adults, 2003

Other books by the same author:
Dreamland, 2000
Keeping the Moon, 1999
Someone Like You, 1998
That Summer, 1996

Other books you might like:
Thom Eberhardt, *Rat Boys: A Dating Experiment*, 2001
    Marci and Summer lie about having dates for the Spring Fling dance, but with the help of a magic ring transform rats into ''hot'' dates.
Louise Rennison, *Angus, Thongs and Full-Frontal Snogging: Confessions of Georgia Nicolson*, 2000
    In her diary Georgia records her interest in kissing, her appearance and her opposition to most of what the adult world thinks is important.
Ellen Wittlinger, *Razzle*, 2001
    Kenyon almost gives up tall, independent Razzle for a self-centered sexpot who throws him aside when he can't help her modeling career.

378

CARL DEUKER

High Heat

(Boston: Houghton Mifflin, 2003)

Subject(s): Sports/Baseball; Family Problems; Fathers and Sons
Age range(s): Grades 7-10
Major character(s): Shane Hunter, 10th Grader, Baseball Player (pitcher); Reese Robertson, Baseball Player
Time period(s): 2000s
Locale(s): Seattle, Washington

Summary: Baseball is Shane's life, or at least it was until his father was arrested for money laundering, committed suicide and left his family penniless. Moving to a duplex in a not-so-desirable neighborhood and attending public school for the first time, Shane and his sister struggle to adapt to their changed circumstances. A minor scrape with the law rewards Shane with a probation officer who requires him to join the school baseball team. Still filled with hostility, pitcher Shane beans Reese, an opposing player who also happens to now be living in Shane's former home. Guilt assails Shane and he works with Reese on pitching and hitting, trying to return both of them to their previous performance levels in another action-filled sports book from a solid author. (277 pages)

Where it's reviewed:
Bulletin of the Center for Children's Books, June 2003, page 396
Library Media Connection, November 2003, page 56
Publishers Weekly, May 19, 2003, page 74
School Library Journal, July 2003, page 128
Voice of Youth Advocates, August 2003, page 222

Other books by the same author:
Night Hoops, 2000
Painting the Black, 1997
On the Devil's Court, 1988

Other books you might like:
Alden R. Carter, *Bull Catcher*, 1997
    Through death, divorce, friendship and the different seasons of the year, Bull and his best friend Jeff play baseball.
John Herman, *Labyrinth*, 2001
    After his father commits suicide, Gregory has difficulty distinguishing between the real world and the fantasy world.
Michael Simmons, *Pool Boy*, 2003
    Brett's stockbroker father is sent to prison for insider trading and Brett finds a job with Alfie, an elderly man who becomes Brett's friend.

379

MAGGIE DEVRIES
SHEENA LOTT, Illustrator

How Sleep Found Tabitha

(Custer, WA: Orca Books, 2002)

Subject(s): Bedtime; Animals; Sleep
Age range(s): Preschool-Kindergarten

Major character(s): Tabitha, Child
Time period(s): 2000s (2002)
Locale(s): Canada

Summary: Try as she might, Tabitha just can't fall asleep. Wild animals (with parallels among her stuffed animals) try to lure her to sleep, but Tabitha has concerns with each in turn. She thinks she might fall out of the nest while sleeping with an eagle and discovers that sleeping on all fours like a horse is uncomfortable. Finally the family cat curls up in bed with her and Tabitha is able to go to sleep. (32 pages)

Where it's reviewed:
Booklist, August 2002, page 1970
Horn Book Guide, Fall 2002, page 325
Quill & Quire, March 2002, page 58
School Library Journal, August 2002, page 149

Other books by the same author:
Chance and the Butterfly, 2001
Once Upon a Golden Apple, 1991

Other books you might like:
Josephine Nobisso, *Shh! The Whale Is Smiling*, 1992
   When a nighttime storm scares a little boy, his big sister takes him on an imaginary midnight swim with a whale.
Maurice Sendak, *Where the Wild Things Are*, 1963
   In this Caldecott Medal winner, Max is sent to bed without supper for misbehaving, but a forest grows in his room and his adventure begins.
Charlotte Zolotow, *Sleepy Book*, 1958
   As this title shows, every living being sleeps—from animals to insects to little girls and boys.

380

BABA WAGUE DIAKITE, Author/Illustrator

The Magic Gourd

(New York: Scholastic Press, 2003)

Subject(s): Folk Tales; Africa; Gifts
Age range(s): Grades K-3
Major character(s): Brother Rabbit, Rabbit, Rescuer; Unnamed Character, Reptile (chameleon); Unnamed Character, Ruler, Thief
Time period(s): Indeterminate Past
Locale(s): Mali

Summary: One day during a famine, while foraging for roots for his family to eat, Brother Rabbit stops to help a chameleon stuck in a thorny bush. As a reward, the chameleon gives him a magic gourd that fills with whatever its owner requests. With the gourd, Brother Rabbit is able to feed his family and neighbors, until a jealous king steals the gourd to increase his wealth. With help from the chameleon, Brother Rabbit gets the gourd back and the king learns a lesson about generosity. (32 pages)

Where it's reviewed:
Booklist, February 15, 2003, page 1088
Bulletin of the Center for Children's Books, March 2003, page 271
Publishers Weekly, December 16, 2002, page 67
School Library Journal, February 2003, page 128

Other books by the same author:
The Pot of Wisdom: Ananse Stories, 2001
The Hatseller and the Monkeys, 1999 (ALA Notable Children's Books)
The Hunterman and the Crocodile: A West African Folktale, 1997

Other books you might like:
Jim Aylesworth, *The Full Belly Bowl*, 1999
   A poor man receives a magic bowl that multiplies whatever is placed inside, but when he gets greedy, disaster ensues.
T. Obinkaram Echewa, *The Magic Tree: A Folktale from Nigeria*, 1999
   Mbi, an orphan boy, is always hungry until he plants a magical seed from which a tree grows that always bears fruit.
Shelley Fowles, *The Bachelor and the Bean*, 2003
   A bachelor receives a magic bowl that fills with food, but a jealous old woman steals it.

381

KATE DICAMILLO
TIMOTHY BASIL ERING, Illustrator

The Tale of Despereaux: Being the Story of a Mouse, a Princess, Some Soup, and a Spool of Thread

(Cambridge, MA: Candlewick Press, 2003)

Subject(s): Animals/Mice; Fairy Tales; Love
Age range(s): Grades 3-6
Major character(s): Despereaux Tilling, Mouse, Hero; Princess Pea, Royalty, 12-Year-Old; Roscuro, Rat; Miggory Sow ''Mig'', Servant, 12-Year-Old
Time period(s): Indeterminate Past
Locale(s): Kingdom of Dor, Fictional Country

Summary: Destiny brings together four characters from disparate backgrounds. Poor, abused Mig longs to be a princess. Despereaux, banished to the dungeon for his unmouselike ways, loves Princess Pea, reading and human conversation. Roscuro, unlike other rats, is fascinated by light and soup but also plans revenge against Princess Pea in a very ratlike way. When they all end up in the dungeon together as Despereaux attempts to rescue Princess Pea, kindness, courage, desire and the promise of soup free them from the dungeon and the conventions that bind them in their separate walks of life. (269 pages)

Where it's reviewed:
Booklist, July 2003, page 1886
Bulletin of the Center for Children's Books, November 2003, page 99
Horn Book, September 2003, page 609
Publishers Weekly, June 11, 2003, page 71
School Library Journal, August 2003, page 126

Awards the book has won:
Newbery Medal, 2004
Booklist Editors' Choice, 2003

Other books by the same author:
The Tiger Rising, 2001
Because of Winn-Dixie, 2000 (Newbery Honor Book)

Other books you might like:
Avi, *Poppy*, 1995
   With help from other animals, a young mouse coura-
   geously journeys into the unknown and defeats an evil owl.
Peggy Christian, *The Bookstore Mouse*, 1995
   The bookstore mouse stumbles into a very old book and
   finds himself immersed in a story about medieval England.
Dick King-Smith, *The School Mouse*, 1995
   In the school building that is her family's home Flora takes
   advantage of the daily lessons and uses her literacy to save
   her family.
Philip Pullman, *I Was a Rat!*, 2000
   Roger missed the midnight deadline and is stuck being a
   boy forever just as a once wishful scullery maid is now
   trapped in her new role as a princess.

382

PETER DICKINSON

The Tears of the Salamander
(New York: Wendy Lamb/Random House, 2003)

Subject(s): Fantasy; Animals/Reptiles; Fires
Age range(s): Grades 6-9
Major character(s): Alfredo DiSala, 13-Year-Old, Orphan;
   Giorgio DiSala, Sorcerer, Uncle
Time period(s): Indeterminate Past
Locale(s): Mt. Etna, Italy (Sicily)

Summary: Choirboy Alfredo also tends the oven fires in his
family's bakery until a freak fire destroys the bakery and
leaves him an orphan. The priests wish to preserve Alfredo's
magnificent singing voice by castrating him, but his estranged
Uncle Giorgio appears and takes him to the DiSala family
home on Mount Etna. There Alfredo learns of his family's tie
to controlling the volcanic fires, the singing ability of the
volcano's salamanders and the healing power of "the tears of
the salamander" in this complex fantasy. (197 pages)

Where it's reviewed:
Booklist, May 15, 2003, page 1659
Horn Book, July 2003, page 453
Kirkus Reviews, July 15, 2003, page 962
Publishers Weekly, August 11, 2003, page 281
School Library Journal, August 2003, page 158

Other books by the same author:
Inside Grandad, 2004
The Ropemaker, 2001 (Michael L. Printz Honor Book)
Noli's Story, 1998
The Lion-Tamer's Daughter and Other Stories, 1997

Other books you might like:
Ann Downer, *The Glass Salamander*, 1989
   While Caitlin searches for their kidnapped son Bram, Bad-
   ger tracks down the evil sorcerer Myrrhlock.
Deborah Ellis, *A Company of Fools*, 2002
   Sent to amuse the citizens of their plague-ridden village,
   the choirboys of St. Luc fear their prize singer is being
   used to fill the abbey's coffers.

Sherryl Jordan, *Winter of Fire*, 1993
   Elsha is a rebellious member of the Quelled race but for
   some reason is chosen as handmaid to the Firelord,
   mightiest of the Chosen.

383

JANE DILLON
DEBORAH NOURSE LATTIMORE, Illustrator

Sasha's Matrioshka Dolls
(New York: Farrar Straus Giroux, 2003)

Subject(s): Dolls and Dollhouses; Russians; Grandparents
Age range(s): Grades K-3
Major character(s): Boxer, Grandfather, Artisan; Sasha, Child
Time period(s): 19th century
Locale(s): Moscow, Russia

Summary: Sasha lives with Grandfather, a box maker, in
Moscow. When mice shred Sasha's only rag doll Boxer
makes her a new doll out of wood as well as a doll-shaped box
in which to keep her. When the mice steal the dolls, he builds
another outer box and so on until there are seven nesting dolls.
Soon everyone wants a set of seven matrioshka dolls and
Boxer's business is booming. (32 pages)

Where it's reviewed:
Booklist, March 15, 2003, page 1331
Horn Book Guide, Fall 2003, page 320
Publishers Weekly, April 14, 2003, page 70
School Library Journal, July 2003, page 89

Other books by the same author:
Upsie Downsie, Are You Asleep?, 2002
Lucky O'Leprechaun, 1998
Jeb Scarecrow's Pumpkin Patch, 1992

Other books you might like:
Corinne Demas Bliss, *The Littlest Matryoshka*, 1999
   After the littlest Matryoshka is lost a long journey ensues
   before she is reunited with her sisters.
Susan Bonners, *The Wooden Doll*, 1991
   Stephanie becomes closer to her Polish grandparents after
   she discovers a set of wooden nesting dolls.
Jacqueline Ogburn, *The Magic Nesting Doll*, 2000
   When Katya's grandmother dies she bequeaths to Katya a
   magical matryoshka doll that will grant her three wishes.

384

GARRY DISHER

The Divine Wind: A Love Story
(New York: Arthur A. Levine/Scholastic, 2002)

Subject(s): Friendship; Prejudice; World War II
Age range(s): Grades 9-12
Major character(s): Hartley "Hart" Penrose, Teenager; Alice
   Penrose, Nurse; Mitsu "Mitsy" Sennosuke, Nurse
Time period(s): 1930s; 1940s
Locale(s): Broome, Australia

Summary: Hart, his sister Alice and Mitsy grow up together in
a small seacoast town where Hart's father runs a pearling
operation and Mitsy's father is one of his divers, which leads

to a natural closeness among the family members. Caught in a cyclone, Hart is badly injured and saved from death by Mitsy's father, before he drowns. Nursed back to health by Mitsy, Hart finally acknowledges his love for her, but it's a love that is tempered by the outbreak of war and Mitsy's Japanese heritage. As resentment builds in Australia against anyone of Japanese extraction, Mitsy and her mother are evicted from their home and given shelter by the Penrose family. Alice and Mitsy both trained to become nurses, but Mitsy faces an internment camp, Alice's duty ship is bombed by the Japanese, and Hart is left to ponder his true feelings for Mitsy. (153 pages)

Where it's reviewed:
Childhood Education, Fall 2002, page 51
Kliatt, May 2002, page 8
Publishers Weekly, June 3, 2002, page 89
School Library Journal, August 2002, page 183
Voice of Youth Advocates, August 2002, page 191

Other books by the same author:
The Half Dead, 2000
The Fallout, 1997
Ratface, 1994
The Bamboo Flute, 1993

Other books you might like:
Jim Anderson, *Billarooby*, 1988
    Young Lindsay's Australian farm is near a prisoner of war camp where he witnesses the escape and brutal recapture of a Japanese prisoner.
Julie Otsuka, *When the Emperor Was Divine*, 2002
    Interment for a Japanese-American family from Berkeley leaves them disheartened even after they're finally allowed to return home.
Graham Salisbury, *Under the Blood-Red Sun*, 1994
    Though Tomi is American, he was born in Hawaii of Japanese parents which means he's regarded with suspicion after Pearl Harbor is bombed.

385

TONY DITERLIZZI, Author/Illustrator
HOLLY BLACK, Co-Author

The Seeing Stone
(New York: Simon & Schuster Books for Young Readers, 2003)

Series: Spiderwick Chronicles. Book 2
Subject(s): Brothers and Sisters; Single Parent Families; Fantasy
Age range(s): Grades 3-5
Major character(s): Jared Grace, 9-Year-Old, Twin; Simon Grace, 9-Year-Old, Kidnap Victim; Mallory Grace, 13-Year-Old, Sister
Time period(s): Indeterminate
Locale(s): Spiderwick Estate, Fictional Country

Summary: In the sequel to *The Field Guide*, Simon is kidnapped by goblins while searching for his missing cat. Using clues from *Arthur Spiderwick's Field Guide to the Fantastical World* Jared convinces Mallory to help rescue Simon. By locating and using the "Seeing Stone," Jared is able to see the goblins and other fantastical creatures they encounter in the

woods. Finally they locate Simon, free him and all the other animals captured by the goblins, lead the goblins to their death at the hands of a troll, and rescue an injured griffin. By the time they finally arrive home, they're in so much trouble that they're grounded for a month. Who would believe their excuse? (108 pages)

Where it's reviewed:
Bulletin of the Center for Children's Books, July 2003, page 442
Publishers Weekly, April 14, 2003, page 70
School Library Journal, July 2003, page 95

Other books by the same author:
The Ironwood Tree, 2004 (Spiderwick Chronicles Book 4)
Lucinda's Secret, 2003 (Spiderwick Chronicles Book 3)
The Field Guide, 2003 (Spiderwick Chronicles Book 1)

Other books you might like:
Susan Cooper, *The Boggart and the Monster*, 1997
    The Boggart tries to rescue his long-forgotten cousin from a scientific expedition to locate the Loch Ness monster.
William Mayne, *Hob and the Peddler*, 1997
    Hob, a friendly household spirit, must solve the perplexing problem lurking in the dark pond of his new home in order to assure everyone's happiness.
Emily Rodda, *Rowan of Rin Series*, 2001-
    A fantasy series pits young Rowan against unknown forces with only his companions and riddles from Rin's old witch to assist him.
Lemony Snicket, *Unfortunate Events Series*, 1999-
    The Baudelaire children live up to the name of the series as their lives go from bad to worse after their parents are killed in a fire.

386

DAYLE ANN DODDS
PIERRE PRATT, Illustrator

Where's Pup?
(New York: Dial Books for Young Readers, 2003)

Subject(s): Animals/Dogs; Circus; Stories in Rhyme
Age range(s): Preschool-Grade 1
Major character(s): Pup, Dog; Unnamed Character, Clown
Time period(s): 2000s
Locale(s): Earth

Summary: A clown searches the circus for his missing dog. He asks each performer the same question, "Where's Pup?" and from each he receives a rhyming response suggesting that he ask someone else. After questioning Jo, who's busy feeding Mo and Ray, who's washing Kay the clown goes to Jess, busy training his dog Bess, and Sue astride her horse Blue. He uses a megaphone to call to Claire and Pierre who are high in the air hanging from a trapeze. Lastly he seeks out Nat, on the mat, and is told to look up, up, up to find Pup. Finally the clown and Pup are reunited. (28 pages)

Where it's reviewed:
Bulletin of the Center for Children's Books, March 2003, page 271
Horn Book, March 2003, page 201
Publishers Weekly, April 7, 2003, page 69

School Library Journal, July 2003, page 95

Awards the book has won:
School Library Journal Best Books, 2003
IRA Children's Choices, 2004

Other books by the same author:
Henry's Amazing Machine, 2004
Kettles Get New Clothes, 2002
Pet Wash, 2001

Other books you might like:
William Cole, *Have I Got Dogs!*, 1996
   This rhyming story introduces different types of dogs.
P.D. Eastman, *Go, Dog, Go!*, 1961
   Simple language describes many kinds of dogs enjoying varied activities.
Eric Hill, *Where's Spot?*, 2000
   During her search for Spot a mother dog finds eight animals hiding before locating her pup in this 20th anniversary edition of the title.

387

JENNIFER DONNELLY

A Northern Light
(San Diego: Harcourt, 2003)

Subject(s): Murder; Hotels and Motels; Farm Life
Age range(s): Grades 9-12
Major character(s): Mattie Gokey, 16-Year-Old; Royal Loomis, Farmer, 18-Year-Old; Weaver Smith, Friend (of Mattie; African American); Grace Brown, 19-Year-Old, Historical Figure
Time period(s): 1900s (1906)
Locale(s): Adirondack Mountains, New York

Summary: As the oldest child, Mattie promised her dying mother that she would care for her family, a promise she now rues as her dream of attending college also seems to be dying. Working long hours at home in order to attend her local school, Mattie begins each day with a new word to learn, an act that increases her vocabulary for the word duels she and her friend Weaver play. Uncharacteristically, Mattie stands her ground and works at a hotel during the summer, an act in defiance of both her father and neighbor Royal who's been courting Mattie. At the Glenmore, Mattie is entrusted with a packet of letters from guest Grace Burns; told to burn them, Mattie reads them instead, hoping to learn why Grace drowns and her boyfriend disappears. This eye-opener to the inequalities in the lives of men and women, accompanied by the realization that Royal woos her only to add farmland, prompts Mattie to choose college rather than a stagnant life stuck at home in a beautifully written first novel. (389 pages)

Where it's reviewed:
Booklist, May 15, 2003, page 1663
Horn Book, May 2003, page 342
Publishers Weekly, March 3, 2002, page 76
School Library Journal, May 2003, page 150
Voice of Youth Advocates, April 2003, page 47

Awards the book has won:
Michael L. Printz Honor Book, 2004
ALA Best Books for Young Adults, 2004

Other books by the same author:
The Tea Rose: A Novel, 2003 (adult novel)

Other books you might like:
Carla Joinson, *Diamond in the Dust*, 2001
   The death of Katy's miner brother encourages her to leave home and a possible life as a coal miner's wife for more opportunities in St. Louis.
Phyllis Reynolds Naylor, *Send No Blessings*, 1990
   Beth doesn't want to spend her whole life in a doublewide trailer in West Virginia and is afraid she'll never achieve her dream of college.
Suzanne Newton, *Where Are You When I Need You?*, 1991
   Missy's determination to attend college overcomes her family's disapproval and boyfriend Jim's reluctance to let her go.

388

ARTHUR DORROS
HENRY COLE, Illustrator

City Chicken
(New York: HarperCollins Publishers, 2003)

Subject(s): Animals/Chickens; City and Town Life; Humor
Age range(s): Grades K-2
Major character(s): Henrietta "Henry", Chicken; Alex, Child; Lucy, Cat
Time period(s): 2000s (2003)
Locale(s): United States

Summary: Henry lives contentedly in the coop behind Alex's house in the city. Know-it-all Lucy wanders over from the house next door and advises Henry that chickens live in the country with cows, horses and pigs. Based on Lucy's descriptions Henry imagines what cows, horses and pigs look like (big chickens in white, brown or pink) and decides to go to the country to learn more about it. Not a skilled flier, Henry opts for a bus ride to the country where she encounters some of the animals described by Lucy though she doesn't know which is which. Then Henry wanders into what she considers a city of chickens each in their own little cage laying eggs. Henry decides that the country is not a place for her and hops a ride back to the city on the egg truck. Alex is happy to have her home again. (36 pages)

Where it's reviewed:
Booklist, March 15, 2003, page 1331
Bulletin of the Center for Children's Books, February 2003, page 233
Horn Book, March 2003, page 202
Publishers Weekly, November 25, 2002, page 66
School Library Journal, February 2003, page 104

Other books by the same author:
When the Pigs Took Over, 2002
Ten Go Tango, 2000
The Fungus That Ate My School, 2000

Other books you might like:
Bob Graham, *Queenie, One of the Family*, 1997
   Queenie, a hen that wanders, has her own ideas about where to lay her daily egg.

Grace Lin, *Olvina Flies*, 2003

Olvina overcomes her fear of flying in order to attend a Bird Convention in Hawaii.

Janet Morgan Stoeke, *Minerva Louise and the Red Truck*, 2002

As usual, Minerva Louise interprets what she sees in the wider world from the viewpoint of her limited experience.

389

SHARON ARMS DOUCET
ANNE WILSDORF, Illustrator

Alligator Sue

(New York: Melanie Kroupa Books/Farrar Straus Giroux, 2003)

Subject(s): Animals/Alligators; Identity; Tall Tales
Age range(s): Grades 1-3
Major character(s): Suzanne Marie Sabine Chicot Thibodeaux, Child, Daughter; Mama Coco, Alligator, Mother
Time period(s): Indeterminate Past
Locale(s): Atchafalaya Swamp, Louisiana

Summary: A sudden hurricane blows young Sue right off her family's houseboat home and that's how she comes to be adopted by Mama Coco. Sue masters some alligator habits such as waddling on all fours and crunching crawfish but she never does grow teeth as long and pointy as her alligator siblings. After a long, cold, hungry winter (hibernating doesn't work for Sue either) she grows tired of her alligator brothers' teasing and heads off through the swamp. When Sue comes upon an abandoned houseboat Mama Coco tells her that it was once her home and explains that Sue is a Girl, not an Alligator. With her parents vanished Sue sets up housekeeping on her own. When another hurricane blows up she helps to save Mama Coco and her nest of eggs. And, in time, she figures out who she is, half Gator, half Girl . . . Alligator Sue. (40 pages)

Where it's reviewed:
Booklist, September 1, 2003, page 128
Publishers Weekly, July 7, 2003, page 72
School Library Journal, September 2003, page 177

Other books by the same author:
Lapin Plays Possum: Trickster Tales from the Louisiana Bayou, 2002
Why Lapin's Ears Are Long: And Other Tales from the Louisiana Bayou, 1997

Other books you might like:
Anne Isaacs, *Swamp Angel*, 1994

An original tall tale describes the achievements of Angelica and how she earns her nickname. Caldecott Honor Book

Steven Kellogg, *Sally Ann Thunder Ann Whirlwind Crockett*, 1995

On her eighth birthday, Sally departs for the frontier where she continues her larger-than-life exploits and eventually marries Davy Crockett.

Tynia Thomassie, *Feliciana Feydra LeRoux: A Cajun Tall Tale*, 1995

In an original bayou tall tale, Feliciana sneaks out to join the menfolk's alligator hunt.

390

SHARON ARMS DOUCET, Adaptor
SCOTT COOK, Illustrator

Lapin Plays Possum: Trickster Tales from the Louisiana Bayou

(New York: Melanie Kroupa/Farrar Straus Giroux, 2002)

Subject(s): Folklore; Trickster Tales; Animals/Rabbits
Age range(s): Grades 3-6
Major character(s): Lapin, Rabbit, Trickster; Bouki, Wolf, Farmer
Time period(s): Indeterminate Past
Locale(s): Louisiana

Summary: Each time Bouki discovers that he's been tricked by Lapin he's determined not to let it happen again. Yet, in three stories, cunning Lapin gets the best of the dim-witted Bouki every time. In the first story Lapin tricks Bouki out of a rum cake, a barrel of butter and half a field of cotton while doing very little of the work he's promised. Next Lapin rents one of Bouki's fields with the agreement to share half the crop with the farmer. It doesn't matter whether Bouki demands the top half of the crop, the bottom half or both the top and the bottom, Lapin manages to select a crop that gives the trickster the profitable and edible portion while Bouki is left with the dregs. Finally Bouki uses a tar baby to catch Lapin, but the wily rabbit manages to trick Bouki into freeing him. A glossary and author's note are included. (64 pages)

Where it's reviewed:
Booklist, April 15, 2002, page 1396
Horn Book, May 2002, page 338
Publishers Weekly, April 15, 2002, page 64
Riverbank Review, Fall 2002, page 51
School Library Journal, April 2002, page 130

Other books by the same author:
Fiddle Fever, 2000
Why Lapin's Ears Are Long: And Other Tales from the Louisiana Bayou, 1997

Other books you might like:
Virginia Hamilton, *A Ring of Tricksters: Animal Tales from America, the West Indies and, Africa*, 1997

Eleven read-aloud tales include spider and rabbit tricksters and the unwitting animals that bear the brunt of their cleverness.

Julius Lester, *More Tales of Uncle Remus: Further Adventures of Brer Rabbit, His Friends, Enemies, and Others*, 1988

Thirty-seven stories relate the activities of famous trickster Brer Rabbit.

Margaret Mayo, *Tortoise's Flying Lesson*, 1995

A collection of retold and adapted folk stories tells of animals supporting, tricking and learning from one another.

391

FRANCES O'ROARK DOWELL

Where I'd Like to Be

(New York: Simon & Schuster/Atheneum, 2003)

Subject(s): Orphans; Foster Homes; Friendship
Age range(s): Grades 4-7
Major character(s): Madeline "Maddie" Byers, 11-Year-Old, Orphan; Emily "Murphy", 11-Year-Old
Time period(s): 2000s
Locale(s): Tennessee

Summary: When her string of foster homes runs out, Maddie moves to the East Tennessee Children's Home where she compiles scrapbooks of her favorite houses. A young girl her own age arrives and Maddie decided to share her *Book of Houses* with Murphy, which leads to the two building a fort behind the Home. Inviting other friends to join them, the group researches houses and decorates the interior while telling stories about their own lives. Murphy tells the best story about her deceased research scientist parents, until her mother belies everything by appearing at the Home and taking Murphy away, in a story filled with children who rethink the meaning of home. (232 pages)

Where it's reviewed:
Booklist, May 15, 2003, page 1660
Bulletin of the Center for Children's Books, June 2003, page 396
Library Media Connection, August 2003, page 76
Publishers Weekly, February 24, 2003, page 73
School Library Journal, April 2003, page 158

Other books by the same author:
The Secret Language of Girls, 2004
Dovey Coe, 2000

Other books you might like:
Christopher Paul Curtis, *Bud, Not Buddy*, 1999
  After being bounced from one foster home to another, Buddy finally runs away and is lucky enough to find his grandfather.
Adrian Fogelin, *Anna Casey's Place in the World*, 2001
  For now, Anna's "place" is a foster home in Florida and adjusting to it is difficult.
E.R. Frank, *Friction*, 2003
  New student Stacy ruins Alex's eighth grade year with her lies and gossip about Alex and their teacher Simon.

392

BRIAN DOYLE

Mary Ann Alice

(Toronto: Groundwood Books/Douglas & McIntyre, 2002)

Subject(s): Small Town Life; Rivers; Teachers
Age range(s): Grades 5-8
Major character(s): Mary Ann Alice McCrank, Writer (poet), 7th Grader; Mickey McGuire Jr., 7th Grader; Patchy Drizzle, Teacher
Time period(s): 1920s (1926)
Locale(s): Martindale, Quebec, Canada

Summary: The life of a small, close-knit farming community changes when plans are announced to dam the Gatineau River. For some families, the dam means jobs, while for others it spells the loss of their homes and farms when the river rises. To Mary Ann Alice, it means no longer exploring for the fossils she's learned to identity thanks to her teacher Patchy Drizzle. Mary Ann Alice describes the impact of this technology on her neighbors while she also plots to kiss Mickey McGuire, Jr., interacts with the eccentric residents of her town, writes poetry about the changes in her town and works at the dam site.(167 pages)

Where it's reviewed:
Bulletin of the Center for Children's Books, June 2002, page 361
Horn Book, May 2002, page 326
School Library Journal, June 2002, page 137
Teacher Magazine, March 2002, page 44
Voice of Youth Advocates, June 2002, page 116

Other books by the same author:
Easy Avenue, 1998
Uncle Ronald, 1997
Spud Sweetgrass, 1996
Spud in Winter, 1996
You Can Pick Me Up at Peggy's Cove, 1991

Other books you might like:
Olive Ann Burns, *Cold Sassy Tree*, 1984
  Young Will Tweedy loves to describe the off-beat characters in his small town of Cold Sassy.
Tony Earley, *Jim the Boy*, 2000
  Raised by his mother and her three bachelor brothers, Jim remembers the day that electricity came to his small town of Aliceville.
L.M. Montgomery, *Anne of Green Gables*, 1935
  First in a series of books about high-spirited, mischievous Anne who lives in Canada.

393

EUGENIE DOYLE

Stray Voltage

(Asheville, NC: Front Street, 2002)

Subject(s): Fathers and Sons; Farm Life; School Life
Age range(s): Grades 5-8
Major character(s): Ian Daley, 6th Grader, 12-Year-Old; Ray Daley, 16-Year-Old; Warren Daley, Farmer
Time period(s): 2000s
Locale(s): Vermont

Summary: An ice storm leaves the Daley family with a perplexing problem on their dairy farm as unexpected electrical currents run through the barn floor, upsetting the cows and hurting their business. Ian's family seems to be falling apart too, for his mother's abandoned them and his father's facing bankruptcy. Never a nice man, Warren is verbally abusive to his son Ian, though tolerant of Ray, who's just as uncommunicative as he is. Ian feels very much alone, but his teacher offers him a gift when she has him summarize news events that he reads in the local paper. Suddenly he realizes he has things he wants to say, even if it's only at school and not at home. One night his father drinks much more than usual and sets the barn on fire, determined it's the best way to end their problems. This is the night Ian stands up to him and rescues the cows, forcing a resolution about the farm that gives everyone a chance for success in a winning first novel. (136 pages)

Where it's reviewed:

Booklist, January 2003, page 880

Bulletin of the Center for Children's Books, January 2003, page 195

Publishers Weekly, November 4, 2002, page 84

School Library Journal, October 2002, page 161

Voice of Youth Advocates, February 2003, page 472

Other books you might like:

Alden R. Carter, *Growing Season*, 1984

Although Rick resents his large family's move to a dairy farm, the physical labor is beneficial for everyone.

Berlie Doherty, *White Peak Farm*, 1984

Several generations are bound together by their ties to the land of White Peak Farm.

Louann Gaeddert, *Breaking Free*, 1994

Enduring the humiliation and cruelty of his Uncle Lyman, as well as the tediousness of farm work, is difficult for city-raised orphan Richard.

Janni Howker, *Isaac Campion*, 1986

At the turn of the 20th century, Isaac's older brother dies and his life on his father's horse farm becomes an ordeal.

394

MALACHY DOYLE

Who Is Jesse Flood?

(New York: Bloomsbury, 2002)

Subject(s): Mothers and Sons; Family Problems; Identity

Age range(s): Grades 5-8

Major character(s): Jesse Flood, 14-Year-Old

Time period(s): 2000s

Locale(s): Greywater, Ireland, Northern

Summary: Reflecting on his life, and the fact that he feels he's such a loser, Jesse realizes his life has been like that of his town—very boring. At school he feels alienated from everyone and at home he can hardly block out the arguments of his parents. One day he even goes so far as to enter a train tunnel and press himself into the side wall when the train goes by, just to escape the sound of his parents' arguing. Though his mother leaves, Jesse realizes she'll always be his friend and he finally understands that the only way to live is to enjoy those good moments while they happen. (173 pages)

Where it's reviewed:

Booklist, October 1, 2002, page 312

Bulletin of the Center for Children's Books, December 2002, page 152

Library Media Connection, March 2003, page 76

Publishers Weekly, July 29, 2002, page 73

School Library Journal, October 2002, page 162

Other books by the same author:

Georgie, 2001

Other books you might like:

Adam Bagdasarian, *First French Kiss and Other Traumas*, 2002

Moments from Will's life trace the years of every boy who safely navigates elementary, middle and high school.

Jack Gantos, *Joey Pigza Loses Control*, 2000

Just as Joey is finally able to control his behavior, he spends the summer with his hyperactive father and loses all the gains he's made.

Sarah Weeks, *Guy Time*, 2000

Guy and his best friend Buzz concoct a scheme to reconcile Guy's mom and dad, but before they can put the plan in effect, Guy loses interest.

395

SHARON M. DRAPER

The Battle of Jericho

(New York: Atheneum/Simon & Schuster, 2003)

Subject(s): Clubs; Cousins; Death

Age range(s): Grades 7-10

Major character(s): Jericho Prescott, 11th Grader; Josh Prescott, Cousin, 11th Grader; Kofi Freeman, 11th Grader; Dana, 11th Grader; Arielle, 11th Grader

Time period(s): 2000s

Locale(s): Cincinnati, Ohio

Summary: Jericho, his cousin Josh and good friend Kofi are thrilled to be asked to join the Warriors of Distinction, the secret society at their school. Jericho's father didn't pledge the Warriors when he was in school, though his brother, Josh's father, did; however, he doesn't forbid Jericho to join the group. The boys have admired the black silk jackets of the upperclassmen Warriors and know they'll be moving in fine circles if they pledge this group. Of course there's the pledging period, but starting off wrapping Christmas presents is not difficult. Jericho starts to have second thoughts about the group when he sees how they treat Dana who snuck into the pledging ceremony and is the first girl that's ever been in the brotherhood. He also doesn't like being asked to steal Christmas ornaments, though he's told it's to test their loyalty to one another. Jericho does, however, like the status it's given him with Arielle who's now real happy to be seen with him. Demeaning hazing, digging through garbage bins and keeping everything secret, all of it seems wrong to him, but then comes initiation when the 15 pledges are asked to jump out a second story window. Jericho's world comes apart when Josh jumps, misses the mat, and lands at a very awkward angle. Suddenly he has to face the reality of telling both his and Josh's parents what's really been happening the last few months. (297 pages)

Where it's reviewed:

Booklist, June 2003, page 1761

Bulletin of the Center for Children's Books, July 2003, page 444

Kirkus Reviews, June 1, 2003, page 802

School Library Journal, June 2003, page 137

Voice of Youth Advocates, August 2003, page 222

Awards the book has won:

Coretta Scott King Honor Book, 2004

Other books by the same author:
Double Dutch, 2002
Darkness Before Dawn, 2001
Romiette and Julio, 1999
Forged by Fire, 1997
Tears of a Tiger, 1994

Other books you might like:
Robert Cormier, *The Chocolate War*, 1974
    Archie and his goons, with the assistance of Brother Leon, control everything that happens at Trinity High School.
Beth Goobie, *The Lottery*, 2002
    The Shadow Council is surprised when Sally stands up to them and refuses to do their bidding or be shunned by the rest of the school.
Neal Shusterman, *The Shadow Club*, 1988
    Tired of being ''second best,'' members of this secret club pull anonymous practical jokes on those students they consider rivals.

396

SHARON M. DRAPER

Double Dutch

(New York: Atheneum/Simon & Schuster, 2002)

Subject(s): Contests; African Americans; Weather
Age range(s): Grades 6-9
Major character(s): Delia Douglas, 8th Grader; Yolanda ''Yo Yo'' Pepper, 8th Grader; Randy Youngblood, 8th Grader; Titan Tolliver, 8th Grader, Twin; Tabu Tolliver, 8th Grader, Twin
Time period(s): 2000s
Locale(s): Cincinnati, Ohio

Summary: So good at Double Dutch that her team is heading for the national championships, held in her hometown of Cincinnati, Delia's not so good at reading and is worried that she won't pass the test to be admitted to ninth grade. Up until now she's hidden her flaw by memorizing, working on projects that don't require writing or being an all-around good kid, but her time's running out and her world is starting to collapse. Randy, manager of the Double Dutch team and admirer of Delia, also has a secret because his truck driver father hasn't been home in several weeks and Randy's money for necessities is running out. But these problems aren't the worst these two young kids have. A bigger problem is twins Tabu and Titan Tolliver, the meanest kids in the eighth grade. Suddenly all worries fly out the window when their middle school is hit by a tornado and people have a chance to show their good side. Tabu and Titan emerge as heroes when they rescue Delia's friend Yolanda, even though they were trying to run away from the storm. Delia asks for help to learn to read, Randy's father is found in a hospital and everyone looks differently at the ''Terrible Tollivers.'' (183 pages)

Where it's reviewed:
Booklist, September 1, 2002, page 127
Bulletin of the Center for Children's Books, October 2002, page 54
Publishers Weekly, July 17, 2002, page 66
School Library Journal, June 2002, page 137
Voice of Youth Advocates, August 2002, page 191

Awards the book has won:
Center for Children's Books Best Books, 2002

Other books by the same author:
The Battle of Jericho, 2003
Darkness Before Dawn, 2001 (ALA Quick Picks for Reluctant Young Adult Readers)
Romiette and Julio, 1999
Forged by Fire, 1997
Tears of a Tiger, 1994

Other books you might like:
Sandra Belton, *Ernestine & Amanda: Members of the C.L.U.B.*, 1997
    Rather than choose between two friends, Amanda includes both of them in her club plans.
Helen Frost, *Keesha's House*, 2003
    Sestinas, sonnets and other verse forms tell of Keesha's House, which offers sanctuary to all who need it.
Walter Dean Myers, *Fast Sam, Cool Clyde and Stuff*, 1975
    Stuff remembers his friends, and their crazy adventures, when they all hung out on 116th Street in New York.

397

ANN L. DREYER

After Elaine

(Chicago: Cricket Books, 2002)

Subject(s): Grief; Sisters; Family Problems
Age range(s): Grades 5-8
Major character(s): Gina Beck, 6th Grader; Elaine Beck, Student—High School (deceased); Brian Beck, Student—High School
Time period(s): 2000s
Locale(s): United States

Summary: Being sent to detention for fighting may be the best thing that happens to Gina as it forces her to write about what led up to the fight. And what happened extends back several months to when her older sister Elaine was killed in a car accident. Elaine was not a nice person: she often made cruel, insulting remarks to Gina, as well as stole her money; argued with their older brother Brian; acted hateful to her parents and skipped school every chance possible. One day she skipped with another student, went joy riding and was killed when their car struck a tree. Gina's left with feelings of relief, guilt and grief and wonders if Elaine ever loved her, or anyone in their family. Of more concern is Gina's increasing anger and her fears of becoming like Elaine, but the fight and reflective time in detention help her see that she's her own person, in this author's first novel. (129 pages)

Where it's reviewed:
Booklist, July 2002, page 1844
Bulletin of the Center for Children's Books, May 2002, page 319
Horn Book Guide, Fall 2002, page 390
School Library Journal, July 2002, page 119
Voice of Youth Advocates, December 2002, page 379

Other books you might like:
Gail Giles, *Dead Girls Don't Write Letters*, 2003
    When her older sister dies in an apartment fire, Sunny's

actually happy for the first time as she didn't think her self-centered sister was wonderful.

Adele Griffin, *The Other Shepards*, 1998

Ever since Holland and Geneva's birth, they've been reminded of the tragic automobile accident that killed their three older siblings.

Colby Rodowsky, *Remembering Mog*, 1996

As Annie prepares to graduate, "remembering Mog" isn't hard to do since her older sister was shot to death in a robbery the night of her graduation.

398

ALLAN DRUMMOND, Author/Illustrator

The Flyers

(New York: Frances Foster/Farrar Straus Giroux, 2003)

Subject(s): Airplanes; Historical; Air Travel
Age range(s): Preschool-Grade 1
Major character(s): Orville Wright, Historical Figure, Pilot; Wilbur Wright, Historical Figure, Pilot
Time period(s): 1900s (1903)
Locale(s): Kitty Hawk, North Carolina

Summary: A group of friends who live in Kitty Hawk watch Orville and Wilbur Wright's preparations for the first flight. The idea of a flying machine is the jumping-off point for a myriad of creative ideas. One child wants to create a machine that can fly to Africa, another to the moon. Together the friends imagine a machine big enough to fly all their friends and families. The book ends with a visual timeline of important moments in flight. (40 pages)

Where it's reviewed:
Booklist, October 1, 2003, page 326
Bulletin of the Center for Children's Books, November 2003, page 99
Horn Book, September/October 2003, page 594
Publishers Weekly, August 25, 2003, page 63
School Library Journal, October 2003, page 118

Awards the book has won:
Notable Social Studies Trade Books for Young People, 2004

Other books by the same author:
Liberty!, 2002
Casey Jones, 2001
The Willow Pattern Story, 1995

Other books you might like:
Andrew Glass, *The Wondrous Whirligig: The Wright Brothers' First Flying Machine*, 2003
This tall tale imagines the inventions of the Wright Brothers when they were children.
Wendie Old, *To Fly: The Story of the Wright Brothers*, 2002
This picture book biography tells the story of the Wright Brothers and their first flight.
Jane Yolen, *My Brothers' Flying Machine: Wilbur, Orville, and Me*, 2003
The story of the Wright Brothers' famous flight is seen through the eyes of their younger sister, Katharine.

399

ALLAN DRUMMOND, Author/Illustrator

Liberty!

(New York: Frances Foster/Farrar Straus Giroux, 2002)

Subject(s): Monuments; Freedom; Historical
Age range(s): Grades 1-4
Major character(s): Unnamed Character, Child; Mr. Bartholdi, Artist (sculptor)
Time period(s): 1880s (1886)
Locale(s): New York, New York

Summary: An author's note provides the historical background to the story of a young boy selected to help Mr. Bartholdi complete the unveiling of the statue given to America by France. Despite a driving rain, crowds of men hurry by ferry to the island while women protest their lack of liberty because they are denied the right to vote. Immigrants line the rail of the ship bringing them to a new country. The boy stands in the crowd near the base of the statue holding Mr. Bartholdi's handkerchief with instructions to drop it to signal the unveiling. (36 pages)

Where it's reviewed:
Booklist, March 15, 2002, page 1256
Bulletin of the Center for Children's Books, May 2002, page 319
Horn Book Guide, Fall 2002, page 326
Publishers Weekly, January 7, 2002, page 64
School Library Journal, May 2002, page 111

Other books by the same author:
Casey Jones, 2001
Moby Dick, 1997
The Willow Pattern Story, 1992

Other books you might like:
Eve Bunting, *A Picnic in October*, 1999
Annually a family of immigrants picnics at the base of the Statue of Liberty on the anniversary of the statue's unveiling.
Dana Meachen Rau, *The Statue of Liberty*, 2002
A nonfiction title relates the history of the Statue of Liberty and its importance as a symbol of freedom.
Alice Ross, *The Copper Lady*, 1997
A Parisian orphan stows away on the ship bringing the "Lady" to America so that he can see the completion of the project he's worked on with M. Bartholdi.

400

DIANE DUANE

Stealing the Elf-King's Roses

(New York: Warner Books, 2002)

Subject(s): Fairies; Detection; Magic
Age range(s): Grades 9-Adult
Major character(s): Lee Enfield, Lawyer, Wizard; Madrin Gelert, Mythical Creature, Lawyer
Time period(s): 2000s
Locale(s): Los Angeles, California

Summary: Human Lee Enfield and Madrin Gelert, member of an intelligent race that to humans resemble wolfhounds, are sworn to uphold Justice—in fact, they can't help it. When invoked, Justice is embodied in Lee. Sudden but temporary god-like powers visit on-the-spot judgment and punishment on the guilty. This same relationship with Justice helps Lee to see truth in the confusion of a crime scene. Unfortunately, there are limits, and when a wealthy and aristocratic elf is murdered in the human world Lee and her inhuman partner Gelert find they're stymied. Gelert senses dangers in the fairy connection and urges Lee to give it up. But Lee won't let go, and ends up in the elves' world, where everyone and everything is beautiful, but something is very wrong. (401 pages)

Where it's reviewed:
Chronicle, April 2003, page 43

Other books by the same author:
Wizard's Holiday, 2003
A Wizard Alone, 2002
The Wizard's Dilemma, 2001

Other books you might like:
Glen Cook, *Angry Lead Skies*, 2002
  Garrett chases down some troublesome elves, with small, skinny bodies, large eyes and slick gray skin.
George Alec Effinger, *When Gravity Fails*, 1987
  Marid feels that he is a perfectly good private investigator, but his new patron thinks some minor modifications to his brain would work wonders.
Tanya Huff, *Long, Hot Summoning*, 2003
  Keepers Clare and Diana are back with Austin, the smart-aleck cat, to try to restore the balance of time and space at . . . the shopping mall?

401

DIANE DUANE

A Wizard Alone

(San Diego: Harcourt, 2002)

Series: Young Wizards. Number 6
Subject(s): Magic; Mental Illness
Age range(s): Grades 6-9
Major character(s): Kit Rodriguez, Wizard, Teenager; Juanita "Nita" Callahan, Wizard, Teenager; Ponch, Dog; Darryl McAllister, Wizard, Autistic
Time period(s): 2000s
Locale(s): New York, New York

Summary: Kit and Nita are back at their jobs of being wizards, although Nita is overwhelmed by her mother's death and not terribly interested in being a wizard, or much of anything else at the moment. While she works through her grief, Kit has been asked to look into the disappearance of the young, potential wizard Darryl who has been missing on his wizardly Ordeal for three months. Kit and Ponch, Kit's increasingly magical dog, have no trouble locating Darryl's body, but as Ponch puts it, he's not all there. Darryl is autistic, but as Kit educates himself about the condition, he's knows there's more to Darryl's absence than just his appearance of not paying attention. His sympathies are engaged as he discovers that Darryl is struggling against the evil Lone Power, and Kit

guesses, his disability. What Kit doesn't know is that Nita's dreams about a scary clown, a malfunctioning robot and a lonely knight have an important message for Kit from Darryl. (319 pages)

Where it's reviewed:
Booklist, November 15, 2002, p. 588
Horn Book Guide, Spring 2003, page 93
Kliatt, January 2004, page 22
School Library Journal, February 2003, p. 140
Voice of Youth Advocates, April 2003, page 62

Other books by the same author:
Wizard's Holiday, 2003
Stealing the Elf-King's Roses, 2002
Honor Blade, 2000

Other books you might like:
Diana Wynne Jones, *Deep Magic*, 2000
  It's difficult to be discrete about magic at a science fiction/ fantasy fan convention.
Tamora Pierce, *Magic Steps*, 2001
  Pasco's magic dancing is just what is needed, despite the disapproval of his military family.
J.K. Rowling, *Harry Potter and the Prisoner of Azkaban*, 2000
  Harry learns some unpleasant truths about himself and his wizardly relations.

402

DIANE DUANE

Wizard's Holiday

(San Diego: Harcourt, 2003)

Series: Young Wizards. Number 7
Subject(s): Fantasy; Wizards; Aliens
Age range(s): Grades 5-8
Major character(s): Dairine Callahan, Wizard; Juanita "Nita" Callahan, Wizard; Kit Rodriguez, Wizard; Ponch, Dog
Time period(s): 2000s
Locale(s): New York; Alaalu, Planet—Imaginary

Summary: Everyone needs a break from time to time, or at least that's what Nita thinks when she signs up for an intergalactic cultural exchange program. Her little sister Dairine thinks she should also be part of the exchange, but is kept at home when her father hears of her plans; he does agree to support half the exchange and they invite three aliens to stay with them for the two weeks that Nita will be gone. Nita, her fellow wizard-in-training Kit and Kit's dog Ponch travel to the planet of Alaalu where life seems wonderful and perfect, although that's not really the case. Back on Earth, Dairine and her father welcome a sentient tree, a purple creature similar to a caterpillar and a humanoid who makes everyone miserable. Since the peacefulness on both planets is just a facade, Nita, Kit, and Dairine must use all their magic to keep their worlds from collapsing in this seventh book in the series. (416 pages)

Where it's reviewed:
Booklist, January 2004, page 854
School Library Journal, December 2003, page 149

Other books by the same author:
A Wizard Alone, 2002 (Young Wizards Number 6)

A Wizard Abroad, 2001 (Young Wizards Number 4)
The Wizard's Dilemma, 2001 (Young Wizards Number 5)
High Wizardry, 1990 (Young Wizards Number 3)
Deep Wizardry, 1985 (Young Wizards Number 2)
So You Want to Be a Wizard, 1983 (Young Wizards Number 1)

Other books you might like:
A.C. Crispin, *Silent Dances*, 1990
    A young deaf girl is the perfect communicator for aliens with loud, thundering voices at an interplanetary space school.
Kate Gilmore, *The Exchange Student*, 1999
    A young alien with an obsessive fondness for animals comes to stay with an Earth family.
William Sleator, *Interstellar Pig*, 1984
    Barney plays Interstellar Pig with three neighbors, though he doesn't realize they're aliens playing for control of Earth.

403

KATHLEEN BENNER DUBLE

Bridging Beyond

(New York: Philomel/Penguin Putnam, 2002)

Subject(s): Grief; Memory; Grandmothers
Age range(s): Grades 7-10
Major character(s): Anna Kelts, 15-Year-Old; Nellie Kelts, Child; Mimi Fairfield, Grandmother (great grandmother); Jessica, Accident Victim (deceased); Dr. Bouchard, Doctor (therapist)
Time period(s): 2000s; 1920s
Locale(s): Illinois

Summary: Anna can't rid herself of the guilt she feels over her role in the automobile accident that took her friend Jessica's life. Though Anna wasn't driving, she was as drunk as Jessica and is certain that if she hadn't suggested going to another party, Jessica would still be alive. Four weeks after the accident, her beloved great grandmother Mimi dies and Anna's mother packs up their belongings and moves Anna and her sister Nellie to Mimi's house to start over. Once there, Anna begins having memories and dreams of times and people who lived during the 1920s. Dr. Bouchard advances the theory that Anna is showing a genetic memory and the dreams are really events from Mimi's younger years. Both Mimi and Anna carry guilt for a friend's death and this chance to forgive is carrying over into Anna's memory, in this author's intriguing first novel. (203 pages)

Where it's reviewed:
Horn Book Guide, Fall 2002, page 390
Kirkus Reviews, May 15, 2002, page 731
Kliatt, May 2002, page 9
School Library Journal, May 2002, page 148
Voice of Youth Advocates, June 2002, page 117

Other books you might like:
Martha Brooks, *Bone Dance*, 1997
    After Alexandra is willed a rustic cabin, her deceased grandfather appears in her dreams and encourages her to travel to that cabin.

Carolyn McCullough, *Falling through Darkness*, 2003
    Ginny feels some guilt over the death of her devil-may-care boyfriend Aidan, though finally realizes she couldn't have prevented his car accident.
Han Nolan, *If I Should Die Before I Wake*, 1994
    In a coma, Neo-Nazi Hilary is hospitalized next to a Holocaust survivor and travels into Chana's mind, reliving her concentration camp experiences.

404

LOIS DUNCAN
MEG CUNDIFF, Illustrator

Song of the Circus

(New York: Philomel Books, 2002)

Subject(s): Circus; Animals/Tigers; Stories in Rhyme
Age range(s): Grades K-3
Major character(s): Gisselda, Child; Bop, Child; Tiger, Tiger
Time period(s): Indeterminate
Locale(s): Fictional Country

Summary: Bop and Gisselda are children of the circus so they know the meaning of the "show must go on," when an unfortunate series of events cause the various acts to crash into each other resulting in an elephant stampede. Unfortunately, one elephant lands on Tiger's cage and hungry Tiger escapes with the hope of fulfilling his desire to dine on a circus child as sweet as Gisselda. Seeing Tiger's intent Bop runs up and shouts to distract Tiger who considers eating Bop when Gisselda yells. Bop and Gisselda give Tiger a loud lecture about circus laws and Tiger slinks away hungry as the children bow to the applauding audience who thought the near catastrophe was all part of the show. (32 pages)

Where it's reviewed:
Booklist, August 2002, page 1970
Bulletin of the Center for Children's Books, May 2002, page 320
Horn Book Guide, Fall 2002, page 32
Publishers Weekly, April 22, 2002, page 68
School Library Journal, April 2002, page 109

Other books by the same author:
I Walk at Night, 2000 (New York Times Best Illustrated Book of the Year)
The Longest Hair in the World, 1999
The Magic of Spider Woman, 1996

Other books you might like:
Lois Ehlert, *Circus*, 1992
    A unique picture book illustrates the colorful excitement of the circus.
Ian Falconer, *Olivia Saves the Circus*, 2001
    According to the story Olivia tells her class last summer she saved the circus by performing all the acts when the entire cast became ill.
Marjorie Priceman, *Emeline at the Circus*, 1999
    An elephant lifts Emeline from her seat into the circus ring where she flies on the trapeze.

405

CLARE B. DUNKLE

The Hollow Kingdom

(New York: Henry Holt, 2003)

Subject(s): Magic; Sisters
Age range(s): Grades 7-10
Major character(s): Kate Winslow, Orphan, 18-Year-Old; Emily Winslow, Orphan, 11-Year-Old; Hugh Roberts, Guardian, Cousin Marak, Mythical Creature, Royalty
Time period(s): 19th century
Locale(s): England

Summary: When they find themselves orphaned, Kate and her younger sister Emily are forced to accept a home with their elderly great-aunts. Although their cousin Hugh is their guardian, he is a cold and calculating man who finds two young ladies a great bother and foists them off on the old ladies. Both sisters find their great-aunts kind and their new home tolerable. In spite of their grief, they enjoy the beauty of their surroundings and the fantastic stories some of the ancient servants tell them. Mysterious disappearances of young girls and goblin kidnappings are part of the heritage of Hallow Hill, their new home. As modern young ladies of the 19th century, Kate and Emily naturally pooh-pooh this nonsense. That is, until the night Kate meets the goblin King Marak, who tells her he intends her for his bride. (230 pages)

Where it's reviewed:
Booklist, November 15, 2003, page 608
Kirkus Reviews, October 1, 2003, page 1223
Publishers Weekly, November 17, 2003, page 66
School Library Journal, December 2003, page 149

Other books by the same author:
Close Kin, 2004

Other books you might like:
Liz Berry, *The China Garden*, 1996
 There is some mystery surrounding the abrupt move to the country, and it seems to involve the odd, locked garden.
Robin McKinley, *Beauty: A Retelling of the Story of Beauty and the Beast*, 1993
 Like Kate, Beauty finds herself married to a monster and like Kate, she discovers that her husband is much more than that.
Patricia C. Wrede, *Sorcery and Cecelia, or the Enchanted Chocolate Pot*, 2003
 An exchange of letters between two young ladies of quality tells the story of their romantic encounter with two single gentlemen who just happen to be wizards.

406

OLIVIER DUNREA, Author/Illustrator

Gossie

(Boston: Houghton Mifflin Company, 2002)

Subject(s): Animals/Geese; Lost and Found; Clothes
Age range(s): Preschool-Kindergarten
Major character(s): Gossie, Goose
Time period(s): Indeterminate

Locale(s): Fictional Country

Summary: Gossie, a bright yellow gosling, sports shiny red boots every day, rain or shine, as she goes about her day on the farm. When Gossie awakens one morning to discover her boots are nowhere in sight, she begins searching. Gossie feels sad because she cannot find her boots. Finally, she spots them on the feet of another gosling! As the book concludes it appears that Gossie has found boots and a friend. (32 pages)

Where it's reviewed:
Booklist, August 2002, page 1970
Bulletin of the Center for Children's Books, December 2002, page 153
Horn Book, January 2003, page 55
Publishers Weekly, July 15, 2002, page 72
School Library Journal, September 2002, page 189

Awards the book has won:
Publishers Weekly Best Children's Books, 2002
School Library Journal Best Books, 2002

Other books by the same author:
Gossie & Gertie, 2002 (ALA Notable Children's Book)
Bear Noel, 2000
The Tale of Hilda Louise, 1996

Other books you might like:
Kevin Henkes, *Lilly's Purple Plastic Purse*, 1996
 A purple plastic purse is just as important to Lilly as the red boots are to Gossie.
Amy Hest, *In the Rain with Baby Duck*, 1995
 When understanding Grampa offers reluctant Baby Duck boots and an umbrella, a walk in the rain begins to seem appealing.
John Schoenherr, *Rebel*, 1995
 One of a clutch of five Canada Goose eggs hatches into a gosling with a mind of his own.
Taro Yashima, *Umbrella*, 1958
 After receiving red boots and an umbrella for her birthday Momo eagerly awaits a rainy day.

407

OLIVIER DUNREA, Author/Illustrator

It's Snowing!

(New York: Farrar Straus Giroux, 2002)

Subject(s): Winter; Mothers; Babies
Age range(s): Preschool-Kindergarten
Major character(s): Mama, Mother; Baby, Baby
Time period(s): Indeterminate Past
Locale(s): Earth

Summary: On a very dark cold night in a small mountain home, Mama rocks the cradle and Baby sucks his thumb. When Mama opens the door and sees the first snow falling she bundles up, wraps Baby in furs and ventures out into the snowy night to smell, feel, taste and enjoy the snow. Mama builds a snow troll for Baby, and together they sled down the hill and ride an ice bear. Then they return to their home, Mama sits before the fire, rocking the cradle and Baby sucks his thumb. (32 pages)

Where it's reviewed:
Booklist, November 15, 2002, page 609
Horn Book, September 2002, page 550
Publishers Weekly, October 21, 2002, page 73
School Library Journal, October 2002, page 103

Other books by the same author:
Boo Boo, 2004
Essie and Myles, 2003
Ollie the Stomper, 2003

Other books you might like:
Cheryl Chapman, *Snow on Snow on Snow*, 1994
  Colorful pictures and playful text celebrate the joy of snow.
Kevin Henkes, *Oh!*, 1999
  All night the snow falls coloring everything white and providing a day of fun for animals and children.
Bruce Hiscock, *When Will It Snow?*, 1995
  A child awaits the answer to his questions while animals simply prepare for the season's first snowfall.
Nancy Van Laan, *When Winter Comes*, 2000
  As snow begins to fall a family walks through the remnants of fallen leaves on the ground.

408

OLIVIER DUNREA, Author/Illustrator

Ollie

(Boston: Houghton Mifflin Company, 2003)

Subject(s): Animals/Geese; Brothers and Sisters; Individuality
Age range(s): Preschool
Major character(s): Ollie, Goose, Brother; Gertie, Goose, Sister (older); Gossie, Goose, Sister (older)
Time period(s): Indeterminate
Locale(s): Fictional Country

Summary: Gossie and Gertie wait and wait and wait for Ollie to emerge from his egg. Ollie is waiting, too, for just the right moment to hatch. Until he's ready, he won't come out and he tells his sisters so. He rolls about, hides, and holds his breath but he won't come out despite pokes from Gossie and attentive listening from Gertie. Finally Gossie and Gertie reply to Ollie's refusal to come out by telling him not to come out. Stubborn, contrary Ollie apparently hears that as a challenge and, in no time, Ollie comes out of the egg! (32 pages)

Where it's reviewed:
Booklist, October 1, 2003, page 326
Bulletin of the Center for Children's Books, November 2003, page 100
Publishers Weekly, July 14, 2003, page 75
School Library Journal, July 2003, page 95

Awards the book has won:
School Library Journal Best Books, 2003

Other books by the same author:
Ollie the Stomper, 2003
Gossie, 2002 (School Library Journal Best Books)
Gossie & Gertie, 2002 (ALA Notable Children's Books)
Bear Noel, 2000

Other books you might like:
Trudi Braun, *My Goose Betsy*, 1999
  After carefully crafting her nest Betsy waits patiently for the eight eggs in the nest to hatch.
John Schoenherr, *Rebel*, 1995
  One of a clutch of five eggs hatches into a gosling with a mind of his own.
Nancy Tafuri, *Silly Little Goose!*, 2001
  Goose ignores the opinions of the other animals and builds a nest in which to incubate eight eggs.

409

JEANNE DUPRAU

The City of Ember

(New York: Random House, 2003)

Subject(s): Future; Post Nuclear Holocaust; Science Fiction
Age range(s): Grades 5-8
Major character(s): Lina Mayfleet, 12-Year-Old; Doon Harrow, 12-Year-Old
Time period(s): Indeterminate Future
Locale(s): Ember, Fictional City

Summary: Assignment Day arrives and Lina and Doon find themselves assigned to tasks the other one covets, so they switch and Lina becomes a messenger around her closed city of Ember while Doon toils underground repairing the aging pipeworks. Founded 241 years ago by the Builders, this subterranean, enclosed city was meant to be occupied for 220 years but instructions for exiting the city have not only been lost but its occupants have also forgotten they even existed. With escalating power blackouts and declining supplies, Lina and Doon are increasingly concerned. They discover not only the remnants of the missing instructions, but also the hoarding of supplies by selected leaders, including their mayor, and the two attempt an escape to save their city in this author's exciting first work of science fiction. (270 pages)

Where it's reviewed:
Booklist, April 15, 2003, page 1466
Horn Book, May 2003, page 343
Publishers Weekly, March 10, 2003, page 72
School Library Journal, May 2003, page 150
Voice of Youth Advocates, June 2003, page 148

Other books by the same author:
The People of Sparks, 2004

Other books you might like:
Joan Aiken, *Is Underground*, 1993
  Searching for her cousin Arun, Is finds him held captive in the underground mines and foundries of Holderness.
Louise Lawrence, *Andra*, 1991
  A glimpse of the aboveground world makes Andra realize her need for freedom, which acts as a rallying point for other teens.
Lois Lowry, *The Giver*, 1993
  Jonas is unsettled in his mind when notified by his society that his life work is to be the Receiver, the one who receives all memories.
Gregory Maguire, *I Feel Like the Morning Star*, 1989
  Five years after an atomic attack forces everyone to live in

a subterranean world, only three teens want to return to life aboveground.

410

WILLIAM DURBIN

The Journal of C.J. Jackson: A Dust Bowl Migrant: Oklahoma to California, 1935

(New York: Scholastic, 2002)

Series: My Name Is America
Subject(s): Depression (Economic); Family Life; Migrant Labor
Age range(s): Grades 5-8
Major character(s): C.J. Jackson, 8th Grader
Time period(s): 1930s (1935-1936)
Locale(s): Cimarron County, Oklahoma; Bakersfield, California; Los Angeles, California

Summary: As C.J. tells about his life on his family's Oklahoma ranch, it becomes obvious why the family is forced to give up their life and move rather than stay and contend with dust storms that strip the fields bare, tear leaves off the trees, and leave no forage for cattle. Once on his way to California, C.J. continues his journal writing in the book given to him by his aunt and records the varied signs and landscapes seen by the family, including the well-known Burma Shave jingles. In California, he's astonished at the difficulty in finding work, the dislike shown by people to the Okies and the meanness of some of their employers. Though C.J.'s father finds work as an automobile mechanic at a dealership, the family never loses sight of their desire to return to Oklahoma and reclaim their farm. (166 pages)

Where it's reviewed:
Kliatt, May 2002, page 9
School Library Journal, September 2002, page 220

Other books by the same author:
The Journal of Otto Peltonen: A Finnish Immigrant, 2000 (My Name Is America)
The Journal of Sean Sullivan: A Transcontinental Railroad Worker, 1999 (My Name Is America)
Wintering, 1999
The Broken Blade, 1997

Other books you might like:
Sue Ellen Bridgers, *Home before Dark*, 1976
When Stella and her migrant farm family return to her father's childhood home in Florida, she never wants to leave its safety.
Patricia A Cochrane, *Purely Rosie Pearl*, 1966
Rosie's family loses their land during the Depression and become migrant workers who follow the crops in the Sacramento Valley.
Emily Crofford, *A Place to Belong*, 1994
After losing the family farm during the Depression, Talmadge's family moves to Alabama until his sister becomes ill.
Kathleen Karr, *The Cave*, 1994
Christine and her brother struggle to survive on their South Dakota farm during the days of the Dust Bowl.

Pieter Van Raven, *A Time of Troubles*, 1990
During the Depression, Roy accompanies his irresponsible father to California to find work, but their differences soon part them.

411

WILLIAM DURBIN

Song of Sampo Lake

(New York: Wendy Lamb Books/Random House, 2002)

Subject(s): Emigration and Immigration; Frontier and Pioneer Life
Age range(s): Grades 6-9
Major character(s): Matti Ojala, 15-Year-Old, Miner; Timo Ojala, Brother (of Matti)
Time period(s): 1900s
Locale(s): Soudan, Minnesota (Lake Sampo)

Summary: The Ojala family immigrates to Minnesota, a spot chosen for its resemblance to their beautiful, beloved country of Finland, but the men are now stuck below ground working in the iron mines. When Matti's uncle is killed in a mine accident, and his aunt returns to Finland, the Ojalas decide to speed up their plans to develop their 160-acre homestead on the shores of Lake Sampo. Matti works hard, whether he's helping build the sauna, log cabin or barn; clearing land for crops; milking the cows or hunting for their food, all to show his father he's equal to his older brother Timo. Matti takes a rescued crow with him to his once-a-week clerking job at the general store; survives a blizzard; and rescues his little sister from drowning when she falls through the ice on the lake. This story of the Ojala family depicts some of the privations and hardships immigrants endured as they struggled to make a new life for themselves in America. (217 pages)

Where it's reviewed:
Booklist, October 15, 2002, page 401
Kliatt, December 2002, page 8
Library Media Connection, March 2003, page 72
Publishers Weekly, November 11, 2002, page 65
School Library Journal, November 2002, page 162

Other books by the same author:
The Darkest Evening, 2004
Blackwater Ben, 2003
The Journal of C.J. Jackson: A Dust Bowl Migrant: Oklahoma to California, 1935, 2002 (My Name Is America)
Wintering, 1999
The Broken Blade, 1997

Other books you might like:
Richard Easton, *A Real American*, 2002
Ignoring the town folk's animosity, Nathan befriends one of the Italian immigrants who's been brought in to work the coalmines.
Kristine L. Franklin, *Grape Thief*, 2003
Mining operations slow down and mobsters enter their town; Slava's brothers accidentally kill a mobster and flee, leaving Slava to support his mother.
N.A. Perez, *Breaker*, 1988
After Pat's father is killed in a mining accident, Pat works

in the mines while his brother fights for improved labor conditions.

Laura Ingalls Wilder, *Farmer Boy*, 1953
Part of the beloved Little House on the Prairie Series, this work tells of Almanzo Wilder's childhood growing up on a farm in upper New York.

412

JANE DYER, Author/Illustrator

Little Brown Bear Won't Go to School!

(New York: Little, Brown and Company, 2003)

Subject(s): Animals/Bears; Schools; Work
Age range(s): Grades K-1
Major character(s): Little Brown Bear, Bear, Student; Mama Bear, Mother, Bear; Papa Bear, Father, Bear
Time period(s): Indeterminate
Locale(s): Fictional Country

Summary: At the breakfast table Little Brown Bear announces that he's not going to school. Mama Bear and Papa Bear insist that Little Brown Bear must go to school just as they go to their jobs every day. Little Brown Bear's job is school. Little Brown Bear wants a "real" job so he skips school and tries working at a variety of establishments in town. It's clear from Little Brown Bear's failed attempts that the jobs require more fine-motor skill than Little Brown Bear has developed. Discouraged, he peeks in the school window and decides to rejoin his class. The teacher is happy to see him because she has a job for him. Fortunately it's a developmentally appropriate one that Little Brown Bear can complete successfully. (32 pages)

Where it's reviewed:
Booklist, August 2003, page 1992
Bulletin of the Center for Children's Books, July 2003, page 444
Publishers Weekly, July 28, 2003, page 97
School Library Journal, August 2003, page 126

Other books by the same author:
Little Brown Bear Won't Take a Nap!, 2002 (IRA Children's Choices)
Animal Crackers: A Delectable Collection of Pictures, Poems, Songs, & Lullabies, 1996

Other books you might like:
Robin Ballard, *My Day, Your Day*, 2001
Pictured activities of working parents parallel those of their children playing at day care.
Jonathan London, *Froggy Goes to School*, 1996
Despite feeling nervous about the first day of school, Froggy not only survives, but also enjoys the day.
Margaret Wild, *Tom Goes to Kindergarten*, 2000
Tom's parents enjoy his first day of school so much that

they are disappointed he does not need them to stay with him the second day also.

413

JANE DYER, Author/Illustrator

Little Brown Bear Won't Take a Nap!

(Boston: Little, Brown and Company, 2002)

Subject(s): Animals/Bears; Sleep; Animals/Geese
Age range(s): Preschool-Grade 1
Major character(s): Little Brown Bear, Bear, Son; Mama Bear, Bear, Mother; Papa Bear, Bear, Father
Time period(s): Indeterminate
Locale(s): Fictional Country

Summary: Little Brown Bear refuses to join Mama and Papa Bear in a winter-long nap just because that's what bears do. He watches the geese flying south and decides to follow them as soon as Mama and Papa are sound asleep. Little Brown Bear walks as far as the train station when he discovers that some geese ride the train south rather than fly so he does too. Months of play on a sandy, sunny beach are fun, but tiring so, with help from some northbound geese, Little Brown Bear returns home and quickly falls asleep in his comfortable bed. This is the first book also written by the well-known children's book illustrator. (32 pages)

Where it's reviewed:
Booklist, September 15, 2002, page 239
Horn Book Guide, Spring 2003, page 10
Kirkus Reviews, August 1, 2002, page 1127
Publishers Weekly, July 1, 2002, page 78
School Library Journal, September 2002, page 189

Awards the book has won:
IRA Children's Choices, 2003

Other books by the same author:
Little Brown Bear and the Bundle of Joy, 2004
Little Brown Bear Won't Go to School!, 2002

Other books you might like:
Gavin Bishop, *Stay Awake, Bear!*, 2000
Old Bear and Brown Bear stay awake all winter rather than waste their time hibernating but then sleep through their summer vacation.
Hans De Beer, *Bernard Bear's Amazing Adventure*, 1994
Rather than hibernating alone, Bernard Bear tries a sparrow's advice to head south for the winter.
Denise Fleming, *Time to Sleep*, 1997
Bear passes the word through the animal grapevine that it's time to settle in for the winter; eventually the news comes back to awaken him.

E

414

RICHARD EASTON

A Real American
(New York: Clarion Books, 2002)

Subject(s): Miners and Mining; Emigration and Immigration; Farm Life
Age range(s): Grades 5-8
Major character(s): Nathan McClelland, 11-Year-Old; Arturo Tozzi, 11-Year-Old, Immigrant (Italian)
Time period(s): 1890s
Locale(s): Manorville, Pennsylvania

Summary: In the late 1800s, Nathan watches as the coal-mining companies buy up as much land as they can to put up housing for the immigrant workers they're bringing in to work the mines. Happy to get a good price for their farms, many of Nathan's friends and their families move away. In their place come the Italian immigrants, and animosity and anti-immigrant sentiment rise to the surface. Though warned to stay away from the Italians, Nathan can't help but notice a boy his age who works in the mines and the two become friends. When gangs plan to rout the miners from their shanties, Nathan and his family help the immigrants defend themselves, in this author's first novel. (156 pages)

Where it's reviewed:
Booklist, May 15, 2002, page 1606
Bulletin of the Center for Children's Books, September 2002, page 13
Horn Book Guide, Fall 2002, page 371
Kirkus Reviews, April 15, 2002, page 567
School Library Journal, March 2002, page 230

Other books you might like:
Susan Campbell Bartoletti, *Growing Up in Coal Country*, 1996
   A photo-essay depicts the lives of children who worked in the coal mines of Pennsylvania at the beginning of the 1890s. Nonfiction title.
Ann R. Blakeslee, *A Different Kind of Hero*, 1997
   Concerned that the Chinese will take away their mining

jobs, Renny's father wants to run them out of camp, but Renny stands up for his friend Zi's family.
Kristine L. Franklin, *Grape Thief*, 2003
   Raised in a coal mining town, Slava sees the mines slow down, mobsters infiltrate, and his dreams of attending school diminish.
N.A. Perez, *Breaker*, 1988
   After Pat's father is killed in a mining accident, Pat begins working in the mines while his brother fights for improved labor conditions.

415

ROSEMARY EDGHILL

Paying the Piper at the Gates of Dawn
(Waterville, ME: Five Star, 2003)

Subject(s): Short Stories; Fantasy
Age range(s): Grades 9-Adult

Summary: In this collection, Edghill delivers fairy tales, horror stories, and even science fiction, all with an unusual flavor. "Prince of Exiles" is a sinister, pagan version of one of the familiar Arthurian legends. Two stories, "Maltese Feline" and "Killer in the Reign" involve the familiar hard-boiled detective in fairyland, but this detective is anything but standard. "The Fairy Ring" involves a determined heroine who refuses to give up on the fairy she has fallen in love with, no matter how rough the going gets. A quirky collection that is definitely not like your mother's fairy tales. (333 pages)

Where it's reviewed:
Booklist, June 1, 2003, page 1754
Chronicle, August 2003, page 40
Publishers Weekly, May 26, 2003, page 55

Other books by the same author:
Warslayer: The Incredibly True Adventures of Vixen the Slayer, 2002
The Bowl of Night, 1996
Book of Moons, 1995

183

Other books you might like:

Angela Carter, *The Bloody Chamber*, 1979
 A short story collection that adds a feminist twist to standard fairy tales.
Ellen Datlow, *Snow White, Blood Red*, 1994
 A series of retellings of classic fairytales. Teri Windling, co-editor.
Charles de Lint, *Waifs and Strays*, 2002
 A collection that includes stories of all types, many of which use mythology as background.

416

JULIE ANDREWS EDWARDS
EMMA WALTON HAMILTON, Co-Author
TONY WALTON, Illustrator

Dumpy and the Big Storm
(New York: Hyperion Books for Children, 2002)

Series: Dumpy the Dump Truck
Subject(s): Weather; Transportation; Resourcefulness
Age range(s): Preschool-Kindergarten
Major character(s): Charlie, Child; Dumpy, Object (dump truck)
Time period(s): 2000s (2002)
Locale(s): Apple Harbor

Summary: A big storm is coming to Apple Harbor and Charlie and his family hurry to get their truck in the barn and complete other preparations. When a particularly loud thunderclap wakes him up, Charlie notices that the barn door has flown open and he and his grandfather head out to check on the truck. The radio in the truck has somehow turned itself on and they hear that the light and horn in the lighthouse have gone out. With his family, Charlie races to the scene. Other neighbors join in the rescue effort and, by using the headlights and horns of Dumpy the Dump Truck and other trucks they manage to steer a ship to safety. (32 pages)

Where it's reviewed:
Booklist, December 1, 2002, page 673
Horn Book Guide, Spring 2003, page 32

Other books by the same author:
Dumpy's Apple Shop, 2004
Dumpy Saves Christmas, 2001
Dumpy at School, 2000

Other books you might like:

Virginia Lee Burton, *Katy and the Big Snow*, 1943
 When a blizzard paralyzes the town of Geoppolis snow plow Katy saves the day.
Kate McMullan, *I'm Mighty!*, 2003
 A little tugboat helps boats in trouble, even when they're twice his size!
Watty Piper, *The Little Engine That Could*, 1930
 When bigger, stronger engines refuse to help get food and toys for children over the mountain the little blue engine proves that she is up to the task.

417

MICHELLE EDWARDS, Author/Illustrator

The Talent Show
(San Diego: Harcourt, Inc., 2002)

Series: Jackson Friends. Book 3
Subject(s): Talent; Schools; Grandmothers
Age range(s): Grades 2-4
Major character(s): Howie Smith, 2nd Grader, Singer; Calliope James, 2nd Grader, Friend; Pa Lia Vang, 2nd Grader, Friend; Grandma Gardenia, Grandmother
Time period(s): 2000s (2002)
Locale(s): United States (Jackson Magnet School)

Summary: Howie is looking forward to tonight's talent show with such excitement that she struggles to focus on the class math lesson right before the final rehearsal at school. When it's her turn to take the stage, Howie looks out over the audience, listens to the musical accompaniment and freezes. Unable to breath, let alone sing, Howie stands there as Calliope and Pa Lia encourage her, to no avail. Quietly Grandma Gardenia walks Howie from the stage, out the door and to the car to drive her home. At home Howie feels comfortable and she goes into the yard and sings her song flawlessly to Grandma Gardenia's applause. As her confidence returns, Howie knows that she'll be able to don her beautiful new dress and take the stage in the evening to perform during the school's talent show and she does. Concluding information about stage fright suggests different strategies that people use to overcome it. (56 pages)

Where it's reviewed:
Booklist, August 2002, page 1958
Horn Book Guide, Spring 2003, page 66
Kirkus Reviews, July 15, 2002, page 1030
Riverbank Review, Winter 2002-2003, page 44
School Library Journal, October 2002, page 104

Other books by the same author:
What's That Noise, 2002
Zero Grandparents, 2001 (Jackson Friends Book 2)
Pa Lia's First Day, 1999 (Jackson Friends Book 1)

Other books you might like:

Judy Delton, *Stage Frightened*, 1997
 Problems crop up for the Pee Wee Scouts when they plan a Talent Show as a fund-raising event in this Pee Wee Scouts series #32.
Betsy Duffey, *Spotlight on Cody*, 1998
 Nothing goes right for Cody as he tries to find some "talent" to perform for the school's talent show.
Elissa Haden Guest, *Iris and Walter: The School Play*, 2002
 Walter develops stage fright during the dress rehearsal for the class play and Iris whispers his lines to him.
Steven Kroll, *I'm George Washington and You're Not!*, 1994
 Too nervous to star in the class play, Eric lets the role go to the class bully and then has to step into the spotlight at the last minute.

418

PAMELA DUNCAN EDWARDS
DARCIA LABROSSE, Illustrator

Little Brown Hen's Shower

(New York: Hyperion Books for Children, 2002)

Subject(s): Animals/Chickens; Animals; Stories in Rhyme
Age range(s): Grades K-1
Major character(s): Brown Hen, Chicken, Mother
Time period(s): Indeterminate
Locale(s): Fictional Country

Summary: As Little Brown Hen prepares to go out she hears word of a shower and quickly gathers her umbrella in order to protect her egg from any rainfall. Other animals, finding it strange that Little Brown Hen is using her umbrella on a sunny day, imagine various other reasons for her use of the umbrella such as practicing for a circus act. When Little Brown Hen finally reaches her destination, the farmhouse, she discovers that the rumors of a shower were correct. In the farmhouse is a surprise party for Little Brown Hen and her egg that obligingly hatches during the event. (32 pages)

Where it's reviewed:
Booklist, April 1, 2002, page 1332
Horn Book Guide, Fall 2002, page 300
Publishers Weekly, March 18, 2002, page 101
School Library Journal, July 2002, page 88

Other books by the same author:
Clara Caterpillar, 2001 (IRA Children's Choice)
Bravo, Livingstone Mouse!, 2000
Some Smug Slug, 1996

Other books you might like:
David Martin, *Little Chicken Chicken*, 1996
    Imaginative Little Chicken Chicken entertains the other birds in the henhouse with her juggling and tightrope walking.
Jenny Nimmo, *Something Wonderful*, 2001
    Little Hen surprises the farmer and the other chickens by locating the eggs abandoned in the woods and staying with them until they all hatch.
Mary Wormell, *Hilda Hen's Search*, 1994
    Hilda Hen confidently searches until she finds a perfectly original spot for her nest.

419

PAMELA DUNCAN EDWARDS
HENRY COLE, Illustrator

Muldoon

(New York: Hyperion Books for Children, 2002)

Subject(s): Animals/Dogs; Pets; Family Life
Age range(s): Grades K-2
Major character(s): Muldoon, Dog; Anna West, Sister, Student; Tom West, Brother, Student
Time period(s): 2000s (2002)
Locale(s): United States

Summary: When Muldoon is selected by the West family from all the other dogs at the pet store he considers that he's been hired to do a job at the West's large blue kennel. Muldoon likes his working conditions and the extra perks such as tummy scratches. He takes seriously his responsibility as the family alarm clock and finder of lost sneakers. He even keeps the cat slim by eating her food. Muldoon protects Anna and Tom by putting them on a leash while they're out walking and he sorts the trash so nothing valuable is discarded. Muldoon loves his job! (32 pages)

Where it's reviewed:
Booklist, February 15, 2003, page 1073
Horn Book Guide, Spring 2003, page 32
Publishers Weekly, September 16, 2002, page 67
School Library Journal, December 2002, page 94

Other books by the same author:
Gigi & Lulu's Gigantic Fight, 2004
Leprechaun's Gold, 2004
Rosie's Roses, 2003

Other books you might like:
Glenna Lang, *Looking Out for Sarah*, 2001
    Perry enjoys his days of work as a guide dog for Sarah.
Madeleine L'Engle, *The Other Dog*, 2001
    It's difficult for Touche to comprehend why her family chose to acquire another dog, especially one as inadequate as baby Jo.
Alice Provensen, *A Day in the Life of Murphy*, 2003
    With a terrier's frantic energy Murphy describes his busy day caring for his family.
Harriet Ziefert, *Pushkin Minds the Bundle*, 2000
    Pushkin is understandably jealous of the bundle named Pierre who receives so much attention and even claims Pushkin's favorite seat in the car.

420

RICHARD EDWARDS
SUSAN WINTER, Illustrator

Always Copycub

(New York: HarperCollins Publishers, 2002)

Subject(s): Animals/Bears; Mothers; Games
Age range(s): Preschool-Grade 1
Major character(s): Copycub, Bear, Son; Unnamed Character, Bear, Mother
Time period(s): Indeterminate
Locale(s): Fictional Country

Summary: Copycub's favorite game is hiding. No matter how hard he tries, his mother always finds him, but Copycub never stops trying. From each new hiding place he calls, "Can't find me here!" and his mother replies, "Oh, yes, I can!" and indeed she does. Or she does until the day they are deep in an unfamiliar part of the woods and Copycub sneaks away and hides in a hollow tree. He waits and waits, but his mother doesn't find him. He tries to walk home, but the woods are dark and he is lost. As Copycub quietly whimpers, "Can't find me here!" his mother replies, "Oh, yes, I can." Happily Copycub returns to his cave with his mother and promises never to run away again. Originally published in England in 2001. (28 pages)

Where it's reviewed:
Horn Book Guide, Fall 2002, page 300
Publishers Weekly, February 4, 2002, page 78
School Library Journal, February 2002, page 100

Other books by the same author:
Copy Me, Copycub, 1999
You're Safe Now, Waterdog, 1997
Fly with the Birds: A Word and Rhyme Book, 1996
Moles Can Dance, 1994

Other books you might like:
Jez Alborough, *Where's My Teddy?*, 1992
As Eddie searches the dark woods for his lost teddy bear he encounters a large bear with a similar problem.
Jonathan London, *Honey Paw and Lightfoot*, 1995
A fictionalized account of the life cycle of a brown bear realistically portrays one year in the life of Honeybear and her cub.
Martin Waddell, *Good Job, Little Bear*, 1999
As Little Bear proudly shows Big Bear all he can do in the woods, Big Bear promises to always be near when Little Bear needs him.

421

TIM EGAN, Author/Illustrator

Serious Farm

(Boston: Houghton Mifflin Company, 2003)

Subject(s): Farm Life; Animals; Conduct of Life
Age range(s): Grades K-3
Major character(s): Farmer Fred, Farmer; Edna, Cow
Time period(s): Indeterminate
Locale(s): Fictional Country

Summary: Farmer Fred is a serious farmer because, as he tells the animals, there's no humor in corn or tomatoes. The animals try to be serious too, but after a while they grow tired of it and seek a bit of fun. Edna is the first to do something funny by standing on the fence and attempting to crow. Farmer Fred simply opens the window and reminds Edna that she's not a rooster. All the animals, either singly or in groups, try something silly or humorous but Farmer Fred remains taciturn and the animals become discouraged. Once again Edna leads the way and this time she leads the animals right off the farm. In the morning Farmer Fred searches for his animals. When he finds them walking through the woods he stops to talk and his slight smile convinces them to return. After all, Farmer Fred admits, the thought of animals running wild in the woods is pretty funny to him. (32 pages)

Where it's reviewed:
Bulletin of the Center for Children's Books, December 2003, page 149
Horn Book, September 2003, page 595
Publishers Weekly, November 3, 2003, page 74
School Library Journal, October 2003, page 118

Other books by the same author:
Trial of Cardigan Jones, 2004
The Experiments of Doctor Vermin, 2002
A Mile from Ellington Station, 2001

Burnt Toast on Davenport Street, 1997 (School Library Journal Best Books)
Metropolitan Cow, 1996 (School Library Journal Best Books)

Other books you might like:
Denys Cazet, *Minnie and Moo Series*, 1998-
Minnie and Moo are two earnest cows with well-intentioned plans that usually create havoc for the perennially perplexed farmer.
Paul Brett Johnson, *The Cow Who Wouldn't Come Down*, 1993
Miss Rosemary resorts to an ingenious scheme to convince her flying cow Gertrude to land and resume more typical cow behavior.
James Stevenson, *Don't Make Me Laugh*, 1999
Serious Mr. Frimdimpny has strict rules for the proper way to proceed through the book he narrates; violators must return to the book's beginning.

422

RICHARD EGIELSKI, Author/Illustrator

Slim and Jim

(New York: Laura Geringer Books/HarperCollins Publishers, 2002)

Subject(s): Animals/Rats; Animals/Mice; Animals/Cats
Age range(s): Grades K-3
Major character(s): Slim, Rat, Orphan; Buster, Cat, Criminal; Jim, Mouse, Friend
Time period(s): Indeterminate
Locale(s): Fictional Country

Summary: Buster tries to take advantage of lonely Slim by forcing him to steal. Seeing the commotion outside his bedroom window, Jim tries to intervene and Slim and Jim tumble off the roof into the river. Slim rescues non-swimmer Jim and Jim invites Slim to live with his family. As they make their way through unfamiliar streets they discover a shared love of yo-yos and meet a frog family that gives them a ride home. Jim's family takes Slim in and all is well until Buster kidnaps Slim. Jim searches for his friend and, when he learns Slim's fate uses his yo-yo to overcome Buster until the police arrive. (40 pages)

Where it's reviewed:
Booklist, May 1, 2002, page 1520
Bulletin of the Center for Children's Books, September 2002, page 14
Horn Book, July 2002, page 445
Publishers Weekly, May 6, 2002, page 56
School Library Journal, May 2002, page 112

Other books by the same author:
Three Magic Balls, 2000
Jazper, 1998
The Gingerbread Boy, 1997 (School Library Journal Best Books)

Other books you might like:
Sharleen Collicott, *Toestomper and the Bad Butterflies*, 2002
Toestomper's unusual friendship with caterpillars becomes complicated when they all turn into butterflies that no longer stay in one place.

Todd Starr Palmer, *Rhino and Mouse*, 1994
    Despite their obvious differences, Rhino and Mouse enjoy a close friendship.
Marcus Pfister, *Milo and the Magical Stones*, 1997
    Choices made by Milo and the other mice could have serious environmental consequences depending on their actions.
Ellen Stoll Walsh, *For Pete's Sake*, 1998
    Pete's flamingo friends accept him as the flamingo he thinks he is although others would say the green four-legged creature resembles an alligator.

423

LOIS EHLERT, Author/Illustrator

In My World
(San Diego: Harcourt, Inc., 2002)

Subject(s): Nature; Imagination
Age range(s): Preschool-Grade 1
Time period(s): Indeterminate
Locale(s): Fictional Country

Summary: Brightly colored die-cut shapes illustrate the simple text describing favorite things. As the pages turn the reader begins with bugs, frogs, and birds that are described as creeping, leaping and singing. A variety of simple objects are shown as the concepts grow to include the sun (shining) and stars (glittering) and the moon (glowing). With thanks to the world the book concludes with a rebus filled summary of everything loved in the world. (38 pages)

Where it's reviewed:
Booklist, May 1, 2002, page 1520
Horn Book, July 2002, page 446
Kirkus Reviews, March 1, 2002, page 332
Publishers Weekly, February 18, 2002, page 94
School Library Journal, May 2002, page 112

Awards the book has won:
Parenting's Books of the Year, 2002

Other books by the same author:
Waiting for Wings, 2001 (ALA Notable Children's Book)
Market Day: A Story Told with Folk Art, 2000
Top Cat, 1998
Hands, 1997 (Booklist Editors' Choice)
Color Farm, 1990
Color Zoo, 1989

Other books you might like:
Margaret Wise Brown, *The Important Book*, 1949
    It's clear to anyone that ordinary objects have great importance; grass is green and rain is wet.
Cheryl Willis Hudson, *Hands Can*, 2003
    Simple photos depict the many ways in which young children use their hands as the rhyming text describes the activities.
Bill Martin Jr., *Panda Bear, Panda Bear, What Do You See?*, 2003
    Panda Bear sees ten different animals, each one an endangered species.

Laura Vaccaro Seeger, *The Hidden Alphabet*, 2003
    Objects representing each letter of the alphabet are partially revealed through die-cut holes in a page.
Matthew Van Fleet, *Tails*, 2003
    Animal tails are displayed through die-cut holes and activated with flaps and tabs in this book for the very young.

424

DANIEL EHRENHAFT

The Last Dog on Earth
(New York: Delacorte, 2003)

Subject(s): Animals/Dogs; Stepfathers
Age range(s): Grades 7-10
Major character(s): Logan Moore, 14-Year-Old; Robert, Stepfather; Jack, Dog (mutt)
Time period(s): 2000s
Locale(s): Newburg, Oregon

Summary: Trying to teach Logan a sense of responsibility, his domineering stepfather decides he should have a dog. Rather than the purebred Robert prefers, Logan chooses a mangy mutt he names Jack. Sent away to camp for the summer, Logan runs away but manages to connect with Jack as people on the West Coast become irrational over an outbreak of canine "psychotic outburst syndrome." This syndrome turns dogs into vicious predators before they die, which makes people understandably wary of all dogs. Poor Jack—will she die from the disease or from the vigilante gangs that are tracking down and killing all dogs? (234 pages)

Where it's reviewed:
Kliatt, January 2003, page 7
Library Media Connection, October 2003, page 58
Publishers Weekly, January 27, 2003, page 260
School Library Journal, February 2003, page 141
Voice of Youth Advocates, April 2003, page 47

Other books by the same author:
Tell It to Naomi, 2004

Other books you might like:
James D. Forman, *Cry Havoc*, 1988
    Jim Cooper and his daughter are facing the threat of canine attack from genetically altered dogs.
Dean Koontz, *Watchers*, 1987
    Two animals, altered through genetic experimentation, escape from their lab cages.
David Patneaude, *Framed in Fire*, 1999
    Peter and his stepfather Buck don't get along and Peter often wishes that his real father hadn't died.

425

DAN ELISH

Born Too Short: The Confessions of an Eighth-Grade Basket Case
(New York: Richard Jackson/Simon & Schuster, 2002)

Subject(s): Friendship; Jealousy; Interpersonal Relations
Age range(s): Grades 6-8

Major character(s): Matt Greene, 8th Grader; Keith Livingston, 8th Grader, Basketball Player; Josie Hyde, 8th Grader
Time period(s): 2000s
Locale(s): New York, New York

Summary: It's hard to be the best friend of the "blond Adonis" of the eighth grade at Hannaford School, especially when you walk beside him and realize you're only five feet one and a half inches tall. Keith doesn't mean to excel in everything, he just does, and Matt finally becomes a little jealous as he thinks about the unfairness of life. Matt's a classical guitarist but he isn't selected for the Aspen Music festival, whereas Keith can barely strum four chords and yet writes a rock opera that everyone loves. Matt thought he had a girlfriend, but she falls for Keith. Matt's barely noticed by girls in his class while Keith is being chased by high school girls, and scoring! One night Matt's had it and wishes for all kinds of bad things to happen to his friend; surprisingly enough, his wishes come true. Eventually he starts to worry that his evil intents are the cause of Keith's problems, but how can he stop them? (152 pages)

Where it's reviewed:
Booklist, February 1, 2002, page 938
Bulletin of the Center for Children's Books, May 2002, page 320
Kliatt, March 2002, page 10
Publishers Weekly, January 14, 2002, page 61
School Library Journal, February 2002, page 130

Other books by the same author:
The Worldwide Dessert Contest, 1988

Other books you might like:
Bill Brittain, *All the Money in the World*, 1979
When Quentin's wish for "all the money in the world" comes true, it's more than he ever wanted.
Ellen Conford, *Genie with the Light Blue Hair*, 1989
Jeannie receives an antique lamp complete with a blue Groucho Marx-like genie that's a little rusty in the wish-granting area.
Carol Gorman, *Dork in Disguise*, 1999
Attending a new school, Jerry's ready to blow his dork image and be cool; after a few months, he's glad to be himself and wear his glasses again.
Chris Lynch, *Slot Machine*, 1995
Elvin attends an orientation camp for his private school and sees all his buddies "slotted" for football while he ends up in arts and crafts.

426

LAURA MALONE ELLIOTT
LYNN MUNSINGER, Illustrator

Hunter's Best Friend at School

(New York: HarperCollins Publishers, 2002)

Subject(s): Friendship; Behavior; Schools
Age range(s): Grades K-2
Major character(s): Hunter, Raccoon, Kindergartner; Stripe, Raccoon, Kindergartner; Mr. Ringtail, Teacher, Raccoon
Time period(s): Indeterminate

Locale(s): Fictional Country

Summary: Hunter and Stripe are not only best friends but also the kind of students that Mr. Ringtail is pleased to have in class until the day Stripe arrives in a mood for mischief. Hunter is torn between his interest in the class activities and his desire to be just like his friend. The friendship gets the better of Hunter's judgment and he arrives home from school feeling guilty about his classroom behavior. Hunter's mother suggests that he ignore Stripe's misbehavior and set an example of good behavior, so Stripe is encouraged to change. Hunter tries the suggestion and gradually Stripe returns to the compliant behavior for which he is known. (32 pages)

Where it's reviewed:
Booklist, October 1, 2002, page 334
Bulletin of the Center for Children's Books, October 2002, page 54
Horn Book Guide, Spring 2003, page 33
Publishers Weekly, July 1, 2002, page 78
School Library Journal, September 2002, page 190

Awards the book has won:
IRA Children's Choices, 2003

Other books you might like:
Tony Johnston, *Sparky and Eddie: The First Day of School*, 1997
Best friends learn to adapt to change when they enter school and are assigned to different classrooms.
Alexis O'Neill, *The Recess Queen*, 2002
New student Katie Sue provides a model for cooperative recess behavior that changes Mean Jean's interactions with others.
Amy Schwartz, *The Boys Team*, 2001
Oscar, Eddie and Jacob, inseparable buddies, enjoy their status as kindergarteners.

427

DEBORAH ELLIS
MURIEL WOOD, Illustrator

A Company of Fools

(Allston, MA: Fitzhenry & Whiteside, 2002)

Subject(s): Friendship; Plague; Monasticism
Age range(s): Grades 5-8
Major character(s): Henri, Singer (choirboy); Micah, Orphan, Singer (choirboy)
Time period(s): 14th century (1340s)
Locale(s): Abbey of St. Luc, France

Summary: Henri's quiet, orderly life in the St. Luc monastery changes overnight when one of the monks brings home the filthy street urchin Micah, who was sentenced to death for thievery. Micah's beautiful singing voice has served him in good stead as a street singer, until he added thievery to the mix, but now his voice can be added to those of the other choirboys at St. Luc. Sickly Henri is assigned as Micah's companion and is soon caught up in Micah's mischievous schemes as he sings bawdy street songs, doctors the communion wine and serves up a drugged live pig as the centerpiece for a visiting bishop's meal. The plague also breaks out near St. Luc and the prior sends out the choirboys as a "company of fools'' to sing and ease the dark times faced by the villagers. When the daughter of a nobleman recovers from the plague, it is claimed that Micah's voice was the cause. Suddenly Micah is thrilled by his new importance while Henri worries that Micah's voice is being used to increase the treasury of the abbey in this tale of monastery life during the Plague Year. (191 pages)

Where it's reviewed:
Booklist, January 2003, page 888
Bulletin of the Center for Children's Books, January 2003, page 195
Horn Book, January 2003, page 70
Quill & Quire, October 2002, page 38
Voice of Youth Advocates, February 2003, page 472

Other books by the same author:
Mud City, 2003
Parvana's Journey, 2002
The Breadwinner, 2001

Other books you might like:
Mary Hooper, *At the Sign of the Sugared Plum*, 2003
    Hannah and her sister Sarah keep their confectioner's shop going during the plague by concocting harmless herbal sweets as a disease preventative.
Gary Paulsen, *Harris and Me: A Summer Remembered*, 1994
    A summer of pig wrestling, outmaneuvering a testy barn cat and peeing on an electric fence provide memories for two cousins.
Jill Paton Walsh, *A Parcel of Patterns*, 1983
    In 1665 the inhabitants of a small English town become infected by the plague when a dressmaker receives ''a parcel of patterns'' from London.

428

DEBORAH ELLIS

Mud City

(Toronto: Groundwood Books, 2003)

Series: Breadwinner Trilogy
Subject(s): Refugees; Homeless People
Age range(s): Grades 5-8
Major character(s): Shauzia, Refugee, 14-Year-Old; Jasper, Dog; Mrs. Weera, Leader (of the refugee camp)
Time period(s): 2000s
Locale(s): Peshawar, Pakistan (''Mud City'' refugee camp)

Summary: Afghani Shauzia rebels against the jobs assigned to her in the unsanitary, lice-infested refugee camp in Pakistan. Having left home rather than endure an arranged marriage, Shauzia has few choices of where to live, but dislikes the camp leader Mrs. Weera who is as strong-willed as she is, and elects to live on the streets of Peshawar. With her dog Jasper, Shauzia finds it difficult to survive and when police steal her funds and it becomes difficult to find food, she returns to the camp. A broken leg provides her with quiet time to reflect on her life and she decides to join with Mrs. Weera as the two return to their homeland of Afghanistan. (164 pages)

Where it's reviewed:
Booklist, November 15, 2003, page 597
Kliatt, September 2003, page 7

Resource Links, December 2003, page 14
School Library Journal, November 2003, page 138

Other books by the same author:
Parvana's Journey, 2002 (Breadwinner Trilogy)
The Breadwinner, 2001 (Breadwinner Trilogy)
Looking for X, 2000

Other books you might like:
Anilu Bernardo, *Jumping Off to Freedom*, 1996
    Fleeing from Cuba, David and his father share a raft with two dangerous strangers, which turns their trip into death-defying survival.
Gaye Hicyilmaz, *Smiling for Strangers*, 2000
    Leaving behind her mortally wounded grandfather in war-torn Bosnia, Nina ''smiles for strangers'' as she makes her way to safety in England.
Suzanne Fisher Staples, *Haveli*, 1993
    Forced to become the third wife of elderly Rahim, Shabanu and her daughter run away after Rahim dies.

429

DEBORAH ELLIS

Parvana's Journey

(Toronto, Canada: Groundwood Books/Douglas & McIntyre, 2002)

Subject(s): Survival; Social Conditions; Women
Age range(s): Grades 7-10
Major character(s): Parvana, 13-Year-Old; Asif, Child, Amputee; Leila, Child; Hassan, Baby
Time period(s): 2000s
Locale(s): Afghanistan

Summary: Parvana buries her father and then sets out across Afghanistan to find her remaining family members. She disguises herself as a boy, knowing if the Taliban finds her, they'll force her into the army. If they discover she's a girl, she'll be punished for not wearing a veil or being escorted by a male family member. So Parvana makes her way cautiously, hoping to blend in with other refugees and street children. Along the way she finds a baby and tries to keep it alive, naming it Hassan; then meets Asif, an angry boy who's lost a leg crossing a minefield, but he likes and helps tend the baby. Finally Leila, the only survivor of a bombed out village, joins the trio as the group struggles to avoid the Taliban, hides during bombing raids and searches for food and water until they arrive at a refugee camp that offers some hope for survival. (190 pages)

Where it's reviewed:
Booklist, December 1, 2002, page 662
Kliatt, December 2002, page 8
Quill & Quire, July 2002, page 50
School Library Journal, December 2002, page 137
Voice of Youth Advocates, February 2003, page 472

Awards the book has won:
IRA Children's Choices/Advanced Readers, 2003
ALA Best Books for Young Adults, 2003

Other books by the same author:
Mud City, 2003
The Breadwinner, 2001
Looking for X, 2000

Pick-Up Sticks, 1992
A Family Project, 1988

Other books you might like:

Daniella Carmi, *Samir and Yonatan*, 2000
Palestinian Samir becomes friends with all the children at the Jewish hospital, but especially Yonatan who teaches him how to use the computer.

Gaye Hicyilmaz, *Smiling for Strangers*, 2000
Leaving behind her mortally wounded Bosnian grandfather, Nina ''smiles for strangers'' as she makes her way to safety in England.

John Marsden, *Tomorrow, When the War Began Series*, 1995-2002
Teen friends become guerrillas and assist the army when terrorists overrun their homeland of New Zealand.

Alice Mead, *Girl of Kosovo*, 2001
Zana is caught up in the war between the Serbs and Albanians when family members are killed and her uncle threatens her best friend.

430

SARAH ELLIS
BRUNO ST-AUBIN, Illustrator

The Several Lives of Orphan Jack

(Toronto: Groundwood Books/Douglas & McIntyre, 2003)

Subject(s): Orphans; Apprentices; Runaways
Age range(s): Grades 3-6
Major character(s): Jack, Orphan, 12-Year-Old
Time period(s): Indeterminate Past
Locale(s): Fictional Country (Opportunities School for Orphans and Foundlings); Aberbog, Fictional Country

Summary: One day as apprentice to a bookkeeper is all the exposure to drudgery Jack needs to finally break out of the safety of conformance and free himself from the Opportunities School for Orphans and Foundlings. Memories of cook's stories about life at sea, overheard by Jack as he worked in the scullery, lead Jack to set a path for the coast as he runs away from the orphanage. Good luck, quick wit and the knowledge gained from years of reading his only book, a dictionary with the first two letters missing, bring Jack to Aberbog and enable him to make a living at the town fair as an ''ideas peddler'' selling whims, ideas, impressions and notions to townspeople without an original thought of their own. By putting such concepts into the complacent people's heads Jack runs afoul of the local political leadership and once more finds himself a runaway, but one with a better plan for surviving the life of a ''wandering boy'' this time. (84 pages)

Where it's reviewed:
Booklist, December 1, 2003, page 668
Horn Book, November 2003, page 742
Publishers Weekly, August 11, 2003, page 280

Other books by the same author:
Out of the Blue, 1995
Next-Door Neighbors, 1990
A Family Project, 1988

Other books you might like:

Christopher Paul Curtis, *Bud, Not Buddy*, 1999
In a Newbery Medal winner, orphaned Bud relies on a self-made set of rules to guide his life and his search for a father he's never known.

Gail Carson Levine, *Dave at Night*, 1999
Each night Dave escapes from the Hebrew Home for Boys and enjoys the sights and sounds of Harlem during its Renaissance time.

Barbara Brooks Wallace, *Sparrows in the Scullery*, 1997
Kidnappers deliver Colley, a wealthy but sickly orphan, to the Broggin Home for Boys where other boys befriend him until all are rescued.

431

SUSAN MIDDLETON ELYA
FELIPE DAVALOS, Illustrator

Home at Last

(New York: Lee & Low Books, 2002)

Subject(s): Mexican Americans; Moving, Household; Language
Age range(s): Grades 1-3
Major character(s): Ana Patino, 8-Year-Old, Immigrant; Mama, Mother, Immigrant; Papa, Father, Worker
Time period(s): 2000s (2002)
Locale(s): United States

Summary: An employment opportunity for Papa in a canning factory brings Ana's family to America. Mama misses her home in Mexico and struggles in a land where she cannot speak the language. When one of Ana's younger twin brothers becomes ill while Papa is at work, Mama realizes that she must not depend on Ana and Papa as translators and she enrolls in a night class to study English. Knowing the language helps her feel more comfortable and finally Mama feels that she is ''home at last.'' (32 pages)

Where it's reviewed:
Booklist, May 1, 2002, page 1532
Bulletin of the Center for Children's Books, September 2002, page 15
Horn Book Guide, Fall 2002, page 326
Reading Teacher, December 2002, page 413
School Library Journal, July 2002, page 90

Awards the book has won:
Notable Social Studies Trade Books for Young People, 2003

Other books by the same author:
Eight Animals Play Ball, 2003
Eight Animals Bake a Cake, 2002
Say Hola to Spanish, 1996

Other books you might like:

Tony Johnston, *Uncle Rain Cloud*, 2001
Although Tio Tomas is a masterful storyteller in his native Spanish he depends on Carlos to interpret when English is needed.

Jane Medina, *My Name Is Jorge: On Both Sides of the River*, 1999
A collection of bilingual poems describes the varied experiences of a Mexican child attending an American school.

Pat Mora, *The Rainbow Tulip*, 1999
    A young Mexican American student bridges two cultures as she learns English in school while using Spanish at home.

432

SUSAN MIDDLETON ELYA
G. BRIAN KARAS, Illustrator

Oh No, Gotta Go!

(New York: Penguin Putman, 2003)

Subject(s): Hispanic Americans; Bilingualism; Stories in Rhyme
Age range(s): Preschool-Grade 1
Major character(s): Unnamed Character, Child, Daughter
Time period(s): 2000s (2003)
Locale(s): United States

Summary: On a Sunday drive with her parents, a young girl asks, ''Where is un bano?'' A bilingual search for the nearest bathroom follows. Most of the stores are closed on Sunday and the family ends up at a fancy restaurant with a long line of people waiting to use the bathroom. The other patrons are nice enough to let the little girl go ahead and the family stays to eat. Too much ''Limonade'' starts the problem all over again. (32 pages)

Where it's reviewed:
Booklist, November 15, 2003, page 599
Bulletin of the Center for Children's Books, July 2003, page 444
Publishers Weekly, May 26, 2003, page 69
School Library Journal, July 2003, page 95

Awards the book has won:
Center for Children's Books Best Books, 2003

Other books by the same author:
Geez Louise, 2003
Eight Animals on the Town, 2000
Say Hola to Spanish, 1996

Other books you might like:
Alana Frankel, *Once Upon a Potty*, 1999
    A little girl learns to use the potty.
Wendy Cheyette Lewison, *The Princess and the Potty*, 1994
    A princess refuses to be potty trained until she finds the perfect potty.
Inger Lindahl, *Bertil and the Bathroom Elephants*, 2003
    Bertil stops using the toilet in the bathroom when he becomes convinced mean elephants are living in there.

433

ED EMBERLEY, Author/Illustrator

Thanks, Mom

(Boston: Little, Brown and Company, 2003)

Subject(s): Circus; Animals; Mothers
Age range(s): Preschool-Grade 1
Major character(s): Kiko, Mouse; Koko, Mouse, Mother; Mumbo, Elephant
Time period(s): Indeterminate

Locale(s): Fictional Country

Summary: Kiko grabs a piece of cheese and starts running. Uh oh, he's been spotted and other, increasingly larger animals are soon in pursuit of Kiko and the cheese, or maybe they're after the other animals. Through the circus, run the costumed animals until last-in-line Mumbo comes face to face with Koko and quickly turns to run the other way. Relieved, Kiko and Koko run all the way home where Kiko gives Koko a hug, saying ''Thanks, Mom.'' Then they sit down to dine on the cheese. (32 pages)

Where it's reviewed:
Bulletin of the Center for Children's Books, June 2003, page 398
Publishers Weekly, March 24, 2003, page 74
School Library Journal, May 2003, page 112

Other books by the same author:
Ed Emberley's Drawing Book of Trucks and Trains, 2002
Wing on a Flea: A Book about Shapes, 2001
Ed Emberley's Fingerprint Drawing Book, 2000

Other books you might like:
Lois Ehlert, *Circus*, 1992
    A unique picture book illustrates the colorful excitement of the circus.
Leslie McGuirk, *Tucker Over the Top*, 2000
    Tucker, a daredevil terrier, tries to apply his skateboarding skills to a circus act.
Dr. Seuss, *If I Ran the Circus*, 1956
    Morris McGurk has grand plans for Circus McGurkus on the empty lot behind Mr. Sneelock's store.
Bernard Waber, *A Lion Named Shirley Williamson*, 2000
    Other zoo lions are jealous of the new lion with a fancy name until they're given new names too.

434

LOUISE ERDRICH
STEVE JOHNSON, Illustrator
LOU FANCHER, Illustrator

The Range Eternal

(New York: Hyperion, 2002)

Subject(s): Native Americans; Memory; Childhood
Age range(s): Grades K-3
Major character(s): Mama, Mother; Unnamed Character, Narrator, Daughter
Time period(s): 20th century
Locale(s): Turtle Mountains, North Dakota

Summary: An unnamed narrator remembers with fondness the Range Eternal—the blue enamel stove of her childhood. The narrator remembers Mama cooking soup on the stove, warming herself beside it after chores, getting potatoes from the stove in the morning to carry to school to keep her fingers warm and learning to read from its raised lettering. As electricity spreads through the prairie, the Range Eternal is replaced with an electric stove. The narrator misses the range and its pleasant associations and when she finds it in an antique shop as an adult, she buys it and brings it home. (32 pages)

Where it's reviewed:
Booklist, October 1, 2002, page 334
Bulletin of the Center for Children's Books, December 2002, page 153
Kirkus Reviews, August 15, 2002, page 1222
Publishers Weekly, September 9, 2002, page 67
School Library Journal, October 2002, page 104

Other books by the same author:
The Birchbark House, 1999 (ALA Notable Children's Books)
Grandmother's Pigeon, 1996 (Smithsonian's Notable Books for Children)

Other books you might like:
Margaret Bateson-Hill, *Shota and the Star Quilt*, 2001
    The family and friends of a young Lakota girl, living in the city, use Lakota traditions to save their homes.
Donald Hall, *Lucy's Christmas*, 1994
    In 1909 the Christmas gift of a new kitchen range from Sears is such an event that neighbors and relatives stop by Lucy's home to marvel at it.
Alice Schertle, *Maisie*, 1994
    The story of 90-year-old Maisie's life is also a record of the changes in America during her lifetime and a celebration of family ties.
Cynthia Leitich Smith, *Jingle Dancer*, 2000
    Jenna, a Muscogee girl, wants to jingle dance at her tribe's next pow-wow.
Jan Bourdeau Waboose, *Skysisters*, 2000
    Two young Ojibway girls view the Northern Lights.

435

HELEN ERICSON

Harriet Spies Again

(New York: Delacorte, 2002)

Subject(s): Mystery and Detective Stories; Humor; School Life
Age range(s): Grades 4-7
Major character(s): Harriet M. Welsch, 7th Grader, Spy; Simon "Sport" Rocque, 7th Grader; Catherine "Ole Golly" Waldenstein, Child-Care Giver (nanny); George Waldenstein, Spouse (of Ole Golly)
Time period(s): 1960s
Locale(s): New York, New York

Summary: Approved by the estate of Louise Fitzhugh, Harriet continues her spy business. Her parents travel to Paris for three months and her former nanny Ole Golly returns from Montreal to care for her, which leaves Harriet wondering what happened to Ole Golly's husband, Mr. Waldenstein. Warned not to mention his name, Harriet ends up spying on Ole Golly who makes several trips to the doctors living in the brownstone across the street. Harriet overhears her nanny claiming to be innocent during a phone conversation and is certain Old Golly's murdered her husband. Recruiting her good friend Sport, the two snoop around and arrange for Mr. Waldenstein to make a surprise visit to Harriet's home. The visit turns into a disaster in this companion to the original *Harriet the Spy*. (230 pages)

Where it's reviewed:
Booklist, March 15, 2002, page 1258
Bulletin of the Center for Children's Books, April 2002, page 278
Horn Book, May 2002, page 328
Publishers Weekly, February 11, 2002, page 188
School Library Journal, May 2002, page 148

Other books you might like:
Linda Bailey, *How Can I Be a Detective If I Have to Baby-Sit?*, 1996
    Stuck with watching young Alexander while camping, Stevie and Jesse revert to their detecting work when Alexander's trailer is ransacked.
Betsy Byars, *The Dark Stairs*, 1994
    With a policeman father and a private investigator mother, Herculeah Jones has no choice but to be a female Sherlock Holmes.
Willo Davis Roberts, *Twisted Summer*, 1996
    As Cici snoops around to find a murderer, the trail appears to point toward her step grandfather.
Wendelin Van Draanen, *Sammy Keyes and the Skeleton Man*, 1998
    Out trick-or-treating, Sammy runs into someone dressed in a skeleton costume; when she needs to uncover his identity, she works with police officer Borsch.

436

JENNIFER A. ERICSSON
NADINE BERNARD WESTCOTT, Illustrator

She Did It!

(New York: Melanie Kroupa Books/Farrar Straus Giroux, 2002)

Subject(s): Sisters; Family Life; Stories in Rhyme
Age range(s): Grades K-3
Major character(s): Mother, Mother
Time period(s): 2000s (2002)
Locale(s): United States

Summary: Each time a frustrated mother confronts her four daughters to ask who caused a mess they respond by pointing at each other and claiming that, "She did it!" The responsibility for feathers from a pillow fight covering the bedroom floor, toothpaste on the vanity counter, water splashed on the bathroom floor and food spills in the kitchen making Mother's chair sticky is foisted onto any sister but the one Mother confronts. Finally, Mother sends all the girls to their shared room where they concoct a plan to make Mother happy again. When she sees their sparkling room it's apparent who cleaned up, because "We did it!" is the girls' reply. (32 pages)

Where it's reviewed:
Booklist, February 15, 2002, page 1019
Horn Book Guide, Fall 2002, page 326
Publishers Weekly, January 14, 2002, page 59
School Library Journal, March 2002, page 176

Other books by the same author:
The Most Beautiful Kid in the World, 1996
No Milk!, 1993 (IRA Children's Choice)

Other books you might like:
Mem Fox, *Harriet, You'll Drive Me Wild!*, 2000
Quite unintentionally, or so she says, Harriet is at the center of an escalating series of messes that frustrate her patient mother.
Elise Petersen, *Tracy's Mess*, 1998
Tracy appear to be fastidious— but wait until you see what's behind her bedroom door!
Judith Viorst, *Super-Completely and Totally the Messiest*, 2001
Olivia, neat older sister and perfect role model, cannot understand how her sister Sophie can be such a clumsy, messy person.

437

LISA CAMPBELL ERNST, Author/Illustrator

Hannah Mae O'Hannigan's Wild West Show

(New York: Simon & Schuster Books for Young Readers, 2003)

Subject(s): Cowboys/Cowgirls; Animals/Hamsters; American West
Age range(s): Grades K-3
Major character(s): Hannah Mae O'Hannigan, Cowgirl, Daughter; Coot, Uncle, Rancher; Sassafras, Horse (pony)
Time period(s): Indeterminate Past
Locale(s): United States

Summary: To celebrate Hannah Mae's birth Uncle Coot sends her a big cowboy hat. From that moment on Hannah Mae feels destined to be a cowgirl. As a city girl it's a bit challenging to find a way to practice the skills needed for that career, but Hannah Mae's parents support her in any way they can. They buy Sassafras for her and allow her to herd hamsters in the apartment. Finally, Hannah Mae's parents think she's ready to visit Uncle Coot on his ranch way out west, so they put her on a train with Sassafras. Hannah Mae is assigned ranch chores because Uncle Coot considers her too young to help on the range. However, when a herd of wild hamsters terrifies the cattle and the cowhands, Hannah Mae and Sassafras have just the skills to ride to the rescue. (40 pages)

Where it's reviewed:
Booklist, August 2003, page 1988
Horn Book, July 2003, page 441
Publishers Weekly, May 12, 2003, page 67
School Library Journal, July 2003, page 95

Other books by the same author:
Wake Up, It's Spring!, 2004
Three Spinning Fairies: A Tale from the Brothers Grimm, 2002
Bear's Day, 2000
Goldilocks Returns, 2000

Other books you might like:
Steve Gulbis, *Cowgirl Rosie and Her Five Baby Bison*, 2001
Snakey Jake tries to rustle Cowgirl Rosie's bison, but her tears help the sheriff solve the crime and apprehend the thief.
Steve Sanfield, *The Great Turtle Drive*, 1996
Considering the high cost of turtle soup, a cowboy thinks he's found a way to strike it rich.
Diane Stanley, *Saving Sweetness*, 1996
A sheriff trying to catch an orphanage escapee is instead rescued by the runaway.

438

ERIK E. ESCKILSEN

The Last Mall Rat

(Boston: Walter Lorraine Books/Houghton Mifflin, 2003)

Subject(s): Shopping; Bullies
Age range(s): Grades 7-10
Major character(s): Mitch Grant, 15-Year-Old
Time period(s): 2000s
Locale(s): Shunpike Falls, New England

Summary: Enjoying being at the Onion River Mall, but too poor to buy anything, Mitch doesn't hesitate to accept a ten-dollar bill from an unscrupulous shoe salesman who wants an obnoxious customer hassled in the parking lot. As word of Mitch's deed spreads, other salespeople request his services and soon Mitch has to hire friends to assist him. Donning masks, they follow customers to their cars and yell "caveat emptor," or buyer beware, at them. Mitch enjoys the extra money he makes, as well as the thrill of intimidation, but knows he has a problem when one of his "Mall Mafia" members goes beyond yelling and strikes a customer in this author's first novel. (182 pages)

Where it's reviewed:
Booklist, April 1, 2003, page 1386
Bulletin of the Center for Children's Books, June 2003, page 398
Publishers Weekly, May 26, 2003, page 71
School Library Journal, June 2003, page 138
Voice of Youth Advocates, June 2003, page 126

Other books by the same author:
Iron Rain, 2004

Other books you might like:
Joan Bauer, *Rules of the Road*, 1998
Earning recognition for her salesmanship, teen Jenna is hired to drive elderly Mrs. Gladstone, of Gladstone Shoes, to her conference in Dallas.
Sarah Dessen, *That Summer*, 1996
It's bad enough that her father plans to remarry, but Haven's also stuck working this summer at a kid's shoe store at the mall.
Richard Peck, *Secrets of the Shopping Mall*, 1979
Staying well hidden, two eighth graders spend the night at the shopping mall where they discover inhabitants who "come to life" when the shoppers leave.

439

ELENA YATES EULO

Mixed-Up Doubles

(New York: Holiday House, 2003)

Subject(s): Sports/Tennis; Divorce; Friendship
Age range(s): Grades 6-9
Major character(s): Sarah, Child; Jerome ''Jerry'', 12th Grader, Tennis Player; Hank, 9th Grader, Tennis Player; Tremont ''Monty'' Singer, 9th Grader
Time period(s): 2000s
Locale(s): Alamar, California

Summary: After their parents divorce, Hank, Jerome and Sarah live with their father while their mother continues as a tennis coach, having chosen her profession over her family. Sarah is sad, Jerome gives up his promising tennis start, and Hank braces himself for his geeky, next-door neighbor Tremont's friendship. However Tremont, who now wishes to be known as Monty, becomes an asset to Hank with his academic help and tennis prodding. Though Hank's scheme to reunite his parents in a mixed doubles tennis match fails, he and Jeremy are triumphant in their club's doubles tournament. (185 pages)

Where it's reviewed:
Booklist, May 15, 2003, page 1654
Bulletin of the Center for Children's Books, July 2003, page 446
Publishers Weekly, April 14, 2003, page 71
School Library Journal, July 2003, page 129
Voice of Youth Advocates, June 2003, page 128

Other books by the same author:
Southern Woman, 1993 (adult fiction)

Other books you might like:
Robert Lehrman, *Separations*, 1990
    Her parents divorce and Kim is left in a new city with a new tennis coach, one who doesn't see eye-to-eye with her father.
Gretchen Olson, *Joyride*, 1998
    After a summer working rather than playing tennis, Jeff finds a new group of friends who prove to be warm and caring.
Randy Powell, *The Whistling Toilets*, 1996
    When the game of nationally ranked tennis champion Ginny falls apart, she returns home to work with her friend Stan to regain her focus.

F

IAN FALCONER, Author/Illustrator

Olivia Counts

(New York: Atheneum Books for Young Readers/Simon and Schuster, 2002)

Subject(s): Animals/Pigs; Toys; Mathematics
Age range(s): Preschool
Major character(s): Olivia, Pig
Time period(s): Indeterminate
Locale(s): Fictional Country

Summary: Olivia proudly displays her knowledge of the numbers one to ten in this board book. Beginning by holding one beach ball, then showing off the two red bows tied to her ears, Olivia continues by pondering three pots of paint and introducing four aunts and eight cousins. Her seven accessories are in her trademark red. Olivia carries five books, sports a paper bag mask with six teeth, shows off nine toys and concludes with ten Olivias doing ten different activities. (14 pages)

Where it's reviewed:
Booklist, July 2002, page 1857
Bulletin of the Center for Children's Books, June 2002, page 362
Horn Book Guide, Fall 2002, page 300
Publishers Weekly, May 5, 2002, page 60
School Library Journal, June 2002, page 94

Awards the book has won:
Parenting's Books of the Year, 2002

Other books by the same author:
Olivia's Opposites, 2002
Olivia Saves the Circus, 2001 (School Library Journal Best Books)
Olivia, 2000 (Caldecott Honor Book)

Other books you might like:
John Burningham, *Numbers*, 2003
  In a board book rendition of a title originally published in 1985, children climb a tree individually to demonstrate the numbers one to ten.

Martin Kelly, *Five Green and Speckled Frogs*, 2000
  Five bug-eating frogs on a speckled log leap into the water until none remain in this board book illustration of a familiar child's song.
Lynn Reiser, *Ten Puppies*, 2003
  Any way these ten puppies are sorted, they still total ten cute bundles of fur.

IAN FALCONER, Author/Illustrator

Olivia . . . and the Missing Toy

(New York: Anne Schwartz Book/Atheneum Books for Young Readers, 2003)

Subject(s): Lost and Found; Animals/Pigs; Toys
Age range(s): Grades K-3
Major character(s): Olivia, Pig, Sister (oldest); Perry, Dog; Daddy, Pig, Father; Mommy, Pig, Mother
Time period(s): Indeterminate
Locale(s): Fictional Country

Summary: Poor Olivia! Her absolutely best ever, favorite toy is missing. Olivia knows she put it on her bed while reading a book, but now it's gone. She searches everywhere and, when she can't find it, accuses her little brothers of taking it. Then, during an evening storm, while practicing the piano, Olivia hears a strange sound. Following the sound she enters a room and, alas, she discovers the true culprit. Perry has taken her stuffed animal toy and chewed it into many pieces. Mommy tells her not to worry, Daddy promises to buy her a new toy and Olivia dries her tears before taking needle and thread to repair the toy until she's satisfied that it's better than ever. Then Olivia settles down with Mommy for bedtime stories about cats. (36 pages)

Where it's reviewed:
Booklist, September 1, 2003, page 122
Bulletin of the Center for Children's Books, December 2003, page 150
Horn Book, January 2004, page 69
School Library Journal, October 2003, page 118

Awards the book has won:
Publishers Weekly Best Children's Books, 2003
IRA Children's Choices, 2004

Other books by the same author:
Olivia Saves the Circus, 2001 (School Library Journal Best Books)
Olivia, 2000 (Caldecott Honor Book)

Other books you might like:
Emma Chichester Clark, *Where Are You, Blue Kangaroo?*, 2001
After a week of being forgotten by Lily atop a slide in the park, on the bus, and at the zoo, Blue Kangaroo hides rather than risk a trip to the beach.
Jules Feiffer, *I Lost My Bear*, 1998
A little girl who loses her favorite bear gets very little help from her family with her search for it.
Marie-Louise Fitzpatrick, *Lizzy and Skunk*, 2000
When Skunk becomes lost Lizzy has to conquer her fears in order to find her treasured puppet.

442

ELIZABETH FAMA

Overboard

(Chicago: Cricket books, 2002)

Subject(s): Survival; Shipwrecks; Muslims
Age range(s): Grades 5-8
Major character(s): Emily Slake, 14-Year-Old; Isman, Child
Time period(s): 2000s
Locale(s): Banda Aceh, Indonesia (island of Sumatra); At Sea (adrift in the Indian Ocean)

Summary: Accompanying her parents to Sumatra in their work for World Physicians for Children, Emily helps in their clinic by changing sheets or cleaning up. Tired of living overseas and wishing only to return to Boston to complete her school year, Emily decides to meet her vacationing Uncle Matt on the neighboring island of Weh. Hoping she can return home with him, she clambers aboard the overloaded ferry. Listing before it even leaves the dock, the ferry sinks midway through the voyage and Emily is tumbled out in the ocean. Staying clear of drowning passengers and an overloaded raft, she spends the next seventeen hours in the sea concentrating on staying afloat. Sometime during the night she and the child Isman meet up. Emily's strength and survival skill, coupled with Isman's faith in Allah, keeps them both alive in this first novel, which is based on a true incident. (158 pages)

Where it's reviewed:
Booklist, July 2002, page 1844
Bulletin of the Center for Children's Books, June 2002, page 362
Kliatt, July 2002, page 9
Publishers Weekly, May 13, 2002, page 71
School Library Journal, July 2002, page 119

Awards the book has won:
ALA Best Books for Young Adults, 2003
Center for Children's Books Best Books, 2002

Other books you might like:
Hilary Hyland, *The Wreck of the Ethie*, 1999
The passengers on board the *SSEthie* are rescued when a dog swims out with a cable for their life-saving breeches buoy.
Gary Paulsen, *Hatchet*, 1987
Enroute to visit his father, Brian's plane crashes in the Canadian Northwoods; as the sole survivor, he relies on his hatchet to stay alive.
Theodore Taylor, *The Cay*, 1969
Timothy, an old black sailor, is shipwrecked on a coral island with spoiled, blind Phillip, a young white boy.

443

TERRY FARISH
BARRY ROOT, Illustrator

The Cat Who Liked Potato Soup

(Cambridge, MA: Candlewick Press, 2003)

Subject(s): Animals/Cats; Pets; Friendship
Age range(s): Grades 1-3
Major character(s): Unnamed Character, Aged Person, Fisherman; Unnamed Character, Cat
Time period(s): Indeterminate Past
Locale(s): Texas

Summary: The old man isn't one to let on that he's actually fond of a worthless old cat, but he does enjoy a conversation with his pet now and then especially since the cat is at least wise enough to be fond of his potato soup. Together they fish, but the cat never catches anything and the man doesn't catch much worth keeping either. One morning the cat doesn't want to rise from the new electric blanket and the impatient man goes off without her. After a miserable fishing trip, the man arrives home to find the cat missing. She slipped out when she awakened to an empty house and stays gone for a few days. One day the man arrives home to find her on the porch angrily guarding a large fish and howling the story of how she's caught it. A fresh pot of potato soup begins to heal the rift between them and there's hope the two might just feel a tad more respect for each other in the future. (36 pages)

Where it's reviewed:
Booklist, April 15, 2003, page 1477
Bulletin of the Center for Children's Books, June 2003, page 387
Horn Book Guide, Fall 2003, page 322
Publishers Weekly, May 5, 2003, page 221
School Library Journal, July 2003, page 95

Awards the book has won:
Bulletin of the Center for Children's Books Blue Ribbons, 2003
Center for Children's Books Best Books, 2003

Other books you might like:
Jennifer Armstrong, *Chin Yu Min and the Ginger Cat*, 1993
A ginger cat changes the fortunes of a haughty widow and teaches her the value of companionship over wealth.
Robert J. Blake, *Dog*, 1994
Initially, an elderly man rebuffs a dog's attempts to make a

home with him, but the man eventually reconsiders and accepts Dog as a pet.

Minna Jung, *William's Ninth Life*, 1993

For his ninth life William is offered many choices but he remains with elderly Elizabeth.

Cynthia Rylant, *Mr. Putter and Tabby Pour the Tea*, 1994

At an animal shelter, lonely Mr. Putter finds a lonely old cat with creaking bones and thinning fur—just the match for him!

444

NANCY FARMER

The House of the Scorpion
(New York: Atheneum, 2002)

Subject(s): Cloning; Growing Up

Age range(s): Grades 7-10

Major character(s): Matteo Alacran, Clone; Matteo ''El Patron'' Alacran, Drug Dealer; Tam Lin, Bodyguard; Celia, Cook; Maria, Friend

Time period(s): Indeterminate Future

Locale(s): Opium, Fictional Country (somewhere in Central America)

Summary: Young Matt lives a sheltered life, meeting no one and going nowhere. When he's very young, Matt is content, but as he gets older, his curiosity about his surroundings grows. The encounter he forces with Maria and some other children eventually leads to the terrifying truth about Matt: he is a clone. Treasured by the elderly El Patron, whose clone he is, Matt is feared and despised by others. Maria alternately likes and hates Matt, and Matt's existence is a series of ups and downs as he is tormented when El Patron is not looking and pampered when he is. The bodyguard Tam Lin is one of the few who treats Matt like a real person, but he insists on teaching him some survival skills Matt frankly doesn't think he needs. But when El Patron reveals his ultimate plan for Matt, running away suddenly seems like a very good idea. (380 pages)

Where it's reviewed:

Booklist, September 15, 2002, page 232

Bulletin of the Center for Children's Books, November 2002, page 104

Horn Book, November 2002, page 253

New York Times Book Review, November 17, 2002, page 39

Voice of Youth Advocates, October 2002, page 293

Awards the book has won:

ALA Best Books for Young Adults, 2003

National Book Award, Young People's Literature, 2002

Other books by the same author:

The Sea of Trolls, 2004

A Girl Named Disaster, 1996

The Ear, the Eye and the Arm: A Novel, 1994

Other books you might like:

Lois McMaster Bujold, *Mirror Dance*, 1994

Miles has known about his clone Mark for a long time, but he's never understood the pain that Mark undergoes to be shaped to match Miles in every way.

Eva Hoffman, *The Secret*, 2002

When Iris finally finds out why people have been staring at her and her mother, it precipitates an identity crisis.

William Sleator, *The Duplicate*, 1988

David's life becomes more complex after he finds a gadget on the beach that he uses to duplicate himself.

445

JAN FEARNLEY, Author/Illustrator

A Perfect Day for It
(San Diego: Harcourt, Inc., 2002)

Subject(s): Animals/Bears; Friendship; Winter

Age range(s): Preschool-Grade 1

Major character(s): Bear, Bear, Friend; Badger, Badger, Friend

Time period(s): 2000s (2002)

Locale(s): United States

Summary: When Bear heads up the mountain one winter morning, his friend Badger asks him why he's going. ''Because it's the perfect day for it,'' Bear responds. Thinking that ''it'' must be a secret stash of honeycomb, Badger follows. Soon other animals join the trek up the hill, each one thinking of a different adventure or treasure. At the top however, they all discover what Bear had in mind was some sledding and they spend an enjoyable and exhausting day doing just that. (32 pages)

Where it's reviewed:

Horn Book Guide, Spring 2003, page 33

School Library Journal, December 2002, page 95

Other books by the same author:

Watch Out!, 2004

Just Like You, 2001

Mr. Wolf's Pancakes, 2000

Other books you might like:

Jan Brett, *The Mitten*, 1989

When Nicki loses his white mitten in the snow it is inhabited by a series of successively larger woodland creatures.

Mary Calhoun, *Cross-Country Cat*, 1979

When Henry, a Siamese cat, gets left behind after a family vacation he heads off on his own to ski cross-country to his home.

Emily Arnold McCully, *First Snow*, 1987

After the first snow of the season, the Mouse family goes sledding.

446

JULES FEIFFER, Author/Illustrator

By the Side of the Road
(New York: Michael Di Capua Books/Hyperion Books for Children, 2002)

Subject(s): Family Life; Behavior; Parent and Child

Age range(s): Grades 3-5

Major character(s): Richard, Son, Brother (older); Rudy, Son, Brother (younger); Mom, Mother; Dad, Father

Time period(s): Indeterminate Past

Locale(s): United States; Seattle, Washington

Summary: Mom and Dad become so frustrated with Richard and Rudy's backseat fighting on a car trip that Dad threatens to leave Richard beside the road if he cannot behave. Richard calls his bluff, Dad stops the car, and Richard begins life by the side of the road. Too stubborn to give in to his equally stubborn father Richard grows up beside the road with support from his family who provide food, shelter and a tutor. When Richard is a teenager another teen takes up residence in a tunnel near him and later they marry and raise their family by the side of the road. The home becomes intergenerational when empty nesters Mom and Dad move in. For vacations they visit Rudy in Seattle where he lives underground in a technically-superior tunnel. (64 pages)

Where it's reviewed:
Booklist, June 2002, page 1742
Bulletin of the Center for Children's Books, September 2002, page 15
Publishers Weekly, May 13, 2002, page 69
Riverbank Review, Fall 2002, page 29
School Library Journal, May 2002, page 152

Other books by the same author:
Bark, George, 1999 (Booklist Editors' Choice)
I Lost My Bear, 1998 (ALA Notable Children's Books)
Meanwhile . . ., 1997

Other books you might like:
Stephen Gammell, *Ride*, 2001
   On an afternoon ride to nowhere the happy parents use sandwiches rather than threats to calm the commotion of sibling battles in the back seat.
William Steig, *Grown-Ups Get to Do All the Driving*, 1995
   From a child's viewpoint adults have many privileges.
James Stevenson, *Are We Almost There?*, 1985
   On a car trip fighting puppy brothers must learn to coexist or lose the opportunity to go to the beach.

447

JULES FEIFFER, Author/Illustrator

The House Across the Street

(New York: Michael di Capua/Hyperion Books for Children, 2002)

Subject(s): Fantasy; Neighbors and Neighborhoods; Imagination
Age range(s): Grades K-3
Major character(s): Unnamed Character, Child, Neighbor (imaginary); Unnamed Character, Child, Narrator
Time period(s): 2000s (2002)
Locale(s): United States

Summary: An unnamed narrator imagines living in the big house across the street where everything is better. He is sure that any boy living there would have everything he wants including four dogs, a pet shark, and a pool full of dolphins. He's convinced that in the house across the street a boy's parents would cater to his every whim and not require school attendance on rainy days. In short, life in the house across the street is the dream life of every boy (or at least our narrator). (32 pages)

Where it's reviewed:
Booklist, December 1, 2002, page 673
Bulletin of the Center for Children's Books, January 2003, page 197
Publishers Weekly, October 14, 2002, page 82
School Library Journal, February 2003, page 111

Other books by the same author:
By the Side of the Road, 2002
I'm Not Bobby!, 2001
I Lost My Bear, 1998

Other books you might like:
Chih-Yuan Chen, *On My Way to Buy Eggs*, 2003
   Shau-yu's active imagination makes her trip to the store an adventure.
Marie-Louise Fitzpatrick, *I'm a Tiger, Too!*, 2002
   A lonely boy tries to make believe with the animals near his house, becoming a tiger with a cat, a wolf with his dog, and a sailor with a fish.
Maurice Sendak, *The Sign on Rosie's Door*, 1960
   One day when Katie goes to play with her friend Rosie, she discovers an alter ego, a lovely lady singer named Alinda, who comes to play instead.

448

CAROL FENNER
AMANDA HARVEY, Illustrator

Snowed in with Grandmother Silk

(New York: Dial, 2003)

Subject(s): Grandparents; Weather; Self-Reliance
Age range(s): Grades 2-4
Major character(s): Ruddy, Child, Relative (grandson); Grandmother Silk, Grandmother
Time period(s): 2000s (2003)
Locale(s): Silver Lake

Summary: When Ruddy's parents go on an autumn cruise he must stay with his Grandmother Silk, who is very proper and not very much fun. The one thing Ruddy is looking forward to is going to a Halloween party at the Zoo, but on Halloween morning, Ruddy wakes up to find a snowstorm has blanketed Silver Lake. With no power and the roads closed off, thus keeping the cook and the handy man away, Grandmother Silk and Ruddy learn to fend for themselves and have a little fun in the process. (80 pages)

Where it's reviewed:
Booklist, December 15, 2003, page 352
Bulletin of the Center for Children's Books, November 2003, page 101
School Library Journal, November 2003, page 91

Awards the book has won:
Bulletin of the Center for Children's Books Blue Ribbons, 2003
ALA Notable Children's Books, 2004

Other books by the same author:
Yolonda's Genius, 1995 (Newbery Honor Book)
Randall's Wall, 1991
A Summer of Horses, 1989

Other books you might like:

Steven Kroll, *Patrick's Tree House*, 1994
> When Patrick heads to Maine to spend a week with his grandfather, he is happy to find a newly built tree house waiting for him.

Barbara Park, *Junie B. Jones Is a Party Animal*, 1997
> Junie is excited to visit her friend Lucille, who lives with her rich grandmother, but she finds the many rules to be no fun at all.

Jane Resh Thomas, *The Snoop*, 1999
> When Ellen spends the weekend at her grandmother's farmhouse, her grandmother warns her not to snoop.

449

EUGENIE FERNANDES
KIM FERNANDES, Illustrator

Busy Little Mouse

(Tonawanda, NY: Kids Can Press, 2002)

Subject(s): Animals/Mice; Animals; Bedtime
Age range(s): Preschool
Major character(s): Little Mouse, Mouse
Time period(s): Indeterminate
Locale(s): Fictional Country

Summary: In his overalls and clutching his hat busy Little Mouse runs out the door to play so fast that he bumps into a dog. The woofing dog is on his way to play with the oinking pig. One by one Little Mouse meets the animals of the farm and hears their sounds. The sheep is timid, the cow friendly and the cat happy. Little Mouse is simply busy galloping on the horse's back or splashing with the duck. By day's end, busy Little Mouse is tired and content to settle into bed with his toy farm animals for a good night's sleep. (24 pages)

Where it's reviewed:
Horn Book Guide, Fall 2002, page 301
Quill & Quire, Fall 2002, page 40
School Library Journal, August 2002, page 155

Awards the book has won:
IRA Children's Choices, 2003

Other books by the same author:
One More Pet, 2002
Ordinary Amos and the Amazing Fish, 2000
Baby Dreams, 1999

Other books you might like:

Jane Cowan-Fletcher, *Farmer Will*, 2001
> Will plays with his toy animals, pretending he is a farmer. At the end of a busy day, the animals join Will at bedtime.

Diana Hendry, *The Very Noisy Night*, 1999
> The night is filled with too many strange sounds and Little Mouse cannot sleep.

Kevin Henkes, *Wemberly Worried*, 2000
> Unlike carefree Little Mouse, Wemberly is a mouse that worries about everything, especially the first day of school.

Bethany Roberts, *A Mouse Told His Mother*, 1997
> A young mouse's plans do not include sleep but his creative mother's responses to each of his ideas allows the bedtime ritual to conclude happily.

450

ANTON FERREIRA

Zulu Dog

(New York: Frances Foster Books/Farrar Straus Giroux, 2002)

Subject(s): Animals/Dogs; Friendship; Race Relations
Age range(s): Grades 4-8
Major character(s): Vusi Ngugu, 11-Year-Old (Zulu); Shirley Montgomery, 12-Year-Old; Gillette, Dog
Time period(s): 2000s
Locale(s): Msinga, South Africa

Summary: Following a short overview of South African history, the reader is introduced to Vusi who lives with his poor Zulu family in a kraal, alongside wealthy white neighbors, in a post-apartheid South Africa. Vusi has two secrets, the first of which is his dog, named Gillette because his teeth remind Vusi of his father's sharp razor. Gillette is kept hidden for Vusi's mother hates dogs and can't be told until Gillette has proven himself in the hunt; though handicapped by the loss of one leg to a leopard, Gillette's superior tracking skills compensate. Vusi's other secret is that he's met and become friends with Shirley, the daughter of the white racist living near them. When Shirley's parents decide to send her to boarding school to prevent attending school with black students, she refuses and runs away into the bush. Vusi and Gillette find her just in time as she's turned her ankle and is being stalked by a leopard in this first novel that also shows the politics of South Africa. (193 pages)

Where it's reviewed:
Booklist, September 15, 2002, page 230
Horn Book, November 2002, page 754
Publishers Weekly, September 9, 2002, page 69
School Library Journal, September 2002, page 224
Voice of Youth Advocates, February 2003, page 473

Awards the book has won:
Smithsonian's Notable Books for Children/Older Readers, 2002

Other books you might like:

Marty Crisp, *Private Captain: A Novel of Gettysburg*, 2001
> When Ben can't find his brother Reuben at Gettysburg, he returns home but leaves Reuben's dog behind to search for him.

Natale Ghent, *Piper*, 2001
> Though it's unusual for a breeding farm to keep a runt, Aunt Cindy does; trained by Wesley, one day Piper defends the two of them against coyotes.

Sheila Gordon, *Waiting for the Rain*, 1987
> The truth of apartheid hits childhood friends Tengo and Frikkie. One is a white soldier, the other a black student trying to escape South Africa.

Hazel Rochman, *Somehow Tenderness Survives: Stories of Southern Africa*, 1988
> Growing up in South Africa under apartheid is captured in this collection of short stories and autobiographical sketches.

AMY SCHOR FERRIS

A Greater Goode

(New York: Houghton Mifflin, 2002)

Subject(s): Small Town Life; Pregnancy; Friendship
Age range(s): Grades 5-8
Major character(s): Addie Goode, 12-Year-Old; Luke, Friend (of Addie's), 12-Year-Old; Jessie, Housekeeper; Rachel Batalin, Runaway (pregnant)
Time period(s): 2000s
Locale(s): Lumberland, Pennsylvania

Summary: Addie just naturally tries to help people, even though her father warns her that often times people want to be left alone. One day she and her good friend Luke come upon Rachel, a pregnant woman with an abusive boyfriend; sensing she needs help, Addie feeds, clothes and offers her shelter in their unused barn. Eventually Addie decides Rachel reminds her too much of her own mother, who abandoned her years ago, and sends her on her way. But Addie's life is about to change as her father plans to remarry; her friend Luke, who's very smart, is off to Princeton for a special camp over the summer; and Addie locates Rachel's parents. Soon she, Luke, her housekeeper Jessie and many other members of the community become involved in searching for Rachel as they try to achieve a "greater Goode" in this fetching first novel. (183 pages)

Where it's reviewed:
Book Report, November 2002, page 46
Booklist, June 2002, page 1706
Publishers Weekly, April 1, 2002, page 83
School Library Journal, April 2002, page 148
Voice of Youth Advocates, June 2002, page 117

Other books you might like:
John Armistead, *The $66 Summer*, 2000
    George's sense of fairness overrides his need to keep his summer earnings and he gives his money to Esther so she can attend high school.
Kimberly Willis Holt, *When Zachary Beaver Came to Town*, 1999
    Abandoned by his manager, obese Zachary is befriended by Toby and Cal who learn that everyone deserves sympathy and respect.
Sylvia Hossack, *Green Mango Magic*, 1998
    Maile discovers "ho'oponopono," or "making everything right," as she feeds her new friend Brooke a healthy diet of poi to strengthen her after chemotherapy.

452

JEAN FERRIS

Once Upon a Marigold

(San Diego: Harcourt, 2002)

Subject(s): Fairy Tales; Humor; Princes and Princesses
Age range(s): Grades 6-10
Major character(s): Christian, 17-Year-Old, Servant; Edric, Mythical Creature (troll); Marigold, Royalty (princess); Swithbert, Royalty (king); Olympia, Royalty (queen)
Time period(s): Indeterminate Past
Locale(s): Fictional Country

Summary: Running away to the forest when he's just a lad, Christian is found and taken Edric, where he enjoys a happy life with the troll and his two dogs and devotes some of his time to tinkering with his inventions. One day when he's in his teens he spots Princess Marigold through his telescope and is instantly smitten. Once again he leaves home, only this time he travels to the castle where he takes a job as a servant just to see Princess Marigold. Unfortunately she's betrothed to a most unsuitable candidate, which is almost a moot point as her wicked mother Queen Olympia wants to dispose of both Marigold and her father King Swithbert and claim the throne for herself. A jealous guard throws Christian into the dungeon where he uses the time to build an airplane and escapes just in time to save Princess Marigold from her potentially wretched marriage. The queen drowns in the river, Christian marries Marigold and everyone lives happily ever after. (266 pages)

Where it's reviewed:
Booklist, September 15, 2002, page 226
Horn Book, September 2002, page 571
Publishers Weekly, October 28, 2002, page 72
School Library Journal, November 2002, page 164
Voice of Youth Advocates, December 2002, page 396

Awards the book has won:
Smithsonian's Notable Books for Children/Older Readers, 2002
ALA Best Books for Young Adults, 2003

Other books by the same author:
Of Sound Mind, 2001
Eight Seconds, 2000
Love Among the Walnuts, 1998
All That Glitters, 1996
Across the Grain, 1990

Other books you might like:
E.D. Baker, *The Frog Princess*, 2002
    When Princess Emeralda kisses the proverbial frog, she becomes one and now the two frogs search for a witch to remove the frog spells.
William Goldman, *The Princess Bride*, 1987
    This humorous adventure stars a perfect hero and a beautiful heroine, complete with princes and daring friends.
Patrice Kindl, *Goose Chase*, 2001
    A tart-tongued goose girl is determined to save her beloved geese no matter how many kings or princes want to marry her.
Donna Jo Napoli, *Spinners*, 1999
    In this replay of the fairy tale, Rumplestiltskin doesn't realize that this time he loses to his daughter.

453

JASPER FFORDE

The Eyre Affair: A Novel
(New York: Viking, 2002)

Subject(s): Detection; Literature; Alternate History
Age range(s): Grades 10-Adult
Major character(s): Thursday Next, Detective; Acheron Hades, Criminal; Landen Parke-Laine, Writer
Time period(s): 1980s (1985)
Locale(s): England

Summary: The English are still fighting the Russians in the Crimean, airships are the common means of long distance travel and Special Operations includes the LiteraTecs, those agents assigned to protect the integrity of literature. Thursday Next is one of those agents, and when the original manuscript of *Martin Chuzzlewit* is stolen, it's obvious that serious consequences could follow. Thursday is assigned to the case and begins chasing the third most dangerous criminal in the world, Acheron Hades, whom she suspects of the villainy. With Hades disappearing constantly, her time traveling father popping in and out and stopping time, literally, Thursday has her hands full. But an invention that lets Thursday chase Hades into *Jane Eyre* really upsets things. Thursday will be hard-pressed to find a time and place to tell that abominable Landen Parke-Laine exactly what she thinks of him. (374 pages)

Where it's reviewed:
New York Times Book Review, February 12, 2002, page E8
Publishers Weekly, March 4, 2002, page 41
School Library Journal, October 2002, page 196
Voice of Youth Advocates, December 2002, page 339
Wall Street Journal, February 12, 2002, page A20

Other books by the same author:
Something Rotten, 2004
The Well of Lost Plots, 2003
Lost in a Good Book, 2002

Other books you might like:
Douglas Adams, *The Hitchhiker's Guide to the Galaxy*, 1979
    Even crazier than Thursday's manic world is the universe of poor Arthur, who wakes up to discover his planet has been slated for demolition.
Charlotte Bronte, *Jane Eyre*, 1987
    Thursday is more fun for those who are familiar with the background of this classic tale of love and gothic suspense.
Peter David, *Sir Apropos of Nothing*, 2001
    Knowing literary conventions lead to laughter as Apropos insists on turning them all on their heads, with panache and a bitter humor.

454

JASPER FFORDE

Lost in a Good Book
(New York: Penguin Putnam, 2002)

Subject(s): Literature; Alternate History; Detection
Age range(s): Grades 10-Adult
Major character(s): Thursday Next, Detective, Spouse; Landen Parke-Laine, Writer, Spouse; Miss Havisham, Teacher
Time period(s): 1980s (1985)
Locale(s): England

Summary: Now blissfully married to Landen, Thursday hopes that the publicity surrounding her happy-ending change to *Jane Eyre* will soon be over so that she and Landen can spend more time together. But Thursday's actions in the old case have exposed the Goliath Corporation, and they want to see Thursday back down, something at which Thursday is decidedly not good. After all, she stranded one of Goliath's people in *The Raven* when he got in her way. Determined to get the best of Thursday, Goliath erases Landen by letting him die in childhood, a simple trick for time travelers. Thursday is distraught but somehow, Goliath has contrived to preserve her memories. They offer to reverse the process, if Thursday will only retrieve their lost operative. Alas, the machine that allowed Thursday access to *Jane Eyre* is no more. Undeterred, Thursday turns to book hopping as her next resource. When she finally makes contact with Jurisfiction, the organization of book-hoppers, she is assigned a teacher, the redoubtable Miss Havisham of *Great Expectations*. (416 pages)

Where it's reviewed:
Kirkus Reviews, February 1, 2003, page 161
Kliatt, September 2003, page 54
Library Journal, March 15, 2003, page 114
Publishers Weekly, February 24, 2003, page 53
School Library Journal, June 2003, page 175

Other books by the same author:
Something Rotten, 2004
The Well of Lost Plots, 2003
The Eyre Affair: A Novel, 2001

Other books you might like:
Kage Baker, *Black Projects, White Knights: The Company Dossiers*, 2002
    The Company's time traveling operatives trap Shakespeare in a theme park and visit an ailing Robert Louis Stevenson to try and wrangle a movie script.
Max Barry, *Jennifer Government*, 2003
    Jennifer, a government agent in a near-future world, is out to get the nefarious John Nike in this satire on commercialism
Charles Dickens, *Great Expectations*, 1964
    Read about a different Miss Havisham, the embittered, jolted bride in this classic, and enjoy her character more in *Lost in a Good Book*.

455

ANNE FINE
PENNY DALE, Illustrator

The Jamie and Angus Stories
(Cambridge, MA: Candlewick Press, 2002)

Subject(s): Toys; Family Life; Imagination
Age range(s): Grades 1-3
Major character(s): Jamie, Child, Son; Angus, Bull, Toy (stuffed animal)

Time period(s): 2000s
Locale(s): England

Summary: Six stories tell of the relationship between Jamie and Angus from the moment Jamie first spots the toy bull in a shop window. Jamie discovers the importance of ''dry clean only'' tags when a very dirty Angus is washed in the machine. Jamie overcomes his initial horror to love the bedraggled Angus too. Together Jamie and Angus attend the babysitter's wedding, go to the hospital and listen to family stories. It's a perfect relationship. (110 pages)

Where it's reviewed:
Booklist, November 15, 2002, page 609
Bulletin of the Center for Children's Books, October 2002, page 55
Horn Book, January 2003, page 71
Publishers Weekly, July 29, 2002, page 72
School Library Journal, September 2002, page 190

Awards the book has won:
Center for Children's Books Best Books, 2002
Boston Globe-Horn Book Award, Fiction, 2003

Other books by the same author:
The True Story of Christmas, 2003
Up on Cloud Nine, 2002
The Chicken Gave It to Me, 1993

Other books you might like:
Ann Cameron, *More Stories Julian Tells*, 1986
    Julian describes typical childhood activities in this award-winning sequel to *The Stories Julian Tells*.
A.A. Milne, *Winnie the Pooh*, 1926
    Christopher Robin and his stuffed bear, Winnie the Pooh, share humorous adventures and daring feats in the Hundred Acre Wood.
Philippa Pearce, *Here Comes Tod!*, 1994
    Six adventures showcase the everyday activities of curious, imaginative, sometimes outspoken Tod.

456

CAROLYN FISHER, Author/Illustrator

A Twisted Tale

(New York: Alfred A. Knopf, 2002)

Subject(s): Animals; Weather; Humor
Age range(s): Grades K-3
Major character(s): Bailey Tarbell, Farmer, Daughter; Ma, Mother, Farmer; Pa, Father, Farmer
Time period(s): 2000s
Locale(s): Tornado Alley

Summary: The aftermath of a tornado at the Tarbell farm includes something odd about the animals' behavior. Apparently, as the twister spun them in the air, the characteristics of the animals became mixed. Now the cow says cluck and sits on a nest in the chicken coop. The pigs quack and live in the pond while the chickens wallow in the mud. Ma and Pa call the vet, but his solutions don't cure anything so Bailey tries to figure out how to solve this problem. Several ideas fail, but when Bailey convinces Ma and Pa to load up the animals and drive to a carnival it seems she's found a solution. After a ride on the ''Twister,'' the animals seem dazed, but

they're making the right sounds. Bailey, however, seems a bit twisted from the experience. (38 pages)

Where it's reviewed:
Bulletin of the Center for Children's Books, July 2002, page 401
Publishers Weekly, April 8, 2002, page 227
School Library Journal, June 2002, page 94

Other books you might like:
Darleen Bailey Beard, *Twister*, 1999
    Protected in a cellar, frightened siblings endure the terror of a tornado passing over while their mom tries to help a neighbor.
Stella Blackstone, *There's a Cow in the Cabbage Patch*, 2001
    What should the farmer do when he discovers that all the animals are in the wrong place?
Sharon Darrow, *Old Thunder and Miss Raney*, 2000
    Miss Raney and her horse Old Thunder are swept up by a tornado with unexpected results.
Phyllis Root, *One Windy Wednesday*, 1997
    One Wednesday on the farm the wind is so strong that the sound blows from one animal to another making the cows oink and the ducks moo.

457

VALERIE FISHER, Author/Illustrator

My Big Brother

(New York: Anne Schwartz Book/Atheneum Books for Young Readers, 2002)

Subject(s): Brothers; Babies; Love
Age range(s): Preschool-Kindergarten
Major character(s): Unnamed Character, Brother (older), Child; Unnamed Character, Baby, Narrator
Time period(s): 2000s (2002)
Locale(s): United States

Summary: From the perspective of a baby crawling on the floor, a big brother is really, really big. His actions also reflect larger-than-life importance in the narrator's opinion. Despite his important responsibilities this big brother finds time to play with and help feed his young sibling. It's clear from the photographs that the big brother does not appreciate the baby's effort to return the favor. Still, it's clear that the feelings of affection are mutual. The author's children inspired her first picture book. (36 pages)

Where it's reviewed:
Booklist, September 15, 2002, page 239
Bulletin of the Center for Children's Books, July 2002, page 402
Publishers Weekly, May 20, 2002, page 64
School Library Journal, July 2002, page 90

Other books you might like:
Joanna Cole, *I'm a Big Brother*, 1997
    A big brother proudly explains all about new babies and how he can help care for the one at his house.
William H. Hooks, *Mr. Big Brother*, 1999
    Eli looks forward to being ''Mr. Big Brother,'' but he doesn't anticipate that the baby will be a sister.

Harriet Ziefert, *Talk, Baby!*, 1999

Max waits more than a year for his sister to grow enough to play with and talk to him. Finally she says her first word and he's sure it's his name.

458

SHARON G. FLAKE

Begging for Change
(New York: Hyperion/Jump at the Sun, 2003)

Subject(s): African Americans; Poverty; Fathers and Daughters
Age range(s): Grades 7-10
Major character(s): Raspberry Hill, 14-Year-Old; Zora Mitchell, Friend (of Raspberry's); Mai Kim, Friend (of Raspberry's)
Time period(s): 2000s
Locale(s): United States

Summary: Raspberry's concern about money hasn't changed since her introduction in *Money Hungry*. She still looks for work, often going door-to-door in her neighborhood to seek odd jobs, always worried that she and her mother will once again be homeless. When her mother is hit over the head with a lead pipe and hospitalized, Raspberry's concerns increase and she even steals money from her wealthy best friend Zora just because she thinks she deserves it. This act, and her no-count, drug addict father's stealing from Raspberry and her mother, makes Raspberry worry that she's like him. Worry about her mother, her biracial friend Mai who tattoos "100% black" on her arm, finances, and stealing from friends and neighbors forces Raspberry to rethink some of her ways. (235 pages)

Where it's reviewed:
Booklist, August 2003, page 1980
Bulletin of the Center for Children's Books, July 2003, page 446
Library Media Connection, August 2003, page 79
School Library Journal, July 2003, page 129
Voice of Youth Advocates, June 2003, page 129

Awards the book has won:
ALA Quick Picks for Reluctant Young Adult Readers, 2004
Bulletin of the Center for Children's Books Blue Ribbons, 2003

Other books by the same author:
Money Hungry, 2001 (Coretta Scott King Honor Book)
The Skin I'm In, 1998 (ALA Best Books for Young Adults)

Other books you might like:
Janet McDonald, *Spellbound*, 2001
After becoming pregnant, Raven tries to win a college scholarship through a spelling contest.
Virginia Euwer Wolff, *True Believer*, 2001
Though facing poverty and violence every day in her inner city neighborhood, LaVaughn keeps her attention on college.
Sharon Dennis Wyeth, *A Piece of Heaven*, 2001
Her brother's in jail for stealing, her mother's in the hospital for depression and Haley's only peace comes from working in Jackson's back yard.

459

PAUL FLEISCHMAN
BAGRAM IBATOULLINE, Illustrator

The Animal Hedge
(Cambridge, MA: Candlewick Press, 2003)

Subject(s): Farm Life; Drought; Animals
Age range(s): Grades K-3
Major character(s): Unnamed Character, Farmer, Father
Time period(s): 19th century
Locale(s): United States

Summary: A farmer who lives with his three young sons loves nothing more than to care for his animals. However, when a drought strikes the land, the farmer is forced to sell his farm and move the family to a cottage surrounded by a hedge. While trimming the hedge one day, the farmer begins to see animal shapes in it and trims the hedge to fit them. When the boys become old enough to learn a trade he tells them to carve the hedge into whatever shape they see and that will tell them what to be. (48 pages)

Where it's reviewed:
Booklist, September 15, 2003, page 244
Bulletin of the Center for Children's Books, November 2003, page 102
Publishers Weekly, September 8, 2003, page 76
School Library Journal, October 2003, page 119

Awards the book has won:
Publishers Weekly Best Children's Books, 2003

Other books by the same author:
Weslandia, 1999 (ALA Notable Children's Books)
Dateline: Troy, 1996 (ALA Best Book for Young Adults)
Joyful Noise: Poems for Two Voices, 1988 (Newbery Medal winner)

Other books you might like:
Valerie Coursen, *Mordant's Wish*, 1997
Mordant the Mole wishes that a turtle-shaped cloud would become real.
Elizabeth Friedrich, *Leah's Pony*, 1996
To save her family's farm, threatened by Dust Bowl conditions, Leah sells her beloved pony and bids on her father's tractor.
David Small, *George Washington's Cows*, 1994
Demands of George Washington's livestock supposedly lead him to try politics.

460

PAUL FLEISCHMAN

Breakout
(Chicago: Cricket Books/Marcato, 2003)

Subject(s): Runaways; Self-Perception; Traffic Accidents
Age range(s): Grades 9-12
Major character(s): Audelia "Del" Thigpen, 17-Year-Old; Elena Franco, Writer (playwright)
Time period(s): 1990s; 2000s
Locale(s): Los Angeles, California

Summary: Tired of the endless stream of foster homes she's occupied, Del fakes her own death and then takes off for Taos in an old car she's secretly bought. Unfortunately she doesn't even make it out of town before being trapped in a daylong traffic jam. Using the time to clean her car and make it homey, she observes her neighbors and, uncharacteristically, even talks to some of them. Eight years go by and Del is now Elena Franco, a successful playwright, who turns the traffic jam experience into a one-woman play using her maturity as a filter for that memorable day. (124 pages)

Where it's reviewed:
Bulletin of the Center for Children's Books, October 2003, page 58
Horn Book, November 2003, page 743
Publishers Weekly, July 28, 2003, page 96
School Library Journal, September 2003, page 209

Other books by the same author:
Seek, 2003
Mind's Eye, 2001
Bull Run, 1993
Joyful Noise: Poems for Two Voices, 1988
Graven Images, 1982

Other books you might like:
Julie Johnston, *Adam and Eve and Pinch-Me*, 1994
    Sara arrives at her latest foster home determined to stay detached, but the eccentric, unique Huddlestons refuse to comply with her plan.
Paul Many, *My Life, Take Two*, 2000
    Shooting a film documentary that turns into an award-winner helps Neal grieve for his deceased father and allows him to meet free-spirit Claire.
Matthew Olshan, *Finn: A Novel*, 2001
    When her crazy mother tries to kidnap her, Chloe fakes her death and heads to California with her grandparent's pregnant maid.

461

SID FLEISCHMAN

Disappearing Act

(New York: Greenwillow/HarperCollins, 2003)

Subject(s): Brothers and Sisters; Humor; Stalking
Age range(s): Grades 5-8
Major character(s): Kevin Kidd, 12-Year-Old; Holly Kidd, Sister, Singer; The Toad, Criminal (stalker)
Time period(s): 2000s
Locale(s): Albuquerque, New Mexico; Venice Beach, California

Summary: With no sign of their archaeologist mother after an earthquake destroys her expedition's camp, and realization that a stalker has burglarized their home, Kevin and his older sister Holly flee, landing in Venice Beach. Kevin and Holly hide in the open by calling themselves Pepe and Chickadee Gomez and finding jobs on the Boardwalk, surrounded by all the movie star wannabes. Kevin helps a watermelon juggling med student and tells fortunes with a borrowed crystal ball while Holly sings her beloved opera. Landing the lead in a local operatic production, her opening night becomes chaotic when the mysterious stalker appears with a gun in a rollicking adventure. (144 pages)

Where it's reviewed:
Booklist, June 2003, page 1774
Bulletin of the Center for Children's Books, June 2003, page 399
Horn Book, May 2003, page 345
School Library Journal, May 2003, page 150
Voice of Youth Advocates, August 2003, page 223

Other books by the same author:
The Giant Rat of Sumatra, or, Pirates Galore, 2005
The Midnight Horse, 1990
The Whipping Boy, 1986

Other books you might like:
Peg Kehret, *I'm Not Who You Think I Am*, 1999
    When she's only 13, Ginger is stalked by mentally ill Mrs. Enderly who claims to be her mother.
Jane Kendall, *Miranda Goes to Hollywood: Adventures in the Land of Palm Trees, Cowboys and Moving Pictures*, 1999
    When Miranda and her Aunt Lucy travel to Hollywood for Miranda to appear in a movie, they discover the project hasn't materialized.
Ron Koertge, *The Harmony Arms*, 1992
    Gabriel and his father spend a summer in Los Angeles while his father adapts his children's picture book for television.

462

CANDACE FLEMING
STACEY DRESSEN-MCQUEEN, Illustrator

Boxes for Katje

(New York: Melanie Kroupa Books/Farrar Straus Giroux, 2003)

Subject(s): World War II; Letters; Sharing
Age range(s): Grades 1-4
Major character(s): Katje Van Stegeran, Child (Dutch), Friend; Rosie Johnson, Child (American), Friend
Time period(s): 1940s (1945-1947)
Locale(s): Olst, Netherlands; Mayfield, Indiana

Summary: As part of a Children's Aid Society project at the conclusion of World War II, Rosie sends a box of soap, socks and chocolate to Holland. The recipient, Katje, shares the chocolate with her mother and the postman and then writes Rosie to express her appreciation for the gift box. Each letter prompts Rosie to gather more needed items to mail to Katje. As the letter exchange continues and Rosie shares what she learns about Katje's village with her neighbors and friends, in same way that Katje is sharing the contents of the boxes, the collection truly becomes a community effort. Finally, in the midst of a harsh winter, Katje receives a shipment of multiple boxes as Rosie's hometown sends enough soap, chocolate, socks and food to help Katje's entire town. In the spring Katje sends Rosie a box of tulip bulbs from her yard to thank the American community for their generosity. A concluding author's note tells the factual basis for the story. (40 pages)

Where it's reviewed:
Booklist, September 1, 2003, page 128

Bulletin of the Center for Children's Books, October 2003, page 58
Horn Book, September 2003, page 596
Publishers Weekly, August 18, 2003, page 77
School Library Journal, September 2003, page 177

Awards the book has won:
Publishers Weekly Best Children's Books, 2003
IRA Children's Choices, 2004

Other books by the same author:
Smile, Lily!, 2004
Muncha! Muncha! Muncha!, 2002 (ALA Notable Children's Books)
Who Invited You?, 2001

Other books you might like:
Milly Lee, *Nim and the War Effort*, 1997
Nim participates in the school newspaper drive in support of the war effort to show that an American-born child of Chinese immigrants is truly American.
James Stevenson, *Don't You Know There's a War On?*, 1992
A nonfiction picture book presents the author's childhood recollections of life on the home front during World War II.
Valerie Tripp, *Meet Molly: An American Girl*, 1986
The first book in a series introduces Molly and the daily life and sacrifices of a family during the 1940s as war rages in Europe and the Pacific.

463

CANDACE FLEMING
G. BRIAN KARAS, Illustrator

Muncha! Muncha! Muncha!

(New York: An Anne Schwartz Book/Atheneum Books for Young Readers, 2002)

Subject(s): Animals/Rabbits; Gardens and Gardening; Problem Solving
Age range(s): Grades K-2
Major character(s): Mr. McGreely, Gardener
Time period(s): 2000s
Locale(s): United States

Summary: After years of dreaming about a garden Mr. McGreely finally plants one and eagerly awaits the opportunity to dine on his delicious produce. Every night three little bunnies visit Mr. McGreely's garden and every morning the frustrated gardener discovers only gnawed sprouts in place of vegetables. Daily he builds an increasingly larger and more impenetrable barrier to keep the bunnies out of his garden. Although Mr. McGreely finally succeeds in protecting his garden through the night it's obvious his troubles are not completely over. (32 pages)

Where it's reviewed:
Booklist, January 1, 2002, page 851
Bulletin of the Center for Children's Books, March 2002, page 239
Horn Book Guide, Fall 2002, page 327
Publishers Weekly, December 10, 2001, page 69
School Library Journal, February 2002, page 100

Awards the book has won:
ALA Notable Children's Books, 2003

Other books by the same author:
When Agnes Caws, 1999 (School Library Journal Best Book)
Westward Ho, Carlotta!, 1998
Gabriella's Song, 1997 (ALA Notable Children's Book)

Other books you might like:
Jane Cutler, *Mr. Carey's Garden*, 1996
Mr. Carey explains why he is so tolerant of the hungry snails in his garden.
Beatrix Potter, *The Tale of Peter Rabbit*, 1902
Mr. McGregor does not look kindly on curious Peter Rabbit's visit to his garden.
Janet Stevens, *Tops and Bottoms*, 1995
Industrious Hare is a gardening partner to slumbering Bear in a contemporary interpretation of a trickster tale.

464

DENISE FLEMING, Author/Illustrator

Alphabet under Construction

(New York: Henry Holt and Company, 2002)

Subject(s): Animals/Mice; Construction; Letters
Age range(s): Preschool-Grade 1
Major character(s): Mouse, Mouse
Time period(s): Indeterminate
Locale(s): Fictional Country

Summary: Eagerly Mouse begins a month-long project to make each letter of the alphabet. By airbrushing, buttoning, carving, dying and folding the project begins. Mouse's calendar indicates when he needs to buy tile or hanging wire as well as the letter to be completed on each date. After 26 days of work, Mouse has a lot to show for his effort as the entire alphabet unfolds at the end of the book. (32 pages)

Where it's reviewed:
Booklist, August 2002, page 1962
Bulletin of the Center for Children's Books, October 2002, page 56
Horn Book, September 2002, page 550
Publishers Weekly, June 24, 2002, page 54
School Library Journal, September 2002, page 190

Awards the book has won:
Booklist Editors' Choice, 2002
ALA Notable Children's Books, 2003

Other books by the same author:
Pumpkin Eye, 2001
The Everything Book, 2000
Mama Cat Has Three Kittens, 1998 (ALA Notable Chilren's Books)
In the Small, Small Pond, 1993 (Caldecott Honor Book)

Other books you might like:
Virginia Kroll, *Busy, Busy Mouse*, 2003
A rhyming story describes the nighttime activities of a very busy mouse.
Chris Raschka, *Talk to Me about the Alphabet*, 2003
An alphabet book with "A for Attitude" uses illustrations

and text to explore both the letters and sounds of the alphabet.

Laura Vaccaro Seeger, *The Hidden Alphabet*, 2003
Pictorial clues on die-cut flaps suggest the letters of the alphabet that will be found beneath.

Audrey Wood, *Alphabet Adventure*, 2001
When the lower case ''i'' trips and falls off a bridge while walking to school the other letters link together to save her.

465

DENISE FLEMING, Author/Illustrator

Buster

(New York: Henry Holt and Company, 2003)

Subject(s): Animals/Dogs; Animals/Cats; Pets
Age range(s): Grades K-2
Major character(s): Buster, Dog; Betty, Cat
Time period(s): 2000s
Locale(s): United States

Summary: Buster is a contented dog. He has a perfect dog life until the big box arrives. Buster hopes the box contains steak, cheese or sausage, but in fact it holds Betty. Poor Buster, he's afraid of cats. He tries ignoring Betty, hoping she'll go away, but it doesn't work. Betty obviously adores Buster . . . and his personalized bowls and his favorite tree and his sandpit and even the flap on the door that lets Buster go in and out. Buster runs away to a park, not one he's been to before and he has a perfect day until he realizes that he's lost. With no idea how to get home, Buster begins to feel a bit sad until he sees, in the distance, a ball of white fur, high in a tree, waving at him. By keeping an eye on Betty, Buster finds his way home to resume his life as a happy dog. (36 pages)

Where it's reviewed:
Booklist, September 2003, page 128
Bulletin of the Center for Children's Books, October 2003, page 59
Horn Book, September 2003, page 597
Publishers Weekly, July 14, 2003, page 75
School Library Journal, September 2003, page 178

Awards the book has won:
Publishers Weekly Best Children's Books, 2003
Center for Children's Books Best Books, 2003

Other books by the same author:
Pumpkin Eye, 2001
The Everything Book, 2000
Mama Cat Has Three Kittens, 1998 (ALA Notable Children's Books)
In the Small, Small Pond, 1993 (Caldecott Medal)

Other books you might like:
Paul Fehlner, *Dog and Cat*, 1990
An elderly dog and an overweight cat have learned to coexist peacefully.
Donald Hall, *I Am the Dog, I Am the Cat*, 1994
Poetically, a dog and a cat describe their separate interests.
Lyn Rossiter McFarland, *Widget*, 2001
A stray dog imitates cat behavior in order to be accepted into a home with six cats that don't like dogs.

Lydia Monks, *The Cat Barked?*, 1999
A cat considers the far better life that a dog appears to have and decides that she still prefers being a feline; the dog however might switch places.

466

VERLYN FLIEGER

Pig Tale

(New York: Hyperion, 2002)

Subject(s): Animals/Pigs; Mythology; Orphans
Age range(s): Grades 9-12
Major character(s): Mokie ''Little Pig-Girl'', Orphan; Apple, Pig
Time period(s): Indeterminate Past
Locale(s): Little Wicken, Fictional Country

Summary: Abandoned by her mother after birth, Mokie is taken in by the villagers of Little Wicken and allowed to remain only because of her affinity to animals, especially pigs. She becomes the pig herder and eventually a pig mistress when she cares for a little pig unwanted by its mother. Naming it Apple, she worries that it will become part of the pattern of her village whereby a pig is stoned each season to ensure a good harvest. Attacked and raped by villagers when she is 15, Mokie escapes into the forest where magical people who know her fate befriend her. Celtic mythology and imagery abound in this author's first novel as Mokie becomes part of the village pattern and goes on to a better world. (321 pages)

Where it's reviewed:
Booklist, November 15, 2002, page 590
Bulletin of the Center for Children's Books, January 2003, page 198
Publishers Weekly, November 11, 2002, page 65
School Library Journal, December 2002, page 137
Voice of Youth Advocates, February 2003, page 486

Other books by the same author:
A Question of Time: J.R.R. Tolkien's Road to Faerie, 1997 (adult nonfiction)
Splintered Light: Logos and Language in Tolkien's World, 1983 (adult nonfiction)

Other books you might like:
Karen Cushman, *The Midwife's Apprentice*, 1995
A nameless orphan calls herself Alyce and apprentices to the local midwife, though not without lots of teasing from the village children.
Shirley Jackson, *The Lottery*, 1948
This classic short story describes a small New England village that conducts a yearly lottery to choose one sacrificial victim to be stoned.
Robin McKinley, *Deerskin*, 1993
Forced to flee into the wilderness to escape her father's evil intentions, a princess is accompanied by her faithful dog, Ash.

467

ALEX FLINN

Breaking Point

(New York: HarperCollins, 2002)

Subject(s): Peer Pressure; Schools/High Schools; Friendship
Age range(s): Grades 7-10
Major character(s): Paul Richmond, 10th Grader; Charlie Goode, Tennis Player
Time period(s): 2000s
Locale(s): Miami, Florida

Summary: As a new scholarship student at ritzy Gate-Bricknell Christian, affordable only because his mother is a secretary there, Paul is ignored on good days and hassled and taunted on bad days. His isolation at school carries over to his home life as he turns to his computer to avoid his mother's clinging ways and his now-divorced father's lack of interest in him. Charlie Good is Mr. Popularity at school and takes a surprising interest in Paul, though only off school grounds. Desperate to be part of a group, Paul goes along with whatever Charlie wants and soon is vandalizing mailboxes, hacking into the school's computer system to change one of Charlie's grades and even looking up bomb-making information on the Internet. Paul is oblivious to the warning signs of being set up for one of Charlie's pranks, setting a bomb in a classroom. Who gets caught and who goes to jail? As you can imagine, it's not Mr. Popularity in this tale of peer pressure and wanting to belong. (241 pages)

Where it's reviewed:
Bulletin of the Center for Children's Books, June 2002, page 363
Kliatt, May 2002, page 9
Publishers Weekly, May 20, 2002, page 68
School Library Journal, May 2002, page 152
Voice of Youth Advocates, June 2002, page 117

Awards the book has won:
ALA Quick Picks for Reluctant Young Adult Readers, 2003

Other books by the same author:
Breathing Underwater, 2001

Other books you might like:
Gail Giles, *Shattering Glass*, 2002
  As the alpha male in his new school, Rob decides to transform nerdy Simon Glass, but underestimates Simon's deviousness.
Alice Hoffman, *The River King*, 2000
  August Pierce is too much of an individual for some of the boys at his elite prep school and an attempt to put him in his place turns to tragedy.
Patrick Redmond, *Something Dangerous*, 1999
  Feeling out of place, Jonathan is thrilled when befriended by Richard, unaware that he'll be used to unleash evil against other students.

468

ROBERT FLORCZAK, Author/Illustrator

Yikes!!!

(New York: Blue Sky Press/Scholastic, Inc., 2003)

Subject(s): Animals; Adventure and Adventurers; Imagination
Age range(s): Preschool-Kindergarten
Major character(s): Unnamed Character, Child
Time period(s): 2000s (2003)
Locale(s): Earth

Summary: A young child dressed as an ''alligator hunter-type'' explorer sets off on a worldwide adventure. He swings with orangutans, comes face-to-face with a gorilla, and nearly steps on a scorpion. In the end, the boy is shown napping outside his house with a ''Wild and Dangerous Animals of the World'' book. The wild animals are identified at the end of the book. This the first book that this illustrator has also written. (32 pages)

Where it's reviewed:
Booklist, November 15, 2003, page 600
Publishers Weekly, September 8, 2003, page 75

Awards the book has won:
IRA Children's Choices, 2004

Other books you might like:
Keith Baker, *Who Is the Beast?*, 1990
  As a tiger makes its way through the jungle, animals flee at the sight of the ''beast,'' which the tiger is surprised to learn is him!
Jonathan Emmett, *Through the Heart of the Jungle*, 2003
  In this cumulative tale, a spider eats a fly, starting a food chain that leads up to the King of the Jungle, the lion.
David McPhail, *Edward in the Jungle*, 2002
  Edward becomes so enthralled by his favorite book, *Tarzan*, that he soon finds himself part of the action.

469

MADELEINE FLOYD, Author/Illustrator

Captain's Purr

(San Diego: Harcourt, Inc., 2003)

Subject(s): Animals/Cats; Secrets; Romance
Age range(s): Grades K-2
Major character(s): Captain, Cat
Time period(s): 2000s (2003)
Locale(s): United Kingdom

Summary: By day, Captain, a pampered cat, leads a normal existence—napping, eating and grooming. At night, however, Captain heads down to the river and rows over to his sweetheart's house to visit. By dawn, Captain has returned home for a day of contented purring. (24 pages)

Where it's reviewed:
Booklist, September 1, 2003, page 128
Bulletin of the Center for Children's Books, November 2003, page 103
Publishers Weekly, October 6, 2003, page 82
School Library Journal, November 2003, page 92

Other books you might like:
Barbara Abercrombie, *Charlie Anderson*, 1990
  A cat lives with one family by day and another by night.
Lois Duncan, *I Walk at Night*, 2000
  A household pet becomes a feline adventurer at night.
Bruce Ingman, *A Night on the Tiles*, 1999
  Each night while his owner sleeps Lionel attends the Cat Academy, taking classes in sewing, mechanics and woodworking.
Ann M. Martin, *Leo the Magnificat*, 1996
  A cat wanders into a churchyard one morning and stays for twelve years.

470
ADRIAN FOGELIN

My Brother's Hero
(Atlanta: Peachtree, 2002)

Subject(s): Family Life; Vacations; Christmas
Age range(s): Grades 5-8
Major character(s): Ben Floyd, 13-Year-Old; Cody Floyd, Child; Mica Delano, 11-Year-Old; Dr. Robin Michael Delano, Scientist (Marine biologist)
Time period(s): 2000s
Locale(s): Islamorado, Florida (Florida Keys)

Summary: Unused to traveling, Ben is surprised but excited to hear that his family will spend Christmas in the Florida Keys, helping out at his uncle's marina. He thinks his trip is a real adventure until he meets Mica, daughter of an alcoholic marine biologist, who's spent her life aboard ships, island hopping and taking her classes via correspondence. At first Ben's a little jealous of Mica, as he sees his younger brother Cody become enamored of her, but gradually Ben softens, especially when Mica zips them all around the Keys in her little Zodiac. Though she seems like a show-off, it becomes obvious to Ben that she's only trying for her father's attention. Ben and Cody have a great vacation, but when it's time to return home, Ben looks forward to seeing his friends, especially Cass who's becoming very special to him. (200 pages)

Where it's reviewed:
Booklist, February 1, 2003, page 993
Horn Book Guide, Fall 2003, page 366
Library Media Connection, March 2003, page 73
School Library Journal, February 2003, page 141

Other books by the same author:
The Big Nothing, 2004
Sister Spider Knows All, 2003
Anna Casey's Place in the World, 2001
Crossing Jordan, 2000

Other books you might like:
Helen Cavanaugh, *Panther Glade*, 1993
  Bill learns to overcome many fears while staying in Florida and needs this strength when he's stranded overnight on an island.
Cynthia DeFelice, *Lostman's River*, 1994
  Guiding a photographer around a secret rookery in the Everglades, Tyler is astounded when Mr. Strawbridge begins shooting the birds.

Ellen Wittlinger, *Noticing Paradise*, 1995
  Set amidst the ecology of "orphaned tortoises" in the Galapagos Islands, two teens fall in love when they meet on an international expedition.

471
ADRIAN FOGELIN

Sister Spider Knows All
(Atlanta: Peachtree Publishers, 2003)

Subject(s): Grandmothers; Family Life; Business Enterprises
Age range(s): Grades 5-8
Major character(s): Roxanne Piermont, 7th Grader, 12-Year-Old; Marilyn "Mimi" Piermont, Grandmother; Helen Piermont, Mother; John Martin, Cousin; Lucy Everhart, Student—College
Time period(s): 2000s
Locale(s): Tallahassee, Florida

Summary: Roxanne, her grandmother Mimi and her cousin John Martin are a family whose dynamics are about to change for several reasons. First John Martin brings home a girlfriend who's unlike them, or anyone else they know, for she's thin, blonde, pretty and rich. Then her teachers asks her to write an essay about her mother, but Roxanne is unable to complete the assignment as her mother abandoned her when she was only three months old. Finding her mother's old diary offers Roxanne a chance to know her, though she discovers Helen's not a very nice person. The one piece of Roxanne's life that keeps her focused and feeling good about herself is "the show," the weekly flea market at which she and Mimi set up their wares to make a little bit extra to help with the bills. Roxanne is a natural born salesperson and makes many friends among the other flea market sellers. Eventually John Martin and Lucy sort out their differences; Mimi and Roxanne weather a tornado that temporarily wipes out the flea market; and Roxanne pieces together her mother's story so that she's able to accept Helen and still feel good about herself. (209 pages)

Where it's reviewed:
Booklist, December 15, 2003, page 746
Bulletin of the Center for Children's Books, February 2004, page 228
Kliatt, November 2003, page 5
Library Media Connection, February 2004, page 68
School Library Journal, December 2003, page 150

Other books by the same author:
My Brother's Hero, 2002
Anna Casey's Place in the World, 2001
Crossing Jordan, 2000

Other books you might like:
Nina Bawden, *Granny the Pag*, 1996
  Raised by her grandmother, Cat doesn't want to return to her parents and hires a lawyer to fight the custody battle.
Jack Gantos, *What Would Joey Do?*, 2002
  Joey discovers that all his family members need more help than he can give, including his beloved grandma who tells him to make a friend.

Gary Paulsen, *Alida's Song*, 1999
Once again his grandmother saves him from his drunken parents as she finds him a job on the farm where she's the cook.

472

DENNIS FOON

Skud

(Toronto: Groundwood Books, 2003)

Subject(s): Gangs; Sports/Hockey; Violence
Age range(s): Grades 9-12
Major character(s): Tommy, 12th Grader, Military Personnel (cadet); Andy, 12th Grader, Actor; Brad, 12th Grader; Shane, 12th Grader, Gang Member
Time period(s): 2000s
Locale(s): Vancouver, British Columbia, Canada

Summary: Four seniors have set their goals for life after high school. Tommy is an A-student and cadet who dreams of flight school and a career in the military. His best friend Brad has been pushed by his father to be an aggressive ice hockey player who aims for an NHL career. Andy wants to continue with his acting while Shane wishes to break free from his gang. Their lives intersect, and begin to fall apart, when Tommy sees his former girlfriend kiss Andy while the two are rehearsing a scene. A challenge to Andy to fight; intervention by Shane on Andy's behalf; Brad's loss of playing time on the hockey team and Tommy's rape of his ex-girlfriend contribute to the boys' downward spiral in a book marked by grittiness. (171 pages)

Where it's reviewed:
Kliatt, July 2003, page 10
Library Media Connection, November 2003, page 56
Quill & Quire, March 2003, page 51
School Library Journal, July 2003, page 130
Voice of Youth Advocates, August 2003, page 223

Other books by the same author:
Dirt Eaters, 2003
Double or Nothing, 2000
War, 1995
Mirror Game, 1992

Other books you might like:
Walter Dean Myers, *Monster*, 1999
Sixteen-year-old Steve narrates his trial from a jail cell, a trial held to establish his role in the murder of a Harlem drugstore owner.
Kristen D. Randle, *Breaking Rank*, 1999
Baby defies his gang, and Casey her place in the school's social scene, when they are in the same honors class.
Adam Rapp, *The Buffalo Tree*, 1997
Incarcerated in Hamstock Boys Center for stealing hood ornaments, Sura is the only white boy and faces a six-month sentence.
D. James Smith, *Fast Company*, 1999
An accidental murder, a failed pregnancy and revenge fill the lives of Jason and Cat, two teens who love each other.

473

MICHAEL FOREMAN, Author/Illustrator

Saving Sinbad!

(La Jolla, CA: Kane/Miller, 2002)

Subject(s): Boats and Boating; Animals/Dogs; Rescue Work
Age range(s): Grades K-2
Major character(s): Unnamed Character, Dog; Sinbad, Dog
Time period(s): 2000s (2002)
Locale(s): England

Summary: A dog in a small fishing village accompanies his owner everywhere. When a distress signal goes off and people from the village head out to rescue a sinking sailboat, the dog follows closely behind. The villagers manage to rescue the family, but not their small dog that has washed overboard. Luckily the village dog is able to rescue Sinbad and the family is reunited. (32 pages)

Where it's reviewed:
Book for Keeps, March 2002, page 19
Booklist, December 15, 2002, page 766
Children's Bookwatch, October 2002, page 6
Horn Book Guide, Spring 2003, page 66
Kirkus Reviews, October 1, 2002, page 1469

Other books by the same author:
War and Peas, 2002
Cat in the Manger, 2001
Michael Foreman's Mother Goose, 1991

Other books you might like:
Lisa Desimini, *Dot the Fire Dog*, 2001
When the firefighters are called to a blaze, Dot rescues a kitten trapped inside the burning house.
Margaret Mahy, *Dashing Dog!*, 2002
A French poodle enjoys a day on the beach with his family; when the baby wanders off, the dog must rescue her from the ocean.
Angeli Perrow, *Lighthouse Dog to the Rescue*, 2000
Based on a true story, a dog helps save a boat during a winter storm when the lighthouse's horn is frozen.

474

MICHAEL FOREMAN, Author/Illustrator

Wonder Goal!

(New York: Farrar Straus Giroux, 2003)

Subject(s): Sports/Soccer; Games; Dreams and Nightmares
Age range(s): Grades 1-3
Major character(s): Unnamed Character, Soccer Player, Son
Time period(s): 2000s (2003); Indeterminate Past
Locale(s): England

Summary: The new player on a youth soccer team wants to gain the respect of his teammates. When the chance comes, he shoots the perfect goal yet still feels upset because his father isn't there to see it. Fast forward a decade or so and the player is once again making the perfect goal. This time it happens in the finals of the World Cup with his father in the audience. (32 pages)

Where it's reviewed:
Booklist, April 15, 2003, page 1477
Bulletin of the Center for Children's Books, June 2003, page 399
Horn Book, March/April 2003, page 202
Riverbank Review, Summer 2003, page 34
School Library Journal, April 2003, page 118

Other books by the same author:
A Trip to Dinosaur Time, 2003
Cat in the Manger, 2001
War Boy, 2000 (Kate Greenaway Medal Winner)

Other books you might like:
Anthony Browne, *Willy the Wizard*, 1996
  Chimpanzee Willy joins the soccer team, but is convinced his skill is due to magic shoes, which he forgets on the day of the big game.
Sandra Gilbert Brug, *Soccer Beat*, 2003
  Two animal teams compete in a soccer match.
Jonathan London, *Froggy Plays Soccer*, 1999
  Froggy joins the soccer team, but can he remember not to use his hands?
Pat Posner, *Princess Fidgety Feet*, 2002
  Princess Bridget is very fidgety. With the help of her kingly father, she finds an outlet for her nervous energy playing soccer.

475

SHELLEY FOWLES, Author/Illustrator

The Bachelor and the Bean

(New York: Farrar Straus Giroux, 2003)

Subject(s): Folk Tales; Genies; Wishes
Age range(s): Grades K-3
Major character(s): Unnamed Character, Aged Person, Bachelor; Unnamed Character, Mythical Creature (genie); Unnamed Character, Aged Person, Thief
Time period(s): Indeterminate Past
Locale(s): Morocco

Summary: An old man accidentally drops his last bean in a well and unexpectedly awakens a genie who gives him a magical bowl to quiet him. The bowl fills up with whatever food the old man requests. The man shares his good fortune with his neighbors, but a jealous old lady switches the bowl in the middle of the night. When the old bachelor complains to the genie about the broken bowl the genie gives him a bowl that produces cups and dishes. The jealous old lady steals that bowl as well and the man complains once again to the genie. The third and final pot the bachelor is given reveals the thief's identity and when the cantankerous bachelor goes to confront her, he is entranced by her nasty temper so like his own and his single days are soon over. This is the author's first book. (32 pages)

Where it's reviewed:
Booklist, March 15, 2003, page 1328
Bulletin of the Center for Children's Books, April 2003, page 312

Awards the book has won:
Center for Children's Books Best Books, 2003

Other books you might like:
Jim Aylesworth, *The Full Belly Bowl*, 1999
  An old man learns to use a magic bowl so that it is a blessing rather than a burden until his greed leads to chaos.
Baba Wague Diakite, *The Magic Gourd*, 2003
  In a retelling of a folk tale from Mali, a greedy king steals a rabbit's gourd that magically refills with food but the rabbit retrieves it.
T. Obinkaram Echewa, *The Magic Tree: A Folktale from Nigeria*, 1999
  Mbi, an orphan boy, is always hungry. When he plants a magical seed, a tree grows that always bears fruit.
Lily Toy Hong, *Two of Everything*, 1993
  In an award winning retelling of a Chinese folktale a poor farmer finds a magic pot and learns to live with the unexpected consequences of his good fortune.
Yoshiko Uchida, *The Magic Purse*, 2002
  After a young Japanese farmer helps a ghostly maiden she gives him a purse that magically fills with money.

476

FRANK G. FOX
SCOTT COOK, Illustrator

Jean Laffite and the Big Ol' Whale

(New York: Farrar Straus Giroux, 2003)

Subject(s): Tall Tales; Rivers; Animals/Whales
Age range(s): Grades 1-4
Major character(s): Jean Lafitte, Historical Figure
Time period(s): 19th century
Locale(s): New Orleans, Louisiana

Summary: Jean Lafitte is made of strong stuff. As a baby he drinks hot chicory coffee. At the age of seven, Jean swims the Mississippi from Louisiana to Minnesota and back again. With his experience, when the river dries up one day, Jean isn't scared like all the other river folk. He marches right up the river until he finds a whale that is blocking the water flow. With the help of a little cayenne pepper, Jean frees the whale and gets the river flowing again. On the way home, Jean creates Lake Pontchartrain—in case the whale should ever want to come back for a visit. This is the first children's book for this author of adult mysteries. (32 pages)

Where it's reviewed:
Booklist, February 15, 2003, page 1073
Bulletin of the Center for Children's Books, May 2003, page 359
Horn Book, May/June 2003, page 360
Publishers Weekly, March 3, 2003, page 75
School Library Journal, April 2003, page 118

Awards the book has won:
Center for Children's Books Best Books, 2003

Other books you might like:
Ezra Jack Keats, *John Henry: An American Legend*, 1965
  John Henry competes against (and beats) a steam drill to build a railroad.
Steven Kellogg, *Johnny Appleseed*, 1998
  Larger-than-life American folk hero, Johnny Appleseed

befriends pioneers and spreads apple orchards all over the country.

Audrey Wood, *The Bunyans*, 1996

The jumbo-sized Bunyan family makes its way across the US, creating landmarks such as Niagara Falls and Old Faithful.

Catherine Wright, *Steamboat Annie and the Thousand-Pound Catfish*, 2001

Steamboat Annie promises to rid the town of Pleasant of its Thousand-Pound Catfish.

477

MEM FOX
TRICIA TUSA, Illustrator

The Magic Hat

(San Diego: Harcourt, Inc., 2002)

Subject(s): Magic; Wizards; Stories in Rhyme
Age range(s): Grades K-2
Major character(s): Unnamed Character, Wizard, Traveler
Time period(s): Indeterminate
Locale(s): Fictional Country

Summary: The wind carries a magical hat into a town and, as it spins through the air, it drops onto the heads of various people, changing that person into an animal. A very large wizard skips into town carrying a stop sign, pulls a magic wand from his pocket, and transforms the animals back into the people they had originally been. Leaving the awestruck crowd with one last trick, the wizard quietly skips out of town, puts the hat on his head and continues on his way looking very much like a small child. (32 pages)

Where it's reviewed:

Booklist, April 15, 2002, page 1408
Bulletin of the Center for Children's Books, July 2002, page 402
Horn Book Guide, Fall 2002, page 301
Publishers Weekly, February 11, 2002, page 184
School Library Journal, April 2002, page 110

Other books by the same author:

Harriet, You'll Drive Me Wild!, 2000
Sleepy Bears, 1999
A Bedtime Story, 1996
Feathers and Fools, 1996

Other books you might like:

Catherine Ann Cullen, *The Magical, Mystical, Marvelous Coat*, 2001

Daily, a girl gives away one of the six buttons on her coat to assist a giant, a wizard, three rabbits, an elf, a swan and a wind-tossed sailboat.

Richard Egielski, *Three Magic Balls*, 2000

Rudy discovers that three balls in his uncle's toyshop have magical properties.

Liz Rosenberg, *Eli and Uncle Dawn*, 1997

The curtain that Uncle Dawn gives Eli becomes a magic flying carpet that takes Eli for a quick ride.

478

JERON ASHFORD FRAME
R. GREGORY CHRISTIE, Illustrator

Yesterday I Had the Blues

(Berkeley, CA: Tricycle Press, 2003)

Subject(s): Family Life; African Americans; Relatives
Age range(s): Grades 1-4
Major character(s): Unnamed Character, Narrator, Son; Daddy, Father; Mama, Mother; Gram, Grandmother
Time period(s): 2000s (2003)
Locale(s): United States

Summary: In the author's first picture book colors describe the moods of a boy, his sisters, parents and other relatives. Just yesterday the narrator had the blues, the "deep down in my shoes blues" but today he's got the greens and is feeling much more positive. A parking ticket gives Daddy the grays and when the kids jump on the bed Mama gets the reds. When Gram has the yellows, he hopes it means oatmeal raisin cookies will be coming soon. The changing color of the individuals is interesting, but ultimately unimportant because through it all he can count on a loving family and that's a golden feeling. (28 pages)

Where it's reviewed:

Booklist, November 1, 2003, page 500
Bulletin of the Center for Children's Books, December 2003, page 151
Horn Book, January 2004, page 69
Publishers Weekly, September 15, 2003, page 64
School Library Journal, October 2003, page 119

Awards the book has won:

Bulletin of the Center for Children's Books Blue Ribbon, 2003

Other books you might like:

Aliki, *Feelings*, 1984

Through pictures, poems and stories in a nonfiction title accessible to children Aliki catalogs a broad range of emotions.

Melrose Cooper, *I Got a Family*, 1993

A young girl describes the unique affection she receives from each individual in her caring family.

Dr. Seuss, *My Many Colored Days*, 1996

In a rhyming story color names are used to describe the emotions and behavior of children on a particularly colored day.

479

E.R. FRANK

America

(New York: Atheneum/Simon & Schuster, 2002)

Subject(s): Racially Mixed People; Emotional Problems; Abuse
Age range(s): Grades 9-12
Major character(s): America, Teenager, Abuse Victim; Mrs. Harper, Foster Parent; Dr. B., Doctor (therapist)
Time period(s): 2000s

Locale(s): Nyack, New York; New York, New York

Summary: Born to a crack-addicted mother, and named because so many different men could have been his father, American has been bounced back and forth from his mother's home to foster homes, residential treatment centers and an adopted family. Given up by his adopted parents when his biracial identity became obvious, America lives happily with their nanny Mrs. Harper until he visits his mother one weekend and is never returned. At the age of fifteen, after enduring sexual abuse and time within the social services system, his attempt at suicide lands him at a residential treatment facility where he meets Dr B. Slowly and painfully Dr. B makes him think and talk about all the bad things that have happened to him, a way of life that America does not want to remember. And slowly and painfully America begins to heal, learns that there is worth to him and his life and is reunited with his beloved Mrs. Harper, now older and living in a nursing home, in a tale of forgiveness. (242 pages)

Where it's reviewed:
Booklist, February 15, 2002, page 1013
Bulletin of the Center for Children's Books, March 2002, page 239
New York Times Book Review, May 19, 2002, page 24
Publishers Weekly, January 7, 2002, page 66
School Library Journal, March 2002, page 230

Awards the book has won:
School Library Journal Best Books, 2002
ALA Best Books for Young Adults, 2003

Other books by the same author:
Life Is Funny, 2000

Other books you might like:
Joanne Greenberg, *I Never Promised You a Rose Garden*, 1964
　Deborah has her own fantasy world to which she retreats when she's tired of lies and anti-Semitism; a stay in an asylum helps her face reality.
Monte Killingsworth, *Circle Within a Circle*, 1994
　After a fight with his latest set of foster parents, Chris runs away and is picked up by Chopper, a Vietnam vet with his own set of problems.
Patricia McCormick, *Cut*, 2000
　Callie won't talk, either during group sessions or with the therapist, until another patient is admitted who has the same self-cutting problem as Callie.
Adam Rapp, *The Buffalo Tree*, 1997
　Incarcerated in Hamstock Boys Center for stealing hood ornaments, Sura's goal is to survive his six-month sentence.

480

E.R. FRANK

Friction

(New York: Richard Jackson/Atheneum, 2003)

Subject(s): Teacher-Student Relationships; Child Abuse; Coming-of-Age
Age range(s): Grades 6-10

Major character(s): Alexandra "Alex" Crocker, 8th Grader; Stacy Janice, 8th Grader; Simon, Teacher
Time period(s): 2000s
Locale(s): United States

Summary: Until the arrival of new student Stacy, Alex has loved Forest Alternative School, with its small classes and family atmosphere, and her teacher Simon who is also her soccer coach. But Stacy disrupts the class dynamics with her assertion that Simon "likes" Alex, as in really likes her, and spreads ugly rumors about them. Naive Alex is disturbed by Stacy's continuing comments, but she doesn't understand some of Simon's actions, either, especially on the school camping trip. When Stacy accuses Simon of molesting her, Alex is initially unprepared to defend him, though she knows he would never abuse anyone in this work that explores gossip and school relationships. (197 pages)

Where it's reviewed:
Bulletin of the Center for Children's Books, June 2003, page 400
Horn Book, July 2003, page 455
Publishers Weekly, April 7, 2003, page 68
School Library Journal, June 2003, page 138
Voice of Youth Advocates, August 2003, page 223

Awards the book has won:
ALA Best Books for Young Adults, 2004

Other books by the same author:
Life Is Funny, 2002

Other books you might like:
Margaret Peterson Haddix, *Don't You Dare Read This, Mrs. Dunphrey*, 1996
　Tish fills her English journal with all the problems in her life, finally inviting Mrs. Dunphrey to read it, which leads to help for Tish's family.
Rose Levit, *With Secrets to Keep*, 1991
　Adrianna finally summons the courage to tell her friend Jenny's parents about her father's abusive ways.
Jacqueline Woodson, *Lena*, 1999
　When Lena's sexually abusive father shows interest in her younger sister, Lena and Dion run away.

481

HILLARY FRANK

Better than Running at Night

(Boston: Houghton Mifflin Co., 2002)

Subject(s): Interpersonal Relations; Universities and Colleges; Art
Age range(s): Grades 9-12
Major character(s): Ladybug "Ellie" Yelinski, Student—College (freshman art major); Nate Finerman, Student—College (sophomore art major)
Time period(s): 2000s
Locale(s): New England

Summary: Ellie leaves behind her hippie mother and stepfather as she heads off to the fictional New England College of Art Design. Her mother has no idea who Ellie's biological father might be and her stepfather thinks if Ellie will just smoke a little weed, she'll be able to relax. Understandably,

Ellie looks forward to college life and meeting many new people. One of her first encounters is with good-looking fellow art student Nate and she loses her virginity just one week after meeting him. As Ellie discovers, Nate likes all women and has an open relationship with his girlfriend, something that becomes harder and harder for her to rationalize. But Ellie is there for the education, learns a lot from her exuberant art teacher, and by the end of the fall semester is ready to leave Nate behind in this author's first novel. (263 pages)

Where it's reviewed:
Booklist, October 1, 2002, page 322
Bulletin of the Center for Children's Books, October 2002, page 56
Library Media Connection, April 2003, page 75
Publishers Weekly, August 5, 2002, page 74
School Library Journal, January 2003, page 138

Awards the book has won:
Booklist Editors' Choice/Books for Youth, 2002
ALA Best Books for Young Adults, 2003

Other books you might like:
Catherine Clark, *Wurst Case Scenario*, 2001
It takes awhile for Colorado native Courtney to adjust to campus life in rural Wisconsin, but gradually she becomes used to the different lifestyle.
Chip Kidd, *The Cheese Monkeys: A Novel in Two Semesters*, 2001
Taking the path of least resistance and becoming an art major, this unnamed narrator is surprised to be well challenged by his commercial art teacher.
Tom Perrotta, *Joe College*, 2000
Raised in a blue-collar home, Danny sometimes wonders what he's doing at Yale among all these wealthy students.

482

KRISTINE L. FRANKLIN

Grape Thief

(Cambridge, MA: Candlewick Press, 2003)

Subject(s): City and Town Life; Miners and Mining
Age range(s): Grades 5-9
Major character(s): Slava "Cuss" Petrovich, 12-Year-Old, Immigrant (Croatian American); Skinny Giombetti, Friend; Percival Lincoln "Perks" Perkins, Friend
Time period(s): 1920s (1925)
Locale(s): Roslyn, Washington

Summary: As coal mining operations slow down and mobsters infiltrate their small town, Slava's chances to remain in school decrease. His two older brothers work the mines, which provides the income his widowed mother needs to feed her family. Slava, along with his friends Perks and Skinny, enjoy the waning years of their childhood and reenact the annual ritual of stealing grapes from the "grape train," source for local wine production. Slava is also the bearer of the moniker "Cuss" for his ability to swear in fourteen different languages. When Slava's older brothers attack and kill a mobster, they flee to California leaving Slava deciding whether to

stay in school, drop out to support his mother, or join his brothers in this coming-of-age tale. (295 pages)

Where it's reviewed:
Booklist, October 1, 2003, page 310
Bulletin of the Center for Children's Books, September 2003, page 14
Publishers Weekly, October 6, 2003, page 85
School Library Journal, September 2003, page 209

Other books by the same author:
Dove Song, 1999
Lone Wolf, 1999
The Gift, 1999

Other books you might like:
Judie Angell, *One-Way to Ansonia*, 1985
For 1890s immigrant Rose Olshansky, the only way to achieve her dreams is to attend night school after working all day in a factory.
Robert Lehrman, *The Store That Mama Built*, 1992
After being widowed, Mama surprises everyone by adapting to life in America and running the store her husband had just bought.
N.A. Perez, *Breaker*, 1988
After Pat's father is killed in a mining accident, Pat works in the mines while his brother fights for improved labor conditions.
Gloria Skurzynski, *Rockbuster*, 2001
Orphaned young, Tommy toils in the mines but resists being involved in the labor movement, choosing instead to become a lawyer and help all people.

483

LISA ROWE FRAUSTINO, Editor

Soul Searching: Thirteen Stories about Faith and Belief

(New York: Simon & Schuster, 2002)

Subject(s): Short Stories; Religion; Spirituality
Age range(s): Grades 7-10

Summary: The commonalities and differences of the varied faith and belief systems are well illustrated in this collection of 13 stories. When her grandmother dies, a young Chinese girl assumes her role in tending the family altar, which helps her understand its importance in Minfong Ho's "The See-Far Glasses." The quandary of a pregnant Amish teen is explored in "The Shunning of Sadie B. Zook," by Linda Oatman High. "A Daughter of Abraham," by Dianne Hess recounts a Jewish girl's reaction to learning her great-grandmother died in Auschwitz. William Sleator tells of a monk in Thailand, Dian Curtis Regan of a Venezuelan cult and Elsa Marston of a Palestinian Muslim in stories that take the reader far beyond the United States. Other authors include Jennifer Armstrong, Shonto Begay, Nancy Flynn, editor Lisa Rowe Fraustino, Uma Krishnaswami, David Lubar, and John Slayton. (267 pages)

Where it's reviewed:
Bulletin of the Center for Children's Books, December 2002, page 154
Horn Book, January 2003, page 72

Publishers Weekly, November 25, 2003, page 64
School Library Journal, December 2002, page 137
Voice of Youth Advocates, February 2003, page 482

Other books by the same author:
Don't Cramp My Style: Stories about That Time of the Month, 2004
I Walk in Dread: The Diary of Deliverance Trembley, Witness to the Salem Witch Trials, 2004
Dirty Laundry: Stories about Family Secrets, 1998

Other books you might like:
Fran Arrick, *God's Radar*, 1983
    Roxie undergoes a difficult time when her parents join a fundamentalist church.
Sandy Asher, *With All My Heart, With All My Mind*, 1999
    Thirteen stories examine the issue of growing up Jewish, especially when trying to reconcile centuries of tradition with the modern world.
Bruce Brooks, *Asylum for Nightface*, 1996
    Zim's spirituality is in direct contrast to his parent's carefree lifestyle, until they find God and decide Zim needs to be their poster boy.
Marilyn Singer, *I Believe in Water: Twelve Brushes with Religion*, 2000
    Thirteen stories examine faith and religion from the perspective of young people.

484

MARLA FRAZEE, Author/Illustrator

Roller Coaster

(San Diego: Harcourt, Inc., 2003)

Subject(s): Amusement Parks; Fear; Self-Confidence
Age range(s): Grades K-2
Major character(s): Unnamed Character, Child
Time period(s): 2000s (2003)
Locale(s): United States

Summary: A long line of people waits to ride the roller coaster. One of them is a little girl just tall enough to meet the height restrictions for the ride. Some people change their mind and get out of line, but not the little girl waiting to ride the Rocket for the first time. Though she's a little hesitant to get in the car and sits with wide-eyed wonder (or is that apprehension?) as the ride begins, by the time it stops she's ready to get in line again. (32 pages)

Where it's reviewed:
Booklist, June 2003, page 1768
Bulletin of the Center for Children's Books, June 2003, page 401
Horn Book, May 2003, page 328
Publishers Weekly, April 21, 2003, page 61
School Library Journal, July 2003, page 96

Awards the book has won:
ALA Notable Children's Books, 2004
Riverbank Review Books of Distinction, 2004

Other books by the same author:
Hush Little Baby: A Folk Song with Pictures, 1999

Other books you might like:
Nancy Carlson, *Harriet and the Roller Coaster*, 2003
    George teases Harriet that she's too scared to ride the roller coaster, but it's Harriet, not George, who wants to go again when the ride concludes.
Donald Crews, *Night at the Fair*, 1998
    The excitement of a trip to the fair is displayed in bright illustrations and simple text including a view from the top of the ferris wheel.
June Sobel, *B Is for Bulldozer: A Construction ABC*, 2003
    Rhyming description of a yearlong construction project of an amusement park concludes with ''Z'' for ''Z-O-O-M'' on the new roller coaster.

485

HEATHER VOGEL FREDERICK

The Voyage of Patience Goodspeed

(New York: Simon & Schuster, 2002)

Subject(s): Sea Stories; Animals/Whales; Fathers and Daughters
Age range(s): Grades 5-8
Major character(s): Patience Goodspeed, 12-Year-Old; Thaddeus ''Tad'' Goodspeed, Brother (of Patience); Pardon Sprigg, Steward; Captain Goodspeed, Father, Sea Captain
Time period(s): 1830s
Locale(s): *Morning Star*, At Sea; Nantucket, Massachusetts

Summary: Though Patience objects to her father's decision that she and her brother Thaddeus accompany him on his next three-year whaling voyage, she's unable to convince him of her need to stay in Nantucket and study with Miss Mitchell, her math teacher. Their mother has recently died and their father wants to develop a relationship with them, which is difficult unless they are with him aboard the *Morning Star*. Heading out to the Pacific, Patience wants to put her math to use in navigation, but her father is slow to respond to her abilities. Finally realizing her competence, he brings her up on deck one night and begins by teaching her the stars and the constellations; a birthday present of a sextant from her aunt solidifies her interest. Tad and Patience have their own share of lessons to complete, a process watched over by the ship's steward Sprigg, though he moans and complains about it. Two sailors lead a mutiny against Captain Goodspeed and his officers and set the men and Tad out to sea in an open boat. Once the other seamen retake their ship, it's up to Patience to put her navigating skills to use to locate her father and brother in an exciting, well-researched first novel. (220 pages)

Where it's reviewed:
Booklist, June 2002, page 1722
Horn Book, September 2002, page 571
New York Times Book Review, August 11, 2002, page 19
Publishers Weekly, July 17, 2002, page 65
School Library Journal, July 2002, page 119

Other books you might like:
Avi, *The True Confessions of Charlotte Doyle*, 1990
    Charlotte's adventures aboard the sailing ship *Seahawk* turn her from a proper Victorian lady into a real sailor.
Corinne Demas, *If Ever I Return Again*, 2000
    Celia's adventure aboard her father's whaling ship be-

comes one of survival when her father dies and she uses her navigation lessons to reach New Bedford.

Peg Kehret, *The Secret Journey*, 1999
  Emma disguises herself as a boy and plans to stow away on her parents' ship but lands on a slave ship by mistake.

Douglas Kelly, *The Captain's Wife*, 2001
  With her husband injured in a mutiny attempt, it's up to Mary Ann to navigate his clipper ship.

486

MARIAH FREDERICKS

The True Meaning of Cleavage

(New York: Richard Jackson/Atheneum, 2003)

Subject(s): Friendship; Schools/High Schools; Interpersonal Relations
Age range(s): Grades 7-10
Major character(s): Sari Aaronsohn, 9th Grader; Jessica "Jess" Horvath, 9th Grader; David Cole, 12th Grader
Time period(s): 2000s
Locale(s): New York, New York (Manhattan)

Summary: The beginning of high school, in Jess's mind, is something to be endured. She hopes the four years will go quickly and that she can remain below the radar screen of cliques, boyfriends and popularity. Her best friend Sari, however, falls instantly, maniacally in love with David Cole, a popular senior who already sports an equally popular girlfriend. When David pays a little attention to Sari at a party, she thinks they have a budding romance. Jess figures out that David is only using Sari and, as she feels the changes in her friendship with Sari, she mistakenly blabs about Sari and David to the biggest gossip in the school, which further cleaves their closeness. Sari finally realizes that David's real interest in her is only physical and, when she most needs a friend, Jess is there beside her in this author's insightful, first novel. (211 pages)

Where it's reviewed:
Booklist, March 15, 2003, page 1322
Bulletin of the Center for Children's Books, March 2003, page 273
Publishers Weekly, December 9, 2002, page 85
School Library Journal, February 2003, page 141
Voice of Youth Advocates, April 2003, page 47

Awards the book has won:
Booklist Editors' Choice/Books for Youth, 2003

Other books you might like:
Ann Brashares, *The Sisterhood of the Traveling Pants*, 2001
  Four friends, apart for the summer, decide that a pair of pants, accompanied by the rules and a schedule for wearing them, will keep them united.
Catherine Clark, *Truth or Dairy*, 2000
  Courtney looks forward to her senior year but finds she'll be on her own when her boyfriend breaks up with her.
Ellen Wittlinger, *Razzle*, 2001
  Kenyon almost gives up tall, independent Razzle for a self-centered sexpot who throws him aside when he can't help her modeling career.

487

CLAIRE FREEDMAN
JOHN BENDALL-BRUNELLO, Illustrator

Hushabye Lily

(New York: Orchard Books/Scholastic, Inc., 2003)

Subject(s): Animals/Rabbits; Bedtime; Farm Life
Age range(s): Preschool-Grade 1
Major character(s): Lily, Rabbit, Daughter
Time period(s): 2000s (2003)
Locale(s): England

Summary: Lily is having trouble falling asleep because of the barnyard noises. Some of the offenders, including ducks, cows and hens, offer their sleep solutions. The ducks sing Lily a lullaby. The cows tell her a bedtime story and the hens give Lily straw for her bed. Finally Lily is able to fall asleep, only to have her loud snoring wake up a slumbering foal. (32 pages)

Where it's reviewed:
Publishers Weekly, June 2, 2003, page 50
School Library Journal, November 2003, page 93

Other books by the same author:
Oops-a-Daisy, 2004
Gooseberry Goose, 2003
Where's Your Smile, Crocodile?, 2001

Other books you might like:
Maggie de Vries, *How Sleep Found Tabitha*, 2002
  When Tabitha has trouble sleeping she imagines all the different ways that animals sleep.
Mingfong Ho, *Hush!: A Thai Lullaby*, 2000
  As a mother puts her baby to sleep, she implores the nearby animals to be quiet.
Sylvia Long, *Hush Little Baby*, 1997
  In this reworked version of the lullaby, a mother rabbit sings her baby to sleep by telling her all the things she'll show her.

488

MARTHA FREEMAN
CAT BOWMAN SMITH, Illustrator

The Trouble with Babies

(New York: Holiday House, 2002)

Subject(s): Moving, Household; Stepfathers; Neighbors and Neighborhoods
Age range(s): Grades 3-5
Major character(s): Holly Garland, 9-Year-Old, Daughter; Xavier, Neighbor, Inventor; Annie Cohen-Liu, 9-Year-Old, Neighbor
Time period(s): 2000s (2002)
Locale(s): San Francisco, California

Summary: Holly interrupts the unpacking of boxes to search for one of the family's cats. While retrieving it from the neighbor's yard, Holly meets Xavier and discovers that the strange contraption in his yard is a "de-yucka-ma-box" that Xavier invented in hopes of wooing Annie, hater of all things yucky, including her baby sister. Because Xavier's crush on

Annie renders him speechless he sends Holly with the proposal that she put her baby sister into the box to get rid of her yuckiness. Annie seems willing to try it, but changes her mind when she recognizes that this little bundle is a person with feelings. Xavier's disappointment with his failed plan helps him get over his crush so he can go back to just being Annie's friend. Holly looks forward to being included in neighborly friendship, especially when she learns that a baby will soon be coming to her family, too. She'll need Annie's experience. (121 pages)

Where it's reviewed:
Booklist, July 2002, page 1844
Bulletin of the Center for Children's Books, November 2002, page 105
Kirkus Reviews, June 15, 2002, page 880
Publishers Weekly, August 26, 2002, page 71
School Library Journal, August 2002, page 155

Other books by the same author:
The Spy Wore Shades, 2001
The Trouble with Cats, 2000
Fourth Grade Weirdo, 1999
The Polyester Grandpa, 1998

Other books you might like:
Judy Delton, *Angel Spreads Her Wings*, 1999
Slowly adjusting to a stepfather and a new baby sister, now worrywart Angel has to face family plans to spend the summer in Greece with Rudy's family.
Adele Geras, *The Cats of Cuckoo Square: Two Stories*, 2001
Two stories introduce four cats living with families in homes surrounding Cuckoo Square and feature their everyday adventures.
Eileen Spinelli, *Lizzie Logan, Second Banana*, 1998
Having a stepfather is an adjustment, but then Lizzie learns her mom is pregnant and she fears she'll never be loved as much as the new baby.

489

MARTHA FREEMAN

Who Is Stealing the Twelve Days of Christmas?

(New York: Holiday House, 2003)

Subject(s): Mystery and Detective Stories; Christmas; Animals/Cats
Age range(s): Grades 3-5
Major character(s): Alex Parakeet, 9-Year-Old; Yasmeen Popp, 9-Year-Old
Time period(s): 2000s (2003)
Locale(s): Chickadee Court

Summary: Every year the families on Alex's street put up "Twelve Days of Christmas" decorations but this year the birds have started disappearing. First to go is the rubber ducky. Alex's mom, the town's lone police detective, is busy with a toy store robbery, so Alex and best friend Yasmeen try to solve the mystery. The case becomes even more confusing when the thief starts returning the birds. Finally a late night face off with the culprit solves both the mystery of the disappearing decorations and the toy store robbery. (200 pages)

Where it's reviewed:
Bulletin of the Center for Children's Books, January 2003, page 190
Horn Book, November 2003, page 744

Other books by the same author:
The Trouble with Babies, 2002
Fourth Grade Weirdo, 2000
The Year My Parents Ruined My Life, 1997

Other books you might like:
Laura Lee Hope, *The Bobbsey Twins' Wonderful Winter Secret*, 1962
The Bobbsey twins try to find the perfect Christmas present for their parents.
Barbara Robinson, *The Best Christmas Pageant Ever*, 1972
When the incorrigible Herdman kids (who don't know the Christmas story) take over the Christmas Pageant, the result is surprising.
Gertrude Chandler Warner, *The Mystery in the Snow*, 1992
The Boxcar Children try to solve the mystery of who is wreaking havoc on the Snow Haven winter carnival.

490

JACKIE FRENCH
BRUCE WHATLEY, Illustrator

Diary of a Wombat

(New York: Clarion Books, 2003)

Subject(s): Animals; Diaries; Human Behavior
Age range(s): Grades K-3
Major character(s): Unnamed Character, Wombat
Time period(s): 2000s
Locale(s): Australia

Summary: A wombat's diary entries begin with simple recitations of eating, sleeping, scratching, and more sleeping. Then the wombat discovers new neighbors—humans. The illustrations expand the straightforward diary entries. When wombat describes a battle with a flat, hairy creature, the picture shows it wrestling with the welcome mat. After subduing the creature, the wombat expects a reward from the humans and receives one carrot. The carrot is so delicious that wombat returns later to beg for more, receives no response and chews a hole in the door. Life with the new neighbors offers wombat new scratching posts, new food sources, and soft ground for digging. The wombat finds humans to be quite easy to train. In fact, they are such good pets that the wombat digs a new hole (right under their house) in order to be closer to them. First published in Australia in 2002. (30 pages)

Where it's reviewed:
Bulletin of the Center for Children's Books, November 2003, page 103
Magpies, November 2002, page 29
Publishers Weekly, July 21, 2003, page 193
School Library Journal, August 2003, page 128

Awards the book has won:
CBCA Children's Picture Book of the Year, Honour Book, 2003
ALA Notable Children's Books, 2004

Other books by the same author:
Too Many Pears!, 2003
How to Guzzle Your Garden, 1999

Other books you might like:
Doreen Cronin, *Diary of a Worm*, 2003
  A worm records the trials, tribulations and advantages of a worm's life—no gum chewing, but no complaints about mud in the house either.
Candace Fleming, *Muncha! Muncha! Muncha!*, 2002
  Three bunnies seem able to get around each plan that Mr. McGreely devises to keep them from eating his vegetable garden.
Mem Fox, *Wombat Divine*, 1996
  After auditioning for a Nativity play Wombat is not sure which is the right part.
Michael Morpurgo, *Wombat Goes Walkabout*, 2000
  With a fire rapidly approaching, Wombat digs a hole large enough to save not only himself but also all the other animals that have no time to flee.
Rod Trinca, *One Wooly Wombat*, 1985
  A humorous rhyming tale introduces fourteen Australian animals.

491

SIMON FRENCH

Where in the World

(Atlanta: Peachtree, 2003)

Subject(s): Grandfathers; Music and Musicians
Age range(s): Grades 5-8
Major character(s): Ari Huber, Musician (violinist), 11-Year-Old; Opa, Grandfather; James "Jamie" Nicol, Stepfather
Time period(s): 2000s
Locale(s): Hattorf, Germany; Australia (near Sydney)

Summary: Young Ari is a musical prodigy who grows from playing his violin to composing musical pieces for it. His father died when Ari was only three and he and his mother moved to his beloved Opa's farm in Hattorf. Music and Opa are juxtaposed memories for Ari, for it was from his Opa that he learned to play the violin. But he and his mother move to Australia, his mother marries Jamie, and Ari settles into life near Sydney, not wishing for his classmates to know of his musical talent. When Ari learns of Opa's death, he is devastated and even turns away from his violin. Luckily Jamie helps him see that through composing and playing his violin, Ari will be better able to retain memories of both his father and Opa. (174 pages)

Where it's reviewed:
Booklist, December 15, 2003, page 666
Bulletin of the Center for Children's Books, February 2004, page 230
Publishers Weekly, December 8, 2003, page 62
School Library Journal, December 2003, page 151

Other books by the same author:
Change the Locks, 1993
All We Know, 1987

Other books you might like:
Betty Levin, *Shadow-Catcher*, 2000
  Jonathan travels with his grandfather on his summer photography shoot when he captures some underhanded shenanigans at a logging camp.
Richard Mosher, *Zazoo: A Novel*, 2001
  Zazoo has lived happily with her grandfather for the last 11 years, but a stranger makes her realize she doesn't really know him.
Alison Smith, *Billy Boone*, 1989
  When Billy decides she wants to play the trumpet, only her grandmother supports the idea of girls playing this instrument.

492

GINA FRESCHET, Author/Illustrator

Winnie and Ernst

(New York: Farrar Straus Giroux, 2003)

Subject(s): Friendship; Animals; Birthdays
Age range(s): Grades 1-3
Major character(s): Winnie, Opossum, Friend; Ernst, Otter, Friend
Time period(s): 2000s (2002)
Locale(s): United States

Summary: Winnie and Ernst are best friends who share a variety of adventures in the four stories in this early chapter book. In the first story, Ernst helps Winnie find the misplaced gift she bought for a friend's birthday party. In the following stories, Winnie and Ernst bake nut loaf for a bake sale and have a spring garden party. In the final story, Ernst breaks Winnie's mirror and then helps her turn that bad luck into good. (48 pages)

Where it's reviewed:
Booklist, October 1, 2003, page 327
School Library Journal, November 2003, page 94

Other books by the same author:
Beto and the Bone Dance, 2001
Naty's Parade, 2000
The Lute's Tune, 1992

Other books you might like:
Russell Hoban, *Best Friends for Frances*, 1969
  When Frances's friend Albert excludes her from his Boys-Only baseball game Frances discovers that little sisters can indeed be good friends.
Arnold Lobel, *Frog and Toad Together*, 1972
  In this Newberry Honor Book, best friends Frog and Toad enjoy spending time together, doing everything from planting a flower garden to eating cookies.
Else Holmelund Minarik, *Little Bear's Friend*, 1960
  One summer Little Bear makes friends with a little girl and her doll.

493

GARRET FREYMANN-WEYR

The Kings Are Already Here

(Boston: Houghton Mifflin, 2003)

Subject(s): Ballet; Games; Interpersonal Relations
Age range(s): Grades 7-10
Major character(s): Phebe Knight, 15-Year-Old, Dancer (ballerina); Nikolai Kotalev, 16-Year-Old, Chess Player; Clarence Knight, Father (of Phebe); Stas Vlajnik, Chess Player, Teacher
Time period(s): 2000s
Locale(s): New York, New York (Manhattan); Geneva, Switzerland

Summary: Two teens, each with a specific goal, eventually meet over the summer. Phebe dedicated her life to ballet, but now realizes that she needs a break, and so comes to Geneva to stay with her father. Nikolai, however, is consumed with becoming a grandmaster in chess and stays with Phebe's father Clarence while he searches for a coach. Stas, a famous chess master, promised to coach Nikolai whenever he left his domineering father; now that he's done so, Stas is nowhere to be found. Clarence and Nikolai travel around Europe to find Stas, allowing Nikolai to play in some chess exhibitions and Phebe to take an occasional ballet class to keep her form. The two teens become friends, linked not by romance, but by their tremendous drive and single-minded dedication to one art. As Nikolai narrows his vision even more toward his chess, seeking to play quickly and beautifully, Phebe realizes that she's ready to expand her horizons and not let ballet be what defines her in another well-written work by a former Printz winner. (149 pages)

Where it's reviewed:
Booklist, February 15, 2003, page 1065
Bulletin of the Center for Children's Books, April 2003, page 313
Horn Book, March 2003, page 211
School Library Journal, April 2003, page 158
Voice of Youth Advocates, April 2003, page 48

Other books by the same author:
My Heartbeat, 2002 (Printz Honor Book)
When I Was Older, 2000

Other books you might like:
Donald P. Ladew, *Stradivarius*, 1995
  Given the opportunity to play a Stradivarius, rather than his usual fiddle, Ailey begins his climb into the world of classical music.
Madeleine L'Engle, *The Small Rain*, 1945
  Katherine is a musician extraordinaire whose piano playing comes above everything, including the man she loves.
Walter Tevis, *The Queen's Gambit*, 1983
  Beth is a brilliant chess player who eventually challenges the world chess champion.

494

GARRET FREYMANN-WEYR

My Heartbeat

(New York: Houghton Mifflin, 2002)

Subject(s): Homosexuality/Lesbianism; Brothers and Sisters; Interpersonal Relations
Age range(s): Grades 9-12
Major character(s): Link McConnell, 12th Grader, Homosexual; James Wentworth, 12th Grader; Ellen McConnell, 9th Grader, Sister (of Link)
Time period(s): 2000s
Locale(s): New York, New York (Manhattan)

Summary: Ever since she was in seventh grade Ellen has adored her brother Link's friend James. The two boys remain friends even though they argue and fight, and they include Ellen in their activities, treating her as an equal. When she's a freshman at their private school, a friend asks her if James and Link are a couple, but Ellen doesn't really know and so asks them. Link denies it and is angry that Ellen would even ask, though James says they are and admits to being bisexual. This seemingly-innocent question causes a rift between Link and James and drives Link to date a girl, while James turns to Ellen in a relationship that heats up quickly. Shaken by what's happened, Ellen wants to find out who her brother really is and how each of them fits within her family in this well-crafted second novel. (154 pages)

Where it's reviewed:
Booklist, June 2002, page 1708
Bulletin of the Center for Children's Books, May 2002, page 322
Horn Book, May 2002, page 328
Publishers Weekly, March 18, 2002, page 105
School Library Journal, April 2002, page 148

Awards the book has won:
Michael L. Printz Honor Book, 2003
School Library Journal Best Books, 2002

Other books by the same author:
When I Was Older, 2000

Other books you might like:
Kelly Easton, *The Life History of a Star*, 2001
  Kristin's whole family is affected when her former All-American brother David returns from Vietnam physically and mentally challenged.
Alex Sanchez, *Rainbow Boys*, 2001
  Jason, Kyle and Nelson face their senior year, and life-changing decisions, as they deal with their sexual identity.
Laura Torres, *November Ever After*, 1999
  At first Amy is disturbed that Sara has a lesbian relationship with Anita, but eventually realizes that Sara will always be her best friend.

495

APRIL YOUNG FRITZ

Praying at the Sweetwater Motel

(New York: Hyperion, 2003)

Subject(s): Abuse; Family Problems; Alcoholism
Age range(s): Grades 5-8
Major character(s): Sarah Jane Otis, 12-Year-Old; Alice Otis, Child, Sister; Muriel Sweetwater, Businesswoman (motel owner); Arthur Proctor, 12-Year-Old; Fredericka "Fred", 12-Year-Old
Time period(s): 2000s
Locale(s): Dublin, Ohio; Macon, Georgia

Summary: When Sarah Jane's alcoholic father hits her, her abused mother flees with Sarah Jane and her little sister Alice. Leaving behind their home in Georgia, the trio settles in at the Sweetwater Motel where Mrs. Sweetwater swaps room charges for chores. Already miserable without her father, Sarah's Jane's agony is compounded by attending school with snotty girls who call her "Motel Girl." Her two outcast friends, Fred and Arthur, bolster her belief that her father has quit drinking and help her travel to Georgia to see him, a trip that Sarah Jane realizes is a big mistake. (266 pages)

Where it's reviewed:
Booklist, October 15, 2003, page 412
Bulletin of the Center for Children's Books, November 2003, page 104
Horn Book, November 2003, page 744
School Library Journal, November 2003, page 139

Other books by the same author:
Prom Diaries, 2005
Waiting to Disappear, 2002

Other books you might like:
Nancy Antle, *Playing Solitaire*, 2000
   Vowing to kill her alcoholic father for cutting off three of her fingers, Ellie has control of her feelings by the time he reappears in her life.
Carolyn Coman, *What Jamie Saw*, 1995
   Jamie's mother finally leaves his father the night he hurls Jamie's little sister across the room.
Aileen Kilgore Henderson, *Treasure of Panther Peak*, 1998
   Page and her mother leave her abusive father and settle in Texas; when her father shows up, her mother stands up to him and refuses to move.
John Marsden, *So Much to Tell You*, 1987
   Through her journal Marina reveals the sad story of her facial disfigurement, caused when her father accidentally threw acid at her.

496

APRIL YOUNG FRITZ

Waiting to Disappear

(New York: Hyperion, 2002)

Subject(s): Grief; Mental Illness; Aunts and Uncles
Age range(s): Grades 6-9

Major character(s): Elizabeth "Buddy" Mullen, 9th Grader, 13-Year-Old; Sherry, Aunt; Verna Kaye Sanford, 9th Grader; Ginger, 9th Grader
Time period(s): 1960s (1960)
Locale(s): Moodus, South

Summary: Buddy's older brother died two years ago in a car accident and her mother's been grieving ever since, but this is the summer she has her "episode" and is hospitalized. Buddy's worried enough about starting her first year of high school, especially with her best friend Ginger acting boy crazy and Verna having to help out at home so much, that her mother's plight places an extra burden on her. At first Buddy doesn't want anyone else to know, so the family tells everyone that her mother's visiting a cousin out of state; gradually she includes Verna and Ginger in the news which makes their friendship easier. Her mother's youngest sister, Sherry, stays with Buddy, her father and her grandmother which gives a spark to Buddy's life, but Buddy can't shake the idea that she just wants her mother home. She runs through various plans to kidnap her, but eventually realizes her mother will be home when she's ready in this author's charming first novel. (316 pages)

Where it's reviewed:
Booklist, November 15, 2002, page 594
Library Media Connection, February 2003, page 74
Publishers Weekly, September 23, 2002, page 73
School Library Journal, October 2002, page 163
Voice of Youth Advocates, February 2003, page 474

Other books you might like:
Sue Ellen Bridgers, *Notes for Another Life*, 1981
   Kevin and Wren have lived with their grandparents since they were young as their mother has a career in Chicago and their father is often hospitalized.
Sarah Dessen, *Keeping the Moon*, 1999
   Spending a summer with her eccentric, free-spirited aunt helps Colie grow in confidence.
Sally Warner, *How to Be a Real Person (in Just One Day)*, 2001
   Kara thinks if she lies and follows her made-up rules, no one will know how unhinged her mother has become.

497

DEBORAH FROESE

Out of the Fire

(Toronto: Sumach Press, 2002)

Subject(s): Fires; Hospitals; Guilt
Age range(s): Grades 7-10
Major character(s): Dayle Meryk, 11th Grader, 17-Year-Old; Keith Hutton, 12th Grader, Boyfriend (of Dayle); Pete Wallace, 12th Grader; Amy, 11th Grader
Time period(s): 2000s
Locale(s): Selkirk, Canada

Summary: Until their junior year, Dayle and Amy have been good friends; neither dated much so their free time was spent with one another. But that changes when Dayle starts dating Keith and suddenly the two girls aren't speaking anymore. Amy tries to apologize and gives her two tickets for a Chameleon concert for her birthday, but Dayle returns them as she's already accepted a date with Keith to attend the season's first party out in the Meadow. Part of the party is a bonfire but since the wood's wet, partygoer Pete tosses gasoline on the fire which ignites leaving Dayle badly burned on 45% of her body and Pete critically burned. Dayle's recuperation is lengthy and her therapy and surgeries numerous. Time in the hospital allows her to think about friendships, how she really feels about Pete's actions and even where Keith fits in her life in a poignant, satisfying tale of courage. (282 pages)

Where it's reviewed:
Booklist, July 2002, page 1837
Canadian Book Review Annual, 2001, page 489
Kliatt, July 2002, page 18
School Library Journal, August 2002, page 184
Voice of Youth Advocates, October 2002, page 274

Awards the book has won:
ALA Best Books for Young Adults, 2003

Other books you might like:
Priscilla Cummings, *A Face First*, 2001
  Wearing a plastic facial mask to reduce the scarring from her third-degree burns, Kelley wonders if she'll ever again be able to face her classmates.
Wendy Orr, *Peeling the Onion*, 1997
  For Anna, rediscovering who she is following her accident is like peeling back the layers of an onion.
Cynthia Voigt, *Izzy, Willy-Nilly*, 1986
  Cheerleader Izzy's life changes when an automobile accident leaves her an amputee.

498

HELEN FROST

Keesha's House

(New York: Frances Foster Books/Farrar Straus Giroux, 2003)

Subject(s): Poetry; Family Problems
Age range(s): Grades 7-10
Major character(s): Joe, Landlord; Keesha, Teenager
Time period(s): 2000s
Locale(s): United States

Summary: Rather than free verse or blank verse, Keesha's story, and that of her friends, is told in the more difficult to write sestinas, sonnets of English and Italian derivation, and blendings of the two. When Joe was twelve, he found protection in the house in which he now lives, but it's too big for just one person. When Keesha needs a place to stay, Joe remembers his difficult growing-up years and allows her to choose a room and stay. Gradually the house becomes known as "Keesha's House" and she carefully screens potential occupants. Kids in trouble, kids who need to be free of abuse, those struggling with pregnancy, homosexuality, addiction or neglect—all can find a place of safety here. (116 pages)

Where it's reviewed:
Booklist, March 1, 2003, page 1192
Bulletin of the Center for Children's Books, April 2003, page 313
Publishers Weekly, April 21, 2003, page 63
School Library Journal, March 2003, page 232

Voice of Youth Advocates, April 2003, page 48

Awards the book has won:
Michael L. Printz Honor Book, 2004
ALA Best Books for Young Adults, 2004

Other books you might like:
Carolyn Coman, *What Jamie Saw*, 1995
  Jamie's mother finally leaves his father the night he hurls Jamie's little sister across the room.
Jean Thesman, *In the House of the Queen's Beasts*, 2001
  Emily shares her tree house with Rowan, who obviously needs a friend and a place to hide to escape her father's abusive ways.
Lori Aurelia Williams, *When Kambia Elaine Flew in from Neptune*, 2000
  Shayla worries about her neighbor Kambia, who's thin, wears raggedy second-hand clothes and tells stories to cover up the sexual abuse she's enduring.

499

CORNELIA FUNKE
ANTHEA BELL, Translator

Inkheart

(New York: Chicken House/Scholastic, 2003)

Subject(s): Fantasy; Books and Reading; Magic
Age range(s): Grades 6-12
Major character(s): Dustfinger, Villain; Meggie, 12-Year-Old; Capricorn, Murderer; Aunt Elinor, Aunt (of Meggie); Mo "Silvertongue", Father (of Meggie)
Time period(s): Indeterminate Past
Locale(s): Germany

Summary: Meggie's father Mo is a mender of books but, like his daughter, a person who also loves to read books. Mo has one little trait that he's kept hidden from Meggie and that's his ability to literally read a character out of a book. Several years ago he did just that when he was reading *Inkheart* and managed to read the evil Dustfinger and Capricorn out and his wife in to the book. Now Dustfinger returns with Capricorn's demand for the book, which he plans to keep so that he can remain free. Mo asks Aunt Elinor to watch Meggie, but soon all three of them are busy trying to hide from Dustfinger and Capricorn. Mo manages to outwit all the evil guys when he finds *Inkheart's* author and has him rewrite the plot so Capricorn is eliminated. (534 pages)

Where it's reviewed:
Booklist, September 1, 2003, page 114
Library Media Connection, January 2004, page 64
Publishers Weekly, July 21, 2003, page 196
School Library Journal, October 2003, page 164
Voice of Youth Advocates, December 2003, page 412

Awards the book has won:
ALA Notable Children's Books, 2004
Publishers Weekly Best Children's Books, 2003

Other books by the same author:
Dragon Rider, 2004
The Thief Lord, 2002

Other books you might like:

Michael Ende, *The Neverending Story*, 1984

An overweight boy enters the book he's reading to save the land of Fantastica from devastation.

Jasper Fforde, *The Eyre Affair: A Novel*, 2002

In this tongue-in-cheek romp, a criminal threatens great works of fiction; to stop him, special agent Thursday Next alters the ending to *Jane Eyre*.

Roderick Townsend, *The Great Good Thing*, 2001

Sylvie and other characters residing in her book enter reader Claire's subconscious where they enjoy adventures far beyond anything in their book.

500

CORNELIA FUNKE
OLIVER LATSCH, Translator

The Thief Lord

(New York: Chicken House/Scholastic, 2002)

Subject(s): Brothers; Runaways; Robbers and Outlaws
Age range(s): Grades 6-9
Major character(s): Prosper, 12-Year-Old, Runaway; Bo Boniface, Child, Runaway; Victor Getz, Detective—Private; Scipio Massimo "The Thief Lord", 13-Year-Old, Wealthy; Ida Spavento, Artist
Time period(s): 2000s
Locale(s): Venice, Italy

Summary: Orphaned Prosper and Bo flee from Hamburg, and their humorless aunt and uncle, to the city of Venice, which had been their mother's favorite city. Once in Venice they are lucky enough to fall in with a gang of street urchins, living in an abandoned theater and overseen by the Thief Lord. Though they sometimes resort to stealing wallets or food, the Thief Lord tries to leave them food and money in exchange for their help with stolen articles. Meanwhile Victor, who's been hired by the aunt and uncle, locates Prosper and Bo. After observing the boys and their gang for a while, he transfers his affections to the boys, especially when they care for his pet tortoises. The Thief Lord agrees to steal the wooden wing of a lion, which is located in Ida's home; she's eager to help to see the magical carousel from which the wing was taken. By books' end a suitable orphan's been found for the aunt to adopt; the Thief Lord has been unmasked; and the magic of the carousel still works in this enchanting tale from a popular German author. (349 pages)

Where it's reviewed:

Booklist, October 15, 2002, page 401
Bulletin of the Center for Children's Books, November 2002, page 106
Horn Book, November 2002, page 754
School Library Journal, October 2002, page 163
Voice of Youth Advocates, April 2003, page 49

Awards the book has won:

Mildred L. Batchelder Award, 2003
School Library Journal Best Books, 2002

Other books by the same author:

Inkheart, 2003

Other books you might like:

Ray Bradbury, *Something Wicked This Way Comes*, 1962

A fun trip to the Pandemonium Shadow Show leaves Will and Jim at the mercy of an evil presence that threatens to overtake them.

Charles Dickens, *Oliver Twist*, 1837-1838

An abused runaway, Oliver joins up with the nefarious team of The Artful Dodger and Fagin.

Sid Hite, *Those Darn Dithers*, 1996

Stilt walking, a dancing pig and an uncle who floats out to sea are just a few of the adventures of the Dithers family.

Mary Hoffman, *City of Masks*, 2002

Lucien falls asleep with a notebook in his hands and awakens in 16th-century Bellezza, a city modeled after Venice.

501

JONATHON SCOTT FUQUA

Darby

(Cambridge, MA: Candlewick Press, 2002)

Subject(s): Race Relations; Prejudice; Journalism
Age range(s): Grades 4-6
Major character(s): Darby Carmichael, 9-Year-Old, Writer; Evette, Friend (Darby's), Daughter (of tenant farmer); Beth Fairchild, Friend (Darby's), Classmate (Darby's)
Time period(s): 1920s (1926)
Locale(s): Marlboro County, South Carolina; Bennettsville, South Carolina

Summary: Blind to the societal expectations of a child of her class or skin color, open-minded Darby chooses as her best friends Beth, daughter of a lawyer who supports civil rights for all, and the daughter of one of her family's tenant farmers. From Evette, Darby learns that black people in New York City not only drive, but also own cars and are allowed to write articles for the newspaper. Darby then aspires to be a journalist and Evette helps by editing her writing. Darby's truthful, but naive articles published in the local paper begin with simple observations of life. When her observations turn to race relations in her community, the prejudices of some and the outside influence of the Ku Klux Klan threaten to divide the town. A concluding author's note explains the oral history project that inspired his first novel for young readers. (242 pages)

Where it's reviewed:

Booklist, March 15, 2002, page 1255
Bulletin of the Center for Children's Books, July 2002, page 402
Horn Book, March 2002, page 212
Reading Teacher, November 2002, page 312
School Library Journal, March 2002, page 230

Awards the book has won:

Notable Social Studies Trade Books for Young People, 2003

Other books by the same author:

The Reappearance of Sam Webber, 1999 (Alex Award)

Other books you might like:

Karen Hesse, *Witness*, 2001

Eleven members of a small Vermont community react to

the insidious introduction of the Ku Klux Klan into their town.

Ann M. Martin, *Belle Teal*, 2001

The crowds protesting the entrance of three colored stu-

dents to her school surprise Belle Teal who has learned tolerance of others in her home.

Ronder Thomas Young, *Learning by Heart*, 1993

In the 1960s Rachel becomes aware of racial prejudices and their impact on friendships in her small southern town.

G

502

NEIL GAIMAN
DAVE MCKEAN, Illustrator

Coraline

(New York: HarperCollins, 2002)

Subject(s): Fantasy; Family; Horror
Age range(s): Grades 6-9
Major character(s): Coraline, Child; Mother, Mythical Creature
Time period(s): Indeterminate
Locale(s): Fictional Country

Summary: Coraline is distressed over her family's move to a new house. Wandering disconsolately through the house one day while she is alone, she discovers a mysterious passage that leads to another house. This house seems to be a dream-like mirror image of Coraline's, complete with an ''other mother.'' This other mother uses treats and entertainment to entice Coraline into staying to be her little girl. Coraline is mistrustful, however, and insists on returning to her own side. There she discovers that her parents have been kidnapped by the other mother in hopes of forcing Coraline to stay in the other world. Coraline has little choice but to return to the increasingly creepy other house. Now that bribes haven't worked, the nightmare quality of the place is unveiled. Fortunately, Coraline is befriended by a cat that knows his way around, and she never loses her wits or determination. (176 pages)

Where it's reviewed:
Booklist, August 2002, page 1948
Horn Book, November 2002, page 755
New York Times Book Review, August 11, 2002, page 18
Publishers Weekly, August 5, 2002, page 28
School Library Journal, August 2002, page 184

Awards the book has won:
ALA Best Books for Young Adults, 2003
School Library Journal Best Books, 2002

Other books by the same author:
The Wolves in the Walls, 2003
American Gods: A Novel, 2001
Stardust, 1998

Other books you might like:
Tanith Lee, *Black Unicorn*, 2002
    Tanaquil creates a unicorn and follows it to freedom in this dreamlike tale.
Meredith Ann Pierce, *Treasure at the Heart of the Tanglewood*, 2001
    Hannah undertakes a journey of self-discovery that leads to treasure she has unknowingly guarded.
Sally Prue, *Cold Tom*, 2003
    Tom falls into the stars whenever humans seek to trap him.

503

NEIL GAIMAN
DAVE MCKEAN, Illustrator

The Wolves in the Walls

(New York: HarperCollins Publishers, 2003)

Subject(s): Animals/Wolves; Dwellings; Fantasy
Age range(s): Grades 3-5
Major character(s): Lucy, Child, Daughter
Time period(s): Indeterminate
Locale(s): Fictional Country

Summary: Lucy hears the wolves in the walls but only her stuffed pig toy agrees; no one in her family believes Lucy's claim. The others think the house is old and maybe Lucy is hearing mice or rats or bats. Lucy knows the sounds are coming from wolves and wonders what her parents mean by, '' . . . it's all over'' if wolves come out of the walls. Soon enough the wolves come out and the family flees to the garden. Lucy sneaks back into the house to retrieve her pig by climbing through the walls. The sight of the wolves and their behavior in the house so offends her that she convinces her family to abandon their plans to seek shelter elsewhere and take back the house. Together they sneak into the house's walls and burst through, alarming the wolves. At the sight of people, the wolves flee yelling, " . . . it's all over!" Lucy is content to return to the normalcy of her home and then she hears . . . the elephants in the walls. (56 pages)

Where it's reviewed:
Booklist, August 2003, page 1989
Bulletin of the Center for Children's Books, September 2003, page 14
School Library Journal, September 2003, page 178

Awards the book has won:
New York Times Best Illustrated Books, 2003
IRA Children's Choices, 2004

Other books by the same author:
Coraline, 2002
The Day I Swapped My Dad for 2 Goldfish, 1998

Other books you might like:
Lauren Child, *Beware of the Storybook Wolves*, 2001
   Herb's fears that the characters in his bedtime story will spring to life come true and now he faces two wolves planning to eat him.
Jean Craighead George, *The Moon of the Gray Wolves*, 1991
   A reissue of a youth nonfiction title describes the behavior of an Arctic wolf pack as they hunt caribou during the November full moon.
David Wiesner, *The Three Pigs*, 2001
   Three pigs take control of events in the story by simply walking (or flying) off the page and into another tale where they seek refuge from the wolf.

504

DONALD R. GALLO, Editor

Destination Unexpected
(Cambridge, MA: Candlewick Press, 2003)

Subject(s): Short Stories; Coming-of-Age; Travel
Age range(s): Grades 7-10

Summary: Journeys to places to which one didn't expect to arrive provide the impetus for these ten stories. On a European school trip, Aly unbelievably shares a latte with Seb, the heir apparent, but doesn't know who he is until she spots him riding in the royal carriage in Richard Peck's "The Kiss in the Carryon Bag." Darius's trip is shorter, though emotionally more distant, as he follows a bus route across town to arrive at a library used by rich, white people where he receives an award for his writing in "Something Old, Something New" by Joyce Sweeney. In "August Lights" by Kimberly Willis Holt, Mick takes his adopted younger sister on a trip to the heavens as they share a backyard family tradition and view the Perseid meteor showers. Other authors include Ron Koertge, Margaret Peterson Haddix, Ellen Wittlinger, Alex Flinn, Graham Salisbury, David Lubar and Will Weaver in this anthology of ten short stories. (221 pages)

Where it's reviewed:
Booklist, April 1, 2003, page 1396
Bulletin of the Center for Children's Books, May 2003, page 360
Publishers Weekly, May 5, 2003, page 68
School Library Journal, May 2003, page 151
Voice of Youth Advocates, June 2003, page 127

Other books by the same author:
From There to Here: Short Stories about Immigrant Teens, 2004
On the Fringe, 2001
Time Capsule: Short Stories about Teenagers Throughout the Twentieth Century, 1999
Within Reach: Ten Stories, 1993

Other books you might like:
Jill Davis, *Open Your Eyes: Extraordinary Experiences in Faraway Places*, 2003
   In essays, short stories and letters, ten authors describe their experiences living with, or meeting, people of different cultures.
David Gifaldi, *Rearranging and Other Stories*, 1998
   Teenagers mature in many ways and the author captures the essence of coming-of-age in these stories.
Margaret Peterson Haddix, *Takeoffs and Landings*, 2001
   Chuck and Lori see a different side to their mother as they accompany her on one of her motivational speaking trips.
Joyce Carol Thomas, *A Gathering of Flowers: Stories about Being Young in America*, 1993
   A collection of stories that reflects the ethnic diversity of young people in America.

505

PRISCILLA GALLOWAY

The Courtesan's Daughter
(New York: Delacorte, 2002)

Subject(s): Family Life; Politics; Ancient History
Age range(s): Grades 9-12
Major character(s): Phano, 14-Year-Old, Stepdaughter (of Nera, former courtesan); Nera, Stepmother, Courtier (former, to Phrynion); Stephanos, Father (of Phano); Theo, Political Figure; Phrynion, Wealthy; Philip II of Macedon, Royalty (king)
Time period(s): 4th century B.C. (350s)
Locale(s): Athens, Greece

Summary: The politics and intrigue of ancient Athens form the backdrop for the story of Phano, "the courtesan's daughter." Phano attracts the attention of Theo, a rising politician, because of her lively interest in and knowledge of politics, skills she's learned from Nera, a former courtesan who's now married to Stephanos. Phano and Theo marry but as Theo rises to leadership positions, Phrynion decides he wants revenge against Nera, once his courtesan, and by association against Phano also. Kidnapping both women, they manage to escape and reveal not only Phrynion's plans for revenge, but also his treacherous dealings with King Philip II of Macedon who wishes to overtake Athens. Complicated but fascinating historical tale filled with aspects of Athenian life. (259 pages)

Where it's reviewed:
Booklist, September 15, 2002, page 226
Bulletin of the Center for Children's Books, December 2002, page 155
Publishers Weekly, September 16, 2002, page 69
School Library Journal, September 2002, page 224
Voice of Youth Advocates, December 2002, page 379

Other books by the same author:
Snake Dreamer, 1998
Truly Grim Tales, 1995

Other books you might like:
Gillian Bradshaw, *Imperial Purple*, 1988
   Asked to weave a purple cloak too large for the current ruler, Demetrias knows there's a conspiracy afoot against Emperor Theodosius II.
Gillian Bradshaw, *The Sand-Reckoner*, 2000
   Using the few facts known about Archimedes, the author crafts a tale about the personal side of this brilliant man.
Mary Renault, *Fire from Heaven*, 1969
   The story of the early years of Alexander the Great, up until the death of his father, Philip of Macedonia.

506

JACK GANTOS

Jack Adrift: Fourth Grade without a Clue

(New York: Farrar Straus Giroux, 2003)

Subject(s): Moving, Household; Military Children; Teacher-Student Relationships
Age range(s): Grades 4-7
Major character(s): Jack Henry, 4th Grader, Brother
Time period(s): Indeterminate Past
Locale(s): Cape Hatteras, North Carolina

Summary: When Jack's father joins the Navy, the entire Henry family must move from Pittsburgh to Cape Hatteras, Nort Carolina. Jack worries about making friends, but he fits in with no difficulty. The school year moves quickly with Jack falling in love with his fourth grade teacher, being assigned by the principal to report on other students' bad behavior (an assignment Jack must find a way out of) and refereeing a "genius" contest between his little brother and a neighbor. (208 pages)

Where it's reviewed:
Booklist, August 1, 2003, page 1983
Bulletin of the Center for Children's Books, October 2003, page 60
Horn Book, November/December 2003, page 745
Publishers Weekly, July 21, 2003, page 198
School Library Journal, September 2003, page 210

Other books by the same author:
Jack on the Tracks: Four Seasons of Fifth Grade, 1999
Jack's New Power: Stories from a Caribbean Year, 1995
Heads or Tails: Stories from the Sixth Grade, 1994

Other books you might like:
David A. Adler, *School Trouble for Andy Russell*, 1999
   When a substitute teacher takes over Andy's fourth grade class, he finds himself in the principal's office for a prank he didn't do.
Roald Dahl, *Matilda*, 1988
   Genius Matilda must figure out a way to deal with evil school principal, Mrs. Trunchbull.
Henry Winkler, *Niagara Falls or Does It?*, 2003
   Hank's first assignment in fourth grade turns into a disaster when his "living essay" on Niagara Falls springs a leak.

507

JACK GANTOS
NICOLE RUBEL, Illustrator

Practice Makes Perfect for Rotten Ralph

(New York: Farrar Straus Giroux, 2002)

Series: Rotten Ralph Rotten Reader. Book 2
Subject(s): Animals/Cats; Carnivals; Cheating
Age range(s): Grades 1-3
Major character(s): Ralph, Cat, Cousin (Percy's); Sarah, Child; Percy, Cat, Cousin (Ralph's)
Time period(s): 2000s
Locale(s): United States

Summary: Percy may think that practice is the way to winning prizes at the carnival but Ralph has his own plans for being a winner. Each time perfect Percy wins a contest he gives the prize to Sarah and Ralph becomes just a bit more jealous and desperate. Finally, Ralph resorts to cheating in order to win some prizes for Sarah, but Sarah suspects that he didn't win the prizes honestly and makes him return them. Before they leave the carnival Ralph and Percy try the dunking booth and Ralph legitimately meets with success while Percy practices his swimming. (48 pages)

Where it's reviewed:
Booklist, March 1, 2002, page 1136
Horn Book Guide, Fall 2002, page 351
Horn Book, May 2002, page 330
Publishers Weekly, March 25, 2002, page 66
School Library Journal, March 2002, page 187

Other books by the same author:
Rotten Ralph Helps Out, 2001 (Rotten Ralph Rotten Reader Book 1)
Wedding Bells for Rotten Ralph, 1999
Back to School for Rotten Ralph, 1998

Other books you might like:
Patti Beiling Murphy, *Elinor and Violet: The Story of Two Naughty Chickens*, 2001
   When mischievous Violet befriends slightly naughty Elinor both find themselves in trouble most of the time.
James Stevenson, *Worse than the Worst*, 1994
   When Warren arrives uninvited at Uncle Worst's doorstep the original "worst" appears to have met his match.
Mike Thaler, *The Bully Brothers Trick the Tooth Fairy*, 1993
   Twins Bubba and Bumpo go to extreme measures to make money from the Tooth Fairy until she does some extracting of her own.

508

JACK GANTOS

What Would Joey Do?

(New York: Farrar Straus Giroux, 2002)

Subject(s): Grandmothers; Family Problems; Schools
Age range(s): Grades 5-8
Major character(s): Joey Pigza, Student (home schooler); Olivia Lapp, Blind Person, Student (home schooler); Grandma, Grandmother

Time period(s): 2000s
Locale(s): United States

Summary: In this last book of the *Joey Pigza* trilogy, Joey's hyperactivity is under control and now he tries to be "Mr. Helpful;" unfortunately, his family members need more help than any one person can provide. Grandma tires of living with her son, Joey's father, and moves into Joey's living room, with only a shower curtain for privacy. Though dying, Grandma's content with her oxygen and her smokes. She also gives Joey advice so he'll survive when she's gone, especially the importance of making a friend. Wanting to please, Joey tries to befriend his blind home school partner, Olivia, but she's mean as a snake. By book's end Joey learns he must first help himself before he can help anyone else. (240 pages)

Where it's reviewed:
Booklist, October 1, 2002, page 323
Bulletin of the Center for Children's Books, November 2002, page 107
Horn Book, November 2002, page 757
School Library Journal, September 2002, page 225
Voice of Youth Advocates, December 2002, page 380

Awards the book has won:
Bulletin of the Center for Children's Books Blue Ribbons, 2002

Other books by the same author:
Hole in My Life, 2002
Joey Pigza Loses Control, 2000
Joey Pigza Swallowed the Key, 1998
Jack's Black Book, 1997

Other books you might like:
Lynn McElfresh, *Can You Feel the Thunder?*, 1999
    Self conscious about his sister who's blind and deaf, Mic's too quick to judge other people; the kid Mic thinks is a nerd is the best pitcher he's ever seen.
Gary Paulsen, *Alida's Song*, 1999
    Once again his grandmother saves him from his drunken parents as she finds him a job on the farm where she's the cook.
Patrick J. Quinn, *Matthew Pinkowski's Special Summer*, 1991
    Though Matthew and his friends all have a handicap of some sort, that doesn't stop them from having an adventure-filled summer.

509

LUIS GARAY, Author/Illustrator

The Kite

(Plattsburgh, NY: Tundra Books, 2002)

Subject(s): Poverty; Wishes; Love
Age range(s): Grades 1-4
Major character(s): Francisco, Son, Brother (older); Mama, Mother, Widow(er); Guadalupe, Baby, Sister (younger)
Time period(s): 2000s
Locale(s): Nicaragua

Summary: As Francisco goes to the market to peddle newspapers every morning he passes a vendor with a kite and wishes that he could afford to buy it. The kite symbolizes happy times with his recently deceased father. Instead Francisco dutifully turns over his meager earnings to Mama and wishes for his baby brother's safe birth. When the baby is born, Francisco is more surprised than disappointed to greet a sister, Guadalupe, rather than a brother. While his wish for a brother doesn't come true, Francisco does realize his wish for the kite when the vendor gives it to him in celebration of Guadalupe's birth. (32 pages)

Where it's reviewed:
Booklist, August 2002, page 1971
School Library Journal, December 2002, page 95

Other books by the same author:
Pedrito's Day, 1997 (CLASP Americas Commended Book)
The Long Road, 1997

Other books you might like:
Patricia Grossman, *Saturday Market*, 1994
    A Mexican marketplace is busy on Saturday with vendors selling everything from hand-woven rugs to parrots and sandals.
Mary Kay Kroeger, *Paperboy*, 1996
    In 1927, Willie stands on assigned corners and hawks newspapers in order to earn some money for his family. Louise Borden, co-author.
Tololwa M. Mollel, *My Rows and Piles of Coins*, 1999
    Saruni secretly saves the few coins he earns in hopes of buying a bicycle to help transport his mother's goods to market.

510

PATRICIA LEE GAUCH
SATOMI ICHIKAWA, Illustrator

Tanya and the Red Shoes

(New York: Philomel Books, 2002)

Subject(s): Ballet; Dancing; Sisters
Age range(s): Grades K-3
Major character(s): Tanya, Child, Dancer; Elise, Sister (older), Dancer; Ms. Foley, Teacher, Dancer
Time period(s): 2000s (2002)
Locale(s): United States

Summary: Tanya is eager to progress to dancing *sur pointes*, a level of skill Elise has achieved but for which Ms. Foley says she's not yet ready. So Tanya dreams. In her dreams she is the ballerina in *The Red Shoes* whirling on the tips of her toes in beautiful red shoes. Elise affirms that Tanya is too young for toe, but assures her that one day her turn will come. And, in time, it does. Tanya discovers that the reality of toe shoes includes blisters and sore feet, something she's never experienced in her imagination, but Elise helps her when she's discouraged and Tanya feels confident that she will achieve her dreams. (40 pages)

Where it's reviewed:
Booklist, March 1, 2002, page 1141
Horn Book, May 2002, page 314
Kirkus Reviews, February 15, 2002, page 255
Publishers Weekly, February 4, 2002, page 78
School Library Journal, March 2002, page 187

Other books by the same author:
Tanya Treasury, 2002

Presenting Tanya, the Ugly Duckling, 1999 (Booklist Editors' Choice)
Tanya and the Magic Wardrobe, 1997

Other books you might like:
Naia Bray-Moffatt, *Ballet School*, 2003
In this nonfiction title, photographs illustrate a story of young dancers in class and observing a class of older students.
Rachel Isadora, *On Your Toes: A Ballet ABC*, 2003
Dancers make their way through an alphabet of ballet terms.
Barbara Samuels, *Dolores on Her Toes*, 2003
Since Dolores does everything with her pet cat she mistakenly thinks that Duncan will enjoy her love of ballet, but he is a reluctant partner.

511

GAIL GAUTHIER

Saving the Planet & Stuff

(New York: Putnam, 2003)

Subject(s): Ecology; Summer; Publishing
Age range(s): Grades 7-10
Major character(s): Michael Peter Racine III, 16-Year-Old, Worker (intern); Nora Blake, Publisher (ecology journal); Walt Marcello, Publisher (ecology journal); Todd Mylnarski, Editor
Time period(s): 2000s
Locale(s): Vermont

Summary: Michael's landscaping business goes belly-up and suddenly he has no summer job, unlike all his friends who seem to be doing important things. A typical teenage consumer, he has no idea what he's gotten himself into when he agrees to work for aging hippie friends of his grandparents who own the ecological journal *The Earth's Wife*. Living with Nora and Walt, Michael is dismayed to discover they practice what they write about after he walks into his bedroom and finds it filled with potentially recyclable junk. Turning off lights, using a composting toilet and riding his bicycle to work are all new adventures for Michael and he questions his decision. But the more he's around Nora and Walt and realizes the importance of their ecological decisions, the better able he is to stand up to Todd, the recently hired aggressive, deceitful managing editor. Thanks to Michael's intervention, a takeover of the magazine and cancellation of an important exposé are averted in this ecological work. (232 pages)

Where it's reviewed:
Booklist, May 15, 2003, page 1656
Horn Book, July 2003, page 456
Publishers Weekly, June 16, 2003, page 72
School Library Journal, June 2003, page 138
Voice of Youth Advocates, June 2003, page 129

Other books by the same author:
Hero of Ticonderoga, 2001
Club Earth, 1999
Year with Butch and Spike, 1998
My Life Among the Aliens, 1996

Other books you might like:
Ann Brashares, *The Sisterhood of the Traveling Pants*, 2001
Separated for the summer, four friends rely on a pair of jeans to keep them in touch.
Jean Craighead George, *The Case of the Missing Cutthroats: An Ecological Mystery*, 1996
On a trip to discover why the cutthroat species is declining, Spinner and her cousin Al discover how easily the balance of nature can be disturbed.
Sarah Sargent, *Seeds of Change*, 1989
Rachel's father buys swampland to build a theme park, but Rachel loves the beauty of the swamp and must show her dad how wrong development will be.

512

MARIE-LOUISE GAY, Author/Illustrator

Good Morning, Sam

(Toronto: Groundwood Books/Douglas & McIntyre, 2003)

Subject(s): Brothers and Sisters; Independence; Self-Reliance
Age range(s): Preschool-Grade 1
Major character(s): Sam, Child, Brother (younger); Stella, Child, Sister (older)
Time period(s): 2000s (2003)
Locale(s): Canada

Summary: Stella wakens Sam and offers to help him get dressed. Confident that he can do it himself, Sam refuses Stella's assistance. Assuring Stella that he is hurrying, Sam is, instead, playing happily with his dog. When he does try to get dressed he calls for Stella because his head is stuck in his pajama top and he can't find his underpants. Stella is so busy helping Sam find his shoes and reminding him to put his pants on before he goes out that she seems to have forgotten an important part of her morning routine. (28 pages)

Where it's reviewed:
Booklist, March 15, 2003, page 1331
Bulletin of the Center for Children's Books, May 2003, page 361
Horn Book, July 2003, page 442
School Library Journal, April 2003, page 120

Other books by the same author:
Good Night Sam, 2003
Stella, Fairy of the Forest, 2002 (School Library Journal Best Books)
Stella, Queen of the Snow, 2000
Stella, Star of the Sea, 1999 (Bulletin of the Center for Children's Books Blue Ribbon)

Other books you might like:
Shirley Hughes, *Annie Rose Is My Little Sister*, 2003
Annie Rose is lucky to have a big brother who understands her interests and helps her in any way he can.
Angela Johnson, *Do Like Kyla*, 1990
Kyla's younger sister follows her all day, imitating her behavior.
Rosemary Wells, *Max Cleans Up*, 2000
Max is sure he can clean his room without Ruby's help and Ruby is just as sure that Max will need assistance from his big sister.

513

MARIE-LOUISE GAY, Author/Illustrator

Good Night Sam

(Berkeley, CA: Groundwood Books/Douglas & McIntyre, 2003)

Subject(s): Brothers and Sisters; Bedtime; Sleep
Age range(s): Preschool-Grade 1
Major character(s): Stella, Child, Sister (older); Sam, Child, Brother (younger); Fred, Dog
Time period(s): 2000s (2003)
Locale(s): Canada

Summary: Unable to sleep without the family pet Sam enlists Stella's help in a nighttime search for Fred in the dark house. Sam is confident that Fred wouldn't be in the closet with the monster or downstairs with the strange noises, but Stella looks in all those places anyway. Finally, the tired, unsuccessful children return to bed and that's where Sam finds Fred, sleeping under his quilt. (28 pages)

Where it's reviewed:
Bulletin of the Center for Children's Books, September 2003, page 15
School Library Journal, November 2003, page 94

Awards the book has won:
Center for Children's Books Best Books, 2003

Other books by the same author:
Good Morning, Sam, 2003
Stella, Queen of the Snow, 2000
Stella, Star of the Sea, 1999 (Bulletin of the Center for Children's Books Blue Ribbon)

Other books you might like:
Nicola Edwards, *Goodnight Baxter*, 2002
    Charlie's new puppy can't sleep until Charlie comforts Baxter with lots of love.
Mary Beth Lundgren, *Seven Scary Monsters*, 2003
    In a rhyming tale a little boy uses his wits and his brand of magic to vanquish the monsters in his bedrooms.
Fran Manushkin, *Peeping and Sleeping*, 1994
    The distant and continuous sound of peeping keeps Barry from sleeping so he and his father go to investigate the source.
Veronica Uribe, *Buzz Buzz Buzz*, 2001
    Juliana and Andres are tucked in bed but unable to sleep because of the buzzing of a mosquito.

514

MARIE-LOUISE GAY, Author/Illustrator

Stella, Fairy of the Forest

(Toronto: A Groundwood Book/Douglas & McIntyre, 2002)

Subject(s): Brothers and Sisters; Fairies; Imagination
Age range(s): Grades K-2
Major character(s): Stella, Child, Sister (Older); Sam, Child, Brother (Younger)
Time period(s): 2000s (2002)
Locale(s): Canada

Summary: Confident Stella leads slightly timid, but definitely observant Sam into the forest on a quest for fairies. Stella has a matter-of-fact, comforting answer for each of Sam's many questions. Though Stella's plans do not always work out exactly as she assures Sam they will, the siblings enjoy a shared adventure, make a house of ferns in the forest and settle back to quietly look for fairies on which to make a wish. (32 pages)

Where it's reviewed:
Booklist, March 15, 2002, page 1261
Bulletin of the Center for Children's Books, March 2002, page 240
Horn Book Guide, Fall 2002, page 328
Publishers Weekly, March 18, 2002, page 106
School Library Journal, June 2002, page 96

Awards the book has won:
School Library Journal Best Books, 2002

Other books by the same author:
Stella, Queen of the Snow, 2000
Stella, Star of the Sea, 1999 (Bulletin of the Center for Children's Books Blue Ribbon)
Fat Charlie's Circus, 1997

Other books you might like:
Ian Falconer, *Olivia*, 2000
    Olivia, a pig with a mind of her own, tolerates her younger brother while pursuing her interests independently.
Maurice Sendak, *Outside Over There*, 1981
    In a Caldecott Honor Book, Ida bravely goes ''outside over there'' to search for her baby sister who's been taken by goblins.
Rosemary Wells, *Max Cleans Up*, 2000
    Ruby, the bossy big sister, directs the clean up of Max's messy room as Max quietly asserts himself when Ruby is not looking.

515

ARTHUR GEISERT, Author/Illustrator

The Giant Ball of String

(Boston: Walter Lorraine Books/Houghton Mifflin Company, 2002)

Subject(s): Lost and Found; Problem Solving; Floods
Age range(s): Grades K-3
Time period(s): Indeterminate
Locale(s): Rumpus Ridge, Wisconsin; Cornwall

Summary: Citizens of Rumpus Ridge are mighty proud of their giant ball of string so when a spring flood washes it away the children of Rumpus Ridge go in search of it. They find it in Cornwall where the floodwaters carried it and it's obvious that the Cornwall citizens plan to keep it and display it as their own. Returning to Rumpus Ridge the youngsters devise an elaborate plan to retrieve the string and then set out to implement it. Their scheme succeeds and they sail back upstream with the famous ball of string and celebrate its homecoming. (32 pages)

Where it's reviewed:
Booklist, September 15, 2002, page 232
Horn Book Guide, Spring 2003, page 34
Kirkus Reviews, July 1, 2002, page 954

Publishers Weekly, July 22, 2002, page 177
School Library Journal, September 2002, page 192

Awards the book has won:
Publishers Weekly Best Children's Books, 2002

Other books by the same author:
Nursery Crimes, 2001
The Etcher's Studio, 1997 (Publishers Weekly Best Children's Books)
After the Flood, 1994

Other books you might like:
Paul Fleischman, *Lost!: A Story in String*, 2000
    After a storm causes a power outage Grandmother entertains her granddaughter with a story of a girl and a piece of string, her only toy.
Carole Lexa Schaefer, *The Squiggle*, 1996
    Finding a "squiggle" of red string on the ground inspires the imagination of a child.
Tasha Tudor, *The Great Corgiville Kidnapping*, 1997
    A gang kidnaps Babe, the town's prize rooster, and Caleb, local detective, must come up with an ingenious rescue plan.

516

BONNIE GEISERT
ARTHUR GEISERT, Illustrator

Prairie Summer

(Boston: Walter Lorraine Books/Houghton Mifflin Company, 2002)

Subject(s): Farm Life; Sisters; Growing Up
Age range(s): Grades 3-5
Major character(s): Rachel, 10-Year-Old, Sister; Tony "Dad" Johnson, Father, Farmer; Mom, Mother, Spouse
Time period(s): 1950s (1954)
Locale(s): Cresbard, South Dakota

Summary: Life as a farmer's daughter is a lot of hard work. With her two older sisters, Rachel repairs fences, feeds cattle, rakes hay, and hopes to do something to Dad's satisfaction. Rachel would prefer to stay in the house with Mom and her younger sister since she doesn't enjoy farm work, is afraid of the cattle and tends to daydream so she makes mistakes, sometimes with serious consequences. After her assignment to burn the trash leads to a grass fire that threatens the family's home, Rachel is not allowed to accompany Dad and her sisters to town on a Saturday night. Instead, she's expected to pull weeds. As she works, Rachel hears her pregnant mother calling her. Mom is in labor and needs Rachel to drive her to the hospital. Although Rachel has never driven Dad's pick-up she has experience with tractors and, with Mom's guidance, she succeeds in getting to the county hospital eight minutes before her brother is born. Finally, she's done something right! (114 pages)

Where it's reviewed:
New Advocate, Spring 2003, page 221
New York Times Book Review, June 2, 2002, page 30
Publishers Weekly, March 4, 2002, page 80
Riverbank Review, Summer 2002, page 39
School Library Journal, May 2002, page 114

Other books by the same author:
Desert Town, 2001
Mountain Town, 2000
Prairie Town, 1998

Other books you might like:
Mary Downing Hahn, *Anna on the Farm*, 2001
    For Anna farm work is a summer novelty and an opportunity to wear overalls and braid her hair during the visit with her aunt and uncle.
Patricia MacLachlan, *Sarah, Plain and Tall*, 1985
    In a Newbery Medal winning title Sarah travels from Maine to the prairie farm of a widower and his two children in hopes she can "make a difference."
Laura Ingalls Wilder, *Little Town on the Prairie*, 1953
    The Wilder family settles on a prairie homestead, breaking sod to establish a farm and participating in the building of the town.

517

JEAN CRAIGHEAD GEORGE
WENDELL MINOR, Illustrator

Fire Storm

(New York: Katherine Tegen Books/HarperCollins Publishers, 2003)

Series: Outdoor Adventures. Book 2
Subject(s): Fires; Rafting; Sports/Kayaking
Age range(s): Grades 1-4
Major character(s): Axel, Nephew, Child; Charlotte, Aunt, Spouse; Paul, Uncle, Ranger (forester)
Time period(s): 2000s (2000)
Locale(s): Salmon River, Idaho

Summary: With Aunt Charlotte and Uncle Paul as guides Axel enjoys a vacation trip down the Middle Fork of the Salmon River. He paddles a kayak with his small dog as a companion and follows his aunt and uncle around boulders and down rapids. The summer is dry and forest fires rage in the mountains hundreds of miles from the river as the trip begins. After three days of wilderness beauty the travelers see the first signs of fire encroaching on the nearby hills. Dry lightning ignites more fires as trees explode in flames. When smoke makes continued travel on the river treacherous, Axel, Aunt Charlotte and Uncle Paul beach at a small campground thinking they are safe from the flames on the other side of the river. A shift of wind proves them wrong as a firestorm explodes and flames leap the river forcing them to continue downstream to safety. (32 pages)

Where it's reviewed:
Booklist, December 1, 2003, page 684
Publishers Weekly, September 15, 2003, page 67
School Library Journal, November 2003, page 94

Awards the book has won:
IRA Children's Choices, 2004

Other books by the same author:
Cliff Hanger, 2002 (Outdoor Adventures Book 1)
Nutik & Amaroq Play Ball, 2001
Nutik, the Wolf Pup, 2001 (Notable Social Studies Trade Books for Young People)

Other books you might like:
Patrick Cone, *Wildfire*, 1997
This entry in the nonfiction Nature in Action series describes different types of wildfires and tells how to fight and prevent such fires.
Teddy Jam, *The Year of Fire*, 1993
Grandfather tells of an extinguished fire that continued to burn underground in a Canadian forest all winter, causing the loss of 10,000 trees.
Laurence Pringle, *Fire in the Forest: A Cycle of Growth and Renewal*, 1994
This nonfiction title describes a 300-year cycle of fire and regrowth in a Western lodgepole pine forest.
Ginger Wadsworth, *River Discoveries*, 2002
A nonfiction picture book describes 24 hours in the life of the Salmon River ecosystem.

518

JEAN CRAIGHEAD GEORGE
DANIEL SAN SOUCI, Illustrator

Frightful's Daughter

(New York: Dutton Children's Books, 2002)

Subject(s): Animals/Falcons; Individuality; Survival
Age range(s): Grades 1-3
Major character(s): Sam Gribley, Animal Lover, Naturalist; Frightful, Bird (falcon), Mother; Oksi, Bird (falcon), Daughter
Time period(s): 2000s
Locale(s): Catskill Mountains

Summary: Frightful, watching a man climb the bridge girders to her nest, warns her three chicks of the danger approaching. Oksi's brothers do the natural thing and freeze in place, but independent Oksi hides in the shadows far from the girder's edge. Her individuality saves her from the thief who, despite Frightful's attacks, manages to grab her brothers. Sam sees what happens but can do nothing except rescue Oksi. He brings her to the nesting box near his treehouse home where Frightful finds her. Temporarily, the two peregrine falcons live in the forest until Oksi develops the ability to fly and hunt. Then they return to their natural, open habitat but Oksi remains the individual living life on her own terms. When independent Oksi refuses to fly south for the winter, she almost dies for lack of food, but makes her way back to Sam who shelters her and feeds her until spring. (32 pages)

Where it's reviewed:
Booklist, September 1, 2002, page 136
Publishers Weekly, June 24, 2002, page 59
School Library Journal, September 2002, page 192

Other books by the same author:
Fire Storm, 2003
Cliff Hanger, 2002
Nutik, the Wolf Pup, 2001

Other books you might like:
Robert J. Blake, *Fledgling*, 2000
On her first attempt at flight Fledgling, a kestral, evades a hawk by racing into a crowded subway car.

Madeline Dunphy, *The Peregrine's Journey*, 2000
This picture book describes a peregrine falcon's 8,000-mile migration from Alaska to Argentina.
Suzie Gilbert, *Hawk Hill*, 1996
Pete volunteers at a rehabilitation facility for injured birds and cares for a hawk with an injured wing until she is ready for release.
Lola M. Schaefer, *Arrowhawk*, 2004
Wounded by a poacher's arrow, a red-tailed hawk survives alone for eight weeks before being rescued by wildlife rehabilitators.

519

MORDICAI GERSTEIN, Author/Illustrator

Sparrow Jack

(New York: Frances Foster Books/Farrar Straus Giroux, 2003)

Subject(s): Animals/Birds; Emigration and Immigration; Historical
Age range(s): Grades 1-3
Major character(s): John Bardsley, Immigrant, Animal Lover
Time period(s): 1860s (1868)
Locale(s): Ashton, England; Philadelphia, Pennsylvania

Summary: Long before John Bardsley immigrated to America he befriended sparrows in his hometown. As a newly arrived immigrant he experiences the problems of Philadelphia residents each spring when inchworms are active. The local birds refuse to eat the inchworms so John Bardsley sails back to England, gathers 1,000 sparrows and returns to America. Through the winter John shelters them in his house and in the spring they are released. At first they do not appear to be eating inchworms but once their babies hatch, the inchworms become the primary diet of the infant birds. Although the people appreciate the efforts of ''Sparrow Jack'' they do think, for all their good, the sparrows are actually noisy pests. (32 pages)

Where it's reviewed:
Booklist, April 1, 2003, page 1402
Bulletin of the Center for Children's Books, June 2003, page 401
Horn Book, March 2003, page 202
Riverbank Review, Spring 2003, page 35
School Library Journal, June 2003, page 99

Awards the book has won:
Notable Social Studies Trade Books for Young People, 2004

Other books by the same author:
Fox Eyes, 2004
The Man Who Walked Between the Towers, 2003 (Caldecott Medal)
What Charlie Heard, 2002

Other books you might like:
Caroline Arnold, *House Sparrows Everywhere*, 1992
This nonfiction book describes the habitat and physical characteristics of the sparrow.
Joy Cowley, *The Video Shop Sparrow*, 1999
In order to free a sparrow trapped inside a video shop two boys get help from the mayor.

Leyla Torres, *Subway Sparrow*, 1993
> Passengers on a subway train work together to try to help a trapped sparrow escape.

520

FAYE GIBBONS
SHERRY MEIDELL, Illustrator

The Day the Picture Man Came
(Honesdale, PA: Boyds Mills Press, 2003)

Subject(s): Photography; Rural Life; Family Life
Age range(s): Grades K-2
Major character(s): Emily Howard, Child, Sister; Cecil Bramlett, Photographer
Time period(s): 1900s
Locale(s): Georgia

Summary: Emily Howard is having a bad day. The goat eats her sister's bonnet; the dogs spill her jar of freckle remover; and bugs bite Emily as she picks blackberries. But the arrival of ''C. Bramlett, Photographer,'' brings new excitement. The Howard family poses for a portrait with all of their animals and a ruckus ensues. Mr. Bramlett agrees to sell the family two portraits for the price of one and the Howards manage to get a second, dignified family portrait. (32 pages)

Where it's reviewed:
Booklist, February 15, 2003, page 1074
Horn Book Guide, Fall 2003, page 323
Publishers Weekly, December 16, 2002
School Library Journal, March 2003, page 192

Other books by the same author:
Emma Jo's Song, 2001
Mama and Me and the Model T, 1999
Hook Moon Night: Spooky Tales from the Georgia Mountains, 1997
Night in the Barn, 1995
Mighty Close to Heaven, 1985

Other books you might like:
Larry Dane Brimner, *Max and Felix*, 1995
> Two frogs, Max and Felix, get into some interesting situations when Felix is trying to take a picture of Max with his new camera.
Denis Roche, *The Best Class Picture Ever!*, 2003
> It's class picture day, but Class 202 is missing a teacher, their class pet has run away and Olivia refuses to smile.
Joan Sandin, *Pioneer Bear*, 1995
> When a photographer comes to the Irwin farm to photograph Andrew's trained bear cub no one can find Bearly—until the family picture is developed.
Judith Viorst, *Alexander and the Terrible, Horrible, No Good, Very Bad Day*, 1972
> Alexander has a bad day starting when he wakes up with gum in his hair.

521

FAYE GIBBONS
SHERRY MEIDELL, Illustrator

Full Steam Ahead
(Honesdale, PA: Boyds Mills Press, 2002)

Subject(s): Trains; Grandparents; Rural Life
Age range(s): Grades K-3
Major character(s): Sammy, Child; Grandpa, Grandfather, Farmer
Time period(s): 19th century
Locale(s): Turkey Creek, Georgia

Summary: Sammy loves trains and is excited when he hears that the train is finally coming to Turkey Creek. He sets off with Grandpa to warn all the other townsfolk, but then finds they're too late to make it to the crossing. Sammy and Grandpa take a short cut to the track where they are offered a ride after Sammy tells the engineer their story. Sammy's siblings and the other town folk are surprised to see them get off at the next crossing. (32 pages)

Where it's reviewed:
Booklist, April 1, 2002, page 1332
Horn Book Guide, Fall 2002, page 329
Publishers Weekly, February 4, 2002, page 76
School Library Journal, July 2002, page 90

Other books by the same author:
Emma Jo's Song, 2001
Mama and Me and the Model T, 1999
Mountain Wedding, 1996

Other books you might like:
Marsha Wilson Chall, *Prairie Train*, 2003
> A young girl is excited by her first train ride across the prairie to visit her grandmother.
Angela Johnson, *I Dream of Trains*, 2003
> A young African-American boy dreams of being an engineer like the legendary 19th-century engineer Casey Jones.
Tony Johnston, *How Many Miles to Jacksonville?*, 1996
> For residents of a small, isolated east Texas town the train that passes through symbolizes wealth and adventure.
Patrick O'Brien, *Steam, Smoke and Steel: Back in Time With Trains*, 2000
> A history of trains seen from the perspective of a young boy who comes from a long line of locomotive engineers. Non-fiction.
Watty Piper, *The Little Engine That Could*, 1978
> The Little Blue Engine traverses a mountain that other engines couldn't, in order to deliver toys to good girls and boys.

522

WILLIAM GIBSON

Pattern Recognition
(New York: G.P. Putnam's Sons, 2003)

Subject(s): Popular Culture; Business
Age range(s): Grades 10-Adult

Major character(s): Cayce Pollard, Businesswoman; Humbertus Bigend, Businessman; Peter "Parkaboy" Gilbert, Friend, Computer Expert; Boone Chu, Computer Expert; Wingrove Pollard, Father
Time period(s): Indeterminate Future
Locale(s): London, England; Tokyo, Japan; Moscow, Russia

Summary: Cayce Pollard has turned her eerie talent for spotting trends and fashion into a flourishing consultancy. When she is hired by the cutting-edge Blue Ant advertising firm to vet a new logo, Cayce comes in contact with Humbertus Bigend, the steamrolling Belgian entrepreneur at the head of Big Ant. Bigend has an ulterior motive for hiring Cayce for he is aware of her deep interest in *the footage*, those mysterious pieces of filmmaking being released anonymously over the Internet. In spite of worldwide fascination with these seconds-long sections, no one knows anything about the maker, or whether the bits are part of a whole, how they might fit together, or if it exists complete somewhere. Bigend wants to know. Although she is less than comfortable with Bigend, Cayce takes the job. Aided by her fellow footagehead, Parkaboy, and Boone Chu, a hacker hired by Bigend, Cayce finds herself pursuing the mystery to Tokyo and Moscow. And, unnervingly, it seems to have a connection with her ex-CIA father, who disappeared on 9/11. (356 pages)

Where it's reviewed:
Booklist, November 15, 2002, page 548
Entertainment Weekly, February 7, 2003, page 86
Library Journal, February 1, 2003, page 116
School Library Journal, May 2003, page 179
Time, February 10, 2003, page 80

Other books by the same author:
All Tomorrow's Parties, 1999
Idoru, 1996
Virtual Light, 1993

Other books you might like:
Max Barry, *Jennifer Government*, 2003
    This satire lampoons the all-pervasive commercial culture that triggers Cayce's panic attacks.
Elizabeth Moon, *The Speed of Dark*, 2003
    An autistic man in the near future has to face a choice between his unique perceptions and normalcy.
Connie Willis, *Remake*, 1995
    In a future world where all filmmaking is digitized, a mysterious young woman keeps appearing unexpectedly in the movies.

523

PATRICIA REILLY GIFF

Maggie's Door
(New York: Wendy Lamb/Random House Books, 2003)

Subject(s): Emigration and Immigration; Irish Potato Famine
Age range(s): Grades 5-8
Major character(s): Nory Ryan, Immigrant; Sean Red Mallon, Immigrant
Time period(s): 19th century
Locale(s): Ireland; New York, New York

Summary: In this sequel to *Nory Ryan's Song*, Nory and her boyfriend Sean both head to Galway to take a ship to America, but travel separately from Maidin Bay. Nory's late leaving and then is robbed by a reckless child whose discarded walking stick enables Nory to travel on her injured foot. Sean aids a farmer, but that leaves him lagging behind the others in his group. The two sweethearts don't realize they're aboard the same ship to America, for Sean's in the hold acting as human ballast and Nory's above board. They meet just in time to head to Maggie's door in Brooklyn, where they stay with Nory's sister Maggie who's married to Sean's brother. (158 pages)

Where it's reviewed:
Bulletin of the Center for Children's Books, February 2004, page 230
Horn Book, September 2003, page 610
Library Media Connection, March 2004, page 63
Publishers Weekly, August 25, 2003, page 65
School Library Journal, September 2003, page 210

Other books by the same author:
Don't Tell the Girls: A Family Memoir, 2005
A House of Tailors, 2004
Pictures of Hollis Woods, 2002
All the Way Home, 2001
Nory Ryan's Song, 2000

Other books you might like:
Barry Denenberg, *So Far from Home: The Diary of Mary Driscoll, an Irish Mill Girl*, 1997
    Though America is not as she imagined, Mary is just happy to be out of Ireland and the misery of the potato crop famine.
Elizabeth Lutzier, *The Coldest Winter*, 1991
    Evicted from their home when their crops fail in the coldest winter ever in Ireland, the only hope for the Kennedy family is to sail to America.
Clare Pastore, *Fiona McGilray's Story: A Voyage from Ireland in 1849*, 2001
    In this first of a series, Fiona and Patrick travel to America but are surprised to be referred to as the "dirty Irish."

524

PATRICIA REILLY GIFF

Pictures of Hollis Woods
(New York: Wendy Lamb Books/Random House, 2002)

Subject(s): Foster Homes; Artists and Art; Old Age
Age range(s): Grades 4-8
Major character(s): Hollis Woods, 12-Year-Old, Orphan; Josie Cahill, Aged Person, Artist
Time period(s): 2000s
Locale(s): Long Island, New York

Summary: Named for the place where she was found, Hollis Woods has been in one foster home after another. Recently she lived with the Regan family and thought they would adopt her; when that didn't happen, Hollis once again ran away. Now she's been placed with the eccentric Josie, a retired art teacher, and the two find instant compatibility in their mutual artistic talents. As Josie becomes more and more forgetful their roles are reversed and Hollis becomes the caregiver, afraid now she'll be taken away from Josie. Because Hollis knows that Josie can't survive on her own, she convinces Josie to run away to Hollis's favorite spot, the Regans' summer home. Taking that big step sets up a move for both Hollis and Josie. (166 pages)

Where it's reviewed:
Bulletin of the Center for Children's Books, December 2002, page 156
Horn Book, January 2003, page 72
Publishers Weekly, July 15, 2002, page 74
Riverbank Review, Spring 2003, page 44
School Library Journal, September 2002, page 225

Awards the book has won:
ALA Best Books for Young Adults, 2003
Newbery Honor Book, 2003

Other books by the same author:
A House of Tailors, 2004
Maggie's Door, 2003
All the Way Home, 2001
Nory Ryan's Song, 2000
Lily's Crossing, 1997

Other books you might like:
Adrian Fogelin, *Anna Casey's Place in the World*, 2001
    For now, Anna's "place" is a foster home in Florida and adjusting to it is difficult.
Polly Horvath, *Everything on a Waffle*, 2001
    Primrose's parents are lost at sea but only Primrose is convinced they're waiting for rescue; for now she's shuttled between foster homes.
Katherine Paterson, *The Great Gilly Hopkins*, 1978
    Eleven-year-old Gilly longs to live with her mother and rejects those who reach out to her in friendship.
Katherine Paterson, *The Same Stuff as Stars*, 2002
    Dumped by her mother on her great-grandmother's doorstep, Angel once again assumes responsibility for running a household.
Zilpha Keatley Snyder, *Gib Rides Home*, 1998
    Gib leaps at the chance to leave the orphanage and work on Mr. Thornton's ranch, but an error in judgment sends him back.

525

GAIL GILES

Dead Girls Don't Write Letters

(Brookfield, CT: Roaring Brook Press, 2003)

Subject(s): Sisters; Death; Mystery and Detective Stories
Age range(s): Grades 7-10
Major character(s): Sunny Reynolds, 14-Year-Old; Jasmine "Jazz" Reynolds, Sister (deceased, of Sunny); Debra Hallard, Imposter; Mrs. Reynolds, Mother (of Sunny and Jazz)
Time period(s): 2000s
Locale(s): Angleton, Texas

Summary: Sunny's older sister Jazz dies in an apartment fire in New York City and Sunny's left to pick up the pieces from her father's descent into alcoholism and her mother's into depression. The only person who didn't think self-centered Jazz was

wonderful is Sunny, so for the first time in her life, she's pretty happy. Then her life turns upside down with the receipt of a letter from Jazz saying she wasn't killed in the fire and will be coming home for a visit. The girl who shows up looks like Jazz and knows some family history, which is enough to convince Mrs. Reynolds of her identity, but Sunny and her father quickly realize the girl is an imposter. Who is this girl and what's Sunny to do? (136 pages)

Where it's reviewed:
Booklist, March 15, 2003, page 1317
Bulletin of the Center for Children's Books, March 2003, page 274
Publishers Weekly, January 13, 2003, page 60
School Library Journal, May 2003, page 152
Voice of Youth Advocates, June 2003, page 129

Awards the book has won:
ALA Quick Picks for Reluctant Young Adult Readers, 2004

Other books by the same author:
Playing in Traffic, 2004
Shattering Glass, 2002

Other books you might like:
Lois Duncan, *The Twisted Window*, 1987
    When Tracy agrees to help a young man kidnap his half-sister, she has no idea how much she'll regret her decision.
Sonya Sones, *Stop Pretending: What Happened When My Big Sister Went Crazy*, 1999
    Cookie's life begins to crumble when her sister is hospitalized following a mental breakdown.
Sally Warner, *Sister Split*, 2001
    Until her parents separate, Ivy has no idea that her older sister hates her.
Carol Lynch Williams, *Carolina Autumn*, 2000
    Caroline misses her older sister Madelaine, killed a year earlier in a plane crash, and writes letters to her about her new adventures.

526

GAIL GILES

Shattering Glass

(Brookfield, CT: Roaring Brook/Millbrook, 2002)

Subject(s): Popularity; Violence; Schools/Junior High School
Age range(s): Grades 9-12
Major character(s): Simon Glass, Student—High School; Robert Haynes "Rob" Baddeck Jr., Student—High School; Lance Anstey, Bully, Student—High School; Thaddeus R. "Young" Steward IV, Student—High School, Narrator
Time period(s): 1990s
Locale(s): Texas

Summary: Manipulative Rob transfers to a new high school and quickly assumes Lance Anstey's former alpha position, charms teachers, acquires a harem of 'wannabe' girlfriends and leads a group of popular guys. Rob decides to transform Simon Glass, consummate nerd, object of constant bullying and easily the most hated guy in the high school, into someone as popular as he is. Rob and his friends, including narrator Young Steward, change Simon's dress, teach him how to drive and find him a great girlfriend, who just happens to be the love of Young's life. As introductory chapter comments portend, something terrible occurs, especially when Simon becomes self-confident and fights Rob's manipulation with his own deviousness in this chilling, page-turning first novel. (215 pages)

Where it's reviewed:
Booklist, March 1, 2002, page 1133
Bulletin of the Center for Children's Books, May 2002, page 324
Kliatt, July 2002, page 10
School Library Journal, April 2002, page 148
Voice of Youth Advocates, June 2002, page 118

Awards the book has won:
ALA Best Books for Young Adults, 2003
ALA Quick Picks for Reluctant Young Adult Readers, 2003

Other books by the same author:
Dead Girls Don't Write Letters, 2003

Other books you might like:
Alex Flinn, *Breaking Point*, 2002
  Paul's delight at Charlie's friendship leads to vandalism, cheating and finally leaving a bomb in a classroom.
Alice Hoffman, *The River King*, 2000
  August Pierce is too much of an individual for some of the boys at his elite prep school and an attempt to put him in his place turns to tragedy.
Patrick Redmond, *Something Dangerous*, 1999
  Feeling out of place, Jonathan is thrilled when befriended by Richard, unaware that he'll be used to unleash evil against other students.
Nancy Werlin, *Black Mirror*, 2001
  When her brother commits suicide through a heroin overdose, Frances feels something's amiss and searches for a campus drug group.

527

JAMIE GILSON

Stink Alley

(New York: HarperCollins, 2002)

Subject(s): Puritans; Christian Life; Artists and Art
Age range(s): Grades 4-7
Major character(s): William Brewster, Religious (Puritan leader), Historical Figure; Lizzy Tinker, 12-Year-Old, Orphan; Rembrandt Harmensz van Rijn, Child, Historical Figure (artist)
Time period(s): 17th century (1614)
Locale(s): Leiden, Netherlands

Summary: Six years earlier Lizzy, her parents and other Separatists fled England for Holland, accompanied by their leader William Brewster, prior to their eventual journaey to America. Lizzy's parents died and the Brewsters took her in rather than sending her to the Leiden orphanage. Though Lizzy is grateful for their care, she's an outspoken child who recognizes the contrast between the carefree way Dutch children are raised and the stern, work-filled life she is expected to lead. Lizzy takes a job in the kitchen of the well-to-do van Rijn family where she meets their mischievous son with

whom she gets into alot of trouble. By book's end, Lizzy arranges to live with a different family knowing she'll be able to maintain her friendship with Rembrandt. (183 pages)

Where it's reviewed:
Booklist, April 15, 2002, page 1401
Bulletin of the Center for Children's Books, September 2002, page 17
Horn Book, September 2002, page 472
School Library Journal, July 2002, page 120
Tribune Books (Chicago), June 16, 2002, page 5

Other books by the same author:
Wagon Train 911, 1996
Hobie Hanson, Greatest Hero of the Mall, 1989
Thirteen Ways to Sink a Sub, 1982
Do Bananas Chew Gum?, 1980

Other books you might like:
Sandra Forrester, *Wheel of the Moon*, 2000
  Living with a group of fellow orphans, Pen's group is caught, tossed onboard ship and sent to Jamestown as indentured servants.
Ann Rinaldi, *The Journal of Jasper Jonathan Pierce: A Pilgrim Boy*, 2000
  Jasper is happy to have the chance to sail aboard the *Mayflower* until he realizes his brother has been left behind.
G. Clifton Wisler, *This New Land*, 1987
  Fleeing religious persecution in England, the Woodley family escapes to the Netherlands before setting sail for America.

528

MIRIAM GLASSMAN
VICTORIA ROBERTS, Illustrator

Halloweena

(New York: Atheneum Books for Young Readers, 2002)

Subject(s): Witches and Witchcraft; Halloween; Babies
Age range(s): Grades K-3
Major character(s): Hepzibah, Witch, Mother; Zillah, Witch, Sister; Halloweena, Child, Adoptee
Time period(s): Indeterminate
Locale(s): Fictional Country

Summary: Hepzibah's not sure what to do with Zillah's plan to deliver a human baby to her. Certainly she's never raised a child, but she follows her sister's instructions and goes to the cornfield on Halloween and there, indeed, is a baby. Using her magic to assist her with the challenges of parenting, Hepzibah copes and keeps Halloweena away from humans as Zillah requests. As Halloweena grows she becomes bored with the games of goblins and asks to play with the children she sees in the area. A taste of Halloween candy convinces Halloweena of her need to take action so she puts her magic to good use and creates a cornfield with plants that grow candy corn and attract the friends she seeks. (36 pages)

Where it's reviewed:
Booklist, September 1, 2002, page 139
Bulletin of the Center for Children's Books, October 2002, page 57

Publishers Weekly, September 23, 2002, page 23
School Library Journal, September 2002, page 192

Other books by the same author:
Box Top Dreams, 1998

Other books you might like:
Kevin Somers, *Meaner than Meanest*, 2001
  A mean old hag tries to create a monster that is meaner than the meanest thing she knows but instead she accidentally makes a sweet little girl.
James Stevenson, *Emma*, 1985
  Not a typical witch, Emma even needs flying lessons.
Anne Wilsdorf, *Philomene*, 1992
  Captured by a disagreeable witch, Philomene takes her by surprise when she befriends the witch's monster and they create their own spell.

529

SUSAN GLICK

One Shot
(New York: Holt, 2003)

Subject(s): Photography; Interpersonal Relations; Old Age
Age range(s): Grades 7-10
Major character(s): Lorrie Taylor, 15-Year-Old; Elaine Taylor, Stepmother, Lawyer; Molly Price, Aged Person, Photographer; Sarah O'Connell, 15-Year-Old, Friend
Time period(s): 2000s
Locale(s): Bethesda, Maryland

Summary: When Lorrie's erratic mother takes off to live in California, she chooses to move to her father's home in Maryland, spend the summer lazing by his pool, hook up with her best friend Sarah and even get to know her stepmother Elaine. These plans change quickly when Elaine talks Lorrie into helping her client Molly organize and catalog her noted photographs. Initially intimidated by the crotchety, reclusive older woman, Lorrie's respect and admiration for her work grows. She finally asks to learn some of Molly's trade, but achieving a similar emotional draw in her photos doesn't come easily for Lorrie. In this pivotal summer, Lorrie has a brush with romance, learns to accept her failures, and develops a wonderful relationship with Molly in this author's first novel. (218 pages)

Where it's reviewed:
Bulletin of the Center for Children's Books, June 2003, page 402
Kirkus Reviews, May 15, 2003, page 750
Publishers Weekly, April 28, 2003, page 71
School Library Journal, April 2003, page 158
Voice of Youth Advocates, June 2003, page 129

Other books by the same author:
The Natural World, 2004
Heroes of the Holocaust, 2003

Other books you might like:
Joan Bauer, *Rules of the Road*, 1998
  Earning respect for her salesmanship ability, teen Jenna is hired to drive elderly Mrs. Gladstone to the Gladstone Shoes conference in Dallas.

Rebecca Busselle, *A Frog's-Eye View*, 1990
  When Neela's strategy for romance doesn't work, she gladly accepts her Great Aunt Amelia's offer of photography lessons.
Joan Lowery Nixon, *Nobody's There*, 2000
  Assigned to a community service project, Abbie is paired with a curmudgeonly woman who fancies herself an amateur detective.
Ellen Wittlinger, *Razzle*, 2001
  Ken's interest in photography provides a natural introduction to Razzle, an independent teen whose face is a great portrait study.

530

DEBI GLIORI, Author/Illustrator

Debi Gliori's Bedtime Stories: Bedtime Tales with a Twist
(New York: DK Publishing, Inc., 2002)

Subject(s): Bedtime; Folklore; Animals
Age range(s): Grades K-2
Time period(s): Indeterminate
Locale(s): Fictional Country

Summary: A collection of retold tales includes nine familiar children's stories. An overworked "Little Red Hen" makes a lemon meringue pie rather than bread from the fruits of her labors but still refuses to share with her lazy friends who haven't helped her with any of the work. The tale of the "The Town Mouse and the Country Mouse" is retold in rhyme with the naive country mouse gratefully rescued just in time. "The Three Little Pigs" are builders not brothers but the wolf still blows down the straw and wood houses though his plans to topple the stone house where all three pigs are seeking refuge backfires. (80 pages)

Where it's reviewed:
Booklist, December 15, 2002, page 764
Horn Book Guide, Spring 2003, page 166
Publishers Weekly, September 23, 2002, page 71
Smithsonian, December 2002, page 123

Awards the book has won:
Smithsonian's Notable Books for Children, 2002

Other books by the same author:
Flora's Blanket, 2001 (Smithsonian's Notable Books for Children)
Polar Bolero: A Bedtime Dance, 2001
Mr. Bear to the Rescue, 2000

Other books you might like:
Mary Ann Hoberman, *You Read to Me, I'll Read to You: Very Short Stories to Read Together*, 2001
  A collection of brief stories and poems is designed for shared reading.
Sam McBratney, *In the Light of the Moon & Other Bedtime Stories*, 2001
  Bears, mice, pigs and even the tooth fairy are characters in this collection of eight original stories.
Judy Sierra, *Nursery Tales around the World*, 1996
  Eighteen multicultural tales are grouped into six thematic

categories such as ''Runaway Cookies'' and ''Fooling the Big Bad Wolf.''

531

DEBI GLIORI, Author/Illustrator

Flora's Surprise!

(New York: Orchard Books/Scholastic, Inc., 2003)

Subject(s): Animals/Rabbits; Family; Gardens and Gardening
Age range(s): Grades K-2
Major character(s): Flora, Rabbit, Sister (younger)
Time period(s): Indeterminate
Locale(s): Fictional Country

Summary: Everyone in Flora's family enjoys gardening and each grows something different. Flora's siblings plant a variety of flowers and vegetables. Although Flora is the youngest her dad gives her a pot and suggests that she grow something too. Flora plants a brick and explains that she's growing a house. Flora waits for her house to grow as the family enjoys the garden products planted by her siblings. Flora looks forlornly at her snow-covered pot all winter, but she does not give up hope. In the spring Flora excitedly calls her family to see the house that has grown on her pot. A bird thinks it's just a perfect spot for a nest. First published in Great Britain in 2002. (28 pages)

Where it's reviewed:
Bulletin of the Center for Children's Books, March 2003, page 274
Kirkus Reviews, December 15, 2002, page 1850
School Library Journal, March 2003, page 193

Awards the book has won:
Center for Children's Books Best Books, 2003

Other books by the same author:
Debi Gliori's Bedtime Stories: Bedtime Tales with a Twist, 2002 (Smithsonian's Notable Books for Children)
Penguin Post, 2002
Tickly Under There, 2002
Flora's Blanket, 2001 (Smithsonian's Notable Books for Children)

Other books you might like:
Ruth Brown, *Ten Seeds*, 2001
    A boy plants ten seeds and one develops into a flower from which he harvests ten more seeds.
Eve Bunting, *Sunflower House*, 1996
    A young boy plants his sunflower seeds in a circle and creates a summer play ''house'' to share with friends.
Eric Carle, *The Tiny Seed*, 1970
    One tiny seed sprouts and develops into a flowering plant that produces seeds and so the cycle continues.
Ruth Krauss, *The Carrot Seed*, 1945
    This little boy's family has doubts that the seeds he plants will grow, but they do.

532

DEBI GLIORI, Author/Illustrator

Penguin Post

(San Diego: Harcourt, Inc., 2002)

Subject(s): Babies; Animals/Penguins; Brothers
Age range(s): Preschool-Grade 1
Major character(s): Milo, Penguin, Postal Worker
Time period(s): 2000s (2002)
Locale(s): Polar Regions

Summary: When Milo's mother goes out in search of food, someone has to keep the new baby (still in egg form) warm and someone has to deliver the mail. None too enamored of the egg, Milo offers to deliver all the packages and he heads off, bringing baby presents to his North Pole neighbors. At the end of his journey, Milo hears a cracking sound. It turns out the packages were switched and he's been carrying the egg around all day. He arrives home just as his baby brother makes it out of the egg. (40 pages)

Where it's reviewed:
Booklist, December 15, 2002, page 766
Kirkus Reviews, October 1, 2002, page 1470
Publishers Weekly, September 9, 2002, page 66
School Library Journal, November 2002, page 124

Other books by the same author:
Polar Bolero: A Bedtime Dance, 2001
No Matter What, 1999
The Snow Child, 1994

Other books you might like:
Allan Ahlberg, *The Jolly Postman*, 1986
    The jolly postman travels around delivering mail to fairy tale characters.
Berkeley Breathed, *A Wish for Wings that Work*, 1991
    Santa helps fulfill penguin Opus's Christmas wish to be able to fly.
Vicky Rubin, *Ralphie and the Swamp Baby*, 2004
    Ralphie is excited about his mud-wrestling trophy, but a hatching egg preoccupies his parents.
Brigitte Weninger, *Will You Mind the Baby, Davy?*, 1998
    Youngest child, Davy, is apprehensive about the arrival of a new baby, but once he meets his new baby sister, he is won over.

533

K.L. GOING

Fat Kid Rules the World

(New York: Putnam, 2003)

Subject(s): Weight Control; Music and Musicians; Drugs
Age range(s): Grades 9-12
Major character(s): Troy ''Big T'' Billings, 17-Year-Old, Musician (drummer); Curt MacCrae, Musician (guitarist)
Time period(s): 2000s
Locale(s): New York, New York (Manhattan)

Summary: Obese Troy wonders if anyone would care if he threw himself in front of a subway, but before he can find out, he's ''saved'' by Curt MacCrae, a high school legend. Curt is as thin as Troy is fat, so the request for a meal as his reward sounds logical to Troy. Curt is a high-energy, brilliant guitarist who's usually homeless, hooked on cough medicine and the son of dysfunctional parents. For some reason Curt decides that Troy should be the drummer for his new band Rage/Tectonic, and an odd, symbiotic friendship develops. Troy befriends, feeds and even provides a bed for Curt, while Curt's insistence that Troy can play the drums gives Troy the self-confidence he needs to accept himself in this author's first novel. (183 pages)

Where it's reviewed:
Booklist, May 15, 2003, page 1659
Bulletin of the Center for Children's Books, June 2003, page 402
Horn Book, July 2003, page 456
School Library Journal, May 2003, page 152
Voice of Youth Advocates, June 2003, page 130

Awards the book has won:
Michael L. Printz Honor Book, 2004
School Library Journal Best Books, 2003

Other books you might like:
Chris Lynch, *Extreme Elvin*, 1999
    Chubby Elvin decides he'd rather date the plump girl he's attracted to rather than the slender one his buddies recommend.
Carolyn Mackler, *The Earth, My Butt, and Other Big Round Things*, 2003
    After Virginia's favored brother is suspended from college for date rape, she learns to shed worries about her weight and stand up to her family.
Rebecca O'Connell, *Myrtle of Willendorf*, 2000
    In contrast to her heavily made-up, super-thin college roommate, Myrtle is very satisfied with her round, and some would say obese, body.
Todd Strasser, *Rock 'n' Roll Nights*, 1982
    As lead guitarist, Gary works hard with the rest of his band members to "make it" in the music world.

534

THERESA GOLDING

The Secret Within

(Honesdale, PA: Boyds Mills Press, 2002)

Subject(s): Fathers and Daughters; Abuse; Loneliness
Age range(s): Grades 5-8
Major character(s): Carly Chambers, 8th Grader
Time period(s): 2000s
Locale(s): Oceanside, New Jersey

Summary: Every year Carly's father seems to have a new job that requires them to move from one city to another. At the moment, she enjoys being in a beach town along the New Jersey coast, though she tries to stay away from her father who verbally and physically abuses both Carly and her mother. Because of the abuse, Carly never questions why her father sends her to some strange and disreputable neighborhoods carrying a wrapped package to be passed off to a stranger. Their next door neighbor, who was abused as a foster child, suspects what's going on with the Chambers

family, though Carly denies everything. When the police intervene and arrest her father for counterfeiting, Carly finally discovers what it's like to feel free around her own home. (240 pages)

Where it's reviewed:
Booklist, September 15, 2002, page 231
Library Media Connection, March 2003, page 74
School Library Journal, August 2002, page 184
Voice of Youth Advocates, February 2003, page 475

Other books by the same author:
The Truth about Twelve, 2004
Kat's Surrender, 1999

Other books you might like:
Chimamanda Ngozi Adichie, *Purple Hibiscus*, 2003
    Everyone in their village honors Kambili's father, but she knows that at home he's mean and abusive to his wife and his children.
Margaret Dickson, *Maddy's Song*, 1985
    Maddy's gift of music is her only hope of release from a home dominated by a psychotic, abusive father.
Nina Kiriki Hoffman, *A Stir of Bones*, 2003
    Living in a household controlled by her father, Susan has learned to always be good lest her mother be beaten for her infractions.
Graham McNamee, *Hate You*, 1999
    When her father's dying of cancer, Alice discovers she's able to forgive him even though he ended her singing career by choking her.
Joyce Carol Oates, *Freaky Green Eyes*, 2003
    Franky finds a secret, inner strength that enables her to survive her parent's disintegrating marriage and break free of her controlling father.

535

LISA GOLDSTEIN

The Alchemist's Door

(New York: Tor, 2002)

Subject(s): Magic; Religion; Alternate History
Age range(s): Grades 10-Adult
Major character(s): John Dee, Scientist, Wizard; Judah Loew, Religious (rabbi); Edward Kelley, Criminal
Time period(s): 16th century
Locale(s): Prague, Czechoslovakia; London, England

Summary: Dr. John Dee, alchemist and astrologer to Elizabeth I, is an unendingly curious man. His curiosity sometimes takes him into danger as happens when he takes on Edward Kelley as an assistant. Kelley claims to receive communication from angels, and Dr. Dee longs to establish contact. In spite of some suspicious revelations about Kelley, Dee agrees to perform a spell with him which Kelley says will allow Dee to speak to the angels as well. Disaster ensues, and the spell releases a demon who pursues Dee, his family and Kelley across Europe. In Prague, with nowhere else to go, Dee finds himself consulting with another famous student of the occult, Rabbi Judah Loew. The two are drawn to one another as scholars with similar interests and talents, but wary because of their religious differences. Loew has his own problems, but he is willing to help Dee, for a price. Thus, Dee ends up assisting at the creation of a golem, a soulless creature animated from clay. (256 pages)

Where it's reviewed:
Kirkus Reviews, May 1, 2002, page 624
Kliatt, July 2003, page 32
Library Journal, August 2002, page 151
Publishers Weekly, July 8, 2002, page 36

Other books by the same author:
Dark Cities Underground, 1999
Walking the Labyrinth, 1996
The Red Magician, 1995

Other books you might like:
Sarah A. Hoyt, *Ill Met by Moonlight*, 2001
    Will Shakespeare is drawn into the disputes of the fairy court when his beloved Nan disappears.
Benjamin Wooley, *The Queen's Conjurer: the Science and Magic of Dr. John Dee, Advisor to Queen Elizabeth I*, 2001
    Based on Dr. Dee's diaries, this book tells the real story of his experiments with magic and the supernatural.
Patricia C. Wrede, *Snow White and Rose Red*, 1989
    When two girls disappear into Faerie, their mother suspects the sorcerer Dr. Dee may have had something to do with it.

536

BETH GOOBIE

Sticks and Stones

(Custer, WA: Orca Book Publishers, 2002)

Series: Soundings
Subject(s): Peer Pressure; Interpersonal Relations; School Life
Age range(s): Grades 7-10
Major character(s): Trudy "Jujube" Gelb, 9th Grader, 15-Year-Old; Brent Floyd, 9th Grader; Carlos Rojas, 9th Grader; Sophie, 12th Grader
Time period(s): 2000s
Locale(s): Canada

Summary: When Jujube accepts a date with Brent for the Valentine's Dance, she doesn't have any idea there will be intense repercussions. Even when he asks her to walk to the car with him to get something for the band, and then tries to put the make on her, she doesn't think saying no to him will backfire, but it does. First there's a nudge, then a wink, then a laugh and then the graffiti goes up in the bathrooms, graffiti that reads, "Jujube is a slut." Jujube can't believe that boys she was friends with a week earlier are now vilifying her and so she fights back. With the help of her friends Carlos and Sophie, she completes a slide show for English about graffiti, including the slides of "Jujube is a slut," and stuns her class, and Brent, into humiliation. Forming the "slut club" with all the other girls who've been named on the bathroom walls results in the school finally painting over this vile graffiti in a striking story of a courageous young teen. (86 pages)

Where it's reviewed:
Canadian Living, November 2002, page 157
Kliatt, July 2002, page 19

Quill & Quire, June 2002, page 53
Resource Links, October 2002, page 34
Voice of Youth Advocates, October 2002, page 279

Awards the book has won:
ALA Quick Picks for Reluctant Young Adult Readers, 2003

Other books by the same author:
Who Owns Kelly Paddik?, 2003
The Lottery, 2002
Before Wings, 2000
The Colours of Carol Molev, 1998
Scars of Light, 1994

Other books you might like:
Mary Hooper, *Amy*, 2002
    In need of a friend, Amy finds Zed in an online chatroom and agrees to meet him, but later finds he's used a date rape drug to photograph her naked.
Elizabeth-Ann Sachs, *Kiss Me, Janie Tannenbaum*, 1992
    Janie is impressed by sophisticated Steve but a little time with him shows what a cad he is and teaches her the importance of her good friend Harold.
Barbara Shoup, *Wish You Were Here*, 1994
    Jax tries to figure out who he is after his mother remarries, his father is critically injured, and his inexperience with girls ruins some friendships.
Karen Romano Young, *Video*, 1999
    When a fisherman exposes himself to Janine, her friend Eric records the fisherman's actions to try and apprehend him.

537

BETH GOOBIE

Who Owns Kelly Paddik?

(Custer, WA: Orca Book Publishers, 2003)

Subject(s): Sexual Abuse; Fathers and Daughters
Age range(s): Grades 7-10
Major character(s): Kelly Paddick, 15-Year-Old; Sister Mary, Religious; Chris, 15-Year-Old
Time period(s): 2000s
Locale(s): Winnipeg, Manitoba, Canada

Summary: Marymound School for Girls becomes the place from which Kelly can't run, though she tries to escape as her social worker drives her to the school for admittance. Once caught, she's taken inside, introduced to Sister Mary and assigned her room. Kelly's been running ever since her father abused her and her mother didn't stop him; though he's died, he still exerts influence over Kelly's life. Gradually Kelly opens up, becomes friends with Chris who was also abused by her father, and reflects on a poster that says "Love Yourself," given to her by Sister Mary. By book's end she's able to write about her feelings, speak to her mother and learn to "love herself." (89 pages)

Where it's reviewed:
Kliatt, May 2003, page 9
Resource Links, June 2003, page 25
School Library Journal, July 2003, page 124

Other books by the same author:
Flux, 2004

Kicked Out, 2002
The Lottery, 2002
Sticks and Stones, 2002

Other books you might like:

Cathleen Twomey, *Charlotte's Choice*, 2001
Charlotte doesn't know what to do when her orphaned friend Jesse kills Mr. Phelps for she promised Jesse she wouldn't tell about the sexual abuse.

Cynthia Voigt, *When She Hollers*, 1994
After years of being sexually abused by her stepfather, Tish comes to the breakfast table with a knife; by the end of the day, she has a plan to stop him.

Lori Aurelia Williams, *When Kambia Elaine Flew in from Neptune*, 2000
Shayla slowly realizes that Kambia Elaine's wild stories are cover-ups for the sexual abuse she endures.

538

DIANE GOODE, Author/Illustrator

Monkey Mo Goes to Sea
(New York: Blue Sky Press/Scholastic, 2002)

Subject(s): Cruise Ships; Voyages and Travels; Animals/Monkeys

Age range(s): Preschool-Grade 1

Major character(s): Bertie, Child; Mo, Monkey; Grandfather, Grandfather, Sea Captain

Time period(s): 1920s

Locale(s): Blue Star, At Sea

Summary: When Grandfather invites Bertie and his pet monkey, Mo, to join him for lunch on his luxury liner he admonishes Mo to behave "like a gentleman." Mo tries to imitate the gentlemen on the boat, but with little success. However, when a passenger falls overboard, Mo manages to rescue him by following suit. (40 pages)

Where it's reviewed:

Booklist, March 15, 2003, page 1256
Horn Book Guide, Fall 2002, page 302
Horn Book, March 2002, page 202
Publishers Weekly, February 25, 2002, page 66
School Library Journal, March 2002, page 187

Other books by the same author:

Thanksgiving Is Here!, 2003
Tiger Trouble!, 2001
The Dinosaur's New Clothes, 1999

Other books you might like:

H.A. Rey, *Curious George Takes a Train*, 2002
Curious George gets in trouble at the train station before helping a little boy whose toy has rolled onto the tracks. Margaret Rey, co-author.

John Rowe, *Monkey Trouble*, 1999
Little Monkey keeps getting in trouble because he doesn't listen.

Peter Selgin, *S.S. Gigantic Across the Atlantic: The Story of the World's Biggest Ocean Liner Ever! and Its Disastrous Maiden Voyage*, 1999
In this story that parodies the sinking of the Titanic, Pip-

squeak tells the story of the S.S. Gigantic's maiden voyage.

539

PIPPA GOODHART
CAROLINE JAYNE CHURCH, Illustrator

Pudgy: A Puppy to Love
(New York: Chicken House/Scholastic, Inc., 2003)

Subject(s): Animals/Dogs; Pets; Friendship

Age range(s): Preschool-Grade 1

Major character(s): Pudgy, Dog; Lucy, Child

Time period(s): 2000s (2003)

Locale(s): United Kingdom

Summary: Puppy Pudgy and little girl Lucy are both lonely and want playmates. One day Pudgy runs away from his home and Lucy finds him. The girl and the dog become friends and Pudgy moves in with Lucy. Now neither one will be lonely anymore. (26 pages)

Where it's reviewed:

Bulletin of the Center for Children's Books, May 2003, page 361
School Library Journal, April 2003, page 120

Awards the book has won:

Center for Children's Books Best Books, 2003

Other books by the same author:

Arthur's Tractor: A Fairy Tale with Mechanical Parts, 2003
Slow Magic, 2003
Row, Row, Row Your Boat, 1997

Other books you might like:

Norman Bridwell, *Clifford the Big Red Dog*, 1963
Emily Elizabeth is proud to introduce her neighbors to her new dog, Clifford.

Alexandra Day, *Good Dog, Carl*, 1985
When baby Madeleine's mother steps out for a moment, Carl the rottweiler is in charge of babysitting.

Ezra Jack Keats, *Whistle for Willie*, 1964
Peter wants to learn how to whistle so that he can call his dog, Willie.

540

ALISON GOODMAN

Singing the Dogstar Blues
(New York: Viking, 2003)

Subject(s): Time Travel; Science Fiction; Music and Musicians

Age range(s): Grades 8-12

Major character(s): Joss Aaronson, 18-Year-Old, Student—College; Mavkel, Alien

Time period(s): Indeterminate Future

Locale(s): Australia

Summary: Conceived in a Petri dish, Joss doesn't know who her father is and seldom sees her newscaster mother. Unable to deal with authority figures, Joss has been expelled from several schools but is now attending the Centre for Neo-

Historical Studies. Her school has accepted the Chorian alien Mavkel whose society is composed of telepathically linked pairs; because his twin has died, it is decided to partner him with Joss. The two make an interesting pair who eventually learn to cooperate with one another; when Mavkel becomes sick it's up to Joss to learn to pair with him telepathically. Mavkel returns the favor by helping Joss time travel illegally so she can learn the identity of her father in this Australian import. (261 pages)

Where it's reviewed:
Booklist, April 15, 2003, page 1464
Bulletin of the Center for Children's Books, July 2003, page 447
Publishers Weekly, March 3, 2003, page 76
School Library Journal, April 2003, page 162
Voice of Youth Advocates, February 2003, page 486

Awards the book has won:
School Library Journal Best Books, 2003
ALA Best Books for Young Adults, 2004

Other books you might like:
Kate Gilmore, *The Exchange Student*, 1999
   Fen, a seven-foot alien with an obsessive fondness for animals, comes to stay with an Earth family.
Annette Curtis Klause, *Alien Secrets*, 1993
   A girl traveling between planets befriends an alien with a secret treasure.
Kathryn Lasky, *Star Split*, 1999
   A genetically enhanced person, Darci is intrigued by the "original ones," those without the 48th chromosome, until she meets her own duplicate.

541

JOAN ELIZABETH GOODMAN

Paradise
(Boston: Houghton Mifflin, 2002)

Subject(s): Survival; Romance; Islands
Age range(s): Grades 7-10
Major character(s): Marguerite de la Rocque, 16-Year-Old, Historical Figure; Damienne, 17-Year-Old, Servant; Pierre, Boyfriend (of Marguerite), Sailor
Time period(s): 16th century (1540s)
Locale(s): Demon Island, Canada

Summary: Sent by her uncle to help colonize Canada, Marguerite gladly leaves the gloom of her father's Protestant household and hopes to start a new life with her Catholic boyfriend Pierre. Sailing to Canada with her servant Damienne, and Pierre on board as a deckhand, the two lovers are caught kissing. Marguerite and Damienne are left on an island in the St. Lawrence River with only meager supplies while Pierre joins them after jumping ship. The three build a shelter and forage for food, relying for survival on the Indians who sometimes help them, but by winter Pierre dies from eating poisonous mushrooms and Marguerite realizes she is pregnant. Marguerite and Damienne survive the winter, though tragedy strikes again in a work based on historical fact. (209 pages)

Where it's reviewed:
Booklist, November 15, 2002, page 588
Bulletin of the Center for Children's Books, November 2002, page 107
Kliatt, September 2002, page 9
School Library Journal, December 2002, page 138
Voice of Youth Advocates, December 2002, page 380

Other books by the same author:
Peregrine, 2000
Hope's Crossing, 1998
The Winter Hare, 1996

Other books you might like:
Tracy Barrett, *Anna of Byzantium*, 1999
   Raised as heir to her father's throne, political winds change and Anna's brother comes in favor; Anna's now in a convent for trying to poison him.
Mette Newth, *The Abduction*, 1989
   On their tribe's first walrus hunt, three Inuit Eskimos are kidnapped by sailors and taken to Norway to be exhibited as curiosity items.
Mary Pope Osborne, *Adaline Falling Star*, 2000
   Adaline learns to survive without the help of her famous father Kit Carson by disguising herself as a boy and working on a steamboat.
Joan Weir, *The Brideship*, 1999
   Sarah is thrilled to leave the orphanage, not realizing she's aboard a Brideship bound for the goldfields of British Columbia.

542

VALERI GORBACHEV, Author/Illustrator

One Rainy Day
(New York: Philomel Books, 2002)

Subject(s): Animals/Pigs; Weather; Animals
Age range(s): Grades K-2
Major character(s): Pig, Pig, Friend; Unnamed Character, Goat, Friend
Time period(s): Indeterminate
Locale(s): Fictional Country

Summary: Soaking wet Pig arrives at his friend's home after a heavy downpour. When the goat asks why he didn't seek shelter under a tree, Pig explains that he did. Other animals, including four leopards, ten elephants and three buffaloes joined him but still there was room for all to stay dry. When the rain stopped and the sun came out Pig ran so hurriedly to tell his friend about his experience that he dashed through every puddle on the way and that's how he got so wet. (40 pages)

Where it's reviewed:
Booklist, May 15, 2002, page 1600
Publishers Weekly, June 24, 2002, page 59
Riverbank Review, Spring 2002, page 32
School Library Journal, August 2002, page 156

Other books by the same author:
Big Trip, 2004
Whose Hat Is It?, 2004
Chicken Chickens Go to School, 2003

Other books you might like:

Kathi Appelt, *Rain Dance*, 2001
  Simple rhyming text describes the reactions of animals to rainfall numbering from one to ten.
Lola M. Schaefer, *This Is the Rain*, 2001
  A rhyming cumulative story explains the water cycle.
Janet Morgan Stoeke, *Rainy Day*, 1999
  Unable to find dry shelter, silly chicken Minerva Louise makes the best of her wet day on the farm.

543

CAROL GORMAN

Dork on the Run

(New York: HarperCollins, 2002)

Subject(s): Elections; Popularity; Bullies
Age range(s): Grades 4-7
Major character(s): Jerry Flack, 6th Grader; Gabe Marshall, 6th Grader, Bully; Brenda McAdams, 6th Grader
Time period(s): 2000s
Locale(s): Spencer Lake

Summary: Enrolled in a new school and convinced he's left his dorkiness behind, Jerry agrees to run for class president. With the support of his girlfriend Brenda, and many of her friends, Jerry is all set for his race against Gabe, though he's unprepared for all Gabe does to make his life miserable. When Jerry good-naturedly tries ice skating, his awkward attempts are added to Gabe's web page, then he's held out a second floor window by his opponent and even endures a literal close shave by Gabe just before they're due to give their campaign speeches. Jerry finds that the bullying, classroom cliques, and limited powers of elected officials are worse than being a dork. (184 pages)

Where it's reviewed:

Booklist, June 2002, page 1722
Bulletin of the Center for Children's Books, September 2002, page 17
Horn Book, September 2002, page 572
Publishers Weekly, June 10, 2002, page 62
School Library Journal, June 2002, page 138

Other books by the same author:

A Midsummer Night's Dork, 2004
Dork in Disguise, 1999

Other books you might like:

James Howe, *The Misfits*, 2001
  Tired of being called names, four friends decide to run for office at their school; though they don't win, they focus attention on the problem.
Doug Wilhelm, *The Revealers*, 2003
  Three seventh graders offer other students an online forum to discuss the bullying they've encountered at their school.
Laurence Yep, *Cockroach Cooties*, 2000
  When Bobby finds out the bully who bothers his brother is scared of cockroaches, he borrows a huge one from an entomologist.

544

BOB GRAHAM, Author/Illustrator

Jethro Byrd, Fairy Child

(Cambridge, MA: Candlewick Press, 2002)

Subject(s): Fairies; Imagination; Family
Age range(s): Grades K-2
Major character(s): Annabelle, Child, Daughter; Jethro Byrd, Son, Mythical Creature (fairy); Mommy, Mother
Time period(s): 2000s (2002)
Locale(s): England

Summary: Imaginative Annabelle's search for fairies is finally rewarded when she notices something hitting the other side of the backyard fence. Poking her head through a broken slat Annabelle meets Jethro and his family. The ice cream truck in which they were traveling to the Fairy Travelers Picnic has landed none too gently in the cement and weeds of the lot next door. Annabelle brings Jethro and his family home to her doubting parents for tea. Though Mommy can't see the fairies, she plays along with Annabelle's game and serves tea and fairy cakes. The fairies fiddle, dance and sing all afternoon to Annabelle's delight. When the fairies depart with a reluctant Jethro in tow they promise to come again soon, in fairy time. (32 pages)

Where it's reviewed:

Booklist, May 1, 2002, page 1532
Bulletin of the Center for Children's Books, October 2002, page 57
Publishers Weekly, April 29, 2002, page 69
Riverbank Review, Winter 2002, page 34
School Library Journal, June 2002, page 96

Awards the book has won:

School Library Journal Best Books, 2002
Smithsonian's Notable Books for Children, 2002

Other books by the same author:

Let's Get a Pup! Said Kate, 2001 (ALA Notable Children's Book)
Max, 2000 (Publishers Weekly Best Children's Books)
Benny: An Adventure Story, 1999 (School Library Journal Best Books)

Other books you might like:

Tanya Robyn Batt, *A Child's Book of Faeries*, 2002
  Stories, poems and folklore give an overview of faeries in the British Isles.
Gilly Sergier, *How to Catch Fairies*, 2002
  Annabelle could use this survey of the magical world of fairies the next time she wants to learn more.
Jane Simmons, *The Dreamtime Fairies*, 2002
  A young storyteller creates a bedtime tale about finding the Dreamtime Fairies.

545

ROSEMARY GRAHAM

My Not-So-Terrible Time at the Hippie Hotel

(New York: Viking, 2003)

Subject(s): Divorce; Parent and Child; Vacations
Age range(s): Grades 7-10
Major character(s): Tracy Forrester, 14-Year-Old, Musician (pianist); Kevin, Teenager
Time period(s): 2000s
Locale(s): Cape Cod, Massachusetts

Summary: This summer Tracy's father brings his family to "Together Time," a retreat at Farnsworth House that is set up for single parent families to eat and go sightseeing together in a semblance of family units. The kids immediately call the house Hippie Hotel, in homage to its owner and retreat leader, and realize their one commonality is anger over their parent's divorce. Tracy hasn't played the piano in a year and never thinks about writing songs anymore, plus she's been so unhappy that she overeats and now is too heavy. On a field trip to Plimouth Plantation, Tracy meets Kevin and begins her first romance, though she worries about whether he really likes her. By summer's end, in this author's first novel, Tracy's learned not to judge people by the way they appear for she finds they're often struggling with their own problems in this author's first novel. (214 pages)

Where it's reviewed:
Booklist, August 2003, page 1970
Kliatt, May 2003, page 9
Library Media Connection, February 2004, page 69
School Library Journal, July 2003, page 130
Voice of Youth Advocates, December 2003, page 392

Other books you might like:
Steve Atinsky, *Tyler on Prime Time*, 2002
    His mother vacations with her boyfriend and his lawyer father's too busy to watch him, so Tyler goes to Hollywood to stay with his screenwriter uncle.
Barbara Dana, *Necessary Parties*, 1986
    When his parents file for divorce, Chris Mills hires an unconventional lawyer for $1 and files suit against his parents to block their action.
Susan Haven, *Maybe I'll Move to the Lost and Found*, 1988
    Life's awful! Gilly's parents are divorcing and her best friend doesn't care about her.
Gloria Velasquez, *Maya's Divided World*, 1995
    Maya's charmed life falls to pieces when her parents announce their divorce and her father moves out.

546

LOIS G. GRAMBLING
JUDY LOVE, Illustrator

The Witch Who Wanted to Be a Princess

(Watertown, MA: Whispering Coyote/Charlesbridge, 2002)

Subject(s): Fairy Tales; Witches and Witchcraft; Problem Solving

Age range(s): Grades K-2
Major character(s): Bella, Witch; Franklyn, Royalty
Time period(s): Indeterminate Past
Locale(s): Kingdom of Styne, Fictional Country

Summary: Bella is a witch skilled in many spells but the one intended to turn her into a princess never works because the grand wizard, declaring witches to be an endangered species, forbids it. Not willing to give up her dreams of silk gowns, a jeweled crown and glass slippers Bella scans the personal ads seeking a prince to marry. When she finds an ad that suits her she jumps on her broom and flies to Styne Castle for an interview. Her meeting with Prince Franklyn of Styne is one of love at first sight for both and soon the couple wed making Bella the Princess of Styne. (32 pages)

Where it's reviewed:
Horn Book Guide, Spring 2003, page 35
Kirkus Reviews, June 15, 2002, page 881
Publishers Weekly, June 3, 2002, page 87
School Library Journal, August 2002, page 156

Awards the book has won:
IRA Children's Choices, 2003

Other books by the same author:
Abigail Muchmore: An Original Tale, 2003
This Whole Tooth Fairy Thing's Nothing but a Big Rip-Off!, 2002
Grandma Tells a Story, 2001
Miss Hildy's Missing Cape Caper, 2000
Can I Have a Stegosaurus, Mom? Can I? Please!?, 1995 (IRA/CBC Children's Choice)

Other books you might like:
Deborah Nourse Lattimore, *Cinderhazel: The Cinderella of Halloween*, 1997
    Hazel impresses Prince Alarming with her ability to make a dirty mess of anything including the Witches' Halloween Ball.
Lauren Mills, *The Dog Prince*, 2001
    Eliza, a goatherd, has no aspirations to marry a prince but does so when her love for the stray dog she befriends releases a prince from a spell.
Alain Vaes, *The Princess and the Pea*, 2001
    Seeking a princess to marry, Prince Ralph instead finds a mechanic and tow truck driver who also happens to be a crown princess.

547

BONNIE GRAVES
ROBIN PREISS GLASSER, Illustrator

Taking Care of Trouble

(New York: Dutton Children's Books, 2002)

Subject(s): Babysitters; Humor; Self-Confidence
Age range(s): Grades 3-5
Major character(s): Joel Maccarone, 5th Grader, Babysitter; Tucker "Trouble" Goodchild, Child; Rachel Rottenberger, Babysitter
Time period(s): 2000s
Locale(s): United States

Summary: Joel is known for being so incompetent in emergency situations that he's unable to pass the Junior Adventurer's Emergency Preparedness test. When he hears Rachel calling his name to help her with an "emergency," he tries to hide. Rachel has just learned that a popular band is playing at the mall and she wants Joel to take over her babysitting job with Tucker, the toddler she's nicknamed Trouble. Joel tries every excuse he can think of to avoid Rachel and her plot but he soon finds himself alone with Tucker and clueless about childcare. Inevitably, everything from feeding Tucker to changing his diaper creates an enormous mess, but Joel calmly handles everything. By the time he and Tucker survive the afternoon Joel has the confidence to face his Emergency Preparedness drill with the expectation that passing it will be easier than taking care of Trouble. (70 pages)

Where it's reviewed:
Booklist, March 15, 2002, page 1255
Bulletin of the Center for Children's Books, June 2002, page 365
Horn Book Guide, Fall 2002, page 357
School Library Journal, April 2002, page 110

Other books by the same author:
No Copycats Allowed!, 1998
Mystery of the Tooth Gremlin, 1997
The Best Worst Day, 1996

Other books you might like:
Lynn Cullen, *The Three Lives of Harris Harper*, 1996
    Harris learns that baby-sitting Jamey is not the easy, clean job he thought it would be for the summer.
James Howe, *The New Nick Kramer, or My Life as a Babysitter*, 1995
    Determined to impress Jennifer with his sensitivity, Nick enrolls in a babysitting class, only to be stuck watching a seven-year-old terror.
Claudia Mills, *You're a Brave Man, Julius Zimmerman*, 1999
    Julius's mother fills his summer with unexpected plans including a job babysitting for a three-year-old.

548

KEITH GRAVES, Author/Illustrator

Loretta: Ace Pinky Scout

(New York: Scholastic Press, 2002)

Subject(s): Self-Esteem; Scouting; Self-Acceptance
Age range(s): Grades 1-3
Major character(s): Loretta, Scout, Child; Gran, Grandmother, Scout (former)
Time period(s): Indeterminate
Locale(s): Fictional Country

Summary: Loretta comes from a long-line of perfect Pinky Scouts. Pictures of her relatives in their Pinky uniforms adorn her home with none more accomplished than Gran. Loretta is practically perfect and has the medals to prove it, with one exception; Loretta lacks the Golden Marshmallow badge. Despite diligent preparation for the contest, Loretta fails to achieve her goal when her marshmallows burst into flames. Despondent, Loretta hangs up her Pinky beret and weeps at Gran's picture. Gran's voice comes from the picture to inform Loretta of the imperfections of each of her esteemed relatives and to encourage her to take up her beret and continue to achieve all that she can as a Pinky Scout. (36 pages)

Where it's reviewed:
Booklist, October 15, 2002, page 412
Bulletin of the Center for Children's Books, December 2002, page 157
Newsweek, October 28, 2002, page 75
Publishers Weekly, September 9, 2002, page 68
School Library Journal, December 2002, page 96

Awards the book has won:
Center for Children's Books Best Books, 2002

Other books by the same author:
Pet Boy, 2000
Frank Was a Monster Who Wanted to Dance, 1999

Other books you might like:
Kathi Appelt, *Incredible Me!*, 2002
    A rhyming story depicts one young girl's exuberant celebration of her uniqueness.
Stan Berenstain, *The Berenstain Bear Scouts and the Missing Merit Badges*, 1998
    Scouts Sister Bear and Brother Bear assemble clues needed to help them locate their merit badges.
Deborah Blumenthal, *Aunt Claire's Yellow Beehive Hair*, 2001
    Inspired by family stories of relatives she's never known, Annie creates a scrapbook of mementos and anecdotes about each one.
Judy Katscke, *Take a Hike, Snoopy!*, 2002
    A camping trip with his troop of bird scouts has an unexpected outcome in this beginning reader based on the characters of Charles Schulz.

549

KEITH GRAVES, Author/Illustrator

Three Nasty Gnarlies

(New York: Scholastic Press, 2003)

Subject(s): Cleanliness; Self-Perception; Stories in Rhyme
Age range(s): Grades K-3
Major character(s): Grubby Gurgle, Monster; Stanky Stoo, Monster; Ooga-Mooga, Monster; Snooty Judy Butterfly, Insect (butterfly)
Time period(s): Indeterminate
Locale(s): Fictional Country

Summary: Grubby, Stanky and Ooga-Mooga are chagrined to learn from Snooty Judy that they are not the perfect creatures they believe themselves to be. When the three Nasty Gnarlies learn that, in Snooty Judy's opinion, they are stinky, messy and unattractive they ask for the beauty secret that transformed her from a muddy worm to a beautiful butterfly. Wrapping themselves in junk to mimic Snooty Judy's silk wrap treatment they hang upside down all winter dreaming of butterflies. In May they emerge from their self-imposed cocoons to the disappointing discovery that they are unchanged. Ooga Mooga helps Grubby and Stanky realize that, as Gnarlies, they are already the perfect creatures they are meant to be. Their new self-perception brings happiness. (40 pages)

Where it's reviewed:
Booklist, November 15, 2003, page 600
Publishers Weekly, January 5, 2004, page 61
School Library Journal, December 2003, page 113

Other books by the same author:
Loretta: Ace Pinky Scout, 2002
Uncle Blubbafink's Seriously Ridiculous Stories, 2001
Pet Boy, 2000

Other books you might like:
Patty Lovell, *Stand Tall, Molly Lou Melon*, 2001
  Molly Lou's ability to accept her unique physical charac-
  teristics helps her ignore a bully's taunts and gain accep-
  tance in a new school.
Todd Parr, *It's OK to Be Different*, 2001
  Differences in appearance, talents and family structure are
  all acceptable.
Dan Yaccarino, *Unlovable*, 2001
  So convinced is pug Alfred that he is ugly and unlovable
  that he hides in his fenced yard and fears revealing his
  breed to Rex, a new neighbor.

550

DIANNE E. GRAY

Together Apart
(Boston: Houghton Mifflin, 2002)

Subject(s): Weather; Grief; Women's Rights
Age range(s): Grades 6-9
Major character(s): Hannah Barnett, 14-Year-Old; Isaac Brad-
  shaw, 15-Year-Old; Eliza Moore, Widow(er)
Time period(s): 1880s (1888)
Locale(s): Prairie Hill, Nebraska

Summary: In January of 1888 a fierce blizzard sweeps down
the prairie states, killing so many young people it's often
referred to as the "School Children's Blizzard." Feeling
guilty about surviving the blizzard when her two younger
brothers hadn't, Hannah applies for a job in town with the
widow Moore. Unbeknownst to her, Isaac, wanting to escape
from his abusive stepfather, also applies for the apprentice
job. The lives of these two, who sheltered together in a
haystack to endure the blizzard, are again united, with Hannah
working in Eliza's home and Isaac helping run the printing
press. A young widow with a strong sense of women's rights,
Eliza needs help with her press to produce a weekly edition of
the *Women's Gazette*. While the two young people tiptoe
around their growing affection for one another, Eliza also
opens a "resting room" for women and children to wait in
while their farmer husbands conduct business in town, as she
continues to take those small first steps for women's rights.
(193 pages)

Where it's reviewed:
Booklist, September 15, 2002, page 226
Horn Book, November 2002, page 757
Kliatt, September 2002, page 9
Riverbank Review, Winter 2002, page 46
School Library Journal, December 2002, page 138

Other books by the same author:
Holding Up the Earth, 2000

Other books you might like:
Gretel Ehrlich, *A Blizzard Year: Timmy's Almanac of the
  Seasons*, 1999
  A terrible blizzard destroys most of their cattle and Timmy
  worries that her parents will lose their ranch.
Trudy Krisher, *Uncommon Faith*, 2003
  Able to speak her mind when most women are sedate and
  soft-spoken, one knows Faith won't spend her life darning
  socks or spinning and weaving.
Jim Murphy, *My Face to the Wind: The Diary of Sarah Jane
  Price, a Prairie Teacher, Broken Bow, Nebraska, 1881*,
  2001
  After saving all her schoolchildren when a storm blows the
  roof off Sarah's sod school, the townspeople vote to build
  a proper school.
Richard Peck, *Voices After Midnight*, 1989
  Chad and his younger brother Luke are drawn back in time
  to the Great Blizzard of 1888 where they help save the
  former owners of their townhouse.
Jean Thesman, *The Ornament Tree*, 1996
  Bonnie loves being part of a female-dominated household
  where the women work proactively for women's suffrage,
  birth control and an end to child labor.

551

KES GRAY
MARY MCQUILLAN, Illustrator

Our Twitchy
(New York: Henry Holt and Company, 2003)

Subject(s): Adoption; Parent and Child; Animals/Rabbits
Age range(s): Grades K-2
Major character(s): Twitchy, Rabbit, Adoptee; Milfoil
  "Mom", Mother, Cow; Sedge "Pop", Father, Horse
Time period(s): Indeterminate
Locale(s): Fictional Country

Summary: Twitchy wants to know why his Mom and Pop
don't hop as he does. The answer is the unexpected story of
his adoption. Now Twitchy begins to notice the differences in
appearance, telling evidence that Milfoil and Sedge are not his
real parents. Confused, Twitchy runs away with Milfoil and
Sedge in pursuit. After dark, Milfoil and Sedge abandon their
unsuccessful search and return to their home where they find a
little bunny with ears shortened by clothespins and a twig for
a tail trying to say "moo" and "neigh." Twitchy promises to
change if only Milfoil and Sedge will agree to be his real mom
and pop. Milfoil and Sedge explain that they are Twitchy's
real parents and they love him just the way he is. Their
answers satisfy Twitchy who happily asks, "What's for supper, Mom and Pop?" (32 pages)

Where it's reviewed:
Publishers Weekly, October 20, 2003, page 53
School Library Journal, December 2003, page 114

Other books by the same author:
Cluck O'Clock, 2004
Billy's Bucket, 2003
Eat Your Peas, 2000

Other books you might like:
Jan M. Czech, *An American Face*, 2000
Adopted Korean American Jesse expects his face to change into an ''American'' one when he becomes a naturalized citizen.
Deborah Hodge, *Emma's Story*, 2003
When Emma becomes upset because she looks different from others in her family Grandma assures her of the family's love.
Allen Say, *Allison*, 1997
Allison, wondering why she looks more like her doll than her parents, struggles to understand the story of her adoption.

552

LULI GRAY

Timespinners

(Boston: Houghton Mifflin Company, 2003)

Subject(s): Brothers and Sisters; Twins; Time Travel
Age range(s): Grades 4-7
Major character(s): Alice ''Allie'' Cadwallader-Newton, 10-Year-Old, Twin; Thadeus ''Fig'' Cadwallader-Newton, 10-Year-Old, Twin; Mim, Mother, Archaeologist; Oomor, Prehistoric Human, Friend
Time period(s): 2000s (2003); 1910s (1913)
Locale(s): New York, New York

Summary: On an archeological expedition to France, Mim is injured when a cave she's exploring collapses on her. After months of watching her in a coma, Allie and Fig decide that the only way to heal her is to travel back in time to the cave and somehow prevent the accident. They succeed in doing so by spinning through a diorama at a natural history museum and arrive in 1913 France with the expedition collecting the animals and artifacts now displayed in the exhibit. When Allie and Fig try to return home they instead go farther back in time to the Ice Age. Oomor befriends them, they learn a great deal about Neanderthal culture and they meet another time traveler, the artist who painted the background of the diorama. Sure that they've been away from home for weeks, Allie and Fig gather their courage and, with help from Oomor, try once more to get home. (152 pages)

Where it's reviewed:
Booklist, March 1, 2003, page 1197
Publishers Weekly, May 12, 2003, page 69
School Library Journal, April 2003, page 162

Other books by the same author:
Falcon and the Carousel of Time, 2005
Falcon and the Charles Street Witch, 2002
Falcon's Egg, 1995 (School Library Journal Best Books)

Other books you might like:
Graham Coleman, *Neanderthal*, 1996
A nonfiction title for youth discusses scientific knowledge about Neanderthals and how the information is acquired.
Jane Langton, *The Time Bike*, 2000
An old, unimpressive-looking bike has the magical power to allow the rider to travel back through time.

Jon Scieszka, *Your Mother Was a Neanderthal*, 1993
The Time Warp Trio travel back to the Stone Age in this humorous series entry.

553

SIMON R. GREEN

Drinking Midnight Wine

(New York: NAL/Roc, 2002)

Subject(s): Adventure and Adventurers; Good and Evil; Fantasy
Age range(s): Grades 9-Adult
Major character(s): Toby Dexter, Clerk; Gayle ''Gaia'', Deity; Nicholas Hobb, Demon; Jimmy Thunder, Detective—Private, Deity
Time period(s): Indeterminate
Locale(s): Mysterie, Fictional Country

Summary: Toby Dexter, the most ordinary of men, embarks on a most extraordinary adventure. His life changes when he falls in love at first sight and follows the object of his affections through a doorway. That doorway is the portal between Veritie, the everyday world that Toby knows, and Mysterie, the magical world of deities and demons. Gayle, the woman of Toby's dreams, is seriously annoyed at his intrusion, and tries to send him back. But Toby is wound up in the tangle of fate that is about to play out, and Gayle, despite her powers, is unable to return him. Nicholas Hobb, leader of the fallen angels, plans destruction for both worlds and it falls to Toby and Gayle to stop him. Along the way, they will receive help from a number of Gayle's supernatural friends, including Jimmy Thunder, a former god who has turned private detective. (304 pages)

Where it's reviewed:
Booklist, February 1, 2002, page 930
Library Journal, February 15, 2002, page 181
Publishers Weekly, January 14, 2002, page 45
Science Fiction Chronicle, April 2002, page 50

Other books by the same author:
Deathstalker Return, 2004
Agents of Light and Darkness, 2003
Something from the Nightside, 2003

Other books you might like:
Charles de Lint, *Spirits in the Wires*, 2003
When the Wordwood literary web site goes amiss and users disappear, a peculiar assortment of talents tries to put matters right.
Neil Gaiman, *American Gods: A Novel*, 2001
Shadow's early release from prison is not the good fortune he hopes; it seems the gods have need of a hero . . . or a sacrifice.
Robert Holdstock, *Mythago Wood*, 1984
Steven Huxley follows his father's footsteps when he disappears into Ryhope Woods, that tiny bit of primeval forest that generates living myths.

554

RHONDA GOWLER GREENE
KARLA FIREHAMMER, Illustrator

At Grandma's

(New York: Henry Holt and Company, 2003)

Subject(s): Grandmothers; Sleep; Stories in Rhyme
Age range(s): Preschool-Grade 1
Major character(s): Grandma, Dog, Grandmother; Unnamed Character, Dog
Time period(s): Indeterminate
Locale(s): Fictional Country

Summary: A visit to Grandma's includes such happy activities as eating fresh-baked cinnamon buns for breakfast, canoeing, picking berries, and gardening. In the evening, Grandma and grandchild follow quieter pursuits such as watching fireflies, reading books, and sharing a good night kiss. (32 pages)

Where it's reviewed:
Booklist, June 2003, page 1768
Publishers Weekly, June 2, 2003, page 50
School Library Journal, July 2003, page 96

Other books by the same author:
Santa's Stuck, 2004
This Is the Teacher, 2003
The Beautiful World that God Made, 2002

Other books you might like:
Marthe Jocelyn, *A Day with Nellie*, 2002
    Nellie enjoys a typical toddler day playing dress-up, enjoying a picnic, resisting a nap and splashing in the bathtub.
Laura Joffe Numeroff, *What Grandmas Do Best/What Grandpas Do Best*, 2000
    Grandmas and Grandpas each have unique ways to share their love with their grandchildren.
Caroline Uff, *Lulu's Busy Day*, 2000
    Lulu's active day concludes with a bubble bath, brushing her teddy bear's teeth and hearing a story before snuggling into bed with her bear.

555

ELAINE GREENSTEIN, Author/Illustrator

Ice-Cream Cones for Sale!

(New York: Arthur A. Levine/Scholastic, Inc., 2003)

Subject(s): Food; History; Inventors and Inventions
Age range(s): Grades K-3
Major character(s): Italo Marchiony, Inventor, Immigrant
Time period(s): 1900s (1903-1904)
Locale(s): St. Louis, Missouri; New York, New York

Summary: Who can claim to be the inventor of the ice cream cone? There are several vendors and attendees from the 1904 St. Louis World's Fair who believe they should have the title. However, a little research shows that a New York ice cream vendor, Italo Marchiony received a patent for an ice cream cone mold a year before the St. Louis World's Fair. (32 pages)

Where it's reviewed:
Horn Book Guide, Spring 2004, page 168
Publishers Weekly, May 12, 2003, page 66

Other books by the same author:
One Little Lamb, 2004
Dreaming, 2000
Mrs. Rose's Garden, 1996

Other books you might like:
Elisha Cooper, *Ice Cream*, 2002
    From cow to carton, this book explains all the steps involved in making ice cream.
Daniel Pinkwater, *Ice Cream Larry*, 1999
    Polar bear Larry becomes the spokesman for Iceberg Ice Cream.
H.A. Rey, *Curious George Goes to an Ice Cream Shop*, 1989
    Curious George makes a mess at the ice cream shop, but then redeems himself by luring customers in when he builds a massive sundae.

556

SHEILA GREENWALD, Author/Illustrator

Rosy Cole's Worst Ever, Best Yet Tour of New York City

(New York: Melanie Kroupa/Farrar Straus Giroux, 2003)

Subject(s): Cousins; Travel; City and Town Life
Age range(s): Grades 3-6
Major character(s): Rosy Cole, Student—Elementary School, Cousin; Duncan Cole, Cousin, Tourist
Time period(s): 2000s (2003)
Locale(s): New York, New York

Summary: When Rosy Cole learns that her country cousin, Duncan, is coming to visit her family in Manhattan for a week, she plans an exciting tour of all of New York's biggest attractions. However, when Duncan arrives he is concerned about germs, traffic and spicy food but not particularly interested in Rosy's tour. Through a week of mishaps, Duncan does find two things that he loves about New York: music and food. In the end, Rosy comes to realize that even though Duncan didn't get the grand tour, he did discover all the common, everyday things about New York that make it her home. (122 pages)

Where it's reviewed:
Booklist, July 2003, page 1890
Horn Book, July/August, page 457
School Library Journal, November 2003, page 95

Other books by the same author:
Stucksville, 2000
The Mariah Delaney Lending Library Disaster, 2000
Rosy Cole: She Grows and Graduates, 1997
Rosy Cole: She Walks in Beauty, 1994
Give Us a Great Big Smile, Rosy Cole, 1981

Other books you might like:
Paula Danziger, *Amber Brown Is Not a Crayon*, 1995
    Amber has to deal with the divorce of her parents and the upcoming move of her best friend, Justin.

Louise Fitzhugh, *Harriet the Spy*, 1964
  Harriet records her observations of her neighborhood and neighbors.

Lois Lowry, *Anastasia Krupnik*, 1984
  Fourth-grader Anastasia tracks her life, including the impending arrival of her new baby brother, in her little green notebook.

557

KRISTIANA GREGORY

Eleanor: Crown Jewel of Aquitaine, France, 1136

(New York: Scholastic, 2002)

Series: Royal Diaries
Subject(s): Kings, Queens, Rulers, etc.; Diaries
Age range(s): Grades 5-8
Major character(s): Eleanor, Royalty (queen); Louis the Younger, Royalty (king); Duke William X of Aquitaine, Father (of Eleanor)
Time period(s): 12th century (1136-1137)
Locale(s): Poitiers, France

Summary: Filled with notes of daily living, including the dreadful odors and flies that always hover around the latrines in summer, Eleanor's diary covers the first two years of her teens, ending as she becomes the Queen of France. Living in Poitiers with her father, sister and grandmother, her life is filled with needlework, which she dislikes, and discussions about finding a suitable husband. Banquets, court gossip, riding and lessons also occupy her days until she is engaged to Louis the Younger, son of the King of France. Going on to become the queen, she enjoys a place in history as the independent, politically active Eleanor of Aquitaine. (187 pages)

Where it's reviewed:
Booklist, February 1, 2003, page 994
School Library Journal, January 2003, page 138
Voice of Youth Advocates, April 2003, page 50

Other books by the same author:
Seeds of Hope: The Gold Rush Diary of Susanna Fairchild, California Territory, 1849, 2001
Cleopatra VII: Daughter of the Nile, 1999
The Great Railroad Race: The Diary of Libby West, 1999
The Winter of Red Snow: The Revolutionary War Diary of Abigail Jane Stewart, 1996

Other books you might like:
Karen Cushman, *Catherine, Called Birdy*, 1994
  Although she knows her opinion means nothing, Birdy fights to control her destiny and marriage during the Middle Ages.
E.L. Konigsburg, *A Proud Taste for Scarlet and Miniver*, 1973
  Eleanor of Aquitaine narrates the events of her life from her home in Heaven.
Kathryn Lasky, *Marie Antoinette: Princess of Versailles*, 2000
  Two years of Marie Antoinette's life are revealed when she is engaged to the Dauphin of France and gives up childhood ways to become a young wife.

558

KRISTIANA GREGORY

We Are Patriots

(New York: Scholastic Press, 2002)

Series: My America. Hope's Revolutionary War Diary Book 2
Subject(s): Revolutionary War; Diaries; War
Age range(s): Grades 2-4
Major character(s): Hope Potter, 10-Year-Old, Daughter
Time period(s): 1770s (1777)
Locale(s): Valley Forge, Pennsylvania; Philadelphia, Pennsylvania

Summary: As the Revolutionary War rages in Pennsylvania, Hope, her mother and baby sister struggle to survive under many pressures. Hope's brother finally escapes from the British prison where he's been held him captive, but her father remains away from home, fighting with George Washington. Although the family is eventually forced to house British soldiers and Hope's best friend is forbidden to speak to her because her family sides with the British, Hope remains hopeful for the future and a free America. (108 pages)

Where it's reviewed:
Horn Book Guide, Fall 2002, page 358
School Library Journal, August 2002, page 156

Other books by the same author:
When Freedom Comes, 2004 (My America: Hope's Revolutionary War Diary Book 3)
Five Smooth Stones, 2001 (My America: Hope's Revolutionary War Diary Book 1)
Jenny of the Tetons, 1989

Other books you might like:
Avi, *The Fighting Ground*, 1984
  Thirteen-year-old Jonathan heads off to fight in the Revolutionary War, unprepared for the reality of combat.
Dorothy Hoobler, *The Sign Painter's Secret: The Story of a Revolutionary Girl*, 1991
  A young girl in Philadelphia spies on the British during the Revolutionary War. Thomas Hoobler, co-author.
Bryna Stevens, *Deborah Sampson Goes to War*, 1984
  This biography tells the story of Deborah Sampson who posed as a man to fight in the American Revolution.

559

NAN GREGORY
KADY MACDONALD DENTON, Illustrator

Amber Waiting

(Calgary, AB: Red Deer Press, 2003)

Subject(s): Schools; Fathers and Daughters; Imagination
Age range(s): Grades K-2
Major character(s): Amber, Kindergartner, Daughter; Dad, Father
Time period(s): 2000s (2002)
Locale(s): Canada

Summary: Amber can name many good things about kindergarten such as swinging, picture books and learning to tie shoes. Kindergarten has one bad thing, one very bad thing and that thing is Dad's lack of punctuality. Daily, Amber sees the other children go home with their parents while she sits with all her belongings ready to leave but unable to do so. While waiting, Amber imagines sending her Dad to the moon to sit all alone while he waits for her to come back for him. Maybe then he'd realize how important it is to arrive on time. Originally published in Canada in 2002. (32 pages)

Where it's reviewed:
Booklist, May 15, 2003, page 1659
Publishers Weekly, April 7, 2003, page 64
School Library Journal, July 2003, page 96

Awards the book has won:
Booklist Editors' Choice, 2003

Other books by the same author:
Wild Girl & Gran, 2000
How Smudge Came, 1995 (Booklist Editors' Choice)

Other books you might like:
Nancy Carlson, *Look Out Kindergarten, Here I Come!*, 1999
    Henry's enthusiasm for school wanes as he approaches the building.
Taro Gomi, *I Lost My Dad*, 2001
    While shopping in the toy department of a large store a young boy ''loses'' his father.
Laura Joffe Numeroff, *What Mommies Do Best/What Daddies Do Best*, 1998
    Parents have unique and special ways to express love to their children.
Douglas Wood, *What Dads Can't Do*, 2000
    Since dads are unable to read books alone or sleep late in the morning they really need their kids for company at such times.

560

VALISKA GREGORY
BRUCE DEGEN, Illustrator

Shirley's Wonderful Baby

(New York: HarperCollins, 2002)

Subject(s): Babies; Sibling Rivalry; Babysitters
Age range(s): Grades K-2
Major character(s): Shirley, Hippopotamus, Sister; Stanley, Hippopotamus, Brother; Mrs. Mump, Hippopotamus, Child-Care Giver
Time period(s): 2000s (2002)
Locale(s): United States

Summary: Shirley is not happy that every one thinks her new baby brother, Stanley, is so wonderful. When Mrs. Mump comes to care for the children, she seems to agree with Shirley, noting that babies are notorious for waking up, being hungry and burping. With a little urging from Mrs. Mump, Shirley begins to take more responsibility for Stanley and soon she can see what's wonderful about him too. (32 pages)

Where it's reviewed:
Bulletin of the Center for Children's Books, January 2003, page 199
Horn Book Guide, Spring 2003, page 12
Kirkus Reviews, August 15, 2002, page 1224
Publishers Weekly, July 8, 2002, page 48

School Library Journal, November 2002, page 124

Other books by the same author:
The Mystery of the Grindlecat, 2003
A Valentine for Norman Noggs, 1999
Kate's Giants, 1992

Other books you might like:
Jane Cutler, *Darcy and Gran Don't Like Babies*, 1993
    Big sister Darcy is relieved when Gran professes to share her lack of interest in the new baby and spends time alone with Darcy.
Candace Fleming, *Smile, Lily!*, 2004
    Baby Lily won't stop crying, until her big brother gives her a big smile.
Ezra Jack Keats, *Peter's Chair*, 1967
    When Peter learns that his blue furniture is being painted pink for his new baby sister, he runs away.
Heidi Stetson Mario, *I'd Rather Have an Iguana*, 1998
    A young girl is not happy when her new brother comes home and declares that she'd rather have an iguana.
Mercer Mayer, *The New Baby*, 1985
    Little Critter tries to figure out what things she can do with her new baby sister.

561

ANN GRIFALCONI
KADIR NELSON, Illustrator

The Village That Vanished

(New York: Dial Books for Young Readers, 2002)

Subject(s): Storytelling; Slavery; Folklore
Age range(s): Grades 2-5
Major character(s): Abikanile, Child, Daughter; Njemile, Mother; Chimwala, Grandmother
Time period(s): Indeterminate Past
Locale(s): Yao, Africa

Summary: Word reaches a small village sheltered deep in the forest that slavers from the north are coming. Abikanile knows the tales of these marauders who capture entire villages and sell them into slavery. Njemile presents a plan to the village elders to save the village by making it and the inhabitants disappear. Chimwala supports the plan but refuses to accompany the others. Each hut and every possession is scattered or buried in the surrounding forest. Taking only what they can carry, the villagers follow Njemile through the forest to the river's edge where Abikanile's prayer reveals a way across the river allowing the villagers to reach a safe hiding place. (40 pages)

Where it's reviewed:
Booklist, September 15, 2002, page 231
Bulletin of the Center for Children's Books, November 2002, page 109
Horn Book, September 2002, page 550
Publishers Weekly, August 26, 2002, page 68
School Library Journal, December 2002, page 97

Awards the book has won:
Notable Social Studies Trade Books for Young People, 2003

Other books by the same author:
Tiny's Hat, 1999

The Bravest Flute: A Story of Courage in the Mayan Tradition, 1994
Kinda Blue, 1993
The Village of Round and Square Houses, 1986 (Caldecott Honor Book)

Other books you might like:
Virginia Hamilton, *The People Could Fly: American Black Folktales*, 1985
 An award-winning collection of folktales includes those describing ways in which slaves achieved freedom.
Tom Monaghan, *The Slave Trade*, 2003
 A non-fiction title for youth describes the practice of trading in human cargo, its consequences and eventual abolition.
Kim Siegelson, *In the Time of the Drums*, 1999
 Drumming announces the arrival of a slave ship, carrying an entire captured Ibo village, to a Georgia island.

`562`

ADELE GRIFFIN

Hannah, Divided

(New York: Hyperion, 2002)

Subject(s): Mental Illness; Depression (Economic); Mathematics
Age range(s): Grades 5-8
Major character(s): Hannah Bennett, 13-Year-Old, Student (gifted in mathematics); Granddad McNaughton, Grandfather; Joe Elway, Student (gifted in verbal skills); Theodora Ann ''Teddy'' Sweet, Philanthropist
Time period(s): 1930s
Locale(s): Chadds Ford, Pennsylvania; Philadelphia, Pennsylvania

Summary: Hannah enjoys milking the cows and using her incredible math ability to invoice the customers for her family's dairy farm. Though her teacher thinks mathematical ability is just for boys, Granddad McNaughton has always played number games with her as he realizes her ability will take her far beyond Chadds Ford. The opportunity to study comes when benefactor Mrs. Sweet offers Hannah a chance to board with her in Philadelphia and attend the Ottley Friends School to improve her chances at a scholarship. Hannah is miserable away from the farm and becomes obsessive about counting and tapping which bothers everyone, except for the other boarding student, Joe Elway, who becomes her only friend. It's also Joe who's finally able to teach Hannah to read by using newspaper accounts of gangsters rather than the classics. Hannah's obsessive compulsiveness hampers her efforts on the scholarship, but not her determination for further study. (264 pages)

Where it's reviewed:
Horn Book, November 2002, page 758
Publishers Weekly, August 26, 2002, page 69
Riverbank Review, Winter 2002, page 38
School Library Journal, December 2002, page 138
Voice of Youth Advocates, December 2002, page 380

Awards the book has won:
Booklist Editors' Choice/Books for Youth, 2002

Other books by the same author:
Where I Want to Be, 2004
Overnight, 2003
Amandine, 2001
Dive, 1999
The Other Shepards, 1998

Other books you might like:
Terry Spencer Hesser, *Kissing Doorknobs*, 1998
 It's hard to help Tara when her behavior becomes so obsessive that it takes her 30 minutes to complete her doorknob ritual to leave the house.
Natalie Kinsey-Warnock, *In the Language of Loons*, 1998
 A summer with his grandfather strengthens Arlis so that after he returns home, he's able to face the news of his grandfather's death.
Gail Carson Levine, *Dave at Night*, 1999
 Miserable living in the Hebrew Home for Boys, Dave escapes each night into the art and music of the Harlem Renaissance.
Walter Tevis, *The Queen's Gambit*, 1983
 Orphaned Beth Harmon is a chess genius who wins her first tournament when she's 14.

`563`

ADELE GRIFFIN

Overnight

(New York: Putnam, 2003)

Subject(s): Interpersonal Relations; Kidnapping; Peer Pressure
Age range(s): Grades 4-7
Major character(s): Gray ''Mouse'' Rosenfeld, 11-Year-Old; Martha Van Riet, 11-Year-Old; Caitlin Donnelly, 11-Year-Old; Katrina, Mentally Ill Person; Drew, Kidnapper
Time period(s): 2000s
Locale(s): United States

Summary: Told from the perspective of four of its members, the Lucky Seven celebrate Caitlin's birthday with a sleepover at her house. Gray calls home to demand her mother bring her the correct sleeping bag, an outburst probably caused by her insecurity. Gray's convinced she's part of this group only because her mother has cancer and the girls feel sorry for her. In the kitchen obtaining a drink of water, Gray admits a disheveled woman who she thinks her mother has sent about her sleeping bag; unfortunately Katrina takes Gray to an isolated house where a man named Drew is waiting. Back at the sleepover, the self-centeredness of the girls is apparent, especially leader Martha, as they're more concerned with their standing in the group than Gray's whereabouts. (151 pages)

Where it's reviewed:
Bulletin of the Center for Children's Books, February 2003, page 235
Kirkus Reviews, February 1, 2003, page 229
Publishers Weekly, December 16, 2002, page 68
School Library Journal, February 2003, page 141
Voice of Youth Advocates, April 2003, page 50

Other books by the same author:
Where I Want to Be, 2004
Amandine, 2001
Dive, 1999
Sons of Liberty, 1997
Split Just Right, 1997

Other books you might like:
Amy Goldman Koss, *The Girls*, 2000
   Ringleader Candace manages to whittle her clique from five to four when she decides Maya is out; now the others wonder, who's next?
Elizabeth Laird, *Secret Friends*, 1999
   Wanting to be accepted by the popular kids, Lucy joins in teasing Rafaella, but never reveals that she and Rafaella are friends outside of school.
Rachel Vail, *The Friendship Ring Series*, 1991-1998
   Friends learn that growing up can be tough, even when it's just choosing ballet or a social life, wanting a best friend or learning to be yourself.

564

ADELE GRIFFIN
JACQUELINE ROGERS, Illustrator

Witch Twins at Camp Bliss

(New York: Hyperion Books for Children, 2002)

Subject(s): Twins; Camps and Camping; Witches and Witch-craft
Age range(s): Grades 3-5

Summary: Claire and Luna may look exactly alike but their feelings about spending five weeks at Camp Bliss are completely different. Luna approaches her first camping experience reluctantly while Claire is not only eager to go but also plans to excel in all activities so she will leave camp as the proud recipient of the ''Camp Bliss Girl'' trophy. In order to give Luna a little ''zest'' for camp life Grandy gives her a small bottle of a magic powder with strict instructions to keep it well hidden. Luna tries but someone, who believes Luna's story that it actually is foot powder, steals it and strange things begin to happen at camp. Believing there is another witch doing unauthorized spells Claire and Luna attempt to track down the thief. By the time the trail leads them to the bottle, it is empty and camp life returns to normal. (138 pages)

Where it's reviewed:
Booklist, July 2002, page 1844
Bulletin of the Center for Children's Books, July 2002, page 404
Horn Book Guide, Fall 2002, page 373
Publishers Weekly, June 10, 2002, page 62
School Library Journal, June 2002, page 96

Other books by the same author:
Witch Twins, 2001
Split Just Right, 1997
Rainy Season, 1996

Other books you might like:
Betsy Duffey, *Cody Unplugged*, 1999
   TV addict and reluctant camper Cody learns that real experiences are actually more interesting than the vicarious ones of television and video games.
Jahnna N. Malcolm, *Camp Clodhopper*, 1990
   Characters in the Bad News Ballet series entry soon learn that the camp they're attending will not improve their ballet skills as they'd expected.
Daniel Pinkwater, *Fat Camp Commandos*, 2001
   Ralph and Sylvia run away from Camp Noo Yoo and hide out with Mavis, another disgruntled camper, for the summer.

565

NIKKI GRIMES

Bronx Masquerade

(New York: Dial/Penguin Putnam, 2002)

Subject(s): Poetry; Heritage; Schools/High Schools
Age range(s): Grades 8-12
Major character(s): Mr. Ward, Teacher
Time period(s): 2000s
Locale(s): New York, New York (the Bronx)

Summary: While studying the Harlem Renaissance, Mr. Ward assigns his students to write poetry and then gives them a chance to perform their poems during Friday ''Open Mike'' nights in his classroom at their high school. What a revelation for these 18 students as they examine their lives and openly share them with their classmates. Bit by bit, African Americans, Latinos and white students find common bonds and form a sense of community as they hear the stories told in poetry by their colleagues. (167 pages)

Where it's reviewed:
Bulletin of the Center for Children's Books, March 2002, page 231
Horn Book, March 2002, page 213
Publishers Weekly, December 17, 2001, page 92
School Library Journal, January 2002, page 132
Voice of Youth Advocates, February 2002, page 435

Awards the book has won:
ALA Best Books for Young Adults, 2003
Coretta Scott King, 2003

Other books by the same author:
Dark Sons, 2005
What Is Goodbye?: Poems on Grief, 2005
Jazmin's Notebook, 1998

Other books you might like:
E.R. Frank, *Life Is Funny*, 2000
   This portrayal of a group of 11 students over their six-year high school careers illustrates all possible meanings of the phrase ''life is funny.''
Helen Frost, *Keesha's House*, 2003
   A combination of sestinas, sonnets and other verse forms tell of Keesha's House that offers sanctuary to all who need it.
Mel Glenn, *Class Dismissed! High School Poems*, 1991
   Poems reveal the reality of high school life for these 70 students.

566

NIKKI GRIMES
FLOYD COOPER, Illustrator

Danitra Brown Leaves Town

(New York: Amistad/HarperCollins Publishers, 2002)

Subject(s): Friendship; Poetry; Vacations
Age range(s): Grades 2-4
Major character(s): Zuri Jackson, Child, Friend; Danitra Brown, Child, Friend
Time period(s): 2000s (2003)
Locale(s): United States

Summary: Zuri is upset to learn that her best friend Danitra will be visiting out-of-town relatives all summer. Feelings are smoothed after Danitra leaves and writes Zuri telling her how much she misses her. The girls share their summer adventures with each other through letters and both are glad to be together again at the end of the summer. (32 pages)

Where it's reviewed:
Booklist, February 15, 2002, page 1033
Bulletin of the Center for Children's Books, April 2002, page 280
School Library Journal, February 2002, page 101

Other books by the same author:
Talkin' about Bessie: The Story of Aviator Elizabeth Coleman, 2002 (Coretta Scott King Award)
Jazmin's Notebook, 1998
Meet Danitra Brown, 1994 (Coretta Scott King Honor Book)

Other books you might like:
Karen Hesse, *Come On, Rain!*, 1999
    A steamy city block waits for a summer storm to cool things off a little.
Nancy Poydar, *Cool Ali*, 1996
    During a hot summer day, Ali distracts her neighbors by drawing refreshingly cool scenes on the sidewalk.
Jacqueline Woodson, *The Other Side*, 2001
    Separated by segregation, neighbors Clover and Annie nonetheless become friends.

567

JEANNE MARIE GRUNWELL

Mind Games

(Boston: Houghton Mifflin, 2003)

Subject(s): Scientific Experiments; Lottery; School Life
Age range(s): Grades 5-8
Major character(s): Benjamin D. ''Ben'' Lloyd, 7th Grader; Claire Phelps, 7th Grader, Twin; Kathleen Phelps, 7th Grader, Twin; Ji Eun Oh, 7th Grader; Marina Krenina, Immigrant (Russian), 7th Grader; Brandon Kelly, 7th Grader
Time period(s): 2000s
Locale(s): Maryland

Summary: Six students, members of ''The Mad Science Club,'' decide to explore ESP for their science fairy project, but wind up learning more about themselves during their experiment. Nerdy Ben feels rejected by his mother after she remarries and has a baby; Claire is popular and in academic classes; while her twin Kathleen, brain damaged at birth, attends special education classes. Ji's friendship with Claire subsides during middle school; Russian immigrant Marina knows little English; and Brandon, whose mother died recently in an accident, is certain that some people have ESP since his little brother predicted their mother's accident. After winning $500 in the Maryland lottery, they're all believers in ESP. Chapters alternate among these six students as their notes, journal entries, newspaper clippings and reports describe their project and their lives in this author's first novel. (133 pages)

Where it's reviewed:
Booklist, May 15, 2003, page 1661
Horn Book, May 2003, page 345
Kliatt, July 2003, page 12
Publishers Weekly, April 28, 2003, page 71
School Library Journal, May 2003, page 152

Other books you might like:
E.L. Konigsburg, *The View from Saturday*, 1996
    Chosen by their teacher for the Academic Bowl, four sixth-graders relate their own, intriguingly interwoven, stories.
Anne Peters, *How Do You Spell G-E-E-K?*, 1996
    Kim and Ann's plans to compete in the National Spelling Bee are almost ruined by new student Lurlene, who is a natural speller.
Zilpha Keatley Snyder, *Libby on Wednesday*, 1990
    Libby hates meeting on Wednesdays with four other writing contest winners, but eventually the four help one another with writing and family problems.

568

ELISSA HADEN GUEST
CHRISTINE DAVENIER, Illustrator

Iris and Walter and Baby Rose

(San Diego: Gulliver Books/Harcourt, Inc., 2002)

Series: Iris and Walter. Book 3
Subject(s): Babies; Sisters; Sibling Rivalry
Age range(s): Grades 1-3
Major character(s): Iris, Child, Friend (Walter's); Walter, Child, Friend (Iris's); Rose, Baby, Sister (Iris's); Grandpa, Grandfather
Time period(s): 2000s
Locale(s): United States

Summary: The news that she will become a big sister fills Iris with excited anticipation. Eagerly Iris shares with Walter her plans for the new baby. After a long, impatient wait for the baby's birth, Iris is disappointed to discover that, though Baby Rose looks like a doll, she's actually a noisy intruder. Walter offers earmuffs to Iris but still the time and attention a fussy baby demands is frustrating. After Grandpa takes Iris to a carnival for a ''day away'' from the baby, she feels more understanding of her parents and Baby Rose. Eventually, Iris gives up the earmuffs and begins to enjoy her role as a big sister, most of the time. (44 pages)

Where it's reviewed:
Booklist, March 15, 2002, page 1261

Bulletin of the Center for Children's Books, April 2002, page 281
Horn Book Guide, Fall 2002, page 351
Publishers Weekly, March 25, 2002, page 66
School Library Journal, April 2002, page 110

Other books by the same author:
Iris and Walter: The Sleepover, 2002 (Book 4)
Iris and Walter: True Friends, 2001 (Book 2)
Iris and Walter, 2000 (Book 1)

Other books you might like:
Joyce Champion, *Emily and Alice Baby-Sit Burton*, 2001
  Disappointed that the only response to their baby-sitting ads is a job for dog care, Emily and Alice make the most of it by babying Burton.
Amy Hest, *Nannies for Hire*, 1994
  Three friends who offer to be "nannies" for an infant discover how difficult baby care can be.
James Howe, *Pinky and Rex and the New Baby*, 1993
  Rex becomes so involved in her new role as a big sister that she neglects her friendship with Pinky.

569

ELISSA HADEN GUEST
CHRISTINE DAVENIER, Illustrator

Iris and Walter and Cousin Howie

(San Diego: Gulliver Books/Harcourt, Inc., 2003)

Series: Iris and Walter. Book 6
Subject(s): Friendship; Cousins; Magic
Age range(s): Grades 1-3
Major character(s): Iris, Child, Friend; Walter, Friend, Child; Howie, Cousin, Child
Time period(s): 2000s (2003)
Locale(s): United States

Summary: A visit from Walter's favorite cousin leaves Iris feeling left out as Howie is understandably more interested in Walter than Iris. Howie wants to go fishing rather than teach magic tricks to Iris and Walter as they'd hoped and he obviously doesn't want Iris around. Iris's family assures her that Walter is still her best friend and, once Howie leaves, Iris and Walter learn how to do magic tricks from library books. (44 pages)

Where it's reviewed:
Booklist, September 15, 2003, page 244
Publishers Weekly, September 8, 2003, page 78
School Library Journal, December 2003, page 114

Other books by the same author:
Iris and Walter and Baby Rose, 2002 (Iris and Walter Book 3)
Iris and Walter: True Friends, 2001 (Iris and Walter Book 2)
Iris and Walter, 2000 (Iris and Walter Book 1)

Other books you might like:
Sheila Greenwald, *Rosy Cole's Worst Ever, Best Yet Tour of New York City*, 2003
  When Rosy's cousin Duncan comes to visit, she wants to show him Manhattan, but things don't go as she had hoped.
Russell Hoban, *Best Friends for Frances*, 1969
  After Frances is left out of her best friend Albert's boys-only baseball game she discovers that sisters can be friends.

James Howe, *Pinky and Rex and the Perfect Pumpkin*, 1998
  When Rex accompanies her best friend Pinky on a pumpkin-picking trip, she feels excluded by his cousin Abby.

570

ELISSA HADEN GUEST
CHRISTINE DAVENIER, Illustrator

Iris and Walter: The School Play

(San Diego: Gulliver Books/Harcourt, Inc., 2003)

Series: Iris and Walter. Book 5
Subject(s): Theater; Schools; Illness
Age range(s): Grades 1-3
Major character(s): Iris, Student, Friend; Walter, Student, Friend; Miss Cherry, Teacher
Time period(s): 2000s (2003)
Locale(s): United States

Summary: Walter is cast as a dragonfly and Iris as a cricket in a school play about bugs. Almost as exciting as the play is Miss Cherry's promise of an ice cream party after the performance. Together Iris and Walter paint their costumes and practice their lines until everything is ready for the dress rehearsal. On stage during rehearsal Walter forgets his lines so Iris whispers to him when he falters. The morning of the show Iris awakens with a sore throat and fever. Although she protests, her parents will not allow her to go to school so she misses the play and the ice cream party. Iris can barely hide her disappointment when she's able to return to school but by the end of the day she's able to look forward to the next play about the solar system with Iris cast as the sun. (44 pages)

Where it's reviewed:
Horn Book Guide, Fall 2003, page 349
Horn Book, May 2003, page 346
Publishers Weekly, February 17, 2003, page 78
School Library Journal, April 2003, page 121

Other books by the same author:
Iris and Walter and the Substitute Teacher, 2004 (Iris and Walter Book 8)
Iris and Walter, Lost and Found, 2004 (Iris and Walter Book 7)
Iris and Walter and Cousin Howie, 2003 (Iris and Walter Book 6)
Iris and Walter and Baby Rose, 2002
Iris and Walter: The Sleepover, 2002 (Iris and Walter Book 4)

Other books you might like:
Fred Ehrlich, *A Class Play with Ms. Vanilla*, 1992
  Rhyming text in this Hello Reader! series entry describes Ms. Vanilla's class production of "Little Red Riding Hood."
Maggie Stern, *George*, 1999
  Three stories tell of eager-to-please but impetuous George who can't wait his turn in class yet has the patience to track down a lost class pet.
Rosemary Wells, *The School Play*, 2001
  In the second entry in the Yoko and Friends School Days series kindergartener Yoko and her classmates perform in a play.

571

ELISSA HADEN GUEST
CHRISTINE DAVENIER, Illustrator

Iris and Walter: The Sleepover

(San Diego: Gulliver Books/Harcourt, Inc., 2002)

Series: Iris and Walter. Book 4
Subject(s): Homesickness; Friendship; Sleep
Age range(s): Grades 2-3
Major character(s): Iris, Child, Friend; Walter, Child, Friend; Benny, Child, Classmate
Time period(s): 2000s (2002)
Locale(s): United States

Summary: With eager anticipation Iris tells family and classmates about her planned first sleepover. The glow that surrounds her plans for puppet shows and sleeping on Walter's front porch dims a bit when Benny tells Iris about the homesickness he felt during his first sleepover. That seed of doubt emerges after Iris and Walter enjoy their planned activities and settle down on the porch to tell stories and stay awake all night. As Iris tells the first story, Walter falls asleep and lonely Iris realizes how much she misses the routine of her family's bedtime. She wakes Walter and his parents drive Iris home. Her loving family greets her, tucks her into bed and assures her that she can sleep at Walter's house another time. And one day she does. (44 pages)

Where it's reviewed:
Booklist, November 1, 2002, page 508
Bulletin of the Center for Children's Books, October 2002, page 58
Horn Book Guide, Spring 2003, page 61
Publishers Weekly, September 9, 2002, page 70
School Library Journal, October 2002, page 112

Other books by the same author:
Iris and Walter and Baby Rose, 2002 (Iris and Walter Book 3)
Iris and Walter: True Friends, 2001 (Iris and Walter Book 2)
Iris and Walter, 2000 (Iris and Walter Book 1)

Other books you might like:
Paula Danziger, *What a Trip, Amber Brown*, 2001
  In an entry in the A Is for Amber beginning reader series, Amber and Justin enjoy sleeping out in a tent during their families' shared vacation.
James Howe, *Pinky and Rex*, 1990
  Pinky and Rex, inseparable friends, embark on the first of many shared adventures in this initial book in their series.
Karen Gray Ruelle, *Easy as Apple Pie*, 2002
  Baking an apple pie and spending the night at his grandparents' home is appealing to Harry, but not his younger sister, Emily.

572

JOHN STEVEN GURNEY, Author/Illustrator

Dinosaur Train

(New York: HarperCollins, Inc., 2002)

Subject(s): Dinosaurs; Trains; Bedtime
Age range(s): Preschool-Grade 1

Major character(s): Jesse, Child
Time period(s): 2000s (2002)
Locale(s): United States

Summary: Jesse loves playing with trains and dinosaurs. As he draws a picture incorporating his two interests, a dinosaur train fantastically arrives in his room one night at bedtime. Thrilled, Jesse climbs aboard and joins the dinosaurs on their travels. After an enjoyable ride, the dinosaurs return him to his bedroom. This is the first picture book also written by this longtime illustrator. (32 pages)

Where it's reviewed:
Booklist, November 15, 2002, page 610
Kirkus Reviews, July 15, 2002, page 1031
Publishers Weekly, September 30, 2002, page 70
School Library Journal, December 2002, page 97

Other books you might like:
Kevin Lewis, *Chugga-Chugga Choo-Choo*, 1999
  A boy's toy train set comes alive at night.
Deb Lund, *Dinosailors*, 2003
  After trying a sailing adventure, group of dinosaurs decides to take a train next time.
Mary Lyn Ray, *All Aboard!*, 2002
  A girl and her stuffed rabbit travel overnight on the train to Grandma and Grandpa's house.
Robert Spence, *Clickety Clack*, 1999
  As the animal passengers of a train board, the noise level gets louder and louder. Amy Spence, co-author.

573

ANNE GUTMAN
GEORG HALLENSLEBEN, Illustrator

Gaspard and Lisa's Rainy Day

(New York: Alfred A. Knopf, 2003)

Series: Misadventures of Gaspard and Lisa
Subject(s): Vacations; Behavior; Friendship
Age range(s): Grades K-1
Major character(s): Gaspard, Friend, Dog; Lisa, Friend, Dog; Grandma, Grandmother, Dog
Time period(s): Indeterminate
Locale(s): Fictional Country

Summary: Vacation at Lisa's grandma's house should be fun, but it rains every day and the two friends are a bit bored. Eagerly they try Grandma's suggestion to make a cake, so eagerly that they don't wait for Grandma's instructions and make a mess rather than a cake. Then Gaspard and Lisa plan their own activities such as a haunted house in the bedroom, tennis in the dining room, and making a jigsaw puzzle out of one of Grandma's paintings. Fortunately the sun comes out before Lisa and Gaspard have any more ideas. Originally published in France in 2001. (26 pages)

Where it's reviewed:
Booklist, April 15, 2003, page 1477
Bulletin of the Center for Children's Books, April 2003, page 314
School Library Journal, May 2003, page 120

Other books by the same author:
Gaspard and Lisa's Ready-for-School Words, 2004

Daddy Kisses, 2003
Lisa in the Jungle, 2003

Other books you might like:
Jonathan London, *Puddles*, 1997
  A brother and sister delight in the puddles and mud that await after a storm.
Jack Prelutsky, *Rainy, Rainy Saturday*, 1980
  Fourteen poems celebrate the fun to be had on a rainy day, even if you're stuck inside.
Mary Lyn Ray, *Red Rubber Boot Day*, 2000
  Tiring of indoor activities on a rainy day, a young child dons a yellow raincoat and red rubber boots and heads outside for some fun.

574

ANNE GUTMAN
GEORG HALLENSLEBEN, Illustrator

Lisa's Baby Sister

(New York: Alfred A. Knopf, 2003)

Series: Misadventures of Gaspard and Lisa
Subject(s): Babies; Change; Family Relations
Age range(s): Grades K-1
Major character(s): Lisa, Dog, Sister; Gaspard, Dog, Friend; Victoria, Sister (older), Dog; Lila, Sister (younger), Baby
Time period(s): Indeterminate
Locale(s): Fictional Country

Summary: Lisa is not happy with her mother's pregnancy because it means Lisa has to carry her own schoolbag and has no one to seesaw with her. Gaspard faithfully promises not to speak to the baby. After Lila is born Lisa is really miserable. Victoria thinks the baby is so cute she invites friends over to see Lila while Lisa hides in her room and makes annoying noises on her flute. When no one is around Lisa sneaks into Lila's room and looks her over carefully, picks her up and decides maybe she's not so bad after all. (26 pages)

Where it's reviewed:
Booklist, April 15, 2003, page 1477
Bulletin of the Center for Children's Books, April 2003, page 314
School Library Journal, May 2003, page 120

Other books by the same author:
Gaspard and Lisa, Friends Forever, 2003
Mommy Hugs, 2003
Gaspard and Lisa's Christmas Surprise, 2002

Other books you might like:
Jane Cutler, *Darcy and Gran Don't Like Babies*, 1993
  Big sister Darcy is relieved when Gran professes to share her lack of interest in the new baby and spends time alone with Darcy.
Holly Keller, *Geraldine's Baby Brother*, 1994
  It takes time for Geraldine to adjust to her noisy baby brother and all the attention he receives.
Clara Vulliamy, *Ellen and Penguin and the New Baby*, 1996
  Ellen agrees with her stuffed Penguin's observation that having a new baby in the house is not such a good idea.

575

DAN GUTMAN

Qwerty Stevens Stuck in Time with Benjamin Franklin

(New York: Simon & Schuster, 2002)

Series: Qwerty Stevens, Back in Time. Number 2
Subject(s): Time Travel; Revolutionary War; Schools/Middle Schools
Age range(s): Grades 5-8
Major character(s): Robert Edward ''Qwerty'' Stevens, 13-Year-Old; Benjamin Franklin, Historical Figure; Joey Dvorak, 13-Year-Old
Time period(s): 2000s; 1770s (1776)
Locale(s): West Orange, New Jersey; Philadelphia, Pennsylvania

Summary: Qwerty's at it again! This time he's in a panic for a report on the American Revolution so he goes online, finds info on the web and suddenly Ben Franklin's sitting on Qwerty's bed. The irascible old gentleman is as charming and womanizing as he's been portrayed. Entranced with 21st century inventions, he visits Qwerty's classroom, provides background on the Revolution, and flirts with every woman he meets. To further explain the Revolution, Ben decides that Qwerty and his friend Joey should accompany him back in time to the signing of the Declaration of Independence in 1776 Philadelphia. In the excitement of the travel, Qwerty forgets to set up their return trip but luckily his older sister Barbara ensures that they're not left in time. (183 pages)

Where it's reviewed:
Booklist, September 15, 2002, page 235
Kirkus Reviews, August 1, 2002, page 1130
School Library Journal, August 2002, page 188

Other books by the same author:
The Million Dollar Strike, 2004
Mickey and Me: A Baseball Card Adventure, 2003
The Edison Mystery, 2001 (Qwerty Stevens, Back in Time Number 1)
The Secret Life of Dr. Demented, 2001
Johnny Hangtime, 2000

Other books you might like:
Robert J. Favole, *Through the Wormhole*, 2001
  Michael and Kate work for the CyberTimeSurfingInstitute and are sent to the Revolutionary War to search for one of Michael's ancestors.
Robert Lee Hall, *London Blood: Further Adventures of the American Agent Abroad: A Benjamin Franklin Mystery*, 1997
  Benjamin Franklin and his illegitimate son Nick use their detecting skills when several women are found dead with their hearts cut out. Adult mystery.
Arvella Whitmore, *Trapped: Between the Lash and the Gun*, 1999
  Bad boy Jordan winds up in the pre-Civil War South and discovers there are worse things in life than living in the 'burbs.

H

576

JESSIE HAAS

Shaper

(New York: Greenwillow/HarperCollins, 2002)

Subject(s): Animals/Dogs; Animals, Treatment of; Grief
Age range(s): Grades 5-8
Major character(s): Chad Holloway, 14-Year-Old; David Burton, Animal Trainer; Louise Burton, 15-Year-Old; Jeep Houghton, Grandfather (of Chad); Queenie, Dog
Time period(s): 2000s
Locale(s): Vermont

Summary: The death of his dog Shep leaves Chad angry at his older sister and not speaking to Jeep, his grandfather, who put Shep out of his misery after he was hit by a car. Chad feels as though he doesn't even belong with his family anymore, doesn't want to play summer baseball and certainly doesn't like energetic Queenie, the dog bought to replace Shep. Chad is intrigued by the work of his new neighbor David Burton, who is writing a book about positive reinforcement and the use of a clicker in shaping the behavior of animals. When David offers him a job, Chad accepts partly out of curiosity, but mostly out of interest in David's teenage daughter Louise. As Chad and Queenie work together using David's training method, Chad realizes that David's methods are altering his behavior as much as they're modifying Queenie's and is happy to leave his grief behind, accept Queenie as his new dog and feel part of his family again. (186 pages)

Where it's reviewed:
Booklist, July 2002, page 1844
Horn Book, May 2002, page 330
Kliatt, July 2002, page 10
School Library Journal, May 2002, page 152
Voice of Youth Advocates, June 2002, page 118

Other books by the same author:
Will You, Won't You, 2001
Unbroken, 1999
Westminster West, 1997
Uncle Daney's Way, 1994

Other books you might like:
Lynn Hall, *The Soul of the Silver Dog*, 1992
   Cory pours her heart into training the blind, former champion, Bedlington terrier Sterling for competition on the obstacle course.
Libby Hathorn, *Thunderwith*, 1991
   Lara is convinced her deceased mother has sent her a companion in the form of the magnificent dog she meets in the outback.
Sylvia McNicoll, *Bringing Up Beauty*, 2000
   In return for teaching black lab Beauty the guide commands, Beauty showers Elizabeth with the love and devotion she needs.

577

MARGARET PETERSON HADDIX

Among the Barons

(New York: Simon & Schuster, 2003)

Series: Shadow Children. Book 4
Subject(s): Schools/Boarding Schools; Brothers; Science Fiction
Age range(s): Grades 6-9
Major character(s): Luke "Lee Grant" Garnet, 13-Year-Old; Smithfield William "Smits" Grant, Brother (of Lee)
Time period(s): Indeterminate
Locale(s): United States

Summary: In an overpopulated world, it is illegal to have more than two children per family and the Population Police are noted for hunting down and executing those third children. Luke Garner is a third child who's been in hiding for twelve years, but has assumed the identity of deceased Lee Grant, son of wealthy parents, and is now in boarding school. Posing as Lee hadn't been a problem until Lee's disturbed younger brother Smits is sent to Hendrick's School for Boys; when he sets fire to the school, the Grants request that both boys be sent home. The wealthy Grants, whose class is known to the rest of the population as the Barons, live in a style to which Luke is not accustomed. Not only is it difficult for him to adjust to this manner of living, but Luke also finds himself embroiled in a political plot that could be dangerous, or even fatal. (182 pages)

Where it's reviewed:
Booklist, May 15, 2003, page 1661
Horn Book Guide, Fall 2003, page 367
Publishers Weekly, April 28, 2003, page 71
School Library Journal, June 2003, page 142
Voice of Youth Advocates, August 2003, page 236

Other books by the same author:
Among the Enemy, 2005 (Shadow Children Book 6)
Among the Brave, 2004 (Shadow Children Book 5)
Among the Betrayed, 2002 (Shadow Children Book 3)
Among the Imposters, 2001 (Shadow Children Book 2)
Among the Hidden, 1998 (Shadow Children Book 1)

Other books you might like:
Jennifer Armstrong, *Fire-Us Series*, 2002-2003
  In a world where adults have been killed by a virus, a group of teens and children struggle to survive in Florida.
David Lubar, *Hidden Talents*, 1999
  At the alternative school, Martin helps his roommates use their special abilities of telekinesis and precognition to stop bullies from sabotage.
John Marsden, *Tomorrow When the War Began Series*, 1995-2003
  Five teenagers use guerrilla tactics to fight their country's takeover, even turning to killing if it means saving a friend.
Gary Paulsen, *The White Fox Chronicles: Escape, Return, Breakout*, 2000
  Cody is part of a resistance group of Americans fighting to regain control of their country from the Confederation of Consolidated Republics.

578

MARGARET PETERSON HADDIX

Among the Betrayed
(New York: Simon & Schuster, 2002)

Subject(s): Science Fiction; Conduct of Life; Fear
Age range(s): Grades 6-10
Major character(s): Nina Idi, 13-Year-Old; Alia, Child; Matthias, Child; Percy, Child
Time period(s): Indeterminate Future
Locale(s): United States

Summary: Living in a world where only two children are allowed per family, Nina is one of the "shadow children," those third children who exist on false identity papers or are kept hidden. Falsely accused of treason, Nina is arrested at her boarding school and taken to jail where she faces execution unless she agrees to find out the real identity of her three cellmates. Struggling with what to do, Nina sees an opportunity to escape and takes Alia, Matthias and Percy with her; unfortunately, Nina is recaptured when she forages for food and then must decide whether or not to reveal the whereabouts of the others in this sequel to *Among the Imposters*. (156 pages)

Where it's reviewed:
Bulletin of the Center for Children's Books, October 2002, page 58
Library Media Connection, February 2003, page 80
Publishers Weekly, June 10, 2002, page 61
School Library Journal, June 2002, page 138
Voice of Youth Advocates, June 2002, page 126

Awards the book has won:
IRA Children's Choices/Advanced Readers, 2003
ALA Quick Picks for Reluctant Young Adult Readers, 2003

Other books by the same author:
Among the Brave, 2004
Among the Barons, 2003
Among the Imposters, 2001
Among the Hidden, 1998

Other books you might like:
Thomas Baird, *Smart Rats*, 1990
  Because of overpopulation, the government has decreed that every family with two progeny must send one to be relocated in "disinhabited areas."
Monica Hughes, *Invitation to the Game*, 1990
  Lisse and seven of her friends think they're invited to a role-playing computer game, but are actually sent to colonize a new planet.
Gary Paulsen, *The White Fox Chronicles: Escape, Return, Breakout*, 2000
  Cody is part of a resistance group of Americans fighting to regain control of their country from the Confederation of Consolidated Republics.
Robert Westall, *Futuretrack 5*, 1984
  In a Britain of the future, people either live privileged lives in the Est class or lawless lives outside society's protection in the Unnem group.

579

MARGARET PETERSON HADDIX

Because of Anya
(New York: Simon & Schuster, 2002)

Subject(s): Illness; Hair; Schools
Age range(s): Grades 3-6
Major character(s): Anya Seaver, 10-Year-Old, Student—Elementary School; Keely Michaels, 10-Year-Old, Student—Elementary School
Time period(s): 2000s (2002)
Locale(s): United States

Summary: Keely and her bossier friends notice that classmate Anya returns from winter break wearing a wig. While the classmates wonder if Anya has cancer, Anya worries about people discovering her secret. Anya has alopecia areata, an autoimmune disease that causes hair to fall out. When Anya's wig falls off during gym class, she runs home and refuses to return to school. Keely reaches out to her long-time classmate by cutting off her own hair to be made into a wig. (128 pages)

Where it's reviewed:
Horn Book Guide, Spring 2003, page 81
Kirkus Reviews, November 1, 2002, page 1611
Publishers Weekly, November 11, 2002, page 64

School Library Journal, November 2002, page 168

Other books by the same author:
Among the Brave, 2004
Just Ella, 1999
Running Out of Time, 1995

Other books you might like:
Virginia Hamilton, *Bluish*, 1999
Dreenie befriends a classmate with leukemia, whose treatments are making her so pale that she appears bluish in color.
Angela Johnson, *A Cool Moonlight*, 2003
Nine-year-old Lila has a rare medical condition that makes her allergic to sunlight. Able to go outside only at night, Lila develops a rich fantasy life.
Sally Warner, *Sort of Forever*, 1998
Cady's best friend, Nana, is diagnosed with terminal bone cancer.

580

MARGARET PETERSON HADDIX

Escape from Memory

(New York: Simon & Schuster, 2003)

Subject(s): Memory; Computers; Kidnapping
Age range(s): Grades 6-9
Major character(s): Kira Landon, 15-Year-Old; Lynne Robertson, 15-Year-Old; Sophia Landon, Mother (of Kira); Rona ''Aunt Memory'' Cummins, Kidnapper
Time period(s): 2000s
Locale(s): Willistown, Ohio; Crythe, California

Summary: It all started with being hypnotized at her best friend Lynne's sleepover when Kira talked about being rescued from a war-devastated area as a baby and spoke in a language no one, including Kira, knew. Questioning her mother, Kira receives evasive answers and then her mother disappears. Someone called Aunt Memory appears telling Kira she will need to travel to California to rescue her mother. Lynne hides in Kira's suitcase and the two head to California with Aunt Memory where they're taken to Crythe. Years before the entire old-world town of Crythe was secretly moved to California, in a deal worked out by the Soviet Union and the United States, following the Chernobyl explosion. Kira's parents were noted scientists who'd invented a memory storing computer chip to be implanted in the brain, a chip important to Crythians who believe ones memories shape a person. Aunt Memory wants to make a profit from this computer chip and thinks she'll obtain the necessary information from Kira in a suspense filled story. (220 pages)

Where it's reviewed:
Booklist, September 1, 2003, page 114
Bulletin of the Center for Children's Books, November 2003, page 105
Library Media Connection, March 2004, page 64
Publishers Weekly, October 13, 2003, page 80
Voice of Youth Advocates, October 2003, page 324

Other books by the same author:
Among the Brave, 2004
Say What?, 2004

The House on the Gulf, 2004
Because of Anya, 2002
Takeoffs and Landings, 2001

Other books you might like:
M.T. Anderson, *Feed*, 2002
Computer implants replace the need for people to talk, read, write, or even go to a store to shop, as everything is done mentally.
Nancy Farmer, *The House of the Scorpion*, 2002
El Patron works his poppy fields with clones whose brains were replaced at birth with computer chips.
Lois Lowry, *The Giver*, 1993
Set in a futuristic community, which values sameness, Jonas is assigned his life-task; meeting the Giver helps him see another world.

581

MARY DOWNING HAHN

Hear the Wind Blow: A Novel of the Civil War

(New York: Clarion Books, 2003)

Subject(s): Survival; Civil War; Brothers and Sisters
Age range(s): Grades 5-8
Major character(s): James Marshall, Military Personnel (Confederate soldier); Haswell Colby Magruder, 13-Year-Old; Rachel Magruder, Child, Sister (of Haswell); Avery Magruder, 16-Year-Old, Military Personnel (Confederate soldier)
Time period(s): 1860s
Locale(s): Shenandoah Valley, Virginia

Summary: An act of kindness leads to tragedy for Haswell and his family. In the final days of the Civil War, Haswell convinces his mother to shelter a wounded Confederate soldier, though doing so is tantamount to a death sentence if discovered. Unfortunately the good deed is discovered, their farm is burned, his mother dies following a rape attempt and Haswell flees with his younger sister Rachel. His plan is to leave his sister with his grandparents while he searches for their older brother Avery, a Confederate soldier who's been wounded at Petersburg. To Haswell, war had seemed a noble, valiant event but as he travels the countryside he sees the pillage and destruction caused by battle and realizes that war is horrendous, not heroic. (212 pages)

Where it's reviewed:
Booklist, May 15, 2003, page 1663
Bulletin of the Center for Children's Books, July 2003, page 448
Horn Book, May 2003, page 346
Publishers Weekly, May 19, 2003, page 74
School Library Journal, May 2003, page 152

Other books by the same author:
Promises to the Dead, 2000
As Ever, Gordy, 1998
Following My Own Footsteps, 1996
Wind Blows Backward, 1993
December Stillness, 1988

Other books you might like:
Paul Fleischman, *Bull Run*, 1993
In a unique snapshot of the Civil War, 16 characters offer their accounts of the war from its beginning to the first battle at Bull Run.
Mauriel Phillips Joslyn, *Shenandoah Autumn: Courage under Fire*, 1998
Weary of the war between the Confederacy and the Union, Matilda wants to care for the wounded soldiers, but isn't allowed in the hospitals.
Gary Paulsen, *Soldier's Heart*, 1998
Not wanting to be left out, 15-year-old Charley lies about his age and joins the Union Army, but after being wounded, dies of "soldier's heart."
Ann Rinaldi, *Amelia's War*, 1999
Amelia is forced to choose sides in the Civil War when a Confederate general demands a huge ransom from the residents of her town.

582

ANN HALAM (Pseudonym of Gwyneth Jones)

Dr. Franklin's Island

(New York: Random House/Wendy Lamb, 2002)

Subject(s): Genetic Engineering; Science Fiction; Survival
Age range(s): Grades 7-10
Major character(s): Semirah "Semi" Garson, Teenager; Miranda Fallow, Teenager; Arnie Pullman, Teenager; Dr. George Franklin, Scientist
Time period(s): 2000s
Locale(s): Pacific Ocean (deserted island)

Summary: A group of British teens, prizewinners in a Planet Savers TV competition, are on a charter flight to Ecuador where they'll take tour a wildlife conservation project. Their plane makes an emergency ocean landing and explodes, leaving three survivors who struggle to safety on an isolated island. Shy Semi, confident Miranda and obnoxious Arnie find themselves dependent on one another as they evaluate their situation, hunt for food and build shelter. When Arnie flees with their supplies, the two girls search for him but instead find the laboratory of the mad Dr. Franklin who's working on transgenic treatments. Dr. Franklin captures the two girls, and the missing Arnie, and uses them as human experiments. He injects them with the DNA from various creatures and subsequently turns Semi into a manta ray, Miranda into a bird and Arnie into a snake. The three can communicate through radio telepathy brain implants, but now escaping from the island isn't their first worry, it's how to change back to their former selves in this gripping tale of science and survival. (247 pages)

Where it's reviewed:
Booklist, July 2002, page 1838
Bulletin of the Center for Children's Books, May 2002, page 325
Kliatt, July 2002, page 10
Publishers Weekly, May 6, 2002, page 58
School Library Journal, May 2002, page 152

Awards the book has won:
ALA Best Books for Young Adults, 2003

Other books by the same author:
Transformations, 1988
The Daymaker, 1987

Other books you might like:
Andrew Clements, *Things Not Seen*, 2002
Bobby wakes up one morning, takes a shower and discovers he's invisible.
James DeVita, *Blue*, 2001
Bored and dreaming of the blue marlin fish that leap out of the water, Morgan awakens to find he's turning into one.
Charlotte Kerner, *Blueprint*, 2000
Siri resents being a clone of her talented concert pianist mother Iris.
H.G. Wells, *The Island of Dr. Moreau*, 1896
A South Seas island hosts a crazed doctor whose experiments on animals lead to horrible, semi-human results.

583

BRUCE HALE, Author/Illustrator

The Hamster of the Baskervilles

(San Diego: Harcourt, Inc., 2002)

Series: Chet Gecko Mystery. Case #5
Subject(s): Animals; Schools; Mystery and Detective Stories
Age range(s): Grades 3-5
Major character(s): Chet Gecko, Reptile (gecko), Detective—Amateur, 4th Grader; Natalie Attired, Bird (mockingbird), 4th Grader; Mr. Ratnose, Teacher, Rat
Time period(s): Indeterminate
Locale(s): Fictional Country (Emerson Hicky Elementary)

Summary: Once again a problem at school gives Chet Gecko an opportunity to test his detective skills and earn an edible reward if he succeeds. This time it's a mess in Mr. Ratnose's classroom and Chet's job is to figure out who trashed the unpopular teacher's room over the weekend. With Natalie's help, Chet searches for clues by questioning a bully tarantula, rummaging in a stinky dumpster and trying to infiltrate the Dirty Rotten Stinkers gang. When another room and then another are vandalized and rumors of a werewolf begin circulating, Chet realizes he has only a little time to solve the case. (115 pages)

Where it's reviewed:
Booklist, May 1, 2002, page 1460
Children's Bookwatch, June 2002, page 3
Horn Book Guide, Fall 2002, page 373
Kirkus Reviews, February 15, 2002, page 257
School Library Journal, May 2002, page 116

Awards the book has won:
IRA Children's Choices, 2003

Other books by the same author:
The Malted Falcon, 2002 (Chet Gecko Mystery, Case #7)
Farewell, My Lunchbag, 2001 (Chet Gecko Mystery, Case #3)
The Chameleon Wore Chartreuse, 2000 (Chet Gecko Mystery, Case #1)

Other books you might like:
Linda Bailey, *What's a Serious Detective Like Me Doing in Such a Silly Movie?*, 2002

While working as an extra in a movie, Stevie solves the mystery of suspicious accidents on the set with help from partner Jesse.

Elizabeth Levy, *Night of the Living Gerbil*, 2001
Sam wonders if his recently deceased gerbil has been turned into a zombie.

Michele Torrey, *The Case of the Gasping Garbage*, 2001
Several problems require the services of fifth-grade science detectives Drake and Nell.

584

BRUCE HALE

The Malted Falcon

(San Diego: Harcourt, Inc., 2003)

Series: Chet Gecko Mystery. Case #7
Subject(s): Animals/Reptiles; Mystery and Detective Stories; Schools
Age range(s): Grades 3-5
Major character(s): Chet Gecko, Detective—Private, 4th Grader
Time period(s): 2000s (2003)
Locale(s): United States

Summary: Chet Gecko, grade-school private eye, is flush with clients: a frog, who wants him to find her valentine and a ferret, looking for a lost winning ticket for the Malted Falcon, a dessert. All roads end up leading to the same place, as both customers are working for the bad guy who wants to keep the sweets all to himself. (107 pages)

Where it's reviewed:
Publishers Weekly, March 10, 2003, page 74
School Library Journal, June 2003, page 100

Other books by the same author:
Give My Regrets to Broadway, 2004 (Chet Gecko Mystery Case #9)
Trouble Is My Beeswax, 2003 (Chet Gecko Mystery Case #8)
This Gum for Hire, 2002 (Chet Gecko Mystery Case #6)
The Chameleon Wore Chartreuse, 2000 (Chet Gecko Mystery Case #1)

Other books you might like:
E.A. Hass, *Incognito Mosquito Flies Again*, 1985
A mosquito detective tells a class of FBI agents about his exploits while on the case.

Holm & Hammel, *The Postman Always Brings Mice*, 2004
In the first book of a series featuring cat detective James Edward Bristlefur, James's owner is murdered and he must find the killer.

Deborah Howe, *Bunnicula*, 1979
The Monroes' dog Harold suspects that the new pet rabbit is really a vampire. Co-written by James Howe.

585

BRUCE HALE

Trouble Is My Beeswax

(San Diego: Harcourt, Inc., 2003)

Series: Chet Gecko Mystery. Case #8

Subject(s): Animals/Reptiles; Mystery and Detective Stories; Journalism
Age range(s): Grades 3-5
Major character(s): Chet Gecko, Detective—Private, 4th Grader
Time period(s): 2000s (2003)
Locale(s): United States

Summary: Business is getting personal for Chet Gecko. When a cheating ring at Emerson Hicky Elementary infiltrates his class, Chet must solve the mystery in order to clear his own name. A nosy reporter makes Chet's investigation difficult and he suspects she may know more about the cheaters than she's revealing. (111 pages)

Where it's reviewed:
Publishers Weekly, July 21, 2003, page 198
School Library Journal, November 2003, page 95

Other books by the same author:
The Malted Falcon, 2003 (Chet Gecko Mystery Case #7)
This Gum for Hire, 2002 (Chet Gecko Mystery Case #6)
The Big Nap, 2001 (Chet Gecko Mystery Case #4)
The Chameleon Wore Chartreuse, 2000 (Chet Gecko Mystery Case #1)

Other books you might like:
John Erickson, *The Original Adventures of Hank the Cowdog*, 1988
When Hank is suspected in the murder of a chicken, he must find the real killer in order to clear his name.

E.A. Hass, *Incognito Mosquito: Private Insective*, 1982
A mosquito detective tells a reporter about his exploits while on the case.

James Howe, *The Celery Stalks at Midnight*, 1983
Bunnicula is missing and it's up to the other family pets to save the neighborhood from a vampire rabbit.

586

SHANNON HALE

The Goose Girl

(New York: Bloomsbury, 2003)

Subject(s): Fairy Tales; Coming-of-Age
Age range(s): Grades 6-12
Major character(s): Anidori-Kiladra Talianna "Ani" Isillee, Royalty; Selia, Noblewoman, Servant
Time period(s): Indeterminate
Locale(s): Kildenree, Fictional Country

Summary: This faithful retelling of the fairy tale is by turns poetic, horrifying and inspiring. Princess Ani is uncomfortable being a princess, unhappy with the need for constant display and formality, and more at home outdoors than in the palace. As a small child, she discovers that all things have a language and learns to speak with the royal swans. Her mother the queen is appalled and after the king, Ani's father, dies, the queen reveals that she has arranged a distant marriage for Ani instead of allowing her to inherit the kingdom that is Ani's right. A band of bodyguard soldiers, many of them mysterious volunteers, and Ani's maid-in-waiting Selia, are chosen to accompany Ani over the mountains to her new home. On the way, Selia and her volunteer accomplices rebel, kill the other guards and replace Ani with Selia as the princess. Ani barely escapes and eventually, she follows them to the capital, where she hides as a goose girl, waiting for the opportunity to right the wrongs that have been done. Her childhood gift of bird speech comes back to her and Ani learns other languages as she waits. Hidden among the peasants, Ani learns what a princess really needs to know in this author's first novel. (388 pages)

Where it's reviewed:
Booklist, August 2003, page 1971
Kirkus Reviews, July 1, 2003, page 910
Kliatt, July 2003, page 12
Publishers Weekly, June 30, 2003, page 80
School Library Journal, August 2003, page 160

Other books by the same author:
Enna Burning, 2004

Other books you might like:
Patrice Kindl, *Goose Chase*, 2001
    For a very different take on the princess who hides as a goose girl, try this delirious tale with a heroine who refuses to take anything lying down.
Patricia McKillip, *In the Forests of Serre*, 2003
    When the princess discovers that her prince has disappeared into the enchanted forest of Serre, she goes after him and bargains with a witch.
Robin McKinley, *Deerskin*, 1993
    This is the ugly story of a king so obsessed with beauty that he rapes his own daughter in this powerful story of maturation and self-healing.

587

JOHN HALLIDAY

Shooting Monarchs

(New York: Simon & Schuster/Margaret K. McElderry Books, 2003)

Subject(s): Physically Handicapped; Violence; Crime and Criminals
Age range(s): Grades 9-12
Major character(s): Macy, Criminal; Danny Driscoll, 16-Year-Old, Handicapped (scoliosis); Leah Henderson, Student—High School
Time period(s): 2000s
Locale(s): Shiloh

Summary: Unloved and abused as a child, Macy drops out of high school for a life of crime. Released from jail, he steals a car and a gun and takes off, intent on murdering teenage girls. In the town of Shiloh, he spots a potential victim and forces her into his trunk. Leah's classmate Danny, in the woods to photograph monarch butterflies, sees her being kidnapped and, having loved her from afar, rushes to rescue her in this author's suspenseful first novel. (135 pages)

Where it's reviewed:
Booklist, March 15, 2003, page 1322
Bulletin of the Center for Children's Books, May 2003, page 362
Publishers Weekly, February 17, 2003, page 76
School Library Journal, June 2003, page 143
Voice of Youth Advocates, June 2003, page 130

Awards the book has won:
ALA Quick Picks for Reluctant Young Adult Readers, 2004

Other books by the same author:
Predicktions, 2003

Other books you might like:
Elaine Marie Alphin, *Counterfeit Son*, 2000
    When his serial killer father is shot by police, Cameron escapes; he claims to be Neil Lacey but worries that his real identity will be discovered.
Fran Arrick, *Where'd You Get the Gun, Billy?*, 1991
    Billy finds a Smith and Wesson .38 Chief Special and stuns his community when he shoots his girlfriend Lisa.
Robert Cormier, *Tenderness*, 1997
    When a girl he cares for accidentally drowns, a serial killer knows the police will claim he murdered her.
Alice Hoffman, *The River King*, 2000
    Though Gus is befriended by beautiful Carlin at posh Haddon School, he is disliked by his fellow students, with tragic results.
Patrick Redmond, *Something Dangerous*, 1999
    Two boys use a Ouija board for evil doings at their boarding school.

588

MARILYN HALVORSON

Bull Rider

(Custer, WA: Orca Publishers, 2003)

Series: Orca Soundings
Subject(s): Rodeos; Animals/Bulls
Age range(s): Grades 8-10
Major character(s): Layne McQueen, 16-Year-Old; Rhino, Bull; Jana Kelvin, 16-Year-Old; Chase Kincaid, Grandfather (of Jana)
Time period(s): 2000s
Locale(s): Alberta, Canada

Summary: Six years earlier Layne's father was killed when a bull he'd been riding trampled him; now Layne wants to sign up for the rodeo and his mother's set against it. Because he can't sign up for the rodeo, he practices on the bulls over at his friend Jana's family arena. His riding isn't the best and when Jana's grandfather sees him go flying off the one-horned bull Rhino, he offers to help Layne learn to ride. Though Layne doesn't make it through the required eight seconds when he has his first chance at the rodeo, he rides enough for his mother to see and be proud of him. (92 pages)

Where it's reviewed:
Kliatt, May 2003, page 9
Resource Links, June 2003, page 25
School Library Journal, July 2003, page 130
Voice of Youth Advocates, August 2003, page 213

Awards the book has won:
ALA Quick Picks for Reluctant Young Adult Readers, 2004

Other books by the same author:
Blue Moon, 2004 (Orca Soundings)
Brothers and Strangers, 1996
Cowboys Don't Quit, 1994

Other books you might like:

Jean Ferris, *Eight Seconds*, 2000

Attending rodeo camp and riding a bull are thrilling, but now John has to weigh his feelings for a fellow cowboy.

Lynn Hall, *Flying Changes*, 1991

When Denny's womanizing rodeo rider father is paralyzed, her mother returns home to care for him, which upsets Denny's life.

Chad Henry, *Dogbreath Victorious*, 1999

Tim and his alternate-rock band Dogbreath can't believe they're competing against his mother's band, ''The Angry Housewives.''

589

VIRGINIA HAMILTON
JAMES E. RANSOME, Illustrator

Bruh Rabbit and the Tar Baby Girl

(New York: Blue Sky Press/Scholastic, Inc., 2003)

Subject(s): Animals/Rabbits; Animals; Folklore
Age range(s): Grades 1-4
Major character(s): Bruh Rabbit, Rabbit, Trickster; Bruh Wolf, Wolf, Farmer
Time period(s): Indeterminate Past
Locale(s): South

Summary: Lazy Bruh Rabbit does no work and helps himself to crops grown by Bruh Wolf. Spotting the rabbit's tracks in his field, Bruh Wolf devises a plan to stop the thief. First Bruh Wolf builds a ''scarey-crow,'' but Bruh Rabbit soon figures out that the shadowy form he sees in the moonlight is not a danger and helps himself to peanuts. Bruh Wolf, angered by what he sees in the peanut patch at daybreak, next constructs a tar baby rabbit girl. When Bruh Rabbit returns for more peanuts he sees the girl rabbit and speaks to her. When he hears no response Bruh Rabbit threatens to hit her first with his right paw, then his left. Of course, the tar baby never responds and as Bruh Rabbit follows through with his threats he becomes totally stuck to the tar baby girl. Bruh Wolf finds him in the morning and announces his intention to eat the trickster. Bruh Rabbit agrees to being eaten, but begs not to be thrown in the briar bush. Bruh Wolf does just that, inadvertently freeing the rascal. A concluding author's note about the story gives the Gullah background for this retelling of a familiar tale. (36 pages)

Where it's reviewed:

Booklist, October 15, 2003, page 413
Bulletin of the Center for Children's Books, December 2003, page 153
Horn Book, January 2004, page 94
Publishers Weekly, October 13, 2003, page 77
School Library Journal, November 2003, page 126

Awards the book has won:

School Library Journal Best Books, 2003
ALA Notable Children's Books, 2004

Other books by the same author:

The Girl Who Spun Gold, 2000 (Booklist Editors' Choice)

A Ring of Tricksters: Animal Tales from America, the West Indies, and Africa, 1997 (Publishers Weekly Best Children's Books)
When Birds Could Talk & Bats Could Sing: The Adventures of Bruh Sparrow, Sis Wren, and Their Friends, 1996 (ALA Notable Children's Books)

Other books you might like:

Julius Lester, *More Tales of Uncle Remus: Further Adventures of Brer Rabbit, His Friends, Enemies, and Others*, 1988

Thirty-seven stories feature the activities of famous trickster Brer Rabbit.

Gayle Ross, *How Rabbit Tricked Otter: And Other Cherokee Trickster Stories*, 1994

Fifteen stories about Rabbit show him to be a trickster, outsmarting many animals and being responsible for some of their physical characteristics.

Janet Stevens, *Tops and Bottoms*, 1995

Industrious Hare is a gardening partner to slumbering Bear in a contemporary interpretation of a trickster tale.

590

VIRGINIA HAMILTON

Time Pieces: The Book of Times

(New York: Blue Sky/Scholastic, 2002)

Subject(s): Family Life; Country Life; African Americans
Age range(s): Grades 5-8
Major character(s): Valena McGill, 11-Year-Old; Harriet Harper McGill, Mother (of Valena); Laddie, Dog
Time period(s): 1940s
Locale(s): Ohio

Summary: The summer before her sixth grade year, Valena enjoys the circus, is scared when a tornado touches down, finds the aurora borealis frightening but beautiful, and mourns the loss of the family dog Laddie. It's also the summer she hears the stories of her ancestors and begins to discover her place in family history. Thanks to her mother Harriet, the summer is spent telling the stories that have been passed down in her family, especially the one about her Graw Luke who crosses to freedom thanks to the Underground Railroad in this final, semi-autobiographical novel by a gifted writer. (199 pages)

Where it's reviewed:

Booklist, December 15, 2002, page 761
Bulletin of the Center for Children's Books, December 2002, page 159
Publishers Weekly, November 4, 2002, page 85
School Library Journal, December 2002, page 140
Voice of Youth Advocates, April 2003, page 50

Other books by the same author:

Bluish, 1999
Plain City, 1993
Cousins, 1991
The People Could Fly: American Black Folktales, 1985
M.C. Higgins the Great, 1974
The House of Dies Drear, 1969

Other books you might like:

Christopher Paul Curtis, *The Watsons Go to Birmingham—1963*, 1995

> Heading south to visit Grandmother, the Watson family's high spirits falter when a church in Birmingham blows up and four children are killed.

Gloria Houston, *Bright Freedom's Song: A Story of the Underground Railroad*, 1998

> Bright Freedom's father was an indentured servant, which explains his commitment to using the Underground Railroad to save slaves.

Walter Dean Myers, *The Glory Field*, 1994

> The saga of the Lewis family, who went from slaves to freedmen, is firmly rooted in the family plot of land.

Mildred D. Taylor, *The Land*, 2001

> This prequel to *Roll of Thunder, Hear My Cry* provides a look at the life of former slaves during Reconstruction.

591

MARY HANSON
DEBBIE TILLEY, Illustrator

The Difference Between Babies & Cookies

(San Diego: Silver Whistle/Harcourt, Inc., 2002)

Subject(s): Babies; Mothers and Daughters; Family
Age range(s): Preschool-Kindergarten
Major character(s): Mom, Mother; Unnamed Character, Child, Sister (older); Unnamed Character, Baby, Sister (younger)
Time period(s): 2000s
Locale(s): United States

Summary: A savvy older sister quickly learns the truth about babies despite Mom's pre-birth lessons to her about their characteristics. Obviously, to the sister, babies drool more than cuddly puppies and are not as hungry as bears if they face something they don't want to eat. Despite Mom's claim that babies are as "playful as tiger cubs," the little girl soon learns that painting stripes on them is not allowed. According to Mom a baby may be "sweet as cookies," but sisters can't dip them in milk the way they can a cookie. This baby is fortunate to have an older sister to help her learn the truth about babies or she might grow up with the wrong ideas about what she is. (32 pages)

Where it's reviewed:
Booklist, March 1, 2002, page 1141
Horn Book Guide, Fall 2002, page 330
Publishers Weekly, April 22, 2002, page 68
School Library Journal, May 2002, page 116

Other books by the same author:
The Old Man and the Flea, 2001
Snug, 1998

Other books you might like:

Bruce Coville, *The Lapsnatcher*, 1997

> Jacob is disillusioned by the arrival of his time-consuming, loud baby sister; she is no fun, but his parents assure him she will be.

Marisabina Russo, *Hannah's Baby Sister*, 1998

> Hannah looks forward to a new baby in the family.

Susan Winter, *A Baby Just Like Me*, 1994

> Martha is disappointed that her baby sister is unable to be her playmate immediately.

592

CLEA HANTMAN

Goddesses Series

(New York: Avon/HarperCollins, 2002-)

Subject(s): Mythology; School Life; Sisters
Age range(s): Grades 7-10
Major character(s): Erato "Era", Deity (goddess of love poetry); Polyhymnia "Polly", Deity (goddess of sacred poetry); Thalia, Deity (goddess of comedy); Zeus, Deity; Hera, Deity, Stepmother; Apollo, Deity
Time period(s): 2000s; Indeterminate Past
Locale(s): Athens, Georgia; Mount Olympus, Mythical Place

Summary: Though Thalia likes Apollo, she's not ready for marriage no matter what her father Zeus wants. When she, with a little help from two of her sister Muses, Era and Polly, stops the wedding, Zeus retaliates and banishes them from Mount Olympus to Athens. Unfortunately Zeus is a little distracted and the three sisters end up in contemporary Athens, Georgia where they now attend high school. In this series they must earn their way back to Mount Olympus, which becomes very difficult since school parties, gorgeous guys and the evil Furies, which their stepmother Hera sent down, easily distract them. Zeus sends Apollo as "Dylan from Denver" to help the sisters learn their lesson and return to Mount Olympus, but the sisters' good intentions go awry and now, with Thanksgiving vacation ahead of them, Thalia, Era and Polly are off to explore the United States.

Where it's reviewed:
Booklist, February 15, 2002, page 1010
Bulletin of the Center for Children's Books, March 2002, page 241
Kliatt, May 2002, page 26
Publishers Weekly, December 24, 2001, page 65
School Library Journal, March 2002, page 231

Other books by the same author:
Heaven Sent, 2002 (Goddesses Book 1)
Love or Fate, 2002 (Goddesses Book 4)
Muses on the Move, 2002 (Goddesses Book 3)
Three Girls and a God, 2002 (Goddesses Book 2)

Other books you might like:

Vivien Alcock, *Singer to the Sea God*, 1993

> Perseus needs a way to kill the dreadful Gorgon, a creature with snakes for hair.

Isobel Bird, *Circle of Three Series*, 2001-

> Kate befriends Annie and Cooper as they try to put into practice spells they found when researching sixteenth century witchcraft.

Caroline B. Cooney, *Goddess of Yesterday*, 2002

> Kidnapped by King Nicander as a companion for his daughter Callisto, Anaxandra eventually witnesses the beginning of the Trojan War.

Elsa Marston, *The Ugly Goddess*, 2002

> When Princess Meret is kidnapped, Hector and Bata res-

cue her with the help of the ugly goddess Taweret who comes to life when danger threatens.

593

NIRA HAREL
YOSSI ABULAFIA, Illustrator
THE INSTITUTE FOR TRANSLATION OF HEBREW, Translator

The Key to My Heart

(La Jolla, CA: Kane/Miller Publishers, 2003)

Subject(s): Fathers and Sons; Lost and Found; Family
Age range(s): Grades K-2
Major character(s): Jonathan, Child, Son; Dad, Father, Spouse; Mom, Mother, Spouse
Time period(s): 2000s (2003)
Locale(s): Israel

Summary: Dad's errands cause him to be a little late to pick up Jonathan from school. Though they play for a bit on the playground they still arrive home before Mom and discover they are locked out because Dad has lost his keys. Jonathan and Dad retrace his steps asking in each place if a key chain with a picture of Jonathan on it has been found. While they don't locate the keys Jonathan is able to get a haircut and some pizza as they make the rounds. When they finally return home, late and keyless, Mom greets them, ably guessing where they've been from Jonathan's appearance. Then she displays the missing keys. A teacher found them on the playground and, recognizing Jonathan's picture, returned them. Dad is relieved to once again have the photo key chain, the key to his heart, safely in his pocket. Originally published in Israel. (24 pages)

Where it's reviewed:
Booklist, April 15, 2003, page 1477
Bulletin of the Center for Children's Books, April 2003, page 314
Horn Book, July 2003, page 443
School Library Journal, June 2003, page 100

Other books you might like:
Thierry Courtin, *Daddy and Me*, 1997
    One Daddy plus one child equals lots of fun on Daddy's day off.
Mercer Mayer, *Just Me and My Dad*, 1977
    Illustrations depict what actually happens during a father-and-son camping adventure.
Douglas Wood, *What Dads Can't Do*, 2000
    Since dads are unable to read books alone or sleep late in the morning they really need their kids for company at such times.

594

LESLEY HARKER, Author/Illustrator

Annie's Ark

(New York: Chicken House/Scholastic, Inc., 2002)

Subject(s): Boatbuilding; Religion; Floods
Age range(s): Preschool-Grade 1

Major character(s): Annie, Child, Daughter; Noah, Grandfather, Biblical Figure
Time period(s): Indeterminate Past
Locale(s): Ancient Civilization

Summary: There's no place on Noah's ark that little Annie can find peace and quiet. Her relatives are always asking for her help with the animals, her boots are full of water and every seemingly quiet corner is taken. Finally Annie finds a place to rest, but Noah finds her to make sure she sees that the rain has stopped and a rainbow has appeared. (32 pages)

Where it's reviewed:
Horn Book Guide, Spring 2003, page 104
Publishers Weekly, September 30, 2002, page 69
School Library Journal, January 2003, page 96

Other books by the same author:
Twinkle, Twinkle, Little Star, 2000
Wishing Moon, 1996

Other books you might like:
Joan Paley, *One More River: A Noah's Ark Counting Book*, 2002
    Based on the song, the book looks at Noah as he counts his passengers.
Charles Santore, *A Stowaway on Noah's Ark*, 2000
    Achbar stows away as the third mouse on Noah's ark.
Peter Spier, *Noah's Ark*, 1977
    This Caldecott winner tells the story of Noah and God's command that he build an ark.

595

JESSICA HARPER
LINDSAY HARPER DUPONT, Illustrator

Lizzy's Do's and Don'ts

(New York: HarperCollins Publishers, 2002)

Subject(s): Behavior; Mothers and Daughters; Stories in Rhyme
Age range(s): Grades K-2
Major character(s): Lizzy, Child, Daughter; Unnamed Character, Mother
Time period(s): 2000s (2002)
Locale(s): United States

Summary: To Lizzy, the only word she hears from her mother is "Don't!" Lizzy can list all the behaviors that are proscribed and she's a bit tired of the very long list so she announces her own list of "don'ts" for her mother. After listening to her, Lizzy's mom understands that Lizzy is simply tired of hearing "don't!" and she admits to being tired of saying it. Together they develop a list of things to "Do" that expresses the positive activities they enjoy sharing. (32 pages)

Where it's reviewed:
Booklist, March 15, 2002, page 1262
Detroit Free Press, April 28, 2002, page 5E
Horn Book Guide, Fall 2002, page 330
Publishers Weekly, March 25, 2002, page 64
School Library Journal, July 2002, page 92

Other books by the same author:
Four Boys Named Jordan, 2004

Lizzy's Ups and Downs: Not an Ordinary School Day, 2004
I Like Where I Am, 2004

Other books you might like:
Stan Berenstain, *The Berenstain Bears Forget Their Manners*, 1985
  Mama Bear has a plan to change the family's rude behavior. Jan Berenstain, co-author.
Cressida Cowell, *Don't Do That, Kitty Kilroy!*, 2000
  Kitty is tired of hearing the same admonition from her mother all day long.
Mem Fox, *Harriet, You'll Drive Me Wild!*, 2000
  After a series of messes, Harriet's mom loses her temper but quickly apologizes just as Harriet does when she misbehaves.
David Shannon, *No, David!*, 1998
  In a Caldecott Honor Book, David's mom expresses her love for her son despite his behavior.

596

GEORGE HARRAR

Not as Crazy as I Seem

(Boston: Houghton Mifflin, 2003)

Subject(s): Vandalism; Schools/High Schools; Mental Illness
Age range(s): Grades 7-10
Major character(s): Devon Brown, 15-Year-Old, 10th Grader; Ben Cavendish, 10th Grader; Tanya, 10th Grader; Dr. Wasserman, Doctor (therapist)
Locale(s): Boston, Massachusetts

Summary: Devon prefers orderliness, which explains why he carefully buttons his shirts before putting them in the closet; eats sandwiches cut in fourths, or four of an item; and washes his hands to keep the germs away. When his parents move to Boston to give Devon yet another fresh start, Devon sees Dr. Wasserman who works with him on his obsessive compulsive disorder. Becoming friends with Tanya and Ben, he is even accused of tagging school lockers, which was Ben's misadventure. This incident, which disrupts his parents, school officials and his own carefully controlled life, forces him to learn to manage his obsessive mannerisms. (202 pages)

Where it's reviewed:
Booklist, February 15, 2003, page 1064
Bulletin of the Center for Children's Books, June 2003, page 403
Publishers Weekly, April 7, 2003, page 67
School Library Journal, April 2003, page 162
Voice of Youth Advocates, June 2003, page 130

Other books by the same author:
The Spinning Man, 2003
The Trouble with Jeremy Chance, 2003
First Tiger, 1999

Other books you might like:
Margaret Buffie, *Angels Turn Their Backs*, 1998
  A combination of counseling, a parrot and an incomplete needlepoint angel help Addy overcome her panic attacks.
Terry Spencer Hesser, *Kissing Doorknobs*, 1998
  Tara's behavior becomes so obsessive that it takes 30 minutes to complete the doorknob ritual when leaving her house.
Betty Hyland, *The Girl with the Crazy Brother*, 1987
  Attending a new school is difficult for Dana, but she's more concerned about her brother who's developing signs of schizophrenia.
Janet Tashjian, *Multiple Choice*, 1999
  Neat, orderly and in control describes Monica and her obsessive-compulsiveness; when it becomes out of control, she's compelled to seek help.

597

GEORGE HARRAR
ELIZABETH THAYER, Illustrator

The Trouble with Jeremy Chance

(Minneapolis: Milkweed, 2003)

Subject(s): Fathers and Sons; Country Life; Coming-of-Age
Age range(s): Grades 4-8
Major character(s): Jeremy Theopoulos Chance, 12-Year-Old; David "Davey" Chance, Military Personnel; James "Pa" Chance, Father; Mr. Cutter, Aged Person
Time period(s): 1910s (1919)
Locale(s): Derry, New Hampshire; Boston, Massachusetts

Summary: With his older brother Davey serving in World War I, Jeremy lives with his dad and cousin, his mother having died in the influenza epidemic. One of Jeremy's favorite neighbors is Mr. Cutter, but he's forbidden to visit him after his dad fights with Mr. Cutter over a walnut tree. Not understanding why his father would do this, Jeremy speaks his mind and is whipped in return. Angry and hurt, Jeremy runs away to Boston, hoping to meet Davey's ship, which is due to return from Europe. He arrives just in time to be part of the Great Molasses Flood when a distillery erupts and millions of gallons of molasses spew out, trapping people and animals. Jeremy uses knowledge he's learned from his dad and rescues one trapped man, which puts his father in a better mood when he arrives in Boston in search of Jeremy. The two men forgive one another and then set out to find Davey in this appealing historical tale. (143 pages)

Where it's reviewed:
Booklist, October 1, 2003, page 320
Publishers Weekly, October 27, 2003, page 70
School Library Journal, March 2004, page 212

Other books by the same author:
Not as Crazy as I Seem, 2003
The Spinning Man, 2003
Parents Wanted, 2001

Other books you might like:
Joan Hiatt Harlow, *Joshua's Song*, 2001
  Faced with financial problems after the Influenza Epidemic, Joshua sells newspapers which puts him on the scene of the Great Molasses Flood in Boston.
Carol Flynn Harris, *A Place for Joey*, 2001
  Joey saves a policeman from the syrup of an exploding molasses tank and realizes he will always stay in Boston, and maybe become a policeman.

Gloria Skurzynski, *Good-Bye, Billy Radish*, 1992
  Hank can't believe it when his friend Bazyli, nicknamed Billy Radish, dies during the influenza epidemic.

598

ROBIE H. HARRIS
MICHAEL EMBERLEY, Illustrator

Hello Benny! What It's Like to Be a Baby
(New York: Margaret K. McElderry Books, 2002)

Series: Growing Up Stories
Subject(s): Babies; Behavior; Growing Up
Age range(s): Grades 1-3
Major character(s): Benny, Baby, Son
Time period(s): 2000s
Locale(s): United States

Summary: From the moment of his birth, Benny is loved. In the embrace of a caring family, Benny experiences a joyful first year of life. Each action, reaction, and developmental milestone of Benny's first year is portrayed with an inset factual explanation supporting the story's text and illustrations. (32 pages)

Where it's reviewed:
Booklist, October 15, 2002, page 407
Bulletin of the Center for Children's Books, November 2002, page 110
Horn Book, November 2002, page 776
Publishers Weekly, July 15, 2002, page 72
School Library Journal, September 2002, page 193

Awards the book has won:
Parenting's Books of the Year, 2002
Bulletin of the Center for Children's Books Blue Ribbons, 2002

Other books by the same author:
Goodbye Mousie, 2001 (Publishers Weekly Best Children's Books)
Hi, New Baby!, 2000
Happy Birth Day!, 1996

Other books you might like:
Kathy Henderson, *The Baby Dances*, 1999
  As the seasons change, a baby grows under the watchful eyes of a loving family.
Peter McCarty, *Baby Steps*, 2000
  Month by month baby Suki grows and changes until she takes her first steps.
Amy Schwartz, *A Teeny Tiny Baby*, 1994
  The many needs of a teeny tiny baby are immediately met by doting parents and grandparents.

599

ROBIE H. HARRIS
JAN ORMEROD, Illustrator

I Am NOT Going to School Today!
(New York: Margaret K. McElderry Books, 2003)

Subject(s): Schools; Independence; Parent and Child
Age range(s): Grades K-1

Major character(s): Hank, Monkey (stuffed animal); Unnamed Character, Child, Student; Daddy, Father, Spouse; Mommy, Mother, Spouse
Time period(s): 2000s (2003)
Locale(s): United States

Summary: The night before the first day of school a little boy carefully prepares by laying out supplies and clothes for the morning. Next, Daddy reads to him, Mommy kisses him good night and Hank snuggles close as the boy tries to sleep. It's then that the child decides not to go to school on the first day. As he explains in the morning to Mommy and Daddy, no one knows anyone on the first day, but by the second day everything will be familiar. Mommy and Daddy do not quite buy their son's logic and continue with the morning routine. Once it becomes clear that Hank is able to go along to school, the first day looks less foreboding and the boy and his pal gather the backpack and depart for a successful first day. (32 pages)

Where it's reviewed:
Booklist, August 2003, page 1992
Bulletin of the Center for Children's Books, September 2003, page 16
Publishers Weekly, May 26, 2003, page 69
School Library Journal, July 2003, page 98

Awards the book has won:
Center for Children's Books Best Books, 2003

Other books by the same author:
Goodbye Mousie, 2001 (Publishers Weekly Best Children's Book)
Hi, New Baby!, 2000
Happy Birth Day!, 1996

Other books you might like:
Nancy Carlson, *Look Out Kindergarten, Here I Come!*, 1999
  Henry's enthusiasm for school wanes as he approaches the building.
Nancy Bo Flood, *I'll Go to School, If . . .* , 1997
  A frightened little boy offers conditions under which he'll go to school for the first time; his practical mom suggests more realistic alternatives.
Kevin Henkes, *Wemberly Worried*, 2000
  Wemberly worries about everything, especially beginning school.
Amy Hest, *Off to School, Baby Duck!*, 1999
  With Grandpa Duck's support Baby Duck overcomes her fears, enters school for the first time and makes a friend before the day is over.
Vera Rosenberry, *Vera's First Day of School*, 1999
  Vera's eager for the first day of school until she sees the crowded schoolyard; then she has second thoughts about entering the building.

600

METTE IVIE HARRISON

The Monster in Me
(New York: Holiday House, 2003)

Subject(s): Foster Homes; Sports/Running; Interpersonal Relations
Age range(s): Grades 5-8

Major character(s): Natalie Wills, 13-Year-Old, Runner; John Parker, Foster Parent; Alice Parker, Foster Parent; Ms. Eugenie Beck, Social Worker
Time period(s): 2000s
Locale(s): Heber, Utah

Summary: While her mother's in rehab for drug addiction, Natalie's moved from a group home to live with a foster family, the Parkers. No one in Natalie's life has ever proved to be reliable, so she holds back her feelings for the Parkers even though she and John share a love of running. In her new school, a friend finally convinces Natalie to try out for the cross-country team and it's running that keeps Natalie centered and free from dreaming that she's a monster, just like the one created by Dr. Frankenstein. Afraid to live without her mother, Natalie's also afraid to live with her, and she knows that when her mother hascompleted rehab, the worker assigned to her case will recommend that Natalie return, in this author's first novel. (156 pages)

Where it's reviewed:
Booklist, April 1, 2003, page 1397
Bulletin of the Center for Children's Books, June 2003, page 404
Publishers Weekly, April 14, 2003, page 72
School Library Journal, June 2003, page 143
Voice of Youth Advocates, October 2003, page 305

Other books by the same author:
Mira, Mirror, 2004

Other books you might like:
Alice Childress, *Rainbow Jordan*, 1981
  Many women help Rainbow recognize her self worth as she is continually abandoned by her mother and placed in foster homes.
Adrian Fogelin, *Anna Casey's Place in the World*, 2001
  Anna and Eb are staying with first-time foster parent Miss Riley and spend a wonderful summer together befriending some of the neighborhood children.
Julie Johnston, *Adam and Eve and Pinch-Me*, 1994
  Sara arrives at her latest foster home determined to stay detached, but the eccentric, highly individual Huddlestonsrefuse to comply with Sara's plan.
Katherine Paterson, *The Great Gilly Hopkins*, 1978
  Eleven-year-old Gilly longs to live with her mother and rejects those who reach out to her in friendship.
Jacqueline Woodson, *Hush*, 2002
  Evie's miserable living under the Witness Protection Plan, but running track proves a life-saver for her in her new school.

601

ALISON HART
JEAN-PAUL TIBBLES, Illustrator
GREG DEARTH, Illustrator

Danger at the Wild West Show

(Middleton, WI: American Girl/Pleasant Company, 2003)

Series: History Mysteries
Subject(s): Indians of North America; Mystery and Detective Stories; Entertainment

Age range(s): Grades 5-7
Major character(s): Rose Taylor, 12-Year-Old, Entertainer; Zane Taylor, Brother, Entertainer (sharpshooter); White Bear, Indian; General Judson, Military Personnel, Victim
Time period(s): 1880s
Locale(s): Louisville, Kentucky

Summary: Rose and her brother Zane both perform in a Wild West show, though Rose has to content herself with the boring acting role of a settler while she'd rather be assisting her sharpshooter brother. When her brother is accused of shooting General Judson, Rose sets out to clear his name, especially because she thinks Senator North was the intended target because of his unpopular advocacy for Indian rights. She turns to Chief White Bear who helps in her investigation, though it's Rose who solves the murder, including a harrowing horseback ride to stop a stagecoach bearing Senator North when she realizes the assassin is trying for a second attempt. (163 pages)

Where it's reviewed:
Horn Book Guide, Fall 2003, page 363
School Library Journal, October 2003, page 166

Other books by the same author:
Fires of Jubilee, 2003
Return of the Gypsy Witch, 2003
Shadow Horse, 1999

Other books you might like:
Judy Alter, *Cherokee Rose*, 1996
  Taught trick roping by her father, Tommy Jo signs up with Buffalo Bill's Wild West Show where she's known as Cherokee Rose.
Sherry Garland, *The Last Rainmaker*, 1997
  Running away from a cruel aunt, Carline joins Shawnee Sam's Wild West Extravaganza where she meets her Native American grandfather, "the last rainmaker."
Kathryn Reiss, *Riddle of the Prairie Bride*, 2001
  Ida Kate can hardly wait for the arrival of her father's mail-order bride and her young son, but the woman who arrives isn't like the one in the letter.
Lisa Waller Rogers, *Get Along, Little Doggies: The Chisholm Trail Diary of Hallie Lou Wells: South Texas, 1878*, 2001
  Hallie Lou's diary entries provide a record of life on their cattle ranch and the hardships and travails that accompany a cattle drive.

602

BRENT HARTINGER

Geography Club

(New York: HarperCollins, 2003)

Subject(s): Homosexuality/Lesbianism; Clubs; Schools/High Schools
Age range(s): Grades 9-12
Major character(s): Russel Middlebrook, 10th Grader, Homosexual; Kevin Land, Baseball Player, Homosexual; Min, Lesbian, 10th Grader; Terese Buckman, Lesbian, Soccer Player; Belinda Sherman, 11th Grader
Time period(s): 2000s
Locale(s): United States

Summary: Locating a fellow Goodkind High School student in an online gay chatroom, Russel arranges a face-to-face meeting, but is dismayed when he realizes his chatroom partner is jock Kevin Land. Becoming braver about his sexual orientation, Russel reveals his discovery to his best friend Min, only to find out she's been enjoying a lesbian relationship with Terese. Suddenly these gay teens realize they need to all meet and support one another, which leads to forming the "Geography Club," a boring-sounding cover for their weekly get-togethers. Russel is happier than he's ever been, but soon a few obstacles arise. First a junior named Belinda joins them because she really does like geography, but is content to stay as the token straight. Eventually Kevin can't handle the stress of keeping his relationship with Russel a secret, but by then Russel's more than able to stand on his own in this author's first novel. (226 pages)

Where it's reviewed:
Booklist, April 1, 2003, page 1387
Horn Book, March 2003, page 209
Publishers Weekly, February 3, 2003, page 76
School Library Journal, February 2003, page 141
Voice of Youth Advocates, April 2003, page 51

Other books by the same author:
The Last Chance Texaco, 2004

Other books you might like:
M.E. Kerr, *Hello, I Lied*, 1997
Though Lang finds himself attracted to Huguette, he realizes only Eric makes him truly happy, a confirmation of his homosexuality.
Alex Sanchez, *Rainbow Boys*, 2001
Jason, Kyle and Nelson face their senior year, and life-changing decisions, as they deal with their sexual identity.
Laura Torres, *November Ever After*, 1999
At first Amy is disturbed that her friend Sara has a lesbian relationship with Anita, but eventually accepts that Sara will still be her best friend.
Ellen Wittlinger, *Hard Love*, 1999
John thinks he's found the love for which he's been searching when he meets Marisol, only to discover she's in love with another girl.

603

BOB HARTMAN
TIM RAGLIN, Illustrator

The Wolf Who Cried Boy
(New York: G.P. Putnam's Sons, 2002)

Subject(s): Animals/Wolves; Food; Parent and Child
Age range(s): Grades 1-3
Major character(s): Little Wolf, Wolf, Son; Father Wolf, Wolf, Father; Mother Wolf, Wolf, Mother
Time period(s): Indeterminate
Locale(s): Fictional Country

Summary: Little Wolf is so tired of Mother Wolf's cooking that he calls "Boy!" in order to lead his parents on a futile chase through the woods for a nonexistent boy. Then, because dinner is ruined, Little Wolf dines on junk food. The strategy works so well the first night, Little Wolf tries it again with the same results. By the third night Father Wolf and Mother Wolf are wise to Little Wolf's tricks and studiously ignore his cries as an entire troop of boys in scout uniforms marches through the woods. (32 pages)

Where it's reviewed:
Booklist, July 2002, page 1860
Bulletin of the Center for Children's Books, July 2002, page 404
Horn Book, May 2002, page 314
Publishers Weekly, May 6, 2002, page 58
School Library Journal, June 2002, page 97

Awards the book has won:
IRA Children's Choices, 2003
Center for Children's Books Best Books, 2002

Other books by the same author:
Grumblebunny, 2003
Granny Mae's Christmas Play, 2001
Cheer Up Chicken, 1998

Other books you might like:
Marie-Odile Judes, *Max, the Stubborn Wolf*, 2001
Papa Wolf cannot interest Max in such proper wolf careers as chasing pigs. Max aspires to be a florist.
Gail Carson Levine, *Betsy Who Cried Wolf!*, 2002
In an effort to be a good shepherdess Betsy decides that befriending the hungry wolf lurking about works better than calling for help.
Margie Palatini, *Piggie Pie*, 1995
Hungry witch Gritch is so frustrated by her unsuccessful quest for eight piggies to put in a pie that she accepts a wolf's invitation to lunch.

604

SONYA HARTNETT

What the Birds See
(Cambridge, MA: Candlewick Press, 2003)

Subject(s): Loneliness; Missing Persons; Grandmothers
Age range(s): Grades 7-10
Major character(s): Adrian, Child; Beattie "Grandmonster" McPhee, Grandmother; Clinton Tull, Friend (of Adrian); Nicole, Child
Time period(s): 1970s
Locale(s): Australia

Summary: Taken from his mother and father who are unable to care for him, Adrian lives with his grandmother and housebound uncle. Timid, afraid of everything from quicksand to sea monsters to being left waiting at school, he tries to be unnoticed, both at home and at school. One night he hears on the television news that three children have disappeared while walking to the ice cream store and he wonders why anyone even cares enough about children to take them. To Adrian, it's just another item to add to his list of worries. At school his best friend Clinton abandons him for another friend, while at home three children move into the house across the street and he thinks they're the missing children from the ice cream store. His mind changes when he meets the oldest child, Nicole, and the two team up to find the abducted children who Nicole is convinced can be found near water. Their trek takes them to a covered pool where Nicole falls in and Adrian tries to save her with tragic results for both of them in a haunting, lyrical work. (196 pages)

Where it's reviewed:
Booklist, April 15, 2003, page 1462
Horn Book, May 2003, page 347
Publishers Weekly, January 27, 2003, page 261
School Library Journal, May 2003, page 153
Voice of Youth Advocates, June 2003, page 130

Other books by the same author:
Forest, 2001
All My Dangerous Friends, 1998
Prince, 1998
Sleeping Dogs, 1995

Other books you might like:
David Almond, *Kit's Wilderness*, 2000
    If the spin of the knife chooses you in the game of ''Death,'' you ''die'' in an underground den while your friends wait for you outside.
Lillian Eige, *Dangling*, 2001
    Ring walks into the river one day but keeps going, leaving Ben ''dangling'' not knowing for certain what happened to his good friend.
Susan Beth Pfeffer, *The Year Without Michael*, 1987
    Michael leaves home to play softball and never returns. Was he kidnapped? Did he run away? No one ever knows.

605

AMANDA HARVEY, Author/Illustrator

Dog Eared
(New York: Doubleday Books for Young Readers, 2002)

Subject(s): Animals/Dogs; Teasing; Self-Acceptance
Age range(s): Grades K-2
Major character(s): Lucy, Child; Otis, Dog
Time period(s): 2000s
Locale(s): England

Summary: A caustic comment by a passing dog causes Otis to worry about his appearance. Maybe, he wonders, his ears really are too big? Otis tries various strategies such as curls and bows, but nothing seems to solve the problem of his overly large ears. Finally, he sulks to bed but his sleep is troubled by nightmares about the calamities awaiting a dog with such large ears. During the night Lucy comes down to see her pet and tells him how much she loves his warm, soft, silky ears. The next day as Otis and Lucy walk home from the park the same mean dog calls Otis ''Fat Face'' but this time Otis has the self-confidence to ignore him. (32 pages)

Where it's reviewed:
Booklist, March 1, 2002, page 1141
Bulletin of the Center for Children's Books, February 2002, page 207
Publishers Weekly, January 14, 2002, page 59
School Library Journal, March 2002, page 188

Other books by the same author:
Dog Gone, 2004
Dog Days, 2003
Iron Needle, 1994

Stormy Weather, 1992 (Mother Goose Award)

Other books you might like:
Caroline Church, *Do Your Ears Hang Low?*, 2002
    The lyrics of a folk song are illustrated by two long-eared dogs.
Shana Corey, *First Graders from Mars: Episode 2: The Problem with Pelly*, 2002
    Pelly is teased about the fluffernobbins atop her head; a classroom visitor helps Pelly feel pride in her appearance.
Birte Muller, *Giant Jack*, 2002
    Adopted Jack feels different and out of place in his mouse family. A talk with his mother helps the rat accept his size.
John Richardson, *Grunt*, 2001
    Siblings tease a little pig about his looks. After meeting an old boar he learns the importance of inner beauty.

606

DENNIS HASELEY

The Amazing Thinking Machine
(New York: Dial Books, 2002)

Subject(s): Depression (Economic); Inventors and Inventions; Brothers
Age range(s): Grades 4-6
Major character(s): Patrick, 8-Year-Old, Brother; Roy, 13-Year-Old, Inventor
Time period(s): 1920s (1929)
Locale(s): United States

Summary: Patrick doesn't quite comprehend the full extent of the impact of the country's economic Depression but he's aware that his father leaves the family in search of work and homeless men come to the home begging for food. Inventive Roy focuses his energy on building a machine out of spare lumber, tubing and lights that he scavenges around town. He depends on Patrick for help but doesn't tell him what he's building until the ''Amazing Thinking Machine'' is completed. Then it's apparent that Roy has found a way to help his family. The neighborhood children ''feed'' the machine with canned goods or pennies in order to ask it a question written on a slip of paper. The machine types out a response, with a little help from Roy hidden inside. Roy's machine not only provides food for the family but it also offers a diversion for the community's children from the ever-present threat of loss of home, job, fathers or a way of life. A concluding author's note gives background information to the time period. (117 pages)

Where it's reviewed:
Booklist, May 15, 2002, page 1607
Bulletin of the Center for Children's Books, May 2002, page 326
Horn Book, July 2002, page 461
School Library Journal, May 2002, page 153
Voice of Youth Advocates, April 2002, page 41

Other books by the same author:
Dr. Gravity, 1992
Ghost Catcher, 1991
Shadows, 1991

Other books you might like:

David A. Adler, *The Babe & I*, 1999
  In 1932 a young boy spots his father selling apples on the street corner and decides to sell newspapers to help support his family.

Christopher Paul Curtis, *Bud, Not Buddy*, 1999
  On the run during the Depression, Bud misses the train west and decides to walk to Grand Rapids to find the father he's never known. Newbery Medal winner.

C. Coco De Young, *A Letter to Mrs. Roosevelt*, 1999
  Margo uses a class assignment in letter writing to request that Eleanor Roosevelt help save her family's home.

Candice R. Ransom, *Jimmy Crack Corn*, 1994
  When Jimmy's family falls on hard times during the Great Depression, he and his father join the veteran's march on Washington.

607

DENNIS HASELEY
JIM LAMARCHE, Illustrator

A Story for Bear

(San Diego: Silver Whistle/Harcourt, Inc., 2002)

Subject(s): Literacy; Books and Reading; Animals/Bears
Age range(s): Grades 1-3
Major character(s): Bear, Bear; Unnamed Character, Young Woman, Friend (Bear's)
Time period(s): 2000s
Locale(s): United States

Summary: At first Bear hides out of sight while silently observing a woman as she sits in a chair under the trees surrounded by books. Her expression changes as she reads and sometimes she laughs aloud. Watching her gives Bear a sense of calm. When the woman notices him nearby every day she invites him to come closer and she begins to read aloud to him. Daily he returns to listen to the stories spilling from the pages of her many books. When summer ends, the woman closes up her cabin for the winter and leaves the books for Bear. One by one he carefully carries them to his cave and all winter long, in his dreams, he hears the woman's voice as he sleeps atop the heap of books. (32 pages)

Where it's reviewed:
Booklist, May 1, 2002, page 1533
Horn Book Guide, Fall 2002, page 331
School Library Journal, March 2002, page 188

Other books by the same author:
Crosby, 1996
My Father Doesn't Know About the Woods and Me, 1988
Kite Flier, 1986
The Old Banjo, 1983

Other books you might like:

Deborah Bruss, *Book! Book! Book!*, 2001
  Bored farm animals head to the library in search of a book to read.

Ian Whybrow, *Wish, Change, Friend*, 2002
  A pig's wish for change and friendship come true after he reads the words in a book.

John Winch, *The Old Woman Who Loved to Read*, 1997
  Seeking more time for reading, an old woman who loves books moves away from the noisy distractions of the city to the country.

608

JOHN HASSETT, Author/Illustrator
ANN HASSETT, Co-Author
ANN HASSETT, Illustrator

The Three Silly Girls Grubb

(Boston: Walter Lorraine Books/Houghton Mifflin Company, 2002)

Subject(s): Fairy Tales; Folklore; Sisters
Age range(s): Grades K-3
Major character(s): Ugly-Boy Bobby, Child; Grubb, Sister (biggest), Student
Time period(s): Indeterminate
Locale(s): Fictional Country

Summary: In this adaptation of *The Three Billy Goats Gruff*, an ill-mannered truant lurks in the troll's place under the bridge to steal the lunches of the Grubb sisters as they walk to school. Lunch consists of jelly doughnuts and the smallest sister carries only one. She suggests that Ugly-Boy Bobby wait for the middle-sized sister because she carries six doughnuts in her lunch. Ugly-Boy Bobby does, but that sister tells him the biggest one is yet to come and she has a dozen jelly doughnuts. When the biggest Grubb sister skips over the bridge Ugly-Boy Bobby demands the doughnuts. The biggest sister agrees to hand them over as soon as she plants a dozen kisses on Ugly-Boy Bobby's nose. Disgusted, Ugly-Boy Bobby runs to school as fast as he can and he never returns to his place under the bridge. (32 pages)

Where it's reviewed:
Booklist, September 15, 2002, page 236
Bulletin of the Center for Children's Books, November 2002, page 110
Horn Book, September 2002, page 588
Publishers Weekly, August 19, 2002, page 89
School Library Journal, November 2002, page 144

Other books by the same author:
Father Sun, Mother Moon, 2001
Cat Up a Tree, 1998
We Got My Brother at the Zoo, 1993

Other books you might like:

P.C. Asbjornsen, *The Three Billy Goats Gruff*, 1991
  Marcia Brown illustrates a reissue of the classic Scandinavian tale of three clever goats outwitting the horrid troll. J.E. Moe, co-author.

Stephen Carpenter, *The Three Billy Goats Gruff*, 1998
  An adaptation of the Norwegian tale for younger readers uses illustrations and simple, repetitive language to explain how the goats outwit the troll.

Rebecca Emberley, *Three Cool Kids*, 1995
  This take-off of the familiar fairy tale uses an urban setting with a sewer-living rat as the threat to the goat brothers as they cross the street.

609

GERALD HAUSMAN, Co-Author
LORETTA HAUSMAN, Co-Author

Escape from Botany Bay: The True Story of Mary Bryant

(New York: Scholastic/Orchard, 2003)

Subject(s): Prisoners and Prisons; Survival
Age range(s): Grades 7-10
Major character(s): Mary Broad Bryant, 19-Year-Old, Prisoner; Will Bryant, Prisoner
Time period(s): 1780s; 1790s (1786-1994)
Locale(s): Cornwall, England; Botany Bay, Australia; Timor, Pacific Ocean

Summary: Stealing a bonnet carries a death sentence in 18th-century England for Mary Broad, a sentence later commuted to transport to the penal colony in Australia. Relieved to still be alive, Mary finds the sea trip harrowing as she and other convicts are crowded cheek to jowl in the hold of the ship. A kindly seaman offers bits of sanity with an orange or a chance at fresh air, though Mary learns there are trade-offs for this freedom which leads to her pregnancy by the time the ship lands at Botany Bay. Once on land Mary weds fellow convict Will Bryant and hopes that her life will improve as together they help to build the colony. But life is almost unbearable and Will and Mary conspire to escape aboard a small fishing boat. Finally reaching Timor, after a trip of three thousand miles, Mary thinks they've reached safety only to have Will's boasting lead to their imprisonment. Though Will and her two children die while in prison, Mary is finally able to reach Cornwall in this story based on a real person's life. (220 pages)

Where it's reviewed:
Booklist, March 1, 2003, page 1206
Bulletin of the Center for Children's Books, March 2003, page 276
Kirkus Reviews, March 1, 2003, page 386
School Library Journal, April 2003, page 162
Voice of Youth Advocates, June 2003, page 130

Other books by the same author:
Castaways: Stories of Survival, 2003
The Jacob Ladder, 2001
Tom Cringle: The Pirate and the Patriot, 2001
Metaphysical Cat: Tales of Cats and Their Humans, 2000
Doctor Moledinky's Castle: A Hometown Tale, 1995

Other books you might like:
James Hall, *Botany Bay*, 1941
   Hugh Tallant describes his experiences as one of the first convicts sent to the penal colony in Botany Bay. Adult fiction.
Kathleen Karr, *The Boxer*, 2000
   Arrested for illegally fighting in the 1880s, Johnny's six months in prison provides the training grounds for his becoming a professional fighter.
David Malouf, *The Conversations at Curlow Creek*, 1996
   A guard and his recaptured prisoner from the penal colony talk during the night as the prisoner awaits death by hanging in the morning. Adult fiction.

610

PETE HAUTMAN

Sweetblood

(New York: Simon & Schuster, 2003)

Subject(s): Diabetes; Vampires; Schools/High Schools
Age range(s): Grades 8-12
Major character(s): Lucy Szabo, 16-Year-Old, Diabetic; Wayne "Draco" Smith, Con Artist
Time period(s): 2000s
Locale(s): United States

Summary: Former blonde, A-student Lucy Szabo bedevils her parents and her teachers with her dyed black hair, black Goth outfits and lack of interest in school. When she advances a theory linking diabetes and vampirism, her teacher decides she's "too weird" and calls in Lucy's parents. Restrictions are imposed and Lucy's computer is taken away, depriving her of access to a vampire chat room where Draco has noticed her comments. Though Lucy and Draco eventually meet, Draco is not as formidable an enemy as Lucy's diabetes. (180 pages)

Where it's reviewed:
Booklist, May 1, 2003, page 1595
Bulletin of the Center for Children's Books, July 2003, page 449
Publishers Weekly, June 2, 2003, page 53
School Library Journal, July 2003, page 130
Voice of Youth Advocates, October 2003, page 395

Awards the book has won:
ALA Best Books for Young Adults, 2004
Center for Children's Books Best Books, 2003

Other books by the same author:
Hole in the Sky, 2001
Stone Cold, 1998
Mr. Was, 1996

Other books you might like:
Tracy Briery, *The Vampire Journals*, 1993
   Eighteenth-century vampire Maria Theresa discloses how she chose vampirism as a way to overcome women's second-class status.
Hanna Lutzen, *Vlad the Undead*, 1998
   This chilling retelling of *Dracula* finds Lucia absorbed in the century-old story of a Romanian stranger who now seems to have absconded with her.
Sheri Cooper Sinykin, *Next Thing to Strangers*, 1991
   Visiting her grandparents, Cass meets and is attracted to Jody, but doesn't understand his reluctance to admit he's a diabetic.

611

ESTHER HAUTZIG
BETH PECK, Illustrator

A Picture of Grandmother

(New York: Frances Foster/Farrar Straus and Giroux, 2002)

Subject(s): Jews; Stepmothers; Secrets
Age range(s): Grades 2-5

Major character(s): Sara, Child, Niece; Benjamin, Uncle
Time period(s): 1930s (1939)
Locale(s): Vilna, Poland

Summary: Sara, a Jewish girl living in Poland, looks forward to her Uncle Benjamin's letters from America. When her uncle invites her mother and grandmother to visit him and attend the World's Fair, Sara is confused by a request for a specific photograph of a grandmother that she has never seen and that her mother doesn't want to talk about. Sara investigates and discovers the photo and the family secret that her grandmother is actually her step-grandmother. With some reassurance from her mother, Sara comes to terms with this discovery. (82 pages)

Where it's reviewed:
Booklist, October 2002, page 325
Bulletin of the Center for Children's Books, October 2002, page 112
Kirkus Reviews, August 15, 2002, page 1225
Publishers Weekly, September 16, 2002, page 68
School Library Journal, October 2002, page 112

Other books by the same author:
A Gift for Mama, 1992 (ALA Notable Children's Books)
Riches, 1992 (Sydney Taylor Book Award)
The Endless Steppe: Growing Up in Siberia, 1968 (National Book Award Finalist)

Other books you might like:
Charlotte Herman, *The House on Walenska Street*, 1991
    Leah, a Russian Jewish girl, enjoys reading and responding to letters from her cousins in America.
Karen Hesse, *Letters from Rifka*, 1992
    Rifka tells the story of her difficult immigration from Russia to the United States through letters to her family.
Johanna Hurwitz, *The Rabbi's Girls*, 2002
    Carrie Levin has a rough year in which her family moves, her sister is born and her father dies.

612

JUANITA HAVILL
ANNE SIBLEY O'BRIEN, Illustrator

Brianna, Jamaica, and the Dance of Spring

(Boston: Houghton Mifflin Company, 2002)

Subject(s): Dancing; Friendship; Illness
Age range(s): Grades K-3
Major character(s): Brianna, Sister (younger), Dancer; Nikki, Sister (older), Dancer; Jamaica, Friend, Dancer
Time period(s): 2000s (2002)
Locale(s): United States

Summary: As parts are cast for the spring dance recital Jamaica and Brianna hope to be butterflies. Alas, their class is assigned to be flowers and bees and both of them are flowers. Nikki, though, is chosen to be the butterfly queen and Brianna watches her daily rehearsals wishing that she could have a costume with wings too. At home she secretly practices all the leaps and twirls of Nikki's part. When a bumblebee becomes ill Jamaica quickly volunteers to take her place so she'll have wings rather than petals on her costume. On the day of the

dress rehearsal Nikki is sent home sick from school and Brianna has a chance to take her place. Brianna's fleeting hopes of being the butterfly queen vanish when she too awakens with symptoms of strep throat and the dance goes on without either sister. (32 pages)

Where it's reviewed:
Booklist, March 15, 2002, page 1262
School Library Journal, April 2002, page 110

Other books by the same author:
Jamaica and the Substitute Teacher, 1999
Jamaica's Blue Marker, 1995
Jamaica and Brianna, 1993
Jamaica's Find, 1986 (IRA Children's Choices)

Other books you might like:
Patricia Lee Gauch, *Tanya and Emily in a Dance for Two*, 1994
    Tanya's free-spirited, unconventional dance technique inspires creativity in Emily, a proper ballerina.
Rachel Isadora, *Lili at Ballet*, 1993
    Four times a week Lili attends dance classes in order to realize her dream of becoming a ballerina.
Jane O'Connor, *Nina, Nina Ballerina*, 1993
    Although she is one of a flock of butterflies, Nina stands out from the crowd during the performance.

613

LOUISE HAWES

Waiting for Christopher

(Cambridge, MA: Candlewick Press, 2002)

Subject(s): Child Abuse; Mothers and Sons; Kidnapping
Age range(s): Grades 7-10
Major character(s): Feena Harvey, 14-Year-Old; Christopher Pierson, Child; Raylene Watson, 9th Grader
Time period(s): 2000s
Locale(s): Florida

Summary: Bookish and new at her school, Feena is lonely and still saddened by the death of her brother Christopher ten years earlier. She notices a mother repeatedly spanking her toddler son at the amusement park near her home and, when the child is left alone, Feena snatches him away. Determined to keep this Christopher safe from abuse, Feena hides him in an abandoned boat and, with the help of popular student Raylene, tries to raise him. The good intentions of the teens are thwarted when it becomes obvious that not only does Christopher miss his mother, but it's also very hard to be secretive about raising a kidnapped child. Feena makes a very adult decision when she returns Christopher to his mother, though she worries whether that it was in Christopher's best interest. (224 pages)

Where it's reviewed:
Booklist, July 2002, page 1838
Bulletin of the Center for Children's Books, September 2002, page 18
Horn Book, September 2002, page 573
Publishers Weekly, May 20, 2002, page 66
Voice of Youth Advocates, April 2002, page 41

Other books by the same author:
Vanishing Point: A Story of Lavinia Fontana, 2004
Rosey in the Present Tense, 1999

Other books you might like:
A.E. Cannon, *Amazing Gracie*, 1991
  Gracie hopes her mother's remarriage will help her overcome depression, but even Gracie doesn't know how to prevent another suicide attempt.
Glen Huser, *Touch of the Clown*, 1999
  Though Cosmo's dying of cancer, he's able to help Barbara and her younger sister when they need a safe haven from their abusive father.
Cynthia Voigt, *Homecoming*, 1981
  After abandonment by their mother, Dicey and her younger siblings make the long journey on foot to their eccentric grandmother's home.

614

TOREY HAYDEN

The Very Worst Thing

(New York: HarperCollins, 2003)

Subject(s): Animals/Owls; Foster Homes; Friendship
Age range(s): Grades 5-8
Major character(s): David, 5th Grader, Foster Child; Madeleine Stopes, 5th Grader
Time period(s): 2000s
Locale(s): United States

Summary: David keeps a list of the "very worst things" and in the number one position is having no one who cares about you, which is an accurate representation of David's life after being sent to six foster homes. Now he lives with kindhearted, loving Granny and becomes friends with classmate Mab who's two years younger than everyone else in the class. David's stutter and his difficulty in school sets him up for teasing by the other kids and often causes him to lash out in anger, which unfortunately happens when he discovers an owl nest. Chasing away the mother owl, he breaks one egg but decides to keep the other one and raise the owl. Mab helps, though she and her father encourage him to return the bird, named King Arthur, to the wild. Though the owl dies, the friendship of Mab and David continues in this first novel for young people by a noted adult author. (169 pages)

Where it's reviewed:
Kirkus Reviews, May 15, 2003, page 751
Library Media Connection, January 2004, page 62
School Library Journal, October 2003, page 166

Other books by the same author:
Beautiful Child, 2002 (adult nonfiction)
The Tiger's Child, 1995 (adult nonfiction)
Just Another Kid, 1988 (adult nonfiction)

Other books you might like:
Melvin Burgess, *Kite*, 2000
  Told to destroy the eggs of an endangered kite, Tom keeps them; when one hatches, he raises the bird but needs help to train her.
George Harrar, *Parents Wanted*, 2001
  Andy's attention deficit disorder makes it hard for him to adjust to foster homes; when he finds the perfect family, past behavior almost ruins it for him.
Mary Quattlebaum, *Grover C. Graham and Me*, 2001
  Headed for his eighth foster home, Ben tries to remain distant, but at the Torgles there's chaos, love and Grover, an abandoned 14-month-old baby.

615

GEOFFREY HAYES, Author/Illustrator

Patrick at the Circus

(New York: Hyperion Books for Children, 2002)

Subject(s): Circus; Animals/Bears; Parent and Child
Age range(s): Grades K-2
Major character(s): Patrick Brown, Son, Bear
Time period(s): 2000s (2002)
Locale(s): Puttyville

Summary: Patrick Brown's excitement about the circus coming to town increases when he learns that his father used to be a clown. On a trip to the circus grounds to watch the set up, Patrick and his family learn the show will have to be canceled because the clown has quit. Patrick's father agrees to fill in, but Patrick is jealous that he won't get to be in the show. However, when a monkey steals Patrick's father's hat during the show, Patrick manages to save the hat and join the show too. (32 pages)

Where it's reviewed:
Horn Book Guide, Fall 2002, page 302
Kirkus Reviews, May 1, 2002, apge 656
Publishers Weekly, May 27, 2002, page 61
School Library Journal, July 2002, page 92

Other books by the same author:
Patrick and the Get-Well Day, 2003
Patrick and the Big Bully, 2001
Patrick and His Grandpa, 1986
Bear by Himself, 1976

Other books you might like:
Ian Falconer, *Olivia Saves the Circus*, 2001
  After the circus performers fall ill, Olivia saves the day by doing all the acts solo, or so she says.
Hilary Knight, *The Circus Is Coming*, 1979
  Circus entertainers on parade cause excitement about the show.
Marjorie Priceman, *Emeline at the Circus*, 1999
  During Emeline's class field trip to the circus, she gets caught up in the act.
Dr. Seuss, *If I Ran the Circus*, 1956
  Morris McGurk imagines all the amazing acts he'd have if he created the Circus McGurkus.
Peter Spier, *Circus!*, 1992
  This book explores what goes on in front of the audience and behind the scenes at the circus.

616

BARBARA SHOOK HAZEN
EMILY ARNOLD MCCULLY, Illustrator

Katie's Wish

(New York: Dial Books for Young Readers, 2002)

Subject(s): Historical; Famine Victims; Emigration and Immigration
Age range(s): Grades K-3
Major character(s): Katie, Child; Grand Da, Grandfather, Aged Person; Brian, Cousin; Da, Father, Immigrant
Time period(s): Indeterminate Past
Locale(s): Ireland; Boston

Summary: Poor, lonely Katie misses her deceased mother and her Da, who has gone to America. Is it any wonder that when she faces the same plain potatoes for dinner yet again that she mutters a wish for them to ''go away?'' Soon after, a potato rot begins killing all the potatoes and famine afflicts everyone in Ireland. Without the income from potatoes farmers cannot pay rent money to the masters and are forced to move. Katie, believing her words caused the potatoes to rot, feels responsible. Grand Da announces that Da has sent money for Brian and Katie to travel to America and so they are sent away from the hardship. Not until Katie reaches the safety of Da's arms is she able to confess the guilt she feels for her wish and receive Da's assurance that Katie's words did not cause the famine. A brief author's note gives historical background to the story. (32 pages)

Where it's reviewed:
Booklist, October 15, 2002, page 410
Publishers Weekly, August 26, 2002, page 68
School Library Journal, September 2002, page 193

Other books by the same author:
Noah's Ark, 2003
City Cats, Country Cats, 1999
Road Hog, 1998

Other books you might like:
Eve Bunting, *Dreaming of America: An Ellis Island Story*, 2000
    In 1892 Annie and her brothers leave their Irish home and journey to America to join their parents.
Brian Hasler, *Casper and Catherine Move to America: An Immigrant Family's Adventures, 1849-1850*, 2003
    Family history provides the basis for this story of a journey from Europe to the American Midwest.
Don Nardo, *The Irish Potato Famine*, 1990
    A nonfiction title explores multiple factors contributing to the great famine in 19th-century Ireland.

617

SUE HEAP, Author/Illustrator

Four Friends Together

(Cambridge, MA: Candlewick Press, 2003)

Subject(s): Books and Reading; Friendship; Problem Solving
Age range(s): Preschool-Kindergarten

Major character(s): Seymour, Sheep, Friend; Rachel, Rabbit, Friend; Mary Claire, Child, Friend; Florentina, Bear, Friend
Time period(s): Indeterminate
Locale(s): Fictional Country

Summary: Seymour and Rachel have a big problem. It's story time and Mary Claire has fallen asleep holding the book. When Florentina arrives, another problem quickly becomes obvious. Mary Claire is sleeping in Florentina's chair and Mary Claire's little chair simply won't hold the big flowery bear. The three friends wait patiently for Mary Claire to wake up and when she does, they are ready to begin the story. Unfortunately, more problems soon become apparent. First one and then another friend complain about being unable to see the pictures so Mary Claire, Rachel and Seymour move to Florentina's lap. Now everyone is happy. (28 pages)

Where it's reviewed:
Booklist, October 1, 2003, page 327
Five Owls, 2004, page 82
Publishers Weekly, July 28, 2003, page 93

Other books by the same author:
Four Friends in the Garden, 2004
What Shall We Play?, 2002
Cowboy Baby, 1998

Other books you might like:
Deborah Bruss, *Book! Book! Book!*, 2001
    Even bored farm animals enjoy reading a story now and then.
Jessica Spanyol, *Carlo Likes Reading*, 2001
    Carlo enjoys being read to by his mom as much as he likes reading to his cat, a friend or ducks at the park.
Rosemary Wells, *Read to Your Bunny*, 1998
    The importance of reading daily is emphasized in brief text and cozy pictures of mother and father bunnies reading to their youngsters.

618

SUE HEAP, Author/Illustrator

What Shall We Play?

(Cambridge, MA: Candlewick Press, 2002)

Subject(s): Playing; Imagination; Friendship
Age range(s): Preschool-Grade 1
Major character(s): Lily May, Child, Friend; Matt, Child, Friend; Martha, Child, Friend
Time period(s): 2000s
Locale(s): United States

Summary: Lily May suggests playing fairies, but Matt wants to play trees so they do. Lily May suggests playing fairies, but Martha wants to play cars so they do. Then the imaginative children play cats and jello. Finally, Matt and Martha accept Lily May's idea to play fairies so they do and it is fun. (28 pages)

Where it's reviewed:
Booklist, June 2002, page 1737
Bulletin of the Center for Children's Books, August 2002, page 405
Publishers Weekly, April 1, 2002, page 82

School Library Journal, April 2002, page 112

Other books by the same author:
Four Friends in the Garden, 2004
Four Friends Together, 2003
Baby Bill and Little Lil, 1999
Cowboy Baby, 1998

Other books you might like:
Joan Anderson, *Sally's Submarine*, 1995
   Sally uses a cardboard submarine and her vivid imagination to enjoy a day under the sea.
Jane Cowan-Fletcher, *Farmer Will*, 2001
   Will likes to pretend that he is a farmer, imagining that his toy animals are life-size.
Lindsey Gardiner, *When Poppy and Max Grow Up*, 2001
   Imaginatively, Poppy and Max demonstrate the many possibilities for their future activities or careers.
Peter Sis, *Ballerina!*, 2001
   Terry combines her imagination with her love of dance and colorful costumes to transform a simple mirror into a succession of famous ballets.

619

BETSY HEARNE

The Canine Connection: Stories about Dogs and People

(New York: Margaret K. McElderry/Simon & Schuster, 2003)

Subject(s): Short Stories; Animals/Dogs
Age range(s): Grades 5-8

Summary: The unique bond that forms between a dog and its owner is captured here in a collection of twelve stories with dogs playing their usual subservient role. Tears brim over in ''Bones'' when a young boy has to put his aging Newfoundlander to sleep or ''Room 313'' when a teen realizes she and her therapy dog were privileged to spend time with an ailing child in the hour before her death. Balancing those tears are the chuckles in ''Lab'' where Willa collects strays as easily as her mother bears children. And a little suspense enters for Walter in ''Cargo'' when his beloved Xoloitcuinti, a hairless Mexican dog, is inadvertently placed in the cargo hold of his plane. Both human and canine characters will linger with readers. (113 pages)

Where it's reviewed:
Booklist, April 15, 2003, page 1471
Horn Book, May 2003, page 348
Library Media Connection, August 2003, page 76
Publishers Weekly, February 10, 2003, page 188
School Library Journal, April 2003, page 164

Awards the book has won:
Center for Children's Books Best Books, 2003

Other books by the same author:
Wishes, Kisses, and Pigs, 2001
Eli's Ghost, 1987
Love Lines: Poetry in Person, 1987

Other books you might like:
Phyllis Reynolds Naylor, *Shiloh*, 1991
   In a Newbery Medal winner, Marty tries to hide a beagle from the dog's abusive owner.
Barbara Ann Porte, *Beauty and the Serpent: Thirteen Tales of Unnatural Animals*, 2001
   Whenever students at Wild Alternative HS misbehave, they're sent to the library where Ms. Drumm tells them a story about unnatural, unexpected animals.
Sheila Kelly Welch, *A Horse for All Seasons*, 1995
   Divided into the seasons of the year, this collection of twelve contemporary stories features horses and their young owners.

620

LORRAINE HEATH

Samantha and the Cowboy

(New York: Avon/HarperCollins, 2002)

Subject(s): Romance; Cattle Drives; Gender Roles
Age range(s): Grades 8-12
Major character(s): Samantha ''Sam'' Reynolds, 16-Year-Old; Matthew ''Matt'' Hart, 18-Year-Old, Cowboy; Jake Vaughn, Cowboy (trail boss)
Time period(s): 1860s (1866)
Locale(s): Faithful, Texas; West

Summary: Her older brother's back from the Civil War missing an arm, her mother and younger siblings are hungry, the family's living on credit from the general store and Sam feels as though it's up to her to find the money for them to survive. When she sees a sign advertising for boys 14-years-old and up to help drive cattle to Missouri and earn $100, she doesn't see why she can't do that. Disguised as a boy, she applies but is turned down by the trail boss Jake when she lies about her experience. Feeling sorry for Sam, Matt overrides Jake and hires her, though Jake insists he then has to keep an eye on Sam. Though Matt's father owns the herd, he's training to be the trail boss and is in no position to argue with Jake. Matt would rather not be friends with anyone after burying too many during the Civil War, but becomes used to Sam. Sam, meanwhile, is trying to work as hard as anybody else so that when her gender is discovered, they'll want to keep her anyway. Unfortunately, she feels herself growing interested in Matt, a feeling he doesn't reciprocate when he realizes she's a girl in this sweet, historical romance. (241 pages)

Where it's reviewed:
Kliatt, September 2002, page 18

Other books by the same author:
Amelia and the Outlaw, 2003
Hard Lovin' Man, 2003
To Marry an Heiress, 2002
Always to Remember, 1998

Other books you might like:
Ric Lynden Hardman, *Sunshine Rider: The First Vegetarian Western*, 1998
   Wylie signs up as an assistant cook on a cattle drive where he's put in charge of Roselle, a pet that's part buffalo and part longhorn.

Kathleen Karr, *Gold-Rush Phoebe*, 1998

Phoebe cuts her hair, dresses as a boy and, with her good friend Robbie, runs away for the gold fields of California.

Theodore Taylor, *Walking Up a Rainbow*, 1986

To settle her deceased parent's debts, Susan drives a herd of sheep to California and falls in love with her drover along the way.

621

JAMES HENEGHAN

Flood

(New York: Farrar Straus Giroux, 2002)

Subject(s): Fathers and Sons; Fairies; Aunts and Uncles
Age range(s): Grades 5-8
Major character(s): Andrew "Andy" Flynn, 11-Year-Old; Vincent "Vinny" Flynn, Father, Alcoholic; Mona Hogan, Aunt
Time period(s): 2000s
Locale(s): Halifax, Nova Scotia, Canada

Summary: The rains keep falling, the rivers overflow their banks and landslides obliterate homes. Luckily the Sheehogue, also known as fairies, heed the command of their Old Ones to save the children and pluck Andy Flynn from harm's way. Though happy to be alive, Andy loses his mother and stepfather and now, facing life with his formidable Aunt Mona, learns the truth about his real father. Vinny is alive and lives in Halifax, close to Aunt Mona. That's all Andy needs to hear and off he scampers to live with his well meaning but irresponsible, hard-drinking father. Saying he'll do better, Vinny never finds a job, cleans up the apartment or gives up drinking; instead he sells stolen cigarettes and leads a life of petty crime. When Vinny breaks his leg, Andy moves back to Aunt Mona's home where he realizes the importance of wearing clean clothes, not living in squalor and having an aunt and uncle who love and care for him. As for the Sheehogue who saved Andy, they continue to watch over him until they know he is safe in his new life. (182 pages)

Where it's reviewed:
Booklist, March 15, 2002, page 1258
Bulletin of the Center for Children's Books, April 2002, page 281
Horn Book, July 2002, page 461
Quill & Quire, May 2002, page 34
School Library Journal, April 2002, page 150

Other books by the same author:
Hit Squad, 2003 (Orca Soundings)
The Grave, 2000
Wish Me Luck, 1997
Torn Away, 1994

Other books you might like:
Cat Bauer, *Harley, Like a Person*, 2000
Harley searches for Sean who may be her father; when the truth comes out, Harley realizes she's stronger than any of the adults in her life.
Sharon Creech, *Walk Two Moons*, 1994
It takes a journey across America with her Gram and

Gramps to make Salamanca realize she can't bring her mother back from that fatal bus crash.

Mary E. Lyons, *Knockabeg: A Famine Tale*, 2001
Good fairies, known as the Trooping Ones, fight the Nuckelevee fairies that have destroyed the potato crop.

Joyce Sweeney, *The Tiger Orchard*, 1993
Zack has nightmares of apple orchards and a shadowy man. When he discovers his mother lied about his father's death, he searches for him.

622

KEVIN HENKES, Author/Illustrator

Julius's Candy Corn

(New York: Greenwillow Books/HarperCollins, 2003)

Subject(s): Halloween; Food; Behavior
Age range(s): Preschool
Major character(s): Julius, Mouse, Son
Time period(s): Indeterminate
Locale(s): Fictional Country

Summary: Julius has been forewarned not to eat the cupcakes that have been made for the party. So, Julius counts them instead by counting the single candy corn decorating each cupcake. Julius counts one candy corn and another one and another one until he's counted every one. As he counts, he eats so by the time the party starts the cupcakes are intact, but the candy corn decorations, having been counted, are gone. (24 pages)

Where it's reviewed:
Booklist, September 15, 2003, page 245
Publishers Weekly, August 4, 2003, page 81
School Library Journal, August 2003, page 129

Other books by the same author:
Lilly's Chocolate Heart, 2003
Wemberly's Ice-Cream Star, 2003
Sheila Rae's Peppermint Stick, 2001 (ALA Notable Children's Books)

Other books you might like:
Ellen Jareckie, *A House-Mouse Party: House-Mouse Tales*, 2003
A rhyming board book tells the story of five friends preparing for a party.
Laura Joffe Numeroff, *The Best Mouse Cookie*, 1999
A mouse bakes cookies in a simple board book for younger readers.
Rosemary Wells, *Max's Chocolate Chicken*, 1989
It looks as if older sister Ruby will find the most Easter eggs but Max makes off with the chocolate chicken prize anyway.

623

KEVIN HENKES

Olive's Ocean

(New York: Greenwillow, 2003)

Subject(s): Coming-of-Age; Grandmothers; Self-Perception
Age range(s): Grades 5-8

Major character(s): Olive Barstow, Accident Victim; Martha Boyle, 12-Year-Old; Dorothy "Godbee" Boyle, Grandmother (of Martha)
Time period(s): 2000s
Locale(s): Madison, Wisconsin; Cape Cod, Massachusetts

Summary: One day the mother of Olive Barstow, a young girl who was killed in a bicycle accident just a few weeks before, visits Martha to share with her a page from Olive's journal. Olive had three wishes: to see the ocean, to become a writer and to be friends with Martha, who's the "nicest person" in her class. Martha didn't know Olive, but that summer discovers how Olive has touched her life. As Martha travels to Cape Cod to visit her grandmother, she thinks about how she wants to be a writer, too. Collecting seawater for Olive, and almost drowning while doing so, she is reminded of the fragility of life. In this growing-up summer for Martha she enjoys a kiss, a boyfriend, and a special relationship with her grandmother Godbee. During this time, she also thinks a lot about Olive and how she might have reacted to all these new pieces of Martha's life. (217 pages)

Where it's reviewed:
Booklist, September 1, 2003, page 122
Bulletin of the Center for Children's Books, September 2003, page 17
Horn Book, November 2003, page 745
Publishers Weekly, August 18, 2003, page 80
School Library Journal, August 2003, page 160

Awards the book has won:
ALA Notable Children's Books, 2004
ALA Best Books for Young Adults, 2004

Other books by the same author:
The Birthday Room, 1999
Protecting Marie, 1995
Words of Stone, 1992

Other books you might like:
V.M. Caldwell, *The Ocean Within*, 1999
    After living in various foster homes, it takes Grandma Martha's patience to make Elizabeth feel secure in her new adoptive family.
Sid Hite, *A Hole in the World*, 2001
    Helping at a farm for the summer, Paul puzzles over a hired hand he is said to resemble, a man who is remembered for his integrity and goodness.
Richard Peck, *A Long Way from Chicago*, 1998
    Warm and funny stories of the summers Joey and his sister spent with their grandmother fill this work.

624

KEVIN HENKES, Author/Illustrator

Owen's Marshmallow Chick
(New York: Greenwillow, 2002)

Subject(s): Animals/Mice; Holidays; Friendship
Age range(s): Preschool-Kindergarten
Major character(s): Owen, Mouse
Time period(s): Indeterminate
Locale(s): Fictional Country

Summary: Owen finds many favorites in his Easter basket and one by one he devours them all. Owen eats jellybeans, gumdrops, buttercream eggs and the big chocolate bunny. When only the little marshmallow chick remains Owen notices how the chick's color matches that of his special blanket and he plays with the chick all day. At bedtime he lovingly places the chick with his very best toys, kisses it good night and takes his special blanket to bed. (24 pages)

Where it's reviewed:
Booklist, January 1, 2002, page 864
Bulletin of the Center for Children's Books, February 2002, page 207
Horn Book Guide, Fall 2002, page 303
Publishers Weekly, December 24, 2001, page 66
School Library Journal, February 2002, page 107

Awards the book has won:
Parenting's Books of the Year, 2002

Other books by the same author:
Sheila Rae's Peppermint Stick, 2001 (ALA Notable Children's Books)
Wemberly Worried, 2000 (School Library Journal Best Books)
Owen, 1993 (Caldecott Honor Book)

Other books you might like:
Denise Fleming, *Lunch*, 1992
    By the time a very hungry mouse finishes eating it's devoured foods of every color.
Laura Joffe Numeroff, *If You Give a Mouse a Cookie*, 1985
    Be careful! Giving a cookie to a mouse can lead to many more requests from the mouse for milk and a napkin and. . . .
Rosemary Wells, *Max's Chocolate Chicken*, 1989
    Max doesn't find the most Easter eggs but he manages to claim the chocolate chicken prize anyway.

625

KEVIN HENKES, Author/Illustrator

Wemberly's Ice-Cream Star
(New York: Greenwillow Books/HarperCollins Publishers, 2003)

Subject(s): Food; Summer; Dolls and Dollhouses
Age range(s): Preschool
Major character(s): Wemberly, Child, Mouse
Time period(s): 2000s (2003)
Locale(s): United States

Summary: On a hot summer day Wemberly is given a cool treat, an ice-cream star. She worries, however, that the treat will drip on her dress and that she doesn't have another star to share with her stuffed animal. Wemberly comes up with a solution though: she gets two bowls and allows the star to melt. Then Wemberly and her stuffed animal can share ice cream soup, without getting dirty. (24 pages)

Where it's reviewed:
Booklist, September 15, 2003, page 245
Publishers Weekly, April 7, 2003, page 69
School Library Journal, May 2003, page 120

Other books by the same author:

Julius's Candy Corn, 2003

Lilly's Chocolate Heart, 2003

Wemberly Worried, 2000 (Publishers Weekly Best Children's Books)

Owen, 1993 (Caldecott Honor Book)

Other books you might like:

Elisha Cooper, *Ice Cream*, 2002

From cow to carton, the book explains all the steps involved in making ice cream.

Elaine Greenstein, *Ice-Cream Cones for Sale!*, 2003

This book looks at the invention of the first ice cream cone.

Daniel Pinkwater, *Ice Cream Larry*, 1999

Polar bear Larry becomes the spokesman for Iceberg Ice Cream.

H.A. Rey, *Curious George Goes to an Ice Cream Shop*, 1989

Curious George makes a mess at the ice cream shop, but then redeems himself by luring customers in when he builds a massive sundae.

626

HEATHER HENSON

Making the Run

(New York: HarperCollins, 2002)

Subject(s): Fathers and Daughters; Coming-of-Age; Friendship

Age range(s): Grades 10-12

Major character(s): Lucinda Larrimore ''Crazy Lu'' McClellan, 18-Year-Old, Waiter/Waitress; Jay Shepard, Boyfriend (of Lu); Ginny Cavanaugh, 18-Year-Old

Time period(s): 2000s

Locale(s): Rainey, Kentucky

Summary: ''Making the run'' for the teens of a small town in Kentucky means driving 45 miles to the town of Huntsville, slowing to negotiate Dead Man Bend, and buying booze for their weekend parties. Stuck in small-town America, Lu waits tables until she graduates from high school and reaches her 18th birthday. In the meantime, she pretends not to grieve over the death of her mother and buries her sorrow in alcohol and drugs. She and her friend Ginny don't look much beyond escaping their small town, though Lu knows she will pursue her interest in photography. The return of her older brother's friend Jay leads to a relationship for Lu that quickly becomes intimate; her best friend Ginny announces her pregnancy by a college student; and a terrible automobile wreck makes Lu realize how short life really is in this author's first novel. (227 pages)

Where it's reviewed:

Booklist, April 15, 2002, page 1395

Kliatt, May 2002, page 10

Publishers Weekly, April 29, 2002, page 72

School Library Journal, May 2002, page 154

Voice of Youth Advocates, August 2002, page 192

Other books you might like:

Susan Finch, *The Intimacy of Indiana*, 2001

The pangs of leaving high school affect Olivia, Neil and Adam in different ways.

Alice Hoffman, *Local Girls*, 1999

Interconnected stories follow Gretel's life from preteen years to career woman status and reflect the ups and downs of a suburban family.

Alan Watt, *Diamond Dogs*, 2000

Neil and his father become locked in a silent bond after Neil drinks too much at a party and drives home, but hits and kills a freshman from his high school.

627

PATRICIA HERMES

A Perfect Place

(New York: Scholastic, Inc., 2002)

Series: My America. Joshua's Oregon Trail Diary Book 2

Subject(s): Diaries; Death; Growing Up

Age range(s): Grades 3-5

Major character(s): Joshua McCullough, 9-Year-Old

Time period(s): 1840s (1848)

Locale(s): Willamette Valley, Oregon

Summary: Joshua's family has made it to Oregon, but their struggles are not over. Winter rains and floods lead to an accident in which Joshua's beloved grandfather drowns. Eventually the rest on the family is able to build a small house on their homestead in time for the birth of Joshua's baby brother, bringing hope in this perfect place at journey's end. (112 pages)

Where it's reviewed:

Booklist, January 2003, page 890

Horn Book Guide, Spring 2003, page 67

Kirkus Reviews, October 15, 2002, page 1530

School Library Journal, November 2002, page 124

Other books by the same author:

The Wild Year, 2003 (My America: Joshua's Oregon Trail Diary Book 3)

Westward to Home, 2001 (My America: Joshua's Oregon Trail Diary Book 1)

Kevin Corbett Eats Flies, 1987

Other books you might like:

Kathleen Karr, *Oregon, Sweet Oregon*, 1997

Phoebe Brown and her family have finally arrived in Oregon; after the excitement of the trail, it seems downright boring.

Ellen Levine, *The Journal Of Jedediah Barstow: An Emigrant On The Oregon Trail*, 2002

When his parents and sister die while fording a river on the Oregon Trail, Jedediah decides to complete the journey on his own.

Honore Morrow, *On to Oregon!*, 1946

After their parents die during the Oregon Trail journey to the Willamette Valley, the seven, orphaned Sager children finish the trip alone.

PATRICIA HERMES

Season of Promise

(New York: Scholastic Press, 2002)

Series: My America. Elizabeth's Jamestown Colony Diary Book 3
Subject(s): American Colonies; Diaries; History
Age range(s): Grades 3-5
Major character(s): Lizzie Barker, 10-Year-Old, Daughter
Time period(s): 1610s (1610-1611)
Locale(s): Jamestown, Virginia

Summary: Lizzie, her father and siblings, have survived the Starving Time in the Jamestown settlement and life is beginning to look up. Although Lizzie misses her mother, who died during the winter, she is happy that her brother has arrived and that things in Jamestown are moving more smoothly. Although their new leader has gotten the settlers working again and there is now enough food for everyone, Lizzie feels that his punishments are too harsh and when she gets the chance, she tells him so. Also during this six-month period, Lizzie's father marries a fellow settler whose husband and child died during the harsh winter. (108 pages)

Where it's reviewed:
Horn Book Guide, Spring 2003, page 67
School Library Journal, February 2003, page 112

Other books by the same author:
The Starving Time, 2001 (My America: Elizabeth's Jamestown Diary Book 2)
Our Strange New Land, 2000 (My America: Elizabeth's Jamestown Diary Book 1)
When Snow Law Soft on the Mountain, 1996 (Smithsonian's Notable Books for Children)

Other books you might like:
Tracy Barrett, *Growing Up in Colonial America*, 1995
   This non-fiction book describes what it was like to grow up in the Plymouth and Virginia colonies in the 17th and 18th centuries.
Mary R. Furbee, *Outrageous Women of Colonial American*, 2001
   This non-fiction book provides biographical sketches of fourteen amazing colonial-era women.
Anne Holler, *Pocahontas: Powhatan Peacemaker*, 1993
   This non-fiction book details the life of Pocahontas, including her friendship with the Jamestown settlers.
Gail Langer Karwoski, *Surviving Jamestown: The Adventures of Young Sam Collier*, 2001
   Samuel Collier assists John Smith on his voyage to America and subsequent settlement of Jamestown.
Joan Lowery Nixon, *Ann's Story, 1747*, 1999
   Ann, daughter of Williamsburg's apothecary, rebels against Colonial expectations and wants to be a doctor.

PATRICIA HERMES

Sweet By and By

(New York: HarperCollins, 2002)

Subject(s): Grandmothers; Mountain Life; Music and Musicians
Age range(s): Grades 4-7
Major character(s): Blessing, 11-Year-Old, Orphan; Monnie, Grandmother
Time period(s): 1940s
Locale(s): Star Mountain, Tennessee

Summary: Blessing has been brought up by her beloved grandmother Monnie after her father and grandfather died in a mining accident before she was born and her mother died when Blessing was only two. For the last nine years Monnie and Blessing have made music together, with Monnie playing the violin and Blessing singing. There isn't much money, but there's always a lot of love; now Monnie's heart is wearing out so that some days she doesn't even have the strength to play the violin. Even after meeting with Monnie's doctor, Blessing prays for a miracle though that doesn't seem likely. Blessing spies on the mountain families her grandmother has chosen as possible new homes for her, but one has too many children and not enough beds, one has a child who gives Blessing the creeps and the last family, just a brother and sister, talk to their animals. When the time is right, Blessing will make her decision and she'll always have Monnie's memory beside her in this tear-jerker. (192 pages)

Where it's reviewed:
Booklist, October 1, 2002, page 341
Kirkus Reviews, October 15, 2002, page 1531
Publishers Weekly, November 11, 2002, page 64
School Library Journal, October 2002, page 164

Other books by the same author:
Summer Secrets, 2004
The Wild Year, 2003
A Perfect Place, 2002
Season of Promise, 2002
Westward to Home, 2001

Other books you might like:
Katherine Jay Bacon, *Shadow and Light*, 1987
   Emma's delight at spending the summer with her grandmother Gee diminishes when she realizes how ill Gee is.
Katherine Paterson, *The Same Stuff as Stars*, 2002
   Dumped off at her great-grandmother's house, Angel ends up taking care of her younger brother as well as Grandma.
Barbara A. Smith, *Somewhere Just Beyond*, 1993
   When Callie sees how frail her grandmother is, she adjusts to the inevitability of death and learns to say goodbye to Gramma.
Cynthia Voigt, *Homecoming*, 1981
   After being abandoned by their mother, Dicey and her younger brothers and sister make the long journey on foot to their eccentric grandmother's home.

630

ESTHER HERSHENHORN
ROSANNE LITZINGER, Illustrator

Chicken Soup by Heart

(New York: Simon & Schuster Books for Young Readers, 2002)

Subject(s): Babysitters; Illness; Food
Age range(s): Grades K-3
Major character(s): Mrs. Gittel, Babysitter, Aged Person; Rudie Dinkins, Child
Time period(s): 2000s
Locale(s): United States

Summary: When Rudie learns that his favorite babysitter is sick with the flu he decides to treat Mrs. Gittel just as she treats him when he's sick. That means, making her a pot of chicken soup. With his mother's help, Rudie mixes and stirs and adds the secret ingredients because he knows that Mrs. Gittel likes her soup just a wee bit sweet. In addition to the sweets that Rudie secretly drops into the pot, the soup is sweetened with stories Rudie tells about the recipient while waiting for the soup to cook. When the soup's ready, Rudie helps his mother deliver it and then he waits for the magic. Sure enough, Mrs. Gittel is soon well enough to babysit and just in time because Rudie has a stomachache and needs her "snug-a-bugging." (32 pages)

Where it's reviewed:
Booklist, September 1, 2002, page 120
Bulletin of the Center for Children's Books, January 2003, page 202
School Library Journal, November 2002, page 124

Other books by the same author:
Fancy That, 2003
There Goes Lowell's Party!, 1998

Other books you might like:
Karen English, *Just Right Stew*, 1998
    Only granddaughter Victoria knows the secret ingredient to add to the stew cooking for Big Mama's birthday to assure that it tastes just right.
Sylvia Rosa-Casanova, *Mama Provi and the Pot of Rice*, 1997
    Each neighbor in Mama Provi's apartment building offers an ethnic food for her to take to her sick granddaughter.
Joan Rothenberg, *Matzah Ball Soup*, 1999
    While helping Grandma make matzah balls for the family's Seder, Rosie learns the tradition behind the four matzah balls in each bowl of chicken soup.

631

KAREN HESSE

Aleutian Sparrow

(New York: McElderry/Simon & Schuster, 2003)

Subject(s): World War II; Racially Mixed People; Moving, Household
Age range(s): Grades 6-10
Major character(s): Vera, Teenager
Time period(s): 1940s (1942-1945)
Locale(s): Unalaska Island, Alaska (Kashega village); Ward Lake, Alaska (near Ketchikan)

Summary: During World War II the Japanese attacks the Aleutian Islands, which prompts the United States government to move all the Aleutian Islanders to relocation camps more than a thousand miles away from their homes. Young Vera narrates the trek of her people as they leave their open, coastal homes to live in unsanitary conditions in forests that overwhelm them with leaves, water and gloom. One out of every four Aleuts dies in these camps, either from disease or alcoholism, and Vera watches as her mother leaves the camps for the honky tonk joints where she tries to earn a living. After three years in the camp, Vera finally returns to her home on Unalaska Island, but minus her mother and her best friend. Luckily there's a romantic interest in her life which, coupled with her joy at returning, outweighs the misery of the replacement camps in this novel in verse form. (158 pages)

Where it's reviewed:
Booklist, October 15, 2003, page 405
Horn Book, January 2004, page 82
Publishers Weekly, September 22, 2003, page 104
School Library Journal, October 2003, page 166
Voice of Youth Advocates, December 2003, page 394

Other books by the same author:
Witness, 2001
Stowaway, 2000
A Light in the Storm: The Civil War Diary of Amelia Martin, 1999

Other books you might like:
Margaret Craven, *I Heard the Owl Call My Name*, 1973
    A minister who's battling cancer finds that living among the Kwakiutl Indians helps him accept the inevitability of his death.
Gary Paulsen, *Dogsong*, 1985
    Russell Susskit, a young Eskimo boy, comes of age as he undertakes a perilous dogsled journey seeking the heritage of his ancestors.
Yoshiko Uchida, *Journey Home*, 1978
    Following relocation during World War II, a Japanese American family finally returns to their home and their normal lifestyle.
Eric Walters, *Caged Eagles*, 2000
    Tadashi's family is rounded up, with other Japanese-Canadians, and held at a detention camp in Vancouver.

632

AMY HEST
ANITA JERAM, Illustrator

Don't You Feel Well, Sam?

(Cambridge, MA: Candlewick Press, 2002)

Subject(s): Illness; Mothers and Sons; Animals/Bears
Age range(s): Grades K-2
Major character(s): Sam, Bear, Son; Mrs. Bear, Mother, Bear
Time period(s): Indeterminate
Locale(s): Fictional Country

Summary: As Mrs. Bear tucks Sam into bed on a cold, cold night she notices a little cough. Sam denies having a cough although he admits he doesn't feel well. Reluctantly, he swallows the cough medicine and then enjoys a cup of tea with honey. Then Sam sits in the big chair with his mama, listening to a story and waiting for snow. All night they wait, sleeping in the chair and in the morning they go out to make a snow bear. (32 pages)

Where it's reviewed:
Booklist, November 15, 2002, page 602
Publishers Weekly, July 22, 2002, page 176
School Library Journal, September 2002, page 193

Other books by the same author:
You Can Do It, Sam, 2003
The Friday Nights of Nana, 2001 (Smithsonian's Notable Books for Children)
Off to School, Baby Duck!, 1999 (Booklist Editors' Choice)

Other books you might like:
Vera Rosenberry, *When Vera Was Sick*, 1998
    Vera is miserable when she's sick, but as soon as she's better she's eager to play outside.
Rosemary Wells, *Felix Feels Better*, 2001
    After two spoonfuls of Dr. Duck's ''Happy Tummy'' medicine and a long nap, Felix is ready to make plans for an exciting day.
Jane Yolen, *How Do Dinosaurs Get Well Soon?*, 2003
    Parents care lovingly for their sick offspring.

633

AMY HEST
JILL BARTON, Illustrator

Make the Team, Baby Duck!

(Cambridge, MA: Candlewick Press, 2002)

Subject(s): Animals/Ducks; Self-Confidence; Sports/Swimming
Age range(s): Grades K-1
Major character(s): Baby Duck, Duck, Sister (older); Grampa, Duck, Grandfather
Time period(s): Indeterminate
Locale(s): Fictional Country

Summary: No amount of encouragement from her parents can get Baby Duck into the water this summer. She sits on the edge of the pool and longingly watches the swim team, wishing she had arms that didn't become tired so she, too, could be on the team. Grampa joins her and compliments the way that her strong feet make ripples in the water. He assures her that even champion swimmers sometimes have tired arms or swallow water and cough. Feeling more confident, Baby Duck leaps into the pool to join the team and she doesn't swallow any water. She swims and swims and her arms do not become tired. Baby Duck makes the team! (28 pages)

Where it's reviewed:
Booklist, August 2002, page 1971
Publishers Weekly, June 17, 2002, page 67
School Library Journal, September 2002, page 193

Other books by the same author:
Baby Duck and the Photo Album, 2004
Baby Duck and the Cozy Blanket, 2002

Off to School, Baby Duck!, 1999 (School Library Journal Best Books)
In the Rain with Baby Duck, 1995 (Boston Globe/Horn Book Fanfare Award)

Other books you might like:
Toni Buzzeo, *Little Loon and Papa*, 2004
    With support from Papa Little Loon masters a critical life skill, diving.
Anne Gutman, *Gaspard at the Seashore*, 2002
    Gaspard goes to camp to achieve his goal of being a champion windsurfer but learns he must know how to swim first.
Anne Rockwell, *Katie Catz Makes a Splash*, 2003
    Patsy Polarbear helps Katie overcome her fear of the water so she can enjoy a pool party with friends.

634

JAMES A. HETLEY

The Summer Country

(New York: Ace, 2002)

Subject(s): Fantasy; Magic; Self-Acceptance
Age range(s): Grades 10-Adult
Major character(s): Maureen Anne ''Mo'' Pierce, Sister; Cynthia Josephine ''Jo'' Pierce, Sister; Brian Albion, Knight
Time period(s): 2000s (2002)
Locale(s): Naskeag Falls, Maine (Summer Country)

Summary: Maureen works at a dead end job as a night clerk in a convenience store, but she tells herself it's really for the best as her emotional scars have left her unsuited for anything more. Walking home one night, Maureen is attacked by a stranger. When her gun misfires, Mo is ready for the worst, but a second man appears out of the darkness, kills the stranger and is unfazed when the dead man bursts into flames. Her rescuer introduces himself as Brian Albion and tells Maureen that she has the old blood, the blood of magic that makes her a target for those who would use any untrained magic carrier. Maureen is reluctant to believe any man, but as the threats multiply, and her sister Jo becomes a target as well, Mo comes to see Brian as her best ally. (368 pages)

Where it's reviewed:
Booklist, October 1, 2002, page 309
Chronicle, November 2002, page 30
Kliatt, March 2003, page 34
Library Journal, October 15, 2002, page 98
Publishers Weekly, October 7, 2002, page 57

Other books by the same author:
The Winter Oak, 2004

Other books you might like:
Holly Black, *Tithe: A Modern Faerie Tale*, 2002
    Tough girl Kaye finds herself in over her head when she returns to her childhood home, discovers the fairies are still there and learns that she is a pixie.
Pamela Green, *Tam Lin*, 1992
    Janet is an ordinary college student who ends up dueling with the Queen of Faerie.

Simon R. Green, *Drinking Midnight Wine*, 2002

Toby goes from bookstore clerk to knight-errant in one fatal walk when he passes into the land of Mysterie.

635

KIMBERLEY HEUSTON

Dante's Daughter

(Asheville, NC: Front Street Books, 2003)

Subject(s): Fathers and Daughters; Family Life
Age range(s): Grades 9-12
Major character(s): Antonia ''Bice'' Alighieri, Artist, Daughter (of Dante); Dante Alighieri, Writer (poet), Historical Figure; Ambrogio Lorenzetti, Spouse (of Antonia)
Time period(s): 14th century
Locale(s): Florence, Italy; Siena, Italy; Paris, France

Summary: When political upheaval occurs in Florence, Dante is exiled for his views, his wife moves to her parents and his children are scattered among relatives. Antonia, called Bice, is sent to live with an artist uncle in Siena where her talent and love for painting are awakened in this protective, stable family. All that changes when her father decides to travel to Paris and Bice accompanies him, staying in a convent while he studies and writes. Used to her inattentive parents, though disliking their lack of concern, Bice marries a childhood sweetheart, Ambrogio, and then raises three daughters until tragedy strikes. At that point Bice returns to a convent and spends the rest of her life there in this fictionalized account of ''Dante's daughter.'' (302 pages)

Where it's reviewed:
Booklist, January 2004, page 844
Library Media Connection, March 2004, page 67
Publishers Weekly, December 15, 2003, page 74
School Library Journal, February 2004, page 148
Voice of Youth Advocates, April 2004, page 46

Other books by the same author:
The Shakeress, 2002

Other books you might like:
Deborah Ellis, *A Company of Fools*, 2002
Sent to amuse the citizens of their plague-ridden village, the choirboys of St. Luc fear their prize singer is being used to fill the abbey's coffers.
Tiffany Grace, *My Father Had a Daughter: Judith Shakespeare's Tale*, 2003
Judith and her twin brother Hamnet adjust to their capricious father William Shakespeare who's seldom home and when he is, scribbles on parchment.
Mirjam Pressler, *Shylock's Daughter*, 2001
The desire to escape her Jewish ghetto is so strong that Jessica leaves behind her religion and her father, though not his savings.

636

KIMBERLEY HEUSTON

The Shakeress

(Asheville, NC: Front Street, 2002)

Subject(s): Religion; Orphans; Mormons
Age range(s): Grades 7-10
Major character(s): Naomi Hull, Orphan, Teenager; Joseph Fairweather, Wealthy, Fiance(e)
Time period(s): 1820s; 1830s (1828-1835)
Locale(s): Portsmouth, New Hampshire; St. Johnsbury, Vermont

Summary: Orphaned after her parents and youngest brother are killed in a fire, Naomi and her three remaining siblings move in with their aunt who promptly decides to send Naomi to work in the mills. Realizing this is not the life they wish to lead, the four orphans join a Shaker community where they each thrive. Though Naomi becomes an accomplished herbalist, after several years she decides she needs to have more purpose in her life and travels to Vermont to continue as an herbalist while she lives with a family there. After witnessing several miraculous healings, Naomi finds herself drawl to the new religion of the Mormon. Now she must choose between staying with her fianci Joseph or serving God's purpose by joining a newly established Mormon community in Ohio in this first novel. (216 pages)

Where it's reviewed:
Booklist, June 2002, page 1706
New York Times Book Review, May 19, 2002, page 19
Publishers Weekly, April 1, 2002, page 84
School Library Journal, July 2002, page 120
Voice of Youth Advocates, August 2002, page 192

Other books you might like:
Louann Gaeddert, *Hope*, 1995
When they're left alone, Hope and John are given to a Shaker community; John thrives, but Hope leaves as soon as her father shows up.
Janet Hickman, *Susannah*, 1998
After Susannah's mother dies, she and her father move to a Shaker community, but Susannah isn't happy and asks to leave.
Jane Yolen, *The Gift of Sarah Barker*, 1981
Although marriage is forbidden in their Shaker community, Sister Sarah Barker and brother Able meet and fall in love.

637

CARL HIAASEN

Hoot

(New York: Knopf/Random House, 2002)

Subject(s): Endangered Species; Environmental Problems; Animals/Owls
Age range(s): Grades 6-9
Major character(s): Roy Eberhardt, Student—Middle School; Dana Matherson, Student—Middle School, Bully; Beatrice Leep, Soccer Player, Student—Middle School; Na-

poleon ''Mullet Fingers'', Stepbrother (of Beatrice), Runaway

Time period(s): 2000s

Locale(s): Coconut Cove, Florida

Summary: Newly arrived in Florida, Roy's not ready to admit that Florida could be better than Montana, the last state his family lived in, though he notes that all bullies are the same. Riding the school bus, he searches daily for ways to deflect the bullying tactics of Dana Matherson, though he's not always successful. Roy notices a barefoot boy who often runs beside the bus and later, after befriending Beatrice, finds out the boy is her stepbrother and is known as ''Mullet Fingers'' for his ability to catch mullet fish. Roy and Mullet Fingers become unlikely allies as each fights to protect the burrowing owls who live on a plot of land being developed by Mother Paula's All-American Pancake House. Mullet Fingers wages an all-out battle, pulling up the survey stakes, putting alligators in the portable toilets and releasing cottonmouth snakes to scare the guard dogs. Eventually Roy takes their battle to the local government and enlists the aid of his parents, Beatrice's soccer team and a former Miss America runner-up to halt construction of Mother Paula's All-American Pancake House. (292 pages)

Where it's reviewed:

Booklist, October 15, 2002, page 405

Bulletin of the Center for Children's Books, November 2002, page 11

Horn Book, November 2002, page 759

School Library Journal, August 2002, page 188

Voice of Youth Advocates, October 2002, page 279

Awards the book has won:

Newbery Honor Book, 2003

ALA Best Books for Young Adults, 2003

Other books by the same author:

Skinny Dip, 2004 (adult title)

Basket Case, 2002 (adult title)

Sick Puppy, 2000 (adult title)

Lucky You, 1997 (adult title)

Tourist Season, 1996 (adult title)

Other books you might like:

Sheila Cole, *The Canyon*, 2002

Zach organizes petition signing in his community to fight development in their canyon; when that doesn't work, his friend Trevor pulls up the survey stakes.

David Klass, *California Blue*, 1994

Thrilled to discover a new species of butterfly, John's delight ends when he realizes the butterfly's rarity will cost his father his lumber job.

Gloria Skurzynski, *Deadly Waters*, 1999

The theft of a camera belonging to three young people sets off an investigation into the deaths of some manatees.

638

JANET HICKMAN

Ravine

(New York: Greenwillow, 2002)

Subject(s): Fantasy; Space and Time; Animals/Dogs

Age range(s): Grades 4-7

Major character(s): Jeremy Ervin, Time Traveler; Quinn DaSilva, Time Traveler; Austin Ervin, Brother (of Jeremy), Time Traveler; Richelle DaSilva, Sister (of Quinn), Time Traveler; Ulf, Slave; Harket, Wizard; Old Berta, Wizard

Time period(s): Indeterminate

Locale(s): United States; Alternate Universe

Summary: Warned by his mother not to enter the ravine near their home, Jeremy doesn't know what to do when his beloved collie Duchess slips away into the fog surrounding the off-limits place. Worry over his dog outweighs worry over his mother's possible anger and Jeremy follows, only to slip into an opening to a parallel world. There he finds Ulf, a lonely young boy about his age, who's forced to labor for King Ludwig. Befriended by the wizard Harket and his wife Old Berta, Ulf has a place to sleep but not much else of his own. When he first sees Duchess, whom he calls Magic, he pets and talks to her until she disappears back up the ravine, returning to Jeremy's world. When Jeremy, Quinn, Austin, Richelle and Duchess are trapped in the parallel world, they are unable to return home unless they leave behind something of value in this tale of time travel. (215 pages)

Where it's reviewed:

Booklist, July 2002, page 1846

Horn Book, May 2002, page 331

School Library Journal, October 2002, page 164

Other books by the same author:

Susannah, 1998

Jericho, 1994

Other books you might like:

Gillian Chan, *The Carved Box*, 2001

Newly arrived in Canada, Callum buys a large Newfoundland dog and the carved box that accompanies this magical creature.

Lesley Howarth, *Maphead*, 1994

Maphead leaves his parallel universe to travel to Earth to find his human mother, but first must learn to speak English.

Brian Jacques, *Castaways of the Flying Dutchman*, 2001

Saved from the curse of an avenging angel, Ben and his dog Ned communicate telepathically as they travel the world doing good.

Diana Wynne Jones, *The Lives of Christopher Chant*, 1988

As he dreams, Christopher travels to distant and fascinating worlds.

639

TANUJA DESAI HIDIER

Born Confused

(New York: Scholastic, 2002)

Subject(s): Identity; Photography

Age range(s): Grades 9-12

Major character(s): Dimple Rohitbhai Lala, 17-Year-Old, Photographer; Gwyndolyne ''Gwyn'', 17-Year-Old; Karshum ''Karsh'' Kapoor, Student—College

Time period(s): 2000s

Locale(s): Springfield, New Jersey

Summary: Born feet first, Dimple is certain this is why she's always confused, when in reality it's her double heritage of being born in India yet raised in New Jersey. This confusion spills over into her photography where she doubts her ability and isn't encouraged to pursue her hobby. Her best friend Gwyn is the antithesis of Dimple for she's confident, blonde-haired, blue-eyed and rich, but none of that has mattered to either girl until this summer. Dimple's parents feel she needs to meet a suitable boy so they introduce her to Karsh, whom she immediately rejects. By the time Gwyn decides he's wonderful and asks for background on the Indian culture, Dimple realizes that Karsh is more than suitable, he's perfect, but what is she to do about Gwyn? (413 pages)

Where it's reviewed:
Booklist, December 15, 2002, page 753
Bulletin of the Center for Children's Books, February 2003, page 237
Publishers Weekly, October 28, 2002, page 72
School Library Journal, December 2002, page 136
Voice of Youth Advocates, February 2003, page 472

Awards the book has won:
Bulletin of the Center for Children's Books Blue Ribbons, 2003

Other books you might like:
Chitra Civakaruni, *Arranged Marriage*, 1995
    A collection of short stories that explores the differences between the lives of women living in India and in the United States.
Rachna Gilmore, *A Group of One*, 2001
    When Tara's grandmother comes to visit, her teachings about Tara's East Indian heritage help her understand why her parents immigrated to Canada.
Melita Perkins, *The Sunita Experiment*, 1993
    Just as East Indian Sunita begins to feel totally Americanized, her grandparents arrive for a yearlong visit and change Sunita's whole life.
Indi Rana, *The Roller Birds of Kampur*, 1993
    Raised in Britain but of East Indian heritage, Sheila is caught between Eastern and Western cultures.

640

ELIZABETH STARR HILL
LESLEY LIU, Illustrator

Chang and the Bamboo Flute
(New York: Farrar Straus Giroux, 2002)

Subject(s): Animals/Birds; Mutism; Resourcefulness
Age range(s): Grades 2-5
Major character(s): Chang, Child (mute), Friend; Mei Mei, Child, Friend; Bo Won, Blind Person, Storyteller
Time period(s): Indeterminate Past
Locale(s): Li River, China

Summary: A rainy summer create problems for Chang's family when debris carried downstream in the flood waters of the rising river on which they live destroys part of the cabin on their houseboat. For a few days they find shelter in the barn of Mei Mei's family but once the sun shines, again they return to their home on the river. The damage is more extensive than they originally realized—for many of their meager belongings, including their wok, have been carried away by the floodwaters. Seeking to replace the wok, Chang is willing to trade away his flute, the means by which this mute boy communicates with family, friends and the family's cormorants. At the market, Bo Won encourages Chang to play his flute and, to his surprise, listeners gather and throw coins at his feet. When he stops playing, Chang discovers that his gift for self-expression through music has earned enough money to purchase a new wok for his family. (60 pages)

Where it's reviewed:
Booklist, October 15, 2002, page 405
Horn Book Guide, Spring 2003, page 67
Kirkus Reviews, October 1, 2002, page 1470
Publishers Weekly, October 28, 2002, page 75

Awards the book has won:
Notable Social Studies Trade Books for Young People, 2003

Other books by the same author:
Bird Boy, 1999 (Parent's Choice Gold Award Winner)
Broadway Chances, 1992
Evan's Corner, 1991

Other books you might like:
Jan Brett, *Daisy Comes Home*, 2002
    Mei Mei's favorite hen Daisy floats away in a market basket on the rain-swollen Li River.
Marjorie Flack, *The Story about Ping*, 1933
    Ping, alone on the Yangtze River, searches for his family's boat and finds new friends and adventure with fishing boats and their trained birds.
Eleanor Frances Lattimore, *Little Pear: The Story of a Little Chinese Boy*, 1991
    This reissue of a 1931 classic tells of five-year-old Little Pear growing up in China in the early 1900s.

641

KIRKPATRICK HILL
PATRICK FARICY, Illustrator

Minuk: Ashes in the Pathway
(Middleton, WI: American Girl/Pleasant Company, 2002)

Series: Girls of Many Lands
Subject(s): Eskimos; Missionaries; Gender Roles
Age range(s): Grades 4-8
Major character(s): Minuk, 12-Year-Old; Mr. Hoff, Religious (missionary); Mrs. Hoff, Spouse
Time period(s): 1890s
Locale(s): Alaska (along the Kuskokwim River)

Summary: The United States has recently bought Alaska from Russia and the first white missionary couple arrives in Minuk's Yup'ik village. Though the villagers have seen a white man before, they are very curious about Mrs. Hoff and their child. Minuk assists the Hoffs with household chores and learns a little about the white culture, which seems exceedingly strange to her. Though the villagers exhibit tolerance of the missionaries, the same cannot be said for the Hoffs who disapprove of the Yup'ik customs and life style. When an influenza epidemic rages through Minuk's village, it forces everyone to decide whether to become Americanized or return to their original way of life. (198 pages)

Where it's reviewed:
Booklist, October 1, 2002, page 326
Horn Book, January 2003, page 73
Publishers Weekly, August 26, 2002, page 69
School Library Journal, October 2002, page 164
Voice of Youth Advocates, February 2003, page 476

Other books by the same author:
Dancing at the Odinochka, 2005
The Year of Miss Agnes, 2000
Winter Camp, 1993

Other books you might like:
Jennifer Owings Dewey, *Minik's Story*, 2003
    Minik is curious about the white men who have come to her village, but when a missionary arrives, he is soon banished.
Mette Newth, *The Abduction*, 1989
    On their tribe's first walrus hunt of the season, three Inuit Eskimos are kidnapped by sailors and taken to Norway to be exhibited as curiosity items.
Paul Sullivan, *Maata's Journal*, 2003
    Raised a nomadic Inuit living near the Arctic, Maata witnesses the change in her people's culture when the white men force the Inuits from their land.

642

JUDY HINDLEY
IVAN BATES, Illustrator

Do Like a Duck Does!

(Cambridge, MA: Candlewick Press, 2002)

Subject(s): Animals/Ducks; Animals/Foxes; Stories in Rhyme
Age range(s): Preschool-Grade 1
Major character(s): Mama, Duck, Mother; Unnamed Character, Fox
Time period(s): Indeterminate
Locale(s): United States

Summary: Mama Duck proudly leads her five offspring as the ducklings imitate each of Mama's behaviors. Fox's attempt to pass himself off as a duck does not fool Mama. In order to protect her babies she sets tasks for Fox to show that he can "Do like a duck does . . . ," as Mama demands that Fox quack, eat bugs, and swim. The final test proves to be Fox's undoing as the ducklings swim to safety and bedraggled Fox struggles off the bottom of the pond and slinks home. (34 pages)

Where it's reviewed:
Booklist, March 1, 2002, page 1133
Bulletin of the Center for Children's Books, April 2002, page 282
Horn Book Guide, Fall 2002, page 331
Publishers Weekly, January 28, 2002, page 289
School Library Journal, April 2002, page 112

Awards the book has won:
Booklist Editors' Choice, 2002

Other books by the same author:
Does a Cow Say Boo?, 2002
The Best Thing about a Puppy, 1998
Isn't It Time?, 1996

Other books you might like:
Mem Fox, *Hattie and the Fox*, 1987
    When Hattie, a large hen, spots a fox lurking in the bushes and alerts the barnyard, the animals react in different ways.
Pat Hutchins, *Rosie's Walk*, 1968
    Unaware that a fox is following her Rosie enjoys her walk around the farmyard.
Martin Waddell, *Webster J. Duck*, 2001
    As newly hatched Webster searches for his mother, none of the animals he meets sound quite right until he hears a loud quack.

643

JUDY HINDLEY
BRITA GRANSTROM, Illustrator

Does a Cow Say Boo?

(Cambridge, MA: Candlewick Press, 2002)

Subject(s): Animals; Farm Life
Age range(s): Preschool-Kindergarten
Time period(s): 2000s
Locale(s): United States

Summary: Five children explore a farm seeking the animal that says boo. By·listening carefully they discover it's not a cow, a pig, or a dog. Cats, horses and owls don't make a "boo!" sound either. Finally, after they rule out ducks, sheep, the rooster, chickens and birds they realize they are the only creatures on the farm that say, "Boo!" (28 pages)

Where it's reviewed:
Booklist, June 2002, page 1738
Bulletin of the Center for Children's Books, October 2002, page 60
Publishers Weekly, May 13, 2002, page 69
School Library Journal, September 2002, page 194

Awards the book has won:
Center for Children's Books Best Books, 2002

Other books by the same author:
What's in Baby's Morning?, 2004
Can You Move Like an Elephant?, 2003
Rosy's Visitors, 2002

Other books you might like:
Stella Blackstone, *There's a Cow in the Cabbage Patch*, 2001
    In a rhyming story a farmer finds all the animals out of their assigned places.
Bernard Most, *Cock-a-Doodle-Moo!*, 1996
    When rooster loses his voice and is unable to awaken the farm a helpful cow almost masters the art of crowing.
Phyllis Root, *One Windy Wednesday*, 1997
    One Wednesday on the farm the wind is so strong that the sound blows from one animal to another making the cows oink and the ducks moo.

644

ODO HIRSCH

Hazel Green

(New York: Bloomsbury USA Children's Books, 2003)

Subject(s): Friendship; City and Town Life; Apartments
Age range(s): Grades 3-5
Major character(s): Hazel Green, Student—Elementary School, Neighbor; Yakov Plonsk, Student—Elementary School, Neighbor; Mr. Winkel, Aged Person
Time period(s): Indeterminate Past
Locale(s): Australia

Summary: Hazel cannot understand why children do not march in the annual Frogg Day parade. At least children from the Moodey Building, the very apartment building in which the parade's famous namesake was born many years ago, should be allowed to participate. When Hazel learns that children did at one time march in the parade she promotes the idea to the other young residents of the building and courageously faces grumpy Mr. Winkel in order to gain permission for their inclusion. Reluctantly Mr. Winkel agrees and the children develop a plan to build a replica of the Moodey Building atop a handcart. Yakov sees the plan and declares that it will be blown over in the slightest breeze because it is too tall. Hazel cannot understand Yakov's mathematical proof but she recognizes he's probably right in his calculations. No one else believes her, Mr. Winkel bans her from the parade for causing trouble by even suggesting the float might fail and Hazel has to figure out how to get herself and the float into the parade, ready to march. Originally published in Australia in 2000. (190 pages)

Where it's reviewed:
Booklist, June 2003, page 1776
Bulletin of the Center for Children's Books, October 2003, page 63
School Library Journal, June 2003, page 100

Other books by the same author:
Bartlett and the City of Flames, 2004
Bartlett and the Forest of Plenty, 2004
Yoss, 2004
Have Courage, Hazel Green!, 2001
Something's Fishy, Hazel Green!, 2000

Other books you might like:
Mary Haynes, *The Great Pretenders*, 1990
    As the new kid in town Molly unwittingly offends the mayor's daughter and now may be unable to march in the Fourth of July parade.
Gertrude Chandler Warner, *The Mystery of the Stolen Boxcar*, 1995
    The Alden children have a problem when they discover the boxcar they plan to use in the town's parade has been stolen.
Laurence Yep, *When the Circus Came to Town*, 2001
    A community effort helps Ursula, recovering from smallpox, celebrate the Chinese New Year in the small town of Whistle, MT.

645

RON HIRSCH
PIERRE PRATT, Illustrator

No, No, Jack!

(New York: Dial Books for Young Readers, 2002)

Subject(s): Animals/Dogs; Games; Family
Age range(s): Preschool-Kindergarten
Major character(s): Jack, Dog
Time period(s): 2000s (2002)
Locale(s): United States

Summary: Jack plays a game with his family by hiding things in a closet. Each time a family member opens the door, Jack grabs the missing object and runs away while his family calls for him to return it. The last item found is a kitten and this time Jack is allowed to keep it. The next day both Jack and the kitten hide in the closet until the family finds them. (20 pages)

Where it's reviewed:
Booklist, January 1, 2002, page 864
Horn Book Guide, Fall 2002, page 303
Kirkus Reviews, January 15, 2002, page 106
Publishers Weekly, April 22, 2002, page 72
School Library Journal, July 2002, page 92

Awards the book has won:
IRA Children's Choices, 2003

Other books you might like:
Alyssa Satin Capucilli, *Biscuit's Big Friend*, 2003
    Although Biscuit is a small puppy he becomes friends with Sam, a much larger dog, and tries to follow his actions.
Dayle Ann Dodds, *Where's Pup?*, 2003
    A clown searches the circus grounds for his missing dog.
Eric Hill, *Where's Spot?*, 2000
    During her search for Spot a mother dog finds eight animals hiding before locating her pup in this 20th anniversary edition of the title.

646

MINFONG HO

The Stone Goddess

(New York: Orchard, 2003)

Series: First Person Fiction
Subject(s): Sisters; Emigration and Immigration; Dancing
Age range(s): Grades 6-10
Major character(s): Nakri Sokha, Immigrant, Teenager; Teeda Sokha, Sister, Dancer; Boran Sokha, Brother (of Teeda and Nakri)
Time period(s): 1970s
Locale(s): Phnom Penh, Cambodia; Thailand (refugee camp along border); Philadelphia, Pennsylvania

Summary: Nakri and her older sister Teeda learn Cambodian classical dance, though Nakri feels that she'll never be as good as her sister who performs her hand and foot movements effortlessly. Their lives are disrupted when the Khmer Rouge take over Cambodia and force all educated people out of Phnom Penh, sending Nakri and her family to the country to stay with her grandparents. Her father is taken away and never seen again while Nakri, Teeda and their older brother Boran are sent to labor camps, leaving behind their mother and younger brother. After four years of near-starvation and bouts of malaria, only Nakri and Boran are left for Teeda has died, but not before once more dancing the forbidden role of the goddess of the sea, who picks up dewdrops one by one. Nakri's life dissolves after her adored sister dies, though her memories sustain her during the labor camp days. When the Khmer Rouge are finally defeated, Nakri and Boran return to their mother; together again, the family decides to leave their native country in this work originally titled *Gathering the Dew*. (201 pages)

Where it's reviewed:
Bulletin of the Center for Children's Books, April 2003, page 315
Horn Book, May 2003, page 348
Kliatt, January 2003, page 8
Riverbank Review, Spring 2003, page 42
School Library Journal, March 2003, page 233

Other books by the same author:
The Clay Marble, 1991
Rice without Rain, 1990

Other books you might like:
Allan Baillie, *Little Brother*, 1992
   Escaping from their Khmer Rouge work camp, Vithy and his older brother are separated, leaving "little brother" Vithy to survive on his own.
Sook Nyul Choi, *Gathering of Pearls*, 1994
   A freshman in college in New York, Korean Sookan adjusts to cultural differences, homesickness, and the loss of her dear mother.
An Na, *A Step from Heaven*, 2001
   Young Ju overcomes cultural norms and steps forward to save her mother from her father's harsh beatings.

647

ROBIN HOBB

Fool's Errand
(New York: Bantam/Spectra, 2002)

Series: Tawny Man. Book 1
Subject(s): Fantasy; Adventure and Adventurers
Age range(s): Grades 10-Adult
Major character(s): FitzChivalry Farseer, Spy; Fool, Psychic; Chade Fallstar, Spy; Dutiful Farseer, Royalty
Time period(s): Indeterminate
Locale(s): Six Duchies, Fictional Country

Summary: FitzChivalry Farseer, prince's bastard and former royal assassin, has retreated to a small cottage in the woods determined to give up the political intrigues he has come to see as hopeless. His decision is made easier by his bond to his Wit companion, Nighteyes, the wolf with whom he communicates mind-to-mind. Nighteyes approves of their almost wild life and is content in the pack of two. The flaw is Fitz's constant craving for the Skill, the magic he has inherited from the royal line, but rejected as too dangerous. The near-idyll comes to an end with the arrival of the enigmatic Fool, Fitz's friend from his days of service to the old king. The Fool brings a summons from another old acquaintance, Chade. It was Chade who trained Fitz as an assassin and it is as assassin that he calls him now, for the prince has disappeared and the kingdom hangs by a thread. (496 pages)

Where it's reviewed:
Booklist, December 15, 2001, page 709
Kirkus Reviews, October 15, 2001, page 1461
Publishers Weekly, December 10, 2001, page 56
Voice of Youth Advocates, February 2002, page 446

Other books by the same author:
Golden Fool, 2003 (Tawny Man Book 2)
Ship of Destiny, 2000
The Mad Ship, 1999

Other books you might like:
Mercedes Lackey, *Mad Maudlin*, 2003
   Another royal runaway, this time an elven prince, has hidden himself in the cold iron of New York City.
Robin McKinley, *Spindle's End*, 2000
   Briar Rose has a special ability to communicate with animals, which helps her to avoid the effects of her curse.
Martha Wells, *The Death of the Necromancer*, 1998
   Nicholas Valiarde, like FitzChivalry, should be a noble, but instead finds himself surviving in an unsavory occupation.

648

ROBIN HOBB

Golden Fool
(New York: Bantam/Spectra, 2003)

Series: Tawny Man. Book 2
Subject(s): Fantasy; Adventure and Adventurers; Friendship
Age range(s): Grades 10-Adult
Major character(s): FitzChivalry Farseer, Spy; Fool, Psychic; Chade Fallstar, Spy; Dutiful Farseer, Royalty
Time period(s): Indeterminate
Locale(s): Six Duchies, Fictional Country

Summary: FitzChivary Farseer has loyally served two kings and now seeks to do the same for the current Queen and Prince. Fitz is a royal bastard himself who, denied any legitimate role in the kingdom, finds himself thrust into actions that, again and again, are decisive for the kingdom. Maybe the weird beliefs of the mysterious Fool, who insists that he and Fitz are the pivotal figures for the direction the future will take, are true. The Fool has been around almost as long as Fitz, and certainly knows things to which not even master-spy Chade. The Fool is currently disguised as Lord Golden, and Fitz, whom most believe dead, masquerades as Tom Badgerlock, Golden's servant cum bodyguard. Prince Dutiful is pressured to marry a princess from the barbaric Out Islands; violence is directed at those with Wit-magic, the ability to communicate with animals; and Chade demands a coterie of Skill magic-users for the Prince. It is Fitz, with his Wit and Skill, who can uncover the Fool's secret knowledge of the Islands. But can he maintain his bond with the Fool if he breaks the trust that has supported their friendship? (520 pages)

Where it's reviewed:
Booklist, November 15, 2002, page 584
Kirkus Reviews, November 1, 2002, page 1578
Library Journal, January 2003, page 164
Publishers Weekly, November 18, 2002, page 46

Other books by the same author:
Fool's Errand, 2002 (Tawny Man Book 1)
Ship of Magic, 1998
Assassin's Quest, 1997

Other books you might like:
Noel-Anne Brennan, *The Sword of the Land*, 2003
    Though Sithli saved Rislin's life, Rislin may need to break her promise to Sithli to be true to herself.
James A. Hetley, *The Summer Country*, 2002
    When Maureen starts talking about their magical abilities in the Summer Country, her sister Jo is convinced their whole relationship is in jeopardy.
Ursula K. Le Guin, *The Left Hand of Darkness*, 1969
    A visitor to an alien world finds himself estranged from his only friend when he is confronted with his friend's sexual bimorphism.

649

HOLLY HOBBIE, Author/Illustrator

Toot & Puddle: Charming Opal

(New York: Little, Brown and Company, 2003)

Subject(s): Fairies; Animals/Pigs; Cousins
Age range(s): Preschool-Grade 1
Major character(s): Puddle, Pig, Cousin (older); Opal, Pig, Cousin (younger); Toot, Pig, Friend
Time period(s): Indeterminate
Locale(s): Woodcock Pocket, Fictional Country

Summary: Opal arrives for a vacation in Woodcock Pocket with a very loose tooth. While swimming in Pocket Pond, Opal loses the tooth, but unfortunately she doesn't know where it is. Puddle, Toot and Opal search the sandy shores of the pond and Toot dives to the pond's bottom until he locates and retrieves the tooth. That night Opal goes to bed expecting the Tooth Fairy to visit while Toot and Puddle worry that the fairy may not know to look for Opal in Woodcock Pocket. Determined to stay awake all night and substitute if the Tooth Fairy does not appear, Toot and Puddle instead fall asleep and awaken to Opal's cry. Nervously, Toot and Puddle approach Opal's room. With relief they see her excitedly showing off her shiny new quarter. (32 pages)

Where it's reviewed:
Publishers Weekly, July 21, 2003, page 194
School Library Journal, December 2003, page 114

Awards the book has won:
New York Times Best Illustrated Books, 2003

Other books by the same author:
Toot & Puddle: The New Friend, 2004
Toot & Puddle: The Top of the World, 2002
Toot & Puddle: Welcome to Woodcock Pocket, 2001

Other books you might like:
Pamela Duncan Edwards, *Dear Tooth Fairy*, 2003
    Concerned that she has not yet lost a tooth six-year-old Claire writes letters to the Tooth Fairy about her worries.
Charlotte Middleton, *Tabitha's Terrifically Tough Tooth*, 2001
    Tabitha's strategies for removing a loose tooth are creative but ineffective. A sneeze, however, propels the tooth across the room.
Jane O'Connor, *Dear Tooth Fairy*, 2002
    In a beginning reader Robby writes to the Tooth Fairy in hopes that she can help him lose a tooth before Class Picture Day.
Hans Wilhelm, *I Lost My Tooth!*, 1999
    Although Puppy swallows his loose tooth while eating he verifies the loss to the Tooth Fairy by leaving a photograph of his smile under his pillow.

650

VALERIE HOBBS

Sonny's War

(New York: Frances Foster/Farrar Straus Giroux, 2002)

Subject(s): Vietnam War; Brothers and Sisters; Small Town Life
Age range(s): Grades 7-10
Major character(s): Corin ''Cory'' Davies, 15-Year-Old; Sonny Davies, Brother (of Cory), Military Personnel; Marion Taylor Lawrence, Teacher
Time period(s): 1960s
Locale(s): Ojala, California

Summary: Struggling to make ends meet, Cory helps her mother in her family's small restaurant while her brother Sonny decides enlisting in the army will add more funds to the family coffers, while removing another mouth to feed. Cory's dad has just died unexpectedly of a heart attack and she feels as though her safe world is gone, especially when Sonny receives orders for Vietnam. At school, Mr. Lawrence is her new social studies teacher and he revs up his students, inspiring them to read the newspaper, watch the TV news and protest the Vietnam War. Mr. Lawrence's ideas are a little too liberal for Cory's small town and he's released from his contract by the school board. Cory has a crush on Mr. Lawrence and attends an antiwar demonstration in hopes of seeing him. Unfortunately, she sees him torch an army recruiting office, which crumples her crush as she realizes that Mr. Lawrence is not all good. Later she finds that his wealthy family used their connections to keep him from being prosecuted for his act. She rethinks her feelings about the war, especially when Sonny returns home wounded, but alive. (215 pages)

Where it's reviewed:
Booklist, November 1, 2002, page 484
Bulletin of the Center for Children's Books, November 2002, page 111
Horn Book, November 2002, page 760
School Library Journal, November 2002, page 168
Voice of Youth Advocates, December 2002, page 382

Awards the book has won:
Horn Book Fanfare, 2002

Other books by the same author:
Letting Go of Bobby James, or, How I Found My Self of Steam, 2004
Stefan's Story, 2003
Tender, 2001

Other books you might like:
Nancy Antle, *Lost in the War*, 1998
    The Vietnam War cost Lisa dearly, from her father's death to her mother's nightmares, and she doesn't relish having to study it in school.
Kelly Easton, *The Life History of a Star*, 2001
    Kristin's whole family is affected when her former All-American brother David returns from Vietnam physically and mentally disabled.
Garret Freymann-Weyr, *My Heartbeat*, 2002
    Shaken by someone asking Ellen if her brother Link and his friend James are a couple, Ellen wants to find out who her brother really is.
Theresa Nelson, *And One for All*, 1989
    Geraldine's world changes forever when her brother enlists in the Marines and heads for Vietnam.
Margaret I. Rostkowski, *The Best of Friends*, 1989
    Three good friends react to the Vietnam War in different ways: one enlists, one burns his draft card and one participates in protest marches.

651

VALERIE HOBBS

Stefan's Story

(New York: Frances Foster Books/Farrar Straus Giroux, 2003)

Subject(s): Environmental Problems; Physically Handicapped; Friendship
Age range(s): Grades 6-8
Major character(s): Stefan Millington Crouch III, Handicapped, 13-Year-Old; Carolina Lewis, 8th Grader; Hank, Fiance(e) (of Melanie), Lumberjack; Melanie Lewis, Mother (of Carolina)
Time period(s): 2000s
Locale(s): Haskell's Bay, Oregon

Summary: It's been two years since Carolina and Stefan saw one another and Stefan worries that their friendship might have changed as he flies to Oregon for the marriage of Carolina's mother Melanie. Stefan has reason to worry as he's older and he's seen how the girls react to him in his wheelchair, but the minute he's with Carolina's family, he realizes that their feelings for him haven't changed at all. Melanie is so happy with her fiance Hank, and Hank's great with Stefan, quietly assisting him without calling attention to his deeds. Carolina and Stefan become embroiled in another environmental controversy when Hank's company, Coastal Lumber, is about to cut down an old-growth forest. The two teens protest against this cutting, even though they know Hank needs the job. When someone cuts the brake lines in Hank's truck, he's injured and police consider the action attempted murder. Carolina and Stefan continue their protest with Stefan even resorting to physical action to halt the saws. (165 pages)

Where it's reviewed:
Booklist, September 15, 2003, page 236
Journal of Adolescent and Adult Literacy, May 2004, page 707
Kirkus Reviews, August 15, 2003, page 1074
School Library Journal, August 2003, page 160
Voice of Youth Advocates, February 2004, page 491

Other books by the same author:
Sonny's War, 2002
Charlie's Run, 2001
Tender, 2001
Carolina Crow Girl, 1999

Other books you might like:
Patricia Calvert, *Picking Up the Pieces*, 1993
    Filled with pity at being in a wheelchair after a motorcycle accident, Megan regains her self-confidence after meeting Harris.
Elizabeth Feuer, *Paper Doll*, 1990
    Leslie's interest in Jeff, a young man with cerebral palsy, leads to family arguments.
Cynthia Voigt, *Izzy, Willy-Nilly*, 1986
    Cheerleader Izzy's life changes when an automobile accident leaves her an amputee.

652

WILL HOBBS

Jackie's Wild Seattle

(New York: HarperCollins, 2003)

Subject(s): Aunts and Uncles; Brothers and Sisters; Wildlife Rescue
Age range(s): Grades 5-8
Major character(s): Shannon Young, 14-Year-Old; Cody Young, Child; Neal, Animal Lover, Cancer Patient; Tyler Tucker, 15-Year-Old, Abuse Victim; Jackie, Animal Lover
Time period(s): 2000s
Locale(s): Seattle, Washington

Summary: With their physician parents in Pakistan and Afghanistan aiding Doctors without Borders, Shannon and her brother Cody are in Seattle with their Uncle Neal. He currently volunteers for a wildlife rescue and rehabilitation center rather than working for Boeing as an aeronautical engineer. The three live with owner Jackie at the rehab center Jackie's Wild Seattle and spend their days rescuing wild animals. If they're not picking up injured animals from vets, they're looking for raccoons and possums trapped in houses, picking up an injured seal before the tide can take it away, or retrieving a hawk caught in a net. Uncle Neal is injured during the hawk rescue and Shannon and Cody, under Neal's tutelage, take over many subsequent rescues. It's a good summer for all as Cody overcomes his obsession with disasters, caused by the events of 9/11; Uncle Neal reveals his battle with cancer, which is now in remission; and fellow volunteer Tyler, doing community service at the shelter, finally opens up about his abusive home life in this spirited tale of adventure. (200 pages)

Where it's reviewed:
Booklist, June 2003, page 1776
Bulletin of the Center for Children's Books, May 2003, page 363
Kirkus Reviews, March 15, 2003, page 468
School Library Journal, May 2003, page 153
Voice of Youth Advocates, August 2003, page 224

Other books by the same author:
Leaving Protection, 2004
Wild Man Island, 2003
Down the Yukon, 2001
Jason's Gold, 1999
Maze, 1998

Other books you might like:
Melvin Burgess, *Kite*, 2000
   Told to destroy the eggs of an endangered bird called a kite, Tom keeps them; when one hatches, he raises the bird but needs help to train her.
M.E. Kerr, *Snakes Don't Miss Their Mothers*, 2003
   The animals at the Critters shelter offer their opinions about adoptions, potential owners and one another.
Deborah Savage, *Summer Hawk*, 1999
   Finding an injured hawk, Taylor takes it to a doctor who runs a rehabilitation center and follows up her visit with an article about the center's work.
Bill Wallace, *Coyote Autumn*, 2000
   Though Brad raises a coyote pup to be the dog he wants, he realizes that Scooter is a wild animal and takes him to a wildlife refuge.

653

WILL HOBBS

Wild Man Island

(New York: HarperCollins, 2002)

Subject(s): Animals/Dogs; Wilderness Survival; Sports/Kayaking
Age range(s): Grades 6-9
Major character(s): Andy Galloway, 14-Year-Old; David ''Wild Man'' Atkins, Recluse, Scientist; Bear, Dog (Newfoundland)
Time period(s): 2000s
Locale(s): Admiralty Island, Alaska

Summary: Enjoying his kayaking vacation, Andy realizes he's near the spot where his father died nine years ago while searching for signs of early man in Alaska. He slips away from his group and easily kayaks to the site where his father died, only to be blown off course when a sudden gale arises on his return. Landing on wild and primitive Admiralty Island, Andy dines on fiddlehead ferns, berries and a fish dropped from a bird's talons. Lacking modern tools and additional clothes, he never gives up hope of signaling a plane. Delighted when a Newfoundland dog finds him, he's unsure about the cave to which the dog leads him, and even more concerned about the wild man who lives in that cave. Andy's growing friendship with the wild man, David, helps David attempt a small, tenuous relationship with civilization in order to continue the research begun by Andy's dad. (184 pages)

Where it's reviewed:
Booklist, April 15, 2002, page 1395
Horn Book, July 2002, page 462
Kliatt, March 2002, page 11
School Library Journal, May 2002, page 154
Voice of Youth Advocates, June 2002, page 118

Other books by the same author:
Jackie's Wild Seattle, 2003
Down the Yukon, 2001
Jason's Gold, 1999
Ghost Canoe, 1997
Far North, 1996

Other books you might like:
Ben Mikaelsen, *Touching Spirit Bear*, 2001
   Cole inherited his father's meanness and arrogance and finds he's been sent to an isolated Alaska island to rethink his ways.
Gary Paulsen, *Hatchet*, 1987
   Enroute to visit his father, Brian's plane crashes in the Canadian Northwoods; as the sole survivor, he relies on his hatchet to stay alive.
Will Weaver, *Memory Boy*, 2001
   Escaping falling volcanic ash, Miles and his family survive on the woodland lore he learned from an older man he once interviewed for a history project.

654

MARY ANN HOBERMAN
LAURA FORMAN, Illustrator

The Marvelous Mouse Man

(San Diego: Gulliver Books/Harcourt, Inc., 2002)

Subject(s): Animals/Mice; Problem Solving; Stories in Rhyme
Age range(s): Grades 1-4
Major character(s): Mouse Man, Aged Person, Trickster; Unnamed Character, Child
Time period(s): Indeterminate Past
Locale(s): Fictional Country

Summary: To rid the town of an infestation of mice the mayor offers a reward to anyone who can assure the mice leave the town forever. A peculiar old man accepts the challenge and soon the mice come from all around to follow the man and his odiferous fan out of town. A young girl and her cat watch Mouse Man suspiciously and, in the morning, lead the town's children in pursuit of the man. When they find him they also discover that all the pets have followed the man and the mice out of town. The town's people hasten to accost the man for taking their children and reluctantly agree to allow him to lead the mice back into town in order to have the children return. Now the town is back to its original problem for which the girl has a solution that satisfies everyone and solves a problem for the Mouse Man too. (40 pages)

Where it's reviewed:
Booklist, March 15, 2002, page 1262
Bulletin of the Center for Children's Books, May 2002, page 326
Horn Book Guide, Fall 2002, page 331
Publishers Weekly, March 18, 2002, page 102

School Library Journal, May 2002, page 117

Other books by the same author:
It's Simple, Said Simon, 2001
You Read to Me, I'll Read to You: Very Short Stories to Read Together, 2001
One of Each, 1997 (School Library Journal Best Books)

Other books you might like:
Robert Browning, *The Pied Piper of Hamelin*, 1993
  Illustrator Kate Greenaway retells the poem of a mysterious Pied Piper who frees a village of rats and takes revenge when he's not paid for the service.
Judy Waite, *Mouse, Look Out!*, 1998
  Seeking shelter, a hungry mouse explores an abandoned house, unaware that a cat stalks it while the cat doesn't notice the dog following.
Wong Herbert Yee, *Eek! There's a Mouse in the House*, 1992
  In a rhyming tale a little girl tries to catch a mouse in the house by sending in larger and larger animals.

655

DEBORAH HODGE
SONG NAN ZHANG, Illustrator

Emma's Story

(Plattsburgh, NY: Tundra Books, 2003)

Subject(s): Adoption; Family; Difference
Age range(s): Grades K-2
Major character(s): Emma, Adoptee, Daughter; Grandma, Grandmother, Storyteller
Time period(s): 2000s (2003)
Locale(s): Canada

Summary: One day while Emma bakes family-shaped cookies with her brother and Grandma, she feels upset that her cookie with its black licorice hair and black raisin eyes looks different. To make her feel better, Emma's grandmother tells her the story of how the family adopted Emma from China and how much her entire family wanted her and loves her. This is the first fiction book from this author of children's non-fiction. (32 pages)

Where it's reviewed:
Horn Book Guide, Spring 2004, page 45
Publishers Weekly, November 3, 2003, page 74

Other books you might like:
Ying Ying Fry, *Kids Like Me in China*, 2001
  Eight-year-old Ying Ying goes back to China to visit the orphanage from which she was adopted.
Keiko Kasza, *A Mother for Choco*, 1992
  Little bird, Choco, wants a mother, but he thinks all families must look alike. However, when Mrs. Bear adopts him, he learns what a real family is.
Karen Katz, *Over the Moon: An Adoption Tale*, 1997
  Parents await the birth of the baby girl they are adopting from Central America.
Rose Lewis, *I Love You Like Crazy Cakes*, 2000
  A mother travels to China to adopt a baby. Based on the author's real life experience.

656

MARGARET HODGES, Adaptor
AKI SOGABE, Illustrator

The Boy Who Drew Cats

(New York: Holiday House, 2002)

Subject(s): Fairy Tales; Folklore; Animals/Cats
Age range(s): Grades K-3
Major character(s): Sesshu Toyo, Child, Artist; Unnamed Character, Religious
Time period(s): 15th century
Locale(s): Japan

Summary: The youngest child of a large, poor family, Sesshu does not seem physically able to withstand the labor of the family's life so his parents send him to a temple to become a priest. The elderly priest attempts to teach Sesshu, a capable student with one serious fault: he draws cats everywhere. Finally, the frustrated priest sends Sesshu away to try his life as an artist with one last bit of advice, "avoid large places at night—keep to small." Although Sesshu doesn't understand the advice he remembers it when he seeks shelter in a large, abandoned temple. Sesshu paints the walls with cats until darkness falls and then he huddles in a small cabinet all night while listening to the sounds of fighting in the temple. What Sesshu discovers in the morning helps him understand and appreciate the priest's advice. A concluding author's note gives the background of the legend. (32 pages)

Where it's reviewed:
Booklist, June 2002, page 1726
Horn Book, May 2002, page 339
Publishers Weekly, January 28, 2002, page 290
Riverbank Review, Summer 2002, page 28
School Library Journal, March 2002, page 214

Other books by the same author:
Joan of Arc: The Lily Maid, 1999
Silent Night: The Song and Its Story, 1997
Comus, 1996
Gulliver in Lilliput, 1995

Other books you might like:
Rafe Martin, *Mysterious Tales of Japan*, 1996
  Ten traditional tales from Japan are retold in an illustrated, award-winning collection.
Judy Sierra, *Tasty Baby Belly Buttons*, 1999
  In this retelling of a Japanese legend Uriko, born of a melon, saves the children of a village from oni determined to savor their tasty belly buttons.
Nadia Wheatley, *Luke's Way of Looking*, 2001
  Luke's imaginative paintings make him the odd one out in a classroom of conformists who all see the world the same way.

657

MICHAEL HOEYE

Time Stops for No Mouse

(New York: Putnam, 2000)

Subject(s): Animals/Mice; Adventure and Adventurers

Age range(s): Grades 5-9
Major character(s): Hermux Tantamoq, Mouse, Artisan (watchmaker); Linka Perflinger, Mouse, Pilot; Tucka Mertslin, Mouse, Businesswoman (cosmetics); Hiril Mennus, Mole, Scientist
Time period(s): Indeterminate
Locale(s): Pinchester, Fictional Country

Summary: Hermux's orderly life is thrown helter skelter when the well-known aviatrix Linka Perflinger walks into his shop and requests that her watch be repaired. Disappointed when she doesn't return for it, and then worried about what may have happened to Linka, Hermux marches to the police station to report a missing person. Receiving no help from the police, Hermux embarks on a very unlikely path as he searches for Linka himself. He soon finds himself in the clutches of Tucka Mertslin, a cosmetics tycoon and neighbor, who is obsessed with finding the secret of everlasting life and beauty. Helping her is the nefarious Dr. Hiril Mennus, in charge of the spa called Last Resort; together they will stop at nothing to discover the secret of eternal youth. Quiet, meek Hermux, who wants only to return home to his pet ladybug, discovers that "time stops for no mouse" in this delightful fantasy. (279 pages)

Where it's reviewed:
Booklist, March 15, 2002, page 1257
Horn Book, July 2002, page 462
Kliatt, June 16, 2002, page 21
School Library Journal, May 2002, page 154
Voice of Youth Advocates, June 2002, page 128

Other books by the same author:
The Sands of Time, 2001

Other books you might like:
Nina Bawden, Henry, 1988
    The antics of Henry the squirrel keep everyone living on the Jones's British farm from thinking about the horror of World War II.
Aeron Clement, The Cold Moons, 1989
    A badger colony encounters peril on their journey for a new home after an eradication program to prevent the spread of TB to cattle is begun.
Robin Hawdon, A Rustle in the Grass, 1985
    A tranquil colony of black ants must defend itself against ferocious red ants who could easily overwhelm them.
Brian Jacques, Redwall Series, 1987-
    This charming series features the mice of Redwall who not only defend their abbey against scurrilous animals but also offer refuge to their friends.
Tad Williams, Tailchaser's Song, 1984
    The ginger cat Tailchaser searches for his missing mate in this quest fantasy.

658

ALICE HOFFMAN

Green Angel

(New York: Scholastic, 2003)

Subject(s): Grief; Gardens and Gardening
Age range(s): Grades 7-10

Major character(s): Green, 15-Year-Old, Gardener
Time period(s): Indeterminate Future
Locale(s): Fictional Country

Summary: Though it's Green's turn to go to the city, it's her younger sister who accompanies their parents as they leave to sell vegetables while she stays home to tend to the garden. Suddenly the ground shakes, ashes fall around Green, flames from the city dance across the sky and she knows her family is lost to her. Desolate, she attaches thorns to her clothes, wears nail-studded boots and tattoos vines and black roses on her body as she struggles with her grief. Gradually, though, her heart opens, a bit at a time, and she offers safety and shelter to an injured hawk, a mysterious dog and a mute fire victim. With time, her tattoos revert to their normal green color and her garden tries to once again blossom in this fanciful young adult work by an adult author. (116 pages)

Where it's reviewed:
Booklist, April 15, 2003, page 1462
Bulletin of the Center for Children's Books, April 2003, page 316
Horn Book, March 2003, page 211
Publishers Weekly, January 6, 2003, page 60
School Library Journal, March 2003, page 234

Awards the book has won:
Publishers Weekly Best Children's Books, 2003

Other books by the same author:
Indigo, 2002
Aquamarine, 2001

Other books you might like:
Liz Berry, The China Garden, 1996
    Young Clare and her new boyfriend Mark learn they are the guardians of Ravensmere, which is located in the mysterious China Garden.
Franny Billingsley, The Folk Keeper, 1999
    Inexplicable magical powers inherent in her enable orphaned Corinna to masquerade as Corin, a folk keeper.
Brooks Hansen, Caesar's Antlers, 1997
    Thanks to the reindeer Caesar, Bette the sparrow is able to attach her nest to his antlers as together they search for her mate Piorello.
Mary Wesley, Speaking Terms, 1994
    Two sisters spend the summer preventing animals from being hunted, all because they discover that animals can talk.

659

ALICE HOFFMAN

Indigo

(New York: Scholastic, 2002)

Subject(s): Friendship; Runaways; Self-Perception
Age range(s): Grades 6-9
Major character(s): Martha Glimmer, 13-Year-Old; Trevor "Trout" McGill, Adoptee, 13-Year-Old; Eli "Eel" McGill, 11-Year-Old, Adoptee
Time period(s): 2000s
Locale(s): Oak Grove

Summary: In the tiny town of Oak Grove, Martha mourns the death of her mother and doesn't know how to console her sad father. Her two best friends are Trevor and Eli, nicknamed Trout and Eel for the webbing between their fingers and toes and their desire to travel to the sea. The three leave home one day heading for the seashore but are halted by a horrific rainstorm that threatens the town. Luckily Trout and Eel are excellent swimmers and able to remove a rock from a wall built to keep water out of the town, but at the moment retaining the trapped water. The town is saved from flooding and, once the McGill parents see how much their sons need water, they sell their home and move to the beach in Ocean City. Martha, on the other hand, decides to remain after her father returns to his old self in this novella. (84 pages)

Where it's reviewed:
Booklist, August 2002, page 1961
Bulletin of the Center for Children's Books, June 2002, page 367
Publishers Weekly, March 11, 2002, page 73
School Library Journal, August 2002, page 188
Voice of Youth Advocates, August 2002, page 202

Other books by the same author:
Green Angel, 2003
Aquamarine, 2001
Blue Diary, 2001
The River King, 2000

Other books you might like:
Mollie Hunter, *The Mermaid Summer*, 1988
Eric laughs at the idea of mermaids, until mermaids wreck his boat and leave him stranded for three years.
Janet Taylor Lisle, *The Lampfish of Twill*, 1991
Eric dreams of single-handedly catching a lampfish, but this obsession pulls him down a whirlpool into another world.
Mary Pope Osborne, *Haunted Waters*, 1994
Lord Huldbrand marries the mysterious Undine but their lives are changed forever by the lure of the sea in this retelling of a German fairy tale.

660

EVA HOFFMAN

The Secret

(New York: Public Affairs, 2002)

Subject(s): Cloning; Coming-of-Age; Mothers and Daughters
Age range(s): Grades 9-Adult
Major character(s): Iris Surrey, Daughter, Clone; Elizabeth Surrey, Mother
Time period(s): 2020s (2022)
Locale(s): United States

Summary: Iris has an idyllic childhood, sharing a special awareness of her connection with her mother. As a child, Iris attributes this to the fact that the two are together almost constantly, but as she reaches her teens, Iris begins to question her relationship with her mother. Why is her mother so restrictively possessive? Who is Iris's father, and where is he? What disturbs Iris the most is that she and her mother have such an uncanny resemblance that people often stare at them.

Finally, Iris discovers that she is a clone of her mother. Iris is devastated. How can she be a man-made artifact, a non-person, a monster? To survive, Iris will need to discover in herself a sense of self-worth that has nothing to do with her parent. (272 pages)

Where it's reviewed:
Booklist, December 1, 2002, page 646
Kirkus Reviews, August 1, 2002, page 1061
Library Journal, September 15, 2002, page 91
New York Times Book Review, November 10, 2002, page 18
Publishers Weekly, September 23, 2002, page 47

Other books by the same author:
After Such Knowledge: Reflections on the Aftermath of the Holocaust, 2004 (adult nonfiction)
Shtetl: The Life and Death of a Small Town and the World of Polish Jews, 1997 (adult nonfiction)

Other books you might like:
Caroline B. Cooney, *The Face on the Milk Carton*, 1990
Janey recognizes the lost child on the milk carton as herself, and realizes she has no idea who she is.
Nancy Farmer, *The House of the Scorpion*, 2002
A wealthy drug lord has a clone made to prolong his life, but Matt wants a life of his own.
Uri Orlev, *Run, Boy, Run*, 2003
A young Jewish boy survives the Holocaust by denying his identity, but ends up not knowing who he is.

661

MARY HOFFMAN

City of Masks

(New York: Bloomsbury, 2002)

Series: Stravaganza Book 1
Subject(s): Space and Time; Friendship; Gender Roles
Age range(s): Grades 7-10
Major character(s): Lucien "Luciano" Mulholland, Time Traveler, Cancer Patient; Arianna Gasparini, 15-Year-Old; Count Rodolfo, Philosopher; Duchessa Arianna Silvia, Ruler
Time period(s): 2000s; 16th century
Locale(s): England; Bellezza, Fictional Country (a country called Talia)

Summary: Recovering from the effects of chemo for his cancer, Lucien's throat is so sore that he can't speak. To help his son communicate, his father gives him a beautiful journal covered with marbled paper. Falling asleep that night with the journal in his hand, Lucien unknowingly stravigates to Bellezza, a 16th century city similar to Venice. There he meets Arianna, who wants nothing more than to join the Scuola Mandoliera, the rowing society forbidden to girls. Arianna is furious when Lucien is befriended by Count Rodolfo, special friend of the Duchessa, and admitted to the Scuola Mandoliera. For Lucien, his friendship with Count Rololfo is critical as it helps him understand the concept of stravigation and gives him a passageway to and from Bellezza. Lucien doesn't want to leave his parents, but in England he's very sick and certain to die; in Bellezza, he's healthy again with a head full of curly blonde hair, though he knows he's left behind his body in a coma-like state. The excitement of life in Bellezza, the political intrigues, Lucien's saving of the Duchessa from an assassination attempt, all contribute to his decision to remain in Bellezza in this captivating first of a trilogy. (345 pages)

Where it's reviewed:
Booklist, October 15, 2002, page 407
Bulletin of the Center for Children's Books, February 2003, page 238
Publishers Weekly, September 30, 2002, page 72
School Library Journal, November 2002, page 168
Voice of Youth Advocates, December 2002, page 396

Awards the book has won:
Booklist Editors' Choice/Books for Youth, 2002

Other books by the same author:
City of Flowers, 2005 (Stravaganza Book 3)
City of Stars, 2004 (Stravaganza Book 2)

Other books you might like:
Tracy Barrett, *Anna of Byzantium*, 1999
    When Anna proves the perfect heir to her father's throne, her grandmother's status is threatened and she switches allegiance to Anna's younger brother.
Dorothy Sharp Carter, *His Majesty, Queen Hatshepsut*, 1987
    This work offers a fictionalized look at the life of Queen Hatshepsut, one of the female leaders of Egypt.
Sonia Levitin, *The Cure*, 1999
    Gemm 16884 is different so he's sent back to 14th century Strasbourg for the cure; when he returns, he tosses away his silk mask of conformity.

662

MARY HOFFMAN

City of Stars

(New York: Bloomsbury, 2003)

Series: Stravaganza. Book 2
Subject(s): Space and Time; Animals/Horses; Self-Confidence
Age range(s): Grades 7-10
Major character(s): Georgia "Giorgia Gredi" O'Grady, Time Traveler; Falco, Handicapped; Lucien "Luciano" Mulholland, Time Traveler; Arianna Silvia, Ruler
Time period(s): 2000s; 16th century
Locale(s): England; Remora, Fictional Country (Talia)

Summary: Once again Georgia sneaks up to her room, hoping to escape the taunts and abuse of her stepbrother and knowing she must hide the miniature winged horse she just bought at an antique shop. Ever since her mother remarried, Georgia's life has been miserable; the only way she can escape is through her horseback riding where she's free of her stepbrother's wickedness. That night when she falls asleep clutching her horse, she is transported to Remora, one of the city-states of Talia introduced in *Stravaganza: City of Masks*. Georgia is amazed to learn that she's a stravagante, just like her classmate Lucien who she discovers is alive in Talia, and delighted to realize she's arrived just at the start of their annual horse race, the Stellata. Lucien is involved in the political maneuverings that become sinister with the di Chimici family trying to usurp power from the Duchess of

Bellezza; they plan to win the Stellata to enhance their standing and increase their power. Georgia finds herself involved when Falco, one of the di Chimici sons is crippled in a horse race, learns that Georgia can stravagate, and talks her into bringing him to 20th-century England in hopes his disability can be cured. (459 pages)

Where it's reviewed:
Journal of Adolescent and Adult Literacy, May 2004, page 409
Kirkus Reviews, September 15, 2003, page 1175
Publishers Weekly, November 24, 2003, page 66
School Library Journal, January 2004, page 130
Voice of Youth Advocates, December 2003, page 412

Awards the book has won:
Booklist Editors' Choice/Books for Youth, 2003

Other books by the same author:
City of Flowers, 2005 (Stravaganza Book 3)
City of Masks, 2003 (Stravaganza Book 2)

Other books you might like:
Ann Cheetham, *The Pit*, 1990
    Oliver finds himself drawn to the time when a newly excavated pit was used to bury plague victims.
Sherryl Jordan, *The Juniper Game*, 1991
    Dylan uses his artistic ability to draw Juniper's dreams, which transport them to a scene of presumed 15th-century witchcraft.
Richard Peck, *Voices After Midnight*, 1989
    Chad and his younger brother Luke are drawn back in time to the Great Blizzard of 1888 when they help save the former owners of their townhouse.
Chelsea Quinn Yarbro, *Monet's Ghost*, 1997
    Geena discovers she can "think" herself into a painting and explores Monet's "Water Lilies," but now can't find the moat she needs to return.

663

MARY HOFFMAN
KARIN LITTLEWOOD, Illustrator

The Color of Home

(New York: Phyllis Fogelman Books, 2002)

Subject(s): Refugees; Emigration and Immigration; Homesickness
Age range(s): Grades K-2
Major character(s): Hassan, Refugee, Student; Miss Kelly, Teacher; Fela, Linguist
Time period(s): 2000s (2002)
Locale(s): Somalia; United States

Summary: An American school is a strange place for Hassan, accustomed to sitting outside in the hot sun for lessons. Though Hassan cannot understand Miss Kelly's words her smile expresses friendliness and through her gestures and the actions of the other students, Hassan realizes he is to paint a picture, another new experience. Hassan creates a brightly colored picture of his Somalian home that he then covers with the colors of fire, carnage and death. The next day, Fela greets Hassan when he arrives at school so he can tell Miss Kelly about his picture. When he finishes his story of escape, he asks to paint another picture, a happy one in the colors of his home in Somalia. (32 pages)

Where it's reviewed:
Booklist, October 15, 2002, page 410
Bulletin of the Center for Children's Books, October 2002, page 60
Horn Book Guide, Spring 2003, page 37
Kirkus Reviews, August 15, 2002, page 1225
School Library Journal, September 2002, page 194

Awards the book has won:
IRA Teachers' Choices, 2003

Other books by the same author:
Starring Grace, 2000
Boundless Grace, 1995
Amazing Grace, 1991 (ALA Notable Children's Book)

Other books you might like:
Aliki, *Painted Words/Spoken Memories*, 1998
    Through painted pictures immigrant Marianthe communicates her feelings until she learns enough English to speak of her past.
Eve Bunting, *Gleam and Glow*, 2001
    When a refugee family returns to their destroyed village they find a sign of hope, the pet fish they left in their pond.
Luis Garay, *The Long Road*, 1997
    When a civil war breaks out in Jose's village, he must flee to America with his mother.
Robert Munsch, *From Far Away*, 1995
    Saoussan and her family move to Canada from war-torn Lebanon.

664

ROBERT HOLDSTOCK

Celtika

(New York: Tor, 2003)

Series: Merlin Codex. Book 1
Subject(s): Fantasy; Mythology; Magic
Age range(s): Grades 10-Adult
Major character(s): Merlin, Wizard; Jason, Warrior; Medea, Wizard
Time period(s): Indeterminate Past
Locale(s): Earth

Summary: Long before he aided Arthur in his quest to unite the Britons, Merlin time traveled while studying magic. One of his early encounters is with Jason, and Merlin aids in the quest for the Golden Fleece. He is also present for the horrifying end of Jason's relationship with Medea, during which both men believe she murders Jason's sons. Centuries later, Merlin hears about a ship which screams from the bottom of a frozen lake and goes to investigate. It is the magical *Argo*, Jason's ship, and Jason is the screamer, still howling for his lost sons. Merlin employs his carefully hoarded magic and resurrects both ship and man. The two collect other followers and set off on a search for the sons Jason is certain still exist somewhere. On the journey, Merlin discovers there is another student of magic traveling through time—Medea. (368 pages)

Where it's reviewed:
Booklist, March 15, 2003, page 1286

Kirkus Reviews, February 15, 2003, page 276
Library Journal, March 15, 2003, page 120
Publishers Weekly, March 10, 2003, page 58
Voice of Youth Advocates, June 2003, page 150

Other books by the same author:
The Iron Grail, 2002 (Merlin Codex Book 2)
Gate of Ivory, Gate of Horn, 1997
Ancient Echoes, 1996

Other books you might like:
A.A. Attanasio, *The Eagle and the Sword*, 1997
    This version of Merlin and Arthur's story combines elements of Celtic and Norse mythology.
J. Robert King, *Mad Merlin*, 2000
    A blend of Greek and Roman mythology and the Arthurian legend, this time with an amnesic Merlin who can't remember that he is actually the god Jupiter.
Fred Saberhagen, *God of the Golden Fleece*, 2001
    Jason and the Argonauts may be searching for the fleece in the mists of the past, or perhaps in the infinitely far future.

665

LINDA HOLEMAN

Search of the Moon King's Daughter

(Toronto: Tundra, 2002)

Subject(s): Brothers and Sisters; City and Town Life
Age range(s): Grades 8-11
Major character(s): Emmaline Roke, 16-Year-Old, Servant; Tommy Roke, Chimneysweep, Deaf Person; Cat Roke, Mother
Time period(s): 1830s
Locale(s): Tibbing, England; London, England

Summary: Until she's in her mid-teens, Emmaline's life is spent in her small English village with her father, a shopkeeper who likes to read aloud to her. When he dies of cholera, Emmaline's family moves to a mill town where her mother Cat takes a job in a factory while Emmaline sews for her wealthy aunt. The little family, including Emmaline's deaf-mute brother Tommy, manages to survive until Cat becomes addicted to laudanum to mask the pain of her hand, badly mangled in an accident. When Cat is forced to sell Tommy to a chimneysweep for money for laudanum, Emmaline leaves home and travels to London in search of him. Finding a position at Thorn House as a scullery maid, she spends the early mornings searching for Tommy in this descriptive tale of life in industrialized England. (309 pages)

Where it's reviewed:
Booklist, December 15, 2002, page 753
Kirkus Reviews, November 15, 2002, page 1694
Quill & Quire, September 2002, page 59
School Library Journal, March 2003, page 234
Voice of Youth Advocates, February 2003, page 476

Awards the book has won:
ALA Best Books for Young Adults, 2003

Other books by the same author:
Raspberry House Blues, 2000
Devil's Darning Needle, 1999
Mercy's Birds, 1998

Other books you might like:

Malcolm Bosse, *Captives of Time*, 1987
Two siblings struggle across medieval Europe, driven by outlaws, disease and developing technology.

Charles Dickens, *Oliver Twist*, 1837
This portrayal of a youngster's life in 19th-century Britain led to much needed social change.

Anna Kirwan, *Victoria: May Blossom of Britannia, England, 1829*, 2001
The thoughts of the future Queen Victoria reside in a record book she steals from the stable.

666

JENNIFER L. HOLM

Boston Jane: Wilderness Days

(New York: HarperCollins, 2002)

Subject(s): Frontier and Pioneer Life; Indians of North America

Age range(s): Grades 6-10

Major character(s): Jane "Boston Jane" Peck, 16-Year-Old; Jehu Scudder, Boyfriend (of Jane's); Mrs. Frink, Pioneer; Mr. Russell, Landlord (of Jane); Sally Biddle, Gentlewoman

Time period(s): 1850s

Locale(s): Shoalwater Bay, Washington (Washington Territory)

Summary: Having realized what a skunk her fiance is, Jane breaks their engagement and, as the only woman in Shoalwater Bay, thinks of returning to Philadelphia, especially after learning of her father's death. Luckily Jane changes her mind and remains where she has an interest in an oyster concern, takes in laundry and bakes wonderful pies. These frontier skills she's worked so hard to acquire suddenly seem to be of no merit when Mrs. Frink arrives and all those unwashed, unshaven men once again find their manners. That irritates Jane to no end and her prickliness even affects her relationship with Jehu, a former seaman who's obviously in love with her. But there's no time to waste on silly jealousy as she and Jehu travel to the Stevens Negotiations between the Indians and the territorial government representatives where they must warn her bedraggled landlord Mr. Russell that someone wants to kill him. When Jane's worst enemy from her Philadelphia days, the ever-proper Sally Biddle, shows up in Shoalwater Bay, the reader knows there's a sequel afoot. (242 pages)

Where it's reviewed:

Booklist, September 1, 2002, page 123
Horn Book, September 2002, page 574
Kirkus Reviews, July 15, 2002, page 1033
School Library Journal, October 2002, page 164
Voice of Youth Advocates, October 2002, page 279

Other books by the same author:

Boston Jane: The Claim, 2004
The Creek, 2003
Boston Jane: An Adventure, 2001
Our Only May Amelia, 1999

Other books you might like:

Kristiana Gregory, *Seeds of Hope: The Gold Rush Diary of Susanna Fairchild, California Territory, 1849*, 2001
Rather than going to Oregon after the death of their mother, the Fairchild family decides to remain in California and hunt for gold.

Barbara Riefe, *Westward Hearts: The Amelia Dale Archer Story*, 1998
Knowing she'll never get ahead in Philadelphia, Doctor Archer and her grandchildren head to California, which she hopes will be better for her.

Ann Turner, *Third Girl from the Left*, 1986
Young, adventureous Sary answers an ad for a mail-order bride and winds up in Montana married to a 60-year-old rancher.

667

JENNIFER L. HOLM

The Creek

(New York: HarperCollins, 2003)

Subject(s): Mystery and Detective Stories; Fear; Murder

Age range(s): Grades 6-9

Major character(s): Penny Carson, 12-Year-Old; Caleb Devlin, 17-Year-Old, Criminal

Time period(s): 2000s

Locale(s): Philadelphia, Pennsylvania

Summary: It's summertime and Penny and her neighborhood group of boys look forward to returning to the creek where they spend hours playing and building forts. But danger enters their world when local hoodlum Caleb returns from reform school and pets once again disappear. Everyone immediately suspects Caleb of these deeds so when he comes after Penny by the creek, she pushes him away and he falls over the edge and into the swirling water. Scared to tell anyone what she's done, Penny acts as though nothing has happened, but when a neighbor's child is killed and everyone suspects Caleb, Penny knows someone else is the criminal. Quietly investigating, she uncovers the real killer when he comes after her with a kitchen knife in this chilling tale. (232 pages)

Where it's reviewed:

Booklist, August 2003, page 1973
Bulletin of the Center for Children's Books, July 2003, page 450
Publishers Weekly, July 7, 2003, page 73
School Library Journal, July 2003, page 131
Voice of Youth Advocates, October 2003, page 306

Other books by the same author:

Boston Jane: The Claim, 2004
Boston Jane: Wilderness Days, 2002
Boston Jane: An Adventure, 2001 (ALA Best Books for Young Adults)
Our Only May Amelia, 1999

Other books you might like:

Caroline B. Cooney, *Wanted!*, 1997
Alice finds herself in a nightmare when she tries to help her father, but the police claim she murdered him and left an e-mail confession.

Robert Cormier, *The Rag and Bone Shop*, 2001
As the last to have seen murdered Alicia, Jason begins to wonder if he did indeed kill her.
E.L. Konigsburg, *Silent to the Bone*, 2000
Falsely accused of hurting his sister, mute Branwell is not able to defend himself until his best friend devises a way to break through his silence.

668

SHERI HOLMAN

Sondok: Princess of the Moon and Stars, Korea, A.D. 595
(New York: Scholastic, 2002)

Series: Royal Diaries
Subject(s): Princes and Princesses; Astronomy; Diaries
Age range(s): Grades 5-8
Major character(s): Sondok, Royalty (princess); Chajang, Friend, Religious (Buddhist monk)
Time period(s): 7th century (595-647)
Locale(s): Silla, Republic of Korea

Summary: At the age of fourteen, Sondok is given responsibility for her grandmother's ashes, kept in the family's Ancestor jar, and thus writes notes to her almost daily telling of the family activities. As a female, and a member of royalty, Sondok must follow a narrow path and thus isn't allowed to indulge in her passion to study astronomy. Her childhood friend Chajang is not a member of the Holy Bone rank, to which Sondok's family belongs, thus is ineligible to be consort of a queen, a role to which Sondok will eventually ascend upon the death of her father. In later years, she will be able to attain many of her dreams as recorded in the epilogue to this stirring tale of the first female queen of an Asian nation. (187 pages)

Where it's reviewed:
School Library Journal, August 2002, page 188
Voice of Youth Advocates, October 2002, page 280

Other books by the same author:
The Mammoth Cheese, 2003 (adult title)
The Dress Lodger, 2000 (adult title)
A Stolen Tongue, 1997 (adult title)

Other books you might like:
Kristiana Gregory, *Cleopatra VII: Daughter of the Nile*, 1999
Diary entries for Cleopatra, ruler of Egypt, cover her early teen years when she was preparing to be Egypt's ruler.
Linda Sue Park, *A Single Shard*, 2001
Orphan Tree-Ear is entranced by the celadon pottery made by his village's artisans and is finally entrusted to carry two pots to the royal court.
Laurence Yep, *Lady of Ch'iao Kuo: Warrior of the South, Southern China, A.D. 531*, 2001
A member of the Hsien tribe, Princess Redbird is schooled in China and later uses her logic to help create alliances to defeat her tribe's enemies.

669

KIMBERLY WILLIS HOLT

Keeper of the Night
(New York: Holt, 2003)

Subject(s): Grief; Suicide; Family Problems
Age range(s): Grades 7-10
Major character(s): Isabel Moreno, 13-Year-Old, 8th Grader; Tata Moreno, Father, Fisherman; Frank Moreno, 12-Year-Old, Brother; Olivia Moreno, Sister, Child
Time period(s): 2000s
Locale(s): Malesso, Guam

Summary: After her mother commits suicide, Isabel's grief prevents her from sleeping and she becomes "the keeper of the night" as she watches over her father and her siblings. Isabel's entire family is altered by the loss of their beautiful but sad mother as her little sister Olivia wets the bed, her father Tata sleeps beside his wife's bed, and her brother Frank carves the words "I hate you" in his bedroom wall. Though the entire family is grieving, it takes Frank's carving "I hate you" into his arm for them to seek out the counseling help they need and return to their former, happier days. (308 pages)

Where it's reviewed:
Booklist, April 15, 2003, page 1462
Bulletin of the Center for Children's Books, June 2003, page 405
Horn Book, May 2003, page 349
Publishers Weekly, May 5, 2003, page 68
School Library Journal, May 2003, page 153

Awards the book has won:
ALA Best Books for Young Adults, 2004
School Library Journal Best Books, 2003

Other books by the same author:
Dancing in Cadillac Light, 2001
When Zachary Beaver Came to Town, 1999
My Louisiana Sky, 1998

Other books you might like:
Katherine Holubitsky, *Alone at Ninety Foot*, 1999
Pam's drawn to the spot where her mother committed suicide; gradually time and solitude help her adjust to her changed life.
Patricia McCormick, *Cut*, 2000
Hospitalized for self-abuse, Callie begins to speak only when a new girl who cuts herself joins her group therapy program.
Carol Lynch Williams, *Carolina Autumn*, 2000
Caroline misses her older sister Madelaine, killed a year earlier in a plane crash, and writes letters to her about her new adventures.
Jacqueline Woodson, *Miracle's Boys*, 2000
Sons Ty'ree, Charlie and Lafayette grieve in their own, separate ways following the death of their mother, Miracle.

670

ELIZABETH HONEY, Author/Illustrator

Remote Man

(New York: Knopf, 2002)

Subject(s): Mystery and Detective Stories; Internet; Smuggling
Age range(s): Grades 6-9
Major character(s): Edward Huon ''Ned'' Spinner, 13-Year-Old, Animal Lover; Kate Spokes, Cousin; Cleverton Lee, Computer Expert; Yvette Claverlous, Student—Boarding School; Cabot ''Rocky'' Brotherbum, 13-Year-Old, Animal Lover
Time period(s): 2000s
Locale(s): Australia; Concord, Massachusetts

Summary: Ned's either watching TV or chatting online with friends so it's a while before he realizes how depressed his mother is. While his mother receives some help before they both fly to Massachusetts for her recovery, Ned stays with his cousin Kate in the Outback. In Concord, Ned and Rocky become friends as they share a mutual interest in animals, especially reptiles and bears. Ned gets an inkling that something's amiss when he learns that a rare python he spotted in Australia has been snatched, then he and Rocky stumble over the site of a bear killing. Both times he'd mentioned sighting these specific animals to a different man and he starts to wonder if somehow he's to blame. Ned puts his computer knowledge to work under his moniker ''Remote Man'' and links up internationally with Cleverton in Jamaica and Yvette in France as the two boys put up bogus web sites and lurk in chat rooms. They finally combine all their knowledge and uncover an international smuggling ring in this fast-paced adventure. (260 pages)

Where it's reviewed:
Booklist, October 15, 2002, page 405
Bulletin of the Center for Children's Books, October 2002, page 61
Library Media Connection, January 2003, page 90
School Library Journal, August 2002, page 189
Voice of Youth Advocates, August 2002, page 193

Awards the book has won:
Smithsonian's Notable Books for Children/Older Readers, 2002

Other books by the same author:
Fiddleback, 2001
Don't Pat the Wombat, 2000
45 47 Stella Street and Everything That Happened, 1995

Other books you might like:
Aileen Kilgore Henderson, *The Monkey Thief*, 1997
    Determined to have a monkey for a pet while he's in Costa Rica, Steve unwittingly helps a smuggler.
Hester Mundis, *My Chimp Friday: The Nana Banana Chronicles*, 2002
    Asked to watch a baby chimp that has mastered Rubik's cube, the Stelson family finds they're protecting Friday from kidnappers.
Rob Thomas, *Green Thumb*, 1999
    High school student Grady Jacobs is thrilled to be part of

Dr. Carter's rain forest research until he discovers Carter's secret and has to dodge machetes.

671

TOM HOOBLER, Co-Author
DOROTHY HOOBLER, Co-Author

The 1980s: Earthsong

(Brookfield, CT: The Millbrook Press, 2002)

Series: Century Kids
Subject(s): Environmental Problems; Pollution
Age range(s): Grades 6-8
Major character(s): Jason Woods, Cousin; Eric Woods, Cousin; Suzanne Woods, Cousin; Nell Aldrich, Aunt
Time period(s): 1980s
Locale(s): Lake Chohobee, Maine

Summary: A long, boring summer in Maine unfolds for Suzanne and she wonders how long her mother can stay retired, which is what brought them both here to Great-aunt Nell's from Beverly Hills. Suzanne's mother was one of the original singers in the 1980s rock group the Whatevers, who plan a reunion tour this summer, but Suzanne's mother declines to travel with them. One bright spot is the family wedding of Nell's adopted son and Suzanne waits for her cousins Jason and Eric to arrive. A little exploring of Lake Chohobee reveals a fish kill, which leads the cousins to photograph the pollution and take water samples to uncover its source. But when Suzanne and her cousins trace the source of contamination to a prominent family living in the village, they decide to put their musical talents to work and host a benefit concert instead that outlines the pollution dangers, in this continuing series. (158 pages)

Where it's reviewed:
Horn Book Guide, Spring 2003, page 82
Voice of Youth Advocates, February 2003, page 477

Other books by the same author:
1970s: Arguments, 2002 (Century Kids)
1990s: Families, 2002 (Century Kids)
1960s: Rebels, 2001 (Century Kids)

Other books you might like:
Grace Dent, *LBD: It's a Girl Thing*, 2003
    When the parents of Les Bambinos Dangereuses refuse to let their daughters attend the Astlebury Music Festival, the girls bring the music to their town.
Jean Craighead George, *The Case of the Missing Cutthroats: An Ecological Mystery*, 1996
    Spinner and her cousin Allen follow the Snake River to find out what has happened to the cutthroats, a fish which hasn't been caught on this river in years.
Tim Winton, *Lockie Leonard, Scumbuster*, 1999
    Finding gray scum floating in the harbor, Lockie and his friend Egg top an effluent cap, which forces the sludge back into the factory and makes the national news.

672

BELL HOOKS
CHRIS RASCHKA, Illustrator

Be Boy Buzz

(New York: Jump at the Sun/Hyperion Books for Children, 2002)

Subject(s): African Americans; Poetry; Self-Esteem
Age range(s): Preschool-Kindergarten
Time period(s): 2000s (2002)
Locale(s): United States

Summary: In a celebration of all things BOY, African-American boys show all their sides. From misbehaving boys to running, jumping, active boys to quiet boys wanting a hug, tribute is paid to boys for being just who they are. (32 pages)

Where it's reviewed:
Bulletin of the Center for Children's Books, December 2002, page 160
Five Owls, 2003, page 16
Publishers Weekly, September 30, 2002, page 71
Riverbank Review, Winter 2002/2003, page 33
School Library Journal, December 2002, page 97

Awards the book has won:
Center for Children's Books Best Books, 2003

Other books by the same author:
Skin Again, 2004
Homemade Love, 2002
Happy to Be Nappy, 1999

Other books you might like:
Donald Crews, *Bigmama's*, 1991
   Every summer, the narrator and his siblings descend on Bigmama's house in Florida.
Karen Katz, *The Colors of Us*, 1999
   When Lena walks around her neighborhood with her artist mother, she discovers that her friends and neighbors are many different shades of brown.
Faith Ringgold, *Tar Beach*, 1991
   Based on a story quilt, a girl in 1939 Harlem imaginatively turns the rooftop of her apartment building into a tar beach.

673

BELL HOOKS
SHANE W. EVANS, Illustrator

Homemade Love

(New York: Jump at the Sun/Hyperion Books for Children, 2002)

Subject(s): African Americans; Poetry; Self-Esteem
Age range(s): Preschool-Kindergarten
Major character(s): Girlpie, Child, Daughter
Time period(s): 2000s (2002)
Locale(s): United States

Summary: Girlpie (as her mother calls her) talks about how much her parents love her even when she sometimes misbehaves. Once she's snuggled in bed at night she remembers being hugged by her mother and tossed high by her father. Girlpie feels safe and secure at home with her family. (32 pages)

Where it's reviewed:
Booklist, February 1, 2003, page 1001
Bulletin of the Center for Children's Books, February 2003, page 238
Publishers Weekly, November 18, 2002, page 59
Riverbank Review, Winter 2002-2003, page 33
School Library Journal, December 2002, page 97

Awards the book has won:
Center for Children's Books Best Books, 2003

Other books by the same author:
Skin Again, 2004
Be Boy Buzz, 2002
Happy to Be Nappy, 1999

Other books you might like:
Sylviane Diouf, *Bintou's Braids*, 2001
   Bintou dreams of having braids like the women in her African village do.
Spike Lee, *Please, Baby, Please*, 2002
   African American parents urge their baby girl to go to sleep.
Joyce Carol Thomas, *Joy!*, 2001
   An African American mother celebrates her love for her child throughout the seasons.

674

MARY HOOPER

Amy

(New York: Bloomsbury, 2002)

Subject(s): Interpersonal Relations; Crime and Criminals; Internet
Age range(s): Grades 7-10
Major character(s): Amy, 15-Year-Old; Serena "Beaky", 15-Year-Old; Zed, Con Artist
Time period(s): 2000s
Locale(s): Watford, England

Summary: First there were four friends who always hung out together, but then one moved to Scotland leaving Amy with Lou and Bethany in a threesome that didn't work for friendship. Once Amy realizes that she's the one left out, she looks for a friend in Internet chat rooms. There she finds Zed, exchanges photographs and decides to meet him. Enjoying a picnic lunch on the beach with him, Amy becomes sleepy and wakes up three hours later. Returning home, she notices that some of her clothing is on backwards, has dreams about the afternoon and finally opens up to her new friend Beaky. The two girls realize that Amy has been slipped a date rape drug and decide to set Zed up before Amy makes a statement to police in this cautionary tale. (171 pages)

Where it's reviewed:
Booklist, September 15, 2002, page 226
Bulletin of the Center for Children's Books, December 2002, page 160
Publishers Weekly, August 19, 2002, page 90
School Library Journal, September 2002, page 226
Voice of Youth Advocates, December 2002, page 382

Other books by the same author:
Petals in the Ashes, 2004

At the Sign of the Sugared Plum, 2003
Megan 3, 2001
Megan, 1999
Megan 2, 1999

Other books you might like:

Jordan Cray, *Gemini7*, 1997
Jonah becomes nervous about his ''cyber girlfriend'' Nicole for, after meeting her, his father has a car accident and a former girlfriend is almost killed.

Beth Goodie, *Sticks and Stones*, 2002
What Jujube thinks is an innocent date for the Valentine's Dance leads to a nightmare when Brent intimates that she's easy.

Cheryl Zach, *Secret Admirer*, 1999
Brittany foolishly agrees to meet ''Randall45,'' someone she's been e-mailing thanks to an online chat room.

675

MARY HOOPER

At the Sign of the Sugared Plum

(New York: Bloomsbury, 2003)

Subject(s): Plague; Sisters
Age range(s): Grades 5-9
Major character(s): Sarah, Teenager, Businesswoman (sweetshop owner); Hannah, Sister (of Sarah), Teenager; Tom, Apprentice (to apothecary)
Time period(s): 17th century (1660s)
Locale(s): London, England

Summary: Arriving in London to help her older sister Sarah with her sweetmeats shop, Hannah is dismayed when she's asked to return home because of the plague. Having lived in a small village, Hannah is thrilled at the sights and sounds of London and doesn't want to miss anything in the big city, especially after meeting Tom, apprentice at the apothecary shop. The plague spreads and it becomes dangerous to remain in London, but impossible to leave without a pass, usually available only to the wealthy. When Sarah and Hannah have a chance to escort a young infant out of the city, they seize the opportunity to escape in this authentic tale of plague-ridden London. (176 pages)

Where it's reviewed:

Booklist, September 15, 2003, page 236
Bulletin of the Center for Children's Books, October 2003, page 63
Publishers Weekly, August 25, 2003, page 65
School Library Journal, August 2003, page 160
Voice of Youth Advocates, October 2003, page 306

Other books by the same author:

Amy, 2002

Other books you might like:

Malcolm Bosse, *Captives of Time*, 1987
Two siblings struggle across medieval Europe, driven by outlaws, disease and developing technology.

Deborah Ellis, *A Company of Fools*, 2002
Sent to amuse the citizens of their plague-ridden village, the choirboys of St. Luc fear their prize singer is being used to fill the abbey's coffers.

Jill Paton Walsh, *A Parcel of Patterns*, 1983
In 1665 the inhabitants of a small English town become infected by the plague when a dressmaker receives ''a parcel of patterns'' from London.

676

CATHY HOPKINS

Mates, Dates and Inflatable Bras

(New York: Pulse/Simon & Schuster, 2003)

Series: Mates, Dates
Subject(s): Interpersonal Relations; Schools/High Schools; Friendship
Age range(s): Grades 6-9
Major character(s): Lucy Luvering, 14-Year-Old; Izzie Foster, 14-Year-Old; Nesta Williams, 14-Year-Old
Time period(s): 2000s
Locale(s): London, England

Summary: Friends Lucy, Izzie and Nesta confront the usual teenage problems but do so with humor and flamboyance. Lucy is stumped by a ''what do you want to be'' class assignment and, thinking about herself, feels like a child next to glamorous Izzie and Nesta, especially with her latest, dreadful haircut. A long talk with her mother, a gift of an inflatable bra from her friends, and the ability to design and sew some marvelous clothes renews her self-esteem. (164 pages)

Where it's reviewed:

Booklist, February 1, 2003, page 981
Kliatt, September 2003, page 17
Publishers Weekly, December 9, 2002, page 85
School Library Journal, April 2003, page 164
Voice of Youth Advocates, April 2003, page 36

Awards the book has won:

ALA Quick Picks for Reluctant Young Adult Readers, 2004

Other books by the same author:

Mates, Dates and Cosmic Kisses, 2003 (Mates, Dates)
Mates, Dates and Sleepover Secrets, 2003 (Mates, Dates)
Mates, Dates and Designer Divas, 2003 (Mates, Dates)

Other books you might like:

Ann Herrick, *The Perfect Guy*, 1989
Rebecca's plan for her new stepbrother to fall for her backfires and she almost loses out on the best guy of all.

Louise Rennison, *Angus, Thongs and Full-Frontal Snogging: Confessions of Georgia Nicolson*, 2000
In her diary, Georgia records her interest in kissing, her appearance and her opposition to most of what the adult world thinks is important.

Cynthia Voigt, *Bad Girls in Love*, 2002
''Bad girls'' Mikey and Margalo have fallen in love, Mikey openly with Shawn and Margalo secretly with her teacher.

Cherry Whytock, *My Cup Runneth Over: The Life of Angelica Cookson Potts*, 2003
With eight of her favorite recipes, Angel shows how she manages to combine her love of eating and cooking with a flair for modeling.

677

DEBORAH HOPKINSON
PATRICK FARICY, Illustrator

Pioneer Summer

(New York: Aladdin/Simon & Schuster Books for Young Readers, 2002)

Series: Prairie Skies. Book 1
Subject(s): Historical; Abolition; Emigration and Immigration
Age range(s): Grades 2-4
Major character(s): Charlie Keller, Son, Brother; Ida Jane Keller, 10-Year-Old, Sister (older); Sadie Keller, Sister, 4-Year-Old
Time period(s): 1850s (1855)
Locale(s): Massachusetts; Kansas

Summary: Charlie's the one who doesn't want to leave the family's Massachusetts home and set off for the prairie. His abolitionist parents think it's their responsibility to help settle the Kansas territory so it will enter the Union as a free state. Charlie wants to hold on to the familiar but Ida Jane and Sadie seem ready for the adventure of a new life. A long, dirty ride on a train and even more days on a steamboat bring them close enough to complete the journey with oxen and wagon. Then the real work begins of breaking the prairie sod, planting the crops, building a house, and hauling water from the creek. Finding a stray dog helps to ease Charlie's loneliness a bit and gives him hope that he'll find a way to feel at home under the prairie sky just as Ida Jane and Sadie do. Brief historical notes conclude the book giving background to the story. (74 pages)

Where it's reviewed:
Booklist, May 1, 2002, page 1526
Publishers Weekly, April 15, 2002, page 65
School Library Journal, October 2002, page 112

Other books by the same author:
Sailing for Gold, 2004 (Klondike Kid Trilogy Book 1)
Our Kansas Home, 2003 (Prairie Skies Book 3)
Cabin in the Snow, 2002 (Prairie Skies Book 2)

Other books you might like:
E. Cody Kimmel, *One Sky Above Us*, 2002
    The abolitionist beliefs of Bill's father threaten the peaceful life the family seeks to build on their claim in Kansas Territory.
Kate McMullan, *As Far as I Can See: Meg's Prairie Diary*, 2002
    To protect Meg and her brother from a cholera outbreak in 1856 St. Louis her father sends them to safety with relatives in Kansas.
Joan Lowery Nixon, *In the Face of Danger*, 1988
    After poverty forces her family to separate, Megan needs time to settle into a home on the Kansas prairie with an adoptive family.

678

DEBORAH HOPKINSON
JAMES E. RANSOME, Illustrator

Under the Quilt of Night

(New York: An Anne Schwartz Book/Atheneum Books for Young Readers, 2002)

Subject(s): Underground Railroad; Slavery; African Americans
Age range(s): Grades 2-5
Major character(s): Unnamed Character, Narrator, Slave (runaway)
Time period(s): Indeterminate Past
Locale(s): United States

Summary: A group of escaping slaves runs for their lives and their freedom under the cover of the night's darkness. A boat hidden in reeds helps them to cross a river and get away from pursuers on horseback and their dogs. By day they hide in bushes trying to sleep, ignoring the heat, the mosquitoes and the briars. When they near a town they look for a signal and bravely the young runaway leaves the group and approaches a home with a quilt draped over its fence. With assistance from the Underground Railroad they are sheltered and carried farther north, hidden in a wagon, until they finally reach their goal of freedom. A concluding author's note gives background information to the story. (32 pages)

Where it's reviewed:
Booklist, February 15, 2002, page 1034
Bulletin of the Center for Children's Books, February 2002, page 208
Horn Book, July 2002, page 447
Publishers Weekly, November 26, 2001, page 61
School Library Journal, January 2002, page 102

Awards the book has won:
IRA Children's Choices, 2003

Other books by the same author:
A Band of Angels, 1999 (ALA Notable Children's Book)
Birdie's Lighthouse, 1997 (Bulletin of the Center for Children's Books Blue Ribbon)
Sweet Clara and the Freedom Quilt, 1993 (IRA Children's Choices)

Other books you might like:
Pamela Duncan Edwards, *Barefoot: Escape on the Underground Railroad*, 1997
    A runaway slave finds food, water and a safe house by observing the animals along a trail.
Jeanette Winter, *Follow the Drinking Gourd*, 1988
    Escaped slaves use a song about the Big Dipper for the information they need to find a safe route to the North.
Sharon Dennis Wyeth, *Freedom's Wings: Corey's Diary*, 2001
    With help from the Underground Railroad runaway slaves Corey and Mama reach Canada to join Daddy who escaped first.

679

JOANNE HORNIMAN

Mahalia

(New York: Knopf, 2003)

Subject(s): Fathers and Daughters; Single Parent Families; Teen Parents

Age range(s): Grades 9-12

Major character(s): Matt, 17-Year-Old, Father (of Mahalia); Emmy, Mother (of Mahalia); Eliza, Singer, Student—College; Mahalia, Baby

Time period(s): 2000s

Locale(s): Lismore, Australia (New South Wales)

Summary: Emmy becomes pregnant and Matt and Emmy both drop out of school with every intention of keeping and loving their child. When Mahalia is five months old, Emmy can't cope with motherhood and leaves Matt on his own to care for their little girl. Though he knows it would be easier, he doesn't want his mother to raise Mahalia, so Matt rents a room from Eliza and tries to exist on the state's "single-parent pension." Though he's always tired and able to work only odd jobs, he adores Mahalia; when Emmy reappears to claim her, Matt knows he can't relinquish his daughter to Emmy. (184 pages)

Where it's reviewed:
Booklist, July 2003, page 1881
Bulletin of the Center for Children's Books, June 2003, page 405
Horn Book, July 2003, page 458
School Library Journal, April 2003, page 164
Voice of Youth Advocates, June 2003, page 134

Other books you might like:

Margaret Bechard, *Hanging on to Max*, 2002
    Sam's senior year isn't quite what he used to dream about as he's filling baby bottles, changing diapers and playing with Max, his son.

Angela Johnson, *The First Part Last*, 2003
    Told in alternating "then" and "now" chapters, teenager Bobby describes how his life changes after the birth of his daughter Feather.

Norma Klein, *No More Saturday Nights*, 1988
    Though college becomes more difficult, Tim Weber fights to keep his son rather than let his girlfriend give him up for adoption.

Marilyn Reynolds, *Too Soon for Jeff*, 1994
    Jeff finally leaves college to return home and split the parenting responsibilities for his newborn son Ethan.

680

ANTHONY HOROWITZ

Point Blank

(New York: Putnam/Philomel, 2002)

Subject(s): Spies; Schools/Boarding Schools; Cloning

Age range(s): Grades 6-10

Major character(s): Alexander "Alex" Rider, 14-Year-Old, Spy

Time period(s): 2000s

Locale(s): London, England; France (Point Blanc school)

Summary: After two noted businessmen die in different accidents, Alex is once again sent by M16 to investigate. This time the inquiry takes him to Point Blanc, an elite finishing school in the French Alps, where he enrolls to become a confidante of the sons of the two deceased businessmen. What Alex finds in the school are dull, studious boys who are not anything like the wealthy, juvenile delinquents he'd expected to meet. Further searching reveals a crazed scientist who wants to replace the sons of important men with docile clones who will do his bidding. Alex again carries James-Bond type weapons, but finds himself hanging onto an ironing board to escape down a mountain, in this continuing adventure series. (215 pages)

Where it's reviewed:
Booklist, April 1, 2002, page 1319
Kirkus Reviews, February 15, 2002, page 258
Kliatt, March 2002, page 11
School Library Journal, March 2002, page 232
Voice of Youth Advocates, February 2002, page 446

Other books by the same author:
Stormbreaker, 2000
The Devil and His Boy, 2000
Night of the Scorpion, 1988
The Devil-s Door-Bell, 1983

Other books you might like:

Anthony Dana Arkin, *Captain Hawaii*, 1994
    Exploding rafts, swarming spiders and a severed hand aren't what Arron expects to find when he and his parents vacation in Hawaii.

Norma Howe, *The Adventures of Blue Avenger*, 1999
    David decides to become the cartoon superhero he's always drawn and so performs good deeds, ends handgun violence and makes a weepless lemon meringue pie.

Rob McGregor, *Indiana Jones and the Dance of the Giants*, 1991
    Indiana and one of his students head off on a dangerous quest to locate a scroll that proves Merlin's existence.

Walter Dean Myers, *The Nicholas Factor*, 1983
    Spying for the government, a college student becomes part of a secret organization.

681

ANTHONY HOROWITZ

Skeleton Key

(New York: Philomel/Putnam Penguin, 2003)

Series: Alex Rider Adventure

Subject(s): Adventure and Adventurers; Spies; Orphans

Age range(s): Grades 6-10

Major character(s): Alexander "Alex" Rider, 14-Year-Old, Spy; Alexei Sarov, Military Personnel (retired), Terrorist

Time period(s): 2000s

Locale(s): Cayo Esquelto/Skeleton Key, Fictional Country (off the coast of Cuba)

Summary: On the small island of Cayo Esquelto, off the coast of Cuba, a former Russian general buys uranium he plans to use to set off a nuclear attack. His goal is to create enough chaos and tumult that he can seize power in Russia and return it to its glory days as the Soviet Union. Young spy Alex Rider is sent as a tourist to that island to collect information and try to halt Sarov's plan. Taking an instant liking to Rider, General Sarov regards him as his own son, even offering to adopt him. Alex takes advantage of this friendship and, using all the technology at his disposal, is in the right place at the right time to thwart Sarov's nuclear takeover in another spy adventure. (264 pages)

Where it's reviewed:
Booklist, May 15, 2003, page 1656
Kirkus Reviews, May 1, 2003, page 677
School Library Journal, May 2003, page 154
Voice of Youth Advocates, June 2003, page 150

Awards the book has won:
ALA Quick Picks for Reluctant Young Adult Readers, 2004

Other books by the same author:
Eagle Strike, 2004 (Alex Rider Adventure)
Point Blank, 2002 (Alex Rider Adventure)
Stormbreaker, 2001 (Alex Rider Adventure)
Mindgame, 2000

Other books you might like:
Ian Fleming, *Doctor No*, 1958
    James Bond tromps across a Caribbean island trying to stop the maniacal Doctor No's plan of world conquest.
Gary Paulsen, *The White Fox Chronicles: Escape, Return, Breakout*, 2000
    Cody is part of a resistance group of Americans fighting to regain control of their country from the Confederation of Consolidated Republics.
Paul Zindel, *The Gadget*, 2001
    Determined to find out about the "gadget" his Los Alamos-based father is working on, Stephen accidentally stumbles onto some Russian spies.

682

HARRY HORSE, Author/Illustrator

Little Rabbit Lost

(Atlanta, GA: Peachtree Publishers, 2002)

Subject(s): Animals/Rabbits; Birthdays; Missing Persons
Age range(s): Grades K-2
Major character(s): Little Rabbit, Rabbit, 4-Year-Old; Mama, Rabbit, Mother; Papa, Father, Rabbit
Time period(s): Indeterminate
Locale(s): Fictional Country

Summary: On a birthday trip to Rabbit World with his family, Little Rabbit is disappointed to discover that he is still too little to ride some of the rides. He was sure that he could now be considered a big rabbit, one that doesn't need to stay close to his parents while at Rabbit World. When he loses sight of Mama and Papa in the crowds at the amusement park, Little Rabbit realizes that maybe he's not quite ready to be alone in the world. Fortunately, Little Rabbit is carrying his big, red, helium birthday balloon and, as he searches for his parents, the balloon helps his family locate him. (32 pages)

Where it's reviewed:
Booklist, December 1, 2002, page 674
Horn Book Guide, Spring 2003, page 13
Publishers Weekly, September 2, 2002, page 74
School Library Journal, October 2002, page 112

Awards the book has won:
Publishers Weekly Best Children's Books, 2002

Other books by the same author:
Little Rabbit Goes to School, 2004
A Friend for Little Bear, 1996

Other books you might like:
Joyce Dunbar, *Tell Me What It's Like to Be Big*, 2001
    After talking with her older brother about what the future holds as she grows up, Willa's not sure if she wants to be bigger or not.
Diane Johnston Hamm, *Laney's Lost Mama*, 1991
    Following a plan helps Laney and her mom find each other when Laney's mom becomes "lost" while shopping.
Frances Minters, *Too Big, Too Small, Just Right*, 2001
    Rabbit friends discover how to enjoy some toys despite the fact that some are too big and some too small; by playing together everything is just right.
Rosemary Wells, *Bunny Party*, 2001
    Ruby invites Max to help her prepare a birthday party for Grandma but, as usual, they do not agree on anything.

683

POLLY HORVATH

The Canning Season

(New York: Farrar Straus Giroux, 2003)

Subject(s): Aunts and Uncles; Twins; Family Life
Age range(s): Grades 7-10
Major character(s): Tilly Menuto, Aged Person, Twin; Penelope "PenPen" Menuto, Aged Person, Twin; Ratchet Clark, 13-Year-Old; Harper, 14-Year-Old; Henriette Clark, Mother (of Ratchet)
Time period(s): 2000s
Locale(s): Glen Rosa, Maine

Summary: Living in a below-ground apartment in Pensacola, with an uncaring mother who's never home, Ratchet is nevertheless taken aback when Henriette sends her by train, minus her suitcase, to spend the summer in a remote area of Maine with her great-aunts. Tilly and PenPen are past old, and have become more than eccentric along the way, but are delighted to have an audience in Ratchet as they spin the weird stories of their family. The trio becomes a quartet when Harper's pregnant aunt drops her off at the door of Glen Rosa, thinking it's an orphanage; unable to explain the difference, PenPen and Tilly welcome the outspoken Harper into their midst. Though bizarre, Glen Rosa and the eccentric aunts are just the loving, caring components that Ratchet and Harper need in their lives. Even after Tilly dies, Ratchet and Harper stay on with PenPen, living surrounded by man-eating bears and picking blueberries for "canning season." (196 pages)

Where it's reviewed:
Booklist, April 1, 2003, page 1387

Bulletin of the Center for Children's Books, July 2003, page 451

Horn Book, May 2003, page 350

Quill & Quire, March 2003, page 51

School Library Journal, May 2003, page 154

Awards the book has won:

National Book Award, Young People's Literature, 2003

ALA Best Books for Young Adults, 2004

Other books by the same author:

Everything on a Waffle, 2001

Trolls, 1999

When the Circus Came to Town, 1996

Other books you might like:

Debi Gliori, *Pure Dead Magic*, 2001

Titus, Pandora and Damp adjust to a new nanny, their mother's return to witchcraft school and their fathers kidnapping by his evil half-brother.

Sid Hite, *Dither Farm*, 1992

Dither Farm becomes really lively after Great-Aunt Emma arrives.

Eva Ibbotson, *Island of the Aunts*, 2000

When Aunts Etta, Coral and Myrtle need help caring for their animals, they return to England and kidnap several children to be their assistants.

Richard Peck, *A Long Way from Chicago*, 1998

Warm and funny stories are shared during the summer Joey and his sister Mary Alice spend with their grandmother.

684

ARTHUR HOWARD, Author/Illustrator

Serious Trouble

(San Diego: Harcourt, Inc., 2003)

Subject(s): Fairy Tales; Dragons; Kings, Queens, Rulers, etc.

Age range(s): Grades K-2

Major character(s): Ernest, Son, Royalty; Olaf, Royalty (king), Father; Olive, Royalty (queen), Mother

Time period(s): Indeterminate Past

Locale(s): Fictional Country

Summary: Serious King Olaf and Queen Olive consider their son's ideas about what he will be when he grows up to be a bit preposterous. Ernest refuses to be serious, has no plans to be king and tells his parents that he aspires to be a jester. King Olaf reminds Ernest the kingdom is troubled by a three-headed, fire-breathing, people-eating dragon, a serious situation indeed. When Ernest, quite by chance, finds himself "face-to-face-to-face-to-face" with the dragon he recognizes just how serious it is. Still, Ernest uses his strengths to get out of the predicament and his talent is humor. The three heads aren't in agreement as to their approach to Ernest, but the dragon's feet succumb to his tickle attack. Ernest only stops tickling when the dragon promises to stop eating people. Then Ernest and the dragon get together to perform for King Olaf and Queen Olive. (32 pages)

Where it's reviewed:

Horn Book, November 2003, page 730

Publishers Weekly, November 3, 2003, page 72

School Library Journal, November 2003, page 96

Other books by the same author:

Hoodwinked, 2001 (School Library Journal Best Books)

Cosmo Zooms, 1999 (IRA Children's Choices)

When I Was Five, 1996 (IRA Children's Choices)

Other books you might like:

Ogden Nash, *The Tale of Custard the Dragon*, 1995

In an illustrated reissue of the 1936 tale, Belinda lives with a cowardly dragon that, fortunately, finds the courage to save her from a vicious pirate.

Shelley Moore Thomas, *Get Well, Good Knight*, 2002

The Good Knight comes to the aid of his young dragon friends with a mom-made potion to treat their colds.

Kathy Tucker, *The Seven Chinese Sisters*, 2003

Each of six sisters uses her unique talent to aid in rescuing their youngest sister from a dragon.

685

JAMES HOWE, Editor

13: Thirteen Stories That Capture the Agony and Ecstasy of Being Thirteen

(New York: Atheneum/Simon & Schuster, 2003)

Subject(s): Short Stories; Teen Relationships

Age range(s): Grades 6-9

Summary: The trials and tribulations of being 13 are captured by authors who well remember those early years. Lori Aurelia Williams tells of Malik who seriously considers joining a gang just to get those shoes he wants in "Black Holes and Basketball Sneakers." Wondering and worrying about what happens if a boy kisses another boy is explored in Alex Sanchez's "If You Kiss a Boy." "Noodle Soup for Nincompoops" by Ellen Wittlinger features Maggie in her new, anonymous role as advice columnist for her school's newspaper. Wanting his bar mitzvah to mean something, Jeremy invites a homeless man to attend and participate in James Howe's "Jeremy Goldblatt Is So Not Moses." Other young adult authors included are Meg Cabot, Bruce Coville, Maureen Ryan Griffin, Ron Koertge, Carolyn Mackler, Ann M. Martin, Laura Godwin, Stephen Roos, Todd Strasser and Rachel Vail. Each story includes a photo of the author at 13. (281 pages)

Where it's reviewed:

Booklist, January 2004, page 843

Bulletin of the Center for Children's Books, January 2004, page 193

Publishers Weekly, November 17, 2003, page 65

School Library Journal, October 2003, page 167

Voice of Youth Advocates, December 2003, page 388

Other books by the same author:

The Color of Absence: Twelve Stories about Loss and Hope, 2001

The Watcher, 1997

The New Nick Kramer, or My Life as a Baby-sitter, 1995

Other books you might like:

Michael Cart, *Love and Sex: Ten Stories of Truth*, 2001

All the angst of being in love is captured here, from

worries about being gay to "doing it," to infatuation and crushes.

Donald R. Gallo, *No Easy Answers: Short Stories about Teenagers Making Tough Choices*, 1997

A strong collection of short stories featuring teens who face a moral crisis, such as peer pressure, computer blackmail or gangs.

Barbara Ann Porte, *Beauty and the Serpent: Thirteen Tales of Unnatural Animals*, 2001

Whenever students at Wild Alternative HS misbehave, they're sent to the library where Ms. Drumm tells them a story about unnatural, unexpected animals.

686

JAMES HOWE
AMY WALROD, Illustrator

Horace and Morris Join the Chorus (but what about Dolores?)

(New York: Atheneum Books for Young Readers, 2002)

Subject(s): Animals/Mice; Singing; Friendship
Age range(s): Grades K-2
Major character(s): Horace, Mouse, Student; Morris, Mouse, Student; Dolores, Mouse, Student; Moustro Provolone, Mouse, Teacher
Time period(s): Indeterminate
Locale(s): Fictional Country

Summary: When Horace, Morris and Dolores see a notice for chorus tryouts they attend in anticipation of singing together in a performance. Horace likes to sing high notes while Morris prefers low notes and Dolores sings notes that not many have ever heard before. When the results of the tryouts are posted Dolores is sad to see her name is not listed. Dolores unsuccessfully pleads her case with Moustro Provolone and when she can find nothing else to do she pours her heart out to him in a letter. Moustro Provolone sees Dolores's potential as a songwriter and decides to give her voice instructions so that, by the night of the concert, she's hitting the right note most of the time. (32 pages)

Where it's reviewed:
Booklist, November 15, 2002, page 610
Horn Book, January 2003, page 56
Publishers Weekly, October 14, 2002, page 83
School Library Journal, November 2002, page 126

Other books by the same author:
Amazing Odorous Adventures of Stinky Dog, 2003
Pinky and Rex and the Just-Right Pet, 2001
Horace and Morris but Mostly Dolores, 1999 (Booklist Editors' Choice)

Other books you might like:
Mary Jane Auch, *Bantam of the Opera*, 1997
Born to sing, Luigi angers the head rooster by creating variations on the cock-a-doodle-doo theme so he turns to opera.
Carolyn Crimi, *Tessa's Tip-Tapping Toes*, 2002
A mouse that can't stop dancing joins up with a housecat that loves to sing for a lively duet.

Dayle Ann Dodds, *Sing, Sophie!*, 1997
No one on the family farm seems to appreciate Sophie's singing talents until her loud song is able to calm Baby Jacob during a thunderstorm.
Faye Gibbons, *Emma Jo's Song*, 2001
Emma Jo feels like the outcast in a musical family because she just can't seem to carry a tune.
Linda Goss, *The Frog Who Wanted to Be a Singer*, 1996
Determined to be a singer, Frog goes to Brother Fox's Big Time Weekly Concert to perform before an audience.

687

JAMES HOWE
BRETT HELQUIST, Illustrator

Howie Monroe and the Doghouse of Doom

(New York: Atheneum Books for Young Readers, 2002)

Series: Tales from the House of Bunnicula
Subject(s): Animals/Dogs; Writing; Humor
Age range(s): Grades 3-5
Major character(s): Howie Monroe, Dog, Writer; Toby Monroe, Child; Uncle Harold, Dog, Writer
Time period(s): 2000s (2002)
Locale(s): Centerville; Dogwiz Academy, Fictional Country

Summary: As Howie approaches his third book he realizes he's running out of ideas and finds inspiration in a story that Toby's reading Howie and Uncle Harold. Casting himself as the mistreated orphan, Howie sets his third adventure at the Dogwiz Academy for Canine Conjurers. Soon after his arrival Howie's warned to stay away from the Doghouse of Doom. However, in order for the story to develop as the author intends, eventually Howie must enter the Doghouse of Doom and face the evil, unnamed force determined to destroy him. Just when it appears that Howie is a goner he saves himself by calling out the real name of the evil force and transforms it back into the innocent kitten it once was. (90 pages)

Where it's reviewed:
Booklist, October 1, 2002, page 326
School Library Journal, November 2002, page 169

Other books by the same author:
Bud Barkin, Private Eye, 2003
Invasion of the Mind Swappers from Asteroid 6!, 2002
It Came from Beneath the Bed, 2002

Other books you might like:
Patricia Finney, *I, Jack*, 2004
Jack relates the routine events of life and the excitement generated when an attractive female dog moves into the neighborhood.
Lois Lowry, *Gooney Bird Greene*, 2002
New student Gooney Bird is quite a storyteller and all her improbable tales are true.
Daniel Pinkwater, *Mush's Jazz Adventure*, 2002
Alien dog Mush adds the job title jazz musician to her lengthy list of accomplishments.

688

JAMES HOWE
BRETT HELQUIST, Illustrator

It Came from Beneath the Bed

(New York: Atheneum Books for Young Readers, 2002)

Series: Tales from the House of Bunnicula
Subject(s): Authors and Writers; Scientific Experiments; Animals/Dogs
Age range(s): Grades 3-6
Major character(s): Howie Monroe, Dog (dachshund), Writer; Delilah, Dog, Friend; Pete Monroe, 11-Year-Old, 6th Grader
Time period(s): 2000s
Locale(s): Centerville

Summary: Howie tries his hand (or should that be paw?) at writing this episode in the Bunnicula series. Inserted between the chapters are paw-written entries from Howie's writing journal that contain critiques of his progress as a writer. The story develops in fits and starts as Howie responds to suggestions but throughout it involves his growing affection for Delilah, Pete's messy room and Howie's idea that Pete is developing a potion to assure his domination of the world. (90 pages)

Where it's reviewed:
Booklist, August 2002, page 1961
Bulletin of the Center for Children's Books, October 2002, page 61
Publishers Weekly, July 8, 2002, page 50
School Library Journal, November 2002, page 169

Other books by the same author:
Bud Barkin, Private Eye, 2003 (Tales from the House of Bunnicula)
Howie Monroe and the Doghouse of Doom, 2002 (Tales from the House of Bunnicula)
Invasion of the Mind Swappers from Asteroid 6!, 2002 (Tales from the House of Bunnicula)

Other books you might like:
Mary Jane Auch, *I Was a Third Grade Science Project*, 1998
Brian's plan to hypnotize his dog doesn't work out in quite the way he hypothesizes.
Jim Benton, *Lunch Walks Among Us*, 2003
The first entry in the Franny K. Stein Mad Scientist series introduces Franny as she tries to make friends in a new school.
Mary Blount Christian, *The Sebastian (Super Sleuth) Series*, 1982-
Sebastian, an English sheepdog, is the case-solving sidekick of his master John Jones.
Elizabeth Levy, *The Something Queer Series*, 1971-
Gwen, Jill and basset hound Fletcher enjoy adventures as they solve mysteries.

689

NORMA HOWE

Blue Avenger and the Theory of Everything

(Chicago: Marcato/Cricket, 2002)

Subject(s): Interpersonal Relations; Contests; Identity
Age range(s): Grades 7-10
Major character(s): David Bruce ''Blue Avenger'' Schumacher, 16-Year-Old; Omaha Nebraska Brown, 16-Year-Old
Time period(s): 2000s
Locale(s): Oakland, California

Summary: When David Schumacher changed his name to Blue Avenger, he also found the courage to tell his girlfriend Omaha that he loved her, but now there's a problem. Omaha's single mother is in financial difficulties, which may force them to move away, Blue Avenger can't bear to think about their move, especially because he's not able to change anything monetarily. Suddenly he has a chance to earn some money by helping encode the word ''suck'' so that it will pass unchallenged by the license plate censor. It seems a wealthy movie producer never had a chance to deliver his valedictory speech at San Pablo High because of the word suck and he now wishes to retaliate against the student who turned him in, the same student who is now a license plate censor. Along with this quandary, Blue also faces the challenge of oversimplified reading programs, his divorced mother's boyfriend and his brother's school projects in this third Blue Avenger adventure. (225 pages)

Where it's reviewed:
Booklist, May 15, 2001, page 1592
Bulletin of the Center for Children's Books, July 2002, page 405
Kirkus Reviews, April 1, 2002, page 493
Kliatt, July 2002, page 10
School Library Journal, July 2002, page 120

Awards the book has won:
Center for Children's Books Best Books, 2002

Other books by the same author:
Blue Avenger Cracks the Code, 2000
The Adventures of Blue Avenger, 1999
Shoot for the Moon, 1992
God, the Universe, and Hot Fudge Sundaes, 1984

Other books you might like:
A.E. Cannon, *Cal Cameron by Day, Spider-Man by Night*, 1988
Although Cal tries to play the role of popular football hero, he really looks for a deeper meaning to life.
Dan Gutman, *The Million Dollar Kick*, 2001
Whisper wins a slogan contest for a women's soccer team, but is horrified to discover she has to kick a twenty-yard penalty shot.
Anne C. LeMieux, *All the Answers*, 2000
Being a teen-ager is difficult for Jason as he struggles with algebra, his messiness and a going-nowhere romance.

MARY HOWITT
TONY DITERLIZZI, Illustrator

The Spider and the Fly

(New York: Simon & Schuster Books for Young Readers, 2002)

Subject(s): Animals/Spiders; Animals/Insects; Stories in Rhyme
Age range(s): Grades 3-6
Major character(s): Spider, Spider, Villain; Fly, Fly
Time period(s): Indeterminate Past
Locale(s): Fictional Country

Summary: In the newly illustrated version of Howitt's 1829 poem villainous Spider invites naive, but skeptical Fly into his parlor. Ghostly creatures seek to warn Fly by displaying cutlery while pointing to a cookbook entitled "The Joy of Cooking Bugs." Repeatedly, demure Fly declines before eventually succumbing to Spider's enticements and meeting the same fate as the specters flitting about. As Spider's concluding letter notes, what other ending could one expect from such a tale. (32 pages)

Where it's reviewed:
Booklist, October 1, 2002, page 316
Bulletin of the Center for Children's Books, November 2002, page 112
Horn Book Guide, Spring 2003, page 169
Publishers Weekly, July 1, 2002, page 79
School Library Journal, September 2002, page 214

Awards the book has won:
Caldecott Honor Book, 2003
School Library Journal Best Books, 2002

Other books you might like:
David Kirk, *Miss Spider's Tea Party*, 1994
    Bugs are reluctant to accept Miss Spider's invitation to tea although she's only interested in eating the floral centerpiece and not her guests.
Simms Taback, *There Was an Old Lady Who Swallowed a Fly*, 1997
    A Caldecott Honor Book follows the traditional tale with inventive illustrations.
Jeanette Winter, *The Itsy-Bitsy Spider*, 2000
    The well-known children's song provides the text for this illustrated board book.

691

SARAH A. HOYT

All Night Awake

(New York: Ace Books, 2002)

Subject(s): Fantasy; Fairies
Age range(s): Grades 9-Adult
Major character(s): Silver "Quicksilver", Mythical Creature (fairy), Noblewoman; William "Will" Shakespeare, Writer, Historical Figure; Kit Marlowe, Writer, Historical Figure; Sylvanus, Mythical Creature (fairt), Criminal
Time period(s): Indeterminate
Locale(s): London, England

Summary: Starving poet Will Shakespeare has just had a stunning dream. In it, three weird women have promised him his poetry will be remembered down the ages if he will stop Sylvanus and restore the balance of the human and fairy worlds. Shakespeare has had dealings with fairy kind before when he was drawn into the machinations of the fairy court. There he struggled to save his beloved Nan and to extricate himself from the seductions of Lady Silver. Silver is the changeling fairy that currently rules the fairies, in his feminine aspect. His brother Sylvanus lost the kingdom while Silver toyed with Will, and now Sylvanus is condemned to serve the Hunter in punishment. But Sylvanus has not given up his evil ways and he has learned from the Hunter how to draw power from death. This ability, meant to be used to dispense justice, is now corrupted and allows Sylvanus to escape to London, where there are many humans upon which to prey. Quicksilver follows, desperate to bring Sylvanus back under control. In London, Will has met a man he hopes will further his career, the famous playwright Kit Marlowe, but Marlowe has troubles of his own and hopes Will can help him. Quicksilver arrives as Lady Silver and the complications are multiplied, for Kit is also one of her former lovers and those who have had dealings with Faerie are Sylvanus's first choice of victim in this sequel to *Ill Met by Moonlight*. (311 pages)

Where it's reviewed:
Booklist, September 15, 2002, page 212
Chronicle, November 2002, page 28
Library Journal, October 15, 2002, page 97
Publishers Weekly, September 23, 2002, page 55
Voice of Youth Advocates, April 2003, page 65

Other books by the same author:
Any Man So Daring, 2003
Ill Met by Moonlight, 2001

Other books you might like:
Anne Crompton, *Merlin's Harp*, 1995
    Merlin visits the faeries as a tutor for the Lady of the Lake's children.
Lisa Goldstein, *Strange Devices of the Sun and Moon*, 1993
    The entire Seelie Court invades Renaissance London.
Grace Tiffany, *My Father Had a Daughter: Judith Shakespeare's Tale*, 2003
    Teenaged Judith is furious with her famous father after he uses her emotions in one of his plays.

692

SHELLEY HRDLITSCHKA

Dancing Naked

(Custer, WA: Orca Book Publishers, 2002)

Subject(s): Pregnancy; Adoption
Age range(s): Grades 8-12
Major character(s): Kia Hazelwood, 16-Year-Old, Pregnant Teenager; Derek Klassen, 17-Year-Old; Justin Reid, Counselor (youth counselor), Homosexual
Time period(s): 2000s
Locale(s): Canada

Summary: Kia makes a mistake, a big mistake, when she makes love with Derek for her first sexual experience. Not only does she become pregnant, but Kia also discovers what a selfish jerk Derek is; his only concern is that Kia not tell anyone she's pregnant before she can have an abortion and remove all the evidence. Thankfully Kia has her family, friends and Justin, the youth counselor from her church, who support her during her pregnancy and through the decision-making process of keeping her child or allowing it to be adopted. (250 pages)

Where it's reviewed:
Booklist, March 15, 2002, page 1250
Kliatt, July 2002, page 21
Resource Links, February 2002, page 27
School Library Journal, March 2002, page 232
Voice of Youth Advocates, April 2001, page 44

Awards the book has won:
ALA Quick Picks for Reluctant Young Adult Readers, 2003

Other books by the same author:
Kat's Fall, 2004
Tangled Web, 2000
Beans on Toast, 1998
Disconnected, 1998

Other books you might like:
Patricia Calvert, *Stranger, You and I*, 1987
    When Hughie's best friend reveals her pregnancy after a fling with a rich guy, Hughie helps her through the birth and subsequent adoption.
Sarah Dessen, *Someone Like You*, 1998
    During Halley's junior year, she and her best friend Scarlett become very close, especially after Scarlett discovers she's pregnant.
Geraldine Kaye, *Someone Else's Baby*, 1992
    Raped by a stranger while in a drunken haze at a party, Terry makes the difficult decision to give up the baby for adoption.
Marilyn Reynolds, *Detour for Emmy*, 1993
    Deserted by the father of her child, Emmy decides to have her baby and make the best life she can for both of them.
Beatrice Sparks, *Annie's Baby: The Diary of Anonymous, a Pregnant Teenager*, 1998
    Annie can't believe that good-looking Danny has fallen for her, but he abuses her and when confronted with her pregnancy, denies he's the father.

693

PAT HUGHES

Guerrilla Season
(New York: Farrar Straus Giroux, 2003)

Subject(s): Civil War; Farm Life; Underground Resistance Movements
Age range(s): Grades 7-10
Major character(s): Matt Howard, 15-Year-Old, Farmer; Jesse James, Friend (of Matt's), Historical Figure; William Clark Quantrill, Historical Figure, Military Personnel
Time period(s): 1860s (1863)
Locale(s): Missouri

Summary: In the western part of Missouri, neighbor turns against neighbor depending upon whom they favor, the Un-

ions and the Northern jayhawkers or the Rebels and the Southern bushwhackers. Since the death of his father, Matt isn't interested in fighting for either side and wants to spend his time farming to care for his mother and five siblings. His best friend Jesse is firmly for the Southerners and can hardly wait to join his older brother in Quantrill's forces. Matt feels continually buffeted by the various factions in his neighborhood so that soon he's forced to take a stand in this author's first novel. (329 pages)

Where it's reviewed:
Booklist, August 2003, page 1971
Kirkus Reviews, July 15, 2003, page 964
Publishers Weekly, August 11, 2003, page 281
School Library Journal, November 2003, page 140
Voice of Youth Advocates, December 2003, page 402

Other books by the same author:
Breaker Boys, 2004

Other books you might like:
Jennifer Johnson Garrity, *The Bushwhackers: A Civil War Adventure*, 1999
    Because their father is a Union man, Jacob and Eliza's farm is burned down by Confederate sympathizers called "bushwhackers."
Pamela Smith Hill, *A Voice from the Border*, 1998
    Reeves doesn't understand the Civil War or the various causes espoused by the secessionists, slaves, slave owners, Jayhawkers and those loyal to the union.
Carolyn Reeder, *Shades of Gray*, 1989
    Orphan Will Page has a hard time living with his Uncle Jed knowing that Jed didn't fight for either side during the Civil War when Will's father was killed.

694

SHIRLEY HUGHES, Author/Illustrator

Annie Rose Is My Little Sister
(Cambridge, MA: Candlewick Press, 2003)

Subject(s): Brothers and Sisters; Playing; Family
Age range(s): Grades K-1
Major character(s): Annie Rose, Child, Sister (younger); Unnamed Character, Brother, Narrator
Time period(s): 2000s (2002)
Locale(s): England

Summary: Annie Rose's big brother knows her interests and patiently reads to her, plays hide and seek and takes on roles in her make-believe games. While it's a bit annoying when Annie Rose wants to play with his toys, he tolerates her and adapts by using a table higher than she can reach for his trains. They enjoy different activities at the beach and different friends at home. If Annie Rose wakes up from a nap feeling grumpy only her big brother can make her happy. That's how it is and will be for a big brother and a little sister in a loving family. Originally published in the United Kingdom in 2002. (32 pages)

Where it's reviewed:
Booklist, March 1, 2003, page 1201
Bulletin of the Center for Children's Books, April 2003, page 317

Publishers Weekly, February 24, 2003, page 74
School Library Journal, April 2003, page 122

Other books by the same author:
Olly and Me, 2004
Alfie and the Birthday Surprise, 1997
Rhymes for Annie Rose, 1995
Alfie Gets in First, 1982

Other books you might like:
Ian Falconer, *Olivia*, 2000
   Olivia, a pig with a mind of her own, tolerates her younger brother, tries on every outfit before making up her mind, and dances during naptime.
Anne Rockwell, *Long Ago Yesterday*, 1999
   Ten brief stories describe everyday family activities that are important to young children.
Caroline Uff, *Hello, Lulu*, 1999
   Lulu's favorite things include the color red, a special teddy bear, her best friend, three pets and her family.

695

JAN HULING
PHIL HULING, Illustrator

Puss in Cowboy Boots

(New York: Simon & Schuster Books for Young Readers, 2002)

Subject(s): Fairy Tales; Folklore; American West
Age range(s): Grades 1-3
Major character(s): Dan, Brother, Young Man; Puss, Cat, Trickster; Mr. Patoot, Businessman, Father
Time period(s): Indeterminate Past
Locale(s): Texas

Summary: In this adaptation of the French fairy tale Puss is an old scrawny Texas cat sporting red cowboy boots. Puss has a plan to make Dan rich and he begins by delivering a wild turkey to Mr. Patoot as a gift from "Rancher Dan." On a regular basis over a few months' time Puss makes deliveries of animals that remind Mr. Patoot of his country upbringing. With his daughter, an art student home on vacation, Mr. Patoot drives into the countryside for a picnic. Puss arranges the circumstances for Mr. Patoot and his daughter to meet Dan, to provide him with new clothes and boots and to believe that Dan truly is rich with vast land holdings. The plan works as Puss hopes and the story ends on a happy note for everyone, including a contented Puss, as the author's first book concludes. (36 pages)

Where it's reviewed:
Booklist, August 2002, page 1968
Bulletin of the Center for Children's Books, October 2002, page 62
Horn Book, July 2002, page 475
Publishers Weekly, April 29, 2002, page 70
School Library Journal, June 2002, page 120

Other books you might like:
Steve Light, *Puss in Boots*, 2002
   In this adaptation of the folktale, illustrated with collages, Puss is portrayed as female.
Charles Perrault, *Puss in Boots*, 1990
   In this translation of the French fairy tale illustrated by

Marcellino, a cat uses only a sack and a pair of boots to acquire wealth for its master.
Anne Rockwell, *Puss in Boots and Other Stories*, 1988
   The illustrated collection of 12 stories includes a retelling of Puss in Boots.

696

ERIN HUNTER

Warriors Series

(New York: HarperCollins, 2003-)

Series: Warriors
Subject(s): Animals/Cats; Fantasy
Age range(s): Grades 5 and Up
Major character(s): Bluestar, Leader, Cat; Firepaw "Fireheart", Cat, Apprentice
Time period(s): Indeterminate
Locale(s): Fictional Country

Summary: The Warriors Series follows four clans of cats, RiverClan, ShadowClan, ThunderClan and WindClan, who live in the forest and observe territorial boundaries, but align with one another when necessary. The teen tomcat Rusty decides he's had enough of the world of "twolegs" and is ready to abandon his "kittypet" position for life in the wild. Lacking proven hunting skills, he's found by Bluestar, leader of the ThunderClan, and is adopted into their group. Now called Firepaw to designate his apprentice role, he joins with his fellow clan members and other apprentices to learn new rules for living. As the series continues, Firepaw becomes a warrior and is renamed Fireheart, the various clans jockey for territory and position in the forest and Fireheart learns that some of the worst danger occurs from cats within his own clan.

Where it's reviewed:
Booklist, February 15, 2003, page 1064
Bulletin of the Center for Children's Books, March 2003, page 277
Library Media Connection, November 2003, page 53
Publishers Weekly, December 23, 2002, page 72
School Library Journal, May 2003, page 154

Other books by the same author:
Fire and Ice, 2003 (Warriors Book 2)
Forest of Secrets, 2003 (Warriors Book 3)
Into the Wild, 2003 (Warriors Book 1)

Other books you might like:
Clare Bell, *Ratha's Creature*, 1983
   Ratha, an intelligent feline, is forced out of her clan until she discovers the use of fire and can help her clanmates. Sequels.
Shirley Rousseau Murphy, *The Catswold Portal*, 1992
   In a strange, underground landscape, cats who are able to shape shift must save their world from an evil queen.
Phyllis Reynolds Naylor, *The Grand Escape*, 1993
   Brother cats Marco and Polo plan their "grand escape" after Marco reads all about ranches in the newspapers lining his litter box.

rzweil, *Leon and the Spitting Image*, 2003
d to stitch a doll, Leon designs one that resembles his
r Miss Hagmeyer and finds manipulating the doll
manipulates her.

ox Mazer, *Out of Control*, 1993
spirited physical revenge for an imagined insult
the victim and her attackers, even when they all try
tend nothing happened.

704

HAZEL HUTCHINS

T.J. and the Cats

(Custer, WA: Orca Book Publishers)

rca Young Reader
): Animals/Cats; Grandmothers; Vacations
e(s): Grades 3-4
character(s): T.J. Barnes, Student—Elementary
l, Friend; Seymour, Student—Elementary School,
; Gran, Grandmother
iod(s): 2000s (2002)
: Canada

y: Clearly T.J.'s love of Gran overpowered his com-
se or he would never have agreed to care for her four
le she vacationed in Hawaii. T.J. fears cats and now
rounded by them with no idea what to do. After
ing Seymour to change their school project topic from
s to cats, T.J. begins to learn from their research the
r cats' behavior and his fear decreases. By the time
turns from her trip to reclaim her pets, T.J. and
r have earned an "A" on their project, lost and found
, and become sufficiently fond of them to agree to
e two kittens resulting from one cat's three-day esca-
hile lost. (103 pages)

it's reviewed:
t, December 15, 2002, page 759
Library Journal, February 2003, page 114

books by the same author:
s Art Attack, 2001
nce of Tarn, 1997
ree and Many Wishes of Jason Reid, 1988

books you might like:
Freeman, *The Trouble with Cats*, 2000
e her mother's remarriage, Holly is having a hard time
sting to life with a stepfather and his four cats.
hitehead Nagda, *Meow Means Mischief*, 2003
riending a stray kitten helps Rana adjust to a new
ool.

Phyllis Reynolds Naylor, *Danny's Desert Rats*, 1998
Danny and his brother T.R. help their new friend Paul hide
his pet cat from the apartment manager.

705

PAT HUTCHINS, Author/Illustrator

We're Going on a Picnic!

(New York: Greenwillow Books, 2002)

Subject(s): Animals/Birds; Food; Animals
Age range(s): Preschool-Grade 1
Major character(s): Hen, Chicken; Duck, Duck; Goose, Goose
Time period(s): Indeterminate
Locale(s): Fictional Country

Summary: Hen, Duck and Goose decide it's a perfect day for a
picnic so each picks a favorite fruit and packs it into a picnic
basket. They take turns carrying the basket as they search for
just the right spot to eat. None realize that the basket is so
heavy because of a succession of animals hopping in and out
to eat the fruit. When Hen, Duck and Goose finally reach a
spot to eat, they discover that the basket is empty so they pick
more fruit and set out again to find the perfect picnic location.
(32 pages)

Where it's reviewed:
Booklist, March 1, 2002, page 1142
Bulletin of the Center for Children's Books, July/August
2002, page 40
Horn Book Guide, Fall 2002, page 304
Publishers Weekly, January 21, 2002, page 89
School Library Journal, March 2002, page 190

Other books by the same author:
It's MY Birthday!, 1999
Titch and Daisy, 1996
Three-Star Billy, 1994

Other books you might like:
Jez Alborough, *Duck in the Truck*, 2000
When Duck gets his red truck stuck a frog a goat and a
sheep help to free the truck from the muck. Yuck!
Ruth Brown, *The Picnic*, 1993
After rain causes a family to hurriedly leave their picnic in
a meadow animals come out of hiding to enjoy the re-
mains.
Jane Yolen, *Off We Go!*, 2000
The various animals in this picture book have one destina-
tion as they set out—Grandma's house.

697

THACHER HURD, Author/Illustrator

Moo Cow Kaboom!

(New York: HarperCollins Publishers, 2003)

Subject(s): Animals/Cows; Farm Life; Space Travel
Age range(s): Grades K-2
Major character(s): Farmer George, Farmer; Moo Cow, Cow,
Kidnap Victim; Zork, Kidnapper, Alien
Time period(s): Indeterminate
Locale(s): Earth; Planet—Imaginary

Summary: In the middle of the night a loud "kaboom!"
awakens Farmer George. When he rushes out to investigate,
he can't find Moo Cow. Zork, a space cowboy who wants to
have an unusual entry in the Inter-Galactic Rodeo, has kidnapped Moo Cow. The befuddled animal is not familiar with
rodeos so she initially stands and does nothing while the
increasingly irate Zork shouts at her. Moo Cow understands
the insults and does not appreciate them so she begins whirling, twirling, bouncing and bucking until Zork is propelled
back to his farm. The other aliens, horrified by this wild
animal, put Moo Cow in a spaceship and send her back to
Earth where she lands with a "kaboom!" on Farmer George's
farm. (32 pages)

Where it's reviewed:
Booklist, July 2003, page 1897
Horn Book, May 2003, page 329
Publishers Weekly, April 21, 2003, page 61
School Library Journal, June 2003, page 107

Awards the book has won:
Center for Children's Books Best Books, 2003

Other books by the same author:
Santa Mouse and the Ratdeer, 1998
Zoom City, 1998
Art Dog, 1996

Other books you might like:
Chris Babcock, *No Moon, No Milk!*, 1993
Martha refuses to give her owner any milk until she fulfills
her dream to be a "cowsmonaut" and walk on the moon.
Denys Cazet, *Minnie and Moo Go to the Moon*, 1998
Cows Minnie and Moo "borrow" the farmer's tractor.
After crashing into the pigsty and becoming airborne they
think they've landed on the moon.
Paul Brett Johnson, *The Cow Who Wouldn't Come Down*,
1993
Gertrude, a cow with a mind of her own, has a mind to fly.
After she succeeds, she has no interest in returning to the
barn.
Toby Speed, *Two Cool Cows*, 1995
Maude and Millie, two cool cows in borrowed boots and
sunglasses, jump to the moon to frolic with their bovine
buddies.

698

CAROL OTIS HURST

In Plain Sight

(Boston: Houghton Mifflin/A Walter Lorraine Book, 2002)

Subject(s): Farm Life; Gold Discoveries; Fathers and Daugh-
ters
Age range(s): Grades 4-7
Major character(s): Sarah Corbin, 11-Year-Old; Robin
Corbin, Child, Brother; Delina Corbin, Mother; Miles
Corbin, Father, Prospector
Time period(s): 1850s
Locale(s): Westfield, Massachusetts

Summary: When Sarah's father leaves their farm to try his
luck in California's gold fields, she feels that all the fun has
gone out of her life. Though her quiet mother works to keep
the family and farm flourishing, her efforts aren't appreciated
until Sarah's badly burned in a fire while rescuing her brother.
Sarah has even more to weather besides her burns when the
family hears of her father's drowning, her grandfather's
stroke, and the startling reappearance of her father, who faked
his death after failing to make his fortune in gold. Sarah
struggles with her new understanding of her parents and wonders how she'll ever forgive her father for lying to his family.
(154 pages)

Where it's reviewed:
Booklist, March 1, 2002, page 1147
Horn Book, May 2002, page 331
Kirkus Reviews, March 1, 2002, page 337
School Library Journal, March 2002, page 232

Other books by the same author:
Through the Lock, 2001

Other books you might like:
Louann Gaeddert, *Hope*, 1995
With their father prospecting for gold, and their mother
dead, Hope and her brother are taken in by the Shaker
community.
Pamela Smith Hill, *A Voice from the Border*, 1998
Reeves has difficulty understanding why the North and
South are fighting, a difficulty compounded by the death of
her soldier father.
Sonia Levitin, *Clem's Chances*, 2001
When his mother dies, Clem takes a chance, leaves his
Missouri farm and heads west on foot to find his gold-
seeking father.

699

CAROL OTIS HURST

The Wrong One

(Boston: Walter Lorraine/Houghton Mifflin Books, 2003)

Subject(s): Moving, Household; Brothers and Sisters; Dolls
and Dollhouses
Age range(s): Grades 4-6
Major character(s): Kate Spencer, 11-Year-Old; Jesse
Spencer, Child; Sookhan Spencer, Adoptee, Child; Agatha
Paran, Collector (of dolls)

Time period(s): 2000s
Locale(s): Massachusetts

Summary: The death of their father leaves the Spencer family grieving, as well as quite a bit poorer, so they move from their home in Brooklyn to a farmhouse. Almost from the moment they arrive, strange events occur beginning with Sookhan's fear at staying in her room because of the wallpaper imprinted with a doll motif; finding an antique doll in the barn that matches the wallpaper is eerie. But there are other strange happenings, from a TV that turns on by itself, to a shimmery blue light and that antique doll that Sookhan keeps saying is "the wrong one." A burst water pipe unveils a hole in the wall that leads them to the "right" doll, a doll that fetches them $100,000 from Agatha Paran who once lived in their old farmhouse. Are there ghosts in that farmhouse? Perhaps, but only the Spencers know for sure. (156 pages)

Where it's reviewed:
Booklist, March 1, 2003, page 1198
Bulletin of the Center for Children's Books, July 2003, page 452
Kirkus Reviews, May 1, 2003, page 678
Publishers Weekly, May 5, 2003, page 67
School Library Journal, May 2003, page 154

Other books by the same author:
A Killing in Plymouth Colony, 2003
In Plain Sight, 2002
Through the Lock, 2001

Other books you might like:
Mary Downing Hahn, *The Doll in the Garden*, 1989
 Finding an antique doll in an overgrown rose garden links Ashley with the present and the past.
Sylvia Waugh, *The Mennyms*, 1994
 After she dies, life-size dolls that Kate Penshaw created 40 years ago, come to life and enjoy residing in her home.
Betty Ren Wright, *The Dollhouse Murders*, 1983
 The clues left by a pair of dolls in the attic help Amy solve the murder of her aunt's grandparents.

700

DAVIDA WILLS HURWIN

The Farther You Run
(New York: Viking, 2003)

Subject(s): Grief; Friendship; Death
Age range(s): Grades 9-12
Major character(s): Samantha Russell, 18-Year-Old; Mona Brocato, 19-Year-Old; Juliana, Friend (of Samantha; deceased)
Time period(s): 1990s
Locale(s): San Francisco, California

Summary: It's now summer and Samantha's taking an English class in order to graduate, having failed English after her best friend Juliana died of cancer in May. In class she meets Mona, also trying to graduate, who failed English because of caring for her bipolar mother during her manic episodes. While Samantha struggles with her grief and Mona with her relationship with her mother, the two decide to rent an apartment together and look for jobs. Suddenly a fresh world opens for

Samantha as she meets new people and tries to move on, but it's hard to forget. At times even her friendship with Mona suffers, especially when Mona sleeps with a boy Sam's been dating. On her nineteenth birthday, Sam makes a special attempt to come to terms with her grief as she takes a ballet class in fulfillment of a promise to Juliana. (217 pages)

Where it's reviewed:
Booklist, August 2003, page 1980
Kirkus Reviews, June 15, 2003, page 859
Library Media Connection, March 2004, page 67
School Library Journal, August 2003, page 160
Voice of Youth Advocates, August 2003, page 225

Other books by the same author:
A Time for Dancing, 1995

Other books you might like:
Bruce Brooks, *All That Remains*, 2001
 Three novellas offer different takes on death from creative coffins and burial spots to looking after a cousin.
Julie Reece Deaver, *Say Goodnight, Gracie*, 1988
 Morgan's life comes to an abrupt halt when her dear friend Jimmy is killed in an automobile accident.
Carolyn McCullough, *Falling through Darkness*, 2003
 Ginny reflects on her adventures with her devil-may-care boyfriend Aidan, before his abusive home situation overwhelmed his life.

701

JOHANNA HURWITZ
BARBARA GARRISON, Illustrator

Dear Emma
(New York: HarperCollins, 2002)

Subject(s): Friendship; Letters; Russian Americans
Age range(s): Grades 4-6
Major character(s): Hadassah "Dossi" Rabinowitz, 12-Year-Old, Orphan; Ruth "Ruthi" Rabinowitz, Sister (of Dossi), Orphan; Emma Meade, Friend (of Dossi); Meyer Reisman, Pharmacist
Time period(s): 1910s (1910-1911)
Locale(s): New York, New York (Lower East Side)

Summary: A friendship begun when Dossi attended summer camp in Vermont, thanks to the Clean Air Fund, continues once Dossi returns to the Lower East Side of New York and writes to Emma. Her letters are filled with stories of her life after her older sister Ruthi marries Meyer and both sisters move into his apartment. Though Dossi and her brother-in-law often butt heads, Dossi feels more kindly toward him when she learns her sister is pregnant. Their neighborhood is hit by a double tragedy when a diphtheria epidemic breaks out and then the Triangle Shirtwaist Factory fire erupts, killing over 100 seamstresses, including one of their friends. The year ends well when her niece is born and Dossi considers studying for a medical career after she graduates from grammar school in this sequel to *Faraway Summer*. (150 pages)

Where it's reviewed:
Booklist, December 1, 2002, page 666
Kirkus Reviews, October 15, 2002, page 1531
Publishers Weekly, November 11, 2002, page 66

School Library Journal, December 2002, page 140

Other books by the same author:
Faraway Summer, 1998
Spring Break, 1997
Even Stephen, 1996
Ozzie on His Own, 1995
A Llama in the Family, 1994

Other books you might like:
Judie Angell, *One-Way to Ansonia*, 1985
 For 1890s immigrant Rose Olshansky, the only way to achieve her dream is to attend night school after working all day at the Griffin Cap Factory.
Kathryn Lasky, *Dreams in the Golden Country: The Diary of Zipporah Feldman, a Jewish Immigrant Girl*, 1998
 At the turn of the century, Zipporah and her family join thousands of other immigrants when they leave Russia for New York's Lower East Side.
Joan Lowery Nixon, *Land of Hope*, 1992
 Fleeing the Russian pograms, Rebekah and her family find life hard in New York City, though Rebekah loves attending school and dreams of teaching.

702

JOHANNA HURWITZ
DEBBIE TILLEY, Illustrator

Elisa Michaels, Bigger & Better
(New York: HarperCollins Publishers, 2003)

Series: Riverside Kids
Subject(s): Brothers and Sisters; Short Stories; Family Life
Age range(s): Grades 2-3
Major character(s): Elisa Michaels, 7-Year-Old, 2nd Grader; Grandma, Grandmother; Marshall, Brother, 2-Year-Old
Time period(s): 2000s (2003)
Locale(s): New York, New York; Florida

Summary: An episodic early chapter book describes Elisa's growing independence. When the three children are left in the care of a babysitter more interested in playing chess with her older brother than caring for Marshall, Elisa takes care of his dirty diaper and sings a song to help him sleep. Elisa eats breakfast with Grandma in Florida by talking to her on the phone as each dines in their respective homes. Cleverly, during a trip to the zoo, Elisa figures out how to get Marshall to give up pacifiers. An opportunity to travel to Florida in the company of Grandma's friends gives Elisa the chance to fly for the first time and to courageously do something without her family present. Although Elisa gets her wish to eat only chocolate for a day, she quickly learns that such a restricted diet grows tiresome and doesn't satisfy her hunger. Elisa is growing, bigger and better. (128 pages)

Where it's reviewed:
Booklist, December 15, 2003, page 753
Horn Book, November 2003, page 747
Publishers Weekly, December 1, 2003, page 58

Other books by the same author:
Fourth Grade Fuss, 2004
E Is for Elisa, 2003
Ever Clever Elisa, 2002

Other books you might like:
Ann Cameron, *Gloria's Way*, 20[...]
 Gloria faces the trials and tri[...] support from friends and fam[...]
Beverly Cleary, *The Ramona Se*[...]
 Irrepressible Ramona and her [...] lems and sibling squabbles wit[...]
Paula Danziger, *It's Justin Time,*[...]
 Amber eagerly counts the days[...] while hoping to receive a wat[...]
Maud Hart Lovelace, *Betsy-Tacy*[...]
 The warmth of small town neigh[...] ties of close friends make this[...]

703

GLEN HUS[...]

Stitches
(Toronto: Groundwoo[...]

Subject(s): Friendship; Sewing; Phy[...]
Age range(s): Grades 7-10
Major character(s): Chantelle Bosco[...] dent—High School; Travis, Sea[...] School; Gentry, Singer, Mother [...]
Time period(s): 2000s
Locale(s): Alberta, Canada

Summary: Two misfits, Chantelle an[...] school together since first grade. C[...] facial and body deformities, yet seem[...] problems and get on with her life. Th[...] six older, muscular, hoodlum brothers[...] child of a single mother, Gentry, who'[...] and is seldom home. Instead, his n[...] abusive husband raise him in their t[...] children. Because Travis has effemina[...] to sew puppets, he's been teased a[...] bullies through elementary, middle an[...] friendship Chantelle and Travis enjo[...] ignore the class bullies and together[...] which Travis sews his puppets and Ch[...] performance in this charming, heart[...] pages)

Where it's reviewed:
Bulletin of the Center for Children's [...] page 233
Horn Book, November 2003, page 748
Resource Links, February 2004, page [...]
School Library Journal, December 200[...]

Other books by the same author:
Grace Lake: A Novel, 1990

Other books you might like:
Gail Giles, *Shattering Glass*, 2002
 Rob's attempt to transform consumma[...] into Mr. Cool, backfires and leads to[...]
Alice Hoffman, *The River King*, 2000[...]
 August Pierce is too much of an indivi[...] boys at his elite prep school and an a[...] his place turns to tragedy.

Allen Ku[...]
 Force[...]
 teache[...]
 also [...]
Norma [...]
 Mean[...]
 haunt[...]
 to pr[...]

Series: [...]
Subject([...]
Age ran [...]
Major [...]
 Scho[...]
 Frien[...]
Time pe[...]
Locale(s [...]

Summa[...]
 mon se[...]
 cats wh[...]
 he's su[...]
 convinc[...]
 dinosau[...]
 basis f[...]
 Gran r[...]
 Seymou[...]
 the cats[...]
 adopt t[...]
 pade w[...]

Where [...]
Booklis[...]
School[...]

Other [...]
Robyn [...]
The P[...]
The T[...]

Other [...]
Martha[...]
 Sin[...]
 adj[...]
Ann V[...]
 Be[...]
 sch[...]

I

706

EVA IBBOTSON
KEVIN HAWKES, Illustrator

The Great Ghost Rescue
(New York: Dutton, 2002)

Subject(s): Ghosts
Age range(s): Grades 4-7
Major character(s): Rick Henderson, Student—Boarding School; Humphrey the Horrible, Spirit; Lord Bullhaven, Nobleman
Time period(s): 1970s
Locale(s): Scotland; England

Summary: One by one the great ghosts of Britain are being turned out of their castles by the renovations for the tourists. Homeless, Humphrey and his ghost family search for another spot and, attracted by the smell of dirty socks, stumble across Norton Castle School where Humphrey is seen by student Rick Henderson. Luckily Rick is an activist and after hearing Humphrey's tale of woe, decides to do something about this ghost problem. Traveling to London, he convinces the Prime Minister to establish a ''ghost sanctuary'' for all the homeless ghosts. Lord Bullhaven donates his deserted Scottish castle, Insleyfarne, and the ghosts merrily settle in. When it's discovered that Bullhaven plans to collect all the homeless ghosts in one spot and then exorcise them, Rick and his friends take charge once again in a delightfully macabre work originally written in 1975. (167 pages)

Where it's reviewed:
Booklist, July 2002, page 1846
Bulletin of the Center for Children's Books, November 2002, page 113
Horn Book, September 2002, page 574
Publishers Weekly, July 22, 2002, page 182
School Library Journal, August 2002, page 189

Other books by the same author:
The Haunting of Granite Falls, 2005
Not Just a Witch, 2003
Journey to the River Sea, 2002

Dial-a-Ghost, 2001
Island of the Aunts, 2000

Other books you might like:
Eileen Dunlop, *The Ghost by the Sea*, 1996
  Two cousins try to solve the mysterious drowning of an ancestor so Milly's spirit can finally rest and stop haunting their grandparents' home.
Peni R. Griffin, *The Ghost Sitter*, 2001
  Promising her sister that she won't leave, Susie waits for her family to return until two young girls help release her from her pledge.
Betty Ren Wright, *A Ghost in the Family*, 1998
  Chad accompanies a friend on a two-week stay at her aunt's boarding house and discovers a ghost haunting his room.

707

EVA IBBOTSON
KEVIN HAWKES, Illustrator

Journey to the River Sea
(New York: Dutton, 2002)

Subject(s): Adventure and Adventurers; Orphans
Age range(s): Grades 5-8
Major character(s): Maia Fielding, Orphan; Gwendolyn Carter, Twin; Beatrice Carter, Twin; Miss Minton, Governess; Finn Taverner, Orphan; Jimmy ''Clovis King'' Bates, Orphan, Adoptee
Time period(s): 1910s
Locale(s): England; Manaus, Brazil (along the Amazon River (the River Sea))

Summary: While at boarding school in England, Maia learns that her parents have died and her trustee arranges for her to live with the Carters, her relatives on a rubber plantation in Brazil. Excited at this adventure, and accompanied by her new governess Miss Minton, Maia travels to Manaus on the Amazon River where she finds the Carters hate everything Brazilian, never go outside, and try to pretend they're still in England. Mr. Carter is a thief on the run, Mrs. Carter wishes to rid her house of every insect and their twin daughters Beatrice and Gwendolyn are snobby, nasty girls; the family has only taken her in because of Maia's quarterly allotment. Whenever Maia can escape from the house, she goes exploring and so meets Finn, a young boy who'd like to stay with the Indians and not return to England. Maia also runs into Clovis, a young actor she met on her trip over, who wants desperately to return to England. Two detectives show up in search of Finn, heir to a fortune in England, and Maia uses this opportunity to switch some identities and make everyone happy. (298 pages)

Where it's reviewed:
Bulletin of the Center for Children's Books, April 2002, page 283
Horn Book, January 2002, page 78
Publishers Weekly, November 26, 2001, page 62
School Library Journal, January 2002, page 132
Voice of Youth Advocates, December 2001, page 359

Awards the book has won:
ALA Notable Children's Books, 2003
School Library Journal Best Books, 2002

Other books by the same author:
The Haunting of Granite Falls, 2005
Not Just a Witch, 2003
The Great Ghost Rescue, 2002
Dial-a-Ghost, 2001
Island of the Aunts, 2000

Other books you might like:
Avi, *The True Confessions of Charlotte Doyle*, 1990
   Charlotte's adventures aboard the sailing ship *Seahawk* turn her from a proper Victorian lady into a real sailor.
Sharon Creech, *The Wanderer*, 2000
   Sophie never wants to be left out so talks her relatives into letting her accompany them on a sea journey aboard their 45-foot sailboat.
Philip Pullman, *The Ruby in the Smoke*, 1987
   Sally, an orphaned 16-year-old, outmaneuvers a host of villainous 19th-century figures to claim her inheritance and her independence.

708

EVA IBBOTSON
KEVIN HAWKES, Illustrator

Not Just a Witch
(New York: Dutton, 2003)

Subject(s): Witches and Witchcraft; Animals; Humor
Age range(s): Grades 4-7
Major character(s): Hecate ''Heckie'' Tenbury-Smith, Witch; Lionel Knapsack, Businessman (furrier); Daniel, Child
Time period(s): 2000s
Locale(s): Wellbridge, England

Summary: Graduating from Witch School, Heckie settles down in Wellbridge and, because of her ability to turn evildoers into animals, runs the local pet shop. Aided by young Daniel; her ''dragworm,'' a combination of dragon and worm; and various other witches and wizards, she forms the Wellbridge Wickedness Hunters. She successfully transforms the evil nursing home director into a warthog, a cruel chicken

farmer into a fish and a bank robber into a mouse. Unfortunately for Heckie, this last deed is seen by the furrier Lionel who wants her to transform 300 prisoners into snow leopards that he can then kill, skin and make into matching coats for a wealthy sheik's harem. She disregards the warnings of Daniel and her dragworm as Lionel adds soft-center chocolates to his courting repertoire and her two friends worry that Heckie's heart will be broken during this merry adventure. (185 pages)

Where it's reviewed:
Booklist, April 15, 2003, page 1466
Bulletin of the Center for Children's Books, September 2003, page 17
Kirkus Reviews, June 15, 2003, page 859
Publishers Weekly, July 21, 2003, page 195
School Library Journal, October 2003, page 168

Other books by the same author:
The Haunting of Hiram, 2004 (Kevin Hawkes, illustrator)
The Star of Kazan, 2004 (Kevin Hawkes, illustrator)
The Great Ghost Rescue, 2002 (Kevin Hawkes, illustrator)
Dial-a-Ghost, 2001 (Kevin Hawkes, illustrator)

Other books you might like:
Debi Gliori, *Pure Dead Magic*, 2001
   Siblings Titus and Pandora have their hands full when they try to rescue baby Damp from cyberspace.
Patrice Kindl, *Goose Chase*, 2001
   A tart-tongued goose girl is determined to save her beloved geese no matter how many kings or princes want to marry her.
Terry Pratchett, *The Wee Free Men: A Novel of Discworld*, 2003
   Tiffany marches forth to save her brother from the Fairy Queen, armed with a sheep diseases manual and an iron frying pan.
Dian Curtis Regan, *Monsters in Cyberspace*, 1997
   Rilla loves belonging to the Monster-of-the-Month Club, but only she and a friend know that the monsters occasionally come to life.

709

SATOMI ICHIKAWA, Author/Illustrator

My Pig Amarillo
(New York: Philomel Books, 2002)

Subject(s): Animals/Pigs; Pets; Lost and Found
Age range(s): Grades K-2
Major character(s): Amarillo, Pig; Pablito, Child, Student; Grandpa, Grandfather
Time period(s): 2000s
Locale(s): Guatemala

Summary: The baby pig that Grandpa gives Pablito as a pet becomes, in Pablito's eyes, his best friend. Pablito makes a hut to shelter Amarillo, they play together daily, and, as the pig grows, Amarillo follows Pablito wherever he goes. Pablito's happiness ends the afternoon he returns home from school to find Amarillo's hut empty. Pablito searches in vain until finally he cries himself to sleep. Days later, Grandpa brings Pablito a small wooden pig that he has carved and talks to Pablito about the possibility that Amarillo could have met with a fatal accident. Grandpa reminds Pablito of the custom of flying kites on All Saints Day to send a message to those who have died, inspiring Pablito to make a kite for Amarillo. (32 pages)

Where it's reviewed:
Booklist, April 1, 2003, page 1396
Horn Book Guide, Fall 2003, page 326
Publishers Weekly, May 12, 2003, page 66
Riverbank Review, Spring 2003, page 32
School Library Journal, May 2003, page 122

Awards the book has won:
Booklist Editors' Choice, 2003

Other books by the same author:
First Bear in Africa, 2001
What the Little Fir Tree Wore to the Christmas Party, 2001
Nora's Surprise, 1994

Other books you might like:
Robie H. Harris, *Goodbye Mousie*, 2001
    A little boy wakes up to find his pet mouse lifeless and his parents sensitively help him accept Mousie's death and grieve for his loss.
Angela Johnson, *Julius*, 1993
    Maya knows that Granddaddy is bringing her a special gift from Alaska but she doesn't expect it to be a pet pig.
Ezra Jack Keats, *Maggie and the Pirate*, 1979
    Maggie searches for her stolen pet cricket; death claims her pet, but Maggie finds a friend.
Antonio Hernandez Madrigal, *Blanca's Feather*, 2000
    After Rosalia's pet chicken vanishes Rosalia brings one of Blanca's feathers to church for the blessing of the animals.

710

WITI IHIMAERA

The Whale Rider
(San Diego: Harcourt, 2003)

Subject(s): Animals/Whales; Relationships; Kings, Queens, Rulers, etc.
Age range(s): Grades 6-12
Major character(s): Kahu, Child; Rawiri, Uncle (of Kahu); Koro Apirana, Grandfather (of Kahu), Chieftain; Nanny Flowers, Grandmother (of Kahu); Kahutia Te Rangi ''Whale Rider'', Mythical Creature
Time period(s): Indeterminate Past; 1980s
Locale(s): Whangara, New Zealand

Summary: In the long ago, a whale beached and atop his back was a heavily tattooed man, the mythical whale rider, who launched spear after spear upon New Zealand's shores. One spear became pigeons, another became eels and so on until one spear remained. Refusing to leave the rider's hand, he blessed it and it flew away, to wait a thousand years until it was needed. Thus began the Maori tribe living in Whangara and now, with Koro Apirana as its chief, the male line of succession appears broken when his great-granddaughter Kahu is born. Narrated by her uncle Rawiri, Kahu strives in vain to please Koro, though it's only her Nanny who believes in her. When whales beach themselves near the tribe, it's

Kahu who resurrects the role of the whale rider and saves the pod. (152 pages)

Where it's reviewed:
Booklist, July 2003, page 1881
Kirkus Reviews, May 1, 2003, page 678
Kliatt, November 2003, page 15
School Library Journal, September 2003, page 214
Voice of Youth Advocates, October 2003, page 311

Other books by the same author:
Ihimaera: His Best Stories, 2003 (adult title)
Sky Dancer, 2003 (adult fiction)
The Uncle's Story, 2000 (adult fiction)
Growing Up Maori, 1998 (adult nonfiction)
The Dream Swimmer, 1997 (adult fiction)

Other books you might like:
Welwyn Wilton Katz, *Whalesinger*, 1990
    A teen working on a research project at Point Reyes hears the sounds of a mother whale and swims out to help its sickly calf.
Rafe Martin, *The World Before This One*, 2002
    Once outcasts, Crow and his grandmother are welcomed back into their village when he is chosen as the first storyteller for the Seneca Indians.
Tom Shachtman, *Driftwhistler: A Story of Daniel Au Fond*, 1991
    Driftwhistler and his sea lions emphasize concern about pollution, exploitation of animals and resources, and the need for cooperative living.

711

GENEVA COBB IIJIMA
PAIGE BILLIN-FRYE, Illustrator

The Way We Do It in Japan
(Morton Grove, IL: Albert Whitman & Company, 2002)

Subject(s): Family; Multicultural; Moving, Household
Age range(s): Grades K-3
Major character(s): Gregory, Child, Son; Hidiaki ''Dad'', Father, Businessman; Jane ''Mom'', Mother
Time period(s): 2000s
Locale(s): San Francisco, California; Tokyo, Japan

Summary: When Dad announces that he's received a job transfer the family makes plans to move to Japan. As they pack, Gregory wonders about life in Japan and the kinds of toys used by the children as well as the clothes they wear. Gregory's introduction to the Japanese way of life begins on the airplane as he learns Japanese phrases for ''good morning'' and eats his lunch with chopsticks. Upon arrival, Gregory soon learns about the monetary system and discovers that the cars are not really going down the ''wrong'' side of the road because in Japan cars drive on the left side. Mom and Dad help Gregory become accustomed to Japanese furnishings and customs before he begins school. Factual information about Japan concludes the story. (32 pages)

Where it's reviewed:
Booklist, May 15, 2002, page 1600
Bulletin of the Center for Children's Books, March 2002, page 244

School Library Journal, April 2002, page 112

Other books by the same author:
The First Christmas Origami, 1993
Object Lessons with Origami, 1990

Other books you might like:
Elaine Hosozawa-Nagano, *Chopsticks from America*, 1995
    Japanese-American siblings move to Japan with their family and find the adjustment more difficult than they expected.
Mari Takabayashi, *I Live in Tokyo*, 2001
    A Tokyo schoolgirl introduces readers to Japanese culture through a year of traditionally observed events.
Karen B. Winnick, *The Night of the Fireflies*, 2004
    On one special night school children in Japan gather for the release of fireflies; briefly caught in paper lanterns, the bugs then are released.

712

BRUCE INGMAN, Author/Illustrator

Bad News! I'm in Charge!

(Cambridge, MA: Candlewick Press, 2003)

Subject(s): Behavior; Parent and Child; Humor
Age range(s): Grades K-3
Major character(s): Danny, Son, Child
Time period(s): 2000s
Locale(s): Fictional Country

Summary: Danny is sent outside and told to take his metal detector with him. In addition to bottle caps, spoons and assorted other metal items Danny locates a chest containing a suit of armor and a charter naming the finder the "new owner and ruler of this land." Danny quickly adopts his new role and gets to work ruling his land. His changes include kid-friendly ideas such us staying up late, eating snacks and initiating an 8 o'clock bedtime for parents. Life is great for Danny until he discovers that rulers have responsibilities that are not completely to his liking so Danny calls a meeting of his cabinet and delegates the duties that he doesn't like. Danny keeps the best duty for himself, "President of Fun!" (32 pages)

Where it's reviewed:
Booklist, April 1, 2003, page 1402
Bulletin of the Center for Children's Books, June 2003, page 406
Publishers Weekly, March 10, 2003, page 71
School Library Journal, August 2003, page 129

Other books by the same author:
A Night on the Tiles, 1999
Lost Property, 1998
When Martha's Away, 1995

Other books you might like:
Babette Cole, *Bad Habits!*, 1999
    Lucretzia Crum's parents work to curb her bad habits.
Nathalie Dieterle, *I Am the King!*, 2001
    After receiving a toy crown Little Louis begins behaving as if he truly is the ruler of all he surveys—but his parents have other expectations.

Fred Hiatt, *If I Were Queen of the World*, 1997
    A young girl imagines that as queen she could eat lollipops without sharing and stay up as late as she wants.
Suzanne Williams, *My Dog Never Says Please*, 1997
    Ginny Mae envies the family dog because he has no chores and never is told to mind his manners.

713

JEANETTE INGOLD

The Big Burn

·(San Diego: Harcourt, 2002)

Subject(s): Fires; Survival; Frontier and Pioneer Life
Age range(s): Grades 6-10
Major character(s): Celia Whitcomb, Guardian (of Lizbeth), Aunt (of Lizbeth); Lizbeth, 16-Year-Old; Jarrett Logan, 16-Year-Old, Ranger (forest service); Samuel Logan, Ranger (forest service); Seth Brown, Military Personnel (private in 25th infantry)
Time period(s): 1910s (1910)
Locale(s): Coeur D'Alene National Forest, Idaho

Summary: Three teens find their lives intertwined when the "big burn" forest fire blazes through the Northwest. Seth is a Buffalo soldier, part of the all-black 25th infantry, who's sent west to help put out the forest fires. Lizbeth lives with her Aunt Celia on a homestead that is a struggle for two women to maintain, but one Lizbeth loves. Jarrett has been let go by the railroad and kicked out of his house by his father, so he joins the Forest Service to fight the fires and coincidentally meets up with his estranged brother Samuel. Seth is influenced by a fellow soldier to use the fire as a ruse to escape army life, but is convinced by Jarrett to stay and help fight the fires. Lizbeth and her aunt are finally forced to flee their homestead for town where they meet up with Jarrett and Seth in a story based on a forest fire that devastated parts of Montana and Idaho in the summer of 1910. (295 pages)

Where it's reviewed:
Booklist, June 2002, page 1708
Bulletin of the Center for Children's Books, July 2002, page 406
Publishers Weekly, July 1, 2002, page 80
School Library Journal, August 2002, page 190
Voice of Youth Advocates, August 2002, page 193

Other books by the same author:
Mountain Solo, 2003
Airfield, 1999
Pictures, 1918, 1998
The Window, 1996

Other books you might like:
Cameron Dokey, *Washington Avalanche, 1910*, 2000
    Two teens meet on a train heading to Seattle, never thinking that an avalanche will change their lives.
Maurice Gee, *The Fire-Raiser*, 1992
    A group of young New Zealanders brings to justice the pyromaniac terrorizing their small town.
Libby Gleeson, *Eleanor, Elizabeth*, 1990
    Reading her grandmother's diary provides Eleanor with

knowledge about a cave that saves her life during a brush fire.

Colin Thiele, *Jodie's Journey*, 1990

Though disabled by rheumatoid arthritis, which ends her riding career, Jodie is able to save herself from a brushfire.

Lee Wardlaw, *Corey's Fire*, 1990

Corey's had enough of her sullen neighbor Topher until the Santa Ana winds sweep up their canyon and the two must work together to save their homes.

714

JEANETTE INGOLD

Mountain Solo

(San Diego: Harcourt, 2003)

Subject(s): Mothers and Daughters; Frontier and Pioneer Life; Music and Musicians
Age range(s): Grades 6-9
Major character(s): Tess Thaler, 16-Year-Old, Musician (violinist); Frederik Bottner, Immigrant, Musician (violinist); Meg Thaler, Stepmother
Time period(s): 2000s; 1900s
Locale(s): New York, New York; Missoula, Montana

Summary: Playing the violin since she was three, Tess has developed into quite a musical prodigy until the awful night she plays with an orchestra in Germany, a performance for which she proves she isn't emotionally ready. Returning to New York with her aggressive mother, Tess decides to get away from her music and heads to Montana for quiet time with her veterinarian father and his new wife. Meg is a Forest Service historian who's researching Frederick Bottner, the former occupant of an old homesteader cabin, who was also a violinist. Frederick's story is told in juxtaposition to Tess's as both young musicians struggle to make music an integral component of their lives. (309 pages)

Where it's reviewed:
Booklist, December 15, 2003, page 659
Bulletin of the Center for Children's Books, January 2004, page 194
Publishers Weekly, September 8, 2003, page 77
School Library Journal, November 2003, page 140
Voice of Youth Advocates, February 2004, page 492

Other books by the same author:
The Big Burn, 2002
Airfield, 1999
Pictures, 1918, 1998
The Window, 1996

Other books you might like:
Bruce Brooks, *Midnight Hour Encores*, 1986
Musical prodigy Sibilance T. Spooner, helped by her ex-hippie father, travels to California to meet the mother who abandoned her just after she was born.
Jane Leslie Conly, *What Happened on Planet Kid*, 2000
Though Dawn stays busy with piano playing and pitching practice, she's not so busy that she overlooks the abuse her friend Charlotte endures.

Maurine F. Dahlberg, *Play to the Angel*, 2000
Greta's piano recital occurs the same night the Nazis riot in the streets of Vienna, forcing her piano teacher to flee.
Virginia Euwer Wolff, *The Mozart Season*, 1991
Softball practice and violin lessons overlap in Allegra's mind as she prepares to play in a musical competition.

715

MICK INKPEN, Author/Illustrator

Kipper's Monster

(San Diego: Red Wagon/Harcourt, Inc., 2002)

Subject(s): Fear; Animals/Dogs; Camps and Camping
Age range(s): Preschool-Kindergarten
Major character(s): Kipper, Dog, Friend; Tiger, Dog, Friend
Time period(s): 2000s (2002)
Locale(s): United States

Summary: Tiger is very excited about his new flashlight and encourages Kipper to go camping with him so that they can try it out. The great outdoors proves to be a little scarier than expected. A screeching owl makes them drop the flashlight, which causes a shadow that turns a little snail into a big monster. Finally Kipper and Tiger decide to take their tent back to Tiger's house and set it up in his bedroom. (32 pages)

Where it's reviewed:
Horn Book Guide, Fall 2002, page 304
Kirkus Reviews, April 1, 2002, page 493
Publishers Weekly, April 8, 2002, page 229
School Librarian, Winter 2002, page 187
School Library Journal, July 2002, page 93

Other books by the same author:
Kipper and Roly, 2001
Wibbly Pig Can Make a Tent, 2000
Kipper, 1992

Other books you might like:
Lena Arro, *Good Night, Animals*, 2002
Best friends go camping; with each strange noise they invite another animal into their tent.
Tom Birdseye, *Oh Yeah!*, 2003
Two boys, camping out in the backyard, boast that nothing could scare them—at least not until the family dog startles them.
Mercer Mayer, *Just Camping Out*, 1989
Little Critter and his sister go camping in the back yard, but they don't make it through the night.

716

KARIN IRELAND
DAVID CATROW, Illustrator

Don't Take Your Snake for a Stroll

(San Diego: Harcourt, Inc., 2003)

Subject(s): Pets; Animals; Stories in Rhyme
Age range(s): Grades K-2
Major character(s): Unnamed Character, Child, Animal Lover
Time period(s): 2000s
Locale(s): United States

Summary: A youngster with a lot of unusual pets offers instructions about the various activities one should avoid with certain animals. Avoid the mall with your pig and realize bringing your elephant to the beach requires way too much sunscreen. Walking a snake alarms others and taking a rabbit to a dance means doing the bunny-hop because a rabbit doesn't want to waltz. Definitely avoid airplanes when traveling with a skunk and never bring a moose to the movies because other patrons can't see through his antlers. In fact, if you really want to enjoy a walk, just bring your family and leave the animals at home. (32 pages)

Where it's reviewed:
Booklist, May 15, 2003, page 1670
Publishers Weekly, May 5, 2003, page 219
School Library Journal, October 2003, page 126

Other books by the same author:
Wonderful Nature, Wonderful You, 1996

Other books you might like:
Lauren Child, *I Want a Pet*, 1999
  A little girl desperately wants a pet but has some difficulty choosing one that meets the requirements of her family.
Lee Harris, *Never Let Your Cat Make Lunch for You*, 1999
  This cautionary tale advises why one should not allow a cat, even one with culinary skills, to pack a school lunch.
Laura Joffe Numeroff, *If You Give a Pig a Pancake*, 1998
  If an uninvited pig shows up at breakfast to share your pancakes, be prepared for a busy day.
Tres Seymour, *I Love My Buzzard*, 1994
  A young boy who loves his buzzard as well as his squid, slugs and warthog reconsiders his priorities when his mom moves out to escape the menagerie.
Dan Yaccarino, *An Octopus Followed Me Home*, 1997
  As a young girl explains to her overwhelmed dad, the octopus simply followed her home just as the crocodile, seals and penguins did previously.

717

RACHEL ISADORA, Author/Illustrator

Bring on That Beat

(New York: G.P. Putnam's Sons, 2002)

Subject(s): Music and Musicians; African Americans; Stories in Rhyme
Age range(s): Grades 1-4
Time period(s): 1930s
Locale(s): New York, New York (Harlem)

Summary: The late night sound of jazz notes brings the beat to the darkened streets of Harlem and attracts a crowd of young and old. Joyously children dance and swing to the beat they hear. The musicians move to a roof top and the dancers do too as the sound, represented by colorful geometric shapes overlaid on the black and white illustrations, spreads all over the city. (32 pages)

Where it's reviewed:
Booklist, February 15, 2002, page 1034
Bulletin of the Center for Children's Books, January 2002, page 175
Kirkus Reviews, November 15, 2001, page 1612
Publishers Weekly, December 10, 2001, page 69
School Library Journal, January 2002, page 102

Other books by the same author:
Nick Plays Baseball, 2001
123 Pop!, 2000
Listen to the City, 2000
Ben's Trumpet, 1979 (Caldecott Honor Book)

Other books you might like:
Robert Burleigh, *Lookin' for Bird in the Big City*, 2001
  While searching for Charlie "Bird" Parker in New York, Miles Davis plays his trumpet, incorporating the sounds of the city into his music.
Jonathan London, *Hip Cat*, 1993
  Oobie-do John, a sax-playing cat, hops the night train to San Francisco where he feels free to play the jazz that he loves.
Walter Dean Myers, *The Blues of Flats Brown*, 2000
  A guitar-playing dog escapes its cruel master in order to fulfill its dream of playing and writing the blues.
Chris Raschka, *Charlie Parker Played Be Bop*, 1992
  A picture book biography tells of the life of a famous jazz saxophonist.

718

RACHEL ISADORA, Author/Illustrator

Not Just Tutus

(New York: G.P. Putnam's Sons, 2003)

Subject(s): Dancing; Ballet; Stories in Rhyme
Age range(s): Grades K-3
Time period(s): 2000s
Locale(s): United States

Summary: In two sections labeled "Dreams and Practice" and "Makeup and Lights," the aspirations, challenges, hard work and success of children hoping to dance on stage is portrayed through illustrations and text. The diverse dance students include those who persevere despite body shapes that may not seem natural to the art. Dealing with costumes that don't fit, broken ribbons during a show and last minute stage fright are all possibilities for the dancer in training. Still, the show must go on and the students realize that the thrill of being under the lights makes all the practice worthwhile. (40 pages)

Where it's reviewed:
Booklist, January 2003, page 907
Bulletin of the Center for Children's Books, April 2003, page 318
Publishers Weekly, December 16, 2002, page 67
School Library Journal, April 2003, page 122

Other books by the same author:
On Your Toes: A Ballet ABC, 2003
Sophie Skates, 1999
Isadora Dances, 1998

Other books you might like:
Naia Bray-Moffatt, *Ballet School*, 2003
  A nonfiction title describes a ballet studio, various classes and the work of student dancers.

knowledge about a cave that saves her life during a brush fire.

Colin Thiele, *Jodie's Journey*, 1990
 Though disabled by rheumatoid arthritis, which ends her riding career, Jodie is able to save herself from a brushfire.

Lee Wardlaw, *Corey's Fire*, 1990
 Corey's had enough of her sullen neighbor Topher until the Santa Ana winds sweep up their canyon and the two must work together to save their homes.

714

JEANETTE INGOLD

Mountain Solo
(San Diego: Harcourt, 2003)

Subject(s): Mothers and Daughters; Frontier and Pioneer Life; Music and Musicians
Age range(s): Grades 6-9
Major character(s): Tess Thaler, 16-Year-Old, Musician (violinist); Frederik Bottner, Immigrant, Musician (violinist); Meg Thaler, Stepmother
Time period(s): 2000s; 1900s
Locale(s): New York, New York; Missoula, Montana

Summary: Playing the violin since she was three, Tess has developed into quite a musical prodigy until the awful night she plays with an orchestra in Germany, a performance for which she proves she isn't emotionally ready. Returning to New York with her aggressive mother, Tess decides to get away from her music and heads to Montana for quiet time with her veterinarian father and his new wife. Meg is a Forest Service historian who's researching Frederick Bottner, the former occupant of an old homesteader cabin, who was also a violinist. Frederick's story is told in juxtaposition to Tess's as both young musicians struggle to make music an integral component of their lives. (309 pages)

Where it's reviewed:
Booklist, December 15, 2003, page 659
Bulletin of the Center for Children's Books, January 2004, page 194
Publishers Weekly, September 8, 2003, page 77
School Library Journal, November 2003, page 140
Voice of Youth Advocates, February 2004, page 492

Other books by the same author:
The Big Burn, 2002
Airfield, 1999
Pictures, 1918, 1998
The Window, 1996

Other books you might like:
Bruce Brooks, *Midnight Hour Encores*, 1986
 Musical prodigy Sibilance T. Spooner, helped by her ex-hippie father, travels to California to meet the mother who abandoned her just after she was born.
Jane Leslie Conly, *What Happened on Planet Kid*, 2000
 Though Dawn stays busy with piano playing and pitching practice, she's not so busy that she overlooks the abuse her friend Charlotte endures.

Maurine F. Dahlberg, *Play to the Angel*, 2000
 Greta's piano recital occurs the same night the Nazis riot in the streets of Vienna, forcing her piano teacher to flee.
Virginia Euwer Wolff, *The Mozart Season*, 1991
 Softball practice and violin lessons overlap in Allegra's mind as she prepares to play in a musical competition.

715

MICK INKPEN, Author/Illustrator

Kipper's Monster
(San Diego: Red Wagon/Harcourt, Inc., 2002)

Subject(s): Fear; Animals/Dogs; Camps and Camping
Age range(s): Preschool-Kindergarten
Major character(s): Kipper, Dog, Friend; Tiger, Dog, Friend
Time period(s): 2000s (2002)
Locale(s): United States

Summary: Tiger is very excited about his new flashlight and encourages Kipper to go camping with him so that they can try it out. The great outdoors proves to be a little scarier than expected. A screeching owl makes them drop the flashlight, which causes a shadow that turns a little snail into a big monster. Finally Kipper and Tiger decide to take their tent back to Tiger's house and set it up in his bedroom. (32 pages)

Where it's reviewed:
Horn Book Guide, Fall 2002, page 304
Kirkus Reviews, April 1, 2002, page 493
Publishers Weekly, April 8, 2002, page 229
School Librarian, Winter 2002, page 187
School Library Journal, July 2002, page 93

Other books by the same author:
Kipper and Roly, 2001
Wibbly Pig Can Make a Tent, 2000
Kipper, 1992

Other books you might like:
Lena Arro, *Good Night, Animals*, 2002
 Best friends go camping; with each strange noise they invite another animal into their tent.
Tom Birdseye, *Oh Yeah!*, 2003
 Two boys, camping out in the backyard, boast that nothing could scare them—at least not until the family dog startles them.
Mercer Mayer, *Just Camping Out*, 1989
 Little Critter and his sister go camping in the back yard, but they don't make it through the night.

716

KARIN IRELAND
DAVID CATROW, Illustrator

Don't Take Your Snake for a Stroll
(San Diego: Harcourt, Inc., 2003)

Subject(s): Pets; Animals; Stories in Rhyme
Age range(s): Grades K-2
Major character(s): Unnamed Character, Child, Animal Lover
Time period(s): 2000s
Locale(s): United States

Summary: A youngster with a lot of unusual pets offers instructions about the various activities one should avoid with certain animals. Avoid the mall with your pig and realize bringing your elephant to the beach requires way too much sunscreen. Walking a snake alarms others and taking a rabbit to a dance means doing the bunny-hop because a rabbit doesn't want to waltz. Definitely avoid airplanes when traveling with a skunk and never bring a moose to the movies because other patrons can't see through his antlers. In fact, if you really want to enjoy a walk, just bring your family and leave the animals at home. (32 pages)

Where it's reviewed:
Booklist, May 15, 2003, page 1670
Publishers Weekly, May 5, 2003, page 219
School Library Journal, October 2003, page 126

Other books by the same author:
Wonderful Nature, Wonderful You, 1996

Other books you might like:
Lauren Child, *I Want a Pet*, 1999
   A little girl desperately wants a pet but has some difficulty choosing one that meets the requirements of her family.
Lee Harris, *Never Let Your Cat Make Lunch for You*, 1999
   This cautionary tale advises why one should not allow a cat, even one with culinary skills, to pack a school lunch.
Laura Joffe Numeroff, *If You Give a Pig a Pancake*, 1998
   If an uninvited pig shows up at breakfast to share your pancakes, be prepared for a busy day.
Tres Seymour, *I Love My Buzzard*, 1994
   A young boy who loves his buzzard as well as his squid, slugs and warthog reconsiders his priorities when his mom moves out to escape the menagerie.
Dan Yaccarino, *An Octopus Followed Me Home*, 1997
   As a young girl explains to her overwhelmed dad, the octopus simply followed her home just as the crocodile, seals and penguins did previously.

717

RACHEL ISADORA, Author/Illustrator

Bring on That Beat

(New York: G.P. Putnam's Sons, 2002)

Subject(s): Music and Musicians; African Americans; Stories in Rhyme
Age range(s): Grades 1-4
Time period(s): 1930s
Locale(s): New York, New York (Harlem)

Summary: The late night sound of jazz notes brings the beat to the darkened streets of Harlem and attracts a crowd of young and old. Joyously children dance and swing to the beat they hear. The musicians move to a roof top and the dancers do too as the sound, represented by colorful geometric shapes overlaid on the black and white illustrations, spreads all over the city. (32 pages)

Where it's reviewed:
Booklist, February 15, 2002, page 1034
Bulletin of the Center for Children's Books, January 2002, page 175
Kirkus Reviews, November 15, 2001, page 1612

Publishers Weekly, December 10, 2001, page 69
School Library Journal, January 2002, page 102

Other books by the same author:
Nick Plays Baseball, 2001
123 Pop!, 2000
Listen to the City, 2000
Ben's Trumpet, 1979 (Caldecott Honor Book)

Other books you might like:
Robert Burleigh, *Lookin' for Bird in the Big City*, 2001
   While searching for Charlie ''Bird'' Parker in New York, Miles Davis plays his trumpet, incorporating the sounds of the city into his music.
Jonathan London, *Hip Cat*, 1993
   Oobie-do John, a sax-playing cat, hops the night train to San Francisco where he feels free to play the jazz that he loves.
Walter Dean Myers, *The Blues of Flats Brown*, 2000
   A guitar-playing dog escapes its cruel master in order to fulfill its dream of playing and writing the blues.
Chris Raschka, *Charlie Parker Played Be Bop*, 1992
   A picture book biography tells of the life of a famous jazz saxophonist.

718

RACHEL ISADORA, Author/Illustrator

Not Just Tutus

(New York: G.P. Putnam's Sons, 2003)

Subject(s): Dancing; Ballet; Stories in Rhyme
Age range(s): Grades K-3
Time period(s): 2000s
Locale(s): United States

Summary: In two sections labeled ''Dreams and Practice'' and ''Makeup and Lights,'' the aspirations, challenges, hard work and success of children hoping to dance on stage is portrayed through illustrations and text. The diverse dance students include those who persevere despite body shapes that may not seem natural to the art. Dealing with costumes that don't fit, broken ribbons during a show and last minute stage fright are all possibilities for the dancer in training. Still, the show must go on and the students realize that the thrill of being under the lights makes all the practice worthwhile. (40 pages)

Where it's reviewed:
Booklist, January 2003, page 907
Bulletin of the Center for Children's Books, April 2003, page 318
Publishers Weekly, December 16, 2002, page 67
School Library Journal, April 2003, page 122

Other books by the same author:
On Your Toes: A Ballet ABC, 2003
Sophie Skates, 1999
Isadora Dances, 1998

Other books you might like:
Naia Bray-Moffatt, *Ballet School*, 2003
   A nonfiction title describes a ballet studio, various classes and the work of student dancers.

School Library Journal, April 2002, page 112

Other books by the same author:
The First Christmas Origami, 1993
Object Lessons with Origami, 1990

Other books you might like:
Elaine Hosozawa-Nagano, *Chopsticks from America*, 1995
　　Japanese-American siblings move to Japan with their family and find the adjustment more difficult than they expected.
Mari Takabayashi, *I Live in Tokyo*, 2001
　　A Tokyo schoolgirl introduces readers to Japanese culture through a year of traditionally observed events.
Karen B. Winnick, *The Night of the Fireflies*, 2004
　　On one special night school children in Japan gather for the release of fireflies; briefly caught in paper lanterns, the bugs then are released.

712

BRUCE INGMAN, Author/Illustrator

Bad News! I'm in Charge!

(Cambridge, MA: Candlewick Press, 2003)

Subject(s): Behavior; Parent and Child; Humor
Age range(s): Grades K-3
Major character(s): Danny, Son, Child
Time period(s): 2000s
Locale(s): Fictional Country

Summary: Danny is sent outside and told to take his metal detector with him. In addition to bottle caps, spoons and assorted other metal items Danny locates a chest containing a suit of armor and a charter naming the finder the ''new owner and ruler of this land.'' Danny quickly adopts his new role and gets to work ruling his land. His changes include kid-friendly ideas such us staying up late, eating snacks and initiating an 8 o'clock bedtime for parents. Life is great for Danny until he discovers that rulers have responsibilities that are not completely to his liking so Danny calls a meeting of his cabinet and delegates the duties that he doesn't like. Danny keeps the best duty for himself, ''President of Fun!'' (32 pages)

Where it's reviewed:
Booklist, April 1, 2003, page 1402
Bulletin of the Center for Children's Books, June 2003, page 406
Publishers Weekly, March 10, 2003, page 71
School Library Journal, August 2003, page 129

Other books by the same author:
A Night on the Tiles, 1999
Lost Property, 1998
When Martha's Away, 1995

Other books you might like:
Babette Cole, *Bad Habits!*, 1999
　　Lucretzia Crum's parents work to curb her bad habits.
Nathalie Dieterle, *I Am the King!*, 2001
　　After receiving a toy crown Little Louis begins behaving as if he truly is the ruler of all he surveys—but his parents have other expectations.

Fred Hiatt, *If I Were Queen of the World*, 1997
　　A young girl imagines that as queen she could eat lollipops without sharing and stay up as late as she wants.
Suzanne Williams, *My Dog Never Says Please*, 1997
　　Ginny Mae envies the family dog because he has no chores and never is told to mind his manners.

713

JEANETTE INGOLD

The Big Burn

(San Diego: Harcourt, 2002)

Subject(s): Fires; Survival; Frontier and Pioneer Life
Age range(s): Grades 6-10
Major character(s): Celia Whitcomb, Guardian (of Lizbeth), Aunt (of Lizbeth); Lizbeth, 16-Year-Old; Jarrett Logan, 16-Year-Old, Ranger (forest service); Samuel Logan, Ranger (forest service); Seth Brown, Military Personnel (private in 25th infantry)
Time period(s): 1910s (1910)
Locale(s): Coeur D'Alene National Forest, Idaho

Summary: Three teens find their lives intertwined when the ''big burn'' forest fire blazes through the Northwest. Seth is a Buffalo soldier, part of the all-black 25th infantry, who's sent west to help put out the forest fires. Lizbeth lives with her Aunt Celia on a homestead that is a struggle for two women to maintain, but one Lizbeth loves. Jarrett has been let go by the railroad and kicked out of his house by his father, so he joins the Forest Service to fight the fires and coincidentally meets up with his estranged brother Samuel. Seth is influenced by a fellow soldier to use the fire as a ruse to escape army life, but is convinced by Jarrett to stay and help fight the fires. Lizbeth and her aunt are finally forced to flee their homestead for town where they meet up with Jarrett and Seth in a story based on a forest fire that devastated parts of Montana and Idaho in the summer of 1910. (295 pages)

Where it's reviewed:
Booklist, June 2002, page 1708
Bulletin of the Center for Children's Books, July 2002, page 406
Publishers Weekly, July 1, 2002, page 80
School Library Journal, August 2002, page 190
Voice of Youth Advocates, August 2002, page 193

Other books by the same author:
Mountain Solo, 2003
Airfield, 1999
Pictures, 1918, 1998
The Window, 1996

Other books you might like:
Cameron Dokey, *Washington Avalanche, 1910*, 2000
　　Two teens meet on a train heading to Seattle, never thinking that an avalanche will change their lives.
Maurice Gee, *The Fire-Raiser*, 1992
　　A group of young New Zealanders brings to justice the pyromaniac terrorizing their small town.
Libby Gleeson, *Eleanor, Elizabeth*, 1990
　　Reading her grandmother's diary provides Eleanor with

with a fatal accident. Grandpa reminds Pablito of the custom of flying kites on All Saints Day to send a message to those who have died, inspiring Pablito to make a kite for Amarillo. (32 pages)

Where it's reviewed:
Booklist, April 1, 2003, page 1396
Horn Book Guide, Fall 2003, page 326
Publishers Weekly, May 12, 2003, page 66
Riverbank Review, Spring 2003, page 32
School Library Journal, May 2003, page 122

Awards the book has won:
Booklist Editors' Choice, 2003

Other books by the same author:
First Bear in Africa, 2001
What the Little Fir Tree Wore to the Christmas Party, 2001
Nora's Surprise, 1994

Other books you might like:
Robie H. Harris, *Goodbye Mousie*, 2001
   A little boy wakes up to find his pet mouse lifeless and his parents sensitively help him accept Mousie's death and grieve for his loss.
Angela Johnson, *Julius*, 1993
   Maya knows that Granddaddy is bringing her a special gift from Alaska but she doesn't expect it to be a pet pig.
Ezra Jack Keats, *Maggie and the Pirate*, 1979
   Maggie searches for her stolen pet cricket; death claims her pet, but Maggie finds a friend.
Antonio Hernandez Madrigal, *Blanca's Feather*, 2000
   After Rosalia's pet chicken vanishes Rosalia brings one of Blanca's feathers to church for the blessing of the animals.

710

WITI IHIMAERA

The Whale Rider

(San Diego: Harcourt, 2003)

Subject(s): Animals/Whales; Relationships; Kings, Queens, Rulers, etc.
Age range(s): Grades 6-12
Major character(s): Kahu, Child; Rawiri, Uncle (of Kahu); Koro Apirana, Grandfather (of Kahu), Chieftain; Nanny Flowers, Grandmother (of Kahu); Kahutia Te Rangi "Whale Rider", Mythical Creature
Time period(s): Indeterminate Past; 1980s
Locale(s): Whangara, New Zealand

Summary: In the long ago, a whale beached and atop his back was a heavily tattooed man, the mythical whale rider, who launched spear after spear upon New Zealand's shores. One spear became pigeons, another became eels and so on until one spear remained. Refusing to leave the rider's hand, he blessed it and it flew away, to wait a thousand years until it was needed. Thus began the Maori tribe living in Whangara and now, with Koro Apirana as its chief, the male line of succession appears broken when his great-granddaughter Kahu is born. Narrated by her uncle Rawiri, Kahu strives in vain to please Koro, though it's only her Nanny who believes in her. When whales beach themselves near the tribe, it's

Kahu who resurrects the role of the whale rider and saves the pod. (152 pages)

Where it's reviewed:
Booklist, July 2003, page 1881
Kirkus Reviews, May 1, 2003, page 678
Kliatt, November 2003, page 15
School Library Journal, September 2003, page 214
Voice of Youth Advocates, October 2003, page 311

Other books by the same author:
Ihimaera: His Best Stories, 2003 (adult title)
Sky Dancer, 2003 (adult fiction)
The Uncle's Story, 2000 (adult fiction)
Growing Up Maori, 1998 (adult nonfiction)
The Dream Swimmer, 1997 (adult fiction)

Other books you might like:
Welwyn Wilton Katz, *Whalesinger*, 1990
   A teen working on a research project at Point Reyes hears the sounds of a mother whale and swims out to help its sickly calf.
Rafe Martin, *The World Before This One*, 2002
   Once outcasts, Crow and his grandmother are welcomed back into their village when he is chosen as the first storyteller for the Seneca Indians.
Tom Shachtman, *Driftwhistler: A Story of Daniel Au Fond*, 1991
   Driftwhistler and his sea lions emphasize concern about pollution, exploitation of animals and resources, and the need for cooperative living.

711

GENEVA COBB IIJIMA
PAIGE BILLIN-FRYE, Illustrator

The Way We Do It in Japan

(Morton Grove, IL: Albert Whitman & Company, 2002)

Subject(s): Family; Multicultural; Moving, Household
Age range(s): Grades K-3
Major character(s): Gregory, Child, Son; Hidiaki "Dad", Father, Businessman; Jane "Mom", Mother
Time period(s): 2000s
Locale(s): San Francisco, California; Tokyo, Japan

Summary: When Dad announces that he's received a job transfer the family makes plans to move to Japan. As they pack, Gregory wonders about life in Japan and the kinds of toys used by the children as well as the clothes they wear. Gregory's introduction to the Japanese way of life begins on the airplane as he learns Japanese phrases for "good morning" and eats his lunch with chopsticks. Upon arrival, Gregory soon learns about the monetary system and discovers that the cars are not really going down the "wrong" side of the road because in Japan cars drive on the left side. Mom and Dad help Gregory become accustomed to Japanese furnishings and customs before he begins school. Factual information about Japan concludes the story. (32 pages)

Where it's reviewed:
Booklist, May 15, 2002, page 1600
Bulletin of the Center for Children's Books, March 2002, page 244

rid her house of every insect and their twin daughters Beatrice and Gwendolyn are snobby, nasty girls; the family has only taken her in because of Maia's quarterly allotment. Whenever Maia can escape from the house, she goes exploring and so meets Finn, a young boy who'd like to stay with the Indians and not return to England. Maia also runs into Clovis, a young actor she met on her trip over, who wants desperately to return to England. Two detectives show up in search of Finn, heir to a fortune in England, and Maia uses this opportunity to switch some identities and make everyone happy. (298 pages)

Where it's reviewed:
Bulletin of the Center for Children's Books, April 2002, page 283
Horn Book, January 2002, page 78
Publishers Weekly, November 26, 2001, page 62
School Library Journal, January 2002, page 132
Voice of Youth Advocates, December 2001, page 359

Awards the book has won:
ALA Notable Children's Books, 2003
School Library Journal Best Books, 2002

Other books by the same author:
The Haunting of Granite Falls, 2005
Not Just a Witch, 2003
The Great Ghost Rescue, 2002
Dial-a-Ghost, 2001
Island of the Aunts, 2000

Other books you might like:
Avi, *The True Confessions of Charlotte Doyle*, 1990
Charlotte's adventures aboard the sailing ship *Seahawk* turn her from a proper Victorian lady into a real sailor.
Sharon Creech, *The Wanderer*, 2000
Sophie never wants to be left out so talks her relatives into letting her accompany them on a sea journey aboard their 45-foot sailboat.
Philip Pullman, *The Ruby in the Smoke*, 1987
Sally, an orphaned 16-year-old, outmaneuvers a host of villainous 19th-century figures to claim her inheritance and her independence.

708

EVA IBBOTSON
KEVIN HAWKES, Illustrator

Not Just a Witch
(New York: Dutton, 2003)

Subject(s): Witches and Witchcraft; Animals; Humor
Age range(s): Grades 4-7
Major character(s): Hecate "Heckie" Tenbury-Smith, Witch; Lionel Knapsack, Businessman (furrier); Daniel, Child
Time period(s): 2000s
Locale(s): Wellbridge, England

Summary: Graduating from Witch School, Heckie settles down in Wellbridge and, because of her ability to turn evil-doers into animals, runs the local pet shop. Aided by young Daniel; her "dragworm," a combination of dragon and worm; and various other witches and wizards, she forms the Wellbridge Wickedness Hunters. She successfully transforms the evil nursing home director into a warthog, a cruel chicken

farmer into a fish and a bank robber into a mouse. Unfortunately for Heckie, this last deed is seen by the furrier Lionel who wants her to transform 300 prisoners into snow leopards that he can then kill, skin and make into matching coats for a wealthy sheik's harem. She disregards the warnings of Daniel and her dragworm as Lionel adds soft-center chocolates to his courting repertoire and her two friends worry that Heckie's heart will be broken during this merry adventure. (185 pages)

Where it's reviewed:
Booklist, April 15, 2003, page 1466
Bulletin of the Center for Children's Books, September 2003, page 17
Kirkus Reviews, June 15, 2003, page 859
Publishers Weekly, July 21, 2003, page 195
School Library Journal, October 2003, page 168

Other books by the same author:
The Haunting of Hiram, 2004 (Kevin Hawkes, illustrator)
The Star of Kazan, 2004 (Kevin Hawkes, illustrator)
The Great Ghost Rescue, 2002 (Kevin Hawkes, illustrator)
Dial-a-Ghost, 2001 (Kevin Hawkes, illustrator)

Other books you might like:
Debi Gliori, *Pure Dead Magic*, 2001
Siblings Titus and Pandora have their hands full when they try to rescue baby Damp from cyberspace.
Patrice Kindl, *Goose Chase*, 2001
A tart-tongued goose girl is determined to save her beloved geese no matter how many kings or princes want to marry her.
Terry Pratchett, *The Wee Free Men: A Novel of Discworld*, 2003
Tiffany marches forth to save her brother from the Fairy Queen, armed with a sheep diseases manual and an iron frying pan.
Dian Curtis Regan, *Monsters in Cyberspace*, 1997
Rilla loves belonging to the Monster-of-the-Month Club, but only she and a friend know that the monsters occasionally come to life.

709

SATOMI ICHIKAWA, Author/Illustrator

My Pig Amarillo
(New York: Philomel Books, 2002)

Subject(s): Animals/Pigs; Pets; Lost and Found
Age range(s): Grades K-2
Major character(s): Amarillo, Pig; Pablito, Child, Student; Grandpa, Grandfather
Time period(s): 2000s
Locale(s): Guatemala

Summary: The baby pig that Grandpa gives Pablito as a pet becomes, in Pablito's eyes, his best friend. Pablito makes a hut to shelter Amarillo, they play together daily, and, as the pig grows, Amarillo follows Pablito wherever he goes. Pablito's happiness ends the afternoon he returns home from school to find Amarillo's hut empty. Pablito searches in vain until finally he cries himself to sleep. Days later, Grandpa brings Pablito a small wooden pig that he has carved and talks to Pablito about the possibility that Amarillo could have met

I

706

EVA IBBOTSON
KEVIN HAWKES, Illustrator

The Great Ghost Rescue

(New York: Dutton, 2002)

Subject(s): Ghosts
Age range(s): Grades 4-7
Major character(s): Rick Henderson, Student—Boarding School; Humphrey the Horrible, Spirit; Lord Bullhaven, Nobleman
Time period(s): 1970s
Locale(s): Scotland; England

Summary: One by one the great ghosts of Britain are being turned out of their castles by the renovations for the tourists. Homeless, Humphrey and his ghost family search for another spot and, attracted by the smell of dirty socks, stumble across Norton Castle School where Humphrey is seen by student Rick Henderson. Luckily Rick is an activist and after hearing Humphrey's tale of woe, decides to do something about this ghost problem. Traveling to London, he convinces the Prime Minister to establish a "ghost sanctuary" for all the homeless ghosts. Lord Bullhaven donates his deserted Scottish castle, Insleyfarne, and the ghosts merrily settle in. When it's discovered that Bullhaven plans to collect all the homeless ghosts in one spot and then exorcise them, Rick and his friends take charge once again in a delightfully macabre work originally written in 1975. (167 pages)

Where it's reviewed:
Booklist, July 2002, page 1846
Bulletin of the Center for Children's Books, November 2002, page 113
Horn Book, September 2002, page 574
Publishers Weekly, July 22, 2002, page 182
School Library Journal, August 2002, page 189

Other books by the same author:
The Haunting of Granite Falls, 2005
Not Just a Witch, 2003
Journey to the River Sea, 2002

Dial-a-Ghost, 2001
Island of the Aunts, 2000

Other books you might like:
Eileen Dunlop, *The Ghost by the Sea*, 1996
  Two cousins try to solve the mysterious drowning of an ancestor so Milly's spirit can finally rest and stop haunting their grandparents' home.
Peni R. Griffin, *The Ghost Sitter*, 2001
  Promising her sister that she won't leave, Susie waits for her family to return until two young girls help release her from her pledge.
Betty Ren Wright, *A Ghost in the Family*, 1998
  Chad accompanies a friend on a two-week stay at her aunt's boarding house and discovers a ghost haunting his room.

707

EVA IBBOTSON
KEVIN HAWKES, Illustrator

Journey to the River Sea

(New York: Dutton, 2002)

Subject(s): Adventure and Adventurers; Orphans
Age range(s): Grades 5-8
Major character(s): Maia Fielding, Orphan; Gwendolyn Carter, Twin; Beatrice Carter, Twin; Miss Minton, Governess; Finn Taverner, Orphan; Jimmy "Clovis King" Bates, Orphan, Adoptee
Time period(s): 1910s
Locale(s): England; Manaus, Brazil (along the Amazon River (the River Sea))

Summary: While at boarding school in England, Maia learns that her parents have died and her trustee arranges for her to live with the Carters, her relatives on a rubber plantation in Brazil. Excited at this adventure, and accompanied by her new governess Miss Minton, Maia travels to Manaus on the Amazon River where she finds the Carters hate everything Brazilian, never go outside, and try to pretend they're still in England. Mr. Carter is a thief on the run, Mrs. Carter wishes to

697

THACHER HURD, Author/Illustrator

Moo Cow Kaboom!

(New York: HarperCollins Publishers, 2003)

Subject(s): Animals/Cows; Farm Life; Space Travel
Age range(s): Grades K-2
Major character(s): Farmer George, Farmer; Moo Cow, Cow, Kidnap Victim; Zork, Kidnapper, Alien
Time period(s): Indeterminate
Locale(s): Earth; Planet—Imaginary

Summary: In the middle of the night a loud "kaboom!" awakens Farmer George. When he rushes out to investigate, he can't find Moo Cow. Zork, a space cowboy who wants to have an unusual entry in the Inter-Galactic Rodeo, has kidnapped Moo Cow. The befuddled animal is not familiar with rodeos so she initially stands and does nothing while the increasingly irate Zork shouts at her. Moo Cow understands the insults and does not appreciate them so she begins whirling, twirling, bouncing and bucking until Zork is propelled back to his farm. The other aliens, horrified by this wild animal, put Moo Cow in a spaceship and send her back to Earth where she lands with a "kaboom!" on Farmer George's farm. (32 pages)

Where it's reviewed:
Booklist, July 2003, page 1897
Horn Book, May 2003, page 329
Publishers Weekly, April 21, 2003, page 61
School Library Journal, June 2003, page 107

Awards the book has won:
Center for Children's Books Best Books, 2003

Other books by the same author:
Santa Mouse and the Ratdeer, 1998
Zoom City, 1998
Art Dog, 1996

Other books you might like:
Chris Babcock, *No Moon, No Milk!*, 1993
    Martha refuses to give her owner any milk until she fulfills her dream to be a "cowsmonaut" and walk on the moon.
Denys Cazet, *Minnie and Moo Go to the Moon*, 1998
    Cows Minnie and Moo "borrow" the farmer's tractor. After crashing into the pigsty and becoming airborne they think they've landed on the moon.
Paul Brett Johnson, *The Cow Who Wouldn't Come Down*, 1993
    Gertrude, a cow with a mind of her own, has a mind to fly. After she succeeds, she has no interest in returning to the barn.
Toby Speed, *Two Cool Cows*, 1995
    Maude and Millie, two cool cows in borrowed boots and sunglasses, jump to the moon to frolic with their bovine buddies.

698

CAROL OTIS HURST

In Plain Sight

(Boston: Houghton Mifflin/A Walter Lorraine Book, 2002)

Subject(s): Farm Life; Gold Discoveries; Fathers and Daughters
Age range(s): Grades 4-7
Major character(s): Sarah Corbin, 11-Year-Old; Robin Corbin, Child, Brother; Delina Corbin, Mother; Miles Corbin, Father, Prospector
Time period(s): 1850s
Locale(s): Westfield, Massachusetts

Summary: When Sarah's father leaves their farm to try his luck in California's gold fields, she feels that all the fun has gone out of her life. Though her quiet mother works to keep the family and farm flourishing, her efforts aren't appreciated until Sarah's badly burned in a fire while rescuing her brother. Sarah has even more to weather besides her burns when the family hears of her father's drowning, her grandfather's stroke, and the startling reappearance of her father, who faked his death after failing to make his fortune in gold. Sarah struggles with her new understanding of her parents and wonders how she'll ever forgive her father for lying to his family. (154 pages)

Where it's reviewed:
Booklist, March 1, 2002, page 1147
Horn Book, May 2002, page 331
Kirkus Reviews, March 1, 2002, page 337
School Library Journal, March 2002, page 232

Other books by the same author:
Through the Lock, 2001

Other books you might like:
Louann Gaeddert, *Hope*, 1995
    With their father prospecting for gold, and their mother dead, Hope and her brother are taken in by the Shaker community.
Pamela Smith Hill, *A Voice from the Border*, 1998
    Reeves has difficulty understanding why the North and South are fighting, a difficulty compounded by the death of her soldier father.
Sonia Levitin, *Clem's Chances*, 2001
    When his mother dies, Clem takes a chance, leaves his Missouri farm and heads west on foot to find his gold-seeking father.

699

CAROL OTIS HURST

The Wrong One

(Boston: Walter Lorraine/Houghton Mifflin Books, 2003)

Subject(s): Moving, Household; Brothers and Sisters; Dolls and Dollhouses
Age range(s): Grades 4-6
Major character(s): Kate Spencer, 11-Year-Old; Jesse Spencer, Child; Sookhan Spencer, Adoptee, Child; Agatha Paran, Collector (of dolls)

Time period(s): 2000s
Locale(s): Massachusetts

Summary: The death of their father leaves the Spencer family grieving, as well as quite a bit poorer, so they move from their home in Brooklyn to a farmhouse. Almost from the moment they arrive, strange events occur beginning with Sookhan's fear at staying in her room because of the wallpaper imprinted with a doll motif; finding an antique doll in the barn that matches the wallpaper is eerie. But there are other strange happenings, from a TV that turns on by itself, to a shimmery blue light and that antique doll that Sookhan keeps saying is "the wrong one." A burst water pipe unveils a hole in the wall that leads them to the "right" doll, a doll that fetches them $100,000 from Agatha Paran who once lived in their old farmhouse. Are there ghosts in that farmhouse? Perhaps, but only the Spencers know for sure. (156 pages)

Where it's reviewed:
Booklist, March 1, 2003, page 1198
Bulletin of the Center for Children's Books, July 2003, page 452
Kirkus Reviews, May 1, 2003, page 678
Publishers Weekly, May 5, 2003, page 67
School Library Journal, May 2003, page 154

Other books by the same author:
A Killing in Plymouth Colony, 2003
In Plain Sight, 2002
Through the Lock, 2001

Other books you might like:
Mary Downing Hahn, *The Doll in the Garden*, 1989
    Finding an antique doll in an overgrown rose garden links Ashley with the present and the past.
Sylvia Waugh, *The Mennyms*, 1994
    After she dies, life-size dolls that Kate Penshaw created 40 years ago, come to life and enjoy residing in her home.
Betty Ren Wright, *The Dollhouse Murders*, 1983
    The clues left by a pair of dolls in the attic help Amy solve the murder of her aunt's grandparents.

700

DAVIDA WILLS HURWIN

The Farther You Run

(New York: Viking, 2003)

Subject(s): Grief; Friendship; Death
Age range(s): Grades 9-12
Major character(s): Samantha Russell, 18-Year-Old; Mona Brocato, 19-Year-Old; Juliana, Friend (of Samantha; deceased)
Time period(s): 1990s
Locale(s): San Francisco, California

Summary: It's now summer and Samantha's taking an English class in order to graduate, having failed English after her best friend Juliana died of cancer in May. In class she meets Mona, also trying to graduate, who failed English because of caring for her bipolar mother during her manic episodes. While Samantha struggles with her grief and Mona with her relationship with her mother, the two decide to rent an apartment together and look for jobs. Suddenly a fresh world opens for Samantha as she meets new people and tries to move on, but it's hard to forget. At times even her friendship with Mona suffers, especially when Mona sleeps with a boy Sam's been dating. On her nineteenth birthday, Sam makes a special attempt to come to terms with her grief as she takes a ballet class in fulfillment of a promise to Juliana. (217 pages)

Where it's reviewed:
Booklist, August 2003, page 1980
Kirkus Reviews, June 15, 2003, page 859
Library Media Connection, March 2004, page 67
School Library Journal, August 2003, page 160
Voice of Youth Advocates, August 2003, page 225

Other books by the same author:
A Time for Dancing, 1995

Other books you might like:
Bruce Brooks, *All That Remains*, 2001
    Three novellas offer different takes on death from creative coffins and burial spots to looking after a cousin.
Julie Reece Deaver, *Say Goodnight, Gracie*, 1988
    Morgan's life comes to an abrupt halt when her dear friend Jimmy is killed in an automobile accident.
Carolyn McCullough, *Falling through Darkness*, 2003
    Ginny reflects on her adventures with her devil-may-care boyfriend Aidan, before his abusive home situation overwhelmed his life.

701

JOHANNA HURWITZ
BARBARA GARRISON, Illustrator

Dear Emma

(New York: HarperCollins, 2002)

Subject(s): Friendship; Letters; Russian Americans
Age range(s): Grades 4-6
Major character(s): Hadassah "Dossi" Rabinowitz, 12-Year-Old, Orphan; Ruth "Ruthi" Rabinowitz, Sister (of Dossi), Orphan; Emma Meade, Friend (of Dossi); Meyer Reisman, Pharmacist
Time period(s): 1910s (1910-1911)
Locale(s): New York, New York (Lower East Side)

Summary: A friendship begun when Dossi attended summer camp in Vermont, thanks to the Clean Air Fund, continues once Dossi returns to the Lower East Side of New York and writes to Emma. Her letters are filled with stories of her life after her older sister Ruthi marries Meyer and both sisters move into his apartment. Though Dossi and her brother-in-law often butt heads, Dossi feels more kindly toward him when she learns her sister is pregnant. Their neighborhood is hit by a double tragedy when a diphtheria epidemic breaks out and then the Triangle Shirtwaist Factory fire erupts, killing over 100 seamstresses, including one of their friends. The year ends well when her niece is born and Dossi considers studying for a medical career after she graduates from grammar school in this sequel to *Faraway Summer*. (150 pages)

Where it's reviewed:
Booklist, December 1, 2002, page 666
Kirkus Reviews, October 15, 2002, page 1531
Publishers Weekly, November 11, 2002, page 66

School Library Journal, December 2002, page 140

Other books by the same author:
Faraway Summer, 1998
Spring Break, 1997
Even Stephen, 1996
Ozzie on His Own, 1995
A Llama in the Family, 1994

Other books you might like:
Judie Angell, *One-Way to Ansonia*, 1985
For 1890s immigrant Rose Olshansky, the only way to achieve her dream is to attend night school after working all day at the Griffin Cap Factory.
Kathryn Lasky, *Dreams in the Golden Country: The Diary of Zipporah Feldman, a Jewish Immigrant Girl*, 1998
At the turn of the century, Zipporah and her family join thousands of other immigrants when they leave Russia for New York's Lower East Side.
Joan Lowery Nixon, *Land of Hope*, 1992
Fleeing the Russian pograms, Rebekah and her family find life hard in New York City, though Rebekah loves attending school and dreams of teaching.

702

JOHANNA HURWITZ
DEBBIE TILLEY, Illustrator

Elisa Michaels, Bigger & Better

(New York: HarperCollins Publishers, 2003)

Series: Riverside Kids
Subject(s): Brothers and Sisters; Short Stories; Family Life
Age range(s): Grades 2-3
Major character(s): Elisa Michaels, 7-Year-Old, 2nd Grader; Grandma, Grandmother; Marshall, Brother, 2-Year-Old
Time period(s): 2000s (2003)
Locale(s): New York, New York; Florida

Summary: An episodic early chapter book describes Elisa's growing independence. When the three children are left in the care of a babysitter more interested in playing chess with her older brother than caring for Marshall, Elisa takes care of his dirty diaper and sings a song to help him sleep. Elisa eats breakfast with Grandma in Florida by talking to her on the phone as each dines in their respective homes. Cleverly, during a trip to the zoo, Elisa figures out how to get Marshall to give up pacifiers. An opportunity to travel to Florida in the company of Grandma's friends gives Elisa the chance to fly for the first time and to courageously do something without her family present. Although Elisa gets her wish to eat only chocolate for a day, she quickly learns that such a restricted diet grows tiresome and doesn't satisfy her hunger. Elisa is growing, bigger and better. (128 pages)

Where it's reviewed:
Booklist, December 15, 2003, page 753
Horn Book, November 2003, page 747
Publishers Weekly, December 1, 2003, page 58

Other books by the same author:
Fourth Grade Fuss, 2004
E Is for Elisa, 2003
Ever Clever Elisa, 2002

Other books you might like:
Ann Cameron, *Gloria's Way*, 2000
Gloria faces the trials and tribulations of childhood with support from friends and family.
Beverly Cleary, *The Ramona Series*, 1952-1999
Irrepressible Ramona and her family endure school problems and sibling squabbles with love and a sense of humor.
Paula Danziger, *It's Justin Time, Amber Brown*, 2001
Amber eagerly counts the days until her seventh birthday while hoping to receive a watch as a present.
Maud Hart Lovelace, *Betsy-Tacy and Tib*, 1941
The warmth of small town neighbors and the shared activities of close friends make this work a timeless classic.

703

GLEN HUSER

Stitches

(Toronto: Groundwood, 2003)

Subject(s): Friendship; Sewing; Physically Handicapped
Age range(s): Grades 7-10
Major character(s): Chantelle Boscombe, Handicapped, Student—High School; Travis, Seamstress, Student—High School; Gentry, Singer, Mother (of Travis)
Time period(s): 2000s
Locale(s): Alberta, Canada

Summary: Two misfits, Chantelle and Travis, have gone to school together since first grade. Chantelle was born with facial and body deformities, yet seems able to overlook these problems and get on with her life. The fact that she also has six older, muscular, hoodlum brothers helps, too. Travis is the child of a single mother, Gentry, who's a country music singer and is seldom home. Instead, his mother's sister and her abusive husband raise him in their trailer, along with their children. Because Travis has effeminate tendencies and loves to sew puppets, he's been teased unmercifully by the class bullies through elementary, middle and high school. But the friendship Chantelle and Travis enjoy helps each of them ignore the class bullies and together they write plays for which Travis sews his puppets and Chantelle helps with the performance in this charming, heart-warming story. (198 pages)

Where it's reviewed:
Bulletin of the Center for Children's Books, February 2004, page 233
Horn Book, November 2003, page 748
Resource Links, February 2004, page 34
School Library Journal, December 2003, page 152

Other books by the same author:
Grace Lake: A Novel, 1990

Other books you might like:
Gail Giles, *Shattering Glass*, 2002
Rob's attempt to transform consummate nerd Simon Glass into Mr. Cool, backfires and leads to tragedy.
Alice Hoffman, *The River King*, 2000
August Pierce is too much of an individual for some of the boys at his elite prep school and an attempt to put him in his place turns to tragedy.

Allen Kurzweil, *Leon and the Spitting Image*, 2003
Forced to stitch a doll, Leon designs one that resembles his teacher Miss Hagmeyer and finds manipulating the doll also manipulates her.
Norma Fox Mazer, *Out of Control*, 1993
Mean-spirited physical revenge for an imagined insult haunts the victim and her attackers, even when they all try to pretend nothing happened.

704

HAZEL HUTCHINS

T.J. and the Cats

(Custer, WA: Orca Book Publishers)

Series: Orca Young Reader
Subject(s): Animals/Cats; Grandmothers; Vacations
Age range(s): Grades 3-4
Major character(s): T.J. Barnes, Student—Elementary School, Friend; Seymour, Student—Elementary School, Friend; Gran, Grandmother
Time period(s): 2000s (2002)
Locale(s): Canada

Summary: Clearly T.J.'s love of Gran overpowered his common sense or he would never have agreed to care for her four cats while she vacationed in Hawaii. T.J. fears cats and now he's surrounded by them with no idea what to do. After convincing Seymour to change their school project topic from dinosaurs to cats, T.J. begins to learn from their research the basis for cats' behavior and his fear decreases. By the time Gran returns from her trip to reclaim her pets, T.J. and Seymour have earned an ''A'' on their project, lost and found the cats, and become sufficiently fond of them to agree to adopt the two kittens resulting from one cat's three-day escapade while lost. (103 pages)

Where it's reviewed:
Booklist, December 15, 2002, page 759
School Library Journal, February 2003, page 114

Other books by the same author:
Robyn's Art Attack, 2001
The Prince of Tarn, 1997
The Three and Many Wishes of Jason Reid, 1988

Other books you might like:
Martha Freeman, *The Trouble with Cats*, 2000
Since her mother's remarriage, Holly is having a hard time adjusting to life with a stepfather and his four cats.
Ann Whitehead Nagda, *Meow Means Mischief*, 2003
Befriending a stray kitten helps Rana adjust to a new school.

Phyllis Reynolds Naylor, *Danny's Desert Rats*, 1998
Danny and his brother T.R. help their new friend Paul hide his pet cat from the apartment manager.

705

PAT HUTCHINS, Author/Illustrator

We're Going on a Picnic!

(New York: Greenwillow Books, 2002)

Subject(s): Animals/Birds; Food; Animals
Age range(s): Preschool-Grade 1
Major character(s): Hen, Chicken; Duck, Duck; Goose, Goose
Time period(s): Indeterminate
Locale(s): Fictional Country

Summary: Hen, Duck and Goose decide it's a perfect day for a picnic so each picks a favorite fruit and packs it into a picnic basket. They take turns carrying the basket as they search for just the right spot to eat. None realize that the basket is so heavy because of a succession of animals hopping in and out to eat the fruit. When Hen, Duck and Goose finally reach a spot to eat, they discover that the basket is empty so they pick more fruit and set out again to find the perfect picnic location. (32 pages)

Where it's reviewed:
Booklist, March 1, 2002, page 1142
Bulletin of the Center for Children's Books, July/August 2002, page 40
Horn Book Guide, Fall 2002, page 304
Publishers Weekly, January 21, 2002, page 89
School Library Journal, March 2002, page 190

Other books by the same author:
It's MY Birthday!, 1999
Titch and Daisy, 1996
Three-Star Billy, 1994

Other books you might like:
Jez Alborough, *Duck in the Truck*, 2000
When Duck gets his red truck stuck a frog a goat and a sheep help to free the truck from the muck. Yuck!
Ruth Brown, *The Picnic*, 1993
After rain causes a family to hurriedly leave their picnic in a meadow animals come out of hiding to enjoy the remains.
Jane Yolen, *Off We Go!*, 2000
The various animals in this picture book have one destination as they set out—Grandma's house.

Adele Geras, *Time for Ballet*, 2003
  Tilly and the others in her dance class practice for an important recital.
Alexander Stadler, *Lila Bloom*, 2004
  Lila reconsiders her decision to stop ballet lessons when she admits the positive benefits of dancing to her frame of mind.

719

RACHEL ISADORA, Author/Illustrator

Peekaboo Morning
(New York: G.P. Putnam's Sons, 2002)

Subject(s): Playing; Family; Games
Age range(s): Preschool
Major character(s): Unnamed Character, Child
Time period(s): 2000s
Locale(s): United States

Summary: From the moment a little child's eyes first open and peep out from under the covers to see waking parents, ''Peekaboo!'' becomes the game of the day. Peeking in a mirror shows the child's reflection, peeking behind the door reveals the family's puppy and peeking outside finds grandparents under a hat and behind a newspaper. A happy child in a loving family enjoys a sunny day with a friend who likes to play peekaboo, too. (28 pages)

Where it's reviewed:
Booklist, March 1, 2002, page 1142
Bulletin of the Center for Children's Books, July 2002, page 407
Publishers Weekly, April 15, 2002, page 62
School Library Journal, July 2002, page 93

Other books by the same author:
In the Beginning, 2003
Mr. Moon, 2002
ABC Pop!, 1999

Other books you might like:
Janet Ahlberg, *Peek-a-Boo!*, 1981
  A rhyming story follows a baby playfully enjoying the day from beginning to end. Allan Ahlberg, co-author.
Roberta Grobel Intrater, *Peek-a-Boo!*, 1997
  Photographs of happy babies illustrate this board book.
Jan Ormerod, *Peek-a-Boo!*, 1997
  Where's the baby? Hiding behind mittens, bibs and teddy bears. Peek-a-boo!

J

720

CHRIS JACKSON, Author/Illustrator

The Gaggle Sisters River Tour

(Montreal: Lobster Press, 2002)

Subject(s): Animals/Geese; Sisters; Rivers
Age range(s): Grades K-2
Major character(s): Dorothy Gaggle, Goose, Sister; Sadie Gaggle, Goose, Sister
Time period(s): Indeterminate
Locale(s): Wriggle River, Fictional Country

Summary: Hard-working Dorothy loads the sisters' raft while Sadie selects jewelry and paints a banner giving her singing top billing and relegating Dorothy and her accordion to the fine print. Self-centered Sadie, with her frequent complaints and criticisms, appears to be unappreciative of patient Dorothy but it's clear she depends on Dorothy to solve any problem that comes up with the journey or the performance. Dorothy understands and supports her sister and the humorous story ends on a note of sisterly tolerance and love. (32 pages)

Where it's reviewed:
Booklist, December 15, 2002, page 768
Publishers Weekly, August 5, 2002, page 71
School Library Journal, January 2003, page 97

Other books by the same author:
The Gaggle Sisters Sing Again, 2004
Edmund for Short: A Tale from China Plate Farm, 2000
Edmund and Hillary: A Tale from China Plate Farm, 1997

Other books you might like:
Jef Kaminsky, *Poppy & Ella: 3 Stories about 2 Friends*, 2000
   Poppy and Ella are great friends who agree about everything and even when they disagree they are still friends.
James Marshall, *Wings: A Tale of Two Chickens*, 1986
   Adventurous Winnie accepts a ride in a fox's hot air balloon forcing her sensible friend Harriet to plan a rescue mission.

Laura Joffe Numeroff, *The Chicken Sisters*, 1997
   The three chicken sisters share a home with each one tolerating the others' hobbies in a humorous look at individuality and acceptance.

721

SHELLEY JACKSON, Author/Illustrator

Sophia: The Alchemist's Dog

(New York: Richard Jackson Book/Atheneum Books for Young Readers, 2002)

Subject(s): Alchemy; Animals/Dogs; Artists and Art
Age range(s): Grades 2-5
Major character(s): Sophia, Dog; Unnamed Character, Artist; Unnamed Character, Royalty
Time period(s): Indeterminate Past
Locale(s): Fictional Country

Summary: Though Sophia's master serves as alchemist to the king he's actually an artist at heart. Sensitive by nature and attentive to his pet's needs, he spends his days drawing the dreams he recalls from his night's sleep, sure that they hold the answer to creating gold. For several years Sophia and her master share this contented life but when word comes that the king will be coming in two weeks to see the result of the alchemist's work, life changes. Sophia is so concerned to see the worry and stress in her master that, as he sleeps, she secretly labors to create gold. After several nights, Sophia is successful but chooses not to reveal her product when the king visits for he is so taken by the master's art that he changes her master's job title from alchemist to ''painter for the king.'' Now the only ''gold'' the painter is required to create is that needed for his paintings. (48 pages)

Where it's reviewed:
Booklist, October 1, 2002, page 336
Publishers Weekly, August 5, 2002, page 72
School Library Journal, October 2002, page 166

Other books by the same author:
The Old Woman and the Wave, 1998

Other books you might like:

Diane Stanley, *Rumpelstiltskin's Daughter*, 1997
  In a take-off on the original tale, a greedy king still expects straw to be spun into gold.
William Steig, *The Toy Brother*, 1996
  Preoccupied with efforts to turn donkey dung into gold Yorick ignores his father's warning to stay out of the lab and suffers unfortunate consequences.
Colin Thompson, *The Last Alchemist*, 1999
  Apprentice Arthur sees and enjoys gold in nature and cannot understand Spinifex's obsession with creating the metallic substance.

722

BRIAN JACQUES
DAVID ELLIOTT, Illustrator

The Angel's Command: A Tale from the Castaways of the Flying Dutchman

(New York: Philomel/Penguin Putnam, 2003)

Subject(s): Sea Stories; Heroes and Heroines; Pirates
Age range(s): Grades 5 and Up
Major character(s): Nebuchadnezzer ''Ben'', Immortal; Denmark ''Ned'', Dog (black Labrador), Immortal; Raphael Thuron, Sea Captain; Adamo Bregon, Nobleman; Maguda Razan, Gypsy; Karay, Gypsy, Singer
Time period(s): 17th century (1628)
Locale(s): *La Petite Marie*, Caribbean; Pyrenees, France; Pyrenees, Spain

Summary: First introduced in *Castaways of the Flying Dutchman*, where Ben and his dog Ned received immortality by an angel that damned the rest of the ship's crew, they meet up with Captain Thuron when Ben helps him beat a cheating card player. On board *La Petite Marie*, they join the good-natured pirate as he sails around the Caribbean trying to evade two mean ship's captains who pursue him. When Captain Thuron is killed, Ben and Ned depart and travel to the Pyrenees where they continue their charge of forever wandering to help others, this time rescuing the nobleman Adamo who's in the clutches of the evil Maguda Razan. Aided by Karay, and with their ability to communicate telepathically, Ben and Ned face the wicked Maguda and her Razan tribe who live high in the Pyrenees Mountains, in another adventure complete with swashbucklers, pirates, gypsies and crooks. (374 pages)

Where it's reviewed:
Booklist, February 1, 2003, page 982
Horn Book, March 2003, page 212
Kliatt, January 2003, page 8
School Library Journal, March 2003, page 235
Voice of Youth Advocates, April 2003, page 65

Other books by the same author:
Castaways of the Flying Dutchman, 2001

Other books you might like:
Iain Lawrence, *The Buccaneers*, 2001
  Picking up a drifting sailor proves advantageous for John Spencer when the schooner *Dragon* is later attacked by pirates.

Robin Moore, *The Man with the Silver Oar*, 2002
  Quaker Daniel's in an ethical quandary when he's aboard a pirate hunting ship, but even more so when he recognizes the captured pirate Scarfield.
J.R.R. Tolkien, *The Lord of the Rings Trilogy*, 1954-1956
  The epic battle between good and evil begins when the hobbit Frodo takes on the burden of the destruction of the Ring of Power.

723

BRIAN JACQUES
ALEXI NATCHEV, Illustrator

The Tale of Urso Brunov: Little Father of All Bears

(New York: Philomel Books, 2003)

Subject(s): Animals/Bears; Animals; Tall Tales
Age range(s): Grades 1-4
Major character(s): Urso Brunov, Bear
Time period(s): Indeterminate Past
Locale(s): Fictional Country

Summary: Urso Brunov, leader of a tribe of thumb-sized bears, sets off on a winter quest to find four of his young bears that decided to sneak south for the winter while the others hibernated. Confidently Urso faces mountain goats, high mountains, wild boars, deep rivers, and vast deserts as he trudges along. He learns that men have captured the four bears along with relatives of some of the wild animals he meets along the way. Urso promises to bring all the captured animals back in exchange for assistance with his journey. Urso finally locates them in the place of the ''Lightning Flash and Two Cartwheels,'' known to readers as a zoo. Because he is Urso Brunov, he fulfills his promise, frees the animals, imprisons the hunters and brings the four tiny bears safely home. (48 pages)

Where it's reviewed:
Booklist, September 1, 2003, page 128
Publishers Weekly, October 6, 2003, page 83
School Library Journal, September 2003, page 180

Other books by the same author:
A Redwall's Winter Tale, 2001
The Great Redwall Feast, 1996

Other books you might like:
Virginia Hamilton, *When Birds Could Talk & Bats Could Sing: The Adventures of Bruh Sparrow, Sis Wren, and Their Friends*, 1996
  A collection of eight stories based on African American folklore is set in the time long ago when animals could talk and sport fancy clothes.
Julius Lester, *More Tales of Uncle Remus: Further Adventures of Brer Rabbit, His Friends, Enemies, and Others*, 1988
  Thirty-seven stories feature the activities of famous trickster Brer Rabbit.
Paul Peabody, *Blackberry Hollow*, 1993
  Parnussus, a kindly bear, tries to ease the homesickness of Tom, a Scottish frog, in hopes he'll stop playing his bagpipes.

Cynthia Rylant, *Thimbleberry Stories*, 2000
  Four stories chronicle the peaceful life of the animal residents of Thimbleberry Lane.
James Stevenson, *Mud Flat Spring*, 1999
  Each of the many animals of Mud Flat enjoys a particular feature of spring and has a unique way to celebrate it.

724

LISA JAHN-CLOUGH, Author/Illustrator

Alicia's Best Friends

(Boston: Houghton Mifflin Company, 2003)

Subject(s): Friendship; Individuality; Pets
Age range(s): Preschool-Grade 1
Major character(s): Alicia, Child; Neptune, Dog
Time period(s): 2000s (2003)
Locale(s): United States

Summary: In addition to Neptune, Alicia has four great friends. To show her appreciation she plans a party but then the friends want her to choose which is her best friend. Alicia tries but since each friend has a unique gift or talent, choosing one means losing out on another's special qualities. For a while Alicia selects Neptune as her best friend, but that is not a completely satisfying solution. Finally Alicia realizes that she has five best friends: a best dog friend, a best athlete friend, a best artist friend, a best jokester friend, and a best bug-loving friend. Lucky Alicia! (32 pages)

Where it's reviewed:
Booklist, March 15, 2003, page 1332
Publishers Weekly, February 24, 2003, page 74
School Library Journal, March 2003, page 196

Other books by the same author:
Country Girl, City Girl, 2004
On the Hill, 2004
Missing Molly, 2000
Alicia Has a Bad Day, 1994

Other books you might like:
Jef Kaminsky, *Poppy & Ella: 3 Stories about 2 Friends*, 2000
  Poppy and Ella are great friends who agree about everything and even when they disagree they are still friends.
Kim Lewis, *Friends*, 1997
  Sam and Alice squabble briefly over a dropped egg but put their differences aside when they hear the hen clucking again.
Sam McBratney, *I'm Sorry*, 2000
  Angry words pass between two good friends leaving them each feeling sad and lonely until the words "I'm sorry" bring smiles to their faces.
Megan McDonald, *Reptiles Are My Life*, 2001
  Maggie and Amanda's shared interest forms the basis of a friendship that is threatened by the arrival of a new student.
Lynn Reiser, *Best Friends Think Alike*, 1997
  Beryl and Ruby resolve a brief disagreement and continue their imaginative play knowing that best friends really do think alike.

725

BRIAN JAMES

Tomorrow, Maybe

(New York: Push/Scholastic, Inc., 2003)

Subject(s): Runaways; Homeless People
Age range(s): Grades 7-10
Major character(s): Gretchen "Chan", 15-Year-Old, Streetperson; Elizabeth, 10-Year-Old, Streetperson; Jef, Streetperson
Time period(s): 2000s
Locale(s): New York, New York

Summary: Two years before, Gretchen lived in a nice house with clean sheets, heat and bathtubs, but then her father remarried, her stepmother was abusive and Gretchen ran away. Ever since then she's known as Chan and lives in drafty basements or crashes with friends whenever and wherever she can. One night a child named Elizabeth shows up in their squat and, though everyone else wants the child to leave, Chan feels she needs to take care of her. The two girls specialize in begging and begin to save their money in order to move away from New York City. Invited to a concert by their friend Jef, the two girls find they're in a trap to obtain prostitutes and barely manage to escape. The next day Chan wakes up to find that Elizabeth has stolen all their money and left. That's when Chan realizes she needs to return to the world of Gretchen and calls her father for help. (248 pages)

Where it's reviewed:
Kliatt, May 2003, page 18
Library Media Connection, October 2003, page 60
School Library Journal, June 2003, page 144
Voice of Youth Advocates, August 2003, page 226

Other books you might like:
Margaret Clark, *Care Factor Zero*, 2000
  After Larceny hears voices and attacks a man, she runs away to Melbourne and lives on the streets until she meets social worker Kaz.
Ineke Holtwijk, *Asphalt Angels*, 1999
  Kicked out of his house by his abusive stepfather, Alex joins the gang Asphalt Angels but feels himself pulling away from their criminal lifestyle.
Diane Silvey, *Raven's Flight*, 2001
  Searching for her sister, Raven's afraid that Marcie's been taken by a kidnapping ring that steals children and sends them to work in sweatshops.

726

SIMON JAMES, Author/Illustrator

The Birdwatchers

(Cambridge, MA: Candlewick Press, 2002)

Subject(s): Animals/Birds; Grandfathers; Hobbies
Age range(s): Grades K-3
Major character(s): Jess, Relative (granddaughter); Granddad, Grandfather
Time period(s): 2000s
Locale(s): United States

Summary: Jess isn't sure what to make of Granddad's tales about birds drawing pictures of him as he sketches them and helping him identify them in his bird book. To find out the real truth, Jess accompanies him one day. At first, the most amazing thing Jess sees is nothing. Using Granddad's binoculars doesn't help; the woods seem empty. Then Granddad takes Jess to the bird watching hut and when she looks out the hatch a huge variety of birds are visible. After spending the day sketching birds and taking notes just as Granddad does, Jess walks out of the woods with him while sharing a little bird watching tale of her own. (28 pages)

Where it's reviewed:
Booklist, August 2002, page 1972
Bulletin of the Center for Children's Books, June 2002, page 368
Publishers Weekly, April 15, 2002, page 63
Riverbank Review, Fall 2002, page 29
School Library Journal, May 2002, page 117

Awards the book has won:
Smithsonian's Notable Books for Children, 2002

Other books by the same author:
Leon and Bob, 1997 (New York Times Best Illustrated Children's Book)
The Wild Woods, 1993
Dear Mr. Blueberry, 1991

Other books you might like:
Candace Fleming, *When Agnes Caws*, 1999
    Agnes, a gifted mimicker of birdcalls, travels the globe with her ornithologist mother in search of rare species.
Jane B. Mason, *River Day*, 1994
    A serene day on the river with her grandfather seems incomplete until Alex spots a bald eagle.
Cynthia Rylant, *The Bird House*, 1998
    Birds spell the word ''girl'' in the sky in order to alert a bird lover to the plight of homeless girl hiding nearby.

727

SIMON JAMES, Author/Illustrator

Little One Step

(Cambridge, MA: Candlewick Press, 2003)

Subject(s): Animals/Ducks; Brothers; Games
Age range(s): Grades K-2
Major character(s): Little One Step, Duck (duckling), Brother (youngest); Mama, Duck, Mother; Unnamed Character, Duck (duckling), Brother (oldest)
Time period(s): Indeterminate
Locale(s): Fictional Country

Summary: When three brother ducklings realize they are lost in the woods and don't know where Mama is, they begin walking in the direction of home. Soon the youngest duckling complains that his legs are too wobbly to continue. His oldest brother teaches him a game called One Step that requires the player to lift one foot while saying ''one,'' put it down and then lift the other while saying ''step'' and put that one down in front of the first foot. By using the game each time he feels tired the littlest duckling not only walks all the way but he's

the first to find Mama and tell her his new name, Little One Step. (32 pages)

Where it's reviewed:
Booklist, March 15, 2003, page 1332
Bulletin of the Center for Children's Books, April 2003, page 318
Horn Book Guide, Fall 2003, page 303
Publishers Weekly, March 3, 2003, page 75
School Library Journal, April 2003, page 129

Awards the book has won:
School Library Journal Best Books, 2003
ALA Notable Children's Books, 2004

Other books by the same author:
The Birdwatchers, 2002
Leon and Bob, 1997 (New York Times Best Illustrated Book)
The Wild Woods, 1993

Other books you might like:
Frank Asch, *Baby Duck's New Friend*, 2001
    Baby Duck befriends a rubber duck and follows it so far from home that he wonders how he'll find his mama.
Lisa Westberg Peters, *Cold Little Duck, Duck, Duck*, 2000
    Positive thinking frees a determined little duck that returns too early to the pond and becomes stuck to the frozen surface.
Nancy Tafuri, *Have You Seen My Duckling?*, 1984
    In a Caldecott Honor Book ducklings follow their mother as she searches a pond for her one missing offspring.
Martin Waddell, *Webster J. Duck*, 2001
    As a newly hatched duck looks for his mother she hears his persistent, quiet quacking over the sounds of the other animals.

728

KATELAN JANKE

Survival in the Storm: The Dust Bowl Diary of Grace Edwards

(New York: Scholastic, 2002)

Series: Dear America
Subject(s): Depression (Economic); Farm Life; Diaries
Age range(s): Grades 4-8
Major character(s): Grace Edwards, 12-Year-Old
Time period(s): 1930s (1935)
Locale(s): Dalhart, Texas

Summary: The diary of Grace Edwards details the difficulties of day-to-day living that afflict so many people during the Dust Bowl, when there is no rain and anytime the wind blows the dirt from the fields scatters everywhere. The fine dust grains blow into houses forcing people to wear damp handkerchiefs over their noses and mouths; cover everything on the kitchen counter so that bread is kneaded in a drawer; and causing the deaths of many people from dust pneumonia. Farms fail and many people migrate to California to make a living as migrant workers. Grace finds some joy during this time, when she has a new dress made from a pretty flour sack or finds a newborn rabbit. This book won the 1998 Arrow Book Club/Dear America Student Writing Contest, written when the author was only 15. (189 pages)

Where it's reviewed:
Booklist, February 15, 2003, page 1069
Detroit Free Press, November 24, 2002, page 5E
School Library Journal, December 2002, page 142

Other books you might like:
Clayton Bess, *Tracks*, 1986
Blue Roan and his brother Monroe leave their Oklahoma home to ride the rails looking for work.
Karen Hesse, *Out of the Dust*, 1997
During the Dust Bowl Days, Billie Jo tosses a burning pail of kerosene out the kitchen door and accidentally douses her mother, who later dies.
Kathleen Karr, *The Cave*, 1994
Christine and her brother struggle to survive on their South Dakota farm during the Dust Bowl Days.

729

WILLIAM JASPERSOHN
VERNON THORNBLAD, Illustrator

The Scrimshaw Ring

(Middlebury, VT: The Vermont Folklife Center, 2002)

Series: Family Heritage Book
Subject(s): Historical; Pirates; Family
Age range(s): Grades 2-5
Major character(s): William Bateman, 6-Year-Old, Son; Unnamed Character, Pirate
Time period(s): 1700s (1710)
Locale(s): Newport, Rhode Island, American Colonies

Summary: Imaginative William's experience with pirates provides the basis for a family story that is passed down for generations along with a scrimshaw ring. Hiding in his house on a day when his parents have gone to town in the buggy William watches pirates coming ashore. They bury two bodies on his family's farm and then steal all the farm animals. One pirate comes into the house, but when he sees William is only a boy he gives him the ring, pats his cheek and returns to his ship with the others. At first William's parents think his tale is another of his imaginative stories but the graves and the scrimshaw ring convince them otherwise. A concluding note about the tale verifies the family history on which the story is based. (32 pages)

Where it's reviewed:
Booklist, November 15, 2002, page 604
Publishers Weekly, November 4, 2002, page 83
School Library Journal, December 2002, page 98

Other books by the same author:
Two Brothers, 2000
Timber!, 1996
How the Forest Grew, 1980 (Boston Globe/Horn Book Award)

Other books you might like:
Ginger Howard, *William's House*, 2001
Upon arrival in New England in 1637 William builds a replica of his father's English home, modifying it as he experiences this new land.
Patricia Kirkpatrick, *Plowie: A Story from the Prairie*, 1994
The porcelain doll found by a little girl in the newly turned

earth behind her father's plow is passed along for succeeding generations to enjoy.
Carole Lexa Schaefer, *The Copper Tin Cup*, 2000
Sammy enjoys imagining his forebears as he sips cocoa from a copper tin cup passed down for generations in his family.
Anne Shelby, *Homeplace*, 1995
While rocking a grandchild, a grandmother traces the history of the family from the building of the family homestead to the present.

730

ALISON JAY, Author/Illustrator

ABC: A Child's First Alphabet Book

(New York: Dutton, 2003)

Subject(s): Adventure and Adventurers; Animals; Zoos
Age range(s): Grades K-2
Major character(s): Unnamed Character, Artist; Unnamed Character, Explorer
Time period(s): 2000s (2003)
Locale(s): Earth

Summary: Pictures tell the complete story in this seemingly straightforward alphabet book. While the text is limited to simple "A is for Apple" type statements, the illustrations show a woman saying farewell to a man, who then goes on a worldwide adventure, finding unique animals and buried treasure. In the end, man and woman are reunited and start a zoo with the animals they've both come to know during their separation. Although each letter only gets one statement, more objects starting with the same letter can be found in each illustration. (40 pages)

Where it's reviewed:
Five Owls, 2004, page 80
Publishers Weekly, August 11, 2003, page 277
School Library Journal, September 2003, page 181

Other books by the same author:
Picture This . . ., 2000

Other books you might like:
Graeme Base, *Animalia*, 1987
This alphabet book features rich illustrations of animals while the text includes lots of alliteration.
Bruno Munari, *ABC*, 1960
In this alphabet book, the fly takes off from his F page and visits all the other letters.
George Shannon, *Tomorrow's Alphabet*, 1996
This alphabet book challenges readers with such puzzles as why A is for seed (it's tomorrow's apple, of course).

731

SUSAN JEFFERS, Author/Illustrator

My Pony

(New York: Hyperion Books for Children, 2003)

Subject(s): Animals/Horses; Imagination; Artists and Art
Age range(s): Grades K-3

Major character(s): Unnamed Character, Child, Daughter; Unnamed Character, Mother; Unnamed Character, Father
Time period(s): 20th century
Locale(s): United States

Summary: A young girl longs for her pony, but her mother tells her they are too expensive and her father says they don't have space for a pony. Instead the girl draws pictures of her dream horse. The drawing turns into her imaginary friend, taking her on a journey through the mountains, visiting other horses and then back to her own room. (32 pages)

Where it's reviewed:
Booklist, November 1, 2003, page 501
School Library Journal, November 2003, page 102

Other books by the same author:
Little Book of Confidence, 2004
I'm Okay . . . You're a Brat!, 2000
Wild Swans, 1990
Three Jovial Huntsmen, 1989
Black Beauty, 1986

Other books you might like:
Carol Lee Cohen, *The Mud Pony*, 1989
    A Native American boy, too poor to own a horse, fashions a pony out of mud and it comes to life.
Cynthia Cotten, *Snow Ponies*, 2001
    When Old Man Winter lets his snow ponies out of the barn they bring the winter's first snowfall.
Gudrun Ongman, *The Sleep Ponies*, 2000
    At bedtime, the sleep ponies come to carry children off to dreamland.

732

A.M. JENKINS

Out of Order
(New York: HarperCollins, 2003)

Subject(s): Sports/Baseball; Schools/High Schools; Interpersonal Relations
Age range(s): Grades 8-12
Major character(s): Colt Trammel, 10th Grader, Baseball Player; Grace Garcetti, 10th Grader; Corinne "Chlorophyll" Hecht, 10th Grader
Time period(s): 2000s
Locale(s): Texas

Summary: Nice, mean, sweet, dumb, aggressive, scared. Any one of these terms could describe Colt, who excels on the baseball field but chokes on the academics. As the only sophomore on the varsity baseball team, he feels he's "someone" on his school's social scene and enhances that image by always dressing correctly and hanging out with the right people, but has passing grades only by using cheat sheets. He's also in love with Grace who's attracted to him physically, but way ahead of him in brain power. Grace jilts him for an older student who's been eager to add her to his stable, while Colt's left to pine and feel sorry for himself. New student Corinne, whom he tags as Chlorophyll for her green hair, is in accelerated English and through sharing a free fifth period, begins to explain the romance poets to Colt. Though he'll never be a gifted student, some of Chlo's teachings make sense to him

and he's able to pass an English test without surreptitious help. By book's end he's also gained a little better understanding of himself and has become friends, of a sort, with Chlo. (247 pages)

Where it's reviewed:
Booklist, September 1, 2003, page 115
Bulletin of the Center for Children's Books, October 2003, page 64
Horn Book, November 2003, page 749
School Library Journal, September 2003, page 214
Voice of Youth Advocates, October 2003, page 311

Awards the book has won:
Bulletin of the Center for Children's Books Blue Ribbons, 2003
ALA Best Books for Young Adults, 2004

Other books by the same author:
Damage, 2001
Breaking Boxes, 1997

Other books you might like:
James Bennett, *Plunking Reggie Jackson*, 2001
    Failing grades, a possibly pregnant girlfriend and a domineering father combine to upend Coley's pitching and any potential baseball scholarships.
Daniel Handler, *The Basic Eight*, 1999
    Part of a clique, Flannery and her high school friends go overboard in their dislike of a teacher and now she's facing jail time. Adult fiction.
Kristen D. Randle, *Breaking Rank*, 1999
    Baby defies his gang, and Casey her place in the school's social scene, when they are in the same honors class.
Ellen Wittlinger, *Razzle*, 2001
    Kenyon almost gives up tall, independent Razzle for a self-centered sexpot who throws him aside when he can't help her with a modeling career.

733

PATRICK JENNINGS
ANNA ALTER, Illustrator

The Tornado Watches
(New York: Holiday House, 2002)

Series: Ike and Mem Story
Subject(s): Weather; Family; Sleep
Age range(s): Grades 2-4
Major character(s): Ike Nunn, Brother (older), Student—Elementary School; Buzzy Starzinsky, Friend, Neighbor; Mem Nunn, Sister (younger), Student (preschooler)
Time period(s): Indeterminate Past
Locale(s): United States

Summary: Ike's family seeks shelter in the basement each time a tornado warning is announced. Ike wonders how the family will know if a warning is posted while they're asleep so, to assure the safety of his family, he puts a portable television in his bed and stays awake all night watching old movies and waiting for another warning. Mem discovers what he's doing but promises not to tell but the signs of sleeplessness are evident in Ike's appearance, his sleeping in class and his after school naps. On the fourth night of Ike's vigil he falls asleep in bed and awakens in the basement. His parents have carried him down when increasing winds awakened them. The tornado hits close to home that night, blowing the roof off Buzzy's house and destroying Ike and Buzzy's tree house. (64 pages)

Where it's reviewed:
Booklist, August 2002, page 1961
Horn Book, January 2003, page 75
School Library Journal, December 2002, page 98

Other books by the same author:
Ears of Corn, 2003 (Ike and Mem Story)
The Lightning Bugs, 2003 (Ike and Mem Story)
The Bird Shadow, 2001 (Ike and Mem Story)

Other books you might like:
P.M. Boekhoff, *Tornadoes*, 2003
　A nonfiction title explains how tornadoes form and describes different types of tornadoes.
Kate McMullan, *A Fine Start: Meg's Prairie Diary*, 2003
　Life on the Kansas prairie at a time of political turmoil is further complicated by a tornado.
Ann Schreiber, *Twister Trouble*, 2000
　In a Magic School Bus Science Chapter Book Ms. Frizzle and her class, on a trip to an amusement park, fly into the heart of a tornado.

734

PATRICK JENNINGS
ANNA ALTER, Illustrator

The Weeping Willow
(New York: Holiday House, 2002)

Series: Ike and Mem Story
Subject(s): Interpersonal Relations; Brothers and Sisters; Friendship
Age range(s): Grades 2-4
Major character(s): Mem Nunn, Child, Sister (younger); Ike Nunn, Child, Brother (older); Buzzy Starzinsky, Child, Friend (Ike's)
Time period(s): Indeterminate Past
Locale(s): United States

Summary: As they walk home from the pond Ike and Buzzy agree to Mem's suggestion to go inside the weeping willow tree. Once inside the cool space they realize it would be a good location for a tree house to replace the one recently damaged by a tornado. Using lumber from the old tree house, Ike and Buzzy try to construct a new one. The frustrating process of building in a swaying tree creates friction between the friends. After the boys angrily abandon the half-built tree house, Ike uses the lumber to build a playhouse for Mem. As friends do, Ike and Buzzy get over their differences, move Mem's playhouse into the cool shade of the willow tree and return to the pond to fish. (56 pages)

Where it's reviewed:
Booklist, December 15, 2002, page 759
Horn Book, January 2003, page 75
School Library Journal, February 2003, page 114

Other books by the same author:
Ears of Corn, 2003 (Ike and Mem Story)

The Lightning Bugs, 2003 (Ike and Mem Story)
The Bird Shadow, 2001 (Ike and Mem Story)

Other books you might like:
David Elliott, *The Cool Crazy Crickets to the Rescue!*, 2000
　Four friends start a club for the purpose of being friends for life.
James Howe, *Pinky and Rex*, 1990
　Pinky and Rex, inseparable friends, embark on the first of many shared adventures in this initial book in their series.
Cynthia Rylant, *Blue Hill Meadows*, 1997
　For Willie, each season of the year holds a special memory of his family and their rural home near the small community of Blue Hill.
Marilyn Sachs, *JoJo & Winnie Again: More Sister Stories*, 2000
　The rivalry between JoJo and Winnie is obvious in eight episodic chapters but so is the support the sisters offer one another.

735

PATRICK JENNINGS

The Wolving Time
(New York: Scholastic, 2003)

Subject(s): Werewolves; Animals/Wolves; Religion
Age range(s): Grades 7-10
Major character(s): Laszlo Emberek, 13-Year-Old, Shepherd; Muno, Orphan; Pere Raoul, Religious (priest)
Time period(s): 16th century
Locale(s): Saint-Eustache, France (in the French Pyrenees)

Summary: In France in the late 16th century, the church seeks out and executes anyone who is accused of being a witch or, even worse, a ''loup-garou'' or werewolf. Living outside the town because of their ability to shape shift into a loup-garou, the Emberek family makes its living as shepherds and works together with natural wolves to protect their flock. One day when his mother shape-shifts, Muno, the orphaned ward of the zealous priest Pere Raoul, witnesses the event and Laszlo fears she will disclose their secret. As time passes and she doesn't, Laszlo relaxes but then the priest tortures the information out of Muno, arrests the Emberek family and throws them into the dungeon. Luckily they are able to shape shift, escape, and free Muno to accompany them to a different village and a new life as Laszlo ponders who in this scenario is really the beast. (197 pages)

Where it's reviewed:
Bulletin of the Center for Children's Books, February 2004, page 235
Library Media Connection, January 2004, page 67
Publishers Weekly, December 1, 2003, page 57
School Library Journal, January 2004, page 130
Voice of Youth Advocates, December 2003, page 413

Other books by the same author:
Out Standing in My Field, 2005
The Beastly Arms, 2001
Faith and the Rocket Cat, 1998
Faith and the Electric Dogs, 1996

Other books you might like:
Annette Curtis Klause, *Blood and Chocolate*, 1997
Love is no easy matter for Vivian, a teenage werewolf.
Pamela Melnikoff, *Plots and Players: The Lopez Conspiracy*, 1988
Forced to practice their religion in secret, Robin's family hides the fact they're Jewish and worships as Catholics.
Pat Murphy, *Nadya: The Wolf Chronicles*, 1996
A young werewolf travels west and, despite her better judgment, uses her abilities to shelter two less able travelers.
Patricia Windsor, *The Blooding*, 1996
Maris's summer as an au pair takes a terrifying turn when she discovers she's working for a werewolf.

736
RICHARD W. JENNINGS
My Life of Crime
(Boston: Walter Lorraine Books/Houghton Mifflin, 2002)

Subject(s): Animals/Birds; Stealing; School Life
Age range(s): Grades 5-8
Major character(s): Fowler Young, 6th Grader; Mrs. Picklestain, Teacher
Time period(s): 2000s
Locale(s): United States

Summary: Following a trail of bright green feathers, Fowler finds a parrot sadly confined in Mrs. Picklestain's third grade classroom. Worried about this dejected looking bird, Fowler stages a heist set up to frame the nerdiest boy in his sixth grade classroom. Continually tripped up by his ill-conceived plan, he somehow winds up taking oboe lessons from the bird's previous owner, Mrs. Picklestain. By the time he takes part in his school's musical recital, accompanied by the parrot, the audience figures out that Fowler is the thief, but by that time no one is too upset in this quixotic, humorous tale. (147 pages)

Where it's reviewed:
Booklist, January 2003, page 890
Horn Book Guide, Fall 2003, page 83
Journal of Adolescent and Adult Literacy, May 2003, page 700
Publishers Weekly, October 28, 2002, page 71
Voice of Youth Advocates, February 2003, page 477

Other books by the same author:
Scribble: A Dog Story, a Ghost Story, a Love Story, 2004
Mystery in Mt. Mole, 2003
The Great Whale of Kansas, 2001
Orwell's Luck, 2000

Other books you might like:
Mary Amato, *The Word Eater*, 2000
Life in her new school becomes easier for Lerner when she finds a magical worm that eats printed words instead of dirt.
Gordon Korman, *No More Dead Dogs*, 2000
Wallace tells the truth, as he always does, when he informs his English teacher that he's tired of reading books where the dog dies.

Sonia Levitin, *The Mark of Conte*, 1976
Imagine the fun when Conte receives two school schedules, one for Conte Mark and the other for Mark Conte.

737
RICHARD W. JENNINGS
Mystery in Mt. Mole
(Boston: Walter Lorraine Books/Houghton Mifflin, 2003)

Subject(s): City and Town Life; Volcanoes; Mystery and Detective Stories
Age range(s): Grades 5-9
Major character(s): Andrew J. "Andy" Forrest, 12-Year-Old; Georgia Wayne, 12-Year-Old, Girlfriend (of Andy); Jacob Farley, Principal (assistant); Eagle Talon, Police Officer (Chief of police)
Time period(s): 2000s
Locale(s): Mt. Mole, Kansas

Summary: It's hard to believe that no one seems to care that Mr. Farley has disappeared. Andy realizes that Mr. Farley is the least popular person at his school, but shouldn't someone care? Thinking about it, Andy decides he does care and, since he knows the police chief spends more time napping than sleuthing, investigates on his own. With some help from his classmate Georgia, upon whom he has a major crush, he travels all over town on his little Pegasus electric scooter and interviews possible suspects, including his own mother. Andy quickly realizes that he doesn't have many clues to go on besides the fact that Mr. Farley likes popcorn and is intrigued by volcanoes. Meanwhile the little town of Mt. Mole suffers from strange geological rumblings and disastrous weather complications that hamper Andy's investigations in another humorous offering from this author. (144 pages)

Where it's reviewed:
Booklist, September 15, 2003, page 238
Bulletin of the Center for Children's Books, November 2003, page 108
Kirkus Reviews, September 1, 2003, page 1125
Publishers Weekly, October 13, 2003, page 80
School Library Journal, December 2003, page 152

Other books by the same author:
Scribble: A Dog Story, a Ghost Story, a Love Story, 2004
My Life of Crime, 2002
The Great Whale of Kansas, 2001
Orwell's Luck, 2000

Other books you might like:
Sid Hite, *Those Darn Dithers*, 1996
The Dithers family experiences stilt walking, a dancing pig and an uncle who floats out to sea.
Daniel Pinkwater, *The Snarkout Boys and the Avocado of Death*, 1982
Sneaking out to midnight movies lands the boys in trouble when they run into a mad scientist with a deadly supercomputer disguised as an avocado.
Lemony Snicket, *Unfortunate Events Series*, 1999-
The Baudelaire children live up to the name of the series as their lives go from bad to worse after their parents are killed in a fire.

738

JI-LI JIANG
HUI HUI SU-KENNEDY, Illustrator

The Magical Monkey King: Mischief in Heaven

(New York: HarperCollins Publishers, 2002)

Subject(s): Folklore; Animals/Monkeys; Trickster Tales
Age range(s): Grades 3-6
Major character(s): Monkey King, Monkey, Trickster
Time period(s): Indeterminate Past
Locale(s): China

Summary: Eighteen episodes chronicle the adventures of Monkey King beginning with his birth as a small stone monkey emerging from a stone egg warmed by a dragon's breath. The energetic and fearless trickster brings as much mischief as he does joy to the monkey clan he rules yet he is sad that for each, life will end. So he begins a quest for the secret of life that takes him on a long journey filled with adventures. An introductory Author's Note gives background information about Monkey King and his place in Chinese cultural history. (122 pages)

Where it's reviewed:
Booklist, April 15, 2002, page 1397
Bulletin of the Center for Children's Books, September 2002, page 20
Horn Book, September 2002, page 588
Publishers Weekly, June 10, 2002, page 63
School Library Journal, May 2002, page 139

Other books by the same author:
Red Scarf Girl, 1997

Other books you might like:
Linda Fang, *The Ch'i-lin Purse: A Collection of Ancient Chinese Stories*, 1995
  This collection includes illustrated retellings of nine folktales from China.
Sherry Garland, *Children of the Dragon: Selected Tales from Vietnam*, 2001
  A summary of Vietnamese history and folkloric tradition complements the retelling of six Vietnamese folktales.
Virginia Hamilton, *A Ring of Tricksters: Animal Tales from America, the West Indies, and Africa*, 1997
  Eleven tales grouped by geographic area of origin and united by the trickster theme include the familiar Anansi and the less well-known Cunnie Rabbit.
Ed Young, *Monkey King*, 2001
  A picture book adaptation of one portion of a Chinese epic tells of Monkey's years of study with a master and his developing magical skill.

739

CATHERINE JINKS

Pagan's Crusade

(Cambridge, MA: Candlewick Press, 2003)

Subject(s): Crusades; Knights and Knighthood; Orphans
Age range(s): Grades 7-10
Major character(s): Pagan Kidrouk, Orphan, Servant (squire); Roland de Bram, Knight; Saladin, Historical Figure, Leader (Sultan of Egypt)
Time period(s): 12th century
Locale(s): Jerusalem, Israel

Summary: Pagan needs to repay some gambling debts and seeks work with the Templar Knights. This orphan has been raised among some of the seamier inhabitants of Jerusalem but finds he's now squire to Lord Roland, one of the more virtuous, spiritual knights of the Crusades. Though Pagan polishes armor and tends the horses, he also offers many opinions about the foolishness of these knights, as well as the tourists who've come to view the religious landmarks and buy artifacts. When Saladin besieges Jerusalem and Lord Roland is taken hostage, it's Pagan's streetwise fast-talk that manages to spring his Lord in this first of several adventures. (246 pages)

Where it's reviewed:
Bulletin of the Center for Children's Books, February 2004, page 236
Horn Book, September 2003, page 611
Publishers Weekly, November 10, 2003, page 63
School Library Journal, December 2003, page 153
Voice of Youth Advocates, December 2003, page 402

Other books by the same author:
Pagan in Exile, 2004
The Inquisitor, 2002 (adult title)
Bella Vista, 2001 (adult title)

Other books you might like:
Michael Cadnum, *The Leopard Sword*, 2002
  Following the battle of Acre in the 12th century, Squire Hubert accompanies his knight back to England where more problems await.
Joan Elizabeth Goodman, *The Winter Hare*, 1996
  Will has always wanted to be a knight; his dream comes true when he helps Empress Matilda escape and is allowed to use the winter hare on his shield.
Gerald Morris, *The Squire, His Knight & His Lady*, 1999
  The squire to one of the knights of the Round Table hopes that someday he can be a bit more important.
Frances Temple, *The Ramsay Scallop*, 1994
  In the aftermath of the Crusades, two young people go on a pilgrimage on behalf of their village.

740

MARTHE JOCELYN
ABBY CARTER, Illustrator

The Invisible Enemy

(New York: Dutton, 2002)

Subject(s): School Life; Humor; Scientific Experiments
Age range(s): Grades 4-6
Major character(s): Billie Stoner, 6th Grader; Alyssa Morgan, 6th Grader
Time period(s): 2000s
Locale(s): New York, New York

Summary: Returning to school after winter break, Billie is determined to not let her enemy Alyssa bother her. That resolution quickly changes when Alyssa pointedly doesn't share her homemade brownies with Billie, leaving her as the only one excluded. On a field trip to the Cloisters Museum, Alyssa intentionally swaps backpacks with Billie and discovers her vanishing powder. Sprinkling it all over herself, Alyssa disappears, but leaves Billie with a problem. Should she be nice and help Alyssa, or make her own life more pleasant by leaving Alyssa vanished? (167 pages)

Where it's reviewed:
Booklist, June 2002, page 1723
Horn Book Guide, Fall 2002, page 375
Publishers Weekly, May 13, 2002, page 72
Resource Links, April 2002, page 23
School Library Journal, May 2002, page 154

Other books by the same author:
The Invisible Harry, 1998
The Invisible Day, 1997

Other books you might like:
Steven Cousins, *Frankenbug*, 2001
    Fed up with Jeb's teasing about his interest in insects, Adam creates the monster "Frankenbug," brings it to life with fireflies and scares Jeb.
Richard W. Jennings, *My Life of Crime*, 2002
    Fowler's "life of crime" is really a life of good deeds as he steals the poorly caged parrot from Mrs. Picklestain's third grade classroom.
Tim Kennemore, *The Circle of Doom*, 2003
    When Lizzie's potion seems to work and her disagreeable neighbors the Potwards move away, she is inspired to try more magical solutions.

741

ANGELA JOHNSON

A Cool Moonlight

(New York: Dial, 2003)

Subject(s): Sisters; Diseases
Age range(s): Grades 4-7
Major character(s): Lila, Child; Monk, 18-Year-Old, Sister (of Lila)
Time period(s): 2000s
Locale(s): United States

Summary: Born with xeroderma pigmentosum, a rare sensitivity to sunlight and some UV lights, Lila is blessed with parents and an older sister who adjust their lives to make hers as normal as possible. Her mother home schools her and her father often takes her to the grocery at night, while Monk drives Lila and her friend David to chic coffee shops in the late hours. Though Lila longs for all things connected to the sun, and even hopes to go outside some day, the night of her ninth birthday party, she begins to see life differently. Standing outside in the moonlight, with fireflies twinkling around her, for the first time Lila sees how lucky she is to be a "moon girl." (133 pages)

Where it's reviewed:
Booklist, October 1, 2003, page 324
Horn Book, September 2003, page 611
Publishers Weekly, October 20, 2003, page 55

School Library Journal, September 2003, page 215
Voice of Youth Advocates, October 2003, page 311

Other books by the same author:
Bird, 2004
The First Part Last, 2003
Looking for Red, 2002
Gone from Home: Short Takes, 1998
Heaven, 1998

Other books you might like:
Mette Newth, *The Dark Light*, 1998
    Stuck in a leprosy hospital, Tora reads to all the patients, helping them to leave the hospital by a way other than death.
Kenneth Oppel, *Dead Water Zone*, 1993
    Sam suffers from a debilitating genetic disorder, but can usually count on his brother Paul the body-builder for protection from bullies.

742

ANGELA JOHNSON
LOREN LONG, Illustrator

I Dream of Trains

(New York: Simon & Schuster Books for Young Readers, 2003)

Subject(s): Trains; Heroes and Heroines; Fathers and Sons
Age range(s): Grades 2-4
Major character(s): Unnamed Character, Son, Narrator; Papa, Father; Casey Jones, Historical Figure, Engineer
Time period(s): 1900s (1900)
Locale(s): Mississippi

Summary: A train runs past cotton fields where a young boy, from a family of sharecroppers, daydreams as he picks cotton. Papa tells him Casey Jones dreamed of trains from the days when he was young too. The boy imagines he's in the engine with Casey Jones and his crew heading for the mountains and the ocean beyond. Papa understands the dreams of his son's soul and knows they mean one day he'll be leaving on the train that roars past the fields. Until then the boy is content with Papa as his hero and dreams of what lies ahead. A brief author's note gives background to the story. (32 pages)

Where it's reviewed:
Bulletin of the Center for Children's Books, November 2003, page 108
Publishers Weekly, October 20, 2003, page 53
School Library Journal, October 2003, page 126

Awards the book has won:
Notable Social Studies Trade Books for Young People, 2004

Other books by the same author:
Just Like Josh Gibson, 2004
Violet's Music, 2004
Those Building Men, 2001

Other books you might like:
Allan Drummond, *Casey Jones*, 2001
    Casey Jones is a legend in his own time as a train engineer with a reputation for being on time and having a distinctive steam whistle.

Nancy Farmer, *Casey Jones's Fireman: The Story of Sim Webb*, 1999
As fireman to the legendary Casey Jones, Sim Webb follows orders to increase power despite sensing impending danger.
Tony Johnston, *How Many Miles to Jacksonville?*, 1996
The train that passes through a small Texas town symbolizes wealth and adventure to residents of the small isolated community.

743

ANGELA JOHNSON

Looking for Red
(New York: Simon & Schuster, 2002)

Subject(s): Brothers and Sisters; Grief; African Americans
Age range(s): Grades 7-10
Major character(s): Michaela "Mike", 14-Year-Old; Red, 17-Year-Old; Mark Hollywood, Student—High School; Mona, Student—High School
Time period(s): 2000s
Locale(s): Cape Cod, Massachusetts

Summary: Mike's brother is missing and everyone in her community on Cape Cod is grieving. Mike and Red were always together for Red was the biggest part of her life; now she doesn't know what to do half the time. She clings to Mark and Mona, Red's best friends, for together it seems easier to handle their grief. Memories of Red and Mark and Mona fill her mind as she endures her daily routine. But worse than their grief is their guilt, for only the three of them know exactly what happened to Red and that he isn't ever coming back. (116 pages)

Where it's reviewed:
Booklist, April 15, 2002, page 1395
Bulletin of the Center for Children's Books, September 2002, page 20
Publishers Weekly, May 27, 2002, page 60
School Library Journal, July 2002, page 120
Voice of Youth Advocates, June 2002, page 119

Other books by the same author:
Bird, 2004
The First Part Last, 2003
Heaven, 1998
Songs of Faith, 1998
Toning the Sweep, 1993

Other books you might like:
Marion Dane Bauer, *On My Honor*, 1986
Good friends Joel and Tony swim in a river off limits to them; when Tony drowns, Joel is terrified to tell either set of parents.
Paul Fleischman, *Whirligig*, 1998
Brent wants to kill himself, but instead kills Lea Zamora in a car accident; as penance he agrees to set up whirligigs in the four corners of America.
Barbara Park, *Mick Harte Was Here*, 1995
Phoebe wants to tell everyone how wonderful and impish Mick was and how, if he'd only warn his bicycle helmet, he could tell you himself.

Susan Beth Pfeffer, *The Year Without Michael*, 1987
Michael leaves home to play softball and never returns. Was he kidnapped? Did he run away? No one ever knows.
Ingrid Tomey, *Nobody Else Has to Know*, 1999
Webber realizes that he was driving the car that caused the terrible accident, but fears telling the truth will have dreadful consequences.

744

D.B. JOHNSON, Author/Illustrator

Henry Builds a Cabin
(Boston: Houghton Mifflin Company, 2002)

Subject(s): Housing; Construction; Problem Solving
Age range(s): Grades K-2
Major character(s): Henry, Bear, Historical Figure
Time period(s): Indeterminate Past
Locale(s): Massachusetts

Summary: Based on an episode in the life of Henry David Thoreau, this sequel to *Henry Hikes to Fitchburg* describes the construction of a small home near the shores of a pond. As Henry builds, his friends stop by to comment on the small size of the cabin he's constructing. Henry sees no problem with the size because he has a bean patch for his dining area, a sunny spot in the woods for his library and the path to the pond as his ballroom. When it rains, he "wears" his small house. A concluding note gives the historical background to the story. (32 pages)

Where it's reviewed:
Booklist, March 15, 2002, page 1257
Horn Book, July 2002, page 448
Publishers Weekly, February 4, 2002, page 76
Riverbank Review, Summer 2002, page 46
School Library Journal, March 2002, page 190

Awards the book has won:
Publishers Weekly Best Children's Books, 2002

Other books by the same author:
Henry Climbs a Mountain, 2003
Henry Hikes to Fitchburg, 2000 (Boston Globe-Horn Book Award)

Other books you might like:
Julie Dunlap, *Louisa May and Mr. Thoreau's Flute*, 2002
Visiting with naturalist and teacher Henry David Thoreau inspires seven-year-old Louisa May Alcott to write her first poem.
Ginger Howard, *William's House*, 2001
William, newly arrived from England, builds a replica of his father's home, modifying it as he learns more about the climate in the New World.
Henry David Thoreau, *Henry David's House*, 2002
Editor Steven Schnur selects excerpts from *Walden* to tell the story of Thoreau building his cabin in this illustrated picture book.

745

D.B. JOHNSON, Author/Illustrator

Henry Climbs a Mountain

(Boston: Houghton Mifflin Company, 2003)

Subject(s): Animals/Bears; Historical; Imagination
Age range(s): Grades 1-3
Major character(s): Henry, Bear; Sam, Government Official
Time period(s): Indeterminate Past
Locale(s): Massachusetts

Summary: Before Henry can climb a mountain he has to stop by the shoemaker's and pick up a shoe that's being repaired. As Henry walks to the shoemaker's shop Sam, the tax collector, stops him because his taxes are past due. Because Henry refuses to pay taxes to a government that supports slavery, Sam puts him in jail. Now Henry's left to climb the mountain in his imagination. He pulls crayons from his pocket and begins drawing, first the missing shoe, then a flower, a hummingbird, a tree, a path and a mountain. Henry passes his jail time by drawing and hiking through his creation all night. In the morning he's released because someone paid his taxes for him. A concluding note gives factual information about Henry David Thoreau on whom the story is based. (32 pages)

Where it's reviewed:
Booklist, October 1, 2003, page 324
Kirkus Reviews, September 1, 2003, page 1125
Publishers Weekly, September 1, 2003, page 91
School Library Journal, September 2003, page 181

Other books by the same author:
Henry Works, 2004
Henry Builds a Cabin, 2002 (Publishers Weekly Best Children's Books)
Henry Hikes to Fitchburg, 2000 (Boston Globe/Horn Book Award)

Other books you might like:
Martha Alexander, *You're a Genius, Blackboard Bear*, 1995
With help from Blackboard Bear, Anthony builds a spaceship to the moon.
Anthony Browne, *Bear Goes to Town*, 1989
Using his magic pencil Bear is able to create all that he needs and come to the assistance of other animals too.
Judith Heide Gilliland, *Not in the House, Newton!*, 1995
When Newton discovers that his new red crayon creates drawings that become real he hops on his paper airplane and flies out the window.
Crockett Johnson, *Harold and the Purple Crayon*, 1958
Harold has a magic purple crayon, a vivid imagination, and a talent for drawing himself into and out of trouble.

746

DOUG JOHNSON
TAMMY SMITH, Illustrator

Substitute Teacher Plans

(New York: Henry Holt and Company, 2002)

Subject(s): Teachers; Schools; Humor
Age range(s): Grades 1-3

Major character(s): Miss Huff, Teacher; Mrs. Martin, Teacher (substitute)
Time period(s): 2000s (2002)
Locale(s): United States

Summary: When Miss Huff decides to take a day off the tired teacher mixes up her substitute plans with her list of activities for her day off. While Miss Huff is at home relaxing by reading a book, writing letters to family, and practicing spelling by playing Scrabble with the cat, Mrs. Martin is dutifully following the sub plans. The students ride a roller coaster, go skydiving, scuba diving, skiing and attend the circus where Mrs. Martin tames the lions. Mrs. Martin appreciates the innovative substitute plans but when Miss Huff returns to school the next day, the principal is not happy so Miss Huff makes some plans to include him in the class's next activity. (32 pages)

Where it's reviewed:
Booklist, September 15, 2002, page 240
Bulletin of the Center for Children's Books, October 2002, page 62
Publishers Weekly, June 10, 2002, page 60
School Library Journal, August 2002, page 158

Other books by the same author:
James and the Dinosaurs, 1995
Never Ride Your Elephant to School, 1995
Never Babysit the Hippopotamuses!, 1993

Other books you might like:
Harry Allard, *Miss Nelson Is Missing!*, 1977
Fed up with the misbehavior of her students Miss Nelson vanishes. The substitute is so strict that the students wish Miss Nelson would return.
Juanita Havill, *Jamaica and the Substitute Teacher*, 1999
Mrs. Duval follows traditional lesson plans when she substitutes in Jamaica's class.
Grace Maccarone, *Mr. Rover Takes Over*, 2000
When Mrs. Katz is ill the principal sends Mr. Rover, a dog, to substitute in this beginning reader.

747

KATHLEEN JEFFRIE JOHNSON

Target

(Brookfield, CT: Roaring Brook/Deborah Brodie, 2003)

Subject(s): Rape; Race Relations; Homosexuality/Lesbianism
Age range(s): Grades 10-12
Major character(s): Grady West, 16-Year-Old, 11th Grader; Jess Williams, 11th Grader; Pearl, 11th Grader; Gwendolyn, 11th Grader, Journalist (school newspaper)
Time period(s): 2000s
Locale(s): United States

Summary: Since last spring, Grady's divided his life into before and after "the night of," which is the night two men abducted, beat and raped him, leaving him ashamed, broken and wondering if he's gay. Now attending a new school, Grady wants only to keep a low profile and attend his classes, but his wishes aren't to be. First there's Jess, a talkative, energized classmate whose constant cajoling and wisecracking becomes a rhythmic normalcy for Grady. Then there's

Pearl, a pleasantly overweight, tenderhearted girl who seems to touch Grady's core. And finally there's Gwendolyn, malicious reporter for the school newspaper, who is determined to uncover Grady's secret. Slowly, ever so slowly, Grady is able to answer in class, eat a little bit, and even able to share his secret with his new friends in this gut-wrenching novel. (175 pages)

Where it's reviewed:
Booklist, November 15, 2003, page 593
Bulletin of the Center for Children's Books, November 2003, page 109
Kirkus Reviews, August 1, 2003, page 1018
Publishers Weekly, November 3, 2003, page 76
School Library Journal, December 2003, page 153

Awards the book has won:
ALA Best Books for Young Adults, 2004

Other books by the same author:
The Parallel Universe of Liars, 2002

Other books you might like:
Catherine Atkins, *When Jeff Comes Home*, 1999
  Returned to his family after two and a half years of degradation at the hands of a kidnapper, Jeff finds it hard to adjust to normal life.
Judith Clarke, *The Lost Day*, 1999
  Leaving a club with friends one night, Vinny disappears for thirty hours during which time he's drugged, robbed and molested.
David Klass, *You Don't Know Me*, 2001
  John endures two lives, one as a normal high school student, the other as the victim of abuse from his mother's live-in boyfriend.

748

LINDSAY LEE JOHNSON

Soul Moon Soup

(Asheville, NC: Front Street, 2002)

Subject(s): Grandmothers; Homeless People; Single Parent Families
Age range(s): Grades 6-9
Major character(s): Phoebe Rose, 11-Year-Old, Streetperson; Ruby, Adoptee; Gram, Grandmother
Time period(s): 2000s
Locale(s): Full Moon Lake

Summary: When her father leaves, Phoebe Rose and her mother are left homeless, caught in the cycle of urban poverty. Living in shelters with all their possessions in one small suitcase, Phoebe tries to maintain her interest in art, which her father had always encouraged. But then that one small suitcase is stolen and Phoebe's mother sends her to Full Moon Lake to live with her grandmother. Now, deprived of both parents, Phoebe even loses her interest in drawing. The beauty of the lake, the neighbor Ruby who seems like an older sister to Phoebe, and the family truths Gram reveals through her stories help Phoebe begin to feel like a person again in this author's first novel for teens written in poetry. (134 pages)

Where it's reviewed:
Booklist, November 15, 2002, page 598

Horn Book, January 2003, page 76
Publishers Weekly, November 4, 2002, page 85
School Library Journal, November 2002, page 169
Voice of Youth Advocates, February 2003, page 477

Other books you might like:
Adrian Fogelin, *Anna Casey's Place in the World*, 2001
  When Anna runs out of relatives who can care for her, she's sent to a first-time foster mother and finally finds a place she can call home.
Paula Fox, *The Western Wind*, 1993
  Elizabeth stops being resentful about spending the summer with her grandmother as she enjoys hearing the family stories her grandmother shares.
Jonathan Nasaw, *Shakedown Street*, 1993
  Homeless, Caro meets many eccentric people who provide support and love to her and her mother, but all she wants is to live in her own house.

749

PAUL BRETT JOHNSON, Author/Illustrator

Jack Outwits the Giants

(New York: Margaret K. McElderry Books/Simon & Schuster, 2002)

Subject(s): Folklore; Humor; Giants
Age range(s): Grades 2-4
Major character(s): Jack, Child, Trickster
Time period(s): Indeterminate Past
Locale(s): Appalachians

Summary: Caught in a sudden storm, Jack seeks shelter at a farmhouse that is occupied by a giantess and her husband. Realizing that he is destined to become breakfast, Jack uses his wits to trick the giants. Each time Jack thinks he'll be released the giant gives him another impossible task to complete and Jack figures out another way to trick the giants until finally he frees himself from their threat and safely continues his journey home. (32 pages)

Where it's reviewed:
Booklist, June 2002, page 1726
Bulletin of the Center for Children's Books, July 2002, page 407
Horn Book, July 2002, page 476
Publishers Weekly, April 22, 2002, page 69
School Library Journal, November 2002, page 144

Other books by the same author:
Fearless Jack, 2001
Bearhide and Crow, 2000
Old Dry Frye: A Deliciously Funny Tall Tale, 1999

Other books you might like:
Tom Birdseye, *Look Out, Jack! The Giant !s Back!*, 2001
  Jack escapes the angry brother of a giant he's slain atop a beanstalk, but Mr. Giant finds him so Jack thinks of another trick to get rid of the giant.
Gail E. Haley, *Mountain Jack Tales*, 1992
  This collection of stories about the inimitable Jack of folklore is set in the North Carolina mountains.
M.C. Helldorfer, *Jack, Skinny Bones and the Golden Pancakes*, 1996
  Jack learns all of dishonest Granny's tricks and one day

uses them to save himself and his pal Skinny Bones from Granny and the devil.

750

TIM JOHNSTON

Never So Green

(New York: Farrar Straus Giroux, 2002)

Subject(s): Sports/Baseball; Child Abuse; Physically Handicapped
Age range(s): Grades 8-10
Major character(s): Davy "Tex" Donleavy, 7th Grader, Handicapped (deformed hand); Jacob Donleavy, Lawyer; Caroline Dickerson, Librarian; Farley Dickerson, Coach; Jack Dickerson, Stepsister
Time period(s): 1970s (1974)
Locale(s): Big River, Iowa

Summary: After his parents divorce, Tex loves living with his father Jacob and his young girlfriend, but when they go on a vacation, he's sent to live with his alcoholic mother Caroline and her new husband Farley. At first it's not too bad living there as Farley has a tomboy daughter named Jack, a good baseball player, who takes time to work with Tex to improve his pitching skills and help him learn to make better use of his deformed hand. And it's a big thrill to Tex when Farley asks him to pitch for his Little League team. But this is also the summer that Tex discovers he can have romantic, lustful feelings for a girl and, worse yet, sees Farley exhibit his lustful feelings for Jack. Though Jack makes him promise not to tell, Tex talks to his own father about the problem and together they try to help in a realistic, disturbing first novel. (228 pages)

Where it's reviewed:
Booklist, September 1, 2002, page 127
Bulletin of the Center for Children's Books, December 2002, page 162
Publishers Weekly, October 14, 2002, page 85
School Library Journal, October 2002, page 167
Voice of Youth Advocates, October 2002, page 280

Other books you might like:
Peggy King Anderson, *Safe at Home!*, 1992
    A dysfunctional family life leaves Tony feeling secure only when he's on the baseball diamond.
Rose Levit, *With Secrets to Keep*, 1991
    Adrianna finally summons the courage to tell her friend's parents about her father's abusive ways.
Stephen Roos, *The Gypsies Never Came*, 2001
    Augie keeps his deformed left hand covered with a flesh-colored glove and endures the jibes and comments of some of his classmates.

751

TONY JOHNSTON
TONY DITERLIZZI, Illustrator

Alien & Possum: Hanging Out

(New York: Simon & Schuster Books for Young Readers, 2002)

Subject(s): Animals/Opossums; Aliens; Friendship
Age range(s): Grades 2-3
Major character(s): Alien, Robot, Friend; Possum, Opossum, Friend
Time period(s): Indeterminate
Locale(s): Fictional Country

Summary: As only friends can, Alien and Possum cheer each other when feelings of discouragement are overwhelming. Possum does such a good job convincing Alien that being different is special because it is one of a kind that Possum becomes sad because he's just one of many oppossums. Alien has a helpful response to that idea, too. When Possum awakens on his birthday morning excitedly making plans for a party Alien learns the meaning of birthdays and parties and then becomes unhappy because it doesn't have a birthday. Possum has a solution for that problem. When Possum needs some "hang" time, upside down in a tree, Alien tries to join him, but becomes dizzy and falls. Alien wants to share the experience with Possum so he climbs the tree again but this time he hangs right side up not upside down. (48 pages)

Where it's reviewed:
Publishers Weekly, April 15, 2002, page 66
School Library Journal, August 2002, page 158

Other books by the same author:
Sparky and Eddie: Trouble with Bugs, 2003 (Hello Reader!)
Alien & Possum: Friends No Matter What, 2001
Sparky and Eddie: Wild, Wild Rodeo!, 1998 (Hello Reader!)

Other books you might like:
James Howe, *Pinky and Rex*, 1990
    Pinky and Rex begin their friendship in the first book of the series.
Arnold Lobel, *Frog and Toad Are Friends*, 1970
    The award-winning celebration of friendship shows the give-and-take necessary to make a relationship successful.
Arnold Lobel, *Frog and Toad Together*, 1972
    The Newbery Honor book is one of four titles describing the adventures and misadventures of loyal friends Frog and Toad.
Cynthia Rylant, *Poppleton Forever*, 1998
    Three glimpses of Poppleton's life show the efforts of his supportive friends to help him with different problems.

752

TONY JOHNSTON
TIM RAGLIN, Illustrator

Go Track a Yak!

(New York: Simon & Schuster Books for Young Readers, 2003)

Subject(s): Animals; Babies; Stories in Rhyme
Age range(s): Grades K-3

Major character(s): Baby, Baby; Unnamed Character, Aged Person; Unnamed Character, Father; Unnamed Character, Mother
Time period(s): Indeterminate Past
Locale(s): Asia

Summary: When Baby won't eat his parents just don't know what to do. A crone offers the solution, in return for her "heart's desire." When Baby's parents agree, she tells them that Baby needs yak juice. With some help from the crone, Baby's father is able to track a yak and bring it home for the mother to milk. The crone then comes to collect her fee, which turns out to be Baby, and the yak kicks her over the mountain. (32 pages)

Where it's reviewed:
Bulletin of the Center for Children's Books, September 2003, page 18
School Library Journal, November 2003, page 102

Awards the book has won:
Bulletin of the Center for Children's Books Blue Ribbons, 2003
Center for Children's Books Best Books, 2003

Other books by the same author:
Bigfoot Cinderrrrrella, 1998
The Iguana Brothers: A Tale of Two Lizards, 1995
The Quilt Story, 1985

Other books you might like:
Robert Munsch, *A Promise Is a Promise*, 1988
When an Inuit monster captures Allashua, she promises to bring him her siblings. Once free she must find a way to trick him out of the promise.
Judy Sierra, *Tasty Baby Belly Buttons*, 1999
The oni (Japanese ogres) love to eat babies' belly buttons, but Uriko, a young villager, decides to fight back.
Paul O. Zelinsky, *Rumpelstiltskin*, 1986
In this Caldecott Honor Book, Rumplestiltskin helps the Miller's daughter spin straw into gold and then demands her first-born child as payment.

`753`

TONY JOHNSTON

The Mummy's Mother
(New York: Blue Sky/Scholastic, 2003)

Subject(s): Egyptian Antiquities; Mummies; Mothers and Sons
Age range(s): Grades 3-6
Major character(s): Ramose, Supernatural Being (mummy), 10-Year-Old
Time period(s): 2000s (2003)
Locale(s): Egypt; New York, New York

Summary: When grave robbers steal Ramose's mother, Ramose knows that he must save her. He escapes his tomb and heads off (with the help of a camel) to a port city, where he sees his mother being loaded onto a ship. Ramose manages to sneak aboard the ship where he is befriended by a group of American students. Although the boys are able to rescue his mother, she is rediscovered and again sent on her journey to the Central Museum of Art in New York City. Finally, Ra-

mose develops another plan and with the help of a pigeon and the friendly students, he manages to free his mother and begin the trip back to their tomb. (160 pages)

Where it's reviewed:
Booklist, November 3, 2003, page 497
Horn Book, January 2004, page 195
School Library Journal, October 2003, page 168

Other books by the same author:
Any Small Goodness: A Novel of the Barrio, 2001 (NCTE Notable Children's Book)
Day of the Dead, 1997
The Quilt Story, 1985

Other books you might like:
E.L. Konigsburg, *From the Mixed-Up Files of Mrs. Basil E. Frankweiler*, 1968
Claudia and her brother run away from home and live at the Metropolitan Museum of Art.
David Stewart, *You Wouldn't Want to be an Egyptian Mummy!*, 2000
This short non-fiction book explains the embalming and mummification process.
Cynthia Voigt, *The Vandemark Mummy*, 1991
When a mummy vanishes from their father's museum, a 12-year-old boy and his sister must solve the mystery.

`754`

TONY JOHNSTON
TED LEWIN, Illustrator

Sunsets of the West
(New York: G.P. Putnam's Sons, 2002)

Subject(s): Frontier and Pioneer Life; American West; Historical
Age range(s): Grades 1-3
Major character(s): Ma, Mother, Pioneer; Pa, Father, Pioneer
Time period(s): Indeterminate Past
Locale(s): United States

Summary: Pa decides to leave the family's comfortable New England home and head to the West. He and Ma load the belongings in a covered wagon, gather their children and supplies and begin the long, arduous journey. Ma is especially sad to leave their home behind but eventually feels the anticipation of a new beginning. Along the way they join with other families, suffer hardship, meet Indians, endure severe weather, and lose animals and belongings. They cross the vast prairie and the arid desert and finally reach the mountains where they settle to enjoy the sunsets of the west. (36 pages)

Where it's reviewed:
Booklist, June 2002, page 1738
Publishers Weekly, May 13, 2002, page 70
School Library Journal, July 2002, page 94

Other books by the same author:
Harmonica, 2004
Ten Fat Turkeys, 2004
Ancestors Are Singing, 2003

Other books you might like:

Raymond Bial, *Frontier Home*, 1993
> Diary excerpts enliven descriptions of the homes and tools used by pioneer families in this nonfiction view of life long ago.

Verla Kay, *Covered Wagons, Bumpy Trails*, 2000
> Life in a covered wagon is described in a rhyming tale of parents with an infant son trekking west to California.

Jean Van Leeuwen, *A Fourth of July on the Plains*, 1997
> On the journey to Oregon a wagon train stops to rest and celebrate the Fourth of July.

755

TONY JOHNSTON
BARRY MOSER, Illustrator

That Summer

(San Diego: Harcourt, Inc., 2002)

Subject(s): Summer; Death; Quilts
Age range(s): Grades 2-5
Major character(s): Joey, Brother (younger); Unnamed Character, Brother (older), Narrator; Gram, Grandmother
Time period(s): Indeterminate Past
Locale(s): United States

Summary: Two brothers celebrate the start of summer with enthusiasm, but too soon Joey falls ill and it becomes clear that he is dying. That summer Gram teaches Joey to quilt and together they create patches with images that he cherishes, the family dog, baseball, an owl, and a fishing pole. When Joey dies, his big brother helps to finish the quilt. (32 pages)

Where it's reviewed:
Booklist, May 15, 2002, page 1594
Bulletin of the Center for Children's Books, September 2002, page 21
Publishers Weekly, March 18, 2002, page 103
School Library Journal, May 2002, page 118

Other books by the same author:
It's about Dogs, 2000
Day of the Dead, 1997
Very Scary, 1995

Other books you might like:

Eleanor Coerr, *Sadako*, 1993
> When Sadako is dying of leukemia, she decides to try to make 1,000 origami cranes before she dies.

Tomie De Paola, *Nana Upstairs and Nana Downstairs*, 1973
> Tommy loves visiting his great-grandmother, Nana Upstairs, but when she dies, he must learn to say goodbye.

Miska Miles, *Annie and the Old One*, 1972
> When Annie learns that her grandmother is dying she tries to find a way to prevent it in a Newberry Honor Book.

756

LYNNE JONELL
PETRA MATHERS, Illustrator

When Mommy Was Mad

(New York: G.P. Putnam's Sons, 2002)

Subject(s): Anger; Mothers; Brothers
Age range(s): Grades K-2
Major character(s): Mommy, Mother, Spouse; Robbie, Son, Brother (younger); Christopher, Son, Brother (older); Daddy, Father, Spouse
Time period(s): 2000s
Locale(s): United States

Summary: Christopher and Robbie wonder what they've done to make Mommy so mad that she forgets to kiss Daddy goodbye, bangs the pots, and burns the toast. They review the possibilities and do all they can to modify their behavior but still Mommy is too noisy and unsmiling. Robbie makes a picture for Mommy and when she doesn't receive it with a smile, Robbie begins to feel as prickly as Mommy seems to be. In fact, Robbie feels a little mad and he begins to bump Mommy while saying "Bork." By pretending to be a prickly "borkupine" Robbie finally gets Mommy's attention. Now that Mommy is able to hear Robbie they work together to smooth down the prickles so the family can be happy again. When Daddy arrives home from work looking a little prickly they help him too. (28 pages)

Where it's reviewed:
Booklist, May 15, 2002, page 1601
Bulletin of the Center for Children's Books, September 2002, page 22
Publishers Weekly, April 8, 2002, page 229
School Library Journal, June 2002, page 98

Awards the book has won:
Center for Children's Books Best Books, 2002

Other books by the same author:
Mom Pie, 2001
It's My Birthday, Too!, 1999 (Booklist Editors' Choice)
I Need a Snake, 1998 (School Library Journal Best Books)
Mommy Go Away!, 1997

Other books you might like:

Molly Bang, *When Sophie Gets Angry—Really, Really Angry . . .*, 1999
> Sophie's anger explodes in a temper tantrum. She runs to her favorite tree to let the branches soothe her before returning home. Caldecott Honor Book.

Betsy Everitt, *Mean Soup*, 1992
> After a bad day Horace helps his mother make Mean Soup and he begins to feel better.

Mem Fox, *Harriet, You'll Drive Me Wild!*, 2000
> After a day of patiently dealing with Harriet's misbehavior the girl's mother loses her temper and yells. Harriet apologizes and the two share a hug and a laugh.

757

DIANA WYNNE JONES

The Merlin Conspiracy

(New York: Greenwillow Books, 2003)

Subject(s): Fantasy; Magic
Age range(s): Grades 6-10
Major character(s): Arianrhod ''Roddy'' Hyde, Wizard, Teenager; Grundo, Wizard; Nicholas ''Nick'' Mallory, Teenager
Time period(s): Indeterminate
Locale(s): Blest, Fictional Country

Summary: Arianrhod Hyde is just another hanger-on, traveling through Blest following the King's Progress. Actually, it's rather boring for any teen that happens to be forced to follow, but since both of Roddy's parents are court mages, she really has no choice. Things are made worse by the fact that Roddy is the youngest follower, except for Grundo who is her best friend. The two are teased mercilessly by the others, but it only makes them appreciate each other more. Things change dramatically for the worse when Roddy and Grundo overhear a magical conspiracy and the old Merlin dies; the new Merlin is one of the plotters, but no one will believe them. Meanwhile in another part of the multiverse, Nick Mallory has blundered into wizard territory. When Roddy magically summons a wizard, Nick arrives in Blest. Too bad he doesn't know anything about magic, because Nick would very much like to impress Roddy by saving the world. (438 pages)

Where it's reviewed:
Booklist, April 15, 2003, page 1464
Bulletin of the Center for Children's Books, May 2003, page 364
Horn Book, May 2003, page 359
Kirkus Reviews, March 15, 2003, page 469
Publishers Weekly, March 10, 2003, page 73

Awards the book has won:
ALA Notable Children's Books, 2004

Other books by the same author:
Power of Three, 2003
The Time of the Ghost, 2002
Dogsbody, 2001

Other books you might like:
Charles de Lint, *Seven Wild Sisters*, 2002
  When one sister falls afoul of the fairies, all her sisters bring their varied talents to bear to try to free her, but some get snared themselves.
Kate Gilmore, *Enter Three Witches*, 1990
  A teen boy finds his flamboyant and magical female relations to be a burden.
Margaret Mahy, *The Changeover: A Supernatural Romance*, 1984
  When an evil, ancient spirit begins to suck away her little brother's life, Laura decides to changeover and become a witch to save him.

758

URSULA JONES
RUSSELL AYTO, Illustrator

The Witch's Children

(New York: Henry Holt and Company, 2003)

Subject(s): Witches and Witchcraft; Magic; Humor
Age range(s): Grades K-3
Major character(s): Eldest One, Brother, Son; Middle One, Sister, Daughter; Little One, Sister, Daughter; Gemma, Child
Time period(s): Indeterminate
Locale(s): Fictional Country

Summary: On a visit to the park Eldest One helps Gemma retrieve her boat from the pond by changing her into a frog that can swim to get the boat. Gemma is happy to do so but cries when she learns that Eldest One hasn't learned the spell to change her back into a little girl. Middle One then changes trees, pigeons, squirrels, the ice cream truck and ice cream lady into a palace, footmen, soldiers, a coach and a princess and commands the princess to kiss the frog thus creating a prince. Of course, Gemma wants to be Gemma not a prince so she and the other changed people and animals turn to Little One for help. Little One knows only one piece of magic, but she tries it, yelling ''Mommy!'' as loudly as she can. Sure enough, Little One's magic works and gets everyone out of trouble as the author's first picture book concludes. (32 pages)

Where it's reviewed:
Booklist, June 2003, page 1785
Bulletin of the Center for Children's Books, May 2003, page 365
Horn Book, July 2003, page 443
Publishers Weekly, March 17, 2003, page 75
School Library Journal, July 2003, page 99

Awards the book has won:
Bulletin of the Center for Children's Books Blue Ribbons, 2003
Center for Children's Books Best Books, 2003

Other books you might like:
Margie Palatini, *Zoom Broom*, 1998
  Gritch's broom seems to be beyond repair, even with magic, so she's shopping for a new one.
Kevin Somers, *Meaner than Meanest*, 2001
  Too late, a mean old hag realizes she's forgotten a critical ingredient in the concoction she intended to result in a really mean monster.
James Stevenson, *Emma*, 1985
  Not a typical witch, Emma even needs flying lessons.

759

BARBARA M. JOOSSE
R. GREGORY CHRISTIE, Illustrator

Stars in the Darkness

(San Francisco: Chronicle Books, 2002)

Subject(s): Gangs; Brothers; Mothers and Sons
Age range(s): Grades 2-5

Major character(s): Mama, Single Mother, Activist; Richard, Son, Brother (older); Unnamed Character, Child, Brother (younger)
Time period(s): 2000s (2002)
Locale(s): United States

Summary: Mama and her youngest son like to pretend that the nightly sounds of shots in their inner city neighborhood are "stars cracking in the darkness." Richard helps his little brother feel safe at night simply by being with him. Sleeping becomes hard though when Richard begins to stay out all night and his brother worries he's joined a gang. When Richard comes home early one morning with a bloody bandage on his arm, Mama and his brother can no longer ignore the obvious and they develop a plan to organize the little brothers, sisters and the mamas of the neighborhood to participate in evening peace walks. Now the night is not as scary and the stars in the darkness are the flashlights of the walkers. A concluding author's note gives background to the story and a list of resources for gang prevention. (32 pages)

Where it's reviewed:
Booklist, May 15, 2002, page 1601
Bulletin of the Center for Children's Books, September 2002, page 22
New York Times Book Review, August 11, 2002, page 19
Publishers Weekly, April 22, 2002, page 69
School Library Journal, August 2002, page 159

Awards the book has won:
New York Times Best Illustrated Children's Books, 2002

Other books by the same author:
A Houseful of Christmas, 2001
Ghost Wings, 2001
I Love You the Purplest, 1996 (Golden Kite Award)

Other books you might like:
Eve Bunting, *Your Move*, 1998
    James learns an important lesson when he brings his younger brother along as he fulfills his initiation rite into a gang.
Marybeth Lorbiecki, *Just One Flick of a Finger*, 1996
    To protect himself from a bully, Jack brings his father's gun to school and accidentally shoots his friend.
Luis J. Rodriguez, *It Doesn't Have to Be This Way: A Barrio Story*, 1999
    A bilingual picture book chronicles a young boy's reluctant involvement with a gang and the tragic events that ensue.

760

SANDRA JORDAN, Author/Illustrator

Frog Hunt

(Brookfield, CT: Roaring Brook Press, 2002)

Subject(s): Animals/Frogs and Toads; Nature; Summer
Age range(s): Grades K-2
Major character(s): Unnamed Character, Child; Unnamed Character, Child
Time period(s): 2000s
Locale(s): United States

Summary: Two boys spend a summer day at a pond searching for a frog. They observe tadpoles, minnows, a muskrat, a turtle and fish. They see a toad hopping by and hear a frog's croaking but do not see a frog, although alert readers might spot one in some of the photographs illustrating the text. Finally, just as they are ready to call it quits for the day they snare a frog in their net, take turns holding it and then release it into the pond so they can search for it again another day. Factual information about ponds concludes the book. (32 pages)

Where it's reviewed:
Booklist, June 2002, page 1738
Publishers Weekly, March 11, 2002, page 70
School Library Journal, April 2002, page 113

Other books by the same author:
Pond Book, 1999
Down on Casey's Farm, 1996
Christmas Tree Farm, 1993

Other books you might like:
Alyssa Satin Capucilli, *Good Morning, Pond*, 1994
    Early in the morning, three children observe the many animals of the pond awakening.
Vivian French, *Growing Frogs*, 2000
    With Mom's help a little girl collects frog spawn from a pond and watches the frogs' development in her home aquarium.
Kathryn Lasky, *Pond Year*, 1995
    Two best friends enjoy the seasonal changes observed in the pond near their homes.

761

SHERRYL JORDAN

The Hunting of the Last Dragon

(New York: HarperCollins, 2002)

Subject(s): Dragons; Fantasy; Middle Ages
Age range(s): Grades 6-9
Major character(s): Jude, Orphan; Jing-wei "Lizzie", Captive; Lan, Herbalist
Time period(s): 14th century
Locale(s): England (alternate England)

Summary: Jude returns to his village one day to find it destroyed and his family killed, the work of a dragon when it was thought that all dragons were exterminated. Needing shelter, he attaches himself to a traveling carnival where part of his job is to look after Jing-wei, a captured Chinese girl whose bound feet make her part of the freak exhibit. Becoming friends, the two escape and travel to the home of an old Chinese wise woman who urges them to find and kill the dragon. After they agree, she teaches them the use of kites and gunpowder and sends them off on their mission, an adventure which is later told by Jude to a monastery brother in this alternate England. (186 pages)

Where it's reviewed:
Booklist, April 15, 2002, page 1416
Bulletin of the Center for Children's Books, September 2002, page 23
Kliatt, July 2002, page 11
School Library Journal, July 2002, page 120
Voice of Youth Advocates, August 2002, page 202

Awards the book has won:
ALA Best Books for Young Adults, 2003

Other books by the same author:
Secret Sacrament, 2000
The Raging Quiet, 1999
Sign of the Lion, 1995

Other books you might like:
Lynne Reid Banks, *The Dungeon*, 2002
Blaming Peony for a loss to his hated neighbor, Scotsman Bruce MacLennan throws his Chinese servant into the dungeon and leaves her.
T.A. Barron, *The Fires of Merlin*, 1998
Though his magic's untried, Merlin can't turn down Urnalda's request to help the dwarves combat the dragon Valdearg.
Robin McKinley, *The Hero and the Crown*, 1984
Aerin proves her worth as daughter of the Damarian King when, using the Blue Sword, she slays the Black Dragon.

762

WILLIAM JOYCE, Author/Illustrator

Big Time Olie

(New York: Laura Geringer/HarperCollins, 2002)

Subject(s): Growing Up; Self-Acceptance; Family
Age range(s): Grades K-2
Major character(s): Rolie Polie Olie, Robot, Child; Spot, Dog, Robot; Pappy, Grandfather, Robot; Mom, Mother, Robot; Dad, Father, Robot
Time period(s): 2000s (2002)
Locale(s): Planet—Imaginary

Summary: Rolie Polie Olie thinks he is growing up quite nicely, but then Mom and Dad tell him he is too small to go to Mount Big Ball and Pappy tells him he is too big to jump on his bed. Olie decides to use the shrink-and-grow-olator to become the perfect size, but he accidentally shrinks himself to doll-size. Spot helps him back to the shrink-and-grow-olator, but then Olie grows larger than his house. One jump and he's in outer space. Mom and Dad find him and help him shrink back to his normal size, which Olie decides is just right for the time being. (40 pages)

Where it's reviewed:
Booklist, October 1, 2002, page 336
Horn Book Guide, Spring 2003, page 14
Kirkus Reviews, October 1, 2002, page 1472
Publishers Weekly, October 7, 2002, page 75
School Library Journal, November 2002, page 128

Other books by the same author:
Sleepy Time Olie, 2001
Rolie Polie Olie, 1999
George Shrinks, 1985

Other books you might like:
Larry Dane Brimner, *The Littlest Wolf*, 2002
A young wolf cub worries that he can't do all the things his older siblings do, but his father helps him see that Little Wolf is just what he should be.

Syd Hoff, *Bernard on His Own*, 1993
Bernard's parents assure the young bear that one day he'll be able to accomplish, on his own, the many tasks that frustrate him now.
Janie Jasin, *The Littlest Christmas Tree: A Tale of Growing and Becoming*, 2003
A seedling can't wait to grow up and become a beautiful Christmas tree.
Miriam Monnier, *Just Right*, 2001
A little girl is upset by expectations of "big girl" behavior, while only being allowed to do "little girl" activities.

763

SUSAN JUBY

Alice, I Think

(New York: HarperTempest, 2003)

Subject(s): Coming-of-Age; Family Life; Self-Perception
Age range(s): Grades 7-10
Major character(s): Alice MacLeod, 15-Year-Old
Time period(s): 2000s
Locale(s): Smithers, British Columbia, Canada

Summary: Wearing a hobbit costume to her first day of school pretty much sets the stage for Alice and causes her bohemian, protective parents to home school her instead. But everyone, and that includes Alice, her parents, and her therapist, agrees that Alice needs to return to public school, even an alternative high school. In her journal, Alice records the daily events of her school life, including encountering her archenemy. This is the year she decides she's in love with Aubrey, and then tries to figure out how to get rid of him, learns to drive by chauffeuring her father's drunken poker club to a memorial service for Princess Diana and comes of age in this witty, sometimes acerbic first novel. (290 pages)

Where it's reviewed:
Booklist, August 2003, page 1971
Bulletin of the Center for Children's Books, September 2003, page 19
Horn Book, July 2003, page 459
School Library Journal, July 2003, page 131
Voice of Youth Advocates, August 2003, page 226

Awards the book has won:
ALA Best Books for Young Adults, 2004

Other books by the same author:
Miss Smithers, 2004

Other books you might like:
Beth Goobie, *Sticks and Stones*, 2002
Besmirched by a boy she dated for the Valentine's Dance, and tired of the school not painting over any libelous graffiti, Jujube fights back.
Polly Horvath, *Canning Season*, 2003
Ratchet spends the summer with her two great aunts, Tilly and PenPen, whose eccentricities match their age.
Jerry Spinelli, *Loser*, 2002
Pegged as a loser early in his school career, Donald is oblivious of the labeling and skips through life, supported by his great family.

K

764

G. BRIAN KARAS, Author/Illustrator

Atlantic

(New York: G.P. Putnam's Sons, 2002)

Subject(s): Nature; Geography; Environment
Age range(s): Grades K-3
Major character(s): Atlantic Ocean, Narrator
Time period(s): Indeterminate
Locale(s): Atlantic Ocean

Summary: The Atlantic Ocean describes itself as beginning "where the land runs out" and stretching from one pole to another. The narration follows the travels, colors and smells of the waters comprising the Atlantic as they pass continents, reach into bays and inlets along coastlines, and change color and shape with the weather and the pull of the lunar cycle. The Atlantic Ocean recognizes its important place in the world's water cycle as well as its role as a home for marine life and an inspiration to artists and poets. In conclusion, the Atlantic pleads for respect and sensitivity to the need to reduce the wastes that pollute its waters. (32 pages)

Where it's reviewed:
Book Links, December 2002-January 2003, page 12
Booklist, April 15, 2002, page 1398
Bulletin of the Center for Children's Books, April 2002, page 282
Horn Book Guide, Fall 2002, page 333
School Library Journal, June 2002, page 98

Awards the book has won:
Book Links Lasting Connections, 2002
ALA Notable Children's Books, 2003

Other books by the same author:
The Class Artist, 2001 (Smithsonian's Notable Books for Children)
Bebe's Bad Dream, 2000
Home on the Bayou: A Cowboy's Story, 1996 (Boston Globe-Horn Book Honor Book)

Other books you might like:
Kate Banks, *A Gift from the Sea*, 2001
A boy finds a rock, made smooth by years of being tumbled by wave action, unaware of the rock's geologic origin from a volcano.
Kathleen W. Kranking, *The Ocean Is . . .* , 2003
Rhyming quatrains complemented by photographs of each species introduce a variety of marine life.
Martin Waddell, *The Big, Big Sea*, 1994
Mother and daughter walk along the shore of a big, big sea on a moonlit night savoring a moment that will live in their memories.

765

KATHLEEN KARR

The 7th Knot

(Tarrytown, NY: Marshall Cavendish, 2003)

Subject(s): Brothers; Adventure and Adventurers; Art
Age range(s): Grades 5-8
Major character(s): Chadwick Hoving "Wick" Forrester III, 15-Year-Old; Miles Forrester, 12-Year-Old; Eustace Forrester, Uncle, Wealthy; Jose Gregorio, Servant (valet), Art Historian
Time period(s): 1890s
Locale(s): Europe

Summary: After another school year filled with hijinks that almost lead to expulsion, Wick and Miles spend the summer with their Uncle Eustace, who's on a tour of Europe buying enough art masterpieces to rival the collections of J.P. Morgan and the Rockefellers. Uncle Eustace's valet is an art expert and provides tutoring for the boys on this topic while they sail to Europe. The woodcuts of Albrecht Durer's missing "knot series" capture their interest, especially after Jose is kidnapped. As Wick and Miles try to find him, they become entangled with the Durerbund, a German secret society that seems a precursor to Nazism. For two boys who like mischief and adventure, Wick and Miles find enough to satisfy them as they travel to Mad Ludwig's castle, escape in airships and eventually find Jose on their quest to stop the work of the Durerbund. (149 pages)

Where it's reviewed:
Booklist, July 2003, page 1881
Bulletin of the Center for Children's Books, July 2003, page 45
Horn Book Guide, Fall 2003, page 385
Library Media Connection, October 2003, page 58
School Library Journal, August 2003, page 161

Other books by the same author:
Exiled: Memoirs of a Camel, 2004
Gilbert & Sullivan Set Me Free, 2003
Bone Dry, 2002

Other books you might like:
Lloyd Alexander, *The El Dorado Adventure*, 1987
  Vesper and her guardian Brinnie travel to Central America to look at property she's inherited, but instead face an erupting volcano.
Carol Hughes, *Jack Black & the Ship of Thieves*, 2000
  Jack is proud to join his father, captain of the airship *Bellerophon*, on its maiden voyage, until he falls off and lands on a pirate ship.
Caroline Stevermer, *River Rats*, 1992
  Orphans Tomcat, Esteban and Toby ply the now polluted Mississippi River on an old paddlewheel, swapping mail and freight for food and clothing.

766

KATHLEEN KARR

Bone Dry

(New York: Hyperion, 2002)

Subject(s): Adventure and Adventurers
Age range(s): Grades 5-8
Major character(s): Matthew Morrisey, 15-Year-Old, Orphan; Asa B. Cornwall, Doctor (phrenologist); Gin, Dog
Time period(s): 1840s
Locale(s): Sahara Desert, Africa (northern part)

Summary: Matthew and his employer, the noted phrenologist Dr. Cornwall, who searched for the skull of Napoleon in *Skullduggery*, have now set their sights on the skull of Alexander the Great, said to be buried in Siwa. Dr. Cornwall hypothesizes that the size and shape of a person's skull determines their personality and hopes, by studying the skulls of noted men, to prove his theory. To travel to Siwa, Matthew and Dr. Cornwall, accompanied by Gin, travel by camel caravan across the Sahara, which is filled with more dangers than they realized, from scorpions to slave traders and sand storms. Luckily Matthew manages to get into, and out of, trouble with ease and finds more than a skull in this historical adventure. (220 pages)

Where it's reviewed:
Booklist, September 15, 2002, page 235
Bulletin of the Center for Children's Books, October 2002, page 63
Kirkus Reviews, July 1, 2002, page 957
School Library Journal, August 2002, page 190
Voice of Youth Advocates, August 2002, page 193

Awards the book has won:
Center for Children's Books Best Books, 2002

Other books by the same author:
Exiled: Memoirs of a Camel, 2004
Gilbert & Sullivan Set Me Free, 2003
The Seventh Knot, 2003
Skullduggery, 2000
The Boxer, 2000

Other books you might like:
Lloyd Alexander, *The Drackenberg Adventure*, 1988
  Vesper Holly and her guardian Brinnie don't let the dangers of earthquakes or volcanoes keep them from saving the Chirica Indians.
Gerald Hausman, *Tom Cringle: Battle on the High Seas*, 2000
  Off to sea aboard the *Bream*, Tom's eyesight makes him a perfect lookout for spotting pirate ships, though he never expects to sail aboard one.
Robin McKinley, *The Blue Sword*, 1982
  Bored with her proper life, when Harry is kidnapped by a king, she discovers magic she never knew she had.

767

KATHLEEN KARR

Gilbert & Sullivan Set Me Free

(New York: Hyperion, 2003)

Subject(s): Prisoners and Prisons; Theater; Orphans
Age range(s): Grades 7-10
Major character(s): Libby Dodge, Prisoner, Singer; Belle "Ma" McCreary, Prisoner, Singer; Quintus Wylie Gill, Con Artist
Time period(s): 1910s (1914)
Locale(s): Sherborn Women's Prison, Massachusetts

Summary: Libby is serving time at Sherborn Women's Prison where she's living with arsonists, prostitutes, murderers and other criminals, though she doesn't reveal the reason for her imprisonment. Singing in the laundry room with her good friend and protector Mother McCreary, the two are discovered by the new chaplain, Mrs. Wilkinson, who promptly transfers them to garden duty to keep their voices from being ruined by the laundry steam. Libby and Ma sing *The Messiah* at Easter and then try out for, and win, the leading roles in the operetta *The Pirates of Penzance*. For the first time Libby feels there's some purpose to her life and is even able to share her reason for being in prison, which was simple thievery. Libby's beautiful singing voice, coupled with a confession from her "guardian" Quintus Wylie Gill about using young orphans as thieves, lead to Libby's release from prison and admission to the New England Conservatory of Music in a book based on a true incident. (231 pages)

Where it's reviewed:
Booklist, May 15, 2003, page 1663
Bulletin of the Center for Children's Books, September 2003, page 20
Horn Book, July 2003, page 460
School Library Journal, July 2003, page 131
Voice of Youth Advocates, June 2003, page 136

Other books by the same author:
Exiled: Memoirs of a Camel, 2004
The Seventh Knot, 2003
Bone Dry, 2002
Skullduggery, 2000
The Boxer, 2000

Other books you might like:
James Lincoln Collier, *My Crooked Family*, 1991
    Thrown in jail for stealing food worth 60 cents, Roger accepts ''Circus's'' offer to make some money, though not by any legal means.
Gillian Cross, *The Dark Behind the Curtain*, 1981
    The school Drama Club's production of *Sweeney Todd* has as much mystery around it as the actual play does.
Maurice Gee, *The Fat Man*, 1997
    Caught when he steals a chocolate bar from the ''fat man,'' it's really a set-up to enable Herbert Muskie to retaliate against Colin's parents.
Jean Thesman, *The Ornament Tree*, 1996
    Bonnie loves being part of a female-dominated household where the women work proactively for women's suffrage, birth control and an end to child labor.

768

KEIKO KASZA, Author/Illustrator

My Lucky Day

(New York: G.P. Putnam's Sons, 2003)

Subject(s): Animals/Pigs; Animals/Foxes; Problem Solving
Age range(s): Grades K-2
Major character(s): Mr. Fox, Fox; Unnamed Character, Pig, Trickster
Time period(s): Indeterminate
Locale(s): Fictional Country

Summary: A piglet knocks on Mr. Fox's door, ostensibly in error. Mr. Fox is thrilled to open the door and see that dinner has arrived with so little effort and makes plans to begin cooking a pork roast dinner. The piglet thinks fast and convinces Mr. Fox to bathe him before putting him in the roasting pan. Still stalling, the piglet suggests that Mr. Fox fatten him up a bit so Mr. Fox cooks dinner for the piglet. Then, to assure a tender pork roast, the piglet recommends a massage and, once again, Mr. Fox obliges until, completely exhausted, he collapses. The piglet races home, excited about the lucky day he's had with dinner, a bath and a massage. Then, he begins planning another lucky visit. (32 pages)

Where it's reviewed:
Booklist, October 15, 2003, page 419
Horn Book, September 2003, page 598
Publishers Weekly, October 6, 2003, page 84
School Library Journal, September 2003, page 182

Other books by the same author:
The Mightiest, 2001 (Storytelling World Award Book)
Dorothy & Mikey, 2000 (Parenting's Reading Magic Award)
Don't Laugh, Joe, 1997 (IRA Children's Choices)

Other books you might like:
Steven Kellogg, *The Three Little Pigs*, 1997
    Three pigs, in this humorous retelling, face a tough-look-

ing hungry wolf trying to order piglet from their waffle wagon.
Colin McNaughton, *Yum!: A Preston Pig Story*, 1999
    Noticing Mr. Wolf nearby, waiting to capture and eat him, clever Preston tries to interest Mr. Wolf in finding a job to earn money to purchase food.
Susan Meddaugh, *Hog-Eye*, 1995
    A literate, confident pig uses her reading ability to outwit a wolf intent on making her his next meal.
Tony Ross, *Stone Soup*, 1987
    A hen cleverly avoids becoming a wolf's dinner by offering him a taste of her stone soup.
Janet Stevens, *Tops and Bottoms*, 1995
    Industrious Hare is a gardening partner to slumbering Bear in a contemporary interpretation of a trickster tale.

769

NANCY KAUFMANN
JUNG-HEE SPETTER, Illustrator

Bye, Bye!

(Asheville, NC: Front Street, 2003)

Subject(s): Animals/Pigs; Schools; Parent and Child
Age range(s): Preschool-Kindergarten
Major character(s): Piggy, Pig, Student (preschooler); Daddy, Pig, Father
Time period(s): Indeterminate
Locale(s): Fictional Country

Summary: Piggy, reluctant to go to school, asks Daddy to stay in the room, play, read a story and paint. Daddy does all these activities and then the teacher indicates that it really is time for Daddy to go. After sadly watching Daddy's departure, Piggy plays with the other students and in no time at all it's time for the students to pack up and get ready to home with the waiting parents. Bye, bye! Spetter's character Piggy has previously appeared in *Just a Minute!* and *Piggy's Birthday Dream*, written by other authors. (28 pages)

Where it's reviewed:
Booklist, October 15, 2003, page 419
Publishers Weekly, September 8, 2003, page 79
School Library Journal, October 2003, page 128

Other books you might like:
Dandi Daley Mackall, *First Day*, 2003
    After overcoming her apprehension about the first day of school, a little girl looks forward to day two.
Francesca Rusackas, *I Love You All Day Long*, 2003
    A mama pig assures her fearful son Owen that she will love him all the long first day of preschool.
Lauren Thompson, *Mouse's First Day of School*, 2003
    By hiding in a backpack, Mouse discovers the fun of a kindergarten classroom.

770
ELIZABETH KAY

The Divide

(New York: The Chicken House/Scholastic, 2003)

Subject(s): Fantasy; Adventure and Adventurers
Age range(s): Grades 5-8
Major character(s): Felix Sanders, 13-Year-Old; Betony, Mythical Creature (elf); Snakeweed, Mythical Creature (evil pixie)
Time period(s): 2000s
Locale(s): Costa Rica; Tiratattle, Fictional City; Geddon, Fictional City

Summary: Vacationing with his parents in Costa Rica, Felix worries that this might be his last vacation for his heart condition indicates a very short life. While on a walk with them, he runs ahead and as he's straddling the Continental Divide, falls into a rift to enter a fantasy world of unicorns, pixies, griffins, elves and many other legendary creatures. To his amazement, Felix discovers that magic is considered real here and science a mythical fable. Betony, an elf who's on a quest to fulfill the wish of a dying unicorn, and Felix, hunting for a cure for his ailment, join forces. When Snakeweed hears of Felix, he wants to use him as a means of entering Felix's world to sell bogus medicine. (318 pages)

Where it's reviewed:
Booklist, June 2003, page 1762
Bulletin of the Center for Children's Books, December 2003, page 154
Publishers Weekly, July 28, 2003, page 95
School Library Journal, September 2003, page 215
Voice of Youth Advocates, August 2003, page 237

Other books you might like:
Franny Billingsley, *The Folk Keeper*, 1999
    Inexplicable magical powers inherent in her enable orphaned Corinna to masquerade as Corin, a folk keeper.
Tom Birdseye, *The Eye of the Stone*, 2002
    Unable to replicate guns and electricity to aid the Timmran, Jackson feels he's just as much a wimp in this mythical world as he is at home.
Darcy Pattison, *The Wayfinder*, 2000
    In search of healing water, Win and telepathic Lady Kala must cross the Rift, where they encounter strange beasts and animals.

771
VERLA KAY
TED RAND, Illustrator

Homespun Sarah

(New York: G.P. Putnam's Sons, 2003)

Subject(s): Historical; Farm Life; Stories in Rhyme
Age range(s): Grades 1-4
Major character(s): Sarah, Daughter, Sister; Father, Father, Farmer; Mother, Mother, Seamstress
Time period(s): 1700s
Locale(s): Pennsylvania, American Colonies

Summary: An author's note giving historical facts on which Sarah's tale is based introduces this story in verse. With the rooster's crow Sarah and family members rise to begin the work of the day. Sarah struggles into her homespun dress that grows snugger and shorter daily. As Sarah watches Father in the fields or shearing sheep, she hauls water and pulls weeds. Inside she helps Mother with the cooking and puts out fires ignited by popping cinders. Sarah hangs out laundry as Mother scrubs clothes, makes candles, picks berries, and dyes wool. When enough wool is carded and spun the weaver sets to work at the loom, Mother measures, sews and eventually Sarah has a new red dress. (32 pages)

Where it's reviewed:
Booklist, March 1, 2003, page 1208
Bulletin of the Center for Children's Books, June 2003, page 407
Publishers Weekly, February 17, 2003, page 74
School Library Journal, June 2003, page 110

Other books by the same author:
Tattered Sails, 2001 (Notable Social Studies Trade Books for Young People)
Covered Wagons, Bumpy Trails, 2000
Iron Horses, 1999 (Notable Social Studies Trade Books for Young People)

Other books you might like:
Esla Beskow, *Pelle's New Suit*, 1929
    Pelle observes the progress of his new suit from the shearing of the fleece to the final tailoring.
Tomie De Paola, *Charlie Needs a Cloak*, 1973
    A shepherd shears the sheep to begin the process of preparing the wool needed to create a cloak.
Andrea Spalding, *Sarah May and the New Red Dress*, 1999
    Sarah May's wish for a red dress comes true after a rainstorm washes the blue dye from her new dress and she selects the dye to recolor the garment.

772
SALLY M. KEEHN

Anna Sunday

(New York: Philomel Books/Penguin Putnam, 2002)

Subject(s): Civil War; Gender Roles
Age range(s): Grades 5-8
Major character(s): Anna "Adam" Sunday, 12-Year-Old; Jed Sunday, Child; Samson, Horse; Katherine McDowell, Widow(er); Abraham Sunday, Father, Military Personnel (Union soldier)
Time period(s): 1860s
Locale(s): Gettysburg, Pennsylvania; Winchester, Virginia

Summary: Receiving word that their father has been wounded and lies near death, Anna and her younger brother Jed take their cousin's horse Samson, who responds only to Bible sayings such as "Praise the Lord" or "Love thy neighbor," and set off to find him. Anna disguises herself as a boy called Adam and quickly learns how much more she can do in trousers rather than a dress. They find their father being tended by the widow Mrs. McDowell, a Rebel, and are surprised to discover she's nice and not the "she devil" they'd imagined a Confederate supporter would be. Before they can smuggle their father home, word is received that Confederate troops are headed their way. Anna and Jed seek shelter in the Union fort, but are captured and sent to Richmond as prisoners. Finally exchanged for other prisoners, they return home where Mrs. McDowell, in her disguise as a man, awaits them along with their father. (265 pages)

Where it's reviewed:
Booklist, June 2002, page 1723
Bulletin of the Center for Children's Books, September 2002, page 23
Publishers Weekly, July 17, 2002, page 65
School Library Journal, June 2002, page 140
Voice of Youth Advocates, August 2002, page 193

Other books by the same author:
Gnat Stokes and the Foggy Bottom Swamp Queen, 2005
The First Horse I See, 1999
Moon of Two Dark Horses, 1995
I Am Regina, 1991

Other books you might like:
Gloria Houston, *Mountain Valor*, 1994
   After their farm is raided by Union soldiers, Valor dresses as a boy, rides into the Union camp, and rescues her family's belongings.
Ann Rinaldi, *Girl in Blue*, 2001
   Sick of her father's abuse, and unwilling to marry the widower to whom she's been promised, Sarah leaves home dressed as a boy and joins the Union Army.
Laura Jan Shore, *The Sacred Moon Tree*, 1986
   Disguised as a boy, Phoebe and her friend Jotham cross through enemy territory to rescue Phoebe's brother during the Civil War.
G. Clifton Wisler, *Red Cap*, 1991
   Young Union drummer Ransom J. Powell, who lies about his age to join the army, is one of the few to survive the rigors of Andersonville Prison.

773

PEG KEHRET, Co-Author
PETE THE CAT, Co-Author

Spy Cat
(New York: Dutton, 2003)

Subject(s): Burglary; Kidnapping; Animals/Cats
Age range(s): Grades 4-7
Major character(s): Alex Kendrill, 6th Grader; Benjie Kendrill, Child; Pete, Cat
Time period(s): 2000s
Locale(s): Hilltop

Summary: The Kendrills enjoy an amazing cat, for Pete can understand and read English though his verbalization skills are limited to meowing. Their Valley View Estates community has been plagued recently by a series of burglaries and when their neighbor's house is robbed, Alex and Benjie worry about their own house. One day Benjie enters his home to find a burglary in progress with Pete howling away. Benjie runs after the burglars to rescue Pete, but the burglars kidnap him

instead and toss Pete out. Between Pete's ingenuity and Benjie's bravery, all turns out well. (181 pages)

Where it's reviewed:
Booklist, January 2003, page 890
Kirkus Reviews, February 1, 2003, page 233
School Library Journal, January 2003, page 140

Other books by the same author:
Abduction!, 2004
Escaping the Giant Wave, 2003
The Stranger Next Door, 2002
Hideout, 2001
Don't Tell Anyone, 2000

Other books you might like:
Shirley Rousseau Murphy, *Cat Spitting Mad*, 2001
   Those cats that talk and read are back again with another crime to solve, this time clearing the name of a friend who's being framed for murder. Adult fiction.
Phyllis Reynolds Naylor, *The Grand Escape*, 1993
   Two housecats, Marco and his brother Polo, escape one day, meet tomcat Texas Jack, explore the sewer system and follow two-legged automobile drivers.
Susan Shreve, *Ghost Cats*, 1999
   Peter's not adjusting well to his new home in Boston, and losing his cat isn't helping, but then some ghost cats appear that brighten his life.

774

PEG KEHRET, Co-Author
PETE THE CAT, Co-Author

The Stranger Next Door
(New York: Dutton/Penguin Putnam, 2002)

Subject(s): Animals/Cats; Identity, Concealed; Arson
Age range(s): Grades 4-8
Major character(s): Alex Kendrill, 12-Year-Old, 6th Grader; Clifford ''Rocky'' Lexton, 12-Year-Old; Pete, Cat
Time period(s): 2000s
Locale(s): Hilltop

Summary: Alex is overjoyed to see the for sale sign gone in front of the house next door. Maybe someone who's his age will move in and they can walk to school together and have protection from the bullies. Not only do some of the kids at his new school think he's rich, but they're also mad because the houses in Alex's development were built atop their old dirt bike trails. To Alex's delight, Rocky and his family move in but though Rocky is his age, he acts very standoffish; Alex doesn't know that Rocky can't disclose that his family is part of the witness protection program. At the same time, incidents of vandalism occur and Alex wonders if Rocky's involved. Then there's a fire and Pete, Alex's cat, decides it's time someone besides himself figures out what's going on, so he meows enough and drops a few clues and an insurance scam is uncovered. Alex also finds out that Rocky's not a bad kid; he's just upset about moving and leaving behind his friends and his dog. (162 pages)

Where it's reviewed:
Booklist, February 1, 2002, page 938
Horn Book Guide, Fall 2002, page 375

Kirkus Reviews, March 15, 2002, page 415
School Library Journal, March 2002, page 232
Voice of Youth Advocates, February 2002, page 447

Other books by the same author:
Abduction!, 2004
Escaping the Giant Wave, 2003
Spy Cat, 2003
Hideout, 2001
Don't Tell Anyone, 2000

Other books you might like:
Maurice Gee, *The Fire-Raiser*, 1992
    A group of young New Zealanders is responsible for bringing to justice the pyromaniac terrorizing their small town.
Robert Westall, *Yaxley's Cat*, 1992
    Their former owner's cat saves the lives of Rose and her children when they rent an isolated beach house.
Jacqueline Woodson, *Hush*, 2002
    Since having to move under the witness protection program, Toswiah/Evie is saddened by the changes in her family.

775

GARRET KEIZER

God of Beer

(New York: HarperCollins, 2002)

Subject(s): Drunk Driving; Friendship; Schools/High Schools
Age range(s): Grades 9-12
Major character(s): Kyle, 12th Grader; Christopher "Quaker" Oats, 12th Grader, Pacifist; David Logan, 12th Grader; Diana LaValley, Basketball Player; Condor Christy, Boyfriend (of Diana)
Time period(s): 2000s
Locale(s): Salmon Falls, Vermont

Summary: Prompted by a class study of protests and protestors, and their teacher's quote of Gandhi who felt that if God were to be meaningful to India, he'd have to return as bread, Kyle and his friends Quaker and Diana decide that beer is the most meaningful object for their high school crowd. Calling their class project SUDS: Students Undermining a Drunk Society, they want to show the hypocrisy between the rules and the reality and host a party where no one knows whether or not they're being served alcohol. Their plan goes awry when sober Diana gives drunken Condor a ride home and he causes an accident that leads to her death. Other repercussions follow and David is arrested for destroying bottles of beer at the mini-mart while Quaker does the same at David's trial. Watching his friends David and Quaker work through their community service hours, Kyle has to decide about his own choices in this author's first teen novel. (242 pages)

Where it's reviewed:
Bulletin of the Center for Children's Books, May 2002, page 328
Horn Book, May 2002, page 332
Publishers Weekly, January 28, 2002, page 292
School Library Journal, February 2002, page 134
Voice of Youth Advocates, April 2002, page 44

Other books by the same author:
The Enigma of Anger: Essays on a Sometimes Deadly Sin, 2002 (adult nonfiction)
A Dresser of Sycamore Trees: The Finding of a Ministry, 1993 (adult nonfiction)
No Place but Here: A Teacher's Vocation in a Rural Community, 1988 (adult nonfiction)

Other books you might like:
Jake Coburn, *Prep*, 2003
    Nick's pulled away from his former days of tagging, but reenters the world of gangs to save his best friend Kris's younger brother Danny.
Dennis Foon, *Skud*, 2003
    Three of four seniors see their life-long plans fall apart before they graduate: one dies, one is jailed and one loses a chance at pro ice hockey.
Gordon Korman, *Jake, Reinvented*, 2003
    In an attempt to win the hand of DiDi, Jacob reinvents himself as Jake, cool long snapper of the football team and fabulous party thrower.
Alex Sanchez, *Rainbow Boys*, 2001
    Jason, Kyle and Nelson face their senior year, and life-changing decisions, as they deal with their sexual identity.

776

HOLLY KELLER, Author/Illustrator

Cecil's Garden

(New York: Greenwillow/HarperCollins, 2002)

Subject(s): Gardens and Gardening; Animals/Rabbits; Food
Age range(s): Preschool-Grade 1
Major character(s): Cecil, Rabbit, Gardener
Time period(s): 2000s (2002)
Locale(s): United States

Summary: Cecil is looking forward to planting a garden with his friends. However, when the friends discover that there are only five rows in which to plant vegetables and six seed packets, they can't agree on which vegetables to plant. Cecil visits his friends the mice and the moles but both are busy with their own silly arguments. Cecil solves the problem by enlarging the garden to fit the sixth row of vegetables. When it comes time to harvest the crops, the rabbits enjoy a yummy vegetable stew, but the mice and the moles are too busy fighting to come and enjoy. (32 pages)

Where it's reviewed:
Booklist, February 1, 2002, page 947
Horn Book Guide, Fall 2002, page 333
Kirkus Reviews, December 15, 2001, page 1759
Publishers Weekly, December 24, 2001, page 64
School Library Journal, March 2002, page 190

Other books by the same author:
What a Hat!, 2003
Farfallina & Marcel, 2002
Horace, 1991

Other books you might like:
Lynne Cherry, *How Groundhog's Garden Grew*, 2003
    Groundhog is always eating vegetables from Squirrel's garden, so Squirrel offers to help him plant his own.

Lois Ehlert, *Growing Vegetable Soup*, 1987
From planting to harvesting to cooking, this book shows the cycle of gardening vegetables.

Ruth Krauss, *The Carrot Seed*, 1945
A young boy plants and carefully tends a carrot seed.

Grace Lin, *The Ugly Vegetables*, 1999
A young Chinese girl is disappointed when her mother plants vegetables instead of a beautiful flower garden.

777

HOLLY KELLER, Author/Illustrator

Farfallina & Marcel

(New York: Greenwillow Books/HarperCollins Publishers, 2002)

Subject(s): Growing Up; Change; Friendship
Age range(s): Preschool-Kindergarten
Major character(s): Farfallina, Caterpillar, Friend; Marcel, Goose, Friend
Time period(s): Indeterminate
Locale(s): Fictional Country

Summary: Farfallina and Marcel meet on a rainy day when Marcel complains that Farfallina is eating the leaf he's using as an umbrella. Sensitive to each other's needs and abilities the two play together every day until Farfallina begins feeling a need to rest on a branch in a tree. Marcel waits patiently for her to return, but she does not. Feeling sad that he has lost his friend he spends his days idly swimming in the pond and changing from a gosling to a goose. When Farfallina emerges from her chrysalis as a beautiful butterfly she cannot find Marcel and sadly flies over the pond wondering about the new goose she sees. As the two kindred spirits share their tale of lost friends they realize that they've found each other again. In the fall they fly south, together. (32 pages)

Where it's reviewed:
Booklist, September 15, 2002, page 240
Horn Book Guide, Spring 2003, page 40
Kirkus Reviews, July 15, 2002, page 1035
Publishers Weekly, July 29, 2002, page 71
School Library Journal, October 2002, page 114

Awards the book has won:
Publishers Weekly Best Children's Books, 2002

Other books by the same author:
What a Hat!, 2003
Cecil's Garden, 2002
Geraldine and Mrs. Duffy, 2000

Other books you might like:
Frank Asch, *Moonbear's Pet*, 1997
The changes that happen to a pet "fish" strain Moonbear's friendship with Little Bird until Splash completes his development into a frog.

Lois Ehlert, *Waiting for Wings*, 2001
An award-winning nonfiction title introduces the life cycle of butterflies.

Lisa Campbell Ernst, *Bubba and Trixie*, 1997
Trixie, an outgoing ladybug, befriends Bubba, a fearful caterpillar, and helps him become more adventurous.

Sam Swope, *Gotta Go! Gotta Go!*, 2000
A caterpillar with an urgent need to go to Mexico inter-

rupts the trip for a nap and when it awakens as a butterfly continues the journey.

Nancy Tafuri, *Will You Be My Friend?*, 2000
Bunny befriends Bird although Bird is, at first, too shy to respond.

778

HOLLY KELLER, Author/Illustrator

What a Hat!

(New York: Greenwillow Books/HarperCollins Publishers, 2003)

Subject(s): Clothes; Cousins; Animals/Rabbits
Age range(s): Grades K-2
Major character(s): Henry, Rabbit, Brother (older); Wizzie, Rabbit, Sister (younger); Newton, Rabbit, Cousin (younger)
Time period(s): Indeterminate
Locale(s): Fictional Country

Summary: Henry tries to follow directions by taking Newton's hat and coat when he arrives for a week's stay but Newton won't part with the hat. Newton wears his hat at dinner, in the bath and while he sleeps. Henry grows tired of the hat and teases Newton by taking it. Wizzie retrieves it and gently returns it to Newton's head. After that, Henry studiously ignores Newton but, later, when a bully at the park destroys Newton and Wizzie's sand house, Henry defends them. Wizzie cries and Newton comforts her by placing his hat on her head. (24 pages)

Where it's reviewed:
Booklist, September 15, 2003, page 246
Bulletin of the Center for Children's Books, November 2003, page 110
Horn Book, November 2003, page 731
Publishers Weekly, October 6, 2003, page 84
School Library Journal, October 2003, page 128

Other books by the same author:
Geraldine and Mrs. Duffy, 2000
Jacob's Tree, 1999
Brave Horace, 1998

Other books you might like:
Catherine Bancroft, *Felix's Hat*, 1993
Felix loses his beloved orange baseball cap on a trip to the pond and even his caring siblings can't make up for his loss.

Debi Gliori, *Flora's Blanket*, 2001
Poor Flora can't sleep because she can't find her blanket.

John Wallace, *Tiny Rabbit Goes to a Birthday*, 2000
Tiny Rabbit has mixed feelings about attending a friend's birthday party.

779

LAURIE KELLER, Author/Illustrator

Arnie the Doughnut

(New York: Henry Holt and Company, 2003)

Subject(s): Food; Cooks and Cooking; Humor
Age range(s): Grades 1-4

Major character(s): Arnie, Object (doughnut), Friend; Mr. Bing, Gentleman, Friend
Time period(s): 2000s
Locale(s): United States

Summary: Arnie is grateful for the baking and decorating process that enables him to become a chocolate-covered doughnut with multi-colored sprinkles. As Arnie sits in the baker's case surrounded by a variety of baked goods and watches the other doughnuts being sold, either singly or by the dozen, he wonders with whom he will depart. Mr. Bing selects Arnie and leaves the store carrying his purchase in a paper bag. Arnie's excitement at traveling in a car to Mr. Bing's apartment ends abruptly when Mr. Bing opens the bag, takes Arnie out and prepares to bite him. Arnie yells, startling Mr. Bing and beginning a discussion of Mr. Bing's behavior toward houseguests. After his conversation with Arnie, Mr. Bing loses his appetite for doughnuts and the two devise an alternate plan that is mutually satisfying. (40 pages)

Where it's reviewed:
Booklist, May 1, 2003, page 1605
Horn Book Guide, Fall 2003, page 328
Publishers Weekly, February 17, 2003, page 73
School Library Journal, May 2003, page 122

Awards the book has won:
Publishers Weekly Best Children's Books, 2003

Other books by the same author:
Open Wide: Tooth School Inside, 2000
The Scrambled States of America, 1999 (Publishers Weekly Best Children's Book)

Other books you might like:
Maira Kalman, *What Pete Ate from A-Z*, 2001
    Arnie is fortunate not to be in the home of Pete, a dog that devours everything (no matter how inedible) in sight, in alphabetical order.
Toby Speed, *Brave Potatoes*, 2000
    Unlike the other vegetables, the potatoes have no intention of willingly complying with Chef Hackemup's plans to add them to his pot of chowder.
Bruce Whatley, *Detective Donut and the Wild Goose Chase*, 1997
    Fortunately for dimwitted Detective Donut his partner Mouse is clever enough to retrieve the Maltese Dodo from the nefarious Goose.
David Wisniewski, *Tough Cookie*, 1999
    Detective Tough Cookie decides to put an end to Fingers once and for all before any more of his friends get hurt at the Top of the Jar.

780

KATHARINE KENAH
PETER CATALANOTTO, Illustrator

The Dream Shop

(New York: HarperCollins Publishers, 2002)

Subject(s): Dreams and Nightmares; Cousins; Farm Life
Age range(s): Grades K-3
Major character(s): Pip, Child, Cousin; Joseph, Cousin, Child
Time period(s): 2000s (2002)

Locale(s): United States

Summary: One night when Pip can't sleep, she remembers what her cousin, Joseph, told her about the Dream Shop. By imagining wooden horses prancing backwards as Joseph told her, she finds herself in the shop. After picking out a few dream items, including a pig and a sunset, she runs into Joseph, who tells her he prefers scarier items and more exciting dreams. Joseph and Pip both want a small dragon, but when he escapes and wreaks havoc, they have to work together to capture him. Once they do, both wake up. In the morning, Joseph surprises Pip with the baby pig. (32 pages)

Where it's reviewed:
Booklist, February 15, 2002, page 1120
Horn Book Guide, Fall 2002, page 334
Kirkus Reviews, December 1, 2001, page 1685
Publishers Weekly, December 10, 2001
School Library Journal, January 2002, page 104

Other books by the same author:
Eggs Over Easy, 1993

Other books you might like:
Gudrun Ongman, *The Sleep Ponies*, 2000
    A little girl closes her eyes and is carried off to sleep by the Sleep Ponies.
Chris Van Allsburg, *The Polar Express*, 1985
    When a young boy can't sleep on Christmas Eve, a magical train ride takes him to the North Pole.
Audrey Wood, *Sweet Dream Pie*, 1998
    The Brindles bake a delicious pie which leads to sweet dreams.

781

TIM KENNEMORE
TIM ARCHBOLD, Illustrator

The Circle of Doom

(New York: Farrar Straus Giroux, 2003)

Subject(s): Magic; Brothers and Sisters; Family Life
Age range(s): Grades 4-6
Major character(s): Lizzie Sharp, 13-Year-Old; Max Sharp, Child, Brother; Dan Sharp, 10-Year-Old, Brother
Time period(s): 2000s
Locale(s): England

Summary: Lizzie's opinion of their next-door neighbors the Potwards as the grumpiest, least fun-loving people in the world is confirmed when they complain about the noise from her thirteenth birthday party. Furious with their continual kevetching, Lizzie decides to brew up a potion that will make them move. After sprinkling the disgusting mess around their house, Mrs. Potward injures her arthritic hip and the couple is never seen again. Max is delighted with the success of the potion while Dan is skeptical of its actual effect, but this big success encourages Lizzie, who thinks she now has magical powers. Her brothers, however, watch and learn as the magic sometimes works, and sometimes doesn't, in this amusing story of family life. (203 pages)

Where it's reviewed:
Booklist, May 1, 2003, page 1594
Horn Book, September 2003, page 613

Kirkus Reviews, May 1, 2003, page 678
Publishers Weekly, May 5, 2003, page 221
School Library Journal, May 2003, page 156

Other books by the same author:
Changing Times, 1984
Here Today, Gone Tomorrow, 1983
The Fortunate Few, 1983

Other books you might like:
Helen Cresswell, *The Bagthorpe Series*, 1978-
    The peculiar members of the Bagthorpe family confront one crisis after another.
Roald Dahl, *James and the Giant Peach*, 1961
    With a fantastic assortment of insects, James travels in a giant peach far away from his unhappy home.
Hilary McKay, *The Amber Cat*, 1997
    Two friends, recovering from the chicken pox, meet a ghost named Harriet who returns periodically to visit them.

782

JUDITH KERR, Author/Illustrator

The Other Goose

(New York: HarperCollins Publishers, 2001)

Subject(s): Animals/Geese; Loneliness; Robbers and Outlaws
Age range(s): Grades K-2
Major character(s): Katerina, Goose
Time period(s): 2000s (2002)
Locale(s): United Kingdom

Summary: Katerina is the only goose at her pond and she is very lonely. She sees another goose reflected in the banker's shiny car, but he never comes out to live on the pond with her. After a snowstorm, Katerina notices the other goose has disappeared from the snow-covered car so Katerina searches for him. When she spots a man carrying a goose-sized bag, she gives chase and inadvertently foils a bank robber. As a reward, the banker, at the suggestion of his observant daughter, buys a goose for Katerina and delivers it to the pond in his shiny car. (32 pages)

Where it's reviewed:
Booklist, April 1, 2001, page 1333
Horn Book, July/August 2002, page 448
Kirkus Reviews, May 15, 2002, page 735
Publishers Weekly, April 29, 2002, page 70
School Library Journal, June 2002, page 98

Other books by the same author:
The Tiger Who Came to Tea, 2002
When Hitler Stole Pink Rabbit, 1989
Mog the Forgetful Cat, 1970

Other books you might like:
Florence Page Jacques, *There Once Was a Puffin*, 1956
    A lonely puffin looks for someone with whom to play.
Nancy Tafuri, *Silly Little Goose!*, 2001
    A goose wanders around her farm, looking for a place to build a nest.
Ellen Stoll Walsh, *You Silly Goose!*, 1992
    A goose confuses a mouse that has come to visit her goslings with a fox, intent on eating them.

783

M.E. KERR)

Snakes Don't Miss Their Mothers

(New York: HarperCollins, 2003)

Subject(s): Animals, Treatment of
Age range(s): Grades 4-6
Major character(s): Placido, Cat (Siamese); Rex, Dog (yellow Lab); Catherine, Dog (greyhound); Marshall, Snake (King snake); Irving, Dog (German shorthair)
Time period(s): 2000s
Locale(s): New York, New York (The Hamptons)

Summary: As Christmas approaches, the animals at Critters hope for adoption, though most are resigned to life at the shelter. When the notoriously grouchy, one-eyed Siamese Placido is adopted by young Jimmie and her father, hope rises for the others. Irving, an aging dog, watches as Catherine departs for a holiday visit, Rex is brought in as a stray and Marshall complains about never knowing his mother. By book's end, all the animals have new homes except for Irving, who's content to curl up on his cot with his new cedar-filled pillow. (195 pages)

Where it's reviewed:
Booklist, September 15, 2003, page 237
Bulletin of the Center for Children's Books, November 2003, page 110
Publishers Weekly, November 3, 2003, page 75
School Library Journal, October 2003, page 169
Voice of Youth Advocates, October 2003, page 312

Other books by the same author:
Slap Your Sides: A Novel, 2001
What Became of Her: A Novel, 2000
Deliver Us from Evie, 1994

Other books you might like:
Kelly Easton, *Trouble at Betts Pets*, 2002
    Aaron solves both his problems, failing math and pets disappearing from his parents' store, when Sharon tutors him.
Hester Mundis, *My Chimp Friday: The Nana Banana Chronicles*, 2002
    Asked to watch a baby chimp that has mastered Rubik's cube, the Stelson family finds they're protecting Friday from kidnappers.
Sally Warner, *Bad Girl Blues*, 2001
    Quinney can't understand why neither of her friends are excited about volunteering at the new animal shelter.

784

RUKHSANA KHAN
R. GREGORY CHRISTIE, Illustrator

Ruler of the Courtyard

(New York: Viking, 2003)

Subject(s): Animals/Chickens; Fear; Problem Solving
Age range(s): Grades K-3
Major character(s): Saba, Child
Time period(s): Indeterminate Past

Locale(s): Pakistan

Summary: Saba must cross the courtyard to reach the bath-house, a simple task complicated by chickens, creatures that simply terrify Saba. While bathing Saba can relax and forget her fears, but eventually she must get back to the house. Then she sees something in the bathhouse that is even more frightening than chickens. A snake lies curled on the floor between her and the door. Saba searches the bathhouse for something to use as a weapon or a trap. Finally, Saba courageously slams the bucket over the snake and then waits, but she hears nothing. Curiously she uses a stick to raise the bucket and discovers that the snake she's trapped is actually a drawstring from a pair of pants. Relief floods her, laughter fills her and Saba roars confidently from the bathhouse as chickens scatter in all directions before mighty Saba, ruler of the courtyard. (36 pages)

Where it's reviewed:
Booklist, February 15, 2003, page 1074
Bulletin of the Center for Children's Books, May 2003, page 365
Horn Book, March 2003, page 204
Riverbank Review, Spring 2003, page 35
School Library Journal, February 2003, page 114

Other books by the same author:
Muslim Child: Understanding Islam through Stories and Poems, 2002
The Roses in My Carpets, 1998

Other books you might like:
Katie Davis, *Scared Stiff*, 2001
  Frightened of the dog next door, monsters behind the fence and snakes in her closet, a little girl decides to be brave and confront her fears.
Eileen Spinelli, *A Safe Place Called Home*, 2001
  A boy encounters so many scary things as he tries to reach his house after school that he is relieved to finally be safely home.
Ian Whybrow, *Little Farmer Joe*, 2001
  Away from home for the first time, Joe tries to overcome his fear of the farm animals by helping his uncle with some of the baby ones.

785

K.M. KIMBALL

The Secret of the Red Flame

(New York: Aladdin/Simon & Schuster, 2002)

Subject(s): Mystery and Detective Stories; Gangs; Fires
Age range(s): Grades 4-7
Major character(s): Jozef Chapski, 12-Year-Old, Immigrant (Polish); Bridget, Gang Member; Frank Fryderyk Chapski, Amputee, Veteran (of the Civil War)
Time period(s): 1870s (1871)
Locale(s): Chicago, Illinois (Polish immigrant settlement)

Summary: While taking his father's receipts from his butcher shop to the bank, Jozef is rubbed by a young girl and boy, which leaves him angry and humiliated but determined to retrieve his money. At first he's not sure what to do, especially when he hears of other merchants who had money or goods stolen from their shops, but he's determined to try something. Gathering together some of his friends, the boys set up the Red Flame, a secret society that allows them to penetrate a gang of thieves. Jozef even becomes friends with Bridget, one of the gang members, and when she is accused of murder, Jozef and his handicapped brother Frank are determined to find the real killer and prove Bridget's innocence. Unfortunately, the night they track down the real murderer is also the night the Great Chicago Fire breaks out. (226 pages)

Where it's reviewed:
Booklist, July 2002, page 1846
School Library Journal, August 2002, page 190

Other books by the same author:
The Star-Spangled Secret, 2001

Other books you might like:
James Lincoln Collier, *Chipper*, 2001
  In order to survive on the streets of New York City, orphaned Chipper joins the Midnight Rats, though he hates having to steal.
Isabelle Holland, *Paperboy*, 1999
  Caught snitching a newspaper, Kevin is challenged to read the news, which leads to a career in journalism.
Elizabeth Massie, *1870: Not with Our Blood*, 2000
  After the Civil War, Patrick's family moves north to work in the factories and have a better life, but factory conditions are terrible.

786

E. CODY KIMMEL

Lily B. on the Brink of Cool

(New York: HarperCollins, 2003)

Subject(s): Family Life; Diaries; Crime and Criminals
Age range(s): Grades 4-8
Major character(s): Lily Blennerhassett, 13-Year-Old; Charles "Charlie White" LeBlanc, Con Artist; Veronique "Vera White" LeBlanc, Con Artist; Karma "Kay White" LeBlanc, Teenager
Time period(s): 2000s
Locale(s): New York

Summary: Boring life, boring parents and boring summer thinks Lily, until she attends a family wedding and meets some distant relatives, the LeBlancs and their daughter Karma. Wow! These people are exciting and worldly, at least to Lily's naive eyes, though her parents warn her to stay away from them. Flattered by their attention and impressed with the non-profit environmental group they've founded, Lily gullibly arranges for them to stay at her parent's beach house. Even when Lily and her parents find their beach house trashed, Lily doesn't recognize how she's been conned. But a $1.6 million lawsuit filed against her parents by the Whites, whose LeBlanc name is just another sham, awakens Lily to reality. (245 pages)

Where it's reviewed:
Booklist, December 15, 2003, page 666
Bulletin of the Center for Children's Books, February 2004, page 237
Publishers Weekly, December 8, 2003, page 62

School Library Journal, October 2003, page 169
Voice of Youth Advocates, October 2003, page 312

Other books by the same author:
To the Frontier, 2001
Visiting Miss Caples, 2000
In the Stone Circle, 1998

Other books you might like:
James Lincoln Collier, *Chipper*, 2001
    Orphan Chipper is being asked to pass himself off as the
    son of a wealthy man, but Chipper thinks there may be
    some truth to this scam.
Dennis Foon, *Double or Nothing*, 2000
    Set for college with money he's saved, Kip loses it all
    when he dates Joey who introduces him to her father, a
    high-stakes gambler.
Phyllis Reynolds Naylor, *All but Alice*, 1992
    Just piercing her ears seems to have made Alice popular,
    but she quickly realizes it's boring to be like everyone else.

787

E. CODY KIMMEL
SCOTT SNOW, Illustrator

One Sky Above Us

(New York: HarperCollins Publishers, 2002)

Series: Adventures of Young Buffalo Bill. #2
Subject(s): Historical; Abolition; Frontier and Pioneer Life
Age range(s): Grades 4-6
Major character(s): William Frederick "Bill" Cody, 8-Year-
    Old, Son; Isaac "Pa" Cody, Farmer, Father; Doc Hatha-
    way, Doctor, Settler
Time period(s): 1850s (1854)
Locale(s): Kansas (Kansas Territory)

Summary: Alongside Pa and Doc, Bill works to get the crops
planted on the family's new homestead. In addition, he hauls
water and wood to the cabin so his mother and sisters can do
the chores and, when time permits, he enjoys his horse. Bill
and Pa work on completing the barn so it'll be weather and
wolf-proof before winter. The troubles that they left behind in
Iowa crop up in Kansas Territory as those favoring slavery
threaten violence against abolitionists or "free-soilers." As
an election to decide the issue nears, Pa is stabbed for his anti-
slavery beliefs and Bill takes on all the responsibility for the
family, farm and animals with support from Doc and a young
Indian friend. An afterword gives the historical basis for the
story. (177 pages)

Where it's reviewed:
Booklist, September 1, 2002, page 124
Horn Book Guide, Fall 2003, page 369
Publishers Weekly, September 30, 2002, page 74
School Library Journal, November 2002, page 169

Awards the book has won:
Notable Social Studies Trade Books for Young People, 2003

Other books by the same author:
In the Eye of the Storm, 2003 (Adventures of Young Buffalo
    Bill, #3)
West on the Wagon Train, 2003 (Adventures of Young Buf-
    falo Bill, #4)

To the Frontier, 2002 (Adventures of Young Buffalo Bill,
    #1)

Other books you might like:
Kate McMullan, *A Fine Start: Meg's Prairie Diary*, 2003
    In this third title about Meg and her family's life in Kansas
    Territory, her father is injured during the fight to make
    Kansas a free state.
Bonnie Pryor, *Luke: 1849-On the Golden Trail*, 1999
    Eleven-year-old Luke helps his father break the sod and
    put in crops for the farm they are establishing on the Iowa
    prairie.
Laura Ingalls Wilder, *Farmer Boy*, 1953
    Almanzo and his siblings live on an established farm rather
    than the prairie but still have farm chores to complete.

788

ERIC A. KIMMEL
ANDREW GLASS, Illustrator

The Erie Canal Pirates

(New York: Holiday House, 2002)

Subject(s): Pirates; Tall Tales; Boats and Boating
Age range(s): Grades K-3
Major character(s): Captain Flynn, Sea Captain
Time period(s): Indeterminate Past
Locale(s): Erie Canal, New York

Summary: As Captain Flynn and his men travel along the Erie
Canal to deliver the mail to Buffalo, New York, pirates attack
their mule-drawn barge. A fierce battle ensues and Captain
Flynn tries to take an alternate route around the pirates. The
pirate crew ends up at the bottom of Niagara Falls, but in true
tall tale fashion, Captain Flynn and his men sail straight up the
falls, leaving the pirates to their watery doom. An author's
note explains the artistic license used by the author with the
geographic features of the area in order to resolve the tale as
he does. (32 pages)

Where it's reviewed:
Booklist, October 15, 2002, page 412
Bulletin of the Center for Children's Books, November 2002,
    page 113
Publishers Weekly, October 28, 2002, page 74
School Library Journal, November 2002, page 128

Other books by the same author:
The Brass Serpent, 2002
Hershel and the Hanukkah Goblins, 1989
Anansi and the Moss Covered Rock, 1988

Other books you might like:
Colin McNaughton, *Captain Abdul's Pirate School*, 1994
    Maisie attends Captain Abdul's pirate school and orga-
    nizes a mutiny.
David McPhail, *Edward and the Pirates*, 1997
    After Edward reads a book about pirates, they invade his
    bedroom.
Peter Spier, *The Erie Canal*, 1970
    This book is an illustrated version of the folk song, "The
    Erie Canal."

789

ERIC A. KIMMEL
MORDICAI GERSTEIN, Illustrator

Three Samurai Cats: A Story from Japan

(New York: Holiday House, 2003)

Subject(s): Folklore; Animals/Cats; Problem Solving
Age range(s): Grades K-3
Major character(s): Unnamed Character, Rat, Bully; Unnamed Character, Nobleman (daimyo); Neko Roshi, Cat, Warrior
Time period(s): Indeterminate Past
Locale(s): Japan

Summary: A daimyo whose castle is overtaken by an enormous bullying rat seeks help in getting rid of the villain. The rat outwits each of the first two samurai cats sent to evict it before they can use any of the fighting skills of which they seem proud. The third cat is old, physically feeble and apparently uninterested in the rat. Neko Roshi sleeps and eats while the rat becomes bolder. Each time the rat asks Neko Roshi if he wants to fight, Neko Roshi declines. Finally, the rat's gluttony is his downfall and, when he's trapped beneath the gigantic rice ball he's rolled by taking all the rice for himself, Neko Roshi comes to his aid on the condition that he leave the palace. The rat complies, demonstrating the truth of Neko Roshi's training, "draw strength from stillness." A concluding author's note gives background and sources for the folktale. (32 pages)

Where it's reviewed:
Booklist, April 15, 2003, page 1473
Horn Book, July 2003, page 470
Publishers Weekly, March 17, 2003, page 76
School Library Journal, June 2003, page 129

Other books by the same author:
A Cloak for the Moon, 2001 (Sidney Taylor Honor Book for Younger Readers)
Gershon's Monster, 2000 (ALA Notable Children's Books)
Hershel and the Hanukkah Goblins, 1989 (Caldecott Honor Book)

Other books you might like:
Margaret Hodges, *The Boy Who Drew Cats*, 2002
Cats drawn on the walls of an abandoned temple come to life at night and protect the young artist from the hungry rat goblin haunting the temple.
Rafe Martin, *Mysterious Tales of Japan*, 1996
Ten traditional tales are retold in an illustrated, award-winning collection.
Tim Myers, *Tanuki's Gift: A Japanese Tale*, 2003
A kindly priest shelters a Tanuki, a disliked animal in Japanese lore, and learns the true value of friendship.

790

HAVEN KIMMEL
ROBERT ANDREW PARKER, Illustrator

Orville: A Dog Story

(New York: Clarion Books, 2003)

Subject(s): Animals/Dogs; Animals, Treatment of; Farm Life

Age range(s): Grades 3-6
Major character(s): Orville, Dog; Sally Macintosh, Neighbor, Worker (night shift); Maybelle, Spouse, Neighbor (Sally's); Herbert, Farmer, Spouse
Time period(s): 2000s
Locale(s): United States

Summary: Maybelle and Herbert discover an ugly stray and decide to take him to their farm as a watchdog. Though they name him Orville, the dog knows that's not his real name, but he's been homeless for so long he's no longer sure of his real name. Unfortunately, Herbert chains Orville near the barn and the chain brings back old memories causing Orville to become more and more angry every day. Then he sees a girl with cotton candy hair move in across the street and Orville returns to his chain-breaking ways. He dashes to Sally's house, sneaks inside and lies down to sleep right next to the couch on which Sally sleeps. Orville's attraction to Sally leads to Sally's friendship with Maybelle, the fulfillment of one of Herbert's dreams and a potential relationship with one of the volunteer firefighters that come to the rescue each time Sally calls for help when she discovers Orville in her house. Philosophical Orville realizes that he's not the only one to slip his chains and leave his loneliness behind. (32 pages)

Where it's reviewed:
Booklist, September 15, 2003, page 246
Bulletin of the Center for Children's Books, November 2003, page 111
Publishers Weekly, September 8, 2003, page 76
School Library Journal, November 2003, page 102

Awards the book has won:
Bulletin of the Center for Children's Books Blue Ribbons, 2003

Other books by the same author:
A Girl Named Zippy: Growing up Small in Mooreland, Indiana, 2001

Other books you might like:
Gloria Rand, *A Home for Spooky*, 1998
Annie secretly feeds an abandoned dog until the dog's health deteriorates and he needs medical treatment to save his life.
Tres Seymour, *Pole Dog*, 1993
An abandoned dog sits forlornly near a telephone pole until rescued by a sympathetic family.
Rosemary Wells, *Lassie Come Home*, 1995
The picture book adaptation of Eric Knight's classic story tells of the power of love binding pet to owner and Lassie's determination to return to Joe.

791

ROBERT KINERK
STEVEN KELLOGG, Illustrator

Clorinda

(New York: Simon & Schuster Books for Young Readers, 2003)

Subject(s): Animals/Cows; Ballet; Stories in Rhyme
Age range(s): Grades K-3
Major character(s): Clorinda, Cow, Dancer; Leonard P. "Len" Cage, Farmer

Time period(s): Indeterminate
Locale(s): United States; New York, New York (Manhattan)

Summary: On her annual trip into town to cast her ballot, Clorinda somehow ends up watching a ballet. The experience sparks a desire to become a ballerina. Len builds a stage in the back of the barn and Clorinda practices until she decides she has to fly to Manhattan to seek her fortunes with a professional troupe. It takes lots of auditions and a lucky break before Clorinda actually dons a tutu in a performance, one that requires the leaping ballerinas to be caught by their partners. A cow floating light as air still packs enough power to flatten a dancer's partner. Clorinda realizes she's done her best, but still she needs to return to the farm. There, Len enlarges the stage, Clorinda gives lessons and soon all the animals are dancing. (36 pages)

Where it's reviewed:
Booklist, November 1, 2003, page 513
Horn Book Guide, Spring 2004, page 47
Publishers Weekly, October 13, 2003, page 77
School Library Journal, November 2003, page 102

Other books by the same author:
Clorinda the Fearless, 2005
Timothy Cox Will Not Change His Socks, 2005
Slim and Miss Prim, 1998

Other books you might like:
Mary Jane Auch, *Hen Lake*, 1995
    Poulette, a determined hen ballerina, challenges a conceited barnyard peacock to a talent contest.
Mary Palatini, *Mary Had a Little Ham*, 2003
    Encouraged by his friend Mary, Stanley Snoutowski travels to New York City to achieve his dream of seeing his name in lights.
Rachel Vail, *Over the Moon*, 1998
    Director Hi Diddle Diddle tries to make the cow follow the nursery rhyme script and jump over (not under or through) the moon.

792

DICK KING-SMITH
JILL BARTON, Illustrator

Clever Lollipop

(Cambridge, MA: Candlewick Press, 2003)

Subject(s): Animals/Pigs; Princes and Princesses; Magicians
Age range(s): Grades 3-4
Major character(s): Penelope, Royalty (princess), Student; Lady Lollipop, Pig; Johnny Skinner, Student, Animal Lover; Collie Cob, Teacher, Magician
Time period(s): Indeterminate Past
Locale(s): Fictional Country

Summary: In this sequel to *Lady Lollipop*, Princess Penelope's pet pig continues to be the inspiration for change and growth in her young owner. Penelope is unable to read and sees little reason to learn, but Johnny and Lady Lollipop manage to convince her of the value of literacy. After the first tutor quits, and none to soon in the opinion of her students, Collie Cob takes over with his unconventional instructional style. Together, Collie and Lady Lollipop cure Princess Penelope's

father from a loss of appetite and plan an unforgettable birthday surprise for the little princess. (143 pages)

Where it's reviewed:
Booklist, September 15, 2003, page 240
Publishers Weekly, July 21, 2003, page 197
School Library Journal, October 2003, page 128

Other books by the same author:
Funny Frank, 2002
Billy the Bird, 2001
Lady Lollipop, 2001

Other books you might like:
Anita Briggs, *Hobart*, 2002
    Four little farm pigs save their lives and the farm by following their dreams and developing their theatrical talents.
Deitlof Reiche, *I, Freddy*, 2003
    Freddy, a golden hamster, learns to read while observing its young owner do her homework. Then it masters the computer and writes its life story.
E.B. White, *Charlotte's Web*, 1952
    A runt pig, saved by a young farm girl, becomes a spider's best friend on the farm. Charlotte uses her talented web-making to save Wilber's life.

793

DICK KING-SMITH
JOHN EASTWOOD, Illustrator

Funny Frank

(New York: Alfred A. Knopf, 2002)

Subject(s): Animals/Chickens; Animals/Ducks; Individuality
Age range(s): Grades 2-4
Major character(s): Frank, Chicken; Jemima Tabb, 8-Year-Old, Daughter; Ted Tabb, Uncle, Veterinarian
Time period(s): 2000s (2001)
Locale(s): England

Summary: A newly hatched chick, more interested in the ducks in the pond than the other chicks scratching in the dirt, actually goes into the pond to try to swim. Fortunately Jemima is near enough to hear his "frank!" squawk and rescue him from drowning. Dubbing the chick Frank, Jemima tries in vain to keep him out of the water. Finally, she enlists the help of Uncle Ted and her mother to improvise flippers and a wetsuit for Frank so he can achieve his desire to be a swimmer. As Frank matures into the rooster he is to become, he begins to notice more than the pond and the ducks. The introduction of an unusually colored pullet to the farm allows the natural course of events to compel Frank to give up his life as a duck and settle into his destiny. Originally published in Great Britain in 2001. (108 pages)

Where it's reviewed:
Booklist, January 1, 2002, page 858
Publishers Weekly, December 10, 2001, page
School Library Journal, March 2002, page 190

Other books by the same author:
Charlie Muffin's Miracle Mouse, 1999
Mr. Potter's Pet, 1996
The School Mouse, 1995 (School Library Journal Best Books)

Other books you might like:
Kate DiCamillo, *The Tale of Despereaux: Being the Story of a Mouse, a Princess, Some Soup, and a Spool of Thread*, 2003
Different from other mice in the castle, Despereaux is banished to the dungeon because of his appearance and love of both reading and a princess.
Philip Pullman, *I Was a Rat!*, 2000
Though Roger looks like a boy he behaves like a rat; a product of a magical spell gone awry when he missed the midnight pumpkin deadline.
Colby Rodowsky, *Jason Rat-a-Tat*, 2002
Jason just doesn't fit in with his athletic family. Fortunately Grandpa notices and nurtures Jason's musical talent.

794
DICK KING-SMITH
BOB GRAHAM, Illustrator

The Nine Lives of Aristotle
(Cambridge, MA: Candlewick Press, 2003)

Subject(s): Animals/Cats; Witches and Witchcraft; Accidents
Age range(s): Grades 2-4
Major character(s): Aristotle, Cat (kitten); Bella Donna, Witch
Time period(s): Indeterminate Past
Locale(s): Fictional Country

Summary: For a change of pace, Bella Donna chooses a small white kitten rather than a black one for her new pet. Curious and adventurous, Aristotle rapidly begins using up his nine lives before he even nears adulthood. Fortunately, Bella Donna is usually nearby to rescue him from his forays into the unknown, but she does caution him that he has only nine lives so he needs to stop going through them so quickly. After eight near misses with certain death, Aristotle settles into a quieter life and he and Bella Donna live contentedly in their little thatched cottage for many years. (77 pages)

Where it's reviewed:
Booklist, December 1, 2003, page 667
Bulletin of the Center for Children's Books, November 2003, page 111
Publishers Weekly, August 4, 2003, page 80
School Library Journal, October 2003, page 128

Awards the book has won:
IRA Children's Choices, 2004

Other books by the same author:
Clever Lollipop, 2003
Mysterious Miss Slade, 2000
Mr. Potter's Pet, 1996

Other books you might like:
Julie Andrews Edwards, *Little Bo: The Story of Bonnie Boadicea*, 1999
An abandoned kitten faces cold and hunger before being found by a sailor who sneaks her aboard his ship.
James Howe, *Pinky and Rex and the Just-Right Pet*, 2001
Dog-lover Pinky doesn't want to like the family's new pet, but it's hard to resist a playful kitten.
Ursula K. Le Guin, *Wonderful Alexander and the Catwings*, 1994
A big, bossy kitten's unexpected adventures lead to his introduction to cats with wings.

795
NATALIE KINSEY-WARNOCK
JAMES BERNARDIN, Illustrator

A Doctor Like Papa
(New York: HarperCollins Publishers, 2002)

Subject(s): Illness; Doctors; Rural Life
Age range(s): Grades 2-4
Major character(s): Margaret, 11-Year-Old; Colin, Child, Brother; Owen, Uncle, Military Personnel
Time period(s): 1910s (1918)
Locale(s): Northeast Kingdom, Vermont

Summary: Margaret dreams of being a doctor like her father but she must overcome her mother's concerns that doctoring is too hard a profession. After Margaret's Uncle Owen comes back injured from World War I, Margaret is worried about his recovery and about her father who is battling the influenza epidemic of 1918. When Margaret and her brother Colin are sent to her aunt's house to wait out the epidemic, Margaret has a chance to do some doctoring of her own with a sick family. In the end, the demands of the epidemic test and strengthen the entire family. (72 pages)

Where it's reviewed:
Booklist, April 1, 2002, page 1328
Horn Book Guide, Fall 2002, page 359
Kirkus Reviews, April 15, 2002, page 572
School Library Journal, July 2002, page 94

Other books by the same author:
If Wishes Were Horses, 2000
In the Language of Loons, 1998
The Canada Geese Quilt, 1989 (ALA Notable Children's Books)

Other books you might like:
Laurie Halse Anderson, *Fever 1793*, 2000
Mattie tells the story of the yellow fever epidemic of 1793 that killed ten percent of Philadelphia's residents.
Karen Hesse, *A Time for Angels*, 1995
Hannah's life is touched by the dual tragedies of World War I and the Influenza epidemic of 1918-1919.
Laura Ingalls Wilder, *By the Shores of Silver Lake*, 1941
The Ingalls family moves to the unsettled Dakota Territory where they are tested by various hardships, including scarlet fever.

796
NATALIE KINSEY-WARNOCK
MARY AZARIAN, Illustrator

From Dawn till Dusk
(Boston: Houghton Mifflin Company, 2002)

Subject(s): Farm Life; Family Life; Seasons
Age range(s): Grades 1-3

Major character(s): Natalie Kinsey, Sister (younger), Narrator
Time period(s): Indeterminate Past
Locale(s): Vermont

Summary: On a snowy evening, sitting around the wood stove, Natalie listens to her siblings as they discuss where they will move when they grow up. Natalie can't imagine leaving the area and asks repeatedly, ''Won't you miss . . . sugaring time, or sledding off the barn roof, or fishing after a long day, or finding baby kittens in the haymow?'' While her brothers and sister agree they would miss the things of which they are most fond, they think they could happily do with less than seven months of snow, less work than a rocky farm requires, and a lot less mud during mud season. (40 pages)

Where it's reviewed:
Booklist, November 15, 2002, page 602
Publishers Weekly, September 2, 2002, page 76
School Library Journal, October 2002, page 115

Other books by the same author:
A Farm of Her Own, 2001
The Summer of Stanley, 1997 (Smithsonian's Notable Books for Children)
The Fiddler of the Northern Lights, 1996 (Smithsonian's Notable Books for Children)

Other books you might like:
Patricia MacLachlan, *All the Places to Love*, 1994
 Three generations live on a family farm that holds ''all the places to love'' anyone could ever want.
Cynthia Rylant, *When I Was Young in the Mountains*, 1982
 Set in Appalachia the book celebrates the needed support of family to endure the hardship of life in the simple beauty of the mountain world.
Rosemary Wells, *Waiting for the Evening Star*, 1993
 Young Berty appreciates the simple pleasures of life in rural Vermont while his older brother is eager to see beyond the distant mountains.

797

NATALIE KINSEY-WARNOCK
JUDY PEDERSEN, Illustrator

Gifts from the Sea
(New York: Borzoi/Knopf, 2003)

Subject(s): Fathers and Daughters; Babies; Lighthouses
Age range(s): Grades 4-6
Major character(s): Aquila Jane ''Quila'' MacKinnon, 12-Year-Old; Cecelia ''Celia'' MacKinnon, Baby; Margaret Malone, Aunt (of Celia)
Time period(s): 1850s
Locale(s): Devil's Rock Island, Maine

Summary: Quila is 12 when her mother dies, and their lighthouse on Devil's Rock Island seems lonely without her mother's singing and storytelling. About six months later, following a storm, Quila notices two mattresses tied together drifting toward shore. Pulling in the bundle, she finds a child tucked inside, well protected from the water. Naming her Cecelia, meaning ''gift from the sea,'' Quila and her dad enjoy this baby who always brings a smile to their faces. When a young woman appears asking to say good-bye to her sister who died in a shipwreck, Quila realizes this Margaret is probably Celia's aunt who'll take Celia away. Quila tries to hide Celia by heading to sea in a boat, but they capsize and almost drown before being miraculously rescued by a group of seals in this work based on a true incident. (112 pages)

Where it's reviewed:
Booklist, June 1, 2003, page 1777
Kirkus Reviews, June 1, 2003, page 806
Kliatt, July 2003, page 14
Publishers Weekly, May 5, 2003, page 68
School Library Journal, June 2003, page 144

Other books by the same author:
If Wishes Were Horses, 2000
In the Language of Loons, 1998
As Long as There Are Mountains, 1997

Other books you might like:
Cynthia Copeland, *Elin's Island*, 2003
 Found floating in a box following the sinking of a schooner, Elin is raised by lighthouse keepers and helps them maintain the light.
Katherine Kirkpatrick, *Keeping the Good Light*, 1995
 The isolation of living with her family in Stepping Stones lighthouse changes for Eliza when a ship's captain finds a note she placed in a bottle.
Patricia Curtis Pfitsch, *Keeper of the Light*, 1997
 After her lighthouse keeper father dies, Faith's family moves back to town, though she returns during a storm to provide light for a foundering schooner.

798

NATALIE KINSEY-WARNOCK
JAMES BERNARDIN, Illustrator

Lumber Camp Library
(New York: HarperCollins Publishers, 2002)

Subject(s): Death; Lumber Industry; Books and Reading
Age range(s): Grades 2-6
Major character(s): Ruby Sawyer, 10-Year-Old, Sister; Aurora Graham, Blind Person, Aged Person
Time period(s): 1920s (1922)
Locale(s): Vermont

Summary: Ruby Sawyer loves her life in the lumber camp. Her father encourages her to keep up with her schooling, so that she can become a teacher. However, when her father is killed in a logging accident, Ruby, her mother and her ten brothers and sisters are forced to move into town. When Ruby's mother gets a job cooking at the lumber camp, Ruby has to stay home and take care of her younger brothers and sisters. One day, Ruby meets Aurora Graham, a blind woman in town with a house full of books. Ruby starts teaching the loggers to read and begins on her life's path of becoming a teacher and founding a lumber camp library. (96 pages)

Where it's reviewed:
Booklist, April 15, 2002, page 1401
Horn Book Guide, Fall 2002, page 359
Kirkus Reviews, April 15, 2002, page 572
School Library Journal, May 2002, page 118

Other books by the same author:
Gifts from the Sea, 2003
As Long as There Are Mountains, 2001
The Night the Bells Rang, 2000

Other books you might like:
Avi, *Prairie School*, 2001
When Noah's Aunt Dora comes out to the Colorado prairie and tries to teach him to read, he resists at first but soon discovers a love of books.
Bill Cleaver, *Where the Lilies Bloom*, 1969
After her father dies, Mary Call tries to keep her brothers and sisters together.
Patricia MacLachlan, *Sarah, Plain and Tall*, 1985
Sarah travels to the Midwest from Maine to marry a widowed farmer and be a mother to his two children.

799

DANIEL KIRK, Author/Illustrator

Jack and Jill
(New York: G.P. Putnam's Sons, 2003)

Subject(s): Brothers and Sisters; Wishes; Stories in Rhyme
Age range(s): Grades K-2
Major character(s): Jack, Brother, Son; Jill, Sister, Daughter; Magic Sam, Crocodile
Time period(s): Indeterminate
Locale(s): Fictional Country

Summary: A broken sink and a pet fish in need of water propel Jack and Jill up the hill to fetch a pail of water from the well. Unexpectedly, Magic Sam pops out of the well, startling them so much that Jack falls, breaks his crown and tumbles down the hill with Jill right behind. Sent back to the well, the children again face Magic Sam who demands food in exchange for water. After the children comply, Magic Sam wants to grant a wish before giving any water. Finally, in frustration Jack exclaims that he wishes their missing dad could help them and Magic Sam vanishes. In the crocodile's place is the missing father, freed from a witch's spell. (32 pages)

Where it's reviewed:
Booklist, June 2003, page 1787
Publishers Weekly, May 19, 2003, page 73
School Library Journal, November 2003, page 104

Other books by the same author:
Bus Stop, Bus Go!, 2001
Humpty Dumpty, 2000
Snow Family, 2000 (IRA Children's Choice)

Other books you might like:
David T. Greenburg, *Whatever Happened to Humpty Dumpty?: And Other Surprising Sequels to Mother Goose Rhymes*, 1999
Retellings of traditional nursery rhymes conclude with new, humorous endings suggesting what really happened to the characters.
Joanne Oppenheim, *Eency Weency Spider*, 1991
In an expanded tale of the spider washed down the waterspout, Eency Weency meets other nursery rhyme characters.

Janet Stevens, *And the Dish Ran Away with the Spoon*, 2001
Cat, Dog and Cow try to find missing Dish and Spoon before it's time for their nursery rhyme to be read again.

800

DAVID KIRK, Author/Illustrator

Little Bunny, Biddle Bunny
(New York: Callaway/Scholastic Press, 2002)

Series: Biddle Books
Subject(s): Animals/Rabbits; Stories in Rhyme; Babies
Age range(s): Preschool-Kindergarten
Major character(s): Little Bunny, Rabbit, Baby
Time period(s): 2000s (2002)
Locale(s): United States

Summary: As Little Bunny explores the new, springtime world he discovers flowers, insects and food. When the day comes to an end, Little Bunny heads home to sleep with his mother and the rest of his siblings, tired after a satisfying day. (32 pages)

Where it's reviewed:
Horn Book Guide, Fall 2002, page 305
Publishers Weekly, March 18, 2002, page 106
School Library Journal, April 2002, page 113

Other books by the same author:
Little Pig, Biddle Pig, 2001
Little Bird, Biddle Bird, 1999
Little Miss Spider, 1999

Other books you might like:
Margaret Wise Brown, *The Runaway Bunny*, 1942
In this reassuring classic, each time a young bunny runs away, his mother finds him.
Sam McBratney, *Guess How Much I Love You*, 1994
Little Nutbrown Hare's father reassures his young son of just how much he loves him.
Rick Walton, *Bunny Day*, 2002
A loving bunny family spends their day together.

801

KATHERINE KIRKPATRICK

The Voyage of the Continental
(New York: Holiday House, 2002)

Subject(s): Orphans; Frontier and Pioneer Life; Diaries
Age range(s): Grades 6-9
Major character(s): Asa Mercer, Businessman; Emeline "Emmy" McCullough, 17-Year-Old; Ruby Shaw, Runaway
Time period(s): 1860s (1866)
Locale(s): Lowell, Massachusetts; *Continental*, At Sea; Seattle, Northwest Territories

Summary: Tired of life as a mill girl in Lowell, Emmy decides to take a chance and become a "Mercer's girl," sailing with other widows and orphans to the Washington Territory. Asa Mercer's claim to want to resettle those left widowed or orphaned from the Civil War is actually an attempt to bring potential brides to the Northwest Territory, as well as make a profit for him from the frontier settlers. On the sea voyage around South America, Emmy becomes friends with Ruby who's traveling under an alias as she flees from an abusive husband. With attempts on Ruby's life, the trip to the Washington Territory is never dull; best of all, upon arrival, Emmy finds a special person to love. (297 pages)

Where it's reviewed:
Booklist, December 15, 2002, page 753
Kirkus Reviews, October 14, 2002, page 82
Publishers Weekly, October 14, 2002, page 85
School Library Journal, November 2002, page 170
Voice of Youth Advocates, December 2002, page 384

Other books by the same author:
The Adventures of Daniel Bonnet, 2004
Trouble's Daughter: The Story of Susanna Hutchinson, Indian Captive, 1998
Keeping the Good Light, 1995

Other books you might like:
Jennifer L. Holm , *Boston Jane: An Adventure*, 2001
    Miss Heppelwhite's training doesn't help Jane at all as she struggles to adapt to her new life in the Washington Territory.
Philip Pullman, *The Ruby in the Smoke*, 1987
    Sally, an orphaned 16-year-old, outmaneuvers a host of villainous 19th-century characters to claim her inheritance and her independence.
Jocelyn Reekie, *Tess*, 2002
    Forced to leave the family estate in Scotland, Tess and her father travel to British Columbia where they will begin new lives in the wilderness.
Joan Weir, *The Brideship*, 1999
    It's not until Sarah's aboard ship that the 48 orphans are told they're sailing on a brideship heading for the goldfields of British Columbia.

802

SATOSHI KITAMURA, Author/Illustrator

Comic Adventures of Boots

(New York: Farrar Straus Giroux, 2002)

Subject(s): Animals/Cats; Cartoons and Comics; Graphic Novel
Age range(s): Grades 1-4
Major character(s): Boots, Cat
Time period(s): 2000s (2002)
Locale(s): Fictional Country

Summary: Boots is the hero of three comic-strip adventures. In the first, "Operation Fish Biscuits," Boots tries to regain his sleeping spot on the neighborhood wall with the help of some delicious-smelling fish biscuits. In "Pleased to Meet You, Madam Quark" a duck teaches him how to swim. Finally, Boots and his friends play a game of charades in "Let's Play a Guessing Game." (32 pages)

Where it's reviewed:
Booklist, October 1, 2002, page 326
Horn Book Guide, Fall 2003, page 329
Kirkus Reviews, June 1, 2002, page 806
Publishers Weekly, June 24, 2002, page 57

School Library Journal, August 2002, page 159

Other books by the same author:
Me and My Cat?, 2000
A Friend for Boots, 1998
Bathtime Boots, 1998
Lily Takes a Walk, 1987

Other books you might like:
Jules Feiffer, *Meanwhile . . .* , 1997
    A little boy becomes so engrossed in his comic book that he becomes a part of the adventures.
Marilyn Haffner, *A Year with Molly and Emmett*, 1997
    Stars of a comic strip first featured in *Ladybug* magazine appear in this book that highlights a year in their life.
Art Spiegelman, *Little Lit: Folklore & Fairy Tale Funnies*, 2000
    This anthology tells classic folklore and fairy tale stories in comic-book format.

803

DAVID KLASS

Home of the Braves

(New York: Frances Foster Books/Farrar Straus Giroux, 2002)

Subject(s): Sports/Soccer; Schools/High Schools; School Life
Age range(s): Grades 9-12
Major character(s): Joe Brickman, 12th Grader, Soccer Player; Antonio "the Phenom" Silva, Soccer Player; Ed "the Mouse" McBean, 12th Grader; Kris, 12th Grader
Time period(s): 2000s
Locale(s): Lawndale, New Jersey

Summary: Though neither team is outstanding, Joe looks forward to his senior year when he'll be captain of both the wrestling and the soccer team. When "the Phenom," the outstanding Brazilian soccer player Antonio Silva, transfers to Lawndale High, the soccer team's chances for winning look up. Though Joe extends a hand in friendship and invites him to join the team, Antonio is too cool for such an amateur player and not only spurns the soccer team but also proceeds to date Kris, the girl Joe wanted to ask out. Cajoling by the staff and faculty changes Antonio's mind and he joins the team, but his career is limited by his arrogant attitude. Up until now Joe's been a good enough athlete that he manages to stay out of the mainstream and isn't bullied by the football players, most of whom are bused into the school from Bankside, a tough area by the Hudson River. However his "don't become involved" attitude changes when his good friend Ed "the Mouse" is beaten up by the football crowd. Balancing the conceited Antonio, the meek Ed, and the unattainable Kris are an effort for Joe, but his growing maturity helps him keep everyone at the right distance in another strong offering by a talented author. (312 pages)

Where it's reviewed:
Bulletin of the Center for Children's Books, December 2002, page 162
Horn Book, January 2003, page 77
Publishers Weekly, October 14, 2002, page 85
School Library Journal, September 2002, page 226
Voice of Youth Advocates, October 2002, page 280

Other books by the same author:
You Don't Know Me, 2001
Screen Test, 1997
Danger Zone, 1996
California Blue, 1994
Wrestling with Honor, 1989

Other books you might like:
Nancy Garden, *Peace, O River*, 1986
Kate tries but fails to stop the silly feuding between the white- and blue-collar segments of her community.
Gordon Korman, *Jake, Reinvented*, 2001
Trying to woo Didi away from football star Todd, Jake remakes himself and throws great parties, until one gets out of hand.
Robert Lehrman, *Juggling*, 1982
Howie learns to juggle life, just as he learns to juggle soccer balls, especially when the girl he thinks he loves dates two other guys.

804

LISA WILLIAMS KLINE

The Princesses of Atlantis
(Chicago: Cricket Books, 2002)

Subject(s): Friendship; Identity; Authorship
Age range(s): Grades 5-7
Major character(s): Carly Lewis, 12-Year-Old, 7th Grader; Arlene Welch, 12-Year-Old, 7th Grader; Zack Wingo, 7th Grader; Whitney, 7th Grader (new student)
Time period(s): 2000s
Locale(s): North Carolina

Summary: Friends since second grade, Carly and Arlene find their interests diverging as they begin their seventh grade year. Though the two write a novel about the last days of Atlantis that stars two young princesses, the project seems to be their only mutual interest as the school year moves along. Carly has a crush on Zack and befriends Whitney, a new student who seems poised to bring Carly along into the popular crowd. Arlene bemoans her glasses, ears that stick out and "pleasingly plump" body and always has the correct, sometimes lengthy, answer in class. As the two friends meet in Carly's room to continue their novel, the activities of the two princesses parallel their lives; luckily Carly gets herself into some trouble and reevaluates what it means to be a friend in these confusing days of middle school. (174 pages)

Where it's reviewed:
Booklist, April 15, 2002, page 1401
Horn Book Guide, Fall 2002, page 375
Kirkus Reviews, April 1, 2002, page 494
School Library Journal, July 2002, page 122

Other books by the same author:
Floods, 2004
Eleanor Hill, 1999

Other books you might like:
Andrew Clements, *The School Story*, 2001
Twelve-year-old Natalie and her friend Zoe work on a plan to get Natalie's novel published.

Amy Goldman Koss, *The Girls*, 2000
A group of five friends reduces itself to four as leader Candace decides Maya is out of the clique.
Richard Peck, *Princess Ashley*, 1987
New student Chelsea is thrilled to be included in Ashley's "in" group, not realizing she's just being used.
Karen Salmansohn, *One Puppy, Three Tales*, 2001
Alexandra has lots to say about her family and her life, including deciding which school clique is right for her.
Rachel Vail, *The Friendship Ring Series*, 1991-1998
CJ, Zoe and Morgan face middle school worries, including whom to please, wanting a best friend or speaking up in class.

805

SUZY KLINE

Herbie Jones Moves On
(New York: Putnam, 2003)

Series: Herbie Jones. Book 9
Subject(s): Friendship; Moving, Household; Change
Age range(s): Grades 2-4
Major character(s): Herbie Jones, 4th Grader, Friend; Raymond Martin, 4th Grader, Friend
Time period(s): 2000s (2003)
Locale(s): Connecticut

Summary: Herbie has a hard time adjusting when he learns that Ray is moving to Texas. After attempts to sabotage the sale of the Martin's home fail, Herbie resigns himself to Ray's departure. He even helps plan Ray's farewell party at school. However, after all the moving plans and goodbyes, Ray shows up unexpectedly in class on Monday morning. His family decided to stay in town after all. (78 pages)

Where it's reviewed:
Publishers Weekly, June 9, 2003, page 54
School Library Journal, June 2003, page 110

Other books by the same author:
Horrible Harry Goes to the Moon, 2000
Herbie Jones and Hamburger Head, 1989 (Herbie Jones Book 5)
Herbie Jones, 1985 (Herbie Jones Book 1)

Other books you might like:
Paula Danziger, *Amber Brown Is Not a Crayon*, 1994
Amber has a hard time adjusting to the idea of her best friend Justin moving away.
Patricia Reilly Giff, *Sunny-Side Up*, 1986
After learning that his friend Matthew is moving Beast develops a plan to hide Matthew in his garage.
Bernard Waber, *Ira Says Goodbye*, 1988
Ira's best friend Reggie and his family are moving. Ira worries that Reggie isn't as upset about the changes the move brings as Ira is.

806

SUZY KLINE
FRANK REMKIEWICZ, Illustrator

Horrible Harry and the Dragon War

(New York: Viking, 2002)

Subject(s): Friendship; Schools; Korean Americans
Age range(s): Grades 2-3
Major character(s): Doug, 3rd Grader, Narrator; Song Lee Park, 3rd Grader, Friend; Harry Spooger, 3rd Grader, Friend
Time period(s): 2000s
Locale(s): United States

Summary: No one in class 3B expects a class project to create a war between Harry and Song Lee, each of whom selects a dragon as the literary animal for the project. Doug feels stuck in the middle between Harry and his vision of a terrifying, fire-breathing dragon and Song Lee with her image of a beautiful, gentle dragon. Losing a kickball game helps Harry finally realize how hurtful it was to Song Lee when he called her dragon stupid and he apologizes. Online research reveals that both Harry and Song Lee are right about their interpretation of dragons: western cultures portray dragons as Harry knows them and Eastern cultures recognize wise and friendly dragons. (51 pages)

Where it's reviewed:
Booklist, June 2002, page 1740
School Library Journal, August 2002, page 159

Other books by the same author:
Horrible Harry and the Locked Closet, 2004
Horrible Harry and the Mud Gremlins, 2003
Horrible Harry's Holiday Story, 2003

Other books you might like:
Andrew Clements, Jake Drake, Know-It-All, 2001
   Third grader Jake's desire to win a science fair is so strong that it keeps him from enjoying either the project or his friendship with Willie.
Betsy Duffey, How to Be Cool in the Third Grade, 1993
   Robbie views third grade as an opportunity to grow and change.
Patricia Reilly Giff, The Secret at the Polk Street School, 1987
   One title in a series tells about the many adventures of students at Polk Street School.
Colleen O'Shaughnessy McKenna, Good Grief . . . Third Grade, 1993
   Marsha's goal to improve her behavior this year is challenged when troublesome Roger is assigned as her classroom buddy.

807

JOAN MACPHAIL KNIGHT
MELISSA SWEET, Illustrator

Charlotte in Paris

(San Francisco: Chronicle Books, 2003)

Subject(s): Artists and Art; Diaries; Travel
Age range(s): Grades 2-5
Major character(s): Charlotte Glidden, Child, Daughter
Time period(s): 1890s (1893)
Locale(s): Paris, France

Summary: American expatriate Charlotte lives with her painter parents in Giverny. When the family moves to Paris for six months to study at the Academie Julian, Charlotte is thrilled to explore the big city. She enjoys visiting the Louvre, the Eiffel Tower, and other Parisian landmarks and strikes up a friendship with another painter's daughter. (52 pages)

Where it's reviewed:
Booklist, November 1, 2003, page 510
Publishers Weekly, October 6, 2003, page 86
School Library Journal, January, 2004, page 100

Other books by the same author:
Charlotte in Giverny, 2000

Other books you might like:
Anni Axworthy, Anni's Diary of France, 1994
   In her diary Anni describes a family trip to France.
Christina Bjork, Linnea in Monet's Garden, 1987
   Linnea travels to France with an elderly neighbor to see Monet's garden.
Claudia Mauner, Zoe Sophia's Scrapbook: An Adventure in Venice, 2003
   Zoe Sophia documents in a scrapbook a trip to visit her great-aunt in Venice.

808

LEE KOCHENDERFER

The Victory Garden

(New York: Delacorte/Random House, 2002)

Subject(s): World War II; Gardens and Gardening
Age range(s): Grades 4-6
Major character(s): Teresa Marks, 11-Year-Old; Tom Burt, Aged Person, Gardener
Time period(s): 1940s (1943)
Locale(s): Kansas

Summary: With her older brother a bomber pilot overseas during World War II, Teresa's father and their neighbor Mr. Burt have a friendly competition over who can grow the best tomatoes, a competition that helps take their minds off the war. One day Mr. Burt is hurt in a tractor accident and is hospitalized for a long stay. Teresa worries that the plants in his huge victory garden will die or be plowed under so she rallies her classmates to help tend the garden. At season's end they sell the vegetables and buy war stamps to aid the war effort in a charming first novel. (166 pages)

Where it's reviewed:
Booklist, March 1, 2002, page 1147
Bulletin of the Center for Children's Books, March 2002, page 245
Kirkus Reviews, December 1, 2001, page 1686
Publishers Weekly, January 14, 2002, page 61
School Library Journal, January 2002, page 136

Other books you might like:
Patricia Baird Greene, The Sabbath Garden, 1993
   African-American teen Opie and her Jewish neighbor Sol-

omon Leshko form an unlikely friendship as they build a ''Sabbath Garden'' for their community.

Carol Matas, *The Garden*, 1997
Living on a kibbutz in the late 1940s, Ruth loves tending her peaceful, serene garden and is crushed when it's destroyed.

Mary Pope Osborne, *My Secret War: The World War II Diary of Madeline Beck*, 2000
Maddie feels better when she helps the war effort by collecting scrap metal and newspapers.

809

RON KOERTGE

Shakespeare Bats Cleanup

(Cambridge, MS: Candlewick Press, 2003)

Subject(s): Poetry; Sports/Baseball; Authorship
Age range(s): Grades 6-9
Major character(s): Kevin Boland, Baseball Player (1st baseman), 14-Year-Old; Mira Hidalgo, 14-Year-Old
Time period(s): 2000s
Locale(s): Los Angeles, California

Summary: The Most Valuable Player on his junior high's baseball team shouldn't have mono, but he does. Kevin rests, and rests, and rests some more as he tries to regain his strength after being ill. His father is a writer so it's no surprise that he tries to keep Kevin occupied by giving him a black and white marbled notebook and suggesting he keep a journal. As Kevin writes some thoughts, he sneaks into the den and removes a book on how to write poetry from his father's shelves. Back in his bedroom he tries a little haiku, mainly because it is short; then switches to a sonnet, which with its fourteen syllables and need to rhyme, is too hard; then Kevin even tries a sestina. More than anything, though, he enjoys the free verse where he lets his thoughts wander from his grief over his mother's recent death to a potential girlfriend named Mira, and from his supportive dad to his baseball teammates. Kevin discovers that poetry is ''almost as cool as baseball.'' (116 pages)

Where it's reviewed:
Bulletin of the Center for Children's Books, July 2003, page 453
Horn Book, July 2003, page 461
Publishers Weekly, February 17, 2003, page 76
School Library Journal, May 2003, page 156
Voice of Youth Advocates, August 2003, page 226

Awards the book has won:
Center for Children's Books Best Books, 2003

Other books by the same author:
Margaux with an X, 2004
Stoner & Spaz, 2002
The Brimstone Journals, 2001
Confess-O-Rama, 1996
Tiger, Tiger, Burning Bright: A Novel, 1994
The Arizona Kid, 1988

Other books you might like:
Chris Crutcher, *The Crazy Horse Electric Game*, 1987
After being hit by a pitch, Willie's sense of balance is

---

impaired and, unable to accept his disability, he runs away from home.

Helen Frost, *Keesha's House*, 2003
A combination of sestinas, sonnets and other verse forms tell of Keesha's House, which offers sanctuary to all who need it.

Robert Newton Peck, *Extra Innings*, 2001
Unable to play baseball anymore, Tate is inspired to write a book about Aunt Vidalia's life traveling with the all-black baseball team Ethiopia's Clowns.

810

RON KOERTGE

Stoner & Spaz

(Cambridge, MA: Candlewick Press, 2002)

Subject(s): Drugs; Physically Handicapped; Movies
Age range(s): Grades 9-12
Major character(s): Ben ''Spaz'' Bancroft, 16-Year-Old, Handicapped (cerebral palsy); Colleen ''Stoner'' Minou, 16-Year-Old, Addict; Marcie Sorrels, Filmmaker
Time period(s): 2000s
Locale(s): Los Angeles, California

Summary: Living with his caring but overly protective grandmother, Ben's cerebral palsy so embarrasses him that he avoids classmates and looks forward to Saturdays watching old movies at the Rialto Theatre. One afternoon at the theater, he is startled when Colleen sits next to him and falls asleep with her head on his shoulder. His grandmother doesn't approve of this tattooed, usually stoned classmate of Ben's, especially after she throws up on her Cadillac, but Ben loves having a friend and doesn't care that the friendship is a little one-sided. At the same time, his neighbor Marcie interests him in filmmaking and all of a sudden Ben has to talk to people in order to create a film about high school life. His grandmother changes from protective to displeased; Colleen sobers up now and then, though she eventually returns to her old ways; and Ben finds new friends among other film fans, once he learns to let them become friends. (169 pages)

Where it's reviewed:
Booklist, May 1, 2002, page 1521
Bulletin of the Center for Children's Books, March 2002, page 246
Horn Book, July 2002, page 464
School Library Journal, April 2002, page 150
Voice of Youth Advocates, April 2002, page 44

Awards the book has won:
ALA Best Books for Young Adults, 2003
ALA Quick Picks for Reluctant Young Adult Readers, 2003

Other books by the same author:
Margaux with an X, 2004
Shakespeare Bats Cleanup, 2003
The Brimstone Journals, 2001

Other books you might like:
Elizabeth Feuer, *Paper Doll*, 1990
Leslie's interest in Jeff, a young man with cerebral palsy, leads to family arguments.

David Hill, *See Ya, Simon*, 1994

Though confined to a wheelchair due to muscular dystrophy, and with only a few more years to life, Simon makes the most of every moment.

Terry Trueman, *Stuck in Neutral*, 2000

Unable to speak because of cerebral palsy, no one can appreciate Shawn's wonderful sense of humor and gift of total recall.

811

KATHE KOJA

Buddha Boy

(New York: Frances Foster Books/Farrar Straus Giroux, 2003)

Subject(s): Conduct of Life; Peer Pressure; Schools/High Schools
Age range(s): Grades 7-10
Major character(s): Michael/Jinsen ''Buddha Boy'' Martin, 10th Grader, Artist; Justin, 10th Grader
Time period(s): 2000s
Locale(s): United States

Summary: Preferring to stay under the radar of his high school classmates, Justin is noticed when he's paired with Jinsen for an economics project. Jinsen, nicknamed ''Buddha Boy'' by the school thugs, shaves his head, begs for lunch money and tries to lead a life according to Buddhist principles, all of which sets him up as a target for bullies. Justin sees another side to Jinsen when his artistic talent becomes apparent as they work on their joint project. Gradually Jinsen reveals his need to remain calm, a discipline he learned from his Buddhist teacher after his parents died and he became catatonic. Even Jinsen's new-found strength is tested when the school bullies destroy one of his art projects. (117 pages)

Where it's reviewed:
Bulletin of the Center for Children's Books, June 2003, page 407
Horn Book, May 2003, page 350
Publishers Weekly, January 6, 2003, page 60
School Library Journal, February 2003, page 142
Voice of Youth Advocates, April 2003, page 52

Awards the book has won:
Bulletin of the Center for Children's Books Blue Ribbons, 2003
ALA Best Books for Young Adults, 2004

Other books by the same author:
Talk, 2005
The Blue Mirror, 2004
Straydog, 2002

Other books you might like:
Robert Cormier, *We All Fall Down*, 1991

After Jane's house is wantonly trashed, she and her new boyfriend, ironically a culprit in the crime, both become victims of the Avenger.

Chris Crutcher, *Ironman*, 1995

A domineering, sadistic father works hard to make a ''man'' of Bo, but instead turns him into a teen who resists authority.

Norma Fox Mazer, *Out of Control*, 1993

Mean-spirited physical revenge for an imagined insult haunts the victim and her attackers, even when they all try to pretend nothing happened.

Gary Paulsen, *The Boy Who Owned the School*, 1990

Jacob's quest to pass through high school undetected fails when he falls for Maria who plays the Wicked Witch of the West in the school play.

Mark Salzman, *The Laughing Sutra*, 1991

In a rollicking adventure, Hsun-ching, accompanied by an ancient warrior, travels to America to locate a Buddhist document for his guardian.

812

KATHE KOJA

Straydog

(New York: Farrar Straus Giroux, 2002)

Subject(s): Animals/Dogs; Individuality; Writing
Age range(s): Grades 7-10
Major character(s): Rachel, Student—High School, Writer; Griffin, Student—High School, Writer; Mrs. Cruzzelle, Teacher (language arts); Grrl, Dog (collie)
Time period(s): 2000s
Locale(s): United States

Summary: A loner at school, smart but an outcast because she's different, Rachel survives through her writing and by volunteering at the animal shelter. One day a beautiful, feral collie is brought in that touches Rachel's heart and she is determined to adopt her, though she knows feral dogs are usually euthanized. Calling the collie Grrl, Rachel incorporates the dog into a competitive essay her advanced language arts teacher encourages her to write. Mrs. Cruzzelle also asks Rachel to become the writing partner of Griffin, a new student, with whom she gradually becomes friends. When Grrl attacks shelter workers and has to be euthanized, Rachel takes her anger out on the shelter office and is asked to stop volunteering. It's difficult for Rachel to trust anyone or let them enter her world, but after Grrl dies she reassesses her life and tries to rebuild her friendship with Griffin and with her mother, whom she's always considered overprotective. Adopting a dog at Pet Depot helps a lot, too. (106 pages)

Where it's reviewed:
Booklist, April 15, 2002, page 1395
Horn Book, May 2002, page 333
Publishers Weekly, March 25, 2002, page 66
School Library Journal, April 2002, page 150
Voice of Youth Advocates, June 2002, page 119

Other books by the same author:
Talk, 2005
The Blue Mirror, 2004
Buddha Boy, 2003

Other books you might like:
Lynn Hall, *Windsong*, 1992

Marty saves a greyhound that's the runt of the litter, but then has to find a home for Windsong when her brother's allergies act up.

John Marsden, *Checkers*, 1998
Upset about the unfavorable publicity Warner's dog Checkers brings his family, her father stabs the dog, which breaks Warner's heart.

Rob Thomas, *Rats Saw God*, 1996
One English credit shy of graduation, Steve's guidance counselor suggests he write a 100-page essay about anything he knows.

813

BOB KOLAR, Author/Illustrator

Racer Dogs

(New York: Dutton Children's Books, 2003)

Subject(s): Animals/Dogs; Automobiles; Stories in Rhyme
Age range(s): Grades K-2
Time period(s): Indeterminate
Locale(s): Fictional Country

Summary: Eight dogs prepare for a motorcar race. The excitement mounts; each driver is eager to win. Problems arise during the race and there is a pile-up on the track until a tow truck clears the way. As they near the finish line the wrong-way driver causes another accident and no one can agree on a winner since all the cars are in a heap. The dogs finish the day by washing the cars and the drivers. (32 pages)

Where it's reviewed:
Bulletin of the Center for Children's Books, April 2003, page 318
Publishers Weekly, December 23, 2002, page 69
School Library Journal, March 2003, page 198

Other books by the same author:
Do You Want to Play?: A Book about Friends, 1999
Stomp, Stomp!, 1997

Other books you might like:
P.D. Eastman, *Go, Dog, Go!*, 1961
Dogs of many hues enjoy going places by car and other means of transportation too in this lively beginning reader.
Richard Scarry, *Richard Scarry's Cars and Trucks and Things that Go*, 1974
As the Pig family drives to the beach they see many kinds of vehicles on the road.
James Stevenson, *The Mud Flat Olympics*, 1994
Annually a competitive group of animal friends hold their own wacky version of the Olympics.

814

JACKIE FRENCH KOLLER
JANET PEDERSEN, Illustrator

Baby for Sale

(New York: Marshall Cavendish, 2002)

Subject(s): Brothers and Sisters; Babies; Behavior
Age range(s): Grades K-3
Major character(s): Peter, Rabbit, Brother (older); Emily, Rabbit, Sister (younger)
Time period(s): Indeterminate
Locale(s): Fictional Country

Summary: Peter's tolerated a lot from Emily since her birth but finding his new baseball cap in the toilet is more than he can handle. So, Peter loads Emily in the wagon and sets off to sell her to anyone willing to buy her. To each community member Peter meets he pitches one of Emily's attributes. Her behavior is usually contradictory to the positive quality Peter is promoting but Peter continues through the neighborhood. As Peter is trying to convince one neighbor to buy Emily she toddles away and Peter has to hurry to grab her before she steps into the street in front of car. After that Peter puts Emily back in the wagon and pulls her home. (32 pages)

Where it's reviewed:
Booklist, September 1, 2002, page 136
Publishers Weekly, August 12, 2002, page 299
School Library Journal, September 2002, page 196

Other books by the same author:
Bouncing on the Bed, 1999
One Monkey Too Many, 1999
No Such Thing, 1997

Other books you might like:
Martha Alexander, *Nobody Asked Me If I Wanted a Baby Sister*, 1977
Despite the fact that too much attention is paid to his baby sister, a little boy begrudgingly admits to feeling some affection for her.
Jane Cutler, *Darcy and Gran Don't Like Babies*, 1993
Darcy and Gran expect to like Darcy's baby brother better when he's a little older.
Anne Gutman, *Lisa's Baby Sister*, 2003
At first Lisa is not at all happy with the new baby because she gets all the attention that Lisa needs.
Kevin Henkes, *Julius, the Baby of the World*, 1990
Lilly does not share her parents' high opinion of baby brother Julius but defends him when cousin Garland makes disparaging remarks about him.
Jonathan London, *Froggy's Baby Sister*, 2003
Froggy hoped for a brother but plans to make the best of the situation as soon as his baby sister grows big enough to play.

815

JACKIE FRENCH KOLLER

Someday: A Novel

(New York: Orchard/Scholastic, 2002)

Subject(s): Family Life; Friendship; Grandmothers
Age range(s): Grades 6-8
Major character(s): Cecelia "Celie" Wheeler, 14-Year-Old, 8th Grader; Randall "Chubby" Miller, 8th Grader
Time period(s): 1930s
Locale(s): Enfield, Massachusetts

Summary: Celie, her mother and grandmother have always know that "someday" would come when they'd have to leave their homes in the Swift River Valley before it was flooded for the proposed reservoir for Boston's water supply. The notice arrives and Celie watches how her mother and grandmother react: her mother can hardly wait to move to a city to live while her grandmother refuses to sell the land that's been in their family for over two hundred years. The "last" of every event is described, from Celie and Chubby's graduation to the last wedding ever held in the town and the last town social. When Celie's best friend Chubby tells her how much he cares for her, she realizes that "lasts" can sometimes be "firsts" for she's never before been interested in a boy. This delightful coming-of-age tale is based on a true incident when the Quabbin Reservoir was built. (215 pages)

Where it's reviewed:
Booklist, June 2002, page 1723
Bulletin of the Center for Children's Books, October 2002, page 64
Publishers Weekly, July 1, 2002, page 80
School Library Journal, July 2002, page 122
Voice of Youth Advocates, June 2002, page 119

Other books by the same author:
Falcon, 1998
A Place to Call Home, 1995
The Last Voyage of the Misty Day, 1992
The Primrose Way, 1992
Nothing to Fear, 1991

Other books you might like:
Brian Doyle, *Mary Ann Alice*, 2002
    The life of a small, close-knit farming community changes when plans are announced to dam the Gatineau River.
Tony Earley, *Jim the Boy*, 2000
    Raised by his mother and her three bachelor brothers, Jim remembers the day that electricity came to his small town of Aliceville.
L.M. Montgomery, *Anne of Green Gables*, 1935
    First in a series of books about high-spirited, mischievous Anne who lives in Canada.

816

GORDON KORMAN

Jake, Reinvented
(New York: Hyperion, 2003)

Subject(s): Peer Pressure; Self-Perception
Age range(s): Grades 9-12
Major character(s): Jacob "Jake" Garrett, 12-Year-Old, Football Player; Didi Ray, Girlfriend (of Todd); Todd Buckley, 12th Grader, Football Player (quarterback); Richard "Rick" Paradis, Narrator, Football Player (kicker)
Time period(s): 2000s
Locale(s): United States

Summary: With a wink at F. Scott Fitzgerald's *The Great Gatsby*, this book introduces Jake Garrett, who emerges on the high school scene as the coolest guy around. He drives a BMW, stars on the football field, throws great parties and dresses better than anyone else around. Prepared to dislike any student this cool, narrator Rick discovers as he watches the guy in action that he likes him. It soon becomes obvious that Jake has a plan to lure Didi away from football quarterback Todd, a plan that began several years earlier when he was a nerd who tutored Didi in mathematics. Now he's remade himself to attract her attention. When one of Jake's

parties gets out of hand, Jake takes the blame for Didi and reverts to his former self. (213 pages)

Where it's reviewed:
Booklist, December 15, 2003, page 659
Bulletin of the Center for Children's Books, November 2003, page 112
Kliatt, January 2004, page 8
Publishers Weekly, October 6, 2003, page 86
School Library Journal, February 2004, page 148

Awards the book has won:
ALA Best Books for Young Adults, 2004

Other books by the same author:
Son of the Mob: Hollywood Hustle, 2004
Maxx Comedy: The Funniest Kid in America, 2003
Son of the Mob, 2002
No More Dead Dogs, 2000
Chicken Doesn't Skate, 1996

Other books you might like:
F. Scott Fitzgerald, *The Great Gatsby*, 1925
    Jay Gatsby hosts lavish parties as he attempts to woo Daisy Buchanan away from her crass husband.
Kathe Koja, *Buddha Boy*, 2003
    Jinsen tries to live by Buddhist principles, which makes him different from his classmates and sets him up for their bullying.
Jerry Spinelli, *Stargirl*, 2000
    Stargirl rocks Mica High School, but she isn't prepared for the fickle roller coaster of popularity for nonconformists.

817

GORDON KORMAN

Maxx Comedy: The Funniest Kid in America
(New York: Hyperion, 2003)

Subject(s): Comedians; Contests; Stepfamilies
Age range(s): Grades 4-6
Major character(s): Max "Maxx Comedy" Carmody, 6th Grader, Entertainer
Time period(s): 2000s
Locale(s): Bartonsville, Ohio

Summary: Ever since he was young, Max has dreamed of being a stand-up comedian and it looks as though his chance for discovery has finally arrived. Reading of a talent search to find "The Funniest Kid in America," which pays $1000 and provides a television appearance, Max knows this is his moment. To even be considered he must submit a video of his comedy routine and for that he needs his friends, not only for the comedy scenes but also to provide the laugh track. Unfortunately, as bumbling as Max is, now renamed Maxx Comedy for the contest, so are his friends which means that no scene ever goes perfectly. Matter of fact, Maxx is such a bumbler that he shows up late for the contest and then, when given a second chance, muffs up again in another humorous tale from a talented author. (153 pages)

Where it's reviewed:
Booklist, June 2003, page 1777

Kirkus Reviews, June 1, 2003, page 806
Owl, September 2003, page 11
Publishers Weekly, June 16, 2003, page 71
School Library Journal, September 2003, page 216

Other books by the same author:
Discovery, 2003
Jake, Reinvented, 2003
Son of the Mob, 2002
No More Dead Dogs, 2000
Chicken Doesn't Skate, 1996

Other books you might like:
Robin Brancato, *Come Alive at 505*, 1980
    Danny is a first-rate DJ who doesn't care that his radio station doesn't extend beyond the walls of his room; it doesn't matter, he's having fun.
Ellen Conford, *Strictly for Laughs*, 1985
    Comedienne wannabe Joey can't understand why her friend Peter invites Dinah ''the warbler'' on his late-night radio show instead of her.
Jean Davies Okimoto, *Talent Night*, 1995
    Rodney has one goal that's driving his life: becoming the first Asian rap star, even though he's actually part Polish as well as part Asian.
Carol Lynch Williams, *My Angelica*, 1999
    Hoping to follow the same path as her romance writer mother, Sage is mortified when told she's won the school prize for best satire of romance novels.

818

GORDON KORMAN

Son of the Mob

(New York: Hyperion, 2002)

Subject(s): Organized Crime; Humor; Dating (Social Customs)
Age range(s): Grades 7-10
Major character(s): Vincent ''Vince'' Luca, 12th Grader, 17-Year-Old; Kendra Bightly, Girlfriend (of Vince), Journalist (school newspaper); Anthony ''Honest Abe'' Luca, Organized Crime Figure, Father (of Vince); Agent Bightly, FBI Agent
Time period(s): 2000s
Locale(s): New York

Summary: No matter how he tries to escape it, Vince can't avoid the ''family business,'' which is his father, ''Honest Abe,'' being the crime boss for New York. Vince makes it perfectly clear to his father and older brother that he is not part of the business and just wants to lead a typical high school life. When he finally falls for Kendra Bightly, little does he know that her father is FBI Agent ''Bite Me,'' to whom his father has said good night for the last two years, taunting him via all the wiretaps and bugs that fill their house. Some intricate timing is required to keep Kendra from meeting his father, and Vince from meeting hers, and he never wants the two fathers to be together. Vince is inadvertently involved in the ''family business'' when his older brother turns Vince's class project, a cat lover's website, into a site for betting or when he feels sorry for two losers who work for his dad and

need money to pay off some loan sharks. Vince's actions are hilarious and guaranteed to draw a guffaw. (262 pages)

Where it's reviewed:
Booklist, November 1, 2002, page 485
Publishers Weekly, October 28, 2002, page 73
Quill & Quire, July 2002, page 49
School Library Journal, November 2002, page 170
Voice of Youth Advocates, February 2003, page 477

Awards the book has won:
ALA Best Books for Young Adults, 2003
ALA Quick Picks for Reluctant Young Adult Readers, 2003

Other books by the same author:
Son of the Mob: Hollywood Hustle, 2004
Discovery, 2003
Maxx Comedy: The Funniest Kid in America, 2003
Jake, Reinvented, 2003
No More Dead Dogs, 2000

Other books you might like:
Jay Bennett, *Say Hello to the Hit Man*, 1977
    When Fred receives a strange phone call warning him of his upcoming death, he's convinced it's because his father's a gangster.
Richard Peck, *Through a Brief Darkness*, 1973
    Karen's never been sure whether or not her father's affiliated with the Mafia, until his enemies kidnap her.
Susan Beth Pfeffer, *Most Precious Blood*, 1991
    Val learns she's adopted and her father's criminal ties may have forced her real parents to give her up for adoption.

819

MARC KORNBLATT

Izzy's Place

(New York: Margaret K. McElderry/Simon & Schuster, 2003)

Subject(s): Family Problems; Death; Grandparents
Age range(s): Grades 4-6
Major character(s): Henry Stone, 5th Grader; Mr. Fine, Aged Person; Grandma Martha, Grandmother
Time period(s): 2000s
Locale(s): Indiana

Summary: The constant bickering of his parents upsets Henry so much that the psychiatrist suggests he spend the summer with his grandmother. Henry's not too excited about the idea, for his beloved Grandpa Jay died recently, but he's not too thrilled about being at home, either. So it's off to Indiana for Henry while his parents try to sort out their marriage. Unfortunately, there aren't any nice kids to play with and his grandmother drags him to her jewelry shop each day. When Henry's befriended by a neighbor, Mr. Fine, he learns a valuable lesson in controlling one'ss sadness. Just as Mr. Fine practices his violin daily to ease his sorrow over the death of his son, so too does Henry practice his juggling to ease the stress over his turbulent life. (118 pages)

Where it's reviewed:
Booklist, June 1, 2003, page 1777
Bulletin of the Center for Children's Books, June 2003, page 407
Horn Book Guide, Fall 2003, page 369

Kirkus Reviews, May 15, 2003, page 752
School Library Journal, July 2003, page 131

Other books by the same author:
Understanding Buddy, 2001

Other books you might like:
W.E. Butterworth, *LeRoy and the Old Man*, 1980
  Sent to live with his grandfather after some trouble in his Chicago projects, LeRoy learns more from him than just the shrimp trade.
Betsy Byars, *Coast to Coast*, 1992
  Faced with going into a retirement home, Pop and his granddaughter Birch sneak off for one last cross-country flight in his Piper J-3 Cub.
Michelle Magorian, *Goodnight, Mr. Tom*, 1982
  Reclusive widower Tom Oakley and an abused eight-year-old boy form a lasting friendship during World War II.

820

AMY GOLDMAN KOSS

The Cheat

(New York: Dial, 2003)

Subject(s): Cheating; School Life
Age range(s): Grades 6-8
Major character(s): Katie, 8th Grader; Sarah Collier, 8th Grader; Jake Broder, 8th Grader; Daniel "Dan" Brand, 8th Grader; Robert "Rob" King, 8th Grader
Time period(s): 2000s
Locale(s): United States

Summary: Wanting to impress Sarah, Jake offers her a copy of the geography midterm exam from last year. Sarah, in turn, provides a copy to her best friend Katie, as well as Dan and Rob. Together Sarah and Katie memorize the multiple choice answers, even making up a song so they can remember the A, B, C order. During the exam Katie panics and doesn't use their device though Sarah, Dan and Rob complete theirs with the purloined answers; unfortunately, this exam is different from last year's. What follows varies among the individuals: Sarah's mother blames everything on her ex-husband; Dan's father laughs off the incident; Rob runs away rather than face a beating from his father; Katie and Sarah face some glitches in their friendship; and Jake just hopes his role isn't revealed. (176 pages)

Where it's reviewed:
Booklist, January 2003, page 890
Bulletin of the Center for Children's Books, February 2003, page 240
Publishers Weekly, December 9, 2002, page 85
School Library Journal, January 2003, page 140
Voice of Youth Advocates, April 2003, page 52

Other books by the same author:
Gossip Times Three, 2003
Stolen Words, 2001
Stranger in Dadland, 2001
Strike Two, 2001
The Girls, 2000
The Ashwater Experiment, 1999

Other books you might like:
Linda Ellerbee, *Girl Reporter Sinks School!*, 2000
  Reporter Casey has her investigative work cut out for her when she discovers the editor of her school newspaper bought answers to a math test.
Elizabeth Levy, *Cheater, Cheater*, 1993
  Lucy lies about her bowling score and finds that silly mistake comes back to haunt her when classmates nickname her "cheater."
P.J. Petersen, *Liars*, 1992
  When someone is lying, Sam's arms tingle, but what surprises him is how many people lie, including his own father!

821

AMY GOLDMAN KOSS

Gossip Times Three

(New York: Dial, 2003)

Subject(s): Friendship; Interpersonal Relations
Age range(s): Grades 5-8
Major character(s): Abby, 7th Grader; Bess, 7th Grader; Cristy, 7th Grader; Zack, 7th Grader; Gilda, 16-Year-Old
Time period(s): 2000s
Locale(s): United States

Summary: Abby, Bess and Cristy are good friends, similar in that they each live with divorced mothers, dissimilar in that Cristy's not yet interested in boys, Bess is boy crazy and Abby has had a crush on Zack forever. Their friendship hits rocky ground after Bess comments that Zack is cute and then, three days later, dumps Max so she can go out with Zack. Abby's crushed and Cristy's not sure what to do. Narrated by Gilda, Bess's older sister, this story has been written to complete an assignment for her writing teacher and explores the world of love triangles, romances and friendship. (170 pages)

Where it's reviewed:
Bulletin of the Center for Children's Books, September 2003, page 20
Horn Book, July 2003, page 461
Publishers Weekly, July 17, 2003, page 73
School Library Journal, September 2003, page 216
Voice of Youth Advocates, October 2003, page 312

Other books by the same author:
The Cheat, 2003
Stolen Words, 2001
Strike Two, 2001
Stranger in Dadland, 2001
The Girls, 2000

Other books you might like:
Elizabeth Levy, *Seventh Grade Tango*, 2000
  Paired with her childhood friend Scott for ballroom dancing, Rebecca realizes there's a little chemistry between them.
Phyllis Reynolds Naylor, *The Alice Series*, 1985-
  Motherless Alice and her friends Pamela, Elizabeth and Patrick survive all the traumas of junior high, peer pressure and dating, but now await high school.

Rachel Vail, *The Friendship Ring Series*, 1991-1998

CJ, Zoe, and Morgan know that growing up is tough, even if it's just choosing ballet or a social life, wanting a best friend, or learning to be yourself.

Sally Warner, *Bad Girl Blues*, 2001

Best friends since they were little, Quinney realizes as they've gotten older that she's growing apart from Marguerite and Brynnie.

822

JAN DALE KOUTSKY, Author/Illustrator

My Grandma, My Pen Pal

(Honesdale, PA: Boyds Mill Press, 2002)

Subject(s): Letters; Grandmothers; Love
Age range(s): Grades K-3
Major character(s): Grandma, Grandmother; Unnamed Character, Child (grandchild)
Time period(s): 2000s
Locale(s): United States

Summary: From the moment of a child's birth, Grandma begins building a loving relationship that will span the miles between them. Grandma and grandchild correspond for years in letters with drawings and photos. Over time their correspondence and their shared activities change as they both grow older, one becoming a young adult and one, an elderly person, whose age shows in her shaky handwriting. Not long after Grandma becomes a great-grandmother she dies and her grandchild discovers a scrapbook of all the letters they've exchanged. A concluding author's note encourages correspondence between children and their grandparents. (28 pages)

Where it's reviewed:
Booklist, May 15, 2002, page 1596
Horn Book Guide, Fall 2002, page 335
School Library Journal, June 2002, page 98

Awards the book has won:
IRA Teachers' Choices, 2003

Other books you might like:
Judy Caseley, *Dear Annie*, 1992

A story unfolds in the correspondence between Annie and her grandfather.

Soyung Pak, *Dear Juno*, 1999

Though they live in different countries and speak different languages Juno and his Grandma correspond in a way that each understands.

Eric Valasquez, *Grandma's Records*, 2001

For this grown grandchild, memories of Grandma include summers listening to her collection of records and watching her dance.

Gina Willner-Pardo, *Hunting Grandma's Treasures*, 1996

Grandma leaves a fitting legacy for her grandchildren by planning the annual vacation treasure hunt prior to her death.

823

ERIK P. KRAFT, Author/Illustrator

Lenny and Mel

(New York: Simon & Schuster Books for Young Readers, 2002)

Subject(s): Holidays; Twins; Humor
Age range(s): Grades 2-5
Major character(s): Lenny, Student—Elementary School, Brother; Mel, Student—Elementary School, Brother
Time period(s): 2000s
Locale(s): United States

Summary: Lenny and Mel try to start the new school year on the right foot but their efforts seem to backfire. The same could be said for their Halloween costumes and their plan, the week after Thanksgiving, to leave the leftover turkey under Mel's pillow for the "Leftover Fairy" who, alas, never comes. After Lenny decides that Santa is a vegetarian the boys select a healthy snack for him and decorate a block of jalapeno cheese to leave on Christmas Eve. According to the note Santa leaves, the cheese is now a hood ornament on the sleigh. The dedicated students spend so much time creating papier-mache heads for President's Day that they forget to write the oral report. At least they get double duty from the papier-mache heads when they turn them into pinatas for Cinco de Mayo. (60 pages)

Where it's reviewed:
Booklist, March 1, 2002, page 1136
Horn Book, May 2002, page 333
Publishers Weekly, January 21, 2002, page 90
School Library Journal, February 2002, page 107

Other books by the same author:
Lenny and Mel After-School Confidential, 2004
Lenny and Mel's Summer Vacation, 2003

Other books you might like:
James Marshall, *The Cut-Ups Cut Loose*, 1987

Spud and Joe may have to change their ways; the school principal sees no humor in their antics.

Dav Pilkey, *Captain Underpants and the Wrath of the Wicked Wedgie Woman*, 2001

George and Harold's cartoon, once again, earns them a trip to the principal's office where they begin their usual pranks.

Jon Scieszka, *It's All Greek to Me*, 1999

The intrepid Time Warp trio, while playing their parts in a class play based on Greek mythology, accidentally travel back in time to Mount Olympus.

824

ERIK P. KRAFT, Author/Illustrator

Lenny and Mel's Summer Vacation

(New York: Simon & Schuster Books for Young Readers, 2003)

Subject(s): Twins; Brothers; Vacations
Age range(s): Grades 2-4
Major character(s): Lenny, Brother, Twin; Mel, Brother, Twin
Time period(s): 2000s (2003)
Locale(s): United States

Summary: Lenny and Mel don't share their parents' belief that inactivity leads to a boring summer vacation. To Lenny and Mel doing nothing is the entire reason for a vacation thus they are grateful the camp refused to allow their return this summer. The heat does convince them to get up and create personalized swimming pools out of trash bags and the water hose. Begrudgingly, the boys are dragged to the library, Animal Town, and a family vacation in a small cabin when they are content to stay home and sleep. Before they've reached their nap quota, vacation is over and the beginning of a new school year is only two days away. (58 pages)

Where it's reviewed:

Bulletin of the Center for Children's Books, June 2003, page 408

Publishers Weekly, May 12, 2003, page 69

School Library Journal, August 2003, page 135

Awards the book has won:

Center for Children's Books Best Books, 2003

Other books by the same author:

Lenny and Mel After-School Confidential, 2004

Lenny and Mel, 2002

Chocolatina, 1999

Other books you might like:

Elizabeth Levy, *Take Two, They're Small*, 2002
  Eve probably wishes that her younger twin sisters wanted to sleep all the time; her life would be simpler.

Daniel Pinkwater, *Fat Camp Commandos*, 2001
  Resentful that their parents sent them to despised Camp Noo Yoo, Sylvia and Ralph sneak away with friend Mavis and hide at her house for the summer.

Todd Strasser, *Help! I'm Trapped in the First Day of Summer Camp*, 1997
  Jake is bored by continually reliving the events of the first day of camp.

825

LAURIE KREBS

MELISSA IWAI, Illustrator

The Beeman

(Washington, D.C.: National Geographic, 2002)

Subject(s): Animals/Bees; Grandfathers; Stories in Rhyme

Age range(s): Grades K-2

Major character(s): Grandpa, Grandfather, Beekeeper; Unnamed Character, Child, Relative (granddaughter)

Time period(s): 2000s

Locale(s): United States

Summary: A young girl describes Grandpa's work as the ''Beeman'' in town. The girl understands everything from the protective clothing to the function and structure of the bee's hives. As he works with his granddaughter by his side, Grandpa points out the queen bee, the drone bees, the house bees, and the workers, explaining the role of each. Then, with his granddaughter's help Grandpa extracts the honey, fills jars for the family and returns some to the hives to provide food for the bees during the winter. (32 pages)

Where it's reviewed:

Booklist, October 1, 2002, page 336

Publishers Weekly, September 16, 2002, page 70

School Library Journal, September 2002, page 196

Other books by the same author:

A Day in the Life of a Colonial Doctor, 2004

A Day in the Life of a Colonial Shipwright, 2004

A Day in the Life of a Colonial Miller, 2004

Other books you might like:

Andrea Cheng, *When the Bees Fly Home*, 2002
  Jonathan, son of a beekeeper, receives support from his mother to identify a way that he's able to help his father's work.

Joanna Cole, *The Magic School Bus Inside a Beehive*, 1996
  Mrs. Frizzle takes her class for a closer look at the workings of a beehive colony.

Linda Oatman High, *Beekeepers*, 1998
  On a fine spring morning a little girl helps her grandfather tend his bees.

Mary Thompson, *Gran's Bees*, 1996
  Jessie and her father help Gran, the beekeeper, harvest honey from the frames of honeycombs.

826

STEPHEN KRENSKY

SUSANNA NATTI, Illustrator

Lionel's Birthday

(New York: Dial Books for Young Readers, 2003)

Subject(s): Birthdays; Brothers and Sisters; Humor

Age range(s): Grades 1-3

Major character(s): Lionel, Brother, Son; Louise, Sister, Daughter; Jeffrey, Friend, Child

Time period(s): 2000s

Locale(s): United States

Summary: In four brief stories, Lionel prepares for his birthday. He searches for hidden presents and, when he learns Louise has not yet purchased his present, makes a suggestion about what he wants. To assure he doesn't forget this birthday Lionel creates a time capsule and then discusses with Jeffrey just where to bury it so he'll be able to locate it in the future. The thought of growing older leads Lionel to apply makeup to his face and powder to his hair so he can get an idea about his future appearance. Finally, Lionel's birthday arrives and, after lots of practice, he succeeds in blowing out all the candles with one breath, assuring, he thinks, that for the first time a birthday wish will come true. (48 pages)

Where it's reviewed:

Booklist, July 2003, page 1899

School Library Journal, October 2003, page 129

Other books by the same author:

Lionel at School, 2000

Louise, Soccer Star, 2000

Louise Goes Wild, 1999

Lionel in the Summer, 1998

Lionel and Louise, 1997

Other books you might like:

Paula Danziger, *It's Justin Time, Amber Brown*, 2001
  Amber counts the days until her seventh birthday while fervently hoping to receive a watch as one of her gifts.

Jonathan London, *Shawn and Keeper and the Birthday Party*, 1999

Shawn and his dog Keeper share the same birthday in this book for beginning readers.

Joan Robins, *Addie's Bad Day*, 1993

Good friend Max helps Addie get over her bad hair day and enjoy his birthday party.

827

TRUDY KRISHER

Uncommon Faith

(New York: Holiday House, 2003)

Subject(s): Abolition; Women's Rights; Christian Life
Age range(s): Grades 7-10
Major character(s): Faith Common, 14-Year-Old
Time period(s): 1830s (1837-38)
Locale(s): Millbrook, Massachusetts

Summary: In a small New England town, a fire in a livery stable has killed six citizens, disrupted the townspeople and signaled the beginning of change, a change that often involves the "uncommon Faith." Ten different townspeople, both old and young, offer their understanding of events and people in Millbrook and, through this, readers learn of the strongly opinionated, yet very fair, young lady called Faith. Daughter of a Methodist minister, Faith is not sedate and soft-spoken, as are most women of this time period, but speaks her mind as she thinks necessary. She's the one who makes her classmates see the chauvinism of their teacher who thinks it's unwise to teach women geometry; she's the one who points out the unfairness in pricing by the owner of the general store; and she's the one who supports the abolitionist Quakers who help with the underground railroad. Assured of a spot at the new Mount Holyoke Female Seminary, one knows that Faith won't spend the rest of her life darning socks or spinning and weaving. (263 pages)

Where it's reviewed:
Booklist, October 15, 2003, page 405
Kirkus Reviews, September 15, 2003, page 1176
Publishers Weekly, November 10, 2003, page 63
School Library Journal, October 2003, page 169
Voice of Youth Advocates, October 2003, page 313

Awards the book has won:
ALA Best Books for Young Adults, 2004

Other books by the same author:
Kinship, 1997
Spite Fences, 1994

Other books you might like:
Jennifer L. Holm, *Boston Jane: An Adventure*, 2001
Miss Heppelwhite's proper training doesn't matter now to Jane as she embarks on her new life in the Washington territory.
Philip Pullman, *The Ruby in the Smoke*, 1987
Sally, an orphaned 16-year-old, outmaneuvers a host of villainous 19th-century figures to claim her inheritance and her independence.
Jean Thesman, *The Ornament Tree*, 1996
Bonnie loves being part of a female-dominated household

where the women work proactively for women's suffrage, birth control and an end to child labor.

828

UMA KRISHNASWAMI
SOUMYA SITARAMAN, Illustrator

Chachaji's Cup

(San Francisco: Children's Book Press, 2003)

Subject(s): Aunts and Uncles; Storytelling; Historical
Age range(s): Grades 1-4
Major character(s): Neel, Child, Nephew; Chachaji, Uncle, Storyteller; Daniel, Child, Friend
Time period(s): 2000s; 1940s (1947)
Locale(s): United States; India

Summary: Teatime is a special time at Neel's home. Often Daniel joins the family and Chachaji pours the tea, serves the food and tells the stories. The story about the old teacup Chachaji uses daily for his tea informs Daniel and Neel of the life of refuges after the partition of India in 1947. Neel understands how precious the cup is to Chachaji and he is filled with sorrow and guilt when he drops it while washing dishes one evening. Neel secretly glues the pieces together and presents the repaired cup to his great-uncle, knowing that a broken cup can still hold memories even if it's unable to hold tea. (32 pages)

Where it's reviewed:
Booklist, March 15, 2003, page 1332
Bulletin of the Center for Children's Books, June 2003, page 408
School Library Journal, June 2003, page 110

Other books by the same author:
Monsoon, 2003
Shower of Gold: Girls and Women in the Stories of India, 1999
Broken Tusk: Stories of the Hindu God Ganesha, 1996

Other books you might like:
Sherry Garland, *The Lotus Seed*, 1993
An immigrant to America uses a lotus seed to connect to her birthplace and share her heritage with her children and grandchildren.
Marissa Moss, *The Ugly Menorah*, 1996
After learning the history of Grandma's ugly menorah Rachel understands why it is so important to her recently widowed grandmother.
George Shannon, *This Is the Bird*, 1997
A young girl explains the origins of a simply carved wooden bird that has been in her family for many generations.

829

UMA KRISHNASWAMI
JAMEL AKIB, Illustrator

Monsoon

(New York: Farrar Straus Giroux, 2003)

Subject(s): Weather; Family

Age range(s): Grades K-3
Major character(s): Unnamed Character, Child, Daughter; Mummy, Mother; Papa, Father
Time period(s): 2000s
Locale(s): India

Summary: The hot dry summer wears on people. Papa reminds the family that the heat is needed for the mangoes to ripen and after the monsoon arrives, the dust will be washed away. A little girl worries that the soothing monsoon rains will not come or, if they do, could cause floods. Mummy cautions her to stay close by and not to stay outside too long when playing. Everyone watches the sky for signs of rain clouds and listens to hear thunder over the sounds of traffic. Then one day, the clouds gather, the wind increases and the sound of thunder can be heard in the distance. The soothing, cleansing monsoon rains begin! (32 pages)

Where it's reviewed:
Bulletin of the Center for Children's Books, January 2004, page 196
School Library Journal, December 2003, page 118

Other books by the same author:
Naming Maya, 2004
Chachaji's Cup, 2003
Shower of Gold: Girls and Women in the Stories of India, 1999

Other books you might like:
Verna Aardema, *Bringing the Rain to Kapiti Plain: A Nandi Tale*, 1981
  A rhyming retelling of an African folktale explains how Ki-pat brings the rain to the dry Kapiti Plain and its wildlife.
Joy Cowley, *Singing Down the Rain*, 1997
  Is it coincidence or does a stranger's rhythmic rain song bring the soothing rain to a dry community?
Karen Hesse, *Come On, Rain!*, 1999
  Everyone in Tessie's neighborhood welcomes the cooling rain when it finally comes to soothe their heat-induced irritability.
Manya Stojic, *Rain*, 2000
  A dry African plain is transformed by a rainstorm.

830

STEVEN KROLL
CHRISTINE DAVENIER, Illustrator

That Makes Me Mad!

(New York: SeaStar Books, 2002)

Subject(s): Parent and Child; Behavior; Family Life
Age range(s): Preschool-Grade 1
Major character(s): Nina, Daughter, Sister (older); Mom, Mother; Dad, Father; Tony, Brother (younger), Son
Time period(s): 2000s
Locale(s): United States

Summary: A newly illustrated reissue of a title first published in 1976 presents the many frustrations of Nina. Trying to get dressed without help makes her mad when she can't find the armholes and the buttons don't line up right with the button-holes. Being blamed for making a mess in the bath when it really is Tony's fault makes Nina mad too. Even Mom and Dad make her mad when they promise something and then don't do it or they talk to others about her as if she isn't there or they don't respond quickly when she calls. However, Mom and Dad can also help Nina feel better when they are willing to listen to her anger and frustration. Then she feels very grateful. (32 pages)

Where it's reviewed:
New York Times Book Review, September 29, 2002, page 26
Publishers Weekly, June 10, 2002, page 60
School Library Journal, August 2002, page 160

Other books by the same author:
Tale of Two Dogs, 2004
Patches Lost and Found, 2001 (Booklist Editors' Choice)
Eat!, 1995

Other books you might like:
Molly Bang, *When Sophie Gets Angry—Really, Really Angry . . .*, 1999
  When Sophie's anger explodes in a temper tantrum she runs to her favorite tree and allows the branches to soothe her before returning home.
Mercer Mayer, *I Was So Mad*, 1983
  A child tries different techniques to dissipate angry feelings.
David Shannon, *No, David!*, 1998
  In a Caldecott Honor book David hears, "No, David!" when he misbehaves. After breaking a vase the sad, remorseful boy finally hears, "I love you!"

831

VIRGINIA KROLL
TIM LADWIG, Illustrator

Especially Heroes

(Grand Rapids, MI: Eerdman's Books for Young Readers, 2003)

Subject(s): Heroes and Heroines; Racism; Courage
Age range(s): Grades 3-5
Major character(s): Ginny, 4th Grader, Daughter; Geri Hall, Neighbor, Widow(er); Daddy, Father, Hero
Time period(s): 1960s (1962)
Locale(s): United States

Summary: A class lesson on the Revolutionary War leads to a discussion of martyrs and heroes. After school, while enjoying cocoa and cookies with Mrs. Hall, Ginny is still wondering about the teacher's comment that some heroes are willing to die for a cause in which they believe. Following dinner the family receives a phone call and Daddy rushes out the door with a baseball bat. From the window Ginny can hear men yelling hateful words at Mrs. Hall's home and can see broken windows and racist words painted on Mrs. Hall's car. Two other neighbors arrive with bats to confront the six younger men. Some run off but some are caught as the police cars arrive. Having seen heroes in action, Ginny now has a better understanding of the class lesson on heroism. (32 pages)

Where it's reviewed:
Booklist, February 1, 2003, page 996
Horn Book Guide, Fall 2003, page 329

School Library Journal, April 2003, page 130

Other books by the same author:
Boy, You're Amazing!, 2004
Busy, Busy Mouse, 2003 (IRA Children's Choices)
Butterfly Boy, 2002
Girl, You're Amazing!, 2001

Other books you might like:
Evelyn Coleman, *White Socks Only*, 1996
  In 1950s Mississippi a young black child wearing white socks naively drinks from the ''whites only'' water fountain with unexpected consequences.
Margaree King Mitchell, *Granddaddy's Gift*, 1997
  Despite threats and humiliation in the segregated 1960s, Granddaddy stands up for his constitutional right to vote.
Jacqueline Woodson, *The Other Side*, 2001
  Two girls, one white and one black, refuse to let a fence, or local prejudice, keep them from playing together.

832
PAUL KROPP

The Countess and Me
(Allston, MA: Fitzhenry & Whiteside, 2002)

Subject(s): Trust; Friendship; Moving, Household
Age range(s): Grades 6-9
Major character(s): Jordan Bellemare, 13-Year-Old; Countess von Loewen, Aged Person
Time period(s): 2000s
Locale(s): Surrey, British Columbia, Canada

Summary: New at school, Jordan doesn't yet have any friends so is happy when the eccentric Mrs. von Loewen asks him to help her around the house and in her garden. Said to be a European countess, she also has a cursed quartz skull that she asks Jordan to bury for her in the garden. At school, Jordan has become part of a rather bad group of boys who up to this point only want his homework. But as Jordan brags about burying the skull, and exaggerates about the countess's riches, he inadvertently puts too many ideas into the heads of these boys and they ransack her home. Jordan must now choose between his friendship with the countess or the group of boys in this coming-of-age tale. (142 pages)

Where it's reviewed:
Booklist, October 1, 2002, page 313
Quill & Quire, May 2002, page 34
Resource Links, October 2002, page 35
School Library Journal, November 2002, page 172

Other books by the same author:
Moonkid and Liberty, 1990
Take Off, 1987
Micro Man, 1986

Other books you might like:
Pat Derby, *Visiting Miss Pierce*, 1986
  As part of a school project, Barry visits nursing home resident Miss Pierce and finds his life changed by her stories.
Kenneth E. Ethridge, *Viola, Furgy, Bobbi, and Me*, 1989
  Old Mrs. Viola Spencer hires Stephen to do his yard work,

but their mutual interest in baseball quickly leads to friendship.
Scott Johnson, *One of the Boys*, 1992
  Eric likes being noticed as one of the ''Benbow Boys,'' until their school pranks become malicious.

833
JARRETT J. KROSOCZKA, Author/Illustrator

Annie Was Warned
(New York: Alfred A. Knopf, 2003)

Subject(s): Haunted Houses; Halloween; Birthdays
Age range(s): Grades K-3
Major character(s): Annie, Child, Friend; James, Child, Friend
Time period(s): 2000s
Locale(s): United States

Summary: Her family warns Annie to stay away from the old Montgomery Mansion on Halloween night but James dares her to go and that's all the additional incentive Annie needs. Annie's not scared even as she hurries along the path lit by her flashlight, even as the wind howls, and even as the trees sway menacingly. Born on Halloween, Annie is afraid of nothing! As she nears the mansion Annie begins to see, hear and feel suspicious things but each time she discovers the simple truth that it is not something menacing. Finally she reaches the mansion, ignores the warning signs and opens the door to the big surprise awaiting her. (30 pages)

Where it's reviewed:
Booklist, October 15, 2003, page 420
Bulletin of the Center for Children's Books, September 2003, page 21
Publishers Weekly, August 4, 2003, page 78
School Library Journal, September 2003, page 182

Awards the book has won:
IRA Children's Choices, 2004

Other books by the same author:
Max for President, 2004
Bubble Bath Pirates!, 2003
Good Night, Monkey Boy, 2001

Other books you might like:
Alyssa Satin Capucilli, *Inside a House that Is Haunted: A Rebus Read-Along Story*, 1998
  A trick-or-treater knocking on the door startles the inhabitants of a haunted house.
Patricia Polacco, *The Graves Family*, 2003
  When the Graves family moves into the local haunted house, Sara and Seth courageously reach out in friendship to them.
Martha Weston, *Tuck's Haunted House*, 2002
  For his Halloween party, Tuck makes a haunted house in his garage.

834

JARRETT J. KROSOCZKA, Author/Illustrator

Baghead

(New York: Alfred A. Knopf, 2002)

Subject(s): Hair; Humor; Problem Solving
Age range(s): Grades K-2
Major character(s): Josh, Student—Elementary School, Son; Unnamed Character, Sister (younger), Daughter
Time period(s): 2000s (2002)
Locale(s): United States

Summary: One look in the mirror gives Josh an idea. He grabs a brown grocery bag, cuts holes for eyes and his mouth and covers his head. All day he hears adults telling him he can't eat, go to school, or play soccer with a bag on his head, but Josh does just that. At dinner, only his little sister asks why Josh is wearing a bag so he removes it to reveal the haircut he gave himself. The next morning Josh's sister has an idea that keeps Josh from wearing a bag again. (36 pages)

Where it's reviewed:
Booklist, November 15, 2002, page 611
Five Owls, 2003, page 39
Newsweek, October 28, 2002, page 75
Publishers Weekly, August 12, 2002, page 299

Other books by the same author:
Annie Was Warned, 2003
Bubble Bath Pirates!, 2003
Good Night, Monkey Boy, 2001

Other books you might like:
Damon Burnard, *Dave's Haircut*, 2003
   An inattentive barber leaves Dave with a messy haircut that he tries unsuccessfully to improve before seeking professional help.
Olof Landstrom, *Will Gets a Haircut*, 1993
   While waiting his turn for a haircut, Will selects an unusual new hairstyle from a picture in a magazine.
Natasha Anastasia Tarpley, *Bippity Bop Barbershop*, 2002
   A little boy approaches his first trip to the barbershop with mixed feelings.

835

JARRETT J. KROSOCZKA, Author/Illustrator

Bubble Bath Pirates!

(New York: Viking, 2003)

Subject(s): Cleanliness; Pirates; Imagination
Age range(s): Preschool-Grade 1
Major character(s): Unnamed Character, Child; Unnamed Character, Child; Unnamed Character, Mother
Time period(s): 2000s (2002)
Locale(s): United States

Summary: Making a game of bath time, a mother pretending to be a "pirate mommy" calls her two young pirates and orders them to "walk the plank" into the tub. Pirate jargon enlivens the youngsters scrubbing and playing in the bubble-filled bath. As a treat for completing the journey, the children are allowed to find the "buried treasure" in the kitchen. After devouring the chocolate fudge ice cream it appears that they both need to "walk the plank" again. (36 pages)

Where it's reviewed:
Bulletin of the Center for Children's Books, March 2003, page 263
Publishers Weekly, November 25, 2002, page 65
School Library Journal, June 2003, page 111

Awards the book has won:
IRA Children's Choices, 2004

Other books by the same author:
Annie Was Warned, 2003
Baghead, 2002
Good Night, Monkey Boy, 2001

Other books you might like:
Kevin Henkes, *Clean Enough*, 1982
   A young boy finds the bath is useful for many things other than washing oneself.
Steven Kroll, *The Pigrates Clean Up*, 1993
   In a rhyming story Captain Dan and his crew of pig pirates work on their personal cleanliness as well as that of their ship.
Jerry Palotta, *Dory Story*, 2000
   While bathing, a boy imagines being in his new toy dory, alone in the ocean.
Simon Puttock, *Squeaky Clean*, 2002
   Mrs. Pig makes bath time so much fun that her children try to get dirty again so they can have another bath right away!

836

LORETTA KRUPINSKI, Author/Illustrator

Christmas in the City

(New York: Hyperion Books for Children, 2002)

Subject(s): Christmas; City and Town Life; Animals/Mice
Age range(s): Grades K-2
Major character(s): Mr. Mouse, Mouse, Father; Mrs. Mouse, Mouse, Mother
Time period(s): 2000s
Locale(s): New York, New York (Manhattan)

Summary: Mr. and Mrs. Mouse are a bit alarmed to peep out of their home in the trunk of an evergreen and discover that it's been moved to Rockefeller Plaza and decorated with colored lights and ornaments. Once they recover from the initial shock, Mr. and Mrs. Mouse enjoy nightly forays around the city, appreciating the new sights. On one such evening, as they pass a church, Mrs. Mouse senses that she will soon deliver their babies and they seek shelter in the hay of a manger scene in the courtyard. The mice are unaware that it is Christmas Eve until animals bring presents to them. Not long after they return to their tree home, it is removed, hauled to the country and dumped in an area near an old barn where the mouse family finds an old dollhouse in which to take up residence. (40 pages)

Where it's reviewed:
Booklist, September 15, 2002, page 246
Publishers Weekly, September 23, 2002, page 36
School Library Journal, October 2002, page 60

Other books by the same author:
Royal Mice: The Sword and the Horn, 2004
Best Friends, 1998
Into the Woods: A Woodland Scrapbook, 1997

Other books you might like:
Michael Garland, *The Mouse Before Christmas*, 2001
  Curiosity lands a young mouse in Santa's sack giving him an unexpected yet exciting trip on Christmas Eve.
Katharine Holabird, *Angelina's Christmas*, 2002
  Happy Angelina's kindness assures that no one in the village will have a lonely holiday.
Bethany Roberts, *Christmas Mice!*, 2000
  Four mice happily prepare for Christmas in this story in rhyme.

837

JANE KURTZ
BETH PECK, Illustrator

Bicycle Madness
(New York: Holt, 2003)

Subject(s): Bicycles and Bicycling; Gender Roles; Friendship
Age range(s): Grades 4-6
Major character(s): Lillie Applewood, Child; Frances Willard, Historical Figure
Time period(s): 1890s
Locale(s): United States

Summary: After her mother dies, Lillie's life turns upside-down. She not only misses her mother but, after her father decides to move across town to escape the sadness of their old house, she no longer sees her best friend Minerva every day after school. Miss Frances Willard, her new next-door neighbor, intrigues Lillie though her father disapproves of this high-spirited suffragette. Considering her to be a terrible influence on Lillie, he forbids his daughter to visit her, but Miss Willard is trying to ride a safety-bicycle and Lillie really wants to help her. The two befriend one another, though Lillie hides this from her father, as Lillie gives Miss Willard a hand with her bicycle and Miss Willard helps Lillie become a better speller. Lillie and her father finally have a good talk, Lillie shares her unhappiness about moving away from Minerva, and wins permission to spend time with Miss Willard. (122 pages)

Where it's reviewed:
Booklist, October 15, 2003, page 412
Bulletin of the Center for Children's Books, November 2003, page 113
Horn Book, September 2003, page 613
Publishers Weekly, September 22, 2003, page 104
School Library Journal, October 2003, page 170

Awards the book has won:
Notable Social Studies Trade Books for Young People, 2004

Other books by the same author:
In the Sunbird's Claw, 2004
Jakarta Missing, 2001
The Storyteller's Beads, 1998

Other books you might like:
Kathryn Lasky, *A Time for Courage: The Suffragette Diary of Kathleen Bowen, Washington, DC, 1917*, 2002
  Kat's diary records the efforts by her mother and her aunt to march for the suffragette movement, even though her uncle forbids it.
N.A. Perez, *One Special Year*, 1985
  The slower pace of the early 20th century is captured in this coming-of-age tale of Jen who gets her first kiss as well as her first corset.
Rhea Beth Ross, *The Bet's On, Lizzie Bingman!*, 1988
  When Lizzie's brothers claim that women require sheltering, Lizzie lets them know that she doesn't need their protection.
Jean Thesman, *The Ornament Tree*, 1996
  Bonnie is happy to join her cousin's family where the female-dominated household works for women's suffrage, birth control and an end to child labor.

838

JANE KURTZ
CHRISTOPHER KURTZ, Co-Author
LEE CHRISTIANSEN, Illustrator

Water Hole Waiting
(New York: Greenwillow/HarperCollins Publishers, 2002)

Subject(s): Africa; Animals; Animals/Monkeys
Age range(s): Grades K-2
Major character(s): Monkey, Monkey
Time period(s): 2000s (2002)
Locale(s): Africa

Summary: On the African savannah, Monkey wakes up and heads for the water hole. His mother catches him repeatedly thus saving him from swimming hippopotami, splashing elephants, a lurking crocodile and other dangers. Finally at the end of the day, Monkey and the entire pack are able to go to the water hole to drink. (32 pages)

Where it's reviewed:
Booklist, May 15, 2002, page 1601
Bulletin of the Center for Children's Books, June 2002, page 369
Horn Book Guide, Fall 2002, page 335
Kirkus Reviews, March 1, 2002, page 337
School Library Journal, May 2002, page 120

Other books by the same author:
Only a Pigeon, 1997

Other books you might like:
Jim Arnosky, *A Manatee Morning*, 2000
  As a manatee mother and her baby swim in Florida's crystal river, they must avoid the dangers of alligators and passing motorboats.
Anne Laurel Carter, *Under a Prairie Sky*, 2002
  Through a young Canadian boy's search for his little brother before a storm, readers are able to experience the Canadian grasslands.
Lynne Cherry, *The Great Kapok Tree*, 1990
  When a man falls asleep while cutting down a kapok tree

rainforest animals whisper its importance to them in his ear.

LAURA MCGEE KVASNOSKY

One Lucky Summer

(New York: Dutton Children's Books, 2002)

Subject(s): Moving, Household; Friendship; Summer
Age range(s): Grades 3-6
Major character(s): Steven Bennett, 10-Year-Old, Baseball Player; Lucinda Capuletto, 10-Year-Old, Dancer
Time period(s): 2000s (2002)
Locale(s): Sacramento, California; Twain Harte, California

Summary: Bummer summer! Steven's family moves to Sacramento, forcing him to leave his baseball team and leaving him with no friends other than next-door neighbor Lucinda. Although they have totally opposite interests, the science geek and the ballerina build a friendship during a vacation with their mothers in Twain Harte. The discovery, after a storm, of an orphaned baby flying squirrel gives them a common goal. Not only do they want to rescue the squirrel but they also plan to sneak it back to Sacramento so they can care for it until it is old enough to return to its forest home. This is the first novel for the picture book author. (148 pages)

Where it's reviewed:
Booklist, March 1, 2002, page 1137
Bulletin of the Center for Children's Books, May 2002, page 329
Horn Book Guide, Fall 2002, page 360
Publishers Weekly, April 8, 2002, page 228
School Library Journal, April 2002, page 114

Other books by the same author:
Zelda and Ivy One Christmas, 2000
Zelda and Ivy and the Boy Next Door, 1999
Zelda and Ivy, 1998 (Booklist Editors' Choice)

Other books you might like:
David Elliott, *The Cool Crazy Crickets to the Rescue!*, 2000
    Four friends start a club for the purpose of being friends for life.
Johanna Hurwitz, *Lexi's Tale*, 2001
    Lexi, a squirrel, befriends PeeWee, a guinea pig now living in Central Park, and tries to teach him how to survive in the wild.
Cynthia Rylant, *Gooseberry Park*, 1995
    A dog, a bat and a hermit crab are stuck babysitting for young squirrels whose mother is lost after an ice storm destroys their tree home.

839

ALLEN KURZWEIL

Leon and the Spitting Image

(New York: Greenwillow, 2003)

Subject(s): Humor; Magic; Sewing
Age range(s): Grades 4-6
Major character(s): Leon Zeisel, 4th Grader; Miss Hagmeyer, Teacher; Phya Winit ''P.W.'' Dhabanandana, 4th Grader; Lily-Matisse, 4th Grader; Henry ''Lumpkin the Pumpkin'' Lumpkin, Bully
Time period(s): 2000s
Locale(s): New York, New York

Summary: Leon is miserable. His teacher Miss Hagmeyer is a beanpole who dresses all in black, wears a cape fastened shut with eyeballs and bases her entire curriculum around stitchery. Since Leon lacks fine motor skills, stitching is very hard for him and he manages only two stitches per inch while his teacher requires eleven per inch. But he's determined to succeed and somehow manages to stitch a doll that resembles Miss Hagmeyer. Best of all, when the school bully soaks the doll in their coach's tobacco spit, Leon discovers that manipulating the doll also manipulates Miss Hagmeyer, which opens up a world of possibilities for Leon and his friends. (302 pages)

Where it's reviewed:
Booklist, October 15, 2003, page 412
Bulletin of the Center for Children's Books, June 2003, page 407
Horn Book, January 2004, page 83
Kirkus Reviews, August 1, 2003, page 1019
Voice of Youth Advocates, February 2004, page 504

Other books you might like:
Steven Cousins, *Frankenbug*, 2001
    Fed up with Jeb's teasing about his interest in insects, Adam creates the monster ''Frankenbug,'' brings it to life with fireflies, and scares Jeb.
Richard W. Jennings, *My Life of Crime*, 2002
    Fowler's ''life of crime'' is really a life of good deeds as he steals the poorly caged parrot from Mrs. Picklestain's third grade classroom.
Tim Kennemore, *The Circle of Doom*, 2003
    When Lizzie's potion seems to work and her disagreeable neighbors the Potwards move away, she is inspired to try more magical solutions.

L

841

R.L. LA FEVERS

The Falconmaster

(New York: Dutton, 2003)

Subject(s): Magic; Grandfathers; Animals/Falcons
Age range(s): Grades 6-8
Major character(s): Wat, Handicapped, 10-Year-Old; Griswold, Grandfather, Wizard; Lord Sherborne, Nobleman
Time period(s): 11th century
Locale(s): England

Summary: Born blind in one eye and with a deformed leg, Wat finds himself an outcast of his village, thought by the villagers to be affiliated with the devil who caused his handicap. Though handicapped physically, Wat has a strong sense of right and wrong and is at home with nature. Seeing two young falcons seized by Lord Sherborne's men, who plan to tame them by sewing their eyes shut, Wat snatches the birds and runs into the forest. There he meets Griswold, mystical keeper of the forest, who also happens to be his grandfather. Working together, Wat learns how to tend to the forest, keeping it in balance and protecting it when necessary. This knowledge, plus his ability to shape shift, allows him to foil Lord Sherbourne's hunters when they enter his forest in this author's first novel written for young people. (167 pages)

Where it's reviewed:
Booklist, November 1, 2003, page 490
Bulletin of the Center for Children's Books, December 2003, page 156
Kirkus Reviews, November 1, 2003, page 1312
Publishers Weekly, November 24, 2003, page 64
School Library Journal, January 2004, page 132

Other books by the same author:
The Forging of the Blade, 2004

Other books you might like:
Melvin Burgess, *Kite*, 2000
    Told to destroy the eggs of an endangered kite, Tom keeps

them; when one hatches, he raises the bird but must have help to train her.
William Mayne, *Antar and the Eagles*, 1990
    Stolen by eagles to help them retrieve a special golden egg, Antar learns eagle ways, even how to fly by attaching feathers to his garments.
Theresa Tomlinson, *The Forestwife*, 1995
    In a retelling of Robin Hood, Mary runs away from an arranged marriage, finds shelter with the Forestwife and learns to be an herbalist.

842

CHARLOTTE LABARONNE, Author/Illustrator

Best Friends

(New York: Orchard Books/Scholastic, Inc., 2003)

Subject(s): Friendship; Shyness; Animals/Alligators
Age range(s): Grades K-3
Major character(s): Alexander, Alligator; Louise, Lion
Time period(s): 2000s (2003)
Locale(s): France

Summary: Shy Alexander doesn't have any friends. When a new girl, Louise, joins his class he hopes that she will be his friend, but he doesn't know how to get her attention. Alexander tries squirting her teddy bear with juice, knocking over her blocks and painting on her drawing. All Alexander succeeds in doing is upsetting Louise. Finally, Louise asks Alexander why he doesn't like her, and they make up and play together. (32 pages)

Where it's reviewed:
Horn Book Guide, Spring 2004, page 18
Publishers Weekly, May 26, 2003, page 69

Other books by the same author:
Just One Roar!, 2002

Other books you might like:
Rigoberto Gonzalez, *Soledad Sigh-Sighs*, 2003
    Soledad comes home to an empty apartment everyday, but

her loneliness subsides when she makes friends with her neighbors.

Florence Page Jaques, *There Once Was a Puffin*, 1956
A lonely puffin makes friends with the fish he had been eating.

Jillian Lund, *Two Cool Coyotes*, 1999
When Frank's best friend moves away he is lonely until he meets the new coyote in town, Larry.

843

MERCEDES LACKEY

The Gates of Sleep
(New York: DAW, 2002)

Subject(s): Fantasy; Magic; Coming-of-Age
Age range(s): Grades 9-Adult
Major character(s): Marina Roeswood, Wizard, Niece; Arachne Chamberten, Wizard, Aunt
Time period(s): Indeterminate Past
Locale(s): England

Summary: Marina grows up pampered by good friends, but mystified by the absence of her parents. For some reason that no one will explain, they have sent Marina away and never visit her. Both Marina's parents and the friends who raise Marina are magically gifted, but Marina is carefully sheltered and sees only the gentlest of magic. As she approaches her 18th birthday, the date on which she is to be reunited with her parents, some of the restrictions on magic are lifted and Marina happily anticipates a fuller life. But before any of it can come to fruition, Marina's parents are killed in an apparent accident and Aunt Arachne Chamberten asserts her rights as guardian. Marina is forced to go live with her cold and calculating aunt, whom she never even heard of before the accident. Some mischief is afoot, and Marina will need all of her magical inheritance to survive. (352 pages)

Where it's reviewed:
Booklist, April 15, 2002, page 389
Bookwatch, June 2002, page 8
Kliatt, May 2003, page 26
Publishers Weekly, March 11, 2002, page 55
School Library Journal, September 2002, page 256

Other books by the same author:
To Light a Candle, 2004
Charmed Destinies, 2003
Exile's Valor: A Novel of Valdemar, 2003
The Gates of Sleep, 2002
Serpent's Shadow, 2001

Other books you might like:
Adele Geras, *Watching the Roses*, 1992
This variation on the Sleeping Beauty fairy tale takes place in modern times.

Robin McKinley, *Spindle's End*, 2000
What if Sleeping Beauty was spirited away for protection and grew up just wanting a simple life, without magic kisses?

Patricia C. Wrede, *Sorcery and Cecelia, or the Enchanted Chocolate Pot*, 2003

Two proper young English ladies of 1817 meet two charming bachelors who just happen to be wizards in trouble.

844

MERCEDES LACKEY, Co-Author
ROSEMARY EDGHILL, Co-Author

Mad Maudlin
(Riverdale, NY: Baen, 2003)

Series: Bedlam's Bard. Number 5
Subject(s): Fantasy; Runaways; Music and Musicians
Age range(s): Grades 9-Adult
Major character(s): Eric Banyon, Musician; Magnus Banyon, Runaway; Grace ''Ace'' Fairchild, Runaway; Jachiel ''Jaycie'' ap Gabrevys, Runaway, Royalty; Hosea Songmaster, Musician
Time period(s): 2000s (2003)
Locale(s): New York, New York

Summary: Three teenage runaways hide in an abandoned New York City squat. Ace, once known as Heavenly Grace, is the daughter of a fundamentalist preacher who exploited her for her singing abilities. Ace has a touch of magic in her singing voice that made her father a wealthy man. Magnus Banyon is also a musical prodigy, the trophy child of parents who want to keep him as a wind-up, performing boy. But Magnus had ideas of his own about what sort of music he'd like to play, inspired partly by the bardic magic that runs in his veins. Magnus doesn't know it, but his parents are duplicating the mistakes they made with his older brother, Eric. In fact, Magnus doesn't even know he has a brother, since Eric ran away before Magnus was born. Eric now lives in Underhill, the fairy realms where his magic as a bard was recognized and trained. Eric searches frantically for his brother to protect him, but the hunt is complicated by the third runaway, Jaycie. Quiet, sick Jaycie doesn't want anyone to know that he is the elf prince Jachiel, hiding amid the cold iron of New York. Eric needs to find the three teens immediately his fellow bard Hosea has just alerted him to the killer phantom Bloody Mary, who stalks the streets in search of homeless children. (439 pages)

Where it's reviewed:
Booklist, August 2003, page 1968
Library Journal, August 2003, page 142
Publishers Weekly, July 21, 2003, page 179

Other books by the same author:
Beyond World's End, 2001
Spirits White as Lightning (2001)

Other books you might like:
Holly Black, *Tithe: A Modern Faerie Tale*, 2002
Kaye is as tough as they come, but is she ready to find out the truth about herself?

Charles de Lint, *The Onion Girl*, 2001
Two sisters, united and alienated by their shared history of child abuse, are trapped in the Other World.

James A. Hetley, *The Summer Country*, 2002
Untrained magic users are fair game for anyone unscrupulous enough to use them, and a family of them is a real find.

845

A. LAFAYE

The Strength of Saints

(New York: Simon & Schuster, 2002)

Subject(s): Race Relations; City and Town Life; Remarriage
Age range(s): Grades 6-9
Major character(s): Nissa Bergen, 14-Year-Old; Heirah Bergen, Mother; Lara Bergen, Stepmother; Lily Maeve Bergen, Baby, Sister (of Nissa)
Time period(s): 1930s (1936)
Locale(s): Harper, Louisiana

Summary: Nissa faces all kinds of challenges this year, beginning with the return of her mother Heirah who vowed she'd never again live in Harper. Remaining with her father, stepmother and their new baby, Nissa is aware of the tensions caused by her mother's return. Another problem is of more concern to Nissa, and that's the town library that she operates. Taking her stepmother's old house, she divides it in half and has two libraries, one for black and one for white customers, which are separate but equal, as Nissa feels strongly about the "equal" piece. Workable at first, when Nissa expands her services by taking books to the newly opened cannery, owned by Northerners who employ both blacks and whites, she runs into difficulty. Tensions mount in the town and when a fire is inadvertently started in the cannery, the economic hope for her little town is destroyed in this sequel to *Nissa's Place*. (183 pages)

Where it's reviewed:
Booklist, June 2002, page 1724
Horn Book Guide, Fall 2002, page 376
Publishers Weekly, June 10, 2002, page 62
School Library Journal, June 2002, page 140
Voice of Youth Advocates, August 2002, page 194

Other books by the same author:
Worth, 2004
Dad, in Spirit, 2001
Nissa's Place, 1999
Strawberry Hill, 1999
The Year of the Sawdust Man, 1998

Other books you might like:
Karen English, *Francie*, 1999
    Francie learns to survive and keep her self-esteem intact while living in the South before the days of Civil Rights and integration.
Harper Lee, *To Kill a Mockingbird*, 1960
    The lives of Scout and her younger brother change when their father defends a black man accused of raping a white woman in 1930s Alabama.
Mildred D. Taylor, *Roll of Thunder, Hear My Cry*, 1976
    Cassie and the rest of her black family struggle to keep up their land payments in the South during the Depression.

846

KATE LAING
R.W. ALLEY, Illustrator

Best Kind of Baby

(New York: Dial Books for Young Readers, 2003)

Subject(s): Babies; Sibling Rivalry; Animals
Age range(s): Preschool-Grade 1
Major character(s): Sophie, Child, Daughter; Mommy, Mother
Time period(s): 2000s (2003)
Locale(s): United States

Summary: Sophie is less than excited to learn that her mom is pregnant. When her four friends inquire about Mommy's expanding frame and voracious eating habits, Sophie explains, in turn, that her mom is having a mouse, a dog, a monkey, and a dolphin. Her parents patiently correct her by saying that they are having a human baby although that idea doesn't sound quite as fun to Sophie. However, when her baby brother arrives, Sophie discovers that he is somewhat the same as what she imagined considering the drool and spitting that he does, so maybe he isn't quite so bad after all. (32 pages)

Where it's reviewed:
Booklist, August 2003, page 1989
Bulletin of the Center for Children's Books, September 2003, page 21
Publishers Weekly, May 26, 2003, page 70
School Library Journal, July 2003, page 100

Other books you might like:
Candace Fleming, *Smile, Lily!*, 2004
    Baby Lily won't stop crying, until her big brother gives her a big smile.
Valiska Gregory, *Shirley's Wonderful Baby*, 2002
    Shirley's not too fond of her new baby brother and all the attention he's getting, until a babysitter helps her see some of his charms.
Kevin Henkes, *Julius, the Baby of the World*, 1990
    Lily thinks her new baby brother is disgusting, until her cousin insults him.
Ezra Jack Keats, *Peter's Chair*, 1967
    When Peter learns that his blue furniture is being painted pink for his new baby sister, he runs away.
Heidi Stetson Mario, *I'd Rather Have an Iguana*, 1998
    A young girl is not happy when her new brother arrives and declares that she'd rather have an iguana.
Mercer Mayer, *The New Baby*, 1985
    Little Critter tries to figure out what things he can do with her new baby sister.

847

LENA LANDSTROM, Author/Illustrator
JOAN SANDIN, Translator

The Little Hippos' Adventure

(New York: R & S Books/Farrar Straus Giroux, 2002)

Subject(s): Animals/Hippos; Adventure and Adventurers; Rivers
Age range(s): Grades K-2
Major character(s): Mrs. Hippopotamus, Hippopotamus
Time period(s): 2000s (2002)
Locale(s): Africa

Summary: Little hippos like to play in the river every day, splashing around, and jumping off their diving board. The little hippos wish that their diving board equaled the height of Tall Cliff, a spot forbidden to them because of the dangers of the jungle. One day, after wheedling permission from another adult in the village they go to Tall Cliff and dive off. On the way back, exhilaration over their feat causes them to forget the caution necessary for a safe journey in the jungle and a crocodile follows the unobservant little hippos. Luckily, Mrs. Hippopotamus is alert and scares off the crocodile, saving the little hippos. The next day, she helps them enlarge their diving board so they won't need to travel to Tall Cliff for excitement. (28 pages)

Where it's reviewed:
Booklist, March 15, 2002, page 1263
Horn Book Guide, Fall 2002, page 306
Publishers Weekly, April 8, 2002, page 225
Riverbank Review, Summer 2002, page 31
School Library Journal, April 2002, page 114

Other books by the same author:
Boo and Baa Get Wet, 2000 (Olof Landstrom, co-author)
Boo and Baa at Sea, 1997 (Olof Landstrom, co-author)
Will Gets a Haircut, 1993 (Olof Landstrom, co-author)

Other books you might like:
Richard Fowler, *Little Chick's Big Adventure*, 1996
    Despite warnings from his mother, Little Chick wanders off and must find his way home.
Joanne Partis, *Stripe*, 2000
    Although little tiger Stripe is warned by his parents not to explore the jungle by himself he sets off on his own anyway.
Tony Payne, *Hippo-NOT-amus*, 2004
    Portly finds being a hippopotamus boring, so he takes off on an adventure to determine what animal to be.

848

LENA LANDSTROM, Author/Illustrator
JOAN SANDIN, Translator

The New Hippos

(New York: R&S Books, 2003)

Subject(s): Animals/Hippos; Change; Neighbors and Neighborhoods
Age range(s): Grades K-2
Major character(s): Mrs. Hippopotamus, Hippopotamus, Neighbor; Unnamed Character, Hippopotamus, Mother; Unnamed Character, Hippopotamus, Baby
Time period(s): Indeterminate
Locale(s): Fictional Country

Summary: When a new hippo and her baby move to the riverbank, the longtime residents are upset by the change. The young hippos won't let the new child use their diving board and the older hippos are skeptical of the way the mother makes her house. Once the baby hippo shows off on the diving board by doing amazing summersaults, the reception warms. When the new hippos disappear, the little hippos go searching (with a little encouragement from Mrs. Hippopotamus), but eventually mother and child return, bringing fruit for their new neighbors. (32 pages)

Where it's reviewed:
Booklist, April 15, 2003, page 1478
Publishers Weekly, February 24, 2003, page 74
School Library Journal, April 2003, page 130

Other books by the same author:
The Little Hippos' Adventure, 2002
Boo and Baa Get Wet, 2000 (Olof Landstrom, co-author)
Boo and Baa at Sea, 1997 (Olof Landstrom, co-author)

Other books you might like:
Katherine Couric, *The Brand New Kid*, 2000
    After Lazlo starts a new school his classmates make fun of him, until one starts to see all that is wonderful about this immigrant.
Claudia Fries, *A Pig Is Moving In*, 2000
    A pig moves into an apartment building, prompting concern from his neighbors, but at his housewarming party, everyone gets to know the real pig.
Patricia Lakin, *Fat Chance Thanksgiving*, 2001
    When Carla and her mother move into a new apartment, Carla organizes a potluck Thanksgiving with all her new neighbors.

849

LAURA LANGSTON

A Taste of Perfection

(Niagara Falls, NY: Stoddart Kids, 2002)

Subject(s): Animals/Dogs; Grandmothers
Age range(s): Grades 5-8
Major character(s): Erin Morris, 12-Year-Old; Lavender Blue, Dog (black Lab)
Time period(s): 2000s
Locale(s): Nanaimo, British Columbia, Canada; Courtenay, British Columbia, Canada

Summary: When her father loses his job, Erin is sent to spend the summer at her grandmother's while her folks work out their financial problems. Though not thrilled at giving up her SPCA volunteering, Erin is delighted when told she'll train Lavender Blue, her grandmother's black Lab, for the upcoming dog show. She's always wanted a dog and this should help her learn what to do. Her life seems great when Blue takes first place at the show, but everything comes apart when a puppy she's been hoping to adopt is put down because of its deformed leg. Angry at what she thinks is an injustice, Erin rides her bike to a friend's house, taking Blue with her, but off his lead. A car accident leaves Blue minus one leg and Erin with some important lessons to learn in this dog lover's story. (219 pages)

Where it's reviewed:
Resource Links, June 2003, page 27
School Library Journal, May 2003, page 156
Voice of Youth Advocates, June 2003, page 136

Other books you might like:
Natale Ghent, *Piper*, 2001
   Allowed to raise a runt Australian shepherd dog, Wesley feeds and cares for Piper until the day the two are attacked by coyotes.
Lynn Hall, *The Soul of the Silver Dog*, 1992
   Cory pours her heart into training blind, former Bedlington terrier champion Sterling for competition on the obstacle course.
Sylvia McNicoll, *Bringing Up Beauty*, 2000
   Sometimes feeling friendless, Elizabeth finds a perfect companion in the black Lab Beauty whom she trains as a guide dog for Canine Vision Canada.

850

KATHRYN LASKY
LEUYEN PHAM, Illustrator

Before I Was Your Mother

(San Diego: Harcourt, Inc., 2003)

Subject(s): Mothers and Daughters; Mothers; Bedtime
Age range(s): Grades K-3
Major character(s): Katie, Daughter; Unnamed Character, Mother
Time period(s): 2000s (2003); 1960s
Locale(s): United States

Summary: When Katie's mother tucks her in one night, she tells her about what she was like as a little girl. Not always a mother who shushes her daughter while she's on the phone, Katie's mom was once a little girl who liked tap-dancing on garbage can lids, eating the sugar roses off cakes, roller-skating with her best friend, and dreaming of a little girl of her own to love. (40 pages)

Where it's reviewed:
Booklist, March 15, 2003, page 40
School Library Journal, March 2003, page 122

Other books by the same author:
Sophie and Rose, 1998
Marven of the Great North Woods, 1997 (ALA Notable Children's Books)
The Librarian Who Measured the Earth, 1994

Other books you might like:
Libba Moore Gray, *My Mama Had a Dancing Heart*, 1995
   A ballerina remembers how her mother would celebrate each new season with dance.
Karen Hesse, *Come On, Rain!*, 1999
   Tessie and her friends hope for rain in the hot city summer and when it comes their mothers join them to dance in streets.

Lynn Reiser, *Cherry Pies and Lullabies*, 1998
   Four generations of women pass down family traditions from mother to daughter.

851

KATHRYN LASKY

The Capture

(New York: Scholastic, 2003)

Series: Guardians of Ga'Hoole. Book 1
Subject(s): Animals/Owls; Adventure and Adventurers
Age range(s): Grades 5-9
Major character(s): Soren, Owl, Orphan; Gylfie, Owl, Orphan
Time period(s): Indeterminate
Locale(s): Tyto Forest, Fictional Country

Summary: Soren is born to a pleasant family of barn owls and seems destined for a full and happy life. Respectful of all owl traditions, he carefully follows his parents' lead in spite of his older brother's teasing and his younger sister's eager pushing. Soren is especially fond of the stories his father tells about the great Ga'Hoole tree, and the knight owls that live there and champion justice. Then, when his parents are off hunting, the unthinkable happens and Soren falls from the nest. He has not yet learned to fly and it seems Soren is about to be some animal's dinner, when an adult owl swoops him up, but doesn't return him to the nest. Although he protests until threatened, Soren is taken to the St. Aegolius Academy for Orphaned Owls. This so-called school is a home of terrible cruelty and the owls living there seem to have no will of their own. Luckily Soren meets Gylfie, a tiny elf owl with enormous courage and together they struggle to maintain their wits and wills until they are fledged and able to escape. This is the first in a series about Soren, Gylfie and the noble owl guardians of Ga'Hoole. (226 pages)

Where it's reviewed:
Booklist, September 15, 2003, page 240
Library Media Connection, January 2004, page 65
Publishers Weekly, July 7, 2003, page 72
School Library Journal, October 2003, page 170
Voice of Youth Advocates, December 2003, page 414

Other books by the same author:
The Journey, 2003 (Guardians of Ga'Hoole Book 2)
The Rescue, 2003 (Guardians of Ga'Hoole Book 3)
Beyond the Burning Time, 1994

Other books you might like:
Michael Hoeye, *The Sands of Time*, 2002
   Three independent-minded mice set out to prove that the past included a lost Kingdom of Cats.
Brian Jacques, *Redwall*, 1987
   This is the first of the epic series that chronicles the adventures of the many creatures living at the sanctuary of Redwall Abbey.
Kate Thompson, *Switchers*, 1998
   Two Irish teens are able to switch into animal form and find the ability is key to human survival.

852

KATHRYN LASKY

Home at Last

(New York: Scholastic Press, 2003)

Series: My America. Sofia's Immigrant Diary, Book Two
Subject(s): Emigration and Immigration; Italian Americans; Diaries
Age range(s): Grades 3-5
Major character(s): Sofia Monari, 9-Year-Old, Immigrant; Maureen O'Malley, 9-Year-Old, Immigrant
Time period(s): 1900s (1903)
Locale(s): Boston, Massachusetts

Summary: Italian immigrant Sofia Monari settles with her family in the North End of Boston. Sofia's dad gets a job working in another immigrant's grocery store and Sofia and her siblings start school. Sofia learns quickly and loves her teacher, although her older sister struggles. Difficulties arise when Sofia contracts infantile paralysis, which leaves her with a weakened leg and a limp. Sofia also worries about her friend Maureen, still back in New York, whose family is struggling after the death of her mother. Eventually Maureen comes to live with the Monari family. With a lot of hard work the Monari family is doing well in Boston. A historical note follows the text, providing background on the immigrant community in the North End of Boston. (108 pages)

Where it's reviewed:
Booklist, December 15, 2003, page 751
School Library Journal, February 2004, page 116

Other books by the same author:
An American Spring, 2004 (Sofia's Immigrant Diary, Book Three)
Jahanara: Princess of Princesses, India 1627, 2002 (Royal Diaries Series)
Beyond the Burning Time, 1994

Other books you might like:
Richard Easton, *A Real American*, 2002
   When immigrant miners move into Nathan McClelland's small Pennsylvania town, Nathan befriends a young Italian boy.
Johanna Hurwitz, *Dear Emma*, 2002
   Dossi Rabinowitz describes her life in the tenements of New York through letters to her friend Emma.
Marie Raphael, *Streets of Gold*, 1995
   Polish immigrant girl Marisia Bolinski fights to survive on New York's Lower East Side.

853

KATHRYN LASKY

Hope in My Heart

(New York: Scholastic Press, 2003)

Series: My America. Sofia's Immigrant Diary, Book One
Subject(s): Emigration and Immigration; Italian Americans; Diaries
Age range(s): Grades 3-5

Major character(s): Sofia Monari, 9-Year-Old, Immigrant; Maureen O'Malley, 9-Year-Old, Immigrant
Time period(s): 1900s (1903)
Locale(s): New York, New York

Summary: Sofia immigrates to America from Italy with her entire family. On Ellis Island Sofia is kept in quarantine, while the rest of her family is allowed into the country. Alone and speaking almost no English, Sofia survives with the help of her new friend, Maureen O'Malley, an immigrant girl from Ireland. Eventually, assisted by a kind nurse and a priest, Maureen and Sofia are able to leave quarantine and reunite with their families. An historical afterword provides background on the events that occurred. (106 pages)

Where it's reviewed:
Booklist, December 15, 2003, page 751
School Library Journal, February 2004, page 116

Other books by the same author:
A Journey to the New World, 1996 (Dear America Series)
True North: A Novel of the Underground Railroad, 1996
Sugaring Time, 1986 (Newbery Honor Book)

Other books you might like:
Kathleen Duey, *Nell Dunne: Ellis Island, 1904*, 2000
   In this addition to the American Diaries series, Nell Dunne immigrates to America through Ellis Island in 1904.
Patricia Reilly Giff, *Maggie's Door*, 2003
   Twelve-year-old Nory Ryan struggles to follow the rest of her family from famine-ridden Ireland to the United States.
Veronica Lawlor, *I Was Dreaming to Come to America: Memories from the Ellis Island Oral History Project*, 1995
   This non-fiction book includes excerpts of 15 different interviews with children who immigrated through Ellis Island between 1900 and 1925.
Marissa Moss, *Hannah's Journal*, 2000
   As life in Lithuania at the turn of the century becomes more difficult for Jewish people ten-year-old Hannah and her cousin Esther immigrate to America.

854

KATHRYN LASKY
MARYLIN HAFNER, Illustrator

Lucille Camps In

(New York: Knopf, 2003)

Subject(s): Animals/Pigs; Camps and Camping; Sibling Rivalry
Age range(s): Grades K-2
Major character(s): Lucille, Child, Pig; Dad, Pig, Father; Mom, Pig, Mother
Time period(s): 2000s (2003)
Locale(s): United States

Summary: Lucille's dad is taking her older brother and sister camping, but says that Lucille is too young to go. Initially inconsolable, Lucille begins to feel better after she decides to "camp in" at home. With Mom's help, Lucille sets up a tent in the living room and together they roast marshmallows in the fireplace and watch the stars out the window. Lucille has a really great time and doesn't even have to suffer from pesky mosquitoes. (32 pages)

Where it's reviewed:
Booklist, July 2003, page 1897
Bulletin of the Center for Children's Books, July 2003, page 453
Publishers Weekly, May 5, 2003, page 224
School Library Journal, July 2003, page 100

Awards the book has won:
Center for Children's Books Best Books, 2003

Other books by the same author:
Starring Lucille, 2001
Lucille's Snowsuit, 2000
Lunch Bunnies, 1996

Other books you might like:
Lena Arro, *Good Night, Animals*, 2002
  Best friends go camping and with each strange noise they invite another animal into their tent.
Tom Birdseye, *Oh Yeah!*, 2003
  Two boys, camping out in the backyard, boast that nothing could scare them, until the family dog startles them.
Kevin Henkes, *Bailey Goes Camping*, 1985
  When Bailey isn't allowed to go camping with his older siblings he sets up his own camp in the living room.
Mick Inkpen, *Kipper's Monster*, 2002
  Kipper can't wait to go camping, but when the outdoors proves scary, he decides to camp out in his bedroom.
Mercer Mayer, *Just Camping Out*, 1989
  Little Critter and his sister go camping in the back yard, but they don't make it through the night.

855

KATHRYN LASKY
JANE KAMINE, Co-Author
DARCIA LABROSSE, Illustrator

Mommy's Hands
(New York: Hyperion Books for Children, 2002)

Subject(s): Mothers; Mothers and Daughters; Mothers and Sons
Age range(s): Preschool-Kindergarten
Time period(s): 2000s (2002)
Locale(s): United States

Summary: A trio of preschool-aged children proclaim their love for their mother's hands and all the great things they can do. An Asian girl loves the braid her mommy makes in her hair. An African-American boy is impressed by his mom's ability to pick the knots out of his shoelaces. Finally, a little strawberry-blond boy loves his mother's hands when they tuck him in at night. (32 pages)

Where it's reviewed:
Booklist, June 2002, page 1740
School Library Journal, July 2002, page 94

Other books by the same author:
Love That Baby!, 2003
Starring Lucille, 2001
Sugaring Time, 1983 (Newberry Honor Book)

Other books you might like:
Rebecca Kai Dotlich, *Mama Loves*, 2004
  Mama Pig loves doing many different activities with her young daughter.
Laura Joffe Numeroff, *What Mommies Do Best*, 2002
  Mommies are good at lots of things; the most important one is love.
Susan Paradis, *My Mommy*, 2002
  A young girls marvels at all her mommy can do.

856

KATHRYN LASKY
DAVID JARVIS, Illustrator

Porkenstein
(New York: Blue Sky Press/Scholastic, Inc., 2002)

Subject(s): Inventors and Inventions; Loneliness; Halloween
Age range(s): Grades 1-3
Major character(s): Smart Pig, Pig, Inventor; Porkenstein, Monster, Friend; Big Bad Wolf, Wolf
Time period(s): Indeterminate
Locale(s): Fictional Country

Summary: Dr. Smart Pig faces a lonely Halloween. Big Bad Wolf ate his brothers and now he has no one to trick-or-treat with him. To solve the problem, Dr. Pig invents a friend. His first attempt is a bat-pig—not exactly what he wanted so he tries again. The second attempt creates an enormous (and hungry) pig that devours everything in sight, including the Halloween candy. Dr. Pig is overwhelmed with this Porkenstein he's made until the doorbell rings to signal the first trick-or-treater. Peering out the window, Dr. Pig sees Big Bad Wolf who has seen news reports of Dr. Pig's invention and is eager to satisfy his hunger for pork. Porkenstein opens the door to greet Big Bad Wolf. In moments, the problem of no Halloween candy and the menace of Big Bad Wolf are solved and Dr. Pig, with his new friend Porkenstein, goes out to trick-or-treat. (32 pages)

Where it's reviewed:
Booklist, September 15, 2002, page 246
Bulletin of the Center for Children's Books, October 2002, page 64
Horn Book Guide, Spring 2003, page 41
Publishers Weekly, September 23, 2002, page 22
School Library Journal, September 2002, page 197

Other books by the same author:
Humphrey, Albert and the Flying Machine, 2004
Before I Was Your Mother, 2003
Lucille Camps In, 2003
Man Who Made Time Travel, 2003 (ALA Notable Children's Books)

Other books you might like:
Addie Adams, *Hilda and the Mad Scientist*, 1995
  Helpful Hilda's do-good housekeeping plans unintentionally foil Dr. Weinerstein's monster-making experiments.
Pamela Jane, *Monster Mischief*, 2001
  After Little Moe tips over the stew pot, five unhappy,

hungry monsters are relieved when a sixth monster arrives with a bag of Halloween candy.

Kim Kennedy, *Frankenfrog*, 1999

Dr. Franken invents Frankenfrog to get rid of Hyperfly, a creature produced when an ordinary fly lands in some of Dr. Franken's growth tonic.

857

KATHRYN LASKY

A Time for Courage: The Suffragette Diary of Kathleen Bowen, Washington, DC, 1917

(New York: Scholastic, 2002)

Series: Dear America
Subject(s): Women's Rights; World War I; Family Life
Age range(s): Grades 4-8
Major character(s): Kathlee "Kat" Bowen, 8th Grader; Alma Minette, Cousin (of Kat); Nell Bowen, Teenager
Time period(s): 1910s
Locale(s): Washington, District of Columbia

Summary: When her mother gives Kat a diary for Christmas, she uses it to record her boring life during the suffragette movement. Attending a private school in Washington, D.C., with Alma, her cousin and her best friend, the two watch as their mothers participate in the fight to earn the vote for women. Though Kat's dad supports her mother's efforts, Alma's father forbids his wife to take part, even threatening divorce if she continues to march and picket. Alma is eventually sent away to school to curtail her activities and Kat misses her terribly. World War I breaks out, the influenza epidemic takes one of Kat's sisters and Nell, her other sister, heads to Europe to become an ambulance driver. Kat finally realizes her life is anything but boring, especially when her mother is arrested for picketing and sent to jail, in this diary filled with historical details. (217 pages)

Where it's reviewed:
Horn Book Guide, Fall 2002, page 376
Kliatt, May 2002, page 11
School Library Journal, August 2003, page 190

Other books by the same author:
Kazunomiya: Prisoner of Heaven, 2004 (Royal Diaries)
Christmas After All: The Great Depression Diary of Minnie Swift, 2001 (Dear America)
Dreams in the Golden Country: The Diary of Zipporah Feldman, a Jewish Immigrant Girl, 1998 (Dear America)

Other books you might like:
Rhea Beth Ross, *The Bet's On, Lizzie Bingman!*, 1988
When Lizzie's brothers claim that women require sheltering, Lizzie lets them know that she doesn't need their protection.
Gloria Skurzynski, *Good-Bye, Billy Radish*, 1992
Hank thinks he'll lose his friend Bazyli to the steel mills or World War I, but he never dreams his friend will die from influenza.
Jean Thesman, *The Ornament Tree*, 1996
Bonnie is happy to join her cousin's family where the female-dominated household works for women's suffrage, birth control and an end to child labor.

858

WILLIAM LAVENDER

Just Jane: The Story of a Daughter of England Caught in the Struggle for Independence in Revolutionary America

(San Diego: Gulliver/Harcourt, 2002)

Series: Great Episodes
Subject(s): Revolutionary War; Orphans; Loyalty
Age range(s): Grades 6-10
Major character(s): Jane Prentice, 16-Year-Old, Orphan; Clarissa Prentice, Aunt; Robert Prentice, Uncle, Plantation Owner; Hugh Prentice, Cousin, Artisan (cabinetmaker); Simon Cordwyn, Teacher
Time period(s): 1770s; 1780s (1776-1782)
Locale(s): Charleston, South Carolina; Rosewall Plantation, South Carolina

Summary: When Lady Jane is orphaned, she's sent to the colonies to live with her only relatives, Uncle Robert and Aunt Clarissa. It's 1776 and the colonists are embroiled in war, with tensions high between those who want to remain loyal to Britain and those who wish for independence. Jane tries to leave behind all pretensions of class, asking to be called "just Jane," as well as loyalties to one side of the other. Staying neutral is more difficult than she imagines, especially when Loyalist Uncle Robert forbids her to have anything to do with her Patriot cousin Hugh. Though several men seem interested in Jane, she finds her heart is taken with Simon, a young schoolmaster, which sends her loyalties squarely over to the side of the colonists who fight for independence in this author's first novel. (277 pages)

Where it's reviewed:
Booklist, November 1, 2002, page 485
Bulletin of the Center for Children's Books, December 2002, page 163
Kirkus Reviews, July 15, 2002, page 1036
School Library Journal, December 2002, page 143
Voice of Youth Advocates, December 2002, page 386

Other books you might like:
Ann Rinaldi, *Cast Two Shadows: The American Revolution in the South*, 1998
Caroline sees her Camden, South Carolina home commandeered by the British, her friend's brother whipped and her best friend hanged in the 1780s.
Ann Rinaldi, *Or Give Me Death*, 2003
With her father speaking around the countryside about the possibility of war with England, Patsy Henry is left to take care of her siblings and their home.
G. Clifton Wisler, *Kings Mountain*, 2002
Francis would prefer to stay out of talk about the war, but can't when he finds his community divided between the loyalists and the patriots.

859

LAURIE LAWLOR
JOHN WINCH, Illustrator

Old Crump: The True Story of a Trip West
(New York: Holiday House, 2002)

Subject(s): Pioneers; Survival; American West
Age range(s): Grades 1-4
Major character(s): Old Crump, Ox; Charlie, 2-Year-Old, Brother; Martha, 4-Year-Old, Sister; Ma, Mother, Pioneer
Time period(s): 1850s (1850)
Locale(s): West

Summary: A family heading for California travels with a group that chooses a route taking them through Death Valley. After burning the wagons and all their possessions they continue on with only the oxen and the supplies they can carry. When it's obvious that Charlie and Martha can walk no further Ma sews two shirts together to make packs to carry the youngest children on Old Crump's back. Despite a shortage of water and food Old Crump never wavers or falters with his important cargo and eventually the family successfully gets through the arid land. Once established in California, Old Crump lives out his years with the family. An introductory author's note gives the historical background for the story. (36 pages)

Where it's reviewed:
Booklist, March 15, 2002, page 1263
Bulletin of the Center for Children's Books, April 2002, page 284
New Advocate, Spring 2003, page 218
Publishers Weekly, February 11, 2002, page 186
School Library Journal, June 2002, page 98

Other books by the same author:
Crooked Creek, 2004
Worst Kid Who Ever Lived on Eighth Avenue, 1998
Addie's Forever Friend, 1997

Other books you might like:
Verla Kay, *Covered Wagons, Bumpy Trails*, 2000
  Life in a covered wagon is described in a rhyming tale of parents with an infant son trekking west to California.
Marissa Moss, *Rachel's Journal: The Story of a Pioneer Girl*, 1998
  A fictionalized diary gives an account of daily life for a family traveling to California in 1850.
Ann Turner, *Red Flower Goes West*, 1999
  Gold fever and the promise of free land convince James and Jenny's father to sell their belongings, buy oxen and a wagon and head west.

860

IAIN LAWRENCE

The Lighthouse Keeper's Daughter
(New York: Delacorte/Random House, 2002)

Subject(s): Islands; Lighthouses; Brothers and Sisters
Age range(s): Grades 9-12

Major character(s): Elizabeth ''Squid'' McCrae, 17-Year-Old; Alastair McCrae, Brother (deceased); Hannah McCrae, Mother; Murray McCrae, Father, Lighthouse Keeper; Tatiana McCrae, Child (of Squid)
Time period(s): 2000s
Locale(s): Lizzie Island, British Columbia, Canada

Summary: After four years away, Squid returns to the island with her three-year-old daughter Tatiana, determined to come to terms with the grief that drove her away. Squid's father is a lighthouse keeper who worries that his job will become obsolete as lighthouses become fully automated. In addition he's a possessive man who wanted nothing more than to keep Squid and her brother Alastair close at hand. Both children are now gone, perhaps by choice. Alastair loved animals and had become enamored with whales, convinced that he could understand their whale song, but one day he doesn't return in his kayak from a whale observation trip. Was Squid to blame? She's not sure as her brother had just indicated his deep love for her before he set out to sea; finding his journals helps Squid understand her role in his life and his death. Tatiana seems to be the key to help all the family members work through their memories and their deep grief in a stirring, contemporary novel. (246 pages)

Where it's reviewed:
Booklist, January 2003, page 870
Bulletin of the Center for Children's Books, November 2002, page 114
Publishers Weekly, August 5, 2002, page 74
Riverbank Review, Spring 2003, page 42
School Library Journal, September 2002, page 226

Awards the book has won:
ALA Best Books for Young Adults, 2003

Other books by the same author:
B for Buster, 2004
Lord of the Nutcracker Men, 2001
The Buccaneers, 2001
Smugglers, 1999
Wreckers, 1998

Other books you might like:
Welwyn Wilton Katz, *Whalesinger*, 1991
  While on a conservation project on the California coast, Marty is attracted to a mother whale and her sickly calf.
Katherine Kirkpatrick, *Keeping the Good Light*, 1995
  The isolation of living with her family in Stepping Stones lighthouse changes for Eliza when a ship's captain finds a note she placed in a bottle.
Patricia Curtis Pfitsch, *Keeper of the Light*, 1997
  After her lighthouse keeper father dies, Faith's family moves back to town, though she returns during a storm to provide light for a foundering schooner.

861

JOHN LAWRENCE, Author/Illustrator

This Little Chick
(Cambridge, MA: Candlewick Press, 2002)

Subject(s): Animals/Chickens; Animals; Stories in Rhyme
Age range(s): Preschool-Kindergarten

Major character(s): Unnamed Character, Chicken, Baby
Time period(s): Indeterminate
Locale(s): Fictional Country

Summary: A little chick wanders the barnyard greeting each animal in its own language. The chick oinks at the pigs, quacks to the ducks and moos with the cows. When the little chick goes home, it greets its mother with all the sounds of the farm animals, including the cheep of a little chick. This is the first picture book written by the well-known illustrator. (32 pages)

Where it's reviewed:
Booklist, February 1, 2002, page 949
Bulletin of the Center for Children's Books, April 2002, page 285
Horn Book Guide, Fall 2002, page 306
Kirkus Reviews, January 1, 2002, page 48
School Library Journal, March 2002, page 192

Awards the book has won:
New York Times Best Illustrated Children's Books, 2002
School Library Journal Best Books, 2002

Other books you might like:
Laura Godwin, *What Baby Hears*, 2002
    A rhyming story presents the sounds baby animals hear from their parents.
Kirsten Hall, *Who Says?*, 2003
    Animals sing their unique sounds for a musical conductor.
Judy Hindley, *Does a Cow Say Boo?*, 2002
    As children search a farm for the animal that says ''boo'' they learn the sounds of all the barnyard creatures.
David McPhail, *The Day the Cow Said, ''Cock-a-Doodle-Doo!''*, 1997
    On a particularly windy day, the sounds of the farm animals get mixed up so that each is making another's sound.

862

MICHAEL LAWRENCE

The Poltergoose

(New York: Dutton/Penguin Putnam, 2002)

Series: Jiggy McCue Story
Subject(s): Humor; Ghosts; Animals/Geese
Age range(s): Grades 4-7
Major character(s): Jiggy McCue, 12-Year-Old; Pete Garrett, 12-Year-Old; Angie Mint, 12-Year-Old; Linus Brooks, Aged Person; Aunt Hetty, Goose
Time period(s): 2000s
Locale(s): England

Summary: Moving to a new subdivision after his father finally finds a job, Jiggy is stalked and harassed by a dead goose he and his friends Pete and Angie call a poltergoose. First the goose destroys his miniature rocking horse collection, then it follows him to school and even to the therapist his parents think he needs to visit. Goose droppings fill their stair landing, a beak continually stabs at his legs accompanied by a constant hissing sound. Jiggy and his friends finally discover that the former owner, Linus Brooks, had a pet goose named Aunt Hetty that was accidentally run over by a bulldozer and buried in Jiggy's yard. Hetty wants to be reburied by her old farm-

house, but a new mall has been built atop the old site. Luckily Jiggy, Pete and Angie find a way to provide Aunt Hetty a peaceful rest in this funny British import. (132 pages)

Where it's reviewed:
Booklist, January 2002, page 858
Horn Book Guide, Fall 2002, page 376
Kirkus Reviews, December 15, 2001, page 1760
Library Talk, September 2002, page 44
School Library Journal, March 2002, page 232

Other books by the same author:
Killer Underpants, 2002
The Toilet of Doom, 2002

Other books you might like:
Marianne Carus, *That's Ghosts for You!*, 2000
    If ghost stories are what you like to read, here's a collection of 13 deliciously terrifying ones.
David Ives, *Monsieur Eek*, 2001
    Emmaline finds a chimpanzee in a deserted ship, but the town bailiff decides he's a thief and Emmaline appoints herself as Monsieur Eek's lawyer.
Barbara Timberlake Russell, *Blue Lightning*, 1997
    A ghost who aims to make his life miserable haunts young baseball player Calvin.

863

JANET LAWSON, Author/Illustrator

Audrey and Barbara

(New York: Atheneum Books for Young Readers, 2002)

Subject(s): Animals/Cats; Imagination; Pets
Age range(s): Grades K-2
Major character(s): Audrey, Child, Adventurer; Barbara, Cat
Time period(s): 2000s (2002)
Locale(s): United States

Summary: Barbara prefers sleeping on her comfortable pillow but Audrey's ready for adventure. As Audrey plans a trip to India to ride an elephant Barbara questions Audrey's plans and Audrey begins revising them. First she abandons the idea of riding her bike to India and turns the bathtub into a boat. Audrey plans to sail or row to India but Barbara suggests using whale power and that's just what they do. This imaginative tale is the author's first picture book. (32 pages)

Where it's reviewed:
Booklist, September 15, 2002, page 240
Bulletin of the Center for Children's Books, May 2002, page 315
Publishers Weekly, April 8, 2002, page 226
School Library Journal, July 2002, page 94

Other books you might like:
Isabelle Harper, *My Cats Nick and Nora*, 1995
    Two cousins while away a Sunday afternoon playing dress-up with their patient cats.
Barbara M. Joosse, *Nugget and Darling*, 1997
    Nugget thinks life with Nell is just perfect until they find a stray kitten in the yard that Nell takes in as another pet.
Barbara Samuels, *Duncan & Dolores*, 1986
    Dolores includes her pet cat Duncan in all her imaginative

plans despite the fact that he isn't always eager to participate.

864

JULIE LAWSON
KASIA CHARKO, Illustrator

Arizona Charlie and the Klondike Kid

(Custer, WA: Orca Book Publishers, 2003)

Subject(s): American West; Theater; Crime and Criminals
Age range(s): Grades K-3
Major character(s): Ben, Child; Arizona Charlie, Cowboy, Entertainer
Time period(s): 1890s (1899)
Locale(s): Dawson City, Yukon Territory, Canada

Summary: Ben is entranced when Wild West star Arizona Charlie comes to live in Dawson City. He follows the entertainer around, practices lasso tricks and dreams of being just like Arizona Charlie. When Arizona Charlie notices Ben and asks him to be a part of his closing act, Ben is thrilled. Unfortunately, he gets stage fright, is unable to perform any of his tricks and runs from the theater in shame—right into a robbery. Ben is then able to capture the escaping thief with his lasso. (32 pages)

Where it's reviewed:
Horn Book Guide, Fall 2003, page 330
School Library Journal, September 2003, page 182

Other books by the same author:
The Klondike Cat, 2002
Destination Gold, 2000
The Dragon's Pearl, 1993

Other books you might like:
Eleanor Coerr, *Buffalo Bill and the Pony Express*, 1995
  Before Buffalo Bill toured the country with his Wild West Show he was a rider on the Pony Express.
Lisa Campbell Ernst, *Hannah Mae O'Hannigan's Wild West Show*, 2003
  Hannah dreams of being a cowgirl and, despite her urban locale, develops skills that help Uncle Coot when she visits him way out West.
April Pulley Sayre, *Noodle Man: The Pasta Superhero*, 2002
  Al Dente starts a not completely successful door-to-door pasta business, but the pasta comes in handy for capturing bank robbers.

865

URSULA K. LE GUIN

The Birthday of the World and Other Stories

(New York: HarperCollins, 2002)

Subject(s): Short Stories; Science Fiction
Age range(s): Grades 9-Adult

Summary: Individual identity, the individual's place in society and the role that love plays in discovering these things have long been preoccupations of Le Guin. In this collection of short stories, she revisits these themes, which have special resonance for young adults. As always she brings her special insight and compassion to bear. In the first story, "Coming-of-Age in Karhide," the mysteries of that most mysterious world, gender-changing Gethen (the setting of *Left Hand of Darkness*) are investigated, with messages for those us with fixed gender. "Solitude" visits a rural society in which knowing one's self is the highest good, but is this society selfishly primitive or has it evolved beyond busy industrial societies? "Old Music and the Slave Women" is the story of an elderly off-worlder who finds himself trapped in the chaos of a war of liberation. Le Guin's quiet tone is misleading for these gentle stories raise questions that will disturb the reader long after the book is closed. (362 pages)

Where it's reviewed:
Booklist, January 1, 2002, page 776
Kirkus Reviews, January 1, 2002, page 22
Library Journal, March 15, 2002, page 112
New York Review of Books, September 26, 2002, page 23
Publishers Weekly, January 14, 2002, page 45

Other books by the same author:
Changing Planes, 2003
Tales from Earthsea, 2001
The Other Wind, 2001

Other books you might like:
Terry Bisson, *Bears Discover Fire: And Other Stories*, 1993
  The bears are just the beginning of the familiar turned unpredictable in this collection.
Nancy Kress, *Beaker's Dozen*, 1998
  Most of the stories in this collection relate to the author's interest in medicine and anthropology as sources for science fiction.
Connie Willis, *Impossible Things*, 1993
  Award-winning author Willis takes you on a guided tour of her quirky vision of the present and the future.

866

URSULA K. LE GUIN
ERIC BEDDOWS, Illustrator

Changing Planes

(New York: Harcourt, 2003)

Subject(s): Science Fiction; Short Stories
Age range(s): Grades 9-Adult

Summary: It's an experience practically everyone is familiar with, the slightly anxious boredom that one experiences while waiting to change planes in an airport. One gifted soul harnesses her discomfort and really changes planes, finding herself in a different world where she explores another reality. The technique turns out to be teachable and soon travelers in airports everywhere are visiting some truly exotic places. This short story collection is the record of the planes visited and the experiences of the visitors. In one, a newfound friend is discovered to be part corn plant; in another, the denizens of the visited world have wings. On another plane, a defeated people build a palace of small rooms that serves no purpose yet covers a mountain, insisting it is dedicated to their enemies. Although there are light-hearted visits, like the plane of holidays where Christmas and Easter are perpetual, most are dark and enigmatic. (246 pages)

Where it's reviewed:
Booklist, April 15, 2003, page 1428
Kirkus Reviews, May 1, 2003, page 633
Library Journal, April 1, 2003, page 133
New York Times Book Review, July 27, 2003, page 17
Publishers Weekly, April 14, 2003, page 45

Other books by the same author:
The Birthday of the World and Other Stories, 2002
The Other Wind, 2001
The Telling, 2000

Other books you might like:
Orson Scott Card, *Future on Ice*, 1998
  Card is the editor of this collection of science fiction stories by a variety of famous authors.
James Patrick Kelly, *Think Like a Dinosaur*, 1997
  Dinosaurs supervise human space travel due to our emotional instability in one story in this unpredictable collection.
Nancy Kress, *The Aliens of Earth*, 1993
  We are the aliens in this collection of futures in which humanity behaves in ways scarcely human.

867

URSULA K. LE GUIN
JULIE DOWNING, Illustrator

Tom Mouse

(Brookfield, CT: Roaring Brook Press, 2002)

Subject(s): Animals/Mice; Railroads; Travel
Age range(s): Grades K-3
Major character(s): Tom Mouse, Mouse, Traveler; Ms. Powers, Aged Person, Traveler
Time period(s): 2000s
Locale(s): United States

Summary: Not content to live out his life in the diner at the train station, Tom Mouse longs for the freedom of travel and sneaks aboard a train in hopes of fulfilling his dream. Unfamiliar with trains, Tom is not able to locate the recommended boxcar and scurries into the first empty room with a closet that he finds. Roomette Nine is soon occupied by Ms. Powers who quickly deduces the presence of a mouse and quietly appreciates the companionship. She talks to Tom Mouse and offers him a way off the train when it arrives in Chicago. More importantly, she promises future travel to San Francisco and Japan as well as more carrot sticks and molasses cookies if Tom can travel quietly and out of sight. A dream comes true for Tom! (40 pages)

Where it's reviewed:
Booklist, March 15, 2002, page 1263
Bulletin of the Center for Children's Books, May 2002, page 329
Horn Book, May 2002, page 316
Publishers Weekly, March 11, 2002, page 71
School Library Journal, May 2002, page 120

Other books by the same author:
A Ride on the Red Mare's Back, 1992

Fire and Stone, 1989
A Visit from Dr. Katz, 1988

Other books you might like:
Mary Lyn Ray, *All Aboard!*, 2003
  A girl and her toy rabbit travel by train to Grandma and Grandpa's house.
Marjorie Weinman Sharmat, *Nate the Great on the Owl Express*, 2003
  Nate's cousin depends on him to safely escort her owl on a train trip. When the owl vanishes Nate and Sludge use their detective skills to find it.
James Stevenson, *All Aboard!*, 1995
  On a trip to the World's Fair, Hubie gets aboard the wrong train after a brief stop and heads for California while his family goes to New York.

868

MARY LEARY, Author/Illustrator

Karate Girl

(New York: Farrar Straus Giroux, 2003)

Subject(s): Martial Arts; Bullies; Brothers and Sisters
Age range(s): Grades K-2
Major character(s): Unnamed Character, Sister
Time period(s): 2000s (2003)
Locale(s): United States

Summary: In the author's first picture book a young girl feels helpless when bullies pick on her little brother. She begins going to karate lessons with a friend in the hopes of being able to get back at the bullies. The lessons teach her self-defense, self-confidence, and the importance of being strong enough to avoid a fight. In the fall, she is able to stand up to the bullies and her brother begins taking karate lessons as well. (32 pages)

Where it's reviewed:
Booklist, December 15, 2003, page 753
School Library Journal, November 2003, page 105

Other books you might like:
Emily Arnold McCully, *Beautiful Warrior: The Legend of the Nun's Kung Fu*, 1998
  McCully imagines the life of two legendary female Kung Fu masters who lived in 17th-century China.
Ann Morris, *Karate Boy*, 1996
  A boy prepares for his test to be promoted from blue belt to green belt.
Brian Pinkney, *JoJo's Flying Side Kick*, 1995
  Tae Kwon Do student JoJo worries that she will not be able to do the flying side kick required to earn her yellow belt.

869

HO BAEK LEE, Author/Illustrator

While We Were Out

(La Jolla, CA: Kane/Miller Book Publishers, 2003)

Subject(s): Animals/Rabbits; Playing; Apartments
Age range(s): Preschool-Grade 1
Major character(s): Unnamed Character, Rabbit

Time period(s): 2000s
Locale(s): Korea, South

Summary: Through an unlocked balcony door, a rabbit quietly enters an empty apartment. She helps herself to food from the refrigerator, dines at the table, and watches a video while snacking like a couch potato. The curious rabbit continues with her imitative behavior by trying on clothes, sampling make-up, and playing with toys. After a good night's sleep the rabbit returns to the balcony, closing the door behind her and lies down as if nothing has happened. She's confident that no one will suspect she's been in the apartment, but the family may find some clues when they return in a title originally published in South Korea. (32 pages)

Where it's reviewed:
Booklist, April 15, 2003, page 1469
Bulletin of the Center for Children's Books, March 2003, page 278
Horn Book, July 2003, page 444
School Library Journal, June 2003, page 111

Awards the book has won:
Bulletin of the Center for Children's Books Blue Ribbons, 2003
New York Times Best Illustrated Books, 2003

Other books you might like:
Margaret Wise Brown, *Home for a Bunny*, 2003
  A new edition of a 1956 classic tells of a rabbit's search for a home and the satisfaction of finding one to share with another rabbit.
Lindsay Barrett George, *My Bunny and Me*, 2001
  After drawing a picture of a rabbit, Luis imagines the activities he would share with the bunny if it were only real.
Joan Holub, *Why Do Rabbits Hop?: And Other Questions about Rabbits, Guinea Pigs, Hamsters, and Gerbils*, 2003
  A nonfiction title in the Dial Easy-to-Read series uses answers to questions to explain the behavior and characteristics of rabbits and other small animals.

870

JEANNE M. LEE, Author/Illustrator

Bitter Dumplings

(New York: Farrar Straus Giroux, 2002)

Subject(s): Orphans; Outcasts; Poverty
Age range(s): Grades 1-4
Major character(s): Mei Mei, Orphan, Young Woman; Po Po, Aged Person
Time period(s): 15th century
Locale(s): China

Summary: After Mei Mei's father dies, her dowry is spent to pay for his funeral and she is left destitute and alone. The only person in her village who takes pity on her is the old, outcast dumpling seller, Po Po. Po Po teaches Mei Mei to make dumplings from shrimp and bitter melon to sell in the village. One day, the emperor's treasure fleet lands in the village harbor. A slave with the fleet tastes the bitter dumplings and realizes that this is the village he was kidnapped from as a

child. Mei Mei and Po Po help the slave escape and they start a happy new life together. (32 pages)

Where it's reviewed:
Booklist, May 15, 2002, page 1602
Bulletin of the Center for Children's Books, May 2002, page 329
Horn Book, May/June 2002, page 315
Publishers Weekly, February 4, 2002, page 77
School Library Journal, May 2002, page 120

Other books by the same author:
I Once Was a Monkey: Stories Buddha Told, 1999
Silent Lotus, 1991
Toad Is the Uncle of Heaven: A Vietnamese Folktale, 1989

Other books you might like:
Ai-Ling Louie, *Yeh-Shen: A Cinderella Story from China*, 1982
  Yeh-Shen overcomes her evil stepsister and stepmother to marry a prince.
Kathy Tucker, *The Seven Chinese Sisters*, 2003
  After a dragon kidnaps a baby, her six sisters use their individual talents to rescue her.
Ed Young, *Lon Po Po: A Red-Riding Hood Story from China*, 1990
  In this Caldecott Medal winner, three sisters band together to fight off a wolf.

871

JEFFREY LEE

True Blue

(New York: Delacorte/Random House, 2003)

Subject(s): Animals/Insects; Fathers and Daughters; Schools/Middle Schools
Age range(s): Grades 4-7
Major character(s): Molly O'Connor, Student—Middle School; Chrys Lepida, Student—Middle School; Rick O'Connor, Handicapped
Time period(s): 2000s
Locale(s): United States

Summary: A car accident leaves Molly with a terrible scar above her knee and, even worse, puts her journalist father in a wheelchair and impairs his ability to speak. With their family income reduced and her mother working as a waitress, Molly switches schools in the middle of the year where the only person who's nice to her is Chrys, a strange boy who always wears a bulky black overcoat. Working together on a science project, Molly is surprised to learn how much Chrys knows about butterflies and other insects. She's astounded when Chrys takes off his coat and displays his butterfly wings, a necessary feat to save their damaged science project. They win the top prize which helps buy computer software so Molly's father can once again communicate. (132 pages)

Where it's reviewed:
Bulletin of the Center for Children's Books, November 2003, page 114
Kirkus Reviews, July 15, 2003, page 965
Library Media Connection, March 2004, page 67
Publishers Weekly, September 8, 2003, page 77

School Library Journal, September 2003, page 216

Other books you might like:
David Almond, *Skellig*, 1999
  Michael and his neighbor Mina befriend a winged creature hiding in their garage who helps heal Michael's sister.
Bill Brittain, *Wings*, 1991
  Until Ian sprouts bat-like wings, six-fingered Anita has been the class oddity.
John LeVert, *The Flight of the Cassowary*, 1986
  John becomes so obsessed with animal characteristics in humans that he actually flies.
Laurel Winter, *Growing Wings*, 2000
  Turning 11, Linnet grows wings and finds happiness when her grandmother takes her to a hidden refuge where she meets others with wings.

872

TANITH LEE

A Bed of Earth: The Gravedigger's Tale
(Woodstock, NY: Overlook Press, 2002)

Series: Secret Books of Venus. Book Three
Subject(s): Fantasy; Love; Death
Age range(s): Grades 9-Adult
Major character(s): Meralda della Scorpia, Noblewoman; Beatrixa Barbaron, Noblewoman; Bartolome da Loura di An'Santa, Morgue Attendant (gravedigger)
Time period(s): Indeterminate Past
Locale(s): Venus, Fictional City

Summary: Two noble families squabble over a small plot of land. It appears of little significance, but is one of the few places in Venus in which a body may truly be buried; under most of the land, the water is too close and bodies must be entombed. Tragedy follows the della Scorpia and Barbaron houses as a result of their quarrel. When a della Scorpia flees from an arranged marriage, a Barbaron makes certain that the outcome is both horrible and deadly. Meralda della Scorpia's child, given spirit form, haunts the next generation and enacts a terrible revenge on the Barbarons. Bartolome is ignorant of his connection to the feuding noble houses, but eventually he discovers that he is no simple gravedigger and has been drawn to this burial ground by connections of flesh and spirit. This is a dark but elegant tale of star-crossed lovers and the reverberation of their pain down the generations. (330 pages)

Where it's reviewed:
Booklist, August 2002, page 1938
Library Journal, September 5, 2002, page 96
Publishers Weekly, August 19, 2002, page 71

Other books by the same author:
Mortal Suns, 2003
Wolf Queen, 2002
Wolf Wing, 2002

Other books you might like:
Mercedes Lackey, *The Shadow of the Lion*, 2002
  The shadow of the winged lion of St. Mark's falls on Marco and designates him as the future ruler of a magical, alternate-history Venice.

Patricia McKillip, *Ombria in Shadow*, 2002
  Many strange allies aid the king's mistress when she's turned out on the streets by the new regent of mysterious, shadowy Ombria.
Michaela Roessner, *The Stars Dispose*, 1997
  An apprentice finds himself caught up in the intrigues of the Medici family.

873

TANITH LEE

Mortal Suns
(Woodstock, NY: The Overlook Press, 2003)

Subject(s): Fantasy; Coming-of-Age
Age range(s): Grades 10-Adult
Major character(s): Calistra "Cemira" or "Sirai", Royalty, Handicapped; Klyton, Royalty, Warrior; Udrombis, Royalty
Time period(s): Indeterminate Past
Locale(s): Akhemony, Fictional Country

Summary: Now an elderly woman in a foreign land, Sirai tells the story of her youth, a time so distant even her name has changed. Sirai, one of the many king's children, was born to a minor wife of his. Born without feet, her horrified mother called her Cemira and exiled her to the shrine of the Dead God. Here the servers are virtually entombed and kept locked away from the world until their deaths. But Cemira is not forgotten, as her mother intends, for the high queen Udrombis hears of the child and makes inquiries. When she becomes a widow, Udrombis retains power and decides that no child of her husband's can be wasted; recalling Cemira, she renames her Calistra. A patient woman, Udrombis now waits to see what will come of this action. Her warrior brother Klyton notices her beauty and sends for an army veteran with a wooden leg to teach his sister to stand. Calistra, who has fallen in love with her handsome brother, determines she will learn to walk and, on her silver feet, defy any obstacles to marry Klyton. Her journey is longer and stranger than she can possibly imagine. (335 pages)

Where it's reviewed:
Booklist, September 1, 2003, page 75
Kirkus Reviews, June 1, 2003, page 783
Library Journal, July 2003, page 133
Publishers Weekly, August 4, 2003, page 61

Other books by the same author:
Venus Preserved, 2003
A Bed of Earth: The Gravedigger's Tale, 2002
Wolf Wing, 2002

Other books you might like:
Roberta Gellis, *Bull God*, 2000
  Ariadne is the unhappy sister of the Minotaur, a monster who is half bull and half man.
Adele Geras, *Troy*, 2002
  As the ancient city of Troy falls, the gods are still playing with its inhabitants.
Donna Jo Napoli, *The Great God Pan*, 2003
  Pan falls in love with a human girl whose father is willing to do anything to sail for Troy.

874

TANITH LEE

Wolf Queen

(New York: Dutton Children's Books, 2002)

Series: Claidi Journals. Book III
Subject(s): Fantasy; Adventure and Adventurers; Romance
Age range(s): Grades 7-10
Major character(s): Claidi, Rebel; Argul, Leader
Time period(s): Indeterminate
Locale(s): Fictional Country

Summary: Claidi has her freedom again, and she immediately sets out in the mechanical Star to find the Hulta and her beloved Argul. The nearly omniscient and all-powerful Star makes short work of discovering the Hulta tribe, but all is not well. The people have been led to believe that Claidi left willingly and Argul gave up leadership of the tribe and disappeared. Claidi is distraught, but soon decides to find and convince him of her innocence. Unfortunately, shortly after she begins this mission, the Star fails and both it and its mechanical guardian shut down for repairs. Claidi has no recourse but to begin her search on foot. Intending to reach a town called Panther's Halt, her first night outdoors finds her in the middle of a forest. Out of the darkness appears a speaking panther, which, although scornful, insists on setting her on her way. Obviously, Claidi is destined for something, and in this final volume of the trilogy she may finally discover what it is. (216 pages)

Where it's reviewed:
Booklist, April 15, 2002, page 1418
Bulletin of the Center for Children's Books, June 2002, page 370
Kirkus Reviews, May 1, 2002, page 659
School Library Journal, June 2002, page 141
Voice of Youth Advocates, August 2002, page 203

Other books by the same author:
Mortal Suns, 2003
Wolf Wing, 2002 (Claidi Journals Book IV)
Wolf Tower, 1998 (Claidi Journals Book II)

Other books you might like:
Clare B. Dunkle, *The Hollow Kingdom*, 2003
    When he is trapped by a sorcerer, the human wife of the goblin king follows to find and rescue him.
Laura Williams McCaffrey, *Alia Waking*, 2003
    Alia shares the dreams of all the girls in her village to join the warrior women, but she painfully discovers that her destiny lies elsewhere.
Tamora Pierce, *Trickster's Choice*, 2003
    To be the chosen of a god is an uncomfortable thing, Aly finds, but it does give one a certain direction.

875

ALISON LESTER

The Snow Pony

(Boston: Walter Lorraine Books/Houghton Mifflin, 2003)

Subject(s): Animals/Horses; Adventure and Adventurers; Ranch Life
Age range(s): Grades 6-10
Major character(s): Dusty Riley, 14-Year-Old; Snow Pony, Horse; Stewie Riley, Brother (of Dusty)
Time period(s): 2000s
Locale(s): Australia (cattle farm)

Summary: The daughter of fourth generation Australian cattle farmers, Dusty is proud of her mother, who trains horses and was once a show jumper, and happiest when working alongside her father who considers her his "right hand man." Three years of drought have altered her once happy father until now he looks for his happiness in alcohol, which sends Dusty to her beloved horse Snow Pony for companionship. Dusty and her father found Snow Pony in the wild and after her mother trained the horse, Dusty's been the only one able to ride Snow Pony. Heading up to the high plains to bring in the cattle for the winter, Dusty, Stewie and their father are suddenly faced with a heavy snowstorm. Dusty's father is badly injured by a cow and now it's up to Dusty to ride Snow Pony through the storm and the snow-covered terrain to find help for her father. (194 pages)

Where it's reviewed:
Booklist, March 15, 2003, page 1317
Kirkus Reviews, April 15, 2003, page 609
Publishers Weekly, March 31, 2003, page 67
School Library Journal, April 2003, page 164
Voice of Youth Advocates, June 2003, page 136

Other books by the same author:
The Quicksand Pony, 1998

Other books you might like:
Noel Ackerman, *Spirit Horse*, 1998
    Running Crane overcomes his fear of horses to befriend, tame and ride the stallion called the "spirit horse" because of his legendary color.
Walt Morey, *The Year of the Black Pony*, 1976
    In Oregon in the early 1900s, young Christopher owns and loves his black stallion.
K.M. Peyton, *Darkling*, 1990
    Jenny's grandfather buys her a gangly colt and Jenny transforms that colt into a winning racehorse.

876

HELEN LESTER
LYNN MUNSINGER, Illustrator

Something Might Happen

(Boston: Walter Lorraine Books/Houghton Mifflin Company, 2003)

Subject(s): Fear; Animals; Aunts and Uncles
Age range(s): Grades K-3
Major character(s): Twitchly Fidget, Animal (lemur); Bridget, Aunt, Animal (lemur)

Time period(s): Indeterminate
Locale(s): Fictional Country

Summary: Twitchly sits in his windowless, doorless, roofless hut afraid to go out, afraid to use shampoo, fearful of something getting in and frightening him. He refuses to go to parades with the other lemurs because he might get hit with a drumstick or sucked into a trombone. Twitchly imagines disasters everywhere. One day Aunt Bridget drops in through the nonroof and notes that Twitchly needs ''a fixin'.'' She shampoos his fur, feeds him cereal, and insists he put his shoes on his feet and—nothing happens. When Aunt Bridget is ready to leave she can't get out so the newly confident Twitchly creates a door and windows for her. Then he strolls out in search of parades and marshmallow roasts. (32 pages)

Where it's reviewed:
Booklist, September 15, 2003, page 246
Bulletin of the Center for Children's Books, October 2003, page 67
School Library Journal, September 2003, page 183

Other books by the same author:
Score One for the Sloths, 2001
Hooway for Wodney Wat, 1999 (ALA Notable Children's Books)
Princess Penelope's Parrot, 1996

Other books you might like:
Katie Davis, *Scared Stiff*, 2001
    A timid, overly imaginative girl is scared of many things until she dons a witch's hat to give her confidence.
Valiska Gregory, *Kate's Giants*, 1995
    When Kate imagines scary things behind the attic door her parents help her find the courage to confront her fears.
Kevin Henkes, *Wemberly Worried*, 2000
    Wemberly worries about everything, imagining the worst for every situation although in reality the anticipated problems do not materialize.

877

HELEN LESTER
LYNN MUNSINGER, Illustrator

Tackylocks and the Three Bears

(Boston: Walter Lorraine Books/Houghton Mifflin Company, 2002)

Subject(s): Schools; Animals/Penguins; Acting
Age range(s): Grades K-2
Major character(s): Tacky, Penguin
Time period(s): Indeterminate
Locale(s): Fictional Country

Summary: By the luck of the draw, Tacky gets the lead role in a play that he and his friends will put on for a class of younger penguins. Everyone practices in preparation for the big day. On stage the three bears go out on a walk right on cue. Tackylocks enters and immediately the play goes in an unrehearsed direction. He knocks over the table, eats all the porridge in every bowl and piles the chairs up to reach a cookie jar so in the ensuing crash all the chairs break. Feeling very tired, Tackylocks is grateful the next scene involves beds. He pulls the bedding off the big, hard bed and the soft middle-sized bed revealing the reality of the stage props

beneath. Then he snuggles into the just-right little bed and goes to sleep under all the blankets. When the three bears return the props no longer match their lines, but they try to carry on with the show. The audience considers it the best play ever! (32 pages)

Where it's reviewed:
Booklist, October 1, 2002, page 337
Bulletin of the Center for Children's Books, December 2002, page 164
Publishers Weekly, August 19, 2002, page 92
School Library Journal, September 2002, page 197

Other books by the same author:
Hurty Feelings, 2004
Score One for the Sloths, 2001
Tacky and the Emperor, 2000
Tacky in Trouble, 1998

Other books you might like:
Susan Lowell, *Dusty Locks and the Three Bears*, 2001
    This retelling casts a dirty little girl avoiding a bath as the intruder in the bears' home.
James Marshall, *Goldilocks and the Three Bears*, 1988
    In a humorous version of the tale, three bears returning from a walk discover someone sleeping in Baby Bear's bed.
Alan Osmond, *Just Right*, 1998
    This story tells what happens to Goldilocks and the Three Bears as grown-ups.

878

JULIUS LESTER
JOHN CLAPP, Illustrator

Shining

(San Diego: Silver Whistle/Harcourt, Inc., 2003)

Subject(s): Africa; Mutism; Difference
Age range(s): Grades 1-4
Major character(s): Shining, Child, Daughter
Time period(s): Indeterminate Past
Locale(s): Africa

Summary: A baby girl born in a mountain village is named Shining because her skin is so black that it shines like the sun. Shining is mute, however, and this causes fear in her parents and the other villagers. When Shining is two, her mother takes her to a wise woman to find out the cause of her muteness. Shining's mother is reassured, but the villagers continue to shun her. Shining finally gains acceptance when the wise woman appears in the village, anointing Shining as her successor. (32 pages)

Where it's reviewed:
Bulletin of the Center for Children's Books, December 2003, page 156
Publishers Weekly, December 22, 2003, page 60

Other books by the same author:
Black Cowboy, Wild Horses: A True Story, 1998
John Henry, 1994
To Be a Slave, 1968 (Newbery Honor Book)

Other books you might like:

Meshack Asare, *Sosu's Call*, 2001
   Sosu's Ghanian neighbors shun him because he can't walk, but when a storm threatens the village, Sosu saves the day.
Jeanne M. Lee, *Silent Lotus*, 1991
   Lotus was born deaf and mute; the other children in her Cambodian village don't want to play with her.
Stephanie Stuve-Bodeen, *Babu's Song*, 2003
   Babu and his mute grandfather sell toys that the grandfather makes in their Tanzanian village.

879

JULIUS LESTER
JOE CEPEDA, Illustrator

Why Heaven Is Far Away

(New York: Scholastic, 2002)

Subject(s): Religion; Folk Tales; Animals/Reptiles
Age range(s): Grades K-3
Major character(s): Shaniqua, Angel; God, Deity; Mrs. God, Spouse
Time period(s): Indeterminate
Locale(s): Heaven

Summary: One day, Shaniqua, the "angel in charge of everybody's business," notices that the snakes down on earth are being eaten up, because they are not able to defend themselves. God sends Shaniqua back down to earth with poison to give to the snakes. Once that happens though, the snakes start biting everything that moves and all the humans and animals begin climbing up the ladders into Heaven. Shaniqua and Mrs. God go down to talk to the snakes and discover that the snakes can't see or hear much, so they're biting to be on the safe side. Shaniqua and Mrs. God come up with a solution and all the ladders from heaven to earth are pulled up to prevent another mass migration. (40 pages)

Where it's reviewed:
Booklist, October 2002, page 345
Bulletin of the Center for Children's Books, December 2002, page 164
Horn Book, November/December 2002, page 735
Publishers Weekly, October 28, 2002, page 75
School Library Journal, October 2002, page 118

Other books by the same author:
Ackamarackus: Julius Lester's Sumptuously Silly Fantastically Funny Fables, 2001 (Parenting's Reading Magic Award)
What a Truly Cool World, 1999 (Bulletin of the Center for Children's Books Blue Ribbons)
Black Cowboy, Wild Horses: A True Story, 1998
John Henry, 1994

Other books you might like:
Verna Aardema, *Why Mosquitoes Buzz in People's Ears: A West African Tale*, 1975
   This Caldecott winner tells how mosquitoes developed their annoying buzz.

Lily Toy Hong, *How the Ox Star Fell From Heaven*, 1995
   This Chinese legend tells how oxen first came to live on Earth.
Jeanne M. Lee, *Toad Is the Uncle of Heaven: A Vietnamese Folktale*, 1989
   Toad travels to heaven to ask for rain.

880

LAURA LEUCK
NIGEL MCMULLEN, Illustrator

Goodnight, Baby Monster

(New York: HarperCollins, Inc., 2002)

Subject(s): Bedtime; Monsters; Stories in Rhyme
Age range(s): Preschool-Grade 1
Major character(s): Unnamed Character, Mother; Unnamed Character, Child
Time period(s): 2000s (2002)
Locale(s): United States

Summary: A human mother reads her child a bedtime story which describes how monsters and other spooky creatures sleep. The baby mummy wraps up in its tomb and the baby swamp thing snuggles in slime. A final good night finds mother and child in bed surrounded by the spooky creatures, now revealed to be stuffed animals. (32 pages)

Where it's reviewed:
Bulletin of the Center for Children's Book, October 2002, page 65
School Library Journal, September 2002, page 198

Other books by the same author:
My Beastly Brother, 2003
My Monster Mama Loves Me So, 1999
My Baby Brother Has Ten Tiny Toes, 1997

Other books you might like:
Maggie de Vries, *How Sleep Found Tabitha*, 2002
   One night, when Tabitha can't sleep she imagines her stuffed animals coming alive and asking her to sleep with each of them in their natural habitats.
Preston McClear, *The Boy Under the Bed*, 1998
   Monster Giles is scared of the boy he thinks lives under his bed.
Frances Thomas, *What If*, 1999
   Little Monster has typical childish fears, but Mother Monster soothes them.

881

LAURA LEUCK
S.D. SCHINDLER, Illustrator

One Witch

(New York: Walker & Company, 2003)

Subject(s): Witches and Witchcraft; Halloween; Stories in Rhyme
Age range(s): Grades K-2
Major character(s): Unnamed Character, Witch
Time period(s): Indeterminate
Locale(s): Fictional Country

Summary: One witch stands atop a hill with a large, empty caldron. To fill it she visits two cats, three scarecrows and four goblins. Each makes a contribution. Five vampires, six mummies and seven owls pitch in too as do eight ghosts, nine skeletons and ten werewolves. The witch's bats deliver invitations to each of those giving ingredients to the witch's concoction. The stew of moths, snakes, spiders, bones, bird's claws, hair, blood, slugs, and fish tails boils, brews and oozes. The witch's friends come to enjoy the stew, saving one bowl for . . . who? You! (32 pages)

Where it's reviewed:
Booklist, September 1, 2003, page 136
Bulletin of the Center for Children's Books, October 2003, page 67
Publishers Weekly, August 4, 2003, page 77
School Library Journal, August 2003, page 136

Awards the book has won:
Center for Children's Books Best Books, 2003

Other books by the same author:
My Creature Teacher, 2004
My Beastly Brother, 2003
Goodnight, Baby Monster, 2002

Other books you might like:
Charlotte Huck, *A Creepy Countdown*, 1998
   Halloween symbols appear in a rhyming tale that uses the numbers one to ten and back again.
Judy Sierra, *The House That Drac Built*, 1995
   A rhyming cumulative tale introduces such unusual creatures as a manticore and the fiend of Bloodygore living in the house that Drac built.
Kevin Somers, *Meaner than Meanest*, 2001
   By forgetting one critical ingredient in a recipe a witch creates a sweet little girl rather than the mean creature she's trying to make.

882

GAIL CARSON LEVINE
SCOTT NASH, Illustrator

Betsy Who Cried Wolf!
(New York: HarperCollins Publishers, 2002)

Subject(s): Animals/Sheep; Animals/Wolves; Humor
Age range(s): Grades K-2
Major character(s): Betsy, 8-Year-Old, Shepherd; Zimmo, Wolf; Farmer Woolsey, Farmer
Time period(s): Indeterminate Past
Locale(s): Bray Valley, Fictional Country

Summary: As novice shepherd Betsy heads up the mountain for her first day on the job she's unaware that Zimmo is waiting with a plan to satisfy his loneliness and his hunger. Although Betsy confirms Zimmo's identity as a wolf with her Wolf Checklist, her attempts to secure help fail because Zimmo vanishes each time she blows her whistle. After hurrying to the rescue twice, Farmer Woolsey scolds Betsy for the false alarms and sends her back to Shepherd School. The next day Betsy is allowed to shepherd the flock again, but she knows better than to whistle when she sees a wolf. Instead, she shares her lunch with the hungry creature thus fulfilling her obligation to the sheep and Zimmo's plan too as the wolf acquires a home and a job with Betsy. (36 pages)

Where it's reviewed:
Booklist, July 2002, page 1860
Bulletin of the Center for Children's Books, October 2002, page 65
New York Times Book Review, June 2, 2002, page 30
Publishers Weekly, May 6, 2002, page 57
School Library Journal, June 2002, page 98

Other books you might like:
Sara Fanelli, *Wolf*, 1997
   Friendly Wolf's intentions are misunderstood by the fearful townspeople who chase Wolf away from their city.
Bob Hartman, *The Wolf Who Cried Boy*, 2002
   Seeking a more varied dinner menu Little Wolf tries to trick his parents by calling ''Boy!'' but when one finally appears, they refuse to heed his call.
Jerry Pinkney, *Aesop's Fables*, 2000
   An award-winning illustrated collection of Aesop's work includes a retelling of ''The Shepherd Boy and the Wolf.''

883

GAIL CARSON LEVINE
MARK ELLIOT, Illustrator

The Fairy's Return
(New York: HarperCollins Publishers, 2002)

Series: Princess Tales
Subject(s): Princes and Princesses; Fairies; Fairy Tales
Age range(s): Grades 3-5
Major character(s): Lark, Royalty (princess); Robin, Young Man
Time period(s): Indeterminate Past
Locale(s): Fictional Country

Summary: Princess Lark longs to be treated like a regular person and Robin, a baker's son, wants to find someone to laugh at his jokes. It's love at first sight when they meet, although their families try to keep them apart. Finally, after Robin is able to complete three seemingly impossible tasks with the help of a fairy, Robin and Princess Lark marry and live happily ever after. (112 pages)

Where it's reviewed:
Booklist, August 2002, page 1964
School Library Journal, September 2002, page 198

Other books by the same author:
The Wish, 2000
The Fairy's Mistake, 1999 (Princess Tales)
The Princess Test, 1999 (Princess Tales)

Other books you might like:
Donna Jo Napoli, *The Prince of the Pond: Otherwise Known As De Fawg Pin*, 1992
   This humorous tale tells the story of the Frog Prince from the frog's perspective.
E. Nesbit, *Melisande*, 1992
   When Princess Melisande is born a fairy godmother casts a spell that makes her bald.

Vivian Vande Velde, *A Hidden Magic*, 1985
> Ordinary but spirited Princess Jennifer must save the conceited Prince Alexander.

Patricia C. Wrede, *Searching for Dragons*, 1991
> Sensible Princess Cimorene meets her match in sensible King Mendanbar when the two investigate a series of dragon-nappings.

884

GAIL CARSON LEVINE
MARK ELLIOT, Illustrator

For Biddle's Sake

(New York: HarperCollins, 2002)

Series: Princess Tales
Subject(s): Princes and Princesses; Fairies; Fairy Tales
Age range(s): Grades 3-5
Major character(s): Parsley, Young Woman, Adoptee; Bombina, Mythical Creature (fairy), Mother; Tansy, Royalty (prince), Brother (younger)
Time period(s): Indeterminate Past
Locale(s): Snettering-on-Snoakes, Fictional Country

Summary: Unable to resist Parsley's smile, Bombina adopts him at a young age, a puzzling situation since Bombina usually only wants to turn humans into toads. When Bombina sees Parsley smiling at the long-suffering Prince Tansy, her jealousy prompts her to try to turn the prince into a toad. However, Parsley steps in the way of the spell and she gets turned into a toad instead. Only a marriage proposal from a human can turn her back. As a toad, fortunately, Parsley gains magical powers and is able to help Prince Tansy beat his older twin brothers in the quest to be king. Prince Tansy falls in love with the toady Parsley and, once she is human again, they marry. (112 pages)

Where it's reviewed:
Booklist, August 2002, page 1964
School Library Journal, September 2002, page 198

Other books by the same author:
The Fairy's Return, 2002 (Princess Tales)
The Two Princesses of Bamarre, 2001
Ella Enchanted, 1997 (Newbery Honor Book)

Other books you might like:
M.M. Kaye, *The Ordinary Princess*, 1984
> When her godmother's wish makes the seventh princess of Phantasmorania ordinary, she becomes a kitchen maid in a neighboring kingdom.

Vivian Vande Velde, *Wizard at Work*, 2003
> A young wizard wants to have an ordinary summer vacation, but he is drawn into adventures with unicorns, ghosts, and far too many princesses.

Patricia C. Wrede, *Dealing with Dragons*, 1990
> Tomboy Princess Cimorene is tired of etiquette and embroidery so she runs away to be the princess for a dragon.

885

DAVID LEVITHAN

Boy Meets Boy

(New York: Knopf, 2003)

Subject(s): Homosexuality/Lesbianism; Romance
Age range(s): Grades 9-12
Major character(s): Paul, 10th Grader, Homosexual; Noah, Homosexual, Student—High School; Kyle, Student—High School
Time period(s): 2000s
Locale(s): United States

Summary: Happily gay Paul meets new kid Noah, the boy of his dreams, in the local bookstore and immediately falls in love with him. In Paul's town, where the Boy Scouts become the Joy Scouts to show their displeasure with the national organization and the cheerleaders ride motorcycles, no one looks askance if Paul and Noah walk through town down the street holding hands. The entire town is filled with intriguing individuals, such as janitors who operate as day traders but keep cleaning because they enjoy it, and customs such as the journal affixed to each gravestone so one can write to the occupant. When Paul's former boyfriend Kyle tries to reenter his life, Paul has to prove his loyalty to Noah in this quirkily entertaining first novel by this author. (185 pages)

Where it's reviewed:
Bulletin of the Center for Children's Books, September 2003, page 3
Horn Book, January 2004, page 83
Publishers Weekly, October 6, 2003, page 85
School Library Journal, September 2003, page 216
Voice of Youth Advocates, October 2003, page 314

Awards the book has won:
Booklist Editors' Choice/Books for Youth, 2003
ALA Best Books for Young Adults, 2004

Other books by the same author:
The Realm of Possibility, 2004

Other books you might like:
Francesca Lia Block, *Weetzie Bat*, 1989
> Offbeat Weetzie and Dirk each find their true love, though not with one another, in this witty, bizarre, modern-day fairy tale.

Stephen Chbosky, *The Perks of Being a Wallflower*, 1999
> In Charlie's freshman year in high school, he helps his pregnant sister, adjusts to the suicide of a best friend and is hospitalized for depression.

Alex Sanchez, *Rainbow Boys*, 2001
> Jason, Kyle and Nelson face their senior year, and life-changing decisions, as they deal with their sexual identity.

Ellen Wittlinger, *Hard Love*, 1999
> John thinks he's found the love for which he's been searching when he meets Marisol, only to discover she's in love with another girl.

886

SONIA LEVITIN

Room in the Heart

(New York: Dutton, 2003)

Subject(s): Holocaust; Jews; World War II
Age range(s): Grades 7-10
Major character(s): Julie Weinstein, 13-Year-Old; Ingrid Nelson, 13-Year-Old; Niels Nelson, 15-Year-Old, Resistance Fighter; Emil Hansen, 15-Year-Old
Time period(s): 1940s (1940-1943)
Locale(s): Copenhagen, Denmark

Summary: Though Julie and her family are Jewish, living in Copenhagen they have never felt the persecution experienced by other Jews in Europe, until the spring of 1940 when Germans drop leaflets letting the Danish know they're invading for "their protection." For the next three years Julie and her good friend Ingrid, who's Christian, worry about what will happen to the Jews in Denmark. Ingrid's brother Niels does more than worry; he joins the resistance movement and delivers anti-Nazi leaflets around the city. His good friend Emil takes a different stance for he likes the Nazis and would like to keep Denmark "pure." When word is received that the Nazis plan to round up all the Jews in Copenhagen, Julie works to find a way to escape while Niels wishes he could do more to help, a task his father has already taken on without Niels's knowledge. In an amazing success story, 7000 of Copenhagen's 8000 Jews are boat-lifted to safety in Sweden with Julie's family among those successfully rescued, and Emil as one of the rescuers. (290 pages)

Where it's reviewed:
Booklist, November 1, 2003, page 490
Horn Book, January 2004, page 85
Publishers Weekly, September 8, 2003, page 77
School Library Journal, December 2003, page 156
Voice of Youth Advocates, February 2004, page 493

Other books by the same author:
Clem's Chances, 2001
Dream Freedom, 2000
The Cure, 1999
Yesterday's Child, 1997
Escape from Egypt: A Novel, 1994

Other books you might like:
Lois Lowry, *Number the Stars*, 1989
    Annemarie fears for her Jewish friend's life when the Germans occupy her Copenhagen neighborhood.
Johanna Reiss, *The Upstairs Room*, 1972
    Staying in the homes of farmers has kept a Jewish family from Nazi persecution, but now it's time to face the future together.
Bjarne B. Reuter, *The Boys of St. Petri*, 1994
    Sons of a local minister, Lars and Gunnar lead their Danish classmates in acts of resistance against the Nazis.

887

ELIZABETH LEVY
SALLY WERN COMPORT, Illustrator

Vampire State Building

(New York: HarperCollins Publishers, 2002)

Series: Sam and Robert
Subject(s): Contests; Vampires; Games
Age range(s): Grades 2-5
Major character(s): Sam Bamford, 11-Year-Old, Chess Player; Robert Bamford, Brother (younger), 9-Year-Old; Mabel, Cousin, 9-Year-Old; Vlad Clinciu, 12-Year-Old, Chess Player
Time period(s): 2000s (2002)
Locale(s): New York, New York

Summary: Learning from Mabel that Vlad and his family are coming to America for a chess tournament, Sam feels betrayed to discover that his online chess partner is Romania's grand master and not the beginner he portrays himself to be to Sam. Mabel is sure that anyone from Bucharest must be a vampire and she convinces Robert that Vlad's actions assure that not only is Vlad a vampire but that he's also turned Sam into one. As it turns out, Mabel is wrong, as she usually is when she jumps to conclusions. Vlad wins the tournament and, after seeing the pressure of a tournament, Sam is able to forgive Vlad for his online deception. (100 pages)

Where it's reviewed:
Booklist, August 2002, page 1950
Horn Book Guide, Spring 2003, page 70
Publishers Weekly, August 26, 2002, page 71
School Library Journal, November 2002, page 129

Other books by the same author:
Night of the Living Gerbil, 2001
Gorgonzola Zombies in the Park, 1993
Dracula Is a Pain in the Neck, 1983

Other books you might like:
Tony Abbott, *Dracula: Trapped in Transylvania*, 2002
    A humorous time travel journey by two sixth graders to 1897 Transylvania gives the students an unexpected research opportunity for an assignment.
Dan Greenburg, *Don't Count on Dracula*, 2000
    The prize Zack wins in a contest is to meet horror film star Mella Bugosi whose odd habits make Zack wonder if the actor is actually a vampire.
Daniel Pinkwater, *The Werewolf Club Meets Dorkula*, 2001
    Lucy's suspicions about club member Henry lead to the discovery that he is a "fruitpire" because he changes into a fruit bat rather than a vampire bat.
David Wisniewski, *Halloweenies*, 2002
    Five brief chapters spoof classic horror movies.

888

TED LEWIN, Author/Illustrator

Big Jimmy's Kum Kau Chinese Take Out

(New York: HarperCollins Publishers, 2002)

Subject(s): Restaurants; Cooks and Cooking; Fathers and Sons

Age range(s): Grades 1-3
Major character(s): Big Jimmy, Father, Restaurateur; Unnamed Character, Son, Narrator
Time period(s): 2000s (2002)
Locale(s): New York, New York (Brooklyn)

Summary: A young boy is excited when Saturday dawns because then he can help his family in their restaurant. The boy knows the routine and eagerly greets the deliveryman, helping him with boxes of fresh vegetables. Although he's not allowed in the dangerous kitchen he understands the specific assignments of each of the eight cooks that Big Jimmy oversees. The boy's job is to fold and stack menus neatly before the shuttered building is opened at eleven o'clock. Now it's time for his mother and aunt to begin taking orders as customers begin to arrive or call in their orders. Now his job assignment changes for he's in charge of the orders, stuffing each bag with napkins, utensils, condiments, and fortune cookies and taking the drink orders. All day long the family works together until finally, the hungry boy can sit down for his favorite meal, pizza. (36 pages)

Where it's reviewed:
Booklist, January 1, 2002, page 866
Horn Book Guide, Spring 2002, page 50
Publishers Weekly, February 25, 2002, page 68
School Library Journal, April 2002, page 114

Awards the book has won:
Notable Social Studies Trade Books for Young People, 2003

Other books by the same author:
Tooth and Claw: Animal Adventures in the Wild, 2003
Red Legs: A Drummer Boy of the Civil War, 2001
Gorilla Walk, 1999

Other books you might like:
Grace Lin, *Dim Sum for Everyone!*, 2001
    In a dim sum restaurant a family selects their favorite dishes from the appetizing offerings on the cart.
William Low, *Chinatown*, 1997
    Daily a young boy walks with Grandma through the crowded streets of Chinatown.
Amy Wilson Sanger, *Yum Yum Dim Sum*, 2003
    An illustrated rhyming story describes the process of created a dim sum meal with each dish identified by its Chinese name.
Janet S. Wong, *Apple Pie 4th of July*, 2002
    While helping her parents in their grocery story, a young Chinese-American girl worries that no one will buy the take-out food on an American holiday.

889

KEVIN LEWIS
DANIEL KIRK, Illustrator

My Truck Is Stuck!

(New York: Hyperion Books for Children, 2002)

Subject(s): Transportation; Stories in Rhyme; Problem Solving
Age range(s): Preschool-Kindergarten
Major character(s): Unnamed Character, Dog, Truck Driver; Unnamed Character, Dog, Truck Driver

Time period(s): Indeterminate
Locale(s): Fictional Country

Summary: A dump truck loaded with bones is stuck in a hole in the road. While the driver laments, hollers for help and tries to extricate the truck, prairie dogs (the creators of the hole) are quietly unloading the truck's cargo. The driver and his partner stop a car, a moving van, a jeep, and a school bus, but still the dump truck is stuck fast in the hole. Finally a tow truck arrives and the driver hoists the dump truck out of the hole so it can continue its journey just as the little critters toss the last bone out the back. (32 pages)

Where it's reviewed:
Booklist, November 1, 2002, page 508
Horn Book Guide, Spring 2003, page 15
Kirkus Reviews, August 15, 2002, page 1228
Publishers Weekly, September 2, 2002, page 74
School Library Journal, October 2002, page 118

Other books by the same author:
The Runaway Pumpkin, 2003
The Lot at the End of My Block, 2001
Chugga-Chugga Choo-Choo, 1999

Other books you might like:
Jez Alborough, *Duck in the Truck*, 2000
    Duck's truck is stuck in the muck. With assistance from helpful friends Duck's truck is finally free but what about Sheep, Frog and Goat?
Paul Collicutt, *This Truck*, 2004
    A nonfiction picture book for truck lovers includes small toy trucks, big forklifts and really enormous dump trucks.
Nancy Shaw, *Sheep in a Jeep*, 1986
    A group of exuberant sheep take off in a jeep and, as usual, find themselves in a bit of a predicament in this rhyming picture book.

890

KEVIN LEWIS
S.D. SCHINDLER, Illustrator

The Runaway Pumpkin

(New York: Orchard Books/Scholastic, Inc., 2003)

Subject(s): Halloween; Pumpkins; Stories in Rhyme
Age range(s): Preschool-Kindergarten
Major character(s): Granny Baxter, Grandmother, Cook
Time period(s): 2000s (2003)
Locale(s): United States

Summary: On Halloween the Baxter children find an enormous pumpkin, but when they cut it loose it starts a rapid decent down the hill on its own. As the pumpkin crashes through the pigsty and henhouse before landing in a plowed field, the family can only think of Granny Baxter's delicious pumpkin recipes. Luckily, that night Granny makes Halloween supper from the pumpkin, which joins the family at the table as a gigantic Jack-o-Lantern. (32 pages)

Where it's reviewed:
Booklist, November 15, 2003, page 601
Publishers Weekly, August 4, 2003, page 77
School Library Journal, October 2003, page 129

Other books by the same author:
My Truck Is Stuck!, 2002
The Lot at the End of My Block, 2001
Chugga-Chugga Choo-Choo, 1999

Other books you might like:
Margaret Wise Brown, *The Fierce Yellow Pumpkin*, 2003
A small green pumpkin gets its wish to be able to scare away the field mice when it grows into a large orange pumpkin that is made into a Jack-o-Lantern.
Erica Silverman, *Big Pumpkin*, 1992
A witch grows herself a pumpkin to make into pumpkin pie for Halloween, but it becomes so large she can't move it by herself.
Tasha Tudor, *Pumpkin Moonshine*, 1938
Seeking the very best pumpkin in her grandparents' patch, a little girl selects a big one that rolls down the hill and arrives home ahead of her.
Linda White, *Too Many Pumpkins*, 1996
Rebecca has hated pumpkins since childhood, but when a bumper crop grows in her yard, she digs out the old recipes and invites the neighbors.

891

ERIK L'HOMME

Quadehar the Sorcerer

(New York: Chicken House/Scholastic, 2003)

Series: Book of the Stars. Book 1
Subject(s): Fantasy; Magic; Wizards
Age range(s): Grades 6-9
Major character(s): Robin Penmarch, 12-Year-Old, Apprentice; Quadehar, Sorcerer; Agatha Balangru, Kidnap Victim, Bully
Time period(s): Indeterminate
Locale(s): Fictional Country

Summary: Robin lives on magical Lost Isle, which floats between The Uncertain World, a place to avoid, and The Real World, which resembles the world we know. Picked on by bullies and unaware of his magical powers, Robin is taken on as an apprentice by the powerful wizard Quadehar who one night witnesses his ability. Gradually Robin responds to the instructions of Quadehar so that he's able to harness the power that controls the universe. Gommons, monsters from The Uncertain World, come to Lost Isle and accidentally kidnap the wrong person, bullying Agatha, and take her back to their homeland. Robin realizes they meant to kidnap him and, though he doesn't like Agatha, feels responsible for her kidnapping so heads out with some of his friends to rescue her. (275 pages)

Where it's reviewed:
Kirkus Reviews, September 15, 2003, page 1177
Publishers Weekly, September 29, 2003, page 65
School Librarian, Spring 2004, page 24
School Library Journal, December 2003, page 156

Other books you might like:
Tamora Pierce, *Sandry's Book*, 1997
This entry in the Circle of Magic Series features Sandry, a young magician in training at the Winding Circle Temple.

J.K. Rowling, *Harry Potter and the Sorcerer's Stone*, 1997
In order to save Hogwarts from the evil sorcerer who killed his parents, Harry and his friends must find the hidden sorcerer's stone.
Cynthia Voigt, *Jackaroo*, 1985
To help the People through hard times, an innkeeper's daughter goes on a quest to learn the truth behind the legend of the hero Jackaroo.

892

REBECCA LICKISS

Never After

(New York: Ace, 2002)

Subject(s): Fantasy; Fairy Tales; Humor
Age range(s): Grades 8-Adult
Major character(s): Vevila, Royalty (princess), Cousin; Althestan, Royalty (prince), Cousin; Urticacea, Witch
Time period(s): Indeterminate
Locale(s): Fictional Country

Summary: Prince Althestan is flummoxed; instead of a castle containing a sleeping princess for him to awaken with a kiss, he has stumbled on a castle containing three sleeping princes. Downstairs is an enchanted girl so lovely, Althestan knows she must be a princess. Not the most creative thinker, Althestan knows just the person to help him, his clever cousin, the princess Vevila, but she is having difficulties of her own. A series of doltish suitors are being paraded before her, and in spite of her general irritation, she decides that taking off with Althestan has got to be better. Unfortunately the plan is overheard by a trio of greedy, gluttonous or just plain misguided wizards, who insist on coming along to get in the way. The princes turn out to be one prince, split into three by his over-protective fairy godmother, the witch Urticacea. Urticacea is not about to let Vevila kiss her princes without proving that she is a princess and constructs a series of tests that take the reader romping and laughing through a variety of familiar fairy tales. (261 pages)

Where it's reviewed:
Booklist, June 1, 2002, page 1696
Kliatt, November 2002, page 24
Voice of Youth Advocates, December 2002, page 398

Other books by the same author:
Eccentric Circles, 2001

Other books you might like:
Patrice Kindl, *Goose Chase*, 2001
Like Vevila, the heroine of this story refuses to let events boss her around, proving she's a take-charge kind of girl.
Patricia C. Wrede, *Dealing with Dragons*, 1990
Cimorene, a stubborn princess with a mind of her own, decides to keep house for a dragon before one kidnaps her.
Diana Wynne Jones, *Dark Lord of Derkholm*, 1998
Fairytale lands make ends meet by hosting tourist groups from the more mundane dimensions; join the current tour, which is unusual by anyone's standards.

893

GRACE LIN, Author/Illustrator

Olvina Flies

(New York: Henry Holt and Company, 2003)

Subject(s): Fear; Voyages and Travels; Air Travel
Age range(s): Grades K-3
Major character(s): Olvina Alice Rhea, Chicken, Traveler; Will Gelato, Pig, Friend; Hailey, Penguin, Traveler
Time period(s): Indeterminate
Locale(s): Pacyworks Village, Fictional Country; Hawaii

Summary: When an invitation to the Tenth Annual Bird Convention first arrives Olvina tells Will she can't go because chickens don't fly. Will protests, explaining that Olvina simply needs to fly by plane. That idea is a bit scary for Olvina, but she realizes she's missing out on life by not traveling so she agrees to go. Will offers reassurance each time Olvina reconsiders and drives her to the airport for the flight. Once aloft Olvina begins to feel less nervous and strikes up a conversation with seatmate Hailey. As it turns out, Hailey is also going to the convention so the two non-flying birds share a taxi and enjoy their new friendship as well as the sights of Hawaii during their visit. (32 pages)

Where it's reviewed:
Booklist, February 1, 2003, page 1001
Horn Book, May 2003, page 329
Publishers Weekly, March 10, 2003, page 71
School Library Journal, April 2003, page 132

Other books by the same author:
Robert's Snow, 2004
Dim Sum for Everyone!, 2001
The Ugly Vegetables, 1999 (Notable Social Studies Trade Books for Young People)

Other books you might like:
Mary Calhoun, *Hot-Air Henry*, 1981
   Henry's hiding place takes flight giving the surprised Siamese cat an unexpected hot air balloon ride across the mountains.
Anne Gutman, *Lisa's Airplane Trip*, 2001
   On little dog Lisa's first solo plane trip she naps, eats and spills her juice while trying to watch the movie.
Amy Hest, *Make the Team, Baby Duck!*, 2002
   With encouragement from Grandpa Duck, Baby Duck overcomes her fear of the water to compete for a place on the swim team.
Rafik Schami, *Albert & Lila*, 1999
   Albert, the pig, and Lila, the hen, share a farmyard friendship and gain the respect of the other animals.

894

INGER LINDAHL
EVA LINDSTROM, Illustrator
ELISABETH KALLICK DYSSEGAARD, Translator

Bertil and the Bathroom Elephants

(New York: R&S Books/Farrar Straus Giroux, 2003)

Subject(s): Animals/Elephants; Imagination; Fear

Age range(s): Preschool
Major character(s): Bertil, 3-Year-Old, Son; Unnamed Character, Mother; Unnamed Character, Father
Time period(s): 2000s (2003)
Locale(s): Sweden

Summary: After Bertil's mother scolds him for flooding the bathroom floor Bertil blames the problem on the bathroom elephants. The elephants keep the family amused. They eat raisins and flush Bertil's dad's underpants down the toilet. One day though Bertil hears the elephants growling and decides that the elephants have turned against the family and are now after him. Bertil refuses to use the bathroom and takes to using his old potty in the hallway. However, his dad comes up with the perfect solution allowing the elephants to move in with a neighbor who wants them. This is the first English translation of any works by this Swedish children's book author. (32 pages)

Where it's reviewed:
Horn Book, September/October 2003, page 599
Publishers Weekly, September 8, 2003, page 75
School Library Journal, December 2003, page 118

Other books you might like:
Rick Brown, *The Princess and the Potty*, 1998
   A picky princess searches for the perfect potty.
Eve Bunting, *Too Many Monsters*, 1999
   A young boy is frightened by bedtime monsters until his family scares them away by quacking like ducks.
Mercer Mayer, *There's a Monster in my Closet*, 1968
   A young boy confronts the monster in his closet.
David McPhail, *Andrew's Bath*, 1984
   The first time Andrew is allowed to bathe himself an elephant drinks the shampoo and a hippo sits on the soap.
Nanette Newman, *There's a Bear in the Bath!*, 1994
   Liza's day is enlivened when she finds Jam in her garden and invites the friendly bear into the house.

895

PIJA LINDENBAUM, Author/Illustrator
KJERSTI BOARD, Translator

Bridget and the Muttonheads

(New York: R&S Books/Farrar Straus Giroux, 2002)

Subject(s): Animals/Sheep; Vacations; Beaches
Age range(s): Preschool-Grade 1
Major character(s): Bridget, Child
Time period(s): 2000s (2002)
Locale(s): Sweden

Summary: Bridget is bored stiff on vacation at a fancy resort with her parents. When she wanders off to play in the sand on the beach, she notices a small island that looks as if little clouds inhabit it. Bridget wades out to explore the island and discovers that the clouds are really sheep, overheated in their wooly coats. Bridget sets about milking them, feeding them and shearing them. Then she teaches them to swim so that they can get to the mainland. (28 pages)

Where it's reviewed:
Booklist, August 2002, page 1973
Horn Book, November/October 2002, page 735

Publishers Weekly, October 7, 2002, page 75
School Library Journal, January 2003, page 105

Other books by the same author:
Bridget and the Moose Brothers, 2004
Bridget and the Gray Wolves, 2001
Boodil My Dog, 1992

Other books you might like:
Judith Enderle, *Six Sandy Sheep*, 1997
   Six sheep spend a day at the seashore.
Nancy Shaw, *Sheep in a Jeep*, 1986
   Five sheep take an ill-fated road trip.
Teri Sloat, *Farmer Brown Shears His Sheep: A Yarn About Wool*, 2000
   Farmer Brown shears his sheep, but when he realizes they're cold, he knits them sweaters from the wool.

896

ASTRID LINDGREN
PIJA LINDENBAUM, Illustrator
ELISABETH KALLICK DYSSEGAARD, Translator

Mirabelle
(New York: R&S Books/Farrar Straus Giroux, 2003)

Subject(s): Dolls and Dollhouses; Poverty; Wishes
Age range(s): Grades K-2
Major character(s): Britta, Child, Daughter; Mirabelle, Doll
Time period(s): 1940s (1949)
Locale(s): Sweden

Summary: More than anything else, Britta wants a doll, but her parents are too poor to buy one for her. One day when her parents have gone into town to sell their produce, Britta opens the gate near their farm for a strange old man, and he gives her a magic seed as thanks. Britta is surprised when, instead of flowers, the seed grows into a beautiful doll that she names Mirabelle. Mirabelle turns out to have a mind of her own and she comes alive when she and Britta are alone, ending Britta's loneliness. This book was first published in Sweden in 1949. (32 pages)

Where it's reviewed:
Booklist, May 15, 2003, page 1672
Bulletin of the Center for Children's Books, May 2003, page 367
Publishers Weekly, May 5, 2003, page 223
Riverbank Review, Spring 2003, page 29
School Library Journal, August 2003, page 136

Other books by the same author:
Most Beloved Sister, 2002
Lotta on Troublemaker Street, 1962
Pippi Longstocking, 1950

Other books you might like:
Don Freeman, *Corduroy*, 1968
   Teddy bear, Corduroy, dreams of being adopted from his department store.
Johnny Gruelle, *Raggedy Ann Stories*, 1918
   Raggedy Ann comes to life in Marcella's nursery.
Pija Lindenbaum, *Bridget and the Muttonheads*, 2002
   Bridget's family vacation is boring, until she stumbles across some sheep that need her help.

897

ASTRID LINDGREN
HANS ARNOLD, Illustrator
ELISABETH KALLICK DYSSEGAARD, Translator

Most Beloved Sister
(New York: R&S Books/Farrar Straus Giroux, 2002)

Subject(s): Sibling Rivalry; Imagination; Animals/Dogs
Age range(s): Grades K-3
Major character(s): Barbara, 7-Year-Old, Sister (older); Lalla-Lee, Twin (imaginary)
Time period(s): 1940s (1949)
Locale(s): Sweden

Summary: Barbara's parents may be paying a lot of attention to her new baby brother, but Barbara knows her secret twin sister, Lalla-Lee likes her best. Lalla-Lee lives beneath the rosebush in Barbara's yard and together the girls have all sorts of secret adventures. One day Lalla-Lee tells Barbara that when the roses die she will be gone. That evening, Barbara's mother expresses the worry she feels during Barbara's lengthy absences and her father gives her the little black poodle she's always wanted. With her fears assuaged, Barbara wakes up the next morning to find the rose bush withered and Lalla-Lee gone. (32 pages)

Where it's reviewed:
Booklist, July 2002, page 1846
Horn Book Guide, Fall 2002, page 306
New York Times Book Review, June 2, 2002, page 36
Publishers Weekly, June 2, 2002, page 30
School Library Journal, August 2002, page 160

Other books by the same author:
Mirabelle, 2003
Mio, My Son, 1956
Pippi Longstocking, 1950

Other books you might like:
Valiska Gregory, *Shirley's Wonderful Baby*, 2002
   Shirley's not too fond of her new baby brother and the attention he gets, but a babysitter who doesn't like babies helps her see some of his charms.
Kevin Henkes, *Julius, the Baby of the World*, 1990
   Lily thinks her new baby brother is disgusting, until her cousin insults him.
Ezra Jack Keats, *Peter's Chair*, 1967
   Peter is none too thrilled by the arrival of his new baby sister, especially since it means all of his baby furniture is being repainted pink.

898

BARBRO LINDGREN
OLOF LANDSTROM, Illustrator
ELISABETH KALLICK DYSSEGAARD, Translator

Benny and the Binky
(New York: R&S Books, 2002)

Subject(s): Animals/Pigs; Brothers; Babies
Age range(s): Preschool-Grade 1

Major character(s): Benny, Pig, Brother (older); Unnamed Character, Pig, Brother (younger); Little Piggy, Toy (stuffed animal)
Time period(s): Indeterminate
Locale(s): Fictional Country

Summary: Although Benny wanted a baby brother, now that he has one he's soon tired of this crying baby who's pacified with a binky. Benny wants a binky too but he's told that he's ''too big'' to use one. The sight of his baby brother sucking on his binky becomes too much for Benny and he takes his brother outside, sets him by the front door and gives him Little Piggy in exchange for the binky. Benny runs away with the binky feeling momentary satisfaction that soon ends when three bullies chase him. Fortunately, Benny makes it home, with the binky, in time to soothe his little brother. Originally published in Sweden in 2001. (32 pages)

Where it's reviewed:
Bulletin of the Center for Children's Books, May 2002, page 330
Horn Book, May 2002, page 317
Publishers Weekly, February 4, 2002, page 78
Riverbank Review, Summer 2002, page 28
School Library Journal, April 2002, page 116

Awards the book has won:
Bulletin of the Center for Children's Books Blue Ribbons, 2002
Horn Book Fanfare, 2002

Other books by the same author:
Benny's Had Enough!, 1999 (Horn Book Fanfare)
Shorty Takes Off, 1990
Sam's Wagon, 1986

Other books you might like:
Ian Falconer, *Olivia*, 2000
　Olivia is an independent, creative pig that tolerates her younger brother and challenges her mom.
Holly Keller, *Geraldine's Baby Brother*, 1994
　It takes some time for Geraldine to adjust to her noisy baby brother and all the attention he receives.
Jill Murphy, *The Last Noo-Noo*, 1995
　Marlon is attached to his pacifier until neighborhood bullies convince him to do what his family couldn't; still, he has an emergency plan.

899

BARBRO LINDGREN
EVA ERIKSSON, Illustrator
ELISABETH KALLICK DYSSEGAARD, Translator

Julia Wants a Pet

(New York: R&S Books/Farrar Straus Giroux, 2003)

Subject(s): Pets; Animals; Imagination
Age range(s): Grades K-2
Major character(s): Julia, 7-Year-Old, Child of Divorced Parents
Time period(s): 2000s (2002)
Locale(s): Sweden

Summary: Daily Julia wonders if this is the day she will finally be given a pet. Until that day actually arrives, Julia settles for finding bugs in the yard that she calls pets until they die and then she adds them to the bug cemetery she's made behind the apartment building. One day while pushing her baby carriage and searching for a pet, Julia spots a dog outside a store. Although the dog's leash is tied, Julia decides he's in need of a home and she adds him to her carriage and begins to stroll away. She doesn't get far before the angry owner claims the dog. Alas, Julia goes back to imagining and finds a beautiful green beetle. Before the beetle can die and be added to the cemetery, it flies away. Oh well, Julia's eighth birthday comes and with it the fulfillment of her wish for a pet.

Where it's reviewed:
Horn Book, September 2003, page 599
Publishers Weekly, September 29, 2003, page 65
School Library Journal, November 2003, page 106

Other books by the same author:
Benny and the Binky, 2002
Andrei's Search, 2000
Rosa Goes to Daycare, 2000

Other books you might like:
Lauren Child, *I Want a Pet*, 1999
　A little girl desperately wants a pet but has some difficulty choosing one that meets the requirements of her family.
Lynne Jonell, *I Need a Snake*, 1998
　Robbie is convinced that he needs a pet snake and his mother is just as sure that he doesn't.
Mary Packard, *The Pet That I Want*, 1995
　In the rhyming text of a book in the ''My First Hello Reader'' series a young boy visiting a pet store describes the pet he seeks.

900

ROBERT LIPSYTE

Warrior Angel

(New York: HarperCollins, 2003)

Subject(s): Sports/Boxing; Mental Illness; Depression
Age range(s): Grades 8-10
Major character(s): George Harrison ''Sonny Bear'' Bayer, Boxer; Navy Crockett, Boxer; Richard Starkey, Teenager; Alfred Brooks, Coach
Time period(s): 2000s
Locale(s): Las Vegas, Nevada; New York, New York

Summary: At 20, Sonny Bear is a young heavyweight champ who successfully defends his title against Navy Crockett, though his sluggishness leads to speculation that he was drugged. He wasn't drugged, but he is tired of everybody telling him what to do and when to do it, which has led to his apathy and depression. He receives e-mails signed by ''Warrior Angel'' telling him to hang on, that he'll be there soon to help him. Warrior Angel is Richard Starkey, a schizophrenic who lives in a group home for emotionally disturbed teens, and is convinced that he can save Sonny's career. The two coordinate to meet at Donatelli's Gym, where Sonny's career began. Sonny dresses as a waiter to escape his handlers and Richard hot-wires cars to drive to New York. Having arranged for Alfred Brooks, Sonny's mentor, to meet them, Richard does seem to know just what's needed for Sonny. These two unlikely men manage to help one another in this fourth book in Lipsyte's boxing saga that began with *The Contender*. (186 pages)

Where it's reviewed:
Booklist, January 2003, page 871
Bulletin of the Center for Children's Books, February 2003, page 242
Horn Book, March 2003, page 212
School Library Journal, March 2003, page 235
Voice of Youth Advocates, April 2003, page 52

Other books by the same author:
The Chief, 1995
The Brave, 1993
The Contender, 1967

Other books you might like:
William Kelly, *The Sweet Summer*, 2000
  The only white member on the 1940s Army boxing team, Cully endures the virulence of racism from outsiders as he grows to love and respect his teammates.
Leonard Todd, *Squaring Off*, 1990
  When a gigantic boxer is about to make mincemeat of Willy, his father's girlfriend's secret weapons save him.
Peter Weston Wood, *To Swallow a Toad*, 1987
  A miserable home life makes Pete Wood hungry for boxing's Golden Gloves title.

901

JANET TAYLOR LISLE

The Crying Rocks

(New York: Atheneum/Simon & Schuster, 2003)

Subject(s): Orphans; Identity; Indians of North America
Age range(s): Grades 6-9

Summary: Joelle knows little about her life before she was adopted when she was five, though she vaguely remembers odd snippets here and there. She's been told she was born in Chicago, thrown from a window, and then brought to Connecticut where she lived in a box with an old woman. Now adopted and living with Mary Louise and Vernon, whom she calls Aunt and Uncle, Joelle wonders who she really is. Researching the Narragansett Indians with Carlos, he suggests that she resembles them and oddly enough, when Joelle looks at the Indians in an old mural in the library, she does! When they hike in the woods, Carlos tells her about the Crying Rocks where many Indians were said to have died and where Carlos's own brother was killed in a climbing accident. Aunt Mary Louise dies unexpectedly and bits of Joelle's past come to the surface, especially when some very tall Native American men show up at the funeral. Eventually Joelle learns enough about herself to solve her origin and be at peace with who she is. (199 pages)

Where it's reviewed:
Booklist, October 15, 2003, page 405
Bulletin of the Center for Children's Books, December 2003, page 157
Publishers Weekly, November 17, 2003, page 65
School Library Journal, December 2003, page 156
Voice of Youth Advocates, February 2004, page 494

Other books by the same author:
How I Became a Writer and Oggie Learned to Drive, 2002
The Art of Keeping Cool, 2000
The Lampfish of Twill, 1991
Sirens and Spies, 1990
Afternoon of the Elves, 1989

Other books you might like:
Ann Cameron, *Colibri*, 2003
  Stolen from her parents when she was young, Tzunun, now called Rosa, can barely remember her early life.
Caroline B. Cooney, *What Janie Found*, 2000
  Kidnapped and living with the family that raised her rather than her biological one, Janie has finally come to terms with her own feelings.
Sherry Garland, *Indio*, 1995
  Captured by the Spanish when Ipa's tribe is attacked, Ipa escapes and returns to her village where pottery and weaving help everyone survive.

902

JANET TAYLOR LISLE

How I Became a Writer and Oggie Learned to Drive

(New York: Philomel/Putnam, 2002)

Subject(s): Brothers; Divorce; Gangs
Age range(s): Grades 4-8
Major character(s): James Archer "Archie" Jones, 11-Year-Old; Ogden Jackson "Oogie" Jones, Child, Brother (of Archie)
Time period(s): 2000s
Locale(s): United States

Summary: Shuttling back and forth between their mother's home and their father's apartment, Archie and his little brother Oogie have to walk through a neighborhood ruled by the Night Riders, a gang that's hard to avoid. Once they're safe with either parent, Archie tries to distract Oogie from the stress of the divorce by telling him stories about the Mole People, strange creatures who were once human but are now covered with fur, have claws and live underground. A brush with the Night Riders results in Oogie's wallet being stolen and Archie running errands for the gang while he tries to retrieve the wallet. On his deliveries one night, a shootout occurs and to get away, Archie and Oogie flee in a Pontiac Bonneville with Oogie driving. Heartened by all their adventures, Archie decides he's finished with the book *The Mysterious Mole People* and ready to begin writing *How I Became a Writer and Oogie Learned to Drive*. (155 pages)

Where it's reviewed:
Booklist, February 1, 2002, page 939
Bulletin of the Center for Children's Books, May 2002, page 331
Horn Book, March 2002, page 214
Publishers Weekly, March 11, 2002, page 73
School Library Journal, March 2002, page 234

Other books by the same author:
The Crying Rocks, 2003
The Art of Keeping Cool, 2000

The Lampfish of Twill, 1991

Other books you might like:

Paula Danziger, *The Divorce Express*, 1982
  Phoebe feels as though she's on the "divorce express," as she divides her time between her divorced parents.
Lulu Delacre, *Salsa Stories*, 2000
  Carmen Teresa uses the gift of a blank book to record the stories told by family members around the New Year's dinner table.
Barbara Brooks Wallace, *Secret in St. Something*, 2001
  At the mercy of their stepfather, Robin grabs his little brother Danny and they run away, meeting a group of street boys who take them in.

903

JEAN LITTLE

Willow and Twig

(New York: Viking/Penguin Group, 2003)

Subject(s): Family Problems; Grandmothers; Abandonment
Age range(s): Grades 5-8
Major character(s): Willow Wind Jones, 12-Year-Old; Calypso "Twig" Jones, Child, Deaf Person; Nell "Gram" Jones, Grandmother; Constance "Con" Gordon, Aunt; Humphrey "Hum" Gordon, Uncle, Writer (children's books)
Time period(s): 2000s
Locale(s): Vancouver, British Columbia, Canada; Toronto, Ontario, Canada

Summary: Once again their drug-addicted mother abandons Willow and her half-brother Twig; this time she leaves them with an elderly, sick woman at their welfare hotel. When the woman collapses, and probably dies, Willow knows it's time to contact her mother's mother and heads to the local police station to explain their situation. Calling their grandmother, the police put Willow and Twig on a plane to Toronto where they meet their grandmother, then travel to their ten-acre farm where Uncle Hum and Aunt Constance wait for them. For the first time in many years, Willow can relax and let others help with Twig, who was born addicted and suffered deafness from a beating from one of their mother's friends. Uncle Hum, a children's writer, becomes an instant friend, though it takes longer for Aunt Constance to warm up to them, and vice-versa. Gram loves them instantly and works to provide the first warm, comforting home these two children have ever enjoyed. (227 pages)

Where it's reviewed:
Booklist, July 2003, page 1891
Bulletin of the Center for Children's Books, March 2003, page 279
Kirkus Reviews, March 1, 2003, page 390
Publishers Weekly, April 7, 2003, page 67
School Library Journal, August 2003, page 161

Other books by the same author:
Dear Canada, Brothers Far from Home: The World War I Diary of Eliza Bates, 2003
Orphan at My Door: The Home Child Diary of Victoria Cope, 2001

Belonging Place, 1997
His Banner over Me, 1995
Mine for Keeps, 1994

Other books you might like:

Patricia Hermes, *Cheat the Moon*, 1998
  With her mother dead, her father an alcoholic and the responsibility of her brother Will on her shoulders, young Gabby grows up quickly.
Katherine Paterson, *The Same Stuff as Stars*, 2002
  Dumped by her mother on her great-grandmother's doorstep, Angel once again assumes responsibility for running a household.
Cynthia Voigt, *Homecoming*, 1981
  After abandonment by their mother, Dicey and her younger brothers and sister make the long journey on foot to their eccentric grandmother's home.

904

CLAUDIA LOGAN
MELISSA SWEET, Illustrator

The 5,000-Year-Old Puzzle: Solving a Mystery of Ancient Egypt

(New York: Melanie Kroupa/Farrar Straus Giroux, 2002)

Subject(s): Egyptian Antiquities; Archaeology; Mystery
Age range(s): Grades 2-5
Major character(s): Will Hunt, Preteen, Explorer
Time period(s): 1920s (1924)
Locale(s): Giza, Egypt

Summary: Will Hunt is fascinated with ancient Egypt. When his father joins the (real-life) Reisner archeological dig at Giza, Will is thrilled to go along. Through a series of diary entries and postcards to his best friend back home, Will tells the story of the discovery of a burial chamber, the identification of whose tomb it was, and the mystery of the missing mummy. The book then offers two different archeologist's alternate theories as to why the mummy is missing from the tomb. (48 pages)

Where it's reviewed:
Booklist, April 15, 2002, page 1401
Bulletin of the Center for Children's Books, June 2002, page 371
Horn Book Guide, Fall 2002, page 360
Publishers Weekly, April 29, 2002, page 71
School Library Journal, June 2002, page 100

Awards the book has won:
Center for Children's Books Best Books, 2002

Other books by the same author:
Scruffy's Museum Adventure, 1996

Other books you might like:

Linda Bailey, *Adventures in Ancient Egypt*, 2000
  The Binkerton children are transported back in time to ancient Egypt.
Sandra Bower, *The Shipwrecked Sailor: An Egyptian Tale with Hieroglyphs*, 2000
  Based on a 4,000-year-old papyrus scroll, the sole survivor

of a shipwreck finds himself on an island paradise, inhabited only by a serpent.

Joanna Cole, *Ms. Frizzle's Adventures: Ancient Egypt*, 2001
Mrs. Frizzle (star of the Magic School Bus series) takes a vacation to Egypt, where her tour group suddenly finds itself transported back in time.

James Rumford, *Seeker of Knowledge: The Man Who Deciphered Egyptian Hieroglyphs*, 2000
This picture book biography tells the story of Jean Francois Champollion, the man who first deciphered hieroglyphs.

905

JONATHAN LONDON
FRANK REMKIEWICZ, Illustrator

Froggy Goes to the Doctor
(New York: Viking, 2002)

Subject(s): Doctors; Animals/Frogs and Toads; Humor
Age range(s): Preschool-Grade 1
Major character(s): Froggy, Frog, Patient; Dr. Mugwort, Doctor, Frog
Time period(s): Indeterminate
Locale(s): Fictional Country

Summary: Froggy's joy at missing school for a doctor's appointment vanishes quickly when he realizes that the doctor might be planning to give him a shot. Froggy sits anxiously in the doctor's waiting room, making a paper airplane as a distraction. That just causes him to start off on the wrong foot with Dr. Mugwort when his paper airplane hits her in the eye. Then he realizes as Dr. Mugwort is looking in his mouth that he forgot to brush his teeth, next he yells into her stethoscope, and finally as she checks his reflexes he kicks so hard that he knocks her over. Dr. Mugwort is probably even more relieved than Froggy when the appointment is over and Froggy leaves with a clean bill of health and no shots. (32 pages)

Where it's reviewed:
Booklist, January 2003, page 908
Horn Book Guide, Spring 2003, page 43
Kirkus Reviews, August 1, 2002, page 1135
Publishers Weekly, June 24, 2002, page 59

Awards the book has won:
IRA Children's Choices, 2003

Other books by the same author:
Froggy's Day with Dad, 2004
Froggy's Baby Sister, 2003
Froggy Takes a Bath, 2001

Other books you might like:
Claire Masurel, *Too Big*, 1999
Charlie's large toy dinosaur is just the right size to comfort him on a trip to the doctor's office.

Herman Parish, *Calling Doctor Amelia Bedelia*, 2002
Amelia Bedelia's idea of helping out at her doctor's office creates humorous challenges for the nurse but the patients are happy.

Rosemary Wells, *Felix Feels Better*, 2001
Felix's fear of visiting Dr. Duck's office vanishes when his mother is allowed to remain with him.

906

JONATHAN LONDON
FRANK REMKIEWICZ, Illustrator

Froggy Plays in the Band
(New York: Viking, 2002)

Subject(s): Bands; Contests; Music and Musicians
Age range(s): Grades K-2
Major character(s): Froggy, Frog, Musician (novice); Miss Martin, Teacher (music), Bird; Frogilina, Frog, Student—Elementary School
Time period(s): Indeterminate
Locale(s): Fictional Country

Summary: After spotting a poster for a marching band contest with a "big prize" Froggy gets more information from Miss Martin. Determined to win the secret prize, Froggy locates his father's old saxophone and convinces some friends to join the contest with him. Unable to play an instrument, Frogilina twirls her baton and leads the small band in the parade. Diligently following Miss Martin's marching instructions: "Don't look left, don't look right and don't stop for anything!" Froggy doesn't see Frogilina's tossed baton heading for his head just as the band reaches the viewing stand. Knocked off his feet, Froggy quickly scrambles up again and keeps marching while wailing a jazzy tune on his sax. When prizes are awarded, Froggy's Ragtag Band wins a special award for "coolest" marching band. (32 pages)

Where it's reviewed:
Bulletin of the Center for Children's Books, April 2002, page 287
Horn Book Guide, Fall 2002, page 337
Kirkus Reviews, December 1, 2001, page 1686
Publishers Weekly, January 28, 2002, page 293
School Library Journal, April 2002, page 116

Awards the book has won:
IRA Children's Choices, 2003

Other books by the same author:
Froggy Goes to the Doctor, 2002 (IRA Children's Choices)
Froggy Eats Out, 2001 (IRA Children's Choices)
Froggy's Best Christmas, 2000
Froggy Plays Soccer, 1999 (IRA Children's Choices)

Other books you might like:
Norman Bridwell, *Clifford and the Big Parade*, 1998
Enjoying the town's birthday with Emily Elizabeth, Clifford, the big red dog, helps to assure the parade's success in a way only a dog his size can.

Lloyd Moss, *Our Marching Band*, 2001
With a lot of practice, a group of novice musicians is able to come together as a marching band.

Harriet Ziefert, *Animal Music*, 1999
Rhyming stories describe animal marching bands.

907

MELINDA LONG
DAVID SHANNON, Illustrator

How I Became a Pirate
(San Diego: Harcourt, Inc., 2003)

Subject(s): Pirates; Humor; Adventure and Adventurers
Age range(s): Grades K-3
Major character(s): Jeremy Jacob, Child, Son; Braid Beard, Pirate
Time period(s): Indeterminate
Locale(s): Fictional Country

Summary: As Jeremy Jacob builds a sandcastle Braid Beard and his crew row ashore, admire his digging ability and realize he has just the skills needed for burying a treasure chest. Braid Beard invites Jeremy to join the crew. Jeremy's confident that he doesn't need his parents' permission to sail away as long as he returns in time for soccer practice. Initially, the life of a pirate appeals to Jeremy: no table manners, no changing into pajamas and no brushing teeth. However, when Jeremy discovers pirates also have no books thus eliminating bedtime stories the appeal of their lifestyle diminishes. After a fierce storm blows them off course and breaks the ship's mast they row ashore to bury their treasure chest in Jeremy's backyard and he is home in time for soccer practice with his team, the Pirates. (40 pages)

Where it's reviewed:
Booklist, September 15, 2003, page 238
Bulletin of the Center for Children's Books, January 2004, page 197
Publishers Weekly, July 7, 2003, page 70
School Library Journal, September 2003, page 184

Awards the book has won:
School Library Journal Best Books, 2003
ALA Notable Children's Books, 2004

Other books by the same author:
Hiccup Snickup, 2001
When Papa Snores, 2000

Other books you might like:
Colin McNaughton, *Captain Abdul's Pirate School*, 1994
  Maisie organizes a mutiny, overtakes wicked Captain Abdul and his crew and sails with the other students to the West Indies.
David McPhail, *Edward and the Pirates*, 1997
  As Edward reads the stories come alive for him so vividly he's kidnapped by the pirates in his book and must be saved by other literary heroes.
Kathy Tucker, *Do Pirates Take Baths*, 1994
  A story in rhyme provides details about the daily life of pirates.

908

CELIA BARKER LOTTRIDGE
ELSA MYOTTE, Illustrator

Berta: A Remarkable Dog
(Toronto: Groundwood, 2002)

Subject(s): Animals/Dogs; Babies; Animals
Age range(s): Grades 3-5
Major character(s): Marjory Miller, 9-Year-Old, Daughter; Berta, Dog
Time period(s): 2000s (2002)
Locale(s): Middle Westfield, Canada

Summary: Marjory's family has a perfectly ordinary dachshund, but Marjory knows that Berta is really a remarkable dog. One spring, Berta's maternal instincts strongly influence her behavior and she tries to mother, in turn, chicks, piglets and a tiny, newborn kitten. However, when a local farmer brings the family a lamb rejected by its mother and asks the family's help in raising it, Berta has found the answer to her mothering needs. Berta cares for the lamb until it is grown and, before she can get too lonely, she has puppies all her own. (104 pages)

Where it's reviewed:
Booklist, May 1, 2002, page 1525
Horn Book, July/August 2002, page 464
Quill & Quire, May 2002, page 34

Other books by the same author:
The Wind Wagon, 1995
The Name of the Tree, 1989
One Watermelon Seed, 1988

Other books you might like:
Betsy Byars, *Tornado*, 1996
  During a tornado, Pete tells the story of how he acquired his dog with the help of another storm.
Wolfram Hanel, *Abby*, 1996
  When Moira's dog, Abby, accidentally eats some poisoned meat, Moira cares for her through the night.
Dick King-Smith, *The Invisible Dog*, 1993
  Janie's family can't afford to get a dog so she imagines one.

909

D. ANNE LOVE

The Puppeteer's Apprentice
(New York: Simon & Schuster, 2003)

Subject(s): Orphans; Middle Ages; Entertainment
Age range(s): Grades 4-7
Major character(s): Mouse, Child, Apprentice (to a puppeteer)
Time period(s): 18th century
Locale(s): England

Summary: Left on the doorsteps of Dunston Manor when she was a baby, Mouse is raised as scullery maid to the cook from whom she endures much verbal and physical abuse, until the day she's struck with a meat hook and runs away. Accompanying a group of minstrels to York, Mouse spots a puppet show, watches, becomes entranced with the entertainment, and asks the puppeteer to take her on as an apprentice. The puppeteer finally relents and Mouse travels along, learning to carve the puppets, manipulate their strings and help the puppeteer with the performances, though she's aware that something odious hangs over her new master. For a young orphan living in medieval England, it's enough for Mouse that she has a place to sleep, a job to do and the puppeteer as her friend, though sadness will beset her before Mouse becomes her own person. (185 pages)

Where it's reviewed:
Booklist, March 15, 2003, page 1327
Bulletin of the Center for Children's Books, May 2003, page 367
Kirkus Reviews, March 15, 2003, page 472
Publishers Weekly, March 17, 2003, page 77
School Library Journal, May 2003, page 156

Other books by the same author:
Hypatia: Her Story, 2005
The Secret Prince, 2005
A Year without Rain, 2000
I Remember the Alamo, 1999
Three Against the Tide, 1998

Other books you might like:
Malcolm Bosse, *Captives of Time*, 1987
    Two siblings struggle across medieval Europe, driven by outlaws, disease and developing technology.
Karen Cushman, *The Midwife's Apprentice*, 1995
    Orphaned Brat, found in a dung heap, struggles to satisfy Jane the midwife, names herself Alyce and knows she has skills and a future.
Elizabeth Gray, *Adam of the Road*, 1942
    This Newbery winner portrays a 13th-century minstrel lad who searches for both his father and his dog.

910

BRIGID LOWRY

Guitar Highway Rose
(New York: Holiday House, 2003)

Subject(s): Runaways; School Life; Coming-of-Age
Age range(s): Grades 8-12
Major character(s): Rosie Moon, 15-Year-Old, Runaway; Asher Fielding, Student—High School, Runaway
Time period(s): 2000s
Locale(s): Perth, Australia

Summary: Rosie, who has a flower name just like all the other women in her family, wishes for a "juicy life" and a nose ring. The nose ring she does on her own though the juicy life waits until new student Asher arrives. Asher is the son of former hippies who have now split and he seems determined to disregard the school's dress code, which doesn't sit well with the teachers. When a teacher's wallet is stolen, Asher's accused of the theft and he and Rosie decide to take off for a while. They have the adventure of their lives as they discover the landscape of their own country and one another, all of which is recorded in their distinctive voices. Other people share observations of these two, from their parents, bus driv-

ers, teachers and other people they meet along the way in an uplifting narrative by a New Zealand author. (196 pages)

Where it's reviewed:
Booklist, February 15, 2004, page 1051
Kirkus Reviews, November 15, 2003, page 1361
Publishers Weekly, December 15, 2003, page 74
School Library Journal, December 2003, page 146

Other books by the same author:
Follow the Blue, 2004

Other books you might like:
Eve Bunting, *If I Asked You, Would You Stay?*, 1984
    Runaway Crow lives in a secret apartment above a carousel. One day he rescues a drowning girl but then worries that she'll reveal his hiding place.
Margaret Clark, *Care Factor Zero*, 2000
    When Larceny thinks she's killed a man, she runs away to the streets of Melbourne but luckily meets a social worker who helps her put her life in order.
Louise Rennison, *Angus, Thongs and Full-Frontal Snogging: Confessions of Georgia Nicolson*, 2000
    In her diary, Georgia records her interest in kissing, her appearance and her opposition to most of what the adult world thinks is important.

911

LOIS LOWRY
MIDDY THOMAS, Illustrator

Gooney Bird Greene
(Boston: Walter Lorraine Books/Houghton Mifflin Company, 2002)

Subject(s): Storytelling; Schools; Humor
Age range(s): Grades 2-4
Major character(s): Gooney Bird Greene, 2nd Grader, Storyteller; Mrs. Pidgeon, Teacher
Time period(s): 2000s (2002)
Locale(s): Watertower

Summary: Gooney Bird's unusual outfits garner attention from the moment she enters Mrs. Pidgeon's second grade classroom. However, it is with her creative, but "absolutely true," stories that Gooney Bird easily achieves her goal of being "right smack in the middle of everything." Coincidentally Mrs. Pidgeon is introducing a storytelling unit on Gooney Bird's first day at Watertower Elementary School. Gooney Bird, through her truthful stories and imaginative presentations, models the attributes of a good storyteller and encourages the other students to recognize that they, too, have stories to tell the class. (88 pages)

Where it's reviewed:
Booklist, September 1, 2002, page 125
Bulletin of the Center for Children's Books, October 2002, page 66
Horn Book, September 2002, page 575
Publishers Weekly, August 12, 2002, page 300
School Library Journal, November 2002, page 129

Awards the book has won:
ALA Notable Children's Books, 2003
Center for Children's Books Best Books, 2002

Other books by the same author:
The Silent Boy, 2003
Zooman Sam, 1999
Stay!: Keeper's Story, 1997
See You around, Sam!, 1996 (School Library Journal Best Books)

Other books you might like:
Beverly Cleary, *The Ramona Series*, 1952-1999
Irrepressible Ramona and her family endure school problems and sibling squabbles with love and a sense of humor.
Astrid Lindgren, *Pippi Longstocking*, 1950
Independent Pippi tells stories of her life sailing the seven seas before settling down with a monkey and a horse for companions.
Rafe Martin, *The Storytelling Princess*, 2001
After surviving a storm at sea a princess tells the story of her adventure to a prince and they all live happily ever after.

912

DAVID LUBAR

Dunk
(New York: Clarion Books, 2002)

Subject(s): Humor; Amusement Parks; Beaches
Age range(s): Grades 7-10
Major character(s): Chad Turner, 15-Year-Old, 11th Grader; Malcolm Vale, Teacher (drama), Entertainer (clown); Guinevere "Gwen" O'Sullivan, Teenager; Jason Lahasca, 15-Year-Old, Friend (of Chad)
Time period(s): 2000s
Locale(s): Atlantic City, New Jersey

Summary: Chad worries about his mother, working as a waitress to make ends meet after his miserable dad abandoned them; tires of always feeling like a loser; wishes his mom would let him get a job; and hopes he's not like his father. Wandering the boardwalk, he notices Bozo, the clown who sits over a tub of water and hurls insults to lure people into paying to throw a ball at a target, which in turn dunks the clown. Being able to use humor to disguise the taunts and barbs thrown at people, while still protected in a cage, appeals to Chad. To his surprise, Bozo turns out to be his mother's new tenant, Malcolm Vale, who's moonlighting from his real job teaching drama. Then Chad's best friend Jason becomes ill with a disease that's untreatable and the girl he'd like to date turns him down, which sends Chad in to a funk where he doesn't leave the couch. Malcolm finally convinces him to use the gift of laughter in a nice way to not only help his friend Jason but also to pursue the girl of his dreams, as the two being a relationship that approximates that of father and son. (249 pages)

Where it's reviewed:
Booklist, September 1, 2002, page 116
Bulletin of the Center for Children's Books, December 2002, page 165
Horn Book, November 2002, page 762
School Library Journal, August 2002, page 192
Voice of Youth Advocates, October 2002, page 281

Awards the book has won:
Center for Children's Books Best Books, 2002

Other books by the same author:
Flip, 2003
In the Land of the Lawn Weenies: And Other Misadventures, 2003
Wizards of the Game, 2003
Hidden Talents, 1999

Other books you might like:
Chris Crutcher, *Staying Fat for Sarah Byrnes*, 1993
When his friend Sarah's fear of her father sends her to the hospital, it's up to Eric to make sure she gets the correct help.
Sid Fleischman, *Disappearing Act*, 2003
Being stalked, Kevin and Holly run away to Venice Beach where they find jobs on the Boardwalk.
A.M. Jenkins, *Damage*, 2001
As a football star in his senior year of high school, Austin should be happy but he's battling depression and has little energy for anything.

913

DAVID LUBAR

Flip
(New York: Tor, 2003)

Subject(s): Fantasy; Twins; Peer Pressure
Age range(s): Grades 6-8
Major character(s): Ryan McKenzie, Twin, 8th Grader; Taylor McKenzie, Twin, 8th Grader; Ellis Izbecki, 8th Grader; Billy Snooks, Bully
Time period(s): 2000s
Locale(s): United States

Summary: The planet Nexula is the "entertainment hub of the universe" and when aliens from Nexula discovered humans on Earth, they knew they had a ready-made source of entertainment. Having recorded a series entitled "Legends of Earth," they head back to Nexula only to encounter space debris, which rips a hole in the side of their craft and releases their Earth legend disks. Seeing the flash in the sky, Ryan searches for the spacecraft the next morning but instead finds over fifty discs in the weeds near his school. He shows his perfect twin Taylor that he can activate the disc by flipping it so that it lands in his palm where it's absorbed and for a few hours he then becomes the person of the legendary event. Hopeless at baseball, when he becomes Babe Ruth, he hits one home run after another. The flip of a new disk changes him into Albert Einstein in time to ace a math test; Queen Victoria, Gandhi and Spartacus follow. Unfortunately his buddy Ellis manages to ruin the remaining disks so that when he faces bully Billy Snooks he relies on his new found self-confidence in another humorous tale by a popular author. (300 pages)

Where it's reviewed:
Bulletin of the Center for Children's Books, October 2003, page 68
Kliatt, July 2003, page 14
Publishers Weekly, July 14, 2003, page 77

School Library Journal, August 2003, page 162
Voice of Youth Advocates, August 2003, page 238

Other books by the same author:
Wizards of the Game, 2003
Dunk, 2002
Hidden Talents, 1999

Other books you might like:
Bruce Coville, *Bruce Coville's Alien Visitors*, 1999
    An anthology that features an alien in every short story.
Richard Scrimger, *The Nose from Jupiter*, 1998
    Alan appreciates the help he receives from the alien who
    lives in his nose; when Norbert's no longer needed, one
    giant sneeze sends him to Jupiter.
William Sleator, *The Night the Heads Came*, 1996
    The alien invasion seems silly at first, but it slowly be-
    comes clear that humans are no longer in charge.
Sheila Kelly Welch, *The Shadowed Unicorn*, 2000
    Moving into an old farmhouse, twins Brendan and Nick
    depart from their "twinness" and elect to have separate
    bedrooms for the first time in their lives.

914

DAVID LUBAR

Wizards of the Game

(New York: Philomel/Penguin Putnam, 2003)

Subject(s): Fantasy; Computer Games; Wizards
Age range(s): Grades 5-8
Major character(s): Mercer Dickensen, 8th Grader; Ed Bing-
    ham, 8th Grader; Chuck, Religious (pastor)
Time period(s): 2000s
Locale(s): United States

Summary: Master game player Mercer convinces his social
studies teacher that the eighth graders should host a weekend
game-playing tournament as their fundraiser for the local
homeless shelter. All seems on course until committee member Ed speaks up against the idea, following up with an article
for the school newspaper about gaming and its link to Sa-
tanism and devil worship. Now the fundamentalists enter the
fray as they speak in opposition to the weekend tournament,
even though Pastor Chuck, who runs the shelter, disagrees
with them. Mercer is really surprised when some occupants of
the shelter come to him, convinced he's a super wizard, and
ask for help to return to their home of Gliphidetsia. Mercer's
not sure what to do next, except that he and some of his game-
playing friends need to find the portal that connects Earth with
Gliphidetsia, in this blend of fantasy, humor and a few social
issues. (166 pages)

Where it's reviewed:
Booklist, February 15, 2003, page 1065
Bulletin of the Center for Children's Books, June 2003, page
    409
Publishers Weekly, March 31, 2003, page 68
School Library Journal, March 2003, page 235
Voice of Youth Advocates, April 2003, page 66

Other books by the same author:
Flip, 2003

In the Land of the Lawn Weenies: And Other Misadventures,
    2003
Dunk, 2002
Hidden Talents, 1999

Other books you might like:
Robert Norman, *Albion's Game: A Novel of Terror*, 1992
    Playing the board game Albion's Dream propels Edward
    into a struggle between good and evil.
Vivian Vande Velde, *User Unfriendly*, 1991
    A fantasy quest computer game becomes too real when the
    computer takes over as dungeon master and threatens the
    players.
Mary Frances Zambreno, *A Plague of Sorcerers*, 1991
    Jeremy's first attempt to be a wizard is not very promising,
    especially after a skunk elects to be his familiar.

915

DEB LUND
HOWARD FINE, Illustrator

Dinosailors

(San Diego: Harcourt, Inc., 2003)

Subject(s): Dinosaurs; Boats and Boating; Sailing
Age range(s): Grades K-2
Time period(s): 20th century
Locale(s): At Sea

Summary: A group of dinosaurs head to sea, but when a storm
hits, so does the seasickness. By morning the storm is over,
the boatload of dinosaurs heads back to solid land and quickly
sell their boat. The desire for adventure sends them out again,
but this time they decide to travel by train. (40 pages)

Where it's reviewed:
Booklist, September 2003, page 129
Bulletin of the Center for Children's Books, January 2004,
    page 197
Publishers Weekly, September 8, 2003, page 75
School Library Journal, September 2003, page 184

Other books by the same author:
Tell Me My Story, Mama, 2004
Me & God, 2003
Play & Pray, 2002

Other books you might like:
Michael Chesworth, *Alphaboat*, 2002
    The alphabet takes off on a boating adventure.
Nancy Shaw, *Sheep on a Ship*, 1989
    A group of sheep go for an adventure on a pirate ship, but
    soon are glad to be back on land.
Jane Yolen, *How Do Dinosaurs Say Good Night?*, 2000
    Ten sleepy dinosaurs get ready for bed in an award-win-
    ning title.

916

APRIL LURIE

Dancing in the Streets of Brooklyn

(New York: Delacorte, 2002)

Subject(s): World War II; Norwegian Americans; Stepfathers

Age range(s): Grades 6-9
Major character(s): Judy Strand, 13-Year-Old; Jacob Jacobsen, Boyfriend
Time period(s): 1940s
Locale(s): New York, New York (Brooklyn)

Summary: As the rest of the world struggles with the events of World War II, Judy has her own internal battle when she learns that her Pa is really her stepfather. Upset about this misinformation, she's very distressed when told that her real father is an alcoholic who abandoned his family in Norway, prompting her mother to immigrate to America. For a while her feelings taint her growing relationship with Jacob, as his father is also an alcoholic. Having Jacob join her family on a vacation in the Catskill Mountains, and witnessing the ending of the war, help Judy as she joins others "dancing in the streets of Brooklyn" in this author's first novel. (194 pages)

Where it's reviewed:
Booklist, November 15, 2002, page 595
Bulletin of the Center for Children's Books, December 2002, page 165
Kirkus Reviews, October 15, 2002, page 1533
Publishers Weekly, October 21, 2002, page 76
School Library Journal, September 2002, page 226

Other books you might like:
Morse Hamilton, *The Garden of Eden Motel*, 1999
    Del enjoys getting to know his stepfather, a seed company inspector, the summer they travel together to Idaho.
Christa Laird, *But Can the Phoenix Sing?: A Compelling Story of Unrelenting Courage in Nazi-Occupied Poland*, 1995
    Learning about his stepfather Misha's life as a partisan fighter in Warsaw helps Rich appreciate him.
Ida Vos, *Dancing on the Bridge at Avignon*, 1995
    Rosa's dream of "dancing on the bridge at Avignon" is shattered when her family is arrested and sent to the concentration camps.

917

KEVIN LUTHARDT, Author/Illustrator

Peep!

(Atlanta: Peachtree Publishers, Ltd., 2003)

Subject(s): Animals/Ducks; Pets; Animals, Treatment of
Age range(s): Preschool-Grade 1
Major character(s): Unnamed Character, Child, Son; Unnamed Character, Duck
Time period(s): 2000s (2003)
Locale(s): United States

Summary: Few words are exchanged between a young boy and a newly hatched duck. The boy's simple "Peep!" in response to the duck's peep seems a sufficient invitation in the duck's mind to follow the boy home and become his pet. Together they watch television and play soccer. The duck is the boy's show-and-tell at school. On a walk one fall day the duck sees and hears a flock of ducks flying south and his peep changes to "Quack!!" Puzzled, the boy seeks help from his parents and they drive to a duck pond where they release the pet duck, freeing it to join others for the flight to warmer

climes. The boy is lonely, but hears a "mew" while walking, suggesting another animal may follow him home. (36 pages)

Where it's reviewed:
Booklist, May 15, 2003, page 1672
Bulletin of the Center for Children's Books, April 2003, page 320
Horn Book, July 2003, page 445
School Library Journal, May 2003, page 124

Awards the book has won:
IRA Children's Choices, 2004

Other books by the same author:
You're Weird!, 2005
Hats!, 2004
Larrabee, 2004
Mine!, 2001

Other books you might like:
Jonathan Emmett, *Ruby in Her Own Time*, 2004
    The last of five ducks to hatch, Ruby also learns to fly at her own pace.
Ezra Jack Keats, *Clementina's Cactus*, 1999
    Silently walking in the desert with her father after a rainstorm, Clementina discovers "her" cactus holds a surprise.
Emily Arnold McCully, *Four Hungry Kittens*, 2001
    In a wordless picture book a mother cat hunting for mice in the feed room becomes accidentally trapped inside, leaving her kittens temporarily hungry.
Arthur Yorinks, *Quack!*, 2003
    Illustrations expand the minimal dialogue telling the story of a young duck's adventure to the moon.

918

CHRIS LYNCH

Who the Man

(New York: HarperCollins, 2002)

Subject(s): Family Problems; Violence; Interpersonal Relations
Age range(s): Grades 6-9
Major character(s): Earl Pryor, 13-Year-Old
Time period(s): 2000s
Locale(s): United States

Summary: Big for his age with a stubbly growth on his chin, everyone expects Earl to be older than he is, which gets him into situations that are beyond his knowledge to handle. He still looks at life simply, right is right and wrong is wrong, and hasn't yet discovered that gray area in between. After one fight too many in school, he's suspended for a week and quickly realizes his reliance on the structure of school to keep him focused. Now he sees the disharmony in his parent's relationship; wonders why his former babysitter, upon whom he has a crush, always asks him to buy liquor for her boyfriend; and finally loses his temper with his father. Following that outburst, Earl realizes that he can't fight anymore, either for himself or for others, and will have to adjust to a divided lifestyle between his parents in a gritty coming of age tale. (186 pages)

Where it's reviewed:

Booklist, November 15, 2002, page 588

Bulletin of the Center for Children's Books, January 2003, page 204

Publishers Weekly, November 11, 2002, page 65

School Library Journal, December 2002, page 144

Voice of Youth Advocates, February 2003, page 478

Other books by the same author:

Gravedigger's Cottage, 2004

All the Old Haunts, 2001

Freewill, 2001

Extreme Elvin, 1999

Whitechurch, 1999

Other books you might like:

Joan Bauer, *Stand Tall*, 2002

At six feet three inches, Tree's still growing but doesn't know quite what to do with himself as he's not as grown up as everyone expects.

Chris Crutcher, *Ironman*, 1995

A domineering, sadistic father works hard to make a ''man'' of Bo, but instead turns him into a young man who resists any and all authority.

John Steinbeck, *Of Mice and Men*, 1937

Traveling together from one ranch job to another are George and his not-as-smart friend Lennie.

Peter Weston Wood, *To Swallow a Toad*, 1987

A miserable home life has made Pete Wood hungry for boxing's Golden Gloves title.

919

TRACY LYNN

Snow

(New York: Simon Pulse/Simon & Schuster, 2003)

Subject(s): Fantasy; Fairy Tales

Age range(s): Grades 7-10

Major character(s): Jessica Abigail Danvers ''Snow'' Kenigh, Noblewoman; Alan, Musician; Anne of Mandagor, Stepmother, Royalty (duchess)

Time period(s): 19th century

Locale(s): Wales; London, England

Summary: Jessica's mother dies in childbirth leaving her father the Duke so grief struck that he ignores her. Brought up in the kitchen of the castle and learning to bake bread, turn the meat on the spit, churn butter or make jam, Jessica is a happy child until her father remarries. As she approaches her teen years, her beauty causes jealousy in her stepmother Anne, who in turn keeps Jessica confined to the castle. Anne wishes to be considered a scientist and wants to use her unusual skills to produce an heir for the Duke, an act that requires Jessica's heart. Luckily Alan, Anne's musician and personal servant, knows of the plan and helps Jessica escape to London where she falls in with a strange group of thieves, part human and part animal hybrid, called the Lonely Ones. Though Duchess Anne tries to extend her powers over Jessica, a little ''modern science'' and the help of friends returns Jessica to her real place in the world in this retelling of *Snow White*. (259 pages)

Where it's reviewed:

Bulletin of the Center for Children's Books, May 2003, page 369

Kliatt, July 2003, page 33

Publishers Weekly, March 10, 2003, page 73

School Library Journal, August 2003, page 162

Voice of Youth Advocates, August 2003, page 238

Other books you might like:

Francesca Lia Block, *The Rose and the Beast: Fairy Tales Retold*, 2000

These nine fairy tales are wonderfully, magically reworked so they're only tangentially similar to their original form.

Gail Carson Levine, *Ella Enchanted*, 1997

The Cinderella theme weaves through this fantasy of an orphaned girl and her quest to remove a fairy's curse.

Donna Jo Napoli, *Zel*, 1996

In this retelling of Rapunzel, a young girl is held prisoner while her lover struggles through magical barriers to rescue her.

920

GEORGE ELLA LYON

Gina.Jamie.Father.Bear

(New York: Richard Jackson/Atheneum, 2002)

Subject(s): Supernatural; Fathers; Secrets

Age range(s): Grades 6-9

Major character(s): Gina Ourisman, 9th Grader; Jamie, 12-Year-Old

Time period(s): 2000s; Indeterminate Past

Locale(s): Cleveland, Ohio; Fictional Country

Summary: The worlds of Gina and Jamie intersect in a blending of fantasy and reality. Gina lives in Cleveland with her rather proper father and older brother, while Jamie lives in the past in an unnamed, Celtic-type world with his father and sisters. Concerned about her father's behavior, Gina follows him to a McDonald's where he meets and leaves with Esther, a psychic. Gina and Esther eventually meet and Esther suggests that she journey to Jamie's world to help him track his father who also exhibits strange behavior. Both fathers have lost their wives and seem to be transforming into bears, but Gina's meeting with Jamie turns everything around in a strange, yet enticing tale. (135 pages)

Where it's reviewed:

Booklist, December 15, 2002, page 754

Bulletin of the Center for Children's Books, December 2002, page 165

Publishers Weekly, September 9, 2002, page 69

School Library Journal, August 2002, page 194

Voice of Youth Advocates, October 2002, page 298

Other books by the same author:

Sonny's House of Spies, 2004

The Stranger I Left Behind, 1997

With a Hammer for My Heart, 1996

Here and Then, 1994

Borrowed Children, 1988

Other books you might like:

Michael Chabon, *Summerland*, 2002

When his father is kidnapped, Ethan travels through the gate at Summerland and crosses to another world in search of him.

Judith Clarke, *Starry Nights*, 2003

Moving into a new house, Clem falls into conversation with a ghostly presence named Amy in a relationship that blends the real and the spiritual.

Elizabeth Kay, *The Divide*, 2003

Straddling the Continental Divide, Felix lands in a fantasy world of unicorns, pixies and griffins and hunts for a cure for his damaged heart.

M

921

DAVID MACAULAY, Author/Illustrator

Angelo

(Boston: Walter Lorraine Books/Houghton Mifflin Company, 2002)

Subject(s): Art Restoration; Animals/Birds; Wildlife Rescue
Age range(s): Grades 1-4
Major character(s): Angelo, Artisan, Aged Person; Sylvia, Pigeon, Friend
Time period(s): Indeterminate Past
Locale(s): Rome, Italy

Summary: As Angelo prepares to restore the plaster facade of a church by removing old pigeon nests and other debris he comes upon an ill bird, barely breathing. At the end of the day, the pigeon is still alive and begrudgingly Angelo carries her home and nurses her back to health. In time the two develop a mutually supportive relationship and Angelo names his companion Sylvia, shares his pasta with her in the evenings and regales her with tales of his life, his work and his dreams for the church restoration. Through the heat and cold for more than two years, the restoration continues. Sylvia notices that Angelo is growing slower, weaker and more worried as the project nears completion. His final act assures that Sylvia and her descendants will always have a home high on the facade of the restored church. (48 pages)

Where it's reviewed:
Bulletin of the Center for Children's Books, June 2002, page 372
Horn Book, May 2002, page 318
Publishers Weekly, January 21, 2002, page 88
Riverbank Review, Fall 2002, page 28
School Library Journal, May 2002, page 121

Awards the book has won:
School Library Journal Best Books, 2002

Other books by the same author:
Building Big, 2000 (Booklist Editors' Choice)
The New Way Things Work, 1998 (Parents' Choice Gold Award)

Rome Antics, 1997
Shortcut, 1995 (ALA Notable Children's Book)
Black and White, 1990 (Caldecott Medal)

Other books you might like:
Tomie De Paola, *Days of the Blackbird: A Tale of Northern Italy*, 1997
  Throughout a harsh winter, a white bird stays to sing for a gravely ill Duke, sacrificing its beauty to repay the Duke's kindness.
Donna Jo Napoli, *Albert*, 2001
  Reclusive Albert becomes more outgoing in order to accommodate the needs of a pair of birds that builds a nest on his hand.
Oscar Wilde, *The Happy Prince*, 1995
  An illustrated adaptation by Jane Ray retells Wilde's 1888 tale of sacrifice by a sparrow to bring happiness to the little prince statue.

922

AMY MACDONALD
EMILY LISKER, Illustrator

Please, Malese

(New York: Melanie Kroupa Books/Farrar Straus Giroux, 2002)

Subject(s): Folklore; Trickster Tales; Conduct of Life
Age range(s): Grades 2-5
Major character(s): Malese, Trickster
Time period(s): Indeterminate Past
Locale(s): Haiti

Summary: Lazy Malese's conniving manner enables him to get something for nothing by tricking the other villagers so many times that they finally throw him in jail. Soon the villagers learn that an imprisoned Malese is more work than a free one so they beg him to go home. Malese refuses to leave the "comfort" of the mud hut jail until the villagers promise to repair his home's leaky roof, broken gate and damaged wall. And so, once again, Malese gets what he wants at no expense to himself. The book concludes with an "Author's

Note'' explaining sources and background for the story. (32 pages)

Where it's reviewed:
Booklist, August 2002, page 1968
Bulletin of the Center for Children's Books, October 2002, page 67
Horn Book, September 2002, page 590
Publishers Weekly, May 27, 2002, page 59
School Library Journal, September 2002, page 215

Other books by the same author:
Quentin Fenton Herter III, 2002
Cousin Ruth's Tooth, 1996 (IRA Children's Choices)
The Spider Who Created the World, 1996
Little Beaver and the Echo, 1990
Rachel Fister's Blister, 1990

Other books you might like:
Virginia Hamilton, *A Ring of Tricksters: Animal Tales from America, the West Indies, and Africa*, 1997
  Eleven read-aloud tales include tricksters as diverse as spiders and rabbits and the unwitting animals that bear the brunt of their cleverness.
Julius Lester, *More Tales of Uncle Remus: Further Adventures of Brer Rabbit, His Friends, Enemies, and Others*, 1988
  Thirty-seven stories feature the activities of the famous trickster Brer Rabbit.
Gayle Ross, *How Rabbit Tricked Otter: And Other Cherokee Trickster Stories*, 1994
  Fifteen stories about Rabbit show him to be a trickster, outsmarting animals and being responsible for some of their physical characteristics.

923

AMY MACDONALD
GISELLE POTTER, Illustrator

Quentin Fenton Herter III
(New York: Melanie Kroupa Books/Farrar Straus Giroux, 2002)

Subject(s): Behavior; Humor; Stories in Rhyme
Age range(s): Grades K-3
Major character(s): Quentin Fenton ''Quentin'' Herter III, Child, Nephew; Quentin Fenton ''Shad'' Herter Three, Friend (imaginary, Quentin's)
Time period(s): Indeterminate Past
Locale(s): Fictional Country

Summary: Well-behaved Quentin Fenton Herter Third has a shadow known as Quentin Fenton Herter Three. Though ''seldom seen and never heard'' Quentin Third is polite, conscientious and mannerly while Quentin Three is a selfish, uncooperative, ill-behaved, mischievous bully. Each would secretly like to be just a bit like the other and finally they reconcile just enough to become pals so that neither Quentin nor Shad is too good or too bad but each is a blend of traits. (32 pages)

Where it's reviewed:
Booklist, May 15, 2002, page 1602
Bulletin of the Center for Children's Books, September 2002, page 25

Horn Book, May 2002, page 318
Publishers Weekly, January 14, 2002, page 58
School Library Journal, May 2002, page 122

Other books by the same author:
Cousin Ruth's Tooth, 1996 (IRA Children's Choices)
The Spider Who Created the World, 1996
Little Beaver and the Echo, 1990

Other books you might like:
Diane Cuneo, *Mary Louise Loses Her Manners*, 1999
  After Mary Louise's manners run away she needs help finding them again.
Lawrence David, *Peter Claus and the Naughty List*, 2001
  With Santa's ''naughty'' list in hand, Peter locates each child and helps them atone for their misbehavior until only his name remains on the list.
David Small, *Fenwick's Suit*, 1996
  A new suit rather than a shadow takes on an identity of its own, behaving in a way that Fenwick never would.

924

ROSS MACDONALD, Author/Illustrator

Achoo! Bang! Crash!: The Noisy Alphabet
(Brookfield, CT: Neal Porter Book/Roaring Brook Press, 2003)

Subject(s): Language; Humor
Age range(s): Grades K-3
Time period(s): Indeterminate
Locale(s): Fictional Country

Summary: Sounds rather than objects represent the letters of the alphabet in this lively text. The picture of a little girl bestowing a kiss on a young boy does not grace the ''K'' page but demonstrates the letter ''I'' for ''ICK!'' A cow and a cat portray ''M'' because of the sounds the animals make rather than the initial letter of their names. A beak of a peeping bird pops a balloon on the ''P'' page. To illustrate ''V'' a little girl on a tricycle ''Vrooooomms'' with such speed past a man that he's knocked off his feet and his coffee and newspaper go flying. A concluding author's note describes the 19th century wood type technique used in creating the book. (32 pages)

Where it's reviewed:
Booklist, November 1, 2003, page 502
Horn Book, January 2004, page 71
Publishers Weekly, August 11, 2003, page 277

Awards the book has won:
Publishers Weekly Best Children's Books, 2003

Other books by the same author:
Another Perfect Day, 2002 (Publishers Weekly Best Children's Book)

Other books you might like:
Michael Chesworth, *Alphaboat*, 2002
  Letters sail away in search of treasure in this rhyming tale.
Jerry Pallotta, *The Beetle Alphabet Book*, 2004
  Humorous and educational, this nature ABC book has a beetle for every letter.
Dr. Seuss, *Dr. Seuss's ABC*, 1963
  Nonsense verse introduces the letters and their sounds in this I Can Read title.

925

ROSS MACDONALD, Author/Illustrator

Another Perfect Day

(Brookfield, CT: Roaring Brook Press, 2002)

Subject(s): Heroes and Heroines; Dreams and Nightmares; Sleep

Age range(s): Grades K-3

Major character(s): Jack, Child, Son

Time period(s): Indeterminate Past

Locale(s): United States

Summary: In his dreams Jack is a superhero hurrying to work as a flavor tester at an ice cream factory. Because his day is so perfect he decides to walk home (by leaps and bounds atop buildings) when suddenly his suit changes into a pink tutu, clown shoes sprout on his feet, a large baby bonnet is tied to his head and a rattle appears in his hand. His private plane is now a tricycle and police are chasing him. When he wonders what became of his perfect day, a young Jack tells him he has not yet awakened so he unsuccessfully tries to wake up. Young Jack explains that he's going about the process the wrong way and tells him to imagine sunlight, birds, and the smell of breakfast. Sure enough, the plan works and Jack wakes up in his bedroom where all the toys that have been a larger-than-life part of his superhero dream are waiting to be played with on another perfect day. (32 pages)

Where it's reviewed:
Booklist, November 1, 2002, page 509
Horn Book Guide, Spring 2003, page 44
Kirkus Reviews, July 1, 2002, page 958
Publishers Weekly, August 19, 2002, page 89
School Library Journal, September 2002, page 201

Awards the book has won:
Publishers Weekly Best Children's Books, 2002

Other books by the same author:
Achoo! Bang! Crash!: The Noisy Alphabet, 2003

Other books you might like:
Laurence Anholt, *Jack and the Dreamsack*, 2003
  Jack's plan to stay awake all night and stuff his dreams in a sack so he can enjoy them more doesn't work.
Maya Gottfried, *Last Night I Dreamed a Circus*, 2003
  Colorful images of a dream adorn the pages of a lyrical fantasy.
Maurice Sendak, *Kenny's Window*, 2002
  In a reissue of a 1956 title the reality of a little boy's daily activity blends with the fantasy of his dreams.

926

TODD MACK
JULIA GRAN, Illustrator

Princess Penelope

(New York: Scholastic, Inc., 2003)

Subject(s): Princes and Princesses; Parent and Child; Imagination

Age range(s): Grades K-2

Major character(s): Penelope, Child, Royalty (princess)

Time period(s): 2000s (2003)

Locale(s): United States

Summary: Penelope is a princess—of that she is quite certain. She changes her outfits several times a day, sits on many thrones (a dining room chair, a potty), rides in a chariot (stroller), and is quite demanding. Penelope's imagination turns a day's ordinary activities into royal adventures. (32 pages)

Where it's reviewed:
Bulletin of the Center for Children's Books, March 2003, page 280
School Library Journal, April 1, 2003, page 1403

Other books by the same author:
Baby for Princess Penelope, 2005

Other books you might like:
Carmela Lavigna Coyle, *Do Princesses Wear Hiking Boots?*, 2003
  A young girl wonders if princesses do ordinary things like play in the dirt, eat vegetables and follow rules.
Cynthia DeFelice, *The Real, True Dulcie Campbell*, 2002
  Farm girl Dulcie is convinced that she is really the Princess Dulcinea.
Lisa McCourt, *Good Night Princess Pruney Toes*, 1999
  While a little girl gets out of her bath, she is dubbed Princess Pruney Toes and Sir Daddy sets about putting her to bed.
Richard Scrimger, *Princess Bun Bun*, 2002
  Winifred and baby sister Bun Bun, go to visit their uncle in the Castle Apartments.

927

TRACY MACK

Birdland

(New York: Scholastic, 2003)

Subject(s): Brothers; Grief; Movies

Age range(s): Grades 7-10

Major character(s): Joseph Eli ''Jed'' Diamond, 8th Grader; Zeke ''Bird'' Diamond, Brother (deceased); Flyer, 8th Grader

Time period(s): 2000s

Locale(s): New York, New York

Summary: Assigned to portray their neighborhoods any way they see them, either through writing, painting, singing or any other medium, Jed and his good friend Flyer decide to film their East Village community. Jed's older brother Zeke was a diabetic who died after consuming too much alcohol and Jed feels guilty because he wasn't home to help him. Jed's parents have withdrawn in their grief, leaving him to struggle with his own feelings. Finding Zeke's journal, Jed uses his brother's writing to search for and record the sights and sounds that he describes. As he does so, he draws comfort from the familiar pieces of his neighborhood in a beautifully written novel. (198 pages)

Where it's reviewed:
Booklist, October 15, 2003, page 409
Bulletin of the Center for Children's Books, November 2003, page 114

Publishers Weekly, November 17, 2003, page 66
School Library Journal, October 2003, page 172
Voice of Youth Advocates, February 2004, page 494

Awards the book has won:
Booklist Editors' Choice/Books for Youth, 2003
ALA Best Books for Young Adults, 2004

Other books by the same author:
Drawing Lessons, 2000

Other books you might like:
Charles Butler, *Timon's Tide*, 2000
 Daniel has felt guilty ever since his brother Timon's drug related activities caught up with him and he was killed.
James D. Forman, *The Big Bang*, 1989
 The only survivor of a van accident, Chris has to live with the grief and guilt associated with losing his brother and seven of his brother's friends.
James Howe, *The Color of Absence: Twelve Stories about Loss and Hope*, 2001
 Though one can be sad, these stories show there's no need for loss and hope to be dismal.
Paul Many, *My Life, Take Two*, 2000
 To complete requirements for his film class, Neal films the estate where his deceased father used to work which alleviates his sadness.
Pamela Walker, *Pray Hard*, 2001
 Convinced it's her fault that her father's crop duster plane crashed, Amelia's happy to learn a toy of hers didn't distract him.

928

DANDI DALEY MACKALL
TIPHANIE BEEKE, Illustrator

First Day
(San Diego: Silver Whistle/Harcourt, Inc., 2003)

Subject(s): Schools; Fear; Stories in Rhyme
Age range(s): Preschool-Kindergarten
Major character(s): Mom, Mother; Dad, Father; Unnamed Character, Daughter, Student
Time period(s): 2000s (2003)
Locale(s): United States

Summary: No amount of preparation seems to remove the mixture of excitement and apprehension on the first day of school for the pig-tailed narrator. Clinging to Mom and Dad in the schoolyard, she considers making a getaway, but gathers the courage to enter the building. Realizing that it's the first day for everyone helps her overcome the setback of a broken crayon and a clock that doesn't seem to be ticking. By lunchtime and recess on the first day of school, the possibility of a successful day seems clear. By the end of the first day, the departing girl declares that school is cool and eagerly anticipates returning for day two. (32 pages)

Where it's reviewed:
Booklist, August 2003, page 1994
Publishers Weekly, August 25, 2003, page 62
School Library Journal, September 2003, page 184

Other books by the same author:
Merry Creature Christmas!, 2004

Animal Babies, 2003
Are We There Yet?, 2003

Other books you might like:
Nancy Carlson, *Look Out Kindergarten, Here I Come!*, 1999
 Henry's enthusiasm for school wanes as he approaches the building.
Anne Rockwell, *Welcome to Kindergarten*, 2001
 A preview visit to his classroom helps prepare Tim for entry into kindergarten.
Vera Rosenberry, *Vera's First Day of School*, 1999
 Vera's eager for the first day of school until she sees the crowded schoolyard; then she has second thoughts about entering the building.

929

KATHY MACKEL

From the Horse's Mouth
(New York: HarperCollins, 2002)

Subject(s): School Life; Aliens; Space and Time
Age range(s): Grades 5-7
Major character(s): Nicholas "Nick" Thorpe, 13-Year-Old; Albert Michael "Mike" Pillsbury, 13-Year-Old; Jill Pillsbury, Student—High School
Time period(s): 2000s
Locale(s): United States

Summary: The good news about time warps is that Nick and Jill, his best friend Mike's gorgeous older sister, become better friends when they're both trapped in a warp; the bad news is that it introduces him to more aliens. The first time Nick is sucked into a time warp, it's just as he's on the receiving end of a punch. Suddenly he's several hours behind everyone else and is invisible, a plight that could allow some interesting observations for Nick. Instead he discovers that a fast-moving creature, a Zephyr from the planet Grayle, is using his horn to disrupt space and time as he tries to escape the dreaded Draconians. Nick must come to the rescue and reunite this Zephyr with his rider, a rescue in which Mike refuses to participate because he's afraid to have any more interactions with aliens. This time Nick's adventures with aliens include volunteering in a homeless shelter, learning more about friendship and accepting his parents' divorce in this sequel to *Eggs in One Basket*. (214 pages)

Where it's reviewed:
Booklist, May 1, 2002, page 1526
Kirkus Reviews, May 1, 2002, page 660
Publishers Weekly, June 10, 2002, page 62
School Library Journal, July 2002, page 122

Other books by the same author:
Eggs in One Basket, 2000
Can of Worms, 1999
A Season of Comebacks, 1997

Other books you might like:
Vivien Alcock, *The Red-Eared Ghosts*, 1997
 Because of the resemblance between Mary and her grandmother, aliens lure her into a parallel universe.
Bruce Coville, *Bruce Coville's Alien Visitors*, 1999
 Aliens are everywhere, at least in every short story in this

new anthology, which features such authors as Ray Bradbury, Sherwood Smith and Mel Gilden.

Gail Gauthier, *Club Earth*, 1999

When Will and Robby's alien guests return, the Denis home becomes an intergalactic tourist spot, a lodge for Club Earth.

William Sleator, *Boltzmon!*, 1999

In order to save his life, Chris travels to an alternate world.

930

CAROLYN MACKLER

The Earth, My Butt, and Other Big Round Things

(Cambridge, MA: Candlewick Press, 2003)

Subject(s): Self-Perception; Weight Control; Family Problems
Age range(s): Grades 7-12
Major character(s): Virginia Shreves, 15-Year-Old; Byron Shreves, Student—College; Anais Shreves, Sister (of Virginia and Byron); Shannon, 15-Year-Old; Froggy Welsh, Student—High School
Time period(s): 2000s
Locale(s): New York, New York (Manhattan)

Summary: Virginia is convinced that she was switched at birth. How else can one explain a blonde, overweight teenager in a family of slender, dark-haired, overachievers? Uncomfortable with her weight and lacking self-confidence, she allows Froggy the Fourth to grope her on Monday afternoons, but never expects him to speak to her at their school. Her older sister Anais joins the Peace Corps to escape their noted psychologist mother, her perfect brother Byron's at Columbia, and her father's not often home. Her world changes when Byron's accused of date rape and, found guilty, expelled from school. Virginia can't believe that her adored brother has done such a thing and, after daring to meet and talk with his victim, she looks at her family and herself differently as she realizes that people aren't perfect. Armed with this knowledge, she flies to Seattle to visit her friend Shannon, pierces her eyebrow, asks her dad to quit commenting on her weight, buys fun, teenager clothes and learns to like herself. And Froggy likes her, too. (246 pages)

Where it's reviewed:
Booklist, September 1, 2003, page 115
Horn Book, September 2003, page 614
Publishers Weekly, July 21, 2003, page 197
School Library Journal, September 2003, page 218
Voice of Youth Advocates, October 2003, page 314

Awards the book has won:
Michael L. Printz Honor Book, 2004
ALA Best Books for Young Adults, 2004

Other books by the same author:
Vegan Virgin Valentine, 2004
Love and Other Four-Letter Words, 2000

Other books you might like:
Sarah Dessen, *Keeping the Moon*, 1999
Though Colie loses 45 pounds, she hasn't shed her insecurity, especially when a classmate tries to say she has an "easy" reputation.

Anna Fienberg, *Borrowed Light*, 2000
In Cally's life, people are either moons, borrowers of light like she is; or stars, those who make light.

Cherry Whytock, *My Cup Runneth Over: The Life of Angelica Cookson Potts*, 2003
With thin friends, and a mother who's a former model, Angel's set apart by her "wobbly bits," which are growing thanks to her love for food.

931

ERIN MACLELLAN

Run from the Nun!

(New York: Holiday House, 2003)

Subject(s): Friendship; Humor; Schools/Catholic Schools
Age range(s): Grades 4-6
Major character(s): Kara McKinney, 5th Grader; Sister Mary Francis, Principal, Religious
Time period(s): 2000s
Locale(s): Philadelphia, Pennsylvania

Summary: In an attempt to impose some structure on their daughter's life, her parents decide to send Kara to St. Joan of Arc Catholic School. Kara, however, has other ideas and tries to do whatever she can to be expelled in order to return to her former school and her best friend. On her first day, she runs away from the school principal, though Sister Mary Francis catches up with her when Kara trips over her shoelaces. Then she wears too much makeup, in direct violation of the dress code, but only ends up in detention. When put in charge of the food drive, she promises the winning class a day off of school, a promise that is later honored. No matter what Kara tries to do, she's not expelled! Finally her parents agree to return her to Bingham Elementary, but Kara realizes that's not really what she wants to do; instead, she stays at St. Joan of Arc where she's made many new and different friends. (165 pages)

Where it's reviewed:
Bulletin of the Center for Children's Books, January 2004, page 199
Publishers Weekly, December 15, 2003, page 73
School Library Journal, February 2004, page 149

Other books you might like:
Gordon Korman, *Macdonald Hall Goes Hollywood*, 1991
Boots and Bruno stir up trouble as they try to entice a moviemaker into using their campus for his new production.

Sonia Levitin, *The Mark of Conte*, 1976
Humor abounds as Conte receives two school schedules, one for Conte Mark and the other for Mark Conte.

Susan Wojciechowski, *Patty Dillman of Hot Dog Fame*, 1989
Selling hot dogs to raise money for the homeless, Patty takes time to become friends with some of the street people.

932

CATHERINE MACPHAIL

Dark Waters

(New York: Bloomsbury, 2003)

Subject(s): Brothers; Heroes and Heroines; Conduct of Life
Age range(s): Grades 7-10
Major character(s): Col McCann, Teenager; Mungo McCann, Brother (of Col), Juvenile Delinquent; Dominic Sampson, 10-Year-Old; Klaus, Accident Victim, Spirit
Time period(s): 2000s
Locale(s): Scotland

Summary: Growing up, Col idolizes his older brother Mungo just as Mungo idolized their father, shot when he was driving the getaway car during a robbery. Mungo is a small-time criminal who has been in trouble with the law several times but Col hasn't lost his loyalty for his brother, even going so far as to provide an alibi for him one night. Then Col's perception of himself changes when he rescues young Dominic from an ice-covered loch and the townspeople regard him as a hero, rather than the brother of a hood. Dominic and his family befriend Col, even bringing him to London to receive a heroism award. But memories and bad dreams plague Col as he realizes a face he remembers seeing underwater is actually attached to the body of Klaus, an illegal immigrant his brother Mungo might have killed, and Col's loyalty is severely tested. (176 pages)

Where it's reviewed:
Booklist, March 15, 2003, page 1317
Bulletin of the Center for Children's Books, March 2003, page 280
Publishers Weekly, January 27, 2003, page 260
School Library Journal, June 2003, page 146
Voice of Youth Advocates, June 2003, page 139

Awards the book has won:
Center for Children's Books Best Books, 2002

Other books by the same author:
Missing, 2002

Other books you might like:
David Almond, *Kit's Wilderness*, 2000
   If the spin of the knife chooses you in the game of Death, you are left behind to ''die'' in an underground den while your friends wait outside.
Peter Blauner, *Man of the House*, 1999
   Saving a pregnant student from an explosion, David's first called a hero and then questioned as to his role in the blast.
Eoin Colfer, *The Wish List*, 2003
   Neither Beelzebub nor St. Peter can decide who gets Meg, so she's sent back to earth to help a victim attain everything on his wish list.

933

CATHERINE MACPHAIL

Missing

(New York: Bloomsbury, 2002)

Subject(s): Missing Persons; Runaways; Bullies

Age range(s): Grades 5-8
Major character(s): Maxine ''Maxie'' Moody, 13-Year-Old; Derek Moody, Brother (of Maxine), Runaway; Cam, Student—High School, Immigrant (Chinese); Sweeney, Bully
Time period(s): 2000s
Locale(s): Scotland

Summary: Maxine is convinced that her parents don't love her for all they do is worry about where Derek might be. It's been ten months since she saw her brother and no one knows where he is, until the day her father's asked to identify a body and he says it's his son Derek. After Derek's burial, her mother seeks out psychics to hold seances to speak with him while her father refuses to speak about his son. Maxine is befriended by Cam, an immigrant Chinese student two years ahead of her, who's picked on by Sweeney as much as Derek was. At the same time, Maxine receives strange phone calls from a person who claims to be Derek, but she doesn't feel she can tell her parents about the calls. Coming upon Sweeney and his gang beating up Cam in the cemetery, Maxine springs to his defense, but it's the help from Derek that finally thwarts the bullying of Sweeney. (191 pages)

Where it's reviewed:
Kirkus Reviews, October 15, 2002, page 1533
Kliatt, November 2002, page 12
Publishers Weekly, October 28, 2002, page 72
School Library Journal, November 2002, page 173
Voice of Youth Advocates, February 2003, page 478

Other books by the same author:
Dark Waters, 2003

Other books you might like:
Michael Cadnum, *Calling Home*, 1991
   While drunk, Peter accidentally kills his best friend Mead, then calls Mead's parents daily pretending to be their son.
Lois Duncan, *Killing Mr. Griffin*, 1978
   Kidnapping Mr. Griffin begins as a prank; his students never meant to kill him.
Susan Beth Pfeffer, *The Year Without Michael*, 1987
   Michael leaves home to play softball and never returns. Was he kidnapped or did he run away? Will anyone ever know?

934

DANIEL J. MAHONEY, Author/Illustrator

The Saturday Escape

(New York: Clarion Books, 2002)

Subject(s): Behavior; Responsibility; Animals
Age range(s): Grades K-2
Major character(s): Jack, Bear, Friend; Angie, Rabbit, Friend; Melden, Mouse, Friend
Time period(s): Indeterminate
Locale(s): Fictional Country

Summary: The lure of Saturday morning story hour at the library outweighs Jack's usual approach to chores. He ''cleans'' his room by shoving everything under the bed and then encourages Angie and Melden to shirk their responsibilities and accompany him to story hour. The plot of the first story they hear causes each to feel so guilty that they excuse themselves and hurry away to help each other correctly complete the neglected chores. Then, with clear consciences, they have their own story hour in Jack's clean bedroom as the author's first book concludes. (32 pages)

Where it's reviewed:
Book Links, December 2002/January 2003, page 12
Booklist, March 15, 2002, page 1263
Horn Book, May 2002, page 320
Publishers Weekly, February 11, 2002, page 187
School Library Journal, March 2002, page 193

Awards the book has won:
Book Links Lasting Connections, 2002

Other books you might like:
Marc Brown, *D.W.'s Library Card*, 2001
  It takes a week of practice before D.W. masters the writing of her complete name so she can get her own library card.
Judith Caseley, *Sammy and Sophie's Library Sleepover*, 1993
  Sophie tries to help younger brother Sammy learn how to treat library books so he can come with her the next time the library has a special program.
Carl Meister, *Tiny Goes to the Library*, 2000
  When Tiny accompanies his owner to the library the big dog waits outside to pull home the wagon loaded with books.

935

MARGARET MAHY

Alchemy

(New York: Margaret K. McElderry Books, 2003)

Subject(s): Fantasy; Magic; Friendship
Age range(s): Grades 8-12
Major character(s): Roland Fairfield, Teenager, Student; Jess Ferret, Teenager, Student; Mr. Hudson, Teacher; Quando, Wizard
Time period(s): 2000s (2003)
Locale(s): New Zealand

Summary: Roland's life seems very close to perfect. His mother and little brothers love him, he's a decent student who is also popular, so what is Roland doing shoplifting? He really doesn't know himself, and when his teacher Mr. Hudson knows all about it, Roland is ready to agree to just about anything in exchange for his silence. But Mr. Hudson's request is as bizarre as Roland's petty crime; he wants Roland to pretend to be friends with another student, Jess Ferret, and find out what is going on with him. Having no choice, Roland imposes himself on Jess and discovers things are indeed odd at Jess's home, but he also discovers a deep connection with Jess. Roland's terrifying dream of a sinister magician and a magical siege at Jess's house seem to be related. The two will need to untangle memory from dream to defeat the greedy wizard who wants to prey on both of them. (207 pages)

Where it's reviewed:
Booklist, March 15, 2003, page 1317
Horn Book, May 2003, page 352
Publishers Weekly, April 7, 2003, page 68
School Library Journal, May 2003, page 157

Voice of Youth Advocates, June 2003, page 150

Other books by the same author:
The Other Side of Silence, 1995
Underrunners, 1992
Dangerous Spaces, 1991

Other books you might like:
Peter S. Beagle, *Tamsin*, 1999
  Jenny tries to help her friend Tamsin, who died 300 years ago.
Pamela Dean, *Juniper, Gentian and Rosemary*, 1998
  Three sisters are protected by their names during a magical assault.
Rita Murphy, *Night Flying*, 2000
  Georgia finds that her grandmother's strict rules about using the family talent may be arbitrary when rebellious Aunt Carmen shows up.

936

PATRICIA MALONE

The Legend of Lady Ilena

(New York: Delacorte, 2002)

Subject(s): Identity; Historical
Age range(s): Grades 6-9
Major character(s): Ilena, Orphan, 15-Year-Old; Ryamen, Aged Person; Durant, Knight (to King Arthur)
Time period(s): 5th century
Locale(s): Dun Alyn, England (now part of Scotland)

Summary: Heeding her father's dying words, Ilena leaves the home she's always known in Vale of Enfert and heads east toward Dun Alyn where she is to locate Ryamen. Trained in weaponry, Ilena dresses as a boy to undertake the dangerous journey to a spot she knows nothing about. Meeting Durant along the way, the two travel to Dun Alyn, which is ruled by the Christian Belert who is being opposed by the Druid Ogern. Ilena becomes caught up in the conflict between these two strong men until she's captured by Ogern and is slated to become the next human sacrifice. Ilena's peril forces Ryamen to reveal the truth behind Ilena's birth, a truth which leads to Ilena assuming the role of leader of Dun Alyn in this first novel. (232 pages)

Where it's reviewed:
Booklist, January 2002, page 842
Bulletin of the Center for Children's Books, April 2002, page 287
Kirkus Reviews, December 15, 2001, page 1760
Publishers Weekly, January 7, 2002, page 65
School Library Journal, January 2002, page 137

Other books you might like:
Henrietta Branford, *The Fated Sky*, 1999
  Though Ran is scheduled to be sacrificed to Odin, she is rescued by the blind harper Toki and taken to Iceland where the two fall in love.
Chris Eboch, *The Well of Sacrifice*, 1999
  Eveningstar is unsuccessful in her attempt to save her brother from being thrown into the "well of sacrifice."
Rebecca Tingle, *The Edge on the Sword*, 2001
  Pledged to wed Ethelred of Mercia, Flaed resists the assis-

tance of her bodyguard Red until the day she eludes him and travels straight into disaster.

937

MAURIE J. MANNING, Author/Illustrator

The Aunts Go Marching
(Honesdale, PA: Boyds Mills Press, 2003)

Subject(s): Aunts and Uncles; Music and Musicians; Weather
Age range(s): Preschool-Grade 1
Major character(s): Unnamed Character, Child, Niece; Unnamed Character, Aunt
Time period(s): 2000s (2003)
Locale(s): United States

Summary: In a twist on the song ''The Ants Go Marching,'' a little girl and her aunt go marching into town joined by more and more aunts as they go along. As they march, the drumbeat, provided by the little girl, is joined with the loud percussive sound of thunder and they march back home. (32 pages)

Where it's reviewed:
Booklist, February 1, 2003, page 1001
Horn Book, May 2003, page 330
School Library Journal, April 2003, page 133

Other books you might like:
Alan Katz, *Take Me Out of the Bathtub and Other Silly Dilly Songs*, 2001
 Fifteen traditional songs (including ''Take Me Out to the Ballgame'') get a playful rewrite in this book.
Steven Kellogg, *A-Hunting We Will Go!*, 1998
 Based on the traditional folk song, this version tells of two kids' reluctant bedtime preparations.
Jama Kim Rattigan, *Truman's Aunt Farm*, 1994
 When Truman orders an ant farm there is a mix-up and he is overrun with aunts.

938

CELESTE DAVIDSON MANNIS
SUSAN KATHLEEN HARTUNG, Illustrator

One Leaf Rides the Wind
(New York: Viking, 2002)

Subject(s): Gardens and Gardening; Nature; Poetry
Age range(s): Grades K-3
Major character(s): Unnamed Character, Child
Time period(s): Indeterminate
Locale(s): Japan

Summary: One leaf, two carved temple dogs, five roofs atop a pagoda and six wooden sandals are described in haiku and illustrated with the young child observing and counting each item. Factual footnotes on each page give more information about Japanese customs relating to each haiku and picture from seven sweets on a tea tray to eight pink lotus blossoms and nine shiny koi in a pond. A conclusion to the author's first book gives additional information about Japanese gardens and haiku. (28 pages)

Where it's reviewed:
Five Owls, 2003, page 17
Horn Book Guide, Spring 2003, page 169
Kirkus Reviews, August 1, 2002, page 1136
Publishers Weekly, September 2, 2002, page 75
School Library Journal, October 2002, page 149

Awards the book has won:
IRA Children's Choices, 2003

Other books you might like:
Miriam Chaikin, *Don't Step on the Sky: A Handful of Haiku*, 2002
 A collection of haiku in a picture book reflects the simplicity of nature in both urban and rural settings.
Matthew Gollub, *Cool Melons—Turn to Frogs!: The Life and Poems of Issa*, 1998
 This biography for young readers of the 18th-century poet includes translations of more than thirty of Issa's haiku.
George Shannon, *Spring: A Haiku Story*, 1996
 Illustrations of children on a walk provide continuity linking individual haiku in this collection of poems.

939

NICK MANNS

Operating Codes
(Boston: Little, Brown and Company, 2001)

Subject(s): Ghosts; Trials; Family Problems
Age range(s): Grades 6-9
Major character(s): Mathilda Emily Hayton, Child; Graham Hayton, 15-Year-Old; Brian Hayton, Father, Computer Expert; Paul Whitaker, Spirit, Military Personnel
Time period(s): 2000s
Locale(s): New Barton, England

Summary: Graham and Matty join their parents as the family moves into Sentinel House, an historic home that turns out to be haunted by the ghost of a World War II soldier. Graham's father is working on a top-secret design for a fighter plane that would be used to cause destruction and death, a fact that's disturbing to his family. When Graham's father is accused of espionage for posting information on the Internet about his secret design, the family realizes his plans were also disturbing to others. But when it appears that the person who sent the classified aircraft information over the Internet was the resident ghost Paul Whitaker, a conscientious objector who was killed for sharing information about poison gas research, Graham's not sure anyone will believe his father's innocence. (182 pages)

Where it's reviewed:
Book Report, May 2002, page 56
Booklist, December 15, 2001, page 723
Children's Bookwatch, December 2001, page 2
School Library Journal, January 2002, page 138
Science Fiction Chronicle, December 2001, page 45

Other books by the same author:
Control Shift, 2001

Other books you might like:

Robert Hawks, *This Stranger, My Father*, 1988
Patty flees from her foster home to reunite with her father, a prison escapee, who sold secrets to the Russians.

Walter Dean Myers, *The Nicholas Factor*, 1983
Spying for the government, a college student becomes part of a secret organization.

David Patneaude, *Haunting at Home Plate*, 2000
The ghost of a fan killed 50 years earlier inspires a new team by leaving baseball tips written in the dirt of their infield.

Robert Westall, *The Promise*, 1990
Valerie dies during World War II, a bomb obliterates her grave and her ghost reminds Bob of the promise he made to find her if she's ever lost.

940

PAUL MANY

Walk Away Home

(New York: Walker, 2002)

Subject(s): Family Problems; Aunts and Uncles; Coming-of-Age
Age range(s): Grades 8-11
Major character(s): Diana Lawson, Teenager, Abuse Victim; Wanda, Aunt; Nick Doran, 11th Grader
Time period(s): 2000s
Locale(s): Ohio

Summary: Nick is a walker who not only walks away from problems but also walks to sort out problems. Recently kicked out of school, Nick wants to get away from his distant parents as well as avoid military school, so he walks halfway across Ohio to his Aunt Wanda's home. Hoping to stay for the year, he settles down with Wanda in her hippie commune, which consists of a gaggle of older cottages next to a recently built, wealthy housing development. One day Nick meets Diana, who lives next to them, and soon a relationship develops. Diana has her own problems with a sexually abusive father and, fearing that he's starting on her younger sisters, the three flee their home and, with Nick's help, find a more permanent solution for their lives. (240 pages)

Where it's reviewed:
Horn Book, January 2003, page 78
Kliatt, November 2002, page 12
Publishers Weekly, November 25, 2002, page 69
School Library Journal, September 2002, page 228
Voice of Youth Advocates, December 2002, page 387

Other books by the same author:
My Life, Take Two, 2000
These Are the Rules, 1997

Other books you might like:

Joan Bauer, *Hope Was Here*, 2000
Living a nomadic lifestyle with her guardian aunt, Hope helps out in the diners where Aunt Addie cooks, and inscribes "Hope was here" in each one.

Dudley J. Delffs, *Forgiving August*, 1993
This is the summer Bounty's parents' marriage disintegrates and he breaks free of past parental restraints.

C.D. Payne, *Youth in Revolt: The Journals of Nick Twisp*, 1996
Nick's diaries reveal his struggle to deal with his parents' divorce, figure out what high school's all about, and examine his widening world.

941

JULIET MARILLIER

Child of the Prophecy

(New York: Tor, 2002)

Series: Sevenwaters Trilogy. Book 3
Subject(s): Fantasy; Mythology; Family
Age range(s): Grades 9-Adult
Major character(s): Ciaran, Father, Wizard; Fainne, Daughter, Wizard; Darraugh Walker, Gypsy; Johnny, Cousin; Oonagh, Sorceress, Grandmother, Wizard
Time period(s): Indeterminate Past
Locale(s): Ireland

Summary: Raised in solitude by her wizard father, Fainne knows almost nothing about her family or the world beyond her cove. Ciaran is a strict but patient teacher and he shares all his druidic knowledge with his daughter Fainne, a talented and hard-working student of the supernatural arts. Her only escape is her summer friendship with Darraugh, one of the Travelers who summers at the seaside. As she reaches her teens, Ciaran reveals the secrets of Fainne's family to her: she is the child of a forbidden union because her parents were half siblings. As if that were not enough for Fainne to absorb, she learns further that her grandmother is the awful sorceress Oonagh who seeks to bring down the clan of Sevenwaters. Ciaran proposes that Fainne should make herself ready to go and live with her family at Sevenwaters. Fainne is still reeling when Ciaran disappears and Oonagh appears announcing that she has come to further Fainne's education. She drives the girl mercilessly, and then reveals that she has a death spell on Ciaran. Fainne can save him only by going to Sevenwaters and finishing the destruction Oonagh began so long ago. Oonagh believes that Fainne's cousin Johnny is the child foretold in prophecy, who will heal the wounds of the land. It is Fainne's task to be sure he does not. (528 pages)

Where it's reviewed:
Booklist, February 15, 2002, page 999
Library Journal, March 15, 2002, page 111
Publishers Weekly, February 4, 2002, page 58
Teacher Librarian, December 2002, page 60
Voice of Youth Advocates, August 2002, page 204

Other books by the same author:
Wolfskin, 2002
Son of the Shadows, 2001 (Sevenwaters Trilogy Book 2)
Daughter of the Forest, 2000 (Sevenwaters Trilogy Book 1)

Other books you might like:

Morgan Llywelyn, *Strongbow: The Story of Richard and Aoife*, 1996
Richard falls in love with Aoife and decides to fight with the Irish against his native land.

Robin McKinley, *Spindle's End*, 2000
> Hidden away to escape a dire curse, Briar Rose comes to believe that everyone has misinterpreted the prophecy.

Rosalind Miles, *Isolde: Queen of the Western Isle: The First of the Tristan and Isolde Novels*, 2002
> Like Fainne, Isolde struggles to avert the disaster a powerful female seems bent on creating; but for Isolde, the problem is her mother.

942

CAROLYN MARSDEN

The Gold-Threaded Dress

(Cambridge, MA: Candlewick Press, 2002)

Subject(s): Identity; Prejudice; Moving, Household
Age range(s): Grades 3-5
Major character(s): Oy Chaisang, 4th Grader, Bullied Child; Frankie, 4th Grader; Liliandra, 4th Grader, Bully
Time period(s): 2000s
Locale(s): United States

Summary: When Oy's family moves to a new neighborhood she enters a classroom in which the teacher calls her Olivia and she is the only Thai American. Oy feels frustrated that Frankie considers her Chinese and she does not recognize his awkward attempts to reach out in friendship. Oy really wants to join the popular group controlled by Liliandra and finally complies with the bully's command to bring her gold-threaded dress to school. At recess, the girls in Liliandra's club fight to try on the dress, creating such a scene that Oy and others are sent to the office and the dress is ruined. Ashamed to have caused trouble, Oy finally confesses to her mother about the adjustment problems she is having. With her mother's help she washes and repairs the dress. Following the incident Oy learns that Frankie is actually a much better friend than Liliandra ever could be. The author's first book is based on the school experiences of her daughter. (73 pages)

Where it's reviewed:
Booklist, May 1, 2002, page 1521
Bulletin of the Center for Children's Books, June 2002, page 373
Horn Book Guide, Spring 2003, page 70
Publishers Weekly, March 4, 2002, page 79
School Library Journal, April 2002, page 117

Awards the book has won:
Booklist Editors' Choice, 2002

Other books you might like:
Alma Flor Ada, *My Name Is Maria Isabel*, 1993
> After moving to a ''better'' neighborhood, Maria attends a new school where she is the third Maria in the class so the teacher calls her Mary.

Margaret Peterson Haddix, *The Girl with 500 Middle Names*, 2001
> Janie's wardrobe looks dated in comparison to the wealthier kids in her new school making it difficult for her to be accepted.

Suzy Kline, *Song Lee in Room 2B*, 1993
> Korean-American Song Lee's kindness toward her classmates shows that friendship knows no language barriers.

943

JOHN MARSDEN

Winter

(New York: Scholastic, 2002)

Subject(s): Orphans; Mystery and Detective Stories
Age range(s): Grades 7-10
Major character(s): Winter De Salis, 16-Year-Old, Orphan
Time period(s): 2000s
Locale(s): Warriewood, Australia

Summary: Orphaned when she was only four and living with relatives for the last twelve years, Winter has had enough of her guardians and returns to her childhood home, determined to make it a thriving ranch once again. When she arrives, she discovers that the estate managers have sold off the expensive furniture and stole other profits from the land, so Winter dismisses them. Finding her parents' grave, she finds her mother died six months after her father, not together in the sailing accident as she'd been told. Neighbors talk around matters as if they're concealing something from her, which makes Winter determined to solve the mystery of her mother's death. (147 pages)

Where it's reviewed:
Bulletin of the Center for Children's Books, November 2002, page 115
Kliatt, July 2002, page 12
Publishers Weekly, August 5, 2002, page 73
School Library Journal, August 2002, page 194
Voice of Youth Advocates, October 2002, page 282

Other books by the same author:
Checkers, 1996
Tomorrow, When the War Began Series, 1995-2002
Letters from the Inside, 1994
So Much to Tell You, 1989

Other books you might like:
Sharon Creech, *Chasing Redbird*, 1997
> A project to clean up a 20-mile trail helps Zinny accept her aunt's death and other mysterious aspects of her family.

Melina Marchetta, *Looking for Alibrandi*, 1999
> Josephine feels set apart at her posh Catholic girls school, from her illegitimacy and status as scholarship student, to life in a female-dominated household.

Richard Mosher, *Zazoo: A Novel*, 2001
> Orphaned and living with her grandfather, Zazoo realizes one day that she knows little of his earlier life and resolves to learn that missing piece.

944

ELSA MARSTON

The Ugly Goddess

(Chicago: Cricket, 2002)

Subject(s): Mythology; Kidnapping; Adventure and Adventurers
Age range(s): Grades 5-8
Major character(s): Meret, Royalty (daughter of Pharaoh), 14-Year-Old; Hector, Military Personnel (Greek soldier);

Bata, Servant (to a sculptor); Amun, Deity; Taweret, Deity (goddess of protection)

Time period(s): 5th century B.C.

Locale(s): Thebes, Egypt

Summary: A triangle of teens become part of Egyptian history in this blend of fiction and fantasy. Princess Meret, daughter of a Pharaoh, is promised as the next Divine Wife of Amun, a powerful political figure, in a move to help her father's kingdom. Resigned to a future life spent residing in Amun's temple, she's on her way to Thebes accompanied by a statue of Taweret, the ugly goddess who protects women. In love with Meret is Hector, a young soldier in the Greek army, who's part of the mercenaries who help the Pharaoh against the Persians. Serving the master who carved the statue of Taweret is Bata who ensures its delivery to Meret. The princess is kidnapped on her journey and Hector and Bata unite to save Meret, aided by Taweret who comes to life with Bata's help, in this adventure of desert travel, disguises and deities. (218 pages)

Where it's reviewed:
Booklist, January 2003, page 891
Kliatt, January 2003, page 10
School Library Journal, December 2002, page 144

Other books by the same author:
The Byzantine Empire, 2003 (nonfiction)
Women in the Middle East: Tradition and Change, 2003 (nonfiction)
The Phoenicians, 2002 (nonfiction)
The Ancient Egyptians, 1996 (nonfiction)

Other books you might like:
Dorothy Sharp Carter, *His Majesty, Queen Hatshepsut*, 1987
In ancient Egypt, this bold female declares herself as pharaoh and rules for more than two decades.
Jane Louise Curry, *The Egyptian Box*, 2002
An inherited carved wooden statue, called a Shabti, comes to life and Tee sends it to school in her place.
Kate McMullan, *Under the Mummy's Spell*, 1992
Kissing the 3,000-year-old mummy mask of Princess Nephia, Peter accidentally releases the spirit of the princess's evil Aunt Tachu.

945

ANN M. MARTIN

A Corner of the Universe
(New York: Scholastic, 2002)

Subject(s): Aunts and Uncles; Mental Illness; Family Life

Age range(s): Grades 5-8

Major character(s): Hattie Owen, 12-Year-Old; Adam Mercer, Uncle, Mentally Ill Person; Leila Cahn, 12-Year-Old

Time period(s): 1960s

Locale(s): Millerton

Summary: For Hattie, summer is a time to enjoy all the familiar and comfortable parts of her small town, from chatting with her parents' boarders, to watching her artist father paint, to lying around reading library books. This is also the summer that shy Hattie makes two new friends, one of whom is her Uncle Adam whom she's never met. Adam

returns home when his special school for people with mental problems closes down and Hattie enjoys his friendship, though his conversations don't always make sense, especially when he reverts to *I Love Lucy* dialogue. The carnival also comes to town and Hattie befriends Leila whose mother is the Pretzel Woman of the show. Wanting Adam to enjoy himself without always having to be on his best behavior, Hattie and Leila arrange for him to join them at the carnival one night but that act of kindness ultimately leads to tragedy in a tender story of friendship. (191 pages)

Where it's reviewed:
Booklist, December 1, 2002, page 659
Horn Book, January 2003, page 79
Kliatt, November 2002, page 12
Publishers Weekly, July 22, 2002, page 180
School Library Journal, September 2002, page 228

Awards the book has won:
Newbery Honor Book, 2003
Horn Book Fanfare, 2002

Other books by the same author:
Here Today, 2004
The Meanest Doll in the World, 2003 (Laura Godwin, co-author)
Belle Teal, 2001 (IRA Young Adult's Choices)
Snail Mail No More, 2000 (Paula Danziger, co-author)

Other books you might like:
Hadley Irwin, *So Long at the Fair*, 1988
Joel takes a job at the fair grounds to figure out why Ashley killed herself there.
Celia Rees, *The Truth Out There*, 2000
Joshua wonders why no one ever talks about deceased Uncle Patrick, until he discovers he's institutionalized with a form of autism.
June Rae Wood, *The Man Who Loved Clowns*, 1992
After her parents die, Delrita learns not to feel ashamed about her kind, loving Uncle Punky who has Down syndrome.

946

ANN M. MARTIN
LAURA GODWIN, Co-Author
BRIAN SELZNICK, Illustrator

The Meanest Doll in the World
(New York: Hyperion Books for Children, 2003)

Subject(s): Dolls and Dollhouses; Fantasy; School Life

Age range(s): Grades 3-6

Major character(s): Annabelle Doll, Doll, Friend; Tiffany Funcraft, Doll, Friend; Kate Palmer, 4th Grader, Sister (older); Mimi, Doll, Bully

Time period(s): 2000s (2002)

Locale(s): United States

Summary: To avoid being seen by humans and risk being placed in "Doll State" or, worse, "Permanent Doll State" (PDS) Annabelle and Tiffany dive into Kate's backpack to hide and thus take an inadvertent trip to school. When their curiosity leads them on an exploration in the school they are unable to get back in the backpack until the next day and then they climb into the wrong one. Discovering that they are in a strange house on a Friday afternoon is scary enough but learning that Mean Mimi terrorizes the other dolls all weekend is truly frightening. Annabelle and Tiffany recognize that Mean Mimi is a threat to all dolls and as soon as they can get back to school and find Kate's backpack they rush home to tell the others about the problem. Too late—they discover that the problem has followed them. Vengeful Mimi climbs out of Kate's backpack and spends several days trying to ruin the dolls' peaceful life in Kate's home before Mimi's reckless nature propels her into PDS, confirming Annabelle's worst fears: that the condition truly exists. (260 pages)

Where it's reviewed:
Booklist, October 15, 2003, page 412
Horn Book, November 2003, page 751
Publishers Weekly, August 11, 2003, page 280
School Library Journal, October 2003, page 130

Awards the book has won:
Publishers Weekly Best Children's Books, 2003
School Library Journal Best Books, 2003

Other books by the same author:
The Doll People, 2000 (ALA Notable Children's Books)

Other books you might like:
Rumer Godden, *The Doll's House*, 1976
    Two little girls enjoy adventures with their Victorian dollhouse and the family of dolls living in it.
Melodye Benson Rosales, *Minnie Saves the Day*, 2001
    While Hester sleeps her new doll Minnie comes to life and socializes with the other dolls and toys in Hester's room.
Rosemary Wells, *Rachel Field's Hitty, Her First Hundred Years: A New Edition*, 1999
    This newly illustrated adaptation of the 1930 Newbery Award winner describes the adventurous first hundred years of a doll's life.

947

JACQUELINE BRIGGS MARTIN
DAVID A. JOHNSON, Illustrator

On Sand Island
(Boston: Houghton Mifflin Company, 2003)

Subject(s): Islands; Boats and Boating; Norwegian Americans
Age range(s): Grades 1-3
Major character(s): Carl Dahl, 10-Year-Old, Sailor
Time period(s): 1910s (1916)
Locale(s): Sand Island, Wisconsin (Lake Superior)

Summary: Carl longs to have a boat of his own in which to enjoy the quiet of water and sky, away from his home that's become too sad and quiet since his mother's death. As luck would have it, Carl finds boards floating in off the lake one day and he pulls them ashore to use in making a boat. Each task and additional item that Carl needs he acquires by trading with a neighbor. He picks strawberries, moves rocks and mends fishing nets in exchange for having the boards cut, and getting nails and paint. When Carl finally launches his boat a celebration is held to recognize the newest boat on the island. A concluding Author's Note gives factual information about

Sand Island and the resident on whom the story is based. (32 pages)

Where it's reviewed:
Booklist, August 2003, page 1981
Bulletin of the Center for Children's Books, October 2003, page 70
Publishers Weekly, July 21, 2003, page 194
School Library Journal, November 2003, page 110

Awards the book has won:
Publishers Weekly Best Children's Books, 2003

Other books by the same author:
The Lamp, the Ice and the Boat Called Fish, 2001
Snowflake Bentley, 1998 (Caldecott Medal)
Grandmother Bryant's Pocket, 1996 (School Library Journal Best Books)

Other books you might like:
Margaret Wise Brown, *The Little Island*, 1946
    On a small island seasons and storms bring changes that are depicted in a Caldecott Medal winner.
Robert McCloskey, *One Morning in Maine*, 1952
    One day along the shores of Maine's Penobscot Bay, Sal loses her first tooth and it's all portrayed in a Caldecott Honor Book.
Barbara Mitchell, *Waterman's Child*, 1997
    Despite changes over time, Annie's family has made a living on the water for generations and Annie hopes to continue the tradition.

948

JACQUELINE BRIGGS MARTIN
LINDA S. WINGERTER, Illustrator

The Water Gift and the Pig of the Pig
(Boston: Houghton Mifflin, 2003)

Subject(s): Grandparents; Animals/Pigs; Boats and Boating
Age range(s): Grades 1-4
Major character(s): Isabel, Child, Daughter; Grandfather, Grandfather, Aged Person; Pig of the Pig, Pig
Time period(s): 2000s (2003)
Locale(s): Waldo County, New England

Summary: Shy Isabel's grandfather is still considered a waterman despite leaving the sea years ago when he married. Grandfather loves to tell tales of the sea and he still has the water gift, the ability to find underground water sources using a divining rod. In a spell of bad luck, Grandfather hurts himself while searching for water and he stops telling tales and trying to find water or other precious things. Then, the family's beloved Pig of the Pig (the descendant of a pig that sailed on the grandfather's schooner) goes missing. In her search for Pig of the Pig, Isabel discovers within herself the ability to find lost things whether they are Grandfather's spirits or family pets. (32 pages)

Where it's reviewed:
Booklist, June 2003, page 1787
Bulletin of the Center for Children's Books, May 2003, page 369
Horn Book, May/June 2003, page 331
School Library Journal, June 2003, page 112

Awards the book has won:
Bulletin of the Center for Children's Books Blue Ribbons, 2003
Center for Children's Books Best Books, 2003

Other books by the same author:
The Finest Horse in Town, 2003
Snowflake Bentley, 1998 (Caldecott Medal winner)
Grandmother Bryant's Pocket, 1996 (ALA Notable Children's Books)

Other books you might like:
Laurie Krebs, *The Beeman*, 2002
  A young girl loves to assist her grandfather with his beekeeping.
Kathy May, *Molasses Man*, 2000
  A young African-American boy helps his grandfather make and sell molasses.
Roni Schotter, *In the Piney Woods*, 2003
  Ella loves exploring the piney woods around her beach home with her grandfather.

949

NORA MARTIN

Flight of the Fisherbird
(New York: Bloomsbury, 2003)

Subject(s): Aunts and Uncles; Prejudice; Chinese Americans
Age range(s): Grades 4-7
Major character(s): Clementine "Clem" Nesbitt, 13-Year-Old; Sarah Hersey, 15-Year-Old, Orphan; Doran, Uncle; Jed, Teenager; Tong-Ling, Immigrant (Chinese)
Time period(s): 1880s (1889)
Locale(s): San Juan Islands, Washington

Summary: With passage of the Exclusion Act, the Chinese are no longer admitted to America and this catches many by surprise, especially those Chinese with homes and jobs in America who just happen to be out of the country. On her dory the *Fisherbird*, Clem's emptying the family lobster pots when she hears objects being tossed in the ocean. Sailing over, she finds Tong-Ling trussed in a burlap bag and saves him from drowning. She's disheartened to find that her favorite uncle Doran tossed the men overboard rather than face arrest for smuggling. Hiding Tong-Ling on an island, she returns home to figure out what to do next. Staying with her family is orphaned Sarah, a prissy girl who loves to remind Clem of her engagement to Doran. Clem and her neighbor Jed set out to retrieve Tong-Ling but somehow Sarah ends up in their boat and suddenly the three are pursued by Doran who will do anything to prevent arrest, even killing his own family, in this taut adventure. (150 pages)

Where it's reviewed:
Booklist, April 1, 2003, page 1397
Horn Book, May 2003, page 370
Publishers Weekly, April 28, 2003, page 71
School Library Journal, May 2003, page 157
Voice of Youth Advocates, June 2003, page 139

Other books by the same author:
A Perfect Snow, 2002
The Eagle's Shadow, 1997

Other books you might like:
Avi, *The True Confessions of Charlotte Doyle*, 1990
  Charlotte's adventures on the sailing ship *Seahawk* turn her from a proper young Victorian lady to a real sailor.
Rhea Beth Ross, *The Bet's On, Lizzie Bingman!*, 1988
  When Lizzie's brothers claim that women need sheltering, Lizzie lets them all know that she doesn't require their protection.
Paul Yee, *Tales from Gold Mountain: Stories of the Chinese in the New World*, 1990
  When Chinese immigrants came to America, they combined their beliefs and folklore as they adapted to new life and work.

950

RAFE MARTIN
CALVIN NICHOLL, Illustrator

The World Before This One
(New York: Arthur A. Levine/Scholastic, 2002)

Subject(s): Indians of North America; Folklore
Age range(s): Grades 5-8
Major character(s): Crow, Indian (Seneca); Grandmother, Indian (Seneca)
Time period(s): Indeterminate Past
Locale(s): United States

Summary: People think that his grandmother is a witch, so Crow and Grandmother live as outcasts outside their Seneca village with Crow trying to become a good hunter so the two of them will survive. One day while tracking game in the woods, a boulder speaks to him; Crow is so enthralled that he listens and hears the stories of the "Long-Ago Time." Each day he returns to hear about Sky Woman falling to the Earth, or the brothers who hunt the bear up in the heavens, or the boy who becomes a buffalo and flees to safety, stories that explain the creation, survival and existence of the Seneca Indians. Crow and his Grandmother are welcomed back into the village when he is chosen as his village's first storyteller. Exquisite paper cutouts illustrate some of the stories. (195 pages)

Where it's reviewed:
Bulletin of the Center for Children's Books, February 2003, page 243
Kliatt, November 2002, page 12
Library Media Connection, February 2003, page 75
School Library Journal, December 2002, page 165
Voice of Youth Advocates, February 2003, page 490

Other books you might like:
Joseph Bruchac, *The Heart of a Chief*, 1998
  Living on the Penacook Reservation with elderly relatives, Chris learns about his culture and discovers his leadership potential.
Joseph Bruchac, *Skeleton Man*, 2001
  After her parents disappear and an unknown uncle shows up, Molly wonders why he looks like the Skeleton Man of her father's Mohawk Indian tales.
Margaret Peterson Haddix, *Memory*, 2003
  Kira is surprised to learn she's associated with the Crythians who believe memories shape a person.

Lois Lowry, *The Giver*, 1993
Set in a futuristic community that values sameness, Jonas is assigned his life-task but meeting the Giver helps him seek another world.

951

JEAN MARZOLLO
SHANE W. EVANS, Illustrator

Shanna's Teacher Show

(New York: Jump at the Sun/Hyperion, 2002)

Subject(s): Teachers; Education; Brothers and Sisters
Age range(s): Preschool-Grade 1
Major character(s): Shanna, Sister, Child
Time period(s): 2000s (2002)
Locale(s): United States

Summary: Shanna pretends to be a teacher and offers clues to her profession. Books, numbers, the alphabet and crayons are all a part of what makes her the teacher. In the end, however, Shanna's mother comes in to get her and her brother ready for school where they will work with a real teacher. (24 pages)

Where it's reviewed:
Horn Book Guide, Spring 2003, page 15
Kirkus Reviews, June 1, 2002, page 807
Publishers Weekly, June 17, 2002, page 67

Other books by the same author:
Shanna's Ballerina Show, 2003
I See a Star, 2002
Shanna's Doctor Show, 2001

Other books you might like:
Dolores Johnson, *My Mom Is My Show-and-Tell*, 1999
When David brings his mom, a teacher, to show-and-tell he is worried about what his classmates will think.
Daniel Liebman, *I Want to Be a Teacher*, 2001
This book, illustrated with photographs, looks at what teachers do all day.
Mercer Mayer, *When I Grow Up*, 1991
Little Critter thinks about all the different careers she could have when she grows up.

952

SIMON MASON
HELEN STEPHENS, Illustrator

The Quigleys

(Oxford, NY: David Fickling Books, 2002)

Subject(s): Family; Humor; Brothers and Sisters
Age range(s): Grades 2-4
Major character(s): Dad, Father, Spouse; Mum, Mother, Spouse; Lucy Quigley, Daughter, Sister; Will Quigley, Brother, Son
Time period(s): 2000s
Locale(s): England

Summary: Four stories introduce each of four members of the Quigley family. When Lucy is asked to be a bridesmaid in a wedding she rejects all the styles of bridesmaid dresses and insists on being a bumblebee. Mum and Dad try bribes and threats to convince Lucy that she must wear the dress of the bride's choice in the wedding. Lucy secretly makes the bee costume that she wants and dresses in it for the wedding to her parents' chagrin. Dad, while caring for the neighbor's children, loses one of them, but only temporarily. Will and Lucy try to make up for their bad behavior on Mum's birthday by planning a surprise for her. Finally, Will tries to decide how to convince Mum and Dad to give him a special Christmas gift. This is the first children's book for the British novelist. (148 pages)

Where it's reviewed:
Booklist, July 2002, page 1848
Bulletin of the Center for Children's Books, September 2002, page 26
Horn Book, July 2002, page 468
Publishers Weekly, April 15, 2002, page 64
School Library Journal, June 2002, page 104

Awards the book has won:
Center for Children's Books Best Books, 2002

Other books by the same author:
The Quigleys: Not for Sale, 2004
The Quigleys at Large, 2003

Other books you might like:
Allan Ahlberg, *The Better Brown Stories*, 1996
The Brown family visits the writer of their stories to suggest he liven their boring lives with some better adventures.
Roald Dahl, *The Wonderful Story of Henry Sugar and Six More*, 1977
Seven fantastic short stories include Henry Sugar's story as well as one about a boy who talks to animals and another about a hitchhiker.
Roddy Doyle, *The Giggler Treatment*, 2000
Gigglers, small, unseen beings, punish adults they consider mean to children with a pile of dog poop left in the path of the unsuspecting victim.

953

SIMON MASON
HELEN STEPHENS, Illustrator

The Quigleys at Large

(New York: David Fickling/Random House, 2003)

Subject(s): Family; Animals/Birds; Camps and Camping
Age range(s): Grades 2-4
Major character(s): Lucy Quigley, Sister, Child; Will Quigley, Brother, Child; Dad, Father, Spouse; Mum, Mother, Spouse
Time period(s): 2000s (2003)
Locale(s): England

Summary: The Quigley family manages to turn every day events into hilarious adventures in this sequel to *The Quigleys*. In the first chapter, Dad loses Will's beloved parakeet while cleaning out the cage and goes to great lengths to recapture the pet. Then, Will forgets his jacket at school and when he goes back to retrieve it, he's locked inside the building. In the third chapter, Mum has her wisdom teeth out and her family enforces rest even though she feels fine and wants to participate in the local fete. Finally, on a family vacation to France, Lucy finds friends for the rest of her family, but has a hard time overcoming the language barrier to make her own. (148 pages)

Where it's reviewed:
Booklist, December 1, 2003, page 667
Bulletin of the Center for Children's Books, December 2003, page 159
Horn Book, September/October 2003, page 615
Publishers Weekly, December 1, 2003, page 58
School Library Journal, December 2003, page 120

Other books by the same author:
The Quigleys: Not for Sale, 2004
The Quigleys, 2002

Other books you might like:
Beverly Cleary, *Ramona Forever*, 1984
   Life is changing in the Quimby family, with Dad worrying about finding a new job and Ramona worrying about having to move.
Johanna Hurwitz, *Aldo Peanut Butter*, 1990
   When their parents have to go out of town for two weeks, Aldo and his older sisters are in charge, with hilarious results.
Ann M. Martin, *The Doll People*, 2000
   Annabelle Doll is bored with her life, the same for 100 years, but when the Funcraft family moves in, life becomes exciting.

954

CAROL MATAS

Sparks Fly Upward

(New York: Clarion Books, 2002)

Subject(s): Jews; Prejudice; Family Life
Age range(s): Grades 4-8
Major character(s): Rebecca Bernstein, 12-Year-Old; Sophie Kostaniuk, 12-Year-Old
Time period(s): 1910s
Locale(s): Oxbow, Saskatchewan, Canada; Winnipeg, Manitoba, Canada

Summary: Having fled from Russia because of their Jewish religion, Rebecca and her extended family live in very close quarters on a farm in Saskatchewan, with Rebecca sharing her bedroom with four aunts and her sister. Though crowded, the family is happy until their farmhouse burns to the ground and they must move to Winnipeg. Her father can't find work and their new quarters are too small to hold everyone, so Rebecca is fostered to a Ukrainian family. Ukrainians have been natural enemies of the Jews in her native land so Rebecca isn't sure what to expect when she moves in with this Christian family. The Kostaniuk's daughter Sophie becomes her good friend, but the anti-Semitic father and brother make her life miserable until her grandfather brings her home and forbids her to see the Kostaniuks. Luckily Rebecca's rabbi offers her words of comfort and common sense as she learns to be her own person in this work based on the life of the author's family. (180 pages)

Where it's reviewed:
Booklist, April 1, 2002, page 1328
Bulletin of the Center for Children's Books, July 2002, page 409
Library Talk, September 2002, page 44
School Library Journal, March 2002, page 234
School Library Journal, March 2002, page 234

Other books by the same author:
War Within: A Novel of the Civil War, 2001
In My Enemy's House, 1999
Greater than Angels, 1998
The Garden, 1997

Other books you might like:
Johanna Hurwitz, *Faraway Summer*, 1998
   Used to New York City living, Dossie maintains her kosher diet while enjoying two weeks in Vermont on a Fresh Air Fund vacation.
Kathryn Lasky, *Dreams in the Golden Country: The Diary of Zipporah Feldman, a Jewish Immigrant Girl*, 1998
   Immigrating from Russia, Zipporah's family settles on New York's Lower East Side where Zipporah's dream is to become an actress.
Robert Lehrman, *The Store That Mama Built*, 1992
   After moving to America, the Fried family adapts to the death of their father and their mother becoming a storeowner.

955

PETRA MATHERS, Author/Illustrator

Herbie's Secret Santa

(New York: Anne Schwartz/Atheneum, 2002)

Subject(s): Christmas; Stealing; Guilt
Age range(s): Grades K-2
Major character(s): Herbie, Duck, Friend; Lottie, Friend, Chicken
Time period(s): 2000s (2002)
Locale(s): Oysterville

Summary: Herbie is so full of the Christmas Spirit that when he and Lottie go into town to get a Christmas tree, Herbie can't resist eating a Christmas cookie from the bakery. Herbie feels guilty about eating a cookie without paying for it and his actions weigh on him heavily. Finally, after he confesses his deeds to Lottie and the bakery owners, he feels better and he finds forgiveness. (32 pages)

Where it's reviewed:
Booklist, September 1, 2002, page 140
Publishers Weekly, September 23, 2002, page 34
School Library Journal, October 2002, page 60

Other books by the same author:
Dodo Gets Married, 2001
A Cake for Herbie, 2000 (Horn Book Fanfare)
Lottie's New Friend, 1999
Sophie and Lou, 1991

Other books you might like:
Stan Berenstain, *The Berenstain Bears and the Truth*, 1983
   When Brother and Sister Bear accidentally break their

mother's lamp they have a hard time admitting the truth. Jan Berenstain, co-author.

Sally Grindley, *Will You Forgive Me?*, 2001
  After losing her best friend's tickling stick Figgy Twosocks is scared to tell him the truth.

Holly Keller, *That's Mine, Horace*, 2000
  When Horace takes another child's truck on the playground, he feels so guilty about it that he makes himself sick and can't go to school.

956

ANDREW MATTHEWS

The Flip Side

(New York: Delacorte, 2003)

Subject(s): Gender Roles; Identity; School Life
Age range(s): Grades 8-10
Major character(s): Robert "Rob" Hunt, 15-Year-Old, 10th Grader; Milena Griffin, 10th Grader; Kevin Robert "Kev" Davies, 15-Year-Old, Homosexual
Time period(s): 2000s
Locale(s): England

Summary: Studying *As You Like It* in English class, Rob's selected by his teacher to play the part of Rosalind, just as was done in Shakespeare's time with men playing the female parts. The love of his life, Milena, is assigned the male role of Orlando, which enables the two to act opposite one another. Rob's surprised to discover than when he dresses as Rosalind, he feels very comfortable, even somewhat more confident, than when he's just plain Rob. Both Milena and Rob explore their gender identity and, after attending a cross-dressing party, realize they're pretty happy with who they already are, though very supportive of their friend Kev who reveals he's gay, in this British import. (147 pages)

Where it's reviewed:
Bulletin of the Center for Children's Books, October 2003, page 70
Publishers Weekly, August 4, 2003, page 81
School Library Journal, October 2003, page 172

Other books by the same author:
Stiks and Stoans, 1999

Other books you might like:
Francesca Lia Block, *Weetzie Bat*, 1989
  Offbeat Weetzie and Dirk each find their true love, though not with one another, in this witty, bizarre, modern-day fairy tale.
Nancy Garden, *Annie on My Mind*, 1982
  Lisa and Annie fall in love but are afraid to tell anyone of their relationship.
Carol Plum-Ucci, *What Happened to Lani Garver*, 2002
  Claire doesn't care that her new friend Lani isn't concerned about his gender identity; she just knows that he helps her forget her problems.

957

CLAUDIA MAUNER, Author/Illustrator
ELISA SMALLEY, Co-Author

Zoe Sophia's Scrapbook: An Adventure in Venice

(San Francisco: Chronicle Books, 2003)

Subject(s): Travel; Aunts and Uncles; Animals/Dogs
Age range(s): Grades 1-4
Major character(s): Zoe Sophia, 9-Year-Old, Niece; Mickey, Dog; Dorothy Pomander, Aunt (great-aunt), Writer
Time period(s): 2000s (2003)
Locale(s): New York, New York; Venice, Italy

Summary: Native New Yorker Zoe Sophia travels with Mickey to Venice to see her great-aunt, Dorothy. During her visit, Zoe Sophia takes advantage of all that Venice has to offer. With her great-aunt, she tours museums, rides gondolas, looks at Carnevale masks and eats lots of yummy Italian food. When Mickey goes missing, a helpful gondolier returns him. Finally, after an enjoyable week, Zoe Sophia feels a bit disappointed to have to return to New York so soon. (34 pages)

Where it's reviewed:
Booklist, May 15, 2003, page 1661
Bulletin of the Center for Children's Books, September 2003, page 24
Publishers Weekly, May 19, 2003, page 72
School Library Journal, August 2003, page 139

Other books you might like:
Christina Bjork, *Vendela in Venice*, 1999
  Vendela tours Venice with her father.
Candace Fleming, *Gabriella's Song*, 1997
  Inspired by the sounds of Venice, Gabriella hums a tune wherever she walks; a composer uses Gabriella's song to write a symphony.
Joan MacPhail Knight, *Charlotte in Paris*, 2003
  Charlotte and her artist parents travel to Paris.
Kay Thompson, *Eloise in Moscow*, 1959
  Eloise visits Moscow with Nanny.

958

SUE MAYFIELD

Drowning Anna

(New York: Hyperion Books, 2002)

Subject(s): Bullies; Self-Mutilation; School Life
Age range(s): Grades 7-10
Major character(s): Anna Goldsmith, 15-Year-Old; Hayley Parkin, Bully; Melanie Blackwood, 15-Year-Old
Time period(s): 2000s
Locale(s): Yorkshire, England

Summary: An attractive pianist who also plays sports, Anna leaves London with her family and moves to a small town in Yorkshire. Popular Hayley immediately latches on to Anna and quickly establishes herself as "best friend." Melanie watches all this from the sidelines as she'd like to be Anna's friend, too, but accepts that Hayley wouldn't permit it. After Hayley's initial friendship with Anna, she slowly but surely turns on her, and begins to bully and tease her. This harass-ment continues for two years as Anna loses her self-confi-dence and turns into a self-mutilator until she finally over-doses on vodka and pills, but not without first writing a letter to Hayley, which Melanie delivers. Though Anna suffers a heart attack while in the hospital, by book's end she's improv-ing mentally and physically while Melanie waits to be the friend she wanted to be two years earlier. (316 pages)

Where it's reviewed:
Bulletin of the Center for Children's Books, December 2002, page 166
Library Media Connection, February 2003, page 81
Publishers Weekly, October 7, 2002, page 73
School Library Journal, December 2002, page 145
Voice of Youth Advocates, February 2003, page 478

Other books by the same author:
I Carried You on Eagle's Wings, 1991

Other books you might like:
Alex Flinn, *Breaking Point*, 2002
    Paul's delight at Charlie's friendship leads to vandalism, cheating and finally leaving a bomb in a classroom.
Gail Giles, *Shattering Glass*, 2002
    Manipulative Rob charms teachers, acquires a harem of 'wannabe' girlfriends and decides to transform nerd Simon Glass, which leads to disaster.
Patrick Redmond, *Something Dangerous*, 1999
    Feeling out of place, Jonathan is thrilled when befriended by Richard, unaware that he's being used to unleash evil against other students.

959

MARGARET MAYO
ALEX AYLIFFE, Illustrator

Emergency!

(Minneapolis: Carolrhoda Books, Inc., 2002)

Subject(s): Community Helpers; Rescue Work; Stories in Rhyme
Age range(s): Preschool-Kindergarten
Time period(s): 2000s
Locale(s): England

Summary: Originally published in England in 2002, this book describes 11 situations which could be found in any country. Rhyming verse and the repetitive refrain, ''Help is coming. It's on the way!'' reassure young readers that the appropriate emergency vehicle will arrive to take care of hazardous situa-tions on land, water, road, train track, or mountain trail. When the emergency passes then each rescue vehicle returns to port, hanger, or garage to await another 911 call. (32 pages)

Where it's reviewed:
Booklist, August 2002, page 1974
Horn Book Guide, Spring 2003, page 16
Kirkus Reviews, August 15, 2002, page 1229
Publishers Weekly, August 5, 2002, page 71
School Library Journal, October 2002, page 120

Awards the book has won:
IRA Children's Choices, 2003

Other books by the same author:
Dig Dig Digging, 2002
Wiggle Waggle Fun: Stories and Rhymes for the Very Young, 2002
Magical Tales from Many Lands, 1993

Other books you might like:
Gail Gibbons, *Emergency!*, 1994
    Simple pictures support the descriptions of various emer-gency personnel and their vehicles.
Arlene Bourgeois Molzahn, *Police and Emergency Vehicles*, 2002
    A nonfiction title uses photographs to expand the informa-tion about the history of emergency vehicles and their current use.
Peter Sis, *Trucks Trucks Trucks*, 1999
    In an award-winning title, as Matt cleans up, he imagines the real work done by each of his toy vehicles.

960

MARGARET MCALLISTER

Ghost at the Window

(New York: Dutton, 2002)

Subject(s): Ghosts; Fear; Time Travel
Age range(s): Grades 5-8
Major character(s): Ewan Dart, Student; Mick McPherson, Student; Elspeth Cooper, Child, Spirit; Lizzie Dart, Mother (of Ewan), Interior Decorator; Simon Dart, Father (of Ewan), Artist; Alex Sutherland, Cousin (of Elspeth's)
Time period(s): 2000s
Locale(s): Loch Treen, Scotland

Summary: Ewan's parents buy and move into Ninian House, a thousand-year-old stone dwelling that has been inhabited by warriors, saints, hermits and regular people like the Dart family. Ninian House, however, is not a regular house; when Ewan walks into a room, he never knows if he'll be in a Victorian living room, a stable, a great banquet hall or some-one else's bedroom. Luckily these emergences into the vari-ous time periods of the house last only a few seconds before the house reverts to Ewan's time and any people that Ewan spots don't see him. Well, that is until he meets Elspeth, a girl who died from diphtheria in 1937, who cannot only see him but also wants his help to leave the house. Though Ewan wants to assist her, the evil force in his closet prevents Elspeth from passing to the other side. Ewan and his friend Mick consult with several older village inhabitants and track down Elspeth's cousin, Alex Sutherland. Alex arrives at Ninian House with the answers to setting Elspeth free in a tale of fear and forgiveness, love and hate. (119 pages)

Where it's reviewed:
Booklist, May 1, 2002, page 1429
Bulletin of the Center for Children's Books, June 2002, page 373
Kirkus Reviews, July 1, 2002, page 958
School Library Journal, August 2002, page 194
Voice of Youth Advocates, August 2002, page 204

Other books by the same author:
The Octave of Angels, 2002

Hold My Hand and Run, 2000

Other books you might like:

Avi, *Something Upstairs: A Tale of Ghosts*, 1988
Kenny's new bedroom is haunted by the ghost of a slave who was murdered more than 100 years earlier.

Judd Holt, *A Promise to Catie*, 1992
Billy falls in love with a young girl he sees around his Texas farmhouse, not realizing she's a ghost.

Diana Wynne Jones, *Howl's Moving Castle*, 1986
Cursed by a witch and turned into an old woman, Sophie enters the moving castle of the Wizard Howl, but is never sure where its exit doors will lead.

Betty Ren Wright, *A Ghost in the Family*, 1998
Chad accompanies a friend on a two-week stay at her aunt's boarding house and discovers a ghost haunting his room.

961

BRUCE MCBAY, Co-Author
JAMES HENEGHAN, Co-Author

Waiting for Sarah

(Custer, WA: Orca Publishers, 2003)

Subject(s): Supernatural; Ghosts; Physically Handicapped
Age range(s): Grades 7-10
Major character(s): Mike Scott, 12th Grader; Sarah Francis, 8th Grader; Mr. Dorfman, Teacher (social studies)
Time period(s): 2000s
Locale(s): Vancouver, British Columbia, Canada

Summary: In his sophomore year, Mike loses his parents, his sister and his legs to a drunk driver. The next year is spent living with his Aunt Norma and receiving rehabilitation, though his desire to do more than that is gone. Aunt Norma finally convinces him to return to Carlton High School though he wants nothing to do with former friends. Leaping at the chance to get out of Mr. Dorfman's deadly dull history class, Mike agrees to write the 50-year history of Carlton HS. Enjoying his daily quiet time in the library, Mike resents the appearance of eighth grader Sarah Francis as she shows up to help him, but gradually he looks forward to seeing and talking to her. Imagine his surprise when he tries to find more information about her and is told she doesn't exist, and hasn't since 1982 when she was murdered. Sarah slowly reveals the identity of her killer and Mike makes sure that justice is done. (170 pages)

Where it's reviewed:
Booklist, September 15, 2003, page 231
Kliatt, March 2004, page 27
Library Media Connection, November 2003, page 57
Publishers Weekly, September 29, 2003, page 66
School Library Journal, October 2003, page 171

Other books you might like:

Catherine Dexter, *I Dream of Murder*, 1997
For years Jere has been haunted by a dream of a man killing a young girl, then one day she meets the man from her dreams.

Judd Holt, *A Promise to Catie*, 1992
Billy falls in love with a young girl he sees around his Texas farmhouse, not realizing she's a ghost.

Patricia Windsor, *The Christmas Killer*, 1991
Victims of a serial killer reappear in Rose Potter's dreams, asking for help and giving clues to locate their bodies.

962

LAURA WILLIAMS MCCAFFREY

Alia Waking

(New York: Clarion Books, 2003)

Subject(s): Friendship; Coming-of-Age
Age range(s): Grades 6-9
Major character(s): Alia, Teenager; Kay, Teenager; Mari, Cousin, Healer
Time period(s): Indeterminate
Locale(s): Trantia, Fictional Country

Summary: Alia and Kay have always been best friends, and like most young Trantian girls their age, they are obsessed with being chosen by the Keenteens to join the band of warrior women. When Kay and Alia capture two young enemies trespassing near the village, they find they're responsible for the welfare of these captive men. Kay is without mercy, but Alia finds herself unable to deny the sympathy she feels for the captive Beechans. As she becomes more familiar with them a rift between the two friends grows. Alia's cousin, Mari, who's also a healer, helps Alia explore the unfamiliar emotions and sensations she is experiencing. And it is Mari who recognizes that Alia has a special gift granted by the magical Raven Wood. (214 pages)

Where it's reviewed:
Booklist, March 1, 2003, page 1199
Horn Book Guide, Fall 2003, page 371
Kirkus Reviews, March 1, 2003, page 392
Publishers Weekly, January 20, 2003, page 83
School Library Journal, June 2003, page 146

Other books you might like:

Shannon Hale, *The Goose Girl*, 2003
A betrayed princess finds friends among her enemies, and a special connection with nature.

Tamora Pierce, *Briar's Book*, 1999
Briar is uncertain about his ability as a healer; is it a lesser magical ability?

Jane Yolen, *Sister Light, Sister Dark*, 1988
The sisters who aid these warrior women can only appear in the dark.

963

MEGHAN MCCARTHY, Author/Illustrator

George Upside Down

(New York: Viking/Penguin Putnam, 2003)

Subject(s): Individuality; Behavior; Imagination
Age range(s): Grades K-2
Major character(s): George, Child, Student—Elementary School

Time period(s): 2000s (2003)
Locale(s): United States

Summary: George loves to be upside down. He watches TV upside down, reads books upside down, and even paints pictures upside down. But sometimes being upside down gets him in trouble: when he is riding in the car, sitting at the dinner table, and especially when he's at school. George's teacher sends him to the tutor, who sends him to the nurse, who sends him to the principal, who finds a solution. The principal invites other adults to his office and they all spend their time in the office upside down, causing George to find something new to do in this first book by the author. (40 pages)

Where it's reviewed:
Booklist, February 15, 2003, page 1075
Bulletin of the Center for Children's Books, April 2003, page 321
Publishers Weekly, December 9, 2002, page 82
School Library Journal, March 2003, page 198

Other books by the same author:
Adventures of Patty and the Big Red Bus, 2005
Show Dog, 2004

Other books you might like:
Ross Collins, *Alvie Eats Soup*, 2002
   Alvie eats soup and only soup, until a visit from his Grandmother leads him to discover a new favorite food—peas.
Philip Heckman, *Waking Upside Down*, 1996
   Morton tours his house at night by walking on the ceiling.
David Shannon, *A Bad Case of Stripes*, 1998
   Camilla Cream loves to please; her inability to express her own opinion leads to some interesting problems.

964

PETER MCCARTY, Author/Illustrator

Hondo & Fabian

(New York: Henry Holt and Company, 2002)

Subject(s): Animals/Dogs; Animals/Cats; Pets
Age range(s): Preschool-Grade 1
Major character(s): Hondo, Dog; Fabian, Cat
Time period(s): Indeterminate
Locale(s): United States

Summary: While Hondo goes to the beach Fabian stays home. Hondo frolics in the waves and Fabian tries to avoid the family's toddler. Fabian is happy to see Hondo return from his adventure so the pets will finally be able to satisfy their hunger. Then, feeling full, they settle once again into their favorite places and bid each other good night. (32 pages)

Where it's reviewed:
Booklist, February 15, 2002, page 1021
Horn Book Guide, Fall 2002, page 308
New York Times Book Review, December 8, 2002, page 74
Publishers Weekly, November 4, 2002, page 39
School Library Journal, June 2002, page 100

Awards the book has won:
Caldecott Honor Book, 2003

New York Times Best Illustrated Children's Books, 2002

Other books by the same author:
Baby Steps, 2000
Little Bunny on the Move, 1999 (New York Times Best Illustrated Children's Book)

Other books you might like:
Ruth Brown, *Copycat*, 1994
   Buddy, the family cat, tries to imitate the behaviors of the other family pets and hurts himself when he gnaws the dog's bone.
Paul Fehlner, *Dog and Cat*, 1990
   An elderly dog and an overweight cat have learned to coexist peacefully.
Donald Hall, *I Am the Dog, I Am the Cat*, 1994
   Poetically, a dog and a cat describe their separate interests.
Lydia Monks, *The Cat Barked?*, 1999
   A cat considers the far better life that a dog appears to have but decides she still prefers being a feline; the dog however might switch places.

965

GERALDINE MCCAUGHREAN

The Kite Rider

(New York: HarperCollins, 2002)

Subject(s): Circus; Family; Adventure and Adventurers
Age range(s): Grades 5-9
Major character(s): Gou Haoyou, 12-Year-Old, Entertainer (circus kite rider); Mipeng, Cousin (of Haoyou); Kublai Khan, Historical Figure, Warrior; Miao Jie, Wealthy
Time period(s): 13th century (1280s)
Locale(s): China

Summary: In the last 13th century in China, it was the custom for sailors to test the potential outcome of their voyage by having a man ride a kite up into the sky; a successful kite flight indicated a successful voyage. Young Haoyou witnesses the death of his father when he flies high into the sky, an unexpected fatality caused by an order from the ship's first mate, a man who is in love with Haoyou's mother. To prevent his mother from marrying his father's murderer, Haoyou joins a circus where he performs as a kite rider, one whom the audience believes is soaring into the sky to commune with the spirits. Accompanied by his cousin Mipeng, who keeps an eye on Haoyou and tries to keep him out of trouble, the two travel with the circus master Miao Jie to the court of Kublai Khan. The death-defying flights of Haoyou earn him a living and eventually reconnect him with his mother in this fast-paced adventure. (272 pages)

Where it's reviewed:
Bulletin of the Center for Children's Books, July 2002, page 409
Horn Book, July 2002, page 465
Publishers Weekly, July 8, 2002, page 50
School Library Journal, June 2002, page 142
Voice of Youth Advocates, June 2002, page 120

Awards the book has won:
ALA Best Books for Young Adults, 2003
School Library Journal Best Books, 2002

Other books by the same author:
Stop the Train!, 2003
The Stones Are Hatching, 2000
The Pirate's Son, 1998

Other books you might like:
Malcolm Bosse, *The Examination*, 1994
  Brothers Hong, the practical one, and Chen, the scholar, travel to Beijing for Chan to take an examination that will determine their futures.
Linda Sue Park, *The Kite Fighters*, 2000
  Pooling their talents in making and flying kites helps Young-sup and Kee-sup learn to be brothers who are also friends.
Barbara Ann Porte, *Hearsay: Strange Tales from the Middle Kingdom*, 1998
  A collection of fifteen stories based on legend, Chinese lore and the author's own imagination.

966

GERALDINE MCCAUGHREAN
STEPHEN LAMBERT, Illustrator

My Grandmother's Clock

(New York: Clarion, 2002)

Subject(s): Grandparents; Family; Childhood
Age range(s): Grades K-3
Major character(s): Unnamed Character, Child, Relative (granddaughter); Grandmother, Grandmother
Time period(s): 2000s (2002)
Locale(s): England

Summary: A young girl asks Grandmother why she doesn't fix her broken grandfather clock. In reply, Grandmother explains all the ways she can tell time. She can count seconds by listening to her heartbeat. She can tell the time of day by the sun's shadows and the days of the week by local goings-on (baking is on Mondays). Grandmother lengthens the periods of time to those beyond the limitations of a clock until she describes lifetimes (measured in birthdays and friends) and the eternity of the stars. (32 pages)

Where it's reviewed:
Booklist, September 15, 2002, page 241
Horn Book, January/February 2003, page 59
Publishers Weekly, July 15, 2002, page 73
School Library Journal, September 2002, page 200

Other books by the same author:
Stop the Train!, 2003
The Kite Rider, 2002
Blue Moon Mountain, 1994

Other books you might like:
Eric Carle, *Today Is Monday*, 1993
  Hungry children can tell what day of the week it is by what's for dinner.
Kes Gray, *Cluck O'Clock*, 2004
  A mother hen gives an hour-by-hour account of the goings-on on the farm.
Penny Pollock, *When the Moon Is Full: A Lunar Year*, 2001
  This collection of poems looks at 12 months of full moons.

967

GERALDINE MCCAUGHREAN
PAUL HOWARD, Illustrator

One Bright Penny

(New York: Viking, 2002)

Subject(s): Money; Problem Solving; Parent and Child
Age range(s): Grades K-3
Major character(s): Pa, Father, Farmer; Bob, Brother, Son; Bill, Brother, Son; Penny, Sister, Daughter
Time period(s): Indeterminate Past
Locale(s): United States

Summary: As Pa distributes the weekly penny to each of his three children he expounds on the days when a penny actually had value. Bill offers Pa the challenge of filling the barn for one penny. Pa accepts and agrees to give the children the farm if any one of them succeeds in filling the barn for a penny. Bill tries first by cleaning up turkey feathers from a nearby farm and dumping them into the barn. The place looks full until Pa sneezes and Bill loses the bet. Bob uses his penny to buy string and wax so he can fill the barn with light but a draft blows out a candle and Pa wins again. Penny tries a different approach and even Pa has to admit that every corner of the barn is filled with the sound of music. (32 pages)

Where it's reviewed:
Booklist, November 1, 2002, page 509
Bulletin of the Center for Children's Books, February 2003, page 244
Publishers Weekly, October 7, 2002, page 72
School Library Journal, February 2003, page 115

Other books by the same author:
Epic of Gilgamesh, 2003
My Grandmother's Clock, 2002
Six Storey House, 2002

Other books you might like:
Phillis Gershator, *Only One Cowry: A Dahomean Tale*, 2000
  A successful series of trades begins with only one cowry and concludes with enough goods to win the hand of a village chief's daughter.
Eric A. Kimmell, *Bernal & Florinda: A Spanish Tale*, 1994
  Poor but clever Bernal uses a grasshopper-infested field and skillful trading to acquire wealth in hopes of marrying Florinda.
Margaret Willey, *Clever Beatrice*, 2001
  Poor but clever Beatrice solves her family's money problems by challenging and outsmarting Mister Giant.

968

GERALDINE MCCAUGHREAN

Stop the Train!

(New York: HarperCollins, 2003)

Subject(s): Frontier and Pioneer Life; Railroads
Age range(s): Grades 5-8
Major character(s): Cissy Sissney, 12-Year-Old; Clifford T. Rimm, Businessman (railroad owner)
Time period(s): 1890s (1893)

Locale(s): Florence, Oklahoma

Summary: The Oklahoma Land Rush is on and Cissy and her parents feel fortunate to have made a claim in the flat prairie town of Florence. Unfortunately, Clifford T. Rimm wants to acquire all the claims in Florence to erect a company town for his railroad the Red Rock Runner. When the homesteaders refuse to relinquish their claims for his $50 offer, he threatens to have his railroad pass the town by. Without a stop on the train line, these pioneers know their town will dry up financially and their claims will be worthless. It's time for battle as the townspeople come up with one plan after another to "stop the train!" (287 pages)

Where it's reviewed:
Booklist, August 2003, page 1981
Horn Book, July 2003, page 462
Publishers Weekly, May 26, 2003, page 71
School Library Journal, August 2003, page 163
Voice of Youth Advocates, October 2003, page 315

Awards the book has won:
School Library Journal Best Books, 2003

Other books by the same author:
The Kite Rider, 2002
The Stones Are Hatching, 1999
The Pirate's Son, 1998

Other books you might like:
Debbie Dadey, *Cherokee Sister*, 2000
    While visiting her friend Leaf, Allie is swept up in the Cherokee removal and marches to Oklahoma; luckily Allie's father finds and rescues both girls.
Jennifer L. Holm, *Boston Jane: An Adventure*, 2001
    Neither Miss Heppelwhite's training, nor William's nice looks, matters to Jane when she compares either to her new life in the Washington Territory.
Kathleen Karr, *Oh, Those Harper Girls! Or Young and Dangerous*, 1992
    Lily and her five sisters try to earn money to help their father save his ranch, but unfortunately all their schemes are illegal.
Gary Paulsen, *Call Me Francis Tucket*, 1995
    Captured by Pawnee Indians and then rescued by Mr. Grimes, Francis continues west across the prairie looking for his parents' wagon train.

969

GEORGE MCCLEMENTS, Author/Illustrator

Jake Gander, Storyville Detective: The Case of the Greedy Granny
(New York: Hyperion Books for Children, 2002)

Subject(s): Mystery and Detective Stories; Fairy Tales; Animals/Wolves
Age range(s): Grades K-3
Major character(s): Jake Gander, Detective; Red R. Hood, Child
Time period(s): 2000s (2002)
Locale(s): Storyville

Summary: When private detective Jake Gander fields a call from one Red R. Hood, he takes on the case of the impostor granny. Jake looks through all the clues, including pointy ears, bulging eyes, and sharp teeth, and comes to the conclusion that the granny is really a wolf. While the wolf is arrested (on one count of impersonating a granny and four of shedding), Red learns that her real granny is off on vacation as the author's first book concludes. (32 pages)

Where it's reviewed:
Horn Book Guide, June 10, 2002, page 59
Kirkus Reviews, May 15, 2002, page 736
New York Times Book Review, October 20, 2002, page 23
Publishers Weekly, June 10, 2002, page 59
School Library Journal, September 2002, page 201

Other books you might like:
Margie Palatini, *The Web Files*, 2001
    In this parody of *Dragnet*, two duck detectives try to solve several robberies on the farm.
Jon Scieszka, *The True Story of the 3 Little Pigs!*, 1989
    In this retelling of the classic tale, the wolf tells his side of the story.
David Wisniewski, *Tough Cookie*, 1999
    PI Tough Cookie has to find his ex-partner, Chips.

970

BARBARA MCCLINTOCK, Author/Illustrator

Dahlia
(New York: Frances Foster/Farrar Straus Giroux, 2002)

Subject(s): Dolls and Dollhouses; Toys; Playing
Age range(s): Grades K-3
Major character(s): Charlotte, Child, Niece; Bruno, Toy, Bear; Dahlia, Doll, Toy; Edme, Aunt, Aged Person
Time period(s): Indeterminate Past
Locale(s): New England

Summary: Tomboyish Charlotte and her pal Bruno are not interested in the fragile, lace-trimmed, beribboned doll that arrives in a package from Aunt Edme. Charlotte has no use for dolls but she gives this one a lecture on her ideas of proper doll behavior and carries her out with Bruno for an afternoon of mud cakes, boat sailing, fishing, and planting stones in the flowerbed. Charlotte, Dahlia and Bruno even win a downhill wagon race over a bunch of doubting boys. Alas, Dahlia climbs too high in a tree and falls to the ground but Charlotte tends her lovingly so by the time Aunt Edme arrives for tea Dahlia looks as well loved as Aunt Edme hoped she would. (32 pages)

Where it's reviewed:
Booklist, September 1, 2002, page 121
Horn Book, September 2002, page 555
Publishers Weekly, June 24, 2002, page 55
Riverbank Review, Fall 2002, page 30
School Library Journal, November 2002, page 130

Awards the book has won:
Horn Book Fanfare, 2002
School Library Journal Best Books, 2002

Other books by the same author:
Molly and the Magic Wishbone, 2001

The Fantastic Drawings of Danielle, 1996 (Smithsonian's Notable Books for Children)

The Heartaches of a French Cat, 1989 (New York Times Best Illustrated Book)

Other books you might like:

Patricia Kirkpatrick, *Plowie: A Story from the Prairie*, 1994
    The porcelain doll found by a little girl in the newly turned earth behind her father's plow is passed along for succeeding generations to enjoy.

Kathryn Lasky, *Sophie and Rose*, 1998
    The very old doll that becomes Sophie's constant companion and playmate once belonged to her mother and grandmother.

Shulamith Levey Oppenheim, *I Love You, Bunny Rabbit*, 1995
    Micah's well-worn Bunny Rabbit is soiled with applesauce, chocolate milk and puddle mud, making it irreplaceable.

971

GLENN MCCOY, Author/Illustrator

Penny Lee and Her TV

(New York: Hyperion Books for Children, 2002)

Subject(s): Television; Animals/Dogs; Humor
Age range(s): Grades K-3
Major character(s): Penny Lee, Child; Mr. Barkley, Dog
Time period(s): 2000s
Locale(s): United States

Summary: Penny Lee loves TV. She loves it so much that all she does all day, every day is watch TV despite everything her pet, Mr. Barkley, does to get her attention. One day when her TV breaks, Mr. Barkley suggests taking it to a TV repair shop. To do so Penny Lee must go outside where the sight of the bright colors and children at play amazes her. She and Mr. Barkley have so much fun playing outside, that by the time they return to the repair shop, it's closed. Once Penny Lee has gone to bed, Mr. Barkley "fixes" the TV by putting the batteries back in the remote. (32 pages)

Where it's reviewed:

Bulletin of the Center for Children's Books, June 2002, page 374
Horn Book Guide, Fall 2002, page 337
Kirkus Reviews, March 15, 2002, page 419
Publishers Weekly, February 25, 2002, page 66
School Library Journal, June 2002, page 100

Awards the book has won:

Center for Children's Books Best Books, 2002

Other books you might like:

Stan Berenstain, *The Berenstain Bears and Too Much TV*, 1984
    When Mama Bear decides to ban TV for one week the Berenstains find other ways to have fun. Jan Berenstain, co-author.

Matt Novak, *Mouse TV*, 1994
    The Mouse family loves watching TV, but when their TV breaks one day, they discover other fun activities that they can do together.

Patricia Polacco, *Aunt Chip and the Great Triple Creek Dam Affair*, 1996
    The town of Triple Creek watches so much TV they've forgotten that books are for reading.

972

CAROLYN MCCULLOUGH

Falling through Darkness

(Brookfield, CT: Roaring Brook, 2003)

Subject(s): Grief; Death; Guilt
Age range(s): Grades 9-12
Major character(s): Ginny, 17-Year-Old; Aidan, Boyfriend (of Ginny); Caleb Lamb, Artisan (toy maker)
Time period(s): 2000s
Locale(s): United States

Summary: Aidan loves the night, or at least he seems to, for much of their dating revolves around out-of-the-ordinary late night activities, like an impromptu poetry slam at a Laundromat, visiting a tattoo parlor or just going for long drives in the night air. Ginny reflects back on her adventures with this devil-may-care boyfriend, before his abusive home life took a toll on his life. Killed in an automobile accident, Aidan almost took Ginny with him, but now she's left chain-smoking and unsure what to do. Caleb, a new tenant for her father's little apartment, occupies some of Ginny's interest and she feels comfortable talking with him, but undoes their friendship by letting romance filter into her thoughts. By book's end Ginny has accepted Aidan's death and just might be ready to start communicating with her worried father in this author's first novel. (151 pages)

Where it's reviewed:

Booklist, November 15, 2003, page 607
Horn Book, November 2003, page 750
Library Media Connection, February 2004, page 72
Publishers Weekly, October 13, 2003, page 80
School Library Journal, November 2003, page 142

Other books you might like:

Eve Bunting, *Jumping the Nail*, 1991
    Dru's friend Elisa jumps off a 90-foot cliff with her boyfriend; they survive the jump but peer pressure drives her to try it again.

Patrick Jones, *Things Change*, 2004
    Johanna's first love is Paul and, though she knows he's not the right boy for her, she's so happy to feel part of her school's social scene.

Richard Peck, *Remembering the Good Times*, 1995
    Two friends try to understand why their best friend committed suicide.

973

EMILY ARNOLD MCCULLY, Author/Illustrator

The Battle for St. Michaels

(New York: HarperCollins Publishers, 2002)

Series: I Can Read Book
Subject(s): Historical; War of 1812; Heroes and Heroines

Age range(s): Grades 2-4
Major character(s): Caroline Banning, 9-Year-Old, Runner; Mrs. Banning, Mother; Robert, Friend
Time period(s): 1800s (1813)
Locale(s): St. Michaels, Maryland

Summary: Caroline races home with news that the British have burned Havre de Grace. Citizens of St. Michaels fear that their town will be the next to be attacked and make preparations by burying valuables and sending women and children to safety. Because Mrs. Banning provides housing for soldiers she is allowed to stay and insists on keeping Caroline with her. The local military leaders are grateful to have Caroline, for she's well known to be the fastest runner in town and they use her and her friend Robert as messengers. The town devises a plan that, with the help of a foggy night, fools the British enough to save the town and its occupants. A concluding author's note gives historical background for the story. (64 pages)

Where it's reviewed:
Booklist, September 15, 2002, page 235
Horn Book Guide, Spring 2003, page 70
Kirkus Reviews, August 1, 2002, page 1137
School Library Journal, September 2002, page 201

Other books by the same author:
Grandmas Trick-or-Treat, 2001 (I Can Read Book)
The Orphan Singer, 2001 (Notable Social Studies Books for Young People)
Grandmas at Bat, 1993 (I Can Read Book)
Mirette on the High Wire, 1992 (Caldecott Medal)

Other books you might like:
Carl R. Green, The War of 1812, 2002
    A nonfiction title for youth includes information about major battles of the war with internet links to additional sources.
John A. Monahan, Abigail's Drum, 1995
    When British forces take their father hostage, Rebecca and Abigail play their fife and drum in the lighthouse; the amplified sound convinces the British to retreat.
Brenda Seabrooke, The Boy Who Saved the Town, 1990
    In this interpretation of events in St. Michaels during the War of 1812 a young boy is the town's hero.

974

LURLENE MCDANIEL

Telling Christina Goodbye

(New York: Bantam, 2002)

Subject(s): Grief; Automobile Accidents; Dating (Social Customs)
Age range(s): Grades 7-10
Major character(s): Tucker Hanson, 12th Grader; Christina Eckloe, 12th Grader, Accident Victim; Trisha Thompson, 12th Grader; Cody McGuire, 12th Grader
Time period(s): 2000s
Locale(s): Mooresville, Indiana

Summary: Trisha can't believe that her best friend Christina enables her boyfriend Tucker to control her so much. On the one hand he tells Christina he loves her, while on the other he

doesn't trust her at all; if a boy at school talks to her, Tucker blows it all out of proportion. Trisha spends most of her time drying Christina's tears and being grateful that her boyfriend Cody is so much nicer. In an effort to prevent Christina from attending the University of Vermont on scholarship, Tucker decides to ask her to marry him after they graduate from high school. Before he has a chance to give her an engagement ring, the two couples are in a terrible automobile accident. Tucker is driving and escapes without a scratch, while Trisha is injured, Cody left in a coma and Christina killed. In addition to their grief over losing Christina, the survivors must rethink all their plans for life after high school in another gripping story from a popular author. (224 pages)

Where it's reviewed:
Book Report, September 2002, page 55
Booklist, March 15, 2002, page 1251
School Library Journal, July 2002, page 122

Other books by the same author:
How Do I Love Thee?, 2001
To Live Again, 2001
Angel of Hope, 2000
Angel of Mercy, 1999
The Girl Death Left Behind, 1999

Other books you might like:
Julie Reece Deaver, Say Goodnight, Gracie, 1988
    Morgan's life comes to an abrupt halt when her dear friend Jimmy is killed in an automobile accident.
Wendy Orr, Peeling the Onion, 1997
    An automobile accident leaves former karate champion Anna Duncan unsure of who she is or what's happening in her life.
Todd Strasser, The Accident, 1988
    When Matt's best friend is killed in a car accident, everyone blames it on alcoholic Chris Walsh, though there's really a police cover-up involved.

975

JANET MCDONALD

Chill Wind

(New York: Farrar Straus Giroux, 2003)

Subject(s): African Americans; Teen Parents; Work
Age range(s): Grades 8-12
Major character(s): Aisha Ingram, 19-Year-Old, Single Mother; Kevin Vinker, Boyfriend (of Aisha)
Time period(s): 2000s
Locale(s): New York, New York

Summary: With two children to raise, and her lifetime welfare benefits coming to an end, teen mother Aisha is desperate to find a source of income. Thinking the workfare jobs are too demeaning, she tries to talk her children's father into marriage, then pleads insanity, but none of these ploys is successful. Even when plus size modeling seems a possibility, Aisha's attitude leads to an argument with the president of the company, which nixes her job. Resigned to a workfare job, she agrees to subway patrol, but "Lady Luck" intervenes and a new career awaits her in this continuation of Spellbound. (134 pages)

Where it's reviewed:
Booklist, September 1, 2002, page 121
Horn Book, September 2002, page 576
Publishers Weekly, November 11, 2002, page 65
School Library Journal, November 2002, page 173
Voice of Youth Advocates, October 2002, page 282

Other books by the same author:
Brother Hood, 2004
Twists and Turns, 2003
Spellbound, 2001
Project Girl, 1999

Other books you might like:
Sharon G. Flake, *Money Hungry*, 2001
    A few weeks on the streets for Raspberry and her mother before moving into the projects leads Raspberry to be obsessive about money.
Nikki Grimes, *Jazmin's Notebook*, 1998
    Though Jazmin has a tough life, reading her journal makes one realize she'll succeed and never again be homeless.
Connie Porter, *Imani All Mine*, 1999
    Single mother Tasha juggles schoolwork and parenting classes to care for her beloved son, Imani. Adult title.

976

MEGAN MCDONALD
PETER H. REYNOLDS, Illustrator

Judy Moody Saves the World!

(Cambridge, MA: Candlewick Press, 2002)

Subject(s): Environmental Problems; Brothers and Sisters; Humor
Age range(s): Grades 2-4
Major character(s): Judy Moody, 3rd Grader, Sister (older); Stink Moody, 7-Year-Old, Brother; Mr. Todd, Teacher
Time period(s): 2000s (2002)
Locale(s): Virginia

Summary: Inspired by Mr. Todd's science lessons about the rain forest and endangered species Judy Moody initiates several projects in order to save the world. She enters a contest to design a band-aid in hopes that her message to heal the world will be seen on scraped knees everywhere, she liberates Stink's pet frog, and she collects all the household items made from products that contribute to the decline of the rain forests. Judy meets with little success or support and Stink's design wins the band-aid contest. After admitting to collecting all the pencils in the classroom in order to save the cedar trees in the rain forest, Judy inspires her classmates to join her in a rain forest fund-raising activity that is also a recycling project. The proceeds will purchase trees in the rain forests of Costa Rica. Finally, Judy has a winning idea and feels satisfied that she's done her part to save the world. (145 pages)

Where it's reviewed:
Booklist, September 1, 2002, page 125
Five Owls, 2003, page 44
Horn Book Guide, Spring 2003, page 70
Kirkus Reviews, July 1, 2002, page 958
Publishers Weekly, July 8, 2002, page 51

Awards the book has won:
IRA Children's Choices, 2003

Other books by the same author:
Judy Moody, M.D., 2004
Judy Moody Predicts the Future, 2003
Judy Moody Gets Famous!, 2001 (ALA Notable Children's Books)
Judy Moody, 2000 (Publishers Weekly Best Children's Books)

Other books you might like:
Beverly Cleary, *Ramona Quimby, Age 8*, 1981
    One of several titles about energetic Ramona and life in the Quimby household is a Newbery Honor Book.
Jane Cutler, *Leap, Frog*, 2002
    Third grader Edward plans to enter the First Annual Mark Twain Memorial Jumping Frog Contest, but first he needs to find a frog.
Diane DeGroat, *Annie Pitts, Burger Kid*, 2000
    Annie Pitts, aspiring actress, feels confident that she'll win the Burger Barn poster contest and fulfill her desire for fame.

977

FLORA MCDONNELL, Author/Illustrator

Giddy-up! Let's Ride!

(Cambridge, MA: Candlewick Press, 2002)

Subject(s): Horsemanship; Animals/Horses; Transportation
Age range(s): Preschool-Kindergarten
Time period(s): 2000s (2002)
Locale(s): Earth

Summary: Costumed children saddle up to ride a variety of steeds. From a knight who rides with a "clankety-clank," to a raja riding an elephant with a "rumpetta-trump," to a fairy riding a unicorn with a "whish swish," each pair makes a unique sound. Finally all the children are shown riding together on their toy steeds. (32 pages)

Where it's reviewed:
Booklist, May 1, 2002, page 1534
Bulletin of the Center for Children's Books, October 2002, page 69
Publishers Weekly, May 6, 2002, page 56
School Library Journal, July 2002, page 95

Awards the book has won:
Center for Children's Books Best Books, 2002

Other books by the same author:
Sparky, 2004
Splash!, 1999
I Love Animals, 1994

Other books you might like:
Deborah Chandra, *A Is for Amos*, 1999
    On her rocking horse Amos, a young girl, goes for an imaginary ride across a farm.
Jessie Haas, *Appaloosa Zebra*, 2002
    Although she dreams of having a horse farm, for now a little girl uses her imagination to conjure up all types of horses.

Susan Jeffers, *My Pony*, 2003
A little girl draws a longed-for horse that comes alive and takes her for a ride.

978

ALISON MCGHEE
HARRY BLISS, Illustrator

Countdown to Kindergarten
(San Diego: Silver Whistle/Harcourt, Inc., 2002)

Subject(s): Fear; Schools; Growing Up
Age range(s): Preschool-Kindergarten
Major character(s): Unnamed Character, Kindergartner, Daughter
Time period(s): 2000s (2002)
Locale(s): United States

Summary: With only 10 days until the opening day of kindergarten a young girl awakens with worries about the three rules a first grader has told her are strictly enforced. The future student thinks she can adjust to leaving her stuffed animals and her pet cat at home, but there is no way to hide the fact that she cannot tie her shoes. With fears of embarrassing moments in her mind as she counts down the days, the girl tries to master the fine art of tying shoelaces, but to no avail. She feels relieved on the first day to learn that many students had help from their parents in order to make the perfect bows she sees on their shoes and, when the teacher announces the day's activities, she realizes the first grader's report may not have been completely accurate. This is the first children's book for novelist McGhee. (32 pages)

Where it's reviewed:
Booklist, August 2002, page 1974
Bulletin of the Center for Children's Books, October 2002, page 69
Kirkus Reviews, July 1, 2002, page 959
Publishers Weekly, July 8, 2002, page 48
School Library Journal, September 2002, page 201

Awards the book has won:
Center for Children's Books Best Books, 2002

Other books you might like:
Nancy Carlson, *Look Out Kindergarten, Here I Come!*, 1999
Henry's enthusiasm for school wanes as he approaches the building on the first day.
Nancy Poydar, *First Day, Hooray!*, 1999
As she prepares for school to begin, Ivy worries, but the first day turns out to be just terrific!
Vera Rosenberry, *Vera's First Day of School*, 1999
Vera's eager for the first day of school until she sees the crowded schoolyard; then she has second thoughts about entering the building.

979

ALICE MCGILL
SHANE W. EVANS, Illustrator

Here We Go Round
(Boston: Houghton Mifflin Company, 2002)

Subject(s): African Americans; Babies; Grandparents
Age range(s): Grades 2-4
Major character(s): Roberta Louise Robinson, 7-Year-Old, Daughter; Gramma Louise, Grandmother; Grandpa Dave, Grandfather, Farmer
Time period(s): 1940s (1946)
Locale(s): Washington, District of Columbia; Scotland Neck, North Carolina

Summary: While her mother is bedridden for the final weeks of a difficult pregnancy, Roberta is sent to live with Gramma and Grandpa. Being isolated from her parents seems to contribute to her feeling that the new baby will be loved while she'll be pushed out of the family. During the hot summer month she stays with her grandparents Roberta helps on the farm and plays with a nearby family that has many children, including a four-month-old baby. Finally she's able to share some of her feelings about the new baby with Gramma and Grandpa and Grandpa helps her understand that families are circles that go round and create new circles as they enlarge and mature. By the time a letter comes announcing the birth of her brother, Roberta feels more confident about her new role as big sister. (115 pages)

Where it's reviewed:
Booklist, February 15, 2002, page 1032
Bulletin of the Center for Children's Books, July 2002, page 410
The New Advocate, Spring 2003, page 221
Publishers Weekly, January 7, 2002, page 65
School Library Journal, April 2002, page 117

Other books by the same author:
Sure as Sunrise: Stories of Bruh Rabbit and His Walkin 'n Talkin Friends, 2004
In the Hollow of Your Hand: Slave Lullabies, 1999
Molly Bannaky, 1999 (ALA Notable Children's Books)

Other books you might like:
Ann Cameron, *Gloria's Way*, 2000
Gloria learns important lessons about promises, friendship and the importance of being herself in a book about the everyday events of childhood.
Dorothy Carter, *Wilhe'mina Miles After the Stork Night*, 1999
Wilhe'mina's pregnant mother sends her seven-year-old daughter out into the night to fetch the midwife, Mis' Hattie.
Martha Freeman, *The Trouble with Babies*, 2002
After meeting neighbor Annie and the new baby at her house Holly doesn't feel particularly excited to learn of her mother's pregnancy.

HILARY MCKAY

Saffy's Angel

(New York: Simon & Schuster/Margaret K. McElderry Books, 2002)

Subject(s): Family Life; Artists and Art; Adoption
Age range(s): Grades 5-8
Major character(s): Cadmium Gold "Caddy" Casson, 18-Year-Old; Saffron "Saffy" Casson, 13-Year-Old, Adoptee; Indigo Charles Casson, 11-Year-Old; Rose Casson, Child; Eve Casson, Artist, Mother; Sarah Warbeck, Handicapped, 13-Year-Old; Bill Casson, Artist, Father
Time period(s): 2000s
Locale(s): Siena, Italy; England; Wales

Summary: Cadmium, Saffron, Indigo and Rose are children of artists who have been named after colors, though Saffy discovers she's adopted when she realizes her color isn't part of the color wheel. Orphaned when Eve Casson's sister died in an automobile accident in Italy, Saffy's really the Casson's cousin, though Caddy, Indigo and Rose consider her their sister. When their grandfather dies, he leaves his worldly goods to the four children: his cottage in Wales to Caddy, his aging Bentley to Indigo, his remaining pounds to Rose and a stone angel to Saffy. Though the cottage, car and money are easily found, no one knows the location of the stone angel. Saffy talks her way into a trip to Italy with her wheel-chair bound friend Sarah's family to see if the angel's there. Meanwhile, Caddy finally gets her driver's license and takes off for Wales, with Rose in the back seat writing signs for the impatient drivers lining up behind them and Indigo navigating the hapless Caddy up the unfamiliar roads to their grandfather's cottage. Though they find bits and pieces of Saffy's angel, Caddy puts everything to rights in this touching story of a charmingly eccentric family. (152 pages)

Where it's reviewed:
Booklist, May 15, 2002, page 1594
Bulletin of the Center for Children's Books, May 2002, page 332
Horn Book, July 2002, page 466
Publishers Weekly, March 18, 2002, page 104
School Library Journal, May 2002, page 156

Awards the book has won:
School Library Journal Best Books, 2002
Booklist Editors' Choice/Books for Youth, 2002

Other books by the same author:
Dolphin Luck, 1999
The Exiles in Love, 1998
The Amber Cat, 1997
The Exiles at Home, 1994

Other books you might like:
Helen Cresswell, *The Bagthorpe Series*, 1978-
  The peculiar members of the Bagthorpe family confront one crisis after another.
Sid Hite, *Those Darn Dithers*, 1996
  Stilt walking, a dancing pig and an uncle who floats out to sea are just a few of the eccentric characters and adventures shared by the Dithers' family.

Dorothy Gladys Smith, *I Capture the Castle*, 1948
  Reading Cassandra's journal reveals the life of her eccentrically genteel but impoverished family who live in a crumbling castle.

HILARY MCKAY
AMANDA HARVEY, Illustrator

Was That Christmas?

(New York: Margaret K. McElderry Books, 2002)

Subject(s): Christmas; Animals/Cats; Santa Claus
Age range(s): Grades K-2
Major character(s): Bella, 3-Year-Old, Daughter; Black Jack, Cat
Time period(s): 2000s (2001)
Locale(s): England

Summary: In preschool Bella's understanding of Christmas begins to reach a new level. Assured by her parents that Santa will bring a gift to Black Jack too, she's distraught when the Santa Claus that comes to preschool has no present for her pet. She's a bit relieved to learn that Santa's visit to school was not THE Christmas. As she participates in the family's preparations for Christmas Bella, learns that baking, decorating the tree, singing carols and wrapping gifts are only the beginning of Christmas. Finally, it's Christmas Eve. Bella hangs her stocking and one for Black Jack; then she sleeps because her wait for Christmas is almost over. Originally published in London in 2001. (32 pages)

Where it's reviewed:
Booklist, September 1, 2002, page 138
Bulletin of the Center for Children's Books, November 2002, page 116
Horn Book, November 2002, page 736
Publishers Weekly, September 23, 2002, page 32
School Library Journal, October 2002, page 60

Awards the book has won:
Center for Children's Books Best Books, 2002

Other books by the same author:
Pirates Ahoy!, 2000
Where's Bear?, 1998

Other books you might like:
Vivian French, *A Christmas Star Called Hannah*, 1997
  Hannah has an important role in her preschool's Christmas play.
Marianna, *Miss Flora McFlimsey's Christmas Eve*, 1949
  With help from Timothy Mouse, an angel, and her own belief, Miss Flora has a joyful Christmas that proves wishes do come true.
James Stevenson, *Christmas at Mud Flat*, 2000
  All the animal residents of Mud Flat busily prepare for their communal holiday celebration.

982

COLLEEN O'SHAUGHNESSY MCKENNA
STEPHANIE ROTH, Illustrator

Doggone . . . Third Grade!

(New York: Holiday House, 2002)

Subject(s): Friendship; Animals/Dogs; Talent
Age range(s): Grades 2-4
Major character(s): Gordie Barr, 3rd Grader; Scratch, Dog; Lamont, 3rd Grader; Red, 3rd Grader
Time period(s): 2000s (2002)
Locale(s): United States

Summary: Gordie's love of third grade begins fading when the teacher announces a Talent Show. Gordie is embarrassed to admit he has no talents so he enters Scratch, a dog who knows no tricks. Although Lamont initially offers to help Gordie, the moment the new student, Red, enters the room Lamont ignores Gordie and gives all his attention to Red. Gordie feels torn between sadness and anger about losing his friend. By the day of the show Scratch has mastered enough tricks to save Gordie from embarrassment and Lamont is finding a way to include Gordie while developing a new friendship with Red too. (82 pages)

Where it's reviewed:
Booklist, July 2002, page 1848
Horn Book Guide, Fall 2002, page 361
Publishers Weekly, June 10, 2002
School Library Journal, July 2002, page 95

Other books by the same author:
Third Grade Ghouls!, 2001
Third Grade Stinks!, 2001
Good Grief . . . Third Grade, 1993

Other books you might like:
Betsy Duffey, *Spotlight on Cody*, 1998
    Nothing goes right for Cody as he tries to find some "talent" to perform for the school's talent show.
Michelle Edwards, *The Talent Show*, 2002
    Stage fright threatens to silence Howie's performance of a song at the Jackson Magnet School Talent Show.
Megan McDonald, *Judy Moody Gets Famous!*, 2001
    Judy's quest for fame runs into one stumbling block after another as her plans go awry until, anonymously, she achieves her goal.

983

NANCY MCKENZIE

The Grail Prince

(New York: Del Rey, 2003)

Subject(s): Arthurian Legends; Adventure and Adventurers; Coming-of-Age
Age range(s): Grades 9-Adult
Major character(s): Galahad, Royalty (prince), Son; Lancelot, Royalty (king); Percival, Royalty (prince), Brother; Dandran, Royalty (princess), Sister
Time period(s): Indeterminate Past
Locale(s): England

Summary: McKenzie recasts the story of the quest for the Holy Grail as a torturous coming-of-age story. Young Galahad's famous father, Lancelot, is often absent and Galahad worships his mother, a bitter woman disappointed in life who hopes her son will avenge her regrets. With this background, it is no surprise that when his father arrives to take him to the court at Camelot, Galahad is sullen and difficult. Having internalized his mother's lessons that she is a wronged woman, and that Lancelot and Guinevere are sinners, he must be pure at all costs. Galahad is a difficult young man, talented in battle, but unbending and without mercy. He loves Arthur but cannot bear the company of those Arthur loves best. Percival of Gwynedd becomes his friend, and as Arthur's kingdom begins to dissolve after his death, Galahad takes the wounded Percival home. Once there, he meets Percival's twin sister, Dandrane. He falls in love, but cannot admit it even to himself. Galahad spends years avoiding this realization, hunting sporadically for the grail, unable to find himself or the holy object he is seeking. (510 pages)

Where it's reviewed:
Booklist, December 1, 2002, page 646
Chronicle, April 2003, page 41
Library Journal, November 15, 2002, page 102
Publishers Weekly, December 23, 2002, page 50
Voice of Youth Advocates, June 2003, page 151

Other books by the same author:
Prince of Dreams: A Tale of Tristan and Essylte, 2003
Queen of Camelot, 2002

Other books you might like:
J. Robert King, *Lancelot du Lethe*, 2001
    Galahad is not the only member of his family to wander in a kind of madness; this is the story of his father's lost years.
Steve Lawhead, *Grail*, 1997
    This is the final book of Lawhead's *Pendragon* cycle; in it Galahad narrates the story of the theft of the Grail and the ensuing search.
Rosalind Miles, *The Child of the Holy Grail: The Third of the Guenevere Novels*, 2001
    Galahad challenges Mordred for a seat at the Round Table.

984

PATRICIA MCKILLIP

In the Forests of Serre

(New York: Berkley/Ace, 2003)

Subject(s): Fantasy; Love
Age range(s): Grades 9-Adult
Major character(s): Ronan, Royalty (prince); Sidonis, Royalty (princess); Brume, Witch
Time period(s): Indeterminate
Locale(s): Serre, Fictional Country

Summary: Prince Ronan is a broken man. His beloved wife and child have died and his only wish is to follow them. He pursues his royal duties in hopes that they will afford him the opportunity to die. His carelessness on the way home proves more nearly fatal than any battle, for it takes him through the magical forest of Serre. Ronan's horse accidentally crushes the white hen that is the special pet of the witch Brume and, when cursed by her, he's certain the worst has already happened. Ronan discovers almost immediately that he is wrong, for on arriving home, he finds that his father has arranged a marriage for him that will take place as soon as Princess Sidonis arrives. Before she appears at the palace, however, Ronan is enchanted by a glimpse of a magical bird flitting through the forest of Serre and is enticed into its enchanted depths. Now Sidonis, discovering herself without a prince, must brave Brume if she is to regain him. (304 pages)

Where it's reviewed:
Booklist, May 15, 2003
Chronicle, May 2003, page 38
Library Journal, May 15, 2003, page 131
Publishers Weekly, May 12, 2003, page 49

Other books by the same author:
Alphabet of Thorn, 2004
Song for the Basilisk, 1998
Winter Rose, 1996

Other books you might like:
Shannon Hale, *The Goose Girl*, 2003
    Ani is betrayed, but her knowledge of the secrets of the woods will help her regain her prince.
Mercedes Lackey, *The Firebird*, 1996
    The firebird has been luring unwary princes into the forest for a long time, but in this version, a younger son is determined to get the best of her.
Meredith Ann Pierce, *Treasure at the Heart of the Tanglewood*, 2001
    Hannah has always known her forest had a treasure hidden within it, but she will have a long quest before she learns its true nature.

985

ROBIN MCKINLEY, Co-Author
PETER DICKINSON , Co-Author

Water: Tales of Elemental Spirits
(New York: Putnam, 2002)

Subject(s): Fantasy; Short Stories
Age range(s): Grades 6-10

Summary: The mysterious power of water unites the six stories in this collection. The authors alternate stories, so each tale is followed by a contrasting one. McKinley's stories generally end on a hopeful note, while Dickinson's tend to involve some of the miseries of ordinary life, though some element of fantasy is present in each. Mer-people, the mythic Kraken of the deep, and water horses all make an appearance, as well as more unusual characters such as the woman who escapes her unhappy life by traveling through a pool, and the rivermen who struggle to defeat the sea serpent that will cost them their livelihoods. There is something here for every fantasy lover. (272 pages)

Where it's reviewed:
Booklist, April 15, 2002, page 1416
Bulletin of the Center for Children's Books, July 2002, page 410
Horn Book, July 2002, page 466

School Library Journal, June 2002, page 142
Voice of Youth Advocates, June 2002, page 130

Other books by the same author:
Sunshine, 2003

Other books you might like:
Mercedes Lackey, *Flights of Fantasy*, 1999
    Birds are the subject of these stories, which range from science fiction to fantasy.
Ursula K. Le Guin, *Tales from Earthsea*, 2001
    Return to Earthsea in this collection of stories that tell of times both before and after the wizard Ged.
William Sleator, *Oddballs*, 1993
    Author Sleator claims these stories about his childhood are all true, but they seem suspiciously like his novels.

986

PATRICIA C. MCKISSACK
SUSAN KEETER, Illustrator

Tippy Lemmey
(New York: Aladdin, 2003)

Series: Ready-for-Chapters
Subject(s): Animals/Dogs; Fear; Neighbors and Neighborhoods
Age range(s): Grades 2-4
Major character(s): Tippy Lemmey, Dog (chow); Leandra Martin, 7-Year-Old, Friend; Jeannie, Friend, 8-Year-Old; Paul, Friend, 8-Year-Old
Time period(s): 1950s (1951)
Locale(s): Templeton, Tennessee

Summary: The arrival of Tippy Lemmey strikes fear into Leandra and her friends each time they pedal past the house on their bicycles. In order to go to school or to some of their favorite play spots in town, Paul, Jeannie and Leandra have to think of alternate routes. Finally, Leandra tells her parents about the problem and they speak to the owners. After that Tippy is tied in the yard. As Leandra and her friends come to know Tippy better they feel less fear and come to his rescue when he's dognapped. Tippy returns the favor by getting help for them when a sudden storm traps the children in a creek bed rapidly filling with water. (60 pages)

Where it's reviewed:
Booklist, January 2003, page 892
Bulletin of the Center for Children's Books, March 2003, page 281
Horn Book, March 2003, page 213
School Library Journal, January 2003, page 106

Awards the book has won:
Center for Children's Books Best Books, 2003

Other books by the same author:
Goin' Someplace Special, 2001 (Coretta Scott King Illustrator Award)
A Picture of Freedom: The Diary of Clotee, a Slave Girl, 1997 (Dear America Series)
Mirandy and Brother Wind, 1988 (Caldecott Honor Book)

Other books you might like:

Betsy Duffey, *Throw-Away Pets*, 1993

Evie and Megan have 24 hours to find homes for abandoned pets at the animal shelter or the animals will be destroyed.

Karen Hesse, *Lester's Dog*, 1993

Lester's dog has a home and a reputation for meanness that suggests he is mistreated or neglected.

Bill Wallace, *A Dog Called Kitty*, 1980

Ricky overcomes his fear of dogs and the taunts of a bully to save a starving stray pup found in his barn.

987

CHESLEY MCLAREN, Author/Illustrator

Zat Cat! A Haute Couture Tail

(New York: Scholastic, 2002)

Subject(s): Animals/Cats; Fashion Design; Stories in Rhyme
Age range(s): Grades 1-4
Major character(s): Etoile, Cat; Monsieur Pierre, Designer
Time period(s): 2000s (2002)
Locale(s): Paris, France

Summary: A Parisian stray enjoys all that Paris has to offer from the gardens to the cafes to the Louvre. One day, while happening by a Parisian hotel, the cat notices a fashion show and decides to take a closer look. When a wayward sash tosses the cat in the air, he panics and shreds all of the clothes. Critics love the new "frayed" look and the fashion designer, Monsieur Pierre, adopts the cat and renames her Etoile (Star). This is the first book this illustrator has written. (40 pages)

Where it's reviewed:
Booklist, March 1, 2002, page 1142
Horn Book Guide, Fall 2002, page 338
Kirkus Reviews, February 1, 2002, page 184
Publishers Weekly, February 4, 2002, page 75
School Library Journal, April 2002, page 117

Other books you might like:

Leslie Baker, *Paris Cat*, 1999

Alice, the cat, gets a tour of Paris when she gets lost going to visit her aunt.

Ludwig Bemelmans, *Madeline*, 1939

Madeline lives in Paris with Miss Clavel and 12 other girls.

Maira Kalman, *Ooh-la-la (Max in Love)*, 1991

Max, the millionaire poet dog, falls in love while on a trip to Paris.

Kay Thompson, *Eloise in Paris*, 1957

Eloise turns Paris upside down during a visit.

988

SARAH MCMENEMY, Author/Illustrator

Waggle

(Cambridge, MA: Candlewick Press, 2003)

Subject(s): Animals/Dogs; Pets; Behavior
Age range(s): Grades K-2
Major character(s): Rosie, Child, Daughter; Dad, Father; Waggles, Dog

Time period(s): 2000s
Locale(s): England

Summary: In the author's first children's book Dad surprises Rosie with a little brown and white puppy. Happily Rosie follows the puppy as it plays with flip-flops, digs in the garden, and burrows into a wastepaper basket. She considers naming the puppy Digger or Basket or Flip-Flop but finally settles on Waggle because she and Dad notice that the puppy's tail has waggled nonstop since he arrived. (28 pages)

Where it's reviewed:
Booklist, May 15, 2003, page 1672
Publishers Weekly, April 21, 2003, page 60
School Library Journal, August 2003, page 138

Other books by the same author:
Jack's New Boat, 2004

Other books you might like:

Alyssa Satin Capucilli, *Biscuit*, 1996

New puppy Biscuit has difficulty sleeping until his owner brings him just one more thing.

Pippa Goodhart, *Pudgy: A Puppy to Love*, 2003

Lonely Lucy and sad Pudgy find each other and develop a friendship that will last forever and ever.

Bob Graham, *Let's Get a Pup! Said Kate*, 2001

Kate and her parents visit an animal shelter looking for a pup and also find an appealing older dog.

Martine Schaap, *Mop to the Rescue*, 1999

The puppy Justin and Julie receive as a birthday gift earns the name "Mop" after eagerly lapping up Julie's spilled milk.

989

KATE MCMULLAN

As Far as I Can See: Meg's Prairie Diary

(New York: Scholastic, Inc., 2002)

Series: My America. Book One
Subject(s): Historical; Diaries; Illness
Age range(s): Grades 3-4
Major character(s): Margaret Cora "Meg" Wells, 9-Year-Old, Sister (older); Preston "Pres" Wells, 7-Year-Old, Brother; Father, Father, Businessman
Time period(s): 1850s (1856)
Locale(s): St. Louis, Missouri; Kansas

Summary: When Meg's younger sister and mother are taken ill with cholera, Father arranges for a friend bound for the Kansas Territory to escort Meg and Pres to the prairie homestead of relatives. While Meg doesn't want to leave St. Louis and her family, Pres is eager for adventure. The long steamboat ride followed by four days in an oxcart is exciting to Pres, but a disaster for Meg's city wardrobe. Although the mail service has not yet brought Father's letter about their arrival, the children's aunt, uncle and cousins welcome them and make room in the tiny cabin for the visitors. (106 pages)

Where it's reviewed:
Booklist, October 1, 2002, page 326
Horn Book Guide, Spring 2003, page 70
Kirkus Reviews, July 1, 2002, page 959
School Library Journal, August 2002, page 161

Other books by the same author:
For This Land: Meg's Prairie Diary, 2003 (My America
   Book Two)
Have a Hot Time, Hades!, 2002 (Myth-O-Mania)
Wheel of Misfortune, 1999

Other books you might like:
Patricia Hermes, *Westward to Home*, 2001
   Joshua records the monotony, hardship, and danger of his
   family's cross-country trek by wagon train.
Jane Kurtz, *I'm Sorry, Almira Ann*, 1999
   The tedium of Sarah's Oregon Trail journey with her
   family tests her patience and threatens her friendship with
   Almira Anne.
Laura Ingalls Wilder, *Little House on the Prairie*, 1935
   Seeking a better life, the Wilder family settles on a prairie
   homestead.

990

KATE MCMULLAN

A Fine Start: Meg's Prairie Diary

()

Series: My America. Book Three
Subject(s): Rural Life; Schools; Diaries
Age range(s): Grades 3-5
Major character(s): Margaret Cora "Meg" Wells, 9-Year-
   Old, Daughter
Time period(s): 1850s (1856)
Locale(s): Lawrence, Kansas

Summary: Meg's family manages to make it to the Kansas
territory, but her father's injured arm will make it difficult for
him to farm their claim. Instead, the family moves into the
town of Lawrence to set up a general store. Meg is happy that
she will be able to attend the school that is opening in town.
Then a tornado rips through the prairie damaging Meg's
cousin's house and they come to town to live with Meg and
her family. (106 pages)

Where it's reviewed:
Horn Book Guide, Spring 2004, page 82
School Library Journal, January 2004, page 132

Other books by the same author:
For This Land: Meg's Prairie Diary, 2003 (My America
   Book Two)
As Far as I Can See: Meg's Prairie Diary, 2002 (My America
   Book One)
I Stink!, 2002 (ALA Notable Children's Books)

Other books you might like:
Carol Ryrie Brink, *Caddie Woodlawn*, 1935
   Eleven-year-old Caddie Woodlawn loves running wild
   with her brothers in the Wisconsin woods.
Andrea Warren, *Pioneer Girl: Growing Up on the Prairie*,
   2000
   Based on a true story, three-year-old Grace's family moves
   to the Nebraska Territory where growing up on the prairie
   is hard but rewarding.
Laura Ingalls Wilder, *Little House on the Prairie*, 1935
   The Ingalls family moves from Wisconsin to the new
   Kansas Territory where they set up house.

991

KATE MCMULLAN
DAVID LAFLEUR, Illustrator

Have a Hot Time, Hades!

(New York: Volo/Hyperion Books for Children, 2002)

Series: Myth-O-Mania. Book 1
Subject(s): Mythology; Sibling Rivalry; Legends
Age range(s): Grades 3-6
Major character(s): Hades, Deity; Zeus, Deity
Time period(s): Indeterminate Past
Locale(s): Greece

Summary: In a humorous take on Greek mythology Hades
decides to set the record straight about the rise of the Greek
gods and how they assumed their different roles. Youngest
child, Zeus, helps rescue the other gods from their father's
stomach after he swallows them in an attempt to retain power,
but Zeus isn't the hero he claims to be. Working together, the
gods manage to overthrow the Titans (their father and his
siblings), but they can't agree on who should rule. Zeus finally
wins by cheating at cards and the roles we know today
become established. (144 pages)

Where it's reviewed:
Booklist, November 1, 2002, page 497
Horn Book, December 2002, page 166
Kirkus Reviews, June 15, 2002, page 885
Publishers Weekly, July 29, 2002, page 72
School Library Journal, January 2003, page 140

Other books by the same author:
For This Land: Meg's Prairie Diary, 2003 (My America
   Book Two)
Phone Home, Persephone!, 2002 (Myth-O-Mania Book 2)
Say Cheese, Medusa!, 2002 (Myth-O-Mania Book 3)

Other books you might like:
Priscilla Galloway, *Daedalus and the Minotaur*, 1997
   In the addition to the Tales from Ancient Lands series,
   Galloway retells the story of Daedalus and his son Icarus
   who try to fly with wings of feathers and wax.
Clea Hantman, *Heaven Sent*, 2002
   As punishment for a prank played on their stepmother,
   Hera, Zeus sends three of his Muse daughters to a high
   school in Athens, Georgia.
Mary Pope Osborne, *The One-Eyed Giant*, 2002
   In this retelling of the Odyssey, the men begin their jour-
   ney home from the Trojan War and encounter Cyclops.

992

KATE MCMULLAN
JIM MCMULLAN, Illustrator

I Stink!

(New York: Joanna Cotler Books/HarperCollins Publishers, 2002)

Subject(s): Community Helpers; City and Town Life; Work
Age range(s): Grades K-2
Major character(s): Unnamed Character, Narrator (garbage
   truck)
Time period(s): 2000s (2002)

Locale(s): New York, New York

Summary: A city garbage truck proclaims its many attributes, including ten wide tires, lights and no air conditioning. With its crew aboard it boldly takes to the night streets sniffing out breakfast, squealing to the curb and loading up with bags of trash until the full hopper must be compacted in order to make room for more. The truck describes the "alphabet soup" it carries daily causing the incredible stink of which the truck is rightfully proud. When the truck is full it travels to the river, backs up to the sound of blasting beeps and dumps its contents onto a barge before returning to the garage to be hosed off and gassed up in preparation for a day of rest and the next night's run. (40 pages)

Where it's reviewed:
Bulletin of the Center for Children's Books, June 2002, page 374
Horn Book, May 2002, page 319
Publishers Weekly, February 18, 2002, page 95
Riverbank Review, Fall 2002, page 30
School Library Journal, May 2002, page 122

Awards the book has won:
Boston Globe-Horn Book Picture Book Honor Book, 2002
School Library Journal Best Books, 2002

Other books by the same author:
Papa's Song, 2000
Noel the First, 1996
Hey, Pipsqueak!, 1995

Other books you might like:
Jean Eick, *Garbage Trucks*, 1999
    A nonfiction title describes how garbage trucks work.
Daniel Kirk, *Trash Trucks!*, 1997
    In a rhyming story trash trucks travel the city streets doing their job.
Paul Showers, *Where Does the Garbage Go?*, 1994
    A revision of the 1974 nonfiction title promotes recycling and alternative solutions to trash disposal such as energy-producing incineration.
Andrea Zimmerman, *Trashy Town*, 1999
    Mr. Gilly drives his trash truck all over town, collecting the garbage from residents and businesses.

993

KATE MCMULLEN
JIM MCMULLEN, Illustrator

I'm Mighty!

(New York: Joanna Cotler Books/HarperCollins Publishers, 2003)

Subject(s): Ships; Work; Self-Confidence
Age range(s): Grades K-2
Major character(s): Unnamed Character, Object (tugboat)
Time period(s): 2000s
Locale(s): At Sea

Summary: A confident tugboat may be small but he's MIGHTY! Large ships do not intimidate him. He begins each day by checking his gear, pulling away from the tug dock and heading to the ship anchorage. Then he tugs his first assignment, a loaded oil tanker, to its proper dock and parks her. Next he pulls a six-decker container ship to the unloading

dock and last he maneuvers a large cruise ship to Pier 92. One more check of the gear situation and the mighty tired tugboat goes back to the tug dock to rest and prepare for another big day. (36 pages)

Where it's reviewed:
Booklist, November 1, 2003, page 504
Bulletin of the Center for Children's Books, December 2003, page 160
Horn Book, November 2003, page 731
Publishers Weekly, October 20, 2003, page 53
School Library Journal, November 2003, page 107

Other books by the same author:
Nubby Bear, 2003
Nubby Cat, 2003
I Stink!, 2002 (School Library Journal Best Books)
Papa's Song, 2000

Other books you might like:
Virginia Lee Burton, *Mike Mulligan and His Steam Shovel*, 1939
    Age does not prevent Mike Mulligan's steam shovel Mary Anne from doing the work that the newer power shovels cannot.
Joy Cowley, *The Rusty, Trusty Tractor*, 1999
    Granpappy's tractor may not look like much but for 50 years it's helped plow the fields, plant the crops and bring in the harvest.
Watty Piper, *The Little Engine That Could*, 1930
    The Little Engine proves that gumption is more important than size if there is a job to be done.

994

SEAN MCMULLEN

Voyage of the Shadowmoon

(New York: Tor, 2002)

Subject(s): Adventure and Adventurers; War; Vampires
Age range(s): Grades 9-Adult
Major character(s): Laron Alisialar, Vampire; Velander, Religious; Warsovran, Royalty (emperor)
Time period(s): Indeterminate
Locale(s): Verral, Planet—Imaginary

Summary: Emperor Warsovran discovers an ancient device known as Silverdeath and sets about testing it. As he is currently in the middle of conquering one of the planet's continents, the next city on his menu of conquest makes a spectacular test site. Silverdeath performs beyond expectation, essentially vaporizing in flame everything within its limited sphere of influence. Unfortunately, it is now out of control and will continue to strike in ever-doubling circles of fire, with constantly increasing frequency. On the ship *Shadowmoon*, a diverse group of religious men, warriors and spies, all opposed to Warsovran, watch and speculate as the circle of destruction grows closer. At the last possible moment, Velander, a member of the religious order of the Metrologans, realizes that the next strike is imminent and will encompass the harbor in which the *Shadowmoon* is docked. The *Shadowmoo* is more than it seems and is saved when it dives to the bottom of the harbor. The continent of Torea is annihilated, but Silverdeath is satiated and the danger is over until Warsovran chooses to use it again. Led by Laron, an ancient vampire trapped in the body of a boy, the *Shadowmoon* and its passengers and crew set off for distant Helion to recruit others to the cause of separating Warsoveran and Silverdeath, but this noble goal is endangered by Laron's need to feed. (496 pages)

Where it's reviewed:
Booklist, December 1, 2002, page 652
Kirkus Reviews, November 1, 2002, page 1578
Library Journal, December 2002, page 184
Publishers Weekly, November 18, 2002, page 46
Voice of Youth Advocates, June 2003, page 151

Other books by the same author:
Eyes of the Calculor, 2001
The Miocene Arrow, 2000
Soul in the Great Machine, 1999

Other books you might like:
Barbara Hambly, *Traveling with the Dead*, 1995
  Lydia Asher takes special precautions when she asks a vampire to help her find her missing husband.
Robin Hobb, *Ship of Magic*, 1998
  Like the *Shadowmoon*, the ships of Bingtown are more than they seem and the living figureheads give their captains a decisive edge.
Robert Silverberg, *Lord Prestimion*, 1999
  Prestimion finally becomes ruler of Majipoor and must immediately solve the crisis of murderous insanity that is spreading everywhere.

995

GRAHAM MCNAMEE

Acceleration

(New York: Wendy Lamb Books/Random House, 2003)

Subject(s): Mystery and Detective Stories; Serial Killers; Diaries
Age range(s): Grades 7-10
Major character(s): Duncan, 17-Year-Old
Time period(s): 2000s
Locale(s): Toronto, Ontario, Canada

Summary: Spending the summer months working underground in the subway system's lost and found office is not Duncan's idea of a fun job, but he finds ways to amuse himself when business is slow. Lost items are kept for three months and then sent to the YMCA for sale, but as Duncan discovers, some items have been kept for several years. At the moment, he's got his eye on a great leather jacket whose time is up at the end of the week, and he also finds a leather-bound journal. Reading the journal, he finds information and articles about drowning mice, dismemberment of pets, arson and then notes about three women the journal's owner is stalking and planning to kill. Duncan notifies the police, but they dismiss his concerns about the madman's intentions. Instead, Duncan decides to track down the killer himself, based on the notes he reads in the man's journal, but receives an earlier break when the man reclaims the journal. Following him, Duncan finds

himself in a cat-and-mouse game that becomes scarier and scarier. (210 pages)

Where it's reviewed:
Booklist, September 15, 2003, page 232
Bulletin of the Center for Children's Books, November 2003, page 116
Kliatt, January 2004, page 10
Publishers Weekly, November 10, 2003, page 63
School Library Journal, November 2003, page 142

Awards the book has won:
ALA Best Books for Young Adults, 2004
ALA Quick Picks for Reluctant Young Adult Readers, 2004

Other books by the same author:
Sparks, 2002
Nothing Wrong with a Three-Legged Dog, 2000
Hate You, 1999

Other books you might like:
Sharon E. Heisel, *Eyes of a Stranger*, 1996
  As Melissa investigates the empty, whirling carousel, she is caught by a serial killer who has eliminated four other young girls.
Marsha Qualey, *Close to a Killer*, 1999
  Barrie lives with his mother, recently released from prison and owner of a beauty salon called Killer Looks, and finds they're in the middle of murder.
Patricia Windsor, *The Christmas Killer*, 1991
  Victims of a serial killer reappear in Rose Potter's dreams, asking for help and giving clues to the location of their bodies.

996

LAURA MCNEAL, Co-Author
TOM MCNEAL, Co-Author

Zipped

(New York: Knopf/Random House, 2003)

Subject(s): Stepfamilies; Interpersonal Relations; Dating (Social Customs)
Age range(s): Grades 9-12
Major character(s): Mick Nichols, 15-Year-Old; Nora Mercer-Nichols, Stepmother, Teacher (art); Lisa Doyle, 15-Year-Old; Myra Vidal, Student—College
Time period(s): 2000s
Locale(s): United States

Summary: While searching the family computer for the file with his history paper, Mick stumbles across some of his stepmother Nora's e-mail and correctly deduces that she's having an affair. Stunned, Mick is furious with her, protective of his father and determined to identify her lover. At the same time, he tries to summon his courage to date Lisa, upon whom he has a crush, while he's also becoming friends with Myra, a beautiful college student. Mick's life becomes more complicated when he begins to date Lisa, watches Lisa's good friend date a chauvinist, and vandalizes the beloved sports car of Nora's paramour in this challenging, meaty novel. (283 pages)

Where it's reviewed:
Bulletin of the Center for Children's Books, March 2003, page 281
Kliatt, January 2003, page 10
Publishers Weekly, February 10, 2003, page 188
School Library Journal, February 2003, page 142
Voice of Youth Advocates, April 2003, page 54

Other books by the same author:
Crooked, 1999

Other books you might like:
Catherine Dexter, *Driving Lessons*, 2000
    Mattie resents being sent to stay with a family friend and decides to be a little bad, not realizing her mother needs quiet time to finish her dissertation.
Barbara Shoup, *Wish You Were Here*, 1994
    Jax tries to figure out who he is after his mother remarries, his father is critically injured, and his own inexperience with girls ruins some friendships.
Karen Romano Young, *Video*, 1999
    Once-popular Janine and new-kid Eric share a class and a bus stop, but it takes longer for them to share a friendship.

997

CLIFF MCNISH
GEOFF TAYLOR, Illustrator

The Doomspell
(New York: Phyllis Fogelman Books/Penguin Putnam, 2002)

Subject(s): Fantasy; Good and Evil
Age range(s): Grades 5-8
Major character(s): Rachel, Child; Eric, Child, Brother (of Rachel); Dragwena, Witch; Morpeth, Dwarf
Time period(s): 2000s
Locale(s): Ithrea, Fictional Country; England

Summary: Many years ago the evil witch Dragwena was exiled to the cold, snowy planet of Ithrea for trying to wrest authority from the wizards. Ever since she has been kidnapping Earth children, searching for one with magical power strong enough to help her return to Earth. Thinking she's found that person in Rachel, she kidnaps both Rachel and her brother. This time the witch may have kidnapped the wrong person, for Rachel soon learns to fly and shape shift, skills that may make her more powerful than Dragwena. Dragwena's assistant, the dwarf Morpeth, helps Rachel develop these magical skills as he hopes to be freed from Dragwena's spell in this author's first fantasy. (214 pages)

Where it's reviewed:
Book Report, September 2002, page 55
Booklist, April 15, 2002, page 1418
Bulletin of the Center for Children's Books, October 2002, page 70
Publishers Weekly, July 17, 2002, page 65
School Library Journal, June 2002, page 142

Other books you might like:
Debi Gliori, *Pure Dead Magic*, 2001
    Siblings Pandora and Titus evade assassins as they search for and try to rescue their kidnapped father.

Eva Ibbotson, *Island of the Aunts*, 2000
    When Aunts Etta, Coral and Myrtle need help caring for their creatures, they return to England and kidnap several children to be assistants.
Philip Pullman, *The Subtle Knife*, 1997
    A magical tool that can cut between universes draws an innocent into a battle between good and evil.

998

DAVID MCPHAIL, Author/Illustrator

Big Brown Bear's Up and Down Day
(San Diego: Harcourt, Inc., 2003)

Subject(s): Animals/Bears; Animals/Rats; Sharing
Age range(s): Grades K-2
Major character(s): Big Brown Bear, Bear; Rat, Rat
Time period(s): Indeterminate
Locale(s): Fictional Country

Summary: Big Brown Bear awakens one morning to see Rat carrying away one of his slippers. Rat wants the slipper for a bed, but Big Brown Bear has two feet and he wants two slippers to wear on them. Rat tries various schemes but Big Brown Bear is steadfast in his determination to keep both his slippers. He does befriend Rat by sharing his breakfast and, when he later finds an odd slipper in a box tucked away in his closet, he gives it to Rat along with a small windup car from the box. Problem solved and everyone's happy. (48 pages)

Where it's reviewed:
Booklist, November 15, 2003, page 602
Bulletin of the Center for Children's Books, October 2003, page 71
Publishers Weekly, August 11, 2003, page 278
School Library Journal, November 2003, page 107

Other books by the same author:
My Little Brother, 2004
Rick Is Sick, 2004
Henry Bear's Christmas, 2003

Other books you might like:
Diane Marcial Fuchs, *A Bear for All Seasons*, 1995
    For Bear, any time of year is great when it's shared with a friend.
Kathy Mallat, *Brave Bear*, 1999
    A young bear helps a little lost bird return to its home high in a tree.
Martin Waddell, *Can't You Sleep, Little Bear?*, 1988
    Big Bear comforts Little Bear when a fear of the dark keeps him from dozing off.

999

DAVID MCPHAIL, Author/Illustrator

Edward in the Jungle
(Boston: Little, Brown and Company, 2002)

Subject(s): Imagination; Books and Reading; Animals
Age range(s): Grades K-3
Major character(s): Edward, Child; Tarzan, Animal Lover, Rescuer

Time period(s): Indeterminate
Locale(s): Fictional Country

Summary: Stories about Tarzan are Edward's favorites. Using his toy jungle animals Edward reenacts the adventures as he reads. One afternoon Edward's imaginary play becomes so real he's almost devoured by a crocodile. Tarzan saves him and teaches Edward how to call the animals in a loud Tarzan yell. When the animals appear Tarzan introduces Edward. Soon, Edward discovers that poachers have captured the crocodile and he uses that newly learned yell to get help. In appreciation, the crocodile takes Edward back across the river so he can get home in time for dinner. (32 pages)

Where it's reviewed:
Booklist, April 1, 2002, page 1334
Bulletin of the Center for Children's Books, April 2002, page 289
Publishers Weekly, March 18, 2002, page 106
School Library Journal, March 2002, page 193

Other books by the same author:
Big Brown Bear's Up and Down Day, 2003
The Teddy Bear, 2002
Edward and the Pirates, 1997

Other books you might like:
Lauren Child, *Beware of the Storybook Wolves*, 2001
    Big Wolf and Little Wolf climb out of Herb's bedtime story with plans to make him their evening meal.
Jules Feiffer, *Meanwhile . . .* , 1997
    Raymond can't seem to find a way out of the comic book he's reading.
Robert D. San Souci, *Tarzan*, 1999
    A picture book adaptation of the classic novel by Burroughs relates the life of an orphaned baby adopted and raised by a gorilla.

1000

DAVID MCPHAIL, Author/Illustrator

Piggy's Pancake Parlor

(New York: Dutton Children's Books, 2002)

Subject(s): Animals/Pigs; Animals/Foxes; Food
Age range(s): Grades 2-3
Major character(s): Piggy, Pig, Cook; Fox, Fox, Friend; Mrs. Farmer Todd, Aged Person, Cook
Time period(s): Indeterminate Past
Locale(s): West Wee, Fictional Country

Summary: When Piggy is born the runt of a litter Mrs. Farmer Todd raises him to be a kind pig and teaches him to make pancakes using her secret ingredient. One day, while gathering eggs, Piggy finds hungry Fox in the henhouse. Piggy invites Fox in for breakfast and then includes him in his plans to operate Piggy's Pancake Parlor. Brief chapters describe the events of setting up the restaurant, serving the customers, trying new ideas, and facing temptations. Through it all Piggy remains positive and Fox becomes such a loyal friend and helper that Piggy entrusts him with the secret pancake recipe. (48 pages)

Where it's reviewed:
Booklist, August 2002, page 1974

Bulletin of the Center for Children's Books, July 2002, page 411
Publishers Weekly, May 20, 2002, page 64
School Library Journal, June 2002, page 103

Other books by the same author:
Drawing Lessons from a Bear, 2000 (Smithsonian's Notable Books for Children)
Mole Music, 1999 (Publishers Weekly Best Children's Books)
Pigs Aplenty, Pigs Galore!, 1993 (ALA Notable Children's Books)

Other books you might like:
Tim Egan, *Friday Night at Hodges' Cafe*, 1994
    Hodges's pet duck helps to save the restaurant's patrons from three tigers that obviously have plans to dine on something that's not on the menu.
Laura Joffe Numeroff, *If You Give a Pig a Pancake*, 1998
    If an uninvited pig shows up at breakfast to share your pancakes, be prepared for a busy day.
Tamson Weston, *Hey, Pancakes!*, 2003
    While their parents sleep, three lively siblings concoct a pancake breakfast and clean up too!

1001

DAVID MCPHAIL, Author/Illustrator

The Teddy Bear

(New York: Henry Holt and Company, 2002)

Subject(s): Lost and Found; Homeless People; Love
Age range(s): Grades K-2
Major character(s): Unnamed Character, Toy (teddy bear); Unnamed Character, Child, Son; Unnamed Character, Streetperson, Aged Person
Time period(s): 2000s
Locale(s): United States

Summary: As a sleepy little boy and his parents leave a restaurant the boy's beloved teddy bear is left behind. By the time the family returns, the bear has been swept into the trash where an elderly man finds it. The boy grieves for his lost bear and the bear misses his boy but in time each adjusts. The bear is satisfied because it is still loved and carried everywhere in the pocket of the homeless man's coat. On a spring day, the old man sets the bear on a park bench as he rummages through a nearby trash can just as the boy and his parents walk by. The boy grabs his bear and continues walking until he hears the wails of the old man looking for his bear. The boy then realizes that he must love his bear enough to give it away to someone who needs it more so he hurries back to do just that. (32 pages)

Where it's reviewed:
Booklist, May 1, 2002, page 1521
Horn Book Guide, Fall 2002, page 309
Kirkus Reviews, April 1, 2002, page 496
Publishers Weekly, April 22, 2002, page 69
School Library Journal, June 2002, page 103

Awards the book has won:
Booklist Editors' Choice, 2002
Notable Social Studies Trade Books for Young People, 2003

Other books by the same author:
Drawing Lessons from a Bear, 2000 (Smithsonian's Notable Books for Children)
Big Brown Bear, 1999
Tinker and Tom and the Star Baby, 1998

Other books you might like:
Ian Beck, *Home Before Dark*, 2001
   A teddy bear, dropped in the park by its owner, attempts to find his way home while it is still daylight.
Don Freeman, *Corduroy*, 1968
   A lonely, department store bear with a missing button eventually is purchased and given a loving home.
Tony Johnston, *My Best Friend Bear*, 2001
   Bear is such a cherished old friend to a young girl that he's literally been loved until he's unrecognizable.
Barbro Lindgren, *Sam's Teddy Bear*, 1982
   Sam's dog helps recover his special teddy bear.
Marjorie Newman, *Mole and the Baby Bird*, 2002
   Mole wants to keep the baby bird he's rescued but he realizes that he loves it so much he must set it free to fly.
Marjorie Williams, *The Velveteen Rabbit*, 1926
   A toy rabbit is so loved by a little boy that the rabbit, in time, becomes real.
Selina Young, *Ned*, 1993
   Emily and Ned, a green cloth donkey, are inseparable until Ned is lost, and then found again, on the first day of school.

`1002`

ALICE MEAD

Junebug in Trouble

(New York: Farrar Straus Giroux, 2002)

Subject(s): Friendship; Gangs; Single Parent Families
Age range(s): Grades 4-7
Major character(s): Reeve "Junebug" McClain Jr., 10-Year-Old, Friend; Robert, Friend (Junebug's), Neglected Child; Trevor, Gang Member, 12-Year-Old
Time period(s): 1990s
Locale(s): New Haven, Connecticut

Summary: Because Junebug has not been allowed to return to his former home in the projects to visit Robert, meeting him for a family outing to the beach is an eagerly anticipated summer treat. What Junebug discovers, sadly, is a friend on the threshold of being sucked into gang life with Trevor because Robert sees no other options in his life for food or companionship. On a trip to the Mall, Robert circumvents Junebug's mother's rules by secretly bringing Trevor along. Following an argument, Trevor shoots a rival gang member and hands the gun to Junebug before running away, leaving Junebug trapped between loyalty to Robert and fear that he will be joining his father in jail. (135 pages)

Where it's reviewed:
Booklist, April 15, 2002, page 1402
Bulletin of the Center for Children's Books, June 2002, page 374
Horn Book, May 2002, page 334
New Advocate, Summer 2002, page 240
School Library Journal, March 2002, page 235

Other books by the same author:
Soldier Mom, 1999
Junebug and the Reverend, 1998
Junebug, 1995 (Book Links Good Book)

Other books you might like:
Eve Bunting, *Riding the Tiger*, 2001
   A picture book for older readers metaphorically describes the appeal of gangs to Danny and his efforts to resist the allure.
Janet Taylor Lisle, *How I Became a Writer and Oggie Learned to Drive*, 2002
   Attempting to retrieve his younger brother Oggie's wallet Archie becomes unwittingly involved in a gang's activities.
Marybeth Lorbiecki, *Just One Flick of a Finger*, 1996
   Despite the disapproval of his friend Sherm, Jack takes his father's gun to school to intimidate a bully, with unexpected results.

`1003`

SUSAN MEDDAUGH, Author/Illustrator

Lulu's Hat

(Boston: Walter Lorraine Books/Houghton Mifflin Company, 2002)

Subject(s): Magicians; Adoption; Family
Age range(s): Grades 2-5
Major character(s): Lulu, Adoptee, 12-Year-Old; Jerry, Uncle, Magician
Time period(s): 2000s
Locale(s): Upper Parkington, New Jersey; Deep Magic Space, Fictional Country

Summary: Everyone in Lulu's adoptive family agrees that she can't be the one family member of this generation to have inherited the true magic gene. Nonetheless, Uncle Jerry takes someone on tour with him every summer and this year it is Lulu's turn. Indeed, Lulu appears to be hopelessly clumsy until she finds a top hat in Uncle Jerry's trunk that she uses for a costume. When Lulu wears the hat, she really does have the gift of magic. To find her dog and learn more about the hat, Lulu jumps into Deep Magic Space. Lulu locates her dog, a brother she didn't know she had, and the key to returning to the real world. She also discovers that she's from a magical family and she is, indeed, the one member of her generation to have the true magic gene. (74 pages)

Where it's reviewed:
Booklist, May 1, 2002, page 1527
Bulletin of the Center for Children's Books, May 2002, page 333
Publishers Weekly, February 11, 2002, page 187
School Library Journal, May 2002, page 123

Other books by the same author:
Perfectly Martha, 2004
Harry on the Rocks, 2003
Cinderella's Rat, 1997

Other books you might like:
Jon Agee, *Milo's Hat Trick*, 2001
   Bungling magician Milo will lose his job if he's not able to pull a rabbit out of a hat.

Cary Fagan, *Daughter of the Great Zandini*, 2001
 The Great Zandini expects his son to carry on the magical family tradition but it's his daughter Fanny who shows both interest and talent.

James Howe, *Rabbit-Cadabra!*, 1993
 Bunnicula, suspected of being a vampire rabbit, appears onstage as the rabbit in a magician's hat.

1004

LAURA KRAUSS MELMED
HENRY COLE, Illustrator

Fright Night Flight

(New York: HarperCollins Publishers, 2002)

Subject(s): Halloween; Witches and Witchcraft; Stories in Rhyme
Age range(s): Preschool-Kindergarten
Major character(s): Unnamed Character, Witch
Time period(s): 2000s (2002)
Locale(s): United States

Summary: A witch flies through the neighborhood, picking up passengers. A vampire hops on her broom from a haunted castle; a skeleton joins from the cemetery; and they also pick up a mummy from the museum. All the scary pals end up at ''your house'' to trick or treat. (32 pages)

Where it's reviewed:
Booklist, September 1, 2002, page 140
Horn Book Guide, Spring 2003, page 45
Kirkus Reviews, August 15, 2002, page 1229
Publishers Weekly, September 23, 2002, page 22
School Library Journal, September 2002, page 201

Other books by the same author:
This First Thanksgiving Day, 2001
Little Oh, 1997 (ALA Notable Children's Books)
The Rainbabies, 1992

Other books you might like:
Julia Donaldson, *Room on the Broom*, 2001
 After a witch drops her hat and wand helpful animals find them for her in return for a ride on her broom.
Don Freeman, *Space Witch*, 1979
 One Halloween, Tilly Ipswich decides to frighten creatures on other planets.
Arthur Howard, *Hoodwinked*, 2001
 Witch Mitzi adopts a kitten despite her initial concerns that he's not creepy enough.
Howard Reeves, *There Was An Old Witch*, 2000
 In this cumulative tale, a witch gathers items to adorn her Halloween hat.

1005

LAURA KRAUSS MELMED
BETSY LEWIN, Illustrator

A Hug Goes Around

(New York: HarperCollins Publishers, 2002)

Subject(s): Family Life; Rural Life; Farm Life
Age range(s): Preschool-Kindergarten

Major character(s): Ma, Mother; Pa, Father
Time period(s): 2000s (2002)
Locale(s): United States

Summary: A hug works its way through a family, starting with Ma hugging the baby when she wakes up. As the day's mishaps occur—syrup is spilled, chickens get out, a thunderstorm ruins a fishing trip—Ma and Pa are there to offer a hug and make everything better. As the day ends Ma and Pa hug on the porch after the kids settle into bed. (32 pages)

Where it's reviewed:
Booklist, June 2002, page 1742
Horn Book Guide, Fall 2002, page 309
School Library Journal, July 2002, page 95

Other books by the same author:
Moishe's Miracle: A Hanukkah Story, 2000
Little Oh, 1997 (ALA Notable Children's Books)
The Rainbabies, 1992

Other books you might like:
Jez Alborough, *Hug*, 2000
 Bobo searches the jungle for just one thing—a hug from his mother.
Natalie Babbitt, *Bub: Or the Very Best Thing*, 1994
 A King and Queen seek the ''very best thing'' to give their child but no understands that, to Prince, ''bub'' means love.
Sharon Jennings, *Into My Mother's Arms*, 2003
 A little girl recounts her day's activities with her mother.
Lois Lenski, *The Little Family*, 1932
 Set in the 1930s, the Little family enjoys spending their day together, doing routine activities.

1006

CAROLYN MEYER

Doomed Queen Anne

(San Diego: Gulliver/Harcourt, 2002)

Series: Young Royals
Subject(s): Kings, Queens, Rulers, etc.; Middle Ages
Age range(s): Grades 6-10
Major character(s): Anne Boleyn, Royalty (queen), Mother (of Elizabeth I); Henry VIII, Royalty (king); Mary Tudor, Royalty (princess)
Time period(s): 16th century (1520-1536)
Locale(s): London, England

Summary: Schooled in France, Anne is sixteen before King Henry VIII notices her. Anne has watched her sister in the role of Henry's mistress and knows she wants only a legitimate relationship with him. She uses her feminine wiles to captivate him, while also encouraging him to assume authority for the church in England so he can divorce his wife Catherine, mother of Princess Mary. After attaining her goal, and bearing Elizabeth but no male heir, Anne's fate is sealed at the age of twenty-nine when she's confined to the Tower of London and faces execution on the charge of unfaithfulness. (230 pages)

Where it's reviewed:
Booklist, September 15, 2002, page 222
Kirkus Reviews, October 15, 2002, page 1534

Library Media Connection, March 2003, page 78
School Library Journal, October 2002, page 168
Voice of Youth Advocates, December 2002, page 388

Other books by the same author:
Patience, Princess Catherine, 2004 (Young Royals)
Kristina, the Girl King: Sweden, 1638, 2003 (Royal Diaries)
Beware, Princess Elizabeth, 2001 (Young Royals)
Anastasia, the Last Grand Duchess, 2000 (Royal Diaries)
Mary, Bloody Mary, 1999 (The Young Royals)

Other books you might like:
Kathryn Lasky, *Elizabeth I: Red Rose of the House of Tudor*, 1999
    A series of fictionalized diary entries provides a look at Elizabeth's life during her early teen years as she strives for her father's attention.
Mary Stolz, *Bartholomew Fair*, 1990
    Queen Elizabeth I visits Bartholomew Fair and, in so doing, benefits the lives of five others.
Jane Yolen, *Queen's Own Fool: A Novel of Mary Queen of Scots*, 2000
    After Nicola performs for Queen Mary, she is invited to be Mary's personal "fool," a job she accepts for she knows she can tell Queen Mary the truth.

1007

L.A. MEYER

Bloody Jack: Being an Account of the Curious Adventures of Mary "Jacky" Faber, Ship's Boy

(San Diego: Harcourt, Inc., 2002)

Subject(s): Sea Stories; Pirates; Gender Roles
Age range(s): Grades 7-10
Major character(s): Mary "Jacky" Faber, Orphan, Sailor; Jaimy, Sailor
Time period(s): 19th century
Locale(s): HMS *Dolphin*, Atlantic Ocean

Summary: Orphaned at the age of eight, Mary survives London's streets by joining a gang, but when her leader is killed several years later, opts for a life at sea. Donning the leader's clothes and renaming herself Jacky, Mary signs on as a ship's boy on the *HMS Dolphin* where her street survival skills come in useful. Her ship's orders are to hunt down pirates and, after she shoots one in the chest, earns the moniker "Bloody Jack." It becomes harder to conceal her identity when she reaches puberty, especially when she falls for fellow ship's boy Jaimy, in a first novel that brims with adventure. (278 pages)

Where it's reviewed:
Booklist, November 15, 2002, page 595
Horn Book, January 2003, page 81
Publishers Weekly, October 7, 2002, page 74
School Library Journal, September 2002, page 229
Voice of Youth Advocates, December 2002, page 388

Awards the book has won:
ALA Best Books for Young Adults, 2003
Booklist Editors' Choice/Books for Youth, 2002

Other books by the same author:
Curse of the Blue Tattoo: Being an Account of the Misadventures of Jacky Faber, Midshipman and Fine Lady, 2004

Other books you might like:
Avi, *The True Confessions of Charlotte Doyle*, 1990
    Charlotte's adventures aboard the sailing ship *Seahawk* turn her from a proper Victorian lady into a real sailor.
Iain Lawrence, *The Buccaneers*, 2001
    Picking up a drifting sailor proves advantageous for John Spencer, aboard the schooner *Dragon*, when they're later attacked by pirates.
Celia Rees, *Pirates!: The True and Remarkable Adventures of Minerva Sharpe and Nancy Kington, Female Pirates*, 2003
    Two young girls join a shipload of pirates, one to escape a planned marriage and the other a life of slavery.
Robert Louis Stevenson, *Treasure Island*, 1882
    After finding a treasure map, Jim Hawkins receives help to outfit a ship and sail to the treasure, but among the crew are pirates who also want the spoils.

1008

BEN MIKAELSEN

Red Midnight

(New York: HarperCollins, 2002)

Subject(s): Survival; Emigration and Immigration; Voyages and Travels
Age range(s): Grades 5-9
Major character(s): Santiago Cruz, 12-Year-Old; Angelina Cruz, Child
Time period(s): 1980s
Locale(s): Dos Vias, Guatemala; Lake Izabal, Guatemala; Florida

Summary: Santiago is awakened by his mother who tells him to run as the soldiers have come to kill them. Snatching up his sister Angelina, the two escape the killings of their parents, siblings and grandfather. Told by their dying uncle to use his boat to travel to the United States and tell their story, the two ride on horseback to Lake Izabal where they find his home-made kayak. A neighbor helps stock it with food and, receiving some sailing instructions, the two children sail past Belize into the Gulf of Mexico and then to Florida. The three weeks on the sea are filled with terror as they battle storms, pirates, and the lack of food until finally landing on a Florida beach. Told to leave the private beach, Santiago and Angelina are eventually taken in by more kindly Americans and tell their story to immigration officials of events that occurred often in Central America during the 1980s. (212 pages)

Where it's reviewed:
Horn Book Guide, Fall 2002, page 378
Kirkus Reviews, March 15, 2002, page 419
Kliatt, July 2002, page 12
School Library Journal, May 2002, page 157
Voice of Youth Advocates, June 2002, page 120

Other books by the same author:
Tree Girl, 2004
Touching Spirit Bear, 2001
Petey, 1998

Countdown, 1996
Stranded, 1995

Other books you might like:
Sonia Levitin, *The Return*, 1987
Ethiopian Jews Desta, Almaz and Joas flee to Israel to escape harassment by their countrymen.
Louise Moeri, *The Forty-Third War*, 1989
Teen Uno and two of his friends become battle initiates in the eight days they help the revolutionaries of their Central American country.
Beverley Naidoo, *Chain of Fire*, 1990
The members of Naledi's African village resist the government's decision to move them to "the homeland."

1009

GLORIA D. MIKLOWITZ

The Enemy Has a Face

(Grand Rapids, MI: Eerdman's Publishing Co., 2003)

Subject(s): Missing Persons; Jews; Arab-Israeli Wars
Age range(s): Grades 7-10
Major character(s): Netta Hoffman, 14-Year-Old; Adam Hoffman, 17-Year-Old; Laith al Salaam, Student—Middle School
Time period(s): 2000s
Locale(s): Los Angeles, California

Summary: Recent emigres from Israel, where her father and brother were both outspoken Israelis, Netta has barely adjusted to life in America when Adam disappears. She is certain that Palestinian terrorists have kidnapped Adam and now plan to harm him, though there's never a ransom request or any political statement from a terrorist group. Determined to find out what happened to her brother, Netta uses his computer to trace Adam's e-mail and see what chat rooms he's been in, as well as talks to some of his friends at the high school. Laith, a Palestinian boy at her school, is as concerned as she is about Adam, though Netta isn't sure whether or not to trust him. One thing she does know is that she feels more comfortable with Laith than any of her American friends. When the Hoffmans finally learn what really happened to Adam, they're devastated yet in some small way relieved that, this time, Palestinians aren't to blame. (139 pages)

Where it's reviewed:
Booklist, June 2003, page 1778
Kliatt, May 2003, page 11
Library Media Connection, November 2003, page 58
School Library Journal, July 2003, page 133
Voice of Youth Advocates, August 2003, page 226

Other books by the same author:
Secrets in the House of Delgado, 2001
Masada: The Last Fortress, 1998
Standing Tall, Looking Good, 1991

Other books you might like:
Danielle Carmi, *Samir and Yonatan*, 2000
Initially terrified to have surgery at a Jewish hospital, Palestinian Samir befriends all the children on his ward.
Cathryn Clinton, *A Stone in My Hand*, 2002
Devastated when the Islamic Jihad blow up her father's

bus as he rides into Israel to find work, Malaak can't believe her brother wants to join the Jihad.
Alice Mead, *Girl of Kosovo*, 2001
Zana is caught up in the war between Serbs and Albanians when family members are killed and her uncle threatens her best friend.

1010

ROSALIND MILES

Isolde: Queen of the Western Isle: The First of the Tristan and Isolde Novels

(New York: Crown, 2002)

Subject(s): Love; Magic
Age range(s): Grades 9-Adult
Major character(s): Isolde, Royalty; Tristan, Royalty; Mark, Royalty (king)
Time period(s): Indeterminate Past
Locale(s): Ireland; England

Summary: Before Romeo and Juliet, Tristan and Isolde may have been the most famous star-crossed lovers. Here their story is retold with full romantic trappings within the setting of the Arthurian legend. As Isolde, a princess of Ireland, has become older, she realizes that her mother has shortcomings as a leader. Isolde is determined to do better, to see that her people come first and that she remains faithful to her gifts of healing. Tristan is a prince without a country, sent away by his father to protect him from an ambitious stepmother. Tristan's weak Uncle Mark is king of Cornwall, but a king in name only, who's easily swayed by the venial and self-seeking with whom he surrounds himself. When the Irish Queen's consort decides to impress her by conquering Cornwall by right of combat, neither Mark nor any of his knights are up to the challenge. The Camelot court rides to the rescue, but before they can arrive, Tristan appears and vanquishes the Irish hero. Tristan is deeply wounded and Merlin, who knows of Isolde's gifts as a healer, sends Tristan to her to be healed. They fall in love and the tragedy is set in motion. (368 pages)

Where it's reviewed:
Booklist, July 2002, page 1822
Kirkus Reviews, May 15, 2002, page 692
Library Journal, July 2002, page 121
Publishers Weekly, June 24, 2002, page 39

Other books by the same author:
The Lady of the Sea: The Third of the Tristan and Isolde Novels, 2004
The Maid of the White Hands: The Second of the Tristan and Isolde Novels, 2003
The Child of the Holy Grail: The Third of the Guenevere Novels, 2001
Knight of the Sacred Lake: The Second of the Guenevere Novels, 2000

Other books you might like:
Marion Zimmer Bradley, *The Mists of Avalon*, 1982
The Arthurian legend is retold by Morgaine, whose perspective is very different, and focuses on people and relationships rather than battles.

Nancy McKenzie, *Queen of Camelot*, 2002
  A shy orphan from a northern kingdom becomes Arthur's queen and her noble cousin reacts with dangerous jealousy.
Steven Millhauser, *The King in the Tree: Three Novellas*, 2003
  The final story in this collection is a very different version of Isolde's tale.

1011

MARY BETH MILLER

Aimee

(New York: Dutton, 2002)

Subject(s): Suicide; Friendship; Mental Illness
Age range(s): Grades 9-12
Major character(s): Zoe, 17-Year-Old; Aimee, Victim (of suicide)
Time period(s): 2000s
Locale(s): United States

Summary: Miserable over her stepmother's obvious dislike and needling of her, and molested by a minister, Aimee has many reasons to dislike her life and threaten to end it. Zoe and her friends try, as best they know how, to keep Aimee from committing suicide, even going so far as to arrange a suicide watch where one of them is always with her. Even with all their efforts, Aimee still manages to kill herself and she does it when Zoe is on duty. Though Zoe tells her side of the night watching Aimee to the police, she's arrested, tried and acquitted. Her parents move to another town and old friends are not allowed to see her. Ordered to see a psychologist, Zoe won't speak to her but does keep a journal where she finally records the events of that fateful night and begins to break through her wall of grief and guilt, in an intense first novel. (276 pages)

Where it's reviewed:
Booklist, May 1, 2002, page 1518
Kliatt, May 2002, page 11
Publishers Weekly, May 20, 2002, page 68
School Library Journal, April 2002, page 153
Voice of Youth Advocates, June 2002, page 120

Awards the book has won:
ALA Best Books for Young Adults, 2003

Other books you might like:
James Bennett, *I Can Hear the Mourning Dove*, 1990
  Shaken by her father's death, Grace attempts suicide but is hospitalized instead.
Lisa Rowe Fraustino, *Ash*, 1995
  Again and again Ash and his family try to save his older, schizophrenic brother from suicide attempts.
Mary Beth Lundgren, *Love, Sara*, 2001
  When her best friend Dulcie is pregnant and her boyfriend Jon is kicked out of his house, Sara is unable to prevent their suicide.
Zibby Oneal, *The Language of Goldfish*, 1980
  For teen Carrie Stokes, growing up is filled with so much uncertainty and difficulty that she suffers a nervous breakdown.

1012

ISAAC MILLMAN, Author/Illustrator

Moses Goes to the Circus

(New York: Frances Foster Books/Farrar Straus Giroux, 2003)

Subject(s): Deafness; Communication; Circus
Age range(s): Grades K-2
Major character(s): Moses, Brother (older), Deaf Person; Renee, Sister (younger)
Time period(s): 2000s (2003)
Locale(s): United States

Summary: With their parents Moses and Renee go to an interpreted performance of the Big Apple Circus. Too young to speak, Renee is still able to communicate in American Sign Language although her youthful experience with animals seems to be limited to cats. Moses chuckles over Renee's errors in identification and corrects her with signs for bear, dog, elephant and seal. During the clown act, Moses is selected as the audience participant. After Moses dons a red clown nose and a funny costume, Renee doesn't recognize her brother. At home that evening, Moses and Renee reenact some of their favorite parts of today's show for their parents' enjoyment. An introductory author's note gives background information about American Sign Language and explains how to read the illustrations of the pictured signs. (32 pages)

Where it's reviewed:
Booklist, April 15, 2003, page 1479
Horn Book Guide, Fall 2003, page 333
Kirkus Reviews, December 15, 2002, page 1853
Publishers Weekly, December 16, 2002, page 69
School Library Journal, March 2003, page 199

Other books by the same author:
Moses Goes to School, 2000
Moses Goes to a Concert, 1998 (Bank Street Best Children's Book of 1998)

Other books you might like:
Jamee Riggio Heelan, *Can You Hear a Rainbow?: The Story of a Deaf Boy Named Chris*, 2002
  Through the similarities and differences of a hearing friend and a deaf friend Chris explains his deafness and the strategies he uses to be successful.
Joan Holub, *My First Book of Sign Language*, 1996
  Simple illustrated text in a nonfiction title provides a guide to fingerspelling and basic signs.
Dorothy Hoffman Levi, *A Very Special Friend*, 1989
  When Frannie learns that her new neighbor Laura is deaf she tries to learn enough sign language to make communication easier.

1013

CLAUDIA MILLS
G. BRIAN KARAS, Illustrator

7 x 9 = Trouble!

(New York: Farrar Straus Giroux, 2002)

Subject(s): Mathematics; Schools; Brothers
Age range(s): Grades 2-4

Major character(s): Wilson Williams, 3rd Grader, Brother (older); Kipper Williams, Kindergartner, Brother (younger); Josh Hernandez, 3rd Grader, Friend
Time period(s): 2000s (2002)
Locale(s): Colorado

Summary: Multiplication facts threaten to end Wilson's enjoyment of school! If he cannot pass all of his times tables in three weeks he'll not only be the only student not to get an ice-cream cone reward but he also may no longer be allowed to bring the class hamster home for a weekend visit. As Wilson's parents help him master his multiplication facts, math-lover Kipper demonstrates the ability to comprehend multiplication and to remember the times tables more easily than Wilson does. Josh devotes part of every play date with Wilson to completion of some of his practice tests. Initially resentful, Wilson soon accepts that his family and Josh are only trying to help him and just in the nick of time the hard work pays off. (103 pages)

Where it's reviewed:
Booklist, April 1, 2002, page 1328
Bulletin of the Center for Children's Books, April 2002, page 289
Horn Book, March 2002, page 215
Riverbank Review, Summer 2002, page 41
School Library Journal, April 2002, page 118

Awards the book has won:
ALA Notable Children's Books, 2003
Bulletin of the Center for Children's Books Blue Ribbons, 2002

Other books by the same author:
Gus and Grandpa at Basketball, 2001 (ALA Notable Children's Books)
You're a Brave Man, Julius Zimmerman, 1999
Losers, Inc., 1997

Other books you might like:
David A. Adler, *The Many Troubles of Andy Russell*, 1998
One of Andy's many troubles is figuring out how to locate and capture all his pet gerbils after they escape from their cage.
Kate Banks, *Howie Bowles and Uncle Sam*, 2000
Howie's troubles with numbers go beyond math lessons when a letter from an Uncle Sam he doesn't know he has threatens him with jail for unpaid taxes.
Patricia Reilly Giff, *Shark in School*, 1994
With help from an understanding teacher and a compassionate classmate Matthew begins to overcome his reading problem.
Suzy Kline, *Song Lee and the Hamster Hunt*, 1994
During a visit to Song Lee's classroom, her pet hamster gets out of the cage.

1014

CLAUDIA MILLS
CATHERINE STOCK, Illustrator

Gus and Grandpa and the Halloween Costume

(New York: Farrar Straus Giroux, 2002)

Series: Gus and Grandpa. Book 8
Subject(s): Halloween; Grandfathers; Fathers and Sons
Age range(s): Grades 2-3
Major character(s): Gus, 2nd Grader, Son; Grandpa, Grandfather; Daddy, Father
Time period(s): 2000s
Locale(s): Colorado

Summary: Halloween is approaching and Gus feels his annual disappointment knowing that his parents will not allow a store-bought costume. Just once he'd like to have fake teeth and blood instead of an old sheet with holes cut for eyes. As usual, Gus turns to Grandpa for help. A search through an old trunk reveals a Canadian Mountie costume and a photograph of Daddy as a boy, wearing the outfit. Now, wearing his unique costume, Gus has an extra reason to be excited about Halloween because he'll look exactly the same as his Daddy did as a boy. (48 pages)

Where it's reviewed:
Booklist, September 1, 2002, page 140
Horn Book Guide, Spring 2003, page 71
Kirkus Reviews, August 1, 2002, page 1138
Publishers Weekly, September 23, 2002, page 24
Tribune Books, October 20, 2002, page 5

Other books by the same author:
Gus and Grandpa at Basketball, 2001 (Gus and Grandpa Book 7)
Gus and Grandpa and Show-and-Tell, 2000 (Gus and Grandpa Book 6)
Gus and Grandpa and the Two-Wheeled Bike, 1999 (Gus and Grandpa Book 3)

Other books you might like:
Marion Dane Bauer, *Alison's Fierce and Ugly Halloween*, 1997
Alison's attempt to be scary on Halloween creates friction with her friend Cindy who has different ideas about the holiday.
Emily Arnold McCully, *Grandmas Trick-or-Treat*, 2001
Grandma Sal, wearing a mummy costume, encourages Pip and her friends to be a bit scarier as they trick-or-treat.
Karen Gray Ruelle, *Spookier than a Ghost*, 2001
In a beginning reader, Harry and Emily create original costumes for Halloween with varying degrees of success.

1015

CLAUDIA MILLS
CATHERINE STOCK, Illustrator

Gus and Grandpa Go Fishing

(New York: Farrar Straus Giroux, 2003)

Series: Gus and Grandpa. Book 9

Subject(s): Fishing; Grandparents; Family
Age range(s): Grades 1-3
Major character(s): Gus, Child, Relative (grandson); Grandpa, Grandfather, Aged Person; Mom, Mother; Dad, Father
Time period(s): 2000s (2003)
Locale(s): United States

Summary: Gus's family is going fishing. While Mom busies herself with the details of the picnic and Dad goofs around trying to learn how to use his fancy new fishing pole, Gus and Grandpa get right down to the business at hand. It takes Gus awhile to learn how to cast, but he eventually does and both he and Grandpa manage to catch a fish. (48 pages)

Where it's reviewed:
Booklist, September 1, 2003, page 130
Bulletin of the Center for Children's Books, October 2003, page 72
School Library Journal, October 2003, page 131

Other books by the same author:
Gus and Grandpa at Basketball, 2001 (Gus and Grandpa Book 7)
Gus and Grandpa and Show-and-Tell, 2000 (Gus and Grandpa Book 6)
Gus and Grandpa, 1997 (Gus and Grandpa Book 1)

Other books you might like:
Margaret Carney, *The Biggest Fish in the Lake*, 2001
A young girl goes on a summer fishing trip with her grandfather, but she has a hard time catching a fish.
Andrea Davis Pinkney, *Fishing Day*, 2003
In the segregated South, Reenie and her mother go fishing on Jim Crow River.
Dr. Seuss, *McElligot's Pool*, 1947
Despite his nay-saying neighbors, a young boy is sure that he will be able to catch a fish in a small puddle.

1016

NANCY MINCHELLA
KEIKO NARAHASHI, Illustrator

Mama Will Be Home Soon
(New York: Scholastic, Inc., 2003)

Subject(s): Mothers and Daughters; Grandparents; Family
Age range(s): Grades K-2
Major character(s): Lili, Child, Daughter
Time period(s): 2000s (2003)
Locale(s): United States

Summary: Lili stays with her grandmother while her mother travels for a few days. Lili's mother tells her to be on the lookout for a yellow hat as that's what she'll be wearing when she returns. For the next few days, Lili sees yellow everywhere—yellow balloons, yellow beach umbrellas and yellow sunflowers. Finally Lili's grandmother takes her back to the ferry to pick up her mother and Lili receives her own yellow hat as the author's first book concludes. (32 pages)

Where it's reviewed:
Booklist, June 2003, page 1787
Publishers Weekly, April 28, 2003, page 68
School Library Journal, August 2003, page 139

Other books you might like:
Susi Fowler, *I'll See You When the Moon Is Full*, 1994
When Abe's father has to go out of town for a two week business trip, he tells Abe that he'll be back when the moon is full.
Natalie Honeycutt, *Whistle Home*, 1993
When a little girl is left with her Aunt Whistle while her mama goes into town, she wants Aunt Whistle to whistle her mama home again.
Mindy Pelton, *When Dad's at Sea*, 2004
Emily's Dad is in the Navy and she misses him when he's out on deployment.

1017

FRANCES MINTERS
G. BRIAN KARAS, Illustrator

Princess Fishtail
(New York: Viking/Penguin, 2002)

Subject(s): Princes and Princesses; Mermaids; Stories in Rhyme
Age range(s): Grades K-2
Major character(s): Mer-Princess, Mythical Creature, Royalty; Burt, Swimmer
Time period(s): 2000s (2002)
Locale(s): Pacific Ocean; Los Angeles, California

Summary: When a thoroughly modern Mer-Princess falls in love with a California surfer, she enlists the help of a sneaky troll. In exchange for her fish tail, the troll gives her legs. At first Mer-Princess and surfer Burt have a great time exploring Los Angeles (Mer-Princess has to buy a lot of shoes of course), but after a month, Mer-Princess becomes homesick. When the troll offers to give her back her fishtail in return for her voice, Mer-Princess thinks she can get a better deal. In the end Burt buys them both scuba gear so that they can visit her family any time they want. (32 pages)

Where it's reviewed:
Booklist, October 15, 2002, page 412
Bulletin of the Center for Children's Books, December 2002, page 167
Publishers Weekly, August 26, 2002, page 66
School Library Journal, September 2002, page 202

Other books by the same author:
Too Big, Too Small, Just Right, 2001
Sleepless Beauty, 1996
Cinder-Elly, 1994

Other books you might like:
Hans Christian Andersen, *The Little Mermaid*, 1959
After falling in love with a human, the little mermaid sacrifices her voice to be able to live with him on land in this adaptation of a classic.
Shirley Climo, *A Treasury of Mermaids: Mermaid Tales from around the World*, 1997
Mermaids fill the water in eight folktales from around the world.
Marilyn Singer, *In the Palace of the Ocean King*, 1995
Princess Marianna is scared of the ocean, but when the Ocean King captures her beloved she dives in to save him.

1018

MARIANNE MITCHELL
NORMAND CHARTIER, Illustrator

Gullywasher Gulch

(Honesdale, PA: Boyds Mills Press, 2002)

Subject(s): Gold Discoveries; Floods; Collectors and Collecting
Age range(s): Grades K-3
Major character(s): Ebenezer Overall, Prospector
Time period(s): 20th century
Locale(s): Dry Gulch

Summary: Ebenezer Overall's shack and land is covered with "junk." His family and neighbors tell him to get rid of it, but Old Eb claims he is saving it for a "rainy day." Such a day comes and flash floods wash away his shack and the entire town. Old Eb generously gives his building materials and bags of gold to rebuild the town, renamed Gullywasher Gulch. (32 pages)

Where it's reviewed:
Horn Book Guide, Spring 2003, page 46
Kirkus Reviews, September 15, 2002, page 1396
School Library Journal, November 2002, page 132

Other books by the same author:
Joe Cinders, 2002
Maya Moon, 1995

Other books you might like:
Michael Brownlow, *Way Out West With a Baby*, 2000
    After three cowboys discover a baby in the midst of a cattle drive they try to return him to his mother.
Verla Kay, *Gold Fever*, 1999
    Jasper seeks his fortune in the 1849 California Gold Rush.
Chad Stuart, *The Ballymara Flood*, 1996
    A young boy in a small Irish town floods Ballymara with his overflowing bathtub.

1019

TONY MITTON
GUY PARKER-REES, Illustrator

Dinosaurumpus

(New York: Orchard/Scholastic, Inc., 2003)

Subject(s): Dinosaurs; Dancing; Stories in Rhyme
Age range(s): Preschool-Grade 1
Time period(s): Indeterminate Past
Locale(s): Earth

Summary: Dinosaurs are coming, but not to hunt; they want to dance! A variety of dinosaur species are introduced, each making their own unique sound and adding to the overall rhythm. Finally late in the night, the exhausted dinosaurs all fall asleep and add a new sound, snoring. (32 pages)

Where it's reviewed:
Booklist, January 2003, page 908
Magpies, September 2002, page 27
School Library Journal, March 2003, page 200

Other books by the same author:
Plum: Poems, 2003
Amazing Airplanes, 2002
Down by the Cool of the Pool, 2002

Other books you might like:
Kathi Appelt, *Piggies in a Polka*, 2003
    While the farmers are sleeping, the pigs all gather for a hootenanny.
Carol Diggory Shields, *Saturday Night at the Dinosaur Stomp*, 2002
    Dinosaurs get ready for the Saturday night Dinosaur Stomp.
Paul Stickland, *Dinosaur Stomp!*, 1996
    Dinosaurs all head to a big celebration in the swamp.

1020

TONY MITTON
GUY PARKER-REES, Illustrator

Down by the Cool of the Pool

(New York: Orchard Books/Scholastic, Inc., 2002)

Subject(s): Animals; Dancing; Stories in Rhyme
Age range(s): Preschool-Grade 1
Major character(s): Frog, Frog, Dancer
Time period(s): Indeterminate
Locale(s): Fictional Country

Summary: An exuberant frog calls other animals to join in a dance down by the cool of the pool. While the others can't dance quite like Frog each does whatever motion it can. As the day goes on the pond fills with flapping, wiggling, stamping, bounding, frisking, skipping, hopping, prancing, drumming and capering creatures. The good time ends when the sun sets bringing the dance to conclusion. Originally published in Great Britain in 2001. (28 pages)

Where it's reviewed:
Horn Book Guide, Fall 2002, page 309
Kirkus Reviews, May 1, 2002, page 662
Publishers Weekly, April 15, 2002, page 62
School Librarian, Summer 2002, page 76
School Library Journal, July 2002, page 96

Awards the book has won:
IRA Children's Choices, 2003

Other books by the same author:
Spooky Hour, 2004
Tale of Tales, 2004
Dinosaurumpus, 2003

Other books you might like:
Rhonda Gowler Greene, *Jamboree Day*, 2001
    Animals hop, float, fly, bounce, march and leap to the jungle spot where the annual jamboree is being held.
Ellen Stoll Walsh, *Hop Jump*, 1993
    Other frogs may hop but an independently minded blue frog learns to dance instead.
Elizabeth Winthrop, *Dumpy La Rue*, 2001
    Dumpy's got so much rhythm the little pig is soon joined by all the other animals swinging and swaying to their individual inner beats.

1021

KEN MOCHIZUKI

Beacon Hill Boys

(New York: Scholastic, 2002)

Subject(s): Japanese Americans; Individuality
Age range(s): Grades 7-10
Major character(s): Dan Inagki, 16-Year-Old; Brad Inagki, 18-Year-Old
Time period(s): 1970s
Locale(s): Seattle, Washington

Summary: Young Dan is not content to be the academic scholar his brother Brad is, a brother Dan calls yellow because ''he's white on the inside but yellow on the outside.'' Instead Dan wants to know about his heritage and what life was like for his father in the internment camps, a topic his father won't discuss. He's tired of being called ''Oriental'' and wishes the Asians had a movement similar to the current one of ''black pride.'' At school he manages to convince the principal to offer a class comparing the various American cultures in this author's first novel. (201 pages)

Where it's reviewed:
Booklist, November 15, 2002, page 595
Kliatt, November 2002, page 12
Publishers Weekly, November 11, 2002, page 65
School Library Journal, January 2003, page 140
Voice of Youth Advocates, February 2003, page 479

Other books by the same author:
Different Battle: Stories of Asian Pacific American Veterans, 1999
Baseball Saved Us, 1993

Other books you might like:
Barry Denenberg, *The Journal of Ben Uchida: Citizen 13559 Mirror Lake Internment Camp*, 1999
   Using a journal given him by a friend, Ben records his family's life at their internment camp following the bombing of Pearl Harbor.
Jean Davies Okimoto, *Talent Night*, 1995
   Rodney has one major goal that drives his life: becoming the first Asian rap star, even though he's part Asian and part Polish.
Yoshiko Uchida, *Journey Home*, 1978
   Following relocation during World War II, a Japanese American family finally returns to their home and their normal lifestyle.

1022

MICHAEL MOLLOY
DAVID WYATT, Illustrator

The Time Witches

(New York: Scholastic, 2002)

Series: Witch Trade
Subject(s): Fantasy; Witches and Witchcraft; Adventure and Adventurers
Age range(s): Grades 5-8

Major character(s): Abby Clover, Witch (Light Witch); Wolfbane, Witch (Night Witch); Baal, Spider; Sir Chadwick Street, Witch; Hilda Bluebell, Fiance(e)
Time period(s): Indeterminate
Locale(s): Speller, England

Summary: Wolfbane, leader of the Night Witches, was defeated by the young Light Witch Abby Clover in *The Witch Trade*, but he returns, along with his evil mother and the nasty jumbo spider Baal. He concocts a plot of revenge against Abby by eliminating one of her ancestors, which in turn will eliminate her. To add an extra dollop of evil to his scheme, he kidnaps Hilda, fiancee of the Grand Master of the Light Witches, Sir Chadwick Street, and takes her back in time with him. Securing permission to time travel from the Wizards, Abby and Sir Street set off in pursuit of Wolfbane and manage to lose him in the depths of time, save Abby's forbear, watch Baal be squished by a train and rescue Hilda. The wedding of Sir Street and Hilda goes on as planned while Abby wonders what else is in store for her. (257 pages)

Where it's reviewed:
Booklist, January 2003, page 892
Journal of Adolescent and Adult Literacy, May 1, 2003, page 699
Kliatt, January 2003, page 22
School Library Journal, August 2003, page 164

Other books by the same author:
The House on Falling Star Hill, 2004
Wild West Witches, 2003 (Witch Trade)
Witch Trade, 2001 (Witch Trade)

Other books you might like:
Eva Ibbotson, *Which Witch?*, 1999
   All the witches are nervous as they gather for the spell competition and a chance for the hand of the wizard Arriman the Awful who's looking for a wife.
Ursula K. Le Guin, *A Wizard of Earthsea*, 1968
   An apprentice wizard accidentally releases an evil power.
J.K. Rowling, *Harry Potter and the Sorcerer's Stone*, 1998
   Raised by his aunt and uncle, Harry is thrilled to be selected for the Hogwarts School of Witchcraft and Wizardry.
Vivian Vande Velde, *Magic Can Be Murder*, 2000
   Witches are usually executed if discovered, so Nola practices her magic quietly, until she sees her former employer murdered and must investigate.

1023

MARISA MONTES

A Circle of Time

(San Diego: Harcourt, Inc., 2002)

Subject(s): Time Travel; Family Problems
Age range(s): Grades 6-9
Major character(s): Allison Blair, 14-Year-Old, Accident Victim; Rebecca Lee ''Becky'' Thompson, 14-Year-Old; Joshua Winthrop, 14-Year-Old
Time period(s): 1900s (1906); 1990s (1996)
Locale(s): California

Summary: Riding her bike on a deserted road, Allison is struck by a roadster and is now hospitalized in a coma. Somehow Becky, who lived one hundred years earlier, enters Allison's body and promises to keep it alive until Allison returns to California and prevents the deaths of Becky and her boyfriend Joshua in the San Francisco earthquake. Allison doesn't have much of a choice in all this as her comatose body lies in the hospital bed awaiting brain surgery, but she also doesn't like being Becky whose stepmother is extremely mean. The suspense builds as Allison also battles the time constraints of the impending earthquake and the fear that she might die on the operating table with Becky still inhabiting her body in this "time travel mystery." (261 pages)

Where it's reviewed:
Booklist, May 1, 2002, page 1459
Horn Book Guide, Fall 2002, page 378
Kirkus Reviews, May 1, 2002, page 662
School Library Journal, August 2002, page 195
Voice of Youth Advocates, June 2002, page 130

Other books by the same author:
Something Wicked's in Those Woods, 2000

Other books you might like:
Caroline B. Cooney, *Both Sides of Time*, 1995
    Annie falls back in time, meets the young heir to the Stratton mansion and, though she witnesses a murder, keeps returning to the past.
Peni R. Griffin, *Switching Well*, 1993
    When a fairy hears their wishes, she sends Ada forward in time and Amber back, but each quickly realizes she's traded one set of problems for another.
Gary Paulsen, *Canyons*, 1990
    Brennan Cole finds the skull of Coyote Runs, an Indian boy killed on a raid, and is drawn across time in a mystical bond with the Indian.

1024

MARISA MONTES
JOE CEPEDA, Illustrator

A Crazy, Mixed-Up Spanglish Day
(New York: Scholastic Press, 2003)

Series: Get Ready for Gabi!. Book 1
Subject(s): Bilingualism; Hispanic Americans; Schools
Age range(s): Grades 2-4
Major character(s): Gabi Morales, 3rd Grader, Daughter; Johnny Wiley, 3rd Grader, Bully
Time period(s): 2000s (2003)
Locale(s): United States

Summary: Gabi Morales only has one problem—Johnny Wiley, a fellow third-grader who teases her constantly. When they are assigned to work on a project together, the discord intensifies. Not only can they not agree on an animal for their project, but Gabi also gets so stressed out that she begins mixing up English and Spanish, the language she speaks at home. With a little advice from her dad and some help from her visiting grandmother, Gabi comes up with a solution to both the teasing and the project. (120 pages)

Where it's reviewed:
Booklist, September 1, 2003, page 121
Bulletin of the Center for Children's Books, June 2003, page 413
Publishers Weekly, April 7, 2003, page 66
School Library Journal, November 2003, page 110

Awards the book has won:
Center for Children's Books Best Books, 2003

Other books by the same author:
No More Spanish!, 2004 (Get Ready for Gabi! Book 3)
Please Don't Go, 2004 (Get Ready for Gabi! Book 4)
Who's That Girl?, 2003 (Get Ready for Gabi! Book 2)

Other books you might like:
Alma Flor Ada, *My Name Is Maria Isabel*, 1993
    When Maria Lopez starts a new school, the teacher calls her Mary and Maria must find a way to get the teacher to call her by her correct name.
Julia Alvarez, *How Tia Lola Came to Visit/Stay*, 2001
    When Miguel moves to Vermont from New York City after his parents divorce, Tia Lola comes from the Dominican Republic to help the family.
Beverly Cleary, *Ramona Quimby, Age 8*, 1981
    Ramona enters third grade where her boisterous personality sometimes leads to trouble.
Nicholasa Mohr, *Felita*, 1979
    When Felita moves to a new neighborhood, she is able to adjust with the help of her close-knit family.

1025

ELIZABETH MOON

The Speed of Dark
(New York: Ballantine Books, 2003)

Subject(s): Mentally Handicapped; Medicine; Change
Age range(s): Grades 9-Adult
Major character(s): Lou Arrendale, Autistic
Time period(s): Indeterminate Future
Locale(s): United States

Summary: Lou is autistic, which says both everything and nothing about him. By choice, Lou lives a very orderly existence where deviation from the routine bothers him. He works for a company that recognizes when autistic workers are provided with a sheltering environment and allowed to work at their own pace, they are able to see patterns in data and thus advance research much more quickly that ordinary scientists. Lou's other interest is fencing where the patterns in the fencing style of his opponents give him a mysterious edge. Change is Lou's great fear, and change is suddenly everywhere. An ambitious new boss at work begins pressuring Lou and all the autistics in the section to be guinea pigs for an experimental procedure that is supposed to make them more normal. At his fencing group, Lou meets a woman who is highly sympathetic. As he becomes closer to his new friend, Lou wonders what normalcy would mean; will he lose himself if he becomes normal? And will he have a chance to make a choice, or will he be threatened into being part of the experiment? (340 pages)

Where it's reviewed:
Booklist, February 1, 2003, page 972
Chronicle, January 2003, page 26
Library Journal, January 2003, page 157
Publishers Weekly, December 16, 2002, page 45
Voice of Youth Advocates, February 2003, page 490

Other books by the same author:
Marque and Reprisal, 2004
Trading in Danger, 2003
Heris Serrano, 2002

Other books you might like:
William Gibson, *Pattern Recognition*, 2003
   Cayce's fear of certain recognizable trademarks, and her enhanced sensitivity to patterns in behavior, are both a curse and a talent.
Eli Gottlieb, *The Boy Who Went Away*, 1997
   Denny's coming-of-age summer teaches him some difficult truths about family, especially his autistic brother, Fad.
Mark Haddon, *The Curious Incident of the Dog in the Night-time: A Novel*, 2003
   Autistic Christopher is disturbed when a dog is murdered, so he begins an investigation.

1026

ELIZABETH MOON

Trading in Danger
(New York: DelRey, 2003)

Subject(s): Coming-of-Age; Adventure and Adventurers
Age range(s): Grades 8-Adult
Major character(s): Kylara "Ky" Vatta, Businesswoman, Daughter
Time period(s): Indeterminate Future
Locale(s): *Glennys Jones*, Spaceship

Summary: Her wealthy family would like nothing better than for Ky to join them in the shipping business, but Ky has other ideas. She's made her way into the space academy and is doing well, when she's betrayed by her own kindness. Ky just can't stand to see someone in trouble and not help, but this time the cadet abuses Ky's kindness and the result is that both are kicked out of the academy. Ky is stunned to realize her dreams of military distinction are over. Her family closes ranks to protect her, and before she knows quite what has happened, Ky finds herself captaining one of the family's spaceships, albeit one that is taking its final voyage to be sold as scrap. It doesn't take long before Ky sees an opportunity to do some business on the way, and she seizes the chance to return home acknowledged at least as a sharp business-woman. Unfortunately, the deal takes Ky and her crew to a planet under attack, and in the ensuing chaos, Ky will need to use everything she's ever learned. (294 pages)

Where it's reviewed:
Booklist, September 1, 2003, page 75
Library Journal, September 2003, page 142
Publishers Weekly, September 29, 2003, page 48
School Library Journal, January 2004, page 163

Other books by the same author:
The Speed of Dark, 2002
Against the Odds, 2000
Change of Command, 1999

Other books you might like:
Hilari Bell, *A Matter of Profit*, 2001
   Ahvrem comes from a culture that glorifies war, but a forced interaction with an alien teaches him that there is more than one way to conquer.
Lois McMaster Bujold, *Cordelia's Honor*, 1996
   Captain Cordelia Naismith has her hands full when she crosses paths with a man from the conflict-prone planet of Barrayar.
David Weber, *Honor Among Enemies*, 1996
   Honor commands a fleet of Q-ships, freighters outfitted to fight pirates and privateers.

1027

MARTHA MOORE

Matchit
(New York: Delacorte, 2002)

Subject(s): Fathers and Sons; Self-Esteem; Emotional Problems
Age range(s): Grades 4-7
Major character(s): Matchit McCarty, 7th Grader; Babe Clark, Dealer (junkyard dealer); Zebedee "Zebby", Artist (sculptor); Sister, Taxidermist
Time period(s): 2000s
Locale(s): Texas

Summary: Matchit feels like his bad luck is continuing when his father, eager to take a trip with his girlfriend, dumps Matchit on an old friend who owes him a favor. Though Babe's been given no advance warning, she opens her arms, and her junkyard, to Matchit, who's a little put off by Babe's surroundings. Afraid his father will never return, just like his mother who left and never came back, it takes a while for Matchit to open up to Babe's good heartedness. He also comes to enjoy her eccentric friends and neighbors, like Zebby who lives in an old school bus and uses the junkyard to select car parts for his sculpture, and Sister, a taxidermist living next door to the junkyard. Though Babe buys the book *How to Raise a Kid in Ten Easy Lessons*, her common sense more than makes up for her lack of maternal experience. Matchit gains self-confidence as he furnishes an old van to make his own private space, convinces Zebby his sculpture is worth doing, learns to ride a bike and helps an injured pigeon that he names Dog. (197 pages)

Where it's reviewed:
Booklist, February 15, 2002, page 1015
Bulletin of the Center for Children's Books, June 2002, page 375
Kirkus Reviews, March 15, 2002, page 420
Publishers Weekly, April 8, 2002, page 228
School Library Journal, April 2002, page 153

Other books by the same author:
Angels on the Roof, 1997
Under the Mermaid Angel, 1995

Other books you might like:

Patricia Calvert, *When Morning Comes*, 1989
  Runaway Cat finally hits upon a home with foster mother Annie Bowen, a middle-aged, frumpy bee farmer, whose heart is 100% honey.

Carole Crowe, *Groover's Heart*, 2001
  Charlotte discovers the plain lifestyle of her recovering alcoholic Uncle Charlie is more suitable than life with her wealthy Aunt Viola and Uncle Ed.

Ellen Wittlinger, *Razzle*, 2001
  Kenyon locates a wonderful subject for his portrait photography when he meets Razzle who runs the recycling center at the town dump.

1028

PETER MOORE

Blind Sighted

(New York: Viking/Penguin Putnam, 2002)

Subject(s): Coming-of-Age; Alcoholism; Blindness
Age range(s): Grades 9-12
Major character(s): Kirk Tobak, 11th Grader; Glenn, Musician (guitarist), 11th Grader; Lauren, 11th Grader; Callie, Blind Person
Time period(s): 2000s
Locale(s): New Jersey

Summary: Though bright, Kirk's bored with school and works only if the topic interests him, which pushes him out of honors English into a remedial class. Short and shy, he's pretty much an outsider, and is usually left alone because his alcoholic mother has a new boyfriend. In his English class Kirk insults "Big Glenn" who he thinks will turn on him, but Glenn, a great guitarist who writes music, realizes Kirk has the writing ability he needs to add lyrics to his music and an unlikely friendship develops between these two. Working in the public library, Kirk's offered a job reading to a blind woman; he accepts but is surprised to see that Callie is only thirty and doesn't look or act blind. Kirk's life goes smoothly until his mother moves to California with her obnoxious boyfriend and puts their house up for sale; that's when Kirk learns to make some very mature decisions about his future in this author's first novel. (262 pages)

Where it's reviewed:
Booklist, September 1, 2002, page 116
Kliatt, September 2002, page 12
Publishers Weekly, August 5, 2002, page 74
School Library Journal, September 2002, page 230
Voice of Youth Advocates, October 2002, page 283

Other books by the same author:
Rebel on Wheels, 1990 (biography)

Other books you might like:

Alden R. Carter, *Up Country*, 1989
  Though Carl Stagger has a love-hate relationship with his mother, he supports her when she finally seeks help from an alcohol rehab center.

Dennis Foon, *Skud*, 2003
  Three of four seniors see their life-long plans fall apart

before they graduate: one dies, one is jailed and one loses a chance at pro ice hockey.

Kristen D. Randle, *Breaking Rank*, 1999
  Baby defies his gang, and Casey her place in the school's social scene, when they are in the same honors class.

1029

ROBIN MOORE

The Man with the Silver Oar

(New York: HarperCollins, 2002)

Subject(s): Pirates; Adventure and Adventurers; Sea Stories
Age range(s): Grades 6-10
Major character(s): Daniel Collins, 15-Year-Old, Religious (Quaker); Elias Collins, Uncle, Shipowner; James Mainwaring, Sea Captain; Jack Scarfield, Pirate
Time period(s): 1710s (1718)
Locale(s): Philadelphia, Pennsylvania; *Sea Turtle*, At Sea

Summary: Though longing to follow in his deceased father's footsteps, Daniel knows he'll always be a ship's carpenter, or at least that's the career his Uncle Elias has chosen for him. One day Daniel sneaks away from the shipyard to witness the hanging of two pirates, but hearing one of them say "Be bold! Take of the sea!," puts an idea in his head and when given the chance, he stows away aboard Lt. Mainwaring's pirate hunting ship. Once he actually faces pirates, Daniel's in a quandary for Quaker boys are non-violent, and yet he sees the death and destruction that follow in the wake of these buccaneers. Lt. Mainwaring, aboard his ship the *Sea Turtle*, searches for the legendary pirate Scarfield. Once Scarfield is captured, Daniel is amazed to discover the pirate is someone he knows in an exciting tale of adventure. (183 pages)

Where it's reviewed:
Booklist, June 2002, page 1708
Kirkus Reviews, May 1, 2002, page 662
Kliatt, July 2002, page 13
School Library Journal, July 2002, page 122
Voice of Youth Advocates, August 2002, page 195

Other books by the same author:
The Cherry Tree Buck, and Other Stories, 1995
When the Moon Is Full: Supernatural Stories from the Old Pennsylvania Mountains, 1994
Maggie Among the Seneca, 1990
The Bread Sister of Sinking Creek, 1984

Other books you might like:

Erik Christian Haugaard, *Under the Black Flag*, 1994
  Sailing to England for boarding school, William is captured by Blackbeard, held for ransom, and eventually becomes Blackbeard's cabin boy.

Gerald Hausman, *Tom Cringle: Battle on the High Seas*, 2000
  After a storm interrupts his voyage, Tom finds himself aboard a pirate ship.

Iain Lawrence, *The Buccaneers*, 2001
  Picking up a drifting sailor proves advantageous for John Spencer, aboard the schooner *Dragon*, when they're later attacked by pirates.

Celia Rees, *Pirates!: The True and Remarkable Adventures of Minerva Sharpe and Nancy Kington, Female Pirates*, 2003

Two young girls, one to escape a planned marriage and the other a life of slavery, find themselves with no choice but to join a shipload of pirates.

1030

YUYI MORALES, Author/Illustrator

Just a Minute: A Trickster Tale and Counting Book

(San Francisco: Chronicle Books, 2003)

Subject(s): Folklore; Trickster Tales; Birthdays
Age range(s): Grades 1-4
Major character(s): Grandma Beetle, Aged Person, Grandmother; Senor Calavera, Spirit (skeleton)
Time period(s): Indeterminate Past
Locale(s): Mexico

Summary: Senor Calavera calls on Grandma Beetle but she just doesn't have time to go with him as he signals she should do. First she has to sweep one house and boil two pots of tea and turn three pounds of corn into three stacks of tortillas. By the time Grandma Beetle works her way through four fruits, five cheeses, six pots of food, seven pinatas and eight platters of food Senor Calavera is a bit anxious about the time. Then nine grandchildren arrive to make a total of ten guests at the table. Senor Calavera is so pleased to be included as a guest that he decides to leave without Grandma Beetle so he can come back for her birthday next year. (32 pages)

Where it's reviewed:
Booklist, December 1, 2003, page 668
Publishers Weekly, December 1, 2003, page 55
School Library Journal, December 2003, page 136

Awards the book has won:
ALA Notable Children's Books, 2004
Pura Belpre Award, Illustration, 2004

Other books you might like:
Gina Freschet, *Beto and the Bone Dance*, 2001
　Beto's dream about his grandmother helps him make an offering in her memory at his favorite festival, the Day of the Dead.
Tony Johnston, *Day of the Dead*, 1997
　The annual Day of the Dead holiday is seen through the eyes of children waiting for the preparations to end so the celebration can begin.
Nancy Luenn, *A Gift for Abuelita: Celebrating the Day of the Dead*, 1998
　In a bilingual title Rosita prepares a gift for her grandmother's altar at the family's celebration of the Day of the Dead.

1031

LYDA MOREHOUSE

Fallen Host

(New York: Roc Books, 2002)

Subject(s): Artificial Intelligence; Science Fiction
Age range(s): Grades 9-Adult

Major character(s): Mouse, Computer Expert; Page, Artificial Intelligence; Emmaline, Religious; Morningstar, Demon
Time period(s): Indeterminate
Locale(s): Earth

Summary: In a world dominated by theocracies, you must declare your religion in order to become a citizen. Those too stubborn to do so are not given access to the LINK, a computer network to which citizens are connected by implant. Mouse is the champion of the rights of non-citizens, and to defend them he has created mouse.net, an alternative to LINK. Mouse.net is run partly by Page, an artificial intelligence unintentionally created by Mouse, which enjoys considerable freedom. This freedom has also attracted some unwanted attention. The Pope, concerned about the possibility of AIs having souls, sends Emmaline, his most computer savvy inquisitor, to investigate Page. Emmaline and Mouse aren't the only ones interested in Page. Morningstar, oldest and most powerful of the fallen angels, is fascinated by Page and is busily investigating the possibilities for tempting artificial intelligences to sin in this sequel to *Archangel Protocol*. (339 pages)

Where it's reviewed:
Booklist, April 15, 2002, page 1390
Library Journal, May 15, 2002, page 130

Other books by the same author:
Messiah Node, 2003
Archangel Protocol, 2001

Other books you might like:
M.T. Anderson, *Feed*, 2002
　The implant that links a girl to the networked feed fails and cuts her off from everyone, including her boyfriend Titus.
William Gibson, *Mona Lisa Overdrive*, 1988
　An artificial intelligence amuses herself by creating art objects and distributing them anonymously.
Sharon Shinn, *Angelica: A Novel of Samaria*, 2003
　The world of Samaria is run by an orbiting artificial intelligence, which communicates through the enhanced humans known as angels.

1032

SUSIE MORGENSTERN
SERGE BLOCH, Illustrator
BILL MAY, Translator

Princesses Are People, Too: Two Modern Fairy Tales

(New York: Viking, 2002)

Subject(s): Princes and Princesses; Humor; Fairy Tales
Age range(s): Grades 3-5
Major character(s): Yona, Royalty (princess), 8-Year-Old; Emma, Royalty (princess), Daughter
Time period(s): Indeterminate
Locale(s): Fictional Country

Summary: Originally published in 1991 and 1992 as separate French tales, the translated stories are presented here in one book. In the first spoof, bored Princess Yona longs to be like other children. As a princess she's allowed to do nothing but remember that she is a princess. After her parents fall on hard times and sell the castle, the family moves into an apartment that offers Princess Yona, and eventually her parents, a more realistic and varied view of life that Yona convinces them to accept and enjoy. Princess Emma seeks only one thing, a prince who can satisfy the itch in the middle of her back. Many princes try, but all fail to meet Emma's demands. Finally, common interests join Emma and the future prince of her dreams. (52 pages)

Where it's reviewed:
Booklist, May 1, 2002, page 1527
Bulletin of the Center for Children's Books, May 2002, page 334
Horn Book Guide, Fall 2002, page 362
Publishers Weekly, April 29, 2002, page 71
School Library Journal, May 2002, page 124

Other books by the same author:
A Book of Coupons, 2001 (Mildred L. Batchelder Honor Book)
Secret Letters from 0 to 10, 1998 (Booklist Editors' Choice)

Other books you might like:
E.D. Baker, *The Frog Princess*, 2002
  Kissing a frog not only does not free the trapped prince, but the act also unexpectedly changes a 14-year-old princess into a frog.
Dick King-Smith, *Lady Lollipop*, 2001
  Spoiled Princess Penelope receives not only the pet pig she demands as her birthday gift but also lessons in behavior so she can care for Lollipop.
Gail Carson Levine, *The Princess Test*, 1999
  In this title in the Princess Tales series sensitive Lorelei lacks a royal heritage but has what it takes to pass a demanding queen's princess test.

1033

MICHAEL MORPURGO

Kensuke's Kingdom

(New York: Scholastic, 2003)

Subject(s): Survival; Islands; Animals/Dogs
Age range(s): Grades 4-8
Major character(s): Kensuke, Survivor, Doctor; Michael, 12-Year-Old; Stella, Dog (sheepdog)
Time period(s): 1980s
Locale(s): Pacific Ocean (island in the Coral Sea)

Summary: Laid off from work, Michael's parents combine their severance pay and some savings to buy a 42-foot sail boat on which they take off around the world. Michael and his sheepdog Stella are on watch one night when they're swept overboard; feeling as though he's dying as he battles to stay afloat, Michael awakens on an island with Stella close by. The island is hot, filled with mosquitoes and seems deserted, yet every morning when Michael awakens he finds fresh water and food. Eventually he meets Kensuke, a former Japanese doctor, who's remained on this island since hearing of the attack on Nagasaki. Figuring that his family has all died, he never chose to return home and now, after an initial standoff, becomes friends with Michael as together they paint, protect the orangutans and play soccer. When rescuers arrive for

Michael, Kensuke opts to remain on his island and both realize what a special friendship they've enjoyed. (164 pages)

Where it's reviewed:
Booklist, February 15, 2003, page 1069
Bulletin of the Center for Children's Books, April 2003, page 324
Publishers Weekly, January 20, 2003, page 82
School Library Journal, March 2003, page 237
Voice of Youth Advocates, June 2003, page 140

Awards the book has won:
ALA Notable Children's Books, 2004

Other books by the same author:
Private Peaceful, 2004
Escape from Shangri-La, 1998
The Butterfly Lion, 1997
The Ghost of Grania O'Malley, 1996

Other books you might like:
Gary Paulsen, *Hatchet*, 1987
  Enroute to visit his father, Brian's plane crashes in the Canadian Northwoods; as the sole survivor, he has to rely on his hatchet to stay alive.
Theodore Taylor, *The Cay*, 1960
  Timothy, an old black sailor, is shipwrecked on a coral island with spoiled, blind Phillip, a young white boy.
Johann Wyss, *The Swiss Family Robinson*, 1814
  A much-loved classic about a family that uses all its ingenuity to survive after being shipwrecked on an island.

1034

GERALD MORRIS

The Ballad of Sir Dinadan

(Boston: Houghton Mifflin, 2003)

Subject(s): Knights and Knighthood; Arthurian Legends
Age range(s): Grades 6-9
Major character(s): Dinadan "Dinny", Knight, Minstrel; Culloch, Knight; Tristram, Knight, Brother (of Dinny); Iseult, Lover (of Tristram)
Time period(s): Indeterminate Past
Locale(s): Fictional Country (King Arthur's Court)

Summary: Dinny's father decides that Dinny must uphold the family name and follow in the family tradition of chivalry, so he knights him, though Dinny would rather be a minstrel. Setting out on his steed, with his armor hidden under a blanket and his stringed rebec close at hand, he heads for King Arthur's court. He meets up with Culloch from Wales who is also heading to court to become a knight, though Culloch isn't the "sharpest sword in the armory." Dinny's older brother Tristram loves Iseult and Dinny finds himself playing a role in their romance, in addition to protecting another knight's lands and defending a woman he admires. Dinny finds humor in the tradition and lore ascribed to the knights and notes that many of them don't live up to the exacting standards of chivalry, though he proves to be a most capable knight. (245 pages)

Where it's reviewed:
Booklist, May 1, 2003, page 1589
Bulletin of the Center for Children's Books, April 2003, page 324

Horn Book, May 2003, page 353
School Library Journal, April 2003, page 166
Voice of Youth Advocates, June 2003, page 152

Other books by the same author:
The Knight and the Lioness, 2005
The Princess, the Crone and the Dung-Cart Knight, 2004
Parsifal's Page, 2001
The Savage Damsel and the Dwarf, 2000

Other books you might like:
Michael Cadnum, *The Leopard Sword*, 2002
Hubert enters a trial by combat and his fellow Squire Edmund finds that a previous crime could imprison him, as the two return to 12th-century England.
Marguerite De Angeli, *A Door in the Wall*, 1949
Though Robin is crippled, he dreams of becoming a knight and, in an unexpected way, is able to help the King.
Katherine Paterson, *Parzival: The Quest of the Grail Knight*, 1998
An unsophisticated lad, Parzival mounts a sway-backed nag and goes in search of King Arthur; his desire to excel overcomes his bumbling moments.

1035

MARISSA MOSS, Author/Illustrator

Max's Logbook
(New York: Scholastic Press, 2003)

Subject(s): Divorce; Diaries; Scientific Experiments
Age range(s): Grades 3-5
Major character(s): Max, Child, Son
Time period(s): 2000s (2003)
Locale(s): United States

Summary: Max is interested in science, just like his scientist parents, and he starts a notebook to record his experiments. He also ends up recording his fears (and inventions, such as a ''Prevent-a-Divorce Machine'' or an ''Instant Happiness Robot'') as his parents fight more and more and eventually decide to separate. After his father moves out, Max continues to describe what it's like to have to redefine his family. (48 pages)

Where it's reviewed:
Booklist, October 15, 2003, page 412
Publishers Weekly, July 14, 2003, page 76
School Library Journal, October 2003, page 132

Other books by the same author:
Max's Mystical Logbook, 2004
Mighty Jackie: The Strike-Out Queen, 2004
Amelia's Notebook, 1999

Other books you might like:
Julia Alvarez, *How Tia Lola Came to Visit/Stay*, 2001
When Miguel's parents get divorced, his Tia Lola comes to stay and help his mother.
Beverly Cleary, *Dear Mr. Henshaw*, 1983
In this Newberry-Award-winning book, Leigh writes to a famous author about his parents' divorce.
Paula Danziger, *You Can't Eat Your Chicken Pox, Amber Brown*, 1995

Amber deals with the fact that her parents' separation is becoming permanent.

1036

MIRIAM MOSS
DELPHINE DURAND, Illustrator

Scritch Scratch
(New York: Orchard Books/Scholastic, Inc., 2002)

Subject(s): Health; School Life; Animals/Insects
Age range(s): Grades 1-4
Major character(s): Ms. Calypso, Teacher; Mr. Trout, Principal; Unnamed Character, Insect (louse), Mother
Time period(s): 2000s
Locale(s): England

Summary: No one notices the tiny insect that crawls into Ms. Calypso's classroom, but soon everyone realizes the impact of her presence. The louse settles into Ms. Calypso's curly red hair and carefully attaches an egg at the base of each strand. As the eggs hatch, the louse's children spread from one head to another through the simple interactions of the teacher and her students. Mr. Trout notifies the parents of the infestation of head lice and the children, after undergoing treatment, return to school louse-free, temporarily. The original louse lives on to begin the process again though she does eventually move on to another classroom. Originally published in 2001 in Great Britain. (28 pages)

Where it's reviewed:
Book for Keeps, September 2002, page 26
Bulletin of the Center for Children's Books, November 2002, page 117
Publishers Weekly, June 10, 2002, page 59
School Library Journal, October 2002, page 121
Tribune Books, September 22, 2002, page 5

Awards the book has won:
Center for Children's Books Best Books, 2002

Other books by the same author:
Don't Forget I Love You, 2004
Bad Hare Day, 2003
Wiley and Jasper, 2003

Other books you might like:
Donna Caffey, *Yikes-lice!*, 1998
A rhyming nonfiction title for younger readers describes a family's fight against lice in their home.
Bobbi Katz, *Lots of Lice*, 1998
A rhyming Hello Reader story humorously discusses the nature of lice and how to protect oneself from them.
Angela Royston, *Head Lice*, 2002
This nonfiction title defines head lice, describes how they are transmitted and explains the treatment necessary to get rid of them.

1037

DIANE MULDROW

Dish Series

(New York: Grosset & Dunlap, 2002-)

Subject(s): Cooks and Cooking; Humor
Age range(s): Grades 4-7
Major character(s): Molly Moore, Twin, 11-Year-Old; Amanda Moore, Twin; Shawn Jordan, 11-Year-Old; Natasha Ross, 11-Year-Old; Peichi Cheng, 11-Year-Old
Time period(s): 2000s
Locale(s): New York, New York (Brooklyn)

Summary: With their mother's busy work schedule, twins Molly and Amanda tire of take-out meals and, with summertime ahead of them, decide to cook chicken piccata one night. Though the dinner is delicious, their dad surprises them with chef's hats and cooking lessons as both parents think a few rules for working with knives and hot pans might be useful. At class they're joined by their friends Shawn and Peichi, as well as their archenemy Natasha. Ignoring Natasha, they do improve their culinary skills and soon start their own cooking business in this humorous series filled not only with recipes and cooking tips, but also problems faced by any preteen.

Where it's reviewed:
Booklist, July 2002, page 1848
School Library Journal, August 2002, page 195

Other books by the same author:
Boiling Point, 2002 (Dish Book 3)
Stirring It Up, 2002 (Dish Book 1)
Turning Up the Heat, 2002 (Dish Book 2)

Other books you might like:
Judie Angell, *Leave the Cooking to Me*, 1990
    Shirley helps a friend's mother with her dinner party and winds up forming Vanessa's Catering.
Jeanne Betancourt, *Not Just Party Girls*, 1988
    Anne, Kate and Janet use their business of theme parties to provide support for one another.
David Haynes, *Business as Usual*, 1997
    For their annual spring economics unit, Bobby and his friends decide to bake and sell chocolate chip cookies at "Marketplace Day."

1038

HESTER MUNDIS

My Chimp Friday: The Nana Banana Chronicles

(New York: Simon & Schuster, 2002)

Subject(s): Animals/Chimpanzees; Family Life; Animals/Chimpanzees
Age range(s): Grades 4-7
Major character(s): Rachel Stelson, 6th Grader; Jared Stelson, Child, Brother; Bucky Greene, Scientist; Friday, Chimpanzee
Time period(s): 2000s
Locale(s): New York, New York (Manhattan)

Summary: Early one morning the eccentric scientist Bucky Greene drops off a baby chimp named Friday at the Stelson's apartment, asking that he be kept for a week but not to tell anyone. Rachel and her brother Jared think that's very strange, but not unusual for a scientist who's working on genetically engineered bananas. The week goes by but Bucky dies from slipping on a banana peel, leaving the Stelson family with a chimpanzee. Of course Rachel and Jared are thrilled because Friday's very smart—he's already learned to use the computer, give tummy rubs to their dog and solve a Rubik's cube. Unfortunately, other people know that Friday's very intelligent, specifically the company for whom Bucky worked, and several attempts are made to kidnap him. Luckily the Stelsons reunite Friday with his sister. This story is based on the author's adventures raising a chimpanzee in Manhattan. (169 pages)

Where it's reviewed:
Booklist, June 2002, page 1724
Horn Book Guide, Fall 2002, page 378
Kirkus Reviews, June 1, 2002, page 808
Publishers Weekly, June 10, 2002, page 60
School Library Journal, June 2002, page 142

Other books by the same author:
Heart Songs for Animal Lovers: True Stories of Devotion, Courage and Love, 1999
No, He's Not a Monkey, He's an Ape and He's My Son, 1976

Other books you might like:
Kate DiCamillo, *The Tiger Rising*, 2001
    Taking pity on a caged tiger he's been hired to feed, Rob releases him, but that results in unexpected tragedy.
Peter Dickinson, *Eva*, 1989
    After an automobile accident, Eva's neuron memory is transferred into the body of a young chimpanzee.
M.E. Kerr, *Snakes Don't Miss Their Mothers*, 2003
    The animals at the Critters shelter offer their opinions about adoptions, potential owners, and one another.

1039

ROBERT MUNSCH
JANET WILSON, Illustrator

Lighthouse: A Story of Remembrance

(New York: Cartwheel/Scholastic, Inc., 2003)

Subject(s): Grandparents; Death; Lighthouses
Age range(s): Grades K-3
Major character(s): Sarah, Child, Daughter
Time period(s): 2000s (2003)
Locale(s): United States

Summary: When Sarah's father was a boy, her grandfather used to take him out to visit a nearby lighthouse in the middle of the night. Now that Sarah's grandfather has died, Sarah wakes her father up one night so that he can take her. On their trip, they talk about her grandfather and what he would do if he were with them. When they reach the top of the lighthouse, Sarah throws a flower, saved from her grandfather's funeral, into the ocean. On their way back down, Sarah declares that she will take her child to the lighthouse one day too. (32 pages)

Where it's reviewed:
Publishers Weekly, January 12, 2004, page 52
School Library Journal, January 2004, page 102

Other books by the same author:
Mmm, Cookies!, 2002
Love You Forever, 1986
The Paper Bag Princess, 1980

Other books you might like:
Trish Cooke, *The Grandad Tree*, 2000
When Vin and Leigh's grandfather dies, they remember him through their apple tree, under which he played with them.
Mavis Jukes, *Blackberries in the Dark*, 1994
After Austin's grandfather dies his grandmother continues the tradition of picking blackberries together in the summer.
Jane Yolen, *Grandad Bill's Song*, 1994
With support from family and friends, a young boy begins to accept his feelings following his grandfather's death.
Jane Breskin Zalben, *Pearl's Marigolds for Grandpa*, 1997
When Pearl's grandfather dies, she remembers him by planting marigolds, as he did every year.

`1040`

ROBERT MUNSCH
MICHAEL MARTCHENKO, Illustrator

More Pies!

(New York: Cartwheel/Scholastic, Inc., 2002)

Subject(s): Food; Contests; Brothers
Age range(s): Grades K-2
Major character(s): Samuel, Child, Son; Unnamed Character, Child, Brother (younger); Unnamed Character, Mother, Cook
Time period(s): 2000s (2002)
Locale(s): Toronto, Canada

Summary: One morning, Samuel wakes up famished. He makes quick work of the cereal, milkshakes, pancakes and fried chicken that his mother prepares for him, but when he declares himself still hungry his mother tells him she's not making him anything more to eat until lunch. Samuel's little brother suggests that he take part in the pie-eating contest down in the park, so he does and beats a fireman, a lumberjack and a construction worker. When Samuel returns home, he discovers that his mom's made pies for his lunch. Samuel's soon unable to eat another bite so his brother helps out. (32 pages)

Where it's reviewed:
Children's Bookwatch, November 2002, page 8
Horn Book, January 2003, page 207
Kirkus Reviews, October 15, 2002, page 1534
School Library Journal, March 2003, page 200

Other books by the same author:
Up, Up, Down, 2001
We Share Everything!, 2000
Love You Forever, 1989

Other books you might like:
Eric Carle, *The Very Hungry Caterpillar*, 1983
No matter how much the tiny caterpillar eats, he is still hungry.
Lensey Namioka, *The Hungriest Boy in the World*, 2001
When Jiro swallows the Hunger Monster he begins eating everything in sight from sushi to fishing nets.
Karma Wilson, *Bear Wants More*, 2003
When Bear wakes up from his winter hibernation, he is starving.

`1041`

ROBERT MUNSCH
MICHAEL MARTCHENKO, Illustrator

Zoom!

(New York: Cartwheel/Scholastic, Inc., 2003)

Subject(s): Transportation; Physically Handicapped; Accidents
Age range(s): Grades K-3
Major character(s): Lauretta, Handicapped, Child
Time period(s): 2000s (2003)
Locale(s): United States

Summary: Lauretta feels that it's time for a new wheelchair, so her mother takes her to the wheelchair store. Model after model is determined by Lauretta to be too slow. Finally Lauretta finds a 92-speed wheelchair that the saleswoman encourages her to take home for a test drive. While zooming down the road, Lauretta is given a speeding ticket by the police, quashing her hopes of keeping the wheelchair. When Lauretta's brother cuts his finger, however, and the family car won't start, Lauretta saves the day by rushing him to the hospital in her wheelchair. (32 pages)

Where it's reviewed:
Booklist, February 1, 2003, page 1000
Bulletin of the Center for Children's Books, April 2003, page 325
School Library Journal, April 2003, page 134

Awards the book has won:
Center for Children's Books Best Books, 2003

Other books by the same author:
Boo!, 2004
More Pies!, 2002
Mortimer, 1985

Other books you might like:
Jamee Riggio Heelan, *Rolling Along: The Story of Taylor and His Wheelchair*, 2000
Taylor, a young boy with cerebral palsy, describes what his day is like.
Ellen Senisi, *All Kinds of Friends, Even Green!*, 2002
Moses, in a wheelchair due to spina bifida, chooses to write a school assignment about a neighbor's iguana that has overcome physical challenges.
Jeanne Willis, *Susan Laughs*, 2000
Susan does all the things that other kids do, just from a wheelchair.

1042

CLAIRE RUDOLF MURPHY

Free Radical

(New York: Clarion Books, 2002)

Subject(s): Sports/Baseball; Identity, Concealed
Age range(s): Grades 7-10
Major character(s): Luke McHenry, 15-Year-Old, Baseball Player; Faith/Mary Margaret McHenry/Cunningham, Fugitive, Mother (of Luke)
Time period(s): 2000s
Locale(s): Fairbanks, Alaska; Oakland, California

Summary: Luke is convinced this will be the summer he lands a spot on Alaska's All-Star baseball team and then heads to California for the regional playoffs. Just as he nears his goal, his mother reveals her involvement in a protest incident thirty years ago that resulted in the death of a Berkeley student. Feeling Luke is now old enough to be left under the care of his stepfather, Faith wants to turn herself in, but this action will upset all of Luke's plans for baseball season. While family and friends give her support, Luke must learn to accept and forgive her actions, even as he arranges a meeting between the bombing victim's family and his mother. (198 pages)

Where it's reviewed:
Booklist, March 15, 2000, page 1252
Bulletin of the Center for Children's Books, June 2002, page 375
Publishers Weekly, January 21, 2002
School Library Journal, March 2002, page 235
Voice of Youth Advocates, June 2002, page 121

Other books by the same author:
Children of the Gold Rush, 2001
Gold Rush Dogs, 2001
Gold Rush Women, 1997
Gold Star Sister, 1994
To the Summit, 1992

Other books you might like:
Alden R. Carter, *Bull Catcher*, 1997
  Through death, divorce, friendships and the different seasons of the year, Bull and his best friend Jeff play baseball.
John Gilstrap, *At All Costs*, 1998
  Jake, Carolyn and their son Travis are on the run, fleeing from a government that holds them responsible for the destruction of an ammunition plant.
Mary Elizabeth Ryan, *Alias*, 1997
  Researching the Vietnam War on the Internet, Toby spots a photo of his mother and realizes she was involved in a campus bombing.

1043

MARY MURPHY, Author/Illustrator

I Kissed the Baby!

(Cambridge, MA: Candlewick Press, 2003)

Subject(s): Babies; Animals; Love
Age range(s): Preschool-Kindergarten
Major character(s): Unnamed Character, Duck, Mother

Time period(s): Indeterminate
Locale(s): Fictional Country

Summary: Excitedly a diverse group of animals ask each other if they've seen the baby. Some have not only seen it, but they've fed the baby, sung to the baby and even tickled the baby. The mother duck, of course, has kissed the baby and plans to do it again. The baby's comment is ''Quack, quack.'' (20 pages)

Where it's reviewed:
Booklist, April 1, 2003, page 1403
Bulletin of the Center for Children's Books, June 2003, page 414
Horn Book, July 2003, page 445
Publishers Weekly, April 7, 2003, page 64
School Library Journal, May 2003, page 126

Awards the book has won:
Publishers Weekly Best Children's Books, 2003
School Library Journal Best Books, 2003

Other books by the same author:
The Alphabet Keeper, 2003
How Kind!, 2002
Koala and the Flower, 2002

Other books you might like:
Nancy Tafuri, *Have You Seen My Duckling?*, 1984
  With her ducklings following, a mother duck searches the pond for her one missing offspring in a Caldecott Honor Book.
Martin Waddell, *Webster J. Duck*, 2001
  As newly hatched Webster J. Duck searches for his mother he depends on the sounds of the animals he meets to determine where she is.
Margaret Wild, *Kiss Kiss!*, 2004
  Eagerly running out to play one morning, Baby Hippo forgets to kiss his mother.

1044

RITA MURPHY

Harmony

(New York: Delacorte, 2002)

Subject(s): Magic; Family
Age range(s): Grades 7-12
Major character(s): Harmony McClean, 15-Year-Old; Nettie Mae McClean, Healer; Felix McGillicuddy, Farmer, Inventor
Time period(s): 2000s
Locale(s): Hamlin Mountains, Tennessee

Summary: Harmony's arrival is anything but prosaic for she is found in the chicken coop after it is hit by a falling star. Named Harmony in honor of the harmony of the spheres, she grows up warmly sheltered by both Felix and Nettie Mae in the Tennessee mountains. Nettie Mae is a healer for the local people and seems to have special powers, so when Harmony begins to manifest some powers of her own, no one is overwhelmed, except perhaps Harmony herself. Harmony just wants to be normal, and since her spectacular arrival, everyone considers her odd. When Nettie Mae's Old Ones, some special magical trees left in her trust by Nettie's Cherokee mother, are threatened by a rapacious logging company, Harmony discovers a reason to embrace her special gifts. (128 pages)

Where it's reviewed:
Booklist, April 15, 2002, page 222
Horn Book, January 2003, page 81
Publishers Weekly, September 23, 2002, page 73
School Library Journal, October 2002, page 169
Voice of Youth Advocates, December 2002, page 400

Other books by the same author:
Black Angels, 2001
Night Flying, 2001

Other books you might like:
Holly Black, *Tithe: A Modern Faerie Tale*, 2002
Kaye couldn't be more different from Harmony, and her life is far from Harmony's sheltered situation, but she too has special gifts.
Neil Gaiman, *Stardust*, 1998
After he promises his beloved a falling star, a young man goes looking for one in Faerie and discovers that the star doesn't like the idea.
L.M. Montgomery, *Anne of Green Gables*, 2000
Anne's adoptive aunt and uncle are similar to Felix and Nettie Mae and they give Anne an education in humanity that is comparable to Harmony's.

1045

JAYE MURRAY

Bottled Up

(New York: Dial, 2003)

Subject(s): Family Problems; Brothers; Drugs
Age range(s): Grades 8-12
Major character(s): Phillip "Pip" Downs, 17-Year-Old; Michael "Mikey" Downs, Child, Brother (of Pip); Mr. Giraldi, Principal; Claire Butler, Counselor
Time period(s): 2000s
Locale(s): United States

Summary: Cutting or sleeping through class, smoking pot, drinking liquor and shooting off his mouth seem to be Pip's primary activities. At home his mother eats Valium and his father drinks and is abusive, leaving Pip feeling jaded against both of them. If it weren't for his brother Mikey, it's doubtful there'd be anyone he'd care about. At school Mr. Giraldi delivers an ultimatum: Pip is to talk to the counselor Claire Butler and attend all his classes or he'll contact Pip's father about the class cutting and misbehaving. Pip's not afraid of anyone, except his father, for he knows how violent and abusive his father can become. He agrees to the counseling and he begins attending class, but he doesn't give up his daily oblivion through his drugs. It takes Pip a long time to realize that some people in his life do care about him, but gradually Claire and Mr. Giraldi break through his shell. Pip really turns around when he realizes how his behavior, on top of that of his dad's, affects his little brother Mikey in this author's poignant first novel. (220 pages)

Where it's reviewed:
Bulletin of the Center for Children's Books, July 2003, page 455
Library Media Connection, February 2004, page 72
Publishers Weekly, June 16, 2003, page 72
School Library Journal, June 2003, page 146
Voice of Youth Advocates, August 2003, page 226

Awards the book has won:
ALA Best Books for Young Adults, 2004

Other books you might like:
Ben Mikaelsen, *Touching Spirit Bear*, 2001
Cole's mean, arrogant and vicious, traits he's learned from his abusive father, until he's sent to an isolated Alaskan island to rethink his ways.
Joyce Carol Oates, *Freaky Green Eyes*, 2003
Franky finds a secret, inner strength that helps her survive her parent's disintegrating marriage and break free of her controlling father.
S.L. Rottman, *Stetson*, 2002
Raised by his father who spends all his money and time at the local bar, Stet earns food money by charging to disrupt classes at school.

1046

MARTINE MURRAY, Author/Illustrator

The Slightly True Story of Cedar B. Hartley (Who Planned to Live an Unusual Life)

(New York: Arthur A. Levine/Scholastic, 2002)

Subject(s): Family Life; Friendship; Sports/Gymnastics
Age range(s): Grades 5-8
Major character(s): Cedar B. Hartley, 12-Year-Old; Kite Freeman, Gymnast; Ricci, Aged Person (Yugoslavian); Barnaby Hartley, Brother, Runaway
Time period(s): 2000s
Locale(s): Australia

Summary: Cedar's "green thumb" for people will certainly help her intention of leading an interesting life as she's already collecting friends by the truckload. This summer she meets Kite, the son of circus trainers, and when he offers to teach her acrobatics, she jumps at the chance to learn these routines. Cedar learns enough tumbling tricks that when her friend Ricci's dog needs an operation, she and Kite put on a show to earn money. This is also the summer that she finds out more about her father, who died when she was very young, and why her brother Barnaby ran away from home rather than attend boarding school. Gregarious and a friend to all, Cedar's just beginning what will surely be an unusual, fun-filled life in this author's first novel. (233 pages)

Where it's reviewed:
Booklist, November 15, 2003, page 608
Bulletin of the Center for Children's Books, September 2003, page 25
Horn Book, September 2003, page 615
School Library Journal, August 2003, page 164
Voice of Youth Advocates, October 2003, page 316

Awards the book has won:
Center for Children's Books Best Books, 2003

Other books you might like:
Katherine Holubitsky, *Last Summer in Agatha*, 2001
    Rachel spends the summer with her aunt and uncle and quickly makes friends, including Michael with whom she rides bikes and canoes.
Marilyn Singer, *The Circus Lunicus*, 2000
    A fairy lizard ensures that Solly gets to the Circus Lunicus, his first step in becoming one of its stars in this wonderfully wacky tale.
Jerry Spinelli, *Maniac Magee*, 1990
    Maniac is legendary for bringing together kids from the black East End and the white West End, mixing them in a such a way that prejudices are forgotten.
Jean Thesman, *In the House of the Queen's Beasts*, 2001
    New to the neighborhood, Emily's happy to make friends with Rowan as they share a wonderful tree house in Emily's backyard.

1047

JON J. MUTH, Author/Illustrator

Stone Soup

(New York: Scholastic Press, 2003)

Subject(s): Folklore; Sharing; Cooks and Cooking
Age range(s): Grades 1-3
Major character(s): Hok, Religious; Lok, Religious; Siew, Religious
Time period(s): Indeterminate Past
Locale(s): China

Summary: Three traveling monks come upon a village that has known such hard times that the villagers are suspicious not only of strangers but also of one another. It is clear to Siew that the villagers do not know happiness and, with help from Hok and Lok, he attempts to give them some by teaching them how to make stone soup. In the middle of the vacant village square, Lok gathers twigs so Hok can start a fire under the pot Siew fills with water. A curious young girl helps the monks find three stones and then she runs home to get a bigger pot for Siew. Her actions attract all the other residents who come out of their homes to learn more about the fire and the pot. As Siew, Hok and Lok stir the pot and comment on other times they have made the soup with additional ingredients, the villagers offer some of their hoarded food. By evening, the entire village assembles for a banquet of soup, rice, steamed buns, sweet cakes and lychee nuts and an evening of stories and songs. From the monks the villagers learn the happiness that comes from sharing. (32 pages)

Where it's reviewed:
Booklist, January 2003, page 900
Bulletin of the Center for Children's Books, March 2003, page 282
Five Owls, 2003, page 43
Horn Book, March 2003, page 221
Riverbank Review, Summer 2003, page 30

Awards the book has won:
Riverbank Review Books of Distinction, 2004

Other books by the same author:
The Three Questions, 2002
Swamp Thing: Roots, 1998
Dracula: A Symphony in Moonlight and Nightmares, 1986

Other books you might like:
Marcia Brown, *Stone Soup*, 1986
    In one of many retellings of the tale, three hungry soldiers claiming to make soup from water and a stone outwit villagers hoarding food.
Susan Stevens Crummel, *Tumbleweed Stew*, 2000
    Jack Rabbit has a hankering for tumbleweed stew. In no time other animals contribute enough ingredients to really flavor the pot.
Tony Ross, *Stone Soup*, 1987
    A hen cleverly avoids becoming a wolf's dinner by offering him a taste of her stone soup.

1048

JON J. MUTH, Author/Illustrator

The Three Questions

(New York: Scholastic Press, 2002)

Subject(s): Conduct of Life; Animals
Age range(s): Grades 1-4
Major character(s): Nikolai, Friend, Child; Leo, Turtle
Time period(s): Indeterminate Past
Locale(s): Earth

Summary: Based on a short story of the same name by Leo Tolstoy this story is written for a younger audience. Nikolai seeks to be a good person and decides that the answers to three questions will enable him to achieve that. He first asks the three questions of three animal friends each of whom gives him a different answer. Feeling unsatisfied Nikolai hikes to a mountaintop to ask wise Leo. Although he doesn't realize it, Nikolai's actions while visiting Leo provide the answers to his questions; Leo simply points that out to him. (32 pages)

Where it's reviewed:
Booklist, March 15, 2002, page 1264
Horn Book Guide, Fall 2002, page 362
Kirkus Reviews, March 15, 2002, page 420
Publishers Weekly, February 11, 2002, page 187
School Library Journal, June 2002, page 104

Awards the book has won:
Notable Social Studies Trade Books for Young People, 2003

Other books by the same author:
Stone Soup, 2003

Other books you might like:
Donna Jo Napoli, *Albert*, 2001
    Reclusive Albert learns it's important to become more outgoing so he can accommodate the needs of a pair of birds nesting on his hand.
Ellen Stoll Walsh, *Pip's Magic*, 1994
    In the process of searching for magic answers to his fear of the dark, Pip overcomes his problem on his own.
Douglas Wood, *Old Turtle*, 1991
    Wise Old Turtle stops the incessant arguing on Earth with the observation that all God's creatures must listen if the Earth is to heal.

1049

ANNA MYERS

Flying Blind

(New York: Walker, 2003)

Subject(s): Animals/Birds; Orphans; Wildlife Conservation
Age range(s): Grades 4-8
Major character(s): Ben Riley, 13-Year-Old; Murphy, Bird (macaw); Elisha Riley, Salesman, Father (adoptive father of Ben); Bess Gilbert, 12-Year-Old, Orphan; Enoch Gilbert, 16-Year-Old, Orphan
Time period(s): 1900s
Locale(s): Flamingo, Florida

Summary: Abandoned by his mother when just a baby, Ben is adopted by Elisha Riley who makes his living peddling Professor Riley's Magic Elixir at their Shakespearean Elocution Show. Professor Riley also has a macaw who exhibits premonitions, the latest of which has them traveling to Florida to save birds who are being killed for their feathers. Though Ben is determined to save the beautiful herons and egrets from extermination, his head and heart are confused after meeting siblings Bess and Enoch, orphans who kill birds for their plumage in order to have food to eat. Telling the game warden about these two, Ben also warns them of their likely arrest as he tries to play fair with everyone. As it turns out, Bess and Enoch are only following the orders of Runt Lawson, who uses them as his underlings to acquire the plumage. As the book ends, Professor Riley makes plans to increase the number of travelers in his Elocution Show in a story of hope and caring. (180 pages)

Where it's reviewed:
Booklist, September 15, 2003, page 240
Kirkus Reviews, August 15, 2003, page 1076
School Library Journal, November 2003, page 143
Voice of Youth Advocates, October 2003, page 326

Other books by the same author:
Hoggee, 2004
Stolen by the Sea, 2002
Tulsa Burning, 2002
When the Bough Breaks, 2000
Captain's Command, 1999

Other books you might like:
Cynthia DeFelice, *Lostman's River*, 1994
    Tyler unwittingly betrays the location of a friend's secret rookery in the Everglades, and then must flee the plume hunters who attack.
Jean Craighead George, *The Missing 'Gator of Gumbo Limbo: An Ecological Mystery*, 1992
    A group of homeless people saves Dajun, the 12-foot alligator that keeps the water of Gumbo Limbo Hammock clean by eating the algae.
Ben Mikaelsen, *Stranded*, 1995
    Self-conscious about her prosthesis, Koby feels a new sense of purpose when she helps rescue a whale and its baby.

1050

LAURIE MYERS
MICHAEL DOOLING, Illustrator

Lewis and Clark and Me: A Dog's Tale

(New York: Henry Holt and Company, 2002)

Subject(s): Animals/Dogs; American West; Adventure and Adventurers
Age range(s): Grades 3-6
Major character(s): Seaman, Dog (Newfoundland), Narrator; Meriwether Lewis, Explorer, Animal Lover
Time period(s): 1800s (1803-1806)
Locale(s): United States

Summary: Based on excerpts from Lewis's journal Seaman narrates fictionalized accounts of certain episodes of the Lewis and Clark expedition. Beginning with Lewis's purchase of the large Newfoundland, Seaman relates his utter devotion to his new master and the events of most interest to a dog. In one chapter he hunts squirrels swimming across a river and thus providing food for the travelers; in another his barking causes a rampaging buffalo to alter his path just enough to avoid trampling Lewis, asleep in his tent. A beaver bite threatens Seaman's life and Indians try to kidnap him, but with Lewis's protection, he survives the journey. A concluding "Afterword" gives background to the story. (63 pages)

Where it's reviewed:
Booklist, September 1, 2002, page 125
Bulletin of the Center for Children's Books, October 2002, page 71
Horn Book, September 2002, page 577
Publishers Weekly, July 29, 2002, page 74
School Library Journal, September 2002, page 230

Awards the book has won:
IRA Teachers' Choices, 2003

Other books by the same author:
Surviving Brick Johnson, 2000 (ALA Notable Children's Book)
Guinea Pigs Don't Talk, 1994
Garage Sale Fever, 1993

Other books you might like:
Betsy Byars, *My Dog, My Hero*, 2000
    Eight stories describe the heroics of dogs selected as finalists in a fictional newspaper contest for the "My Hero" award.
Patricia Reeder Eubank, *Seaman's Journal: On the Trail with Lewis and Clark*, 2002
    Seaman records his adventures as a companion to Lewis.
Gail Langer Karwoski, *Seaman: The Dog Who Explored the West with Lewis & Clark*, 1999
    Throughout the long, dangerous journey, Seaman proves a valiant companion to all members of the Corps of Discovery.
Roland Smith, *The Captain's Dog*, 1999
    Seaman tells the story of his travels with the Lewis and Clark expedition.

1051

WALTER DEAN MYERS

The Beast

(New York: Scholastic, 2003)

Subject(s): Interpersonal Relations; Drugs; African Americans
Age range(s): Grades 9-12
Major character(s): Anthony "Spoon" Witherspoon, 12th Grader, 16-Year-Old; Gabi, Girlfriend (of Spoon); Rafael, Brother (of Gabi)
Time period(s): 2000s
Locale(s): New York, New York; Connecticut

Summary: Taking the chance that spending his senior year at Wallingford Academy will help him be accepted at Brown or another prestigious college, Spoon leaves Harlem and his girlfriend Gabi. Returning home for Christmas break, he can't believe how much his old world has changed since he left. He learns that a respected girl is now pregnant, a friend has dropped out of school, Gabi's brother is trying to run with a gang and his beloved Gabi, who wrote unbelievable poetry, has been caught by "the beast," heroin. Gabi blames her addiction on her mother's illness and her blind grandfather moving in with them, but all Spoon knows is that once you're hooked, it's hard to break free. He does what he can to help her, but realizes that his life lies in a different direction for he's determined to attend college, and perhaps even grad school, with or without Gabi. (170 pages)

Where it's reviewed:
Bulletin of the Center for Children's Books, January 2004, page 199
Horn Book, November 2003, page 752
Publishers Weekly, December 1, 2003, page 57
School Library Journal, December 2003, page 157
Voice of Youth Advocates, October 2003, page 316

Other books by the same author:
Shooter, 2004
Voices from Harlem, 2004
The Dream Bearer, 2003
Handbook for Boys: A Novel, 2002
Bad Boy: A Memoir, 2001

Other books you might like:
Sharon M. Draper, *Darkness Before Dawn*, 2001
    Senior Keisha accepts track coach Jonathan's dinner invitation, but regrets it when the dinner turns to a sexual assault.
Linda Glovach, *Beauty Queen*, 1998
    A stint at topless dancing to earn enough money to flee her abusive home leads Samantha into heroin addiction from which there's no escape.
Jess Mowry, *Babylon Boyz*, 1997
    Three young boys from Oakland's inner city, trying to escape from their drug-riddled neighborhood, find a drug dealer's suitcase filled with money.

1052

WALTER DEAN MYERS

The Dream Bearer

(New York: Amistad/HarperCollins, 2003)

Subject(s): African Americans; Fathers and Sons; Family Life
Age range(s): Grades 5-8
Major character(s): David Curry, 12-Year-Old; Reuben Curry, Father; Moses Littlejohn, Aged Person, Streetperson
Time period(s): 2000s
Locale(s): New York, New York (Harlem)

Summary: David senses the tension in his family as his older brother spends more time on the streets, his mother struggles to adapt a building into a homeless shelter and his mentally-unstable father battles his own demons. Then one day on the playground he meets Moses Littlejohn who tells him he's a "dream bearer" and proceeds to share heartfelt stories of the centuries-old experiences of African Americans. By books' end, David has integrated these dreams into his own as he learns about anger and forgiveness, builds his relationship with his troubled father and accepts the loss of his brother to the streets. (181 pages)

Where it's reviewed:
Bulletin of the Center for Children's Books, July 2003, page 455
Kirkus Reviews, May 15, 2003, page 754
Publishers Weekly, June 9, 2003, page 52
School Library Journal, June 2003, page 146
Voice of Youth Advocates, June 2003, page 140

Other books by the same author:
Here in Harlem: Poems in Many Voices, 2004
Shooter, 2004
The Beast, 2003
145th Street: Short Stories, 2000
Motown and Didi: A Love Story, 1984

Other books you might like:
Sharon G. Flake, *Money Hungry*, 2001
    After being temporarily homeless, Raspberry becomes obsessive about saving money to ensure never returning to the streets.
Mildred D. Taylor, *The Land*, 2001
    Paul-Edward, son of a slave and a white master, faces almost insurmountable odds in his attempt to fulfill his dream and buy some land.
Virginia Euwer Wolff, *Make Lemonade*, 1993
    LaVaughn and her single-parent mother make the most of life, though they're surrounded by poverty, gangs, and tenements.

1053

WALTER DEAN MYERS
MATTHEW BANDSUCH, Illustrator

Handbook for Boys: A Novel

(New York: HarperCollins, 2002)

Subject(s): Conduct of Life; African Americans; Juvenile Detention Centers

Age range(s): Grades 7-10

Major character(s): Jimmy Lynch, 16-Year-Old, Juvenile Delinquent; Kevin, 17-Year-Old, Juvenile Delinquent; Duke Wilson, Hairdresser (barber); Edward "Cap" Mills, Aged Person; Claudio "Mister M" Morales, Aged Person

Time period(s): 2000s

Locale(s): New York, New York (Harlem)

Summary: No way did Jimmy want to be in "Duke's Torture Chamber," but he didn't have much choice when the alternative was a juvenile facility. Jimmy's temper lands him in trouble when he punches a student at his school and breaks his nose. Appearing before the judge on assault charges, he opts for six months with Duke in a community-mentoring program. Every afternoon he and Kevin, in trouble for smoking marijuana, arrive at Duke's barbershop to clean up, where they also hear the conversations of Duke, his customers and his two good "side line quarterbacks" Mister M and Cap. There's a lot to learn about living from the dialogue in the barbershop, but it takes Jimmy a while to appreciate the stories he hears from men who either strive for success or just react to the happenings in their life. (179 pages)

Where it's reviewed:

Bulletin of the Center for Children's Books, July 2002, page 412

Kliatt, May 2002, page 12

Publishers Weekly, April 22, 2002, page 70

School Library Journal, May 2002, page 157

Voice of Youth Advocates, August 2002, page 195

Awards the book has won:

Smithsonian's Notable Books for Children/Older Readers, 2002

Other books by the same author:

The Beast, 2003

The Journal of Biddy Owens: The Negro Leagues, Birmingham, Alabama, 1948, 2001 (My Name Is America)

145th Street: Short Stories, 2000

Monster, 1999

Slam!, 1996

Other books you might like:

Will Hobbs, *Bearstone*, 1989

 Cloyd discovers love, along with his Indian heritage, when sent by his social worker to stay with the widowed rancher Walter.

S.L. Rottman, *Hero*, 1997

 Sentenced to community service hours at crusty Mr. Hassler's ranch, Sean learns what's important and how to protect it.

Diana Wieler, *Last Chance Summer*, 1991

 Marl is given one last chance at a group home before being sent to an institution; his friendship with Goat keeps him straight.

1054

LAUREN MYRACLE

Kissing Kate

(New York: Dutton, 2003)

Subject(s): Friendship; Identity; Homosexuality/Lesbianism

Age range(s): Grades 9-12

Major character(s): Kate, 16-Year-Old; Lissa, 16-Year-Old; Kimberly "Ariel" Thomas, 10th Grader

Time period(s): 2000s

Locale(s): Atlanta, Georgia

Summary: Friends for five years, Lissa and Kate find their friendship tested beyond endurance the night they're at a party and inebriated Kate kisses Lissa, and Lissa kisses her back. Lissa wonders about her sexuality while Kate becomes homophobic about their kiss, clinging even more closely to her boyfriend. Lissa gradually spreads her wings beyond Kate, works for Entrees on Trays where she meets offbeat Ariel, spends more time with her little sister, and helps her shy uncle as he embarks on a romance. Is she a lesbian? Lissa's not sure, but she is willing to accept whoever she turns out to be in this author's first novel. (198 pages)

Where it's reviewed:

Booklist, August 2003, page 1972

Bulletin of the Center for Children's Books, May 2003, page 373

Publishers Weekly, March 17, 2003, page 77

School Library Journal, April 2003, page 166

Voice of Youth Advocates, April 2003, page 55

Awards the book has won:

ALA Best Books for Young Adults, 2004

Other books by the same author:

Eleven, 2004

Ttyl, 2004

Other books you might like:

Nancy Garden, *Annie on My Mind*, 1982

 Lisa and Annie fall in love, but are afraid to tell anyone of their relationship.

David Levithan, *Boy Meets Boy*, 2003

 At the local bookstore happily gay Paul meets new kid Noah, the boy of his dreams, and immediately falls in love in this first novel.

Sara Ryan, *Empress of the World*, 2001

 Attending a summer program for gifted students, Nic is amazed when she falls for Battle and moves into a relationship that escalates from kissing to sneaking out.

Alex Sanchez, *Rainbow Boys*, 2001

 Jason, Kyle and Nelson face their senior year, and life-changing decisions, as they deal with their sexual identity.

1055

ANN WHITEHEAD NAGDA
STEPHANIE ROTH, Illustrator

Meow Means Mischief

(New York: Holiday House, 2003)

Subject(s): Animals/Cats; Difference; Grandparents
Age range(s): Grades 2-4
Major character(s): Rana, Student—Elementary School; Grandma, Grandmother; Mom, Mother
Time period(s): 2000s (2003)

Summary: Rana and her family have just moved to a new town and Rana is having a hard time making friends and fitting in at school. To make matters worse, Rana's parents are going on vacation and her grandparents are coming from India to baby-sit. The night of her grandparents' arrival, Rana discovers a stray kitten outside the door that she wants to keep. Mom allows Rana to keep the cat for the week with the understanding a permanent decision will wait until her parents return. The kitten's bad behavior upsets Grandma, but with the help of some of her classmates, Rana is able to turn the tide and get her family to accept the cat. (92 pages)

Where it's reviewed:
Booklist, October 1, 2003, page 321
Bulletin of the Center for Children's Books, January 2004, page 199
School Library Journal, October 2003, page 132

Other books by the same author:
Snake Charmer, 2002
Dear Whiskers, 2000
Bamboo Valley: A Story of a Chinese Bamboo Forest, 1997

Other books you might like:
Kate DiCamillo, *Because of Winn-Dixie*, 2000
    With the help of her dog, Winn-Dixie, Opal is able to meet residents of her new town and learn more about her long-gone mother.
Marisa Montes, *A Crazy, Mixed-Up Spanglish Day*,
    Gabi struggles with the conflict between her Spanish-speaking family and her English-speaking school, but is happy when her grandma comes to visit.
Jyotsna Sreenivasan, *Aruna's Journeys*, 1997
    Aruna's family moved to Ohio from India seven years ago, but she still worries about being "different".

1056

BEVERLEY NAIDOO

Out of Bounds: Seven Stories of Conflict

(New York: HarperCollins, 2003)

Subject(s): Race Relations; Apartheid
Age range(s): Grades 5-8
Time period(s): 20th century (1948-2000)
Locale(s): South Africa

Summary: In seven short stories, one per decade from the 1940s to the present, the author tells the story of apartheid in South Africa. Beginning with "The Dare," in 1948, a white girl steals a poinsettia flower from a neighbor but is untroubled when a young black boy is caned for the same offense. "The Noose," takes place in 1955 with the reclassification of a boy's father as African, which has serious implications for keeping his job or remaining with his family. By 2000 there's some hope in "Out of Bounds," when a young African boy and an Indian boy work together to help a young pregnant woman. A timetable of Apartheid history completes this heart-wrenching book. (175 pages)

Where it's reviewed:
Bulletin of the Center for Children's Books, February 2003, page 246
Horn Book, March 2003, page 214
Publishers Weekly, December 16, 2002, page 68
Riverbank Review, Spring 2003, page 44
School Library Journal, January 2003, page 141

Awards the book has won:
ALA Best Books for Young Adults, 2004

Other books by the same author:
The Other Side of Truth, 2001

No Turning Back: A Novel of South Africa, 1997
Chain of Fire, 1990
Journey to Jo'Burg: A South African Story, 1986

Other books you might like:
Carolyn Coman, *Many Stones*, 2000
Berry's sister is murdered while volunteering in South Africa, making a trip there for the dedication of her sister's memorial especially difficult.
Hazel Rochman, *Somehow Tenderness Survives: Stories of Southern Africa*, 1988
Growing up in South Africa under apartheid is captured in this collection of short stories and autobiographical sketches.
Norman Silver, *An Eye for Color*, 1993
This group of stories reflects Basil's experiences as a Jewish teen in a world organized by apartheid.

1057

KATHERINE RILEY NAKAMURA
LINNEA RILEY, Illustrator

Song of Night: It's Time to Go to Bed
(New York: Blue Sky Press, Scholastic, Inc., 2002)

Subject(s): Animals; Stories in Rhyme; Bedtime
Age range(s): Preschool
Time period(s): Indeterminate
Locale(s): Fictional Country

Summary: Animal parents follow familiar bedtime routines with their offspring. Some oversee bath time; some read stories or sing a song. Some little ones make a mess brushing their teeth while others quietly slumber under a parent's watchful eye. A full moon shines overhead, crickets add a lullaby and with one last, loving, parental kiss, little ones sleep. This collaboration with her mother/illustrator is the author's first book. (40 pages)

Where it's reviewed:
Booklist, February 1, 2002, page 940
Bulletin of the Center for Children's Books, April 2002, page 290
Horn Book Guide, Fall 2002, page 309
Publishers Weekly, January 7, 2002, page 63
School Library Journal, May 2002, page 124

Awards the book has won:
Center for Children's Books Best Books, 2002

Other books you might like:
Kathi Appelt, *Bayou Lullaby*, 1995
A rhyming lullaby about the animals of the bayou soothes a little girl at bedtime.
Margaret Wise Brown, *Goodnight Moon*, 1947
In a classic bedtime story, a little rabbit's evening ritual is to say goodnight to everything in sight, including the moon, shining outside.
John Burningham, *Hushabye*, 2001
Tired creatures from fish to frogs to bears to kittens seek a place to spend the night.
Mem Fox, *Time for Bed*, 1993
Mothers the world over are putting their kittens, lambs, fawns and children to sleep.

1058

LENSEY NAMIOKA

An Ocean Apart, a World Away
(New York: Delacorte, 2002)

Subject(s): College Life; Prejudice; Interpersonal Relations
Age range(s): Grades 7-10
Major character(s): Yanyan "Sheila", Teenager, Student—College; Liang Baoshu, Revolutionary
Time period(s): 1920s (1921)
Locale(s): Nanjing, China; Ithaca, New York

Summary: At a time when most Chinese women have bound feet and think only of marriage, Yanyan refuses to cave in to cultural demands and dreams of studying western medicine in America. Her father, who has lived in Europe, supports her dreams though they almost fall apart when Yanyan meets and falls for Liang. Liang is a rebel who wants to restore the Manchu government and asks her to come with him when he runs off to be part of the political overthrow. Considering his offer, common sense prevails and Yanyan sails to America to enroll at Cornell University. In this work that continues *Ties That Bind, Ties That Break*, Yanyan learns to deal with a different cultural problem—prejudice against the Chinese. (197 pages)

Where it's reviewed:
Booklist, June 2002, page 1708
Kliatt, July 2002, page 13
Publishers Weekly, July 8, 2002, page 50
School Library Journal, July 2002, page 123
Voice of Youth Advocates, July 2002, page 121

Other books by the same author:
Half and Half, 2003
Ties That Bind, Ties That Break, 1999
Den of the White Fox, 1997
April and the Dragon Lady, 1994

Other books you might like:
Pearl Buck, *A House Divided*, 1935
Yuan spends time in America as a student, but returns to China, marries a girl of his own race and resolves to help his people.
Sook Nyul Choi, *Gathering of Pearls*, 1994
After escaping from North Korea, Sookan adapts to American culture when she attends college in New York.
Ruthann Lum McCunn, *The Moon Pearl*, 2000
Three Chinese girls defy tradition when they refuse to become either wives or nuns and so begin the spinsterhood movement of the Pearl River district.

1059

DONNA JO NAPOLI

Breath
(New York: Atheneum/Simon & Schuster, 2003)

Subject(s): Middle Ages; Family Life; Plague
Age range(s): Grades 7-10
Major character(s): Salz, 12-Year-Old; Bertram, Brother (of Salz); Grossmutter, Grandmother (of Salz)

Time period(s): 13th century
Locale(s): Hameln, Germany (Saxony)

Summary: Subject to constant coughing and shortness of breath, Salz's Grossmutter has helped him survive by pounding on his back to break up the phlegm that collects and teaching him to walk on his hands to alleviate the pressure on his lungs. His life has been one constant struggle against pain but, when young and old around him begin to die, he's not affected because he doesn't drink the beer that's been made with ergot poisoned grain. Hallucinating from the ergot, Bertram tries to kill Salz, convinced his brother is the source of his illness, but Grossmutter intervenes and is killed instead. A trial ensues with first Bertram and then Salz as the defendant; only the priest's intervention saves him. The villagers finally hire a piper to draw out the rats from the town, which they think will reduce the amount of sickness, but when the task is complete and they refuse to pay him, he pipes their children away from Hameln. Witnessing all this, Salz and his adopted sister flee their town for a new beginning in this retelling of *The Pied Piper of Hameln*. (260 pages)

Where it's reviewed:
Bulletin of the Center for Children's Books, October 2003, page 72
Horn Book, January 2004, page 85
Kliatt, November 2003, page 8
School Library Journal, November 2003, page 143
Voice of Youth Advocates, December 2003, page 416

Awards the book has won:
ALA Best Books for Young Adults, 2004

Other books by the same author:
Bound, 2004
North, 2004
Song of the Magdalene, 2004
The Great God Pan, 2003
Shelley Shock, 2000

Other books you might like:
Malcolm Bosse, *Captives of Time*, 1987
    Two siblings struggle across medieval Europe, driven by outlaws, disease and developing technology.
Deborah Ellis, *A Company of Fools*, 2002
    Sent to amuse the citizens of their plague-ridden village, the choirboys of St. Luc fear their prize singer is being used to fill the abbey's coffers.
Mary Hooper, *At the Sign of the Sugared Plum*, 2003
    Hannah and her sister Sarah keep their confectioner's shop going during the plague by concocting harmless herbal sweets as a disease preventative.
Tanith Lee, *Red as Blood, or Tales from the Sisters Grimmer*, 1983
    New interpretations of old tales find the unexpected in the familiar.
Jill Paton Walsh, *A Parcel of Patterns*, 1983
    In 1665 the inhabitants of a small English town become infected by the plague when a dressmaker receives "a parcel of patterns" from London.

DONNA JO NAPOLI

Daughter of Venice

(New York: Wendy Lamb/Random House, 2002)

Subject(s): Gender Roles; Family Life; Jews
Age range(s): Grades 7-10
Major character(s): Donata Aurelia Mocenigo, Twin, 14-Year-Old; Laura Mocenigo, Twin, 14-Year-Old; Andriana Mocenigo, Sister (of Donata and Laura); Noe, Teenager
Time period(s): 16th century
Locale(s): Venice, Italy

Summary: Daughter of a nobleman, and raised to be a proper lady, Donata knows her fate. Her older sister Andriana will have an arranged marriage, and maybe she or her twin will also marry, since her father's very wealthy, but the remaining twin will move to a convent or be the spinster aunt who watches after other family members. Donata feels so constrained by society's expectations of her that she dons a set of boys clothing and, with the help of her siblings, slips away from the family palace to explore the alleyways of Venice. She meets the young Jewish boy Noe and even falls in love with him, which she knows is impossible. More than anything Donata wants to study with her brothers' tutor, but realizes that decision lies with her father in this work dedicated to Elena Lucrezia Cornaro Piscopia, the first woman to earn a Doctor of Philosophy degree at the University of Padua in 1678. (274 pages)

Where it's reviewed:
Bulletin of the Center for Children's Books, July 2002, page 413
Horn Book, March 2002, page 216
Kliatt, May 2002, page 12
Publishers Weekly, February 18, 2002, page 97
School Library Journal, March 2002, page 236

Other books by the same author:
Three Days, 2001
Beast, 2000
For the Love of Venice, 1998
Zel, 1996

Other books you might like:
Teri Kanefield, *Rivka's Way*, 2001
    Rivka wonders what lies beyond the walls of her Jewish ghetto in Prague, so she dresses as a boy, removes her yellow Jewish star and goes exploring.
Linda Sue Park, *Seesaw Girl*, 1999
    Jade's life in her Korean family is defined by the walls of their Inner Court where she embroiders, washes the family clothes and prepares meals.
Mirjam Pressler, *Shylock's Daughter*, 2001
    The desire to escape her Venetian Jewish ghetto is so strong that Jessica leaves behind her religion and her father, but not her savings.
Suzanne Fisher Staples, *Shabanu: Daughter of the Wind*, 1989
    Shabanu is told she will marry old, fat Rahim Sahib, which drives her to choose between family honor and her own identity.

1061

DONNA JO NAPOLI
CATHIE FELSTEAD, Illustrator

Flamingo Dream

(New York: Greenwillow Books, 2002)

Subject(s): Death; Fathers and Daughters; Grief
Age range(s): Grades K-3
Major character(s): Daddy, Father, Cancer Patient; Mamma, Mother, Spouse; Unnamed Character, Child, Daughter
Time period(s): 2000s
Locale(s): United States

Summary: After a trip to relatives in Florida, flamingos become an important symbol for a little girl and her dying father. Mamma and Daddy talk with their daughter about the cancer that ravages his body but still his death is difficult and sad. Daddy's friends, following his instructions, bring flamingos to the girl and she puts the flock in the yard where, eventually she and Mamma sprinkle his ashes. Snows come and winter winds blow away the flamingos. The little girl believes that the flamingos flew back to Florida and took Daddy with them. With Mamma's help she gathers all her souvenirs of the past year and creates a book of her memories of the experience, beginning with the trip to Florida and her flamingo dreams. (30 pages)

Where it's reviewed:
Booklist, April 15, 2002, page 1408
Horn Book, July 2002, page 450
Kirkus Reviews, March 15, 2002, page 421
Publishers Weekly, March 11, 2002, page 72
School Library Journal, May 2002, page 124

Other books by the same author:
Albert, 2001 (School Library Journal Best Books)
Rocky: The Cat Who Barks, 2001
How Hungry Are You?, 2001

Other books you might like:
Eve Bunting, *The Memory String*, 2000
    Laura, grieving for her deceased mother, finds comfort in a string of buttons representing important events in her mother's life.
Cindy Klein Cohen, *Daddy's Promise*, 1997
    Cohen bases the text on the experience of helping her son cope with the death of his father. John T. Heiney, co-author.
Cornelia Spelman, *After Charlotte's Mom Died*, 1996
    Counseling helps Charlotte deal with the confusing feelings of grief after her mother's death.

1062

DONNA JO NAPOLI

The Great God Pan

(New York: Wendy Lamb Books/Random House, 2003)

Subject(s): Mythology; Love
Age range(s): Grades 6-11
Major character(s): Pan, Mythical Creature; Iphigenia, Royalty, Daughter

Time period(s): Indeterminate Past
Locale(s): Greece

Summary: Napoli weaves a plot from the various myths involving Pan, the goat-footed god of wild spaces who is responsible for panic. Because the other residents of Mount Olympus make fun of his feet, Pan chooses to live alone, consorting with nymphs in the wilderness. He delights in the beauties of nature and enjoys the simple relationships he has with dryads and maenads. Apollo's demanding nature offends him, and he tries to avoid crossing paths with this greater god. In particular, Pan is angered by Apollo's perfectionism in music since Pan finds a deep pleasure in the simple pipes he fashions from reeds. When he meets the child Iphigenia, Pan is enchanted by her innocence. His feelings deepen as she grows into a beautiful young woman, but Iphigenia has been born into one of ancient Greece's cursed royal houses. She is the daughter of Agamemnon, who is waiting for the winds to turn favorable for his fleet to sail to Troy and avenge the kidnapping of his brother's wife, Helen. The king is desperate and he is willing to sacrifice whatever and whomever some cruel god might request. (149 pages)

Where it's reviewed:
Booklist, April 15, 2003, page 1464
Library Media Connection, January 2004, page 68
Publishers Weekly, May 26, 2003, page 71
School Library Journal, April 2003, page 58
Voice of Youth Advocates, December 2003, page 416

Other books by the same author:
Breath, 2003
Crazy Jack, 1999
Spinners, 1999

Other books you might like:
Patrice Kindl, *Lost in the Labyrinth: A Novel*, 2002
    Princess Xenodice tries to save the Minotaur, while her sister Ariadne works against her.
Clemence McLaren, *Waiting for Odysseus*, 2000
    The Odyssey told through the eyes of the women who wait for the hero.
Stephanie Spinner, *Quiver*, 2002
    Atalanta gives her suitors a series of impossible tasks, hoping to avoid breaking her vow of chastity.

1063

PHYLLIS REYNOLDS NAYLOR

Alice in Blunderland

(New York: Atheneum Books for Young Readers, 2003)

Subject(s): Brothers and Sisters; Single Parent Families; Friendship
Age range(s): Grades 3-6
Major character(s): Alice Kathleen McKinley, 4th Grader, Sister (younger); Lester McKinley, Brother (older), Teenager
Time period(s): 2000s
Locale(s): Silver Spring, Maryland

Summary: In a prequel to the classic Alice series, fourth grader Alice feels like a blunderbuss, someone who never does anything right. It's hard for her to imagine how so many innocent actions turn out to be so embarrassing for such a kind-hearted girl. Having a brother like Lester who takes advantage of her gullibility and then becomes angry when she actually believes him and acts on his misleading information doesn't help. What she can't understand is why he's angry with her when he's the one who tells lies. By the time the year ends Alice can look back on sneezing beans on her best friend at lunch, getting caught in her underwear while retrieving a book from the front porch, having a vitamin pill stuck in her nose and sending a care package to Lester's girlfriend from the perspective of someone who can also recall some successes during the year. Maybe, Alice thinks, she's not totally hopeless after all. (200 pages)

Where it's reviewed:
Booklist, October 1, 2003, page 321
Horn Book, January 2004, page 86
Publishers Weekly, August 25, 2003, page 64
School Library Journal, September 2003, page 218

Awards the book has won:
IRA Children's Choices, 2004

Other books by the same author:
Including Alice, 2004
Starting with Alice, 2002
Shiloh, 1991 (Newbery Medal)
Agony of Alice, 1985

Other books you might like:
David A. Adler, *Andy Russell, NOT Wanted by the Police*, 2001
    Andy is watching the next-door neighbor's house while they travel and calls the police about strange activity (in his mind) too often.
Beverly Cleary, *Ramona's World*, 1999
    Daisy, a new student, becomes fourth-grader Ramona's friend, fulfilling one of her wishes for the school year.
Paula Danziger, *Amber Brown Is Feeling Blue*, 1998
    When Kelly Green joins Amber's fourth grade class, Amber Brown loses her special status as the kid with the colorful name.

1064

PHYLLIS REYNOLDS NAYLOR

Bernie Magruder & the Bats in the Belfry

(New York: Atheneum Books for Young Readers, 2003)

Subject(s): Animals/Bats; Hotels and Motels; Mystery and Detective Stories
Age range(s): Grades 4-7
Major character(s): Bernie Magruder, 6th Grader, Son (of hotel manager); Georgene Riley, 6th Grader, Friend; Wallace "Weasel" Boyd, 6th Grader, Friend
Time period(s): 2000s
Locale(s): Middleburg, Indiana

Summary: Posters warn that a rare species of bat with a fatal bite may invade the town that is already in an uproar because a deceased wealthy resident has willed that the church bells play her favorite hymn every quarter hour. Torn between fear of the bats and frustration with the ringing bells, the town's residents feel hopeless when it appears that the bats are

roosting in the church belfry. Bernie, Georgene and Weasel, hoping to be pictured in the newspaper, use their detective skills to gather clues and contribute to the solution of the mystery. (130 pages)

Where it's reviewed:
Booklist, January 2003, page 892
Bulletin of the Center for Children's Books, April 2003, page 326
Publishers Weekly, February 17, 2003, page 77
School Library Journal, April 2003, page 166

Other books by the same author:
Peril in the Bessledorf Parachute Factory, 2000
The Treasure of Bessledorf Hill, 1998
The Bomb in the Bessledorf Bus Depot, 1996

Other books you might like:
Douglas Evans, *The Elevator Family*, 2000
    The vacationing Wilson family is quite content in a small room just off the lobby with a phone, piped in music and a steady stream of visitors.
Mary Labatt, *A Weekend at the Grand Hotel*, 2001
    Dog detective Sam accompanies Jennie and her family to the Grand Hotel for the weekend. Her snooping lands them in the middle of a mystery.
Gertrude Chandler Warner, *The Mystery at Snowflake Inn*, 1994
    Accidents at an 18th-century Vermont Inn pique the curiosity of the Boxcar children in this mystery series.

1065

PHYLLIS REYNOLDS NAYLOR

Blizzard's Wake

(New York: Atheneum/Simon & Schuster, 2002)

Subject(s): Interpersonal Relations; Weather; Forgiveness
Age range(s): Grades 7-10
Major character(s): Kate Sterling, 15-Year-Old; Jesse Sterling, 11-Year-Old, Brother (of Kate); Doc Sterling, Doctor, Father (of Kate and Jesse); Zeke Dexter, Convict
Time period(s): 1940s (1941)
Locale(s): Grand Forks, North Dakota

Summary: The historical Red River Valley Blizzard of 1941 unleashes more than cold and snow on the Sterling family. Just released from prison, Zeke is traveling back to Grand Forks when he's caught in the blizzard. That same day Kate's father and brother drive home from visiting one of her father's patients. The blizzard strikes, trapping Dr. Sterling and Jesse just as they're nearing their home. Kate manages to rig a line out to their car only to discover they sheltering Zeke Dexter, the drunk driver of the car that killed her mother and the man she's hated for the last four years. Trapped by the storm, the remorseful Zeke and the hate-filled Kate must confront one another, though it's hard for each of them. (212 pages)

Where it's reviewed:
Book World, January 12, 2003, page 11
Booklist, October 15, 2002, page 401
Publishers Weekly, October 28, 2002, page 73
School Library Journal, December 2002, page 146
Voice of Youth Advocates, October 2002, page 283

Other books by the same author:
Including Alice, 2004
Jade Green: A Ghost Story, 2000
Walker's Crossing, 1999
Sang Spell, 1998
Ice, 1995

Other books you might like:
Patricia Calvert, *Glennis, Before and After,* 1996
Crushed to discover that her father really did commit the crime for which he's imprisoned, Glennis must learn to forgive him.
Paul Fleischman, *Whirligig,* 1998
Brent accidentally kills Lia Zamora and after meeting her mother, agrees to set up whirligigs in the four corners of America as penance.
Dianne E. Gray, *Together Apart,* 2002
Feeling guilty about surviving the "School Children's Blizzard" when her two brothers didn't, Hannah escapes the farm and works in town.

1066

PHYLLIS REYNOLDS NAYLOR

Boys in Control

(New York: Delacorte Press, 2003)

Subject(s): Sports/Baseball; Small Town Life; Plays
Age range(s): Grades 3-6
Major character(s): Wally Hatford, 4th Grader, Brother; Caroline Malloy, 4th Grader, Sister
Time period(s): 2000s (2003)
Locale(s): Buckman, West Virginia

Summary: Because Wally likes baseball the least of anyone in his family, he gets stuck watching the women's auxiliary rummage sale because it's scheduled on the same day as his brother's baseball championship. To make matters even worse, Caroline Malloy spends the time he's stuck at the rummage sale to convince Wally to perform in a play she's written for their fourth grade class. Of course, asking is not enough for Caroline. She ensures Wally's agreement by blackmailing him into performing, in exchange for the return of some embarrassing pictures. The rummage sale turns out to be more exciting than expected when two women try to steal a picture before the sale opens. (160 pages)

Where it's reviewed:
Booklist, September 15, 2003, page 241
School Library Journal, October 2003, page 172

Other books by the same author:
The Girls Take Over, 2002
The Girls Get Even, 1993
The Boys Start the War, 1992

Other books you might like:
Judy Blume, *Fudge-a-Mania,* 1991
The Hatcher and Tubman families vacation next door to one another in Maine.
Beverly Cleary, *Mitch and Amy,* 1967
Twins Mitch and Amy are always fighting, but when a bully starts picking on them, they band together.

Nancy Ruth Patterson, *A Simple Gift,* 2003
Aspiring actress Carrie travels to North Carolina to audition for a play based on a children's book by her mother.

1067

PHYLLIS REYNOLDS NAYLOR

The Girls Take Over

(New York: Delacorte, 2002)

Subject(s): Sports/Baseball; Competition; Gender Roles
Age range(s): Grades 3-6
Major character(s): Jake Hatford, 6th Grader, Brother; Eddie Malloy, 6th Grader, Sister; Caroline Malloy, 4th Grader, Sister
Time period(s): 2000s (2002)
Locale(s): Buckman, West Virginia

Summary: The rivalry between the Hatford boys and the Malloy girls continues. Both Jake Hatford and Eddie Malloy makes the sixth grade baseball team, but a conflict arises when they both want to be the pitcher. Meanwhile, all the Hatford boys and Malloy girls decide to do a bottle race in the swollen river. Each one puts their name and phone number in a bottle and throws it into the river. The one getting a call by the end of the month from the longest distance wins. Complications from the bottle race cause Caroline's drama queen tendencies to raise their ugly head again, but she redeems herself by helping to catch a thief. (160 pages)

Where it's reviewed:
Booklist, September 15, 2002, page 235
Publishers Weekly, August 26, 2002, page 71
School Library Journal, September 2002, page 230

Other books by the same author:
Boys in Control, 2003
The Girls Get Even, 1993
The Boys Start the War, 1992

Other books you might like:
Judy Blume, *Tales of a Fourth Grade Nothing,* 1972
Peter's little brother, Fudge, is always messing things up for him.
Beverly Cleary, *Henry Huggins,* 1950
Life is boring for Henry until he adopts a stray dog named Ribsy.
Sheila Greenwald, *Here's Hermione: A Rosy Cole Production,* 1991
When Rosy's best friend, Hermione, decides she wants to be a rock cellist, Rosy becomes her self-appointed manager.

1068

PHYLLIS REYNOLDS NAYLOR

Patiently Alice

(New York: Simon & Schuster, 2003)

Series: Alice
Subject(s): Camps and Camping; Poverty; Friendship
Age range(s): Grades 6-9

Major character(s): Alice Kathleen McKinley, 10th Grader, Counselor (camp); Pamela Jones, 10th Grader, Counselor (camp); Elizabeth Price, 10th Grader, Counselor (camp); Patrick Long, 10th Grader, Boyfriend (former, of Alice); Sylvia Summers, Fiance(e) (of Alice's father)

Time period(s): 2000s

Locale(s): Silver Spring, Maryland

Summary: The summer after her freshman year finds Alice, along with her good friends Pamela and Elizabeth, volunteering as counselors at a nature camp for disadvantaged kids. Camp turns out to be more serious than fun as Alice's young charges don't always know how to work out disagreements and Alice realizes how much more training she needs to be effective. Returning home she finds her world just a little off course, beginning with a visit from her former boyfriend Patrick; an attempt by Pamela's mother to return to her family; and the postponement of the long-awaited wedding of Alice's father and his girlfriend Sylvia in this fifteenth in the *Alice* series. (243 pages)

Where it's reviewed:
Booklist, August 2003, page 1972
Horn Book, July 2003, page 463
School Library Journal, May 2003, page 158
Voice of Youth Advocates, August 2003, page 228

Other books by the same author:
Simply Alice, 2002
Starting with Alice, 2002
Alice Alone, 2001
The Grooming of Alice, 2000
Alice on the Outside, 1999
Achingly Alice, 1998

Other books you might like:
Paula Danziger, *There's a Bat in Bunk Five*, 1980
   Marcy looks at camp differently now that she's a counselor.
Elizabeth Honey, *Don't Pat the Wombat*, 2000
   New student Jonah makes friends in time to ensure that summer camp is fun with its mud fights, leech battles and midnight shenanigans.
Scott Johnson, *Overnight Sensation*, 1994
   Kerry realizes she's made a mistake when she lets her friends lead her away from her old buddy Madeline, an individual who refuses to follow the crowd.
Robert Lipsyte, *Summer Rules*, 1981
   Bobby adjusts to life as a camp counselor, until he meets Sheila, and then none of the camp rules make sense.

`1069`

PHYLLIS REYNOLDS NAYLOR

Simply Alice

(New York: Simon & Schuster, 2002)

Subject(s): School Life; Brothers and Sisters; Interpersonal Relations

Age range(s): Grades 6-9

Major character(s): Alice Kathleen McKinley, 9th Grader; Patrick Long, 9th Grader; Lester McKinley, Brother (of Alice), Student—College; Pamela Jones, 9th Grader; Eliz-

abeth Price, 9th Grader; Sylvia Summers, Fiance(e) (of Alice's father)

Time period(s): 2000s

Locale(s): Silver Spring, Maryland

Summary: Finishing up her first year in high school, Alice enjoys such a busy year that she finally accepts seeing Patrick with his new girlfriend, realizes she's been too busy to see her best friends Elizabeth and Pamela, and is happy that her dad is marrying Miss Summers. Once Alice worried what life would be like without Patrick, but quickly threw herself into the school play and the newspaper, discovering that she could not only stay busy but also enjoy being on her own. Gradually she takes a little more time for her best friends and even supports her brother Les when he and his girlfriend breakup. Now it's summer and Alice awaits her father's marriage to Sylvia, as well as a job as an assistant counselor at camp in this four-teenth title in the *Alice* series. (222 pages)

Where it's reviewed:
Booklist, June 2002, page 1708
Bulletin of the Center for Children's Books, June 2002, page 376
Horn Book, July 2002, page 468
School Library Journal, May 2002, page 158
Voice of Youth Advocates, June 2002, page 1221

Other books by the same author:
Patiently Alice, 2003
Starting with Alice, 2002
Alice Alone, 2001
The Grooming of Alice, 2000
Alice on the Outside, 1999
Achingly Alice, 1998

Other books you might like:
Deborah Kent, *The Courage to Live*, 2001
   Chloe stays so busy doing fifteen things at once that she doesn't realize her headaches might be a sign of illness and not stress.
Lynne Rae Perkins, *All Alone in the Universe*, 1999
   Though hurt when her best friend ditches her, Debbie discovers that it's possible to be friendly with many different people.
Rachel Vail, *Ever After*, 1994
   Molly has trouble with her friends the summer before high school as she realizes one is manipulative and the other gets her into trouble.

`1070`

PHYLLIS REYNOLDS NAYLOR

Starting with Alice

(New York: Atheneum Books for Young Readers, 2002)

Series: Alice

Subject(s): Friendship; Single Parent Families; Family Life

Age range(s): Grades 3-5

Major character(s): Alice Kathleen McKinley, 3rd Grader, Sister (younger); Lester McKinley, Teenager, Brother (older); Rosalind Rodriguez, 3rd Grader, Friend; Sara Evans, 3rd Grader, Friend

Time period(s): 1990s

Locale(s): Takoma Park, Maryland

Summary: When Alice and her family move from Chicago to Maryland so her dad can take a new job as a music store manager Alice becomes more aware of the absence of a mother in her life. She struggles to make friends in her new school, endures driving lessons with Lester, and mourns with her family the death her dad's older brother. When Alice learns that her classmate Rosalind is the younger sister of one of Lester's band members she strikes up a friendship with her and then tries to enlarge it to include Sara. A successful sleepover with Rosalind and Sara helps Alice feel more comfortable in the friend department and by the time her May birthday comes sensitive Alice is confident enough to reach out to other classmates, too. Life is a never-ending challenge for this motherless eight-year-old. (181 pages)

Where it's reviewed:
Booklist, November 15, 2002, page 600
Bulletin of the Center for Children's Books, November 2002, page 118
Horn Book, September 2002, page 579
Publishers Weekly, September 30, 2002, page 74
School Library Journal, September 2002, page 230

Other books by the same author:
Including Alice, 2004
Lovingly Alice, 2004
Alice in Blunderland, 2003

Other books you might like:
Ann Cameron, *Gloria's Way*, 2000
    Gloria faces the trials and tribulations of childhood with support from friends and family.
Beverly Cleary, *Ramona Quimby, Age 8*, 1981
    Spirited Ramona copes with family, friends and entering third grade in this Newbery Honor Book.
Paula Danziger, *Amber Brown Is Not a Crayon*, 1994
    Amber's third grade year is made more difficult when she learns that her best friend Justin is moving.
Susan Wojciechowski, *Beany and the Dreaded Wedding*, 2000
    Worrywart Beany is sure something will go wrong with her cousin's wedding because she is both the flower girl and the ring bearer.

1071
SHIRLEY NEITZEL
NANCY WINSLOW PARKER, Illustrator

Our Class Took a Trip to the Zoo
(New York: Greenwillow Books/HarperCollins Publishers, 2002)

Subject(s): Animals; Zoos; Stories in Rhyme
Age range(s): Grades K-2
Major character(s): Unnamed Character, Child, Student
Time period(s): 2000s (2002)
Locale(s): United States

Summary: During a class trip to the zoo, a young boy has an eventful day. To explain his disheveled appearance, the student relates a cumulative tale of a popped button, lost coat, torn pants, muddy shoes, wet shirt and dropped lunch. The many mishaps do not dampen the boy's enjoyment of the trip, but encourage him to consider a career as a zookeeper. (32 pages)

Where it's reviewed:
Booklist, March 15, 2002, page 1264
Horn Book Guide, Fall 2002, page 340
Kirkus Reviews, March 1, 2002, page 341
Publishers Weekly, April 8, 2002, page 230
School Library Journal, June 2002, page 104

Other books by the same author:
I'm Not Feeling Well Today, 2001
I'm Taking a Trip on My Train, 1999
The House I'll Build for the Wrens, 1997

Other books you might like:
Michael Garland, *Last Night at the Zoo*, 2001
    Bored zoo animals plan and execute a night on the town with no one noticing that they are missing.
Trinka Hakes Noble, *The Day Jimmy's Boa Ate the Wash*, 1987
    What should be an educational field trip to a farm becomes a most unusual adventure for Jimmy's class when his pet boa gets loose.
Peggy Rathmann, *Good Night, Gorilla*, 1994
    Unbeknownst to a zookeeper making his final rounds, a little gorilla steals his keys and releases the animals to follow the unsuspecting man home.

1072
BLAKE NELSON

The New Rules of High School
(New York: Viking, 2003)

Subject(s): Schools/High Schools; Newspapers; Conduct of Life
Age range(s): Grades 9-12
Major character(s): Max Caldwell, 12th Grader; Cynthia "Cindy" Sherman, 11th Grader
Time period(s): 2000s
Locale(s): Portland, Oregon

Summary: At the end of Max's junior year, he seems like a golden boy: a straight-A student, newly named editor of the school paper *The Evergreen Owl*, debate team captain and likely candidate for Yale. But something doesn't feel right to Max and he realizes he's tired of always doing what's expected, so he drops some of his old friends, including his girlfriend Cindy, adds some new, unsuitable ones and makes unwise decisions that get him into trouble. By the end of his senior year, he discovers that the more he tries to change, the more he end up just like himself, in this authentic look at being a teenager. (227 pages)

Where it's reviewed:
Booklist, August 2003, page 1972
Kirkus Reviews, June 1, 2003, page 809
Publishers Weekly, June 23, 2003, page 68
School Library Journal, June 2003, page 148
Voice of Youth Advocates, June 2003, page 142

Other books by the same author:
Rock Star, Superstar, 2004
Girl, 1994

Other books you might like:

E.R. Frank, *Life Is Funny*, 2000
> Eleven students, who relate their high school careers over a period of six years, provide a different perspective on school life.

Donald R. Gallo, *On the Fringe*, 2001
> A collection of eleven short stories about insiders and outsiders in school life.

Rob Thomas, *Slave Day*, 1997
> African American Keena Davenport writes a letter to the school newspaper editor urging students to boycott the demeaning ritual of "slave day."

1073

S.D. NELSON, Author/Illustrator

The Star People: A Lakota Story
(New York: Harry N. Abrams, 2003)

Subject(s): Native Americans; Folk Tales; Fires
Age range(s): Grades 1-4
Major character(s): Sister Girl, Indian, Sister; Young Wolf, Indian, Brother (younger)
Time period(s): 19th century
Locale(s): Great Plains

Summary: Sister Girl and Young Wolf explore the land around their village. During a thunderstorm, they are caught in a prairie fire and barely manage to escape by stumbling into a stream. Once the fire has past, they realize that they have strayed too far from their village and, without the vegetation to mark their way, they can't find their way back. Suddenly, under a night sky, Sister Girl and Young Wolf see the Star People, their Lakota ancestors who now live in the sky. Their recently deceased grandmother is among them and she helps guide Sister Girl and Young Wolf back to their village. (40 pages)

Where it's reviewed:
Booklist, November 15, 2003, page 602
Bulletin of the Center for Children's Books, December 2003, page 160
Five Owls, Number 2, 2004, page 83
School Library Journal, September 2003, page 185

Other books by the same author:
Gift Horse: A Lakota Story, 1999 (Parents' Choice Award)

Other books you might like:

Barbara Esbensen, *The Star Maiden: An Ojibway Tale*, 1988
> This Ojibway tale explains the origin of water lilies. According to the tale, they were formed when a star maiden searched for a home on earth.

Paul Goble, *The Lost Children: The Boys Who Were Neglected*, 1993
> This Blackfoot tale tells of six neglected boys who become the star constellation Pleiades.

Jerrie Oughton, *How the Stars Fell into the Sky: A Navajo Legend*, 1992
> A Navajo woman tries to write the laws of her people in the stars, but is tricked by a coyote.

1074

THERESA NELSON

Ruby Electric
(New York: Richard Jackson/Atheneum, 2003)

Subject(s): Fathers and Daughters; Brothers and Sisters; Single Parent Families
Age range(s): Grades 5-8
Major character(s): Ruby Miller, 12-Year-Old, 7th Grader; Pete Miller, Brother, Child; Vincent "Big Skinny" Bogart, 7th Grader; Matthew "Mouse" Mossbach, 7th Grader, Sidekick (of Big Skinny); Frank P. Miller, Father, Convict
Time period(s): 2000s
Locale(s): Los Angeles, California

Summary: Rewriting her life into a screenplay is Ruby's way of dealing with her missing father, her uprooted life, and the amorous attentions of Big Skinny. Ruby's father disappeared five years ago after which her mother moved the family to Los Angeles into a home beside the concrete culvert of the Los Angeles River. A badly written love poem spray-painted on this culvert results in Ruby, Big Skinny and Mouse working on a community project mural and gives Ruby a chance to revise her opinion of Big Skinny and his wisecracking cohort. When her father returns after serving time in prison, Ruby learns to forgive him, as well as her mother, who was unable to share the truth about his disappearance. (264 pages)

Where it's reviewed:
Bulletin of the Center for Children's Books, July 2003, page 456
Horn Book, July 2003, page 464
Publishers Weekly, May 26, 2003, page 71
School Library Journal, June 2003, page 148
Voice of Youth Advocates, October 2003, page 316

Other books by the same author:
The Empress of Elsewhere, 1998
Earthshine, 1994
The Beggars' Ride, 1992
And One for All, 1989

Other books you might like:

Michael Cadnum, *Heat*, 1998
> When her father's accused of defrauding his clients, Bonnie accepts his word that he's innocent but changes her mind as more information leaks out.

Patricia Calvert, *Glennis, Before and After*, 1996
> When her father's imprisoned and her mother's hospitalized, Glennis and her siblings are parceled out to live with family members.

Phyllis Reynolds Naylor, *Ice*, 1995
> Chrissa doesn't understand why she hasn't seen her father in three years; by the time she's told he's been in jail, she's able to accept the news.

1075

LINDA NEWBERY

The Shell House

(New York: David Fickling Books/Random House, 2002)

Subject(s): Self-Perception; Homosexuality/Lesbianism; World War I
Age range(s): Grades 9-12
Major character(s): Greg Hobbs, 17-Year-Old; Faith Tarrant, Teenager; Jordan, Swimmer, Homosexual; Edmund Pearson, Homosexual, 18-Year-Old (poet); Alex Culworth, Homosexual
Time period(s): 1910s (1917); 2000s
Locale(s): Graveney Hall, England

Summary: Linked by Graveney Hall are two young men whose sexuality affects both their lives. Built in the 1700s, Graveney Hall is to be inherited by Edmund who, at the age of eighteen, heads off to fight in World War I. In the army he meets Alex and the two find themselves romantically involved until Alex's death in battle; returning home his parents urge him to marry to a suitable woman. Upset by their expectations, and the death of his lover, Edmund sets fire to Graveney Hall and tries to commit suicide. Years later volunteers restore the landscape around this shell of a house and it's here that Greg comes to photograph its stark walls. Meeting the daughter of the landscape foreman, Faith, the two share many conversations as Faith explores her Christianity and Greg wonders about his sexuality. In juxtaposed stories, Greg recounts his experience with fellow student Jordan who is openly gay while Edmund describes his time with Alex. Feelings and beliefs change as Greg and Faith trace the history behind Edmund and Graveney Hall. (335 pages)

Where it's reviewed:
Booklist, August 2002, page 1946
Bulletin of the Center for Children's Books, November 2002, page 119
Publishers Weekly, June 24, 2002, page 58
School Library Journal, August 2002, page 196
Voice of Youth Advocates, August 2002, page 195

Other books by the same author:
Sisterland, 2004
The Damage Done, 2001
Riddle Me This, 1993

Other books you might like:
Andrew Matthews, *The Flip Side*, 2003
    After exploring their gender identity, Milena and Rob decide they're happy with themselves, though supportive of their friend Kev who reveals he's gay.
Erich Marie Remarque, *All Quiet on the Western Front*, 1929
    Of four German friends, only Paul survives the battles of World War I.
Alex Sanchez, *Rainbow Boys*, 2001
    Jason, Kyle and Nelson face their senior year, and life-changing decisions, as they deal with their sexual identity.

1076

MARJORIE NEWMAN
PATRICK BENSON, Illustrator

Mole and the Baby Bird

(New York: Bloomsbury Children's Books, 2002)

Subject(s): Love; Animals/Moles; Animals/Birds
Age range(s): Grades K-2
Major character(s): Mole, Mole, Rescuer; Unnamed Character, Bird; Grandad, Mole, Grandfather
Time period(s): Indeterminate
Locale(s): Fictional Country

Summary: Mole's parents are not encouraging when he comes home with a baby bird he's found. Mole, however, is confident that the bird will live and stay with him as a pet despite his parent's reminders that a bird is a wild animal. When the bird survives and grows enough to fly, Mole builds a cage so the bird cannot leave him. Grandad helps Mole realize that he must love the bird enough to set it free to fly, even if it means the bird flies away. (32 pages)

Where it's reviewed:
Booklist, October 15, 2002, page 413
Bulletin of the Center for Children's Books, November 2002, page 120
Publishers Weekly, July 15, 2002, page 72
Riverbank Review, Fall 2002, page 33
School Library Journal, December 2002, page 104

Awards the book has won:
School Library Journal Best Books, 2002

Other books by the same author:
The King and the Cuddly, 2000
Is That What Friends Do?, 1998

Other books you might like:
Molly Bang, *Goose*, 1996
    A gosling feels out of place with her adoptive woodchuck family until she learns to fly—right back to the comfort of her woodchuck home.
David McPhail, *The Teddy Bear*, 2002
    A little boy is happy to see his beloved, lost teddy bear yet he realizes that the old man who found it needs it more than he does.
Tracey Campbell Pearson, *The Purple Hat*, 1997
    When Annie's favorite lost hat is found with a full bird's nest in the crown she decides that the birds need it more than she does for now.

1077

BARBARA NICHOL
ANJA REICHEL, Illustrator

Safe and Sound

(Plattsburgh, NY: Tundra, 2003)

Subject(s): Travel; Animals/Dogs; Stories in Rhyme
Age range(s): Grades K-2
Major character(s): Safe, Dog, Traveler; Sound, Dog, Traveler
Time period(s): 2000s (2003)
Locale(s): Earth

Summary: Inspired by travel books, Safe and Sound decide to take a trip around the world. However they find that the reality of travel is not as glamorous as the books portray. From the very first flight (with planes that fly much too high) to strange foods, languages and modes of transportation, Safe and Sound tour the world, but decide they are happiest staying home. (32 pages)

Where it's reviewed:
Horn Book Guide, Spring 2004, page 54
Publishers Weekly, October 13, 2003, page 77

Other books by the same author:
Dippers, 2001
One Small Garden, 2001
Beethoven Lives Upstairs, 1994

Other books you might like:
Gilles Eduar, *Gigi and Zachary's Around-the-World Adventure*, 2003
  Gigi and Zachary travel around the world to 19 different countries.
Holly Hobbie, *Toot & Puddle*, 1997
  Toot travels the world and writes his homebody friend Puddle all about what he sees.
H.A. Rey, *Whiteblack the Penguin Sees the World*, 2000
  Whiteblack has run out of material for his radio show, so he decides to go on a world tour. Margaret Rey, co-author.

1078

WILLIAM NICHOLSON
PETER SIS, Illustrator

Firesong: An Adventure
(New York: Hyperion, 2002)

Series: Wind on Fire Trilogy. Book 3
Subject(s): Adventure and Adventurers
Age range(s): Grades 6-9
Major character(s): Ira Hath, Mother, Psychic; Hanno Hath, Father; Bowman Hath, Son, Twin; Kestrel Hath, Daughter, Twin
Time period(s): Indeterminate
Locale(s): Fictional Country

Summary: The Manth people leave the enslavement of the city of Mastery and, led by Ira Hath's vision, set out on a journey to their homeland. Ira's husband Hanno is the leader of the group, but the twins Bowman and Kestrel are at the heart of the migration, both because of the contributions they have made to their people's survival in the past, and the roles they are expected to fill in the future. Bowman's sensitivity helps keep the group on course and saves them from threats, like the horrible parasite that tries to prey on the group. When the teenaged girls are kidnapped as brides by a bandit group, Kestrel's quick thinking and daring leadership free them. As the journey drags on, some are disillusioned, some grow ill and all are tempted to quit, but fear of the coming ''Wind on Fire'' drives the Manth to reach their goal despite the obstacles. (422 pages)

Where it's reviewed:
Magpies, July 2002, page 18
Publishers Weekly, August 26, 2002, page 71

School Librarian, Winter 2002, page 215
School Library Journal, January 2003, page 141
Voice of Youth Advocates, December 2002, page 400

Other books by the same author:
Slaves of the Mastery: An Adventure, 2001 (Wind on Fire Trilogy Book 2)
The Wind Singer: An Adventure, 2000 (Wind on Fire Trilogy Book 1)

Other books you might like:
Peter Dickinson, *The Ropemaker*, 2001
  When the magic protecting the valley begins to fail, an odd group sets out on a quest to find the wizard who can renew the spells.
Garth Nix, *Abhorsen*, 2003
  Sam and Lirael travel across the Old Kingdom to try and avert the evil of the Destroyer.
Christopher Paolini, *Eragon*, 2003
  Eragon doesn't set out to be a hero on a quest, but once he finds the dragon egg that hatches Saphira, it seems to be the only course.

1079

SARA NICKERSON
SALLY WERN COMPORT, Illustrator

How to Disappear Completely and Never Be Found
(New York: HarperCollins, 2002)

Subject(s): Mystery and Detective Stories; Family Life; Cartoons and Comics
Age range(s): Grades 5-8
Major character(s): Margaret Clairmont, 12-Year-Old; Sophie Clairmont, Child; Boyd, 12-Year-Old
Time period(s): 2000s
Locale(s): Pacific Northwest

Summary: Since their father died four years ago, Margaret and her little sister Sophie have learned not to ask their depressed mother any questions about him. Answers to family secrets begin to appear the day the three drive to a deserted seaside mansion and her mother posts a ''For Sale by Owner'' sign in the front yard. As they roam around the house, Margaret discovers three things that puzzle her: a swimming medal that belonged to her father, a key, and a comic book with a character named Ratt. Determined to solve the mystery of her father's drowning, made stranger by his swimming medal, Margaret returns to the island where she meets Boyd, a neighbor her age, and locates the town library which includes only unpublished books. In this first novel, comic strips that disclose what did, or could happen, are scattered throughout the book and reveal the identity of Ratt's creator. (281 pages)

Where it's reviewed:
Bulletin of the Center for Children's Books, May 2002, page 335
Horn Book, July 2002, page 469
Publishers Weekly, April 15, 2002, page 65
School Library Journal, April 2002, page 154
Voice of Youth Advocates, June 2002, page 121

Awards the book has won:
Center for Children's Books Best Books, 2002

Other books you might like:
Dayle Campbell Gaetz, *Mystery from History*, 2001
Katie and her friends can't resist exploring their town's deserted mansion, especially when they see mysterious lights inside.
Kate Klise, *Letters from Camp*, 1999
Siblings communicate suspicions about their summer camp's operators in letters home to their parents.
David Patneaude, *Someone Was Watching*, 1993
Though everyone thinks Chris's sister Molly drowned, Chris is convinced she was kidnapped and travels to Florida to rescue her.

1080

SUSIN NIELSEN-FERNLUND
LOUISE-ANDREE LALIBERTE, Illustrator

Hank and Fergus

(Custer, WA: Orca Books, 2003)

Subject(s): Imagination; Pets; Friendship
Age range(s): Preschool-Grade 1
Major character(s): Hank, Child, Neighbor; Fergus, Dog (imaginary); Cooper, Child, Neighbor
Time period(s): 2000s (2003)
Locale(s): Canada

Summary: Hank's imaginary dog, Fergus, is his best friend. Not only do they do everything together, but Fergus also makes Hank feel better about the embarrassing birthmark on his forehead. When a new boy, Cooper, moves into the house next door to Hank he tries to make friends with Hank, but Hank is not interested and the boys start fighting. In the end, however, Hank decides that it is perhaps possible to have two best friends. To make the new relationship with Cooper ideal, Hank gives him an imaginary dog of his own. (32 pages)

Where it's reviewed:
Publishers Weekly, December 15, 2003, page 72
School Library Journal, February 2004, page 120

Other books you might like:
Lindsay Barrett George, *My Bunny and Me*, 2001
The bunny Luis draws becomes his imaginary friend.
Syd Hoff, *The Horse in Harry's Room*, 1970
Only city-living Harry can see the horse in his room.
Dick King-Smith, *The Invisible Dog*, 1993
Wishes come true for Janie when her conscientious care of an imaginary pet leads to her acquisition of a real one with the same characteristics.
Alice McLerran, *Roxaboxen*, 1992
Marian and her sisters create an imaginary town called Roxaboxen.

1081

JENNY NIMMO

Charlie Bone and the Time Twister

(New York: Orchard Books, 2003)

Series: Children of the Red King. Book 2
Subject(s): Magic; Time Travel; Fantasy
Age range(s): Grades 6-9
Major character(s): Charlie Bone, Wizard, Student—Boarding School; Fidelio Gunn, Wizard, Student—Boarding School; Olivia Vertigo, Wizard, Student—Boarding School; Henry Yewbeam, Time Traveler
Time period(s): 2000s
Locale(s): England

Summary: Charlie continues his stressful education at Bloor's Academy, where students with a variety of magical abilities are educated. In this second book in the series, Charlie and his friends Fidelio and Olivia discover an exotic marble that has the ability to take the user through time. Along with the time twister, Charlie discovers his great-uncle Henry who has been lost in time since 1916. It's all the doing of wicked old Ezekiel Bloor, who still resides at the academy. Charlie has his hands full trying to keep the irrepressible Henry hidden while he looks for a way to protect him from the Bloors. Without Fidelio's help and Olivia's distractions, Charlie and Henry will be caught for sure. (402 pages)

Where it's reviewed:
Booklist, September 15, 2003, page 241
Bulletin of the Center for Children's Books, December 2003, page 161
Publishers Weekly, September 29, 2003, page 67
School Library Journal, October 2003, page 172
Voice of Youth Advocates, February 2004, page 506

Other books by the same author:
Midnight for Charlie Bone, 2002 (Children of the Red King Book 1)
Something Wonderful, 2001
Griffin's Castle, 1997

Other books you might like:
Diana Wynne Jones, *The Time of the Ghost*, 2002
A boarding school is haunted by a ghost who doesn't seem to know who she is.
Jane Langton, *The Diamond in the Window*, 1962
Eddy and Eleanor discover a secret attic room in their house, which leads them to another dimension.
Anne Lindbergh, *The People in Pineapple Place*, 1982
Moving to a new home introduces some ordinary kids to a way to travel through time.

1082

JENNY NIMMO

Midnight for Charlie Bone

(New York: Orchard Books, 2002)

Series: Children of the Red King. Book 1
Subject(s): Magic; Growing Up; Schools
Age range(s): Grades 6-9

Major character(s): Charlie Bone, Student—Boarding School; Paton Yewbeam, Uncle, Wizard; Griselda Yewbeam Bone, Grandmother; Fidelio Gunn, Student—Boarding School; Olivia Vertigo, Student—Boarding School

Time period(s): 2000s

Locale(s): England (Bloor's Academy)

Summary: Charlie and his mother have lived with his father's family since the awful day that his father drove into the quarry. It hasn't been a happy choice as the Yewbeams are a tight knit clan with some decidedly odd ideas, and they seem to despise Charlie and his mother. On Charlie's birthday, the Yewbeams, led by Charlie's formidable grandmother, decide he needs to be tested. In spite of the fact that he has no idea what is going on, Charlie passes the test with flying colors, which proves that Charlie has inherited the magical talents of the Yewbeams. Grandma Bone decides that Charlie must begin attending Bloor's Academy where his talents can be properly nurtured. Bloor's Academy turns out to be rather sinister, but Charlie makes two good friends, Fidelio and Olivia, who also suspect that there is more going on at Bloor's than meets the eye. As the three friends begin to uncover the mystery, they find an unexpected ally in Charlie's Uncle Paton. (401 pages)

Where it's reviewed:

Booklist, January 1, 2003, page 892
Kirkus Reviews, December 15, 2002, page 1854
Magpies, July 2002, page 38
Publishers Weekly, December 9, 2002, page 85
School Library Journal, February 2003, page 146

Other books by the same author:

Charlie Bone and the Time Twister, 2003 (Children of the Red King Book 2)
Something Wonderful, 2001
Griffin's Castle, 1997

Other books you might like:

Diane Duane, *So You Want to Be a Wizard*, 1983
  Nita and Kit are young American wizards who live at home, but still find that wizardly gifts make life difficult at times.
J.K. Rowling, *Harry Potter and the Sorcerer's Stone*, 1998
  Like Charlie, Harry is a student at a boarding school for wizards.
Mary Frances Zambreno, *A Plague of Sorcerers*, 1991
  A magical plague challenges the young wizard Jermyn and Delia, his skunk familiar.

1083

CLAIRE A. NIVOLA, Author/Illustrator

The Forest

(New York: Frances Foster Books/Farrar Straus Giroux, 2002)

Subject(s): Animals/Mice; Fear; Courage
Age range(s): Grades K-3
Major character(s): Unnamed Character, Mouse, Adventurer
Time period(s): Indeterminate
Locale(s): Fictional Country

Summary: A mouse lives contentedly in a cozy home, terrified of the forest visible some distance from his village. Deter-

mined to overcome this fear he sets out early one morning to walk to the forest and venture into the unknown wondering what fate awaits him. Initially the sights and sounds of the dark woods frighten the mouse and he begins to flee, when he trips. In that moment when the mouse gives thanks that he lives, he also begins to truly see and appreciate the beauty of the forest. With his fear vanquished the mouse enjoys a relaxing day and then calmly walks back to his village, no longer haunted by the unknown. (32 pages)

Where it's reviewed:

Booklist, April 15, 2002, page 1408
Horn Book Guide, Fall 2002, page 310
Publishers Weekly, March 18, 2002, page 102
Riverbank Review, Spring 2002, page 31
School Library Journal, June 2002, page 106

Other books by the same author:

Elisabeth, 1997

Other books you might like:

Jez Alborough, *Watch Out! Big Bro's Coming!*, 1997
  A little mouse warns all the other animals that rough, tough Big Bro is coming! When he arrives it's obvious that size is relative.
Sam McBratney, *The Dark at the Top of the Stairs*, 1996
  Rejecting the suggestions of a wise, old mouse, three young mice insist on climbing the stairs to see what lurks in the dark at the top.
Gloria Rand, *Willie Takes a Hike*, 1996
  Willie goes on a pretend hike near his new home and soon becomes lost.

1084

GARTH NIX

Abhorsen

(New York: HarperCollins, 2003)

Subject(s): Magic; Death; Fantasy
Age range(s): Grades 7-12
Major character(s): Lirael, Librarian; Sameth, Royalty (prince); Hedge, Wizard; Mogget, Cat; Disreputable Dog, Dog
Time period(s): Indeterminate
Locale(s): Old Kingdom, Fictional Country

Summary: Lirael is the Abhorsen-in-waiting; the one who will maintain the borders between life and death. The charge is a difficult one, and Lirael fears it. Prince Sameth is also afraid of his future. In trying to escape their destinies, the two have found troubles they can only resolve by exercising the very talents they fear. Fortunately, two magical creatures, the Disreputable Dog and Mogget, who appears to be a white cat, are determined not to let Lirael and Sam despair. After they escape from Abhorsen House, where a creature of the evil wizard Hedge had them trapped, the two try to save a friend of Sam's who has been duped into unearthing a massive evil known as Orannis the Destroyer. Lirael ventures into the realm of death, while Sam finds that being a leader in frightening times is an equally fearful task, in this sequel to *Lirael* and *Sabriel*. (358 pages)

Where it's reviewed:
Booklist, January 1, 2003, page 871
Horn Book, March 2003, page 214
Publishers Weekly, November 25, 2002, page 20
School Library Journal, February 2003, page 146
Voice of Youth Advocates, February 2003, page 490

Other books by the same author:
Grim Tuesday, 2004
Mister Monday, 2003
Lirael: Daughter of the Clayr, 2001
Sabriel, 1995

Other books you might like:
Peter Dickinson, *The Ropemaker*, 2001
  When the magic that has always protected her homeland begins to fail, Tilja is called to make the journey to find a wizard who can restore it.
William Nicholson, *The Wind Singer: An Adventure*, 2000
  A rebellious girl is forced to flee the repressive city where she was born and on her travels she discovers some of its frightful history.
Philip Pullman, *The Golden Compass*, 1995
  Lyra has what everyone wants, the magical golden compass and the ability to interpret it, but can she keep the compass out of evil hands?

1085

GARTH NIX

Mister Monday

(New York: Scholastic, 2003)

Series: Keys to the Kingdom. Book 1
Subject(s): Fantasy; Adventure and Adventurers
Age range(s): Grades 6-9
Major character(s): Arthur Penhaligon, 7th Grader, Adoptee; Mister Monday, Supernatural Being; Suzy Turquoise Blue, Worker (ink filler)
Time period(s): Indeterminate
Locale(s): The House, Fictional Country; England

Summary: A new student at his school, Arthur can't make his physical education teacher understand that he shouldn't be running, as he's just recovering from an asthma attack, but his words are worthless, he runs and has another attack. Mister Monday appears and, to conform to the tenets of The Will, gives Arthur a key and an atlas to hold, though he plans to take back both items when Arthur dies his expected early death. The key helps Arthur's asthma and he doesn't die, which poses a problem for Mister Monday, as he needs the key to retain his power. He sends dog-faced Fetchers to retrieve the key, but they also bring a plague virus to Earth, which threatens people Arthur loves. Determined to track down the Fetchers, Arthur enters The House, which only he can see, meets Suzy Turquoise Blue who will be his helpmate, and finds himself in a realm of danger and excitement as the battle is on for control of the key. (361 pages)

Where it's reviewed:
Bulletin of the Center for Children's Books, January 2004, page 200
Publishers Weekly, July 28, 2003, page 95

School Library Journal, December 2003, page 158
Voice of Youth Advocates, February 2004, page 506

Other books by the same author:
Drowned Wednesday, 2005 (Keys to the Kingdom Book 3)
Grim Tuesday, 2004 (Keys to the Kingdom Book 2)
The Ragwitch, 2004
Abhorsen, 2003
The Violet Keystone, 2001 (Seventh Tower Book 6)

Other books you might like:
Lewis Carroll, *Alice's Adventures in Wonderland*, 1865
  Sitting bored upon a riverbank, Alice doesn't hesitate to follow the White Rabbit down his rabbit hole where she enters an amazing world.
Diana Wynne Jones, *The Lives of Christopher Chant*, 1988
  As Christopher dreams, he travels to strange and fascinating worlds.
Darcy Pattison, *The Wayfinder*, 2000
  Able to find anything from a person to clothing, Win enters the fog-shrouded Rift to rescue his sister and locate the Well of Life that combats plague.

1086

JOAN LOWERY NIXON

Nightmare

(New York: Delacorte, 2003)

Subject(s): Mystery and Detective Stories; Dreams and Nightmares; Murder
Age range(s): Grades 6-10
Major character(s): Emily Wood, 16-Year-Old, 10th Grader
Time period(s): 2000s
Locale(s): Hill Country, Texas

Summary: The classic underachiever in a family of overachievers with two valedictorian sisters, a physician father and a lawyer mother, Emily is content to sit in the back of a classroom and remain silent. But this summer her parents decide that Camp Excel, a summer program for underachievers, will benefit her greatly and enroll her. As soon as Emily hears the name of the institute where one of the Camp Excel directors works, Foxworth-Isaacson Educational Center, she blanches and wonders why that name is so familiar to her. Arriving at the camp, she feels a strong sense of deja vu and her recurring nightmare stirs in her mind, the one where she's trapped by vines yet sees a dead body with its mouth open to scream. As it turns out, perhaps Emily has been in this spot before as someone at the camp definitely wants to eliminate her in a work published after the death of this four-time Edgar winning author. (166 pages)

Where it's reviewed:
Booklist, October 15, 2003, page 405
Bulletin of the Center for Children's Books, November 2003, page 117
Publishers Weekly, October 6, 2003, page 85
School Library Journal, October 2003, page 172
Voice of Youth Advocates, October 2003, page 316

Awards the book has won:
ALA Quick Picks for Reluctant Young Adult Readers, 2004

Other books by the same author:
The Trap, 2002
Playing for Keeps, 2001
Caught in the Act, 2000
Nobody's There, 2000
Who Are You?, 1999

Other books you might like:
Lois Duncan, *Down a Dark Hall*, 1974
Four girls, selected for their ESP ability and living in a boarding school, suffer from terrible nightmares and don't know what's real and what isn't.
Dorothy Hoobler, *The Demon in the Teahouse*, 2001
Sent to investigate several suspicious fires, Seikei is now trapped on a rooftop surrounded by flames.
Marsha Qualey, *Close to a Killer*, 1999
Just released from prison, Daria and her daughter Barrie open Killer Looks beauty salon but when two clients are murdered, Daria's a suspect.

1087

JOAN LOWERY NIXON

The Trap

(New York: Delacorte, 2002)

Subject(s): Mystery and Detective Stories
Age range(s): Grades 6-9
Major character(s): Julie Hollister, 16-Year-Old; Gabe Hollister, Uncle, Retiree; Glenda Hollister, Aunt, Retiree
Time period(s): 2000s
Locale(s): Rancho del Oro, Texas

Summary: Julie plans to spend her summer working with her swim team as they prepare for their next season, but her family has other plans for her when her great-uncle Gabe breaks his ankle. Sent to the retirement community Rancho del Oro where her relatives live, Julie is the only one who believes her Uncle Gabe's claim that he didn't fall, but was made to fall, and so broke his ankle. E-mailing to her friend back in Texas, the two discuss investigating the accident, especially when Julie has no end of suspects to consider. When two people die and jewelry shows up missing, Julie begins to connect the clues in another whodunit from a master author. (165 pages)

Where it's reviewed:
Booklist, September 15, 2002, page 224
Kirkus Reviews, August 1, 2002, page 1139
Library Media Connection, March 2003, page 75
School Library Journal, September 2002, page 231
Voice of Youth Advocates, February 2003, page 480

Other books by the same author:
Playing for Keeps, 2001
Caught in the Act, 2000
In the Face of Danger, 2000
The Haunting, 1998
Murdered, My Sweet, 1997

Other books you might like:
Dorothy Hoobler, *The Demon in the Teahouse*, 2001
Adopted by Judge Ooka, Seikei helps with his investiga-

tions and is sent to a teahouse when suspicious fires are set and three people are murdered.
Patricia H. Rushford, *Over the Edge*, 1997
Vacationing at her grandmother's beach cottage, Jennie's not happy to stop her holiday to investigate the murder of the mayor's daughter.
Wendelin Van Draanen, *Sammy Keyes and the Hollywood Mummy*, 2001
Visiting her mother in Hollywood, Sammy digs right into investigating when her mother's competitor for a role is found dead.

1088

TRINKA HAKES NOBLE
STEVEN KELLOGG, Illustrator

Jimmy's Boa and the Bungee Jump Slam Dunk

(New York: Dial Books for Young Readers, 2003)

Subject(s): Animals/Reptiles; Sports/Basketball; Tall Tales
Age range(s): Grades K-3

Summary: Maggie tells her mother about an after-school adventure when Jimmy brings his boa to dance class in the gym. During the class, Jimmy will only dance with his boa, causing the kids end up doing the "Tangle" instead of the Tango because of the boa's long tail. The fancy footwork and bouncing of the dancers attract the attention of the basketball coach and some nearby rabbits as this humorous, exuberant tale concludes. (32 pages)

Where it's reviewed:
Booklist, August, 2003, page 1990
Publishers Weekly, October 27, 2003, page 72
School Library Journal, September 2003, page 186

Other books by the same author:
Jimmy's Boa and the Big Splash Birthday Bash, 1989
Jimmy's Boa Bounces Back, 1984
The Day Jimmy's Boa Ate the Wash, 1980

Other books you might like:
Lynne Jonell, *I Need a Snake*, 1998
Robbie NEEDS a snake, but his mom doesn't want him to have one as a pet.
Steven Kellogg, *Pinkerton, Behave!*, 1982
Great Dane Pinkerton gets sent to obedience school, but he still has trouble behaving.
Rose-Marie Provencher, *Slithery Jake*, 2004
When Sid brings home a snake and asks if he can keep it as his pet, his parents decide to sleep on it. In the morning, the snake is missing.

1089

HAN NOLAN

When We Were Saints

(San Diego: Harcourt, 2003)

Subject(s): Spirituality; Emotional Problems; Christian Life
Age range(s): Grades 8-11

Major character(s): Archibald Lee "Archie" Caswell, 14-Year-Old, Orphan; Clare Simpson, Religious; Silas Benjamin, Grandfather
Time period(s): 2000s
Locale(s): Appalachians; New York, New York

Summary: Archie's lived with his grandfather, the prophet Silas, since he was an orphan, but seems to always make Granddaddy mad. On his deathbed, Granddaddy Silas points a finger at him and says "Young man, you are a saint." Archie's unsure what to make of that until he feels a touch of spiritualism one afternoon while sitting atop a mountain on their farm. Meeting Clare, a teen who thinks the two of them must be related to the original saints Francis and Clare, he considers the possibility that sainthood is his destiny. Clare is ready to give up material possessions and lead a simple life and decides the two need to make a pilgrimage to the Cloisters Museum in New York. Stealing his grandfather's truck, Archie drives them northward though he worries about Clare's fasting and hours of prayer which lead to the stigmata marks that appear on her body. Is Clare deeply religious or a fanatic? Is her institutionalization merely a side trip on her path to sainthood or a sign of mental instability? Join Archie as he accompanies Clare on a search for truth and spirituality in this thought-provoking work. (291 pages)

Where it's reviewed:
Bulletin of the Center for Children's Books, December 2003, page 161
Horn Book, January 2004, page 87
Publishers Weekly, October 20, 2003, page 55
School Library Journal, November 2003, page 144
Voice of Youth Advocates, December 2003, page 404

Other books by the same author:
Born Blue, 2001 (ALA Best Books for Young Adults)
A Face in Every Window, 1999
Dancing on the Edge, 1997 (National Book Award)
Send Me Down a Miracle, 1996
If I Should Die Before I Wake, 1994

Other books you might like:
Cathryn Clinton, *The Calling*, 2001
 Called to the Lord when she's only 12, Esta Lea is amazed to discover she has the gift of healing, too.
Patty Dann, *Mermaids*, 1986
 Charlotte, who wishes to be a saint, secretly lusts after Joe, a caretaker at a nearby convent, in this funny coming-of-age novel.
Michael Morpurgo, *The War of Jenkins' Ear*, 1995
 At boarding school Toby meets Simon Christopher who claims to be the reincarnated Jesus Christ.
Terry Pringle, *Preacher's Boy*, 1988
 The trouble between Michael and his preacher father can be traced to the day Michael has the giggles while in the pulpit during "Youth Day."
Marilyn Singer, *I Believe in Water: Twelve Brushes with Religion*, 2000
 Thirteen short stories examine faith and religion from the perspective of young people.

LUCY NOLAN
LAURA J. BRYANT, Illustrator

A Fairy in a Dairy
(New York: Marshall Cavendish, 2003)

Subject(s): Animals/Cows; Magic; Humor
Age range(s): Grades K-3
Major character(s): Pixie, Cow; Farmer Blue, Farmer; Mayor Clabber, Government Official
Time period(s): Indeterminate Past
Locale(s): Buttermilk Hollow, Fictional Country

Summary: Mayor Clabber's trying to get rich by selling his land to a toothpick factory and encouraging local farmers to also sell theirs. Farmer Blue doesn't think the wealth to be gained from the land sale can compensate for the change of lifestyle and suggests to Pixie that what Buttermilk Hollow needs is a fairy godmother. Not long after their conversation, dairy products begin appearing magically all over town in response to people's wishes. Most citizens are simply pleasantly puzzled but Mayor Clabber is enraged. He wants the wealth from the land sale so he sets a trap to catch the "fairy." When his net captures Pixie, wearing a pink tutu and riding a bicycle Mayor Clabber publicly denounces her as a fraud because she's riding a bicycle and not flying. His plan backfires when Pixie slowly rises into the air, floating over the assembled crowd and continuing to bestow her fairy dairy wishes. (32 pages)

Where it's reviewed:
Booklist, November 1, 2003, page 505
Bulletin of the Center for Children's Books, February 2004, page 241
Publishers Weekly, December 15, 2003, page 72
School Library Journal, November 2003, page 110

Other books by the same author:
Down Girl and Sit: Smarter than Squirrels, 2004
Jack Quack, 2001
Lizard Man of Crabtree County, 1999

Other books you might like:
Doreen Cronin, *Click, Clack, Moo: Cows That Type*, 2000
 Clever cows use an old typewriter rather than magic to achieve their goals by writing letters to Farmer Brown.
Paul Brett Johnson, *The Cow Who Wouldn't Come Down*, 1993
 Gertrude doesn't pretend to be a fairy but she does have a mind to fly and, once she succeeds, she has no interest in returning to the barn.
David Small, *George Washington's Cows*, 1994
 According to this tale Washington's outlandish animals are the reason he gave politics a try.

1091

JERDINE NOLEN
DEBBIE TILLEY, Illustrator

Lauren McGill's Pickle Museum

(San Diego: Harcourt, Inc., 2003)

Subject(s): Collectors and Collecting; Museums; Food
Age range(s): Grades K-3
Major character(s): Lauren McGill, Collector, Child
Time period(s): 2000s (2003)
Locale(s): United States

Summary: Lauren McGill loves pickles so she is thrilled when her class plans a field trip to the pickle factory. However, the class never actually makes it to the factory because an explosion at the factory unleashes a flood of pickles. Lauren saves the day by showing her classmates how to bottle pickles, but instead of feeling heroic, Lauren feels lost. Now that all of her classmates like pickles too, Lauren doesn't feel unique any more. Finally, Lauren manages to find her place again by opening a Pickle Museum. (32 pages)

Where it's reviewed:
Publishers Weekly, April 14, 2003, page 70
School Library Journal, July 2003, page 102

Other books by the same author:
Thunder Rose, 2003
Raising Dragons, 1998
Harvey Potter's Balloon Farm, 1994

Other books you might like:
Judi Barrett, *Pickles to Pittsburgh*, 1997
    Kate and Henry return to the town of Chewandswallow where the Falling Food Company was created to deal with their unusual weather.
Marjorie Priceman, *Emeline at the Circus*, 1999
    During Emeline's class field trip to the circus, she gets caught up in the act.
David Shannon, *A Bad Case of Stripes*, 1998
    Camilla worries so much about other's opinions of her that her skin changes colors and patterns. Admitting her love of unpopular lima beans cures her.

1092

JERDINE NOLEN
DAVID CATROW, Illustrator

Plantzilla

(San Diego: Silver Whistle/Harcourt, Inc., 2002)

Subject(s): Letters; Humor; Vacations
Age range(s): Grades 1-3
Major character(s): Mortimer Henryson, 3rd Grader, Son; Samuel G. Lester, Teacher; Mrs. Henry Henryson, Mother, Spouse; Plantzilla, Plant
Time period(s): Indeterminate
Locale(s): United States; Hawaii

Summary: Through letters, Mortimer requests permission to care for the class plant during the summer, Mrs. Henryson describes the changes in the household due to Plantzilla's growth habits and Mr. Lester responds, from his vacation spot, with scientific information about plants with cilia. Mortimer's joy in the plant never wanes but Mrs. Henryson's letters show her growing alarm at the size and eating habits of Plantzilla as well as the parents' desire to return the plant to Mr. Lester. Mortimer, though, adores Plantzilla and, by the end of summer (and the reappearance of the family dog), his parents reach the conclusion that Plantzilla should be adopted into the family. (32 pages)

Where it's reviewed:
Booklist, October 15, 2002, page 413
Bulletin of the Center for Children's Books, November 2002, page 120
Horn Book Guide, Spring 2003, page 47
Publishers Weekly, August 12, 2002, page 300
School Library Journal, September 2002, page 202

Awards the book has won:
IRA Children's Choices, 2003
Center for Children's Books Best Books, 2002

Other books by the same author:
Big Jabe, 1999 (Publishers Weekly Best Children's Books)
In My Momma's Kitchen, 1999
Raising Dragons, 1998
Harvey Potter's Balloon Farm, 1994 (ALA Notable Children's Book)

Other books you might like:
Paul Fleischman, *Weslandia*, 1999
    Contented nonconformist Wesley plants a garden and transforms his backyard into a new civilization based on the crop he produces.
Walter Lynn Krudop, *Something Is Growing*, 1995
    Unnoticed, Peter plants a seed in an urban neighborhood with results that get everyone's attention.
Nancy Willard, *The Magic Cornfield*, 1997
    Postcards to cousin Bottom document Totem's travels from New York to Minneapolis through a magic cornfield.

1093

JERDINE NOLEN
KADIR NELSON, Illustrator

Thunder Rose

(San Diego: Silver Whistle/Harcourt, Inc., 2003)

Subject(s): Tall Tales; Cowboys/Cowgirls; American West
Age range(s): Grades 1-4
Major character(s): Rose "Thunder Rose" MacGruder, Daughter, Cowgirl
Time period(s): Indeterminate Past
Locale(s): West

Summary: Within moments of her birth during a violent thunderstorm Rose is sitting up, conversing with her parents and rolling lightning into a ball. Clearly, the child who comes to be known as Thunder Rose has the power of thunder and lightning within her. Rose satiates her baby's thirst by drinking straight from a cow and satisfies her two-year-old curiosity by playing with pieces of scrap metal that she twists and bends into rods or fencing. Thunder Rose's greatest challenge comes during her first cattle drive to Abilene. Catching cattle rustlers was easy, but catching the clouds overhead to bring rain to the parched land provokes the anger of the clouds and soon Thunder Rose is facing twin twisters. Reaching deep within Rose calls on the thunder and lightning in her and sings her own song of thunder and lightning. Not only does Thunder Rose calm the tornadoes with her song, but she also causes a gentle rain to pour from the hearts of clouds. (32 pages)

Where it's reviewed:
Booklist, November 1, 2003, page 505
Bulletin of the Center for Children's Books, January 2004, page 200
Publishers Weekly, October 6, 2003, page 84
School Library Journal, September 2003, page 186

Awards the book has won:
Coretta Scott King Illustration Honor Book, 2004
IRA Children's Choices, 2004

Other books by the same author:
Plantzilla, 2002 (IRA Children's Choices)
Big Jabe, 1999 (Publishers Weekly Best Children's Books)
In My Momma's Kitchen, 1999
Raising Dragons, 1998
Harvey Potter's Balloon Farm, 1994 (ALA Notable Children's Books)

Other books you might like:
Anne Isaacs, *Swamp Angel*, 1994
    An original tall tale named a Caldecott Honor Book describes the achievements of Angelica and how she earns her nickname.
Steven Kellogg, *Sally Ann Thunder Ann Whirlwind Crockett*, 1995
    According to this tall tale, Sally Ann departs for the frontier on her eighth birthday to continue her larger than life exploits.
Robert D. San Souci, *Cut from the Same Cloth: American Women of Myth, Legend and Tall Tale*, 1993
    The illustrated collection of 20 tales is drawn from folk tales, ballads and popular stories.
Lisa Wheeler, *Avalanche Annie: A Not-So-Tall Tale*, 2003
    A rhyming tale tells of Annie Halfpint who lassoes an avalanche and rides it from the mountaintop into her town.
Catherine Wright, *Steamboat Annie and the Thousand-Pound Catfish*, 2001
    After Annie hooks Ernie she battles the catfish up and down the Ohio River for a year and a half before landing him and flinging him to California.

1094

MATT NOVAK, Author/Illustrator

No Zombies Allowed

(New York: Richard Jackson Book/Atheneum Books for Young Readers, 2002)

Subject(s): Witches and Witchcraft; Halloween; Problem Solving
Age range(s): Grades K-2
Major character(s): Wizzle, Witch; Woddle, Witch
Time period(s): Indeterminate
Locale(s): Fictional Country

Summary: As Wizzle and Woddle plan for Halloween they look over photographs from the previous year's party. Each photo brings back memories of something unpleasant such as moaning ghosts, silent zombies that dropped their eyes in the punch bowl or swamp monsters tracking in slime. By the time they finish looking at the pictures their yard is full of signs excluding one type of monster or another. When they find photos of each other up to mischief at last year's party they reconsider, take down all the signs and post just one saying "No Photos Allowed." Then they invite everyone to their Halloween party and have a great time. (32 pages)

Where it's reviewed:
Bulletin of the Center for Children's Books, September 2002, page 30
Horn Book, September 2002, page 556
Publishers Weekly, September 23, 2002, page 71
School Library Journal, August 2002, page 162

Other books by the same author:
Too Many Bunnies, 2004
On Halloween Street: A Lift-the-Flap Story, 2001
Little Wolf, Big Wolf, 2000

Other books you might like:
Pamela Jane, *Monster Mischief*, 2001
    Little Moe accidentally spills the pot of stew five monsters are cooking, leaving them nothing to eat but Halloween candy.
Judy Sierra, *The House That Drac Built*, 1995
    A rhyming cumulative tale introduces such unusual creatures as a manticore and the fiend of Bloodygore living in the house that Drac built.
Erica Silverman, *The Halloween House*, 1997
    On Halloween two prison escapees are the uninvited guests in a haunted house.
Michael O. Tunnell, *Halloween Pie*, 1999
    The fragrance of Old Witch's Halloween pie awakens a ghost, a ghoul, a vampire, a zombie, a skeleton, and a banshee.

1095

SHARYN NOVEMBER, Editor

Firebirds: An Anthology of Original Fantasy and Science Fiction

(New York: Firebird/Penguin Putnam, 2003)

Subject(s): Fantasy; Short Stories; Science Fiction
Age range(s): Grades 7-12

Summary: Sixteen delightfully delicious tales of fantasy or science fiction, written by noted authors in the young adult field, fill the pages of this anthology. Garth Nix's brand of Western style justice can be found in "Hope Chest," Delia Sherman retells the Tam Lin story in "Cotillion," while Lloyd Alexander describes the terrifying result of an unsuccessful quest for a job in "Max Mondrosch." A notary public who follows the rules halts the plans of an evil enchantress in "The Baby in the Night Deposit Box," while a cat tells about her human in "Little Dot," by Diana Wynne Jones. The other authors included are Emma Bull, Michael Cadnum, Kara Dalkey, Nancy Farmer, Nina Kiriki Hoffman, Patricia McKillip, Meredith Ann Pierce, Sherwood Smith, Nancy Springer, Elizabeth E. Wein and Laurel Winter. (421 pages)

Where it's reviewed:
Bulletin of the Center for Children's Books, January 2004, page 201
Horn Book, January 2004, page 89
Publishers Weekly, September 1, 2003, page 90
School Library Journal, October 2003, page 172
Voice of Youth Advocates, December 2003, page 411

Awards the book has won:
ALA Best Books for Young Adults, 2004

Other books you might like:
Ursula K. Le Guin, *Tales from Earthsea*, 2001
 Return to Earthsea in this collection of stories that tell of times both before and after the wizard Ged.
Patricia McKillip, *A Knot in the Grain and Other Stories*, 1994
 Fantasy and fairy tale stories each sport a magical twist.
Robin McKinley, *Water: Tales of Elemental Spirits*, 2002
 This anthology explores the mysterious power of water. Peter Dickinson, co-author.

`1096`

LAURA JOFFE NUMEROFF
FELICIA BOND, Illustrator

If You Take a Mouse to School

(New York: Laura Geringer Books/HarperCollins Publishers, 2002)

Subject(s): Animals/Mice; Schools; Humor
Age range(s): Preschool
Major character(s): Unnamed Character, Student—Elementary School; Unnamed Character, Mouse
Time period(s): 2000s
Locale(s): United States

Summary: If a mouse hides in your backpack to get a ride to school he'll try to do all that you do too. He'll try to solve a math problem and follow you to lunch and he might even write a book to read to you. When the bell rings he'll race with you to wait for the bus, but as soon as he feels hungry and reaches for his snack he'll remember the lunch box and you'll have to go back to class. (32 pages)

Where it's reviewed:
Bulletin of the Center for Children's Books, October 2002, page 72
Horn Book Guide, Spring 2003, page 17
Kirkus Reviews, June 15, 2002, page 886
Publishers Weekly, June 24, 2002, page 54
School Library Journal, September 2002, page 202

Awards the book has won:
IRA Children's Choices, 2003

Other books by the same author:
If You Take a Mouse to the Movies, 2000
If You Give a Pig a Pancake, 1998
If You Give a Moose a Muffin, 1991

Other books you might like:
Kathryn Heling, *Mouse Makes Words: A Phonics Reader*, 2002
 In a rhyming story, Mouse (who must have gone to school) shows how to make new words by substituting different first letters.
Jan Ormerod, *Miss Mouse's Day*, 2001
 Miss Mouse and her pal play together outside and build houses in the sandbox.
Brenda Shannon Yee, *Hide & Seek*, 2001
 A little mouse unsuccessfully attempts to cross a room without being noticed.

`1097`

LAURA JOFFE NUMEROFF
NATE EVANS, Illustrator

Laura Numeroff's 10-Step Guide to Living with Your Monster

(New York: Laura Geringer Books/HarperCollins Publishers, 2002)

Subject(s): Monsters; Pets; Humor
Age range(s): Grades K-2
Major character(s): Bob, Monster; Unnamed Character, Child
Time period(s): Indeterminate
Locale(s): Fictional Country

Summary: Illustrations show a young boy's attempts to comply with the ten rules of living with a monster. Advice on the selection, feeding and care of monsters features the boy's experience with his pet Bob. Monsters need a lot of practice with basic commands such as sit, but seem to take to Country and Western music naturally. Teaching Bob to brush his teeth and giving him a monthly bubble bath are challenging, but necessary to proper care of one's monster. Lastly, a bedtime story will assure that everyone sleeps well. (32 pages)

Where it's reviewed:
Horn Book Guide, Fall 2002, page 310
Publishers Weekly, February 25, 2002, page 65
School Library Journal, June 2002, page 106

Awards the book has won:
IRA Children's Choices, 2003

Other books by the same author:
Beatrice Doesn't Want To, 2004
What Mommies Do Best, 2003
If You Give an Author a Pencil, 2002

Other books you might like:
Judy Hindley, *The Perfect Little Monster*, 2001
 To his proud family a baby monster is perfectly horrible but at his first birthday party he scares the relatives away with his smile.
Jackie French Koller, *No Such Thing*, 1997
 Just as Howard's mother refuses to believe his claim that there is a monster under the bed, so Monster's mother will not accept that a boy is in the bed.
Laura Leuck, *My Monster Mama Loves Me So*, 1999
 In a rhyming story Mama expresses the many ways in which she loves her dear little monster.

O

1098

Big Mouth & Ugly Girl

(New York: HarperCollins, 2002)

Subject(s): Friendship; Schools/High Schools; Peer Pressure

Age range(s): Grades 8-12

Major character(s): Matt Donaghy, 11th Grader, Leader (vice president of his class); Ursula Riggs, 11th Grader

Time period(s): 2000s

Locale(s): Westchester County, New York

Summary: The "Big Mouth" of the title, Matt, clowns around in the cafeteria one day and kiddingly makes reference to blowing up the school if his play isn't accepted for the Spring Arts Festival. Overheard by some trouble-making twins who report him to the principal, Matt is dragged out of his class, brought to police headquarters and suspended from school. His friends disavow any knowledge of what he said and pretend they've never heard of Matt. Only Ursula, the "Ugly Girl" of the title, breaks out of her loner solitude to tell the principal exactly what Matt said, emphasizing the teasing nature of his remarks. Matt returns to school, but when his parents sue, he's ostracized. As one who's used to lots of attention, Matt becomes despondent and even considers suicide; once again Ursula comes to his rescue. The two form a hesitant friendship with Matt reconsidering his propensity for silly remarks, and Ursula her inclination to be a loner, in this first young adult novel by a noted adult author. (266 pages)

Where it's reviewed:
Booklist, May 15, 2002, page 1592
New York Times Book Review, May 19, 2002, page 32
Publishers Weekly, April 22, 2002, page 71
School Library Journal, May 2002, page 158
Voice of Youth Advocates, August 2002, page 196

Awards the book has won:
ALA Best Books for Young Adults, 2003
School Library Journal Best Books, 2002

Other books by the same author:
Small Avalanches and Other Stories, 2003

Other books you might like:
Ron Koertge, *The Brimstone Journals*, 2001
   Fifteen seniors reveal their thoughts in a series of poems, but one is so angry he wants to retaliate against anyone who's ever made him mad.
Carol Plum-Ucci, *The Body of Christopher Creed*, 2000
   Geeky Christopher Creed is missing and his classmates buzz with speculation as to whether he was murdered or kidnapped.
Francine Prose, *After*, 2003
   When a Columbine-type shooting occurs at a school near his, Tom realizes that his school days will never be the same.

1099

Freaky Green Eyes

(New York: HarperTempest, 2003)

Subject(s): Fathers and Daughters; Murder; Abuse

Age range(s): Grades 7-10

Major character(s): Francesca "Franky" Pierson, 15-Year-Old; Reid Pierson, Television Personality (sportscaster), Father (of Franky); Krista Pierson, Mother (of Franky); Samantha Pierson, Child, Sister (of Franky)

Time period(s): 2000s

Locale(s): Seattle, Washington; Puget Sound, Washington

Summary: It's hard to be noticed in Franky's house as everything revolves around her sportscaster father, Reid, a former football star and popular television star. As long as everything goes Reid's way, he's happy; when thwarted, he becomes abusive. Franky has ignored all the signs of her father's controlling ways until she's accosted by a drunk at a party and finds an inner reserve to deflect his advances, a reserve she calls her "Freaky Green Eyes." These eyes begin to see the conflict in her home, her mother's move to an artist's cottage in Puget Sound for what it really is, her sister Samantha's worries, and her father's attempt to blame her mother for pulling their family apart. When her mother disappears from the cottage, and Franky finds her journal, she begins to assemble the facts about her father and realizes he's killed Krista, though it takes enormous courage for her to contact the police. (341 pages)

Where it's reviewed:
Booklist, December 15, 2003, page 660
Bulletin of the Center for Children's Books, November 2003, page 117
Horn Book, November 2003, page 752
School Library Journal, October 2003, page 174
Voice of Youth Advocates, October 2003, page 316

Awards the book has won:
Publishers Weekly Best Children's Books, 2003

Other books by the same author:
Big Mouth & Ugly Girl, 2002
Small Avalanches and Other Stories, 2002

Other books you might like:
Deb Caletti, *The Queen of Everything*, 2002
    Jordan watches, unable to help, when her nice, sweet father's obsession with wealthy neighbor Mrs. D'Angelo leads him to kill her husband.
Lois Duncan, *I Know What You Did Last Summer*, 1973
    Four teens that take a vow of silence after they cause a hit-and-run accident are tracked down, though not by the police.
Julius Lester, *When Dad Killed Mom*, 2001
    Jenny and Jeremy erupt in the courtroom when they hear the lies their father tells about their mother, their marriage and his affairs with students.

1100

JOYCE CAROL OATES

Small Avalanches and Other Stories
(New York: HarperCollins, 2003)

Subject(s): Short Stories; Adolescence; Coming-of-Age
Age range(s): Grades 9-Adult
Locale(s): United States

Summary: The temptations, thrills and tempering that all teenage girls face are explored in this collection of adult stories featuring 12 different narrators. "Where Are You Going, Where Have You Been," tells of a teen who is strangely attracted to an older man. A teen finally visits her grandmother, afflicted with Alzheimer's and living in a nursing home, and reflects on its impact in "The Visit." And another girl discovers as she nears adulthood that popularity isn't always the answer as reflected in "Life After High School." This popular adult author has compiled a challenging collection of stories that should appeal to older teen readers. (390 pages)

Where it's reviewed:
Booklist, March 15, 2003, page 1323
Kirkus Reviews, December 15, 2002, page 1855
Kliatt, May 2004, page 31
School Library Journal, July 2003, page 134
Voice of Youth Advocates, June 2003, page 14

Other books by the same author:
Freaky Green Eyes, 2003
Big Mouth & Ugly Girl, 2002

Other books you might like:
Michael Cart, *Love and Sex: Ten Stories of Truth*, 2001
    All aspects of love and sex, from infatuation to homosexuality and virginity, are explored in these stories.
Peter Carver, *Close-ups*, 2000
    Written by Canadian authors of young adult fiction, this rich collection shows that the universal complexities of life are not only for teenagers.
Chris Lynch, *All the Old Haunts*, 2001
    "All the old haunts" appear in these stories of teens as they become aware of the realities of life and have to make personal decisions.

1101

JUDITH O'BRIEN

Timeless Love
(New York: Simon Pulse/Simon & Schuster, 2002)

Subject(s): Time Travel; Romance; Historical
Age range(s): Grades 7-10
Major character(s): Samantha "Sam" McKenna, 16-Year-Old; Edward VI, Royalty (prince); Barnaby Fitzpatrick, Nobleman
Time period(s): 2000s; 16th century
Locale(s): United States; London, England

Summary: Sam's adventures started when her friend permed and highlighted her hair at the same time, leaving a frizzled mess just hours before Sam's sixteenth birthday. They were forced to drive her father's prized BMW to the drugstore for conditioner when a runaway shopping cart damaged its passenger side. Returning home, Sam recovers the car and then, wearing a necklace her mother's given her for her birthday, wishes she could be anywhere but at home when her father returns. Lo and behold, she's now standing in the bedchamber of Edward VI, a sickly boy who history says died before he could claim the throne of England. Putting 21st century medical knowledge to good use, Sam determines he just has allergies and "cures" him. Enjoying her life in Henry VIII's court, she meets and falls for Sir Barnaby Fitzpatrick, but when rumors spread that she and Barnaby are conspiring against Edward, she wishes she could return home. When she returns home, it's not as she left it for she's changed history: there's been no Queen Elizabeth I or the Industrial Revolution, no one understands her English and her school notes are now written in Spanish in this fun, romantic adventure. (231 pages)

Where it's reviewed:
Kliatt, May 2002, page 28
School Library Journal, March 2002, page 236

Other books by the same author:
Mary Jane, 2003
The Forever Bride, 1999
Once upon a Rose, 1996

Other books you might like:

Virginia Farmer, *Blast to the Past*, 2004
  Accidentally blasted to 1300s Scotland, Brian Skelley meets, falls in love with Caira and wonders why he's trying to return home.

Diana Gabaldon, *The Outlander*, 1991
  On a second honeymoon, Claire touches part of an ancient stone circle and travels back to 1740s Scotland where she falls in love with a kilted Scotsman.

Kathryn Lasky, *Elizabeth I: Red Rose of the House of Tudor*, 1999
  These fictionalized diary entries provide a look at Elizabeth's life during her early teen years as she strives for her father's attention.

1102

BARBARA O'CONNOR

Fame and Glory in Freedom, Georgia
(New York: Frances Foster/Farrar Straus Giroux, 2003)

Subject(s): Interpersonal Relations; Contests; Popularity
Age range(s): Grades 4-7
Major character(s): Burdette "Bird" Weaver, 6th Grader; Harlem Tate, 6th Grader; Miss Delphine, Neighbor
Time period(s): 2000s
Locale(s): Freedom, Georgia

Summary: When new boy Harlem moves to Freedom, Georgia, Bird's determined to befriend him before the other kids in her class can tell him nasty things about her. Bird's not very popular, partly because she's so skinny, but also because she wears some strange outfits. Harlem's rather an outcast, too, because he looks both mean and dumb. In the afternoons, Bird goes over to visit with Miss Delphine and shares her wish to become friends with Harlem. The opportunity arises when word of the spelling bee goes around and their teacher says they must work with a partner; Bird's persistence finally wins Harlem over and he becomes her spelling bee cohort. He's really good at spelling so Bird feels like her second dream might come true and that they could win the trip to Disney World. But Bird doesn't know that Harlem needs glasses, which explains why he runs off the stage at the spelling bee and puts them out of competition. As Bird finds out, it's not really important to win the Bee or go to Disney World, but it is important to be a friend. (104 pages)

Where it's reviewed:
Booklist, July 2003, page 887
Bulletin of the Center for Children's Books, March 2003, page 283
Horn Book, July 2003, page 465
Publishers Weekly, May 12, 2003, page 67
School Library Journal, June 2003, page 148

Other books by the same author:
Taking Care of Moses, 2004
Moonpie and Ivy, 2001
Me and Rupert Goody, 1999

Other books you might like:
Kate DiCamillo, *Because of Winn-Dixie*, 2000
  Opal's new pet, a stray found at the Winn-Dixie grocery store, helps her grow out of the loneliness she feels in her new home.

Glen Huser, *Stitches*, 2003
  Two misfits, Chantelle and Travis, have been friends since first grade as Travis sews his puppets and Chantelle helps with their play performances.

Ann M. Martin, *Belle Teal*, 2001
  New student Darryl is heartened by the friendship, acceptance and writing partnership he enjoys with Belle Teal.

1103

KATHLEEN O'DELL
CHARISE MERICLE HARPER, Illustrator

Agnes Parker ... Girl in Progress
(New York: Dial, 2003)

Subject(s): Friendship; Bullies; School Life
Age range(s): Grades 4-6
Major character(s): Agnes Parker, 6th Grader; Prejean, 6th Grader; Peggy Neidermeyer, 6th Grader, Bully; Joe Waldrip, 6th Grader; Mrs. Libonati, Teacher
Time period(s): 2000s
Locale(s): United States

Summary: In this first novel Agnes is thrilled that her best friend Prejean is in her sixth grade class, though she's not happy to see that Peggy, who bullies her all the time, will also have Mrs. Libonati as her teacher. In this last year of elementary school, Agnes realizes that some of her preconceptions are not always correct, and that perhaps Peggy isn't as big a bully as she thought she was. She really likes Prejean, but when new student Joe shows up, she finds he's pretty interesting too; unfortunately, liking Joe puts a crimp in her friendship with Prejean. Agnes also gets glasses for the first time, considers trick or treating all by herself, and realizes that Mrs. Libonati is not a mean teacher, but instead one from whom Agnes learns a lot during this transitional year. (157 pages)

Where it's reviewed:
Bulletin of the Center for Children's Books, April 2003, page 326
Horn Book, March 2003, page 215
Publishers Weekly, April 14, 2003, page 71
School Library Journal, February 2003, page 146
Voice of Youth Advocates, April 2006, page 55

Other books by the same author:
Agnes Parker ... Happy Camper?, 2005 (Charise Mericle Harper, illustrator)

Other books you might like:
James Howe, *The Misfits*, 2001
  Tired of being called names, four friends decide to run for office at their school; though they don't win, they focus attention on the problem.

Martine Murray, *The Slightly True Story of Cedar B. Hartley (Who Planned to Live an Unusual Life)*, 2002
  Gregarious Cedar collects people as friends, which should help her live her "unusual life."

Phyllis Reynolds Naylor, *The Alice Series*, 1985-
  Alice and her friends Pamela, Elizabeth and Patrick sur-

vive the rigors of junior high school thanks to their friendship and support for one another.

1104

MARGARET O'HAIR
THIERRY COURTIN, Illustrator

Twin to Twin

(New York: Margaret K. McElderry/Simon & Schuster, 2003)

Subject(s): Twins; Brothers and Sisters; Stories in Rhyme
Age range(s): Preschool
Major character(s): Unnamed Character, Twin, Brother; Unnamed Character, Twin, Sister
Time period(s): 2000s (2003)
Locale(s): United States

Summary: A pair of fraternal twins grow into toddlers. Walking, talking, playing and eating are all twice the fun because they do everything as a pair. The active twins enjoy their similarity and the many things they do together. The author's first book concludes with a double bedtime. (32 pages)

Where it's reviewed:
Booklist, June 2003, page 1788
Bulletin of the Center for Children's Books, June 2003, page 415
Publishers Weekly, April 21, 2003, page 60
School Library Journal, May 2003, page 126

Other books by the same author:
Star Baby, 2005

Other books you might like:
Charlotte Doyle, *Twins!*, 2003
  This books looks at a day in the life of identical toddler twin girls.
Shelley Rotner, *About Twins*, 1999
  Color photographs of twin siblings illustrate what it's like to be a twin.
Elaine Scott, *Twins!*, 1998
  This book explores the similarities and differences of both fraternal and identical twins.

1105

SUSAN HEYBOER O'KEEFE

My Life and Death by Alexandra Canarsie

(Atlanta, GA: Peachtree Publishers, 2002)

Subject(s): Mystery and Detective Stories; Death; Family Problems
Age range(s): Grades 7-10
Major character(s): Alexandra "Allie" Canarsie, 14-Year-Old, Detective—Amateur; Jimmy Muller, 14-Year-Old (deceased); Dennis Monaghan, 14-Year-Old
Time period(s): 2000s
Locale(s): Nickel Park

Summary: Having moved ten times in six years, and wondering about the father she's never met, Allie is tired of never fitting in, becoming a troublemaker in school and living in trailer parks, especially the one they're in now whose grounds

are either dusty or muddy. The Evergreen Cemetery next to the Lost and Found Acres trailer park reaches out to her, with its cool, green vegetation and Allie starts attending the funerals of strangers. At first she's just an extra mourner, but when a boy her own age is buried, Allie thinks Jimmy's murder has been covered up. Suddenly she has a purpose and, with the help of Jimmy's friend Dennis, she's off and running, trying to find Jimmy's murderer, no matter how outlandish and impossible her suspects might be. Though Allie finally learns the truth about Jimmy's death, she also faces up to some truths in her own life in this author's first novel for teens. (217 pages)

Where it's reviewed:
Book Report, September 2002, page 56
Journal of Adolescent and Adult Literacy, November 2002, page 270
Kliatt, May 2002, page 13
Publishers Weekly, May 13, 2002, page 71
School Library Journal, September 2002, page 231

Other books by the same author:
Death by Eggplant, 2004

Other books you might like:
Barbara Holmes, *Following Fake Man*, 2001
  Homer's mother won't talk about his deceased father, but when Homer meets his father's best friend, it's the breakthrough he and his mother need.
Joan Lowery Nixon, *Murdered, My Sweet*, 1997
  A murder takes place and everyone assumes Jenny's mystery writer mother can solve the crime, but that's not her mother's strength.
Patricia H. Rushford, *Over the Edge*, 1997
  Looking forward to her vacation, Jennie's not sure she wants to find the murderer of the mayor's daughter in this continuing series.
Marcia Wood, *The Search for Jim McGwynn*, 1989
  Jamie decides to spend the summer tracking down his favorite author, P.J. Ross, who's supposed to live in his hometown of Riverton.

1106

JEAN DAVIES OKIMOTO
ELAINE M. AOKI, Co-Author
MEILO SO, Illustrator

The White Swan Express: A Story About Adoption

(New York: Clarion Books, 2002)

Subject(s): Adoption; Babies; Parent and Child
Age range(s): Grades K-3
Time period(s): 2000s
Locale(s): North America; Guangzhou, China

Summary: After long flights from various parts of North America adoptive parents arrive in China and board a bus together to continue their journey to the orphanage. Four babies await the two traditional couples, one non-traditional couple and a single woman. After a night at the White Swan Hotel the weary but excited travelers are led to a government building where they meet the daughters that they know from small photographs. After returning to their respective homes in America and Canada the families correspond annually, sharing photos of their growing daughters. The book is based on the adoption experience of one author; an afterword includes general information about the adoption process. (32 pages)

Where it's reviewed:
Booklist, November 1, 2002, page 509
Bulletin of the Center for Children's Books, January 2003, page 208
Kirkus Reviews, September 15, 2002, page 1397
Publishers Weekly, October 14, 2002, page 83
School Library Journal, February 2003, page 119

Awards the book has won:
Notable Social Studies Trade Books for Young People, 2003
Center for Children's Books Best Books, 2002

Other books you might like:
Lotta Hojer, *Heart of Mine: A Story of Adoption*, 2001
  Prospective parents fly across the world to fulfill their dream of adopting Tu Thi and return to their home as a family. Dan Hojer, co-author.
Karen Katz, *Over the Moon: An Adoption Tale*, 1997
  Receiving news of a baby's birth, a couple travels to another country to complete the process of adopting the child.
Rose Lewis, *I Love You Like Crazy Cakes*, 2000
  An American mother expresses her love for her adopted Chinese daughter by sharing the story of their first meeting and her homecoming.

1107

KEVIN O'MALLEY, Author/Illustrator

Little Buggy

(San Diego: Gulliver Books/Harcourt, Inc., 2002)

Subject(s): Animals/Insects; Fathers and Sons; Determination
Age range(s): Grades K-3
Major character(s): Little Buggy, Insect (ladybug), Son; Unnamed Character, Father, Insect (ladybug); Fred, Neighbor
Time period(s): Indeterminate
Locale(s): Fictional Country

Summary: Once Little Buggy decides he's ready to fly, he can't wait for his dad's ponderous directions. Little Buggy scurries up a plant stalk and takes to the air, falling on top of his dad, as Fred and a friend watch. Undeterred, Little Buggy silently climbs up again for another try and this time he remembers to open his wings. With his father beside him, Little Buggy tries and tries again until he masters both flying and landing. Fred is so inspired by Little Buggy that he plans to teach himself to fly. (32 pages)

Where it's reviewed:
Booklist, October 1, 2002, page 337
Horn Book Guide, Spring 2003, page 48
Kirkus Reviews, August 15, 2002, page 1231
Publishers Weekly, July 1, 2002, page 78
School Library Journal, September 2002, page 203

Awards the book has won:
IRA Children's Choices, 2003

Other books by the same author:
Little Buggy Runs Away, 2003
Bud, 2000
Leo Cockroach . . . Toy Tester, 1999

Other books you might like:
Eric Carle, *The Very Clumsy Click Beetle*, 1999
  A young click beetle tries and tries to learn how to flip himself over so he doesn't stay stuck on his back.
Pamela Duncan Edwards, *Some Smug Slug*, 1996
  Smugly, a slug ignores suspicious surroundings and shouts of warning, slowly slithering to a sudden end to his stroll.
Bob Graham, *Max*, 2000
  Max's superhero parents and grandparents worry about his inability to fly because, without flight, he cannot uphold the family tradition.

1108

KEVIN O'MALLEY, Author/Illustrator

Little Buggy Runs Away

(San Diego: Gulliver Books/Harcourt, Inc., 2003)

Subject(s): Animals/Insects; Runaways; Fathers and Sons
Age range(s): Grades K-3
Major character(s): Little Buggy, Son, Insect (ladybug); Big Buggy, Father, Insect (ladybug); Louie, Ant; Henry, Ant
Time period(s): Indeterminate
Locale(s): Fictional Country

Summary: Henry and Louie notice angry Little Buggy running away from home so they follow him and offer advice. Henry's questions show concern for Little Buggy while Louie's advice suggests that Little Buggy is now footloose and fancy-free. Together they gather some things Little Buggy will need such as a pen cap to use for a house and some not too moldy food. They bring messages from Big Buggy and a comic book to read at bedtime. After the sun sets Henry and Louie go home and Little Buggy is alone with only fireflies to light the night. One firefly stops by to see Little Buggy and mentions how sad Big Buggy seems to be then it lights the way for Little Buggy to walk home. On the way they meet Big Buggy and father and son continue the walk home together. (32 pages)

Where it's reviewed:
Booklist, November 15, 2003, page 602
Publishers Weekly, October 27, 2003, page 67
School Library Journal, November 2003, page 112

Other books by the same author:
Lucky Leaf, 2004
Little Buggy, 2002 (IRA Children's Choice)
Bud, 2000

Other books you might like:
Martha Alexander, *And My Mean Old Mother Will Be Sorry, Blackboard Bear*, 2000
  New illustrations enhance a story first published in 1969 about a little boy who briefly runs away when his mom becomes angry about messy behavior.
Wolfram Hanel, *Little Elephant Runs Away*, 2001
  While running away Little Elephant becomes lost in the jungle but he comes up with plan that gets him safely home again.

Vera Rosenberry, *Vera Runs Away*, 2000
When Vera doesn't receive the recognition she expects for her good report card she leaves home to live in the woods, until she gets hungry.

1109

KEVIN O'MALLEY, Author/Illustrator

Straight to the Pole
(New York: Walker & Company, 2003)

Subject(s): Winter; Weather
Age range(s): Grades K-3
Major character(s): Unnamed Character, Child, Student—Elementary School
Time period(s): 2000s (2002)
Locale(s): United States

Summary: Through a driving snow, a young child trudges with his loaded backpack, feeling isolated, chilled and unsure of his ability to continue his journey. As the storm worsens, the boy slips and falls, determined to reach his destination. Just as he thinks he can go no further in his frozen boots he spots a "wolf" approaching and calls for help. To his rescue come two friends with the news that school is closed. Leaving his backpack at the bus stop, his original destination, the boy runs off to play with his friends and their dog. (32 pages)

Where it's reviewed:
Bulletin of the Center for Children's Books, December 2003, page 162
Publishers Weekly, November 3, 2003, page 73
School Library Journal, November 2003, page 112

Awards the book has won:
School Library Journal Best Books, 2003

Other books by the same author:
Little Buggy Runs Away, 2003
Mount Olympus Basketball, 2003
Bud, 2000

Other books you might like:
Barbara M. Joosse, *Snow Day!*, 1995
After snow forces the cancellation of school Robby and his family have a day to play outside.
Ezra Jack Keats, *The Snowy Day*, 1962
The Caldecott Medal winner portrays a young child's enjoyment of the season's first snowfall.
Lynne Rae Perkins, *Snow Music*, 2003
Daily life goes on for people and animals within the quiet wonder of a snowy day.

1110

ALEXIS O'NEILL
LAURA HULISKA-BEITH, Illustrator

The Recess Queen
(New York: Scholastic Press, 2002)

Subject(s): Schools; Playing; Behavior
Age range(s): Grades K-3
Major character(s): Mean Jean, Student—Elementary School, Bully; Katie Sue, Child, Student—Elementary School (new)
Time period(s): Indeterminate
Locale(s): Fictional Country

Summary: All the students acknowledge that Mean Jean is the queen of recess. No one swings or plays with a ball until Mean Jean has the first turn. No one, that is, until tiny Katie Sue arrives. Oblivious to Mean Jean's power over the others, Katie Sue goes out at recess to have fun. She swings, kicks and bounces with glee and when Mean Jean confronts her, Katie Sue questions why she is so bossy. Then Katie Sue pulls out a jump rope and invites Mean Jean to jump with her. Once the Recess Queen learns how much fun it is to play with others, recess becomes a happier time of day for everyone. (32 pages)

Where it's reviewed:
Booklist, March 1, 2002, page 1143
Bulletin of the Center for Children's Books, March 2002, page 250
Horn Book Guide, Fall 2002, page 340
Publishers Weekly, January 21, 2002, page 89
School Library Journal, March 2002, page 198

Awards the book has won:
Notable Social Studies Trade Books for Young People, 2003

Other books by the same author:
Estela's Swap, 2002
Loud Emily, 1998 (School Library Journal Best Books)

Other books you might like:
Barbara Bottner, *Bootsie Barker Bites*, 1992
Rather than allow obnoxious Bootsie to terrorize her one more time, a young girl carefully plans the activities for Bootsie's next visit.
Judith Caseley, *Bully*, 2001
Mickey can't understand what causes his friend Jack to become a bully, but some understanding and shared cookies help to restore the friendship.
Patty Lovell, *Stand Tall, Molly Lou Melon*, 2001
Molly Lou's self-confidence enables her to ignore Ronald's taunts about her loud voice, clumsiness and prominent teeth.
Susan Meddaugh, *Martha Walks the Dog*, 1998
Martha the talking dog learns from a parrot's example that kind words have a more positive impact on Bad Dog Bob than insults.

1111

KENNETH OPPEL

Firewing
(New York: Simon & Schuster, 2003)

Subject(s): Animals/Bats; Fantasy; Fathers and Sons
Age range(s): Grades 5-8
Major character(s): Griffin Silverwing, Bat; Shade Silverwing, Bat, Father (of Griffin); Cama Zotz, Deity (god of the dead), Bat; Goth, Bat
Time period(s): Indeterminate
Locale(s): Fictional Country

Summary: Son of the legendary bat Shade Silverwing, Griffin fears he'll never live up to the heroics of his father. Mulling this over one day, he's sucked down a crack in the earth and ends up in the realm of Cama Zotz, the bat god of the dead. Nothing living has ever escaped from this realm, though every dead bat would like to return to the world above ground, as Griffin quickly discovers. Shade also enters the underworld to rescue his son but finds he must first defeat his enemy Goth, a bat who was killed but has been promised new life by Cama if he'll kill Shade. Griffin and Shade discover they're also tailed by all the dead bats who want to assume their bodies and a new chance at life in this companion to *Silverwing* and *Sunwing*. (270 pages)

Where it's reviewed:
Bulletin of the Center for Children's Books, April 2003, page 327
Horn Book, March 2003, page 215
Quill & Quire, May 2002, page 33
School Library Journal, January 2003, page 142
Voice of Youth Advocates, June 2003, page 152

Other books by the same author:
Airborn, 2004
Sunwing, 2000
Silverwing, 1997
Dead Water Zone, 1993

Other books you might like:
Barbara Block, *In Plain Sight*, 1996
   Pet storeowner Robin has her hands full when a friend is murdered, a high school student is missing and the bat population explodes.
Garth Nix, *Lirael: Daughter of the Clayr*, 2001
   Lirael has not inherited the psychic gifts of her people, but discovers she has other talents.
Paul Zindel, *Night of the Bat*, 2001
   Jake flies to the Amazon for a research project on bats, but finds a mutated giant bat is snacking on members of the research team.

`1112`

SHULAMITH LEVEY OPPENHEIM
WINSLOW PELS, Illustrator

Ali and the Magic Stew
(Honesdale, PA: Boyds Mills Press, 2002)

Subject(s): Folk Tales; Charity; Social Classes
Age range(s): Grades 1-4
Major character(s): Ali ibn Ali, Child, Wealthy; Unnamed Character, Impoverished, Aged Person
Time period(s): Indeterminate Past
Locale(s): Persia

Summary: Ali, the spoiled son of a rich merchant, looks down on the beggar sitting outside his front gates daily. When Ali's beloved father falls ill, he requests a special stew, shula kalambar. The beggar tells Ali that the stew will only heal his father if its ingredients are bought with money Ali receives from begging. Through his experience, Ali faces the unkindness and name-calling that the poor receive and learns an important lesson. A newly humble Ali makes it home in time to make the stew and heal his father. (32 pages)

Where it's reviewed:
Booklist, April 15, 2002, page 1408
Bulletin of the Center for Children's Books, May 2002, page 336
Horn Book Guide, Fall 2002, page 341
Publishers Weekly, February 18, 2002
School Library Journal, April 2002, page 118

Other books by the same author:
Yanni Rubbish, 1999
The Hundredth Name, 1995
The Lily Cupboard, 1992

Other books you might like:
Shirley Climo, *The Persian Cinderella*, 1999
   Setterah outwits her two evil stepsisters and catches the eye of a prince.
Tomie De Paola, *The Legend of the Persian Carpet*, 1993
   When the king's diamond is stolen, he relies on a poor carpet seller to save the day.
Aaron Shepard, *Forty Fortunes: A Tale of Iran*, 1999
   Ahmed becomes a fortune-teller at his wife's urging and has to solve the mystery of the King's missing treasure.

`1113`

DENISE GOSLINER ORENSTEIN

Unseen Companion
(New York: Katherine Tegen Books/HarperCollins, 2003)

Subject(s): Orphans; Schools/Boarding Schools; Indians of North America
Age range(s): Grades 9-12
Major character(s): Dove Alexie, 16-Year-Old, Prisoner; Lorraine Hobbs, 14-Year-Old, Cook; Annette Weinland, 18-Year-Old, Volunteer; Thelma Cooke, Student—Boarding School, Indian (Yup'ik); Edgar Kwagley, Student—Boarding School, Indian (Yup'ik)
Time period(s): 1960s (1968-1969)
Locale(s): Bethel, Alaska

Summary: Dove is tossed into jail after striking a teacher at the Indian boarding school he attends, but then disappears into the penal system. Lorraine cooks meals for the prisoners and she spots Dove in his cell, bruised and bloody, and worries about him. Then Annette enters the picture through her volunteer work at the jail where she handles clerical records and worries about the discrepancies she sees, but being easily intimidated by the sheriff, remains quiet about the irregularities. The reader learns more about Dove from two other students at his school: Edgar is a Yup'ik who dismisses Dove because he's a half-breed while Thelma, also a Yup'ik, thinks Dove is pretty cute. These four different views of Dove also relate the story of Alaska, with its beauty and isolation as well as its wealth of culture, accompanied by a lack of understanding between whites and Indians about that culture. (357 pages)

Where it's reviewed:
Booklist, October 15, 2003, page 409
Bulletin of the Center for Children's Books, November 2003, page 118

Publishers Weekly, November 24, 2003, page 66
School Library Journal, January 2004, page 134
Voice of Youth Advocates, December 2003, page 405

Awards the book has won:
Booklist Editors' Choice/Books for Youth, 2003

Other books by the same author:
When the Wind Blows Hard, 1982

Other books you might like:
James S. Bryson, *The War Canoe*, 1990
    When a teacher piques his curiosity about his heritage, Mickey gives up drugs and drinking to build a war canoe like the ones used by his ancestors.
Ben Mikaelsen, *Touching Spirit Bear*, 2001
    Cole's mean, arrogant and vicious, traits he's learned from his abusive father, until he's sent to an isolated Alaskan island to rethink his ways.
Deb Vanasse, *A Distant Enemy*, 1997
    Child of an Eskimo mother and a white father who has abandoned the family, Joseph is an angry young man trying to live by the old ways.

1114

URI ORLEV
HILLEL HALKIN, Translator

Run, Boy, Run

(Boston: Walter Lorraine Books/Houghton Mifflin, 2003)

Subject(s): Survival; Jews; Holocaust
Age range(s): Grades 6-10
Major character(s): Srulik "Jurek Staniak" Frydman, Child, Jew
Time period(s): 1940s
Locale(s): Poland

Summary: Some Jews survive the Holocaust because friends hid them or they moved away before the Nazis collected them for the concentration camps, but for a child to be alone and survive requires courage, help from others and plain old luck. Such is the case of Srulik who tries to remember his dying father's words to never forget he's a Jew, but pretend to be a Christian in order to live. Srulik calls himself Jurek, hides his circumcision as best he can, pretends to be Catholic and calls upon Mary and Jesus as he sees fit. He works for farmers in the Polish countryside and when his arm is mangled in farm machinery and a Christian doctor refuses to operate, his arm is later amputated. On the farms his Jewishness is eventually discovered and he's forced to leave and forage for food and shelter in the forests. Srulik eventually reaches Israel but his memories of survival during the war remain excruciatingly painful. (186 pages)

Where it's reviewed:
Booklist, October 15, 2003, page 404
Horn Book, November 2003, page 753
Publishers Weekly, December 22, 2003, page 62
School Library Journal, November 2003, page 144
Voice of Youth Advocates, December 2003, page 405

Awards the book has won:
ALA Notable Children's Books, 2004

Other books by the same author:
The Lady with the Hat, 1995
The Man from the Other Side, 1991
The Island on Bird Street, 1984

Other books you might like:
Renee Roth-Hana, *Touch Wood: A Childhood in Occupied France*, 1988
    Young Renee and her family flee Alsace for Paris and then Normandy, as they seek shelter from the Nazis who seem to be everywhere.
Jerry Spinelli, *Milkweed*, 2003
    A young Gypsy boy is at first enamored of the "jack boots" who take over his city, but later realizes the horror of the Nazis.
Eva Wiseman, *My Canary Yellow Star*, 2002
    When the Nazis occupy her country, Hungarian Marta learns the Swedish diplomat Raoul Wallenberg gives passports to Jews.

1115

NANCY OSA

Cuba 15

(New York: Delacorte, 2003)

Subject(s): Cuban Americans; Cultures and Customs; Schools/High Schools
Age range(s): Grades 6-10
Major character(s): Violet Paz, 15-Year-Old
Time period(s): 2000s
Locale(s): Chicago, Illinois

Summary: Violet's heritage suddenly creates problems for her when she turns fifteen and her Cuban grandmother assumes she will celebrate this milestone with a quinceanero. With a Cuban-American father and a Polish-American mother, Violet knows only that she's first-born American, so the origins of the quinceanero are foreign to her. The best thing Violet's discovered about her family is that it's perfect source material for her speech team's Original Comedy competition, and she makes light of their obsession with playing dominoes, her father's colorful shirts and their anger whenever Fidel Castro's name is mentioned. Gradually Violet learns more about Cuba's history and stops blocking every custom her grandmother wants to include in this author's charming first novel of family life and tradition. (277 pages)

Where it's reviewed:
Bulletin of the Center for Children's Books, September 2003, page 27
Horn Book, July 2003, page 465
School Library Journal, June 2003, page 148
Voice of Youth Advocates, June 2003, page 142

Awards the book has won:
Pura Belpre Honor Book, Narrative, 2004
ALA Best Books for Young Adults, 2004

Other books you might like:
Diane Gonzales Bertrand, *Sweet Fifteen*, 1995
    Seamstress Rita Navarro not only makes Stefanie's quinceanero dress, but also befriends her entire family, including Stefanie's grieving mother.

Veronica Chambers, *Quinceanera Means Sweet 15*, 2001
    Though her best friend Magda has gotten in with a bad group of girls, Marisol doesn't let it spoil her own quinceanera.

Minfong Ho, *The Stone Goddess*, 2003
    Sent to a Khmer Rouge labor camp, Nakri gains strength from her memories of the forbidden Cambodian classical dances.

1116

MARY POPE OSBORNE
GISELLE POTTER, Illustrator

The Brave Little Seamstress

(New York: Anne Schwartz Book/Atheneum Books for Young Readers, 2002)

Subject(s): Fairy Tales; Courage; Giants
Age range(s): Grades K-3
Major character(s): Unnamed Character, Seamstress, Heroine
Time period(s): Indeterminate Past
Locale(s): Fictional Country

Summary: In this retelling of a German tale the character of the tailor is a seamstress with no less pluck and determination. Bothered by flies the seamstress swats at them with a cloth and kills seven in one blow. So impressed is she with her success that she embroiders the phrase "Seven with one blow!" on the back of a coat. When she wears it, a giant thinks it means that she's killed seven giants with one blow and he challenges her to three tasks to prove her strength. After outwitting the giant she proceeds on her journey. Her embroidered coat is threatening to a king who thinks the words mean that she's slain seven knights and now has designs on his kingdom. The brave, confident seamstress accomplishes each seemingly impossible task the king gives her yet still he wishes to kill her. With forewarning from one of the king's knights, the seamstress is able to frighten off the king and his other knights, take over the kingdom and marry the kind knight. (36 pages)

Where it's reviewed:
Booklist, April 1, 2002, page 1335
Bulletin of the Center for Children's Books, May 2002, page 337
Publishers Weekly, March 25, 2002, page 63
Riverbank Review, Spring 2002, page 30
School Library Journal, April 2002, page 118

Other books by the same author:
Happy Birthday, America, 2003
New York's Bravest, 2002 (Publishers Weekly Best Children's Books)
Kate and the Beanstalk, 2000 (School Library Journal Best Books)

Other books you might like:
Jacob Grimm, *The Brave Little Tailor*, 1989
    This retelling by Anthea Bell remains true to the original gender in the tale of a brave tailor outwitting a giant and a king.

Susan L. Roth, *Brave Martha and the Dragon*, 1996
    Martha courageously saves a village from the terrifying nightly visits of a wicked fire-breathing dragon.

Audrey Wood, *Rude Giants*, 1993
    Persuasive Beatrix convinces two rude giants to clean up their act and become good neighbors.

1117

MARY POPE OSBORNE
STEVE JOHNSON, Illustrator
LOU FANCHER, Illustrator

New York's Bravest

(New York: Alfred A. Knopf, 2002)

Subject(s): Fires; Community Helpers; Legends
Age range(s): Grades K-3
Major character(s): Mose Humphreys, Fire Fighter, Hero
Time period(s): 1840s
Locale(s): New York, New York

Summary: This book is dedicated to the memory of the firefighters who gave their lives on September 11, 2001 and its in history and legend is described in an opening historical note. Mose, the most famous firefighter in the city, stands eight feet tall without his stovepipe hat and is known to lead the charge into danger to save people trapped in burning buildings. One morning after fighting a particularly hazardous hotel blaze all night, the firefighters realize they cannot find Mose. Though he's never seen again, the firefighters know that he lives on in spirit as they continue the work to which he dedicated his life. (32 pages)

Where it's reviewed:
Booklist, July 2002, page 1847
Bulletin of the Center for Children's Books, September 2002, page 30
Horn Book, November 2002, page 737
Publishers Weekly, June 24, 2002, page 56
School Library Journal, September 2002, page 203

Awards the book has won:
Booklist Editors' Choice, 2002
Publishers Weekly Best Children's Books, 2002

Other books by the same author:
Happy Birthday, America, 2003
The Brave Little Seamstress, 2002
Kate and the Beanstalk, 2000 (School Library Journal Best Books)

Other books you might like:
Maira Kalman, *Fireboat: The Heroic Adventures of the John J. Harvey*, 2002
    Also written as a tribute to New York, this nonfiction title presents the distinguished history of a fireboat recalled to service on September 11th, 2001.

Lois Lenski, *The Little Fire Engine*, 1946
    Fireman Small is a hero in the little fire engine in Tinytown.

Andrea Zimmerman, *Fire! Fire! Hurry! Hurry!*, 2003
    When the alarm sounds the firefighters rush to duty, leaving their dinner behind.

1118

MARY POPE OSBORNE
TROY HOWELL, Illustrator

The One-Eyed Giant
(New York: Hyperion Books for Children, 2002)

Series: Tales from the Odyssey. Book 1
Subject(s): Adventure and Adventurers; Legends; Mythology
Age range(s): Grades 3-5
Major character(s): Odysseus, Hero, Leader
Time period(s): Indeterminate Past
Locale(s): Ithaca, Greece; At Sea

Summary: Osborne retells Homer's Odyssey in a series of chapter books accessible to middle grade readers. The first book opens with Odysseus plowing his fields while watching his wife and infant son sitting nearby. Called to service by the king, Odysseus reluctantly leaves his family on a journey that takes him to unexpected places and lasts many years longer than he could have imagined. Returning home from a ten-year siege of Troy, Odysseus and his soldiers are caught in a ferocious storm that lasts for many days and drives their ships into unfamiliar territory where they confront Lotus-eaters, a one-eyed giant, and the god of the winds. A glossary, pronunciation guide and general information about the sources conclude the book. (104 pages)

Where it's reviewed:
Booklist, November 15, 2002, page 599
Bulletin of the Center for Children's Books, December 2002, page 169
Kirkus Reviews, September 15, 2002, page 1397
Publishers Weekly, September 9, 2002, page 68
Riverbank Review, Winter 2002-2003, page 46

Awards the book has won:
Publishers Weekly Best Children's Books, 2002

Other books by the same author:
Return to Ithaca, 2004 (Tales from the Odyssey Book 5)
Sirens and Sea Monsters, 2003 (Tales from the Odyssey Book 3)
The Gray-Eyed Goddess, 2003 (Tales from the Odyssey Book 4)
The Land of the Dead, 2002 (Tales from the Odyssey Book 2)

Other books you might like:
Leonard Everett Fisher, *The Olympians: Great Gods and Goddesses of Ancient Greece*, 1984
  Biographical sketches describe twelve gods and goddesses from Greek mythology.
Doris Orgel, *Mother's Daughter: Four Greek Goddesses Speak*, 2003
  Imagined conversations of Leto and Artemis and Demeter and Persephone give one perspective to Greek mythological characters.
Jon Scieszka, *It's All Greek to Me*, 1999
  Time travel adventures of the Time Warp Trio put the students on Mount Olympus instead of on stage as they act in a class play.

1119

MARY POPE OSBORNE
WILL OSBORNE, Co-Author

A Time to Dance
(New York: Scholastic Press, 2003)

Series: My America. Virginia's Civil War Diary Book 3
Subject(s): Civil War; Diaries; Theater
Age range(s): Grades 2-5
Major character(s): Virginia Dickens, 11-Year-Old, Daughter; Pa, Father, Musician
Time period(s): 1860s (1865)
Locale(s): New York, New York

Summary: After the end of the Civil War, Virginia and her family move to New York City. When Pa is unable to find work as a musician, he must take in music students. At the same time, Virginia finds work as a dresser in a theater, a perfect job for her because of her love of the stage. After some initial struggles, the family settles into a comfortable life and Virginia's father even decides to get married again, to the mother of one of his music students. (107 pages)

Where it's reviewed:
Horn Book Guide, Spring 2004, page 83
School Library Journal, February 2004, page 150

Other books by the same author:
After the Rain, 2002 (My America: Virginia's Civil War Diary Book 2)
Knights and Castles: A Nonfiction Companion to The Knight at Dawn, 2000
My Brother's Keeper, 2000 (My America: Virginia's Civil War Diary Book 1)

Other books you might like:
Patricia Beatty, *Be Ever Hopeful, Hannalee*, 1988
  After the end of the Civil War, Hannalee and her family move to Atlanta to start anew.
Joyce Hansen, *I Thought My Soul Would Rise and Fly: The Diary of Patsy, a Freed Girl*, 2003
  With the conclusion of the Civil War, Patsy is freed and decides to become a teacher.
Harriette Gillem Robinet, *Forty Acres and Maybe a Mule*, 1998
  Pascal sets out with his brother to claim the 40 acres of land promised to former slaves after the Civil War ends.

1120

JULIE OTSUKA

When the Emperor Was Divine
(New York: Random House, 2002)

Subject(s): Japanese Americans; World War II; Family Life
Age range(s): Grades 10-Adult
Major character(s): Mother, Immigrant (Japanese American); Father, Immigrant (Japanese American); Daughter, Teenager, Immigrant (Japanese American); Son, Child, Immigrant (Japanese American)
Time period(s): 1940s
Locale(s): Berkeley, California; Topaz, Utah

Summary: Following the bombing of Pearl Harbor by the Japanese, when Americans feared a Japanese attack to the mainland, President Roosevelt ordered all Japanese-Americans to evacuate to interment camps. One such family in Berkeley sees their father taken away one night, still wearing his robe and slippers, to be questioned by the FBI. Following that night, the remaining family members prepare for their evacuation, packing only a few items that can be carried easily. Each family member tells his or her story, which provides varying perspectives on their time in camp. The mother, her daughter and her son return from the camps, able to continue with their lives, while the father comes home a beaten, dispirited man, in this award-winning tale. (144 pages)

Where it's reviewed:

Booklist, September 1, 2002, page 59

Kliatt, January 2004, page 19

Library Journal, March 15, 2002, page 54

Publishers Weekly, August 26, 2002, page 44

Voice of Youth Advocates, June 2003, page 142

Awards the book has won:

Booklist Editors' Choice/Adult Books for Young Adults, 2002

ALA Alex Award, 2003

Other books you might like:

Barry Denenberg, *The Journal of Ben Uchida: Citizen 13559 Mirror Lake Internment Camp*, 1999

Using a journal given him by a friend, Ben records his family's life at their internment camp following the bombing of Pearl Harbor.

Yoshiko Uchida, *Journey Home*, 1978

Following relocation during World War II, a Japanese American family finally returns to their home and their normal lifestyle.

Eric Walters, *Caged Eagles*, 2000

Tadashi's family is rounded up, with other Japanese-Canadians, and held at a detention camp in Vancouver.

P

1121

SOYUNG PAK
MARCELINO TRUONG, Illustrator

A Place to Grow

(New York: Arthur A. Levine Books/Scholastic Press, 2002)

Subject(s): Fathers and Daughters; Emigration and Immigration; Gardens and Gardening
Age range(s): Grades 1-4
Major character(s): Unnamed Character, Father, Gardener; Unnamed Character, Daughter, Child
Time period(s): Indeterminate Past
Locale(s): Asia; Europe

Summary: Using a garden metaphor that compares their family to a seed, a father explains to his daughter the reasons for leaving their homeland in an unspecified Asian country and fleeing to a rural area in what appears, from the illustrations, to be a European village. The girl wonders if some day she will again ''fly with the wind'' as a seed might and her father reassures her that her family will always be a garden in her heart, just as he knows the same is true for the father he left behind. (32 pages)

Where it's reviewed:
Booklist, October 15, 2002, page 410
Horn Book, January 2003, page 60
Kirkus Reviews, October 1, 2002, page 1477
Publishers Weekly, August 12, 2002, page 300
School Library Journal, November 2002, page 132

Other books by the same author:
Dear Juno, 1999

Other books you might like:
Luis Garay, *The Long Road*, 1997
    When a civil war breaks out in Jose's village, he flees to America with his mother.
Robert Munsch, *From Far Away*, 1995
    Saoussan and her family move to Canada from war-torn Lebanon.

Liz Rosenberg, *The Silence in the Mountains*, 1999
    War drives Iskander and his family from their homeland to America.
Mary Watson, *The Butterfly Seeds*, 1995
    When Jake immigrates to America he brings ''butterfly'' seeds from Grandpa to plant in memory of his homeland.

1122

MARGIE PALATINI
BARRY MOSER, Illustrator

Earthquack!

(New York: Simon & Schuster Books for Young Readers, 2002)

Subject(s): Animals; Humor; Animals/Ducks
Age range(s): Grades K-2
Major character(s): Chucky Ducky, Duck; Brewster Rooster, Rooster; Herman Ermine, Weasel
Time period(s): Indeterminate
Locale(s): Fictional Country

Summary: Chucky Ducky is the first to feel the grumble, rumble of the earth that makes him stumble. Instantly he hurries to alert other farm animals to the earthquake. When the animals first ask Brewster Rooster to crow the alarm he refuses but then he too feels the rumble, grumble of the ground and doodle-doos the warning. From the nearby woods Hermine Ermine observes the growing panic and devises a plan to fill his pantry with meals for a month. He dons his white winter coat and approaches the frightened animals that willingly follow him to his quakeproof shelter in the woods. Upon arrival the animals are reluctant to enter what appears to be a deep hole in the ground and, as another rumble is felt, Brewster Rooster yanks off the weasel's coat just as the real cause of the quaking earth becomes obvious to all. The animals return to the farm and Chucky Ducky gets back in the pond where a duck that is obviously all wet belongs. (32 pages)

Where it's reviewed:
Booklist, July 2002, page 1860

Bulletin of the Center for Children's Books, July 2002, page 414

Publishers Weekly, May 6, 2002, page 57

School Library Journal, June 2002, page 106

Other books by the same author:

Moo Who?, 2004

Three Silly Billies, 2004

The Perfect Pet, 2003

Other books you might like:

Sally Hobson, *Chicken Little*, 1994

In a retelling of the classic tale, Chicken Little and her feathered friends are so concerned about the sky falling that they overlook the prowling fox.

Elizabeth MacDonald, *The Wolf Is Coming!*, 1998

With a wolf in pursuit animals race for cover with increasingly larger animals.

Jonathan Meres, *The Big Bad Rumor*, 2000

As animals pass along Goose's warning about a big, bad, mad wolf on the way the message becomes garbled and misunderstood.

1123

MARGIE PALATINI
GUY FRANCIS, Illustrator

Mary Had a Little Ham

(New York: Hyperion Books for Children, 2003)

Subject(s): Animals/Pigs; Farm Life; Talent

Age range(s): Grades 1-3

Major character(s): Mary, Child; Stanley Snoutowski, Pig, Actor

Time period(s): Indeterminate

Locale(s): Fictional Country

Summary: It's clear to see that Stanley is not your typical pig, he's definitely a ham. Mary encourages Stanley to develop his talents though she realizes she'll not be able to keep him down on the farm. Indeed Stanley dreams of seeing the name Snoutkowski in lights on Broadway. He moves to New York to pursue his dreams and, through months of discouraging cattle calls and menial jobs, finds hope in Mary's weekly correspondence. Finally, Stanley gets a lucky break and sees his dream come true! Mary travels to New York to see him star in *Hamlet*, and to hear Stanley quote those famous lines, "To oink, or not to oink, that is the question . . . " (32 pages)

Where it's reviewed:

Booklist, December 15, 2003, page 754

Publishers Weekly, October 6, 2003, page 84

School Library Journal, November 2003, page 112

Other books by the same author:

Moo Who?, 2004

Bad Boys, 2003

The Perfect Pet, 2003

Other books you might like:

Ian Falconer, *Olivia Saves the Circus*, 2001

To hear Olivia tell it, on a family trip to the circus, she takes center stage by performing all the acts solo when the cast is too sick to perform.

Kathryn Lasky, *Starring Lucille*, 2001

On her birthday, Lucille dances for the guests in her new tutu.

Elizabeth Winthrop, *Dumpy La Rue*, 2001

Dumpy achieves his dream to become a dancing pig and inspires some others too.

1124

MARGIE PALATINI
BRUCE WHATLEY, Illustrator

The Perfect Pet

(New York: HarperCollins Publishers, 2003)

Subject(s): Pets; Animals/Insects; Parent and Child

Age range(s): Grades K-3

Major character(s): Elizabeth, Daughter, Animal Lover; Carolyn, Plant (cactus); Doug, Insect

Time period(s): 2000s (2003)

Locale(s): United States

Summary: Elizabeth's parents expect a cactus to satisfy her desire for a pet. Carolyn is nice, though not too cuddly, and Elizabeth would prefer a horse, dog or cat. None of her reasons convince her parents to add an animal to the household. When Elizabeth finds Doug on her rug, she knows he's the perfect pet. Doug is not too big, he doesn't jump on the furniture and he can't scratch or shed. Carolyn, Doug and Elizabeth get along well and Doug grows large on a diet of crumbs. Once his presence is discovered Elizabeth has to point out his virtues in order to keep her pet, but it's clear he's perfect. (32 pages)

Where it's reviewed:

Booklist, July 2003, page 1898

Bulletin of the Center for Children's Books, May 2003, page 374

School Library Journal, May 2003, page 128

Awards the book has won:

IRA Children's Choices, 2004

Other books by the same author:

Bad Boys, 2003

Tub-boo-boo, 2001

Bedhead, 2000

Other books you might like:

Lauren Child, *I Want a Pet*, 1999

A little girl desperately wants a pet but has some difficulty choosing one that meets the requirements of her family.

Mick Inkpen, *Billy's Beetle*, 1992

When Billy loses his beetle he receives a lot of help with his search for it.

Megan McDonald, *Insects Are My Life*, 1995

A new classmate seems to share Amanda's interest in insects.

Tres Seymour, *I Love My Buzzard*, 1994

A young boy who loves his buzzard as well as his squid, slugs and warthog reconsiders his priorities when his mom moves out to escapes his menagerie.

1125

CHRISTOPHER PAOLINI

Eragon

(New York: Knopf, 2003)

Series: Inheritance. Book 1
Subject(s): Adventure and Adventurers; Dragons
Age range(s): Grades 7-12
Major character(s): Eragon, Teenager; Brom, Wizard, Story-teller; Saphira, Dragon
Time period(s): Indeterminate
Locale(s): Alagaesia, Fictional Country

Summary: Hunting in the mountains of the Spine, Eragon is the only witness when a mysterious blue stone appears from nowhere. Clearly, the magic that has made the Spine a fearful place is at work, but Eragon hopes it may do his family a good turn. If he can sell the blue stone, it could provide the meat his family desperately needs to survive. Unfortunately, once it is known that the blue stone comes from the Spine, no one is willing to risk owning it. In fact, the only one who seems interested in it once its origin is known is old Brom, the storyteller. Brom is full of tales of the Dragon Riders, legendary guardians of the realm, and he hints that he knows more about the stone than he is willing to tell. Nothing, however could prepare Eragon for the reality of his blue stone. It is in fact a dragon egg, and the hatching of the dragon will threaten all Eragon holds dear, reveal abilities he has never suspected, and send him on a quest, accompanied by Brom and the blue dragon, Saphira. (497 pages)

Where it's reviewed:
Booklist, August 2003, page 1981
Bulletin of the Center for Children's Books, December 2003, page 163
Publishers Weekly, July 21, 2003, page 196
School Library Journal, September 2003, page 218
Voice of Youth Advocates, August 2003, page 240

Other books by the same author:
Eldest, 2005 (Inheritance Book 2)

Other books you might like:
Anne McCaffrey, *The Chronicles of Pern: First Fall*, 1993
   On the planet Pern, the first defense against the deadly Thread fall are the dragon riders.
Cora Taylor, *On the Wings of a Dragon*, 2001
   Kour'el and her dragon are on a mission to rescue the king.
Jane Yolen, *Dragon's Blood*, 1987
   A young slave steals a dragon egg and secretly raises a fighting dragon in hopes of winning his freedom.

1126

HERMAN PARISH
LYNN SWEAT, Illustrator

Calling Doctor Amelia Bedelia

(New York: Greenwillow Books, 2002)

Subject(s): Medicine; Humor; Language
Age range(s): Grades 1-2
Major character(s): Amelia Bedelia, Housekeeper; Dr. Horton, Doctor
Time period(s): 2000s
Locale(s): United States

Summary: When Amelia Bedelia arrives at Dr. Horton's office the nurse asks for her help until Dr. Horton returns from the hospital. Ever the willing helper, Amelia Bedelia begins answering the phone and tending to patients with her usual misunderstanding of idioms and multiple meaning words. The younger patients enjoy Amelia's approach to checking temperatures or drawing blood, but the adults calling with complaints of hives or being a little hoarse don't appreciate Amelia's responses. Fortunately, just as Dr. Horton arrives to a waiting room of impatient patients, the ice cream Amelia has ordered to treat the patients is delivered and Amelia goes home, leaving the office in Dr. Horton's capable hands. (64 pages)

Where it's reviewed:
Booklist, August 2002, page 1975
Horn Book, November 2002, page 763
Kirkus Reviews, June 15, 2002, page 887
Publishers Weekly, July 1, 2002, page 81
School Library Journal, August 2002, page 164

Other books by the same author:
Amelia Bedelia 4 Mayor, 1999
Bravo, Amelia Bedelia, 1997
Good Driving, Amelia Bedelia, 1995

Other books you might like:
Denys Cazet, *Minnie and Moo and the Musk of Zorro*, 2000
   Inspired by a book about Zorro, Minnie and Moo take on the role of barnyard heroes oblivious to the humor of their misguided heroic actions.
Lane Smith, *The Happy Hocky Family Moves to the Country!*, 2003
   The Hocky family soon learns that living in the country requires a different understanding of the intended meaning of terms.
Inez Snyder, *Doctor Tools*, 2002
   Reading this nonfiction book about Michelle's visit to the doctor might help Amelia Bedelia understand the terminology of a medical check-up.

1127

LINDA SUE PARK

When My Name Was Keoko

(New York: Clarion Books, 2002)

Subject(s): Underground Resistance Movements; Family Life; Courage
Age range(s): Grades 5-8
Major character(s): Sun-hee "Keoko" Kim, Sister (of Tae-yul); Tae-yul "Nobuo" Kim, Teenager; Uncle, Resistance Fighter
Time period(s): 1940s (1940-1945)
Locale(s): Republic of Korea

Summary: Living in an occupied country, Koreans Sun-hee and Tae-yul grow up learning Japanese in school while speaking Korean at home. With the Japanese making every effort to erase Korean culture, the Kim family rebels in quiet but significant ways. Told to dig up all Rose of Sharon trees, they peacefully plant the required cherry trees, but keep a Rose of Sharon shoot alive in their shed. Their father, a learned Korean scholar, is removed as principal of his school while their uncle publishes an underground newspaper as part of the resistance movement. Being required to take Japanese names is the final indignity for the family, leaving Sun-hee as Keoko and Tae-yul called Nobuo. In alternating chapters, each sibling reveals his or her reaction to the occupation, from Sun-hee's writing to Tae-yul's attempt to maintain secrecy about his uncle, in this work by a Newbery winning author. (199 pages)

Where it's reviewed:
Bulletin of the Center for Children's Books, May 2002, page 337
Horn Book, May 2002, page 335
Publishers Weekly, March 4, 2002, page 80
School Library Journal, April 2002, page 154
Voice of Youth Advocates, April 2002, page 46

Awards the book has won:
ALA Best Books for Young Adults, 2003
School Library Journal Best Books, 2002

Other books by the same author:
A Single Shard, 2001
The Kite Fighters, 2000
Seesaw Girl, 1999

Other books you might like:
Sook Nyul Choi, *The Year of Impossible Goodbyes*, 1991
 Young Sookan and her brother are separated from their mother as they flee from North to South Korea to meet their father.
Julie Otsuka, *When the Emperor Was Divine*, 2002
 Internment for a Japanese-American family from Berkeley leaves them disheartened, even after they're finally allowed to return home.
Yoko Kawashima Watkins, *So Far from the Bamboo Grove*, 1986
 A Japanese family from Korea struggles to return to their homeland after World War II.

1128

KATHERINE PATERSON

The Same Stuff as Stars

(New York: Clarion Books, 2002)

Subject(s): Family Problems; Brothers and Sisters; Grandmothers
Age range(s): Grades 5-8
Major character(s): Angel Morgan, 11-Year-Old; Bernie Morgan, Child; Grandma Morgan, Grandmother (of Angel and Bernie); Verna Morgan, Mother (of Angel and Bernie); Wayne Morgan, Father (of Angel and Bernie), Convict; Ray Morgan, Uncle (of Angel and Bernie)
Time period(s): 2000s
Locale(s): Vermont

Summary: As an almost 12-year-old, Angel has more adult responsibility than either of her parents can handle, either singly or together. Her father's in jail for armed robbery and, after one of their dreary weekly visits, Verna drops Angel and Bernie off at their great-grandmother's house. Grandma is 80 years old and scarcely able to take care of herself, much less two children, so once again Angel makes sure there's food on the table, enrolls herself and Bernie in school and locates the library, one of her few pleasures. Her other consolation comes from the "star man," the person Grandma calls "Santy Claus" for he fills their wood bin with chopped logs and often leaves food for them. The "star man," in reality Angel's uncle who's been left damaged by the Vietnam War, gives her hope as together they explore the universe through his telescope and he repeats to her that she's made of "the same stuff as stars." Hope is what she needs when her mother returns and takes Bernie back, her father escapes from jail to try to help and the social workers question Grandma's ability to care for Angel in this outstanding tale of a resilient heroine. (242 pages)

Where it's reviewed:
Booklist, September 15, 2002, page 233
Bulletin of the Center for Children's Books, October 2002, page 72
Horn Book, September 2002, page 579
New York Times Book Review, April 20, 2003, page 21
School Library Journal, August 2002, page 196

Awards the book has won:
School Library Journal Best Books, 2002
IRA Teachers' Choices/Advanced, 2003

Other books by the same author:
Preacher's Boy, 1999
Jip: His Story, 1996
Flip-Flop Girl, 1994
Come Sing, Jimmy Jo, 1985
Jacob Have I Loved, 1980
The Great Gilly Hopkins, 1978

Other books you might like:
Robbie Branscum, *The Girl*, 1986
 Raised by uncaring grandparents on a dirt-poor farm, "the girl" and her siblings gather strength from one another.
Patricia Reilly Giff, *Pictures of Hollis Woods*, 2002
 Living with foster parent Josie, Hollis worries that Josie's increasing senility will mean she has to find another foster home.
Patricia Hermes, *Cheat the Moon*, 1998
 With her mother dead, her father an alcoholic and the responsibility of her brother Will on her shoulders, young Gabby grows up quickly.
Gary Paulsen, *Alida's Song*, 1999
 Once again his grandmother saves him from his drunken parents as she finds him a job on the farm where she's the cook.
Cynthia Voigt, *Homecoming*, 1981
 After being abandoned by their mother, Dicey and her younger brothers and sister make the long journey on foot to their eccentric grandmother's home.

1129

NANCY RUTH PATTERSON

A Simple Gift

(New York: Farrar Straus Giroux, 2003)

Subject(s): Plays; Theater; Growing Up
Age range(s): Grades 3-6
Major character(s): Carrie O'Connor, 10-Year-Old, Actress (aspiring)
Time period(s): 2000s (2003)
Locale(s): Brownsville, North Carolina

Summary: Native New Yorker, Carrie O'Connor dreams of being an actress. When she finds out one of the novels written by her mother, a children's book author, is being turned into a play in her mother's hometown, Carrie begs to be able to go to the town and audition. Carrie wins a role in the play, but when she shares a secret about a cast member, the production is almost ruined. At the end of the experience, Carrie realizes that the book is based on her uncle, who died as a child. (118 pages)

Where it's reviewed:
Booklist, April 15, 2003, page 1472
School Library Journal, May 2003, page 158

Other books by the same author:
The Shiniest Rock of All, 1991
The Christmas Cup, 1989

Other books you might like:
Diane DeGroat, *Annie Pitts, Artichoke*, 1992
    Annie dreams of being an actress, but is disappointed when she is cast as an artichoke in the school play.
Mary Hoffman, *Amazing Grace*, 1991
    When Grace's class does a production of Peter Pan she knows she wants the starring role.
Maryann McDonald, *Secondhand Star (Lots of O'Leary's)*, 1994
    Francie O'Leary is cast as Toto in the school's production of the Wizard of Oz.
Noel Streatfield, *Theatre Shoes*, 1945
    After their father is reported missing in World War II three children are forced by their actress grandmother to go to acting school.

1130

DARCY PATTISON
JOE CEPEDA, Illustrator

The Journey of Oliver K. Woodman

(San Diego: Harcourt, Inc., 2003)

Subject(s): Dolls and Dollhouses; Travel; Letters
Age range(s): Grades K-3
Major character(s): Tameka Schwartz, Niece; Raymond Johnson, Uncle, Carpenter; Oliver K. Woodman, Doll
Time period(s): 2000s (2003)
Locale(s): Rock Hill, South Carolina; Redcrest, California

Summary: Unable to accept Tameka's invitation for a summer visit, Uncle Ray uses his carpentry skills to create Oliver K. Woodman, a large, jointed wooden doll carrying a backpack with an explanatory letter requesting rides across the country. Each traveler that provides a portion of Oliver's transportation sends a letter or postcard to Uncle Ray advising him of Oliver's location and his adventures along the way. The trip that Uncle Ray expects will take two weeks actually takes more than two months, but Oliver does finally reach Tameka and her family. (48 pages)

Where it's reviewed:
Booklist, April 1, 2003, page 1403
Bulletin of the Center for Children's Books, June 2003, page 415
Horn Book, May 2003, page 333
School Library Journal, April 2003, page 134

Awards the book has won:
Bulletin of the Center for Children's Books Blue Ribbons, 2003
Center for Children's Books Best Books, 2003

Other books by the same author:
Searching for Oliver K. Woodman, 2005
The River Dragon, 1991

Other books you might like:
Julie Danneberg, *First Year Letters*, 2003
    First graders write letters to their teacher.
Jerdine Nolen, *Plantzilla*, 2002
    Correspondence with a vacationing science teacher describes the unusual behavior of a plant a student is caring for at his home.
Mark Teague, *Dear Mrs. LaRue: Letters from Obedience School*, 2002
    A dog complains to his owner about the conditions in the school to which he's sent to improve his behavior; the illustrations contradict his reports.
Nancy Willard, *The Magic Cornfield*, 1997
    Postcards to cousin Bottom document Tottem's travels from New York to Minneapolis through a magic cornfield.

1131

EDITH PATTOU

East

(San Diego: Harcourt, 2003)

Subject(s): Fantasy; Animals/Bears; Fairy Tales
Age range(s): Grades 6-10
Major character(s): Ebba Rose "Rose", 15-Year-Old; White Bear, Royalty (prince); Troll Queen, Mythical Creature
Time period(s): Indeterminate Past
Locale(s): Scandinavia

Summary: The seventh child of a large, poor family, Rose agrees to accompany the White Bear when he offers riches for her family in exchange for her being his traveling companion. Accompanying him to a castle in the icy, snowy North, Rose discovers that every night a mysterious companion occupies her bed. By the time she realizes her nighttime partner is the White Bear, the Troll Queen has fallen in love with him and spirited him away. Feeling responsible for the White Bear's kidnapping, Rose undertakes a difficult journey to find him in this retelling of the myth *East of the Sun and West of the Moon*. (498 pages)

Where it's reviewed:
Booklist, September 1, 2003, page 123
Kirkus Reviews, September 15, 2003, page 1180
Kliatt, September 2003, page 10
Publishers Weekly, July 28, 2003, page 96
School Library Journal, December 2003, page 158

Awards the book has won:
School Library Journal Best Books, 2003
ALA Best Books for Young Adults, 2004

Other books by the same author:
Fire Arrow: The Second Song of Eirren, 1998
Hero's Song: The First Song of Eirren, 1991

Other books you might like:
Patrice Kindl, *Goose Chase*, 2001
  A tart-tongued goose girl is determined to save her beloved geese no matter how many kings or princes want to marry her.
Tanith Lee, *Red as Blood, or Tales from the Sisters Grimmer*, 1983
  New interpretations of old tales find the unexpected in the familiar.
Robin McKinley, *Beauty: A Retelling of the Story of Beauty and the Beast*, 1978
  A romantic reworking of the classic story of the young girl who overlooks the beast's ugliness and sees his kind heart.

1132

ANN WHITFORD PAUL
DAVID WALKER, Illustrator

Little Monkey Says Good Night

(New York: Melanie Kroupa/Farrar Straus and Giroux, 2003)

Subject(s): Animals/Monkeys; Bedtime; Circus
Age range(s): Preschool-Grade 1
Major character(s): Little Monkey, Monkey
Time period(s): 2000s (2003)
Locale(s): United States

Summary: It's time for Little Monkey to go to bed, but first he wants to tell everyone in the Big Top good night. Little Monkey is catapulted from performer to performer saying good night until he ends up with his mother (a trapeze artist) who tosses him back down to his father who tucks Little Monkey into bed. (32 pages)

Where it's reviewed:
Booklist, March 15, 2003, page 1333
Bulletin of the Center for Children's Books, June 2003, page 416
Publishers Weekly, March 24, 2003, page 74
School Library Journal, July 2003, page 104

Other books by the same author:
All by Herself: 14 Girls Who Made a Difference, 1999
Hello Toes, Hello Feet, 1998
The Seasons Sewn: A Year in Patchwork, 1996

Other books you might like:
Maya Gottfried, *Last Night I Dreamed a Circus*, 2003
  A young girl dreams that she is a part of the circus.

Amy Hest, *Kiss Good Night*, 2001
  Mrs. Bear has gone through the bedtime routine, but Sam still won't go to sleep. Finally Mrs. Bear realizes she hasn't given Sam his good night kiss.
Jane Yolen, *How Do Dinosaurs Say Good Night?*, 2000
  Dinosaurs show off bad bedtime behaviors and the right way to go to bed.

1133

GARY PAULSEN

Brian's Hunt

(New York: Wendy Lamb Books/Random House, 2003)

Subject(s): Animals/Bears; Animals/Dogs; Hunting
Age range(s): Grades 6-10
Major character(s): Brian Robeson, 16-Year-Old; David, Indian (Cree); Kay-gwa-daush "Susan", Indian (Cree)
Time period(s): 1980s
Locale(s): Canada

Summary: Returning to the northern Canadian wilderness that he loves, Brian canoes through a series of connecting lakes and makes camp at one of them where he hears a dog crying. Seeing that the dog's been mauled by a bear, he patches up the wounds and becomes concerned about the well-being of the Cree family he met last winter, especially their daughter Susan. Heading to their home, he finds the bodies of David and his wife, partially eaten by the bear, and Susan's tracks heading toward the lake where she seems to have gotten away in a canoe. Locating Susan, he then sets out armed with only a bow and arrow to hunt down the bear in this fourth book featuring the hero of *Hatchet*. (103 pages)

Where it's reviewed:
Booklist, January 2004, page 848
Bulletin of the Center for Children's Books, February 2004, page 242
Kliatt, January 2004, page 10
School Library Journal, December 2003, page 158
Voice of Youth Advocates, February 2004, page 497

Other books by the same author:
Brian's Return, 1999
Brian's Winter, 1996
The River, 1991
Hatchet, 1987

Other books you might like:
Earl Fleck, *Chasing Bears*, 1999
  While camping, Danny overcomes his fear of bears and rescues his father and brother who are injured when a tree falls on their tent.
Stephen King, *The Girl Who Loved Tom Gordon*, 1999
  Stepping off the Appalachian Trail, Trisha promptly loses her way and becomes lost in the woods for nine days, fearful that a large bear is tracking her.
Ben Mikaelsen, *Touching Spirit Bear*, 2001
  Cole's mean, arrogant and vicious, traits he's learned from his abusive father, until he's sent to an isolated Alaska island to rethink his ways.

1134

GARY PAULSEN

The Glass Cafe: Or the Stripper and the State: How My Mother Started a War with the System that Made Us Kind of Rich and a Little Bit Famous

(New York: Wendy Lamb/Random House, 2003)

Subject(s): Mothers and Sons; Humor; Dancing
Age range(s): Grades 6-9
Major character(s): Anthony "Tony", 12-Year-Old; Alice "Al", Dancer, Mother (of Tony); Miss Klein, Teacher (art)
Time period(s): 2000s
Locale(s): United States

Summary: Raised by a single mom who's an exotic dancer, Tony and Al enjoy one another's company and their life together. Al dances at the Kitty Kat club to make money to pursue her PhD in literature while Tony attends middle school and discovers he enjoys art. When Miss Klein introduces his art class to figure drawing, Tony is given permission by his mother to draw some of the dancers at the Kitty Kat club. Sketching the women as they leave the dance floor, he captures their weariness and the hard lives some of them have led; he draws so well that Miss Klein asks permission to enter his drawings in an art contest at the museum in town. The contest leads problems as someone complains to a social worker about Tony's pornographic drawings and suddenly there's a police officer at their door to arrest his mother. Luckily Al and Tony can see the humor of the situation, but not without a court fight to prove Tony's innocence and Al's fitness to be a mother. There's also a large settlement from the state that allows Al to quit dancing and become a full-time graduate student in another humorous, yet thoughtful work from a gifted writer. (99 pages)

Where it's reviewed:
Booklist, September 1, 2003, page 115
Library Media Connection, February 2004, page 70
Publishers Weekly, June 30, 2003, page 81
School Library Journal, June 2003, page 150
Voice of Youth Advocates, August 2003, page 228

Other books by the same author:
Time Hackers, 2005
Brian's Hunt, 2003
Shelf Life: Stories by the Book, 2003
How Angel Peterson Got His Name, 2003
The Beet Fields: Memories of a Sixteenth Summer, 2000

Other books you might like:
Avi, *Nothing but the Truth*, 1991
    A student attempts to get out of homeroom by whistling through the National Anthem, but the media blows the incident out of proportion.
Kate Klise, *Trial by Jury/Journal*, 2001
    Lily's selection as the youngest juror in the state of Missouri becomes a humorous assignment when her teacher requires her to keep a journal of her experiences.

Susan Beth Pfeffer, *The Ring of Truth*, 1993
    Because the news that Sloan was pawed by a drunk senator could damage fundraising, everyone wants it kept quiet.

1135

GARY PAULSEN

How Angel Peterson Got His Name

(New York: Wendy Lamb/Random House, 2003)

Subject(s): Short Stories; Humor; Sports
Age range(s): Grades 6-9
Major character(s): Carl "Angel" Peterson, 13-Year-Old; Gary Paulsen, Narrator, 13-Year-Old; Orvis Orvisen, 13-Year-Old
Time period(s): 1950s
Locale(s): Minnesota

Summary: Looking back to the summer the author and his friends were 13, Paulsen narrates their wild adventures as these boys blazon the trail for what will come to be called "extreme sports." Carl becomes known as angel when he tries to break the world speed record by skiing behind their town's fastest hot rod, and experiences the anticipated results. To impress a girl and win $25, Orvis borrows a quarter for the right to wrestle a bear; Paulsen goes over a waterfall in a pickle barrel; Emil rides an old parachute that the boys make into a kite; and the teens, riding their one-speed, fat-tired Schwinn bikes, attempt some daringly stupid jumps in this mad-capped, fictionalized memoir. (111 pages)

Where it's reviewed:
Booklist, December 15, 2002, page 754
Bulletin of the Center for Children's Books, February 2003, page 247
Kirkus Reviews, December 1, 2002, page 1772
Publishers Weekly, January 20, 2003, page 83
School Library Journal, February 2003, page 168

Awards the book has won:
ALA Best Books for Young Adults, 2004
Center for Children's Books Best Books, 2002

Other books by the same author:
Time Hackers, 2005
Brian's Hunt, 2003
Shelf Life: Stories by the Book, 2003
The Beet Fields: Memories of a Sixteenth Summer, 2000
Harris and Me: A Summer Remembered, 1993

Other books you might like:
Chris Lynch, *Johnny Chesthair*, 1997
    Two boys start a club that has only one rule-no girls! Their worst moment comes as they confront archenemy Monica and her cookie-selling Girl Scouts.
Patrick F. McManus, *Never Cry "Arp" and Other Great Adventures*, 1996
    Although the author claims these 12 tales are factual, there's been enough truth stretching that they deserve their fictional designation.
Todd Strasser, *Kidnap Kids*, 1998
    On a rare weekend together, Steven and his brother throw away their parents' beepers, car keys, phones and laptops to ensure their undivided attention.

1136

WON-LDY PAYE
MARGARET H. LIPPERT, Co-Author
JULIE PASCHKIS, Illustrator

Head, Body, Legs: A Story from Liberia
(New York: Henry Holt and Company, 2002)

Subject(s): Folklore; Africa; Problem Solving
Age range(s): Grades K-2
Time period(s): Indeterminate Past
Locale(s): Liberia

Summary: In this retelling of a creation story from the Dan People of Liberia, a solo head is limited to eating food it can gather with its tongue as it rolls along the ground. When the head attracts the attention of a pair of arms in a tree, the head and the arms join together and enjoy cherries from the tree. Then a body bumps into head and arms and agrees to hook up with them so the body can better see where it's going. Even with arms and a body, the head can't get mangos from a tree until it convinces some legs to cooperate with the plan. It takes awhile to get all the body parts connected in the most efficient way, but once that effort is accomplished, the newly created head, body, legs, arms enjoys the mangos it's now able to pick from the tree. (32 pages)

Where it's reviewed:
Book Links, December 2002, page 12
Booklist, August 2002, page 1968
Bulletin of the Center for Children's Books, May 2002, page 338
Horn Book, May 2002, page 340
Publishers Weekly, April 1, 2002, page 82

Awards the book has won:
Bulletin of the Center for Children's Books Blue Ribbons, 2002
ALA Notable Children's Books, 2003

Other books by the same author:
Mrs. Chicken and the Hungry Crocodile, 2003 (School Library Journal Best Books)
Why Leopard Has Spots: Dan Stories from Liberia, 1998

Other books you might like:
Mary-Joan Gerson, *Why the Sky Is Far Away: A Nigerian Folktale*, 1992
Considering itself misused by the peasants, the sky responds by moving farther away.
Walter Dean Myers, *The Story of the Three Kingdoms*, 1995
The wisdom in the People's stories gives them the strength to share the kingdoms of earth, sky and water with the creatures living there.
Isaac O. Olaleye, *In the Rainfield: Who Is the Greatest?*, 2000
Many years ago, according to a Nigerian folktale, Rain, Fire, and Wind argue with each claiming to be the greatest.

1137

WON-LDY PAYE
MARGARET H. LIPPERT, Illustrator

Mrs. Chicken and the Hungry Crocodile
(New York: Henry Holt and Company, 2003)

Subject(s): Folklore; Animals/Chickens; Animals/Crocodiles
Age range(s): Grades K-3
Major character(s): Mrs. Chicken, Chicken, Mother; Crocodile, Crocodile, Mother
Time period(s): Indeterminate Past
Locale(s): Liberia

Summary: While bathing in a puddle Mrs. Chicken decides she needs a larger expanse of water in order to appreciate her full beauty so she walks down to the river. Yet when she leans over, she sees scaly green legs and a long mouth with teeth rather than her beautiful wings. Silently, underwater, Crocodile waits as the tasty morsel moves closer until she's able to grab the startled chicken's leg. When Mrs. Chicken realizes she's to be eaten she protests that Crocodile should not eat her sister. To prove her point, she lays three eggs to match the three that Crocodile has and then, when they are about to hatch, switches them as Crocodile sleeps. Crocodile is shocked by what hatches from her eggs, but pleased by the beautiful babies hatching from Mrs. Chicken's eggs. Kindly, Mrs. Chicken agrees to give Crocodile ''her'' babies and she takes the ugly ones from Crocodile and hurries home where she is, from now on, content to bath in puddles with her chicks. (32 pages)

Where it's reviewed:
Bulletin of the Center for Children's Books, July 2003, page 457
Horn Book, May 2003, page 361
Publishers Weekly, April 14, 2003, page 69
School Library Journal, July 2003, page 116

Awards the book has won:
School Library Journal Best Books, 2003
Notable Social Studies Trade Books for Young People, 2004

Other books by the same author:
Head, Body, Legs: A Story from Liberia, 2002 (ALA Notable Children's Books)
Why Leopard Has Spots: Dan Stories from Liberia, 1998

Other books you might like:
Verna Aardema, *Rabbit Makes a Monkey of Lion*, 1989
With the help of her friends Turtle and Bush-rat, Rabbit outsmarts Lion and devours his honey.
Paul Galdone, *The Monkey and the Crocodile: A Jataka Tale from India*, 1969
When a wily crocodile tries to capture a monkey the monkey must be very clever in order to save himself.
April Pulley Sayre, *Crocodile Listens*, 2001
Crocodile listens for the sounds of her babies, buried in the sand at river's edge, to call for help with removal of the sand so they can emerge from their eggs.
Judy Sierra, *Counting Crocodiles*, 1997
A rhyming story based on a folktale tells how a monkey tricks a crocodile in order to reach the banana tree on a nearby island.

`1138`

PHILIPPA PEARCE

Familiar and Haunting: Collected Stories

(New York: Greenwillow/HarperCollins, 2002)

Subject(s): Short Stories; Supernatural; Family Life
Age range(s): Grades 5-8
Summary: Written across six decades, these 37 stories serve either as a splendid introduction to Philippa Pearce or a chat with an old friend. Some are stories of daily life, relationships with family and friends, and special events in life, from the closeness of a boy and his grandfather to the dread of swinging on a rope over a river. The author's love of the supernatural is evident in stories about a tree with a soul, a child who's caught by a cage made of shadows, unwanted ghosts who materialize uninvited and a ghost dog who appears whenever her favorite ball is tossed. (388 pages)

Where it's reviewed:
Booklist, May 1, 2002, page 1527
Bulletin of the Center for Children's Books, October 2002, page 73
Horn Book, May 2002, page 335
School Library Journal, July 2002, page 124
Voice of Youth Advocates, June 2002, page 130

Other books by the same author:
The Children of Charlecote, 1989
Tom's Midnight Garden, 1984 (Carnegie Medal)
Minnow on the Say, 1955

Other books you might like:
Joan Aiken, *A Fit of Shivers: Tales for Late at Night*, 1992
    Scary stories guaranteed to give the reader "a fit of shivers."
Malka Penn, *Ghosts and Golems: Haunting Tales of the Supernatural*, 2001
    Original short stories by ten different authors offer a look at Jewish culture while also adding a dollop of suspense.
R.L. Stine, *The Haunting Hour: Chills in the Dead of the Night*, 2001
    Voodoo cookies, graveyard romps, and ghostly requests add touches of terror to these ten stories.

`1139`

SHELLEY PEARSALL

Trouble Don't Last

(New York: Knopf/Random House, 2002)

Subject(s): Underground Railroad; Slavery; Old Age
Age range(s): Grades 5-8
Major character(s): Samuel, 11-Year-Old, Slave; Harrison, Aged Person, Slave; Master Hackler, Landowner
Time period(s): 1850s (1850)
Locale(s): Kentucky; Ohio; Chatham, Canada
Summary: Since Master Hackler sold his mother, Samuel's been raised by a variety of slaves on the plantation, including old Harrison. Samuel's pretty surprised when Harrison grabs him off his pallet one night and tells him the two are leaving for "Canaday." Now Samuel would really rather stay behind

where he knows what's expected of him and where he'll sleep indoors each night, but Harrison doesn't give him much choice in the matter. The two depend on the station masters who lead them from one safe house to another; some force them along the route with pistols and knives, another one talks to her dead husband and one white man is in it just for the money. Harrison and Samuel nevertheless make it to Canada on a trip that reveals family secrets to Samuel in this author's first novel. (237 pages)

Where it's reviewed:
Book Report, May 2002, page 58
Bulletin of the Center for Children's Books, March 2002, page 251
Publishers Weekly, December 17, 2001, page 91
School Library Journal, January 2002, page 138

Awards the book has won:
Scott O'Dell Award, 2003
Booklist Editors' Choice/Books for Youth, 2002

Other books by the same author:
Remarkable Ohioans: Stories, 1997 (Nonfiction)

Other books you might like:
Elisa Carbone, *Stealing Freedom*, 1998
    Without her family to support her, Ann Maria's life as a slave is horrible until a stranger helps her escape on the Underground Railroad to Canada.
Gloria Houston, *Bright Freedom's Song: A Story of the Underground Railroad*, 1998
    Bright Freedom's father was an indentured servant, which explains his commitment to using the Underground Railroad to help slaves.
Patricia C. McKissack, *A Picture of Freedom: The Diary of Clotee, a Slave Girl*, 1997
    Clotee, a literate 12-year-old house slave, considers running away in this "Dear America" series entry set in 1859.
Virginia Frances Schwartz, *If I Just Had Two Wings*, 2001
    Hearing she is to be sold, Phoebe joins slave Liney and her four children as they use their limited information to reach the Underground Railroad.

`1140`

TRACEY CAMPBELL PEARSON, Author/Illustrator

Bob

(New York: Farrar Straus Giroux, 2002)

Subject(s): Animals/Roosters; Personal Odyssey; Farm Life
Age range(s): Preschool-Kindergarten
Major character(s): Bob, Rooster
Time period(s): 2000s (2002)
Locale(s): United States
Summary: Bob is a rooster that doesn't know how to crow. One morning, he sets out looking for a rooster to teach him how. On the way, he finds a cat that teaches him to meow, a dog that teaches him to bark and a cow that teaches him to moo. Finally, after wandering all night, Bob is awakened by a rooster teaching him how to crow. That night, Bob puts his new crowing skill and all the other animal sounds he's learned to good use, when he scares away a fox coming to attack the hens. (32 pages)

Where it's reviewed:
Booklist, November 15, 2002, page 611
Horn Book Guide, Spring 2003, page 48
Kirkus Reviews, August 15, 2002, page 1232
Publishers Weekly, July 8, 2002, page 48
School Library Journal, August 2002, page 164

Other books by the same author:
Myrtle, 2004
Where Does Joe Go?, 1999
The Purple Hat, 1997

Other books you might like:
P.D. Eastman, *Are You My Mother?*, 1960
A baby bird falls out of his nest and goes searching for his mother, imitating those he meets including a dog, a cow and a plane.
Jules Feiffer, *Bark, George*, 1999
George is a puppy that can't bark, but instead imitates all the things that other animals say.
John Lawrence, *This Little Chick*, 2002
A little chick makes the rounds on this farm, imitating the noises of the other animals.

1141

RICHARD PECK

The River between Us
(New York: Dial/Penguin Putnam, 2003)

Subject(s): Race Relations; Racially Mixed People; Heritage
Age range(s): Grades 6-10
Major character(s): Howard Leland Hutchings, 15-Year-Old; Tilly Pruitt Hutchings, Grandmother (of Howard); Delphine Duvall Pruitt, Aunt (great aunt); Noah Pruitt, Uncle (great uncle); Calinda, Slave
Time period(s): 19th century; 20th century (1861-1916)
Locale(s): Grand Tower, Illinois; Cairo, Illinois

Summary: Howard, his two younger brothers and his father travel by Model-T from St. Louis to Grand Tower to visit his grandparents, Aunt Delphine, and Uncle Noah. As Howard sees their old house with its peeling wallpaper and lack of indoor plumbing, he wonders about their lives when they were younger and the house freshly built. Grandma Tilly uses their week together to tell Howard his family's history beginning with the arrival of Delphine and her slave Calinda at the beginning of the Civil War. Riding the steamboat up from New Orleans, Delphine is the most sophisticated person to ever set foot in Grand Tower. With no suitable lodgings, Tilly's mother invites them to stay and the two quickly became part of the Pruitt family. It's not until Tilly and Delphine go in search of wounded Noah, Tilly's twin who joined the Union Army, that Delphine is recognized and her ethnic background revealed. Howard listens to Tilly's stories, and his father's addition to the family heritage, and feels great pride in the blood that flows in his veins in another stirring work from this award-winning author. (164 pages)

Where it's reviewed:
Bulletin of the Center for Children's Books, November 2003, page 119
Horn Book, September 2003, page 616

Publishers Weekly, July 14, 2003, page 77
School Library Journal, September 2003, page 218
Voice of Youth Advocates, October 2003, page 317

Awards the book has won:
Scott O'Dell Award for Historical Fiction, 2004
ALA Best Books for Young Adults, 2004

Other books by the same author:
Fair Weather, 2001
Year Down Yonder, 2000
A Long Way from Chicago, 1998
Voices After Midnight, 1989
This Family of Women, 1983

Other books you might like:
James Lincoln Collier, *With Every Drop of Blood*, 1994
White southerner Johnny is captured by black Union soldier Cush, but the two gradually becomes friends and partners as they're caught in a battle.
Virginia Frances Schwartz, *Send One Angel Down*, 2000
Though every slave knows that Eliza is another child fathered by their master, it's Eliza's half-sister who sends her to the fields to work.
Mildred D. Taylor, *The Land*, 2001
With a slave mother and her white master for his father, Paul-Edward walks that fine line of being half white and living in the South after the Civil War.

1142

ROBERT NEWTON PECK

Horse Thief: A Novel
(New York: HarperCollins, 2002)

Subject(s): Rodeos; Animals/Horses; Stealing
Age range(s): Grades 7-10
Major character(s): Tullis Yoder, 17-Year-Old, Orphan; Agnolia Platt, Doctor; Rubin Leviticus "Hitch" Hitchborn, Thief; Clemsa Lou Wetmeadow, Girlfriend (of Tullis)
Time period(s): 1930s (1938)
Locale(s): Chickalookee, Florida; Redworm, Florida

Summary: Orphaned Tullis Yoder works as a stable hand for the Big Bubb Stampede Rodeo and leaps at the chance to ride a bull, a leap that results in an injury to his hand. Stitched together by Dr. Platt, Tullis returns to his work until he learns that the rodeo is shutting down. Concerned only about the rodeo's 13 horses, he decides to steal them when he hears of the plan to sell the horses to a pet food factory. Enlisting the help of the doctor and her card-playing, drunken father Hitch, Tullis sets off on a wild chase around Florida with a corrupt judge and various law enforcement officials in pursuit. All ends well as the horses are saved, Tullis finally rides a bull for the required eight seconds, a new rodeo is formed and Clemsa agrees to be his girlfriend. (231 pages)

Where it's reviewed:
Kliatt, July 2002, page 13
Library Media Connection, January 2003, page 92
Publishers Weekly, June 10, 2002, page 61
School Library Journal, July 2002, page 124
Voice of Youth Advocates, August 2002, page 196

Other books by the same author:
Bro, 2004
Extra Innings, 2001
The Cowboy Ghost, 1999
Nice Man Tree, 1998
A Day No Pigs Would Die, 1973

Other books you might like:
Mary Casanova, *Stealing Thunder*, 1999
When Libby thinks Mr. Porter is harming her favorite horse Thunder, she steals the horse and uncovers Porter's plans to collect insurance money.
Jean Ferris, *Eight Seconds*, 2000
John has the opportunity during rodeo camp to feel the adrenaline rush of riding a bull for eight terrifying, thrilling seconds.
Mark Twain, *The Adventures of Huckleberry Finn*, 1885
The classic adventure of the slave Jim and young Huck, two runaways who flee Huck's abusive father and float down the Mississippi River.

`1143`

SARA PENNYPACKER
MARTIN MATJE, Illustrator

Stuart Goes to School

(New York: Orchard Books/Scholastic, Inc, 2003)

Subject(s): Fear; Clothes; Magic
Age range(s): Grades 2-4
Major character(s): Stuart, 3rd Grader, 8-Year-Old; Mrs. Spindles, Teacher
Time period(s): 2000s
Locale(s): Punbury, Fictional Country

Summary: Although Stuart's many worries about embarrassing moments on the first day of school don't happen exactly as he fears he does suffer embarrassment that he hasn't anticipated. His magical cape is a mixed blessing for Stuart as he cannot anticipate how it will choose to interpret his wishes. Although Stuart thinks his first two days in Mrs. Spindle's classroom are total disasters and he considers throwing away his cape, by the third day, a drawing assignment allows him to use a natural talent—in combination with the cape's magic—to solve his worries about having friends. Maybe this new school will work out after all. (58 pages)

Where it's reviewed:
Booklist, July 2003, page 1892
Publishers Weekly, June 9, 2003, page 54
School Library Journal, September 2003, page 187

Awards the book has won:
IRA Children's Choices, 2004

Other books by the same author:
Stuart's Cape, 2002
Dumbstruck, 1994

Other books you might like:
Allan Ahlberg, *The Woman Who Won Things*, 2002
While their lucky mom wins one contest after another, Gus and Gloria discover that their kindly substitute teacher is not what she seems.

Betsy Duffey, *Virtual Cody*, 1997
Cody fears that when he gives his school report, classmates will laugh to learn he's named after a dog and not the famous Buffalo Bill Cody.
Dav Pilkey, *Captain Underpants and the Attack of the Talking Toilets*, 1999
Mischief makers Harold and George and their principal's alter ego, Captain Underpants, use cafeteria food to vanquish an invention gone awry.

`1144`

SARA PENNYPACKER
MARTIN MATJE, Illustrator

Stuart's Cape

(New York: Orchard Books/Scholastic, Inc., 2002)

Subject(s): Moving, Household; Fear; Fantasy
Age range(s): Grades 2-4
Major character(s): Stuart, 3rd Grader, Son; One-Tooth, Cat; Stanley, Maintenance Worker
Time period(s): Indeterminate
Locale(s): Punbury, Fictional Country

Summary: Moving is boring and creates worries. Stuart wants adventure to distract him from his worrying about a new school and making friends in a new town. Rummaging through a box of discards Stuart finds a purple sock, a stapler and many old ties that he puts together to make a cape, the kind of cape that guarantees adventure. Stuart soon learns the magical power of a cape for just wearing it causes three unusual and exciting events. Unfortunately, after his parents insist that Stuart remove his cape, One-Tooth lies on it for a nap and somehow changes places with Stanley, the driver of a garbage truck. This fourth adventure leads to Stuart finding a friend, Stanley, who has the same hobby as Stuart—junk collecting. (57 pages)

Where it's reviewed:
Booklist, September 1, 2002, page 125
Horn Book Guide, Spring 2003, page 71
Kirkus Reviews, July 1, 2002, page 961
Publishers Weekly, November 4, 2002, page 84
School Library Journal, November 2002, page 133

Other books by the same author:
Stuart Goes to School, 2003
Dumbstruck, 1994

Other books you might like:
Kate Banks, *Howie Bowles, Secret Agent*, 1999
To assure he will make friends easily after his second move in one year, Howie becomes Secret Agent Bean Burger to his classmates.
Adele Geras, *The Fabulous Fantoras: Book One: Family Files*, 1998
The first book in a fantasy series introduces the family members and the unique talents of each.
Dick King-Smith, *Billy the Bird*, 2001
Only Billy's big sister Mary knows that monthly, on the night of the full moon, sleeping Billy becomes lighter than air and soars above the town.

1145

L. KING PEREZ
ROBERT CASILLA, Illustrator

First Day in Grapes

(New York: Lee & Low Books Inc., 2002)

Subject(s): Self-Confidence; Schools; Migrant Labor
Age range(s): Grades 1-3
Major character(s): Chico Padilla, 3rd Grader, Son (of migrant laborers); Mama, Mother; Ms. Andrews, Teacher
Time period(s): 2000s
Locale(s): California

Summary: During the school year as his family follows the crops Chico has many first days of school. At this stop, it's a first day in grapes, the crop that his parents will pick while he is in school. Chico doesn't want to face the teasing and name-calling at yet another school but Mama insists and stands him tall before sending him to the bus. Ms. Andrews helps Chico feel more comfortable and during math class she notes his skill in the subject. Feeling more confident, Chico stands up to the bullies in the cafeteria by challenging them with math problems. By the time Chico's first day in grapes is over he's hoping to stay long enough to participate in the school's math fair. (32 pages)

Where it's reviewed:
Booklist, November 15, 2002, page 612
Horn Book Guide, Spring 2003, page 49
Kirkus Reviews, October 1, 2002, page 1477
School Library Journal, October 2002, page 125
Smithsonian, December 2002, page 126

Awards the book has won:
Smithsonian's Notable Books for Children, 2002
Pura Belpre Honor Book, Illustration, 2004

Other books by the same author:
Ghost Stalking, 1995
Belle: The Great American Lap Dog, 1988

Other books you might like:
Linda Jacobs Altman, *Amelia's Road*, 1993
    Unlike others in her family of migrant laborers Amelia longs for permanence, a house with a yard and a teacher that knows her name.
Arthur Dorros, *Radio Man/Don Radio: A Story in English and Spanish*, 1993
    Diego uses his ever-present radio to keep up with friends as he and his family follow the crops.
Francisco Jimenez, *La Mariposa*, 1998
    Speaking only Spanish, the son of migrant workers has a difficult adjustment to his English-speaking first grade classroom.

1146

LYNNE RAE PERKINS, Author/Illustrator

The Broken Cat

(New York: Greenwillow Books, 2002)

Subject(s): Animals/Cats; Veterinarians; Accidents
Age range(s): Grades K-3
Major character(s): Andy, Child, Son; Frank, Cat; Mom, Mother, Storyteller
Time period(s): 2000s (2002); Indeterminate Past
Locale(s): United States

Summary: While sitting at the vet's awaiting treatment for his injured pet Andy asks his mother to relate the childhood story of her broken arm. The story distracts Andy from his fears for Frank, comforts him and enables the time to pass. After taking a history and examining Frank the vet concludes that Frank was injured in a fight with another cat. She treats his head wound and Andy carries Frank, with his shaved head swathed in bandages, home to recuperate. Mom's responses to Andy's questions about her recovery from her broken arm give Andy hope that one day Frank will be back to normal too. (32 pages)

Where it's reviewed:
Booklist, March 15, 2002, page 1264
Horn Book, May 2002, page 320
Publishers Weekly, April 1, 2002, page 81
Riverbank Review, Summer 2002, page 29
School Library Journal, June 2002, page 107

Awards the book has won:
Horn Book Fanfare, 2002
Smithsonian's Notable Books for Children, 2002

Other books by the same author:
Snow Music, 2003
Clouds for Dinner, 1997 (Riverbank Review Children's Books of Distinction)
Home Lovely, 1995 (Boston Globe-Horn Book Honor Book)

Other books you might like:
Patricia Casey, *One Day at Wood Green Animal Shelter*, 2001
    Stray animals that come to the shelter lack caring owners, but they still receive compassionate treatment from the shelter staff.
Ann M. Martin, *Leo the Magnificat*, 1996
    A fluffy black and white cat wanders into a churchyard and makes himself at home for the rest of his long life.
Patricia Polacco, *Mrs. Katz and Tush*, 1992
    A gift of a kitten begins the intergenerational friendship between an elderly Jewish widow and a young African American neighbor.

1147

LYNNE RAE PERKINS, Author/Illustrator

Snow Music

(New York: Greenwillow Books, 2003)

Subject(s): Winter; Lost and Found; Animals/Dogs
Age range(s): Grades K-2
Major character(s): Unnamed Character, Child, Son; Unnamed Character, Dog
Time period(s): 2000s
Locale(s): United States

Summary: Softly, quietly the snow falls all night as people and animals sleep. When a young boy opens the door to look over the still, snow-covered land his dog bounds out of the house. Bundled against the cold, the boy and his friend go searching; a friend joins him. Deer, birds, squirrels, a curious dog and two children leave tracks on the newly fallen snow. The sounds each makes become music floating over the snowy landscape. By climbing a tree, the boy and his friend spot the dog and bring it home before nightfall when, with a quiet whisper, the snow begins to fall again. (34 pages)

Where it's reviewed:
Booklist, September 1, 2003, page 130
Bulletin of the Center for Children's Books, December 2003, page 164
Horn Book, November 2003, page 734
Publishers Weekly, October 27, 2003, page 67
School Library Journal, November 2003, page 112

Awards the book has won:
Bulletin of the Center for Children's Books Blue Ribbons, 2003
Horn Book Fanfare, 2003

Other books by the same author:
The Broken Cat, 2002 (Horn Book Fanfare)
Clouds for Dinner, 1997 (Smithsonian's Notable Books for Children)
Home Lovely, 1995 (Boston Globe-Horn Book Honor Book)

Other books you might like:
Nancy White Carlstrom, *The Snow Speaks*, 1992
    Two children enjoy the sights and sounds of the season's first snow.
Kevin Henkes, *Oh!*, 1999
    All night snow falls, coloring everything white. All day animals and children run, jump, and play in the bright snow.
Bruce Hiscock, *When Will It Snow?*, 1995
    A child awaits the answer to his question while animals simply prepare for the season's first snowfall.
Ezra Jack Keats, *The Snowy Day*, 1962
    The Caldecott Medal winner portrays a young child's enjoyment of the season's first snowfall.
Steve Sanfield, *Snow*, 1995
    A child marvels at the beauty of the newly fallen snow dotted with the tracks of passing animals.
Manya Stojic, *Snow*, 2002
    Owl announces the coming of snow, geëse fly south, bears hibernate, the snow covers the land until spring when it slowly melts away.

1148

P.J. PETERSEN

Rising Water

(New York: Simon & Schuster, 2002)

Subject(s): Floods; Brothers and Sisters; Rescue Work
Age range(s): Grades 5-8
Major character(s): Kevin Marsh, Juvenile Delinquent, Student—High School; Tracy Barnett, Student—High School, Volunteer; Luke Barnett, Student—High School, Volunteer
Time period(s): 2000s
Locale(s): United States

Summary: Tracy's not happy about working with Kevin who, as part of Operation Start Over, is performing his community service for car theft at the Jefferson Science Center. Feeding

the animals and cleaning their cages are just some of the tasks where Tracy could use Kevin's help, but he's never on time. Kevin has a chance to give his views in alternating chapters and it's soon obvious why he's always late since he has to hitchhike to work. While the two verbally spar with one another, the days of heavy rain force the river over the levees leaving townspeople and their animals stranded in homes suddenly surrounded by water. Tracy, her brother Luke and Kevin travel by boat to rescue a black Lab but run into trouble when they find looters taking advantage of the flood conditions and ransacking a home. The looters grab Luke while Kevin and Tracy motor away to find help. Suddenly the two are forced to work together as they dodge bullets, rescue Luke, and then notify the police as their animosity turns to friendship. (120 pages)

Where it's reviewed:
Booklist, March 1, 2002, page 1131
Bulletin of the Center for Children's Books, February 2002, page 216
Kirkus Reviews, February 1, 2002, page 186
Library Media Connection, May 2002, page 60
School Library Journal, February 2002, page 135

Awards the book has won:
Center for Children's Books Best Books, 2002

Other books by the same author:
Rob&sara.com, 2004
White Water, 1997
Liars, 1992

Other books you might like:
M.E. Kerr, *Snakes Don't Miss Their Mothers*, 2003
    Christmas nears and the animals at Critters hope to be adopted, though most are resigned to life at the shelter.
Willo Davis Roberts, *The Kidnappers: A Mystery*, 1998
    Because he's lied before, Joel knows no one will believe his story of seeing Willie kidnapped.
Ivy Ruckman, *No Way Out*, 1988
    A group of campers hiking through Utah's Zion Narrows is trapped in a canyon by a flash flood.

1149

PATRICIA CURTIS PFITSCH

Riding the Flume

(New York: Simon & Schuster, 2002)

Subject(s): Lumber Industry; Frontier and Pioneer Life; Conservation
Age range(s): Grades 5-8
Major character(s): Frances "Francie" Cavanaugh, 15-Year-Old; Mary Carolyn Cavanaugh, Sister (deceased); Mr. Court, Journalist
Time period(s): 1890s (1894)
Locale(s): Connorsville, California

Summary: For six years the death of Francie's sister has haunted her. When Carrie was killed in a landslide, Francie lost her best friend and has felt ever since that she'll never live up to her parents' expectations. Her town, and her father's hotel, have been built around the logging of the Sierra Lumber Company, which is cutting down the giant sequoia trees.

Counting growth rings for a newspaperman who's writing about these giants, she puts her hand in a hole for balance and finds a mysterious note written by Carrie. As she investigates, she finds Carrie's diary, which is followed by a strange fire in a hermit's cabin and then some information about land ownership. Needing to verify the information in St. Joseph, she decides the fastest way for her to travel is by riding the log flume, a dangerous, wet and scary thirty-mile ride, which allows her to save a very special sequoia called ''Carrie's tree.'' (232 pages)

Where it's reviewed:
Booklist, November 15, 2002, page 604
Kirkus Reviews, September 15, 2002, page 1398
School Library Journal, November 2002, page 174

Other books by the same author:
The Deeper Song, 1998
Keeper of the Light, 1997

Other books you might like:
Linda Crew, *Fire on the Wind*, 1995
    Though asked to fight the blaze, loggers are finally convinced to take the last train to safety before an 18-mile-wide fire destroys their camp.
Monte Killingsworth, *Eli's Song*, 1991
    Upset that an old-growth forest is to be cut, young Eli ''tree sits'' until a lawyer agrees to take his case to court.
Rhea Beth Ross, *The Bet's On, Lizzie Bingman!*, 1988
    When Lizzie's brothers claim that women need sheltering, Lizzie lets them all know that she doesn't require their protection.

1150

TAMORA PIERCE

Lady Knight

(New York: Random House, 2002)

Series: Protector of the Small. Number 4
Subject(s): Fantasy; Adventure and Adventurers; Knights and Knighthood
Age range(s): Grades 6-10
Major character(s): Kelandry ''Kel'', Knight
Time period(s): Indeterminate
Locale(s): Tortall, Fictional Country

Summary: Kelandry of Mindelan passes her Ordeal and becomes a full-fledged knight of the realm. During the mysterious testing known as the Ordeal, Kel is given a destiny to fulfill and it is one guaranteed to appeal to the heroine who has always protected those weaker than herself. Somewhere an evil mage is murdering children to power his war machines and Kel is eager to get to the war's front lines, where she believes she will discover a way to remove this monster. Her orders are otherwise and Kel finds herself in charge of Haven, a refugee camp. Her training stands her in good stead as she brings order to the messy camp and restores self-esteem in the refugees by having them train to defend themselves against future attacks. It all seems a success until Kel is called away and a surprise attack overruns the camp. Many of the refugees, mostly children, are marched as prisoners of war towards a destination Kel can only assume will bring her face-to-face with her destiny. In this conclusion to the quartet, the heroine's more mundane skills play a greater part in her heroism than does her magic. (448 pages)

Where it's reviewed:
Booklist, October 1, 2002, page 313
Children's Bookwatch, October 2002, page 3
Kliatt, November 2002, page 14
Publishers Weekly, July 8, 2002, page 67
School Library Journal, December 2002, page 146

Other books by the same author:
Shatterglass, 2003
Trickster's Choice, 2003
Cold Fire, 2002

Other books you might like:
Laura Williams McCaffrey, *Alia Waking*, 2003
    Alia finds that perhaps the life of a woman warrior is not for her.
Robin McKinley, *The Blue Sword*, 1982
    Harry discovers her true calling as a warrior is to wield the blue sword.
Sherwood Smith, *Wren's Quest*, 1993
    When Wren's best friend is kidnapped, she rushes to the rescue.

1151

TAMORA PIERCE

Shatterglass

(New York: Scholastic, 2003)

Series: Circle Opens. Book 4
Subject(s): Magic; Fantasy; Weather
Age range(s): Grades 6-10
Major character(s): Trisana ''Tris'' Chandler, Wizard (a weather mage), 14-Year-Old; Kethlun ''Keth'' Warder, Artisan (glassmaker); The Ghost, Serial Killer
Time period(s): Indeterminate
Locale(s): Tharios, Fictional Country

Summary: The weather mage Tris travels to Tharios, a medieval city with a strict caste system that ignores the needs of their poorer citizens. She arrives when a serial killer nicknamed The Ghost is methodically removing many of the members of the city's entertainment center. Her primary task is to train Keth, a talented glassmaker whose talent for making weather balls has been enhanced by his being struck by lightning. Teaching him to control his ability is Tris's primary task, though when they realize his weather balls depict The Ghost's upcoming murders, they instantly involve the police. (361 pages)

Where it's reviewed:
Booklist, March 1, 2003, page 1193
Bulletin of the Center for Children's Books, April 2003, page 328
Horn Book, May 2003, page 353
School Library Journal, July 2003, page 134
Voice of Youth Advocates, June 2003, page 152

Other books by the same author:
Cold Fire, 2002 (Circle Opens Book 3)
Street Magic, 2001 (Circle Opens Book 2)

Magic Steps, 2000 (Circle Opens Book 1)

Other books you might like:

Sherryl Jordan, *Secret Sacrament*, 2001
  An amulet given to him by a slave woman brings Gabriel strange visions that help him decide to become a healer.
Philip Pullman, *His Dark Materials Trilogy*, 1996-2000
  When the Dust increases on Lyra's world, evil follows, flowing in from a rift in time and space.
Gillian Rubenstein, *Under the Cat's Eye: A Tale of Morph and Mystery*, 1998
  The headmaster at Jai's boarding school alters the future of his students, but help from a parallel world halts the headmaster's evil plans.

1152

TAMORA PIERCE

Trickster's Choice

(New York: Random House, 2003)

Series: Daughter of the Lioness. Book 1
Subject(s): Fantasy; Adventure and Adventurers
Age range(s): Grades 6-12
Major character(s): Alianne "Aly", Daughter, Spy
Time period(s): Indeterminate
Locale(s): Copper Isles, Fictional Country

Summary: Aly doesn't want to be her mother, and that shouldn't be a crime, but when your mother is Alanna the Lioness, the first lady knight in the kingdom, people just naturally have expectations, especially mothers. Aly's talents are much more like her father's, and although Aly thinks it's obvious, neither of her parents will even consider letting her work as a professional spy. After yet another uncomfortable confrontation with her mother, Aly takes off alone in her sailboat, hoping that when she returns, things will be different. Fate doesn't arrange events for her convenience for Aly is almost immediately captured by pirates and sold into slavery. Her talents give her confidence that she can soon escape, so she bides her time. On the Copper Isles she becomes the property of the noble Balitangs where she's puzzled by the undercurrents of politics and plots surrounding them. Just as Aly is about to escape, the trickster god of the isles, Kyprioth, appears. It seems the god would like to make a wager with Aly if she will keep the Balitang girls alive through the summer, he will help her return home. Since Aly's plans go no further than escape, she decides to accept the god's offer. (446 pages)

Where it's reviewed:
Booklist, December 1, 2003, page 660
Horn Book, January 2004, page 90
Kirkus Reviews, September 1, 2003, page 1129
Publishers Weekly, September 15, 2003, page 66
School Library Journal, December 2003, page 158

Awards the book has won:
ALA Best Books for Young Adults, 2004

Other books by the same author:
Lady Knight, 2002
Squire, 2001
Street Magic, 2001

Other books you might like:

Patricia Briggs, *Dragon Blood*, 2003
  Ward is desperate not to be like his cruel, violent father, but he can't escape the call of the land to become ruler.
Clare B. Dunkle, *The Hollow Kingdom*, 2003
  Like Aly, Kate has no one to turn to when the goblin king proposes marriage, and she must rely on her own wits to survive.
Roberta Gellis, *Bull God*, 2000
  Ariadne has a special relationship with the god Dionysus, but not even a special friendship makes it possible for Ariadne to avert disaster.

1153

DAV PILKEY, Author/Illustrator

The Adventures of Super Diaper Baby: The First Graphic Novel

(New York: Blue Sky Press/Scholastic, Inc., 2002)

Subject(s): Graphic Novel; Humor; Behavior
Age range(s): Grades 2-5
Major character(s): George Beard, 4th Grader, Friend; Harold Hutchins, 4th Grader, Friend; Billy Hoskins, Baby, Hero
Time period(s): Indeterminate
Locale(s): Fictional Country

Summary: To satisfy a requirement that they write an essay on good citizenship as punishment for misbehavior, George and Harold create another cartoon superhero, Super Diaper Baby. When Billy Hoskins is born, he has no superpowers but, in a freak accident, he acquires them and uses them to rid the world of an evil villain who's trying to acquire Billy's superpowers. The principal doesn't appreciate Harold and George's interpretation of the assignment but readers surely will. (125 pages)

Where it's reviewed:
Children's Bookwatch, June 2002, page 3
Horn Book Guide, Fall 2002, page 380
Kirkus Reviews, February 1, 2002, page 187
Publishers Weekly, January 28, 2002, page 291
School Library Journal, June 2002, page 108

Awards the book has won:
IRA Children's Choices, 2003

Other books by the same author:
Ricky Ricotta's Mighty Robot vs. the Jurassic Jackrabbits from Jupiter, 2002 (Fifth Robot Adventure Novel)
Captain Underpants and the Wrath of the Wicked Wedgie Woman, 2001 (Fifth Epic Novel)
The Adventures of Captain Underpants, 1997 (IRA/CBC Children's Choice)

Other books you might like:

Jim Benton, *Lunch Walks Among Us*, 2003
  The first title in the Franny K. Stein, Mad Scientist series introduces Franny, a most unusual child who doesn't quite fit at her new school.
Damon Burnard, *The Amazing Adventures of Soupy Boy!*, 1997
  In a graphic novel, an accidental encounter with radioac-

tive tomatoes changes baby Ashley Fugg into a can of soup with superpowers.

Don Mayne, *Draw Your Own Cartoons*, 2000
This nonfiction title gives instruction to anyone wishing to copy Harold and George's success with cartoon characters.

1154

DAV PILKEY
MARTIN ONTIVEROS, Illustrator

Ricky Ricotta's Mighty Robot vs. the Jurassic Jackrabbits from Jupiter

(New York: Blue Sky Press/Scholastic, Inc., 2002)

Series: Robot Adventure Novel. Number 5
Subject(s): Robots; Heroes and Heroines; Graphic Novel
Age range(s): Grades 2-4
Major character(s): Ricky Ricotta, Mouse; Mighty Robot, Robot; General Jackrabbit, Rabbit, Military Personnel
Time period(s): 2000s (2002)
Locale(s): Fictional Country

Summary: Ricky's excitement about going to the Natural History Museum with Mighty Robot and his parents for his birthday wanes a bit when he learns that his pesky cousin will be coming too. At the museum though, Ricky has bigger things to worry about when evil General Jackrabbit steals the dinosaur skulls to make mutant dinosaur-jackrabbits. Ricky and Mighty Robot manage to outwit the villain, with a little help from Ricky's cousin and they still have time for cake and ice cream. (127 pages)

Where it's reviewed:
Publishers Weekly, September 9, 2002, page 70
School Library Journal, December 2002, page 106

Other books by the same author:
Ricky Ricotta's Mighty Robot vs. the Mecha-Monkeys from Mars, 2002 (IRA Children's Choices)
The Adventures of Super Diaper Baby: The First Graphic Novel, 2002 (IRA Children's Choices)
Ricky Ricotta's Giant Robot vs. the Voodoo Vultures from Venus, 2001 (Robot Adventure Novel Number 3)
Ricky Ricotta's Giant Robot, 2000 (Robot Adventure Novel Number 1)
The Adventures of Captain Underpants, 1997 (IRA Children's Choices)

Other books you might like:
Jules Feiffer, *Meanwhile . . .* , 1997
Raymond becomes a part of the action of the comic book he is reading.
Katherine Pebley O'Neal, *The Reek from Outer Space*, 2003
Gilbreath and his dog, Whiff, have to save the world from alien stinkpots.
James Proimos, *Mutton Soup: More Adventures of Johnny Mutton*, 2004
Johnny Mutton embarks on a series of adventures, including attempting to set a roller coaster-riding world record.

1155

DAV PILKEY
MARTIN ONTIVEROS, Illustrator

Ricky Ricotta's Mighty Robot vs. the Mecha-Monkeys from Mars

(New York: Blue Sky Press/Scholastic, Inc., 2002)

Series: Robot Adventure Novel. Number 4
Subject(s): Robots; Space Travel; Friendship
Age range(s): Grades 2-4
Major character(s): Ricky Ricotta, Mouse, Friend; Mighty Robot, Robot; Major Monkey, Monkey, Alien
Time period(s): Indeterminate
Locale(s): Squeakyville, Earth; Mars

Summary: Determined to conquer Earth, Major Monkey devises a plan to eliminate the one thing that could stop him—Mighty Robot. After luring Mighty Robot to Mars, Major Monkey makes sure the robot is firmly gripped in a giant robot's hand before flying to Earth with a few mecha-monkeys. Earth's space agency flies Ricky to Mars in order to rescue Mighty Robot. They return to Earth and Mighty Robot defeats the mecha-monkeys, who quickly take off for Mars, leaving an angry Major Monkey behind. As payment for saving Earth, Mighty Robot receives a rocket-propelled minivan to replace the family van he damaged while using it as a skateboard. (141 pages)

Where it's reviewed:
Children's Bookwatch, June 2002, page 3
Horn Book Guide, Fall 2002, page 362
School Library Journal, April 2002, page 120

Awards the book has won:
IRA Children's Choices, 2003

Other books by the same author:
Ricky Ricotta's Mighty Robot vs. the Stupid Stinkbugs from Saturn, 2003 (Robot Adventure Novel Number 6)
Ricky Ricotta's Giant Robot vs. the Voodoo Vultures from Venus, 2001 (Robot Adventure Novel Number 3)
Ricky Ricotta's Giant Robot, 2000 (Robot Adventure Novel Number 1)

Other books you might like:
Janet Asimov, *Norby and the Terrified Taxi*, 1997
After traveling to Earth to assist in resolving a problem related to graffiti on orbiting spaceships, robot Norby is kidnapped.
Bonnie Becker, *My Brother, the Robot*, 2001
Chris can't believe his parents have ordered a robot named ''Simon the Perfect Son'' to be his brother and role model.
Stan Berenstain, *The Berenstain Bear Scouts and the Run-Amuck Robot*, 1997
Professor Actual Factual has no control over his latest invention, a supercharged robot destroying Bear Country, if the scouts can't stop it.
L.L. Hench, *Boing-Boing the Bionic Cat*, 2000
Allergies keep Daniel from having a cat until his neighbor uses fiber optics to build one at home for him.

1156

ANDREA DAVIS PINKNEY
SHANE W. EVANS, Illustrator

Fishing Day

(New York: Jump at the Sun/Hyperion Books for Children, 2003)

Subject(s): African Americans; Fishing; Prejudice
Age range(s): Preschool-Grade 1
Major character(s): Reenie, Child, Narrator; Unnamed Character, Mother; Peter ''Pigeon'' Troop, Child, Son
Time period(s): Indeterminate Past
Locale(s): Jim Crow River

Summary: Reenie and her mother like to fish for carp in Jim Crow River and usually have a good catch. A white boy and his father often come fishing there too, but they are usually unsuccessful because they're too noisy and they don't know how to fish. Because of Jim Crow laws, Reenie's mom cautions her not to speak to Peter and his dad, and Reenie complies until the day the boy throws rocks at her. Reenie decides to do something and reaches out to show Peter the trick to catching fish. An author's note explains the term ''Jim Crow'' and the origins of the story. (32 pages)

Where it's reviewed:
Booklist, November 15, 2003, page 602
Bulletin of the Center for Children's Books, January 2004, page 202
Publishers Weekly, November 3, 2003, page 74
School Library Journal, December 2003, page 122

Other books by the same author:
Mim's Christmas Jam, 2001
Duke Ellington: The Piano Prince and His Orchestra, 1998 (Caldecott Honor Book)
Solo Girl, 1997
Alvin Ailey, 1993

Other books you might like:
William Miller, *The Bus Ride*, 1998
  In the segregated South, Sara, an African-American girl, takes a seat at the front of the bus.
Deborah Wiles, *Freedom Summer*, 2001
  After the 1964 Civil Rights Act passes, a public pool is filled in so people of different races such as friends John Henry and Joe cannot swim together.
Jacqueline Woodson, *The Other Side*, 2001
  Despite being warned by their mothers to stay apart, a friendship forms between a white girl and a black girl in the segregated South.

1157

JERRY PINKNEY, Author/Illustrator

The Nightingale

(New York: Phyllis Fogelman Books, 2002)

Subject(s): Fairy Tales; Animals/Birds; Kings, Queens, Rulers, etc.
Age range(s): Grades 1-4
Major character(s): Unnamed Character, Child, Servant; Unnamed Character, Bird; Unnamed Character, Royalty

Time period(s): Indeterminate Past
Locale(s): Morocco

Summary: In an adaptation of Hans Christian Andersen's fairy tale set in northwest Africa, a king learns that somewhere in his kingdom lives a nightingale with a beautiful voice and he demands to hear the bird sing in the palace. None of the palace courtiers is aware of the bird, but a poor kitchen servant knows where to find the bird and she leads the others to the nightingale. The bird's song enchants the king who commands that the nightingale live in the palace so he can hear its beautiful song. After a jeweled mechanical bird is given to the king the nightingale returns to the woods and the king enjoys the mechanized bird until it is worn out from use. The nightingale returns to the palace years later, as the king lies dying, to sing so beautifully for him that he recovers from his illness. (40 pages)

Where it's reviewed:
Booklist, September 1, 2002, page 121
Bulletin of the Center for Children's Books, November 2002, page 98
Horn Book, November 2002, page 733
Riverbank Review, Winter 2002-2003, page 36
School Library Journal, September 2002, page 180

Awards the book has won:
Notable Social Studies Trade Books for Young People, 2003

Other books by the same author:
The Little Match Girl, 1999 (Notable Social Studies Trade Books for Young People)
The Ugly Duckling, 1999 (Caldecott Honor Book)
Rikki-Tikki-Tavi, 1997 (Booklist Editors' Choice)

Other books you might like:
Hans Christian Andersen, *The Fairy Tales of Hans Christian Andersen*, 1995
  Collected and retold by Neil Philip, the title includes twelve classic tales.
Tomie De Paola, *Days of the Blackbird: A Tale of Northern Italy*, 1997
  Throughout the harsh winter, a white bird stays to sing for a gravely ill Duke, sacrificing its beauty to repay the Duke's kindness.
Oscar Wilde, *The Happy Prince*, 1995
  An illustrated adaptation by Jane Ray retells Wilde's 1888 tale of sacrifice by the sparrow to bring happiness to the little prince statue.

1158

JERRY PINKNEY, Author/Illustrator

Noah's Ark

(New York: SeaStar Books, 2002)

Subject(s): Biblical Fiction; Animals; Floods
Age range(s): Grades K-3
Major character(s): Noah, Aged Person, Biblical Figure
Time period(s): Indeterminate Past
Locale(s): Earth

Summary: This picture book rendition of the biblical story of the flood shows Noah's faithfulness to God's instructions. Despite ridicule, Noah and his family build a large ark and stock it with food and water. Then Noah calls the animals as God instructs so that two of each kind of animal on the earth are safely aboard the ark. As promised, the rains begin and continue until the ark floats safely atop the flooded earth. When the water subsides and the wind dries the ground, Noah releases the animals and he and his family resume life on dry ground. (36 pages)

Where it's reviewed:
Booklist, October 1, 2002, page 342
Bulletin of the Center for Children's Books, January 2003, page 188
Horn Book, January 2002, page 103
Publishers Weekly, September 30, 2002, page 69
School Library Journal, November 2002, page 146

Awards the book has won:
Caldecott Honor Book, 2003
ALA Notable Children's Books, 2003

Other books by the same author:
The Nightingale, 2002 (Notable Social Studies Trade Books for Young People)
Aesop's Fables, 2000 (Booklist Editors' Choice)
The Little Match Girl, 1999 (Notable Social Studies Trade Books for Young People)

Other books you might like:
Pippa Goodhart, *Noah Makes a Boat*, 1997
    Although he has no experience in boat-building, Noah is obedient and resourceful so he completes the task God gives him just as the rains begin.
Geraldine McCaughrean, *The Story of Noah and the Ark*, 1989
    Based on the Biblical story, Noah follows God's command to build an ark and load it with two of every animal.
Peter Spier, *Noah's Ark*, 1977
    A Caldecott Medal winner pictorially re-enacts the well-known story of the flood.

1159

DANIEL PINKWATER
ANDY RASH, Illustrator

Fat Camp Commandos Go West

(New York: Scholastic Press, 2002)

Subject(s): Camps and Camping; Humor; Brothers and Sisters
Age range(s): Grades 3-5
Major character(s): Ralph Nebula, Brother, Camper (runaway); Sylvia Nebula, Sister, Camper (runaway); Mavis Goldfarb, Friend
Time period(s): 2000s (2002)
Locale(s): Deepdip Cha-cha's Fun Ashram, West; Horny Toad, West (Rough-Ridin' Rudy's Rootin'-Tootin' Rancho)

Summary: Once again Ralph and Sylvia end up at a summer camp that is really a "fat camp" in disguise so they quickly escape from the daily diet of shredded carrots. Mavis, vacationing at a nearby dude ranch, rescues Ralph and Sylvia and they join her in solving a big problem in the little town of Horny Toad. Mavis, famous for her plans, intends to avert war between the new-fangled health spas and the original dude ranches by advertising a UFO landing in the area and she needs Ralph and Sylvia's help. (89 pages)

Where it's reviewed:
Booklist, June 2002, page 1724
Bulletin of the Center for Children's Books, July 2002, page 415
Horn Book Guide, Fall 2002, page 363
Publishers Weekly, February 11, 2002, page 189
School Library Journal, June 2002, page 108

Other books by the same author:
Fat Camp Commandos, 2001 (IRA Children's Choices)
The Werewolf Club Meets Dorkula, 2001 (Werewolf Club, Number 3)
Mush, A Dog from Space, 1995

Other books you might like:
Dan Greenburg, *The Boy Who Cried Bigfoot*, 2000
    First-time camper Zack and his pal Spencer suspect that the tales of a Bigfoot-type monster at Camp Weno-Wanna-Getta-Wedgee may be true.
Adele Griffin, *Witch Twins at Camp Bliss*, 2002
    Claire is eager to attend camp while her twin sister Luna is reluctant but both find the five-week experience valuable.
Pam Smallcomb, *Camp Buccaneer*, 2002
    A boring summer vacation becomes exciting when Marlon discovers Camp Buccaneer and spends three-weeks learning to be a pirate.

1160

JAIRA PLACIDE

Fresh Girl

(New York: Wendy Lamb/Random House, 2002)

Subject(s): Haitian Americans; Rape; Emigration and Immigration
Age range(s): Grades 9-12
Major character(s): Mardi Desravines, 9th Grader; Perrin, Uncle, Activist
Time period(s): 1990s
Locale(s): New York, New York (Brooklyn); Port-au-Prince, Haiti

Summary: Though born in America, Mardi lived with her grandmother in Haiti from a young age until the 1991 coup when she returned to Brooklyn, along with her older sister and grandmother, while her political activist uncle was confined to a detainee camp in Cuba. Now Mardi tries to adjust to life at her school where the other kids tease her about being a "dumb island" girl, though intellectually she's at the top of her class. The school bully picks on her and if he hasn't hit her, she abuses herself, even going so far as to sleep on rocks to keep the nightmares away. What she's never told her family, and what causes her nightmares, are the soldiers that raped her the last day she was in Haiti, for which she blames Uncle Perrin for not protecting her. When she hears that Perrin is released and coming to Brooklyn, her anger surfaces and she's unable to be kind to this man who was once her favorite uncle. Thankfully Perrin is patient and gradually gets to the heart of Mardi's problems so that she's able to receive counseling in this author's first novel. (216 pages)

Booklist, November 15, 2001, page 566
Bulletin of the Center for Children's Books, March 2002, page 252
Publishers Weekly, December 24, 2001, page 65
School Library Journal, January 2002, page 138
Voice of Youth Advocates, August 2002, page 196

Awards the book has won:
ALA Best Books for Young Adults, 2003
Smithsonian's Notable Books for Children/Older Readers, 2002

Other books you might like:
Julia Alvarez, *How the Garcia Girls Lost Their Accents*, 1991
   A sensitive story of four sisters and their adjustment to life in America after fleeing the Dominican Republic. Adult title.
Laurie Halse Anderson, *Speak*, 1999
   Melinda is ostracized by classmates who think she dialed 911 to break up a party; when the truth comes out, she's finally vindicated.
Anilu Bernardo, *Jumping Off to Freedom*, 1996
   David and his father endure a death-defying trip of survival as they flee from Cuba aboard a raft with two dangerous strangers.
Norma Fox Mazer, *Out of Control*, 1993
   During her junior year Valerie is assaulted in a deserted hallway by three classmates, only one of whom feels any remorse.
Frances Temple, *Tonight, by Sea*, 1995
   Paulie cannot imagine leaving her home in Haiti, but when soldiers kill her best friend, she knows it's time to depart.

1161

CAROL PLUM-UCCI

The She

(San Diego: Harcourt, 2003)

Subject(s): Sea Stories; Brothers; Supernatural
Age range(s): Grades 8-12
Major character(s): Evan Barrett, Orphan, 12th Grader; Grey Shailey, Mentally Ill Person; Emmett Barrett, Brother (of Evan)
Time period(s): 2000s
Locale(s): Philadelphia, Pennsylvania; East Hook, New Jersey

Summary: From a long line of seafaring people, it's been eight years since Evan's parents died at sea while aboard their freighter. It's a night he'll never forget as he heard the shriek of The She, a fabled sea hag who pulls ships down into her greedy jaws. Living with his aunt and older brother ever since, he's put the past behind him until Grey, a classmate of his, asks for him. Last year she was involved in a sailing accident where a friend was drowned and Grey, too, heard the shriek of The She. Unable to bear listening to the sound every time there's a storm, she's now in a mental hospital and has asked for Evan's help. Together the two examine both scientific and supernatural explanations of the night when Evan's parents' drowned, as he also has to come to terms with the news from Emmett that their parents' accident might have been tied in with drug running. (280 pages)

Where it's reviewed:
Bulletin of the Center for Children's Books, November 2003, page 121
Kliatt, September 2003, page 10
Publishers Weekly, November 17, 2003, page 66
School Library Journal, October 2003, page 175
Voice of Youth Advocates, December 2003, page 405

Other books by the same author:
What Happened to Lani Garver, 2002 (ALA Best Books for Young Adults)
The Body of Christopher Creed, 2000 (ALA Best Books for Young Adults)

Other books you might like:
Norma Lehr, *Haunting at Black Water Cove*, 2000
   A request from a ghost, Ruby Faye, leads Kathy to investigate how Ruby was murdered in the early 1900s.
Kathryn Reiss, *Dreadful Sorry*, 1993
   Haunted by a fear of water and the song "Oh My Darling Clementine," Molly summers with her stepfamily in Maine who lives in the house of her nightmares.
Vivian Vande Velde, *Being Dead: Stories*, 2001
   The dead don't always stay dead, as evidenced by this collection of short stories.

1162

CAROL PLUM-UCCI

What Happened to Lani Garver

(San Diego: Harcourt, 2002)

Subject(s): Homosexuality/Lesbianism; Prejudice; Cancer
Age range(s): Grades 8-12
Major character(s): Claire McKenzie, 16-Year-Old, Musician (guitarist); Lani Garver, Student—High School; Macy, Cheerleader, Student—High School
Time period(s): 2000s
Locale(s): Hackett Island, New Jersey

Summary: With an alcoholic mother and a fear that her leukemia has returned, Claire concentrates on hanging with the "in" crowd to keep her worries at bay. Newcomer Lani Garver moves to town and no one is sure if he's a she, though Lani denies being a girl. Well, the cool kids think, if Lani's not a girl, then he must surely be a homosexual, though they never receive a yes or a no to their supposition. Claire and Lani become good friends and Lani helps Claire understand the many talents she has, ones she's not shared with her good friend Macy, as well as deal with her food disorder which she thinks is the return of her leukemia. However, the high school crowd can't accept their friendship or the fact that Lani is different from them and one night kidnaps both Claire and Lani, taking them to the town docks to drown them, in another chilling tale from an award-winning author. (307 pages)

Where it's reviewed:
Booklist, August 2002, page 1947
Kliatt, September 2002, page 13
Publishers Weekly, August 19, 2002, page 91
School Library Journal, October 2002, page 170
Voice of Youth Advocates, December 2002, page 391

Awards the book has won:
ALA Best Books for Young Adults, 2003

Other books by the same author:
The She, 2003
The Body of Christopher Creed, 2000 (Michael L. Printz Honor Book)

Other books you might like:
Kevin Brooks, *Lucas*, 2003
Teenager Lucas appears on an isolated island where he's made the scapegoat for an attack on a young girl and Cait is powerless to halt the mob mentality.
Bette Greene, *The Drowning of Stephan Jones*, 1991
After Carla witnesses violence against a gay couple, she must testify against her boyfriend and his cronies.
Stephanie S. Tolan, *Plague Year*, 1990
New student Bran's ponytail and gold earring set him apart, which leads to torment and tragedy.

1163

PATRICIA POLACCO, Author/Illustrator

Christmas Tapestry

(New York: Philomel/Putnam, 2002)

Subject(s): Christmas; Holocaust; Reunions
Age range(s): Grades 3-6
Major character(s): Jonathan Jefferson Weeks, Child, Son; Reverend Weeks, Religious, Father
Time period(s): 20th century
Locale(s): Detroit, Michigan

Summary: Jonathan Jefferson Weeks is not too happy that his father has moved the entire family to Detroit to take over a run-down church. As the family works together to fix up the church before Christmas, Jonathan's mood gradually improves. He tries to share his dad's belief that everything happens for a reason but then everything seems to go wrong at once. A series of disasters including a roof leak that leads to a hole in the wall and a dead car battery that forces Jonathan and his father to take the bus downtown leads to a happy reunion. The tapestry Reverend Weeks buys to cover the hole in the church's wall, is the wedding chuppah of the old woman waiting with them for the bus. When the plasterer comes to fix the wall, he recognizes the tapestry as well and the couple, separated in a concentration camp many years before, is reunited. (48 pages)

Where it's reviewed:
Booklist, September 1, 2002, page 138
Bulletin of the Center for Children's Books, October 2002, page 74
Publishers Weekly, September 23, 2002, page 30
School Library Journal, October 2002, page 62

Other books by the same author:
Pink and Say, 1994 (Jefferson Cup Award)
The Bee Tree, 1993
The Keeping Quilt, 1991

Other books you might like:
Eve Bunting, *One Candle*, 2002
Every year at Hanukkah, Grandma commemorates her first Hanukkah at Buchenwald.

Barbara Cohen, *Molly's Pilgrim*, 1983
Molly's depiction of a pilgrim as a Russian Jew seeking religious freedom in America as her family did helps others appreciate the pilgrims' hopes.
Susan Wojciechowski, *The Christmas Miracle of Jonathan Toomey*, 1995
A bitter woodcarver finds the Christmas spirit when a local widow asks him to carve a creche for her son.

1164

TRACEY PORTER

A Dance of Sisters

(New York: Joanna Cotler/HarperCollins, 2002)

Subject(s): Sisters; Weight Control; Ballet
Age range(s): Grades 6-8
Major character(s): Delia Ferri, 13-Year-Old, Dancer (ballerina); Pearl Ferri, Sister (of Delia), Student—Boarding School
Time period(s): 2000s
Locale(s): Washington, District of Columbia

Summary: Their mother dies when they are young, their father still grieves over the loss of his wife and sisters Delia and Pearl grow apart from one another. Rebellious Pearl has been expelled from her private day school and now attends a boarding school where she learns to ride horseback and continues to experiment with witchcraft. Delia finds her spot at Elanova School of Dance where she studies ballet under the tutelage of Madame Elanova. Seeking Madame's approval, since she favors the thinner girls, Delia eventually becomes anorexic but her father's so worried about Pearl he doesn't even notice her weight loss. As ballet demands more and more from Delia, she finally realizes that it's okay to give up some of the structure required by ballet and try another form of dance. (276 pages)

Where it's reviewed:
Bulletin of the Center for Children's Books, January 2003, page 209
Horn Book Guide, Spring 2003, page 87
Publishers Weekly, November 18, 2002, page 61
School Library Journal, January 2003, page 142
Voice of Youth Advocates, February 2003, page 481

Other books by the same author:
Treasures in the Dust, 1997

Other books you might like:
Rumer Godden, *Thursday's Children*, 1984
The youngest of six children, Doone is overshadowed by his sister Crystal until it comes to ballet where he quickly outperforms her.
Sally Warner, *Ellie & the Bunheads*, 1997
Ellie reaches the age where she must decide for herself whether or not she wishes to continue her ballet training.
Laurence Yep, *Angelfish*, 2001
Crabby Mr. Cao was once an accomplished ballet dancer in China so Robin enlists his help in costume and set design for her ballet teacher.

1165

ELLEN POTTER
PETER H. REYNOLDS, Illustrator

Olivia Kidney

(New York: Philomel/Penguin Putnam, 2003)

Subject(s): Apartments; Loneliness; Grief
Age range(s): Grades 4-7
Major character(s): Olivia Kidney, 12-Year-Old; Bramwell, 12-Year-Old
Time period(s): 2000s
Locale(s): New York, New York

Summary: One afternoon Olivia returns home from school and discovers, just outside the locked door to her apartment building, that she's lost her house keys. Finally let into the building by Bramwell, a shoeless boy with ten siblings, she's still locked out of her own residence. Invited into other apartments that afternoon, she meets a menagerie of strange occupants and hears their even stranger tales. After meeting the princess who lives in the apartment with the glass floors, she rushes to the apartment below to warn the mother of possible danger to her child. Then it's into the sauna apartment to meet the lizard lady, another encounter with two mean, snotty girls her age and finally a ghost who only Olivia can see. All these meetings help Olivia as she deals with her mother's leaving and her older brother's dying during a phantasmagorical afternoon in this author's first novel. (155 pages)

Where it's reviewed:
Booklist, June 2003, page 1778
Bulletin of the Center for Children's Books, June 2003, page 417
Horn Book, September 2003, page 617
Library Media Connection, January 2004, page 66
School Library Journal, June 2003, page 150

Other books you might like:
Melvin Burgess, *The Ghost Behind the Wall*, 2003
    Crawling through the air ducts of his apartment building, David unknowingly unleashes a malevolent ghost.
Janet Lee Carey, *Wenny Has Wings*, 2002
    When Will survives the runaway truck accident that kills his sister, Will tries to contact Wenny through seances and messages in balloons.
Patrick Jennings, *The Beastly Arms*, 2001
    Moving into a new apartment building, Nickel smells strange, animal-like odors and hears growls and tweets in all the apartments above theirs.

1166

RANDY POWELL

Three Clams and an Oyster

(New York: Farrar Straus Giroux, 2002)

Subject(s): Humor; Friendship; Sports/Football
Age range(s): Grades 7-10
Major character(s): Cade Savage, 11th Grader, Football Player; Rick Beaterson, 11th Grader, Football Player; Dwight Deshutsis, 11th Grader, Football Player; Flint Mc-Callister, 11th Grader, Football Player; Rachel Summerfield, Football Player
Time period(s): 2000s
Locale(s): Seattle, Washington

Summary: For seven years the Three Clams, Rick, Dwight and Flint, have played flag football together. Their first Oyster died in an accident and his spot was taken by Cade, but lately Cade spends more time partying than practicing. The Three Clams are left deciding what to do about Cade, but whom can they get to replace him? Over the weekend, they consider some alternatives, from an athletic womanizer to a very offbeat friend. None of these choices work, so they're left with Rachel, an aggressive athlete whose unshaven legs bother the heck out of them. But if they want a winning team, she's the obvious choice as the Three Clams let go of what was, and move on to what could be. (216 pages)

Where it's reviewed:
Bulletin of the Center for Children's Books, July 2002, page 415
Horn Book, July 2002, page 470
Publishers Weekly, March 11, 2002, page 73
School Library Journal, March 2002, page 236
Voice of Youth Advocates, August 2002, page 196

Awards the book has won:
ALA Best Books for Young Adults, 2003

Other books by the same author:
Run If You Dare, 2001
Tribute to Another Dead Rock Star, 1999
The Whistling Toilets, 1996

Other books you might like:
Alden R. Carter, *Bull Catcher*, 1997
    Through death, divorce, friendships, and the different seasons of the year, Bull and his best friend Jeff play baseball.
A.M. Jenkins, *Damage*, 2001
    Everyone thinks Austin's life should be wonderful, for he's a senior football player, but his partying hides his depression and lack of energy.
Jerry Spinelli, *There's a Girl in My Hammerlock*, 1991
    Maisie finds everyone is against her when she joins the wrestling team, but she's determined to make it through the season.

1167

TERRY PRATCHETT

The Wee Free Men: A Novel of Discworld

(New York: HarperCollins, 2003)

Subject(s): Fairies; Witches and Witchcraft; Fantasy
Age range(s): Grades 6-10
Major character(s): Tiffany Aching, Child, Witch; Wentworth Aching, Brother
Time period(s): Indeterminate
Locale(s): Fairyland, Fictional Country; The Chalk, Fictional Country

Summary: Part of a long line of shepherds, Tiffany lives on the Chalk. Originally protected by her now-deceased Granny, the Chalk is now overrun with monsters that kidnap people for the Fairy Queen. When Tiffany's brother Wentworth is kidnapped, she marches forth armed with a sheep diseases manual and an iron frying pan to find and bring him back home. Unbeknownst to Tiffany, she is as adept a witch as her Granny Aching, which serves her well on her quest. The Nac Mac Feegle, the six-inches-high, blue ''wee free men,'' who specialize in drinking, stealing and fighting, accompany Tiffany in her search for the Fairy Queen. Tiffany's perseverance and determination help her overcome the Fairy Queen and as she returns home, she slams the door between the two worlds with such authority that it's unlikely to be opened anytime soon. (263 pages)

Where it's reviewed:
Booklist, April 15, 2003, page 1465
Bulletin of the Center for Children's Book, July 2003, page 458
Horn Book, May 2003, page 355
Publishers Weekly, May 5, 2003, page 68
School Library Journal, May 2003, page 158

Awards the book has won:
School Library Journal Best Books, 2003
ALA Best Books for Young Adults, 2004

Other books by the same author:
Amazing Maurice and His Educated Rodents: A Novel of Discworld, 2001
The Fifth Elephant: A Novel of Discworld, 2000
The Truth: A Novel of Discworld, 2000
Carpe Jugulum: A Novel of Discworld, 1998

Other books you might like:
Peter Dickinson, *The Ropemaker*, 2001
    A foursome sets off into an unknown land in search of the wizard who can renew their valley's magical protections.
Patrice Kindl, *Goose Chase*, 2001
    A tart-tongued goose girl is determined to save her beloved geese no matter how many kings or princes want to marry her.
J.K. Rowling, *The Harry Potter Series*, 1998-
    Raised by his aunt and uncle, Harry is thrilled to be invited to attend Hogwarts School and begin his wizardry studies.

1168

MIRJAM PRESSLER
BRIAN MURDOCH, Translator

Malka

(New York: Philomel Books, 2003)

Subject(s): Holocaust; Mothers and Daughters; Jews
Age range(s): Grades 6-10
Major character(s): Hannah Mai, Doctor, Mother; Malka Mai, Child; Minna Mai, 16-Year-Old
Time period(s): 1940s (1943-1944)
Locale(s): Lawoczne, Poland

Summary: When Dr. Hannah Mai receives word that the Nazis are rounding up the Jews in her small town in Poland, she escapes through the mountains to Hungary with her two daughters, Minna and Malka. As they near the border, Malka becomes too ill to travel and Hannah decides to leave her with a family who will send her on when she's better. At this point Malka's and Hannah's stories are told in alternating chapters

with Hannah becoming more and more upset that she's left Malka behind and Malka shutting down her emotional ties to her mother and sister in order to survive. Malka is turned out by the family that agreed to keep her and ultimately ends up in a ghetto, until her mother returns and manages a daring rescue of her. Based on a true story, the reader will be glad to know that Malka lives in Tel Aviv where she's the mother of two and grandmother of three. (280 pages)

Where it's reviewed:
Booklist, April 1, 2003, page 1390
Bulletin of the Center for Children's Books, June 2003, page 418
Publishers Weekly, May 5, 2003, page 222
School Library Journal, May 2003, page 160
Voice of Youth Advocates, October 2003, page 317

Other books by the same author:
Shylock's Daughter, 2001
Anne Frank: A Hidden Life, 2000
Halinka, 1998
Diary of a Young Girl: The Definitive Edition, 1995

Other books you might like:
Gila Almagor, *Under the Domin Tree*, 1995
    An autobiographical novel by a noted Israeli actress about her life in an Israeli youth camp with other Holocaust survivors.
Norma Fox Mazer, *Good Night, Maman*, 1999
    Karin and her brother Marc are forced to leave their ill mother behind as they escape from the Nazis; sadly they never again see Maman.
Gudrun Pausewang, *The Final Journey*, 1996
    Sheltered from Nazi terrorism, young Alice rides a cattle car to Auschwitz where she's happy to go to the showers and wash away the grime of the trip.
Jerry Spinelli, *Milkweed*, 2003
    A young Gypsy boy is at first enamored of the ''jack boots'' who take over his city, but later realizes the horror of the Nazis.

1169

CHRIS PRIESTLEY, Author/Illustrator

Death and the Arrow

(New York: Knopf, 2003)

Subject(s): Murder; Mystery and Detective Stories; Historical
Age range(s): Grades 6-9
Major character(s): Tom Marlowe, 15-Year-Old, Apprentice (printer); Dr. Harker, Scientist; Will Piggot, Thief
Time period(s): 1710s (1715)
Locale(s): London, England

Summary: Someone is murdering London residents, shooting them from the rooftops with an Indian arrow and leaving a ''Death and Arrow'' calling card on them. Tom becomes ensnared in the whodunit when his good friend, the pickpocket Will Piggot, is murdered and he teams up with family friend Dr. Harker to track down the murderer. As London tenses for word of the next victim, Tom and Dr. Harker fear they may be next on the murderer's list in a vendetta that is traced back to the French and Indian War fought in the American colonies. (161 pages)

Where it's reviewed:
Bulletin of the Center for Children's Books, July 2003, page 458
Kirkus Reviews, May 1, 2003, page 682
Publishers Weekly, May 19, 2003, page 74
School Library Journal, July 2003, page 134
Voice of Youth Advocates, October 2003, page 318

Awards the book has won:
Center for Children's Books Best Books, 2003

Other books you might like:
Claudio Apone, *My Grandfather, Jack the Ripper*, 2001
Andy lives in the shabby guesthouse called Jack-in-the-Box where Jack the Ripper's last victim supposedly stayed.
Gary Blackwood, *The Shakespeare Stealer*, 1998
Sent to London to steal *The Tragedy of Hamlet*, Widge loses his tablet and ends up joining the cast to find his writings.
Geraldine McCaughrean, *The Pirate's Son*, 1998
Kicked out of school for not paying his fees, Nathaniel is thrilled to travel to Madagascar with Tamo, a pirate's son.
Philip Pullman, *The Ruby in the Smoke*, 1987
Orphaned, 16-year-old Sally must outmaneuver a host of villainous nineteenth-century characters to claim her inheritance and her independence.

1170

MARY SKILLINGS PRIGGER
BETSY LEWIN, Illustrator

Aunt Minnie and the Twister
(New York: Clarion Books, 2002)

Subject(s): Weather; Farm Life; Aunts and Uncles
Age range(s): Grades K-3
Major character(s): Minnie McGranahan, Aunt, Guardian
Time period(s): Indeterminate Past
Locale(s): Kansas

Summary: The sequel to *Aunt Minnie McGranahan* continues the story of the kindly aunt and the nine orphaned nieces and nephews living on her farm. Orderly Aunt Minnie has a routine for the children to follow and uses an old school bell to get their attention when it's time to eat, there's a problem to solve or company's come calling. One spring day when the children respond to the clanging bell Aunt Minnie hurries them into the root cellar. There they stay, listening to the sound of a tornado roaring overhead, until all is quiet. When they emerge they discover that their house has been turned around so that the front door faces the outhouse. Aunt Minnie solves the problem by building a new porch on the new front of the house and enclosing the original porch to make more room for the children. (32 pages)

Where it's reviewed:
Booklist, February 15, 2002, page 1021
Horn Book, May 2002, page 321
Publishers Weekly, March 11, 2002, page 71
School Library Journal, April 2002, page 120

Other books by the same author:
Aunt Minnie McGranahan, 1999

Other books you might like:
Darleen Bailey Beard, *Twister*, 1999
Natt and Lucille huddle in the storm cellar wondering if their mother has reached safety before a tornado rushes over their home.
Sharon Darrow, *Old Thunder and Miss Raney*, 2000
A tornado that whirls Miss Raney and her old horse Thunder through the air also changes Raney's entry in the County Fair.
Phyllis Root, *One Windy Wednesday*, 1997
One Wednesday on the farm the wind is so strong that the sound blows from one animal to another making the cows oink and the ducks moo.

1171

ELISE PRIMAVERA, Author/Illustrator

Auntie Claus and the Key to Christmas
(San Diego: Silver Whistle/Harcourt, Inc., 2002)

Subject(s): Aunts and Uncles; Christmas; Santa Claus
Age range(s): Grades K-3
Major character(s): Christopher Kringle, Child, Nephew; Sophie Kringle, Sister, Niece; Auntie Claus, Aunt
Time period(s): Indeterminate
Locale(s): New York, New York; North Pole, Earth

Summary: Adopting the behavior of famous, spoiled twins staying at the Bing Cherry Hotel, Christopher tries to get his name on the B-B-and-G (bad boys and girls) List that Sophie and Auntie Claus warn him to avoid. Perhaps by doing so he'll be able to figure out the family secret that Sophie and Auntie Claus already seem to know. Christopher is so successful that, when Sophie sends him on a trip to the North Pole, he's locked out of Christmas and discovers he may become a lifetime member of a tiresome group known for bad behavior. Then he discovers the key that unlocks the mystery of the family secret just as Auntie Claus promised. (40 pages)

Where it's reviewed:
Booklist, September 15, 2002, page 246
Bulletin of the Center for Children's Books, November 2002, page 123
Kirkus Reviews, November 1, 2002, page 1624
Publishers Weekly, September 23, 2002, page 36
School Library Journal, October 2002, page 62

Other books by the same author:
Auntie Claus, 1999
Plantpet, 1995
The Three Dots, 1994

Other books you might like:
Lawrence David, *Peter Claus and the Naughty List*, 2001
Discovering his name on Santa's "naughty" list, Peter secretly tries to help remove the names of everyone on the list.
William Joyce, *Santa Calls*, 1993
Accompanied by his sister and best friend, Art Atchinson Aimesworth, boy inventor, visits Santa Claus at the North Pole.

Viveca Larn Sundvall, *Santa's Winter Vacation*, 1994
  While vacationing, three brothers (two naughty, one nice) meet an elderly bearded man and his wife who recall them the next year in December.

1172

LAURENCE PRINGLE
KATE SALLEY PALMER, Illustrator

Bear Hug

(Honesdale, PA: Boyds Mills Press, 2003)

Subject(s): Camps and Camping; African Americans; Animals
Age range(s): Grades K-3
Major character(s): Jesse, Brother, Son; Becky, Sister, Daughter; Dad, Father, Camper
Time period(s): 2000s (2003)
Locale(s): Black Bear Lake

Summary: Dad takes Jesse and Becky camping at Black Bear Lake. While the kids worry that the lake's name is a sign of scary bears, Dad reassures them that there are no bears around. The family explores the area and finds other animals such as a squirrel, an owl and bats. When morning comes, Jesse wishes he had gotten the chance to see a bear. (32 pages)

Where it's reviewed:
Publishers Weekly, February 24, 2003, page 74
School Library Journal, February 2003, page 120

Other books by the same author:
Elephant Woman, 1997
Naming the Cat, 1997
Octopus Hug, 1993

Other books you might like:
Margriet Ruurs, *When We Go Camping*, 2001
  A busy family enjoys getting closer to nature on a camping trip.
Chris Van Dusen, *A Camping Spree with Mr. Magee*, 2003
  On a camping trip, Mr. Magee and his dog have a run-in with a hungry bear.
Ashley Wolff, *Stella and Roy Go Camping*, 1999
  When Stella and Roy go camping with their mother, Roy spots a brown bear in the middle of the night.

1173

JAMES PROIMOS, Author/Illustrator

Cowboy Boy

(New York: Scholastic, Inc., 2003)

Subject(s): Bullies; Schools/Middle Schools; Grandparents
Age range(s): Grades 3-6
Major character(s): Ricky Smootz, 6th Grader; Unnamed Character, Bully
Time period(s): 2000s (2003)
Locale(s): United States

Summary: The start of sixth grade is not going well for Ricky Smootz. An eighth grade bully gives him a superwedgie and then, when Ricky stands up to him, the bully gets him in trouble with his teacher, by making it look as if Ricky has been sending spitballs her way. Ricky does what any kid would do, fakes being sick so he can stay home. While Ricky's home sick, his grandmother inspires him to try again to change the bully's ways. The next day Ricky becomes Cowboy Boy and succeeds in his mission to neutralize the bully. (96 pages)

Where it's reviewed:
Booklist, September 1, 2003, page 121
Publishers Weekly, July 7, 2003, page 72
School Library Journal, November 2003, page 144

Awards the book has won:
IRA Children's Choices, 2004

Other books by the same author:
The Many Adventures of Johnny Mutton, 2001
The Loudness of Sam, 1999
Joe's Wish, 1998

Other books you might like:
Carol Gorman, *A Midsummer Night's Dork*, 2004
  Newly elected class president Jerry tries to plan fun activities for his sixth grade class while standing up to a bully.
Dav Pilkey, *The Adventures of Captain Underpants*, 1997
  George and Harold hypnotize their principal and turn him into Captain Underpants.
Louis Sachar, *The Boy Who Lost His Face*, 1989
  When David's best friend turns on him he doesn't know how he'll make it through middle school.
Carol Sonenklar, *Mighty Boy*, 1999
  Howard wishes he could stand up to a bully, just as he watches Mighty Boy do on a television show.

1174

JAMES PROIMOS, Author/Illustrator

Johnny Mutton, He's So Him!

(San Diego: Harcourt, Inc., 2003)

Subject(s): Animals/Sheep; Humor; Cartoons and Comics
Age range(s): Grades 2-4
Major character(s): Johnny Mutton, Sheep, Student—Elementary School; Momma, Mother
Time period(s): Indeterminate
Locale(s): Fictional Country

Summary: Five humorous stories and an epilogue entitled "Where Are They Now?" describe the current adventures of naive student Johnny. While Johnny's heart is in the right place his actions are enough to infuriate teachers, shopkeepers and most peers. Yet, each time, when it seems that Johnny has really made a mess of what he's doing, someone affirms Johnny for doing just the right thing in that person's estimation. A kind-hearted individual, Johnny is simply so Johnny. (42 pages)

Where it's reviewed:
Bulletin of the Center for Children's Books, May 2003, page 375
Horn Book, May 2003, page 356
Publishers Weekly, February 17, 2003, page 78
School Library Journal, August 2003, page 140

Other books by the same author:
Mutton Soup: More Adventures of Johnny Mutton, 2004

Cowboy Boy, 2003
If I Were in Charge, the Rules Would Be Different, 2002
The Many Adventures of Johnny Mutton, 2001

Other books you might like:

Margie Palatini, *Bad Boys*, 2003
Two wolves masquerading as Bo Peep's lost sheep try to join a flock of sheep to assure a steady supply of food.

Dav Pilkey, *The Adventures of Super Diaper Baby: The First Graphic Novel*, 2002
In George and Harold's latest comic, Super Diaper Baby saves the planet from Deputy Doo-Doo and his evil pet Danger Dog.

Daniel Pinkwater, *The Picture of Morty & Ray*, 2003
Inspired by a movie, Morty and Ray paint a self-portrait and then try various pranks to make the picture change as in *The Picture of Dorian Gray*.

1175

FRANCINE PROSE

After

(New York: HarperCollins/Joanna Cotler Books, 2003)

Subject(s): Schools/High Schools; Conspiracies
Age range(s): Grades 7-10
Major character(s): Tom Bishop, 10th Grader; Henry Willner, Counselor; Silas, 10th Grader; Becca Sawyer, 10th Grader; Mr. Trent, Principal
Time period(s): Indeterminate Future
Locale(s): Massachusetts

Summary: In this adult author's first young adult novel, Central High School students notice gradual, but insidious, adjustments at their school after a shooting at Pleasant Valley High School, located fifty miles away. Tom and his friends, the "Smart Jocks," endure the addition of grief counselor Dr. Henry Willner, who institutes backpack searches, random drug testing, and a dress code. Gradually Dr. Willner shunts aside their beloved principal Mr. Trent and releases some of their favorite teachers. Though Tom, Silas and Becca joke about the e-mails being sent to their parents and the feeling they're being overtaken by a Gestapo-like administration, the situation turns serious as friends are shipped off to survival camps known as Operation Turnaround and never heard from again. Tom realizes that he may be sent away next and turns to his father; together they plan an escape in this chilling National Book Award finalist. (330 pages)

Where it's reviewed:

Booklist, June 2003, page 1762
Horn Book, May 2003, page 357
Publishers Weekly, February 24, 2003, page 73
School Library Journal, May 2003, page 160
Voice of Youth Advocates, June 2003, page 143

Other books you might like:

Ron Koertge, *The Brimstone Journals*, 2001
Fifteen seniors reveal their thoughts in a series of poems, but one is so angry he wants to retaliate against anyone who's ever made him mad.

Joyce Carol Oates, *Big Mouth & Ugly Girl*, 2002
A kidding remark about blowing up the school if his play

isn't accepted for Spring Arts Festival brings Matt suspension and a visit from the police.

Todd Strasser, *Give a Boy a Gun*, 2000
Student interviews, coupled with facts about shootings, tell of two unhappy boys who attend a school dance determined to harm teachers and students.

1176

ALICE PROVENSEN, Author/Illustrator

A Day in the Life of Murphy

(New York: Simon & Schuster Books for Young Readers, 2003)

Subject(s): Animals/Dogs; Farm Life; Pets
Age range(s): Grades K-2
Major character(s): Murphy, Dog (terrier), Narrator
Time period(s): 2000s (2002)
Locale(s): Pleasant Valley, New York

Summary: Murphy describes himself as a terrier that barks at anything and everything, all the time. He thinks his name is "Murphy-Stop-That," since that's what he hears all day. Although Murphy sleeps in the barn with the other pets and the farm animals, he's the first pet in the house every morning and he stays in the kitchen, his favorite place, until he's shooed out. Murphy hates to ride in the car, especially when it brings him to the vet's office. He can't wait to get home, leap out of the car and hurry back to the kitchen because it's dinnertime! At the end of Murphy's busy day, he takes time to bark at the moon on his way to the barn where he curls up on his bed of hay and sighs good night. (34 pages)

Where it's reviewed:

Booklist, May 15, 2003, page 1672
Bulletin of the Center for Children's Books, June 2003, page 419
Horn Book, July 2003, page 447
Publishers Weekly, April 28, 2003, page 68
School Library Journal, July 2003, page 104

Awards the book has won:

Bulletin of the Center for Children's Books Blue Ribbons, 2003
School Library Journal Best Books, 2003

Other books by the same author:

Master Swordsman and the Magic Doorway: Two Legends from Ancient China, 2001
Count on Me, 1995
My Fellow Americans: A Family Album, 1995

Other books you might like:

Marjorie Flack, *Angus and the Ducks*, 1930
Curious Angus investigates the unusual quacking sounds coming from the other side of the hedge.

Steven Kroll, *Oh, Tucker!*, 1998
Despite the chaos Tucker creates in their home, a dog's owners find it difficult to scold him.

Alan Snow, *How Dogs Really Work!*, 1993
A winner of the New York Times Best Illustrated Children's Book Award is a humorous instruction manual for dog owners.

Rosemary Wells, *The McDuff Series*, 1997-
A West Highland terrier finds a home, adjusts to a baby's

arrival and saves Santa Claus from the chimney in an award-winning series.

1177

SALLY PRUE

Cold Tom

(New York: Scholastic Press, 2003)

Subject(s): Fantasy; Fairies
Age range(s): Grades 6-10
Major character(s): Tom, Mythical Creature (fairy); Anna, Sister; Joe, Brother; Edie Mackintosh, Neighbor
Time period(s): 2000s
Locale(s): England

Summary: The Tribe has always lived on the green, coming together for their revels, but remaining essentially solitary. They greatly value their privacy and any member who by word or deed risks revealing their presence to outsiders, such as the human "demons," could be cast out, or worse. Tom is a young member of the Tribe who is different; even his parents seem to despise him. So it is no surprise that when Tom is found guilty of clumsiness for almost being discovered, the punishment is banishment from the green. Tom has no idea where to go or how to survive and wanders aimlessly through the town. Knowing he cannot be found abroad in the daylight, Tom takes refuge in a shed where he is found by Anna, one of the demons the Tribe so fears. Anna is just an ordinary girl and can't believe what she has found, for Tom seems to be a fairy. Tom knows that since the demons have found him, the tribe will kill him. It will take the combined efforts of Anna, her brother Joe and their uncanny neighbor Edie to keep Tom alive. (187 pages)

Where it's reviewed:
Bulletin of the Center for Children's Books, November 2003, page 122
Horn Book, July 2003, page 466
Publishers Weekly, June 16, 2003, page 72
School Library Journal, September 2003, page 219
Voice of Youth Advocates, October 2003, page 326

Other books by the same author:
The Devil's Toenail, 2004

Other books you might like:
Hilari Bell, *The Goblin Wood*, 2003
Makenna's goblin friends are as tricky as a pack of pixies, and just about as much trouble.
Herbie Brennan, *Faerie Wars*, 2003
Pyrgus is sent away from the Purple Kingdom of Faerie for his own protection but nearly winds up under Henry's lawnmower.
Bruce Coville, *Part-Human*, 2001
In this collection of short stories, mermaids, centaurs and other half-human creatures struggle to understand who they are.

1178

ROBIN PULVER
LYNN ROWE REED, Illustrator

Punctuation Takes a Vacation

(New York: Holiday House, 2003)

Subject(s): Literacy; Schools; Humor
Age range(s): Grades 1-3
Major character(s): Mr. Wright, Teacher
Time period(s): 2000s (2003)
Locale(s): United States

Summary: All the punctuation marks in Mr. Wright's classroom are known for their faithful attendance. However, when Mr. Wright declares a brief vacation from punctuation while the class goes outside for recess, the punctuation marks take him literally and rush right out the door. When the class returns, they discover just how critically important punctuation is as Mr. Wright tries to read chapter four in a novel to the class. Conversations don't make much sense either. Postcards begin to arrive from various punctuation marks, bearing the postmark "Take-a-Break Lake." In order to reply to the postcards, the students have to borrow some punctuation from another class. Unfortunately, these marks don't follow the rules so the correspondence is a bit challenging to read. It does communicate the message that the class really misses and needs their punctuation marks so they return from vacation. A list of "Punctuation Rules!" concludes the book. (32 pages)

Where it's reviewed:
Booklist, March 1, 2003, page 1203
Horn Book, May 2003, page 335
School Library Journal, April 2003, page 136

Awards the book has won:
School Library Journal Best Books, 2003

Other books by the same author:
Axle Annie, 1999
Way to Go, Alex!, 1999
Alicia's Tutu, 1997

Other books you might like:
Debra Fraser, *Miss Alaineus: A Vocabulary Disaster*, 2000
Sage misunderstands one of the week's vocabulary words but turns her embarrassing moment into a prize-winning costume.
Loreen Leedy, *There's a Frog in My Throat*, 2003
In a nonfiction picture book, illustrations literally portray idiomatic expressions while the text includes clear explanations of the intended meaning. Pat Street, co-author.
Peggy Parish, *Amelia Bedelia*, 1963
In the first book about beloved Amelia Bedelia her literal interpretation of instructions leads to humorous events.

1179

SIMON PUTTOCK
MARY MCQUILLAN, Illustrator

Squeaky Clean

(Boston: Little, Brown and Company, 2002)

Subject(s): Animals/Pigs; Cleanliness; Mothers

Age range(s): Preschool-Kindergarten
Major character(s): Mama Pig, Pig, Mother
Time period(s): Indeterminate
Locale(s): Fictional Country

Summary: Mama Pig's three mucky little piglets protest her desire to clean them up in a bath. Mama Pig pops them in the tub anyway, ignoring their complaints and adding so many bubbles and toys that the bath becomes a real pleasure. In fact, the piglets enjoy the bath so much that they protest when Mama Pig says it's time to get out and go to bed but again Mama Pig prevails. The piglets think they can outsmart Mama Pig by sneaking outside to get mucky again, but she catches them and promises they can have another bath tomorrow. Originally published in the United Kingdom in 2001. (32 pages)

Where it's reviewed:
Booklist, June 2002, page 1743
Horn Book Guide, Fall 2002, page 311
Kirkus Reviews, February 15, 2002, page 263

Publishers Weekly, February 4, 2002, page 75
School Library Journal, April 2002, page 120

Awards the book has won:
IRA Children's Choices, 2003

Other books by the same author:
Here I Am! Said Smedley, 2002
Ladder to the Stars, 2001
Story for Hippo: A Book About Loss, 2001

Other books you might like:
Janie Bynum, *Otis*, 2000
    A fastidious pig that disdains mud, Otis is unlikely to need a bath, but finding a friend with similar interests is challenging.
Eileen Spinelli, *Bath Time*, 2003
    Rhyming text describes the pleasure a young penguin has in the bath.
Nancy Van Laan, *Scrubba Dub*, 2003
    A rabbit mother uses nonsense phrases and rhyming instructions to coax her young ones into the tub.

Q

1180

MARSHA QUALEY

One Night

(New York: Dial Books/Penguin Putnam, 2002)

Subject(s): Aunts and Uncles; Princes and Princesses; Drugs
Age range(s): Grades 8-12
Major character(s): Kelly Ray, Researcher, 19-Year-Old; Prince Tomas Teronovich, Royalty (crown prince); Kit Carpenter, Aunt, Radio Personality
Time period(s): 2000s
Locale(s): Dakota City, Minnesota

Summary: A former heroin addict, Kelly currently works as a research assistant for her aunt Kit Carpenter, a strong personality who lost part of an arm while a war correspondent in Vietnam and now hosts the number one radio show in America. Kelly is sent off to soothe a movie star snubbed by her aunt when she happens to meet Tomas, the Crown Prince of Lakveria, in town to win support for his country at a peace conference. Thinking that an interview with Tomas might make up for her aunt's cancellation of the movie star, Kelly talks him into spending twenty-four hours with her and the two sneak away from his security. From eating at a diner, to attending a Judy Garland movie marathon, to kayaking at dawn, the two young people enjoy themselves while also discussing their problems and concerns, from Kelly's former addiction to Tomas's efforts to achieve peace for his country. This fantastic night together not only gives Tomas the chance to speak for his country on ''Kit Chat'' and but also provides Kelly with the courage to reconcile with her mother. (170 pages)

Where it's reviewed:
Booklist, April 1, 2002, page 1320
Bulletin of the Center for Children's Books, March 2002, page 253
Kliatt, May 2002, page 13
Publishers Weekly, April 22, 2002, page 71
School Library Journal, June 2002, page 142

Awards the book has won:
Center for Children's Books Best Books, 2002

Other books by the same author:
Close to a Killer, 1999
Thin Ice, 1997
Hometown, 1995
Come in from the Cold, 1994

Other books you might like:
Anonymous, *Go Ask Alice*, 1971
    A chronological journal account tells of a young teen's downfall after running away and becoming a drug addict.
Joan Bauer, *Backwater*, 1999
    Visiting her eccentric Aunt Jo, who lives in the backwater of the Adirondacks, helps Ivy understand more about her family.
Francess Lantz, *A Royal Kiss*, 2000
    Samantha has a whirlwind adventure with Prince Sebastian after a coincidental meeting in a vintage clothing store.

R

1181

VLADIMIR RADUNSKY, Author/Illustrator

Mannekin Pis: A Simple Story of a Boy Who Peed on a War

(New York: Anne Schwartz Book/Atheneum Books for Young Readers, 2002)

Subject(s): War; Historical; Legends
Age range(s): Grades K-2
Major character(s): Unnamed Character, Child, Son
Time period(s): Indeterminate Past
Locale(s): Brussels, Belgium

Summary: A little boy lives happily with his loving parents in a small, walled town until enemies attack. As the terrible war rages the fighting seems to go on constantly and the town becomes sad. The frightened little boy cannot find his parents. As he searches for them he realizes how much he needs to pee and he stands on the town's wall and pees onto the battling soldiers below. The fighting stops and the men begin laughing. The boy finds his parents and the town erects a bronze statue entitled ''Manneken Pis'' in his honor. (32 pages)

Where it's reviewed:
Booklist, October 15, 2002, page 413
Bulletin of the Center for Children's Books, November 2002, page 123
Horn Book, September 2002, page 557
Publishers Weekly, June 24, 2002, page 55
School Library Journal, December 2002, page 106

Other books by the same author:
Mighty Asparagus, 2004
One, 2003
What Does Peace Feel Like?, 2003

Other books you might like:
Jane Cutler, *The Cello of Mr. O.*, 1999
  Undeterred by mortar barrages, Mr. O. defiantly plays his cello daily in his war-ravaged city's open square.
Isabel Pin, *The Seed*, 2001
  As two insect tribes prepare to battle for ownership of a cherry pit wedged into their lands' boundary, a tree grows and provides fruit for all.
Dr. Seuss, *The Butter Battle Book*, 1984
  The stupidity of the war is obvious as Zooks and Yooks take sides against each other because of the different way in which each group butters bread.

1182

GLORIA RAND
R.W. ALLEY, Illustrator

Little Flower

(New York: Henry Holt and Company, 2002)

Subject(s): Animals/Pigs; Pets; Accidents
Age range(s): Grades K-2
Major character(s): Miss Pearl, Aged Person, Accident Victim; Little Flower, Pig, Hero
Time period(s): 2000s
Locale(s): United States

Summary: In the eyes of proud Miss Pearl, Little Flower is one smart pig. She shows all their neighbors Little Flower's trick of playing dead. Those that think it's funny provide an audience for Little Flower and she uses her one trick to get attention. The day that Miss Pearl falls and injures her hip Little Flower turns the trick into a rescue operation by playing dead in the middle of the street. When a car stops Little Flower leads the driver to the house and he calls for help. While Miss Pearl is hospitalized for treatment the neighbors care for Little Flower in a story based on an actual incident. (32 pages)

Where it's reviewed:
Booklist, March, 15, 2002, page 1264
Bulletin of the Center for Children's Books, June 2002, page 378
Publishers Weekly, February 18, 2002, page 95
School Library Journal, August 2002, page 165

Other books by the same author:
Mary Was a Little Lamb, 2004
Fighting for the Forest, 1999

A Home for Spooky, 1998

Other books you might like:

Lisa Hall Huckaby, *Pot-Bellied Pigs and Other Miniature Pet Pigs*, 1992
A photo-illustrated non-fiction title for youth explains the special needs of these exotic pets.

Laura Joffe Numeroff, *If You Give a Pig a Pancake*, 2000
If an uninvited pig shows up for breakfast to share your pancakes, be prepared for a busy day.

Elizabeth Spurr, *A Pig Named Perrier*, 2002
Perrier, a miniature pot-bellied pig, lives a pampered life with a movie actress but longs to roll in mud as other pigs do.

1183

KRISTEN D. RANDLE

Slumming

(New York: HarperTempest/HarperCollins, 2003)

Subject(s): Self-Perception; Interpersonal Relations; Family Problems
Age range(s): Grades 9-12
Major character(s): Nikki Bickerstaff, 12th Grader; Sam Pittman, 12th Grader, Football Player; Alicia, 12th Grader; Brian Camargo, 12th Grader; Morgan Weiss, 12th Grader; Tia Terraletto, 12th Grader
Time period(s): 2000s
Locale(s): United States

Summary: With just a few weeks left during their senior year, Nikki, Alicia and Sam embark on a *Pygmalion*-type project—select someone you don't know and, through kindness and friendship, help that person get a better life. There's a three-week limit on the project and each must take their person to the prom. Nikki selects the stereotypical science nerd, Brian, and quickly discovers that he's not pleased when she selects him as her class project partner. Sam's choice is Tia, a hard-looking young lady whose Goth makeup hides family secrets, including a Down Syndrome brother and a stepfather who blackmails her. Alicia doesn't even want to identify her choice as she's so sure she can remold bad boy Morgan, an assumption even he tries to convince her isn't possible. The three teens mean well but discover their suppositions about people are entirely wrong. (232 pages)

Where it's reviewed:
Booklist, August 2003, page 1973
Horn Book, July 2003, page 466
Publishers Weekly, July 21, 2003, page 196
School Library Journal, August 2003, page 164
Voice of Youth Advocates, August 2003, page 228

Other books by the same author:
Breaking Rank, 1999
The Only Alien on the Planet, 1995
On the Side of Angels, 1989

Other books you might like:

Sarah Dessen, *Someone Like You*, 1998
During her junior year Halley falls for "bad boy" Macon; being forbidden to see him just makes her want him all the more.

Cin Forshay-Lunsford, *Walk through Cold Fire*, 1985
Desiree is a straight-A student who hangs out with the Outlaws, falls in love with Billy and gets mixed up with a murder.

Donald R. Gallo, *On the Fringe*, 2001
A collection of short stories about insiders and outsiders and whether or not that label matters.

David Klass, *You Don't Know Me*, 2001
John endures two lives, one as a normal high school student, the other as the victim of abuse from his mother's live-in boyfriend.

1184

JOAN RANKIN, Author/Illustrator

First Day

(New York: Margaret K. McElderry Books, 2002)

Subject(s): Schools/Preschool; Animals/Dogs; Animals
Age range(s): Preschool-Kindergarten
Major character(s): Haybillybun, Dog, Student; Mom, Mother, Dog
Time period(s): Indeterminate
Locale(s): Fictional Country

Summary: Mom tries to wake Haybillybun for his first day of school but the little pup isn't interested. He frets about his appearance and all the reasons his feet, ears and eyes will keep him from making friends or being able to play. Feeling completely misunderstood, Haybillybun reluctantly allows Mom to lead him to school. All day Mom worries about her little one until she finally sneaks back to school to peer through the playground fence and into the classroom window. What she sees assures her that Haybillybun is doing just fine and so his report at the end of the day confirms. (32 pages)

Where it's reviewed:
Booklist, June 2002, page 1743
New York Times Book Review, August 11, 2002, page 18
Publishers Weekly, May 27, 2002, page 59
School Library Journal, July 2002, page 97

Other books by the same author:
Oh, Mum!, 2002
You're Somebody Special, Walliwigs!, 1999
Wow! It's Great Being a Duck, 1998

Other books you might like:

Nancy Kaufmann, *Bye, Bye!*, 2003
It's hard for Piggy to let go of his father on the first day of school but once he does he enjoys the day.

Dandi Daley Mackall, *First Day*, 2003
Initial misgivings aside, a little girl becomes happily involved in the classroom activities.

Wendy Rouillard, *Barnaby Goes to School*, 2002
On his first day in school Barnaby is relieved to learn that education is just one more adventure for him to enjoy.

Lauren Thompson, *Mouse's First Day of School*, 2003
By hiding in a backpack Mouse learns about a day in kindergarten.

1185

RANULFO

Nirvana's Children

(New York: HarperCollins, 2003)

Subject(s): Runaways; Homeless People
Age range(s): Grades 9-12
Major character(s): Napoleon Taal, 15-Year-Old, Runaway; Sammie, Addict (heroin); Blondie, Gang Member
Time period(s): 2000s
Locale(s): Sydney, Australia

Summary: Napoleon hates Adults, is tired of corporate take-overs, and feels dissatisfied with everything. He's cruel to his girlfriend and absolutely despises his father; after one disastrous fight, he runs away from home and ends up on the streets of Sydney. There a gang of street kids, led by Blondie, share his feelings for Adults, and are glad to take him in, but their protection doesn't last long when the gang is wiped out in a gun battle with police. Luckily Sammie comes into his life and this 15-year-old heroin addict, who prostitutes to buy the drug, loves Napoleon and takes care of him. Though Napoleon would like to think she was murdered by one of her tricks, in reality Sammie overdosed in a public toilet. After Sammie's death he's sent back home and though still filled with adolescent rage and confusion, admits it's nice to be looked after in this first novel by an Australian author. (217 pages)

Where it's reviewed:
Horn Book, November 2003, page 753
Kirkus Reviews, September 15, 2003, page 1181
Kliatt, September 2003, page 11
Publishers Weekly, November 17, 2003, page 66
Voice of Youth Advocates, December 2003, page 406

Other books you might like:
Melvin Burgess, *Smack*, 1998
    Runaway Gemma meets up with Tar and both experiment with heroin, though Gemma is finally able to break away and return home.
Ineke Holtwijk, *Asphalt Angels*, 1999
    Kicked out by his stepfather, Alex runs away to Rio de Janeiro where he falls in with an organized gang who call themselves the Asphalt Angels.
Adam Rapp, *33 Snowfish*, 2003
    Three teens, a prostitute, a murderer and a racist orphan, steal a car and run away, but two of them lack the resources to survive.

1186

ADAM RAPP
TIMOTHY BASIL ERING, Illustrator

33 Snowfish

(Cambridge, MA: Candlewick Press, 2003)

Subject(s): Homeless People; Sexual Abuse; Babies
Age range(s): Grades 9-12
Major character(s): Custis, Orphan, Runaway; Curl, Teenager, Prostitute; Boobie, Teenager, Runaway; Unnamed Child, Baby; Seldom, Aged Person, Widow(er)

Time period(s): 2000s
Locale(s): Midwest; Minnesota

Summary: Three "throwaway" kids are on the run: Custis, Curl and Boobie, along with Boobie's infant brother. Boobie has just killed his parents, stolen their car and taken his younger, unnamed brother in hopes of selling him for some cash. Accompanying him are Curl, a teen prostitute who regards her body as a source of income, and Custis, a racist orphan who's run away from his smutty guardian. The three drive aimlessly through the Midwest, stealing or turning tricks to earn money to survive. Boobie communicates through line drawings while Curl and Custis alternate their narrative. Running out of funds, they park their van in an abandoned field where Curl dies and Boobie walks out into the snow. Custis is caught stealing a chicken and African American Seldom, who becomes his benefactor, takes him in and tries to whittle away the years of abuse and teach him how to relate to others in this gritty and haunting tale. (179 pages)

Where it's reviewed:
Bulletin of the Center for Children's Books, May 2003, page 375
Kirkus Reviews, February 1, 2003, page 237
Publishers Weekly, January 13, 2003, page 61
School Library Journal, April 2003, page 166
Voice of Youth Advocates, April 2003, page 55

Awards the book has won:
ALA Best Books for Young Adults, 2004

Other books by the same author:
Stone Cold Serious and Other Plays, 2004
Little Chicago, 2002
Copper Elephant, 1999
The Buffalo Tree, 1997
Missing the Piano, 1994

Other books you might like:
Francesca Lia Block, *The Hanged Man*, 1994
    Laurel lives in a fast-paced town where drugs, casual sex and tarot cards are all part of life.
Melvin Burgess, *Smack*, 1998
    Runaway Gemma meets up with Tar and both experiment with heroin, though Gemma is finally able to break away and return home.
Brock Cole, *The Facts Speak for Themselves*, 1997
    Though Linda's life is dysfunctional, it's the only one she knows so it doesn't strike her as unusual to have an affair with a much older man.
Ineke Holtwijk, *Asphalt Angels*, 1999
    Kicked out by his stepfather, Alex runs away to Rio de Janeiro where he falls in with an organized gang who call themselves the Asphalt Angels.

1187

PEGGY RATHMANN, Author/Illustrator

The Day the Babies Crawled Away

(New York: G.P. Putnam's Sons, 2003)

Subject(s): Babies; Rescue Work; Stories in Rhyme
Age range(s): Grades K-2
Major character(s): Unnamed Character, Child, Rescuer

Time period(s): 2000s
Locale(s): United States

Summary: Only a young child notices the babies crawl away from a neighborhood fair where the parents are busy with a pie-eating contest. Unable to get any adult attention, the boy follows the babies through woods and a bog and into a cave (the babies loved the bats). At first he simply follows but when the babies crawl too near a ledge he becomes an active rescuer. By the end of the day the babies, led by the boy in his fireman's helmet, crawl back to their waiting parents for fireworks and then a good night's sleep in their own beds. (36 pages)

Where it's reviewed:
Booklist, September 15, 2003, page 248
Bulletin of the Center for Children's Books, December 2003, page 164
Horn Book, September 2003, page 600
School Library Journal, November 2003, page 113

Awards the book has won:
Publishers Weekly Best Children's Books, 2003
Horn Book Fanfare, 2003

Other books by the same author:
10 Minutes till Bedtime, 1998 (School Library Journal Best Books)
Officer Buckle and Gloria, 1995 (Caldecott Medal)
Good Night, Gorilla, 1994 (ALA Notable Children's Books)

Other books you might like:
Adele Aron Greenspun, *Bunny and Me*, 2000
    Baby and Bunny imitate each other's behavior but when Bunny hops away Baby's left feeling sad until Bunny reappears.
Susan Meyers, *Everywhere Babies*, 2001
    Babies of all shapes, sizes and colors are everywhere, playing eating, sleeping and most of all, being loved.
Marisabina Russo, *Come Back, Hannah!*, 2001
    Hannah has learned to crawl but not to come back so Mama chases her a lot.
Margaret Wild, *Midnight Babies*, 2001
    Baby Brenda sneaks out the cat door and crawls to the Midnight Cafe to meet her baby friends for an evening of fun.

1188

DELIA RAY

Ghost Girl: A Blue Ridge Mountain Story

(New York: Clarion Books, 2003)

Subject(s): Schools; Grief; Teachers
Age range(s): Grades 5-8
Major character(s): April Sloane, Teenager; Birdy, Grandmother (of April); Christine Vest, Teacher, Historical Figure; Riley Sloane, Brother (deceased); Herbert Hoover, Historical Figure (President of the United States)
Time period(s): 1930s
Locale(s): Doubletop Mountain, Virginia (Blue Ridge Mountains)

Summary: Raised in the isolated Blue Ridge Mountains, April lives with her depressed mother who still grieves over the loss of her son Riley in a fire. When April hears that President Hoover is building a school in her community, she wants to attend so she can learn to read, but her mother refuses to send her. Aunt Birdy intervenes and April meets the wonderful Miss Vest, the teacher hired by the Hoovers. School is a struggle for April, for not only do the other students call her ghost girl in reference to her pale hair and complexion, but April also finds that reading is difficult. Just as she begins to feel successful, she breaks her arm and is yanked out of school by her mother. When April's role in Riley's death becomes apparent, she's thrown out of her house. Luckily Miss Vest takes April in and lets her see the possibility of a life beyond her Blue Ridge Mountain home. This first novel, which captures the feel of mountain life before the Shenandoah National Park, is based on correspondence between the real Miss Vest and the White House. (216 pages)

Where it's reviewed:
Booklist, November 15, 2003, page 610
Bulletin of the Center for Children's Books, November 2003, page 122
Horn Book, January 2004, page 91
Kirkus Reviews, September 1, 2003, page 1129
School Library Journal, November 2003, page 146

Other books by the same author:
Behind the Blue and Gray: The Soldier's Life in the Civil War, 1991 (Nonfiction)
Nation Torn: The Story of How the Civil War Began, 1990 (Nonfiction)
Gold! The Klondike Adventure, 1989 (Nonfiction)

Other books you might like:
Jennifer Armstrong, *Theodore Roosevelt: Letters from a Young Coal Miner*, 2001
    A feeling of warmth and respect fills the letters between two unlikely correspondents, the coal miner Frank Kovacs and the president Teddy Roosevelt.
Robbie Branscum, *Old Blue Tilley*, 1991
    The circuit minister Old Blue takes in orphaned Hambone and together they visit the Ozark families before the revival meeting.
Christopher Paul Curtis, *Bud, Not Buddy*, 1999
    After being bounced from one foster home to another, Buddy finally runs away and is lucky enough to find his grandfather.
Doris Buchanan Smith, *Return to Bitter Creek*, 1986
    Lacey and her mother return to her mother's home in tiny, rural Bitter Creek, but mending past family differences is a slow process.

1189

HELEN RECORVITS
GABI SWIATKOWSKA, Illustrator

My Name Is Yoon

(New York: Frances Foster Books/Farrar Straus Giroux, 2003)

Subject(s): Korean Americans; Emigration and Immigration; Names, Personal
Age range(s): Grades K-2
Major character(s): Yoon, Immigrant, Student—Elementary School

Time period(s): 2000s (2003)
Locale(s): United States

Summary: Yoon is not happy with the appearance of her name as it is written in English. In Korean the symbols look happy together and show that her name means "Shining Wisdom." In English the lines and circles spelling Yoon look isolated and lonely, just as Yoon feels. In class Yoon refuses to write her name. Each day she chooses a different word to use for her name and she imagines being the object the word represents. One day she is CAT, another BIRD and another CUPCAKE. At home each night she tries to convince her parents to move back to Korea where she had friends and was the teacher's favorite student. After a few days another girl offers Yoon a cupcake and she begins to sense that perhaps she will have friends in this strange new country. The next day she writes YOON on her papers, confident that it still means "Shining Wisdom" even in lines and circles. (32 pages)

Where it's reviewed:
Booklist, March 15, 2003, page 1333
Bulletin of the Center for Children's Books, April 2003, page 3
Horn Book Guide, Fall 2003, page 337
Riverbank Review, Spring 2003, page 31
School Library Journal, May 2003, page 128

Awards the book has won:
Publishers Weekly Best Children's Books, 2003
School Library Journal Best Books, 2003

Other books by the same author:
Where Heroes Hide, 2002
Goodbye, Walter Malinski, 1999 (Notable Social Studies Trade Books for Young People)

Other books you might like:
Yangsook Choi, *The Name Jar*, 2001
    After a week in an American school, a Korean immigrant feels confident enough to use her given name Unhei, meaning grace.
Jan M. Czech, *An American Face*, 2000
    Adopted Korean American Jesse expects his face to change into an "American" one when he becomes a naturalized citizen.
Sandra S. Yamate, *Ashok by Any Other Name*, 1992
    A young Indian-American immigrant feels self-conscious about his foreign-sounding name.

1190

HELEN RECORVITS

Where Heroes Hide

(New York: Frances Foster Books/Farrar Straus Giroux, 2002)

Subject(s): Heroes and Heroines; Friendship; Physically Handicapped
Age range(s): Grades 4-6
Major character(s): Junior Webster, 10-Year-Old, Friend; Lenny, Handicapped, Friend; Joe Webster, Father, Veteran
Time period(s): 1950s (1956)
Locale(s): Mansfield, New England

Summary: Junior, in order to enjoy a summer playing with his friends, including Lenny, a polio survivor, must defy his increasingly volatile father who forbids him to play with Lenny out of fear that Junior may contract the poliovirus. As Joe's mood swings become more pronounced and he ignores his wife's requests to seek help, Junior's play activities are curtailed out of embarrassment over his father's actions and concern for Lenny. When Junior accidentally knocks over a box, spilling the contents over the basement floor, he and his father together confront the memories of war that haunt Joe as they clean up the photos and the medal Joe received for heroism. Later when a fire spreads from the factory where Junior's father and sister work to the home of Junior's friend, Joe rescues the boy while Lenny stands in the street flagging down a speeding fire truck to get help. Though Joe is considered a hero he only recognizes the heroic actions of Lenny who, despite impaired mobility, took a big risk to help a friend. (135 pages)

Where it's reviewed:
Booklist, May 15, 2002, page 1608
Horn Book Guide, Fall 2002, page 380
Publishers Weekly, May 6, 2002, page 58
Riverbank Review, Spring 2002, page 42
School Library Journal, May 2002, page 158

Other books by the same author:
Goodbye, Walter Malinski, 1999 (Notable Social Studies Trade Books for Young People)

Other books you might like:
Janet Lee Carey, *Molly's Fire*, 2000
    News that her father's plane has been shot down over Holland during World War II does not convince Molly that he is dead.
Jane Cutler, *My Wartime Summers*, 1994
    Uncle Bob's service during World War II changes him so much that Ellen and her family are unsure how to relate to him.
Gregory Maguire, *The Good Liar*, 1999
    Although they live in occupied France during World War II, three brothers try to enjoy their usual summer activities.

1191

REBECCA KRAFT RECTOR

Tria and the Great Star Rescue

(New York: Delacorte Press, 2002)

Subject(s): Science Fiction; Futuristic Fiction; Kidnapping
Age range(s): Grades 4-7
Major character(s): Tria, Child, Daughter; Unnamed Character, Mother, Archaeologist
Time period(s): Indeterminate Future
Locale(s): Planet—Imaginary

Summary: Ever since Tria's father died "Outside," she has been terrified to leave the confines of her house and face the real people, animals, and especially germs she would find there. However, when her mother, while on an archeological dig, finds a device desired by criminals she is kidnapped. Before vanishing she instructs Tria to move and attend an "Outside" school. There, Tria must conquer her fears in order to rescue her mother. With the help of two classmates and her holographic best friend, Tria thwarts the bad guys and saves her mother in the author's first book. (184 pages)

Where it's reviewed:

Book Report, September 2002, page 56
Bulletin of the Center for Children's Books, September 2002, page 32
Horn Book, May 2002, page 336
Publishers Weekly, January 28, 2001, page 291
School Library Journal, February 2002, page 135

Other books you might like:

Eoin Colfer, *Artemis Fowl: The Arctic Incident*, 2002
    Artemis Fowl goes in search of his long-missing father, held captive by the Russian Mafia.
Zizou Corder, *Lionboy*, 2003
    When Charlie's parents are kidnapped, he joins up with a passing, floating circus that's heading in their direction.
Gloria Skurzynski, *Cyberstorm*, 1995
    In 2051, Darci Kane tries to avoid the order to get rid of her dog Chip, by hiding in a Rent-a-Memory machine that traps Darci and Chip.

1192

CAROLYN REEDER

Before the Creeks Ran Red

(New York: HarperCollins, 2003)

Subject(s): Civil War; Coming-of-Age
Age range(s): Grades 6-9
Major character(s): Timothy Donovan, Military Personnel (U.S. Army bugler), Orphan; Joseph Schwartz, Student—High School; Gregory Howard, Student—High School
Time period(s): 1860s
Locale(s): Charleston, South Carolina; Baltimore, Maryland; Alexandria, Virginia

Summary: Three teenage boys observe the beginning of the Civil War from vastly different viewpoints. In Charleston, U.S. Army bugler Timothy is unprepared for the violence that erupts when South Carolina secedes from the Union. A few months later in Baltimore, student Joseph witnesses mobs attacking the northern troops and is unsure which side he favors. In northern Virginia, Greg sees how difficult it is to take sides as his father favors the Union troops and his mother tries to help the Confederacy. Adolescent problems diminish as the realities of war confront these boys. (370 pages)

Where it's reviewed:

Booklist, February 15, 2003, page 1065
Bulletin of the Center for Children's Books, March 2003, page 286
Kliatt, January 2003, page 10
Publishers Weekly, December 16, 2002, page 70
School Library Journal, February 2003, page 147

Other books by the same author:

Captain Kate, 1999
Foster's War, 1998
Across the Lines, 1997
Shades of Gray, 1989

Other books you might like:

James Lincoln Collier, *With Every Drop of Blood*, 1994
    White southerner Johnny is captured by black Union soldier Cush, but the two gradually become friends and partners as they stumble into a battle.
Paul Fleischman, *Bull Run*, 1993
    A unique snapshot of the conflict is provided by 16 characters who provide accounts of the Civil War leading up to the Battle of Bull Run.
Ann Rinaldi, *Amelia's War*, 1999
    Though Amelia tries to stay neutral about the Civil War, when her town is threatened with burning, she chooses which side to support.

1193

CELIA REES

Pirates!: The True and Remarkable Adventures of Minerva Sharpe and Nancy Kington, Female Pirates

(New York: Bloomsbury, 2003)

Subject(s): Pirates; Slavery; Adventure and Adventurers
Age range(s): Grades 7-10
Major character(s): Nancy Kington, Heiress, Pirate; Minerva Sharpe, Slave, Pirate; Bartholome, Sea Captain; Vincent Crosby, Sailor; Mr. Broom, Sea Captain
Time period(s): 18th century (1720s)
Locale(s): Bristol, England; Port Royal, Jamaica; *Deliverance*, At Sea

Summary: Nancy's merchant and slave trader father dies leaving the family finances in disarray. To ameliorate the family situation, Nancy's brothers send her to the plantation on Jamaica that she is to inherit, where they've arranged her marriage to the diabolical Brazilian Bartholome. Nancy and her slave Minerva become friends and when Nancy kills the overseer to prevent his raping Minerva, the two don men's clothing and set off for a pirate camp. Sailing on a ship captained by Mr. Broom, whom Nancy met on her voyage to Jamaica, the two more than hold their own in battle though Nancy worries about a recurring dream where Bartholome pursues and eventually finds her. Nancy is still in love with her childhood sweetheart, now a sailor, and wants only to be reunited with him while Minerva falls in love with Vincent, one of the pirates aboard their ship. All is well until the day Bartholome's ship sails toward theirs off the coast of Madagascar in this rousing adventure. (380 pages)

Where it's reviewed:

Booklist, December 15, 2003, page 749
Kirkus Reviews, October 15, 2003, page 1275
Magpies, November 2003, page 44
Publishers Weekly, October 20, 2003, page 55
School Library Journal, October 2003, page 175

Awards the book has won:
ALA Best Books for Young Adults, 2004

Other books by the same author:

Sorceress, 2002
Witch Child, 2001
The Truth Out There, 2000

Other books you might like:

Avi, *The True Confessions of Charlotte Doyle*, 1990
  Charlotte's adventures on the sailing ship *Seahawk* turn her from a proper Victorian lady to a real sailor.

Elizabeth Garrett, *The Sweet Trade*, 2001
  Female pirates Anne Bonny and Mary Read appear in these exciting, illegal adventures on the high seas.

Douglas Kelley, *The Captain's Wife*, 2001
  When her sea captain husband falls ill, Mary Ann has to assume command for she's the only one who knows how to navigate.

Iain Lawrence, *The Buccaneers*, 2001
  Picking up a drifting sailor proves advantageous for John Spencer, aboard the schooner *Dragon*, when they're later attacked by pirates.

1194

DOUGLAS REES

Vampire High

(New York: Delacorte, 2003)

Subject(s): Vampires; Schools/High Schools
Age range(s): Grades 7-10
Major character(s): Cody Elliot, 15-Year-Old; Justin Warrener, Vampire, 15-Year-Old; Ileana Antonescu, Vampire, Royalty (princess); Charon/Dracula, Wolf, Vampire
Time period(s): 2000s
Locale(s): New Sodom, Massachusetts

Summary: Unhappy at his family's move from California to Massachusetts, Cody rebels by failing all his classes, a move that sends him to the public magnet school Vlad Dracul High School. Noticing all the tall, pale students in sunglasses, and escorted to his classes by a wolf named Charon, Cody gradually realizes he's at a vampire school. One of few "gadje" students, Cody's there because he's willing to be a member of the school's water polo team, a position vampires are unable to fill because they dissolve in water. If Cody will just swim, he's guaranteed A's in class and a free ride to a prestigious college. Cody, however, upsets the system when he befriends vampires Justin and Ileana, turns down the easy A's and leads the water polo team to its first-ever success. (226 pages)

Where it's reviewed:
Booklist, August 2003, page 1973
Bulletin of the Center for Children's Books, November 2003, page 122
Horn Book, September 2003, page 617
Publishers Weekly, August 4, 2003, page 81
School Library Journal, November 2003, page 146

Awards the book has won:
ALA Quick Picks for Reluctant Young Adult Readers, 2004

Other books by the same author:
Lightning Time, 1997

Other books you might like:

M.T. Anderson, *Thirsty*, 1997
  As Chris approaches adolescence, he is dismayed by his increasing thirst for blood, a sure sign he's becoming a vampire.

Amelia Atwater-Rhodes, *Demon in My View*, 2000
  Jessica doesn't realize she's about to be caught between vampires who want to claim her as one of their own and good witches who will try to save her.

Hanna Lutzen, *Vlad the Undead*, 1998
  This chilling retelling of *Dracula* finds Lucia absorbed in the century-old story of a Romanian stranger who now seems to have absconded with her.

M.C. Sumner, *The Coach*, 1994
  There's no way Chris can tell the police the reason there are so many dead people is because they were all vampires.

1195

PHILIP REEVE

Mortal Engines

(New York: Eos/HarperCollins, 2003)

Series: Hungry City Chronicles. Book 1
Subject(s): Science Fiction; Orphans
Age range(s): Grades 8-Adult
Major character(s): Tom Natsworthy, 15-Year-Old, Orphan; Thaddeus Valentine, Government Official (head historian); Katherine Valentine, Daughter (of Thaddeus); Hester Shaw, Orphan
Time period(s): Indeterminate Future
Locale(s): Europe

Summary: The traction city of London successfully captures a smaller city and processes its useable materials to provide the power needed to sustain itself and its inhabitants. Following this seizure, Apprentice Historian Natsworthy is in the Gut where the processing takes place, standing near Historian Valentine and his daughter Katherine, who are examining some of the artifacts claimed from the newest prize. Suddenly a facially-scarred girl screams about her murdered parents and attacks Valentine. Tom leaps to defend his hero and is astonished when he's pushed down the same waste chute as the escaped assassin. Left with Hester on the bare Earth, Tom has no choice but to join her on an odyssey of vengeance in this author's debut novel. (310 pages)

Where it's reviewed:
Booklist, November 1, 2003, page 491
Horn Book, November 2003, page 755
Publishers Weekly, October 27, 2003, page 70
School Library Journal, December 2003, page 158
Voice of Youth Advocates, December 2003, page 418

Awards the book has won:
School Library Journal Best Books, 2003
ALA Best Books for Young Adults, 2004

Other books by the same author:
Predator's Gold, 2004 (Hungry City Chronicles Book 2)

Other books you might like:

Mel Odom, *The Rover*, 2001
  Third level librarian Edgewick Lamplighter is shanghaied by pirates, which leads to his unlikely rescue of a damsel and killing of a dragon.

Rodman Philbrick, *The Last Book in the Universe*, 2000
  In a decimated world where acid rain, gangs and cement

abound, Spaz inadvertently becomes the owner of "the last book in the universe."

Philip Pullman, *His Dark Materials Trilogy*, 1996-2000
When the dust increases on Lyra's world, evil follows, flowing from a rift in time and space.

1196

DEITLOF REICHE
JOE CEPEDA, Illustrator
JOHN BROWNJOHN, Translator

I, Freddy
(New York: Scholastic Press, 2003)

Series: Golden Hamster Saga. Book 1
Subject(s): Animals/Hamsters; Pets; Literacy
Age range(s): Grades 3-5
Major character(s): Freddy, Hamster, Narrator; Mr. John, Animal Lover, Linguist; Sophie, Student—Elementary School, Daughter
Time period(s): 1990s (1998)
Locale(s): Germany

Summary: Freddy, as he's quick to point out, is unique even for a golden hamster. Never one to enjoy the hamster games of his littermates, Freddy figures out how to convince a buyer to purchase him so he can get out of the crowded pet store cage. From the moment he becomes Sophie's pet Freddy is caught between Sophie's jealous, allergic mother's dislike of Freddy and kind but lonely Sophie's desire to keep Freddy. While watching Sophie do her homework Freddy teaches himself to read. It's his quest for more challenging reading material that proves to be his undoing at Sophie's and he's sent to live with Mr. John. Already the owner of a cat and two guinea pigs, Mr. John not only welcomes Freddy, but also seems to intuitively understand his needs. With help from the cat Freddy reads the many books on Mr. John's shelves and then figures out how to work Mr. John's new computer. In time, he becomes proficient enough to write his memoirs, originally published in German in 1998. (203 pages)

Where it's reviewed:
Booklist, April 1, 2003, page 1398
Bulletin of the Center for Children's Books, July 2003, page 459
School Library Journal, November 2003, page 113

Other books by the same author:
Freddy to the Rescue, 2005 (Golden Hamster Saga Book 3)
Freddy in Peril, 2004 (Golden Hamster Saga Book 2)

Other books you might like:
Ben Baglio, *Hamster in a Handbasket*, 1996
After the class hamster is stolen from his home during summer vacation James has to figure who did it so he can retrieve the pet.
Betty G. Birney, *The World According to Humphrey*, 2004
Humphrey, class pet in an elementary school, is an astute observer of social interactions in class and in students' homes during weekend visits.
Errol Broome, *Magnus Maybe*, 2002
After escaping from his cage, Magnus, a white pet mouse,

finds relative safety if not complete acceptance with a family of brown wild mice.
Beverly Cleary, *Runaway Ralph*, 1970
Family life seems to confining for Ralph S. Mouse so he takes off on his motorcycle in search of freedom.
Dick King-Smith, *The School Mouse*, 1995
In the school building that is her family's home Flora takes advantage of the daily lessons and uses her literacy to save her family.

1197

KATHRYN REISS

Paint by Magic: A Time Travel Mystery
(San Diego: Harcourt, 2002)

Subject(s): Time Travel; Artists and Art
Age range(s): Grades 5-8
Major character(s): Connor Rigoletti-Chase, 11-Year-Old; Fitzgerald Cotton, Artist; Lorenzo da Padova, Artist
Time period(s): 2000s; 1920s (1926)
Locale(s): Padua, Italy; California

Summary: One day Connor returns from school and finds his mother garbed in old-fashioned clothes, standing in the kitchen cooking dinner and asking about his day at school. Whoa! This can't be his mother; she's usually not even home until much later in the evening. When her actions seem almost robotic, Connor traces the problem to a book his mother's reading about the artist Fitzgerald Cotton. Looking at the photos, he realizes his mom modeled for this 15th-century artist and suddenly Connor travels through time until he arrives at the household of Cotton and his family. There he discovers that the paints of Lorenzo da Padova, an evil contemporary painter of Cotton's, possess both the artist Cotton and his model, Connor's mother. Now it's up to Connor to break the spell and free his mom in this "time travel mystery." (271 pages)

Where it's reviewed:
Booklist, May 1, 2002, page 1460
Bulletin of the Center for Children's Books, September 2002, page 32
Kirkus Reviews, May 1, 2002, page 666
School Library Journal, May 2002, page 158
Voice of Youth Advocates, June 2002, page 131

Other books by the same author:
Sweet Miss Honeywell's Revenge: A Ghost Story, 2004
The Strange Case of Baby H, 2002
Riddle of the Prairie Bride, 2001

Other books you might like:
Caroline B. Cooney, *For All Time*, 2001
Annie finds herself in Egypt when the pyramids are being built, not when they're being excavated as she wanted.
Terry Kretzer-Malvehy, *Passage to Little Bighorn*, 1999
At a reenactment of the Little Bighorn battle, Dakota travels back in time and is captured by Sitting Bull's warriors.
Phyllis Reynolds Naylor, *Jade Green: A Ghost Story*, 2000
Judith's green-framed photo of her mother awakens the

ghost of a former serving girl; luckily the ghost protects Judith from a murderous relative.

1198

LOUISE RENNISON

Dancing in My Nuddy-Pants: Even Further Confessions of Georgia Nicolson

(New York: HarperCollins, 2003)

Subject(s): Dating (Social Customs); Diaries; Humor
Age range(s): Grades 7-10
Major character(s): Georgia Nicolson, Student—High School; Robbie "The Sex God", Boyfriend (Georgia's crush); Dave "The Laugh", Boyfriend (Georgia's crush); Angus, Cat
Time period(s): 2000s
Locale(s): England

Summary: Georgia's breathless, hilarious life continues as she seems to have decided to focus her attentions on Robbie the Sex God, though Dave the Laugh isn't quite out of her daydreams. This is also the year that Georgia and her schoolmates travel to Paris, or "Frogland" as she terms it; she's named captain of her hockey team; and, miracle of miracles, Angus, her very large cat who's recently been spayed, evidently had a timely score with the cat across the street who's now pregnant with his kittens. By book's end, Georgia's despondent to learn that Robbie's off to "Kiwi-a-gogo" land, better known as New Zealand, which means Dave the Laugh might have to suffice. (214 pages)

Where it's reviewed:
Booklist, April 15, 2003, page 1462
Kirkus Reviews, February 15, 2003, page 315
School Library Journal, May 2003, page 160
Voice of Youth Advocates, June 2003, page 144

Other books by the same author:
Knocked Out by My Nunga-Nungas: Further Confessions of Georgia Nicolson, 2002
On the Bright Side, I'm Now the Girlfriend of a Sex God: Further Confessions of Georgia Nicolson, 2001
Angus, Thongs and Full-Frontal Snogging: Confessions of Georgia Nicolson, 2000

Other books you might like:
Grace Dent, *LBD: It's a Girl Thing*, 2003
  Les Bambinos Dangereuses can't believe their ancient parents won't let them attend a music festival, so they host one themselves.
Rosie Rushton, *Just Don't Make a Scene, Mum*, 1999
  In this first of a series, five British teens find their lives connected through a radio show that lets them describe embarrassing moments.
Cherry Whytock, *My Cup Runneth Over: The Life of Angelica Cookson Potts*, 2003
  Though told by her friends otherwise, Angel loves food and knows she is endowed with many "wobbly bits."

1199

LOUISE RENNISON

Knocked Out by My Nunga-Nungas: Further, Further Confessions of Georgia Nicolson

(New York: HarperCollins, 2002)

Subject(s): Humor; Interpersonal Relations; Diaries
Age range(s): Grades 7-10
Major character(s): Georgia Nicolson, 15-Year-Old; Robbie, Boyfriend; Dave, Boyfriend
Time period(s): 2000s
Locale(s): England; Scotland

Summary: Georgia moans loudly but achieves nothing with her protests about the family vacation to Scotland, "Och-aye Land," where she quickly discovers the biggest excitement for teens is going to the 24-hour supermarket. Returning home to Robbie, her "Sex God" boyfriend, she finds snogging (kissing) is just as pleasant as it always was, so she's not sure why she plays "True. Dare. Kiss or Promise" with her former boyfriend "Dave the Laugh" and really enjoys snogging with him, too. Her cute biology teacher gives every pair of students an egg to care for, her little sister is still adorable and her cat Angus continues his feisty ways in a breezy, light-hearted series from England. Glossary included. (183 pages)

Where it's reviewed:
Booklist, April 15, 2002, page 1395
Kliatt, May 2002, page 13
Publishers Weekly, April 8, 2002, page 228
School Library Journal, May 2002, page 160
Voice of Youth Advocates, August 2002, page 197

Awards the book has won:
ALA Quick Picks for Reluctant Young Adult Readers, 2003

Other books by the same author:
Away Laughing on a Fast Camel: Even More Confessions of Georgia Nicolson, 2004
Dancing in My Nuddy-Pants: Even Further Confessions of Georgia Nicolson, 2003
On the Bright Side, I'm Now the Girlfriend of a Sex God: Confessions of Georgia Nicolson, 2001
Angus, Thongs and Full-Frontal Snogging: Confessions of Georgia Nicolson, 2000

Other books you might like:
Cathy Hopkins, *Mates, Dates Series*, 2003-
  With her horrible new haircut, Lucy feels like a child next to her glamorous friends Izzie and Nesta.
Rosie Rushton, *Just Don't Make a Scene, Mum*, 1999
  In this first of a series, five British teens find their lives connected through a radio show that lets them describe embarrassing moments.
Cynthia Voigt, *Bad Girls in Love*, 2002
  "Bad girls" Mikey and Margalo have fallen in love, Mikey openly with Shawn and Margalo secretly with her teacher.

1200

ADRIAN REYNOLDS, Author/Illustrator

Pete and Polo's Farmyard Adventure

(New York: Orchard Books, 2002)

Subject(s): Animals/Ducks; Farm Life; Grandfathers
Age range(s): Preschool-Kindergarten
Major character(s): Pete, Child, Relative (grandson); Polo, Toy (stuffed animal), Bear; Grandpa, Grandfather, Farmer
Time period(s): 2000s (2001)
Locale(s): England

Summary: Pete and Polo can count on an adventure each time they visit Grandpa's farm. On this summer visit, Pete and Polo discover that the hot, dry weather has evaporated all the water in the duck pond and ten ducklings are missing. Pete and Polo track down clusters of ducklings by checking all the farm's sources of water from the dog's bowl to the old water pump. After loading all ten in the trailer Pete pedals the tractor to the duck pond that Grandpa has refilled with water to conclude the best adventure these two pals have had yet. Originally published in Great Britain in 2001. (28 pages)

Where it's reviewed:
Booklist, August 2002, page 1976
Children's Bookwatch, July 2002, page 4
Horn Book Guide, Fall 2002, page 311
Kirkus Reviews, April 1, 2002, page 498
School Library Journal, July 2002, page 97

Other books by the same author:
Pete and Polo's Big School Adventure, 2000

Other books you might like:
June Crebbin, *Danny's Duck*, 1995
    Danny's teacher is able to show him where all the ducks missing from the nest he's been watching have gone.
Robert McCloskey, *Make Way for Ducklings*, 1941
    No ducks are lost in this Caldecott Medal winner but they do stop traffic when they cross a busy Boston street to walk to the pond.
Phyllis Reynolds Naylor, *Ducks Disappearing*, 1997
    As Willie watches a line of baby ducks following their mother he's puzzled by the diminishing number of ducklings he can see.
Nancy Tafuri, *Have You Seen My Duckling?*, 1984
    A mother duck searches the pond for her one missing offspring in a Caldecott Honor Book.

1201

V.A. RICHARDSON

The House of Windjammer

(New York: Bloomsbury, 2003)

Subject(s): Family Problems; Ships
Age range(s): Grades 7-10
Major character(s): Hugo van Helsen, Banker; Abner Heems, Con Artist; Adam Windjammer, 14-Year-Old; Gerrit, Bookkeeper, Heir
Time period(s): 17th century (1630s)
Locale(s): Amsterdam, Netherlands

Summary: The news that the Windjammer's fleet of merchant ships has been lost at sea becomes the portent of doom for that family. Suddenly banker van Helsen is ready to collect every penny owed him and uses the so-called preacher Abner Heems to turn the people of Amsterdam against the Windjammer family. Though Adam is heir to the family business, a lazy, untrustworthy uncle assumes responsibility until Adam is older. Since Adam doesn't have confidence in his uncle, he turns to the family bookkeeper for assurance. Before Gerrit is killed by preacher Heems, he tries to take advantage of "tulipmania" and secure the famous Black Pearl tulip for the Windjammers. Thankfully some creditors come forward to aid the family to complete construction of the sailing ship *Draco* so that Adam can sail to the Americas in this first of a series. (350 pages)

Where it's reviewed:
Booklist, May 15, 2003, page 1666
Bulletin of the Center for Children's Books, September 2003, page 29
Publishers Weekly, July 14, 2003, page 77
School Library Journal, September 2003, page 219
Voice of Youth Advocates, October 2003, page 318

Other books you might like:
Alexandre Dumas, *The Black Tulip*, 1891
    An historical romance involving the Haarlem tulip craze during the late 1600s. Adult title.
Brian Jacques, *Castaways of the Flying Dutchman*, 2001
    Neb and his dog Den are tossed overboard from the *Flying Dutchman* just after an angel curses its crew to forever sail the sea.
Deborah Moggach, *Tulip Fever*, 2000
    Amsterdam in the 1700s teems with artists and tulips, both of which leave lasting memories.
Celia Rees, *Pirates!: The True and Remarkable Adventures of Minerva Sharpe and Nancy Kington, Female Pirates*, 2003
    After her father loses his fortune and subsequently dies, Nancy is promised in marriage to a sadistic man; rather than marry him, she becomes a pirate.

1202

CHRIS RIDDELL, Author/Illustrator

Platypus

(San Diego: Harcourt, 2002)

Subject(s): Collectors and Collecting; Animals; Lost and Found
Age range(s): Preschool-Grade 1
Major character(s): Platypus, Animal (platypus), Collector
Time period(s): 2000s (2002)
Locale(s): Fictional Country

Summary: Platypus likes to collect items that he finds at the beach. One day he finds a shell that is "just right" for his collection. He takes it home and puts it in his collection box, but when he goes to look for it the next day, the shell has disappeared. The same thing happens when Platypus takes the shell home again. Platypus soon discovers that the curly shell he loves is home to a hermit crab and finds another, unoccupied shell, for his collection. (32 pages)

Where it's reviewed:
Booklist, March 1, 2002, page 1143
Horn Book Guide, Fall 2002, page 311
Kirkus Reviews, April 15, 2002, page 577
Publishers Weekly, April 15, 2002, page 62
School Library Journal, June 2002, page 109

Other books by the same author:
Platypus and the Birthday Party, 2003
Platypus and the Lucky Day, 2002
The Bear Dance, 1991

Other books you might like:
Jan Brett, *Goldilocks and the Three Bears*, 1987
    Goldilocks searches for the ''just right'' porridge, chair, and bed.
Dick Bruna, *Miffy at the Beach*, 1984
    Young bunny, Miffy, spends a day at the beach.
Mick Inkpen, *Kipper*, 1992
    Kipper searches for a better place to sleep.
Elisa Kleven, *The Puddle Pail*, 1997
    Brothers take different approaches to collecting items. Sol finds shells, rocks and feathers while Ernst collects puddles, clouds and stars.

1203

CHRIS RIDDELL, Author/Illustrator

Platypus and the Birthday Party

(San Diego: Harcourt, Inc. 2003)

Subject(s): Animals; Birthdays; Toys
Age range(s): Preschool-Kindergarten
Major character(s): Platypus, Animal, Friend; Echidna, Animal, Friend
Time period(s): 2000s (2003)
Locale(s): England

Summary: When Platypus decides to have a birthday party for his favorite stuffed animal he invites his best friend, Echidna. Together the friends bake a cake, blow up balloons and make paper chain decorations. The party is such a success that they decide to have another one the very next day. (32 pages)

Where it's reviewed:
Publishers Weekly, September 8, 2003, page 78
School Library Journal, December 2003, page 124

Other books by the same author:
Platypus, 2002
Platypus and the Lucky Day, 2002
The Trouble with Elephants, 1988

Other books you might like:
Lucy Cousins, *Happy Birthday Maisy*, 1998
    Maisy gets ready for her birthday party.
Mick Inkpen, *Kipper's Birthday*, 1993
    Confusion results when Kipper invites his friends to his birthday party ''tomorrow'' and they all show up a day late.
Cynthia Rylant, *Little Whistle's Dinner Party*, 2001
    Little Whistle throws a midnight dinner party for all his friends.

1204

CHRIS RIDDELL, Author/Illustrator

Platypus and the Lucky Day

(San Diego: Harcourt, Inc., 2002)

Subject(s): Animals; Lost and Found; Artists and Art
Age range(s): Preschool-Grade 1
Major character(s): Platypus, Animal
Time period(s): 2000s (2002)
Locale(s): England

Summary: Platypus is sure that today is his lucky day but when he tries to fly his kite, it gets stuck in a tree. Attempts to paint a picture are ruined by rain and wind and when Platypus trips and falls (on the broken kite string no less), he decides that today is not his day after all and he is going back to bed. The happy discovery of a forgotten banana under his pillow and a lost toy under his blankets turns the day back around and he decides he was right; it is his lucky day. (32 pages)

Where it's reviewed:
Publishers Weekly, July 8, 2002, page 51
School Library Journal, November 2002, page 134

Other books by the same author:
Platypus and the Birthday Party, 2003
Platypus, 2002
The Trouble with Elephants, 1988

Other books you might like:
Lisa Jahn-Clough, *Alicia Has a Bad Day*, 1994
    Alicia's bad day is made better by her dog.
Keiko Kasza, *My Lucky Day*, 2003
    Mr. Fox thinks it's his lucky day when a pig shows up on his doorstep, but things don't go as he expects.
Judith Viorst, *Alexander and the Terrible, Horrible, No Good, Very Bad Day*, 1972
    Alexander's bad day begins when he wakes up with gum in his hair.

1205

ANN RINALDI

Numbering All the Bones

(New York: Jump at the Sun/Hyperion, 2002)

Subject(s): Civil War; Slavery; Prisoners and Prisons
Age range(s): Grades 6-9
Major character(s): Eulinda, 13-Year-Old, Slave; Zeke, Slave, Brother (of Eulinda); Neddy, Military Personnel, Runaway; Hampton Kellogg, Landowner; Clarissa Harlowe ''Clara'' Barton, Historical Figure (founder of Red Cross)
Time period(s): 1860s (1864-1865)
Locale(s): Andersonville, Georgia

Summary: Growing up the daughter of a slave and her white plantation owner, Eulinda doesn't feel as though she fits in anywhere. The other slaves don't want to talk to her and Mr. Kellogg and his second wife treat her like a daughter some days and a slave other days. Her brother Zeke is accused of theft and sold, which makes her older brother Neddy so angry he runs away and joins the Union Army. Her mother, once the cook on the plantation, dies, leaving Eulinda alone and unsure how the Emancipation Proclamation will affect her. Andersonville Prison is built and Eulinda focuses on the thought that Neddy might be imprisoned there. By war's end she's helped Clara Barton care for the wounded and identify and bury all the deceased prisoners; once she realizes Neddy has died, she's ready to accept Miss Barton's job offer. (170 pages)

Where it's reviewed:
Booklist, May 15, 2002, page 1605
Bulletin of the Center for Children's Books, June 2002, page 380
Library Media Connection, February 2003, page 77
School Library Journal, June 2002, page 144
Voice of Youth Advocates, August 2002, page 197

Other books by the same author:
Girl in Blue, 2001
Amelia's War, 1999
An Acquaintance with Darkness, 1997
Mine Eyes Have Seen, 1997
In My Father's House, 1993
The Last Silk Dress, 1988

Other books you might like:
Gary Paulsen, *Sarny: A Life Remembered*, 1997
    Once freed, Sarny travels to New Orleans where she accepts a job with Miss Laura, an octoroon, and enjoys the creature comforts of her home.
Harriette Gillem Robinet, *Forty Acres and Maybe a Mule*, 1998
    When the government's offer of 40 acres and a mule is rescinded, Pascal and Gideon rely on found treasure to buy land on Georgia's Sea Islands.
G. Clifton Wisler, *Red Cap*, 1991
    Young Union drummer Ransom J. Powell, who lies about his age to join the army, is one of the few to survive the rigors of Andersonville Prison.

1206

ANN RINALDI

Or Give Me Death

(San Diego: Harcourt, Inc., 2003)

Series: Great Episodes
Subject(s): Mental Illness; Family Life; Revolutionary War
Age range(s): Grades 7-10
Major character(s): Martha ''Patsy'' Henry, 16-Year-Old, Historical Figure; Sarah Shelton Henry, Mother, Mentally Ill Person; John ''MyJohn'' Fontaine, Fiance(e), Historical Figure; Anne Henry, Sister (of Patsy), Historical Figure; Patrick Henry, Lawyer, Historical Figure
Time period(s): 1770s (1771-1778)
Locale(s): Hanover County, Virginia

Summary: While Patrick Henry travels the countryside speaking of the possibility of war with England, Patsy is left at home to act as mistress of the house, prevent her siblings from going too wild and guard against her mother harming herself or any of the children. When Patsy sees her mother trying to drown the baby because he won't stop crying, she realizes that something must be done to confine Sarah. Patsy and her betrothed MyJohn travel to Williamsburg to inspect its com-

bined jail and hospital, but find it's dismal, rat-infested, and altogether unsuitable for her mother. Eventually, for the safety of everyone, Sarah is kept in their basement where she enjoys light, cheery rooms and is no threat to anyone. When Patsy weds MyJohn, the responsibility for the Henry household passes to Anne, the only child who knows which of the siblings has inherited their mother's mental illness. (226 pages)

Where it's reviewed:
Booklist, May 15, 2003, page 1663
Kirkus Reviews, June 15, 2003, page 863
Publishers Weekly, July 14, 2003, page 77
School Library Journal, July 2003, page 134
Voice of Youth Advocates, August 2003, page 229

Other books by the same author:
Mistress of Dorchester, 2005
Mutiny's Daughter, 2004
Sarah's Ground, 2004
Millicent's Gift, 2002
Numbering All the Bones, 2002

Other books you might like:
Anna Myers, *The Keeping Room*, 1997
    Left in charge when his father marches off to fight against the redcoats, Joseph runs into difficulty when General Cornwallis appropriates his home.
Phyllis Reynolds Naylor, *The Keeper*, 1986
    Teen Nick Karpinski shoulders the arduous task of having his mentally ill father committed for treatment.
Robert Newton Peck, *Hang for Treason*, 1976
    His father's Tory sympathies can't keep a young boy from joining up with Ethan Allen and the Green Mountain Boys.
Sally Warner, *How to Be a Real Person (in Just One Day)*, 2001
    Kara thinks if she lies and follows her made-up rules, no one will know how unhinged her mother has become.

1207

ANN RINALDI

Taking Liberty: The Story of Oney Judge, George Washington's Runaway Slave

(New York: Simon & Schuster, 2002)

Subject(s): Slavery; African Americans; Runaways
Age range(s): Grades 7-10
Major character(s): Oney Judge, Slave, Historical Figure; George Washington, Historical Figure, Political Figure (President of the United States); Martha Washington, Historical Figure
Time period(s): 18th century
Locale(s): Mount Vernon, Virginia; New Hampshire

Summary: It's hard to want your freedom when you're living a life of relative privilege; this is the problem for Oney, the favorite personal servant of Martha Washington, who's used to wearing fine clothes and having her own room. Though Oney's mother has always told her to run for her freedom whenever she gets the chance, she feels so much a part of the Washington family that she doesn't want to leave. Accompanying the new President and Martha to Pennsylvania, Oney meets an abolitionist who tells her about the Underground Railroad, but she merely files this information away. When she learns that she's to be given to Martha Washington's eldest daughter when she marries, Oney realizes that she's only property and makes her plans to escape. Ending up in New Hampshire, she tells her story to a journalist in this novel that is based on the life of the real Oney Judge. (267 pages)

Where it's reviewed:
Kirkus Reviews, October 15, 2002, page 1537
Kliatt, November 2002, page 14
Publishers Weekly, December 2, 2002, page 53
School Library Journal, January 2003, page 143
Voice of Youth Advocates, February 2003, page 481

Other books by the same author:
Brooklyn Rose, 2005
Cast Two Shadows: The American Revolution in the South, 2004
Sarah's Ground, 2004
Mutiny's Daughter, 2004
Millicent's Gift, 2002

Other books you might like:
Mary E. Lyons, *Letters from a Slave Girl: The Story of Harriet Jacobs*, 1992
   After seven years hiding in her grandmother's small storeroom, Harriet escapes along the Underground Railroad.
Gary Paulsen, *Sarny: A Life Remembered*, 1997
   Once freed, Sarny travels to New Orleans where she accepts a job with Miss Laura, an octoroon, and enjoys the creature comforts of her home.
Glennette Tilley Turner, *Running for Our Lives*, 1994
   Separated from their parents as their slave family escapes, Carrie and Luther arrive in Canada but never again see their mother and father.

1208

GEORGIE RIPPER, Author/Illustrator

Brian & Bob: The Tale of Two Guinea Pigs

(New York: Hyperion Books for Children, 2003)

Subject(s): Animals/Guinea Pigs; Friendship; Pets
Age range(s): Grades K-2
Major character(s): Brian, Guinea Pig, Friend; Bob, Guinea Pig, Friend
Time period(s): 2000s (2003)
Locale(s): England

Summary: Best friends Brian and Bob are separated when a little boy adopts Bob from Pete's Pet Palace. Brian is lonely and sad all by himself, until the day he too is adopted. Luckily, the old man adopting Brian is buying him as a gift for his grandson, the same boy who earlier adopted Bob. Unexpectedly, the two friends are happily reunited. (32 pages)

Where it's reviewed:
Publishers Weekly, October 20, 2003, page 52
School Library Journal, December 2003, page 124

Other books by the same author:
My Best Friend, Bob, 2003

The Little Brown Bushrat, 2002 (Macmillan Prize for Picture Book Illustration)

Other books you might like:
Kate Duke, *One Guinea Pig Is Not Enough*, 1998
   This counting book shows the fun guinea pigs have as more and more come to play.
Dick King-Smith, *I Love Guinea Pigs*, 1994
   In addition to paying tribute to guinea pigs, this title provides information on their care and history.
Holly Meade, *John Willy and Freddy McGee*, 1998
   The discovery of an open cage door is the only invitation guinea pigs John Willy and Freddy McGee need to escape and explore their house.
Cynthia Rylant, *Little Whistle*, 2001
   Guinea Pig, Little Whistle, lives in a toy store and enjoys playing with his toy neighbors at night.

1209

JON RIPSLINGER

How I Fell in Love & Learned to Shoot Free Throws

(Brookfield, CT: Roaring Brook Press, 2003)

Subject(s): Sports/Basketball; Dating (Social Customs); Schools/High Schools
Age range(s): Grades 8-12
Major character(s): Danny Henderson, Basketball Player, 17-Year-Old; Angel McPherson, Basketball Player
Time period(s): 2000s
Locale(s): Iowa

Summary: Danny is bested 23-18 by Angel in a free throw shooting contest, but that doesn't bother him for that loss is his attempt to become friends with her. Secretly interested in Angel, who's known around school as a loner, Danny figures he'll ask for help with his free throw shooting. Sports are a safe outlet for Angel so she agrees and, even after breaking her ankle, continues working with Danny. Gradually the two become serious about one another and it's only a matter of time before they're each sharing secrets about their mothers in this romantic sports novel. (170 pages)

Where it's reviewed:
Booklist, April 15, 2003, page 1463
Bulletin of the Center for Children's Books, June 2003, page 419
Publishers Weekly, April 14, 2003, page 71
School Library Journal, April 2003, page 166
Voice of Youth Advocates, June 2003, page 144

Other books by the same author:
Triangle, 1994

Other books you might like:
Carl Deuker, *Night Hoops*, 2000
   Determined to gain his father's attention, Nick hones his skills as he and his neighbor establish a nightly basketball game.
David Klass, *A Different Season*, 1987
   A female second baseman on the boys' baseball team affects star pitcher Jim Roark's usually perfect throw.

Randy Powell, *My Underrated Year*, 1988
Roger finds himself attracted to Mary Jo, the new tennis player who is about to knock him out of his number one spot.

Marilyn Reynolds, *Love Rules*, 2001
During their senior year in high school, Lynn stands by her friend Kit when Kit decides to come out of the closet.

1210

JOHN RITTER

The Boy Who Saved Baseball
(New York: Philomel/Penguin Putnam, 2003)

Subject(s): Sports/Baseball; Small Town Life
Age range(s): Grades 5-8
Major character(s): Thomas ''Tom'' Gallagher, 12-Year-Old; Cruz de la Cruz, Baseball Player; Dante del Gato, Baseball Player, Recluse; Kennesaw Mountain ''Doc'' Altenheimer, Doctor
Time period(s): 2000s
Locale(s): Dillontown, California

Summary: Dillontown has shrunk in size over the last hundred years, and the town's spirit seems to have diminished accordingly. Doc Altenheimer's thinking of selling his 320 acres so that a new baseball field, homes and a golf course can be built until Tom mentions that a new field won't necessarily make a better team, that it's the spirit that counts. Doc agrees with Tom's thinking and proposes a baseball game between the Dillontown Wildcats and their arch rivals, the all-stars from the summer camp. If Dillontown wins, the sale of his land is off; if not, the bulldozers will rev up their engines. That's all very well, but the Dillontown team is coed and doesn't even have nine players, until Cruz de la Cruz rides into town with his bat stuck in a rifle holster on his saddle. Tom first begins to work with Cruz, learning more about his computer program to improve hitting, and then lines up the reclusive Dante del Gato, the former Padres outstanding hitter, to be the team's trainer. Suddenly the town begins taking an interest in the legendary del Gato and the way he's working with their team, as anticipation mounts for the momentous game that will determine whether or not the developers have won in this grand slam of a baseball book. (216 pages)

Where it's reviewed:
Booklist, May 1, 2003, page 1595
Bulletin of the Center for Children's Books, July 2003, page 460
Publishers Weekly, May 19, 2003, page 74
School Library Journal, June 2003, page 150
Voice of Youth Advocates, August 2003, page 240

Other books by the same author:
Over the Wall, 2000
Choosing Up Sides, 1998

Other books you might like:
Bruce Brooks, *Throwing Smoke*, 2000
Baseball team co-captain Whiz prints up a baseball card featuring a longed-for imaginary pitcher; the next day, Ace Jones shows up to hurl his stuff.

W.P. Kinsella, *Shoeless Joe*, 1982
A mixture of fantasy, time travel, and one man's dream combine to produce an incredible baseball game.

David Patneaude, *Haunting at Home Plate*, 2000
A baseball team is inspired by messages left by Andy Kirk who's haunted their park ever since falling to his death while watching his brother play.

Joseph Romain, *The Mystery of the Wagner Whacker*, 1998
Ghosts from the past repair a special baseball bat machine, much to the delight of Matt and the well-being of his uncle.

1211

WILLO DAVIS ROBERTS

Rebel
(New York: Atheneum/Simon & Schuster, 2003)

Subject(s): Mystery and Detective Stories; Grandmothers; Crime and Criminals
Age range(s): Grades 5-8
Major character(s): Amanda Jane ''Rebel'' Keeling, 14-Year-Old; Moses Adams, 15-Year-Old; Gram Keeling, Grandmother; Viola ''Old Vi'', Grandmother (of Moses)
Time period(s): 2000s
Locale(s): Seattle, Washington

Summary: Once Amanda learned to say the word ''No,'' her behavior was downhill. Nicknamed ''Rebel,'' she refused to attend kindergarten when she was five and seems to have acquired her stubbornness from Gram Keeling. Now Gram offers Rebel a chance to help clean a rooming house she's just bought with her friend Vi while Rebel's family heads to Salzburg, Austria for a music competition. Happy to spend time with Gram, Rebel's interest picks up when she finds she'll be working with Vi's grandson Moses who's eight inches taller than her five feet ten inches. An aspiring filmmaker, Moses inadvertently videotapes a counterfeiter's transaction while the two are walking their dogs. Deciding they'd like to solve the crime themselves, Moses and Rebel set up a trap at the rooming house which, thanks to friendly police intervention, doesn't backfire on them in this work from a prolific mystery writer. (153 pages)

Where it's reviewed:
Booklist, July 2003, page 1892
Bulletin of the Center for Children's Books, September 2003, page 30
Kirkus Reviews, June 15, 2003, page 864
School Library Journal, August 2003, page 165

Other books by the same author:
Blood on His Hands, 2004
Undercurrents, 2002
Buddy Is a Stupid Name for a Girl, 2001
Hostage, 2000
The Kidnappers: A Mystery, 1998

Other books you might like:
Michael Dahl, *The Horizontal Man*, 1999
After Finn spots a golden Mayan relic which belongs to his missing parents, he investigates and is kidnapped.

Joachim Friedrich, *4 1/2 Friends and the Secret Cave*, 2001
Collin and Steffi set up a detective agency but have to add

her twin brother Radish when he finds a cave complete with treasure map.

Dayle Campbell Gaetz, *Mystery from History*, 2001
   Katie, Sheila and Rusty of ''Investigations Unlimited'' snoop around and discover their town's chief of police is an art thief.

Wendelin Van Draanen, *Sammy Keyes and the Hotel Thief*, 1998
   Sammy tells the police about a thief she saw, but has difficulty making them believe her.

1212
WILLO DAVIS ROBERTS

Undercurrents
(New York: Atheneum/Simon & Schuster, 2002)

Subject(s): Mystery and Detective Stories; Stepmothers; Haunted Houses
Age range(s): Grades 6-9
Major character(s): Nikki Simons, 14-Year-Old; Crystal Simons, Artist (illustrator), Stepmother
Time period(s): 2000s
Locale(s): Trinidad, California; Seattle, Washington

Summary: It's not even been a year since Nikki's mother died of cancer and her father marries Crystal, a young woman who's an illustrator at the publishing house where he works. After her father and stepmother return from their honeymoon, Crystal discovers she's inherited her aunt's beach house in California and Nikki's dad immediately decides the family needs to vacation there. Oblivious to Crystal's pleas to not vacation there, the family arrives in Trinidad but Dad is called home on a business emergency. Crystal's behavior becomes very erratic: she refuses to be seen in public without a headscarf and forbids Nikki to type up a manuscript for the professor living next door. The story of Crystal's haunted house, her parent's death and a tragic fire finally emerges but not before Nikki almost becomes the next victim in another thriller from a prolific author. (232 pages)

Where it's reviewed:
Booklist, February 15, 2002, page 1010
Bulletin of the Center for Children's Books, April 2002, page 291
Publishers Weekly, March 4, 2002, page 80
School Library Journal, February 2002, page 136
Voice of Youth Advocates, February 2002, page 438

Other books by the same author:
Blood on His Hands, 2004
Rebel, 2003
Hostage, 2000
Pawns, 1998
The Kidnappers: A Mystery, 1998

Other books you might like:
Mary Downing Hahn, *Following the Mystery Man*, 1988
   Madigan has always wanted to know the father who abandoned her and is convinced the stranger who's rented a room from her grandmother is that man.
Eloise McGraw, *Tangled Webb*, 1993
   Juniper decides her new stepmother, who dyes her hair and

has no labels in her clothes, is the perfect main character for the mystery she wants to write.

Kathryn Reiss, *Riddle of the Prairie Bride*, 2001
   Ida Kate's excited about her father's mail-order bride, but when she arrives everything about the bride is wrong from the color of her hair to her height.

1213
HARRIETTE GILLEM ROBINET

Twelve Travelers, Twenty Horses
(New York: Atheneum/Simon & Schuster, 2003)

Subject(s): African Americans; Slavery; Adventure and Adventurers
Age range(s): Grades 6-9
Major character(s): Jacob Israel Christmas, 13-Year-Old, Slave; Clarence ''Honorable Mister'' Higgenboom, Con Artist
Time period(s): 1860s
Locale(s): Kentucky; West

Summary: Sent to the auction block, Jacob can't believe his luck when he's reunited with his mother and then, best of all, the two are bought, along with eight other slaves, by a seemingly-honorable gentleman named Mister Clarence Higgenboom. The ten slaves, Mister Higgenboom and his pregnant wife leave Missouri for California where their new owner plans to prospect for gold. Soon Jacob overhears some worrisome news indicating that Mr. Higgenboom is not as nice as he seems for he plans to rob the stagecoach, which carries the wages for the Pony Express riders. Jacob knows if the Pony Express doesn't carry the news to California of Lincoln's election win, there's a good chance the news about freeing the slaves won't reach there either, consigning all of them to a life of servitude. Whatever happens to Mr. Higgenboom, Jacob is determined that the election news will reach California. (192 pages)

Where it's reviewed:
Booklist, February 15, 2003, page 1082
Kirkus Reviews, December 1, 2002, page 1772
Kliatt, January 2003, page 11
School Library Journal, February 2003, page 147
Voice of Youth Advocates, February 2003, page 481

Other books by the same author:
Missing from Haymarket Square, 2001
Forty Acres and Maybe a Mule, 1998
Washington City Is Burning, 1996
If You Please, President Lincoln, 1995

Other books you might like:
Kristiana Gregory, *Jimmy Spoon and the Pony Express*, 1994
   Tired of working in his father's store, Jimmy responds to an ad for Pony Express riders that asks for a ''young, skinny, wiry fellow.''
Mary Stolz, *Cezanne Pinto: A Memoir*, 1994
   Once the Civil War ends, Cezanne travels to Texas to find his mother; when he's unsuccessful, he first becomes a cowboy and then a teacher.
Sharon Dennis Wyeth, *Freedom's Wings: Corey's Diary*, 2001

Rather than be sold, Corey's father runs away from their master; later Corey and Mama journey on the Underground Railroad to join him.

1214

DENIS ROCHE, Author/Illustrator

The Best Class Picture Ever!

(New York: Scholastic Press, 2003)

Subject(s): Schools; Photography; Pets
Age range(s): Grades K-2
Major character(s): Olivia, 2nd Grader; Mr. Click, Photographer
Time period(s): 2000s (2003)
Locale(s): United States

Summary: Olivia is unhappy. It's Class Picture Day, her class doesn't have a teacher, and now even their class pet, a guinea pig, has disappeared. When her class arrives in the auditorium for their picture, Mr. Click, the photographer, notices Olivia's frown and tries to cheer her up. The class searches for words funnier than "Cheese" to make Olivia smile. They find a word (trombone) and the class pet at the same time and Mr. Click becomes the students' new teacher. (32 pages)

Where it's reviewed:
Booklist, October 15, 2003, page 420
Publishers Weekly, September 8, 2003, page 76

Other books by the same author:
Mim, Gym, and June, 2003
Little Pig Is Capable, 2002
Only One Ollie, 1997

Other books you might like:
Harry Allard, *Miss Nelson Is Missing!*, 1977
    The kids in Miss Nelson's class misbehave until she disappears and a mean substitute replaces her.
Faye Gibbons, *The Day the Picture Man Came*, 2003
    Emily Howard's family tries to sit for a family photograph, but everything goes wrong.
Lynn Plourde, *School Picture Day*, 2002
    Josephina is more interested in how things work than in dressing up for a picture; when the photographer's camera breaks she's able to save the day.

1215

DENIS ROCHE, Author/Illustrator

Little Pig Is Capable

(Boston: Houghton Mifflin Company, 2002)

Subject(s): Animals/Pigs; Animals/Wolves; Scouting
Age range(s): Grades K-2
Major character(s): Little Pig, Pig, Scout; Ravenous, Wolf
Time period(s): Indeterminate
Locale(s): Fictional Country

Summary: Little Pig's overprotective parents send him off on a hike with his scout troop so overloaded with protective gear that he's afraid to look in the mirror and see if he looks as ridiculous as he feels. The troop's leader is absent and Ravenous, a rather thin, gray pig is the substitute leader for the day.

Little Pig is the only member of the troop suspicious of Ravenous. Although he says they're heading home, he's leading them farther up the mountain. When Ravenous instructs the pigs to build a fire to cook dinner only Little Pig remembers that no one has any food left. To save the troop members, Little Pig tricks Ravenous and soon has the wolf wrapped up in some of the protective gear he's been wearing all day. When the troop gets back down the mountain, with Little Pig leading the wolf by its tail, Little Pig's parents are so proud of him that they start calling him "Capable" Pig. (32 pages)

Where it's reviewed:
Booklist, March 1, 2002, page 1144
Horn Book, May 2002, page 322
Publishers Weekly, January 14, 2002, page 60
School Library Journal, August 2002, page 166

Other books by the same author:
Mim, Gym, and June, 2003
The Best Class Picture Ever!, 2003
Ollie All Over, 1997 (Parenting's Reading Magic Award)

Other books you might like:
Alma Flor Ada, *Yours Truly, Goldilocks*, 1998
    Fer O'Cious and his cousin plan to ambush the guests as they depart the little pigs' housewarming party.
Syd Hoff, *Bernard on His Own*, 1993
    Unlike Little Pig's parents, Bernard's are confident that one day he'll be able to do things for himself.
Susan Meddaugh, *Hog-Eye*, 1995
    A literate pig uses her reading ability to outwit a wolf intent on making her into his next meal.

1216

JOANNE ROCKLIN
JOANN ADINOLFI, Illustrator

This Book Is Haunted

(New York: HarperCollins Publishers, 2002)

Series: I Can Read Book
Subject(s): Ghosts; Halloween; Haunted Houses
Age range(s): Grades 1-3
Time period(s): Indeterminate
Locale(s): Fictional Country

Summary: Six brief tales, some in rhyme, offer scary fare for the beginning reader. Greedy trick-or-treaters, hoping for a bit more, knock on the door of a real witch and ghost and are scared out of all their candy. A haunted library book terrifies a big brother who has failed to return his sister's book, making it overdue on Halloween. An echo in a rented house persists after new occupants move in, frightening them away. (48 pages)

Where it's reviewed:
Bulletin of the Center for Children's Books, October 2002, page 75
Horn Book Guide, Spring 2003, page 62
Kirkus Reviews, July 15, 2002, page 1042
School Library Journal, September 2002, page 205

Awards the book has won:
Center for Children's Books Best Books, 2002

Other books by the same author:
Strudel Stories, 1999
The Very Best Hanukkah Gift, 1999
Three Smart Pals, 1994 (Hello Reader! Level 4)

Other books you might like:
Stephanie Calmenson, *Gator Halloween*, 1999
  A good deed sidetracks Amy and Allie so they miss entering the costume contest but they have a happy Halloween anyway.
Dav Pilkey, *Dragon's Halloween*, 1993
  In the fifth easy reader about Dragon, the kindly creature scares himself with his own pumpkin monster and then with sounds from his hungry stomach.
Jean Van Leeuwen, *Amanda Pig and the Awful Scary Monster*, 2003
  Nightly Amanda Pig feels afraid of monsters until she finds a way to use words to help her confront her fears.

1217

EMILY RODDA

Rowan and the Ice Creepers

(New York: Greenwillow Books/HarperCollins Publishers, 2003)

Series: Rowan of Rin. #5
Subject(s): Heroes and Heroines; Fantasy; Quest
Age range(s): Grades 4-6
Major character(s): Rowan, Hero, Friend; Norris, Brother, Hero; Shaaron, Sister, Heroine; Zeel, Heroine, Friend
Time period(s): Indeterminate
Locale(s): Rin, Fictional Country

Summary: At a time of the year when Rin's winter usually abates and signs of spring appear the snow, ice and cold instead seem to worsen. With food supplies and firewood dwindling, the villagers march to the safety of the coast leaving behind one too old to travel, one too injured and Rowan who along with Norris and Shaaron must solve the mystery of the ice creepers and save the village. As the trio trudges up the mountain Zeel flies in with her kite to join the quest, fulfilling the prophesy of the riddle stating that "four must make their sacrifice." Rowan's dreams and visions during the journey provide instructions to the group that, when properly interpreted, assure their safety and the defeat of the ice creepers. Through courage, sacrifice, friendship and the loyalty of the buksah Rowan's group discovers secrets long buried in the mountain, assuring Rin's future survival. (261 pages)

Where it's reviewed:
Booklist, October 1, 2003, page 322
Horn Book Guide, Spring 2004, page 101
School Library Journal, December 2003, page 160

Other books by the same author:
Rowan and the Keeper of the Crystal, 2002 (Rowan of Rin #3)
Rowan and the Zebak, 2002 (Rowan of Rin #4)
Rowan and the Travelers, 2001 (Rowan of Rin #2)
Rowan of Rin, 2001 (CBC of Australia Book of the Year for Younger Readers; Rowan of Rin #1)

Other books you might like:
Susan Cooper, *The Dark Is Rising*, 1973
  As evil begins to overtake the world one English boy has the power to stop it.
Madeleine L'Engle, *A Wrinkle in Time*, 1962
  The first in a four-book series about the Murry family finds the children on an interplanetary search for their father.
J.K. Rowling, *Harry Potter and the Chamber of Secrets*, 1999
  In the second book in the Harry Potter series, Harry and his friends take risks in order to save Hogwarts from He-Who-Can't-Be-Named.

1218

EMILY RODDA

Rowan and the Keeper of the Crystal

(New York: Greenwillow Books, 2002)

Series: Rowan of Rin. #3
Subject(s): Heroes and Heroines; Fantasy; Crystals
Age range(s): Grades 3-6
Major character(s): Rowan, Son, Hero; Jiller, Single Mother, Widow(er); Keeper of the Crystal, Aged Person
Time period(s): Indeterminate
Locale(s): Rin, Fictional Country; Maris, Fictional Country

Summary: The arrival of a messenger from Maris calling for the Chooser to hasten to the coast to select the successor to the Keeper of the Crystal creates great excitement in Rin. Rowan enjoys the novelty of the moment until Jiller steps forward to claim her inherited role as Chooser. As her first-born, Rowan must also journey to Maris into an unfamiliar world of intrigue and danger. Before Jiller begins her task she is poisoned and Rowan is thrust into the role of Chooser. Refusing to allow his mother to die, Rowan ignores the Keeper's warning that time will not allow him to follow his plan to save Jiller. He uses the three candidates vying to replace the Keeper in his quest to locate the ingredients for the antidote to the poison. Together they must complete their mission before sunrise or their world will be overtaken by the dreaded Zebak. Originally published in Australia in 1996. (197 pages)

Where it's reviewed:
Booklist, January 1, 2002, page 859
Bulletin of the Center for Children's Books, April 2002, page 291
Horn Book, March 2002, page 217
Publishers Weekly, April 1, 2002, page 85
School Library Journal, May 2002, page 160

Other books by the same author:
Rowan and the Zebak, 2002 (Rowan of Rin #4)
Rowan and the Travelers, 2001 (Rowan of Rin #2)
Rowan of Rin, 2001 (CBC of Australia Book of the Year for Younger Readers; Rowan of Rin #1)

Other books you might like:
Franny Billingsley, *The Folk Keeper*, 1999
  Inexplicable magical powers inherent in her enable orphaned Corinna to masquerade as Corin, a folk keeper.
Gail Carson Levine, *Ella Enchanted*, 1997
  In the Newbery Honor book Ella is cursed with obedience and must go on a quest to save herself and those she loves.

J.K. Rowling, *Harry Potter and the Sorcerer's Stone*, 1997
In order to save Hogwart's from the evil sorcerer that killed his parents Harry and his friends must find the hidden sorcerer's stone.

J.R.R. Tolkien, *The Hobbit*, 1938
In the first book of a fantasy trilogy a Hobbit finds himself on a journey that grows increasingly treacherous.

1219

EMILY RODDA

Rowan and the Zebak

(New York: Greenwillow Books/HarperCollins Publishers, 2002)

Series: Rowan of Rin. #4
Subject(s): Heroes and Heroines; Quest; Fantasy
Age range(s): Grades 4-6
Major character(s): Rowan, Brother (older), Hero; Zeel, Adventurer, Adoptee; Allun, Baker, Adventurer; Perlain, Sailor, Adventurer
Time period(s): Indeterminate Past
Locale(s): Rin, Fictional Country; Land of the Zebak, Fictional Country

Summary: After a flying Zebak creature snatches Rowan's younger sister and carries her back to the slave-holders long feared by the residents of Rin, Rowan determines to rescue her. Though he intends to go alone, Zeel, Allun, and Perlain recognize that this bold move by the Zebak threatens all citizens of the land and they join the quest. Riddles supplied by the feared witch of Rin help each to recognize how their unique talents are critical to the success of the adventure. Despite shipwreck, hardship, imprisonment and tragedy, they succeed in rescuing Rowan's sister and in solving the mystery of Rin's founding 300 years earlier. First published in Australia in 1999. (198 pages)

Where it's reviewed:
Booklist, March 1, 2002, page 1133
Bulletin of the Center for Children's Books, July 2002, page 417
Horn Book Guide, Fall 2002, page 381
Kirkus Reviews, May 1, 2002, page 666
School Library Journal, July 2002, page 124

Other books by the same author:
Rowan and the Ice Creepers, 2003 (Rowan of Rin #5)
Rowan and the Keeper of the Crystal, 2002 (Rowan of Rin #3)
Rowan and the Travelers, 2001 (Rowan of Rin #2)
Rowan of Rin, 2001 (Rowan of Rin #1)

Other books you might like:
Lloyd Alexander, *Taran Wanderer*, 1999
In the fourth book of the Chronicles of Prydain, Taran searches for answers to his identity.
Jenny Nimmo, *Midnight for Charlie Bone*, 2003
Charlie's discovery that he can hear the thoughts of photographed people leads to unexpected adventure for the ten-year-old student.
Philip Pullman, *His Dark Materials Trilogy*, 1996-2000
When the Dust increases on Lyra's world, evil follows, flowing from a rift in time and space.

J.K. Rowling, *The Harry Potter Series*, 1998-
Harry, a student at Hogwarts School of Witchcraft and Wizardry constantly battles the forces of evil that seek to diminish his potential power.

1220

COLBY RODOWSKY
BETH PECK, Illustrator

Jason Rat-a-Tat

(New York: Farrar Straus Giroux, 2002)

Subject(s): Individuality; Grandfathers; Family Life
Age range(s): Grades 2-4
Major character(s): Jason Miller, 9-Year-Old, Brother; Grandad, Grandfather; Andrew Miller, 11-Year-Old, Baseball Player; Emily Miller, 6-Year-Old, Soccer Player
Time period(s): 2000s (2002)
Locale(s): Maryland

Summary: Sports are a defining feature of the Miller family's life. Andrew and Emily's game and practice schedules determine meal times and menus, usually take-out pizza. Jason doesn't fit into this family pattern because he doesn't enjoy ball games and refuses to join a team despite his parents' insistence. Although Jason tries to express his interests no one really has time to listen to him until Granddad comes for a visit. Granddad sits with Jason at games, listens to him, observes his constant tapping on objects and notes his fascination with the marching bands at a Memorial Day parade. Before his visit ends Granddad buys ''unpresents'' for Andrew, Emily and Jason. Jason receives not only a snare drum, but also lessons. Now Jason has a schedule to post on the refrigerator right beside Andrew and Emily's and an answer for people who ask, ''What do you play, Jason?'' (68 pages)

Where it's reviewed:
Booklist, June 2002, page 1725
Bulletin of the Center for Children's Books, May 2002, page 339
Horn Book Guide, Fall 2002, page 363
Publishers Weekly, February 25, 2002, page 67
School Library Journal, April 2002, page 120

Other books by the same author:
Not Quite a Stranger, 2003
Hannah in Between, 2001
Not My Dog, 1999 (ALA Notable Children's Books)

Other books you might like:
Gail Herman, *Just Like Mike*, 2000
When Mike's mother remarries he becomes Michael Jordan. The kids in his new school expect him to play ball like a pro, but he's interested in acting.
Jennifer Richard Jacobson, *Winnie Dancing on Her Own*, 2001
Vanessa, Winnie and Zoe find a way to maintain their individuality and stay friends despite their different interests.
Mildred Pitts Walter, *Suitcase*, 1999
Because of Xander's height and big hands he's nicknamed Suitcase and expected to be good at basketball when his real love is art.

1221

COLBY RODOWSKY

Not Quite a Stranger

(New York: Farrar Straus Giroux, 2003)

Subject(s): Family Life; Stepfamilies; Brothers and Sisters
Age range(s): Grades 6-9
Major character(s): Charlotte "Tottie" Flannigan, 13-Year-Old; Zachary "Zach" Pearce, 17-Year-Old; David Flannigan, Doctor (pediatrician)
Time period(s): 2000s
Locale(s): Baltimore, Maryland

Summary: Up to the moment Zach appears at her front door, Tottie's life has been marred only by her mother's annoying habit of sharing their family life in her newspaper column, but this boy is another problem altogether. It seems that before Tottie's parents were married, her father David had a brief affair, which resulted in a pregnancy. Though both partners agreed that the baby should be adopted, the mother moved away and unbeknownst to David, raised Zachary herself. Now Zach's mother has died and he has no other family with whom he can live. Though Tottie sees only her side of the story and is bothered by the fact she's no longer oldest, Zach's grief and feelings of discomfort living with the Flannigans are also explored, in a touching story of shifting family relationships. (181 pages)

Where it's reviewed:
Book World, August 24, 2003, page 11
Booklist, November 15, 2003, page 593
Bulletin of the Center for Children's Books, October 2003, page 75
School Library Journal, September 2003, page 220
Voice of Youth Advocates, October 2003, page 318

Other books by the same author:
Clay, 2001
Spindrift, 2000
The Turnabout Shop, 1998
Remembering Mog, 1996
Sydney, Invincible, 1995

Other books you might like:
Sarah Ellis, *Out of the Blue*, 1995
When it's revealed that her mother had a child she put up for adoption, Megan has a hard time accepting her changed status in the family.
Cheryl Foggo, *One Thing That's True*, 1998
Roxanne learns that her older brother Joel's adopted and has run away because his real father, who's been in jail, wants to see him.
Angela Johnson, *Heaven*, 1998
Finding out that she's been raised by her aunt and uncle, Marley's angry to have never been told about her real parents.
Mavis Jukes, *Cinderella 2000*, 1999
Ashley's unhappy giving up her New Year's Eve date to stay home and babysit her twin stepsisters.
Susan Beth Pfeffer, *Most Precious Blood*, 1991
After her mother dies, Val is distressed to hear she's

adopted; the hard part now is to meet her birth mother and siblings.

1222

ERIC ROHMANN, Author/Illustrator

My Friend Rabbit

(Brookfield, CT: Roaring Brook Press, 2002)

Subject(s): Friendship; Animals; Problem Solving
Age range(s): Preschool-Grade 1
Major character(s): Rabbit, Rabbit, Friend; Mouse, Mouse, Friend
Time period(s): Indeterminate
Locale(s): Fictional Country

Summary: Mouse's friend Rabbit has good intentions, but trouble seems to come with each of his ideas. When Rabbit helps Mouse fly his plane, the plane ends up in a tree. Helpful Rabbit carries an assortment of large, disgruntled animals to the tree and then stacks them one atop the other to reach the toy airplane. Alas, the plan does not work exactly as Rabbit plans, but that just means he'll come up with another of his good ideas the next time Mouse needs a little help. (30 pages)

Where it's reviewed:
Booklist, May 15, 2002, page 1602
Children's Bookwatch, July 2002, page 1
Horn Book Guide, Fall 2002, page 342
Publishers Weekly, April 29, 2002, page 69
School Library Journal, May 2002, page 126

Awards the book has won:
Caldecott Medal, 2003
ALA Notable Children's Books, 2003

Other books by the same author:
The Cinder-Eyed Cats, 1997
Time Flies, 1994 (Caldecott Honor Book)

Other books you might like:
Holly Hobbie, *Toot & Puddle: You Are My Sunshine*, 1999
Puddle and Tulip try many ideas to cheer up their moping friend Toot.
Brian Lies, *Hamlet and the Magnificent Sandcastle*, 2001
Quince fashions a boat from his beach chair and umbrella to rescue Hamlet when the tide comes in and destroys Hamlet's sandcastle.
Arnold Lobel, *Frog and Toad Are Friends*, 1970
In an award-winning title Frog and Toad share some of the difficulties as well as the pleasures of friendship.

1223

DIANA REYNOLDS ROOME
JUDE DALY, Illustrator

The Elephant's Pillow

(New York: Farrar Straus Giroux, 2003)

Subject(s): Animals/Elephants; Sleep; Folk Tales
Age range(s): Grades K-2
Major character(s): Sing Lo, Child, Son
Time period(s): Indeterminate Past
Locale(s): Peking, China

Summary: Sing Lo, son of a wealthy merchant, has seen all the great sights in Peking, or so he thinks. When he hears of the imperial elephant, he demands to be taken to it. Sing Lo is told that the elephant has not slept since the death of the emperor. Sing Lo tries to imagine what the elephant would want and he brings it his favorite buns, a special bedtime drink and a soft silk pillow. Finally he scratches the elephant behind its ears until it falls asleep. Unaccustomed to doing things for himself Sing Lo gains a sense of accomplishment from his good deed. (32 pages)

Where it's reviewed:
Booklist, January 2004, page 882
Kirkus Reviews, October 1, 2003, page 1230
Publishers Weekly, December 8, 2003, page 60
School Library Journal, November 2003, page 114

Other books you might like:
Demi, *One Grain of Rice: A Mathematical Folktale*, 1997
  A village girl outsmarts the greedy raja and earns rice for her starving village.
Caroline Heaton, *Yi-Min and the Elephants: A Tale of Ancient China*, 2004
  Yi-Min, daughter of the Chinese emperor, begs her father to take her on an elephant hunt.
Shulamith Levey Oppenheim, *Ali and the Magic Stew*, 2002
  Selfish and spoiled, Ali learns compassion and humility in order to prepare the stew that will save his ill father's life.

1224

STEPHEN ROOS

Recycling George

(New York: Simon & Schuster, 2002)

Subject(s): Wealth; Poverty; Mills and Millwork
Age range(s): Grades 4-8
Major character(s): George Honiker, 12-Year-Old; Rennie Whitfield, 12-Year-Old, Wealthy; "Ga" Whitfield, Grandmother
Time period(s): 2000s
Locale(s): East Siena, Ohio

Summary: Living with his pregnant older sister and her husband while his father's off on another scheme to make money, George learns at school that the town's mill has closed its doors. Returning home, he finds his sister's family has left to find other work, taking the trailer with them and leaving him some money and a note telling where to find them. George uses the money to buy a birthday present for wealthy classmate Rennie and then bunks down in the Whitfield's boathouse. Invited to live with the family, George and Ga hit it off and, when she sees his artistic talent in his art project of recycled materials, offers to provide him with art lessons. Though George enjoys the lifestyle of the Whitfields, with their servants, opulent meals, horses for riding and luxurious home, he realizes his place is with his family. (136 pages)

Where it's reviewed:
Book Report, September 2002, page 57
Booklist, January 2002, page 859
Bulletin of the Center for Children's Books, April 2002, page 293

Horn Book, March 2002, page 218
School Library Journal, March 2002, page 238

Other books by the same author:
The Gypsies Never Came, 2001
You'll Miss Me When I'm Gone, 1988
Confessions of a Wayward Preppie, 1986

Other books you might like:
Priscilla Cummings, *Saving Grace*, 2003
  The Depression splits up her family and Grace lives with the Hammonds, but when they wish to adopt her, she knows it's time to return to her own family.
Alan Davidson, *The Bewitching of Alison Allbright*, 1989
  Ashamed of her poor family, Alison fantasizes about being wealthy, but when a grieving mother showers her with gifts, she appreciates her own shabby home.
Patrick McCabe, *The Butcher Boy*, 1993
  Orphaned when his alcoholic father and mentally ill mother die, Francie takes desperate steps to attain the status of those who are wealthy.

1225

BARRY ROOT, Author/Illustrator

Gumbrella

(New York: G.P. Putnam's Sons, 2002)

Subject(s): Animals, Treatment of; Animals; Animals/Elephants
Age range(s): Grades K-3
Major character(s): Gumbrella, Elephant, Sister; Trumbull, Elephant, Brother
Time period(s): Indeterminate
Locale(s): Fictional Country

Summary: Do-gooder Gumbrella relishes her role as "doctor" to ailing animals. She uses Trumbull as the ambulance to bring any ill or injured animals that he finds to her hospital. There she lavishes attention on them, ignoring their pleas to return to their own homes. In Gumbrella's opinion, no patient is ever quite well enough to depart before she's finished her plans and her ideas are never-ending. Finally, one mouse that has had enough steals the key and leads a bold escape of all the animals. Gumbrella is so depressed that Trumbull has to seek assistance from her former patients. They build a stretcher and carry Gumbrella into the forest where they "doctor" her just as she did them for many months. This is the first book also written by the well-known illustrator. (32 pages)

Where it's reviewed:
Booklist, November 15, 2002, page 612
Bulletin of the Center for Children's Books, December 2002, page 171
Horn Book, September 2002, page 559
Publishers Weekly, September 9, 2002, page 67
School Library Journal, November 2002, page 134

Awards the book has won:
Center for Children's Books Best Books, 2002

Other books you might like:
Quentin Blake, *Loveykins*, 2002
  Angela adores the baby bird she rescues but when it's

apparent that the grown bird is a bird of prey she finally lets it go and finds another hobby.

Joy Cowley, *The Video Shop Sparrow*, 1999
George and Harry have to call on the mayor to open the closed video store so a sparrow trapped inside can be freed.

Marjorie Newman, *Mole and the Baby Bird*, 2002
Mole lovingly cares for a baby bird and, to the surprise of Mole's parents, the bird lives but it wants to be free to fly and Mole must learn to let go.

Charlotte Voake, *Ginger Finds a Home*, 2003
In a prequel to *Ginger*, a stray cat gradually accepts the home offered by a young girl.

1226

PHYLLIS ROOT
HELEN OXENBURY, Illustrator

Big Momma Makes the World

(Cambridge, MA: Candlewick Press, 2003)

Subject(s): Creation; Mothers
Age range(s): Grades K-3
Major character(s): Big Momma, Mother, Inventor; Unnamed Character, Baby
Time period(s): Indeterminate Past
Locale(s): Earth

Summary: Big Momma and her baby burst out of the water calling for some light and then some dark. That's good for the first day according to Big Momma, but she's got more work to do to make the world a proper place. Day by day Big Momma adds sky and sun and moon so she knows day from night and she thinks her work is coming along real good but she's not finished. Big Momma calls for some earth, some grass, some shade trees and fruit to eat too. By the fifth day Big Momma thinks it's a might quiet so she creates fish, birds and other animals. By then Big Momma's housework is piling up so to save time she creates everything else on the sixth day with one big bang. Although she tells the newly created people to take care of this real nice world, she still has to keep an eye on them when the baby and the chores give her time to do so. (44 pages)

Where it's reviewed:
Booklist, January 2003, page 881
Bulletin of the Center for Children's Books, February 2003, page 247
Horn Book, March 2003, page 205
Riverbank Review, Summer 2003, page 28
School Library Journal, March 2003, page 206

Awards the book has won:
School Library Journal Best Books, 2003
Booklist Editors' Choice, 2003

Other books by the same author:
If You Want to See a Caribou, 2004
The Name Quilt, 2003
Oliver Finds His Way, 2002

Other books you might like:
John Burningham, *Whaddayamean*, 1999
When God awakens from his nap he's disappointed to see that his creation has been mistreated and enlists two children to help change things.

Julius Lester, *What a Truly Cool World*, 1999
God thinks he can call it quits after creating Earth but bossy Shaniqua considers it boring and demands a bit more input to make it a truly cool world.

Harriet Ziefert, *First He Made the Sun*, 2000
Simple rhyming text describes the seven days in which God creates the world and its many creatures.

1227

PHYLLIS ROOT
MARGOT APPLE, Illustrator

The Name Quilt

(New York: Farrar Straus Giroux, 2003)

Subject(s): Quilts; Grandparents; Family
Age range(s): Grades K-2
Major character(s): Sadie, Child, Relative (granddaughter); Grandma, Grandmother
Time period(s): 2000s (2003)
Locale(s): United States

Summary: During summer vacations at Grandma's, Sadie looks forward to being tucked in under the name quilt. It features the names of many different family members and Sadie's grandmother will tell her a story about whatever name she picks. One day, Sadie and Grandma wash the quilt and hang it out to dry while they go fishing. A surprise summer storm blows away all the laundry, including the quilt. Sadie is upset, but Grandma remembers all the names and together they make a new name quilt that includes Sadie's name too. (32 pages)

Where it's reviewed:
Booklist, March 15, 2003, page 1333
School Library Journal, May 2003, page 129

Other books by the same author:
Ten Sleepy Sheep, 2004
Big Momma Makes the World, 2002
What's That Noise?, 2002

Other books you might like:
Jeannine Atkins, *A Name on the Quilt: A Story of Remembrance*, 1999
Lauren helps her family make a panel for the NAMES Quilt in honor of her Uncle Ron who died of AIDS.

Pat Brisson, *Star Blanket*, 2003
Laura goes to sleep under the star blanket, which used to belong to her father and features a star for every member of the family.

Patricia Polacco, *The Keeping Quilt*, 1991
A quilt made by a Jewish immigrant family from the family's old clothes is passed down from generation to generation.

1228

PHYLLIS ROOT
CHRISTOPHER DENISE, Illustrator

Oliver Finds His Way

(Cambridge, MA: Candlewick Press, 2002)

Subject(s): Animals/Bears; Missing Persons; Problem Solving
Age range(s): Preschool-Kindergarten
Major character(s): Oliver, Bear, Son; Mama, Bear, Mother; Papa, Bear, Father
Time period(s): Indeterminate
Locale(s): Fictional Country

Summary: As Mama hangs out the wash and Papa rakes the yard Oliver chases a leaf so far that when he stops he realizes he's lost at the edge of the woods. At first Oliver cries when he can't figure out the way home, but then he has a better idea and he begins to roar. Louder and louder he roars until he hears a roar in the distance and then another. Mama and Papa are answering him so that Oliver can follow the sound right back to his own yard and hugs from Mama and Papa. (40 pages)

Where it's reviewed:
Booklist, September 15, 2002, page 242
Bulletin of the Center for Children's Books, December 2002, page 172
Horn Book, January 2003, page 60
Publishers Weekly, August 19, 2002, page 87
School Library Journal, October 2002, page 126

Awards the book has won:
School Library Journal Best Books, 2002
Center for Children's Books Best Books, 2002

Other books by the same author:
Rattletrap Car, 2001 (Booklist Editors' Choice)
Kiss the Cow!, 2000
What Baby Wants, 1998 (School Library Journal Best Books)

Other books you might like:
Jez Alborough, *Where's My Teddy?*, 1992
    As Eddie searches the dark woods for his lost teddy bear he encounters a large bear with a similar problem.
Geoffrey Hayes, *Patrick and the Big Bully*, 2001
    Little bear Patrick uses his loudest roar to frighten away bully Big Bear.
Ursel Scheffler, *Who Has Time for Little Bear?*, 1998
    Mama and Papa are too busy to play with Little Bear so he goes walking in the woods and meets another bear cub that's eager to play.
Martin Waddell, *Small Bear Lost*, 1996
    After Small bear is forgotten on a train he manages to find his way home to the little girl who lost him.

1229

DEBORAH LEE ROSE
LYNN MUNSINGER, Illustrator

Birthday Zoo

(Morton Grove, IL: Albert Whitman & Company, 2002)

Subject(s): Birthdays; Animals; Stories in Rhyme

Age range(s): Grades K-2
Major character(s): Unnamed Character, 7-Year-Old
Time period(s): Indeterminate
Locale(s): United States

Summary: Zoo animals plan a party for one lucky child. They decorate, blow up balloons, wrap presents, act silly, set the table and plan the games. Everyone helps to blow out the candles on the cake and wish the birthday boy a happy birthday. At least, that's what he imagines as he sits, eating cake, surrounded by all his stuffed animals. (24 pages)

Where it's reviewed:
Booklist, September 15, 2002, page 242
Horn Book, November 2002, page 738
Publishers Weekly, September 2, 2002, page 78
School Library Journal, October 2002, page 126

Other books by the same author:
Ocean Babies, 2004
One Nighttime Sea, 2003
Twelve Days of Kindergarten: A Counting Book, 2003

Other books you might like:
Lee Davis, *P.B. Bear's Birthday Party*, 1994
    Stuffed-animal friends gather to help P.B. Bear celebrate his birthday.
Michael Garland, *Last Night at the Zoo*, 2001
    Bored zoo animals sneak away for a night of dinner and dancing.
Helen Oxenbury, *It's My Birthday*, 1993
    Animal friends bring the ingredients needed for a young child to make a birthday cake, assist with the cooking and help to eat the finished product.

1230

LIZ ROSENBERG

17: A Novel in Prose Poems

(Chicago: Marcato/Cricket, 2002)

Subject(s): Romance; Mental Illness; Poetry
Age range(s): Grades 9-12
Major character(s): Stephanie, 17-Year-Old, Writer (poet); Dennis "Denny" Pistil, 11th Grader, Writer (poet); Ben, Wrestler
Time period(s): 2000s
Locale(s): Massachusetts

Summary: Falling in love with a fellow poet, Stephanie is at first in awe of Denny: his father's a famous attorney who's worked for the Queen of England, Denny attended Eton in England the last two years, and he's supposed to go to Oxford for college. Their poetry links them and their relationship blooms, though Stephanie worries about everything, from becoming pregnant to fear she'll become bipolar like her mother, until finally she battles anorexia. The realization that Denny is gay and really in love with a good friend of his sends her spiraling downward until she accepts that she and Denny can't have a relationship. Releasing him also releases her to dare dating Ben, whose wrestling ability and dislike of poetry set him apart from her usual interests, in this compelling prose poem. (142 pages)

Where it's reviewed:

Booklist, November 15, 2002, page 589

Bulletin of the Center for Children's Books, February 2003, page 248

Publishers Weekly, September 30, 2002, page 72

School Library Journal, November 2002, page 174

Voice of Youth Advocates, April 2003, page 59

Other books by the same author:

Roots & Flowers: Poets and Poems on Family, 2001

Light-Gathering Poems, 2000

Earth-Shattering Poems, 1998

Other books you might like:

April Halprin Wayland, *Girl Coming in for a Landing*, 2002
 A young girl writes a series of poems organized around the seasons of the school year and tells of the little and big things in her life.

Margaret Willey, *Saving Lenny*, 1990
 Foregoing college to live with Lenny, Jesse finally realizes his depression is destroying their relationship.

Ellen Wittlinger, *Hard Love*, 1999
 John thinks he's found the love for which he's been searching when he meets Marisol, only to discover she's in love with another girl.

1231

CAROL ROTH
PAMELA PAPARONE, Illustrator

The Little School Bus

(New York: Cheshire Studio Book/North-South Books, 2002)

Subject(s): School Life; Transportation; Stories in Rhyme
Age range(s): Preschool-Kindergarten
Time period(s): Indeterminate
Locale(s): Fictional Country

Summary: In a cumulative tale, a school bus picks up students, each identified by a rhyming characteristic. The bus transports a hairy bear, a pig in a wig, a sleepy sheep, a goat in a coat, a quick chick and a squirmy worm. All day while the students attend school the bus waits. At dismissal the students board the bus and ride it home from school. (32 pages)

Where it's reviewed:

Booklist, August 2002, page 1976

Bulletin of the Center for Children's Books, September 2002, page 33

Publishers Weekly, May 13, 2002, page 69

School Library Journal, July 2002, page 97

Other books by the same author:

Who Will Tuck Me in Tonight?, 2004

My Little Valentine, 2003

Little Bunny's Sleepless Night, 1999

Ten Dirty Pigs; Ten Clean Pigs, 1999

Other books you might like:

Suzanne Bloom, *The Bus for Us*, 2001
 As each of a variety of vehicles nears the bus stop new student Tess asks her older brother, ''Is that the bus for us, Gus?''

Donald Crews, *School Bus*, 1984
 School buses deliver children to school and carry them safely home again in all kinds of weather.

Daniel Kirk, *Bus Stop, Bus Go!*, 2001
 A rhyming tale describes the excitement caused by an escaped hamster in the bus during the morning ride to school.

1232

S.L. ROTTMAN

Shadow of a Doubt

(Atlanta: Peachtree, 2003)

Subject(s): Brothers; Family Problems; Clubs
Age range(s): Grades 7-10
Major character(s): Ernest ''Shadow'' Thompson, 15-Year-Old; Daniel Thompson, Criminal, Brother; Vernon Thomas, 9th Grader
Time period(s): 2000s
Locale(s): Colorado

Summary: The day Shadow turns 15 is a momentous one for his family as that's the age his older brother Daniel was when he ran away. No one has heard from him since and Shadow, who adored his older brother, no longer trusts anyone. Beginning high school, Shadow's ready for a new chapter in his life. He makes friends with Vernon, whose locker is next to his, joins the forensics team to learn to argue, and runs afoul of the disciplinary principal over his black clothes and sunglasses. Then Daniel calls from jail, where he's being held on a murder charge, and Shadow's attempt at a new life dissolves. Every event in his family now revolves around Daniel and Shadow's asked to put aside his plans to let his brother take center stage in this powerful tale of family life. (172 pages)

Where it's reviewed:

Booklist, November 15, 2003, page 593

Bulletin of the Center for Children's Books, January 2004, page 205

Library Media Connection, January 2004, page 68

School Library Journal, January 2004, page 134

Voice of Youth Advocates, December 2003, page 406

Other books by the same author:

Slalom, 2004

Stetson, 2002

Head Above Water, 1999

Hero, 1997

Rough Waters, 1997

Other books you might like:

Caroline B. Cooney, *Don't Blame the Music*, 1986
 Susan and her older rock musician sister don't get along, especially when her sister returns home after her career fails.

Gail Giles, *Dead Girls Don't Write Letters*, 2003
 Supposedly dead, Sunny's sister Jazz shocks the whole family by coming home, though Sunny wonders if this Jazz is an imposter.

Anita Horrocks, *What They Don't Know*, 1999
 Kelly's younger sister Hannah is on a path of self-destruc-

tion, complete with drugs, alcohol and vandalism, and Kelly can't figure out why.

1233

S.L. ROTTMAN

Stetson

(New York: Viking, 2002)

Subject(s): Brothers and Sisters; Alcoholism; Automobiles
Age range(s): Grades 9-12
Major character(s): Stetson "Stet", 17-Year-Old; Jason, Businessman (salvage yard owner); Kayla, 14-Year-Old
Time period(s): 2000s
Locale(s): United States

Summary: Abandoned by his mother when he was only three, Stet's been left to live with his alcoholic father, who spends all his away-from-work time and money at the local bar. Stet earns his own funds in order to eat, so he paints and designs T-shirts, works at a salvage yard refurbishing cars and takes money from schoolmates to disrupt classes. His main goal is to become the first person in his family to graduate from high school, but at times it seems he'll never achieve that goal, though he's certainly smart enough. The only stabilizing influence in his life has been Jason, owner of the salvage yard, who's now dying of cancer. Stet's latest escapade to earn money at school almost gets him expelled. And when he comes home from school one day, he finds he has a sister, born after his mother left him. Kayla has nowhere to go now that their mother has died, so she's sitting in his dad's trailer. Stet and Kayla find a lot in common in a short time and when their father causes an accident that injures Kayla, Stet knows it's time for the two of them to leave and start life anew. Jason's help makes it all possible. (222 pages)

Where it's reviewed:
Booklist, April 1, 2002, page 1320
Bulletin of the Center for Children's Books, March 2002, page 254
Kliatt, March 2002, page 12
School Library Journal, April 2002, page 156
Voice of Youth Advocates, February 2002, page 438

Awards the book has won:
ALA Best Books for Young Adults, 2003

Other books by the same author:
Slalom, 2004
Shadow of a Doubt, 2003
Head Above Water, 1999
Hero, 1997
Rough Waters, 1997

Other books you might like:
Alden R. Carter, *Up Country*, 1989
   When his alcoholic mother finally self-destructs, a teenager finds a haven with distant relatives who live in the country.
Ben Mikaelsen, *Touching Spirit Bear*, 2001
   Cole's mean, arrogant and vicious, traits he's learned from his abusive father, until he's sent to an isolated Alaskan island to rethink his ways.

Gary Paulsen, *The Beet Fields: Memories of a Sixteenth Summer*, 2000
   Escaping from his alcoholic mother, the boy leaves and works in a beet field, then a carnival and finally enlists in the army, maturing with each job.

1234

J.K. ROWLING

Harry Potter and the Order of the Phoenix

(New York: Scholastic, 2003)

Series: Harry Potter. Book 5
Subject(s): Magic; Growing Up; Fantasy
Age range(s): Grades 8-Adult
Major character(s): Harry Potter, 15-Year-Old, Wizard; Professor Snape, Teacher, Wizard; Professor Dumbledore, Teacher, Wizard
Time period(s): Indeterminate
Locale(s): England

Summary: Harry may be a wizard, but that doesn't preclude his having the usual troubles of a teenager. At Hogwarts Academy, all the adults seem to have become stupid or evil. When Harry is sent away for his own protection, he feels even more an outsider, as the adult wizards of the Order of the Phoenix refuse to let him take any part in the plans for the final confrontation with Voldemort. Little wonder that Harry has plenty of time to brood on some ugly revelations about his father and Professor Snape. In fact, Harry resents almost everything, from his treatment by Dumbledore, to his father's imperfections, the secrecy of the Order and his frustrated attempts at romance. Harry is discovering who he is, and it's a painful process. The confrontation with Voldemort is chilling but hardly less so than Dumbledore's final revelations. (870 pages)

Where it's reviewed:
Booklist, July 2003, page 1842
Horn Book, September 2003, page 619
Publishers Weekly, June 30, 2003, page 79
School Library Journal, August 2003, page 165
Voice of Youth Advocates, August 2003, page 240

Awards the book has won:
ALA Best Books for Young Adults, 2004

Other books by the same author:
Fantastic Beasts and Where to Find Them, 2001
Harry Potter and the Goblet of Fire, 2000 (Harry Potter Book 4)
Harry Potter and the Chamber of Secrets, 1999 (Harry Potter Book 2)
Harry Potter and the Prisoner of Azkaban, 1999 (Harry Potter Book 3)
Harry Potter and the Sorcerer's Stone, 1998 (Harry Potter Book 1)

Other books you might like:
Diana Wynne Jones, *The Merlin Conspiracy*, 2003
   An ordinary guy gets caught up in a magical battle and despairs of finding a way to impress the pretty girl who dragged him into the mess.

Caroline Stevermer, *A College of Magics*, 1994
Against her will, Faris is sent off to Greenlaw College to be educated in magic.

Jonathan Stroud, *The Amulet of Samarkand*, 2003
An ancient spirit doesn't think much of the young conjurer who is forcing him to do his bidding.

1235

NICOLE RUBEL, Author/Illustrator

Grody's Not So Golden Rules

(San Diego: Silver Whistle/Harcourt, Inc., 2003)

Subject(s): Animals/Dogs; Behavior; Schools
Age range(s): Grades K-3
Major character(s): Grody, Dog, Child
Time period(s): 2000s (2003)
Locale(s): United States

Summary: Tired of all the seemingly pointless rules he has to follow, Grody decides to make up some rules of his own. Rule number two, for example, is to not brush your teeth, because they will just be dirty again after you eat breakfast. Grody's rules may be more fun, but the book ends with a look at what would happen if Grody followed all his own rules. He'd be dirty, cavity-ridden and failing school. (40 pages)

Where it's reviewed:
Booklist, March 1, 2003, page 1203
Bulletin of the Center for Children's Books, June 2003, page 420
Publishers Weekly, April 14, 2003, page 70
School Library Journal, July 2003, page 105

Other books by the same author:
A Cowboy Named Ernestine, 2001
Swampy Alligator, 1980
Greedy Greeny, 1979
Rotten Ralph, 1976

Other books you might like:
Babette Cole, *Bad Habits!*, 1999
Lucretzia Crum's parents search for ways to calm her bad habits.

Amy MacDonald, *Quentin Fenton Herter III*, 2002
Quentin follows all the rules properly, but his evil shadow has some bad behavior.

David Roberts, *Dirty Bertie*, 2003
Bertie's family tries to teach him good manners.

David Shannon, *No, David!*, 1998
David breaks all of his mother's rules, but is reassured in the end that, yes, she loves him despite his behavior.

1236

NICOLE RUBEL, Author/Illustrator

No More Vegetables!

(New York: Farrar Straus Giroux, 2002)

Subject(s): Food; Gardens and Gardening; Health
Age range(s): Grades K-2
Major character(s): Ruthie, Child, Daughter; Mom, Mother, Gardener

Time period(s): 2000s (2002)
Locale(s): United States

Summary: Ruthie declares that she will eat no more vegetables, unless potato chips and french fries are considered vegetables. Mom takes her to the doctor and the teacher lectures about food groups and healthy eating, but still Ruthie refuses to devour a vegetable. Mom finally agrees that if Ruthie will help her work in the garden then Mom will not put vegetables on her plate. Ruthie loves this arrangement. She enjoys being responsible for planting the seeds, pulling weeds, and saving the garden from slugs. During the summer, Ruthie plans a picnic in the garden but her dog eats her food. Feeling hungry, Ruthie picks first one vegetable, and then another, until she's happily sampled all the fruits (and vegetables) of her labors. Now when she tells Mom "No more vegetables . . ." she means, not until dinner. (32 pages)

Where it's reviewed:
Booklist, December 15, 2002, page 769
Horn Book Guide, Spring 2003, page 52
Kirkus Reviews, June 15, 2002, page 887
Publishers Weekly, July 1, 2002, page 78
School Library Journal, August 2002, page 166

Other books by the same author:
A Cowboy Named Ernestine, 2001
Conga Crocodile, 1993
It Came From the Swamp, 1988

Other books you might like:
Vivian French, *Oliver's Vegetables*, 1995
Although Oliver claims to only eat potatoes Grandpa's idea has him sampling different vegetables from the garden.

Susanna Gretz, *Rabbit Food*, 1999
John thinks he's the only one in his rabbit family that doesn't like vegetables until Uncle Bunny comes to visit.

Russell Hoban, *Bread and Jam for Frances*, 1965
When Frances refuses to eat anything other than bread and jam she is served a steady diet of it until she's eager to try something new.

1237

LAURA RUBY

Lily's Ghosts

(New York: HarperCollins, 2003)

Subject(s): Ghosts; Mothers and Daughters; Secrets
Age range(s): Grades 5-8
Major character(s): Lily Crabtree, 13-Year-Old; Wesley, Uncle (great uncle); Julep, Cat
Time period(s): 2000s
Locale(s): Cape May, New Jersey

Summary: Following the breakup of her mother's latest romance, Lily is dismayed to learn they'll be spending the winter in her great uncle Wesley's summer house, a Victorian in the now-deserted resort town of Cape May. As soon as they move in, Lily stashes a ghastly portrait of one of her ancestors in the closet, after which a series of strange events begins. Though Lily can't see anyone, Julep always seems alert to some mysterious activity; her mother's Kewpie doll disappears and then reappears; Lily's shoes fill with jam; and smoke smells emanate from the attic. It becomes obvious that Uncle Wesley's home is filled with ghosts of past relatives and one of them is trying to reveal family secrets to Lily in this author's first novel. (258 pages)

Where it's reviewed:
Bulletin of the Center for Children's Books, September 2003, page 31
Kirkus Reviews, July 1, 2003, page 914
Publishers Weekly, August 11, 2003, page 281
Publishers Weekly, January 2004, page 66
School Library Journal, December 2003, page 160

Awards the book has won:
Center for Children's Books Best Books, 2003

Other books you might like:
Janice Del Negro, *Lucy Dove*, 1998
    Determination enables Lucy Dove to complete a challenge to sew a pair of trousers in a haunted graveyard so she can win a sack of gold.
Eileen Dunlop, *The Ghost by the Sea*, 1996
    Two cousins try to solve the mysterious drowning of their ancestor Milly so her spirit can rest and stop haunting their grandparent's home.
Betty Ren Wright, *A Ghost in the Family*, 1998
    Chad accompanies a friend on a two-week stay at her aunt's boarding house and discovers a ghost haunting his room.

1238

JAMES RUMFORD, Author/Illustrator

Nine Animals and the Well
(Boston: Houghton Mifflin, 2003)

Subject(s): Birthdays; Friendship; Mathematics
Age range(s): Grades K-3
Major character(s): Unnamed Character, Royalty; Unnamed Character, Monkey, Friend; Unnamed Character, Rhinoceros, Friend
Time period(s): Indeterminate Past
Locale(s): India

Summary: Nine animals receive invitations to the raja-king's birthday and each brings what it thinks will be the perfect gift. However as they meet up along the way, each thinks that the other's present is better. When the monkey, the first animal on the road, meets up with the rhino, the monkey proudly shows off his perfect present, a loaf of bread. Rhino's two ripe mangoes seem more impressive though and so the bread is tossed. This pattern continues until the ninth friend, a peacock brings a present on which they all can agree: nine gold coins. However, as the coins are being shown off they fall into a well and the nine animals arrive at the birthday celebration empty handed. The raja-king assures them that their friendship is the best present of all. (32 pages)

Where it's reviewed:
Booklist, July 2003, page 1898
Bulletin of the Center for Children's Books, June 2003, page 421
Five Owls, 2004, page 83

Horn Book, May/June 2003, page 337
School Library Journal, June 2003, page 115

Other books by the same author:
Calabash Cat and His Amazing Journey, 2003
The Island-Below-the-Star, 1998
The Cloudmakers, 1996

Other books you might like:
Demi, *One Grain of Rice: A Mathematical Folktale*, 1997
    A village girl is able to outsmart a greedy raja and get food for her village by requesting one grain of rice, doubled every day for 30 days.
Ilse Plume, *The Bremen Town Musicians*, 1980
    A donkey, dog, cat and rooster set out together on a journey to their new lives as musicians. Caldecott Honor Book.
Lauren Thompson, *One Riddle, One Answer*, 2001
    When the time comes for Persian princess Aziza to marry she devises a mathematical riddle and declares she will marry the man who can solve it.

1239

KRISTINE KATHRYN RUSCH

The Disappeared
(New York: NAL/Roc, 2002)

Series: Retrieval Artist
Subject(s): Detection; Science Fiction
Age range(s): Grades 9-Adult
Major character(s): Noelle DeRicci, Detective—Police; Miles Flint, Detective—Police
Time period(s): Indeterminate Future
Locale(s): Moon (Earth's) (Armstrong Dome)

Summary: Detective Miles Flint is learning his new job the hard way. His partner Noelle DeRicci is a seasoned officer, but that doesn't mean she knows how to stay out of trouble, it means she knows how to find it. The two are working three cases and Flint tries hard to keep DeRicci from getting herself suspended before they're solved. Their first case involves a female attorney, obviously on the run, who's very good at concealing information from the detectives. Their second case involves two children who appear to be kidnapping victims. In the third case, they are confronted with the bodies of what appears to be an alien vengeance killing. DeRicci surprises Flint when she turns out to be quite adept at negotiating with the three different alien species involved. As Flint and DeRicci dig deeper, they find a common thread in all the killings, Disappearance Inc., which was involved in helping someone escape alien justice in the past. (384 pages)

Where it's reviewed:
Analog Science Fiction and Fact, December 2002, page 131
Booklist, June 1, 2002, page 1698
Science Fiction Chronicle, July 2002, page 52

Other books by the same author:
Extremes, 2003 (Retrieval Artist)
The Retrieval Artist and Other Stories, 2002
Thin Air, 2000

Other books you might like:

Greg Bear, *Slant*, 1997

Detective Mary Choy investigates a series of violent deaths that appear to be connected with virtual reality equipment.

Pat Cadigan, *Tea from an Empty Cup*, 1998

The victims are alone in their virtual reality rooms when they die, so how are they being killed?

Denise Vitola, *The Red Sky File*, 1999

In a future dystopia, a detective finds that the fact that she turns into a werewolf with the full moon is both a handicap and an advantage.

1240

MARISABINA RUSSO

House of Sports
(New York: Greenwillow, 2002)

Subject(s): Sports/Basketball; Grandmothers; Interpersonal Relations
Age range(s): Grades 5-8
Major character(s): Jim Malone, 12-Year-Old, Basketball Player; Nana, Grandmother; Lisa Mondini, Basketball Player
Time period(s): 2000s
Locale(s): New York

Summary: Jim's life revolves around basketball, even though he's a little short and has to be content with a point guard position. Nana refers to his home as the "house of sports" as that's all Jim ever seems to do, even if she'd like him to enjoy a museum now and then. A Holocaust survivor, Nana speaks with a German accent and is sometimes too slow for Jim's energy level, though she loves him and is quick to tell him so. Jim's dog Jake dies, followed by Nana's stroke, and for the first time Jim rethinks some of his goals. His friend Lisa joins Jim as part of their school delegation for an essay reading contest, an experience that helps Jim when he travels to Washington, DC to deliver Nana's speech to a symposium on Holocaust survivors. Realizing that there's a world beyond basketball, and that his Nana was right to try to show it to him, is the first sign that Jim's beginning to grow up. (188 pages)

Where it's reviewed:
Booklist, March 15, 2002, page 1258
Bulletin of the Center for Children's Books, March 2002, page 254
Publishers Weekly, January 21, 2002, page 90
School Library Journal, April 2002, page 156
Voice of Youth Advocates, February 2002, page 438

Other books by the same author:
Always Remember Me: How One Family Survived World War II, 2005 (nonfiction)

Other books you might like:
Bruce Brooks, *The Moves Make the Man*, 1984
Black Jerome and white Bix become friends through their love of basketball in a story that is about more than sports.
Gayle Friesen, *Men of Stone*, 2000
Bullied into giving up his dancing lessons, Ben is strength-

ened by Frieda's visit as he learns of her survival during Stalin's regime.
Sybil Rosen, *Speed of Light*, 1999
Upset by the racism and anti-semitism she sees, Audrey is ready to listen to the Holocaust stories of her distance cousin, Tante Pesel.

1241

PAM MUNOZ RYAN
DAVID MCPHAIL, Illustrator

Mud Is Cake
(New York: Hyperion Books for Children, 2002)

Subject(s): Imagination; Playing; Stories in Rhyme
Age range(s): Preschool-Kindergarten
Time period(s): Indeterminate
Locale(s): Fictional Country

Summary: For an imaginative child mud could be cake just as juice can pass for tea in a pretend game. Imagination can put you on a stage before an appreciative audience or drumming along in a marching band. Ordinary things can take one on extraordinary adventures with just a bit of willingness to believe in the magic of child's play. (32 pages)

Where it's reviewed:
Booklist, June 2002, page 1743
Horn Book Guide, Fall 2002, page 312
Publishers Weekly, February 18, 2002, page 94
Riverbank Review, Summer 2002, page 33
School Library Journal, May 2002, page 126

Other books by the same author:
Mice and Beans, 2001 (ALA Notable Children's Book)
Amelia and Eleanor Go for a Ride, 1999 (ALA Notable Children's Book)
Armadillos Sleep in Dugouts: And Other Places Animals Live, 1997

Other books you might like:
Ruth Brown, *Mad Summer Night's Dream*, 1999
Fantastic illustrations interpret the nonsense of a childish rhyme in which nothing is as it should be.
Eve Bunting, *Little Badger, Terror of the Seven Seas*, 2001
Little Badger uses his imagination to become a pirate who is careful to come home in time for dinner.
Julian Scheer, *Rain Make Applesauce*, 1964
Whimsical illustrations in this Caldecott Honor Book support the rhythmic "silly talk" of the story.

1242

JOANNE RYDER
STEVEN KELLOGG, Illustrator

Big Bear Ball
(New York: HarperCollins Publishers, 2002)

Subject(s): Dancing; Animals/Bears; Stories in Rhyme
Age range(s): Preschool-Kindergarten
Time period(s): Indeterminate
Locale(s): Fictional Country

Summary: Bears of all shapes and sizes gather to dance the night away under a full moon. Arriving by hot air balloon the colorfully dressed bears sway and stomp to the band's lively tunes until the sun begins to rise. As day dawns the bears float away with plans to gather again the next time the moon is full. (32 pages)

Where it's reviewed:
Booklist, May 1, 2002, page 1536
Bulletin of the Center for Children's Books, October 2002, page 77
Horn Book Guide, Fall 2002, page 312
Publishers Weekly, April 29, 2002, page 68
School Library Journal, June 2002, page 110

Other books by the same author:
Mouse Tail Moon, 2002
Bears Out There, 1995
Dancers in the Garden, 1992 (Notable Children's Books in the Language Arts)

Other books you might like:
Debi Gliori, *Polar Bolero: A Bedtime Dance*, 2001
Wide-awake children and animals assemble on a grassy knoll to dance the Polar Bolero until the activity tires them and they drift home to bed.
Dee Lillegard, *The Big Bug Ball*, 1999
Insects of all kinds come together for the Big Bug Ball.
Linda Lowery, *Twist with a Burger, Jitter with a Bug*, 1995
A lively read-aloud tale encourages movement to the syncopated rhythm of the text.

1243

CYNTHIA RYLANT
G. BRIAN KARAS, Illustrator

The Case of the Sleepy Sloth
(New York: Greenwillow/HarperCollins Publishers, 2002)

Series: High-Rise Private Eyes. Case #005
Subject(s): Mystery and Detective Stories; Animals; Humor
Age range(s): Grades 1-2
Major character(s): Bunny Brown, Rabbit, Detective; Jack Jones, Raccoon, Detective; Ramon, Dog
Time period(s): Indeterminate
Locale(s): Fictional Country

Summary: Bunny and Jack head to the docks for a pizza picnic lunch. Despite Bunny's admonition Jack just can't stop himself from feeding the begging seagulls. Soon the pizza is gone and Jack and Bunny are still hungry. A dog snooping on a nearby boat distracts Jack and gives him a new case to solve. Ramon is searching for the lawn chair that vanished from his houseboat. While standing on the dock questioning Ramon, Bunny's notepad blows away in the wind. Seeing the other items that come by gives Bunny the clue she needs to track down Ramon's missing lawn chair. Soon they find it, but it's occupied by a sleeping sloth they are unable to awaken so Ramon will get his chair back when the sloth's nap is completed. (48 pages)

Where it's reviewed:
Booklist, September 15, 2002, page 242
Horn Book Guide, Spring 2003, page 63

Kirkus Reviews, June 15, 2002, page 888
Publishers Weekly, July 1, 2002, page 81
School Library Journal, December 2002, page 108

Other books by the same author:
The Case of the Baffled Bear, 2004 (High-Rise Private Eyes Case 007)
The Case of the Fidgety Fox, 2003 (High-Rise Private Eyes Case 006)
The Case of the Puzzling Possum, 2002 (High-Rise Private Eyes Case 003)

Other books you might like:
David A. Adler, *Young Cam Jansen and the Double Beach Mystery*, 2002
A simple walk on the beach presents Cam with a mystery when an umbrella serving as her location marker seems to have moved from the spot she remembers.
Robert Quackenbush, *Detective Mole and the Circus Mystery*, 1980
On the day of her wedding, Melba the cow vanishes from the circus. Detective Mole finds her in time for the ceremony.
Marjorie Weinman Sharmat, *The Nate the Great Series*, 1972-
In a mystery series for beginning readers, Nate follows one clue after another in the style of Sherlock Holmes.

1244

CYNTHIA RYLANT
DIANE GOODE, Illustrator

Christmas in the Country
(New York: The Blue Sky Press/Scholastic, Inc., 2002)

Subject(s): Christmas; Country Life; Grandparents
Age range(s): Grades K-3
Major character(s): Unnamed Character, Child, Relative (granddaughter); Unnamed Character, Grandmother, Aged Person; Unnamed Character, Grandfather, Aged Person
Time period(s): Indeterminate Past
Locale(s): West Virginia

Summary: Through the eyes of a young girl, a simple Christmas in the country comes alive. Together the girl and her grandparents put lights on the house and hang a wreath. While it is the grandfather's job to cut a tree from the nearby woods, it is the girl and her grandmother collecting the boxes of old ornaments to lovingly unpack and use to decorate the tree. Church services on Christmas Eve and Christmas day are a tradition in the country as is the doll Santa brings each year. All Christmas day neighbors and relatives stop by to visit and share food. With the New Year, the ornaments are packed until the next Christmas in the country. (32 pages)

Where it's reviewed:
Booklist, September 15, 2002, page 247
Horn Book, November 2002, page 738
Kirkus Reviews, November 1, 2002, page 1625
Publishers Weekly, September 23, 2002, page 34
School Library Journal, October 2002, page 63

Other books by the same author:
Little Whistle, 2001

The Great Gracie Chase: Stop That Dog!, 2001 (IRA Children's Choices)

When I Was Young in the Mountains, 1982 (Caldecott Honor Book)

Other books you might like:

Eve Bunting, *Night Tree*, 1991
By the light of the Christmas Eve moon a family decorates a tree in the woods with seeds, apples and popcorn for the animals.

Barbara M. Joosse, *A Houseful of Christmas*, 2001
A houseful of visiting relatives become overnight guests when they become snowed in while celebrating Christmas with Granny.

Andrea Davis Pinkney, *Mim's Christmas Jam*, 2001
Homemade jam and family togetherness make this Christmas celebration complete.

1245

CYNTHIA RYLANT

God Went to Beauty School

(New York: HarperTempest, 2003)

Subject(s): God; Religion
Age range(s): Grades 7-12
Major character(s): God, Deity
Time period(s): 2000s
Locale(s): Earth

Summary: Twenty-three poems humanize God as the author envisions Him in various every day situations, from opening a nail shop to having a head cold with Mother Teresa waiting on him. The sight from atop Mount Everest makes him wonder how anyone can ever feel anger. He acts just like everyone else, but doesn't understand how humans have lost their ability to appreciate the big and little moments in life. God makes spaghetti, roller blades, sees a movie and watches cable. Then like all other humans he dies, and better understands that process, in this humorous rejoicing of God's love and caring. (56 pages)

Where it's reviewed:

Booklist, August 2003, page 1983
Bulletin of the Center for Children's Books, July 2003, page 461
Horn Book, July 2003, page 474
Kirkus Reviews, June 15, 2003, page 864
Voice of Youth Advocates, August 2003, page 229

Awards the book has won:

ALA Best Books for Young Adults, 2004
ALA Quick Picks for Reluctant Young Adult Readers, 2004

Other books by the same author:

The Heavenly Village, 1999
The Islander, 1998
I Had Seen Castles, 1993

Other books you might like:

Michael Morpurgo, *The War of Jenkins' Ear*, 1995
At boarding school Toby meets Simon Christopher, who claims to be the reincarnated Jesus Christ.

Mary E. Pearson, *David v. God*, 2000
David realizes he's supposed to be dead, but he's not ready

so he challenges God to a debate, though he doesn't have a clue how to be a debater.

Lee Smith, *Saving Gracie*, 1995
A serpent-handling preacher raises Gracie, though she never wants to tell him that she doesn't like Jesus.

1246

CYNTHIA RYLANT
TIM BOWERS, Illustrator

Little Whistle's Medicine

(San Diego: Harcourt, Inc., 2002)

Subject(s): Animals/Guinea Pigs; Toys; Illness
Age range(s): Grades K-2
Major character(s): Little Whistle, Guinea Pig; Soldier, Toy
Time period(s): 2000s (2002)
Locale(s): Toytown

Summary: Little Whistle looks forward to exploring Toytown every night after the store closes. One night, when Little Whistle visits Soldier for a bedtime story, Soldier has a headache. Little Whistle searches all over Toytown for a cure and a toy first-aid kit. With medicine and bandages, Soldier is soon feeling better and he reads Little Whistle and the Toytown babies a good night story. (32 pages)

Where it's reviewed:

Booklist, March 1, 2002, page 1144
Horn Book Guide, Fall 2002, page 343
Kirkus Reviews, January 15, 2002, page 108
Publishers Weekly, March 18, 2002, page 105
School Library Journal, April 2002, page 122

Other books by the same author:

Little Whistle, 2001
Little Whistle's Dinner Party, 2001
When I Was Young in the Mountains, 1982 (Caldecott Honor Book)

Other books you might like:

Charlotte Dematons, *The Worry Bear*, 2002
At night when all the bears in the toy store are sleeping, one bear is awake and worrying.

Don Freeman, *Corduroy*, 1976
Corduroy, a teddy bear, explores the department store where he lives after it closes for the night.

Kim Lewis, *Good Night, Harry*, 2004
When Harry, a stuffed elephant, has trouble sleeping the other stuffed animals help him.

1247

CYNTHIA RYLANT
ARTHUR HOWARD, Illustrator

Mr. Putter & Tabby Catch the Cold

(San Diego: Harcourt, Inc., 2002)

Subject(s): Illness; Animals/Cats; Aging
Age range(s): Grades 1-3
Major character(s): Mr. Putter, Aged Person, Neighbor; Tabby, Cat; Mrs. Teaberry, Aged Person, Neighbor; Zeke, Dog

Time period(s): 2000s (2002)
Locale(s): United States

Summary: When Mr. Putter catches a cold he is truly miserable. As he recalls his childhood, being sick in bed with a cold had some advantages, but now that he's older Mr. Putter has no one to take care of him. When he refuses to allow Mrs. Teaberry to come over for fear she will also become sick, Mrs. Teaberry sends Zeke with comfort foods that both Mr. Putter and Tabby enjoy. Mr. Putter needs one thing more—an adventure story to read. Mrs. Teaberry happily sends Zeke over with his book about a brave dog and Zeke joins Tabby to listen to Mr. Putter read the book aloud all day long. (44 pages)

Where it's reviewed:
Booklist, November 1, 2002, page 509
Horn Book Guide, Spring 2003, page 63
Publishers Weekly, September 9, 2002, page 70
School Library Journal, October 2002, page 130
Smithsonian, December 2002, page 123

Awards the book has won:
Smithsonian's Notable Books for Children, 2002

Other books by the same author:
Mr. Putter & Tabby Stir the Soup, 2003
Mr. Putter & Tabby Feed the Fish, 2001
Mr. Putter & Tabby Paint the Porch, 2000

Other books you might like:
Grace Maccarone, *I Have a Cold*, 1998
  In a rhyming story for beginning readers a sick child describes how it feels to have a cold.
Roni Schotter, *Warm at Home*, 1993
  Bunny's too sick to go out on a rainy day but still has enough energy to moan and groan about feeling bored.
Sarah Willson, *Tommy Catches a Cold*, 1998
  Tommy and his Rugrats pals seek to eliminate the ''bug'' causing Tommy's illness.

1248

CYNTHIA RYLANT
ARTHUR HOWARD, Illustrator

Mr. Putter & Tabby Stir the Soup

(San Diego: Harcourt, Inc., 2003)

Subject(s): Food; Cooks and Cooking; Neighbors and Neighborhoods

Age range(s): Grades 1-3
Major character(s): Mr. Putter, Aged Person, Cook; Mrs. Teaberry, Cook, Friend; Tabby, Cat; Zeke, Dog
Time period(s): 2000s (2003)
Locale(s): United States

Summary: When Mr. Putter's stove stops working just as he and Tabby are ready to make soup he brings his ingredients next door and uses Mrs. Teaberry's stove. Mrs. Teaberry is going out but she assures Mr. Putter that Zeke promises not to be a bother in her absence. Zeke's understanding of the word ''bother'' may not be the same as Mrs. Teaberry's as he, in typical dog fashion, interrupts Mr. Putter and Tabby repeatedly. First he brings his leash, then a ball and a stick. When those suggestions don't bring the desired response, Zeke begins carrying in radios, plants, and lamps in a desperate attempt to get some attention. By the time Mrs. Teaberry arrives home, her exhausted neighbors are asleep on the couch and most of her home's moveable objects are piled in the bathtub, out of Zeke's reach. The soup is still unmade, but Mrs. Teaberry completes it and does some baking so a fine dinner is ready for Mr. Putter and Tabby when they awaken. (44 pages)

Where it's reviewed:
Booklist, July 2003, page 1903
School Library Journal, October 2003, page 137

Other books by the same author:
Mr. Putter & Tabby Write the Book, 2004
Mr. Putter & Tabby Feed the Fish, 2001
Mr. Putter & Tabby Paint the Porch, 2000

Other books you might like:
Ross Collins, *Alvie Eats Soup*, 2002
  When Granny Franny, a world-renowned chef, visits Alvie's family discovers that Alvie is not the only finicky eater in the family.
Terry Farish, *The Cat Who Liked Potato Soup*, 2003
  A grumpy old man begrudges the companionship of a cat because the feline has sense enough to enjoy the man's potato soup.
Judith Head, *Mud Soup*, 2003
  In a Step into Reading title Josh is afraid to try the black bean soup his friend Rosa offers because it looks like mud.
Esther Hershenhorn, *Chicken Soup by Heart*, 2002
  When Rudie's elderly sitter gets the flu, Rudie asks his mother to help him make chicken soup for her.

S

1249

MARILYN SACHS
ROSANNE LITZINGER, Illustrator

The Four Ugly Cats in Apartment 3D

(New York: Richard Jackson Book/Atheneum Books for Young Readers, 2002)

Subject(s): Animals/Cats; Neighbors and Neighborhoods; Apartments
Age range(s): Grades 3-5
Major character(s): Lily, 10-Year-Old, Neighbor; Mr. Freeman, Aged Person, Neighbor; Mr. Kaspian, Neighbor
Locale(s): San Francisco, California

Summary: A forgotten key and absent neighbors leaves Lily crying at her apartment door when mean Mr. Freeman opens it to complain about the noise she's making. When he learns of her plight he softens a bit and invites Lily into his apartment. There she meets his four, ugly, loud cats and learns of the grouchy man's affection for the former strays. When Mr. Freeman dies Lily is sad to learn that the landlord plans to send the cats to the SPCA and she decides to repay Mr. Freeman's act of kindness to her by finding homes for each of the four ugly felines. (67 pages)

Where it's reviewed:
Booklist, May 1, 2002, page 1528
Bulletin of the Center for Children's Books, July 2002, page 417
Horn Book, March 2002, page 218
Publishers Weekly, April 8, 2002, page 228
School Library Journal, March 2002, page 200

Awards the book has won:
Center for Children's Books Best Books, 2002

Other books by the same author:
JoJo & Winnie: Sister Stories, 1999
A Pocket Full of Seeds, 1995
The Bears' House, 1987

Other books you might like:
Martha Freeman, *The Trouble with Cats*, 2000
  When her mother remarries, Holly has to adjust to a new home and school as well as life in an apartment with four cats.
Adele Geras, *The Cats of Cuckoo Square: Two Stories*, 2001
  Four cats live with their respective families in homes surrounding Cuckoo Square where they meet daily to swap tales.
Ursula K. Le Guin, *Wonderful Alexander and the Catwings*, 1994
  A big, bossy curious kitten's unexpected adventures lead to his introduction to cats with wings.

1250

S.F. SAID
DAVE MCKEAN, Illustrator

Varjak Paw

(New York: David Finkling Books, 2003)

Subject(s): Fantasy; Animals/Cats; Coming-of-Age
Age range(s): Grades 5-9
Major character(s): Varjak Paw, Cat; Elder Paw, Cat, Grandfather; Jalal Paw, Cat
Time period(s): Indeterminate
Locale(s): Fictional City

Summary: Varjak is a pampered Mesopotamian Blue kitten that lives with his family in comfort supplied by the Contessa; when their mistress dies, everything changes. Although they continue to live in the Contessa's house, privation and punishment, along with two cat bullies, enter their lives. The rest of the family is resigned to their situation, except for Elder Paw who inspires his rebellious grandson with stories of a distant ancestor named Jalal Paw. Jalal taught a Way that allows survival and triumph, even on the outside. When Elder is killed in a confrontation, Varjak leaps the walls to the outside. As he begins to learn how to survive on his own, Varjak is tutored by Jalal himself, who appears and teaches him the mysteries of Slow Time, Moving Circles and Shadow Walking. Now a master of the Way, Varjak must decide whether to return to his family or to stay outside and solve the mysterious disappearances that are decimating the cat population. (254 pages)

Where it's reviewed:
Booklist, June 1, 2003, page 1779
Bulletin of the Center for Children's Books, September 2003, page 32
Horn Book, July 2003, page 467
Library Media Connection, November 2003, page 54
Publishers Weekly, April 28, 2003, page 70

Other books you might like:
Kathryn Lasky, *The Rescue*, 2004
   A group of young owls, newly trained as fighters, decide to rescue a missing professor and discover some horrible truths.
Susan Fromberg Schaeffer, *The Autobiography of Foudini M. Cat*, 1997
   Foudini tells his own story, from foundling kitten to wise elder.
Christopher Stasheff, *The Feline Wizard*, 2000
   Just as you've always suspected—some cats aren't cats at all!

1251

KATE SAKSENA

Hang On in There, Shelley

(New York: Bloomsbury, 2003)

Subject(s): Alcoholism; Bullies; Racially Mixed People
Age range(s): Grades 7-10
Major character(s): Shelley Wright, 14-Year-Old; Ziggy, Musician; Liz Wright, Alcoholic, Mother; Janice, Bully
Time period(s): 2000s
Locale(s): London, England

Summary: On her birthday, Shelley writes her favorite rock star, Ziggy of Arctic 2000, and opens up her heart to him about her life; in return he sends her an upbeat postcard, beginning a habit they continue throughout that school year. She has a lot to write about, for when her parents divorce, biracial Shelley and her younger brother stay with their white mother whose alcoholism keeps her from holding on to a steady job. Shelley and Liz reverse roles as Shelley continually cleans up after her mother, puts her to bed and makes sure that Jake is fed and clothed. At school, she makes a few new friends, but a few enemies, too. Janice is the leader of the clique that harasses her, even going so far as to plant marijuana in her locker to get her expelled. Luckily her West-African father comes to her defense so that it's Janice who's expelled and Shelley's innocence recognized in this author's first novel. (219 pages)

Where it's reviewed:
Kirkus Reviews, June 1, 2003, page 810
Kliatt, May 2003, page 13
Publishers Weekly, June 2, 2003, page 52
School Library Journal, August 2003, page 165
Voice of Youth Advocates, August 2003, page 230

Other books you might like:
Amy Goldman Koss, *The Girls*, 2000
   Ringleader Candace manages to whittle her clique from five to four when she decides Maya is out; now the others wonder who's next.
Kevin Major, *Dear Bruce Springsteen*, 1988
   After Terry's parents' divorce, he pours out his thoughts in unmailed letters to rock star Bruce Springsteen.
Susan Beth Pfeffer, *Family of Strangers*, 1992
   Through letters and other writings, Abby reveals the sad story of her dysfunctional family.
Philip Pullman, *The Broken Bridge*, 1992
   As a biracial child, Ginny's always wondered about the identity of her mother and is relieved to finally learn the truth.

1252

RENE SALDANA JR.

Finding Our Way

(New York: Random House/Wendy Lamb, 2003)

Subject(s): Short Stories; Mexican Americans; School Life
Age range(s): Grades 7-10
Time period(s): 2000s

Summary: In this collection of 11 stories young Latinos reach stages in their lives where they have to make decisions, and sometimes the decisions are grown-up ones and sometimes they're not. Rey learns the hard way that his neighbor always promises payment for Rey's help, but then never follows through. Spotting his neighbor's flat tire, Rey returns to help him, but then wisely turns down the man's facile offer of a barbeque dinner in "The Good Samaritan." Andy, who even fails a grade so that he and Ruthie are in the same classes, has been Ruthie's boyfriend for three years. As prom approaches, he assumes she'll be his date but discovers too late that he should have asked her earlier in "Andy and Ruthie." Though Melly wants to prove she's just as tough as the boys in her hometown who ritually dive off Jensen's Bridge, listening to her grandmother's stories helps her realize she doesn't need to prove herself in "The Dive." Eight more stories complete this coming-of-age anthology. (117 pages)

Where it's reviewed:
Booklist, February 15, 2003, page 1065
Bulletin of the Center for Children's Books, April 2003, page 330
Horn Book, March 2003, page 216
Publishers Weekly, February 3, 2003, page 76
School Library Journal, March 2003, page 237

Other books by the same author:
The Jumping Tree, 2001

Other books you might like:
Rudolfo A. Anaya, *My Land Sings: Stories from the Rio Grande*, 1999
   Original stories are combined with folkloric retellings that continue the tradition of Mexican and Native American folklore.
Carolyn Meyer, *Rio Grande Stories*, 1994
   Seventh graders at Rio Grande Junior High School write

their own stories to assemble into a book for a school fundraiser.

David Rice, *Crazy Loco*, 2001

The importance of family is featured in this collection of short stories about Mexican Americans living in a small south Texas town.

Gary Soto, *Baseball in April: And Other Stories*, 1990

Day-to-day life for young Hispanics is related in these 11 short stories.

1253

GRAHAM SALISBURY

Island Boyz

(New York: Wendy Lamb/Random House, 2002)

Subject(s): Short Stories; Adolescence; Islands
Age range(s): Grades 7-10
Locale(s): Hawaii

Summary: These 11 stories of boys growing up on the Hawaiian Islands find them facing concerns both similar to, and yet vastly different from, boys on the mainland, including fear of sharks, the sight and smell of lava flows, and the tremendous diversity in ethnicity of the island people. Respect for the many military personnel on their island during World War II is realized by two teens in "Waiting for the War;" a decision to jump or walk away from a scary dive into a pond is made in "The Ravine;" while a group of sixth graders retaliates against Frankie Diamond in "Frankie Diamond Is Robbing Us Blind." The feel of the island and its people is described in the opening poem "Island Boyz." (260 pages)

Where it's reviewed:
Booklist, April 15, 2002, page 1399
Bulletin of the Center for Children's Books, March 2002, page 255
Horn Book, March 2002, page 219
School Library Journal, March 2002, page 238
Voice of Youth Advocates, October 2002, page 285

Awards the book has won:
Booklist Editors' Choice/Books for Youth, 2002

Other books by the same author:
Eyes of the Emperor, 2005
Jungle Dogs, 1998
Shark Bait, 1997
Under the Blood-Red Sun, 1994

Other books you might like:
James Berry, *A Thief in the Village and Other Stories of Jamaica*, 1988
The quiet simplicity of Caribbean life is depicted in these nine stories.

Jack Gantos, *Jack's New Power: Stories from a Caribbean Year*, 1995
Eight semi-autobiographical stories take place on Barbados when Jack indulges in pepper eating contests and falls in love with an older woman.

Harry Mazer, *A Boy at War: A Novel of Pearl Harbor*, 2001
Adam's life turns upside down the Sunday he goes fishing with friends in Pearl Harbor and sees his father's ship, and others, go up in flames.

1254

COLEEN SALLEY
JANET STEVENS, Illustrator

Epossumondas

(San Diego: Harcourt, Inc., 2002)

Subject(s): Folklore; Animals/Opossums; Humor
Age range(s): Grades K-3
Major character(s): Epossumondas, Opossum; Mama, Mother; Auntie, Aunt
Time period(s): Indeterminate
Locale(s): Fictional Country

Summary: In this adaptation of a classic "noodlehead" tale, defined in a concluding "Storyteller's Note," the fool is a young diaper-wearing opossum. Each time Mama sends her "sweet little patootie" on an errand to Auntie's house, he receives a treat to bring home. By the time he arrives home the item has been destroyed by his method of carrying it and Mama instructs Epossumondas as to how to carry it the next time. Of course, each treat is different and by using the technique appropriate for carrying the previous item, Epossumondas manages to damage what he's transporting the next day. Finally Mama gives up and goes to Auntie's house herself leaving Epossumondas with instructions about how to behave in her absence that mean something different to Epossumondas than what Mama intends. (36 pages)

Where it's reviewed:
Booklist, August 2002, page 1976
Bulletin of the Center for Children's Books, October 2002, page 77
Horn Book, November 2002, page 767
Publishers Weekly, June 17, 2002, page 63
School Library Journal, September 2002, page 217

Awards the book has won:
Center for Children's Books Best Books, 2002

Other books by the same author:
Who's That Tripping Over My Bridge?, 2002

Other books you might like:
Joanne Compton, *Sody Salleratus*, 1995
In this retelling of the tale, Jack tries to outsmart the bear that has swallowed his family.

Vivian French, *Lazy Jack*, 1995
Jack's mother sends her sleepy son off to work but he can't seem to remember to bring his wages home to her.

Steve Sanfield, *The Feather Merchants and Other Tales of the Fools of Chelm*, 1991
Thirteen tales drawn from Jewish folklore offer another perspective on "noodlehead" stories.

1255

BARNEY SALTZBERG, Author/Illustrator

Hip, Hip, Hooray Day!

(San Diego: Gulliver Books/Harcourt, Inc., 2002)

Series: Hip & Hop Story. Book 2
Subject(s): Friendship; Birthdays; Wishes
Age range(s): Grades K-2

Major character(s): Hip, Hippopotamus, Friend; Hop, Rabbit, Friend
Time period(s): 2000s (2002)
Locale(s): United States

Summary: Hip's birthday is coming soon and she gives Hop lots of hints that she wants to go skating at the Royal Roller Rink. Hop is planning a big surprise, with help from other friends, but when Hip shows up at his house early, the elaborate plans are spoiled. Then Hop presents two ''decoy'' gifts, a promise to rearrange Hip's sock drawer and a coupon for tooth polish and floss. Feeling angry and disappointed that her best friend doesn't seem to know her at all, Hip goes home. Other friends are able to coax her back to Hop's house for the big surprise, a gift of roller skates so Hip can go skating whenever she likes. (32 pages)

Where it's reviewed:
Publishers Weekly, March 18, 2002, page 106
School Library Journal, April 2002, page 122

Other books by the same author:
Crazy Hair Day, 2003
The Problem with Pumpkins, 2001 (Hip & Hop Story Book 1)
Soccer Mom from Outer Space, 2000

Other books you might like:
Holly Hobbie, *Toot & Puddle: A Present for Toot*, 1998
    Puddle is having a hard time finding the perfect present for best friend Toot's birthday.
Lore Segal, *Morris the Artist*, 2003
    For Benjamin's birthday, Morris buys him a present that he really wants for himself: a paint set.
Paul Stewart, *The Birthday Presents*, 2000
    Best friends, Rabbit and Hedgehog, decide to celebrate their birthdays together and each starts searching for the perfect present.

1256

BARBARA SAMUELS, Author/Illustrator

Dolores on Her Toes

(New York: Melanie Kroupa Books/Farrar Straus Giroux, 2003)

Subject(s): Ballet; Animals/Cats; Sisters
Age range(s): Grades K-2
Major character(s): Dolores, Child, Dancer; Duncan, Cat; Faye, Sister (older)
Time period(s): 2000s (2002)
Locale(s): New York, New York

Summary: Dolores considers Duncan her best friend and thus makes sure that Duncan does everything with her. Duncan may enjoy reading, eating and playing with Dolores but when she takes up ballet, Duncan seems less enthusiastic. Though Faye notes that Duncan doesn't seem to like ballet, Dolores disagrees. When Dolores puts her tutu on Duncan the cat has suffered enough and he runs, unnoticed, out the open apartment door. Dolores searches everywhere, puts up notices in the neighborhood and sprinkles cat treats on the sidewalk. Finally, Dolores tries thinking like Duncan and imitates his favorite behaviors. That strategy leads her to Duncan, happily hiding under her bed. (36 pages)

Where it's reviewed:
Booklist, April 1, 2003, page 1397
Horn Book Guide, Fall 2003, page 340
Publishers Weekly, March 24, 2003, page 78
School Library Journal, June 2003, page 116

Awards the book has won:
Booklist Editors' Choice, 2003

Other books by the same author:
Aloha, Dolores, 2000
Happy Birthday, Dolores, 1989
Duncan & Dolores, 1986
Faye & Dolores, 1985

Other books you might like:
Leslie Baker, *Paris Cat*, 1999
    Annie's cat becomes lost while chasing a mouse and tours Paris as she searches for the way home.
Holly Keller, *A Bed Full of Cats*, 1999
    Lee worries when he can't find his pet Flora but she reappears leading the reason for her absence.
Kathryn Lasky, *Starring Lucille*, 2001
    A tutu received as an early birthday present inspires Lucille to plan a performance for her family.

1257

DANIEL SAN SOUCI
EUJIN KIM NEILAN, Illustrator

The Rabbit and the Dragon King

(Honesdale, PA: Boyds Mills Press, 2002)

Subject(s): Folk Tales; Fairy Tales; Illness
Age range(s): Grades 1-4
Major character(s): Dragon King, Mythical Creature, Dragon
Time period(s): 7th century (Shila Dynasty)
Locale(s): Republic of Korea

Summary: The hypochondriac Dragon King who rules under the sea seeks relief for his many ailments. His court advisors convince him that eating the heart of a rabbit will cure all of his ills, so the king sends a turtle to locate a rabbit. The turtle finds a rabbit and brings her to the underwater kingdom with the help of some magic sand that enables her to breathe under water. The rabbit convinces the Dragon King that her heart is stored elsewhere and he sends her off with the turtle to retrieve it. The rabbit gives the turtle a piece of persimmon, claiming it is her heart. The king eats it and is miraculously cured of all his maladies. (32 pages)

Where it's reviewed:
Bulletin of the Center for Children's Books, February 2003, page 248
Children's Bookwatch, September 2002, page 7
Kirkus Reviews, September 15, 2002, apge 1399
Publishers Weekly, October 28, 2002, page 75
School Library Journal, November 2002, page 148

Other books by the same author:
The Dangerous Snake and Reptile Club, 2004
In the Moonlight Mist: A Korean Tale, 1999
Country Road, 1993
North Country Night, 1990

Other books you might like:

Oki Han, *Sir Whong and the Golden Pig*, 1993
   When Mr. Oh tricks Sir Whong out of his money Sir Whong devises an ingenious plan to get his money back.

Suzanne Crowder Han, *The Rabbit's Judgment*, 1994
   A tiger freed from a pit forgets his promise to his rescuer and considers eating the man; a passing rabbit tricks the tiger back into the pit.

Janie Jaehyun Park, *The Tiger and the Dried Persimmon: A Korean Folk Tale*, 2002
   A tiger hunting food misunderstands an overheard conversation about a dried persimmon and flees the village for fear of a beast.

1258

ROBERT D. SAN SOUCI
KIMBERLY BULCKEN ROOT, Illustrator

The Birds of Killingworth

(New York: Dial Books for Young Readers, 2002)

Subject(s): Animals/Birds; Ecology; Conservation
Age range(s): Grades 1-3
Major character(s): Almira Case, Daughter, Animal Lover; Squire Case, Father, Gentleman; Noah Arden, Teacher
Time period(s): Indeterminate Past
Locale(s): Killingworth, Connecticut, American Colonies

Summary: In a story based on Longfellow's poem by the same name, sensitive Almira's desire to save the birds and their sweet music is at odds with her father's wish to preserve his crops. Despite the protests of Noah Arden that the birds play a role in the balance of nature, Squire Case convinces the townspeople to offer a reward for each dead bird. Soon hunters have eliminated every adult bird in the area and miserable Almira hurriedly tries to rescue the nests of avian infants. She enlists the help of Noah and his students who fashion cages and tend to the birds in the schoolhouse. With the arrival of summer, insects wreak far more damage on the local crops than the birds ever did and the community faces a long winter with few provisions. In the spring Squire Case realizes the error of his actions and wishes he could bring the birds back to Killingworth. Thanks to Almira, Noah and the school children, the birds are able to return and the balance of nature is restored. (32 pages)

Where it's reviewed:

Booklist, April 1, 2002, page 1335
Bulletin of the Center for Children's Books, May 2002, page 340
Horn Book Guide, Fall 2002, page 344
Publishers Weekly, April 15, 2002, page 63
School Library Journal, August 2002, page 168

Other books by the same author:

Callie Ann and Mistah Bear, 2000 (Notable Social Studies Trade Books for Young People)
Peter and the Blue Witch Baby, 2000
Cinderella Skeleton, 2000

Other books you might like:

Holly Keller, *Grandfather's Dream*, 1994
   Grandfather's dream is to see the wetlands restored to their

pre-war condition so the Sarus Cranes can return to their habitat.

Donna Jo Napoli, *Albert*, 2001
   Unlike the squire, Albert is so sensitive to birds that when a pair builds a nest in his hand he rearranges his life style to accommodate the birds.

Helen Ward, *The Tin Forest*, 2001
   An old man living in a barren wasteland sees his dream of a beautiful forest come true thanks to his initiative and one live bird.

1259

ROBERT D. SAN SOUCI
DAVID CATROW, Illustrator

Little Pierre: A Cajun Story from Louisiana

(San Diego: Silver Whistle/Harcourt, Inc., 2003)

Subject(s): Fairy Tales; Folklore; Brothers
Age range(s): Grades 1-4
Major character(s): Little Pierre, Son, Brother (youngest); Marie-Louise, Daughter (of rich man), Kidnap Victim; Swamp Ogre, Monster, Kidnapper
Time period(s): Indeterminate Past
Locale(s): Louisiana

Summary: Although he's the youngest and smallest of five boys, Little Pierre has more brains, energy, and initiative than his four brothers put together. Learning that Marie-Louise's rich father is offering a reward to anyone rescuing her from Swamp Ogre, the four brothers decide to take action to win the reward and assure their future comfort. Ignoring their objections, Little Pierre follows secretly. When they become lost in the swamp at dusk and seek refuge in a house that, too late, they discover is Swamp Ogre's home, Little Pierre has the gumption needed to save them and Marie-Louise. For Little Pierre and Marie-Louise the story ends happily, but the brothers are forced to actually do some work. A concluding "Author's Note" gives sources and background for the tale originating in European Tom Thumb lore. (32 pages)

Where it's reviewed:

Bulletin of the Center for Children's Books, November 2003, page 123
Horn Book, January 2004, page 95
Publishers Weekly, October 13, 2002, page 77
School Library Journal, January 2004, page 122

Awards the book has won:
IRA Children's Choices, 2004

Other books by the same author:

Dare to Be Scared: Thirteen Stories to Chill and Thrill, 2003
Callie Ann and Mistah Bear, 2000 (Notable Social Studies Trade Books for Young People)
Peter and the Blue Witch Baby, 2000

Other books you might like:

Mike Artell, *Petite Rouge: A Cajun Red Riding Hood*, 2001
   In this retelling of a familiar tale an alligator plays the role of the wolf and Petite Rouge foils his dinner plans with Cajun sausage and hot sauce.

Coleen Salley, *Who's That Tripping Over My Bridge?*, 2002
    In this Cajun version of "Three Billy Goats Gruff," three brother goats living north of Baton Rouge face a familiar problem with a troll.
Tynia Thomassie, *Feliciana Meets d'Loup Garou: A Cajun Tall Tale*, 1998
    Courageous Feliciana meets the dreaded swamp monster and learns Loup Garou's remedy for a bad day.

1260

ROBERT D. SAN SOUCI
TERRY WIDENER, Illustrator

The Twins and the Bird of Darkness: A Hero Tale from the Caribbean
(New York: Simon & Schuster Books for Young Readers, 2002)

Subject(s): Folklore; Twins; Kidnapping
Age range(s): Grades 2-6
Major character(s): Marie, Royalty (princess), Kidnap Victim; Bird of Darkness, Kidnapper, Mythical Creature; Soliday, Twin, Brother; Salacota, Twin, Brother
Time period(s): Indeterminate Past
Locale(s): Antilles, West Indies

Summary: To save the people of her island home from the misery of the Bird of Darkness, Marie allows the seven-headed creature to take her captive. Her distraught father makes three promises to any man who can slay the beast and bring his daughter safely home. Many try, none succeed. Kind-hearted Soliday determines to rescue Marie. Lazy Salacota mocks his brother, but accompanies him on the trip anyway. By following the advice of a sorcerer, Soliday locates the island home of the Bird of Darkness and slays it. As Soliday returns to his boat to get an ax in order to free Marie, he runs into Salacota on the path and tumbles into a ravine. Salacota refuses to help Soliday and instead frees the princess and sails back with her to claim the reward. Suspicious, Marie delays the marriage for one year. Resourceful Soliday frees himself, builds a raft and returns to his home bearing the golden beaks of the Bird of Darkness and a token from Princess Marie to prove that he, not Salacota, met the king's challenge. Everyone, even Salacota, lives happily ever after. A concluding author's note gives background for the tale. (40 pages)

Where it's reviewed:
Booklist, August 2002, page 1968
Bulletin of the Center for Children's Books, October 2002, page 78
Kirkus Reviews, September 1, 2002, page 1319
Publishers Weekly, July 22, 2002, page 178
School Library Journal, September 2002, page 218

Awards the book has won:
Notable Social Studies Trade Books for Young People, 2003

Other books by the same author:
Callie Ann and Mistah Bear, 2000 (Notable Social Studies Trade Books for Young People)
The Hired Hand, 1997 (Aesop Prize)
The Faithful Friend, 1995 (Caldecott Honor Book)

Other books you might like:
Mary-Joan Gerson, *How Night Came from the Sea: A Story from Brazil*, 1994
    A Brazilian folktale tells the origins of darkness long ago at a time of relentless daylight for those living on land.
Eric A. Kimmel, *Onions and Garlic*, 1996
    Although his older brothers consider Getzel a fool he is able to trade onions for diamonds while his brothers receive only garlic in exchange.
Ruth Sanderson, *The Golden Mare, the Firebird, and the Magic Ring*, 2001
    Elements from several Russian folktales contribute to this original story of Alexi, seeker of adventure and fortune.

1261

RYAN SANANGELO
JACKIE URBANOVIC, Illustrator

Spaghetti Eddie
(Honesdale, PA: Boyds Mills Press, 2002)

Subject(s): Food; Heroes and Heroines; Resourcefulness
Age range(s): Grades K-2
Major character(s): Eddie, Child, Son
Time period(s): 2000s (2002)
Locale(s): United States

Summary: Eddie loves spaghetti so much that when he's sent to the store to buy chocolate frosting for a birthday cake, he brings his bowl of spaghetti and meatballs with him. When he runs into a neighbor with a broken shoelace, he offers her a noodle to use instead. Noodles also help make a net for fishing and fix broken guitar strings for other neighbors. Once Eddie finally makes it to the store he is able to stop a robbery with the only thing he has left—a meatball. (32 pages)

Where it's reviewed:
Booklist, August 2002, page 1976
School Library Journal, September 2002, page 205

Other books you might like:
Judi Barrett, *Cloudy with a Chance of Meatballs*, 1982
    In the town of Chewandswallow, meals rain from the sky and then the weather takes a turn for the worse.
John Vernon Lord, *The Giant Jam Sandwich*, 1987
    When the residents of Itching Down are overrun with wasps, they build a giant jam sandwich to combat the problem.
April Pulley Sayre, *Noodle Man: The Pasta Superhero*, 2002
    Al Dente saves the day with his pasta-making machine.

1262

ALEX SANCHEZ

Rainbow High
(New York: Simon & Schuster, 2003)

Subject(s): Homosexuality/Lesbianism; Interpersonal Relations; Schools/High Schools
Age range(s): Grades 9-12
Major character(s): Nelson Glassman, Homosexual, 12th Grader; Kyle Meeks, Homosexual, 12th Grader; Jason

Carrillo, Basketball Player, Homosexual; Jeremy, Homosexual
Time period(s): 2000s
Locale(s): United States

Summary: Kyle, Nelson and Jason, introduced in *Rainbow Boys*, are back to complete their senior year of high school and resolve some major decisions about life after graduation. Kyle has been out for quite a while and is finally dating the boy he's lusted after all through high school, star basketball player Jason. Now Kyle's biggest decision is whether to attend Tech with Jason or his father's alma mater Princeton, where he's been accepted. Jason finally revealed his homosexuality to his parents, though his mother doesn't believe him and his alcoholic father left home. Harder was telling his coach and basketball team though the coach's reaction set a positive tone for the rest of the players; difficulties may arise over Jason's athletic scholarship when word reaches Tech. And Nelson, who's prone to dying his hair various wild shades and wearing flashy clothes, is dating Jeremy who unfortunately is HIV-positive. At the moment, he's not sure how long he can continue to date Jeremy without confiding in his mom about his health status. (260 pages)

Where it's reviewed:
Bulletin of the Center for Children's Books, January 2004, page 206
Horn Book, January 2004, page 83
Publishers Weekly, November 24, 2003, page 65
School Library Journal, November 2003, page 146
Voice of Youth Advocates, December 2003, page 406

Other books by the same author:
So Hard to Say, 2004
Rainbow Boys, 2001

Other books you might like:
Michael Cart, *My Father's Scar*, 1996
   Adam's friend Evan is beaten for being gay and Adam purposefully stays uninvolved; when Adam falls in love, he realizes he's also gay.
Ron Koertge, *The Arizona Kid*, 1988
   Discovering that his Uncle Wes is gay is hard for Billy to accept, until he realizes that Wes is no different than he's always been.
William Taylor, *The Blue Lawn*, 1999
   Tough guy Theo catches the attention of good-looking David who's able to accept the idea that he's gay, while Theo isn't so sure.
Kate Walker, *Peter*, 1993
   When a gay friend of his older brother's fixes Pete's bike, Pete is labeled a ''poof'' by other dirt bikers and wonders about his conflicting feelings.

1263

RUTH SANDERSON, Author/Illustrator

Cinderella

(Boston: Little, Brown and Company, 2002)

Subject(s): Fairy Tales; Folklore; Conduct of Life
Age range(s): Grades 1-4

Major character(s): Cinderella, Stepdaughter, Abuse Victim; Unnamed Character, Royalty; Unnamed Character, Godmother, Mythical Creature (fairy)
Time period(s): Indeterminate Past
Locale(s): Fictional Country

Summary: This retelling of Perrault's tale also includes elements from the Brothers Grimm. Cinderella, mistreated by her stepmother and stepsisters finds solace under a magical hazel tree in which resides a white bird. The setting comforts Cinderella when she is not allowed to accompany her family to the prince's ball. When her fairy godmother appears, Cinderella's dreams come true, she attends the ball and captures the prince's attention. Heeding the fairy godmother's warning Cinderella hurriedly leaves the ball before midnight, losing one glass slipper as she runs away. The prince uses the slipper to locate Cinderella so he can bring her to the palace to begin their ''happily-ever-after'' life. The birds assure that the wicked stepmother and her daughters never leave their house again. (32 pages)

Where it's reviewed:
Booklist, April 15, 2002, page 1399
Bulletin of the Center for Children's Books, May 2002, page 339
Horn Book Guide, Fall 2002, page 413
Publishers Weekly, April 15, 2002, page 67
School Library Journal, June 2002, page 124

Other books by the same author:
The Golden Mare, the Firebird, and the Magic Ring, 2001
The Crystal Mountain, 1999 (Notable Social Studies Trade Books for Young People)
Rose Red & Snow White, 1997

Other books you might like:
Jude Daly, *Fair, Brown & Trembling: An Irish Cinderella Story*, 2000
   Jealous sisters try to prevent the beautiful Trembling from being seen in public out of fear that she will marry first but magic changes their plans.
Rebecca Hickox, *The Golden Sandal: A Middle Eastern Cinderella Story*, 1998
   Maha's loss of a golden sandal after a party leads to her discovery by a well-to-do villager interested in marrying her.
Charles Perrault, *Cinderella*, 1954
   In a retelling of a classic tale of love and inner beauty Cinderella, after years of torment from her stepfamily, marries a prince.

1264

LEIGH SAUERWEIN

Song for Eloise

(Asheville, NC: Front Street, 2003)

Subject(s): Middle Ages; Marriage
Age range(s): Grades 9-12
Major character(s): Eloise, 15-Year-Old; Merle, Blind Person, Mother (of Robert); Robert of Rochefort, Spouse (of Eloise); Thomas, Entertainer (troubadour)
Time period(s): 12th century

Locale(s): France

Summary: Because one of his retainers saves his life, Eloise's father promises her in marriage to Robert of Rochefort, a man who is twice her age. A kind but gruff man, Robert lacks the words to tell Eloise how he loves the sparkle in her eye and her love of life. Though she doesn't want to marry Robert, a girl in France can't refuse her father so Eloise leaves her home to marry and live with Robert. Though sad, she remains and bears him a son. Thinking to cheer his wife, Robert hires the troubadour Thomas to sing and tell her stories for a few days, but he's unknowingly brought a childhood friend of Eloise's into his castle. In Eloise's loneliness, she falls into a passionate affair with Thomas that finally comes to closure thanks to the efforts of Merle, who sees more than many sighted people. Alas, happily ever after doesn't come for Eloise and Robert in this beautifully written tragedy. (133 pages)

Where it's reviewed:
Booklist, December 15, 2003, page 660
Bulletin of the Center for Children's Books, January 2004, page 206
Horn Book, January 2004, page 92
Publishers Weekly, December 22, 2003, page 62
School Library Journal, December 2003, page 160

Other books by the same author:
The Way Home, 1994

Other books you might like:
Karen Cushman, *Catherine, Called Birdy*, 1994
    Though she knows her opinion means nothing, Birdy fights to control her destiny and marriage during the Middle Ages.
Joan Elizabeth Goodman, *Peregrine*, 2000
    Recovering from the death of her older husband, and unwilling to be part of an arranged marriage, Lady Edith goes on pilgrimage to the Holy Land.
Gloria Skurzynski, *Spider's Voice*, 1999
    Unable to speak because his tongue is fused to the bottom of his mouth, Aran becomes the perfect servant for the lovers Eloise and Abelard.

1265

DEBORAH SAVAGE

Kotuku

(Boston: Houghton Mifflin, 2002)

Subject(s): Coming-of-Age; Identity; Aunts and Uncles
Age range(s): Grades 7-10
Major character(s): Charlotte Williamson "Wim" Thorpe, 17-Year-Old; Aunt Kia, Aunt, Aged Person; Tangi, 15-Year-Old; David Te Makara, Professor
Time period(s): 2000s
Locale(s): Provincetown, Massachusetts

Summary: Wim still grieves for her friend who died from anorexia and is content to work at the stables where the horses and stray dogs offer her a sense of security. However, two new people arrive and shake up her life. First to come is her elderly Aunt Kia who, like Wim, has visions of a tattooed Maori man; knowing their commonality helps Wim accept the extra duties her aunt Kia requires. Then Professor Te Makara

arrives with a coded journal written by an aide to an 18th-century family member, Captain Charles Williamson Thorpe, which reveals secrets and leads to an open discussion of the Maori line in the Thorpe family. The supernatural feel of the book is enhanced by the sighting of a rare white heron, a kotuku, and the unexpected romance between Wim and the professor. (291 pages)

Where it's reviewed:
Booklist, May 15, 2002, page 1592
Kliatt, March 2002, page 12
Publishers Weekly, March 25, 2002, page 66
School Library Journal, March 2002, page 238
Voice of Youth Advocates, April 2002, page 46

Awards the book has won:
ALA Best Books for Young Adults, 2003

Other books by the same author:
Summer Hawk, 1999
Under a Different Sky, 1997
To Race a Dream, 1994
A Rumour of Otters, 1984

Other books you might like:
Liz Berry, *The China Garden*, 1996
    Clare's mother drags her off to an estate in the English countryside where the mysterious China Garden heightens Clare's psychic abilities.
Margaret Buffie, *The Dark Garden*, 1997
    Traumatic amnesia leads Thea to dream, melding her thoughts with those of the young girl who used to live in Thea's house.
Philip Pullman, *His Dark Materials Trilogy*, 1996-2000
    When the Dust increases on Lyra's world, evil follows, flowing from a rift in time and space.

1266

APRIL PULLEY SAYRE
STEPHEN COSTANZA, Illustrator

Noodle Man: The Pasta Superhero

(New York: Orchard Books/Scholastic, Inc., 2002)

Subject(s): Business Enterprises; Heroes and Heroines; Food
Age range(s): Grades K-2
Major character(s): Al Dente, Son, Hero; Mama Dente, Mother, Businesswoman; Grandma Dente, Grandmother, Hero; Mari Nara, Driver (Pizza Delivery), Young Woman
Time period(s): 2000s (2002)
Locale(s): Durum

Summary: The Dente family's pasta business is not doing well. Everyone in Durum wants pizza for dinner. So Al Dente decides to save the family business by selling pasta door-to-door with his portable pasta-maker. Nobody's buying, but Al manages to catch bank thieves with sticky spaghetti, save children from a burning building by creating a lasagna slide and help Durum residents bounce across a flooded street with fusilli for their shoes. Finally, after Mari Nara, a pizza delivery driver, crashes in the town fountain and Al saves her with the help of Mama, Grandma and some linguine, perciatelli and ravioli, the town takes another look at pasta for dinner. (40 pages)

Where it's reviewed:
Booklist, February 15, 2002, page 1021
Horn Book Guide, Fall 2002, page 344
Kirkus Reviews, February 15, 2002
Publishers Weekly, April 8, 2002, page 226
School Library Journal, March 2002, page 200

Other books by the same author:
Shadows, 2002
It's My City!: A Singing Map, 2001
Turtle, Turtle, Watch Out!, 2000

Other books you might like:
Judi Barrett, *Cloudy with a Chance of Meatballs*, 1982
    In the town of Chewandswallow, meals rain from the sky.
    But one day, the weather takes a turn for the worse.
Tomie De Paola, *Strega Nona: An Old Tale*, 1975
    When Strega Nona heads out of town, she cautions An-
    thony against using her magical pasta pot, however An-
    thony cannot resist and disaster ensues.
John Vernon Lord, *The Giant Jam Sandwich*, 1987
    When the residents of Itching Down are overrun with
    wasps, they build a giant jam sandwich to combat the
    problem.
Paul Many, *The Great Pancake Escape*, 2002
    A magician father makes pancakes for his hungry kids, but
    they all escape and the kids have to round them up.

1267

APRIL PULLEY SAYRE
JEFF SAYRE, Co-Author
RANDY CECIL, Illustrator

One Is a Snail, Ten Is a Crab: A Counting by Feet Book

(Cambridge, MA: Candlewick Press, 2003)

Subject(s): Mathematics; Animals; Beaches
Age range(s): Grades K-3
Time period(s): Indeterminate
Locale(s): Fictional Country

Summary: Numbers from one to ten and multiples up to 100
are identified by the number of feet animals commonly found
at a beach have. A snail, with only one foot is indispensable
for making odd numbers. Three is a person and a snail while
five is a dog and a snail. Because crabs have ten feet (considering the two with an extra job as claws) they can be easily
used to teach multiples of ten. Eighty, for example, could be
eight crabs or ten spiders. Seventy is six insects and a crab.
One hundred could be ten crabs, floating on inner tubes, or, if
you've lots of time to count, 100 snails. (36 pages)

Where it's reviewed:
Bulletin of the Center for Children's Books, July 2002, page
    461
Horn Book Guide, Fall 2003, page 340
Publishers Weekly, April 28, 2003, page 69
School Library Journal, July 2003, page 117

Awards the book has won:
ALA Notable Children's Books, 2004
Bulletin of the Center for Children's Books Blue Ribbons,
    2003

Other books by the same author:
Trout, Trout, Trout!: A Fish Chant, 2003
Army Ant Parade, 2002
Crocodile Listens, 2001
Dig, Wait, Listen: A Desert Toad's Tale, 2001 (Booklist
    Editors' Choice)

Other books you might like:
Betsy Lewin, *Cat Count*, 2003
    A rhyming story originally published in 1981 and reissued
    in color describes the pets of the young narrator's family
    and friends.
Claire Masurel, *Ten Dogs in the Window: A Countdown Book*,
    1997
    Rhythmic text describes dogs and the owners who pur-
    chase them, one at a time, from a pet shop.
Julia Noonan, *Mouse by Mouse: A Counting Adventure*, 2003
    Mice exploring the remains of a picnic introduce the num-
    bers one to ten.
Lynn Reiser, *Ten Puppies*, 2003
    After adopting ten puppies from a shelter a mother dog
    places them in groups of varying size according to their
    characteristics.

1268

CAROLE LEXA SCHAEFER
PIERR MORGAN, Illustrator

Someone Says

(New York: Viking, 2003)

Subject(s): Schools/Preschool; Imagination; Bedtime
Age range(s): Preschool-Kindergarten
Major character(s): Mei Lin, Student (preschooler); Unnamed
    Character, Teacher
Time period(s): 2000s (2003)
Locale(s): China

Summary: Imagination adds excitement to the routine of a day
in preschool. Beginning with the line to enter that someone
suggests become a leapfrog game to something as simple as
pretending to be a tiger slurping noodles for lunch, the children find an innovative way to approach each task. In response to the teacher's suggestion that they sing songs, someone suggests creating some new songs, and they do. To the
direction to draw Mei Lin on a large sheet of paper someone
adds, ''Let's draw her dancing like a pony,'' since everyone
knows Mei Lin can't stay still. As they leave class for the day
they agree to dream up another great day for tomorrow and at
bedtime, that's just what they do. (32 pages)

Where it's reviewed:
Booklist, November 15, 2003, page 603
Publishers Weekly, September 8, 2003, page 75
School Library Journal, November 2003, page 115

Awards the book has won:
School Library Journal Best Books, 2003

Other books by the same author:
Biggest Soap, 2004
One Wheel Wobbles, 2003
Snow Pumpkin, 2000
The Squiggle, 1996 (ALA Notable Children's Books)

Other books you might like:

Lindsey Gardiner, *Here Come Poppy and Max*, 2000
  Poppy imagines being like different animals and she tries stretching tall as a giraffe, splashing like a duck and waddling like a penguin.

Marthe Jocelyn, *A Day with Nellie*, 2002
  Nellie enjoys a day of simple activities including play, a nap and a bath.

Caroline Uff, *Hello, Lulu*, 1999
  Lulu's favorite things include the color red, a special teddy bear, her best friends, three pets and her family.

1269

ALICE SCHERTLE
BARBARA LAVALLEE, Illustrator

All You Need for a Snowman

(San Diego: Silver Whistle/Harcourt, Inc., 2002)

Subject(s): Winter; Construction; Children
Age range(s): Preschool-Kindergarten
Time period(s): Indeterminate
Locale(s): Fictional Country

Summary: A group of industrious children proves the point that all you need to construct a snowman is one snowflake, followed by six or eight million or billion more. While that amount might be sufficient for the first large ball, more is needed for the medium-sized and small balls. Then, of course, there's a need for a hat, bottle caps for eyes, a carrot nose, buttons, belts and boots and . . . if the snowman is to have a friend . . . you'll have to begin again with one snowflake. That's all you need. (32 pages)

Where it's reviewed:
Booklist, November 15, 2002, page 612
Bulletin of the Center for Children's Books, January 2003, page 210
Horn Book, November 2002, page 739
Publishers Weekly, October 21, 2002, page 73
School Library Journal, December 2002, page 108

Awards the book has won:
Center for Children's Books Best Books, 2002

Other books by the same author:
Good Night, Hattie, My Dearie, My Dove, 2002
Down the Road, 1995 (ALA Notable Children's Book)
How Now, Brown Cow?, 1994 (ALA Notable Children's Book)

Other books you might like:

Raymond Briggs, *The Snowman*, 1978
  In a wordless picture book a young boy enjoys the companionship of the snowman he builds.

Lucille Colandro, *There Was a Cold Lady Who Swallowed Some Snow!*, 2003
  A cold lady swallows snow, a pipe, some coal and many other odd objects with surprising results when she hiccups.

Mick Inkpen, *Kipper's Snowy Day*, 1996
  With his friend Tiger, Kipper plays all day in the snow.

Jean Van Leeuwen, *Oliver and Amanda and the Big Snow*, 1995
  Siblings Oliver and Amanda enjoy the day romping in the snow with their parents.

1270

RONI SCHOTTER
KIMBERLY BULCKEN ROOT, Illustrator

In the Piney Woods

(New York: Melanie Kroupa/Farrar Straus Giroux, 2003)

Subject(s): Grandparents; Death; Nature
Age range(s): Grades K-3
Major character(s): Ella, Child, Daughter; Unnamed Character, Grandfather, Aged Person
Time period(s): 2000s (2003)
Locale(s): United States

Summary: Ella loves to explore the nearby piney woods with her grandfather. Although her grandfather has gotten old and can't walk very far, he still tells her about the pine trees and how there will need to be a fire to enable the pinecones to open and to make enough room for new pine trees to grow. Finally a fire burns through the woods, but Ella's grandfather is too ill to venture out exploring. After her grandfather dies, Ella plants a pine seed by his grave. (32 pages)

Where it's reviewed:
Booklist, July 2003, page 1898
Bulletin of the Center for Children's Books, March 2003, page 287
Publishers Weekly, November 25, 2002, page 67
School Library Journal, April 2003, page 137

Other books by the same author:
Room for Rabbit, 2003
Nothing Ever Happens on 90th Street, 2002
Warm at Home, 1993

Other books you might like:

Eve Bunting, *I Have an Olive Tree*, 1999
  Sophia's puzzled by her grandfather's gift of an olive tree symbolizing her Greek heritage but after her grandfather's death she comes to treasure it.

Trish Cooke, *The Grandad Tree*, 2000
  When Vin and Leigh's grandfather dies, they cherish memories of time playing with him under an apple tree.

Barbara Santucci, *Anna's Corn*, 2002
  Anna enjoys walking through the cornfields with her grandfather, but after his death she is reluctant to plant the corn kernels he left her.

1271

ELLEN SCHREIBER

Vampire Kisses

(New York: HarperCollins, 2003)

Subject(s): Vampires; Interpersonal Relations; Haunted Houses
Age range(s): Grades 7-10
Major character(s): Raven Madison, 16-Year-Old; Trevor Mitchell, Soccer Player; Alexander Sterling, 17-Year-Old; Jameson, Servant (butler)

Time period(s): 2000s
Locale(s): United States

Summary: With her former hippie parents now in the corporate world and her schoolmates permanent conformists, Raven is out of step with her black fingernails, scuffed combat boots and Anne Rice novels. Ever since Raven was in kindergarten and announced that she wanted to be a vampire, she and Trevor have had a long-standing hatred of one another, which creates problems for becoming a vampire. On her sixteenth birthday, Raven's dreams appear to be coming true when she hears that the Sterling family has moved into the abandoned, supposedly haunted mansion on Benson Hill. Their simply gorgeous son Alexander, who seldom comes out of his attic bedroom, catches Raven's attention and she knows he could be her soul mate. Rumors quickly spread that he's a vampire and Raven worries that, for all her bragging about wishing to become a vampire, dating one might be a little more than she anticipated. (197 pages)

Where it's reviewed:
Booklist, November 15, 2003, page 593
Bulletin of the Center for Children's Books, October 2003, page 76
Publishers Weekly, August 4, 2003, page 81
School Library Journal, August 2003, page 166
Voice of Youth Advocates, February 2004, page 498

Awards the book has won:
ALA Quick Picks for Reluctant Young Adult Readers, 2004

Other books by the same author:
Comedy Girl, 2004
Teenage Mermaid, 2003

Other books you might like:
Amelia Atwater-Rhodes, *Shattered Mirror*, 2001
    Sarah's interest in Christopher leaves her caught between the witch world and the vampire world.
Mary Downing Hahn, *Look for Me by Moonlight*, 1995
    Attracted to Victor, a pale, aristocratic-looking poet, Cynda never connects him to the legends about their old house being haunted.
Pete Hautman, *Sweetblood*, 2003
    Lucy's theory linking diabetes and vampirism, judged too weird by her teacher, leads to parental restrictions.
Annette Curtis Klause, *Silver Kiss*, 1990
    In this ultimate romance, a young girl falls in love with a 300-year-old vampire.
Anne Rice, *Interview with the Vampire*, 1986
    A two-hundred-year-old vampire's life is recounted, detail by gory detail.

1272

AMY SCHWARTZ, Author/Illustrator

What James Likes Best

(New York: Richard Jackson Book/Atheneum Books for Young Readers, 2003)

Subject(s): Transportation; Family; City and Town Life
Age range(s): Preschool-Grade 1
Major character(s): James, Child, Son; Mommy, Mother; Daddy, Father; Angela, Friend

Time period(s): 2000s (2003)
Locale(s): United States

Summary: Four brief stories describe the way James travels and the activities he enjoys at various locations. With Mommy and Daddy, James boards a bus to visit a family friend with young twins. On the bus ride home James ponders what he likes best about the visit. On another day, James travels by taxi with Mommy and Daddy to visit his grandmother and on the taxi ride home he wonders what was best about this day. To go to the County Fair, James, Mommy and Daddy travel by car. They visit the petting zoo, ride a little train and eat a lot. What does James like best about this trip? Finally, James and Mommy walk to Angela's house for a play date with his friend. After a busy morning, James and Mommy walk home thinking about what James likes best. (32 pages)

Where it's reviewed:
Booklist, March 1, 2003, page 1196
Bulletin of the Center for Children's Books, March 2003, page 288
Horn Book, May 2003, page 337
Publishers Weekly, February 24, 2003, page 70
Riverbank Review, Spring 2003, page 40

Awards the book has won:
Booklist Editors' Choice, 2003
Charlotte Zolotow Award, 2004

Other books by the same author:
Glorious Day, 2004
Things I Learned in Second Grade, 2004
The Boys Team, 2001

Other books you might like:
Julie Brillhart, *Molly Rides the School Bus*, 2002
    Molly rides the bus to school for the first time, feeling a little apprehensive about the experience.
Marilyn Singer, *Diddi and Daddy on the Promenade*, 2001
    Diddi loves her Sunday morning walks on the Promenade with Daddy so much that even rain doesn't deter her pleasure.
Caroline Uff, *Lulu's Busy Day*, 2000
    Preschooler Lulu's busy day includes going to the park until rain forces her to return home.

1273

HOWARD SCHWARTZ
STEPHEN FIESER, Illustrator

Invisible Kingdoms: Jewish Tales of Angels, Spirits, and Demons

(New York: HarperCollins Publishers, 2002)

Subject(s): Supernatural; Jews; Folk Tales
Age range(s): Grades 3-5
Time period(s): Indeterminate
Locale(s): Fictional Country

Summary: The nine tales in this collection are divided equally between sections entitled ''The Kingdom of Angels,'' ''The Kingdom of Spirits,'' and ''The Kingdom of Demons.'' Each retelling concludes with a notation of its date and country of origin. In the first tale an angel grants the desire of childless couple for a baby. In ''A Roomful of Ghosts'' young Jacob learns a lesson about the spirit world when a wise rabbi sends him to the cemetery at night. The author's introduction to the book gives background to the tales. (67 pages)

Where it's reviewed:
Booklist, October 1, 2002, page 342
Horn Book, November 2002, page 769
Publishers Weekly, October 28, 2002, page 69
School Library Journal, October 2002, page 150
Smithsonian, December 2002, page 125

Awards the book has won:
Smithsonian's Notable Books for Children, 2002

Other books by the same author:
The Day the Rabbi Disappeared: Jewish Holiday Tales of Magic, 2000
A Coat for the Moon and Other Jewish Tales, 1999
Lilith's Cave: Jewish Tales of the Supernatural, 1991

Other books you might like:
Adele Geras, *My Grandmother's Stories: A Collection of Jewish Folk Tales*, 1990
   An award-winning collection of stories told by a grandmother to her granddaughter includes customs and recipes.
Malka Penn, *Ghosts and Golems: Haunting Tales of the Supernatural*, 2001
   Original short stories by ten different authors offer a look at Jewish culture.
Steve Sanfield, *The Feather Merchants and Other Tales of the Fools of Chelm*, 1991
   Thirteen tales reflect the humorous side of Jewish folklore rather than the supernatural.

1274

RICHARD SCRIMGER
GILLIAN JOHNSON, Illustrator

Eugene's Story

(Plattsburgh, NY: Tundra Books, 2003)

Subject(s): Sibling Rivalry; Storytelling; Brothers and Sisters
Age range(s): Preschool-Grade 1
Major character(s): Eugene, Brother, Child; Winifred, Sister (older), Child
Time period(s): 2000s (2003)
Locale(s): Canada

Summary: Eugene is stuck in the middle between two sisters. As Eugene tries to tell his own story one morning, his bossy older sister repeatedly interrupts him. When Eugene writes of walking the dog, Winifred interrupts to say that they don't have a dog. When Eugene writes of a trip to the candy store, Winifred reminds him that he's not allowed to cross that street by himself. Finally, Eugene tunes Winifred out as he begins the story and this time, in his tale, he's an only child. (32 pages)

Where it's reviewed:
Booklist, December 1, 2003, page 684
Bulletin of the Center for Children's Books, February 2004, page 244
Publishers Weekly, November 17, 2003, page 67

Other books by the same author:
Princess Bun Bun, 2002
Bun Bun's Birthday, 2001
The Nose from Jupiter, 1998

Other books you might like:
Mary Ann Hoberman, *And to Think That We Thought We'd Never Be Friends*, 1999
   A brother and sister can't stop arguing, until their little sister brokers a truce.
Steven Kellogg, *Much Bigger than Martin*, 1976
   A young boy tries to think of ways to grow bigger than his bossy older brother.
William Steig, *Grown-Ups Get to Do All the Driving*, 1995
   A young child describes how he sees grown-ups.

1275

MARCUS SEDGWICK, Author/Illustrator

The Dark Horse

(New York: Random House/Wendy Lamb, 2003)

Subject(s): Mythology; Adventure and Adventurers; Survival
Age range(s): Grades 6-9
Major character(s): Sigurd ''Sig'' Olafsson, 16-Year-Old; Mouse, Foundling; Ragnald, Traveler
Time period(s): Indeterminate Past
Locale(s): Storn, Europe

Summary: Sigurd discovers a young girl, living in a cave with wolves as her companions, and rescues her. His family raises the child they now call Mouse and Sig and Mouse develop a special bond. They explore the countryside together and find a wooden box that only Mouse is able to open. The stranger Ragnald enters Sigurd's village in search of the box, but upon meeting Mouse he reveals information about their shared heritage, for both are members of the raiding Dark Horse tribe. Sig, Mouse and a few other members of the Storn tribe manage to escape from the Dark Horse, but Mouse betrays them which leads to their capture. Offered a choice between death or life as a slave, all the Storn tribe members choose death in this tale of ancient tribes. (217 pages)

Where it's reviewed:
Booklist, February 1, 2003, page 995
Bulletin of the Center for Children's Books, June 2003, page 421
Horn Book, March 2003, page 217
School Library Journal, March 2003, page 237
Voice of Youth Advocates, April 2003, page 68

Awards the book has won:
School Library Journal Best Books, 2003

Other books by the same author:
Floodland, 2001
Witch Hill, 2001

Other books you might like:
Henrietta Bradford, *The Fated Sky*, 1999
   Ran is scheduled to be sacrificed to Odin, but she's rescued by the blind harper Toki and taken to Iceland where the two fall in love.
Michael Cadnum, *Raven of the Waves*, 2001
   Vikings overrun his village but Wiglaf, a young boy with a

withered arm, is saved; he in turn helps the wounded man who just killed his family.

Eloise McGraw, *The Striped Ships*, 1991
Young Jilly tells the story of the Norman invasion of Saxon England through her work on the famed Bayeux Tapestry.

Rosemary Sutcliff, *Sword Song*, 1998
Banished from his village, Bjarni offers his services as a mercenary to Thorstein the Red, but eventually settles down at Rafnglas with a wife.

1276

LORE SEGAL
BORIS KULIKOV, Illustrator

Morris the Artist

(New York: Frances Foster Books/Farrar Straus Giroux, 2003)

Subject(s): Birthdays; Gifts; Artists and Art
Age range(s): Grades K-3
Major character(s): Morris, Child, Friend; Benjamin, Child, Friend
Time period(s): Indeterminate Past
Locale(s): United States

Summary: Reluctantly Morris leaves his paints to accompany his mother on a shopping trip to buy a birthday gift for Benjamin. At the party, Benjamin opens the gifts from all the guests except Morris, who will not relinquish the small box he clutches. The partiers move on to eat birthday cake but Morris is unable to enjoy his as the box he holds grows to such large proportions that it fills his lap and his arms cannot reach around it. When the children begin playing, Morris tries to give the box to Benjamin but the birthday boy is busy playing with his other gifts and has no interest in the box. Finally, Morris opens the gift for Benjamin and when no one is interested in the paints, Morris begins painting alone. Soon the others join him to create works of art, first on paper and then on each other. (32 pages)

Where it's reviewed:

Booklist, August 2003, page 1990
Bulletin of the Center for Children's Books, July 2003, page 462
Publishers Weekly, April 7, 2003, page 66
School Library Journal, June 2003, page 116

Awards the book has won:
School Library Journal Best Books, 2003

Other books by the same author:
Why Mole Shouted & Other Stories, 2004
Tell Me a Trudy, 1977
All the Way Home, 1973
Tell Me a Mitzi, 1970

Other books you might like:

Peter Catalanotto, *Emily's Art*, 2001
Emily's disappointed that her picture loses a school art contest because the judge does not like her choice of subject.

Barbara McClintock, *The Fantastic Drawings of Danielle*, 1996
Papa does not approve of Danielle's fanciful drawings but

they do lead to a paid position as an assistant to Madame Beton.

Nancy Poydar, *Cool Ali*, 1996
Ali uses chalk and her artistic ability to create pictures on the sidewalk.

Sara Yamaka, *The Gift of Driscoll Lipscomb*, 1995
Annual gifts from an artist-neighbor teach Molly to see the colors in the world around her.

1277

TOR SEIDLER
PETER MCCARTY, Illustrator

Brothers Below Zero

(New York: HarperCollins, 2002)

Subject(s): Brothers; Artists and Art; Self-Esteem
Age range(s): Grades 4-8
Major character(s): Tim Tuttle, 7th Grader; Winifred V. Tuttle, Aunt (great-aunt); John Henry Tuttle, 6th Grader
Time period(s): 2000s
Locale(s): Williston, Vermont

Summary: Pudgy, unathletic Tim's learned to accept his subservient role in deference to his younger brother John Henry who's always been in the spotlight for he's better looking, athletic and smarter. His great-aunt Winifred spends a lot of time with Tim and encourages him to continue with his art, an area in which he has incredible talent. Suddenly John Henry's not in the spotlight and he's unhappy with the recognition Tim now receives. Though Aunt Winifred dies, Tim continues with his art and plans a special portrait of his parents for their Christmas present. John Henry vindictively ruins the portraits by adding a wart to his father's face and a mustache to his mother's. Upset because his parents think he's purposefully damaged their portraits, Tim runs away but is caught in a blizzard. Feeling guilty over the way he's behaved, John Henry comes out to rescue him in a story of rivalry between two brothers. (137 pages)

Where it's reviewed:

Booklist, January 2002, page 845
Bulletin of the Center for Children's Books, March 2002, page 255
Library Media Connection, September 2002, page 58
Publishers Weekly, January 14, 2002, page 61
School Library Journal, April 2002, page 157

Other books by the same author:
Brainboy and the Deathmaster, 2003
The Dulcimer Boy, 2003 (Brian Selznick, illustrator)
The Tar Pit, 2001

Other books you might like:

Paula Fox, *Radiance Descending*, 1997
It isn't until Jacob's birthday party that Paul learns to let go of the loathing he feels for his handicapped brother and sees him in another light.

Caroline Janover, *How Many Days Until Tomorrow?*, 2000
Josh senses Gramps's preference for his gifted brother Simon, yet when Gramps breaks his hip, it's Josh who knows how to help him.

Chris Westwood, *Brother of Mine*, 1994

Twins Nick and Tony have hated one another since they were born; just as they reach an understanding with one another, a car hits Nick.

1278

LUIS SEPULVEDA
CHRIS SHEBAN, Illustrator
MARGARET SAYERS PEDEN, Translator

The Story of a Seagull and the Cat Who Taught her to Fly

(New York: Arthur A. Levine/Scholastic, Inc., 2003)

Subject(s): Animals/Cats; Animals/Birds; Promises
Age range(s): Grades 3-6
Major character(s): Zorba, Cat; Lucky, Seagull
Time period(s): 2000s (2003)
Locale(s): Hamburg, Germany

Summary: Zorba is looking forward to peace and quiet when his owner leaves on vacation. Instead, an oil-covered seagull lands on his balcony and makes the dying request that Zorba protect the egg she will lay, care for the hatched chick and finally teach the grown gull to fly. Promises are sacred to port cats and Zorba soon enlists the aid of his friends and neighbors to fulfill the one he's made. Too soon, Lucky hatches and Zorba must find a solution to the most difficult promise he made, teaching Lucky to fly. This is the Spanish author's first children's book. (128 pages)

Where it's reviewed:
Booklist, September 1, 2003, page 121
Horn Book Guide, Spring 2004, page 102

Other books you might like:
Kate DiCamillo, *The Tale of Despereaux: Being the Story of a Mouse, a Princess, Some Soup, and a Spool of Thread*, 2003
Castle mouse Despereaux is determined to save the princess that he loves from sure death in the castle dungeon. Newbery Medal winner.
Dick King-Smith, *Martin's Mice*, 1988
Farm cat Martin loves mice, but he doesn't want to eat them. When he captures a pregnant mouse, he makes her his pet.
Evelyn Wilde Mayerson, *The Cat Who Escaped from Steerage*, 1990
On her family's travel to America, Chanah adopts a stray cat.

1279

BARBARA SEULING
PAUL BREWER, Illustrator

Robert and the Weird & Wacky Facts

(Chicago: Cricket Books, 2002)

Subject(s): Contests; Schools; Self-Confidence
Age range(s): Grades 2-4
Major character(s): Robert Dorfman, 8-Year-Old, 3rd Grader; Paul Felcher, 3rd Grader, Friend; Mrs. Bernthal, Teacher

Time period(s): 2000s (2002)
Locale(s): River Edge, New Jersey

Summary: Confident that memorizing all the arcane information in the Weird and Wacky Facts series will enable him to win lots of money on a television game show, Robert is disappointed to learn that he's ineligible for the contest because of his age. Determined to pick a winner, Robert tries to enter Mrs. Bernthal. Although she, too, is ineligible, Robert's idea prompts Mrs. Bernthal to plan a trivia contest in the classroom. Robert and Paul use the books to coach the other boys so they can defeat the girls. Alas, Robert's plans don't work out to be the moneymaker that he expects. (112 pages)

Where it's reviewed:
Booklist, April 1, 2002, page 1329
Horn Book, July 2002, page 471
Kirkus Reviews, March 15, 2002, page 426
Publishers Weekly, April 1, 2002, page 86
School Library Journal, July 2002, page 98

Other books by the same author:
Robert and the Great Pepperoni, 2001
Oh No, It's Robert, 1999
Winter Lullaby, 1998

Other books you might like:
Diane DeGroat, *Annie Pitts, Burger Kid*, 2000
Annie, aspiring actress, feels confident that she'll win the Burger Barn poster contest and fulfill her desire for fame.
Betsy Duffey, *Spotlight on Cody*, 1998
Nothing goes right for Cody as he tries to find some "talent" to perform for the school's talent show.
David Elliott, *The Cool Crazy Crickets to the Rescue!*, 2001
Everyone in the Cool Crazy Crickets Club has an own idea for earning money as well for spending it.
Stephanie Greene, *Owen Foote, Money Man*, 2000
Owen and his pal Joseph try various ways to make money so they can order neat products such as fake vomit from a catalog.

1280

PHYLLIS SHALANT

When Pirates Came to Brooklyn

(New York: Dutton, 2002)

Subject(s): Jews; Friendship; Prejudice
Age range(s): Grades 4-6
Major character(s): Lee Bloom, 6th Grader; Polly Burke, 6th Grader
Time period(s): 1960s
Locale(s): New York, New York (Brooklyn)

Summary: When her best friend moves away, Lee is heartbroken until she meets Polly with whom she can create and play wonderful fantasy games. Lee's mother distrusts anyone who isn't Jewish and doesn't really want her daughter playing with Polly who is Catholic. Polly's mother, on the other hand, leaves tracts around for Lee in an attempt to convert her and thus save her from Hell. This religious intolerance is the first time Lee confronts prejudice and she finally realizes that she is sometimes guilty of it, too. Though their mothers try to keep the girls apart, their friendship wins out as both girls understand the need to look beyond appearances. (213 pages)

Where it's reviewed:
Booklist, October 15, 2002, page 407
Bulletin of the Center for Children's Books, December 2002, page 173
Kirkus Reviews, August 1, 2002, page 1142
Publishers Weekly, August 12, 2002, page 301
School Library Journal, October 2002, page 170

Other books by the same author:
The Great Eye, 1996
Beware of Kissing Lizard Lips, 1995
Shalom, Geneva Peace, 1992
Transformation of Faith Futterman, 1990

Other books you might like:
J.M. Barrie, *Peter Pan*,
   The classic story of the boy who wants to remain forever young and his escapades with the Darling children.
Anna Fienberg, *Ariel, Zed & the Secret of Life*, 1994
   Ariel's writer mother sends her unruly characters to the Island, but one year has to send Ariel and her friend Zed in hopes they'll cheer up.
Jack Gantos, *What Would Joey Do?*, 2002
   Joey agrees to be home schooled with mean-as-a-snake, blind Olivia whose mother always asks Joey "What would Jesus do?"

1281

NTOZAKE SHANGE

Daddy Says

(New York: Simon & Schuster, 2003)

Subject(s): Rodeos; African Americans; Fathers and Daughters
Age range(s): Grades 6-9
Major character(s): Lucie-Marie Brown, 12-Year-Old; Annie Sharon Brown, 14-Year-Old, Rodeo Rider; Tie-Down Brown, Rodeo Rider, Father (of Annie Sharon and Lucie-Mari); Cassie Caruthers, Girlfriend (of Tie-Down); Twanda Rochelle Johnson-Brown, Rodeo Rider, Mother (of Annie Sharon and Lucie-Mari)
Time period(s): 2000s
Locale(s): Texas

Summary: Lucie-Marie and Annie Sharon both miss their mother Twanda, a rodeo star killed several years earlier in a riding accident; to commemorate her name, they each have learned to rope and ride. They're also a little concerned about their father's growing interest in Cassie, a slender young woman whom they fear will try to take the place of their mother. In an act of rebellion, or maybe just to emulate her deceased mother, Annie Sharon competes against a friend in an informal bronco riding contest. Though her father saves her from the enraged horse, Tie-Down's left with a bad head injury that forces Tie-Down and his daughters to talk about their future life with Cassie. (183 pages)

Where it's reviewed:
Booklist, March 15, 2003, page 1317

Bulletin of the Center for Children's Books, March 2003, page 288
Publishers Weekly, November 25, 2002, page 68
School Library Journal, February 2003, page 148
Voice of Youth Advocates, February 2003, page 482

Other books by the same author:
Betsey Brown: A Novel, 1985
Daughter's Geography, 1983
Sassafrass, Cypress and Indigo: A Novel, 1982
For Colored Girls Who Have Considered Suicide When the Rainbow Is Enuf, 1975

Other books you might like:
Jean Ferris, *Eight Seconds*, 2000
   Living in "cowboy country," John attends rodeo camp where he feels the adrenalin rush of riding a bull for eight terrifying, exciting seconds.
Lynn Hall, *Flying Changes*, 1991
   Denny's life is upset when her womanizing rodeo father is paralyzed and her mother returns home to care for him.
Mary Stolz, *Cezanne Pinto: A Memoir*, 1994
   Escaping from a life of slavery, Cezanne travels to Texas where's he's unable to locate his mother, but finds work as a cowboy.

1282

DAVID SHANNON, Author/Illustrator

David Gets in Trouble

(New York: The Blue Sky Press/Scholastic, Inc., 2002)

Subject(s): Behavior; Responsibility; Self-Perception
Age range(s): Preschool-Grade 1
Major character(s): David, Child, Son
Time period(s): 2000s
Locale(s): United States

Summary: David is not a troublemaker but he is a kid who seems to always be in trouble. Of course, from David's perspective, it's not his fault that his ball accidentally breaks the window or he falls off his skateboard and knocks over the table. David proudly strides to school alone, oblivious to the fact that he's not completely dressed because he forgot his pants. Being hungry seems a good reason for David to help himself to the dog's biscuits and he's positive that the cat enjoys having its tail pulled. After a pajama-clad David denies taking a bite from a newly decorated cake the guilt awakens him and he confesses, apologizes and expresses his love for his very patient mother. (32 pages)

Where it's reviewed:
Booklist, September 15, 2002, page 233
Horn Book, January 2003, page 61
New York Times Book Review, November 17, 2002, page 42
Publishers Weekly, June 24, 2002, page 55
School Library Journal, September 2002, page 206

Awards the book has won:
Booklist Editors' Choice, 2002
IRA Children's Choices, 2003

Other books by the same author:
The Rain Came Down, 2000

David Goes to School, 1999 (Publishers Weekly Best Children's Books)
No, David!, 1998 (Caldecott Honor Book)

Other books you might like:
Tom Birdseye, *A Regular Flood of Mishap*, 1994
In her efforts to be helpful Ima Bean sets in motion a series of events that trigger "a regular flood of mishap" for her family.
Steven Kroll, *Oh, Tucker!*, 1998
A family's very large, exuberant dog unwittingly leaves a trail of disaster wherever he goes.
Phyllis Reynolds Naylor, *I Can't Take You Anywhere!*, 1997
Clumsy Amy Audrey is so apt to accidentally create a major mess that her parents stay home rather than take her out in public.

1283

DAVID SHANNON, Author/Illustrator

Duck on a Bike
(New York: Blue Sky Press/Scholastic, 2002)

Subject(s): Animals/Ducks; Bicycles and Bicycling; Animals
Age range(s): Preschool-Grade 1
Major character(s): Duck, Duck; Mouse, Mouse
Time period(s): Indeterminate
Locale(s): Fictional Country

Summary: The other animals on the farm have varied opinions about Duck's bike riding, but only Mouse seems interested in sharing the experience. Opportunity knocks when a group of bike-riding kids arrives and hurries inside. The sight of all the parked bicycles inspires all the farm animals to put their skepticism aside and join Duck on a bike. (32 pages)

Where it's reviewed:
Booklist, February 15, 2002, page 1013
Bulletin of the Center for Children's Books, March 2002, page 256
Horn Book, March 2002, page 203
Kirkus Reviews, January 15, 2002, page 109
School Library Journal, March 2002, page 201

Awards the book has won:
Parenting's Books of the Year, 2002
School Library Journal Best Books, 2002

Other books by the same author:
The Rain Came Down, 2000
David Goes to School, 1999 (School Library Journal Best Books)
A Bad Case of Stripes, 1998
No, David!, 1998 (Caldecott Honor Book)

Other books you might like:
Doreen Cronin, *Click, Clack, Moo: Cows That Type*, 2000
A farm's ducks note the effectiveness of the cows' use of an old typewriter to submit requests to Farmer Brown and try to learn to type also.
Amy Ehrlich, *Parents in the Pigpen, Pigs in the Tub*, 1993
The farm animals move into the house and the family heads for the barn in a humorous reversal of roles.

Paul Brett Johnson, *The Pig Who Ran a Red Light*, 1999
George commandeers Miss Rosemary's truck and drives to town, but not without an accident.
Martin Waddell, *Webster J. Duck*, 2001
Baby Webster isn't interested in bike riding; the newly hatched duck just wants to find his mother.

1284

GEORGE SHANNON
LAURA DRONZEK, Illustrator

Tippy-Toe Chick, Go!
(New York: Greenwillow/HarperCollins, 2003)

Subject(s): Animals/Chickens; Animals/Dogs; Gardens and Gardening
Age range(s): Preschool-Grade 1
Major character(s): Little Chick, Chicken; Unnamed Character, Mother, Hen
Time period(s): 2000s (2003)
Locale(s): United States

Summary: Every day a mother hen and her three chicks make an early morning trip to the garden to snack on beans and potato bugs. One day, a big barking dog blocks the path and the mother hen declares that they'll all have to go back home and wait for the chicken feed to be passed out. The chicks aren't ready to give up yet and one by one try to get past the dog. Finally, the youngest, Little Chick, figures out a successful way by getting the dog tangled around the tree to which it's tied. (32 pages)

Where it's reviewed:
Booklist, January 2003, page 910
Bulletin of the Center for Children's Books, March 2003, page 289
Horn Book, January/February 2003, page 62
Publishers Weekly, November 18, 2002, page 59
School Library Journal, February 2003, page 122

Other books by the same author:
Tomorrow's Alphabet, 1996
Climbing Kansas Mountains, 1993 (School Library Journal Best Books)
Lizard's Song, 1981

Other books you might like:
Scott Beck, *Pepito the Brave*, 2001
Pepito is afraid to fly like his avian siblings, so he learns to hop, swim and burrow instead.
Mary Finch, *The Three Billy Goats Gruff*, 2001
Three goats outsmart a troll blocking their way in order to reach the tasty food on the other side of the bridge.
Pat Hutchins, *Rosie's Walk*, 1968
On her walk, Rosie unknowingly foils a fox that is trying to eat her.

1285

MARGARET SHANNON, Author/Illustrator

The Red Wolf

(Boston: Houghton Mifflin Company, 2002)

Subject(s): Fairy Tales; Princes and Princesses; Problem Solving
Age range(s): Grades K-3
Major character(s): Roselupin, Royalty, 7-Year-Old; Unnamed Character, Royalty, Father
Time period(s): Indeterminate Past
Locale(s): Fictional Country

Summary: Roselupin's father protects his precious daughter by locking her in a tall tower, a residence that Roselupin would happily escape in order to experience the dangerous world beyond the tower. On Roselupin's birthday a mysterious jeweled box appears at the castle gate as a gift for the young princess. Inside are balls of yarn and a note saying, "Knit what you want." Roselupin's father requests a scarf but Roselupin instead selects all the red yarn and knits a red wolf suit. While wearing the suit Roselupin magically grows until she bursts out of the tower and escapes into the countryside. Alas, the magic unravels along with the knitted suit; Roselupin is found in the forest and returned to a newly built, taller tower with another box of yarn. This time she does knit something for her father, but it's not the scarf he's expecting. (32 pages)

Where it's reviewed:
Bulletin of the Center for Children's Books, May 2002, page 340
Horn Book, March 2002, page 204
Kirkus Reviews, February 15, 2002, page 265
Publishers Weekly, January 21, 2002, page 89
School Library Journal, May 2002, page 126

Awards the book has won:
Center for Children's Books Best Books, 2002

Other books by the same author:
Gullible's Troubles, 1998
Elvira, 1993

Other books you might like:
Alma Flor Ada, *The Malachite Palace*, 1998
    Shut away in the palace for protection, a lonely princess cannot be given what she truly wants, a friend, so she frees herself.
Vivian French, *The Thistle Princess*, 1998
    The wall that a king and queen build to protect their beloved child actually stifles her and deprives her of happiness.
Maurice Sendak, *Where the Wild Things Are*, 1963
    Max is angry to be sent to his room and takes an imaginary, temporary journey to the Land of the Wild Things.
Paul O. Zelinsky, *Rapunzel*, 1997
    This retelling of the classic story of the pain and power of love captured the Caldecott Medal.

1286

NICK SHARRATT, Author/Illustrator

Shark in the Park!

(Oxford, NY: David Fickling Books, 2002)

Subject(s): Humor; Animals/Sharks; Stories in Rhyme
Age range(s): Preschool-Grade 1
Major character(s): Timothy Pope, Child
Time period(s): 2000s
Locale(s): United States

Summary: Timothy takes his new toy, a telescope, to the park to try it out. Die-cut holes in the page allow the reader to have the same circumscribed view of the park that Timothy has each time he spies something and cries "There's a shark in the park!" Turning the page gives the broader view that Timothy has when he looks without the telescope to see his innocent mistake. (20 pages)

Where it's reviewed:
Booklist, September 1, 2002, page 137
Books for Keeps, September 2002, page 24
Publishers Weekly, October 21, 2002, page 77
School Library Journal, December 2002, page 108
Smithsonian, December 2002, page 123

Awards the book has won:
Smithsonian's Notable Books for Children, 2002

Other books by the same author:
Ahoy, Pirate Pete, 2003
Once upon a Time . . ., 2002
Buzz, Buzz, Bumble Kitty, 2000

Other books you might like:
Eric Hill, *Spot Goes to the Park*, 1991
    Spot enjoys a day at the park playing with his friends; no sharks are seen.
Astrid Lindgren, *Pippi Longstocking in the Park*, 2004
    Pippi moves into the city park with her friends Tommy and Annika.
John Schindel, *What Did They See?*, 2003
    Woodland animals are excited to see what Raccoon finds in an Antique and Curiosities Shop.

1287

SUSAN SHAW

Black-Eyed Suzie

(Honesdale, PA: Boyds Mills Press, 2002)

Subject(s): Mothers and Daughters; Mental Illness; Child Abuse
Age range(s): Grades 6-9
Major character(s): Suzie, 12-Year-Old, Mentally Ill Person; Elliott, Uncle; Deanna, Sister (of Suzie)
Time period(s): 2000s
Locale(s): United States

Summary: Unable to deal with her verbally and physically abusive mother, Suzie has pulled herself into a fetal position with her chin on her knees, her "safety box," and is unable to make herself talk or eat, though she can't stop crying. Her mother claims Suzie's going through a stage while her father doesn't realize the problem as his job as a salesman finds him often away from home. When Uncle Elliott stops by for a visit, he refuses to listens to any of the family excuses and takes Suzie to the hospital where she's transferred to a mental hospital. Though the staff works with her to build trust, Suzie won't relate any of the home problems until her sister comes to visit and she discovers their mother has transferred the physical abuse to Deanna. Only then does Suzie begin to talk, disclose the abuse from her alcoholic mother, and finally start to heal in this author's first novel. (167 pages)

Where it's reviewed:
Booklist, May 15, 2002, page 1592
Bulletin of the Center for Children's Books, September 2002, page 34
Library Media Connection, September 2002, page 59
School Library Journal, May 2002, page 160
Voice of Youth Advocates, August 2002, page 197

Other books by the same author:
The Boy in the Basement, 2004

Other books you might like:
Kate Saksena, *Hang On in There, Shelley*, 2003
    After her parents divorce, Shelley becomes the parent as her mother's alcoholism prevents her holding a steady job.
Kim Taylor, *Cissy Funk*, 2001
    Cissy doesn't understand why her mother beats her and not her brother, but her Aunt Vera's news offers some explanation.
Sally Warner, *How to Be a Real Person (in Just One Day)*, 2001
    As long as Kara's mother takes her medication, she's lots of fun, but now she stays in her bedroom and Kara doesn't know what to do.
Amy Bronwen Zemser, *Beyond the Mango Tree*, 1998
    Sarina's obsessive, overprotective mother often ties her to the mango tree to prevent her leaving the yard.

1288

TUCKER SHAW

Flavor of the Week

(New York: Hyperion, 2003)

Subject(s): Love; Cooks and Cooking; Weight Control
Age range(s): Grades 7-10
Major character(s): Cyril Bartholomew, Cook, 12th Grader; Rose Mulligan, 12th Grader; Nick Garbacchio, 12th Grader
Time period(s): 2000s
Locale(s): New York

Summary: In a romance evocative of *Cyrano de Bergerac*, Cyril pines for Rose, who is infatuated with Nick. Senior Cyril, a talented cook, has his heart set on attending the American Institute of Culinary Arts after high school. Rose is Cyril's lab partner and likes him as a friend, but that's all. Since breaking up with her former boyfriend, she's crossed off boys altogether. Nick moved away a few years ago and has just returned, but immediately resumes his friendship with Cyril. When Cyril bakes some kitchen sink cookies and gives

some to Nick, who in turn shares them with Rose, a pattern of deception is set for Rose immediately thinks Nick is the great cook. Because Cyril is so in love with Rose, he bakes gourmet dinners for her but goes along with the myth that Nick cooked them. The humor of this story isn't lost among all the recipes that end each chapter, and when Nick wins his acceptance to the American Institute of Culinary Arts, along with the girl of his dreams, stand by for cheering in this author's first novel. (220 pages)

Where it's reviewed:
Booklist, November 15, 2003, page 607
Publishers Weekly, October 6, 2003, page 85
School Library Journal, December 2003, page 160
Voice of Youth Advocates, February 2004, page 498

Other books you might like:
Judie Angell, *Leave the Cooking to Me*, 1990
    Shirley helps a friend's mother with her dinner party and ends up forming Vanessa's Catering.
Sarah Dessen, *Keeping the Moon*, 1999
    Though Colie loses 45 pounds, she hasn't shed her insecurity, especially when a classmate tries to say she has an "easy" reputation.
Ann Herrick, *The Perfect Guy*, 1989
    Rebecca's plan for her new stepbrother to fall for her backfires and she almost loses out on the best guy of all.
Cherry Whytock, *My Cup Runneth Over: The Life of Angelica Cookson Potts*, 2003
    With eight of her favorite recipes, Angel shows how she manages to combine her love of eating and cooking with a flair for modeling.

1289

PEGI DEITZ SHEA

Tangled Threads: A Hmong Girl's Story

(New York: Clarion Books, 2003)

Subject(s): Refugees; Grandmothers; Sewing
Age range(s): Grades 6-10
Major character(s): Mai Yang, 13-Year-Old, Orphan; See Cua "Heather", Cousin; Pa Cua "Lisa", Cousin
Time period(s): 2000s
Locale(s): Thailand; Providence, Rhode Island

Summary: After her parents are killed in Laos, Mai and her grandmother cross over into Thailand where they live in a refugee camp for ten years. She writes her cousins who live in Rhode Island, practices her English and looks forward to moving to America. Her grandmother is reluctant to leave Thailand and stitches life events on her pa'ndua, or story cloth. Arriving in America her grandmother's unable to understand English, so Mai remains by her side to translate. Mai is shocked at the changes in her cousins who have become disrespectful of their elders. When her cousin Heather runs away with her boyfriend, Mai reconsiders her life and realizes the importance of blending her Hmong customs with the good aspects of American life in this author's first novel. (236 pages)

Where it's reviewed:
Bulletin of the Center for Children's Books, December 2003, page 165
Library Media Connection, November 2003, page 60
Publishers Weekly, September 22, 2003, page 105
School Library Journal, November 2003, page 148
Voice of Youth Advocates, December 2003, page 407

Other books you might like:
Fran Leeper Buss, *Journey of the Sparrows*, 1991
    Although life in America is difficult for illegal aliens, young Marie knows it's still better than the terror and killings that occur in El Salvador.
Linda Crew, *Children of the River*, 1989
    Forced by the Khymer Rouge to give up her life in Cambodia, moving to America is equally hard for Sundara.
Sherry Garland, *Shadow of the Dragon*, 1993
    Danny has difficulty reconciling his Vietnamese heritage with life in America.
Minfong Ho, *The Stone Goddess*, 2003
    After losing her father and sister to the Khmer Rouge, Nakri and her brother locate their mother and together leave their native country.

1290

ALEX SHEARER

The Great Blue Yonder

(New York: Clarion Books, 2002)

Subject(s): Death; Future; Fantasy
Age range(s): Grades 5-9
Major character(s): Harry, Spirit; Tina, Sister (of Harry); Arthur, Friend (of Harry's)
Time period(s): 2000s
Locale(s): England; Other Lands, Fictional Country

Summary: After yelling at his sister that she'll be sorry when he's dead, Harry leaps on his bike, pedals away and is struck and killed by a lorry. Now in the Other Lands, Harry worries that his sister will think she caused his death and he searches for a way to comfort her. Meeting Arthur, who's been in the Other Lands searching for his mother for well over a century, Harry learns the requirements to pass over to the "Great Blue Yonder." The boys return to the Land of the Living to see how everyone is reacting to Harry's death, and Harry is suitable impressed with the depth of their sadness. Since he wants to cross over, Harry exerts great effort to leave Tina a note asking for her forgiveness for their argument. Back in the Other Lands, Arthur has finally found his mother and now the three can cross over to the Great Blue Yonder. (184 pages)

Where it's reviewed:
Bulletin of the Center for Children's Books, June 2002, page 382
Horn Book Guide, Fall 2002, page 382
Library Media Connection, January 2003, page 87
School Library Journal, April 2002, page 157
Voice of Youth Advocates, June 2002, page 131

Other books by the same author:
Sea Legs, 2004

Other books you might like:
Cherie Bennett, *Heaven Can't Wait*, 1996
    Teens Cisco, Nicole and Melody die before learning life's lessons and must now help other teens before being admitted to Ultimate Heaven.
Meg Cabot, *Haunted: A Tale of the Mediator*, 2003
    The Mediator is a little distracted by the fact that she has fallen for one of the spirits she should be helping to move on.
Lael Littke, *Haunted Sister*, 1998
    Janine "dies" in an automobile accident, but instead has a near-death experience; when she returns to earth, her dead twin Lenore comes back with her.
Gary Soto, *The Afterlife*, 2003
    Stabbed to death over a compliment about yellow shoes, Chuy separates from his body and begins his afterlife as a ghost.
Rich Wallace, *Restless: A Ghost's Story*, 2003
    Frank hasn't moved on since his death, so he tries to connect with his little brother, now a high school senior.

1291

DYAN SHELDON

Planet Janet

(Cambridge, MA: Candlewick Press, 2003)

Subject(s): Family Problems; Interpersonal Relations; Diaries
Age range(s): Grades 7-10
Major character(s): Janet Foley Bandry, 16-Year-Old; Disha Paski, 16-Year-Old
Time period(s): 2000s
Locale(s): England

Summary: Tired of her family and determined to pursue the artistic side of life, Janet and her best friend Disha make a pact to enter their "Dark Phase." Using her journal, Janet plans to explore her creative side through daily entries while she limits her wardrobe to purple and black items. Day by day she records her parents' arguments, which ultimately lead to their separation; her fruitless quest of Elvin, for whom she becomes a vegetarian; and her forays into yoga and nose piercings, which are more humorous than successful in this offering from a British author. (231 pages)

Where it's reviewed:
Booklist, March 15, 2003, page 1319
Bulletin of the Center for Children's Books, March 2003, page 289
Library Media Connection, August 2003, page 82
Publishers Weekly, January 6, 2003, page 60
School Library Journal, May 2003, page 160

Other books by the same author:
Confessions of a Teenage Drama Queen, 1999
The Boy of My Dreams, 1997
Save the Last Dance for Me, 1995
Tall, Thin and Blonde, 1993

Other books you might like:
Meg Cabot, *All-American Girl*, 2002
    In protest Samantha dyes her clothes black, wishes she

were like her sister, and, while cutting her art class, saves the president from assassination.

Louise Rennison, *Angus, Thongs and Full-Frontal Snogging: Confessions of Georgia Nicolson*, 2000

In her diary, Georgia records her interest in kissing, her appearance and her opposition to most of what the adult worlds thinks is important.

Sue Townsend, *The Secret Diary of Adrian Mole, Aged 13 3/ 4*, 1982

Adrian Mole, who often feels beleaguered and put upon, begins his diary the day his first zit erupts.

1292

CAROL DIGGORY SHIELDS
SCOTT NASH, Illustrator

The Bugliest Bug

(Cambridge, MA: Candlewick Press, 2002)

Subject(s): Animals/Insects; Contests; Stories in Rhyme
Age range(s): Grades K-2
Major character(s): Dilly, Insect (damselfly), Heroine
Time period(s): Indeterminate
Locale(s): Fictional Country

Summary: A contest to choose the "bugliest bug" attracts insects of all kinds. Dilly has no plans to compete but she does want to watch so she joins the six-legged creatures hurrying toward the stage. Observant Dilly notices something odd about the judges—their wings appear to be attached with string. When she notices their fangs she sounds the alarm to one and all that the judges are not insects but arachnids! Dilly rallies the fearful insects encouraging each to do whatever they do best. Into the fray march ants as mantises pray until the stinkbugs carry the day as the spiders hurry away from their awful smell. Though the contest hasn't turned out as expected, it's easy for all the participants to see which bug is the bugliest—little Dilly. (32 pages)

Where it's reviewed:
Bulletin of the Center for Children's Books, April 2002, page 294
Children's Bookwatch, April 2002, page 3
Horn Book Guide, Fall 2002, page 345
Publishers Weekly, March 11, 2002, page 72
School Library Journal, May 2002, page 128

Awards the book has won:
IRA Children's Choices, 2003

Other books by the same author:
Lucky Pennies and Hot Chocolate, 2000
Martian Rock, 1999
I Wish My Brother Was a Dog, 1997
Saturday Night at the Dinosaur Stomp, 1997

Other books you might like:
Jerry Booth, *Big Bugs*, 1994
A factual look at many bugs describes habitats and characteristics.
Mary Howitt, *The Spider and the Fly*, 2002
An illustrated version of Howitt's 1829 poem shows the consequences of being overly trusting of an arachnid.

David Kirk, *Miss Spider's Tea Party*, 1994
Bugs don't accept lonely Miss Spider's invitation to tea because they think she plans to eat them.
Dee Lillegard, *The Big Bug Ball*, 1999
Insects of all kinds gather for the Big Bug Ball.

1293

SHARON SHINN

Angelica: A Novel of Samaria

(New York: Berkley/Ace, 2003)

Subject(s): Science Fiction; Romance; Cultural Conflict
Age range(s): Grades 9-Adult
Major character(s): Susannah, Spouse; Gabriel Aaron "Gaaron", Spouse
Time period(s): Indeterminate Future
Locale(s): Samaria, Planet—Imaginary

Summary: Samaria is guided by an orbiting artificial intelligence known as the god, and the winged humans, called angels, who communicate with it. Gaaron, soon to become the leader of the angels, expects god to communicate with him about his choice of Angelica, the woman who will be both his wife and helper. He is astonished when the god chooses Susannah, a member of the wandering Edori tribe. This high honor is no honor to Susannah, who loves her life of travel and simplicity, but her disillusionment with her unfaithful Edori lover makes her willing to abandon everything. She finds her new life at the angels' aerie to be difficult as her assigned role in it is much more formal than anything with which she is familiar, and Gaaron seems distant. The two struggle to establish a relationship, especially since Gaaron feels his responsibilities to Samaria and the god must come first. But when Samaria is threatened by incomprehensible enemies with powerful weapons, who disappear leaving only smoking ruins, Susannah is the one the god needs to help put things right. (485 pages)

Where it's reviewed:
Booklist, March 1, 2003, page 1153
Publishers Weekly, February 17, 2003, page 61
Voice of Youth Advocates, August 2003, page 242

Other books by the same author:
Angel-Seeker, 2004
Jenna Starborn, 2002
Summers at Castle Auburn, 2001

Other books you might like:
Catherine Asaro, *The Phoenix Code*, 2000
A researcher finds her relationship with an android turns difficult as he becomes more and more human.
Orson Scott Card, *The Ships of Earth*, 1994
A space colony is dependent on artificial intelligence for everything.
Tanya Huff, *The Second Summoning*, 2001
Claire inadvertently calls an angel to earth, where he becomes a problem.

1294

SHARON SHINN

Jenna Starborn

(New York: Ace, 2002)

Subject(s): Science Fiction; Romance
Age range(s): Grades 8-Adult
Major character(s): Jenna Starborn, Orphan; Everett Ravenbeck, Businessman
Time period(s): Indeterminate Future
Locale(s): Planet—Imaginary

Summary: An orphan, rejected by her relations, is sent away to boarding school. She does well there and finds a job on the remote estate of a wealthy man. He is seldom there, but the orphan gets along well with his ward and the housekeeper who live there. When the owner pays a visit, she finds his abrasive personality oddly compelling. Weird accidents begin to happen, but the owner brushes them off, despite the appearance that one of his lesser employees is to blame. Meanwhile, it is clear that there is a growing romantic attraction between the orphan and her employer. Jenna Starborn is Jane Eyre in space, complete with her own Mr. Rochester, now christened Ravenbeck, and Thornfield Hall has become Thorrastone Park on a desolate mining planet. Like Jane, Jenna is a no-nonsense type, but romance and gothic thrills will find her anyway. (381 pages)

Where it's reviewed:
Booklist, April 1, 2002, page 1313
Library Journal, April 15, 2002, page 127
Publisher's Weekly, March 4, 2002, page 62
Science Fiction Chronicle, June 2002, page 32
Voice of Youth Advocates, August 2002, page 205

Other books by the same author:
Angelica: A Novel of Samaria, 2003
Heart of Gold, 2000
Wrapt in Crystal, 1999

Other books you might like:
Jasper Fforde, *The Eyre Affair: A Novel*, 2001
    A violent criminal takes refuge in the pages of *Jane Eyre* and Special Agent Thursday Next enlists the help of characters to catch the bad guy.
Pat Murphy, *There and Back Again by Max Merriwell*, 1999
    Max is a space-going version of Bilbo Baggins, and his adventures parallel *The Hobbit*.
Sheri S. Tepper, *Beauty: A Novel*, 1991
    Beauty wakes up without the benefit of a prince's kiss, and her subsequent life follows the plot of several familiar fairytales.

1295

JOCELYN SHIPLEY

Getting a Life

(Toronto: Sumach Press, 2003)

Subject(s): Friendship; School Newspapers; Coming-of-Age
Age range(s): Grades 8-10
Major character(s): Carly Lark, 15-Year-Old; Tanya Petrovski, 15-Year-Old; Dawn Radford, Teenager
Time period(s): 2000s
Locale(s): Northington, Canada

Summary: Carly's best friend Tanya and her family move to Australia and, though Carly writes her every day, it's 49 days before she receives a reply. Though it's certainly not the letter she expected, it turns out that Tanya's advice to "get a life" is just what Carly needs to hear. Motherless, Carly didn't realize that she'd been treating Tanya's mother as her own and acting like a "clone of Tanya." Now she embarks on a one-sided friendship with her new neighbor Dawn who works in a clothing store and doesn't attend school. Carly also baby-sits each afternoon without pay for Dawn's little sisters so the social services agency won't find out they're left alone. At school she writes an advice column for her newspaper and though her advice is logical, it doesn't always match her actions. Eventually she tires of the shallow, vapid friendships that she's turned to as she tries to "get a life." Dumping some these new "friends," she also calls the social services agency and reports Dawn's mother as she slowly discovers who her real friends are. (223 pages)

Where it's reviewed:
Kliatt, September 2003, page 22
School Library Journal, August 2003, page 166

Other books by the same author:
Cross My Heart, 2004

Other books you might like:
Paula Danziger, *Snail Mail No More*, 2000
    When Tara moves away, she and Elizabeth correspond by e-mail and find it's easier to stay in touch, though not necessarily easier to stay friends.
Rosie Rushton, *Just Don't Make a Scene, Mum*, 1999
    Five British teens find their lives connected through a radio show that lets them describe embarrassing moments in this first of a series.
Don Trembath, *A Fly Named Alfred*, 1997
    Harper writes an anonymous column about high school life for his school paper, but when he makes fun of Veronica, he's challenged by her thug boyfriend.

1296

LISA SHULMAN
ASHLEY WOLFF, Illustrator

Old MacDonald Had a Woodshop

(New York: G.P. Putnam's Sons, 2002)

Subject(s): Farm Life; Animals; Stories in Rhyme
Age range(s): Preschool-Grade 1
Major character(s): Old MacDonald, Sheep, Carpenter
Time period(s): Indeterminate
Locale(s): Fictional Country

Summary: In this take-off on a familiar children's rhyme Old MacDonald lives on a farm with animals for companions but her passion is her woodshop. In this woodshop she has a saw, a drill, a hammer, a chisel, a file, a screwdriver and a paintbrush. As Old MacDonald teaches each of the various animals how to use their assigned tool the shop fills with the sounds of the many tools being used at once. When the work is done and the shop is quiet, the animals proudly unveil the toy farm they've made. E-I-E-I-O! (28 pages)

Where it's reviewed:
Booklist, September 15, 2002, page 243
Horn Book, September 2002, page 559
Publishers Weekly, August 19, 2002, page 87
School Library Journal, September 2002, page 206

Other books by the same author:
Unbelievable!, 2001

Other books you might like:
Judi Barrett, *Old MacDonald Had an Apartment House*, 1998
    The super of a city apartment building turns the vacant apartments into a farm.
Rosemary Wells, *Old MacDonald*, 1998
    The illustrated song begins the ''Bunny Reads Back'' line of books, designed to encourage the development of reading skills.
Suzanne Williams, *Old MacDonald in the City*, 2002
    In an urban park, Old MacDonald operates a food cart described in a rhyming, counting book.

1297

NEAL SHUSTERMAN

Full Tilt: A Novel

(New York: Simon & Schuster, 2003)

Subject(s): Brothers; Near-Death Experience; Carnivals
Age range(s): Grades 7-10
Major character(s): Blake, 16-Year-Old; Quinn, Brother (of Blake)
Time period(s): 2000s
Locale(s): United States

Summary: Brothers Blake and Quinn are opposite in their take on life: Blake is quiet, steady, and definitely Ivy League bound while Quinn holds nothing back and acts on impulse. At a carnival one night a mysterious woman approaches and tempts Blake with an offer to come to a special carnival, open only to invitees. He turns her down but realizes Quinn has stolen the invitation so is forced to follow him. At the special amusement park, open only from midnight to dawn, he discovers the price of admission is ones soul. All guests must go on seven rides before dawn or they become absorbed by the park, unable to leave. Blake has no choice but to take a seat on a ride, each of which reflects a terrifying moment from his life. The seventh and last ride whirls him back into the school bus accident where he was the only survivor, an event he's successfully squashed until now. (201 pages)

Where it's reviewed:
Booklist, May 15, 2003, page 1656
Bulletin of the Center for Children's Books, September 2003, page 35
Horn Book, July 2003, page 468
School Library Journal, June 2003, page 152
Voice of Youth Advocates, October 2003, page 328

Other books by the same author:
Schwa Was Here, 2004
Mind Storms: Stories to Blow Your Mind, 2002

Shattered Sky, 2002
The Shadow Club Rising, 2002
Thief of Souls, 1999

Other books you might like:
Charles Grant, *The Black Carousel*, 1995
    The Pilgrim's Travelers come to town and their carousel takes each rider into a different world, a world no one can explain.
Sharon E. Heisel, *Eyes of a Stranger*, 1996
    As Merissa investigates the empty, whirling carousel, she is caught by a serial killer who has already murdered four young girls.
William W. Johnstone, *Carnival*, 1989
    Killings begin in the town soon after the Carnival of Dread arrives; only the mayor and his daughter try to stop the evil powers.

1298

NEAL SHUSTERMAN

The Shadow Club Rising

(New York: Dutton/Penguin Putnam, 2002)

Subject(s): Clubs; Schools/High Schools
Age range(s): Grades 7-10
Major character(s): Jared Mercer, 9th Grader; Alec Smartz, 9th Grader
Time period(s): 1980s
Locale(s): United States

Summary: No one at his school has forgotten Jared's involvement with the Shadow Club, a group of wannabes who played practical jokes until a fire and the loss of a house halted their increasingly dangerous shenanigans. Jared tries to put the club behind him and start over, but when self-confident Alex Smartz arrives at his school, those practical jokes start up again and Jared's the primary suspect. Knowing that he's not involved and eager to clear up the suspicion around his name, Jared goes so far as to work with the school administration to find out who is stirring up havoc in this sequel to *The Shadow Club*. (200 pages)

Where it's reviewed:
Bulletin of the Center for Children's Books, April 2002, page 294
Kirkus Reviews, December 15, 2001, page 1762
Kliatt, January 2002, page 8
School Library Journal, February 2002, page 136
Voice of Youth Advocates, February 2002, page 439

Other books by the same author:
Schwa Was Here, 2004
Full Tilt: A Novel, 2003
Mind Storms: Stories to Blow Your Mind, 2002
Thief of Souls, 1999

Other books you might like:
Scott Johnson, *One of the Boys*, 1992
    Eric likes being noticed as one of the ''Benbow Boys,'' until their school pranks become malicious.
Paul Kropp, *The Countess and Me*, 2002
    New at school, Jordan's pleased to help some boys with

their homework, but rebels when they ransack the home of an older woman for whom he gardens.

Chris Lynch, *Slot Machine*, 1995

Elvin attends an orientation camp for his private school and realizes the camp is just an attempt to find the right ''slot'' for each potential student.

`1299`

MARLENE FANTA SHYER

The Rainbow Kite

(Tarrytown, NY: Marshall Cavendish, 2002)

Subject(s): Homosexuality/Lesbianism; Prejudice; Brothers
Age range(s): Grades 7-10
Major character(s): Matthew Cummings, 12-Year-Old; Bennett Lawson Cummings, 15-Year-Old, Homosexual; Jeremy, 8th Grader, Homosexual
Time period(s): 2000s
Locale(s): United States

Summary: Bennett's younger brother Matthew wonders why his brother doesn't have friends anymore and why he quit his swim team, though he never is brave enough to ask. He begins to figure it out, though, when he hears the names Bennett's classmates call him at school and the mean tricks they play on him: his brother is gay! Though initially upset at Bennett, Matthew reverts to his role as brother and sticks up for him whenever he can. New student Jeremy befriends Bennett and together the two decide to make a rainbow kite for their eighth grade graduation, but the kite is called a ''fag flag'' and their home is defaced. Bennett is so upset that he even attempts suicide, but luckily fails. Two elderly lesbians intervene and help to bring Bennett out of his despair, even giving him a puppy with six toes. Though painful for everyone, Bennett decides to attend graduation where the principal apologizes to Bennett and his classmates cheer for him, taking off their caps and exhibiting their rainbow-colored hair. (205 pages)

Where it's reviewed:
Booklist, December 15, 2002, page 754
Bulletin of the Center for Children's Books, December 2002, page 174
Horn Book Guide, Spring 2003, page 99
School Library Journal, November 2002, page 176
Voice of Youth Advocates, June 2003, page 144

Other books by the same author:
Two Daughters, 2002
Second Chances, 2001
Me & Joey Pinstripe, the King of Rock, 1988

Other books you might like:
Michael Cart, *My Father's Scar*, 1996
After Evan is beaten up for announcing his homosexuality, Andy worries that he did nothing to help.
Garret Freymann-Weyr, *My Heartbeat*, 2002
Ellen has never questioned her brother Link's friendship with James until a classmate asks her if they're a couple.
Alex Sanchez, *Rainbow Boys*, 2001
Jason, Kyle and Nelson face their senior year, and life-changing decisions, as they deal with their sexual identity.

`1300`

KIM SIEGELSON
LISA COHEN, Illustrator

Dancing the Ring Shout!

(New York: Jump at the Sun/Hyperion Books for Children, 2003)

Subject(s): African Americans; Traditions; Music and Musicians
Age range(s): Grades K-3
Major character(s): Toby, Child, Son; Grand, Grandfather
Time period(s): Indeterminate Past
Locale(s): Appling Farm

Summary: With the completion of harvest at Appling Farm it's time for the ''ring shout'' celebration. This is the first year that Toby has been old enough to participate and he doesn't know what noisemaker to bring that will speak ''from your heart to the ears of God.'' Everyone in his family has an instrument of some sort—his grandfather uses his cane, his father a hoop drum, his mother tin pans and his sister a dried gourd. When Toby approaches Grand with his dilemma, he is told that he can use his bare hands to show his gratitude and so he does. A historical note on the ring shouting tradition follows the text. (32 pages)

Where it's reviewed:
Booklist, December 1, 2003, page 685
Publishers Weekly, October 27, 2003, page 68
School Library Journal, December 2003, page 126

Other books by the same author:
Trembling Earth, 2004
Escape South, 2000
In the Time of the Drums, 1999 (Coretta Scott King Illustrator Award)

Other books you might like:
Jerry Pinkney, *Mirandy and Brother Wind*, 1988
Mirandy is sure that she will win the cakewalk if only she can catch Brother Wind to be her partner.
Irene Smalls, *Irene Jennie and the Christmas Masquerade: The Johnkankus*, 1996
The Johnkankus Parade is a Christmas tradition for North Carolina slaves.
Courtni Wright, *Jumping the Broom*, 1994
Lettie describes an African-American tradition, rooted in slavery, of jumping a broom at a wedding.

`1301`

JUDY SIERRA
WILL HILLENBRAND, Illustrator

'Twas the Fright Before Christmas

(San Diego: Gulliver Books/Harcourt, Inc., 2002)

Subject(s): Haunted Houses; Animals/Mice; Stories in Rhyme
Age range(s): Grades K-2
Major character(s): Unnamed Character, Mouse
Time period(s): Indeterminate
Locale(s): Fictional Country

Summary: On Christmas Eve the residents of a haunted house doze in the decorated living room until one awakens complaining that its tail has been mangled. Then the accusations begin as the ghoul, zombie, fiend, mummy, cat, manticore, bat, and dragon each blame the other for beginning the chain reaction that led to the werewolf's tail being mangled. By the time the tale is done, it's clear to all that a mouse (in Santa hat) that dropped down the chimney is responsible for the melee. To make things right, the mouse makes cocoa for all, reads a bedtime story then scurries back up the chimney wishing all a good night. (32 pages)

Where it's reviewed:
Horn Book Guide, Spring 2003, page 54
Kirkus Reviews, November 1, 2002, page 1625
New York Times Book Review, December 8, 2002, page 76
Publishers Weekly, September 23, 2002, page 30
School Library Journal, October 2002, page 63

Awards the book has won:
IRA Children's Choices, 2003

Other books by the same author:
Preschool to the Rescue, 2001
The Beautiful Butterfly: A Folktale from Spain, 2000
There's a Zoo in Room 22, 2000
The House That Drac Built, 1995

Other books you might like:
Clement C. Moore, *The Night Before Christmas: A Goblin Tale*, 2003
    The classic poem comprises the text of this edition in which illustrator Jacqueline Rogers portrays the characters as goblins.
Laura Joffe Numeroff, *If You Take a Mouse to the Movies*, 2000
    If you take a mouse to the movies during the holidays and buy him popcorn, he's going to think about decorating the Christmas tree.
Sandy Turner, *Silent Night*, 2001
    As a family sleeps, the dog barks in vain to alert them to the fat, red guy coming down the chimney.

1302

JUDY SIERRA
STEFANO VITALE, Illustrator

Can You Guess My Name?: Traditional Tales around the World

(New York: Clarion Books, 2002)

Subject(s): Folk Tales; Folklore; Multicultural
Age range(s): Grades 3-6
Time period(s): Indeterminate Past
Locale(s): Earth

Summary: The selector and reteller of fifteen folktales arranges them in five chapters based on their similarities to commonly known European tales such as ''The Three Pigs,'' ''Hansel and Gretel'' and ''Rumpelstiltskin.'' Each section begins with an explanation of the cultural variants of the section's theme. An ''Introduction'' explains the format and concluding ''Notes'' and bibliography provide more information about the selected tales. (110 pages)

Where it's reviewed:
Booklist, November 15, 2002, page 599
Bulletin of the Center for Children's Books, January 2003, page 211
Horn Book, January 2003, page 87
Publishers Weekly, September 30, 2002, page 74
School Library Journal, November 2002, page 149

Awards the book has won:
Notable Social Studies Trade Books for Young People, 2003
Smithsonian's Notable Books for Children, 2002

Other books by the same author:
Silly & Sillier: Read-Aloud Tales from around the World, 2002
Preschool to the Rescue, 2001
Nursery Tales around the World, 1996 (ALA Notable Children's Books)

Other books you might like:
Virginia Hamilton, *A Ring of Tricksters: Animal Tales from America, the West Indies, and Africa*, 1997
    Eleven tales grouped by geographic area of origin are united by the trickster theme.
Margaret Mayo, *Tortoise's Flying Lesson*, 1995
    A collection of retold and adapted folktales tells of animals supporting, tricking and learning from one another.
Howard Norman, *The Girl Who Dreamed Only Geese and Other Tales of the Far North*, 1997
    An illustrated collection of ten Inuit stories records the oral history of a people and their harsh environment.
Neil Philip, *Stockings of Buttermilk: American Folktales*, 1999
    Sixteen tales from the European tradition are retold as they evolved after reaching America's shores.

1303

WENDI SILVANO
RICARDO GAMBOA, Illustrator

Just One More

(San Jose, CA: All About Kids Publishing, 2002)

Subject(s): Travel; Transportation; Accidents
Age range(s): Grades K-3
Major character(s): Hector, Child, Passenger
Time period(s): Indeterminate
Locale(s): Andes Mountains, Peru

Summary: When Hector boards the bus it is so full there are no available seats yet the driver continues to stop each time someone is standing beside the road. To those trying to board Hector yells that the bus is packed, but each time the driver insists there is room for one more. Passengers carrying chickens, pigs and assorted bundles struggle onto the bus until finally the driver admits the bus is full. Then, a passenger in the back of the bus burps beginning a chain reaction that ends with the bus crashing into a ditch. The passengers get off and begin walking to their destinations as the driver pulls a bike off the bus roof and Hector asks, ''Just one more?'' (32 pages)

Where it's reviewed:
Children's Bookwatch, August 2002, page 6
Horn Book Guide, Spring 2003, page 54

School Library Journal, September 2002, page 206

Other books by the same author:
Hey Diddle Riddle, 2003

Other books you might like:
Suzanne Bloom, *The Bus for Us*, 2001
As each of a variety of vehicles nears the bus stop new student Tess asks her older brother, ''Is that the bus for us, Gus?''
Mary Casanova, *One-Dog Canoe*, 2003
Over a girl's protests each animal she meets on the lake climbs into her small canoe until the leap of a frog causes it to capsize.
Sarah Ellis, *Next Stop*, 2000
On Saturday Claire rides the bus, sitting behind and helping the driver (her father), as she watches the passengers come and go.
Mirra Ginsburg, *Mushroom in the Rain*, 1974
In an adaptation of a Russian tale an ant seeking refuge from the rain is joined under a mushroom by many other animals with the same idea.
Judy Hindley, *The Big Red Bus*, 1995
After a wheel on the big red bus gets stuck in a pothole no traffic can get past.

`1304`

JANE SIMMONS, Author/Illustrator

Ebb & Flo and the Baby Seal

(New York: Margaret K. McElderry Books, 2002)

Subject(s): Animals/Dogs; Pets; Lost and Found
Age range(s): Preschool-Grade 1
Major character(s): Ebb, Dog; Flo, Child, Daughter; Mom, Mother
Time period(s): 2000s
Locale(s): England

Summary: Hearing a cry from up the beach, bored Ebb hopefully races off the houseboat looking for something to do on a rainy day. Ebb locates the baby seal making the noise and together they play all day in the sand, the rock pools and the water. When hungry Ebb heads home the baby seal follows, crying. Ebb cannot understand why the seal simply doesn't go home so she hurries back to Flo and Mom, barking for help. Mom knows what to do to lead the lost baby seal back to Seal Island and her mother. Contented, Ebb concludes her day with a nice long nap. Originally published in Great Britain in 2000. (32 pages)

Where it's reviewed:
Booklist, January 1, 2002, page 868
Bulletin of the Center for Children's Books, March 2002, page 256
Horn Book Guide, Fall 2002, page 313
Publishers Weekly, January 28, 2002, page 292
School Library Journal, March 2002, page 201

Other books by the same author:
Ebb & Flo & the Greedy Gulls, 2000
Quack, Daisy, Quack, 2000
Ebb & Flo & the New Friend, 1999
Daisy & the Egg, 1998

Other books you might like:
Marjorie Flack, *Angus and the Ducks*, 1930
Curious Angus investigates the unusual quacking sounds coming from the other side of the hedge.
Stephen Huneck, *Sally Goes to the Beach*, 2000
Sally, a black lab, loves a day at the beach with her family.
Nancy Tafuri, *Have You Seen My Duckling?*, 1984
Followed by her other ducklings, a mother duck searches the pond for her one missing offspring in a Caldecott Honor book.

`1305`

MICHAEL SIMMONS

Pool Boy

(Brookfield, CT: Roaring Brook/Millbrook, 2003)

Subject(s): Fathers and Sons; Prisoners and Prisons; Wealth
Age range(s): Grades 7-10
Major character(s): Brett Gerson, 15-Year-Old; Alfie Moore, Aged Person
Time period(s): 2000s
Locale(s): California

Summary: All of a sudden, Brett, his mother and his sister are living with an aunt in a tiny house in the wrong section of town, he no longer expects a car for his birthday or listens to his expensive stereo, and he can't begin to forgive his father for the insider trading that led to his imprisonment. Humiliated at his loss in status, and laying low at school, Brett wallows in his misery and takes his anger out on his father, saying ugly things to him during prison visits when he knows the Plexiglas pane separates and protects him. Fired from his job at a fast-food restaurant, Brett accepts a position as an assistant pool cleaner with eccentric, energetic 70-year-old Alfie. In his own offbeat way, Alfie encourages Brett to be kinder to his father and consider forgiving him, though Brett isn't quite ready to change his stance. It takes Alfie's heart attack for Brett to realize that being a self-absorbed, bratty pool boy isn't the way he wants to live in this author's first novel. (164 pages)

Where it's reviewed:
Booklist, April 1, 2003, page 1391
Bulletin of the Center for Children's Books, June 2003, page 422
Publishers Weekly, May 5, 2003, page 222
School Library Journal, April 2003, page 168
Voice of Youth Advocates, June 2003, page 144

Awards the book has won:
Center for Children's Books Best Books, 2003

Other books you might like:
Carl Deuker, *High Heat*, 2003
Shane Hunter's father commits suicide rather than face prison for money laundering, leaving Shane doubting whether he's even able to play baseball.
Robert Hawks, *This Stranger, My Father*, 1988
Patty flees her foster home to reunite with her father, an escapee from prison where he was sent for selling secrets to the Russians.

Paul Many, *These Are the Rules*, 1997

As Colm begins his senior year, he begins to learn the rules for life; most importantly, that "there are no rules."

Randy Powell, *Run If You Dare*, 2001

When his father loses his job, it takes Gardner a while to realize that his mother's working for two and his once-idolized father's doing nothing.

1306

JAN SIMOEN
JOHN NIEUWENHUIZEN, Translator

And What about Anna?

(New York: Walker, 2002)

Subject(s): Brothers and Sisters; Family Problems; Grief
Age range(s): Grades 9-12
Major character(s): Anna Bracke, 16-Year-Old; Hugo Vandamme, Businessman (music promoter); Michael Lupovic, Brother (of Anna's); Marta Ugresio, Spouse (of Michael's); Irina Bracke, Mother (of Anna and Michael)
Time period(s): 1990s
Locale(s): Belgium; Balkan Peninsula

Summary: Two years after the supposed deaths of Michael and his wife Marta in a bomb blast while working for UNICED in Bosnia, his half-sister Anna receives a letter from Michael's friend Hugo that mentions the possibility that her brother is alive. As Anna finds out, and finally reveals to her parents, Michael and Marta were forced into hiding because of their relationship with Michael's Serbian father. As the war criminals are captured and brought to trial, it becomes safer for Marta to emerge from hiding. Michael has harder decisions to make partly because of his hearing loss from the bomb blast in this work translated from Dutch. (254 pages)

Where it's reviewed:
Booklist, May 1, 2002, page 1518
Kliatt, May 2002, page 14
Publishers Weekly, May 20, 2002, page 68
School Library Journal, June 2002, page 146
Voice of Youth Advocates, June 2002, page 123

Other books you might like:
Gaye Hicyilmaz, *Smiling for Strangers*, 2000

Soldiers mortally wound Nina's grandfather as they flee Yugoslavia, but he urges her to continue to England and seek shelter with a family friend.

Ellen Howard, *A Different Kind of Courage*, 1996

Two young refugees, terrified to leave their parents behind, meet on a train heading across Europe that will take them to America.

Alice Mead, *Adem's Cross*, 1996

After seeing his sister killed, his father beaten, and a large Orthodox cross carved on his chest by soldiers, Adem knows he must leave Kosovo to find peace.

1307

PETER SIS, Author/Illustrator

Madlenka's Dog

(New York: Frances Foster Books/Farrar Straus Giroux, 2002)

Subject(s): Animals/Dogs; Imagination; Neighbors and Neighborhoods
Age range(s): Grades K-3
Major character(s): Madlenka, Child, Friend; Cleopatra, Child, Friend
Time period(s): 2000s
Locale(s): New York, New York

Summary: Madlenka's parents refuse to satisfy her desire for a dog, any dog. Fortunately, Madlenka's active imagination gives her a dog to walk through the neighborhood that sparks memories of former canine pets in every passerby. When Madlenka meets Cleopatra who's out walking her "horse" the two friends run to the courtyard to play. Their versatile imaginary pets take on the shape, size and coloring needed for their various roles until the children are called home. Madlenka runs down the block, followed by real dogs of every description all the way to her front door. (40 pages)

Where it's reviewed:
Booklist, April 1, 2002, page 1323
Bulletin of the Center for Children's Books, June 2002, page 383
Horn Book, March 2002, page 205
Riverbank Review, Summer 2002, page 32
School Library Journal, April 2002, page 122

Awards the book has won:
Booklist Editors' Choice, 2002
Parenting's Books of the Year, 2002

Other books by the same author:
Madlenka, 2000 (Horn Book Fanfare)
Tibet through the Red Box, 1998 (Caldecott Honor Book)
Starry Messenger, 1996 (Caldecott Honor Book)

Other books you might like:
Lauren Child, *I Want a Pet*, 1999

A little girl desperately wants a pet but has some difficulty choosing one that meets the requirements of her family.

Bob Graham, *Let's Get a Pup! Said Kate*, 2001

Kate and her parents visit an animal shelter looking for a puppy and also find an appealing older dog to adopt.

Marc Simont, *The Stray Dog*, 2001

The stray dog that joins a family picnic is not imaginary but the children pretend he's their family's pet in order to save him from the dog warden.

1308

ARTHUR SLADE

Dust

(New York: Random/Wendy Lamb Books, 2003)

Subject(s): Supernatural; Depression (Economic); Missing Persons
Age range(s): Grades 7-10

Major character(s): Robert Steelgate, 11-Year-Old, Brother (of Matthew); Matthew Steelgate, Child, Brother (of Robert); Abram Harsich, Con Artist; Alden, Farmer, Uncle (of Robert)

Time period(s): 1930s

Locale(s): Horshoe, Saskatchewan, Canada

Summary: Living in a dust-choked farming town, Robert understands the worry of his family and his neighbors as the need for rain preoccupies them. Adding to his family's worry is the disappearance of his younger brother Matthew, who vanishes while walking to the store for some chewing gum. At the same time the mesmerizing stranger Abram Harsich arrives with a magical mirror and soon convinces the townspeople to build a "rainmill" and forget about the disappearance of three children. Only Robert and his uncle remain unimpressed by Harsich. When strange maladies beset some of the townspeople and Uncle Alden's farm is beset by calamity, Robert steals onto Harsich's property to investigate in this Canadian import. (183 pages)

Where it's reviewed:
Booklist, February 15, 2003, page 1065
Bulletin of the Center for Children's Books, March 2003, page 291
Horn Book, March 2003, page 217
School Library Journal, March 2003, page 240
Voice of Youth Advocates, February 2003, page 492

Awards the book has won:
ALA Best Books for Young Adults, 2004

Other books by the same author:
Tribes, 2002
Loki Wolf, 2000
The Haunting of Drang Island, 1999
Draugr, 1998

Other books you might like:
Ray Bradbury, *Something Wicked This Way Comes*, 1962
  When James and William discover the wonderful Pandemonium Shadow Show, they quickly wish they hadn't.
Susan Cooper, *The Dark Is Rising*, 1973
  As evil overtakes the world, one English boy has the power to stop it.
Philip Pullman, *His Dark Materials Trilogy*, 1996-2000
  When the Dust increases on Lyra's world, evil follows, flowing from a rift in time and space.

`1309`

ARTHUR SLADE

Tribes

(New York: Wendy Lamb/Random House, 2002)

Subject(s): Schools/Junior High School; Anthropology; Fathers and Sons

Age range(s): Grades 9-12

Major character(s): Percival "Percy" Montmount Jr., 17-Year-Old; Elissa, 12th Grader; Percival Montmount Sr., Anthropologist

Time period(s): 2000s

Locale(s): Saskatoon, Saskatchewan, Canada

Summary: According to Percy, his famous father the anthropologist died three years ago in the Congo when a tsetse fly bit him. Percy adapts some of his father's training to a study of his high school years as he keeps a field journal and records his observations of the various tribes he encounters, including the Jocks, Logo, Digerati and Born-Agains, to name a few. His only friend is Elissa who shares observations with him; together the two also constitute a tribe, which he refers to as "quasi-omniscient Observers." Occasionally he runs afoul of one of the members of the Jock tribe in which case he's usually pummeled. But as graduation night nears, he seems to become more aware of reality; when his father appears at the ceremony, Percy finally has to admit what he's denied to himself-his father didn't die but left his family for another woman. From this acceptance, with a little extra help from his counselor, Percy heads into the real world, far away from the tribes of his high school years. (134 pages)

Where it's reviewed:
Booklist, October 15, 2002, page 402
Publishers Weekly, September 23, 2002, page 74
Quill & Quire, August 2002, page 30
School Library Journal, October 2002, page 170
Voice of Youth Advocates, February 2003, page 482

Other books by the same author:
Dust, 2003
Loki Wolf, 2000
The Haunting of Drang Island, 1998
Draugr, 1997

Other books you might like:
Daniel Handler, *The Basic Eight*, 1999
  Being part of a clique called "the basic eight" sends Flannery to jail when a biology teacher is killed and she's accused of murder.
Ron Koertge, *The Brimstone Journals*, 2001
  Through short poems, 15 students at Branston High School reveal problems experienced during their senior year in high school.
Joy Nicholson, *The Tribes of Palos Verdes*, 1997
  New in Palos Verdes, Medina surfs, braves the "no girls" land of the waves and tries to save her twin from their possessive mother.
Kristen D. Randle, *Breaking Rank*, 1999
  As a member of "the Clan," Baby wears black and attends class, but doesn't speak or participate until he's placed in an honors class.

`1310`

WILLIAM SLEATOR

Parasite Pig

(New York: Dutton, 2002)

Subject(s): Science Fiction; Aliens

Age range(s): Grades 6-10

Major character(s): Barney, 16-Year-Old; Katie, Teenager; Toxoplasma Gondii, Alien

Time period(s): 2000s

Locale(s): Cambridge, Massachusetts; J'Koot, Planet—Imaginary

Summary: Just when Barney thought it was safe to play the game again, here comes a sequel to *Interstellar Pig*, complete with aliens ready to gobble up humankind, after a brief fattening. Barney foolishly brings out the gameboard and advertises for players, though he should have suspected that disguised aliens would show up. Barney and his almost-girlfriend Katie find themselves kidnapped to the planet J'Koot, where Barney sent the Piggy at the end of the last game. A giant wasp captures Katie and threatens to lay eggs in her, Barney's being fattened up by some crab-creatures and escape seems impossible with the parasitic Madame Toxoplasma Gondii residing in Barney's brain, where she muddles up his thinking. (212 pages)

Where it's reviewed:
Booklist, November 15, 2002, page 589
Horn Book, November 2002, page 764
Kliatt, November 2002, page 15
School Library Journal, October 2002, page 172
Voice of Youth Advocates, December 2002, page 402

Other books by the same author:
The Boy Who Couldn't Die, 2004
Marco's Millions, 2001
Rewind, 1999
The Boxes, 1998

Other books you might like:
Quentin Dodd, *Beatnik Rutabagas from Beyond the Stars*, 2001
    Best friends Walter and Yselle find themselves on opposite sides when they are kidnapped by aliens looking for military leaders.
Diane Duane, *Wizard's Holiday*, 2003
    Nita and Kit travel across the galaxy on what turns out to be only partly a holiday.
Alison Goodman, *Singing the Dogstar Blues*, 2003
    Joss is the lucky student who gets the alien as her partner.

1311

PAM SMALLCOMB

The Last Burp of Mac McGerp

(New York: Bloomsbury, 2003)

Subject(s): Schools; Behavior; Friendship
Age range(s): Grades 4-6
Major character(s): Mac McGerp, 10-Year-Old, 5th Grader; Lido Katz, 5th Grader, Friend; Mrs. Goodbody, Principal
Time period(s): 2000s (2003)
Locale(s): Withersberg

Summary: Champion burper Mac, in training for the Nationals, meets his nemesis when Mrs. Goodbody is transferred to his school. The harsh principal bans just about everything fun about a school day, including burping. Lido worries about Mac's ability to contain his burps for an entire school day, but he underestimates Mac's determination and sense of justice. Unwilling to succumb to Mrs. Goodbody's repressive measures, Mac follows the rules to the letter, leading Mrs. Goodbody to become more and more controlling. One thing she cannot control is Mac's final burp and the positive changes it brings to the school. (117 pages)

Where it's reviewed:
Booklist, February 15, 2004, page 1060
Publishers Weekly, October 6, 2003, page 84
School Library Journal, September 2003, page 220

Other books by the same author:
Trimoni Twins and the Changing Coin, 2004
Camp Buccaneer, 2002

Other books you might like:
Dav Pilkey, *Captain Underpants and the Attack of the Talking Toilets*, 1999
    Mischief makers Harold and George assisted by their principal's alter ego, Captain Underpants, use cafeteria food to vanquish an invention gone awry.
Don Trembath, *Frog Face and the Three Boys*, 2000
    A principal reduces the number of referrals to his office received by three boys by requiring them to enroll in a karate class.
Ross Venokur, *Meatball*, 2001
    When a vegetarian discovers that eating meatballs gives him magical powers he uses the ability to overcome the principal's plot to eliminate fun.

1312

CYNTHIA LEITICH SMITH
JIM MADSEN, Illustrator

Indian Shoes

(New York: HarperCollins Publishers, 2002)

Subject(s): Grandfathers; Indians of North America; Family Life
Age range(s): Grades 3-5
Major character(s): Ray Halfmoon, Indian (Seminole-Cherokee), Child; Grampa Halfmoon, Grandfather, Indian
Time period(s): 2000s
Locale(s): Chicago, Illinois; Oklahoma

Summary: Together Ray and Grampa enjoy baseball games at Wrigley Field, celebrate Christmas despite a storm that causes a power outage, and travel to Oklahoma to visit relatives and fish. Unable to afford a pair of moccasins spotted in an antique store, Ray trades the purchaser his own guaranteed Indian-worn shoes (high-tops with orange laces) for the moccasins. Then he gives the moccasins to Grampa for whom the moccasins provide a memory of home. Through Grampa's stories and visits to relatives in Oklahoma Ray learns about his heritage. (66 pages)

Where it's reviewed:
Booklist, June 2002, page 1725
Bulletin of the Center for Children's Books, September 2002, page 35
Horn Book Guide, Fall 2002, page 365
Publishers Weekly, April 1, 2002, page 83
School Library Journal, May 2002, page 128

Awards the book has won:
Center for Children's Books Best Books, 2002

Other books by the same author:
Rain Is Not My Indian Name, 2001
Jingle Dancer, 2000

Other books you might like:

Joseph Bruchac, *Eagle Song*, 1997
> When unemployment on their Iroquois reservation forces Danny's family to move to Brooklyn he depends on his cultural heritage to overcome prejudice.

Kimberley Griffiths Little, *Enchanted Runner*, 1999
> Seen as an outsider and a half-breed, Kendall must prove worthy of his Acoma heritage when he visits his deceased mother's village for the first time.

Craig Kee Strete, *The World in Grandfather's Hands*, 1995
> After his father's death, Jimmy's family moves to a noisy, confining city and Jimmy misses the quiet of his desert pueblo home.

1313

JANE DENITZ SMITH

Fairy Dust

(New York: HarperCollins Publishers, 2002)

Subject(s): Babysitters; Fairies; Honesty
Age range(s): Grades 3-6
Major character(s): Ruthie Reynolds, 9-Year-Old, Daughter; Alice, Babysitter, Teenager
Time period(s): 2000s (2002)
Locale(s): United States

Summary: When her dad interviews new after-school caretakers, lonely Ruthie insists that he hire magical, mysterious Alice who sprinkles her with "fairy dust" as she departs. The routine of Ruthie's life quickly comes to an end for a few hours every day as Alice tells her tales of fairies and leads her in the construction of a fairy village in the woods near her home. Ruthie becomes so caught up in Alice's fantasies and the magical ability of "fairy dust" to make all things right that she doesn't see the distortions of truth in Alice's thinking and actions until, on a trip to the mall, they are apprehended for shoplifting. Gradually, a sad, disillusioned Ruthie comes to recognize that Alice is a troubled teen who has not been truthful with her and has encouraged her to steal from her teacher and her father under the guise of serving the fairies. (152 pages)

Where it's reviewed:

Bulletin of the Center for Children's Books, April 2002, page 295
Horn Book Guide, Fall 2002, page 383
Kirkus Reviews, January 1, 2002, page 51
Publishers Weekly, December 17, 2001, page 91
School Library Journal, January 2002, page 140

Other books by the same author:
Charlie Is a Chicken, 1998
Mary by Myself, 1994

Other books you might like:

Kimberly Burke-Weiner, *The Maybe Garden*, 1992
> In her imagination a little girl changes her mother's garden into one filled with fairies.

Katherine Paterson, *The Great Gilly Hopkins*, 1978
> Eleven-year-old Gilly longs to live with her mother and rejects those who reach out to her in friendship.

Linda Leopold Strauss, *A Fairy Called Hilary*, 1999
> As if to prove a point, Hilary appears out of nowhere as Caroline muses about the possible existence of fairies.

Jacqueline Wilson, *Bad Girls*, 2001
> Mandy's brief friendship with Tanya ends when Tanya is caught shoplifting during a shopping trip with the younger girl.

1314

LANE SMITH, Author/Illustrator

Pinocchio the Boy: Incognito in Collodi

(New York: Viking, 2002)

Subject(s): Identity; Humor; Fathers and Sons
Age range(s): Grades 1-4
Major character(s): Pinocchio, Toy (puppet), Adoptee; Geppetto, Father, Artisan; Hershabel, Child, Daughter; Blue Fairy, Mythical Creature, Mother
Time period(s): Indeterminate
Locale(s): Collodi City, Fictional Country

Summary: Unbeknownst to Pinocchio the Blue Fairy changes him into a real boy as he sleeps. When he awakens he sets off, thinking he's still a puppet, to get some chicken soup for ailing Geppetto. None of his moneymaking ideas succeed but his efforts attract the attention of Hershabel who follows him around all day. Just when Pinocchio feels complete despair he notices Geppetto on television pleading for Pinocchio's return. Beside him on the TV screen is the Blue Fairy delivering soup to Geppetto. Hershabel recognizes her mother and finally understands that her work as a fairy explains her frequent absences. Pinocchio returns home, but Geppetto doesn't know this real boy so Blue Fairy has to explain what she's done. Then they all go skating at Collodi Rink. (44 pages)

Where it's reviewed:

Booklist, August 2002, page 1974
Bulletin of the Center for Children's Books, November 2002, page 126
Horn Book, September 2002, page 561
Publishers Weekly, July 22, 2002, page 177
School Library Journal, September 2002, page 206

Other books by the same author:
The Happy Hocky Family Moves to the Country!, 2003
The Happy Hocky Family, 1993
Glasses: Who Needs 'Em?, 1991
The Big Pets, 1991

Other books you might like:

Margaret Hillert, *Pinocchio*, 1982
> Retold as an early reader, the classic story of a wooden marionette with a lie-detector nose describes trials and adventures leading to being a real boy.

Jon Scieszka, *The Stinky Cheese Man: And Other Fairly Stupid Tales*, 1992
> Classic fairy tales take on a new look in these humorous retellings comprising a Caldecott Honor Book.

1315

LINDA SMITH
MARLA FRAZEE, Illustrator

Mrs. Biddlebox

(New York: HarperCollins Publishers, 2002)

Subject(s): Food; Problem Solving; Stories in Rhyme
Age range(s): Grades 1-3
Major character(s): Mrs. Biddlebox, Witch
Time period(s): Indeterminate
Locale(s): Fictional Country

Summary: Faced with a dreary morning, Mrs. Biddlebox decides to gather up the gloomy day and bake it into a cake. Toting pot and broom, Mrs. Biddlebox snatches bits of this and that and dumps them in her pot. With the broom she twirls the fog and yanks a ray of sun from the sky. She rolls the dark sky and crams it into the overflowing pot of bad day. After whipping, beating, rolling and kneading the day Mrs. Biddlebox stomps it into a tin and bakes it. The finished product is delicious with a cup of tea and Mrs. Biddlebox eats the entire cake before settling down to sleep on a beautiful night. (32 pages)

Where it's reviewed:
Booklist, November 15, 2002, page 612
Horn Book, November 2002, page 739
Publishers Weekly, July 15, 2002, page 73
Riverbank Review, Fall 2002, page 33
School Library Journal, October 2002, page 132

Other books by the same author:
When Moon Fell Down, 2001 (Booklist Editors' Choice)

Other books you might like:
Patricia Hooper, *How the Sky's Housekeeper Wore Her Scarves*, 1995
  A week of rain keeps the sky's housekeeper from her daily chores, necessitating her use of all her colored scarves on one day thus making a rainbow.
William Steig, *Pete's a Pizza*, 1998
  Pete's parents put the giggles back in his disappointing day by pretending to transform him into a pizza.
Judith Viorst, *Alexander and the Terrible, Horrible, No Good, Very Bad Day*, 1972
  Alexander is having a day in which everything that can possibly go wrong does.

1316

SHERRI L. SMITH

Lucy the Giant

(New York: Delacorte, 2002)

Subject(s): Runaways; Coming-of-Age; Family Problems
Age range(s): Grades 7-10
Major character(s): Lucy "Lucy the Giant" Otsego, 15-Year-Old, Runaway
Time period(s): 2000s
Locale(s): Sitka, Alaska; Kodiak, Alaska; *Miranda Lee*, At Sea (Bering Sea)

Summary: Tired of dragging her alcoholic father home from the bar each night; being called "Lucy the Giant" by her classmates; and feeling totally alone after her stray dog dies, Lucy doesn't correct anyone when it's assumed she's part of a work crew and winds up in Kodiak aboard a crabbing boat. Her height becomes an asset as everyone takes for granted she's an adult named Barbara, and her strength endears her to the captain and most of the crew for she doesn't mind the twenty-hour workdays. When a disgruntled crewmate reveals her true identity, Lucy has learned to like herself and earned enough money, so that she doesn't complain about being sent back to live with her drunken dad in this author's adventurous first novel. (217 pages)

Where it's reviewed:
Booklist, February 15, 2002, page 1010
Bulletin of the Center for Children's Books, April 2002, page 296
Publishers Weekly, December 24, 2001, page 65
School Library Journal, February 2002, page 140
Voice of Youth Advocates, October 2002, page 286

Awards the book has won:
ALA Best Books for Young Adults, 2003

Other books you might like:
Rodman Philbrick, *Max the Mighty*, 1998
  Just like knights of old, Max fights for the underdog; this time he kidnaps Worm from her abusive stepfather and together they search for her real father.
Randall Beth Platt, *The Likes of Me*, 2000
  Running away with a no-good logger, albino Cordy realizes he's only interested in the money she makes from the sideshow, so she heads back home.
Dana Stabenow, *Killing Grounds*, 1998
  While helping her uncle haul in salmon and halibut aboard his fishing boat, Kate Shugak also hauls in the body of a dead fisherman. Adult title.

1317

ETHEL FOOTMAN SMOTHERS
JOHN HOLYFIELD, Illustrator

The Hard-Times Jar

(New York: Frances Foster Books/Farrar Straus Giroux, 2003)

Subject(s): Migrant Labor; Books and Reading; African Americans
Age range(s): Grades 1-3
Major character(s): Emma Jean Turner, 8-Year-Old, Sister (older); Mama, Mother, Migrant Worker; Miss Miller, Teacher
Time period(s): Indeterminate Past
Locale(s): Pennsylvania

Summary: More than anything Emma Jean wants a real store-bought book of her very own. Until the family's hard-times jar has enough money for extras she has to be content with the books she writes with paper and pencil. When the family travels to Pennsylvania to pick apples Emma Jean is surprised when Mama tells her she'll not be working daily. In this community she'll go to school. This is the first time Emma Jean's ever gone to school up north so she's a bit intimidated by Miss Miller's classroom of white children. In Florida this would not be allowed. The sight of the class library is all it takes to convince Emma Jean to stay. She can read any book in the library, but none can leave the class. Emma Jean does well with that rule until the first weekend and then she sneaks two books home to read. Mama makes her return them with apologies on Monday morning. Recognizing that Emma Jean has done a hard thing, Mama reaches into the hard-times jar after school and picks out six quarters for Emma Jean, knowing she'll spend them on her first store-bought book. (32 pages)

Where it's reviewed:
Booklist, August 2003, page 1995
Bulletin of the Center for Children's Books, September 2003, page 36
Publishers Weekly, July 28, 2003, page 94
School Library Journal, October 2003, page 138

Awards the book has won:
Notable Social Studies Trade Books for Young People, 2004

Other books by the same author:
Auntee Edna, 2001

Other books you might like:
Tololwa M. Mollel, *My Rows and Piles of Coins*, 1999
  Each time Saruni earns a few coins helping his mother, he saves them in neat piles in order to buy his own bicycle.
Pat Mora, *Tomas and the Library Lady*, 1997
  While Tomas and his family of migrant workers pick corn in Iowa he is befriended by a librarian and introduced to the wider world through books.
Vera B. Williams, *A Chair for My Mother*, 1982
  In a Caldecott Honor book, Rosa and her grandmother save coins in a big jar until they have enough to buy a comfortable chair for her hard-working mother.

1318

MIDORI SNYDER

Hannah's Garden

(New York: Viking, 2002)

Subject(s): Mothers and Daughters; Grandfathers; Magic
Age range(s): Grades 7-10
Major character(s): Cassiopeia Emma "Cassie" Brittman, 17-Year-Old, Musician (violinist); Anne Brittman, Mother; Daniel "Poppie" Brittman, Grandfather, Artist; Hannah, Grandmother (great-grandmother)
Time period(s): 2000s
Locale(s): Rose Bay; Ashland

Summary: Preparing for both her prom and a violin recital, Cassie drops everything to accompany her mother Anne to her grandfather's farm when they receive word that Poppie's dying. The two women are shocked and disturbed to see the terrible shape of the farmhouse and Cassie's great-grandmother Hannah's garden. Both are nearly destroyed with fungus growing in the house, bats in the attic and plants lying damaged in the garden. Though Cassie has always known that her family's home was a little strange, for the first time she's really seeing it, as well as some strange creatures lurking around the grounds. Eventually her mother reveals some

family secrets that explain the two clans of faeries who are now fighting over Hannah's garden, the entryway to another world. It seems that Cassie's family are the green faeries while the new clan that wishes to take over are the red faeries in a delightful tale of humans with a touch of nature in them. (247 pages)

Where it's reviewed:
Booklist, October 15, 2002, page 402
Bulletin of the Center for Children's Books, February 2003, page 250
Publishers Weekly, October 21, 2002, page 77
School Library Journal, October 2002, page 172
Voice of Youth Advocates, December 2002, page 402

Other books by the same author:
Innamorati, 1998 (adult title)
Hatchling, 1995
The Flight of Michael McBride, 1994 (adult title)

Other books you might like:
Lynn Abbey, *Jerlayne*, 1999
  Jerlayne's insistence on uncovering all the secrets of Fairie leads her to some unpleasant truths about the relationship of humans and goblins.
Rebecca Lickiss, *Eccentric Circles*, 2001
  In addition to her great-grandmother's house, Piper also inherits the old lady's relationship with Fairie.
Mary E. Lyons, *Knockabeg: A Famine Tale*, 2001
  The Nuckelevee fairies destroy the East Isle and now turn to Ireland, where they curse the potato crop, and in turn the good fairies.
Josepha Sherman, *Windleaf*, 1993
  Thierry falls in love with a girl who's half human and half faerie; to win her hand, he must accomplish three dangerous quests.

1319

JUNE SOBEL
MELISSA IWAI, Illustrator

B Is for Bulldozer: A Construction ABC

(San Diego: Gulliver Books/Harcourt, Inc., 2003)

Subject(s): Construction; Amusement Parks; Stories in Rhyme
Age range(s): Preschool-Kindergarten
Major character(s): Unnamed Character, Child, Friend; Unnamed Character, Child, Friend
Time period(s): 2000s (2003)
Locale(s): United States

Summary: Two young friends watch the construction of an amusement park in this alphabet book. From the pouring of Asphalt to the Scaffolding coming down, the year-long process is fun to watch. The opening of the park is even more fun as the friends enjoy a Zoom on the roller coaster as the author's first book concludes. (32 pages)

Where it's reviewed:
Publishers Weekly, April 21, 2003, page 60
School Library Journal, July 2003, page 106

Other books you might like:
Virginia Lee Burton, *Mike Mulligan and His Steam Shovel*, 1939

Mike and his steam shovel Mary Anne dig the basement of Popperville's new town hall in just one day.

Don Carter, *Get to Work, Trucks!*, 2002

A road crew, using a wide variety of construction equipment builds a bridge over a pond.

Denise Fleming, *Alphabet under Construction*, 2002

Mouse works hard building each letter of the alphabet.

Kevin Lewis, *The Lot at the End of My Block*, 2001

A young boy watches while the lot at the end of his block is transformed into an apartment building.

1320

GARY SOTO

The Afterlife

(San Diego: Harcourt, 2003)

Subject(s): Death; Ghosts
Age range(s): Grades 7-12
Major character(s): Jesus "Chuy", Spirit, 17-Year-Old; Crystal, Teenager, Spirit
Time period(s): 2000s
Locale(s): Fresno, California

Summary: Chuy is just an ordinary guy who's excited to be meeting a girl at a club; his mistake is to compliment a man on his yellow shoes. In the next minute, Chuy is bleeding to death on the restroom floor, stabbed by Yellow Shoes, a hothead who found Chuy's innocent compliment insulting. Chuy is stunned as he separates from his body and begins his afterlife as a ghost. He visits his high school haunts, attempts to contact his parents, and even encounters his killer. Then he meets another ghost, Crystal, whose suicide seems as pointless as Chuy's murder. As the two become friends, Chuy realizes that he is slowly fading. (158 pages)

Where it's reviewed:
Booklist, August 2003, page 1981
Bulletin of the Center for Children's Books, October 2003, page 77
Horn Book, November 2003, page 755
Publishers Weekly, August 25, 2003, page 65
School Library Journal, November 2003, page 148

Awards the book has won:
Booklist Editors' Choice/Books for Youth, 2003
ALA Quick Picks for Reluctant Young Adult Readers, 2004

Other books by the same author:
Help Wanted: Stories, 2005
Local News, 2003
Petty Crimes, 1998
Buried Onions, 1997
Jesse, 1994

Other books you might like:
Eve Bunting, *The Presence: A Ghost Story*, 2003

Catherine meets someone who says he can help her reach the friend whose death Catherine feels she caused.

Meg Cabot, *Haunted: A Tale of the Mediator*, 2003

The Mediator is a little distracted by the fact that she has fallen for one of the spirits she should be helping to move on.

Rich Wallace, *Restless: A Ghost's Story*, 2003

Frank hasn't moved on since his death, so he tries to connect with his little brother, now a high school senior.

1321

GARY SOTO
TERRY WIDENER, Illustrator

If the Shoe Fits

(New York: G.P. Putnam's Sons, 2002)

Subject(s): Aunts and Uncles; Teasing; Mexican Americans
Age range(s): Grades 1-4
Major character(s): Rigo, 9-Year-Old, Brother (youngest); Celso, Uncle, Immigrant
Time period(s): 2000s
Locale(s): California

Summary: As the youngest of five children and the fourth boy, Rigo's clothes are always torn, faded hand-me-downs from his older brothers. When he receives a new pair of loafers for his birthday he is so thrilled that he puts nickels rather than pennies into their slits and goes for a walk. At the playground a local bully ridicules Rigo's shoes and steals the nickels from them so Rigo puts them in the closet, refusing to wear them. Some months later he takes them out to wear to a birthday party and discovers that he's outgrown them. Rigo also notices that he's grown larger than Uncle Celso so he passes the shoes on to him and learns that some people are happy to receive hand-me-downs. (32 pages)

Where it's reviewed:
Booklist, January 1, 2002, page 868
Bulletin of the Center for Children's Books, March 2002, page 258
Horn Book, July 2002, page 451
Publishers Weekly, December 24, 2001, page 64
School Library Journal, January 2002, page 110

Other books by the same author:
Chato and the Party Animals, 2000 (ALA Notable Children's Books)
Snapshots from the Wedding, 1997 (Booklist Editors' Choice)
The Old Man and His Door, 1996
Too Many Tamales, 1993 (Booklist Editors' Choice)

Other books you might like:
Johanna Hurwitz, *New Shoes for Silvia*, 1993

Silvia finds many new uses for her new red shoes while she waits to grow into them.

Mary Serfozo, *Benjamin Bigfoot*, 1993

Wearing his dad's big, old shoes helps Benjamin feels braver about beginning school.

Amanda Vesey, *Hector's New Sneakers*, 1993

The sneakers Hector receives for his birthday teach him to adjust his expectations and accept something that is a little different.

1322

JESSICA SOUHAMI, Author/Illustrator

Mrs. McCool and the Giant Cuhullin: An Irish Tale

(New York: Henry Holt and Company, 2002)

Subject(s): Legends; Folklore; Giants
Age range(s): Grades K-3
Major character(s): Cuhullin, Mythical Creature (giant); Finn McCool, Mythical Creature (giant), Spouse; Oona McCool, Spouse, Trickster
Time period(s): Indeterminate Past
Locale(s): Ireland

Summary: By sucking on his magic thumb Finn McCool learns that Cuhullin seeks to defeat him in order to establish his position as the strongest of all giants. While Finn's magic thumb gives him the ability to see what will be it doesn't provide him the wits to deal with what's coming. For the solution to the impending problems Finn turns to Oona who has a plan concocted in time for Cuhullin's four o'clock arrival. Oona tricks Cuhullin into believing that Finn is a larger, stronger giant than he expects thus saving Finn's life and relieving Cuhullin of his magic finger in the process. (32 pages)

Where it's reviewed:
Booklist, February 15, 2002, page 1018
Bulletin of the Center for Children's Books, March 2002, page 258
Horn Book, May 2002, page 340
Publishers Weekly, January 21, 2002, page 89
School Library Journal, March 2002, page 221

Other books by the same author:
In the Dark, Dark Wood, 2002
No Dinner: The Story of the Old Woman and the Pumpkin, 2000
One Potato, Two Potato, 1999
The Leopard's Drum: An Asante Tale from West Africa, 1995

Other books you might like:
Robert Byrd, *Finn Maccoul and His Fearless Wife: A Giant of a Tale from Ireland*, 1999
  Finn depends on the wisdom of his wife Oonagh to defeat the villainous giant Cucullin.
Tomie De Paola, *Fin M'Coul, the Giant of Knockmany Hill*, 1981
  With his wife, Oonagh's help, Fin outwits his rival Cucullin.
Pat O'Shea, *Finn MacCool*, 1987
  The legendary Irish hero appears in another retelling of one of his many exploits.

1323

BEATRICE SPARKS, Editor

Kim: Empty Inside

(New York: Avon/HarperCollins, 2002)

Subject(s): Eating Disorders; School Life; Self-Perception
Age range(s): Grades 7-10

Major character(s): Kim, Gymnast, 17-Year-Old; Lawrence, Student—College
Time period(s): 2000s
Locale(s): Arizona; Los Angeles, California (UCLA)

Summary: Is she too fat? Would she be a better gymnast if she weren't so heavy? Kim struggles with the feeling that she looks fat, yet she also likes to eat. What to do? Kim discovers that bingeing and purging allow her to eat and then get rid of her food, but Kim still thinks she's either too fat or too skinny. Just as her weight is out of control, so are her attempts to have relationships with others, but she's unable to help herself. After graduating from high school, she's thrilled to attend UCLA, where her mother and twin sisters all went, but her weight concerns follow her to California. At school Kim eventually admits her eating problems, begins therapy treatment and works out her relationship with Lawrence. (165 pages)

Where it's reviewed:
Kliatt, July 2002, page 24
School Library Journal, September 2002, page 234
Voice of Youth Advocates, October 2002, page 286

Awards the book has won:
ALA Quick Picks for Reluctant Young Adult Readers, 2003

Other books by the same author:
Treacherous Love: The Diary of an Anonymous Teenager, 2000
Annie's Baby: The Diary of Anonymous, a Pregnant Teenager, 1998
Almost Lost: The True Story of an Anonymous Teen's Life on the Streets, 1996
It Happened to Nancy, 1994

Other books you might like:
Cherie Bennett, *Life in the Fat Lane*, 1998
  Lara suddenly puts on weight; when she weighs over 200 pounds, she sees life from the ''fat side'' as her social standing plummets.
Liza F. Hall, *Perk! The True Story of a Teenager with Bulimia*, 1997
  After people comment on how good she looks after being sick with bronchitis and losing weight, Perk veers into bulimia.
Steven Levenkron, *The Best Little Girl in the World*, 1978
  Though Francesca feels fat, at five-feet-four she weighs only 98 pounds and doesn't realize she's killing herself.
Leslea Newman, *Fat Chance*, 1994
  To lose weight Judi tries her friend Nancy's method of bingeing and purging to stay slim, until Nancy's hospitalized.

1324

MARK SPERRING
ALEXANDRA STEELE-MORGAN, Illustrator

Find-a-Saurus

(New York: The Chicken House/Scholastic, Inc., 2003)

Subject(s): Imagination; Dinosaurs; Fantasy
Age range(s): Preschool-Grade 1

Major character(s): Marty, Child, Son; Unnamed Character, Mother
Time period(s): 2000s (2003)
Locale(s): United States

Summary: After Marty's mother tells him about dinosaurs, he decides that he wants to meet one. Marty refuses to believe his mother when she says that dinosaurs are extinct and decides instead that they are simply very good at hiding. Marty begins an exhaustive search of his house and finds a monster (under the bed, of course), some elves, a dodo bird and a wide variety of other fantastic creatures but, alas, no dinosaurs. (32 pages)

Where it's reviewed:
Publishers Weekly, December 15, 2003, page 71
School Library Journal, January 2004, page 106

Other books by the same author:
Wanda's First Day, 2004

Other books you might like:
Carol Carrick, *Patrick's Dinosaurs*, 1983
    During a trip to the zoo Patrick's big brother tells him about dinosaurs and Patrick begins to see the creatures everywhere.
John Steven Gurney, *Dinosaur Train*, 2002
    Jesse loves two things: dinosaurs and trains. So when a train of dinosaurs picks him up one night at bedtime, he has an exciting ride.
Peter Sis, *Dinosaur!*, 2000
    While bathing with his toy dinosaur, a little boy finds himself in a prehistoric pond with even more company.
Jan Wahl, *I Met a Dinosaur*, 1997
    After a trip to the Natural History Museum, a little girl begins seeing dinosaurs all around.

1325

JERRY SPINELLI

Loser

(New York: HarperCollins, 2002)

Subject(s): Self-Acceptance; Family Life; School Life
Age range(s): Grades 5-8
Major character(s): Donald Zinkoff, Student—Middle School
Time period(s): 2000s
Locale(s): United States

Summary: Pegged a loser by his fourth-grade classmates, Donald seems oblivious of their labeling as he skips through life. He's not particularly athletic, or very smart, or able to act "cool" like his classmates expect, but he has a great family and enjoys his neighbors, hoping one day to become a mailman like his father. Though he tends to throw up too often and is never picked first for a school team, he doesn't see himself as a loser. When a little girl is lost and he continues to hunt for her, unaware that she's already been found, some of his loser status begins to dissipate and his classmates regard him a little more kindly. (218 pages)

Where it's reviewed:
Booklist, May 15, 2002, page 1597
Bulletin of the Center for Children's Books, May 2002, page 342
Horn Book, July 2002, page 472

Publishers Weekly, February 11, 2002, page 188
School Library Journal, May 2002, page 160

Awards the book has won:
Publishers Weekly Best Children's Books, 2002

Other books by the same author:
Milkweed, 2003
Stargirl, 2000
Wringer, 1997
Crash, 1996
Maniac Magee, 1990

Other books you might like:
Steven Cousins, *Frankenbug*, 2001
    Fed up with Jed's teasing about his insects, Adam creates Frankenburg, brings it to life with fireflies and uses "Frankie" to scare Jed.
Jack Gantos, *Joey Pigza Swallowed the Key*, 1998
    Unless he takes his medication, Joey is an out-of-control kid who sticks his finger in the pencil sharpener, swallows his house key or careens off desks.
Ross Venokur, *The Autobiography of Meatball Finkelstein*, 2001
    Vegetarian Meatball is tired of being teased about his eating, so one day swallows a meatball in the school cafeteria which gives him secret powers.

1326

JERRY SPINELLI

Milkweed

(New York: Knopf, 2003)

Subject(s): Holocaust; World War II; Orphans
Age range(s): Grades 6-10
Major character(s): Misha "Stopthief" Pilsudski, Orphan, Streetperson; Uri, Streetperson; Janina Milgrom, Child
Time period(s): 1930s; 1940s
Locale(s): Warsaw, Poland

Summary: Young "Stopthief" wanders the streets of Warsaw, not knowing if he's a Jew or a gypsy, orphaned or lost, surviving by stealing what food he can. Taken in by Uri, ringleader of a group of Jewish boys, he's given the name Misha along with a suitable Gypsy family history that, after repeated tellings, becomes fact to Misha. With a surplus of abandoned stores, Uri and Misha dine on caviar and candy; Misha befriends Janina; and is awestruck when the Nazis parade through town, completely bewitched by their marching boots. Party time ends when the Jews are herded into the ghetto and Misha accompanies Janina's family, through the two children sneak out at night to scavenge whatever food they can. The trains arrive to "resettle" the Jews and only Uri's intervention prevents Misha from traveling to the concentration camps in an unforgettable tale. (208 pages)

Where it's reviewed:
Booklist, October 15, 2003, page 404
Horn Book, November 2003, page 756
Publishers Weekly, September 1, 2003, page 90
School Library Journal, November 2003, page 149
Voice of Youth Advocates, February 2004, page 498

Awards the book has won:
ALA Best Books for Young Adults, 2004

Other books by the same author:
Loser, 2002
Stargirl, 2000
Wringer, 1997
Maniac Magee, 1993

Other books you might like:
Kimberly Brubaker Bradley, *For Freedom: The Story of a French Spy*, 2003
Intent upon a career singing opera, Suzanne is oblivious to the war until the Germans gain control of her French town and evict her family.
Uri Orlev, *Run, Boy, Run*, 2003
Orphaned Jew Srulik survives the Holocaust due to his courage, help from others and plain old luck.
Eva Wiseman, *My Canary Yellow Star*, 2002
When the Nazis occupy her country, Hungarian Marta contacts Swedish diplomat Raoul Wallenberg who is giving passports to Jews.

1327

STEPHANIE SPINNER

Quiver
(New York: Knopf/Random House, 2002)

Subject(s): Mythology; Gender Roles; Hunting
Age range(s): Grades 7-10
Major character(s): Atalanta, 16-Year-Old; Artemis, Deity (goddess of the hunt); Hippomenes, Spouse (husband of Atalanta); Eros, Son (of Aphrodite), Deity (god of love); Aphrodite, Deity (goddess of love); Iasus, Royalty (king), Father (of Atalanta)
Time period(s): Indeterminate Past
Locale(s): Greece

Summary: King Iasus is so disappointed that his first child is a girl that he leaves her exposed on the mountainside as was the custom of that time. Atalanta is saved by the goddess of the hunt, Artemis, and grows up to be a swift runner and a good hunter. Hearing of her prowess while hunting the Calydonian boar, her father demands that she return to his kingdom, marry and produce an heir for him. Because Atalanta has taken a vow of chastity for Artemis, she agrees to come back but will only marry a man who can beat her in a foot race. Thinking she has a foolproof contest, Atalanta is unprepared for the intervention of Eros and Aphrodite who send love arrows her way and upset the race with golden apples, all so she will be united with her soul mate Hippomenes in the retelling of the Atalanta myth in this author's first young adult novel. (177 pages)

Where it's reviewed:
Booklist, January 2003, page 870
Bulletin of the Center for Children's Books, February 2003, page 251
Horn Book, January 2003, page 85
Publishers Weekly, November 4, 2002, page 86
Voice of Youth Advocates, December 2002, page 402

Other books you might like:
Priscilla Galloway, *Atalanta: The Fastest Runner in the World*, 1995
This version of the myth of Atalanta also examines the motive for abandoning female children in ancient Greece.
Clemence McLaren, *Aphrodite's Blessings*, 2001
The mythical tales of the tribulations of marriage for Atalanta, Andromeda and Psyche are retold in these three love stories.
Jane Yolen, *Atalanta and the Arcadian Beast*, 2003
Aided by the bear that found her, young Atalanta hunts the winged lion that killed her guardian in this third of the *Young Heroes* series.

1328

GENNADY SPIRIN, Author/Illustrator
TATIANA POPOVA, Translator

The Tale of the Firebird
(New York: Philomel/Penguin Putnam, 2002)

Subject(s): Folk Tales; Princes and Princesses; Russians
Age range(s): Grades 1-4
Major character(s): Ivan-Tsarevitch, Royalty
Time period(s): Indeterminate Past
Locale(s): Russia

Summary: Ivan-Tsarevitch reports seeing a firebird stealing his father's golden apples. His father tells Ivan-Tsarevitch and his other two sons that whoever brings him the bird shall have half his kingdom. With the help of a gray wolf, Ivan-Tsarevitch begins his quest, which eventually takes him to three kingdoms and wins him three prizes: the firebird, a horse with a golden mane, and the love of a beautiful princess. This retelling combining several traditional tales is the first book also written by this children's book illustrator. (32 pages)

Where it's reviewed:
Booklist, November 15, 2002, page 606
Bulletin of the Center for Children's Books, November 2002, page 126
Publishers Weekly, August 5, 2002, page 72
School Library Journal, September 2002, page 218

Other books you might like:
Demi, *The Firebird*, 1994
A quest started by archer Dimitri when he finds a firebird feather eventually leads to him becoming a prince.
J. Patrick Lewis, *The Frog Princess: A Russian Folktale*, 1994
Prince Ivan is forced to marry a frog, but the frog turns out to be Vasilisa the Wise, under a curse from her evil father.
Alison Lurie, *Black Geese: A Baba Yaga Story from Russia*, 1999
When Elena discovers her baby brother is missing, she knows she must rescue him from Baba Yaga.
Ruth Sanderson, *The Golden Mare, the Firebird, and the Magic Ring*, 2001
When young Alexi heads off to seek his fortune the jealous tsar sends him on several seemingly impossible tasks.
Aaron Shepard, *The Sea King's Daughter: A Russian Legend*, 1997

The story of a poor musician whose luck changes after he plays at the Sea King's palace is an ALA Notable Book.

Jane Yolen, *The Firebird*, 2002

With the help of the firebird, Prince Ivan is able to free the nine princesses that Kotschei the Deathless has held captive.

1329

NANCY SPRINGER

Blood Trail

(New York: Holiday, 2003)

Subject(s): Murder; Grief; Mystery and Detective Stories
Age range(s): Grades 7-10
Major character(s): Jeremy ''Booger'' Davis, 17-Year-Old; Aaron Gingrich, 17-Year-Old, Victim; Nathan Gingrich, Twin (of Aaron)
Time period(s): 2000s
Locale(s): Pinto River

Summary: Playing down at the swimming hole, Aaron and Jeremy suddenly realize they each need to go home and finish chores, though surprisingly Aaron admits to being afraid of his twin brother Nathan. Reaching Jeremy's house, he agrees to call Aaron in ten minutes, though thinks it's a strange request. The ten minutes elapse and Jeremy calls but Nathan answers and says that no one's home. When he hears an ambulance, Jeremy knows that something is wrong at Aaron's house. His worst fears are realized when he learns that Aaron is dead, stabbed more than 70 times. But who did it? Was it Nathan, who was found covered in blood? Or perhaps Aaron's sister who is later sent away? Aaron wonders if he'll ever learn what did happen on that terrible afternoon. (105 pages)

Where it's reviewed:
Booklist, May 1, 2003, page 1528
Horn Book Guide, Fall 2003, page 288
School Library Journal, May 2003, page 161
Voice of Youth Advocates, August 2003, page 231

Awards the book has won:
ALA Quick Picks for Reluctant Young Adult Readers, 2004

Other books by the same author:
Separate Sisters, 2001
Secret Star, 1997
Fair Peril, 1996

Other books you might like:
Robert Cormier, *Tenderness*, 1997
    When a girl he cares for accidentally drowns, a serial killer knows the police will claim he murdered her.
E.L. Konigsburg, *Silent to the Bone*, 2000
    Falsely accused of hurting his sister, mute Branwell is not able to defend himself until his best friend devises a way to break through his silence.
Alan Watt, *Diamond Dogs*, 2000
    When Neil's sheriff father hides the evidence of an accidental death caused by Neil, they are forever linked in a chilling, destructive bond.
Paul Zindel, *The Square Root of Murder*, 2002
    When their disliked professor of calculus is murdered, P.C.

and Mackenzie find themselves running to track down the professor's murderer.

1330

NANCY SPRINGER

Lionclaw: A Tale of Rowan Hood

(New York: Philomel/Penguin Putnam, 2002)

Subject(s): Courage; Middle Ages; Adventure and Adventurers
Age range(s): Grades 5-8
Major character(s): Rowan Hood, 14-Year-Old; Lionel, Musician (minstrel); Robin Hood, Outlaw; Roderick Lionclaw, Royalty (lord); Guy of Gisborn, Bounty Hunter
Time period(s): 12th century
Locale(s): Sherwood Forest, England

Summary: At seven feet tall, young Lionel is nothing but a disappointment to his father Lord Lionclaw, who envisioned a brave warrior of a son; instead Lionel is a gentle minstrel who prefers his music and lute-playing to battle. Belonging to Rowan's band, the minstrel lives in Sherwood Forest, along with Robin Hood and his band. When Lionel hears that Robin has captured Lord Lionclaw, he mistakenly thinks that playing his music for his father will reconcile them; instead his father is so angered that he calls for Lionel's head. With the bounty hunter Guy of Gisborn setting traps throughout the woods to capture Lionel, even Robin Hood and his men disappear from the forest. When Rowan refuses to leave and is caught in one of the bear traps, Lionel discards his whining ways and rushes to her rescue, finding a way to use his music to heal her in this sequel to *Rowan Hood*. (122 pages)

Where it's reviewed:
Booklist, October 1, 2002, page 327
Bulletin of the Center for Children's Books, February 2003, page 251
Kirkus Reviews, September 1, 2002, page 1321
Kliatt, September 2002, page 14
Voice of Youth Advocates, December 2002, page 403

Other books by the same author:
Wild Boy: A Tale of Rowan Hood, 2004
Outlaw Princess of Sherwood: A Tale of Rowan Hood, 2003
Rowan Hood: Outlaw Girl of Sherwood Forest, 2001

Other books you might like:
Michael Cadnum, *Forbidden Forest: The Story of Little John and Robin Hood*, 2002
    Continuing the retelling of Robin Hood's adventures, this describes John Little's admittance to the ''band of merry men.''
Robin McKinley, *The Outlaws of Sherwood*, 1988
    A realistic reworking of the story of Robin Hood with Robin as a more ordinary man.
Jane Yolen, *Sherwood: Original Stories from the World of Robin Hood*, 2000
    Eight stories explore the life around Sherwood Forest, though not necessarily from the original Robin Hood's perspective.

`1331`

ELIZABETH SPURR
MARTIN MATJE, Illustrator

A Pig Named Perrier

(New York: Hyperion Books for Children, 2002)

Subject(s): Animals/Pigs; Movie Industry; Wealth
Age range(s): Grades K-2
Major character(s): Perrier, Pig; Marbella, Actress
Time period(s): 2000s (2002)
Locale(s): California; France

Summary: Perrier, adopted from a Beverly Hills pet store by movie starlet Marbella, lives a pampered, carefree existence. Then, on a trip to Marbella's country house, Perrier discovers what is missing in his life—mud! Marbella is horrified at Perrier's messy appearance and, to please her, he promises to stay clean. Still, Perrier pines for mud, getting thinner and thinner until the night he discovers Marbella using a mud facial mask. Once Marbella figures out what's been ailing Perrier they take a trip together to a Palm Desert spa for a day in the mud baths. (32 pages)

Where it's reviewed:
Booklist, April 15, 2002, page 1409
Bulletin of the Center for Children's Books, September 2002, page 36
Horn Book Guide, March 18, 2002, page 102
Publishers Weekly, March 18, 2002, page 102
School Library Journal, July 2002, page 100

Other books by the same author:
The Peterkins' Christmas, 2004
Two Bears Beneath the Stairs, 2002
The Long, Long Letter, 1996

Other books you might like:
Andre Dahan, *Squiggle's Tale*, 2000
   Squiggle writes his parents about his adventures while visiting his cousins in Paris.
Ian Falconer, *Olivia*, 2000
   The introduction to the energetic, irrepressible pig that is Olivia is a Caldecott Honor Book.
Barbro Lindgren, *Benny's Had Enough!*, 1999
   A dirt-loving pig runs away after his mother tries to clean him up.
Simon Puttock, *Squeaky Clean*, 2002
   Mama Pig convinces her three piglets to take a bath.

`1332`

ELIZABETH SPURR

Surfer Dog

(New York: Dutton, 2002)

Subject(s): Animals/Dogs; Sports/Surfing; Moving, Household
Age range(s): Grades 4-6
Major character(s): Peter "Pete" Fox, 11-Year-Old, Surfer; Blackie "Surfer Dog", Dog (black Lab)
Time period(s): 2000s
Locale(s): Whaler's Cove, California (Central Coast)

Summary: Moving from his friends in Los Angeles to the central coast of California is hard on Pete. He surfs but is yelled at for getting in the way of the older kids, but is too good to surf in the beginner's area. To find the good waves he needs to go off by himself, but he's not allowed to surf alone. That first day help comes in the form of Blackie, a black Lab who loves to ride the waves and seems to know instinctively when a good swell comes rolling in. Pete's thrilled to have this dog adopt him and even happier when his mother likes Blackie. Though his schoolwork suffers because of his surfing, and he has to attend summer school, Pete's still happy until Blackie's owner claims him. But sometimes a dog adopts a boy, and nothing can change that. (103 pages)

Where it's reviewed:
Booklist, June 2002, page 1725
Bulletin of the Center for Children's Books, September 2002, page 36
Horn Book Guide, Fall 2002, page 383
School Library Journal, July 2002, page 124

Other books you might like:
Marty Crisp, *Ratzo*, 1998
   Dreams of allowing his rescued greyhound Ratzo to race again change when Josh sees the conditions under which the racing occurs.
Theresa Tomlinson, *Riding the Waves*, 1993
   Visiting an elderly friend of his grandmother's leads Matt to an introduction to the surfing group of Seaburn Bay and a chance to "ride the waves."
Tim Winton, *Lockie Leonard, Human Torpedo*, 1991
   A tryst with popular Vicki doesn't pan out and Lockie's soon back on his surfboard where he's happiest.

`1333`

ALEXANDER STADLER, Author/Illustrator

Beverly Billingsly Borrows a Book

(San Diego: Silver Whistle/Harcourt, Inc., 2002)

Subject(s): Books and Reading; Libraries; Dreams and Nightmares
Age range(s): Grades K-3
Major character(s): Beverly Billingsly, Bear, Daughter; Mrs. Del Rubio, Bird, Librarian
Time period(s): Indeterminate
Locale(s): Fictional Country

Summary: In the author's first book, Beverly Billingsly proudly receives her very own library card and uses it to check out a book about dinosaurs which she reads whenever she has time to spare. Finally, as she reads the last page and closes the book she notices the due date-yesterday. Beverly, with suggestions from classmates, imagines the terrible consequences facing a library patron with an overdue book so she delays returning it another day. When a nightmare about the predicament awakens Beverly, her mother realizes what's happened and helps Beverly resolve the problem. (32 pages)

Where it's reviewed:
Booklist, March 15, 2002, page 1265
Bulletin of the Center for Children's Books, April 2002, page 296

Horn Book Guide, Spring 2003, page 55
Publishers Weekly, March 11, 2002, page 70
School Library Journal, April 2002, page 124

Other books you might like:
Marc Brown, *D.W.'s Library Card*, 2001
    D.W. learns to write her name in order to get her own
    library card.
Lisa Campbell Ernst, *Stella Louella's Runaway Book*, 1998
    Stella searches frantically for the library book that is due
    by five o'clock today.
Barbara Ann Porte, *Harry in Trouble*, 1989
    Harry really has problems; he's lost his library card for the
    third time.

1334

ALEXANDER STADLER, Author/Illustrator

Beverly Billingsly Takes a Bow
(San Diego: Silver Whistle/Harcourt Inc., 2003)

Subject(s): Plays; Theater; Acting
Age range(s): Grades K-2
Major character(s): Beverly Billingsly, Student—Elementary
    School, Actress (amateur); Unnamed Character, Lion,
    Teacher; Unnamed Character, Student—Elementary
    School, Actress (amateur)
Time period(s): 2000s (2003)
Locale(s): United States

Summary: Beverly Billingsly loves to play dress up, so when
her teacher announces the upcoming school musical, Beverly
can't wait to audition. When her turn comes though, Beverly
freezes and can't say a word. She is cast in two minor roles
and concentrates on doing as well as possible. When the lead
actress gets stage fright on opening night, Beverly helps feed
her lines to her and the show goes on. (32 pages)

Where it's reviewed:
Publishers Weekly, February 24, 2003, page 70
School Library Journal, April 2003, page 138

Other books by the same author:
Beverly Billingsly Can't Catch, 2004
Lila Bloom, 2004
Beverly Billingsly Borrows a Book, 2002

Other books you might like:
Cari Best, *Shrinking Violet*, 2001
    Shy Violet saves the show during her school play.
James Howe, *Horace and Morris Join the Chorus (but what
    about Dolores?)*, 2002
    When Dolores isn't chosen to join the chorus she searches
    for a way to let the conductor know how much participa-
    tion means to her.
Nancy Poydar, *Bunny Business*, 2003
    Harry saves the day when the star of the school play gets
    stage fright.
Mark Shulman, *Stella the Star*, 2004
    Stella is cast as a star in her school play.

1335

SANNA STANLEY, Author/Illustrator

Monkey for Sale
(New York: Frances Foster Books/Farrar Straus Giroux, 2002)

Subject(s): Shopping; Wildlife Rescue; Problem Solving
Age range(s): Grades K-3
Major character(s): Luzolo, Daughter, Friend; Kiese, Friend;
    Mama Lusufu, Neighbor, Saleswoman
Time period(s): Indeterminate Past
Locale(s): Republic of the Congo

Summary: Luzolo learns the fine art of bartering on Market
Day. With her five-franc piece she purchases nail polish and
snacks that she shares with Kiese as they make bracelets from
Kiese's purchases. Then they discover that Mama Lusufu has
captured a monkey and is selling it for 15 francs. In order to
rescue the monkey they have to negotiate a series of bartered
exchanges to meet Mama Lusufu's demands. By using their
nail polish and bracelets for the first trade they negotiate their
way through several vendors and finally receive the water pot
needed to trade for the monkey that they set free in the nearby
jungle. (32 pages)

Where it's reviewed:
Booklist, December 1, 2002, page 679
Bulletin of the Center for Children's Books, February 2003,
    page 252
Kirkus Reviews, October 1, 2002, page 1481
Publishers Weekly, October 7, 2002, page 75
School Library Journal, December 2002, page 110

Awards the book has won:
Notable Social Studies Trade Books for Young People, 2003

Other books by the same author:
Monkey Sunday: A Story from a Congolese Village, 1998
The Rains Are Coming, 1993

Other books you might like:
Polly Alakija, *Catch that Goat!*, 2002
    Ayoka is responsible for watching the family goat that,
    unfortunately, escapes into the town market creating
    havoc.
Patricia Grossman, *Saturday Market*, 1994
    A Mexican marketplace is busy on Saturday with vendors
    selling everything from hand-woven rugs to parrots and
    sandals.
Katrin Tchana, *Oh, No, Toto!*, 1997
    As Toto's grandmother shops in the Cameroon market, the
    hungry two-year-old helps himself to any food within his
    reach.
Leyla Torres, *Saturday Sancocho*, 1995
    Maria Lili and Mama Ana visit the market to barter their
    eggs for the ingredients needed to make a special dinner.

1336

SUZANNE FISHER STAPLES

The Green Dog: A Mostly True Story
(New York: Frances Foster Books/Farrar Straus Giroux, 2003)

Subject(s): Animals/Dogs; Summer; Family

Age range(s): Grades 3-6
Major character(s): Suzanne Fisher, 5th Grader, Sister; Karen Fisher, Sister (younger); Bobby Fisher, Brother (older), Asthmatic; Jeff, Dog
Time period(s): 1950s
Locale(s): Lackawanna County, Pennsylvania (near Scranton)

Summary: In her frequent daydreams Suzanne sees the dog she's always wanted and never been allowed to have because of Bobby's allergies and asthma. During the summer between fourth and fifth grade, Suzanne's dreams become reality when a stray appears on the family's doorstep. Begrudgingly at first, Suzanne shares the care of Jeff, as she names her dream dog, with Karen. As Jeff's reputation as an escape artist known for getting into trouble causes problems with the neighbors and in the family, Suzanne and Karen accept responsibility for him and thus spend more time together than they have during any previous summer. Each time Jeff causes a problem, Suzanne worries that his days in their family have come to an end. Unexpectedly, one day they do. (120 pages)

Where it's reviewed:
Booklist, October 1, 2003, page 322
Bulletin of the Center for Children's Books, November 2003, page 126
Horn Book, September 2003, page 620
Publishers Weekly, July 28, 2003, page 95
School Library Journal, September 2003, page 220

Other books by the same author:
Shiva's Fire, 2000 (Publishers Weekly Best Children's Books)
Dangerous Skies, 1996 (ALA Best Book for Young Adults)
Haveli, 1993

Other books you might like:
Sharon Creech, *Love That Dog*, 2001
Inspired by Walter Dean Myers's poem "Love That Boy," Jack writes a poem celebrating the joy his deceased dog brought to his life.
Kate DiCamillo, *Because of Winn-Dixie*, 2000
The summer Opal claims a stray found in the Winn-Dixie grocery store as her own pet she grows out of the loneliness she feels in her new home.
Karen Hesse, *Sable*, 1994
In order to keep the stray dog that wanders into the yard of her mountain home, Tate must demonstrate the ability to care for it responsibly.

1337

SUE STAUFFACHER

Donuthead

(New York: Alfred A. Knopf, 2003)

Subject(s): Courage; Fear; Friendship
Age range(s): Grades 4-6
Major character(s): Franklin Delano Donuthead, 5th Grader, Son; Sarah Kervick, 5th Grader, Friend; Julia Donuthead, Single Mother, Friend
Time period(s): 2000s (2003)
Locale(s): Pelican View

Summary: The day Sarah arrives as a new student in Franklin's class the neurotic boy knows immediately from the girl's disheveled appearance that he doesn't want to be anywhere near such a collection of germs. Circumstances do place compulsively clean, anxious Franklin in proximity with fearless, dirty Sarah and the mix changes both of the students. In exchange for helping Julia develop Franklin into a baseball player, Sarah, a natural at the sport, receives support to achieve her desire to be a "regular" fifth grader and an ice skater. Franklin begins to understand others as being something more than a bundle of contagion and teaches Sarah to read. It's possible that Franklin, too, may become a "regular" student one day. (141 pages)

Where it's reviewed:
Booklist, September 1, 2003, page 124
School Library Journal, November 2003, page 149

Other books by the same author:
Angel and Other Stories, 2002
S'gana the Black Whale, 1992

Other books you might like:
Jeanne Betancourt, *My Name Is Brian/Brain*, 1993
Sixth grader Brian comes to a new understanding of friendship and school, resolving to be better in both areas.
Patricia Reilly Giff, *Shark in School*, 1994
With help from an understanding teacher and a compassionate classmate Matthew begins to overcome his reading problem.
Susie Morgenstern, *Secret Letters from 0 to 10*, 1998
Ernest's sheltered, monotonous life changes dramatically when outgoing Victoria joins his class and becomes his friend.

1338

WILLIAM STEIG
JON AGEE, Illustrator

Potch & Polly

(New York: Farrar Straus Giroux, 2002)

Subject(s): Love; Courtship; Humor
Age range(s): Grades 1-4
Major character(s): Potch, Gentleman, Wealthy; Polly Pumpernickel, Gentlewoman
Time period(s): Indeterminate Past
Locale(s): Fictional Country

Summary: Potch, lover of life, is born happy. As an adult he discovers that his life is incomplete when he sees Polly at a masquerade ball and realizes that love is the ingredient needed to make his life complete. Smitten with Polly, Potch enjoys the evening dancing with her, but then klutzy Potch makes his first mistake when he tries a bit too hard to impress her. Trying to undo the harm the next day, his attempts to win Polly's admiration flop. The fireworks he plans for that evening begin well, but a stray one adds to Polly's ire as well as the mess in her house. Despondent, Potch confides in his clown-faced guardian angel. With a bit of influence from Potch's angel, Polly decides to become the pursuer rather than the pursued and soon Potch and Polly are dancing and laughing together. (32 pages)

Where it's reviewed:
Booklist, September 1, 2002, page 137
Bulletin of the Center for Children's Books, October 2002, page 80
Kirkus Reviews, June 1, 2002, page 811
Publishers Weekly, June 24, 2002, page 56
School Library Journal, August 2002, page 170

Other books by the same author:
Toby, What Are You?, 2001
Wizzil, 2000
Pete's a Pizza, 1998 (Booklist Editors' Choice)

Other books you might like:
Ellen Jackson, *Cinder Edna*, 1994
Neighbors Cinderella and Cinder Edna have different philosophies of life yet each meets the prince of her dreams at the ball.
Alain Vaes, *The Princess and the Pea*, 2001
Smitten with the mechanic who helps him when his car breaks down, Prince Ralph is relieved to learn that she is also Princess Opal.
Jane Yolen, *Sleeping Ugly*, 1981
In a clever retelling of a classic fairy tale, inner beauty triumphs and the deserving live happily ever after.

1339

WILLIAM STEIG
HARRY BLISS, Illustrator

Which Would You Rather Be?

(New York: Joanna Cotler/HarperCollins Publishers, 2002)

Subject(s): Animals/Rabbits; Magicians; Magic
Age range(s): Grades K-2
Major character(s): Unnamed Character, Child; Unnamed Character, Child; Unnamed Character, Rabbit, Magician
Time period(s): 2000s (2002)
Locale(s): United States

Summary: A boy and girl sit watching as a rabbit pulls objects out of his top hat. With each trick, he offers the children a choice, asking, "Which would you rather be?" The children get ten separate options, including, cat or dog, thunder or lighting and so on, but only express an opinion on three of the pairs, leaving readers plenty of room to plug in their favorite. (32 pages)

Where it's reviewed:
Booklist, August 2002, page 1977
Publishers Weekly, May 20, 2002, page 64
School Library Journal, June 2002, page 110

Other books by the same author:
Toby, Who Are You?, 2004
Pete's a Pizza, 1998 (Booklist Editors' Choice)
CDC?, 1984
Sylvester and the Magic Pebble, 1969 (Caldecott Medal)

Other books you might like:
Linda Ashman, *Maxwell's Magic Mix-Up*, 2001
Maxwell's bungled magic tricks transform the birthday girl into a rock, her dad into a broom and the guests into animals.

Judi Barrett, *Which Witch Is Which?*, 2001
Children are encouraged to find the "right" witch among the groups of witches.
John Burningham, *Would You Rather . . .*, 1978
Given various choices children decide between such options as being crushed by a snake or swallowed by a fish—the one they would prefer.
John O'Brien, *Poof!*, 1999
With a wave of their wands two wizards tackle their chores by transforming each job and each other into something else.

1340

HELEN STEPHENS, Author/Illustrator

Blue Horse

(New York: Scholastic, Inc., 2003)

Subject(s): Shyness; Loneliness; Friendship
Age range(s): Preschool-Kindergarten
Major character(s): Tilly, Child; Blue Horse, Toy (stuffed animal)
Time period(s): 2000s (2003)
Locale(s): United States

Summary: Shy Tilly is reluctant to make friends after moving to a new town. Blue Horse becomes her imaginary playmate. During a visit to the playground Blue Horse encourages Tilly to make friends with a little girl playing alone. The little girl also has a stuffed doll and the four end up playing together happily. (32 pages)

Where it's reviewed:
Booklist, March 15, 2003, page 1334
Publishers Weekly, February 17, 2003, page 73
School Library Journal, March 2003, page 208

Other books by the same author:
Ahoyty-Toyty, 2004
Poochie Poo, 2003
Twinkly Night, 2003

Other books you might like:
Lindsay Barrett George, *My Bunny and Me*, 2001
The bunny Luis draws becomes his imaginary friend.
Syd Hoff, *The Horse in Harry's Room*, 1970
Only city-living Harry can see the horse in his room.
Susin Nielsen-Fernlund, *Hank and Fergus*, 2003
Hank's best friend is his imaginary dog, Fergus, but when a new neighbor moves in, Hank warms to the idea of both real and imaginary friends.

1341

RICKI STERN
HEIDI P. WORCESTER, Co-Author
AMY JUNE BATES, Illustrator

Might Adventurer of the Planet!

(New York: HarperCollins Publishers, 2002)

Series: Beryl E. Bean. Book 1
Subject(s): Adventure and Adventurers; Museums; Friendship
Age range(s): Grades 3-5

Major character(s): Beryl E. Bean, 10-Year-Old, Soccer Player; Mary Priscilla "Mary P" Barofsky, 10-Year-Old, Friend; Warren, Stepfather

Time period(s): 2000s (2002)

Locale(s): United States

Summary: Beryl E. Bean loves soccer, so she is quite depressed when she breaks her arm the week before the All-City Junior-Juniors Soccer Championship. Being out of commission proves to have it's upside though when Beryl befriends Mary Priscilla Barofsky (Mary P) on the sidelines. To keep Beryl's mind off her injury, Warren plans a museum-based adventure for the day of the championship. Beryl and Mary P have a great time working in the Paleontology department and Beryl makes an accidental, but important discovery just in time for Beryl and Mary P to get to the championships and cheer on Beryl's team. (64 pages)

Where it's reviewed:

Booklist, July 2002, page 1849

Publishers Weekly, June 17, 2002, page 64

School Library Journal, January 2003, page 112

Other books by the same author:

Mission: Impossible Friendship, 2004 (Beryl E. Bean Book 4)

Adventure: Lonely Leader, 2003 (Beryl E. Bean Book 3)

Expedition Sleepaway Camp, 2002 (Beryl E. Bean Book 2)

Other books you might like:

Paula Danziger, *Amber Brown Goes Fourth*, 1995

When Amber starts fourth grade without her best friend Max, she is worried, but she manages to make a new friend.

Louise Fitzhugh, *Harriet the Spy*, 1960

Harriet isn't a real spy, but she does like to write down everything she knows about her friends and classmates in her notebook.

E.L. Konigsburg, *From the Mixed-Up Files of Mrs. Basil E. Frankweiler*, 1967

Claudia and her brother, Jamie, run away from home to the Metropolitan Museum of Art.

Marissa Moss, *Amelia's Notebook*, 1999

Nine-year-old Amelia writes about her family's move to a new town in her notebook.

1342

JANET STEVENS, Author/Illustrator

SUSAN STEVENS CRUMMEL, Co-Author

Jackalope

(San Diego: Harcourt, Inc., 2003)

Subject(s): Animals/Extinct; Tall Tales; Wishes

Age range(s): Grades K-3

Major character(s): Jack, Rabbit; Unnamed Character, Armadillo, Narrator; Unnamed Character, Rabbit, Mythical Creature (fairy godmother)

Time period(s): Indeterminate Past

Locale(s): United States

Summary: An unnamed Armadillo, given to speaking in rhyme, tells the tale of Jack, an ordinary hare, who wants only to be fierce and scary. A wish on a star brings his punning fairy "godrabbit" who grants his one wish, to have horns, on

the condition that Jack not tell lies. Lying causes the horns to grow as Jack discovers when he tries to escape from a coyote by diving into his hole and the horns get stuck. In the ensuing confusion, Jack escapes, the fairy godrabbit ends up with the horns and gets stuck and Jack rescues her. The two end up living happily (and un-scarily) ever after. (56 pages)

Where it's reviewed:

Booklist, March 15, 2003, page 1334

School Library Journal, July 2003, page 108

Awards the book has won:

IRA Children's Choices, 2004

Other books by the same author:

And the Dish Ran Away with the Spoon, 2001 (ALA Notable Children's Books)

Cook-a-Doodle-Doo!, 1999

My Big Dog, 1999

Other books you might like:

Anne Isaacs, *Swamp Angel*, 1994

A original tall tale and Caldecott Honor Book describes the achievements of Angelica and how she earns her nickname.

Paul Brett Johnson, *Old Dry Frye: A Deliciously Funny Tall Tale*, 1999

When Preacher Frye chokes to death while eating chicken, the scared hosts panic and hilarious results follow.

Steven Kellogg, *Pecos Bill: A Tall Tale*, 1986

Texas cowboy Pecos Bill becomes a folk hero of legendary proportions.

Helen Ketteman, *The Christmas Blizzard*, 1995

In this tall tale when things at the North Pole heat up, Santa moves his workshop to the frigid town of Lizzard, Indiana.

1343

JAMES STEVENSON, Author/Illustrator

The Castaway

(New York: Greenwillow Books/HarperCollins, 2002)

Subject(s): Islands; Vacations; Cartoons and Comics

Age range(s): Grades 2-4

Major character(s): Hubie, Mouse, Castaway; Leo, Porcupine, Castaway

Time period(s): 1930s (1937)

Locale(s): Barabooda Island, Fictional Country

Summary: On this family vacation, traveler Hubie falls out of the dirigible transporting his family to Barabooda Island. He lands in a pelican's voluminous beak and is flown to a nearby island where he finds Leo, marooned since he fell off a boat 10 years earlier. Imagining that he'll never see his family again, Hubie accepts Leo's offer of a tour of the island. When Hubie and Leo accidentally land in the river they're swept over the waterfall and land on the top of the dirigible that has closed in for a close view of the uninhabited island thus inadvertently reuniting Hubie with his unsuspecting family. (32 pages)

Where it's reviewed:

Booklist, June 2002, page 1726

Horn Book, July 2002, page 452

Publishers Weekly, April 29, 2002, page 72

School Library Journal, May 2002, page 128
Smithsonian, December 2002, page 124

Awards the book has won:
Smithsonian's Notable Books for Children, 2002

Other books by the same author:
The Most Amazing Dinosaur, 2000
Don't Make Me Laugh, 1999
All Aboard!, 1995

Other books you might like:
Tomie De Paola, *Strega Nona Takes a Vacation*, 2000
 Strega Nona ends her seashore vacation early because of the problems caused in her home village by her assistants.
Cooper Edens, *Santa Cow Island*, 1994
 On the day after Christmas Ruby's wish lands her family on a South Sea Island for an unexpected vacation.
Jules Feiffer, *Meanwhile . . .*, 1997
 Raymond settles down for a quiet afternoon of reading and finds himself in a comic book adventure that seems to have no way out.

1344

JOHN WARREN STEWIG
KEVIN O'MALLEY, Illustrator

Making Plum Jam
(New York: Hyperion, 2002)

Subject(s): Aunts and Uncles; Farm Life; Cooks and Cooking
Age range(s): Grades 1-4
Major character(s): Jackie, Child, Nephew; Farmer Wilson, Farmer, Neighbor
Time period(s): 2000s (2002)
Locale(s): Minnesota

Summary: Jackie looks forward to visiting his aunts on their farm every summer. While he's there his aunts decide to make jam with the plums from their neighbor's farm. However Farmer Wilson, the new owner of the farm, chases them off for stealing. That night, Jackie sneaks several jars of the finished jam back to the neighbor with an explanatory note. A few days later the aunts find a basket of fresh plums on their porch. (32 pages)

Where it's reviewed:
Booklist, August 2002, page 1977
Bulletin of the Center for Children's Books, July 2002, page 419
Horn Book Guide, Fall 2002, page 347
Kirkus Reviews, May 15, 2002, page 741
School Library Journal, June 2002, page 112

Other books by the same author:
Mother Holly, 2001
King Midas: A Golden Tale, 1999
Princess Florecita and the Iron Shoes, 1995
The Fisherman and His Wife, 1988

Other books you might like:
Natalie Kinsey-Warnock, *A Farm of Her Own*, 2001
 A young city girl enjoys spending her summers on her aunt and uncle's Vermont farm.

Andrea Davis Pinkney, *Mim's Christmas Jam*, 2001
 Mim's special Christmas jam is so delicious that just a taste convinces Pap's bosses to give the work crew the day off for the holiday.
Ann Purmell, *Apple Cider-Making Days*, 2002
 Alex, Abigail and the entire family help make apple cider at Grandpa's apple farm.
Gloria Whelan, *Jam and Jelly by Holly and Nellie*, 2002
 Holly and her mom pick berries and make jam to raise money for a winter coat for Holly.

1345

R.L. STINE

Dangerous Girls
(New York: Parachute Press/HarperCollins, 2003)

Subject(s): Vampires; Twins; Sisters
Age range(s): Grades 7-10
Major character(s): Destiny Weller, Twin, 12th Grader; Livy Weller, Twin, 12th Grader; Lorenzo ''Renz'' Angelini, Vampire
Time period(s): 2000s
Locale(s): United States

Summary: Spending the summer as camp counselors is a good way for twins Destiny and Livy to keep their mind off their mother's recent suicide. Their head counselor Renz is a hottie and both twins find themselves attracted to him. Unbeknownst to them, Renz is really a centuries-old vampire who bites both twins, but is stopped before Destiny can return his bite and drink his blood. The twins return home and each is consumed with the desire to drink blood, which leads to the killing of small animals and eventually their friends. Renz returns to convert Destiny to full vampire status but is killed when she spears him with a tent pole. When the twins' father is revealed as a ''restorer,'' Destiny realizes she can be saved, though her twin Livy will remain forever a vampire in another chiller from a popular author. (247 pages)

Where it's reviewed:
Publishers Weekly, August 4, 2003, page 30
School Library Journal, August 2003, page 166
Voice of Youth Advocates, October 2003, page 329

Awards the book has won:
ALA Quick Picks for Reluctant Young Adult Readers, 2004

Other books by the same author:
Little Camp of Horrors, 2005
One Night in Doom House, 2005
Dangerous Girls: The Taste of Night, 2004
Beware, 2002
Fear Games, 2001

Other books you might like:
Amelia Atwater-Rhodes, *Demon in My View*, 2000
 Jessica doesn't realize she's about to be caught between vampires who want to claim her as one of their own, and good witches who will try to save her.
Mary Downing Hahn, *Look for Me by Moonlight*, 1995
 Attracted to pale, aristocratic-looking Victor, Cynda never connects him to the legends about her old house being haunted.

Annette Curtis Klause, *Silver Kiss*, 1990

In this ultimate romance, a young girl falls in love with a 300-year-old vampire.

Douglas Rees, *Vampire High*, 2003

Cody is one of the few non-vampire students at Vlad Dracul High School only because of his swimming prowess.

Ellen Schreiber, *Vampire Kisses*, 2003

Having always wanted to be a vampire, Raven knows that gorgeous Alexander, who's moved into a supposedly haunted mansion, could be her soul mate.

1346

MANYA STOJIC, Author/Illustrator

Snow

(New York: Alfred A. Knopf, 2002)

Subject(s): Animals; Seasons; Winter
Age range(s): Preschool-Kindergarten
Major character(s): Moose, Moose; Bear, Bear; Owl, Owl
Time period(s): Indeterminate
Locale(s): Fictional Country

Summary: All the animals agree that snow is in the offing. Moose smells it, Bear looks forward to sleeping through it, and Owl senses its impending arrival. Soon the forest is still, covered in a coating of white. The rabbits are happy to change the color of their coats to match the snow but the fox thinks he stands out too much against the white land. Bear happily sleeps, geese fly south and Owl waits for spring. (32 pages)

Where it's reviewed:
Booklist, December 1, 2002, page 679
Bulletin of the Center for Children's Books, December 2002, page 175
Publishers Weekly, October 28, 2002, page 75
School Library Journal, December 2002, page 110

Awards the book has won:
School Library Journal Best Books, 2002
Center for Children's Books Best Books, 2002

Other books by the same author:
Hello World!: Greeting in 42 Languages Around the Globe!, 2002
Wet Pebbles under Our Feet, 2002
Rain, 2000

Other books you might like:
Cheryl Chapman, *Snow on Snow on Snow*, 1994
Colorful pictures and playful text celebrate the joy of snow.
Piers Harper, *Snow Bear*, 2003
On the first day of spring a young polar bear ventures out into the snowy land and becomes lost.
Steve Sanfield, *Snow*, 1995
A young boy marvels at the beauty of the newly fallen snow dotted with the tracks of passing animals.
Martin Waddell, *Snow Bears*, 2002
Three bear cubs playing in the snow become so covered that they tell their mother they are "snow bears."

1347

TODD STRASSER

Thief of Dreams

(New York: Putnam, 2003)

Subject(s): Aunts and Uncles; Burglary; Family Problems
Age range(s): Grades 6-8
Major character(s): Lawrence Hunter, Uncle, Thief; Martin Hunter, 8th Grader, 13-Year-Old; Elka, Child-Care Giver; Idahlia Rodriguez, Psychologist
Time period(s): 2000s
Locale(s): Deep Meadow

Summary: Martin's not at all disturbed when his parents announce a business trip to China over Christmas and leave Martin at home under the care of his nanny and his father's brother, Uncle Lawrence, whom he's met only once before. Uncle Lawrence is a likable soul, though his odd habits of sleeping late and being out until all hours of the night seem a little strange. Martin's therapist, Dr. Rodriguez, who talks to Martin more than his parents do, and his nanny, Elka, are equally charmed by Lawrence, and Martin delights in the mall visits and the video games Lawrence plays with him. However, it's pretty obvious that Lawrence is up to no good, especially when Martin discovers a black wet suit and night vision goggles in his uncle's room. Now Martin's in a dilemma as he decides what to do—turn in his uncle or keep his mouth shut? (160 pages)

Where it's reviewed:
Bulletin of the Center for Children's Books, March 2003, page 292
Library Media Connection, January 2004, page 63
Publishers Weekly, February 24, 2003, page 73
School Library Journal, March 2003, page 241
Voice of Youth Advocates, August 2003, page 231

Other books by the same author:
Give a Boy a Gun, 2000
Gator Prey, 1999
Here Comes Heavenly, 1999
The Accident, 1988

Other books you might like:
Tony Earley, *Jim the Boy*, 2000
From his uncles Jim learns about growing up, keeping promises, laughing at himself and being loved.
Dayle Campbell Gaetz, *Mystery from History*, 2001
Katie, Sheila and Rusty follow their inclinations and discover their chief of police is part of an art thievery ring.
Celia Rees, *The Truth Out There*, 2000
Joshua has often wondered about his never-mentioned Uncle Patrick and is amazed to discover that he's alive, though institutionalized.

1348

BRAD STRICKLAND, Co-Author
THOMAS E. FULLER, Co-Author
DOMINIC SAPONARO, Illustrator

Pirate Hunter Series

(New York: Aladdin/Simon & Schuster, 2002-)

Subject(s): Pirates; Sea Stories; Adventure and Adventurers
Age range(s): Grades 4-8
Major character(s): Davy Shea, Orphan, 12-Year-Old; Patrick ''Dr. Patch'' Shea, Doctor, Uncle; William Hunter, Military Personnel (British Navy); Jack Steele, Pirate
Time period(s): 17th century (1680s)
Locale(s): HMS *Retribution*, Caribbean

Summary: Orphaned Davy Shea is shipped to Jamaica to live with his Uncle Patch but, before he can find him, encounters hooligans who beat and rob him. When he does locate Dr. Patch, his uncle is not happy to see him, though he lets Davy act as his assistant on house calls. Shipping out on the *HMS Retribution*, his uncle is ship's surgeon and Davy is his assistant. A fake mutiny leaves Davy confused and his uncle scheduled to hang, until he realizes that his uncle and Lt. Hunter are really agents trying to catch pirates. Their goal is to capture the noted pirate Jack Steele before he unites the pirates into a formidable armada in this continuing series.

Where it's reviewed:
Booklist, December 1, 2002, page 668
Booklist, February 1, 2003, page 995
Publishers Weekly, November 18, 2002, page 60
School Library Journal, March 2003, page 241
School Library Journal, November 2002, page 176

Other books by the same author:
Heart of Steele, 2003 (Pirate Hunter Book 3)
The Guns of Tortuga, 2003 (Pirate Hunter Book 2)
Mutiny, 2002 (Pitrate Hunter Book 1)

Other books you might like:
Iain Lawrence, *The Buccaneers*, 2001
    Picking up a drifting sailor proves advantageous for John Spencer when the schooner *Dragon* is later attacked by pirates.
Robin Moore, *The Man with the Silver Oar*, 2002
    Quaker Daniel's in an ethical quandary when he's aboard a pirate hunting ship, but even more so when he recognizes the captured pirate Scarfield.
Celia Rees, *Pirates!: The True and Remarkable Adventures of Minerva Sharpe and Nancy Kington, Female Pirates*, 2003
    Rather than endure an arranged marriage, Nancy and her slave Minerva join a company of pirates where each finds her niche.

1349

BRAD STRICKLAND

The Whistle, the Grave, and the Ghost

(New York: Dial, 2003)

Subject(s): Supernatural; Magic; Adventure and Adventurers
Age range(s): Grades 5-8

Major character(s): Lewis Barnavelt, 13-Year-Old, Orphan; Jonathan Barnavelt, Uncle, Sorcerer; Rose Rita Pottinger, Student—Junior High; Stan Peters, Bully; Billy Fox, Bully; Father Foley, Religious (priest); Florence Zimmerman, Witch
Time period(s): 1950s
Locale(s): Michigan (Richardson's woods in southern Michigan); New Zebedee, Michigan

Summary: On a camping trip with his Boy Scout troop, Lewis is hassled by Stan and Billy who are always up to no-good. Sent to find flat rocks for the fire, Lewis finds a ten-foot long stone with an inscription on it, just as a grave would have, and beside it is a silver whistle. Returning home, he and Rose Rita translate the inscription on the whistle realizing it says ''Hiss and I will come.'' Lewis has unknowingly found a means of calling a Lamia, a wraith-like woman in a serpent's body. When Stan and Billy try to beat him up, the whistle appears in Lewis's hand and blowing it stops them in their tracks. Unfortunately having the whistle exerts itself in strange ways on his family with Uncle Jonathan having horrible dreams and Lewis becoming more withdrawn. Mrs. Zimmerman, Father Foley and Uncle Jonathan use a combination of magic and religion to destroy the Lamia and rescue Lewis in this continuation of Lewis Barnavelt's adventures, begun by the late John Bellairs. (152 pages)

Where it's reviewed:
Booklist, August 2003, page 1984
School Library Journal, August 2003, page 168

Other books by the same author:
The Tower at the End of the World, 2001
The Beast under the Wizard's Bridge, 2000
The Wrath of the Grinning Ghost, 1999
The Bell, the Book, and the Spellbinder, 1997

Other books you might like:
Jane Louise Curry, *The Egyptian Box*, 2002
    An inherited carved wooden statue, called a Shabti, comes to life and Tee sends it to school in her place.
R.L. Stine, *The Haunting Hour: Chills in the Dead of the Night*, 2001
    Voodoo cookies, graveyard romps and ghostly requests add touches of terror to these ten stories.
Mark London Williams, *Ancient Fire*, 2001
    Eli accidentally stumbles into one of his father's time spheres and lands in the middle of a riot in ancient Alexandria.

1350

JONATHAN STROUD

The Amulet of Samarkand

(New York: Hyperion, 2003)

Series: Bartimaeus Trilogy. Book 1
Subject(s): Magic; Magicians; Apprentices
Age range(s): Grades 6-10
Major character(s): Bartimaeus, Demon (djinni); Nathaniel Underwood, Apprentice, Magician; Simon Lovelace, Magician
Time period(s): 2000s

Locale(s): London, England

Summary: Taken from his parents when he was only five and apprenticed to a rather middling magician, Nathaniel has been left with enough free time that he reads all the books in his master's library. His ability soars beyond that of his master so when the visiting magician Simon Lovelace makes fun of him, Nathaniel plots revenge. He summons a 5000-year-old djinni named Bartimaeus to do his bidding and steal the Amulet of Samarkand from Simon Lovelace, who murdered the previous owner to obtain this valuable magical artifact. Stealing it is easy, but keeping it is something else as Simon stalks the Amulet to repossess it. This sets in motion danger and tragedy as Nathaniel's house and master are blown to bits; now he's left on his own with only Bartimaeus to help prove Lovelace's plans to assume control of the government in this first of a trilogy. (462 pages)

Where it's reviewed:
Booklist, September 1, 2003, page 123
Horn Book, November 2003, page 757
Publishers Weekly, July 21, 2003, page 196
School Library Journal, January 2004, page 136
Voice of Youth Advocates, December 2003, page 416

Awards the book has won:
Booklist Editors' Choice/Books for Youth, 2003
ALA Best Books for Young Adults, 2004

Other books by the same author:
Buried Fire, 2004
The Leap, 2004
The Golem's Eye, 2004 (Bartimaeus Trilogy Book 2)

Other books you might like:
Diana Wynne Jones, *Dark Lord of Derkholm*, 1998
    With Derk roasted by an elderly dragon, his children are in charge of events until evil armies and Dark Elves threaten to run out of control.
Tamora Pierce, *Circle of Magic*, 1997-1999
    Four teens are brought together and taught to combine their magical talents, which makes them an extremely powerful unit.
J.K. Rowling, *The Harry Potter Series*, 1998-
    Raised by his aunt and uncle, Harry is thrilled to be invited to attend Hogwarts School and begin his studies of wizardry.
Caroline Stevermer, *A College of Magics*, 1994
    Magical competition at a school for wizards has unanticipated consequences.

1351

CAROLINE STUTSON
KATHERINE TILLOTSON, Illustrator

Night Train

(Brookfield, CT: Roaring Brook Press, 2002)

Subject(s): Railroads; Travel; Stories in Rhyme
Age range(s): Preschool-Grade 1
Major character(s): Unnamed Character, Child, Traveler
Time period(s): Indeterminate Past
Locale(s): United States

Summary: As a train approaches the station a young boy and his father eagerly wait to board. Through the train's windows the boy views the passing countryside, the darkness of the tunnels, the lights of stations and towns as they speed along, faster than cars and trucks. After eating in the dining car, they return to their seats by walking the length of the train and passing through the "hissing" doors linking the cars. Sleeping intermittently through the night, the boy is alertly peering out the window as the train enters the station so he's first to glimpse his grandmother waiting happily to greet them. (32 pages)

Where it's reviewed:
Booklist, May 1, 2002, page 1536
Bulletin of the Center for Children's Books, July 2002, page 419
Horn Book Guide, Fall 2002, page 314
Publishers Weekly, March 18, 2002, page 102
School Library Journal, May 2002, page 128

Other books by the same author:
Prairie Primer: A to Z, 1996
By the Light of the Halloween Moon, 1993 (Golden Kite Award)
On the River ABC, 1993

Other books you might like:
Margaret Wise Brown, *Two Little Trains*, 2001
    A 1949 title with new illustrations shows two trains, a real, streamlined one on the tracks heading West and a child's toy train on an imaginary journey.
Donald Crews, *Freight Train*, 1978
    Colorful train cars gather speed as they're pulled along the tracks in this Caldecott Honor Book.
Harriet Ziefert, *Train Song*, 1999
    While playing with his toy train a young boy listens to the song of the train whistle as the daily train passes by on tracks below.

1352

STEPHANIE STUVE-BODEEN
CHRISTY HALE, Illustrator

Elizabeti's School

(New York: Lee & Low Books Inc., 2002)

Subject(s): Schools; Family Life; Learning
Age range(s): Grades K-2
Major character(s): Elizabeti, Daughter, Student—Elementary School; Pendo, Sister (older), Student; Moshi, Cat
Time period(s): 2000s
Locale(s): Tanzania

Summary: Eagerly Elizabeti takes Pendo's hand and sets out for her first day of school. The day away from her family and Moshi seems so long that she considers not returning. When she arrives home she discovers that Moshi has delivered kittens that Elizabeti is able to correctly count in Swahili. Later she writes some of the letters she's learned in the dirt for her parents and plays a game that she's learned at school. Seeing the pride her parents have in her accomplishments makes Elizabeti realize that she should give school another try. (32 pages)

Where it's reviewed:
Booklist, September 15, 2002, page 243
Bulletin of the Center for Children's Books, December 2002, page 175
Horn Book, November 2002, page 741
Publishers Weekly, August 19, 2002, page 92
School Library Journal, September 2002, page 206

Other books by the same author:
Babu's Song, 2003
Mama Elizabeti, 2000
Elizabeti's Doll, 1998 (ALA Notable Children's Books)

Other books you might like:
Laurie Halse Anderson, *Ndito Runs*, 1996
    Joyfully, Ndito runs across the Kenyan countryside to her schoolhouse.
Page McBrier, *Beatrice's Goat*, 2001
    In her Ugandan village, Beatrice's goat provides her family with enough income to allow her to go to school for the first time.
Clifton L. Taulbert, *Little Cliff's First Day of School*, 2001
    Mama Pearl and Poppa Joe proudly look forward to Little Cliff's first day of school while Little Cliff would prefer to stay home.

1353

PAUL SULLIVAN

Maata's Journal

(New York: Simon & Schuster/Atheneum, 2003)

Subject(s): Indians of North America; Survival
Age range(s): Grades 7-10
Major character(s): Maata, Indian (Inuit); Tiitaa, Indian (Inuit); Daniel Morgan, Explorer; Frank Nicolson, Explorer; Avery Smith, Explorer
Time period(s): 1920s
Locale(s): Arctic; Foster's Bay, Canada

Summary: Brought up a nomadic Inuit living near the Arctic, Maata witnesses the change in her people's culture when the white men force the Inuits from their land to a government settlement in Foster's Bay. Sent to boarding school in Quebec City, Maata learns to speak and write English which, coupled with her knowledge of the land, makes her an invaluable member of a mapping expedition when her brother Tiitaa opts to remain with his family. Maata joins four men, including their friend Morgan, as they head north to map her homeland. After a fire kills one member of the party, two others head across the tundra to safety, leaving Maata and Morgan behind. In her journal Maata records the time she and Morgan await the return of their supply ship *Venture*, using this time to collect her thoughts about the changes in herself and the culture of her people. (221 pages)

Where it's reviewed:
Bulletin of the Center for Children's Books, April 2003, page 332
Library Media Connection, October 2003, page 59
Publishers Weekly, January 27, 2003

School Library Journal, April 2003, page 168
Voice of Youth Advocates, February 2003, page 484

Other books by the same author:
The Spirit Walker, 1997
Keewatin, 1996

Other books you might like:
Jean Craighead George, *Julie of the Wolves*, 1971
    Julie loses her way while looking for her father, but her Inuit heritage and the survival skills of the wolves keep her alive.
Karen Hesse, *Aleutian Sparrow*, 2003
    Japanese attack the Aleutian Islands in 1942 and for their protection the native Aleuts are moved to camps, but three years of misery await them.
Mette Newth, *The Transformation*, 2000
    After three summers of cold and famine, young Inuit Navarana decides to help by hunting the polar bear and training to become a shaman.

1354

KITOBA SUNAMI
AMIKO HIRAO, Illustrator

How the Fisherman Tricked the Genie

(New York: Atheneum Books for Young Readers, 2002)

Subject(s): Fairy Tales; Revenge; Storytelling
Age range(s): Grades 3-5
Major character(s): Unnamed Character, Fisherman, Storyteller; Unnamed Character, Mythical Creature (genie)
Time period(s): Indeterminate Past
Locale(s): Arabian Sea, Arabia

Summary: A fisherman pulling a heavy brass bottle out of his net initially thinks his luck has changed for the better. After opening the bottle he discovers that he's freed an evil genie angry after 3000 years of entrapment and determined to kill the person releasing him. To convince the genie that his plan to repay a good deed with an evil one is foolhardy the fisherman tells him a story about the fate that awaits someone that does so whether by design or accident. The genie is not convinced and, in his vanity, he seals his fate at the conclusion of the first book for author and illustrator. (36 pages)

Where it's reviewed:
Booklist, August 2002, page 1977
Bulletin of the Center for Children's Books, October 2002, page 81
Horn Book, September 2002, page 563
Publishers Weekly, May 27, 2002, page 59
School Library Journal, August 2002, page 170

Other books you might like:
Teresa Bateman, *The Ring of Truth*, 1997
    After the king of the leprechauns gives Patrick a ring of truth he loses his gift for blarney but still wins a storytelling contest.
J. Patrick Lewis, *Night of the Goat Children*, 1999
    Princess Birgitta, disguised as a hag, tells a convincing story to a group of outlaws and saves her town and her people.

Rafe Martin, *The Storytelling Princess*, 2001
> A princess, by telling the story of the adventure that brings her to a prince's kingdom, unwittingly fulfills his dreams for marriage as well as her own.

Geraldine McCaughrean, *One Thousand and One Arabian Nights*, 1982
> To avoid the fate of King Shahryar's previous wives Shahrazad tells him stories nightly thus postponing her execution.

1355

SUSAN MARIE SWANSON
CHRISTINE DAVENIER, Illustrator

The First Thing My Mama Told Me
(San Diego: Harcourt, Inc., 2002)

Subject(s): Names, Personal; Identity; Mothers and Daughters
Age range(s): Grades K-2
Major character(s): Lucy, 7-Year-Old, Daughter; Mama, Mother; Madeleine, Sister (younger), Daughter
Time period(s): Indeterminate
Locale(s): United States

Summary: From the perspective of her seventh birthday, Lucy looks back over her life and speaks of events of importance. Mama gives her the name Lucy at her birth, an uncle paints her name on a stepstool and her father cooks her name in pancakes. When Madeleine is born, she's not able to eat her long name in pancakes so Lucy helps. Her name designates the hook on which she hangs her sweater when she goes to school for the first time and, written on the label, Lucy's name helps her locate the lost sweater in the school's lost and found. With the flashlight she receives on her seventh birthday, Lucy writes her name in the night sky. (34 pages)

Where it's reviewed:
Booklist, July 2002, page 1861
Bulletin of the Center for Children's Books, May 2002, page 342
Horn Book Guide, Fall 2002, page 314
Publishers Weekly, April 22, 2002, page 68
School Library Journal, August 2002, page 170

Awards the book has won:
New York Times Best Illustrated Books, 2002

Other books by the same author:
Letter to the Lake, 1998
Getting Used to the Dark: 26 Night Poems, 1997

Other books you might like:
Kevin Henkes, *Chrysanthemum*, 1991
> Unhappy Chrysanthemum arrives home from her first day of school feeling humiliated by teasing from classmates about her unusual name.

Pat Hutchins, *There's Only One of Me!*, 2003
> As family gathers to celebrate her birthday a young girl notes that while she may be someone's daughter, sister or stepsister, she's still unique.

Belinda Rochelle, *When Jo Louis Won the Title*, 1994
> Jo Louis begins to appreciate the significance of her name after her grandfather explains its meaning in his life.

1356

JOYCE SWEENEY

Waiting for June
(Tarrytown, NY: Marshall Cavendish, 2003)

Subject(s): Pregnancy; Racially Mixed People; Mothers and Daughters
Age range(s): Grades 8-11
Major character(s): Sophie Cooper, 12th Grader, Pregnant Teenager; June Cooper, Baby; Joshua, 12th Grader
Time period(s): 2000s
Locale(s): Florida

Summary: Pregnant during her senior year, Sophie angers everyone when she refuses to name the father of her baby. Many think Joshua is the culprit, including his girlfriend, but Joshua really is just a very good friend of Sophie's. He even agrees to help her in the delivery room with her Lamaze, but brings his girlfriend along. Sophie's pregnancy leads her to wonder about her own father, whom she's never known. When she gives birth to a black baby, her mother finally reveals details of her pregnancy with Sophie's black father. Though Sophie's future may be filled with unknowns, when June is born she's able to welcome her into a family whose secrets have finally been revealed. (145 pages)

Where it's reviewed:
Booklist, September 1, 2003, page 115
Bulletin of the Center for Children's Books, February 2004, page 246
Kirkus Reviews, October 1, 2003, page 123
Publishers Weekly, November 3, 2003, page 75
School Library Journal, October 2003, page 180

Other books by the same author:
Takedown, 2004
Players, 2000
Split Window, 1998

Other books you might like:
Berlie Doherty, *Dear Nobody*, 1992
> Teenager Helen finds herself unexpectedly pregnant and she and Chris record their thoughts as they try to decide whether or not to keep their child.

Joanne Horniman, *Mahalia*, 2003
> As Matt raises his daughter Mahalia, he finds how much he loves her; when mother Emmy returns to claim her, he knows he can't give up his child.

Rita Williams-Garcia, *Like Sisters on the Homefront*, 1995
> After becoming pregnant a second time, Gayle's mother marches her to the abortion clinic and then to Georgia to live with her grandparents.

1357

RUTH LOUISE SYMES
DAVID SIM, Illustrator

The Sheep Fairy: When Wishes Have Wings
(New York: The Chicken House/Scholastic, Inc., 2003)

Subject(s): Animals/Sheep; Fairies; Wishes

Age range(s): Grades K-1
Major character(s): Wendy Woolcoat, Sheep; Unnamed Character, Mythical Creature (fairy)
Time period(s): Indeterminate
Locale(s): Fictional Country

Summary: While eating grass (her favorite activity) Wendy hears a cry for help. A fairy is stuck in a brambly bush. Wendy sets the fairy free and the fairy offers to grant one wish. Wendy has a secret dream, to fly, and the fairy promises that when the moon and stars appear, her wish will come true. That night, quite unexpectedly Wendy finds herself floating in the air with large fairy wings on her back. Wendy has a great time soaring over the field full of sleeping sheep. From the air Wendy sees a wolf sneaking into the field. Unable to awaken the flock she flies at the wolf and scares it away as the author's first book concludes. (32 pages)

Where it's reviewed:
Booklist, October 1, 2003, page 329
Publishers Weekly, November 24, 2003, page 63
School Library Journal, December 2003, page 128

Other books you might like:
Tanya Robyn Batt, *A Child's Book of Faeries*, 2002
    A collection of tales from English literature introduces a variety of fairies.
Anik McGrory, *Mouton's Impossible Dream*, 2000
    Mouton's dream of flying comes true when she and two other farm animals hide in a basket that is attached to a hot air balloon.
Jane Simmons, *The Dreamtime Fairies*, 2002
    Three children and a toy rabbit fly across the ocean to ask the Dreamtime Fairies to help them fall asleep.

T

1358

SIMMS TABACK, Author/Illustrator

This Is the House That Jack Built

(New York: G.P. Putnam's Sons, 2002)

Subject(s): Poetry; Dwellings; Humor
Age range(s): Grades K-2
Time period(s): Indeterminate
Locale(s): Fictional Country

Summary: The house that Jack built is for sale. As the cumulative nursery rhyme unfolds, the illustrations give a more extensive picture of Jack's house and the frenetic activity in it. As children have chanted the rhythmic story for centuries in this version the rat still eats the cheese in the house and in turn is killed by a cat. After following the traditional version with the dog, a cow with a crumpled horn, a maiden all forlorn, a man all tattered and torn, a judge all shaven and shorn, the rooster that crows in the morn and the farmer planting corn, a new character appears. The artist "who first had drawn" all the pictures draws himself into the concluding sequence of things in the house that Jack built with a sold sign in the yard. (28 pages)

Where it's reviewed:

Booklist, October 1, 2002, page 323
Bulletin of the Center for Children's Books, October 2002, page 81
Horn Book, November 2002, page 769
Publishers Weekly, July 22, 2002, page 176
School Library Journal, September 2002, page 218

Other books by the same author:

Joseph Had a Little Overcoat, 1999 (Caldecott Medal)
There Was an Old Lady Who Swallowed a Fly, 1997 (Caldecott Honor Book)

Other books you might like:

Nina Crews, *The Neighborhood Mother Goose*, 2004
    Photographs of an urban neighborhood illustrate a collection of nursery rhymes.

Wayne Montgomery, *Over the Candlestick: Classic Nursery Rhymes and the Real Stories Behind Them*, 2002
    The historical background for each rhyme in this collection provides context for the entry.
Liz Underhill, *This Is the House That Jack Built*, 1987
    An illustrated interpretation of the nursery rhyme describes the house that Jack builds and the events he experiences.

1359

NANCY TAFURI, Author/Illustrator

The Donkey's Christmas

(New York: Scholastic Press, 2002)

Subject(s): Animals/Donkeys; Christmas; Shyness
Age range(s): Preschool-Kindergarten
Major character(s): Jesus, Baby
Time period(s): Indeterminate Past
Locale(s): Jerusalem, Israel

Summary: After the baby Jesus is born, the barnyard animals come to welcome him in the stable. Cows, goats, even mice sing a welcome, but the donkey is too shy. Finally, after the baby Jesus smiles at the donkey, it has the courage to bray a noisy song, making Jesus laugh. (32 pages)

Where it's reviewed:

Booklist, September 15, 2002, page 247
School Library Journal, October 2002, page 64

Other books by the same author:

You Are Special, Little One, 2003
Spots Feathers and Curly Tails, 1988
Have You Seen My Duckling?, 1986 (Caldecott Honor winner)

Other books you might like:

Margaret Wise Brown, *A Child Is Born*, 2000
    Realistic illustrations celebrate the story of the birth of Jesus.
John Herman, *One Winter's Night*, 2003
    A pregnant cow searching for a safe place to have her baby

is welcomed by Joseph and Mary to the stable where Jesus is also being born.

Ezra Jack Keats, *The Little Drummer Boy*, 1968
Unable to afford a gift for the baby Jesus, the little drummer boy plays him a song on his drum.

1360

NANCY TAFURI, Author/Illustrator

Mama's Little Bears

(New York: Scholastic Press, 2002)

Subject(s): Animals/Bears; Animals; Mothers
Age range(s): Preschool
Major character(s): Mama, Bear, Mother
Time period(s): Indeterminate
Locale(s): Earth

Summary: Three curious bear cubs tire of fishing with Mama and wander off to explore. They spot other baby animals in their homes under a mother's watchful eye. After climbing a tree and discovering an owl's nest the frightened cubs scurry back to the ground calling for their mother. Mama has been discreetly following her cubs so she's close by to give them a reassuring hug. (36 pages)

Where it's reviewed:
Booklist, March 1, 2002, page 1144
Horn Book, March 2002, page 206
Kirkus Reviews, March 1, 2002, page 346
Publishers Weekly, January 14, 2002, page 58
School Library Journal, April 2002, page 126

Other books by the same author:
Silly Little Goose!, 2001 (Parenting's Reading Magic Award)
Will You Be My Friend?, 2000
Have You Seen My Duckling?, 1984 (Caldecott Honor Book)

Other books you might like:
Stella Blackstone, *Bear in Sunshine*, 2001
Through all types of weather and in any season, Bear is actively having fun!
Reeve Lindbergh, *North Country Spring*, 1997
The natural world awakens to the call of spring as bear cubs tumble, geese fly and frogs begin their spring peeping.
Jonathan London, *Honey Paw and Lightfoot*, 1995
A fictionalized account of the life cycle of a brown bear realistically portrays one year in the life of a mother bear and her cub.

1361

NANCY TAFURI, Author/Illustrator

You Are Special, Little One

(New York: Scholastic, Inc., 2003)

Subject(s): Animals; Parent and Child; Love
Age range(s): Preschool-Kindergarten
Time period(s): 2000s (2003)
Locale(s): Earth

Summary: Six baby animals in a variety of habitats ask their parents what makes them special. From lions to humans, each

parent tells their individual child all the ways that they are special. The parents assure the offspring of their love forever. (32 pages)

Where it's reviewed:
Booklist, November 1, 2003, page 506
Publishers Weekly, September 15, 2003, page 67
School Library Journal, October 2003, page 140

Other books by the same author:
Mama's Little Bears, 2002
Silly Little Goose!, 2001 (Parenting's Reading Magic Award)
I Love You, Little One, 1998
Have You Seen My Duckling?, 1984 (Caldecott Honor Book)

Other books you might like:
Linda Ashman, *Babies on the Go*, 2003
Babies get around in many unique ways.
Sebastien Braun, *I Love My Mommy*, 2004
A variety of young animals describe why they love their mothers.
Paul Carrick, *Mothers Are Like That*, 2000
Different animal mothers take care of their babies.
Ashley Wolff, *My Somebody Special*, 2002
As parents pick up their different animal babies from daycare they celebrate what makes them special.

1362

NATASHA ANASTASIA TARPLEY
E.B. LEWIS, Illustrator

Bippity Bop Barbershop

(Boston: Little, Brown and Company, 2002)

Subject(s): Hair; Fathers and Sons; African Americans
Age range(s): Grades K-2
Major character(s): Charles "Daddy", Father; Miles "Little Man", Son, Child; Mr. Seymour, Hairdresser (barber)
Time period(s): 2000s (2002)
Locale(s): United States

Summary: Early on a Saturday morning Little Man and Daddy embark on an important journey. The road to becoming "one of the guys" leads through a doughnut shop and into Seymour's Barbershop where Little Man is to receive his first professional haircut. While waiting for service the many men in the shop converse, play checkers, watch sports on television and offer Little Man advice. Miles sees a variety of hairstyles and gives careful consideration to the style that will suit him. Mr. Seymour goes to work with pick, scissors and clippers and soon Daddy and Miles walk out of the shop hand-in-hand looking like twins. (32 pages)

Where it's reviewed:
Booklist, February 15, 2002, page 1036
Bulletin of the Center for Children's Books, March 2002, page 259
Kirkus Reviews, December 2001, page 1690
Publishers Weekly, January 28, 2002, page 293
School Library Journal, February 2002, page 114

Awards the book has won:
Booklist Editors' Choice, 2002
Center for Children's Books Best Books, 2002

Other books by the same author:
I Love My Hair!, 1998 (BlackBoard Book of the Year for Children)

Other books you might like:
Gwendolyn Battle-Lavert, *The Barber's Cutting Edge*, 1994
Rashaad visits Mr. Bigalow, the proprietor of a barbershop that is also a local gathering spot.
Margaree King Mitchell, *Uncle Jed's Barbershop*, 1993
In an award-winning story, Sarah Jean recalls the determination of her Uncle Jed to save enough money to open his own barbershop.
Michael R. Strickland, *Haircuts at Sleepy Sam's*, 1998
Despite Mom's instructions, her three sons come home from their trip to the barber with the haircuts that they want.

1363
NIKKI TATE
STEPHEN MCCALLUM, Illustrator

Jo's Triumph
(Custer, WA: Orca Publishers, 2002)

Subject(s): Frontier and Pioneer Life; Orphans; Robbers and Outlaws
Age range(s): Grades 4-6
Major character(s): Joselyn Whyte, 12-Year-Old, Orphan; Sarah Winnemucca, Indian (Paiute)
Time period(s): 1850s; 1860s (1859-1860)
Locale(s): Carson City, Nevada

Summary: Joselyn's brothers dump her at the Carson City Home for Unfortunate Girls while they scoot off to the gold fields of California. Unhappy about her new life as an orphan, and wishing her parents were still alive, she makes friends with Sarah, a Paiute Indian. The relationship between the settlers and the Paiutes becomes tense so Joselyn cuts off her braids, dons boy's clothes, palms herself off as Joe and becomes a rider for the Pony Express. All goes well until another rider figures out she's a girl and tries to blackmail her into committing a robbery with him. Joselyn manages to outwit him and save the money, which earns her enough of a reward that she's able to travel to California to find those rascally brothers of hers. (139 pages)

Where it's reviewed:
Quill & Quire, July 2002, page 50
Resource Links, June 2002, page 15
School Library Journal, December 2002, page 150

Other books by the same author:
Caves of Departure, 2001
Raven's Revenge, 1999

Other books you might like:
Mary Downing Hahn, *The Gentleman Outlaw and Me—Eli: A Story of the Old West*, 1996
Eliza finds herself on a wild adventure when she tires of her abusive aunt and uncle, runs away and teams up with Calvin, the Gentleman Outlaw.
Ann Rinaldi, *The Staircase*, 2000
Lizzy's not prepared for the cruel treatment she receives

when she attends the boarding school run by the Sisters of Loretto in Santa Fe.
Willo Davis Roberts, *Jo and the Bandit*, 1992
Jo is used as bait to catch stagecoach robbers.

1364
THEODORE TAYLOR

The Boy Who Could Fly Without a Motor
(San Diego: Harcourt, Inc., 2002)

Subject(s): Lighthouses; Magicians; Fantasy
Age range(s): Grades 3-6
Major character(s): Jon Jeffers, 9-Year-Old, Son; Ling Wu, Magician, Spirit
Time period(s): 1930s (1935)
Locale(s): Clementine Rock, California

Summary: Jon Jeffers lives alone with his parents in a lighthouse on an island off the coast of California. It's a lonely and boring existence and Jon wishes he could learn to fly so that he could escape the tedium of his isolated life. Jon begins to practice telepathy and conjures up Ling Wu, the great Chinese magician, who died in a shipwreck near Jon's island. Ling Wu teaches Jon how to levitate, but Jon ignores Ling Wu's warnings and soon he is unable to stop levitating. After Jon is seen by some fishermen, a government investigation ensues, culminating in a trip to Washington to show President Roosevelt his skill. Finally, Jon is able to get back in touch with Ling Wu and learns how to free himself from his newfound skill. (144 pages)

Where it's reviewed:
Booklist, June 2002, page 1726
Horn Book Guide, Fall 2002, page 384
Kirkus Reviews, April 15, 2002, page 580
Publishers Weekly, May 13, 2002, page 71
School Library Journal, May 2002, page 161

Other books by the same author:
Timothy of the Cay, 1993
The Maldonado Miracle, 1973
The Cay, 1969 (ALA Notable Children's Books)

Other books you might like:
Dick King-Smith, *Billy the Bird*, 2001
Mary's little brother becomes weightless during the full moon and flies over their town.
Jane Langton, *The Fledgling*, 1981
Georgie wants to learn how to fly and takes lessons from a goose in the middle of the night.
Mallory Loehr, *Wind Spell*, 2000
Three siblings find magic feathers that enable them to fly.

1365
THEODORE TAYLOR
MARGARET CHODOS-IRVINE, Illustrator

Hello, Arctic!
(San Diego: Harcourt, Inc., 2002)

Subject(s): Seasons; Wilderness; Nature
Age range(s): Preschool-Grade 1

Time period(s): 2000s (2002)
Locale(s): Arctic

Summary: Muted prints highlight the changing seasons in the Arctic. When summer arrives, life blooms in the Arctic, the sun shines, birds arrive, flowers grow, and polar cubs play. Summer is quickly over with the setting of the sun; birds migrate to warmer climates and the animals that remain settle down to hibernate for the winter. This is the first picture book for the children's novelist. (40 pages)

Where it's reviewed:
Booklist, October 1, 2002, page 339
Kirkus Reviews, July 15, 2002, page 1045
Publishers Weekly, July 29, 2002, page 70
School Library Journal, November 2002, page 138

Other books by the same author:
The Boy Who Could Fly Without a Motor, 2002
Timothy of the Cay, 1993
The Cay, 1969

Other books you might like:
Lydia Dabcovich, *The Polar Bear Son: An Inuit Tale*, 1997
   In this traditional Inuit folktale, a lonely old woman adopts a polar cub as her son, but the jealous villagers force her to send him away.
Debbie Miller, *A Polar Bear Journey*, 1997
   This nonfiction title explores the life cycle of a polar bear and her cubs.
Jane Yolen, *Welcome to the Ice House*, 1998
   This title explores the Arctic seasons.

1366

THEODORE TAYLOR

Lord of the Kill

(New York: Blue Sky/Scholastic, 2003)

Subject(s): Animals/Tigers; Gangs; Mystery and Detective Stories
Age range(s): Grades 6-9
Major character(s): Ben Jepson, 16-Year-Old; Lord of the Kill, Tiger
Time period(s): 2000s
Locale(s): Orange County, California (Los Coyotes Preserve)

Summary: With his animal rights activist parents in India concerned about the poaching of the Bengal tiger, Ben's in charge of their wild cat sanctuary, Los Coyotes Preserve. He feels comfortable in this role, as he's been around the big cats since he was six, but is unprepared for the partially-eaten body of a young woman that's found in the jaguar compound. While he's trying to help the police with this matter, the Siberian tiger named "Lord of the Kill" is stolen and a note asking for payment is received. There are several suspects in these two cases, from people living in nearby developments, to poachers of endangered species to owners of ranches that sponsor "canned hunts," where exotic zoo animals are "sitting ducks" waiting to be shot by a hunter. While Ben worries about the tiger and the body of the woman, the disappearance of his parents in India becomes of even greater concern in a fast-paced adventure. (246 pages)

Where it's reviewed:
Booklist, January 2003, page 872
Bulletin of the Center for Children's Books, January 2003, page 212
Kliatt, January 2003, page 11
School Library Journal, January 2003, page 144
Voice of Youth Advocates, April 2003, page 60

Other books by the same author:
The Taming of Billy the Kid: A Novel, 2005
Ice Drift, 2004
The Odyssey of Ben O'Neal, 2004
Rogue Wave: And Other Red-Blooded Sea Stories, 1996
Sniper, 1989

Other books you might like:
Nevada Barr, *Hunting Season*, 2002
   Investigating an illegal hunting stand leads ranger Anna Pigeon into murder, a ring of poachers and an unhappy park ranger in this adult title.
Kate DiCamillo, *The Tiger Rising*, 2001
   Taking pity on a caged tiger he's been hired to feed, Rob releases him but that act leads to unexpected tragedy.
Ron Koertge, *Tiger, Tiger, Burning Bright: A Novel*, 1994
   When Jesse's beloved grandfather claims to have seen tiger tracks while on a camping trip in California, Jesse rounds up friends to search for the animal.

1367

THOMAS TAYLOR, Author/Illustrator

The Loudest Roar

(New York: Arthur A. Levine/Scholastic, Inc., 2003)

Subject(s): Animals; Animals/Tigers; Behavior
Age range(s): Preschool-Grade 1
Major character(s): Clovis, Tiger
Time period(s): 2000s (2003)
Locale(s): Africa

Summary: Clovis may be a small tiger, but he has a loud roar. He's always sneaking up on the other animals in the jungle and surprising them. Finally all the animals get together to develop a plan to make him stop. One day while Clovis is drinking at the water hole, all the animals sneak up on him and make their loudest sounds. Alarmed, Clovis jumps right up a tree. When he calms down, he agrees to a truce. (32 pages)

Where it's reviewed:
Publishers Weekly, March 24, 2003, page 74
School Library Journal, March 2003, page 208

Other books you might like:
Paul Bright, *Quiet!*, 2003
   Papa Lion orders the other jungle animals to be quiet so that his son can nap, but then his growling stomach wakes his son.
Robert Kraus, *Leo the Late Bloomer*, 1971
   Father is impatient for Leo to learn to do things for himself, but Mother knows that Leo will bloom in his own time.
Karma Wilson, *Hilda Must Be Dancing*, 2004
   When Hilda the hippo's enthusiastic dancing disturbs her jungle neighbors, they come up with a compromise.

1368

KATRIN TCHANA
TRINA SCHART HYMAN, Illustrator

Sense Pass King: A Story from Cameroon

(New York: Holiday House, 2002)

Subject(s): Folklore; Folk Tales; Conduct of Life
Age range(s): Grades 1-4
Major character(s): Ma'antah, Heroine
Time period(s): Indeterminate Past
Locale(s): Cameroon

Summary: This retelling depicts a girl as the precocious child so wise she is known to the villagers as ''Sense Pass King'' because her wisdom surpasses that of the king. Her ability to talk to animals, cook dinner for her parents, and speak the languages of all seven villages in her area before her fourth birthday attracts the king's attention. He orders her killed but she saves herself so he has her captured but she gets away. Finally the king forces Ma'antah to live in the palace serving him and listening to his problems each night. In time the people of the kingdom grow tired of the king's ways, recognize Ma'antah as their ruler and drive the king out of the palace. During Ma'antah's reign as queen the villages know peace and prosperity. A concluding author's note gives background information about the story. (32 pages)

Where it's reviewed:
Booklist, November 1, 2002, page 502
Bulletin of the Center for Children's Books, January 2003, page 213
Horn Book, November 2002, page 770
Publishers Weekly, July 22, 2002, page 176
School Library Journal, September 2002, page 218

Awards the book has won:
Parenting's Books of the Year, 2002
Notable Social Studies Trade Books for Young People, 2003

Other books by the same author:
The Serpent Slayer, 2000
Oh, No, Toto!, 1997

Other books you might like:
Baba Wague Diakite, *The Hunterman and the Crocodile: A West African Folktale*, 1997
An award-winning title retells the story of Donso who learns to appreciate the need for mutual cooperation among all creatures.
Phillis Gershator, *Only One Cowry: A Dahomean Tale*, 2000
The clever daughter of a village chief extracts a greater reward from a stingy king than the one cowry he planned to pay as a bride gift.
Ann Grifalconi, *The Village That Vanished*, 2002
The plans and actions of three generations of strong women save the people of their remote village from capture by slave traders.

1369

MARK TEAGUE, Author/Illustrator

Dear Mrs. LaRue: Letters from Obedience School

(New York: Scholastic Press, 2002)

Subject(s): Animals/Dogs; Pets; Letters
Age range(s): Grades K-3
Major character(s): Ike LaRue, Dog, Student; Gertrude R. LaRue, Animal Lover (pet owner), Aged Person
Time period(s): Indeterminate Past
Locale(s): Snort City; Igor Brotweiler Canine Academy

Summary: Frustrated by Ike's unruly behavior, Mrs. LaRue enrolls him in the Igor Brotweiler Canine Academy. Ike is unhappy with the discipline there and writes to Mrs. LaRue to question her response to his behavior and complain about the regimen at the Academy. The illustrations portray a story contrary to the conditions Ike describes in his correspondence. Nothing deters Ike from writing, not the confiscation of his manual typewriter or being on the lam from obedience school. When Ike runs away he simply takes pencil to paper and continues writing. Ike makes his way back to Snort City just in time to save Mrs. LaRue from being run over by a truck and assure the unrepentant pet's return to his former life. (32 pages)

Where it's reviewed:
Booklist, November 1, 2002, page 494
Horn Book Guide, Spring 2003, page 56
Newsweek, October 28, 2002, page 75
Publishers Weekly, July 22, 2002, page 177
School Library Journal, September 2002, page 207

Awards the book has won:
Booklist Editors' Choice, 2002
Publishers Weekly Best Children's Books, 2002

Other books by the same author:
One Halloween Night, 1999
The Lost and Found, 1998
Baby Tamer, 1997

Other books you might like:
Steven Kroll, *Oh, Tucker!*, 1998
Despite the chaos Tucker creates in their home, the dog's owners find it difficult to scold him.
Peggy Rathmann, *Officer Buckle and Gloria*, 1995
Behind Officer Buckle's back, police dog Gloria acts out his safety tips, bringing new life to his dull assemblies. Caldecott Medal winner.
Rosemary Wells, *McDuff Goes to School*, 2001
McDuff's owners take him to obedience school, but do not complete their homework so he fails to graduate.

1370

CHRISTOPHER TEBBETTS

The Viking Series

(New York: Puffin/Penguin Putnam, 2003-)

Subject(s): Time Travel; Fathers and Sons; Vikings

Age range(s): Grades 5-8
Major character(s): Zack Gilman, 9th Grader
Time period(s): 2000s; 9th century
Locale(s): Minneapolis, Minnesota; Scandinavia

Summary: Living with a father obsessed with the Minnesota Vikings football team, Zack often has no choice but to accompany him to the game, though he'd rather be home working on his inventive projects. Heading to the concession stand one football afternoon, he trips over a metal object obscured by the snow and is transported back to the land of the real Viking warriors. This quartet of books finds Zack in a world parallel to his own, filled with Vikings similar to his family, friends, enemies and girlfriend who encounter some of the same problems that Zack does. Whether Zack's leading the Vikings in battle, traveling to the land of the giants or searching for treasure, the action and adventure continues at a fast pace.

Where it's reviewed:
Booklist, September 1, 2003, page 124
Kliatt, September 2003, page 28
School Library Journal, December 2003, page 161

Other books by the same author:
Land of the Dead, 2003 (Vikings Saga Three)
Quest for Faith, 2003 (Vikings Saga Two)
Viking Pride, 2003 (Vikings Saga One)

Other books you might like:
Scott Ciencin, *Dinoverse*, 1999
    Bertram uses his science fair project to send himself and three others back to prehistoric times where they blend in as human-dinosaurs.
Welwyn Wilton Katz, *Out of the Dark*, 1996
    Miserable over his mother's accidental death, Ben retreats to the ruins of a Viking site near his home and immerses himself in the Norse legends.
Mark London Williams, *Ancient Fire*, 2001
    Eli stumbles into one of his father's time spheres and lands in the middle of a riot in ancient Alexandria.

1371

HEATHER TEKAVEC
MARGARET SPENGLER, Illustrator

Storm Is Coming!

(New York: Dial Books for Young Readers, 2002)

Subject(s): Weather; Animals; Farm Life
Age range(s): Preschool-Grade 1
Major character(s): Dog, Dog; Unnamed Character, Farmer, Aged Person; Duck, Duck
Time period(s): 2000s (2002)
Locale(s): United States

Summary: After hearing the weather report on the radio a farmer tells Dog to help him get the animals into the shelter of the barn. Dog rounds up the sheep that call to Duck as they run to the barn. The cows follow suit and the farmer shuts them all in the barn where they waken the cat. Cat wants to know, "Who's Storm?," and that gets all the animals wondering. They decide that Storm must be big, mean and scary so they get Duck to fly to the barn window and keep a lookout. Throughout the storm the animals misinterpret the weather

resulting from the storm as actions that will protect them from Storm. Finally all is silent until they hear a thump at the barn door. It's the farmer coming to let them out as the author's first book concludes. (32 pages)

Where it's reviewed:
Booklist, March 1, 2002, page 1144
Horn Book Guide, Fall 2002, page 314
Kirkus Reviews, December 15, 2001, page 1763
Publishers Weekly, February 11, 2002, page 187
School Library Journal, March 2002, page 204

Awards the book has won:
IRA Children's Choices, 2003

Other books you might like:
Betsy Byars, *Tornado*, 1996
    While sheltered in a storm cellar, a farmhand tells a family about a dog blown into his life by a tornado.
Libba Moore Gray, *Is There Room on the Feather Bed?*, 1997
    During a storm the farm animals seek shelter in the teeny, tiny house of the wee fat woman and her wee fat husband.
Jane Simmons, *Daisy and the Beastie*, 2000
    Daisy and Pip search the farm for the scary Beastie Grandpa tells about in a story.

1372

RICK TELANDER

String Music

(Chicago: Marcato/Cricket, 2002)

Subject(s): Sports/Basketball; Family Problems; School Life
Age range(s): Grades 4-6
Major character(s): Robbie Denwood, 11-Year-Old, Basketball Player; Jasper Jasmine, Basketball Player
Time period(s): 2000s
Locale(s): Chicago, Illinois

Summary: Loser—that's the way Robbie feels about himself, for his father's abandoned the family, his mother's always arguing with his sister, and his coach calls him "dimwit" for being so uncoordinated. His retreat when he's feeling low is his fort in the woods and it's there that he keeps his treasures, including his pictures of Jasper Jasmine, the great basketball player for the Thunder. Fed up one day with home, school and basketball, Robbie runs away and manages to get into a Thunders game. To his great delight, he meets Jasper and realizes later that somehow he's touched Jasper's heart. The two become friends with Jasper stopping by Robbie's practice, which shuts up the cruel coach, and Robbie becoming the ball boy for the Thunders in this heart-warming story by a sportswriter. (138 pages)

Where it's reviewed:
Booklist, May 1, 2002, page 144
Bulletin of the Center for Children's Books, July 2002, page 419
Kirkus Reviews, May 15, 2002, page 742
Publishers Weekly, May 27, 2002, page 60
School Library Journal, June 2002, page 146

Awards the book has won:
Center for Children's Books Best Books, 2002

Other books you might like:

Jan Cheripko, *Rat*, 2002
Rat earns the disdain of all his teammates when he tells the judge about their basketball coach's attempt to rape a cheerleader.

Dan Gutman, *Honus and Me: A Baseball Card Adventure*, 1997
Finding an Honus Wagner baseball card leads Joe to a meeting with the legendary player and time travel to the 1909 World Series.

Paul Kropp, *Moonkid and Prometheus*, 1998
In exchange for tutoring Prometheus in reading and writing skills, Prometheus helps klutzy Moonkid learn a few basketball moves.

1373

SHERI S. TEPPER

The Companions
(New York: EOS/HarperCollins, 2003)

Subject(s): Animals/Dogs; Ecology; Cultural Conflict
Age range(s): Grades 9-Adult
Major character(s): Jewel Delis, Sister, Activist; Paul Delis, Brother, Linguist
Time period(s): Indeterminate Future
Locale(s): Mossen, Planet—Imaginary

Summary: Jewel is part of an underground movement that seeks to preserve the diversity of Earth's animal life. The current political climate is completely human-centric and animals are threatened because they take resources away from humans. Jewel's group is investigating possibilities for creating havens for animals on other worlds. Jewel is especially valuable in this work because of her brother Paul who, though completely absorbed in his own pleasures, is a gifted translator whose work takes him to distant worlds. He demands that his sister accompany him to cater to his whims, which is useful to the movement as it brings Jewel into contact with a variety of aliens. Self-effacing by nature, Jewel's quiet ways serve her well in interacting with alien species and in her relationships with her *dogs*, genetically modified animals with abilities no natural dog could possess. Jewel believes she and the dogs love one another, but her faith will be tested when they travel to Mossen, a world that may provide a haven in which canines can survive. (452 pages)

Where it's reviewed:
Booklist, September 15, 2003, page 218
Bookpage, September 2003, page 8
Kirkus Reviews, June 15, 2003, page 840
Library Journal, July 2003, page 131
Publishers Weekly, July 21, 2003, page 178

Other books by the same author:
The Visitor, 2002
The Fresco, 2000
Singer from the Sea, 1999

Other books you might like:
Kirsten Bakis, *The Lives of the Monster Dogs*, 1997
Transformed into a parody of humans, the monster dogs find their lives difficult.

Kate Gilmore, *The Exchange Student*, 1999
The alien student's interest in animals stems from a dreadful secret about his home world.

Gabriel King, *The Golden Cat*, 1999
An escape from an experimental lab releases a cat with an important part to play in the discovery of the promised golden cat.

1374

STANLEY TODD TERASAKI
SHELLY SHINJO, Illustrator

Ghosts for Breakfast
(New York: Lee & Low Books, Inc., 2002)

Subject(s): Ghosts; Food; Humor
Age range(s): Grades 1-3
Major character(s): Papa, Father; Unnamed Character, Son, Narrator; Mr. Omi, Neighbor, Aged Person; Mr. Omaye, Neighbor, Aged Person; Mr. Ono, Neighbor, Aged Person
Time period(s): 1920s
Locale(s): California

Summary: One foggy night Mr. Omi, Mr. Omaye and Mr. Ono report the sighting of ghosts in a nearby farmer's fields. Papa makes light of this report as "The Troublesome Triplets" are known for seeing danger everywhere. Taking his son in hand Papa goes in search of the ghosts and discovers the source of Mr. Omi, Mr. Omaye, and Mr. Ono's fears. Gathering some of the "ghosts," Papa and his son walk home to show the daikon, a long white radish hung to dry in the farmer's field to the fearful trio. A few days later Mr. Omi, Mr. Omaye and Mr. Ono return with pickled daikon and the boy and his family enjoy the gift of "ghosts" for breakfast. This first children's book for the author and illustrator is based on family stories. (32 pages)

Where it's reviewed:
Booklist, January 2003, page 910
Horn Book Guide, Spring 2003, page 56
Kirkus Reviews, October 1, 2002, page 1481
Publishers Weekly, September 16, 2002, page 68
School Library Journal, October 2002, page 132

Awards the book has won:
Smithsonian's Notable Books for Children, 2002

Other books you might like:
James Howe, *There's a Monster under My Bed*, 1986
Monster noises coming from under a boy's bed are really made by little brother Alex.

Polly Powell, *Just Dessert*, 1996
In her dark house, everyday objects appear to be dangers lurking in Patsy's path as she tries to sneak to the kitchen for a piece of cake.

Maggie Smith, *There's a Witch under the Stairs*, 1991
Imaginative Frances is certain that a witch lives under the basement stairs.

1375

JEAN THESMAN

Between

(New York: Viking, 2002)

Subject(s): Fairy Tales; Brothers and Sisters; Good and Evil
Age range(s): Grades 5-9
Major character(s): Charlotte Thacker, 14-Year-Old; Will Thacker, Brother (of Charlotte), Adoptee
Time period(s): 1940s
Locale(s): Puget Sound, Washington; Darkwood, Fictional Country

Summary: With their mother in a sanitarium fighting tuberculosis and their father recalled to Naval Service after Pearl Harbor, the Thacker children stay with friends at Gull Walk, a down-at-the-heel guesthouse near Puget Sound. Charlotte is worried about her adopted brother Will who occasionally has no shadow and is drawn to the Darkwood, which she's been warned not to enter. Gradually Charlotte discovers that Darkwood is the home of mythical creatures such as griffins and unicorns and Will is its prophesized Fair Prince, sent to save these creatures from humans, called evil mudwalkers. Will is greatly conflicted as he wants to stay with his human family yet doesn't want to abandon the denizens of the Darkwood, who face the loss of their forest. Charlotte is known as a "Between" and helps Will and the Darkwood occupants in a fantasy of good versus evil. (197 pages)

Where it's reviewed:
Booklist, June 2002, page 1709
Bulletin of the Center for Children's Books, May 2002, page 343
Kliatt, May 2002, page 14
School Library Journal, May 2002, page 162
Voice of Youth Advocates, June 2002, page 132

Other books by the same author:
Singer, 2005
Rising Tide, 2003
In the House of the Queen's Beasts, 2001
Calling the Swan, 2000
The Tree of Bells, 1999

Other books you might like:
Elizabeth Kay, *The Divide*, 2003
 Vacationing in Costa Rica, Felix falls into a rift and enters a fantasy world of unicorns, pixies, griffins, elves and many other legendary creatures.
Patricia McKillip, *The Forgotten Beasts of Eld*, 1974
 From a long line of wizards, Sybel lives in an idyllic world where she interacts telepathically with the magical animals surrounding her home.
Darcy Pattison, *The Wayfinder*, 2000
 In search of healing water, Win and telepathic Lady Kala cross the Rift, where they encounter strange beasts and animals.

1376

JEAN THESMAN

Rising Tide

(New York: Viking, 2003)

Subject(s): Gender Roles; Boarding Houses; Business Enterprises
Age range(s): Grades 6-9
Major character(s): Kate Keely, Businesswoman, 17-Year-Old; Ellen Flannery, Businesswoman; Jolie Logan, Wealthy (deceased)
Time period(s): 1900s
Locale(s): San Francisco, California

Summary: In this continuation of *A Sea So Far*, Kate returns to San Francisco after serving as a companion to terminally ill Jolie in Ireland. Jolie's father presents Kate with a generous bequest, which provides her share of a shop she and her friend Ellen plan to stock with handmade Irish linen items to sell. Both girls are excited about their venture and their independence, yet Ellen squanders some of her share of the startup funds to buy clothes to entice the son of their boss, who proves to be a cad. While Kate seems the more independent of the two, the landlord at her boarding house shows interest in her, and one wonders what the future holds for these two young businesswomen. (228 pages)

Where it's reviewed:
Booklist, January 2004, page 848
Bulletin of the Center for Children's Books, November 2003, page 127
Kirkus Reviews, October 1, 2003, page 1232
School Library Journal, December 2003, page 161
Voice of Youth Advocates, December 2003, page 407

Other books by the same author:
Singer, 2005
Between, 2002
A Sea So Far, 2001

Other books you might like:
Lisa Williams Kline, *Eleanor Hill*, 1999
 Eleanor Hill's not like the other girls in her small home town as she learns to drive a car, goes to the movies and leaves home to live with her aunt.
Roger Lea MacBride, *Bachelor Girl*, 1999
 Eager to prove that she can earn a living, Rose learns telegraphy, moves to San Francisco and meets dapper Gillette Lane.
Diane Smith, *Letters from Yellowstone*, 1999
 Botanist Alexandria, who goes by A.L., is invited to join a field study in Yellowstone National Park but surprises the team when they find A.L. is a she.
Florida Ann Town, *With a Silent Companion*, 2000
 When Margaret and her mother are left with no man to support them, Margaret dons men's clothing and attends medical school to become a British surgeon.

`1377`

SHELLEY MOORE THOMAS
JENNIFER PLECAS, Illustrator

Get Well, Good Knight

(New York: Dutton Children's Books, 2002)

Series: Dutton Easy Reader
Subject(s): Dragons; Knights and Knighthood; Illness
Age range(s): Grades 2-3
Major character(s): Good Knight, Knight; Unnamed Character, Wizard; Unnamed Character, Mother, Cook
Time period(s): Indeterminate
Locale(s): Fictional Country

Summary: On his daily ride through the forest Good Knight discovers that his three little dragon friends are ill. He rides quickly to the wizard's home for help. The "scaly snail-y" soup concocted by the wizard is so bad the dragons will not eat it and, after trying it, Good Knight can understand why. After a second trip to the wizard, Good Knight brings "slimy, grimy" soup to the dragons with the same results. On his third try, Good Knight avoids the wizard and rides to his mother's home. The delicious soup she makes is just what the dragons need to get well. (48 pages)

Where it's reviewed:
Booklist, January 2003, page 910
Bulletin of the Center for Children's Books, December 2002, page 176
Horn Book, September 2002, page 581
Kirkus Reviews, September 15, 2002, page 1402
School Library Journal, November 2002, page 139

Awards the book has won:
ALA Notable Children's Books, 2003

Other books by the same author:
Good Night, Good Knight, 2000 (Horn Book Fanfare)
Somewhere Today: A Book of Peace, 1998
Putting the World to Sleep, 1995

Other books you might like:
Teresa Bateman, *Farm Flu*, 2001
    When the cow sneezes a young boy treats it with the same care that he's accustomed to receiving from his mother when he is ill.
H.M. Ehrlich, *Dr. Duck*, 2000
    When dedicated Dr. Duck falls ill his patients arrive to care for him until he's able to return to work.
Herman Parish, *Calling Doctor Amelia Bedelia*, 2002
    When Amelia Bedelia fills in briefly at her doctor's office she not only creates turmoil but also soothes fraying nerves in her inimitable way.

`1378`

JULIAN F. THOMPSON

Hard Time

(New York: Atheneum/Simon & Schuster, 2003)

Subject(s): Interpersonal Relations; Schools/High Schools; Magic
Age range(s): Grades 7-10

Major character(s): Ann "Annie" Ireland, 9th Grader; Pantagruel Primo Esq., Mythical Creature (leprechaun); Nemo "Arby the Roach Boy" Skank, 9th Grader
Time period(s): 2000s
Locale(s): United States

Summary: Annie realizes the inequalities of life, especially hers, since she always seems to be in trouble and having to do "hard time." She carries around a doll for her Life Skills class but the night her home catches on fire Annie discovers the doll's inhabited by a leprechaun. It seems that Pantagruel Primo, Esquire, has been magically placed inside her doll, which is helpful to escape the fire. Her house burns, her parents escape to a fat farm and Annie is left with an aunt and uncle to continue her school life. When Primo helps her write a paper for English class, she gets in trouble for advocating violence and an aggressive D.A. sentences her to jail for five days. Her friend Arby protests the conviction and he's sent to jail along with her. After release from jail, she and Arby are sent off to a behavior modification camp in this wildly satirical fantasy, as campers worry that their parents want to eliminate them. (243 pages)

Where it's reviewed:
Booklist, December 15, 2003, page 746
Bulletin of the Center for Children's Books, January 2004, page 208
Kirkus Reviews, October 15, 2003, page 1277
Publishers Weekly, December 15, 2003, page 74
School Library Journal, January 2004, page 137

Other books by the same author:
Terry and the Pirates, 2000
Ghost Story, 1997
Simon Pure, 1987
Band of Angels, 1986
The Grounding of Group 6, 1983

Other books you might like:
Thom Eberhardt, *Rat Boys: A Dating Experiment*, 2001
    Marci and Summer lie about dates for the Spring Fling dance but, with the help of a magic ring, enjoy "hot" dates with transformed rats.
Scarlett Macdougal, *Have a Nice Life Series*, 2001-
    Four girls, shown their not-too-pretty karmic destinies by an intergalactic angel, have a chance to change their behavior.
Francine Prose, *After*, 2003
    When a Columbine-type shooting occurs at a high school near his, Tom realizes that his school days will never be the same.

`1379`

KAY THOMPSON
HILARY KNIGHT, Illustrator

Eloise Takes a Bawth

(New York: Simon & Schuster Books for Young Readers, 2002)

Subject(s): Cleanliness; Behavior; Hotels and Motels
Age range(s): Grades 1-4
Major character(s): Eloise, 6-Year-Old; Nanny, Child-Care Giver; Mr. Salomone, Manager
Time period(s): Indeterminate Past
Locale(s): New York, New York

Summary: Nanny instructs Eloise to quickly clean up in the "bawth" before Mr. Salomone comes to tea. Eloise knows all the requirements for being extra careful while bathing in a hotel, but she also has a lively imagination. Soon the tub is filled to the brim while Eloise, with lots of exuberant splashing, pretends to be a mermaid, a speedboat driver, and a pirate. Meanwhile, Mr. Salomone discovers that the preparations for the evening's Venetian Masked Ball are awash in water. A little investigation reveals that the plumbing problem originates on the upper floor of the Plaza Hotel in the suite occupied by Eloise. (50 pages)

Where it's reviewed:
Booklist, December 1, 2002, page 679
Bulletin of the Center for Children's Books, January 2003, page 63
Publishers Weekly, September 23, 2002, page 72
School Library Journal, December 2002, page 110

Awards the book has won:
Publishers Weekly Best Children's Books, 2002

Other books by the same author:
Eloise in Moscow, 1960
Eloise at Christmastime, 1958
Eloise in Paris, 1957
Kay Thompson's Eloise, 1955

Other books you might like:
Tedd Arnold, *No More Water in the Tub*, 1995
  William's bathwater overflows and carries William, still in the tub, out the door and down the apartment stairs.
Margie Palatini, *Tub-boo-boo*, 2001
  Henry's toe is the first appendage to become stuck in the faucet as his parents, a policeman and a plumber hurry to the rescue.
Chad Stuart, *The Ballymara Flood*, 1996
  Stuck faucets turn a simple bath into a flood that quickly covers the town in a humorous rhyming story.

1380

PAT THOMSON
AILIE BUSBY, Illustrator

Drat That Fat Cat!

(New York: Arthur A. Levine/Scholastic, Inc., 2003)

Subject(s): Animals/Cats; Traditional Stories; Animals/Bees
Age range(s): Preschool-Grade 1
Major character(s): Fat Cat, Cat
Time period(s): 2000s (2003)
Locale(s): United Kingdom

Summary: Fat Cat is always hungry and always eating. As he travels he eats everything he meets—a rat, a duck, a dog and even an old lady. However, after he swallows a bee, he gets the hiccups and the accumulation of things he's devoured pops back out. The old lady takes pity on the cat and takes him home with her to fatten him up even more. (32 pages)

Where it's reviewed:
Booklist, January 2004, page 883
Bulletin of the Center for Children's Books, January 2004, page 209
Horn Book, January/February 2004, page 73

Publishers Weekly, January 5, 2004, page 59
School Library Journal, December 2003, page 128

Other books by the same author:
The Squeaky, Creaky Bed, 2003
A Cauldron of Magical Stories, 2000
Beware of the Aunts!, 1992

Other books you might like:
Henrik Drescher, *The Boy Who Ate Around*, 1994
  Mo eats around his unappetizing dinner until he's consumed the world and is left with his plate, heartburn and the inevitable burp.
Alison Jackson, *I Know An Old Lady Who Swallowed a Pie*, 1997
  A Thanksgiving retelling of the classic "old lady who swallowed a fly" story substitutes a seasonal menu for the swallowed items.
Margaret Read MacDonald, *Fat Cat: A Danish Folktale*, 2001
  A voracious cat eats its way through the Danish countryside.
David McPhail, *The Glerp*, 1972
  While walking, the Glerp swallows everything in its path until the elephant's tusks get stuck and the Glerp coughs up all the swallowed animals.
Lensey Namioka, *The Hungriest Boy in the World*, 2001
  After swallowing the Hunger Monster, Jiro develops an insatiable appetite in order to satisfy the Hunger Monster's demands for food.
Simms Taback, *There Was an Old Lady Who Swallowed a Fly*, 1997
  Inventive illustrations in a Caldecott Honor Book tell of the many animals swallowed by the old lady to counteract the tickling fly inside her.

1381

GRACE TIFFANY

My Father Had a Daughter: Judith Shakespeare's Tale

(New York: Berkley, 2003)

Subject(s): Twins; Fathers and Daughters; Theater
Age range(s): Grades 10-Adult
Major character(s): Judith Shakespeare, Twin, Historical Figure; Hamnet Shakespeare, Twin, Historical Figure; William Shakespeare, Historical Figure, Writer (dramatist)
Time period(s): 16th century
Locale(s): London, England; Stratford on Avon, England

Summary: In this fictionalized "memoir," Judith and her twin brother Hamnet adjust to William Shakespeare, their capricious father who flits in and out of their lives. The few times he comes home from London, he's either scribbling away on parchment or regaling them with fantastic stories. When Judith is eleven, her twin drowns in the Avon River, but worse follows when she thinks her father has written about her grief in his new play. Determined to spoil the debut of the performance, she travels to London disguised as the boy Castor Popworthy determined to be cast as a character in her father's latest endeavor. However, the theater sweeps up Judith and soon she's cast as Viola in *Twelfth Night*, and is eager to begin a career on the stage. Discovering Judith in her disguise, Will sends her home, which ends her acting career but leaves her with wonderful memories as she settles into a quiet life married to a local vintner in this author's first novel. (291 pages)

Where it's reviewed:
Booklist, May 1, 2003, page 1582
Kirkus Reviews, April 1, 2003, page 505
Library Journal, May 15, 2003, page 127
Publishers Weekly, April 21, 2003, page 40
School Library Journal, October 2003, page 208

Other books by the same author:
Will, 2004

Other books you might like:
Anthony Burgess, *Nothing Like the Sun: A Story of Shakespeare's Love-Life*, 1964
 Working with the few facts known about Shakespeare, the author spins a story revolving around the mysterious "dark lady" of the sonnets.
Faye Kellerman, *The Quality of Mercy*, 1989
 Shakespeare and Rebecca Lopez meet when each is burying a loved one; their paths cross again when they seek retaliation for those unfortunate deaths.
Robert Nye, *The Late Mr. Shakespeare*, 1999
 Writing in a garret located above a bawdy house, Pickleherring decides to share his memories of William Shakespeare and the times in which he wrote.

1382

AMY TIMBERLAKE
ADAM REX, Illustrator

The Dirty Cowboy
(New York: Farrar Straus Giroux, 2003)

Subject(s): Cowboys/Cowgirls; Cleanliness; Animals/Dogs
Age range(s): Grades 1-4
Major character(s): Eustace Shackleford Montana, Dog; Unnamed Character, Cowboy
Time period(s): Indeterminate Past
Locale(s): New Mexico

Summary: This tall tale from a first-time author features an odiferous cowboy and his faithful dog. When the dirt, vermin and stench become too much for even the tough cowboy he calls his loyal "dawg," Eustace, mounts his horse and rides to the nearest river. After disrobing, the cowboy puts Eustace in charge of the pile of stinky clothes, grabs his soap and jumps in the river to scrub and splash until he's wrinkled as a "prickly pear." Thinking his clothes could do with a bit of soap too, the cowboy goes to gather them from the bank but vigilant Eustace doesn't recognize by either sight or smell the naked man trying to grab them and he guards the clothes, ignoring the stranger's commands. As the sun sets the cowboy and his pet wrestle for the clothes, raising a cloud of dust that includes bits and pieces of the attire. Finally, the cowboy is once again so dirty that Eustace recognizes him, but the only identifiable clothing left is a pair of boots and a hat. (32 pages)

Where it's reviewed:
Booklist, September 1, 2003, page 131

Bulletin of the Center for Children's Books, September 2003, page 37
Publishers Weekly, July 14, 2003, page 75
School Library Journal, September 2003, page 192

Awards the book has won:
Bulletin of the Center for Children's Books Blue Ribbons, 2003
Center for Children's Books Best Books, 2003

Other books you might like:
Helen Ketteman, *Shoeshine Whittaker*, 1999
 In this tall tale, Sheriff Blackstone expects Shoeshine to honor his guarantee of clean boots. It takes some quick thinking to get out of town.
Nicole Rubel, *A Cowboy Named Ernestine*, 2001
 The sight of a grizzly dirty groom awaiting mail-order bride Ernestine convinces her to disguise herself as a cowboy and quickly sneak away.
Eric Jon Slangerup, *Dirt Boy*, 2000
 Fister Farnello comes home so dirty that his mother doesn't recognize him until she hoses off some of the dirt with a garden hose.
Janice Lee Smith, *Jess and the Stinky Cowboys*, 2004
 It's up to Deputy Jess to enforce Snake Gulf's No-Stink Law when four smelly cowboys ride into town.

1383

STEPHANIE S. TOLAN

Surviving the Applewhites
(New York: HarperCollins, 2002)

Subject(s): Humor; Family Life
Age range(s): Grades 6-9
Major character(s): Jake Semple, 13-Year-Old; Edith Wharton "E.D." Applewhite, 12-Year-Old
Time period(s): 2000s
Locale(s): North Carolina (Wit's End Farm)

Summary: When Jake's thrown out of Traybridge Middle School and his parents are sent to jail for growing marijuana, he's run out of schools that will take him and has no place to live. Luckily, the Applewhite family's home school Creative Academy, located on their farm Wit's End, accepts him and Jake moves to North Carolina. There he walks into a school staffed by a family that believes your education is self-education, which means that Jake either teaches himself or doesn't learn. He's paired with the Applewhite daughter E.D. who is the only organized Applewhite and she resents someone sharing the curriculum that she's designed. Jake's not too worried, though, as he doesn't plan to stay long at this school. When E.D.'s father decides to produce *The Sound of Music*, Jake's given a singing part and all of a sudden he belongs! Happier than he's ever been, and blessed with a great singing voice, Jake has found his niche. Surprisingly, E.D. also finds her niche when her organizational skills help her become the perfect stage manager in this robust, rollicking comedy. (216 pages)

Where it's reviewed:
Booklist, November 1, 2002, page 494
Bulletin of the Center for Children's Books, October 2002, page 82

Publishers Weekly, August 5, 2002, page 73
School Library Journal, September 2002, page 235
Voice of Youth Advocates, October 2002, page 286

Awards the book has won:
Newbery Honor Book, 2003
ALA Best Books for Young Adults, 2003

Other books by the same author:
Flight of the Raven, 2001
Ordinary Miracles, 1999
Welcome to the Ark, 1996

Other books you might like:
Sue Ellen Bridgers, *Permanent Connections*, 1987
Alienation and self-hatred characterize Rob until staying a few months at the North Carolina family homestead makes him realize his worth.
Helen Cresswell, *The Bagthorpe Series*, 1978-
The peculiar members of the Bagthorpe family confront one crisis after another.
Sid Hite, *Dither Farm*, 1992
Dither Farm is fairly quiet until Aunt Emma arrives and then the family witnesses a kidnapping, a flying carpet and several romances.

1384

MICHELE TORREY
BARBARA JOHANSEN NEWMAN, Illustrator

The Case of the Graveyard Ghost
(New York: Dutton Children's Books, 2002)

Series: Doyle and Fossey, Science Detectives. Book 3
Subject(s): Science; Scientific Experiments; Mystery and Detective Stories
Age range(s): Grades 3-5
Major character(s): Drake Doyle, 5th Grader, Detective—Amateur; Nell Fossey, 5th Grader, Detective—Amateur; Dr. Livingston, Dog
Time period(s): 2000s (2002)
Locale(s): Mossy Lake

Summary: Science Detectives Drake and Nell solve each puzzling problem by using the Scientific Method. They rely on scientific investigation, the formulation of a hypothesis and laboratory experiments before informing the client of the resolution of the problem. By following his nose Dr. Livingston helps them solve some cases including the mystery of the graveyard ghost. Using science Nell and Drake also free a classmate stuck in a laundry chute, discover the cause of discoloration in roses at a garden show, and investigate the smuggling of endangered parrots. The book concludes with a section of activities and experiments. (85 pages)

Where it's reviewed:
Booklist, October 15, 2002, page 405
Horn Book Guide, Fall 2003, page 359
Kirkus Reviews, July 15, 2002, page 1046
School Library Journal, August 2002, page 171

Other books by the same author:
The Case of the Mossy Lake Monster, 2002 (Doyle and Fossey, Science Detectives Book 2)

The Case of the Gasping Garbage, 2001 (Doyle and Fossey, Science Detectives Book 1)
Bottle of Eight and Pieces of Rum, 1998

Other books you might like:
Mary Blount Christian, *The Sebastian (Super Sleuth) Series*, 1982-
Although his owner considers himself to be the detective, the sheepdog Sebastian knows who really solves the mysteries.
Barbara M. Joosse, *Ghost Trap*, 1998
In the third entry in the Wild Willie Mystery series, three friends solve the mystery of a talking ghost and form a detective agency.
Donald J. Sobol, *Encyclopedia Brown, Boy Detective*, 1979
Confident and affordable, Encyclopedia Brown opens a detective agency in this first book in a popular series.

1385

MICHELE TORREY

To the Edge of the World
(New York: Knopf, 2003)

Subject(s): Voyages and Travels; Sea Stories; Orphans
Age range(s): Grades 5-8
Major character(s): Mateo Macias de Avila, Orphan, 14-Year-Old; Fernando de/Ferdinand Magallanes/Magellan, Historical Figure, Explorer; Espinosa, Sailor
Time period(s): 16th century
Locale(s): Trinidad, At Sea; Spain

Summary: After his parents die of the plague and Mateo burns their farm, he wanders around Spain for two months while trying to find a place where he will fit in. Luckily he's found by Espinosa who's recruiting sailors for Magellan's secret voyage to find a route to the West Indies. Agreeing to sign on for two years as cabin boy, Mateo finds he loves life at sea, even with its rigors and deprivations. There is more political infighting among the crew and the officers than Mateo imagined, but he manages to withstand storms, mutinies, illness and lack of decent food until he finally returns to Spanish soil, three years and thousands of miles later. Though Magellan was killed while on the voyage, this journey marked the first time a ship circumnavigated the globe and this fictionalized sea adventure realistically portrays the voyage and life aboard ship. (233 pages)

Where it's reviewed:
Booklist, February 1, 2003, page 996
Bulletin of the Center for Children's Books, April 2003, page 333
Publishers Weekly, January 27, 2003, page 260
School Library Journal, February 2003, page 148
Voice of Youth Advocates, April 2003, page 60

Awards the book has won:
Notable Social Studies Trade Books for Young People, 2004

Other books by the same author:
Voyage of Ice, 2004

Other books you might like:
Erik Christian Haugaard, *Under the Black Flag*, 1994
Sailing to England for boarding school, William is cap-

tured by Blackbeard, held for ransom and eventually becomes Blackbeard's cabin boy.

Karen Hesse, *Stowaway*, 1999
Running away from his abusive master, young butcher's apprentice Nicholas stows away on the *Endeavor* and has the adventure of his life.

Iain Lawrence, *The Buccaneers*, 2001
Picking up a drifting sailor proves advantageous for John Spencer, aboard the schooner *Dragon*, when they're later attacked by pirates.

1386
TERRY TRUEMAN

Inside Out
(New York: HarperCollins, 2003)

Subject(s): Mental Illness; Suicide; Hostages
Age range(s): Grades 8-12
Major character(s): Zachary McDaniel "Zach" Wahhsted, Mentally Ill Person (schizophrenic), 16-Year-Old; Alan "Frosty" Mender, 17-Year-Old, Criminal; Joseph "Stormy" Mender, 14-Year-Old, Criminal
Time period(s): 2000s
Locale(s): Spokane, Washington

Summary: For several years Zach's been battling the demons in his head, demons he calls Rat and Dirtbag, as they encourage him to commit suicide. He's had one unsuccessful attempt and now every day after school he waits for his mother to bring him his meds when she picks him up from the coffee shop. Today she doesn't arrive in time because two brothers, worried about their mother's cancer, decide to hold up the coffee shop and take some of the customers hostage. Zach's held the longest, but during the extra time he develops empathy for the brothers as he realizes they're more messed up than he is. Finally Zach calls his psychiatrist to act as a mediator between the brothers and the police and the hostage situation is resolved. The two brothers are eventually sentenced to some jail time; tragically, Zach finally listens to the voices in his head. (117 pages)

Where it's reviewed:
Booklist, September 1, 2003, page 116
Horn Book, September 2003, page 37
Publishers Weekly, August 18, 2003, page 80
School Library Journal, September 2003, page 222
Voice of Youth Advocates, October 2003, page 320

Awards the book has won:
ALA Best Books for Young Adults, 2004
ALA Quick Picks for Reluctant Young Adult Readers, 2004

Other books by the same author:
Cruise Control, 2004
Stuck in Neutral, 2000

Other books you might like:
Robert Cormier, *I Am the Cheese*, 1977
Adam struggles to survive against unidentified captors who keep him drugged and unable to remember his former life.
Lisa Rowe Fraustino, *Ash*, 1995
Over and over, Ash and his family try to save his older, schizophrenic brother from suicide attempts.

Betty Hyland, *The Girl with the Crazy Brother*, 1987
Attending a new school is difficult for Dana, but she's more concerned about her brother who develops signs of schizophrenia.
Angela Johnson, *Humming Whispers*, 1995
Though Sophie worries that her older, schizophrenic sister forgets to take her medicine, she worries more that she'll begin hearing the "humming whispers."

1387
DIANE TULLSON

Saving Jasey
(Custer, WA: Orca Books, 2002)

Subject(s): Drugs; Family Problems; Diseases
Age range(s): Grades 7-9
Major character(s): Gavin, 8th Grader, Artist; Tristan "Trist" McVeigh, 8th Grader; Jasey McVeigh, 15-Year-Old; Blake, 15-Year-Old, Brother (of Gavin)
Time period(s): 2000s
Locale(s): Canada

Summary: Gavin can hardly wait to escape his home life where his father is abusive to both Gavin and his mother while his older brother Blake emulates his dad. Gavin's refuge is his friend Trist's home not only because he and Trist are good friends, but also because Gavin has a crush on Jasey, Trist's older sister. Friday nights are always reserved for donuts and Monopoly at the McVeigh home, though Gavin wonders why Jasey begins missing their Friday night tradition. When he realizes she's dating Blake, who's been hanging out with the local drug dealer, he becomes very worried, not realizing much of Jasey's behavior is caused by concern that she'll end up with the Huntington's disease that led to her father's suicide and her uncle's institutionalization. Matters come to a crisis when Blake is dumped by both Jasey and the drug dealer and thinks he can solve his problems with a gun in this author's first novel. (172 pages)

Where it's reviewed:
Kliatt, May 2002, page 23
Publishers Weekly, January 28, 2002, page 292
Resource Links, February 2002, page 36
School Library Journal, April 2002, page 159
Voice of Youth Advocates, April 2002, page 48

Other books by the same author:
Edge, 2002

Other books you might like:
Charles Butler, *Timon's Tide*, 2000
Daniel has suffered guilt ever since his brother Timon's drug-related activities caught up with him and led to his death.
Anita Horrocks, *What They Don't Know*, 1999
Kelly's younger sister Hannah is on a path of self-destruction and Kelly doesn't know why.
Elizabeth Wennick, *Changing Jareth*, 2000
Jareth knows his life is out of control, especially when his alcoholic mother beats to death his sickly brother, but he doesn't know what to do.

U

1388

ANDREA U'REN, Author/Illustrator

Mary Smith

(New York: Farrar Straus Giroux, 2003)

Subject(s): City and Town Life; Sleep; Work
Age range(s): Grades K-3
Major character(s): Mary Smith, Mother, Worker; Rose Smith, Daughter, Student
Time period(s): 1920s (1927)
Locale(s): London, England

Summary: Mary Smith, a knocker-up, leaves her home in the darkness of early morning with her trusty peashooter and a pocket full of dried peas. Mary walks through the nearby town stopping to blow a pea or two at the windows of sleeping citizens that have arranged for her services as a human alarm clock. As soon as she sees signs of life in the room, Mary hurries to the next home. By the time the community helpers are awake and heading for the bakery, the train station, the laundry or the Town Hall, Mary has returned to her home where she is horrified to discover Rose. Initially fearful that her own daughter has overslept Mary is relieved to learn the real reason that Rose is under the covers. The book concludes with the factual basis for the story. (32 pages)

Where it's reviewed:
Booklist, August 2003, page 1991

Bulletin of the Center for Children's Books, September 2003, page 38
Horn Book, September 2003, page 603
Publishers Weekly, August 11, 2003, page 279
School Library Journal, September 2003, page 193

Awards the book has won:
Bulletin of the Center for Children's Books Blue Ribbons, 2003
Horn Book Fanfare, 2003

Other books by the same author:
Pugdog, 2001

Other books you might like:
Elisa Bartone, *Peppe the Lamplighter*, 1993
    In a Caldecott Honor Book Peppe helps to support his immigrant family by lighting the city's street lamps each day at dusk.
Robert Burleigh, *Messenger, Messenger*, 2000
    Early in the morning Calvin Curbhopper begins his day as a bicycle messenger in a large city.
Glenna Lang, *Looking Out for Sarah*, 2001
    Daily, Perry performs the very important job of serving as the seeing-eye guide dog for Sarah.
Ian Wallace, *Boy of the Deeps*, 1999
    Proudly James goes to his first day of work in the mines with his father, an experienced coal miner.

V

1389

RACHEL VAIL
YUMI HEO, Illustrator

Sometimes I'm Bombaloo

(New York: Scholastic Press, 2002)

Subject(s): Brothers and Sisters; Anger; Parent and Child
Age range(s): Grades K-2
Major character(s): Katie Honors, Sister (older), Daughter; Unnamed Character, Baby, Brother; Unnamed Character, Mother
Time period(s): 2000s
Locale(s): United States

Summary: Cheerful, obedient Katie admits that sometimes she is simply ''Bombaloo.'' Katie acknowledges that such anger is frightening and she understands her mother's request that she go to her room for a tim -out. When Katie's temper subsides she share hugs with her mom and baby brother and resumes her more typical cooperative demeanor—after cleaning up the ''Bombaloo'' mess in her room, of course. (32 pages)

Where it's reviewed:
Booklist, February 1, 2002, page 940
Bulletin of the Center for Children's Books, April 2002, page 298
Horn Book Guide, Fall 2002, page 315
Kirkus Reviews, January 1, 2002, page 53
School Library Journal, March 2002, page 204

Awards the book has won:
Booklist Editors' Choice, 2002

Other books by the same author:
Mama Rex and T: Homework Trouble, 2002
Mama Rex and T: The Horrible Play Date, 2002
Over the Moon, 1998

Other books you might like:
Molly Bang, *When Sophie Gets Angry—Really, Really Angry . . .*, 1999
Sophie's anger explodes in a temper tantrum. She runs to her favorite tree and allows the branches to soothe her before returning home.
Betsy Everitt, *Mean Soup*, 1992
After a bad day, Horace helps his mother make Mean Soup and he begins to feel better.
Mem Fox, *Harriet, You'll Drive Me Wild!*, 2000
Even Harriet's patient mother loses her temper sometimes, but she apologizes and hugs Harriet when the mood passes.
David Shannon, *No, David!*, 1998
In a Caldecott Honor book David hears ''No, David!'' when he misbehaves. After breaking a vase, the sad, remorseful boy finally hears, ''I love you!''

1390

CHRIS VAN ALLSBURG, Author/Illustrator

Zathura: A Space Adventure

(Boston: Houghton Mifflin Company, 2002)

Subject(s): Playing; Games; Fantasy
Age range(s): Grades 1-4
Major character(s): Danny Budwing, Child, Brother (younger); Walter Budwing, Child, Brother (older)
Time period(s): Indeterminate
Locale(s): Earth; Outer Space

Summary: One evening after their parents go out, Danny and Walter are left home alone. Danny opens a game box he found in the park that afternoon. Underneath the board game labeled ''Jumanji'' Danny finds another with a path of squares leading from Earth to Zathura and back again. That game looks interesting so Danny rolls the dice. A card pops out of the game and instantly the event announced by the card begins. Walter thinks it's hail, but Danny knows from the card it is a meteor shower. One look out the front door and Walter realizes the house is now in outer space. The brothers play the game, trying to get back to Earth before their parents return. When a black hole swallows Walter it looks as if the game is over . . . or perhaps it's not yet begun. (32 pages)

Where it's reviewed:
Book World, November 10, 2002, page 12

Booklist, November 15, 2002, page 603
Horn Book, November 2002, page 741
Publishers Weekly, June 24, 2002, page 54
School Library Journal, November 2002, page 139

Other books by the same author:
All Aboard the Polar Express, 2004
Bad Day at Riverbend, 1995
The Sweetest Fig, 1993 (ALA Notable Children's Books)
Jumanji, 1981 (Caldecott Medal)

Other books you might like:
Raul Colon, *Orson Blasts Off!*, 2004
After Orson's computer crashes a talking jack-in-the-box encourages him to try a more imaginative adventure.
Erica Silverman, *Follow the Leader*, 2000
An older brother controls an imaginative game until the younger one stops playing and his brother realizes it's more fun to let him lead than to play alone.
Bruce Whatley, *Captain Pajamas: Defender of the Universe*, 2000
When Brian's "Remote-Control Techno-Robotic Alien Communicator" indicates the presence of an alien he becomes Captain Pajamas to save his sister.

1391

WENDELIN VAN DRAANEN

Sammy Keyes and the Search for Snake Eyes

(New York: Knopf/Borzoi, 2002)

Subject(s): Mystery and Detective Stories; Abandonment; Sports/Softball
Age range(s): Grades 5-8
Major character(s): Samantha Jo "Sammy" Keyes, Detective—Amateur; Officer Borsch, Police Officer; Marissa McKenze, 7th Grader
Time period(s): 2000s
Locale(s): Santa Martina, California

Summary: Exploring the mall with her friend Marissa while they take their minds off the upcoming Junior Sluggers' Cup baseball tournament, Sammy is given a bag to hold by a young girl. Told she'll return for the bag that evening, the girl takes off, pursued by an evil-looking man with "snake eyes." The bag contains a baby and the mother doesn't return; after being peed and puked on, the next day Sammy turns the baby over to her friend Officer Borsch. Worried and concerned, Sammy can't leave the situation alone and, though warned not to intervene, investigates and finds herself in the midst of Mexican-American street gangs. As if that weren't bad enough, her grandmother's new neighbor threatens to report Sammy for living in a senior-only residence; her enemy at school tries to get her kicked off the softball team; and, perhaps worst of all, her enemy's brother has a crush on Sammy as she rollicks through her seventh adventure. (277 pages)

Where it's reviewed:
Booklist, May 1, 2002, page 1460
Bulletin of the Center for Children's Books, June 2002, page 473

Kirkus Reviews, April 1, 2002, page 500
School Library Journal, April 2002, page 159
Voice of Youth Advocates, August 2002, page 198

Other books by the same author:
Sammy Keyes and the Curse of Moustache Mary, 2000
Sammy Keyes and the Runaway Elf, 1999
Sammy Keyes and the Sisters of Mercy, 1999
Sammy Keyes and the Hotel Thief, 1998

Other books you might like:
Linda Bailey, *How Can I Be a Detective If I Have to Baby-Sit?*, 1996
Stuck with watching young Alexander while camping, Stevie and Jesse revert to their detecting work when Alexander's trailer is ransacked.
Betsy Byars, *The Dark Stairs*, 1994
With a policeman father and a private investigator mother, Herculeah Jones has no choice but to be a female Sherlock Holmes.
Helen Ericson, *Harriet Spies Again*, 2002
Fearing her nanny has murdered her husband, Harriet investigates and discovers that her nanny is pregnant.
Laurence Yep, *The Case of the Goblin Pearls*, 1998
While riding on the Lion Salve float for the Chinese New Year's parade, Lily is helpless to prevent the Goblin Pearls from being stolen.

1392

WENDELIN VAN DRAANEN

Swear to Howdy

(New York: Knopf, 2003)

Subject(s): Family Problems; Brothers and Sisters; Friendship
Age range(s): Grades 5-8
Major character(s): Russell "Rusty" Cooper, 12-Year-Old; Joey Banks, 12-Year-Old; Amanda Jane Banks, Sister (of Joey)
Time period(s): 2000s
Locale(s): Lost River

Summary: Rusty can't believe his good luck when his family moves and he becomes instant pals with his next-door neighbor Joey. They spend their days that summer swimming in the creek where they produce spectacular farts in the water, hide a huge front in the underwear drawer of Joey's sister and secretly add bugs to the soft drinks their sisters sell at the baseball game. After every prank or embarrassing moment, they pledge secrecy beginning with the refrain "I swear to howdy, if you tell. . . . " Their pranks continue but become a little more devious each time, though Joey lives in fear of the beatings he receives from his alcoholic father. The night they fake the Legendary Ghost of Lost River leads to a car crash that kills Joey's sister Amanda Jane. The boys once again pledge secrecy, but they're so guilt-ridden that when Joey tries to commit suicide, Rusty knows it's time to break their pact and tell their parents of their involvement. (126 pages)

Where it's reviewed:
Booklist, October 1, 2003, page 324
Bulletin of the Center for Children's Books, February 2004, page 248

Kirkus Reviews, September 15, 2003, page 1184
Publishers Weekly, October 27, 2003, page 70
School Library Journal, November 2003, page 150

Other books by the same author:
Sammy Keyes and the Art of Deception, 2003
Flipped, 2001
How I Survived Being a Girl, 1997

Other books you might like:
Marion Dane Bauer, *On My Honor*, 1986
　　Good friends Joel and Tony swim in a river off limits to
　　them; when Tony drowns, Joel is terrified to tell either set
　　of parents.
Ron Carlson, *The Speed of Light*, 2003
　　The trio of Larry, Witt and Rafferty devour summer with
　　baseball games, bike rides, sleep outs in weedy fields and
　　dangerous experiments.
Gary Paulsen, *Harris and Me: A Summer Remembered*, 1994
　　A summer of pig wrestling, outmaneuvering a testy barn
　　cat and peeing on an electric fence make many memories
　　for ''Harris and me.''
Bill Wallace, *Skinny-Dipping at Monster Lake*, 2003
　　Skinny dipping one night with his friends, Kent notices
　　huge yellow eyes glowing at him under water and is sure
　　there's a monster in the lake.

1393

JEAN VAN LEEUWEN

Lucy Was There . . .

(New York: Jean Fogelman Books/Penguin Putnam, 2002)

Subject(s): Grief; Animals/Dogs; Mothers and Daughters
Age range(s): Grades 4-7
Major character(s): Morgan, 12-Year-Old; Isabella Pratt, 12-
　　Year-Old; Cassie, Sister (of Morgan); Lucy, Dog (imagi-
　　nary)
Time period(s): 2000s
Locale(s): United States

Summary: Missing her mother and younger brother who left
her last November, Morgan is comforted only when she
sleeps. It's then that Lucy, the ''magic dog,'' appears in her
dreams, singing lullabies to her and speaking just as her
mother would. Her days are lonely because her grieving father
is at work and her older sister Cassie has immersed herself in
the school's social scene. Without her mother to help, Morgan's mascara ends up looking as though she has a black eye;
an attempt at cutting her own hair is a disaster; and if she
polishes her nails, they never match. Her classmate Isabella
offers to help fix her hair and the two become friends. When
Morgan finally accepts the fact that her mother and brother
were both killed in a plane crash, she lets go of the ''magic
dog'' Lucy, returns to her music by playing a favorite piano
piece of her mother's, and begins to heal. (165 pages)

Where it's reviewed:
Booklist, September 1, 2002, page 126
Bulletin of the Center for Children's Books, March 2002,
　　page 260
Publishers Weekly, May 27, 2002, page 60
School Library Journal, May 2002, page 162

Voice of Youth Advocates, June 2002, page 123

Other books by the same author:
Cabin on Trouble Creek, 2004
Blue Sky, Butterfly, 1996
Bound for Oregon, 1994
The Great Summer Catastrophe, 1992

Other books you might like:
Sharon Creech, *Walk Two Moons*, 1994
　　It takes a trip across America to the site of the bus crash for
　　Salamanca to accept her mother's death.
Karen Hesse, *Out of the Dust*, 1997
　　Billie Jo accidentally tosses a burning pail of kerosene out
　　the kitchen door and onto her mother, who later dies.
Cynthia Rylant, *Missing May*, 1992
　　After Aunt May dies, Uncle Ob's hand-carved whirligigs
　　stop and both he and Summer take time to grieve.

1394

SUSANNA VANCE

Deep

(New York: Delacorte, 2003)

Subject(s): Kidnapping; Sailing; Interpersonal Relations
Age range(s): Grades 7-10
Major character(s): Birdie Sidwell, 13-Year-Old; Morgan
　　Bera, 17-Year-Old; Nicholas, Kidnapper
Time period(s): 2000s
Locale(s): Riverton, Oregon; Calista Island, Caribbean

Summary: Two very different teenage girls find their lives
intertwined in this chilling tale. Young, upbeat Birdie is the
only child of two intellectual parents who decide to give up
their jobs and live for a year on a Caribbean island, an idyll
they've always dreamed of doing. Morgan has never lived
anywhere except aboard a sailboat in the Caribbean but after
her older sister drowns, her parents spend all their time
drinking rum in the bars. Disgusted with them, Morgan leaves
them ashore and sails away in their boat. She searches for
Nicholas to buy fake owner papers, not realizing he's a
psychopath who's just kidnapped Birdie and taken her to his
island. Once Morgan is on Nicholas's island, she's also kept
as a captive. Both girls are eventually placed in a cage
suspended in an old, unused well. Though their former lives
differed, each girl is feisty and bright and together figure out a
way to escape from certain death. (261 pages)

Where it's reviewed:
Booklist, April 15, 2003, page 1463
Horn Book, May 2003, page 357
Library Media Connection, February 2004, page 73
Publishers Weekly, May 19, 2003, page 76
School Library Journal, June 2003, page 152

Awards the book has won:
ALA Best Books for Young Adults, 2004

Other books by the same author:
Sights, 2001

Other books you might like:
Catherine Atkins, *When Jeff Comes Home*, 1999
　　Finally returned to his family after two and a half years of a

degrading existence at the hands of a kidnapper, Jeff has trouble adjusting to normal life.

Donna Jo Napoli, *Three Days*, 2001
    Taken away from the scene of her father's car accident, Jackie realizes she's being held captive in an old farm-house by a woman who's just lost a daughter.

Joan Lowery Nixon, *Playing for Keeps*, 2001
    Aboard a cruise ship in the Caribbean, Rose agrees to help handsome Ricky who's headed for asylum in the US but right now is a suspect in a murder.

Nancy Werlin, *Locked Inside*, 2000
    Kidnapped by her deranged chemistry teacher, Marnie and her online friend Elf are both tossed into the cellar.

1395

VIVIAN VANDE VELDE

Heir Apparent

(San Diego: Harcourt, 2002)

Subject(s): Virtual Reality; Science Fiction
Age range(s): Grades 7-10
Major character(s): Giannine ''Janine'' Bellisario, 14-Year-Old; Nigel ''Kenric'' Rasmussen, 16-Year-Old
Time period(s): Indeterminate Future
Locale(s): Rochester, New York

Summary: Giannine simply wants to play the virtual reality game at Rasmussen Gaming Center. Just because angry pick-eters from Citizens to Protect Our Children (CPOC) surround the place is no reason not to go in and play, as far as Giannine is concerned. Once inside, Giannine quickly opts to go to Shelby, where she is eager to take on the character of Janine de St. Jehan in a medieval world. Gamers learn by making mistakes, and quite soon Giannine makes a fatal error and finds herself back at the beginning of the game. In fact things don't seem to be quite right in the game as oddities that shouldn't have fatal consequences are making Giannine start over more often than seems reasonable. Then a voice from outside informs her that someone has tampered with the gaming equipment and if she cannot win the game, she may be trapped there until her real self is brain damaged. She needs help, but whom can she trust? Meanwhile, Nigel Rasmussen, inventor of the gaming system, wonders how far CPOC will go to close him down as he struggles to find a way to help Giannine. (315 pages)

Where it's reviewed:
Bulletin of the Center for Children's Books, December 2002, page 177
Horn Book, November 2002, page 764
Kirkus Reviews, September 15, 2002, page 1403
School Library Journal, October 2002, page 174
Voice of Youth Advocates, December 2002, page 403

Awards the book has won:
ALA Best Books for Young Adults, 2004
Center for Children's Books Best Books, 2002

Other books by the same author:
Being Dead: Stories, 2001
Never Trust a Dead Man, 1999
Curses, Inc: And Other Stories, 1997

Other books you might like:
Pat Cadigan, *Tea from an Empty Cup*, 1999
    Bodies are turning up in virtual reality booths, and a po-liceman and a bereaved girlfriend team up to discover the truth.
Diana Wynne Jones, *Hexwood*, 1993
    Aliens have placed a machine that manipulates reality in the English woods outside Ann's village, but no one will believe her.
Delia Marshall Turner, *Of Swords and Spells*, 1999
    Malka is the kind of seasoned warrior Giannine emulates to win her way free of Shelby, but Malka's freedom is much more elusive.

1396

VIVIAN VANDE VELDE

Witch's Wishes

(New York: Holiday House, 2003)

Subject(s): Witches and Witchcraft; Halloween; Wishes
Age range(s): Grades 2-5
Major character(s): Sarah Gonnella, Kindergartner, Sister (younger); Justin Gonnella, Brother (older), 5th Grader; Unnamed Character, Witch, Aged Person
Time period(s): 2000s (2003)
Locale(s): Irondequoit

Summary: The old witch's talking broom tries to warn her not to take chances but it's Halloween and she's in a hurry so she rides the broom to the store. Sarah spots her and, thinking she's someone in costume, engages the witch in conversation despite Justin's admonitions. Feeling kindly toward Sarah, the witch puts a spell on the magic wand that is part of her fairy costume to make all Sarah's wishes come true for one night. Instead of being helpful, the witch creates major prob-lems for the town as Sarah innocently wishes everyone could have a dog and every night could be Halloween and Christ-mas, too. Finally, the witch has to magically play reruns of the evening not once but twice in order to undo what she uninten-tionally wrought. (91 pages)

Where it's reviewed:
Booklist, December 1, 2003, page 669
Bulletin of the Center for Children's Books, January 2004, page 210
School Library Journal, November 2003, page 116

Other books by the same author:
Wizard at Work, 2003
Heir Apparent, 2002
There's a Dead Person Following My Sister Around, 1999
Smart Dog, 1998

Other books you might like:
Ruth Chew, *The Witch and the Ring*, 1992
    Two unsuspecting siblings find a magic ring that leads them to unexpected adventure.
Catherine Dexter, *A Is for Apple, W Is for Witch*, 1996
    Apple ignores her mother's guidance and tries out an over-heard spell with troubling consequences.
Anne Mazer, *The Accidental Witch*, 1995
    Clumsy Bee tumbles into a circle of witches absorbing

some of their power, but none of their experience; the results are disastrous.

`1397`

VIVIAN VANDE VELDE

Wizard at Work

(San Diego: Harcourt, Inc., 2003)

Subject(s): Wizards; Fantasy; Fairy Tales
Age range(s): Grades 3-6
Major character(s): Unnamed Character, Wizard, Teacher
Time period(s): Indeterminate
Locale(s): Saint Wayne the Stutterer, Fictional Country

Summary: A young wizard is very much looking forward to his summer vacation and a break from his students at wizard school. However his vacation is filled with a series of pleas for his help from rescuing princesses to saving a village from wild unicorns. A request to rid a castle of its ghost explains the mystery of the Loch Ness monster (the wizard takes the sea monster out of the castle and gives him a new home in Loch Ness). Finally a quest to find a husband for the princess of his very own kingdom leads to a little romance for the wizard himself. (134 pages)

Where it's reviewed:
Booklist, April 15, 2003, page 1466
School Library Journal, May 2003, page 132

Other books by the same author:
Witch's Wishes, 2003
Never Trust a Dead Man, 1999 (ALA Best Book for Young Adults)
A Hidden Magic, 1985

Other books you might like:
Eva Ibbotson, *Which Witch?*, 1999
    Arriman the Awful needs a wife and, as a wizard, he can only marry a witch, but which one should he choose?
M.M. Kaye, *The Ordinary Princess*, 1984
    When seventh princess, Amy, turns out ordinary, she embarks on an adventure rather than marry a prince.
Jane Yolen, *Wizard's Hall*, 1991
    Henry is a poor student at Wizard's Hall, but when a cruel sorcerer threatens the school, he must save the day.

`1398`

MARCIA VAUGHAN
LISA DESIMINI, Illustrator

Night Dancer: Mythical Piper of the Native American Southwest

(New York: Orchard Books/Scholastic, Inc., 2002)

Subject(s): Native Americans; Folk Tales; Music and Musicians
Age range(s): Grades K-3
Major character(s): Kokopelli, Mythical Creature
Time period(s): Indeterminate Past
Locale(s): United States

Summary: In the moonlight, Kokopelli uses his flute to call the desert animals to come and dance with him. One by one all the animals, from the coyote to the jackrabbit to the tarantula join Kokopelli. Finally even the Native American children wake from their slumber and come out to dance. An historical note on the significance of Kokopelli among the Hopi, Zuni and Pueblo follows the text. (32 pages)

Where it's reviewed:
Publishers Weekly, October 14, 2002, page 82
School Library Journal, October 2002, page 134

Other books by the same author:
Up the Learning Tree, 2003
Kissing Coyotes, 2002
The Secret to Freedom, 2001

Other books you might like:
Robert Browning, *The Pied Piper of Hamelin*, 1987
    A piper lures away not only the town's rats, but also their children.
Gerald McDermott, *Coyote: A Trickster Tale from the American Southwest*, 1994
    Coyote decides that he wants to fly like a crow and he does so with limited success.
Jerrie Oughton, *How the Stars Fell into the Sky: A Navajo Legend*, 1992
    First Woman decides to write the laws in the sky, but when Coyote agrees to finish the job he just throws the stars up randomly.
Nancy Van Laan, *Rainbow Crow: A Lenape Tale*, 1989
    After the rainbow-colored crow saves his animal friends from a snowstorm he loses his brilliant colors.

`1399`

ROBIN VAUPEL

My Contract with Henry

(New York: Holiday, 2003)

Subject(s): Friendship; Schools/Middle Schools; Nature
Age range(s): Grades 5-8
Major character(s): Beth Gardner, 13-Year-Old; Stuart Garfield, 13-Year-Old; Hollis Robbins, 13-Year-Old; Rachel Haygen, 13-Year-Old
Time period(s): 2000s
Locale(s): Wayburn Woods, Michigan

Summary: New student Beth is unprepared for choosing a partner for her eighth grade English teacher's assignment entitled "The Henry Contract," a project about Thoreau and his time spent at Walden Pond. As the popular kids choose up their groups, Beth finds she's left with three losers, grouchy Rachel, energetic Stuart and skinny Hollis. The group decides to recreate Thoreau's cabin in nearby Wayburn Woods and emulate the time the author would have spent there. As the cabin is built, their enthusiasm for the project also climbs and soon Hollis produces beautiful drawings of the surrounding plants and animals, Rachel cooks using natural materials and Stuart spins off on his own to assume control of the newspaper. Writing in Thoreau's style, Beth records their activities at the cabin in a school newspaper column that serves as a rallying point when Wayburn Woods is sold to a developer in this author's thoughtful first novel. (244 pages)

Where it's reviewed:
Booklist, July 2003, page 1892
Bulletin of the Center for Children's Books, September 2003, page 38
Publishers Weekly, June 30, 2003, page 80
School Library Journal, July 2003, page 135
Voice of Youth Advocates, October 2003, page 320

Other books by the same author:
Austin's Orbit, 2004

Other books you might like:
James Howe, *The Misfits*, 2001
Tired of being called names, four friends decide to run for office at their school; though they don't win, they focus attention on the problem.
E.L. Konigsburg, *The View from Saturday*, 1996
Mrs. Olinski chooses four sixth graders as class representatives to the Academic Bowl, but as the story shows, maybe these four chose her.
Zilpha Keatley Snyder, *Libby on Wednesday*, 1990
Libby hates meeting on Wednesdays with four other writing contest winners, but finds they help one another with both school and family problems.

1400

ANA VECIANA-SUAREZ

Flight to Freedom
(New York: Orchard/Scholastic, 2002)

Series: First Person Fiction
Subject(s): Cuban Americans; Emigration and Immigration; Diaries
Age range(s): Grades 6-10
Major character(s): Yara Garcia, 13-Year-Old; Ileana Garcia, 16-Year-Old
Time period(s): 1960s
Locale(s): Havana, Cuba; Miami, Florida

Summary: Because of her family's anti-Castro feelings, Yara's Papi is sent out of town to harvest crops while the family waits for permission to leave. The food rationing, youth work camps and the spying of neighbors on one another disturb Yara while she lives in Cuba, yet when she arrives in Miami she worries about her lack of English, unfamiliarity with people at school, and the constant family tenseness. Gradually all her family members adapt to their new life: Mami learns to drive and goes to work, Papi joins a pseudo-military group who want to retake Cuba, her older sister Ileana sneaks out to date a boy and Yara learns English and adjusts to her new life. Though the Garcia family slowly becomes Americanized, they keep alive their hope of returning to Cuba in this *First Person Fiction* title. (213 pages)

Where it's reviewed:
Booklist, November 15, 2003, page 596
Bulletin of the Center for Children's Books, February 2003, page 253
Kliatt, November 2002, page 16
School Library Journal, October 2002, page 174

Voice of Youth Advocates, February 2003, page 484

Other books by the same author:
Birthday Parties in Heaven: Thoughts on Love, Grief and Other Matters of the Heart, 2000 (adult title)
The Chin Kiss King, 1997 (adult title)

Other books you might like:
Julia Alvarez, *How the Garcia Girls Lost Their Accents*, 1991
A sensitive story of four sisters and their adjustment to life in America after fleeing the Dominican Republic. Adult title.
Anilu Bernardo, *Jumping Off to Freedom*, 1996
David and his father endure a death-defying trip of survival as they flee from Cuba on a raft with two dangerous strangers.
Joan Lowery Nixon, *Playing for Keeps*, 2001
Smuggled out of Cuba to Haiti, and then placed aboard a cruise ship, Ricky hopes to be granted asylum in America but suddenly he's a suspect in a murder.

1401

CHARLOTTE VOAKE, Author/Illustrator

Pizza Kittens
(Cambridge, MA: Candlewick Press, 2002)

Subject(s): Animals/Cats; Food; Behavior
Age range(s): Grades K-1
Major character(s): Mom, Mother, Cat; Dad, Father, Cat; Bert, Cat, Brother
Time period(s): Indeterminate
Locale(s): Fictional Country

Summary: In an effort to broaden the food preferences of their three offspring and introduce some table manners Mom and Dad institute family dinners. Each of the kittens is expected to help by setting the table and eating what is served. The first night Mom serves water rather than soda for beverages and Dad has the audacity to expect them to eat peas. Bert tips his chair, causing a chain reaction spill that makes the meal even more unappetizing. The next night Mom and Dad try a different approach and offer pizza. Finally, it looks as if they'll have a perfect meal, if Bert's chair can stay balanced on one leg. (34 pages)

Where it's reviewed:
Booklist, May 1, 2002, page 1537
Bulletin of the Center for Children's Books, June 2002, page 384
Horn Book Guide, Fall 2002, page 315
Publishers Weekly, April 8, 2002, page 225
School Library Journal, May 2002, page 129

Other books by the same author:
Here Comes the Train, 1998
Ginger, 1997 (ALA Notable Children's Book)
Mr. Davies and the Baby, 1996

Other books you might like:
Marc Brown, *D.W., the Picky Eater*, 1995
D.W. learns to be more willing to try new foods in order to join the family when they go out to eat.

Susanna Gretz, *Rabbit Food*, 1999
John does not share his rabbit family's appreciation of vegetables.

Jane Read Martin, *Now I Will Never Leave the Dinner Table*, 1996
In order to eat the detested spinach on her plate, Patty Jane adds chips, grape juice and ketchup to make it more palatable.

1402

CYNTHIA VOIGT

Bad Girls in Love

(New York: Anne Schwartz Books/Atheneum, 2002)

Subject(s): Interpersonal Relations; Friendship; School Life
Age range(s): Grades 5-8
Major character(s): Mikey Elsinger, 8th Grader; Margalo Epps, 8th Grader; Shawn Macavity, 8th Grader
Time period(s): 2000s
Locale(s): United States

Summary: Those "bad girls" Mikey and Margalo, who aren't popular or part of the social scene, are now in eighth grade and find they're both in love, though luckily not with the same person. Mikey has flipped over Shawn and doesn't hold back in her attempts to let him know. Though she does try to dress with a little more femininity, she scares him away with her aggressiveness as she showers him with cookies, decorates blackboards with their initials and gives him a special T-shirt. After four weeks, the mad crush passes on. Margalo, however, keeps the object of her romantic thoughts to herself, which is sensible because she's crazy about the wonderfully unattainable Mr. Schramm, her biology teacher. First love is memorable and difficult and important, as Mikey and Margalo discover, and when it's over, it's great to have your best friend waiting for you. (233 pages)

Where it's reviewed:
Booklist, August 2002, page 1964
Bulletin of the Center for Children's Books, October 2002, page 84
Horn Book, September 2002, page 582
School Library Journal, July 2002, page 126
Voice of Youth Advocates, October 2002, page 286

Awards the book has won:
IRA Children's Choices/Advanced Readers, 2003

Other books by the same author:
It's Not Easy Being Bad, 2000
Bad, Badder, Baddest!, 1997
Bad Girls, 1996

Other books you might like:
Ellen Conford, *If This Is Love, I'll Take Spaghetti*, 1983
These stories relate the humorous aspects of love, from dating a best friend's boyfriend to discovering that "dream boat" is a dud.

Ann Herrick, *The Perfect Guy*, 1989
Rebecca's view of her new stepbrother as the "perfect guy" does not mesh with his image of her as a sister.

Phyllis Reynolds Naylor, *The Alice Series*, 1985-
Alice and her friends Pamela, Elizabeth and Patrick survive all the rigors of being a teenager, from dating to peer pressure, schoolwork and family problems.

Rachel Vail, *The Friendship Ring Series*, 1991-1998
The teens in this series can attest to the rigors of middle school life.

1403

CLARA VULLIAMY, Author/Illustrator

Small

(New York: Clarion Books, 2002)

Subject(s): Toys; Animals/Mice; Bedtime
Age range(s): Preschool-Kindergarten
Major character(s): Tom, Child; Granny, Grandmother; Small, Toy (stuffed animal), Mouse
Time period(s): 2000s (2001)
Locale(s): England

Summary: Tom carefully packs and repacks the many items he needs for an overnight stay at Granny's house. At bedtime Tom realizes that Small is missing and must have been left at home. When darkness falls and Tom does not return home to Small the little mouse climbs out Tom's window and shinnies down the drain spout. Small runs through the dark city streets, climbing obstacles, enduring rain, and ignoring fear. After he leaves the city Small continues on through the dark, scary woods until he reaches Granny's house. Unable to sleep, Tom tiptoes downstairs to look for Small and finds him in a soggy puddle just below the mail slot near the front door. Granny thinks Tom dropped Small when he arrived but Tom knows differently. Originally published in 2001 in England. (28 pages)

Where it's reviewed:
Booklist, April 15, 2002, page 1409
Bulletin of the Center for Children's Books, April 2002, page 298
Kirkus Reviews, February 1, 2002, page 190
Publishers Weekly, February 18, 2002, page 94
School Library Journal, April 2002, page 126

Other books by the same author:
Ellen and Penguin and the New Baby, 1996
Wide Awake!, 1996
Good Night, Baby, 1996

Other books you might like:
Ian Beck, *Home before Dark*, 2001
A teddy bear, dropped in the park by its owner, attempts to find his way home while it is still daylight.

Debi Gliori, *Flora's Blanket*, 2001
Flora knows she will not be able to sleep until she finds her special blanket.

Martin Waddell, *Small Bear Lost*, 1996
After Small Bear is forgotten on a train he manages to find his way home to the little girl who lost him.

W

1404

LEA WAIT

Seaward Born

(New York: Margaret K. McElderry/Simon & Schuster, 2003)

Subject(s): Slavery; Ships; Runaways
Age range(s): Grades 4-7
Major character(s): Michael ''Noah Brown'' Lautrec, Slave
Time period(s): 1800s
Locale(s): Charleston, South Carolina; Massachusetts; Maine

Summary: Working on the docks of Charleston aboard a lighter, part of a crew that sails out to larger ships to unload their cargo, orphaned Michael is happy to work as his father once did. When his mistress dies, he seizes the chance to flee rather than be sold elsewhere, and stows away aboard a ship headed to Massachusetts. Changing his name to Noah Brown to elude the slave hunters, he finds he can't escape from their tentacles even when he moves up to Maine to work. Finally the desire for freedom and living without fear become so overwhelming that he moves to Canada in this work filled with details of sea life. (156 pages)

Where it's reviewed:
Booklist, February 15, 2003, page 1082
Kirkus Reviews, December 15, 2002, page 1859
Publishers Weekly, January 6, 2003, page 61
School Library Journal, January 2003, page 144

Awards the book has won:
Notable Social Studies Trade Books for Young People, 2004

Other books by the same author:
Wintering Well, 2004
Stopping to Home, 2001

Other books you might like:
Elisa Carbone, *Stealing Freedom*, 1998
   Without her family to support her, Ann Maria's life as a slave is horrible until a stranger helps her escape on the Underground Railroad to Canada.

James Lincoln Collier, *Jump Ship to Freedom*, 1981
   Young slave Daniel tries to save enough money to buy freedom for himself and his mother.
Carolyn Reeder, *Across the Lines*, 1997
   Edward and Simon have been more than master and slave, but when Union soldiers overtake Edward's plantation, Simon seizes the chance to escape.

1405

JUDY WAITE

Shopaholic

(New York: Atheneum/Simon & Schuster, 2003)

Subject(s): Stealing; Shopping; Family Problems
Age range(s): Grades 6-10
Major character(s): Taylor, 14-Year-Old; Kat, 16-Year-Old
Time period(s): 2000s
Locale(s): England

Summary: Taylor's life changes after her young sister accidentally drowns and her mother's depression sends her to her bedroom, which in turn piles household responsibilities onto Taylor and deprives her of time to spend with her best friends. Shopping one day, Taylor meets glamorous Kat and is thrilled to spend time with her. Taylor's so desperate to have a friend that she overlooks the ways Kat mistreats her, from stealing her money and letting her be accused of shoplifting, to leaving her with a credit card debt. Stealing from her family's household money to finance all the shopping eventually catches up with Taylor and she confesses her misdoings to her mother in this British import. (211 pages)

Where it's reviewed:
Booklist, May 1, 2003, page 1589
Bulletin of the Center for Children's Books, June 2003, page 425
Publishers Weekly, May 5, 2003, page 222
School Library Journal, July 2003, page 135
Voice of Youth Advocates, August 2003, page 232

Awards the book has won:
Center for Children's Books Best Books, 2003

Other books by the same author:
Trick of the Mind, 2005

Other books you might like:
Kevin Brooks, *Martyn Pig*, 2002
   Alex helps Martyn cover up his father's death, but then
   steals his money and turns him in to the police.
Peg Kehret, *Cages*, 1999
   Caught shoplifting, Kit is humiliated over having to per-
   form community service work and resolves to get her life
   under control.
Sophie Kinsella, *Confessions of a Shopaholic*, 2001
   Becky Bloomwood is a financial journalist whose credit
   cards are maxed out and checking account overdrawn, but
   whose closet bulges with designer clothes.

1406

BILL WALLACE

Skinny-Dipping at Monster Lake
(New York: Simon & Schuster, 2003)

Subject(s): Fathers and Sons; Rescue Work; Monsters
Age range(s): Grades 5-8
Major character(s): Kent Morgan, 12-Year-Old; Mrs. Baum,
   Aged Person
Time period(s): 2000s
Locale(s): United States

Summary: Kent and his friends all ride horses and spend their
summer days pretending to be members of "The Seventh
Cavalry," attacking one another with pretend spears, and
playing at being knights or cowboys or soldiers. One night
they decide to fish and then camp overnight at Cedar Lake,
which has a reputation of hiding a large creature. When Kent
goes skinny-dipping and notices huge yellow eyes glowing at
him under the water, he's certain there's a monster in the lake.
The next time Kent's at the lake, he and a friend discover a
submarine in the lake; trapped inside is their grouchy, older
neighbor Mrs. Baum. Kent's dad helps rescue Mrs. Baum and
she eventually tells the whole story about the submarine, a
platinum mine and silver dollars buried by her grandfather in
another warm-hearted adventure. (212 pages)

Where it's reviewed:
Booklist, May 15, 2003, page 166
School Library Journal, August 2003, page 168

Other books by the same author:
Pick of the Litter, 2005
No Dogs Allowed!, 2004
Coyote Autumn, 2000

Other books you might like:
Bruce Coville, *The Monsters of Morley Manor: A Madcap
   Adventure*, 2001
   Anthony and Sarah buy a carved wooden box at Morley
   Manor's yard sale and discover five brass monsters that
   come alive when wet.
Anna Fienberg, *The Witch in the Lake*, 2002
   Leo uses his wizardry skills to challenge the witch in the
   lake and retrieve the children she's said to steal.
Elizabeth Honey, *Fiddleback*, 2001
   On a neighborhood camping trip, the kids sleep in one

huge tent and spend their days skinny-dipping and playing
games.

1407

IAN WALLACE, Author/Illustrator

The True Story of Trapper Jack's Left Big Toe
(Brookfield, CT: Roaring Brook Press, 2002)

Subject(s): Legends; Frontier, Canada; Anatomy
Age range(s): Grades 2-5
Major character(s): Joshua "Josh" Yew, Student, Friend;
   Gabe Kidder, Student, Friend; Trapper Jack, Aged Person,
   Trapper
Time period(s): 2000s (2002)
Locale(s): Dawson City, Yukon Territory, Canada

Summary: Josh has only been in town a week when his new
friend Gabe tells him the story of Trapper Jack's toe. Doubting the story, Josh wants to sneak into the Sourdough Saloon
to look for the can with the toe inside, but they're caught
trying to enter. The next day they go to Trapper Jack's cabin
to get the story from the source. Sure enough, Trapper Jack's
left big toe is missing. According to Trapper Jack's story,
frostbite caused its loss ten years earlier. When the Sourdough
Saloon opens, Gabe and Josh meet Trapper Jack and he brings
out the tobacco can from which he pulls a black, shriveled
object. Before Josh can get a closer look a stray dog snatches
it and runs off. Though Gabe, Josh and Trapper Jack chase the
dog, they can't find the toe. Truth is, Trapper Jack still has ten
toes because his right foot has six toes and that's a true story
too. A concluding Author's Note informs the reader of the
location of Trapper Jack's toe and the procedure for becoming
a member of the Sourdough's Sourtoe Cocktail Club. (36
pages)

Where it's reviewed:
Booklist, June 2002, page 1744
Bulletin of the Center for Children's Books, July 2002, page
   420
Horn Book, May 2002, page 323
The New Advocate, Spring 2003, page 219
Publishers Weekly, March 18, 2002, page 104

Other books by the same author:
Boy of the Deeps, 1999 (Smithsonian's Notable Books for
   Children)
A Winter's Tale, 1997
Morgan the Magnificent, 1988

Other books you might like:
Shutta Crum, *Who Took My Hairy Toe?*, 2001
   The retelling of a Southern folktale explains how a greedy
   man comes to possess an ogre's toe and the consequences
   when the ogre finds it.
Cynthia DeFelice, *Cold Feet*, 2000
   A bagpiper with newly found boots is surprised by a knock
   at the door from a corpse seeking the return of his feet.
Nancy Lamb, *The World's Greatest Toe Show*, 1994
   In hopes of winning a prize at the fair Emily Anderson
   displays her father's severed toe in a matchbox.

1408

KAREN WALLACE

Raspberries on the Yangtze

(New York: Delacorte, 2002)

Subject(s): Friendship; Summer
Age range(s): Grades 5-8
Major character(s): Nancy, Child; Amy Linklater, Child; Clare Linklater, Child; Tracy Wilkins, Pregnant Teenager; Sandra Wilkins, Child
Time period(s): 1950s
Locale(s): Quebec, Canada (along the Gatineau River)

Summary: Nancy spends a delightful summer with her good friends Amy and Clare: they enjoy life on the Gatineau River, picking raspberries and swinging on the wire pasture fence they call the Yangtze, but it turns out to be a more complicated summer than Nancy ever imagined. She and her two friends experience one adventure after another, yet are never malicious in their escapades, unlike Nancy's enemy Sandra who always lies when she gets in trouble and tries to blame it on Nancy. Nancy, Amy and Clare don't particularly like any of the Wilkins family as Mrs. Wilkins is a snob who judges everyone by their social status, Sandra is a tattletale and Tracy, the oldest sister, rebels against her mother's strictures and becomes pregnant. Mr. Chevrolet is also a bit of a puzzle to the girls for they can't pronounce his real last name, but they know he likes children, makes lemonade for them and decides to marry widowed Mrs. Linklater, Amy and Clare's mother. Gossip and secrets, love and playing on a wire pasture fence, idyllic summer days and complicated months, all fill this story based on the author's childhood. (134 pages)

Where it's reviewed:
Horn Book, September 2002, page 583
Journal of Adolescent and Adult Literacy, March 2003, page 530
Kirkus Reviews, May 15, 2002, page 743
Resource Links, October 2001, page 56
School Library Journal, July 2002, page 127

Other books by the same author:
Wendy, 2004

Other books you might like:
Robert Cormier, *Frenchtown Summer*, 1999
    In free verse Eugene thinks over all the occurrences during the summer he was 12 and how they all contributed to his growing up.
Gerald Hausman, *Doctor Moledinky's Castle: A Hometown Tale*, 1995
    One summer Andy and his friend Pauly explore their town of Berkeley Bend and discover the strange yet heart-warming characters who live there.
Robin Klein, *Dresses of Red and Gold*, 1993
    The three sisters and cousin of the Australian Melling family fill their summer with rich activities as they endure World War II.
Gary Paulsen, *Harris and Me: A Summer Remembered*, 1994
    A summer on the Larson's farm forges a bond between an unnamed narrator and Harris as each day brings a new set of adventures for the two boys.

1409

NANCY ELIZABETH WALLACE, Author/Illustrator

Pumpkin Day!

(New York: Marshall Cavendish, 2002)

Subject(s): Animals/Rabbits; Pumpkins; Family
Age range(s): Grades K-2
Major character(s): Trudy, Rabbit, Sister; Jack, Rabbit, Brother; Mrs. Bell, Rabbit, Farmer
Time period(s): Indeterminate
Locale(s): Fictional Country

Summary: Pumpkin Day is an annual tradition in Trudy and Jack's family. After eating pumpkin pancakes for breakfast they walk with their parents to Pumpkin Hollow Farm where Mrs. Bell answers all their questions about pumpkins. Informative signs in Mrs. Bell's pumpkin patch educate the visitors to interesting facts about pumpkins. Mrs. Bell shows pictures of the pumpkin's life cycle to help Trudy and Jack understand how the pumpkins grow from seed to maturity. Trudy and Jack select the pumpkins they want to bring home and carve into jack-o'-lanterns before they eat a special Pumpkin Day supper. (32 pages)

Where it's reviewed:
Book Links, December 2002, page 13
Booklist, August 2002, page 1963
Bulletin of the Center for Children's Books, October 2002, page 84
Publishers Weekly, September 16, 2002, page 70
School Library Journal, November 2002, page 140

Awards the book has won:
Book Links Lasting Connections, 2002
Center for Children's Books Best Books, 2002

Other books by the same author:
Apples, Apples, Apples, 2000
Paperwhite, 2000
Rabbit's Bedtime, 1999

Other books you might like:
Zoe Hall, *It's Pumpkin Time!*, 1994
    Siblings describe the growth of the pumpkins in their specially planted jack-o'-lantern patch.
Joan Holub, *The Garden That We Grew*, 2001
    Children carefully plant and tend a garden. After harvesting their pumpkins they stay busy making pies, cookies and jack-o'-lanterns.
Teri Sloat, *Patty's Pumpkin Patch*, 1999
    Patty plants her seeds and watches the pumpkins grow in this rhyming alphabet story.

1410

RICH WALLACE

Losing Is Not an Option

(New York: Borzoi/Knopf, 2003)

Subject(s): Short Stories; Sports/Running; Family Life
Age range(s): Grades 8-12
Major character(s): Ron, Runner, 12th Grader
Time period(s): 2000s

Locale(s): Sturbridge, Pennsylvania

Summary: Nine short stories follow Ron from sixth grade through his graduation from high school as he finds his spot in the world as a track star. Appropriately, the book begins with "Night Game," as Ron and his friend Gene sneak into a night football game, but Ron realizes his friend is growing up and away from him when Gene leaves with a girl. In the intervening stories, Ron focuses on running, meeting girls and relating to his father. He spends time at the county fair with his family, discovers his deceased grandfather's lode of old "Playboys" and even attends a weeklong conference on the arts where he shares some of his poetry. In the last story, "Losing Is Not an Option," Ron concentrates all his energies and talent on winning a state championship which leaves the reader wondering where he'll go next. (127 pages)

Where it's reviewed:
Booklist, August 2003, page 1973
Horn Book, September 2003, page 621
Publishers Weekly, August 18, 2003, page 80
School Library Journal, September 2003, page 222
Voice of Youth Advocates, October 2003, page 320

Other books by the same author:
Fast Company, 2004
Technical Foul, 2004 (Winning Season #2)
The Roar of the Crowd, 2004 (Winning Season #1)

Other books you might like:
Rick Book, *Necking with Louise*, 1999
 Seven chapters capture a memorable year in Eric's life as he vacillates between boyhood and manhood, dates Louise and adores his grandfather.
Jeanne Schinto, *Show Me a Hero: Great Contemporary Stories about Sports*, 1995
 The emotions, lifestyles and backgrounds found in any athletic activity are portrayed in this collection of 21 stories.
Don Trembath, *The Tuesday Cafe*, 1996
 Enrolled in a writing class, Harper doesn't realize he's in a section for newly literate and learning disabled, for it's the best class he's ever taken.

1411

RICH WALLACE

Restless: A Ghost's Story

(New York: Viking, 2003)

Subject(s): Ghosts; Supernatural; Brothers
Age range(s): Grades 9-12
Major character(s): Warren "Herbie" Herbert, Football Player, Runner (cross country); Frank Herbert, Narrator, Brother; Eamon Connolly, Spirit
Time period(s): 2000s
Locale(s): Sturbridge, Pennsylvania

Summary: Tired of undeserved riding by his soccer coach, in the fall Herbie joins both the football and cross-country teams. He's exhausted from participating in two sports, plus his full-time job, but would never admit this to anyone. One night while running through the cemetery, he feels a presence behind him and ultimately traces it to Eamon Connolly, a very

distant relative who's been dead since the late 1800s but hasn't yet left Earth. It's not only Eamon who's restless, but also Herbie's older brother Frank who died when he was only 17. To compensate for all he's missed, he follows Herbie and vicariously enjoys his little brother's life, in addition to serving as the narrator for this tale. The combination of Herbie, Frank and Eamon eventually allows the ghosts to leave Earth and find their natural peace. (167 pages)

Where it's reviewed:
Booklist, September 15, 2003, page 232
Bulletin of the Center for Children's Books, October 2003, page 79
Kliatt, September 2003, page 14
School Library Journal, November 2003, page 150
Voice of Youth Advocates, October 2003, page 329

Other books by the same author:
Technical Foul, 2004
The Roar of the Crowd, 2004
Losing Is Not an Option, 2003
Playing without the Ball: A Novel in Four Quarters, 2000
Shots on Goal, 1997
Wrestling Sturbridge, 1996

Other books you might like:
Victor Kelleher, *Baily's Bones*, 1988
 When their handicapped brother is possessed by a deceased convict, two siblings must prevent him from reenacting a long-past tragedy.
Lael Littke, *Lake of Secrets*, 2002
 Traveling to Lake Isadora, site of her brother's drowning, Carlene finds herself caught up in disturbing memories of this unfamiliar lake.
Markus Zusak, *Fighting Ruben Wolfe*, 2001
 To earn extra money for their family, two brothers agree to fight for an organized boxing racket not realizing they'll have to fight each other.

1412

RUTH WALLACE-BRODEUR

Blue Eyes Better

(New York: Dutton Children's Books, 2002)

Subject(s): Death; Grief; Family
Age range(s): Grades 4-6
Major character(s): Tessa Drummond, 10-Year-Old, Daughter; Ms. Dunn, Teacher, Coach; Mrs. Hirsch, Aged Person, Neighbor
Time period(s): 2000s
Locale(s): Wardsboro, Massachusetts; Truro, Massachusetts

Summary: The death of Tessa's teen-aged brother in a car accident dramatically changes the dynamics of her family. Brown-eyed Tessa feels rejected and abandoned by her mother, who is so consumed by her grief that she moves to Truro for the summer to help her sister run a gift shop, leaving Tessa and her father home alone with their memories. The guilt that Tessa feels about her brother's death burdens her and, with no one at home in whom to confide, she turns to Mrs. Hirsch when she needs a "grandmother" and Ms. Dunn, an empathic teacher and summer track coach. Tessa finds peace as she runs and learns coping skills from conversations with Mrs. Hirsch and Ms. Dunn. Though her life will always be changed, by summer's end, Tessa knows her family will survive. (106 pages)

Where it's reviewed:
Booklist, April 1, 2002, page 1323
Bulletin of the Center for Children's Books, March 2002, page 260
Horn Book Guide, Fall 2002, page 384
Publishers Weekly, November 4, 2002, page 40
School Library Journal, January 2002, page 140

Awards the book has won:
Publishers Weekly Best Children's Books, 2002

Other books by the same author:
The Godmother Tree, 1992
Callie's Way, 1990
Steps in Time, 1986

Other books you might like:
Susan Katz, *Snowdrops for Cousin Ruth*, 1998
　After her younger brother dies in a tragic accident, Josie grieves for all her family has lost; Cousin Ruth brings hope for healing and happiness.
Deborah Wiles, *Love, Ruby Lavender*, 2001
　Newcomers in a small town, a teacher and student, help grieving members of the community heal following a deadly single-car accident.
Nancy Hope Wilson, *Flapjack Waltzes*, 1998
　An elderly neighbor helps Natalie cope following her brother's death in an automobile accident.

1413

ELLEN STOLL WALSH, Author/Illustrator

Dot & Jabber and the Mystery of the Missing Stream

(San Diego: Harcourt, Inc., 2002)

Subject(s): Rivers; Mystery; Animals/Mice
Age range(s): Grades K-2
Major character(s): Dot, Mouse, Detective; Jabber, Mouse, Detective
Time period(s): Indeterminate
Locale(s): Fictional Country

Summary: The day after a big storm Dot and Jabber hurry to float sticks in the stream and discover that the stream has vanished. Since they expected it to be running full of water they proceed to follow the dry bed upstream searching for clues to the mystery of the missing water. They find minnows crowded into a puddle, leaves and sticks. Dot is sure that the sticks must be an important clue. The farther upstream they travel the more leaves and branches litter the ground and streambed. Finally they discover a dam made, not by beavers, but by the accumulation of storm debris. Before they can figure out how to free the water, the force of the dammed up water breaks the makeshift dam and the stream quickly fills again as Dot and Jabber scramble up the bank to safety. The book concludes with facts about storms and dams. (32 pages)

Where it's reviewed:
Horn Book Guide, Spring 2003, page 21
Kirkus Reviews, August 15, 2002, page 1238
Publishers Weekly, September 9, 2002, page 70
School Library Journal, November 2002, page 140

Other books by the same author:
Dot & Jabber and the Big Bug Mystery, 2003
Dot & Jabber and the Great Acorn Mystery, 2001
Mouse Magic, 2000

Other books you might like:
Debi Gliori, *Mr. Bear to the Rescue*, 2000
　On a stormy night Mr. Bear responds to Mr. Rabbit-Bunn's plea for help after the destruction of a tree that housed his family.
Kathy Henderson, *The Storm*, 1999
　The day after a coastal storm Jim observes the changes wrought by the power of wind and water.
Lynn Plourde, *Pigs in the Mud in the Middle of the Rud*, 1997
　A large mud puddle blocks the road when it becomes full of pigs and other farm animals attracted by the commotion.

1414

VIVIAN WALSH
J. OTTO SEIBOLD, Illustrator

Gluey: A Snail Tale

(San Diego: Harcourt, Inc., 2002)

Subject(s): Animals/Rabbits; Animals, Treatment of; Dwellings
Age range(s): Grades K-3
Major character(s): Celerina, Rabbit; Gluey, Snail
Time period(s): Indeterminate
Locale(s): Fictional Country

Summary: Celerina happens upon a lovely, apparently unoccupied house and claims it as her own without noticing the home's resident snail. Gluey sees her and hopes to become her friend so, in addition to his constant repair of the house's cracks, he also fixes anything Celerina breaks. Celerina, thinking the repairs are magical, plans a party to show the house off to her friends. While preparing, she spots Gluey for the first time and heaves him (and unwittingly her "magic") into the meadow. The Wee people rescue Gluey, repair his cracked shell and help him return to his home where Celerina greets him with a bit more understanding as together they face the house, damaged by Celerina's partying friends. (40 pages)

Where it's reviewed:
Booklist, October 15, 2002, page 413
Horn Book Guide, Spring 2003, page 74
Newsweek, October 28, 2002, page 75
Publishers Weekly, September 2, 2002, page 74
School Library Journal, December 2002, page 112

Other books by the same author:
Penguin Dreams, 1999 (New York Times Best Illustrated Children's Book)
Free Lunch, 1996
Monkey Business, 1995

Other books you might like:

Linda Ashman, *Castles, Caves, and Honeycombs*, 2001
A rhyming story reflects on the concept of homes. No matter the shape or size they are safe, cozy places to sleep and play for their occupants.

Kate Banks, *The Bird, the Monkey, and the Snake in the Jungle*, 1999
When their tree home topples over in a storm, a bird, a monkey and a snake search for another dwelling place.

Mary Ann Hoberman, *A House Is a House for Me*, 1978
Rhyming text lists various objects that can be used as dwelling by different animals.

Leo Lionni, *It's Mine!*, 1986
Three selfish frogs argue about ownership of a pond and island until a storm threatens their safety and they begin to work together.

1415

HELEN WARD, Author/Illustrator

The Rooster and the Fox

(Brookfield, CT: The Millbrook Press, 2003)

Subject(s): Animals/Roosters; Animals/Foxes; Fables
Age range(s): Grades 1-4
Major character(s): Chanticleer, Rooster; Mr. Fox, Fox
Time period(s): Indeterminate Past
Locale(s): Fictional Country

Summary: Proudly Chanticleer crows each morning to awaken the farm animals to another day. When hungry Mr. Fox visits the farm, Chanticleer, strutting in self-importance, inquires why Mr. Fox has come. Flattered by Mr. Fox's compliments of his fine voice, Chanticleer willingly throws back his head to crow thus giving Mr. Fox the opportunity to grab his neck and race away with the barnyard leader. The animals follow until Mr. Fox enters the wood and they dare go no further. During the run, Chanticleer thinks of a plan that tricks Mr. Fox into opening his mouth, freeing Chanticleer who flies into a tree, out of the fox's reach. Basing the story on "The Nun's Priest's Tale" from Chaucer's *Canterbury Tales*, the author provides background information from other tales and fables as well as information about the rare breeds of animals pictured. Originally published in Great Britain in 2002. (40 pages)

Where it's reviewed:
Booklist, January 2003, page 911
Bulletin of the Center for Children's Books, February 2003, page 255
Horn Book Guide, Fall 2003, page 345
School Library Journal, February 2003, page 124

Other books by the same author:
The Tin Forest, 2001
The King of the Birds, 1997
The Golden Pear, 1991

Other books you might like:
Barbara Cooney, *Chanticleer and the Fox*, 1958
Cooney's illustrated adaptation of Chaucer's tale of a sly fox and a proud rooster received the Caldecott Medal.

Bill Martin Jr., *Chicken Chuck*, 2000
A rooster's inflated sense of self-importance shatters when he spots a circus poster with a horse that has not one, but two, blue feathers on his head.

Mary Wormell, *Bernard the Angry Rooster*, 2001
To Bernard, the installation of a rooster-shaped weather vane threatens his position as the "top" rooster at the farm.

1416

RICHARD WARING
CAROLINE JAYNE CHURCH, Illustrator

Hungry Hen

(New York: HarperCollins Publishers, 2002)

Subject(s): Animals/Chickens; Animals/Foxes; Greed
Age range(s): Grades K-2
Major character(s): Unnamed Character, Hen; Unnamed Character, Fox
Time period(s): Indeterminate
Locale(s): Fictional Country

Summary: Each morning as a hen with a voracious appetite emerges from the hen house to begin a day of eating, a fox living on a nearby hill watches her and plans for the day when he will make her his meal. Being a greedy fox, he realizes that the longer he waits, the larger the hungry hen will grow and so the fox waits and watches. The hen grows while the fox becomes thinner daily. Finally the skinny fox makes his move and leaps through the henhouse window to devour the hen that has grown so large she can no longer get out the door. Too late, the fox discovers that he's waited just a bit too long to make his move on this very hungry hen. The author's first book was originally published in England in 2001. (28 pages)

Where it's reviewed:
Booklist, January 1, 2002, page 868
Bulletin of the Center for Children's Books, March 2002, page 261
Horn Book Guide, Fall 2002, page 316
Publishers Weekly, November 26, 2001, page 60
School Library Journal, January 2002, page 112

Awards the book has won:
Center for Children's Books Best Books, 2002

Other books you might like:
Judith Ross Enderle, *What Would Mama Do?*, 1995
Little Lily Goose depends on her mother's teachings to outsmart a fox that is following her. Stephanie Gordon Tessler, co-author.

Vivian French, *Red Hen and Sly Fox*, 1995
A clever hen outwits a fox who had hoped to enjoy her for dinner.

Pat Hutchins, *Rosie's Walk*, 1968
Unaware that a hungry fox is following her, Rosie enjoys her walk around the farmyard.

Gerald McDermott, *The Fox and the Stork*, 1999
Fox's trick on Stork backfires when she returns his dinner invitation and Fox goes home hungry.

1417

SALLY WARNER

This Isn't about the Money

(New York: Viking, 2002)

Subject(s): Death; Grief; Orphans
Age range(s): Grades 5-8
Major character(s): Jane Elizabeth ''Janey'' Bishop, 12-Year-Old, Accident Victim; Yolanda ''YoYo'' Bishop, Child; Howard Bishop, Grandfather; Irene ''Baby'' Bishop, Aunt (great-aunt)
Time period(s): 2000s
Locale(s): Flagstaff, Arizona; Phoenix, Arizona; Glendale, California

Summary: On a summer trip to visit relatives in California, her parents' car is hit by a drunk driver, Janey and her younger sister YoYo are thrown from the car and their parents are killed when the car flares and burns. Badly burned on her face, Janey spends time in the hospital and then accompanies Grandpa and Aunt Baby back to their home in California. Each person reacts to the accident differently, yet each is badly affected by it. Grandpa must now work past retirement to support everyone; Aunt Baby is saddled with children when she's never had any of her own; YoYo is happy with the attention she receives as the ''miracle child,'' unscathed from the accident; and Janey, who doesn't know how to grieve, desperately misses her parents. Overriding everything is Aunt Baby's determination to bring a civil suit against the drunk driver, even though she keeps saying ''This isn't about the money.'' Bit by bit each of the four learns to adjust to the other and slowly the horror of what they've each experienced diminishes. (209 pages)

Where it's reviewed:
Booklist, September 1, 2002, page 126
Bulletin of the Center for Children's Books, December 2002, page 177
Publishers Weekly, October 7, 2002, page 73
School Library Journal, September 2002, page 236
Voice of Youth Advocates, October 2002, page 287

Other books by the same author:
Long Time Ago Today, 2003
Bad Girl Blues, 2001
Sister Split, 2001
How to Be a Real Person (in Just One Day), 2001
Totally Confidential, 2000

Other books you might like:
Tony Earley, *Jim the Boy*, 2000
   A week before Jim is born, his father dies unexpectedly and he's raised by his still-grieving mother and her three bachelor brothers.
Adrienne Ross, *In the Quiet*, 2000
   Sammy keeps digging holes, trying to find something of his mother's so he can reconnect with her spirit, lost when she was killed in a bus accident.
Ruth White, *Belle Prater's Boy*, 1996
   Two cousins learn to live with the loss of a parent, supported by the help each gives to the other.

1418

APRIL HALPRIN WAYLAND
ELAINE CLAYTON, Illustrator

Girl Coming in for a Landing

(New York: Knopf/Random House, 2002)

Subject(s): Schools/High Schools; Teen Relationships; Poetry
Age range(s): Grades 7-10
Major character(s): Unnamed Girl, Narrator, Teenager
Time period(s): 2000s
Locale(s): United States

Summary: A young girl writes a series of poems organized around the seasons of the school year and tells of the little and big things in her life. These experiences include walking on the beach with her mother to relations with her older sister; fighting with her best friend to wishing vile things on that same friend; anticipating and actually beginning her first period; and finally, moving from spin the bottle to falling in love. Intriguing illustrations further illume every poem, from photo cutouts and woodcuts to stitchery and real objects. Tips for writing and being published conclude the book. (134 pages)

Where it's reviewed:
Horn Book, September 2002, page 584
Kliatt, July 2002, page 14
Library Media Connection, January 2003, page 92
Publishers Weekly, July 8, 2002, page 50
Voice of Youth Advocates, August 2002, page 198

Other books you might like:
Robert Cormier, *Frenchtown Summer*, 1999
   In free verse Eugene thinks over all the occurrences during the summer he was twelve and how they all contributed to his growing up.
Helen Frost, *Keesha's House*, 2003
   A combination of sestinas, sonnets and other verse forms tell of Keesha's House that offers sanctuary to all who need it.
Ron Koertge, *Shakespeare Bats Cleanup*, 2003
   Recovering from mono, Kevin tries writing a little haiku, then a sonnet and even a sestina, discovering that poetry is ''almost as cool as baseball.''
Sonya Sones, *What My Mother Doesn't Know*, 2001
   Sophie finally meets Mr. Right and can hardly wait to tell all her friends in this novel written in free verse.

1419

LEE WEATHERLY

Child X

(New York: David Fickling/Random House, 2002)

Subject(s): Family Problems; Fathers and Daughters; Identity
Age range(s): Grades 6-9
Major character(s): Juliet ''Jules'' Cheney, 13-Year-Old; Ben Cheney, Father; Holly Cheney, Mother
Time period(s): 2000s
Locale(s): England

Summary: Her parents are so opposite that Jules is never surprised at their continual arguing. Her mother is a successful international financier who's always in suits and traveling around the world while her father Ben is usually jeans-clad and can be found either on his motorcycle or writing. When one particularly vicious argument leads to her father walking out and filing for divorce, Jules is surprised only that her father has no contact with her, but she immerses herself in the part of Lyra in Philip Pullman's *Northern Lights* being put on by her school. When the media stalk her, she learns that she is "Child X" and her father is suing her mother for divorce because Jules is not his natural child and he wants compensation for the cost of raising her these past thirteen years. Jules can't believe her beloved father has disowned her, especially because he was her nurturer, in this author's first novel. (211 pages)

Where it's reviewed:
Booklist, July 2002, page 1850
Bulletin of the Center for Children's Books, October 2002, page 84
Publishers Weekly, July 29, 2002, page 72
School Library Journal, June 2002, page 148
Voice of Youth Advocates, August 2002, page 198

Other books by the same author:
Missing Abby, 2004

Other books you might like:
Caroline B. Cooney, *Tune in Anytime*, 1999
   Sophie can't believe that her life has been like a soap opera ever since her father fell in love with her sister's college roommate.
Barbara Dana, *Necessary Parties*, 1986
   When his parents file for divorce, Chris Mills hires an unconventional lawyer for $1 and files suit against his parents to block their action.
Susan Beth Pfeffer, *Make Believe*, 1993
   Carrie and Jill have been best friends for their entire 12 years, so when Jill's father announces he's leaving both families are devastated.

1420

WILL WEAVER

Claws

(New York: HarperCollins, 2003)

Subject(s): Family Problems; Divorce; Runaways
Age range(s): Grades 7-10
Major character(s): Jed Berg, 11th Grader; Laura Sanborn, 11th Grader; Jenny Sanborn, Sister (of Laura)
Time period(s): 2000s
Locale(s): Duluth, Minnesota; Boundary Waters

Summary: Jed is startled when a pink-haired girl dressed in Goth clothes arranges a meeting with him and reveals that his father is having an affair with her mother, information that she backs up with revealing photographs. The Goth girl, who Jed finally identifies as Laura, demands that Jed tell his father to leave her mother alone, or else she'll do the telling. Their good intentions are the breaking point for both the Sanborn and the Berg marriage, though increased visits between Jed and Laura lead to their falling in love with one another. Jed's perfect life is slowly getting back on track when Laura's sister Jessie runs away to the Boundary Waters and Jed and Laura pack sleeping bags and a tent to find her. Telling no one of their plan, the two track Jessie down but before everyone can get to safety, a storm comes up and Jed's perfect life is shattered once again. (232 pages)

Where it's reviewed:
Booklist, April 15, 2003, page 1463
Bulletin of the Center for Children's Books, April 2003, page 335
Publishers Weekly, January 13, 2003, page 61
School Library Journal, March 2003, page 242
Voice of Youth Advocates, June 2003, page 144

Other books by the same author:
Memory Boy, 2001
Hard Ball, 1998
Farm Team, 1995
Striking Out, 1993

Other books you might like:
Laurie Halse Anderson, *Catalyst*, 2002
   An unlikely friendship develops during Kate's senior year when Teri Litch is burned out of her home and moves in with Kate's family.
Alex Flinn, *Breaking Point*, 2002
   Paul's delight at Charlie's friendship leads to vandalizing, cheating and finally leaving a bomb in a classroom.
Laura McNeal, *Zipped*, 2003
   Mick is furious with his stepmother for having an affair, determined to identify her lover and protective of his father.

1421

DAVID WEBER

War of Honor

(Riverdale, NY: Baen, 2002)

Series: Honor Harrington. Book 10
Subject(s): Politics; War; Love
Age range(s): Grades 9-Adult
Major character(s): Honor Harrington, Military Personnel; Earl Hamish Alexander of Whitehaven, Nobleman
Time period(s): Indeterminate Future
Locale(s): Outer Space

Summary: After their defeat in the war, everyone expects the Havenites will simply agree peacefully to whatever demands Manticore makes for peace, but several factions have determined that peace is not in their best interest. No terms have been forthcoming from Manticore so the defeated Peep Navy rebuilds their fleet, making it better, which they hope will allow them to negotiate terms more to their liking. Honor and Hamish are in the forefront of the political maneuverings to get things moving as they sense the danger of the present situation. There are like-minded individuals in the Peep government as well, but messages are intercepted, deliberately reworded to insult or lost altogether. As negotiations break down, Honor is ordered to the Andermani borders, where it seems the Empire is trying to take advantage of the chaos.

While war looms on two fronts, Honor and Hamish struggle with their passion for one another, though the treecats complicate that situation. (864 pages)

Where it's reviewed:
Booklist, September 1, 2002, page 70
Library Journal, October 15, 2002, page 97
Publishers Weekly, October 14, 2002, page 69

Other books by the same author:
Ashes of Victory, 2000 (Honor Harrington Book 9)
In Enemy Hands, 1997 (Honor Harrington Book 7)
Honor Among Enemies, 1996 (Honor Harrington Book 6)

Other books you might like:
Lois McMaster Bujold, *Miles, Mystery and Mayhem*, 2001
    Several of Bujold's novels about the handicapped military genius Miles Vorkosigan are collected in this volume.
Jack McDevitt, *The Engines of God*, 1994
    Priscilla Hutchins pilots the shipload of archaeologists that will investigate a mysterious city about to be lost in a terraforming operation.
Elizabeth Moon, *Heris Serrano*, 2002
    Heris comes from a family of career space navy officers, but her adventures may outdo them all.

1422

SARAH WEEKS
ASHLEY WOLFF, Illustrator

My Somebody Special

(San Diego: Gulliver/Harcourt, Inc., 2002)

Subject(s): Schools/Preschool; Parent and Child; Animals
Age range(s): Preschool-Grade 1
Major character(s): Unnamed Character, Dog, Child
Time period(s): 2000s (2002)

Summary: A little puppy and his friends in daycare wait for their parents to pick them up at the end of the day. One by one their "someone special" comes to take them home until, finally, only the little puppy is left. Worried that he's been forgotten, the puppy is soon greeted by his mother, breathless after running from the bus stop. (40 pages)

Where it's reviewed:
Booklist, August 2002, page 1977
Horn Book Guide, Fall 2002, page 316
Publishers Weekly, April 15, 2002, page 62
School Library Journal, May 2002, page 130
Tribune Books, June 16, 2002, page 5

Other books by the same author:
If I Were a Lion, 2004
Two Eggs, Please, 2003
Mrs. McNosh and the Great Big Squash, 2000

Other books you might like:
Nancy Minchella, *Mama Will Be Home Soon*, 2003
    Lili stays with her grandmother while her mother travels and worries about when Mama will return and how she'll recognize her.
Audrey Penn, *The Kissing Hand*, 1993
    Chester worries about being away from his mom when he starts school, so she gives him the kissing hand.

Ann Tompert, *Will You Come Back for Me?*, 1989
    When Suki starts day care she worries that her mother will forget to come get her.

1423

SARAH WEEKS
NADINE BERNARD WESTCOTT, Illustrator

Oh My Gosh, Mrs. McNosh!

(New York: Laura Geringer Books/HarperCollins Publishers, 2002)

Subject(s): Animals/Dogs; Humor; Stories in Rhyme
Age range(s): Grades K-2
Major character(s): Nelly McNosh, Animal Lover; George, Dog
Time period(s): 2000s
Locale(s): United States

Summary: Nelly McNosh's walk in the park turns into a comical chase when George bolts after a squirrel and his leash breaks. As Nelly chases her errant pet through the park she catches a trout, a bride's bouquet, a fly ball and a cold, but she doesn't catch George. Finally, tired and defeated, Nelly trudges home, missing her mischievous pet. Unbeknownst to Nelly, George has scampered home, entered through the pet door and presents her slippers as she opens the door. (32 pages)

Where it's reviewed:
Booklist, May 1, 2002, page 1537
Bulletin of the Center for Children's Books, May 2002, page 344
Horn Book Guide, Fall 2002, page 316
Publishers Weekly, April 8, 2002, page 230
School Library Journal, June 2002, page 114

Awards the book has won:
IRA Children's Choices, 2003

Other books by the same author:
Mrs. McNosh and the Great Big Squash, 2000
Splish, Splash!, 1999
Mrs. McNosh Hangs Up Her Wash, 1998

Other books you might like:
Paulette Bogan, *Spike in Trouble*, 2003
    Misjudged by the family as the perpetrator of mischief at home, Spike is sent to obedience school and graduates with honors.
Alice Provensen, *A Day in the Life of Murphy*, 2003
    An active farm dog believes his name to be "Murphy-Stop-That" because that's what he hears all day.
Cynthia Rylant, *The Great Gracie Chase: Stop That Dog!*, 2001
    Gracie leads an increasingly long line of people on a merry chase through town until she reaches the comfort of her quiet home.

1424

ELIZABETH E. WEIN

A Coalition of Lions

(New York: Viking, 2003)

Subject(s): Princes and Princesses; Arthurian Legends
Age range(s): Grades 8-12
Major character(s): Artos, Royalty (deceased); Goewin, Royalty (princess); Priamos, Diplomat (Aksumite ambassador to Britain); Constantine, Diplomat (British ambassador to Aksum), Heir (to the British throne); Telemakos, Nephew (of Goewin)
Time period(s): 6th century
Locale(s): Aksum, Africa (ancient Ethiopia)

Summary: After her father King Artos, twin brother and half-brother are all killed in battle, Princess Goewin and Priamos, the Aksumite ambassador to Britain, travel to Aksum where Goewin seeks sanctuary. Her cousin and betrothed Constantine, now viceroy of Aksum, proves haughty and distant and Goewin realizes there are enough political intrigues in Aksum to rival those of the royal court in Britain. When she meets her nephew Telemakos, son of her deceased half-brother, she agrees to marry Constantine if she can be allowed to name Telemakos heir to the throne of Britain. Constantine does not approve of the contacts Goewin makes, or her stipulations for marriage, and keeps her under guard until she and Telemakos escape to safety through the tunnel of a tomb in this sequel to *The Winter Prince*. (210 pages)

Where it's reviewed:
Booklist, February 15, 2003, page 1065
Bulletin of the Center for Children's Books, April 2003, page 336
Horn Book, March 2003, page 218
School Library Journal, April 2003, page 170
Voice of Youth Advocates, December 2003, page 420

Other books by the same author:
The Sunbird, 2004
The Winter Prince, 1993

Other books you might like:
Marion Zimmer Bradley, *The Mists of Avalon*, 1982
   The sorceress Morgan offers her perspective on the rise and fall of her brother Arthur.
Robin McKinley, *The Blue Sword*, 1982
   Bored with her proper life, when Harry is kidnapped by a king, she discovers magic she never knew she had.
Jane Yolen, *Passenger*, 1996
   Arthur's magician Merlin is the protagonist of the trilogy that begins with this book.

1425

ROSEMARY WELLS
TOM WELLS, Co-Author
DAN ANDREASEN, Illustrator

The House in the Mail

(New York: Viking, 2002)

Subject(s): Dwellings; Historical; Family

Age range(s): Grades 2-5
Major character(s): Emily Cartwright, 12-Year-Old, Sister; Homer Cartwright, 9-Year-Old, Brother; Joseph Cartwright, Baby, Brother
Time period(s): 1920s (1927-1928)
Locale(s): Enfield, Kentucky

Summary: Emily and Homer pore over the pages of a catalog helping their parents select the house they will build to provide more room for their growing family than is available in the home they share with their grandparents. Investing their entire life savings of $2,500 the family orders a house kit from Sears, Roebuck & Company and eagerly awaits its arrival by train. Although the new home comes with some assembly required, it also has modern conveniences such as electricity and indoor plumbing. Emily and Homer are happy to have such amenities but they feel a tad sorry for Joseph who will never know what life was like in the "old days." (32 pages)

Where it's reviewed:
Booklist, March 1, 2002, page 1137
Bulletin of the Center for Children's Books, February 2002, page 223
Horn Book Guide, Fall 2002, page 366
Publishers Weekly, January 14, 2002, page 60
School Library Journal, March 2002, page 205

Other books by the same author:
Wingwalker, 2002
Streets of Gold, 1999
Mary on Horseback: Three Mountain Stories, 1998
   (Riverbank Review Children's Book of Distinction)

Other books you might like:
Mary Calhoun, *Flood*, 1997
   A broken levee forces Sarajean and her family to flee from their home as the Mississippi River threatens to destroy all she knows and loves.
Cynthia Rylant, *Let's Go Home: The Wonderful Things about a House*, 2002
   The component parts of a house add up to a happy home when a loving family dwells within.
Anne Shelby, *Homeplace*, 1995
   A grandmother traces the history of the family from the building of the family homestead by the great-great-great grandpa to the present.

1426

ROSEMARY WELLS
SUSAN JEFFERS, Illustrator

McDuff Saves the Day

(New York: Hyperion Books for Children, 2002)

Subject(s): Animals/Dogs; Food; Problem Solving
Age range(s): Grades K-3
Major character(s): McDuff, Dog; Fred, Spouse, Father; Lucy, Spouse, Mother
Time period(s): Indeterminate Past
Locale(s): Lake Ocarina

Summary: While Fred is unloading the car and Lucy is playing with the baby McDuff is in charge of watching the picnic basket. McDuff guards the basket diligently but he doesn't hear or smell the ants that silently invade the basket and carry off every morsel. Lucy and Fred stare at the empty basket while McDuff springs into action. He visits the other picnickers until he finds one lone man with food to spare. Of course the man is not happy to have a dog stealing his meatballs but after Lucy and Fred explain their situation he invites them to join his picnic. As they watch the sunset and await the Fourth of July fireworks they agree that McDuff saved the day for his family by finding food and for the solo picnicker by saving him from being alone. (28 pages)

Where it's reviewed:
Booklist, July 2002, page 1861
Horn Book Guide, Fall 2002, page 316
Kirkus Reviews, May 15, 2002, page 743
Publishers Weekly, April 29, 2002, page 72
School Library Journal, August 2002, page 172

Other books by the same author:
McDuff Steps Out, 2004
Timothy's Tales from Hilltop School, 2002 (Bulletin of the Center for Children's Books Blue Ribbon)
McDuff Goes to School, 2001
McDuff's New Friend, 1998

Other books you might like:
Alyssa Satin Capucilli, *Biscuit's Picnic*, 1998
    Biscuit returns in a My First I Can Read Book chasing a cat and ending up in the middle of a cake at a picnic.
Pat Hutchins, *We're Going on a Picnic!*, 2002
    Hen, Duck and Goose fail to notice that smaller animals are eating the contents of their picnic basket as they search for the perfect picnic spot.
Martine Schaap, *Mop and the Birthday Picnic*, 2001
    Twins Justine and Julie celebrate their birthday with a picnic for their dog Mop.

1427

ROSEMARY WELLS, Author/Illustrator

Ruby's Beauty Shop
(New York: Viking, 2002)

Subject(s): Beauty; Brothers and Sisters; Animals/Rabbits
Age range(s): Preschool-Grade 1
Major character(s): Ruby, Rabbit, Sister (older); Max, Rabbit, Brother (younger); Louise, Rabbit, Friend
Time period(s): Indeterminate
Locale(s): Fictional Country

Summary: Louise brings her ''Deluxe Beauty Kit'' when she comes to visit Ruby. They use Max as their first customer. Soon Max sports bright red fingernails, a bouffant blond wig, and lots of makeup. While Louise and Ruby move on to their next pretend customers, Max removes the fake nails, makeup and wig. Then, he explores the Deluxe Beauty Kit and selects some bottles of hair color. Soon Max's fur is Lizard Green with Sunflower Yellow and Ocean Blue feet. Max is ready now for the next customer. (26 pages)

Where it's reviewed:
Booklist, August 2002, page 1977
Bulletin of the Center for Children's Books, November 2002, page 130

Publishers Weekly, October 7, 2002, page 75
School Library Journal, October 2002, page 134

Other books by the same author:
Bunny Mail, 2004
Max's Christmas Stocking, 2003
Only You, 2003
Max Cleans Up, 2002

Other books you might like:
Barbara E. Barber, *Saturday at the New You*, 1994
    Saturday is the day Shauna helps her mother work at The New You Beauty Parlor.
Denys Cazet, *Minnie and Moo and the Attack of the Easter Bunnies*, 2004
    Minnie & Moo convince other farm animals to join them in dressing up as Easter bunnies for the farmer's Easter egg hunt.
Barbara Park, *Junie B. Jones Is a Beauty Shop Guy*, 1998
    When Junie B. sets her mind on being a hair stylist she hones her scissors skills on her dog, her bunny slippers and her own hair.

1428

ROSEMARY WELLS, Author/Illustrator
JODY WHEELER, Illustrator

Timothy's Tales from Hilltop School
(New York: Viking, 2002)

Subject(s): Schools; Animals; Teacher-Student Relationships
Age range(s): Grades K-3
Major character(s): Charles, Student, Mouse; Nora, Student, Mouse; Yoko, Friend, Cat
Time period(s): Indeterminate
Locale(s): Fictional Country

Summary: The students and teachers of Hilltop School, introduced in *Timothy Goes to School*, return in six short stories. Whether the students are planning an entry for the Science Fair or a costume for the celebration of Bug Week they meet with typical unanticipated challenges and receive support from their teachers and parents as they resolve problems. Nora faces a dilemma about Yoko's birthday gift and shy Charles figures out how to screech like an eagle, in fact ten eagles, despite his quiet voice. (64 pages)

Where it's reviewed:
Book World, August 11, 2002, page 11
Bulletin of the Center for Children's Books, October 2002, page 85
Horn Book, January 2003, page 64
Kirkus Reviews, June 15, 2002, page 890
School Library Journal, October 2002, page 134

Awards the book has won:
Bulletin of the Center for Children's Books Blue Ribbons, 2002
Center for Children's Books Best Books, 2002

Other books by the same author:
Read Me a Story, 2002
The Secret Birthday, 2002
Yoko's Paper Cranes, 2001

Emily's First 100 Days of School, 2000 (Bulletin of the Center for Children's Books Blue Ribbon)
Timothy Goes to School, 1992

Other books you might like:

Tomie De Paola, *Meet the Barkers: Morgan and Moffat Go to School*, 2001
Twins Morgie and Moffie take different approaches to the beginning of the school year but both conclude that school is terrific!

Diane DeGroat, *We Gather Together . . . Now Please Get Lost!*, 2001
Gilbert's stuck with a partner he doesn't like for a school field trip, but he learns to be grateful for Philip's ability to follow directions.

Amy Schwartz, *The Boys Team*, 2001
Jacob, Oscar and Eddie revel in their status as kindergartners, take after-school karate classes and trick-or-treat, all together of course.

1429

ROSEMARY WELLS
BRIAN SELZNICK, Illustrator

Wingwalker

(New York: Hyperion Books for Children, 2002)

Subject(s): Fairs; Fear; Depression (Economic)
Age range(s): Grades 3-6
Major character(s): Reuben, 2nd Grader, Son; Father, Father, Teacher (of dance); Dixie Belle, Pilot
Time period(s): 1930s (1933-1934)
Locale(s): Ambler, Oklahoma; St. Paul, Minnesota

Summary: Reuben's contented life in Ambler ends with the dust storms and Depression that cause his parents to lose their jobs. Seeking work, Father answers Dixie Belle's ad for a "wingwalker." As a former dancing teacher, Father has the skills to perform on the wing of a biplane high above the ground and the desire to soar above the earth. Reuben, who plans to never go higher than the attic window, fears for his father and the family's future if an accident should happen as Father performs. Instead, something happens inside Reuben as he comes to know the other carnival workers for the people they are beneath the persona of their acts. Gradually his courage grows until he's able to join his father on Dixie Belle's wing. (64 pages)

Where it's reviewed:

Booklist, March 15, 2002, page 1257
Bulletin of the Center for Children's Books, May 2002, page 345
Horn Book, July 2002, page 474
Publishers Weekly, March 25, 2002, page 65
School Library Journal, May 2002, page 162

Other books by the same author:

The House in the Mail, 2002 (Tom Wells, co-author)
Streets of Gold, 1999
Mary on Horseback: Three Mountain Stories, 1998 (Riverbank Review Children's Book of Distinction)

Other books you might like:

Patricia MacLachlan, *Skylark*, 1994
Drought causes crop failure and forces many families to leave their prairie homes.

Marissa Moss, *Rose's Journal: The Story of a Girl in the Great Depression*, 2001
In her diary, Rose recounts the challenges of living through three years of drought and dust storms and the changes in her family as a result.

Pam Munoz Ryan, *Amelia and Eleanor Go for a Ride*, 1999
In 1933, Amelia Earhart takes Eleanor Roosevelt for her first night flight to see the lights of the nation's capital.

1430

VALERIE WILSON WESLEY
MARYN ROOS, Illustrator

How to Lose Your Class Pet

(New York: Jump at the Sun/Hyperion Books for Children, 2003)

Series: Willimena Rules!. Rule Book 1
Subject(s): Schools; Pets; Teacher-Student Relationships
Age range(s): Grades 2-4
Major character(s): Willimena "Willie" Thomas, 3rd Grader; Mrs. Sweetly, Teacher
Time period(s): 2000s (2003)
Locale(s): United States

Summary: On the first day of third grade, Willimena learns that the teacher she thought she was going to have is out on maternity leave and that she will be in Mrs. Sweetly's class instead. Known as the meanest teacher at Harriet Tubman Elementary, Mrs. Sweetly is one teacher Willie would like to avoid. Willie tries to get on her teacher's good side by volunteering to take home the class's pet guinea pig for the weekend. When the guinea pig runs away, Willie is worried what Mrs. Sweetly and the other kids in her class will think, but Mrs. Sweetly is kind and reassuring, proving that she's not so mean after all. (96 pages)

Where it's reviewed:

Publishers Weekly, December 1, 2003, page 58
School Library Journal, January 2004, page 107

Other books by the same author:

How to Fish for Trouble, 2004 (Willimena Rules! Rule Book 2)
How to Lose Your Cookie Money, 2004 (Willimena Rules! Rule Book 3)

Other books you might like:

Colleen O'Shaughnessy McKenna, *Good Grief . . . Third Grade*, 1993
As Marsha starts third grade, she vows to stay out of trouble, but when she's paired with the class bully for a school project, the trouble starts.

Marisa Montes, *A Crazy, Mixed-Up Spanglish Day*, 2003
Third-grader Gabi has to deal with a class bully and other problems in the first book in the "Get Ready for Gabi" series.

Laurie Myers, *Earthquake in Third Grade*, 1993
When John's favorite teacher announces that he's leaving, John and his friends try to convince him to stay.

1431

CARRIE WESTON
CHARLOTTE MIDDLETON, Illustrator

Lucky Socks

(New York: Phyllis Fogelman Books, 2002)

Subject(s): Clothes; Superstition; Lost and Found
Age range(s): Grades K-2
Major character(s): Kevin, Student—Elementary School
Time period(s): 2000s (2001)

Summary: On the days that Kevin wears red socks, green socks, blue socks or even striped socks he experiences one calamity after another. However, on the days that he wears his yellow socks everything seems to go his way. So convinced is Kevin in the power of his yellow socks that he plans to wear them on the school's field day to assure success. The problem is, he can't find them and has to settle for old yellow underpants. The underpants don't have the same positive effect as the socks but still Kevin receives a medal for trying very hard. That experience convinces Kevin that the color of his socks doesn't matter, but he's quite particular about his underwear. This book, the author's first, was originally published in Great Britain in 2001. (32 pages)

Where it's reviewed:
Booklist, February 15, 2002, page 1023
Horn Book Guide, Fall 2002, page 348
Kirkus Reviews, January 1, 2002, page 53
Publishers Weekly, November 26, 2001, page 61
School Library Journal, March 2002, page 206

Awards the book has won:
IRA Children's Choices, 2003

Other books you might like:
Catherine Bancroft, *Felix's Hat*, 1993
    Sensitive parents and supportive siblings help Felix overcome the loss of his favorite orange hat. Hannah Coale Gruenberg, co-author.
Marc Brown, *D.W.'s Lost Blankie*, 1998
    D.W.'s relieved to learn that her blankie is not lost, but in the laundry. She's not sure, however, that a clean blankie has the same effect.
Kevin Henkes, *Owen*, 1993
    Owen's blanket is so special to him that his mother makes part of it into a handkerchief that he can carry to school each day.

1432

TAMSON WESTON
STEPHEN GAMMELL, Illustrator

Hey, Pancakes!

(San Diego: Silver Whistle/Harcourt, Inc., 2003)

Subject(s): Food; Family Life; Stories in Rhyme
Age range(s): Preschool-Grade 1
Major character(s): Unnamed Character, Child, Brother; Unnamed Character, Child, Brother (older); Unnamed Character, Sister, Cook
Time period(s): 2000s (2003)

Locale(s): United States

Summary: A ringing alarm clock awakens two boys who stumble into the kitchen where their sister is already busy creating pancakes. The younger brother adds blueberries to the batter and the older one carries plates and a pitcher of juice to the table. Teetering on a chair the girl begins cooking, flipping the pancakes through the air with panache. After cooking stacks and stacks of pancakes, the girl joins her brothers to eat. Together the three wash dishes and clean up the kitchen. The older brother carries a stack of leftover pancakes to the basement to hide for a snack later and then they all go out to play. A recipe for "Grandma's Pancakes" is included to end the published poet's first picture book. (32 pages)

Where it's reviewed:
Booklist, August 2003, page 1981
Bulletin of the Center for Children's Books, October 2003, page 80
Publishers Weekly, August 18, 2003, page 77
School Library Journal, September 2003, page 193

Awards the book has won:
IRA Children's Choices, 2004

Other books you might like:
Eric Carle, *Pancakes, Pancakes!*, 1970
    In order to make pancakes for breakfast Jack begins by cutting the wheat and grinding it into flour.
M.C. Helldorfer, *Jack, Skinny Bones and the Golden Pancakes*, 1996
    In this tall tale Jack uses all he's learned from wicked Granny Trick, including how to make pancakes, to free himself and Skinny Bones.
Laura Joffe Numeroff, *If You Give a Pig a Pancake*, 1998
    If an uninvited pig shows up at breakfast to share your pancakes, be prepared for a busy day.
H.A. Rey, *Curious George Makes Pancakes*, 1998
    At a fundraiser for the Children's Hospital, Curious George tries to help by making pancakes.

1433

LISA WHEELER
KURT CYRUS, Illustrator

Avalanche Annie: A Not-So-Tall Tale

(San Diego: Harcourt, Inc., 2003)

Subject(s): Tall Tales; Stories in Rhyme; Rescue Work
Age range(s): Grades K-2
Major character(s): Annie Halfpint, Rescuer, Heroine
Time period(s): Indeterminate Past
Locale(s): Yoohoo Valley

Summary: Annie Halfpint is leading the Yoohoo Valley snowshoe race, when her yodeling causes an avalanche. After a bit of a struggle, Annie manages to lasso the avalanche and ride it down the mountain. It stops just short of town and that's how Twin Antler Lake is formed. (32 pages)

Where it's reviewed:
Booklist, October 15, 2003, page 420
School Library Journal, December 2003, page 130

Other books by the same author:
Bubble Gum, Bubble Gum, 2004
One Dark Night, 2003
Sixteen Cows, 2002

Other books you might like:
Marguerite W. Davol, *The Loudest, Fastest, Best Drummer in Kansas*, 2000
    Maggie loves to drum, but her relentless rhythm drives her entire town crazy until she uses her drumming to save the town from killer wasps.
Sharon Arms Doucet, *Alligator Sue*, 2003
    After Sue blows off her family's bayou houseboat as a baby an alligator mom finds and raises her along with her own offspring.
Anne Isaacs, *Swamp Angel*, 1994
    A original tall tale and Caldecott Honor Book describes the achievements of Angelica and how she earns her nickname.
Steven Kellogg, *Sally Ann Thunder Ann Whirlwind Crockett*, 1995
    Sally Ann, future wife of Davy Crockett, leads an adventuresome, tall-tale-worthy life.

1434

LISA WHEELER
PONDER GOEMBEL, Illustrator

Old Cricket

(New York: Richard Jackson Book/Atheneum Books for Young Readers, 2003)

Subject(s): Animals/Insects; Animals/Birds; Behavior
Age range(s): Grades K-2
Major character(s): Old Cricket, Cricket, Spouse; Doc Hopper, Doctor, Insect (grasshopper); Old Crow, Crow
Time period(s): Indeterminate
Locale(s): Fictional Country

Summary: To avoid household chores, Old Cricket complains of a creak in his knee and hobbles off to see Doc Hopper. On the way he meets first a katydid and then ants that are busy gathering food for the coming winter. At each encounter he's invited to help and each time he adds another ailment to his list of excuses. Kindly, everyone from his wife to the friends he meets gives him one item of food for his lunch bundle. Before completing his tiring journey to the doctor's office, Old Cricket falls asleep and is awakened by the cawing of Old Crow, ready to eat him for lunch. As he runs from Old Crow, Old Cricket tosses out the food items he's been given. The final one sticks in Old Crow's throat and Old Cricket is able to get away. As he runs, he also trips and falls so that, by the time he reaches Doc Hopper, he really does have the very ailments he's been faking all along. (32 pages)

Where it's reviewed:
Booklist, May 15, 2003, page 1674
Horn Book Guide, Fall 2003, page 346
Publishers Weekly, April 7, 2003, page 65
School Library Journal, May 2003, page 132

Awards the book has won:
School Library Journal Best Books, 2003

Other books by the same author:
Farmer Dale's Red Pickup Truck, 2004
Who's Afraid of Granny Wolf, 2004
One Dark Night, 2003
Sailor Moo: Cow at Sea, 2002

Other books you might like:
Kay Chorao, *Pig and Crow*, 2000
    Crow's slightly deceptive trades of "magic" items for Pig's culinary treats actually prove to magically improve Pig's lonely life.
Virginia Hamilton, *A Ring of Tricksters: Animal Tales from America, the West Indies, and Africa*, 1997
    Eleven tales united by the trickster theme include the familiar Anansi and the less well-known Cunnie Rabbit.
Amy Lowry Poole, *The Ant and the Grasshopper*, 2000
    In this retelling of Aesop's fable a colony of industrious ants and a lazy grasshopper approach winter with different ideas of preparation.

1435

LISA WHEELER
KURT CYRUS, Illustrator

Sixteen Cows

(San Diego: Harcourt, Inc., 2002)

Subject(s): Animals/Cows; Ranch Life; Romance
Age range(s): Grades K-2
Major character(s): Gene, Cowboy, Rancher; Sue, Cowboy, Rancher
Time period(s): 20th century
Locale(s): United States

Summary: Cowboy Gene and Cowgirl Sue live on adjoining ranches. They have eight cows each that they adore. When a tornado tears down the fence between the two farms, their cows get all mixed up. They try to separate the herds, but when that doesn't work, they come up with a solution to get married and combine ranches. (32 pages)

Where it's reviewed:
Booklist, June 2002, page 1744
Horn Book Guide, Fall 2002, page 316
Los Angeles Times Book Review, May 12, 2002, page 7
Publishers Weekly, March 25, 2002, page 63
School Library Journal, April 2002, page 128

Other books by the same author:
Porcupining: A Prickly Love Story, 2003
Sailor Moo: Cow at Sea, 2002
Wool Gathering: A Sheep Family Reunion, 2001

Other books you might like:
Stephen Gulbis, *Cowgirl Rosie and Her Five Baby Bison*, 2001
    When Rosie's five baby bison wander off in town, she has to round them up.
Helen Ketteman, *Bubba the Cowboy Prince: A Fractured Texas Tale*, 1997
    In this Cinderella story, Bubba wins the heart of Miz Lurleen, despite the interference of his evil stepfather and two stepbrothers.

Caroline Stutson, *Cowpokes*, 1999
Ten cowboys are busy from dusk until dawn.

1436

GLORIA WHELAN

The Impossible Journey

(New York: HarperCollins, 2003)

Subject(s): Voyages and Travels; Brothers and Sisters; Political Prisoners
Age range(s): Grades 5-8
Major character(s): Marya Mikhailovna Gnedich, 13-Year-Old; Georgi Gnedich, Brother (of Marya); Mikhail Sergeyevich "Misha" Gnedich, Father (of Marya and Georgi), Prisoner; Katya Gnedich, Mother (of Marya and Georgi)
Time period(s): 1930s
Locale(s): Dudinka, Russia (Siberia); Leningrad, Russia

Summary: During the time of Stalin's rule, aristocrats are viewed with great suspicion so when an important Communist leader in Leningrad is assassinated, Misha and Katya are arrested with Misha sent to prison and Katya exiled to Siberia. Marya and Georgi are left with neighbors who don't really want to care for them, but are happy to receive the Gnedich's furniture from their abandoned apartment. Fearing they'll be sent to an orphanage, Marya sells her paintings and collects enough money for railroad tickets to Siberia where, once they reach the Yenisey River, the youngsters face a 1,000-mile-walk to reach Dudinka where their mother has been sent. Armed with their train tickets, blankets, a little food and lots of courage, the two children set out, careful to avoid anyone who tries to turn them over to the Communist party, and leeringly accepting aid from those who try to help them. As their journey nears completion, the nomadic Samoyed offer the last generous bit of help as the children ride their reindeer to Dudinka and reunion with their mother in this follow up volume to *Angel on the Square*. (249 pages)

Where it's reviewed:
Booklist, December 15, 2002, page 761
Horn Book, March 2003, page 218
Publishers Weekly, December 16, 2002, page 68
Riverbank Review, Spring 2003, page 42
School Library Journal, January 2003, page 146

Awards the book has won:
Notable Social Studies Trade Books for Young People, 2004

Other books by the same author:
Burying the Sun, 2004
Chu Ju's House, 2004
The Wanigan: A Life on the River, 2002
Angel on the Square, 2001

Other books you might like:
Felice Holman, *The Wild Children*, 1983
    After the Bolshevik Revolution, Eric and other homeless children beg and rob to survive.
Kathryn Lasky, *The Night Journey*, 1981
    Rachel recounts the story of her great-grandmother's family's escape from the cruelty of Tsarist Russia.

Cynthia Voigt, *Homecoming*, 1981
    After being abandoned by their mother, Dicey and her younger brothers and sister make the long journey on foot to their eccentric grandmother's home.

1437

ELLEN EMERSON WHITE

Where Have All the Flowers Gone?: The Diary of Molly Mackenzie Flaherty

(New York: Scholastic, 2002)

Series: Dear America
Subject(s): Vietnam War; Diaries; Brothers and Sisters
Age range(s): Grades 7-10
Major character(s): Molly MacKenzie Flaherty, 15-Year-Old; Patrick Seamus Flaherty, Military Personnel, Brother (of Molly)
Time period(s): 1960s (1967-1968)
Locale(s): Boston, Massachusetts; Vietnam, South

Summary: With her brother serving in Vietnam in an area that receives heavy artillery fire, Molly is understandably concerned about his fate, just as she worries about whether or not America should even be in this war. Though many people demonstrate against the war, none of them seems to know a great deal about it, so Molly tries to learn as much as she can. Her eyes really open when, against her parent's wishes, she volunteers at the VA hospital and sees firsthand the wounds these young military men receive, all of which is set against the backdrop of events from the 1960s era. This is a companion volume to *The Journal of Patrick Seamus Flaherty, United States Marine Corps*. (188 pages)

Where it's reviewed:
Booklist, August 2002, page 1947
Kirkus Reviews, June 1, 2002, page 813
Kliatt, May 2002, page 15
School Library Journal, July 2002, page 128
Voice of Youth Advocates, October 2002, page 287

Other books by the same author:
The Journal of Patrick Seamus Flaherty, United States Marine Corps., 2002 (My Name Is America)
Kaiulani: The People's Princess, 2001 (Royal Diaries)
Voyage on the Great Titanic: The Diary of Margaret Ann Brady, 1998 (Dear America)
The Road Home, 1995
Long Live the Queen, 1989

Other books you might like:
Nancy Antle, *Lost in the War*, 1998
    The Vietnam War costs Lisa dearly, from her father's death to her mother's continuing nightmares, and she doesn't relish having to study it in school.
Kelly Easton, *The Life History of a Star*, 2001
    Kristin's whole family is affected when her former All-American brother David returns from Vietnam physically and mentally challenged.
Bobbie Ann Mason, *In Country*, 1985
    Sam loses her father in the Vietnam War and now sees her uncle suffer from the effects of Agent Orange, all from a war Sam doesn't understand.

1438

RUTH WHITE

Tadpole

(New York: Farrar Straus Giroux, 2003)

Subject(s): Orphans; Cousins; Child Abuse
Age range(s): Grades 4-8
Major character(s): Carolina "Carol" Collins, Narrator, 10-Year-Old; Serilda Collins, Mother; Winston Churchill "Tadpole" Birch, 13-Year-Old, Singer; Kentucky Collins, 14-Year-Old; Virginia Collins, 12-Year-Old; Georgia Collins, 11-Year-Old
Time period(s): 1950s (1955)
Locale(s): Polly's Fork, Kentucky

Summary: With three older sisters, Kentucky who's popular, Virginia who's pretty and Georgia who's smart, Carol often feels like the overlooked runt, so it's she who's probably the happiest when their cousin Tadpole shows up on their porch. Tad makes them all feel better, with his singing and guitar playing and his overall nice ways. As they soon discover, however, he's run away from his aunt and uncle who have beaten him, taken away his guitar and made him work long hours on their farm. Serilda would love to have custody of Tad, but as a single parent with four girls of her own, she barely has enough money to feed them. The threat from Tad's uncle is overwhelming and Serilda eventually goes to court to obtain custody of Tad. When that fails, Tad runs away and ends up in Nashville where he immediately finds a job. When he sends his guitar to Carol, he reminds her of the talent she has and urges her to continue playing and singing in another heart-warming story set in Appalachia. (198 pages)

Where it's reviewed:
Booklist, May 1, 2003, page 1598
Horn Book, May 2003, page 358
Publishers Weekly, December 23, 2002, page 71
Riverbank Review, Spring 2003, page 44
School Library Journal, March 2003, page 242

Awards the book has won:
School Library Journal Best Books, 2003

Other books by the same author:
Buttermilk Hill, 2004
The Search for Belle Prater, 2004
Memories of Summer, 2000
Belle Prater's Boy, 1996

Other books you might like:
Janni Howker, *Isaac Campion*, 1986
    At the turn of the century, Isaac's older brother dies and life on his father's horse farm becomes an ordeal.
Katherine Paterson, *Come Sing, Jimmy Jo*, 1985
    Though Jimmy Jo becomes a famous singer with his blues family, he'd rather be doing something else.
P.L. Whitney, *This Is Graceanne's Book*, 1999
    Weary of her mother's beatings, Graceanne and her handicapped friend Charlie toss her diary in the Mississippi River and leave home.

1439

IAN WHYBROW
OLIVIA VILLET, Illustrator

Sissy Buttons Takes Charge!

(New York: The Chicken House/Scholastic, Inc., 2002)

Subject(s): Cleanliness; Toys; Self-Reliance
Age range(s): Preschool-Grade 1
Major character(s): Sissy Buttons, Child, Daughter; Unnamed Character, Mother
Time period(s): 2000s (2002)
Locale(s): United Kingdom

Summary: Sissy Buttons is full of energy until it's time to clean up her toys, then, she's always too tired. Her mother assures her that there is nothing she can't do if she just tries, but the message doesn't hit home until Sissy's imagination takes her on a picnic with her teddy bears. The bears create a mess and make Sissy do all the work until she teaches them to "try and try." (32 pages)

Where it's reviewed:
Booklist, December 1, 2002, page 680
School Library Journal, December 2002, page 112

Other books by the same author:
Harry and the Bucketful of Dinosaurs, 2003
Sammy and the Robots, 2001
Jump In!, 1999

Other books you might like:
Jerry Garcia, *The Teddy Bears' Picnic*, 1992
    An illustrated retelling of the popular children's song shows a little boy spying on the teddy bears' picnic.
Amy Hest, *You Can Do It, Sam*, 2003
    Sam is scared to help his mother deliver cakes to their neighbors, but his mother reassures him that he can do it.
Daniel Kamish, *Diggy Dan: A Room-Cleaning Adventure*, 2001
    Dan doesn't want to clean his room, but with a little imagination, he gets the job done.

1440

IAN WHYBROW
TIPHANIE BEEKE, Illustrator

Wish, Change, Friend

(New York: Margaret K. McElderry Books, 2002)

Subject(s): Animals/Pigs; Books and Reading; Wishes
Age range(s): Grades K-2
Major character(s): Little Pig, Pig; Unnamed Character, Friend; Penguin, Penguin
Time period(s): Indeterminate
Locale(s): Fictional Country

Summary: Little Pig leads a contented, solitary life reading books in his home under an oak tree until the day he reads three words: wish, change and friend. Endeavoring to understand the meaning of the words Little Pig formulates the sentence, "I wish for a change and a friend." As snow begins to fall Little Pig realizes a wish has been granted because the snow is a pleasant change. Then he creates a snow friend that walks with him to a small igloo where Little Pig finds a penguin reading a book. Penguin asks for help reading the words ''pig'' and ''together'' and suddenly Little Pig has found fulfilled wishes, changes, friends and, best of all, togetherness. (32 pages)

Where it's reviewed:
Booklist, February 15, 2002, page 1023
Bulletin of the Center for Children's Books, February 2002, page 224
Horn Book Guide, Fall 2002, page 316
Publishers Weekly, November 26, 2001, page 61
School Library Journal, January 2002, page 112

Other books by the same author:
Sammy and the Robots, 2001
Sammy and the Dinosaurs, 1999 (Smithsonian's Notable Books for Children)
A Baby for Grace, 1998

Other books you might like:
Deborah Bruss, *Book! Book! Book!*, 2001
  Even the bored farm animals enjoy reading a story now and then.
P.K. Hallinan, *Just Open a Book*, 1995
  A rhyming story tells how simple it is to have an adventure: open a book.
Mick Inkpen, *Kipper's Snowy Day*, 1996
  With his friend Tiger, Kipper plays all day in the snow.
Jessica Spanyol, *Carlo Likes Reading*, 2001
  Giraffe Carlo sees opportunities for reading all around him.

`1441`

CHERRY WHYTOCK, Author/Illustrator

My Cup Runneth Over: The Life of Angelica Cookson Potts

(2003)

Subject(s): Weight Control; Interpersonal Relations; School Life
Age range(s): Grades 7-10
Major character(s): Angelica Cookson ''Angel'' Potts, 14-Year-Old; Adam, Student—Middle School; Flossie, Housekeeper
Time period(s): 2000s
Locale(s): England

Summary: Though her friends tell her otherwise, Angel knows she's plump and that she can never manage to get her large breasts under control. But that doesn't stop her love of food nor the housekeeper's efforts to prepare her favorites. Spotting Adam, a hunk at her school who drives a motorcycle, Angel decides to go on the cabbage diet, hoping to lose her extra weight so that he'll ask her to the Valentine disco. The cabbage diet proves a little windy, so Angel discards it and tries kickboxing instead, but at the party, Adam asks one of her good friends to dance. The chance to show herself off isn't over yet as Angel is asked to model a very expensive dress for her school's Fashion Fair. A trip to the lingerie department and a good supporting undergarment are just what Angel needs to model the beautiful dress and let her family and

friends see how gorgeous she is. Recipes included. (163 pages)

Where it's reviewed:
Booklist, November 15, 2003, page 607
Bulletin of the Center for Children's Books, November 2003, page 129
Kliatt, September 2003, page 14
Library Media Connection, March 2004, page 65
Publishers Weekly, September 1, 2003, page 90

Other books by the same author:
My Scrumptious Scottish Dumplings: The Life of Angelica Cookson Potts, 2004

Other books you might like:
Sarah Dessen, *Keeping the Moon*, 1999
  Though Colie loses 45 pounds, she hasn't shed her insecurity, especially when a classmate tries to say she has an ''easy'' reputation.
Louise Rennison, *Angus, Thongs and Full-Frontal Snogging: Confessions of Georgia Nicolson*, 2000
  Georgia's witty observations pepper her diary as she begins the process of growing up.
Tucker Shaw, *Flavor of the Week*, 2003
  In this triangular romance, Cyril is an overweight, talented cook who loves Rose, but Rose loves Cyril's best friend Nick who pretends to cook.

`1442`

CHRISTINE WIDMAN
PIERR MORGAN, Illustrator

Cornfield Hide-and-Seek

(New York: Melanie Kroupa/Farrar Straus Giroux, 2003)

Subject(s): Farm Life; Family; Summer
Age range(s): Grades K-2
Major character(s): Mamaw, Mother
Time period(s): 21st century
Locale(s): United States

Summary: One by one, Mamaw's three children sneak off into the cornfield on a hot summer day to avoid the heat. Mamaw's father soon joins them and, with her entire family shirking their chores in hopes of getting some relief from the baking sun, Mamaw gives up on getting them to come out and decides to join them in the field where it's nice and cool indeed. (40 pages)

Where it's reviewed:
Booklist, May 1, 2003, page 1606
Publishers Weekly, March 20, 2003, page 70
School Library Journal, July 2003, page 109

Other books by the same author:
The Hummingbird Garden, 1993
The Willow Umbrella, 1993
The Lemon Drop Jar, 1992

Other books you might like:
Cari Best, *When Catherine the Great and I Were Eight!*, 2003
  On a sizzling summer day, Sara and her neighbors decide to head to the beach.

Karen Hesse, *Come On, Rain!*, 1999

During a sweltering summer, inner city residents hope for rain to bring cooler temperatures.

Helen Ketteman, *Heat Wave*, 2001

When a heat wave descends on a Kansas farm, a young girl tries to find a way to cool things down a bit.

1443

DOUG WILHELM

The Revealers

(New York: Farrar Straus Giroux, 2003)

Subject(s): Bullies; Internet; Friendship
Age range(s): Grades 5-7
Major character(s): Russell Trainor, 7th Grader; Elliot Gekewicz, 7th Grader; Catalina Aarons, 7th Grader; Richie Tucker, 8th Grader, Bully
Time period(s): 2000s
Locale(s): United States

Summary: As Russell begins seventh grade, he slowly realizes that he doesn't really fit in. As he looks around, it seems that all his previous friends know just what to do in middle school, while he always says or does the wrong thing. For the first time in his life, he doesn't have anyone to sit with or talk to, until Richie picks him out as a victim for his bullying. Since he doesn't know what to do about Richie, either, Russell talks to the school nerd Elliott to find out any special techniques he uses. This leads to a conversation with Catalina, a new student who's being victimized by the popular girl clique. The three decide to fight back and use their school's internal e-mail for Catalina to put out a message about her background and why she moved from the Philippines to the United States. Suddenly other kids pipe in with stories of bullying treatment they've received until Russell, Elliott and Catalina create *The Revealer*, a forum for all students to relate their stories about mistreatment. Slowly the amount of pestering drops, though enough remains for the three seventh graders to collect data for an amazing science fair project that objectively analyzes the degree of harassment in their school. (207 pages)

Where it's reviewed:
Booklist, November 1, 2003, page 497
Bulletin of the Center for Children's Books, October 2003, page 81
Publishers Weekly, November 3, 2003, page 75
School Library Journal, November 2003, page 150
Voice of Youth Advocates, February 2004, page 499

Other books by the same author:
Raising the Shades, 2001

Other books you might like:
James Howe, *The Misfits*, 2001
Tired of being called names, four friends decide to run for office at their school; though they don't win, they call attention to the problem.
Amy Goldman Koss, *The Girls*, 2000
Ringleader Candace manages to whittle her clique from five to four when she decides Maya is out; now the other girls wonder who's next.

Elizabeth Laird, *Secret Friends*, 1999
Wanting to be part of the popular clique, Lucy teases Rafaella about her ears, but doesn't reveal that she and Rafaella are friends outside of school.

1444

NANCY WILLARD
JANE DYER, Illustrator

Cinderella's Dress

(New York: Blue Sky Press/Scholastic, Inc., 2003)

Subject(s): Fairy Tales; Clothes; Stories in Rhyme
Age range(s): Grades K-3
Major character(s): Cinderella, Servant, Stepdaughter; Unnamed Character, Bird (magpie), Collector; Unnamed Character, Bird (magpie), Collector
Time period(s): Indeterminate Past
Locale(s): Fictional Country

Summary: Two magpies nest in a tree just outside Cinderella's home, observing the cruel treatment of the girl with the beautiful singing voice. They decide to adopt Cinderella and when an invitation comes for a ball at the palace the magpies immediately begin making a dress out of the trinkets and paper they've collected. Cinderella is pleased with the beauty of a garment and quickly dons it to join her stepsisters. Alas, the stepsisters tear the dress as they rip off items they recognize having lost and Cinderella is left to forlornly rue the day she lost a ring given her by her deceased mother. Hearing Cinderella's lament the magpie realizes that the ring she prizes and wears on her tail is in fact Cinderella's and she lets it fall to floor to be found. It is this magic ring that brings the fairy godmother to create the final magic that allows Cinderella to go to the ball and meet the prince. (32 pages)

Where it's reviewed:
Booklist, September 15, 2003, page 249
Bulletin of the Center for Children's Books, December 2003, page 168
Horn Book, January 2004, page 74
Publishers Weekly, November 17, 2003, page 64
School Library Journal, November 2003, page 118

Other books by the same author:
Sweep Dreams, 2004
The Mouse, the Cat and Grandmother's Hat, 2003
Shadow Story, 1999
The Tale I Told Sasha, 1999

Other books you might like:
Shirley Climo, *The Persian Cinderella*, 1999
Settareh, the Persian Cinderella, finds a fairy in a cracked jug she buys in the market and thus is able to get to the palace and meet the prince.
Oki S. Han, *Kongi and Potgi: A Cinderella Story from Korea*, 1996
Kongi's ability to treat others kindly despite her mistreatment by her stepmother and stepsister is eventually rewarded.
Charles Perrault, *Cinderella*, 1954
In one of many retellings of a classic tale of love and inner

beauty Cinderella survives years of torment to win a prince's hand in marriage.

1445

MO WILLEMS, Author/Illustrator

Don't Let the Pigeon Drive the Bus!
(New York: Hyperion Books for Children, 2003)

Subject(s): Transportation; Animals/Birds; Community Helpers
Age range(s): Grades K-3
Major character(s): Unnamed Character, Pigeon; Unnamed Character, Driver (bus)
Time period(s): Indeterminate
Locale(s): Fictional Country

Summary: As a bus driver leaves on a brief break he requests that no one allow the pigeon to drive the bus. The pigeon has other ideas and begins wheedling for permission. It promises to be careful, it tries negotiating by agreeing only to steer, it claims that its cousin drives a bus as if that guarantees a pigeon's ability to undertake the task. When none of its efforts work, the pigeon loses all control and screams, ''LET ME DRIVE THE BUS!'' The bus driver returns before the discouraged pigeon succeeds with its goal, but the pigeon perks up when an 18-wheeler drives past and a new dream becomes to form in its mind as the author's first book concludes. (38 pages)

Where it's reviewed:
Booklist, September 1, 2003, page 123
Bulletin of the Center for Children's Books, May 2003, page 378
Horn Book, July 2003, page 449
School Library Journal, May 2003, page 132

Awards the book has won:
Caldecott Honor Book, 2004
Bulletin of the Center for Children's Books Blue Ribbons, 2003

Other books you might like:
Jez Alborough, *Duck in the Truck*, 2000
   Duck merrily drives a bright red truck until, yuck, it becomes stuck in muck.
Doreen Cronin, *Click, Clack, Moo: Cows That Type*, 2000
   Seeing the effectiveness of the cows and hens' typed demands of the farmer, the ducks learn to type also in a Caldecott Honor Book.
James Stevenson, *Don't Make Me Laugh*, 1999
   Mr. Frimdimpny has strict rules for the proper way to proceed through the book he narrates; violators must return to the book's beginning.

1446

LINDA WILLIAMS
MEGAN LLOYD, Illustrator

Horse in the Pigpen
(New York: HarperCollins Publishers, 2002)

Subject(s): Farm Life; Mothers and Daughters; Stories in Rhyme
Age range(s): Grades K-2
Major character(s): Ma, Mother, Farmer; Unnamed Character, Child, Daughter
Time period(s): 2000s
Locale(s): United States

Summary: A young girl tells her busy mother that the horse is in the pigpen, but Ma has no time to tend to the horse and sends the girl to tell the pigs. Well, the pigs are in the chicken coop and the hens are in the doghouse but Ma's on the phone. Not until the cow ends up in the girl's bed does Ma have time to set the farm to rights. With her broom she shoos the cow out the door and back to the barn causing a domino effect as ducks, the cat, the rabbit, the dog, the hens, the pigs and the horse scurry back to their respective, proper places. (32 pages)

Where it's reviewed:
Booklist, July 2002, page 1861
Bulletin of the Center for Children's Books, May 2002, page 346
Horn Book Guide, Fall 2002, page 317
Publishers Weekly, March 18, 2002, page 101
School Library Journal, June 2002, page 116

Other books by the same author:
The Little Old Lady Who Was Not Afraid of Anything, 1986

Other books you might like:
Amy Ehrlich, *Parents in the Pigpen, Pigs in the Tub*, 1993
   When Ma allows Bossy the cow to move into the house, she doesn't realize that she's starting a trend.
Paul Brett Johnson, *The Pig Who Ran a Red Light*, 1999
   George, jealous of Gertrude the farm's flying cow, takes the pick-up and drives to town for a little adventure.
Lynn Plourde, *Pigs in the Mud in the Middle of the Rud*, 1997
   Grandma needs to get down the road, but first the pigs and other animals have to move out of the muddy way.

1447

SUE WILLIAMS
KERRY ARGENT, Illustrator

Dinnertime!
(San Diego: Harcourt, Inc., 2002)

Subject(s): Animals; Suspense; Stories in Rhyme
Age range(s): Preschool-Grade 1
Major character(s): Unnamed Character, Fox
Time period(s): Indeterminate
Locale(s): Fictional Country

Summary: A hungry fox pounces on six rabbits as six sheep, six ducks and six mice sound the alarm. The rabbits scatter each time the other animals warn of the fox's presence but in each succeeding scene there is one less rabbit. The number of animals giving warning also diminishes by one each time the fox pounces as a call of ''Dinnertime!'' rings in the air. As the last rabbit dives down the burrow hole he's reunited with his siblings who race to the dinner table and a scolding from their mother because they did not come the first time she called them to dinner. The story was first published in Australia in 2001. (32 pages)

Where it's reviewed:
Booklist, April 1, 2002, page 1323
Bulletin of the Center for Children's Books, April 2002, page 299
Horn Book Guide, Fall 2002, page 317
Publishers Weekly, March 11, 2002, page 70
School Library Journal, May 2002, page 131

Awards the book has won:
Center for Children's Books Best Books, 2002

Other books by the same author:
Let's Go Visiting, 1998
I Went Walking, 1990

Other books you might like:
Jim Arnosky, *Rabbits and Raindrops*, 1997
    A mother rabbit watches over her five babies as they hop out of the nest to munch grass for the first time.
Peter McCarty, *Little Bunny on the Move*, 1999
    Little Bunny, determined to reach his destination, ignores everything in his path until his reaches his goal-home.
Beatrix Potter, *The Tale of Peter Rabbit*, 1902
    Peter Rabbit is grateful for the sanctuary of his home after his ill-advised visit to Mr. McGregor's garden.

1448

JACQUELINE WILSON

Girls in Love

(New York: Delacorte, 2002)

Series: Girlfriends Trilogy. Book 1
Subject(s): Friendship; Interpersonal Relations; Humor
Age range(s): Grades 7-10
Major character(s): Eleanor ''Ellie'' Allard, 9th Grader; Magda, 9th Grader; Nadine, 9th Grader; Dan, 9th Grader
Time period(s): 2000s
Locale(s): London, England

Summary: Ellie can hardly wait for school to begin and see her friends Magda and Nadine, but when they get together the first day, she discovers that Nadine has a boyfriend and that Magda enjoyed a flirty summer vacation. Poor Ellie. She doesn't like her hair or her weight and she'd give anything to have a boyfriend. Well, maybe she does have a boyfriend—she met nerdy Dan this summer. Pretty soon Ellie's built up a boyfriend who is perfect, a mixture of Dan's brains and the looks of a cute boy she noticed over the summer. Suddenly Dan appears in London and Ellie realizes that he's not so bad after all; he may not be as cute as she wants, but he's awfully nice and likes her for who she is. Ellie finally decides that maybe ninth grade isn't going to be too terrible. (181 pages)

Where it's reviewed:
Booklist, May 15, 2002, page 1592

Kliatt, September 2002, page 14
Library Media Connection, September 2002, page 59
Publishers Weekly, December 3, 2001, page 61
School Library Journal, January 2002, page 141

Awards the book has won:
ALA Quick Picks for Reluctant Young Adult Readers, 2003

Other books by the same author:
The Illustrated Mum, 2005
Girls in Tears, 2003
Girls Out Late, 2002
Girls Under Pressure, 2002

Other books you might like:
Ann Herrick, *The Perfect Guy*, 1989
    Rebecca's plan for her new stepbrother to fall for her backfires and she almost loses out on the best guy of all.
Louise Rennison, *Angus, Thongs and Full-Frontal Snogging: Confessions of Georgia Nicolson*, 2000
    In her diary, Georgia records her interest in kissing, her appearance and her opposition to most of what the adult world thinks is important.
Cynthia Voigt, *Bad Girls in Love*, 2002
    ''Bad girls'' Mikey and Margalo have fallen in love, Mikey openly with Shawn and Margalo secretly with her teacher.
Cherry Whytock, *My Cup Runneth Over: The Life of Angelica Cookson Potts*, 2003
    With eight of her favorite recipes, Angel shows how she manages to combine her love of eating and cooking with a flair for modeling.

1449

KARMA WILSON
JANE CHAPMAN, Illustrator

Bear Snores On

(New York: Margaret K. McElderry Books, 2002)

Subject(s): Animals/Bears; Animals; Stories in Rhyme
Age range(s): Grades K-1
Major character(s): Mouse, Mouse; Hare, Rabbit; Bear, Bear
Time period(s): Indeterminate
Locale(s): Fictional Country

Summary: As a hibernating bear snores away in his den, Mouse arrives, lights a fire and brews tea. Hare joins Mouse and the friends make popcorn. As more animals arrive, the party gets lively, but Bear snores on and on until a bit of pepper makes him sneeze. Bear wakes up grumpy and sadly complains that the others have had all the fun while he's been sleeping. Mouse brews more tea and cooks more popcorn and everyone sits up late listening to Bear's stories until only Bear is awake and his friends snore on. Originally published in London in 2001, this is Karma Wilson's first book. (36 pages)

Where it's reviewed:
Booklist, January 1, 2002, page 868
Horn Book Guide, Fall 2002, page 317
Kirkus Reviews, November 15, 2001, page 1616
Publishers Weekly, November 6, 2001, page 60
School Library Journal, January 2002, page 114

Awards the book has won:
ALA Notable Children's Books, 2003

Other books by the same author:
A Frog in the Bog, 2003
Sweet Briar Goes to School, 2003
Bear Wants More, 2003

Other books you might like:
Mem Fox, *Sleepy Bears*, 1999
   As winter nears Mother Bear calls her children inside for a bedtime rhyme before they sleep.
Don Freeman, *Bearymore*, 1976
   Bearymore has a new circus act to plan but winter calls and he settles down to hibernate instead.
Diane Marcial Fuchs, *A Bear for All Seasons*, 1995
   For Bear, any time of year is great if it's shared with a friend.
James Preller, *Wake Me in Spring*, 1994
   A mouse is sad that he will not be able to play with his friend Bear again until winter ends.
Don Wood, *Merry Christmas, Big Hungry Bear!*, 2002
   Mouse tiptoes up the snowy hill to Bear's cave to quietly decorate a tree and leave Christmas gifts for his hibernating neighbor. Audrey Wood, co-author.

1450

DAVID WINKLER

The Return of Calico Bright
(New York: Farrar Straus Giroux, 2003)

Subject(s): Divorce; Race Relations; Militia Movements
Age range(s): Grades 7-10
Major character(s): Calico "Callie" Weston, 16-Year-Old Trotter, 11th Grader; Jeff Froehlich, Basketball Player; Calico Warrenfield Bright, Grandmother
Time period(s): 2000s
Locale(s): Colorado

Summary: Periodically Callie's mother reads to her from the journal of Calico Bright, her infamous relative, whom legend says fought against Indians, shot her weak-kneed husband, and held off a grizzly bear. Wanting to emulate her feisty great-great-great-great-grandmother, after whom she's named, and to catch the attention of basketball star Jeff, Callie decides it's time to take off some weight, which she does with an increase in exercise and dieting. Callie's happiness is short-lived when she realizes that everything she's believed in is fake. Jeff loses interest in her when it's clear that Callie's professor father can't guarantee his acceptance at the local university. Most heinous of all, Callie is twice betrayed by her mother, first when she realizes that Calico Bright's journal is a fictional piece written by her mother and secondly when she discovers her mother in the arms of another man. Frustrated and upset, she joins her biracial friend Trotter in a camping trip for their social studies class where they run into a group of white supremacists who would like nothing better than getting rid of Trotter, permanently. Luckily Callie is just as strong as she believed her namesake was and she fights to save Trotter. (344 pages)

Where it's reviewed:
Booklist, September 15, 2003, page 232
Bulletin of the Center for Children's Books, October 2003, page 81
Kirkus Reviews, September 1, 2003, page 1133
School Library Journal, October 2003, page 180

Other books by the same author:
Scotty and the Gypsy Bandit, 2000

Other books you might like:
Gloria D. Miklowitz, *Camouflage*, 1998
   Kyle enjoys vacations with his divorced father's gun club until he realizes the members are part of a militia movement for which his father is the general.
Colby Rodowsky, *Spindrift*, 2000
   Cassie loves summer at Bethany Beach, until this year when she sees her sister's husband Mickey kissing another woman at a party.
Julian F. Thompson, *Brothers*, 1998
   When his brother Cam disappears, Chris finds him with a white militia group whose members are happy to have Cam's money.

1451

G. CLIFTON WISLER

Kings Mountain
(New York: HarperCollins, 2002)

Subject(s): Revolutionary War; Fathers and Sons
Age range(s): Grades 5-8
Major character(s): Francis Hugh Livingstone, 14-Year-Old, Artist; Kate Livingstone, 16-Year-Old
Time period(s): 1780s
Locale(s): Watauga Settlements, North Carolina; Camden, South Carolina; Kings Mountain, South Carolina

Summary: Growing up in the mountains of North Carolina Francis received a Dickert rifle on his ninth birthday, which he learned to shoot accurately, but he preferred drawing to killing animals or people. The colonies in America agitate to leave Britain's rule and Francis finds his community divided between the loyalists, who feel allegiance to Britain, and the patriots who wish to establish their own government. Francis is disinclined to take either side until he and his sister Kate are sent to South Carolina to help their grandmother run her tavern where they see the cruelty of the British troops and their allies. Returning home, he agrees to help the patriots and puts his sketching skills to use by drawing the enemy camps and positions before taking part in the decisive battle of Kings Mountain in this historical coming of age tale. (154 pages)

Where it's reviewed:
Booklist, March 15, 2002, page 1258
Horn Book Guide, Fall 2002, page 385
Kirkus Reviews, June 1, 2002, page 813
Kliatt, July 2002, page 14
School Library Journal, July 2002, page 128

Other books by the same author:
When Johnny Went Marching: Young Americans Fight the Civil War, 2001
Run the Blockade, 2000

Mustang Flats, 1997
Ross's Gap, 1988
This New Land, 1987

Other books you might like:
Avi, *The Fighting Ground*, 1984
In 1778 13-year-old Jonathan goes to war, returning home the next day, but not before witnessing fear, horror, pain and death.
Anna Myers, *The Keeping Room*, 1997
Left in charge when his father marches off to fight against the redcoats, Joseph runs into difficulty when General Cornwallis appropriates his home.
Seymour Reit, *Guns for General Washington: A Story of the American Revolution*, 1990
Colonel Know and his brother volunteer to bring the guns from Fort Ticonderoga to Boston to help General Washington.
Ann Rinaldi, *Cast Two Shadows: The American Revolution in the South*, 1998
Caroline sees her Camden, South Carolina home commandeered by the British, her friend's brother whipped and her best friend hanged in the 1780s.

1452

DAVID WISNIEWSKI, Author/Illustrator

Halloweenies

(New York: HarperCollins Publishers, 2002)

Subject(s): Humor; Short Stories; Movies
Age range(s): Grades 2-4
Time period(s): Indeterminate
Locale(s): Fictional Country

Summary: Classic horror films form the basis for five short stories. More humorous than scary these spoofs include ''The Curse of the Werewuss,'' in which a lost and rather clueless beautician gives a makeover to a werewolf and one glance in the mirror scares the creature right out of town. ''Frankenstein's Hamster,'' wreaks revenge on his owner's creator in the second story. An alien spaceship lands in Washington, D.C. in ''Attack of the Space Toupees,'' disgorging mind-controlling toupees that land on government officials' heads. In ''I Forgot What You Did Last Summer,'' the Atlantic Ocean carries a forgetful, nutty fisherman into the apartment of aspiring actress Buffy. While climbing Mt. Everest Sir Percy awakens ''The Abominable Showman'' and ignores his guide's advice not to encourage the jokester. (71 pages)

Where it's reviewed:
Booklist, September 1, 2002, page 138
Horn Book Guide, Spring 2003, page 74
Publishers Weekly, September 23, 2002, page 23
School Library Journal, October 2002, page 136

Other books by the same author:
Sumo Mouse, 2002
Tough Cookie, 1999 (Parents' Choice Gold Award)
The Secret Knowledge of Grown-Ups, 1998
Golem, 1996 (Caldecott Medal)

Other books you might like:
Kevin O'Malley, *Velcome*, 1997
The host of this tale ''velcomes'' you to a little Halloween fun in a collection of short stories that combine scary and humorous elements.
Dav Pilkey, *Captain Underpants and the Attack of the Talking Toilets*, 1999
Mischief makers Harold and George and their principal's alter ego, Captain Underpants, use cafeteria food to vanquish an invention gone awry.
Daniel Pinkwater, *The Hoboken Chicken Emergency*, 1977
In lieu of a turkey for Thanksgiving dinner, a mad inventor sells Arthur a 6-foot, 266 pound chicken that gets loose in town and causes a panic.
Jon Scieszka, *The Stinky Cheese Man: And Other Fairly Stupid Tales*, 1992
Classic fairy tales take on a new look in these humorous retellings comprising a Caldecott Honor Book.
Judith Bauer Stamper, *Five Goofy Ghosts*, 1996
Five brief stories featuring ghosts in a Level 4 Hello Reader! title combine humor and horror.

1453

ELLEN WITTLINGER

The Long Night of Leo and Bree

(New York: Simon & Schuster, 2002)

Subject(s): Murder; Kidnapping; Emotional Problems
Age range(s): Grades 8-12
Major character(s): Leo, 17-Year-Old; Michelle, Sister (deceased); Breeze ''Bree'', 17-Year-Old, Kidnap Victim
Time period(s): 2000s
Locale(s): Fenton, Massachusetts; Hawthorn, Massachusetts

Summary: Four years ago tonight Leo's sister was stabbed to death by a sadistic boyfriend. Since then his father's disappeared, his mother's turned into an alcoholic and he's dropped out of school and works in a garage. Angry at his mother for wanting him to look at the crime scene photos of his sister, Leo runs from the house, hops in his car and begins to drive around, ready to vent his rage and frustration on someone. That same night Bree has had enough of her overprotective mother and heads to Leo's part of town looking for a game of pool. As Leo spots Bree in her short skirt and high heels, he thinks she should have died instead of his saintly sister and abducts her. Back in his basement, where she's bound and blindfolded, the two begin to talk and, slowly but surely, each becomes a person to the other. Each is able to share their terrible demons with the other and by night's end, Leo has no desire to kill Bree and Bree doesn't plan to turn in Leo for kidnapping. (111 pages)

Where it's reviewed:
Bulletin of the Center for Children's Books, March 2002, page 261
Horn Book, March 2002, page 221
Publishers Weekly, February 18, 2002, page 97
School Library Journal, March 2002, page 240
Voice of Youth Advocates, February 2002, page 441

Awards the book has won:
ALA Quick Picks for Reluctant Young Adult Readers, 2003

Other books by the same author:
Heart on My Sleeve, 2004
Zigzag, 2003
Razzle, 2001
What's in a Name?, 2000
Hard Love, 1999

Other books you might like:
Robert Cormier, *Tenderness*, 1997
   When a girl he cares for accidentally drowns, a serial killer knows the police will claim he murdered her.
Julius Lester, *When Dad Killed Mom*, 2001
   Siblings Jeremy and Jenna struggle to understand why their father killed their mother and then lied about it in the courtroom.
Nancy Werlin, *The Killer's Cousin*, 1998
   Though his cousin Lily taunts and harasses him, David doesn't give up on her and eventually saves her from an attempt at suicide.

1454

PATRICIA RAE WOLFF
LYNNE CRAVATH, Illustrator

A New Improved Santa
(New York: Orchard/Scholastic, Inc., 2002)

Subject(s): Santa Claus; Christmas; Weight Control
Age range(s): Grades K-3
Major character(s): Santa Claus, Mythical Creature, Aged Person
Time period(s): 2000s (2002)
Locale(s): Polar Regions

Summary: One Christmas Santa notices that the chimneys seem a little tighter so he begins a year-long, self-improvement project. He loses weight, changes his clothes, dyes his hair, updates his mode of transportation and even changes his catchphrase. However when Santa unveils his new and improved look in November, none of the children like it, so Mrs. Claus helps him get back to his former appearance. (32 pages)

Where it's reviewed:
Bulletin of the Center for Children's Books, November 2002, page 131
Kirkus Reviews, November 1, 2002, page 1627
Publishers Weekly, September 23, 2002, page 34
School Library Journal, October 2002, page 65

Other books by the same author:
Cackle Cook's Monster Stew, 2001
The Toll-Bridge Toll, 1995

Other books you might like:
Stephen Krensky, *How Santa Got His Job*, 1998
   This story offers a look at how Santa acquired all the skills necessary to do his gift-delivering, child-pleasing job.
Elise Primavera, *Auntie Claus*, 1999
   Sophie Kringle is determined to figure out just where her eccentric Auntie Claus disappears each Christmas Eve.
Mike Reiss, *Santa Claustrophia*, 2002
   When Santa needs a vacation the other seasonal celebrities, from Cupid to the Easter Bunny, fill in for him.

1455

JANET S. WONG
MARGARET CHODOS-IRVINE, Illustrator

Apple Pie 4th of July
(San Diego: Harcourt, Inc., 2002)

Subject(s): Holidays; Food; Chinese Americans
Age range(s): Grades K-2
Major character(s): Unnamed Character, Daughter, Narrator; Mother, Store Owner, Cook; Father, Store Owner, Cook
Time period(s): 2000s (2002)
Locale(s): United States

Summary: A young Chinese-American does not understand why her parents insist on opening their store and preparing take-out Chinese food on the Fourth of July. Mother and Father should know that on this American holiday they should be selling apple pie. Indeed, it is a slow day in the store as the girl listens to a parade in the distance and smells an apple pie baking at a neighbor's, mingling with the odor from her parents cooking chow mein and sweet and sour pork. All day customers buy chips, soda, ice cream and ice but no Chinese food so the family dines on the prepared food. By late afternoon, as customers enter the store, the girl is grateful that Mother and Father have cooked more food for the people eager to purchase take-out Chinese food as part of their celebration of an American holiday. (40 pages)

Where it's reviewed:
Booklist, August 2002, page 1963
Horn Book Guide, Fall 2002, page 317
Kirkus Reviews, April 15, 2002, page 582
Publishers Weekly, April 8, 2002, page 226
School Library Journal, May 2002, page 132

Awards the book has won:
Booklist Editors' Choice, 2002

Other books by the same author:
Buzz, 2000 (School Library Journal Best Books)
The Trip Back Home, 2000 (Asian Pacific American Award for Literature)
This Next New Year, 2000

Other books you might like:
Betty G. Birney, *Pie's in the Oven*, 1996
   The fragrant odor of Grandma's apple pie attracts neighbors, friends and relatives eager for a taste.
Sook Nyul Choi, *Halmoni and the Picnic*, 1993
   Yunmi's grandmother prepares traditional Korean food for a class picnic.
Grace Lin, *The Ugly Vegetables*, 1999
   Compared to the neighbor's flowers, the ugly Chinese vegetables in Mommy's garden are embarrassing but the neighbors enjoy the vegetable soup.
Rosemary Wells, *Yoko*, 1998
   For International Food Day Yoko brings homemade sushi to share with her classmates.

1456

JANET S. WONG
GENEVIEVE COTE, Illustrator

Minn and Jake

(New York: Frances Foster Books/Farrar Straus Giroux, 2003)

Subject(s): Friendship; Individuality; Self-Confidence
Age range(s): Grades 3-5
Major character(s): Minn, 5th Grader, Friend; Jake, 5th Grader, Friend
Time period(s): 2000s (2003)
Locale(s): Santa Brunella, California

Summary: It's easy to spot Jake, the new kid in class, because he's so short, the opposite of Minn, who is the tallest girl Jake has ever seen. Circumstances force the two together during Jake's first days at Santa Brunella Elementary and very gradually—and a bit reluctantly—a friendship develops. As a city boy, Jake never develops a liking for lizards and worms, Minn's favorite activities, but the classmates come to respect each other as unique individuals and in the process learn a greater appreciation of the meaning of friendship. (146 pages)

Where it's reviewed:
Bulletin of the Center for Children's Books, October 2003, page 83
Publishers Weekly, August 2003, page 79
School Library Journal, October 2003, page 142

Awards the book has won:
Bulletin of the Center for Children's Books Blue Ribbons, 2003

Other books by the same author:
Knock on Wood: Poems about Superstitions, 2003
Night Garden: Poems from the World of Dreams, 2000
Behind the Wheel: Poems about Driving, 1999

Other books you might like:
Judith Caseley, *Jorah's Journal*, 1997
    Jorah records her unhappy thoughts about her new home and school and her difficulty making friends.
Ralph Fletcher, *Spider Boy*, 1997
    After moving from the Midwest to New York Bobby has difficulty finding friends and feeling at home in his new community.
Phyllis Reynolds Naylor, *The Boys Return*, 2001
    The modern day feud between the Malloy sisters and the Hatford brothers heats up when the Benson brothers return to town for vacation.

1457

AUDREY WOOD
BRUCE WOOD, Illustrator

Alphabet Mystery

(New York: Blue Sky Press/Scholastic, Inc., 2003)

Subject(s): Mystery; Missing Persons; Birthdays
Age range(s): Grades K-2
Major character(s): Charley, Child
Time period(s): 2000s (2003)
Locale(s): United States

Summary: The letter "x" is missing from Charley's alphabet, so the other letters set off in search of it. They locate "x" in the castle of capital M, playing a lullaby on a xylophone. The letter x has run away because he is never used, but the other letters assure him that Charley needs him for his mother's birthday tomorrow, so x agrees to go home. The next day, Charley uses the letters to write a message on his mother's birthday cake: "I love you Mom xxxx." (40 pages)

Where it's reviewed:
Booklist, December 1, 2003, page 687
School Library Journal, November 2003, page 120

Other books by the same author:
Alphabet Adventure, 2001
The Tickleoctopus, 1994
The Napping House, 1984

Other books you might like:
Michael Chesworth, *Alphaboat*, 2002
    The alphabet sets off on a pun-filled sailing adventure.
Andy Rash, *Agent A to Agent Z*, 2004
    Agent A is on a mission to find the letter whose actions don't match his name.
William Steig, *CDC?*, 1984
    The story is created from word puzzles in which letters form sentences. CDC?, for example, is "See the Sea?"

1458

AUDREY WOOD
NED BITTINGER, Illustrator

When the Root Children Wake Up

(New York: Scholastic Press, 2002)

Subject(s): Folklore; Nature; Seasons
Age range(s): Grades 1-4
Major character(s): Root Children, Mythical Creature; Mother Earth, Mythical Creature
Time period(s): Indeterminate
Locale(s): Earth

Summary: In this retelling of a 1906 German tale, winter retires and Mother Earth awakens the Root Children who fashion blossom clothes from bits of rainbow and paint sparkles on the bugs. When all is ready, Mother Earth releases them to begin the masquerade. The children awaken spring before racing across the land to spread the perfume of their blossoms. As the growing warmth makes spring drowsy, the children turn their attention to summer until the cool winds of fall quiet the land and Mother Nature calls the Root Children back to their underground home. (32 pages)

Where it's reviewed:
Booklist, February 15, 2002, page 1017
Bulletin of the Center for Children's Books, July 2002, page 422
Horn Book Guide, Fall 2002, page 348
Publishers Weekly, March 4, 2002, page 79
School Library Journal, May 2002, page 132

Other books by the same author:
Jubal's Wish, 2000
Sweet Dream Pie, 1998
The Flying Dragon Room, 1996

Other books you might like:
David Christiana, *The First Snow*, 1996
  Mother Nature tries to scare Winter away by painting the leaves bright colors but she comes to appreciate Winter when he learns to make snow.
Reeve Lindbergh, *North Country Spring*, 1997
  The natural world awakens to the call of spring as bear cubs tumble, geese fly and frogs begin their spring peeping.
Lynn Plourde, *Wild Child*, 1999
  Mother Nature is ready for her wild child to settle down for a nap but her offspring has other plans.

`1459`

DON WOOD, Author/Illustrator
AUDREY WOOD, Co-Author

Merry Christmas, Big Hungry Bear!
(New York: Blue Sky Press/Scholastic, Inc., 2002)

Subject(s): Animals/Mice; Christmas; Gifts
Age range(s): Preschool-Grade 1
Major character(s): Mouse, Mouse
Time period(s): Indeterminate
Locale(s): Fictional Country

Summary: Mouse is unable to truly enjoy his pile of Christmas gifts when he's reminded of the big hungry bear hibernating in his cave atop the hill. Realizing that the bear never receives gifts, Mouse abandons his attempts to protect his presents from an imagined assault by the deprived bear, gathers his courage, dresses in a Santa suit and struggles up the hill with a large bag. Bravely, Mouse decorates a nearby snow-covered tree and places gifts under it. To his surprise, he receives a package in return for his kindness. (42 pages)

Where it's reviewed:
Booklist, September 15, 2002, page 247
Bulletin of the Center for Children's Books, November 2002, page 131
Horn Book Guide, Spring 2003, page 22
Publishers Weekly, September 23, 2002, page 32
School Library Journal, October 2002, page 65

Other books by the same author:
Jubal's Wish, 2000
The Little Mouse, the Red Ripe Strawberry, and the Big, Hungry Bear, 1998
The Napping House, 1984 (New York Times Best Illustrated Book)

Other books you might like:
Olivier Dunrea, *Bear Noel*, 2000
  One by one the clues mount telling the animals of the north woods to gather in anticipation of Bear Noel's arrival.
Laura Joffe Numeroff, *If You Take a Mouse to the Movies*, 2000
  Taking a mouse to the movies is the start of unexpected holiday preparations when the popcorn inspires the mouse to string some for a tree decoration.
Brigitte Weninger, *Merry Christmas, Davy!*, 1998
  Animals offer future foraging help in gratitude for Davy's

generous gift of most of his family's winter food supply to ease their hunger.

`1460`

DOUGLAS WOOD
DAN ANDREASEN, Illustrator

A Quiet Place
(New York: Simon & Schuster Books for Young Readers, 2002)

Subject(s): Imagination; Nature; Childhood
Age range(s): Grades 1-4
Major character(s): Unnamed Character, Child
Time period(s): 2000s (2003)
Locale(s): United States

Summary: A boy searches for a quiet place, someplace away from the hustle and bustle and, especially, the "grown-ups talking." Imaginatively, the boy explores a wide variety of "quiet places" from a desert, where one can be a Pony Express rider, to a cavern, where one can be a cave dweller, to a library, where books can take one to other lands. In the end, the boy decides that the best quiet place is the one inside oneself because it's always there. (32 pages)

Where it's reviewed:
Booklist, February 15, 2002, page 1023
Publishers Weekly, February 4, 2002, page 75
School Library Journal, July 2002, page 102

Awards the book has won:
IRA Teachers' Choices, 2003

Other books by the same author:
Old Turtle and the Broken Truth, 2003
What Dads Can't Do, 2000
Grandad's Prayers of the Earth, 1999
Old Turtle, 1991

Other books you might like:
Sharon Creech, *Fishing in the Air*, 2000
  A boy and his father use their time on a fishing trip to imaginatively journey beyond the river and into an exploration of family history.
Charlotte Dematons, *Let's Go*, 2001
  A young boy turns a walk to the grocery store into an imaginative adventure.
Kevin Henkes, *All Alone*, 1981
  According to one young boy, sometimes it's good to alone.

`1461`

CHRIS WOODING

Kerosene
(New York: Scholastic/Push, 2002)

Subject(s): Fires; Friendship; School Life
Age range(s): Grades 9-12
Major character(s): Cal Sampson, 11th Grader; Joel Manning, 11th Grader; Emma Cohen, 11th Grader; Abby Cobley, 11th Grader; Ben Deerborn, Police Officer (fire investigator)
Time period(s): 2000s
Locale(s): England

Summary: Cal hates his shyness, wishing he could just speak up now and then, but it's no use, even though he knows people often mistake his shyness for snobbery or simply not caring. Without his best friend Joel, he'd probably never make it through a school day, but suddenly Joel's in trouble with some drug dealers and doesn't have much time for Cal. Then Cal angers Emma and Abby, two popular girls at school, and they turn around and make life miserable for him. Suddenly the matches he used to light to calm himself down don't seem to be enough, and he begins to set fires to buildings, a barn and then a factory. To help his friend, Cal decides to set a spectacular blaze that will eliminate the drug dealers who are bothering Joel, but luckily Abby and fire investigator Mr. Deerborn intervene before any damage is done. (195 pages)

Where it's reviewed:
Booklist, July 2002, page 1838
Kliatt, July 2002, page 26
Publishers Weekly, February 18, 2002, page 98
School Library Journal, July 2002, page 128
Voice of Youth Advocates, August 2002, page 199

Other books by the same author:
Haunting of Alaizabel Clay, 2004
Crashing, 2003
Poison, 2003
Endgame, 2000

Other books you might like:
Kate Banks, *Walk Softly, Rachel*, 2003
    Rachel's so caught up in her brother's death that she forgets about her friend who likes to play with matches, until some fires grab her attention.
Michael Cadnum, *Breaking the Fall*, 1992
    "It's only a game," Stanley tells himself before he and Jared break into yet another occupied house and steal something from the bedroom.
Deborah Froese, *Out of the Fire*, 2002
    Badly burned when a bonfire ignites suddenly, Dayle recuperates and rethinks her life until she's able to forgive the boy who tossed the gasoline.
Karen Hesse, *Out of the Dust*, 1997
    Billie Jo accidentally tosses a burning pail of kerosene out the kitchen door and onto her mother, who later dies.
Tim Wynne-Jones, *Stephen Fair*, 1998
    Stephen has strange dreams of a fire and a baby crying, dreams that are finally explained when he understands a family secret.

1462

ELVIRA WOODRUFF

The Ravenmaster's Secret

(New York: Scholastic, 2003)

Subject(s): Prisoners and Prisons; Animals/Birds; Prejudice
Age range(s): Grades 5-8
Major character(s): Forrest Harper, 11-Year-Old; Maddy Stewart, 12-Year-Old, Rebel; Rat, Apprentice (to a ratcatcher), Orphan; Tuck, Raven
Time period(s): 1730s (1735)
Locale(s): London, England (Tower of London)

Summary: Living in the Tower of London where his father is Ravenmaster, in charge of the legendary ravens and an occasional prisoner, Forrest often finds he's lonely with only his raven Tuck and his friend Rat as companions. Scottish rebels are captured and Forrest's family is given the task of caring for Maddy, daughter of the rebel leader, who's about Forrest's age. Brought up to believe all Scots are devils, Forrest is prepared to dislike Maddy but as they become acquainted and she tells of her life in Scotland, he realizes she's a person just like him, not an evil person as he's been led to believe. When her father and uncle are killed trying to escape, Forrest realizes Maddy is to be executed and decides he can't let that happen. With help from Rat, Forrest manages to help Maddy escape from the Tower and Rat from his life of menial labor, in a work filled with historical details and notes. (225 pages)

Where it's reviewed:
Booklist, January 2004, page 864
Kirkus Reviews, October 15, 2003, page 1277
Publishers Weekly, January 5, 2004, page 62
School Library Journal, January 2004, page 138

Other books by the same author:
The Christmas Doll, 2000
The Ghost of Lizard Light, 1999
Dear Austin: Letters from the Underground Railroad, 1998
The Orphan of Ellis Island: A Time Travel Adventure, 1997
Dear Levi: Letters from the Overland Trail, 1994

Other books you might like:
Jamila Gavin, *Coram Boy*, 2001
    In 18th-century England, many mothers hire the "Coram Man" to take their offspring to a hospital for abandoned children, not realizing he's unscrupulous.
Anthony Horowitz, *The Devil and His Boy*, 2000
    Brought to London, Tom evades the beggar gang leader who wants to hire him and joins a group of actors who perform for Queen Elizabeth.
Laura E. Williams, *The Executioner's Daughter*, 2000
    After her protective mother's death, Lily realizes she will inherit her father's job and knows she must escape before she becomes the executioner.

1463

BRENDA WOODS

The Red Rose Box

(New York: G.P. Putnam's Sons, 2002)

Subject(s): Segregation; African Americans; Sisters
Age range(s): Grades 4-6
Major character(s): Leah Jean Hopper, 10-Year-Old, Sister; Ruth Hopper, 8-Year-Old, Sister; Olivia Chapel, Aunt
Time period(s): 1950s (1953-1955)
Locale(s): Sulphur, Louisiana; Los Angeles, California; New York, New York

Summary: No one foresees the changes that will come because of the "red rose box" Leah receives as a birthday gift from Aunt Olivia, her mother's estranged sister. A letter to Leah's mother, enclosed with the gift, contains four train tickets. The journey from rural Louisiana to Los Angeles heals the estrangement of two sisters and propels Leah, Ruth, their mother and grandmother from a world of ''Jim Crow'' discriminatory treatment to a city in which Leah experiences equality for the first time in her life. Wealthy, childless Aunt Olivia and her husband also invite Leah and Ruth on a trip to New York the following summer. While they travel, a hurricane devastates their small home community, killing their parents and ending the life they know. The wealth, privilege and respect that Leah and Ruth gain and enjoy when they move in with Aunt Olivia and her husband do not relieve the pain of their loss in the author's first novel. (136 pages)

Where it's reviewed:
Booklist, June 2002, page 1726
Bulletin of the Center for Children's Books, July 2002, page 422
Publishers Weekly, May 20, 2002, page 66
School Library Journal, June 2002, page 149
Voice of Youth Advocates, June 2002, page 124

Awards the book has won:
Coretta Scott King Honor Book, 2003
Center for Children's Books Best Books, 2002

Other books you might like:
Kristi Collier, *Jericho Walls*, 2002
  Northerner Jo moves into a small South Carolina town where navigating socially in an unfamiliar segregated society determines her acceptance by peers.
Christopher Paul Curtis, *Bud, Not Buddy*, 1999
  After four years in foster homes, Bud runs away in search of his father and finds, instead, the missing pieces of his life story. Newbery Medal.
Michael Dorris, *The Window*, 1997
  When 11-year-old Rayona meets her father's family for the first time, she discovers long-hold family secrets that help her understand herself.
Ronder Thomas Young, *Learning by Heart*, 1993
  In the 1960s, Rachel becomes aware of racial prejudices and their impact on friendships in her small southern town.

1464

RON WOODS

The Hero

(New York: Knopf, 2002)

Subject(s): Fathers and Sons; Rafting; Conduct of Life
Age range(s): Grades 5-9
Major character(s): James ''Jamie'' West, 14-Year-Old; Jerry, 15-Year-Old, Cousin; Dennis Leeper, Abuse Victim (of teasing); Arlie Leeper, Father (of Dennis)
Time period(s): 1950s (1957)
Locale(s): Payette River, Idaho

Summary: Summer's running out and Jamie still hasn't finished building his raft, so he asks his cousin Jerry to give him a hand. As the two work on it, they try to avoid their neighbor Dennis who wants desperately to be their friend, hiding from him or teasing him by calling him ''Denise.'' Finally the raft is finished and, at his mother's cajoling, Jamie lets Dennis ride on the raft with them, though they've been warned not to go outside the logjam into the swift current. A day swimming in the shallows isn't very exciting and pretty soon they inch their

way out into the current, which is swifter than they can handle with no paddles. Jerry swims to shore to try to get help while Dennis and Jamie head over the dam; Jamie's rescued but Dennis drowns. Mr. Leeper is so angry that he threatens revenge against Jamie's family, which prompts Jamie to stand up at his funeral and tell the mourners that Dennis lost his life trying to save Jamie's. Though Jamie must learn to live with his lie, he does talk to his parents about the moral implications of his deed in this author's first novel. (215 pages)

Where it's reviewed:
Booklist, February 1, 2002, page 934
Horn Book, March 2002, page 221
Publishers Weekly, January 28, 2002, page 292
School Library Journal, January 2002, page 141
Voice of Youth Advocates, August 2002, page 199

Awards the book has won:
Center for Children's Books Best Books, 2002

Other books you might like:
Marion Dane Bauer, *On My Honor*, 1986
  Good friends Joel and Tony swim in a river off limits to them; when Tony drowns, Joel is terrified to tell either set of parents.
Don Brown, *Our Time on the River*, 2003
  Before David leaves for Vietnam, two brothers embark on a canoe trip where they learn to care for and appreciate one another.
Eve Bunting, *Blackwater*, 1999
  Trying to impress Pauline, upon whom he has a crush, leads to tragedy when Brodie accidentally pulls her off a rock and she's swept away in the current.
Alden R. Carter, *Between a Rock and a Hard Place*, 1995
  A rite-of-passage canoe trip for two cousins almost turns to disaster when Randy loses his insulin and Mark must find help fast.

1465

JACQUELINE WOODSON

Hush

(New York: Penguin Putnam, 2002)

Subject(s): African Americans; Identity, Concealed; Sports/Track
Age range(s): Grades 6-9
Major character(s): Toswiah ''Evie Thomas'' Green, 13-Year-Old; Cameron ''Anne Thomas'' Green, 11th Grader, Sister
Time period(s): 2000s
Locale(s): Denver, Colorado

Summary: Life in Denver was very nice, or at least that's how Toswiah, now called Evie, remembers it. There she had friends and her family was happy, but now her sister Cameron, now called Anne, wants to attend college early, her mother becomes too religious and her father tries to commit suicide. Her family is living under the witness protection program because her father followed his conscience, broke the code of silence and testified against two fellow white policemen who shot an unarmed African American teen. Life for Toswiah/Evie doesn't get better until she loses herself in track at her new school and finds that when she's running, she can forget how miserable she is. Track also gives her some friends, one who even calls her "spider" because of her long legs, and provides Toswiah/Evie the hope that her new life will become better. (180 pages)

Where it's reviewed:
Booklist, January 2002, page 851
Bulletin of the Center for Children's Books, March 2002, page 262
Horn Book, January 2002, page 87
School Library Journal, February 2002, page 138
Voice of Youth Advocates, February 2002, page 442

Awards the book has won:
ALA Best Books for Young Adults, 2003
School Library Journal Best Books, 2002

Other books by the same author:
Behind You, 2004
Locomotion, 2003
Miracle's Boys, 2000
Lena, 1999
If You Come Softly, 1998

Other books you might like:
Robert Cormier, *In the Middle of the Night*, 1995
  Because of an incident years ago, Denny's family moves often, changing houses, phone numbers and schools.
Lois Duncan, *Don't Look Behind You*, 1989
  Though April's family is part of a Witness Security Program, April inadvertently reveals their whereabouts and places her family in danger.
Roland Smith, *Zach's Lie*, 2001
  Though he knows he shouldn't keep a journal with references to his past life, Zach does, an act he later regrets when it compromises his family's safety.
James Stevenson, *The Unprotected Witness*, 1997
  Pete, his grandmother and his best friend Rollie travel to the Ozarks for the funeral of his father, killed while part of the Witness Protection Program.

1466

JACQUELINE WOODSON

Locomotion

(New York: Putnam, 2003)

Subject(s): Brothers and Sisters; Orphans; Poetry
Age range(s): Grades 4-8
Major character(s): Lonnie Collins "Locomotion" Motion, 11-Year-Old, Orphan; Miss Edna, Foster Parent; Lili Motion, Sister (of Lonnie)
Time period(s): 2000s
Locale(s): United States

Summary: When Lonnie was only seven, his parents were killed in a fire, his sister Lili adopted and he was sent to the foster home of Miss Edna. Now his teacher assigns his class to keep a poetry journal and Lonnie's troubles over the last four years pour out in haiku, sonnets and free verse. Though he writes that Miss Edna always says "Be quiet" to him, he also describes her many kindnesses. Through his poetry journal,

Lonnie continues to heal his grief and becomes positive about the days ahead. (100 pages)

Where it's reviewed:
Bulletin of the Center for Children's Books, March 2003, page 294
Horn Book, March 2003, page 219
Publishers Weekly, November 25, 2002, page 68
Riverbank Review, Summer 2003, page 36
Voice of Youth Advocates, February 2003, page 484

Awards the book has won:
Boston Globe-Horn Book Honor Book, 2003
ALA Best Books for Young Adults, 2004

Other books by the same author:
Behind You, 2004
Miracle's Boys, 2000
Lena, 1999
If You Come Softly, 1997
From the Notebooks of Melanin Sun, 1995

Other books you might like:
Helen Frost, *Keesha's House*, 2003
  A combination of sestinas, sonnets and other verse forms tell of Keesha's House that offers sanctuary to all who need it.
Nikki Grimes, *Bronx Masquerade*, 2002
  Students of Mr. Ward enjoy "Open Mike" nights where they read their poetry and watch as their writings gradually draw them all together.
Ron Koertge, *Shakespeare Bats Cleanup*, 2003
  Recovering from mono, Kevin tries writing a little haiku, then a sonnet and even a sestina, discovering that poetry is "almost as cool as baseball."

1467

JACQUELINE WOODSON
JON J. MUTH, Illustrator

Our Gracie Aunt

(New York: Jump at the Sun/Hyperion Books for Children, 2002)

Subject(s): Brothers and Sisters; Foster Homes; African Americans
Age range(s): Grades K-3
Major character(s): Beebee, Sister (older), Niece; Johnson, Brother (younger), Nephew; Miss Roy, Social Worker; Gracie, Aunt, Foster Parent
Time period(s): 2000s (2002)
Locale(s): United States

Summary: On Miss Roy's third visit to their apartment, Beebee finally and reluctantly opens the door. Having received a report that Beebee and Johnson are alone, Miss Roy has come to take them to foster care in the home of their mother's sister, Grace. Johnson has no memory of Aunt Gracie, but Beebee recalls that their mother doesn't like her. Into her home Aunt Gracie welcomes the children with love, cookies, regular meals and lullabies at bedtime. Miss Roy returns one day and takes the children to visit their mother who is still not able to care for them so they return to their Gracie aunt's home where they are welcomed with a big hug. (32 pages)

Where it's reviewed:

Booklist, September 1, 2002, page 137
Bulletin of the Center for Children's Books, September 2002, page 37
Horn Book Guide, Spring 2003, page 59
Publishers Weekly, March 4, 2002, page 79
School Library Journal, December 2002, page 114

Awards the book has won:

IRA Teachers' Choices, 2003
Notable Social Studies Trade Books for Young People, 2003

Other books by the same author:

The Other Side, 2001 (School Library Journal Best Books)
Sweet, Sweet Memory, 2000
We Had a Picnic This Sunday Past, 1997

Other books you might like:

Lucille Clifton, *One of the Problems of Everett Anderson*, 2001
 Mama helps Everett determine his responsibility to a class-mate he suspects is being abused at home.
Patricia Polacco, *Welcome Comfort*, 1999
 Foster child Welcome Comfort finds relief from class-mates' teasing in a friendship with the school's custodian.
Maria Testa, *Nine Candles*, 1996
 When Raymond visits his incarcerated mother on his sev-enth birthday she promises to be home with him when his cake has nine candles.
Vera B. Williams, *Amber Was Brave, Essie Was Smart*, 2001
 Sisters Amber and Essie depend on each other for com-pany, solace and nurture as their mother works long hours during their father's imprisonment.

`1468`

JACQUELINE WOODSON
JAMES E. RANSOME, Illustrator

Visiting Day

(New York: Scholastic Press, 2002)

Subject(s): Prisoners and Prisons; Prisoner's Families; Fathers and Daughters
Age range(s): Grades K-3
Major character(s): Grandma, Grandmother, Mother; Un-named Character, Daughter; Daddy, Father, Prisoner
Time period(s): 2000s
Locale(s): United States

Summary: When the smell of frying chicken awakens a little girl she knows it is Visiting Day. As the contented little girl lies in bed she imagines Daddy waking and getting ready for the day too. With Grandma the little girl waits patiently for the bus and then enjoys the ride, the camaraderie of the passen-gers and the shared food until the bus reaches its destination, a big old building where, Grandma says, "Daddy is doing a little time." The little girl eagerly sits on Daddy's lap to tell him about her activities of the past month before she and Grandma sadly must say goodbye. Grandma assures her that one day Daddy will be waking up in his own home again and the bus rides will not be necessary but, until then, there is Visiting Day to count on each month. (32 pages)

Where it's reviewed:

Booklist, November 1, 2002, page 504
Bulletin of the Center for Children's Books, December 2002, page 178
Horn Book, November 2002, page 743
Publishers Weekly, September 16, 2002, page 68
School Library Journal, September 2002, page 208

Awards the book has won:

Center for Children's Books Best Books, 2002

Other books by the same author:

Our Gracie Aunt, 2002 (IRA Teachers' Choice)
The Other Side, 2001 (School Library Journal Best Books)
Sweet, Sweet Memory, 2000

Other books you might like:

Angela Shelf Medearis, *Our People*, 1994
 Father and daughter playfully share a history lesson and a hope for the future in a nonfiction picture book.
Maria Testa, *Nine Candles*, 1996
 On Raymond's seventh birthday, while visiting his incar-cerated mother, he receives her promise to be home when his cake has nine candles.
Vera B. Williams, *Amber Was Brave, Essie Was Smart*, 2001
 Two sisters depend on each other for company, solace and nurture as their mother works long hours during their father's imprisonment.

`1469`

VIKI WOODWORTH, Author/Illustrator

Daisy the Dancing Cow

(Honesdale, PA: Boyd Mills Press, 2003)

Subject(s): Animals/Cows; Dancing; Theater
Age range(s): Grades K-3
Major character(s): Daisy, Cow
Time period(s): 2000s (2003)
Locale(s): United States

Summary: After reading an announcement seeking "hoofers" for a new musical Daisy decides to try out. The director tells Daisy that she is not interested in casting cows, but Daisy is allowed to stay on as a "gofer." She learns a lot about the theater and the dances as well. When a performer sprains her ankle on opening night, Daisy steps in and saves the day. (32 pages)

Where it's reviewed:

Publishers Weekly, September 8, 2003, page 78
School Library Journal, October 2003, page 142

Other books by the same author:

Daisy the Firecow, 2001
Do Cows Turn Colors in the Fall?, 1997
Does a Dinosaur Check Your Teeth? Learn About Community Helpers, 1996

Other books you might like:

Kathi Appelt, *Piggies in a Polka*, 2003
 At the yearly hootenanny, all the pigs get together to dance.
Robert Kinerk, *Clorinda*, 2003
 With a lot of work Clorinda the cow achieves her dream of

dancing professionally in a ballet and learns that performing may not be for her.

James Marshall, *Swine Lake*, 1999
A porcine dance troupe performs Swine Lake.

Bill Martin Jr., *Barn Dance*, 1986
A young farm boy discovers the barnyard animals having a dance in the middle of the night. John Archambault, co-author.

Carole Lexa Schaefer, *Full Moon Barnyard Dance*, 2003
One night when the farm animals can't sleep, they decide to have a dance by the pond.

Elizabeth Winthrop, *Dumpy La Rue*, 2001
Dumpy La Rue wants to be a ballerina, but he's told, "Pigs don't dance."

1470

PATRICIA C. WREDE, Co-Author
CAROLINE STEVERMER, Co-Author

Sorcery and Cecelia, or the Enchanted Chocolate Pot
(San Diego: Harcourt, 2003)

Subject(s): Fantasy; Magic; Love
Age range(s): Grades 7-12
Major character(s): Cecelia "Cecy" Rushton, Cousin; Kate Talgarth, Cousin; Marquis Thomas of Sch, Wizard, Nobleman; James Tarleton, Military Personnel
Time period(s): 1810s
Locale(s): Essex, England; London, England

Summary: In an England recognizable except for the presence of wizardry, two young ladies of the upper class exchange letters relating their adventures. When Kate goes off to London for the season, she and her cousin Cecy, left at home in Essex, begin an exchange of letters. Cecy is convinced that Kate's life in London will be much more exciting than hers in the country, and at first she appears to be correct. Kate attends the investiture of a country neighbor into London's College of Wizards, and encounters a sinister little woman who appears to mistake her for some wizardly enemy. In short order, Kate meets the mysterious Marquis of Schoefield, while Cecy encounters his friend James Tarleton in Essex. Then Kate becomes engaged to the Marquis, Cecy is magically threatened, and both girls reveal a talent for magic that seems to run in families. Can two well-bred young ladies enjoy balls, teas and romance despite the machinations of two unscrupulous wizards? If it can be done, energetic Cecy and sensible Kate intend to try. (316 pages)

Where it's reviewed:
Bulletin of the Center for Children's Books, July 2003, page 466
Chronicle, May 2003, page 41
Horn Book, September 2003, page 586
Magazine of Fantasy and Science Fiction, October 2003, page 55
Voice of Youth Advocates, June 2003, page 154

Awards the book has won:
ALA Best Books for Young Adults, 2004

Other books by the same author:
The Grand Tour, 2004

Other books you might like:
Teresa Edgerton, *The Queen's Necklace*, 2001
Will abandons his rakish ways when the kingdom is threatened and he learns that his wife is a gifted wizard.
Martha Wells, *The Death of the Necromancer*, 1998
A nobleman turned thief finds his gang, livelihood and life threatened by a wizard who deals in death.
Elizabeth Wiley, *A Sorcerer and a Gentleman*, 1995
Two young lovers try to avoid angering anyone in either of their two magical families; it doesn't help that war has been declared.

1471

SHARON DENNIS WYETH

Flying Free: Corey's Underground Railroad Diary
(New York: Scholastic, Inc., 2002)

Series: My America. Book Two
Subject(s): African Americans; Diaries; Historical
Age range(s): Grades 2-5
Major character(s): Corey Birdsong, 9-Year-Old, Runaway; George Davis, 11-Year-Old, Friend; Mingo, Friend, Runaway
Time period(s): 1850s (1858)
Locale(s): Amherstburg, Canada

Summary: In the sequel to *Freedom's Wings: Corey's Diary* Corey and his family are settling into life as free people. They find work in the community and eventually are able to acquire land for a small farm and build a home. Corey makes friends with George and attends school. He longs to see Mingo again and does what he can to encourage his Kentucky friend to flee slavery and run away to Canada. Diary entries record Corey's observations, document the family's new life and reveal Mingo's successful trip to Canada. (100 pages)

Where it's reviewed:
Booklist, June 2002, page 1726
Horn Book Guide, Fall 2002, page 366
Kirkus Reviews, April 15, 2002, page 582
School Library Journal, August 2002, page 156

Other books by the same author:
Freedom's Wings: Corey's Diary, 2001 (Notable Social Studies Trade Books for Young People)
Tomboy Trouble, 1998
The Winning Stroke, 1996

Other books you might like:
James Haskins, *Following Freedom's Star: The Story of the Underground Railroad*, 2001
This nonfiction title for youth describing the Underground Railroad includes excerpts from diaries and newspapers of the time.
Shelley Pearsall, *Trouble Don't Last*, 2002
Harrison, an elderly slave, takes 11-year-old Samuel with him when he escapes their Kentucky plantation and flees to Canada.

Roni Schotter, *F Is for Freedom*, 2000

Accidentally discovering her parents' involvement with the Underground Railroad, 10-year-old Amanda offers what help she can to the runaways.

1472

THELMA HATCH WYSS

Ten Miles from Winnemucca

(New York: HarperCollins, 2002)

Subject(s): Runaways; Stepfamilies; Self-Reliance
Age range(s): Grades 7-10
Major character(s): Martin J. "Marty" Miller, 16-Year-Old, Runaway; Diantha Dragon, 11th Grader; Mom Miller, Mother (of Marty); Joe Wonderful, Stepfather (of Marty); Burgess, 16-Year-Old, Stepbrother
Time period(s): 2000s
Locale(s): Winnemucca, Nevada; Seattle, Washington; Red Rock, Idaho

Summary: Though his father died when he was only five, Marty and his mother have enjoyed their life in Winnemucca until the summer his mother meets Mr. Joe Wonderful. In Reno to renew her teaching certificate, she meets Mr. Wonderful who's attending the car auction and soon after, Marty and his mother have moved to Seattle. She's now Mrs. Joe Wonderful and off for a European honeymoon. Marty's stepbrother takes advantage of their absence and tosses Marty's belongings out his bedroom window, which prompts Marty to take off in his red jeep and head back to Winnemucca. Running out of money in Idaho, he stops in Red Rock, enrolls in school and finds a job cooking hamburgers.

Hiding his jeep on a back canyon road, he's befriended by all the little animals at his campsite and by Diantha Dragon, a new student who wears only black. After three months of hideout living, Marty realizes that though his heart will always be in Winnemucca, he needs to return home to his family. (129 pages)

Where it's reviewed:
Bulletin of the Center for Children's Books, July 2002, page 423
Horn Book, July 2002, page 475
Publishers Weekly, January 7, 2002, page 66
School Library Journal, June 2002, page 150
Voice of Youth Advocates, February 2002, page 442

Awards the book has won:
Center for Children's Books Best Books, 2002

Other books by the same author:
A Stranger Here, 1993
Here at the Scenic-Vu Motel, 1988
Show Me Your Rocky Mountains, 1982

Other books you might like:
Ron Koertge, *The Harmony Arms*, 1992

When Ron and his father stay at The Harmony Arms in Los Angeles, he meets so many eccentric people that his own father seems normal.

Carolyn Mackler, *The Earth, My Butt, and Other Big Round Things*, 2003

Virginia learns that you can't run away from family problems in this Printz Honor Book.

Matthew Olshan, *Finn: A Novel*, 2001

To escape her crazy mother, Finn takes off with her grandparents' pregnant maid and the two head for California in search of the baby's father.

Y

1473

DAN YACCARINO, Author/Illustrator

The Big Science Fair

(New York: Hyperion Books for Children, 2002)

Series: Blast Off Boy and Blorp
Subject(s): Space Travel; Schools; Aliens
Age range(s): Grades 2-4
Major character(s): Blorp, Alien, Student—Exchange; Blast Off Boy, Student—Exchange
Time period(s): Indeterminate
Locale(s): Earth; Meep, Planet—Imaginary

Summary: On Earth, Blorp excitedly begins planning his science project confident that he will win awards while, on Meep, Blast Off Boy, known for being a poor student of science, dreads the approaching science fair. Classmates are excitedly talking about models of molecules and homemade atom splitters while Blast Off Boy frets. Meanwhile Blorp busily proceeds with his project while his host parents notice that important household appliances such as the blender and pieces to the dryer are missing. On the day of the fair Blorp is amazed to discover that his elaborate contraption designed to open cans has already been invented and is available in a much simpler form. Desperately, Blast Off Boy grabs some beans from lunch, mixes them with soda and proceeds to his fair. Prior to the judging, his last-minute project begins to grow and Blast Off Boy wins a prize for experimentation. (34 pages)

Where it's reviewed:
Kirkus Reviews, October 1, 2002, page 1484
Publishers Weekly, September 9, 2002, page 70
School Library Journal, December 2002, page 114

Other books by the same author:
New Pet, 2001 (Blast Off Boy and Blorp)
The Lima Bean Monster, 2001
First Day on a Strange New Planet, 2000 (Blast Off Boy and Blorp)

Other books you might like:
Shana Corey, *First Graders from Mars: Episode 3: Nergal and the Great Space Race*, 2002
  Nergal, not a skilled runner, is nervous about the culminating event to Martian Health Week, the space race.
Beverly Lewis, *The Stinky Sneakers Mystery*, 1996
  After Jason sees the science fair entries planned by the other students he doubts that his project will win a prize.
Janice Lee Smith, *Serious Science: An Adam Joshua Story*, 1993
  Two days before the science fair, Adam Joshua discovers that his younger sister and his dog have eaten his science project.

1474

LAURENCE YEP

The Tiger's Apprentice

(New York: HarperCollins, 2003)

Series: Tiger's Apprentice. Book 1
Subject(s): Magic; Orphans; Chinese Americans
Age range(s): Grades 5-7
Major character(s): Tom Lee, 8th Grader, Orphan; Lee ''Grandmom'', Grandmother; Mr. Hu, Shape-Shifter
Time period(s): 2000s
Locale(s): San Francisco, California

Summary: Living with his grandmother in San Francisco, Tom arrives home one day to find a strange visitor and discovers his grandmother's other role. For years Mistress Lee has been a Guardian whose job is to protect a Phoenix egg that is disguised as a coral rose. Mr. Hu is a shape shifter who reverts to his tiger form when he and Tom flee from the apartment while his grandmother remains to fight the invading monsters. Mistress Lee is killed and Mr. Hu assumes her place as the Guardian, with Tom serving as his apprentice. Aided by a dragon, a yellow rat and a golden monkey, the two strive to keep the Phoenix egg out of evil hands in a fantasy that merges Chinese mythology with everyday life. (184 pages)

Where it's reviewed:
Booklist, July 2003, page 1893
Kirkus Reviews, March 1, 2003, page 402
Library Media Connection, November 2003, page 55
Publishers Weekly, April 14, 2003, page 71
School Library Journal, April 2003, page 170

Other books by the same author:
Sweetwater, 2004
Tiger's Blood, 2004 (Tiger's Apprentice Book 2)
Sea Glass, 2002

Other books you might like:
Susan Cooper, *The Dark Is Rising*, 1973
    As evil begins to overtake the world, one English boy has the power to stop it.
Eva Ibbotson, *Not Just a Witch*, 2003
    Heckie's ability to transform evil persons into animals catches the eye of a con artist furrier who has nefarious plans for her talent.
Tamora Pierce, *Wolf-Speaker*, 1994
    Daine leaves mage training and finds her ability to read minds and shape-change will help her save her valley from destruction.

1475

LAURENCE YEP

The Traitor: Golden Mountain Chronicles: 1885

(New York: HarperCollins, 2003)

Series: Golden Mountain Chronicles
Subject(s): Prejudice; Chinese Americans; Miners and Mining
Age range(s): Grades 6-9
Major character(s): Joseph Young, 12-Year-Old; Michael Purdy, Bastard Son, 12-Year-Old
Time period(s): 1880s
Locale(s): Rock Springs, Wyoming (Wyoming Territory)

Summary: Considered outcasts by their community, two young boys meet in a fossil-rich cave and become friends while the adults of their world view one another with suspicion, hatred and fear of losing their jobs. Michael is the illegitimate son of the local laundrywoman and is teased and taunted by the other boys. Though Joseph feels more American than Chinese, he works alongside his father Otter in the coalmines of the Wyoming Territory and is interested in fossils. Hounded one day by bullies, Michael seeks shelter in the cave where Joseph is searching for fossils and the two boys discover a mutual interest in fossils that sparks their friendship. It's their friendship that helps them survive the horrible massacre of the Chinese miners by the Western miners. (310 pages)

Where it's reviewed:
Booklist, January 2003, page 894
Bulletin of the Center for Children's Books, March 2003, page 295
Horn Book, March 2003, page 219
School Library Journal, March 2003, page 244
Voice of Youth Advocates, October 2003, page 320

Awards the book has won:
Notable Social Studies Trade Books for Young People, 2004

Other books by the same author:
Thief of Hearts, 1995 (Golden Mountain Chronicles)
Dragon's Gate, 1993 (Golden Mountain Chronicles)
Mountain Light, 1985 (Golden Mountain Chronicles)
Serpent's Children, 1984 (Golden Mountain Chronicles)
Sea Glass, 1979 (Golden Mountain Chronicles)
Child of the Owl, 1977 (Golden Mountain Chronicles)
Dragonwings, 1975 (Golden Mountain Chronicles)

Other books you might like:
Ann R. Blakeslee, *A Different Kind of Hero*, 1997
    Concerned that the Chinese will take away mining jobs, his father wants to run them out of camp, but Renny stands up for his Chinese friend's family.
Mary Casanova, *Riot*, 1996
    Bryan is relieved when his father admits he was wrong to set fire to homes of non-union workers who replaced him at the paper mill.
Paul Yee, *Tales from Gold Mountain: Stories of the Chinese in the New World*, 1990
    Eight original stories that reflect the lives of Chinese immigrants who often left wealthy backgrounds only to be menial laborers in America.

1476

LAURENCE YEP
SULING WANG, Illustrator

When the Circus Came to Town

(New York: HarperCollins Publishers, 2002)

Subject(s): Self-Esteem; Frontier and Pioneer Life; Circus
Age range(s): Grades 3-5
Major character(s): Ursula, 10-Year-Old, Daughter; Ah Sam, Cook, Immigrant
Time period(s): 20th century (early)
Locale(s): Whistle, Montana

Summary: Imaginative Ursula leads the children in her small town in imaginative games, casting herself as ''Pirate Ursula,'' until she contracts smallpox. At first she is too sick to play but when her health returns she is so embarrassed by her appearance that she refuses to leave her room or see any of her friends. During her illness, her parents hired Ah Sam to assist with the chores of the stagecoach station and it is Ah Sam who gradually draws Ursula out of her self-pity and seclusion. Secretly, he arranges for his friends, a traveling troupe of performers, to come to town and present their circus acts. After they perform, a blizzard stops all stage travel, keeping the troupe from reaching San Francisco for the Chinese New Year celebration. Grateful Ursula enlists the townspeople's help to make a dragon and stage a New Year's celebration for the stranded Chinese immigrants. An ''Afterword'' identifies the historical incident on which the story is based. (115 pages)

Where it's reviewed:
Booklist, December 15, 2001, page 732
Bulletin of the Center for Children's Books, February 2002, page 225

Horn Book Guide, Fall 2001, page 366
Publishers Weekly, December 24, 2001, page 64
School Library Journal, December 2001, page 149

Other books by the same author:
Angelfish, 2001
Cockroach Cooties, 2000
The Cook's Family, 1998

Other books you might like:
Polly Horvath, *When the Circus Came to Town*, 1996
    A family of former circus performers that moves in next door provides a diversion to their bored neighbor, Ivy, as she recovers from double pneumonia.
Jane Kurtz, *I'm Sorry, Almira Ann*, 1999
    Tedium of a journey on the Oregon Trail rather than illness tests Sarah's patience and threatens her friendship with Almira Ann.
Margaret Mahy, *The Greatest Show Off Earth*, 1994
    Delphinium initiates some action that relieves the monotony of life at Space Station Vulnik.

1477

THOMAS F. YEZERSKI, Author/Illustrator

A Full Hand

(New York: Farrar Straus Giroux, 2002)

Subject(s): Canals; Transportation; Historical
Age range(s): Grades 1-3
Major character(s): Asa, 9-Year-Old, Son; Captain, Father
Time period(s): 19th century
Locale(s): Morris Canal, New Jersey

Summary: Unexpectedly Asa is called on to assist his father when Captain's mule driver quits. Early one morning they begin the journey with an empty canal boat, Captain at the tiller and Asa walking the towpath with the mules. After getting the two-sectioned boat loaded with coal they continue on the Morris Canal through locks, over an aqueduct, and up an inclined plane. When a lightning storm blows up suddenly Asa is unable to control the mules, but he does rescue his father from the canal after Captain's efforts to assist Asa put him in the way of a kicking mule. When the storm subsides it's obvious that the boat needs repair and the mules have run off but Asa and Captain are safe and able to deal with those problems after a good night's sleep. The author's "Foreword" gives background information that inspired the story. (32 pages)

Where it's reviewed:
Booklist, January 2003, page 911
Bulletin of the Center for Children's Books, December 2002, page 178
Kirkus Reviews, July 15, 2002, page 1048
Publishers Weekly, September 16, 2002, page 71
School Library Journal, September 2002, page 209

Awards the book has won:
Notable Social Studies Trade Books for Young People, 2003

Other books by the same author:
Queen of the World, 2000
Together in Pinecone Patch, 1999 (Riverbank Review Children's Books of Distinction)

Other books you might like:
Candace Christiansen, *The Ice Horse*, 1993
    Proudly, young Jack helps his uncle harvest the blocks of ice from the frozen Hudson River.
Peter Spier, *The Erie Canal*, 1970
    With the words of a folk song as text, Spier illustrates a mid-1850s journey on the Erie Canal from Albany to Buffalo.
Ian Wallace, *Boy of the Deeps*, 1999
    James is proud that he's old enough to begin working underground with his father, an experienced coal miner.

1478

JANE YOLEN

The Bagpiper's Ghost

(San Diego: Harcourt, 2002)

Series: Tartan Magic. Book 3
Subject(s): Ghosts; Magic; Twins
Age range(s): Grades 4-7
Major character(s): Jennifer, Twin; Peter, Twin; Mary MacFadden, Spirit, Twin; Ewan McGregory, Spirit; Andrew MacFadden, Spirit, Twin; Gran, Cousin (of Peter and Jennifer)
Time period(s): 2000s
Locale(s): Scotland

Summary: Continuing on their Scottish vacation, Peter and Jennifer meet the ghost of Mary MacFadden in a cemetery. This "Lady in White" longs to be reunited with the ghost of her lover Ewan, killed centuries ago at the famous battle at Culloden. Ewan stands outside the cemetery gates piping on his bagpipe, kept apart in death just as he was kept apart in life by Mary's vengeful twin brother Andrew. Peter becomes possessed by Andrew's ghost and Jennifer and her Gran know they have only 24 hours to free Peter from Andrew's grasp, or they'll lose him forever, in this third volume of the *Tartan Magic* series. (129 pages)

Where it's reviewed:
Booklist, April 15, 2002, page 1418
Horn Book Guide, Fall 2002, page 386
Kirkus Reviews, March 1, 2002, page 349
School Library Journal, March 2002, page 240
Voice of Youth Advocates, June 2002, page 133

Other books by the same author:
Sword of the Rightful King: A Novel of King Arthur, 2003
Boots and the Seven Leaguers: A Rock-and-Troll Novel, 2000
Sister Emily's Lightship and Other Stories, 2000
The Pictish Child, 1999 (Tartan Magic Book 2)
The Wizard's Map, 1999 (Tartan Magic Book 1)
Child of Faerie, Child of Earth, 1997

Other books you might like:
James M. Deem, *The Very Real Ghost Book of Christina Rose*, 1996
    Christina and Danny's father moves them cross country to escape memories of their mother's death, not realizing that he's bought a haunted house.
Eileen Dunlop, *The Ghost by the Sea*, 1996
    Two cousins try to solve the mysterious drowning of an

ancestor so Milly's spirit can finally rest and quit haunting their grandparent's home

Michael Hague, *Kate Culhane: A Ghost Story*, 2001
  Accidentally stepping on the dirt of a newly covered grave, Kate is trapped and compelled to do the bidding of the grave's occupant.

Vivian Vande Velde, *There's a Dead Person Following My Sister Around*, 1999
  A ghost seeking to return to life takes over Vicki's body and Ted has to figure out how to evict the ghost so his sister can return.

1479

JANE YOLEN
VLADIMIR VAGIN, Illustrator

The Firebird
(New York: HarperCollins Publishers, 2002)

Subject(s): Folk Tales; Ballet; Princes and Princesses
Age range(s): Grades K-3
Major character(s): Kotschei the Deathless, Wizard; Ivan, Royalty (prince); Firebird, Mythical Creature
Time period(s): Indeterminate Past
Locale(s): Russia

Summary: Kotschei the Deathless keeps a princess and her nine maidens trapped in his beautiful garden. Whenever princes try to rescue them, Kotschei turns the princes to stone. One day, lost near the garden while hunting, Prince Ivan captures the Firebird. In exchange for its freedom the Firebird leaves the prince with a magical feather and a wish. While battling Kotschei and his demons, Prince Ivan turns to the Firebird for help and receives a magic sword. Prince Ivan is able to kill the evil wizard and marry the princess. Vagin's illustrations show the story's two traditions: the classic Russian folktale and the Balanchine-Stravinsky ballet. (32 pages)

Where it's reviewed:
Booklist, June 2002, page 1732
Bulletin of the Center for Children's Books, July/August 2002, page 42
Horn Book Guide, Fall 2002, page 413
Publishers Weekly, April 29, 2002, page 68
School Library Journal, June 2002, page 127

Other books by the same author:
How Do Dinosaurs Say Good Night?, 2000
The Devil's Arithmetic, 1998
Owl Moon, 1987 (Caldecott Medal)

Other books you might like:
Demi, *The Firebird*, 1994
  In one of many retellings of a classic Russian tale, Dimitri searches for the beautiful but elusive firebird.
J. Patrick Lewis, *The Frog Princess: A Russian Folktale*, 1994
  Prince Ivan is forced to marry a frog, but the frog turns out to be Vasilisa the Wise, under a curse from her evil father.
Loriot, *Peter and the Wolf: A Musical Fairy Tale by Sergei Prokofiev*, 1986
  Peter ignores his father's warning and captures a wolf. Illustrations of the orchestra accompany the story's scenes.

Alison Lurie, *Black Geese: A Baba Yaga Story from Russia*, 1999
  When Elena discovers her baby brother is missing, she knows she must rescue him from Baba Yaga.
Aaron Shepard, *The Sea King's Daughter: A Russian Legend*, 1997
  The story of a poor musician whose luck changes after he plays at the Sea King's palace.

1480

JANE YOLEN, Co-Author
ROBERT J. HARRIS, Co-Author

Girl in a Cage
(New York: Philomel Books/Penguin Putnam, 2002)

Subject(s): Princes and Princesses; Kidnapping
Age range(s): Grades 6-10
Major character(s): Marjorie Bruce, Royalty (princess), Historical Figure; Robert Bruce, Royalty (king of Scotland), Historical Figure; Edward "Longshanks" I, Royalty (king of England), Historical Figure; William "Braveheart" Wallace, Historical Figure, Patriot
Time period(s): 14th century (1306)
Locale(s): Scotland; Lanercost, England

Summary: Thrilling though it is to see her father be crowned King of Scotland, and herself be called a princess, Marjorie learns only too quickly how a real princess must act. A year after the Scottish patriot Braveheart is executed, Robert the Bruce is crowned Scotland's king, an act that King Edward I of England challenges. The Bruce family is forced to run, continually hiding from Edward's armies as the English invade Scotland while also trying to rally supporters. Marjorie is captured by Edward's men and taken to England where she is caged and hung in a public square for twenty days, subject to the taunts of townspeople, the vagaries of the weather and the scorn of Longshanks who visits her daily. Quickly losing her spoiled behavior, Marjorie determines to remain loyal to her father and act as she thinks a princess must act, with regal spirit and pride, a behavior she masters as she returns the taunts of Longshanks in this work based on historical fact. (234 pages)

Where it's reviewed:
Booklist, September 15, 2002, page 233
Bulletin of the Center for Children's Books, February 2003, page 255
Horn Book, January 2003, page 86
School Library Journal, October 2002, page 178
Voice of Youth Advocates, October 2002, page 288

Awards the book has won:
School Library Journal Best Books, 2002
ALA Best Books for Young Adults, 2003

Other books by the same author:
Atalanta and the Arcadian Beast, 2003
Hippolyta and the Curse of the Amazons, 2002
Odysseus in the Serpent Maze, 2001
Queen's Own Fool: A Novel of Mary Queen of Scots, 2000

Other books you might like:

Khephra Burns, *Mansa Musa: The Lion of Mali*, 2001
In 14th-century Africa, Tariq rescues the future king of Mali from slave traders and spends the next seven years teaching him survival skills.

Karen Cushman, *Matilda Bone*, 2000
Orphan Matilda is deposited on Blood and Bone Alley to help Red Peg, but has difficulty adjusting and prays to every saint she knows to save her.

Deborah Lisson, *Red Hugh*, 1998
Elizabeth I of England captures Red Hugh, plus other Irish noblemen, to prevent Ireland from allying itself with England's enemy Spain.

John Morressy, *The Juggler*, 1996
Leaving behind his life as a peasant, Beran makes a pact with a stranger to be the best juggler in the world, not caring what he must give up in return.

1481

JANE YOLEN
GREG SHED, Illustrator

Harvest Home
(San Diego: Silver Whistle/Harcourt, Inc., 2002)

Subject(s): Farm Life; Stories in Rhyme; Rural Life
Age range(s): Grades 1-4
Major character(s): Bess, Child, Sister
Time period(s): 19th century
Locale(s): United States

Summary: Bess narrates the story of her family's wheat harvest. Brothers, sisters, parents, grandparents and neighbors all work hard to bring in the golden wheat. Although the work is difficult and the weather is very hot, the family manages to finish the harvest. With the last stalk of wheat, Bess's mother makes her a harvest doll and then family and friends celebrate with food and music. A note about harvest dolls follows the text. (32 pages)

Where it's reviewed:
Booklist, October 15, 2002, page 413
Kirkus Reviews, August 15, 2002, page 1240
School Library Journal, November 2002, page 140

Other books by the same author:
The Flying Witch, 2003
The Firebird, 2002
Raising Yoder's Barn, 1998

Other books you might like:
Jessie Haas, *Hurry!*, 2000
Nora and her Grandpa hurry to harvest all the hay before a big storm comes.

Ann Purmell, *Apple Cider-Making Days*, 2002
When it's harvest time on Grandpa's farm, Alex and Abigail help the family pick apples and make cider.

Michele Benoit Slawson, *Apple Picking Time*, 1994
Apples are ready for harvesting and Anna is determined to pick a whole bin by herself this year.

1482

JANE YOLEN, Co-Author
ROBERT J. HARRIS, Co-Author

Hippolyta and the Curse of the Amazons
(New York: HarperCollins, 2002)

Subject(s): Mythology; Adventure and Adventurers
Age range(s): Grades 5-8
Major character(s): Hippolyta, 13-Year-Old; Laomedon of Troy, Royalty (king); Otrere of Amazon, Royalty (queen), Mother (of Hippolyta and Tithonus); Tithonus, Child, Brother (half-brother of Hippolyta)
Time period(s): Indeterminate Past
Locale(s): Greece

Summary: When Amazon Queen Otrere has a second son, she defies tradition and refuses to sacrifice him. Jailed, she sends her daughter Hippolyta with her son to his father, King Laomedon of Troy, hoping to save the baby. Hippolyta offends King Laomedon and finds herself tied to a post as bait for a sea monster until her half-brother Tithonus rescues her, after which Hippolyta and Tithonus return to the Amazon capital where they discover a curse has been laid on the Amazons and the only way to remove the curse is to travel to the ancient city of Arimaspa. The two youngsters travel once more and upon reaching Arimaspa, Hippolyta must decide whether or not to sacrifice Tithonus, as commanded by the goddess Athena, in this second of the *Young Heroes* series. (248 pages)

Where it's reviewed:
Bulletin of the Center for Children's Books, April 2002, page 300
Horn Book Guide, Fall 2002, page 386
Kirkus Reviews, January 1, 2002, page 54
Publishers Weekly, April 1, 2002, page 85
School Library Journal, March 2002, page 240

Other books by the same author:
Jason and the Gorgon's Blood, 2004 (Young Heroes series)
Atalanta and the Arcadian Beast, 2003 (Young Heroes series)
Odysseus in the Serpent Maze, 2001 (Young Heroes series)

Other books you might like:
Vivien Alcock, *Singer to the Sea God*, 1993
Perseus needs a way to kill the dreadful Gorgon, a creature with snakes for hair.

Priscilla Galloway, *Snake Dreamer*, 1998
Claiming to cure people who suffer from dreams of snakes, two sisters are actually Gorgons searching for Medusa.

Brian Keaney, *No Need for Heroes*, 1989
Daughter of King Minos, Ariadne tells her version of the Minotaur myth, starting with the arrival of Daedalus and Icarus on her island.

Donna Jo Napoli, *Sirena*, 1998
The mermaid Sirena falls in love with a wounded sailor, but her wish to be mortal isn't granted.

1483

JANE YOLEN
KAREN LEE SCHMIDT, Illustrator

Hoptoad

(San Diego: Silver Whistle/Harcourt, Inc., 2003)

Subject(s): Animals/Frogs and Toads; Automobiles; Stories in Rhyme
Age range(s): Preschool-Kindergarten
Major character(s): Unnamed Character, Toad
Time period(s): 2000s (2003)
Locale(s): United States

Summary: In the desert Southwest, a toad attempts to cross a highway. A middle-of-the-road rest stop almost leads to disaster when a truck comes barreling down the road. Fortunately, the driver sees the toad and is able to stop the truck. Father and son emerge and are relieved to find the toad alive and well under the vehicle. (32 pages)

Where it's reviewed:
Booklist, May 15, 2003, page 1674
School Library Journal, June 2003, page 122

Other books by the same author:
The Flying Witch, 2003
The Devil's Arithmetic, 1988
Owl Moon, 1987 (Caldecott Medal winner)

Other books you might like:
Barbara Shook Hazen, *That Toad Is Mine!*, 1998
  Two young friends who find a toad fight for so long about who will get it that the toad hops away.
Robert Kalan, *Jump, Frog, Jump!*, 1981
  In this cumulative tale, a frog tries to catch a fly, but ends up having to escape becoming dinner himself.
George Shannon, *Frog Legs: A Picture Book of Action Verse*, 2000
  In a series of 24 poems, frogs do all sorts of activities.

1484

JANE YOLEN
MARK TEAGUE, Illustrator

How Do Dinosaurs Get Well Soon?

(New York: Blue Sky Press/Scholastic, Inc., 2003)

Subject(s): Dinosaurs; Illness; Imagination
Age range(s): Preschool-Grade 1
Time period(s): Indeterminate
Locale(s): Fictional Country

Summary: Imagine what would happen if a dinosaur became sick at school and had to leave. Would a dinosaur leave used tissues on the floor, refuse to take his medication or whine all the time? Of course not, a dinosaur would go cooperatively to the doctor and follow instructions. He'd cover his mouth when he sneezes and quietly snuggle into bed after taking his medicine. Then the sick little dinosaur would go to sleep so he could get well soon. (36 pages)

Where it's reviewed:
Booklist, January 2003, page 881

Bulletin of the Center for Children's Books, April 2003, page 338
Five Owls, 2003, page 39
Horn Book, March 2003, page 208
Publishers Weekly, December 23, 2002, page 68

Other books by the same author:
How Do Dinosaurs Clean Their Rooms?, 2004
How Do Dinosaurs Count to Ten?, 2004
Felix Feels Better, 2001 (Bulletin of the Center for Children's Books Blue Ribbon)
How Do Dinosaurs Say Good Night?, 2000 (Booklist Editors' Choice)

Other books you might like:
Patricia MacLachlan, *The Sick Day*, 2001
  In a reissue of a 1979 title Emily is initially alarmed to hear Father say she has a "bug" when she tells him how poorly she's feeling.
Claire Masurel, *Too Big*, 1999
  His parents don't agree but Charlie knows his large toy dinosaur is just the right size to comfort him on a trip to the doctor's office.
Shirley Neitzel, *I'm Not Feeling Well Today*, 2001
  A child, who announces upon awakening to feeling ill, suddenly becomes better upon learning that school is closed due to snow.

1485

JANE YOLEN
RAUL COLON, Illustrator

Mightier than the Sword: World Folktales for Strong Boys

(San Diego: Silver Whistle/Harcourt, Inc., 2003)

Subject(s): Folk Tales; Courage; Heroes and Heroines
Age range(s): Grades 3-6
Time period(s): Indeterminate Past
Locale(s): Earth

Summary: In this collection of 14 folktales from around the world, boys save the day with their brains rather than their brawn. In the Israeli folktale "And Who Cured the Princess?" three brothers work together to save a princess who has fallen ill. In "The Magic Brocade" from China, the youngest son of a weaver must rescue his mother's favorite brocade after it blows away. Yolen includes thorough notes on the origin and variations of each story. (112 pages)

Where it's reviewed:
Booklist, April 1, 2003, page 1394
Bulletin of the Center for Children's Books, July 2003, page 466
Horn Book, May 2003, page 362
Publishers Weekly, April 14, 2003, page 72
School Library Journal, May 2003, page 143

Other books by the same author:
Not One Damsel in Distress: World Folktales for Strong Girls, 2000 (Notable Social Studies Trade Books for Young People)
Merlin and the Dragons, 1995
Owl Moon, 1987 (Caldecott Medal winner)

Other books you might like:

Joanna Cole, *Best-Loved Folktales of the World*, 1982
This collection contains over 200 folk and fairy tales from around the world.

Heather Forest, *Wisdom Tales from around the World*, 1996
This collection of brief parables, proverbs and folktales imparts lessons for living.

Nina Jaffe, *The Cow of No Color: Riddle Stories and Justice Tales from World Traditions*, 1998
This collection of folktales from around the world focuses on the theme of justice. Co-written with Steve Zeitlin.

1486

JANE YOLEN

Sword of the Rightful King: A Novel of King Arthur
(San Diego: Harcourt, 2003)

Subject(s): Arthurian Legends; Magic
Age range(s): Grades 6-10
Major character(s): Arthur, Royalty (king); Merlinnus, Wizard; Gawaine, Knight, Son; Morgause, Mother, Wizard; Gawen, Servant
Time period(s): Indeterminate Past
Locale(s): England

Summary: The mage Merlinnus plots to secure Arthur's kingdom with a magical display that will convince all disbelievers of Arthur's right to the throne. At the same time, Morgause, the Witch of the North, plans the black magic that will place one of her sons on the throne instead. While he is arranging the magical sword in the stone, Merlinnus meets a mysterious boy, Gawen, who quickly becomes his helper. Merlinnus is troubled by the boy's secrecy, but delighted by his cleverness and aptitude. Gawen is not only indispensable to Merlinnus, he quickly becomes a favorite of the king as well. In fact, Gawen gets along with everyone except the knight Gawaine, Morgause's son, for whom he seems to have an aversion. When Morgause appears for the midsummer celebration at which the sword-pulling ceremony is to be the climax, uncovering Gawen's secrets suddenly becomes critical. (350 pages)

Where it's reviewed:
Booklist, April 15, 2003, page 1464
Horn Book, May 2003, page 359
Publishers Weekly, April 14, 2003, page 72
School Library Journal, July 2003, page 135
Voice of Youth Advocates, June 2003, page 154

Awards the book has won:
Booklist Editors' Choice/Books for Youth, 2003
ALA Best Books for Young Adults, 2004

Other books by the same author:
Merlin, 1997
Hobby, 1996
Passenger, 1996

Other books you might like:
N.M. Browne, *Warriors of Camlann*, 2003
Two time travelers meet a king they suspect is Arthur and are surprised to find they don't like him very much.

Kevin Crossley-Holland, *At the Crossing Places*, 2002
A young man about to go off to the Crusades has a magical stone that shows him glimpses of King Arthur's life.

T.H. White, *The Once and Future King*, 1958
The first part of White's classic retelling of the Arthurian legend ends with Wart pulling the sword from the stone.

1487

CATHY YOUNG, Editor

One Hot Second: Stories about Desire
(New York: Knopf/Random House, 2002)

Subject(s): Short Stories; Love; Teen Relationships
Age range(s): Grades 9-12
Time period(s): 2000s
Locale(s): United States

Summary: Desire comes in all shapes and sizes and promises different experiences for different people, as evidenced in this collection that embraces first kisses, first love and first relationships. For Rachel Vail's heroine, that first highly anticipated and eagerly awaited kiss becomes nothing but concern over germs in "One Hot Second." In Angela Johnson's "A Kind of Music," a first experience filled with love becomes one that will always contain good memories. Though Sarah Dessen's main character in "Someone Bold" loses 45 pounds, she doesn't yet feel that she's desirable, but then maybe something's wrong with her boyfriend. Krystal deals with a drunken mother and an abusive grandmother until she meets a fellow shoplifter and realizes that he might be interested in her in "Who Hears the Fish Cry" by Norma Fox Mazer. Other authors included in this anthology include Jennifer Armstrong, Victor Martinez, Nancy Garden, Rich Wallace, Ellen Wittlinger and Emma Donoghue. (218 pages)

Where it's reviewed:
Booklist, June 2002, page 1708
Library Media Connection, January 2003, page 91
Publishers Weekly, June 10, 2002, page 61
School Library Journal, June 2002, page 150
Voice of Youth Advocates, June 2002, page 122

Other books you might like:
Francesca Lia Block, *Girl Goddess #9: Nine Stories*, 1996
Stories that range from the deliciously different and funky to the whimsical and haunting fill the pages of this work.

Rick Book, *Necking with Louise*, 1999
From his first date with Louise to his love for his grandfather and his final ice hockey game of the season, 1965 is a turning point in Eric's life.

Michael Cart, *Love and Sex: Ten Stories of Truth*, 2001
"All ranges of the interrelationships of love and sex," including virginity, lesbianism and infatuation, are found in this collection of short stories.

1488

ED YOUNG, Author/Illustrator

What About Me?

(New York: Philomel Books, 2002)

Subject(s): Folklore; Sufism; Folk Tales
Age range(s): Grades 2-4
Major character(s): Unnamed Character, Child; Grand Master, Aged Person
Time period(s): Indeterminate Past
Locale(s): Middle East

Summary: In this retelling of a Sufi tale, a young boy desiring knowledge seeks it from the Grand Master, confident that the wise man has enough knowledge to share. The Grand Master sends the boy on a quest for a small carpet that he needs in order to do his work. The boy hastens to acquire a carpet but the artisan also has needs for the boy to fulfill. Each errand leads to another and soon the boy wonders if he'll ever achieve his original goal of acquiring a carpet for the Grand Master. The cumulative tale leads the boy far from his original goal and then brings him back to the Grand Master, carpet in hand, wondering if the knowledge he seeks awaits him. (32 pages)

Where it's reviewed:
Booklist, May 1, 2002, page 1521
Bulletin of the Center for Children's Books, July 2002, page 424
Horn Book, July 2002, page 477
Publishers Weekly, April 22, 2002, page 69
School Library Journal, June 2002, page 127

Other books by the same author:
Monkey King, 2001 (Notable Social Studies Trade Books for Young People)
The Lost Horse: A Chinese Folktale, 1998
Mouse Match: A Chinese Folktale, 1997 (Booklist Editors' Choice)

Other books you might like:
Eric A. Kimmel, *The Old Woman and Her Pig*, 1992
　　When an old woman's pig refuses to go over the stile, the woman calls for help in a lively retelling of a traditional cumulative tale.
Lauren Thompson, *One Riddle, One Answer*, 2001
　　Aziza, daughter of a Persian sultan, devises a riddle to test suitors, agreeing to marry only the man who answers it correctly.
Ellen Stoll Walsh, *Pip's Magic*, 1994
　　As Pip seeks a wizard's magic to overcome his fear of the dark he unwittingly solves his problem as he searches.

1489

KAREN ROMANO YOUNG

Outside In

(New York: Greenwillow, 2002)

Subject(s): Coming-of-Age; Friendship; Family Life
Age range(s): Grades 6-9

Major character(s): Cherie Witkowski, 13-Year-Old, Newspaper Carrier; Dave Asconti, 13-Year-Old
Time period(s): 1960s (1968)
Locale(s): Bridgefield, Connecticut

Summary: Her newly won paper route is fast becoming a downer as Cherie folds the papers and can't miss seeing the headlines listing the casualties from the Vietnam War, the hunger in Biafra, and then the assassinations of Martin Luther King, Jr. and Robert F. Kennedy. In a nearby town a girl her own age is missing and later found dead, adding to the worries confronting Cherie. 1968 is becoming a very bad year for Cherie as her mother's pregnancy means they may have to sell their home; her best friend relationship with her neighbor Dave may be moving beyond its comfortable status into a more romantic one; and arguments in neighbors' homes sometimes result in divorces and more change. Though spunky and always able to laugh, Cherie finds all the changes in her young world just a little overwhelming in this coming-of-age novel. (201 pages)

Where it's reviewed:
Booklist, April 1, 2002, page 1320
Bulletin of the Center for Children's Books, September 2002, page 37
Publishers Weekly, May 13, 2002, page 71
School Library Journal, May 2002, page 164
Voice of Youth Advocates, October 2002, page 288

Other books by the same author:
Cobwebs from the Sky, 2002
The Beetle and Me: A Love Story, 1999
Video, 1999

Other books you might like:
Kristine L. Franklin, *Dove Song*, 1999
　　Bobbie Lynn's father is sent to Vietnam and her mother has a nervous breakdown, leaving Bobbie Lynn and her brother to scrounge for themselves.
Linda Oatman High, *The Summer of the Great Divide*, 1996
　　Wheezie runs away to try to halt her parent's divorce and to escape the grief over her uncle's death in Vietnam.
Patrice Kindl, *The Woman in the Wall*, 1997
　　Terrified to attend school, Anna builds a room for herself in her family's large, rambling house and remains hidden for seven years.
Natalie Kinsey-Warnock, *In the Language of Loons*, 1998
　　A terrible school year, a pregnant mother and a bully always waiting for her make Arlis's summer spent with her grandfather especially wonderful.

1490

KAZUMI YUMOTO
CATHY HIRANO, Translator

The Letters

(New York: Farrar Straus Giroux, 2002)

Subject(s): Grief; Death; Old Age
Age range(s): Grades 7-10
Major character(s): Chiaki Hoshino, Child; Mrs. Yanagi, Landlord
Time period(s): 1980s

Locale(s): Japan

Summary: After the sudden death of Chiaki's father, she and her mother move to an apartment in Poplar House where Mrs. Yanagi reigns as the landlady. To young Chiaki, unnerved by her father's death, everything outside her home is suddenly scary and she remains inside resting. Since her mother works, she's under the care of Mrs. Yanagi who offers a clever plan to ease Chiaki's grief and worries. Mrs. Yanagi explains that she's been entrusted with carrying letters to the deceased and that when she dies, all the letters she keeps in a special drawer will go with her to heaven where she'll distribute them. Chiaki writes one letter, and then another, and then more and more until she's eased the grief from her heart. Years later, after losing a lover and miscarrying, she hears of Mrs. Yanagi's death and returns to her former home in Poplar House to attend the funeral. There Chiaki meets many other friends of Mrs. Yanagi who have also filled the special drawer with letters to their deceased loved ones; that simple knowledge gives Chiaki the strength to once again go forward with her life instead of ruing her recent losses. (165 pages)

Where it's reviewed:

Booklist, April 1, 2002, page 1320
Bulletin of the Center for Children's Books, July 2002, page 424

Horn Book, September 2002, page 585
School Library Journal, May 2002, page 164
Voice of Youth Advocates, October 2002, page 290

Other books by the same author:

The Spring Tone, 1999
The Friends, 1996

Other books you might like:

Emily Rhoads Johnson, *Write Me If You Dare!*, 2000
   Receiving word that her aged pen pal Pearl is dying, Maddie's grandfather drives her to be with Pearl for the last few hours of her life.

E. Cody Kimmel, *Visiting Miss Caples*, 2000
   Jenna discovers her elderly friend Miss Caples had the same problem she has: a manipulative friend who is unkind to others.

Margaret Mahy, *Memory*, 1988
   Young Jonny and aged Sophie are two people with confused memories who help each other survive.

Ben Mikaelsen, *Petey*, 1998
   Lonely teenager Trevor and cerebral palsy patient Petey form an unlikely bond with each growing and learning from the other.

Z

Manta's Gift

(New York: Tor, 2002)

Subject(s): Science Fiction; Aliens; Coming-of-Age
Age range(s): Grades 9-Adult
Major character(s): Matthew ''Manta'' Raimey, Handicapped (quadriplegic); Drusni, Alien; Pranlo, Alien
Time period(s): Indeterminate Future
Locale(s): Jupiter

Summary: Exploration of Jupiter reveals an intelligent alien race swimming through the gas seas of the giant planet. Humans make contact only to discover how difficult true communication is. A solution is proposed by the Qanska, who will provide the brain-injured body of one of their own species and assist in helping a paralyzed human migrate to it. Young quadriplegic Matthew Raimey is enlisted. Matt was recently injured and is not only full of grief for his lost future but also angry at the blow fate has dealt him. When he joins the Qanska, he is full of turbulent human emotions that make it difficult for him to fit in. Matt also alienates the humans who are counting on him to provide the crucial link to communicate with and understand the Qanska. Despite himself, Matt becomes friendly with two of the young Qanska, Drusni, a female and Pranlo, a young male like Matt himself. Slowly he begins to think like a Qanska and become the being called Manta. But some of the humans in Manta's past want something from the Qanska, and they count on Manta to help them get it. Does he remember enough of human thinking to help protect the Qanska? (427 pages)

Where it's reviewed:
Analog Science Fiction and Fact, April 2003, page 135
Booklist, November 1, 2002, page 481
Kirkus Reviews, October 1, 2002, page 1435
Library Journal, December 2002, page 184
New York Times Book Review, March 2, 2003, page 19

Other books by the same author:
Survivor's Quest, 2004

Dragon and Thief: A Dragonback Adventure, 2003
Angelmass, 2001

Other books you might like:
Lois McMaster Bujold, *Falling Free*, 1988
    Born in the free fall of space, the four-armed Quaddies have never missed having legs.
Nancy Kress, *Nothing Human*, 2003
    Genetic manipulation of several generations of teens may leave little that can be called human in the resulting offspring.
Ian Stewart, *Wheelers*, 2000
    The alien Jovians look like little gears, but have technologies humans have only dreamed of.

Bringing Up the Bones

(New York: Delacorte, 2002)

Subject(s): Grief; Depression; Interpersonal Relations
Age range(s): Grades 9-12
Major character(s): Bridget Edelstein, 18-Year-Old, Waiter/Waitress; Benjamin ''Benji'' Gilbert, 18-Year-Old (deceased); Jasper Douglas, Student—College
Time period(s): 2000s
Locale(s): New Castle, Delaware

Summary: In this author's first novel, Bridget doesn't know how she'll get along in life without her best friend and recent, though reluctant, boyfriend Benji, who died in a car accident just after he'd written a letter expressing his wish to break up with her. Dropping out of college to try to get herself back on track, Bridget works as a waitress at a truckstop in addition to receiving therapy thanks to the generosity of her stepfather. She's been unhappy since her parents divorced when she was young, has almost no relationship with her mother and doesn't know where her father is. For seven years Benji's been her best friend and life without him overwhelms her. Her brief fling with Jasper forces her to rethink who she is and what she wants her life to be, rather than doing what everyone else expects of her. (213 pages)

Where it's reviewed:
Booklist, November 15, 2002, page 596
Bulletin of the Center for Children's Books, January 2003, page 215
Publishers Weekly, October 7, 2002, page 74
School Library Journal, November 2002, page 178
Voice of Youth Advocates, December 2002, page 393

Other books by the same author:
Contents under Pressure, 2004

Other books you might like:
Julie Reece Deaver, *Say Goodnight, Gracie*, 1988
    Morgan's life comes to an abrupt halt when her dear friend Jimmy is killed in an automobile accident.
Heather Henson, *Making the Run*, 2002
    Living in a small town makes Lu ache to escape, but a terrible automobile wreck causes her to realize how short life really is.
Chris Lynch, *Freewill*, 2001
    Grieving over the deaths of his father and stepmother, Will is numb to everything until he builds his own memorial to his dad.

1493

KAETHE ZEMACH, Author/Illustrator

Just Enough and Not Too Much
(New York: Arthur A. Levine/Scholastic, Inc., 2003)

Subject(s): Possessions; Greed; Music and Musicians
Age range(s): Grades K-2
Major character(s): Simon, Musician
Time period(s): 2000s (2003)
Locale(s): United States

Summary: Simon lives in a perfect little house with everything he needs, until the day he decides that he needs more—more chairs, more hats, and more toys. He acquires more and more possessions until his house is so crowded that he can hardly move. Longing for the simple life, Simon throws a party and, as his friends leave, he sends each home with a chair, a hat and a stuffed animal. (32 pages)

Where it's reviewed:
Booklist, November 1, 2003
Publishers Weekly, October 2003, page 59
School Library Journal, October 10, 2003, page 143

Other books by the same author:
The Question Song, 2003
The Character in the Book, 1998
The Funny Dream, 1988

Other books you might like:
Stan Berenstain, *The Berenstain Bears Get the Gimmies*, 1988
    Granny and Gramps figure out a solution to their grandchildren's case of the gimmies. Jan Berenstain, co-author.
Beatrice Schenk de Regniers, *Was It a Good Trade?*, 2002
    In this story, based on a folksong, a man trades everything he can, eventually ending up with what he started with.

Joseph Theobald, *Marvin Wanted More!*, 2003
    Unhappy being the smallest sheep, Marvin eats more and more, but he's never satisfied.

1494

BENJAMIN ZEPHANIAH

Face
(New York: Bloomsbury, 2002)

Subject(s): Prejudice; Automobile Accidents; School Life
Age range(s): Grades 7-10
Major character(s): Martin Turner, 15-Year-Old
Time period(s): 2000s
Locale(s): London, England (East London)

Summary: Heading home from a dance club one night, popular Martin accepts a ride with a former schoolmate not realizing the car is stolen and the police might be after it. The police chase it, the car bursts into flames, and Martin is horribly burned on his face. After a month in hospital, his injuries have healed enough for him to go home, but the scars are deep and dreadful. Resolved to go on with life, Martin returns to school but is bothered by his friends who are too kind and careful around him. His tenure on the gymnastics team is shortened when younger kids call him ''Dog Face'' and his girlfriend rejects him, but rather than stay in his room and feel sorry for himself, he returns to the team. Elected captain, he works up a winning gymnastics routine and after a competition realizes that just showing up and taking part is more important than winning. (207 pages)

Where it's reviewed:
Booklist, November 15, 2002, page 589
Kirkus Reviews, November 15, 2002, page1704
Publishers Weekly, November 11, 2002, page 65
School Library Journal, December 2002, page 151
Voice of Youth Advocates, December 2002, page 393

Other books by the same author:
Gangster Rap, 2004
Refugee Boy, 2001

Other books you might like:
Priscilla Cummings, *A Face First*, 2001
    Wearing a plastic facial mask to reduce the scarring from her third degree burns, Kelley wonders if she'll ever again be able to face her classmates.
Deborah Froese, *Out of the Fire*, 2002
    Badly burned·when a bonfire ignites suddenly, Dayle recuperates and rethinks her life until she's able to forgive the boy who tossed the gasoline.
Karen Hesse, *Out of the Dust*, 1997
    Billie Jo accidentally tosses a burning pail of kerosene out the kitchen door and onto her mother, who later dies.
Robert Lipsyte, *The Contender*, 1967
    Alfred learns that in boxing, as in life, it's more important to be a contender than a winner.

1495

HARRIET ZIEFERT
TODD MCKIE, Illustrator

Egad Alligator!

(Boston: Walter Lorraine Books/Houghton Mifflin Company, 2002)

Subject(s): Animals/Alligators; Animals; Fear
Age range(s): Preschool-Grade 1
Major character(s): Little Gator, Alligator, Brother
Time period(s): Indeterminate
Locale(s): Fictional Country

Summary: While Little Gator's brother naps, Little Gator explores. Discovering people for the first time, Little Gator greets them with his friendliest voice, but the people shout, ''Egad alligator!'' and run away. The same thing happens when Little Gator finds nesting herons and a baseball game in progress. Exhausted by his trek Little Gator settles down on a big floating log to rest when the log raises its head and Little Gator screams, ''Egad python!'' before swimming home as fast as he can. (36 pages)

Where it's reviewed:
Booklist, April 15, 2002, page 1410
Bulletin of the Center for Children's Books, September 2002, page 38
Horn Book Guide, Fall 2002, page 349
Publishers Weekly, February 18, 2002, page 95
School Library Journal, April 2002, page 128

Other books by the same author:
No Kiss for Grandpa, 2001
Someday We'll Have Very Good Manners, 2001
Pushkin Minds the Bundle, 2000

Other books you might like:
Sara Fanelli, *Wolf*, 1997
   Friendly Wolf's intentions are misunderstood by the fearful townspeople who chase Wolf away from their city.
Claire Freedman, *Where's Your Smile, Crocodile?*, 2001
   Wandering through the jungle in search of his smile, young Kyle finds a lost lion cub in need of cheering.
Florence Parry Heide, *Some Things Are Scary*, 2000
   The illustrations in this book include many scary things but none are alligators.

1496

PAUL ZINDEL

The Square Root of Murder

(New York: Hyperion, 2002)

Series: P.C. Hawke Mysteries. Book 5
Subject(s): Mystery and Detective Stories; Murder
Age range(s): Grades 5-8
Major character(s): P.C. Hawke, 11th Grader, Detective—Amateur; Mackenzie Riggs, 11th Grader, Detective—Amateur; Eva Marie Dunaway, Teacher (calculus), Crime Victim
Time period(s): 2000s
Locale(s): New York, New York

Summary: Students P.C. and Mackenzie take calculus at Columbia University as part of a cooperative plan with their high school. Though younger than most of their classmates, they join in the mutual dislike of their calculus professor who often makes snide, uncalled for comments about her students. When Professor Dunaway is found stuck to her blackboard by a bolt from a crossbow, it means no homework for a week. Well, it does mean more than that as P.C. and Mackenzie investigate this murder. From crossbow research to embezzling schemes to chases through darkened classrooms, P.C. and Mackenzie are continually on the run in this popular mystery series. (131 pages)

Where it's reviewed:
Booklist, May 1, 2002, page 1461
Kliatt, January 2004, page 50
School Library Journal, April 2002, page 159

Other books by the same author:
Death on the Amazon, 2002 (P.C. Hawke Mysteries Book 6)
The Phantom of 86th Street, 2002 (P.C. Hawke Mysteries Book 8)
The E-Mail Murders, 2001 (P.C. Hawke Mysteries Book 3)
The Lethal Gorilla, 2001 (P.C. Hawke Mysteries Book 4)
The Scream Museum, 2001 (P.C. Hawke Mysteries Book 1)
The Surfing Corpse, 2001 (P.C. Hawke Mysteries Book 2)

Other books you might like:
Michael Dahl, *The Viking Claw*, 2001
   Searching for his missing parents, Finn and his uncle find eight buried Viking ships in Iceland and what may be a clue left by his mom and dad.
Anthony Horowitz, *Stormbreaker*, 2001
   After his uncle dies, Alex agrees to take his place helping British Intelligence as he investigates the computer giant Sayle Enterprises.
T.M. Murphy, *The Secrets of Code Z*, 2001
   Amateur detective Orville contends with the CIA, a Russian scientist, a rookie newspaper reporter and too many murders in this fifth adventure.

1497

GERMANO ZULLO
ALBERTINE, Illustrator

Marta and the Bicycle

(La Jolla, CA: Kane/Miller, 2002)

Subject(s): Animals/Cows; Bicycles and Bicycling; Competition
Age range(s): Grades K-3
Major character(s): Marta, Cow
Time period(s): 2000s (2002)
Locale(s): Switzerland

Summary: The sight of bicycle racers as they pass by her farm gives Marta the idea to learn to ride a bicycle. The next day she scrounges through the dump for bicycle parts and builds a bike. It takes some effort to learn how to ride but, eventually, Marta figures it out and soon she is a biking champ. The next year, when the time comes for the same bike race, Marta enters and even wins! This is the first book by this Swiss author to have been translated into English. (32 pages)

Where it's reviewed:
Kirkus Reviews, October 1, 2002, page 1484
Publishers Weekly, October 21, 2002, page 74

Other books you might like:
David Goldin, *Go-Go-Go!*, 2000
  Maurice is determined to win the annual bike race, but some unusual obstacles pop up unexpectedly.
Vera Rosenberry, *Vera Rides a Bike*, 2004
  When Vera's bicycle is stolen she decides it's time to learn how to ride a bike.
David Shannon, *Duck on a Bike*, 2002
  Duck decides to try out a bicycle that he sees on their farm, but the other farm animals are skeptical of his idea.
Audrey Wood, *The Red Racer*, 1996
  After bullies tease Nona about her beat up old bike she devises a plan to get a new one.

1498

MARKUS ZUSAK

Getting the Girl

(New York: Arthur Levine/Scholastic, 2003)

Subject(s): Brothers; Interpersonal Relations; Family Life
Age range(s): Grades 9-12
Major character(s): Cameron "Cam" Wolfe, Student—High School; Ruben Wolfe, Brother; Octavia, Girlfriend
Time period(s): 2000s
Locale(s): Australia

Summary: In *Fighting Ruben Wolfe*, both brothers stepped into the boxing ring after discovering they could be paid for their fights. Though Ruben is still a fighter, Cam is searching for his own identity and knows it's not someone like his "love 'em and leave 'em" brother. Ruben still plays the field while Cam wishes he had one girlfriend; when Ruben dumps Octavia, Cam steps in and, surprisingly, Octavia invites him to stay. Cam has also discovered an ability and desire to write, so he walks around with his pants pockets stuffed with little scraps of paper upon which he's written all kinds of thoughts. Though Ruben will likely remain a fighter all his life, Cam knows there's more that he wants to do and will probably have to leave Ruben behind. (261 pages)

Where it's reviewed:
Booklist, May 15, 2003, page 1656
Bulletin of the Center for Children's Books, July 2003, page 467
Horn Book, May 2003, page 360
School Library Journal, April 2003, page 171
Voice of Youth Advocates, August 2003, page 232

Awards the book has won:
Center for Children's Books Best Books, 2003

Other books by the same author:
I Am the Messenger, 2005
Fighting Ruben Wolfe, 2001

Other books you might like:
Ethan Howland, *The Lobster War*, 2001
  Seeking support from his older brother, Dain discovers it's his brother and his disreputable friend who have been cutting his lobster traps.
Alan Watt, *Diamond Dogs*, 2000
  When Neil's sheriff father hides the evidence of an accidental death cause by Neil, they are forever locked in a chilling, destructive bond.
Jacqueline Woodson, *Miracle's Boys*, 2000
  Three brothers, each very different from the other, find they need to stay close and help one another after their mother dies.

Series Index

This index alphabetically lists series to which books featured in the entries belong. Beneath each series name, book titles are listed alphabetically, with author names, age-level code(s) and entry numbers also included. The age-level codes are as follows: *p* Preschool, *b* Beginning Reader, *e* Elementary School (Grades 2-5), *m* Middle School (Grades 5-8), *h* High School (Grades 9-12), and *a* Adult.

Award Index

This index lists major awards given to books featured in the entries. Books are listed alphabetically beneath the name of the award, with author name, age-level code(s) and entry numbers also included. The age-level codes are as follows: *p* Preschool, *b* Beginning Reader, *e* Elementary School (Grades 2-5), *m* Middle School (Grades 5-8), *h* High School (Grades 9-12), and *a* Adult.

ALA Alex Award

When the Emperor Was Divine - Julie Otsuka   *h, a* 1120

ALA Best Books for Young Adults

33 Snowfish - Adam Rapp   *h* 1186
Abarat - Clive Barker   *h* 80
Acceleration - Graham McNamee   *m, h* 995
Aimee - Mary Beth Miller   *h* 1011
Alice, I Think - Susan Juby   *m, h* 763
America - E.R. Frank   *h* 479
The Amulet of Samarkand - Jonathan Stroud   *m, h* 1350
Before We Were Free - Julia Alvarez   *m, h* 24
Better than Running at Night - Hillary Frank   *h* 481
Big Mouth & Ugly Girl - Joyce Carol Oates   *h* 1098
Birdland - Tracy Mack   *m, h* 927
Bloody Jack: Being an Account of the Curious Adventures of Mary ''Jacky'' Faber, Ship's Boy - L.A. Meyer   *m, h* 1007
Bottled Up - Jaye Murray   *m, h* 1045
Boy Meets Boy - David Levithan   *h* 885
Breath - Donna Jo Napoli   *h* 1059
Bronx Masquerade - Nikki Grimes   *m, h* 565
Buddha Boy - Kathe Koja   *m, h* 811
The Canning Season - Polly Horvath   *m, h* 683
Catalyst - Laurie Halse Anderson   *h* 28
Coraline - Neil Gaiman   *m* 502
Cuba 15 - Nancy Osa   *m, h* 1115
Deep - Susanna Vance   *m, h* 1394
Dr. Franklin's Island - Ann Halam   *m, h* 582
Dust - Arthur Slade   *m, h* 1308
The Earth, My Butt, and Other Big Round Things - Carolyn Mackler   *m, h* 930
East - Edith Pattou   *m, h* 1131
Faerie Wars - Herbie Brennan   *h* 141
Feed - M.T. Anderson   *h* 29
Firebirds: An Anthology of Original Fantasy and Science Fiction - Sharyn November   *m, h* 1095
Fresh Girl - Jaira Placide   *h* 1160
Friction - E.R. Frank   *h* 480
Gingerbread - Rachel Cohn   *h* 272
Girl in a Cage - Jane Yolen   *m, h* 1480
The Goblin Wood - Hilari Bell   *m, h* 98
God Went to Beauty School - Cynthia Rylant   *m, h* 1245
A Great and Terrible Beauty - Libba Bray   *h* 138
The Green Man: Tales from the Mythic Forest - Ellen Datlow   *m, h* 349
Hanging on to Max - Margaret Bechard   *h* 94

Harry Potter and the Order of the Phoenix - J.K. Rowling   *m, h* 1234
Heir Apparent - Vivian Vande Velde   1395
Hoot - Carl Hiaasen   *m, h* 637
The House of the Scorpion - Nancy Farmer   *m, h* 444
How Angel Peterson Got His Name - Gary Paulsen   *m, h* 1135
The Hunting of the Last Dragon - Sherryl Jordan   *m, h* 761
Hush - Jacqueline Woodson   *m, h* 1465
Inside Out - Terry Trueman   *h* 1386
Jake, Reinvented - Gordon Korman   *h* 816
Keeper of the Night - Kimberly Willis Holt   *m, h* 669
Keesha's House - Helen Frost   *m, h* 498
Kissing Kate - Lauren Myracle   *h* 1054
The Kite Rider - Geraldine McCaughrean   *m, h* 965
Kotuku - Deborah Savage   *m, h* 1265
The Lighthouse Keeper's Daughter - Iain Lawrence   *h* 860
Locomotion - Jacqueline Woodson   *e, m* 1466
Lucas - Kevin Brooks   *h* 159
Lucy the Giant - Sherri L. Smith   *m, h* 1316
Milkweed - Jerry Spinelli   *m, h* 1326
Mississippi Trial, 1955 - Chris Crowe   *m, h* 320
Mortal Engines - Philip Reeve   *h, a* 1195
A Northern Light - Jennifer Donnelly   *h* 387
Olive's Ocean - Kevin Henkes   *m* 623
Once Upon a Marigold - Jean Ferris   *m, h* 452
Out of Bounds: Seven Stories of Conflict - Beverley Naidoo   *m* 1056
Out of Order - A.M. Jenkins   *h* 732
Out of the Fire - Deborah Froese   *m, h* 497
Overboard - Elizabeth Fama   *m, h* 442
Parvana's Journey - Deborah Ellis   *m, h* 429
Pictures of Hollis Woods - Patricia Reilly Giff   *e, m* 524
Pirates!: The True and Remarkable Adventures of Minerva Sharpe and Nancy Kington, Female Pirates - Celia Rees   *m, h* 1193
Postcards from No Man's Land - Aidan Chambers   *h* 237
Prep - Jake Coburn   *h* 266
Remembrance - Theresa Breslin   *m, h* 143
The River between Us - Richard Peck   *m, h* 1141
Search of the Moon King's Daughter - Linda Holeman   *m, h* 665
Shattered: Stories of Children and War - Jennifer Armstrong   *m, h* 39
Shattering Glass - Gail Giles   *h* 526

Singing the Dogstar Blues - Alison Goodman   *h* 540
Son of the Mob - Gordon Korman   *m, h* 818
Sorcery and Cecelia, or the Enchanted Chocolate Pot - Patricia C. Wrede   *m, h* 1470
Stetson - S.L. Rottman   *h* 1233
Stoner & Spaz - Ron Koertge   *h* 810
Surviving the Applewhites - Stephanie S. Tolan   *m, h* 1383
Sweetblood - Pete Hautman   *h* 610
Sword of the Rightful King: A Novel of King Arthur - Jane Yolen   *m, h* 1486
Target - Kathleen Jeffrie Johnson   *h* 747
Things Not Seen - Andrew Clements   *m* 261
Three Clams and an Oyster - Randy Powell   *m, h* 1166
Tithe: A Modern Faerie Tale - Holly Black   *h* 111
Trickster's Choice - Tamora Pierce   *m, h* 1152
True Confessions of a Heartless Girl - Martha Brooks   *h* 161
Uncommon Faith - Trudy Krisher   *m, h* 827
The Wee Free Men: A Novel of Discworld - Terry Pratchett   *m, h* 1167
What Happened to Lani Garver - Carol Plum-Ucci   *h* 1162
When My Name Was Keoko - Linda Sue Park   *m* 1127
White Midnight - Dia Calhoun   *m, h* 203
The Year of the Hangman - Gary Blackwood   *m, h* 115

ALA Notable Children's Books

7 x 9 = Trouble! - Claudia Mills   *e* 1013
Alphabet under Construction - Denise Fleming   *p* 464
Atlantic - G. Brian Karas   *p* 764
Bear Snores On - Karma Wilson   *p* 1449
Before We Were Free - Julia Alvarez   *m, h* 24
Bruh Rabbit and the Tar Baby Girl - Virginia Hamilton   *p* 589
Colibrí - Ann Cameron   *m* 206
Diary of a Wombat - Jackie French   *p* 490
Ella Sarah Gets Dressed - Margaret Chodos-Irvine   *p* 253
Georgie Lee - Sharon Phillips Denslow   *e* 374
Get Well, Good Knight - Shelley Moore Thomas   *b* 1377
Goddess of Yesterday - Caroline B. Cooney   *m, h* 292
Gooney Bird Greene - Lois Lowry   *e* 911
Head, Body, Legs: A Story from Liberia - Won-Ldy Paye   *p* 1136
How I Became a Pirate - Melinda Long   *p* 907

Time Index

This index chronologically lists the time settings in which the featured books take place. Main headings refer to a century; where no specific time is given, the headings MULTIPLE TIME PERIODS, INDETERMINATE PAST, INDETERMINATE FUTURE, AND INDETERMINATE are used. The 18th through 21st centuries are broken down into decades when possible. (Note: 1800s, for example, refers to the first decade of the 19th century.) Featured titles are listed alphabetically beneath time headings, with author names, age-level code(s) and entry numbers also included. The age-level codes are as follows: *p* Preschool, *b* Beginning Reader, *e* Elementary School (Grades 2-5), *m* Middle School (Grades 5-8), *h* High School (Grades 9-12), and *a* Adult.

Time Index

Time Index

Geographic Index

This index provides access to all featured books by geographic settings—such as countries, continents, oceans, and planets. States and provinces are indicated for the United States and Canada. Also interfiled are headings for fictional place names (Spaceships, Imaginary Planets, etc.). Sections are further broken down by city or the specific name of the imaginary locale. Book titles are listed alphabetically under headings, with author names, age-level code(s) and entry numbers also included. The age-level codes are as follows: *p* Preschool, *b* Beginning Reader, *e* Elementary School (Grades 2-5), *m* Middle School (Grades 5-8), *h* High School (Grades 9-12), and *a* Adult.

AFGHANISTAN

Parvana's Journey - Deborah Ellis   *m, h* 429

AFRICA

Birdbrain Amos - Michael Delaney   *e* 371
The Little Hippos' Adventure - Lena Landstrom
    p 847
The Loudest Roar - Thomas Taylor   *p* 1367
Quiet! - Paul Bright   *p* 153
Shining - Julius Lester   *p* 878
Water Hole Waiting - Jane Kurtz   *p* 838

Aksum
A Coalition of Lions - Elizabeth E. Wein   *h* 1424

Sahara Desert
Bone Dry - Kathleen Karr   *m* 766

Yao
The Village That Vanished - Ann Grifalconi   *p* 561

ALTERNATE UNIVERSE

Ravine - Janet Hickman   *m* 638

AMERICAN COLONIES

CONNECTICUT

Killingworth
The Birds of Killingworth - Robert D. San Souci
    p 1258

PENNSYLVANIA

Homespun Sarah - Verla Kay   *p* 771

RHODE ISLAND

Newport
The Scrimshaw Ring - William Jaspersohn   *p* 729

ANCIENT CIVILIZATION

Annie's Ark - Lesley Harker   *p* 594

ARABIA

Arabian Sea
How the Fisherman Tricked the Genie - Kitoba
Sunami   *p* 1354

ARCTIC

Hello, Arctic! - Theodore Taylor   *p* 1365
Kumak's House: A Tale of the Far North - Michael
    Bania   *p* 73
Maata's Journal - Paul Sullivan   *m, h* 1353

ASIA

Go Track a Yak! - Tony Johnston   *p* 752
A Place to Grow - Soyung Pak   *p* 1121

AT SEA

Alphaboat - Michael Chesworth   *p* 245
Dinosailors - Deb Lund   *p* 915
I'm Mighty! - Kate McMullan   *p* 993
The One-Eyed Giant - Mary Pope Osborne   *e* 1118
Overboard - Elizabeth Fama   *m, h* 442

Blue Star
Monkey Mo Goes to Sea - Diane Goode   *p* 538

Continental
The Voyage of the Continental - Katherine Kirkpatrick
    m 801

Deliverance
*Pirates!: The True and Remarkable Adventures of
    Minerva Sharpe and Nancy Kington, Female Pirates*
    - Celia Rees   *m, h* 1193

Miranda Lee
Lucy the Giant - Sherri L. Smith   *m, h* 1316

Morning Star
The Voyage of Patience Goodspeed - Heather Vogel
    Frederick   *m* 485

San Raffaello
The Leopard Sword - Michael Cadnum   *m, h* 201

Sea Turtle
The Man with the Silver Oar - Robin Moore   *m,*
    h 1029

Trinidad
To the Edge of the World - Michele Torrey
    m 1385

ATLANTIC OCEAN

Atlantic - G. Brian Karas   *p* 764

HMS *Amity*
The Year of the Hangman - Gary Blackwood   *m,*
    h 115

HMS *Dolphin*
*Bloody Jack: Being an Account of the Curious
    Adventures of Mary "Jacky" Faber, Ship's Boy* -
    L.A. Meyer   *m, h* 1007

AUSTRALIA

The Dark - Marianne Curley   *m, h* 328
Diary of a Wombat - Jackie French   *p* 490
Fifteen Love - Robert Corbet   *m, h* 299
Getting the Girl - Markus Zusak   *h* 1498
Hazel Green - Odo Hirsch   *e* 644
Jennifer Government - Max Barry   *h, a* 85
The Named - Marianne Curley   *m, h* 329
Remote Man - Elizabeth Honey   *m, h* 670
Singing the Dogstar Blues - Alison Goodman
    h 540
*The Slightly True Story of Cedar B. Hartley (Who
    Planned to Live an Unusual Life)* - Martine Murray
    m 1046
The Snow Pony - Alison Lester   *m, h* 875
Starry Nights - Judith Clarke   *m, h* 258
The Terrible Underpants - Kaz Cooke   *p* 290
What the Birds See - Sonya Hartnett   *m, h* 604
Where in the World - Simon French   *m* 491
Wolf on the Fold - Judith Clarke   *h* 259

Botany Bay
*Escape from Botany Bay: The True Story of Mary
    Bryant* - Gerald Hausman   *m, h* 609

Broome
The Divine Wind: A Love Story - Garry Disher
    h 384

Lismore
Mahalia - Joanne Horniman   *h* 679

Melbourne
The Earthborn - Paul Collins   *h, a* 282

Perth
Guitar Highway Rose - Brigid Lowry   *h*   910

Sydney
Nirvana's Children - Ranulfo   *h*   1185
The Steps - Rachel Cohn   *m*   273

Warriewood
Winter - John Marsden   *m, h*   943

AUSTRIA

Bad Ischl
Elisabeth: The Princess Bride - Barry Denenberg
   m   372

BAHAMAS

Long Pond Cay
Green Boy - Susan Cooper   *m*   297

Lucaya Island
Green Boy - Susan Cooper   *m*   297

BALKAN PENINSULA

And What about Anna? - Jan Simoen   *h*   1306

BELGIUM

And What about Anna? - Jan Simoen   *h*   1306

Brussels
*Mannekin Pis: A Simple Story of a Boy Who Peed on
   a War* - Vladimir Radunsky   *p*   1181

BRAZIL

Amazon Jungle
Rosa Raposa - F. Isabel Campoy   *p*   209

Manaus
Journey to the River Sea - Eva Ibbotson   *m*   707

CAMBODIA

Phnom Penh
The Stone Goddess - Minfong Ho   *m, h*   646

CAMEROON

Sense Pass King: A Story from Cameroon - Katrin
   Tchana   *p*   1368

CANADA

Amber Waiting - Nan Gregory   *p*   559
A Brave Soldier - Nicholas Debon   *p*   365
Brian's Hunt - Gary Paulsen   *m, h*   1133
Cairo Kelly and the Mann - Kristin Butcher   *e,*
   m   185
Dancing Naked - Shelley Hrdlitschka   *h*   692
Emma's Story - Deborah Hodge   *p*   655
Eugene's Story - Richard Scrimger   *p*   1274
Good Morning, Sam - Marie-Louise Gay   *p*   512
Good Night Sam - Marie-Louise Gay   *p*   513
Hank and Fergus - Susin Nielsen-Fernlund
   p   1080
How Sleep Found Tabitha - Maggie deVries
   p   379
Saving Jasey - Diane Tullson   *m, h*   1387
Stanley's Party - Linda Bailey   *p*   65
Stella, Fairy of the Forest - Marie-Louise Gay
   p   514
Sticks and Stones - Beth Goobie   *m, h*   536
T.J. and the Cats - Hazel Hutchins   *e*   704
Under a Prairie Sky - Anne Laurel Carter   *p*   221

Amherstburg
Flying Free: Corey's Underground Railroad Diary -
   Sharon Dennis Wyeth   *e*   1471

Chatham
Trouble Don't Last - Shelley Pearsall   *m*   1139

Demon Island
Paradise - Joan Elizabeth Goodman   *m, h*   541

Foster's Bay
Maata's Journal - Paul Sullivan   *m, h*   1353

Middle Westfield
Berta: A Remarkable Dog - Celia Barker Lottridge
   e   908

Northington
Getting a Life - Jocelyn Shipley   *m, h*   1295

Perambulator Park
Gregory and Alexander - William Barringer   *p*   84

Selkirk
Out of the Fire - Deborah Froese   *m, h*   497

Toronto
More Pies! - Robert Munsch   *p*   1040

ALBERTA

Bull Rider - Marilyn Halvorson   *m, h*   588
Stitches - Glen Huser   *m, h*   703

BRITISH COLUMBIA

Courtenay
A Taste of Perfection - Laura Langston   *m*   849

Lizzie Island
The Lighthouse Keeper's Daughter - Iain Lawrence
   h   860

Nanaimo
A Taste of Perfection - Laura Langston   *m*   849

Smithers
Alice, I Think - Susan Juby   *m, h*   763

Surrey
The Countess and Me - Paul Kropp   *m, h*   832

Sutter's Crossing
The Trouble with Liberty - Kristin Butcher   *m,*
   h   187

Vancouver
Skud - Dennis Foon   *h*   472
Waiting for Sarah - Bruce McBay   *m, h*   961
Willow and Twig - Jean Little   *m*   903

MANITOBA

Pembina Lake
True Confessions of a Heartless Girl - Martha Brooks
   h   161

Winnipeg
The Hemingway Tradition - Kristin Butcher
   m   186
Sparks Fly Upward - Carol Matas   *e, m*   954
Who Owns Kelly Paddik? - Beth Goobie   *m, h*   537

NOVA SCOTIA

Cape Breton
Sea Gift - John Ashby   *m, h*   47

Halifax
Flood - James Heneghan   *m*   621

ONTARIO

You Can't Rush a Cat - Karleen Bradford   *p*   133

Barrie
Death Wind - William Bell   *m, h*   99

Ottawa
Death Wind - William Bell   *m, h*   99

Toronto
Acceleration - Graham McNamee   *m, h*   995
Willow and Twig - Jean Little   *m*   903

QUEBEC

Raspberries on the Yangtze - Karen Wallace
   m   1408

Martindale
Mary Ann Alice - Brian Doyle   *m*   392

St. Francis
The Winter People - Joseph Bruchac   *m, h*   171

SASKATCHEWAN

Horshoe
Dust - Arthur Slade   *m, h*   1308

Oxbow
Sparks Fly Upward - Carol Matas   *e, m*   954

Saskatoon
Tribes - Arthur Slade   *h*   1309

YUKON TERRITORY

Dawson City
Arizona Charlie and the Klondike Kid - Julie Lawson
   p   864
The True Story of Trapper Jack's Left Big Toe - Ian
   Wallace   *p*   1407

CARIBBEAN

Calista Island
Deep - Susanna Vance   *m, h*   1394

HMS *Retribution*
Pirate Hunter Series - Brad Strickland   *e, m*   1348

La Petite Marie
*The Angel's Command: A Tale from the Castaways of
   the Flying Dutchman* - Brian Jacques   *m, h*   722

CHINA

Bitter Dumplings - Jeanne M. Lee   *p*   870
The Dungeon - Lynne Reid Banks   *m, h*   79
The Kite Rider - Geraldine McCaughrean   *m,*
   h   965
The Magical Monkey King: Mischief in Heaven - Ji-Li
   Jiang   *e*   738
Paper Mage - Leah Cutter   *h, a*   333
Ruby's Wish - Shirin Yim Bridges   *p*   148
Someone Says - Carole Lexa Schaefer   *p*   1268
Stone Soup - Jon J. Muth   *p*   1047
Wandering Warrior - Da Chen   *m, h*   240

Guangzhou
The White Swan Express: A Story About Adoption -
   Jean Davies Okimoto   *p*   1106

Li River
Chang and the Bamboo Flute - Elizabeth Starr Hill
   e   640
Daisy Comes Home - Jan Brett   *p*   144

Nanjing
An Ocean Apart, a World Away - Lensey Namioka
   m, h   1058

UNITED STATES

Oakland
Blue Avenger and the Theory of Everything - Norma Howe   m, h   689
Free Radical - Claire Rudolf Murphy   m, h   1042

Ojala
Sonny's War - Valerie Hobbs   m, h   650

Orange County
Lord of the Kill - Theodore Taylor   m, h   1366

Pasadena
The Presence: A Ghost Story - Eve Bunting   m, h   181

Redcrest
The Journey of Oliver K. Woodman - Darcy Pattison   p   1130

Sacramento
One Lucky Summer - Laura McGee Kvasnosky   e   840

San Francisco
The Farther You Run - Davida Wills Hurwin   h   700
The Four Ugly Cats in Apartment 3D - Marilyn Sachs   e   1249
Gingerbread - Rachel Cohn   h   272
Rising Tide - Jean Thesman   m, h   1376
The Tiger's Apprentice - Laurence Yep   m   1474
The Trouble with Babies - Martha Freeman   e   488
The Way We Do It in Japan - Geneva Cobb Iijima   p   711

San Ramon
The Canyon - Sheila Cole   e, m   275

Santa Brunella
Minn and Jake - Janet S. Wong   e   1456

Santa Martina
Sammy Keyes and the Search for Snake Eyes - Wendelin Van Draanen   m   1391

Sawville
Picture Perfect - Elaine Marie Alphin   m, h   22

Timberville
Falling from Fire - Teena Booth   m, h   126

Trinidad
Undercurrents - Willo Davis Roberts   m, h   1212

Twain Harte
One Lucky Summer - Laura McGee Kvasnosky   e   840

Venice Beach
Disappearing Act - Sid Fleischman   m   461

Whaler's Cove
Surfer Dog - Elizabeth Spurr   e, m   1332

COLORADO
7 x 9 = Trouble! - Claudia Mills   e   1013
Gus and Grandpa and the Halloween Costume - Claudia Mills   b   1014
The Return of Calico Bright - David Winkler   m, h   1450
Shadow of a Doubt - S.L. Rottman   m, h   1232

Denver
Hush - Jacqueline Woodson   m, h   1465

CONNECTICUT
The Beast - Walter Dean Myers   h   1051
Goose's Story - Cari Best   p   106
Herbie Jones Moves On - Suzy Kline   e   805

Bridgefield
Outside In - Karen Romano Young   m, h   1489

New Haven
Junebug in Trouble - Alice Mead   e   1002

DELAWARE

New Castle
Bringing Up the Bones - Lara M. Zeises   h   1492

DISTRICT OF COLUMBIA

Washington
All-American Girl - Meg Cabot   m, h   195
A Dance of Sisters - Tracey Porter   m   1164
Double Fudge - Judy Blume   e, m   120
Here We Go Round - Alice McGill   e   979
The Pack - Elisa Carbone   m, h   214
Pictures for Miss Josie - Sandra Belton   p   100
Saving Grace - Priscilla Cummings   e, m   327
A Time for Courage: The Suffragette Diary of Kathleen Bowen, Washington, DC, 1917 - Kathryn Lasky   e, m   857

FLORIDA
Elisa Michaels, Bigger & Better - Johanna Hurwitz   e   702
Red Midnight - Ben Mikaelsen   m, h   1008
Waiting for Christopher - Louise Hawes   m, h   613
Waiting for June - Joyce Sweeney   h   1356

Chickalookee
Horse Thief: A Novel - Robert Newton Peck   m, h   1142

Coconut Cove
Hoot - Carl Hiaasen   m, h   637

Flamingo
Flying Blind - Anna Myers   e, m   1049

Islamorado
My Brother's Hero - Adrian Fogelin   m   470

Lazarus
The Kindling - Jennifer Armstrong   m, h   38

Miami
Breaking Point - Alex Flinn   m, h   467
Flight to Freedom - Ana Veciana-Suarez   m, h   1400

Redworm
Horse Thief: A Novel - Robert Newton Peck   m, h   1142

Singer Island
Amaryllis - Craig Crist-Evans   m, h   315

Tallahassee
Sister Spider Knows All - Adrian Fogelin   m   471

GEORGIA
The Day the Picture Man Came - Faye Gibbons   p   520

Andersonville
Numbering All the Bones - Ann Rinaldi   m   1205

Athens
Goddesses Series - Clea Hantman   m, h   592

Atlanta
Kissing Kate - Lauren Myracle   h   1054

Freedom
Fame and Glory in Freedom, Georgia - Barbara O'Connor   e, m   1102

Macon
Praying at the Sweetwater Motel - April Young Fritz   m   495

Turkey Creek
Full Steam Ahead - Faye Gibbons   p   521

GREAT PLAINS
The Star People: A Lakota Story - S.D. Nelson   p   1073

HAWAII
Island Boyz - Graham Salisbury   m, h   1253
Olvina Flies - Grace Lin   p   893
Plantzilla - Jerdine Nolen   p   1092

Kalaupapa Leprosy Colony
In the Shadow of the Pali: A Story of the Hawaiian Leper Colony - Lisa Cindrich   m, h   255

IDAHO

Coeur D'Alene National Forest
The Big Burn - Jeanette Ingold   m, h   713

Payette River
The Hero - Ron Woods   m, h   1464

Red Rock
Ten Miles from Winnemucca - Thelma Hatch Wyss   m, h   1472

Salmon River
Fire Storm - Jean Craighead George   p   517

ILLINOIS

Bridging Beyond
Bridging Beyond - Kathleen Benner Duble   m, h   403

Cairo
The River between Us - Richard Peck   m, h   1141

Camp Shaddai
Faith Wish - James Bennett   h   102

Chicago
Artemis Fowl: The Eternity Code - Eoin Colfer   m   277
Cuba 15 - Nancy Osa   m, h   1115
Faith Wish - James Bennett   h   102
Indian Shoes - Cynthia Leitich Smith   e   1312
The Night I Disappeared - Julie Reece Deaver   m, h   364
The Secret of the Red Flame - K.M. Kimball   e, m   785
String Music - Rick Telander   e, m   1372
Things Not Seen - Andrew Clements   m   261

Grand Tower
The River between Us - Richard Peck   m, h   1141

INDIANA
Izzy's Place - Marc Kornblatt   e, m   819
Nelly in the Wilderness - Lynn Cullen   m   325

Mayfield
Boxes for Katje - Candace Fleming   p   462

Middleburg
Bernie Magruder & the Bats in the Belfry - Phyllis Reynolds Naylor   e   1064

Mooresville
Telling Christina Goodbye - Lurlene McDaniel   m, h   974

IOWA
How I Fell in Love & Learned to Shoot Free Throws - Jon Ripslinger   h   1209

Dakota City
One Night - Marsha Qualey   h   1180

Duluth
Claws - Will Weaver   m, h   1420

International Falls
When Eagles Fall - Mary Casanova   m   226

Minneapolis
The Viking Series - Christopher Tebbetts   m   1370

St. Paul
Wingwalker - Rosemary Wells   e   1429

Soudan
Song of Sampo Lake - William Durbin   m, h   411

MISSISSIPPI

I Dream of Trains - Angela Johnson   p   742

Greenwood
Mississippi Trial, 1955 - Chris Crowe   m, h   320

MISSOURI

Guerrilla Season - Pat Hughes   m, h   693

St. Joseph
Betrayed! - Patricia Calvert   m   205

St. Louis
As Far as I Can See: Meg's Prairie Diary - Kate McMullan   e   989
A Chapel of Thieves - Bruce Clements   m   263
Ice-Cream Cones for Sale! - Elaine Greenstein   p   555

Valley Junction
Butterflies and Lizards, Beryl and Me - Ruth Lercher Bornstein   e, m   127

MONTANA

Fort Benton
Betrayed! - Patricia Calvert   m   205

Missoula
Mountain Solo - Jeanette Ingold   m, h   714

Whistle
When the Circus Came to Town - Laurence Yep   e   1476

NEBRASKA

Prairie Hill
Together Apart - Dianne E. Gray   m, h   550

NEVADA

Carson City
Jo's Triumph - Nikki Tate   e, m   1363

Las Vegas
Warrior Angel - Robert Lipsyte   h   900

Winnemucca
Ten Miles from Winnemucca - Thelma Hatch Wyss   m, h   1472

NEW ENGLAND

Better than Running at Night - Hillary Frank   h   481
Dahlia - Barbara McClintock   p   970

Mansfield
Where Heroes Hide - Helen Recorvits   e   1190

Shunpike Falls
The Last Mall Rat - Erik E. Esckilsen   m, h   438

Waldo County
The Water Gift and the Pig of the Pig - Jacqueline Briggs Martin   p   948

NEW HAMPSHIRE

Taking Liberty: The Story of Oney Judge, George Washington's Runaway Slave - Ann Rinaldi   m, h   1207

Derry
The Trouble with Jeremy Chance - George Harrar   e, m   597

Portsmouth
The Shakeress - Kimberley Heuston   m, h   636

Rock Falls
Dillon Dillon - Kate Banks   e   75

Whitson
A Week in the Woods - Andrew Clements   e   262

NEW JERSEY

Blind Sighted - Peter Moore   h   1028
Tithe: A Modern Faerie Tale - Holly Black   h   111

Atlantic City
Dunk - David Lubar   m, h   912

Cape May
Lily's Ghosts - Laura Ruby   m   1237

Chelsea
United Tates of America - Paula Danziger   e, m   347

East Hook
The She - Carol Plum-Ucci   m, h   1161

Hackett Island
What Happened to Lani Garver - Carol Plum-Ucci   h   1162

Lawndale
Home of the Braves - David Klass   h   803

Morris Canal
A Full Hand - Thomas F. Yezerski   p   1477

Oceanside
The Secret Within - Theresa Golding   m   534

River Edge
Robert and the Weird & Wacky Facts - Barbara Seuling   e   1279

Springfield
Born Confused - Tanuja Desai Hidier   h   639

Upper Parkington
Lulu's Hat - Susan Meddaugh   e   1003

West Orange
Qwerty Stevens Stuck in Time with Benjamin Franklin - Dan Gutman   m   575

NEW MEXICO

The Dirty Cowboy - Amy Timberlake   p   1382

Albuquerque
Disappearing Act - Sid Fleischman   m   461

NEW YORK

Amber Brown Is Green with Envy - Paula Danziger   e   345
Flavor of the Week - Tucker Shaw   m, h   1288
House of Sports - Marisabina Russo   m   1240
Lily B. on the Brink of Cool - E. Cody Kimmel   e, m   786
Son of the Mob - Gordon Korman   m, h   818

Souperchicken - Mary Jane Auch   p   57
Under the Same Sky - Cynthia DeFelice   m, h   368
Who Will Tell My Brother? - Marlene Carvell   m, h   223
Wizard's Holiday - Diane Duane   m   402

Adirondack Mountains
A Northern Light - Jennifer Donnelly   h   387

Brooklyn
When Marcus Moore Moved In - Rebecca Bond   p   123

Delaware River
Hill Hawk Hattie - Clara Gillow Clark   e, m   257

Erie Canal
The Erie Canal Pirates - Eric A. Kimmel   p   788

Ithaca
An Ocean Apart, a World Away - Lensey Namioka   m, h   1058

Long Island
Pictures of Hollis Woods - Patricia Reilly Giff   e, m   524
Quit It - Marcia Byalick   e, m   191

New Paltz
Almost Home - Nora Raleigh Baskin   e, m   87

New York
America - E.R. Frank   h   479
Auntie Claus and the Key to Christmas - Elise Primavera   p   1171
The Beast - Walter Dean Myers   h   1051
Behind the Mountains: The Diary of Celiane Esperance - Edwidge Danticat   m, h   343
Big Jimmy's Kum Kau Chinese Take Out - Ted Lewin   p   888
Birdland - Tracy Mack   m, h   927
Born Too Short: The Confessions of an Eighth-Grade Basket Case - Dan Elish   m   425
Bring on That Beat - Rachel Isadora   p   717
Bronx Masquerade - Nikki Grimes   m, h   565
Chill Wind - Janet McDonald   h   975
Christmas in the City - Loretta Krupinski   p   836
Clorinda - Robert Kinerk   p   791
Dancing in the Streets of Brooklyn - April Lurie   m, h   916
Dear Emma - Johanna Hurwitz   e, m   701
Dish Series - Diane Muldrow   e, m   1037
Dolores on Her Toes - Barbara Samuels   p   1256
Dolores: Seven Stories about Her - Bruce Brooks   m, h   158
Double Fudge - Judy Blume   e, m   120
The Dream Bearer - Walter Dean Myers   m   1052
The Earth, My Butt, and Other Big Round Things - Carolyn Mackler   m, h   930
Elisa Michaels, Bigger & Better - Johanna Hurwitz   e   702
Eloise Takes a Bawth - Kay Thompson   p   1379
Fat Kid Rules the World - K.L. Going   h   533
Fresh Girl - Jaira Placide   h   1160
Gingerbread - Rachel Cohn   h   272
Gregor the Overlander - Suzanne Collins   m   284
Handbook for Boys: A Novel - Walter Dean Myers   m, h   1053
Harriet Spies Again - Helen Ericson   e, m   435
Hope in My Heart - Kathryn Lasky   e   853
I Stink! - Kate McMullan   p   992
Ice-Cream Cones for Sale! - Elaine Greenstein   p   555
The Invisible Enemy - Marthe Jocelyn   e, m   740
The Kings Are Already Here - Garret Freymann-Weyr   m, h   493
Leon and the Spitting Image - Allen Kurzweil   e, m   839
Liberty! - Allan Drummond   p   399
Mad Maudlin - Mercedes Lackey   h, a   844
Madlenka's Dog - Peter Sis   p   1307
Maggie's Door - Patricia Reilly Giff   m   523

The Mayor of Central Park - Avi   *e* 59
Melonhead - Michael de Guzman   *m* 354
Milly and the Macy's Parade - Shana Corey
    p 303
Morning Glory Monday - Arlene Alda   *p* 16
Mountain Solo - Jeanette Ingold   *m, h* 714
The Mummy's Mother - Tony Johnston   *e* 753
My Chimp Friday: The Nana Banana Chronicles -
    Hester Mundis   *e, m* 1038
My Heartbeat - Garret Freymann-Weyr   *h* 494
New York's Bravest - Mary Pope Osborne   *p* 1117
Olivia Kidney - Ellen Potter   *e, m* 1165
Prep - Jake Coburn   *h* 266
Princess in Love - Meg Cabot   *m, h* 197
Princess in Waiting - Meg Cabot   *m, h* 198
The Red Rose Box - Brenda Woods   *e* 1463
*Rosy Cole's Worst Ever, Best Yet Tour of New York
    City* - Sheila Greenwald   *e* 556
Say Yes - Audrey Couloumbis   *m, h* 306
Silent Movie - Avi   *p* 60
Snakes Don't Miss Their Mothers - M.E. Kerr   *e,
    m* 783
The Square Root of Murder - Paul Zindel   *m* 1496
The Steps - Rachel Cohn   *m* 273
A Time to Dance - Mary Pope Osborne   *e* 1119
Timespinners - Luli Gray   *e* 552
Tomorrow, Maybe - Brian James   *m, h* 725
The True Meaning of Cleavage - Mariah Fredericks
    m, h 486
Vampire State Building - Elizabeth Levy   *e* 887
Warrior Angel - Robert Lipsyte   *h* 900
When Catherine the Great and I Were Eight! - Cari
    Best   *p* 107
When Pirates Came to Brooklyn - Phyllis Shalant   *e,
    m* 1280
When We Were Saints - Han Nolan   *h* 1089
A Wizard Alone - Diane Duane   *m, h* 401
Zoe Sophia's Scrapbook: An Adventure in Venice -
    Claudia Mauner   *p* 957

Nyack

America - E.R. Frank   *h* 479

Pleasant Valley

A Day in the Life of Murphy - Alice Provensen
    p 1176

Rochester

Heir Apparent - Vivian Vande Velde   1395

Scarsdale

A Week in the Woods - Andrew Clements   *e* 262

Smiths Mills

The Last Treasure - Janet S. Anderson   *m, h* 26

Sparrowburg

Rat - Jan Cheripko   *m, h* 242

Susquehanna River

Our Time on the River - Don Brown   *m, h* 162

Westchester County

Big Mouth & Ugly Girl - Joyce Carol Oates
    h 1098

NORTH CAROLINA

The Princesses of Atlantis - Lisa Williams Kline
    m 804
Surviving the Applewhites - Stephanie S. Tolan   *m,
    h* 1383

Brownsville

A Simple Gift - Nancy Ruth Patterson   *e* 1129

Cape Hatteras

Jack Adrift: Fourth Grade without a Clue - Jack
    Gantos   *e* 506

Greensboro

Gravel Queen - Tea Benduhn   *h* 101

Kitty Hawk

The Flyers - Allan Drummond   *p* 398

Scotland Neck

Here We Go Round - Alice McGill   *e* 979

Watauga Settlements

Kings Mountain - G. Clifton Wisler   *m* 1451

Williamston College

The Second Summer of the Sisterhood - Ann Brashares
    m, h 137

NORTH DAKOTA

Grand Forks

Blizzard's Wake - Phyllis Reynolds Naylor   *m,
    h* 1065

Turtle Mountains

The Range Eternal - Louise Erdrich   *p* 434

NORTHWEST TERRITORIES

Seattle

The Voyage of the Continental - Katherine Kirkpatrick
    m 801

OHIO

Shoeless Joe & Black Betsy - Phil Bildner   *p* 108
Time Pieces: The Book of Times - Virginia Hamilton
    m 590
Trouble Don't Last - Shelley Pearsall   *m* 1139
Walk Away Home - Paul Many   *h* 940

Bartonsville

Maxx Comedy: The Funniest Kid in America - Gordon
    Korman   *e, m* 817

Cincinnati

The Battle of Jericho - Sharon M. Draper   *m,
    h* 395
Double Dutch - Sharon M. Draper   *m, h* 396

Cleveland

Gina.Jamie.Father.Bear - George Ella Lyon   *m,
    h* 920

Dublin

Praying at the Sweetwater Motel - April Young Fritz
    m 495

East Siena

Recycling George - Stephen Roos   *e, m* 1224

Willistown

Escape from Memory - Margaret Peterson Haddix
    m, h 580

OKLAHOMA

Indian Shoes - Cynthia Leitich Smith   *e* 1312

Ambler

Wingwalker - Rosemary Wells   *e* 1429

Babbs Switch

The Babbs Switch Story - Darleen Bailey Beard
    m 93

Cimarron County

*The Journal of C.J. Jackson: A Dust Bowl Migrant:
    Oklahoma to California, 1935* - William Durbin
    m 410

Florence

Stop the Train! - Geraldine McCaughrean   *e,
    m* 968

OREGON

Azalea

Hoop Girlz - Lucy Jane Bledsoe   *e, m* 118

Benton

Attack of the Mutant Underwear - Tom Birdseye
    e 109

Haskell's Bay

Stefan's Story - Valerie Hobbs   *m* 651

Newburg

The Last Dog on Earth - Daniel Ehrenhaft   *m,
    h* 424

Portland

The New Rules of High School - Blake Nelson
    h 1072

Riverton

Deep - Susanna Vance   *m, h* 1394

Willamette Valley

A Perfect Place - Patricia Hermes   *e* 627

PACIFIC NORTHWEST

How to Disappear Completely and Never Be Found -
    Sara Nickerson   *m* 1079
Taf: A Novel - Annie Callan   *h* 204

PENNSYLVANIA

The Hard-Times Jar - Ethel Footman Smothers
    p 1317
Shoeless Joe & Black Betsy - Phil Bildner   *p* 108

Chadds Ford

Hannah, Divided - Adele Griffin   *m* 562

Delaware River

Hill Hawk Hattie - Clara Gillow Clark   *e, m* 257

Gettysburg

Anna Sunday - Sally M. Keehn   *m* 772

Lackawanna County

The Green Dog: A Mostly True Story - Suzanne Fisher
    Staples   *e* 1336

Lumberland

A Greater Goode - Amy Schor Ferris   *m* 451

Manorville

A Real American - Richard Easton   *m* 414

Philadelphia

The Creek - Jennifer L. Holm   *m, h* 667
Hannah, Divided - Adele Griffin   *m* 562
The Man with the Silver Oar - Robin Moore   *m,
    h* 1029
Qwerty Stevens Stuck in Time with Benjamin Franklin
    - Dan Gutman   *m* 575
Run from the Nun! - Erin MacLellan   *e, m* 931
The She - Carol Plum-Ucci   *m, h* 1161
Sparrow Jack - Mordicai Gerstein   *p* 519
The Stone Goddess - Minfong Ho   *m, h* 646
We Are Patriots - Kristiana Gregory   *e* 558
Witch Twins at Camp Bliss - Adele Griffin   *e* 564

Pittsburgh

Macaroni Boy - Katherine Ayres   *e, m* 62

Sturbridge

Losing Is Not an Option - Rich Wallace   *m,
    h* 1410
Restless: A Ghost's Story - Rich Wallace   *h* 1411

Susquehanna River

Our Time on the River - Don Brown   *m, h* 162

Valley Forge

We Are Patriots - Kristiana Gregory   *e* 558

RHODE ISLAND

Mansfield
The Crying Rocks - Janet Taylor Lisle   *m, h* 901

Providence
Tangled Threads: A Hmong Girl's Story - Pegi Deitz Shea   *m, h* 1289

SOUTH

Bruh Rabbit and the Tar Baby Girl - Virginia Hamilton   *p* 589

Moodus
Waiting to Disappear - April Young Fritz   *m, h* 496

SOUTH CAROLINA

Camp of the Angel - Aileen Arrington   *e, m* 42
Shoeless Joe & Black Betsy - Phil Bildner   *p* 108

Bennettsville
Darby - Jonathon Scott Fuqua   *e* 501

Camden
Kings Mountain - G. Clifton Wisler   *m* 1451

Charleston
Before the Creeks Ran Red - Carolyn Reeder   *m, h* 1192
Just Jane: The Story of a Daughter of England Caught in the Struggle for Independence in Revolutionary America - William Lavender   *m, h* 858
Seaward Born - Lea Wait   *e, m* 1404

Jericho
Jericho Walls - Kristi Collier   *m, h* 280

Kings Mountain
Kings Mountain - G. Clifton Wisler   *m* 1451

Marlboro County
Darby - Jonathon Scott Fuqua   *e* 501

Rock Hill
The Journey of Oliver K. Woodman - Darcy Pattison   *p* 1130

Rosewall Plantation
Just Jane: The Story of a Daughter of England Caught in the Struggle for Independence in Revolutionary America - William Lavender   *m, h* 858

SOUTH DAKOTA

Prairie Whispers - Frances Arrington   *m* 43

Cresbard
Prairie Summer - Bonnie Geisert   *e* 516

SOUTHWEST

Oasis Wells
The Egyptian Box - Jane Louise Curry   *e, m* 330

TENNESSEE

Where I'd Like to Be - Frances O'Roark Dowell   *e, m* 391

Bristol
Halfway to the Sky - Kimberly Brubaker Bradley   *m* 135

Dobbin
Cold in Summer - Tracy Barrett   *e, m* 83

Hamlin Mountains
Harmony - Rita Murphy   *m, h* 1044

Star Mountain
Sweet By and By - Patricia Hermes   *e, m* 629

Templeton
Tippy Lemmey - Patricia C. McKissack   *e* 986

TEXAS

Bubba and Beau, Best Friends - Kathi Appelt   *p* 34
The Cat Who Liked Potato Soup - Terry Farish   *p* 443
Daddy Says - Ntozake Shange   *m* 1281
Matchit - Martha Moore   *e, m* 1027
Out of Order - A.M. Jenkins   *h* 732
Puss in Cowboy Boots - Jan Huling   *p* 695
Shattering Glass - Gail Giles   *h* 526

Angleton
Dead Girls Don't Write Letters - Gail Giles   *m, h* 525

Comfort
Comfort - Carolee Dean   *m, h* 363

Dalhart
Survival in the Storm: The Dust Bowl Diary of Grace Edwards - Katelan Janke   *e, m* 728

Faithful
Samantha and the Cowboy - Lorraine Heath   *h* 620

Hill Country
Nightmare - Joan Lowery Nixon   *m, h* 1086

Houston
Simon Says - Elaine Marie Alphin   *h* 23

Rancho del Oro
The Trap - Joan Lowery Nixon   *m, h* 1087

San Antonio
Just One More Story - Jennifer Brutschy   *p* 173

UTAH

Heber
The Monster in Me - Mette Ivie Harrison   *m* 600

Topaz
When the Emperor Was Divine - Julie Otsuka   *h, a* 1120

VERMONT

From Dawn till Dusk - Natalie Kinsey-Warnock   *p* 796
Lumber Camp Library - Natalie Kinsey-Warnock   *e* 798
The Rudest Alien on Earth - Jane Leslie Conly   *e, m* 286
The Same Stuff as Stars - Katherine Paterson   *m* 1128
Saving the Planet & Stuff - Gail Gauthier   *m, h* 511
Shaper - Jessie Haas   *m* 576
Stray Voltage - Eugenie Doyle   *m* 393

Northeast Kingdom
A Doctor Like Papa - Natalie Kinsey-Warnock   *e* 795

St. Johnsbury
The Shakeress - Kimberley Heuston   *m, h* 636

Salmon Falls
God of Beer - Garret Keizer   *h* 775

Williston
Brothers Below Zero - Tor Seidler   *e, m* 1277

VIRGINIA

Evvy's Civil War - Miriam Brenaman   *m, h* 140
Judy Moody Saves the World! - Megan McDonald   *e* 976

Alexandria
Before the Creeks Ran Red - Carolyn Reeder   *m, h* 1192

Bluefly
Witch Twins at Camp Bliss - Adele Griffin   *e* 564

Doubletop Mountain
Ghost Girl: A Blue Ridge Mountain Story - Delia Ray   *m* 1188

Glencaren Plantation
The Spirit and Gilly Bucket - Maurine F. Dahlberg   *m* 337

Hanover County
Or Give Me Death - Ann Rinaldi   *m, h* 1206

Jamestown
Season of Promise - Patricia Hermes   *e* 628
Virginia Bound - Amy Butler   *e, m* 188

Mount Vernon
Taking Liberty: The Story of Oney Judge, George Washington's Runaway Slave - Ann Rinaldi   *m, h* 1207

Richmond
The Watch - Dennis Danvers   *h, a* 344

Shenandoah Valley
Hear the Wind Blow: A Novel of the Civil War - Mary Downing Hahn   *m* 581

Winchester
Anna Sunday - Sally M. Keehn   *m* 772

WASHINGTON

Clam Island
Summerland - Michael Chabon   *m, h* 236

Parrish Island
The Queen of Everything - Deb Caletti   *h* 202

Puget Sound
Between - Jean Thesman   *m, h* 1375
Freaky Green Eyes - Joyce Carol Oates   *m, h* 1099

Roslyn
Grape Thief - Kristine L. Franklin   *m, h* 482

San Juan Islands
Flight of the Fisherbird - Nora Martin   *e, m* 949

Seattle
Beacon Hill Boys - Ken Mochizuki   *m, h* 1021
By the Side of the Road - Jules Feiffer   *p* 446
Freaky Green Eyes - Joyce Carol Oates   *m, h* 1099
High Heat - Carl Deuker   *m, h* 378
Jackie's Wild Seattle - Will Hobbs   *m* 652
Melonhead - Michael de Guzman   *m* 354
Rebel - Willo Davis Roberts   *m* 1211
Ten Miles from Winnemucca - Thelma Hatch Wyss   *m, h* 1472
Three Clams and an Oyster - Randy Powell   *m, h* 1166
Undercurrents - Willo Davis Roberts   *m, h* 1212

Shoalwater Bay
Boston Jane: Wilderness Days - Jennifer L. Holm   *m, h* 666

Spokane
Inside Out - Terry Trueman   *h* 1386

WEST

Old Crump: The True Story of a Trip West - Laurie
   Lawlor   *p*   859
Rodzina - Karen Cushman   *m*   331
Samantha and the Cowboy - Lorraine Heath   *h*   620
*This Vast Land: A Young Man's Journal of the Lewis
   and Clark Expedition* - Stephen E. Ambrose   *m,
   h*   25
Thunder Rose - Jerdine Nolen   *p*   1093
Twelve Travelers, Twenty Horses - Harriette Gillem
   Robinet   *m, h*   1213

Deepdip Cha-cha's Fun Ashram
Fat Camp Commandos Go West - Daniel Pinkwater
   e   1159

Horny Toad
Fat Camp Commandos Go West - Daniel Pinkwater
   e   1159

WEST VIRGINIA

Christmas in the Country - Cynthia Rylant   *p*   1244

Buckman
Boys in Control - Phyllis Reynolds Naylor   *e*   1066

The Girls Take Over - Phyllis Reynolds Naylor
   e   1067

Clay
Up Molasses Mountain - Julie Baker   *m, h*   68

WISCONSIN

Madison
Olive's Ocean - Kevin Henkes   *m*   623

Rumpus Ridge
The Giant Ball of String - Arthur Geisert   *p*   515

Sand Island
On Sand Island - Jacqueline Briggs Martin   *p*   947

WYOMING

Rock Springs
The Traitor: Golden Mountain Chronicles: 1885 -
   Laurence Yep   *m, h*   1475

Saddlestring
Savage Run - C.J. Box   *h, a*   130

VIETNAM

Amaryllis - Craig Crist-Evans   *m, h*   315

VIETNAM, SOUTH

*Where Have All the Flowers Gone?: The Diary of
   Molly Mackenzie Flaherty* - Ellen Emerson White
   m, h   1437

WALES

Saffy's Angel - Hilary McKay   *m*   980
Snow - Tracy Lynn   *m, h*   919

WEST INDIES

Antilles
*The Twins and the Bird of Darkness: A Hero Tale
   from the Caribbean* - Robert D. San Souci
   e   1260

Subject Index

This index lists subjects which are covered in the featured titles. These can include such things as family life, animals, personal and social problems, historical events, ethnic groups, and story types, e.g. Mystery and Detective Stories. Beneath each subject heading, titles are arranged alphabetically with author names, age-level code(s) and entry numbers also included. The age-level codes are as follows: *p* Preschool, *b* Beginning Reader, *e* Elementary School (Grades 2-5), *m* Middle School (Grades 5-8), *h* High School (Grades 9-12), and *a* Adult.

Abandonment

Sammy Keyes and the Search for Snake Eyes - Wendelin Van Draanen   *m* 1391
Willow and Twig - Jean Little   *m* 903

Abolition

One Sky Above Us - E. Cody Kimmel   *e* 787
Pioneer Summer - Deborah Hopkinson   *e* 677
Uncommon Faith - Trudy Krisher   *m, h* 827

Abortion

Gingerbread - Rachel Cohn   *h* 272

Abuse

America - E.R. Frank   *h* 479
Freaky Green Eyes - Joyce Carol Oates   *m, h* 1099
Picture Perfect - Elaine Marie Alphin   *m, h* 22
Praying at the Sweetwater Motel - April Young Fritz   *m* 495
The Secret Within - Theresa Golding   *m* 534

Accidents

The Broken Cat - Lynne Rae Perkins   *p* 1146
Just One More - Wendi Silvano   *p* 1303
Little Flower - Gloria Rand   *p* 1182
The Nine Lives of Aristotle - Dick King-Smith   *e* 794
Zoom! - Robert Munsch   *p* 1041

Acting

Beverly Billingsly Takes a Bow - Alexander Stadler   *p* 1334
Tackylocks and the Three Bears - Helen Lester   *p* 877

Actors and Actresses

Annabel the Actress, Starring in Hound of the Barkervilles - Ellen Conford   *e* 285
Shakespeare's Spy - Gary Blackwood   *m* 114

Adolescence

Island Boyz - Graham Salisbury   *m, h* 1253
Rat - Jan Cheripko   *m, h* 242

Small Avalanches and Other Stories - Joyce Carol Oates   *h, a* 1100

Adoption

The Angel Factor - Terence Blacker   *m, h* 113
Dancing Naked - Shelley Hrdlitschka   *h* 692
Dillon Dillon - Kate Banks   *e* 75
Emma's Story - Deborah Hodge   *p* 655
Lulu's Hat - Susan Meddaugh   *e* 1003
A New Barker in the House - Tomie De Paola   *p* 359
Our Twitchy - Kes Gray   *p* 551
Saffy's Angel - Hilary McKay   *m* 980
The White Swan Express: A Story About Adoption - Jean Davies Okimoto   *p* 1106

Adventure and Adventurers

The 7th Knot - Kathleen Karr   *m* 765
ABC: A Child's First Alphabet Book - Alison Jay   *p* 730
Artemis Fowl: The Eternity Code - Eoin Colfer   *m* 277
Bone Dry - Kathleen Karr   *m* 766
The Capture - Kathryn Lasky   *m* 851
Daisy Comes Home - Jan Brett   *p* 144
The Dark - Marianne Curley   *m, h* 328
The Dark Horse - Marcus Sedgwick   *m* 1275
Daughter of the Wind - Michael Cadnum   *m, h* 199
Devlin's Luck - Patricia Bray   *h, a* 139
The Divide - Elizabeth Kay   *m* 770
Drinking Midnight Wine - Simon R. Green   *h, a* 553
Eragon - Christopher Paolini   *m, h* 1125
Firesong: An Adventure - William Nicholson   1078
Fool's Errand - Robin Hobb   *h, a* 647
Golden Fool - Robin Hobb   *h, a* 648
The Grail Prince - Nancy McKenzie   *h, a* 983
Hippolyta and the Curse of the Amazons - Jane Yolen   *m* 1482
How I Became a Pirate - Melinda Long   *p* 907
Isabel: Taking Wing - Annie Dalton   *m* 339
Journey to the River Sea - Eva Ibbotson   *m* 707
The Kite Rider - Geraldine McCaughrean   *m, h* 965
Lady Knight - Tamora Pierce   *m, h* 1150
Lewis and Clark and Me: A Dog's Tale - Laurie Myers   *e* 1050

Lionclaw: A Tale of Rowan Hood - Nancy Springer   *m* 1330
The Little Hippos' Adventure - Lena Landstrom   *p* 847
Little Horse - Betsy Byars   *e* 193
The Man with the Silver Oar - Robin Moore   *m, h* 1029
Midwinter Nightingale - Joan Aiken   *m* 13
Might Adventurer of the Planet! - Ricki Stern   *e* 1341
Mister Monday - Garth Nix   *m, h* 1085
The One-Eyed Giant - Mary Pope Osborne   *e* 1118
Pirate Hunter Series - Brad Strickland   *e, m* 1348
Pirates!: The True and Remarkable Adventures of Minerva Sharpe and Nancy Kington, Female Pirates - Celia Rees   *m, h* 1193
The Rope Trick - Lloyd Alexander   *e, m* 18
Sidekicks - Dan Danko   *m* 342
Skeleton Key - Anthony Horowitz   *m, h* 681
The Snow Pony - Alison Lester   *m, h* 875
Time Stops for No Mouse - Michael Hoeye   *m, h* 657
The Time Witches - Michael Molloy   *m* 1022
Trading in Danger - Elizabeth Moon   *h, a* 1026
Trickster's Choice - Tamora Pierce   *m, h* 1152
Twelve Travelers, Twenty Horses - Harriette Gillem Robinet   *m, h* 1213
The Ugly Goddess - Elsa Marston   *m* 944
Voyage of the Shadowmoon - Sean McMullen   *h, a* 994
Wandering Warrior - Da Chen   *m, h* 240
The Whistle, the Grave, and the Ghost - Brad Strickland   *m* 1349
Wolf Queen - Tanith Lee   *m, h* 874
Yikes!!! - Robert Florczak   *p* 468

Africa

Head, Body, Legs: A Story from Liberia - Won-Ldy Paye   *p* 1136
The Magic Gourd - Baba Wague Diakite   *p* 380
Shining - Julius Lester   *p* 878
Water Hole Waiting - Jane Kurtz   *p* 838

African Americans

Be Boy Buzz - bell hooks   *p* 672
Bear Hug - Laurence Pringle   *p* 1172
The Beast - Walter Dean Myers   *h* 1051
Begging for Change - Sharon G. Flake   *m, h* 458
Bippity Bop Barbershop - Natasha Anastasia Tarpley   *p* 1362

Bring on That Beat - Rachel Isadora   *p* 717
Chill Wind - Janet McDonald   *h* 975
Daddy Says - Ntozake Shange   *m* 1281
Dancing the Ring Shout! - Kim Siegelson   *p* 1300
Double Dutch - Sharon M. Draper   *m, h* 396
The Dream Bearer - Walter Dean Myers   *m* 1052
Fishing Day - Andrea Davis Pinkney   *p* 1156
Flying Free: Corey's Underground Railroad Diary - Sharon Dennis Wyeth   *e* 1471
Full, Full, Full of Love - Trish Cooke   *p* 291
Gloria Rising - Ann Cameron   *e* 207
Handbook for Boys: A Novel - Walter Dean Myers   *m, h* 1053
The Hard-Times Jar - Ethel Footman Smothers   *p* 1317
Here We Go Round - Alice McGill   *e* 979
Homemade Love - bell hooks   *p* 673
Hush - Jacqueline Woodson   *m, h* 1465
Jericho Walls - Kristi Collier   *m, h* 280
Looking for Red - Angela Johnson   *m, h* 743
Our Gracie Aunt - Jacqueline Woodson   *p* 1467
Pictures for Miss Josie - Sandra Belton   *p* 100
The Red Rose Box - Brenda Woods   *e* 1463
Taking Liberty: The Story of Oney Judge, George Washington's Runaway Slave - Ann Rinaldi   *m, h* 1207
Time Pieces: The Book of Times - Virginia Hamilton   *m* 590
Twelve Travelers, Twenty Horses - Harriette Gillem Robinet   *m, h* 1213
Under the Quilt of Night - Deborah Hopkinson   *p* 678
Yesterday I Had the Blues - Jeron Ashford Frame   *p* 478

Aging

Mr. Putter & Tabby Catch the Cold - Cynthia Rylant   *b* 1247

Air Travel

The Flyers - Allan Drummond   *p* 398
Olvina Flies - Grace Lin   *p* 893

Airplanes

The Flyers - Allan Drummond   *p* 398

Alchemy

Sophia: The Alchemist's Dog - Shelley Jackson   *p* 721

Alcoholism

Blind Sighted - Peter Moore   *h* 1028
Comfort - Carolee Dean   *m, h* 363
Hang On in There, Shelley - Kate Saksena   *m, h* 1251
Lady: My Life as a Bitch - Melvin Burgess   *h* 183
Martyn Pig - Kevin Brooks   *m, h* 160
Praying at the Sweetwater Motel - April Young Fritz   *m* 495
Stetson - S.L. Rottman   *h* 1233

Aliens

Alien & Possum: Hanging Out - Tony Johnston   *e* 751
The Angel Factor - Terence Blacker   *m, h* 113
Beegu - Alexis Deacon   *p* 360
The Big Science Fair - Dan Yaccarino   *e* 1473
Explorer - C.J. Cherryh   *h, a* 244
From the Horse's Mouth - Kathy Mackel   *m* 929
Manta's Gift - Timothy Zahn   *h, a* 1491

Minnie and Moo and the Potato from Planet X - Denys Cazet   *b* 233
Parasite Pig - William Sleator   *m, h* 1310
The Rudest Alien on Earth - Jane Leslie Conly   *e, m* 286
Wizard's Holiday - Diane Duane   *m* 402

Alternate History

The Alchemist's Door - Lisa Goldstein   *h, a* 535
The Eyre Affair: A Novel - Jasper Fforde   *h, a* 453
Lion's Blood: A Novel of Slavery and Freedom in an Alternate America - Steven Barnes   *h, a* 81
Lost in a Good Book - Jasper Fforde   *h, a* 454
The Year of the Hangman - Gary Blackwood   *m, h* 115
Zulu Heart - Steven Barnes   *h, a* 82

American Colonies

Season of Promise - Patricia Hermes   *e* 628

American West

Arizona Charlie and the Klondike Kid - Julie Lawson   *p* 864
Hannah Mae O'Hannigan's Wild West Show - Lisa Campbell Ernst   *p* 437
Lewis and Clark and Me: A Dog's Tale - Laurie Myers   *e* 1050
Old Crump: The True Story of a Trip West - Laurie Lawlor   *p* 859
Puss in Cowboy Boots - Jan Huling   *p* 695
Sunsets of the West - Tony Johnston   *p* 754
This Vast Land: A Young Man's Journal of the Lewis and Clark Expedition - Stephen E. Ambrose   *m, h* 25
Thunder Rose - Jerdine Nolen   *p* 1093

Amusement Parks

B Is for Bulldozer: A Construction ABC - June Sobel   *p* 1319
Dunk - David Lubar   *m, h* 912
Roller Coaster - Marla Frazee   *p* 484

Anatomy

The True Story of Trapper Jack's Left Big Toe - Ian Wallace   *p* 1407

Ancient History

The Courtesan's Daughter - Priscilla Galloway   *h* 505

Angels

The Angel Factor - Terence Blacker   *m, h* 113

Anger

Sometimes I'm Bombaloo - Rachel Vail   *p* 1389
When Mommy Was Mad - Lynne Jonell   *p* 756
Wild Boy - James Lincoln Collier   *m* 279

Animals

ABC: A Child's First Alphabet Book - Alison Jay   *p* 730
The Animal Hedge - Paul Fleischman   *p* 459
Armadillo's Orange - Jim Arnosky   *p* 40
Babies on the Go - Linda Ashman   *p* 49
Bear Hug - Laurence Pringle   *p* 1172
Bear Snores On - Karma Wilson   *p* 1449
Berta: A Remarkable Dog - Celia Barker Lottridge   *e* 908

Best Kind of Baby - Kate Laing   *p* 846
Birthday Zoo - Deborah Lee Rose   *p* 1229
Bruh Rabbit and the Tar Baby Girl - Virginia Hamilton   *p* 589
Busy Little Mouse - Eugenie Fernandes   *p* 449
Can You Make a Piggy Giggle? - Linda Ashman   *p* 50
Captain Duck - Jez Alborough   *p* 14
The Case of the Sleepy Sloth - Cynthia Rylant   *b* 1243
Cock-a-Moo-Moo - Juliet Dallas-Conte   *p* 338
Debi Gliori's Bedtime Stories: Bedtime Tales with a Twist - Debi Gliori   *p* 530
Diary of a Wombat - Jackie French   *p* 490
Dinnertime! - Sue Williams   *p* 1447
Does a Cow Say Boo? - Judy Hindley   *p* 643
Don't Take Your Snake for a Stroll - Karin Ireland   *p* 716
Down by the Cool of the Pool - Tony Mitton   *p* 1020
Duck on a Bike - David Shannon   *p* 1283
Earthquack! - Margie Palatini   *p* 1122
Edward in the Jungle - David McPhail   *p* 999
Egad Alligator! - Harriet Ziefert   *p* 1495
First Day - Joan Rankin   *p* 1184
Giggle, Giggle, Quack - Doreen Cronin   *p* 317
Go Track a Yak! - Tony Johnston   *p* 752
Good Night, Animals - Lena Arro   *p* 44
Good Night, Sleep Tight, Don't Let the Bedbugs Bite! - Diane DeGroat   *p* 369
Good Night, Sleep Tight, Little Bunnies - Dawn Apperley   *p* 37
Gumbrella - Barry Root   *p* 1225
The Hamster of the Baskervilles - Bruce Hale   *e* 583
Hobbledy-Clop - Pat Brisson   *p* 155
How Groundhog's Garden Grew - Lynne Cherry   *p* 243
How Sleep Found Tabitha - Maggie deVries   *p* 379
I Kissed the Baby! - Mary Murphy   *p* 1043
Jazzy in the Jungle - Lucy Cousins   *p* 307
Julia Wants a Pet - Barbro Lindgren   *p* 899
Little Badger's Just-About Birthday - Eve Bunting   *p* 179
Little Brown Hen's Shower - Pamela Duncan Edwards   *p* 418
The Loudest Roar - Thomas Taylor   *p* 1367
Mama's Little Bears - Nancy Tafuri   *p* 1360
The Mayor of Central Park - Avi   *e* 59
My Friend Rabbit - Eric Rohmann   *p* 1222
My Somebody Special - Sarah Weeks   *p* 1422
Noah's Ark - Jerry Pinkney   *p* 1158
Not Just a Witch - Eva Ibbotson   *e, m* 708
Old MacDonald Had a Woodshop - Lisa Shulman   *p* 1296
One-Dog Canoe - Mary Casanova   *p* 225
One Is a Snail, Ten Is a Crab: A Counting by Feet Book - April Pulley Sayre   *p* 1267
One Rainy Day - Valeri Gorbachev   *p* 542
Our Class Took a Trip to the Zoo - Shirley Neitzel   *p* 1071
Platypus - Chris Riddell   *p* 1202
Platypus and the Birthday Party - Chris Riddell   *p* 1203
Platypus and the Lucky Day - Chris Riddell   *p* 1204
Poultrygeist - Mary Jane Auch   *p* 55
The Rudest Alien on Earth - Jane Leslie Conly   *e, m* 286
The Saturday Escape - Daniel J. Mahoney   *p* 934
Secret Heart - David Almond   *m, h* 21
Serious Farm - Tim Egan   *p* 421
Slow Loris - Alexis Deacon   *p* 361
Slowly, Slowly, Slowly, said the Sloth - Eric Carle   *p* 217
Snow - Manya Stojic   *p* 1346
Something Might Happen - Helen Lester   *p* 876

Big Jimmy's Kum Kau Chinese Take Out - Ted Lewin
p 888
Dish Series - Diane Muldrow   *e, m* 1037
Flavor of the Week - Tucker Shaw   *m, h* 1288
Making Plum Jam - John Warren Stewig   *p* 1344
Mr. Putter & Tabby Stir the Soup - Cynthia Rylant
b 1248
Stone Soup - Jon J. Muth   *p* 1047

Country Life

Christmas in the Country - Cynthia Rylant   *p* 1244
The Painters of Lexieville - Sharon Darrow   *m,*
h 348
Time Pieces: The Book of Times - Virginia Hamilton
m 590
The Trouble with Jeremy Chance - George Harrar   *e,*
m 597
Welcome Home or Someplace Like It - Charlotte Agell
m 7

Courage

The Brave Little Seamstress - Mary Pope Osborne
p 1116
A Brave Soldier - Nicholas Debon   *p* 365
Donuthead - Sue Stauffacher   *e* 1337
Especially Heroes - Virginia Kroll   *p* 831
The Forest - Claire A. Nivola   *p* 1083
Francis the Scaredy Cat - Ed Boxall   *p* 131
Goddess of Yesterday - Caroline B. Cooney   *m,*
h 292
Good Night, Sleep Tight, Don't Let the Bedbugs Bite! -
Diane DeGroat   *p* 369
Lionclaw: A Tale of Rowan Hood - Nancy Springer
m 1330
*Mightier than the Sword: World Folktales for Strong
Boys* - Jane Yolen   *e* 1485
When My Name Was Keoko - Linda Sue Park
m 1127

Courtship

Potch & Polly - William Steig   *p* 1338

Cousins

The Battle of Jericho - Sharon M. Draper   *m,*
h 395
The Dream Shop - Katharine Kenah   *p* 780
Iris and Walter and Cousin Howie - Elissa Haden
Guest   *b* 569
*Rosy Cole's Worst Ever, Best Yet Tour of New York
City* - Sheila Greenwald   *e* 556
Tadpole - Ruth White   *e, m* 1438
Toot & Puddle: Charming Opal - Holly Hobbie
p 649
What a Hat! - Holly Keller   *p* 778

Cowboys/Cowgirls

The Dirty Cowboy - Amy Timberlake   *p* 1382
Hannah Mae O'Hannigan's Wild West Show - Lisa
Campbell Ernst   *p* 437
*Little Old Big Beard and Big Young Little Beard: A
Short and Tall Tale* - Remy Charlip   *p* 238
Thunder Rose - Jerdine Nolen   *p* 1093

Creation

Big Momma Makes the World - Phyllis Root
p 1226

Crime and Criminals

Amy - Mary Hooper   *m, h* 674

Arizona Charlie and the Klondike Kid - Julie Lawson
p 864
Lily B. on the Brink of Cool - E. Cody Kimmel   *e,*
m 786
Rebel - Willo Davis Roberts   *m* 1211
Shooting Monarchs - John Halliday   *h* 587

Cruise Ships

Monkey Mo Goes to Sea - Diane Goode   *p* 538

Crusades

At the Crossing Places - Kevin Crossley-Holland   *m,*
h 319
The Leopard Sword - Michael Cadnum   *m, h* 201
Pagan's Crusade - Catherine Jinks   *m, h* 739

Crystals

Rowan and the Keeper of the Crystal - Emily Rodda
e 1218

Cuban Americans

Cuba 15 - Nancy Osa   *m, h* 1115
Flight to Freedom - Ana Veciana-Suarez   *m,*
h 1400

Cults

Faith Wish - James Bennett   *h* 102
I Am Not Esther - Fleur Beale   *m, h* 91

Cultural Conflict

Angelica: A Novel of Samaria - Sharon Shinn   *h,*
a 1293
The Companions - Sheri S. Tepper   *h, a* 1373
Diplomatic Immunity: A Comedy of Terrors - Lois
McMaster Bujold   *h, a* 176
Explorer - C.J. Cherryh   *h, a* 244

Cultures and Customs

Cuba 15 - Nancy Osa   *m, h* 1115

Dancing

The Alley Cat's Meow - Kathi Appelt   *p* 32
Big Bear Ball - Joanne Ryder   *p* 1242
Brianna, Jamaica, and the Dance of Spring - Juanita
Havill   *p* 612
Daisy the Dancing Cow - Viki Woodworth
p 1469
Dinosaurumpus - Tony Mitton   *p* 1019
Down by the Cool of the Pool - Tony Mitton
p 1020
*The Glass Cafe: Or the Stripper and the State: How
My Mother Started a War with the System that
Made Us Kind of Rich and a Little Bit Famous* -
Gary Paulsen   *m, h* 1134
Not Just Tutus - Rachel Isadora   *p* 718
Sailor Boy Jig - Margaret Wise Brown   *p* 167
The Stone Goddess - Minfong Ho   *m, h* 646
Tanya and the Red Shoes - Patricia Lee Gauch
p 510
Tessa's Tip-Tapping Toes - Carolyn Crimi   *p* 314

Dating (Social Customs)

*Dancing in My Nuddy-Pants: Even Further
Confessions of Georgia Nicolson* - Louise Rennison
m, h 1198
How I Fell in Love & Learned to Shoot Free Throws -
Jon Ripslinger   *h* 1209
Princess in Waiting - Meg Cabot   *m, h* 198

Son of the Mob - Gordon Korman   *m, h* 818
Telling Christina Goodbye - Lurlene McDaniel   *m,*
h 974
This Lullaby - Sarah Dessen   *h* 377
Zipped - Laura McNeal   *h* 996

Deafness

Moses Goes to the Circus - Isaac Millman   *p* 1012
Saving Grace - Priscilla Cummings   *e, m* 327

Death

Abhorsen - Garth Nix   *m, h* 1084
The Afterlife - Gary Soto   *m, h* 1320
The Battle of Jericho - Sharon M. Draper   *m,*
h 395
A Bed of Earth: The Gravedigger's Tale - Tanith Lee
h, a 872
Blue Eyes Better - Ruth Wallace-Brodeur   *e* 1412
Dead Girls Don't Write Letters - Gail Giles   *m,*
h 525
Falling through Darkness - Carolyn McCullough
h 972
The Farther You Run - Davida Wills Hurwin
h 700
Flamingo Dream - Donna Jo Napoli   *p* 1061
The Great Blue Yonder - Alex Shearer   *m, h* 1290
In the Piney Woods - Roni Schotter   *p* 1270
Izzy's Place - Marc Kornblatt   *e, m* 819
The Letters - Kazumi Yumoto   *m, h* 1490
Lighthouse: A Story of Remembrance - Robert Munsch
p 1039
Lumber Camp Library - Natalie Kinsey-Warnock
e 798
Martyn Pig - Kevin Brooks   *m, h* 160
My Life and Death by Alexandra Canarsie - Susan
Heyboer O'Keefe   *m, h* 1105
A Perfect Place - Patricia Hermes   *e* 627
That Summer - Tony Johnston   *p* 755
This Isn't about the Money - Sally Warner
m 1417
United Tates of America - Paula Danziger   *e,*
m 347

Dentistry

Mabel the Tooth Fairy and How She Got Her Job -
Katie Davis   *p* 350

Department Stores

Milly and the Macy's Parade - Shana Corey
p 303

Depression

Bringing Up the Bones - Lara M. Zeises   *h* 1492
Warrior Angel - Robert Lipsyte   *h* 900

Depression (Economic)

The Amazing Thinking Machine - Dennis Haseley
e 606
Butterflies and Lizards, Beryl and Me - Ruth Lercher
Bornstein   *e, m* 127
Dust - Arthur Slade   *m, h* 1308
Hannah, Divided - Adele Griffin   *m* 562
*The Journal of C.J. Jackson: A Dust Bowl Migrant:
Oklahoma to California, 1935* - William Durbin
m 410
Macaroni Boy - Katherine Ayres   *e, m* 62
Saving Grace - Priscilla Cummings   *e, m* 327
*Survival in the Storm: The Dust Bowl Diary of Grace
Edwards* - Katelan Janke   *e, m* 728
Wingwalker - Rosemary Wells   *e* 1429

Subject Index

Subject Index

Water: Tales of Elemental Spirits - Robin McKinley
m, h 985

The Wee Free Men: A Novel of Discworld - Terry Pratchett m, h 1167

Wizard at Work - Vivian Vande Velde e 1397

Wizard's Holiday - Diane Duane m 402

Wizards of the Game - David Lubar m 914

Wolf Queen - Tanith Lee m, h 874

The Wolves in the Walls - Neil Gaiman p 503

Zathura: A Space Adventure - Chris Van Allsburg
p 1390

Farm Life

The Animal Hedge - Paul Fleischman p 459

Aunt Minnie and the Twister - Mary Skillings Prigger
p 1170

Bob - Tracey Campbell Pearson p 1140

Cornfield Hide-and-Seek - Christine Widman
p 1442

Daniel's Pet - Alma Flor Ada b 1

A Day in the Life of Murphy - Alice Provensen
p 1176

Does a Cow Say Boo? - Judy Hindley p 643

The Dream Shop - Katharine Kenah p 780

From Dawn till Dusk - Natalie Kinsey-Warnock
p 796

Georgie Lee - Sharon Phillips Denslow e 374

Giggle, Giggle, Quack - Doreen Cronin p 317

Guerrilla Season - Pat Hughes m, h 693

Harvest Home - Jane Yolen p 1481

Hobart - Anita Briggs e 149

Homespun Sarah - Verla Kay p 771

Horse in the Pigpen - Linda Williams p 1446

A Hug Goes Around - Laura Krauss Melmed
p 1005

Hushabye Lily - Claire Freedman p 487

In Plain Sight - Carol Otis Hurst e, m 698

Jake Riley: Irreparably Damaged - Rebecca Fjelland
Davis m, h 352

Making Plum Jam - John Warren Stewig p 1344

Mary Had a Little Ham - Margie Palatini p 1123

Minnie and Moo and the Seven Wonders of the World
- Denys Cazet e 234

Moo Cow Kaboom! - Thacher Hurd p 697

A Northern Light - Jennifer Donnelly h 387

Old MacDonald Had a Woodshop - Lisa Shulman
p 1296

Once Upon a Farm - Marie Bradby p 132

Orville: A Dog Story - Haven Kimmel p 790

Party Animals - Katie Davis p 351

Pete and Polo's Farmyard Adventure - Adrian
Reynolds p 1200

Piggies in a Polka - Kathi Appelt p 35

Prairie Summer - Bonnie Geisert e 516

A Real American - Richard Easton m 414

Serious Farm - Tim Egan p 421

Storm Is Coming! - Heather Tekavec p 1371

Stray Voltage - Eugenie Doyle p 393

*Survival in the Storm: The Dust Bowl Diary of Grace
Edwards* - Katelan Janke e, m 728

Under the Same Sky - Cynthia DeFelice m, h 368

Wake Up, Big Barn! - Suzanne Tanner Chitwood
p 252

What Did You Do Today? - Kerry Arquette p 41

Fashion Design

Miss Hunnicutt's Hat - Jeff Brumbeau p 172

Zat Cat! A Haute Couture Tail - Chesley McLaren
p 987

Fathers

Gina.Jamie.Father.Bear - George Ella Lyon m,
h 920

Keeper of the Doves - Betsy Byars e 192

Spitting Image - Shutta Crum m 321

Fathers and Daughters

Amber Waiting - Nan Gregory p 559

Begging for Change - Sharon G. Flake m, h 458

Catalyst - Laurie Halse Anderson h 28

Child X - Lee Weatherly m, h 1419

Daddy Says - Ntozake Shange m 1281

Dante's Daughter - Kimberley Heuston h 635

Flamingo Dream - Donna Jo Napoli p 1061

Freaky Green Eyes - Joyce Carol Oates m,
h 1099

Gifts from the Sea - Natalie Kinsey-Warnock e,
m 797

Hill Hawk Hattie - Clara Gillow Clark e, m 257

In Plain Sight - Carol Otis Hurst e, m 698

Mahalia - Joanne Horniman h 679

Making the Run - Heather Henson h 626

My Father Had a Daughter: Judith Shakespeare's Tale
- Grace Tiffany h, a 1381

A Place to Grow - Soyung Pak p 1121

Ruby Electric - Theresa Nelson m 1074

The Secret Within - Theresa Golding m 534

True Blue - Jeffrey Lee e, m 871

Two Old Potatoes and Me - John Coy p 311

Visiting Day - Jacqueline Woodson p 1468

The Voyage of Patience Goodspeed - Heather Vogel
Frederick m 485

Who Owns Kelly Paddik? - Beth Goobie m, h 537

Fathers and Sons

Amaryllis - Craig Crist-Evans m, h 315

Big Jimmy's Kum Kau Chinese Take Out - Ted Lewin
p 888

Bippity Bop Barbershop - Natasha Anastasia Tarpley
p 1362

The Dream Bearer - Walter Dean Myers m 1052

Dream Carver - Diana Cohn p 271

Firewing - Kenneth Oppel m 1111

Flood - James Heneghan m 621

Gus and Grandpa and the Halloween Costume -
Claudia Mills b 1014

Hanging on to Max - Margaret Bechard h 94

The Hemingway Tradition - Kristin Butcher
m 186

The Hero - Ron Woods m, h 1464

High Heat - Carl Deuker m, h 378

I Dream of Trains - Angela Johnson p 742

The Key to My Heart - Nira Harel p 593

Kings Mountain - G. Clifton Wisler m 1451

Little Buggy - Kevin O'Malley p 1107

Little Buggy Runs Away - Kevin O'Malley p 1108

Matchit - Martha Moore e, m 1027

Mississippi Trial, 1955 - Chris Crowe m, h 320

Pinocchio the Boy: Incognito in Collodi - Lane Smith
p 1314

Pool Boy - Michael Simmons m, h 1305

Skinny-Dipping at Monster Lake - Bill Wallace
m 1406

Stray Voltage - Eugenie Doyle m 393

Tribes - Arthur Slade h 1309

The Trouble with Jeremy Chance - George Harrar e,
m 597

Under the Same Sky - Cynthia DeFelice m, h 368

The Viking Series - Christopher Tebbetts m 1370

Wild Boy - James Lincoln Collier m 279

Fear

Among the Betrayed - Margaret Peterson Haddix m,
h 578

Bertil and the Bathroom Elephants - Inger Lindahl
p 894

Bravery Soup - Maryann Cocca-Leffler p 267

Countdown to Kindergarten - Alison McGhee
p 978

The Creek - Jennifer L. Holm m, h 667

Donuthead - Sue Stauffacher e 1337

Egad Alligator! - Harriet Ziefert p 1495

First Day - Dandi Daley Mackall p 928

The Forest - Claire A. Nivola p 1083

Francis the Scaredy Cat - Ed Boxall p 131

Get Ready for Second Grade, Amber Brown - Paula
Danziger b 346

Ghost at the Window - Margaret McAllister e,
m 960

Kipper's Monster - Mick Inkpen p 715

Little Rat Sets Sail - Monika Bang-Campbell b 72

Olvina Flies - Grace Lin p 893

Roller Coaster - Marla Frazee p 484

Ruler of the Courtyard - Rukhsana Khan p 784

The Scaredy Cats - Barbara Bottner p 128

Something Might Happen - Helen Lester p 876

Stuart Goes to School - Sara Pennypacker e 1143

Stuart's Cape - Sara Pennypacker e 1144

Tippy Lemmey - Patricia C. McKissack e 986

The Turtle and the Hippopotamus - Kate Banks
p 77

Wingwalker - Rosemary Wells e 1429

Feral Children

The Earthborn - Paul Collins h, a 282

The Pack - Elisa Carbone m, h 214

Fires

The Babbs Switch Story - Darleen Bailey Beard
m 93

The Big Burn - Jeanette Ingold m, h 713

Falling from Fire - Teena Booth m, h 126

Fire Storm - Jean Craighead George p 517

Kerosene - Chris Wooding h 1461

New York's Bravest - Mary Pope Osborne p 1117

Out of the Fire - Deborah Froese h 497

The Secret of the Red Flame - K.M. Kimball e,
m 785

The Star People: A Lakota Story - S.D. Nelson
p 1073

The Tears of the Salamander - Peter Dickinson m,
h 382

Fishing

Fishing Day - Andrea Davis Pinkney p 1156

Gus and Grandpa Go Fishing - Claudia Mills
b 1015

Sea Gift - John Ashby m, h 47

Floods

Annie's Ark - Lesley Harker p 594

The Giant Ball of String - Arthur Geisert p 515

Gullywasher Gulch - Marianne Mitchell p 1018

Little Scraggly Hair: A Dog on Noah's Ark - Lynn
Cullen p 324

Noah's Ark - Jerry Pinkney p 1158

Rising Water - P.J. Petersen m 1148

Folk Tales

Ali and the Magic Stew - Shulamith Levey Oppenheim
p 1112

The Bachelor and the Bean - Shelley Fowles
p 475

*Can You Guess My Name?: Traditional Tales around
the World* - Judy Sierra e 1302

The Elephant's Pillow - Diana Reynolds Roome
p 1223

The Firebird - Jane Yolen p 1479

*Invisible Kingdoms: Jewish Tales of Angels, Spirits,
and Demons* - Howard Schwartz e 1273

The Magic Gourd - Baba Wague Diakite p 380

*Mightier than the Sword: World Folktales for Strong
Boys* - Jane Yolen e 1485

*Night Dancer: Mythical Piper of the Native American
Southwest* - Marcia Vaughan p 1398

Subject Index

Interpersonal Relations

Alt Ed - Catherine Atkins   *m, h* 52

Amy - Mary Hooper   *m, h* 674

Attack of the Mutant Underwear - Tom Birdseye   *e* 109

Bad Girls in Love - Cynthia Voigt   *m* 1402

The Beast - Walter Dean Myers   *h* 1051

Better than Running at Night - Hillary Frank   *h* 481

Blizzard's Wake - Phyllis Reynolds Naylor   *m, h* 1065

Blue Avenger and the Theory of Everything - Norma Howe   *m, h* 689

Born Too Short: The Confessions of an Eighth-Grade Basket Case - Dan Elish   *m* 425

Bringing Up the Bones - Lara M. Zeises   *h* 1492

Deep - Susanna Vance   *m, h* 1394

Fame and Glory in Freedom, Georgia - Barbara O'Connor   *e, m* 1102

Getting the Girl - Markus Zusak   *h* 1498

Girls in Love - Jacqueline Wilson   *m, h* 1448

Gossip Times Three - Amy Goldman Koss   *m* 821

Hard Time - Julian F. Thompson   *m, h* 1378

House of Sports - Marisabina Russo   *m* 1240

The Kings Are Already Here - Garret Freymann-Weyr   *m, h* 493

Knocked Out by My Nunga-Nungas: Further, Further Confessions of Georgia Nicolson - Louise Rennison   *m, h* 1199

Mates, Dates and Inflatable Bras - Cathy Hopkins   *m, h* 676

The Monster in Me - Mette Ivie Harrison   *m* 600

My Cup Runneth Over: The Life of Angelica Cookson Potts - Cherry Whytock   *m, h* 1441

My Heartbeat - Garret Freymann-Weyr   *h* 494

An Ocean Apart, a World Away - Lensey Namioka   *m, h* 1058

One Shot - Susan Glick   *m, h* 529

Out of Order - A.M. Jenkins   *h* 732

Overnight - Adele Griffin   *e, m* 563

Planet Janet - Dyan Sheldon   *m, h* 1291

Prep - Jake Coburn   *h* 266

Rainbow High - Alex Sanchez   *h* 1262

Remembrance - Theresa Breslin   *m, h* 143

Simply Alice - Phyllis Reynolds Naylor   *m* 1069

Slumming - Kristen D. Randle   *h* 1183

Sticks and Stones - Beth Goobie   *m, h* 536

True Confessions of a Heartless Girl - Martha Brooks   *h* 161

The True Meaning of Cleavage - Mariah Fredericks   *m, h* 486

Vampire Kisses - Ellen Schreiber   *m, h* 1271

The Weeping Willow - Patrick Jennings   *e* 734

Who the Man - Chris Lynch   *m, h* 918

Zipped - Laura McNeal   *h* 996

Inventors and Inventions

The Amazing Thinking Machine - Dennis Haseley   *e* 606

Ice-Cream Cones for Sale! - Elaine Greenstein   *p* 555

Porkenstein - Kathryn Lasky   *p* 856

Irish Potato Famine

Maggie's Door - Patricia Reilly Giff   *m* 523

Islands

Camp of the Angel - Aileen Arrington   *e, m* 42

The Castaway - James Stevenson   *p* 1343

The Fattening Hut - Pat Lowery Collins   *h* 281

Island Boyz - Graham Salisbury   *m, h* 1253

Kensuke's Kingdom - Michael Morpurgo   *e* 1033

The Lighthouse Keeper's Daughter - Iain Lawrence   *h* 860

Lucas - Kevin Brooks   *h* 159

On Sand Island - Jacqueline Briggs Martin   *p* 947

Paradise - Joan Elizabeth Goodman   *m, h* 541

The Sea Chest - Toni Buzzeo   *p* 190

Italian Americans

Home at Last - Kathryn Lasky   *e* 852

Hope in My Heart - Kathryn Lasky   *e* 853

Morning Glory Monday - Arlene Alda   *p* 16

Japanese Americans

Beacon Hill Boys - Ken Mochizuki   *m, h* 1021

When the Emperor Was Divine - Julie Otsuka   *h, a* 1120

Jealousy

Born Too Short: The Confessions of an Eighth-Grade Basket Case - Dan Elish   *m* 425

Jews

Daughter of Venice - Donna Jo Napoli   *m, h* 1060

The Enemy Has a Face - Gloria D. Miklowitz   *m, h* 1009

Invisible Kingdoms: Jewish Tales of Angels, Spirits, and Demons - Howard Schwartz   *e* 1273

Malka - Mirjam Pressler   *m, h* 1168

Marika - Andrea Cheng   *m, h* 241

One Candle - Eve Bunting   *p* 180

A Picture of Grandmother - Esther Hautzig   *e* 611

Room in the Heart - Sonia Levitin   *m, h* 886

Run, Boy, Run - Uri Orlev   *m, h* 1114

Sparks Fly Upward - Carol Matas   *e, m* 954

When Pirates Came to Brooklyn - Phyllis Shalant   *e, m* 1280

Journalism

Darby - Jonathon Scott Fuqua   *e* 501

Trouble Is My Beeswax - Bruce Hale   *e* 585

Juvenile Detention Centers

Handbook for Boys: A Novel - Walter Dean Myers   *m, h* 1053

Kidnapping

Artemis Fowl: The Arctic Incident - Eoin Colfer   *m* 276

Colibri - Ann Cameron   *m* 206

Deep - Susanna Vance   *m, h* 1394

Escape from Memory - Margaret Peterson Haddix   *m, h* 580

Girl in a Cage - Jane Yolen   *m, h* 1480

The Long Night of Leo and Bree - Ellen Wittlinger   *m, h* 1453

Overnight - Adele Griffin   *e, m* 563

Spy Cat - Peg Kehret   *e, m* 773

Storm Catchers - Tim Bowler   *m, h* 129

Tria and the Great Star Rescue - Rebecca Kraft Rector   *e* 1191

The Twins and the Bird of Darkness: A Hero Tale from the Caribbean - Robert D. San Souci   *e* 1260

The Ugly Goddess - Elsa Marston   *m* 944

Waiting for Christopher - Louise Hawes   *m, h* 613

Kings, Queens, Rulers, etc.

Cecile: Gates of Gold - Mary Casanova   *e, m* 224

Doomed Queen Anne - Carolyn Meyer   *m, h* 1006

Eleanor: Crown Jewel of Aquitaine, France, 1136 - Kristiana Gregory   *m* 557

Midwinter Nightingale - Joan Aiken   *m* 13

The Nightingale - Jerry Pinkney   *p* 1157

Serious Trouble - Arthur Howard   *p* 684

The Warhorse - Don Bolognese   *m* 122

The Whale Rider - Witi Ihimaera   *m, h* 710

Knights and Knighthood

The Ballad of Sir Dinadan - Gerald Morris   *m, h* 1034

Get Well, Good Knight - Shelley Moore Thomas   *b* 1377

The Goblin Wood - Hilari Bell   *m, h* 98

Lady Knight - Tamora Pierce   *m, h* 1150

The Leopard Sword - Michael Cadnum   *m, h* 201

Pagan's Crusade - Catherine Jinks   *m, h* 739

Korean Americans

Horrible Harry and the Dragon War - Suzy Kline   *e* 806

My Name Is Yoon - Helen Recorvits   *p* 1189

Language

Achoo! Bang! Crash!: The Noisy Alphabet - Ross MacDonald   *p* 924

Calling Doctor Amelia Bedelia - Herman Parish   *b* 1126

Home at Last - Susan Middleton Elya   *p* 431

Learning

Elizabeti's School - Stephanie Stuve-Bodeen   *p* 1352

Legends

Ananse and the Lizard: A West African Tale - Pat Cummings   *p* 326

Have a Hot Time, Hades! - Kate McMullan   *e* 991

Mannekin Pis: A Simple Story of a Boy Who Peed on a War - Vladimir Radunsky   *p* 1181

Mrs. McCool and the Giant Cuhullin: An Irish Tale - Jessica Souhami   *p* 1322

New York's Bravest - Mary Pope Osborne   *p* 1117

The One-Eyed Giant - Mary Pope Osborne   *e* 1118

The True Story of Trapper Jack's Left Big Toe - Ian Wallace   *p* 1407

Letters

Alphabet under Construction - Denise Fleming   *p* 464

Boxes for Katje - Candace Fleming   *p* 462

Dear Emma - Johanna Hurwitz   *e, m* 701

Dear Mrs. LaRue: Letters from Obedience School - Mark Teague   *p* 1369

The Journey of Oliver K. Woodman - Darcy Pattison   *p* 1130

My Grandma, My Pen Pal - Jan Dale Koutsky   *p* 822

Plantzilla - Jerdine Nolen   *p* 1092

Z Goes Home - Jon Agee   *p* 6

Libraries

Beverly Billingsly Borrows a Book - Alexander Stadler   *p* 1333

Lighthouses

The Boy Who Could Fly Without a Motor - Theodore Taylor   *e* 1364

One Lucky Summer - Laura McGee Kvasnosky
   e   840

Sliding into Home - Dori Hillstad Butler   m   189

Stuart's Cape - Sara Pennypacker   e   1144

Surfer Dog - Elizabeth Spurr   e, m   1332

The Trouble with Babies - Martha Freeman   e   488

The Trouble with Liberty - Kristin Butcher   m,
   h   187

The Way We Do It in Japan - Geneva Cobb Iijima
   p   711

When Marcus Moore Moved In - Rebecca Bond
   p   123

The Wrong One - Carol Otis Hurst   e, m   699

Multicultural

*Can You Guess My Name?: Traditional Tales around
   the World* - Judy Sierra   e   1302

The Way We Do It in Japan - Geneva Cobb Iijima
   p   711

Multiple Personalities

Picture Perfect - Elaine Marie Alphin   m, h   22

Mummies

The Mummy's Mother - Tony Johnston   e   753

Murder

Blood Trail - Nancy Springer   m, h   1329

The Creek - Jennifer L. Holm   m, h   667

Death and the Arrow - Chris Priestley   m, h   1169

Freaky Green Eyes - Joyce Carol Oates   m,
   h   1099

The Long Night of Leo and Bree - Ellen Wittlinger
   m, h   1453

Nightmare - Joan Lowery Nixon   m, h   1086

A Northern Light - Jennifer Donnelly   h   387

The Queen of Everything - Deb Caletti   h   202

The Square Root of Murder - Paul Zindel   m   1496

Museums

Lauren McGill's Pickle Museum - Jerdine Nolen
   p   1091

Might Adventurer of the Planet! - Ricki Stern
   e   1341

Music and Musicians

The Alley Cat's Meow - Kathi Appelt   p   32

The Aunts Go Marching - Maurie J. Manning
   p   937

Bring on That Beat - Rachel Isadora   p   717

Dancing the Ring Shout! - Kim Siegelson   p   1300

Fat Kid Rules the World - K.L. Going   h   533

Froggy Plays in the Band - Jonathan London
   p   906

Just Enough and Not Too Much - Kaethe Zemach
   p   1493

Just One More Story - Jennifer Brutschy   p   173

LBD: It's a Girl Thing - Grace Dent   m, h   375

Mad Maudlin - Mercedes Lackey   h, a   844

Making Music - Susan Bonners   e   124

Mountain Solo - Jeanette Ingold   m, h   714

*Night Dancer: Mythical Piper of the Native American
   Southwest* - Marcia Vaughan   p   1398

Piggies in a Polka - Kathi Appelt   p   35

Singing the Dogstar Blues - Alison Goodman
   h   540

Sweet By and By - Patricia Hermes   e, m   629

This Lullaby - Sarah Dessen   h   377

Where in the World - Simon French   m   491

Muslims

Overboard - Elizabeth Fama   m, h   442

Mutism

Chang and the Bamboo Flute - Elizabeth Starr Hill
   e   640

Green Boy - Susan Cooper   m   297

Shining - Julius Lester   p   878

Mystery

*The 5,000-Year-Old Puzzle: Solving a Mystery of
   Ancient Egypt* - Claudia Logan   p   904

Alphabet Mystery - Audrey Wood   p   1457

Dot & Jabber and the Mystery of the Missing Stream -
   Ellen Stoll Walsh   p   1413

Mystery and Detective Stories

Acceleration - Graham McNamee   m, h   995

Bernie Magruder & the Bats in the Belfry - Phyllis
   Reynolds Naylor   e   1064

Blood Trail - Nancy Springer   m, h   1329

The Case of the Graveyard Ghost - Michele Torrey
   e   1384

The Case of the Sleepy Sloth - Cynthia Rylant
   b   1243

The Creek - Jennifer L. Holm   m, h   667

Danger at the Wild West Show - Alison Hart
   m   601

Dead Girls Don't Write Letters - Gail Giles   m,
   h   525

Death and the Arrow - Chris Priestley   m, h   1169

The Hamster of the Baskervilles - Bruce Hale
   e   583

Harriet Spies Again - Helen Ericson   e, m   435

How to Disappear Completely and Never Be Found -
   Sara Nickerson   m   1079

*Jake Gander, Storyville Detective: The Case of the
   Greedy Granny* - George McClements   p   969

The Last Treasure - Janet S. Anderson   m, h   26

Lord of the Kill - Theodore Taylor   m, h   1366

The Malted Falcon - Bruce Hale   e   584

My Life and Death by Alexandra Canarsie - Susan
   Heyboer O'Keefe   m, h   1105

Mystery in Mt. Mole - Richard W. Jennings   m,
   h   737

Nightmare - Joan Lowery Nixon   m, h   1086

Phoning a Dead Man - Gillian Cross   m, h   318

Rebel - Willo Davis Roberts   m   1211

Remote Man - Elizabeth Honey   m, h   670

Sammy Keyes and the Search for Snake Eyes -
   Wendelin Van Draanen   m   1391

Savage Run - C.J. Box   h, a   130

The Secret of the Red Flame - K.M. Kimball   e,
   m   785

The Square Root of Murder - Paul Zindel   m   1496

The Trap - Joan Lowery Nixon   m, h   1087

Trouble Is My Beeswax - Bruce Hale   e   585

Undercurrents - Willo Davis Roberts   m, h   1212

Where's the Big Bad Wolf? - Eileen Christelow
   p   254

Who Is Stealing the Twelve Days of Christmas? -
   Martha Freeman   e   489

Winter - John Marsden   m, h   943

Mythology

Celtika - Robert Holdstock   h, a   664

Child of the Prophecy - Juliet Marillier   h, a   941

The Dark Horse - Marcus Sedgwick   m   1275

Goddess of Yesterday - Caroline B. Cooney   m,
   h   292

Goddesses Series - Clea Hantman   m, h   592

The Great God Pan - Donna Jo Napoli   m, h   1062

Have a Hot Time, Hades! - Kate McMullan   e   991

Hippolyta and the Curse of the Amazons - Jane Yolen
   m   1482

Juliet Dove, Queen of Love - Bruce Coville   e,
   m   308

The One-Eyed Giant - Mary Pope Osborne   e   1118

Pig Tale - Verlyn Flieger   h   466

Quiver - Stephanie Spinner   m, h   1327

The Ugly Goddess - Elsa Marston   m   944

Names, Personal

City of Names - Kevin Brockmeier   e   157

The First Thing My Mama Told Me - Susan Marie
   Swanson   p   1355

Matthew A.B.C. - Peter Catalanotto   p   229

My Name Is Yoon - Helen Recorvits   p   1189

That Pesky Rat - Lauren Child   p   248

Native Americans

*Night Dancer: Mythical Piper of the Native American
   Southwest* - Marcia Vaughan   p   1398

The Range Eternal - Louise Erdrich   p   434

The Star People: A Lakota Story - S.D. Nelson
   p   1073

Nature

Atlantic - G. Brian Karas   p   764

Frog Hunt - Sandra Jordan   p   760

Hello, Arctic! - Theodore Taylor   p   1365

In My World - Lois Ehlert   p   423

In the Piney Woods - Roni Schotter   p   1270

My Contract with Henry - Robin Vaupel   m   1399

My World of Color - Margaret Wise Brown   p   165

One Leaf Rides the Wind - Celeste Davidson Mannis
   p   938

A Quiet Place - Douglas Wood   p   1460

When the Root Children Wake Up - Audrey Wood
   p   1458

Near-Death Experience

Full Tilt: A Novel - Neal Shusterman   m, h   1297

Wenny Has Wings - Janet Lee Carey   e, m   216

Neighbors and Neighborhoods

The Big Cheese of Third Street - Laurie Halse
   Anderson   p   27

Catalyst - Laurie Halse Anderson   h   28

The Four Ugly Cats in Apartment 3D - Marilyn Sachs
   e   1249

The House Across the Street - Jules Feiffer   p   447

It Feels Like Snow - Nancy Cote   p   305

Madlenka's Dog - Peter Sis   p   1307

Mr. Putter & Tabby Stir the Soup - Cynthia Rylant
   b   1248

The New Hippos - Lena Landstrom   p   848

No Place for a Pig - Suzanne Bloom   p   119

On the Town: A Community Adventure - Judith
   Caseley   p   227

Tippy Lemmey - Patricia C. McKissack   e   986

The Trouble with Babies - Martha Freeman   e   488

When Catherine the Great and I Were Eight! - Cari
   Best   p   107

When Marcus Moore Moved In - Rebecca Bond
   p   123

Newspapers

The New Rules of High School - Blake Nelson
   h   1072

Subject Index

Breath - Donna Jo Napoli   *m, h*   1059
A Company of Fools - Deborah Ellis   *m*   427

Playing

Annie Rose Is My Little Sister - Shirley Hughes
    p   694
Dahlia - Barbara McClintock   *p*   970
Like a Windy Day - Frank Asch   *p*   46
Mr. Basset Plays - Dominic Catalano   *p*   228
Mud Is Cake - Pam Munoz Ryan   *p*   1241
On My Way to Buy Eggs - Chih-Yuan Chen   *p*   239
Peekaboo Morning - Rachel Isadora   *p*   719
The Recess Queen - Alexis O'Neill   *p*   1110
Treasure Hunt - Allan Ahlberg   *p*   10
What Shall We Play? - Sue Heap   *p*   618
While We Were Out - Ho Baek Lee   *p*   869
Zathura: A Space Adventure - Chris Van Allsburg
    p   1390

Plays

Beverly Billingsly Takes a Bow - Alexander Stadler
    p   1334
Boys in Control - Phyllis Reynolds Naylor   *e*   1066
A Simple Gift - Nancy Ruth Patterson   *e*   1129

Poetry

17: A Novel in Prose Poems - Liz Rosenberg
    h   1230
Be Boy Buzz - bell hooks   *p*   672
Bronx Masquerade - Nikki Grimes   *m, h*   565
Comfort - Carolee Dean   *m, h*   363
Danitra Brown Leaves Town - Nikki Grimes
    p   566
Girl Coming in for a Landing - April Halprin Wayland
    m, h   1418
Homemade Love - bell hooks   *p*   673
Keesha's House - Helen Frost   *m, h*   498
Locomotion - Jacqueline Woodson   *m, h*   1466
One Leaf Rides the Wind - Celeste Davidson Mannis
    p   938
Shakespeare Bats Cleanup - Ron Koertge   *m,*
    h   809
This Is the House That Jack Built - Simms Taback
    p   1358

Police Procedural

Policeman Lou and Policewoman Sue - Lisa Desimini
    p   376

Political Prisoners

The Impossible Journey - Gloria Whelan   *m*   1436

Political Thriller

Shadow Puppets - Orson Scott Card   *h, a*   215

Politics

The Courtesan's Daughter - Priscilla Galloway
    h   505
War of Honor - David Weber   *h, a*   1421
The Watch - Dennis Danvers   *h, a*   344

Pollution

The 1980s: Earthsong - Tom Hoobler   *m*   671

Popular Culture

Pattern Recognition - William Gibson   *h, a*   522

Popularity

Dork on the Run - Carol Gorman   *e, m*   543
Fame and Glory in Freedom, Georgia - Barbara
    O'Connor   *e, m*   1102
Shattering Glass - Gail Giles   *h*   526

Possessions

Just Enough and Not Too Much - Kaethe Zemach
    p   1493

Post Nuclear Holocaust

The City of Ember - Jeanne DuPrau   *m*   409

Poverty

Begging for Change - Sharon G. Flake   *m, h*   458
Bitter Dumplings - Jeanne M. Lee   *p*   870
The Kite - Luis Garay   *p*   509
Mirabelle - Astrid Lindgren   *p*   896
The Painters of Lexieville - Sharon Darrow   *m,*
    h   348
Patiently Alice - Phyllis Reynolds Naylor   *m,*
    h   1068
Recycling George - Stephen Roos   *e, m*   1224
Spitting Image - Shutta Crum   *m*   321

Pregnancy

Dancing Naked - Shelley Hrdlitschka   *h*   692
Faith Wish - James Bennett   *h*   102
A Greater Goode - Amy Schor Ferris   *m*   451
True Confessions of a Heartless Girl - Martha Brooks
    h   161
Waiting for June - Joyce Sweeney   *h*   1356

Prejudice

Darby - Jonathon Scott Fuqua   *e*   501
The Divine Wind: A Love Story - Garry Disher
    h   384
Face - Benjamin Zephaniah   *m, h*   1494
Fishing Day - Andrea Davis Pinkney   *p*   1156
Flight of the Fisherbird - Nora Martin   *e, m*   949
The Gold-Threaded Dress - Carolyn Marsden
    e   942
Lucas - Kevin Brooks   *h*   159
An Ocean Apart, a World Away - Lensey Namioka
    m, h   1058
The Rainbow Kite - Marlene Fanta Shyer   *m,*
    h   1299
The Ravenmaster's Secret - Elvira Woodruff
    m   1462
Shadows and Light - Anne Bishop   *h, a*   110
Sparks Fly Upward - Carol Matas   *m, h*   954
The Traitor: Golden Mountain Chronicles: 1885 -
    Laurence Yep   *m, h*   1475
Up Molasses Mountain - Julie Baker   *m, h*   68
What Happened to Lani Garver - Carol Plum-Ucci
    h   1162
When Pirates Came to Brooklyn - Phyllis Shalant   *e,*
    m   1280

Presidents

All-American Girl - Meg Cabot   *m, h*   195

Princes and Princesses

Clever Lollipop - Dick King-Smith   *e*   792
A Coalition of Lions - Elizabeth E. Wein   *h*   1424
Elisabeth: The Princess Bride - Barry Denenberg
    m   372
The Fairy's Return - Gail Carson Levine   *e*   883
The Firebird - Jane Yolen   *p*   1479

For Biddle's Sake - Gail Carson Levine   *e*   884
The Frog Princess - E.D. Baker   *m*   67
Girl in a Cage - Jane Yolen   *m, h*   1480
Once Upon a Marigold - Jean Ferris   *m, h*   452
One Night - Marsha Qualey   *h*   1180
The Princess and the Pauper - Kate Brian   *m*   147
The Princess and the Pizza - Mary Jane Auch
    p   56
Princess Fishtail - Frances Minters   *p*   1017
Princess in Love - Meg Cabot   *m, h*   197
Princess in Waiting - Meg Cabot   *m, h*   198
Princess Penelope - Todd Mack   *p*   926
Princesses Are People, Too: Two Modern Fairy Tales
    - Susie Morgenstern   *e*   1032
The Real, True Dulcie Campbell - Cynthia DeFelice
    p   367
The Red Wolf - Margaret Shannon   *p*   1285
Sleeping Beauty - Mahlon F. Craft   *p*   312
Sondok: Princess of the Moon and Stars, Korea, A.D.
    595 - Sheri Holman   *m*   668
The Tale of the Firebird - Gennady Spirin   *p*   1328

Prisoners and Prisons

Escape from Botany Bay: The True Story of Mary
    Bryant - Gerald Hausman   *m, h*   609
Gilbert & Sullivan Set Me Free - Kathleen Karr   *m,*
    h   767
Numbering All the Bones - Ann Rinaldi   *m,*
    h   1205
Pool Boy - Michael Simmons   *m, h*   1305
The Ravenmaster's Secret - Elvira Woodruff
    m   1462
Visiting Day - Jacqueline Woodson   *p*   1468

Prisoner's Families

Visiting Day - Jacqueline Woodson   *p*   1468

Problem Solving

Baghead - Jarrett J. Krosoczka   *p*   834
Bravery Soup - Maryann Cocca-Leffler   *p*   267
Fix-It Duck - Jez Alborough   *p*   15
Four Friends Together - Sue Heap   *p*   617
Frog - Susan Cooper   *p*   296
The Giant Ball of String - Arthur Geisert   *p*   515
Head, Body, Legs: A Story from Liberia - Won-Ldy
    Paye   *p*   1136
Henry Builds a Cabin - D.B. Johnson   *p*   744
Kumak's House: A Tale of the Far North - Michael
    Bania   *p*   73
Martin MacGregor's Snowman - Lisa Broadie Cook
    p   289
The Marvelous Mouse Man - Mary Ann Hoberman
    p   654
McDuff Saves the Day - Rosemary Wells   *p*   1426
Monkey for Sale - Sanna Stanley   *p*   1335
Mr. Tanen's Tie Trouble - Maryann Cocca-Leffler
    p   268
Mrs. Biddlebox - Linda Smith   *p*   1315
Muncha! Muncha! Muncha! - Candace Fleming
    p   463
My Friend Rabbit - Eric Rohmann   *p*   1222
My Lucky Day - Keiko Kasza   *p*   768
My Truck Is Stuck! - Kevin Lewis   *p*   889
No Zombies Allowed - Matt Novak   *p*   1094
Oliver Finds His Way - Phyllis Root   *p*   1228
One Bright Penny - Geraldine McCaughrean
    p   967
The Red Wolf - Margaret Shannon   *p*   1285
Ruler of the Courtyard - Rukhsana Khan   *p*   784
Skeleton Hiccups - Margery Cuyler   *p*   334
Three Samurai Cats: A Story from Japan - Eric A.
    Kimmel   *p*   789
The Turtle and the Hippopotamus - Kate Banks
    p   77

Rodeos

Bull Rider - Marilyn Halvorson   *m, h*   588
Daddy Says - Ntozake Shange   *m*   1281
Horse Thief: A Novel - Robert Newton Peck   *m, h*   1142

Romance

17: A Novel in Prose Poems - Liz Rosenberg   *h*   1230
Angelica: A Novel of Samaria - Sharon Shinn   *h, a*   1293
Boy Meets Boy - David Levithan   *h*   885
Captain's Purr - Madeleine Floyd   *p*   469
Dragon Blood - Patricia Briggs   *h, a*   150
Fifteen Love - Robert Corbet   *m, h*   299
Haunted: A Tale of the Mediator - Meg Cabot   *m, h*   196
Jenna Starborn - Sharon Shinn   *h, a*   1294
Paradise - Joan Elizabeth Goodman   *m, h*   541
Samantha and the Cowboy - Lorraine Heath   *h*   620
Sixteen Cows - Lisa Wheeler   *p*   1435
Timeless Love - Judith O'Brien   *m, h*   1101
When the War Is Over - Martha Attema   *m, h*   53
Wolf Queen - Tanith Lee   *m, h*   874

Runaways

Breakout - Paul Fleischman   *h*   460
Claws - Will Weaver   *m, h*   1420
Death Wind - William Bell   *m, h*   99
The Fattening Hut - Pat Lowery Collins   *h*   281
Guitar Highway Rose - Brigid Lowry   *h*   910
Indigo - Alice Hoffman   *m, h*   659
Little Buggy Runs Away - Kevin O'Malley   *p*   1108
Lucy the Giant - Sherri L. Smith   *m, h*   1316
Mad Maudlin - Mercedes Lackey   *h, a*   844
Melonhead - Michael de Guzman   *m*   354
Missing - Catherine MacPhail   *m*   933
Nirvana's Children - Ranulfo   *h*   1185
The No Place Cat - C.S. Adler   *e, m*   4
Otto: The Story of a Mirror - Ali Bahrampour   *p*   64
Seaward Born - Lea Wait   *e, m*   1404
The Several Lives of Orphan Jack - Sarah Ellis   *e*   430
Taf: A Novel - Annie Callan   *h*   204
Taking Liberty: The Story of Oney Judge, George Washington's Runaway Slave - Ann Rinaldi   *m, h*   1207
Ten Miles from Winnemucca - Thelma Hatch Wyss   *m, h*   1472
The Thief Lord - Cornelia Funke   *m, h*   500
Tomorrow, Maybe - Brian James   *m, h*   725

Rural Life

The Day the Picture Man Came - Faye Gibbons   *p*   520
A Doctor Like Papa - Natalie Kinsey-Warnock   *e*   795
A Fine Start: Meg's Prairie Diary - Kate McMullan   *e*   990
Full Steam Ahead - Faye Gibbons   *p*   521
Harvest Home - Jane Yolen   *p*   1481
A Hug Goes Around - Laura Krauss Melmed   *p*   1005
The Secret Remedy Book: A Story of Comfort and Love - Karin Cates   *p*   231

Russian Americans

Dear Emma - Johanna Hurwitz   *e, m*   701

Russians

Sasha's Matrioshka Dolls - Jane Dillon   *p*   383

The Tale of the Firebird - Gennady Spirin   *p*   1328

Sailing

Deep - Susanna Vance   *m, h*   1394
Dinosailors - Deb Lund   *p*   915
Little Rat Sets Sail - Monika Bang-Campbell   *b*   72
Stanley, Flat Again! - Jeff Brown   *e*   163

Santa Claus

Auntie Claus and the Key to Christmas - Elise Primavera   *p*   1171
A New Improved Santa - Patricia Rae Wolff   *p*   1454
Was That Christmas? - Hilary McKay   *p*   981

Satire

Jennifer Government - Max Barry   *h, a*   85

School Life

Agnes Parker . . . Girl in Progress - Kathleen O'Dell   *e, m*   1103
Attack of the Mutant Underwear - Tom Birdseye   *e*   109
Bad Girls in Love - Cynthia Voigt   *m*   1402
The Cheat - Amy Goldman Koss   *m*   820
Drowning Anna - Sue Mayfield   *m, h*   958
Face - Benjamin Zephaniah   *m, h*   1494
Finding Our Way - Rene Saldana Jr.   *m, h*   1252
The Flip Side - Andrew Matthews   *m*   956
From the Horse's Mouth - Kathy Mackel   *m*   929
The Ghost of P.S. 42 - Frank Asch   *e*   45
Goddesses Series - Clea Hantman   *m, h*   592
Guitar Highway Rose - Brigid Lowry   *h*   910
Harriet Spies Again - Helen Ericson   *e, m*   435
Home of the Braves - David Klass   *h*   803
I'm Not Invited? - Diane Cain Bluthenthal   *p*   121
The Invisible Enemy - Marthe Jocelyn   *e, m*   740
Jake Drake, Class Clown - Andrew Clements   *e*   260
Kerosene - Chris Wooding   *h*   1461
Kim: Empty Inside - Beatrice Sparks   *m, h*   1323
The Little School Bus - Carol Roth   *p*   1231
Loser - Jerry Spinelli   *m*   1325
Lunch Walks Among Us - Jim Benton   *e*   103
The Meanest Doll in the World - Ann M. Martin   *e*   946
Mind Games - Jeanne Marie Grunwell   *m*   567
My Cup Runneth Over: The Life of Angelica Cookson Potts - Cherry Whytock   *m, h*   1441
My Life of Crime - Richard W. Jennings   *m*   736
Rat - Jan Cheripko   *m, h*   242
Scritch Scratch - Miriam Moss   *p*   1036
Simply Alice - Phyllis Reynolds Naylor   *m*   1069
Sticks and Stones - Beth Goobie   *m, h*   536
Stray Voltage - Eugenie Doyle   *m*   393
String Music - Rick Telander   *e, m*   1372

School Newspapers

Getting a Life - Jocelyn Shipley   *m, h*   1295
The Hemingway Tradition - Kristin Butcher   *m*   186

Schools

7 x 9 = Trouble! - Claudia Mills   *e*   1013
Amber Waiting - Nan Gregory   *p*   559
Because of Anya - Margaret Peterson Haddix   *e*   579
The Best Class Picture Ever! - Denis Roche   *p*   1214
The Big Science Fair - Dan Yaccarino   *e*   1473

Biscuit Goes to School - Alyssa Satin Capucilli   *p*   213
Bye, Bye! - Nancy Kaufmann   *p*   769
Cool Cat, School Cat - Judy Cox   *e*   310
Countdown to Kindergarten - Alison McGhee   *p*   978
A Crazy, Mixed-Up Spanglish Day - Marisa Montes   *e*   1024
Elizabeti's School - Stephanie Stuve-Bodeen   *p*   1352
A Fine Start: Meg's Prairie Diary - Kate McMullan   *e*   990
First Day - Dandi Daley Mackall   *p*   928
First Day in Grapes - L. King Perez   *p*   1145
First Graders from Mars: Episode 2: The Problem with Pelly - Shana Corey   *b*   301
First Graders from Mars: Episode 3: Nergal and the Great Space Race - Shana Corey   *e*   302
Get Ready for Second Grade, Amber Brown - Paula Danziger   *b*   346
Ghost Girl: A Blue Ridge Mountain Story - Delia Ray   *m*   1188
Gloria Rising - Ann Cameron   *e*   207
Gooney Bird Greene - Lois Lowry   *e*   911
Grody's Not So Golden Rules - Nicole Rubel   *p*   1235
The Hamster of the Baskervilles - Bruce Hale   *e*   583
Horrible Harry and the Dragon War - Suzy Kline   *e*   806
How to Lose Your Class Pet - Valerie Wilson Wesley   *e*   1430
Hunter's Best Friend at School - Laura Malone Elliott   *p*   426
I Am NOT Going to School Today! - Robie H. Harris   *p*   599
If You Take a Mouse to School - Laura Joffe Numeroff   *p*   1096
Iris and Walter: The School Play - Elissa Haden Guest   *b*   570
The Last Burp of Mac McGerp - Pam Smallcomb   *e*   1311
Little Brown Bear Won't Go to School! - Jane Dyer   *p*   412
The Malted Falcon - Bruce Hale   *e*   584
Matthew A.B.C. - Peter Catalanotto   *p*   229
Midnight for Charlie Bone - Jenny Nimmo   *m*   1082
Mr. Tanen's Tie Trouble - Maryann Cocca-Leffler   *p*   268
Once Upon a Time - Niki Daly   *p*   341
Punctuation Takes a Vacation - Robin Pulver   *p*   1178
The Recess Queen - Alexis O'Neill   *p*   1110
Robert and the Weird & Wacky Facts - Barbara Seuling   *e*   1279
Substitute Teacher Plans - Doug Johnson   *p*   746
Tackylocks and the Three Bears - Helen Lester   *p*   877
The Talent Show - Michelle Edwards   *e*   417
Timothy's Tales from Hilltop School - Rosemary Wells   *p*   1428
Utterly Me, Clarice Bean - Lauren Child   *e*   249
What Planet Are You from, Clarice Bean? - Lauren Child   *p*   250
What Would Joey Do? - Jack Gantos   *m*   508

Schools/Boarding Schools

Among the Barons - Margaret Peterson Haddix   *m, h*   577
A Great and Terrible Beauty - Libba Bray   *h*   138
Point Blank - Anthony Horowitz   *m, h*   680
Simon Says - Elaine Marie Alphin   *h*   23
Unseen Companion - Denise Gosliner Orenstein   *h*   1113
The Warriors - Joseph Bruchac   *m*   170

Schools/Catholic Schools

Run from the Nun! - Erin MacLellan   *e, m*   931
St. Michael's Scales - Neil Connelly   *m, h*   287

Schools/High Schools

After - Francine Prose   *m, h*   1175
Big Mouth & Ugly Girl - Joyce Carol Oates
   h   1098
Breaking Point - Alex Flinn   *m, h*   467
Bronx Masquerade - Nikki Grimes   *m, h*   565
Buddha Boy - Kathe Koja   *m, h*   811
Catalyst - Laurie Halse Anderson   *h*   28
Cheating Lessons - Nan Willard Cappo   *m, h*   212
Cuba 15 - Nancy Osa   *m, h*   1115
Geography Club - Brent Hartinger   *h*   602
Girl Coming in for a Landing - April Halprin Wayland
   m, h   1418
God of Beer - Garret Keizer   *h*   775
Happenings - Katie Cobb   *m, h*   265
Hard Time - Julian F. Thompson   *m, h*   1378
Home of the Braves - David Klass   *h*   803
How I Fell in Love & Learned to Shoot Free Throws -
   Jon Ripslinger   *h*   1209
LBD: It's a Girl Thing - Grace Dent   *m, h*   375
Mates, Dates and Inflatable Bras - Cathy Hopkins
   m, h   676
The New Rules of High School - Blake Nelson
   h   1072
Not as Crazy as I Seem - George Harrar   *m, h*   596
Out of Order - A.M. Jenkins   *h*   732
Rainbow High - Alex Sanchez   *h*   1262
The Shadow Club Rising - Neal Shusterman   *m,*
   h   1298
Sweetblood - Pete Hautman   *h*   610
The True Meaning of Cleavage - Mariah Fredericks
   m, h   486
Vampire High - Douglas Rees   *m, h*   1194
Who Will Tell My Brother? - Marlene Carvell   *m,*
   h   223

Schools/Junior High School

Alt Ed - Catherine Atkins   *m, h*   52
Jake Riley: Irreparably Damaged - Rebecca Fjelland
   Davis   *m, h*   352
Shattering Glass - Gail Giles   *h*   526
Tribes - Arthur Slade   *h*   1309

Schools/Middle Schools

Cowboy Boy - James Proimos   *e*   1173
My Contract with Henry - Robin Vaupel   *m*   1399
Qwerty Stevens Stuck in Time with Benjamin Franklin
   - Dan Gutman   *m*   575
True Blue - Jeffrey Lee   *e, m*   871

Schools/Preschool

First Day - Joan Rankin   *p*   1184
My Somebody Special - Sarah Weeks   *p*   1422
Someone Says - Carole Lexa Schaefer   *p*   1268

Science

The Case of the Graveyard Ghost - Michele Torrey
   e   1384

Science Fiction

Among the Barons - Margaret Peterson Haddix   *m,*
   h   577
Among the Betrayed - Margaret Peterson Haddix   *m,*
   h   578
Angelica: A Novel of Samaria - Sharon Shinn   *h,*
   a   1293

The Birthday of the World and Other Stories - Ursula
   K. Le Guin   *h, a*   865
Black Projects, White Knights: The Company Dossiers
   - Kage Baker   *h, a*   69
Changing Planes - Ursula K. Le Guin   *h, a*   866
The City of Ember - Jeanne DuPrau   *m*   409
Diplomatic Immunity: A Comedy of Terrors - Lois
   McMaster Bujold   *h, a*   176
The Disappeared - Kristine Kathryn Rusch   *h,*
   a   1239
Dr. Franklin's Island - Ann Halam   *m, h*   582
The Earthborn - Paul Collins   *h, a*   282
Fallen Host - Lyda Morehouse   *h, a*   1031
*Firebirds: An Anthology of Original Fantasy and
   Science Fiction* - Sharyn November   *m, h*   1095
Heir Apparent - Vivian Vande Velde   1395
Jenna Starborn - Sharon Shinn   *h, a*   1294
Manta's Gift - Timothy Zahn   *h, a*   1491
Mortal Engines - Philip Reeve   *h, a*   1195
Parasite Pig - William Sleator   *m, h*   1310
The Rudest Alien on Earth - Jane Leslie Conly   *e,*
   m   286
Singing the Dogstar Blues - Alison Goodman
   h   540
Tria and the Great Star Rescue - Rebecca Kraft Rector
   e   1191

Scientific Experiments

The Case of the Graveyard Ghost - Michele Torrey
   e   1384
The Invisible Enemy - Marthe Jocelyn   *e, m*   740
It Came from Beneath the Bed - James Howe
   e   688
Lunch Walks Among Us - Jim Benton   *e*   103
Max's Logbook - Marissa Moss   *e*   1035
Mind Games - Jeanne Marie Grunwell   *m*   567
The Speed of Light - Ron Carlson   *m, h*   218

Scouting

Little Pig Is Capable - Denis Roche   *p*   1215
Loretta: Ace Pinky Scout - Keith Graves   *p*   548
Pig Enough - Janie Bynum   *p*   194

Sea Stories

*The Angel's Command: A Tale from the Castaways of
   the Flying Dutchman* - Brian Jacques   *m, h*   722
*Bloody Jack: Being an Account of the Curious
   Adventures of Mary "Jacky" Faber, Ship's Boy* -
   L.A. Meyer   *m, h*   1007
The Man with the Silver Oar - Robin Moore   *m,*
   h   1029
Pirate Hunter Series - Brad Strickland   *e, m*   1348
The She - Carol Plum-Ucci   *m, h*   1161
To the Edge of the World - Michele Torrey
   m   1385
The Voyage of Patience Goodspeed - Heather Vogel
   Frederick   *m*   485

Seasons

From Dawn till Dusk - Natalie Kinsey-Warnock
   p   796
Gregory and Alexander - William Barringer   *p*   84
Hello, Arctic! - Theodore Taylor   *p*   1365
Snow - Manya Stojic   *p*   1346
When the Root Children Wake Up - Audrey Wood
   p   1458

Secrets

Captain's Purr - Madeleine Floyd   *p*   469
Gina.Jamie.Father.Bear - George Ella Lyon   *m,*
   h   920
Lily's Ghosts - Laura Ruby   *m*   1237
A Picture of Grandmother - Esther Hautzig   *e*   611

Walk Softly, Rachel - Kate Banks   *m, h*   78
Whistler's Hollow - Debbie Dadey   *e, m*   336

Segregation

Jericho Walls - Kristi Collier   *m, h*   280
The Red Rose Box - Brenda Woods   *e*   1463

Self-Acceptance

Almost Home - Nora Raleigh Baskin   *e, m*   87
Big Time Olie - William Joyce   *p*   762
Dog Eared - Amanda Harvey   *p*   605
*First Graders from Mars: Episode 2: The Problem
   with Pelly* - Shana Corey   *b*   301
Loretta: Ace Pinky Scout - Keith Graves   *p*   548
Loser - Jerry Spinelli   *m*   1325
Shadow Puppets - Orson Scott Card   *h, a*   215
The Summer Country - James A. Hetley   *h, a*   634

Self-Awareness

Gloria Rising - Ann Cameron   *e*   207

Self-Confidence

City of Stars - Mary Hoffman   *m, h*   662
First Day in Grapes - L. King Perez   *p*   1145
Hoop Girlz - Lucy Jane Bledsoe   *e, m*   118
I'm Mighty! - Kate McMullan   *p*   993
Make the Team, Baby Duck! - Amy Hest   *p*   633
Minn and Jake - Janet S. Wong   *m*   1456
Miss Hunnicutt's Hat - Jeff Brumbeau   *p*   172
Robert and the Weird & Wacky Facts - Barbara
   Seuling   *e*   1279
Roller Coaster - Marla Frazee   *p*   484
Taking Care of Trouble - Bonnie Graves   *e*   547

Self-Esteem

Be Boy Buzz - bell hooks   *p*   672
The Big Cheese of Third Street - Laurie Halse
   Anderson   *p*   27
Brothers Below Zero - Tor Seidler   *e, m*   1277
Christmas Cricket - Eve Bunting   *p*   178
*First Graders from Mars: Episode 3: Nergal and the
   Great Space Race* - Shana Corey   *e*   302
Homemade Love - bell hooks   *p*   673
The Littlest Wolf - Larry Dane Brimner   *p*   154
Loretta: Ace Pinky Scout - Keith Graves   *p*   548
Matchit - Martha Moore   *e, m*   1027
Pictures for Miss Josie - Sandra Belton   *p*   100
Sahara Special - Esme Raji Codell   *e, m*   269
When the Circus Came to Town - Laurence Yep
   e   1476

Self-Mutilation

Drowning Anna - Sue Mayfield   *m, h*   958

Self-Perception

Alice, I Think - Susan Juby   *m, h*   763
Breakout - Paul Fleischman   *h*   460
David Gets in Trouble - David Shannon   *p*   1282
The Earth, My Butt, and Other Big Round Things -
   Carolyn Mackler   *m, h*   930
Indigo - Alice Hoffman   *m, h*   659
Jake, Reinvented - Gordon Korman   *h*   816
Kim: Empty Inside - Beatrice Sparks   *m, h*   1323
Olive's Ocean - Kevin Henkes   *m*   623
Prep - Jake Coburn   *h*   266
Secret Heart - David Almond   *m, h*   21
The Shell House - Linda Newbery   *h*   1075
Slumming - Kristen D. Randle   *h*   1183
Three Nasty Gnarlies - Keith Graves   *p*   549

Subject Index

Jake Drake, Class Clown - Andrew Clements
   e 260

Sahara Special - Esme Raji Codell   e, m 269

Timothy's Tales from Hilltop School - Rosemary Wells
   p 1428

The Trouble with Liberty - Kristin Butcher   m,
   h 187

A Week in the Woods - Andrew Clements   e 262

Teachers

Get Ready for Second Grade, Amber Brown - Paula
   Danziger   b 346

Ghost Girl: A Blue Ridge Mountain Story - Delia Ray
   m 1188

Happenings - Katie Cobb   m, h 265

Mary Ann Alice - Brian Doyle   m 392

Shanna's Teacher Show - Jean Marzollo   p 951

Substitute Teacher Plans - Doug Johnson   p 746

Teasing

The Big Cheese of Third Street - Laurie Halse
   Anderson   p 27

Dog Eared - Amanda Harvey   p 605

If the Shoe Fits - Gary Soto   p 1321

Teen Parents

Chill Wind - Janet McDonald   h 975

Hanging on to Max - Margaret Bechard   h 94

Mahalia - Joanne Horniman   h 679

Teen Relationships

*13: Thirteen Stories That Capture the Agony and
   Ecstasy of Being Thirteen* - James Howe   m,
   h 685

Girl Coming in for a Landing - April Halprin Wayland
   m, h 1418

One Hot Second: Stories about Desire - Cathy Young
   h 1487

Television

Penny Lee and Her TV - Glenn McCoy   p 971

Theater

Arizona Charlie and the Klondike Kid - Julie Lawson
   p 864

Beverly Billingsly Takes a Bow - Alexander Stadler
   p 1334

Daisy the Dancing Cow - Viki Woodworth
   p 1469

Gilbert & Sullivan Set Me Free - Kathleen Karr   m,
   h 767

Iris and Walter: The School Play - Elissa Haden Guest
   b 570

Isabel: Taking Wing - Annie Dalton   m 339

My Father Had a Daughter: Judith Shakespeare's Tale
   - Grace Tiffany   h, a 1381

Shakespeare's Spy - Gary Blackwood   m 114

A Simple Gift - Nancy Ruth Patterson   e 1129

A Time to Dance - Mary Pope Osborne   e 1119

Time Travel

Black Projects, White Knights: The Company Dossiers
   - Kage Baker   h, a 69

Charlie Bone and the Time Twister - Jenny Nimmo
   m 1081

A Circle of Time - Marisa Montes   m, h 1023

Ghost at the Window - Margaret McAllister   e,
   m 960

Paint by Magic: A Time Travel Mystery - Kathryn
   Reiss   m 1197

Qwerty Stevens Stuck in Time with Benjamin Franklin
   - Dan Gutman   m 575

Singing the Dogstar Blues - Alison Goodman
   h 540

Timeless Love - Judith O'Brien   m, h 1101

Timespinners - Luli Gray   e 552

The Viking Series - Christopher Tebbetts   m 1370

Warriors of Camlann - N.M. Browne   m, h 169

The Watch - Dennis Danvers   h, a 344

Tolerance

White Midnight - Dia Calhoun   m, h 203

Toys

Dahlia - Barbara McClintock   p 970

The Jamie and Angus Stories - Anne Fine   e 455

Little Whistle's Medicine - Cynthia Rylant   p 1246

Olivia Counts - Ian Falconer   p 440

Olivia . . . and the Missing Toy - Ian Falconer
   p 441

Platypus and the Birthday Party - Chris Riddell
   p 1203

Sissy Buttons Takes Charge! - Ian Whybrow
   p 1439

Small - Clara Vulliamy   p 1403

Tatty Ratty - Helen Cooper   p 295

Teddy's Snowy Day - Ian Beck   p 95

What Shall We Do, Blue Kangaroo? - Emma
   Chichester Clark   p 247

Traditional Stories

Drat That Fat Cat! - Pat Thomson   p 1380

Traditions

Dancing the Ring Shout! - Kim Siegelson   p 1300

Traffic Accidents

Breakout - Paul Fleischman   h 460

Trains

Dinosaur Train - John Steven Gurney   p 572

Full Steam Ahead - Faye Gibbons   p 521

I Dream of Trains - Angela Johnson   p 742

Transportation

Don't Let the Pigeon Drive the Bus! - Mo Willems
   p 1445

Dumpy and the Big Storm - Julie Andrews Edwards
   p 416

A Full Hand - Thomas F. Yezerski   p 1477

Get to Work, Trucks! - Don Carter   p 222

Giddy-up! Let's Ride! - Flora McDonnell   p 977

Just One More - Wendi Silvano   p 1303

The Little School Bus - Carol Roth   p 1231

Mrs. Armitage: Queen of the Road - Quentin Blake
   p 116

My Truck Is Stuck! - Kevin Lewis   p 889

What James Likes Best - Amy Schwartz   p 1272

Zoom! - Robert Munsch   p 1041

Travel

All the Way Lhasa: A Tale from Tibet - Barbara Helen
   Berger   p 104

Charlotte in Paris - Joan MacPhail Knight   e 807

Destination Unexpected - Donald R. Gallo   m,
   h 504

The Journey of Oliver K. Woodman - Darcy Pattison
   p 1130

Just One More - Wendi Silvano   p 1303

Night Train - Caroline Stutson   p 1351

Otto: The Story of a Mirror - Ali Bahrampour
   p 64

Pancake Dreams - Ingmarie Ahvander   p 12

*Rosy Cole's Worst Ever, Best Yet Tour of New York
   City* - Sheila Greenwald   e 556

Safe and Sound - Barbara Nichol   p 1077

That's Good! That's Bad! In The Grand Canyon -
   Margery Cuyler   p 335

Tom Mouse - Ursula K. Le Guin   p 867

Zoe Sophia's Scrapbook: An Adventure in Venice -
   Claudia Mauner   p 957

Treasure

Alphaboat - Michael Chesworth   p 245

Treasure, Buried

The Last Treasure - Janet S. Anderson   m, h 26

Sea Gift - John Ashby   m, h 47

Trials

Operating Codes - Nick Manns   m, h 939

Trickster Tales

Just a Minute: A Trickster Tale and Counting Book -
   Yuyi Morales   p 1030

*Lapin Plays Possum: Trickster Tales from the
   Louisiana Bayou* - Sharon Arms Doucet   e 390

The Magical Monkey King: Mischief in Heaven - Ji-Li
   Jiang   e 738

Please, Malese - Amy MacDonald   p 922

Rosa Raposa - F. Isabel Campoy   p 209

Trust

The Countess and Me - Paul Kropp   m, h 832

Twins

The Bagpiper's Ghost - Jane Yolen   e, m 1478

The Canning Season - Polly Horvath   m, h 683

Dangerous Girls - R.L. Stine   m, h 1345

Flip - David Lubar   m 913

Lenny and Mel - Erik P. Kraft   e 823

Lenny and Mel's Summer Vacation - Erik P. Kraft
   e 824

*Mirror, Mirror on the Wall: The Diary of Bess
   Brennan* - Barry Denenberg   e, m 373

My Father Had a Daughter: Judith Shakespeare's Tale
   - Grace Tiffany   h, a 1381

A New Barker in the House - Tomie De Paola
   p 359

Ruby Holler - Sharon Creech   e, m 313

Timespinners - Luli Gray   e 552

Twin to Twin - Margaret O'Hair   p 1104

*The Twins and the Bird of Darkness: A Hero Tale
   from the Caribbean* - Robert D. San Souci
   e 1260

Witch Twins at Camp Bliss - Adele Griffin   e 564

Underground Railroad

Evvy's Civil War - Miriam Brenaman   m, h 140

The Spirit and Gilly Bucket - Maurine F. Dahlberg
   m 337

Trouble Don't Last - Shelley Pearsall   m 1139

Under the Quilt of Night - Deborah Hopkinson
   p 678

Underground Resistance Movements

For Freedom: The Story of a French Spy - Kimberly
   Brubaker Bradley   m, h 134

Guerrilla Season - Pat Hughes   *m, h*   693
When My Name Was Keoko - Linda Sue Park
   m   1127

Underwater Exploration

Rub-a-Dub Sub - Linda Ashman   *p*   51

Universities and Colleges

Better than Running at Night - Hillary Frank
   h   481

Unmarried Mothers

Postcards from No Man's Land - Aidan Chambers
   h   237

Vacations

Bridget and the Muttonheads - Pija Lindenbaum
   p   895
The Castaway - James Stevenson   *p*   1343
Danitra Brown Leaves Town - Nikki Grimes
   p   566
Gaspard and Lisa's Rainy Day - Anne Gutman
   p   573
Lenny and Mel's Summer Vacation - Erik P. Kraft
   e   824
My Brother's Hero - Adrian Fogelin   *m*   470
My Not-So-Terrible Time at the Hippie Hotel -
   Rosemary Graham   *m, h*   545
Plantzilla - Jerdine Nolen   *p*   1092
T.J. and the Cats - Hazel Hutchins   *e*   704

Vampires

Dangerous Girls - R.L. Stine   *m, h*   1345
Sweetblood - Pete Hautman   *h*   610
Vampire High - Douglas Rees   *m, h*   1194
Vampire Kisses - Ellen Schreiber   *m, h*   1271
Vampire State Building - Elizabeth Levy   *e*   887
Voyage of the Shadowmoon - Sean McMullen   *h,*
   a   994

Vandalism

Not as Crazy as I Seem - George Harrar   *m, h*   596

Veterinarians

The Broken Cat - Lynne Rae Perkins   *p*   1146

Victorian Period

A Great and Terrible Beauty - Libba Bray   *h*   138

Vietnam War

Amaryllis - Craig Crist-Evans   *m, h*   315
Sonny's War - Valerie Hobbs   *m, h*   650
*Where Have All the Flowers Gone?: The Diary of
   Molly Mackenzie Flaherty* - Ellen Emerson White
   m, h   1437

Vikings

Daughter of the Wind - Michael Cadnum   *m,*
   h   199
The Viking Series - Christopher Tebbetts   *m*   1370

Violence

The Pack - Elisa Carbone   *m, h*   214
Shattering Glass - Gail Giles   *h*   526
Shooting Monarchs - John Halliday   *h*   587

Skud - Dennis Foon   *h*   472
Who the Man - Chris Lynch   *m, h*   918

Virtual Reality

Heir Apparent - Vivian Vande Velde   1395

Volcanoes

Mystery in Mt. Mole - Richard W. Jennings   *m,*
   h   737

Voyages and Travels

A Chapel of Thieves - Bruce Clements   *m*   263
The Dungeon - Lynne Reid Banks   *m, h*   79
The Impossible Journey - Gloria Whelan   *m*   1436
Melonhead - Michael de Guzman   *m*   354
Monkey Mo Goes to Sea - Diane Goode   *p*   538
Olvina Flies - Grace Lin   *p*   893
Red Midnight - Ben Mikaelsen   *m, h*   1008
Ruby Holler - Sharon Creech   *e, m*   313
*This Vast Land: A Young Man's Journal of the Lewis
   and Clark Expedition* - Stephen E. Ambrose   *m,*
   h   25
To the Edge of the World - Michele Torrey
   m   1385

War

*Mannekin Pis: A Simple Story of a Boy Who Peed on
   a War* - Vladimir Radunsky   *p*   1181
Shattered: Stories of Children and War - Jennifer
   Armstrong   *m, h*   39
Voyage of the Shadowmoon - Sean McMullen   *h,*
   a   994
War of Honor - David Weber   *h, a*   1421
Warriors of Alavna - N.M. Browne   *m, h*   168
We Are Patriots - Kristiana Gregory   *e*   558

War of 1812

The Battle for St. Michaels - Emily Arnold McCully
   b   973
Crossing the Panther's Path - Elizabeth Alder   *m,*
   h   17

Wealth

Hard Cash - Kate Cann   *h*   210
Mr. Basset Plays - Dominic Catalano   *p*   228
A Pig Named Perrier - Elizabeth Spurr   *p*   1331
Pool Boy - Michael Simmons   *m, h*   1305
Recycling George - Stephen Roos   *e, m*   1224

Weather

Aunt Minnie and the Twister - Mary Skillings Prigger
   p   1170
The Aunts Go Marching - Maurie J. Manning
   p   937
Blizzard's Wake - Phyllis Reynolds Naylor   *m,*
   h   1065
Chimp and Zee and the Big Storm - Laurence Anholt
   p   31
Death Wind - William Bell   *m, h*   99
Double Dutch - Sharon M. Draper   *m, h*   396
Dumpy and the Big Storm - Julie Andrews Edwards
   p   416
It Feels Like Snow - Nancy Cote   *p*   305
Like a Windy Day - Frank Asch   *p*   46
Martin MacGregor's Snowman - Lisa Broadie Cook
   p   289
Monsoon - Uma Krishnaswami   *p*   829
One Rainy Day - Valeri Gorbachev   *p*   542
Shatterglass - Tamora Pierce   *m, h*   1151

Snowed in with Grandmother Silk - Carol Fenner
   e   448
Storm Is Coming! - Heather Tekavec   *p*   1371
Straight to the Pole - Kevin O'Malley   *p*   1109
Together Apart - Dianne E. Gray   *m, h*   550
The Tornado Watches - Patrick Jennings   *e*   733
A Twisted Tale - Carolyn Fisher   *p*   456

Weight Control

A Dance of Sisters - Tracey Porter   *m*   1164
The Earth, My Butt, and Other Big Round Things -
   Carolyn Mackler   *m, h*   930
Fat Kid Rules the World - K.L. Going   *h*   533
Flavor of the Week - Tucker Shaw   *m, h*   1288
*My Cup Runneth Over: The Life of Angelica Cookson
   Potts* - Cherry Whytock   *m, h*   1441
A New Improved Santa - Patricia Rae Wolff
   p   1454

Werewolves

The Wolving Time - Patrick Jennings   *m, h*   735

Wilderness

Hello, Arctic! - Theodore Taylor   *p*   1365

Wilderness Survival

When Eagles Fall - Mary Casanova   *m*   226
Wild Man Island - Will Hobbs   *m, h*   653

Wildlife Conservation

Flying Blind - Anna Myers   *e, m*   1049

Wildlife Rescue

Angelo - David Macaulay   *p*   921
Jackie's Wild Seattle - Will Hobbs   *m*   652
Monkey for Sale - Sanna Stanley   *p*   1335
When Eagles Fall - Mary Casanova   *m*   226

Winter

All You Need for a Snowman - Alice Schertle
   p   1269
It's Snowing! - Olivier Dunrea   *p*   407
A Perfect Day for It - Jan Fearnley   *p*   445
Snow - Manya Stojic   *p*   1346
Snow Music - Lynne Rae Perkins   *p*   1147
Straight to the Pole - Kevin O'Malley   *p*   1109
Teddy's Snowy Day - Ian Beck   *p*   95

Wishes

12 Again - Sue Corbett   *e, m*   300
The Bachelor and the Bean - Shelley Fowles
   p   475
The Faerie's Gift - Tanya Robyn Batt   *p*   88
Hip, Hip, Hooray Day! - Barney Saltzberg   *p*   1255
Jack and Jill - Daniel Kirk   *p*   799
Jackalope - Janet Stevens   *p*   1342
The Kite - Luis Garay   *p*   509
Mirabelle - Astrid Lindgren   *p*   896
Sandmare - Helen Cooper   *e*   294
The Sheep Fairy: When Wishes Have Wings - Ruth
   Louise Symes   *p*   1357
Wish, Change, Friend - Ian Whybrow   *p*   1440
Witch's Wishes - Vivian Vande Velde   *e*   1396

Witches and Witchcraft

Curse in Reverse - Tom Coppinger   *p*   298
Fright Night Flight - Laura Krauss Melmed
   p   1004

Character Name Index

This index alphabetically lists the major characters in each featured title. Each character name is followed by a description of the character. Citations also provide titles of the books featuring the character, listed alphabetically if there is more than one title, with author names, age-level code(s) and entry numbers also included. The age-level codes are as follows: *p* Preschool, *b* Beginning Reader, *e* Elementary School (Grades 2-5), *m* Middle School (Grades 5-8), *h* High School (Grades 9-12), and *a* Adult.

A

Aana Lulu (Eskimo; Aged Person)
Kumak's House: A Tale of the Far North - Michael Bania   *p*   73

Aarons, Catalina (7th Grader)
The Revealers - Doug Wilhelm   *m*   1443

Aaronsohn, Sari (9th Grader)
The True Meaning of Cleavage - Mariah Fredericks   *m, h*   486

Aaronson, Joss (18-Year-Old; Student—College)
Singing the Dogstar Blues - Alison Goodman   *h*   540

Abby (7th Grader)
Gossip Times Three - Amy Goldman Koss   *m*   821

Abikanile (Child; Daughter)
The Village That Vanished - Ann Grifalconi   *p*   561

Abuelita (Grandmother)
I Love Saturdays Y Domingos - Alma Flor Ada   *p*   2

Aching, Tiffany (Child; Witch)
The Wee Free Men: A Novel of Discworld - Terry Pratchett   *m, h*   1167

Aching, Wentworth (Brother)
The Wee Free Men: A Novel of Discworld - Terry Pratchett   *m, h*   1167

Adam (Student—Middle School)
My Cup Runneth Over: The Life of Angelica Cookson Potts - Cherry Whytock   *m, h*   1441

Adams, Moses (15-Year-Old)
Rebel - Willo Davis Roberts   *m*   1211

Adrian (Child)
What the Birds See - Sonya Hartnett   *m, h*   604

Agneeza (Witch; Aged Person)
Curse in Reverse - Tom Coppinger   *p*   298

Ah Sam (Cook; Immigrant)
When the Circus Came to Town - Laurence Yep   *e*   1476

Aidan (Boyfriend)
Falling through Darkness - Carolyn McCullough   *h*   972

Aiden (Mythical Creature)
Shadows and Light - Anne Bishop   *h, a*   110

Aimee (Victim)
Aimee - Mary Beth Miller   *h*   1011

Akarian (Kidnap Victim; Wizard)
The Dark - Marianne Curley   *m, h*   328

Al (Insect; Friend)
Gregory and Alexander - William Barringer   *p*   84

Alacran, Matteo (Clone)
The House of the Scorpion - Nancy Farmer   *m, h*   444

Alacran, Matteo "El Patron" (Drug Dealer)
The House of the Scorpion - Nancy Farmer   *m, h*   444

Alan (Musician)
Snow - Tracy Lynn   *m, h*   919

Albion, Brian (Knight)
The Summer Country - James A. Hetley   *h, a*   634

Alden (Farmer; Uncle)
Dust - Arthur Slade   *m, h*   1308

Aldrich, Nell (Aunt)
The 1980s: Earthsong - Tom Hoobler   *m*   671

Alex (Child)
City Chicken - Arthur Dorros   *p*   388

Alexander (Alligator)
Best Friends - Charlotte Labaronne   *p*   842

Alexander of Whitehaven, Hamish (Nobleman)
War of Honor - David Weber   *h, a*   1421

Alexie, Dove (16-Year-Old; Prisoner)
Unseen Companion - Denise Gosliner Orenstein   *h*   1113

Alia (Teenager)
Alia Waking - Laura Williams McCaffrey   *m, h*   962

Alia (Child)
Among the Betrayed - Margaret Peterson Haddix   *m, h*   578

Alianne "Aly" (Daughter; Spy)
Trickster's Choice - Tamora Pierce   *m, h*   1152

Alice (Babysitter; Teenager)
Fairy Dust - Jane Denitz Smith   *e*   1313

Alice (Aged Person; Neighbor)
It Feels Like Snow - Nancy Cote   *p*   305

Alice (Grandmother)
Melonhead - Michael de Guzman   *m*   354

Alice "Al" (Dancer; Mother)
The Glass Cafe: Or the Stripper and the State: How My Mother Started a War with the System that Made Us Kind of Rich and a Little Bit Famous - Gary Paulsen   *m, h*   1134

Alicia (Child)
Alicia's Best Friends - Lisa Jahn-Clough   *p*   724

Alicia (12th Grader)
Slumming - Kristen D. Randle   *h*   1183

Alien (Robot; Friend)
Alien & Possum: Hanging Out - Tony Johnston   *e*   751

Alighieri, Antonia "Bice" (Artist; Daughter)
Dante's Daughter - Kimberley Heuston   *h*   635

Alighieri, Dante (Writer; Historical Figure)
Dante's Daughter - Kimberley Heuston   *h*   635

Alisialar, Laron (Vampire)
Voyage of the Shadowmoon - Sean McMullen   *h, a*   994

Allard, Eleanor "Ellie" (9th Grader)
Girls in Love - Jacqueline Wilson   *m, h*   1448

Allie (Runaway)
Death Wind - William Bell   *m, h*   99

Allita (Daughter; Sister)
The Snake's Tales - Marguerite W. Davol   *p*   353

Allun (Baker; Adventurer)
Rowan and the Zebak - Emily Rodda   *e*   1219

Altenheimer, Kennesaw Mountain "Doc" (Doctor)
The Boy Who Saved Baseball - John Ritter   *m*   1210

Althestan (Royalty; Cousin)
Never After - Rebecca Lickiss   *h, a*   892

Alveston, Robert (Aged Person)
The Ghost Behind the Wall - Melvin Burgess   *m*   182

Alvie (Child; Brother)
Alvie Eats Soup - Ross Collins   *p*   283

Amarillo (Pig)
My Pig Amarillo - Satomi Ichikawa   *p*   709

Amber (Kindergartner; Daughter)
Amber Waiting - Nan Gregory   *p*   559

America (Teenager; Abuse Victim)
America - E.R. Frank   *h*   479

Amoeba (Bird)
Birdbrain Amos - Michael Delaney   *e*   371

Amos (Hippopotamus)
Birdbrain Amos - Michael Delaney   e   371

Amun (Deity)
The Ugly Goddess - Elsa Marston   m   944

Amy (15-Year-Old)
Amy - Mary Hooper   m, h   674

Amy (5th Grader)
Attack of the Mutant Underwear - Tom Birdseye
   e   109

Amy (Child; Daughter)
Mama Played Baseball - David A. Adler   p   5

Amy (11th Grader)
Out of the Fire - Deborah Froese   m, h   497

Ananse (Spider)
Ananse and the Lizard: A West African Tale - Pat
   Cummings   p   326

Anaxandra (12-Year-Old)
Goddess of Yesterday - Caroline B. Cooney   m,
   h   292

Anchorman "Angerman" (Teenager)
The Kindling - Jennifer Armstrong   m, h   38

Andrews (Teacher)
First Day in Grapes - L. King Perez   p   1145

Andy (Child; Son)
The Broken Cat - Lynne Rae Perkins   p   1146

Andy (12th Grader; Actor)
Skud - Dennis Foon   h   472

Angela (Friend)
What James Likes Best - Amy Schwartz   p   1272

Angelini, Lorenzo "Renz" (Vampire)
Dangerous Girls - R.L. Stine   m, h   1345

Angelo (Artisan; Aged Person)
Angelo - David Macaulay   p   921

Angie (Rabbit; Friend)
The Saturday Escape - Daniel J. Mahoney   p   934

Angus (Cat)
*Dancing in My Nuddy-Pants: Even Further
   Confessions of Georgia Nicolson* - Louise Rennison
   m, h   1198

Angus (Bull; Toy)
The Jamie and Angus Stories - Anne Fine   e   455

Angus (14-Year-Old; Fisherman)
Sea Gift - John Ashby   m, h   47

Anna (Sister)
Cold Tom - Sally Prue   m, h   1177

Anna (Aunt)
Once Upon a Time - Niki Daly   p   341

Annabel (Child; Actress)
*Annabel the Actress, Starring in Hound of the
   Barkervilles* - Ellen Conford   e   285

Annabelle (Child; Daughter)
Jethro Byrd, Fairy Child - Bob Graham   p   544

Anne of Mandagor (Stepmother; Royalty)
Snow - Tracy Lynn   m, h   919

Annie (Child; Friend)
Annie Was Warned - Jarrett J. Krosoczka   p   833

Annie (Child; Daughter)
Annie's Ark - Lesley Harker   p   594

Annie (Stepsister; Child)
The No Place Cat - C.S. Adler   e, m   4

Annie Rose (Child; Sister)
Annie Rose Is My Little Sister - Shirley Hughes
   p   694

Anstey, Lance (Bully; Student—High School)
Shattering Glass - Gail Giles   h   526

Anthony (Child; Friend)
I'll Never Share You, Blackboard Bear - Martha
   Alexander   p   19

Anthony "Tony" (12-Year-Old)
*The Glass Cafe: Or the Stripper and the State: How
   My Mother Started a War with the System that
   Made Us Kind of Rich and a Little Bit Famous* -
   Gary Paulsen   m, h   1134

Antonelli, Little Benny (Child; Bullied Child)
The Big Cheese of Third Street - Laurie Halse
   Anderson   p   27

Antonescu, Ileana (Vampire; Royalty)
Vampire High - Douglas Rees   m, h   1194

ap Gabrevys, Jachiel "Jaycie" (Runaway; Royalty)
Mad Maudlin - Mercedes Lackey   h, a   844

Aphrodite (Deity)
Quiver - Stephanie Spinner   m, h   1327

Apollo (Deity)
Goddesses Series - Clea Hantman   m, h   592

Apple (Pig)
Pig Tale - Verlyn Flieger   h   466

Apple (Administrator)
Mr. Tanen's Tie Trouble - Maryann Cocca-Leffler
   p   268

Applewhite, Edith Wharton "E.D." (12-Year-Old)
Surviving the Applewhites - Stephanie S. Tolan   m,
   h   1383

Applewood, Lillie (Child)
Bicycle Madness - Jane Kurtz   e, m   837

Arden, Noah (Teacher)
The Birds of Killingworth - Robert D. San Souci
   p   1258

Argul (Leader)
Wolf Queen - Tanith Lee   m, h   874

Arielle (11th Grader)
The Battle of Jericho - Sharon M. Draper   m,
   h   395

Aristotle (Cat)
The Nine Lives of Aristotle - Dick King-Smith
   e   794

Arizona Charlie (Cowboy; Entertainer)
Arizona Charlie and the Klondike Kid - Julie Lawson
   p   864

Arkanian, Petra (Genius)
Shadow Puppets - Orson Scott Card   h, a   215

Armadillo (Armadillo)
Armadillo's Orange - Jim Arnosky   p   40

Armitage, Anastasia (Niece; Driver)
Mrs. Armitage: Queen of the Road - Quentin Blake
   p   116

Armstrong, Delbert "Del" (Farmer)
True Confessions of a Heartless Girl - Martha Brooks
   h   161

Armstrong-Barnes, Charlotte (15-Year-Old; Nurse)
Remembrance - Theresa Breslin   m, h   143

Armstrong-Barnes, Francis (Military Personnel;
Pacifist)
Remembrance - Theresa Breslin   m, h   143

Arnie (Object; Friend)
Arnie the Doughnut - Laurie Keller   p   779

Arnold, Benedict (Historical Figure)
The Year of the Hangman - Gary Blackwood   m,
   h   115

Arrendale, Lou (Autistic)
The Speed of Dark - Elizabeth Moon   h, a   1025

Arrighi, Lorenzo (Apprentice; Artist)
The Warhorse - Don Bolognese   m   122

Arrighi, Renato (Artisan; Father)
The Warhorse - Don Bolognese   m   122

Artemis (Deity)
Quiver - Stephanie Spinner   m, h   1327

Arthur (Friend)
The Great Blue Yonder - Alex Shearer   m, h   1290

Arthur (Royalty)
Sword of the Rightful King: A Novel of King Arthur -
   Jane Yolen   m, h   1486

Artos (Royalty)
A Coalition of Lions - Elizabeth E. Wein   h   1424

Arturus (Royalty)
Warriors of Camlann - N.M. Browne   m, h   169

Asa (9-Year-Old; Son)
A Full Hand - Thomas F. Yezerski   p   1477

Asconti, Dave (13-Year-Old)
Outside In - Karen Romano Young   m, h   1489

Ashk (Mythical Creature)
Shadows and Light - Anne Bishop   h, a   110

Asif (Child; Amputee)
Parvana's Journey - Deborah Ellis   m, h   429

Atalanta (16-Year-Old)
Quiver - Stephanie Spinner   m, h   1327

Atami Baba (Religious; Martial Arts Expert)
Wandering Warrior - Da Chen   m, h   240

Atherton, Henry (Teenager)
Faerie Wars - Herbie Brennan   h   141

Atkins, David "Wild Man" (Recluse; Scientist)
Wild Man Island - Will Hobbs   m, h   653

Atlantic Ocean (Narrator)
Atlantic - G. Brian Karas   p   764

Atlee, Amy (Spirit)
Starry Nights - Judith Clarke   m, h   258

Attired, Natalie (Bird; 4th Grader)
The Hamster of the Baskervilles - Bruce Hale
   e   583

Audrey (Child; Adventurer)
Audrey and Barbara - Janet Lawson   p   863

Auntie (Aunt)
Epossumondas - Coleen Salley   p   1254

Auntie Claus (Aunt)
Auntie Claus and the Key to Christmas - Elise
   Primavera   p   1171

Aurora (Royalty; Daughter)
Sleeping Beauty - Mahlon F. Craft   p   312

Austin (Child; Son)
Just One More Story - Jennifer Brutschy   p   173

Avila, Mateo Macias de (Orphan; 14-Year-Old)
To the Edge of the World - Michele Torrey
   m   1385

Axel (Nephew; Child)
Fire Storm - Jean Craighead George   p   517

Aycliff, John (Steward)
Crispin: The Cross of Lead - Avi   m, h   58

B

B. (Doctor)
America - E.R. Frank   h   479

B (Teacher)
Attack of the Mutant Underwear - Tom Birdseye
   e   109

Baal (Spider)
The Time Witches - Michael Molloy   m   1022

Baby (Baby)
Go Track a Yak! - Tony Johnston   *p   752*
It's Snowing! - Olivier Dunrea   *p   407*

Baby Jazzy (Animal)
Jazzy in the Jungle - Lucy Cousins   *p   307*

Baby Leo (Lion; Baby)
Quiet! - Paul Bright   *p   153*

Baddeck, Robert Haynes "Rob" Jr. (Student—High School)
Shattering Glass - Gail Giles   *h   526*

Badger (Badger; Friend)
A Perfect Day for It - Jan Fearnley   *p   445*

Baer, Annie (Stepsister)
Almost Home - Nora Raleigh Baskin   *e, m   87*

Baer, Gail (Stepmother)
Almost Home - Nora Raleigh Baskin   *e, m   87*

Baer, Karen (Stepmother)
Almost Home - Nora Raleigh Baskin   *e, m   87*

Baer, Leah (6th Grader)
Almost Home - Nora Raleigh Baskin   *e, m   87*

Bailey, Claire (Single Mother; 12th Grader)
Hanging on to Max - Margaret Bechard   *h   94*

Balangru, Agatha (Kidnap Victim; Bully)
Quadehar the Sorcerer - Erik L'Homme   *m, h   891*

Bamford, Robert (Brother; 9-Year-Old)
Vampire State Building - Elizabeth Levy   *e   887*

Bamford, Sam (11-Year-Old; Chess Player)
Vampire State Building - Elizabeth Levy   *e   887*

Bancroft, Ben "Spaz" (16-Year-Old; Handicapped)
Stoner & Spaz - Ron Koertge   *h   810*

Bandry, Janet Foley (16-Year-Old)
Planet Janet - Dyan Sheldon   *m, h   1291*

Banks, Amanda Jane (Sister)
Swear to Howdy - Wendelin Van Draanen   *m   1392*

Banks, Joey (12-Year-Old)
Swear to Howdy - Wendelin Van Draanen   *m   1392*

Banning (Mother)
The Battle for St. Michaels - Emily Arnold McCully   *b   973*

Banning, Caroline (9-Year-Old; Runner)
The Battle for St. Michaels - Emily Arnold McCully   *b   973*

Banyon, Eric (Musician)
Mad Maudlin - Mercedes Lackey   *h, a   844*

Banyon, Magnus (Runaway)
Mad Maudlin - Mercedes Lackey   *h, a   844*

Barbara (Cat)
Audrey and Barbara - Janet Lawson   *p   863*

Barbara (7-Year-Old; Sister)
Most Beloved Sister - Astrid Lindgren   *p   897*

Barbaron, Beatrixa (Noblewoman)
A Bed of Earth: The Gravedigger's Tale - Tanith Lee   *h, a   872*

Bardsley, John (Immigrant; Animal Lover)
Sparrow Jack - Mordicai Gerstein   *p   519*

Bark (Dog)
Agapanthus Hum and the Angel Hoot - Joy Cowley   *b   309*

Barker, Lizzie (10-Year-Old; Daughter)
Season of Promise - Patricia Hermes   *e   628*

Barkley (Dog)
Penny Lee and Her TV - Glenn McCoy   *p   971*

Barnavelt, Jonathan (Uncle; Sorcerer)
The Whistle, the Grave, and the Ghost - Brad Strickland   *m   1349*

Barnavelt, Lewis (13-Year-Old; Orphan)
The Whistle, the Grave, and the Ghost - Brad Strickland   *m   1349*

Barnes, T.J. (Student—Elementary School; Friend)
T.J. and the Cats - Hazel Hutchins   *e   704*

Barnes, Zachary James "Zach" (6th Grader)
The Canyon - Sheila Cole   *e, m   275*

Barnett, Hannah (14-Year-Old)
Together Apart - Dianne E. Gray   *m, h   550*

Barnett, Luke (Student—High School; Volunteer)
Rising Water - P.J. Petersen   *m   1148*

Barnett, Tracy (Student—High School; Volunteer)
Rising Water - P.J. Petersen   *m   1148*

Barney (16-Year-Old)
Parasite Pig - William Sleator   *m, h   1310*

Barofsky, Mary Priscilla "Mary P" (10-Year-Old; Friend)
Might Adventurer of the Planet! - Ricki Stern   *e   1341*

Baron (Werewolf)
Midwinter Nightingale - Joan Aiken   *m   13*

Barr, Gordie (3rd Grader)
Doggone . . . Third Grade! - Colleen O'Shaughnessy McKenna   *e   982*

Barrett, Emmett (Brother)
The She - Carol Plum-Ucci   *m, h   1161*

Barrett, Evan (Orphan; 12th Grader)
The She - Carol Plum-Ucci   *m, h   1161*

Barstow, Olive (Accident Victim)
Olive's Ocean - Kevin Henkes   *m   623*

Bartholdi (Artist)
Liberty! - Allan Drummond   *p   399*

Bartholome (Sea Captain)
Pirates!: The True and Remarkable Adventures of Minerva Sharpe and Nancy Kington, Female Pirates - Celia Rees   *m, h   1193*

Bartholomew, Cyril (Cook; 12th Grader)
Flavor of the Week - Tucker Shaw   *m, h   1288*

Bartimaeus (Demon)
The Amulet of Samarkand - Jonathan Stroud   *m, h   1350*

Barton, Clarissa Harlowe "Clara" (Historical Figure)
Numbering All the Bones - Ann Rinaldi   *m, h   1205*

Basket, Amos (Father; Lumberjack)
Hill Hawk Hattie - Clara Gillow Clark   *e, m   257*

Basket, Hattie (11-Year-Old)
Hill Hawk Hattie - Clara Gillow Clark   *e, m   257*

Basset, Reginald E. (Dog; Wealthy)
Mr. Basset Plays - Dominic Catalano   *p   228*

Bata (Servant)
The Ugly Goddess - Elsa Marston   *m   944*

Batalin, Rachel (Runaway)
A Greater Goode - Amy Schor Ferris   *m   451*

Bateman, William (6-Year-Old; Son)
The Scrimshaw Ring - William Jaspersohn   *p   729*

Bates, Jimmy "Clovis King" (Orphan; Adoptee)
Journey to the River Sea - Eva Ibbotson   *m   707*

Bates, Julian (4th Grader; Friend)
Gloria Rising - Ann Cameron   *e   207*

Baum (Aged Person)
Skinny-Dipping at Monster Lake - Bill Wallace   *m   1406*

Bayer, George Harrison "Sonny Bear" (Boxer)
Warrior Angel - Robert Lipsyte   *h   900*

BBW (Wolf)
Where's the Big Bad Wolf? - Eileen Christelow   *p   254*

Bean, Beryl E. (10-Year-Old; Soccer Player)
Might Adventurer of the Planet! - Ricki Stern   *e   1341*

Bean, Clarice (Student—Elementary School; Friend)
Utterly Me, Clarice Bean - Lauren Child   *e   249*

Bean, Clarice (Sister; Student)
What Planet Are You from, Clarice Bean? - Lauren Child   *p   250*

Bean, Kurt (Brother; Environmentalist)
What Planet Are You from, Clarice Bean? - Lauren Child   *p   250*

Bear (Bear)
Bear Snores On - Karma Wilson   *p   1449*

Bear (Entertainer)
Crispin: The Cross of Lead - Avi   *m, h   58*

Bear (Bear; Friend)
A Perfect Day for It - Jan Fearnley   *p   445*

Bear (Bear)
Snow - Manya Stojic   *p   1346*
A Story for Bear - Dennis Haseley   *p   607*

Bear (Dog)
Wild Man Island - Will Hobbs   *m, h   653*

Bear (Mother; Bear)
Don't You Feel Well, Sam? - Amy Hest   *p   632*

Beard, George (4th Grader; Friend)
The Adventures of Super Diaper Baby: The First Graphic Novel - Dav Pilkey   *e   1153*

Beasley, John "Johnny" (Football Player)
Up Molasses Mountain - Julie Baker   *m, h   68*

Beaterson, Rick (11th Grader; Football Player)
Three Clams and an Oyster - Randy Powell   *m, h   1166*

Beatrice (Teenager)
The Warhorse - Don Bolognese   *m   122*

Beau (Dog; Friend)
Bubba and Beau, Best Friends - Kathi Appelt   *p   34*

Beau (Dog)
Bubba and Beau Go Night-Night - Kathi Appelt   *p   33*

Becaharuvic, Mabel (Mythical Creature)
Mabel the Tooth Fairy and How She Got Her Job - Katie Davis   *p   350*

Becha, Rislin sae (Noblewoman)
The Sword of the Land - Noel-Anne Brennan   *h, a   142*

Beck, Brian (Student—High School)
After Elaine - Ann L. Dreyer   *m   397*

Beck, Elaine (Student—High School)
After Elaine - Ann L. Dreyer   *m   397*

Beck, Eugenie (Social Worker)
The Monster in Me - Mette Ivie Harrison   *m   600*

Beck, Gina (6th Grader)
After Elaine - Ann L. Dreyer   *m   397*

Becket, Isabel (16-Year-Old; Healer)
The Dark - Marianne Curley   *m, h   328*

Becket, Isabel (16-Year-Old; Student—High School)
The Named - Marianne Curley   *m, h   329*

Becket, Matt (Brother)
The Dark - Marianne Curley   *m, h   328*

Becky (Sister; Daughter)
Bear Hug - Laurence Pringle   *p   1172*

Bedelia, Amelia (Housekeeper)
Calling Doctor Amelia Bedelia - Herman Parish   *b   1126*

Blackboard Bear (Bear)
I'll Never Share You, Blackboard Bear - Martha Alexander   p   19

Blackie "Surfer Dog" (Dog)
Surfer Dog - Elizabeth Spurr   e, m   1332

Blackwell, Kelsey Gene (12th Grader)
Happenings - Katie Cobb   m, h   265

Blackwell, Russ (Guardian; Police Officer)
Happenings - Katie Cobb   m, h   265

Blackwood, Melanie (15-Year-Old)
Drowning Anna - Sue Mayfield   m, h   958

Blair, Allison (14-Year-Old; Accident Victim)
A Circle of Time - Marisa Montes   m, h   1023

Blake (16-Year-Old)
Full Tilt: A Novel - Neal Shusterman   m, h   1297

Blake (15-Year-Old; Brother)
Saving Jasey - Diane Tullson   m, h   1387

Blake, Nora (Publisher)
Saving the Planet & Stuff - Gail Gauthier   m, h   511

Blast Off Boy (Student—Exchange)
The Big Science Fair - Dan Yaccarino   e   1473

Blennerhassett, Lily (13-Year-Old)
Lily B. on the Brink of Cool - E. Cody Kimmel   e, m   786

Blessing (11-Year-Old; Orphan)
Sweet By and By - Patricia Hermes   e, m   629

Blondie (Gang Member)
Nirvana's Children - Ranulfo   h   1185

Bloom, Lee (6th Grader)
When Pirates Came to Brooklyn - Phyllis Shalant   e, m   1280

Blorp (Alien; Student—Exchange)
The Big Science Fair - Dan Yaccarino   e   1473

Blue Fairy (Mythical Creature; Mother)
Pinocchio the Boy: Incognito in Collodi - Lane Smith   p   1314

Blue Horse (Toy)
Blue Horse - Helen Stephens   p   1340

Blue Kangaroo (Toy)
What Shall We Do, Blue Kangaroo? - Emma Chichester Clark   p   247

Bluebell, Hilda (Fiance(e))
The Time Witches - Michael Molloy   m   1022

Bluestar (Leader; Cat)
Warriors Series - Erin Hunter   m, h   696

Bo Won (Blind Person; Storyteller)
Chang and the Bamboo Flute - Elizabeth Starr Hill   e   640

Bob (Rooster)
Bob - Tracey Campbell Pearson   p   1140

Bob (Guinea Pig; Friend)
Brian & Bob: The Tale of Two Guinea Pigs - Georgie Ripper   p   1208

Bob (Brother)
Giggle, Giggle, Quack - Doreen Cronin   p   317

Bob (Monster)
Laura Numeroff's 10-Step Guide to Living with Your Monster - Laura Joffe Numeroff   p   1097

Bob (Brother; Son)
One Bright Penny - Geraldine McCaughrean   p   967

Bogart, Vincent "Big Skinny" (7th Grader)
Ruby Electric - Theresa Nelson   m   1074

Bohannon, Tyler (14-Year-Old)
Betrayed! - Patricia Calvert   m   205

Boland, Kevin (Baseball Player; 14-Year-Old)
Shakespeare Bats Cleanup - Ron Koertge   m, h   809

Boleyn, Anne (Royalty; Mother)
Doomed Queen Anne - Carolyn Meyer   m, h   1006

Bombina (Mythical Creature; Mother)
For Biddle's Sake - Gail Carson Levine   e   884

Bone, Charlie (Wizard; Student—Boarding School)
Charlie Bone and the Time Twister - Jenny Nimmo   m   1081

Bone, Charlie (Student—Boarding School)
Midnight for Charlie Bone - Jenny Nimmo   m   1082

Bone, Griselda Yewbeam (Grandmother)
Midnight for Charlie Bone - Jenny Nimmo   m   1082

Boniface, Bo (Child; Runaway)
The Thief Lord - Cornelia Funke   m, h   500

Boo (Cat)
Rembrandt's Hat - Susan Blackaby   p   112

Boobie (Teenager; Runaway)
33 Snowfish - Adam Rapp   h   1186

Boots (Cat)
Comic Adventures of Boots - Satoshi Kitamura   p   802

Boots (Sister; Child)
Gregor the Overlander - Suzanne Collins   m   284

Bop (Child)
Song of the Circus - Lois Duncan   p   404

Boris (Hamster)
Boris's Glasses - Peter Cohen   p   270

Borowitz-Jacobs, River (11-Year-Old; Basketball Player)
Hoop Girlz - Lucy Jane Bledsoe   e, m   118

Borowitz-Jacobs, Zacj (Coach; Brother)
Hoop Girlz - Lucy Jane Bledsoe   e, m   118

Borsch (Police Officer)
Sammy Keyes and the Search for Snake Eyes - Wendelin Van Draanen   m   1391

Boscombe, Chantelle (Handicapped; Student—High School)
Stitches - Glen Huser   m, h   703

Bottner, Frederik (Immigrant; Musician)
Mountain Solo - Jeanette Ingold   m, h   714

Bouchard (Doctor)
Bridging Beyond - Kathleen Benner Duble   m, h   403

Bouki (Wolf; Farmer)
Lapin Plays Possum: Trickster Tales from the Louisiana Bayou - Sharon Arms Doucet   e   390

Bovey, Jessica Kay "Jessie" (12-Year-Old)
Spitting Image - Shutta Crum   m   321

Bowen, Kathlee "Kat" (8th Grader)
A Time for Courage: The Suffragette Diary of Kathleen Bowen, Washington, DC, 1917 - Kathryn Lasky   e, m   857

Bowen, Nell (Teenager)
A Time for Courage: The Suffragette Diary of Kathleen Bowen, Washington, DC, 1917 - Kathryn Lasky   e, m   857

Boxer (Grandfather; Artisan)
Sasha's Matrioshka Dolls - Jane Dillon   p   383

Boyd (12-Year-Old)
How to Disappear Completely and Never Be Found - Sara Nickerson   m   1079

Boyd, Wallace "Weasel" (6th Grader; Friend)
Bernie Magruder & the Bats in the Belfry - Phyllis Reynolds Naylor   e   1064

Boyle, Dorothy "Godbee" (Grandmother)
Olive's Ocean - Kevin Henkes   m   623

Boyle, Martha (12-Year-Old)
Olive's Ocean - Kevin Henkes   m   623

Brace, Gwendolyn Mary "Gwen" (12-Year-Old; Mentally Ill Person)
The Earth Kitchen - Sharon Bryant   m   174

Bracke, Anna (16-Year-Old)
And What about Anna? - Jan Simoen   h   1306

Bracke, Irina (Mother)
And What about Anna? - Jan Simoen   h   1306

Brackett, Rob (13-Year-Old; Orphan)
Virginia Bound - Amy Butler   e, m   188

Brad (12th Grader)
Skud - Dennis Foon   h   472

Bradley, Lynda (Restaurateur)
True Confessions of a Heartless Girl - Martha Brooks   h   161

Bradley, Seth (Child)
True Confessions of a Heartless Girl - Martha Brooks   h   161

Bradshaw, Ann (Student—Boarding School)
A Great and Terrible Beauty - Libba Bray   h   138

Bradshaw, Isaac (15-Year-Old)
Together Apart - Dianne E. Gray   m, h   550

Brae (Landowner)
White Midnight - Dia Calhoun   m, h   203

Brae, Raymont (Teenager)
White Midnight - Dia Calhoun   m, h   203

Braid Beard (Pirate)
How I Became a Pirate - Melinda Long   p   907

Bramlett, Cecil (Photographer)
The Day the Picture Man Came - Faye Gibbons   p   520

Bramwell (12-Year-Old)
Olivia Kidney - Ellen Potter   e, m   1165

Brand, Daniel "Dan" (8th Grader)
The Cheat - Amy Goldman Koss   m   820

Brandt, Graeme (12th Grader; Writer)
Simon Says - Elaine Marie Alphin   h   23

Brattle (Teacher)
Jake Drake, Class Clown - Andrew Clements   e   260

Braxton, Elizabeth (15-Year-Old)
Up Molasses Mountain - Julie Baker   m, h   68

Breakspear (Dog)
Mrs. Armitage: Queen of the Road - Quentin Blake   p   116

Breeze "Bree" (17-Year-Old; Kidnap Victim)
The Long Night of Leo and Bree - Ellen Wittlinger   m, h   1453

Bregon, Adamo (Nobleman)
The Angel's Command: A Tale from the Castaways of the Flying Dutchman - Brian Jacques   m, h   722

Brenna (Witch; Sister)
Shadows and Light - Anne Bishop   h, a   110

Brennan, Bess (Blind Person; 12-Year-Old)
Mirror, Mirror on the Wall: The Diary of Bess Brennan - Barry Denenberg   e, m   373

Brennan, Elin (Twin; 12-Year-Old)
Mirror, Mirror on the Wall: The Diary of Bess Brennan - Barry Denenberg   e, m   373

Brewster, William (Religious; Historical Figure)
Stink Alley - Jamie Gilson   e, m   527

Brewster Rooster (Rooster)
Earthquack! - Margie Palatini   p   1122

Brian (Guinea Pig; Friend)
Brian & Bob: The Tale of Two Guinea Pigs - Georgie Ripper   p   1208

Brian (Cousin)
Katie's Wish - Barbara Shook Hazen   p   616

Brianna (Sister; Dancer)
Brianna, Jamaica, and the Dance of Spring - Juanita Havill   p   612

Brickman, Joe (12th Grader; Soccer Player)
Home of the Braves - David Klass   h   803

Bridget (Child)
Bridget and the Muttonheads - Pija Lindenbaum   p   895

Bridget (Gang Member)
The Secret of the Red Flame - K.M. Kimball   e, m   785

Bridget (Aunt; Animal)
Something Might Happen - Helen Lester   p   876

Bright, Calico Warrenfield (Grandmother)
The Return of Calico Bright - David Winkler   m, h   1450

Britta (Child; Daughter)
Mirabelle - Astrid Lindgren   p   896

Brittman, Anne (Mother)
Hannah's Garden - Midori Snyder   m, h   1318

Brittman, Cassiopeia Emma "Cassie" (17-Year-Old; Musician)
Hannah's Garden - Midori Snyder   m, h   1318

Brittman, Daniel "Poppie" (Grandfather; Artist)
Hannah's Garden - Midori Snyder   m, h   1318

Brocato, Mona (19-Year-Old)
The Farther You Run - Davida Wills Hurwin   h   700

Broder, Jake (8th Grader)
The Cheat - Amy Goldman Koss   m   820

Brodski, Rodzina Clara Jadqiga Anastozy (Orphan; 12-Year-Old)
Rodzina - Karen Cushman   m   331

Brom (Wizard; Storyteller)
Eragon - Christopher Paolini   m, h   1125

Brooks, Alfred (Coach)
Warrior Angel - Robert Lipsyte   h   900

Brooks, Linus (Aged Person)
The Poltergoose - Michael Lawrence   e, m   862

Broom (Sea Captain)
Pirates!: The True and Remarkable Adventures of Minerva Sharpe and Nancy Kington, Female Pirates - Celia Rees   m, h   1193

Brother Rabbit (Rabbit; Rescuer)
The Magic Gourd - Baba Wague Diakite   p   380

Brotherbum, Cabot "Rocky" (13-Year-Old; Animal Lover)
Remote Man - Elizabeth Honey   m, h   670

Brown, Amber (Child of Divorced Parents; 4th Grader)
Amber Brown Is Green with Envy - Paula Danziger   e   345

Brown, Amber (2nd Grader)
Get Ready for Second Grade, Amber Brown - Paula Danziger   b   346

Brown, Annie Sharon (14-Year-Old; Rodeo Rider)
Daddy Says - Ntozake Shange   m   1281

Brown, Bunny (Rabbit; Detective)
The Case of the Sleepy Sloth - Cynthia Rylant   b   1243

Brown, Creighton (17-Year-Old; Spy)
The Year of the Hangman - Gary Blackwood   m, h   115

Brown, Danitra (Child; Friend)
Danitra Brown Leaves Town - Nikki Grimes   p   566

Brown, Devon (15-Year-Old; 10th Grader)
Not as Crazy as I Seem - George Harrar   m, h   596

Brown, Grace (19-Year-Old; Historical Figure)
A Northern Light - Jennifer Donnelly   h   387

Brown, Katahdin "Dani" (12-Year-Old)
Halfway to the Sky - Kimberly Brubaker Bradley   m   135

Brown, Katherine "Kate" (Child)
When Marcus Moore Moved In - Rebecca Bond   p   123

Brown, Lucie-Marie (12-Year-Old)
Daddy Says - Ntozake Shange   m   1281

Brown, Omaha Nebraska (16-Year-Old)
Blue Avenger and the Theory of Everything - Norma Howe   m, h   689

Brown, Patrick (Son; Bear)
Patrick at the Circus - Geoffrey Hayes   p   615

Brown, Ringfinger (Aged Person)
Summerland - Michael Chabon   m, h   236

Brown, Seth (Military Personnel)
The Big Burn - Jeanette Ingold   m, h   713

Brown, Springer (13-Year-Old; Handicapped)
Halfway to the Sky - Kimberly Brubaker Bradley   m   135

Brown, Susan (Mother)
Halfway to the Sky - Kimberly Brubaker Bradley   m   135

Brown, Tie-Down (Rodeo Rider; Father)
Daddy Says - Ntozake Shange   m   1281

Brown Hen (Chicken; Mother)
Little Brown Hen's Shower - Pamela Duncan Edwards   p   418

Bruce (Teacher)
Jake Drake, Class Clown - Andrew Clements   e   260

Bruce, Marjorie (Royalty; Historical Figure)
Girl in a Cage - Jane Yolen   m, h   1480

Bruce, Robert (Royalty; Historical Figure)
Girl in a Cage - Jane Yolen   m, h   1480

Bruh Rabbit (Rabbit; Trickster)
Bruh Rabbit and the Tar Baby Girl - Virginia Hamilton   p   589

Bruh Wolf (Wolf; Farmer)
Bruh Rabbit and the Tar Baby Girl - Virginia Hamilton   p   589

Brume (Witch)
In the Forests of Serre - Patricia McKillip   h, a   984

Bruno (Toy; Bear)
Dahlia - Barbara McClintock   p   970

Bruno (Bear; Friend)
Where Does Thursday Go? - Janeen Brian   p   146

Brunov, Urso (Bear)
The Tale of Urso Brunov: Little Father of All Bears - Brian Jacques   p   723

Bryant, Mary Broad (19-Year-Old; Prisoner)
Escape from Botany Bay: The True Story of Mary Bryant - Gerald Hausman   m, h   609

Bryant, Will (Prisoner)
Escape from Botany Bay: The True Story of Mary Bryant - Gerald Hausman   m, h   609

Bubba (Baby; Son)
Bubba and Beau, Best Friends - Kathi Appelt   p   34

Bubba and Beau Go Night-Night - Kathi Appelt   p   33

Bubble (Child)
Good Night, Animals - Lena Arro   p   44

Bucket, Mary Gillian "Gilly" (11-Year-Old)
The Spirit and Gilly Bucket - Maurine F. Dahlberg   m   337

Buckley, Todd (12th Grader; Football Player)
Jake, Reinvented - Gordon Korman   h   816

Buckman, Terese (Lesbian; Soccer Player)
Geography Club - Brent Hartinger   h   602

Budwing, Danny (Child; Brother)
Zathura: A Space Adventure - Chris Van Allsburg   p   1390

Budwing, Walter (Child; Brother)
Zathura: A Space Adventure - Chris Van Allsburg   p   1390

Bugg, Kevin (5th Grader; Friend)
City of Names - Kevin Brockmeier   e   157

Bullhaven (Nobleman)
The Great Ghost Rescue - Eva Ibbotson   m, h   706

Bulumba, Kaninda (Orphan)
Little Soldier - Bernard Ashley   m, h   48

Bunting, Bartholomew (Producer; Businessman)
Silent Movie - Avi   p   60

Burden, Mary "Many Horses" (Captive)
Betrayed! - Patricia Calvert   m   205

Burgess (16-Year-Old; Stepbrother)
Ten Miles from Winnemucca - Thelma Hatch Wyss   m, h   1472

Burke, Polly (6th Grader)
When Pirates Came to Brooklyn - Phyllis Shalant   e, m   1280

Burt (Swimmer)
Princess Fishtail - Frances Minters   p   1017

Burt, Tom (Aged Person; Gardener)
The Victory Garden - Lee Kochenderfer   e, m   808

Burton, David (Animal Trainer)
Shaper - Jessie Haas   m   576

Burton, Louise (15-Year-Old)
Shaper - Jessie Haas   m   576

Buster (Dog)
Buster - Denise Fleming   p   465

Buster (Cat; Criminal)
Slim and Jim - Richard Egielski   p   422

Butler (Servant)
Artemis Fowl: The Arctic Incident - Eoin Colfer   m   276
Artemis Fowl: The Eternity Code - Eoin Colfer   m   277

Butler, Claire (Counselor)
Bottled Up - Jaye Murray   m, h   1045

Butler, Juliet (Sister)
Artemis Fowl: The Eternity Code - Eoin Colfer   m   277

Butler, May (Spirit)
Cold in Summer - Tracy Barrett   e, m   83

Butterfly, Snooty Judy (Insect)
Three Nasty Gnarlies - Keith Graves   p   549

Buttons, Sissy (Child; Daughter)
Sissy Buttons Takes Charge! - Ian Whybrow   p   1439

Buzzy Bear (Bear; Teacher)
Little Rat Sets Sail - Monika Bang-Campbell   b   72

Byers, Madeline "Maddie" (11-Year-Old; Orphan)
Where I'd Like to Be - Frances O'Roark Dowell   e, m   391

Character Name Index

Chambers, Carly (8th Grader)
The Secret Within - Theresa Golding   m   534

Chamberten, Arachne (Wizard; Aunt)
The Gates of Sleep - Mercedes Lackey   h, a   843

Chance, David "Davey" (Military Personnel)
The Trouble with Jeremy Chance - George Harrar   e,
   m   597

Chance, James "Pa" (Father)
The Trouble with Jeremy Chance - George Harrar   e,
   m   597

Chance, Jeremy Theopoulos (12-Year-Old)
The Trouble with Jeremy Chance - George Harrar   e,
   m   597

Chandler, Jeremy "Rat" (15-Year-Old)
Rat - Jan Cheripko   m, h   242

Chandler, Rose (15-Year-Old)
White Midnight - Dia Calhoun   m, h   203

Chandler, Trisana "Tris" (Wizard; 14-Year-Old)
Shatterglass - Tamora Pierce   m, h   1151

Chang (Child; Friend)
Chang and the Bamboo Flute - Elizabeth Starr Hill
   e   640

Chango-monkey (Monkey; Friend)
Rosa Raposa - F. Isabel Campoy   p   209

Chanticleer (Rooster)
The Rooster and the Fox - Helen Ward   p   1415

Chapel, Olivia (Aunt)
The Red Rose Box - Brenda Woods   e   1463

Chapman, John "Johnny Appleseed" (Frontiersman)
Nelly in the Wilderness - Lynn Cullen   m   325

Chapski, Frank Fryderyk (Amputee; Veteran)
The Secret of the Red Flame - K.M. Kimball   e,
   m   785

Chapski, Jozef (12-Year-Old; Immigrant)
The Secret of the Red Flame - K.M. Kimball   e,
   m   785

Charles (Student—Elementary School; Friend)
I'm Not Invited? - Diane Cain Bluthenthal   p   121

Charles (Student; Mouse)
Timothy's Tales from Hilltop School - Rosemary Wells
   p   1428

Charles "Daddy" (Father)
Bippity Bop Barbershop - Natasha Anastasia Tarpley
   p   1362

Charley (Child)
Alphabet Mystery - Audrey Wood   p   1457

Charlie (Child)
Dumpy and the Big Storm - Julie Andrews Edwards
   p   416

Charlie (2-Year-Old; Brother)
Old Crump: The True Story of a Trip West - Laurie
   Lawlor   p   859

Charlie (Student—Elementary School; Son)
On the Town: A Community Adventure - Judith
   Caseley   p   227

Charlotte (Child; Niece)
Dahlia - Barbara McClintock   p   970

Charlotte (Aunt; Spouse)
Fire Storm - Jean Craighead George   p   517

Charon/Dracula (Wolf; Vampire)
Vampire High - Douglas Rees   m, h   1194

Chelmsley, Mark Robert (5th Grader; Son)
A Week in the Woods - Andrew Clements   e   262

Cheney, Ben (Father)
Child X - Lee Weatherly   m, h   1419

Cheney, Holly (Mother)
Child X - Lee Weatherly   m, h   1419

Cheney, Juliet "Jules" (13-Year-Old)
Child X - Lee Weatherly   m, h   1419

Cheng, Peichi (11-Year-Old)
Dish Series - Diane Muldrow   e, m   1037

Cherry (Teacher)
Iris and Walter: The School Play - Elissa Haden Guest
   b   570

Chicken (Chicken; Mother)
Mrs. Chicken and the Hungry Crocodile - Won-Ldy
   Paye   p   1137

Chimp (Chimpanzee; Twin)
Chimp and Zee and the Big Storm - Laurence Anholt
   p   31

Chimwala (Grandmother)
The Village That Vanished - Ann Grifalconi   p   561

Chris (15-Year-Old)
Who Owns Kelly Paddik? - Beth Goobie   m, h   537

Christian (17-Year-Old; Servant)
Once Upon a Marigold - Jean Ferris   m, h   452

Christmas, Jacob Israel (13-Year-Old; Slave)
Twelve Travelers, Twenty Horses - Harriette Gillem
   Robinet   m, h   1213

Christopher (Son; Brother)
When Mommy Was Mad - Lynne Jonell   p   756

Christy, Condor (Boyfriend)
God of Beer - Garret Keizer   h   775

Chu, Boone (Computer Expert)
Pattern Recognition - William Gibson   h, a   522

Chuck (Religious)
Wizards of the Game - David Lubar   m   914

Chucky Ducky (Duck)
Earthquack! - Margie Palatini   p   1122

Chumil, Tzunun "Rosa Garcia" (12-Year-Old;
   Crime Victim)
Colibri - Ann Cameron   m   206

Ciaran (Father; Wizard)
Child of the Prophecy - Juliet Marillier   h, a   941

Cinderella (Stepdaughter; Abuse Victim)
Cinderella - Ruth Sanderson   p   1263

Cinderella (Servant; Stepdaughter)
Cinderella's Dress - Nancy Willard   p   1444

Clabber (Government Official)
A Fairy in a Dairy - Lucy Nolan   p   1090

Claidi (Rebel)
Wolf Queen - Tanith Lee   m, h   874

Claire (Mother)
The Queen of Everything - Deb Caletti   h   202

Clairmont, Margaret (12-Year-Old)
How to Disappear Completely and Never Be Found -
   Sara Nickerson   m   1079

Clairmont, Sophie (Child)
How to Disappear Completely and Never Be Found -
   Sara Nickerson   m   1079

Clarissa (Cow)
Poultrygeist - Mary Jane Auch   p   55

Clark, Babe (Dealer)
Matchit - Martha Moore   e, m   1027

Clark, Henriette (Mother)
The Canning Season - Polly Horvath   m, h   683

Clark, Ratchet (13-Year-Old)
The Canning Season - Polly Horvath   m, h   683

Clark, William (Historical Figure; Explorer)
*This Vast Land: A Young Man's Journal of the Lewis
   and Clark Expedition* - Stephen E. Ambrose   m,
   h   25

Claverlous, Yvette (Student—Boarding School)
Remote Man - Elizabeth Honey   m, h   670

Clawson, Josephine "Jo" (11-Year-Old)
Jericho Walls - Kristi Collier   m, h   280

Cleopatra (Child; Friend)
Madlenka's Dog - Peter Sis   p   1307

Click (Photographer)
The Best Class Picture Ever! - Denis Roche
   p   1214

Clinciu, Vlad (12-Year-Old; Chess Player)
Vampire State Building - Elizabeth Levy   e   887

Clorinda (Cow; Dancer)
Clorinda - Robert Kinerk   p   791

Clover, Abby (Witch)
The Time Witches - Michael Molloy   m   1022

Clovis (Tiger)
The Loudest Roar - Thomas Taylor   p   1367

Cob, Collie (Teacher; Magician)
Clever Lollipop - Dick King-Smith   e   792

Cobley, Abby (11th Grader)
Kerosene - Chris Wooding   h   1461

Cobriana, Zane (Shape-Shifter)
Hawksong - Amelia Atwater-Rhodes   m, h   54

Cody, Isaac "Pa" (Farmer; Father)
One Sky Above Us - E. Cody Kimmel   e   787

Cody, William Frederick "Bill" (8-Year-Old; Son)
One Sky Above Us - E. Cody Kimmel   e   787

Cogswallop (Mythical Creature)
The Goblin Wood - Hilari Bell   m, h   98

Cohen, Emma (11th Grader)
Kerosene - Chris Wooding   h   1461

Cohen-Liu, Annie (9-Year-Old; Neighbor)
The Trouble with Babies - Martha Freeman   e   488

Cole, David (12th Grader)
The True Meaning of Cleavage - Mariah Fredericks
   m, h   486

Cole, Duncan (Cousin; Tourist)
*Rosy Cole's Worst Ever, Best Yet Tour of New York
   City* - Sheila Greenwald   e   556

Cole, Rosy (Student—Elementary School; Cousin)
*Rosy Cole's Worst Ever, Best Yet Tour of New York
   City* - Sheila Greenwald   e   556

Colin (Child; Brother)
A Doctor Like Papa - Natalie Kinsey-Warnock
   e   795

Collier, Sarah (8th Grader)
The Cheat - Amy Goldman Koss   m   820

Collins, Carolina "Carol" (Narrator; 10-Year-Old)
Tadpole - Ruth White   e, m   1438

Collins, Daniel (15-Year-Old; Religious)
The Man with the Silver Oar - Robin Moore   m,
   h   1029

Collins, Elias (Uncle; Shipowner)
The Man with the Silver Oar - Robin Moore   m,
   h   1029

Collins, Georgia (11-Year-Old)
Tadpole - Ruth White   e, m   1438

Collins, Kentucky (14-Year-Old)
Tadpole - Ruth White   e, m   1438

Collins, Serilda (Mother)
Tadpole - Ruth White   e, m   1438

Collins, Virginia (12-Year-Old)
Tadpole - Ruth White   e, m   1438

Common, Faith (14-Year-Old)
Uncommon Faith - Trudy Krisher   m, h   827

Connolly, Eamon (Spirit)
Restless: A Ghost's Story - Rich Wallace   h   1411

Constantine (Diplomat; Heir)
A Coalition of Lions - Elizabeth E. Wein   h   1424

Conway, Daniel H. "Danny" (9th Grader)
Prep - Jake Coburn   *h* 266

Conway, Kris (Student—High School)
Prep - Jake Coburn   *h* 266

Cooke, Thelma (Student—Boarding School; Indian)
Unseen Companion - Denise Gosliner Orenstein
    h 1113

Cooper (Child; Neighbor)
Hank and Fergus - Susin Nielsen-Fernlund
    p 1080

Cooper, Elspeth (Child; Spirit)
Ghost at the Window - Margaret McAllister   *e,*
    m 960

Cooper, June (Baby)
Waiting for June - Joyce Sweeney   *h* 1356

Cooper, Russell "Rusty" (12-Year-Old)
Swear to Howdy - Wendelin Van Draanen   *m* 1392

Cooper, Sophie (12th Grader; Pregnant Teenager)
Waiting for June - Joyce Sweeney   *h* 1356

Coot (Uncle; Rancher)
Hannah Mae O'Hannigan's Wild West Show - Lisa
    Campbell Ernst   *p* 437

Copycub (Bear; Son)
Always Copycub - Richard Edwards   *p* 420

Coraline (Child)
Coraline - Neil Gaiman   *m* 502

Corbin, Delina (Mother)
In Plain Sight - Carol Otis Hurst   *e, m* 698

Corbin, Miles (Father; Prospector)
In Plain Sight - Carol Otis Hurst   *e, m* 698

Corbin, Robin (Child; Brother)
In Plain Sight - Carol Otis Hurst   *e, m* 698

Corbin, Sarah (11-Year-Old)
In Plain Sight - Carol Otis Hurst   *e, m* 698

Cordwyn, Simon (Teacher)
*Just Jane: The Story of a Daughter of England Caught
    in the Struggle for Independence in Revolutionary
    America* - William Lavender   *m, h* 858

Corinna (Entertainer)
Secret Heart - David Almond   *m, h* 21

Cornwall, Asa B. (Doctor)
Bone Dry - Kathleen Karr   *m* 766

Cosmo (Uncle; Motorcyclist)
Mrs. Armitage: Queen of the Road - Quentin Blake
    p 116

Costa, Mike (6th Grader)
Macaroni Boy - Katherine Ayres   *e, m* 62

Costa "Grandpap" (Grandfather)
Macaroni Boy - Katherine Ayres   *e, m* 62

Cotton, Fitzgerald (Artist)
Paint by Magic: A Time Travel Mystery - Kathryn
    Reiss   *m* 1197

Court (Journalist)
Riding the Flume - Patricia Curtis Pfitsch   *m* 1149

Cox, Hayley (Student—High School)
Phoning a Dead Man - Gillian Cross   *m, h* 318

Cox, John (Brother; Amnesiac)
Phoning a Dead Man - Gillian Cross   *m, h* 318

Coyote (Mythical Creature)
Summerland - Michael Chabon   *m, h* 236

Crabtree, Lily (13-Year-Old)
Lily's Ghosts - Laura Ruby   *m* 1237

Craiky, Simon (Plantation Owner)
The Spirit and Gilly Bucket - Maurine F. Dahlberg
    m 337

Cranston, Nell (Child; Orphan)
Virginia Bound - Amy Butler   *e, m* 188

Cricket (Cricket)
Christmas Cricket - Eve Bunting   *p* 178

Crispin "Asta's son" (13-Year-Old)
Crispin: The Cross of Lead - Avi   *m, h* 58

Cristy (7th Grader)
Gossip Times Three - Amy Goldman Koss   *m* 821

Crocker, Alexandra "Alex" (8th Grader)
Friction - E.R. Frank   *m, h* 480

Crockett, Navy (Boxer)
Warrior Angel - Robert Lipsyte   *h* 900

Crocodile (Crocodile; Mother)
Mrs. Chicken and the Hungry Crocodile - Won-Ldy
    Paye   *p* 1137

Crosby, Vincent (Sailor)
*Pirates!: The True and Remarkable Adventures of
    Minerva Sharpe and Nancy Kington, Female Pirates*
    - Celia Rees   *m, h* 1193

Crosswell, Angus (Child; Stepbrother)
The Steps - Rachel Cohn   *m* 273

Crosswell, Lucy (12-Year-Old; Stepsister)
The Steps - Rachel Cohn   *m* 273

Crouch, Stefan Millington III (Handicapped; 13-
    Year-Old)
Stefan's Story - Valerie Hobbs   *m* 651

Crow (Indian)
The World Before This One - Rafe Martin   *m* 950

Cruz, Angelina (Child)
Red Midnight - Ben Mikaelsen   *m, h* 1008

Cruz, Santiago (12-Year-Old)
Red Midnight - Ben Mikaelsen   *m, h* 1008

Cruzzelle (Teacher)
Straydog - Kathe Koja   *m, h* 812

Crystal (Teenager; Spirit)
The Afterlife - Gary Soto   *m, h* 1320

Cuhullin (Mythical Creature)
Mrs. McCool and the Giant Cuhullin: An Irish Tale -
    Jessica Souhami   *p* 1322

Culloch (Knight)
The Ballad of Sir Dinadan - Gerald Morris   *m,*
    h 1034

Culworth, Alex (Homosexual)
The Shell House - Linda Newbery   *h* 1075

Cummings, Bennett Lawson (15-Year-Old;
    Homosexual)
The Rainbow Kite - Marlene Fanta Shyer   *m,*
    h 1299

Cummings, Matthew (12-Year-Old)
The Rainbow Kite - Marlene Fanta Shyer   *m,*
    h 1299

Cummins, Rona "Aunt Memory" (Kidnapper)
Escape from Memory - Margaret Peterson Haddix
    m, h 580

Cunningham, Joelle (Baseball Player; 13-Year-Old)
Sliding into Home - Dori Hillstad Butler   *m* 189

Cupid (Deity)
Juliet Dove, Queen of Love - Bruce Coville   *e,*
    m 308

Curl (Teenager; Prostitute)
33 Snowfish - Adam Rapp   *h* 1186

Curry, David (12-Year-Old)
The Dream Bearer - Walter Dean Myers   *m* 1052

Curry, Reuben (Father)
The Dream Bearer - Walter Dean Myers   *m* 1052

Custis (Orphan; Runaway)
33 Snowfish - Adam Rapp   *h* 1186

Cuthand, Wesley (Indian; Boyfriend)
True Confessions of a Heartless Girl - Martha Brooks
    h 161

Cutter (Aged Person)
The Trouble with Jeremy Chance - George Harrar   *e,*
    m 597

Cyd Charisse (16-Year-Old)
Gingerbread - Rachel Cohn   *h* 272

D

Da (Father; Immigrant)
Katie's Wish - Barbara Shook Hazen   *p* 616

da Loura di An'Santa, Bartolome (Morgue
    Attendant)
A Bed of Earth: The Gravedigger's Tale - Tanith Lee
    h, a 872

da Padova, Lorenzo (Artist)
Paint by Magic: A Time Travel Mystery - Kathryn
    Reiss   *m* 1197

Dad (Father)
Amber Waiting - Nan Gregory   *p* 559

Dad (Father; Camper)
Bear Hug - Laurence Pringle   *p* 1172

Dad (Father; Robot)
Big Time Olie - William Joyce   *p* 762

Dad (Father)
By the Side of the Road - Jules Feiffer   *p* 446
Christmas Cricket - Eve Bunting   *p* 178
First Day - Dandi Daley Mackall   *p* 928
Gus and Grandpa Go Fishing - Claudia Mills
    b 1015

Dad (Musician; Storyteller)
Just One More Story - Jennifer Brutschy   *p* 173

Dad (Father; Spouse)
The Key to My Heart - Nira Harel   *p* 593

Dad (Pig; Father)
Lucille Camps In - Kathryn Lasky   *p* 854

Dad (Father; Spouse)
Musical Beds - Mara Bergman   *p* 105

Dad (Father; Cat)
Pizza Kittens - Charlotte Voake   *p* 1401

Dad (Father; Spouse)
The Quigleys - Simon Mason   *e* 952
The Quigleys at Large - Simon Mason   *e* 953

Dad (Father; Farmer)
The Real, True Dulcie Campbell - Cynthia DeFelice
    p 367

Dad (Father; Spouse)
Tatty Ratty - Helen Cooper   *p* 295

Dad (Father)
That Makes Me Mad! - Steven Kroll   *p* 830

Dad (Father; Divorced Person)
Two Old Potatoes and Me - John Coy   *p* 311

Dad (Father)
Waggle - Sarah McMenemy   *p* 988

Daddy (Father; Spouse)
Agapanthus Hum and the Angel Hoot - Joy Cowley
    b 309

Daddy (Pig; Father)
Bye, Bye! - Nancy Kaufmann   *p* 769

Daddy (Father; Hero)
Especially Heroes - Virginia Kroll   *p* 831

Daddy (Father; Cancer Patient)
Flamingo Dream - Donna Jo Napoli   *p* 1061

Daddy (Father)
Gus and Grandpa and the Halloween Costume -
    Claudia Mills   *b* 1014

Daddy (Father; Spouse)
I Am NOT Going to School Today! - Robie H. Harris
p 599

Daddy (Pig; Father)
Olivia . . . and the Missing Toy - Ian Falconer
p 441

Daddy (Father; Farmer)
Once Upon a Farm - Marie Bradby   p 132

Daddy (Father; Prisoner)
Visiting Day - Jacqueline Woodson   p 1468

Daddy (Father)
What James Likes Best - Amy Schwartz   p 1272

Daddy (Father; Spouse)
When Mommy Was Mad - Lynne Jonell   p 756

Daddy (Father)
Yesterday I Had the Blues - Jeron Ashford Frame
p 478

Dahl, Carl (10-Year-Old; Sailor)
On Sand Island - Jacqueline Briggs Martin   p 947

Dahlia (Doll; Toy)
Dahlia - Barbara McClintock   p 970

Daisy (Chicken; Runaway)
Daisy Comes Home - Jan Brett   p 144

Daisy (Cow)
Daisy the Dancing Cow - Viki Woodworth
p 1469

Daley, Ian (6th Grader; 12-Year-Old)
Stray Voltage - Eugenie Doyle   m 393

Daley, Ray (16-Year-Old)
Stray Voltage - Eugenie Doyle   m 393

Daley, Warren (Farmer)
Stray Voltage - Eugenie Doyle   m 393

DaLuna, Madama (Singer)
*First Graders from Mars: Episode 2: The Problem
with Pelly* - Shana Corey   b 301

Damienne (17-Year-Old; Servant)
Paradise - Joan Elizabeth Goodman   m, h 541

Dan (9th Grader)
Girls in Love - Jacqueline Wilson   m, h 1448

Dan (Brother; Young Man)
Puss in Cowboy Boots - Jan Huling   p 695

Dan (Teenager; Warrior)
Warriors of Camlann - N.M. Browne   m, h 169

Dan "Bear Sark" (Warrior)
Warriors of Alavna - N.M. Browne   m, h 168

Dana (11th Grader)
The Battle of Jericho - Sharon M. Draper   m,
h 395

Dandran (Royalty; Sister)
The Grail Prince - Nancy McKenzie   h, a 983

D'Angelo, Gayle (Neighbor; Wealthy)
The Queen of Everything - Deb Caletti   h 202

Daniel (Child; Friend)
Chachaji's Cup - Uma Krishnaswami   p 828

Daniel (Child; Son)
Daniel's Pet - Alma Flor Ada   b 1

Daniel (Child)
Not Just a Witch - Eva Ibbotson   e, m 708

Daniella (Orphan; Psychic)
The Rope Trick - Lloyd Alexander   e, m 18

Daniels, Justin (Friend; 2nd Grader)
Get Ready for Second Grade, Amber Brown - Paula
Danziger   b 346

Danny (Son; Child)
Bad News! I'm in Charge! - Bruce Ingman   p 712

Danny (Stepbrother)
Gingerbread - Rachel Cohn   h 272

Dart, Ewan (Student)
Ghost at the Window - Margaret McAllister   e,
m 960

Dart, Lizzie (Mother; Interior Decorator)
Ghost at the Window - Margaret McAllister   e,
m 960

Dart, Simon (Father; Artist)
Ghost at the Window - Margaret McAllister   e,
m 960

DaSilva, Quinn (Time Traveler)
Ravine - Janet Hickman   m 638

DaSilva, Richelle (Sister; Time Traveler)
Ravine - Janet Hickman   m 638

Daughter (Teenager; Immigrant)
When the Emperor Was Divine - Julie Otsuka   h,
a 1120

Dave (Boyfriend)
*Knocked Out by My Nunga-Nungas: Further, Further
Confessions of Georgia Nicolson* - Louise Rennison
m, h 1199

Dave "The Laugh" (Boyfriend)
*Dancing in My Nuddy-Pants: Even Further
Confessions of Georgia Nicolson* - Louise Rennison
m, h 1198

David (Artist; Teenager)
All-American Girl - Meg Cabot   m, h 195

David (Indian)
Brian's Hunt - Gary Paulsen   m, h 1133

David (Child; Son)
David Gets in Trouble - David Shannon   p 1282

David (19-Year-Old; Military Personnel)
Our Time on the River - Don Brown   m, h 162

David (5th Grader; Foster Child)
The Very Worst Thing - Torey Hayden   m 614

David, Suzanne (Spy; Singer)
For Freedom: The Story of a French Spy - Kimberly
Brubaker Bradley   m, h 134

Davies, Corin "Cory" (15-Year-Old)
Sonny's War - Valerie Hobbs   m, h 650

Davies, Kevin Robert "Kev" (15-Year-Old;
Homosexual)
The Flip Side - Andrew Matthews   m 956

Davies, Sonny (Brother; Military Personnel)
Sonny's War - Valerie Hobbs   m, h 650

Davis, George (11-Year-Old; Friend)
Flying Free: Corey's Underground Railroad Diary -
Sharon Dennis Wyeth   e 1471

Davis, Jeremy "Booger" (17-Year-Old)
Blood Trail - Nancy Springer   m, h 1329

de Bram, Roland (Knight)
Pagan's Crusade - Catherine Jinks   m, h 739

de la Cruz, Cruz (Baseball Player)
The Boy Who Saved Baseball - John Ritter
m 1210

de la Rocque, Marguerite (16-Year-Old; Historical
Figure)
Paradise - Joan Elizabeth Goodman   m, h 541

de la Torre, Anita (12-Year-Old)
Before We Were Free - Julia Alvarez   m, h 24

de la Torre, Mundin (Brother)
Before We Were Free - Julia Alvarez   m, h 24

De Salis, Winter (16-Year-Old; Orphan)
Winter - John Marsden   m, h 943

De Silva, Hector "Jesse" (Spirit)
Haunted: A Tale of the Mediator - Meg Cabot   m,
h 196

de Vere (Healer)
Isabel: Taking Wing - Annie Dalton   m 339

Dean (Boyfriend)
Martyn Pig - Kevin Brooks   m, h 160

Deanna (Sister)
Black-Eyed Suzie - Susan Shaw   m, h 1287

Dee, John (Scientist; Wizard)
The Alchemist's Door - Lisa Goldstein   h, a 535

Deerborn, Ben (Police Officer)
Kerosene - Chris Wooding   h 1461

del Gato, Dante (Baseball Player; Recluse)
The Boy Who Saved Baseball - John Ritter
m 1210

Del Rubio (Bird; Librarian)
Beverly Billingsly Borrows a Book - Alexander Stadler
p 1333

Delano, Mica (11-Year-Old)
My Brother's Hero - Adrian Fogelin   m 470

Delano, Robin Michael (Scientist)
My Brother's Hero - Adrian Fogelin   m 470

Delilah (Child; Sister)
Alvie Eats Soup - Ross Collins   p 283

Delilah (Dog; Friend)
It Came from Beneath the Bed - James Howe
e 688

Delis, Jewel (Sister; Activist)
The Companions - Sheri S. Tepper   h, a 1373

Delis, Paul (Brother; Linguist)
The Companions - Sheri S. Tepper   h, a 1373

della Scorpia, Meralda (Noblewoman)
A Bed of Earth: The Gravedigger's Tale - Tanith Lee
h, a 872

Delphiki, Julian "Bean" (Genius)
Shadow Puppets - Orson Scott Card   h, a 215

Delphine (Neighbor)
Fame and Glory in Freedom, Georgia - Barbara
O'Connor   e, m 1102

Denmark "Ned" (Dog; Immortal)
*The Angel's Command: A Tale from the Castaways of
the Flying Dutchman* - Brian Jacques   m, h 722

Dente, Al (Son; Hero)
Noodle Man: The Pasta Superhero - April Pulley
Sayre   p 1266

Dente, Grandma (Grandmother; Hero)
Noodle Man: The Pasta Superhero - April Pulley
Sayre   p 1266

Dente, Mama (Mother; Businesswoman)
Noodle Man: The Pasta Superhero - April Pulley
Sayre   p 1266

Denwood, Robbie (11-Year-Old; Basketball Player)
String Music - Rick Telander   e, m 1372

DeRicci, Noelle (Detective—Police)
The Disappeared - Kristine Kathryn Rusch   h,
a 1239

Desant, Clayton (Religious; Brother)
A Chapel of Thieves - Bruce Clements   m 263

Desant, Henry (15-Year-Old; Brother)
A Chapel of Thieves - Bruce Clements   m 263

Deshutsis, Dwight (11th Grader; Football Player)
Three Clams and an Oyster - Randy Powell   m,
h 1166

Desravines, Mardi (9th Grader)
Fresh Girl - Jaira Placide   h 1160

Devlin, Caleb (17-Year-Old; Criminal)
The Creek - Jennifer L. Holm   m, h 667

Dexter, Toby (Clerk)
Drinking Midnight Wine - Simon R. Green   h,
a 553

Dundas, John Malcolm (Twin; Military Personnel)
Remembrance - Theresa Breslin   m, h   143

Dundas, Maggie (Twin; Nurse)
Remembrance - Theresa Breslin   m, h   143

Dunn (Teacher; Coach)
Blue Eyes Better - Ruth Wallace-Brodeur   e   1412

Durant (Knight)
The Legend of Lady Ilena - Patricia Malone   m, h   936

Dustfinger (Villain)
Inkheart - Cornelia Funke   m, h   499

Dusty (Child; Artisan)
The Beloved Dearly - Doug Cooney   e, m   293

Dvorak, Joey (13-Year-Old)
Qwerty Stevens Stuck in Time with Benjamin Franklin - Dan Gutman   m   575

E

Eadric (Royalty)
The Frog Princess - E.D. Baker   m   67

Eagle Talon (Police Officer)
Mystery in Mt. Mole - Richard W. Jennings   m, h   737

Ebb (Dog)
Ebb & Flo and the Baby Seal - Jane Simmons   p   1304

Ebba Rose "Rose" (15-Year-Old)
East - Edith Pattou   m, h   1131

Eberhardt, Roy (Student—Middle School)
Hoot - Carl Hiaasen   m, h   637

Echidna (Animal; Friend)
Platypus and the Birthday Party - Chris Riddell   p   1203

Eckloe, Christina (12th Grader; Accident Victim)
Telling Christina Goodbye - Lurlene McDaniel   m, h   974

Eddie (Child; Son)
Spaghetti Eddie - Ryan SanAngelo   p   1261

Edelstein, Bridget (18-Year-Old; Waiter/Waitress)
Bringing Up the Bones - Lara M. Zeises   h   1492

Edme (Aunt; Aged Person)
Dahlia - Barbara McClintock   p   970

Edmund (Servant)
The Leopard Sword - Michael Cadnum   m, h   201

Edna (Cow)
Serious Farm - Tim Egan   p   421

Edna (Foster Parent)
Locomotion - Jacqueline Woodson   e, m   1466

Edric (Mythical Creature)
Once Upon a Marigold - Jean Ferris   m, h   452

Edward (Child)
Edward in the Jungle - David McPhail   p   999

Edward, VI (Royalty)
Timeless Love - Judith O'Brien   m, h   1101

Edward "Longshanks", I (Royalty; Historical Figure)
Girl in a Cage - Jane Yolen   m, h   1480

Edwards, Grace (12-Year-Old)
Survival in the Storm: The Dust Bowl Diary of Grace Edwards - Katelan Janke   e, m   728

Elaine "Lainey" (14-Year-Old)
Jake Riley: Irreparably Damaged - Rebecca Fjelland Davis   m, h   352

Eldest One (Brother; Son)
The Witch's Children - Ursula Jones   p   758

Eleanor (Royalty)
Eleanor: Crown Jewel of Aquitaine, France, 1136 - Kristiana Gregory   m   557

Elinor (Aunt)
Isabel: Taking Wing - Annie Dalton   m   339
Inkheart - Cornelia Funke   m, h   499

Elisabeth Amelie Eugenie "Sisi" (Royalty)
Elisabeth: The Princess Bride - Barry Denenberg   m   372

Elise (Sister; Dancer)
Tanya and the Red Shoes - Patricia Lee Gauch   p   510

Elissa (12th Grader)
Tribes - Arthur Slade   h   1309

Elives, S.H. (Magician)
Juliet Dove, Queen of Love - Bruce Coville   e, m   308

Eliza (Singer; Student—College)
Mahalia - Joanne Horniman   h   679

Elizabeth (Daughter; Animal Lover)
The Perfect Pet - Margie Palatini   p   1124

Elizabeth (10-Year-Old; Streetperson)
Tomorrow, Maybe - Brian James   m, h   725

Elizabeth "Jordan" (11-Year-Old)
Camp of the Angel - Aileen Arrington   e, m   42

Elizabeti (Daughter; Student—Elementary School)
Elizabeti's School - Stephanie Stuve-Bodeen   p   1352

Elka (Child-Care Giver)
Thief of Dreams - Todd Strasser   m   1347

Ella (Child; Daughter)
In the Piney Woods - Roni Schotter   p   1270

Ella Sarah (Child; Sister)
Ella Sarah Gets Dressed - Margaret Chodos-Irvine   p   253

Elliot, Cody (15-Year-Old)
Vampire High - Douglas Rees   m, h   1194

Elliott (Uncle)
Black-Eyed Suzie - Susan Shaw   m, h   1287

Ellison, Tracee (11th Grader; Cheerleader)
Alt Ed - Catherine Atkins   m, h   52

Eloise (6-Year-Old)
Eloise Takes a Bawth - Kay Thompson   p   1379

Eloise (15-Year-Old)
Song for Eloise - Leigh Sauerwein   h   1264

Elsinger, Mikey (8th Grader)
Bad Girls in Love - Cynthia Voigt   m   1402

Elvis (Rooster)
Elvis the Rooster Almost Goes to Heaven - Denys Cazet   b   232

Elway, Joe (Student)
Hannah, Divided - Adele Griffin   m   562

Emberek, Laszlo (13-Year-Old; Shepherd)
The Wolving Time - Patrick Jennings   m, h   735

Emeralda (14-Year-Old; Royalty)
The Frog Princess - E.D. Baker   m   67

Emily (Rabbit; Sister)
Baby for Sale - Jackie French Koller   p   814

Emily "Murphy" (11-Year-Old)
Where I'd Like to Be - Frances O'Roark Dowell   e, m   391

Emma (Adoptee; Daughter)
Emma's Story - Deborah Hodge   p   655

Emma (Child; Daughter)
Old Bob's Brown Bear - Niki Daly   p   340

Emma (Royalty; Daughter)
Princesses Are People, Too: Two Modern Fairy Tales - Susie Morgenstern   e   1032

Emmaline (Religious)
Fallen Host - Lyda Morehouse   h, a   1031

Emmy (Mother)
Mahalia - Joanne Horniman   h   679

Enfield, Lee (Lawyer; Wizard)
Stealing the Elf-King's Roses - Diane Duane   h, a   400

Epossumondas (Opossum)
Epossumondas - Coleen Salley   p   1254

Epps, Margalo (8th Grader)
Bad Girls in Love - Cynthia Voigt   m   1402

Eragon (Teenager)
Eragon - Christopher Paolini   m, h   1125

Erato "Era" (Deity)
Goddesses Series - Clea Hantman   m, h   592

Eric (Child; Brother)
The Doomspell - Cliff McNish   m   997

Ernest (Son; Royalty)
Serious Trouble - Arthur Howard   p   684

Ernst (Otter; Friend)
Winnie and Ernst - Gina Freschet   e   492

Eros (Son; Deity)
Quiver - Stephanie Spinner   m, h   1327

Ervin, Austin (Brother; Time Traveler)
Ravine - Janet Hickman   m   638

Ervin, Jeremy (Time Traveler)
Ravine - Janet Hickman   m   638

Esperance, Celiane (13-Year-Old; Immigrant)
Behind the Mountains: The Diary of Celiane Esperance - Edwidge Danticat   m, h   343

Esperance, Moy (19-Year-Old; Immigrant)
Behind the Mountains: The Diary of Celiane Esperance - Edwidge Danticat   m, h   343

Esperanza (Aged Person; Servant)
Adelita: A Mexican Cinderella Story - Tomie De Paola   p   358

Espinosa (Sailor)
To the Edge of the World - Michele Torrey   m   1385

Etoile (Cat)
Zat Cat! A Haute Couture Tail - Chesley McLaren   p   987

Eugene (Brother; Child)
Eugene's Story - Richard Scrimger   p   1274

Eulinda (13-Year-Old; Slave)
Numbering All the Bones - Ann Rinaldi   m, h   1205

Evans, Sara (3rd Grader; Friend)
Starting with Alice - Phyllis Reynolds Naylor   e   1070

Everhart, Lucy (Student—College)
Sister Spider Knows All - Adrian Fogelin   m   471

Evette (Friend; Daughter)
Darby - Jonathon Scott Fuqua   e   501

Ezzie (Child; Friend)
Who's Afraid of the Big Bad Book? - Lauren Child   p   251

F

Faber, Mary "Jacky" (Orphan; Sailor)
Bloody Jack: Being an Account of the Curious Adventures of Mary "Jacky" Faber, Ship's Boy - L.A. Meyer   *m, h*   1007

Fabian (Cat)
Hondo & Fabian - Peter McCarty   *p*   964

Fainne (Daughter; Wizard)
Child of the Prophecy - Juliet Marillier   *h, a*   941

Fairchild, Beth (Friend; Classmate)
Darby - Jonathon Scott Fuqua   *e*   501

Fairchild, Grace "Ace" (Runaway)
Mad Maudlin - Mercedes Lackey   *h, a*   844

Fairfield, Mimi (Grandmother)
Bridging Beyond - Kathleen Benner Duble   *m, h*   403

Fairfield, Roland (Teenager; Student)
Alchemy - Margaret Mahy   *m, h*   935

Fairweather, Joseph (Wealthy; Fiance(e))
The Shakeress - Kimberley Heuston   *m, h*   636

Falco (Handicapped)
City of Stars - Mary Hoffman   *m, h*   662

Fall, Sebastian "Uncle Bass" (Uncle)
The Egyptian Box - Jane Louise Curry   *e, m*   330

Fallow, Miranda (Teenager)
Dr. Franklin's Island - Ann Halam   *m, h*   582

Fallstar, Chade (Spy)
Fool's Errand - Robin Hobb   *h, a*   647
Golden Fool - Robin Hobb   *h, a*   648

Farfallina (Caterpillar; Friend)
Farfallina & Marcel - Holly Keller   *p*   777

Farley, Jacob (Principal)
Mystery in Mt. Mole - Richard W. Jennings   *m, h*   737

Farmer, Queenie (Single Mother)
Queenie Farmer Had Fifteen Daughters - Ann Campbell   *p*   208

Farmer Blue (Farmer)
A Fairy in a Dairy - Lucy Nolan   *p*   1090

Farmer Brown (Farmer; Brother)
Giggle, Giggle, Quack - Doreen Cronin   *p*   317

Farmer Fred (Farmer)
Serious Farm - Tim Egan   *p*   421

Farmer George (Farmer)
Moo Cow Kaboom! - Thacher Hurd   *p*   697

Farmer Todd (Aged Person; Cook)
Piggy's Pancake Parlor - David McPhail   *e*   1000

Farmer Wilson (Farmer; Neighbor)
Making Plum Jam - John Warren Stewig   *p*   1344

Farmer Woolsey (Farmer)
Betsy Who Cried Wolf! - Gail Carson Levine   *p*   882

Farrell, Peggy Fleming (17-Year-Old)
Frozen Rodeo - Catherine Clark   *m, h*   256

Farseer, Dutiful (Royalty)
Fool's Errand - Robin Hobb   *h, a*   647
Golden Fool - Robin Hobb   *h, a*   648

Farseer, FitzChivalry (Spy)
Fool's Errand - Robin Hobb   *h, a*   647
Golden Fool - Robin Hobb   *h, a*   648

Fat Cat (Cat)
Drat That Fat Cat! - Pat Thomson   *p*   1380

Father (Store Owner; Cook)
Apple Pie 4th of July - Janet S. Wong   *p*   1455

Father (Father; Businessman)
As Far as I Can See: Meg's Prairie Diary - Kate McMullan   *e*   989

Father (Father; Farmer)
Homespun Sarah - Verla Kay   *p*   771

Father (Immigrant)
When the Emperor Was Divine - Julie Otsuka   *h, a*   1120

Father (Father; Teacher)
Wingwalker - Rosemary Wells   *e*   1429

Father Wolf (Wolf; Father)
The Wolf Who Cried Boy - Bob Hartman   *p*   603

Faye (Sister)
Dolores on Her Toes - Barbara Samuels   *p*   1256

Fela (Linguist)
The Color of Home - Mary Hoffman   *p*   663

Felcher, Paul (3rd Grader; Friend)
Robert and the Weird & Wacky Facts - Barbara Seuling   *e*   1279

Feld, Ethan (11-Year-Old; Baseball Player)
Summerland - Michael Chabon   *m, h*   236

Fellowes, Ariadne "Addy" (7th Grader)
Cold in Summer - Tracy Barrett   *e, m*   83

Fergus (Dog)
Hank and Fergus - Susin Nielsen-Fernlund   *p*   1080

Ferguson (Alligator)
The Speed of Light - Ron Carlson   *m, h*   218

Ferguson, Charlie (Artisan; Aged Person)
Shoeless Joe & Black Betsy - Phil Bildner   *p*   108

Ferramondo (Magician)
The Rope Trick - Lloyd Alexander   *e, m*   18

Ferret, Jess (Teenager; Student)
Alchemy - Margaret Mahy   *m, h*   935

Ferri, Delia (13-Year-Old; Dancer)
A Dance of Sisters - Tracey Porter   *m*   1164

Ferri, Pearl (Sister; Student—Boarding School)
A Dance of Sisters - Tracey Porter   *m*   1164

Fidget, Twitchly (Animal)
Something Might Happen - Helen Lester   *p*   876

Fielding, Asher (Student—High School; Runaway)
Guitar Highway Rose - Brigid Lowry   *h*   910

Fielding, Maia (Orphan)
Journey to the River Sea - Eva Ibbotson   *m*   707

Fierch, Kaye (Teenager; Mythical Creature)
Tithe: A Modern Faerie Tale - Holly Black   *h*   111

Fine (Aged Person)
Izzy's Place - Marc Kornblatt   *e, m*   819

Finerman, Nate (Student—College)
Better than Running at Night - Hillary Frank   *h*   481

Finn, Meg (14-Year-Old; Spirit)
The Wish List - Eoin Colfer   *m, h*   278

Finotta, Jim (Rancher)
Savage Run - C.J. Box   *h, a*   130

Firebird (Mythical Creature)
The Firebird - Jane Yolen   *p*   1479

Firepaw "Fireheart" (Cat; Apprentice)
Warriors Series - Erin Hunter   *m, h*   696

Fisher, Bobby (Brother; Asthmatic)
The Green Dog: A Mostly True Story - Suzanne Fisher Staples   *e*   1336

Fisher, Karen (Sister)
The Green Dog: A Mostly True Story - Suzanne Fisher Staples   *e*   1336

Fisher, Suzanne (5th Grader; Sister)
The Green Dog: A Mostly True Story - Suzanne Fisher Staples   *e*   1336

Fitzpatrick, Barnaby (Nobleman)
Timeless Love - Judith O'Brien   *m, h*   1101

Flack, Jerry (6th Grader)
Dork on the Run - Carol Gorman   *e, m*   543

Flaherty, Molly MacKenzie (15-Year-Old)
Where Have All the Flowers Gone?: The Diary of Molly Mackenzie Flaherty - Ellen Emerson White   *m, h*   1437

Flaherty, Patrick Seamus (Military Personnel; Brother)
Where Have All the Flowers Gone?: The Diary of Molly Mackenzie Flaherty - Ellen Emerson White   *m, h*   1437

Flandres, Achilles (Genius)
Shadow Puppets - Orson Scott Card   *h, a*   215

Flannery, Ellen (Businesswoman)
Rising Tide - Jean Thesman   *m, h*   1376

Flannery, Keegan (15-Year-Old; Twin)
St. Michael's Scales - Neil Connelly   *m, h*   287

Flannery, Michael (Twin)
St. Michael's Scales - Neil Connelly   *m, h*   287

Flannigan, Charlotte "Tottie" (13-Year-Old)
Not Quite a Stranger - Colby Rodowsky   *m, h*   1221

Flannigan, David (Doctor)
Not Quite a Stranger - Colby Rodowsky   *m, h*   1221

Flint, Miles (Detective—Police)
The Disappeared - Kristine Kathryn Rusch   *h, a*   1239

Flo (Child; Daughter)
Ebb & Flo and the Baby Seal - Jane Simmons   *p*   1304

Flood, Jesse (14-Year-Old)
Who Is Jesse Flood? - Malachy Doyle   *m*   394

Flora (Rabbit; Sister)
Flora's Surprise! - Debi Gliori   *p*   531

Florentina (Bear; Friend)
Four Friends Together - Sue Heap   *p*   617

Flossie (Housekeeper)
My Cup Runneth Over: The Life of Angelica Cookson Potts - Cherry Whytock   *m, h*   1441

Flowers, Nanny (Grandmother)
The Whale Rider - Witi Ihimaera   *m, h*   710

Floyd, Ben (13-Year-Old)
My Brother's Hero - Adrian Fogelin   *m*   470

Floyd, Brent (9th Grader)
Sticks and Stones - Beth Goobie   *m, h*   536

Floyd, Cody (Child)
My Brother's Hero - Adrian Fogelin   *m*   470

Fly (Fly)
The Spider and the Fly - Mary Howitt   *p*   690

Flyer (8th Grader)
Birdland - Tracy Mack   *m, h*   927

Flynn (Sea Captain)
The Erie Canal Pirates - Eric A. Kimmel   *p*   788

Flynn, Andrew "Andy" (11-Year-Old)
Flood - James Heneghan   *m*   621

Flynn, Vincent "Vinny" (Father; Alcoholic)
Flood - James Heneghan   *m*   621

Fogarty, Alan (Criminal; Scientist)
Faerie Wars - Herbie Brennan   *h*   141

Foley (Religious)
The Whistle, the Grave, and the Ghost - Brad Strickland   *m*   1349

Foley (Teacher; Dancer)
Tanya and the Red Shoes - Patricia Lee Gauch
p 510

Foley, Mia (Musician; 15-Year-Old)
Fifteen Love - Robert Corbet   m, h   299

Fontaine, John "MyJohn" (Fiance(e); Historical Figure)
Or Give Me Death - Ann Rinaldi   m, h   1206

Fool (Psychic)
Fool's Errand - Robin Hobb   h, a   647
Golden Fool - Robin Hobb   h, a   648

Forrest, Andrew J. "Andy" (12-Year-Old)
Mystery in Mt. Mole - Richard W. Jennings   m, h   737

Forrest, Jake (Indian; Sports Figure)
The Warriors - Joseph Bruchac   m   170

Forrester, Chadwick Hoving "Wick" III (15-Year-Old)
The 7th Knot - Kathleen Karr   m   765

Forrester, Eustace (Uncle; Wealthy)
The 7th Knot - Kathleen Karr   m   765

Forrester, Miles (12-Year-Old)
The 7th Knot - Kathleen Karr   m   765

Forrester, Tracy (14-Year-Old; Musician)
My Not-So-Terrible Time at the Hippie Hotel - Rosemary Graham   m, h   545

Fortesque (Aged Person)
That Pesky Rat - Lauren Child   p   248

Fossey, Nell (5th Grader; Detective—Amateur)
The Case of the Graveyard Ghost - Michele Torrey   e   1384

Foster, Izzie (14-Year-Old)
Mates, Dates and Inflatable Bras - Cathy Hopkins   m, h   676

Fowl, Artemis (Teenager; Con Artist)
Artemis Fowl: The Eternity Code - Eoin Colfer   m   277

Fowl, Artemis Jr. (13-Year-Old)
Artemis Fowl: The Arctic Incident - Eoin Colfer   m   276

Fowl, Artemis Sr. (Father; Kidnap Victim)
Artemis Fowl: The Arctic Incident - Eoin Colfer   m   276

Fox (Fox; Trickster)
Fox Tale Soup - Tony Bonning   p   125

Fox (Fox; Friend)
Piggy's Pancake Parlor - David McPhail   e   1000

Fox (Fox)
My Lucky Day - Keiko Kasza   p   768
The Rooster and the Fox - Helen Ward   p   1415

Fox, Billy (Bully)
The Whistle, the Grave, and the Ghost - Brad Strickland   m   1349

Fox, Peter "Pete" (11-Year-Old; Surfer)
Surfer Dog - Elizabeth Spurr   e, m   1332

Francis (Cat)
Francis the Scaredy Cat - Ed Boxall   p   131

Francis, Sarah (8th Grader)
Waiting for Sarah - Bruce McBay   m, h   961

Francisco (Son; Brother)
The Kite - Luis Garay   p   509

Franco, Elena (Writer)
Breakout - Paul Fleischman   h   460

Francy, Sandra "Lady" (17-Year-Old; Dog)
Lady: My Life as a Bitch - Melvin Burgess   h   183

Frank (Military Personnel)
A Brave Soldier - Nicholas Debon   p   365

Frank (Cat)
The Broken Cat - Lynne Rae Perkins   p   1146

Frank (Chicken)
Funny Frank - Dick King-Smith   e   793

Frank (Father)
Gingerbread - Rachel Cohn   h   272

Frank (Raccoon; Friend)
Good Night, Sleep Tight, Don't Let the Bedbugs Bite! - Diane DeGroat   p   369

Frankie (4th Grader)
The Gold-Threaded Dress - Carolyn Marsden   e   942

Franklin, Benjamin (Historical Figure)
Qwerty Stevens Stuck in Time with Benjamin Franklin - Dan Gutman   m   575
The Year of the Hangman - Gary Blackwood   m, h   115

Franklin, George (Scientist)
Dr. Franklin's Island - Ann Halam   m, h   582

Franklyn (Royalty)
The Witch Who Wanted to Be a Princess - Lois G. Grambling   p   546

Franny, Gourmet Granny (Cook; Grandmother)
Alvie Eats Soup - Ross Collins   p   283

Franz Joseph, I (Royalty)
Elisabeth: The Princess Bride - Barry Denenberg   m   372

Fraser, Edward (3rd Grader; Brother)
Leap, Frog - Jane Cutler   e   332

Fraser, Jason (Brother; 6th Grader)
Leap, Frog - Jane Cutler   e   332

Fred (Dog)
Good Night Sam - Marie-Louise Gay   p   513

Fred (Neighbor)
Little Buggy - Kevin O'Malley   p   1107

Fred (Spouse; Father)
McDuff Saves the Day - Rosemary Wells   p   1426

Freddy (Hamster; Narrator)
I, Freddy - Deitlof Reiche   e   1196

Fredericka "Fred" (12-Year-Old)
Praying at the Sweetwater Motel - April Young Fritz   m   495

Freeman (Aged Person; Neighbor)
The Four Ugly Cats in Apartment 3D - Marilyn Sachs   e   1249

Freeman, Alexandra "Alex" (17-Year-Old)
Martyn Pig - Kevin Brooks   m, h   160

Freeman, Kite (Gymnast)
The Slightly True Story of Cedar B. Hartley (Who Planned to Live an Unusual Life) - Martine Murray   m   1046

Freeman, Kofi (11th Grader)
The Battle of Jericho - Sharon M. Draper   m, h   395

Friday (Chimpanzee)
My Chimp Friday: The Nana Banana Chronicles - Hester Mundis   e, m   1038

Frightful (Bird; Mother)
Frightful's Daughter - Jean Craighead George   p   518

Frink (Pioneer)
Boston Jane: Wilderness Days - Jennifer L. Holm   m, h   666

Froehlich, Jeff (Basketball Player)
The Return of Calico Bright - David Winkler   m   1450

Frog (Frog)
Captain Duck - Jez Alborough   p   14

Frog (Frog; Dancer)
Down by the Cool of the Pool - Tony Mitton   p   1020

Frog (Frog; Friend)
Fix-It Duck - Jez Alborough   p   15

Frog (Frog)
Frog - Susan Cooper   p   296

Froggy (Frog; Patient)
Froggy Goes to the Doctor - Jonathan London   p   905

Froggy (Frog; Musician)
Froggy Plays in the Band - Jonathan London   p   906

Frogilina (Frog; Student—Elementary School)
Froggy Plays in the Band - Jonathan London   p   906

Frosya (Care Giver)
Phoning a Dead Man - Gillian Cross   m, h   318

Frydman, Srulik "Jurek Staniak" (Child; Jew)
Run, Boy, Run - Uri Orlev   m, h   1114

Funcraft, Tiffany (Doll; Friend)
The Meanest Doll in the World - Ann M. Martin   e   946

Furnival (Nobleman; Father)
Crispin: The Cross of Lead - Avi   m, h   58

G

Gabi (Girlfriend)
The Beast - Walter Dean Myers   h   1051

Gabriel Aaron "Gaaron" (Spouse)
Angelica: A Novel of Samaria - Sharon Shinn   h, a   1293

Gaggle, Dorothy (Goose; Sister)
The Gaggle Sisters River Tour - Chris Jackson   p   720

Gaggle, Sadie (Goose; Sister)
The Gaggle Sisters River Tour - Chris Jackson   p   720

Galahad (Royalty; Son)
The Grail Prince - Nancy McKenzie   h, a   983

Gallagher, Thomas "Tom" (12-Year-Old)
The Boy Who Saved Baseball - John Ritter   m   1210

Galloway, Andy (14-Year-Old)
Wild Man Island - Will Hobbs   m, h   653

Gander, Jake (Detective)
Jake Gander, Storyville Detective: The Case of the Greedy Granny - George McClements   p   969

Garbacchio, Nick (12th Grader)
Flavor of the Week - Tucker Shaw   m, h   1288

Garcetti, Grace (10th Grader)
Out of Order - A.M. Jenkins   h   732

Garcia, Ileana (16-Year-Old)
Flight to Freedom - Ana Veciana-Suarez   m, h   1400

Garcia, Yara (13-Year-Old)
Flight to Freedom - Ana Veciana-Suarez   m, h   1400

Gardner, Beth (13-Year-Old)
My Contract with Henry - Robin Vaupel   m   1399

Garfield, Stuart (13-Year-Old)
My Contract with Henry - Robin Vaupel   m   1399

Garland, Holly (9-Year-Old; Daughter)
The Trouble with Babies - Martha Freeman   e   488

Garnet, Luke "Lee Grant" (13-Year-Old)
Among the Barons - Margaret Peterson Haddix   *m,
h*   577

Garrett (Detective—Private)
Angry Lead Skies - Glen Cook   *h, a*   288

Garrett, Jacob "Jake" (12-Year-Old; Football
Player)
Jake, Reinvented - Gordon Korman   *h*   816

Garrett, Paul (Student—Middle School; Neighbor)
Whistler's Hollow - Debbie Dadey   *e, m*   336

Garrett, Pete (12-Year-Old)
The Poltergoose - Michael Lawrence   *e, m*   862

Garson, Semirah "Semi" (Teenager)
Dr. Franklin's Island - Ann Halam   *m, h*   582

Garver, Lani (Student—High School)
What Happened to Lani Garver - Carol Plum-Ucci
h   1162

Gaskitt (Mother; Spouse)
The Woman Who Won Things - Allan Ahlberg
e   11

Gaskitt, Gloria (Sister; Student—Elementary School)
The Cat Who Got Carried Away - Allan Ahlberg
e   9

Gaskitt, Gloria (9-Year-Old; Twin)
The Woman Who Won Things - Allan Ahlberg
e   11

Gaskitt, Gus (Brother; Student—Elementary School)
The Cat Who Got Carried Away - Allan Ahlberg
e   9

Gaskitt, Gus (9-Year-Old; Twin)
The Woman Who Won Things - Allan Ahlberg
e   11

Gaspard (Friend; Dog)
Gaspard and Lisa's Rainy Day - Anne Gutman
p   573

Gaspard (Dog; Friend)
Lisa's Baby Sister - Anne Gutman   *p*   574

Gasparini, Arianna (15-Year-Old)
City of Masks - Mary Hoffman   *m, h*   661

Gauk (17-Year-Old)
Daughter of the Wind - Michael Cadnum   *m,
h*   199

Gavin (8th Grader; Artist)
Saving Jasey - Diane Tullson   *m, h*   1387

Gawaine (Knight; Son)
Sword of the Rightful King: A Novel of King Arthur -
Jane Yolen   *m, h*   1486

Gawen (Servant)
Sword of the Rightful King: A Novel of King Arthur -
Jane Yolen   *m, h*   1486

Gayle "Gaia" (Deity)
Drinking Midnight Wine - Simon R. Green   *h,
a*   553

Gecko, Chet (Reptile; Detective—Amateur; 4th
Grader)
The Hamster of the Baskervilles - Bruce Hale
e   583

Gecko, Chet (Detective—Private; 4th Grader)
The Malted Falcon - Bruce Hale   *e*   584
Trouble Is My Beeswax - Bruce Hale   *e*   585

Gekewicz, Elliot (7th Grader)
The Revealers - Doug Wilhelm   *m*   1443

Gelato, Will (Pig; Friend)
Olvina Flies - Grace Lin   *p*   893

Gelb, Trudy "Jujube" (9th Grader; 15-Year-Old)
Sticks and Stones - Beth Goobie   *m, h*   536

Gelert, Madrin (Mythical Creature; Lawyer)
Stealing the Elf-King's Roses - Diane Duane   *h,
a*   400

Gemma (Child)
The Witch's Children - Ursula Jones   *p*   758

Gene (Cowboy; Rancher)
Sixteen Cows - Lisa Wheeler   *p*   1435

Gentry (Singer; Mother)
Stitches - Glen Huser   *m, h*   703

George (Child; Student—Elementary School)
George Upside Down - Meghan McCarthy   *p*   963

George (Dog)
Oh My Gosh, Mrs. McNosh! - Sarah Weeks
p   1423

Georgie (Child; Son)
The Magic Bed - John Burningham   *p*   184

Georgie Lee (Cow)
Georgie Lee - Sharon Phillips Denslow   *e*   374

Geppetto (Father; Artisan)
Pinocchio the Boy: Incognito in Collodi - Lane Smith
p   1314

Gerrit (Bookkeeper; Heir)
The House of Windjammer - V.A. Richardson   *m,
h*   1201

Gerson, Brett (15-Year-Old)
Pool Boy - Michael Simmons   *m, h*   1305

Gertie (Goose; Sister)
Ollie - Olivier Dunrea   *p*   408

Getz, Victor (Detective—Private)
The Thief Lord - Cornelia Funke   *m, h*   500

Ghost (Spirit)
Skeleton Hiccups - Margery Cuyler   *p*   334

Ghost (Serial Killer)
Shatterglass - Tamora Pierce   *m, h*   1151

Gianini, Frank (Stepfather; Teacher)
Princess in Love - Meg Cabot   *m, h*   197

Gilbert (Opossum; Camper)
Good Night, Sleep Tight, Don't Let the Bedbugs Bite! -
Diane DeGroat   *p*   369

Gilbert, Benjamin "Benji" (18-Year-Old)
Bringing Up the Bones - Lara M. Zeises   *h*   1492

Gilbert, Bess (12-Year-Old; Orphan)
Flying Blind - Anna Myers   *e, m*   1049

Gilbert, Enoch (16-Year-Old; Orphan)
Flying Blind - Anna Myers   *e, m*   1049

Gilbert, Peter "Parkaboy" (Friend; Computer
Expert)
Pattern Recognition - William Gibson   *h, a*   522

Gilda (16-Year-Old)
Gossip Times Three - Amy Goldman Koss   *m*   821

Gill, Quintus Wylie (Con Artist)
Gilbert & Sullivan Set Me Free - Kathleen Karr   *m,
h*   767

Gillette (Dog)
Zulu Dog - Anton Ferreira   *e, m*   450

Gilman, Zack (9th Grader)
The Viking Series - Christopher Tebbetts   *m*   1370

Gin (Dog)
Bone Dry - Kathleen Karr   *m*   766

Ginger (Cat)
The Alley Cat's Meow - Kathi Appelt   *p*   32

Ginger (9th Grader)
Waiting to Disappear - April Young Fritz   *m,
h*   496

Gingrich, Aaron (17-Year-Old; Victim)
Blood Trail - Nancy Springer   *m, h*   1329

Gingrich, Nathan (Twin)
Blood Trail - Nancy Springer   *m, h*   1329

Ginny (4th Grader; Daughter)
Especially Heroes - Virginia Kroll   *p*   831

Ginny (17-Year-Old)
Falling through Darkness - Carolyn McCullough
h   972

Gino (Hamster; Spirit)
The Ghost of P.S. 42 - Frank Asch   *e*   45

Giombetti, Skinny (Friend)
Grape Thief - Kristine L. Franklin   *m, h*   482

Giraldi (Principal)
Bottled Up - Jaye Murray   *m, h*   1045

Girlpie (Child; Daughter)
Homemade Love - bell hooks   *p*   673

Gisselda (Child)
Song of the Circus - Lois Duncan   *p*   404

Gittel (Babysitter; Aged Person)
Chicken Soup by Heart - Esther Hershenhorn
p   630

Glasgow, Annie (Fiance(e); Handicapped)
Phoning a Dead Man - Gillian Cross   *m, h*   318

Glass, Simon (Student—High School)
Shattering Glass - Gail Giles   *h*   526

Glassman, Nelson (Homosexual; 12th Grader)
Rainbow High - Alex Sanchez   *h*   1262

Glenda (Animal)
The Terrible Underpants - Kaz Cooke   *p*   290

Glenn (Musician; 11th Grader)
Blind Sighted - Peter Moore   *h*   1028

Glidden, Charlotte (Child; Daughter)
Charlotte in Paris - Joan MacPhail Knight   *e*   807

Glimmer, Martha (13-Year-Old)
Indigo - Alice Hoffman   *m, h*   659

Gloria (Child; Friend)
I'll Never Share You, Blackboard Bear - Martha
Alexander   *p*   19

Gluey (Snail)
Gluey: A Snail Tale - Vivian Walsh   *p*   1414

Gnedich, Georgi (Brother)
The Impossible Journey - Gloria Whelan   *m*   1436

Gnedich, Katya (Mother)
The Impossible Journey - Gloria Whelan   *m*   1436

Gnedich, Marya Mikhailovna (13-Year-Old)
The Impossible Journey - Gloria Whelan   *m*   1436

Gnedich, Mikhail Sergeyevich "Misha" (Father;
Prisoner)
The Impossible Journey - Gloria Whelan   *m*   1436

Goat (Goat)
Captain Duck - Jez Alborough   *p*   14

God (Deity)
God Went to Beauty School - Cynthia Rylant   *m,
h*   1245
Why Heaven Is Far Away - Julius Lester   *p*   879

God (Spouse)
Why Heaven Is Far Away - Julius Lester   *p*   879

Goewin (Royalty)
A Coalition of Lions - Elizabeth E. Wein   *h*   1424

Gokey, Mattie (16-Year-Old)
A Northern Light - Jennifer Donnelly   *h*   387

Goldfarb, Mavis (Friend)
Fat Camp Commandos Go West - Daniel Pinkwater
e   1159

Goldilocks (Child; Daughter)
Goldilocks and the Three Bears - Jim Aylesworth
p   61

Goldsmith, Anna (15-Year-Old)
Drowning Anna - Sue Mayfield   *m, h*   958

Gondii, Toxoplasma (Alien)
Parasite Pig - William Sleator   *m, h*   1310

Gonnella, Justin (Brother; 5th Grader)
Witch's Wishes - Vivian Vande Velde   *e*   1396

Gonnella, Sarah (Kindergartner; Sister)
Witch's Wishes - Vivian Vande Velde   *e*   1396

Good Knight (Knight)
Get Well, Good Knight - Shelley Moore Thomas
   b   1377

Goodbody (Principal)
The Last Burp of Mac McGerp - Pam Smallcomb
   e   1311

Goodchild, Tucker "Trouble" (Child)
Taking Care of Trouble - Bonnie Graves   *e*   547

Goode, Addie (12-Year-Old)
A Greater Goode - Amy Schor Ferris   *m*   451

Goode, Charlie (Tennis Player)
Breaking Point - Alex Flinn   *m, h*   467

Goodspeed (Father; Sea Captain)
The Voyage of Patience Goodspeed - Heather Vogel
   Frederick   *m*   485

Goodspeed, Patience (12-Year-Old)
The Voyage of Patience Goodspeed - Heather Vogel
   Frederick   *m*   485

Goodspeed, Thaddeus "Tad" (Brother)
The Voyage of Patience Goodspeed - Heather Vogel
   Frederick   *m*   485

Goose (Goose)
We're Going on a Picnic! - Pat Hutchins   *p*   705

Gordon, Charlotte "Charley" (11-Year-Old; Artist)
Butterflies and Lizards, Beryl and Me - Ruth Lercher
   Bornstein   *e, m*   127

Gordon, Constance "Con" (Aunt)
Willow and Twig - Jean Little   *m*   903

Gordon, Humphrey "Hum" (Uncle; Writer)
Willow and Twig - Jean Little   *m*   903

Gossie (Goose)
Gossie - Olivier Dunrea   *p*   406

Gossie (Goose; Sister)
Ollie - Olivier Dunrea   *p*   408

Goth (Bat)
Firewing - Kenneth Oppel   *m*   1111

Gou Haoyou (12-Year-Old; Entertainer)
The Kite Rider - Geraldine McCaughrean   *m,
   h*   965

Government, Jennifer (Government Official;
   Mother)
Jennifer Government - Max Barry   *h, a*   85

Gower, Hugh (Uncle; Government Official)
The Year of the Hangman - Gary Blackwood   *m,
   h*   115

Grace (Cow)
*Little Old Big Beard and Big Young Little Beard: A
   Short and Tall Tale* - Remy Charlip   *p*   238

Grace, Jared (9-Year-Old; Twin)
The Seeing Stone - Tony DiTerlizzi   *e*   385

Grace, Mallory (13-Year-Old; Sister)
The Seeing Stone - Tony DiTerlizzi   *e*   385

Grace, Simon (9-Year-Old; Kidnap Victim)
The Seeing Stone - Tony DiTerlizzi   *e*   385

Gracie (Aunt; Foster Parent)
Our Gracie Aunt - Jacqueline Woodson   *p*   1467

Graham, Aurora (Blind Person; Aged Person)
Lumber Camp Library - Natalie Kinsey-Warnock
   e   798

Gram (Grandmother)
Soul Moon Soup - Lindsay Lee Johnson   *m, h*   748
That Summer - Tony Johnston   *p*   755
Yesterday I Had the Blues - Jeron Ashford Frame
   p   478

Gramma (Grandmother)
Falling from Fire - Teena Booth   *m, h*   126

Gramma Louise (Grandmother)
Here We Go Round - Alice McGill   *e*   979

Grampa (Duck; Grandfather)
Make the Team, Baby Duck! - Amy Hest   *p*   633

Gran (Cousin)
The Bagpiper's Ghost - Jane Yolen   *e, m*   1478

Gran (Grandmother; Scout)
Loretta: Ace Pinky Scout - Keith Graves   *p*   548

Gran (Grandmother)
T.J. and the Cats - Hazel Hutchins   *e*   704

Grand (Grandfather)
Dancing the Ring Shout! - Kim Siegelson   *p*   1300

Grand Da (Grandfather; Aged Person)
Katie's Wish - Barbara Shook Hazen   *p*   616

Grand Master (Aged Person)
What About Me? - Ed Young   *p*   1488

Grandad (Grandfather)
Jason Rat-a-Tat - Colby Rodowsky   *e*   1220

Grandad (Mole; Grandfather)
Mole and the Baby Bird - Marjorie Newman
   p   1076

Granddad (Grandfather)
The Birdwatchers - Simon James   *p*   726

Granddaddy (Grandfather)
You Can't Rush a Cat - Karleen Bradford   *p*   133

Grandfather (Grandfather; Sea Captain)
Monkey Mo Goes to Sea - Diane Goode   *p*   538

Grandfather (Grandfather; Aged Person)
Ruby's Wish - Shirin Yim Bridges   *p*   148
The Water Gift and the Pig of the Pig - Jacqueline
   Briggs Martin   *p*   948

Grandma (Dog; Grandmother)
At Grandma's - Rhonda Gowler Greene   *p*   554

Grandma (Grandmother)
Elisa Michaels, Bigger & Better - Johanna Hurwitz
   e   702

Grandma (Grandmother; Storyteller)
Emma's Story - Deborah Hodge   *p*   655

Grandma (Grandmother; Dog)
Gaspard and Lisa's Rainy Day - Anne Gutman
   p   573

Grandma (Grandmother)
Hobbledy-Clop - Pat Brisson   *p*   155
Meow Means Mischief - Ann Whitehead Nagda
   e   1055
My Grandma, My Pen Pal - Jan Dale Koutsky
   p   822
The Name Quilt - Phyllis Root   *p*   1227
One Candle - Eve Bunting   *p*   180

Grandma (Grandmother; Mother)
Visiting Day - Jacqueline Woodson   *p*   1468

Grandma (Grandmother)
What Would Joey Do? - Jack Gantos   *m*   508

Grandma Beetle (Aged Person; Grandmother)
Just a Minute: A Trickster Tale and Counting Book -
   Yuyi Morales   *p*   1030

Grandma Gardenia (Grandmother)
The Talent Show - Michelle Edwards   *e*   417

Grandma Martha (Grandmother)
Izzy's Place - Marc Kornblatt   *e, m*   819

Grandma Morgan (Grandmother)
The Same Stuff as Stars - Katherine Paterson
   m   1128

Grandmere (Grandmother)
Princess in Love - Meg Cabot   *m, h*   197
Princess in Waiting - Meg Cabot   *m, h*   198

Grandmother (Grandmother; Seamstress)
A Far-Fetched Story - Karin Cates   *p*   230

Grandmother (Grandmother; Aged Person)
Georgie Lee - Sharon Phillips Denslow   *e*   374

Grandmother (Grandmother)
My Grandmother's Clock - Geraldine McCaughrean
   p   966

Grandmother (Indian)
The World Before This One - Rafe Martin   *m*   950

Grandmother Morrow (Grandmother)
The Kingfisher's Gift - Susan Williams Beckhorn   *e,
   m*   96

Grandmother Silk (Grandmother)
Snowed in with Grandmother Silk - Carol Fenner
   e   448

Grandpa (Grandfather; Beekeeper)
The Beeman - Laurie Krebs   *p*   825

Grandpa (Grandfather; Farmer)
Full Steam Ahead - Faye Gibbons   *p*   521

Grandpa (Grandfather)
Gus and Grandpa and the Halloween Costume -
   Claudia Mills   *b*   1014

Grandpa (Grandfather; Aged Person)
Gus and Grandpa Go Fishing - Claudia Mills
   b   1015

Grandpa (Grandfather)
I Love Saturdays Y Domingos - Alma Flor Ada
   p   2
Iris and Walter and Baby Rose - Elissa Haden Guest
   b   568
My Pig Amarillo - Satomi Ichikawa   *p*   709

Grandpa (Grandfather; Farmer)
Pete and Polo's Farmyard Adventure - Adrian
   Reynolds   *p*   1200

Grandpa (Grandfather)
Thirsty Baby - Catherine Ann Cullen   *p*   323

Grandpa Dave (Grandfather; Farmer)
Here We Go Round - Alice McGill   *e*   979

Grandy (Grandmother; Witch)
Witch Twins at Camp Bliss - Adele Griffin   *e*   564

Granger, Robert (Student; Classmate)
What Planet Are You from, Clarice Bean? - Lauren
   Child   *p*   250

Grannie (Grandmother; Cook)
Full, Full, Full of Love - Trish Cooke   *p*   291

Granny (Grandmother)
Small - Clara Vulliamy   *p*   1403

Granny Baxter (Grandmother; Cook)
The Runaway Pumpkin - Kevin Lewis   *p*   890

Granpere (Grandfather; Fisherman)
Where, Where Is Swamp Bear? - Kathi Appelt
   p   36

Grant, Mitch (15-Year-Old)
The Last Mall Rat - Erik E. Esckilsen   *m, h*   438

Grant, Smithfield William "Smits" (Brother)
Among the Barons - Margaret Peterson Haddix   *m,
   h*   577

Grassina (Aunt; Witch)
The Frog Princess - E.D. Baker   *m*   67

Grayson, Grant (Cousin)
Gravel Queen - Tea Benduhn   *h*   101

Green (15-Year-Old; Gardener)
Green Angel - Alice Hoffman   *m, h* 658

Green (Alligator)
Meet Mr. and Mrs. Green - Keith Baker   *p* 70
Meet Mr. and Mrs. Green - Keith Baker   *p* 70

Green, Cameron "Anne Thomas" (11th Grader; Sister)
Hush - Jacqueline Woodson   *m, h* 1465

Green, Hazel (Student—Elementary School; Neighbor)
Hazel Green - Odo Hirsch   *e* 644

Green, Toswiah "Evie Thomas" (13-Year-Old)
Hush - Jacqueline Woodson   *m, h* 1465

Greene, Bucky (Scientist)
My Chimp Friday: The Nana Banana Chronicles - Hester Mundis   *e, m* 1038

Greene, Gooney Bird (2nd Grader; Storyteller)
Gooney Bird Greene - Lois Lowry   *e* 911

Greene, Matt (8th Grader)
Born Too Short: The Confessions of an Eighth-Grade Basket Case - Dan Elish   *m* 425

Greenland, Ellen (Widow(er); Nurse)
I Am Not Esther - Fleur Beale   *m, h* 91

Greenland, Kirby "Esther Pilgrim" (14-Year-Old)
I Am Not Esther - Fleur Beale   *m, h* 91

Gregor (11-Year-Old)
Gregor the Overlander - Suzanne Collins   *m* 284

Gregorio, Jose (Servant; Art Historian)
The 7th Knot - Kathleen Karr   *m* 765

Gregory (Mouse; Friend)
Gregory and Alexander - William Barringer   *p* 84

Gregory (Child; Son)
The Way We Do It in Japan - Geneva Cobb Iijima   *p* 711

Gretchen "Chan" (15-Year-Old; Streetperson)
Tomorrow, Maybe - Brian James   *m, h* 725

Gribley, Sam (Animal Lover; Naturalist)
Frightful's Daughter - Jean Craighead George   *p* 518

Griffin (Student—High School; Writer)
Straydog - Kathe Koja   *m, h* 812

Griffin, Milena (10th Grader)
The Flip Side - Andrew Matthews   *m* 956

Griswold (Grandfather; Wizard)
The Falconmaster - R.L. La Fevers   *m* 841

Grody (Dog; Child)
Grody's Not So Golden Rules - Nicole Rubel   *p* 1235

Grossmutter (Grandmother)
Breath - Donna Jo Napoli   *m, h* 1059

Grrl (Dog)
Straydog - Kathe Koja   *m, h* 812

Grubb (Sister; Student)
The Three Silly Girls Grubb - John Hassett   *p* 608

Grubby Gurgle (Monster)
Three Nasty Gnarlies - Keith Graves   *p* 549

Grundo (Wizard)
The Merlin Conspiracy - Diana Wynne Jones   *m, h* 757

Guadalupe (Baby; Sister)
The Kite - Luis Garay   *p* 509

Gulan (Religious; Martial Arts Expert)
Wandering Warrior - Da Chen   *m, h* 240

Gumbrella (Elephant; Sister)
Gumbrella - Barry Root   *p* 1225

Gunn, Fidelio (Wizard; Student—Boarding School)
Charlie Bone and the Time Twister - Jenny Nimmo   *m* 1081

Gunn, Fidelio (Student—Boarding School)
Midnight for Charlie Bone - Jenny Nimmo   *m* 1082

Gus (2nd Grader; Son)
Gus and Grandpa and the Halloween Costume - Claudia Mills   *b* 1014

Gus (Child; Relative)
Gus and Grandpa Go Fishing - Claudia Mills   *b* 1015

Gustave (Immigrant; Son)
Silent Movie - Avi   *p* 60

Guy of Gisborn (Bounty Hunter)
Lionclaw: A Tale of Rowan Hood - Nancy Springer   *m* 1330

Gwendolyn (11th Grader; Journalist)
Target - Kathleen Jeffrie Johnson   *h* 747

Gwyndolyne "Gwyn" (17-Year-Old)
Born Confused - Tanuja Desai Hidier   *h* 639

Gylfie (Owl; Orphan)
The Capture - Kathryn Lasky   *m* 851

H

Hackenschmidt "Lion of Russia" (Wrestler)
Secret Heart - David Almond   *m, h* 21

Hackett (Doctor)
The Night I Disappeared - Julie Reece Deaver   *m, h* 364

Hackett, Morgan (18-Year-Old)
The Night I Disappeared - Julie Reece Deaver   *m, h* 364

Hackler (Landowner)
Trouble Don't Last - Shelley Pearsall   *m* 1139

Hades (Deity)
Have a Hot Time, Hades! - Kate McMullan   *e* 991

Hades, Acheron (Criminal)
The Eyre Affair: A Novel - Jasper Fforde   *h, a* 453

Hagmeyer (Teacher)
Leon and the Spitting Image - Allen Kurzweil   *e, m* 839

Hailey (Penguin; Traveler)
Olvina Flies - Grace Lin   *p* 893

Halfmoon, Grampa (Grandfather; Indian)
Indian Shoes - Cynthia Leitich Smith   *e* 1312

Halfmoon, Ray (Indian; Child)
Indian Shoes - Cynthia Leitich Smith   *e* 1312

Halfpint, Annie (Rescuer; Heroine)
Avalanche Annie: A Not-So-Tall Tale - Lisa Wheeler   *p* 1433

Hall, Geri (Neighbor; Widow(er))
Especially Heroes - Virginia Kroll   *p* 831

Hallard, Debra (Imposter)
Dead Girls Don't Write Letters - Gail Giles   *m, h* 525

Hallgerd (Kidnap Victim)
Daughter of the Wind - Michael Cadnum   *m, h* 199

Halloweena (Child; Adoptee)
Halloweena - Miriam Glassman   *p* 528

Hana (Friend)
In the Shadow of the Pali: A Story of the Hawaiian Leper Colony - Lisa Cindrich   *m, h* 255

Hank (Child; Neighbor)
Hank and Fergus - Susin Nielsen-Fernlund   *p* 1080

Hank (Monkey)
I Am NOT Going to School Today! - Robie H. Harris   *p* 599

Hank (9th Grader; Tennis Player)
Mixed-Up Doubles - Elena Yates Eulo   *m, h* 439

Hank (Fiance(e); Lumberjack)
Stefan's Story - Valerie Hobbs   *m* 651

Hannah (Sister; Teenager)
At the Sign of the Sugared Plum - Mary Hooper   *m, h* 675

Hannah (Grandmother)
Hannah's Garden - Midori Snyder   *m, h* 1318

Hansen, Emil (15-Year-Old)
Room in the Heart - Sonia Levitin   *m, h* 886

Hanson, Tucker (12th Grader)
Telling Christina Goodbye - Lurlene McDaniel   *m, h* 974

Hare (Rabbit)
Bear Snores On - Karma Wilson   *p* 1449

Hargraves, Emily (Basketball Player)
Hoop Girlz - Lucy Jane Bledsoe   *e, m* 118

Harker (Scientist)
Death and the Arrow - Chris Priestley   *m, h* 1169

Harket (Wizard)
Ravine - Janet Hickman   *m* 638

Harkin, Molly (10-Year-Old)
The Rudest Alien on Earth - Jane Leslie Conly   *e, m* 286

Harper (14-Year-Old)
The Canning Season - Polly Horvath   *m, h* 683

Harper (Foster Parent)
America - E.R. Frank   *h* 479

Harper, Dolores (Waiter/Waitress; Aged Person)
True Confessions of a Heartless Girl - Martha Brooks   *h* 161

Harper, Forrest (11-Year-Old)
The Ravenmaster's Secret - Elvira Woodruff   *m* 1462

Harriet (Dog)
Fifteen Love - Robert Corbet   *m, h* 299

Harrington, Honor (Military Personnel)
War of Honor - David Weber   *h, a* 1421

Harrison (Aged Person; Slave)
Trouble Don't Last - Shelley Pearsall   *m* 1139

Harrison, William Henry (Government Official)
Crossing the Panther's Path - Elizabeth Alder   *m, h* 17

Harrow, Doon (12-Year-Old)
The City of Ember - Jeanne DuPrau   *m* 409

Harry (Spirit)
The Great Blue Yonder - Alex Shearer   *m, h* 1290

Harsich, Abram (Con Artist)
Dust - Arthur Slade   *m, h* 1308

Hart, Matthew "Matt" (18-Year-Old; Cowboy)
Samantha and the Cowboy - Lorraine Heath   *h* 620

Hartley, Barnaby (Brother; Runaway)
The Slightly True Story of Cedar B. Hartley (Who Planned to Live an Unusual Life) - Martine Murray   *m* 1046

Hartley, Cedar B. (12-Year-Old)
The Slightly True Story of Cedar B. Hartley (Who Planned to Live an Unusual Life) - Martine Murray   *m* 1046

Harvey, Feena (14-Year-Old)
Waiting for Christopher - Louise Hawes   *m, h* 613

Idi, Nina (13-Year-Old)
Among the Betrayed - Margaret Peterson Haddix   m, h   578

Ilena (Orphan; 15-Year-Old)
The Legend of Lady Ilena - Patricia Malone   m, h   936

Ilisidi (Alien; Noblewoman)
Explorer - C.J. Cherryh   h, a   244

Inagki, Brad (18-Year-Old)
Beacon Hill Boys - Ken Mochizuki   m, h   1021

Inagki, Dan (16-Year-Old)
Beacon Hill Boys - Ken Mochizuki   m, h   1021

Ingram, Aisha (19-Year-Old; Single Mother)
Chill Wind - Janet McDonald   h   975

Ingrid (16-Year-Old; Friend)
The Princess and the Pauper - Kate Brian   m   147

Ingvoldsson, Markus (16-Year-Old; Friend)
The Princess and the Pauper - Kate Brian   m   147

Iphigenia (Royalty; Daughter)
The Great God Pan - Donna Jo Napoli   m, h   1062

Ireland, Ann "Annie" (9th Grader)
Hard Time - Julian F. Thompson   m, h   1378

Irene (Rhinoceros)
Minnie and Moo and the Seven Wonders of the World - Denys Cazet   e   234

Iris (Child; Friend)
Iris and Walter and Baby Rose - Elissa Haden Guest   b   568

Iris and Walter and Cousin Howie - Elissa Haden Guest   b   569

Iris (Student; Friend)
Iris and Walter: The School Play - Elissa Haden Guest   b   570

Iris (Child; Friend)
Iris and Walter: The Sleepover - Elissa Haden Guest   b   571

Iris (Deity)
Juliet Dove, Queen of Love - Bruce Coville   e, m   308

Iris (Mythical Creature)
The Kingfisher's Gift - Susan Williams Beckhorn   e, m   96

Iron Shell (Chieftain; Indian)
Betrayed! - Patricia Calvert   m   205

Irving (Dog)
Snakes Don't Miss Their Mothers - M.E. Kerr   e, m   783

Isabel (Child; Daughter)
The Water Gift and the Pig of the Pig - Jacqueline Briggs Martin   p   948

Iseult (Lover)
The Ballad of Sir Dinadan - Gerald Morris   m, h   1034

Isillee, Anidori-Kiladra Talianna "Ani" (Royalty)
The Goose Girl - Shannon Hale   m, h   586

Isman (Child)
Overboard - Elizabeth Fama   m, h   442

Isolde (Royalty)
Isolde: Queen of the Western Isle: The First of the Tristan and Isolde Novels - Rosalind Miles   h, a   1010

Ivan (Royalty)
The Firebird - Jane Yolen   p   1479

Ivan-Tsarevitch (Royalty)
The Tale of the Firebird - Gennady Spirin   p   1328

Izbecki, Ellis (8th Grader)
Flip - David Lubar   m   913

J

J.D. (8-Year-Old)
Georgie Lee - Sharon Phillips Denslow   e   374

Jabber (Mouse; Detective)
Dot & Jabber and the Mystery of the Missing Stream - Ellen Stoll Walsh   p   1413

Jack (Child; Son)
Another Perfect Day - Ross MacDonald   p   925

Jack (Brother; Son)
Jack and Jill - Daniel Kirk   p   799

Jack (Child; Trickster)
Jack Outwits the Giants - Paul Brett Johnson   p   749

Jack (Rabbit)
Jackalope - Janet Stevens   p   1342

Jack (Dog)
The Last Dog on Earth - Daniel Ehrenhaft   m, h   424

No, No, Jack! - Ron Hirsch   p   645

Jack (Rabbit; Brother)
Pumpkin Day! - Nancy Elizabeth Wallace   p   1409

Jack (Bear; Friend)
The Saturday Escape - Daniel J. Mahoney   p   934

Jack (Orphan; 12-Year-Old)
The Several Lives of Orphan Jack - Sarah Ellis   e   430

Jackie (Animal Lover)
Jackie's Wild Seattle - Will Hobbs   m   652

Jackie (Child; Nephew)
Making Plum Jam - John Warren Stewig   p   1344

Jackrabbit (Rabbit; Military Personnel)
Ricky Ricotta's Mighty Robot vs. the Jurassic Jackrabbits from Jupiter - Dav Pilkey   e   1154

Jackson (Religious)
Faith Wish - James Bennett   h   102

Jackson, C.J. (8th Grader)
The Journal of C.J. Jackson: A Dust Bowl Migrant: Oklahoma to California, 1935 - William Durbin   m   410

Jackson, Joseph "Shoeless Joe" (Baseball Player)
Shoeless Joe & Black Betsy - Phil Bildner   p   108

Jackson, Zuri (Child; Friend)
Danitra Brown Leaves Town - Nikki Grimes   p   566

Jacob, Jeremy (Child; Son)
How I Became a Pirate - Melinda Long   p   907

Jacobsen, Jacob (Boyfriend)
Dancing in the Streets of Brooklyn - April Lurie   m, h   916

Jaguar (Jaguar)
Rosa Raposa - F. Isabel Campoy   p   209

Jaimy (Sailor)
Bloody Jack: Being an Account of the Curious Adventures of Mary "Jacky" Faber, Ship's Boy - L.A. Meyer   m, h   1007

Jake (Mouse; Brother)
The Ghost of P.S. 42 - Frank Asch   e   45

Jake (5th Grader; Friend)
Minn and Jake - Janet S. Wong   e   1456

Jake (Brother)
Walk Softly, Rachel - Kate Banks   m, h   78

Jakoven (Royalty)
Dragon Blood - Patricia Briggs   h, a   150

Jamaica (Friend; Dancer)
Brianna, Jamaica, and the Dance of Spring - Juanita Havill   p   612

James (Child; Friend)
Annie Was Warned - Jarrett J. Krosoczka   p   833

James (Child; Son)
What James Likes Best - Amy Schwartz   p   1272

James (Religious)
Wenny Has Wings - Janet Lee Carey   e, m   216

James, Calliope (2nd Grader; Friend)
The Talent Show - Michelle Edwards   e   417

James, Jesse (Friend; Historical Figure)
Guerrilla Season - Pat Hughes   m, h   693

Jameson (Servant)
Vampire Kisses - Ellen Schreiber   m, h   1271

Jamie (12-Year-Old)
Gina.Jamie.Father.Bear - George Ella Lyon   m, h   920

Jamie (Child; Son)
The Jamie and Angus Stories - Anne Fine   e   455

Jane "Mom" (Mother)
The Way We Do It in Japan - Geneva Cobb Iijima   p   711

Janice (Bully)
Hang On in There, Shelley - Kate Saksena   m, h   1251

Janice, Stacy (8th Grader)
Friction - E.R. Frank   m, h   480

Jasmine, Jasper (Basketball Player)
String Music - Rick Telander   e, m   1372

Jason (Warrior)
Celtika - Robert Holdstock   h, a   664

Jason (Businessman)
Stetson - S.L. Rottman   h   1233

Jasper (Dog)
Mud City - Deborah Ellis   m   428

Javier (Young Man; Friend)
Adelita: A Mexican Cinderella Story - Tomie De Paola   p   358

Jay Jay (Child; Son)
Full, Full, Full of Love - Trish Cooke   p   291

Jeannie (Friend; 8-Year-Old)
Tippy Lemmey - Patricia C. McKissack   e   986

Jed (Teenager)
Flight of the Fisherbird - Nora Martin   e, m   949

Jef (Streetperson)
Tomorrow, Maybe - Brian James   m, h   725

Jeff (Dog)
The Green Dog: A Mostly True Story - Suzanne Fisher Staples   e   1336

Jeffers, Jon (9-Year-Old; Son)
The Boy Who Could Fly Without a Motor - Theodore Taylor   e   1364

Jefferson, Abilene (Housekeeper)
Jericho Walls - Kristi Collier   m, h   280

Jefferson, Lucas (12-Year-Old)
Jericho Walls - Kristi Collier   m, h   280

Jeffrey (Friend; Child)
Lionel's Birthday - Stephen Krensky   b   826

Jen (Chicken)
Daniel's Pet - Alma Flor Ada   b   1

Jennifer (Twin)
The Bagpiper's Ghost - Jane Yolen   e, m   1478

Jeoffry (Cat; Friend)
Jeoffry's Halloween - Mary Bryant Bailey   p   66

Jepson, Ben (16-Year-Old)
Lord of the Kill - Theodore Taylor   m, h   1366

Jeremy (Homosexual)
Rainbow High - Alex Sanchez   h   1262

Jeremy (8th Grader; Homosexual)
The Rainbow Kite - Marlene Fanta Shyer   m, h   1299

Jericho (Worker)
The Rope Trick - Lloyd Alexander   e, m   18

Jerome (Rat)
Juliet Dove, Queen of Love - Bruce Coville   e, m   308

Jerome "Jerry" (12th Grader; Tennis Player)
Mixed-Up Doubles - Elena Yates Eulo   m, h   439

Jerry (15-Year-Old; Cousin)
The Hero - Ron Woods   m, h   1464

Jerry (Uncle; Magician)
Lulu's Hat - Susan Meddaugh   e   1003

Jess (Relative)
The Birdwatchers - Simon James   p   726

Jesse (Brother; Son)
Bear Hug - Laurence Pringle   p   1172

Jesse (Child)
Dinosaur Train - John Steven Gurney   p   572

Jesse (12-Year-Old)
Wild Boy - James Lincoln Collier   m   279

Jessica (Accident Victim)
Bridging Beyond - Kathleen Benner Duble   m, h   403

Jessica (Child)
You Can't Rush a Cat - Karleen Bradford   p   133

Jessie (Child; Sister)
The Bones of Fred McFee - Eve Bunting   p   177

Jessie (Housekeeper)
A Greater Goode - Amy Schor Ferris   m   451

Jesus (Baby)
The Donkey's Christmas - Nancy Tafuri   p   1359

Jesus "Chuy" (Spirit; 17-Year-Old)
The Afterlife - Gary Soto   m, h   1320

Jewell, Sapphire (Slave; Aunt)
Evvy's Civil War - Miriam Brenaman   m, h   140

Jiaan (Bastard Son; 17-Year-Old)
Flame - Hilari Bell   m, h   97

Jill (Sister; Daughter)
Jack and Jill - Daniel Kirk   p   799

Jiller (Single Mother; Widow(er))
Rowan and the Keeper of the Crystal - Emily Rodda   e   1218

Jim (Mouse; Friend)
Slim and Jim - Richard Egielski   p   422

Jimmy (Brother)
Dolores: Seven Stories about Her - Bruce Brooks   m, h   158

Jing-wei "Lizzie" (Captive)
The Hunting of the Last Dragon - Sherryl Jordan   m, h   761

Joe (Brother)
Cold Tom - Sally Prue   m, h   1177

Joe (Landlord)
Keesha's House - Helen Frost   m, h   498

Joe (Frog; Son)
Let's Clean Up! - Peggy Perry Anderson   p   30

Joe (Pirate)
On the Go with Pirate Pete and Pirate Joe - A.E. Cannon   b   211

Joey (Brother)
That Summer - Tony Johnston   p   755

John (Royalty)
The Leopard Sword - Michael Cadnum   m, h   201

John (Farmer)
Minnie and Moo: The Night Before Christmas - Denys Cazet   b   235

John (Animal Lover; Linguist)
I, Freddy - Deitlof Reiche   e   1196

John Martin (Cousin)
Sister Spider Knows All - Adrian Fogelin   m   471

Johnny (Cousin)
Child of the Prophecy - Juliet Marillier   h, a   941

Johnson (Brother; Nephew)
Our Gracie Aunt - Jacqueline Woodson   p   1467

Johnson, Julia (16-Year-Old)
The Princess and the Pauper - Kate Brian   m   147

Johnson, Raymond (Uncle; Carpenter)
The Journey of Oliver K. Woodman - Darcy Pattison   p   1130

Johnson, Rosie (Child; Friend)
Boxes for Katje - Candace Fleming   p   462

Johnson, Tony "Dad" (Father; Farmer)
Prairie Summer - Bonnie Geisert   e   516

Johnson-Brown, Twanda Rochelle (Rodeo Rider; Mother)
Daddy Says - Ntozake Shange   m   1281

Jonah (Slave; Time Traveler)
The Watch - Dennis Danvers   h, a   344

Jonathan (Child; Son)
The Key to My Heart - Nira Harel   p   593

Jondiss, Aurin (12th Grader; Lesbian)
Gravel Queen - Tea Benduhn   h   101

Jones, Calypso "Twig" (Child; Deaf Person)
Willow and Twig - Jean Little   m   903

Jones, Casey (Historical Figure; Engineer)
I Dream of Trains - Angela Johnson   p   742

Jones, Dexter (Singer)
This Lullaby - Sarah Dessen   h   377

Jones, Gloria (4th Grader; Friend)
Gloria Rising - Ann Cameron   e   207

Jones, Herbie (4th Grader; Friend)
Herbie Jones Moves On - Suzy Kline   e   805

Jones, Jack (Raccoon; Detective)
The Case of the Sleepy Sloth - Cynthia Rylant   b   1243

Jones, James Archer "Archie" (11-Year-Old)
How I Became a Writer and Oggie Learned to Drive - Janet Taylor Lisle   e, m   902

Jones, Nell "Gram" (Grandmother)
Willow and Twig - Jean Little   m   903

Jones, Ogden Jackson "Oogie" (Child; Brother)
How I Became a Writer and Oggie Learned to Drive - Janet Taylor Lisle   e, m   902

Jones, Pamela (10th Grader; Counselor)
Patiently Alice - Phyllis Reynolds Naylor   m, h   1068

Jones, Pamela (9th Grader)
Simply Alice - Phyllis Reynolds Naylor   m   1069

Jones, Sahara "Sahara Special" (5th Grader)
Sahara Special - Esme Raji Codell   e, m   269

Jones, Willow Wind (12-Year-Old)
Willow and Twig - Jean Little   m   903

Jordan (Swimmer; Homosexual)
The Shell House - Linda Newbery   h   1075

Jordan, Shawn (11-Year-Old)
Dish Series - Diane Muldrow   e, m   1037

Jorge (Royalty)
The Frog Princess - E.D. Baker   m   67

Joseph (Cousin; Child)
The Dream Shop - Katharine Kenah   p   780

Josh (Student—Elementary School; Son)
Baghead - Jarrett J. Krosoczka   p   834

Joshua (12th Grader)
Waiting for June - Joyce Sweeney   h   1356

Josie (Child; Daughter)
Musical Beds - Mara Bergman   p   105

Jude (Orphan)
The Hunting of the Last Dragon - Sherryl Jordan   m, h   761

Judge, Oney (Slave; Historical Figure)
Taking Liberty: The Story of Oney Judge, George Washington's Runaway Slave - Ann Rinaldi   m, h   1207

Judson (Military Personnel; Victim)
Danger at the Wild West Show - Alison Hart   m   601

Julep (Cat)
Lily's Ghosts - Laura Ruby   m   1237

Julia (7-Year-Old; Child of Divorced Parents)
Julia Wants a Pet - Barbro Lindgren   p   899

Julian (Farmer)
The Rope Trick - Lloyd Alexander   e, m   18

Juliana (Friend)
The Farther You Run - Davida Wills Hurwin   h   700

Julius (Mouse; Son)
Julius's Candy Corn - Kevin Henkes   p   622

Justin (10th Grader)
Buddha Boy - Kathe Koja   m, h   811

K

Kaalani (Bully)
In the Shadow of the Pali: A Story of the Hawaiian Leper Colony - Lisa Cindrich   m, h   255

Kahu (Child)
The Whale Rider - Witi Ihimaera   m, h   710

Kahutia Te Rangi "Whale Rider" (Mythical Creature)
The Whale Rider - Witi Ihimaera   m, h   710

Kaligaris, Lena (16-Year-Old; Clerk)
The Second Summer of the Sisterhood - Ann Brashares   m, h   137

Kapoor, Karshum "Karsh" (Student—College)
Born Confused - Tanuja Desai Hidier   h   639

Karay (Gypsy; Singer)
The Angel's Command: A Tale from the Castaways of the Flying Dutchman - Brian Jacques   m, h   722

Kaspian (Neighbor)
The Four Ugly Cats in Apartment 3D - Marilyn Sachs   e   1249

Kat (16-Year-Old)
Shopaholic - Judy Waite   m, h   1405

Kate (16-Year-Old)
Kissing Kate - Lauren Myracle   h   1054

Katerina (Goose)
The Other Goose - Judith Kerr   p   782

Katie (Daughter)
Before I Was Your Mother - Kathryn Lasky   p   850

Katie (8th Grader)
The Cheat - Amy Goldman Koss   m   820

Katie (Child)
Katie's Wish - Barbara Shook Hazen   p   616

Katie (Teenager)
Parasite Pig - William Sleator   m, h   1310

Katie Sue (Child; Student—Elementary School)
The Recess Queen - Alexis O'Neill   *p*   1110

Katrina (Mentally Ill Person)
Overnight - Adele Griffin   *e, m*   563

Katz, Lido (5th Grader; Friend)
The Last Burp of Mac McGerp - Pam Smallcomb
   e   1311

Kavi (Spy; 19-Year-Old)
Flame - Hilari Bell   *m, h*   97

Kay (Teenager)
Alia Waking - Laura Williams McCaffrey   *m,
h*   962

Kay-gwa-daush "Susan" (Indian)
Brian's Hunt - Gary Paulsen   *m, h*   1133

Kayla (14-Year-Old)
Stetson - S.L. Rottman   *h*   1233

Keeling (Grandmother)
Rebel - Willo Davis Roberts   *m*   1211

Keeling, Amanda Jane "Rebel" (14-Year-Old)
Rebel - Willo Davis Roberts   *m*   1211

Keely, Kate (Businesswoman; 17-Year-Old)
Rising Tide - Jean Thesman   *m, h*   1376

Keeper of the Crystal (Aged Person)
Rowan and the Keeper of the Crystal - Emily Rodda
   e   1218

Keesha (Teenager)
Keesha's House - Helen Frost   *m, h*   498

Kelandry "Kel" (Knight)
Lady Knight - Tamora Pierce   *m, h*   1150

Keller, Charlie (Son; Brother)
Pioneer Summer - Deborah Hopkinson   *e*   677

Keller, Ida Jane (10-Year-Old; Sister)
Pioneer Summer - Deborah Hopkinson   *e*   677

Keller, Sadie (Sister; 4-Year-Old)
Pioneer Summer - Deborah Hopkinson   *e*   677

Kelley, Edward (Criminal)
The Alchemist's Door - Lisa Goldstein   *h, a*   535

Kellogg, Hampton (Landowner)
Numbering All the Bones - Ann Rinaldi   *m,
h*   1205

Kelly (Teacher)
The Color of Home - Mary Hoffman   *p*   663

Kelly, Brandon (7th Grader)
Mind Games - Jeanne Marie Grunwell   *m*   567

Kelts, Anna (15-Year-Old)
Bridging Beyond - Kathleen Benner Duble   *m,
h*   403

Kelts, Nellie (Child)
Bridging Beyond - Kathleen Benner Duble   *m,
h*   403

Kelvin, Jana (16-Year-Old)
Bull Rider - Marilyn Halvorson   *m, h*   588

Kendrill, Alex (6th Grader)
Spy Cat - Peg Kehret   *e, m*   773

Kendrill, Alex (12-Year-Old; 6th Grader)
The Stranger Next Door - Peg Kehret   *e, m*   774

Kendrill, Benjie (Child)
Spy Cat - Peg Kehret   *e, m*   773

**Kenigh, Jessica Abigail Danvers
"Snow"** (Noblewoman)
Snow - Tracy Lynn   *m, h*   919

Kennedy, Pamela (Student—Elementary School;
Animal Lover)
Cool Cat, School Cat - Judy Cox   *e*   310

Kenney (12th Grader)
Gravel Queen - Tea Benduhn   *h*   101

Kenny (Boyfriend)
Princess in Love - Meg Cabot   *m, h*   197

Kensuke (Survivor; Doctor)
Kensuke's Kingdom - Michael Morpurgo   *e,
m*   1033

Kervick, Sarah (5th Grader; Friend)
Donuthead - Sue Stauffacher   *e*   1337

Ketchum, Robert E. (12-Year-Old)
Spitting Image - Shutta Crum   *m*   321

Kevin (17-Year-Old; Juvenile Delinquent)
Handbook for Boys: A Novel - Walter Dean Myers
   m, h   1053

Kevin (Student—Elementary School)
Lucky Socks - Carrie Weston   *p*   1431

Kevin (Teenager)
My Not-So-Terrible Time at the Hippie Hotel -
   Rosemary Graham   *m, h*   545

Keyes, Samantha Jo "Sammy" (Detective—
Amateur)
Sammy Keyes and the Search for Snake Eyes -
   Wendelin Van Draanen   *m*   1391

Kia (Aunt; Aged Person)
Kotuku - Deborah Savage   *m, h*   1265

Kidd, Holly (Sister; Singer)
Disappearing Act - Sid Fleischman   *m*   461

Kidd, Kevin (12-Year-Old)
Disappearing Act - Sid Fleischman   *m*   461

Kidder, Gabe (Student; Friend)
The True Story of Trapper Jack's Left Big Toe - Ian
   Wallace   *p*   1407

Kidney, Olivia (12-Year-Old)
Olivia Kidney - Ellen Potter   *e, m*   1165

Kidrouk, Pagan (Orphan; Servant)
Pagan's Crusade - Catherine Jinks   *m, h*   739

Kiese (Friend)
Monkey for Sale - Sanna Stanley   *p*   1335

Kiko (Mouse)
Thanks, Mom - Ed Emberley   *p*   433

Kim (Gymnast; 17-Year-Old)
Kim: Empty Inside - Beatrice Sparks   *m, h*   1323

Kim, Mai (Friend)
Begging for Change - Sharon G. Flake   *m, h*   458

Kim, Sun-hee "Keoko" (Sister)
When My Name Was Keoko - Linda Sue Park
   m   1127

Kim, Tae-yul "Nobuo" (Teenager)
When My Name Was Keoko - Linda Sue Park
   m   1127

Kincaid, Chase (Grandfather)
Bull Rider - Marilyn Halvorson   *m, h*   588

King (Wolf; Father)
Runt - Marion Dane Bauer   *e, m*   90

King, Robert "Rob" (8th Grader)
The Cheat - Amy Goldman Koss   *m*   820

Kington, Nancy (Heiress; Pirate)
*Pirates!: The True and Remarkable Adventures of
   Minerva Sharpe and Nancy Kington, Female Pirates*
   - Celia Rees   *m, h*   1193

Kinsey, Natalie (Sister; Narrator)
From Dawn till Dusk - Natalie Kinsey-Warnock
   p   796

Kipper (Dog; Friend)
Kipper's Monster - Mick Inkpen   *p*   715

Klassen, Derek (17-Year-Old)
Dancing Naked - Shelley Hrdlitschka   *h*   692

Klaus (Accident Victim; Spirit)
Dark Waters - Catherine MacPhail   *m, h*   932

Klein (Teacher)
*The Glass Cafe: Or the Stripper and the State: How
   My Mother Started a War with the System that
   Made Us Kind of Rich and a Little Bit Famous* -
   Gary Paulsen   *m, h*   1134

Klyton (Royalty; Warrior)
Mortal Suns - Tanith Lee   *h, a*   873

Knapsack, Lionel (Businessman)
Not Just a Witch - Eva Ibbotson   *e, m*   708

Knight, Clarence (Father)
The Kings Are Already Here - Garret Freymann-Weyr
   m, h   493

Knight, Phebe (15-Year-Old; Dancer)
The Kings Are Already Here - Garret Freymann-Weyr
   m, h   493

Kohn, Charles "Kodak" (Student—High School)
Prep - Jake Coburn   *h*   266

Koko (Mouse; Mother)
Thanks, Mom - Ed Emberley   *p*   433

Kokopelli (Mythical Creature)
*Night Dancer: Mythical Piper of the Native American
   Southwest* - Marcia Vaughan   *p*   1398

Koro Apirana (Grandfather; Chieftain)
The Whale Rider - Witi Ihimaera   *m, h*   710

Kostaniuk, Sophie (12-Year-Old)
Sparks Fly Upward - Carol Matas   *e, m*   954

Kotalev, Nikolai (16-Year-Old; Chess Player)
The Kings Are Already Here - Garret Freymann-Weyr
   m, h   493

Kotschei the Deathless (Wizard)
The Firebird - Jane Yolen   *p*   1479

Kramer, Kal (Boyfriend)
The Queen of Everything - Deb Caletti   *h*   202

Krasner, Kale (Bully)
Alt Ed - Catherine Atkins   *m, h*   52

Kravitz, Carrie (7th Grader; Handicapped)
Quit It - Marcia Byalick   *e, m*   191

Krenina, Marina (Immigrant; 7th Grader)
Mind Games - Jeanne Marie Grunwell   *m*   567

Kringle, Christopher (Child; Nephew)
Auntie Claus and the Key to Christmas - Elise
   Primavera   *p*   1171

Kringle, Sophie (Sister)
Auntie Claus and the Key to Christmas - Elise
   Primavera   *p*   1171

Kris (12th Grader)
Home of the Braves - David Klass   *h*   803

Kropotnik, Peter (Philosopher; Time Traveler)
The Watch - Dennis Danvers   *h, a*   344

Kublai Khan (Historical Figure; Warrior)
The Kite Rider - Geraldine McCaughrean   *m,
h*   965

Kumak (Spouse; Eskimo)
Kumak's House: A Tale of the Far North - Michael
   Bania   *p*   73

Kumba (Bird; Mother)
Birdbrain Amos - Michael Delaney   *e*   371

Kwagley, Edgar (Student—Boarding School; Indian)
Unseen Companion - Denise Gosliner Orenstein
   h   1113

Kyle (Student—High School)
Boy Meets Boy - David Levithan   *h*   885

Kyle (12th Grader)
God of Beer - Garret Keizer   *h*   775

Kyri (Child; Daughter)
Who's That Knocking on Christmas Eve? - Jan Brett
   p   145

Lovelace, Simon (Magician)
The Amulet of Samarkand - Jonathan Stroud   *m,
h*   1350

Lowell, Carmen Lucille (16-Year-Old; Babysitter)
The Second Summer of the Sisterhood - Ann Brashares
m, h   137

Luca, Anthony "Honest Abe" (Organized Crime
Figure; Father)
Son of the Mob - Gordon Korman   *m, h*   818

Luca, Vincent "Vince" (12th Grader; 17-Year-Old)
Son of the Mob - Gordon Korman   *m, h*   818

Lucas (Teenager; Drifter)
Lucas - Kevin Brooks   *h*   159

Lucille (Child; Pig)
Lucille Camps In - Kathryn Lasky   *p*   854

Lucky (Seagull)
*The Story of a Seagull and the Cat Who Taught her to
Fly* - Luis Sepulveda   *e*   1278

Lucy (Cat)
City Chicken - Arthur Dorros   *p*   388

Lucy (Child)
Dog Eared - Amanda Harvey   *p*   605

Lucy (7-Year-Old; Daughter)
The First Thing My Mama Told Me - Susan Marie
Swanson   *p*   1355

Lucy (Dog)
Lucy Was There . . . - Jean Van Leeuwen   *e,
m*   1393

Lucy (Spouse; Mother)
McDuff Saves the Day - Rosemary Wells   *p*   1426

Lucy (Child)
Pudgy: A Puppy to Love - Pippa Goodhart   *p*   539

Lucy (Child; Daughter)
The Wolves in the Walls - Neil Gaiman   *p*   503

Luka (11-Year-Old; Warrior)
Wandering Warrior - Da Chen   *m, h*   240

Luke (Friend; 12-Year-Old)
A Greater Goode - Amy Schor Ferris   *m*   451

Lulu (Adoptee; 12-Year-Old)
Lulu's Hat - Susan Meddaugh   *e*   1003

Lumpkin, Henry "Lumpkin the Pumpkin" (Bully)
Leon and the Spitting Image - Allen Kurzweil   *e,
m*   839

Lupovic, Michael (Brother)
And What about Anna? - Jan Simoen   *h*   1306

Luvering, Lucy (14-Year-Old)
Mates, Dates and Inflatable Bras - Cathy Hopkins
m, h   676

Luzolo (Daughter; Friend)
Monkey for Sale - Sanna Stanley   *p*   1335

Lynch, Jimmy (16-Year-Old; Juvenile Delinquent)
Handbook for Boys: A Novel - Walter Dean Myers
m, h   1053

Lyrra (Mythical Creature)
Shadows and Light - Anne Bishop   *h, a*   110

M

Ma (Mother; Farmer)
Horse in the Pigpen - Linda Williams   *p*   1446

Ma (Mother)
A Hug Goes Around - Laura Krauss Melmed
p   1005

Ma (Mother; Pioneer)
Old Crump: The True Story of a Trip West - Laurie
Lawlor   *p*   859

Sunsets of the West - Tony Johnston   *p*   754

Ma (Mother; Farmer)
A Twisted Tale - Carolyn Fisher   *p*   456

Ma'antah (Heroine)
Sense Pass King: A Story from Cameroon - Katrin
Tchana   *p*   1368

Maata (Indian)
Maata's Journal - Paul Sullivan   *m, h*   1353

Mabel (Cousin; 9-Year-Old)
Vampire State Building - Elizabeth Levy   *e*   887

Macavity, Shawn (8th Grader)
Bad Girls in Love - Cynthia Voigt   *m*   1402

Maccarone, Joel (5th Grader; Babysitter)
Taking Care of Trouble - Bonnie Graves   *e*   547

MacCrae, Curt (Musician)
Fat Kid Rules the World - K.L. Going   *h*   533

MacFadden, Andrew (Spirit; Twin)
The Bagpiper's Ghost - Jane Yolen   *e, m*   1478

MacFadden, Mary (Spirit; Twin)
The Bagpiper's Ghost - Jane Yolen   *e, m*   1478

MacGregor, Martin (Child; Son)
Martin MacGregor's Snowman - Lisa Broadie Cook
p   289

MacGruder, Rose "Thunder Rose" (Daughter;
Cowgirl)
Thunder Rose - Jerdine Nolen   *p*   1093

MacInnes, Archibald (Laird)
The Dungeon - Lynne Reid Banks   *m, h*   79

Macintosh, Sally (Neighbor; Worker)
Orville: A Dog Story - Haven Kimmel   *p*   790

MacKinnon, Aquila Jane "Quila" (12-Year-Old)
Gifts from the Sea - Natalie Kinsey-Warnock   *e,
m*   797

MacKinnon, Cecelia "Celia" (Baby)
Gifts from the Sea - Natalie Kinsey-Warnock   *e,
m*   797

Mackintosh, Edie (Neighbor)
Cold Tom - Sally Prue   *m, h*   1177

MacLean, Finlay "Fin" (Servant)
The Dungeon - Lynne Reid Banks   *m, h*   79

MacLennan, Bruce (Laird)
The Dungeon - Lynne Reid Banks   *m, h*   79

MacLeod, Alice (15-Year-Old)
Alice, I Think - Susan Juby   *m, h*   763

MacQueen, Cody (Brother)
The Trouble with Liberty - Kristin Butcher   *m,
h*   187

MacQueen, Valerie Gail "Val" (15-Year-Old)
The Trouble with Liberty - Kristin Butcher   *m,
h*   187

Macsen (Warrior)
Warriors of Alavna - N.M. Browne   *m, h*   168

Macy (Criminal)
Shooting Monarchs - John Halliday   *h*   587

Macy (Cheerleader; Student—High School)
What Happened to Lani Garver - Carol Plum-Ucci
h   1162

Macy (Businessman)
Milly and the Macy's Parade - Shana Corey
p   303

Madding, Saskia (Mythical Creature; Writer)
Spirits in the Wires - Charles de Lint   *h, a*   355

Madeleine (Sister; Daughter)
The First Thing My Mama Told Me - Susan Marie
Swanson   *p*   1355

Madison, Lucy (Sister; Cheerleader)
All-American Girl - Meg Cabot   *m, h*   195

Madison, Raven (16-Year-Old)
Vampire Kisses - Ellen Schreiber   *m, h*   1271

Madison, Rebecca (Sister)
All-American Girl - Meg Cabot   *m, h*   195

Madison, Samantha "Sam" (10th Grader; Artist)
All-American Girl - Meg Cabot   *m, h*   195

Madlenka (Child; Friend)
Madlenka's Dog - Peter Sis   *p*   1307

**Magallanes/Magellan, Fernando de/
Ferdinand** (Historical Figure; Explorer)
To the Edge of the World - Michele Torrey
m   1385

Magda (9th Grader)
Girls in Love - Jacqueline Wilson   *m, h*   1448

Magic Sam (Crocodile)
Jack and Jill - Daniel Kirk   *p*   799

Magruder, Avery (16-Year-Old; Military Personnel)
Hear the Wind Blow: A Novel of the Civil War - Mary
Downing Hahn   *m*   581

Magruder, Bernie (6th Grader; Son)
Bernie Magruder & the Bats in the Belfry - Phyllis
Reynolds Naylor   *e*   1064

Magruder, Haswell Colby (13-Year-Old)
Hear the Wind Blow: A Novel of the Civil War - Mary
Downing Hahn   *m*   581

Magruder, Rachel (Child; Sister)
Hear the Wind Blow: A Novel of the Civil War - Mary
Downing Hahn   *m*   581

Mahalia (Baby)
Mahalia - Joanne Horniman   *h*   679

Mahur, Anchee (Time Traveler)
The Watch - Dennis Danvers   *h, a*   344

Mai, Hannah (Doctor; Mother)
Malka - Mirjam Pressler   *m, h*   1168

Mai, Malka (Child)
Malka - Mirjam Pressler   *m, h*   1168

Mai, Minna (16-Year-Old)
Malka - Mirjam Pressler   *m, h*   1168

Mai Yang (13-Year-Old; Orphan)
Tangled Threads: A Hmong Girl's Story - Pegi Deitz
Shea   *m, h*   1289

Mainwaring, James (Sea Captain)
The Man with the Silver Oar - Robin Moore   *m,
h*   1029

Maita (Aged Person; Aunt)
The Sea Chest - Toni Buzzeo   *p*   190

Maita (10-Year-Old; Relative)
The Sea Chest - Toni Buzzeo   *p*   190

Makenna (Witch; 16-Year-Old)
The Goblin Wood - Hilari Bell   *m, h*   98

Malese (Trickster)
Please, Malese - Amy MacDonald   *p*   922

Mallon, Sean Red (Immigrant)
Maggie's Door - Patricia Reilly Giff   *m*   523

Mallory, Nicholas "Nick" (Teenager)
The Merlin Conspiracy - Diana Wynne Jones   *m,
h*   757

Malloy, Caroline (4th Grader; Sister)
Boys in Control - Phyllis Reynolds Naylor   *e*   1066
The Girls Take Over - Phyllis Reynolds Naylor
e   1067

Malloy, Eddie (6th Grader; Sister)
The Girls Take Over - Phyllis Reynolds Naylor
e   1067

Malone, Jack (Religious; Father)
Catalyst - Laurie Halse Anderson   *h*   28

Malone, Jim (12-Year-Old; Basketball Player)
House of Sports - Marisabina Russo   *m*   1240

Malone, Kate (12th Grader; 18-Year-Old)
Catalyst - Laurie Halse Anderson   *h*   28

Malone, Margaret (Aunt)
Gifts from the Sea - Natalie Kinsey-Warnock   *e, m*   797

Maloney, Joe (Handicapped)
Secret Heart - David Almond   *m, h*   21

Malory (Teacher)
Cheating Lessons - Nan Willard Cappo   *m, h*   212

Malvae, Pyrgus (Mythical Creature; Royalty)
Faerie Wars - Herbie Brennan   *h*   141

Mama (Mother; Photographer)
The Berry-Picking Man - Jane Buchanan   *e*   175

Mama (Mother)
Daniel's Pet - Alma Flor Ada   *b*   1

Mama (Duck; Mother)
Do Like a Duck Does! - Judy Hindley   *p*   642

Mama (Mother)
Epossumondas - Coleen Salley   *p*   1254
First Day in Grapes - L. King Perez   *p*   1145
The First Thing My Mama Told Me - Susan Marie Swanson   *p*   1355

Mama (Mother; Spouse)
Full, Full, Full of Love - Trish Cooke   *p*   291

Mama (Mother; Migrant Worker)
The Hard-Times Jar - Ethel Footman Smothers   *p*   1317

Mama (Mother; Immigrant)
Home at Last - Susan Middleton Elya   *p*   431

Mama (Mother)
It's Snowing! - Olivier Dunrea   *p*   407

Mama (Mother; Widow(er))
The Kite - Luis Garay   *p*   509

Mama (Duck; Mother)
Little One Step - Simon James   *p*   727

Mama (Rabbit; Mother)
Little Rabbit Lost - Harry Horse   *p*   682

Mama (Mother; Businesswoman)
Mama's Coming Home - Kate Banks   *p*   76

Mama (Bear; Mother)
Mama's Little Bears - Nancy Tafuri   *p*   1360

Mama (Mother)
Morning Glory Monday - Arlene Alda   *p*   16

Mama (Bear; Mother)
Oliver Finds His Way - Phyllis Root   *p*   1228

Mama (Mother)
On the Town: A Community Adventure - Judith Caseley   *p*   227
The Range Eternal - Louise Erdrich   *p*   434

Mama (Mother; Immigrant)
Silent Movie - Avi   *p*   60

Mama (Mother; Spouse)
The Snake's Tales - Marguerite W. Davol   *p*   353

Mama (Single Mother; Activist)
Stars in the Darkness - Barbara M. Joosse   *p*   759

Mama (Mother)
Yesterday I Had the Blues - Jeron Ashford Frame   *p*   478

Mama Bear (Mother; Bear)
Little Brown Bear Won't Go to School! - Jane Dyer   *p*   412

Mama Bear (Bear; Mother)
Little Brown Bear Won't Take a Nap! - Jane Dyer   *p*   413

Mama Coco (Alligator; Mother)
Alligator Sue - Sharon Arms Doucet   *p*   389

Mama JoJo (Mother; Animal)
Jazzy in the Jungle - Lucy Cousins   *p*   307

Mama Lion (Lion; Mother)
Quiet! - Paul Bright   *p*   153

Mama Lusufu (Neighbor; Saleswoman)
Monkey for Sale - Sanna Stanley   *p*   1335

Mama Pearl (Mother; Housewife)
Bubba and Beau, Best Friends - Kathi Appelt   *p*   34

Mama Pearl (Mother)
Bubba and Beau Go Night-Night - Kathi Appelt   *p*   33

Mama Pig (Pig; Mother)
Squeaky Clean - Simon Puttock   *p*   1179

Mamaw (Mother)
Cornfield Hide-and-Seek - Christine Widman   *p*   1442

Mamma (Mother; Spouse)
Flamingo Dream - Donna Jo Napoli   *p*   1061

Mann, Harold "the Mann" (Maintenance Worker; Sports Figure)
Cairo Kelly and the Mann - Kristin Butcher   *e, m*   185

Manning, Joel (11th Grader)
Kerosene - Chris Wooding   *h*   1461

Manuel (16-Year-Old; Migrant Worker)
Under the Same Sky - Cynthia DeFelice   *m, h*   368

Manukekua (Friend)
In the Shadow of the Pali: A Story of the Hawaiian Leper Colony - Lisa Cindrich   *m, h*   255

Marbella (Actress)
A Pig Named Perrier - Elizabeth Spurr   *p*   1331

Marcel (Goose; Friend)
Farfallina & Marcel - Holly Keller   *p*   777

Marcello, Walt (Publisher)
Saving the Planet & Stuff - Gail Gauthier   *m, h*   511

Marchiony, Italo (Inventor; Immigrant)
Ice-Cream Cones for Sale! - Elaine Greenstein   *p*   555

Marcos (3-Year-Old; Adoptee)
A New Barker in the House - Tomie De Paola   *p*   359

Margaret (11-Year-Old)
A Doctor Like Papa - Natalie Kinsey-Warnock   *p*   795

Margaret (Aunt)
The Fattening Hut - Pat Lowery Collins   *h*   281

Mari (Cousin; Healer)
Alia Waking - Laura Williams McCaffrey   *m, h*   962

Maria (Friend)
The House of the Scorpion - Nancy Farmer   *m, h*   444

Marie (Royalty; Kidnap Victim)
The Twins and the Bird of Darkness: A Hero Tale from the Caribbean - Robert D. San Souci   *e*   1260

Marie-Louise (Daughter; Kidnap Victim)
Little Pierre: A Cajun Story from Louisiana - Robert D. San Souci   *p*   1259

Marigold (Royalty)
Once Upon a Marigold - Jean Ferris   *m, h*   452

Mark (Royalty)
Isolde: Queen of the Western Isle: The First of the Tristan and Isolde Novels - Rosalind Miles   *h, a*   1010

Marks, Teresa (11-Year-Old)
The Victory Garden - Lee Kochenderfer   *e, m*   808

Marlowe, Kit (Writer; Historical Figure)
All Night Awake - Sarah A. Hoyt   *h, a*   691

Marlowe, Tom (15-Year-Old; Apprentice)
Death and the Arrow - Chris Priestley   *m, h*   1169

Marsh, Kevin (Juvenile Delinquent; Student—High School)
Rising Water - P.J. Petersen   *m*   1148

Marshall (Brother; 2-Year-Old)
Elisa Michaels, Bigger & Better - Johanna Hurwitz   *e*   702

Marshall (Snake)
Snakes Don't Miss Their Mothers - M.E. Kerr   *e, m*   783

Marshall, Gabe (6th Grader; Bully)
Dork on the Run - Carol Gorman   *e, m*   543

Marshall, James (Military Personnel)
Hear the Wind Blow: A Novel of the Civil War - Mary Downing Hahn   *m*   581

Marta (Cow)
Marta and the Bicycle - Germano Zullo   *p*   1497

Martha (4-Year-Old; Sister)
Old Crump: The True Story of a Trip West - Laurie Lawlor   *p*   859

Martha (Child; Friend)
What Shall We Play? - Sue Heap   *p*   618

Martin (Teacher; Bird)
Froggy Plays in the Band - Jonathan London   *p*   906

Martin (Teacher)
Substitute Teacher Plans - Doug Johnson   *p*   746

Martin, Guy "Speedy" (13-Year-Old; Hero)
Sidekicks - Dan Danko   *m*   342

Martin, Leandra (7-Year-Old; Friend)
Tippy Lemmey - Patricia C. McKissack   *e*   986

Martin, Michael/Jinsen "Buddha Boy" (10th Grader; Artist)
Buddha Boy - Kathe Koja   *m, h*   811

Martin, Raymond (4th Grader; Friend)
Herbie Jones Moves On - Suzy Kline   *e*   805

Martinez, Adelita Mercado (Stepdaughter; Servant)
Adelita: A Mexican Cinderella Story - Tomie De Paola   *p*   358

Marty (Child; Son)
Find-a-Saurus - Mark Sperring   *p*   1324

Mary (Child)
Mary Had a Little Ham - Margie Palatini   *p*   1123

Mary (Religious)
Who Owns Kelly Paddik? - Beth Goobie   *m, h*   537

Mary Claire (Child; Friend)
Four Friends Together - Sue Heap   *p*   617

Mary Francis (Principal; Religious)
Run from the Nun! - Erin MacLellan   *e, m*   931

Mary Louise (Mother)
The Crying Rocks - Janet Taylor Lisle   *m, h*   901

Massimo "The Thief Lord", Scipio (13-Year-Old; Wealthy)
The Thief Lord - Cornelia Funke   *m, h*   500

Mateo (Son; Artisan)
Dream Carver - Diana Cohn   *p*   271

Matherson, Dana (Student—Middle School; Bully)
Hoot - Carl Hiaasen   *m, h*   637

Matt (17-Year-Old; Father)
Mahalia - Joanne Horniman   *h*   679

Matt (Child; Friend)
What Shall We Play? - Sue Heap   *p*   618

McVeigh, Jasey (15-Year-Old)
Saving Jasey - Diane Tullson   m, h   1387

McVeigh, Tristan "Trist" (8th Grader)
Saving Jasey - Diane Tullson   m, h   1387

Meade, Emma (Friend)
Dear Emma - Johanna Hurwitz   e, m   701

Meadowsweet (Mythical Creature)
The Kingfisher's Gift - Susan Williams Beckhorn   e, m   96

Mean Jean (Student—Elementary School; Bully)
The Recess Queen - Alexis O'Neill   p   1110

Medea (Wizard)
Celtika - Robert Holdstock   h, a   664

Meeks, Kyle (Homosexual; 12th Grader)
Rainbow High - Alex Sanchez   h   1262

Meggie (9-Year-Old; Daughter)
The Berry-Picking Man - Jane Buchanan   e   175

Meggie (12-Year-Old)
Inkheart - Cornelia Funke   m, h   499

Mei Lin (Student)
Someone Says - Carole Lexa Schaefer   p   1268

Mei Mei (Orphan; Young Woman)
Bitter Dumplings - Jeanne M. Lee   p   870

Mei Mei (Child; Friend)
Chang and the Bamboo Flute - Elizabeth Starr Hill   e   640

Mei Mei (Child)
Daisy Comes Home - Jan Brett   p   144

Mel (Student—Elementary School; Brother)
Lenny and Mel - Erik P. Kraft   e   823

Mel (Brother; Twin)
Lenny and Mel's Summer Vacation - Erik P. Kraft   e   824

Melden (Mouse; Friend)
The Saturday Escape - Daniel J. Mahoney   p   934

Mellon, Sidney T. (12-Year-Old)
Melonhead - Michael de Guzman   m   354

Mender, Alan "Frosty" (17-Year-Old; Criminal)
Inside Out - Terry Trueman   h   1386

Mender, Joseph "Stormy" (14-Year-Old; Criminal)
Inside Out - Terry Trueman   h   1386

Menelaus (Royalty; Spouse)
Goddess of Yesterday - Caroline B. Cooney   m, h   292

Mennus, Hiril (Mole; Scientist)
Time Stops for No Mouse - Michael Hoeye   m, h   657

Menuto, Penelope "PenPen" (Aged Person; Twin)
The Canning Season - Polly Horvath   m, h   683

Menuto, Tilly (Aged Person; Twin)
The Canning Season - Polly Horvath   m, h   683

Mer-Princess (Mythical Creature; Royalty)
Princess Fishtail - Frances Minters   p   1017

Merahb (Military Personnel; Father)
Flame - Hilari Bell   m, h   97

Mercer, Adam (Uncle; Mentally Ill Person)
A Corner of the Universe - Ann M. Martin   m   945

Mercer, Asa (Businessman)
The Voyage of the Continental - Katherine Kirkpatrick   m   801

Mercer, Jared (9th Grader)
The Shadow Club Rising - Neal Shusterman   m, h   1298

Mercer-Nichols, Nora (Stepmother; Teacher)
Zipped - Laura McNeal   h   996

Meret (Royalty; 14-Year-Old)
The Ugly Goddess - Elsa Marston   m   944

Merle (Blind Person; Mother)
Song for Eloise - Leigh Sauerwein   h   1264

Merlin (Wizard)
Celtika - Robert Holdstock   h, a   664

Merlinnus (Wizard)
Sword of the Rightful King: A Novel of King Arthur - Jane Yolen   m, h   1486

Mertslin, Tucka (Mouse; Businesswoman)
Time Stops for No Mouse - Michael Hoeye   m, h   657

Meryk, Dayle (11th Grader; 17-Year-Old)
Out of the Fire - Deborah Froese   m, h   497

Metzger, Kyle (Bully)
The Pack - Elisa Carbone   m, h   214

Miao Jie (Wealthy)
The Kite Rider - Geraldine McCaughrean   m, h   965

Micah (Orphan; Singer)
A Company of Fools - Deborah Ellis   m   427

Michael (12-Year-Old)
Kensuke's Kingdom - Michael Morpurgo   e, m   1033

Michaela "Mike" (14-Year-Old)
Looking for Red - Angela Johnson   m, h   743

Michaels, Elisa (7-Year-Old; 2nd Grader)
Elisa Michaels, Bigger & Better - Johanna Hurwitz   e   702

Michaels, Keely (10-Year-Old; Student—Elementary School)
Because of Anya - Margaret Peterson Haddix   e   579

Michelle (Sister)
The Long Night of Leo and Bree - Ellen Wittlinger   m, h   1453

Mickey (Dog)
Zoe Sophia's Scrapbook: An Adventure in Venice - Claudia Mauner   p   957

Middle One (Sister; Daughter)
The Witch's Children - Ursula Jones   p   758

Middlebrook, Russel (10th Grader; Homosexual)
Geography Club - Brent Hartinger   h   602

Miggory Sow "Mig" (Servant; 12-Year-Old)
The Tale of Despereaux: Being the Story of a Mouse, a Princess, Some Soup, and a Spool of Thread - Kate DiCamillo   e   381

Mighty Robot (Robot)
Ricky Ricotta's Mighty Robot vs. the Jurassic Jackrabbits from Jupiter - Dav Pilkey   e   1154
Ricky Ricotta's Mighty Robot vs. the Mecha-Monkeys from Mars - Dav Pilkey   e   1155

Miles "Little Man" (Son; Child)
Bippity Bop Barbershop - Natasha Anastasia Tarpley   p   1362

Milfoil "Mom" (Mother; Cow)
Our Twitchy - Kes Gray   p   551

Milgrom, Janina (Child)
Milkweed - Jerry Spinelli   m, h   1326

Miller (Teacher)
The Hard-Times Jar - Ethel Footman Smothers   p   1317

Miller, Andrew (11-Year-Old; Baseball Player)
Jason Rat-a-Tat - Colby Rodowsky   e   1220

Miller, Catherine (17-Year-Old)
The Presence: A Ghost Story - Eve Bunting   m, h   181

Miller, Collin (Teenager)
The Presence: A Ghost Story - Eve Bunting   m, h   181

Miller, Emily (6-Year-Old; Soccer Player)
Jason Rat-a-Tat - Colby Rodowsky   e   1220

Miller, Frank P. (Father; Convict)
Ruby Electric - Theresa Nelson   m   1074

Miller, Jason (9-Year-Old; Brother)
Jason Rat-a-Tat - Colby Rodowsky   e   1220

Miller, Marjory (9-Year-Old; Daughter)
Berta: A Remarkable Dog - Celia Barker Lottridge   e   908

Miller, Martin J. "Marty" (16-Year-Old; Runaway)
Ten Miles from Winnemucca - Thelma Hatch Wyss   m, h   1472

Miller, Mom (Mother)
Ten Miles from Winnemucca - Thelma Hatch Wyss   m, h   1472

Miller, Pete (Brother; Child)
Ruby Electric - Theresa Nelson   m   1074

Miller, Randall "Chubby" (8th Grader)
Someday: A Novel - Jackie French Koller   m   815

Miller, Ruby (12-Year-Old; 7th Grader)
Ruby Electric - Theresa Nelson   m   1074

Mills, Edward "Cap" (Aged Person)
Handbook for Boys: A Novel - Walter Dean Myers   m, h   1053

Milly (Immigrant; Child)
Milly and the Macy's Parade - Shana Corey   p   303

Milo (Penguin; Postal Worker)
Penguin Post - Debi Gliori   p   532

Mim (Mother; Archaeologist)
Timespinners - Luli Gray   e   552

Mimi (Doll; Bully)
The Meanest Doll in the World - Ann M. Martin   e   946

Min (Lesbian; 10th Grader)
Geography Club - Brent Hartinger   h   602

Minette, Alma (Cousin)
A Time for Courage: The Suffragette Diary of Kathleen Bowen, Washington, DC, 1917 - Kathryn Lasky   e, m   857

Mingo (Friend; Runaway)
Flying Free: Corey's Underground Railroad Diary - Sharon Dennis Wyeth   e   1471

Minn (5th Grader; Friend)
Minn and Jake - Janet S. Wong   e   1456

Minnie (Student—Elementary School; Friend)
I'm Not Invited? - Diane Cain Bluthenthal   p   121

Minnie (Cow)
Minnie and Moo and the Potato from Planet X - Denys Cazet   b   233
Minnie and Moo and the Seven Wonders of the World - Denys Cazet   b   234
Minnie and Moo: The Night Before Christmas - Denys Cazet   b   235

Minou, Colleen "Stoner" (16-Year-Old; Addict)
Stoner & Spaz - Ron Koertge   h   810

Minsky (Neighbor; Driver)
When Catherine the Great and I Were Eight! - Cari Best   p   107

Mint, Angie (12-Year-Old)
The Poltergoose - Michael Lawrence   e, m   862

Minton (Governess)
Journey to the River Sea - Eva Ibbotson   m   707

Minuk (12-Year-Old)
Minuk: Ashes in the Pathway - Kirkpatrick Hill   e, m   641

Mipeng (Cousin)
The Kite Rider - Geraldine McCaughrean   m, h   965

Mirabelle (Doll)
Mirabelle - Astrid Lindgren   p   896

Miranda (Object)
Otto: The Story of a Mirror - Ali Bahrampour   p   64

Mischief, John (Mythical Creature)
Abarat - Clive Barker   h   80

Mitchell, Trevor (Soccer Player)
Vampire Kisses - Ellen Schreiber   m, h   1271

Mitchell, Zora (Friend)
Begging for Change - Sharon G. Flake   m, h   458

Mo (Monkey)
Monkey Mo Goes to Sea - Diane Goode   p   538

Mo "Silvertongue" (Father)
Inkheart - Cornelia Funke   m, h   499

Mocenigo, Andriana (Sister)
Daughter of Venice - Donna Jo Napoli   m, h   1060

Mocenigo, Donata Aurelia (Twin; 14-Year-Old)
Daughter of Venice - Donna Jo Napoli   m, h   1060

Mocenigo, Laura (Twin; 14-Year-Old)
Daughter of Venice - Donna Jo Napoli   m, h   1060

Moffat "Moffie" (Dog; Sister)
A New Barker in the House - Tomie De Paola   p   359

Mogget (Cat)
Abhorsen - Garth Nix   m, h   1084

Mokie "Little Pig-Girl" (Orphan)
Pig Tale - Verlyn Flieger   h   466

Mole (Mole; Rescuer)
Mole and the Baby Bird - Marjorie Newman   p   1076

Molloy, Jack (10-Year-Old)
The Rudest Alien on Earth - Jane Leslie Conly   e, m   286

Molly (Mouse; Sister)
The Ghost of P.S. 42 - Frank Asch   e   45

Molly (Child; Daughter)
Tatty Ratty - Helen Cooper   p   295

Mom (Mother; Robot)
Big Time Olie - William Joyce   p   762

Mom (Mother; Storyteller)
The Broken Cat - Lynne Rae Perkins   p   1146

Mom (Mother)
By the Side of the Road - Jules Feiffer   p   446
The Difference Between Babies & Cookies - Mary Hanson   p   591
Ebb & Flo and the Baby Seal - Jane Simmons   p   1304

Mom (Mother; Dog)
First Day - Joan Rankin   p   1184

Mom (Mother)
First Day - Dandi Daley Mackall   p   928
Gus and Grandpa Go Fishing - Claudia Mills   b   1015

Mom (Mother; Singer)
Just One More Story - Jennifer Brutschy   p   173

Mom (Mother; Spouse)
The Key to My Heart - Nira Harel   p   593

Mom (Pig; Mother)
Lucille Camps In - Kathryn Lasky   p   854

Mom (Mother)
Meow Means Mischief - Ann Whitehead Nagda   e   1055

Mom (Mother; Gardener)
No More Vegetables! - Nicole Rubel   p   1236

Mom (Mother; Cat)
Pizza Kittens - Charlotte Voake   p   1401

Mom (Mother; Spouse)
Prairie Summer - Bonnie Geisert   e   516
Tatty Ratty - Helen Cooper   p   295

Mom (Mother)
The Terrible Underpants - Kaz Cooke   p   290
That Makes Me Mad! - Steven Kroll   p   830

Momma (Mother)
Johnny Mutton, He's So Him! - James Proimos   e   1174

Mommy (Mother)
Best Kind of Baby - Kate Laing   p   846

Mommy (Mother; Spouse)
I Am NOT Going to School Today! - Robie H. Harris   p   599

Mommy (Mother)
I Used to Be the Baby - Robin Ballard   p   71
Jethro Byrd, Fairy Child - Bob Graham   p   544

Mommy (Teenager)
The Kindling - Jennifer Armstrong   m, h   38

Mommy (Pig; Mother)
Olivia . . . and the Missing Toy - Ian Falconer   p   441

Mommy (Mother)
What James Likes Best - Amy Schwartz   p   1272

Mommy (Mother; Spouse)
When Mommy Was Mad - Lynne Jonell   p   756

Momo (Monkey; Brother)
No More Kissing! - Emma Chichester Clark   p   246

Mona (Student—High School)
Looking for Red - Angela Johnson   m, h   743

Monaghan, Dennis (14-Year-Old)
My Life and Death by Alexandra Canarsie - Susan Heyboer O'Keefe   m, h   1105

Monari, Sofia (9-Year-Old; Immigrant)
Home at Last - Kathryn Lasky   e   852
Hope in My Heart - Kathryn Lasky   e   853

Monday (Supernatural Being)
Mister Monday - Garth Nix   m, h   1085

Mondini, Lisa (Basketball Player)
House of Sports - Marisabina Russo   m   1240

Monk (18-Year-Old; Sister)
A Cool Moonlight - Angela Johnson   e, m   741

Monkey (Monkey)
Water Hole Waiting - Jane Kurtz   p   838

Monkey (Monkey; Alien)
Ricky Ricotta's Mighty Robot vs. the Mecha-Monkeys from Mars - Dav Pilkey   e   1155

Monkey King (Monkey; Trickster)
The Magical Monkey King: Mischief in Heaven - Ji-Li Jiang   e   738

Monnie (Grandmother)
Sweet By and By - Patricia Hermes   e, m   629

Monroe, Howie (Dog; Writer)
Howie Monroe and the Doghouse of Doom - James Howe   e   687
It Came from Beneath the Bed - James Howe   e   688

Monroe, Pete (11-Year-Old; 6th Grader)
It Came from Beneath the Bed - James Howe   e   688

Monroe, Toby (Child)
Howie Monroe and the Doghouse of Doom - James Howe   e   687

Montana, Eustace Shackleford (Dog)
The Dirty Cowboy - Amy Timberlake   p   1382

Montgomery, Shirley (12-Year-Old)
Zulu Dog - Anton Ferreira   e, m   450

Montmount, Percival Sr. (Anthropologist)
Tribes - Arthur Slade   h   1309

Montmount, Percival "Percy" Jr. (17-Year-Old)
Tribes - Arthur Slade   h   1309

Moo (Cow)
Minnie and Moo and the Potato from Planet X - Denys Cazet   b   233
Minnie and Moo and the Seven Wonders of the World - Denys Cazet   e   234
Minnie and Moo: The Night Before Christmas - Denys Cazet   b   235

Moo Cow (Cow; Kidnap Victim)
Moo Cow Kaboom! - Thacher Hurd   p   697

Moody, Betty (Student—Elementary School; Friend)
Utterly Me, Clarice Bean - Lauren Child   e   249

Moody, Derek (Brother; Runaway)
Missing - Catherine MacPhail   m   933

Moody, Judy (3rd Grader; Sister)
Judy Moody Saves the World! - Megan McDonald   e   976

Moody, Maxine "Maxie" (13-Year-Old)
Missing - Catherine MacPhail   m   933

Moody, Stink (7-Year-Old; Brother)
Judy Moody Saves the World! - Megan McDonald   e   976

Moon, Rosie (15-Year-Old; Runaway)
Guitar Highway Rose - Brigid Lowry   h   910

Moore, Alfie (Aged Person)
Pool Boy - Michael Simmons   m, h   1305

Moore, Amanda (Twin)
Dish Series - Diane Muldrow   e, m   1037

Moore, Eliza (Widow(er))
Together Apart - Dianne E. Gray   m, h   550

Moore, Logan (14-Year-Old)
The Last Dog on Earth - Daniel Ehrenhaft   m, h   424

Moore, Marcus (Child)
When Marcus Moore Moved In - Rebecca Bond   p   123

Moore, Molly (Twin; 11-Year-Old)
Dish Series - Diane Muldrow   e, m   1037

Moose (Moose)
Snow - Manya Stojic   p   1346

Morales, Claudio "Mister M" (Aged Person)
Handbook for Boys: A Novel - Walter Dean Myers   m, h   1053

Morales, Gabi (3rd Grader; Daughter)
A Crazy, Mixed-Up Spanglish Day - Marisa Montes   e   1024

Moreno, Frank (12-Year-Old; Brother)
Keeper of the Night - Kimberly Willis Holt   m, h   669

Moreno, Isabel (13-Year-Old; 8th Grader)
Keeper of the Night - Kimberly Willis Holt   m, h   669

Moreno, Olivia (Sister; Child)
Keeper of the Night - Kimberly Willis Holt   m, h   669

Moreno, Tata (Father; Fisherman)
Keeper of the Night - Kimberly Willis Holt   m, h   669

Morey, Sairy (Aged Person; Artisan)
Ruby Holler - Sharon Creech   e, m   313

Morey, Tiller (Aged Person; Artisan)
Ruby Holler - Sharon Creech   e, m   313

Morgan (12-Year-Old)
Lucy Was There . . . - Jean Van Leeuwen   e, m   1393

Morgan, Alyssa (6th Grader)
The Invisible Enemy - Marthe Jocelyn   e, m   740

Morgan, Angel (11-Year-Old)
The Same Stuff as Stars - Katherine Paterson   m   1128

Morgan, Anne-Marie (12th Grader; Cheerleader)
Faith Wish - James Bennett   h   102

Morgan, Bernie (Child)
The Same Stuff as Stars - Katherine Paterson   m   1128

Morgan, Daniel (Explorer)
Maata's Journal - Paul Sullivan   m, h   1353

Morgan, Kent (12-Year-Old)
Skinny-Dipping at Monster Lake - Bill Wallace   m   1406

Morgan, Ray (Uncle)
The Same Stuff as Stars - Katherine Paterson   m   1128

Morgan, Verna (Mother)
The Same Stuff as Stars - Katherine Paterson   m   1128

Morgan, Wayne (Father; Convict)
The Same Stuff as Stars - Katherine Paterson   m   1128

Morgan "Morgie" (Dog; Brother)
A New Barker in the House - Tomie De Paola   p   359

Morgause (Mother; Wizard)
Sword of the Rightful King: A Novel of King Arthur - Jane Yolen   m, h   1486

Morningstar (Demon)
Fallen Host - Lyda Morehouse   h, a   1031

Morpeth (Dwarf)
The Doomspell - Cliff McNish   m   997

Morris (Mouse; Student)
Horace and Morris Join the Chorus (but what about Dolores?) - James Howe   p   686

Morris (Child; Friend)
Morris the Artist - Lore Segal   p   1276

Morris, Erin (12-Year-Old)
A Taste of Perfection - Laura Langston   m   849

Morrisey, Matthew (15-Year-Old; Orphan)
Bone Dry - Kathleen Karr   m   766

Morrow, Fanny (12-Year-Old)
The Kingfisher's Gift - Susan Williams Beckhorn   e, m   96

Mort "GUM" (Uncle)
United Tates of America - Paula Danziger   e, m   347

Moscovitz, Lilly (9th Grader; Entertainer)
Princess in Love - Meg Cabot   m, h   197

Moscovitz, Michael (12th Grader)
Princess in Love - Meg Cabot   m, h   197

Moses (Brother; Deaf Person)
Moses Goes to the Circus - Isaac Millman   p   1012

Moshi (Cat)
Elizabeti's School - Stephanie Stuve-Bodeen   p   1352

Moskowitz, Michael (Boyfriend)
Princess in Waiting - Meg Cabot   m, h   198

Mossbach, Matthew "Mouse" (7th Grader; Sidekick)
Ruby Electric - Theresa Nelson   m   1074

Mother (Store Owner; Cook)
Apple Pie 4th of July - Janet S. Wong   p   1455

Mother (Mythical Creature)
Coraline - Neil Gaiman   m   502

Mother (Mother; Seamstress)
Homespun Sarah - Verla Kay   p   771

Mother (Frog; Mother)
Let's Clean Up! - Peggy Perry Anderson   p   30

Mother (Mother)
She Did It! - Jennifer A. Ericsson   p   436

Mother (Immigrant)
When the Emperor Was Divine - Julie Otsuka   h, a   1120

Mother Earth (Mythical Creature)
When the Root Children Wake Up - Audrey Wood   p   1458

Mother Wolf (Wolf; Mother)
The Wolf Who Cried Boy - Bob Hartman   p   603

Motion, Lili (Sister)
Locomotion - Jacqueline Woodson   e, m   1466

Motion, Lonnie Collins "Locomotion" (11-Year-Old; Orphan)
Locomotion - Jacqueline Woodson   e, m   1466

Mouse (Mouse)
Alphabet under Construction - Denise Fleming   p   464
Bear Snores On - Karma Wilson   p   1449

Mouse (Foundling)
The Dark Horse - Marcus Sedgwick   m   1275

Mouse (Mouse)
Duck on a Bike - David Shannon   p   1283

Mouse (Computer Expert)
Fallen Host - Lyda Morehouse   h, a   1031

Mouse (Mouse)
Merry Christmas, Big Hungry Bear! - Don Wood   p   1459

Mouse (Mouse; Friend)
My Friend Rabbit - Eric Rohmann   p   1222

Mouse (Child; Apprentice)
The Puppeteer's Apprentice - D. Anne Love   e, m   909

Mouse (Mouse; Father)
Christmas in the City - Loretta Krupinski   p   836

Mouse (Mouse; Mother)
Christmas in the City - Loretta Krupinski   p   836

Mouse, Tom (Mouse; Traveler)
Tom Mouse - Ursula K. Le Guin   p   867

Mouse Man (Aged Person; Trickster)
The Marvelous Mouse Man - Mary Ann Hoberman   p   654

Moustro Provolone (Mouse; Teacher)
Horace and Morris Join the Chorus (but what about Dolores?) - James Howe   p   686

Mugwort (Doctor; Frog)
Froggy Goes to the Doctor - Jonathan London   p   905

Muldoon (Dog)
Muldoon - Pamela Duncan Edwards   p   419

Mulholland, Lucien "Luciano" (Time Traveler; Cancer Patient)
City of Masks - Mary Hoffman   m, h   661

Mulholland, Lucien "Luciano" (Time Traveler)
City of Stars - Mary Hoffman   m, h   662

Mullen, Elizabeth "Buddy" (9th Grader; 13-Year-Old)
Waiting to Disappear - April Young Fritz   m, h   496

Muller, Jimmy (14-Year-Old)
My Life and Death by Alexandra Canarsie - Susan Heyboer O'Keefe   m, h   1105

Mulligan, Rose (12th Grader)
Flavor of the Week - Tucker Shaw   m, h   1288

Mum (Mother; Spouse)
The Quigleys - Simon Mason   e   952
The Quigleys at Large - Simon Mason   e   953

Mumbo (Elephant)
Thanks, Mom - Ed Emberley   p   433

Mumkey (Mother; Chimpanzee)
Chimp and Zee and the Big Storm - Laurence Anholt   p   31

Mummy (Mother)
Monsoon - Uma Krishnaswami   p   829

Mump (Hippopotamus; Child-Care Giver)
Shirley's Wonderful Baby - Valiska Gregory   p   560

Muno (Orphan)
The Wolving Time - Patrick Jennings   m, h   735

Murphy (Dog; Narrator)
A Day in the Life of Murphy - Alice Provensen   p   1176

Murphy (Bird)
Flying Blind - Anna Myers   e, m   1049

Mutton, Johnny (Sheep; Student—Elementary School)
Johnny Mutton, He's So Him! - James Proimos   e   1174

Mylnarski, Todd (Editor)
Saving the Planet & Stuff - Gail Gauthier   m, h   511

N

Nadine (9th Grader)
Girls in Love - Jacqueline Wilson   m, h   1448

Nana (Grandmother)
House of Sports - Marisabina Russo   m   1240

Nancy (Child)
Raspberries on the Yangtze - Karen Wallace   m   1408

Nanny (Child-Care Giver)
Eloise Takes a Bawth - Kay Thompson   p   1379

Napoleon "Mullet Fingers" (Stepbrother; Runaway)
Hoot - Carl Hiaasen   m, h   637

Nara, Mari (Driver; Young Woman)
Noodle Man: The Pasta Superhero - April Pulley Sayre   m   1266

Natsworthy, Tom (15-Year-Old; Orphan)
Mortal Engines - Philip Reeve   h, a   1195

Neal (Animal Lover; Cancer Patient)
Jackie's Wild Seattle - Will Hobbs   m   652

Nebuchadnezzer "Ben" (Immortal)
The Angel's Command: A Tale from the Castaways of the Flying Dutchman - Brian Jacques   m, h   722

Nebula, Ralph (Brother; Camper)
Fat Camp Commandos Go West - Daniel Pinkwater   e   1159

Nebula, Sylvia (Sister; Camper)
Fat Camp Commandos Go West - Daniel Pinkwater   e   1159

Neddy (Military Personnel; Runaway)
Numbering All the Bones - Ann Rinaldi   m, h   1205

Neel (Child; Nephew)
Chachaji's Cup - Uma Krishnaswami   p   828

Neidermeyer, Peggy (6th Grader; Bully)
Agnes Parker . . . Girl in Progress - Kathleen O'Dell   e, m   1103

Neko Roshi (Cat; Warrior)
Three Samurai Cats: A Story from Japan - Eric A. Kimmel   *p*   789

Nelia (Lesbian)
Gravel Queen - Tea Benduhn   *h*   101

Nelson, Ingrid (13-Year-Old)
Room in the Heart - Sonia Levitin   *m, h*   886

Nelson, Niels (15-Year-Old; Resistance Fighter)
Room in the Heart - Sonia Levitin   *m, h*   886

Neptune (Dog)
Alicia's Best Friends - Lisa Jahn-Clough   *p*   724

Nera (Stepmother; Courtier)
The Courtesan's Daughter - Priscilla Galloway   *h*   505

Nergal (1st Grader; Alien)
First Graders from Mars: Episode 3: Nergal and the Great Space Race - Shana Corey   *e*   302

Nesbitt, Clementine "Clem" (13-Year-Old)
Flight of the Fisherbird - Nora Martin   *e, m*   949

Newton (Rabbit; Cousin)
What a Hat! - Holly Keller   *p*   778

Next, Thursday (Detective)
The Eyre Affair: A Novel - Jasper Fforde   *h, a*   453

Next, Thursday (Detective; Spouse)
Lost in a Good Book - Jasper Fforde   *h, a*   454

Ngugu, Vusi (11-Year-Old)
Zulu Dog - Anton Ferreira   *e, m*   450

Nicholas (Kidnapper)
Deep - Susanna Vance   *m, h*   1394

Nichols, Mick (15-Year-Old)
Zipped - Laura McNeal   *h*   996

Nick (Student—High School)
Prep - Jake Coburn   *h*   266

Nicol, James "Jamie" (Stepfather)
Where in the World - Simon French   *m*   491

Nicole (Child)
What the Birds See - Sonya Hartnett   *m, h*   604

Nicolson, Frank (Explorer)
Maata's Journal - Paul Sullivan   *m, h*   1353

Nicolson, Georgia (Student—High School)
Dancing in My Nuddy-Pants: Even Further Confessions of Georgia Nicolson - Louise Rennison   *m, h*   1198

Nicolson, Georgia (15-Year-Old)
Knocked Out by My Nunga-Nungas: Further, Further Confessions of Georgia Nicolson - Louise Rennison   *m, h*   1199

Nigel (Knight)
The Leopard Sword - Michael Cadnum   *m, h*   201

Nike, Hack (Office Worker)
Jennifer Government - Max Barry   *h, a*   85

Nike, John (Businessman)
Jennifer Government - Max Barry   *h, a*   85

Nikki (Sister; Dancer)
Brianna, Jamaica, and the Dance of Spring - Juanita Havill   *p*   612

Nikolai (Friend; Child)
The Three Questions - Jon J. Muth   *p*   1048

Nina (Daughter; Sister)
That Makes Me Mad! - Steven Kroll   *p*   830

Njemile (Mother)
The Village That Vanished - Ann Grifalconi   *p*   561

Noah (Grandfather; Biblical Figure)
Annie's Ark - Lesley Harker   *p*   594

Noah (Homosexual; Student—High School)
Boy Meets Boy - David Levithan   *h*   885

Noah (Biblical Figure)
Little Scraggly Hair: A Dog on Noah's Ark - Lynn Cullen   *p*   324

Noah (Aged Person; Biblical Figure)
Noah's Ark - Jerry Pinkney   *p*   1158

Noe (Teenager)
Daughter of Venice - Donna Jo Napoli   *m, h*   1060

Nora (Student; Mouse)
Timothy's Tales from Hilltop School - Rosemary Wells   *p*   1428

Norris (Brother; Hero)
Rowan and the Ice Creepers - Emily Rodda   *e*   1217

North, Wenny (Child; Sister)
Wenny Has Wings - Janet Lee Carey   *e, m*   216

North, Will (11-Year-Old)
Wenny Has Wings - Janet Lee Carey   *e, m*   216

Nozzet (Principal)
Matthew A.B.C. - Peter Catalanotto   *p*   229

Nunn, Ike (Brother; Student—Elementary School)
The Tornado Watches - Patrick Jennings   *e*   733

Nunn, Ike (Child; Brother)
The Weeping Willow - Patrick Jennings   *e*   734

Nunn, Mem (Sister; Student)
The Tornado Watches - Patrick Jennings   *e*   733

Nunn, Mem (Child; Sister)
The Weeping Willow - Patrick Jennings   *e*   734

O

Oats, Christopher "Quaker" (12th Grader; Pacifist)
God of Beer - Garret Keizer   *h*   775

O'Brien, Clay (Father)
Prairie Whispers - Frances Arrington   *m*   43

O'Brien, Mary Kathleen (Mother)
Prairie Whispers - Frances Arrington   *m*   43

O'Connell, Sarah (15-Year-Old; Friend)
One Shot - Susan Glick   *m, h*   529

O'Connor, Carrie (10-Year-Old; Actress)
A Simple Gift - Nancy Ruth Patterson   *e*   1129

O'Connor, Mary (Artist)
Rat - Jan Cheripko   *m, h*   242

O'Connor, Molly (Student—Middle School)
True Blue - Jeffrey Lee   *e, m*   871

O'Connor, Patrick (Coach; Teacher)
Rat - Jan Cheripko   *m, h*   242

O'Connor, Rick (Handicapped)
True Blue - Jeffrey Lee   *e, m*   871

Octavia (Girlfriend)
Getting the Girl - Markus Zusak   *h*   1498

O'Dere, Aidan (Slave)
Lion's Blood: A Novel of Slavery and Freedom in an Alternate America - Steven Barnes   *h, a*   81
Zulu Heart - Steven Barnes   *h, a*   82

O'Doyle, Brendan (Child)
Hobbledy-Clop - Pat Brisson   *p*   155

Odysseus (Hero; Leader)
The One-Eyed Giant - Mary Pope Osborne   *e*   1118

O'Grady, Georgia "Giorgia Gredi" (Time Traveler)
City of Stars - Mary Hoffman   *m, h*   662

Oh, Ji Eun (7th Grader)
Mind Games - Jeanne Marie Grunwell   *m*   567

O'Hannigan, Hannah Mae (Cowgirl; Daughter)
Hannah Mae O'Hannigan's Wild West Show - Lisa Campbell Ernst   *p*   437

O'Hara, Charley (1st Grader; Neighbor)
Leap, Frog - Jane Cutler   *e*   332

Ojala, Matti (15-Year-Old; Miner)
Song of Sampo Lake - William Durbin   *m, h*   411

Ojala, Timo (Brother)
Song of Sampo Lake - William Durbin   *m, h*   411

Oksi (Bird; Daughter)
Frightful's Daughter - Jean Craighead George   *p*   518

Olaf (Royalty; Father)
Serious Trouble - Arthur Howard   *p*   684

Olafsson, Sigurd "Sig" (16-Year-Old)
The Dark Horse - Marcus Sedgwick   *m*   1275

Old Badger (Badger; Grandfather)
Little Badger's Just-About Birthday - Eve Bunting   *p*   179

Old Berta (Wizard)
Ravine - Janet Hickman   *m*   638

Old Bob (Grandfather; Aged Person)
Old Bob's Brown Bear - Niki Daly   *p*   340

Old Cricket (Cricket; Spouse)
Old Cricket - Lisa Wheeler   *p*   1434

Old Crow (Crow)
Old Cricket - Lisa Wheeler   *p*   1434

Old Crump (Ox)
Old Crump: The True Story of a Trip West - Laurie Lawlor   *p*   859

Old Granny (Aged Person; Grandmother)
Old Granny and the Bean Thief - Cynthia DeFelice   *p*   366

Old MacDonald (Sheep; Carpenter)
Old MacDonald Had a Woodshop - Lisa Shulman   *p*   1296

Old Sam (Aged Person; Mentally Ill Person)
The Berry-Picking Man - Jane Buchanan   *e*   175

Olive (Royalty; Mother)
Serious Trouble - Arthur Howard   *p*   684

Oliver (Cat)
Night Cat - Margaret Beames   *p*   92

Oliver (Bear; Son)
Oliver Finds His Way - Phyllis Root   *p*   1228

Olivia (2nd Grader)
The Best Class Picture Ever! - Denis Roche   *p*   1214

Olivia (Pig)
Olivia Counts - Ian Falconer   *p*   440

Olivia (Pig; Sister)
Olivia . . . and the Missing Toy - Ian Falconer   *p*   441

Ollie (Goose; Brother)
Ollie - Olivier Dunrea   *p*   408

Oluu (Alien; Shape-Shifter)
The Rudest Alien on Earth - Jane Leslie Conly   *e, m*   286

Olympia (Royalty)
Once Upon a Marigold - Jean Ferris   *m, h*   452

Om, Baltasar (Kidnapper; Con Artist)
Colibri - Ann Cameron   *m*   206

O'Malley, Maureen (9-Year-Old; Immigrant)
Home at Last - Kathryn Lasky   *e*   852
Hope in My Heart - Kathryn Lasky   *e*   853

Omar (9th Grader)
The Pack - Elisa Carbone   *m, h*   214

Omaye (Neighbor; Aged Person)
Ghosts for Breakfast - Stanley Todd Terasaki   *p*   1374

Omi (Neighbor; Aged Person)
Ghosts for Breakfast - Stanley Todd Terasaki
   p 1374

One-Tooth (Cat)
Stuart's Cape - Sara Pennypacker   e 1144

Ono (Neighbor; Aged Person)
Ghosts for Breakfast - Stanley Todd Terasaki
   p 1374

Ooga-Mooga (Monster)
Three Nasty Gnarlies - Keith Graves   p 549

Oomor (Prehistoric Human; Friend)
Timespinners - Luli Gray   e 552

Oonagh (Sorceress)
Child of the Prophecy - Juliet Marillier   h, a 941

Opa (Grandfather)
Where in the World - Simon French   m 491

Opal (Pig; Cousin)
Toot & Puddle: Charming Opal - Holly Hobbie
   p 649

Oreg (Wizard; Dragon)
Dragon Blood - Patricia Briggs   h, a 150
Dragon Bones - Patricia Briggs   h, a 151

Orville (Child; Friend)
Agapanthus Hum and the Angel Hoot - Joy Cowley
   b 309

Orville (Dog)
Orville: A Dog Story - Haven Kimmel   p 790

Orvisen, Orvis (13-Year-Old)
How Angel Peterson Got His Name - Gary Paulsen
   m, h 1135

Oscar (Cat; Singer)
Tessa's Tip-Tapping Toes - Carolyn Crimi   p 314

O'Sullivan, Guinevere "Gwen" (Teenager)
Dunk - David Lubar   m, h 912

Otis (Dog)
Dog Eared - Amanda Harvey   p 605

Otis, Alice (Child; Sister)
Praying at the Sweetwater Motel - April Young Fritz
   m 495

Otis, Sarah Jane (12-Year-Old)
Praying at the Sweetwater Motel - April Young Fritz
   m 495

Otrere of Amazon (Royalty; Mother)
Hippolyta and the Curse of the Amazons - Jane Yolen
   m 1482

Otsego, Lucy "Lucy the Giant" (15-Year-Old;
   Runaway)
Lucy the Giant - Sherri L. Smith   m, h 1316

Otto (Object)
Otto: The Story of a Mirror - Ali Bahrampour
   p 64

Ourisman, Gina (9th Grader)
Gina.Jamie.Father.Bear - George Ella Lyon   m,
   h 920

Overall, Ebenezer (Prospector)
Gullywasher Gulch - Marianne Mitchell   p 1018

Owen (Uncle; Military Personnel)
A Doctor Like Papa - Natalie Kinsey-Warnock
   e 795

Owen (Mouse)
Owen's Marshmallow Chick - Kevin Henkes
   p 624

Owen, Hattie (12-Year-Old)
A Corner of the Universe - Ann M. Martin   m 945

Owl (Owl)
Snow - Manya Stojic   p 1346

P

Pa (Father)
A Hug Goes Around - Laura Krauss Melmed
   p 1005

Pa (Father; Farmer)
One Bright Penny - Geraldine McCaughrean
   p 967

Pa (Father; Pioneer)
Sunsets of the West - Tony Johnston   p 754

Pa (Father; Musician)
A Time to Dance - Mary Pope Osborne   e 1119

Pa (Father; Farmer)
A Twisted Tale - Carolyn Fisher   p 456

Pa Cua "Lisa" (Cousin)
Tangled Threads: A Hmong Girl's Story - Pegi Deitz
   Shea   m, h 1289

Pablito (Child; Student)
My Pig Amarillo - Satomi Ichikawa   p 709

Paddick, Kelly (15-Year-Old)
Who Owns Kelly Paddik? - Beth Goobie   m, h 537

Padilla, Chico (3rd Grader; Son)
First Day in Grapes - L. King Perez   p 1145

Page (Artificial Intelligence)
Fallen Host - Lyda Morehouse   h, a 1031

Palmer, Kate (4th Grader; Sister)
The Meanest Doll in the World - Ann M. Martin
   e 946

Pan (Mythical Creature)
The Great God Pan - Donna Jo Napoli   m, h 1062

Papa (Father)
Ghosts for Breakfast - Stanley Todd Terasaki
   p 1374

Papa (Father; Worker)
Home at Last - Susan Middleton Elya   p 431

Papa (Father)
I Dream of Trains - Angela Johnson   p 742

Papa (Father; Rabbit)
Little Rabbit Lost - Harry Horse   p 682

Papa (Father; Spouse)
Mama's Coming Home - Kate Banks   p 76

Papa (Father; Immigrant)
Milly and the Macy's Parade - Shana Corey
   p 303

Papa (Father)
Monsoon - Uma Krishnaswami   p 829

Papa (Bear; Father)
Oliver Finds His Way - Phyllis Root   p 1228

Papa (Father)
On the Town: A Community Adventure - Judith
   Caseley   p 227

Papa (Father; Immigrant)
Silent Movie - Avi   p 60

Papa (Father; Spouse)
The Snake's Tales - Marguerite W. Davol   p 353

Papa Bear (Father; Bear)
Little Brown Bear Won't Go to School! - Jane Dyer
   p 412

Papa Bear (Bear; Father)
Little Brown Bear Won't Take a Nap! - Jane Dyer
   p 413

Papa Lion (Lion; Father)
Quiet! - Paul Bright   p 153

Papakey (Father; Chimpanzee)
Chimp and Zee and the Big Storm - Laurence Anholt
   p 31

Pappy (Grandfather; Robot)
Big Time Olie - William Joyce   p 762

Paradis, Richard "Rick" (Narrator; Football Player)
Jake, Reinvented - Gordon Korman   h 816

Parakeet, Alex (9-Year-Old)
Who Is Stealing the Twelve Days of Christmas? -
   Martha Freeman   e 489

Paran, Agatha (Collector)
The Wrong One - Carol Otis Hurst   e, m 699

Paris (Lover)
Goddess of Yesterday - Caroline B. Cooney   m,
   h 292

Park, Song Lee (3rd Grader; Friend)
Horrible Harry and the Dragon War - Suzy Kline
   e 806

Parke-Laine, Landen (Writer)
The Eyre Affair: A Novel - Jasper Fforde   h, a 453

Parke-Laine, Landen (Writer; Spouse)
Lost in a Good Book - Jasper Fforde   h, a 454

Parker, Agnes (6th Grader)
Agnes Parker . . . Girl in Progress - Kathleen O'Dell
   e, m 1103

Parker, Alice (Foster Parent)
The Monster in Me - Mette Ivie Harrison   m 600

Parker, John (Foster Parent)
The Monster in Me - Mette Ivie Harrison   m 600

Parkin, Hayley (Bully)
Drowning Anna - Sue Mayfield   m, h 958

Parnell, Ella (13-Year-Old; Kidnap Victim)
Storm Catchers - Tim Bowler   m, h 129

Parnell, Fin (Teenager; Brother)
Storm Catchers - Tim Bowler   m, h 129

Parnell, Sam (Child)
Storm Catchers - Tim Bowler   m, h 129

Parsley (Young Woman; Adoptee)
For Biddle's Sake - Gail Carson Levine   e 884

Parvana (13-Year-Old)
Parvana's Journey - Deborah Ellis   m, h 429

Paski, Disha (16-Year-Old)
Planet Janet - Dyan Sheldon   m, h 1291

Paskoff, Clyde (6th Grader)
Quit It - Marcia Byalick   e, m 191

Patino, Ana (8-Year-Old; Immigrant)
Home at Last - Susan Middleton Elya   p 431

Patoot (Businessman; Father)
Puss in Cowboy Boots - Jan Huling   p 695

Patrick (8-Year-Old; Brother)
The Amazing Thinking Machine - Dennis Haseley
   e 606

Paul (10th Grader; Homosexual)
Boy Meets Boy - David Levithan   h 885

Paul (Uncle; Ranger)
Fire Storm - Jean Craighead George   p 517

Paul (Friend; 8-Year-Old)
Tippy Lemmey - Patricia C. McKissack   e 986

Paulie (16-Year-Old; Foster Child)
Say Yes - Audrey Couloumbis   m, h 306

Paulina (Royalty)
The Princess and the Pizza - Mary Jane Auch
   p 56

Paulsen, Gary (Narrator; 13-Year-Old)
How Angel Peterson Got His Name - Gary Paulsen
   m, h 1135

Paw, Elder (Cat; Grandfather)
Varjak Paw - S.F. Said   m 1250

Paw, Jalal (Cat)
Varjak Paw - S.F. Said   m 1250

Paw, Varjak (Cat)
Varjak Paw - S.F. Said   *m*   1250

Paz, Violet (15-Year-Old)
Cuba 15 - Nancy Osa   *m, h*   1115

Pea (Royalty; 12-Year-Old)
The Tale of Despereaux: Being the Story of a Mouse, a Princess, Some Soup, and a Spool of Thread - Kate DiCamillo   *e*   381

Pearce, Zachary "Zach" (17-Year-Old)
Not Quite a Stranger - Colby Rodowsky   *m, h*   1221

Pearl (Child)
Good Night, Animals - Lena Arro   *p*   44

Pearl (11th Grader)
Target - Kathleen Jeffrie Johnson   *h*   747

Pearl (Aged Person; Accident Victim)
Little Flower - Gloria Rand   *p*   1182

Pearson, Edmund (Homosexual; 18-Year-Old)
The Shell House - Linda Newbery   *h*   1075

Peck, Jane "Boston Jane" (16-Year-Old)
Boston Jane: Wilderness Days - Jennifer L. Holm   *m, h*   666

Pedersen, Joe (14-Year-Old)
Under the Same Sky - Cynthia DeFelice   *m, h*   368

Pederson, Rachel (Government Official)
The Watch - Dennis Danvers   *h, a*   344

Peerce, Isaac (Slave)
Betrayed! - Patricia Calvert   *m*   205

Pelly (1st Grader)
First Graders from Mars: Episode 2: The Problem with Pelly - Shana Corey   *b*   301

Peme (Indian)
This Vast Land: A Young Man's Journal of the Lewis and Clark Expedition - Stephen E. Ambrose   *m, h*   25

Pendo (Sister; Student)
Elizabeti's School - Stephanie Stuve-Bodeen   *p*   1352

Penelope (Royalty; Student)
Clever Lollipop - Dick King-Smith   *e*   792

Penelope (Child; Royalty)
Princess Penelope - Todd Mack   *p*   926

Penguin (Penguin)
Wish, Change, Friend - Ian Whybrow   *p*   1440

Penhaligon, Arthur (7th Grader; Adoptee)
Mister Monday - Garth Nix   *m, h*   1085

Penmarch, Robin (12-Year-Old; Apprentice)
Quadehar the Sorcerer - Erik L'Homme   *m, h*   891

Penny (Sister; Daughter)
One Bright Penny - Geraldine McCaughrean   *p*   967

Penrose, Alice (Nurse)
The Divine Wind: A Love Story - Garry Disher   *h*   384

Penrose, Hartley "Hart" (Teenager)
The Divine Wind: A Love Story - Garry Disher   *h*   384

Peony (Child; Servant)
The Dungeon - Lynne Reid Banks   *m, h*   79

Pepper, Yolanda "Yo Yo" (8th Grader)
Double Dutch - Sharon M. Draper   *m, h*   396

Percival (Royalty; Brother)
The Grail Prince - Nancy McKenzie   *h, a*   983

Percy (Child)
Among the Betrayed - Margaret Peterson Haddix   *m, h*   578

Percy (Cat; Cousin)
Practice Makes Perfect for Rotten Ralph - Jack Gantos   *b*   507

Perflinger, Linka (Mouse; Pilot)
Time Stops for No Mouse - Michael Hoeye   *m, h*   657

Perkins, Percival Lincoln "Perks" (Friend)
Grape Thief - Kristine L. Franklin   *m, h*   482

Perlain (Sailor; Adventurer)
Rowan and the Zebak - Emily Rodda   *e*   1219

Perrier (Pig)
A Pig Named Perrier - Elizabeth Spurr   *p*   1331

Perrin (Uncle; Activist)
Fresh Girl - Jaira Placide   *h*   1160

Perry (Dog)
Olivia . . . and the Missing Toy - Ian Falconer   *p*   441

Pete (Pirate)
On the Go with Pirate Pete and Pirate Joe - A.E. Cannon   *b*   211

Pete (Child; Relative)
Pete and Polo's Farmyard Adventure - Adrian Reynolds   *p*   1200

Pete (Cat)
Spy Cat - Peg Kehret   *e, m*   773
The Stranger Next Door - Peg Kehret   *e, m*   774

Peter (Rabbit; Brother)
Baby for Sale - Jackie French Koller   *p*   814

Peter (Twin)
The Bagpiper's Ghost - Jane Yolen   *e, m*   1478

Peter (Child)
The Good Little Bad Little Pig - Margaret Wise Brown   *p*   164

Peter (Religious)
The Wish List - Eoin Colfer   *m, h*   278

Peters, Rebecca (6th Grader)
Quit It - Marcia Byalick   *e, m*   191

Peters, Stan (Bully)
The Whistle, the Grave, and the Ghost - Brad Strickland   *m*   1349

Petersen, Tess (11th Grader)
The Hemingway Tradition - Kristin Butcher   *m*   186

Peterson, Carl "Angel" (13-Year-Old)
How Angel Peterson Got His Name - Gary Paulsen   *m, h*   1135

Petrovich, Slava "Cuss" (12-Year-Old; Immigrant)
Grape Thief - Kristine L. Franklin   *m, h*   482

Petrovski, Tanya (15-Year-Old)
Getting a Life - Jocelyn Shipley   *m, h*   1295

Pettigrew, Max (Baby)
Hanging on to Max - Margaret Bechard   *h*   94

Pettigrew, Sam (17-Year-Old; Single Father)
Hanging on to Max - Margaret Bechard   *h*   94

Peyton (Pig; Bully)
Pig Enough - Janie Bynum   *p*   194

Phano (14-Year-Old; Stepdaughter)
The Courtesan's Daughter - Priscilla Galloway   *h*   505

Phelps, Claire (7th Grader; Twin)
Mind Games - Jeanne Marie Grunwell   *m*   567

Phelps, Kathleen (7th Grader; Twin)
Mind Games - Jeanne Marie Grunwell   *m*   567

Philip II of Macedon (Royalty)
The Courtesan's Daughter - Priscilla Galloway   *h*   505

Phillips (Scientist)
Things Not Seen - Andrew Clements   *m*   261

Phillips, Bobby (15-Year-Old)
Things Not Seen - Andrew Clements   *m*   261

Phillips, Emily (Mother)
Things Not Seen - Andrew Clements   *m*   261

Phoebe Rose (11-Year-Old; Streetperson)
Soul Moon Soup - Lindsay Lee Johnson   *m, h*   748

Phrynion (Wealthy)
The Courtesan's Daughter - Priscilla Galloway   *h*   505

Pickett, Joe (Game Warden)
Savage Run - C.J. Box   *h, a*   130

Pickett, Marybeth (Spouse)
Savage Run - C.J. Box   *h, a*   130

Picklestain (Teacher)
My Life of Crime - Richard W. Jennings   *m*   736

Pidgeon (Teacher)
Gooney Bird Greene - Lois Lowry   *e*   911

Pierce, Cynthia Josephine "Jo" (Sister)
The Summer Country - James A. Hetley   *h, a*   634

Pierce, Maureen Anne "Mo" (Sister)
The Summer Country - James A. Hetley   *h, a*   634

Piermont, Helen (Mother)
Sister Spider Knows All - Adrian Fogelin   *m*   471

Piermont, Marilyn "Mimi" (Grandmother)
Sister Spider Knows All - Adrian Fogelin   *m*   471

Piermont, Roxanne (7th Grader; 12-Year-Old)
Sister Spider Knows All - Adrian Fogelin   *m*   471

Pierre (Boyfriend; Sailor)
Paradise - Joan Elizabeth Goodman   *m, h*   541

Pierre (Child; Relative)
Where, Where Is Swamp Bear? - Kathi Appelt   *p*   36

Pierre (Designer)
Zat Cat! A Haute Couture Tail - Chesley McLaren   *p*   987

Pierson, Christopher (Child)
Waiting for Christopher - Louise Hawes   *m, h*   613

Pierson, Francesca "Franky" (15-Year-Old)
Freaky Green Eyes - Joyce Carol Oates   *m, h*   1099

Pierson, Krista (Mother)
Freaky Green Eyes - Joyce Carol Oates   *m, h*   1099

Pierson, Reid (Television Personality; Father)
Freaky Green Eyes - Joyce Carol Oates   *m, h*   1099

Pierson, Samantha (Child; Sister)
Freaky Green Eyes - Joyce Carol Oates   *m, h*   1099

Pig (Pig; Friend)
One Rainy Day - Valeri Gorbachev   *p*   542

Pig, Jean (Aunt)
Martyn Pig - Kevin Brooks   *m, h*   160

Pig, Martyn (15-Year-Old)
Martyn Pig - Kevin Brooks   *m, h*   160

Pig, Smart (Pig; Inventor)
Porkenstein - Kathryn Lasky   *p*   856

Pig, William (Alcoholic)
Martyn Pig - Kevin Brooks   *m, h*   160

Pig Figwort (Pig)
Little Pig Figwort Can't Get to Sleep - Henrietta Branford   *p*   136

Pig of the Pig (Pig)
The Water Gift and the Pig of the Pig - Jacqueline Briggs Martin   *p*   948

Piggot, Will (Thief)
Death and the Arrow - Chris Priestley   *m, h*   1169

Quando (Wizard)
Alchemy - Margaret Mahy   *m, h*   935

Quantrill, William Clark (Historical Figure; Military Personnel)
Guerrilla Season - Pat Hughes   *m, h*   693

Queenie (Dog)
Shaper - Jessie Haas   *m*   576

Quigley, Lucy (Daughter; Sister)
The Quigleys - Simon Mason   *e*   952

Quigley, Lucy (Sister; Child)
The Quigleys at Large - Simon Mason   *e*   953

Quigley, Will (Brother; Son)
The Quigleys - Simon Mason   *e*   952

Quigley, Will (Brother; Child)
The Quigleys at Large - Simon Mason   *e*   953

Quinn (Brother)
Full Tilt: A Novel - Neal Shusterman   *m, h*   1297

Quinn, Welkin (14-Year-Old; Military Personnel)
The Earthborn - Paul Collins   *h, a*   282

R

Rabbit (Rabbit; Friend)
My Friend Rabbit - Eric Rohmann   *p*   1222

Rabinowitz, Hadassah "Dossi" (12-Year-Old; Orphan)
Dear Emma - Johanna Hurwitz   *e, m*   701

Rabinowitz, Ruth "Ruthi" (Sister; Orphan)
Dear Emma - Johanna Hurwitz   *e, m*   701

Rachel (Child)
The Doomspell - Cliff McNish   *m*   997

Rachel (Rabbit; Friend)
Four Friends Together - Sue Heap   *p*   617

Rachel (10-Year-Old; Sister)
Prairie Summer - Bonnie Geisert   *e*   516

Rachel (Student—High School; Writer)
Straydog - Kathe Koja   *m, h*   812

Rachel One (Grandmother)
Walk Softly, Rachel - Kate Banks   *m, h*   78

Rachel Three (14-Year-Old)
Walk Softly, Rachel - Kate Banks   *m, h*   78

Rachel Two (Mother)
Walk Softly, Rachel - Kate Banks   *m, h*   78

Racine, Michael Peter III (16-Year-Old; Worker)
Saving the Planet & Stuff - Gail Gauthier   *m, h*   511

Radford, Dawn (Teenager)
Getting a Life - Jocelyn Shipley   *m, h*   1295

Rafael (Brother)
The Beast - Walter Dean Myers   *h*   1051

Rafferty (12-Year-Old)
The Speed of Light - Ron Carlson   *m, h*   218

Ragnald (Traveler)
The Dark Horse - Marcus Sedgwick   *m*   1275

Raimey, Matthew "Manta" (Handicapped)
Manta's Gift - Timothy Zahn   *h, a*   1491

Ralph (Rooster; Friend)
Poultrygeist - Mary Jane Auch   *p*   55

Ralph (Cat; Cousin)
Practice Makes Perfect for Rotten Ralph - Jack Gantos   *b*   507

Ramon (Dog)
The Case of the Sleepy Sloth - Cynthia Rylant   *b*   1243

Ramose (Supernatural Being; 10-Year-Old)
The Mummy's Mother - Tony Johnston   *e*   753

Rana (Student—Elementary School)
Meow Means Mischief - Ann Whitehead Nagda   *e*   1055

Randall (Child of Divorced Parents; 3rd Grader)
The Hero of Third Grade - Alice DeLaCroix   *e*   370

Randolph (Rat; Kidnap Victim)
The Cat Who Got Carried Away - Allan Ahlberg   *e*   9

Rannulf (Knight)
The Leopard Sword - Michael Cadnum   *m, h*   201

Raoul (Religious)
The Wolving Time - Patrick Jennings   *m, h*   735

Raptor (Dog)
The Wish List - Eoin Colfer   *m, h*   278

Rashid, Kai ibn Jallaleddinibn (Nobleman)
Lion's Blood: A Novel of Slavery and Freedom in an Alternate America - Steven Barnes   *h, a*   81
Zulu Heart - Steven Barnes   *h, a*   82

Rasmussen, Nigel "Kenric" (16-Year-Old)
Heir Apparent - Vivian Vande Velde   1395

Rat (Rat)
Big Brown Bear's Up and Down Day - David McPhail   *p*   998

Rat (Apprentice; Orphan)
The Ravenmaster's Secret - Elvira Woodruff   *m*   1462

Ratnose (Teacher; Rat)
The Hamster of the Baskervilles - Bruce Hale   *e*   583

Ravenbeck, Everett (Businessman)
Jenna Starborn - Sharon Shinn   *h, a*   1294

Ravenous (Wolf)
Little Pig Is Capable - Denis Roche   *p*   1215

Rawiri (Uncle)
The Whale Rider - Witi Ihimaera   *m, h*   710

Ray, Didi (Girlfriend)
Jake, Reinvented - Gordon Korman   *h*   816

Ray, Kelly (Researcher; 19-Year-Old)
One Night - Marsha Qualey   *h*   1180

Razan, Maguda (Gypsy)
The Angel's Command: A Tale from the Castaways of the Flying Dutchman - Brian Jacques   *m, h*   722

Razz (17-Year-Old; Sports Figure)
Death Wind - William Bell   *m, h*   99

Red (Cat)
The Alley Cat's Meow - Kathi Appelt   *p*   32

Red (3rd Grader)
Doggone . . . Third Grade! - Colleen O'Shaughnessy McKenna   *e*   982

Red (17-Year-Old)
Looking for Red - Angela Johnson   *m, h*   743

Red Roger (Outlaw)
Forbidden Forest: The Story of Little John and Robin Hood - Michael Cadnum   *m, h*   200

Reed, Russell (Scientist)
When Eagles Fall - Mary Casanova   *m*   226

Reenie (Child; Narrator)
Fishing Day - Andrea Davis Pinkney   *p*   1156

Reid, Justin (Counselor; Homosexual)
Dancing Naked - Shelley Hrdlitschka   *h*   692

Reisman, Meyer (Pharmacist)
Dear Emma - Johanna Hurwitz   *e, m*   701

Rembrandt (Bear)
Rembrandt's Hat - Susan Blackaby   *p*   112

Renaldo, Amelia "Mia" (Royalty; 9th Grader)
Princess in Love - Meg Cabot   *m, h*   197

Renaldo, Amelia "Mia" (Royalty; 14-Year-Old)
Princess in Waiting - Meg Cabot   *m, h*   198

Renee (Sister)
Moses Goes to the Circus - Isaac Millman   *p*   1012

Reuben (2nd Grader; Son)
Wingwalker - Rosemary Wells   *e*   1429

Revel, Cecile (12-Year-Old)
Cecile: Gates of Gold - Mary Casanova   *e, m*   224

Rex (Dog)
Snakes Don't Miss Their Mothers - M.E. Kerr   *e, m*   783

Reynolds (Mother)
Dead Girls Don't Write Letters - Gail Giles   *m, h*   525

Reynolds, Jasmine "Jazz" (Sister)
Dead Girls Don't Write Letters - Gail Giles   *m, h*   525

Reynolds, Ruthie (9-Year-Old; Daughter)
Fairy Dust - Jane Denitz Smith   *e*   1313

Reynolds, Samantha "Sam" (16-Year-Old)
Samantha and the Cowboy - Lorraine Heath   *h*   620

Reynolds, Sunny (14-Year-Old)
Dead Girls Don't Write Letters - Gail Giles   *m, h*   525

Rhea, Olvina Alice (Chicken; Traveler)
Olvina Flies - Grace Lin   *p*   893

Rhino (Bull)
Bull Rider - Marilyn Halvorson   *m, h*   588

Rhonda (Stepsister)
Gingerbread - Rachel Cohn   *h*   272

Rhonwen (Sorceress)
Warriors of Alavna - N.M. Browne   *m, h*   168

Ricci (Aged Person)
The Slightly True Story of Cedar B. Hartley (Who Planned to Live an Unusual Life) - Martine Murray   *m*   1046

Richard (Son; Brother)
By the Side of the Road - Jules Feiffer   *p*   446
Stars in the Darkness - Barbara M. Joosse   *p*   759

Richard, IV (Royalty)
Midwinter Nightingale - Joan Aiken   *m*   13

Richmond, Paul (10th Grader)
Breaking Point - Alex Flinn   *m, h*   467

Rickman, Andrew (Child; Brother)
Falling from Fire - Teena Booth   *m, h*   126

Ricotta, Ricky (Mouse)
Ricky Ricotta's Mighty Robot vs. the Jurassic Jackrabbits from Jupiter - Dav Pilkey   *e*   1154

Ricotta, Ricky (Mouse; Friend)
Ricky Ricotta's Mighty Robot vs. the Mecha-Monkeys from Mars - Dav Pilkey   *e*   1155

Riddel, Christy (Musician)
Spirits in the Wires - Charles de Lint   *h, a*   355

Rideout, Jennifer T. (Baseball Player)
Summerland - Michael Chabon   *m, h*   236

Rider, Alexander "Alex" (14-Year-Old; Spy)
Point Blank - Anthony Horowitz   *m, h*   680
Skeleton Key - Anthony Horowitz   *m, h*   681

Ridge, Michael "Midge" (13-Year-Old; Baseball Player)
Cairo Kelly and the Mann - Kristin Butcher   *e, m*   185

Riggs, Mackenzie (11th Grader; Detective—Amateur)
The Square Root of Murder - Paul Zindel   *m*   1496

S

Saba (Child)
Ruler of the Courtyard - Rukhsana Khan   *p* 784

Sadie (Child; Relative)
The Name Quilt - Phyllis Root   *p* 1227

Safe (Dog; Traveler)
Safe and Sound - Barbara Nichol   *p* 1077

Salacota (Twin; Brother)
The Twins and the Bird of Darkness: A Hero Tale from the Caribbean - Robert D. San Souci   *e* 1260

Saladin (Historical Figure; Leader)
Pagan's Crusade - Catherine Jinks   *m, h* 739

Salomone (Manager)
Eloise Takes a Bawth - Kay Thompson   *p* 1379

Salz (12-Year-Old)
Breath - Donna Jo Napoli   *m, h* 1059

Sam (Bear; Son)
Don't You Feel Well, Sam? - Amy Hest   *p* 632

Sam (Child; Brother)
Good Morning, Sam - Marie-Louise Gay   *p* 512
Good Night Sam - Marie-Louise Gay   *p* 513

Sam (Government Official)
Henry Climbs a Mountain - D.B. Johnson   *p* 745

Sam (Child; Brother)
Stella, Fairy of the Forest - Marie-Louise Gay   *p* 514

Sameth (Royalty)
Abhorsen - Garth Nix   *m, h* 1084

Sammie (Addict)
Nirvana's Children - Ranulfo   *h* 1185

Sammy (Child)
Full Steam Ahead - Faye Gibbons   *p* 521

Sampson, Cal (11th Grader)
Kerosene - Chris Wooding   *h* 1461

Sampson, Dominic (10-Year-Old)
Dark Waters - Catherine MacPhail   *m, h* 932

Samson (Horse)
Anna Sunday - Sally M. Keehn   *m* 772

Samuel (Child; Son)
More Pies! - Robert Munsch   *p* 1040

Samuel (11-Year-Old; Slave)
Trouble Don't Last - Shelley Pearsall   *m* 1139

Sanborn, Jenny (Sister)
Claws - Will Weaver   *m, h* 1420

Sanborn, Laura (11th Grader)
Claws - Will Weaver   *m, h* 1420

Sanchez, Gip (Alien)
The Angel Factor - Terence Blacker   *m, h* 113

Sanders, Felix (13-Year-Old)
The Divide - Elizabeth Kay   *m* 770

Sandmare (Horse)
Sandmare - Helen Cooper   *e* 294

Sanford, Verna Kaye (9th Grader)
Waiting to Disappear - April Young Fritz   *m, h* 496

Santa Claus (Mythical Creature; Aged Person)
A New Improved Santa - Patricia Rae Wolff   *p* 1454

Santack, Sophia "Sophie" (8th Grader)
Stand Tall - Joan Bauer   *m* 89

Saphira (Dragon)
Eragon - Christopher Paolini   *m, h* 1125

Sara (Child; Niece)
A Picture of Grandmother - Esther Hautzig   *e* 611

Sara (Daughter; 8-Year-Old)
When Catherine the Great and I Were Eight! - Cari Best   *p* 107

Sarah (Teenager; Businesswoman)
At the Sign of the Sugared Plum - Mary Hooper   *m, h* 675

Sarah (Teenager)
The Earthborn - Paul Collins   *h, a* 282

Sarah (Daughter; Sister)
Homespun Sarah - Verla Kay   *p* 771

Sarah (Child; Daughter)
Lighthouse: A Story of Remembrance - Robert Munsch   *p* 1039

Sarah (Child)
Mixed-Up Doubles - Elena Yates Eulo   *m, h* 439
Practice Makes Perfect for Rotten Ralph - Jack Gantos   *b* 507

Sarie (Child; Student—Elementary School)
Once Upon a Time - Niki Daly   *p* 341

Sarov, Alexei (Military Personnel; Terrorist)
Skeleton Key - Anthony Horowitz   *m, h* 681

Sasha (Child)
Sasha's Matrioshka Dolls - Jane Dillon   *p* 383

Sassafras (Horse)
Hannah Mae O'Hannigan's Wild West Show - Lisa Campbell Ernst   *p* 437

Savage, Cade (11th Grader; Football Player)
Three Clams and an Oyster - Randy Powell   *m, h* 1166

Sawyer, Becca (10th Grader)
After - Francine Prose   *m, h* 1175

Sawyer, Ruby (10-Year-Old; Sister)
Lumber Camp Library - Natalie Kinsey-Warnock   *e* 798

Saxso (Indian)
The Winter People - Joseph Bruchac   *m, h* 171

Scaredy Cat (Father; Cat)
The Scaredy Cats - Barbara Bottner   *p* 128

Scaredy Cat (Mother; Cat)
The Scaredy Cats - Barbara Bottner   *p* 128

Scaredy Cat, Baby (Cat; Child)
The Scaredy Cats - Barbara Bottner   *p* 128

Scarfield, Jack (Pirate)
The Man with the Silver Oar - Robin Moore   *m, h* 1029

Schnurmacher, Andras (Brother)
Marika - Andrea Cheng   *m, h* 241

Schnurmacher, Apa (Father; Stock Broker)
Marika - Andrea Cheng   *m, h* 241

Schnurmacher, Maria "Marika" (Teenager)
Marika - Andrea Cheng   *m, h* 241

Schubert, Annabel Whoopi (12-Year-Old)
The Steps - Rachel Cohn   *m* 273

Schubert, Beatrice (Baby)
The Steps - Rachel Cohn   *m* 273

Schubert, Jack (Father)
The Steps - Rachel Cohn   *m* 273

Schumacher, David Bruce "Blue Avenger" (16-Year-Old)
Blue Avenger and the Theory of Everything - Norma Howe   *m, h* 689

Schwartz, Joseph (Student—High School)
Before the Creeks Ran Red - Carolyn Reeder   *m, h* 1192

Schwartz, Tameka (Niece)
The Journey of Oliver K. Woodman - Darcy Pattison   *p* 1130

Scott (Coach)
The Warriors - Joseph Bruchac   *m* 170

Scott, Mike (12th Grader)
Waiting for Sarah - Bruce McBay   *m, h* 961

Scratch (Dog)
Doggone . . . Third Grade! - Colleen O'Shaughnessy McKenna   *e* 982

Scudder, Jehu (Boyfriend)
Boston Jane: Wilderness Days - Jennifer L. Holm   *m, h* 666

Seaborne (Adoptee; Sister)
The Sea Chest - Toni Buzzeo   *p* 190

Seaman (Dog; Narrator)
Lewis and Clark and Me: A Dog's Tale - Laurie Myers   *e* 1050

Seaver, Anya (10-Year-Old; Student—Elementary School)
Because of Anya - Margaret Peterson Haddix   *e* 579

Sebring, Shaw (16-Year-Old; Volleyball Player)
The Hemingway Tradition - Kristin Butcher   *m* 186

Sedge "Pop" (Father; Horse)
Our Twitchy - Kes Gray   *p* 551

See Cua "Heather" (Cousin)
Tangled Threads: A Hmong Girl's Story - Pegi Deitz Shea   *m, h* 1289

Seinfeld, Susie (Cousin; 6th Grader)
United Tates of America - Paula Danziger   *e, m* 347

Seldom (Aged Person; Widow(er))
33 Snowfish - Adam Rapp   *h* 1186

Selia (Noblewoman; Servant)
The Goose Girl - Shannon Hale   *m, h* 586

Semple, Jake (13-Year-Old)
Surviving the Applewhites - Stephanie S. Tolan   *m, h* 1383

Sennosuke, Mitsu "Mitsy" (Nurse)
The Divine Wind: A Love Story - Garry Disher   *h* 384

Seppala, Leonhard (Animal Trainer)
Togo - Robert J. Blake   *p* 117

Serena (Pig)
No Place for a Pig - Suzanne Bloom   *p* 119

Serena "Beaky" (15-Year-Old)
Amy - Mary Hooper   *m, h* 674

Sesshu Toyo (Child; Artist)
The Boy Who Drew Cats - Margaret Hodges   *p* 656

Seymour (Sheep; Friend)
Four Friends Together - Sue Heap   *p* 617

Seymour (Student—Elementary School; Friend)
T.J. and the Cats - Hazel Hutchins   *e* 704

Seymour (Hairdresser)
Bippity Bop Barbershop - Natasha Anastasia Tarpley   *p* 1362

Shaaron (Sister; Heroine)
Rowan and the Ice Creepers - Emily Rodda   *e* 1217

Shailey, Grey (Mentally Ill Person)
The She - Carol Plum-Ucci   *m, h* 1161

Shakespeare, Hamnet (Twin; Historical Figure)
My Father Had a Daughter: Judith Shakespeare's Tale - Grace Tiffany   *h, a* 1381

Shakespeare, Judith (Twin; Historical Figure)
My Father Had a Daughter: Judith Shakespeare's Tale - Grace Tiffany   *h, a* 1381

Thaler, Meg (Stepmother)
Mountain Solo - Jeanette Ingold   *m, h* 714

Thaler, Tess (16-Year-Old; Musician)
Mountain Solo - Jeanette Ingold   *m, h* 714

Thalia (Deity)
Goddesses Series - Clea Hantman   *m, h* 592

Theo (Political Figure)
The Courtesan's Daughter - Priscilla Galloway
    h 505

Theodore, Simpson III (Bully; Basketball Player)
Rat - Jan Cheripko   *m, h* 242

Thibodeaux, Suzanne Marie Sabine Chicot (Child;
    Daughter)
Alligator Sue - Sharon Arms Doucet   *p* 389

Thigpen, Audelia "Del" (17-Year-Old)
Breakout - Paul Fleischman   *h* 460

Thomas (Entertainer)
Song for Eloise - Leigh Sauerwein   *h* 1264

Thomas, of Sch (Wizard; Nobleman)
Sorcery and Cecelia, or the Enchanted Chocolate Pot -
    Patricia C. Wrede   *m, h* 1470

Thomas, Kimberly "Ariel" (10th Grader)
Kissing Kate - Lauren Myracle   *h* 1054

Thomas, Vernon (9th Grader)
Shadow of a Doubt - S.L. Rottman   *m, h* 1232

Thomas, Willimena "Willie" (3rd Grader)
How to Lose Your Class Pet - Valerie Wilson Wesley
    e 1430

Thompson, Daniel (Criminal; Brother)
Shadow of a Doubt - S.L. Rottman   *m, h* 1232

Thompson, Ernest "Shadow" (15-Year-Old)
Shadow of a Doubt - S.L. Rottman   *m, h* 1232

Thompson, Rebecca Lee "Becky" (14-Year-Old)
A Circle of Time - Marisa Montes   *m, h* 1023

Thompson, Trisha (12th Grader)
Telling Christina Goodbye - Lurlene McDaniel   *m,*
    h 974

Thorpe, Charlotte Williamson "Wim" (17-Year-
    Old)
Kotuku - Deborah Savage   *m, h* 1265

Thorpe, Nicholas "Nick" (13-Year-Old)
From the Horse's Mouth - Kathy Mackel   *m* 929

Throckmorton, Dudley "Big Daddy Duds" (Rat;
    Organized Crime Figure)
The Mayor of Central Park - Avi   *e* 59

Throckmorton, Maud (Rat; Daughter)
The Mayor of Central Park - Avi   *e* 59

Thunder, Jimmy (Detective—Private; Deity)
Drinking Midnight Wine - Simon R. Green   *h,*
    a 553

Thuron, Raphael (Sea Captain)
The Angel's Command: A Tale from the Castaways of
    the Flying Dutchman - Brian Jacques   *m, h* 722

Tiger (Dog; Friend)
Kipper's Monster - Mick Inkpen   *p* 715

Tiger (Tiger)
Song of the Circus - Lois Duncan   *p* 404

Tiitaa (Indian)
Maata's Journal - Paul Sullivan   *m, h* 1353

Till, Emmett (14-Year-Old; Historical Figure)
Mississippi Trial, 1955 - Chris Crowe   *m, h* 320

Tilling, Despereaux (Mouse; Hero)
The Tale of Despereaux: Being the Story of a Mouse,
    a Princess, Some Soup, and a Spool of Thread -
    Kate DiCamillo   *e* 381

Tillman, Daphne Sue (16-Year-Old; Mentally Ill
    Person)
The Babbs Switch Story - Darleen Bailey Beard
    m 93

Tillman, Ruth Ann "Ruthie" (12-Year-Old)
The Babbs Switch Story - Darleen Bailey Beard
    m 93

Tilly (Child)
Blue Horse - Helen Stephens   *p* 1340

Tilly (Child; Daughter)
Treasure Hunt - Allan Ahlberg   *p* 10

Tina (Sister)
The Great Blue Yonder - Alex Shearer   *m, h* 1290

Tinker, Lizzy (12-Year-Old; Orphan)
Stink Alley - Jamie Gilson   *e, m* 527

Tiny Teddy (Toy; Bear)
What Shall We Do, Blue Kangaroo? - Emma
    Chichester Clark   *p* 247

Tip (Rabbit)
Rembrandt's Hat - Susan Blackaby   *p* 112

Tisala (Noblewoman; Spy)
Dragon Blood - Patricia Briggs   *h, a* 150

Tithonus (Child; Brother)
Hippolyta and the Curse of the Amazons - Jane Yolen
    m 1482

Titus (Teenager)
Feed - M.T. Anderson   *h* 29

Toad (Criminal)
Disappearing Act - Sid Fleischman   *m* 461

Tobak, Kirk (11th Grader)
Blind Sighted - Peter Moore   *h* 1028

Tobin (Knight)
The Goblin Wood - Hilari Bell   *m, h* 98

Toby (Child; Son)
Dancing the Ring Shout! - Kim Siegelson   *p* 1300

Todd (Teacher)
Judy Moody Saves the World! - Megan McDonald
    e 976

Todd, Jacob (17-Year-Old)
Postcards from No Man's Land - Aidan Chambers
    h 237

Togo (Dog)
Togo - Robert J. Blake   *p* 117

Tolliver, Tabu (8th Grader; Twin)
Double Dutch - Sharon M. Draper   *m, h* 396

Tolliver, Titan (8th Grader; Twin)
Double Dutch - Sharon M. Draper   *m, h* 396

Tom (Apprentice)
At the Sign of the Sugared Plum - Mary Hooper   *m,*
    h 675

Tom (Mythical Creature)
Cold Tom - Sally Prue   *m, h* 1177

Tom (Child)
Small - Clara Vulliamy   *p* 1403

Tominski (Recluse; Immigrant)
Keeper of the Doves - Betsy Byars   *e* 192

Tomko-Rollins, Tabitha "Tibby" (Student)
The Second Summer of the Sisterhood - Ann Brashares
    m, h 137

Tommy (12th Grader; Military Personnel)
Skud - Dennis Foon   *h* 472

Tong-Ling (Immigrant)
Flight of the Fisherbird - Nora Martin   *e, m* 949

Tony (Child)
The Beloved Dearly - Doug Cooney   *e, m* 293

Tony (Brother; Son)
That Makes Me Mad! - Steven Kroll   *p* 830

Toot (Pig; Friend)
Toot & Puddle: Charming Opal - Holly Hobbie
    p 649

Tozzi, Arturo (11-Year-Old; Immigrant)
A Real American - Richard Easton   *m* 414

Trainor, Russell (7th Grader)
The Revealers - Doug Wilhelm   *m* 1443

Trammel, Colt (10th Grader; Baseball Player)
Out of Order - A.M. Jenkins   *h* 732

Trapper Jack (Aged Person; Trapper)
The True Story of Trapper Jack's Left Big Toe - Ian
    Wallace   *p* 1407

Travis (Seamstress; Student—High School)
Stitches - Glen Huser   *m, h* 703

Tree, Christiana (Mythical Creature)
Spirits in the Wires - Charles de Lint   *h, a* 355

Trent (Principal)
After - Francine Prose   *m, h* 1175

Trepid (Businessman)
Ruby Holler - Sharon Creech   *e, m* 313

Tretter (Spouse)
Curse in Reverse - Tom Coppinger   *p* 298
Curse in Reverse - Tom Coppinger   *p* 298

Trevor (6th Grader)
The Canyon - Sheila Cole   *e, m* 275

Trevor (Gang Member; 12-Year-Old)
Junebug in Trouble - Alice Mead   *e* 1002

Trey (12-Year-Old)
Green Boy - Susan Cooper   *m* 297

Tria (Child; Daughter)
Tria and the Great Star Rescue - Rebecca Kraft Rector
    e 1191

Trill (Store Owner)
That Pesky Rat - Lauren Child   *p* 248

Tristan (Royalty)
Isolde: Queen of the Western Isle: The First of the
    Tristan and Isolde Novels - Rosalind Miles   *h,*
    a 1010

Tristram (Knight; Brother)
The Ballad of Sir Dinadan - Gerald Morris   *m,*
    h 1034

Troll Queen (Mythical Creature)
East - Edith Pattou   *m, h* 1131

Troop, Peter "Pigeon" (Child; Son)
Fishing Day - Andrea Davis Pinkney   *p* 1156

Trout (Principal)
Scritch Scratch - Miriam Moss   *p* 1036

Trudy (Rabbit; Sister)
Pumpkin Day! - Nancy Elizabeth Wallace   *p* 1409

Truelove (Dog)
Truelove - Babette Cole   *p* 274

Trujillo, Rafael "El Jefe" (Historical Figure)
Before We Were Free - Julia Alvarez   *m, h* 24

Trumbull (Elephant; Brother)
Gumbrella - Barry Root   *p* 1225

Tuc, Celestina (Friend)
Colibri - Ann Cameron   *m* 206

Tuck (Raven)
The Ravenmaster's Secret - Elvira Woodruff
    m 1462

Tucker, Richie (8th Grader; Bully)
The Revealers - Doug Wilhelm   *m* 1443

Tucker, Tyler (15-Year-Old; Abuse Victim)
Jackie's Wild Seattle - Will Hobbs   *m* 652

Tudor, Mary (Royalty)
Doomed Queen Anne - Carolyn Meyer   *m, h* 1006

Unnamed Character (Monkey; Friend)
Nine Animals and the Well - James Rumford
    p 1238

Unnamed Character (Royalty)
Nine Animals and the Well - James Rumford
    p 1238

Unnamed Character (Monkey; Baby)
No More Kissing! - Emma Chichester Clark   p 246

Unnamed Character (Child; Narrator)
Nobody's Nosier Than a Cat - Susan Campbell
    Bartoletti   p 86

Unnamed Character (Child; Daughter)
Oh No, Gotta Go! - Susan Middleton Elya   p 432

Unnamed Character (Raccoon; Thief)
Old Granny and the Bean Thief - Cynthia DeFelice
    p 366

Unnamed Character (Brother; Narrator)
Once Upon a Farm - Marie Bradby   p 132

Unnamed Character (Dog)
One-Dog Canoe - Mary Casanova   p 225

Unnamed Character (Child)
One-Dog Canoe - Mary Casanova   p 225
One Leaf Rides the Wind - Celeste Davidson Mannis
    p 938

Unnamed Character (Goat; Friend)
One Rainy Day - Valeri Gorbachev   p 542

Unnamed Character (Witch)
One Witch - Laura Leuck   p 881

Unnamed Character (Child; Student)
Our Class Took a Trip to the Zoo - Shirley Neitzel
    p 1071

Unnamed Character (Grandmother; Cook)
Pancake Dreams - Ingmarie Ahvander   p 12

Unnamed Character (Insect)
Party Animals - Katie Davis   p 351

Unnamed Character (Child)
Peekaboo Morning - Rachel Isadora   p 719

Unnamed Character (Child; Son)
Peep! - Kevin Luthardt   p 917

Unnamed Character (Duck)
Peep! - Kevin Luthardt   p 917

Unnamed Character (Father; Friend)
Pictures for Miss Josie - Sandra Belton   p 100

Unnamed Character (Son; Artist)
Pictures for Miss Josie - Sandra Belton   p 100

Unnamed Character (Daughter; Child)
A Place to Grow - Soyung Pak   p 1121

Unnamed Character (Father; Gardener)
A Place to Grow - Soyung Pak   p 1121

Unnamed Character (Child)
A Quiet Place - Douglas Wood   p 1460

Unnamed Character (Narrator; Daughter)
The Range Eternal - Louise Erdrich   p 434

Unnamed Character (Brother; Son)
The Real, True Dulcie Campbell - Cynthia DeFelice
    p 367

Unnamed Character (Royalty; Father)
The Red Wolf - Margaret Shannon   p 1285

Unnamed Character (Child)
Roller Coaster - Marla Frazee   p 484
Rub-a-Dub Sub - Linda Ashman   p 51

Unnamed Character (Dog; Sailor)
Sailor Boy Jig - Margaret Wise Brown   p 167

Unnamed Character (Dog)
Saving Sinbad! - Michael Foreman   p 473

Unnamed Character (Pirate)
The Scrimshaw Ring - William Jaspersohn   p 729

Unnamed Character (Insect; Mother)
Scritch Scratch - Miriam Moss   p 1036

Unnamed Character (Mythical Creature)
The Sheep Fairy: When Wishes Have Wings - Ruth
    Louise Symes   p 1357

Unnamed Character (Mother)
Sissy Buttons Takes Charge! - Ian Whybrow
    p 1439

Unnamed Character (Sloth)
Slowly, Slowly, Slowly, said the Sloth - Eric Carle
    p 217

Unnamed Character (Snake; Storyteller)
The Snake's Tales - Marguerite W. Davol   p 353

Unnamed Character (Child; Son)
Snow Music - Lynne Rae Perkins   p 1147

Unnamed Character (Dog)
Snow Music - Lynne Rae Perkins   p 1147

Unnamed Character (Teacher)
Someone Says - Carole Lexa Schaefer   p 1268

Unnamed Character (Mother)
Sometimes I'm Bombaloo - Rachel Vail   p 1389

Unnamed Character (Baby; Brother)
Sometimes I'm Bombaloo - Rachel Vail   p 1389

Unnamed Character (Royalty)
Sophia: The Alchemist's Dog - Shelley Jackson
    p 721

Unnamed Character (Artist)
Sophia: The Alchemist's Dog - Shelley Jackson
    p 721

Unnamed Character (Father)
Star Blanket - Pat Brisson   p 156

Unnamed Character (Child; Brother)
Stars in the Darkness - Barbara M. Joosse   p 759

Unnamed Character (Farmer; Aged Person)
Storm Is Coming! - Heather Tekavec   p 1371

Unnamed Character (Young Woman; Friend)
A Story for Bear - Dennis Haseley   p 607

Unnamed Character (Child; Student—Elementary
    School)
Straight to the Pole - Kevin O'Malley   p 1109

Unnamed Character (Streetperson; Aged Person)
The Teddy Bear - David McPhail   p 1001

Unnamed Character (Child; Son)
The Teddy Bear - David McPhail   p 1001

Unnamed Character (Toy)
The Teddy Bear - David McPhail   p 1001

Unnamed Character (Rat)
That Pesky Rat - Lauren Child   p 248

Unnamed Character (Brother; Narrator)
That Summer - Tony Johnston   p 755

Unnamed Character (Grandmother; Traveler)
That's Good! That's Bad! In The Grand Canyon -
    Margery Cuyler   p 335

Unnamed Character (Child; Traveler)
That's Good! That's Bad! In The Grand Canyon -
    Margery Cuyler   p 335

Unnamed Character (Baby; Son)
Thirsty Baby - Catherine Ann Cullen   p 323

Unnamed Character (Chicken; Baby)
This Little Chick - John Lawrence   p 861

Unnamed Character (Nobleman)
Three Samurai Cats: A Story from Japan - Eric A.
    Kimmel   p 789

Unnamed Character (Rat; Bully)
Three Samurai Cats: A Story from Japan - Eric A.
    Kimmel   p 789

Unnamed Character (Mother; Hen)
Tippy-Toe Chick, Go! - George Shannon   p 1284

Unnamed Character (Mother; Archaeologist)
Tria and the Great Star Rescue - Rebecca Kraft Rector
    e 1191

Unnamed Character (Mouse)
'Twas the Fright Before Christmas - Judy Sierra
    p 1301

Unnamed Character (Twin; Brother)
Twin to Twin - Margaret O'Hair   p 1104

Unnamed Character (Twin; Sister)
Twin to Twin - Margaret O'Hair   p 1104

Unnamed Character (Child of Divorced Parents;
    Daughter)
Two Old Potatoes and Me - John Coy   p 311

Unnamed Character (Child; Brother)
Under a Prairie Sky - Anne Laurel Carter   p 221
Under a Prairie Sky - Anne Laurel Carter   p 221

Unnamed Character (Narrator; Slave)
Under the Quilt of Night - Deborah Hopkinson
    p 678

Unnamed Character (Daughter)
Visiting Day - Jacqueline Woodson   p 1468

Unnamed Character (Child)
What About Me? - Ed Young   p 1488
What Did You Do Today? - Kerry Arquette   p 41

Unnamed Character (Child; Son)
What's That Noise? - William Carman   p 219

Unnamed Character (Clown)
Where's Pup? - Dayle Ann Dodds   p 386

Unnamed Character (Rabbit; Magician)
Which Would You Rather Be? - William Steig
    p 1339

Unnamed Character (Child)
Which Would You Rather Be? - William Steig
    p 1339
Which Would You Rather Be? - William Steig
    p 1339

Unnamed Character (Rabbit)
While We Were Out - Ho Baek Lee   p 869

Unnamed Character (Traveler)
Who's That Knocking on Christmas Eve? - Jan Brett
    p 145

Unnamed Character (Bear)
Who's That Knocking on Christmas Eve? - Jan Brett
    p 145

Unnamed Character (Friend)
Wish, Change, Friend - Ian Whybrow   p 1440

Unnamed Character (Witch; Aged Person)
Witch's Wishes - Vivian Vande Velde   e 1396

Unnamed Character (Wizard; Teacher)
Wizard at Work - Vivian Vande Velde   e 1397

Unnamed Character (Soccer Player; Son)
Wonder Goal! - Michael Foreman   p 474

Unnamed Character (Baby)
The Wriggly, Wriggly Baby - Jessica Clerk   p 264

Unnamed Character (Narrator; Son)
Yesterday I Had the Blues - Jeron Ashford Frame
    p 478

Unnamed Character (Child)
Yikes!!! - Robert Florczak   p 468

Unnamed Child (Baby)
33 Snowfish - Adam Rapp   h 1186

Unnamed Child (Daughter; Narrator)
Goose's Story - Cari Best   p 106

Unnamed Girl (Narrator; Teenager)
Girl Coming in for a Landing - April Halprin Wayland
    m, h 1418

Uri (Streetperson)
Milkweed - Jerry Spinelli   *m, h*   1326

Ursula (15-Year-Old; Sorceress)
Warriors of Alavna - N.M. Browne   *m, h*   168

Ursula (Teenager; Warrior)
Warriors of Camlann - N.M. Browne   *m, h*   169

Ursula (10-Year-Old; Daughter)
When the Circus Came to Town - Laurence Yep   *e*   1476

Urticacea (Witch)
Never After - Rebecca Lickiss   *h, a*   892

V

Vale, Malcolm (Teacher; Entertainer)
Dunk - David Lubar   *m, h*   912

Valentine, Katherine (Daughter)
Mortal Engines - Philip Reeve   *h, a*   1195

Valentine, Thaddeus (Government Official)
Mortal Engines - Philip Reeve   *h, a*   1195

van Helsen, Hugo (Banker)
The House of Windjammer - V.A. Richardson   *m, h*   1201

Van Horn, Alicia (Blind Person; Teenager)
Things Not Seen - Andrew Clements   *m*   261

van Riet, Daan (Homosexual)
Postcards from No Man's Land - Aidan Chambers   *h*   237

Van Riet, Martha (11-Year-Old)
Overnight - Adele Griffin   *e, m*   563

van Rijn, Rembrandt Harmensz (Child; Historical Figure)
Stink Alley - Jamie Gilson   *e, m*   527

Van Stegeran, Katje (Child; Friend)
Boxes for Katje - Candace Fleming   *p*   462

Vandamme, Hugo (Businessman)
And What about Anna? - Jan Simoen   *h*   1306

Vanderhorst, Noah (Spirit)
The Presence: A Ghost Story - Eve Bunting   *m, h*   181

Vandorn, Cornelius (14-Year-Old)
Nelly in the Wilderness - Lynn Cullen   *m*   325

Vandorn, Frank (Father; Trapper)
Nelly in the Wilderness - Lynn Cullen   *m*   325

Vandorn, Margery (Stepmother)
Nelly in the Wilderness - Lynn Cullen   *m*   325

Vandorn, Nelly (12-Year-Old)
Nelly in the Wilderness - Lynn Cullen   *m*   325

Vang, Pa Lia (2nd Grader; Friend)
The Talent Show - Michelle Edwards   *e*   417

Vatta, Kylara "Ky" (Businesswoman; Daughter)
Trading in Danger - Elizabeth Moon   *h, a*   1026

Vaughn, Jake (Cowboy)
Samantha and the Cowboy - Lorraine Heath   *h*   620

Velander (Religious)
Voyage of the Shadowmoon - Sean McMullen   *h, a*   994

Vera (Teenager)
Aleutian Sparrow - Karen Hesse   *m, h*   631

Verdon, Winnie de (Teenager; Noblewoman)
At the Crossing Places - Kevin Crossley-Holland   *m, h*   319

Vernon (Father)
The Crying Rocks - Janet Taylor Lisle   *m, h*   901

Vertigo, Olivia (Wizard; Student—Boarding School)
Charlie Bone and the Time Twister - Jenny Nimmo   *m*   1081

Vertigo, Olivia (Student—Boarding School)
Midnight for Charlie Bone - Jenny Nimmo   *m*   1082

Vest, Christine (Teacher; Historical Figure)
Ghost Girl: A Blue Ridge Mountain Story - Delia Ray   *m*   1188

Vevila (Royalty; Cousin)
Never After - Rebecca Lickiss   *h, a*   892

Victoria (Sister; Dog)
Lisa's Baby Sister - Anne Gutman   *p*   574

Vidal, Myra (Student—College)
Zipped - Laura McNeal   *h*   996

Vinker, Kevin (Boyfriend)
Chill Wind - Janet McDonald   *h*   975

Viola "Old Vi" (Grandmother)
Rebel - Willo Davis Roberts   *m*   1211

Violet (Teenager)
Feed - M.T. Anderson   *h*   29

Violet (Pig; Acrobat)
Hobart - Anita Briggs   *e*   149

Visser, Jan (Brother; Resistance Fighter)
When the War Is Over - Martha Attema   *m, h*   53

Visser, Janke (16-Year-Old; Resistance Fighter)
When the War Is Over - Martha Attema   *m, h*   53

Vlajnik, Stas (Chess Player; Teacher)
The Kings Are Already Here - Garret Freymann-Weyr   *m, h*   493

von Loewen (Aged Person)
The Countess and Me - Paul Kropp   *m, h*   832

Vorkosigan, Ekaterin (Spouse)
Diplomatic Immunity: A Comedy of Terrors - Lois McMaster Bujold   *h, a*   176

Vorkosigan, Miles (Spouse; Government Official)
Diplomatic Immunity: A Comedy of Terrors - Lois McMaster Bujold   *h, a*   176

Vortex (Teacher; Alien)
First Graders from Mars: Episode 3: Nergal and the Great Space Race - Shana Corey   *e*   302

Vreeland, Bridget "Bee" (16-Year-Old)
The Second Summer of the Sisterhood - Ann Brashares   *m, h*   137

Vyas, Akhil (Orphan; Feral Child)
The Pack - Elisa Carbone   *m, h*   214

W

Waggles (Dog)
Waggle - Sarah McMenemy   *p*   988

Wahhsted, Zachary McDaniel "Zach" (Mentally Ill Person; 16-Year-Old)
Inside Out - Terry Trueman   *h*   1386

Waldenstein, Catherine "Ole Golly" (Child-Care Giver)
Harriet Spies Again - Helen Ericson   *e, m*   435

Waldenstein, George (Spouse)
Harriet Spies Again - Helen Ericson   *e, m*   435

Waldrip, Joe (6th Grader)
Agnes Parker . . . Girl in Progress - Kathleen O'Dell   *e, m*   1103

Walker, Darraugh (Gypsy)
Child of the Prophecy - Juliet Marillier   *h, a*   941

Wallace, Fred (12th Grader; Homosexual)
Gravel Queen - Tea Benduhn   *h*   101

Wallace, Pete (12th Grader)
Out of the Fire - Deborah Froese   *m, h*   497

Wallace, William "Braveheart" (Historical Figure; Patriot)
Girl in a Cage - Jane Yolen   *m, h*   1480

Walt (Streetperson)
Butterflies and Lizards, Beryl and Me - Ruth Lercher Bornstein   *e, m*   127

Walter (Child; Friend)
Iris and Walter and Baby Rose - Elissa Haden Guest   *b*   568

Walter (Friend; Child)
Iris and Walter and Cousin Howie - Elissa Haden Guest   *b*   569

Walter (Student; Friend)
Iris and Walter: The School Play - Elissa Haden Guest   *b*   570

Walter (Child; Friend)
Iris and Walter: The Sleepover - Elissa Haden Guest   *b*   571

Wanda (Aunt)
Walk Away Home - Paul Many   *h*   940

Wanda-Linda (Child; Daughter)
The Terrible Underpants - Kaz Cooke   *p*   290

Warbeck, Sarah (Handicapped; 13-Year-Old)
Saffy's Angel - Hilary McKay   *m*   980

Ward (Teacher)
Bronx Masquerade - Nikki Grimes   *m, h*   565

Warder, Kethlun "Keth" (Artisan)
Shatterglass - Tamora Pierce   *m, h*   1151

Wardwick "Ward" (Nobleman)
Dragon Blood - Patricia Briggs   *h, a*   150
Dragon Bones - Patricia Briggs   *h, a*   151

Warren (Stepfather)
Might Adventurer of the Planet! - Ricki Stern   *e*   1341

Warrener, Justin (Vampire; 15-Year-Old)
Vampire High - Douglas Rees   *m, h*   1194

Warsovran (Royalty)
Voyage of the Shadowmoon - Sean McMullen   *h, a*   994

Washington, George (Historical Figure; Political Figure)
Taking Liberty: The Story of Oney Judge, George Washington's Runaway Slave - Ann Rinaldi   *m, h*   1207

Washington, Martha (Historical Figure)
Taking Liberty: The Story of Oney Judge, George Washington's Runaway Slave - Ann Rinaldi   *m, h*   1207

Wasserman (Doctor)
Not as Crazy as I Seem - George Harrar   *m, h*   596

Wat (Handicapped; 10-Year-Old)
The Falconmaster - R.L. La Fevers   *m*   841

Watson, Raylene (9th Grader)
Waiting for Christopher - Louise Hawes   *m, h*   613

Wayne, Georgia (12-Year-Old; Girlfriend)
Mystery in Mt. Mole - Richard W. Jennings   *m, h*   737

Weaver, Burdette "Bird" (6th Grader)
Fame and Glory in Freedom, Georgia - Barbara O'Connor   *e, m*   1102

Webb (Friend)
The Night I Disappeared - Julie Reece Deaver   *m, h*   364

Webster, Joe (Father; Veteran)
Where Heroes Hide - Helen Recorvits   *e*   1190

Webster, Junior (10-Year-Old; Friend)
Where Heroes Hide - Helen Recorvits   *e*   1190

Weeks (Religious; Father)
Christmas Tapestry - Patricia Polacco   *p*   1163

Weeks, Emma (Classmate; Accident Victim)
Stanley, Flat Again! - Jeff Brown   *e*   163

Weeks, Jonathan Jefferson (Child; Son)
Christmas Tapestry - Patricia Polacco   *p*   1163

Weera (Leader)
Mud City - Deborah Ellis   *m*   428

Weinland, Annette (18-Year-Old; Volunteer)
Unseen Companion - Denise Gosliner Orenstein
    h   1113

Weinstein, Julie (13-Year-Old)
Room in the Heart - Sonia Levitin   *m, h*   886

Weiss, Morgan (12th Grader)
Slumming - Kristen D. Randle   *h*   1183

Welch, Arlene (12-Year-Old; 7th Grader)
The Princesses of Atlantis - Lisa Williams Kline
    m   804

Weller, Destiny (Twin; 12th Grader)
Dangerous Girls - R.L. Stine   *m, h*   1345

Weller, Livy (Twin; 12th Grader)
Dangerous Girls - R.L. Stine   *m, h*   1345

**Wellington, Catriona Anabel "Miss
    Doctor"** (Guardian; Doctor)
Rodzina - Karen Cushman   *m*   331

Wells, Margaret Cora "Meg" (9-Year-Old; Sister)
As Far as I Can See: Meg's Prairie Diary - Kate
    McMullan   *e*   989

Wells, Margaret Cora "Meg" (9-Year-Old;
    Daughter)
A Fine Start: Meg's Prairie Diary - Kate McMullan
    e   990

Wells, Preston "Pres" (7-Year-Old; Brother)
As Far as I Can See: Meg's Prairie Diary - Kate
    McMullan   *e*   989

Welsch, Harriet M. (7th Grader; Spy)
Harriet Spies Again - Helen Ericson   *e, m*   435

Welsh, Froggy (Student—High School)
The Earth, My Butt, and Other Big Round Things -
    Carolyn Mackler   *m, h*   930

Wemberly (Child; Mouse)
Wemberly's Ice-Cream Star - Kevin Henkes   *p*   625

Wentworth, James (12th Grader)
My Heartbeat - Garret Freymann-Weyr   *h*   494

Wesley (Uncle)
Lily's Ghosts - Laura Ruby   *m*   1237

Wesseling, Geertrui "Maria" (Aged Person)
Postcards from No Man's Land - Aidan Chambers
    h   237

West, Anna (Sister; Student)
Muldoon - Pamela Duncan Edwards   *p*   419

West, Grady (16-Year-Old; 11th Grader)
Target - Kathleen Jeffrie Johnson   *h*   747

West, James "Jamie" (14-Year-Old)
The Hero - Ron Woods   *m, h*   1464

West, Tom (Brother; Student)
Muldoon - Pamela Duncan Edwards   *p*   419

Westerwit, Oscar (Squirrel)
The Mayor of Central Park - Avi   *e*   59

Weston, Calico "Callie" (16-Year-Old)
The Return of Calico Bright - David Winkler   *m,
    h*   1450

Weston, Charles (11th Grader; Artist)
Simon Says - Elaine Marie Alphin   *h*   23

Wetmeadow, Clemsa Lou (Girlfriend)
Horse Thief: A Novel - Robert Newton Peck   *m,
    h*   1142

Wheeler, Cecelia "Celie" (14-Year-Old; 8th
    Grader)
Someday: A Novel - Jackie French Koller   *m*   815

Whitaker, Paul (Spirit; Military Personnel)
Operating Codes - Nick Manns   *m, h*   939

Whitcomb, Celia (Guardian; Aunt)
The Big Burn - Jeanette Ingold   *m, h*   713

White Bear (Indian)
Danger at the Wild West Show - Alison Hart
    m   601

White Bear (Royalty)
East - Edith Pattou   *m, h*   1131

White Cat (Cat)
Camp of the Angel - Aileen Arrington   *e, m*   42

Whitfield, "Ga" (Grandmother)
Recycling George - Stephen Roos   *e, m*   1224

Whitfield, Rennie (12-Year-Old; Wealthy)
Recycling George - Stephen Roos   *e, m*   1224

Whitney (7th Grader)
The Princesses of Atlantis - Lisa Williams Kline
    m   804

Whyte, Joselyn (12-Year-Old; Orphan)
Jo's Triumph - Nikki Tate   *e, m*   1363

Widge (Actor; Orphan)
Shakespeare's Spy - Gary Blackwood   *m*   114

Wiggin, Peter (Genius)
Shadow Puppets - Orson Scott Card   *h, a*   215

Wignutt, Thor (Baseball Player)
Summerland - Michael Chabon   *m, h*   236

Wiley, Johnny (3rd Grader; Bully)
A Crazy, Mixed-Up Spanglish Day - Marisa Montes
    e   1024

Wilfred (Pig; Singer)
Hobart - Anita Briggs   *e*   149

Wilkins, Sandra (Child)
Raspberries on the Yangtze - Karen Wallace
    m   1408

Wilkins, Tracy (Pregnant Teenager)
Raspberries on the Yangtze - Karen Wallace
    m   1408

Will (Narrator)
First French Kiss and Other Traumas - Adam
    Bagdasarian   *m, h*   63

Willard, Frances (Historical Figure)
Bicycle Madness - Jane Kurtz   *e, m*   837

William X of Aquitaine (Father)
Eleanor: Crown Jewel of Aquitaine, France, 1136 -
    Kristiana Gregory   *m*   557

Williams, Jess (11th Grader)
Target - Kathleen Jeffrie Johnson   *h*   747

Williams, Kipper (Kindergartner; Brother)
7 x 9 = Trouble! - Claudia Mills   *e*   1013

Williams, Nesta (14-Year-Old)
Mates, Dates and Inflatable Bras - Cathy Hopkins
    m, h   676

Williams, Wilson (3rd Grader; Brother)
7 x 9 = Trouble! - Claudia Mills   *e*   1013

Willner, Henry (Counselor)
After - Francine Prose   *m, h*   1175

Wills, Natalie (13-Year-Old; Runner)
The Monster in Me - Mette Ivie Harrison   *m*   600

Willson, Kenny Roy (15-Year-Old; Writer)
Comfort - Carolee Dean   *m, h*   363

Willson, Maggie (Mother)
Comfort - Carolee Dean   *m, h*   363

Willson, Roy (Convict; Father)
Comfort - Carolee Dean   *m, h*   363

Willy (Guinea Pig; Scout)
Pig Enough - Janie Bynum   *p*   194

Wilson, Duke (Hairdresser)
Handbook for Boys: A Novel - Walter Dean Myers
    m, h   1053

Wilton, Wesley (9th Grader)
Falling from Fire - Teena Booth   *m, h*   126

Windjammer, Adam (14-Year-Old)
The House of Windjammer - V.A. Richardson   *m,
    h*   1201

Wing, Aggie (13-Year-Old)
Welcome Home or Someplace Like It - Charlotte Agell
    m   7

Wing, Thorne (15-Year-Old)
Welcome Home or Someplace Like It - Charlotte Agell
    m   7

Wingo, Zack (7th Grader)
The Princesses of Atlantis - Lisa Williams Kline
    m   804

Winifred (Sister; Child)
Eugene's Story - Richard Scrimger   *p*   1274

Winkel (Aged Person)
Hazel Green - Odo Hirsch   *e*   644

Winnemucca, Sarah (Indian)
Jo's Triumph - Nikki Tate   *e, m*   1363

Winnie (Opossum; Friend)
Winnie and Ernst - Gina Freschet   *e*   492

Winslow, Emily (Orphan; 11-Year-Old)
The Hollow Kingdom - Clare B. Dunkle   *m, h*   405

Winslow, Kate (Orphan; 18-Year-Old)
The Hollow Kingdom - Clare B. Dunkle   *m, h*   405

Winthrop, Joshua (14-Year-Old)
A Circle of Time - Marisa Montes   *m, h*   1023

Wisdom, Thomas (12-Year-Old)
The Angel Factor - Terence Blacker   *m, h*   113

Witherspoon, Anthony "Spoon" (12th Grader; 16-
    Year-Old)
The Beast - Walter Dean Myers   *h*   1051

Withington, David (12-Year-Old)
The Ghost Behind the Wall - Melvin Burgess
    m   182

Witkowski, Cherie (13-Year-Old; Newspaper
    Carrier)
Outside In - Karen Romano Young   *m, h*   1489

Wizzie (Rabbit; Sister)
What a Hat! - Holly Keller   *p*   778

Wizzle (Witch)
No Zombies Allowed - Matt Novak   *p*   1094

Woddle (Witch)
No Zombies Allowed - Matt Novak   *p*   1094

Wolf, Big Bad (Wolf)
Porkenstein - Kathryn Lasky   *p*   856

Wolfbane (Witch)
The Time Witches - Michael Molloy   *m*   1022

Wolfe, Cameron "Cam" (Student—High School)
Getting the Girl - Markus Zusak   *h*   1498

Wolfe, Ruben (Brother)
Getting the Girl - Markus Zusak   *h*   1498

Wonderful, Joe (Stepfather)
Ten Miles from Winnemucca - Thelma Hatch Wyss
    m, h   1472

Wood, Emily (16-Year-Old; 10th Grader)
Nightmare - Joan Lowery Nixon   *m, h*   1086

Character Description Index

This index alphabetically lists descriptions of the major characters in featured titles. The descriptions may be occupations (doctor, lawyer, etc.) or may describe persona (amnesiac, runaway, teenager, etc.). For each description, character names are listed alphabetically. Book titles, author names, age-level code(s) and entry numbers are also included. The age-level codes are as follows: *p* Preschool, *b* Beginning Reader, *e* Elementary School (Grades 2-5), *m* Middle School (Grades 5-8), *h* High School (Grades 9-12), and *a* Adult.

2-YEAR-OLD

Charlie
Old Crump: The True Story of a Trip West - Laurie Lawlor   *p* 859

Marshall
Elisa Michaels, Bigger & Better - Johanna Hurwitz   *e* 702

3-YEAR-OLD

Bella
Was That Christmas? - Hilary McKay   *p* 981

Bertil
Bertil and the Bathroom Elephants - Inger Lindahl   *p* 894

Marcos
A New Barker in the House - Tomie De Paola   *p* 359

4-YEAR-OLD

Keller, Sadie
Pioneer Summer - Deborah Hopkinson   *e* 677

Little Rabbit
Little Rabbit Lost - Harry Horse   *p* 682

Martha
Old Crump: The True Story of a Trip West - Laurie Lawlor   *p* 859

5-YEAR-OLD

Dillon, Daisy
Dillon Dillon - Kate Banks   *e* 75

6-YEAR-OLD

Bateman, William
The Scrimshaw Ring - William Jaspersohn   *p* 729

Eloise
Eloise Takes a Bawth - Kay Thompson   *p* 1379

Miller, Emily
Jason Rat-a-Tat - Colby Rodowsky   *e* 1220

Unnamed Character
I Love Saturdays Y Domingos - Alma Flor Ada   *p* 2

7-YEAR-OLD

Barbara
Most Beloved Sister - Astrid Lindgren   *p* 897

Julia
Julia Wants a Pet - Barbro Lindgren   *p* 899

Lucy
The First Thing My Mama Told Me - Susan Marie Swanson   *p* 1355

Martin, Leandra
Tippy Lemmey - Patricia C. McKissack   *e* 986

Michaels, Elisa
Elisa Michaels, Bigger & Better - Johanna Hurwitz   *e* 702

Moody, Stink
Judy Moody Saves the World! - Megan McDonald   *e* 976

Robinson, Roberta Louise
Here We Go Round - Alice McGill   *e* 979

Roselupin
The Red Wolf - Margaret Shannon   *p* 1285

Unnamed Character
Birthday Zoo - Deborah Lee Rose   *p* 1229

Wells, Preston "Pres"
As Far as I Can See: Meg's Prairie Diary - Kate McMullan   *e* 989

8-YEAR-OLD

Betsy
Betsy Who Cried Wolf! - Gail Carson Levine   *p* 882

Cody, William Frederick "Bill"
One Sky Above Us - E. Cody Kimmel   *e* 787

Dorfman, Robert
Robert and the Weird & Wacky Facts - Barbara Seuling   *e* 1279

Hopper, Ruth
The Red Rose Box - Brenda Woods   *e* 1463

J.D.
Georgie Lee - Sharon Phillips Denslow   *e* 374

Jeannie
Tippy Lemmey - Patricia C. McKissack   *e* 986

Patino, Ana
Home at Last - Susan Middleton Elya   *p* 431

Patrick
The Amazing Thinking Machine - Dennis Haseley   *e* 606

Paul
Tippy Lemmey - Patricia C. McKissack   *e* 986

Sara
When Catherine the Great and I Were Eight! - Cari Best   *p* 107

Stuart
Stuart Goes to School - Sara Pennypacker   *e* 1143

Tabb, Jemima
Funny Frank - Dick King-Smith   *e* 793

Turner, Emma Jean
The Hard-Times Jar - Ethel Footman Smothers   *p* 1317

Yona
Princesses Are People, Too: Two Modern Fairy Tales - Susie Morgenstern   *e* 1032

9-YEAR-OLD

Asa
A Full Hand - Thomas F. Yezerski   *p* 1477

Bamford, Robert
Vampire State Building - Elizabeth Levy   *e* 887

Banning, Caroline
The Battle for St. Michaels - Emily Arnold McCully   *b* 973

Birdsong, Corey
Flying Free: Corey's Underground Railroad Diary - Sharon Dennis Wyeth   *e* 1471

Carmichael, Darby
Darby - Jonathon Scott Fuqua   *e* 501

Cartwright, Homer
The House in the Mail - Rosemary Wells   *p* 1425

Cohen-Liu, Annie
The Trouble with Babies - Martha Freeman   *e* 488

Garland, Holly
The Trouble with Babies - Martha Freeman   *e* 488

Gaskitt, Gloria
The Woman Who Won Things - Allan Ahlberg   *e* 11

Gaskitt, Gus
The Woman Who Won Things - Allan Ahlberg   *e* 11

McGill, Eli "Eel"
Indigo - Alice Hoffman   m, h   659

McGill, Valena
Time Pieces: The Book of Times - Virginia Hamilton
   m   590

Miller, Andrew
Jason Rat-a-Tat - Colby Rodowsky   e   1220

Monroe, Pete
It Came from Beneath the Bed - James Howe
   e   688

Moore, Molly
Dish Series - Diane Muldrow   e, m   1037

Morgan, Angel
The Same Stuff as Stars - Katherine Paterson
   m   1128

Motion, Lonnie Collins "Locomotion"
Locomotion - Jacqueline Woodson   e, m   1466

Ngugu, Vusi
Zulu Dog - Anton Ferreira   e, m   450

North, Will
Wenny Has Wings - Janet Lee Carey   e, m   216

Phoebe Rose
Soul Moon Soup - Lindsay Lee Johnson   m, h   748

Rigoletti-Chase, Connor
Paint by Magic: A Time Travel Mystery - Kathryn
   Reiss   m   1197

Rosenfeld, Gray "Mouse"
Overnight - Adele Griffin   e, m   563

Ross, Natasha
Dish Series - Diane Muldrow   e, m   1037

Samuel
Trouble Don't Last - Shelley Pearsall   m   1139

Spencer, Kate
The Wrong One - Carol Otis Hurst   e, m   699

Steelgate, Robert
Dust - Arthur Slade   m, h   1308

Sterling, Jesse
Blizzard's Wake - Phyllis Reynolds Naylor   m,
   h   1065

Tozzi, Arturo
A Real American - Richard Easton   m   414

Van Riet, Martha
Overnight - Adele Griffin   e, m   563

Winslow, Emily
The Hollow Kingdom - Clare B. Dunkle   m, h   405

Worth, Lillie Mae
Whistler's Hollow - Debbie Dadey   e, m   336

12-YEAR-OLD

Anaxandra
Goddess of Yesterday - Caroline B. Cooney   m,
   h   292

Anthony "Tony"
*The Glass Cafe: Or the Stripper and the State: How
   My Mother Started a War with the System that
   Made Us Kind of Rich and a Little Bit Famous* -
   Gary Paulsen   m, h   1134

Applewhite, Edith Wharton "E.D."
Surviving the Applewhites - Stephanie S. Tolan   m,
   h   1383

Banks, Joey
Swear to Howdy - Wendelin Van Draanen   m   1392

Bernstein, Rebecca
Sparks Fly Upward - Carol Matas   e, m   954

Bishop, Jane Elizabeth "Janey"
This Isn't about the Money - Sally Warner
   m   1417

Bovey, Jessica Kay "Jessie"
Spitting Image - Shutta Crum   m   321

Boyd
How to Disappear Completely and Never Be Found -
   Sara Nickerson   m   1079

Boyle, Martha
Olive's Ocean - Kevin Henkes   m   623

Brace, Gwendolyn Mary "Gwen"
The Earth Kitchen - Sharon Bryant   m   174

Bramwell
Olivia Kidney - Ellen Potter   e, m   1165

Brennan, Bess
*Mirror, Mirror on the Wall: The Diary of Bess
   Brennan* - Barry Denenberg   e, m   373

Brennan, Elin
*Mirror, Mirror on the Wall: The Diary of Bess
   Brennan* - Barry Denenberg   e, m   373

Brodski, Rodzina Clara Jadqiga Anastozy
Rodzina - Karen Cushman   m   331

Brown, Katahdin "Dani"
Halfway to the Sky - Kimberly Brubaker Bradley
   m   135

Brown, Lucie-Marie
Daddy Says - Ntozake Shange   m   1281

Cahn, Leila
A Corner of the Universe - Ann M. Martin   m   945

Campion, Isabel
Isabel: Taking Wing - Annie Dalton   m   339

Carson, Penny
The Creek - Jennifer L. Holm   m, h   667

Cartwright, Emily
The House in the Mail - Rosemary Wells   p   1425

Castellano, Ernest "Ernie"
The Beloved Dearly - Doug Cooney   e, m   293

Chance, Jeremy Theopoulos
The Trouble with Jeremy Chance - George Harrar   e,
   m   597

Chapski, Jozef
The Secret of the Red Flame - K.M. Kimball   e,
   m   785

Chumil, Tzunun "Rosa Garcia"
Colibri - Ann Cameron   m   206

Clairmont, Margaret
How to Disappear Completely and Never Be Found -
   Sara Nickerson   m   1079

Clinciu, Vlad
Vampire State Building - Elizabeth Levy   e   887

Collins, Virginia
Tadpole - Ruth White   e, m   1438

Cooper, Russell "Rusty"
Swear to Howdy - Wendelin Van Draanen   m   1392

Crosswell, Lucy
The Steps - Rachel Cohn   m   273

Cruz, Santiago
Red Midnight - Ben Mikaelsen   m, h   1008

Cummings, Matthew
The Rainbow Kite - Marlene Fanta Shyer   m,
   h   1299

Curry, David
The Dream Bearer - Walter Dean Myers   m   1052

Daley, Ian
Stray Voltage - Eugenie Doyle   m   393

de la Torre, Anita
Before We Were Free - Julia Alvarez   m, h   24

Dimmick, Witt
The Speed of Light - Ron Carlson   m, h   218

Drummond, Casey
Say Yes - Audrey Couloumbis   m, h   306

Edwards, Grace
*Survival in the Storm: The Dust Bowl Diary of Grace
   Edwards* - Katelan Janke   e, m   728

Forrest, Andrew J. "Andy"
Mystery in Mt. Mole - Richard W. Jennings   m,
   h   737

Forrester, Miles
The 7th Knot - Kathleen Karr   m   765

Fredericka "Fred"
Praying at the Sweetwater Motel - April Young Fritz
   m   495

Gallagher, Thomas "Tom"
The Boy Who Saved Baseball - John Ritter
   m   1210

Garrett, Jacob "Jake"
Jake, Reinvented - Gordon Korman   h   816

Garrett, Pete
The Poltergoose - Michael Lawrence   e, m   862

Gilbert, Bess
Flying Blind - Anna Myers   e, m   1049

Goode, Addie
A Greater Goode - Amy Schor Ferris   m   451

Goodspeed, Patience
The Voyage of Patience Goodspeed - Heather Vogel
   Frederick   m   485

Gou Haoyou
The Kite Rider - Geraldine McCaughrean   m,
   h   965

Harrow, Doon
The City of Ember - Jeanne DuPrau   m   409

Hartley, Cedar B.
*The Slightly True Story of Cedar B. Hartley (Who
   Planned to Live an Unusual Life)* - Martine Murray
   m   1046

Honiker, George
Recycling George - Stephen Roos   e, m   1224

Jack
The Several Lives of Orphan Jack - Sarah Ellis
   e   430

Jamie
Gina.Jamie.Father.Bear - George Ella Lyon   m,
   h   920

Jefferson, Lucas
Jericho Walls - Kristi Collier   m, h   280

Jesse
Wild Boy - James Lincoln Collier   m   279

Jones, Willow Wind
Willow and Twig - Jean Little   m   903

Kendrill, Alex
The Stranger Next Door - Peg Kehret   e, m   774

Ketchum, Robert E.
Spitting Image - Shutta Crum   m   321

Kidd, Kevin
Disappearing Act - Sid Fleischman   m   461

Kidney, Olivia
Olivia Kidney - Ellen Potter   e, m   1165

Kostaniuk, Sophie
Sparks Fly Upward - Carol Matas   e, m   954

Lawrence "Larry"
The Speed of Light - Ron Carlson   m, h   218

Lewis, Carly
The Princesses of Atlantis - Lisa Williams Kline
   m   804

Lexton, Clifford "Rocky"
The Stranger Next Door - Peg Kehret   e, m   774

Liliha
In the Shadow of the Pali: A Story of the Hawaiian Leper Colony - Lisa Cindrich   *m, h*   255

Luke
A Greater Goode - Amy Schor Ferris   *m*   451

Lulu
Lulu's Hat - Susan Meddaugh   *e*   1003

MacKinnon, Aquila Jane "Quila"
Gifts from the Sea - Natalie Kinsey-Warnock   *e, m*   797

Malone, Jim
House of Sports - Marisabina Russo   *m*   1240

Mattoume
Virginia Bound - Amy Butler   *e, m*   188

Mayfleet, Lina
The City of Ember - Jeanne DuPrau   *m*   409

McBride, Bernadette "Detta"
12 Again - Sue Corbett   *e, m*   300

McBride, Patrick
12 Again - Sue Corbett   *e, m*   300

McCall, Colleen
Prairie Whispers - Frances Arrington   *m*   43

McCue, Jiggy
The Poltergoose - Michael Lawrence   *e, m*   862

Meggie
Inkheart - Cornelia Funke   *m, h*   499

Mellon, Sidney T.
Melonhead - Michael de Guzman   *m*   354

Michael
Kensuke's Kingdom - Michael Morpurgo   *e, m*   1033

Miggory Sow "Mig"
The Tale of Despereaux: Being the Story of a Mouse, a Princess, Some Soup, and a Spool of Thread - Kate DiCamillo   *e*   381

Miller, Ruby
Ruby Electric - Theresa Nelson   *m*   1074

Mint, Angie
The Poltergoose - Michael Lawrence   *e, m*   862

Minuk
Minuk: Ashes in the Pathway - Kirkpatrick Hill   *e, m*   641

Montgomery, Shirley
Zulu Dog - Anton Ferreira   *e, m*   450

Moreno, Frank
Keeper of the Night - Kimberly Willis Holt   *m, h*   669

Morgan
Lucy Was There . . . - Jean Van Leeuwen   *e, m*   1393

Morgan, Kent
Skinny-Dipping at Monster Lake - Bill Wallace   *m*   1406

Morris, Erin
A Taste of Perfection - Laura Langston   *m*   849

Morrow, Fanny
The Kingfisher's Gift - Susan Williams Beckhorn   *e, m*   96

Otis, Sarah Jane
Praying at the Sweetwater Motel - April Young Fritz   *m*   495

Owen, Hattie
A Corner of the Universe - Ann M. Martin   *m*   945

Pea
The Tale of Despereaux: Being the Story of a Mouse, a Princess, Some Soup, and a Spool of Thread - Kate DiCamillo   *e*   381

Penmarch, Robin
Quadehar the Sorcerer - Erik L'Homme   *m, h*   891

Petrovich, Slava "Cuss"
Grape Thief - Kristine L. Franklin   *m, h*   482

Piermont, Roxanne
Sister Spider Knows All - Adrian Fogelin   *m*   471

Pratt, Isabella
Lucy Was There . . . - Jean Van Leeuwen   *e, m*   1393

Proctor, Arthur
Praying at the Sweetwater Motel - April Young Fritz   *m*   495

Prosper
The Thief Lord - Cornelia Funke   *m, h*   500

Purdy, Michael
The Traitor: Golden Mountain Chronicles: 1885 - Laurence Yep   *m, h*   1475

Rabinowitz, Hadassah "Dossi"
Dear Emma - Johanna Hurwitz   *e, m*   701

Rafferty
The Speed of Light - Ron Carlson   *m, h*   218

Revel, Cecile
Cecile: Gates of Gold - Mary Casanova   *e, m*   224

Salz
Breath - Donna Jo Napoli   *m, h*   1059

Schubert, Annabel Whoopi
The Steps - Rachel Cohn   *m*   273

Shea, Davy
Pirate Hunter Series - Brad Strickland   *e, m*   1348

Sissney, Cissy
Stop the Train! - Geraldine McCaughrean   *e, m*   968

Stewart, Maddy
The Ravenmaster's Secret - Elvira Woodruff   *m*   1462

Sunday, Anna "Adam"
Anna Sunday - Sally M. Keehn   *m*   772

Suzie
Black-Eyed Suzie - Susan Shaw   *m, h*   1287

Taylor, Rose
Danger at the Wild West Show - Alison Hart   *m*   601

Tess
The No Place Cat - C.S. Adler   *e, m*   4

Tillman, Ruth Ann "Ruthie"
The Babbs Switch Story - Darleen Bailey Beard   *m*   93

Tinker, Lizzy
Stink Alley - Jamie Gilson   *e, m*   527

Trevor
Junebug in Trouble - Alice Mead   *e*   1002

Trey
Green Boy - Susan Cooper   *m*   297

Vandorn, Nelly
Nelly in the Wilderness - Lynn Cullen   *m*   325

Wayne, Georgia
Mystery in Mt. Mole - Richard W. Jennings   *m, h*   737

Welch, Arlene
The Princesses of Atlantis - Lisa Williams Kline   *m*   804

Whitfield, Rennie
Recycling George - Stephen Roos   *e, m*   1224

Whyte, Joselyn
Jo's Triumph - Nikki Tate   *e, m*   1363

Wisdom, Thomas
The Angel Factor - Terence Blacker   *m, h*   113

Withington, David
The Ghost Behind the Wall - Melvin Burgess   *m*   182

Woods, Hollis
Pictures of Hollis Woods - Patricia Reilly Giff   *e, m*   524

Young, Joseph
The Traitor: Golden Mountain Chronicles: 1885 - Laurence Yep   *m, h*   1475

13-YEAR-OLD

Asconti, Dave
Outside In - Karen Romano Young   *m, h*   1489

Barnavelt, Lewis
The Whistle, the Grave, and the Ghost - Brad Strickland   *m*   1349

Bellemare, Jordan
The Countess and Me - Paul Kropp   *m, h*   832

Bennett, Hannah
Hannah, Divided - Adele Griffin   *m*   562

Birch, Winston Churchill "Tadpole"
Tadpole - Ruth White   *e, m*   1438

Blennerhassett, Lily
Lily B. on the Brink of Cool - E. Cody Kimmel   *e, m*   786

Brackett, Rob
Virginia Bound - Amy Butler   *e, m*   188

Brotherbum, Cabot "Rocky"
Remote Man - Elizabeth Honey   *m, h*   670

Brown, Springer
Halfway to the Sky - Kimberly Brubaker Bradley   *m*   135

Carter, Dallas
Ruby Holler - Sharon Creech   *e, m*   313

Carter, Florida
Ruby Holler - Sharon Creech   *e, m*   313

Casson, Saffron "Saffy"
Saffy's Angel - Hilary McKay   *m*   980

Castille-Reed, Alexis "Alex"
When Eagles Fall - Mary Casanova   *m*   226

Cheney, Juliet "Jules"
Child X - Lee Weatherly   *m, h*   1419

Christmas, Jacob Israel
Twelve Travelers, Twenty Horses - Harriette Gillem Robinet   *m, h*   1213

Clark, Ratchet
The Canning Season - Polly Horvath   *m, h*   683

Crabtree, Lily
Lily's Ghosts - Laura Ruby   *m*   1237

Crispin "Asta's son"
Crispin: The Cross of Lead - Avi   *m, h*   58

Crouch, Stefan Millington III
Stefan's Story - Valerie Hobbs   *m*   651

Cunningham, Joelle
Sliding into Home - Dori Hillstad Butler   *m*   189

Dillon, Didier
Dillon Dillon - Kate Banks   *e*   75

DiSala, Alfredo
The Tears of the Salamander - Peter Dickinson   *m, h*   382

Dvorak, Joey
Qwerty Stevens Stuck in Time with Benjamin Franklin - Dan Gutman   *m*   575

Emberek, Laszlo
The Wolving Time - Patrick Jennings   *m, h*   735

14-YEAR-OLD

Hobbs, Lorraine
Unseen Companion - Denise Gosliner Orenstein
  h 1113

Hoffman, Netta
The Enemy Has a Face - Gloria D. Miklowitz   *m*,
  h 1009

Holloway, Chad
Shaper - Jessie Haas   *m* 576

Hood, Rowan
Lionclaw: A Tale of Rowan Hood - Nancy Springer
  m 1330

Kayla
Stetson - S.L. Rottman   *h* 1233

Keeling, Amanda Jane "Rebel"
Rebel - Willo Davis Roberts   *m* 1211

Lauchie
Sea Gift - John Ashby   *m, h* 47

Livingstone, Francis Hugh
Kings Mountain - G. Clifton Wisler   *m* 1451

Luvering, Lucy
Mates, Dates and Inflatable Bras - Cathy Hopkins
  m, h 676

Mender, Joseph "Stormy"
Inside Out - Terry Trueman   *h* 1386

Meret
The Ugly Goddess - Elsa Marston   *m* 944

Michaela "Mike"
Looking for Red - Angela Johnson   *m, h* 743

Mocenigo, Donata Aurelia
Daughter of Venice - Donna Jo Napoli   *m, h* 1060

Mocenigo, Laura
Daughter of Venice - Donna Jo Napoli   *m, h* 1060

Monaghan, Dennis
My Life and Death by Alexandra Canarsie - Susan
  Heyboer O'Keefe   *m, h* 1105

Moore, Logan
The Last Dog on Earth - Daniel Ehrenhaft   *m*,
  h 424

Muller, Jimmy
My Life and Death by Alexandra Canarsie - Susan
  Heyboer O'Keefe   *m, h* 1105

Pedersen, Joe
Under the Same Sky - Cynthia DeFelice   *m, h* 368

Phano
The Courtesan's Daughter - Priscilla Galloway
  h 505

Potts, Angelica Cookson "Angel"
*My Cup Runneth Over: The Life of Angelica Cookson
Potts* - Cherry Whytock   *m, h* 1441

Quinn, Welkin
The Earthborn - Paul Collins   *h, a* 282

Rachel Three
Walk Softly, Rachel - Kate Banks   *m, h* 78

Renaldo, Amelia "Mia"
Princess in Waiting - Meg Cabot   *m, h* 198

Reynolds, Sunny
Dead Girls Don't Write Letters - Gail Giles   *m*,
  h 525

Rider, Alexander "Alex"
Point Blank - Anthony Horowitz   *m, h* 680
Skeleton Key - Anthony Horowitz   *m, h* 681

Riley, Dusty
The Snow Pony - Alison Lester   *m, h* 875

Ripperton, Veronica "Ronnie"
LBD: It's a Girl Thing - Grace Dent   *m, h* 375

Shauzia
Mud City - Deborah Ellis   *m* 428

Simons, Nikki
Undercurrents - Willo Davis Roberts   *m, h* 1212

Sinclair, Kenny
Wolf on the Fold - Judith Clarke   *h* 259

Sinclair, Vida
Starry Nights - Judith Clarke   *m, h* 258

Slake, Emily
Overboard - Elizabeth Fama   *m, h* 442

Steve
Our Time on the River - Don Brown   *m, h* 162

Swan, Fleur
LBD: It's a Girl Thing - Grace Dent   *m, h* 375

Taylor
Shopaholic - Judy Waite   *m, h* 1405

Thacker, Charlotte
Between - Jean Thesman   *m, h* 1375

Thompson, Rebecca Lee "Becky"
A Circle of Time - Marisa Montes   *m, h* 1023

Till, Emmett
Mississippi Trial, 1955 - Chris Crowe   *m, h* 320

Vandorn, Cornelius
Nelly in the Wilderness - Lynn Cullen   *m* 325

West, James "Jamie"
The Hero - Ron Woods   *m, h* 1464

Wheeler, Cecelia "Celie"
Someday: A Novel - Jackie French Koller   *m* 815

Williams, Nesta
Mates, Dates and Inflatable Bras - Cathy Hopkins
  m, h 676

Windjammer, Adam
The House of Windjammer - V.A. Richardson   *m*,
  h 1201

Winthrop, Joshua
A Circle of Time - Marisa Montes   *m, h* 1023

Wright, Shelley
Hang On in There, Shelley - Kate Saksena   *m*,
  h 1251

Young, Shannon
Jackie's Wild Seattle - Will Hobbs   *m* 652

15-YEAR-OLD

Adams, Moses
Rebel - Willo Davis Roberts   *m* 1211

Amy
Amy - Mary Hooper   *m, h* 674

Armstrong-Barnes, Charlotte
Remembrance - Theresa Breslin   *m, h* 143

Blackwood, Melanie
Drowning Anna - Sue Mayfield   *m, h* 958

Blake
Saving Jasey - Diane Tullson   *m, h* 1387

Bradshaw, Isaac
Together Apart - Dianne E. Gray   *m, h* 550

Braxton, Elizabeth
Up Molasses Mountain - Julie Baker   *m, h* 68

Brown, Devon
Not as Crazy as I Seem - George Harrar   *m, h* 596

Burton, Louise
Shaper - Jessie Haas   *m* 576

Calder, Billy
Crossing the Panther's Path - Elizabeth Alder   *m*,
  h 17

Carlos
The Crying Rocks - Janet Taylor Lisle   *m, h* 901

Cavanaugh, Frances "Francie"
Riding the Flume - Patricia Curtis Pfitsch   *m* 1149

Chandler, Jeremy "Rat"
Rat - Jan Cheripko   *m, h* 242

Chandler, Rose
White Midnight - Dia Calhoun   *m, h* 203

Chris
Who Owns Kelly Paddik? - Beth Goobie   *m, h* 537

Collins, Daniel
The Man with the Silver Oar - Robin Moore   *m*,
  h 1029

Cummings, Bennett Lawson
The Rainbow Kite - Marlene Fanta Shyer   *m*,
  h 1299

Davies, Corin "Cory"
Sonny's War - Valerie Hobbs   *m, h* 650

Davies, Kevin Robert "Kev"
The Flip Side - Andrew Matthews   *m* 956

Desant, Henry
A Chapel of Thieves - Bruce Clements   *m* 263

Dinsmore, Teresa "Teri"
Falling from Fire - Teena Booth   *m, h* 126

Doyle, Lisa
Zipped - Laura McNeal   *h* 996

Ebba Rose "Rose"
East - Edith Pattou   *m, h* 1131

Elliot, Cody
Vampire High - Douglas Rees   *m, h* 1194

Eloise
Song for Eloise - Leigh Sauerwein   *h* 1264

Flaherty, Molly MacKenzie
*Where Have All the Flowers Gone?: The Diary of
Molly Mackenzie Flaherty* - Ellen Emerson White
  m, h 1437

Flannery, Keegan
St. Michael's Scales - Neil Connelly   *m, h* 287

Foley, Mia
Fifteen Love - Robert Corbet   *m, h* 299

Forrester, Chadwick Hoving "Wick" III
The 7th Knot - Kathleen Karr   *m* 765

Gasparini, Arianna
City of Masks - Mary Hoffman   *m, h* 661

Gelb, Trudy "Jujube"
Sticks and Stones - Beth Goobie   *m, h* 536

Gerson, Brett
Pool Boy - Michael Simmons   *m, h* 1305

Goldsmith, Anna
Drowning Anna - Sue Mayfield   *m, h* 958

Grant, Mitch
The Last Mall Rat - Erik E. Esckilsen   *m, h* 438

Green
Green Angel - Alice Hoffman   *m, h* 658

Gretchen "Chan"
Tomorrow, Maybe - Brian James   *m, h* 725

Hansen, Emil
Room in the Heart - Sonia Levitin   *m, h* 886

Hayton, Graham
Operating Codes - Nick Manns   *m, h* 939

Hersey, Sarah
Flight of the Fisherbird - Nora Martin   *e, m* 949

Hillburn, Hiram
Mississippi Trial, 1955 - Chris Crowe   *m, h* 320

Holland, Will
Fifteen Love - Robert Corbet   *m, h* 299

Howard, Matt
Guerrilla Season - Pat Hughes   *m, h* 693

Hunt, Robert "Rob"
The Flip Side - Andrew Matthews   *m* 956

Hutchings, Howard Leland
The River between Us - Richard Peck   *m, h* 1141

Ilena
The Legend of Lady Ilena - Patricia Malone   *m, h* 936

Jerry
The Hero - Ron Woods   *m, h* 1464

Kelts, Anna
Bridging Beyond - Kathleen Benner Duble   *m, h* 403

Knight, Phebe
The Kings Are Already Here - Garret Freymann-Weyr   *m, h* 493

Lahasca, Jason
Dunk - David Lubar   *m, h* 912

Landon, Kira
Escape from Memory - Margaret Peterson Haddix   *m, h* 580

Lark, Carly
Getting a Life - Jocelyn Shipley   *m, h* 1295

MacLeod, Alice
Alice, I Think - Susan Juby   *m, h* 763

MacQueen, Valerie Gail "Val"
The Trouble with Liberty - Kristin Butcher   *m, h* 187

Marlowe, Tom
Death and the Arrow - Chris Priestley   *m, h* 1169

McCann, Caitlin "Cait"
Lucas - Kevin Brooks   *h* 159

McClean, Harmony
Harmony - Rita Murphy   *m, h* 1044

McHenry, Luke
Free Radical - Claire Rudolf Murphy   *m, h* 1042

McVeigh, Jasey
Saving Jasey - Diane Tullson   *m, h* 1387

Moon, Rosie
Guitar Highway Rose - Brigid Lowry   *h* 910

Morrisey, Matthew
Bone Dry - Kathleen Karr   *m* 766

Natsworthy, Tom
Mortal Engines - Philip Reeve   *h, a* 1195

Nelson, Niels
Room in the Heart - Sonia Levitin   *m, h* 886

Nichols, Mick
Zipped - Laura McNeal   *h* 996

Nicolson, Georgia
Knocked Out by My Nunga-Nungas: Further, Further Confessions of Georgia Nicolson - Louise Rennison   *m, h* 1199

O'Connell, Sarah
One Shot - Susan Glick   *m, h* 529

Ojala, Matti
Song of Sampo Lake - William Durbin   *m, h* 411

Otsego, Lucy "Lucy the Giant"
Lucy the Giant - Sherri L. Smith   *m, h* 1316

Paddick, Kelly
Who Owns Kelly Paddik? - Beth Goobie   *m, h* 537

Paz, Violet
Cuba 15 - Nancy Osa   *m, h* 1115

Petrovski, Tanya
Getting a Life - Jocelyn Shipley   *m, h* 1295

Phillips, Bobby
Things Not Seen - Andrew Clements   *m* 261

Pierson, Francesca "Franky"
Freaky Green Eyes - Joyce Carol Oates   *m, h* 1099

Pig, Martyn
Martyn Pig - Kevin Brooks   *m, h* 160

Potter, Harry
Harry Potter and the Order of the Phoenix - J.K. Rowling   *m, h* 1234

Riley, Jake
Jake Riley: Irreparably Damaged - Rebecca Fjelland Davis   *m, h* 352

Robertson, Lynne
Escape from Memory - Margaret Peterson Haddix   *m, h* 580

Serena "Beaky"
Amy - Mary Hooper   *m, h* 674

Shannon
The Earth, My Butt, and Other Big Round Things - Carolyn Mackler   *m, h* 930

Shreves, Virginia
The Earth, My Butt, and Other Big Round Things - Carolyn Mackler   *m, h* 930

Soraya
Flame - Hilari Bell   *m, h* 97

Sterling, Kate
Blizzard's Wake - Phyllis Reynolds Naylor   *m, h* 1065

Taal, Napoleon
Nirvana's Children - Ranulfo   *h* 1185

Tangi
Kotuku - Deborah Savage   *m, h* 1265

Taylor, Lorrie
One Shot - Susan Glick   *m, h* 529

Thompson, Ernest "Shadow"
Shadow of a Doubt - S.L. Rottman   *m, h* 1232

Tucker, Tyler
Jackie's Wild Seattle - Will Hobbs   *m* 652

Turner, Chad
Dunk - David Lubar   *m, h* 912

Turner, Martin
Face - Benjamin Zephaniah   *m, h* 1494

Tuttle, Becky
The Pack - Elisa Carbone   *m, h* 214

Ursula
Warriors of Alavna - N.M. Browne   *m, h* 168

Warrener, Justin
Vampire High - Douglas Rees   *m, h* 1194

Willson, Kenny Roy
Comfort - Carolee Dean   *m, h* 363

Wing, Thorne
Welcome Home or Someplace Like It - Charlotte Agell   *m* 7

16-YEAR-OLD

Alexie, Dove
Unseen Companion - Denise Gosliner Orenstein   *h* 1113

Atalanta
Quiver - Stephanie Spinner   *m, h* 1327

Bancroft, Ben "Spaz"
Stoner & Spaz - Ron Koertge   *h* 810

Bandry, Janet Foley
Planet Janet - Dyan Sheldon   *m, h* 1291

Barney
Parasite Pig - William Sleator   *m, h* 1310

Becket, Isabel
The Dark - Marianne Curley   *m, h* 328
The Named - Marianne Curley   *m, h* 329

Blake
Full Tilt: A Novel - Neal Shusterman   *m, h* 1297

Bracke, Anna
And What about Anna? - Jan Simoen   *h* 1306

Brown, Omaha Nebraska
Blue Avenger and the Theory of Everything - Norma Howe   *m, h* 689

Burgess
Ten Miles from Winnemucca - Thelma Hatch Wyss   *m, h* 1472

Carina
The Princess and the Pauper - Kate Brian   *m* 147

Cyd Charisse
Gingerbread - Rachel Cohn   *h* 272

Daley, Ray
Stray Voltage - Eugenie Doyle   *m* 393

de la Rocque, Marguerite
Paradise - Joan Elizabeth Goodman   *m, h* 541

De Salis, Winter
Winter - John Marsden   *m, h* 943

Dolores "Do"
Dolores: Seven Stories about Her - Bruce Brooks   *m, h* 158

Doyle, Gemma
A Great and Terrible Beauty - Libba Bray   *h* 138

Driscoll, Danny
Shooting Monarchs - John Halliday   *h* 587

Garcia, Ileana
Flight to Freedom - Ana Veciana-Suarez   *m, h* 1400

Gilbert, Enoch
Flying Blind - Anna Myers   *e, m* 1049

Gilda
Gossip Times Three - Amy Goldman Koss   *m* 821

Gokey, Mattie
A Northern Light - Jennifer Donnelly   *h* 387

Hazelwood, Kia
Dancing Naked - Shelley Hrdlitschka   *h* 692

Henry, Martha "Patsy"
Or Give Me Death - Ann Rinaldi   *m, h* 1206

Hollister, Julie
The Trap - Joan Lowery Nixon   *m, h* 1087

Inagki, Dan
Beacon Hill Boys - Ken Mochizuki   *m, h* 1021

Ingrid
The Princess and the Pauper - Kate Brian   *m* 147

Ingvoldsson, Markus
The Princess and the Pauper - Kate Brian   *m* 147

Jepson, Ben
Lord of the Kill - Theodore Taylor   *m, h* 1366

Johnson, Julia
The Princess and the Pauper - Kate Brian   *m* 147

Kaligaris, Lena
The Second Summer of the Sisterhood - Ann Brashares   *m, h* 137

Kat
Shopaholic - Judy Waite   *m, h* 1405

Kate
Kissing Kate - Lauren Myracle   *h* 1054

Kelvin, Jana
Bull Rider - Marilyn Halvorson   *m, h* 588

Kotalev, Nikolai
The Kings Are Already Here - Garret Freymann-Weyr   *m, h* 493

Lea, Margaret
Forbidden Forest: The Story of Little John and Robin Hood - Michael Cadnum   *m, h* 200

Lissa
Kissing Kate - Lauren Myracle   *h* 1054

Livingstone, Kate
Kings Mountain - G. Clifton Wisler   *m*   1451

Lizbeth
The Big Burn - Jeanette Ingold   *m, h*   713

Logan, Jarrett
The Big Burn - Jeanette Ingold   *m, h*   713

Lowell, Carmen Lucille
The Second Summer of the Sisterhood - Ann Brashares   *m, h*   137

Lynch, Jimmy
Handbook for Boys: A Novel - Walter Dean Myers   *m, h*   1053

Madison, Raven
Vampire Kisses - Ellen Schreiber   *m, h*   1271

Magruder, Avery
Hear the Wind Blow: A Novel of the Civil War - Mary Downing Hahn   *m*   581

Mai, Minna
Malka - Mirjam Pressler   *m, h*   1168

Makenna
The Goblin Wood - Hilari Bell   *m, h*   98

Manuel
Under the Same Sky - Cynthia DeFelice   *m, h*   368

McKenna, Samantha "Sam"
Timeless Love - Judith O'Brien   *m, h*   1101

McKenzie, Claire
What Happened to Lani Garver - Carol Plum-Ucci   *h*   1162

McQueen, Layne
Bull Rider - Marilyn Halvorson   *m, h*   588

Miller, Martin J. "Marty"
Ten Miles from Winnemucca - Thelma Hatch Wyss   *m, h*   1472

Minou, Colleen "Stoner"
Stoner & Spaz - Ron Koertge   *h*   810

Olafsson, Sigurd "Sig"
The Dark Horse - Marcus Sedgwick   *m*   1275

Paski, Disha
Planet Janet - Dyan Sheldon   *m, h*   1291

Paulie
Say Yes - Audrey Couloumbis   *m, h*   306

Peck, Jane "Boston Jane"
Boston Jane: Wilderness Days - Jennifer L. Holm   *m, h*   666

Prentice, Jane
Just Jane: The Story of a Daughter of England Caught in the Struggle for Independence in Revolutionary America - William Lavender   *m, h*   858

Racine, Michael Peter III
Saving the Planet & Stuff - Gail Gauthier   *m, h*   511

Rasmussen, Nigel "Kenric"
Heir Apparent - Vivian Vande Velde   1395

Reynolds, Samantha "Sam"
Samantha and the Cowboy - Lorraine Heath   *h*   620

Robert, Ethan
The Dark - Marianne Curley   *m, h*   328
The Named - Marianne Curley   *m, h*   329

Robeson, Brian
Brian's Hunt - Gary Paulsen   *m, h*   1133

Roke, Emmaline
Search of the Moon King's Daughter - Linda Holeman   *m, h*   665

Schumacher, David Bruce "Blue Avenger"
Blue Avenger and the Theory of Everything - Norma Howe   *m, h*   689

Sebring, Shaw
The Hemingway Tradition - Kristin Butcher   *m*   186

Simon, Susannah "Suze"
Haunted: A Tale of the Mediator - Meg Cabot   *m, h*   196

Szabo, Lucy
Sweetblood - Pete Hautman   *h*   610

Thaler, Tess
Mountain Solo - Jeanette Ingold   *m, h*   714

Tillman, Daphne Sue
The Babbs Switch Story - Darleen Bailey Beard   *m*   93

Visser, Janke
When the War Is Over - Martha Attema   *m, h*   53

Vreeland, Bridget "Bee"
The Second Summer of the Sisterhood - Ann Brashares   *m, h*   137

Wahhsted, Zachary McDaniel "Zach"
Inside Out - Terry Trueman   *h*   1386

West, Grady
Target - Kathleen Jeffrie Johnson   *h*   747

Weston, Calico "Callie"
The Return of Calico Bright - David Winkler   *m, h*   1450

Witherspoon, Anthony "Spoon"
The Beast - Walter Dean Myers   *h*   1051

Wood, Emily
Nightmare - Joan Lowery Nixon   *m, h*   1086

17-YEAR-OLD

Beene, Melissa
The Queen of Everything - Deb Caletti   *h*   202

Bera, Morgan
Deep - Susanna Vance   *m, h*   1394

Billings, Troy "Big T"
Fat Kid Rules the World - K.L. Going   *h*   533

Breeze "Bree"
The Long Night of Leo and Bree - Ellen Wittlinger   *m, h*   1453

Brittman, Cassiopeia Emma "Cassie"
Hannah's Garden - Midori Snyder   *m, h*   1318

Brown, Creighton
The Year of the Hangman - Gary Blackwood   *m, h*   115

Christian
Once Upon a Marigold - Jean Ferris   *m, h*   452

Damienne
Paradise - Joan Elizabeth Goodman   *m, h*   541

Davis, Jeremy "Booger"
Blood Trail - Nancy Springer   *m, h*   1329

Devlin, Caleb
The Creek - Jennifer L. Holm   *m, h*   667

Downs, Phillip "Pip"
Bottled Up - Jaye Murray   *m, h*   1045

Duncan
Acceleration - Graham McNamee   *m, h*   995

Farrell, Peggy Fleming
Frozen Rodeo - Catherine Clark   *m, h*   256

Francy, Sandra "Lady"
Lady: My Life as a Bitch - Melvin Burgess   *h*   183

Freeman, Alexandra "Alex"
Martyn Pig - Kevin Brooks   *m, h*   160

Gauk
Daughter of the Wind - Michael Cadnum   *m, h*   199

Gingrich, Aaron
Blood Trail - Nancy Springer   *m, h*   1329

Ginny
Falling through Darkness - Carolyn McCullough   *h*   972

Gwyndolyne "Gwyn"
Born Confused - Tanuja Desai Hidier   *h*   639

Henderson, Danny
How I Fell in Love & Learned to Shoot Free Throws - Jon Ripslinger   *h*   1209

Hobbs, Greg
The Shell House - Linda Newbery   *h*   1075

Hoffman, Adam
The Enemy Has a Face - Gloria D. Miklowitz   *m, h*   1009

Jesus "Chuy"
The Afterlife - Gary Soto   *m, h*   1320

Jiaan
Flame - Hilari Bell   *m, h*   97

Keely, Kate
Rising Tide - Jean Thesman   *m, h*   1376

Kevin
Handbook for Boys: A Novel - Walter Dean Myers   *m, h*   1053

Kim
Kim: Empty Inside - Beatrice Sparks   *m, h*   1323

Klassen, Derek
Dancing Naked - Shelley Hrdlitschka   *h*   692

Lala, Dimple Rohitbhai
Born Confused - Tanuja Desai Hidier   *h*   639

Leo
The Long Night of Leo and Bree - Ellen Wittlinger   *m, h*   1453

Lexie, Pertrisha "Pert"
The Painters of Lexieville - Sharon Darrow   *m, h*   348

Luca, Vincent "Vince"
Son of the Mob - Gordon Korman   *m, h*   818

Matt
Mahalia - Joanne Horniman   *h*   679

McCrae, Elizabeth "Squid"
The Lighthouse Keeper's Daughter - Iain Lawrence   *h*   860

McCullough, Emeline "Emmy"
The Voyage of the Continental - Katherine Kirkpatrick   *m*   801

McKenzie, Jordan
The Queen of Everything - Deb Caletti   *h*   202

Mender, Alan "Frosty"
Inside Out - Terry Trueman   *h*   1386

Meryk, Dayle
Out of the Fire - Deborah Froese   *m, h*   497

Miller, Catherine
The Presence: A Ghost Story - Eve Bunting   *m, h*   181

Montmount, Percival "Percy" Jr.
Tribes - Arthur Slade   *h*   1309

Pearce, Zachary "Zach"
Not Quite a Stranger - Colby Rodowsky   *m, h*   1221

Pettigrew, Sam
Hanging on to Max - Margaret Bechard   *h*   94

Razz
Death Wind - William Bell   *m, h*   99

Red
Looking for Red - Angela Johnson   *m, h*   743

Sinclair, Clement David "Clem"
Starry Nights - Judith Clarke   *m, h*   258

Slater, Paul
Haunted: A Tale of the Mediator - Meg Cabot   *m, h*   196

Stall, Noreen
True Confessions of a Heartless Girl - Martha Brooks   *h*   161

Steele, Richard
Hard Cash - Kate Cann   *h*   210

Stephanie
17: A Novel in Prose Poems - Liz Rosenberg   *h*   1230

Sterling, Alexander
Vampire Kisses - Ellen Schreiber   *m, h*   1271

Stetson "Stet"
Stetson - S.L. Rottman   *h*   1233

Tessman, Jamie
The Night I Disappeared - Julie Reece Deaver   *m, h*   364

Thigpen, Audelia "Del"
Breakout - Paul Fleischman   *h*   460

Thorpe, Charlotte Williamson "Wim"
Kotuku - Deborah Savage   *m, h*   1265

Todd, Jacob
Postcards from No Man's Land - Aidan Chambers   *h*   237

Yoder, Tullis
Horse Thief: A Novel - Robert Newton Peck   *m, h*   1142

Zoe
Aimee - Mary Beth Miller   *h*   1011

18-YEAR-OLD

Aaronson, Joss
Singing the Dogstar Blues - Alison Goodman   *h*   540

Casson, Cadmium Gold "Caddy"
Saffy's Angel - Hilary McKay   *m*   980

Cavanaugh, Ginny
Making the Run - Heather Henson   *h*   626

Dinsmore, Samantha
Falling from Fire - Teena Booth   *m, h*   126

Edelstein, Bridget
Bringing Up the Bones - Lara M. Zeises   *h*   1492

Gilbert, Benjamin "Benji"
Bringing Up the Bones - Lara M. Zeises   *h*   1492

Hackett, Morgan
The Night I Disappeared - Julie Reece Deaver   *m, h*   364

Hart, Matthew "Matt"
Samantha and the Cowboy - Lorraine Heath   *h*   620

Hubert
The Leopard Sword - Michael Cadnum   *m, h*   201

Inagki, Brad
Beacon Hill Boys - Ken Mochizuki   *m, h*   1021

Lexie, Jobe
The Painters of Lexieville - Sharon Darrow   *m, h*   348

Loomis, Royal
A Northern Light - Jennifer Donnelly   *h*   387

Malone, Kate
Catalyst - Laurie Halse Anderson   *h*   28

McClellan, Lucinda Larrimore "Crazy Lu"
Making the Run - Heather Henson   *h*   626

Monk
A Cool Moonlight - Angela Johnson   *e, m*   741

Pearson, Edmund
The Shell House - Linda Newbery   *h*   1075

Russell, Samantha
The Farther You Run - Davida Wills Hurwin   *h*   700

Rydell, R.C.
Mississippi Trial, 1955 - Chris Crowe   *m, h*   320

Staples, Frank
Amaryllis - Craig Crist-Evans   *m, h*   315

Starr, Remy
This Lullaby - Sarah Dessen   *h*   377

Weinland, Annette
Unseen Companion - Denise Gosliner Orenstein   *h*   1113

Winslow, Kate
The Hollow Kingdom - Clare B. Dunkle   *m, h*   405

19-YEAR-OLD

Brocato, Mona
The Farther You Run - Davida Wills Hurwin   *h*   700

Brown, Grace
A Northern Light - Jennifer Donnelly   *h*   387

Bryant, Mary Broad
Escape from Botany Bay: The True Story of Mary Bryant - Gerald Hausman   *m, h*   609

David
Our Time on the River - Don Brown   *m, h*   162

Esperance, Moy
Behind the Mountains: The Diary of Celiane Esperance - Edwidge Danticat   *m, h*   343

Ingram, Aisha
Chill Wind - Janet McDonald   *h*   975

Kavi
Flame - Hilari Bell   *m, h*   97

Ray, Kelly
One Night - Marsha Qualey   *h*   1180

Shardae, Danica
Hawksong - Amelia Atwater-Rhodes   *m, h*   54

1ST GRADER

Horus
First Graders from Mars: Episode 2: The Problem with Pelly - Shana Corey   *b*   301

Nergal
First Graders from Mars: Episode 3: Nergal and the Great Space Race - Shana Corey   *e*   302

O'Hara, Charley
Leap, Frog - Jane Cutler   *e*   332

Pelly
First Graders from Mars: Episode 2: The Problem with Pelly - Shana Corey   *b*   301

Tera
First Graders from Mars: Episode 2: The Problem with Pelly - Shana Corey   *b*   301

2ND GRADER

Brown, Amber
Get Ready for Second Grade, Amber Brown - Paula Danziger   *b*   346

Daniels, Justin
Get Ready for Second Grade, Amber Brown - Paula Danziger   *b*   346

Greene, Gooney Bird
Gooney Bird Greene - Lois Lowry   *e*   911

Gus
Gus and Grandpa and the Halloween Costume - Claudia Mills   *b*   1014

James, Calliope
The Talent Show - Michelle Edwards   *e*   417

Michaels, Elisa
Elisa Michaels, Bigger & Better - Johanna Hurwitz   *e*   702

Olivia
The Best Class Picture Ever! - Denis Roche   *p*   1214

Reuben
Wingwalker - Rosemary Wells   *e*   1429

Smith, Howie
The Talent Show - Michelle Edwards   *e*   417

Vang, Pa Lia
The Talent Show - Michelle Edwards   *e*   417

3RD GRADER

Barr, Gordie
Doggone . . . Third Grade! - Colleen O'Shaughnessy McKenna   *e*   982

Dorfman, Robert
Robert and the Weird & Wacky Facts - Barbara Seuling   *e*   1279

Doug
Horrible Harry and the Dragon War - Suzy Kline   *e*   806

Evans, Sara
Starting with Alice - Phyllis Reynolds Naylor   *e*   1070

Felcher, Paul
Robert and the Weird & Wacky Facts - Barbara Seuling   *e*   1279

Fraser, Edward
Leap, Frog - Jane Cutler   *e*   332

Henryson, Mortimer
Plantzilla - Jerdine Nolen   *p*   1092

Hernandez, Josh
7 x 9 = Trouble! - Claudia Mills   *e*   1013

Lamont
Doggone . . . Third Grade! - Colleen O'Shaughnessy McKenna   *e*   982

Max
The Hero of Third Grade - Alice DeLaCroix   *e*   370

McKinley, Alice Kathleen
Starting with Alice - Phyllis Reynolds Naylor   *e*   1070

Moody, Judy
Judy Moody Saves the World! - Megan McDonald   *e*   976

Morales, Gabi
A Crazy, Mixed-Up Spanglish Day - Marisa Montes   *e*   1024

Padilla, Chico
First Day in Grapes - L. King Perez   *p*   1145

Park, Song Lee
Horrible Harry and the Dragon War - Suzy Kline   *e*   806

Randall
The Hero of Third Grade - Alice DeLaCroix   *e*   370

Red
Doggone . . . Third Grade! - Colleen O'Shaughnessy McKenna   *e*   982

4TH GRADER

Rodriguez, Rosalind
Starting with Alice - Phyllis Reynolds Naylor
  e 1070

Spooger, Harry
Horrible Harry and the Dragon War - Suzy Kline
  e 806

Stuart
Stuart Goes to School - Sara Pennypacker   e 1143
Stuart's Cape - Sara Pennypacker   e 1144

Thomas, Willimena "Willie"
How to Lose Your Class Pet - Valerie Wilson Wesley
  e 1430

Wiley, Johnny
A Crazy, Mixed-Up Spanglish Day - Marisa Montes
  e 1024

Williams, Wilson
7 x 9 = Trouble! - Claudia Mills   e 1013

4TH GRADER

Attired, Natalie
The Hamster of the Baskervilles - Bruce Hale
  e 583

Bates, Julian
Gloria Rising - Ann Cameron   e 207

Beard, George
The Adventures of Super Diaper Baby: The First Graphic Novel - Dav Pilkey   e 1153

Brown, Amber
Amber Brown Is Green with Envy - Paula Danziger
  e 345

Chaisang, Oy
The Gold-Threaded Dress - Carolyn Marsden
  e 942

Dhabanandana, Phya Winit "P.W."
Leon and the Spitting Image - Allen Kurzweil   e,
  m 839

Frankie
The Gold-Threaded Dress - Carolyn Marsden
  e 942

Gecko, Chet
The Hamster of the Baskervilles - Bruce Hale
  e 583
The Malted Falcon - Bruce Hale   e 584
Trouble Is My Beeswax - Bruce Hale   e 585

Ginny
Especially Heroes - Virginia Kroll   p 831

Hatford, Wally
Boys in Control - Phyllis Reynolds Naylor   e 1066

Henry, Jack
Jack Adrift: Fourth Grade without a Clue - Jack Gantos   e 506

Howard, Annie
Making Music - Susan Bonners   e 124

Hutchins, Harold
The Adventures of Super Diaper Baby: The First Graphic Novel - Dav Pilkey   e 1153

Jones, Gloria
Gloria Rising - Ann Cameron   e 207

Jones, Herbie
Herbie Jones Moves On - Suzy Kline   e 805

Liliandra
The Gold-Threaded Dress - Carolyn Marsden
  e 942

Lily-Matisse
Leon and the Spitting Image - Allen Kurzweil   e,
  m 839

Malloy, Caroline
Boys in Control - Phyllis Reynolds Naylor   e 1066

The Girls Take Over - Phyllis Reynolds Naylor
  e 1067

Martin, Raymond
Herbie Jones Moves On - Suzy Kline   e 805

McKinley, Alice Kathleen
Alice in Blunderland - Phyllis Reynolds Naylor
  e 1063

Palmer, Kate
The Meanest Doll in the World - Ann M. Martin
  e 946

Zeisel, Leon
Leon and the Spitting Image - Allen Kurzweil   e,
  m 839

5TH GRADER

Amy
Attack of the Mutant Underwear - Tom Birdseye
  e 109

Bugg, Kevin
City of Names - Kevin Brockmeier   e 157

Carson, Cody Lee
Attack of the Mutant Underwear - Tom Birdseye
  e 109

Chelmsley, Mark Robert
A Week in the Woods - Andrew Clements   e 262

David
The Very Worst Thing - Torey Hayden   m 614

Donuthead, Franklin Delano
Donuthead - Sue Stauffacher   e 1337

Doyle, Drake
The Case of the Graveyard Ghost - Michele Torrey
  e 1384

Fisher, Suzanne
The Green Dog: A Mostly True Story - Suzanne Fisher Staples   e 1336

Fossey, Nell
The Case of the Graveyard Ghost - Michele Torrey
  e 1384

Gonnella, Justin
Witch's Wishes - Vivian Vande Velde   e 1396

Jake
Minn and Jake - Janet S. Wong   e 1456

Jones, Sahara "Sahara Special"
Sahara Special - Esme Raji Codell   e, m 269

Katz, Lido
The Last Burp of Mac McGerp - Pam Smallcomb
  e 1311

Kervick, Sarah
Donuthead - Sue Stauffacher   e 1337

Maccarone, Joel
Taking Care of Trouble - Bonnie Graves   e 547

McGerp, Mac
The Last Burp of Mac McGerp - Pam Smallcomb
  e 1311

McKinney, Kara
Run from the Nun! - Erin MacLellan   e, m 931

Minn
Minn and Jake - Janet S. Wong   e 1456

Quackenbush, Howie
City of Names - Kevin Brockmeier   e 157

Robinson, Casey
City of Names - Kevin Brockmeier   e 157

Stone, Henry
Izzy's Place - Marc Kornblatt   e, m 819

Stopes, Madeleine
The Very Worst Thing - Torey Hayden   m 614

6TH GRADER

Baer, Leah
Almost Home - Nora Raleigh Baskin   e, m 87

Barnes, Zachary James "Zach"
The Canyon - Sheila Cole   e, m 275

Beck, Gina
After Elaine - Ann L. Dreyer   m 397

Bloom, Lee
When Pirates Came to Brooklyn - Phyllis Shalant   e, m 1280

Boyd, Wallace "Weasel"
Bernie Magruder & the Bats in the Belfry - Phyllis Reynolds Naylor   e 1064

Burke, Polly
When Pirates Came to Brooklyn - Phyllis Shalant   e, m 1280

Carmody, Max "Maxx Comedy"
Maxx Comedy: The Funniest Kid in America - Gordon Korman   e, m 817

Costa, Mike
Macaroni Boy - Katherine Ayres   e, m 62

Daley, Ian
Stray Voltage - Eugenie Doyle   m 393

Flack, Jerry
Dork on the Run - Carol Gorman   e, m 543

Fraser, Jason
Leap, Frog - Jane Cutler   e 332

Hatford, Jake
The Girls Take Over - Phyllis Reynolds Naylor
  e 1067

Hiller, Will
Almost Home - Nora Raleigh Baskin   e, m 87

Kendrill, Alex
Spy Cat - Peg Kehret   e, m 773
The Stranger Next Door - Peg Kehret   e, m 774

Magruder, Bernie
Bernie Magruder & the Bats in the Belfry - Phyllis Reynolds Naylor   e 1064

Malloy, Eddie
The Girls Take Over - Phyllis Reynolds Naylor
  e 1067

Marshall, Gabe
Dork on the Run - Carol Gorman   e, m 543

McAdams, Brenda
Dork on the Run - Carol Gorman   e, m 543

Monroe, Pete
It Came from Beneath the Bed - James Howe
  e 688

Morgan, Alyssa
The Invisible Enemy - Marthe Jocelyn   e, m 740

Neidermeyer, Peggy
Agnes Parker . . . Girl in Progress - Kathleen O'Dell   e, m 1103

Parker, Agnes
Agnes Parker . . . Girl in Progress - Kathleen O'Dell   e, m 1103

Paskoff, Clyde
Quit It - Marcia Byalick   e, m 191

Peters, Rebecca
Quit It - Marcia Byalick   e, m 191

Prejean
Agnes Parker . . . Girl in Progress - Kathleen O'Dell   e, m 1103

Riley, Georgene
Bernie Magruder & the Bats in the Belfry - Phyllis Reynolds Naylor   e 1064

Ryan, Joseph "Joe"
Macaroni Boy - Katherine Ayres   *e, m*   62

Seinfeld, Susie
United Tates of America - Paula Danziger   *e,*
m   347

Smootz, Ricky
Cowboy Boy - James Proimos   *e*   1173

Stelson, Rachel
My Chimp Friday: The Nana Banana Chronicles -
Hester Mundis   *e, m*   1038

Stoner, Billie
The Invisible Enemy - Marthe Jocelyn   *e, m*   740

Tate, Harlem
Fame and Glory in Freedom, Georgia - Barbara
O'Connor   *e, m*   1102

Tate, Sarah Kate "Skate"
United Tates of America - Paula Danziger   *e,*
m   347

Trevor
The Canyon - Sheila Cole   *e, m*   275

Tuttle, John Henry
Brothers Below Zero - Tor Seidler   *e, m*   1277

Waldrip, Joe
Agnes Parker . . . Girl in Progress - Kathleen O'Dell
e, m   1103

Weaver, Burdette "Bird"
Fame and Glory in Freedom, Georgia - Barbara
O'Connor   *e, m*   1102

Young, Fowler
My Life of Crime - Richard W. Jennings   *m*   736

7TH GRADER

Aarons, Catalina
The Revealers - Doug Wilhelm   *m*   1443

Abby
Gossip Times Three - Amy Goldman Koss   *m*   821

Benton, Sam "Tree"
Stand Tall - Joan Bauer   *m*   89

Bess
Gossip Times Three - Amy Goldman Koss   *m*   821

Bogart, Vincent "Big Skinny"
Ruby Electric - Theresa Nelson   *m*   1074

Cristy
Gossip Times Three - Amy Goldman Koss   *m*   821

Donleavy, Davy "Tex"
Never So Green - Tim Johnston   *h*   750

Fellowes, Ariadne "Addy"
Cold in Summer - Tracy Barrett   *e, m*   83

Gekewicz, Elliot
The Revealers - Doug Wilhelm   *m*   1443

Hatcher, Fauna
Double Fudge - Judy Blume   *e, m*   120

Hatcher, Flora
Double Fudge - Judy Blume   *e, m*   120

Hatcher, Peter "Pete"
Double Fudge - Judy Blume   *e, m*   120

Kelly, Brandon
Mind Games - Jeanne Marie Grunwell   *m*   567

Kravitz, Carrie
Quit It - Marcia Byalick   *e, m*   191

Krenina, Marina
Mind Games - Jeanne Marie Grunwell   *m*   567

Lewis, Carly
The Princesses of Atlantis - Lisa Williams Kline
m   804

Lloyd, Benjamin D. "Ben"
Mind Games - Jeanne Marie Grunwell   *m*   567

McCarty, Matchit
Matchit - Martha Moore   *e, m*   1027

McCrank, Mary Ann Alice
Mary Ann Alice - Brian Doyle   *m*   392

McGuire, Mickey Jr.
Mary Ann Alice - Brian Doyle   *m*   392

McKenze, Marissa
Sammy Keyes and the Search for Snake Eyes -
Wendelin Van Draanen   *m*   1391

Miller, Ruby
Ruby Electric - Theresa Nelson   *m*   1074

Mossbach, Matthew "Mouse"
Ruby Electric - Theresa Nelson   *m*   1074

Oh, Ji Eun
Mind Games - Jeanne Marie Grunwell   *m*   567

Penhaligon, Arthur
Mister Monday - Garth Nix   *m, h*   1085

Phelps, Claire
Mind Games - Jeanne Marie Grunwell   *m*   567

Phelps, Kathleen
Mind Games - Jeanne Marie Grunwell   *m*   567

Piermont, Roxanne
Sister Spider Knows All - Adrian Fogelin   *m*   471

Rocque, Simon "Sport"
Harriet Spies Again - Helen Ericson   *e, m*   435

Trainor, Russell
The Revealers - Doug Wilhelm   *m*   1443

Tuttle, Tim
Brothers Below Zero - Tor Seidler   *e, m*   1277

Welch, Arlene
The Princesses of Atlantis - Lisa Williams Kline
m   804

Welsch, Harriet M.
Harriet Spies Again - Helen Ericson   *e, m*   435

Whitney
The Princesses of Atlantis - Lisa Williams Kline
m   804

Wingo, Zack
The Princesses of Atlantis - Lisa Williams Kline
m   804

Zack
Gossip Times Three - Amy Goldman Koss   *m*   821

8TH GRADER

Bingham, Ed
Wizards of the Game - David Lubar   *m*   914

Bowen, Kathlee "Kat"
*A Time for Courage: The Suffragette Diary of
Kathleen Bowen, Washington, DC, 1917* - Kathryn
Lasky   *e, m*   857

Brand, Daniel "Dan"
The Cheat - Amy Goldman Koss   *m*   820

Broder, Jake
The Cheat - Amy Goldman Koss   *m*   820

Chambers, Carly
The Secret Within - Theresa Golding   *m*   534

Collier, Sarah
The Cheat - Amy Goldman Koss   *m*   820

Crocker, Alexandra "Alex"
Friction - E.R. Frank   *m, h*   480

Diamond, Joseph Eli "Jed"
Birdland - Tracy Mack   *m, h*   927

Dickensen, Mercer
Wizards of the Game - David Lubar   *m*   914

Douglas, Delia
Double Dutch - Sharon M. Draper   *m, h*   396

Elsinger, Mikey
Bad Girls in Love - Cynthia Voigt   *m*   1402

Epps, Margalo
Bad Girls in Love - Cynthia Voigt   *m*   1402

Flyer
Birdland - Tracy Mack   *m, h*   927

Francis, Sarah
Waiting for Sarah - Bruce McBay   *m, h*   961

Gavin
Saving Jasey - Diane Tullson   *m, h*   1387

Greene, Matt
*Born Too Short: The Confessions of an Eighth-Grade
Basket Case* - Dan Elish   *m*   425

Hunter, Martin
Thief of Dreams - Todd Strasser   *m*   1347

Hyde, Josie
*Born Too Short: The Confessions of an Eighth-Grade
Basket Case* - Dan Elish   *m*   425

Izbecki, Ellis
Flip - David Lubar   *m*   913

Jackson, C.J.
*The Journal of C.J. Jackson: A Dust Bowl Migrant:
Oklahoma to California, 1935* - William Durbin
m   410

Janice, Stacy
Friction - E.R. Frank   *m, h*   480

Jeremy
The Rainbow Kite - Marlene Fanta Shyer   *m,
h*   1299

Katie
The Cheat - Amy Goldman Koss   *m*   820

King, Robert "Rob"
The Cheat - Amy Goldman Koss   *m*   820

Lee, Tom
The Tiger's Apprentice - Laurence Yep   *m*   1474

Lewis, Carolina
Stefan's Story - Valerie Hobbs   *m*   651

Livingston, Keith
*Born Too Short: The Confessions of an Eighth-Grade
Basket Case* - Dan Elish   *m*   425

Macavity, Shawn
Bad Girls in Love - Cynthia Voigt   *m*   1402

McKenzie, Ryan
Flip - David Lubar   *m*   913

McKenzie, Taylor
Flip - David Lubar   *m*   913

McVeigh, Tristan "Trist"
Saving Jasey - Diane Tullson   *m, h*   1387

Miller, Randall "Chubby"
Someday: A Novel - Jackie French Koller   *m*   815

Moreno, Isabel
Keeper of the Night - Kimberly Willis Holt   *m,
h*   669

Pepper, Yolanda "Yo Yo"
Double Dutch - Sharon M. Draper   *m, h*   396

Santack, Sophia "Sophie"
Stand Tall - Joan Bauer   *m*   89

Tolliver, Tabu
Double Dutch - Sharon M. Draper   *m, h*   396

Tolliver, Titan
Double Dutch - Sharon M. Draper   *m, h*   396

Tucker, Richie
The Revealers - Doug Wilhelm   *m*   1443

Wheeler, Cecelia "Celie"
Someday: A Novel - Jackie French Koller   *m*   815

Youngblood, Randy
Double Dutch - Sharon M. Draper   m, h   396

9TH GRADER

Aaronsohn, Sari
The True Meaning of Cleavage - Mariah Fredericks
m, h   486

Allard, Eleanor "Ellie"
Girls in Love - Jacqueline Wilson   m, h   1448

Camden, Teddy
Picture Perfect - Elaine Marie Alphin   m, h   22

Conway, Daniel H. "Danny"
Prep - Jake Coburn   h   266

Dan
Girls in Love - Jacqueline Wilson   m, h   1448

Desravines, Mardi
Fresh Girl - Jaira Placide   h   1160

Dinsmore, Teresa "Teri"
Falling from Fire - Teena Booth   m, h   126

Floyd, Brent
Sticks and Stones - Beth Goobie   m, h   536

Gelb, Trudy "Jujube"
Sticks and Stones - Beth Goobie   m, h   536

Gilman, Zack
The Viking Series - Christopher Tebbetts   m   1370

Ginger
Waiting to Disappear - April Young Fritz   m,
h   496

Hank
Mixed-Up Doubles - Elena Yates Eulo   m, h   439

Horvath, Jessica "Jess"
The True Meaning of Cleavage - Mariah Fredericks
m, h   486

Ireland, Ann "Annie"
Hard Time - Julian F. Thompson   m, h   1378

Jones, Pamela
Simply Alice - Phyllis Reynolds Naylor   m   1069

Long, Patrick
Simply Alice - Phyllis Reynolds Naylor   m   1069

Magda
Girls in Love - Jacqueline Wilson   m, h   1448

McConnell, Ellen
My Heartbeat - Garret Freymann-Weyr   h   494

McKinley, Alice Kathleen
Simply Alice - Phyllis Reynolds Naylor   m   1069

Mercer, Jared
The Shadow Club Rising - Neal Shusterman   m,
h   1298

Moscovitz, Lilly
Princess in Love - Meg Cabot   m, h   197

Mullen, Elizabeth "Buddy"
Waiting to Disappear - April Young Fritz   m,
h   496

Nadine
Girls in Love - Jacqueline Wilson   m, h   1448

Omar
The Pack - Elisa Carbone   m, h   214

Ourisman, Gina
Gina.Jamie.Father.Bear - George Ella Lyon   m,
h   920

Price, Elizabeth
Simply Alice - Phyllis Reynolds Naylor   m   1069

Renaldo, Amelia "Mia"
Princess in Love - Meg Cabot   m, h   197

Rojas, Carlos
Sticks and Stones - Beth Goobie   m, h   536

Sanford, Verna Kaye
Waiting to Disappear - April Young Fritz   m,
h   496

Singer, Tremont "Monty"
Mixed-Up Doubles - Elena Yates Eulo   m, h   439

Skank, Nemo "Arby the Roach Boy"
Hard Time - Julian F. Thompson   m, h   1378

Slater, Ian
Picture Perfect - Elaine Marie Alphin   m, h   22

Smartz, Alec
The Shadow Club Rising - Neal Shusterman   m,
h   1298

Stewart, Doug
Falling from Fire - Teena Booth   m, h   126

Thomas, Vernon
Shadow of a Doubt - S.L. Rottman   m, h   1232

Tuttle, Becky
The Pack - Elisa Carbone   m, h   214

Watson, Raylene
Waiting for Christopher - Louise Hawes   m, h   613

Wilton, Wesley
Falling from Fire - Teena Booth   m, h   126

10TH GRADER

Bishop, Tom
After - Francine Prose   m, h   1175

Brown, Devon
Not as Crazy as I Seem - George Harrar   m, h   596

Callaway, Susan
Alt Ed - Catherine Atkins   m, h   52

Cavendish, Ben
Not as Crazy as I Seem - George Harrar   m, h   596

Garcetti, Grace
Out of Order - A.M. Jenkins   h   732

Griffin, Milena
The Flip Side - Andrew Matthews   m   956

Hayes, Liberty
The Trouble with Liberty - Kristin Butcher   m,
h   187

Hecht, Corinne "Chlorophyll"
Out of Order - A.M. Jenkins   h   732

Hunt, Robert "Rob"
The Flip Side - Andrew Matthews   m   956

Hunter, Shane
High Heat - Carl Deuker   m, h   378

Jones, Pamela
Patiently Alice - Phyllis Reynolds Naylor   m,
h   1068

Justin
Buddha Boy - Kathe Koja   m, h   811

Long, Patrick
Patiently Alice - Phyllis Reynolds Naylor   m,
h   1068

Madison, Samantha "Sam"
All-American Girl - Meg Cabot   m, h   195

Martin, Michael/Jinsen "Buddha Boy"
Buddha Boy - Kathe Koja   m, h   811

McKinley, Alice Kathleen
Patiently Alice - Phyllis Reynolds Naylor   m,
h   1068

Middlebrook, Russel
Geography Club - Brent Hartinger   h   602

Min
Geography Club - Brent Hartinger   h   602

Paul
Boy Meets Boy - David Levithan   h   885

Price, Elizabeth
Patiently Alice - Phyllis Reynolds Naylor   m,
h   1068

Richmond, Paul
Breaking Point - Alex Flinn   m, h   467

Sawyer, Becca
After - Francine Prose   m, h   1175

Silas
After - Francine Prose   m, h   1175

Tanya
Not as Crazy as I Seem - George Harrar   m, h   596

Thomas, Kimberly "Ariel"
Kissing Kate - Lauren Myracle   h   1054

Trammel, Colt
Out of Order - A.M. Jenkins   h   732

Wood, Emily
Nightmare - Joan Lowery Nixon   m, h   1086

11TH GRADER

Amy
Out of the Fire - Deborah Froese   m, h   497

Arielle
The Battle of Jericho - Sharon M. Draper   m,
h   395

Beaterson, Rick
Three Clams and an Oyster - Randy Powell   m,
h   1166

Berg, Jed
Claws - Will Weaver   m, h   1420

Cobley, Abby
Kerosene - Chris Wooding   h   1461

Cohen, Emma
Kerosene - Chris Wooding   h   1461

Dana
The Battle of Jericho - Sharon M. Draper   m,
h   395

Deshutsis, Dwight
Three Clams and an Oyster - Randy Powell   m,
h   1166

Dhillon, Jai
The Hemingway Tradition - Kristin Butcher
m   186

Donaghy, Matt
Big Mouth & Ugly Girl - Joyce Carol Oates
h   1098

Doran, Nick
Walk Away Home - Paul Many   h   940

Dragon, Diantha
Ten Miles from Winnemucca - Thelma Hatch Wyss
m, h   1472

Ellison, Tracee
Alt Ed - Catherine Atkins   m, h   52

Freeman, Kofi
The Battle of Jericho - Sharon M. Draper   m,
h   395

Glenn
Blind Sighted - Peter Moore   h   1028

Green, Cameron "Anne Thomas"
Hush - Jacqueline Woodson   m, h   1465

Gwendolyn
Target - Kathleen Jeffrie Johnson   h   747

Hawke, P.C.
The Square Root of Murder - Paul Zindel   m   1496

Lauren
Blind Sighted - Peter Moore   h   1028

Lawson, Adrian
Simon Says - Elaine Marie Alphin   h   23

Manning, Joel
Kerosene - Chris Wooding   *h*   1461

McCallister, Flint
Three Clams and an Oyster - Randy Powell   *m,*
h   1166

Meryk, Dayle
Out of the Fire - Deborah Froese   *m, h*   497

Pearl
Target - Kathleen Jeffrie Johnson   *h*   747

Petersen, Tess
The Hemingway Tradition - Kristin Butcher
m   186

Pistil, Dennis "Denny"
17: A Novel in Prose Poems - Liz Rosenberg
h   1230

Prescott, Jericho
The Battle of Jericho - Sharon M. Draper   *m,*
h   395

Prescott, Josh
The Battle of Jericho - Sharon M. Draper   *m,*
h   395

Riggs, Mackenzie
The Square Root of Murder - Paul Zindel   *m*   1496

Riggs, Ursula
Big Mouth & Ugly Girl - Joyce Carol Oates
h   1098

Sampson, Cal
Kerosene - Chris Wooding   *h*   1461

Sanborn, Laura
Claws - Will Weaver   *m, h*   1420

Savage, Cade
Three Clams and an Oyster - Randy Powell   *m,*
h   1166

Sherman, Belinda
Geography Club - Brent Hartinger   *h*   602

Sherman, Cynthia "Cindy"
The New Rules of High School - Blake Nelson
h   1072

Simon, Susannah "Suze"
Haunted: A Tale of the Mediator - Meg Cabot   *m,*
h   196

Slater, Brendan
Alt Ed - Catherine Atkins   *m, h*   52

Ternell, Bernadette
Cheating Lessons - Nan Willard Cappo   *m, h*   212

Tobak, Kirk
Blind Sighted - Peter Moore   *h*   1028

Turner, Chad
Dunk - David Lubar   *m, h*   912

West, Grady
Target - Kathleen Jeffrie Johnson   *h*   747

Weston, Charles
Simon Says - Elaine Marie Alphin   *h*   23

Williams, Jess
Target - Kathleen Jeffrie Johnson   *h*   747

12TH GRADER

Alicia
Slumming - Kristen D. Randle   *h*   1183

Andy
Skud - Dennis Foon   *h*   472

Bailey, Claire
Hanging on to Max - Margaret Bechard   *h*   94

Barrett, Evan
The She - Carol Plum-Ucci   *m, h*   1161

Bartholomew, Cyril
Flavor of the Week - Tucker Shaw   *m, h*   1288

Bickerstaff, Nikki
Slumming - Kristen D. Randle   *h*   1183

Blackwell, Kelsey Gene
Happenings - Katie Cobb   *m, h*   265

Brad
Skud - Dennis Foon   *h*   472

Brandt, Graeme
Simon Says - Elaine Marie Alphin   *h*   23

Brickman, Joe
Home of the Braves - David Klass   *h*   803

Buckley, Todd
Jake, Reinvented - Gordon Korman   *h*   816

Caldwell, Max
The New Rules of High School - Blake Nelson
h   1072

Camargo, Brian
Slumming - Kristen D. Randle   *h*   1183

Cole, David
The True Meaning of Cleavage - Mariah Fredericks
m, h   486

Cooper, Sophie
Waiting for June - Joyce Sweeney   *h*   1356

Eckloe, Christina
Telling Christina Goodbye - Lurlene McDaniel   *m,*
h   974

Elissa
Tribes - Arthur Slade   *h*   1309

Garbacchio, Nick
Flavor of the Week - Tucker Shaw   *m, h*   1288

Glassman, Nelson
Rainbow High - Alex Sanchez   *h*   1262

Hanson, Tucker
Telling Christina Goodbye - Lurlene McDaniel   *m,*
h   974

Hill, Evan
Who Will Tell My Brother? - Marlene Carvell   *m,*
h   223

Hutton, Keith
Out of the Fire - Deborah Froese   *m, h*   497

Jerome "Jerry"
Mixed-Up Doubles - Elena Yates Eulo   *m, h*   439

Jondiss, Aurin
Gravel Queen - Tea Benduhn   *h*   101

Joshua
Waiting for June - Joyce Sweeney   *h*   1356

Kenney
Gravel Queen - Tea Benduhn   *h*   101

Kris
Home of the Braves - David Klass   *h*   803

Kyle
God of Beer - Garret Keizer   *h*   775

Litch, Teri
Catalyst - Laurie Halse Anderson   *h*   28

Logan, David
God of Beer - Garret Keizer   *h*   775

Luca, Vincent "Vince"
Son of the Mob - Gordon Korman   *m, h*   818

Malone, Kate
Catalyst - Laurie Halse Anderson   *h*   28

McBean, Ed "the Mouse"
Home of the Braves - David Klass   *h*   803

McConnell, Link
My Heartbeat - Garret Freymann-Weyr   *h*   494

McGuire, Cody
Telling Christina Goodbye - Lurlene McDaniel   *m,*
h   974

Meeks, Kyle
Rainbow High - Alex Sanchez   *h*   1262

Morgan, Anne-Marie
Faith Wish - James Bennett   *h*   102

Moscovitz, Michael
Princess in Love - Meg Cabot   *m, h*   197

Mulligan, Rose
Flavor of the Week - Tucker Shaw   *m, h*   1288

Oats, Christopher "Quaker"
God of Beer - Garret Keizer   *h*   775

Pittman, Sam
Slumming - Kristen D. Randle   *h*   1183

Ron
Losing Is Not an Option - Rich Wallace   *m,*
h   1410

Scott, Mike
Waiting for Sarah - Bruce McBay   *m, h*   961

Shane
Skud - Dennis Foon   *h*   472

Sophie
Sticks and Stones - Beth Goobie   *m, h*   536

Terraletto, Tia
Slumming - Kristen D. Randle   *h*   1183

Thompson, Trisha
Telling Christina Goodbye - Lurlene McDaniel   *m,*
h   974

Tommy
Skud - Dennis Foon   *h*   472

Wallace, Fred
Gravel Queen - Tea Benduhn   *h*   101

Wallace, Pete
Out of the Fire - Deborah Froese   *m, h*   497

Weiss, Morgan
Slumming - Kristen D. Randle   *h*   1183

Weller, Destiny
Dangerous Girls - R.L. Stine   *m, h*   1345

Weller, Livy
Dangerous Girls - R.L. Stine   *m, h*   1345

Wentworth, James
My Heartbeat - Garret Freymann-Weyr   *h*   494

Witherspoon, Anthony "Spoon"
The Beast - Walter Dean Myers   *h*   1051

ABUSE VICTIM

America
America - E.R. Frank   *h*   479

Cinderella
Cinderella - Ruth Sanderson   *p*   1263

Lawson, Diana
Walk Away Home - Paul Many   *h*   940

Leeper, Dennis
The Hero - Ron Woods   *m, h*   1464

Tucker, Tyler
Jackie's Wild Seattle - Will Hobbs   *m*   652

ACCIDENT VICTIM

Barstow, Olive
Olive's Ocean - Kevin Henkes   *m*   623

Bishop, Jane Elizabeth "Janey"
This Isn't about the Money - Sally Warner
m   1417

Blair, Allison
A Circle of Time - Marisa Montes   *m, h*   1023

Eckloe, Christina
Telling Christina Goodbye - Lurlene McDaniel   m,
h   974

Jessica
Bridging Beyond - Kathleen Benner Duble   m,
h   403

Klaus
Dark Waters - Catherine MacPhail   m, h   932

Pearl
Little Flower - Gloria Rand   p   1182

Weeks, Emma
Stanley, Flat Again! - Jeff Brown   e   163

ACROBAT

Violet
Hobart - Anita Briggs   e   149

ACTIVIST

Delis, Jewel
The Companions - Sheri S. Tepper   h, a   1373

Mama
Stars in the Darkness - Barbara M. Joosse   p   759

Perrin
Fresh Girl - Jaira Placide   h   1160

Woods, Stewie
Savage Run - C.J. Box   h, a   130

ACTOR

Andy
Skud - Dennis Foon   h   472

Snoutowski, Stanley
Mary Had a Little Ham - Margie Palatini   p   1123

Widge
Shakespeare's Spy - Gary Blackwood   m   114

ACTRESS

Annabel
*Annabel the Actress, Starring in Hound of the
Barkervilles* - Ellen Conford   e   285

Billingsly, Beverly
Beverly Billingsly Takes a Bow - Alexander Stadler
p   1334

Marbella
A Pig Named Perrier - Elizabeth Spurr   p   1331

O'Connor, Carrie
A Simple Gift - Nancy Ruth Patterson   e   1129

Unnamed Character
Beverly Billingsly Takes a Bow - Alexander Stadler
p   1334

ADDICT

Minou, Colleen "Stoner"
Stoner & Spaz - Ron Koertge   h   810

Sammie
Nirvana's Children - Ranulfo   h   1185

ADMINISTRATOR

Apple
Mr. Tanen's Tie Trouble - Maryann Cocca-Leffler
p   268

ADOPTEE

Bates, Jimmy "Clovis King"
Journey to the River Sea - Eva Ibbotson   m   707

Casson, Saffron "Saffy"
Saffy's Angel - Hilary McKay   m   980

Dillon, Dillon
Dillon Dillon - Kate Banks   e   75

Emma
Emma's Story - Deborah Hodge   p   655

Halloweena
Halloweena - Miriam Glassman   p   528

Lulu
Lulu's Hat - Susan Meddaugh   e   1003

Marcos
A New Barker in the House - Tomie De Paola
p   359

McGill, Eli "Eel"
Indigo - Alice Hoffman   m, h   659

McGill, Trevor "Trout"
Indigo - Alice Hoffman   m, h   659

Parsley
For Biddle's Sake - Gail Carson Levine   e   884

Penhaligon, Arthur
Mister Monday - Garth Nix   m, h   1085

Pinocchio
Pinocchio the Boy: Incognito in Collodi - Lane Smith
p   1314

Ruby
Soul Moon Soup - Lindsay Lee Johnson   m, h   748

Seaborne
The Sea Chest - Toni Buzzeo   p   190

Spencer, Sookhan
The Wrong One - Carol Otis Hurst   e, m   699

Thacker, Will
Between - Jean Thesman   m, h   1375

Twitchy
Our Twitchy - Kes Gray   p   551

Zeel
Rowan and the Zebak - Emily Rodda   e   1219

ADVENTURER

Allun
Rowan and the Zebak - Emily Rodda   e   1219

Audrey
Audrey and Barbara - Janet Lawson   p   863

Perlain
Rowan and the Zebak - Emily Rodda   e   1219

Twite, Dido
Midwinter Nightingale - Joan Aiken   m   13

Unnamed Character
The Forest - Claire A. Nivola   p   1083

Zeel
Rowan and the Zebak - Emily Rodda   e   1219

AGED PERSON

Aana Lulu
Kumak's House: A Tale of the Far North - Michael
Bania   p   73

Agneeza
Curse in Reverse - Tom Coppinger   p   298

Alice
It Feels Like Snow - Nancy Cote   p   305

Alveston, Robert
The Ghost Behind the Wall - Melvin Burgess
m   182

Angelo
Angelo - David Macaulay   p   921

Baum
Skinny-Dipping at Monster Lake - Bill Wallace
m   1406

Big Beard
*Little Old Big Beard and Big Young Little Beard: A
Short and Tall Tale* - Remy Charlip   p   238

Brooks, Linus
The Poltergoose - Michael Lawrence   e, m   862

Brown, Ringfinger
Summerland - Michael Chabon   m, h   236

Burt, Tom
The Victory Garden - Lee Kochenderfer   e, m   808

Cahill, Josie
Pictures of Hollis Woods - Patricia Reilly Giff   e,
m   524

Capotosto, Fran
Say Yes - Audrey Couloumbis   m, h   306

Cutter
The Trouble with Jeremy Chance - George Harrar   e,
m   597

Edme
Dahlia - Barbara McClintock   p   970

Esperanza
Adelita: A Mexican Cinderella Story - Tomie De Paola
p   358

Farmer Todd
Piggy's Pancake Parlor - David McPhail   e   1000

Ferguson, Charlie
Shoeless Joe & Black Betsy - Phil Bildner   p   108

Fine
Izzy's Place - Marc Kornblatt   e, m   819

Fortesque
That Pesky Rat - Lauren Child   p   248

Freeman
The Four Ugly Cats in Apartment 3D - Marilyn Sachs
e   1249

Gittel
Chicken Soup by Heart - Esther Hershenhorn
p   630

Graham, Aurora
Lumber Camp Library - Natalie Kinsey-Warnock
e   798

Grand Da
Katie's Wish - Barbara Shook Hazen   p   616

Grand Master
What About Me? - Ed Young   p   1488

Grandfather
Ruby's Wish - Shirin Yim Bridges   p   148
The Water Gift and the Pig of the Pig - Jacqueline
Briggs Martin   p   948

Grandma Beetle
Just a Minute: A Trickster Tale and Counting Book -
Yuyi Morales   p   1030

Grandmother
Georgie Lee - Sharon Phillips Denslow   e   374

Grandpa
Gus and Grandpa Go Fishing - Claudia Mills
b   1015

Harper, Dolores
True Confessions of a Heartless Girl - Martha Brooks
h   161

Harrison
Trouble Don't Last - Shelley Pearsall   m   1139

Hirsch
Blue Eyes Better - Ruth Wallace-Brodeur   e   1412

Ian
Sea Gift - John Ashby   m, h   47

Keeper of the Crystal
Rowan and the Keeper of the Crystal - Emily Rodda   e   1218

Kia
Kotuku - Deborah Savage   m, h   1265

LaRue, Gertrude R.
Dear Mrs. LaRue: Letters from Obedience School - Mark Teague   p   1369

Littlejohn, Moses
The Dream Bearer - Walter Dean Myers   m   1052

Maita
The Sea Chest - Toni Buzzeo   p   190

McCall, Lowrie
The Wish List - Eoin Colfer   m, h   278

Menuto, Penelope "PenPen"
The Canning Season - Polly Horvath   m, h   683

Menuto, Tilly
The Canning Season - Polly Horvath   m, h   683

Mills, Edward "Cap"
Handbook for Boys: A Novel - Walter Dean Myers   m, h   1053

Moore, Alfie
Pool Boy - Michael Simmons   m, h   1305

Morales, Claudio "Mister M"
Handbook for Boys: A Novel - Walter Dean Myers   m, h   1053

Morey, Sairy
Ruby Holler - Sharon Creech   e, m   313

Morey, Tiller
Ruby Holler - Sharon Creech   e, m   313

Mouse Man
The Marvelous Mouse Man - Mary Ann Hoberman   p   654

Noah
Noah's Ark - Jerry Pinkney   p   1158

Old Bob
Old Bob's Brown Bear - Niki Daly   p   340

Old Granny
Old Granny and the Bean Thief - Cynthia DeFelice   p   366

Old Sam
The Berry-Picking Man - Jane Buchanan   e   175

Omaye
Ghosts for Breakfast - Stanley Todd Terasaki   p   1374

Omi
Ghosts for Breakfast - Stanley Todd Terasaki   p   1374

Ono
Ghosts for Breakfast - Stanley Todd Terasaki   p   1374

Pearl
Little Flower - Gloria Rand   p   1182

Po Po
Bitter Dumplings - Jeanne M. Lee   p   870

Powers
Tom Mouse - Ursula K. Le Guin   p   867

Price, Molly
One Shot - Susan Glick   m, h   529

Putter
Mr. Putter & Tabby Catch the Cold - Cynthia Rylant   b   1247
Mr. Putter & Tabby Stir the Soup - Cynthia Rylant   b   1248

Ricci
The Slightly True Story of Cedar B. Hartley (Who Planned to Live an Unusual Life) - Martine Murray   m   1046

Ryamen
The Legend of Lady Ilena - Patricia Malone   m, h   936

Santa Claus
A New Improved Santa - Patricia Rae Wolff   p   1454

Seldom
33 Snowfish - Adam Rapp   h   1186

Stubbs, Beryl
Butterflies and Lizards, Beryl and Me - Ruth Lercher Bornstein   e, m   127

Teaberry
Mr. Putter & Tabby Catch the Cold - Cynthia Rylant   b   1247

Trapper Jack
The True Story of Trapper Jack's Left Big Toe - Ian Wallace   p   1407

Unnamed Character
Ali and the Magic Stew - Shulamith Levey Oppenheim   p   1112
All the Way Lhasa: A Tale from Tibet - Barbara Helen Berger   p   104
The Bachelor and the Bean - Shelley Fowles   p   475
The Bachelor and the Bean - Shelley Fowles   p   475
The Cat Who Liked Potato Soup - Terry Farish   p   443
Christmas in the Country - Cynthia Rylant   p   1244
Christmas in the Country - Cynthia Rylant   p   1244
Go Track a Yak! - Tony Johnston   p   752
In the Piney Woods - Roni Schotter   p   1270
Storm Is Coming! - Heather Tekavec   p   1371
The Teddy Bear - David McPhail   p   1001
Witch's Wishes - Vivian Vande Velde   e   1396

von Loewen
The Countess and Me - Paul Kropp   m, h   832

Wesseling, Geertrui "Maria"
Postcards from No Man's Land - Aidan Chambers   h   237

Winkel
Hazel Green - Odo Hirsch   e   644

ALCOHOLIC

Flynn, Vincent "Vinny"
Flood - James Heneghan   m   621

Pig, William
Martyn Pig - Kevin Brooks   m, h   160

Wright, Liz
Hang On in There, Shelley - Kate Saksena   m, h   1251

ALIEN

Beegu
Beegu - Alexis Deacon   p   360

Blorp
The Big Science Fair - Dan Yaccarino   e   1473

Drusni
Manta's Gift - Timothy Zahn   h, a   1491

Gondii, Toxoplasma
Parasite Pig - William Sleator   m, h   1310

Ilisidi
Explorer - C.J. Cherryh   h, a   244

Mavkel
Singing the Dogstar Blues - Alison Goodman   h   540

Monkey
Ricky Ricotta's Mighty Robot vs. the Mecha-Monkeys from Mars - Dav Pilkey   e   1155

Nergal
First Graders from Mars: Episode 3: Nergal and the Great Space Race - Shana Corey   e   302

Oluu
The Rudest Alien on Earth - Jane Leslie Conly   e, m   286

Pranlo
Manta's Gift - Timothy Zahn   h, a   1491

Sanchez, Gip
The Angel Factor - Terence Blacker   m, h   113

Spud
Minnie and Moo and the Potato from Planet X - Denys Cazet   b   233

Vortex
First Graders from Mars: Episode 3: Nergal and the Great Space Race - Shana Corey   e   302

Zork
Moo Cow Kaboom! - Thacher Hurd   p   697

ALLIGATOR

Alexander
Best Friends - Charlotte Labaronne   p   842

Ferguson
The Speed of Light - Ron Carlson   m, h   218

Green
Meet Mr. and Mrs. Green - Keith Baker   p   70
Meet Mr. and Mrs. Green - Keith Baker   p   70

Little Gator
Egad Alligator! - Harriet Ziefert   p   1495

Mama Coco
Alligator Sue - Sharon Arms Doucet   p   389

AMNESIAC

Cox, John
Phoning a Dead Man - Gillian Cross   m, h   318

AMPUTEE

Asif
Parvana's Journey - Deborah Ellis   m, h   429

Chapski, Frank Fryderyk
The Secret of the Red Flame - K.M. Kimball   e, m   785

Unnamed Character
Goose's Story - Cari Best   p   106

ANGEL

Shaniqua
Why Heaven Is Far Away - Julius Lester   p   879

ANIMAL

Baby Jazzy
Jazzy in the Jungle - Lucy Cousins   p   307

Bridget
Something Might Happen - Helen Lester   p   876

Echidna
Platypus and the Birthday Party - Chris Riddell   p   1203

Fidget, Twitchly
Something Might Happen - Helen Lester   p   876

Glenda
The Terrible Underpants - Kaz Cooke   p   290

Mama JoJo
Jazzy in the Jungle - Lucy Cousins   p   307

Platypus
Platypus - Chris Riddell   p   1202
Platypus and the Birthday Party - Chris Riddell
    p   1203
Platypus and the Lucky Day - Chris Riddell
    p   1204

Slow Loris
Slow Loris - Alexis Deacon   p   361

ANIMAL LOVER

Bardsley, John
Sparrow Jack - Mordicai Gerstein   p   519

Brotherbum, Cabot "Rocky"
Remote Man - Elizabeth Honey   m, h   670

Case, Almira
The Birds of Killingworth - Robert D. San Souci
    p   1258

Elizabeth
The Perfect Pet - Margie Palatini   p   1124

Gribley, Sam
Frightful's Daughter - Jean Craighead George
    p   518

Jackie
Jackie's Wild Seattle - Will Hobbs   m   652

John
I, Freddy - Deitlof Reiche   e   1196

Kennedy, Pamela
Cool Cat, School Cat - Judy Cox   e   310

LaRue, Gertrude R.
Dear Mrs. LaRue: Letters from Obedience School -
    Mark Teague   p   1369

Lewis, Meriwether
Lewis and Clark and Me: A Dog's Tale - Laurie
    Myers   e   1050

McNosh, Nelly
Oh My Gosh, Mrs. McNosh! - Sarah Weeks
    p   1423

Neal
Jackie's Wild Seattle - Will Hobbs   m   652

Skinner, Johnny
Clever Lollipop - Dick King-Smith   e   792

Spinner, Edward Huon "Ned"
Remote Man - Elizabeth Honey   m, h   670

Tarzan
Edward in the Jungle - David McPhail   p   999

Unnamed Character
Don't Take Your Snake for a Stroll - Karin Ireland
    p   716

Zander, Gus
Cool Cat, School Cat - Judy Cox   e   310

ANIMAL TRAINER

Burton, David
Shaper - Jessie Haas   m   576

Seppala, Leonhard
Togo - Robert J. Blake   p   117

ANT

Henry
Little Buggy Runs Away - Kevin O'Malley   p   1108

Louie
Little Buggy Runs Away - Kevin O'Malley   p   1108

ANTHROPOLOGIST

Montmount, Percival Sr.
Tribes - Arthur Slade   h   1309

APPRENTICE

Arrighi, Lorenzo
The Warhorse - Don Bolognese   m   122

Firepaw "Fireheart"
Warriors Series - Erin Hunter   m, h   696

Marlowe, Tom
Death and the Arrow - Chris Priestley   m, h   1169

Mouse
The Puppeteer's Apprentice - D. Anne Love   e,
    m   909

Penmarch, Robin
Quadehar the Sorcerer - Erik L'Homme   m, h   891

Rat
The Ravenmaster's Secret - Elvira Woodruff
    m   1462

Tom
At the Sign of the Sugared Plum - Mary Hooper   m,
    h   675

Underwood, Nathaniel
The Amulet of Samarkand - Jonathan Stroud   m,
    h   1350

ARCHAEOLOGIST

Mim
Timespinners - Luli Gray   e   552

Unnamed Character
Tria and the Great Star Rescue - Rebecca Kraft Rector
    e   1191

ARMADILLO

Armadillo
Armadillo's Orange - Jim Arnosky   p   40

Unnamed Character
Jackalope - Janet Stevens   p   1342

ART HISTORIAN

Gregorio, Jose
The 7th Knot - Kathleen Karr   m   765

ARTIFICIAL INTELLIGENCE

Page
Fallen Host - Lyda Morehouse   h, a   1031

ARTISAN

Angelo
Angelo - David Macaulay   p   921

Arrighi, Renato
The Warhorse - Don Bolognese   m   122

Boxer
Sasha's Matrioshka Dolls - Jane Dillon   p   383

Dusty
The Beloved Dearly - Doug Cooney   e, m   293

Ferguson, Charlie
Shoeless Joe & Black Betsy - Phil Bildner   p   108

Geppetto
Pinocchio the Boy: Incognito in Collodi - Lane Smith
    p   1314

Hego
Daughter of the Wind - Michael Cadnum   m,
    h   199

Lamb, Caleb
Falling through Darkness - Carolyn McCullough
    h   972

Mateo
Dream Carver - Diana Cohn   p   271

Morey, Sairy
Ruby Holler - Sharon Creech   e, m   313

Morey, Tiller
Ruby Holler - Sharon Creech   e, m   313

Prentice, Hugh
*Just Jane: The Story of a Daughter of England Caught
    in the Struggle for Independence in Revolutionary
    America* - William Lavender   m, h   858

Tantamoq, Hermux
Time Stops for No Mouse - Michael Hoeye   m,
    h   657

Unnamed Character
Dream Carver - Diana Cohn   p   271

Warder, Kethlun "Keth"
Shatterglass - Tamora Pierce   m, h   1151

ARTIST

Alighieri, Antonia "Bice"
Dante's Daughter - Kimberley Heuston   h   635

Arrighi, Lorenzo
The Warhorse - Don Bolognese   m   122

Bartholdi
Liberty! - Allan Drummond   p   399

Brittman, Daniel "Poppie"
Hannah's Garden - Midori Snyder   m, h   1318

Cahill, Josie
Pictures of Hollis Woods - Patricia Reilly Giff   e,
    m   524

Casson, Bill
Saffy's Angel - Hilary McKay   m   980

Casson, Eve
Saffy's Angel - Hilary McKay   m   980

Cotton, Fitzgerald
Paint by Magic: A Time Travel Mystery - Kathryn
    Reiss   m   1197

da Padova, Lorenzo
Paint by Magic: A Time Travel Mystery - Kathryn
    Reiss   m   1197

Dart, Simon
Ghost at the Window - Margaret McAllister   e,
    m   960

David
All-American Girl - Meg Cabot   m, h   195

Gavin
Saving Jasey - Diane Tullson   m, h   1387

Gordon, Charlotte "Charley"
Butterflies and Lizards, Beryl and Me - Ruth Lercher
    Bornstein   e, m   127

Livingstone, Francis Hugh
Kings Mountain - G. Clifton Wisler   m   1451

Madison, Samantha "Sam"
All-American Girl - Meg Cabot   m, h   195

Martin, Michael/Jinsen "Buddha Boy"
Buddha Boy - Kathe Koja   m, h   811

O'Connor, Mary
Rat - Jan Cheripko   m, h   242

Sesshu Toyo
The Boy Who Drew Cats - Margaret Hodges
  p 656

Simons, Crystal
Undercurrents - Willo Davis Roberts   m, h   1212

Spavento, Ida
The Thief Lord - Cornelia Funke   m, h   500

Steele, Richard
Hard Cash - Kate Cann   h   210

Tate, Sarah Kate "Skate"
United Tates of America - Paula Danziger   e,
  m   347

Unnamed Character
ABC: A Child's First Alphabet Book - Alison Jay
  p   730
My World of Color - Margaret Wise Brown   p   165
Pictures for Miss Josie - Sandra Belton   p   100
Sophia: The Alchemist's Dog - Shelley Jackson
  p   721

Weston, Charles
Simon Says - Elaine Marie Alphin   h   23

Zebedee "Zebby"
Matchit - Martha Moore   e, m   1027

ASTHMATIC

Fisher, Bobby
The Green Dog: A Mostly True Story - Suzanne Fisher
  Staples   e   1336

ASTRONAUT

Street, Grace
Gloria Rising - Ann Cameron   e   207

AUNT

Aldrich, Nell
The 1980s: Earthsong - Tom Hoobler   m   671

Anna
Once Upon a Time - Niki Daly   p   341

Auntie
Epossumondas - Coleen Salley   p   1254

Auntie Claus
Auntie Claus and the Key to Christmas - Elise
  Primavera   p   1171

Bishop, Irene "Baby"
This Isn't about the Money - Sally Warner
  m   1417

Bridget
Something Might Happen - Helen Lester   p   876

Carpenter, Kit
One Night - Marsha Qualey   h   1180

Chamberten, Arachne
The Gates of Sleep - Mercedes Lackey   h, a   843

Chapel, Olivia
The Red Rose Box - Brenda Woods   e   1463

Charlotte
Fire Storm - Jean Craighead George   p   517

Edme
Dahlia - Barbara McClintock   p   970

Elinor
Inkheart - Cornelia Funke   m, h   499
Isabel: Taking Wing - Annie Dalton   m   339

Gordon, Constance "Con"
Willow and Twig - Jean Little   m   903

Gracie
Our Gracie Aunt - Jacqueline Woodson   p   1467

Grassina
The Frog Princess - E.D. Baker   m   67

Hayden, Laura
The Spirit and Gilly Bucket - Maurine F. Dahlberg
  m   337

Hogan, Mona
Flood - James Heneghan   m   621

Hollister, Glenda
The Trap - Joan Lowery Nixon   m, h   1087

Jewell, Sapphire
Evvy's Civil War - Miriam Brenaman   m, h   140

Kia
Kotuku - Deborah Savage   m, h   1265

Maita
The Sea Chest - Toni Buzzeo   p   190

Malone, Margaret
Gifts from the Sea - Natalie Kinsey-Warnock   e,
  m   797

Margaret
The Fattening Hut - Pat Lowery Collins   h   281

McGranahan, Minnie
Aunt Minnie and the Twister - Mary Skillings Prigger
  p   1170

Pig, Jean
Martyn Pig - Kevin Brooks   m, h   160

Pilgrim, Naomi
I Am Not Esther - Fleur Beale   m, h   91

Pomander, Dorothy
Zoe Sophia's Scrapbook: An Adventure in Venice -
  Claudia Mauner   p   957

Prentice, Clarissa
*Just Jane: The Story of a Daughter of England Caught
  in the Struggle for Independence in Revolutionary
  America* - William Lavender   m, h   858

Pruitt, Delphine Duvall
The River between Us - Richard Peck   m, h   1141

Sherry
Waiting to Disappear - April Young Fritz   m,
  h   496

Tuttle, Winifred V.
Brothers Below Zero - Tor Seidler   e, m   1277

Unnamed Character
The Aunts Go Marching - Maurie J. Manning
  p   937

Wanda
Walk Away Home - Paul Many   h   940

Whitcomb, Celia
The Big Burn - Jeanette Ingold   m, h   713

Worth, Esther
Whistler's Hollow - Debbie Dadey   e, m   336

Zep
*The Secret Remedy Book: A Story of Comfort and
  Love* - Karin Cates   p   231

AUTISTIC

Arrendale, Lou
The Speed of Dark - Elizabeth Moon   h, a   1025

McAllister, Darryl
A Wizard Alone - Diane Duane   m, h   401

BABY

Baby
Go Track a Yak! - Tony Johnston   p   752
It's Snowing! - Olivier Dunrea   p   407

Baby Leo
Quiet! - Paul Bright   p   153

Benny
Hello Benny! What It's Like to Be a Baby - Robie H.
  Harris   p   598

Bergen, Lily Maeve
The Strength of Saints - A. LaFaye   m, h   845

Bubba
Bubba and Beau, Best Friends - Kathi Appelt
  p   34
Bubba and Beau Go Night-Night - Kathi Appelt
  p   33

Cartwright, Joseph
The House in the Mail - Rosemary Wells   p   1425

Cooper, June
Waiting for June - Joyce Sweeney   h   1356

Guadalupe
The Kite - Luis Garay   p   509

Hassan
Parvana's Journey - Deborah Ellis   m, h   429

Hoskins, Billy
*The Adventures of Super Diaper Baby: The First
  Graphic Novel* - Dav Pilkey   e   1153

Jesus
The Donkey's Christmas - Nancy Tafuri   p   1359

Lila
Lisa's Baby Sister - Anne Gutman   p   574

Little Bunny
Little Bunny, Biddle Bunny - David Kirk   p   800

MacKinnon, Cecelia "Celia"
Gifts from the Sea - Natalie Kinsey-Warnock   e,
  m   797

Mahalia
Mahalia - Joanne Horniman   h   679

McCall, Bonnie
Prairie Whispers - Frances Arrington   m   43

Pettigrew, Max
Hanging on to Max - Margaret Bechard   h   94

Rose
Iris and Walter and Baby Rose - Elissa Haden Guest
  b   568

Schubert, Beatrice
The Steps - Rachel Cohn   m   273

Unnamed Character
Big Momma Makes the World - Phyllis Root
  p   1226
The Difference Between Babies & Cookies - Mary
  Hanson   p   591
I Used to Be the Baby - Robin Ballard   p   71
My Big Brother - Valerie Fisher   p   457
The New Hippos - Lena Landstrom   p   848
No More Kissing! - Emma Chichester Clark   p   246
Sometimes I'm Bombaloo - Rachel Vail   p   1389
Thirsty Baby - Catherine Ann Cullen   p   323
This Little Chick - John Lawrence   p   861
The Wriggly, Wriggly Baby - Jessica Clerk   p   264

Unnamed Child
33 Snowfish - Adam Rapp   h   1186

BABYSITTER

Alice
Fairy Dust - Jane Denitz Smith   e   1313

Gittel
Chicken Soup by Heart - Esther Hershenhorn
  p   630

Lowell, Carmen Lucille
The Second Summer of the Sisterhood - Ann Brashares
  m, h   137

Maccarone, Joel
Taking Care of Trouble - Bonnie Graves   e   547

BACHELOR

Rottenberger, Rachel
Taking Care of Trouble - Bonnie Graves   e   547

BACHELOR

Unnamed Character
The Bachelor and the Bean - Shelley Fowles
   p   475

BADGER

Badger
A Perfect Day for It - Jan Fearnley   p   445

Little Badger
Little Badger's Just-About Birthday - Eve Bunting
   p   179

Old Badger
Little Badger's Just-About Birthday - Eve Bunting
   p   179

BAKER

Allun
Rowan and the Zebak - Emily Rodda   e   1219

BANKER

van Helsen, Hugo
The House of Windjammer - V.A. Richardson   m,
   h   1201

BASEBALL PLAYER

Bennett, Steven
One Lucky Summer - Laura McGee Kvasnosky
   e   840

Boland, Kevin
Shakespeare Bats Cleanup - Ron Koertge   m,
   h   809

Casey, Katie
Players in Pigtails - Shana Corey   p   304

Cunningham, Joelle
Sliding into Home - Dori Hillstad Butler   m   189

de la Cruz, Cruz
The Boy Who Saved Baseball - John Ritter
   m   1210

del Gato, Dante
The Boy Who Saved Baseball - John Ritter
   m   1210

Feld, Ethan
Summerland - Michael Chabon   m, h   236

Hunter, Shane
High Heat - Carl Deuker   m, h   378

Jackson, Joseph "Shoeless Joe"
Shoeless Joe & Black Betsy - Phil Bildner   p   108

Land, Kevin
Geography Club - Brent Hartinger   h   602

McHenry, Luke
Free Radical - Claire Rudolf Murphy   m, h   1042

Miller, Andrew
Jason Rat-a-Tat - Colby Rodowsky   e   1220

Rideout, Jennifer T.
Summerland - Michael Chabon   m, h   236

Ridge, Michael "Midge"
Cairo Kelly and the Mann - Kristin Butcher   e,
   m   185

Robertson, Reese
High Heat - Carl Deuker   m, h   378

Romani, Cairo Kelly
Cairo Kelly and the Mann - Kristin Butcher   e,
   m   185

Trammel, Colt
Out of Order - A.M. Jenkins   h   732

Unnamed Character
Mama Played Baseball - David A. Adler   p   5

Wignutt, Thor
Summerland - Michael Chabon   m, h   236

BASKETBALL PLAYER

Borowitz-Jacobs, River
Hoop Girlz - Lucy Jane Bledsoe   e, m   118

Carrillo, Jason
Rainbow High - Alex Sanchez   h   1262

Denwood, Robbie
String Music - Rick Telander   e, m   1372

Froehlich, Jeff
The Return of Calico Bright - David Winkler   m,
   h   1450

Hargraves, Emily
Hoop Girlz - Lucy Jane Bledsoe   e, m   118

Henderson, Danny
How I Fell in Love & Learned to Shoot Free Throws -
   Jon Ripslinger   h   1209

Jasmine, Jasper
String Music - Rick Telander   e, m   1372

LaValley, Diana
God of Beer - Garret Keizer   h   775

Livingston, Keith
*Born Too Short: The Confessions of an Eighth-Grade
   Basket Case* - Dan Elish   m   425

Malone, Jim
House of Sports - Marisabina Russo   m   1240

McPherson, Angel
How I Fell in Love & Learned to Shoot Free Throws -
   Jon Ripslinger   h   1209

Mondini, Lisa
House of Sports - Marisabina Russo   m   1240

Theodore, Simpson III
Rat - Jan Cheripko   m, h   242

BASTARD SON

Jiaan
Flame - Hilari Bell   m, h   97

Purdy, Michael
The Traitor: Golden Mountain Chronicles: 1885 -
   Laurence Yep   m, h   1475

BAT

Goth
Firewing - Kenneth Oppel   m   1111

Silverwing, Griffin
Firewing - Kenneth Oppel   m   1111

Silverwing, Shade
Firewing - Kenneth Oppel   m   1111

Zotz, Cama
Firewing - Kenneth Oppel   m   1111

BEAR

Bear
Bear Snores On - Karma Wilson   p   1449
Don't You Feel Well, Sam? - Amy Hest   p   632
A Perfect Day for It - Jan Fearnley   p   445
Snow - Manya Stojic   p   1346

A Story for Bear - Dennis Haseley   p   607

Big Bear
Bravery Soup - Maryann Cocca-Leffler   p   267

Big Brown Bear
Big Brown Bear's Up and Down Day - David McPhail
   p   998

Billingsly, Beverly
Beverly Billingsly Borrows a Book - Alexander Stadler
   p   1333

Blackboard Bear
I'll Never Share You, Blackboard Bear - Martha
   Alexander   p   19

Brown, Patrick
Patrick at the Circus - Geoffrey Hayes   p   615

Bruno
Dahlia - Barbara McClintock   p   970
Where Does Thursday Go? - Janeen Brian   p   146

Brunov, Urso
The Tale of Urso Brunov: Little Father of All Bears -
   Brian Jacques   p   723

Buzzy Bear
Little Rat Sets Sail - Monika Bang-Campbell   b   72

Copycub
Always Copycub - Richard Edwards   p   420

Florentina
Four Friends Together - Sue Heap   p   617

Henry
Henry Builds a Cabin - D.B. Johnson   p   744
Henry Climbs a Mountain - D.B. Johnson   p   745

Jack
The Saturday Escape - Daniel J. Mahoney   p   934

Little Brown Bear
Little Brown Bear Won't Go to School! - Jane Dyer
   p   412
Little Brown Bear Won't Take a Nap! - Jane Dyer
   p   413

Mama
Mama's Little Bears - Nancy Tafuri   p   1360
Oliver Finds His Way - Phyllis Root   p   1228

Mama Bear
Little Brown Bear Won't Go to School! - Jane Dyer
   p   412
Little Brown Bear Won't Take a Nap! - Jane Dyer
   p   413

Oliver
Oliver Finds His Way - Phyllis Root   p   1228

Papa
Oliver Finds His Way - Phyllis Root   p   1228

Papa Bear
Little Brown Bear Won't Go to School! - Jane Dyer
   p   412
Little Brown Bear Won't Take a Nap! - Jane Dyer
   p   413

Polo
Pete and Polo's Farmyard Adventure - Adrian
   Reynolds   p   1200

Rembrandt
Rembrandt's Hat - Susan Blackaby   p   112

Sam
Don't You Feel Well, Sam? - Amy Hest   p   632

Teddy
Teddy's Snowy Day - Ian Beck   p   95

Tiny Teddy
What Shall We Do, Blue Kangaroo? - Emma
   Chichester Clark   p   247

Unnamed Character
Always Copycub - Richard Edwards   p   420
Who's That Knocking on Christmas Eve? - Jan Brett
   p   145

BEEKEEPER

Grandpa
The Beeman - Laurie Krebs   p   825

BIBLICAL FIGURE

Noah
Annie's Ark - Lesley Harker   p   594
Little Scraggly Hair: A Dog on Noah's Ark - Lynn
   Cullen   p   324
Noah's Ark - Jerry Pinkney   p   1158

BIRD

Amoeba
Birdbrain Amos - Michael Delaney   e   371

Attired, Natalie
The Hamster of the Baskervilles - Bruce Hale
   e   583

Bert
Where Does Thursday Go? - Janeen Brian   p   146

Del Rubio
Beverly Billingsly Borrows a Book - Alexander Stadler
   p   1333

Frightful
Frightful's Daughter - Jean Craighead George
   p   518

Kumba
Birdbrain Amos - Michael Delaney   e   371

Martin
Froggy Plays in the Band - Jonathan London
   p   906

Murphy
Flying Blind - Anna Myers   e, m   1049

Oksi
Frightful's Daughter - Jean Craighead George
   p   518

Unnamed Character
Cinderella's Dress - Nancy Willard   p   1444
Cinderella's Dress - Nancy Willard   p   1444
Mole and the Baby Bird - Marjorie Newman
   p   1076
The Nightingale - Jerry Pinkney   p   1157

BLACKSMITH

Stonehand, Devlin
Devlin's Luck - Patricia Bray   h, a   139

BLIND PERSON

Bo Won
Chang and the Bamboo Flute - Elizabeth Starr Hill
   e   640

Brennan, Bess
*Mirror, Mirror on the Wall: The Diary of Bess
   Brennan* - Barry Denenberg   e, m   373

Callie
Blind Sighted - Peter Moore   h   1028

Graham, Aurora
Lumber Camp Library - Natalie Kinsey-Warnock
   e   798

Lapp, Olivia
What Would Joey Do? - Jack Gantos   m   508

Merle
Song for Eloise - Leigh Sauerwein   h   1264

Solo, Nanty
Secret Heart - David Almond   m, h   21

Van Horn, Alicia
Things Not Seen - Andrew Clements   m   261

BODYGUARD

Lin, Tam
The House of the Scorpion - Nancy Farmer   m,
   h   444

BOOKKEEPER

Gerrit
The House of Windjammer - V.A. Richardson   m,
   h   1201

BOUNTY HUNTER

Guy of Gisborn
Lionclaw: A Tale of Rowan Hood - Nancy Springer
   m   1330

BOXER

Bayer, George Harrison "Sonny Bear"
Warrior Angel - Robert Lipsyte   h   900

Crockett, Navy
Warrior Angel - Robert Lipsyte   h   900

BOYFRIEND

Aidan
Falling through Darkness - Carolyn McCullough
   h   972

Christy, Condor
God of Beer - Garret Keizer   h   775

Cuthand, Wesley
True Confessions of a Heartless Girl - Martha Brooks
   h   161

Dave
*Knocked Out by My Nunga-Nungas: Further, Further
   Confessions of Georgia Nicolson* - Louise Rennison
   m, h   1199

Dave "The Laugh"
*Dancing in My Nuddy-Pants: Even Further
   Confessions of Georgia Nicolson* - Louise Rennison
   m, h   1198

Dean
Martyn Pig - Kevin Brooks   m, h   160

Dounas, Kostos
The Second Summer of the Sisterhood - Ann Brashares
   m, h   137

Hutton, Keith
Out of the Fire - Deborah Froese   m, h   497

Jacobsen, Jacob
Dancing in the Streets of Brooklyn - April Lurie   m,
   h   916

Kenny
Princess in Love - Meg Cabot   m, h   197

Kramer, Kal
The Queen of Everything - Deb Caletti   h   202

Long, Patrick
Patiently Alice - Phyllis Reynolds Naylor   m,
   h   1068

Moskowitz, Michael
Princess in Waiting - Meg Cabot   m, h   198

Pierre
Paradise - Joan Elizabeth Goodman   m, h   541

Robbie
*Knocked Out by My Nunga-Nungas: Further, Further
   Confessions of Georgia Nicolson* - Louise Rennison
   m, h   1199

Robbie "The Sex God"
*Dancing in My Nuddy-Pants: Even Further
   Confessions of Georgia Nicolson* - Louise Rennison
   m, h   1198

Scudder, Jehu
Boston Jane: Wilderness Days - Jennifer L. Holm
   m, h   666

Shepard, Jay
Making the Run - Heather Henson   h   626

Shrimp
Gingerbread - Rachel Cohn   h   272

Vinker, Kevin
Chill Wind - Janet McDonald   h   975

BROTHER

Aching, Wentworth
The Wee Free Men: A Novel of Discworld - Terry
   Pratchett   m, h   1167

Alvie
Alvie Eats Soup - Ross Collins   p   283

Bamford, Robert
Vampire State Building - Elizabeth Levy   e   887

Barrett, Emmett
The She - Carol Plum-Ucci   m, h   1161

Bean, Kurt
What Planet Are You from, Clarice Bean? - Lauren
   Child   p   250

Becket, Matt
The Dark - Marianne Curley   m, h   328

Benny
Benny and the Binky - Barbro Lindgren   p   898

Beno
The Snake's Tales - Marguerite W. Davol   p   353

Bert
Pizza Kittens - Charlotte Voake   p   1401

Bertram
Breath - Donna Jo Napoli   m, h   1059

Bill
One Bright Penny - Geraldine McCaughrean
   p   967

Blake
Saving Jasey - Diane Tullson   m, h   1387

Bob
Giggle, Giggle, Quack - Doreen Cronin   p   317
One Bright Penny - Geraldine McCaughrean
   p   967

Borowitz-Jacobs, Zacj
Hoop Girlz - Lucy Jane Bledsoe   e, m   118

Budwing, Danny
Zathura: A Space Adventure - Chris Van Allsburg
   p   1390

Budwing, Walter
Zathura: A Space Adventure - Chris Van Allsburg
   p   1390

Cartwright, Homer
The House in the Mail - Rosemary Wells   p   1425

Cartwright, Joseph
The House in the Mail - Rosemary Wells   p   1425

Charlie
Old Crump: The True Story of a Trip West - Laurie
   Lawlor   p   859

Christopher
When Mommy Was Mad - Lynne Jonell   p   756

Character Description Index

Placido
Snakes Don't Miss Their Mothers - M.E. Kerr   e,
m   783

Puss
Puss in Cowboy Boots - Jan Huling   p   695

Ralph
Practice Makes Perfect for Rotten Ralph - Jack Gantos
b   507

Red
The Alley Cat's Meow - Kathi Appelt   p   32

Scaredy Cat
The Scaredy Cats - Barbara Bottner   p   128
The Scaredy Cats - Barbara Bottner   p   128

Scaredy Cat, Baby
The Scaredy Cats - Barbara Bottner   p   128

Tabby
Mr. Putter & Tabby Catch the Cold - Cynthia Rylant
b   1247
Mr. Putter & Tabby Stir the Soup - Cynthia Rylant
b   1248

Unnamed Character
The Cat Who Liked Potato Soup - Terry Farish
p   443

White Cat
Camp of the Angel - Aileen Arrington   e, m   42

Yoko
Timothy's Tales from Hilltop School - Rosemary Wells
p   1428

Zorba
*The Story of a Seagull and the Cat Who Taught her to
Fly* - Luis Sepulveda   e   1278

CATERPILLAR

Farfallina
Farfallina & Marcel - Holly Keller   p   777

CHAUFFEUR

Henry
The Kingfisher's Gift - Susan Williams Beckhorn   e,
m   96

CHEERLEADER

Ellison, Tracee
Alt Ed - Catherine Atkins   m, h   52

Macy
What Happened to Lani Garver - Carol Plum-Ucci
h   1162

Madison, Lucy
All-American Girl - Meg Cabot   m, h   195

Morgan, Anne-Marie
Faith Wish - James Bennett   h   102

CHESS PLAYER

Bamford, Sam
Vampire State Building - Elizabeth Levy   e   887

Clinciu, Vlad
Vampire State Building - Elizabeth Levy   e   887

Kotalev, Nikolai
The Kings Are Already Here - Garret Freymann-Weyr
m, h   493

Vlajnik, Stas
The Kings Are Already Here - Garret Freymann-Weyr
m, h   493

CHICKEN

Brown Hen
Little Brown Hen's Shower - Pamela Duncan Edwards
p   418

Chicken
Mrs. Chicken and the Hungry Crocodile - Won-Ldy
Paye   p   1137

Daisy
Daisy Comes Home - Jan Brett   p   144

Frank
Funny Frank - Dick King-Smith   e   793

Hen
We're Going on a Picnic! - Pat Hutchins   p   705

Henrietta
Souperchicken - Mary Jane Auch   p   57

Henrietta "Henry"
City Chicken - Arthur Dorros   p   388

Jen
Daniel's Pet - Alma Flor Ada   b   1

Little Chick
Tippy-Toe Chick, Go! - George Shannon   p   1284

Little Willie
Elvis the Rooster Almost Goes to Heaven - Denys
Cazet   b   232

Lottie
Herbie's Secret Santa - Petra Mathers   p   955

Rhea, Olvina Alice
Olvina Flies - Grace Lin   p   893

Unnamed Character
This Little Chick - John Lawrence   p   861

CHIEFTAIN

Iron Shell
Betrayed! - Patricia Calvert   m   205

Koro Apirana
The Whale Rider - Witi Ihimaera   m, h   710

Tecumseh
Crossing the Panther's Path - Elizabeth Alder   m,
h   17

CHILD

Abikanile
The Village That Vanished - Ann Grifalconi   p   561

Aching, Tiffany
The Wee Free Men: A Novel of Discworld - Terry
Pratchett   m, h   1167

Adrian
What the Birds See - Sonya Hartnett   m, h   604

Alex
City Chicken - Arthur Dorros   p   388

Alia
Among the Betrayed - Margaret Peterson Haddix   m,
h   578

Alicia
Alicia's Best Friends - Lisa Jahn-Clough   p   724

Alvie
Alvie Eats Soup - Ross Collins   p   283

Amy
Mama Played Baseball - David A. Adler   p   5

Andy
The Broken Cat - Lynne Rae Perkins   p   1146

Annabel
*Annabel the Actress, Starring in Hound of the
Barkervilles* - Ellen Conford   e   285

Annabelle
Jethro Byrd, Fairy Child - Bob Graham   p   544

Annie
Annie Was Warned - Jarrett J. Krosoczka   p   833
Annie's Ark - Lesley Harker   p   594
The No Place Cat - C.S. Adler   e, m   4

Annie Rose
Annie Rose Is My Little Sister - Shirley Hughes
p   694

Anthony
I'll Never Share You, Blackboard Bear - Martha
Alexander   p   19

Antonelli, Little Benny
The Big Cheese of Third Street - Laurie Halse
Anderson   p   27

Applewood, Lillie
Bicycle Madness - Jane Kurtz   e, m   837

Asif
Parvana's Journey - Deborah Ellis   m, h   429

Audrey
Audrey and Barbara - Janet Lawson   p   863

Austin
Just One More Story - Jennifer Brutschy   p   173

Axel
Fire Storm - Jean Craighead George   p   517

Ben
Arizona Charlie and the Klondike Kid - Julie Lawson
p   864
Francis the Scaredy Cat - Ed Boxall   p   131

Benjamin
Morris the Artist - Lore Segal   p   1276

Benny
Iris and Walter: The Sleepover - Elissa Haden Guest
b   571

Bertie
Monkey Mo Goes to Sea - Diane Goode   p   538

Bess
Harvest Home - Jane Yolen   p   1481

Bishop, Yolanda "YoYo"
This Isn't about the Money - Sally Warner
m   1417

Boniface, Bo
The Thief Lord - Cornelia Funke   m, h   500

Boots
Gregor the Overlander - Suzanne Collins   m   284

Bop
Song of the Circus - Lois Duncan   p   404

Bradley, Seth
True Confessions of a Heartless Girl - Martha Brooks
h   161

Bridget
Bridget and the Muttonheads - Pija Lindenbaum
p   895

Britta
Mirabelle - Astrid Lindgren   p   896

Brown, Danitra
Danitra Brown Leaves Town - Nikki Grimes
p   566

Brown, Katherine "Kate"
When Marcus Moore Moved In - Rebecca Bond
p   123

Bubble
Good Night, Animals - Lena Arro   p   44

Budwing, Danny
Zathura: A Space Adventure - Chris Van Allsburg
p   1390

Jonathan
The Key to My Heart - Nira Harel   p   593

Jones, Calypso "Twig"
Willow and Twig - Jean Little   m   903

Jones, Ogden Jackson "Oogie"
How I Became a Writer and Oggie Learned to Drive - Janet Taylor Lisle   e, m   902

Joseph
The Dream Shop - Katharine Kenah   p   780

Josie
Musical Beds - Mara Bergman   p   105

Kahu
The Whale Rider - Witi Ihimaera   m, h   710

Katie
Katie's Wish - Barbara Shook Hazen   p   616

Katie Sue
The Recess Queen - Alexis O'Neill   p   1110

Kelts, Nellie
Bridging Beyond - Kathleen Benner Duble   m, h   403

Kendrill, Benjie
Spy Cat - Peg Kehret   e, m   773

Kringle, Christopher
Auntie Claus and the Key to Christmas - Elise Primavera   p   1171

Kyri
Who's That Knocking on Christmas Eve? - Jan Brett   p   145

Laura
Star Blanket - Pat Brisson   p   156

Lauretta
Zoom! - Robert Munsch   p   1041

Lee, Penny
Penny Lee and Her TV - Glenn McCoy   p   971

Leila
Parvana's Journey - Deborah Ellis   m, h   429

Lila
A Cool Moonlight - Angela Johnson   e, m   741

Lili
Mama Will Be Home Soon - Nancy Minchella   p   1016

Lily
What Shall We Do, Blue Kangaroo? - Emma Chichester Clark   p   247

Lily May
What Shall We Play? - Sue Heap   p   618

Linklater, Amy
Raspberries on the Yangtze - Karen Wallace   m   1408

Linklater, Clare
Raspberries on the Yangtze - Karen Wallace   m   1408

Litch, Michael "Mikey"
Catalyst - Laurie Halse Anderson   h   28

Little Joe
Frog - Susan Cooper   p   296

Little Rick
Musical Beds - Mara Bergman   p   105

Lizzy
Lizzy's Do's and Don'ts - Jessica Harper   p   595

Locks, Brother
Goldie Locks Has Chicken Pox - Erin Dealey   p   362

Locks, Goldie
Goldie Locks Has Chicken Pox - Erin Dealey   p   362

Lolly
The Secret Remedy Book: A Story of Comfort and Love - Karin Cates   p   231

Loretta
Loretta: Ace Pinky Scout - Keith Graves   p   548

Lou
Green Boy - Susan Cooper   m   297

Lucille
Lucille Camps In - Kathryn Lasky   p   854

Lucy
Dog Eared - Amanda Harvey   p   605
Pudgy: A Puppy to Love - Pippa Goodhart   p   539
The Wolves in the Walls - Neil Gaiman   p   503

MacGregor, Martin
Martin MacGregor's Snowman - Lisa Broadie Cook   p   289

Madlenka
Madlenka's Dog - Peter Sis   p   1307

Magruder, Rachel
Hear the Wind Blow: A Novel of the Civil War - Mary Downing Hahn   m   581

Mai, Malka
Malka - Mirjam Pressler   m, h   1168

Martha
What Shall We Play? - Sue Heap   p   618

Marty
Find-a-Saurus - Mark Sperring   p   1324

Mary
Mary Had a Little Ham - Margie Palatini   p   1123

Mary Claire
Four Friends Together - Sue Heap   p   617

Matt
What Shall We Play? - Sue Heap   p   618

Matthias
Among the Betrayed - Margaret Peterson Haddix   m, h   578

Max
Max's Logbook - Marissa Moss   e   1035

McCrae, Tatiana
The Lighthouse Keeper's Daughter - Iain Lawrence   h   860

McGill, Lauren
Lauren McGill's Pickle Museum - Jerdine Nolen   p   1091

Mei Mei
Chang and the Bamboo Flute - Elizabeth Starr Hill   e   640
Daisy Comes Home - Jan Brett   p   144

Miles "Little Man"
Bippity Bop Barbershop - Natasha Anastasia Tarpley   p   1362

Milgrom, Janina
Milkweed - Jerry Spinelli   m, h   1326

Miller, Pete
Ruby Electric - Theresa Nelson   m   1074

Milly
Milly and the Macy's Parade - Shana Corey   p   303

Molly
Tatty Ratty - Helen Cooper   p   295

Monroe, Toby
Howie Monroe and the Doghouse of Doom - James Howe   e   687

Moore, Marcus
When Marcus Moore Moved In - Rebecca Bond   p   123

Moreno, Olivia
Keeper of the Night - Kimberly Willis Holt   m, h   669

Morgan, Bernie
The Same Stuff as Stars - Katherine Paterson   m   1128

Morris
Morris the Artist - Lore Segal   p   1276

Mouse
The Puppeteer's Apprentice - D. Anne Love   e, m   909

Nancy
Raspberries on the Yangtze - Karen Wallace   m   1408

Neel
Chachaji's Cup - Uma Krishnaswami   p   828

Nicole
What the Birds See - Sonya Hartnett   m, h   604

Nikolai
The Three Questions - Jon J. Muth   p   1048

North, Wenny
Wenny Has Wings - Janet Lee Carey   e, m   216

Nunn, Ike
The Weeping Willow - Patrick Jennings   e   734

Nunn, Mem
The Weeping Willow - Patrick Jennings   e   734

O'Doyle, Brendan
Hobbledy-Clop - Pat Brisson   p   155

Orville
Agapanthus Hum and the Angel Hoot - Joy Cowley   b   309

Otis, Alice
Praying at the Sweetwater Motel - April Young Fritz   m   495

Pablito
My Pig Amarillo - Satomi Ichikawa   p   709

Parnell, Sam
Storm Catchers - Tim Bowler   m, h   129

Pearl
Good Night, Animals - Lena Arro   p   44

Penelope
Princess Penelope - Todd Mack   p   926

Peony
The Dungeon - Lynne Reid Banks   m, h   79

Percy
Among the Betrayed - Margaret Peterson Haddix   m, h   578

Pete
Pete and Polo's Farmyard Adventure - Adrian Reynolds   p   1200

Peter
The Good Little Bad Little Pig - Margaret Wise Brown   p   164

Pierre
Where, Where Is Swamp Bear? - Kathi Appelt   p   36

Pierson, Christopher
Waiting for Christopher - Louise Hawes   m, h   613

Pierson, Samantha
Freaky Green Eyes - Joyce Carol Oates   m, h   1099

Pip
The Dream Shop - Katharine Kenah   p   780

Polly
Sandmare - Helen Cooper   e   294

Pope, Timothy
Shark in the Park! - Nick Sharratt   p   1286

Quigley, Lucy
The Quigleys at Large - Simon Mason   e   953

Quigley, Will
The Quigleys at Large - Simon Mason   e   953

Rachel
The Doomspell - Cliff McNish   m   997

Reenie
Fishing Day - Andrea Davis Pinkney   p   1156

Rickman, Andrew
Falling from Fire - Teena Booth   m, h   126

Robin
Robin's Room - Margaret Wise Brown   p   166

Rolie Polie Olie
Big Time Olie - William Joyce   p   762

Rosie
Waggle - Sarah McMenemy   p   988

Ruby
Musical Beds - Mara Bergman   p   105
Ruby's Wish - Shirin Yim Bridges   p   148

Ruddy
Snowed in with Grandmother Silk - Carol Fenner   e   448

Ruthie
No More Vegetables! - Nicole Rubel   p   1236

Saba
Ruler of the Courtyard - Rukhsana Khan   p   784

Sadie
The Name Quilt - Phyllis Root   p   1227

Sam
Good Morning, Sam - Marie-Louise Gay   p   512
Good Night Sam - Marie-Louise Gay   p   513
Stella, Fairy of the Forest - Marie-Louise Gay   p   514

Sammy
Full Steam Ahead - Faye Gibbons   p   521

Samuel
More Pies! - Robert Munsch   p   1040

Sara
A Picture of Grandmother - Esther Hautzig   e   611

Sarah
Lighthouse: A Story of Remembrance - Robert Munsch   p   1039
Mixed-Up Doubles - Elena Yates Eulo   m, h   439
Practice Makes Perfect for Rotten Ralph - Jack Gantos   b   507

Sarie
Once Upon a Time - Niki Daly   p   341

Sasha
Sasha's Matrioshka Dolls - Jane Dillon   p   383

Scaredy Cat, Baby
The Scaredy Cats - Barbara Bottner   p   128

Sesshu Toyo
The Boy Who Drew Cats - Margaret Hodges   p   656

Shanna
Shanna's Teacher Show - Jean Marzollo   p   951

Sharp, Max
The Circle of Doom - Tim Kennemore   e, m   781

Shau-yu
On My Way to Buy Eggs - Chih-Yuan Chen   p   239

Shining
Shining - Julius Lester   p   878

Sinclair, Jess
Starry Nights - Judith Clarke   m, h   258

Sing Lo
The Elephant's Pillow - Diana Reynolds Roome   p   1223

Son
When the Emperor Was Divine - Julie Otsuka   h, a   1120

Sophie
Best Kind of Baby - Kate Laing   p   846

Spencer, Jesse
The Wrong One - Carol Otis Hurst   e, m   699

Spencer, Sookhan
The Wrong One - Carol Otis Hurst   e, m   699

Starzinsky, Buzzy
The Weeping Willow - Patrick Jennings   e   734

Steelgate, Matthew
Dust - Arthur Slade   m, h   1308

Stefan
Pancake Dreams - Ingmarie Ahvander   p   12

Stella
Good Morning, Sam - Marie-Louise Gay   p   512
Good Night Sam - Marie-Louise Gay   p   513
Stella, Fairy of the Forest - Marie-Louise Gay   p   514

Stelson, Jared
My Chimp Friday: The Nana Banana Chronicles - Hester Mundis   e, m   1038

Stewart
I'll Never Share You, Blackboard Bear - Martha Alexander   p   19

Sunday, Jed
Anna Sunday - Sally M. Keehn   m   772

Swimming Pool
The Beloved Dearly - Doug Cooney   e, m   293

Tabitha
How Sleep Found Tabitha - Maggie deVries   p   379

Tanya
Tanya and the Red Shoes - Patricia Lee Gauch   p   510

Thibodeaux, Suzanne Marie Sabine Chicot
Alligator Sue - Sharon Arms Doucet   p   389

Tilly
Blue Horse - Helen Stephens   p   1340
Treasure Hunt - Allan Ahlberg   p   10

Tithonus
Hippolyta and the Curse of the Amazons - Jane Yolen   m   1482

Toby
Dancing the Ring Shout! - Kim Siegelson   p   1300

Tom
Small - Clara Vulliamy   p   1403

Tony
The Beloved Dearly - Doug Cooney   e, m   293

Tria
Tria and the Great Star Rescue - Rebecca Kraft Rector   e   1191

Troop, Peter "Pigeon"
Fishing Day - Andrea Davis Pinkney   p   1156

Ugly-Boy Bobby
The Three Silly Girls Grubb - John Hassett   p   608

Unnamed Character
All the Way Lhasa: A Tale from Tibet - Barbara Helen Berger   p   104
The Aunts Go Marching - Maurie J. Manning   p   937
B Is for Bulldozer: A Construction ABC - June Sobel   p   1319
B Is for Bulldozer: A Construction ABC - June Sobel   p   1319
The Beeman - Laurie Krebs   p   825
The Bones of Fred McFee - Eve Bunting   p   177
Bubble Bath Pirates! - Jarrett J. Krosoczka   p   835

Bubble Bath Pirates! - Jarrett J. Krosoczka   p   835
Can You Make a Piggy Giggle? - Linda Ashman   p   50
Christmas Cricket - Eve Bunting   p   178
Christmas in the Country - Cynthia Rylant   p   1244
The Day the Babies Crawled Away - Peggy Rathmann   p   1187
The Difference Between Babies & Cookies - Mary Hanson   p   591
Don't Take Your Snake for a Stroll - Karin Ireland   p   716
Flamingo Dream - Donna Jo Napoli   p   1061
Frog Hunt - Sandra Jordan   p   760
Frog Hunt - Sandra Jordan   p   760
Good Night, Sleep Tight, Little Bunnies - Dawn Apperley   p   37
Goodnight, Baby Monster - Laura Leuck   p   880
Hey, Pancakes! - Tamson Weston   p   1432
Hey, Pancakes! - Tamson Weston   p   1432
Horse in the Pigpen - Linda Williams   p   1446
The House Across the Street - Jules Feiffer   p   447
The House Across the Street - Jules Feiffer   p   447
I Am NOT Going to School Today! - Robie H. Harris   p   599
Laura Numeroff's 10-Step Guide to Living with Your Monster - Laura Joffe Numeroff   p   1097
Liberty! - Allan Drummond   p   399
Little Horse - Betsy Byars   e   193
Mannekin Pis: A Simple Story of a Boy Who Peed on a War - Vladimir Radunsky   p   1181
The Marvelous Mouse Man - Mary Ann Hoberman   p   654
Monsoon - Uma Krishnaswami   p   829
More Pies! - Robert Munsch   p   1040
Morning Glory Monday - Arlene Alda   p   16
My Big Brother - Valerie Fisher   p   457
My Grandma, My Pen Pal - Jan Dale Koutsky   p   822
My Grandmother's Clock - Geraldine McCaughrean   p   966
My Pony - Susan Jeffers   p   731
My Somebody Special - Sarah Weeks   p   1422
Night Train - Caroline Stutson   p   1351
The Nightingale - Jerry Pinkney   p   1157
Nobody's Nosier Than a Cat - Susan Campbell Bartoletti   p   86
Oh No, Gotta Go! - Susan Middleton Elya   p   432
One-Dog Canoe - Mary Casanova   p   225
One Leaf Rides the Wind - Celeste Davidson Mannis   p   938
Our Class Took a Trip to the Zoo - Shirley Neitzel   p   1071
Peekaboo Morning - Rachel Isadora   p   719
Peep! - Kevin Luthardt   p   917
A Place to Grow - Soyung Pak   p   1121
A Quiet Place - Douglas Wood   p   1460
Roller Coaster - Marla Frazee   p   484
Rub-a-Dub Sub - Linda Ashman   p   51
Snow Music - Lynne Rae Perkins   p   1147
Stars in the Darkness - Barbara M. Joosse   p   759
Straight to the Pole - Kevin O'Malley   p   1109
The Teddy Bear - David McPhail   p   1001
That's Good! That's Bad! In The Grand Canyon - Margery Cuyler   p   335
Under a Prairie Sky - Anne Laurel Carter   p   221
Under a Prairie Sky - Anne Laurel Carter   p   221
What About Me? - Ed Young   p   1488
What Did You Do Today? - Kerry Arquette   p   41
What's That Noise? - William Carman   p   219
Which Would You Rather Be? - William Steig   p   1339
Which Would You Rather Be? - William Steig   p   1339
Yikes!!! - Robert Florczak   p   468

van Rijn, Rembrandt Harmensz
Stink Alley - Jamie Gilson   e, m   527

Van Stegeran, Katje
Boxes for Katje - Candace Fleming   p   462

Walter

Iris and Walter and Baby Rose - Elissa Haden Guest
   b 568

Iris and Walter and Cousin Howie - Elissa Haden
   Guest *b* 569

Iris and Walter: The Sleepover - Elissa Haden Guest
   b 571

Wanda-Linda
The Terrible Underpants - Kaz Cooke   *p* 290

Weeks, Jonathan Jefferson
Christmas Tapestry - Patricia Polacco   *p* 1163

Wemberly
Wemberly's Ice-Cream Star - Kevin Henkes   *p* 625

Wilkins, Sandra
Raspberries on the Yangtze - Karen Wallace
   m 1408

Winifred
Eugene's Story - Richard Scrimger   *p* 1274

Young, Cody
Jackie's Wild Seattle - Will Hobbs   *m* 652

Zee, Matthew
Matthew A.B.C. - Peter Catalanotto   *p* 229

CHILD-CARE GIVER

Elka
Thief of Dreams - Todd Strasser   *m* 1347

Mump
Shirley's Wonderful Baby - Valiska Gregory   *p* 560

Nanny
Eloise Takes a Bawth - Kay Thompson   *p* 1379

Waldenstein, Catherine "Ole Golly"
Harriet Spies Again - Helen Ericson   *e, m* 435

CHILD OF DIVORCED PARENTS

Brown, Amber
Amber Brown Is Green with Envy - Paula Danziger
   e 345

Howard, Annie
Making Music - Susan Bonners   *e* 124

Julia
Julia Wants a Pet - Barbro Lindgren   *p* 899

Randall
The Hero of Third Grade - Alice DeLaCroix
   e 370

Unnamed Character
Two Old Potatoes and Me - John Coy   *p* 311

CHIMNEYSWEEP

Roke, Tommy
Search of the Moon King's Daughter - Linda Holeman
   m, h 665

CHIMPANZEE

Chimp
Chimp and Zee and the Big Storm - Laurence Anholt
   p 31

Friday
My Chimp Friday: The Nana Banana Chronicles -
   Hester Mundis   *e, m* 1038

Mumkey
Chimp and Zee and the Big Storm - Laurence Anholt
   p 31

Papakey
Chimp and Zee and the Big Storm - Laurence Anholt
   p 31

Zee
Chimp and Zee and the Big Storm - Laurence Anholt
   p 31

CLASSMATE

Benny
Iris and Walter: The Sleepover - Elissa Haden Guest
   b 571

Fairchild, Beth
Darby - Jonathon Scott Fuqua   *e* 501

Granger, Robert
What Planet Are You from, Clarice Bean? - Lauren
   Child   *p* 250

Weeks, Emma
Stanley, Flat Again! - Jeff Brown   *e* 163

Wrenbury, Karl
Utterly Me, Clarice Bean - Lauren Child   *e* 249

CLERK

Dexter, Toby
Drinking Midnight Wine - Simon R. Green   *h,*
   a 553

Kaligaris, Lena
The Second Summer of the Sisterhood - Ann Brashares
   m, h 137

CLONE

Alacran, Matteo
The House of the Scorpion - Nancy Farmer   *m,*
   h 444

Surrey, Iris
The Secret - Eva Hoffman   *h, a* 660

CLOWN

Unnamed Character
Where's Pup? - Dayle Ann Dodds   *p* 386

COACH

Borowitz-Jacobs, Zacj
Hoop Girlz - Lucy Jane Bledsoe   *e, m* 118

Brooks, Alfred
Warrior Angel - Robert Lipsyte   *h* 900

Dickerson, Farley
Never So Green - Tim Johnston   *h* 750

Dunn
Blue Eyes Better - Ruth Wallace-Brodeur   *e* 1412

O'Connor, Patrick
Rat - Jan Cheripko   *m, h* 242

Scott
The Warriors - Joseph Bruchac   *m* 170

COLLECTOR

McGill, Lauren
Lauren McGill's Pickle Museum - Jerdine Nolen
   p 1091

Paran, Agatha
The Wrong One - Carol Otis Hurst   *e, m* 699

Platypus
Platypus - Chris Riddell   *p* 1202

Unnamed Character
Cinderella's Dress - Nancy Willard   *p* 1444
Cinderella's Dress - Nancy Willard   *p* 1444

COMPUTER EXPERT

Chu, Boone
Pattern Recognition - William Gibson   *h, a* 522

Gilbert, Peter "Parkaboy"
Pattern Recognition - William Gibson   *h, a* 522

Hayton, Brian
Operating Codes - Nick Manns   *m, h* 939

Lee, Cleverton
Remote Man - Elizabeth Honey   *m, h* 670

Mouse
Fallen Host - Lyda Morehouse   *h, a* 1031

CON ARTIST

Fowl, Artemis
Artemis Fowl: The Eternity Code - Eoin Colfer
   m 277

Gill, Quintus Wylie
Gilbert & Sullivan Set Me Free - Kathleen Karr   *m,*
   h 767

Harsich, Abram
Dust - Arthur Slade   *m, h* 1308

Heems, Abner
The House of Windjammer - V.A. Richardson   *m,*
   h 1201

Higgenboom, Clarence "Honorable Mister"
Twelve Travelers, Twenty Horses - Harriette Gillem
   Robinet   *m, h* 1213

LeBlanc, Charles "Charlie White"
Lily B. on the Brink of Cool - E. Cody Kimmel   *e,*
   m 786

LeBlanc, Veronique "Vera White"
Lily B. on the Brink of Cool - E. Cody Kimmel   *e,*
   m 786

Om, Baltasar
Colibrí - Ann Cameron   *m* 206

Smith, Wayne "Draco"
Sweetblood - Pete Hautman   *h* 610

Zed
Amy - Mary Hooper   *m, h* 674

CONVICT

Dexter, Zeke
Blizzard's Wake - Phyllis Reynolds Naylor   *m,*
   h 1065

Miller, Frank P.
Ruby Electric - Theresa Nelson   *m* 1074

Morgan, Wayne
The Same Stuff as Stars - Katherine Paterson
   m 1128

Willson, Roy
Comfort - Carolee Dean   *m, h* 363

COOK

Ah Sam
When the Circus Came to Town - Laurence Yep
   e 1476

Bartholomew, Cyril
Flavor of the Week - Tucker Shaw   *m, h* 1288

Big Bear
Bravery Soup - Maryann Cocca-Leffler   *p* 267

Celia
The House of the Scorpion - Nancy Farmer   *m,*
   h 444

Farmer Todd
Piggy's Pancake Parlor - David McPhail   *e* 1000

Father
Apple Pie 4th of July - Janet S. Wong   *p*   1455

Franny, Gourmet Granny
Alvie Eats Soup - Ross Collins   *p*   283

Grannie
Full, Full, Full of Love - Trish Cooke   *p*   291

Granny Baxter
The Runaway Pumpkin - Kevin Lewis   *p*   890

Hobbs, Lorraine
Unseen Companion - Denise Gosliner Orenstein
  h   1113

Mother
Apple Pie 4th of July - Janet S. Wong   *p*   1455

Piggy
Piggy's Pancake Parlor - David McPhail   *e*   1000

Putter
Mr. Putter & Tabby Stir the Soup - Cynthia Rylant
  b   1248

Teaberry
Mr. Putter & Tabby Stir the Soup - Cynthia Rylant
  b   1248

Unnamed Character
Get Well, Good Knight - Shelley Moore Thomas
  b   1377
Hey, Pancakes! - Tamson Weston   *p*   1432
More Pies! - Robert Munsch   *p*   1040
Pancake Dreams - Ingmarie Ahvander   *p*   12

COUNSELOR

Butler, Claire
Bottled Up - Jaye Murray   *m, h*   1045

Duffy, Roy
Alt Ed - Catherine Atkins   *m, h*   52

Jones, Pamela
Patiently Alice - Phyllis Reynolds Naylor   *m,*
  h   1068

McKinley, Alice Kathleen
Patiently Alice - Phyllis Reynolds Naylor   *m,*
  h   1068

Price, Elizabeth
Patiently Alice - Phyllis Reynolds Naylor   *m,*
  h   1068

Reid, Justin
Dancing Naked - Shelley Hrdlitschka   *h*   692

Willner, Henry
After - Francine Prose   *m, h*   1175

COURTIER

Nera
The Courtesan's Daughter - Priscilla Galloway
  h   505

COUSIN

Althestan
Never After - Rebecca Lickiss   *h, a*   892

Brian
Katie's Wish - Barbara Shook Hazen   *p*   616

Cole, Duncan
*Rosy Cole's Worst Ever, Best Yet Tour of New York
  City* - Sheila Greenwald   *e*   556

Cole, Rosy
*Rosy Cole's Worst Ever, Best Yet Tour of New York
  City* - Sheila Greenwald   *e*   556

Gran
The Bagpiper's Ghost - Jane Yolen   *e, m*   1478

Grayson, Grant
Gravel Queen - Tea Benduhn   *h*   101

Hatcher, Farley Drexel
Double Fudge - Judy Blume   *e, m*   120

Hatcher, Fauna
Double Fudge - Judy Blume   *e, m*   120

Hatcher, Flora
Double Fudge - Judy Blume   *e, m*   120

Hayden, Edward "Neddy"
The Spirit and Gilly Bucket - Maurine F. Dahlberg
  m   337

Hayden, Sarah
The Spirit and Gilly Bucket - Maurine F. Dahlberg
  m   337

Howie
Iris and Walter and Cousin Howie - Elissa Haden
  Guest   *b*   569

Jerry
The Hero - Ron Woods   *m, h*   1464

John Martin
Sister Spider Knows All - Adrian Fogelin   *m*   471

Johnny
Child of the Prophecy - Juliet Marillier   *h, a*   941

Joseph
The Dream Shop - Katharine Kenah   *p*   780

Mabel
Vampire State Building - Elizabeth Levy   *e*   887

Mari
Alia Waking - Laura Williams McCaffrey   *m,*
  h   962

Minette, Alma
*A Time for Courage: The Suffragette Diary of
  Kathleen Bowen, Washington, DC, 1917* - Kathryn
  Lasky   *e, m*   857

Mipeng
The Kite Rider - Geraldine McCaughrean   *m,*
  h   965

Newton
What a Hat! - Holly Keller   *p*   778

Opal
Toot & Puddle: Charming Opal - Holly Hobbie
  p   649

Pa Cua "Lisa"
Tangled Threads: A Hmong Girl's Story - Pegi Deitz
  Shea   *m, h*   1289

Percy
Practice Makes Perfect for Rotten Ralph - Jack Gantos
  b   507

Pilgrim, Daniel
I Am Not Esther - Fleur Beale   *m, h*   91

Pip
The Dream Shop - Katharine Kenah   *p*   780

Prentice, Hugh
*Just Jane: The Story of a Daughter of England Caught
  in the Struggle for Independence in Revolutionary
  America* - William Lavender   *m, h*   858

Prescott, Josh
The Battle of Jericho - Sharon M. Draper   *m,*
  h   395

Puddle
Toot & Puddle: Charming Opal - Holly Hobbie
  p   649

Ralph
Practice Makes Perfect for Rotten Ralph - Jack Gantos
  b   507

Roberts, Hugh
The Hollow Kingdom - Clare B. Dunkle   *m, h*   405

Rushton, Cecelia "Cecy"
Sorcery and Cecelia, or the Enchanted Chocolate Pot -
  Patricia C. Wrede   *m, h*   1470

See Cua "Heather"
Tangled Threads: A Hmong Girl's Story - Pegi Deitz
  Shea   *m, h*   1289

Seinfeld, Susie
United Tates of America - Paula Danziger   *e,*
  m   347

Smith, Jessica Emily "Jess"
The Last Treasure - Janet S. Anderson   *m, h*   26

Spokes, Kate
Remote Man - Elizabeth Honey   *m, h*   670

Sudit, Sithli sae
The Sword of the Land - Noel-Anne Brennan   *h,*
  a   142

Sutherland, Alex
Ghost at the Window - Margaret McAllister   *e,*
  m   960

Talgarth, Kate
Sorcery and Cecelia, or the Enchanted Chocolate Pot -
  Patricia C. Wrede   *m, h*   1470

Vevila
Never After - Rebecca Lickiss   *h, a*   892

Woods, Eric
The 1980s: Earthsong - Tom Hoobler   *m*   671

Woods, Jason
The 1980s: Earthsong - Tom Hoobler   *m*   671

Woods, Suzanne
The 1980s: Earthsong - Tom Hoobler   *m*   671

COW

Clarissa
Poultrygeist - Mary Jane Auch   *p*   55

Clorinda
Clorinda - Robert Kinerk   *p*   791

Daisy
Daisy the Dancing Cow - Viki Woodworth
  p   1469

Edna
Serious Farm - Tim Egan   *p*   421

Georgie Lee
Georgie Lee - Sharon Phillips Denslow   *e*   374

Grace
*Little Old Big Beard and Big Young Little Beard: A
  Short and Tall Tale* - Remy Charlip   *p*   238

Marta
Marta and the Bicycle - Germano Zullo   *p*   1497

Milfoil "Mom"
Our Twitchy - Kes Gray   *p*   551

Minnie
Minnie and Moo and the Potato from Planet X -
  Denys Cazet   *b*   233
Minnie and Moo and the Seven Wonders of the World
  - Denys Cazet   *e*   234
Minnie and Moo: The Night Before Christmas - Denys
  Cazet   *b*   235

Moo
Minnie and Moo and the Potato from Planet X -
  Denys Cazet   *b*   233
Minnie and Moo and the Seven Wonders of the World
  - Denys Cazet   *e*   234
Minnie and Moo: The Night Before Christmas - Denys
  Cazet   *b*   235

Moo Cow
Moo Cow Kaboom! - Thacher Hurd   *p*   697

Pixie
A Fairy in a Dairy - Lucy Nolan   *p*   1090

COWBOY

Arizona Charlie
Arizona Charlie and the Klondike Kid - Julie Lawson
   p 864

Big Beard
*Little Old Big Beard and Big Young Little Beard: A
   Short and Tall Tale* - Remy Charlip *p* 238

Gene
Sixteen Cows - Lisa Wheeler *p* 1435

Hart, Matthew "Matt"
Samantha and the Cowboy - Lorraine Heath *h* 620

Little Beard
*Little Old Big Beard and Big Young Little Beard: A
   Short and Tall Tale* - Remy Charlip *p* 238

Sue
Sixteen Cows - Lisa Wheeler *p* 1435

Unnamed Character
The Dirty Cowboy - Amy Timberlake *p* 1382

Vaughn, Jake
Samantha and the Cowboy - Lorraine Heath *h* 620

COWGIRL

MacGruder, Rose "Thunder Rose"
Thunder Rose - Jerdine Nolen *p* 1093

O'Hannigan, Hannah Mae
Hannah Mae O'Hannigan's Wild West Show - Lisa
   Campbell Ernst *p* 437

CRICKET

Cricket
Christmas Cricket - Eve Bunting *p* 178

Old Cricket
Old Cricket - Lisa Wheeler *p* 1434

CRIME VICTIM

Chumil, Tzunun "Rosa Garcia"
Colibri - Ann Cameron *m* 206

Dunaway, Eva Marie
The Square Root of Murder - Paul Zindel *m* 1496

CRIMINAL

Belch
The Wish List - Eoin Colfer *m, h* 278

Buster
Slim and Jim - Richard Egielski *p* 422

Devlin, Caleb
The Creek - Jennifer L. Holm *m, h* 667

Fogarty, Alan
Faerie Wars - Herbie Brennan *h* 141

Hades, Acheron
The Eyre Affair: A Novel - Jasper Fforde *h, a* 453

Kelley, Edward
The Alchemist's Door - Lisa Goldstein *h, a* 535

Macy
Shooting Monarchs - John Halliday *h* 587

Mender, Alan "Frosty"
Inside Out - Terry Trueman *h* 1386

Mender, Joseph "Stormy"
Inside Out - Terry Trueman *h* 1386

Sylvanus
All Night Awake - Sarah A. Hoyt *h, a* 691

Thompson, Daniel
Shadow of a Doubt - S.L. Rottman *m, h* 1232

Toad
Disappearing Act - Sid Fleischman *m* 461

CROCODILE

Crocodile
Mrs. Chicken and the Hungry Crocodile - Won-Ldy
   Paye *p* 1137

Magic Sam
Jack and Jill - Daniel Kirk *p* 799

CROW

Old Crow
Old Cricket - Lisa Wheeler *p* 1434

DANCER

Alice "Al"
*The Glass Cafe: Or the Stripper and the State: How
   My Mother Started a War with the System that
   Made Us Kind of Rich and a Little Bit Famous* -
   Gary Paulsen *m, h* 1134

Brianna
Brianna, Jamaica, and the Dance of Spring - Juanita
   Havill *p* 612

Capuletto, Lucinda
One Lucky Summer - Laura McGee Kvasnosky
   e 840

Clorinda
Clorinda - Robert Kinerk *p* 791

Dolores
Dolores on Her Toes - Barbara Samuels *p* 1256

Elise
Tanya and the Red Shoes - Patricia Lee Gauch
   p 510

Ferri, Delia
A Dance of Sisters - Tracey Porter *m* 1164

Foley
Tanya and the Red Shoes - Patricia Lee Gauch
   p 510

Frog
Down by the Cool of the Pool - Tony Mitton
   p 1020

Hobart
Hobart - Anita Briggs *e* 149

Jamaica
Brianna, Jamaica, and the Dance of Spring - Juanita
   Havill *p* 612

Knight, Phebe
The Kings Are Already Here - Garret Freymann-Weyr
   m, h 493

Nikki
Brianna, Jamaica, and the Dance of Spring - Juanita
   Havill *p* 612

Sokha, Teeda
The Stone Goddess - Minfong Ho *m, h* 646

Tanya
Tanya and the Red Shoes - Patricia Lee Gauch
   p 510

Tessa
Tessa's Tip-Tapping Toes - Carolyn Crimi *p* 314

DAUGHTER

Abikanile
The Village That Vanished - Ann Grifalconi *p* 561

Alianne "Aly"
Trickster's Choice - Tamora Pierce *m, h* 1152

Alighieri, Antonia "Bice"
Dante's Daughter - Kimberley Heuston *h* 635

Allita
The Snake's Tales - Marguerite W. Davol *p* 353

Amber
Amber Waiting - Nan Gregory *p* 559

Amy
Mama Played Baseball - David A. Adler *p* 5

Annabelle
Jethro Byrd, Fairy Child - Bob Graham *p* 544

Annie
Annie's Ark - Lesley Harker *p* 594

Aurora
Sleeping Beauty - Mahlon F. Craft *p* 312

Barker, Lizzie
Season of Promise - Patricia Hermes *e* 628

Becky
Bear Hug - Laurence Pringle *p* 1172

Bella
Was That Christmas? - Hilary McKay *p* 981

Billingsly, Beverly
Beverly Billingsly Borrows a Book - Alexander Stadler
   p 1333

Britta
Mirabelle - Astrid Lindgren *p* 896

Buttons, Sissy
Sissy Buttons Takes Charge! - Ian Whybrow
   p 1439

Campbell, Dulcie
The Real, True Dulcie Campbell - Cynthia DeFelice
   p 367

Case, Almira
The Birds of Killingworth - Robert D. San Souci
   p 1258

Dickens, Virginia
A Time to Dance - Mary Pope Osborne *e* 1119

Drummond, Tessa
Blue Eyes Better - Ruth Wallace-Brodeur *e* 1412

Elizabeth
The Perfect Pet - Margie Palatini *p* 1124

Elizabeti
Elizabeti's School - Stephanie Stuve-Bodeen
   p 1352

Ella
In the Piney Woods - Roni Schotter *p* 1270

Emma
Emma's Story - Deborah Hodge *p* 655
Old Bob's Brown Bear - Niki Daly *p* 340
Princesses Are People, Too: Two Modern Fairy Tales
   - Susie Morgenstern *e* 1032

Evette
Darby - Jonathon Scott Fuqua *e* 501

Fainne
Child of the Prophecy - Juliet Marillier *h, a* 941

Flo
Ebb & Flo and the Baby Seal - Jane Simmons
   p 1304

Garland, Holly
The Trouble with Babies - Martha Freeman *e* 488

Ginny
Especially Heroes - Virginia Kroll *p* 831

Girlpie
Homemade Love - bell hooks *p* 673

Glidden, Charlotte
Charlotte in Paris - Joan MacPhail Knight *e* 807

Goldilocks
Goldilocks and the Three Bears - Jim Aylesworth
    p 61

Hath, Kestrel
Firesong: An Adventure - William Nicholson
    1078

Hershabel
Pinocchio the Boy: Incognito in Collodi - Lane Smith
    p 1314

Honors, Katie
Sometimes I'm Bombaloo - Rachel Vail   p 1389

Hum, Agapanthus
Agapanthus Hum and the Angel Hoot - Joy Cowley
    b 309

Iphigenia
The Great God Pan - Donna Jo Napoli   m, h 1062

Isabel
The Water Gift and the Pig of the Pig - Jacqueline
    Briggs Martin   p 948

Jill
Jack and Jill - Daniel Kirk   p 799

Josie
Musical Beds - Mara Bergman   p 105

Katie
Before I Was Your Mother - Kathryn Lasky   p 850

Kyri
Who's That Knocking on Christmas Eve? - Jan Brett
    p 145

Laura
Star Blanket - Pat Brisson   p 156

Lili
Mama Will Be Home Soon - Nancy Minchella
    p 1016

Lily
Hushabye Lily - Claire Freedman   p 487
What Shall We Do, Blue Kangaroo? - Emma
    Chichester Clark   p 247

Little One
The Witch's Children - Ursula Jones   p 758

Little Rat
Little Rat Sets Sail - Monika Bang-Campbell   b 72

Lizzy
Lizzy's Do's and Don'ts - Jessica Harper   p 595

Locks, Goldie
Goldie Locks Has Chicken Pox - Erin Dealey
    p 362

Louise
Lionel's Birthday - Stephen Krensky   b 826

Lucy
The First Thing My Mama Told Me - Susan Marie
    Swanson   p 1355
The Wolves in the Walls - Neil Gaiman   p 503

Luzolo
Monkey for Sale - Sanna Stanley   p 1335

MacGruder, Rose "Thunder Rose"
Thunder Rose - Jerdine Nolen   p 1093

Madeleine
The First Thing My Mama Told Me - Susan Marie
    Swanson   p 1355

Marie-Louise
Little Pierre: A Cajun Story from Louisiana - Robert
    D. San Souci   p 1259

McBee, Amen "Amie"
Keeper of the Doves - Betsy Byars   e 192

Meggie
The Berry-Picking Man - Jane Buchanan   e 175

Middle One
The Witch's Children - Ursula Jones   p 758

Miller, Marjory
Berta: A Remarkable Dog - Celia Barker Lottridge
    e 908

Molly
Tatty Ratty - Helen Cooper   p 295

Morales, Gabi
A Crazy, Mixed-Up Spanglish Day - Marisa Montes
    e 1024

Nina
That Makes Me Mad! - Steven Kroll   p 830

O'Hannigan, Hannah Mae
Hannah Mae O'Hannigan's Wild West Show - Lisa
    Campbell Ernst   p 437

Oksi
Frightful's Daughter - Jean Craighead George
    p 518

Penny
One Bright Penny - Geraldine McCaughrean
    p 967

Potter, Hope
We Are Patriots - Kristiana Gregory   e 558

Quigley, Lucy
The Quigleys - Simon Mason   e 952

Reynolds, Ruthie
Fairy Dust - Jane Denitz Smith   e 1313

Robinson, Roberta Louise
Here We Go Round - Alice McGill   e 979

Rosie
Waggle - Sarah McMenemy   p 988

Ruby
Musical Beds - Mara Bergman   p 105

Ruthie
No More Vegetables! - Nicole Rubel   p 1236

Sara
When Catherine the Great and I Were Eight! - Cari
    Best   p 107

Sarah
Homespun Sarah - Verla Kay   p 771
Lighthouse: A Story of Remembrance - Robert Munsch
    p 1039

Shakespeare, Judith
Shakespeare's Spy - Gary Blackwood   m 114

Shau-yu
On My Way to Buy Eggs - Chih-Yuan Chen   p 239

Shining
Shining - Julius Lester   p 878

Smith, Rose
Mary Smith - Andrea U'Ren   p 1388

Sophie
Best Kind of Baby - Kate Laing   p 846
I, Freddy - Deitlof Reiche   e 1196

Soraya
Flame - Hilari Bell   m, h 97

Sue
Once Upon a Farm - Marie Bradby   p 132

Surrey, Iris
The Secret - Eva Hoffman   h, a 660

Tabb, Jemima
Funny Frank - Dick King-Smith   e 793

Tarbell, Bailey
A Twisted Tale - Carolyn Fisher   p 456

Thibodeaux, Suzanne Marie Sabine Chicot
Alligator Sue - Sharon Arms Doucet   p 389

Throckmorton, Maud
The Mayor of Central Park - Avi   e 59

Tilly
Treasure Hunt - Allan Ahlberg   p 10

Tria
Tria and the Great Star Rescue - Rebecca Kraft Rector
    e 1191

Unnamed Character
Apple Pie 4th of July - Janet S. Wong   p 1455
Baghead - Jarrett J. Krosoczka   p 834
Countdown to Kindergarten - Alison McGhee
    p 978
First Day - Dandi Daley Mackall   p 928
Flamingo Dream - Donna Jo Napoli   p 1061
Horse in the Pigpen - Linda Williams   p 1446
I Love Saturdays Y Domingos - Alma Flor Ada
    p 2
Monsoon - Uma Krishnaswami   p 829
My Pony - Susan Jeffers   p 731
Oh No, Gotta Go! - Susan Middleton Elya   p 432
A Place to Grow - Soyung Pak   p 1121
The Range Eternal - Louise Erdrich   p 434
Two Old Potatoes and Me - John Coy   p 311
Visiting Day - Jacqueline Woodson   p 1468

Unnamed Child
Goose's Story - Cari Best   p 106

Ursula
When the Circus Came to Town - Laurence Yep
    e 1476

Valentine, Katherine
Mortal Engines - Philip Reeve   h, a 1195

Vatta, Kylara "Ky"
Trading in Danger - Elizabeth Moon   h, a 1026

Wanda-Linda
The Terrible Underpants - Kaz Cooke   p 290

Wells, Margaret Cora "Meg"
A Fine Start: Meg's Prairie Diary - Kate McMullan
    e 990

DEAF PERSON

Jones, Calypso "Twig"
Willow and Twig - Jean Little   m 903

Moses
Moses Goes to the Circus - Isaac Millman   p 1012

Roke, Tommy
Search of the Moon King's Daughter - Linda Holeman
    m, h 665

DEALER

Clark, Babe
Matchit - Martha Moore   e, m 1027

DEITY

Amun
The Ugly Goddess - Elsa Marston   m 944

Aphrodite
Quiver - Stephanie Spinner   m, h 1327

Apollo
Goddesses Series - Clea Hantman   m, h 592

Artemis
Quiver - Stephanie Spinner   m, h 1327

Cupid
Juliet Dove, Queen of Love - Bruce Coville   e,
    m 308

Erato "Era"
Goddesses Series - Clea Hantman   m, h 592

Eros
Quiver - Stephanie Spinner   m, h 1327

Gayle "Gaia"
Drinking Midnight Wine - Simon R. Green   h,
    a 553

FATHER

Knight, Clarence
The Kings Are Already Here - Garret Freymann-Weyr
m, h 493

Leeper, Arlie
The Hero - Ron Woods m, h 1464

Lexie, John
The Painters of Lexieville - Sharon Darrow m,
h 348

Luca, Anthony "Honest Abe"
Son of the Mob - Gordon Korman m, h 818

Malone, Jack
Catalyst - Laurie Halse Anderson h 28

Matt
Mahalia - Joanne Horniman h 679

McBee, Albert "Papa"
Keeper of the Doves - Betsy Byars e 192

McCrae, Murray
The Lighthouse Keeper's Daughter - Iain Lawrence
h 860

McKenzie, Vince
The Queen of Everything - Deb Caletti h 202

Merahb
Flame - Hilari Bell m, h 97

Miller, Frank P.
Ruby Electric - Theresa Nelson m 1074

Mo "Silvertongue"
Inkheart - Cornelia Funke m, h 499

Moreno, Tata
Keeper of the Night - Kimberly Willis Holt m,
h 669

Morgan, Wayne
The Same Stuff as Stars - Katherine Paterson
m 1128

Mouse
Christmas in the City - Loretta Krupinski p 836

O'Brien, Clay
Prairie Whispers - Frances Arrington m 43

Olaf
Serious Trouble - Arthur Howard p 684

Pa
A Hug Goes Around - Laura Krauss Melmed
p 1005
One Bright Penny - Geraldine McCaughrean
p 967
Sunsets of the West - Tony Johnston p 754
A Time to Dance - Mary Pope Osborne e 1119
A Twisted Tale - Carolyn Fisher p 456

Papa
Ghosts for Breakfast - Stanley Todd Terasaki
p 1374
Home at Last - Susan Middleton Elya p 431
I Dream of Trains - Angela Johnson p 742
Little Rabbit Lost - Harry Horse p 682
Mama's Coming Home - Kate Banks p 76
Milly and the Macy's Parade - Shana Corey
p 303
Monsoon - Uma Krishnaswami p 829
Oliver Finds His Way - Phyllis Root p 1228
On the Town: A Community Adventure - Judith
Caseley p 227
Silent Movie - Avi p 60
The Snake's Tales - Marguerite W. Davol p 353

Papa Bear
Little Brown Bear Won't Go to School! - Jane Dyer
p 412
Little Brown Bear Won't Take a Nap! - Jane Dyer
p 413

Papa Lion
Quiet! - Paul Bright p 153

Papakey
Chimp and Zee and the Big Storm - Laurence Anholt
p 31

Patoot
Puss in Cowboy Boots - Jan Huling p 695

Pierson, Reid
Freaky Green Eyes - Joyce Carol Oates m,
h 1099

Pollard, Wingrove
Pattern Recognition - William Gibson h, a 522

Riley, Elisha
Flying Blind - Anna Myers e, m 1049

Scaredy Cat
The Scaredy Cats - Barbara Bottner p 128

Schnurmacher, Apa
Marika - Andrea Cheng m, h 241

Schubert, Jack
The Steps - Rachel Cohn m 273

Sedge "Pop"
Our Twitchy - Kes Gray p 551

Silverwing, Shade
Firewing - Kenneth Oppel m 1111

Stephanos
The Courtesan's Daughter - Priscilla Galloway
h 505

Sterling
Blizzard's Wake - Phyllis Reynolds Naylor m,
h 1065

Sunday, Abraham
Anna Sunday - Sally M. Keehn m 772

Unnamed Character
The Animal Hedge - Paul Fleischman p 459
Bertil and the Bathroom Elephants - Inger Lindahl
p 894
Dream Carver - Diana Cohn p 271
Go Track a Yak! - Tony Johnston p 752
Little Buggy - Kevin O'Malley p 1107
Mama Played Baseball - David A. Adler p 5
My Pony - Susan Jeffers p 731
Pictures for Miss Josie - Sandra Belton p 100
A Place to Grow - Soyung Pak p 1121
The Red Wolf - Margaret Shannon p 1285
Star Blanket - Pat Brisson p 156

Vandorn, Frank
Nelly in the Wilderness - Lynn Cullen m 325

Vernon
The Crying Rocks - Janet Taylor Lisle m, h 901

Webster, Joe
Where Heroes Hide - Helen Recorvits e 1190

Weeks
Christmas Tapestry - Patricia Polacco p 1163

William X of Aquitaine
Eleanor: Crown Jewel of Aquitaine, France, 1136 -
Kristiana Gregory m 557

Willson, Roy
Comfort - Carolee Dean m, h 363

FBI AGENT

Bightly
Son of the Mob - Gordon Korman m, h 818

FERAL CHILD

Vyas, Akhil
The Pack - Elisa Carbone m, h 214

FIANCE(E)

Bluebell, Hilda
The Time Witches - Michael Molloy m 1022

Fairweather, Joseph
The Shakeress - Kimberley Heuston m, h 636

Fontaine, John "MyJohn"
Or Give Me Death - Ann Rinaldi m, h 1206

Glasgow, Annie
Phoning a Dead Man - Gillian Cross m, h 318

Hank
Stefan's Story - Valerie Hobbs m 651

Summers, Sylvia
Patiently Alice - Phyllis Reynolds Naylor m,
h 1068
Simply Alice - Phyllis Reynolds Naylor m 1069

FILMMAKER

Sorrels, Marcie
Stoner & Spaz - Ron Koertge h 810

FIRE FIGHTER

Humphreys, Mose
New York's Bravest - Mary Pope Osborne p 1117

FISHERMAN

Angus
Sea Gift - John Ashby m, h 47

Granpere
Where, Where Is Swamp Bear? - Kathi Appelt
p 36

Ian
Sea Gift - John Ashby m, h 47

Lauchie
Sea Gift - John Ashby m, h 47

Moreno, Tata
Keeper of the Night - Kimberly Willis Holt m,
h 669

Unnamed Character
The Cat Who Liked Potato Soup - Terry Farish
p 443
How the Fisherman Tricked the Genie - Kitoba
Sunami p 1354

FLY

Fly
The Spider and the Fly - Mary Howitt p 690

FOOTBALL PLAYER

Beasley, John "Johnny"
Up Molasses Mountain - Julie Baker m, h 68

Beaterson, Rick
Three Clams and an Oyster - Randy Powell m,
h 1166

Buckley, Todd
Jake, Reinvented - Gordon Korman h 816

Callahan, Randy
Alt Ed - Catherine Atkins m, h 52

Deshutsis, Dwight
Three Clams and an Oyster - Randy Powell m,
h 1166

Garrett, Jacob "Jake"
Jake, Reinvented - Gordon Korman h 816

Herbert, Warren "Herbie"
Restless: A Ghost's Story - Rich Wallace h 1411

FOSTER CHILD (continued)

McCallister, Flint
Three Clams and an Oyster - Randy Powell   m, h   1166

Paradis, Richard "Rick"
Jake, Reinvented - Gordon Korman   h   816

Pittman, Sam
Slumming - Kristen D. Randle   h   1183

Savage, Cade
Three Clams and an Oyster - Randy Powell   m, h   1166

Summerfield, Rachel
Three Clams and an Oyster - Randy Powell   m, h   1166

FOSTER CHILD

David
The Very Worst Thing - Torey Hayden   m   614

Paulie
Say Yes - Audrey Couloumbis   m, h   306

FOSTER PARENT

Edna
Locomotion - Jacqueline Woodson   e, m   1466

Gracie
Our Gracie Aunt - Jacqueline Woodson   p   1467

Harper
America - E.R. Frank   h   479

Parker, Alice
The Monster in Me - Mette Ivie Harrison   m   600

Parker, John
The Monster in Me - Mette Ivie Harrison   m   600

Rose, Betty
Little Soldier - Bernard Ashley   m, h   48

FOUNDLING

Mouse
The Dark Horse - Marcus Sedgwick   m   1275

FOX

Fox
Fox Tale Soup - Tony Bonning   p   125
My Lucky Day - Keiko Kasza   p   768
Piggy's Pancake Parlor - David McPhail   e   1000
The Rooster and the Fox - Helen Ward   p   1415

Rosa Raposa
Rosa Raposa - F. Isabel Campoy   p   209

Unnamed Character
Dinnertime! - Sue Williams   p   1447
Do Like a Duck Does! - Judy Hindley   p   642
Hungry Hen - Richard Waring   p   1416

FRIEND

Al
Gregory and Alexander - William Barringer   p   84

Alien
Alien & Possum: Hanging Out - Tony Johnston   e   751

Angela
What James Likes Best - Amy Schwartz   p   1272

Angie
The Saturday Escape - Daniel J. Mahoney   p   934

Annie
Annie Was Warned - Jarrett J. Krosoczka   p   833

Anthony
I'll Never Share You, Blackboard Bear - Martha Alexander   p   19

Arnie
Arnie the Doughnut - Laurie Keller   p   779

Arthur
The Great Blue Yonder - Alex Shearer   m, h   1290

Badger
A Perfect Day for It - Jan Fearnley   p   445

Barnes, T.J.
T.J. and the Cats - Hazel Hutchins   e   704

Barofsky, Mary Priscilla "Mary P"
Might Adventurer of the Planet! - Ricki Stern   e   1341

Bates, Julian
Gloria Rising - Ann Cameron   e   207

Bean, Clarice
Utterly Me, Clarice Bean - Lauren Child   e   249

Bear
A Perfect Day for It - Jan Fearnley   p   445

Beard, George
The Adventures of Super Diaper Baby: The First Graphic Novel - Dav Pilkey   e   1153

Beau
Bubba and Beau, Best Friends - Kathi Appelt   p   34

Ben
Francis the Scaredy Cat - Ed Boxall   p   131

Benjamin
Morris the Artist - Lore Segal   p   1276

Bert
Where Does Thursday Go? - Janeen Brian   p   146

Bing
Arnie the Doughnut - Laurie Keller   p   779

Bob
Brian & Bob: The Tale of Two Guinea Pigs - Georgie Ripper   p   1208

Boyd, Wallace "Weasel"
Bernie Magruder & the Bats in the Belfry - Phyllis Reynolds Naylor   e   1064

Brian
Brian & Bob: The Tale of Two Guinea Pigs - Georgie Ripper   p   1208

Brown, Danitra
Danitra Brown Leaves Town - Nikki Grimes   p   566

Bruno
Where Does Thursday Go? - Janeen Brian   p   146

Bugg, Kevin
City of Names - Kevin Brockmeier   e   157

Chajang
Sondok: Princess of the Moon and Stars, Korea, A.D. 595 - Sheri Holman   m   668

Chang
Chang and the Bamboo Flute - Elizabeth Starr Hill   e   640

Chango-monkey
Rosa Raposa - F. Isabel Campoy   p   209

Charles
I'm Not Invited? - Diane Cain Bluthenthal   p   121

Cleopatra
Madlenka's Dog - Peter Sis   p   1307

Daniel
Chachaji's Cup - Uma Krishnaswami   p   828

Daniels, Justin
Get Ready for Second Grade, Amber Brown - Paula Danziger   b   346

Davis, George
Flying Free: Corey's Underground Railroad Diary - Sharon Dennis Wyeth   e   1471

Delilah
It Came from Beneath the Bed - James Howe   e   688

Doll, Annabelle
The Meanest Doll in the World - Ann M. Martin   e   946

Donuthead, Julia
Donuthead - Sue Stauffacher   e   1337

Duck
Fix-It Duck - Jez Alborough   p   15

Echidna
Platypus and the Birthday Party - Chris Riddell   p   1203

Ernst
Winnie and Ernst - Gina Freschet   e   492

Evans, Sara
Starting with Alice - Phyllis Reynolds Naylor   e   1070

Evette
Darby - Jonathon Scott Fuqua   e   501

Ezzie
Who's Afraid of the Big Bad Book? - Lauren Child   p   251

Fairchild, Beth
Darby - Jonathon Scott Fuqua   e   501

Farfallina
Farfallina & Marcel - Holly Keller   p   777

Felcher, Paul
Robert and the Weird & Wacky Facts - Barbara Seuling   e   1279

Florentina
Four Friends Together - Sue Heap   p   617

Fox
Piggy's Pancake Parlor - David McPhail   e   1000

Frank
Good Night, Sleep Tight, Don't Let the Bedbugs Bite! - Diane DeGroat   p   369

Frog
Fix-It Duck - Jez Alborough   p   15

Funcraft, Tiffany
The Meanest Doll in the World - Ann M. Martin   e   946

Gaspard
Gaspard and Lisa's Rainy Day - Anne Gutman   p   573
Lisa's Baby Sister - Anne Gutman   p   574

Gelato, Will
Olvina Flies - Grace Lin   p   893

Gilbert, Peter "Parkaboy"
Pattern Recognition - William Gibson   h, a   522

Giombetti, Skinny
Grape Thief - Kristine L. Franklin   m, h   482

Gloria
I'll Never Share You, Blackboard Bear - Martha Alexander   p   19

Goldfarb, Mavis
Fat Camp Commandos Go West - Daniel Pinkwater   e   1159

Gregory
Gregory and Alexander - William Barringer   p   84

Hana
In the Shadow of the Pali: A Story of the Hawaiian Leper Colony - Lisa Cindrich   m, h   255

Herb
Who's Afraid of the Big Bad Book? - Lauren Child
p 251

Herbie
Herbie's Secret Santa - Petra Mathers   p 955

Hernandez, Josh
7 x 9 = Trouble! - Claudia Mills   e 1013

Herter, Quentin Fenton "Shad" Three
Quentin Fenton Herter III - Amy MacDonald
p 923

Hip
Hip, Hip, Hooray Day! - Barney Saltzberg   p 1255

Hop
Hip, Hip, Hooray Day! - Barney Saltzberg   p 1255

Horus
*First Graders from Mars: Episode 2: The Problem
with Pelly* - Shana Corey   b 301

Hutchins, Harold
*The Adventures of Super Diaper Baby: The First
Graphic Novel* - Dav Pilkey   e 1153

Ingrid
The Princess and the Pauper - Kate Brian   m 147

Iris
Iris and Walter and Baby Rose - Elissa Haden Guest
b 568
Iris and Walter and Cousin Howie - Elissa Haden
Guest   b 569
Iris and Walter: The School Play - Elissa Haden Guest
b 570
Iris and Walter: The Sleepover - Elissa Haden Guest
b 571

Jack
The Saturday Escape - Daniel J. Mahoney   p 934

Jackson, Zuri
Danitra Brown Leaves Town - Nikki Grimes
p 566

Jake
Minn and Jake - Janet S. Wong   e 1456

Jamaica
Brianna, Jamaica, and the Dance of Spring - Juanita
Havill   p 612

James
Annie Was Warned - Jarrett J. Krosoczka   p 833

James, Calliope
The Talent Show - Michelle Edwards   e 417

James, Jesse
Guerrilla Season - Pat Hughes   m, h 693

Javier
Adelita: A Mexican Cinderella Story - Tomie De Paola
p 358

Jeannie
Tippy Lemmey - Patricia C. McKissack   e 986

Jeffrey
Lionel's Birthday - Stephen Krensky   b 826

Jeoffry
Jeoffry's Halloween - Mary Bryant Bailey   p 66

Jim
Slim and Jim - Richard Egielski   p 422

Johnson, Rosie
Boxes for Katje - Candace Fleming   p 462

Jones, Gloria
Gloria Rising - Ann Cameron   e 207

Jones, Herbie
Herbie Jones Moves On - Suzy Kline   e 805

Juliana
The Farther You Run - Davida Wills Hurwin
h 700

Katz, Lido
The Last Burp of Mac McGerp - Pam Smallcomb
e 1311

Kervick, Sarah
Donuthead - Sue Stauffacher   e 1337

Kidder, Gabe
The True Story of Trapper Jack's Left Big Toe - Ian
Wallace   p 1407

Kiese
Monkey for Sale - Sanna Stanley   p 1335

Kim, Mai
Begging for Change - Sharon G. Flake   m, h 458

Kipper
Kipper's Monster - Mick Inkpen   p 715

Lahasca, Jason
Dunk - David Lubar   m, h 912

Lenny
Where Heroes Hide - Helen Recorvits   e 1190

Lily May
What Shall We Play? - Sue Heap   p 618

Lisa
Gaspard and Lisa's Rainy Day - Anne Gutman
p 573

Little Badger
Little Badger's Just-About Birthday - Eve Bunting
p 179

Little Beard
*Little Old Big Beard and Big Young Little Beard: A
Short and Tall Tale* - Remy Charlip   p 238

Lottie
Herbie's Secret Santa - Petra Mathers   p 955

Louise
Ruby's Beauty Shop - Rosemary Wells   p 1427

Luke
A Greater Goode - Amy Schor Ferris   m 451

Luzolo
Monkey for Sale - Sanna Stanley   p 1335

Madlenka
Madlenka's Dog - Peter Sis   p 1307

Manukekua
*In the Shadow of the Pali: A Story of the Hawaiian
Leper Colony* - Lisa Cindrich   m, h 255

Marcel
Farfallina & Marcel - Holly Keller   p 777

Maria
The House of the Scorpion - Nancy Farmer   m,
h 444

Martha
What Shall We Play? - Sue Heap   p 618

Martin, Leandra
Tippy Lemmey - Patricia C. McKissack   e 986

Martin, Raymond
Herbie Jones Moves On - Suzy Kline   e 805

Mary Claire
Four Friends Together - Sue Heap   p 617

Matt
What Shall We Play? - Sue Heap   p 618

Max
The Hero of Third Grade - Alice DeLaCroix
e 370

McClain, Reeve "Junebug" Jr.
Junebug in Trouble - Alice Mead   e 1002

Meade, Emma
Dear Emma - Johanna Hurwitz   e, m 701

Mei Mei
Chang and the Bamboo Flute - Elizabeth Starr Hill
e 640

Melden
The Saturday Escape - Daniel J. Mahoney   p 934

Mingo
Flying Free: Corey's Underground Railroad Diary -
Sharon Dennis Wyeth   e 1471

Minn
Minn and Jake - Janet S. Wong   e 1456

Minnie
I'm Not Invited? - Diane Cain Bluthenthal   p 121

Mitchell, Zora
Begging for Change - Sharon G. Flake   m, h 458

Moody, Betty
Utterly Me, Clarice Bean - Lauren Child   e 249

Morris
Morris the Artist - Lore Segal   p 1276

Mouse
My Friend Rabbit - Eric Rohmann   p 1222

Nikolai
The Three Questions - Jon J. Muth   p 1048

O'Connell, Sarah
One Shot - Susan Glick   m, h 529

Oomor
Timespinners - Luli Gray   e 552

Orville
Agapanthus Hum and the Angel Hoot - Joy Cowley
b 309

Park, Song Lee
Horrible Harry and the Dragon War - Suzy Kline
e 806

Paul
Tippy Lemmey - Patricia C. McKissack   e 986

Perkins, Percival Lincoln "Perks"
Grape Thief - Kristine L. Franklin   m, h 482

Pig
One Rainy Day - Valeri Gorbachev   p 542

Platypus
Platypus and the Birthday Party - Chris Riddell
p 1203

Porkenstein
Porkenstein - Kathryn Lasky   p 856

Possum
Alien & Possum: Hanging Out - Tony Johnston
e 751

Rabbit
My Friend Rabbit - Eric Rohmann   p 1222

Rachel
Four Friends Together - Sue Heap   p 617

Ralph
Poultrygeist - Mary Jane Auch   p 55

Ricotta, Ricky
*Ricky Ricotta's Mighty Robot vs. the Mecha-Monkeys
from Mars* - Dav Pilkey   e 1155

Riley, Georgene
Bernie Magruder & the Bats in the Belfry - Phyllis
Reynolds Naylor   e 1064

Robert
The Battle for St. Michaels - Emily Arnold McCully
b 973
Junebug in Trouble - Alice Mead   e 1002

Robinson, Casey
City of Names - Kevin Brockmeier   e 157

Rodriguez, Rosalind
Starting with Alice - Phyllis Reynolds Naylor
e 1070

Rowan
Rowan and the Ice Creepers - Emily Rodda
e 1217

GOOSE

Gaggle, Dorothy
The Gaggle Sisters River Tour - Chris Jackson
p 720

Gaggle, Sadie
The Gaggle Sisters River Tour - Chris Jackson
p 720

Gertie
Ollie - Olivier Dunrea   p 408

Goose
We're Going on a Picnic! - Pat Hutchins   p 705

Gossie
Gossie - Olivier Dunrea   p 406
Ollie - Olivier Dunrea   p 408

Hetty
The Poltergoose - Michael Lawrence   e, m 862

Katerina
The Other Goose - Judith Kerr   p 782

Marcel
Farfallina & Marcel - Holly Keller   p 777

Ollie
Ollie - Olivier Dunrea   p 408

Unnamed Character
Goose's Story - Cari Best   p 106

GOVERNESS

Minton
Journey to the River Sea - Eva Ibbotson   m 707

GOVERNMENT OFFICIAL

Clabber
A Fairy in a Dairy - Lucy Nolan   p 1090

Government, Jennifer
Jennifer Government - Max Barry   h, a 85

Gower, Hugh
The Year of the Hangman - Gary Blackwood   m, h 115

Harrison, William Henry
Crossing the Panther's Path - Elizabeth Alder   m, h 17

Pederson, Rachel
The Watch - Dennis Danvers   h, a 344

Sam
Henry Climbs a Mountain - D.B. Johnson   p 745

Valentine, Thaddeus
Mortal Engines - Philip Reeve   h, a 1195

Vorkosigan, Miles
Diplomatic Immunity: A Comedy of Terrors - Lois McMaster Bujold   h, a 176

GRANDFATHER

Belicose, Eugene
Welcome Home or Someplace Like It - Charlotte Agell   m 7

Benjamin, Silas
When We Were Saints - Han Nolan   h 1089

Benton, Leo
Stand Tall - Joan Bauer   m 89

Bishop, Howard
This Isn't about the Money - Sally Warner   m 1417

Boxer
Sasha's Matrioshka Dolls - Jane Dillon   p 383

Brittman, Daniel "Poppie"
Hannah's Garden - Midori Snyder   m, h 1318

Costa "Grandpap"
Macaroni Boy - Katherine Ayres   e, m 62

Grampa
Make the Team, Baby Duck! - Amy Hest   p 633

Grand
Dancing the Ring Shout! - Kim Siegelson   p 1300

Grand Da
Katie's Wish - Barbara Shook Hazen   p 616

Grandad
Jason Rat-a-Tat - Colby Rodowsky   e 1220
Mole and the Baby Bird - Marjorie Newman   p 1076

Granddad
The Birdwatchers - Simon James   p 726

Granddaddy
You Can't Rush a Cat - Karleen Bradford   p 133

Grandfather
Monkey Mo Goes to Sea - Diane Goode   p 538
Ruby's Wish - Shirin Yim Bridges   p 148
The Water Gift and the Pig of the Pig - Jacqueline Briggs Martin   p 948

Grandpa
The Beeman - Laurie Krebs   p 825
Full Steam Ahead - Faye Gibbons   p 521
Gus and Grandpa and the Halloween Costume - Claudia Mills   b 1014
Gus and Grandpa Go Fishing - Claudia Mills   b 1015
I Love Saturdays Y Domingos - Alma Flor Ada   p 2
Iris and Walter and Baby Rose - Elissa Haden Guest   b 568
My Pig Amarillo - Satomi Ichikawa   p 709
Pete and Polo's Farmyard Adventure - Adrian Reynolds   p 1200
Thirsty Baby - Catherine Ann Cullen   p 323

Grandpa Dave
Here We Go Round - Alice McGill   e 979

Granpere
Where, Where Is Swamp Bear? - Kathi Appelt   p 36

Griswold
The Falconmaster - R.L. La Fevers   m 841

Halfmoon, Grampa
Indian Shoes - Cynthia Leitich Smith   e 1312

Hillburn, Earl
Mississippi Trial, 1955 - Chris Crowe   m, h 320

Houghton, Jeep
Shaper - Jessie Haas   m 576

Kincaid, Chase
Bull Rider - Marilyn Halvorson   m, h 588

Koro Apirana
The Whale Rider - Witi Ihimaera   m, h 710

McNaughton
Hannah, Divided - Adele Griffin   m 562

Noah
Annie's Ark - Lesley Harker   p 594

Old Badger
Little Badger's Just-About Birthday - Eve Bunting   p 179

Old Bob
Old Bob's Brown Bear - Niki Daly   p 340

Opa
Where in the World - Simon French   m 491

Pappy
Big Time Olie - William Joyce   p 762

Paw, Elder
Varjak Paw - S.F. Said   m 1250

Unnamed Character
Christmas in the Country - Cynthia Rylant   p 1244
In the Piney Woods - Roni Schotter   p 1270

GRANDMOTHER

Abuelita
I Love Saturdays Y Domingos - Alma Flor Ada   p 2

Alice
Melonhead - Michael de Guzman   m 354

Birdy
Ghost Girl: A Blue Ridge Mountain Story - Delia Ray   m 1188

Bone, Griselda Yewbeam
Midnight for Charlie Bone - Jenny Nimmo   m 1082

Boyle, Dorothy "Godbee"
Olive's Ocean - Kevin Henkes   m 623

Bright, Calico Warrenfield
The Return of Calico Bright - David Winkler   m, h 1450

Catherine "Grandma"
When Catherine the Great and I Were Eight! - Cari Best   p 107

Chimwala
The Village That Vanished - Ann Grifalconi   p 561

Dente, Grandma
Noodle Man: The Pasta Superhero - April Pulley Sayre   p 1266

Fairfield, Mimi
Bridging Beyond - Kathleen Benner Duble   m, h 403

Flowers, Nanny
The Whale Rider - Witi Ihimaera   m, h 710

Franny, Gourmet Granny
Alvie Eats Soup - Ross Collins   p 283

Gram
Soul Moon Soup - Lindsay Lee Johnson   m, h 748
That Summer - Tony Johnston   p 755
Yesterday I Had the Blues - Jeron Ashford Frame   p 478

Gramma
Falling from Fire - Teena Booth   m, h 126

Gramma Louise
Here We Go Round - Alice McGill   e 979

Gran
Loretta: Ace Pinky Scout - Keith Graves   p 548
T.J. and the Cats - Hazel Hutchins   e 704

Grandma
At Grandma's - Rhonda Gowler Greene   p 554
Elisa Michaels, Bigger & Better - Johanna Hurwitz   e 702
Emma's Story - Deborah Hodge   p 655
Gaspard and Lisa's Rainy Day - Anne Gutman   p 573
Hobbledy-Clop - Pat Brisson   p 155
Meow Means Mischief - Ann Whitehead Nagda   e 1055
My Grandma, My Pen Pal - Jan Dale Koutsky   p 822
The Name Quilt - Phyllis Root   p 1227
One Candle - Eve Bunting   p 180
Visiting Day - Jacqueline Woodson   p 1468
What Would Joey Do? - Jack Gantos   m 508

Grandma Beetle
Just a Minute: A Trickster Tale and Counting Book - Yuyi Morales   p 1030

Grandma Gardenia
The Talent Show - Michelle Edwards   *e*   417

Grandma Martha
Izzy's Place - Marc Kornblatt   *e, m*   819

Grandma Morgan
The Same Stuff as Stars - Katherine Paterson
    m   1128

Grandmere
Princess in Love - Meg Cabot   *m, h*   197
Princess in Waiting - Meg Cabot   *m, h*   198

Grandmother
A Far-Fetched Story - Karin Cates   *p*   230
Georgie Lee - Sharon Phillips Denslow   *e*   374
My Grandmother's Clock - Geraldine McCaughrean
    p   966

Grandmother Morrow
The Kingfisher's Gift - Susan Williams Beckhorn   *e,*
    m   96

Grandmother Silk
Snowed in with Grandmother Silk - Carol Fenner
    e   448

Grandy
Witch Twins at Camp Bliss - Adele Griffin   *e*   564

Grannie
Full, Full, Full of Love - Trish Cooke   *p*   291

Granny
Small - Clara Vulliamy   *p*   1403

Granny Baxter
The Runaway Pumpkin - Kevin Lewis   *p*   890

Grossmutter
Breath - Donna Jo Napoli   *m, h*   1059

Hannah
Hannah's Garden - Midori Snyder   *m, h*   1318

Hutchings, Tilly Pruitt
The River between Us - Richard Peck   *m, h*   1141

Jones, Nell "Gram"
Willow and Twig - Jean Little   *m*   903

Keeling
Rebel - Willo Davis Roberts   *m*   1211

Larrimer, Eunice
The Presence: A Ghost Story - Eve Bunting   *m,*
    h   181

Lee "Grandmom"
The Tiger's Apprentice - Laurence Yep   *m*   1474

McPhee, Beattie "Grandmonster"
What the Birds See - Sonya Hartnett   *m, h*   604

Monnie
Sweet By and By - Patricia Hermes   *e, m*   629

Nana
House of Sports - Marisabina Russo   *m*   1240

Old Granny
Old Granny and the Bean Thief - Cynthia DeFelice
    p   366

Piermont, Marilyn "Mimi"
Sister Spider Knows All - Adrian Fogelin   *m*   471

Rachel One
Walk Softly, Rachel - Kate Banks   *m, h*   78

Unnamed Character
Christmas in the Country - Cynthia Rylant   *p*   1244
The Magic Bed - John Burningham   *p*   184
Pancake Dreams - Ingmarie Ahvander   *p*   12
That's Good! That's Bad! In The Grand Canyon -
    Margery Cuyler   *p*   335

Viola "Old Vi"
Rebel - Willo Davis Roberts   *m*   1211

Whitfield, "Ga"
Recycling George - Stephen Roos   *e, m*   1224

GROUNDHOG

Little Groundhog
How Groundhog's Garden Grew - Lynne Cherry
    p   243

GUARDIAN

Blackwell, Russ
Happenings - Katie Cobb   *m, h*   265

McGranahan, Minnie
Aunt Minnie and the Twister - Mary Skillings Prigger
    p   1170

Roberts, Hugh
The Hollow Kingdom - Clare B. Dunkle   *m, h*   405

Wellington, Catriona Anabel "Miss Doctor"
Rodzina - Karen Cushman   *m*   331

Whitcomb, Celia
The Big Burn - Jeanette Ingold   *m, h*   713

GUINEA PIG

Bob
Brian & Bob: The Tale of Two Guinea Pigs - Georgie
    Ripper   *p*   1208

Brian
Brian & Bob: The Tale of Two Guinea Pigs - Georgie
    Ripper   *p*   1208

Little Whistle
Little Whistle's Medicine - Cynthia Rylant   *p*   1246

Willy
Pig Enough - Janie Bynum   *p*   194

GYMNAST

Freeman, Kite
*The Slightly True Story of Cedar B. Hartley (Who
    Planned to Live an Unusual Life)* - Martine Murray
    m   1046

Kim
Kim: Empty Inside - Beatrice Sparks   *m, h*   1323

GYPSY

Karay
*The Angel's Command: A Tale from the Castaways of
    the Flying Dutchman* - Brian Jacques   *m, h*   722

Razan, Maguda
*The Angel's Command: A Tale from the Castaways of
    the Flying Dutchman* - Brian Jacques   *m, h*   722

Walker, Darraugh
Child of the Prophecy - Juliet Marillier   *h, a*   941

HAIRDRESSER

Seymour
Bippity Bop Barbershop - Natasha Anastasia Tarpley
    p   1362

Wilson, Duke
Handbook for Boys: A Novel - Walter Dean Myers
    m, h   1053

HAMSTER

Boris
Boris's Glasses - Peter Cohen   *p*   270

Freddy
I, Freddy - Deitlof Reiche   *e*   1196

Gino
The Ghost of P.S. 42 - Frank Asch   *e*   45

HANDICAPPED

Bancroft, Ben "Spaz"
Stoner & Spaz - Ron Koertge   *h*   810

Boscombe, Chantelle
Stitches - Glen Huser   *m, h*   703

Brown, Springer
Halfway to the Sky - Kimberly Brubaker Bradley
    m   135

Calistra "Cemira" or "Sirai"
Mortal Suns - Tanith Lee   *h, a*   873

Callisto
Goddess of Yesterday - Caroline B. Cooney   *m,*
    h   292

Crouch, Stefan Millington III
Stefan's Story - Valerie Hobbs   *m*   651

Donleavy, Davy "Tex"
Never So Green - Tim Johnston   *h*   750

Driscoll, Danny
Shooting Monarchs - John Halliday   *h*   587

Falco
City of Stars - Mary Hoffman   *m, h*   662

Glasgow, Annie
Phoning a Dead Man - Gillian Cross   *m, h*   318

Kravitz, Carrie
Quit It - Marcia Byalick   *e, m*   191

Lauretta
Zoom! - Robert Munsch   *p*   1041

Lenny
Where Heroes Hide - Helen Recorvits   *e*   1190

Maloney, Joe
Secret Heart - David Almond   *m, h*   21

O'Connor, Rick
True Blue - Jeffrey Lee   *e, m*   871

Raimey, Matthew "Manta"
Manta's Gift - Timothy Zahn   *h, a*   1491

Warbeck, Sarah
Saffy's Angel - Hilary McKay   *m*   980

Wat
The Falconmaster - R.L. La Fevers   *m*   841

HEALER

Becket, Isabel
The Dark - Marianne Curley   *m, h*   328

de Vere
Isabel: Taking Wing - Annie Dalton   *m*   339

Mari
Alia Waking - Laura Williams McCaffrey   *m,*
    h   962

McClean, Nettie Mae
Harmony - Rita Murphy   *m, h*   1044

HEIR

Constantine
A Coalition of Lions - Elizabeth E. Wein   *h*   1424

Gerrit
The House of Windjammer - V.A. Richardson   *m,*
    h   1201

HEIRESS

Kington, Nancy
*Pirates!: The True and Remarkable Adventures of
    Minerva Sharpe and Nancy Kington, Female Pirates
    - Celia Rees   *m, h*   1193

HEN

Unnamed Character
Hungry Hen - Richard Waring   *p*   1416
Tippy-Toe Chick, Go! - George Shannon   *p*   1284

HERBALIST

Lan
The Hunting of the Last Dragon - Sherryl Jordan   *m,*
   h   761

HERO

Daddy
Especially Heroes - Virginia Kroll   *p*   831

Dente, Al
Noodle Man: The Pasta Superhero - April Pulley
   Sayre   *p*   1266

Dente, Grandma
Noodle Man: The Pasta Superhero - April Pulley
   Sayre   *p*   1266

Hoskins, Billy
*The Adventures of Super Diaper Baby: The First
   Graphic Novel* - Dav Pilkey   *e*   1153

Humphreys, Mose
New York's Bravest - Mary Pope Osborne   *p*   1117

Little Flower
Little Flower - Gloria Rand   *p*   1182

Martin, Guy "Speedy"
Sidekicks - Dan Danko   *m*   342

Norris
Rowan and the Ice Creepers - Emily Rodda
   e   1217

Odysseus
The One-Eyed Giant - Mary Pope Osborne   *e*   1118

"Pumpkin" Pete
Sidekicks - Dan Danko   *m*   342

Rowan
Rowan and the Ice Creepers - Emily Rodda
   e   1217
Rowan and the Keeper of the Crystal - Emily Rodda
   e   1218
Rowan and the Zebak - Emily Rodda   *e*   1219

Spelling Beatrice
Sidekicks - Dan Danko   *m*   342

Tilling, Despereaux
*The Tale of Despereaux: Being the Story of a Mouse,
   a Princess, Some Soup, and a Spool of Thread* -
   Kate DiCamillo   *e*   381

HEROINE

Dilly
The Bugliest Bug - Carol Diggory Shields   *p*   1292

Halfpint, Annie
Avalanche Annie: A Not-So-Tall Tale - Lisa Wheeler
   p   1433

Ma'antah
Sense Pass King: A Story from Cameroon - Katrin
   Tchana   *p*   1368

Shaaron
Rowan and the Ice Creepers - Emily Rodda
   e   1217

Unnamed Character
The Brave Little Seamstress - Mary Pope Osborne
   p   1116

Zeel
Rowan and the Ice Creepers - Emily Rodda
   e   1217

HIPPOPOTAMUS

Amos
Birdbrain Amos - Michael Delaney   *e*   371

Hip
Hip, Hip, Hooray Day! - Barney Saltzberg   *p*   1255

Hippopotamus
The Little Hippos' Adventure - Lena Landstrom
   p   847
The New Hippos - Lena Landstrom   *p*   848
The Turtle and the Hippopotamus - Kate Banks
   p   77

Mump
Shirley's Wonderful Baby - Valiska Gregory   *p*   560

Shirley
Shirley's Wonderful Baby - Valiska Gregory   *p*   560

Stanley
Shirley's Wonderful Baby - Valiska Gregory   *p*   560

Unnamed Character
The New Hippos - Lena Landstrom   *p*   848
The New Hippos - Lena Landstrom   *p*   848

HISTORICAL FIGURE

Alighieri, Dante
Dante's Daughter - Kimberley Heuston   *h*   635

Arnold, Benedict
The Year of the Hangman - Gary Blackwood   *m,*
   h   115

Barton, Clarissa Harlowe "Clara"
Numbering All the Bones - Ann Rinaldi   *m,*
   h   1205

Brewster, William
Stink Alley - Jamie Gilson   *e, m*   527

Brown, Grace
A Northern Light - Jennifer Donnelly   *h*   387

Bruce, Marjorie
Girl in a Cage - Jane Yolen   *m, h*   1480

Bruce, Robert
Girl in a Cage - Jane Yolen   *m, h*   1480

Clark, William
*This Vast Land: A Young Man's Journal of the Lewis
   and Clark Expedition* - Stephen E. Ambrose   *m,*
   h   25

de la Rocque, Marguerite
Paradise - Joan Elizabeth Goodman   *m, h*   541

Edward "Longshanks", I
Girl in a Cage - Jane Yolen   *m, h*   1480

Fontaine, John "MyJohn"
Or Give Me Death - Ann Rinaldi   *m, h*   1206

Franklin, Benjamin
Qwerty Stevens Stuck in Time with Benjamin Franklin
   - Dan Gutman   *m*   575
The Year of the Hangman - Gary Blackwood   *m,*
   h   115

Henry
Henry Builds a Cabin - D.B. Johnson   *p*   744

Henry, Anne
Or Give Me Death - Ann Rinaldi   *m, h*   1206

Henry, Martha "Patsy"
Or Give Me Death - Ann Rinaldi   *m, h*   1206

Henry, Patrick
Or Give Me Death - Ann Rinaldi   *m, h*   1206

Hoover, Herbert
Ghost Girl: A Blue Ridge Mountain Story - Delia Ray
   m   1188

Hugo, Victor
A Chapel of Thieves - Bruce Clements   *m*   263

James, Jesse
Guerrilla Season - Pat Hughes   *m, h*   693

Jones, Casey
I Dream of Trains - Angela Johnson   *p*   742

Judge, Oney
*Taking Liberty: The Story of Oney Judge, George
   Washington's Runaway Slave* - Ann Rinaldi   *m,*
   h   1207

Kublai Khan
The Kite Rider - Geraldine McCaughrean   *m,*
   h   965

Lafitte, Jean
Jean Laffite and the Big Ol' Whale - Frank G. Fox
   p   476

Lewis, Meriwether
*This Vast Land: A Young Man's Journal of the Lewis
   and Clark Expedition* - Stephen E. Ambrose   *m,*
   h   25

Magallanes/Magellan, Fernando de/Ferdinand
To the Edge of the World - Michele Torrey
   m   1385

Marlowe, Kit
All Night Awake - Sarah A. Hoyt   *h, a*   691

Quantrill, William Clark
Guerrilla Season - Pat Hughes   *m, h*   693

Saladin
Pagan's Crusade - Catherine Jinks   *m, h*   739

Shakespeare, Hamnet
My Father Had a Daughter: Judith Shakespeare's Tale
   - Grace Tiffany   *h, a*   1381

Shakespeare, Judith
My Father Had a Daughter: Judith Shakespeare's Tale
   - Grace Tiffany   *h, a*   1381
Shakespeare's Spy - Gary Blackwood   *m*   114

Shakespeare, William
My Father Had a Daughter: Judith Shakespeare's Tale
   - Grace Tiffany   *h, a*   1381
Shakespeare's Spy - Gary Blackwood   *m*   114

Shakespeare, William "Will"
All Night Awake - Sarah A. Hoyt   *h, a*   691

Shannon, George
*This Vast Land: A Young Man's Journal of the Lewis
   and Clark Expedition* - Stephen E. Ambrose   *m,*
   h   25

Till, Emmett
Mississippi Trial, 1955 - Chris Crowe   *m, h*   320

Trujillo, Rafael "El Jefe"
Before We Were Free - Julia Alvarez   *m, h*   24

van Rijn, Rembrandt Harmensz
Stink Alley - Jamie Gilson   *e, m*   527

Vest, Christine
Ghost Girl: A Blue Ridge Mountain Story - Delia Ray
   m   1188

Wallace, William "Braveheart"
Girl in a Cage - Jane Yolen   *m, h*   1480

Washington, George
*Taking Liberty: The Story of Oney Judge, George
   Washington's Runaway Slave* - Ann Rinaldi   *m,*
   h   1207

Washington, Martha
*Taking Liberty: The Story of Oney Judge, George
   Washington's Runaway Slave* - Ann Rinaldi   *m,*
   h   1207

Willard, Frances
Bicycle Madness - Jane Kurtz   *e, m*   837

Wright, Orville
The Flyers - Allan Drummond   *p*   398

Wright, Wilbur
The Flyers - Allan Drummond   *p*   398

HOMOSEXUAL

Carrillo, Jason
Rainbow High - Alex Sanchez   *h*   1262

Culworth, Alex
The Shell House - Linda Newbery   *h*   1075

Cummings, Bennett Lawson
The Rainbow Kite - Marlene Fanta Shyer   *m,
h*   1299

Davies, Kevin Robert "Kev"
The Flip Side - Andrew Matthews   *m*   956

Glassman, Nelson
Rainbow High - Alex Sanchez   *h*   1262

Jeremy
Rainbow High - Alex Sanchez   *h*   1262
The Rainbow Kite - Marlene Fanta Shyer   *m,
h*   1299

Jordan
The Shell House - Linda Newbery   *h*   1075

Land, Kevin
Geography Club - Brent Hartinger   *h*   602

McConnell, Link
My Heartbeat - Garret Freymann-Weyr   *h*   494

Meeks, Kyle
Rainbow High - Alex Sanchez   *h*   1262

Middlebrook, Russel
Geography Club - Brent Hartinger   *h*   602

Noah
Boy Meets Boy - David Levithan   *h*   885

Paul
Boy Meets Boy - David Levithan   *h*   885

Pearson, Edmund
The Shell House - Linda Newbery   *h*   1075

Reid, Justin
Dancing Naked - Shelley Hrdlitschka   *h*   692

Slater, Brendan
Alt Ed - Catherine Atkins   *m, h*   52

van Riet, Daan
Postcards from No Man's Land - Aidan Chambers
h · 237

Wallace, Fred
Gravel Queen - Tea Benduhn   *h*   101

HORSE

Little Horse
Little Horse - Betsy Byars   *e*   193

Samson
Anna Sunday - Sally M. Keehn   *m*   772

Sandmare
Sandmare - Helen Cooper   *e*   294

Sassafras
Hannah Mae O'Hannigan's Wild West Show - Lisa
Campbell Ernst   *p*   437

Sedge "Pop"
Our Twitchy - Kes Gray   *p*   551

Snow Pony
The Snow Pony - Alison Lester   *m, h*   875

HOUSEKEEPER

Bedelia, Amelia
Calling Doctor Amelia Bedelia - Herman Parish
b   1126

Flossie
*My Cup Runneth Over: The Life of Angelica Cookson
Potts* - Cherry Whytock   *m, h*   1441

Jefferson, Abilene
Jericho Walls - Kristi Collier   *m, h*   280

Jessie
A Greater Goode - Amy Schor Ferris   *m*   451

HOUSEWIFE

Mama Pearl
Bubba and Beau, Best Friends - Kathi Appelt
p   34

IMMIGRANT

Ah Sam
When the Circus Came to Town - Laurence Yep
e   1476

Bardsley, John
Sparrow Jack - Mordicai Gerstein   *p*   519

Bottner, Frederik
Mountain Solo - Jeanette Ingold   *m, h*   714

Cam
Missing - Catherine MacPhail   *m*   933

Catherine "Grandma"
When Catherine the Great and I Were Eight! - Cari
Best   *p*   107

Celso
If the Shoe Fits - Gary Soto   *p*   1321

Chapski, Jozef
The Secret of the Red Flame - K.M. Kimball   *e,
m*   785

Da
Katie's Wish - Barbara Shook Hazen   *p*   616

Daughter
When the Emperor Was Divine - Julie Otsuka   *h,
a*   1120

Esperance, Celiane
*Behind the Mountains: The Diary of Celiane
Esperance* - Edwidge Danticat   *m, h*   343

Esperance, Moy
*Behind the Mountains: The Diary of Celiane
Esperance* - Edwidge Danticat   *m, h*   343

Father
When the Emperor Was Divine - Julie Otsuka   *h,
a*   1120

Gustave
Silent Movie - Avi   *p*   60

Krenina, Marina
Mind Games - Jeanne Marie Grunwell   *m*   567

Mallon, Sean Red
Maggie's Door - Patricia Reilly Giff   *m*   523

Mama
Home at Last - Susan Middleton Elya   *p*   431
Silent Movie - Avi   *p*   60

Marchiony, Italo
Ice-Cream Cones for Sale! - Elaine Greenstein
p   555

Milly
Milly and the Macy's Parade - Shana Corey
p   303

Monari, Sofia
Home at Last - Kathryn Lasky   *e*   852
Hope in My Heart - Kathryn Lasky   *e*   853

Mother
When the Emperor Was Divine - Julie Otsuka   *h,
a*   1120

O'Malley, Maureen
Home at Last - Kathryn Lasky   *e*   852
Hope in My Heart - Kathryn Lasky   *e*   853

Papa
Milly and the Macy's Parade - Shana Corey
p   303
Silent Movie - Avi   *p*   60

Patino, Ana
Home at Last - Susan Middleton Elya   *p*   431

Petrovich, Slava "Cuss"
Grape Thief - Kristine L. Franklin   *m, h*   482

Ryan, Nory
Maggie's Door - Patricia Reilly Giff   *m*   523

Sokha, Nakri
The Stone Goddess - Minfong Ho   *m, h*   646

Son
When the Emperor Was Divine - Julie Otsuka   *h,
a*   1120

Tominski
Keeper of the Doves - Betsy Byars   *e*   192

Tong-Ling
Flight of the Fisherbird - Nora Martin   *e, m*   949

Tozzi, Arturo
A Real American - Richard Easton   *m*   414

Yoon
My Name Is Yoon - Helen Recorvits   *p*   1189

IMMORTAL

Denmark "Ned"
*The Angel's Command: A Tale from the Castaways of
the Flying Dutchman* - Brian Jacques   *m, h*   722

Nebuchadnezzer "Ben"
*The Angel's Command: A Tale from the Castaways of
the Flying Dutchman* - Brian Jacques   *m, h*   722

IMPOSTER

Hallard, Debra
Dead Girls Don't Write Letters - Gail Giles   *m,
h*   525

IMPOVERISHED

Unnamed Character
Ali and the Magic Stew - Shulamith Levey Oppenheim
p   1112

INDIAN

Cooke, Thelma
Unseen Companion - Denise Gosliner Orenstein
h   1113

Crow
The World Before This One - Rafe Martin   *m*   950

Cuthand, Wesley
True Confessions of a Heartless Girl - Martha Brooks
h   161

David
Brian's Hunt - Gary Paulsen   *m, h*   1133

Forrest, Jake
The Warriors - Joseph Bruchac   *m*   170

Grandmother
The World Before This One - Rafe Martin   *m*   950

Halfmoon, Grampa
Indian Shoes - Cynthia Leitich Smith   *e*   1312

Halfmoon, Ray
Indian Shoes - Cynthia Leitich Smith   *e*   1312

Hill, Evan
Who Will Tell My Brother? - Marlene Carvell   *m,
h*   223

Iron Shell
Betrayed! - Patricia Calvert   *m*   205

Kay-gwa-daush "Susan"
Brian's Hunt - Gary Paulsen   *m, h*   1133

Kwagley, Edgar
Unseen Companion - Denise Gosliner Orenstein
   h   1113

Maata
Maata's Journal - Paul Sullivan   *m, h*   1353

Mattoume
Virginia Bound - Amy Butler   *e, m*   188

Peme
*This Vast Land: A Young Man's Journal of the Lewis
   and Clark Expedition* - Stephen E. Ambrose   *m,
   h*   25

Saxso
The Winter People - Joseph Bruchac   *m, h*   171

Sister Girl
The Star People: A Lakota Story - S.D. Nelson
   p   1073

Tecumseh
Crossing the Panther's Path - Elizabeth Alder   *m,
   h*   17

Tiitaa
Maata's Journal - Paul Sullivan   *m, h*   1353

White Bear
Danger at the Wild West Show - Alison Hart
   m   601

Winnemucca, Sarah
Jo's Triumph - Nikki Tate   *e, m*   1363

Young Wolf
The Star People: A Lakota Story - S.D. Nelson
   p   1073

INSECT

Al
Gregory and Alexander - William Barringer   *p*   84

Big Buggy
Little Buggy Runs Away - Kevin O'Malley   *p*   1108

Butterfly, Snooty Judy
Three Nasty Gnarlies - Keith Graves   *p*   549

Dilly
The Bugliest Bug - Carol Diggory Shields   *p*   1292

Doc Hopper
Old Cricket - Lisa Wheeler   *p*   1434

Doug
The Perfect Pet - Margie Palatini   *p*   1124

Little Buggy
Little Buggy - Kevin O'Malley   *p*   1107
Little Buggy Runs Away - Kevin O'Malley   *p*   1108

Unnamed Character
Little Buggy - Kevin O'Malley   *p*   1107
Party Animals - Katie Davis   *p*   351
Scritch Scratch - Miriam Moss   *p*   1036

INTERIOR DECORATOR

Dart, Lizzie
Ghost at the Window - Margaret McAllister   *e,
   m*   960

INVENTOR

Big Momma
Big Momma Makes the World - Phyllis Root
   p   1226

Marchiony, Italo
Ice-Cream Cones for Sale! - Elaine Greenstein
   p   555

McGillicuddy, Felix
Harmony - Rita Murphy   *m, h*   1044

Pig, Smart
Porkenstein - Kathryn Lasky   *p*   856

Roy
The Amazing Thinking Machine - Dennis Haseley
   e   606

Xavier
The Trouble with Babies - Martha Freeman   *e*   488

JAGUAR

Jaguar
Rosa Raposa - F. Isabel Campoy   *p*   209

JEW

Frydman, Srulik "Jurek Staniak"
Run, Boy, Run - Uri Orlev   *m, h*   1114

JOURNALIST

Bightly, Kendra
Son of the Mob - Gordon Korman   *m, h*   818

Court
Riding the Flume - Patricia Curtis Pfitsch   *m*   1149

Gwendolyn
Target - Kathleen Jeffrie Johnson   *h*   747

JUVENILE DELINQUENT

Kevin
Handbook for Boys: A Novel - Walter Dean Myers
   m, h   1053

Lynch, Jimmy
Handbook for Boys: A Novel - Walter Dean Myers
   m, h   1053

Marsh, Kevin
Rising Water - P.J. Petersen   *m*   1148

McCann, Mungo
Dark Waters - Catherine MacPhail   *m, h*   932

KIDNAP VICTIM

Akarian
The Dark - Marianne Curley   *m, h*   328

Balangru, Agatha
Quadehar the Sorcerer - Erik L'Homme   *m, h*   891

Breeze "Bree"
The Long Night of Leo and Bree - Ellen Wittlinger
   m, h   1453

Fowl, Artemis Sr.
Artemis Fowl: The Arctic Incident - Eoin Colfer
   m   276

Grace, Simon
The Seeing Stone - Tony DiTerlizzi   *e*   385

Hallgerd
Daughter of the Wind - Michael Cadnum   *m,
   h*   199

Horace
The Cat Who Got Carried Away - Allan Ahlberg
   e   9

Marie
*The Twins and the Bird of Darkness: A Hero Tale
   from the Caribbean* - Robert D. San Souci
   e   1260

Marie-Louise
Little Pierre: A Cajun Story from Louisiana - Robert
   D. San Souci   *p*   1259

Moo Cow
Moo Cow Kaboom! - Thacher Hurd   *p*   697

Parnell, Ella
Storm Catchers - Tim Bowler   *m, h*   129

Randolph
The Cat Who Got Carried Away - Allan Ahlberg
   e   9

KIDNAPPER

Bird of Darkness
*The Twins and the Bird of Darkness: A Hero Tale
   from the Caribbean* - Robert D. San Souci
   e   1260

Cummins, Rona "Aunt Memory"
Escape from Memory - Margaret Peterson Haddix
   m, h   580

Drew
Overnight - Adele Griffin   *e, m*   563

Nicholas
Deep - Susanna Vance   *m, h*   1394

Om, Baltasar
Colibri - Ann Cameron   *m*   206

Prescott, Ricky
Storm Catchers - Tim Bowler   *m, h*   129

Swamp Ogre
Little Pierre: A Cajun Story from Louisiana - Robert
   D. San Souci   *p*   1259

Zork
Moo Cow Kaboom! - Thacher Hurd   *p*   697

KINDERGARTNER

Amber
Amber Waiting - Nan Gregory   *p*   559

Gonnella, Sarah
Witch's Wishes - Vivian Vande Velde   *e*   1396

Hunter
Hunter's Best Friend at School - Laura Malone Elliott
   p   426

Stripe
Hunter's Best Friend at School - Laura Malone Elliott
   p   426

Unnamed Character
Countdown to Kindergarten - Alison McGhee
   p   978

Williams, Kipper
7 x 9 = Trouble! - Claudia Mills   *e*   1013

KNIGHT

Albion, Brian
The Summer Country - James A. Hetley   *h, a*   634

Culloch
The Ballad of Sir Dinadan - Gerald Morris   *m,
   h*   1034

de Bram, Roland
Pagan's Crusade - Catherine Jinks   *m, h*   739

Dinadan "Dinny"
The Ballad of Sir Dinadan - Gerald Morris   *m,
   h*   1034

Durant
The Legend of Lady Ilena - Patricia Malone   *m,
   h*   936

MENTALLY ILL PERSON

Brace, Gwendolyn Mary "Gwen"
The Earth Kitchen - Sharon Bryant   m   174

Henry, Sarah Shelton
Or Give Me Death - Ann Rinaldi   m, h   1206

Katrina
Overnight - Adele Griffin   e, m   563

Mercer, Adam
A Corner of the Universe - Ann M. Martin   m   945

Old Sam
The Berry-Picking Man - Jane Buchanan   e   175

Shailey, Grey
The She - Carol Plum-Ucci   m, h   1161

Suzie
Black-Eyed Suzie - Susan Shaw   m, h   1287

Tillman, Daphne Sue
The Babbs Switch Story - Darleen Bailey Beard
   m   93

Wahhsted, Zachary McDaniel "Zach"
Inside Out - Terry Trueman   h   1386

MIGRANT WORKER

Mama
The Hard-Times Jar - Ethel Footman Smothers
   p   1317

Manuel
Under the Same Sky - Cynthia DeFelice   m, h   368

MILITARY PERSONNEL

Armstrong-Barnes, Francis
Remembrance - Theresa Breslin   m, h   143

Brown, Seth
The Big Burn - Jeanette Ingold   m, h   713

Chance, David "Davey"
The Trouble with Jeremy Chance - George Harrar   e,
   m   597

David
Our Time on the River - Don Brown   m, h   162

Davies, Sonny
Sonny's War - Valerie Hobbs   m, h   650

Donovan, Timothy
Before the Creeks Ran Red - Carolyn Reeder   m,
   h   1192

Dundas, Alex
Remembrance - Theresa Breslin   m, h   143

Dundas, John Malcolm
Remembrance - Theresa Breslin   m, h   143

Flaherty, Patrick Seamus
*Where Have All the Flowers Gone?: The Diary of
   Molly Mackenzie Flaherty* - Ellen Emerson White
   m, h   1437

Frank
A Brave Soldier - Nicholas Debon   p   365

Harrington, Honor
War of Honor - David Weber   h, a   1421

Hector
The Ugly Goddess - Elsa Marston   m   944

Helmut
When the War Is Over - Martha Attema   m, h   53

Hunter, William
Pirate Hunter Series - Brad Strickland   e, m   1348

Jackrabbit
*Ricky Ricotta's Mighty Robot vs. the Jurassic
   Jackrabbits from Jupiter* - Dav Pilkey   e   1154

Judson
Danger at the Wild West Show - Alison Hart
   m   601

Magruder, Avery
Hear the Wind Blow: A Novel of the Civil War - Mary
   Downing Hahn   m   581

Marshall, James
Hear the Wind Blow: A Novel of the Civil War - Mary
   Downing Hahn   m   581

Merahb
Flame - Hilari Bell   m, h   97

Neddy
Numbering All the Bones - Ann Rinaldi   m,
   h   1205

Owen
A Doctor Like Papa - Natalie Kinsey-Warnock
   e   795

Quantrill, William Clark
Guerrilla Season - Pat Hughes   m, h   693

Quinn, Welkin
The Earthborn - Paul Collins   h, a   282

Rogers, Robert
The Winter People - Joseph Bruchac   m, h   171

Sarov, Alexei
Skeleton Key - Anthony Horowitz   m, h   681

Staples, Frank
Amaryllis - Craig Crist-Evans   m, h   315

Sunday, Abraham
Anna Sunday - Sally M. Keehn   m   772

Tarleton, James
Sorcery and Cecelia, or the Enchanted Chocolate Pot -
   Patricia C. Wrede   m, h   1470

Tommy
Skud - Dennis Foon   h   472

Unnamed Character
Mama Played Baseball - David A. Adler   p   5

Whitaker, Paul
Operating Codes - Nick Manns   m, h   939

MINER

Ojala, Matti
Song of Sampo Lake - William Durbin   m, h   411

MINSTREL

Dinadan "Dinny"
The Ballad of Sir Dinadan - Gerald Morris   m,
   h   1034

MOLE

Grandad
Mole and the Baby Bird - Marjorie Newman
   p   1076

Mennus, Hiril
Time Stops for No Mouse - Michael Hoeye   m,
   h   657

Mole
Mole and the Baby Bird - Marjorie Newman
   p   1076

MONKEY

Chango-monkey
Rosa Raposa - F. Isabel Campoy   p   209

Hank
I Am NOT Going to School Today! - Robie H. Harris
   p   599

Little Monkey
Little Monkey Says Good Night - Ann Whitford Paul
   p   1132

Mo
Monkey Mo Goes to Sea - Diane Goode   p   538

Momo
No More Kissing! - Emma Chichester Clark   p   246

Monkey
*Ricky Ricotta's Mighty Robot vs. the Mecha-Monkeys
   from Mars* - Dav Pilkey   e   1155
Water Hole Waiting - Jane Kurtz   p   838

Monkey King
The Magical Monkey King: Mischief in Heaven - Ji-Li
   Jiang   e   738

Unnamed Character
Nine Animals and the Well - James Rumford
   p   1238
No More Kissing! - Emma Chichester Clark   p   246

MONSTER

Bob
*Laura Numeroff's 10-Step Guide to Living with Your
   Monster* - Laura Joffe Numeroff   p   1097

Grubby Gurgle
Three Nasty Gnarlies - Keith Graves   p   549

Ooga-Mooga
Three Nasty Gnarlies - Keith Graves   p   549

Porkenstein
Porkenstein - Kathryn Lasky   p   856

Stanky Stoo
Three Nasty Gnarlies - Keith Graves   p   549

Swamp Ogre
Little Pierre: A Cajun Story from Louisiana - Robert
   D. San Souci   p   1259

MOOSE

Moose
Snow - Manya Stojic   p   1346

MORGUE ATTENDANT

da Loura di An'Santa, Bartolome
A Bed of Earth: The Gravedigger's Tale - Tanith Lee
   h, a   872

MOTHER

Alice "Al"
*The Glass Cafe: Or the Stripper and the State: How
   My Mother Started a War with the System that
   Made Us Kind of Rich and a Little Bit Famous* -
   Gary Paulsen   m, h   1134

Banning
The Battle for St. Michaels - Emily Arnold McCully
   b   973

Bear
Don't You Feel Well, Sam? - Amy Hest   p   632

Bergen, Heirah
The Strength of Saints - A. LaFaye   m, h   845

Big Momma
Big Momma Makes the World - Phyllis Root
   p   1226

Blue Fairy
Pinocchio the Boy: Incognito in Collodi - Lane Smith
   p   1314

Boleyn, Anne
Doomed Queen Anne - Carolyn Meyer   m, h   1006

NATURALIST

Gribley, Sam
Frightful's Daughter - Jean Craighead George
p 518

NEGLECTED CHILD

Robert
Junebug in Trouble - Alice Mead   e   1002

NEIGHBOR

Alice
It Feels Like Snow - Nancy Cote   p   305

Bergstrom
Making Music - Susan Bonners   e   124

Cohen-Liu, Annie
The Trouble with Babies - Martha Freeman   e   488

Cooper
Hank and Fergus - Susin Nielsen-Fernlund
p   1080

D'Angelo, Gayle
The Queen of Everything - Deb Caletti   h   202

Delphine
Fame and Glory in Freedom, Georgia - Barbara
O'Connor   e, m   1102

Farmer Wilson
Making Plum Jam - John Warren Stewig   p   1344

Fred
Little Buggy - Kevin O'Malley   p   1107

Freeman
The Four Ugly Cats in Apartment 3D - Marilyn Sachs
e   1249

Garrett, Paul
Whistler's Hollow - Debbie Dadey   e, m   336

Green, Hazel
Hazel Green - Odo Hirsch   e   644

Hall, Geri
Especially Heroes - Virginia Kroll   p   831

Hank
Hank and Fergus - Susin Nielsen-Fernlund
p   1080

Hippopotamus
The New Hippos - Lena Landstrom   p   848

Hirsch
Blue Eyes Better - Ruth Wallace-Brodeur   e   1412

Hunnicutt
Miss Hunnicutt's Hat - Jeff Brumbeau   p   172

Kaspian
The Four Ugly Cats in Apartment 3D - Marilyn Sachs
e   1249

Lily
The Four Ugly Cats in Apartment 3D - Marilyn Sachs
e   1249

Macintosh, Sally
Orville: A Dog Story - Haven Kimmel   p   790

Mackintosh, Edie
Cold Tom - Sally Prue   m, h   1177

Mama Lusufu
Monkey for Sale - Sanna Stanley   p   1335

Maybelle
Orville: A Dog Story - Haven Kimmel   p   790

Minsky
When Catherine the Great and I Were Eight! - Cari
Best   p   107

O'Hara, Charley
Leap, Frog - Jane Cutler   e   332

Omaye
Ghosts for Breakfast - Stanley Todd Terasaki
p   1374

Omi
Ghosts for Breakfast - Stanley Todd Terasaki
p   1374

Ono
Ghosts for Breakfast - Stanley Todd Terasaki
p   1374

Plonsk, Yakov
Hazel Green - Odo Hirsch   e   644

Putter
Mr. Putter & Tabby Catch the Cold - Cynthia Rylant
b   1247

Starzinsky, Buzzy
The Tornado Watches - Patrick Jennings   e   733

Taffy
No Place for a Pig - Suzanne Bloom   p   119

Teaberry
Mr. Putter & Tabby Catch the Cold - Cynthia Rylant
b   1247

Unnamed Character
The House Across the Street - Jules Feiffer   p   447

Xavier
The Trouble with Babies - Martha Freeman   e   488

NEPHEW

Axel
Fire Storm - Jean Craighead George   p   517

Herter, Quentin Fenton "Quentin" III
Quentin Fenton Herter III - Amy MacDonald
p   923

Jackie
Making Plum Jam - John Warren Stewig   p   1344

Johnson
Our Gracie Aunt - Jacqueline Woodson   p   1467

Kringle, Christopher
Auntie Claus and the Key to Christmas - Elise
Primavera   p   1171

Neel
Chachaji's Cup - Uma Krishnaswami   p   828

Telemakos
A Coalition of Lions - Elizabeth E. Wein   h   1424

NEWSPAPER CARRIER

Witkowski, Cherie
Outside In - Karen Romano Young   m, h   1489

NIECE

Armitage, Anastasia
Mrs. Armitage: Queen of the Road - Quentin Blake
p   116

Beebee
Our Gracie Aunt - Jacqueline Woodson   p   1467

Charlotte
Dahlia - Barbara McClintock   p   970

Lolly
*The Secret Remedy Book: A Story of Comfort and
Love* - Karin Cates   p   231

Roeswood, Marina
The Gates of Sleep - Mercedes Lackey   h, a   843

Sara
A Picture of Grandmother - Esther Hautzig   e   611

Schwartz, Tameka
The Journey of Oliver K. Woodman - Darcy Pattison
p   1130

Unnamed Character
The Aunts Go Marching - Maurie J. Manning
p   937

Zoe Sophia
Zoe Sophia's Scrapbook: An Adventure in Venice -
Claudia Mauner   p   957

NOBLEMAN

Alexander of Whitehaven, Hamish
War of Honor - David Weber   h, a   1421

Bregon, Adamo
*The Angel's Command: A Tale from the Castaways of
the Flying Dutchman* - Brian Jacques   m, h   722

Bullhaven
The Great Ghost Rescue - Eva Ibbotson   m, h   706

Caldicott, Arthur de
At the Crossing Places - Kevin Crossley-Holland   m,
h   319

Fitzpatrick, Barnaby
Timeless Love - Judith O'Brien   m, h   1101

Furnival
Crispin: The Cross of Lead - Avi   m, h   58

Holt, Stephen de
At the Crossing Places - Kevin Crossley-Holland   m,
h   319

Liam
Shadows and Light - Anne Bishop   h, a   110

Rashid, Kai ibn Jallaleddinibn
*Lion's Blood: A Novel of Slavery and Freedom in an
Alternate America* - Steven Barnes   h, a   81
Zulu Heart - Steven Barnes   h, a   82

Sherborne
The Falconmaster - R.L. La Fevers   m   841

Simon
Midwinter Nightingale - Joan Aiken   m   13

Thomas, of Sch
Sorcery and Cecelia, or the Enchanted Chocolate Pot -
Patricia C. Wrede   m, h   1470

Unnamed Character
Three Samurai Cats: A Story from Japan - Eric A.
Kimmel   p   789

Wardwick "Ward"
Dragon Blood - Patricia Briggs   h, a   150
Dragon Bones - Patricia Briggs   h, a   151

NOBLEWOMAN

Barbaron, Beatrixa
A Bed of Earth: The Gravedigger's Tale - Tanith Lee
h, a   872

Becha, Rislin sae
The Sword of the Land - Noel-Anne Brennan   h,
a   142

della Scorpia, Meralda
A Bed of Earth: The Gravedigger's Tale - Tanith Lee
h, a   872

d'Orleans, Elizabeth Charlotte "Madame"
Cecile: Gates of Gold - Mary Casanova   e, m   224

Ilisidi
Explorer - C.J. Cherryh   h, a   244

Kenigh, Jessica Abigail Danvers "Snow"
Snow - Tracy Lynn   m, h   919

Selia
The Goose Girl - Shannon Hale   m, h   586

Silver "Quicksilver"
All Night Awake - Sarah A. Hoyt   h, a   691

Tisala
Dragon Blood - Patricia Briggs   h, a   150

Verdon, Winnie de
At the Crossing Places - Kevin Crossley-Holland   *m,*
h   319

NURSE

Armstrong-Barnes, Charlotte
Remembrance - Theresa Breslin   *m, h*   143

Dundas, Maggie
Remembrance - Theresa Breslin   *m, h*   143

Greenland, Ellen
I Am Not Esther - Fleur Beale   *m, h*   91

Penrose, Alice
The Divine Wind: A Love Story - Garry Disher
h   384

Sennosuke, Mitsu "Mitsy"
The Divine Wind: A Love Story - Garry Disher
h   384

OBJECT

Arnie
Arnie the Doughnut - Laurie Keller   *p*   779

Captain T
Alphaboat - Michael Chesworth   *p*   245

Dumpy
Dumpy and the Big Storm - Julie Andrews Edwards
p   416

Miranda
Otto: The Story of a Mirror - Ali Bahrampour
p   64

Otto
Otto: The Story of a Mirror - Ali Bahrampour
p   64

Unnamed Character
I'm Mighty! - Kate McMullan   *p*   993

Z
Z Goes Home - Jon Agee   *p*   6

OFFICE WORKER

Nike, Hack
Jennifer Government - Max Barry   *h, a*   85

OPOSSUM

Epossumondas
Epossumondas - Coleen Salley   *p*   1254

Gilbert
Good Night, Sleep Tight, Don't Let the Bedbugs Bite! -
Diane DeGroat   *p*   369

Possum
Alien & Possum: Hanging Out - Tony Johnston
e   751

Winnie
Winnie and Ernst - Gina Freschet   *e*   492

ORGANIZED CRIME FIGURE

Luca, Anthony "Honest Abe"
Son of the Mob - Gordon Korman   *m, h*   818

Throckmorton, Dudley "Big Daddy Duds"
The Mayor of Central Park - Avi   *e*   59

ORPHAN

Avila, Mateo Macias de
To the Edge of the World - Michele Torrey
m   1385

Barnavelt, Lewis
The Whistle, the Grave, and the Ghost - Brad
Strickland   *m*   1349

Barrett, Evan
The She - Carol Plum-Ucci   *m, h*   1161

Bates, Jimmy "Clovis King"
Journey to the River Sea - Eva Ibbotson   *m*   707

Blessing
Sweet By and By - Patricia Hermes   *e, m*   629

Brackett, Rob
Virginia Bound - Amy Butler   *e, m*   188

Brodski, Rodzina Clara Jadqiga Anastozy
Rodzina - Karen Cushman   *m*   331

Bulumba, Kaninda
Little Soldier - Bernard Ashley   *m, h*   48

Byers, Madeline "Maddie"
Where I'd Like to Be - Frances O'Roark Dowell   *e,*
m   391

Caswell, Archibald Lee "Archie"
When We Were Saints - Han Nolan   *h*   1089

Cranston, Nell
Virginia Bound - Amy Butler   *e, m*   188

Custis
33 Snowfish - Adam Rapp   *h*   1186

Daniella
The Rope Trick - Lloyd Alexander   *e, m*   18

De Salis, Winter
Winter - John Marsden   *m, h*   943

DiSala, Alfredo
The Tears of the Salamander - Peter Dickinson   *m,*
h   382

Donovan, Timothy
Before the Creeks Ran Red - Carolyn Reeder   *m,*
h   1192

Faber, Mary "Jacky"
Bloody Jack: Being an Account of the Curious
Adventures of Mary "Jacky" Faber, Ship's Boy -
L.A. Meyer   *m, h*   1007

Fielding, Maia
Journey to the River Sea - Eva Ibbotson   *m*   707

Gilbert, Bess
Flying Blind - Anna Myers   *e, m*   1049

Gilbert, Enoch
Flying Blind - Anna Myers   *e, m*   1049

Gylfie
The Capture - Kathryn Lasky   *m*   851

Hersey, Sarah
Flight of the Fisherbird - Nora Martin   *e, m*   949

Hull, Naomi
The Shakeress - Kimberley Heuston   *m, h*   636

Ilena
The Legend of Lady Ilena - Patricia Malone   *m,*
h   936

Jack
The Several Lives of Orphan Jack - Sarah Ellis
e   430

Jude
The Hunting of the Last Dragon - Sherryl Jordan   *m,*
h   761

Kidrouk, Pagan
Pagan's Crusade - Catherine Jinks   *m, h*   739

Lee, Tom
The Tiger's Apprentice - Laurence Yep   *m*   1474

Mai Yang
Tangled Threads: A Hmong Girl's Story - Pegi Deitz
Shea   *m, h*   1289

Mei Mei
Bitter Dumplings - Jeanne M. Lee   *p*   870

Micah
A Company of Fools - Deborah Ellis   *m*   427

Mokie "Little Pig-Girl"
Pig Tale - Verlyn Flieger   *h*   466

Morrisey, Matthew
Bone Dry - Kathleen Karr   *m*   766

Motion, Lonnie Collins "Locomotion"
Locomotion - Jacqueline Woodson   *e, m*   1466

Muno
The Wolving Time - Patrick Jennings   *m, h*   735

Natsworthy, Tom
Mortal Engines - Philip Reeve   *h, a*   1195

Pilsudski, Misha "Stopthief"
Milkweed - Jerry Spinelli   *m, h*   1326

Prentice, Jane
Just Jane: The Story of a Daughter of England Caught
in the Struggle for Independence in Revolutionary
America - William Lavender   *m, h*   858

Rabinowitz, Hadassah "Dossi"
Dear Emma - Johanna Hurwitz   *e, m*   701

Rabinowitz, Ruth "Ruthi"
Dear Emma - Johanna Hurwitz   *e, m*   701

Rat
The Ravenmaster's Secret - Elvira Woodruff
m   1462

Shaw, Hester
Mortal Engines - Philip Reeve   *h, a*   1195

Shea, Davy
Pirate Hunter Series - Brad Strickland   *e, m*   1348

Slim
Slim and Jim - Richard Egielski   *p*   422

Soren
The Capture - Kathryn Lasky   *m*   851

Starborn, Jenna
Jenna Starborn - Sharon Shinn   *h, a*   1294

Taverner, Finn
Journey to the River Sea - Eva Ibbotson   *m*   707

Tinker, Lizzy
Stink Alley - Jamie Gilson   *e, m*   527

Vyas, Akhil
The Pack - Elisa Carbone   *m, h*   214

Whyte, Joselyn
Jo's Triumph - Nikki Tate   *e, m*   1363

Widge
Shakespeare's Spy - Gary Blackwood   *m*   114

Winslow, Emily
The Hollow Kingdom - Clare B. Dunkle   *m, h*   405

Winslow, Kate
The Hollow Kingdom - Clare B. Dunkle   *m, h*   405

Woods, Hollis
Pictures of Hollis Woods - Patricia Reilly Giff   *e,*
m   524

Worth, Lillie Mae
Whistler's Hollow - Debbie Dadey   *e, m*   336

Yoder, Tullis
Horse Thief: A Novel - Robert Newton Peck   *m,*
h   1142

OTTER

Ernst
Winnie and Ernst - Gina Freschet   *e*   492

OUTLAW

Hood, Robin
Forbidden Forest: The Story of Little John and Robin Hood - Michael Cadnum   m, h   200
Lionclaw: A Tale of Rowan Hood - Nancy Springer   m   1330

Little, John "Little John"
Forbidden Forest: The Story of Little John and Robin Hood - Michael Cadnum   m, h   200

Red Roger
Forbidden Forest: The Story of Little John and Robin Hood - Michael Cadnum   m, h   200

OWL

Gylfie
The Capture - Kathryn Lasky   m   851

Owl
Snow - Manya Stojic   p   1346

Soren
The Capture - Kathryn Lasky   m   851

OX

Old Crump
Old Crump: The True Story of a Trip West - Laurie Lawlor   p   859

PACIFIST

Armstrong-Barnes, Francis
Remembrance - Theresa Breslin   m, h   143

Oats, Christopher "Quaker"
God of Beer - Garret Keizer   h   775

PARAPLEGIC

Holland, Dave
Fifteen Love - Robert Corbet   m, h   299

PASSENGER

Hector
Just One More - Wendi Silvano   p   1303

PATIENT

Froggy
Froggy Goes to the Doctor - Jonathan London   p   905

PATRIOT

Wallace, William "Braveheart"
Girl in a Cage - Jane Yolen   m, h   1480

PENGUIN

Hailey
Olvina Flies - Grace Lin   p   893

Milo
Penguin Post - Debi Gliori   p   532

Penguin
Wish, Change, Friend - Ian Whybrow   p   1440

Tacky
Tackylocks and the Three Bears - Helen Lester   p   877

PHARMACIST

Reisman, Meyer
Dear Emma - Johanna Hurwitz   e, m   701

PHILANTHROPIST

Sweet, Theodora Ann "Teddy"
Hannah, Divided - Adele Griffin   m   562

PHILOSOPHER

Kropotnik, Peter
The Watch - Dennis Danvers   h, a   344

Rodolfo
City of Masks - Mary Hoffman   m, h   661

PHOTOGRAPHER

Bramlett, Cecil
The Day the Picture Man Came - Faye Gibbons   p   520

Click
The Best Class Picture Ever! - Denis Roche   p   1214

Lala, Dimple Rohitbhai
Born Confused - Tanuja Desai Hidier   h   639

Mama
The Berry-Picking Man - Jane Buchanan   e   175

Price, Molly
One Shot - Susan Glick   m, h   529

Slater, Ian
Picture Perfect - Elaine Marie Alphin   m, h   22

PIG

Amarillo
My Pig Amarillo - Satomi Ichikawa   p   709

Apple
Pig Tale - Verlyn Flieger   h   466

Benny
Benny and the Binky - Barbro Lindgren   p   898

Byron
Hobart - Anita Briggs   e   149

Dad
Lucille Camps In - Kathryn Lasky   p   854

Daddy
Bye, Bye! - Nancy Kaufmann   p   769
Olivia . . . and the Missing Toy - Ian Falconer   p   441

Gelato, Will
Olvina Flies - Grace Lin   p   893

Hobart
Hobart - Anita Briggs   e   149

Little Flower
Little Flower - Gloria Rand   p   1182

Little Pig
Little Pig Is Capable - Denis Roche   p   1215
Wish, Change, Friend - Ian Whybrow   p   1440

Lollipop
Clever Lollipop - Dick King-Smith   e   792

Lucille
Lucille Camps In - Kathryn Lasky   p   854

Mama Pig
Squeaky Clean - Simon Puttock   p   1179

Mom
Lucille Camps In - Kathryn Lasky   p   854

Mommy
Olivia . . . and the Missing Toy - Ian Falconer   p   441

Olivia
Olivia Counts - Ian Falconer   p   440
Olivia . . . and the Missing Toy - Ian Falconer   p   441

Opal
Toot & Puddle: Charming Opal - Holly Hobbie   p   649

Perrier
A Pig Named Perrier - Elizabeth Spurr   p   1331

Peyton
Pig Enough - Janie Bynum   p   194

Pig
One Rainy Day - Valeri Gorbachev   p   542

Pig, Smart
Porkenstein - Kathryn Lasky   p   856

Pig Figwort
Little Pig Figwort Can't Get to Sleep - Henrietta Branford   p   136

Pig of the Pig
The Water Gift and the Pig of the Pig - Jacqueline Briggs Martin   p   948

Piggy
Bye, Bye! - Nancy Kaufmann   p   769
Piggy's Pancake Parlor - David McPhail   e   1000

Porcina
Piggies in a Polka - Kathi Appelt   p   35

Puddle
Toot & Puddle: Charming Opal - Holly Hobbie   p   649

Serena
No Place for a Pig - Suzanne Bloom   p   119

Snoutowski, Stanley
Mary Had a Little Ham - Margie Palatini   p   1123

Sophie
Poultrygeist - Mary Jane Auch   p   55

Toot
Toot & Puddle: Charming Opal - Holly Hobbie   p   649

Unnamed Character
Benny and the Binky - Barbro Lindgren   p   898
Can You Make a Piggy Giggle? - Linda Ashman   p   50
My Lucky Day - Keiko Kasza   p   768

Violet
Hobart - Anita Briggs   e   149

Wilfred
Hobart - Anita Briggs   e   149

PIGEON

Sylvia
Angelo - David Macaulay   p   921

Unnamed Character
Don't Let the Pigeon Drive the Bus! - Mo Willems   p   1445

PILOT

Belle, Dixie
Wingwalker - Rosemary Wells   e   1429

Perflinger, Linka
Time Stops for No Mouse - Michael Hoeye   m, h   657

Wright, Orville
The Flyers - Allan Drummond   p   398

PIONEER

Wright, Wilbur
The Flyers - Allan Drummond   *p* 398

Frink
Boston Jane: Wilderness Days - Jennifer L. Holm
    m, h 666

Ma
Old Crump: The True Story of a Trip West - Laurie
    Lawlor   *p* 859
Sunsets of the West - Tony Johnston   *p* 754

Pa
Sunsets of the West - Tony Johnston   *p* 754

PIRATE

Braid Beard
How I Became a Pirate - Melinda Long   *p* 907

Joe
On the Go with Pirate Pete and Pirate Joe - A.E.
    Cannon   *b* 211

Kington, Nancy
*Pirates!: The True and Remarkable Adventures of
    Minerva Sharpe and Nancy Kington, Female Pirates*
    - Celia Rees   *m, h* 1193

Pete
On the Go with Pirate Pete and Pirate Joe - A.E.
    Cannon   *b* 211

Scarfield, Jack
The Man with the Silver Oar - Robin Moore   *m,
    h* 1029

Sharpe, Minerva
*Pirates!: The True and Remarkable Adventures of
    Minerva Sharpe and Nancy Kington, Female Pirates*
    - Celia Rees   *m, h* 1193

Steele, Jack
Pirate Hunter Series - Brad Strickland   *e, m* 1348

Unnamed Character
The Scrimshaw Ring - William Jaspersohn   *p* 729

PLANT

Carolyn
The Perfect Pet - Margie Palatini   *p* 1124

Plantzilla
Plantzilla - Jerdine Nolen   *p* 1092

PLANTATION OWNER

Craiky, Simon
The Spirit and Gilly Bucket - Maurine F. Dahlberg
    m 337

Hayden, Henry
The Spirit and Gilly Bucket - Maurine F. Dahlberg
    m 337

Prentice, Robert
*Just Jane: The Story of a Daughter of England Caught
    in the Struggle for Independence in Revolutionary
    America* - William Lavender   *m, h* 858

POLICE OFFICER

Blackwell, Russ
Happenings - Katie Cobb   *m, h* 265

Borsch
Sammy Keyes and the Search for Snake Eyes -
    Wendelin Van Draanen   *m* 1391

Deerborn, Ben
Kerosene - Chris Wooding   *h* 1461

Eagle Talon
Mystery in Mt. Mole - Richard W. Jennings   *m,
    h* 737

Lou
Policeman Lou and Policewoman Sue - Lisa Desimini
    p 376

Short, Holly
Artemis Fowl: The Arctic Incident - Eoin Colfer
    m 276
Artemis Fowl: The Eternity Code - Eoin Colfer
    m 277

Sue
Policeman Lou and Policewoman Sue - Lisa Desimini
    p 376

POLITICAL FIGURE

Theo
The Courtesan's Daughter - Priscilla Galloway
    h 505

Washington, George
*Taking Liberty: The Story of Oney Judge, George
    Washington's Runaway Slave* - Ann Rinaldi   *m,
    h* 1207

PORCUPINE

Leo
The Castaway - James Stevenson   *p* 1343

POSTAL WORKER

Milo
Penguin Post - Debi Gliori   *p* 532

PREGNANT TEENAGER

Cooper, Sophie
Waiting for June - Joyce Sweeney   *h* 1356

Hazelwood, Kia
Dancing Naked - Shelley Hrdlitschka   *h* 692

Stall, Noreen
True Confessions of a Heartless Girl - Martha Brooks
    h 161

Wilkins, Tracy
Raspberries on the Yangtze - Karen Wallace
    m 1408

PREHISTORIC HUMAN

Dug
Ug: Boy Genius of the Stone Age - Raymond Briggs
    e 152

Dugs
Ug: Boy Genius of the Stone Age - Raymond Briggs
    e 152

Oomor
Timespinners - Luli Gray   *e* 552

PRETEEN

Hunt, Will
*The 5,000-Year-Old Puzzle: Solving a Mystery of
    Ancient Egypt* - Claudia Logan   *p* 904

PRINCIPAL

Farley, Jacob
Mystery in Mt. Mole - Richard W. Jennings   *m,
    h* 737

Giraldi
Bottled Up - Jaye Murray   *m, h* 1045

Goodbody
The Last Burp of Mac McGerp - Pam Smallcomb
    e 1311

Mary Francis
Run from the Nun! - Erin MacLellan   *e, m* 931

Nozzet
Matthew A.B.C. - Peter Catalanotto   *p* 229

Slater, Chris
Picture Perfect - Elaine Marie Alphin   *m, h* 22

Tanen
Mr. Tanen's Tie Trouble - Maryann Cocca-Leffler
    p 268

Trent
After - Francine Prose   *m, h* 1175

Trout
Scritch Scratch - Miriam Moss   *p* 1036

PRISONER

Alexie, Dove
Unseen Companion - Denise Gosliner Orenstein
    h 1113

Bryant, Mary Broad
*Escape from Botany Bay: The True Story of Mary
    Bryant* - Gerald Hausman   *m, h* 609

Bryant, Will
*Escape from Botany Bay: The True Story of Mary
    Bryant* - Gerald Hausman   *m, h* 609

Daddy
Visiting Day - Jacqueline Woodson   *p* 1468

Dodge, Libby
Gilbert & Sullivan Set Me Free - Kathleen Karr   *m,
    h* 767

Gnedich, Mikhail Sergeyevich "Misha"
The Impossible Journey - Gloria Whelan   *m* 1436

McCreary, Belle "Ma"
Gilbert & Sullivan Set Me Free - Kathleen Karr   *m,
    h* 767

PRODUCER

Bunting, Bartholomew
Silent Movie - Avi   *p* 60

PROFESSOR

Te Makara, David
Kotuku - Deborah Savage   *m, h* 1265

PROSPECTOR

Corbin, Miles
In Plain Sight - Carol Otis Hurst   *e, m* 698

Overall, Ebenezer
Gullywasher Gulch - Marianne Mitchell   *p* 1018

PROSTITUTE

Curl
33 Snowfish - Adam Rapp   *h* 1186

PSYCHIC

Daniella
The Rope Trick - Lloyd Alexander   *e, m* 18

Fool
Fool's Errand - Robin Hobb   *h, a* 647
Golden Fool - Robin Hobb   *h, a* 648

Hath, Ira
Firesong: An Adventure - William Nicholson
1078

PSYCHOLOGIST

Rodriguez, Idahlia
Thief of Dreams - Todd Strasser   *m*   1347

PUBLISHER

Blake, Nora
Saving the Planet & Stuff - Gail Gauthier   *m,*
h   511

Marcello, Walt
Saving the Planet & Stuff - Gail Gauthier   *m,*
h   511

QUAKER

Shipson, Atha
Evvy's Civil War - Miriam Brenaman   *m, h*   140

Shipson, Sophie
Evvy's Civil War - Miriam Brenaman   *m, h*   140

RABBIT

Angie
The Saturday Escape - Daniel J. Mahoney   *p*   934

Bell
Pumpkin Day! - Nancy Elizabeth Wallace   *p*   1409

Brother Rabbit
The Magic Gourd - Baba Wague Diakite   *p*   380

Brown, Bunny
The Case of the Sleepy Sloth - Cynthia Rylant
b   1243

Bruh Rabbit
Bruh Rabbit and the Tar Baby Girl - Virginia
Hamilton   *p*   589

Cecil
Cecil's Garden - Holly Keller   *p*   776

Celerina
Gluey: A Snail Tale - Vivian Walsh   *p*   1414

Emily
Baby for Sale - Jackie French Koller   *p*   814

Flora
Flora's Surprise! - Debi Gliori   *p*   531

Hare
Bear Snores On - Karma Wilson   *p*   1449

Henry
What a Hat! - Holly Keller   *p*   778

Hop
Hip, Hip, Hooray Day! - Barney Saltzberg   *p*   1255

Jack
Jackalope - Janet Stevens   *p*   1342
Pumpkin Day! - Nancy Elizabeth Wallace   *p*   1409

Jackrabbit
*Ricky Ricotta's Mighty Robot vs. the Jurassic
Jackrabbits from Jupiter* - Dav Pilkey   *e*   1154

Lapin
*Lapin Plays Possum: Trickster Tales from the
Louisiana Bayou* - Sharon Arms Doucet   *e*   390

Lily
Hushabye Lily - Claire Freedman   *p*   487

Little Bunny
Little Bunny, Biddle Bunny - David Kirk   *p*   800

Little Rabbit
Little Rabbit Lost - Harry Horse   *p*   682

Louise
Ruby's Beauty Shop - Rosemary Wells   *p*   1427

Mama
Little Rabbit Lost - Harry Horse   *p*   682

Max
Ruby's Beauty Shop - Rosemary Wells   *p*   1427

Newton
What a Hat! - Holly Keller   *p*   778

Papa
Little Rabbit Lost - Harry Horse   *p*   682

Peter
Baby for Sale - Jackie French Koller   *p*   814

Rabbit
My Friend Rabbit - Eric Rohmann   *p*   1222

Rachel
Four Friends Together - Sue Heap   *p*   617

Ruby
Ruby's Beauty Shop - Rosemary Wells   *p*   1427

Tatty Ratty
Tatty Ratty - Helen Cooper   *p*   295

Tip
Rembrandt's Hat - Susan Blackaby   *p*   112

Trudy
Pumpkin Day! - Nancy Elizabeth Wallace   *p*   1409

Twitchy
Our Twitchy - Kes Gray   *p*   551

Unnamed Character
Jackalope - Janet Stevens   *p*   1342
Which Would You Rather Be? - William Steig
p   1339
While We Were Out - Ho Baek Lee   *p*   869

Wizzie
What a Hat! - Holly Keller   *p*   778

RACCOON

Carlin
Bravery Soup - Maryann Cocca-Leffler   *p*   267

Frank
Good Night, Sleep Tight, Don't Let the Bedbugs Bite! -
Diane DeGroat   *p*   369

Hunter
Hunter's Best Friend at School - Laura Malone Elliott
p   426

Jones, Jack
The Case of the Sleepy Sloth - Cynthia Rylant
b   1243

Ringtail
Hunter's Best Friend at School - Laura Malone Elliott
p   426

Stripe
Hunter's Best Friend at School - Laura Malone Elliott
p   426

Unnamed Character
Old Granny and the Bean Thief - Cynthia DeFelice
p   366

RACIST

Hillburn, Earl
Mississippi Trial, 1955 - Chris Crowe   *m, h*   320

RADIO PERSONALITY

Carpenter, Kit
One Night - Marsha Qualey   *h*   1180

RANCHER

Coot
Hannah Mae O'Hannigan's Wild West Show - Lisa
Campbell Ernst   *p*   437

Finotta, Jim
Savage Run - C.J. Box   *h, a*   130

Gene
Sixteen Cows - Lisa Wheeler   *p*   1435

Sue
Sixteen Cows - Lisa Wheeler   *p*   1435

RANGER

Logan, Jarrett
The Big Burn - Jeanette Ingold   *m, h*   713

Logan, Samuel
The Big Burn - Jeanette Ingold   *m, h*   713

Paul
Fire Storm - Jean Craighead George   *p*   517

RAT

Jerome
Juliet Dove, Queen of Love - Bruce Coville   *e,*
m   308

Little Rat
Little Rat Sets Sail - Monika Bang-Campbell   *b*   72

Randolph
The Cat Who Got Carried Away - Allan Ahlberg
e   9

Rat
Big Brown Bear's Up and Down Day - David McPhail
p   998

Ratnose
The Hamster of the Baskervilles - Bruce Hale
e   583

Roscuro
*The Tale of Despereaux: Being the Story of a Mouse,
a Princess, Some Soup, and a Spool of Thread* -
Kate DiCamillo   *e*   381

Roxanne
Juliet Dove, Queen of Love - Bruce Coville   *e,*
m   308

Slim
Slim and Jim - Richard Egielski   *p*   422

Throckmorton, Dudley "Big Daddy Duds"
The Mayor of Central Park - Avi   *e*   59

Throckmorton, Maud
The Mayor of Central Park - Avi   *e*   59

Unnamed Character
That Pesky Rat - Lauren Child   *p*   248
Three Samurai Cats: A Story from Japan - Eric A.
Kimmel   *p*   789

RAVEN

Tuck
The Ravenmaster's Secret - Elvira Woodruff
m   1462

REBEL

Claidi
Wolf Queen - Tanith Lee   *m, h*   874

Duck
Giggle, Giggle, Quack - Doreen Cronin   *p*   317

Stewart, Maddy
The Ravenmaster's Secret - Elvira Woodruff
m   1462

RECLUSE

Atkins, David "Wild Man"
Wild Man Island - Will Hobbs   *m, h*   653

del Gato, Dante
The Boy Who Saved Baseball - John Ritter
    m   1210

Tominski
Keeper of the Doves - Betsy Byars   *e*   192

REFUGEE

Hassan
The Color of Home - Mary Hoffman   *p*   663

Shauzia
Mud City - Deborah Ellis   *m*   428

RELATIVE

Gus
Gus and Grandpa Go Fishing - Claudia Mills
    b   1015

Jess
The Birdwatchers - Simon James   *p*   726

Maita
The Sea Chest - Toni Buzzeo   *p*   190

Pete
Pete and Polo's Farmyard Adventure - Adrian
    Reynolds   *p*   1200

Pierre
Where, Where Is Swamp Bear? - Kathi Appelt
    p   36

Ruby
Ruby's Wish - Shirin Yim Bridges   *p*   148

Ruddy
Snowed in with Grandmother Silk - Carol Fenner
    e   448

Sadie
The Name Quilt - Phyllis Root   *p*   1227

Unnamed Character
The Beeman - Laurie Krebs   *p*   825
Christmas in the Country - Cynthia Rylant   *p*   1244
My Grandmother's Clock - Geraldine McCaughrean
    p   966

RELIGIOUS

Atami Baba
Wandering Warrior - Da Chen   *m, h*   240

Brewster, William
Stink Alley - Jamie Gilson   *e, m*   527

Chajang
*Sondok: Princess of the Moon and Stars, Korea, A.D.
595* - Sheri Holman   *m*   668

Chuck
Wizards of the Game - David Lubar   *m*   914

Collins, Daniel
The Man with the Silver Oar - Robin Moore   *m,
h*   1029

Desant, Clayton
A Chapel of Thieves - Bruce Clements   *m*   263

Emmaline
Fallen Host - Lyda Morehouse   *h, a*   1031

Foley
The Whistle, the Grave, and the Ghost - Brad
    Strickland   *m*   1349

Gulan
Wandering Warrior - Da Chen   *m, h*   240

Hoff
Minuk: Ashes in the Pathway - Kirkpatrick Hill   *e,
m*   641

Hok
Stone Soup - Jon J. Muth   *p*   1047

Jackson
Faith Wish - James Bennett   *h*   102

James
Wenny Has Wings - Janet Lee Carey   *e, m*   216

Lazur
The Goblin Wood - Hilari Bell   *m, h*   98

Loew, Judah
The Alchemist's Door - Lisa Goldstein   *h, a*   535

Lok
Stone Soup - Jon J. Muth   *p*   1047

Malone, Jack
Catalyst - Laurie Halse Anderson   *h*   28

Mary
Who Owns Kelly Paddik? - Beth Goobie   *m, h*   537

Mary Francis
Run from the Nun! - Erin MacLellan   *e, m*   931

Peter
The Wish List - Eoin Colfer   *m, h*   278

Pilgrim, Caleb
I Am Not Esther - Fleur Beale   *m, h*   91

Raoul
The Wolving Time - Patrick Jennings   *m, h*   735

Siew
Stone Soup - Jon J. Muth   *p*   1047

Simpson, Clare
When We Were Saints - Han Nolan   *h*   1089

Unnamed Character
The Boy Who Drew Cats - Margaret Hodges
    p   656

Velander
Voyage of the Shadowmoon - Sean McMullen   *h,
a*   994

Weeks
Christmas Tapestry - Patricia Polacco   *p*   1163

REPTILE

Gecko, Chet
The Hamster of the Baskervilles - Bruce Hale
    e   583

REPTILE

Unnamed Character
The Magic Gourd - Baba Wague Diakite   *p*   380

RESCUER

Brother Rabbit
The Magic Gourd - Baba Wague Diakite   *p*   380

Halfpint, Annie
Avalanche Annie: A Not-So-Tall Tale - Lisa Wheeler
    p   1433

Mole
Mole and the Baby Bird - Marjorie Newman
    p   1076

Prince
Sleeping Beauty - Mahlon F. Craft   *p*   312

Tarzan
Edward in the Jungle - David McPhail   *p*   999

Unnamed Character
The Day the Babies Crawled Away - Peggy Rathmann
    p   1187

RESEARCHER

Ray, Kelly
One Night - Marsha Qualey   *h*   1180

RESISTANCE FIGHTER

Nelson, Niels
Room in the Heart - Sonia Levitin   *m, h*   886

Uncle
When My Name Was Keoko - Linda Sue Park
    m   1127

Visser, Jan
When the War Is Over - Martha Attema   *m, h*   53

Visser, Janke
When the War Is Over - Martha Attema   *m, h*   53

RESTAURATEUR

Big Jimmy
Big Jimmy's Kum Kau Chinese Take Out - Ted Lewin
    p   888

Bradley, Lynda
True Confessions of a Heartless Girl - Martha Brooks
    h   161

RETIREE

Hollister, Gabe
The Trap - Joan Lowery Nixon   *m, h*   1087

Hollister, Glenda
The Trap - Joan Lowery Nixon   *m, h*   1087

REVOLUTIONARY

Liang Baoshu
An Ocean Apart, a World Away - Lensey Namioka
    m, h   1058

RHINOCEROS

Irene
Minnie and Moo and the Seven Wonders of the World
    - Denys Cazet   *e*   234

Unnamed Character
Nine Animals and the Well - James Rumford
    p   1238

ROBOT

Alien
Alien & Possum: Hanging Out - Tony Johnston
    e   751

Dad
Big Time Olie - William Joyce   *p*   762

Mighty Robot
*Ricky Ricotta's Mighty Robot vs. the Jurassic
    Jackrabbits from Jupiter* - Dav Pilkey   *e*   1154
*Ricky Ricotta's Mighty Robot vs. the Mecha-Monkeys
    from Mars* - Dav Pilkey   *e*   1155

Mom
Big Time Olie - William Joyce   *p*   762

Pappy
Big Time Olie - William Joyce   *p*   762

Rolie Polie Olie
Big Time Olie - William Joyce   *p*   762

Spot
Big Time Olie - William Joyce   *p*   762

RODEO RIDER

Brown, Annie Sharon
Daddy Says - Ntozake Shange   m   1281

Brown, Tie-Down
Daddy Says - Ntozake Shange   m   1281

Johnson-Brown, Twanda Rochelle
Daddy Says - Ntozake Shange   m   1281

ROOSTER

Bob
Bob - Tracey Campbell Pearson   p   1140

Brewster Rooster
Earthquack! - Margie Palatini   p   1122

Chanticleer
The Rooster and the Fox - Helen Ward   p   1415

Elvis
Elvis the Rooster Almost Goes to Heaven - Denys Cazet   b   232

Ralph
Poultrygeist - Mary Jane Auch   p   55

Rooster
Cock-a-Moo-Moo - Juliet Dallas-Conte   p   338

Rudy
Poultrygeist - Mary Jane Auch   p   55

ROYALTY

Althestan
Never After - Rebecca Lickiss   h, a   892

Anne of Mandagor
Snow - Tracy Lynn   m, h   919

Antonescu, Ileana
Vampire High - Douglas Rees   m, h   1194

ap Gabrevys, Jachiel "Jaycie"
Mad Maudlin - Mercedes Lackey   h, a   844

Arthur
Sword of the Rightful King: A Novel of King Arthur - Jane Yolen   m, h   1486

Artos
A Coalition of Lions - Elizabeth E. Wein   h   1424

Arturus
Warriors of Camlann - N.M. Browne   m, h   169

Aurora
Sleeping Beauty - Mahlon F. Craft   p   312

Boleyn, Anne
Doomed Queen Anne - Carolyn Meyer   m, h   1006

Bruce, Marjorie
Girl in a Cage - Jane Yolen   m, h   1480

Bruce, Robert
Girl in a Cage - Jane Yolen   m, h   1480

Calistra "Cemira" or "Sirai"
Mortal Suns - Tanith Lee   h, a   873

Callisto
Goddess of Yesterday - Caroline B. Cooney   m, h   292

Carina
The Princess and the Pauper - Kate Brian   m   147

Dandran
The Grail Prince - Nancy McKenzie   h, a   983

Drupert
The Princess and the Pizza - Mary Jane Auch   p   56

Eadric
The Frog Princess - E.D. Baker   m   67

Edward, VI
Timeless Love - Judith O'Brien   m, h   1101

Edward "Longshanks", I
Girl in a Cage - Jane Yolen   m, h   1480

Eleanor
Eleanor: Crown Jewel of Aquitaine, France, 1136 - Kristiana Gregory   m   557

Elisabeth Amelie Eugenie "Sisi"
Elisabeth: The Princess Bride - Barry Denenberg   m   372

Emeralda
The Frog Princess - E.D. Baker   m   67

Emma
Princesses Are People, Too: Two Modern Fairy Tales - Susie Morgenstern   e   1032

Ernest
Serious Trouble - Arthur Howard   p   684

Farseer, Dutiful
Fool's Errand - Robin Hobb   h, a   647
Golden Fool - Robin Hobb   h, a   648

Franklyn
The Witch Who Wanted to Be a Princess - Lois G. Grambling   p   546

Franz Joseph, I
Elisabeth: The Princess Bride - Barry Denenberg   m   372

Galahad
The Grail Prince - Nancy McKenzie   h, a   983

Goewin
A Coalition of Lions - Elizabeth E. Wein   h   1424

Helen
Goddess of Yesterday - Caroline B. Cooney   m, h   292

Henry, VIII
Doomed Queen Anne - Carolyn Meyer   m, h   1006

Iasus
Quiver - Stephanie Spinner   m, h   1327

Iphigenia
The Great God Pan - Donna Jo Napoli   m, h   1062

Isillee, Anidori-Kiladra Talianna "Ani"
The Goose Girl - Shannon Hale   m, h   586

Isolde
Isolde: Queen of the Western Isle: The First of the Tristan and Isolde Novels - Rosalind Miles   h, a   1010

Ivan
The Firebird - Jane Yolen   p   1479

Ivan-Tsarevitch
The Tale of the Firebird - Gennady Spirin   p   1328

Jakoven
Dragon Blood - Patricia Briggs   h, a   150

John
The Leopard Sword - Michael Cadnum   m, h   201

Jorge
The Frog Princess - E.D. Baker   m   67

Klyton
Mortal Suns - Tanith Lee   h, a   873

Lancelot
The Grail Prince - Nancy McKenzie   h, a   983

Laomedon of Troy
Hippolyta and the Curse of the Amazons - Jane Yolen   m   1482

Lark
The Fairy's Return - Gail Carson Levine   e   883

Lionclaw, Roderick
Lionclaw: A Tale of Rowan Hood - Nancy Springer   m   1330

Louis, 14
Cecile: Gates of Gold - Mary Casanova   e, m   224

Louis the Younger
Eleanor: Crown Jewel of Aquitaine, France, 1136 - Kristiana Gregory   m   557

Malvae, Pyrgus
Faerie Wars - Herbie Brennan   h   141

Marie
The Twins and the Bird of Darkness: A Hero Tale from the Caribbean - Robert D. San Souci   e   1260

Marigold
Once Upon a Marigold - Jean Ferris   m, h   452

Mark
Isolde: Queen of the Western Isle: The First of the Tristan and Isolde Novels - Rosalind Miles   h, a   1010

Menelaus
Goddess of Yesterday - Caroline B. Cooney   m, h   292

Mer-Princess
Princess Fishtail - Frances Minters   p   1017

Meret
The Ugly Goddess - Elsa Marston   m   944

Olaf
Serious Trouble - Arthur Howard   p   684

Olive
Serious Trouble - Arthur Howard   p   684

Olympia
Once Upon a Marigold - Jean Ferris   m, h   452

Otrere of Amazon
Hippolyta and the Curse of the Amazons - Jane Yolen   m   1482

Paulina
The Princess and the Pizza - Mary Jane Auch   p   56

Pea
The Tale of Despereaux: Being the Story of a Mouse, a Princess, Some Soup, and a Spool of Thread - Kate DiCamillo   e   381

Penelope
Clever Lollipop - Dick King-Smith   e   792
Princess Penelope - Todd Mack   p   926

Percival
The Grail Prince - Nancy McKenzie   h, a   983

Philip II of Macedon
The Courtesan's Daughter - Priscilla Galloway   h   505

Pleisthenes
Goddess of Yesterday - Caroline B. Cooney   m, h   292

Prince
Sleeping Beauty - Mahlon F. Craft   p   312

Renaldo, Amelia "Mia"
Princess in Love - Meg Cabot   m, h   197
Princess in Waiting - Meg Cabot   m, h   198

Richard, IV
Midwinter Nightingale - Joan Aiken   m   13

Ronan
In the Forests of Serre - Patricia McKillip   h, a   984

Roselupin
The Red Wolf - Margaret Shannon   p   1285

Sameth
Abhorsen - Garth Nix   m, h   1084

Sidonis
In the Forests of Serre - Patricia McKillip   h, a   984

Moody, Judy
Judy Moody Saves the World! - Megan McDonald
e 976

Moreno, Olivia
Keeper of the Night - Kimberly Willis Holt m,
h 669

Motion, Lili
Locomotion - Jacqueline Woodson e, m 1466

Nebula, Sylvia
Fat Camp Commandos Go West - Daniel Pinkwater
e 1159

Nikki
Brianna, Jamaica, and the Dance of Spring - Juanita
Havill p 612

Nina
That Makes Me Mad! - Steven Kroll p 830

North, Wenny
Wenny Has Wings - Janet Lee Carey e, m 216

Nunn, Mem
The Tornado Watches - Patrick Jennings e 733
The Weeping Willow - Patrick Jennings e 734

Olivia
Olivia . . . and the Missing Toy - Ian Falconer
p 441

Otis, Alice
Praying at the Sweetwater Motel - April Young Fritz
m 495

Palmer, Kate
The Meanest Doll in the World - Ann M. Martin
e 946

Pendo
Elizabeti's School - Stephanie Stuve-Bodeen
p 1352

Penny
One Bright Penny - Geraldine McCaughrean
p 967

Pierce, Cynthia Josephine "Jo"
The Summer Country - James A. Hetley h, a 634

Pierce, Maureen Anne "Mo"
The Summer Country - James A. Hetley h, a 634

Pierson, Samantha
Freaky Green Eyes - Joyce Carol Oates m,
h 1099

Quigley, Lucy
The Quigleys - Simon Mason e 952
The Quigleys at Large - Simon Mason e 953

Rabinowitz, Ruth "Ruthi"
Dear Emma - Johanna Hurwitz e, m 701

Rachel
Prairie Summer - Bonnie Geisert e 516

Renee
Moses Goes to the Circus - Isaac Millman p 1012

Reynolds, Jasmine "Jazz"
Dead Girls Don't Write Letters - Gail Giles m,
h 525

Rose
Iris and Walter and Baby Rose - Elissa Haden Guest
b 568

Ruby
Ruby's Beauty Shop - Rosemary Wells p 1427

Sanborn, Jenny
Claws - Will Weaver m, h 1420

Sarah
Homespun Sarah - Verla Kay p 771

Sawyer, Ruby
Lumber Camp Library - Natalie Kinsey-Warnock
e 798

Seaborne
The Sea Chest - Toni Buzzeo p 190

Shaaron
Rowan and the Ice Creepers - Emily Rodda
e 1217

Shanna
Shanna's Teacher Show - Jean Marzollo p 951

Shirley
Shirley's Wonderful Baby - Valiska Gregory p 560

Shreves, Anais
The Earth, My Butt, and Other Big Round Things -
Carolyn Mackler m, h 930

Sister Girl
The Star People: A Lakota Story - S.D. Nelson
p 1073

Sokha, Teeda
The Stone Goddess - Minfong Ho m, h 646

Stella
Good Morning, Sam - Marie-Louise Gay p 512
Good Night Sam - Marie-Louise Gay p 513
Stella, Fairy of the Forest - Marie-Louise Gay
p 514

Sue
Once Upon a Farm - Marie Bradby p 132

Tina
The Great Blue Yonder - Alex Shearer m, h 1290

Trudy
Pumpkin Day! - Nancy Elizabeth Wallace p 1409

Turner, Emma Jean
The Hard-Times Jar - Ethel Footman Smothers
p 1317

Unnamed Character
Baghead - Jarrett J. Krosoczka p 834
The Difference Between Babies & Cookies - Mary
Hanson p 591
The Difference Between Babies & Cookies - Mary
Hanson p 591
Hey, Pancakes! - Tamson Weston p 1432
Karate Girl - Mary Leary p 868
Twin to Twin - Margaret O'Hair p 1104

Victoria
Lisa's Baby Sister - Anne Gutman p 574

Wells, Margaret Cora "Meg"
As Far as I Can See: Meg's Prairie Diary - Kate
McMullan e 989

West, Anna
Muldoon - Pamela Duncan Edwards p 419

Winifred
Eugene's Story - Richard Scrimger p 1274

Wizzie
What a Hat! - Holly Keller p 778

Zillah
Halloweena - Miriam Glassman p 528

SLAVE

Calinda
The River between Us - Richard Peck m, h 1141

Christmas, Jacob Israel
Twelve Travelers, Twenty Horses - Harriette Gillem
Robinet m, h 1213

Eulinda
Numbering All the Bones - Ann Rinaldi m,
h 1205

Harrison
Trouble Don't Last - Shelley Pearsall m 1139

Jewell, Sapphire
Evvy's Civil War - Miriam Brenaman m, h 140

Jonah
The Watch - Dennis Danvers h, a 344

Judge, Oney
*Taking Liberty: The Story of Oney Judge, George
Washington's Runaway Slave* - Ann Rinaldi m,
h 1207

Lautrec, Michael "Noah Brown"
Seaward Born - Lea Wait e, m 1404

O'Dere, Aidan
*Lion's Blood: A Novel of Slavery and Freedom in an
Alternate America* - Steven Barnes h, a 81
Zulu Heart - Steven Barnes h, a 82

Peerce, Isaac
Betrayed! - Patricia Calvert m 205

Rissy
The Spirit and Gilly Bucket - Maurine F. Dahlberg
m 337

Samuel
Trouble Don't Last - Shelley Pearsall m 1139

Sharpe, Minerva
*Pirates!: The True and Remarkable Adventures of
Minerva Sharpe and Nancy Kington, Female Pirates*
- Celia Rees m, h 1193

Ulf
Ravine - Janet Hickman m 638

Unnamed Character
Under the Quilt of Night - Deborah Hopkinson
p 678

Zeke
Numbering All the Bones - Ann Rinaldi m,
h 1205

SLOTH

Unnamed Character
Slowly, Slowly, Slowly, said the Sloth - Eric Carle
p 217

SNAIL

Gluey
Gluey: A Snail Tale - Vivian Walsh p 1414

SNAKE

Marshall
Snakes Don't Miss Their Mothers - M.E. Kerr e,
m 783

Unnamed Character
The Snake's Tales - Marguerite W. Davol p 353

SOCCER PLAYER

Bean, Beryl E.
Might Adventurer of the Planet! - Ricki Stern
e 1341

Brickman, Joe
Home of the Braves - David Klass h 803

Buckman, Terese
Geography Club - Brent Hartinger h 602

Leep, Beatrice
Hoot - Carl Hiaasen m, h 637

Miller, Emily
Jason Rat-a-Tat - Colby Rodowsky e 1220

Mitchell, Trevor
Vampire Kisses - Ellen Schreiber m, h 1271

Silva, Antonio "the Phenom"
Home of the Braves - David Klass h 803

Vorkosigan, Ekaterin
Diplomatic Immunity: A Comedy of Terrors - Lois
    McMaster Bujold   *h, a*   176

Vorkosigan, Miles
Diplomatic Immunity: A Comedy of Terrors - Lois
    McMaster Bujold   *h, a*   176

Waldenstein, George
Harriet Spies Again - Helen Ericson   *e, m*   435

SPY

Alianne "Aly"
Trickster's Choice - Tamora Pierce   *m, h*   1152

Brown, Creighton
The Year of the Hangman - Gary Blackwood   *m,
    h*   115

David, Suzanne
For Freedom: The Story of a French Spy - Kimberly
    Brubaker Bradley   *m, h*   134

Fallstar, Chade
Fool's Errand - Robin Hobb   *h, a*   647
Golden Fool - Robin Hobb   *h, a*   648

Farseer, FitzChivalry
Fool's Errand - Robin Hobb   *h, a*   647
Golden Fool - Robin Hobb   *h, a*   648

Kavi
Flame - Hilari Bell   *m, h*   97

Rider, Alexander "Alex"
Point Blank - Anthony Horowitz   *m, h*   680
Skeleton Key - Anthony Horowitz   *m, h*   681

Tisala
Dragon Blood - Patricia Briggs   *h, a*   150

Welsch, Harriet M.
Harriet Spies Again - Helen Ericson   *e, m*   435

SQUIRREL

Squirrel
How Groundhog's Garden Grew - Lynne Cherry
    p   243

Westerwit, Oscar
The Mayor of Central Park - Avi   *e*   59

STEPBROTHER

Burgess
Ten Miles from Winnemucca - Thelma Hatch Wyss
    m, h   1472

Crosswell, Angus
The Steps - Rachel Cohn   *m*   273

Danny
Gingerbread - Rachel Cohn   *h*   272

Napoleon "Mullet Fingers"
Hoot - Carl Hiaasen   *m, h*   637

STEPDAUGHTER

Cinderella
Cinderella - Ruth Sanderson   *p*   1263
Cinderella's Dress - Nancy Willard   *p*   1444

Martinez, Adelita Mercado
Adelita: A Mexican Cinderella Story - Tomie De Paola
    p   358

Phano
The Courtesan's Daughter - Priscilla Galloway
    h   505

STEPFATHER

Gianini, Frank
Princess in Love - Meg Cabot   *m, h*   197

Nicol, James "Jamie"
Where in the World - Simon French   *m*   491

Robert
The Last Dog on Earth - Daniel Ehrenhaft   *m,
    h*   424

Warren
Might Adventurer of the Planet! - Ricki Stern
    e   1341

Wonderful, Joe
Ten Miles from Winnemucca - Thelma Hatch Wyss
    m, h   1472

STEPMOTHER

Anne of Mandagor
Snow - Tracy Lynn   *m, h*   919

Baer, Gail
Almost Home - Nora Raleigh Baskin   *e, m*   87

Baer, Karen
Almost Home - Nora Raleigh Baskin   *e, m*   87

Bergen, Lara
The Strength of Saints - A. LaFaye   *m, h*   845

Dona Micaela
Adelita: A Mexican Cinderella Story - Tomie De Paola
    p   358

Drummond, Sylvia
Say Yes - Audrey Couloumbis   *m, h*   306

Hera
Goddesses Series - Clea Hantman   *m, h*   592

Mercer-Nichols, Nora
Zipped - Laura McNeal   *h*   996

Nera
The Courtesan's Daughter - Priscilla Galloway
    h   505

Simons, Crystal
Undercurrents - Willo Davis Roberts   *m, h*   1212

Taylor, Elaine
One Shot - Susan Glick   *m, h*   529

Thaler, Meg
Mountain Solo - Jeanette Ingold   *m, h*   714

Vandorn, Margery
Nelly in the Wilderness - Lynn Cullen   *m*   325

STEPSISTER

Annie
The No Place Cat - C.S. Adler   *e, m*   4

Baer, Annie
Almost Home - Nora Raleigh Baskin   *e, m*   87

Crosswell, Lucy
The Steps - Rachel Cohn   *m*   273

Dickerson, Jack
Never So Green - Tim Johnston   *h*   750

Rhonda
Gingerbread - Rachel Cohn   *h*   272

STEWARD

Aycliff, John
Crispin: The Cross of Lead - Avi   *m, h*   58

Sprigg, Pardon
The Voyage of Patience Goodspeed - Heather Vogel
    Frederick   *m*   485

STOCK BROKER

Schnurmacher, Apa
Marika - Andrea Cheng   *m, h*   241

STORE OWNER

Father
Apple Pie 4th of July - Janet S. Wong   *p*   1455

Mother
Apple Pie 4th of July - Janet S. Wong   *p*   1455

Rue, Holly
Spirits in the Wires - Charles de Lint   *h, a*   355

Trill
That Pesky Rat - Lauren Child   *p*   248

STORYTELLER

Bo Won
Chang and the Bamboo Flute - Elizabeth Starr Hill
    e   640

Brom
Eragon - Christopher Paolini   *m, h*   1125

Chachaji
Chachaji's Cup - Uma Krishnaswami   *p*   828

Dad
Just One More Story - Jennifer Brutschy   *p*   173

Grandma
Emma's Story - Deborah Hodge   *p*   655

Greene, Gooney Bird
Gooney Bird Greene - Lois Lowry   *e*   911

Mom
The Broken Cat - Lynne Rae Perkins   *p*   1146

Unnamed Character
How the Fisherman Tricked the Genie - Kitoba
    Sunami   *p*   1354
The Snake's Tales - Marguerite W. Davol   *p*   353

STREETPERSON

Elizabeth
Tomorrow, Maybe - Brian James   *m, h*   725

Gretchen "Chan"
Tomorrow, Maybe - Brian James   *m, h*   725

Jef
Tomorrow, Maybe - Brian James   *m, h*   725

Littlejohn, Moses
The Dream Bearer - Walter Dean Myers   *m*   1052

Phoebe Rose
Soul Moon Soup - Lindsay Lee Johnson   *m, h*   748

Pilsudski, Misha "Stopthief"
Milkweed - Jerry Spinelli   *m, h*   1326

Unnamed Character
The Teddy Bear - David McPhail   *p*   1001

Uri
Milkweed - Jerry Spinelli   *m, h*   1326

Walt
Butterflies and Lizards, Beryl and Me - Ruth Lercher
    Bornstein   *e, m*   127

STUDENT

Bean, Clarice
What Planet Are You from, Clarice Bean? - Lauren
    Child   *p*   250

Bennett, Hannah
Hannah, Divided - Adele Griffin   *m*   562

Charles
Timothy's Tales from Hilltop School - Rosemary Wells
p 1428

Dart, Ewan
Ghost at the Window - Margaret McAllister e,
m 960

Dolores
*Horace and Morris Join the Chorus (but what about
Dolores?)* - James Howe p 686

Elway, Joe
Hannah, Divided - Adele Griffin m 562

Fairfield, Roland
Alchemy - Margaret Mahy m, h 935

Ferret, Jess
Alchemy - Margaret Mahy m, h 935

Granger, Robert
What Planet Are You from, Clarice Bean? - Lauren
Child p 250

Grubb
The Three Silly Girls Grubb - John Hassett p 608

Hassan
The Color of Home - Mary Hoffman p 663

Haybillybun
First Day - Joan Rankin p 1184

Horace
*Horace and Morris Join the Chorus (but what about
Dolores?)* - James Howe p 686

Iris
Iris and Walter: The School Play - Elissa Haden Guest
b 570

Kidder, Gabe
The True Story of Trapper Jack's Left Big Toe - Ian
Wallace p 1407

Lapp, Olivia
What Would Joey Do? - Jack Gantos m 508

LaRue, Ike
Dear Mrs. LaRue: Letters from Obedience School -
Mark Teague p 1369

Little Brown Bear
Little Brown Bear Won't Go to School! - Jane Dyer
p 412

McPherson, Mick
Ghost at the Window - Margaret McAllister e,
m 960

Mei Lin
Someone Says - Carole Lexa Schaefer p 1268

Morris
*Horace and Morris Join the Chorus (but what about
Dolores?)* - James Howe p 686

Nora
Timothy's Tales from Hilltop School - Rosemary Wells
p 1428

Nunn, Mem
The Tornado Watches - Patrick Jennings e 733

Pablito
My Pig Amarillo - Satomi Ichikawa p 709

Pendo
Elizabeti's School - Stephanie Stuve-Bodeen
p 1352

Penelope
Clever Lollipop - Dick King-Smith e 792

Piggy
Bye, Bye! - Nancy Kaufmann p 769

Pigza, Joey
What Would Joey Do? - Jack Gantos m 508

Skinner, Johnny
Clever Lollipop - Dick King-Smith e 792

Smith, Rose
Mary Smith - Andrea U'Ren p 1388

Stein, Franny K.
Lunch Walks Among Us - Jim Benton e 103

Tomko-Rollins, Tabitha "Tibby"
The Second Summer of the Sisterhood - Ann Brashares
m, h 137

Unnamed Character
Diary of a Worm - Doreen Cronin p 316
First Day - Dandi Daley Mackall p 928
I Am NOT Going to School Today! - Robie H. Harris
p 599
Our Class Took a Trip to the Zoo - Shirley Neitzel
p 1071

Walter
Iris and Walter: The School Play - Elissa Haden Guest
b 570

West, Anna
Muldoon - Pamela Duncan Edwards p 419

West, Tom
Muldoon - Pamela Duncan Edwards p 419

Yew, Joshua "Josh"
The True Story of Trapper Jack's Left Big Toe - Ian
Wallace p 1407

Zara
The Three Little Witches Storybook - Georgie Adams
e 3

Ziggy
The Three Little Witches Storybook - Georgie Adams
e 3

Zoe
The Three Little Witches Storybook - Georgie Adams
e 3

STUDENT—BOARDING SCHOOL

Bone, Charlie
Charlie Bone and the Time Twister - Jenny Nimmo
m 1081
Midnight for Charlie Bone - Jenny Nimmo
m 1082

Bradshaw, Ann
A Great and Terrible Beauty - Libba Bray h 138

Claverlous, Yvette
Remote Man - Elizabeth Honey m, h 670

Cooke, Thelma
Unseen Companion - Denise Gosliner Orenstein
h 1113

Ferri, Pearl
A Dance of Sisters - Tracey Porter m 1164

Gunn, Fidelio
Charlie Bone and the Time Twister - Jenny Nimmo
m 1081
Midnight for Charlie Bone - Jenny Nimmo
m 1082

Henderson, Rick
The Great Ghost Rescue - Eva Ibbotson m, h 706

Kwagley, Edgar
Unseen Companion - Denise Gosliner Orenstein
h 1113

Pippa
A Great and Terrible Beauty - Libba Bray h 138

Vertigo, Olivia
Charlie Bone and the Time Twister - Jenny Nimmo
m 1081
Midnight for Charlie Bone - Jenny Nimmo
m 1082

Worthington, Felicity
A Great and Terrible Beauty - Libba Bray h 138

STUDENT—COLLEGE

Aaronson, Joss
Singing the Dogstar Blues - Alison Goodman
h 540

Douglas, Jasper
Bringing Up the Bones - Lara M. Zeises h 1492

Eliza
Mahalia - Joanne Horniman h 679

Everhart, Lucy
Sister Spider Knows All - Adrian Fogelin m 471

Finerman, Nate
Better than Running at Night - Hillary Frank
h 481

Kapoor, Karshum "Karsh"
Born Confused - Tanuja Desai Hidier h 639

Lawrence
Kim: Empty Inside - Beatrice Sparks m, h 1323

McCann, Dominic "Dom"
Lucas - Kevin Brooks h 159

McKinley, Lester
Simply Alice - Phyllis Reynolds Naylor m 1069

Shreves, Byron
The Earth, My Butt, and Other Big Round Things -
Carolyn Mackler m, h 930

Vidal, Myra
Zipped - Laura McNeal h 996

Yanyan "Sheila"
An Ocean Apart, a World Away - Lensey Namioka
m, h 1058

Yelinski, Ladybug "Ellie"
Better than Running at Night - Hillary Frank
h 481

STUDENT—ELEMENTARY
SCHOOL

Barnes, T.J.
T.J. and the Cats - Hazel Hutchins e 704

Bean, Clarice
Utterly Me, Clarice Bean - Lauren Child e 249

Billingsly, Beverly
Beverly Billingsly Takes a Bow - Alexander Stadler
p 1334

Charles
I'm Not Invited? - Diane Cain Bluthenthal p 121

Charlie
On the Town: A Community Adventure - Judith
Caseley p 227

Cole, Rosy
*Rosy Cole's Worst Ever, Best Yet Tour of New York
City* - Sheila Greenwald e 556

Drake, Jake
Jake Drake, Class Clown - Andrew Clements
e 260

Elizabeti
Elizabeti's School - Stephanie Stuve-Bodeen
p 1352

Frogilina
Froggy Plays in the Band - Jonathan London
p 906

Gaskitt, Gloria
The Cat Who Got Carried Away - Allan Ahlberg
e 9

Gaskitt, Gus
The Cat Who Got Carried Away - Allan Ahlberg
e 9

George
George Upside Down - Meghan McCarthy   p 963

Green, Hazel
Hazel Green - Odo Hirsch   e 644

Josh
Baghead - Jarrett J. Krosoczka   p 834

Katie Sue
The Recess Queen - Alexis O'Neill   p 1110

Kennedy, Pamela
Cool Cat, School Cat - Judy Cox   e 310

Kevin
Lucky Socks - Carrie Weston   p 1431

Lenny
Lenny and Mel - Erik P. Kraft   e 823

Mean Jean
The Recess Queen - Alexis O'Neill   p 1110

Mel
Lenny and Mel - Erik P. Kraft   e 823

Michaels, Keely
Because of Anya - Margaret Peterson Haddix   e 579

Minnie
I'm Not Invited? - Diane Cain Bluthenthal   p 121

Moody, Betty
Utterly Me, Clarice Bean - Lauren Child   e 249

Mutton, Johnny
Johnny Mutton, He's So Him! - James Proimos   e 1174

Nunn, Ike
The Tornado Watches - Patrick Jennings   e 733

Plonsk, Yakov
Hazel Green - Odo Hirsch   e 644

Rana
Meow Means Mischief - Ann Whitehead Nagda   e 1055

Sarie
Once Upon a Time - Niki Daly   p 341

Seaver, Anya
Because of Anya - Margaret Peterson Haddix   e 579

Seymour
T.J. and the Cats - Hazel Hutchins   e 704

Sophie
I, Freddy - Deitlof Reiche   e 1196

Unnamed Character
Beverly Billingsly Takes a Bow - Alexander Stadler   p 1334
If You Take a Mouse to School - Laura Joffe Numeroff   p 1096
Straight to the Pole - Kevin O'Malley   p 1109

Wrenbury, Karl
Utterly Me, Clarice Bean - Lauren Child   e 249

Yoon
My Name Is Yoon - Helen Recorvits   p 1189

Zander, Gus
Cool Cat, School Cat - Judy Cox   e 310

Zee, Matthew
Matthew A.B.C. - Peter Catalanotto   p 229

STUDENT—EXCHANGE

Blast Off Boy
The Big Science Fair - Dan Yaccarino   e 1473

Blorp
The Big Science Fair - Dan Yaccarino   e 1473

STUDENT—HIGH SCHOOL

Anstey, Lance
Shattering Glass - Gail Giles   h 526

Baddeck, Robert Haynes "Rob" Jr.
Shattering Glass - Gail Giles   h 526

Barnett, Luke
Rising Water - P.J. Petersen   m 1148

Barnett, Tracy
Rising Water - P.J. Petersen   m 1148

Beck, Brian
After Elaine - Ann L. Dreyer   m 397

Beck, Elaine
After Elaine - Ann L. Dreyer   m 397

Becket, Isabel
The Named - Marianne Curley   m, h 329

Boscombe, Chantelle
Stitches - Glen Huser   m, h 703

Cam
Missing - Catherine MacPhail   m 933

Carmichael, Greg
Prep - Jake Coburn   h 266

Conway, Kris
Prep - Jake Coburn   h 266

Cox, Hayley
Phoning a Dead Man - Gillian Cross   m, h 318

Fielding, Asher
Guitar Highway Rose - Brigid Lowry   h 910

Garver, Lani
What Happened to Lani Garver - Carol Plum-Ucci   h 1162

Glass, Simon
Shattering Glass - Gail Giles   h 526

Griffin
Straydog - Kathe Koja   m, h 812

Hawkins, Amber
Alt Ed - Catherine Atkins   m, h 52

Henderson, Leah
Shooting Monarchs - John Halliday   h 587

Hollywood, Mark
Looking for Red - Angela Johnson   m, h 743

Howard, Gregory
Before the Creeks Ran Red - Carolyn Reeder   m, h 1192

Kohn, Charles "Kodak"
Prep - Jake Coburn   h 266

Kyle
Boy Meets Boy - David Levithan   h 885

Macy
What Happened to Lani Garver - Carol Plum-Ucci   h 1162

Marsh, Kevin
Rising Water - P.J. Petersen   m 1148

Mona
Looking for Red - Angela Johnson   m, h 743

Nick
Prep - Jake Coburn   h 266

Nicolson, Georgia
Dancing in My Nuddy-Pants: Even Further Confessions of Georgia Nicolson - Louise Rennison   m, h 1198

Noah
Boy Meets Boy - David Levithan   h 885

Pillsbury, Jill
From the Horse's Mouth - Kathy Mackel   m 929

Rachel
Straydog - Kathe Koja   m, h 812

Robert, Ethan
The Dark - Marianne Curley   m, h 328
The Named - Marianne Curley   m, h 329

Schwartz, Joseph
Before the Creeks Ran Red - Carolyn Reeder   m, h 1192

Steward, Thaddeus R. "Young" IV
Shattering Glass - Gail Giles   h 526

Travis
Stitches - Glen Huser   m, h 703

Welsh, Froggy
The Earth, My Butt, and Other Big Round Things - Carolyn Mackler   m, h 930

Wolfe, Cameron "Cam"
Getting the Girl - Markus Zusak   h 1498

STUDENT—JUNIOR HIGH

Pottinger, Rose Rita
The Whistle, the Grave, and the Ghost - Brad Strickland   m 1349

STUDENT—MIDDLE SCHOOL

Adam
My Cup Runneth Over: The Life of Angelica Cookson Potts - Cherry Whytock   m, h 1441

Dove, Juliet
Juliet Dove, Queen of Love - Bruce Coville   e, m 308

Eberhardt, Roy
Hoot - Carl Hiaasen   m, h 637

Garrett, Paul
Whistler's Hollow - Debbie Dadey   e, m 336

Laith al Salaam
The Enemy Has a Face - Gloria D. Miklowitz   m, h 1009

Leep, Beatrice
Hoot - Carl Hiaasen   m, h 637

Lepida, Chrys
True Blue - Jeffrey Lee   e, m 871

Matherson, Dana
Hoot - Carl Hiaasen   m, h 637

O'Connor, Molly
True Blue - Jeffrey Lee   e, m 871

Woodie, Charles
The Egyptian Box - Jane Louise Curry   e, m 330

Woodie, Leticia Ann "Tee"
The Egyptian Box - Jane Louise Curry   e, m 330

Zinkoff, Donald
Loser - Jerry Spinelli   m 1325

SUPERNATURAL BEING

Monday
Mister Monday - Garth Nix   m, h 1085

Ramose
The Mummy's Mother - Tony Johnston   e 753

SURFER

Fox, Peter "Pete"
Surfer Dog - Elizabeth Spurr   e, m 1332

Staples, Jimmy
Amaryllis - Craig Crist-Evans   m, h 315

SURVIVOR

Kensuke
Kensuke's Kingdom - Michael Morpurgo   *e, m*   1033

SWIMMER

Burt
Princess Fishtail - Frances Minters   *p*   1017

Jordan
The Shell House - Linda Newbery   *h*   1075

TAXIDERMIST

Sister
Matchit - Martha Moore   *e, m*   1027

TEACHER

Andrews
First Day in Grapes - L. King Perez   *p*   1145

Arden, Noah
The Birds of Killingworth - Robert D. San Souci   *p*   1258

B
Attack of the Mutant Underwear - Tom Birdseye   *e*   109

Bernthal
Robert and the Weird & Wacky Facts - Barbara Seuling   *e*   1279

Brattle
Jake Drake, Class Clown - Andrew Clements   *e*   260

Bruce
Jake Drake, Class Clown - Andrew Clements   *e*   260

Buzzy Bear
Little Rat Sets Sail - Monika Bang-Campbell   *b*   72

Calypso
Scritch Scratch - Miriam Moss   *p*   1036

Cherry
Iris and Walter: The School Play - Elissa Haden Guest   *b*   570

Cob, Collie
Clever Lollipop - Dick King-Smith   *e*   792

Cordwyn, Simon
Just Jane: The Story of a Daughter of England Caught in the Struggle for Independence in Revolutionary America - William Lavender   *m, h*   858

Cruzzelle
Straydog - Kathe Koja   *m, h*   812

Dorfman
Waiting for Sarah - Bruce McBay   *m, h*   961

Drizzle, Patchy
Mary Ann Alice - Brian Doyle   *m*   392

Dumbledore
Harry Potter and the Order of the Phoenix - J.K. Rowling   *m, h*   1234

Dunaway, Eva Marie
The Square Root of Murder - Paul Zindel   *m*   1496

Dunn
Blue Eyes Better - Ruth Wallace-Brodeur   *e*   1412

Father
Wingwalker - Rosemary Wells   *e*   1429

Foley
Tanya and the Red Shoes - Patricia Lee Gauch   *p*   510

Gianini, Frank
Princess in Love - Meg Cabot   *m, h*   197

Hagmeyer
Leon and the Spitting Image - Allen Kurzweil   *e, m*   839

Havisham
Lost in a Good Book - Jasper Fforde   *h, a*   454

Hubbard
The Hero of Third Grade - Alice DeLaCroix   *e*   370

Hudson
Alchemy - Margaret Mahy   *m, h*   935

Huff
Substitute Teacher Plans - Doug Johnson   *p*   746

Kelly
The Color of Home - Mary Hoffman   *p*   663

Klein
The Glass Cafe: Or the Stripper and the State: How My Mother Started a War with the System that Made Us Kind of Rich and a Little Bit Famous - Gary Paulsen   *m, h*   1134

Lawrence, Marion Taylor
Sonny's War - Valerie Hobbs   *m, h*   650

Lester, Samuel G.
Plantzilla - Jerdine Nolen   *p*   1092

Libonati
Agnes Parker . . . Girl in Progress - Kathleen O'Dell   *e, m*   1103

Light
Get Ready for Second Grade, Amber Brown - Paula Danziger   *b*   346

Malory
Cheating Lessons - Nan Willard Cappo   *m, h*   212

Martin
Froggy Plays in the Band - Jonathan London   *p*   906
Substitute Teacher Plans - Doug Johnson   *p*   746

Maxwell
A Week in the Woods - Andrew Clements   *e*   262

Mercer-Nichols, Nora
Zipped - Laura McNeal   *h*   996

Miller
The Hard-Times Jar - Ethel Footman Smothers   *p*   1317

Moustro Provolone
Horace and Morris Join the Chorus (but what about Dolores?) - James Howe   *p*   686

O'Connor, Patrick
Rat - Jan Cheripko   *m, h*   242

Picklestain
My Life of Crime - Richard W. Jennings   *m*   736

Pidgeon
Gooney Bird Greene - Lois Lowry   *e*   911

Plum
The Woman Who Won Things - Allan Ahlberg   *e*   11

Poitier "Miss Pointy"
Sahara Special - Esme Raji Codell   *e, m*   269

Ratnose
The Hamster of the Baskervilles - Bruce Hale   *e*   583

Ringtail
Hunter's Best Friend at School - Laura Malone Elliott   *p*   426

Shelly
Lunch Walks Among Us - Jim Benton   *e*   103

Shipson, Atha
Evvy's Civil War - Miriam Brenaman   *m, h*   140

Shipson, Sophie
Evvy's Civil War - Miriam Brenaman   *m, h*   140

Simon
Friction - E.R. Frank   *m, h*   480

Smith, Josephine Carroll "Miss Josie"
Pictures for Miss Josie - Sandra Belton   *p*   100

Snape
Harry Potter and the Order of the Phoenix - J.K. Rowling   *m, h*   1234

Spindles
Stuart Goes to School - Sara Pennypacker   *e*   1143

Sweetly
How to Lose Your Class Pet - Valerie Wilson Wesley   *e*   1430

Todd
Judy Moody Saves the World! - Megan McDonald   *e*   976

Tuttle
Matthew A.B.C. - Peter Catalanotto   *p*   229

Unnamed Character
Beverly Billingsly Takes a Bow - Alexander Stadler   *p*   1334
Someone Says - Carole Lexa Schaefer   *p*   1268
Wizard at Work - Vivian Vande Velde   *e*   1397

Vale, Malcolm
Dunk - David Lubar   *m, h*   912

Vest, Christine
Ghost Girl: A Blue Ridge Mountain Story - Delia Ray   *m*   1188

Vlajnik, Stas
The Kings Are Already Here - Garret Freymann-Weyr   *m, h*   493

Vortex
First Graders from Mars: Episode 3: Nergal and the Great Space Race - Shana Corey   *e*   302

Ward
Bronx Masquerade - Nikki Grimes   *m, h*   565

Wright
Punctuation Takes a Vacation - Robin Pulver   *p*   1178

Yardley
Gloria Rising - Ann Cameron   *e*   207

TEENAGER

Alia
Alia Waking - Laura Williams McCaffrey   *m, h*   962

Alice
Fairy Dust - Jane Denitz Smith   *e*   1313

America
America - E.R. Frank   *h*   479

Anchorman "Angerman"
The Kindling - Jennifer Armstrong   *m, h*   38

Atherton, Henry
Faerie Wars - Herbie Brennan   *h*   141

Beatrice
The Warhorse - Don Bolognese   *m*   122

Boobie
33 Snowfish - Adam Rapp   *h*   1186

Bowen, Nell
A Time for Courage: The Suffragette Diary of Kathleen Bowen, Washington, DC, 1917 - Kathryn Lasky   *e, m*   857

Brae, Raymond
White Midnight - Dia Calhoun   *m, h*   203

Ervin, Austin
Ravine - Janet Hickman   *m*   638

Ervin, Jeremy
Ravine - Janet Hickman   *m*   638

Jonah
The Watch - Dennis Danvers   *h, a*   344

Kropotnik, Peter
The Watch - Dennis Danvers   *h, a*   344

Mahur, Anchee
The Watch - Dennis Danvers   *h, a*   344

Mulholland, Lucien "Luciano"
City of Masks - Mary Hoffman   *m, h*   661
City of Stars - Mary Hoffman   *m, h*   662

O'Grady, Georgia "Giorgia Gredi"
City of Stars - Mary Hoffman   *m, h*   662

Yewbeam, Henry
Charlie Bone and the Time Twister - Jenny Nimmo
    m   1081

TOAD

Unnamed Character
Hoptoad - Jane Yolen   *p*   1483

TOURIST

Cole, Duncan
*Rosy Cole's Worst Ever, Best Yet Tour of New York
    City* - Sheila Greenwald   *e*   556

TOY

Angus
The Jamie and Angus Stories - Anne Fine   *e*   455

Blue Horse
Blue Horse - Helen Stephens   *p*   1340

Blue Kangaroo
What Shall We Do, Blue Kangaroo? - Emma
    Chichester Clark   *p*   247

Bruno
Dahlia - Barbara McClintock   *p*   970

Dahlia
Dahlia - Barbara McClintock   *p*   970

Little Piggy
Benny and the Binky - Barbro Lindgren   *p*   898

Pinocchio
Pinocchio the Boy: Incognito in Collodi - Lane Smith
    p   1314

Polo
Pete and Polo's Farmyard Adventure - Adrian
    Reynolds   *p*   1200

Small
Small - Clara Vulliamy   *p*   1403

Soldier
Little Whistle's Medicine - Cynthia Rylant   *p*   1246

Tatty Ratty
Tatty Ratty - Helen Cooper   *p*   295

Teddy
Teddy's Snowy Day - Ian Beck   *p*   95

Tiny Teddy
What Shall We Do, Blue Kangaroo? - Emma
    Chichester Clark   *p*   247

Unnamed Character
The Teddy Bear - David McPhail   *p*   1001

TRAPPER

Larry
Wild Boy - James Lincoln Collier   *m*   279

Trapper Jack
The True Story of Trapper Jack's Left Big Toe - Ian
    Wallace   *p*   1407

Vandorn, Frank
Nelly in the Wilderness - Lynn Cullen   *m*   325

TRAVELER

Hailey
Olvina Flies - Grace Lin   *p*   893

Mouse, Tom
Tom Mouse - Ursula K. Le Guin   *p*   867

Powers
Tom Mouse - Ursula K. Le Guin   *p*   867

Ragnald
The Dark Horse - Marcus Sedgwick   *m*   1275

Rhea, Olvina Alice
Olvina Flies - Grace Lin   *p*   893

Safe
Safe and Sound - Barbara Nichol   *p*   1077

Sound
Safe and Sound - Barbara Nichol   *p*   1077

Unnamed Character
All the Way Lhasa: A Tale from Tibet - Barbara Helen
    Berger   *p*   104
The Magic Hat - Mem Fox   *p*   477
Night Train - Caroline Stutson   *p*   1351
That's Good! That's Bad! In The Grand Canyon -
    Margery Cuyler   *p*   335
That's Good! That's Bad! In The Grand Canyon -
    Margery Cuyler   *p*   335
Who's That Knocking on Christmas Eve? - Jan Brett
    p   145

TRICKSTER

Bruh Rabbit
Bruh Rabbit and the Tar Baby Girl - Virginia
    Hamilton   *p*   589

Fox
Fox Tale Soup - Tony Bonning   *p*   125

Jack
Jack Outwits the Giants - Paul Brett Johnson
    p   749

Lapin
*Lapin Plays Possum: Trickster Tales from the
    Louisiana Bayou* - Sharon Arms Doucet   *e*   390

Lizard
Ananse and the Lizard: A West African Tale - Pat
    Cummings   *p*   326

Malese
Please, Malese - Amy MacDonald   *p*   922

McCool, Oona
Mrs. McCool and the Giant Cuhullin: An Irish Tale -
    Jessica Souhami   *p*   1322

Monkey King
The Magical Monkey King: Mischief in Heaven - Ji-Li
    Jiang   *e*   738

Mouse Man
The Marvelous Mouse Man - Mary Ann Hoberman
    p   654

Puss
Puss in Cowboy Boots - Jan Huling   *p*   695

Rosa Raposa
Rosa Raposa - F. Isabel Campoy   *p*   209

Unnamed Character
My Lucky Day - Keiko Kasza   *p*   768

TRUCK DRIVER

Unnamed Character
My Truck Is Stuck! - Kevin Lewis   *p*   889
My Truck Is Stuck! - Kevin Lewis   *p*   889

TURTLE

Leo
The Three Questions - Jon J. Muth   *p*   1048

Turtle
The Turtle and the Hippopotamus - Kate Banks
    p   77

TWIN

Brennan, Elin
*Mirror, Mirror on the Wall: The Diary of Bess
    Brennan* - Barry Denenberg   *e, m*   373

Cadwallader-Newton, Alice "Allie"
Timespinners - Luli Gray   *e*   552

Cadwallader-Newton, Thadeus "Fig"
Timespinners - Luli Gray   *e*   552

Carter, Beatrice
Journey to the River Sea - Eva Ibbotson   *m*   707

Carter, Dallas
Ruby Holler - Sharon Creech   *e, m*   313

Carter, Florida
Ruby Holler - Sharon Creech   *e, m*   313

Carter, Gwendolyn
Journey to the River Sea - Eva Ibbotson   *m*   707

Chimp
Chimp and Zee and the Big Storm - Laurence Anholt
    p   31

Dundas, John Malcolm
Remembrance - Theresa Breslin   *m, h*   143

Dundas, Maggie
Remembrance - Theresa Breslin   *m, h*   143

Flannery, Keegan
St. Michael's Scales - Neil Connelly   *m, h*   287

Flannery, Michael
St. Michael's Scales - Neil Connelly   *m, h*   287

Gaskitt, Gloria
The Woman Who Won Things - Allan Ahlberg
    e   11

Gaskitt, Gus
The Woman Who Won Things - Allan Ahlberg
    e   11

Gingrich, Nathan
Blood Trail - Nancy Springer   *m, h*   1329

Grace, Jared
The Seeing Stone - Tony DiTerlizzi   *e*   385

Hath, Bowman
Firesong: An Adventure - William Nicholson
    1078

Hath, Kestrel
Firesong: An Adventure - William Nicholson
    1078

Jennifer
The Bagpiper's Ghost - Jane Yolen   *e, m*   1478

Lalla-Lee
Most Beloved Sister - Astrid Lindgren   *p*   897

Lenny
Lenny and Mel's Summer Vacation - Erik P. Kraft
    e   824

MacFadden, Andrew
The Bagpiper's Ghost - Jane Yolen   *e, m*   1478

Barnett, Tracy
Rising Water - P.J. Petersen   m 1148

Weinland, Annette
Unseen Companion - Denise Gosliner Orenstein
    h 1113

Woodruff
Spitting Image - Shutta Crum   m 321

WAITER/WAITRESS

Edelstein, Bridget
Bringing Up the Bones - Lara M. Zeises   h 1492

Harper, Dolores
True Confessions of a Heartless Girl - Martha Brooks
    h 161

McClellan, Lucinda Larrimore "Crazy Lu"
Making the Run - Heather Henson   h 626

WARRIOR

Dan
Warriors of Camlann - N.M. Browne   m, h 169

Dan "Bear Sark"
Warriors of Alavna - N.M. Browne   m, h 168

Jason
Celtika - Robert Holdstock   h, a 664

Klyton
Mortal Suns - Tanith Lee   h, a 873

Kublai Khan
The Kite Rider - Geraldine McCaughrean   m,
    h 965

Luka
Wandering Warrior - Da Chen   m, h 240

Macsen
Warriors of Alavna - N.M. Browne   m, h 168

Neko Roshi
Three Samurai Cats: A Story from Japan - Eric A.
    Kimmel   p 789

Sorahb
Flame - Hilari Bell   m, h 97

Ursula
Warriors of Camlann - N.M. Browne   m, h 169

WEALTHY

Basset, Reginald E.
Mr. Basset Plays - Dominic Catalano   p 228

D'Angelo, Gayle
The Queen of Everything - Deb Caletti   h 202

Fairweather, Joseph
The Shakeress - Kimberley Heuston   m, h 636

Forrester, Eustace
The 7th Knot - Kathleen Karr   m 765

ibn Ali, Ali
Ali and the Magic Stew - Shulamith Levey Oppenheim
    p 1112

Logan, Jolie
Rising Tide - Jean Thesman   m, h 1376

Massimo "The Thief Lord", Scipio
The Thief Lord - Cornelia Funke   m, h 500

Miao Jie
The Kite Rider - Geraldine McCaughrean   m,
    h 965

Phrynion
The Courtesan's Daughter - Priscilla Galloway
    h 505

Potch
Potch & Polly - William Steig   p 1338

Tait, Jamie
Lucas - Kevin Brooks   h 159

Whitfield, Rennie
Recycling George - Stephen Roos   e, m 1224

WEASEL

Herman Ermine
Earthquack! - Margie Palatini   p 1122

WEREWOLF

Baron
Midwinter Nightingale - Joan Aiken   m 13

WIDOW(ER)

Greenland, Ellen
I Am Not Esther - Fleur Beale   m, h 91

Hall, Geri
Especially Heroes - Virginia Kroll   p 831

Jiller
Rowan and the Keeper of the Crystal - Emily Rodda
    e 1218

Lea, Margaret
*Forbidden Forest: The Story of Little John and Robin
    Hood* - Michael Cadnum   m, h 200

Mama
The Kite - Luis Garay   p 509

McDowell, Katherine
Anna Sunday - Sally M. Keehn   m 772

Moore, Eliza
Together Apart - Dianne E. Gray   m, h 550

Seldom
33 Snowfish - Adam Rapp   h 1186

WITCH

Aching, Tiffany
The Wee Free Men: A Novel of Discworld - Terry
    Pratchett   m, h 1167

Agneeza
Curse in Reverse - Tom Coppinger   p 298

Bella
The Witch Who Wanted to Be a Princess - Lois G.
    Grambling   p 546

Bella Donna
The Nine Lives of Aristotle - Dick King-Smith
    e 794

Biddlebox
Mrs. Biddlebox - Linda Smith   p 1315

Brenna
Shadows and Light - Anne Bishop   h, a 110

Brume
In the Forests of Serre - Patricia McKillip   h,
    a 984

Clover, Abby
The Time Witches - Michael Molloy   m 1022

Dragwena
The Doomspell - Cliff McNish   m 997

Grandy
Witch Twins at Camp Bliss - Adele Griffin   e 564

Grassina
The Frog Princess - E.D. Baker   m 67

Hepzibah
Halloweena - Miriam Glassman   p 528

Liam
Shadows and Light - Anne Bishop   h, a 110

Makenna
The Goblin Wood - Hilari Bell   m, h 98

Street, Chadwick
The Time Witches - Michael Molloy   m 1022

Tenbury-Smith, Hecate "Heckie"
Not Just a Witch - Eva Ibbotson   e, m 708

Unnamed Character
Fright Night Flight - Laura Krauss Melmed
    p 1004
One Witch - Laura Leuck   p 881
Witch's Wishes - Vivian Vande Velde   e 1396

Urticacea
Never After - Rebecca Lickiss   h, a 892

Wizzle
No Zombies Allowed - Matt Novak   p 1094

Woddle
No Zombies Allowed - Matt Novak   p 1094

Wolfbane
The Time Witches - Michael Molloy   m 1022

Zara
The Three Little Witches Storybook - Georgie Adams
    e 3

Ziggy
The Three Little Witches Storybook - Georgie Adams
    e 3

Zillah
Halloweena - Miriam Glassman   p 528

Zimmerman, Florence
The Whistle, the Grave, and the Ghost - Brad
    Strickland   m 1349

Zoe
The Three Little Witches Storybook - Georgie Adams
    e 3

WIZARD

Akarian
The Dark - Marianne Curley   m, h 328

Bone, Charlie
Charlie Bone and the Time Twister - Jenny Nimmo
    m 1081

Brom
Eragon - Christopher Paolini   m, h 1125

Callahan, Dairine
Wizard's Holiday - Diane Duane   m 402

Callahan, Juanita "Nita"
A Wizard Alone - Diane Duane   m, h 401
Wizard's Holiday - Diane Duane   m 402

Chamberten, Arachne
The Gates of Sleep - Mercedes Lackey   h, a 843

Chandler, Trisana "Tris"
Shatterglass - Tamora Pierce   m, h 1151

Ciaran
Child of the Prophecy - Juliet Marillier   h, a 941

Dee, John
The Alchemist's Door - Lisa Goldstein   h, a 535

Dumbledore
Harry Potter and the Order of the Phoenix - J.K.
    Rowling   m, h 1234

Enfield, Lee
Stealing the Elf-King's Roses - Diane Duane   h,
    a 400

Fainne
Child of the Prophecy - Juliet Marillier   h, a 941

Griswold
The Falconmaster - R.L. La Fevers   m 841

Grundo
The Merlin Conspiracy - Diana Wynne Jones   *m,
h* 757

Gunn, Fidelio
Charlie Bone and the Time Twister - Jenny Nimmo
m 1081

Harket
Ravine - Janet Hickman   *m* 638

Hedge
Abhorsen - Garth Nix   *m, h* 1084

Hyde, Arianrhod "Roddy"
The Merlin Conspiracy - Diana Wynne Jones   *m,
h* 757

Kotschei the Deathless
The Firebird - Jane Yolen   *p* 1479

McAllister, Darryl
A Wizard Alone - Diane Duane   *m, h* 401

Medea
Celtika - Robert Holdstock   *h, a* 664

Merlin
Celtika - Robert Holdstock   *h, a* 664

Merlinnus
Sword of the Rightful King: A Novel of King Arthur -
Jane Yolen   *m, h* 1486

Morgause
Sword of the Rightful King: A Novel of King Arthur -
Jane Yolen   *m, h* 1486

Old Berta
Ravine - Janet Hickman   *m* 638

Oreg
Dragon Blood - Patricia Briggs   *h, a* 150
Dragon Bones - Patricia Briggs   *h, a* 151

Potter, Harry
Harry Potter and the Order of the Phoenix - J.K.
Rowling   *m, h* 1234

Quando
Alchemy - Margaret Mahy   *m, h* 935

Rodriguez, Kit
A Wizard Alone - Diane Duane   *m, h* 401
Wizard's Holiday - Diane Duane   *m* 402

Roeswood, Marina
The Gates of Sleep - Mercedes Lackey   *h, a* 843

Snape
Harry Potter and the Order of the Phoenix - J.K.
Rowling   *m, h* 1234

Taliesin
Warriors of Camlann - N.M. Browne   *m, h* 169

Thomas, of Sch
Sorcery and Cecelia, or the Enchanted Chocolate Pot -
Patricia C. Wrede   *m, h* 1470

Unnamed Character
Get Well, Good Knight - Shelley Moore Thomas
b 1377
The Magic Hat - Mem Fox   *p* 477
Wizard at Work - Vivian Vande Velde   *e* 1397

Vertigo, Olivia
Charlie Bone and the Time Twister - Jenny Nimmo
m 1081

Yen, Xiao
Paper Mage - Leah Cutter   *h, a* 333

Yewbeam, Paton
Midnight for Charlie Bone - Jenny Nimmo
m 1082

WOLF

BBW
Where's the Big Bad Wolf? - Eileen Christelow
p 254

Bider
Runt - Marion Dane Bauer   *e, m* 90

Big Gray
The Littlest Wolf - Larry Dane Brimner   *p* 154

Bouki
*Lapin Plays Possum: Trickster Tales from the
Louisiana Bayou* - Sharon Arms Doucet   *e* 390

Bruh Wolf
Bruh Rabbit and the Tar Baby Girl - Virginia
Hamilton   *p* 589

Charon/Dracula
Vampire High - Douglas Rees   *m, h* 1194

Father Wolf
The Wolf Who Cried Boy - Bob Hartman   *p* 603

King
Runt - Marion Dane Bauer   *e, m* 90

Little One
The Littlest Wolf - Larry Dane Brimner   *p* 154

Little Wolf
The Wolf Who Cried Boy - Bob Hartman   *p* 603

Mother Wolf
The Wolf Who Cried Boy - Bob Hartman   *p* 603

Ravenous
Little Pig Is Capable - Denis Roche   *p* 1215

Runt
Runt - Marion Dane Bauer   *e, m* 90

Wolf, Big Bad
Porkenstein - Kathryn Lasky   *p* 856

Zimmo
Betsy Who Cried Wolf! - Gail Carson Levine
p 882

WOMBAT

Unnamed Character
Diary of a Wombat - Jackie French   *p* 490

WOODSMAN

Unnamed Character
The Faerie's Gift - Tanya Robyn Batt   *p* 88

WORKER

Jericho
The Rope Trick - Lloyd Alexander   *e, m* 18

Lexie, Jobe
The Painters of Lexieville - Sharon Darrow   *m,
h* 348

Lexie, John
The Painters of Lexieville - Sharon Darrow   *m,
h* 348

Lexie, Orris
The Painters of Lexieville - Sharon Darrow   *m,
h* 348

Macintosh, Sally
Orville: A Dog Story - Haven Kimmel   *p* 790

Papa
Home at Last - Susan Middleton Elya   *p* 431

Racine, Michael Peter III
Saving the Planet & Stuff - Gail Gauthier   *m,
h* 511

Smith, Mary
Mary Smith - Andrea U'Ren   *p* 1388

Suzy Turquoise Blue
Mister Monday - Garth Nix   *m, h* 1085

WORM

Unnamed Character
Diary of a Worm - Doreen Cronin   *p* 316

WRESTLER

Ben
17: A Novel in Prose Poems - Liz Rosenberg
h 1230

Hackenschmidt "Lion of Russia"
Secret Heart - David Almond   *m, h* 21

WRITER

Alighieri, Dante
Dante's Daughter - Kimberley Heuston   *h* 635

Brandt, Graeme
Simon Says - Elaine Marie Alphin   *h* 23

Byron
Hobart - Anita Briggs   *e* 149

Carmichael, Darby
Darby - Jonathon Scott Fuqua   *e* 501

Franco, Elena
Breakout - Paul Fleischman   *h* 460

Gordon, Humphrey "Hum"
Willow and Twig - Jean Little   *m* 903

Griffin
Straydog - Kathe Koja   *m, h* 812

Madding, Saskia
Spirits in the Wires - Charles de Lint   *h, a* 355

Marlowe, Kit
All Night Awake - Sarah A. Hoyt   *h, a* 691

McCrank, Mary Ann Alice
Mary Ann Alice - Brian Doyle   *m* 392

Monroe, Howie
Howie Monroe and the Doghouse of Doom - James
Howe   *e* 687
It Came from Beneath the Bed - James Howe
e 688

Parke-Laine, Landen
The Eyre Affair: A Novel - Jasper Fforde   *h, a* 453
Lost in a Good Book - Jasper Fforde   *h, a* 454

Pistil, Dennis "Denny"
17: A Novel in Prose Poems - Liz Rosenberg
h 1230

Pomander, Dorothy
Zoe Sophia's Scrapbook: An Adventure in Venice -
Claudia Mauner   *p* 957

Rachel
Straydog - Kathe Koja   *m, h* 812

Shakespeare, William
My Father Had a Daughter: Judith Shakespeare's Tale
- Grace Tiffany   *h, a* 1381
Shakespeare's Spy - Gary Blackwood   *m* 114

Shakespeare, William "Will"
All Night Awake - Sarah A. Hoyt   *h, a* 691

Stephanie
17: A Novel in Prose Poems - Liz Rosenberg
h 1230

Uncle Harold
Howie Monroe and the Doghouse of Doom - James
Howe   *e* 687

Willson, Kenny Roy
Comfort - Carolee Dean   *m, h* 363

YOUNG MAN

Dan
Puss in Cowboy Boots - Jan Huling   p   695

Javier
Adelita: A Mexican Cinderella Story - Tomie De Paola
    p   358

Robin
The Fairy's Return - Gail Carson Levine   e   883

YOUNG WOMAN

Mei Mei
Bitter Dumplings - Jeanne M. Lee   p   870

Nara, Mari
Noodle Man: The Pasta Superhero - April Pulley
    Sayre   p   1266

Parsley
For Biddle's Sake - Gail Carson Levine   e   884

Unnamed Character
Like a Windy Day - Frank Asch   p   46
A Story for Bear - Dennis Haseley   p   607

Character Description Index

Age Index

This index groups books according to the grade levels for which they are most appropriate. Beneath each grade range, book titles are listed alphabetically, with author names and entry numbers included.

PRESCHOOL

Babies on the Go - Linda Ashman 49
Bertil and the Bathroom Elephants - Inger Lindahl 894
Busy Little Mouse - Eugenie Fernandes 449
Close Your Eyes - Kate Banks 74
If You Take a Mouse to School - Laura Joffe Numeroff 1096
Jazzy in the Jungle - Lucy Cousins 307
Julius's Candy Corn - Kevin Henkes 622
Mama's Little Bears - Nancy Tafuri 1360
Olivia Counts - Ian Falconer 440
Ollie - Olivier Dunrea 408
Peekaboo Morning - Rachel Isadora 719
Song of Night: It's Time to Go to Bed - Katherine Riley Nakamura 1057
Twin to Twin - Margaret O'Hair 1104
Wemberly's Ice-Cream Star - Kevin Henkes 625

PRESCHOOL-KINDERGARTEN

All You Need for a Snowman - Alice Schertle 1269
B Is for Bulldozer: A Construction ABC - June Sobel 1319
Be Boy Buzz - bell hooks 672
Big Bear Ball - Joanne Ryder 1242
Blue Horse - Helen Stephens 1340
Bob - Tracey Campbell Pearson 1140
Bye, Bye! - Nancy Kaufmann 769
Can You Make a Piggy Giggle? - Linda Ashman 50
Countdown to Kindergarten - Alison McGhee 978
The Difference Between Babies & Cookies - Mary Hanson 591
Does a Cow Say Boo? - Judy Hindley 643
The Donkey's Christmas - Nancy Tafuri 1359
Dumpy and the Big Storm - Julie Andrews Edwards 416
Ella Sarah Gets Dressed - Margaret Chodos-Irvine 253
Emergency! - Margaret Mayo 959
Farfallina & Marcel - Holly Keller 777
First Day - Dandi Daley Mackall 928
First Day - Joan Rankin 1184
Four Friends Together - Sue Heap 617
Francis the Scaredy Cat - Ed Boxall 131
Fright Night Flight - Laura Krauss Melmed 1004
Get to Work, Trucks! - Don Carter 222
Giddy-up! Let's Ride! - Flora McDonnell 977
Good Night, Sleep Tight, Little Bunnies - Dawn Apperley 37
Gossie - Olivier Dunrea 406

Hobbledy-Clop - Pat Brisson 155
Homemade Love - bell hooks 673
Hoptoad - Jane Yolen 1483
How Sleep Found Tabitha - Maggie deVries 379
A Hug Goes Around - Laura Krauss Melmed 1005
I Kissed the Baby! - Mary Murphy 1043
I Used to Be the Baby - Robin Ballard 71
It's Snowing! - Olivier Dunrea 407
Kipper's Monster - Mick Inkpen 715
Little Bunny, Biddle Bunny - David Kirk 800
The Little School Bus - Carol Roth 1231
Mommy's Hands - Kathryn Lasky 855
Mud Is Cake - Pam Munoz Ryan 1241
My Big Brother - Valerie Fisher 457
My Truck Is Stuck! - Kevin Lewis 889
No, No, Jack! - Ron Hirsch 645
Oliver Finds His Way - Phyllis Root 1228
Owen's Marshmallow Chick - Kevin Henkes 624
Pete and Polo's Farmyard Adventure - Adrian Reynolds 1200
Platypus and the Birthday Party - Chris Riddell 1203
Robin's Room - Margaret Wise Brown 166
The Runaway Pumpkin - Kevin Lewis 890
Sailor Boy Jig - Margaret Wise Brown 167
Small - Clara Vulliamy 1403
Snow - Manya Stojic 1346
Someone Says - Carole Lexa Schaefer 1268
Squeaky Clean - Simon Puttock 1179
Tatty Ratty - Helen Cooper 295
Thirsty Baby - Catherine Ann Cullen 323
This Little Chick - John Lawrence 861
Treasure Hunt - Allan Ahlberg 10
Wake Up, Big Barn! - Suzanne Tanner Chitwood 252
What Did You Do Today? - Kerry Arquette 41
Yikes!!! - Robert Florczak 468
You Are Special, Little One - Nancy Tafuri 1361

PRESCHOOL-GRADE 1

Alicia's Best Friends - Lisa Jahn-Clough 724
Alphabet under Construction - Denise Fleming 464
Always Copycub - Richard Edwards 420
Annie's Ark - Lesley Harker 594
At Grandma's - Rhonda Gowler Greene 554
The Aunts Go Marching - Maurie J. Manning 937
Baby Business - Mittie Cuetara 322
Benny and the Binky - Barbro Lindgren 898
Best Kind of Baby - Kate Laing 846
A Bit More Bert - Allan Ahlberg 8
Bridget and the Muttonheads - Pija Lindenbaum 895

Bubba and Beau, Best Friends - Kathi Appelt 34
Bubble Bath Pirates! - Jarrett J. Krosoczka 835
Captain Duck - Jez Alborough 14
Cecil's Garden - Holly Keller 776
Cock-a-Moo-Moo - Juliet Dallas-Conte 338
David Gets in Trouble - David Shannon 1282
Dinnertime! - Sue Williams 1447
Dinosaur Train - John Steven Gurney 572
Dinosaurumpus - Tony Mitton 1019
Do Like a Duck Does! - Judy Hindley 642
Down by the Cool of the Pool - Tony Mitton 1020
Drat That Fat Cat! - Pat Thomson 1380
Duck on a Bike - David Shannon 1283
Ebb & Flo and the Baby Seal - Jane Simmons 1304
Egad Alligator! - Harriet Ziefert 1495
Eugene's Story - Richard Scrimger 1274
Find-a-Saurus - Mark Sperring 1324
Fishing Day - Andrea Davis Pinkney 1156
Fix-It Duck - Jez Alborough 15
The Flyers - Allan Drummond 398
Froggy Goes to the Doctor - Jonathan London 905
The Good Little Bad Little Pig - Margaret Wise Brown 164
Good Morning, Sam - Marie-Louise Gay 512
Good Night, Animals - Lena Arro 44
Good Night Sam - Marie-Louise Gay 513
Goodnight, Baby Monster - Laura Leuck 880
Hank and Fergus - Susin Nielsen-Fernlund 1080
Hello, Arctic! - Theodore Taylor 1365
Hey, Pancakes! - Tamson Weston 1432
Hondo & Fabian - Peter McCarty 964
How Do Dinosaurs Get Well Soon? - Jane Yolen 1484
Hushabye Lily - Claire Freedman 487
I'll Never Share You, Blackboard Bear - Martha Alexander 19
In My World - Lois Ehlert 423
It Feels Like Snow - Nancy Cote 305
Let's Clean Up! - Peggy Perry Anderson 30
Little Brown Bear Won't Take a Nap! - Jane Dyer 413
Little Monkey Says Good Night - Ann Whitford Paul 1132
The Littlest Wolf - Larry Dane Brimner 154
The Loudest Roar - Thomas Taylor 1367
Merry Christmas, Big Hungry Bear! - Don Wood 1459
Monkey Mo Goes to Sea - Diane Goode 538
Musical Beds - Mara Bergman 105
My Friend Rabbit - Eric Rohmann 1222
My Somebody Special - Sarah Weeks 1422
My World of Color - Margaret Wise Brown 165
Night Train - Caroline Stutson 1351

869

GRADES 4-8

GRADES 5-7

GRADES 5-8

GRADES 5-9

GRADES 5 AND UP

Age Index

GRADES 9-ADULT

GRADES 10-12

GRADES 10-ADULT

Page Count Index

This index groups books according to their page counts. Beneath each page count range, book titles are listed alphabetically, followed by the author's name, age-level code(s), the exact page count and the entry number. The age-level codes are as follows: *p* Preschool, *b* Beginning Reader, *e* Elementary School (Grades 2-5), *m* Middle School (Grades 5-8), *h* High School (Grades 9-12), and *a* Adult.

LESS THAN 25 PAGES

Olivia Counts - Ian Falconer (14 pages)   *p*   440
Daniel's Pet - Alma Flor Ada (20 pages)   *b*   1
I Kissed the Baby! - Mary Murphy (20 pages)   *p*   1043
No, No, Jack! - Ron Hirsch (20 pages)   *p*   645
Shark in the Park! - Nick Sharratt (20 pages)   *p*   1286
Birthday Zoo - Deborah Lee Rose (24 pages)   *p*   1229
Busy Little Mouse - Eugenie Fernandes (24 pages)   *p*   449
Captain's Purr - Madeleine Floyd (24 pages)   *p*   469
Get to Work, Trucks! - Don Carter (24 pages)   *p*   222
The Good Little Bad Little Pig - Margaret Wise Brown (24 pages)   *p*   164
I Used to Be the Baby - Robin Ballard (24 pages)   *p*   71
Julius's Candy Corn - Kevin Henkes (24 pages)   *p*   622
The Key to My Heart - Nira Harel (24 pages)   *p*   593
Owen's Marshmallow Chick - Kevin Henkes (24 pages)   *p*   624
Shanna's Teacher Show - Jean Marzollo (24 pages)   *p*   951
Thirsty Baby - Catherine Ann Cullen (24 pages)   *p*   323
Treasure Hunt - Allan Ahlberg (24 pages)   *p*   10
Wemberly's Ice-Cream Star - Kevin Henkes (24 pages)   *p*   625
What a Hat! - Holly Keller (24 pages)   *p*   778

25 TO 39 PAGES

Full, Full, Full of Love - Trish Cooke (26 pages)   *p*   291
Gaspard and Lisa's Rainy Day - Anne Gutman (26 pages)   *p*   573
I'll Never Share You, Blackboard Bear - Martha Alexander (26 pages)   *p*   19
Jazzy in the Jungle - Lucy Cousins (26 pages)   *p*   307
Lisa's Baby Sister - Anne Gutman (26 pages)   *p*   574
Pudgy: A Puppy to Love - Pippa Goodhart (26 pages)   *p*   539
Ruby's Beauty Shop - Rosemary Wells (26 pages)   *p*   1427

Always Copycub - Richard Edwards (28 pages)   *p*   420
Baby Business - Mittie Cuetara (28 pages)   *p*   322
The Birdwatchers - Simon James (28 pages)   *p*   726
Boris's Glasses - Peter Cohen (28 pages)   *p*   270
Bridget and the Muttonheads - Pija Lindenbaum (28 pages)   *p*   895
Bye, Bye! - Nancy Kaufmann (28 pages)   *p*   769
Does a Cow Say Boo? - Judy Hindley (28 pages)   *p*   643
Down by the Cool of the Pool - Tony Mitton (28 pages)   *p*   1020
Flora's Surprise! - Debi Gliori (28 pages)   *p*   531
Four Friends Together - Sue Heap (28 pages)   *p*   617
Good Morning, Sam - Marie-Louise Gay (28 pages)   *p*   512
Good Night, Animals - Lena Arro (28 pages)   *p*   44
Good Night Sam - Marie-Louise Gay (28 pages)   *p*   513
Hungry Hen - Richard Waring (28 pages)   *p*   1416
The Little Hippos' Adventure - Lena Landstrom (28 pages)   *p*   847
Make the Team, Baby Duck! - Amy Hest (28 pages)   *p*   633
McDuff Saves the Day - Rosemary Wells (28 pages)   *p*   1426
My Grandma, My Pen Pal - Jan Dale Koutsky (28 pages)   *p*   822
Old MacDonald Had a Woodshop - Lisa Shulman (28 pages)   *p*   1296
One Leaf Rides the Wind - Celeste Davidson Mannis (28 pages)   *p*   938
Pancake Dreams - Ingmarie Ahvander (28 pages)   *p*   12
Peekaboo Morning - Rachel Isadora (28 pages)   *p*   719
Pete and Polo's Farmyard Adventure - Adrian Reynolds (28 pages)   *p*   1200
Scritch Scratch - Miriam Moss (28 pages)   *p*   1036
Slowly, Slowly, Slowly, said the Sloth - Eric Carle (28 pages)   *p*   217
Small - Clara Vulliamy (28 pages)   *p*   1403
This Is the House That Jack Built - Simms Taback (28 pages)   *p*   1358
The Turtle and the Hippopotamus - Kate Banks (28 pages)   *p*   77
Waggle - Sarah McMenemy (28 pages)   *p*   988
What Shall We Play? - Sue Heap (28 pages)   *p*   618
When Mommy Was Mad - Lynne Jonell (28 pages)   *p*   756

Where's Pup? - Dayle Ann Dodds (28 pages)   *p*   386
Yesterday I Had the Blues - Jeron Ashford Frame (28 pages)   *p*   478
Annie Was Warned - Jarrett J. Krosoczka (30 pages)   *p*   833
Diary of a Wombat - Jackie French (30 pages)   *p*   490
Flamingo Dream - Donna Jo Napoli (30 pages)   *p*   1061
My Friend Rabbit - Eric Rohmann (30 pages)   *p*   1222
Ruby's Wish - Shirin Yim Bridges (30 pages)   *p*   148
Achoo! Bang! Crash!: The Noisy Alphabet - Ross MacDonald (32 pages)   *p*   924
Adelita: A Mexican Cinderella Story - Tomie De Paola (32 pages)   *p*   358
Ali and the Magic Stew - Shulamith Levey Oppenheim (32 pages)   *p*   1112
Alicia's Best Friends - Lisa Jahn-Clough (32 pages)   *p*   724
All the Way Lhasa: A Tale from Tibet - Barbara Helen Berger (32 pages)   *p*   104
All You Need for a Snowman - Alice Schertle (32 pages)   *p*   1269
The Alley Cat's Meow - Kathi Appelt (32 pages)   *p*   32
Alphabet under Construction - Denise Fleming (32 pages)   *p*   464
Alphaboat - Michael Chesworth (32 pages)   *p*   245
Alvie Eats Soup - Ross Collins (32 pages)   *p*   283
Amber Waiting - Nan Gregory (32 pages)   *p*   559
Annie Rose Is My Little Sister - Shirley Hughes (32 pages)   *p*   694
Annie's Ark - Lesley Harker (32 pages)   *p*   594
Another Perfect Day - Ross MacDonald (32 pages)   *p*   925
Arizona Charlie and the Klondike Kid - Julie Lawson (32 pages)   *p*   864
Armadillo's Orange - Jim Arnosky (32 pages)   *p*   40
At Grandma's - Rhonda Gowler Greene (32 pages)   *p*   554
Atlantic - G. Brian Karas (32 pages)   *p*   764
Audrey and Barbara - Janet Lawson (32 pages)   *p*   863
Aunt Minnie and the Twister - Mary Skillings Prigger (32 pages)   *p*   1170
The Aunts Go Marching - Maurie J. Manning (32 pages)   *p*   937
Avalanche Annie: A Not-So-Tall Tale - Lisa Wheeler (32 pages)   *p*   1433

Page Count Index

40 TO 60 PAGES

61 TO 100 PAGES

101 TO 150 PAGES

151 TO 200 PAGES

MORE THAN 200 PAGES

The Traitor: Golden Mountain Chronicles: 1885 - Laurence Yep (310 pages)   *m, h*   1475

All Night Awake - Sarah A. Hoyt (311 pages)   *h, a*   691

Diplomatic Immunity: A Comedy of Terrors - Lois McMaster Bujold (311 pages)   *h, a*   176

Gregor the Overlander - Suzanne Collins (311 pages)   *m*   284

Home of the Braves - David Klass (312 pages)   *h*   803

Postcards from No Man's Land - Aidan Chambers (312 pages)   *h*   237

Heir Apparent - Vivian Vande Velde (315 pages)   1395

Drowning Anna - Sue Mayfield (316 pages)   *m, h*   958

Sorcery and Cecelia, or the Enchanted Chocolate Pot - Patricia C. Wrede (316 pages)   *m, h*   1470

Waiting to Disappear - April Young Fritz (316 pages)   *m, h*   496

The Divide - Elizabeth Kay (318 pages)   *m*   770

A Wizard Alone - Diane Duane (319 pages)   *m, h*   401

Tithe: A Modern Faerie Tale - Holly Black (320 pages)   *h*   111

Jennifer Government - Max Barry (321 pages)   *h, a*   85

Pig Tale - Verlyn Flieger (321 pages)   *h*   466

Wandering Warrior - Da Chen (322 pages)   *m, h*   240

Hard Cash - Kate Cann (327 pages)   *h*   210

Guerrilla Season - Pat Hughes (329 pages)   *m, h*   693

After - Francine Prose (330 pages)   *m, h*   1175

A Bed of Earth: The Gravedigger's Tale - Tanith Lee (330 pages)   *h, a*   872

The Named - Marianne Curley (333 pages)   *m, h*   329

Paying the Piper at the Gates of Dawn - Rosemary Edghill (333 pages)   *h, a*   415

The Dark - Marianne Curley (334 pages)   *m, h*   328

Mortal Suns - Tanith Lee (335 pages)   *h, a*   873

The Shell House - Linda Newbery (335 pages)   *h*   1075

Fallen Host - Lyda Morehouse (339 pages)   *h, a*   1031

The Speed of Dark - Elizabeth Moon (340 pages)   *h, a*   1025

Freaky Green Eyes - Joyce Carol Oates (341 pages)   *m, h*   1099

Flame - Hilari Bell (344 pages)   *m, h*   97

The Return of Calico Bright - David Winkler (344 pages)   *m, h*   1450

City of Masks - Mary Hoffman (345 pages)   *m, h*   661

This Lullaby - Sarah Dessen (345 pages)   *h*   377

The Thief Lord - Cornelia Funke (349 pages)   *m, h*   500

The House of Windjammer - V.A. Richardson (350 pages)   *m, h*   1201

Sword of the Rightful King: A Novel of King Arthur - Jane Yolen (350 pages)   *m, h*   1486

The Gates of Sleep - Mercedes Lackey (352 pages)   *h, a*   843

Paper Mage - Leah Cutter (352 pages)   *h, a*   333

Shadow Puppets - Orson Scott Card (352 pages)   *h, a*   215

The Watch - Dennis Danvers (353 pages)   *h, a*   344

Pattern Recognition - William Gibson (356 pages)   *h, a*   522

Unseen Companion - Denise Gosliner Orenstein (357 pages)   *h*   1113

Abhorsen - Garth Nix (358 pages)   *m, h*   1084

Mister Monday - Garth Nix (361 pages)   *m, h*   1085

Shatterglass - Tamora Pierce (361 pages)   *m, h*   1151

The Birthday of the World and Other Stories - Ursula K. Le Guin (362 pages)   *h, a*   865

Faerie Wars - Herbie Brennan (367 pages)   *h*   141

Angry Lead Skies - Glen Cook (368 pages)   *h, a*   288

Celtika - Robert Holdstock (368 pages)   *h, a*   664

Isolde: Queen of the Western Isle: The First of the Tristan and Isolde Novels - Rosalind Miles (368 pages)   *h, a*   1010

The Summer Country - James A. Hetley (368 pages)   *h, a*   634

The Sword of the Land - Noel-Anne Brennan (368 pages)   *h, a*   142

Before the Creeks Ran Red - Carolyn Reeder (370 pages)   *m, h*   1192

The Queen of Everything - Deb Caletti (372 pages)   *h*   202

The Second Summer of the Sisterhood - Ann Brashares (373 pages)   *m, h*   137

The Angel's Command: A Tale from the Castaways of the Flying Dutchman - Brian Jacques (374 pages)   *m, h*   722

The Eyre Affair: A Novel - Jasper Fforde (374 pages)   *h, a*   453

The House of the Scorpion - Nancy Farmer (380 pages)   *m, h*   444

Pirates!: The True and Remarkable Adventures of Minerva Sharpe and Nancy Kington, Female Pirates - Celia Rees (380 pages)   *m, h*   1193

Jenna Starborn - Sharon Shinn (381 pages)   *h, a*   1294

The Disappeared - Kristine Kathryn Rusch (384 pages)   *h, a*   1239

The Green Man: Tales from the Mythic Forest - Ellen Datlow (384 pages)   *m, h*   349

Abarat - Clive Barker (388 pages)   *h*   80

Familiar and Haunting: Collected Stories - Philippa Pearce (388 pages)   *m*   1138

The Goose Girl - Shannon Hale (388 pages)   *m, h*   586

A Northern Light - Jennifer Donnelly (389 pages)   *h*   387

Small Avalanches and Other Stories - Joyce Carol Oates (390 pages)   *h, a*   1100

Waifs and Strays - Charles de Lint (391 pages)   *h, a*   357

At the Crossing Places - Kevin Crossley-Holland (394 pages)   *m, h*   319

Warriors of Camlann - N.M. Browne (396 pages)   *m, h*   169

Midnight for Charlie Bone - Jenny Nimmo (401 pages)   *m*   1082

Stealing the Elf-King's Roses - Diane Duane (401 pages)   *h, a*   400

Charlie Bone and the Time Twister - Jenny Nimmo (402 pages)   *m*   1081

A Great and Terrible Beauty - Libba Bray (403 pages)   *h*   138

Explorer - C.J. Cherryh (408 pages)   *h, a*   244

Born Confused - Tanuja Desai Hidier (413 pages)   *h*   639

Lost in a Good Book - Jasper Fforde (416 pages)   *h, a*   454

Wizard's Holiday - Diane Duane (416 pages)   *m*   402

Shadows and Light - Anne Bishop (420 pages)   *h, a*   110

Firebirds: An Anthology of Original Fantasy and Science Fiction - Sharyn November (421 pages)   *m, h*   1095

Firesong: An Adventure - William Nicholson (422 pages)   1078

Lucas - Kevin Brooks (423 pages)   *h*   159

Manta's Gift - Timothy Zahn (427 pages)   *h, a*   1491

The Merlin Conspiracy - Diana Wynne Jones (438 pages)   *m, h*   757

Mad Maudlin - Mercedes Lackey (439 pages)   *h, a*   844

Trickster's Choice - Tamora Pierce (446 pages)   *m, h*   1152

Lady Knight - Tamora Pierce (448 pages)   *m, h*   1150

Spirits in the Wires - Charles de Lint (448 pages)   *h, a*   355

The Companions - Sheri S. Tepper (452 pages)   *h, a*   1373

City of Stars - Mary Hoffman (459 pages)   *m, h*   662

The Amulet of Samarkand - Jonathan Stroud (462 pages)   *m, h*   1350

Zulu Heart - Steven Barnes (463 pages)   *h, a*   82

Devlin's Luck - Patricia Bray (480 pages)   *h, a*   139

Angelica: A Novel of Samaria - Sharon Shinn (485 pages)   *h, a*   1293

Summerland - Michael Chabon (492 pages)   *m, h*   236

Fool's Errand - Robin Hobb (496 pages)   *h, a*   647

Voyage of the Shadowmoon - Sean McMullen (496 pages)   *h, a*   994

Eragon - Christopher Paolini (497 pages)   *m, h*   1125

East - Edith Pattou (498 pages)   *m, h*   1131

The Grail Prince - Nancy McKenzie (510 pages)   *h, a*   983

Golden Fool - Robin Hobb (520 pages)   *h, a*   648

Child of the Prophecy - Juliet Marillier (528 pages)   *h, a*   941

Lion's Blood: A Novel of Slavery and Freedom in an Alternate America - Steven Barnes (528 pages)   *h, a*   81

Inkheart - Cornelia Funke (534 pages)   *m, h*   499

Tapping the Dream Tree - Charles de Lint (541 pages)   *h, a*   356

War of Honor - David Weber (864 pages)   *h, a*   1421

Harry Potter and the Order of the Phoenix - J.K. Rowling (870 pages)   *m, h*   1234

Illustrator Index

This index lists the illustrators of the featured titles. Illustrators are listed alphabetically, followed by the title, with author names, age-level code(s) and entry numbers also included. The age-level codes are as follows: *p* Preschool, *b* Beginning Reader, *e* Elementary School (Grades 2-5), *m* Middle School (Grades 5-8), *h* High School (Grades 9-12), and *a* Adult.

A

Abulafia, Yossi
The Key to My Heart - Nira Harel   *p*   593

Adinolfi, JoAnn
This Book Is Haunted - Joanne Rocklin   *b*   1216

Agee, Jon
Potch & Polly - William Steig   *p*   1338
Z Goes Home - Jon Agee   *p*   6

Agell, Charlotte
Welcome Home or Someplace Like It - Charlotte Agell   *m*   7

Akib, Jamel
Monsoon - Uma Krishnaswami   *p*   829

Albertine
Marta and the Bicycle - Germano Zullo   *p*   1497

Alborough, Jez
Captain Duck - Jez Alborough   *p*   14
Fix-It Duck - Jez Alborough   *p*   15

Alexander, Martha
I'll Never Share You, Blackboard Bear - Martha Alexander   *p*   19

Alley, R.W.
Best Kind of Baby - Kate Laing   *p*   846
Little Flower - Gloria Rand   *p*   1182
The Real, True Dulcie Campbell - Cynthia DeFelice   *p*   367

Alter, Anna
The Tornado Watches - Patrick Jennings   *e*   733
The Weeping Willow - Patrick Jennings   *e*   734

Anderson, Peggy Perry
Let's Clean Up! - Peggy Perry Anderson   *p*   30

Andreasen, Dan
The House in the Mail - Rosemary Wells   *p*   1425
A Quiet Place - Douglas Wood   *p*   1460
Sailor Boy Jig - Margaret Wise Brown   *p*   167

Andrews, Benny
Pictures for Miss Josie - Sandra Belton   *p*   100

Andriani, Renee W.
Annabel the Actress, Starring in Hound of the Barkervilles - Ellen Conford   *e*   285

Anholt, Catherine
Chimp and Zee and the Big Storm - Laurence Anholt   *p*   31

Apperley, Dawn
Good Night, Sleep Tight, Little Bunnies - Dawn Apperley   *p*   37

Apple, Margot
The Name Quilt - Phyllis Root   *p*   1227

Archbold, Tim
The Circle of Doom - Tim Kennemore   *e, m*   781

Argent, Kerry
Dinnertime! - Sue Williams   *p*   1447

Arnold, Hans
Most Beloved Sister - Astrid Lindgren   *p*   897

Arnosky, Jim
Armadillo's Orange - Jim Arnosky   *p*   40

Aruego, Jose
The Littlest Wolf - Larry Dane Brimner   *p*   154
Rosa Raposa - F. Isabel Campoy   *p*   209

Asch, Frank
Like a Windy Day - Frank Asch   *p*   46

Auch, Mary Jane
Poultrygeist - Mary Jane Auch   *p*   55
The Princess and the Pizza - Mary Jane Auch   *p*   56
Souperchicken - Mary Jane Auch   *p*   57

Avendano, Dolores
Jake Drake, Class Clown - Andrew Clements   *e*   260

Ayliffe, Alex
Emergency! - Margaret Mayo   *p*   959

Ayto, Russell
The Witch's Children - Ursula Jones   *p*   758

Azarian, Mary
From Dawn till Dusk - Natalie Kinsey-Warnock   *p*   796

B

Bahrampour, Ali
Otto: The Story of a Mirror - Ali Bahrampour   *p*   64

Baker, Keith
Meet Mr. and Mrs. Green - Keith Baker   *p*   70

Ballard, Robin
I Used to Be the Baby - Robin Ballard   *p*   71

Bandsuch, Matthew
Handbook for Boys: A Novel - Walter Dean Myers   *m, h*   1053

Bang, Molly
Little Rat Sets Sail - Monika Bang-Campbell   *b*   72

Bania, Michael
Kumak's House: A Tale of the Far North - Michael Bania   *p*   73

Bartlett, Alison
Cock-a-Moo-Moo - Juliet Dallas-Conte   *p*   338

Barton, Jill
Clever Lollipop - Dick King-Smith   *e*   792
Make the Team, Baby Duck! - Amy Hest   *p*   633

Bates, Amy June
Might Adventurer of the Planet! - Ricki Stern   *e*   1341

Bates, Ivan
Do Like a Duck Does! - Judy Hindley   *p*   642

Beck, Ian
Teddy's Snowy Day - Ian Beck   *p*   95

Beddows, Eric
Changing Planes - Ursula K. Le Guin   *h, a*   866

Beeke, Tiphanie
First Day - Dandi Daley Mackall   *p*   928
Wish, Change, Friend - Ian Whybrow   *p*   1440

Bendall-Brunello, John
Hushabye Lily - Claire Freedman   *p*   487

Benson, Patrick
Mole and the Baby Bird - Marjorie Newman   *p*   1076

Benton, Jim
Lunch Walks Among Us - Jim Benton   *e*   103

Berger, Barbara Helen
All the Way Lhasa: A Tale from Tibet - Barbara Helen Berger   *p*   104

Bernardin, James
A Doctor Like Papa - Natalie Kinsey-Warnock   *e*   795
Lumber Camp Library - Natalie Kinsey-Warnock   *e*   798

Billin-Frye, Paige
The Way We Do It in Japan - Geneva Cobb Iijima   *p*   711

Bittinger, Ned
When the Root Children Wake Up - Audrey Wood   *p*   1458

Illustrator Index

Leary, Mary
Karate Girl - Mary Leary   p   868

Lee, Ho Baek
While We Were Out - Ho Baek Lee   p   869

Lee, Jeanne M.
Bitter Dumplings - Jeanne M. Lee   p   870

Lepp, Mati
Pancake Dreams - Ingmarie Ahvander   p   12

Lewin, Betsy
Aunt Minnie and the Twister - Mary Skillings Prigger
    p   1170
Giggle, Giggle, Quack - Doreen Cronin   p   317
A Hug Goes Around - Laura Krauss Melmed
    p   1005

Lewin, Ted
Big Jimmy's Kum Kau Chinese Take Out - Ted Lewin
    p   888
Sunsets of the West - Tony Johnston   p   754

Lewis, E.B.
Bippity Bop Barbershop - Natasha Anastasia Tarpley
    p   1362

Lin, Grace
Olvina Flies - Grace Lin   p   893

Lindenbaum, Pija
Bridget and the Muttonheads - Pija Lindenbaum
    p   895
Mirabelle - Astrid Lindgren   p   896

Lindstrom, Eva
Bertil and the Bathroom Elephants - Inger Lindahl
    p   894

Lippert, Margaret H.
Mrs. Chicken and the Hungry Crocodile - Won-Ldy
    Paye   p   1137

Lisker, Emily
Please, Malese - Amy MacDonald   p   922

Littlewood, Karin
The Color of Home - Mary Hoffman   p   663

Litzinger, Rosanne
Chicken Soup by Heart - Esther Hershenhorn
    p   630
The Four Ugly Cats in Apartment 3D - Marilyn Sachs
    e   1249

Liu, Lesley
Chang and the Bamboo Flute - Elizabeth Starr Hill
    e   640

Lloyd, Megan
Horse in the Pigpen - Linda Williams   p   1446

Long, Loren
I Dream of Trains - Angela Johnson   p   742

Lott, Sheena
How Sleep Found Tabitha - Maggie deVries
    p   379

Love, Judy
The Witch Who Wanted to Be a Princess - Lois G.
    Grambling   p   546

Luthardt, Kevin
Peep! - Kevin Luthardt   p   917

M

Macaulay, David
Angelo - David Macaulay   p   921

MacDonald, Ross
Achoo! Bang! Crash!: The Noisy Alphabet - Ross
    MacDonald   p   924
Another Perfect Day - Ross MacDonald   p   925

Mack, Jeff
Rub-a-Dub Sub - Linda Ashman   p   51

Madsen, Jim
Indian Shoes - Cynthia Leitich Smith   e   1312

Magnus, Erica
Star Blanket - Pat Brisson   p   156

Mahoney, Daniel J.
The Saturday Escape - Daniel J. Mahoney   p   934

Manning, Maurie J.
The Aunts Go Marching - Maurie J. Manning
    p   937

Martchenko, Michael
More Pies! - Robert Munsch   p   1040
Zoom! - Robert Munsch   p   1041

Mathers, Petra
Herbie's Secret Santa - Petra Mathers   p   955
When Mommy Was Mad - Lynne Jonell   p   756

Matje, Martin
A Pig Named Perrier - Elizabeth Spurr   p   1331
Stuart Goes to School - Sara Pennypacker   e   1143
Stuart's Cape - Sara Pennypacker   e   1144

Mauner, Claudia
Zoe Sophia's Scrapbook: An Adventure in Venice -
    Claudia Mauner   p   957

McCallum, Stephen
Jo's Triumph - Nikki Tate   e, m   1363

McCarthy, Meghan
George Upside Down - Meghan McCarthy   p   963

McCarty, Peter
Brothers Below Zero - Tor Seidler   e, m   1277
Hondo & Fabian - Peter McCarty   p   964

McCauley, Adam
Martin MacGregor's Snowman - Lisa Broadie Cook
    p   289

McClements, George
*Jake Gander, Storyville Detective: The Case of the
    Greedy Granny* - George McClements   p   969

McClintock, Barbara
Dahlia - Barbara McClintock   p   970
Goldilocks and the Three Bears - Jim Aylesworth
    p   61

McCoy, Glenn
Penny Lee and Her TV - Glenn McCoy   p   971

McCully, Emily Arnold
The Battle for St. Michaels - Emily Arnold McCully
    b   973
Katie's Wish - Barbara Shook Hazen   p   616

McDonnell, Flora
Giddy-up! Let's Ride! - Flora McDonnell   p   977

McEwen, Katharine
The Cat Who Got Carried Away - Allan Ahlberg
    e   9
The Woman Who Won Things - Allan Ahlberg
    e   11

McKean, Dave
Coraline - Neil Gaiman   m   502
Varjak Paw - S.F. Said   m   1250
The Wolves in the Walls - Neil Gaiman   p   503

McKie, Todd
Egad Alligator! - Harriet Ziefert   p   1495

McLaren, Chesley
Zat Cat! A Haute Couture Tail - Chesley McLaren
    p   987

McMenemy, Sarah
Waggle - Sarah McMenemy   p   988

McMullan, Jim
I Stink! - Kate McMullan   p   992
I'm Mighty! - Kate McMullan   p   993

McMullen, Nigel
Goodnight, Baby Monster - Laura Leuck   p   880

McPhail, David
Big Brown Bear's Up and Down Day - David McPhail
    p   998
Edward in the Jungle - David McPhail   p   999
Little Horse - Betsy Byars   e   193
Mud Is Cake - Pam Munoz Ryan   p   1241
Piggy's Pancake Parlor - David McPhail   e   1000
The Teddy Bear - David McPhail   p   1001
Thirsty Baby - Catherine Ann Cullen   p   323

McQuillan, Mary
Our Twitchy - Kes Gray   p   551
Squeaky Clean - Simon Puttock   p   1179

Meade, Holly
Goose's Story - Cari Best   p   106
Queenie Farmer Had Fifteen Daughters - Ann
    Campbell   p   208

Meddaugh, Susan
Lulu's Hat - Susan Meddaugh   e   1003

Meidell, Sherry
The Day the Picture Man Came - Faye Gibbons
    p   520
Full Steam Ahead - Faye Gibbons   p   521

Middleton, Charlotte
Lucky Socks - Carrie Weston   p   1431

Millman, Isaac
Moses Goes to the Circus - Isaac Millman   p   1012

Minor, Wendell
Fire Storm - Jean Craighead George   p   517

Morales, Yuyi
Just a Minute: A Trickster Tale and Counting Book -
    Yuyi Morales   p   1030

Mordan, C.B.
Silent Movie - Avi   p   60

Morgan, Pierr
Cornfield Hide-and-Seek - Christine Widman
    p   1442
Someone Says - Carole Lexa Schaefer   p   1268

Moser, Barry
Earthquack! - Margie Palatini   p   1122
That Summer - Tony Johnston   p   755

Moss, Marissa
Max's Logbook - Marissa Moss   e   1035

Munoz, Claudio
Little Pig Figwort Can't Get to Sleep - Henrietta
    Branford   p   136

Munsinger, Lynn
Birthday Zoo - Deborah Lee Rose   p   1229
Hunter's Best Friend at School - Laura Malone Elliott
    p   426
Something Might Happen - Helen Lester   p   876
Tackylocks and the Three Bears - Helen Lester
    p   877

Murphy, Mary
I Kissed the Baby! - Mary Murphy   p   1043

Murray, Martine
*The Slightly True Story of Cedar B. Hartley (Who
    Planned to Live an Unusual Life)* - Martine Murray
    m   1046

Muth, Jon J.
Our Gracie Aunt - Jacqueline Woodson   p   1467
Stone Soup - Jon J. Muth   p   1047
The Three Questions - Jon J. Muth   p   1048

Myotte, Elsa
Berta: A Remarkable Dog - Celia Barker Lottridge
    e   908

N

Narahashi, Keiko
Mama Will Be Home Soon - Nancy Minchella
   p 1016

Nash, Scott
Betsy Who Cried Wolf! - Gail Carson Levine
   p 882
The Bugliest Bug - Carol Diggory Shields   p 1292
Stanley, Flat Again! - Jeff Brown   e 163

Natchev, Alexi
The Tale of Urso Brunov: Little Father of All Bears -
   Brian Jacques   p 723

Natti, Susanna
Lionel's Birthday - Stephen Krensky   b 826

Neilan, Eujin Kim
The Rabbit and the Dragon King - Daniel San Souci
   p 1257

Nelson, Kadir
Thunder Rose - Jerdine Nolen   p 1093
The Village That Vanished - Ann Grifalconi   p 561

Nelson, S.D.
The Star People: A Lakota Story - S.D. Nelson
   p 1073

Newman, Barbara Johansen
The Case of the Graveyard Ghost - Michele Torrey
   e 1384

Nicholl, Calvin
The World Before This One - Rafe Martin   m 950

Nivola, Claire A.
The Forest - Claire A. Nivola   p 1083

Novak, Matt
No Zombies Allowed - Matt Novak   p 1094

O

O'Brien, Anne Sibley
Brianna, Jamaica, and the Dance of Spring - Juanita
   Havill   p 612

O'Leary, Chris
Mama Played Baseball - David A. Adler   p 5

O'Malley, Kevin
Little Buggy - Kevin O'Malley   p 1107
Little Buggy Runs Away - Kevin O'Malley   p 1108
Making Plum Jam - John Warren Stewig   p 1344
Straight to the Pole - Kevin O'Malley   p 1109

Ontiveros, Martin
*Ricky Ricotta's Mighty Robot vs. the Jurassic
   Jackrabbits from Jupiter* - Dav Pilkey   e 1154
*Ricky Ricotta's Mighty Robot vs. the Mecha-Monkeys
   from Mars* - Dav Pilkey   e 1155

Ormerod, Jan
I Am NOT Going to School Today! - Robie H. Harris
   p 599

Oxenbury, Helen
Big Momma Makes the World - Phyllis Root
   p 1226

P

Palmer, Kate Salley
Bear Hug - Laurence Pringle   p 1172

Paparone, Pamela
The Little School Bus - Carol Roth   p 1231

Parker, Nancy Winslow
Our Class Took a Trip to the Zoo - Shirley Neitzel
   p 1071

Parker, Robert Andrew
Orville: A Dog Story - Haven Kimmel   p 790

Parker-Rees, Guy
Dinosaurumpus - Tony Mitton   p 1019
Down by the Cool of the Pool - Tony Mitton
   p 1020
Quiet! - Paul Bright   p 153

Paschkis, Julie
Head, Body, Legs: A Story from Liberia - Won-Ldy
   Paye   p 1136

Payne, C.F.
Shoeless Joe & Black Betsy - Phil Bildner   p 108

Pearson, Tracey Campbell
Bob - Tracey Campbell Pearson   p 1140
Leap, Frog - Jane Cutler   e 332

Peck, Beth
Bicycle Madness - Jane Kurtz   e, m 837
Jason Rat-a-Tat - Colby Rodowsky   e 1220
A Picture of Grandmother - Esther Hautzig   e 611

Pedersen, Janet
Baby for Sale - Jackie French Koller   p 814

Pedersen, Judy
Gifts from the Sea - Natalie Kinsey-Warnock   e,
   m 797

Pels, Winslow
Ali and the Magic Stew - Shulamith Levey Oppenheim
   p 1112

Perkins, Lynne Rae
The Broken Cat - Lynne Rae Perkins   p 1146
Georgie Lee - Sharon Phillips Denslow   e 374
Snow Music - Lynne Rae Perkins   p 1147

Pham, LeUyen
Before I Was Your Mother - Kathryn Lasky   p 850
Little Badger's Just-About Birthday - Eve Bunting
   p 179
Piggies in a Polka - Kathi Appelt   p 35

Pilkey, Dav
*The Adventures of Super Diaper Baby: The First
   Graphic Novel* - Dav Pilkey   e 1153

Pinkney, Jerry
The Nightingale - Jerry Pinkney   p 1157
Noah's Ark - Jerry Pinkney   p 1158

Plecas, Jennifer
Agapanthus Hum and the Angel Hoot - Joy Cowley
   b 309
Get Well, Good Knight - Shelley Moore Thomas
   b 1377

Polacco, Patricia
Christmas Tapestry - Patricia Polacco   p 1163

Popp, K. Wendy
One Candle - Eve Bunting   p 180

Potter, Giselle
The Brave Little Seamstress - Mary Pope Osborne
   p 1116
Quentin Fenton Herter III - Amy MacDonald
   p 923
When Catherine the Great and I Were Eight! - Cari
   Best   p 107

Pottie, Marjolein
Musical Beds - Mara Bergman   p 105

Pratt, Pierre
No, No, Jack! - Ron Hirsch   p 645
Where's Pup? - Dayle Ann Dodds   p 386

Priestley, Chris
Death and the Arrow - Chris Priestley   m, h 1169

Primavera, Elise
Auntie Claus and the Key to Christmas - Elise
   Primavera   p 1171

Proimos, James
Cowboy Boy - James Proimos   e 1173
Johnny Mutton, He's So Him! - James Proimos
   e 1174

Provensen, Alice
A Day in the Life of Murphy - Alice Provensen
   p 1176

R

Radunsky, Vladimir
*Mannekin Pis: A Simple Story of a Boy Who Peed on
   a War* - Vladimir Radunsky   p 1181

Raglin, Tim
Go Track a Yak! - Tony Johnston   p 752
The Wolf Who Cried Boy - Bob Hartman   p 603

Rand, Ted
Homespun Sarah - Verla Kay   p 771
Once Upon a Farm - Marie Bradby   p 132

Rankin, Joan
First Day - Joan Rankin   p 1184

Rankin, Laura
The Wriggly, Wriggly Baby - Jessica Clerk   p 264

Ransome, James E.
Bruh Rabbit and the Tar Baby Girl - Virginia
   Hamilton   p 589
Under the Quilt of Night - Deborah Hopkinson
   p 678
Visiting Day - Jacqueline Woodson   p 1468

Raschka, Chris
Be Boy Buzz - bell hooks   p 672

Rash, Andy
Fat Camp Commandos Go West - Daniel Pinkwater
   e 1159

Rathmann, Peggy
The Day the Babies Crawled Away - Peggy Rathmann
   p 1187

Rayner, Mary
Hobart - Anita Briggs   e 149

Reed, Lynn Rowe
Punctuation Takes a Vacation - Robin Pulver
   p 1178

Reichel, Anja
Safe and Sound - Barbara Nichol   p 1077

Remkiewicz, Frank
Froggy Goes to the Doctor - Jonathan London
   p 905
Froggy Plays in the Band - Jonathan London
   p 906
Horrible Harry and the Dragon War - Suzy Kline
   e 806

Rex, Adam
The Dirty Cowboy - Amy Timberlake   p 1382

Reynolds, Adrian
Pete and Polo's Farmyard Adventure - Adrian
   Reynolds   p 1200

Reynolds, Peter H.
Judy Moody Saves the World! - Megan McDonald
   e 976
Olivia Kidney - Ellen Potter   e, m 1165

Riddell, Chris
Platypus - Chris Riddell   p 1202
Platypus and the Birthday Party - Chris Riddell
   p 1203

Platypus and the Lucky Day - Chris Riddell
  p 1204

Riley, Linnea
Song of Night: It's Time to Go to Bed - Katherine
  Riley Nakamura   p 1057

Ripper, Georgie
Brian & Bob: The Tale of Two Guinea Pigs - Georgie
  Ripper   p 1208

Roberts, Victoria
Halloweena - Miriam Glassman   p 528

Roche, Denis
The Best Class Picture Ever! - Denis Roche
  p 1214
Little Pig Is Capable - Denis Roche   p 1215

Rogers, Jacqueline
Little Scraggly Hair: A Dog on Noah's Ark - Lynn
  Cullen   p 324
Witch Twins at Camp Bliss - Adele Griffin   e 564

Rohmann, Eric
My Friend Rabbit - Eric Rohmann   p 1222

Roos, Maryn
How to Lose Your Class Pet - Valerie Wilson Wesley
  e 1430

Root, Barry
The Cat Who Liked Potato Soup - Terry Farish
  p 443
Gumbrella - Barry Root   p 1225

Root, Kimberly Bulcken
The Birds of Killingworth - Robert D. San Souci
  p 1258
In the Piney Woods - Roni Schotter   p 1270

Ross, Tony
Amber Brown Is Green with Envy - Paula Danziger
  e 345
Get Ready for Second Grade, Amber Brown - Paula
  Danziger   b 346

Roth, Stephanie
Doggone . . . Third Grade! - Colleen O'Shaughnessy
  McKenna   e 982
Meow Means Mischief - Ann Whitehead Nagda
  e 1055

Rubel, Nicole
Grody's Not So Golden Rules - Nicole Rubel
  p 1235
No More Vegetables! - Nicole Rubel   p 1236
Practice Makes Perfect for Rotten Ralph - Jack Gantos
  b 507

Rumford, James
Nine Animals and the Well - James Rumford
  p 1238

S

Saltzberg, Barney
Hip, Hip, Hooray Day! - Barney Saltzberg   p 1255

Samuels, Barbara
Dolores on Her Toes - Barbara Samuels   p 1256

San Souci, Daniel
Frightful's Daughter - Jean Craighead George
  p 518

Sanderson, Ruth
Cinderella - Ruth Sanderson   p 1263

Saponaro, Dominic
Pirate Hunter Series - Brad Strickland   e, m 1348

Savadier, Elivia
I Love Saturdays Y Domingos - Alma Flor Ada
  p 2

Sayles, Elizabeth
Jeoffry's Halloween - Mary Bryant Bailey   p 66

Schindler, S.D.
One Witch - Laura Leuck   p 881
The Runaway Pumpkin - Kevin Lewis   p 890
Skeleton Hiccups - Margery Cuyler   p 334

Schmidt, Karen Lee
Hoptoad - Jane Yolen   p 1483

Schories, Pat
Biscuit Goes to School - Alyssa Satin Capucilli
  p 213

Schwartz, Amy
What James Likes Best - Amy Schwartz   p 1272

Sedgwick, Marcus
The Dark Horse - Marcus Sedgwick   m 1275

Seibold, J. Otto
Gluey: A Snail Tale - Vivian Walsh   p 1414

Selznick, Brian
The Meanest Doll in the World - Ann M. Martin
  e 946
Wingwalker - Rosemary Wells   e 1429

Shannon, David
David Gets in Trouble - David Shannon   p 1282
Duck on a Bike - David Shannon   p 1283
How I Became a Pirate - Melinda Long   p 907

Shannon, Margaret
The Red Wolf - Margaret Shannon   p 1285

Sharratt, Nick
Shark in the Park! - Nick Sharratt   p 1286

Sheban, Chris
*The Story of a Seagull and the Cat Who Taught her to
  Fly* - Luis Sepulveda   e 1278

Shed, Greg
Harvest Home - Jane Yolen   p 1481

Shinjo, Shelly
Ghosts for Breakfast - Stanley Todd Terasaki
  p 1374

Sim, David
The Sheep Fairy: When Wishes Have Wings - Ruth
  Louise Symes   p 1357

Simmons, Jane
Ebb & Flo and the Baby Seal - Jane Simmons
  p 1304

Sims, Blanche
Cool Cat, School Cat - Judy Cox   e 310

Sis, Peter
Firesong: An Adventure - William Nicholson
  1078
Madlenka's Dog - Peter Sis   p 1307

Sitaraman, Soumya
Chachaji's Cup - Uma Krishnaswami   p 828

Slavin, Bill
Stanley's Party - Linda Bailey   p 65

Smith, Cat Bowman
Just One More Story - Jennifer Brutschy   p 173
Old Granny and the Bean Thief - Cynthia DeFelice
  p 366
The Trouble with Babies - Martha Freeman   e 488

Smith, Elwood H.
On the Go with Pirate Pete and Pirate Joe - A.E.
  Cannon   b 211

Smith, Lane
Pinocchio the Boy: Incognito in Collodi - Lane Smith
  p 1314

Smith, Tammy
Substitute Teacher Plans - Doug Johnson   p 746

Snow, Scott
One Sky Above Us - E. Cody Kimmel   e 787

So, Meilo
The White Swan Express: A Story About Adoption -
  Jean Davies Okimoto   p 1106

Sogabe, Aki
The Boy Who Drew Cats - Margaret Hodges
  p 656

Souhami, Jessica
Mrs. McCool and the Giant Cuhullin: An Irish Tale -
  Jessica Souhami   p 1322

Spengler, Margaret
Storm Is Coming! - Heather Tekavec   p 1371

Spetter, Jung-Hee
Bye, Bye! - Nancy Kaufmann   p 769

Spirin, Gennady
The Tale of the Firebird - Gennady Spirin   p 1328

St-Aubin, Bruno
The Several Lives of Orphan Jack - Sarah Ellis
  e 430

Stadler, Alexander
Beverly Billingsly Borrows a Book - Alexander Stadler
  p 1333
Beverly Billingsly Takes a Bow - Alexander Stadler
  p 1334

Stanley, Sanna
Monkey for Sale - Sanna Stanley   p 1335

Steele-Morgan, Alexandra
Find-a-Saurus - Mark Sperring   p 1324

Stephens, Helen
Blue Horse - Helen Stephens   p 1340
The Quigleys - Simon Mason   e 952
The Quigleys at Large - Simon Mason   e 953

Stevens, Janet
Epossumondas - Coleen Salley   p 1254
Jackalope - Janet Stevens   p 1342

Stevenson, James
The Castaway - James Stevenson   p 1343

Stock, Catherine
Gus and Grandpa and the Halloween Costume -
  Claudia Mills   b 1014
Gus and Grandpa Go Fishing - Claudia Mills
  b 1015

Stojic, Manya
Snow - Manya Stojic   p 1346

Su-Kennedy, Hui Hui
The Magical Monkey King: Mischief in Heaven - Ji-Li
  Jiang   e 738

Sweat, Lynn
Calling Doctor Amelia Bedelia - Herman Parish
  b 1126

Sweet, Melissa
*The 5,000-Year-Old Puzzle: Solving a Mystery of
  Ancient Egypt* - Claudia Logan   p 904
Charlotte in Paris - Joan MacPhail Knight   e 807

Swiatkowska, Gabi
My Name Is Yoon - Helen Recorvits   p 1189

T

Taback, Simms
This Is the House That Jack Built - Simms Taback
  p 1358

Tafuri, Nancy
The Donkey's Christmas - Nancy Tafuri   p 1359
Mama's Little Bears - Nancy Tafuri   p 1360
You Are Special, Little One - Nancy Tafuri
  p 1361

Taylor, Geoff
The Doomspell - Cliff McNish   m 997

Author Index

This index is an alphabetical listing of the authors of books featured in entries and those listed under "Other books by the author" and "Other books you might like." Editors and co-authors are interfiled with author names. For each author, the titles of books written and entry numbers are also provided. Bold numbers indicate a featured main entry; light-face numbers refer to books recommended for further reading.

A

Aardema, Verna
Bringing the Rain to Kapiti Plain: A Nandi Tale 829
Rabbit Makes a Monkey of Lion 1137
Why Mosquitoes Buzz in People's Ears: A West African Tale 879

Abbey, Lynn
Jerlayne 110, 1318

Abbott, Tony
Dracula: Trapped in Transylvania 887

Abercrombie, Barbara
Charlie Anderson 469

Achebe, Chinua
Girls at War, and Other Stories 48

Ackerman, Karen
By the Dawn's Early Light 76

Ackerman, Noel
Spirit Horse 875

Ada, Alma Flor
Daniel's Mystery Egg 1
Daniel's Pet 1
I Love Saturdays Y Domingos 1, **2**
Jordi's Star 2
The Malachite Palace 1285
My Name Is Maria Isabel 942, 1024
The Three Golden Oranges 2, 298
With Love, Little Red Hen 1, 2
Yours Truly, Goldilocks 1215

Adams, Addie
Hilda and the Mad Scientist 856

Adams, Douglas
The Hitchhiker's Guide to the Galaxy 453

Adams, Georgie
Fish, Fish, Fish 3
Highway Builders 3
Nanny Fox and the Christmas Surprise 3
The Three Little Witches Storybook **3**

Adichie, Chimamanda Ngozi
Purple Hibiscus 534

Adler, C.S.
Her Blue Straw Hat 4
More than a Horse 4

The No Place Cat **4**, 87, 135
Not Just a Summer Crush 4
The Unhappy Horse 4
Winning 4

Adler, David A.
Andy Russell, NOT Wanted by the Police 1063
The Babe & I 5, 606
Cam Jansen and the Mystery of the Stolen Diamonds 5
The Cam Jansen Series 11
Lou Gehrig: The Luckiest Man 5, 108
Mama Played Baseball **5**, 304
The Many Troubles of Andy Russell 1013
One Yellow Daffodil: A Hanukkah Story 180
A Picture Book of Lewis and Clark 5
School Trouble for Andy Russell 207, 249, 506
Young Cam Jansen and the Double Beach Mystery 1243

Agee, Jon
Dmitri the Astronaut 6
Ludlow Laughs 6
Milo's Hat Trick 6, 1003
Z Goes Home **6**

Agell, Charlotte
Welcome Home or Someplace Like It **7**

Ahlberg, Allan
The Adventures of Bert 8
The Better Brown Stories 9, 11, 952
A Bit More Bert **8**
The Bravest Ever Bear 8, 10
The Cat Who Got Carried Away **9**, 234
The Giant Baby 11
It Was a Dark and Stormy Night 173, 353
The Jolly Postman 532
The Man Who Wore All His Clothes 9, 11
Monkey Do! 10
The Snail House 8, 10
Treasure Hunt **10**
The Woman Who Won Things 9, **11**, 1143

Ahlberg, Janet
Peek-a-Boo! 719

Ahvander, Ingmarie
Pancake Dreams **12**

Aiken, Joan
The Cuckoo Tree 13
Dangerous Games 13
Dido and Pa 13
A Fit of Shivers: Tales for Late at Night 1138
Is Underground 284, 409
Midnight Is a Place 13
Midwinter Nightingale **13**
The Witch of Clatteringshaws 13

Alakija, Polly
Catch that Goat! 1335

Alborough, Jez
Captain Duck 14
Duck in the Truck 14, 15, 705, 889, 1445
Fix-It Duck 14, **15**
Hug 15, 1005
My Friend Bear 14, 15
Watch Out! Big Bro's Coming! 1083
Where's My Teddy? 420, 1228

Alcock, Vivien
The Red-Eared Ghosts 929
Singer to the Sea God 292, 592, 1482

Alcott, Louisa May
Little Women 259

Alda, Arlene
Hurry Granny Annie 16
Morning Glory Monday **16**
Pig, Horse, or Cow, Don't Wake Me Now 16
Sheep, Sheep, Sheep, Help Me Fall Asleep 16

Alder, Elizabeth
Crossing the Panther's Path **17**
The King's Shadow 17

Alexander, Lloyd
The Arkadians 18
The Drackenberg Adventure 766
The El Dorado Adventure 765
The Gawgon and the Boy 18, 269
Gypsy Rizka 18
The Iron Ring 18
The Remarkable Journey of Prince Jen 18
The Rope Trick **18**
Taran Wanderer 1219

Alexander, Martha
And My Mean Old Mother Will Be Sorry, Blackboard Bear 19, 1108
I Sure Am Glad to See You, Blackboard Bear 19
I'll Never Share You, Blackboard Bear **19**
Nobody Asked Me If I Wanted a Baby Sister 814
We're in Big Trouble, Blackboard Bear 19
You're a Genius, Blackboard Bear 745

Aliki
Feelings 478
Painted Words/Spoken Memories 663

Allard, Harry
Miss Nelson Is Missing! 746, 1214
The Stupids Step Out 128

Allen, Richard E.
Ozzy on the Outside 135

Allen, Will
Swords for Hire: Two of the Most Unlikely Heroes 277

Almagor, Gila
Under the Domin Tree 1168

Almond, David
Counting Stars **20**, 21
Fire-Eaters 21
Heaven Eyes 20, 21
Kit's Wilderness 20, 21, 604, 932
Secret Heart 20, **21**
Skellig 20, 21, 871

Alper, Ann Fitzpatrick
Harry McNairy, Tooth Fairy 350

Alphin, Elaine Marie
Counterfeit Son 22, 23, 587
The Ghost Cadet 23
Ghost Soldier 22, 23, 83
Picture Perfect **22**
Simon Says 22, **23**

Alter, Judy
Cherokee Rose 601

Altman, Linda Jacobs
Amelia's Road 1145

Alvarez, Julia
Before We Were Free **24**
Finding Miracles 24

*How the Garcia Girls Lost Their
Accents* 24, 343, 1160, 1400
How Tia Lola Came to Visit/Stay 120,
1024, 1035
In the Time of the Butterflies 24
Something to Declare 24
Woman I Kept to Myself: Poems 24

Amato, Mary
The Word Eater 736

Ambrose, Stephen E.
*Lewis & Clark: Voyage of
Discovery* 25
*Mississippi and the Making of a Nation:
From the Louisiana Purchase to
Today* 25
*This Vast Land: A Young Man's
Journal of the Lewis and Clark
Expedition* 25
*To America: Personal Reflections of an
Historian* 25
*Undaunted Courage: Meriwether Lewis,
Thomas Jefferson and the Opening of
the American West* 25

Amoss, Berthe
Lost Magic 339

Anaya, Rudolfo A.
*My Land Sings: Stories from the Rio
Grande* 1252

Andersen, Hans Christian
*The Fairy Tales of Hans Christian
Andersen* 1157
The Little Mermaid 1017
Thumbelina 193

Anderson, Janet S.
Going through the Gate 26
The Last Treasure **26**
The Monkey Tree 26

Anderson, Jim
Billarooby 384

Anderson, Joan
Sally's Submarine 51, 618

Anderson, Laurie Halse
The Big Cheese of Third Street 27
Catalyst **28**, 126, 1420
Fever 1793 28, 795
Ndito Runs 27, 1352
No Time for Mother's Day 27
Speak 28, 1160
Storm Rescue 28
*Thank You Sarah: The Woman Who
Saved Thanksgiving* 27
Turkey Pox 27, 362

Anderson, M.T.
Burger Wuss 29
Feed **29**, 85, 580, 1031
The Game of Sunken Places 29
Thirsty 29, 1194

Anderson, Peggy King
Safe at Home! 750

Anderson, Peggy Perry
Let's Clean Up! **30**
Out to Lunch 30
Time for Bed, the Babysitter Said 30
To the Tub 30

Angell, Judie
Leave the Cooking to Me 1037, 1288
One-Way to Ansonia 482, 701

Anholt, Laurence
Chimp and Zee 31, 307
Chimp and Zee and the Big Storm **31**
Harry's Home 31
Jack and the Dreamsack 925
Sophie and the New Baby 31

Anonymous
Go Ask Alice 1180

Antle, Nancy
Lost in the War 650, 1437
Playing Solitaire 495

Aoki, Elaine M.
*The White Swan Express: A Story About
Adoption* **1106**

Apone, Claudio
*My Grandfather, Jack the
Ripper* 1169

Appelt, Kathi
The Alley Cat's Meow **32**
Bats around the Clock 35
Bayou Lullaby 1057
Bubba and Beau, Best Friends 33, **34**
Bubba and Beau Go Night-Night **33**
*Bubba and Beau Meet the
Relatives* 33
Bubbles, Bubbles 32, 34, 35, 36
Incredible Me! 35, 36, 548
Oh My Baby, Little One 34, 36
Piggies in a Polka 32, 33, **35**, 1019,
1469
Rain Dance 542
Watermelon Day 32
Where, Where Is Swamp Bear? 34,
36

Apperley, Dawn
Don't Wake the Baby 37
Flip and Flop 37
*Good Night, Sleep Tight, Little
Bunnies* 37
Hello Little Lamb 37

Arkin, Alan
Cassie Loves Beethoven 234, 374

Arkin, Anthony Dana
Captain Hawaii 277, 680

Armistead, John
The $66 Summer 451

Armstrong, Jennifer
Chin Yu Min and the Ginger Cat 443
Fire-Us Series 577
The Keepers of the Flame 38
The Kiln 38
The Kindling **38**, 39
Mary Mehan Awake 39
*Shattered: Stories of Children and
War* **39**
Steal Away 39, 337
*Theodore Roosevelt: Letters from a
Young Coal Miner* 1188
*Thomas Jefferson: Letters from a
Philadelphia Schoolgirl* 39

Arnason, Eleanor
Ring of Swords 244

Arnold, Caroline
House Sparrows Everywhere 519

Arnold, Marsha Diane
Prancing, Dancing Lily 314

Arnold, Tedd
No More Water in the Tub 1379

Arnosky, Jim
Armadillo's Orange **40**
Beachcombing 40
Following the Coast 40
Little Lions 40
A Manatee Morning 838
Rabbits and Raindrops 40, 1447
Raccoon on His Own 40

Arquette, Kerry
Daddy Promises 41
What Did You Do Today? **41**

Arrick, Fran
God's Radar 483
Where'd You Get the Gun, Billy? 587

Arrington, Aileen
Camp of the Angel **42**

Arrington, Frances
Bluestem 43, 325
Prairie Whispers 43

Arro, Lena
By Geezers and Galoshes! 44
Good Night, Animals 44, 715, 854

Artell, Mike
*Petite Rouge: A Cajun Red Riding
Hood* 1259

Asare, Meshack
Sosu's Call 878

Asaro, Catherine
The Phoenix Code 1293

Asbjornsen, P.C.
The Three Billy Goats Gruff 608

Asch, Frank
Baby Duck's New Friend 46, 727
Battle in a Bottle 45
The Ghost of P.S. 42 **45**
Hands around Lincoln School 45
Like a Windy Day **46**
Moonbear's Pet 777
Mooncake 146
Mr. Maxwell's Mouse 46
Survival School 45

Ashby, John
Sea Gift **47**

Asher, Sandy
*With All My Heart, With All My
Mind* 483

Ashley, Bernard
Break in the Sun 48
Dodgem 48
Little Soldier 39, **48**
Terry on the Fence 48

Ashman, Linda
Babies on the Go **49**, 51, 1361
Can You Make a Piggy Giggle? 49,
50, 51
Castles, Caves, and Honeycombs 49,
50, 1414
Maxwell's Magic Mix-Up 50, 1339
Rub-a-Dub Sub 49, **51**
Sailing Off to Sleep 50, 51

Asimov, Janet
Norby and the Terrified Taxi 1155

Atinsky, Steve
Tyler on Prime Time 545

Atkins, Catherine
Alt Ed **52**
When Jeff Comes Home 52, 747,
1394

Atkins, Jeannine
*A Name on the Quilt: A Story of
Remembrance* 1227

Attanasio, A.A.
The Eagle and the Sword 664

Attema, Martha
Daughter of Light 53
Hero 53
A Light in the Dunes 53
A Time to Choose 53
When the War Is Over 53

Atwater-Rhodes, Amelia
Demon in My View 1194, 1345
Hawksong **54**

Midnight Predator 54
Shattered Mirror 54, 1271
Snakecharm 54

Auch, Mary Jane
Bantam of the Opera 56, 57, 338,
686
Eggs Mark the Spot 56, 57
Hen Lake 791
*I Was a Third Grade Science
Project* 688
The Nutquacker 55, 56, 57
Poultrygeist **55**
The Princess and the Pizza 55, **56**
Souperchicken 55, **57**

Avi
Abigail Takes the Wheel 59, 60
The Barn 58
Crispin: The Cross of Lead **58**
*Don't You Know There's a War
On?* 58
Ereth's Birthday 371
The Fighting Ground 558, 1451
*Finding Providence: The Story of Roger
Williams* 60
The Mayor of Central Park 58, **59**
Midnight Magic 18
Nothing but the Truth 223, 1134
Perloo the Bold 59
Poppy 45, 59, 381
Prairie School 60, 798
*Second Sight: Stories for a New
Millennium* 58
The Secret School 58
Silent Movie **60**
*Something Upstairs: A Tale of
Ghosts* 960
*The True Confessions of Charlotte
Doyle* 485, 707, 949, 1007, 1193

Axworthy, Anni
Anni's Diary of France 807

Aylesworth, Jim
The Full Belly Bowl 61, 380, 475
The Gingerbread Man 61
Goldilocks and the Three Bears **61**
*The Tale of Tricky Fox: A New England
Trickster Tale* 61, 209

Ayres, Katherine
Macaroni Boy **62**
*North by Night: A Story of the
Underground Railroad* 62
Silver Dollar Girl 62
*Stealing South: A Story of the
Underground Railroad* 62
Under Copp's Hill 62
Voices at Whisper Bend 62

B

Babbitt, Natalie
Bub: Or the Very Best Thing 1005

Babcock, Chris
No Moon, No Milk! 697

Bacon, Katherine Jay
Shadow and Light 629

Baczewski, Paul
Just for Kicks 118

Bagdasarian, Adam
*First French Kiss and Other
Traumas* 63, 394
Forgotten Fire 63

Baglio, Ben
Hamster in a Handbasket 1196

Author Index

D

Dahlberg, Maurine F.
Even the Spiders Fled West 337
Play to the Angel 337, 714
The Spirit and Gilly Bucket **337**

Dallas-Conte, Juliet
Cock-a-Moo-Moo **338**

Dalton, Annie
Flying High 339
Isabel: Taking Wing **339**
Losing the Plot 339
Winging It 339

Daly, Jude
Fair, Brown & Trembling: An Irish Cinderella Story 1263

Daly, Niki
Bravo Zan Angelo! 341
Jamela's Dress 340, 341
Not So Fast, Songololo 340, 341
Old Bob's Brown Bear **340**
Once Upon a Time 340, **341**
What's Cooking, Jamela? 57

Dana, Barbara
Necessary Parties 545, 1419

Danko, Dan
Attack of the Mole Master 342
The Brotherhood of Rotten Baby-sitters 342
The Candy Man Cometh 342
Operation Squish 342
Sidekicks **342**

Dann, Patty
Mermaids 1089

Danneberg, Julie
First Year Letters 1130

Danticat, Edwidge
Behind the Mountains: The Diary of Celiane Esperance **343**
Breath, Eyes, Memory 343
Dew Breaker 343
Krik? Krak! 343

Danvers, Dennis
Circuit of Heaven 344
End of Days 344
The Fourth World 344
The Watch **344**

Danziger, Paula
Amber Brown Goes Fourth 1341
Amber Brown Is Feeling Blue 345, 1063
Amber Brown Is Green with Envy **345**
Amber Brown Is Not a Crayon 345, 370, 556, 805, 1070
Amber Brown Sees Red 345
The Cat Ate My Gymsuit 347
The Divorce Express 902
Get Ready for Second Grade, Amber Brown **346**
It's a Fair Day, Amber Brown 346
It's Justin Time, Amber Brown 346, 702, 826
P.S. Longer Letter Later 347
Snail Mail No More 347, 1295
Thames Doesn't Rhyme with James 347
There's a Bat in Bunk Five 1068
This Place Has No Atmosphere 347
United Tates of America **347**
What a Trip, Amber Brown 346, 571
You Can't Eat Your Chicken Pox, Amber Brown 1035

Darrow, Sharon
Old Thunder and Miss Raney 456, 1170
The Painters of Lexieville **348**

Datlow, Ellen
Black Heart, Ivory Bones 349
Black Swan, White Raven 357
The Green Man: Tales from the Mythic Forest 349
Silver Birch, Blood Moon 349
Snow White, Blood Red 349, 415

D'Aulaire, Ingri
D'Aulaire's Trolls 145

David, Lawrence
Peter Claus and the Naughty List 923, 1171

David, Peter
Sir Apropos of Nothing 453

Davidson, Alan
The Bewitching of Alison Allbright 1224

Davis, Jill
Open Your Eyes: Extraordinary Experiences in Faraway Places 504

Davis, Katie
Mabel the Tooth Fairy and How She Got Her Job **350**
Party Animals 350, **351**
Scared Stiff 131, 351, 784, 876
Who Hoots? 350, 351
Who Hops? 350, 351

Davis, Lee
P.B. Bear's Birthday Party 1229

Davis, Rebecca Fjelland
Jake Riley: Irreparably Damaged **352**

Davol, Marguerite W.
The Loudest, Fastest, Best Drummer in Kansas 353, 1433
The Paper Dragon 353
The Snake's Tales **353**
Why Butterflies Go By on Silent Wings 353

Day, Alexandra
Good Dog, Carl 539

Day, Shirley
Luna and the Big Blur: A Story for Children Who Wear Glasses 270

De Angeli, Marguerite
A Door in the Wall 1034

De Beer, Hans
Bernard Bear's Amazing Adventure 413

De Felice, Cynthia
The Dancing Skeleton 177

de Guzman, Michael
The Bamboozlers 354
Beekman's Big Deal 354
Melonhead **354**

de Lint, Charles
Forests of the Heart 357
The Onion Girl 356, 844
Seven Wild Sisters 355, 356, 757
Someplace to be Flying 111, 357
Spirits in the Wires **355**, 356, 553
Tapping the Dream Tree 355, **356**, 357
Waifs and Strays 349, 355, **357**, 415

De Paola, Tomie
Adelita: A Mexican Cinderella Story **358**
Bill and Pete to the Rescue 359
Charlie Needs a Cloak 771
Days of the Blackbird: A Tale of Northern Italy 358, 921, 1157
Fin M'Coul, the Giant of Knockmany Hill 1322

Jamie O'Rourke and the Pooka 358
The Legend of the Persian Carpet 1112
Meet the Barkers: Morgan and Moffat Go to School 359, 1428
Nana Upstairs and Nana Downstairs 755
A New Barker in the House **359**
Pancakes for Breakfast 12
Strega Nona: An Old Tale 1266
Strega Nona Takes a Vacation 358, 359, 1343

de Regniers, Beatrice Schenk
Was It a Good Trade? 1493

de Vries, Maggie
How Sleep Found Tabitha 487, 880

De Young, C. Coco
A Letter to Mrs. Roosevelt 606

Deacon, Alexis
Beegu 360
Slow Loris 360, **361**

Dealey, Erin
Goldie Locks Has Chicken Pox **362**

Dean, Carolee
Comfort **363**

Dean, Pamela
Juniper, Gentian and Rosemary 935

Deaver, Julie Reece
Chicago Blues 364
First Wedding, Once Removed 364
The Night I Disappeared **364**
Say Goodnight, Gracie 135, 364, 700, 974, 1492

Debon, Nicholas
A Brave Soldier **365**
Four Pictures by Emily Carr 365

Deem, James M.
The Very Real Ghost Book of Christina Rose 1478

DeFelice, Cynthia
The Apprenticeship of Lucas Whitaker 368
Clever Crow 366, 367
Cold Feet 366, 367, 1407
Death at Devil's Bridge 368
The Ghost of Cutler Creek 368
The Ghost of Fossil Glen 368
Lostman's River 470, 1049
Nowhere to Call Home 327, 368
Old Granny and the Bean Thief **366**, 367
The Real, True Dulcie Campbell 366, **367**, 926
Under the Same Sky **368**

Degens, T.
On the Third Ward 255

DeGroat, Diane
Annie Pitts, Artichoke 1129
Annie Pitts, Burger Kid 285, 976, 1279
Good Night, Sleep Tight, Don't Let the Bedbugs Bite! **369**
Happy Birthday to You, You Belong in a Zoo 369
Jingle Bell, Homework Smells 369
We Gather Together . . . Now Please Get Lost! 369, 1428

Deighton, Len
SS-GB 81

Del Negro, Janice
Lucy Dove 1237

Delacre, Lulu
Salsa Stories 902

DeLaCroix, Alice
The Hero of Third Grade **370**
Mattie's Whisper 370

Delaney, Michael
Birdbrain Amos **371**
Deep Doo-Doo 371
Deep Doo-Doo and the Mysterious E-Mail 371
Henry's Special Delivery 371

Delffs, Dudley J.
Forgiving August 940

Delton, Judy
Angel Spreads Her Wings 488
Stage Frightened 417

Demas, Corinne
If Ever I Return Again 485

Dematons, Charlotte
Let's Go 1460
The Worry Bear 1246

Demi
The Firebird 1328, 1479
One Grain of Rice: A Mathematical Folktale 1223, 1238

Denenberg, Barry
Early Sunday Morning: The Pearl Harbor Diary of Amber Billows 372, 373
Elisabeth: The Princess Bride **372**, 373
The Journal of Ben Uchida: Citizen 13559 Mirror Lake Internment Camp 372, 373, 1021, 1120
The Journal of William Thomas Emerson: A Revolutionary War Patriot 372, 373
Mirror, Mirror on the Wall: The Diary of Bess Brennan 372, **373**
One Eye Laughing, the Other Weeping: The Diary of Julie Weiss 372, 373
So Far from Home: The Diary of Mary Driscoll, an Irish Mill Girl 523

Denslow, Sharon Phillips
Big Wolf and Little Wolf 374
Georgie Lee **374**
On the Trail with Miss Pace 374
Woollybear Good-bye 374

Dent, Grace
LBD: It's a Girl Thing **375**, 671, 1198

Derby, Pat
Visiting Miss Pierce 127, 832

Desimini, Lisa
Dot the Fire Dog 376, 473
My Beautiful Child 376
Policeman Lou and Policewoman Sue 376
Sun & Moon 376

Dessen, Sarah
Dreamland 187, 377
Keeping the Moon 52, 377, 496, 930, 1288, 1441
Someone Like You 28, 377, 692, 1183
That Summer 377, 438
This Lullaby **377**

Deuker, Carl
High Heat **378**, 1305
Night Hoops 378, 1209
On the Devil's Court 378
Painting the Black 242, 378

Fuller, Thomas E.
Pirate Hunter Series **1348**

Funke, Cornelia
Dragon Rider 499
Inkheart **499**, 500
The Thief Lord 499, **500**

Fuqua, Jonathon Scott
Darby **501**
The Reappearance of Sam Webber 501

Furbee, Mary R.
Outrageous Women of Colonial American 628

G

Gabaldon, Diana
The Outlander 1101

Gaeddert, Louann
Breaking Free 337, 393
Hope 636, 698

Gaetz, Dayle Campbell
Mystery from History 1079, 1211, 1347

Gaiman, Neil
American Gods: A Novel 502, 553
Coraline 182, **502**, 503
The Day I Swapped My Dad for 2 Goldfish 503
Stardust 355, 502, 1044
The Wolves in the Walls 502, **503**

Galdone, Paul
The Monkey and the Crocodile: A Jataka Tale from India 1137

Gallo, Donald R.
Destination Unexpected **504**
From There to Here: Short Stories about Immigrant Teens 504
No Easy Answers: Short Stories about Teenagers Making Tough Choices 685
On the Fringe 504, 1072, 1183
Time Capsule: Short Stories about Teenagers Throughout the Twentieth Century 504
Within Reach: Ten Stories 504

Galloway, Priscilla
Atalanta: The Fastest Runner in the World 1327
The Courtesan's Daughter **505**
Daedalus and the Minotaur 991
Snake Dreamer 505, 1482
Truly Grim Tales 505

Gammell, Stephen
Ride 446

Gantos, Jack
Back to School for Rotten Ralph 346, 507
Heads or Tails: Stories from the Sixth Grade 506
Hole in My Life 508
Jack Adrift: Fourth Grade without a Clue **506**
Jack on the Tracks: Four Seasons of Fifth Grade 506
Jack's Black Book 508
Jack's New Power: Stories from a Caribbean Year 506, 1253
Joey Pigza Loses Control 394, 508
Joey Pigza Swallowed the Key 508, 1325

Practice Makes Perfect for Rotten Ralph **507**
Rotten Ralph Helps Out 507
Wedding Bells for Rotten Ralph 507
What Would Joey Do? 363, 471, **508**, 1280

Garay, Luis
The Kite **509**
The Long Road 509, 663, 1121
Pedrito's Day 509

Garcia, Eric
Anonymous Rex 288

Garcia, Jerry
The Teddy Bears' Picnic 1439

Garden, Nancy
Annie on My Mind 956, 1054
Lark in the Morning 101
Peace, O River 803

Gardiner, Lindsey
Here Come Poppy and Max 34, 1268
When Poppy and Max Grow Up 618

Garfield, Leon
The Empty Sleeve 287
Footsteps 138

Garland, Michael
Last Night at the Zoo 65, 361, 1071, 1229
The Mouse Before Christmas 836

Garland, Sherry
Children of the Dragon: Selected Tales from Vietnam 738
Indio 901
The Last Rainmaker 601
The Lotus Seed 828
Shadow of the Dragon 1289

Garrett, Elizabeth
The Sweet Trade 1193

Garrity, Jennifer Johnson
The Bushwhackers: A Civil War Adventure 693

Gauch, Patricia Lee
Presenting Tanya, the Ugly Duckling 510
Tanya and Emily in a Dance for Two 612
Tanya and the Magic Wardrobe 510
Tanya and the Red Shoes **510**
Tanya Treasury 510

Gauthier, Gail
Club Earth 511, 929
Hero of Ticonderoga 511
My Life Among the Aliens 511
Saving the Planet & Stuff **511**
Year with Butch and Spike 511

Gavin, Jamila
Coram Boy 1462

Gay, Marie-Louise
Fat Charlie's Circus 514
Good Morning, Sam **512**, 513
Good Night Sam 105, 512, **513**
Stella, Fairy of the Forest 512, **514**
Stella, Queen of the Snow 512, 513, 514
Stella, Star of the Sea 512, 513, 514

Gee, Maurice
The Fat Man 160, 767
The Fire-Raiser 713, 774

Geisert, Arthur
After the Flood 515
The Etcher's Studio 515
The Giant Ball of String **515**
Nursery Crimes 515

Geisert, Bonnie
Desert Town 516
Mountain Town 516
Prairie Summer **516**
Prairie Town 516

Gellis, Roberta
Bull God 873, 1152

Gentle, Mary
The Book of Ash 81

George, Jean Craighead
The Case of the Missing Cutthroats: An Ecological Mystery 511, 671
Cliff Hanger 517, 518
Fire Storm **517**, 518
Frightful's Daughter **518**
Julie of the Wolves 90, 262, 1353
The Missing 'Gator of Gumbo Limbo: An Ecological Mystery 1049
The Moon of the Gray Wolves 503
Nutik & Amaroq Play Ball 517
Nutik, the Wolf Pup 517, 518
On the Far Side of the Mountain 226

George, Lindsay Barrett
My Bunny and Me 869, 1080, 1340

Geras, Adele
The Cats of Cuckoo Square: Two Stories 488, 1249
The Fabulous Fantoras: Book One: Family Files 1144
My Grandmother's Stories: A Collection of Jewish Folk Tales 1273
Time for Ballet 718
Troy 292, 308, 873
Watching the Roses 843

Gerrard, Roy
Rosie and the Rustlers 238

Gershator, Phillis
Only One Cowry: A Dahomean Tale 967, 1368

Gerson, Mary-Joan
How Night Came from the Sea: A Story from Brazil 1260
Why the Sky Is Far Away: A Nigerian Folktale 1136

Gerstein, Mordicai
Fox Eyes 519
The Man Who Walked Between the Towers 519
Sparrow Jack **519**
Victor: A Novel Based on the Life of Victor, the Savage of Aveyron 214
What Charlie Heard 519

Ghent, Natale
Piper 450, 849

Gianetti, Charlene C.
Who Am I?: And Other Questions of Adopted Kids 75

Gibbons, Faye
The Day the Picture Man Came **520**, 1214
Emma Jo's Song 520, 521, 686
Full Steam Ahead **521**
Hook Moon Night: Spooky Tales from the Georgia Mountains 520
Mama and Me and the Model T 116, 520, 521
Mighty Close to Heaven 520
Mountain Wedding 521
Night in the Barn 520

Gibbons, Gail
Emergency! 959

Gibson, William
All Tomorrow's Parties 215, 355, 522
The Difference Engine 82, 115
Idoru 522
Mona Lisa Overdrive 1031
Pattern Recognition 85, **522**, 1025
Virtual Light 522

Gifaldi, David
Rearranging and Other Stories 220, 504

Giff, Patricia Reilly
All the Way Home 523, 524
Don't Tell the Girls: A Family Memoir 523
A House of Tailors 523, 524
Lily's Crossing 524
Maggie's Door **523**, 524, 853
Nory Ryan's Song 523, 524
Pictures of Hollis Woods 313, 523, **524**, 1128
Poopsie Pomerantz, Pick Up You Feet 285
Ronald Morgan Goes to Camp 369
The Secret at the Polk Street School 260, 806
Shark in School 1013, 1337
Sunny-Side Up 805

Gilbert, Suzie
Hawk Hill 518

Gilden, Mel
Harry Newberry and the Raiders of the Red Drink 342

Giles, Gail
Dead Girls Don't Write Letters 397, **525**, 526, 1232
Playing in Traffic 525
Shattering Glass 352, 467, 525, **526**, 703, 958

Gilliland, Judith Heide
Not in the House, Newton! 745

Gilmore, Kate
Enter Three Witches 757
The Exchange Student 286, 402, 540, 1373

Gilmore, Rachna
A Group of One 639

Gilson, Jamie
Do Bananas Chew Gum? 527
Hobie Hanson, Greatest Hero of the Mall 527
Stink Alley **527**
Thirteen Ways to Sink a Sub 527
Wagon Train 911 527

Gilstrap, John
At All Costs 1042

Ginsburg, Mirra
Mushroom in the Rain 1303

Glaser, Shirley
The Alphazeds 6

Glass, Andrew
The Wondrous Whirligig: The Wright Brothers' First Flying Machine 398

Glassman, Miriam
Box Top Dreams 528
Halloweena **528**

Gleeson, Libby
Eleanor, Elizabeth 713

Glenn, Mel
Class Dismissed! High School Poems 565

Author Index

hooks, bell
Be Boy Buzz **672**, 673
Happy to Be Nappy 672, 673
Homemade Love 291, 672, **673**
Skin Again 672, 673

Hooks, William H.
Mr. Big Brother 457

Hooper, Mary
Amy 536, **674**, 675
At the Sign of the Sugared Plum 427, 674, **675**, 1059
Megan 674
Megan 2 674
Megan 3 674
Petals in the Ashes 674

Hooper, Patricia
How the Sky's Housekeeper Wore Her Scarves 1315
A Stormy Ride on Noah's Ark 324

Hope, Laura Lee
The Bobbsey Twins' Wonderful Winter Secret 489

Hopkins, Cathy
Mates, Dates and Cosmic Kisses 676
Mates, Dates and Designer Divas 676
Mates, Dates and Inflatable Bras **676**
Mates, Dates and Sleepover Secrets 676
Mates, Dates Series 1199

Hopkinson, Deborah
A Band of Angels 678
Birdie's Lighthouse 678
Cabin in the Snow 677
Girl Wonder: A Baseball Story in Nine Innings 5, 304
Our Kansas Home 677
Pioneer Summer **677**
Sailing for Gold 677
Sweet Clara and the Freedom Quilt 678
Under the Quilt of Night **678**

Horniman, Joanne
Mahalia **679**, 1356

Horowitz, Anthony
The Devil and His Boy 680, 1462
The Devil-s Door-Bell 680
Eagle Strike 681
Mindgame 681
Night of the Scorpion 680
Point Blank **680**, 681
Point Blank: An Alex Rider Adventure 277
Skeleton Key **681**
Stormbreaker 680, 681, 1496

Horrocks, Anita
What They Don't Know 1232, 1387

Horse, Harry
A Friend for Little Bear 682
Little Rabbit Goes to School 682
Little Rabbit Lost **682**

Horvath, Polly
The Canning Season 7, **683**
Canning Season 763
Everything on a Waffle 524, 683
Trolls 683
When the Circus Came to Town 683, 1476

Hosozawa-Nagano, Elaine
Chopsticks from America 711

Hossack, Sylvia
Green Mango Magic 451

Houston, Gloria
Bright Freedom's Song: A Story of the Underground Railroad 590, 1139
Mountain Valor 772

Howard, Arthur
Cosmo Zooms 684
Hoodwinked 3, 684, 1004
Serious Trouble **684**
When I Was Five 684

Howard, Elizabeth Fitzgerald
Virgie Goes to School with Us Boys 100, 148

Howard, Ellen
A Different Kind of Courage 1306

Howard, Ginger
William's House 729, 744

Howarth, Lesley
Maphead 354, 638

Howe, Deborah
Bunnicula 584

Howe, James
13: Thirteen Stories That Capture the Agony and Ecstasy of Being Thirteen **685**
Amazing Odorous Adventures of Stinky Dog 686
Bud Barkin, Private Eye 687, 688
The Celery Stalks at Midnight 585
The Color of Absence: Twelve Stories about Loss and Hope 39, 685, 927
Horace and Morris but Mostly Dolores 686
Horace and Morris Join the Chorus (but what about Dolores?) **686**, 1334
Howie Monroe and the Doghouse of Doom **687**, 688
Invasion of the Mind Swappers from Asteroid 6! 687, 688
It Came from Beneath the Bed 687, **688**
The Misfits 52, 543, 1103, 1399, 1443
The New Nick Kramer, or My Life as a Baby-sitter 547, 685
Pinky and Rex 571, 734, 751
Pinky and Rex and the Just-Right Pet 686, 794
Pinky and Rex and the New Baby 359, 568
Pinky and Rex and the Perfect Pumpkin 569
Rabbit-Cadabra! 1003
There's a Monster under My Bed 1374
The Watcher 685

Howe, Norma
The Adventures of Blue Avenger 680, 689
Blue Avenger and the Theory of Everything **689**
Blue Avenger Cracks the Code 689
God, the Universe, and Hot Fudge Sundaes 689
Shoot for the Moon 689

Howitt, Mary
The Spider and the Fly **690**, 1292

Howker, Janni
Isaac Campion 393, 1438

Howland, Ethan
The Lobster War 47, 162, 1498

Hoyt, Sarah A.
All Night Awake **691**
Any Man So Daring 691

Ill Met by Moonlight 535, 691

Hrdlitschka, Shelley
Beans on Toast 692
Dancing Naked **692**
Disconnected 692
Kat's Fall 692
Tangled Web 692

Hubbell, Patricia
I Like Cats 86

Huck, Charlotte
A Creepy Countdown 881

Huckaby, Lisa Hall
Pot-Bellied Pigs and Other Miniature Pet Pigs 1182

Hudson, Cheryl Willis
Hands Can 423

Huff, Tanya
Long, Hot Summoning 400
The Second Summoning 1293
Summon the Keeper 288

Hughart, Barry
The Bridge of Birds 333

Hughes, Carol
Jack Black & the Ship of Thieves 765

Hughes, Dean
Team Picture 306

Hughes, Monica
Invitation to the Game 578

Hughes, Pat
Breaker Boys 693
Guerrilla Season **693**

Hughes, Shirley
Alfie and the Birthday Surprise 694
Alfie Gets in First 694
Annie Rose Is My Little Sister 512, **694**
Olly and Me 694
Rhymes for Annie Rose 694

Huling, Jan
Puss in Cowboy Boots **695**

Hume, Lotta Carswell
Favorite Children's Stories from China and Tibet 104

Huneck, Stephen
Sally Goes to the Beach 1304

Hunter, Erin
Fire and Ice 696
Forest of Secrets 696
Into the Wild 696
Warriors Series **696**

Hunter, Mollie
The King's Swift Rider 79
The Mermaid Summer 659

Hurd, Thacher
Art Dog 697
Moo Cow Kaboom! **697**
Santa Mouse and the Ratdeer 697
Zoom City 697

Hurst, Carol Otis
In Plain Sight 698, 699
A Killing in Plymouth Colony 699
Through the Lock 698, 699
The Wrong One **699**

Hurwin, Davida Wills
The Farther You Run **700**
A Time for Dancing 700

Hurwitz, Johanna
Aldo Peanut Butter 953
Dear Emma **701**, 852
E Is for Elisa 702

Elisa Michaels, Bigger & Better **702**
Even Stephen 701
Ever Clever Elisa 702
Faraway Summer 701, 954
Fourth Grade Fuss 702
Hurray for Ali Baba Bernstein 332
Lexi's Tale 59, 840
A Llama in the Family 701
New Shoes for Silvia 1321
Ozzie on His Own 701
The Rabbi's Girls 611
Spring Break 701

Huser, Glen
Grace Lake: A Novel 703
Stitches **703**, 1102
Touch of the Clown 613

Hutchins, Hazel
One Dark Night 92
The Prince of Tarn 704
Robyn's Art Attack 704
T.J. and the Cats **704**
The Three and Many Wishes of Jason Reid 704

Hutchins, Pat
It's MY Birthday! 179, 705
Rosie's Walk 642, 1284, 1416
There's Only One of Me! 1355
Three-Star Billy 705
Titch and Daisy 705
We're Going on a Picnic! **705**, 1426
Where's the Baby? 264

Hyland, Betty
The Girl with the Crazy Brother 364, 596, 1386

Hyland, Hilary
The Wreck of the Ethie 442

I

Ibbotson, Eva
Dial-a-Ghost 182, 706, 707, 708
The Great Ghost Rescue **706**, 707, 708
The Haunting of Granite Falls 706, 707
The Haunting of Hiram 708
Island of the Aunts 313, 683, 706, 707, 997
Journey to the River Sea 706, **707**
Not Just a Witch 706, 707, **708**, 1474
The Star of Kazan 708
Which Witch? 1022, 1397

Ichikawa, Satomi
First Bear in Africa 709
My Pig Amarillo **709**
Nora's Surprise 709
What the Little Fir Tree Wore to the Christmas Party 709

Ihimaera, Witi
The Dream Swimmer 710
Growing Up Maori 710
Ihimaera: His Best Stories 710
Sky Dancer 710
The Uncle's Story 710
The Whale Rider **710**

Iijima, Geneva Cobb
The First Christmas Origami 711
Object Lessons with Origami 711
The Way We Do It in Japan **711**

Ingman, Bruce
Bad News! I'm in Charge! **712**

Author Index

O

Oates, Joyce Carol
Big Mouth & Ugly Girl **1098**, 1099, 1100, 1175
Freaky Green Eyes 534, 1045, **1099**, 1100
Small Avalanches and Other Stories 1098, 1099, **1100**

O'Brien, John
Poof! 1339

O'Brien, Judith
The Forever Bride 1101
Mary Jane 1101
Once upon a Rose 1101
Timeless Love **1101**

O'Brien, Patrick
Steam, Smoke and Steel: Back in Time With Trains 521

O'Callahan, Jay
Herman and Marguerite: An Earth Story 316

O'Connell, Rebecca
Myrtle of Willendorf 533

O'Connor, Barbara
Fame and Glory in Freedom, Georgia **1102**
Me and Rupert Goody 175, 1102
Moonpie and Ivy 1102
Taking Care of Moses 1102

O'Connor, Jane
Dear Tooth Fairy 649
Nina, Nina Ballerina 612

O'Dell, Kathleen
Agnes Parker . . . Girl in Progress **1103**
Agnes Parker . . . Happy Camper? 1103

Odom, Mel
The Rover 1195

Ogburn, Jacqueline
The Magic Nesting Doll 383

O'Hair, Margaret
Star Baby 1104
Twin to Twin **1104**

O'Keefe, Susan Heyboer
Death by Eggplant 1105
My Life and Death by Alexandra Canarsie **1105**

Okimoto, Jean Davies
Molly by Any Other Name 75
Talent Night 817, 1021
The White Swan Express: A Story About Adoption **1106**

Olaleye, Isaac O.
In the Rainfield: Who Is the Greatest? 1136

Old, Wendie
To Fly: The Story of the Wright Brothers 398

Older, Effin
My Two Grandmothers 2

Olshan, Matthew
Finn: A Novel 99, 460, 1472

Olson, Gretchen
Joyride 368, 439

O'Malley, Kevin
Bud 1107, 1108, 1109
Leo Cockroach . . . Toy Tester 1107
Little Buggy **1107**, 1108

Little Buggy Runs Away 1107, **1108**, 1109
Lucky Leaf 1108
Mount Olympus Basketball 1109
Straight to the Pole 289, **1109**
Velcome 1452

O'Neal, Katherine Pebley
The Reek from Outer Space 1154

Oneal, Zibby
The Language of Goldfish 1011

O'Neill, Alexis
Estela's Swap 1110
Loud Emily 1110
The Recess Queen 426, **1110**

Ongman, Gudrun
The Sleep Ponies 731, 780

Oppel, Kenneth
Airborn 1111
Dead Water Zone 741, 1111
Firewing **1111**
Silverwing 1111
Sunwing 1111

Oppenheim, Joanne
Eency Weency Spider 799

Oppenheim, Shulamith Levey
Ali and the Magic Stew **1112**, 1223
The Hundredth Name 1112
I Love You, Bunny Rabbit 970
The Lily Cupboard 1112
Yanni Rubbish 1112

Orenstein, Denise Gosliner
Unseen Companion **1113**
When the Wind Blows Hard 1113

Orgel, Doris
Mother's Daughter: Four Greek Goddesses Speak 1118
The Princess and the God 308

Orlev, Uri
The Island on Bird Street 1114
The Lady with the Hat 1114
The Man from the Other Side 1114
Run, Boy, Run 660, **1114**, 1326

Ormerod, Jan
Miss Mouse's Day 1096
Peek-a-Boo! 719

Orr, Wendy
Peeling the Onion 497, 974

Osa, Nancy
Cuba 15 **1115**

Osborne, Mary Pope
Adaline Falling Star 541
After the Rain 1119
The Brave Little Seamstress **1116**, 1117
The Gray-Eyed Goddess 1118
Happy Birthday, America 1116, 1117
Haunted Waters 659
Kate and the Beanstalk 1116, 1117
Knights and Castles: A Nonfiction Companion to The Knight at Dawn 1119
The Land of the Dead 1118
My Brother's Keeper 1119
My Secret War: The World War II Diary of Madeline Beck 808
New York's Bravest 1116, **1117**
The One-Eyed Giant 991, **1118**
Return to Ithaca 1118
Sirens and Sea Monsters 1118
A Time to Dance 1119

Osborne, Will
A Time to Dance **1119**

O'Shea, Pat
Finn MacCool 1322

Osmond, Alan
Just Right 877

Osterweil, Adam
The Comic Book Kid 157

Otsuka, Julie
When the Emperor Was Divine 384, **1120**, 1127

Oughton, Jerrie
How the Stars Fell into the Sky: A Navajo Legend 1073, 1398

Oxenbury, Helen
It's My Birthday 1229

P

Pace, Sue
The Last Oasis 297

Packard, Mary
The Pet That I Want 899

Pak, Soyung
Dear Juno 822, 1121
A Place to Grow **1121**

Palatini, Margie
Bad Boys 1123, 1124, 1174
Bedhead 1124
Earthquack! **1122**
Mary Had a Little Ham **1123**
Moo Who? 1122, 1123
The Perfect Pet 1122, 1123, **1124**
Piggie Pie 603
Three Silly Billies 1122
Tub-boo-boo 1124, 1379
The Web Files 969
Zoom Broom 758

Palatini, Mary
Mary Had a Little Ham 791

Paley, Joan
One More River: A Noah's Ark Counting Book 594

Pallotta, Jerry
The Beetle Alphabet Book 924

Palmer, Todd Starr
Rhino and Mouse 422

Palotta, Jerry
Dory Story 835

Paolini, Christopher
Eldest 1125
Eragon 1078, **1125**

Paradis, Susan
My Mommy 855

Parish, Herman
Amelia Bedelia 4 Mayor 1126
Bravo, Amelia Bedelia 1126
Calling Doctor Amelia Bedelia 905, **1126**, 1377
Good Driving, Amelia Bedelia 1126

Parish, Peggy
Amelia Bedelia 1178

Park, Barbara
Junie B., First Grader: One Man Band 9
Junie B., First Grader: Toothless Wonder 309
Junie B. Jones Is a Beauty Shop Guy 1427
Junie B. Jones Is a Party Animal 448

Mick Harte Was Here 743

Park, Janie Jaehyun
The Tiger and the Dried Persimmon: A Korean Folk Tale 1257

Park, Linda Sue
The Kite Fighters 965, 1127
Seesaw Girl 1060, 1127
A Single Shard 668, 1127
When My Name Was Keoko **1127**

Park, Ruth
My Sister Sif 297

Parr, Todd
It's OK to Be Different 549
Underwear Do's and Don'ts 290

Partis, Joanne
Stripe 847

Pascal, Francine
Fearless 240
Hangin' Out with Cici 300

Pastore, Clare
Fiona McGilray's Story: A Voyage from Ireland in 1849 523

Paterson, Katherine
Come Sing, Jimmy Jo 1128, 1438
Flip-Flop Girl 1128
The Great Gilly Hopkins 524, 600, 1128, 1313
Jacob Have I Loved 1128
Jip: His Story 1128
Parzival: The Quest of the Grail Knight 201, 1034
Preacher's Boy 192, 1128
Rebels of the Heavenly Kingdom 79
The Same Stuff as Stars 7, 524, 629, 903, **1128**

Patneaude, David
Framed in Fire 424
Haunting at Home Plate 939, 1210
Someone Was Watching 129, 1079

Patron, Susan
Maybe Yes, Maybe No, Maybe Maybe 124

Patterson, Nancy Ruth
The Christmas Cup 1129
The Shiniest Rock of All 1129
A Simple Gift 1066, **1129**

Pattison, Darcy
The Journey of Oliver K. Woodman **1130**
The River Dragon 1130
Searching for Oliver K. Woodman 1130
The Wayfinder 770, 1085, 1375

Pattou, Edith
East **1131**
Fire Arrow: The Second Song of Eirren 1131
Hero's Song: The First Song of Eirren 1131

Paul, Ann Whitford
All by Herself: 14 Girls Who Made a Difference 1132
Hello Toes, Hello Feet 1132
Little Monkey Says Good Night **1132**
The Seasons Sewn: A Year in Patchwork 230, 1132

Paulsen, Gary
Alida's Song 471, 508, 1128
The Beet Fields: Memories of a Sixteenth Summer 162, 1134, 1135, 1233
The Boy Who Owned the School 811
Brian's Hunt 199, **1133**, 1134, 1135

Author Index

Author Index

Author Index

Author Index

Author Index

Title Index

This index alphabetically lists all titles featured in entries and those listed under "Other books by the author" and "Other books you might like." Each title is followed by the author's name and the number of the entry of that title. Bold numbers indicate featured main entries; light-face numbers refer to books recommended for further reading.

Title Index

Title Index

Title Index

Title Index

Title Index

Title Index

Title Index

Four Hungry Kittens
McCully, Emily Arnold   917

Four Pictures by Emily Carr
Debon, Nicholas   365

The Four Ugly Cats in Apartment 3D
Sachs, Marilyn   **1249**

Fourth Grade Fuss
Hurwitz, Johanna   702

Fourth Grade Weirdo
Freeman, Martha   488, 489

A Fourth of July on the Plains
Van Leeuwen, Jean   754

The Fourth World
Danvers, Dennis   344

The Fox and the Stork
McDermott, Gerald   209, 1416

Fox Eyes
Gerstein, Mordicai   519

Fox Tale Soup
Bonning, Tony   **125**

Foxspell
Rubenstein, Gillian   54

Framed in Fire
Patneaude, David   424

Francie
English, Karen   845

Francis the Scaredy Cat
Boxall, Ed   128, **131**

**Frank Was a Monster Who Wanted
   to Dance**
Graves, Keith   548

Frankenbug
Cousins, Steven   740, 839, 1325

Frankenfrog
Kennedy, Kim   856

**Franklin Delano Roosevelt: Letters
   from a Mill Town Girl**
Winthrop, Elizabeth   327

Fran's Flower
Bruce, Lisa   16

Freaky Green Eyes
Oates, Joyce Carol   534, 1045, **1099**,
   1100

Freddy in Peril
Reiche, Deitlof   1196

Freddy to the Rescue
Reiche, Deitlof   1196

Free Lunch
Walsh, Vivian   1414

Free Radical
Murphy, Claire Rudolf   **1042**

Freedom Summer
Wiles, Deborah   1156

Freedom's Wings: Corey's Diary
Wyeth, Sharon Dennis   678, 1213,
   1471

Freewill
Lynch, Chris   918, 1492

Freight Train
Crews, Donald   1351

Frenchtown Summer
Cormier, Robert   20, 1408, 1418

The Fresco
Tepper, Sheri S.   1373

Fresh Girl
Placide, Jaira   **1160**

Friction
Frank, E.R.   187, 191, 391, **480**

Friday Night at Hodges' Cafe
Egan, Tim   1000

The Friday Nights of Nana
Hest, Amy   632

A Friend for Boots
Kitamura, Satoshi   802

A Friend for Little Bear
Horse, Harry   682

Friends
Lewis, Kim   724

The Friends
Yumoto, Kazumi   1490

The Friendship Ring Series
Vail, Rachel   563, 804, 821, 1402

Fright Night Flight
Melmed, Laura Krauss   **1004**

Frightful's Daughter
George, Jean Craighead   **518**

Frindle
Clements, Andrew   109, 261

Frog
Cooper, Susan   **296**

Frog and Toad Are Friends
Lobel, Arnold   70, 751, 1222

Frog and Toad Together
Lobel, Arnold   492, 751

Frog Face and the Three Boys
Trembath, Don   1311

Frog Hunt
Jordan, Sandra   **760**

A Frog in the Bog
Wilson, Karma   1449

**Frog Legs: A Picture Book of Action
   Verse**
Shannon, George   1483

The Frog Princess
Baker, E.D.   **67**, 452, 1032

The Frog Princess: A Russian Folktale
Lewis, J. Patrick   1328, 1479

The Frog Princess of Pelham
Conford, Ellen   67

The Frog Principal
Calmenson, Stephanie   268

**The Frog Who Wanted to Be a
   Singer**
Goss, Linda   686

Froggy Bakes a Cake
London, Jonathan   30

Froggy Eats Out
London, Jonathan   906

Froggy Goes to School
London, Jonathan   412

Froggy Goes to the Doctor
London, Jonathan   **905**, 906

Froggy Plays in the Band
London, Jonathan   **906**

Froggy Plays Soccer
London, Jonathan   474, 906

Froggy Takes a Bath
London, Jonathan   905

Froggy's Baby Sister
London, Jonathan   814, 905

Froggy's Best Christmas
London, Jonathan   906

Froggy's Day with Dad
London, Jonathan   905

A Frog's-Eye View
Busselle, Rebecca   529

From Dawn till Dusk
Kinsey-Warnock, Natalie   **796**

From Far Away
Munsch, Robert   663, 1121

From Miss Ida's Front Porch
Belton, Sandra   100

From the Horse's Mouth
Mackel, Kathy   **929**

**From the Mixed-Up Files of Mrs.
   Basil E. Frankweiler**
Konigsburg, E.L.   753, 1341

From the Notebooks of Melanin Sun
Woodson, Jacqueline   1466

**From the Outside Looking In: Short
   Stories for LDS Teenagers**
Crowe, Chris   320

**From There to Here: Short Stories
   about Immigrant Teens**
Gallo, Donald R.   504

Frontier Home
Bial, Raymond   754

Frozen Rodeo
Clark, Catherine   **256**

Fudge-a-Mania
Blume, Judy   120, 1066

The Full Belly Bowl
Aylesworth, Jim   61, 380, 475

Full, Full, Full of Love
Cooke, Trish   **291**

A Full Hand
Yezerski, Thomas F.   **1477**

Full Moon Barnyard Dance
Schaefer, Carole Lexa   35, 1469

Full Steam Ahead
Gibbons, Faye   **521**

Full Tilt: A Novel
Shusterman, Neal   **1297**, 1298

The Fungus That Ate My School
Dorros, Arthur   388

The Funny Dream
Zemach, Kaethe   1493

Funny Frank
King-Smith, Dick   792, **793**

Future on Ice
Card, Orson Scott   866

Futuretrack 5
Westall, Robert   578

G

Gabriella's Song
Fleming, Candace   463, 957

The Gadget
Zindel, Paul   681

The Gaggle Sisters River Tour
Jackson, Chris   **720**

The Gaggle Sisters Sing Again
Jackson, Chris   720

The Game of Sunken Places
Anderson, M.T.   29

Gangster Rap
Zephaniah, Benjamin   1494

Garage Sale Fever
Myers, Laurie   1050

Garbage Trucks
Eick, Jean   992

The Garden
Matas, Carol   808, 954

The Garden of Eden Motel
Hamilton, Morse   218, 916

The Garden That We Grew
Holub, Joan   311, 1409

The Gardener
Stewart, Sarah   16

Gaspard and Lisa, Friends Forever
Gutman, Anne   574

**Gaspard and Lisa's Christmas
   Surprise**
Gutman, Anne   574

Gaspard and Lisa's Rainy Day
Gutman, Anne   **573**

**Gaspard and Lisa's Ready-for-School
   Words**
Gutman, Anne   573

Gaspard at the Seashore
Gutman, Anne   633

Gate of Ivory, Gate of Horn
Holdstock, Robert   664

The Gates of Sleep
Lackey, Mercedes   843, **843**

**A Gathering of Flowers: Stories
   about Being Young in America**
Thomas, Joyce Carol   504

Gathering of Pearls
Choi, Sook Nyul   646, 1058

'Gator Aid
Cutler, Jane   332

Gator Halloween
Calmenson, Stephanie   1216

Gator Prey
Strasser, Todd   1347

The Gawgon and the Boy
Alexander, Lloyd   18, 269

Geez Louise
Elya, Susan Middleton   432

Title Index

Hello Benny! What It's Like to Be a Baby

Title Index

Title Index

Title Index

Title Index

Title Index

Title Index

Title Index

Title Index

Title Index

The Secret
Hoffman, Eva   215, 444, **660**

Secret Admirer
Zach, Cheryl   674

The Secret at the Polk Street School
Giff, Patricia Reilly   260, 806

The Secret Birthday
Wells, Rosemary   1428

The Secret Diary of Adrian Mole, Aged 13 3/4
Townsend, Sue   1291

Secret Friends
Laird, Elizabeth   563, 1443

The Secret Garden
Burnet, Frances Hodgson   96

Secret Heart
Almond, David   20, **21**

Secret in St. Something
Wallace, Barbara Brooks   902

The Secret Journey
Kehret, Peg   485

The Secret Knowledge of Grown-Ups
Wisniewski, David   1452

The Secret Language of Girls
Dowell, Frances O'Roark   391

Secret Letters from 0 to 10
Morgenstern, Susie   1032, 1337

The Secret Life of Amanda K. Woods
Cameron, Ann   206

The Secret Life of Dr. Demented
Gutman, Dan   575

The Secret of the Missing Grave
Crossman, David A.   26

The Secret of the Red Flame
Kimball, K.M.   **785**

The Secret Prince
Love, D. Anne   909

The Secret Remedy Book: A Story of Comfort and Love
Cates, Karin   230, **231**

Secret Sacrament
Jordan, Sherryl   761, 1151

The Secret School
Avi   58

Secret Star
Springer, Nancy   1329

The Secret to Freedom
Vaughan, Marcia   1398

The Secret Within
Golding, Theresa   **534**

Secrets
Ferguson, Alane   75

Secrets in the House of Delgado
Miklowitz, Gloria D.   1009

The Secrets of Code Z
Murphy, T.M.   1496

Secrets of the Shopping Mall
Peck, Richard   438

See Ya, Simon
Hill, David   810

See You around, Sam!
Lowry, Lois   911

The Seed
Pin, Isabel   1181

Seeds of Change
Sargent, Sarah   511

Seeds of Hope: The Gold Rush Diary of Susanna Fairchild, California Territory, 1849
Gregory, Kristiana   557, 666

The Seeing Stone
Crossley-Holland, Kevin   319

The Seeing Stone
DiTerlizzi, Tony   **385**

Seek
Fleischman, Paul   460

Seeker of Knowledge: The Man Who Deciphered Egyptian Hieroglyphs
Rumford, James   904

Seesaw Girl
Park, Linda Sue   1060, 1127

Send Me Down a Miracle
Nolan, Han   1089

Send No Blessings
Naylor, Phyllis Reynolds   68, 348, 363, 387

Send One Angel Down
Schwartz, Virginia Frances   1141

Sense Pass King: A Story from Cameroon
Tchana, Katrin   **1368**

Separate Sisters
Springer, Nancy   1329

Separations
Lehrman, Robert   439

Serious Farm
Egan, Tim   **421**

Serious Science: An Adam Joshua Story
Smith, Janice Lee   1473

Serious Trouble
Howard, Arthur   **684**

The Serpent Slayer
Tchana, Katrin   1368

Serpent's Children
Yep, Laurence   1475

Serpent's Shadow
Lackey, Mercedes   843

The Seven Chinese Sisters
Tucker, Kathy   684, 870

Seven-Day Magic
Eager, Edward   157

Seven Scary Monsters
Lundgren, Mary Beth   105, 513

The Seven Silly Eaters
Hoberman, Mary Ann   208, 283

Seven Wild Sisters
de Lint, Charles   355, 356, 757

Seventh Grade Tango
Levy, Elizabeth   821

Seventh Grade Weirdo
Wardlaw, Lee   62

The Seventh Knot
Karr, Kathleen   766, 767

Seventh Son
Card, Orson Scott   81, 115

The Several Lives of Orphan Jack
Ellis, Sarah   **430**

S'gana the Black Whale
Stauffacher, Sue   1337

Shabanu: Daughter of the Wind
Staples, Suzanne Fisher   1060

Shacked Up
Cann, Kate   210

Shades of Gray
Reeder, Carolyn   693, 1192

Shadow and Light
Bacon, Katherine Jay   629

The Shadow Brothers
Cannon, A.E.   223

Shadow-Catcher
Levin, Betty   491

The Shadow Club
Shusterman, Neal   395

The Shadow Club Rising
Shusterman, Neal   1297, **1298**

Shadow Horse
Hart, Alison   601

Shadow of a Doubt
Rottman, S.L.   **1232**, 1233

Shadow of the Dragon
Garland, Sherry   1289

The Shadow of the Hegemon
Card, Orson Scott   215

The Shadow of the Lion
Lackey, Mercedes   872

Shadow Puppets
Card, Orson Scott   **215**

Shadow Story
Willard, Nancy   1444

The Shadowed Unicorn
Welch, Sheila Kelly   913

Shadowland
Cabot, Meg   196

Shadows
Haseley, Dennis   606

Shadows
Sayre, April Pulley   1266

Shadows and Light
Bishop, Anne   **110**

Shadows in the Glasshouse
McDonald, Megan   188

Shakedown Street
Nasaw, Jonathan   748

The Shakeress
Heuston, Kimberley   635, **636**

Shakespeare Bats Cleanup
Koertge, Ron   363, **809**, 810, 1418, 1466

The Shakespeare Stealer
Blackwood, Gary   114, 115, 1169

Shakespeare's Scribe
Blackwood, Gary   114, 115

Shakespeare's Spy
Blackwood, Gary   **114**, 115

Shalom, Geneva Peace
Shalant, Phyllis   1280

Shanna's Ballerina Show
Marzollo, Jean   951

Shanna's Doctor Show
Marzollo, Jean   951

Shanna's Teacher Show
Marzollo, Jean   **951**

Shaper
Haas, Jessie   **576**

Shark Bait
Salisbury, Graham   1253

Shark in School
Giff, Patricia Reilly   1013, 1337

Shark in the Park!
Sharratt, Nick   **1286**

Shattered Mirror
Atwater-Rhodes, Amelia   54, 1271

Shattered Sky
Shusterman, Neal   1297

Shattered: Stories of Children and War
Armstrong, Jennifer   **39**

Shatterglass
Pierce, Tamora   1150, **1151**

Shattering Glass
Giles, Gail   352, 467, 525, **526**, 703, 958

Shawn and Keeper and the Birthday Party
London, Jonathan   826

Shawn and Keeper: Show and Tell
London, Jonathan   213

The She
Plum-Ucci, Carol   **1161**, 1162

She Did It!
Ericsson, Jennifer A.   **436**

The Sheep Fairy: When Wishes Have Wings
Symes, Ruth Louise   **1357**

Sheep in a Jeep
Shaw, Nancy   889, 895

Sheep on a Ship
Shaw, Nancy   915

Sheep, Sheep, Sheep, Help Me Fall Asleep
Alda, Arlene   16

Sheila Rae, the Brave
Henkes, Kevin   267

Sheila Rae's Peppermint Stick
Henkes, Kevin   19, 622, 624

Shelf Life: Stories by the Book
Paulsen, Gary   1134, 1135

The Shell House
Newbery, Linda   143, **1075**

Title Index

Title Index

Title Index

Title Index

Z

Z Goes Home
Agee, Jon **6**

Zach's Lie
Smith, Roland 1465

Zack
Bell, William 99

Zat Cat! A Haute Couture Tail
McLaren, Chesley **987**

Zathura: A Space Adventure
Van Allsburg, Chris **1390**

Zazoo: A Novel
Mosher, Richard 89, 491, 943

Zee's Way
Butcher, Kristin 186, 187

Zel
Napoli, Donna Jo 919, 1060

Zelda and Ivy
Kvasnosky, Laura McGee 840

Zelda and Ivy and the Boy Next Door
Kvasnosky, Laura McGee 840

Zelda and Ivy One Christmas
Kvasnosky, Laura McGee 840

Zero Grandparents
Edwards, Michelle 417

Zigzag
Wittlinger, Ellen 256, 1453

Zipped
McNeal, Laura 1420

Zoe Sophia's Scrapbook: An Adventure in Venice
Mauner, Claudia 807, **957**

Zoom!
Munsch, Robert **1041**

Zoom Broom
Palatini, Margie 758

Zoom City
Hurd, Thacher 697

Zooman Sam
Lowry, Lois 911

Zulu Dog
Ferreira, Anton **450**

Zulu Heart
Barnes, Steven 81, **82**